THE GLADSTONE DIARIES

Gladstone reading in the 'Temple of Peace', Hawarden Castle, by Sydney Prior Hall

THE GLADSTONE DIARIES

WITH CABINET MINUTES AND PRIME-MINISTERIAL CORRESPONDENCE

VOLUME XIV
INDEX

Compiled by
H. C. G. MATTHEW

CLARENDON PRESS · OXFORD
1994

Oxford University Press, Walton Street, Oxford OX2 6DP
Oxford New York Toronto
Delhi Bombay Calcutta Madras Karachi
Kuala Lumpur Singapore Hong Kong Tokyo
Nairobi Dar es Salaam Cape Town
Melbourne Auckland Madrid
and associated companies in
Berlin Ibadan

Oxford is a trade mark of Oxford University Press

Published in the United States
by Oxford University Press Inc. New York

British Library Cataloguing in Publication Data
Data available

Library of Congress Cataloging in Publication Data
Data applied for

ISBN 0-19-820465-5

1 3 5 7 9 10 8 6 4 2

Typeset by Joshua Associates Ltd., Oxford
Printed in Great Britain
on acid-free paper by
Biddles Ltd., Guildford and King's Lynn

PREFACE

Preparing this three-part index has proved one of the most interesting and absorbing of editorial tasks. The staccato character of the daily diary and the vast scope of the topics mentioned in it, in the Cabinet Minutes, and in the correspondence printed in Volumes VII to XIII make the index an integral and essential part of the edition: for many readers, no doubt, their point-of-entry to the edition.

I have tried to make the index entertaining and suggestive, as well as being as comprehensive a coverage as is possible of a text which has itself often the character of an index. Gladstone's terse style as a diarist lends itself admirably to the inclusion of his words in the index; but I have not, except in rare cases, distinguished between my words and his.

In the 'Subject Index' I have tried to include analytical entries as well as the required listings.

'Gladstone's Reading' is a very remarkable cultural document in itself. There are many records of the contents of prominent persons' libraries, but I know of no other major figure who attempted to record, day by day, his or her reading over a life-time, let alone a life-time as long as Gladstone's! Since a part of each day was systematically reserved for reading even when Chancellor or Prime Minister (broken only at moments of exceptional crisis) and since Gladstone read as eclectically as any Victorian, the record of his reading is a tour not only of Victorian high culture—and it is certainly that—but also of the by-ways of nineteenth-century political, religious and literary life.

Especially striking is the extent of Gladstone's reading of works in foreign languages, in addition, of course, to Greek and Latin. Gladstone spoke and read well in French and Italian, and his knowledge of the past and contemporary literature of those countries is daunting; he had a working knowledge of German and read many books in German on theology and the classics; he got by in Spanish. Serendipity will yield the reader as much reward as it did the diarist. Of course, we can tell from the footnotes of Gladstone's own publications that there are gaps in this record of his reading. He recorded much—about 17,500 book and pamphlet titles, and, in addition to that figure, many periodical titles—but not everything. Nor did he list newspaper reading. It would have been interesting to have marked in this vast bibliography which titles survive at St Deiniol's Library with Gladstone's annotations. Time and money prevented this, but it would be a formidable task worth undertaking (and databases can be updated!). Gladstone annotated books fairly heavily, and he often made a brief index at the end (few nineteenth-century books having an index of the modern sort), so it is not difficult to see from his annotations when he took a book especially seriously. Now that the core-information on Gladstone's reading is so comprehensively assembled, the base has been laid for a full-scale study of it.

The data for the Index Volume was recorded at Oxford University Computing Centre on an Ingres database named 'Gladstone', designed by Ms. Beth

Crutch. Ms. Crutch's patience, ability and enthusiasm have been central to what has been a complex and demanding task.

The 'Dramatis Personae' data was keyed in partly by Miss Elizabeth Mitchell and Mr. Oliver Matthew, but largely by Ms. Katharine Hugh. It was checked by Mrs. Jean Gilliland.

The second part of the Index, 'Gladstone's Reading', was keyed-in by myself, Ms. Cindy McCreery, Dr. Mary Heimann, and Ms. Hugh, with amendments and corrections by Ms. Tina Stoecklin, Mrs. Jean Gilliland, and Mr. John Palmer.

I designed and keyed-in the data for the Subject Index myself, a fascinating and educative task. Only by indexing does an editor really read a text! Ms. Kim Reynolds and Ms. Hugh helped with the gathering of some of the diary-dates. An early print-out of the Subject Index benefited from the comments of Professor Derek Beales and Mr. Peter Ghosh; an almost complete version was improved by the sharp scrutiny of Sir Keith Thomas.

Ms. Stoecklin very ably co-ordinated the final preparation of the data of the three parts of the index and arranged with Ms. Crutch for its transfer to Dr. Ruth Glynn and Ms. Elizabeth Atkinson of Electronic Publishing at Oxford University Press, who, with the assistance of Mr. John Snepvangers of AND B.V. of Rotterdam, oversaw its translation into text for setting by Joshua Associates, where Mrs. Anne Joshua's experience and ingenuity were invaluable.

I am obliged to Mrs. Jean Gilliland and Ms. Sarah Brolly for assistance with the proofs, and to the National Portrait Gallery for permission to reproduce Sydney Prior Hall's splendid drawing as a frontispiece.

The Marc Fitch Trustees readily and generously agreed to cover the costs of the keying and the checking of the data. I and the Gladstone Diaries Committee are much obliged to Dr. Richard Smith for his help in this matter and to the Marc Fitch Trustees for their prompt and unstinting support, the second occasion on which one of Mr. Fitch's trusts has come to the assistance of the edition at an awkward financial moment. The Rhodes Trustees are also, as ever, to be thanked for their continuing help.

My wife, Sue, has had to live with indexing more than either of us expected when work on it began. Indeed, neither of us realised in June 1970 when I was appointed Lecturer in Gladstone Studies at Christ Church, Oxford, that we were beginning almost a quarter of a century of daily preoccupation with W. E. Gladstone. That this preoccupation has been a delight rather than a burden has been as much due to her as to the diarist.

This Index volume concludes this edition of Gladstone's diaries and their accompanying materials.

COLIN MATTHEW

Oxford
May 1994

CONTENTS

Using the indexes ix

I. Dramatis Personae 1

II. Gladstone's Reading 285

III. Subject Index 611

USING THE INDEXES

The Index to the Diaries is divided into three parts: Dramatis Personae; Gladstone's Reading; Subject Index.

Alphabetization is by all the letters up to the first comma. Thus:

Church Defence Fund
Churchill, Randolph ...
Church of England

People with only a surname, or with a surname and a title (e.g. Mr. Jones), precede those with a surname and a first name. Names starting with Mac, Mc, etc. are alphabetized under their various spellings. Kings and others qualified by a number normally come after others with the same name.

Gladstone is abbreviated to 'G' throughout (except in book-titles and in 'Dramatis Personae').

In all parts, reference to the text is by diary-date, not page-number, and is thus independent of the printed edition. The volume numbers of *The Gladstone Diaries* and the years covered by each volume are given at the foot of each page in the index, for easy reference from date to volume and page.

Diary-dates are given in the form 6/12/32, 18/3/95 and are qualified (e.g. 6/7/73 L, 17/9/84 c) by the following:

a	Appendix
c	Cabinet (i.e. a mention in the Cabinet Minutes)
ff or f	following
fl	fly-leaf of an MS volume of the diary
L	a letter from Gladstone to the correspondent and printed in *The Diaries*
n	foot-note
s	seen (in the entry on Shakespeare's plays in 'Gladstone's Reading')
?	uncertainty about the person mentioned or the book/pamphlet read.

I. *Dramatis Personae*

This lists over 20,000 different people mentioned in the diaries. It supplies their surnames and, where known, their first names and titles and in many cases their dates, with a brief description of their occupation before 1896. 'Rescue' as an occupation indicates a prostitute or courtesan. Every person has at least one diary-date; the first diary-date given is normally that at which a footnote more fully describing the person will be found (though a number of persons are listed for whom there is no footnote, because no further information about them was found). It has not been possible to index all the diary-mentions for all those in the 'Dramatis Personae'. Gladstone used his diary to list his daily correspondents, usually without comment. To have listed every mention of each correspondent would have produced an index almost as long as the edition! I have, however, attempted to list each date on which Gladstone significantly glosses a meeting or a letter (thus 'Wrote Mr. Smith' would not have a diary-date in the 'Dramatis Personae' but ' Wrote Mr. Smith: difficult, on dissenters' would). Sometimes there is ambiguity as to whether entries are or are not duplicates (i.e. two entries for the same person); this often occurs with 'rescue' cases. In such instances, the entries have usually been kept distinct.

'L' after a diary-date indicates a letter written by Gladstone to that person which is printed in the edition (people who have an entry also in the 'Subject Index' have such letters listed there and *not* in the 'Dramatis Personae'). References to books read by Gladstone whose authors are in the 'Dramatis Personae' are *not* included in it; thus references to meetings and correspondence with Charles Dickens are in the 'Dramatis Personae', but Gladstone's reading of Dickens is recorded in 'Gladstone's Reading'.

Almost 200 persons have a full entry in the 'Subject Index'; such people's names (with their first diary-dates only) are in **bold** in the 'Dramatis Personae' to show that the reader should look them up in the 'Subject Index', where their full details will be found. Thus Acland, **Henry Wentworth, Sir** 4/5/48 should be looked up under Acland in the 'Subject Index'. Persons in the 'Dramatis Personae' will be found under their final surname (i.e. Hope-Scott will be found under Scott) and women under their final married name (i.e. Kitty O'Shea will be found under 'Parnell, Katharine', and Lady Lincoln under 'Opdebeck, Lady Susan'; Lady Waldegrave is a unique exception). Peers will be thus found under their surnames, with a cross-reference in most cases from the chief name in their titles (Lord Lorne, 8th Duke of Argyll is therefore under 'Campbell, George Douglas' and Lord Hartington, 8th Duke of Devonshire, under 'Cavendish, Spencer Compton'). Monarchs are under their regnal names ('Victoria', 'Edward VII').

Where there is a cross-reference to another surname, it appears separately *before* the name to which it refers. Thus

Acland *see* Troyte
Acland,
  Arthur Herbert Dyke . . .

On the whole, institutions are in the 'Subject Index' (e.g. the Reform Club is under 'clubs') but some minor institutions are included in the 'Dramatis Personae'.

II. *Gladstone's Reading*

This records by author, by title where the author is unknown, and by journal title, all the reading of books, pamphlets and periodicals noted in the diaries.

The diary-date given is normally that of the start of reading of the work. When that reading is, from the evidence of the diary, consecutive—on a day-to-day basis, with sometimes the odd gap—the subsequent diary-dates are not listed. It is for the reader, having been given the starting-date, to follow the reading through. However, when there is a long gap, or when the book appears to have been set aside and re-started, then a later diary-date or dates will be given. (Gladstone's 'Sunday books' were usually read each Sunday and not on the intervening week-days; such gaps are not recorded.) Where there is a substantive comment on the book or the author, that is recorded.

There are about 21,000 titles (including reading of periodicals), written by over 4,500 authors, in this Index. The largest entries (other than for periodicals and for the works of Gladstone's immediate contemporaries such as Manning and Newman) are, unsurprisingly, those for Scott and Shakespeare (the latter's entry includes plays seen as well as read). Gladstone's notes of his reading and viewing of Shakespeare's plays (the reading and the viewing often being related) is of especial interest as a record of one Victorian's taste. The largest single entry is that for the *Quarterly Review*.

The following details may be useful:

i. The list is arranged by author's surname (i.e. Argyll is under Campbell). There are no cross-references in ' Gladstone's Reading'.

ii. Pseudonymous works are under the author's real name, with the pseudonym also shown, except in the case of certain very well-known authors, e.g. George Sand, George Eliot.

iii. The edition given is that which appears, or is known, to have been used by Gladstone. The date of publication, if known, is given after the title. In cases where there are details further to the date of publication, these are given in brackets after it, e.g.: 1858 (3v. 1858–65). Where Gladstone read, at different times, different editions of the same work, they are treated as distinct titles. '*Opera*' is used to denote Gladstone's reading of works by an identifiable author, but without any particular work being identifiable (as in 'read Aristotle'). Dates of publication are not given for works of major authors first published before *c.*1700 (e.g. Shakespeare, Milton, Marlowe, à Kempis) which were frequently reprinted and for which no particular edition can be established, or for classical authors, except where Gladstone mentions an edition or a translation.

iv. Some biographical and critical works about a person have been gathered under the subject's name as well as the author's name.

v. Periodicals are given under their titles, followed by volume and page numbers (where known), the month and year of publication (in the form 6/1885), a brief description where appropriate of the topic or author mentioned by Gladstone as read, and the diary date (in this instance the diary date's year is given in full: e.g. 12/6/1846). In addition, in a limited number of cases, information about the reading of a periodical article is given under the name of the author of the article, using the usual abbreviations (*C.R.*, *Contemporary Review; E.R.*, *Edinburgh Review*; *F.R.*, *Fortnightly Review*; *N.C.*, *Nineteenth Century*; *Q.R.*, *Quarterly Review*, etc.). Such articles are normally printed at the start of the author's entry.

vi. Names and titles have been taken from the *Printed Catalogue* of the British Library, if found there. Qualifying descriptors, to distinguish between different authors with the same names, are those used in that catalogue. 'Anon.' is barely used; anon. works will be normally found under the title. There is a large number under 'The ...' Where the work has not been traced, it is entered with Gladstone's sometimes odd spelling retained.

vii. Gladstone's own publications are not listed in this section of the Index, but will be found in the Subject Index under 'Publications of Gladstone' and 'letters and articles for the press'.

III. *Subject Index*

This covers all the printed material of the edition, i.e. daily diary text, cabinet minutes and correspondence, but not the Appendices or the Introductions. There is no separate entry for 'Gladstone, William Ewart', since the whole subject index is in effect subordinate to that heading, the diary text being by definition autobiographical. The qualification 'by Gladstone' or 'of Gladstone' applies naturally to many of the headings (thus 'plays seen' implies 'plays seen by Gladstone'). Where there is a distinction to be drawn (e.g. between 'photographs' and ' photographs of Gladstone') it is made explicitly.

I have tried to use the compilation of the 'Subject Index' to draw together information about aspects of Gladstone's life scattered across the diaries. Some large entries of particular interest to Gladstone are:

card games
budgets prepared by Gladstone
busts of Gladstone
cabinets
child-rearing
clubs, Gladstone member of
conservative party
constituencies [of Gladstone]
deputations [to Gladstone]
essays and papers by Gladstone, unpublished
funerals [attended by Gladstone]
galleries visited
God
governments, Gladstone's
Hawarden Castle
Homer
houses occupied by Gladstone
illnesses of Gladstone
Ireland
journal, Gladstone's
letters and articles for the press
memoranda, printed
operas seen
photographs of Gladstone
plays seen
portraits of Gladstone
publications of Gladstone
rescue work, significant cases
resignation
sermons, notable
speeches
speeches, extra-Parliamentary
theatres attended
travels abroad
tree felling
walks, long

Gladstone's publications mentioned in the diaries are in the Subject Index either under 'Publications of Gladstone' (books, articles in periodicals, pamphlets, etc.) or under ' letters and articles for the press' (i.e. for newspapers). Such letters are those written by Gladstone to an editor; they do not include the vast number of letters written by Gladstone to a correspondent and subsequently published in a newspaper.

The 'Subject Index' also acts as an ordinary subject index, attempting to cover all the topics, themes and places mentioned in the text of the edition (except for Gladstone's reading, which has its own index). As such it is in effect a subject index to much of Victorian political, religious and cultural life. To avoid the 'Subject Index' being cluttered with names, only those most prominent in the diaries are included in it, the rest being found in 'Dramatis Personae'.

Almost 200 such persons are included in the 'Subject Index', with full-scale entries. These include the chief members of the Gladstone family, the chief political, religious and cultural persons in the diaries, and others such as Laura

Thistlethwayte. Peers will be found under their surnames, with a cross-reference from their titles (thus Lord Hartington, later 8th Duke of Devonshire, will be found under Cavendish, Spencer Compton).

The following of Gladstone's contemporaries have entries in the 'Subject Index':

Acland, *Sir* H. W.
Acland, *Sir* T. D.
Acton, *Sir* John, *Lord Acton*
Adderley, C. B., *Lord Norton*
Albert, *Prince*
Alexandra, *Princess*
Anstice, J.
Armitstead, G.
Asquith, H. H.
Balfour, A. J.
Baring, T. G., *Lord Northbrook*
Biscoe, R.
Bismarck, *Prince*
Bradlaugh, C. E.
Brand, H. B. W.
Bright, John
Brougham, *Lord*
Bruce, H. A., *Lord Aberdare*
Bryce, James
Campbell, G. D., *Duke of Argyll*
Canning, C. J.
Cardwell, Edward
Carlyle, Thomas
Carnegie, Andrew
Cavendish, *Lord* Frederick
Cavendish, *Lady* Frederick [Lucy]
Cavendish, S. C., *Lord Hartington, Duke of Devonshire*
Cecil, *Lord* Robert, *3rd Marquis of Salisbury*
Chalmers, Thomas
Chamberlain, Joseph
Childers, H. C. E.
Churchill, *Lord* Randolph
Clark, *Sir* Andrew
Clinton, H. P., *4th Duke of Newcastle*
Clinton, H. P., *Lord Lincoln, 5th Duke of Newcastle*
Cobden, Richard
Coutts, Angela Burdett-
Darwin, Charles
Denison, J. E., *Lord Ossington*
Dilke, *Sir* Charles
Disraeli, Benjamin, *Lord Beaconsfield*
Döllinger, J. J. I. von
Dodson, J. G., *Lord Monk Bretton*
Doyle, *Sir* F. H. C.
Drew, Mary, *daughter*
Edward VII
Farquhar, *Sir* W. R.
Fawcett, H.
Forbes, A. P.
Forster, W. E.
Fortescue, C. S. P., *Lord Carlingford*
Garibaldi, G.
Gaskell, J. Milnes
George, *Duke of Cambridge*
Gladstone, Anne, *mother*
Gladstone, Anne, *sister*
Gladstone, Catherine, *wife*
Gladstone, Catherine Jessy, *daughter*
Gladstone, Helen, *daughter*
Gladstone, Helen Jane, *sister*
Gladstone, Henry Neville, *son*
Gladstone, Herbert John, *son*
Gladstone, *Sir* John, *father*
Gladstone, *Sir* John, *brother*
Gladstone, Robertson, *brother*
Gladstone, Stephen, *son*
Gladstone, Thomas, *brother*
Gladstone, William Henry, *son*
Glyn, G. G., *Lord Wolverton*
Glynne, Henry, *brother-in-law*
Glynne, *Sir* Stephen, *brother-in-law*
Gordon, A. Hamilton, *Lord Stanmore*
Gordon, G. Hamilton, *Lord Aberdeen*
Goschen, G. J.
Gower, G. G. Leveson-, *Lord Granville*
Gower, Harriet Leveson-, *Duchess of Sutherland*
Graham, *Sir* James
Greswell, R.
Grey, *General* Charles
Grosvenor, *Lord* Richard
Gurdon, *Sir* W. B.

Hall, C. Newman
Hallam, A. H.
Hamilton, E. W.
Hamilton, W. K.
Harcourt, *Sir* W.
Hawkins, E.
Heathcote, *Sir* W.
Herbert, H. H. M., *Lord Carnarvon*
Herbert, Sidney
Herschell, F.
Hook, W. F.
Hunt, T. L.
Irving, *Sir* Henry
James, W. C., *Lord Northbourne*
Kinnaird, A.
Knowles, J. T.
Labouchere, H.
Lacaita, J. P.
Lambert, J.
Lefevre, G. J., *Lord Eversley*
Liddell, H. G.
Lowe, R., *Lord Sherbrooke*
Lyttelton, G. W., *brother-in-law*
Lyttelton, Mary, *sister-in-law*
MacColl, M.
Macaulay, T. B.
Manning, H. E.
Maurice, J. F. D.
Max Müller, F.
May, *Sir* T. E.
Mill, J. S.
Millais, *Sir* John
Milnes, R. Monckton, *Lord Houghton*
Morley, John
Mundella, A. J.
Murray, John
Newman, J. H.
Northcote, S. H., *Lord Iddesleigh*
Novikoff, Olga
O'Connell, Daniel
Opdebeck, *Lady* Susan (*formerly Lady Lincoln*)
O'Shea, *Capt.* W.
Palmer, R., *Lord Selborne*
Panizzi, A.
Parnell, C. S.
Parnell, *Mrs.* K. (*formerly O'Shea*)
Peel, *Sir* Robert
Peel, A. W.
Phillimore, *Sir* Robert
Ponsonby, *Sir* Henry
Primrose, A. P., *Lord Rosebery*
Pusey, E. B.
Ramsay, E. B.
Rendel, S.
Rhodes, C. J.
Robinson, F. J., *1st Earl of Ripon*
Robinson, G. F. S., *Earl de Grey, 1st Marquis of Ripon*
Rogers, Sir F., *Lord Blachford*
Ruskin, John
Russell, *Lord* John, *Earl Russell*
Russell, Odo, *Lord Ampthill*
Scott, J. Hope-
Scott, *Sir* Walter
Selwyn, G. A.
Spencer, J. P., *Lord Spencer*
Stanley, E. G., *Lord Stanley, 14th Earl of Derby*
Stanley, E. H., *Lord Stanley, 15th Earl of Derby*
Stansfeld, J.
Stead, W. T.
Stowe, H. Beecher
Swinburne, A. C.
Tait, A. C.
Temple, H. J., *Lord Palmerston*
Tennyson, Alfred
Thistlethwayte, Laura
Thring, H.
Trevelyan, *Sir* G. O.
Tupper, M. F.
Victoria, *Queen*
Villiers, G. W. F., *Lord Clarendon*
Wellesley, A., *Duke of Wellington*
Wellesley, G. V.
West, *Sir* Algernon
Whately, Richard
Wickham, Agnes, *daughter*
Wilberforce, Samuel
Wilde, Oscar
Wodehouse, J., *Lord Kimberley*
Wolseley, *Sir* Garnett
Wood, *Sir* C., *1st Viscount Halifax*
Wood, W. Page, *Lord Hatherley*
Wordsworth, William

Letters from Gladstone to such persons printed in the diaries are listed in each case under the sub-heading, 'letters from G to, printed'. Thus to find a consolidated list of Gladstone's letters to Hartington, look under:

Cavendish, Spencer Compton
  letters from G to, printed

It should, however, be noted that the letters to Laura Thistlethwayte printed in the Appendices in Volumes VII and XII are not so listed, since they are not printed together with the daily diary entries; nor are their contents included in the Subject Index.

Great houses are normally followed by the names of the occupants in parentheses, e.g.: 'Chatsworth House (Devonshire)'. Users of the 'Subject Index' should also consult 'Gladstone's Reading', for there is little repetition between the two, e.g. Gladstone's reading of Newman is not recorded in the Newman entry in the 'Subject Index'.

DRAMATIS PERSONAE

Information on some details of this index will be found in 'Using the Indexes' at the start of this volume. Names in **bold** have their substantive entries in the 'Subject Index'.

Abahall, Mr. 21/4/76
Abbas II, Khedive of Egypt 16/1/93 ff
Abbiss, James (-1882), London tea merchant 19/2/53
Abbot,
Charles (1798-1867), 2nd Baron Colchester (1829) 21/2/57
Charles Henry Philip, Rev. 17/7/67
Elizabeth Susan (-1883), née Law, Lady Colchester 24/2/58
Francis Ellingwood, Rev. (1836-1903), of U.S.A. 24/1/76
Abbott,
Charles Stuart Aubrey (1834-1882), 3rd Baron Tenterden (1870), permanent secretary, foreign office 14/1/71, 31/5/82
Edwin Abbott, Rev. Dr. (1838-1926) 8/7/75, 17/9/82 L
James Swift 22/11/67
John, of Newark 10/2/44 ?
Lyman, Rev. Dr. 15/4/89
Abcarius, John, lexicographer 24/8/77 ?, 18/1/78
Abdul Aziz, Sultan (1830-1876) 20/7/67
Abdulhah Bey 24/12/89
Abdul Lutief 1/12/91
Abdur Rahman, ruler of Afghanistan 19/6/80 n, 9/9/80, 10/9/80
Abdy, John Thomas, Prof. (1822-1899) 31/12/72
Abeken, Heinrich, Rev. (1809-1872), preacher to Prussian legation, Rome (1834) 17/12/38, 14/10/41, 15/10/41, 28/10/41, 2/9/43, 26/2/71, 28/2/71
Abel,
C., of Berlin 11/2/78
Frederick, Sir (1827-1902) 1/8/72
Abercorn *see* Hamilton
Abercromby,
George Ralph (1838-1917), 4th Baron Abercromby (1852) 22/12/68
James, Sir (1776-1858), 1st Baron Dunfermline (1839), whig M.P. 19/2/35 n
Ralph (-1868), 2nd Baron Dunfermline (1858), diplomat 1/11/50
Aberdare *see* Bruce
Aberdeen *see* Gordon
Aberdeen and Temair *see* Gordon
Abingdon *see* Norreys
Abinger *see* Scarlett
ab Ithel, Miss 22/3/87
Ablett, W. H. 25/2/78
About, Edmond François Valentin (1828-1885), author 14/6/79
Abraham *see* Bethell
Abraham,
Mr. 3/7/65
Charles John, Bp. (1814-1903) 9/3/50, 12/4/78
Ellen 3/1/75
Abrath, Gustav Adolph, Dr. 28/2/77
Abu Bakar, Maharajah of Johore 26/7/66
Acheson,
Archibald (1806-1864), 3rd Earl of Gosford (1849), liberal M.P. 18/6/60
Archibald Brabazon Sparrow (1841-1922), 4th Earl of Gosford (1864) 8/5/69
Achilli, Giovanni Giacinto, controversialist 30/6/52
Ackers, B. St. J., tory candidate 15/11/85
Ackland, Joseph, of London 23/4/67
Acklom, Mrs. 23/4/41
Ackroyd, Col. 20/3/74
Ackworth, A. 28/5/68
Acland *see* Troyte
Acland,
Arthur Herbert Dyke, Sir (1847-1926), 13th Baronet (1919), liberal M.P., cabinet minister 11/6/79, 27/7/92, 23/10/92 L, 13/1/93 c, 23/9/93, 5/1/94 n, 5/3/94 L
Charles Thomas Dyke, Sir (1842-1919), 12th Baronet (1898), liberal M.P. 18/8/79, 29/5/85 L, 8/2/86, 21/12/87, 22/12/87
Henry Wentworth, Sir 4/5/48
John Barton Arundel Dyke (-1904), barrister 3/1/52
Mary, Lady (-1892), née Erskine 28/7/58
Peter Leopold Dyke, Rev. (1819-1899) 29/12/59
Sarah Angelina, Miss (1849-1930), photographer of G in Oxford 25/10/92
Thomas Dyke, Sir (1787-1871), 10th Baronet, philanthropist 22/9/28 n
Thomas Dyke, Sir 22/9/28
William Alison Dyke, Sir (1847-1924), 2nd Baronet (1900) 29/10/83
A'Court *see* Herbert
A'Court,
Ashe, General 4/3/47 n

A'Court (*cont.*)
Henry, Capt. (1841–1885) 1/4/61 ?
William (1779–1860), 1st Baron Heytesbury 28/6/45
Acquaviva D'Aragona, Carlo, Duca d'Atri 7/1/51
Acrell, Mr. 29/10/86
Acton *see* Gower
Acton,
Ferdinand Richard Edward, Sir (1801–1837), 7th Baronet (1811) 17/10/54 n
Frederick, liberal 23/3/80
John Adams- (1830–1910), sculptor 7/11/64, 18/10/66, 27/1/73, 7/12/78 ff, 26/1/84, 22/9/91, 31/3/92, 16/5/92, 23/6/92, 12/8/92, 12/1/93
John Emerich Edward Dalberg, Sir 9/4/59
Maria Anna, Lady (1841–1923) 17/9/79, 17/2/89
Richard Maximilian (1870–1924), 2nd Baron Acton (1902), diplomatist 8/6/91, 13/10/91
Adair,
Robert, Sir (1763–1855), diplomat 4/2/32
Robert Alexander Shafto, Sir (1811–1886), 2nd Baronet (1869), 1st Baron Waveney (1873) 21/9/69
T., Rev. 20/5/75
Adam,
Andrew Mercer, Dr. (1829–1895), physician 2/7/60 ?
Edmond 18/10/79 n
F. 17/5/75
Frank Forbes, Sir (1846–1926), Bombay merchant and banker; returned to U. K. 1890 29/8/92
Juliette, Madame, political hostess and Gambetta's mistress 18/10/79, 11/1/80 ff, 13/6/85 n
William Patrick (1823–1881), liberal M.P. and chief whip 9/3/70, 6/1/71 L, 23/3/78, 17/6/78, 5/8/78, 3/12/78, 9/7/79, 25/11/79 ff, 6/12/79, 25/4/80, 25/8/80, 12/11/80, 25/11/80
Adams,
A. W. 2/3/80
Cadwallader Coker, Rev. 6/5/71
Charles Francis (1807–1886), American minister in London 3/6/61, 14/2/74 n
Edward Cay, Rev. (–1873) 9/3/68 ?
Elinor Lily Davenport, Miss 14/10/78 ?
Francis (1796–1861), surgeon, translator 3/5/58 ?
Frank Mantell 6/9/74
Frederick Morice, Rev. (–1871) 19/7/51
George Gammon (1820–1898), sculptor 11/6/61
James, Rev. 20/10/76
J. Davenport 31/12/68
John, publican, secretary, Leicester Conservative Society 11/3/36
John Couch, Prof. (1819–1892), astronomer 7/7/81
J. P., journalist 20/9/66
Nicholas, Liverpool broker 13/10/64
W. B. 15/3/87
William, clerk, woods and forests dept. 18/6/50
William Bartholomew, stationer 24/7/75 ?
William Henry Davenport (1828–1891), author 27/3/78
William Pitt, diplomat 3/12/47 ?
W. M., author 6/2/91 n
Adare *see* Quin
Addams, Mrs., hotelier in Oban 26/9/53
Adderley, Charles Bowyer, Sir 8/3/43
Addington *see* Hubbard
Addington,
Henry (1757–1844), 1st Viscount Sidmouth (1805), former prime minister 31/3/34
Henry Unwin, permanent undersecretary, foreign office 11/11/43
Samuel, collector 26/2/58
William Leonard, Rev. (1794–1864), 2nd Viscount Sidmouth (1844) 3/4/61
Addis,
William, Messrs., London ironmongers 24/9/49 ?
William Edward, Rev., Roman Catholic priest 28/1/84
Addison,
Berkley, Rev. (–1882) 15/5/52
Henry Robert (–1876), dramatist 27/9/66
John H., journalist 22/5/78
Joseph Edward, Major 15/2/55
Additional Curates Society 21/12/89 n
Addorio, Sig. 14/1/88
Adelaide, Queen (1792–1849), Queen Consort (1818) 21/3/33
'Adfyfr' *see* Hughes
Adie, C. L., Rev., minister in Edzell 2/11/46
Adin, Charles 7/12/78
Adler, Herman, Rev. (1839–1911), Chief Rabbi 21/11/93, 26/1/94 n
Adlerberg, Madame 30/8/86
Adsetts, Dr. 10/12/85
Ady,
J. C. 14/8/79
William Brice, Ven. (1816–1882) 30/6/71
Adye, John Miller, Gen. Sir (1819–1900), military reformer 21/9/76, 11/11/79 n, 30/4/80, 1/7/80, 6/9/80 c, 18/3/81, 15/10/81, 20/7/82 c, 3/8/82, 15/1/83, 30/5/84, 2/6/84 n
Affghan Committee, Secretary 15/11/78, 21/11/78 n
Affleck, William, merchant 17/12/87 ?

Agar,
Mrs. 31/10/87
Helen M., Mrs. 13/2/73 ?
Welbore Ellis (1778–1868), 2nd Earl of Normanton (1809) 18/11/67
Agelasto, Mme. 5/6/76 n
Ager, rescue 11/6/68
Aglionby, Henry Aglionby (1790–1854), liberal M.P. 10/3/46
Agnew,
Messrs., picture dealers 18/4/72, 20/4/72, 30/10/72
Andrew, Sir (1793–1849), 7th Baronet (1809), whig M.P. 30/4/34
Andrew, Sir (1818–1892), 8th Baronet (1849), liberal M.P. 22/3/66
Philip Peters, Rev. 30/8/79
T. F. A. 5/6/91
William, Sir (1825–1910), 1st Baronet (1895), art dealer, liberal M.P. 9/4/74, 3/11/87, 3/5/89, 17/5/92, 16/5/94
Agostino, P. M. d', Bp., bishop of Girgenti 20/10/38
Agresti,
Misses 29/2/52
D. Michele, Cav., attorney-general of Naples 20/1/51
Agrestini, Sig., Rome dealer 3/11/66
Agstado, Mme. 5/6/76
Ahmed,
Raees Uddin 18/11/76
Rofinndin, of Bournemouth 22/7/91, 24/11/91
Ahmed Khandeel 26/6/83
Aidé, Charles Hamilton (1826–1907), musician 20/11/89
Ailesbury *see* Bruce
Ailsa *see* Kennedy
Ainger,
Arthur Campbell 15/12/77
Thomas, Rev. (1799–1863) 17/9/52
Ainslie,
George, Rev. (–1875) 17/8/52 ?
Robert, lawyer 23/5/28
Ainslie and McAllan, Edinburgh lawyers 23/5/28
Ainsworth,
D. 9/10/90
Elizabeth, née Byrom, Liverpool heiress 14/9/29
Peter (1790–1870), whig M.P. 14/9/29
Sophia, Mrs. 4/9/78 ?
Thomas, educationalist 1/2/67
Aird,
C., Miss 23/8/76
Robert 6/4/78
Airedale *see* Kitson
Airey, Richard, Gen. Sir (1803–1881), 1st Baron Airey (1876) 15/3/65
Airlie *see* Ogilvy
Airy, George Biddel, Sir (1801–1892), Knight (1872), astronomer royal 14/11/62
Aislabie, William John, Rev. (1804–1876) 21/11/74
Aitchison,
C. 14/10/90
David, Ven. (–1859) 20/2/41
James, poet 25/11/87
Thomas (–1894), 2nd Baron Denman (1854), né Denman, solicitor 9/2/49
Aitken,
D. R. 24/10/89
Robert, Rev. (–1875) 6/3/53 ?
William Hay Macdowall Hunter, Rev. 29/4/75
Akbar, Ally 26/3/56
Akmatoff, Mme. 25/4/77
Akroyd,
Edward, Col. (1810–1887) 19/7/58, 11/3/73
Jonathan, of Halifax 27/2/41
Ala, Stefanucci, of Rome 23/11/66
Alagna, G. A. 25/8/75
Alamayu, Prince (1861–1879), Prince of Abyssinia 22/1/72, 20/8/73
Albani,
Emma, Dame (1852–1930), singer 14/9/84, 1/7/86, 9/6/87, 30/6/87, 9/7/87, 23/6/88, 14/11/92
Giuseppe, Cardinal (1750–1834) 11/6/32
Albany *see* Leopold George Duncan Albert
Albemarle *see* Keppel
Albert, Prince 27/1/40
Albert Edward Victor, Prince (1864–1890), Duke of Clarence (1890) 10/3/64, 15/8/82, 7/5/86, 29/5/86
Alberti *see* Monti
Albutt *see* Jones
Albutt, Mrs., egg woman 17/11/28
Alcock, Rutherford, Sir (1809–1897), diplomat in Japan 14/1/63, 25/6/63, 15/1/69
Alden,
E. Wenham, surgeon in Oxford 4/7/85
Henry Mills, editor of *Harper's* 27/9/76, 17/2/90
Aldenham *see* Gibbs
Alder, George, Rev. (–1882) 14/11/75 ?
Alderson,
Miss 29/6/75
Miss, at Albury 13/5/56
Mrs. 23/7/56
Edmund Hall, Sir (–1857), baron of the Exchequer 18/2/53
Frederick Cecil, Rev. (1836–1907) 8/11/73
Georgina, Lady (–1871) 22/1/60
Aldis,
Mrs. 2/2/56

Aldis (*cont.*)
Charles James Berridge (1808–1872), physician and sanitary reformer 28/3/51
J. A. 3/12/66
Osborne 2/1/90
W. S. 5/3/80
Aldreed, T. 7/1/87
Aldress, F. J. 31/5/78
Aldrich, John Cobbold, Rev. 2/1/44
Alee, Jaffir 26/3/56, 13/6/56
Alehurst, J. 20/5/76
Alemani, Sig. 28/6/79
Alexander *see* Canning
Alexander,
Mrs. 4/8/32 ?
Cecil Frances, Mrs., hymnist 27/1/75 ?
Godfrey Alexander, Rev. 7/2/46
Henry, oculist 10/2/37 ?
Henry McClintock, Admiral 8/8/90
James 16/6/46
James Edward, Gen. Sir (1803–1885) 17/3/38
J. B., Prof. 28/5/58
J. E. 15/8/75
L. C. 8/9/76
Michael Solomon, Bp., bishop of Jerusalem 7/11/41
Ramsay 12/9/37
Robert, Mrs. 4/8/32 ?
William (1826–1894), editor, *Aberdeen Free Press* 4/3/72, 20/11/72 L
William, Abp. 27/1/75 n
William, Bp. (1824–1911) 7/5/79
William John, Sir (1797–1873) 15/2/73
William Lindsay, Rev. Dr. (1808–1884), of Edinburgh 7/10/34 ff, 16/4/60
William M., West Indian proprietor 4/1/33 ?
Alexander II (1818–1881), Tsar (1855) 27/8/38, 15/4/74, 6/9/86
Alexander III (1845–1894), Tsar (1881) 19/6/73, 6/9/86
Alexander of Bulgaria, Prince 26/5/81
Alexandra, Princess 10/3/63 n
Alexis, Grand Duke (1850–) 9/3/81
Alford *see* Cust
Alford *see* Egerton
Alford, Daniel Pring, Rev. 1/7/75
Alfred Ernest Albert, Prince (1844–1900), Duke of Edinburgh (1866) 19/3/62, 31/8/93 c, 7/9/93 ff, 18/9/93 ff, 3/11/93 c, 5/11/93
Alfree & Scudamore, Messrs. 12/12/89
Algar,
H., of Billericay 27/8/87
Henry, Rev. 28/5/79
Alhurst, W. S. 14/4/80
Ali,
Mir Anked, Prof., of Trinity College, Dublin 17/7/77, 19/9/77
Moolk Mahdi, Nawab, secretary to the Nizam of Hyderabad 10/9/88, 15/9/88
Alice Maud Mary, Princess (1843–1878), known as Princess Louise 2/6/43, 27/9/71
Ali Murad Khan, of Khypoor 27/4/69
Alinari, Sig., photographer in Florence 31/1/88
Alington *see* Sturt
Aliprandi, Luigi (–1859), Italian actor 11/11/50
Alison,
Archibald, Rev. (1757–1839) 28/11/33
Archibald, Sir (1792–1867), historian 28/11/33, 22/7/40
E. C. 28/4/88
Allan,
Colin 19/7/90
Henry Marsham Havelock-, Sir (1830–1897), soldier 13/5/80
James 2/10/76
James, steam packet owner 14/8/27
John Lloyd, Rev. (1812–1866), head master 4/7/57 ?
Maria Caterina Rosalbina Caradori- (1800–1865), soprano 15/6/31
Allardice,
Margaret Barclay, Mrs. (1816–1903) 11/1/87
Robert Barclay, Capt. (1779–1854), known as Capt. Barclay, Kincardinshire landowner and pedestrian 2/10/43, 1/11/51
Allbeson, John 2/12/75
Allbright,
Mr., of Salisbury 6/9/66
A., Rev. 20/4/78
Allcroft,
Jeremiah M., glove maker 3/5/47 ?
William F. 3/5/47 ?
Allen,
rescue 2/4/59
C. H. 8/10/87
(Charles) Grant Blairfindie (1848–1899) 7/1/78
E. 13/12/56
F. M. 20/10/89
H. J. 16/6/79
Jane, Mrs., of Hawarden 23/4/92
J. Antisell, Rev., of Toronto 24/6/52 ?
John, of G.P.O. 19/9/59
John, Ven. (–1866) 28/2/52
Joseph, stable keeper 19/9/33
Joseph, Bp. (1770–1845), bishop of Bristol (1834), bishop of Ely (1836) 24/4/36
Ralph Shuttleworth (1818–1887), tory M.P. 11/7/68 ?
Robert, Capt., royal navy 20/6/74
Robin (1820–1899), secretary of Trinity House 26/2/76, 9/6/76

T. E. 27/10/79
Thomas, house agent 21/3/50
William Shepherd (1831–1915), liberal M.P. 31/5/67
Allendale *see* Beaumont
Allerhead, R. 27/4/89
Alley,
George, Rev., Wesleyan 21/12/67
J. H. 23/9/89 ?
Allfrey,
C. H., Dr., physician 28/7/69
Henry Wells, J. P. 15/2/73
Allhusen, Christian (–1890), Newcastle broker 8/10/62
Alliance Life Assurance Co. 3/3/49
Allies, Thomas William, Rev. (1813–1903), tractarian 21/5/30
Allin, S. 11/10/77
Allingham, William (1824–1889), editor, *Fraser's Magazine* 16/5/76
Allison,
H. A. 12/5/79
Robert Andrew, Sir (1838–1926), liberal M.P. 17/12/90
Allix, John Peter (1785–), tory M.P. 29/7/44
Allnutt,
F. 28/10/79
W. H., librarian in the Bodleian 25/10/92
Allom, W. T., Rev. 6/11/75
Allon, Henry, Rev. (1818–1892), Congregationalist 3/7/66, 16/3/67, 4/5/68, 5/7/73 L, 28/10/76, 5/12/77, 29/5/78, 13/5/79 n, 30/5/79, 28/3/81 L
Allport, H. A., of Nottinghamshire 29/9/77 ?
Allsop, Henry, Sir (1811–1887), 1st Baronet (1880), 1st Baron Hindlip (1886), tory M.P. 11/2/78 ?
Allworth, Miss 24/6/76
Allwright, Mr. 11/4/78
Almer, rescue 26/3/59
Aloe, Stanislao D', Cav., director, Museo Borbonico, Naples 2/1/51
Alpass, Thomas, translator 21/2/53
Alpiar, A. 30/3/78
Alpine, W., Mons. 31/12/78 fl
Alpiny, S., Mons. 15/6/78
Alspry, Mr. 11/2/57
Alston,
Mr., supplicant 8/12/65
Rowland Gardiner (1812–), whig parliamentary candidate 4/11/30
Althay, Mr., Birmingham magistrate 15/2/73
Althorp *see* Spencer
Altieri, Ludovicus, Cardinal (1805–1867) 30/4/67 fl
Alves *see* Arbuthnot
Amberley *see* Russell
Ambrosini, Charles, Brighton dealer 20/4/65, 6/4/72
Amcotts, Weston Cracroft, Col. (1815–1883), deputy Lord Lieutenant 13/6/72
Amelia, Queen, of Greece 19/12/58
Amerling, Friedrich von (1803–1887), Austrian painter 22/9/38
Amery, J., Stourbridge banker 2/3/47
Amhearst, Frederick Campbell (1807–1829) 24/9/28
Amherst,
William Archer (1836–1910), Viscount Holmesdale (1857), 1st Baron Amherst (1880), 3rd Earl Amherst (1886), tory M.P. 16/2/61
William Pitt (1773–1857), 1st Earl Amherst (1826), Governor-General of India 24/9/28 n
William Pitt (1805–1886), 2nd Earl Amherst (1857) 24/9/28
Amory, John Heathcoat Heathcoat-, Sir (1829–1914), 1st Baronet (1874), liberal M.P. 18/2/74
Amos,
rescue 24/8/83
Mrs. 31/3/82
Sheldon (1835–1886), barrister 1/1/73
Amphlett *see* Butler
Amphlett,
John, of Clent 2/8/53 n
Martin, Rev. (1815–1886) 18/5/78
Ampthill *see* Russell
Amsinck, George Stewart 18/12/77
Amy,
Miss 17/9/66
James L', advocate 26/7/37
Anartomo, Sig. 20/5/59
Anchetill, M. 14/12/76, 8/1/77
Anders,
Henry Smith, Rev. (–1877) 7/11/55
H. S. 19/8/40 ?
James, surgeon 17/1/35
Anderson,
rescue 6/9/70
Archibald, Rev., of Crathie 5/10/64
Charles Henry (1838–1889), liberal M.P. 27/11/85 n
Charles Henry John, Sir (–1891), 9th Baronet (1846), sheriff 19/10/54, 4/9/72, 13/10/73, 16/11/75
David, Bp. (–1885), bishop of Rupert's Land (1849) 25/5/49
Elizabeth Garrett, Dr. (1836–1917), physician 24/5/67
George (1819–1896), liberal M.P. 7/6/67 ?, 9/9/76
Henry Percy, Sir (1831–1896), undersecretary (1894), Foreign Office clerk 17/9/92 ff, 26/9/92
James, retired colonial officer 6/3/79

Anderson (*cont.*)
James, Sir (1824–1898), telegrapher 11/8/66 ?
James Stuart Murray, Rev. (1800–1869) 14/3/30
J. G. S. 24/5/67 n
John, schoolmaster in Mauritius 14/5/40 ?
John Bennet 31/5/76
John Farmworth, Rev. 5/1/87
Mary, Miss (1859–1940), American actress 8/11/84, 23/4/85
P., of Edzell 21/9/34
Patrick (1784–1839), banker, Lord Provost of Edinburgh 30/7/37
Robert, Rev. 6/5/40
Robert, Sir (1841–1918), commissioner of Metropolitan police 19/11/89
Robert Patrick, Maj. Gen. 1/11/85 n, 2/11/85
Thomas, of Aberdeen & London Steam Navigation Co. 7/10/43 n
William George, Sir (1804–1897), Knight (1870), Assistant Paymaster 14/2/53, 18/1/55, 3/10/60 ff, 28/11/60, 21/2/61, 5/3/61, 31/3/63, 15/4/63, 6/3/65, 1/5/75
Andersons, the, of North Wales 28/8/55, 3/9/55
Anderton, William Michael Ince (1825–1884), of Euxton; Roman Catholic supporter 9/9/68
André, Prof. 4/10/83
Andrew,
Mrs. 27/2/55
F., of Rome? 20/10/66
James, Rev. 2/3/58
John Chapman, Rev., fellow of Lincoln, Oxford 9/5/51
John James, author 4/10/77
Samuel, Rev. (–1889) 21/1/52
Andrewes,
Mr. 8/7/64
Mrs., rescue 1/5/63
Nesfield, Rev. (1844–1916) 13/5/76 ?
William (1802–1880), Irish botanist 26/6/63 ?
Andrews,
C. 30/12/86
C. H. 17/8/87
Gerrard Thomas, Rev. (1795–1851) 28/4/39
Richard (1798–1859), Southampton manufacturer 18/4/55
T., Messrs. 10/1/86
William, of Jamaica 9/1/45
Anduaga, M. D. 18/5/89
Angeli, Heinrich von (1840–1925), artist 10/7/75, 12/3/85
Angelini, Tito (1806–1878), Neapolitan sculptor 24/11/38
Angeloni, Sig. 1/2/88
Angerstein, William (1811–1897), liberal M.P. 1/5/61
Anglesey *see* Paget
Anglo-American Committee 15/12/70
Angrisani, Italian carriage organiser 29/11/38
Angst, H., of Scarborough 20/9/87
Anguish, W. 7/7/45
Angus,
J. M. 29/10/88
Joseph, Rev. Dr. (1816–1902), Baptist 15/1/40, 28/12/69, 9/12/89
T. 18/12/79
W. C., secretary of Scottish Home Rule Association 7/12/88
Aniais, Mr. 28/3/60
Anien, Paul D' 14/1/78
Anino,
Count, of Ionia 15/2/59
Paul de 3/9/77
Ankers, Mr. 1/7/86
Anketell, Mr. 18/10/90
Ankey, Mrs. 5/4/80
Annaly *see* White
Annan, Mr. 12/3/87
Annand,
J. 26/4/79
William, of Nova Scotia 14/2/87
Annandale, Thomas, surgeon 24/2/76 ?
Anne, Sister, of Clewer 29/7/63
Annesley *see* Barry
Annesley,
A., 1st Earl of Mountnorris 4/1/33 n
Charles, fellow of All Souls, Oxford 16/12/48 ff
Hugh (1831–1908), 5th Earl Annesley (1874) 2/11/77 n
Mabel Wilhelmina Frances, née Markham, Lady Annesley 2/11/77
Annett, W. F., decorator 5/5/75
Annsberg, Mr. 21/1/75
Ansell, George Frederick (1826–1880), inventor 19/3/66
Anson *see* Douglas, Primrose
Anson,
rescue 26/7/77
Adelbert John Robert, Rev. (1840–1909) 8/3/76
Archibald Edward Harbord, Sir (1826–1925) 5/4/73 n
Fredrick, Rev. (1811–1885), suitor of Catherine Glynne 15/6/39, 19/9/82 L
George (1797–1857), liberal M.P., soldier 3/8/53
George Edward, secretary to Prince Albert 26/1/43

George Henry Grenville, Ven. (-1898) 30/6/52, 10/4/70
Thomas George (1825-1892), 2nd Earl of Lichfield (1854) 27/10/63, 7/6/69 L, 9/6/69
William Reynell, Sir (1843-1914), jurist; Warden of All Souls, Oxford 25/12/89, 31/12/89 ff, 25/7/92
Ansted, David Thomas (-1880), geologist 19/2/49
Anstey, Thomas Chisholme (1816-1873), barrister, radical M.P. 31/12/45
Anstice,
Joseph, Mrs. 26/1/33
Joseph, Prof. 18/10/28
Robert Richard 18/11/31, 31/7/40 ?
Anstruther,
J. H., of Manchester 8/9/59
Robert, Sir (1834-1886), 5th Baronet (1863), liberal M.P. 24/5/77
Antenori, Giuseppe, Dr., G's doctor in Naples 28/1/89, 5/5/89
Anthony, John, Dr., physician 14/2/79 ?
Antislavery Society 19/5/76
Antiss, George William, Rev. 1/7/90
Antkin, Bp. 8/5/79
Anton *see* Szecsen von Temerin
Antonelli, Giacomo, Cardinal (1806-1876), secretary of state to Pius IX 12/10/66, 15/10/66, 19/10/66, 22/10/66, 11/1/69, 12/10/70
Antony, T. A. 13/12/79
Antrobus,
Anne, Lady (1800-1885), née Lindsay 10/4/35
Edmund, Rev. (1811-1884) 10/6/26
Edmund, Sir (1792-1870), 2nd Baronet (1826) 10/4/35 n
Anziani, Abbé 31/1/88
Apjohn, Michael Lloyd, Rev. (1806-1871) 13/4/39 ?
Aplin, Mr. 23/5/83
Apostolides,
Archimandrite 7/12/89
S. 21/4/80
Apperson, C. V. 12/8/90
Appleby, Charles James, author? 2/5/59
Applegarth, Robert (1834-1924), trade unionist and reformer 21/7/68
Applegate,
Miss 31/10/75
Mr. 25/9/88
Mr., coalwhipper 14/5/51
G. 9/12/56
Applestadt, Herr 5/3/80
Appleton, D., Messrs., New York publishers 4/11/76 n
Applex, Mr., Ross-shire election agent 4/7/37
Apponyi,
Mme. 21/3/60
Rudolf, Count (1812-1876), diplomat 21/3/60 n, 23/6/62
Appuzzi, Canon, author 15/2/51
Apthorpe, Rev., at Florence 25/3/32
Aptomas, Mr., Manchester publisher 14/8/68
Arabi Pasha, Ahmad, Egyptian nationalist leader 14/7/82, 23/7/82, 31/7/82 c, 28/8/82 c, 13/9/82 n, 15/9/82, 28/10/82, 3/11/82, 13/11/82 c, 16/11/82 c, 2/12/82, 4/12/82 c, 28/9/83, 17/1/93
Arber, Henry B., public accounts dept. 9/1/54
Arbuthnot *see* Gough, Inglis
Arbuthnot,
Anne, Lady (-1846), née Alves 26/4/28
George (1772-1843), Madras banker 15/10/33 n
George (1802-1865), treasury clerk 30/12/52
George Bingham, General (1804-1867) 14/7/62
Robert Christopher, Maj. 29/7/65
William, Sir (1766-1829), 1st Baronet (1822), Lord Provost of Edinburgh, East India merchant 22/4/28
Arbuthnott,
Hugh, General (1780-1868), tory M.P. 8/10/34
John (1778-1860), 8th Viscount Arbuthnott (1800) 24/1/33
Walter 18/9/47
Arch, Joseph (1826-1919), trade unionist, liberal M.P. 16/12/72, 4/12/73, 6/5/78, 11/8/92, 21/12/92
Archbold, John Frederick (1814-1870), barrister 3/3/65
Archer,
Miss 27/10/79
Henry (-1863), stamp machine inventor 17/3/53
J. 27/12/86
Thomas (1830-1893), author 26/12/81
Thomas Croxen, Prof. (-1885) 27/6/62
Archibald,
John, Rev. 2/4/77 ?
Thomas Dickson, Judge 5/2/73
Arco-Valley, Emmerich, Count (1852-1909), diplomat, Acton's br.-in-law 17/9/79, 10/10/79, 13/10/79, 27/8/86 ff, 11/9/86 n
Arden *see* Perceval
Arden, Henley I. [Henrietta Knight], novelist 11/1/80 ?
Ardilaun *see* Guinness
Arding, Mrs. 15/11/78
Ardmillan *see* Craufurd
Arena, G., of Malta 12/7/90

Argenti, A., Don, of Rome 4/12/66
Argurakis, Christophoris K., of Crete 21/7/77
Argyll *see* Campbell
Argyropulos, Mr. 23/10/83
Aristarches, Demetrios, constitutional author 29/7/76
Aristarchi, Staurace, Turkish attaché 29/3/64, 21/5/80
Arkington, Mr. 10/3/68
Armellini, Sig., Italian language teacher 1/4/32
Armeni, Pièrre B., Greek minister 3/4/69
Armenian Priest, in Venice 21/6/32
Armitage,
 Mrs., rescue 5/12/84
 Benjamin (1823-1899), liberal M.P. 18/2/70
 E., of Liverpool 23/8/79
 Elkanah, Sir (-1876), Knight (1848), manufacturer 14/10/53
 Robert, Rev. (1805-1852), antiquarian 8/2/44
Armitriding *see* Greswell
Armitstead,
 George 20/12/80
 John, Rev. (-1865) 15/4/52
Armour, J. B., Rev. 12/8/93 L
Armstrong,
 rescue 3/12/72
 Alexander, Dr., of the Admiralty 28/2/71
 David, wine merchant 21/8/29
 George, Prof. 15/11/77
 George Francis 30/1/76
 Henry William Gleed, Rev. (1805-1877), vicar of Willesden 1/6/31
 John, Rev. (-1865) 29/9/27
 John, Rev. (1813-1856), bishop of Grahamstown (1853) 20/4/49
 Joseph, mayor of Newcastle-upon-Tyne 16/6/62
 Richard, Serj. (1815-1880), lawyer 12/12/71
 W., journalist? 1/4/80
 William George (1810-1900), 1st Baron Armstrong of Cragside (1887), arms and shipping manufacturer 22/1/89, 25/6/93
Armstrong & Co., at Pozzuoli 22/1/89
Arnaud, Elias (-1860), customs officer in Liverpool 24/5/54 ?
Arnaudo, Giovanni Battista, Prof., writer on nihilism 27/12/79
Arnheim, H. d', Baron, Prussian ambassador in Rome 26/12/66
Arnold *see* Ward
Arnold,
 Edwin, Sir (1832-1904), orientalist, on *Daily Telegraph* 16/10/62, 17/8/69 L, 5/12/84, 21/7/85
 Matthew (1822-1888), poet and critic 24/7/57, 21/3/69, 30/3/69 L, 7/6/70 L, 8/7/76, 8/7/81 L, 27/9/81, 5/4/82 L, 8/8/83 L, 26/9/92
 Robert Arthur, Sir (1833-1902), Knight (1895), liberal M.P. 23/9/65, 16/5/73 L, 19/5/73 L
 Thomas, Dr. (1795-1842), historian, Headmaster of Rugby 17/4/33, 6/4/49, 30/3/69, 19/10/82
Arnot, John, of Greenock 10/1/78
Arnott,
 James, W. S. 21/12/49
 Samuel, Rev. (-1904) 30/5/55
Aronsberg, Woolf 19/5/75
Arouet, François-Marie de Voltaire (1694-1778) 18/2/32
Arrow, Frederick, Sir (1818-1875), Knight (1868), deputy master, Trinity House 31/3/70
Arrowsmith,
 Mr. 27/1/73
 James, Rev. 30/9/51
Arsnett, Mr. 15/5/76
Arthur,
 Mrs. 24/9/92
 Prince (1850-1942), Duke of Connaught and Strathearn 25/6/71, 26/6/71, 21/5/80 n
 William, Rev., Wesleyan 19/11/81
 William Lihon, Rev. 10/12/75
 W. McIntosh, Rev. 12/9/85 ?
Artley, Mr. 18/12/79
Arundel *see* Howard
Arundel and Surrey *see* Howard
Arundell,
 George Edward Arundell Monckton- (1805-1876), 6th Viscount Galway (1834), tory M.P. 25/4/38 n
 Henrietta Eliza Monckton-, Lady Galway (1838), née Milnes 31/3/32, 25/4/38 n
Arundel Society 16/10/78
Arvamtachi, Spiridon, of Ionia 4/12/58
Arvanitojani, G. 30/7/88
Asbury, Kitty 10/7/41
Ash,
 Mr. 22/4/74
 Richard Robert Drummond, Rev. 22/4/80 ?
Ashburnham,
 Bertram (1797-1878), 4th Earl of Ashburnham 14/4/83 n
 Catherine Charlotte (-1894), née Baillie, Lady Ashburnham 13/10/73
Ashburnham collection 12/3/83, 14/4/83, 26/5/83
Ashburton *see* Baring
Ashbury, James Lloyd (1834-1895), tory M.P. 22/3/77
Ashby,
 C. 28/12/78

Edward Quenby, Rev. (1805–1871) 19/1/33
S. D. 18/11/75
Ashcroft, T., Rev. 19/10/76
Ashe, Thomas, Rev. (–1878), merchant and priest 12/1/48 ?
Asher, Alexander (1835–1905), liberal M.P.; Scottish solicitor general 22/2/88
Ashford, John (–1867), poet 14/5/52 ?
Ashley *see* Cooper
Ashley,
rescue 19/6/62
Mrs. 20/4/32
(Anthony) John (1808–1867), barrister 19/4/64
Antony Evelyn Melbourne (1836–1907), liberal M.P. 9/3/58 n, 3/8/87 n, 7/6/89
John, art dealer 29/5/61
John Mark, Rev. (1828–1909) 6/1/76
Ashman, John, miner 10/12/85
Ashton *see* Lewis, Williamson
Ashton,
Ellis, Rev. (–1869) 27/10/44 n
K. S., of Darwen 17/12/67 ?
Richard, Buckley brick manufacturer 19/8/52
Robert Store, author 28/8/79
Samuel, Liverpool merchant 9/9/33 ?
Thomas, of Didsbury 17/8/87, 2/12/89
Ashwell, Arthur Rawson, Rev. (1824–1879), biographer of S. Wilberforce 24/1/76
Ashworth,
Henry (1794–1880), Anti-Corn Law Leaguer 3/5/58
J., jnr., of Oak Farm 1/9/66
Joseph 9/4/79
Askey, R. 10/12/86
Askin, Gabbitas & Killik 16/2/87 n
Aspinall *see* Swinburne
Aspinall,
Clarke (1827–1891), Liverpool solicitor 15/9/68
George, Rev. 19/4/52
James 23/9/33
James, Mrs. 23/9/33
James, Rev. (1797–1861) 10/3/60
Asplit, Maida, Miss 14/3/79
Aspull,
Mr., musician 24/5/28
George (1813–1832), pianist and composer 19/5/28, 24/5/28
Aspward, T. G. 18/11/90
Asquith,
Emma Alice Margaret (Margot) (1864–1928), née Tennant 28/2/81 ?, 26/4/87, 9/7/87, 23/4/88, 19/11/88, 1/10/89, 13/12/89 ff, 17/12/89, 6/11/90, 27/9/93, 19/2/94 L, 5/5/94, 10/5/94
Herbert Henry 2/4/87
Assailly, Charles Phillipe Alfred, Vicomte d'Assailly 30/4/40
Asser, Louisa, baby linen supplier 31/7/45 ?
Assiter, Mr. 14/4/87
Astell, William, né Thornton, tory M.P. 6/6/42
Astle, John George Edmund 9/10/75
Astley, Francis Bickley, Rev. (1782–) 19/3/34
Aston, Joseph Keech, Queen Anne's Bounty 3/4/75
Aston and Wallis, solicitors 12/4/44 n
Astor,
Mary Dahlgren (–1894), née Paul, hostess 15/6/92, 4/11/92
William Waldorf (1848–1919) 15/6/92, 4/11/92
Atherstone,
Capt. 11/2/79
William Guyton, surgeon at the Cape 5/7/38
Atherton, James, of Manchester 28/1/53
Athlumney *see* Somerville
Atkins,
rescue 12/9/79
James (–1834), portrait painter 24/4/32
William, Ven. (–1879), dean of Ferns (1862) 8/10/49
W. J. 19/2/67
Atkinson,
Mr., of U.S.A. 15/11/89
A. 7/7/77
Amos, of Newcastle 29/9/76 ?
James 28/11/76
Jasper, Sir (–1856), of the Mint 15/3/42
Lucy, Mrs., of Hammersmith 26/4/64
Thomas Witlam (1799–1861), architect and traveller 26/7/60
William, author 24/6/40
Atlay, Brownlow Thomas, Ven. (1832–1912) 7/5/92
Attwood,
C. M., of Darlington 29/1/56
J. 22/10/47
Matthias (1779–1851), banker and tory M.P. 22/4/33
Thomas (1783–1856), banker and radical tory M.P. 21/3/33, 22/4/33 n
Auckland *see* Eden
Audisio, Gugliemo, Canon (1800–1882), canon of St. Paul's and author 27/11/66
August, Mrs. 13/8/68
Augusta, Princess (1822–1916) 28/6/43 n
Augusta Catherine (–1890), Princess of Prussia, Empress of Germany 23/1/58
Augusta Sophia (1768–1840), Princess [of England] 18/5/37 n
Augustenburg *see* Frederick Christian Augustus

Augustus Frederick (–1843), 1st Duke of Sussex 3/8/53 n
Auld,
J. 15/6/92
John (–1874), W. S. 31/1/50 ?
Robert, secretary of penitentiary 9/3/36
Auldjo, John (–1852), mountaineer 2/6/49
Auriemma,
Francesco 4/11/76
T. 13/1/77
Austen, Thomas, Col. 9/12/43
Austin,
servant 24/10/47
A. G. 23/12/76
Alfred (1805–1884), secretary to Office of Works 15/3/56 n
Alfred (1835–1913), versifier and Poet Laureate 10/2/75
Charles Edward, author 4/9/79
Edward, Rev. (1824–1870), priest at Broughton 6/12/53, 10/10/69
F. A. 25/3/76
John (1790–1859), jurist 22/9/37 ?
R. B. 9/8/75
Sarah, Mrs. (1793–1867), née Taylor, translator 9/2/39
William Piercy, Bp. 7/4/47
Australian Trade World, editor of 28/5/87
Avebury *see* Lubbock
Aveling, Thomas William Baxter, Rev. (1815–1884) 1/6/78 ?
Avery,
H. 3/4/91
J. F. 5/10/91
Thomas (1812–1894), mayor of Birmingham 15/5/68
Avery & Sons, Messrs. 8/1/84
Awdry,
John Wither, Sir (–1878) 11/3/54
West, of Wiltshire 14/8/66
William, Rev. (1842–1910) 13/12/76
Axon, John William, London bookbinder 29/12/55
Axton, Mr. 12/11/74
Ayerst, William, Rev. (1802–1883) 26/10/56
Ayliff, Edward George, solicitor 3/1/66
Aylmer, John Evans Freke-, tory M.P. 3/11/82
Aylwin, Bevan, Cole & Harris, Messrs. 19/5/51 ?
Aynscough, J. A. 18/11/90
Ayre, W., Messrs. 10/1/86
Ayrton,
Acton Smee (1816–1886), liberal M.P. and minister 3/12/59, 25/11/67, 6/8/69 c, 1/1/70, 28/2/70, 9/4/70 c, 14/5/70 c, 6/9/70 c, 9/7/71, 10/7/71, 20/11/71, 22/1/72 c, 23/2/72, 13/4/72, 28/6/72, 22/7/72, 31/1/73, 4/2/73 c, 23/6/73, 28/6/73 L, 12/7/73, 6/8/73 c, 2/2/74 L, 9/6/77
Frederick (1812–1873) 4/11/57
Ayscough, Rebecca, rescue 31/10/42, 5/10/44
Azene, P., Baron, of Paris 23/3/55
Azzurri, Francesco, author 24/11/66

Babbage, Henry Provost, General (1824–1918) 1/3/80 ?
Babington, Churchill, Rev. (1821–1889) 5/8/76
Babosa, A. 29/1/77
Bache, Kentish, Rev. 3/6/77
Backe, Rev. Mr. 21/3/87
Backhouse,
Miss 18/7/87
Edmund (1824–1906), liberal M.P. 21/7/87
George Canning, Mrs. 28/8/66 ?
John (1783–1845), permanent under secretary, Foreign Office 27/1/32
Bacon,
Lieut. 27/5/75
George Peter (–1878), editor and proprietor of *Sussex Advertiser* (1843) 2/5/53
Hugh, Rev. 17/3/76 ?
James, barrister 12/1/33
Nicholas Henry, Sir (1857–1947), 12th Baronet (1945) 18/2/79
R. B., Rev. 20/11/78 n
Robert William, Rev. (1810–1862) 22/5/27
Thomas Scott, Rev., priest in U.S.A. 25/4/79
Bacon family 4/12/31
Badcock,
Arthur William (1814–), scholar of Pembroke, Oxford 29/1/34 n
John, of Watlington, Oxon. 29/1/34
Badeau, Adam, General, American diplomat in London 10/5/71, 9/3/72 ?
Badeley, Edward Lowth (1803–1868), ecclesiastical lawyer, author 1/7/40, 12/3/50, 14/3/50, 19/3/51
Baden *see* Stephanie Louise Adrienne
Badenoch, George Roy, Rev. Dr. (–1912), of Church of Scotland 24/11/74
Badger, George Percy, Rev. Dr. (1815–1888), Arabist 5/7/58
Badham, Charles, Rev. (1813–1884) 24/11/57
Bagehot,
Eliza, Mrs., née Wilson 12/6/77, 6/2/80, 25/4/81 L
Walter (1826–1877), editor of *The Economist*; author 27/5/59, 4/4/63, 13/11/63, 19/11/63, 4/12/63, 19/2/64, 9/3/64, 14/5/64, 25/2/65, 10/6/65, 5/7/65 n, 24/11/65, 15/5/66, 18/2/67, 15/6/67, 28/11/67, 3/6/69, 7/10/73 n, 16/10/73 L, 29/2/76, 25/4/81

Baggally, Capt., soldier in Sudan 28/5/84 n, 2/6/84
Bagge, James, Rev. 31/10/68 ?
Baggs, Charles Michael, Bp. (1806–1845), Roman Catholic bishop of Pella 1/4/32
Bagnall, Charles, of Whitby 25/8/71 n
Bagot *see* Phillimore
Bagot,
Miss 12/8/78
Charles Walter, Rev. (1812–1884) 24/7/30
Daniel, Rev. 11/12/42
Lewis Francis, Rev. (1813–1870) 24/7/30, 24/6/54
Richard, Bp. (1782–1854), bishop of Oxford (1829), bishop of Bath and Wells (1845) 24/7/30 n
Bagshaw,
Henry Salmon, Rev. (–1913) 7/6/77
John (1784–1861), liberal M.P. 10/3/35
Bagshawe,
Miss, nurse 8/1/46 n
John B., Rev. 31/8/79
Bagster,
Miss 21/4/79
Samuel, Messrs., publisher 12/9/79
Bagwell, John (1811–1883), liberal M.P. 1/8/59
Baildon, Henry Bellyse 16/4/88, 5/8/89
Bailey *see* Herbert
Bailey,
Messrs. 13/12/77
Mrs. 20/11/78
Benjamin, Rev., priest in Ceylon 20/9/44
F. A. 2/9/74
George, of Oldham 26/10/64 ?
Henry, Rev. Dr. (1815–1906), Warden of St. Augustine's, Canterbury 3/9/60 n
J. H. 23/11/78
John, Hawarden joiner 17/4/74, 22/6/74, 14/10/74, 15/10/74, 19/10/74, 9/8/75, 15/8/87 ff, 10/9/87, 29/10/87 ff, 21/11/87, 16/12/87, 24/5/88 ff, 11/8/88 ff
Joshua, Rev., priest in Ceylon 7/8/44
M. J. 20/5/64, 11/11/64
Neale, excise officer 21/1/33
S., of Bath 22/6/78
S., Mrs. 26/11/63
Thomas John, Rev. (–1890) 21/6/79
Bailey's Tea Shop, of Piccadilly 25/4/34
Bailie,
rescue 7/11/64
Mr. 29/8/76
Baillie *see* Gordon
Baillie,
Mr. 11/9/25
Evan 20/11/72 n
Georgina, Lady, née Montagu 20/11/72
Henry James (1804–1885), tory M.P. 17/4/56, 23/5/56, 6/6/56, 13/6/56, 16/6/56, 17/6/56
Hugh Duncan, Col. (1777–1866), of Tarradale, Ross-shire, tory M.P. 12/5/35
John, Rev. 2/1/60
Neil Benjamin Edmonstone (–1883), writer on India 11/5/58
Baillie [or Bailie], David, Hawarden book-keeper 17/11/52
Baillie [or Baillie Cochrane], Alexander Dundas Cochrane-Wishart- (1816–1890), 1st Baron Lamington (1880), known as Baillie-Cochrane, tory M.P. 13/10/43
Baily,
Edward Hodges (–1867), sculptor 28/9/52
H. G. 4/4/91
J., of Nottinghamshire 24/2/46
M., Miss 3/1/65
Bain,
Donald, writer on Corn Laws 29/1/42 ?
Ebenezer 30/11/87
James, Sir (1817–1898), lord provost of Glasgow, tory M.P. 23/11/76, 13/1/87
N., librarian, Royal Physical Society, Edinburgh 20/11/35
Bainbridge, George, draper 16/12/39
Bainbrigge, Philip John, General 1/7/75 ?
Baines,
Edward, Sir (1800–1890), liberal M.P. 18/2/60, 11/5/64, 10/5/80 L
Matthew Talbot (1799–1860), liberal M.P. 2/2/49
T., Prof. 27/5/68
Baines & Andrews, Messrs., jobbers 1/2/65
Baird,
J. R. 11/11/75
William (–1864), iron master, tory M.P. 6/11/43
Baker *see* Pepys
Baker,
Miss 30/3/59
Mrs., nurse 10/9/49
Mrs., rescue 22/5/86
Arthur, Rev. (–1868) 3/6/52
A. W. 26/4/79
B. B., Prof. (–1868), of Corfu 26/1/66 ?
George, mayor of Birmingham 17/5/77 n
George, Sir (1816–1882), 3rd Baronet 16/1/51
Hugh Lefroy, Rev., curate in Armagh 25/6/46
Hugh Ryves, Rev. 12/1/76
Richard Baker Wingfield (1801–1880), liberal M.P. 9/2/69
Samuel White, Sir (1821–1893), explorer 29/5/69, 21/10/82 c, 14/6/84 c
Stephen Cattley, Rev. (–1892) 21/5/49 n
W. 15/7/57
Baker & Symes 7/5/87

Balabanow, Marco D., of Bulgaria 10/10/76
Balcarres *see* Lindsay
Balch, Elizabeth, author 7/4/89 n
Balck, Mr. 6/11/79
Balder, M., Miss 27/5/87
Baldock,
E. H., Messrs., china merchants 8/2/43
Richard, Rev. 24/6/41 n
Baldwin,
Arthur Hugh, of West Didsbury 1/7/67
Charles, owner of *The Standard* 31/5/47
Balfour *see* Herbert, Lyttelton, Sidgwick
Balfour,
Alexander (1824–1886), of Liverpool 11/8/79, 14/8/84
Alice Blanche, Miss 10/8/75
Arthur James 11/7/72
Cecil Charles (1849–1881) 5/10/72
Eustace James Anthony (1854–1911), scientist 5/10/72, 15/9/78, 12/5/79, 15/6/82
Frances, née Campbell 12/5/79
Francis Maitland (1851–1882) 5/10/72
George, Gen. Sir (1809–1894) 12/7/66, 18/1/68
Gerald William (1853–1945), 2nd Earl of Balfour, tory M.P. 5/10/72
James Maitland (–1856), tory M.P. 1/1/49 ?
John (1811–1895), railway director 16/1/50
John Blair (1837–1905), liberal M.P., Scottish solicitor-general and Lord Advocate 15/6/82 L, 20/10/90 ff, 18/7/92 L
John Hutton, Prof. (1808–1884) 13/12/59, 25/1/65, 14/3/68
Robert, soldier, of Balbirnie 7/7/40 n
Thomas (1810–1838), tory M.P. 26/12/34
William, Rev. (1821–1895), United Presbyterian 7/11/85
Balgarnie, R., Rev. 1/12/76
Ball,
Edward (–1865), tory M.P. 28/7/54
Eustace Alfred Reynolds- (–1928) 5/1/89
J. H. 1/1/91
John, solicitor 8/3/41
John (1818–1889), liberal M.P. 19/2/49
John, Rev. (1800–) 21/8/31
John Thomas, Dr. (1815–1898), tory M.P. 13/5/69
Robert Stawell, Prof. Sir (1840–1913), astronomer 9/5/89
Sidney (1857–1918), liberal educationalist and Fabian 6/2/90
W. J. 13/5/79
Ballachey, Arthur Watts, Rev. 21/5/92 ?
Ballantyne,Hansen, Messrs. 21/2/88
Ballard,
Edward, Dr. (–1897), physician 22/9/49
W. 30/7/88
Ballarini, Francesco, Italian economist 28/11/67
Ballasteros, Mons. 17/8/77
Balle, Surrey & Ball, toolcutters 9/7/46 n
Ballerini, Paolo, Roman dealer 19/12/66
Ballingall, G. 14/10/90
Balls, Miss 31/1/91
Bally, J. G. 12/12/79
Balston, Edward (1817–1891), Headmaster of Eton 26/2/41
Baly, William, Dr., physician 31/8/41
Bamber,
Mr., of Hawarden 9/11/61
James, Rev., Roman Catholic 19/3/45
Bamford,
T. A. 12/7/79
T. H. B. 7/12/88
Bammeville, E. Joly de, picture collector 6/6/54
Bampfylde,
Augustus Frederick George Warwick (1837–1908), 2nd Baron Politmore (1858) 28/12/73
Marcia, Lady 9/7/91 ?
Bampt, Dr. 30/5/55
Banbury, Mr. 4/2/76
Bancroft, George, Prof., American historian 11/8/82 L, 30/4/87 ?
Bandinel,
James (1783–1849), Foreign Office clerk 6/5/42
James, Rev. (1814–1893) 6/1/78
Bandini,
Guistiniani, Prince (1818–1908), 8th Earl of Newburgh (1877) 30/4/67 fl
Maria Sophia Angelica, Princess, Lady Newburgh 30/4/67 fl
Bandmann, Tony (1848–1907), German author 2/2/78 ?
Bandon *see* Bernard
Banerjea, J. K., barrister 18/6/87
Banero, Chevalier 22/6/49
Banes, L. W. 14/5/90
Banff, H. 15/7/76
Banfield, E. 29/1/78
Banister, Thomas, barrister 13/3/49
Bankes *see* Boscawen
Bankes,
Edward, Rev. (1795–1867) 14/8/58
George (1788–1856), tory M.P. 12/4/51
John Scott (1826–1894), G's neighbour in Flintshire 28/5/57, 7/4/82 L, 17/12/83, 18/12/83, 7/1/84
Meyrick (1811–1881), Lancashire coal owner 22/6/26
Banks,
Dr., of Llandudno 11/9/61
Mr., of Hawarden 18/12/91, 22/12/91
A. J. H. 16/6/60, 1/8/60

Arthur, of Chester 27/8/52
Louisa, Mrs. 12/6/60
Bannatyne, John Millar, Lieut. Col. (1829–1886) 8/3/67
Banner, A. 10/2/75, 12/2/75
Bannerman,
Alexander (1783–1864), whig M.P. 7/7/42
Alexander, Sir (1823–1877), 9th Baronet (1851) 17/3/75
Henry Campbell, Sir (1836–1908), liberal M.P., Cabinet minister 11/11/79 n, 1/5/80, 4/2/81, 23/9/84, 12/10/84 n, 28/4/85 c, 11/5/85, 18/5/85, 30/5/85 L, 3/2/86, 22/2/86, 12/5/86 L, 26/5/86, 8/6/86 n, 10/12/86 L, 14/5/88, 2/4/89, 27/2/91, 5/3/91, 1/3/92, 19/5/92, 19/7/92, 20/8/92, 1/10/92 L, 2/11/92 L, 21/11/92 c, 21/1/93 ff, 23/1/93 L, 1/7/93 L, 20/7/93 c, 9/12/93, 5/1/94 n, 22/2/94, 5/3/94 L
H. J. 5/11/89
Bannes, De, Marquis 26/11/66
Banning, Charles Barbour, Liverpool postmaster 10/9/59
Bannister,
John, Rev. 13/6/46 ?
Saxe (1790–1877), author 14/7/55
Banting, William & Sons, cabinet makers 20/1/40, 29/5/52
Banton, W. 23/2/81 ?
Barabino, Georgio, Italian journalist 2/4/78
Barante,
Aimable Guillaume Prosper Brugière de (1782–1866), author and diplomat 5/3/32
Césarine Brugière de, née d'Houdetot 5/3/32
Barbar, G. 6/8/60
Barbari, P., Prof. 28/7/75
Barbarisi, Saverio, Neapolitan prisoner 5/12/51
Barber,
Mrs., housekeeper, National Debt Office 16/8/50, 8/10/53, 28/7/60, 18/10/60, 12/11/62, 17/12/70, 25/10/71
Charles, artist 10/3/45
Dean, servant 10/9/45
F. 1/11/45
James & Co., bankers 16/8/68
John, barrister 3/4/48 ?
L. J., vice-consul in Naples 18/12/50
Thomas 17/1/38 ?
William Henry, Rev. (–1872) 8/3/52
Barberini, Carlo Felice, Duke of Castelvecchio 30/4/67
Barcaple *see* Maitland
Barclay,
A., emigration officer 27/2/40 n
Alexander Charles (1823–1893), liberal M.P. 10/4/75
James William (1832–1907), liberal M.P. 7/10/75
John, Canon 30/1/80
Thomas, Rev. Princ. (1792–1873) 30/12/61
Barclay, Bevan, Tritton & Co., bankers 15/6/47
Barclay, Perkins & Co., London brewers 22/1/44
Barden, Mr. 27/3/61
Bardoux, Benjamin Joseph Agenor (1829–1897) 18/10/79
Bardsley,
Joseph 28/1/35
Samuel, Rev. 17/6/67
Bare, H. B. 18/2/87
Baretto, Baron 5/12/69
Barff, Henry Tootal, Rev. 4/2/89
Barff, Bevan & Co., merchants 19/2/67
Barfoot, William, of Leicester 5/1/76 n
Barge, Thomas, Rev. 21/4/42
Barham,
Alfred G. Foster 1/6/87
Francis Foster (1808–1871), author 23/1/43 ?
John Foster 8/3/53 n
Baring *see* Spencer, Thynne
Baring,
Alexander (1774–1848), 1st Baron Ashburton (1835), diplomat and whig M.P. 25/5/32
Anne Louisa, Lady Ashburton 10/5/36
Celia Anne 2/12/62
Charles Thomas (1807–1879), bishop of Gloucester (1856), bishop of Durham (1861) 9/8/28
Evelyn, Sir (1841–1917), 1st Baron Cromer (1892), Proconsul in Egypt (1882) 16/6/80, 28/10/80, 13/11/80, 20/11/80 ff, 3/1/84 c, 22/1/84 c, 8/2/84 c, 10/2/84, 18/2/84 c, 29/4/84, 1/5/84 c, 14/5/84, 24/6/84 c, 6/8/84 c, 6/1/85, 9/1/85, 20/1/85 c, 15/4/85 c, 10/2/86, 13/9/92, 16/1/93 c, 17/1/93 c, 20/1/93 c, 23/1/93 c, 1/2/93 ff, 5/2/93 ff, 15/4/93 ff, 26/7/93, 3/8/93 ff, 12/8/93
Francis Thornhill (1796–1866), 1st Baron Northbrook (1866), liberal M.P. and cabinet minister 18/7/40, 21/9/41, 13/11/41, 29/4/43
Harriet Mary (–1857), née Montagu, Lady Ashburton 4/4/43 n
Henry Bingham (1804–1869), Peelite M.P. 20/2/36
John (1801–1888), banker 13/2/37
Louisa Caroline (–1903), née Mackenzie, Lady Ashburton 4/4/43 n

Baring (*cont.*)
Mary Ursula (-1840), née Sealy 25/6/31
Thomas (1800-1873), tory M.P. 7/2/52
Thomas George; Earl of Northbrook 22/7/61
Walter (1844-1915), diplomat 4/7/77 ?
William Bingham (1799-1864), 2nd Baron Ashburton (1848), tory M.P. 4/4/43
Barker,
Mr., of Western Australia 30/4/90
Alexander (-1873), collector 21/7/63 ?
Charles Spackman (1806-1879), organ builder 24/3/55
Frederick, Rev. 14/1/74
G. F. R. 13/8/89
H. G. 19/3/91
Horace Ross, poet 3/5/91
Joseph, Rev. (-1901) 1/8/57
Richard (-1877), the Glynnes' solicitor in Chester 9/3/40, 9/7/55, 13/5/65, 6/9/73, 24/12/77
R. Longueville, of Hawarden 9/11/75
Thomas Francis, Rev. (1810-1878) 4/4/56
Thomas Holliday (1818-1889), secretary, United Kingdom Alliance 5/10/77
Thomas Jones (1815-1882), artist 21/7/57
William, Rev. (1838-1917) 20/4/84, 22/3/85
William Wilton (-1856), consul at Messina 6/11/38
Barker, George & Co., wine merchants 15/3/61
Barker, W. J. and Co., brokers 9/1/53 ?
Barker & Rogerson, Messrs. 5/6/91
Barkley, Charles Francis 29/1/41, 12/2/41
Barkly, Henry, Sir (1815-1895), Peelite M.P. and colonial governor 3/7/48
Barlow *see* Parke
Barlow,
Mr. 15/5/74
Edward William, Rev. 10/1/48
Elizabeth (-1831), née Robertson, G's cousin 29/7/25
James William, Prof. (1826-1913) 2/1/78 ?
John Emmott, Sir (1857-1932), 1st Baronet (1907), liberal M.P. 1/7/86 L
John Henry (1795-1841), cousin by marriage 29/7/25
Thomas, merchant 4/8/79
Thomas Wotton, Rev. 19/2/53
Barmby, James, Rev. (-1897) 21/4/54
Barnard,
James 16/4/74
S. P., of Festiniog 30/4/62
Barnes,
Alfred, of Farnworth, Bolton 7/9/64, 9/9/64, 11/10/64
B. T. 1/3/80
Frederick, Rev. (1781-), subdean of Christ Church, Oxford 15/11/28
George (1813-), undergraduate 23/4/31
Henry Eugene, Mercer's co. clerk 31/5/59 n
Henry Hickman, solicitor to Exchequer Bill Office 31/1/53
James Bathe, solicitor 24/8/69
J. Howard, actuary 11/6/90 ?
John Wickham 12/2/76 ?
Ralph (1781-1869), attorney, author, secretary to bps.of Exeter 14/5/34
Richard William, Rev. (1811-1885) 11/1/56
Robert (1800-1871), mayor of Manchester 30/3/53
S. 14/11/75
Thomas, editor of *The Times* 10/1/42 n
Thomas (1813-1897), liberal M.P. 3/7/62
W. 21/11/79
Barnett,
Mr. 23/7/41
Henry Crosby Barry, Lieut. Col. 13/11/79
Samuel Augustus, Rev. (1844-1913), social reformer 4/10/77, 2/8/79
Barnewall, Robert, & Sons, merchants 21/4/59
Barney, George, Col., of Van Diemen's Land 11/3/46
Barnum, Phineas Taylor (1810-1891), circus owner 30/1/90
Baron,
Miss, daughter of Dr. John Baron 5/1/26 n, 5/4/26
Mr. 2/8/85
Felix Le, French advocate 12/7/49
John, Dr. (1786-1851), scientist 5/1/26
Robert Benjamin, Rev. 19/3/79
Barone, Raffaele, art dealer in Naples 30/11/50
Baroniau, Mr., Armenian 23/4/80
Barr,
Edward Frederick, secretary in Ionia 21/1/59
James 20/3/80
Barrable, Mrs. 24/7/50, 26/8/87
Barran, John, Sir (1821-1905), 1st Baronet (1895), liberal M.P. 13/6/77, 21/3/78, 8/10/81, 17/3/87
Barratt, Fisher, Gamman, Messrs., cork cutters 7/6/42
Barraud, Henry Rose, Oxford Street photographer 6/5/91
Barreri, Cav. 27/7/49
Barret, G. T., Rev. 12/4/78
Barrett,
Arthur Charles (-1880), private tutor 6/4/40 ?
B. 21/5/90

Elizabeth, Mrs. 13/5/76 ?
George Willoughby, Rev. 17/5/90
G. S., Rev. 19/5/88
John, Bootle manufacturer 8/8/68 ?
William Fletcher, Prof. Sir (1844–1925) 26/5/77
Barrie, James Matthew, Sir (1860–1937), 1st Baronet, author 31/10/88, 1/11/88 n
Barringer, C. Wright, Dr. 25/1/89
Barrington *see* Legge, West
Barrington,
rescue 3/8/67
Eric 8/2/87
George, 5th Viscount Barrington 29/6/44 n
George William (1824–1886), 7th Viscount Barrington (1867), tory M.P. 7/8/67, 29/3/81
Vincent Hunter Kennett-, Sir (1844–1903) 5/6/86
William Keppel (1793–1867), 6th Viscount Barrington (1829), tory M.P. 24/5/56
Barron,
Henry Winston, Sir (1795–1872), 1st Baronet (1841), liberal M.P. 25/11/67
John Henry, journalist 29/6/40, 13/7/40
Barrone, Prof., ophthalmologist in Rome 9/10/38
Barrot, Camille Hyacinthe Odilon (1791–1873), French orator, statesman 21/7/32, 8/8/49
Barrow,
George, Sir (–1876), 2nd Baronet (1848), colonial office 7/7/46
John, Sir, 1st Baronet, admiralty 11/12/48
Joseph Lyon, Gen. 23/5/78 ?
William, Liverpool solicitor 7/11/53
Barry,
Alfred, Rev. Dr. (–1910), schoolmaster and archbishop 23/10/51
Charles, Sir, architect 19/10/42 n
Charles Robert (1824–1897), liberal M.P. (1865), Irish solicitor general 11/12/68, 3/9/71 L
Charles Upham, of Bloomsbury 13/2/33 ?
David Thomas, Rev. 13/2/54
Edward Middleton (1830–1880), architect 19/12/68
Henry Boothby, Rev., school inspector 8/5/55
John Maxwell- (1767–1838), 5th Baron Farnham 4/1/33 n
John Wolfe, engineer 24/3/74 ?
Juliana Lucy Maxwell- (1772–1833), née Annesley, Lady Farnham 4/1/33
Michael Joseph, Irish pamphleteer 29/2/60
Michael Joseph (1817–1889), poet 31/7/75
Octavia, Miss 24/10/70
William Thomas, Rev. (–1908) 23/3/78
Barry & Co., stockbrokers 3/3/49
Barter, Rupert Speckott (1790–1861), Warden of Winchester College 15/5/35, 8/8/53
Bartholomew,
John, Rev. 19/2/48
John George (1860–1920), geographer 29/11/79 ?
Barthorp, H., Mr. 7/3/51, 10/7/56
Bartle, George, Rev. Dr. 29/8/77
Bartlett,
E., Miss 18/3/36 ?
Ellis Ashmead, Sir (1849–1902), tory M.P., active in Bulgarian horrors campaign 6/9/76, 6/12/76, 11/10/83, 29/1/94
G. C., Rev., former vicar of Newark 18/3/36 n
John, author 22/2/89 ?
S. 6/5/36
Symeon Taylor, Rev. 30/10/40
T., Mrs. 23/5/35
T., Rev. 23/5/35 n
Thomas, Rev. (1789–1872) 14/5/67 ?
William, of Liverpool law society 21/6/67
William, Rev., vicar of Newark 7/12/32
Bartley, J. 14/2/80
Bartling, Dr. 13/5/76
Bartolini, Lorenzo, sculptor 12/7/32 n
Bartolotti, Angelo, importer 31/7/83
Bartolozzi *see* Matthews
Barton,
Mr., of Natal 1/7/75
Charles, Rev. 9/6/58
D. F. P. 24/1/66 n
E. 29/1/79
Frederick Bolton 16/3/75
H. 14/3/88
Henry Jonas, Rev. (–1872) 27/2/56 ?
John, Governor, Bank of Ireland 4/7/53
Thomas Henry (1816–1878), Dublin barrister 30/3/58 ?
Victoria Alexandrina Julia, née Peel 24/1/66
Bartrum, Edward, Rev. 24/7/66
Barttelot, Walter Barttelot, Col. Sir (1820–1893), 1st Baronet (1875), tory M.P. 20/2/63, 24/9/92, 26/9/92
Barwick, John, London goldsmith 29/6/55 ?
Barwis, William Cuthbert, Rev. (1824–1889) 7/2/67
Base, Mr., of Corfu 23/7/61
Baself, H. J. 16/7/74
Bashin, Mr. 15/3/78
Bashkirtseff, Maria Babanina-, Mrs. 10/1/90, 9/2/92
Basile, S., Mons. 10/2/90
Basing *see* Booth
Baskham, T. 28/10/74
Bass,
Michael Arthur, Sir (1837–1909), 1st Baronet (1882), 1st Baron Burton (1886), liberal M.P., brewer 14/10/65 n

Bass (*cont.*)
Michael Thomas (1799–1884), brewer, liberal M.P. 7/2/61, 22/5/80 L
Bassano *see* Maret
Bassano, photographer of Gladstone 10/3/83
Bassermann,
F. D., bookseller, politician in Mannheim 16/7/33 n
R. 16/7/33
Bassett, Mr. 26/6/79
Bassiat, J. 26/10/88
Bassini, Achille de (–1881), singer 9/12/50
Batchelor, George Andrew, merchant 11/4/76 ?
Bate,
E. 26/3/57
G., Messrs., involved with Oak Farm 5/2/50
S. Stringer, also called 'W. L. Raleigh' 28/11/75
Bateman *see* Hanbury
Bateman,
Christian Henry, Rev. 19/10/76, 27/11/77, 28/11/77
E. F. 10/6/78
F., Dr., physician 16/5/90 n
J. R. 10/5/78
Richard W., Stourbridge wheelwright 12/3/47
Bates,
Charlotte, china shopkeeper in Oxford 13/5/46 ?
Edward, Sir (1816–1896), 1st Baronet (1880), tory M.P. 16/6/73
J. F., custom house clerk 3/12/44 ?
J. L. 22/4/80
John Ellison (1809–), undergraduate at Christ Church 5/9/30
Joseph Chadwick, Rev. (1826–) 6/7/59
Bateson *see* McMahon
Bateson,
Robert, Sir (1816–1843), tory M.P. 13/7/38 n, 17/9/39, 15/2/42
R. W. 1/1/44
Samuel Stephen, J. N. Gladstone's br.in law, of Golspie 30/10/48, 17/9/58
Thomas, Sir (1819–1890), 2nd Baronet (1863), 1st Baron Deramore (1885), tory M.P. 11/2/63
William Henry, Rev. (1812–1881), don 18/5/70, 28/10/78
Bath *see* Thynne
Bath, W. S. 16/3/87
Bathe,
Mr., publican 10/6/46
Anthony, Rev. 14/8/74
Bathgate, William, Rev. 2/9/78
Bathurst,
Henry George (1790–1866), 4th Earl Bathurst 3/11/58
Louisa Georgina, Lady (–1874) 19/5/56
William Lennox (1791–1878), 5th Earl Bathurst (1866) 1/9/75, 1/10/75, 5/10/75
Batley, W. F., Mr. 8/7/74
Battam, Thomas, sculptor 19/6/62, 4/4/63
Batten,
rescue 15/10/61
Edmund, barrister 9/5/49
Battenberg,
Beatrice M. V. F. of, Princess 24/1/69
Henry of, Prince 24/1/69 n
Battensberger, G. 9/5/76
Batterbury, Henry Charles, Rev. 10/12/75 ?
Battersby,
Capt. 26/6/75
F. 9/10/77
Battersea *see* Flower
Battiscombe,
Henry, Rev. (1802–1871) 11/3/32
Robert, Rev. (1799–1881) 11/3/32
Batty, Councillor 8/9/76
Bauer, Vasily V., Slav author 12/2/79
Baugh, Folliot, Rev. (1809–1889) 26/9/31
Baulf, Mr. 8/7/75
Baum, H. M., Rev. 12/3/90
Baumann, Arthur Anthony (1856–1936), tory M.P. 27/2/86
Bautte, Mr., watchmaker of Geneva 14/7/32
Bavaria *see* Wittelsbach
Baverstock,
Edwin H., National Debt Office 30/3/75
H. 25/7/91
W., supplicant 24/10/61
Baxter,
David, Sir (1793–1872), 1st Baronet (1863), Dundee merchant 4/5/36
Edward (1791–1870), Dundee merchant 4/5/36 ?
Richard 6/9/78
Robert (–1889), parliamentary solicitor 14/6/51
Robert Dudley (1827–1875), political organiser, author and solicitor 4/12/66, 7/3/68, 21/5/68, 1/2/70 n
William Edward (1825–1890), liberal M.P. 10/11/60
Baxter, Rose & Norton, solicitors 14/6/51 n
Baxton, Mr. 28/3/78
Bayard, Thomas Francis (1828–1898), American senator and Secretary of State 25/10/79
Bayden, rescue 19/9/66
Baylee,
Joseph, Mrs. 17/2/57 ?
Joseph, Rev. Dr. (1808–1883) 18/11/54
Bayley, Edric H., of Southwark liberal association 10/10/77, 16/7/78
Bayliffe, Mrs. 11/4/88

Baylis, Thomas Henry, barrister 2/4/50
Bayliss, William Wyke, Rev. (1834–1889) 13/5/68
Bayly,
Ada Ellen, Miss (1857–1903), novelist 27/4/83 L
Francis Turner, Rev. (1774–) 11/9/25
John Bethune, lawyer 12/6/74
Montagu, Rev. 3/6/52
Bayne,
James 1/2/77
Thomas Vere, Rev. (1803–1848), Student of Christ Church 9/4/28
Thomas Vere, Rev. (1829–) 18/5/74
Baynes,
James 10/2/57 ?
Robert Hall, Rev. (1831–1895) 20/5/65
Robert Lambert, Adm. Sir (1796–1869) 21/8/61
Thomas Spencer, Prof. (1823–1887) 1/11/72
Bayning *see* Powlett
Bayonne, Mayor of 10/10/92
Bazeley, Francis Ley, Rev. (–1877) 12/5/52
Bazley, Thomas, Sir (1797–1885), liberal M.P. 13/3/60, 14/3/78
Beach,
Michael Edward Hicks, Sir (1837–1916), 9th Baronet (1854), 1st Viscount St. Aldwyn (1906), tory M.P. and cabinet minister 11/3/78, 18/4/81, 17/5/81, 25/7/81 n, 29/10/84, 31/10/84 c, 5/11/84, 31/5/85, 7/6/85, 21/7/85, 30/12/85, 10/9/86
Michael Hicks Hicks-, Sir (1809–1854), 8th Baronet (1834), tory M.P. 29/10/28
Beachcroft, Thomas 2/9/41
Beaconsfield *see* Disraeli
Beadel, Mrs., rescue 26/10/71
Beadon, Frederick Fleming, Rev. (1806–1880) 16/5/26 ?
Beal, James (1829–1891), London reformer and estate agent 22/9/68, 8/10/68, 3/12/72, 11/3/74
Beale,
A. 21/8/77
Dorothea, Miss (1831–1906), educationalist 26/12/84
Samuel (1803–1874), liberal M.P. 3/10/62
Beales, Edmond (1803–1881), barrister, President of the Reform League 28/7/66, 10/9/70, 27/1/74 L
Beamish,
Francis Bernard (1802–1868), liberal M.P. 1/3/62
Henry Hamilton, Rev. (1795–1870) 8/6/33
Bean, Messrs. 13/12/76
Beanlands, Charles, Rev. (1824–1898) 16/4/65 n
Beard,
Arthur, Rev. 3/7/87
Charles, Rev. (1827–1888), Unitarian 13/4/75, 23/8/84
Beare, Major, of the Reform Club 17/5/69
Bearn, rescue 4/5/55 ?
Bearne, George, tailor 12/7/45 ?
Beasley,
J. 12/1/74
John, of Althorp 8/11/73
William Cole (1816–1888), barrister 25/5/59
Beaston, C., supplicant 27/10/62
Beater, George P., architect in Dublin 10/11/77 ?
Beatley, Thomas Gage, Messrs., shipping owners 16/3/92
Beatrice, Princess 9/6/85 c, 15/6/85 n
Beattie,
Mr. 8/2/68
Henry, Rev. (–1867) 20/10/57
William, Dr. 31/12/40
Beatts, Mr. 11/3/80
Beauchamp *see* Lygon, Pyndar
Beauchamp, James, Rev. (–1891) 10/4/77
Beauclerk *see* Capell, Coventry, Hughan
Beauclerk,
Aubrey, 6th Duke of St Albans 5/4/32 n
Frances Maria, Lady 9/3/90
W., 8th Duke of St. Albans 1/2/31 n
William Amelius Aubrey de Vere (1840–1898), 10th Duke of St. Albans (1849) 17/12/68
Beaufort *see* Somerset
Beaufoy, Mark Hanbury (1854–1922), Kennington liberal M.P., liberal organiser 13/3/89
Beauharnais *see* Stephanie Louise Adrienne
Beauharnais, Eugène de (1781–1824), Viceroy of Italy (1805) 21/9/38
Beaulieu, Alcindor de, Baron, Belgian ambassador 25/2/69, 29/7/70 L, 11/8/70
Beaumont *see* Stapleton
Beaumont,
rescue 2/7/78
A. 1/12/60
Frederick Edward Blackett (1833–1899), liberal M.P. 21/6/76
G., Sir (–1827), 7th Baronet 17/5/36 n
George Howland Willoughby, Sir (1799–1845), 8th Baronet (1827) 17/5/36 n
Margaret, Lady (–1888) 1/3/71
Mary Anne, Lady, née Howley 17/5/36 n
Somerset Archibald (1835–1921), liberal M.P. 14/1/65
Wentworth Blackett (–1907), 1st Baron Allendale (1906), liberal M.P. 24/5/53

Beaumont (*cont.*)
  William Beresford, Rev. (-1901) 20/4/59
Beaupoil,
  Madame de, née du Roure, Comtesse de Sainte-Aulaire 14/11/43
  Louis de (1778-1854), Comte de Sainte-Aulaire, diplomat, writer 30/5/32
Beauregard, Pierre Gustave Toutant, Gen. (1818-1893), Confederate general 16/6/66
Beauvais, M. de, rescue? 14/6/67
Beauvale *see* Lamb
Beauvoir, Ludovic de, travel writer 10/6/60 ?
Beavan, James, of Saltney 1/4/57
Beaven,
  Alfred Beaven, Rev. 5/11/78
  James, Prof. 24/2/50
Beavis,
  E. 22/1/90
  J. R. 16/12/86
Bebbington,
  E. 23/7/79
  J. B. 23/5/67 ?
Becher,
  Elizabeth, Lady 11/8/71
  John Thomas, Rev. 24/1/44
Bechopoulo, Mr. 17/9/81
Beck,
  C. H., German publisher 14/11/75 n
  Edward Josselyn, Rev. (1832-1924) 18/1/66
  James, Rev. (1819-1896) 13/3/68
  J. R. 14/11/75 ?
  Thomas Snow, Dr., physician 12/9/75 ?
Becker,
  Mr. 23/2/90
  Emil, Dr., Victoria's advisor 30/9/63
  Lydia Ernestine 14/7/74
Becket,
  The Misses, sisters of Thomas Becket, draper 4/12/32
  Thomas, draper 4/12/32 n
Beckett,
  Mr., mining engineer 7/11/62
  C. A. 10/10/77
  William (1784-1863), tory M.P. 9/3/43
Beckford *see* Douglas, Seymer
Beckford, William (1759-1844), author 26/4/33 n
Beckhard, Mr. 24/10/77
Beckingsale, Mr. 21/3/87
Beckles, Edward Hyndman, Bp. (-1902) 29/3/91
Beckwith, John Charles, Col. (1789-1862) 6/3/32
Beddard, Frank E., zoologist 4/11/89
Beddoe, John, ornithologist 5/11/68 ?
Beddoes,
  J. 15/8/77
  James 11/5/89
Bedell, Elgwin, printer 2/7/59 ?
Bedford *see* Russell
Bedford,
  Messrs. 25/4/79
  Mrs. 24/1/44
  Henry, Rev. (1824-1906) 5/7/59 ?
Bedford Liberal Association 12/11/78
Bedhook, Mr. 14/4/87
Bedringfield, rescue 1/8/64, 25/11/64
Beebe, J. 8/1/87
Beeby *see* Swamy
Beeby, Robert, Rev. 9/1/80
Beecham, John, secretary of Wesleyan mission 9/3/37
Beechbrooke, Mr. 25/2/80
Beechend, Messrs. 4/7/76
Beecher, Henry Ward, Rev. (1831-1887), American anti-slaver and clergyman 28/6/86
Beecroft, George Skirrow (1809-1869), liberal M.P. 9/4/62
Beer, A. 6/2/80
Beere, Fanny Mary Bernard, Mrs., actress 4/11/85, 31/1/90
Beesley's livery stables 2/5/31
Beesly *see* Lucas
Beet,
  Mr., bookseller 8/3/82
  Mr., of London 18/12/71
Beetham, John Tidy, Rev. 14/2/45 ?
Beg, A., Rev. 14/8/68
Begbie,
  Mrs., attempted authoress 21/7/59, 10/5/64, 9/1/66, 12/1/66
  E. H. 20/11/91
  James, Dr., physician 18/10/50
Begg,
  James, Rev. (-1883), free church minister 11/7/49
  J. H. 14/4/89
Begnis, Giuseppe de (1793-1849), Italian singer 15/6/31
Béhic, Louis Henri Armand (1809-1891), French politician 1/9/65 n
Behr,
  Sig., Neapolitan liberal 29/2/52, 2/1/68
  H., Baron 24/5/77
Behrend, Henry, Dr., physician 1/10/90
Beighton, William, baker 5/9/34
Beilby, Miss 5/7/88
Beith,
  Gilbert (1827-1904), liberal M.P. 19/11/87
  John Alexander, Manchester liberal 8/10/83
  Robert, Dr., physician 5/4/48
Beke,
  Mrs. 12/12/76
  Charles Tilstone (-1874), explorer 11/5/49

Bekker,
A. Immanuel (1785–1871), German classicist 27/2/38 ?
Bertel Petersen (1797–1870), Danish teacher 27/2/38 ?
Belaney, Robert, Rev. (1804–1895), Jesuit 22/2/76 ?
Belasco, A. 15/4/90
Belcher,
Andrew H., Rev., of Fasque 30/6/74 n, 27/1/80, 5/9/85
E. A. C. 9/2/91
Mary M., née Bunting 9/2/77 n
Thomas Waugh, Rev. Dr. (1831–1910) 9/2/77, 6/9/81, 6/9/91
Beldam, Joseph 28/9/41
Belden, Josiah (1815–1892), of U.S.A. 2/5/68 ?
Belford, Mr. 11/3/74
Belgrave *see* Grosvenor
Belhaven *see* Hamilton
Belinfante & Blaauw, paper merchants 25/9/67
Bell *see* Thistlethwayte
Bell,
rescue 25/4/64, 5/8/67
Lady 16/12/75 ?
Andrew (1753–1832), educationalist 16/12/34
David, of Liverpool 11/7/56
E., rescue 16/8/83
E., Rev. 8/1/87
[Isaac] Lothian, Sir (1816–1904), 1st Baronet (1885), liberal M.P. 10/1/90
J. H., jounalist 19/11/76
John, Rev. (–1883) 27/7/77 ?
Kennedy, Rev. 29/6/88
Laura, Mrs., courtesan? 19/2/69 ?
M. R. C., of Leicester 2/3/44
R. H., Capt., father of Laura Thistlethwayte 10/12/64 n
Sydney Smith, Sir (1805–1879), judge 16/12/75 n
T. A. W. 11/3/91
William, correspondent 7/2/53
Bellairs,
Charles, Rev., of Buckley 30/10/61
Edmund Hooke Wilson, consul in Biarritz 16/1/94
Henry Walford, Rev. (1812–1900) 22/5/40, 9/9/73
Bellamy, Henry Thomas, government clerk 20/7/78 ?
Bell and Bradfute, Edinburgh publishers and booksellers 3/11/34
Bellasis, Edward, Serjeant (1800–1873), Roman Catholic lawyer 21/2/45
Belleroche, Edward 22/8/76
Bellew,
John Chippendall Montesquieu, Rev. Dr. (1806–1887) 11/6/68
Thomas Arthur Grattan (–1863), liberal M.P. 15/8/53
Bellewes, George, Rev. 23/6/77
Bellhouse, William, of Leeds 16/10/77
Belliard, Auguste-Daniel (1769–1832), French count, diplomat, general 6/2/32
Bellinger, Mrs. 23/4/77
Bellis,
(–1882), servant 15/1/57, 18/12/82
G., of Chester 8/6/76
Belmont, Perry, American congressman 9/7/87 n
Belmonte, Prince of, Keeper of Archives, Naples 5/2/51
Belmore *see* Corry
Belmore, Mrs., rescue 12/11/61
Belper *see* Strutt
Bembo, Salomon Pier Luigi, Count (1832–1882) 25/2/59
Bembury, H. 11/12/75
Ben Ali, Princess 28/2/78
Benard, Mons. 10/1/71
Benbow, John Henry, solicitor 12/4/49
Bencke,
Mr. 22/7/67
Albert H. 11/10/83 L
Bendall, J. L., Board of Trade clerk 19/11/78 ?
Bendan, David, Dr., of Dresden 14/3/76, 15/6/76
Bendle, James, secretary of Cumberland liberals 4/11/90
Benedict, Julius, Sir (1804–1885), musician 23/3/71
Benfield, S. 15/3/76
Benholme *see* Robertson
Benisch, Abraham, Dr. (1811–1874), editor of *Jewish Chronicle* 23/2/75, 22/7/76
Benison, H. W. 24/5/88
Benjamin *see* Motley
Benjamin,
Benjamin, London curiosity dealer 15/4/56, 13/4/57, 30/6/65
E. 2/5/87
Horace Bernton 29/7/79
Joseph 19/11/74
Judah Philip (1811–1884), barrister in U. K. and in Confederacy 24/10/65
Benn, W. E. 23/6/79
Bennet *see* Harris
Bennet,
rescue 9/11/60
Charles, Lord Ossulston (1822), 7th Earl of Tankerville (1859) 27/5/43
George, solicitor 3/11/51

Bennet (*cont.*)
Henry, Dr., physician 23/6/58
James, Rev., congregationalist minister 11/7/46
Philip (1795–1866), tory M.P. 14/3/57
Bennett *see* Church
Bennett,
rescue 12/11/73, 30/7/75, 20/6/78
Alfred William, botanist 24/6/67
Anne Ramsden, Mrs. (1817–1906), née Gladstone, G's cousin and co-translator 13/9/27, 19/4/60, 5/12/61, 5/1/64, 11/1/64, 30/9/67, 11/4/71 n, 8/6/71 L, 17/11/78
C. E., Hawarden post master 16/12/60
C. E., Miss, rescue 7/1/61, 25/1/61
Dorothy 30/9/67
George Peter, Rev. 3/11/51 ?
George W., author 9/7/67 ?
Henry, Rev. (1795–1874) 29/4/32 ?
Hugh, Rev. (–1860) 6/5/58
John (1773–1852), tory M.P. 21/2/33
John, Sir (1814–1897), Knight (1872) 12/9/76
John G., of Liverpool 11/4/71
John Marsland (1817–1889), of Manchester 30/9/63
Joseph (1829–1908), liberal M.P. 10/2/90
T. J. Wesley 4/2/90
V., rescue 14/5/78
William Cox, Dr. (1820–1895), of Greenwich 11/1/71 L
William James Early 28/1/40 ?
William Sterndale, Sir (1816–1875), musician 5/3/69
W. W. 18/1/68
Benning, W. 19/3/77
Bennion,
rescue 17/9/80
Mrs. 19/9/66
John, Chester tailor 1/10/49 ?
William, Hawarden grocer 25/1/56
Bennock,
E., Miss 10/9/45
J. 9/4/80
Benrath, Karl, Dr. (1845–1924), historian 3/1/77
Benson *see* Pendleton
Benson,
Charles Maunsell, Rev. 11/11/77
Christopher (–1845), Master of the Temple 9/4/45 n
Christopher, Rev. (1789–1868) 26/4/35
Edward Frederic (1867–1940), author 31/10/91
Edward White, Abp. (1829–1896) 9/7/71, 3/9/82 ff, 9/12/82, 11/12/82, 19/3/83 L, 2/4/83, 24/4/83, 30/6/83, 11/1/84 L, 20/4/84 L, 12/5/84 L, 2/7/84 L, 9/7/84 L, 9/1/85 L, 3/7/85, 24/4/86, 13/7/87, 18/7/87, 25/5/89, 11/6/90, 9/4/92, 3/5/92, 17/5/92, 8/12/92 L, 9/12/92 L, 25/4/93 L, 23/1/94 n, 20/10/94
Mary, née Sidgwick 15/11/74
Mary Eleanor, Mrs., author 29/11/91
Bensusan, Manuel, stock broker 21/6/75
Bent,
James Theodore, archaeologist 6/12/89
John, Sir, of Liverpool 29/7/46
Thomas 16/3/68
Bentinck *see* Denison, Sykes
Bentinck,
Adolphe von, Baron (–1868), Dutch Ambassador 26/4/53
W. H. Cavendish-, 3rd Duke of Portland 8/3/36 n
William Cavendish-, Lord (1774–1839), British minister to Sicily 15/10/38 n
William George Frederic Cavendish-, Lord (1802–1848), tory M.P. 23/12/37, 10/7/46, 5/8/46, 24/8/46, 17/9/46, 26/9/46, 26/10/46, 28/1/85, 4/10/92 n
Bentley,
rescue 9/2/91
Miss 19/2/89
George (1828–1895), publisher 2/1/79
Jonathan, of Dewsbury 21/8/68
Richard (1794–1871), publisher 1/8/50
Samuel, Rev. (1823–1908) 18/11/75
Bentrow, Mr. 12/3/68 ?
Benucci, Sig. 6/1/88
Benvenuti, Pietro (1796–1844), director of Academia Reale, Florence (1803) 23/3/32
Benwell,
Elizabeth, schoolmistress 5/8/25
Thomas, coalmerchant in Oxford 25/7/31 ?
Ber, Mr., artist 30/1/87, 31/1/87
Berardi, Giuseppi, Monsignor, of Rome 13/10/66
Bere,
Mr., of Hawarden 24/8/88
Montagu (1824–1887), Recorder 11/8/57
Beredin, A. 11/12/88
Beresford,
Anne, Lady (–1841) 15/6/37
Charles William De La Poer, Lord (1846–1919), tory M.P., sailor 21/5/88
Christiana (–1905), Lady Waterford 12/7/53, 27/5/92
Francis Marcus, Col. (1818–1890), tory M.P. 23/2/72
George de la Poer, 1st Marquis of Waterford 30/5/36 n
George de la Poer, Sir (1811–1873), 2nd Baronet (1844), tory M.P. 22/2/42

Henry de la Poer (–1859), 3rd Marquis of Waterford (1826) 7/7/53 n
John George de la Poer, Abp. Lord (1773–1862), archbishop of Dublin, Primate of all Ireland 30/5/36
Louisa, Lady (–1851), née Beresford 6/3/39
Louisa de la Poer, Lady, née Stuart, Lady Waterford 13/2/36 n, 7/7/53, 26/9/76
Marcus, Capt., tory M.P. 15/6/26
Marcus Gervais, Abp. (1801–1885), archbishop of Armagh 20/8/64
W., Abp., 1st Baron Decies, archbishop of Tuam 6/3/39 n
William Carr (1768–1854), 1st Viscount Beresford (1823) 6/3/39 n
Berettas, Ioannes Philip, Ionian author 22/12/58
Berg, Louis, of Liverpool 8/8/78
Bergami, Bartolomeo (–1845), Queen Caroline's chamberlain 6/7/32
Bergendahl, Miss 15/3/87
Bergne, John Brodribb (1800–1873), Foreign Office treaty superintendent 12/1/60
Beridge *see* Boothby
Berkeley *see* Feilding, Fitzroy
Berkeley,
rescue 10/6/54
Craven Fitzhardinge (1805–1855), liberal M.P. 25/6/53
Francis Henry Fitzhardinge (1784–1870), liberal M.P. 31/3/43
George Campion, Rev. 4/1/53
George Charles Grantley Fitzhardinge (1800–1881), tory M.P., author 14/1/46, 9/5/46
George Cranfield, Sir 31/5/52 n
Grenville Charles Lennox (1806–1896), liberal M.P. 23/12/53
L., Rev. 24/6/79
Maurice Frederick Fitzhardinge (1788–1867), 1st Baron Fitzhardinge (1861) 14/9/65
Bermingham *see* Caulfeild
Bernacs, M. 21/12/60
Bernal *see* Osborne
Bernal, Ralph (–1854), whig M.P. 24/5/33
Bernard,
rescue 6/2/91
Charles Broderick, Bp. (1811–1890), bishop of Tuam 2/12/29
Francis (1810–1877), 3rd Earl of Bandon (1856), styled Viscount Bernard, tory M.P. 23/7/27, 22/5/68
Mountague, Prof. (1820–1882), lawyer 17/6/52, 24/9/80 n
Thomas Dehany, Rev. 13/5/77
William, Hull liberal 15/5/79
Bernays,
Adolphus 25/4/44
Leopold John, Rev. Dr. 25/9/70
Bernetti, Thomasso (1779–1852), Vatican secretary of state 20/4/32
Bernhard, Duke of Saxe-Meiningen 3/2/93
Bernhardt, Sarah, Miss (1845–1923), actress 23/6/79, 17/10/79, 9/6/80, 28/7/87
Bernoux *see* Perronnet
Bernstorff,
Albrecht von, Baron (1809–1873), Prussian ambassador 25/2/56, 29/2/60, 22/7/70 L, 18/8/70 L, 25/9/70, 27/9/70, 30/9/70 c, 1/4/71, 14/7/71, 20/4/72, 27/3/73
Anna von, Countess (–1893) 30/6/57, 23/1/58
Bernt, Rev. Mr. 4/1/90
Berra, J. W. 16/12/86
Berraios, Anastasios, of Greece 3/10/88
Berry *see* Bourbon
Berry,
Mrs. 5/5/49
Charles Albert, Rev. (1842–1897), minister in Wolverhampton 8/11/88
Graham 20/8/77
Joseph Walter, Rev. 14/8/47
M. A., rescue 20/12/71
Berryer, Antoine Pierre (1790–1868), French advocate 8/11/64
Berryman, R. 17/9/77
Bert *see* Bonjour
Bert, Pierre, Pastor of La Tour 6/3/32
Berth, Mr. 27/1/79
Berthomier, Mons., French tutor at Eton 17/9/25, 2/2/26, 22/7/26, 29/7/26, 31/3/27, 7/5/27, 18/5/27, 6/6/27
Berti, Domenico, author 6/7/88
Bertie *see* Bickersteth, Schreiber
Bertie,
G. A. V. 9/12/65 n
Harriet Blanche Elizabeth (–1923), née Farquhar 9/12/65
Henry, fellow of All Souls 7/2/90
Montagu, Lord Norreys, 6th Earl of Abingdon 16/4/43 n
Bertram,
rescue 27/1/56
Mr., conjuror 6/5/85
Robert Aitkin, author 2/5/77 ?
Robert Aitkin, Rev. 27/5/88
William, of Edinburgh 13/3/80
Bertrand, Alexandre, Homeric author 1/5/60
Berwick *see* Hill
Berwick, Edward (–1877), President of Galway college 20/4/53
Besant, Annie, Mrs. (1847–1933), author 24/11/76 n, 25/11/76
Bessborough *see* Ponsonby
Best,
J. H., Rev., missionary 24/8/60 ?

Best (*cont.*)
John (1821–1865), barrister, tory M.P. 27/5/52
T. 25/7/76
William Draper, Sir (1767–1845), 1st Baron Wynford (1829), judge 3/10/31
William Edward, Rev. (–1906) 19/12/79
William Samuel (1798–1869), 2nd Baron Wynford (1845), tory M.P. 21/3/57
Bet, George 1/11/76
Bethell,
Christopher, Bp. (1773–1859) 31/7/25
Ellinor Mary, née Abraham, Lady Westbury 3/7/65 n
George (1779–1857), vice provost of Eton College 27/11/25
Richard, Sir (1800–1873), Knight (1853), 1st Baron Westbury (1861), liberal M.P., Lord Chancellor 15/2/53, 1/7/65, 3/7/65, 5/7/65
Bethmann, D., Dr., translator 14/6/60
Bethune,
Alice Margaret 27/6/33
Gilbert 27/6/33 n
John Elliot Drinkwater (–1851), counsel to Home Office 27/11/43, 27/7/44
John Trotter, Sir (1827–1894), 10th Earl of Lindsay (1851) 29/6/60
Bett, John 30/1/77 ?
Bettany,
George Thomas 10/12/74
J. 20/9/86
Bettridge, William Craddock, Rev. (1791–1879) 5/5/37
Betts,
J. D. 19/6/77
John Thomas, distiller 9/3/55 ?
J. P. 28/8/77
Thomas & Co., brandy distillers 23/2/60
Beust, Friedrich Ferdinand, Baron (1809–1886), Saxon minister 18/6/64
Bevan, W. L., Rev., Welsh author and propagandist 13/5/83 L
Beveridge, James, of Glasgow 8/3/80, 10/12/86
Beverley *see* Percy
Bevington,
Mr., of Hawarden 17/5/83
Mrs., of Hawarden 21/1/82
Bewes, W. A. 17/8/89
Bewick, Mrs. 31/12/78
Bewsher, William Robert, Rev. 16/11/41 ?
Bexley *see* Vansittart
Bhandane, P. F. 21/2/79
Bhumgara, P. 31/8/89
Bianca, F., Mlle. 18/2/79, 6/3/79
Bianchi,
Cav., of London? 5/6/62 ?
Dr. 13/9/79 n
Marchesa 17/6/84
Bibby,
Mrs. 9/5/56
Isaac Henry, Rev. 30/10/76 ?
Thomas (–1863), scholar 29/3/49
Biber, George Edward, Rev. (–1874) 8/3/52
Bickers, Henry, bookseller 23/1/41
Bickers and Bush, booksellers 23/1/41 n
Bickersteth,
Edward, Ven. (1814–1892), archdeacon and dean 21/4/56
Edward Henry, Bp. (1825–1906) 7/12/74
Lavinia Louisa, née Bertie 16/4/43 n
Robert, surgeon 17/9/27
Robert (1847–1923), liberal unionist M.P. 16/4/43 n
Bickerton, Alderman 16/9/76
Bickford, J., Rev. 26/2/79
Bickle, rescue 19/11/60
Bickley,
Mr. 30/7/79
Samuel, Lloyd's broker 15/2/54 ?
Bicknell, Walter L. 17/8/78
Biddescombe, Mrs. 29/5/70
Biddulph,
John, Maj. (1840–1921) 15/12/83
Mary Frederica, Lady 2/10/71
Robert Myddelton (1805–1872), liberal M.P. 13/12/59
Thomas Myddelton, Gen. Sir (1809–1878), Master of Queen's Household 29/3/66, 10/7/71, 10/8/71, 8/7/78
Bidwell, John (–1870) 31/7/61 n
Bienaimé, Luigi (1795–1878), Italian sculptor 29/12/38
Bierle, L. 22/8/87
Biese,
Alfred, Dr., of Kiel 25/3/87
Mary Elinor, née Gladstone 25/3/87 n
Bigelow, John (1817–1911) 23/7/70
Bigg,
Edward Smith, solicitor 9/5/43
William Robert (1804–), barrister 17/7/37 ?
Biggar, Joseph Gillis (1828–1890), home rule M.P. 17/8/82, 24/12/82, 3/2/83
Bigge, Arthur John, Sir (1849–1931), 1st Baron Stamfordham, Queen's (assistant) secretary 29/9/83, 9/8/84, 11/10/90
Biggs, Louis Coutier, Rev. 16/1/65
Bigland, Ernest, merchant 15/7/90 ?
Bignold, Samuel Frederick, Rev. (1820–1873) 22/6/59
Bigsby, John, Dr., physician 13/8/36
Bikelas, D. (1833–1909), Greek trader in London; translator of Shakespeare 19/9/76
Bilia, Sig. 14/1/89
Bilio, Cardinal 30/4/67 ff

Bilkeley, O. T. 20/1/91
Billard, M. 28/3/89
Billemi, Luigi, singing master, Naples 30/4/32
Billing, Miss 1/12/86
Billingham, Mr. 19/6/79
Bills, J. 19/7/77
Billson,
A., Mrs. 24/10/68
Alfred (1839–1907), secretary of Lancashire liberal association 10/12/67
Billyard, William Whalley, Australian judge 14/3/46
Bilson, David, bookkeeper, Newark 24/1/35
Binducci, Sig., actor 1/7/61
Binger, James Owen, manager of Chester Holyhead railway 1/9/52
Bingham,
Charles George (1800–1888), 3rd Earl of Lucan (1839), soldier 6/11/61
William, Senator, of Philadelphia 10/5/36 n
William Philip Strong, Rev. 15/3/75 ?
Bingley,
Henry, assayer 17/11/41, 29/3/43
P. J., of Paris 26/9/66
Binks, L. J. 21/8/91
Binney, Hibbert, Rev. (–1887), bishop of Nova Scotia 8/4/52
Binns,
Miss 14/10/78
H. 29/5/77
J. A., of Bradford 13/8/73
Biograph, editor of 28/1/79
Birch,
Mr. 3/6/39
Frederick, Rev. (–1859) 17/10/56
Henry Mildred, Rev. (–1884) 8/11/52 ?
Samuel, Dr. (1813–1885), egyptologist 16/5/68
Thomas, liberal L. C. C. candidate 13/1/89
Thomas Jacob, Judge (1806–1868) 16/3/59
William Faulkner 29/7/68
Birchell, C. 28/10/87
Bird,
Miss 9/5/78
A., Rev. 28/2/77
James 14/6/79
James Waller, Rev. (1809–1876) 7/3/45
L. J. K., War Office 21/2/57 ?
Nehemiah, Liverpool merchant 18/8/29
Robert James, Rev. 8/5/80 ?
Samuel William Elderfield, Rev. 25/5/68
Birdsall, Mr. 7/1/80
Birdwood, George Christopher Molesworth, Sir (1832–1917) 2/11/80
Birinna, Sig. 3/1/88
Birkbeck,
Edward, Sir (1838–1907), 1st Baronet (1886), tory M.P. 23/5/83, 5/7/83, 24/11/83
H., East Anglian liberal 16/5/90
R. 30/11/88
Birkett, Capt. 17/7/88
Birks,
Mrs., neighbour in 71 Harley Street 25/10/76, 28/10/76, 17/4/77, 1/2/78, 5/2/78, 22/3/78, 16/10/78, 19/10/78, 5/5/79 ff, 13/9/79, 14/9/79, 28/10/79, 4/5/80, 26/6/80 L, 30/9/80, 13/11/80, 28/10/82, 1/1/84, 23/11/84, 14/7/85, 4/7/87
Edward Bickersteth, Rev. 5/9/87
Birkwyn, Mr. 18/10/90
Birley,
rescue 24/1/74
John Shepherd, Rev. (–1883) 8/2/50 ?
William, Rev. 9/12/47 ?
Birmear, T. H. 22/10/74
Birmingham,
Dr. 15/8/78
Mr., of Dover 28/7/32
Birnam, Mr. 10/12/74
Birrell,
Augustine (1850–1933), liberal M.P. 10/4/90
Eleanor, née Locker, formerly Mrs. L. Tennyson 28/2/78
Biscamp, E., Dr. 11/12/78
Biscoe,
Frederick, Rev. (1808–1880) 23/1/28
Robert, Rev. 22/1/28
William Archibald (1811–) 24/12/29
Bisgood, J. J., Eighty Club member 11/6/92
Bishop,
Miss, governess 30/12/63, 9/1/64
Mrs. 11/10/86
Mrs., rescue 12/7/76
J. 26/1/78
John, Rev. (–1838) 14/9/28
M., rescue 15/8/53, 25/4/61
Robert, Newark maltster 2/8/34
William James, Liverpool artist 29/2/68 ?
Bisi, Alexander Calichiopulo 4/12/58
Bismarck,
N. H. F. Herbert von (1849–1904) 2/6/69, 3/8/82 c, 5/3/85, 7/3/85 c, 7/11/85
Otto Eduard Leopold von, Prince 18/8/70
Wilhelm Otto Albrecht von, Count (1852–1901) 2/6/69, 20/7/85
Bissell, J. Broad, liberal candidate 12/11/85
Bisset,
A., author 26/1/86
Charles, Rev. 15/5/47
Bisshopp *see* Maude
Bisson, Frederick Shirley De Carteret, Capt. 5/3/80
Bittleston, Adam, Sir 13/11/40 ?
Blachford *see* Rogers

Black,
Adam (1784–1874), liberal M.P. 10/6/56
A. H., Rev. 25/6/75
D. 22/5/55
James Frederick, Rev., school master 16/3/49 ?
Patrick, Dr. (–1879), physician 24/5/50
Raymond Charles, Rev. 4/4/90 ?
William George, of Glasgow 8/3/78
Blackadder & Co., booksellers 20/6/56
Blackburn,
Messrs. 26/1/76
Messrs. 5/2/87
Mr. 3/4/71
Bewicke 18/12/77
Peter (1811–1870), tory M.P. 7/5/55
Blackburne,
Henry Ireland, Rev. (1826–) 5/7/59
John George, Maj., of Blackburn 17/12/67
John Ireland (1783–1874), tory M.P. 6/5/37
John Ireland, Col. (1817–1893), tory M.P. 21/11/68
Blackett,
Edward, Sir (1805–1885), 6th Baronet 16/5/26
John Fenwick Burgoyne (1821–1856), liberal M.P. 7/4/52
Blackhorn, Mr. 2/4/78
Blackie,
John (1806–1873), publisher, Lord Provost of Glasgow 23/10/65, 31/10/65, 22/1/66 n
John Stuart, Prof. (1809–1895), Professor in Edinburgh (1852), author 13/12/59, 4/1/73 L, 18/10/83, 15/1/85, 30/11/86
Walter Graham, publisher 17/4/80
Blackledge, J. Ernest, Rev. 6/10/88
Blacklock, William James, artist 26/6/47 ?
Blackmore, Mr. 14/6/78
Blackshaw, rescue 9/8/67
Blackstone,
Frederick Charles, Rev. (1795–) 23/11/28
Jane Martha, Miss 31/3/54
William, Prof. Sir (1723–1780), jurist 11/11/28 n
William Seymour (1809–1881), tory M.P. 11/11/28
Blackwell,
L. 19/6/78
Robert Edward, Rev. (1804–1878) 1/3/38
S. H., Lord Ward's agent 8/7/48
William Whitehead, Rev. (1805–1866) 3/2/37, 5/1/44
Blackwood *see* Neville
Blackwood,
Messrs., publishers of the *Gladstone Almanack* 31/12/84 L
A. 9/12/74
Eliza, Mrs. (–1860), née Dupré 5/12/54
Frederick Temple Hamilton- (1826–1902), 1st Earl of Dufferin (1871), 1st Marquis of Dufferin and Ava (1888), Baron Dufferin 31/5/60, 20/12/61, 21/12/61, 8/7/66, 11/10/69, 13/10/69 L, 3/11/69 L, 13/11/69 L, 18/3/80 L, 2/11/80 ff, 12/12/80 L, 29/7/82 c, 3/8/82 c, 31/8/82, 3/11/82, 25/4/83, 6/7/83, 3/8/83 L, 7/8/84, 3/10/84, 4/3/85, 20/3/85, 27/3/85 c, 30/12/88, 11/1/89, 8/2/89, 29/5/89, 6/10/92, 21/12/92, 23/2/93 c, 20/7/93 c, 27/7/93, 11/9/93, 10/12/93
John (–1879), editor 6/6/54
Price Frederick, Capt. 27/7/89 ?
V., Miss 11/9/78
William, publisher 18/11/33
Blades,
Rowland Hill (1826–1898), printer 26/2/80
William (1824–1890), printer 29/6/77
Blagg,
Mr. 29/10/85
J. W. 13/11/88
Blagrove, Mr. 13/5/79
Blaikie, William Garden, Rev. Prof. (1820–1899), Professor of theology, Edinburgh (1868) 16/3/75, 18/10/88
Blaine, James Gillespie (1830–1893), American Secretary of State 1889-92, protectionist 6/10/87
Blair,
Dr. 26/11/39
Edward Stopford (–1885) 10/11/79 ?
Eliza, née Norris 24/4/32
Forbes Cromartie Hunter 4/11/79
Henry Martin, F. R. G. S. 7/8/78
James F., architect 28/10/68
J. Hunter, né Hunter, friend of Burns 2/4/32 n
John 23/5/90
L. S. 7/8/91
O. P. 20/5/89
Robert Hugh, Rev. 4/7/76 ?
Thomas Hunter, Col., retired (1831) 2/4/32
Thomas Richard Arthur, Rev. (1802–1867) 31/3/38 ff, 3/4/38
William, Dr., physician 29/12/79 ?
William Fordyce, railway director 1/3/51
Blaisdell, J., Rev. 23/9/89
Blake,
rescue 5/5/71, 27/5/73
Mrs. 3/9/76
Anthony Richard, Dublin lawyer 13/4/37 n
Charles Carter, Dr. 9/7/79
Edward (1833–1912), Canadian politician, home rule M.P. 21/1/93, 15/2/93 n, 24/4/93, 11/5/93, 1/9/93, 2/9/93 L, 14/10/93 L

Francis, Sir (1774–1860), 3rd Baronet, whig M.P. 15/6/26
H. A., Mrs. 13/12/80
Henry Wollaston (1815–1899), director of the Bank of England 26/1/81
J. L., Rev. 27/2/78
John Aloysius (1826–1887), liberal M.P. 11/3/65
John Henry (–1882), of Ireland 29/6/82
Martin Joseph (–1861), liberal M.P. 15/8/53
Orme, Mr. 4/4/87 ?
P. J. 12/3/75
R. J., Rev. 19/10/76
R. T., Rev. 27/4/78
Sophia Louisa Jex-, Dr. (1840–1912), physician 21/7/77
Thomas (1825–1901), liberal M.P. 25/11/85
William, Rev. (–1905) 18/12/64 n
Blakemore,
Richard, tory M.P. 2/6/44
Thomas William Booker (–1858), tory M.P. 16/3/54
Blakesley, Joseph Williams, Dean (1808–1885) 16/12/31, 21/11/61, 26/6/67, 29/12/68, 23/1/94
Blakey,
James 22/4/80
Robert (1795–1878), journalist 4/1/54
Blakiston, Charles Dendy, Rev. 26/2/80 ?
Blamire, William (–1862), tithe commissioner 14/11/53
Blanch and sons, W. H. 30/8/77
Blanchard, Jonathan (1811–1892), of U.S.A. 8/8/67
Blanco *see* White
Bland, S., Miss 29/12/85
Blandford *see* Churchill
Blantyre *see* Stuart
Blarke, B., autograph hunter 2/1/77
Blathwayt, Mr. 16/11/91
Blayney, Cadwallader Davis (1802–1874), 12th Baron Blayney (1834) 9/1/55
Bleck, Henry, importer 10/1/80 ?
Blenkinsopp, Edward Clennell Leaton, Rev. 26/5/76
Blennerhassett,
Charlotte, Lady 12/10/79, 13/10/79, 27/3/83
Rowland, Sir (1839–1909), 4th Baronet, liberal M.P. 17/12/70, 19/11/72 L, 10/2/73, 15/2/73 c, 11/3/73, 23/5/73, 9/11/74, 17/9/81 L, 10/3/82, 26/3/83, 27/3/83
Bles, Mlle., rescue 21/12/86
Blewitt, Octavian, author 25/4/40, 7/4/41
Bligh,
Edward Veysey, Rev. (1829–1924) 26/10/69
John, Rev. (–1876), headmaster 22/9/59
John Stuart (1827–1896), 6th Earl of Darnley (1835) 3/10/72
Sophia, née Eversfield 4/9/46
Blind, Mathilde, Miss, poet 16/10/89
Bliss,
James, Rev. (1808–1894) 27/5/68 ?
Philip, Rev. (–1857), antiquary, university administrator 19/3/42, 19/4/49
Blissard, William, Rev. 11/10/91
Block, J. N. 29/2/76
Blogg, Henry Birdwood, Rev. 9/6/92
Blomefield, Robert Allan, Rev. (–1877) 13/7/67 ?
Blomfield,
Major 31/12/74
Mr. 29/9/77
Arthur, Rev. 8/2/63
Charles James, Bp. (1786–1857), bishop of London (1828), bishop of Chester 4/1/28, 24/4/32, 28/3/35, 1/3/38, 8/3/38, 14/3/38, 14/2/40, 24/3/40, 31/5/40, 30/7/40, 5/11/41, 17/11/43, 25/11/43, 2/12/43, 6/12/43, 27/7/44, 29/7/44, 6/5/49, 14/9/49, 8/2/50, 16/3/50 ff, 26/3/50, 16/7/50, 5/2/52, 12/11/54
G. B., Mrs. 13/12/61
George Becher, Rev. Canon (–1885) 14/9/49, 7/7/53
Henry J., Cmdr. 2/1/59
Blondin (1824–1897), tightrope walker 24/7/61
Blood, F. 3/1/79
Bloom,
Mr. 28/3/78
John Hague, Rev. (1805–1873) 4/8/59
Bloomfield, J. A. D. (1802–1879), 2nd Baron Bloomfield (Irish peerage) (1846), Baron Bloomfield (British peerage) (1871) 25/3/45
Blount, Walter Aston Edward (1807–1894), Herald 15/3/71 ?
Blowitz, Henri George S. A. Opper de (1832–1903), journalist 4/6/80
Blumenthal, Mr., of Venice 1/10/79
Blum Pasha 21/6/84
Blundell *see* Stonor, Tempest
Blundell,
Benson, barrister 21/7/56
Charles Joseph Weld- (1845–1927) 22/10/89 n
Charles Robert (1761–1837) 9/8/25
Henry, collector 9/8/25 n
John (1824–1896), of Chorley 23/1/55
Thomas Joseph Weld- (1808–1887) 15/1/39 n, 16/9/65, 20/9/65, 8/9/68, 28/3/71 L
Blunson, Messrs. 30/4/91

Blunt,
Anne, Lady (1837-1917), Arabist and author 13/2/88 n, 10/3/88, 28/5/89
Henry, Rev. (1794-1843), writer, preacher 20/3/34
John Henry, Rev. (1823-1884) 7/3/68, 30/11/72 n
John James, Prof. 24/11/41
Richard Lefevre, Ven. (1833-1910) 11/9/81
Samuel Jasper, colonial office clerk 21/4/46
Wilfrid Scawen (1840-1922), radical and writer 14/9/80, 20/1/82 L, 22/3/82, 16/6/83 n, 28/9/83, 25/2/84 c, 5/9/85, 29/9/85, 22/12/87, 13/2/88, 10/3/88
Willis 1/10/87
Blyden, Edward Wilmot, Liberian statesman assisted by G 16/6/60, 8/7/78
Blyffil, Mr., of Oak Farm 24/1/48
Blyth,
Benjamin Hall (1849-1917), Edinburgh engineer 12/4/80
George Francis Popham, Bp. (-1914) 26/11/88
Boardman, E., of Dumfries 6/2/75
Boase, Francis, of Penzance 7/9/67
Bobrinsky, Leo, Count 19/5/63
Bock, Carl 30/6/80
Bockett,
Mr. 30/8/77
Daniel Smith, solicitor to law life ass. soc. 24/9/49
Boddy, J. H. 26/11/87
Bode,
Baron de, French emigré 3/7/28 n
Clement de, Baron 20/6/54, 4/6/61
John Ernest, Rev. (1816-1874), don 13/8/28, 26/2/73
W. 14/8/28 n
Bodkin,
Christopher, of Dublin 16/10/78 ?
Mathias McDonnell (1850-1933) 26/1/90
William Henry, Sir (-1874), Knight (1869), barrister 15/6/53
Bodley,
John Edward Courtney (1853-1925), Dilke's secretary, author 17/10/90
Thomas, secretary to bishop of London's fund 19/1/65
Body,
Elihu Edmund, Rev. 1/11/69 ?
G., Rev. 18/5/70
Boehm, Joseph Edgar, Sir (1834-1890), 1st Baronet (1889), sculptor 25/11/79, 2/2/81 n, 10/5/81, 12/3/85, 3/12/90 ?
Bogindollo, John Gladstone's factor 18/10/37
Bogle *see* Praed
Bogle,
George 13/6/36 n
W. R. 15/8/91
Bogue, David (-1856), bookseller 15/12/52
Boguschevsky, Nicholas De, Baron 28/9/88
Bogy, J. S. 9/7/77
Bohn, Henry George (1796-1884), publisher 14/7/55, 29/4/59, 3/12/73
Boïelle, James, French author 17/3/76, 21/5/87
Boileau, John Peter, Sir 18/11/38 n
Boinville, A. de, French theologian? 2/7/55
Boissevain, Gideon Maria, Dutch economist 11/2/91
Bojanowski, Paul S. A.von 13/9/89 ?
Bok, W. E., of the Transvaal 5/3/81
Bokkell, Mr. 30/8/88
Bolam, C. 7/12/78
Bölckow, Henry William Ferdinand (1806-1878), liberal M.P. 10/7/67
Bold, Hugh, Rev. (1798-1883) 15/4/27
Bold & Co., Liverpool ship owners 20/4/49
Bolden, Samuel Edward (1812-1880), secretary to railway company 15/10/53
Boldero,
Henry George (1797-1873), tory M.P. 26/3/38
Henry Kearney, Rev. (-1900) 30/3/78 ?
Boldero & Forster, printers 20/2/78
Boler, William, Newark merchant 2/8/34
Boles, Richard Henry, Rev. 8/8/90
Bolitho,
Thomas Bedford (1835-1915), liberal unionist M.P. 9/7/89
Thomas Simon (1808-1887), banker 5/7/83
Bolleroy *see* Slade
Bolleroy, E. 5/9/42 n
Boller & Stewart 1/1/87
Bologna, Becca delli, Prince, Prince Camporeale 22/1/64
Bolter, Mrs. 23/4/56
Bolton,
Mrs., rescue 4/4/82, 3/1/84, 19/10/86, 11/5/87, 5/10/87, 23/10/88, 23/11/89, 10/2/91, 31/1/94
Albert John, architect 20/3/78
C. 22/11/79
George, Crown solicitor, Tipperary 23/7/84
J., Mrs. 15/1/27
John, Liverpool West Indian merchant 20/12/26
Thomas Henry (1841-1916), liberal unionist M.P. 23/8/93
William, of Birmingham 10/10/60
Bolton Republican Club 5/8/71
Bombelli, G., Italian artist 8/12/38 n
Bona, Signor 12/5/93
Bonanni, Giuseppe, of Sicily 29/10/38
Bonaparte,
Charles Lucien, Prince (1803-1857), Prince of Canino and Masignano 8/4/32

Louis-Lucien, Prince (1813-1891) 12/11/73, 7/6/75, 26/6/78, 10/7/78
Lucien, Prince 7/4/32 n
Napoleon E. L. J. J., Prince (1856-1879) 6/11/74, 19/6/80 c, 10/7/80 c, 16/7/80
Bonar, Horatius, Rev. (1808-1889), presbyterian minister 13/3/43 ?
Bond,
Charles, bookseller 18/4/48 ?
Edward Augustus, Sir (1856-1918), of British Museum 2/5/81 L, 2/11/82, 5/2/91, 6/2/91, 29/11/93, 22/12/93, 7/3/94 ?
John, Rev. 24/5/78 ?
W. J. 28/8/79
Bone, Henry Pierce (1779-1856), artist 31/3/48 ?
Bonelli, Italian sculptor 1/10/38
Bonesi, Mrs., nurse 7/1/51
Bonghi, Ruggiero (1826-1895) 4/10/79, 14/3/80, 22/1/88 n
Bonham,
Lieut. 13/11/60
Miss (-1863) 14/10/60
Francis Robert (1785-1863), tory M.P. 23/10/35, 24/5/47, 18/3/52, 14/4/52, 10/5/52, 30/6/52, 30/7/52, 14/12/52, 1/1/53, 18/7/53, 4/8/53, 16/8/53, 26/10/53, 26/12/53, 25/11/55, 28/11/55, 20/1/56, 22/5/56, 27/5/56, 28/2/57, 2/3/57, 7/3/57, 21/3/57, 13/4/57, 11/8/57, 20/5/59, 30/6/59, 22/4/60, 15/10/60, 25/4/63, 26/4/63, 2/5/63
T. 14/10/63
Bonheur, Rosa (1822-1899), artist 30/4/57
Boniface, Abp. 10/5/84
Boning and Small, Messrs. 30/3/91
Bonington, Richard Parkes, artist 17/2/43 n
Bonjour,
Mlle. 6/3/32
Mme., née Bert 6/3/32
Rev. Mons., minister to the Vaudois, Switzerland 4/3/32, 6/3/32
Bonner, of Belfast 27/4/38
Bonnor,
C. M. 28/12/89
Richard Bonnnor Maurice, Ven. (1803-1889), dean of St. Asaph 1859-86 6/11/61
Bonsall, C., of London 19/2/58
Bonser, James Armitage, Rev. 19/11/81
Bonsil, Mrs. 29/6/78
Bonsor, Joseph, brewer 5/12/25
Bonwell, Dr. 28/8/89
Bony, F., Rev. 27/6/78
Boode *see* Cust
Boodle,
Adolphus, Rev. 3/4/41 ?
J., conveyancer 17/3/55
William, solicitor 3/7/65 ?
Boodle & Partington, conveyancers 17/3/55, 27/6/68
Book, Mr., of Blackheath 27/1/75
Bookseller, Marseilles 24/1/39
Bookseller, Milan 9/7/32
Boone, James S., Rev. 15/5/47
Boord, Thomas White, Sir (1838-1912), 1st Baronet (1896), distiller, tory M.P. 3/2/74
Boore, William Charles, banker 18/3/65
Boos, Martin, Rev. (1762-1825), Bavarian priest in Rome 17/12/38
Boot, W. O. 16/8/90
Booth,
Benjamin Blaydes Haworth-, Col. (1823-1901) 18/7/58
C. E., Mrs., assistance 28/4/61
C. F. 15/5/78
Charles (1840-1916), ship-owner and writer on social questions 15/9/91 ?
C. J., of Liverpool? 31/1/80
Edwin (1833-1893), American actor 15/6/81
George Sclater- (1826-1894), 1st Baron Basing (1887) 21/11/60 ?
Henry, railway director 10/9/45
James (1796-1880), secretary of Board of Trade 19/4/61
James, Rev. Dr. (1806-1878), educationalist 2/7/45
Lionel 9/1/80 ?
Robert Gore, Sir (1805-1876), 3rd Baronet (1814), tory M.P. 19/6/56
Samuel Harris, Rev., Baptist 4/5/78
William, of Edinburgh 12/1/78 ?
William, Gen. (1829-1912), Salvation Army founder 11/11/90
William Bramwell, Gen. (1856-1929), Salvation Army leader 19/10/91
Williamson, Sir (1808-1877), 2nd Baronet (1850), distiller 16/5/26
Boothby,
Brooke William Robert, Rev. Sir (1809-1865), 10th Baronet 1/1/39
Charles, Rev. (1786-1846) 4/10/32
Charles Edward 26/1/43 n
Georgiana Mary, née Harbord, formerly Mrs. Anson 26/1/43 n
Marianne, née Beridge 4/10/32
W., Sir, 8th Baronet 4/10/32 n
Boothroyd, Mrs. 25/1/76
Bootle Club secretary 23/10/85
Bootle-Wilbraham *see* Caetani, Stanley
Borbona *see* Maria Isabella
Bordogni, Giovanni (1789-1856), Italian tenor 16/2/32
Boreel *see* Northeys

Borel, Jean-Louis (1819–1884) 16/10/79 ?
Borgatti, Francesco, Italian minister 5/1/67, 10/1/67
Borgia, Alessandro, of Ionia 31/5/59
Borlase, William Copeland (1848–1899), liberal M.P. 29/6/76
Borley, M. W. 7/1/87, 25/11/89
Bornford, Mr. 2/7/77
Borowski, Mons. 4/9/77
Borradaile, Henry, lawyer 27/12/48
Borrett,
  Charles William (1810–), barrister 21/3/29
  James, Dr., physician 6/8/52 ?
Borromeo, C., Italian National Leaguer 9/3/58
Borrowdaile, Mr., of *Debrett's Peerage* 28/8/66
Borthwick, Peter (1805–1852), editor of *Morning Post* (1850), tory M.P. 17/4/50
Borthwick, Wark & Co., London brokers 30/1/56, 9/2/66, 2/3/67
Borton, William Key, Rev. (1806–1882) 18/3/56 ?
Boryll, Mrs. 11/7/88
Bosanquet *see* Hunter
Bosanquet,
  Mr., secretary to Charity Organisation Society 7/3/74 ?
  James Whatman (–1877), banker 6/5/42, 4/11/76
  Robert Carr (1871–1935), archaeologist 5/12/89
Boscawen,
  Anne Frances, née Bankes, Lady Falmouth 5/5/40
  Edward, 1st Earl Falmouth 5/5/40 n
  Evelyn (1819–1889), 7th Viscount Falmouth (1862) 17/5/67
  Evelyn Edward Thomas, Col. 30/7/88 n
  George Henry (1811–1852), 2nd Earl of Falmouth (1841), Baron Boscawen 22/11/25
  William St. Chad 10/12/75
Bosemworth, Mr. 30/12/79
Bosomerville, Mr. 21/10/78
Bosphore Egyptien editor 15/4/85, 25/4/85
Bossoli, Carlo (1815–1884), painter 2/8/60
Bosworth,
  Joseph, Rev. (1789–1876), Professor of Anglo-Saxon, Oxford 12/8/38
  Thomas, bookseller 25/11/48 ?
Botha, C. De 11/1/90
Bothmer, Mary von, Countess 11/6/83
Bott, William, builder 5/2/47 ?
Botting,
  Mons. 22/4/74
  Joseph 15/10/74
Botwood, Mr. 25/4/77
Boucheran, Mons. 11/6/64
Boulay, John Du (1811–1895), Dorset J. P., correspondent on Vaticanism 16/4/75
Bouleur, Mr. 10/10/38
Boult,
  Francis, Liverpool author 19/11/59
  Joseph, of Liverpool 16/6/65
  Swinton (–1876), secretary of Life Assurance Co. 18/6/49
Boulting,
  Mr. 17/7/75
  Mrs. 26/1/53
Boulton,
  Henry John (1790–1870), solicitor general of Upper Canada 20/2/38
  M.P.W. 9/4/78 n
Bour, Mons. 25/6/77
Bourbon,
  Caroline (1822–1869), Duchesse d'Aumale 6/3/58, 6/6/59, 11/6/62
  Caroline Ferdinande Louise (1798–1870), Duchesse de Berry 14/3/32
  Charles F. de (1778–1820), Duc de Berry 14/3/32 n
  Henri E. P. L. d'Orléans (1822–), Duc d'Aumale (1822) 6/3/58, 8/5/58, 10/5/58, 12/5/58, 24/6/58, 28/4/59, 29/4/59, 26/5/59, 28/5/59, 10/12/59, 4/1/60, 18/11/60, 11/6/62, 24/7/62, 27/10/63, 22/6/64, 14/6/77
Bourdache, M. 5/1/91
Bourdillon, James Dewar, secretary to Board of Inland Revenue 10/3/49
Bourgas, citizens of 11/7/78
Bourgeau, Madame, governess 5/8/56
Bourgeois, Paul, député 26/5/75 ?
Bourke,
  Canon 16/11/77 n
  Robert (1827–1901), 1st Baron Connemara (1887) 21/5/56 n, 24/7/80 L
Bourne,
  Miss 2/2/87
  A. 23/4/74
  E., Mrs. 17/8/55
  Henry Richard Fox (1837–1909), editor 3/1/73
  John Bury, Rev. 29/1/41
  John Robert, solicitor 21/12/75
  J. P. 2/12/77
  S. 4/5/93
Bousfield, Henry Newham, Rev. 21/5/45 ?
Bousquet, G. de 3/2/69
Boutell, Charles, Rev. (1812–1877), archaeologist 22/2/65
Bouverie,
  Edward Pleydell (1818–1889), liberal M.P. 13/8/48, 14/8/72 L, 11/3/73
  William Pleydell (1779–1869), 3rd Earl of Radnor (1828), social reformer 21/1/57 n

Bovell, J., of Gloucester 1/6/44
Bovey, Mrs., nurse? 10/12/51
Bovill, William, Sir (1814–1873), Knight (1866), tory M.P., judge 6/3/62
Bow, Hugh 24/8/90
Bowater, T. 5/8/56
Bowden,
Ellis Teacher, Rev. (–1896) 5/3/67
James 15/5/68 ?
W. 1/4/59
Bowditch, William Renwick, Rev. (–1884) 26/6/77
Bowdler, Thomas, Rev. 10/5/41
Bowen,
Charles Synge Christopher, Judge (1835–1894), 1st Baron Bowen (1893), liberal friend of G; Rendel's br.-in-law 13/2/88, 18/12/88, 25/7/90 n, 3/12/90, 26/1/91, 30/1/91, 4/3/91, 18/3/92, 18/6/92, 11/2/93, 23/6/93, 14/12/93 c, 9/4/94
Christopher, Rev. (1801–1890) 7/3/49 n
Diamantia, Lady, née Roma 27/11/58
Emily Frances, née Rendel, Lady Bowen 14/11/88
George Ferguson, Sir (1821–1899), secretary to Commissioner, Ionian Islands, colonial governor 4/5/47, 5/8/48, 30/11/58, 4/12/58
H. 4/1/92
Henry Chandler (1813–1896), founder of the *New York Independent* 6/6/90
James Bevan (1828–1905), tory M.P. 9/7/68 ?
Katherine Emily, née Steele 7/3/49 ?
Bower, Miss 18/12/82
Bowers,
George Hull, Rev. 26/10/42
G. H., Mrs. 25/8/71
P., of Burslem 17/9/63
Bowes,
J. L., Japanese consul 10/10/90
John, mayor of Toronto 18/10/54
Bowie,
Miss 25/2/80
Charles Vincent, Gen. 11/6/62
Henry, of the Philosophical Institute 21/4/71
W. Copeland, Rev. 12/10/90
Bowles,
George, Gen. Sir (1787–1876) 19/6/51
Joseph, Rev. Dr. (–1879) 22/12/66
Thomas Gibson (1843–1922), tory M.P. 17/1/78, 7/4/93
William, bookseller 16/6/74
William, Admiral 11/2/43
Bowman,
rescue 10/3/62
William, Newark bookkeeper 19/5/37 ?
William, Sir (1816–1892), 1st Baronet (1884), G's ophthalmic surgeon 26/7/56, 2/3/82, 30/11/83
Bowmar, Henry, Rev., of Surrey 20/7/73 ?
Bowmont *see* Ker
Bownes, J., Rev. 16/11/86
Bowring,
Edgar Alfred (1826–1911), secretary to 1851 commissioners, liberal M.P. 26/5/51
John, Sir (1792–1872), radical M.P., colonial governor 16/9/41, 2/7/63 ?
John Charles (1821–1893) 26/6/67
Bowron, William 3/7/85
Bowyer,
Charlotte (–1864), née Wells 21/6/50
George, Sir (1811–1883), liberal M.P. 1/4/51, 14/10/80 L
William Henry Wentworth, Rev. (1807–1872) 21/6/50 n
Box,
J. 16/11/78
Stephen, of Chester 12/9/49 ?
Boxall, William, Sir (1800–1879), Knight (1871), director of National Gallery (1865) 12/5/70
Boyce,
Messrs. 26/12/78
J. C., Rev. 5/10/86
Boyd,
Andrew Kennedy Hutchison, Rev. Dr. (1825–1899), Church of Scotland 11/5/77 ?
Benjamin, stockbroker 24/10/37
G. T. 29/6/75
Mark, stockbroker 24/10/37
Robert, Dr., physician 27/6/46 ?
Thomas Jamieson, Sir (1818–1902), Knight (1881), Lord Provost of Edinburgh (1877) 19/8/81
W. F. 3/2/76
Boydell,
Francis 29/3/78 ?
James, agent to the Glynne family and Oak Farm Co. 19/7/39, 22/2/40, 23/1/41, 22/11/47, 23/11/47, 30/11/47, 1/12/47, 4/2/48, 8/9/48
Boyer d'Agen, Mons., of Paris 30/6/93
Boyle *see* Tennyson
Boyle,
A., liberal 5/2/79
Camilla Catherine (–1880), née Smythe 10/12/36
Catherine (–1879), née Lawrence, Lady Dungarvan 19/5/58
Courtenay Edmund, Sir (1845–1901) 10/9/73
David (1772–1853), Lord Justice Clerk, lord of justiciary 10/12/36 ff, 4/1/37
D. B. 29/11/89

Boyle (*cont.*)
E., 7th Earl of Cork and Orrery 19/5/36 n
E., 8th Earl of Cork and Orrery 17/3/31 n
George David, Rev. (1828–1901) 1/5/76
George Frederick (1829–1890), 6th Earl of Glasgow (1869), tory M.P. 22/4/58
John, Rev. (–1866) 7/5/55 ?
Mary (1748–1840), née Monckton, Countess of Cork and Orrery 19/5/36
Richard Cavendish Townsend, Rev. (1812–1886) 17/3/31
Richard Edmund St. Lawrence (1829–1904), 9th Earl of Cork (1856) 28/4/68, 11/12/68
Boyman, B. 29/3/77
Boyton,
Charles, Rev. 26/5/79
Charles, Rev., of Belfast 27/11/32
E., rescue 15/5/67
Brabant *see* Leopold II
Brabazon,
Harrriet, Lady (1811–1898), née Brooke 23/7/38
Reginald (1841–1929), 12th Earl of Meath (1887), Lord Brabazon, social reformer 19/10/77, 27/11/90
William, Lord (1803–1887), 11th Earl of Meath (1851), whig M.P. 23/7/38 n
Brabourne *see* Hugessen
Bracciano *see* Torlonia
Bracebridge, Charles Holter (1799–1872), author 6/11/43 ?
Brackenbury,
Edward, Col. Sir 19/6/45 ?
Henry, Gen. Sir (1837–1914), Irish secret service director 28/11/78, 8/5/82 c, 9/6/82, 12/6/82, 18/6/82, 19/6/82 c, 22/6/82, 19/7/82, 21/7/82
Henry, Rev. (1790–1862) 26/1/35 ?
Joseph, chaplain and secretary, Magdalen Hospital 19/6/45 ?
Brackenridge,
Edward, farmer on Seaforth estate 27/12/51
young 15/6/55
Bradford *see* Bridgeman
Bradford,
Gamahil 10/3/75
J. G. 21/11/74
John Fowler, Col. (1805–1889) 8/5/82
Bradlaugh, Charles 2/5/67
Bradley,
Lieut. Col. 13/6/34
Eliza, Mrs. 3/3/58
Emily Tennyson, Miss 22/4/93
George Granville, Rev., Master of University College, Oxford 13/11/72, 31/1/78, 24/9/80, 7/10/80, 9/8/81 ff, 17/8/81
G. M. 9/5/74
Herbert, Capt. 14/5/77 ?
William (1801–1857), portrait painter 2/5/38, 23/2/41
Bradshaw,
Joseph Hoare (–1845), London banker 13/1/36
Thomas Joseph (1824–1884), barrister 30/9/62 ?
Brady,
Antonio 22/3/57
John, liberal M.P. 19/9/76 ?
Maziere, Sir (1796–1871), lord chancellor 25/7/61 n
William Maziere, Rev. Dr. 15/4/65
Braham *see* Fortescue, Waldegrave
Braham, John (1777–1856), tenor and composer 20/4/27, 1/7/34
Braico, Sig., of Naples 13/2/51, 29/2/52 ff
Braidwood, Mr. 31/1/80
Braila, Pietro, Sir, Ionian minister 26/11/58, 31/1/59, 14/2/59, 19/2/59
Braithwaite, George, Rev. (1818–1875) 1/12/68
Brameld, George William, Rev. 7/3/51, 13/5/75
Bramley, Henry Ramsden, Rev. 5/4/88
Brampton *see* Hawkins
Bramston, John, Rev. (1802–1889) 21/4/48
Bramwell,
C. E., Mrs., rescue: received assistance from G 23/5/55, 8/5/61, 26/6/63, 11/12/81
E., assistance 14/7/61
George, of the Radcliffe Trust 25/5/57
George William Wilshere, Sir (1808–1892), Baron Bramwell, judge 10/3/56
Branaforte, G. L., Prince of Butera-Radalì, of Sicily 23/10/38
Brancker,
Henry, Rev. 11/3/76
Thomas, Rev. (1813–1871) 16/3/31
Thomas, Sir, mayor of Liverpool 16/3/31 n
Brand *see* Farquhar
Brand,
Eliza, Lady Hampden 14/3/94 L
Frederica Mary Jane, Miss (–1873) 29/12/66 ?
Henry Bouverie William, Sir 21/11/53
J. A., admiralty clerk 13/5/64 ?
J. D. 28/10/74
Johannes Henricus, Sir (1823–1888), President of Orange Free State 22/3/81, 23/3/81 c, 29/3/81
Brandauer, Mr. 17/9/66
Brande, William Thomas 1/12/41
Brandeis, Ephraim and Co., metal workers 18/12/47 ?
Brandis, G., Dr., of Göttingen 15/1/76
Brandling,
Charles (–1894) 20/1/36 n

Julia (1821-1893), née Peel, formerly Villiers, Lady Jersey 20/1/36 n
Brandon, Mrs., rescue 26/6/63
Brandram,
Andrew, Rev. (-1855) 6/7/50
Samuel (1824-1892), actor 25/7/77
Brandreth *see* Gaskell
Brandreth,
Miss 11/10/32
Frederick, Capt., of Scots Guards 8/8/35
Joseph Pickington, Dr. 9/9/29 n
Thomas, Liverpool cabinetmaker 14/10/32
Thomas, Adm. Sir (1825-1894) 24/7/67
William Harper, Rev. (1812-1885) 4/2/31, 25/11/53
Brandwood, James, of Manchester 10/10/67
Branson, Juliet, Mrs. 28/10/89
Branston,
Henry John, Rev. (-1884) 27/7/67
J., mayor of Newark 1/12/32
Brasier, James (-1864), R. N. 16/6/49 ?
Brasnell, H. G., Rev. 18/4/45
Brassey, Thomas, Sir (1836-1918), 1st Baron Brassey (1886), author, liberal M.P., colonial governor 16/12/73 L, 10/7/77, 2/11/80 L, 8/8/85 ff, 6/10/85, 28/6/86, 23/7/88, 31/7/89, 18/8/92, 20/3/93
Bratiano, Demetrius, of Rumania 30/7/56, 4/5/58
Brauer, O. 5/6/79
Braun, Mons. 21/1/88
Bravo, Charles Delauney Turner (-1876) 21/11/76 n
Braybrooke *see* Neville
Braye *see* Cave
Breadalbane *see* Campbell
Breakey, Andrew, Rev., presbyterian minister 26/6/40
Brearey,
Mad. 6/10/88
C. B., surgeon 3/8/46 ?
Brechan, J. B., of Dundee 4/11/67
Breck, W. 17/12/79
Breckenridge, John Cabell, Gen. (1821-1875), Confederate general 28/3/67
Bredall, Mr., of Thomas Cook's 12/9/79
Bree, William Thomas, Rev. (1787-) 3/8/28
Breedon, F. 20/3/50
Breen, T. 15/3/87
Brehan, Madeleine, actress 22/10/50
Bremner, F. 5/4/80
Bremond, Mons., French opera singer 21/10/50
Brennan,
Miss 17/5/48
Patrick, Rev. 24/6/40 ?
Brenner, Baron, secretary to Austrian embassy 4/7/45
Brenon, E. St. J., poet 9/4/81 n
Brentlinger, Mr. 12/12/77
Brereton,
Andrew Jones (1827-1885), Mold brewer 12/9/77
Charles David, Rev. (1820-1876) 19/11/47
Shovell, Rev. (-1881) 16/5/78 ?
Breteuil, Marquis de 18/3/89
Brethren, Alexander, of London 29/2/68
Breton & Sedger, Messrs., merchants, trading in Canada 26/10/43
Brett,
Mr., Fenian in prison 4/12/73, 27/12/73
Charles, of Bayswater 29/4/68
Reginald Baliol (1852-1930), 2nd Viscount Esher (1899), liberal M.P., courtier 25/10/80, 2/4/85 n, 13/4/85
Robert, Dr. (1808-1874), physician, member of the Engagement 23/2/45 n, 17/12/51
T. 3/11/85
William Baliol, Judge (1815-1899), 1st Baron Esher (1885) 30/3/83
Brewer,
John Sherren, Prof. (1810-1879), historian 7/3/48, 13/7/73
William, Dr. (-1881), liberal M.P. 20/9/70
Brewin, William 3/4/68 ?
Brewster,
Abraham 8/11/71
David, Sir (1781-1868), Vice-chancellor, Edinburgh (1860), scientist, free churchman 15/8/59, 15/4/60, 30/4/63
Waldegrave, Rev. 22/9/42, 11/8/72
Briant, G. H. 13/9/77
Brickel, Robert, Rev. 15/12/74 ?
Brickwood, John Strettell, secretary to Exchequer Bills Office 31/1/53
Bridge,
Cyprian Arthur George, Adm. Sir (1839-1924) 13/12/90
E. A. 16/11/77
Bridgeman,
George A. F. H., 2nd Earl of Bradford 2/4/41
Georgina Elizabeth, née Moncrieffe, Countess of Bradford 2/4/41 n
Helen, née Mackay, Countess of Bradford 2/4/41 n
Bridges,
John 15/10/41
John Henry, Dr. (1832-1906), physician and positivist 3/7/86 L
Bridgett, T. E., Rev. 22/7/88
Bridgewater *see* Egerton
Bridgman, Arthur Alexander, Rev. (-1909) 8/8/65
Bridie, Mr. 12/10/67
Bridle, Mr., of Oak Farm 7/11/48
Bridlington Convent, Superior of 20/12/84
Bridport *see* Hood

Brietzeke *see* Dean
Brigg, T. M. 28/7/79
Briggs *see* Kennedy
Briggs,
Mr. 19/7/65
Cornelius, Rev. 1/6/92 ?
Jeremy 22/8/54
John, Rev. (1771–1840) 12/3/26
John Thomas, Sir (–1865), accountant general 13/2/54 n
Samuel 13/11/38 n
Thomas Graham, Sir (1833–1887) 5/2/75
Brighouse, T. 1/1/42
Bright,
Henry Arthur (1830–1884), shipowner 4/11/75
Jacob (1821–1899), liberal M.P. 22/1/69, 15/4/71 L, 21/6/80 L, 27/3/94, 29/3/94
John 21/10/42 n
John Albert 13/10/64 ?
J. S., Rev., Congregationalist 11/12/74
Samuel, Liverpool shipowner 26/1/36, 21/10/42
Thomas 14/12/65
William, Rev. Prof. (1824–1901) 3/6/58, 30/1/78
William Leatham, liberal M.P. 8/3/90
Brightman, E. W. 26/10/74
Brignal, W. A. 8/6/88
Brigstock,
Mrs. 15/10/61
William Papwell (1788–), barrister 14/4/37 n
W. P., Mrs. 14/4/37 ?
Brimmer, Martin, American historian 26/7/87 ?
Brinckman,
Arthur, author 26/4/91 ?
Theodore Henry Lavington, Sir (1798–1880), supplicant for a peerage 8/12/69
Brindley, Mr. 30/7/79
Brine,
Mrs. 21/9/82
J. E. B., Rev. 21/9/82 n
Brinley, Mr. 28/1/68
Brinton, J. 28/8/79
Brion, Mr. 4/12/75
Briscoe *see* Inglis
Briscoe,
John Ivatt (1791–1870), liberal M.P. 19/3/60
Richard, Rev. Dr. 17/10/53
Thomas, Rev. (–1895), don 21/3/54
William Kyffin Bostock, Rev. 17/6/58
Brisi, Signor 26/8/92, 30/8/92
Bristol *see* Hervey
Bristow,
Henry, Col. (1786–1874) 13/10/41
John William 25/3/76 ?
W. 19/3/77
Britnell, John, of Toronto 26/10/88
Brittain, H., of Birmingham 18/10/74
Broad, Harrington Evans (1844–1927), liberal M.P. 19/8/92
Broadbent,
J. H., of Hawarden 11/12/73
William Henry, Sir (1835–1907), 1st Baronet (1893), G's physician 21/4/94
Broadbridge, Charles, surveyor 11/2/41
Broade, George Edgar, Rev. (1838–1898), of Biarritz 20/12/91 ff, 28/12/92
Broadhurst, Henry (1840–1911), liberal M.P. 17/5/77, 18/2/78, 20/2/78, 8/1/81 L, 4/1/82 L, 7/4/82 L, 4/11/84 n, 5/2/86, 18/2/86, 11/5/86, 12/4/87
Broadwood, John & Sons, piano makers 28/12/57
Broc, R. De 7/9/76
Brock,
John Allen Clutton 28/3/87
Thomas, Sir (1847–1922), sculptor 20/6/76
William, Rev. 26/3/78 ?
William, Rev. (–1875) 28/12/52
Brockhausen, Adolf F.von (–1858), diplomat 28/11/50
Brocklebank, Thomas, Lancashire liberal 2/7/68
Brocklehurst, John (–1870), silk manufacturer, banker, liberal M.P. 22/10/41
Brockman, George, Col. (1807–1864) 31/8/59
Broderick, George Alan, Rev. (1806–1848), 5th Viscount Midleton (1836) 16/5/26
Brodie *see* Gordon
Brodie,
Alexander, merchant 18/12/43 n
Benjamin Collins, Sir (–1862), 1st Baronet (1834), surgeon 3/11/53
James Campbell John (1848–1880) 18/6/73
W. R., of Edinburgh 22/11/86
Brodrick,
Alan, Rev. (1840–1909) 12/8/68
George Charles (1831–1903), barrister; liberal unionist; Warden of Merton 21/10/58, 26/9/72, 16/3/76, 6/12/77, 8/12/80 L, 26/3/83, 18/5/89
William (1830–1907), 8th Viscount Midleton 27/9/81 L
Brogden,
Mr., of Newark 20/8/41
James, Rev. (1804–1864) 10/4/38 ff, 9/9/57
T. J. 30/12/79
Brogi, G., Sig. 27/1/88
Broglie *see* de Broglie
Broglie, Achille Charles L. V. de, 6th Duc de Broglie 3/5/45
Broglio, Emilio, of Turin 3/5/59
Bromage, Richard Raikes, Rev. 12/6/92

Bromby, Charles Henry, Bp. (1814–1907), bishop of Tasmania 15/8/71, 18/11/85
Bromehead, Joseph Crawford, barrister 17/6/48 ff, 1/7/75, 2/7/75
Bromley *see* Campbell
Bromley,
Lady, née Moser 22/1/60
Misses 4/10/32
Mr. 15/5/59
Ann, Lady, née Wilson 4/10/32 n
Davenport, of Badgginton 31/7/28 n
Richard Madox, Sir (–1865), Knight (1858), public accountant 15/4/54
Bromskill, Mr. 24/9/76
Brook,
rescue 7/5/58
Arthur, Rev. (–1890) 10/2/65
G. 24/12/85
Brook and Chrystal, Messrs. 28/10/91
Brooke *see* Greville, Parker, Warburton, Wilbraham
Brooke,
Charles Hyde, Rev. 11/12/79
James, Sir (1803–1868), imperial proconsul 30/11/47 ff, 26/5/77 n
Richard, Sir, 5th Baronet 17/1/40 n
Richard, Sir (–1795), 6th Baronet 23/7/38 n
Richard, Sir (1785–1865), 7th Baronet (1795), Cheshire landowner 25/7/39 n, 6/9/57
Stopford August, Rev. (1832–1916), famous preacher, left Church of England 1880 24/11/67, 19/5/73, 11/6/76
Brookes,
Henry 12/8/57
John Henry, Rev. (1823–1896), don 25/3/57
Warwick (1806–1882), artist 17/7/66, 6/3/71
Brookfield,
Mrs. 9/3/78
William Henry 3/3/41, 30/10/42 n
Brooks,
Miss 24/1/85
Charles William Shirley (1816–1874), editor of *Punch* 6/10/35 ?
George, Rev. 12/4/78
H. 7/7/60
H., headmaster in Cheshire 15/9/41
Henry, Rev. 4/2/47
Henry Jermyn, portrait painter 29/3/89
Jonathan, Rev. (1775–1855) 7/1/29
Maurice (1823–), liberal M.P. 31/10/77, 23/4/79, 25/7/79
W. G., Bank of England, Liverpool branch 20/3/55 ?
William Cunliffe, Sir (1819–1900), 1st Baronet (1886), tory M.P. 13/11/74
Brooksbank,
Thomas, barrister 21/4/53
Thomas Constantine (–1850), treasury official 21/4/53 n
Brooks & Green, London auctioneers 19/1/60
Broomhall, Thomas Taylor, Dr., Duke of Sutherland's physician 5/9/53
Brophy, Charles Albert, Serjeant 6/1/87
Brosnan, Rev. Canon 21/1/89
Bross, T. K. 19/2/68 ?
Broster and March, book manufacturers 12/12/46
Brotherton, Joseph (–1866), cotton manufacturer, liberal M.P. 18/2/53
Brough,
Messrs. 17/10/90
Miss 16/1/89
Mr. 29/8/76
H., Rev. 26/8/58
Thomas, Liverpool merchant 7/4/55 ff, 19/3/57 ?
Tim, guide 25/10/77
W. 8/10/74
William, printer 3/9/75
Brougham,
Emily Frances (–1884), Lady Brougham and Vaux (1868), née Taylor 22/4/68
Henry Peter 8/3/27
Mary Anne, Lady (–1865), née Eden 23/10/57
William (1795–1886), 2nd Baron Brougham & Vaux (1868) 23/10/57, 11/10/64
Broughton *see* Hobhouse
Broughton,
rescue 19/3/69
Rhoda, Miss (1840–1920), novelist 9/5/88
William Grant, Bp. 21/7/47
Broun,
Richard, Sir, 8th Baronet 24/2/48
Susan Georgiana, Lady, née Broun-Ramsay, Mrs. Bourke, Lady Connemara 21/5/56
W. H. 21/5/56 n
Broussali, Jean, Armenian 29/11/88, 31/8/89
Brown *see* Hope
Brown,
rescue 22/2/62
Miss 16/8/45
Mr. 21/4/32
Mr., banker in Messina 15/10/38
Mr., bodyguard 18/10/82
Mrs. 4/12/64
Nurse 21/12/25 n
A., Messrs. 9/1/79
Abner Edmund, Rev. (–1897) 23/2/77
A. E. 15/12/86
Charles John, Rev. 25/3/74
Cornelius, historian of Newark 22/4/78, 13/8/78, 12/4/79, 13/4/79
C. R. 21/7/87, 10/6/92
C. W. Swinfen 28/9/74
David, Rev. Prof. (1803–1897) 16/6/88

Brown (*cont.*)
Edward Chamberlayn 17/7/45 ?
Ernest Faulkner, Rev. (1866–1938) 19/9/89
F., Miss, governess to the Gladstones (1847), governess to the Glynnes 16/8/45, 30/10/47
F. J. 13/3/48
F. W. 9/12/48
George (1818–1880), Canadian politician, editor, *Toronto Globe* 6/12/64, 25/5/65
George, Gen. Sir (1790–1865) 28/6/59
George Hilary, Rev. (–1856), Roman Catholic 23/8/52 ?
Henry Alvin, American Congressman 31/7/75
Henry Drake (–1892), journalist 21/12/50 ?
Henry Edwards, parliamentary agent 6/10/52
James, Rev., of Arniston 26/4/56 ?
James Baldwin, Rev. (1820–1884), Congregationalist minister 15/11/64
J. De M. 18/2/87
J. E. 8/11/78
John, Boroughreeve of Manchester 17/10/37
John (1826–1883), Queen's servant 26/11/83, 10/9/84
John, Capt. 22/7/79
John, Dr. (1810–1882), Edinburgh physician 12/12/59
John, Sir (1816–1896), Knight (1867), steel manufacturer 30/7/62 n
Joseph, Rev. (1800–1867) 26/9/57
Matthew, of Manchester 18/8/58
Michael Charles, Rev. 26/3/79 ?
R. Ainslie, of Edinburgh 4/12/86
Richard Lewis, Rev. (1811–1884) 26/6/55
R. M. 18/12/77
Robert, junior 21/1/79
Robert Erskine, writer on land 29/5/45, 6/6/45
S., Mrs. 13/3/55
Samuel (1812–1875), actuary 1/3/64
Thomas Edward, Rev. (–1897) 26/4/54
T. J. 15/12/86
T. W. 10/4/75
T. W. 30/12/86
W. A., Rev. 1/9/77
W. E. 30/12/79
William, Rev. (1819–1899) 25/6/58
William, Sir (1784–1864), 1st Baronet (1863), liberal M.P., Liverpool banker and benefactor 18/7/45
William Haig-, Rev. (1823–1907) 25/5/67
William Hay, Rev. 21/1/91
William Henry, Chester solicitor 20/8/40 ?
Brown, Shipley & Co., Liverpool bankers 20/9/54
Brown & Barnes, Messrs. 15/7/76
Browne *see* Munro
Browne,
Lieut. 30/12/64
Miss 13/5/92
A. 14/12/77
A. H., Messrs. 24/4/77
C. Rae 2/6/88
Dominick (–1860), 1st Baron Oranmore (1836) 13/7/53
Edward George Stanley, Rev. 10/12/74, 19/1/75, 10/5/88
Edward Harold, Bp. (1811–1891), bishop of Ely (1864), bishop of Winchester (1873) 28/11/41, 16/6/75, 8/9/75, 22/5/76, 17/9/81, 26/8/82, 29/8/82, 3/9/82, 11/12/82, 2/12/83 L
Edward Noyce, journalist in Naples 21/12/50, 17/2/51
Edward Slater-, Canon 28/4/89
Elizabeth, Mrs., née Carlyon 22/8/45 ?
George John (1820–1896), 3rd Marquis of Sligo (1845) 17/12/68
George Osborne-, Rev. (–1892) 15/3/74, 31/12/79
Henry Montague, Rev. (1799–1884), dean of Lismore 12/6/36
Henry Ralph, General 23/11/86
J. A. 14/11/77
John Denis, Rev. 4/2/54
J. W. 2/1/80
Richard Howe, Lord (1834–1912) 14/7/75
Robert W., Ven. (1809–1895) 22/6/42, 16/4/83 L
Thomas Birch Llewelyn, Rev. 2/4/57
Valentine (–1812), 1st Earl of Kenmare 26/7/48 n
Valentine Augustus (1825–1905), Lord Castleross (1853), 4th Earl of Kenmare (1871), liberal M.P. 10/12/68, 2/1/82
William (1791–1876), liberal M.P. 26/7/48 ?
Brownfield, A. 12/1/87, 11/6/92
Browning,
Arthur Henry, poet, distiller 14/10/43
Charles, Dr., physician 3/2/43 ?
Elizabeth Barrett, Mrs. (1806–1861), poet 9/6/31 n
George 7/5/76
Oscar (1837–1923), author, liberal, fellow of King's, Cambridge 14/12/67, 31/5/75, 27/10/78
Reuben, finance writer 3/4/55
Robert (1812–1889), poet 9/6/31 n, 2/1/70, 1/10/79, 7/6/83 ff, 29/6/85, 2/7/85 L, 16/12/89 n
Brownlees, J. 23/10/75
Brownlie, William, of Y.M.C.A. 16/1/76

Brownlow *see* Cust
Brownlow,
  Charles, 1st Baron Lurgan 29/4/46
  Charles (1831-1882), 2nd Baron Lurgan (1847) 15/12/68, 23/7/72 L
Brownrigg *see* Harington, Wood
Brownrigg,
  Elizabeth Rebecca (-1865), née Casamayor 16/6/36
  John Studholme (1786-1853), tory M.P., director of Bank of Australasia 17/2/41, 13/5/47
  J. S. 16/6/36 n
Brownsea, W. 5/2/80
Broya, E. G., Sig. 10/1/90
Bruce *see* Grant, Hamilton, Maxwell, Stanley
Bruce,
  Alexander, Rev. 24/5/56
  Alexander L., of Edinburgh 22/11/79
  Charles Brudenell (-1856), 1st Marquis of Ailesbury (1821) 7/7/52 n
  Charles Lennox Cumming-, Major (1790-1875), tory M.P. 12/4/34, 2/7/56
  Charles William Brudenell-, Lord (1834-1897), liberal M.P. 29/4/80
  Elizabeth, née Oswald, Lady Elgin 14/11/33
  Elizabeth Mary, née Cumming-Bruce, Lady Elgin 12/4/34 n
  Ernest Augustus Charles Brudenell-, Lord, 3rd Marquis of Ailesbury 5/10/76, 6/10/76, 31/1/77 ff
  Frederick William Adolphus, Sir (1814-1867), diplomat 5/4/34, 6/7/46
  Gertrude Florinda Brudenell- (-1892), née Gardiner, Lady Ailesbury 7/7/52, 7/4/79
  Henry Austin 21/4/56
  Henry Hervey, Sir (1820-1907), of Ulster; former tory M.P. 26/4/86
  James (1811-1863), 8th Earl of Elgin (1841) 15/7/27, 3/10/93 L
  James Knight-, Sir (1791-1866), judge 18/5/61
  Katherine Mary (-1889), née Shaw-Stewart, Woman of the Bedchamber to the Queen 25/9/64
  Robert, Gen. (1813-1862), Prince of Wales's treasurer 19/1/60
  Robert B., Rev. 12/6/58
  T., 7th Earl of Elgin 30/11/32 n
  Thomas 22/4/74
  Victor Alexander (1849-1917), 9th Earl of Elgin (1863), politician 16/7/86, 26/7/93 n, 12/8/93, 23/9/93, 29/9/93, 7/10/93
  Wallace 13/1/90
  W. E., of Kirkliston 26/3/80
Brudenell, James Thomas (1797-1868), 7th Earl of Cardigan (1837), soldier, led the Light Brigade 30/3/36 n
Brunetti, L., rescue 25/5/66
Brunner, John Tomlinson, Sir (1842-1919), 1st Baronet, liberal M.P. 9/10/86, 15/8/87
Brünnow,
  Baroness 7/7/43
  Ernst Philip Ivanovich, Baron, Russian ambassador 7/7/43 n, 7/6/53
Bruno,
  F. 9/2/89
  Giordano 27/5/89
Brunswik, Benoît 21/11/78
Bruyere, H. P., of L. N. W. R. 31/5/52
Bryant, William (-1874), match manufacturer of Bryant & May 22/7/64 ff, 10/12/78
Bryce,
  D. 12/12/79
  James, Prof. 10/4/70
  Lloyd Stephens (1851-1917), proprietor & editor, *North American Review* (1889) 20/6/89
Brydom, R., Rev. 3/7/78
Buccleuch *see* Scott
Buch,
  Miss 8/2/90
  Ludwig August von, diplomat 15/12/38
Buchan,
  Mr. 15/10/74
  Charles Forless, minister in Fordoun 6/12/42, 8/10/46
  John, Rev. 21/3/39 ?
  Peter, publisher 12/3/50 ?
Buchanan,
  Andrew, secretary of Russian legation 1/12/53 ?
  Andrew, Sir (1807-1882), 1st Baronet (1878), diplomat 4/9/72, 13/12/73
  C., Miss 17/12/26
  George (1790-1852), civil engineer, classicist 20/11/51 ?
  Gilbert, Rev. Dr. (-1833) 1/1/26
  James 22/3/32 n
  James, journalist 9/1/80
  Janet, née Sinclair 22/3/32 ?
  Robert William (1841-1901), poet and playwright 29/9/78 ff, 12/1/93 L
  Thomas Boughton, Ven. (1833-1924) 30/8/66, 27/3/68
  Thomas Ryburn (1846-1909), liberal M.P. 6/11/85
  Walter (1797-1883), liberal M.P. 6/12/59
Buchheim, Charles Adolphus, Prof. (1828-1900), classicist 22/4/68
Buchholz, Eduard August Wilhelm (1825-1887) 21/8/76, 30/12/81 L
Buck,
  A., of *Hansard* 9/8/66
  Cornelius, of *Hansard* 24/4/57
  James, clerk 31/12/34 ?
  Zacchariah (1798-1879), organist 8/1/38

Buckden, C., Rev. 21/12/78
Buckeridge,
Arthur Nugent, Rev. (1809–) 17/10/25
George, Rev. 31/5/54
Buckey, F. S. 25/7/78
Buckingham, James Silk (1786–1855), journalist, radical M.P. 1/7/34
Buckingham and Chandos *see* Grenville
Buckland,
W. H. 12/10/88
William (1784–1856), dean of Westminster (1845), geologist 18/8/31
Buckle *see* Hawkins
Buckle,
George, London engraver 26/9/53
Henry Thomas (1821–1862), historian 18/4/81
Buckler,
Mrs. 1/1/75
John Chessel, architect 13/3/44
Buckley *see* Watts
Buckley,
Charles Frederick, Rev. (–1892) 16/10/64
Edmund, Manchester iron manufacturer, Peelite M.P. 29/6/46
Edmund, cousin-in-law 21/4/46 n
Henry William (1800–) 18/1/29
Mary Catherine (–1872), née Gladstone, cousin 21/4/46
Nathaniel (1821–1892), liberal M.P. 8/11/68
Theodore Alois William, Rev. (–1856) 5/3/52
William Edward, Rev. Prof. (–1892) 28/6/52
Buckmaster,
Mr. 17/9/75
Mr., of Lancashire 27/9/64
Buckstone, Mr. 28/9/77
Buckworth *see* Scott
Budd, George, Prof. (1808–1882), physician 28/4/45
Budden, Mr. 22/5/77
Buddicom, R. P., Rev. (1780–1846) 14/8/25
Buddicomb, Robert Joseph, Rev. 4/7/65
Buddicorn, Mr., of Hawarden 30/8/75
Buddiley, Miss 11/5/78
Bude, W. 11/4/78
Budett, H. C. 7/3/76
Budge, Ernest Alfred Thompson Wallis, Sir (1857–1934), education funded by G, Egyptologist at British Museum 26/2/78, 18/6/92
Buggin, George, Sir (–1815) 3/8/53 n
Bugni, Giacomo, Baron 6/9/63 ?
Buist, T. 31/5/90
Bulgari, Spiridon, of Ionia 25/11/58
Bulgaris, L. 20/4/88
Bulgarnie, R., Rev. 6/12/77 ff, 14/9/88
Bulgin, R. 1/12/74
Bulkeley,
Elizabeth Harriet Warren-, Lady (–1826), née Warren 31/8/26 n
Thomas James Warren- (1752–1822), 1st Baron Bulkeley of Beaumaris (1784) 31/8/26
Bull,
E. 30/12/78
John, Dr. 29/2/40
Bull & Auvanche, Messrs., booksellers 23/11/87
Bullen,
Edward, Rev. 28/9/74 ?
F., of Chester 15/12/87
George (1816–1894), Keeper of Printed Books, British Museum 26/8/87
Buller,
Anthony, Rev. (1809–1881) 30/9/26, 26/3/63
Arthur William, Sir (1808–1869) 16/5/60
Charles (1806–1848), liberal M.P. 14/6/33
Edward Manningham-, Sir (1800–1882), 1st Baronet (1866), liberal M.P. 3/6/67
Elizabeth Yarde, Lady (–1837), née Wilson-Patten 3/6/35
G., Rev. 27/3/55
George, Gen. Sir (1802–1884) 12/7/55, 27/11/58
Henrietta, Lady, née MacDonald 14/1/59
James (1813–), of Devon 29/11/27
John Yarde, Sir (1799–1871), 1st Baron Churston (1858), tory M.P. 4/6/35, 12/2/53
Redvers Henry, Sir (1839–1908), soldier 2/2/91, 8/3/93 c
William Edmund, Rev. 24/5/63 n
Bullesley, Rev. Mr. 28/9/74
Bullitt, John Christian (1824–1902), American lawyer 19/4/62
Bullock,
Edward (–1857), Common Serjeant 16/5/26 n
J. 22/9/59
James Trevor or Richard 16/5/26
John, Rev. 1/11/86
N. S., Rev. 24/1/75
William Thomas, assistant-secretary of S. P. G. 4/7/52
Bulstrode, George, Rev. (1824–1897) 5/11/75
Bulteel,
Henry Bellenden, Rev. (1800–1866) 15/11/28, 15/2/29, 29/3/29, 6/2/31, 8/2/31, 15/2/31, 1/3/31, 22/5/31, 14/8/31, 25/9/31
Mary 25/2/56
S. D., railway treasurer 27/8/61
Bulwer,
Henry Ernest Gascoyne, Sir (1836–1914),

governor of Natal and Zulu Commissioner 23/5/82, 27/5/82, 31/7/82, 2/10/82, 5/10/82, 27/10/82, 24/11/82, 22/6/83, 21/8/83 c, 2/9/83, 28/9/83, 29/10/83, 19/12/83, 3/1/84 c, 11/6/84
William Henry Lytton Earle, Sir (1801-1872), 1st Baron Dalling (1871), diplomat, historian 2/2/56
Bumpus, John, bookseller 24/4/79 ff, 24/11/85
Bunbury,
Edward Herbert, Sir (1811-1895), 9th Baronet (1886), liberal M.P. 27/2/41 n, 3/3/41
Emily Richardson 13/7/57 ?
Henry Mill 17/11/76 ?
Bunce, J. T. 25/11/75
Bundy, rescue 23/10/65, 14/11/65
Bunker, Mr. 4/2/78
Bunn, Messrs. 10/3/76
Bunsen,
Christian Karl Josias von, Baron (1791-1860), Prussian diplomat, theologian 29/3/32, 5/4/32, 26/5/32, 27/5/32, 1/6/32, 16/2/39, 17/2/39, 1/3/39, 17/3/39, 19/3/39, 18/4/39, 8/2/41, 14/10/41, 29/1/42, 10/10/42, 17/5/43, 24/5/43, 2/9/43, 15/5/47, 17/3/50, 19/6/53, 2/1/54, 30/5/68, 29/12/70
Ernest 3/4/55
Frances, Baroness (-1876), née Waddington 26/7/50
Henry George De, Rev. 5/6/78
Bunting *see* Belcher
Bunting,
Jabez (1779-1856), Wesleyan leader 9/3/35
Percy William, Sir (1836-1911), Knight (1908), editor, *Contemporary Review* 4/6/84, 2/6/88, 17/6/91, 25/7/91, 13/9/91 n
T. W. 24/8/88
Buonaccorsi, Sig., Innkeeper in Messina 22/11/38
Buongiovanni, Sig., Sicilian artist 24/10/38
Buott, C. F., secretary of Income Tax Association 24/1/57 n
Burar, F. 7/8/91
Burbier, J. H. 16/8/78
Burbridge, John, poet 29/8/76 ?
Burchell, Thomas, missionary 3/3/40
Burchnall, A. B. 14/4/92
Burckhardt, Mr. 14/3/78
Burd,
Frederick, Rev. (1826-1915) 18/3/57
P., Rev. 27/10/87
Burdell, rescue 18/4/85
Burden & Dunning, Parliamentary agents 19/6/55, 21/7/55
Burdett,
rescue 8/6/86
Francis, Sir (1770-1844), 5th Baronet (1797), radical M.P. 15/5/28 n
Henry Charles, Sir (1847-1920), physician, author 29/4/89
H. J. 11/3/91
Burdon, John, Rev. 16/3/78 ?
Burge,
Charles, Edinburgh hatter 1/5/33
William (1787-1850), barrister 24/3/36, 8/2/43, 15/4/43, 23/1/44
Burges, George, London solicitor 11/2/48
Burgess,
Mr., of U.S.A. 23/9/88
H., Bankers' agent 20/2/43
Henry, Rev. Dr. (1808-1886) 16/4/54
Richard, Rev. (1796-1881), educationalist, author 1/4/32
Burgh,
Harriet de, née Canning, Marchioness of Clanricarde 29/9/31 n
Maurice T. de, Rev., of Limerick 19/1/58
Ulick Canning de (1827-1867), Lord Dunkellin, liberal M.P. 30/4/66
Ulick John de (1802-1874), 1st Marquis of Clanricarde (1828) 29/9/31
Burghclere *see* Gardner
Burgon, John William, Rev. Prof. (1813-1888), high church controversialist 22/2/54, 30/1/57
Burgoyne,
A., Mrs. 13/10/52
John Fox, Gen. Sir (1782-1871), 1st Baronet (1856), soldier, inspector of fortifications 3/3/46
Burke,
Messrs. 24/6/79
Miss 13/5/82
Barbara Frances, Lady (-1887) 10/11/77
James St. George, barrister 13/7/44
John Bernard, Sir (1814-1892), genealogist 6/11/77
John William, Rev. (1817-1901) 5/6/68 ?
Oliver J., Irish author, land commissioner 18/11/87
Thomas Henry (1829-1882), Irish undersecretary 14/5/69, 6/5/82
Ulick Ralph (1845-1895), barrister, Spanish scholar 3/2/78 ?
Burkitt, W., Rev. 15/5/52
Burleigh, J. C. 29/7/79
Burley, J. 2/9/62
Burlingham, D. C., Dr., physician at Hawarden (1878) 15/8/78 n
Burlinghame, Anson, diplomat 15/1/69
Burlington *see* Cavendish
Burn,
Adam, barrister 2/12/64 ?

Burn (*cont.*)
Ralph, shoemaker 6/2/49 ?
Richard, of Manchester 14/3/57 ?
Burnaby,
Frederick Augustus, Capt. (1824–1885), soldier, traveller, killed at Khartoum 26/7/78
Henry Fowke, Rev. 15/1/79 ?
Robert William, Rev. 5/8/83
R. T. 20/3/74
T. F. S. 17/11/65
Thomas Fowke Andrew (1808–1893), Newark lawyer 26/7/33
Burnand, Francis Cowley, Sir (1836–1917), editor of *Punch* 24/5/84, 7/5/89 n, 12/9/93 L
Burnard, Nevill Northey (1818–1878), sculptor 7/7/65, 16/7/68, 24/7/68, 25/7/68, 20/8/70
Burnell, George Rowden, engineer 18/6/45
Burnes, James, Dr. (1801–1862) 28/4/58 ?
Burnet,
Mr. 2/2/39
R. 18/6/78
Burnett,
Miss 5/5/80
Alexander, Hawarden 11/2/58
Frances Eliza Hodgson (1849–1924), novelist 19/1/88
Gregory (–1874), Hawarden land agent 2/9/45, 15/4/52, 21/7/52, 19/8/52 ff, 31/8/52, 30/9/52, 19/10/53, 21/10/53, 5/1/55, 2/7/55, 19/10/55, 18/1/56, 3/12/56, 24/12/56, 30/3/57, 8/1/58, 11/1/58, 26/7/58, 31/8/59, 1/10/60 ff, 14/3/61, 21/1/62, 8/8/62, 15/8/62, 18/9/62 ff, 7/11/62 ff, 3/8/63 ff, 15/9/63 ff, 19/8/64, 23/8/64, 29/8/64, 31/7/65 ff, 23/10/67, 29/10/67, 17/9/68 ff, 19/3/69, 1/10/69, 11/11/69, 5/1/72, 13/1/72, 18/5/72 ff, 18/7/72 n, 14/8/72, 10/4/73, 13/10/73, 15/10/73, 2/11/73, 18/12/73, 2/1/74, 10/1/74, 15/1/74, 28/11/74
Gregory, Mrs. 12/2/57
Burnetts, The, in rescue work 19/2/52
Burnham *see* Lawson
Burnley, William Hardin, Trinidad proprietor 20/4/36
Burns,
D. 22/7/75
Dawson, Rev. 20/3/58 ?
John, Sir (1829–1901), 2nd Baronet (1890), 1st Baron Inverclyde (1897) 10/1/80
John Elliot (1858–1943), labour leader 21/9/87 ff, 11/8/92
William Chalmers, Rev. (–1868), minister and missionary 8/12/45 ?
Burnside, Ambrose Everette, Gen. (1824–1881), American general, financier, diplomat 12/9/70, 31/10/70, 3/12/70
Burns & Oates, Messrs. 14/5/88
Burnstone, Mr. 6/4/78
Burr,
David Higford Davall (1811–1885), former tory M.P. 1/5/43
Enoch Fitch, Rev., of U.S.A. 26/10/73
John, accountant 16/4/49
Burrell,
rescue 14/5/62
A. 30/3/91
Charles Merrick, Sir (1774–1862), 3rd Baronet (1796) 15/3/34
Frances, Lady, née Wyndham 5/7/45
Frederick William 9/7/75 ?
Burritt, Elihu, of U.S.A. 19/10/76
Burroughs,
George, artist 10/6/29 n
Selina, née Childers 10/6/29
W. Gore, Rev. 28/8/79
Burrowes, E. H., of the colonial office 4/7/46
Burrows,
H. W., Rev. 29/4/47 n
James, of Pimlico 25/5/61
Montagu, Prof. (1819–1905), lawyer 18/3/61 n, 31/1/90
Burston, J. 2/7/75
Burt,
J., Mrs., rescue 16/10/56
John, Glasgow liberal association 27/10/79
John Thomas, Rev. (1811–1892), gaol chaplain 4/1/65
Thomas (1837–1922), liberal M.P. 27/2/77, 1/5/77, 2/8/92
Burton *see* Bass
Burton,
rescue 18/2/52
Alexander Bradly, Rev. (–1888) 3/5/79 ?
Alfred Henry, Rev. (1850–1934) 29/10/78
Charles, Rev. (–1866), author 10/6/46
Charles Henry, Rev. (1818–1885) 17/7/58
Decimus, architect 7/11/42 n
Edward, Rev. Prof. (1794–1836), regius prof. of Divinity at Christ Church, Oxford 9/11/28
E. F. 22/10/75
Frederic William, Sir (1816–1900), director, National Gallery 5/2/91
H. A., rescue 13/3/67
Henry, Capt. 10/6/75
Henry, Rev. (–1873) 24/10/68
John, Rev. 1/8/76 ?
John Hill, historian 14/3/45 ?
J. S. 25/12/77
M., Miss 27/9/78
Burtt, Joseph (1818–1874), archaeologist 12/7/58

Bury *see* Keppel
Busbridge,
Mr. 4/7/77
G. F., Messrs. 31/7/78
Busby, Michael Horton 25/5/54 ?
Busch, Dr., German foreign under-secretary 21/12/84
Bush,
Paul, Rev. 3/12/85
Robert John, bookseller 23/1/41 n
Bushby,
James, of Auckland 25/6/62, 17/8/64
Thomas A., Liverpool merchant 13/10/64 n
W. 10/2/46
Bushe, Gervase Parker, diplomat 5/10/45
Bushell,
E. 8/2/78
R., Rev. 26/10/78
Bushnell,
John Hext, Rev. (1814-) 11/1/34 ?
R. 23/10/76
Buss,
Dr., physician in Nîmes 2/2/92 ?
Septimus, Rev. 14/9/92
Bussell,
Miss 31/5/87
Frederick Vernon, Rev. 14/6/78
John Garrett, Rev. (1804–1874) 11/2/36
Bussey, Harry Findlater, journalist 3/5/79
Bussy, G. M. 19/10/77, 21/11/77
Bustic, Mr. 30/6/81
Butcher,
rescue 28/1/63
Charles Henry, Rev. (1833–1907) 12/5/56, 17/5/59
Bute *see* Stuart
Butera de Rubari, Prince 16/7/50 n
Butler *see* Oppenheim
Butler,
Alfred Stokes, Rev. 4/5/57
Charles 16/4/57
Charles Ewart, Rev. 28/12/76
Charles Robert, Rev. (–1878) 11/7/51 ?
C. P., Rev. 3/3/79
E., 11th Viscount Mountgarret 4/9/35 n
E., 1st Earl of Kilkenny 4/9/35 n
Eliza Maria Anne (–1882), née Amphlett 2/8/53
Fox 2/8/77
George, of Camberwell 2/8/53 n
George, Bp. (1815–1886), Roman Catholic 15/7/69
George, Rev. (1819–1890), principal of Liverpool college (1866), Canon of Winchester (1882) 1/3/54, 21/12/72, 17/1/79, 26/6/82
Henry, Newark draper 5/8/34
Henry Montagu, Rev. (1833–1918), Master of Trinity, Cambridge 9/8/81, 17/8/81, 25/3/82, 31/1/87
James, Rev. Dr. (1811–1876) 5/3/68
James W. 1/6/91
John Judkin, Rev. 12/12/42 ?
Josephine Elizabeth (1828–1906), née Grey, social reformer, author 1/3/54 n, 21/12/72, 13/10/78, 25/6/82, 26/6/82
Miles, exciseman 16/12/39 ?
Percy Archer, of Tipperary 18/4/40
Pierce (1774–1846), liberal (Repeal) M.P. 4/9/35
Slade 23/8/91
T. W. 25/7/87
William Archer, Rev. Prof. 30/12/42, 7/1/43, 26/1/44, 20/2/45
William Francis, Gen. Sir (1838–1910) 11/7/89
William John, Rev. (1818–1894), dean of Lincoln 8/6/57, 9/6/57, 13/3/59, 8/8/80 n
Butlin, Thomas, tax collector 26/11/46
Butt,
Charles Parker, Judge (–1892) 29/3/83
George Medd (–1860), tory M.P. 27/6/54
Isaac (1813–1879), home rule M.P. 13/6/40, 19/1/61, 22/3/64, 20/1/86
John, Rev. (1826–1899), Roman Catholic 9/4/56 ?
Buttemer, Robert William, goldsmith 15/3/43 n
Butteni, Mr., of Athens 22/12/58
Butterfield,
Thomas (–1861), chief justice, Bermuda 15/6/39
William (1814–1900), architect, member of the Engagement 23/2/45 n, 4/7/45 n, 13/4/54, 1/4/59, 30/7/81, 31/7/81, 1/8/81, 8/12/82
Butterwick, William Thomas, commission agent 4/6/79
Butti, J. A., Edinburgh art dealer 13/10/71
Buttress,
Allan, Rev. 29/9/78 ?
W. 26/8/91
Buxton,
Charles (1822–1871), liberal M.P. 9/8/57, 13/3/71 L
Constance (–1892), née Lubbock 15/7/87
Edward North (1840–1924) 20/12/90
Edward North, Sir (1812–1858), 2nd Baronet (1845), liberal M.P. 11/5/46
Sydney Charles (1853–1934), liberal M.P. and author 25/5/86, 29/6/86, 19/5/88
Thomas, Rev. (–1892) 16/4/79
Thomas Fowell, Sir (1786–1845), 1st Baronet (1840), whig M.P., social reformer 24/7/33
Buyers, T. S. 6/12/86
Buzacott, Aaron, Rev., secretary of the anti-slavery society 19/5/76

Buzzard,
Mr. 13/1/91
George, vestry clerk 30/1/41
Bylandt,
Madame 25/5/78
Charles, Count 25/5/78 n
Byles,
John Barnard, Sir (1801–1884), judge 31/1/76
William Pollard, Sir (1839–1917), liberal M.P. 1/1/91
Byng,
Alice (–1928), née Egerton, Lady Enfield, Lady Strafford 25/6/63 n, 5/9/63
Francis Edmund Cecil, Rev. (1835–1918), 5th Earl of Strafford (1899) 13/3/79
George, Sir (–1884), 7th Viscount Torrington (1831) 25/1/53
George Henry Charles (1830–1898), Lord Enfield (1860), 3rd Earl of Strafford (1886), whig M.P. 25/6/63, 5/9/63, 18/2/71 L
Gerald Frederick (1784–1871), known as 'poodle', courtier 24/2/58
John (1772–1860), 1st Earl of Strafford (1835), whig M.P., soldier 11/3/35
Byrne,
C. C. 11/12/89
Henry Barnes, Rev., fellow of Queen's, Oxford 7/2/48
James, Rev., dean of Clonfert 17/10/56 ff, 4/2/67
John Rice, Rev. 19/9/56
John W., accountant 11/10/51
S. 6/10/75
Byrom *see* Ainsworth
Byrom,
Miss 1/6/91
Edward 19/2/79 ?
Byron *see* King
Byron,
George Frederick William (1855–1917), 9th Baron Byron (1870) 5/5/88
George Gordon (1788–1824), 6th Baron Byron, poet 16/4/30 n
James 31/10/89
R. 27/12/67
W. A. 17/3/55
William, of Liverpool 16/6/75
Byrth,
Henry Stewart, Rev. 1/4/77
Thomas, Rev. 25/7/41
Bywater,
Ingram, Prof. (1840–1914) 11/7/61 ?
Jane, rescue 7/2/54

Cable, McLean, Mr. 3/10/87
Cacha, A., Dr. 25/6/79
Cadbury, George (1839–1922), manufacturer 16/1/92
Caddell, W. W. 10/10/88
Cadell, Francis 29/8/79
Cadly, Mr. 30/12/67
Cadman, William, Rev. (1815–1891) 3/6/76, 20/4/84
Cadogan,
Frederick William (1821–1904), liberal M.P. 1/1/38
George (–1864), 3rd Earl of Cadogan 1/1/38 n, 30/3/65 n
George Henry (1840–1915), 5th Earl of Cadogan (1873) 22/1/77 n
Henry Charles (1812–1873), 4th Earl of Cadogan (1864), Viscount Chelsea, tory M.P. 16/1/44
Cadorna, Carlo, Count 25/6/69, 4/5/70
Cadwallader, James, Rev. 20/5/56
Caesar, Julius P. 11/3/78
Caetani,
Ada Constance, Duchess of Sermoneta (1882), née Bootle-Wilbraham, Princess Teano 12/11/66, 30/4/67 ff, 13/7/76, 19/1/88 ?
Margaret (–1872), née Knight, Duchess of Sermoneta 1/11/66 n
Michael Angelo (1804–1882), 14th Duke of Sermoneta (1850) 22/11/66, 3/7/76, 8/7/76, 24/7/76
Onorato (1824–1917), 15th Duke of Sermoneta (1882), Prince of Teano 12/11/66
Caffarelli, Francesco di 29/7/76 ?
Caffin, Benjamin Charles, Rev. 31/3/56
Cafflisch, Mr. 22/11/79
Cahill, Edward, Admiralty clerk 10/5/53
Caianiello *see* Pezzo
Cailler, Mr., banker 7/11/38 ?
Cain, William, master mariner 6/10/29 ?
Caine,
Thomas Henry Hall, Sir (1853–1931), novelist 22/10/91
William Sproston (1842–1903), liberal M.P. 12/3/78, 10/6/84 c, 14/11/84, 12/5/90 n, 24/7/93 ff, 3/8/93 ff, 23/9/93
Caird,
James, Sir (1816–1892), Knight (1882), economist, liberal M.P. 1/5/54, 13/3/68, 16/10/69, 23/8/73 L, 18/11/81
John, Rev. Princ. (1820–1898), principal of Glasgow university (1873), philosopher 27/9/63, 17/11/77, 30/11/79 ?
Cairnes, John Elliot, Prof. (1823–1875), economist 11/12/57, 28/11/72
Cairns,
Hugh McCalmont, Sir (1819–1885), 1st Baron Cairns (1866), 1st Earl Cairns (1878), tory M.P., lawyer, Lord

Chancellor 17/7/58, 20/7/69, 24/6/71, 5/7/73 c, 8/7/84 n
John, Rev. (1818–1892), presbyterian minister 19/3/53
Caithbell, Mrs. 29/12/75
Caithness *see* Sinclair
Caivano, F., Neapolitan advocate 6/10/76
Cajetan, Maria Trigona e Parisi, Cardinal (-1837), Cardinal archbishop of Palermo (1834) 17/10/38
Calagero, Papa 29/1/59
Calcott, W. H. 25/8/77
Calcraft *see* Waldegrave
Calcraft,
Henry G., of the Treasury 17/4/86
John Hales (1796–1880), liberal M.P. 20/4/53
William (1800–1879), executioner 5/8/73
Caldburies, Dr. 11/11/76
Caldecott, John, Chester accountant 17/11/55
Calder, Miss 1/12/85
Calderwood,
Henry, Rev. Prof. (1830–1897), Scottish philosopher 31/5/79, 1/9/84
J., of Toxteth Mechanics Institute 5/10/58
Caldesi, Mr., photographer 9/7/63
Caldicott, John William, Rev. 26/4/77 ?
Caldwell,
Mr. 22/7/74
Mrs. 21/12/38 ?
David, parliamentary agent, secretary to the Forth & Clyde Navigation Co. 2/5/51
Henry Barney 16/5/26, 21/12/38 n
Hugh, Col. (-1882) 2/11/66
Call, R. 5/8/91
Callan, Philip (1837-) 14/5/77
Calland, Frederick 5/2/57
Callander, James Henry (-1851), liberal M.P. 5/6/33
Callaway, Henry, Bp. (1817–1890) 14/2/78 ?
Callcott, William Hutchins 23/4/76 ?
Callendar, William Romaine, pamphleteer 18/2/52
Callender *see* Graham
Caller, J. W. S. 19/11/90
Callimore, Mr. 18/11/87
Callingham, Mr. 10/8/86
Callisporis, Mr. 7/2/90
Callwall, Mr., Hawarden 11/10/52
Calthorpe,
Frederick Henry William Gough-, 5th Baron Calthorpe (1868) 24/4/68
George Gough- (1787–1851), 3rd Baron Calthorpe (1807) 4/8/38
Calton, J. T. 10/6/92
Calvert *see* Verney
Calvert,
Charles George, Rev. 29/8/79 ?
Edmund 13/3/41
Felix, Gen. 20/3/55
Frederick (1806–1891), barrister, pamphleteer, liberal M.P. 5/12/33, 1/7/47, 21/10/53
Harry, Gen. Sir, 1st Baronet 5/12/33 n
James, of Marykirk 20/9/33 n
James, provost of Montrose 10/12/51
John Mitchinson, Dr. (1803–1842) 22/12/38
R., tenant of Hawarden 22/9/49
Thomas, Prof. (1775–1840) 5/4/38
Calvetti, Mr. 15/10/32
Calyer, J. Y. 24/7/74
Cambridge *see* George William Frederick Charles
Camden *see* Pratt
Cameron,
Mr. 16/12/84
Charles, Rev. (1807–1861) 13/11/30
Charles, Sir (1841–1924), 1st Baronet (1893), physician, liberal M.P. 29/5/76 ff, 3/6/80, 7/6/80 n, 24/8/93 L
C. R., Mrs. 5/1/31
C. R., Rev. 5/1/31 n
Ebenezer, of Edinburgh 18/1/87
Francis Marten, Rev. 21/4/89
George Poulett, Col. 17/3/74, 30/9/74, 17/12/74
Murdoch, Dingwall town clerk 12/12/44
V. L. 14/8/88
Camoys *see* Stonor
Campana,
A. Fabio (1815–1882), composer 20/9/54 n
Giampetro (1808-), Marchese di Cavelli, Etruscan art collector 8/1/39
Margaret 20/9/54
Campanella, Guiseppe Maria, Rev. 23/3/77 n
Campbell *see* Balfour, Clavering, Hamilton, McNeill, Percy
Campbell,
rescue 27/8/59, 4/11/69
Miss 12/1/31
A., Sir, 4th Baronet 13/9/33 n
Alma, née Graham, Lady Breadalbane 15/5/76, 8/1/90, 12/1/90, 6/5/90
Andrew Ramsay, Rev. (-1872) 8/7/68
Anne (-1874), Duchess of Argyll 31/8/71
Arabella Georgina, author 10/5/69
Archibald, Sir, 2nd Baronet 12/11/50 n
Arthur Bruce Knight, Rev. (-1881) 26/6/76 ?
Augustus, Rev. 12/8/41
Caroline, Lady, née Bromley 13/9/33 n
Charles, Rev. 7/6/47 ?
Charles Montgomery, banker 5/4/31 ?
Colin, Lord (1853–1895), liberal M.P. 10/10/78, 27/3/79, 28/3/79, 16/11/86
Colin, Sir (1792–1863), 1st Baron Clyde, soldier 21/6/62

Campbell (*cont.*)
D., Greenock liberal 25/1/86
Digby 15/2/75
Donald, of Monzie 1/6/65
Donald A. 22/2/79 ?
Douglas, historian 16/10/92, 17/10/92 L
Dudley (1833–1900), barrister 22/6/77
Elizabeth Georgina (1824–1878), née Leveson-Gower, Duchess of Argyll 25/7/51 n, 6/4/70, 24/5/78, 25/5/78, 5/6/78
Elspeth Angela, Miss 4/4/84
Gavin (1851–1922), 6th Earl of Breadalbane (1871), 1st Marquis of Breadalbane (1885) 15/5/76, 1/12/79, 12/7/82, 8/1/90, 9/5/90, 25/3/93 ff, 7/5/93, 4/6/93, 2/11/93 n
George, of the Engagement 23/2/45 n
George Douglas, Lord; Duke of Argyll 30/4/45
G. J. 31/12/86, 20/9/87
Hugh Purves-Hume-, Sir (1812–1894), 7th Baronet (1833), tory M.P., of Marchmont 27/12/34, 4/12/40
James, Sir (1737–1805), of Inverneill 12/1/31 n
James, Sir (1790–1876), Knight (1842), of Glasgow 9/9/58
James, Sir (1818–1903), 5th Baronet (1824) 13/9/33 n
James Colquhoun, Bp. (1813–1895), bishop of Bangor 13/9/61
James William, Rev. (1810–1879) 12/9/36
Jane Augusta (–1842), née Pocklington 12/1/31
John, 5th Duke of Argyll 25/3/44 n
John (–1862), 2nd Marquis of Breadalbane (1834) 3/6/53
John (1779–1861), 1st Baron Campbell, lord chancellor 26/5/56
John Douglas Edward Henry, 7th Duke of Argyll 9/2/46 n
John Douglas Sutherland (1845–1914), 9th Duke of Argyll (1900), Marquis of Lorne, governor of Canada (1878), hymnist, liberal M.P. 10/12/59, 9/11/71, 16/11/81, 3/2/83, 17/5/83 L, 25/11/84, 17/9/85 L, 1/2/86, 24/3/86
John Frederick Vaughan, Lord (1817–1898), 2nd Earl Cawdor (1860), Viscount Emlyn, tory M.P. 10/7/52, 16/2/53
Lachlan T., lawyer in Jamaica 27/2/35
Margaret, Lady (–1871), née Coldstream 13/9/33 n
Margaret Purves-Hume-, Lady (–1839), née Spottiswoode 27/12/34 n
Patrick William, Midlothian election agent 17/2/79, 29/9/85 L, 8/6/86, 9/6/86 L, 3/7/86, 20/10/90 ff, 28/10/90, 29/6/92 ff, 4/4/93
Peter Colin, Principal (–1876) 23/3/65
Robert, Rev. 15/11/57
Robert B., American consul 17/6/59
Stuart 28/10/87
Walter Frederick, former liberal M.P. 29/5/46 ?
William Frederick, 2nd Baron Stratheden (1860), 2nd Baron Campbell of St. Andrews (1861), liberal M.P. 12/4/48
Campden *see* Noel
Campden, G. J. S., of Chester 26/8/75
Campello, Enrico di, Count 17/9/81, 19/11/81
Camperdown *see* Duncan
Campobasso,
Baron 24/1/72
Baroness 24/1/72
Camuccini, Vicenzo (1771–1844), artist 10/4/32
Canadia, Mrs. 8/4/59
Canadien, T. J. 4/6/92
Canala, G. D. 4/11/76
Canard, L. 18/10/90
Canburoff, Mr. 8/4/79
Candall, Mr. 12/7/83
Candell, H. S. 28/2/79
Candlish,
John (1816–1874), liberal M.P. 11/4/67
Robert Smith, Rev. Dr. (1806–1873), free churchman 25/12/70
Cane,
Charles Du, Sir (1825–1889), Knight (1875), governor of Tasmania (1869), chairman of customs board (1878) 29/12/71, 6/5/80
Edward, income tax commissioner 24/12/52
Cannan, D. A. 26/3/68
Canney, A. S., Rev. 25/1/56
Canning *see* Burgh
Canning,
A. J. 28/5/78
Albert Stratford George (1832–1916) 20/8/75
C., Lady, née Stuart 13/2/36
Charles John 18/10/25
Eliza Charlotte, née Alexander, Lady Stratford de Redcliffe 30/10/52
George (1770–1827), prime minister 10/6/26 n, 7/8/27, 10/8/27
George Charles (1801–1820) 14/9/27
Harriet (–1817), née Raikes 12/7/32
Joan (–1837), Viscountess Canning (1828), née Scott 27/10/27
Louisa, Miss 26/5/79, 18/8/88
Stratford, Sir (1786–1880), Viscount Stratford de Redcliffe (1852), diplomatist, dedicatee of the *Bulgarian Horrors*

12/7/32 n, 28/4/47, 26/10/52, 30/10/52 ff, 23/12/52, 17/12/53, 22/2/58, 31/8/70 L, 22/4/71, 15/1/72, 16/5/73, 20/7/75, 26/5/76, 27/6/76, 26/7/76, 5/9/76 n, 6/9/76, 23/7/77, 2/1/79, 7/6/79 ff, 29/12/96
Cannon, Thomas, of Covent Garden 13/2/58
Canny, Mr. 25/2/87
Cantacuzene, G., Prince, Russian diplomat in London 19/6/83, 18/6/84, 15/9/84
Canterbury *see* Sutton
Canton, William, publisher 4/4/92
Cantwell, Robert, surveyor 30/7/40, 19/7/51
Canville, rescue 15/4/56
Caparn,
  Richard, of Newark 21/8/40, 26/8/41, 13/9/55
  Robert, attorney, G's agent at Newark 1/10/32
  Robert, Mrs. 24/2/43
  Thomas, druggist, mayor of Newark 1/10/32 n
  William, of Newark 16/11/35
  William Barton (-1875) 25/3/52
Cape, Lawson, Dr., physician 4/11/42
Capebianco, Cav. 18/1/89
Capel, Reginald Algernon (1830-1906) 14/7/72
Capel, Cuerton & Lawford, Messrs., brokers 26/3/44
Capell,
  A. A., 6th Earl of Essex 13/7/46 n
  Caroline Janetta, née Beauclerk, Lady Essex 13/7/46
  Louisa (-1876), Lady Essex 5/1/72
Capellini, Giovanni, Prof. 25/9/88 ?
Capes,
  George, solicitor 1/12/41
  John Moore, Rev. (1812-1889) 23/4/71, 18/1/72 L
Caponetto, Sig., dealer 15/5/72
Capper,
  Mr., mind-reader 10/6/85
  John, linen shop owner 18/9/41, 30/7/45
Capra, N. 22/7/75
Caprano, Sig. 26/1/88
Capston, Mr., of U.S.A. 4/11/87
Car, Miss, rescue 18/1/54
Caracciolo *see* Pezzo
Caradoc, John Hobart (1799-1873), 2nd Baron Howden (1839), ambassador 25/2/60
Carapanos, Constantine, Rev. 12/4/78
Caravia, Mrs. 27/7/50
Carburlotti, Sig. 3/10/79
Carbutt,
  Edward Homer (1838-), liberal M.P. 27/7/83
  E. N. 26/2/80
Card, Henry, Rev. (1779-1844) 14/10/29
Carden,
  James, Rev. 14/2/48
  Pamela Elizabeth Edith, Lady (-1874) 5/4/58
  Robert Walter, Sir (1801-1888), 1st Baronet (1887), tory M.P. 5/4/58 n
Cardi, C. B. 31/3/59
Cardigan *see* Brudenell
Cardon, R., Italian legal historian 19/5/83
Cardwell,
  rescue 24/6/68
  Anne, née Parker, Lady Cardwell 2/7/53
  Edward 1/6/44
  Edward, Prof. (1787-1861), church historian 23/10/28, 29/1/57, 3/6/57
Carelli,
  Gabrielli, artist 9/12/50
  Gonsalvo (-1900), artist 9/12/50
Carew,
  Pole-, Miss 29/11/32
  Robert Shapland (1818-1881), 2nd Baron Carew 28/4/69
Carey,
  Adolphus Frederick, Rev. 28/8/56 ?
  George Henry 31/8/32
  J., Rev., of Guernsey 1/12/41
  James 20/2/83 n
Cargill, W. Walter, Silver Stick 12/2/64
Carington,
  Rupert C. G. (1852-1929), 4th Baron Carington (1928) 11/9/76 n
  William Henry Peregrine, Col. (1845-1914), liberal M.P. 10/5/80
Cariss, A., of Liverpool 29/9/64
Caritati, Dr., of Ionia 1/2/59
Carleton, Hiram, Rev., of U.S.A. 28/2/76
Carley, G. C. 3/10/90
Carlingford *see* Fortescue
Carlisle *see* Howard
Carlisle, Henry E., author 28/1/85
Carlyle,
  Mr. 15/9/85
  Gavin, Rev. 11/7/91
  Thomas (1795-1881), author 8/7/45, 21/6/49, 2/4/82, 3/6/82, 2/9/93
Carlyon *see* Browne
Carment, Mr. 23/5/79
Carmichael,
  Mrs. 11/5/49
  J., Liverpool merchant 7/3/54
  J., of Stirling 24/3/43
  James Morse, Sir (1844-1902), 3rd Baronet (1883) 19/12/84, 24/12/84, 11/4/86, 12/4/86 ff, 21/4/86 L, 23/4/86 L, 27/4/86 L, 8/8/86, 21/4/88, 6/11/88, 15/11/88 ff, 18/12/88 ff, 1/8/89 ff, 13/2/90 ff, 28/2/90 ff, 7/7/90 ff, 21/11/90 ff, 15/4/91 ff, 7/3/92 ff, 16/5/92 ff

Carmichael (*cont.*)
Thomas David Gibson-, Sir (1859–1926), 11th Baronet (1891), 1st Baron Carmichael (1912), liberal M.P. 6/4/80, 29/1/94 n
Thomas Gibson-, Sir (–1855), 9th Baronet (1850) 18/11/50
Carnarvon *see* Herbert
Carne, William Inglis, commission agent 6/3/45
Carné, Louis Joseph Marie de (1804–1876), Comte de Carné Marcein, diplomat 16/6/38
Carnegie,
Mr. 12/7/72
Agnes 29/11/48
Andrew 31/7/82
Catherine Hamilton, Lady (–1855), née Noel 4/12/49
Charlotte, Lady (–1848), née Lysons 21/12/33
Christina Mary 29/11/48
David, temperance advocate 18/5/76 ?
David, Sir, 6th Baronet 29/11/48
Elizabeth 29/11/48
Georgina Maria (–1874), née Elliot, Lady Northesk 10/11/66
James (1827–1905), 9th Earl of Southesk 17/9/84
James, Sir, 5th Baronet (1805) 21/12/33 n
James, Sir (–1905), 6th Baronet (1849), 9th Earl of Southesk (1855) 13/1/49, 4/10/49, 1/5/60, 27/10/85 L
Jane 29/11/48
John Hemery, Rev. 11/12/69
Louise, née Whitfield 13/6/87
William Hopetoun (1794–1878), 8th Earl of Northesk (1831) 10/11/66
Carnforth, W., Rev. 29/12/77
Carnot, President 29/12/87
Carodogana, Sig. 29/9/79
Carolsfeld, Julius Veit Hans Schnorr von (1794–1872), artist 11/1/39 n
Carpenter,
Charles Thomas, Rev. 10/2/45 ?
Walter Cecil Talbot (1834–1904) 15/10/63
William Benjamin, Prof. (1813–1885), naturalist 17/7/57, 14/1/73
William Boyd, Bp. (1841–1918) 18/3/81, 17/8/81, 20/4/84, 4/5/84
Carpenter & Westley, Messrs., London opticians 11/4/57, 20/11/79
Carr *see* Hobart, Rolfe
Carr,
D. McC. 8/2/79
Edward, Rev. Dr. 27/9/69 ?
J. D. 9/6/58
J. R., senior magistrate, Oxford 3/2/90
J. T. 1/2/76
Thomas William, Rev. 15/6/75
William, of Leeds 10/8/78 ?
Carre, Walter Riddell- (1807–1905) 31/1/66
Carré, Collings Mauger, Irvingite 2/2/52 ?
Carrel, Mr. 11/12/79
Carretto, Countess 31/1/89
Carrick,
J. P., Rev. 16/7/92
Robert Mallabar, Rev. 7/9/90
Carrington *see* Smith
Carrington,
Alfred, of Barker, Hignett, Carrington, Chester solicitors 20/9/80, 9/9/82
Charles Robert Wynn- (1843–1928), 3rd Baron Carrington (1868), 1st Marquis of Lincolnshire (1912), liberal minister 27/8/76, 6/3/90 n, 8/3/90, 23/9/93, 29/9/93, 7/10/93
Henry, Rev. 11/7/51
John, master mariner 2/12/68 ?
R., of the Admiralty 14/3/59
Carrington & Barker 11/4/91
Carroll,
A. 17/11/87
William, Sir (1819–1890), lord mayor of Dublin (1868) 21/12/68
William George, Rev., of Dublin 18/5/68
Carruthers, John Robert, Rev. (1795–1843) 3/12/25
Carruti, Domenico, historian 28/8/77, 18/12/77
Carse, J. H. 23/11/78
Carson,
Edward Henry, Sir (1854–1935), unionist M.P. 9/6/93, 29/1/94
Elizabeth, of Seaforth 2/1/32 ?
Thomas, attorney 22/2/34
Thomas, Bp. (1805–1874) 12/2/70 n
Carstairs *see* Molesworth
Carswell & Co., wine merchants 15/5/74
Carta, Natale, Italian artist 11/12/38
Carter,
rescue 2/5/65
B. W. 20/2/79
Eccles James, Rev. 9/3/52
John (1804–1878), London clockmaker, alderman 5/4/67
John Bonham- (1817–1884), liberal M.P. 8/8/61, 26/3/72, 4/4/72
Samuel (1805–1878), solicitor 4/6/58
S. M., Rev. 10/8/88
Thomas, Rev., of Liverpool 22/10/57
Thomas, Rev. (1775–1868) 10/6/27
Thomas Thellusson, Rev. 8/12/49
William Allan 13/7/75 ?
Carter & Bonus, London brokers 27/11/46
Carthew, C. 4/12/78
Cartier, George Etienne, Sir (1814–1873), Canadian politician 10/3/69

Cartman, John, Rev., home ruler in Yorkshire 14/1/86
Cartmell, Studholme, of Carlisle 13/3/80
Carton, H. A. 27/1/90
Cartwright,
James Joel, of Public Record Office 11/4/78
Richard Aubrey (1811–1891) 28/11/27 ?
Roma Adelaide Frances, Miss 11/12/72 ?
Samuel (1789–1864), G's dentist 24/7/45
William Chauncy, Sir (1853–1933), British consul in Egypt 19/6/82
William Cornwallis (1825–1915), liberal M.P. 30/9/66, 20/12/66, 26/12/66, 27/8/68, 23/11/69 L, 19/2/78 ?
W. R. (1771–1847), tory M.P. 28/11/27 ?
Caruso, Demetrio, Count, of Ionia 3/12/58
Carver,
Edward Twist, courtier 9/2/47
James, Rev. (1791–1866) 4/5/43 n
Cary,
rescue 8/2/55
Miss 2/1/81
Henry, Rev. 9/5/48 ?
Lucius Bentinck, 10th Viscount Falkland (1809), 1st Baron Hunsdon (1832), colonial governor 3/3/46
Carysfort *see* Proby
Casamayor *see* Brownrigg
Casati, Gabriel, Count (1798–1873), mayor of Milan 21/9/38
Case,
Mr., of Huyton 13/4/32
Mrs. 14/4/32
George, Rev. Dr., Roman Catholic 11/6/75
Thomas (1811–1887) 14/4/32
Casement, Mr. 12/11/85
Casenove, Dr. 7/7/92
Casey, James R., London printer 4/5/48 ?
Caskin, J. F. 1/10/77
Cassacciolo, Giuseppi, Don, Prince Torelli, Neapolitan politician 15/2/51
Cassani, Giacomo, Prof., of Bologna 14/11/75
Cassano, De, Princess 24/8/92
Casse, Mrs. 9/12/43
Cassell, Messrs., publishers 13/4/74, 1/4/90
Cassidy, B. J. 7/4/74
Cassilis *see* Kennedy
Casson,
rescue 29/10/70
R. J., of *Dundee Courier* 14/4/89
Cassons, Mrs. 8/8/68
Castelanni, Augusto, jewellery dealer in Rome 31/12/66
Castelar, Sig. 2/6/92
Castell, A. 21/5/90
Castellaneta, Duca di 1/2/88
Castelvecchio *see* Barberini
Castille, Hippolyte (1820–1856) 9/8/56
Castledale, Mr. 24/9/77
Castledine, Theodore 9/3/77 ?
Castlereagh *see* Stewart
Castleross *see* Browne
Castletown *see* Fitzpatrick
Casto, Julius, Italian author 7/6/52
Castrofiana, Countess 14/1/69
Castromediano, Sigismondo (1811–1895), Duke of Morciano and Caballino 6/4/59, 8/6/59
Caswall,
Alfred, barrister 11/8/45
Henry, Rev. 29/9/42, 18/1/43
Catalani, T., Chevalier 3/5/79
Catchpool, W. 7/5/89
Cathcart, Charles Murray, Gen. (1783–1859), 2nd Earl Cathcart (1843), Lord Greenock, colonial governor 16/12/33 n, 3/1/46 n
Cathen, Rev. Mr. 22/5/77
Cather,
John, Rev. Dr. (1814–1888), archdeacon of Tuam 18/1/69
R. G., Rev. Dr. 2/1/65
Catherall,
Mrs., of Hawarden 5/5/74
J., of Hawarden 15/11/76
N. 16/1/79
Robert, Hawarden shopkeeper 13/8/61
Cathie, Dr. 3/12/75
Catholic Publication Society 24/1/76
Catley, Horace, secretary of G. N. E. railway 10/10/49 n
Catlin, W. 9/4/78
Catlow, Mr. 1/5/79
Cattell, Christopher William, solicitor 19/7/76 ?
Cattermole, Richard, Rev. (1795–1858) 2/5/55 ?
Cattley, Stephen Reed, Rev. 17/6/50
Caudle, W.& C., paper makers 12/4/68
Caudwell, Francis, Rev. 26/11/75
Caught, Thomas, of Chiswick 1/2/76
Caulfeild, Anne (–1876), née Bermingham, Countess of Charlemont 6/1/46
Caussenville, Mlle., singer 9/7/62
Causton,
Richard Knight, liberal chairman 27/7/87
Thomas, Rev. 7/2/40
Cavan *see* Lambart
Cavan,
A. W. 20/7/75 fl
W. L. 20/7/75 fl
Cave *see* Pusey
Cave,
Alfred T. T. Verney- (1849–1928), 5th Baron Braye (1879) 28/5/83
J. A. 23/9/78
Robert Otway (–1844), liberal M.P. 23/9/44
Stephen, Sir (1820–1889), tory M.P. 23/5/56

Cavell, John C., Mayor of Oxford 17/10/65 n
Cavelli *see* Campana
Cavendish *see* Egerton, Gower, Lyttelton
Cavendish,
Ada, Miss, actress 24/4/83 n
Augustus, Rev. (1798–1864) 25/3/35 ?
Beatrice Constance, Lady, née Grosvenor 14/11/77 n
Charles Compton William (1850–1907), 3rd Baron Chesham (1882) 14/11/77 n
Edward, Lord (1838–1891), whig M.P. 7/10/64 n
Emma Elizabeth, Lady, née Lascelles 7/10/64
Frederick Charles, Lord 5/9/41 n
George Henry, Lord (1810–1880), whig M.P. 14/6/44
Henrietta Frances (–1884), Lady Chesham 22/1/84, 6/2/84, 1/3/84
Louisa (–1863), née O'Callaghan 23/2/50
Louise Fredericke Auguste, née von Alten, Duchess of Devonshire, Duchess of Manchester 6/12/68, 12/9/85, 5/6/90 ?
Lucy Caroline, Lady Frederick Cavendish 5/9/41
R., 2nd Baron Westpark 25/3/35 n
Richard, Lord (1812–1873) 23/6/27, 15/10/52, 28/11/55 ff, 19/12/65, 9/6/66, 7/7/72, 14/11/73, 19/11/73
Spencer Compton; Lord Hartington; Duke of Devonshire 7/6/59 n
Thomas, Rev. (1801–1859) 25/3/35 ?
Victor Christian William, Lord (1868–1938), 9th Duke of Devonshire (1908), liberal unionist M.P. 24/5/92
W., 5th Duke of Devonshire 13/2/32 n
William (1808–1891), 5th Earl of Burlington (1834), 7th Duke of Devonshire (1858) 23/6/27 n, 1/5/50, 24/11/65, 30/5/73, 25/11/73, 18/11/75 ff, 20/12/80 L, 30/1/85 ff
William George (1815–1882), 2nd Baron Chesham (1863) 25/2/65, 28/3/72
Caveneagh, James, Lieut. 16/10/78
Caverns, C., Rev., of U.S.A. 6/11/89
Cavour, Camillo Benso di, Count (1810–1861), Italian statesman 6/8/52, 5/12/55, 3/3/59, 25/11/62, 25/12/68, 15/9/70, 29/6/88, 6/7/88 n, 19/7/92, 15/4/93, 28/10/93
Cawbank, rescue 3/1/68
Cawdor *see* Campbell
Cawkwell, William (1808–1897), of L.N.W. railway 5/10/65
Cawnell, T. 3/9/77
Cawthorn & Hutt, Messrs., booksellers 22/11/87
Cay,
Colin, East India civil servant 10/7/35 n
Geddes Elizabeth 10/7/35 n
George (1810–1844) 10/7/35 n
John, Edinburgh advocate 10/7/35 n
Robert Dundas, assistant secretary of the Glenalmond fund 18/9/45
Cayley,
Charles Bagot (1823–1883), translator 9/12/76
Edward Stillingfleet (1802–1862), liberal M.P. 11/1/42, 1/6/61
W., Canadian 23/4/49, 25/5/49
Cazenove, John Gibson, Rev. (–1896) 30/12/54, 21/1/75, 26/4/75 n, 8/5/75, 16/7/75
Cecil *see* Hope, Stewart
Cecil,
Algernon (1879–1853), author 16/3/92 ?
Eustace Brownlow Henry, Lord (1834–1921), tory M.P. 3/1/73
Florence Mary, Lady 4/8/87
Frances Mary Gascoyne- (–1839), née Gascoygne, Lady Salisbury 28/2/35
Georgina Charlotte (–1899), Lady Cranborne, Lady Salisbury 11/3/68, 6/6/83, 30/6/83, 3/12/84, 2/5/90, 9/3/92
J., 1st Marquis of Salisbury 1/12/35 n
James Brownlow William Gascoyne- (1791–1868), 2nd Marquis of Salisbury (1823) 28/2/35 n
James Edward Herbert Gascoyne- (1861–1947), 4th Marquis of Salisbury (1903), Lord Cranborne 29/11/83
Mary Amelia, née Hill, Lady Salisbury 1/12/35
Mary Catherine (–1900), née West, Lady Salisbury (1847), Lady Derby (1870) 18/6/52
Robert Arthur Talbot Gascoyne-, Lord; 3rd Marquis of Salisbury 28/2/35 n
Robert Gascoyne-, Lord (1864–1958) 16/5/80, 5/7/93
Rupert William Ernest Gascoyne-, Rev. Lord (1863–1936) 4/8/87
Celotti, Abate, Florentine art collector 20/3/32
Cephala, A. N., Dr., of Ionia 7/1/59
Cernuschi, Henri, economist 10/3/76
Ceropii, Mr. 15/1/67
Cerreti, Sig. 21/1/88
Cerrito, Francesca (–1909), dancer 21/10/50
Cerruti, Sig. 28/8/77
César, Louis Gabriel (1804–1888), Comte de Kergoulay, French industrialist and legitimist politician 22/2/60
Cesare, Carlo di, political writer 8/1/70, 2/1/88
Cesaresco, Evelyn Martinengo-, Countess (–1931) 18/4/90

Cesnola, Luigi Palma di, Count 19/11/72
Cetewayo, King of the Zulus 4/6/81, 29/8/81, 16/4/82, 27/5/82, 31/5/82 c, 21/6/82 c, 22/7/82, 31/7/82 c, 9/8/82, 12/8/82, 23/8/82, 2/10/82, 5/1/83 n, 30/5/83, 22/6/83, 7/7/83 c, 2/9/83, 28/9/83, 29/10/83, 8/11/83, 10/11/83 c, 20/11/83 c, 19/12/83
Chable, Rev. Mr. 29/10/45
Chabot,
Geraldine, née Foley, Countess Jarnac 24/9/45 n
Philip James (-1868), merchant 13/5/52 ?
Phillippe F. A. de Rohan-, Count Jarnac 24/9/45
Chace, Mr. 6/3/38
Chadwell, C. B., Oxford cutler 23/10/52
Chadwick,
David, solicitor 14/12/81
David (1821-1895), liberal M.P. (1868) 5/3/68
Edwin, Sir (1800-1890), Utilitarian 2/7/54
S. A. 8/6/68
W. H., former Chartist 22/9/88, 19/11/89
Chaffers,
Thomas, Rev. (-1860) 1/6/50
William (1811-1892), art valuer 15/7/61
Chaillu, Paul Belloni Du (1831-1903), explorer 25/2/61, 5/2/90
Chairmen, Mr. 23/8/60
Chalk, James Jell, Sir (1803-1878), secretary to Ecclesiastical Commissioners 15/11/64, 1/7/65
Challemel-Lacour, Paul-Armand (1827-1896) 27/2/83, 28/2/83
Challenger, Samuel Christopher, Rev., Methodist 4/3/80
Challis,
Thomas (-1874), Lord Mayor of London (1852), liberal M.P. 12/2/53
William, of Fasque 28/12/46
Challoner, Messrs., Liverpool timber merchants? 2/1/43
Chalmers,
J. K. 14/7/88
Patrick (-1854), radical M.P. 30/5/50 ?
Thomas, Rev. Prof. 26/5/28
Chamaillard, Henri Pierre Charles De, Royalist advocate 10/8/55
Chamberlain,
Arthur Neville (1869-1940) 1/6/77
Frederick Thomas, Rev., of Hawarden 4/1/69, 14/12/73
Joseph 9/3/70 n
Joseph Austen, Sir (1863-1937), liberal unionist M.P. 1/6/77
Robert, Rev. 13/12/45
Thomas, Rev. (1810-1892) 24/11/31
Chamberlaine, George John, of Chester 14/9/49
Chamberlin, Robert (1804-1876), of Norwich 17/10/56 n
Chambermaid, of Ireland 15/10/38
Chambers,
E., Rev. 4/5/78
Edmund Kerchever, Sir (1866-1954) 28/2/88
J. C., Rev. 10/1/47, 29/6/58
J. J. D., Miss 19/10/54
O. 9/12/76
Thomas, Sir (1814-1891), liberal M.P. 20/5/71, 14/11/72
Violet, Miss 21/8/87
William, Dr., physician 9/8/70
Chambers & Co., Edinburgh publishers 21/7/56
Chambres,
F. J. 24/4/67
W., Liverpool printer 21/10/58
Chambure, Eugene-Andoche Pelletier de (1813-1897) 21/4/41
Chamerovzow, Louis Alexis, pamphleteer 7/8/48
Champion, H. M. L. E., Col. 6/3/77
Champnes, Thomas Weldon, Rev. (1773-1841) 23/4/26
Champneys, William Weldon, Rev. 20/7/47
Chance,
George, barrister 20/6/48
Robert Lucas (-1865), glass manufacturer 19/9/53
William & Co., merchants 26/7/48
Chancellor, Mr., photographer of Dublin 24/10/77, 6/11/77
Chandler,
George, Rev. (1779-1859), dean of Chichester (1830) 23/3/34
J. 9/2/57
Chandos *see* Grenville
Changarnier, Nicholas A. T., General, French general 8/8/49
Channing, Francis Allston, Sir (1841-1926), 1st Baron Channing (1912), liberal M.P. 7/9/77, 30/8/89
Channon, Mr., butler at Bowden 10/2/63
Chant, Mr. 21/3/78, 20/9/81
Chantell, rescue 28/2/72
Chantrey, Francis Legatt, Sir (1781-1842), sculptor 1/4/34 n, 22/7/34, 21/3/38
Chaplin *see* Ellice
Chaplin,
Edward (1772-1858) 24/12/37 n
Edward John, Rev. (-1853), don 11/5/50
George Ayscough, Rev. 4/8/57
Henry (1840-1923), tory M.P. 16/2/77, 12/5/82, 3/1/84, 19/12/85, 29/8/92, 15/4/93, 27/8/93

Chaplin (*cont.*)
William, Rev. (1825–1906) 20/10/56, 8/9/90 ?
Chapman,
rescue 1/6/75
Messrs., solicitors 19/5/77, 23/8/77
Charles, Rev. (1807–1849) 31/1/27
David Barclay, banker 1/3/43, 19/1/54, 24/5/55, 11/3/61
David Ward (1828–1921) 2/2/56
Edward Martin, Rev. 27/7/75 ?
Elizabeth Rachel, Miss 8/1/90, 8/12/90
James, Bp. (1799–1879), bishop of Columbo (1845) 5/3/34, 19/9/61, 24/1/77
J. C., journalist 19/3/77 ?
John, Dr. (–1894), editor of *Western Review*, physician 12/2/52, 29/12/87
Matthew James (–1865), poet 19/2/67 n
Robert, Customs Department 20/6/44 ?
Thomas 8/11/77
Chappel, W. P., Rev. 25/12/84
Chappuis, P. E., Luminarium 18/2/76 ?
Charlemont *see* Caulfeild
Charles,
G's servant in Rome 20/12/66
Archduke 29/11/42 n
Mad., rescue? 21/5/70, 14/7/70
Alexander John Augustus, Grand Duke of Saxe-Weimar-Eisenach 2/11/67
Ludwig Frederick (1786–1819), Grand Duke of Baden 27/10/45 n
Charles-Albert (1798–1849), King of Sardinia-Piedmont (1831) 29/2/32
Charles Felix (1765–1831), King of Sardinia (1821) 29/2/32
Charles I,
(1600–1649) 30/1/26 n
(1823–1891), of Wurtemburg 12/8/53 n
Charles III (1716–1788), King of the Two Sicilies (1734), King of Spain (1759) 22/5/32
Charles IV, King of Spain 20/11/38 n
Charles X, King of France 13/2/32 n
Charles of Denmark, Prince, King Haakon of Norway (1905) 27/7/96
Charlesworth, E. P., Dr., of London, physician 4/12/39
Charley,
H. B. K. 24/12/89
William Thomas, Sir (1833–1904), tory M.P. 15/7/73
Charlotte Augusta,
(–1817), Princess of England 6/2/32 n
(1792–1873), Empress of Austria 30/6/32
Charlotte Frederica (1784–1840), Princess of Mecklenburg-Schwerin 5/4/32
Charlton,
Edmund Lechmere (1785–1845), whig M.P. 3/6/35 n
M. 3/8/66
Charnock, W., shopkeeper of Chester 22/5/51
Charrière,
Miss, of Potters Bar 22/10/31, 2/11/43
Mrs. 10/3/29, 22/10/31
Ernest (1805–1865), French writer 10/12/28 ?
Charrington,
rescue 30/1/73
Mr. 6/4/78
F. N. 2/6/90
Charter, Mrs. 18/7/78
Charteris,
Dr. 11/12/85
Archibald Hamilton, Rev. Prof. (1835–1908) 9/1/87
Chartres *see* Orléans
Chase,
Drummond Percy, Rev. (1820–1902), don 31/12/53
James Compigné, Rev. (1811–1890) 30/11/37
K., Mrs. 29/10/87
Chaster, Albert William, legal writer 16/11/87
Chateaurenard, F., French Ambassador's Secretary 9/11/60, 5/7/61
Chatelain, Jean Baptiste F. E. de (1801–1881) 26/3/70
Chattaway, Charles, merchant 3/12/78 ?
Chatterton,
Elizabeth, of Toxteth Park 29/6/60 ?
Hedges Eyre (1819–1910), barrister 23/4/75 ?
Chatto *see* Saint Clair
Chatto and Windus, publishers 10/4/77
Chaudordy, Jean de, Comte (1826–1899), French diplomat 2/11/70
Chauffonier, M. 12/9/77
Chaver, S. 14/6/88
Chaytor, Mr., coalman 5/7/79
Cheales, Alan Benjamin, Rev. 27/11/77
Cheere, Robert, barrister 6/6/59 ?
Cheeseman, Henry Jordan, Rev. 20/5/89
Cheeswright, James William, frame maker 26/2/79 ?
Cheetham, John (1802–1886), liberal M.P. 6/6/56
Chelmsford *see* Thesiger
Chelsea *see* Cadogan
Chenery, Thomas (1826–1884), editor of *The Times* 13/4/78
Chérif Pasha (1819–1888) 3/1/84, 22/1/84
Chermside,
Herbert Charles, Sir (1850–1929) 29/3/84
H. L., Mrs., authoress 22/12/74
Richard Seymour Conway, Rev. 19/7/52, 1/4/61
Cherriton, E. A. 28/9/88

Cherry, J. R. 22/5/90
Chesham *see* Cavendish
Chesney, Mr. 15/12/75
Chesshire, Humphrey Pountney, Rev. (-1900) 11/3/74 ?
Chesshyre, C. J. 24/6/78
Chesson, F. W. 15/10/76, 5/3/77, 19/2/78, 4/6/84
Chester *see* Childers
Chester,
rescue 6/6/60, 13/2/67
Harry, Privy Council clerk 17/4/47
Joseph Lemuel, Col. (1821-1882) 14/10/76
Robert, Sir 8/12/33 n
Chester Chronicle, reporter of 30/9/84
Chesterfield, Mrs., rescue 12/6/79, 21/6/79
Chesterton, George Laval, Governor of Coldbathfields Prison 4/8/53
Cheston, C. 31/1/91
Chetwoode, Edward Wilmot 10/3/45
Chetwynd *see* Hanmer
Chetwynd, George, Sir, 2nd Baronet (1824) 7/10/44
Chevalier,
Michel (1806-1879), French economist 15/10/59, 22/5/62, 17/1/67, 24/1/67, 1/9/69 L, 13/9/69 L, 29/11/69 L, 27/1/70 L, 25/7/70 L, 6/9/70 L, 14/9/70 L, 21/9/70 L, 25/11/70 L, 16/2/71 L, 24/1/72 L, 14/10/72 L
William 2/12/75
Chevannes, Mad., widow of H. H. Joy 5/8/49
Cheyne, Patrick, Rev., Episcopalian priest 23/2/48, 12/6/58
Chiara, Piero 19/2/80
Chichester *see* Pelham
Chichester,
Arthur, Lord (1808-1840), whig M.P. 26/4/27
Edward, Bp. (1799-1889), 4th Marquis of Donegal (1883) 7/8/58 n
G. A., 2nd Marquis of Donegal 26/4/27 n
Chick, Samuel, Marylebone Liberal association 6/7/77, 24/6/79 n, 27/2/80
Chidlow, Charles, Rev. 1/12/71, 1/9/72, 24/8/74
Chiene, Major 11/5/76
Chignell, Robert, art biographer 15/1/94 L
Child,
Smith, Sir (1808-1869), Baronet (1868), tory M.P. 9/8/54
William Humphrey, Rev. 26/2/77
William S. H. 29/9/75
Child, Coles & Co., coal merchant 22/2/53
Childe,
Miss 11/8/63
Henry Langdon 11/7/41
Childers *see* Burroughs
Childers,
Charles, Rev. (1806-1896) 21/2/29, 17/7/80, 29/1/88
Dulcibella (-1865), née Chester 8/12/33
Emily, née Walker 19/1/71
Hugh Culling Eardley 16/3/60
Childs, George W., American publisher 15/8/90
Chilver, E. 22/6/75
Chintaman, H. 12/4/74
Chiotes, Panagiote, Greek author 23/8/60
Chipham, Mr., librarian of Leicester 6/4/80
Chisholm *see* Robertson
Chisholm,
Mrs., of Bridaig, Dingwall 29/8/53, 3/9/53, 27/9/53, 27/9/58
Alexander, of Chisholm 7/4/37 n
Alexander William (1810-1838), known as The Chisholm, tory M.P. 13/10/27
Archibald (-1877) 22/7/48 n
Caroline (-1877), née Jones, charity worker 22/7/48
Duncan MacDonnell (-1858), The Chisholm (1838) 20/10/27, 23/1/42
Henry Ward, of the Exchequer 17/12/87
James Sutherland (-1885), known as The Chisholm (1859) 20/9/35 n
John, of Dingwall 27/10/47
Roderick, Mrs. 20/9/35 ?
Chittenden, G. R., of Illinois 15/6/81 L
Chitty,
Edward, barrister 18/3/47
Thomas, barrister 18/3/47
Chivers, George 16/12/56, 1/12/57 ?
Cholmeley,
John, Rev. (-1895) 14/1/53
Montague John, Sir (180-1874), 2nd Baronet (1831) 19/8/51
Cholmley, Hannah, of Whitby 28/8/71
Cholmondeley,
Alice Mary (-1868), née Egerton 27/11/68
George Horatio, 2nd Marquis of Cholmondeley (1827) 8/3/37
Hugh, Lord (1811-1887), 2nd Baron Delamere (1855), tory M.P. 17/10/28
Reginald 27/11/68 n
Sarah, Lady, née Hay, Lady Delamere 23/3/48
S. C., Lady, née Somerset 8/3/37 n
Chondry, P. M. 12/10/91
Chopin, A. 15/7/90
Chreptowisch, Count 24/2/58
Christial, Jonathan (1811-1887), Lord justice 22/6/71
Christian,
Prince, Prince of Schleswig-Holstein 25/5/46 n, 29/11/70, 30/11/72, 24/8/73
James, clerk to Kincardine lieutenancy 27/9/49

Christian (*cont.*)
Peter, W. S. 26/1/38
Christian, 'Little' 27/3/85
Christian VIII, King (1839–), King of Denmark 5/4/32 n
Christian IX, King of Denmark 17/9/83
Christian Victor, Prince (1867–), Prince of Schleswig-Holstein 23/9/69
Christich, Mr., Serbian interior minister 24/3/63
Christie,
Miss 1/11/55
Misses 15/3/33
Mrs. 27/5/27
Albany Henry 7/2/39 n
Albany James, Rev. (1818–1891), Jesuit priest 5/9/69, 30/10/89
Albert James 29/11/44
Charles Henry, Rev. (1820–) 7/2/39
George Henry (1817–1887), auctioneer 29/9/25
James, Rev., of Turriff 12/12/56
J. D. 13/10/85
Langham (1789–1861) 15/3/33 n
Margaret Elizabeth (–1866), née Gosling 27/4/33
William Dougal (1816–1874), liberal M.P. 13/6/41
W. P. 3/3/79
Christie, Manson & Woods, Messrs., auctioneers 16/6/43
Christison, Robert, Sir (1797–1882), professor of Edinburgh 17/4/60, 22/10/60, 27/9/61
Christmas *see* Fearn
Christodoulaki, Nicolaos 17/12/89
Christopher, J. S., of London 13/2/60
Christopherson, Henry, Rev. 20/11/64
Christy, J. T., Bond Street hatter 20/11/54 ?
Chrysoveloni, M. J., of Liverpool 7/2/76
Chrystal, R. L., of Munich 1/11/91
Church,
Mr. 30/1/39
Alfred John, Rev. 16/5/74
Arthur Herbert, Sir (1834–1915), professor 15/5/77
Charles Marcus, Rev. 1/4/89
E., Miss 21/11/79
Frederick Edwin (1826–1900), American artist 16/7/63
Helen Frances, née Bennett 13/7/78
Richard, Sir (1784–1873), soldier 18/12/58
Richard William, Dean (1815–1890) 16/8/71, 22/8/71, 10/1/75, 14/2/77, 13/7/78, 20/10/80 ff, 3/12/81, 4/10/82, 3/8/83, 9/1/85, 12/1/85 L, 24/7/85, 21/6/88
Sanford Elias (1815–1880), chief justice of New York 24/6/72
William Montagu Higginson, Rev., priest, Willy's tutor 21/12/47, 30/1/50, 10/4/63, 25/1/65
W. M. H., Mrs. 30/1/50
Church and People, editor of 21/12/89
Church Association 30/5/82
Churchill *see* Marjoribanks
Churchill,
Ada 6/4/66
Frances Anne Emily (–1899), née Vane-Tempest, Dowager Duchess of Marlborough 6/4/91, 8/4/91, 9/4/91, 5/3/92, 27/5/92
Francis George Spencer (1802–1886), 2nd Baron Churchill (1845) 31/1/65 n
George 13/12/69
Jane Conyngham Spencer (–1900), née Conyngham, Lady Churchill, Lady of the Bedchamber 31/1/65
Jennie Spencer-, Lady, née Jerome, author, editor and society beauty 12/3/90
John Winston Spencer (1822–1883), Marquis of Blandford (1840), 7th Duke of Marlborough (1857), tory M.P. 15/3/51
Randolph Henry Spencer, Lord 1/1/78
Church Pastoral Aid Society 21/12/89 n
Church Reform Association 18/9/69
Churchward, Joseph George, of Dover 15/3/67
Churston *see* Buller
Churton,
Edward, Ven. (1800–1874), archdeacon 10/9/51
Henry Burgess Whitaker, Rev. 17/12/75
Thomas Townson, Rev. (1799–) 25/6/31
Chute, William L. W., tory M.P. 19/10/44
Ciana Tempo, Monsignor 11/11/66
Cicerone,
of Albano 26/4/32
of Frascati 23/4/32
of San Germano 21/5/32
of Terni 6/6/32
Cichelli, Sig. 6/2/89
Cieszkowski, K. 6/1/77 n
Cimitile,
Princess, wife of Prince Prospero Cimitile 29/2/52
Prospero, Prince 20/1/51
Cini,
Count 10/4/32, 14/4/32
Countess 14/4/32
Ciocci, Raphael, refugee 31/3/59
Cipriani, F. 20/6/87
Cist, Lewis John, autograph collector of U.S.A. 22/7/67
Cittadini, singing master 29/3/34
City Liberal Club 23/5/76
Clack, T., of the Science & Art Dept. 19/8/71

Claflin, W., Gov. (1818-1905), of U.S.A. 30/3/70
Clancarty *see* Trench
Clancy, John Joseph (1847-1928), home rule M.P. 19/10/88, 5/12/90 n
Clanranald *see* MacDonald
Clanricarde *see* Burgh
Clanwilliam *see* Meade
Clapp, Mr. 24/7/77
Clare *see* Fitzgibbon
Clare,
- Octavius Leigh, barrister 18/7/66 ?
- Peter, anti-slaver 18/4/45

Claremont, Edward Stopford, General (1819-1890) 24/8/80
Clarence *see* Albert Edward Victor
Clarendon *see* Hyde, Villiers
Claridge, John Thomas, Sir, barrister 15/1/48
Clark,
- rescue 8/7/90
- Mrs., landlady of Invercauld Arms, Braemar 15/8/39
- Mrs., nurse 4/6/40, 6/7/40
- Mrs. (1763-), of Hawarden 18/1/64, 23/1/68
- **Andrew, Sir** 30/10/66
- Andrew Rutherford (1828-1899), advocate 2/10/69
- Archibald, mayor of Aukland, New Zealand 26/2/53
- A. S., of Adelaide 13/1/79
- Benjamin 6/10/41
- Charles Cotesworth Pinkney, author of U.S.A. 17/4/79
- David, lawyer of Perth 20/1/38
- Edwin Charles, Prof. (1835-1917), lawyer 1/1/73
- F., rescue 18/10/61
- George, landlord of Invercauld Arms, Braemar 6/9/36
- George, Rev. (1831-1919) 31/12/64
- George B., lawyer of Perth 20/1/38
- H. W., Rev. 14/10/88
- J. A., Mrs. 11/4/92
- James, Sir (1788-1870), 1st Baronet (1837), physician 17/9/69
- J. O. A., Rev. Dr. 7/9/78
- Sidney, Rev. (-1908) 6/4/49
- Thomas (1820-1876), painter of Rome 14/1/67 ?
- W. H., of London 2/12/44
- William (1821-1880), civil engineer 19/8/51
- William Fox, of York 11/10/62 n
- William Fox, Mrs., of York 11/10/62 n
- William George, Rev. (1821-1878) 22/6/58
- William Robinson, Rev. (-1912), professor 30/1/77
- W. W. 20/12/49

Clarke,
- rescue, prostitute 25/5/58, 10/7/66
- Andrew, Clarke-Wardlaw 1837-1842, landowner 11/9/41
- Andrew, Sir (1824-1902), inspector of fortifications 5/7/83
- Archibald 27/4/76
- B., Mr., solicited a post 9/12/43
- C., rescue 20/7/64
- C. C., Rev. 12/1/87
- Charles Pickering, Rev. 31/10/75
- Charles Whitley, Rev. (1822-1913) 14/2/68, 16/3/68
- Edward Francis Channing 13/9/77
- Frederick Kent, Rev. (-1920) 31/8/76 ?
- George Rochfort, barrister 6/7/44
- Harriet Ludlow, Miss (-1866), artist 10/12/57 ?
- Henry William, Rev. 6/3/75
- James Freeman, Rev. (1810-1888), of U.S.A. 6/2/75
- J. L. 3/6/92
- John (1805-1870), of Harberton 19/8/32
- John Algernon (1828-1887), journalist 5/6/68
- John Erskine, Rev. 22/6/77, 19/7/77
- J. Walround, Capt. 18/9/56
- Marlande 24/7/77
- R. T., liberal of Leeds 22/3/78
- Seymour (1814-1876), railway manager 2/2/48
- Simon, Sir 4/7/44
- Stanley 12/7/78
- William Branwhite, Rev. (1798-1878) 8/12/57 ?
- William Wilcox, Rev. (1808-1881) 20/12/49
- W. M. 5/7/77
- W. R., hymnist in Harrogate 5/9/87

Clarkson,
- D. 14/8/74
- Edward, of Highbury 1/9/55
- Mary 13/9/29
- Thomas, Rev. (-1882) 11/7/55 ?

Clater, F. 11/6/78
Claudet, Antoine François Jean (1797-1867), daguerrotypist 28/7/51
Claughton,
- Piers Claverly, Rev. (-1884) 2/9/48, 26/8/51
- Thomas Legh, Bp. (1808-1892), bishop of Rochester (1867), bishop of St Albans (1877) 1/7/29

Claussen, Chevalier 27/6/49 n
Claveley, T. V. 21/4/92
Clavering,
- Augusta, née Campbell 25/3/44
- Henry Mordaunt, Col. 25/3/44

Claxton, Marshall, artist 12/1/58 ?

Clay,
Messrs., publishers 31/8/77
Edmund, Rev. (1822–1872) 19/10/68
E. Randolph 21/1/75
F., journalist 26/11/72
James (1804–1873), liberal M.P. and whist authority 15/8/57, 1/4/67
William, Sir (1791–1869), radical M.P. 20/7/43, 16/5/67
Clayden,
Arthur 12/8/74
Peter William (1827–1902), journalist 1/9/76 n
Claypole, James, bank clerk of Newark 31/8/36
Clayton,
Charles, Rev. (1813–1883) 29/11/63 ?
Henry 12/12/77
J. H. 2/11/78
Cleaver,
Mr., preacher 23/12/38
Harriet, Mrs., bookseller 30/6/55
William, Rev. (1786–) 11/12/38 ?
Cleeve, J. 15/11/76
Clegg, Joseph, of Preston 28/5/68
Cleghorn,
Mr. 25/2/87
Patrick (1785–), of Lincoln's Inn 13/8/35 ?
Peter (–1863), lawyer at Madras 13/8/35 ?
Cleland, James, Rev., presbyterian 11/11/68
Clemence, John, coffin maker 9/4/50
Clémenceau, Georges (1841–1929), politician, later President of France 8/2/83, 9/2/83, 10/2/83 n
Clement, William James, Dr. (1804–1870), liberal M.P. 24/4/67
Clements,
charity case? 7/2/56
Alderman 23/12/86
Robert Bermingham, 4th Earl of Leitrim (1878) 25/5/78
Clementson, William, Rev. 21/1/54
Clement XIV, Pope (1705–1774) 28/12/38
Clerk,
Mr., in Rome 8/7/32
George, Sir (1787–1867), 6th Baronet (1798), tory M.P. 5/1/36
Maria, Lady, née Law 12/7/48
Clerke, Charles Carr, Ven. (1789–1877) 24/5/29, 30/5/53
Clerks' Union Secretary 24/10/78
Clerle, Sig. 2/10/79
Clery, N. E. 31/3/74
Cleve, James 22/1/78
Cleveland *see* Powlett, Vane
Cleveland, Henry, Rev. (–1889) 15/2/67
Clews, Henry, broker in New York 26/5/89 n
Clifden *see* Ellis, Robartes
Cliff, Percy 23/6/79
Clifford,
rescue 19/3/57
Augustus William James, Sir (1788–1877), Knight (1830), Black Rod 29/7/64
Charles Cavendish, Sir (–1895), 4th Baronet (1892), liberal M.P. 25/10/52
Frederick 16/10/56
Robert Cavendish Spencer, Sir, 3rd Baronet (1882), Black Rod (1859) 9/8/83
Clifton,
A. Maud, Mrs., rescue 4/12/84, 5/12/84, 22/3/85, 6/8/87, 25/8/87, 13/9/87
Emma, rescue 23/7/50
Robert Bellamy, Prof. (1836–1921) 1/2/78, 25/4/78
Robert Cox, Rev. 17/11/41
Clint, Edward, of Liverpool 8/5/68 ?
Clinton *see* Pamphilji, Tempest, Trefusis
Clinton,
Albert Sidney Pelham-, Lord (1845–1884) 29/10/64, 24/1/65
Arthur Pelham-, Lord (1840–1870), liberal M.P. 29/10/64
Charles Pelham-, Lord (1813–1894), tory M.P. 9/10/32
Charlotte Pelham-, Lady (1812–1886) 9/10/32, 6/12/77
Edward Pelham-, Lord (1816–1842), Royal Navy 9/10/32
Edward William Pelham-, Lord (1836–1907) 8/2/64, 28/1/81, 23/7/81, 29/6/83, 21/2/84
Frances Evelyn, Lady, née Stotherd 29/10/64 n, 6/11/70
Frederick, Col. 4/4/46 ?
Georgiana Pelham-, Lady (1810–1874) 9/10/32
Henrietta Adela Pelham-, Lady Lincoln, Duchess of Newcastle 21/9/60 n
Henry Fiennes, Rev. 12/2/80
Henry Pelham Alexander Pelham- (1834–1879), 6th Duke of Newcastle (1864), Earl of Lincoln 21/9/60
Henry Pelham Archibald Douglas (1864–1928), 7th Duke of Newcastle (1879) 31/5/79, 25/6/82, 19/12/83
Henry Pelham Fiennes Pelham-; 4th Duke of Newcastle 6/7/32
Henry Pelham Fiennes Pelham-; 5th Duke of Newcastle 8/6/30
Marianne Pelham-, Lady, née Gritton (separated 1865) 19/1/65
Robert Renebald Pelham-, Lord (1820–1867), Peelite M.P. 19/7/54
Thomas Charles Pelham-, Lord (1813–1882) 9/10/32, 19/1/65
William Henry, Sir (1769–1846), general 26/4/33
William Osbert, Rev. (–1921) 8/5/79 ?

William Pelham-, Lord 9/10/32
Clipperton, John, attorney of Ipswich 29/7/35
Clive *see* Herbert, Lyttelton, Percy, Wynn
Clive,
Archer Anthony (1842–1877) 22/4/76
E., 5th Earl of Powis 1/3/38 n
George (1816–1909), liberal M.P. 17/2/60
Harriet, Lady, née Windsor, Lady Windsor 21/5/42 n
Robert, Lord 21/5/41
Robert Henry, Peelite M.P. 21/5/42
Cloak, J. 27/4/88
Clode,
Charles Matthew, solicitor 6/2/49
C. M., author 19/3/69
Clonmell *see* Scott
Clonmell, Mayor of 13/12/78
Close,
Francis, dean of Carlisle (1856) 12/3/41
Maxwell Charles (1828–1903), tory M.P. 10/4/62
W., Rev., nonconformist 28/4/68
Clough,
Anne Jemima (1820–1895), principal 26/10/78
Arthur Hugh (1819–1861) 17/6/59
Charles Butler (1793–1859), dean 15/12/55
James B., merchant of Liverpool 2/1/43
Walter Owen (1846–1922), liberal M.P. 25/11/86 ?
Clouston,
Mr. 5/3/80
Peter, lord provost of Glasgow 16/7/61 n, 20/7/63 n
Clow, William MacCallum, Rev. 20/3/80
Clowes,
Thomas Ball, Capt. (1787–1864) 23/9/62
William, printer 8/3/41, 15/11/49, 20/12/74, 5/9/76 ?
Clunie, Mr. 3/8/26
Clurland, Mr. 22/9/62
Clutterbuck, Thomas, solicitor 21/3/68
Clyde *see* Campbell
Clyne, Mr. 21/10/87
Coachman 29/3/34, 4/4/34
Coatcott, Dr. 5/8/83
Coate, C. H., of Edinburgh; invited G again to stand for Rector 30/12/92
Coates,
George Alexander Augustus, Rev. 3/11/76
James Irwin, Rev. 1/12/89
Thomas (1778–1846) 5/3/36
Coates & Howes, wine merchants 19/1/66
Coats, C. H., of Glasgow University 19/9/93 L
Cobb,
Charles Francis, solicitor 16/4/45 ?
H. 23/6/77
Henry Peyton (1835–1910), liberal M.P. 1/1/86, 23/6/87
J. F. 8/7/79
Cobbe,
Frances Power, Miss 1/3/76
George, soldier 2/2/49 ?
Thomas, historian 15/6/77
Cobbett,
John Morgan (–1877), radical tory M.P. 9/5/53
William (1762–1835), tory M.P. and author 11/2/33, 19/6/35
Cobbold, John Chevalier (1797–1882), tory M.P. 23/7/62
Cobby, Miss 5/4/78, 9/4/78
Cobden,
Catherine Anne, née Williams 12/10/65, 30/12/65, 1/5/66
Ellen M., Miss 20/6/77, 6/5/78, 9/4/90
Richard 23/6/41
Cobham *see* Lyttelton
Cobham, C. Delavel 24/12/75
Cobley, Thomas, Newark lawyer 3/3/37
Cochrane *see* Ramsay
Cochrane,
Miss, of Edinburgh 11/10/71
Mr., of Newcastle 27/5/90
A. B., of Stourbridge 18/5/53
James Henry Dickson, Rev. 3/2/80 ?
John George, bibliographer 3/2/41 n, 12/2/41
Robert 18/1/87 ?
Thomas John, Sir (1789–1872), Knight (1825), admiral, tory M.P. 9/1/35
William George, Col. (–1857) 17/4/43
Cochrane-Baillie *see* Vitelleschi
Cockburn *see* Northcote
Cockburn,
Alexander James Edmund, Sir (1802–1880), 10th Baronet, solicitor general (1851), attorney general (1852), lord chief justice (1859) 15/2/53, 28/6/65, 23/6/73 L
Francis, Sir 3/11/42
George, hotelier of Inverness 26/9/53
George, Sir (–1853), admiral, Peelite M.P. 28/10/42, 5/9/43
Cockell *see* Milman
Cockerell, Charles Robert (1788–1863), architect 18/2/45
Cockett, William, Rev. 10/3/56
Cockle, Rita F. Moss, Mrs. 25/11/86, 12/12/90
Cocks,
Caroline Harriet, Lady, née Yorke 29/11/32, 3/10/45 n
Horrock, Rev. (1818–1888), congregationalist 19/9/68 ?
John Somers (1788–1852), 2nd Earl Somers (1841), Viscount Eastnorr 3/10/45
Cocks and Biddulph, bankers 12/8/39
Cockshutt, Mr. 21/2/79

Codd, Edward Thornton, Rev. (–1878) 5/12/53
Coddington, Joshua William, Capt., secretary of Caledonian Railway Co. (1847) 25/1/49
Code, Mrs. 17/8/64
Codling 22/2/39
Codner, Mr. 18/7/38
Codrington,
 Christopher William, Sir (1805–1864), tory M.P. 3/6/29, 21/6/44
 E., Sir, admiral, 'victor of Navarino' 26/3/33 n
 William, Sir (1804–1884), liberal M.P. 14/3/61
Codronchi, Count 3/5/89
Cody, William ('Buffalo Bill'), rodeo and circus manager 28/4/87 n
Coe, J. Herbert 11/5/55
Coeloegon, Col. 25/1/84 n
Coffey,
 G., Irish author 22/5/88
 James 22/6/75
Coffin, John Townsend, Admiral (1789–1882) 20/11/60
Coffingwell, Mr. 4/12/78
Cogan, William Henry Ford (1823–1894), liberal M.P. 25/2/60, 28/2/68
Cogan & MacLardy, Messrs. 5/2/80
Coghill, Mrs. 13/8/91
Coghlan,
 A. W., Rev. 3/3/79
 D. 18/8/49
 J. C., Rev., physician 8/3/74 ?
Cohen *see* Palgrave
Cohen,
 Arthur (1829–1914), liberal M.P., barrister 18/3/58, 28/2/77, 24/5/82
 Herman Joseph, barrister and editor of G's speeches 26/4/90, 23/10/91, 14/5/92, 11/6/92
Coiffier, Alexandre, Mad. 12/7/59
Coit, S. 3/6/91
Coke,
 Edward Francis, Rev. 6/3/68
 Thomas William (1822–1909), 2nd Earl of Leicester (1842) 14/5/73
Coker, F. 9/8/66
Colam, W. 6/4/78
Colbart, Mr. 18/12/78
Colborne,
 Mr. 12/11/74
 John, Sir (–1868), 1st Baron Seaton (1839), Governor-General of Canada (1839) 10/4/40, 27/5/40, 13/6/40, 30/5/46
 Nicholas William Ridley- (1779–1854), 1st Baron Colborne (1839), liberal M.P. 26/6/37
Colburn,
 G. 28/9/91
 Henry (–1855), publisher 11/12/27
Colchester *see* Abbot
Colchester, Maynard 16/7/25 n
Coldrigh, Mrs. 15/6/59
Coldstream *see* Campbell
Coldstream,
 John, W. S. of Edinburgh 29/9/68
 J. P. 30/9/90
Coldwell,
 William Edward, Rev. 20/7/40 n
 William G., architect 2/7/68
Cole *see* Grey, Medge
Cole,
 A. A., Baptist minister 23/12/32 ?
 A. W. 27/3/56
 Frances Isabella Monck, Lady, née Monck 24/5/36, 23/6/62
 Francis Burton (–1833) 25/1/29
 Francis Burton Owen, Capt. (1838–1912) 28/3/73, 29/11/86
 Galbraith Lowry, Sir (1772–1842), general, M.P. 8/2/36
 George, Rev. (–1876) 15/8/55
 George Vicat (1833–1893), landscape painter 15/1/94
 Henry, Major (–1815) 22/6/30 n
 Henry, Sir (1808–1882), dept. of practical art 21/3/54, 8/4/77
 Henry Arthur, Col. (1809–1890), tory M.P. 30/7/66
 Jane Eliza, née Owen 22/6/30
 Owen Blayney (1808–1886), high sheriff of Co. Monaghan 6/12/28
 T. E., Mrs., of Hawarden 11/9/49
 Thomas Edward, Capt. 11/9/49
 W. W., 1st Earl of Enniskillen 8/6/38 n
Colebrook, William MacBean George, Sir (1787–1870), colonial governor 1/6/58, 31/3/59
Colebrooke,
 Elizabeth, Lady 28/6/79
 Thomas Edward, Sir (1813–1890), 4th Baronet (1838), liberal M.P. 19/2/64
Coleman,
 Charles (–1874), painter & etcher in Rome 2/1/39, 30/11/66
 James Edward, accountant 8/8/48
 John Henry, Rev. (–1907) 27/9/66
Coleman, Turquand & Young, accountants 8/8/48 n
Colenso,
 Miss 19/7/90
 John William, Bp. (1814–1883), bishop of Natal 30/7/31, 4/9/63, 20/6/65, 21/11/65, 22/11/65, 27/10/82
Colentrof, Miss 2/10/75

Coleridge,
Derwent 6/8/42
Edward, Rev. (1800–1883) 21/9/26, 3/12/54
Hartley 6/8/42 n
Henry James, Rev. (1822–1893), S. J. 11/12/74
Henry Nelson 30/11/47 n
John Duke (1820–1894), Knight (1871), 1st Baron Coleridge (1874) 18/4/66, 1/12/70 L, 4/12/70 L, 30/7/82, 2/1/84 L, 10/1/90 ff
John Taylor, Sir (1790–1876), judge, member of the Engagement 10/6/41, 18/11/41, 12/1/42, 23/2/45 n, 2/12/69 ff
Mary, née Keate 21/9/26
R., Rev. 29/8/74
Samuel Taylor 27/2/35 n, 3/6/82
Sarah, née Coleridge 30/11/47
William Hart, Bp. (1789–1849), bishop of Barbados (1824) 27/2/35
Colerrook, Mr. 12/2/78
Coles,
Cowper Phipps, Capt. (1819–1870), Royal Navy 1/2/61
Robert Bartlett, Lieut. Gen. 4/2/34
W. E. 28/12/78
Coleshill, J. 12/12/79
Colet, Louise Révoil (1810–1876) 27/7/68
Colhurst, D. La Touche 20/1/81 L
Coligny, bass of Italy 3/4/32
Coling, James, Rev. (1819–1888) 30/11/76 ?
Collalto, Massimo, author 19/7/88
Collard, Edwin Curwen, Rev. 7/1/78
Coller, Francis, stable owner of London 9/12/40 ?
Collerade, rescue 26/4/79
Collet,
Collet Dobson (1812–1898), newspaper tax reformer 7/4/59
Mark Wilks, banker 18/10/78 ?
Sophia Dobson (1822–1894) 25/12/76, 6/1/78 n
Collett,
Edward, Rev. 11/12/79 ?
William Rickford (1810–), tory M.P. 19/1/44
Collette, Charles Hastings 10/3/75
Colley,
George Pomeroy, Sir (1835–1881), Knight (1879) 24/1/79 n, 5/2/81, 9/2/81, 15/2/81 c, 19/2/81 c, 28/2/81 n, 2/3/81, 5/3/81 c
J., saddler 24/2/37
Thomas, Ven. 10/10/75, 16/1/86
Collie, Alexander, Dr., physician 11/11/76
Collier,
librarian to Lord F. Egerton 21/10/37
Charles, surgeon 13/6/46 ?
Edward, Sir (1783–1872), Knight (1865), admiral 23/1/60
E. H., city merchant 18/4/49 ?
Francis Augustus, Sir (1783–1849), Knight (1830), rear admiral 28/8/32
Henry Theodosius Browne, Admiral (1791–1872) 20/11/60
James Alphonse, Col. 18/2/73 ?
John Payne (1789–1883), editor 26/6/56
Robert Porrett, Sir (1817–1886), Knight (1863), 1st Baron Monkswell (1885), lawyer 25/7/66, 16/10/71 L, 11/12/71 c, 22/1/72 c, 3/2/72 c, 10/2/72 c, 19/2/72, 2/11/72
Collinet, Paul, author 3/12/87
Collings,
Edward J., school teacher 1/9/76
F. 8/4/78
Jesse (1831–1920), liberal (unionist) M.P. 9/6/81, 24/1/86, 25/1/86, 26/1/86, 8/2/86, 5/4/86 L, 8/2/93
Collingwood,
Miss, of Rome 25/12/66
C. 15/12/86
Charles Edward Stuart, Rev. (1831–1898) 26/2/77 ?
William Gershom (1854–1932), author 12/2/75 ff, 14/5/88
Collins,
rescue 8/7/90
Mr. 30/3/29
Charles MacCarthy 23/10/68
Colman 3/10/87
E., rescue 11/6/51
Edward Francis (1807–1872), editor of *Hull Advertiser* 12/3/55
James, House of Commons Vote Officer 19/12/78 n
J. C. 15/1/91
John, chartist 10/7/40 n
John Coombes, Rev. (1798–1867) 9/6/57 ?
Thomas (1775–1856), mayor of Warwick (1832) 2/4/33
Thomas (1825–1884), tory M.P. 13/3/58
William, Rev. (1817–1887) 27/12/56
Collis,
Christopher Annett, brewer & baker of Essex 1/8/34
John Day, Rev. Dr. (1816–1879) 16/11/52
William Blow, solicitor 5/2/48
Collison, Frederick William Portlock, Rev. (1814–1889) 11/1/54
Collman, Mr. 17/4/75
Colloredo, Marie Thérèse, Princess, née Lebzeltern 23/2/53
Colloredo-Mannsfeld, Joseph François Jerome, Prince 23/2/53 n
Colls, John Flowerdew, Rev. 22/1/44

Colman,
Mrs. 19/5/49
Jeremiah James (1830–1898), liberal M.P. (1871) 23/3/68 n, 17/5/90 ff, 26/6/91 ff, 16/7/91 ff, 27/8/91 ff, 20/5/92, 19/7/93
Colmige, W. A. 10/6/92
Colnaghi,
Dominic Ellis, Sir (1838–1908), British consul in Florence 2/1/88, 14/5/88
Dominic Paul (–1879), print seller 20/3/52
Colomb,
Julian Charles Ready, Sir (1838–1909), tory M.P. 5/4/90
W. 15/11/77
Colombine, David Elwin, solicitor 26/10/41
Colonna,
Giovanni, Prince (1820–1894) 30/4/67 fl
Isabella, Princess (1823–1867) 30/4/67 fl
Colonsay *see* Macneill
Colquhoun,
Henrietta Maria, née Powys 14/5/40 n
John Campbell (1802–1870), tory M.P. 14/5/40
Patrick MacChombaich, Sir (1815–1891) 10/1/59, 5/3/77 n
William Lawrence (1810–1861) 21/11/30
Colter, Mr. 12/3/47
Colthurst, David La Touche, Col., liberal M.P. 20/1/81
Colton, William Charles, Rev. (–1884) 25/6/52
Colvile,
rescue 5/6/58
Mrs. 13/3/38
Andrew Wedderburn (–1856) 21/2/35
Charles Robert (1815–1886), liberal M.P. 19/9/43
James William, Sir (1810–1880), judge 14/7/26, 21/2/35 n, 21/10/71
Colville *see* Needham, Simeon
Colville, Charles, Sir (–1843), general 1/11/51 n
Colvin, Sidney, Sir (1845–1927), art critic 2/9/73
Colwell,
Charles 4/12/74 ?
John, Rev. (1840–1887), methodist 2/2/57 ?
Comandi, Sig. 9/1/88
Combe,
E., miniaturist 12/12/37
Henry 12/12/37 n
Thomas (1797–1872), director of the Clarendon Press, Oxford, Pre-Raphaelite sponsor 28/7/59, 2/11/72
Comber,
Mrs., of Clumber 6/6/78
William, Chester and Holyhead Goods Manager 4/9/52
Combes, W. H., editor *Entr'acte* 5/2/78, 23/10/78
Comerford, Thomas F., of Birmingham 25/3/90
Commandi, Sig., of Florence 9/1/88
Comper,
A. F., Rev. 1/9/77
J., Rev. 24/7/79
Compson, John, Rev. 6/6/62 ?
Compston, Rev. 9/7/77
Compton *see* Egerton
Compton,
Alwyne Frederick, Lord (1855–1911), liberal-unionist M.P. 4/4/79, 7/10/79, 31/7/86 n
Charles, Lord, 3rd Marquis of Northampton (1851) 8/5/46
Francis, tory M.P. 5/6/89
Mary, Lady, née Vyner 31/7/86
Mary Violet Isabel, Lady 27/1/86
Spencer Joshua Alwyne, 2nd Marquis of Northampton 3/6/43 n
Compton, Newton & Co. 16/4/57
Compton & Crosby, solicitors of London 17/2/45 ?
Comyn, H. E. Fitzgerald 27/9/87
Comyns, Mrs. 5/5/55
Conant, Mr. 17/4/79
Concanen, George, solicitor 23/4/45
Condari, Signor, of Ionia 7/12/58
Condé, Louis-Henri Joseph de, Prince (1756–1830) 13/2/32
Condenriotes, Mr. 13/4/94
Conder,
Mrs. 2/6/78
E. R., Dr. 2/6/78
G. W., of Leeds Mechanics Institute 13/12/56
Condon, Mrs. 22/4/79
Conestabile, Carlo, Count 9/1/88
Conger, J. W. 16/3/74
Congleton *see* Parnell
Congreve,
Richard (1818–1899), positivist 7/9/76
Richard Jones (–1879), artist 12/6/57 ?
Coningham, William (1815–1884), liberal M.P., picture collector 9/6/49, 9/7/59, 3/4/60
Conington, John, Prof. (1825–1869) 16/2/57
Conliffe, Misses, of Wrexham 3/1/58
Conn, J. L. 14/11/78
Connah, Mrs., musician? 26/7/67
Connal, E. 8/8/88
Connaught *see* Louise
Connaught and Strathearn *see* Arthur
Connell,
Alexander A. 1/8/78
Alexander R. Campbell, Rev. 7/3/78
Connell & Hope, parliamentary agents 5/3/56 n

Connelly, Pierce, Rev., writer 30/9/51
Connemara *see* Bourke, Broun
Conners, Rev. 28/3/79
Connor,
D. 9/2/61
G. F. 21/3/87
James, Rev. 10/7/45
Conolly,
Mrs. 19/9/75
Edward, barrister 25/4/76
Edward Michael (1786–1849), né Pakenham, tory M.P. 8/5/33, 30/12/45
Thomas (–1876), tory M.P. 24/5/53
Consell, L. 10/11/77
Consolo,
Benjamin, Italian living in Brussels 10/5/54
B. jnr., Sig. 23/2/56
Constabile, Marquis 27/7/49
Constable,
Charles, of Symonds Inn 12/2/34 ?
Henry, Rev. 17/5/76
Thomas (1812–1881), publisher 22/6/76
Thomas Kirk, of Symonds Inn 12/2/34 ?
Consterdine, James, Rev. 27/11/68
Conte, Antoine Joseph Xavier, director general of French posts 11/5/41 ?
Contostaulos, Alexander, Greek ambassador 26/5/80
Conway,
Mrs., of Seaforth 15/9/43
E., Miss, of Liverpool 6/1/53
Francis Charles Seymour- (1777–1842), 3rd Marquis of Hertford (1822), diplomat 1/10/35
J., Mrs. (–1830) 5/8/25
John, of Edgehill, Liverpool 25/11/29
Joseph (–1828), clothier of Liverpool 9/8/25
J. S., of Liverpool 10/7/50
Moncure Daniel, Rev. (1832–1907), unitarian 15/6/76
Richard Seymour- (1800–1874), 4th Marquis of Hertford 24/6/67
Conybeare,
Charles Augustus Vansittart (1853–1919) 11/6/89
William Daniel, Dean (1787–1857), Dean of Llandaff (1845), geologist 25/3/52
William John, Rev. (1815–1857) 27/9/42
Conyngham *see* Churchill, Denison
Conyngham,
Mrs. 30/11/38
Francis Nathaniel (1797–1876), 2nd Marquis Conyngham (1832) 3/5/69
G. Lenox-, chief clerk at Foreign Office 15/5/43
Henry (–1832), 1st Marquis Conyngham 21/5/51 n
Jane St. Maur Blanche, née Stanhope, Lady Conyngham 23/1/71
William, Abp. (1828–1897), 4th Baron Plunket (1871) 23/10/77
Coode, George, barrister 19/4/52
Cook,
Col., Royal Engineers 19/6/74
Charles Henry ('John Bickerdyke'), author 12/10/89
Edward Tyas, Sir (1857–1919), editor and biographer 12/1/86 n, 4/3/89, 29/11/90, 1/12/90
G., Rev. 2/3/80
George, wool broker of City 14/2/60 ?
G. H. 2/9/78
James, physician at Brechin 29/6/43
James, victualier 7/12/32 ?
John, Rev. Dr. (1807–1869), presbyterian minister 22/9/44
John Douglas (1808–1868), editor of *Manchester Chronicle* (1848), journalist 27/8/50 n, 15/1/54
S. G. B. 25/1/90
Cooke,
of Peace Society 23/7/50
A. 27/1/79
A. R. 29/12/68
Bella, Mrs. 7/11/91
Bryan George Davies- (1834–1913), of Flintshire 6/1/66
C. A., Rev. 10/10/91
Charles Edward Stephen, banker 13/11/42 n
Charles Wallwyn Radcliffe (1841–1911), tory M.P. 7/6/90
Edward William (1811–1880), Royal Academician 25/5/67
George Robert Davies-, Rev. 8/12/77
Henry Salkeld, Rev. 28/12/76
J. H., Rev. 12/4/94
Mary Louisa, Lady, née Stewart 13/11/42 n
Philip Davies-, of Mold 20/8/50
Robert, of Murray's 5/9/56 ff, 13/2/75
Theophilus Leigh, Rev. (1778–1846) 29/9/30
W., Rev., Dr. 10/10/75
William, Rev. 13/8/51
William Fothergill, Sir (1806–1879), scientist 1/9/69, 18/9/69
William Henry (1811–1894), judge 27/4/59, 10/7/79
William Henry (1843–1921), barrister 7/7/79 n
Cookesley, William Gifford, Rev., school master 25/1/44
Cookfoye, Henry 16/5/74
Cookson,
William Isaac, of Worksop 12/5/75
William Strickland (1810–1877), barrister 17/12/60, 19/12/60
Cooper,
rescue 26/7/77

Cooper (*cont.*)
see also Cowper, rescue? 5/12/62, 14/2/66, 15/6/68
Miss 23/10/71
Mr., of Jamaica 8/11/54
A. F. Ashley- (-1825) 23/10/83, 31/10/83
Allen, Rev. (1793-1851) 26/2/39
Anthony Ashley- (1801-1885), 7th Earl of Shaftesbury (1851), tory philanthropist 20/10/31 n, 7/11/52, 15/3/59 n, 17/6/70 L, 2/9/70 L, 5/5/72 L, 8/12/76 n, 13/3/78, 24/2/87, 27/2/87, 19/3/87
Anthony Evelyn Melbourne Ashley- (1836-1907), Palmerston's secretary, liberal M.P. 2/9/47 n, 30/11/68 ff
Anthony John Ashley- (1808-1867), Queen's Counsel, whig M.P. 11/3/26
Basil Henry (1819-), author 22/11/60
C. Ashley-, 6th Earl of Shaftesbury 11/3/26 n
Charles Alfred (1829-1916), editor of *The Scotsman* 18/11/85, 24/12/85, 21/6/86, 17/2/87 n
Charles F., of New Cross 17/11/87
Charles Purton (1793-1873), barrister 26/8/57
Emily Ashley-, née Cowper, Lady Ashley, Lady Shaftesbury 24/7/48
E. S., Rev. 20/12/79
George, of Bromley 24/7/70
Henry, Rev. 25/2/45
James Hughes, Rev. (-1909) 13/1/69 ?, 11/8/72
John Mawbey, Rev. 12/3/45
John William (-1906), barrister 28/10/78
Joseph 20/7/77
J. W. 28/10/78
Sybella Charlotte Ashley- (-1884), née Farquhar 2/9/47
Thomas, Register Office clerk 15/1/53
(Thomas) Sidney (1803-1902), artist 5/5/70, 11/3/74, 3/7/90
William Samuel, author 20/3/79 ?
William White (1816-1886), surgeon 28/5/86
W. M. 14/8/54 n
W. M., Mrs. 14/8/54
Coote,
Capt. 12/3/70
C. J., landowner of Ireland 18/12/80
Cope,
Anne Charlotte, Mrs. 19/5/64
Charles Henry, Rev. 27/11/90
Charles West (1811-1890), artist 5/3/63
John A. M., of Drumilly 13/4/68
William Henry, Sir (1811-1892), 12th Baronet (1851), Rev. 26/4/79
Copecky, Herr 15/8/90
Copeland,
George Dale, Rev. 22/1/75 ?
William Taylor (1797-1868), lord mayor of London (1835), eminent potter, Peelite M.P. 7/5/36, 31/3/42
Copeman,
J. 6/5/65
Philip Walker, Rev. 1/1/47
Copland, James, Rev. 4/1/79
Copleston,
Edward, Bp. (1776-1849), bishop of Llandaff (1828) 30/6/29
Reginald Stephen, Bp. (1845-1925) 22/1/80
Copley,
Georgiana, née Goldsmith, Lady Lyndhurst 19/6/44, 31/8/83 L
John Singleton (1772-1863), 1st Baron Lyndhurst (1827), tory lord chancellor 3/10/31, 27/2/52, 7/2/56, 17/2/58, 28/4/59, 18/11/62, 28/1/63, 31/8/83, 2/1/84
Coppock,
Charles 30/7/66
Henry, of Stockport 22/4/62
Coquelin, Constant-Benoit, Mons., actor 1/6/83, 30/5/89
Coram, Thomas, patron of Foundling Hospital 28/7/33 n
Corbally, J. H. 13/2/91
Corbet, William Joseph, home rule M.P. 22/7/84 L
Corbett,
A., Mrs., of Beeston 3/12/56, 10/12/56
Charles Joseph, architect 19/3/75
George, Mrs. 1/12/89
William, Inland Revenue Board 9/4/63
Corbin, D. F. Maury, Mrs. 14/1/90
Corbould, Dorothea M., author 30/10/89
Corbyn, Thomas, of New Palace Yard 14/7/36
Corcoran, Mr. 29/12/78
Corden,
Miss, of Newark? 6/3/78
H., Rev. 13/1/87
W., Mrs. 27/9/32
William, linen draper 27/9/32 n
Cordery, Edward, classicist 24/12/70
Cordingley, Mr. 14/5/78
Corfe, A. A. 12/7/76
Corfield,
Mr. 7/6/77
W. H. 24/2/90
Cork and Orrery *see* Boyle
Corke,
Mrs. 19/7/79
John 8/9/76 ?
Corkhill, J. A. 1/5/79

Corkran, John Frazer (-1884), journalist 8/11/59, 12/8/74
Cornel, rescue 27/5/59, 28/5/59
Cornell, Mr., of Nice 14/2/92
Corner,
C., Mrs. 13/9/60
Edward, of Whitby 2/9/71
William Elgie, ship owner 16/4/56
Cornish,
Charles Lewis, Rev. (1810-1870) 24/11/31
Francis Warre, Rev. (1839-1916) 20/2/64
James, Messrs., booksellers 16/10/91
Cornwall *see* Lyttelton
Cornwallis *see* Eliot, Neville, Ross
Cornwallis, C., 2nd Marquis Cornwallis 20/12/34 n
Coroneo, P., of Finsbury Square 19/3/58
Correa, Mrs. 24/6/92
Corrie,
D. 7/7/81
R., merchant 1/12/79
Valentine Bryom, tea broker 16/2/57
Corrie & Co., corn merchants of Liverpool 22/8/39
Corry,
Mrs. 24/4/83
Anne Elizabeth Honoria Lowry-, née Gladstone, Lady Belmore, niece 20/6/61
Henry Thomas Lowry- (1803-1873), tory M.P. 4/2/46
Montagu William Lowry- (1838-1903), 1st Baron Rowton (1880), Disraeli's secretary 19/4/81 L, 15/7/93
Somerset Richard Lowry- (1835-1913), 4th Earl Belmore (1845) 20/6/61
Corsi, Sig., of Florence 13/1/88
Corsini, Neri, Marchese Laiatico 30/7/59
Corstorphine, William 11/12/79
Cortazzi, Frederick, economist 17/1/56
Cortemiglia, Sig. 6/1/88
Corti, Luigi, Count, secretary of Sardinian legation 13/1/54
Cory, William Johnson (1823-1892), took name Cory (1872), master at Eton 4/4/57, 4/5/57
Coscia, F. C. 28/3/76 ?
Cosens,
Edward Hyde, Rev. (-1859) 8/12/57 ff, 12/3/59
Frederick William 9/10/68
Cossa, Sig. 30/6/42
Cosserat,
Mrs. 26/11/52
George Peloquin Graham, Rev. 26/11/52 n, 7/8/65
Cossham,
Mr. 1/11/78
Handel 14/3/76
Costa,
G., Rev. 3/12/50
Giovanni (1833-1903), artist 21/11/66
Michael Andrew Agnus, Sir (1810-1884), Knight (1869), conductor 7/4/69
Costello *see* Costelloe
Costello,
William Birmingham, surgeon 18/5/44
Costelloe, Benjamin Francis Conn (1855-1897), barrister; member of L. C. C. and Eighty Club 15/10/77, 26/9/83 ff, 17/12/92 n
Cotes,
Charles Cecil (1846-1898), liberal M.P. (1874) 26/9/70, 16/3/77, 9/8/84
Louisa, Lady (1814-1887) 4/7/76
Nathaniel Hardcastle, bookseller 31/1/43
Cotgrave, Mr., of Hawarden 11/9/72
Cotgreave, F. 15/11/76
Cotham, George Toulson, Rev. 29/6/58
Cotman, Joseph John, artist 12/9/47 ?
Cottam, John, maltster of Newark 21/1/33 ?
Cottenham *see* Pepys
Cotter, James Lawrence, Rev. 7/6/76 ?
Cotterill,
C. C. 18/6/86
Charles Forster, writer on railways 8/2/49
Henry, Bp. (1812-1886) 11/11/67 n
Cottesloe *see* Fremantle
Cottingham,
Mr. 30/7/79
James, Rev. (1803-1890) 31/12/57
Cottle,
James, Rev., theologian 15/4/43 ?
Robert, author 4/2/52 ?
Cotton,
Miss 26/1/90
Francis Vere, Admiral (1799-1884) 4/12/62
F. V., Major 15/1/46
James Henry, Very Rev. (1781-1862), of Bangor 15/9/61 n
John, chairman of East India Company 21/11/43
M. F. 3/4/91
Richard Lynch (1794-1880), don of Oxford, Provost of Worcester College 7/3/45
Sidney John, Sir (1792-1874) 15/10/69
William (1786-1866), director and governor of Bank of England 11/5/39, 13/1/44 n
Coubertin, Pierre de, Baron (1863-1937) 11/11/88
Coulson,
Hardy 24/3/80
Walter 6/4/43 n
Coultast, Mrs. 1/4/55
Coulthurst, John (1826-1897) 23/11/64 ?
Count, of Rome 23/5/32

Coupland, Charles, solicitor? 14/12/78 ?
Courier,
Austrian 30/11/38
Sicilian 3/11/38
Mr., of Baden 8/10/45
Courlander, Messrs. 30/9/86
Courroux, A. T., of Brussels 8/5/57, 4/9/57
Courtenay *see* Locke, Wood
Courtenay,
Capt. 1/11/87
Elizabeth, Lady (-1867), née Fortescue, Lady Devon 2/7/58
Francis Foljambe, secretary to Lord Dalhousie 15/8/44
John Irving, Sir (1837-1912), Knight (1907), City of London liberal association 21/7/68 ?
Reginald, Bp. (1813-1906), bishop of Jamaica 11/9/62, 3/6/75
Thomas Peregrine (-1861), treasury clerk 24/12/42, 18/8/43
W., 10th Earl of Devon 25/6/39, 15/8/47
W., 2nd Viscount Courtenay 22/3/32 n
William Reginald (1807-1888), 11th Earl of Devon (1859) 10/11/28, 18/11/69 L
Courtney,
Lionel Henry (1832-1918), liberal (unionist) M.P. 25/3/78, 19/12/80 n, 31/12/80 c, 27/7/81, 16/3/82, 16/4/82, 8/5/82, 12/7/82, 27/11/82 L, 1/1/83 L, 10/9/83, 5/3/84 c, 15/4/84 n, 13/6/84 n, 20/11/84 L, 1/12/84 L, 18/12/84, 16/2/85 c, 17/12/85, 29/8/92
T. T., steward 18/8/43
William Leonard (1850-1928), author, philosopher and journalist 18/9/80, 5/9/89
William Prideaux (1845-1913) 7/5/89
Courtown *see* Stopford
Courvoisier, François Bernard, murderer 9/5/40 n
Cousen, Charles (1816-1889), engraver 1/4/51 ?
Cousens, W. 8/2/77
Cousin, Victor (1792-1867), philosopher 24/1/67
Cousins,
rescue 29/6/68
Samuel (1801-1887), artist 25/6/77 ?
William Henry (1833-1917), Inland Revenue 8/2/77 ?
Coussmaker *see* Russell
Coutts,
rescue 26/5/64
Angela Georgina Burdett-, Lady 15/7/40
W. L. A. B. C. Burdett- (1851-1921) 15/7/40 n, 6/9/80 n
Coutts Trotter *see* Lindsay
Couty, David, sec. of S. London Inst. for reform of females 11/7/59 n
Couvreur, Auguste (1827-1894), Belgian deputy 14/3/68
Cove, Edward, Rev. 21/2/49
Coventry,
George (1784-1843), 10th Earl of Coventry, tory M.P. 5/4/32 n
Lady Mary's servant, servant in Rome 2/11/38
Mary, Lady (1791-1845), née Beauclerk 5/4/32
Cowan,
rescue 14/2/74
Charles (1801-1889), liberal M.P. 25/4/53
James (1816-1895) 1/1/73
John, Sir (1814-1900), 1st Baronet (1894) 30/1/79 L, 30/5/81 L, 29/12/83 L, 27/6/85, 29/9/85, 10/4/86 L, 8/6/86 L, 19/6/86 ff, 25/10/90 ff, 4/7/93 L, 18/7/93 L, 20/7/93 L, 13/2/94 L, 18/2/94 L, 19/2/94 L
S. 4/6/68
Thomas C., Rev., of Liverpool 16/11/48
Coward, in hospital 14/3/47
Cowburn, George, solicitor 25/6/57
Cowe, Mrs. 21/7/79
Cowell,
John Clayton, Sir (1832-1894), Knight (1865) 12/10/63, 26/11/83
John Wellsford, author 29/2/60
John William, banker? 19/12/54
Lydia, Miss, actress 24/4/83 n
Cowen,
Joseph (1831-1900), liberal M.P. (1874) 26/4/70
Joseph, Sir (1800-1873), liberal M.P. of Newcastle 22/8/62
Cowie,
Benjamin Morgan, Dean (1816-1900) 10/10/72, 14/10/75
L., of Fasque? 13/4/48
Cowley *see* Wellesley
Cowley,
Mr. 20/3/74
E., Miss 9/6/90
Cowper *see* Cooper, Fane, Jocelyn, Temple
Cowper,
Rev. Mr., non-conformist 2/1/68
Anne Florence, Lady, Lady Cowper 26/5/71, 24/10/78
E., also known as Throckmorton, rescue 27/11/62, 26/7/63
Francis Thomas de Grey (1834-1905), 7th Earl Cowper (1856) 22/4/66, 26/5/71, 30/4/80, 22/10/80 L, 14/11/80 L, 24/11/80 L, 18/12/80, 31/5/81, 4/6/81 L, 22/8/81 L, 1/9/81 L,

5/9/81 L, 9/9/81 L, 20/9/81 ff, 27/10/81, 21/4/82 L, 26/4/82 L, 29/4/82 ff, 1/5/82 L, 2/5/82 L, 3/5/82 L, 20/6/83, 20/8/84, 22/8/84, 13/10/84
Henry Frederick (1836–1887), liberal M.P. 2/2/69
J. M. 15/3/75
P. L. T. F. N. C-, 5th Earl Cowper 24/7/48 n
Thomas Alexander, Capt., E. I. C. S. 8/12/57
W. 14/8/35 n
Cowtan, Robert (1817–1893), of British Museum 8/6/68
Cox,
also known as Stanley, rescue 2/7/73, 6/3/74
Miss 12/10/78
A., Miss 5/5/91
Alfred Treslove, surveyor 28/9/74
Charles C. 18/12/77
Charles Thomas, Sir, of colonial office 27/12/45
Frederic, Rev. 1/12/69
George (–1857), superintendent SPCK depository 12/5/56
George William, Rev. Sir (1827–1902), claimed 14th Baronet (1877) 6/6/66
Hippisley, Mrs. 20/2/41
H. N. 14/2/77
Homersham (1821–1897), barrister/judge 16/12/54, 14/10/63, 19/2/70, 6/3/70
James, Rev. (1769–) 29/1/37 n
James Bell, Rev. Dr. 1/1/90
J. M. 3/5/79
John Charles, Rev. Dr. (1843–1919), historian 7/1/76, 20/9/89
John Edmund, Rev. (1812–1890) 4/6/53
John George Snead, editor of *The Tablet* 25/8/88, 18/11/89
John Mason, Rev. (1825–1870) 25/6/68
Joshua 18/12/78
N. T., picture dealer 14/5/74
Samuel, Rev. (1826–1893), Baptist 21/10/75 ?
William Kipling, Rev. 12/6/77 ?
Coxburgh, J. 29/5/90
Coxe,
Arthur Cleveland, Bp. (1818–1896), of U.S.A. 6/6/61, 7/4/88 n
Henry Octavius, Rev. (1811–1881), Bodley's Librarian 15/7/75
Coxon, W. E. A. 21/9/87
Cozic, Henry, journalist of France 24/2/70 n
Cozzolini, Cav. 6/2/89
Crabb, James, Rev. 22/5/55
Crabbe, J., surgeon of Edinburgh 27/11/33 ?
Crackenthorpe, William (1790–1888) 23/10/57
Cracroft,
Caroline (–1879), née Scott 27/8/38
Peter (–1865), Royal Navy 27/8/38 n
Craddock, S., of Rugely 13/7/68 ?
Crafer, Edward T., clerk 23/1/35
Cragg,
Mary Anne, author 9/1/26 ?
T. 2/1/80
Craib, A., Rev. 10/7/79
Craig,
or Greig, in Sicily 23/10/38
Edward, Rev. 13/4/28, 5/1/34
Edward Thomas, journalist 5/10/87
Edward Thomas (1804–1894) 21/4/77
Henry Vivian Gibson- (1847–) 14/9/84
James, Dr. 11/4/80
Jardine 15/3/80
John, Rev. 5/6/45
William Gibson-, Sir, 2nd Baronet (1850), liberal M.P. 11/2/52
William Young (1827–), liberal M.P. 5/2/81
Craighead, Mr. 16/11/78
Craik, Henry, Sir (1846–1927), 1st Baronet (1926) 26/9/74, 12/12/86 ?
Craine, Edward, Rev. 8/7/47 ?
Crake,
Augustine David, Rev. (1836–1890) 9/3/77
William Hamilton 9/4/78
Cramend, W. 2/11/91
Cramer,
Johann Baptist (1771–1858), German pianist, music teacher 17/12/38
John Anthony (1793–1848), dean of Carlisle (1844) 18/1/29
Crampern, John Callis, corn dealer 7/1/33
Crampton,
Mr., dentist 20/8/49
John Fiennes Twistleton, Sir (1805–1886), 2nd Baronet, diplomatist 30/10/77
Philip, Sir (1777–1858), surgeon 30/10/77 n
Cranborne *see* Cecil
Cranbrook *see* Hardy
Crandell, Mr. 14/8/77
Crane,
Ebenezer 27/3/76
Joseph, auctioneer 23/6/35
Walter (1845–1915), artist 12/8/89
Cranford *see* Dukinfield
Cranston, Messrs. 24/12/79
Cranswick, C. M. 13/11/74
Cranworth *see* Rolfe
Crapp, Mrs. 22/9/78
Crauford,
O. 24/7/76
R., editor 6/12/34
Craufurd,
Edward Henry John (1816–1887), liberal M.P. 12/5/54

Craufurd (*cont.*)
James (1805–1876), Lord Ardmillan (1855), judge 1/12/65
Craven,
Augustus, diplomat 30/9/45
Charles, Rev. (1797–1877) 29/12/59
H., of Buckley 30/3/57
Keppel Richard 30/9/45 n
Pauline M. A. A., née de la Ferronays, novelist 30/9/45 n, 1/3/83, 3/3/83 L, 24/8/83 ?
Craw,
Mrs. 18/1/90
J. A. 26/8/78
Crawford,
Mr., rescue? 29/6/63
Donald (1837–1919), liberal M.P. 18/1/92
Emily, Mrs., French correspondent of the *Daily News* 8/2/83, 15/2/83, 7/9/89
I. V., consul 10/11/73 n
J., of Atherdun 5/7/44
Mabel Sharman, Miss, author 12/1/89, 26/7/92
Robert Wigram (1813–1889), liberal M.P. 19/3/60
W., Mrs. 18/7/39 ?
William, whig M.P. 18/7/39 n
William Sharman, liberal M.P. 15/1/45 ?
Crawford, Colvin & Co., East India merchants 23/12/52
Crawford and Balcarres *see* Lindsay
Crawfurd,
Frances, Mrs. 11/11/82 ?
Lionel Payne, Rev. (1864–1934) 9/2/80
Crawley,
Charles 8/2/79
Henry, Rev. 18/12/76 ?
Henry Owen, Rev. 23/4/76 ?
Samuel, whig M.P. 5/3/33 n
Thomas William, Rev. 29/3/78 ?
Crawshay, George, of Gateshead 14/1/56
Cray, rescue 27/2/86
Creagh,
James 28/5/56 ?
L., Mrs., rescue 30/6/75, 8/7/75
Cream, J. A. 12/10/78
Crease, Orlando 22/2/49
Creasey, Mr., of Sidcup 1/2/90
Creasy, Mr. 21/6/79
Cree,
old, of Hawarden 13/6/57
Edward David, author 7/3/55 ?
Creed,
Edward Richard, barrister 30/6/48 ?
Henry Harris, clerk in House of Commons 18/12/41
H. Herries, author 7/7/68
Richard, secretary LNWR 19/8/49
Creeson, A. 22/11/79
Creeth, Miss 4/8/87
Creighton, Mandell, Bp. (1843–1901) 14/5/78 ?, 13/2/84, 11/4/84, 20/4/84, 20/1/87, 3/2/87 n, 10/2/87
Crellin,
J. H. 22/3/76
P. 20/1/90
Crelly, R., Rev. 5/3/74
Cremer, W. R. 6/4/80
Cremorne *see* Dawson
Crepaz, Adèle, author on motherhood 3/10/92 L
Crespi, Paolo (–1900) 3/10/79 ?
Crespigny,
C. C. de, Sir, 1st Baronet 18/6/73 n
Emma H. D. de 18/6/73 ?
Cresswell, Cresswell, Sir (–1863), judge, tory M.P. 24/9/41
Creswick, Thomas, painter 9/12/40 ?
Creswick & Co., silversmiths 25/4/76
Cresy, Mr. 28/7/68
Crewe *see* Cunliffe, Milnes, Offley
Crewe,
Hungerford, 3rd Baron Crewe 14/7/48
J. R., Rev., non-anglican 6/7/74
W. H. C. 18/2/43
Crews, J. 4/12/78
Creyke, Ralph (1849–1908), liberal M.P. 5/4/80
Cribbes, Mrs. 21/5/89
Crichton *see* Mackenzie
Crichton,
Mr. 9/11/74
James, of Alyth 4/1/33 ?
John (–1828), 1st Earl Erne 15/4/54 n
John Henry (1839–1914), 4th Earl Erne (1885), Viscount Crichton, tory M.P. 12/3/70
Criely, A. 16/3/78
Crigan,
Capt. 29/11/56
Alexander, Rev. Dr. 1/12/39
Crighton, Miss 4/12/78
Crilly, Mr. 23/5/79
Crippin, T. G., Rev. 21/12/78
Cripps,
Henry, Rev. 14/3/47
Joseph (–1843) 15/3/34
Crispi, Francesco (1819–1901), Italian Prime Minister (1887), Sicilian politician, visitor to Hawarden 2/10/77, 6/10/77, 14/2/89, 23/4/90, 25/4/90, 19/3/94
Cristini, Sig. 12/10/77, 14/10/77
Crittendon, John Denton (1834–1877), sculptor 25/1/72, 28/6/72
Croall,
Mr., stone mason of Fasque 24/8/43, 2/9/50 n
Annie, Mrs., of Fasque 12/12/49

Croasdill, Mr. 24/10/77
Croce, Enrico 6/4/76
Crockett, Samuel Rutherford, Rev. (1860-1914), novelist 26/10/90
Croft, John, Sir (1778-1862), 1st Baronet (1818) 24/5/58
Crofts,
Alfred, haberdasher 4/6/42
Christopher, Rev. (-1894), headmaster 7/5/52
Croke, Thomas William, Abp. (1824-1902) 18/4/90
Croker,
J. 5/6/77
John Wilson (1780-1857), journalist and tory M.P. 17/2/35
Croll, James (1821-1890), geologist 13/1/73
Croly, George, Rev. 13/8/49
Cromartie *see* Gower
Crombie,
A., Mrs. 12/9/33
Alexander, of Thornton Castle 12/9/33
John William (1858-1908), author, liberal M.P. 29/10/86 ?
Lewis, advocate of Aberdeen 17/4/34
Lewis, superintendent LSWR 1/12/54
Cromdell, William 11/8/52
Cromer *see* Baring
Cromer, rescue 8/4/62
Crompton,
Richard, coachmaker of Liverpool 7/12/67 ?
Samuel 15/4/72
Cronin, Mr. 9/5/79
Crony, J. S. M. 19/4/90
Cronyn,
Mr., mayor of Kilkenny 5/5/37 n
Benjamin, Bp. (1802-1871), bishop of Huron 5/5/37
Crook,
Henry Simon Charles, Rev. (1806-1884) 17/3/29 ?
Joseph (1809-1884), liberal M.P. 30/11/55
Crooke, Mr. 16/8/58
Cropper,
Alderman 22/9/87
A. E. 23/12/90
James (1823-1900), liberal M.P. 17/10/90
Crosbie,
Howard Augustus, Rev. (1844-1918) 10/1/79
S. H. 28/8/79
W. H. 5/1/42
Crosfield,
Joseph 15/2/42
William, of Lancashire 10/10/65, 23/9/68, 12/10/68
Croskery, Thomas, Rev. (1830-1886), presbyterian 10/6/68
Crosland, T. P., of Huddersfield 2/11/89
Cross,
servant 5/12/91
Alexander, merchant of Glasgow 10/5/38 ?
F. J. 30/11/89
Jane, Mrs. 11/9/77
John, solicitor 25/7/68
John, Sir (1766-1842), Knight (1831), judge 16/5/38 n
John Kynaston (1832-1887), liberal M.P. 7/12/75, 5/1/83, 15/1/83, 5/5/83 c, 8/5/83
John Walter, widower of 'George Eliot'; with G in France 5/2/83, 11/2/85, 2/12/92 L
Katherine Matilda (-1871), née Winn 9/6/51
Margaret, Lady, née Hyde, of Ardwick 16/5/38
Mary Ann [George Eliot] (1819-1880), novelist 11/2/85, 24/2/85, 21/3/85, 29/3/85
Maurice, of Ireland 21/2/53 ?
P. 8/4/64
William Assheton (1818-1883) 9/6/51 n, 16/11/68
Crossley,
Mr. 18/12/85
Francis, Sir (1817-1872), 1st Baronet (1863), liberal M.P. 22/2/60
James, lawyer of Manchester 24/7/37, 4/8/37
Crosthwaite,
Charles, Rev. (1806-1892), of Kildare 6/6/59
John Clarke, Rev. 8/1/40
Crotch, William Robert, Rev. (1799-1877) 14/6/29
Crouch, Henry, of Glastonbury 28/1/77
Croucher, G. B. 22/5/88
Crowder,
John H., Rev. 9/12/40
John Hutton, Rev. (-1883), in Rome 28/10/66
Crowe,
Eyre 17/1/74
G. 14/8/79
Joseph Archer, Sir (1825-1896), consul in Dusseldorf 15/5/76
Crowther,
E. 28/10/85
M. A., rescue 4/3/51
Samuel, Rev. (1802-1879), of Rome 9/1/31, 10/1/31, 28/10/66 ?
Crozier, Robert, of Manchester 11/10/57
Cruddass, Thomas 22/9/76
Cruden, Mrs. 20/5/56
Cruess, J. 23/12/79
Cruickshank,
Mrs., of Brechin 18/10/33 ?

Cruickshank (*cont.*)
Mrs., of Montrose 18/10/33 ?
Alexander, of Brechin 18/10/33 ?
James, of Montrose 18/10/33 ?
Cruikshank,
Alex, hosier of Edinburgh 16/9/45
Alfred Hamilton 2/6/76
Crump *see* Wilkinson
Crump,
Arthur, author 11/1/86
George Hamilton (1801-1876), of Cheshire 9/11/52 n
J. E. 17/11/90
Crunden, Messrs. 30/1/66, 31/7/66
Cruttenden, William Cruttenden, Rev. (1776-1863) 28/1/28 n
Cruttenden family 28/1/28
Cruttwell, Charles Thomas, Rev. (1847-1911) 10/11/79
Cruvelli, Jeanne Sophie, singer 4/11/50
Crybbaer, Mr. 30/10/68
Crymlan, Mr. 15/4/80
Cubitt,
Thomas (-1855), builder 24/12/52
William (1791-1863), tory M.P. 29/5/50
Cubley, William Harold, painter 26/1/41, 9/1/73
Cudingley, C. 25/3/57
Cuff, William, Rev., baptist 30/10/79
Cullen,
J., Rev. 13/10/85
Paul, Cardinal (1803-1878) 29/7/45, 17/4/69 c, 15/7/69 L, 16/2/70, 9/7/72 n, 3/9/72, 6/9/72, 1/3/73, 6/11/77, 3/12/77 n
Cullinan, William Fitzpatrick, parliamentary draftsman in the Irish Office 22/4/81
Cullum *see* Gibson
Cully, Miss 25/1/87
Cumberland *see* Ernest Augustus (Ernest I), George
Cumberland,
Mr., historian, thought-reader 19/6/84
John (-1866), publisher 16/6/59
Stuart C. 25/6/87
Cumbleholme, Mr. 25/5/68
Cumin, Patrick (1823-1890), publisher, civil servant 12/5/63
Cumming,
Miss 17/7/44
Alexander, Rev. 17/1/37 ?
C. 12/12/79
James, Dr., of Glasgow 19/9/72 ?
John, Rev. (1807-1881), presbyterian 26/2/39, 12/7/66
William Gordon-, Sir (1848-1930), of the Tranby Croft affair 4/6/91
William Gordon Gordon-, Col. (1829-1908) 15/6/88
Cunard, Samuel, Sir (-1865), Baronet (1859), shipping 15/8/53
Cundall, Joseph H. (1818-1895), superintendent of publications, South Kensington 6/7/81 ?
Cunliffe *see* Wynn
Cunliffe,
Charlotte (-1856), née Howel 11/4/38 ?
Charlotte (-1875) 9/1/40
Emma (-1850), née Crewe 11/4/40 n
Emma (-1875) 9/1/40
Foster, Sir 17/5/34 n
J. 6/1/87
R. A., Sir, 4th Baronet 11/4/38 n
Robert Alfred, Sir (1839-1905), 5th Baronet 14/9/73, 5/10/77
Robert Ellis (1805-1855) 11/4/38 n
Cunningham,
Charles Thornton (1811-), colonial governor 9/2/30, 1/5/46
H. 23/3/78
J. M. 3/6/65
John, architect of Liverpool 20/10/52
John William (-1901), secretary of King's College, London 21/4/52
John William, Rev. (1780-1861), author 9/2/30 n, 28/2/31
Cunnington, John 16/9/75
Cunynghame, Arthur Augustus Thurlow, Gen. (1812-1884) 29/11/72
Curcumelli, Demetrio, Sir, of Ionia 30/11/58
Cure, Edward Capel, Rev. (1828-1890) 17/4/77
Curè, Sig., of Zante 30/12/58
Cureton, William, Rev. (1808-1864), of the British Museum 21/8/30
Curis, Socrates, of Ionia 1/12/58
Curr, D. 19/8/90
Curran, John James, surgeon in Cork 30/9/86 ?
Currey,
George, Rev. (1816-1885) 17/1/71
William, Hartington's Irish agent 16/3/86 n
Currie *see* Repington
Currie,
Dr., of U.S.A. 28/4/91
Bertram Wodehouse (1827-1896), banker 19/3/84, 23/3/84 ff, 6/4/84, 4/12/84, 18/2/85, 10/3/85, 23/1/86, 25/1/86, 5/2/86, 15/3/86, 1/4/87, 12/4/87, 5/5/87, 27/2/88, 28/11/90, 28/2/91, 21/5/92, 26/5/92, 3/6/92 n, 11/8/92, 29/8/92 n, 10/9/92, 21/9/92, 23/9/92 ff, 25/9/92, 28/9/92 n, 28/10/92, 4/3/93 L, 12/5/93 ff, 15/6/93 ff, 30/11/93
Donald, Sir (1825-1909), ship owner 12/7/76, 10/7/77 n, 12/7/77, 26/8/80 ff, 15/7/81, 18/3/82, 23/9/84, 5/6/86
Edmund Hall, Sir (1834-1913) 26/8/87

Edmund Hay, distiller 4/7/76
Frederick, Sir (1799–1875), of India council 8/3/69
Henry (1798–1873), Peelite M.P. 15/7/53
James, Rev. (–1877) 5/8/67
Jean, Miss 3/9/77
M., Prof., of U.S.A.? 22/4/76
Philip Henry Wodehouse, Sir (1834–1906), 1st Baron Currie (1899), diplomat 8/3/90, 9/4/90
Raikes (1801–1881), liberal M.P., banker 27/3/51, 1/11/79
Curry,
D. J. 12/2/78
Peter Finch, attorney of Liverpool 25/4/55 ?
Cursham,
George, surgeon 27/4/39 ?
Thomas, Rev. (–1868) 27/10/52
Curteis,
A. M. 26/10/85
George Herbert, Rev. (1824–1894), professor 7/3/56, 12/10/81
Curteyne, W. 22/10/90
Curtis,
A., Miss 20/3/91
A. H. 6/1/90
Emma, charity case of Bermondsey 7/1/62 ?
F. H., Rev. 9/6/63, 12/5/68
George William (1824–1892), poet of U.S.A. 28/7/58, 21/8/58
John Harrison, ear specialist 4/3/45
Matthew (–1887), cotton machine manufacturer 12/10/53
Curtius, Julius S. 31/7/88
Curzon,
Emily Julia (–1866), née Horton, Lady Zouche 1/3/52
Francis Nathaniel (1865–1941), Eton schoolboy, later stockbroker 24/6/82
Frank, author 24/11/55
Frederick Emmanuel Hippolytus, Rev. (1795–1871) 22/7/57
George Nathaniel (1859–1925), 1st Baron Curzon (1898), 1st Marquis Curzon (1921) 6/5/78, 6/7/78 n, 7/7/78
Robert (1810–1873), Baron de la Zouche 4/9/41
Cusack,
Miss 4/11/78
Mary Frances, Sister (1830–1899) 23/10/77
P. J. 25/4/89
Cusin, A., Rev. 3/10/89
Cust *see* Egerton, Middleton
Cust,
Adelaide (1868–1917), née Talbot, Lady Brownlow 30/10/63, 20/5/70
Adelbert Wellington Brownlow (1844–1921), 3rd Earl Brownlow (1867) 30/10/63 n, 20/5/70, 25/6/70, 22/7/75, 28/6/83, 16/9/86, 27/3/92
Brownlow, Sir, 1st Baron Brownlow 2/7/42 n
Edward, Sir (1794–1878), Baronet, tory M.P. 18/1/40
John Hume (1812–1851), took name of Egerton, Viscount Alford, tory M.P. 3/6/43 n
John William Spencer Egerton- (1842–1867) 21/1/67
Marianne Margaret Compton (–1888), Lady Brownlow 27/7/72 ff, 17/10/75, 8/5/79, 26/6/79, 10/7/79, 14/12/85, 16/9/86
Mary Anne, Lady (–1882), née Boode 11/12/61
Robert Needham (1821–1909), poet 18/8/79
Custance, Henry Neville 2/1/79
Custode,
of Bologna 12/6/32
of Colosseum 3/4/32
of Milan 22/9/38
of Pompeii 21/11/38
of Taormina 31/10/38
of Venice 19/6/32
Customs, Chairman of, Sir T. Fremantle (1846–1874) 22/12/34
Customs officer 9/2/32
Customs Officer, of Piacenza 24/9/38
Cutborn, T. 14/3/78
Cuthbert,
A. A., of Glasgow 13/6/77 ?
A. J. 14/8/91
Cuthbertson, Dr. 17/8/87
Cuyler,
Mrs. 6/7/89
Theodore Ledyard, Rev. Dr., American clergyman 1/8/85
Cuzner, John Henry, of Hackney 25/8/56
Cwiek, M. 6/1/77 n
Cymrodorion Society 12/5/77
Czarnowski, Jan Nepomucen, Polish historian 7/6/52
Czartoryski *see* Dzialynska

Dabling, Mr., editor of *Lloyd's Weekly* 3/4/90
Dack, C. 8/6/87
Dacosta,
Mr. 19/2/78
John 22/3/79
Dacre *see* Brand
Dacres, Sidney Colpoys, Adm. Sir (1805–1884) 9/12/68
Dadson, Alfred William, barrister 8/1/80
D'Agen, A. J. Boyer 30/1/92

Dagna, Sig., landlord of Naples 13/11/50
Daily Chronicle, (editor of) 24/4/86 L
Daily Review, (publisher of) 28/4/79
Dain, Horatio, solicitor 29/8/78
Dakeyne, John Osmund, Rev., formerly Deakin 27/1/43
Dakin,
Edward, Rev. 3/2/88
Thomas, Sir (1808–1899) 14/11/71
Dalberg *see* Gower
Dalbiac *see* Ker
Dalbiac, James Charles, Sir (1776–1847), Knight (1831), M.P., lieutenant general 23/4/35 n
Dalby, William Bartlett, Sir (1840–1918), Knight (1886), physician 11/6/75, 1/6/81
Daldy, Isbister & Co., publishers 15/6/76, 30/6/76
Dale,
Lawford William Torriano, Rev. (1826–1898) 17/5/63
M., Mrs., née Summerhayes, rescue 30/7/59, 24/3/60, 17/7/61, 3/8/61, 5/3/62, 14/6/67, 20/6/67, 3/5/78, 16/10/86
Robert William, Rev. (1829–1895), Congregationalist minister in Birmingham 23/11/71, 25/11/71, 5/12/77, 24/4/86 L, 29/4/86 L, 8/5/86, 30/12/86
Thomas, Prof. (1797–1870), dean of Rochester (1870) 5/6/36
Thomas Pelham, Rev. (1821–1892) 16/5/70
William 17/3/74
Dalgairns, John Dobree, Rev. (1818–1876), Roman Catholic 7/12/72
Dalgleish, W. S. 24/12/90
Dalglish,
Mr., of Bank of England 8/7/63
Robert, liberal M.P. 29/2/60
Dalhousie *see* Ramsay
d'Alice, Madame, rescue 24/6/72
Dalkeith, Provost of 12/8/88
Dall, Caroline Wells Healey, Mrs., American writer and feminist 8/1/86
Dallas,
Mr. 21/3/81
George Mifflin (1792–1864), minister of U.S.A. in London (1856) 2/6/56, 16/6/56, 17/6/56
Dalley *see* Goschen
D'Alleyn, rescue 21/2/72
Dalling *see* Bulwer
Dallyn, W. 9/9/87
Dalmeny *see* Primrose
d'Alopens *see* Ferronays
D'Aloz, St. 8/10/75
Dalrymple,
Adolphus John, Sir (–1866), 2nd Baronet (1830) 10/8/49
John, oculist 17/3/48
John Hamilton (1819–1903), 10th Earl of Stair (1864) 12/5/70, 22/6/92
John Hew (1848–1914), 11th Earl of Stair (1903), Lord Dalrymple 25/11/79
North Hamilton (–1864), 9th Earl of Stair (1853) 20/9/53
Dalton *see* Young
Dalton,
Mrs., rescue 9/2/76
Charles Browne, Rev. (1810–1893) 23/9/38 ?, 4/5/55
George James, school master 6/4/50
Daly,
Mr. 19/7/78
Charles Patrick, Judge (1816–1899), of U.S.A. 8/7/74 ?
J. Bowles 21/7/87
John Fairley, Rev. 19/5/76
Robert, Bp. (1783–1872), bishop of Cashel (1843) 9/3/34
William, Rev. 9/4/69
Dalyell, Robert Alexander Osborne, Sir (–1886), 8th Baronet (1865) 13/3/51
Dalzell, John E., Dr., physician 1/6/62
Dalziel, J. H. 22/12/89
Damala, Emanuel Michael, of Greece 15/1/79, 19/7/88, 23/4/90
Damalas, Nikolaos M., Greek author 19/6/90
Damen,
A. R. 16/3/78
Arnold, Rev. 16/3/78 ?
Damer,
George Lionel Dawson- (1788–1856), né Dawson, tory M.P. 17/12/32 n, 4/3/52
Henry John Reuben Dawson- (1822–1889), 3rd Earl of Portarlington (1845) 2/9/81 L
d'Amico, Baron 28/4/90
Dammeyer, Mr. 11/4/78
Damoys, Mons. 10/7/83
Dampier,
Augustus, Rev. 28/2/93
William James, Rev. (–1878) 1/12/75 ?
Damrong, Prince, of Siam 25/9/91
Dana, Richard Henry, writer of U.S.A. 15/8/56, 13/1/71 L, 18/10/79 ?
Dandolo, A., of Ionia 3/12/58
Danell, James, Bp., Roman Catholic 17/5/71
Dangerfield, John Howell, Rev. 21/10/58 ?
Daniel,
Charles Henry Oliver 8/11/91 n
William Thomas Shave (1806–1891), judge 25/3/68 ?
Daniell,
Mrs. 27/3/90

John Jeremiah, Rev. (1818–1898) 14/2/56
Raymond Samuel, Rev. 1/2/53
Dankin, Mr. 18/8/86
Dannatt, Thomas William, auctioneer 16/12/79
Danton, A. 2/5/86
Darbishire,
Samuel Dukinfield (1796–1870), of Pendyffryn, Conway, unitarian and G's host 29/9/59 n, 11/9/60, 24/9/60, 10/9/61, 4/9/63, 21/9/63, 30/8/64, 12/9/64, 11/8/67 ff, 2/9/67, 14/8/68, 13/9/68
Vernon 29/9/59
Darby,
Christopher Lovett, Rev. 5/11/42, 8/7/47
E. W. 21/2/89
G., of Flintshire 25/3/56, 12/8/56, 3/6/58
John Wareyn, Rev. (1793–1846) 1/6/39
W. H., of Brymbo Iron Works, Wrexham 30/3/57
Darbyshire, William, coachmaker of Newark 2/7/33
Darcey, John, Rev. 29/1/28
D'Arcy, John Francis, barrister of Ireland 3/5/47 ?
Dare,
Robert Westley Hall (–1836), tory M.P. 29/6/33, 6/3/46
Robert Westley Hall, Mrs. 18/5/46
D'Aristocles, Jean, Mons. 19/6/78
Darke, C. 30/9/87
Darley,
Mr. 4/3/80
George Steel 22/7/80
John Richard, Bp. (–1884) 18/11/53
Darling,
M. 23/7/66
R., merchant of Edinburgh 21/2/79
Ralph, Sir (1775–1858), Knight (1835) 7/8/35
Thomas, Rev. (1816–1893) 17/5/56
Darlington,
Joseph (or James), mining engineer of Wigan 19/8/56, 25/11/56, 9/9/57, 10/10/60, 7/8/62
R. 10/7/88
Darnley *see* Bligh
Darrant, F. 26/11/86
Darrick, C. 29/2/68
D'Arsonval,
J. D. 22/9/45 n
J. D., Mad., friend of Helen 22/9/45
Dart, Joseph Henry (1817–1887), conveyancer, author 16/6/62
Dartmouth *see* Legge
Darton,
F. R. 18/9/89
P. F., bookseller? 6/11/58
Darton & Clark, booksellers 30/12/42
Dartrey *see* Dawson
Darwin *see* Galton
Darwin,
Charles Robert 6/2/41 n
Erasmus 18/1/33 n
William Erasmus (1839–) 6/3/80
Darwin and Pugh, Messrs. 7/10/62
Dasent, George Webbe, Sir (1817–1896), civil servant 11/1/70, 4/4/79, 19/4/84
Dashwood *see* Loftus
Dashwood,
rescue 7/2/76
rescue 4/3/91
H., Sir, 3rd Baronet 11/3/39 n
J. 2/4/78
L. 24/5/89
Dassi, Giuseppe F., economist 7/3/53
Dassj, Sig. 20/5/75
Daubeny, Charles Giles Bridle, Prof. (–1867) 8/3/53
D'Aubigné, Françoise (1635–1719), Marquise de Maintenon 20/2/32
D'Aubigny, Madame 24/2/86
d'Aumale *see* Bourbon
Daunt,
William Joseph O'Neill (1807–1894), Irish politician 25/9/54, 24/1/87
W. J. O'Neill, Mrs. 30/11/68
Dauval, Mr. 25/1/76
Davenport,
Mrs., of Kirkdale, Liverpool 21/7/43
E., merchant of Liverpool 18/2/52 ?
G. A. 30/9/68
John Coltman (1830–1858) 2/11/56 ?
Davey,
C. H., G.P.O. 5/9/78
Horace, Sir (1833–1907), 1st Baron Davey (1894) 22/8/75, 8/6/82
Richard (1799–1884), liberal M.P. 4/2/60
R. S., Dr., physician of Walmer 17/8/69
R. W. 2/11/85, 19/10/89
William Harrison, Rev. 3/3/75
David, servant 16/1/57
Davide, Giovanni (1789–1851), tenor of Italy 23/3/32
David Kalakaua (1836–1891), King of the Sandwich Islands 11/7/81
Davidson,
Miss, of Hawarden 27/8/64, 9/1/87
Mrs., rescue 16/10/86
A. 23/2/77
Alexander, of Manchester 18/8/42
C. F., N. B. Railway 26/12/46 n
Duncan (1800–1882), M.P. 28/12/32 n
Edith Murdoch, née Tait 14/3/91
Elizabeth Diana (1804–1839), née Macdonald 28/12/32 ?
James, of Greenock 16/10/86
James, Rev. 29/5/77 ?

Davidson (*cont.*)
John Morrison, radical and author 28/11/88
Randall Thomas, Abp. (1848–1930) 9/5/83, 14/6/84, 15/6/84, 11/10/84, 22/7/90
William Edward (1853–1923), counsel to the Foreign Office 21/11/93
W. J., banker of London 20/3/48
Davies,
of Liverpool 27/11/76
Mr., of Hawarden 2/11/64
David Jones, Rev. (–1910) 8/10/78
D. E. 30/10/86
D. T. 6/12/86
E. B. 21/6/79
Fox 15/9/91
Henry Thomas (–1869), captain, Royal Navy 21/3/49
James & Son, of Hawarden 29/3/57
Jenkin, Rev., rector of Mold 28/9/56
John, of Hawarden 11/9/75
John, Rev. 2/2/56 ?
John Llewelyn, Rev. (1843–1916) 11/5/73
M. J. 22/2/77
R. A., Rev. 2/4/78
R. E. 25/11/67
Richard (1818–1896), liberal M.P. 29/12/82
R. Rice, author 3/9/78, 12/12/79
Samuel Price, Rev. 29/6/47
Thomas, of Hawarden 11/9/75 n
Thomas Henry Hastings, liberal M.P. 6/6/33 n
W. E. 13/8/77
Davies (Ashmore) & Co, silk merchants of London 12/11/56
d'Avigliano *see* Pamphilji
D'Avignor, Elim Henry (1841–1895) 2/9/78
Davis,
rescue 21/6/70, 26/7/70
Mr., actor in Whitby 28/8/71
Mrs., rescue 17/8/60
C. A. 18/7/74
Charles Henry, Rev. (1823–) 31/3/56
C. T. 13/12/79
E., liberal of Greenwich 29/3/77
Ebenezer, liberal of Woolwich 5/9/76
E. F. 23/12/79
F., picture dealer 22/6/47 ?
F. R., of Hoxton 4/2/52
Frederick, curiosity dealer 24/3/64
Frederick Whylock, Rev. 8/2/67
F. T. 13/11/75
Hart Jr. 15/10/42
J., of Hawarden 3/8/58
John, Rev. 15/11/76 ?
John Francis, Sir, 1st Baronet, colonial governor 23/2/46
Richard Hart, Fellow of Royal Society 16/4/30
Davison,
rescue 5/6/72
Miss 26/4/89
Charles, of Hawarden 13/9/52
Christopher, secretary of Great North of England Junction RR 18/2/52
John Robert (1826–1871), liberal M.P. (1868) 24/3/69 ff, 21/12/70, 20/4/71 n
Davison & Co 11/1/42
Davison & Simpson, merchants of Broad Street, London 22/9/27
Davitt, Michael (1846–1906), founder of the Land League (1879), home rule M.P. (1882) 22/1/81 c, 29/1/81 c, 5/2/81 c, 4/5/82, 7/5/82, 23/5/82 c, 29/8/82, 21/3/90 n, 21/11/90
Davy,
Charles Raikes, Rev. 14/3/68 ?
Humphrey, Sir 1/12/41 n
Jane, Lady, née Kerr 15/6/47
W. J. 18/1/78
Davydow, A. 22/8/77 n
Dawkins, George, baptist 12/12/45 ?
Dawnay, Guy Cuthbert (1848–1889), tory M.P. 1/5/84
Dawson *see* Damer
Dawson,
Augusta, Lady Cremorne, Lady Dartrey 2/6/56
C., lord mayor of Dublin 11/10/82
C. T. 4/11/86
E. B. 1/8/66
Frederick, treasury clerk 24/5/53
George, Rev. (1804–) 20/9/32
George Robert (1790–1856), M.P., Peel's son-in-law 12/1/46 n
J. M., Rev. 13/2/90
John (–1798), 1st Earl of Portarlington 4/3/52 n
John, Rev. (–1913) 23/1/76
Mary, née Peel 12/1/46
P., of Dublin 30/3/44
R., solicitor 8/9/77
R., Dr. 17/7/77
Richard (1783–1850), merchant of Liverpool 6/2/37
Richard (1817–1897), 1st Earl of Dartrey (1866), 2nd Baron Cremorne, liberal 2/6/56 n
Robert Peel (1818–1877), Peelite, Peelite M.P. 12/1/46 n, 13/6/70
Veysey, Baron Cremorne (1866), 2nd Earl of Dartrey (1897), liberal M.P. 29/5/66
W., of Co. Kerry 24/7/43
William, Rev. 27/11/74
William Harbutt (1860–1948), author 31/10/89 ?
Day,
Alfred 3/9/69

Harry 11/12/77
J. B. 2/1/80
Lal Behari, Rev. (1824–1894), Indian Free Churchman 12/12/79, 22/2/80
Philip, reporter 27/4/59
Samuel Phillips (–1880), reporter 22/8/67
S. H., barrister 3/1/91
William Ansell, author 19/6/68 ?
Days, Alfred, secretary of Atrocities Committee 23/8/76
Deacle, Edward Leathes Young, Rev. (1828–1915) 28/12/74
Deacon, of Rome 22/12/38
Deakin *see* Dakeyne
Deakin, Messrs. 3/1/87
Deal, J. G., Rev. 30/4/87
Dealtry,
Thomas, Bp., of Madras 31/1/49
William, Prof. (1775–1847) 31/7/32, 4/8/32
Dean,
Mr., of Hawarden 10/12/60
Richard Betenson, né Brietzeke 27/4/41, 13/10/41, 14/3/42, 18/9/43
Richard Ryder (–1885), barrister 25/3/50
Deane,
Rev. Dr. 20/7/77
John Connellan (1816–1884), exhibition organiser of Manchester 27/8/56, 15/10/56
Ralph 21/6/26
Richard Wallace, Rev. 10/12/75
Deanes, W. 31/5/76
Deans, A. 24/1/77
Deansfield, J. H. 28/8/79
Dearden, George Ferrand, Rev. 17/1/78 ?
Dearle, Edward (–1891), organist 23/7/50
Dease, Edmund Gerald (1829–1904), liberal M.P. 30/11/70 L, 24/12/70 n, 8/1/71, 18/1/71 n, 19/1/71 c, 6/2/71
Deasy, Rickard (1812–1883), liberal M.P., judge 1/8/60
De Beauvoir, Mrs. 23/6/63
Debenham,
Messrs. 18/7/79
William Elliot, photographer 30/7/63
Debidor, Antoine, historian 15/11/90
De Borne, rescue 15/11/80
de Brockdorff *see* Schack
de Broglie, Achille Charles L. V., 6th Duc de Broglie 3/5/45
de Burgh, H., of Dublin 25/1/86
de Caux, J. W. 16/8/90
de Cetto, Baron (–1879), Bavarian ambassador 3/5/79
Dechman, Mr. 22/1/79
Decies *see* Beresford
de Clifford *see* Russell
de Coverley,
Mr. 2/7/81
R. 6/9/90
de Crecy, A., Miss 1/3/80
Deed, John George, Rev. Dr. 14/4/92
Deedes, William, Col. (1796–1862), tory M.P. 14/2/53
Dee Embankment Trust 29/5/90
Deeley, Mr. 28/12/86
Deering, W. W., Rev. 12/2/56
Deevey, W. F. 17/10/90
de Fontaine, Felix Gregory, American author 5/6/89 ?
de Grey *see* Grey, Robinson
de Hagen, Maria, Miss, dressmaker 21/10/87
de Hohsé, Major 26/7/77
D'Eichthal, A. 14/1/91
Deidor, Mr. 28/3/78
Deighton, Messrs., publishers 7/3/83
Deinhardt, Johann Heinrich (1805–1867) 8/9/38 ?
Delabruère, P. B., Speaker, Quebec Legislative Council 1/6/87
de la Ferronays *see* Craven
Delafield, Mad., singer of Naples 23/12/50
de la Fleurière, N. 15/6/77, 18/8/77, 8/2/80
Delafosse, Charles David, Rev. 31/10/42
Delahunty, James (–1885) 21/2/73
Delamere *see* Cholmondeley
Delane, John Thadeus (1817–1877) 10/1/42, 14/10/58, 16/1/66, 22/2/68, 25/4/68, 3/12/68, 3/2/69 L, 4/2/69 L, 27/2/69 L, 19/7/69 L, 6/10/69 L, 21/6/70 L, 18/11/71, 5/2/74 L, 28/4/77
de Laon, Vicomte 25/9/77
Delapryme, Charles (–1899), barrister 28/4/54
Delarive,
Auguste, Swiss ambassador 2/7/60
William (1827–1900), of Switzerland 16/5/60
Delarue, Thomas (1793–1866), printer 5/4/56
Delawarr *see* West
de la Zouche *see* Curzon
Delbert, P., author 10/5/91
de Leon, Thomas Cooper, American author 16/9/90
Delevigne, Harry Brunning Constant, Rev. (–1888) 10/11/76, 15/10/78
Delfosse, Maurice, Belgian diplomat 3/11/58
Delganni, Mons., Greek minister 18/7/78
de Lille,
Mons. 2/11/79
J. D. 21/3/87
de Lisle,
Ambrose Lisle March Phillips (1809–1878) 20/7/71, 21/7/71, 30/9/73, 7/10/73, 24/10/74, 27/10/74, 28/10/74, 29/10/74, 19/4/77, 22/4/77, 12/12/80

de Lisle (*cont.*)
Margaret 20/2/78, 12/12/80 L, 18/6/82 L
Delitzsch, Johannes, Dr. 27/7/75
Della Chiesa della Torre, Camillo (1812–1888), soldier 3/3/59 ?
Dellow, Hugh 30/5/92
Delmath, C. 5/3/80
Delvinotti Barozzi, Achille 27/6/59
Deman, E. F., instructor to royal flax society 23/3/52
de Marzo, Gualberto, of Florence 11/5/86
de Mauley *see* Ponsonby
Demaus, Robert, Rev. (1829–1874) 7/10/64
Dempsey,
Mr. 24/7/43
James 7/11/88
Denbigh *see* Feilding
Denby, Thomas, attorney 4/2/36 ?
de Nino, Sig. 9/1/88
Denison *see* Phillimore
Denison,
rescue 10/5/72
Albert Denison (1805–1860), Baron Londesborough (1850), né Conyngham 21/5/51
Charlotte, Lady, née Bentinck, Lady Ossington 14/3/61, 1/3/66
Edmund Beckett (1816–1905), 1st Baron Grimthorpe (1886), Queen's Counsel 3/5/45
Edward (1801–1854), bishop of Salisbury (1987) 1/5/29
Frank (1813–1843), naval officer 27/8/30 ?
George Anthony, Ven. (1805–1896) 24/6/29, 13/8/56 ff, 1/9/56, 5/11/56 ff, 18/12/85
Henry (1810–1858), fellow of All Souls, Oxford 17/8/30
John, formerly Wilkinson, of Ossington 23/3/33 n
John Evelyn 2/12/30
Louisa Mary, née Seymer 25/9/41 n
N. J. 6/5/48
Stephen Charles (1811–1871) 27/8/30 ?
W. T., Sir, colonial governer 20/6/46, 19/5/83
Denman *see* Aitchison
Denman,
Emma, née Jones 21/5/44
George (1819–1896), liberal M.P., judge 11/3/65
Richard (1814–1883), barrister 21/5/44 n
Thomas, 1st Baron Denman 21/5/44 n
Denneby, W. S., Mr. 25/10/86, 6/8/89, 23/9/90
Dennelly, W. A. 1/11/90
Dennet, Misses 19/6/64
Dennington, A. 16/2/75
Dennis,
Mr. 12/6/39
George (1814–1898), consul 10/12/57
W. R. 18/5/78
Dennistoun, James 10/12/42
Denny, W. H. 16/4/92
Denoon, Alexander, merchant 19/8/51
Denora, Col., of Florence 31/12/87
Dent,
John Dent (1826–1894), liberal M.P. 14/3/61
Robert Kirkup, travel writer 9/10/77
Wilkinson, of London 28/6/58
Dent & Co., clockmakers 21/1/61
Denton,
bookseller 7/11/27
rescue 3/3/76
William, Rev. (–1888) 13/6/51, 24/4/69
Dentrici, Antonio 29/2/52 fl
Denvil, C., Miss 12/3/67, 16/3/67
de Peryer, Mr. 25/11/85
Deramore *see* Bateson
Derby *see* Cecil, Stanley
Derbyshire,
W., gardener 7/8/37
William, brewer of Liverpool 25/11/68
D'Eremas, J. P. Val, Dr. 18/5/88
de Reszke, Jean (1850–1935), opera singer 23/6/88, 15/7/89 n, 12/6/90 n
de Ricci *see* Walewska
de Rinaldi, Sig. 11/4/77
Dering,
Edward Cholmeley, Sir (1807–1896), 8th Baronet, liberal M.P. 23/11/38 n, 3/8/54
Jane, Lady, née Edwardes 23/11/38
Dermott, Miss 25/4/88
de Roque,
Baron 10/5/90
Baroness 10/5/90
de Ros *see* Ros
Derrig, Hugh Carey, Rev. 2/3/80
Derwent *see* Johnstone
Derwentwater *see* Radcliffe
de Salis *see* Salis
de Salis-Soglio *see* Warren
Desborough, Laurence, solicitor 5/5/45 ?
De Simone, Cav. 3/1/89
Desmond, A., rescue 25/4/63, 21/6/63
de Soyres, John, Rev. Princ. (1847–1905) 9/5/79
Despotović, Mileta, Gen. 4/7/78
Dessilla, Mr. 25/10/79
Dessoulavy, T., English landscape painter 11/4/32
D'Este *see* Wilde
de Steding, Mons. 17/11/92
des Voeux, George William, Sir (1834–1909) 6/1/93
de Tabley *see* Warren
D'Etchegoyen, M.& Mad. 20/4/78

Detnore, rescue 25/7/57
Deuce, Mr. 28/2/57
Deutsch, Emanuel Oscar Menahem (1829–1873), assistant librarian at British Museum 20/2/69
Devalle, Walter 12/9/77
Dever & Co., wine shippers of London 10/1/42
de Verdon, Thomas K., author 17/8/77
Deverell,
John Croft, barrister 4/8/91
William Henry, barrister 23/4/74 ?
William Trapnell, historian 17/4/78
Wykeham T., secretary to City Liberal Club 23/5/76 n
Devereux,
Henry Cornwall (1807–1839) 28/6/27 ?
Richard Joseph (1829–), liberal M.P. 23/1/69
Robert (1809–1855), 15th Viscount Hereford (1843), canon of Durham 28/6/27 ?
D'Everton, Charles Sebright, Baron, of Ionia 7/12/58
de Vesci *see* Vesey
De Vesci *see* Vesey
Devey,
Mr., of Hawarden 15/10/77
J. 8/7/56
Devine,
Mr. 19/3/78
J. P. 23/12/79
Devinvenzi, Giuseppi 21/4/59
Devis *see* Tupper
de Vita, Signora 19/1/88
Devon *see* Courtenay
Devonshire *see* Cavendish, Trist
Devonshire, Thomas Harris, solicitor 25/3/79 ?
Devoto, Mr. 11/11/79
Devrient, Wilhelmine Schröder (1804–1860), soprano of Germany 24/5/33
Dewar, James, Dr., physician 19/1/68 ?
Dewdney, Edgar, Lt. Governor of Canada 4/11/86 n
Dewer (Dever), Messrs. 8/1/42, 10/1/42
Dewhurst, Henry William, physician 4/6/52
de Wilde, Mr. 5/3/78
de Winter, Mr. 21/10/87
Dexter,
Messrs., of U.S.A. 1/9/87
A. P. 2/9/74
John Thomas, author 28/2/68 ?
Deym,
Count 18/3/91
Countess 18/3/91
D'Eyncourt,
Charles Tennyson (1784–1861), né Tennyson, liberal M.P. 18/8/29
E. C. Tennyson-, Adm. (–1903) 9/10/32
Henrietta, Lady (1819–1890), née Pelham-Clinton 9/10/32
d'Houdetot *see* Barante
D'Houne, Mlle. 11/5/81
Dibdin,
Charles (1849–1910), of savings bank 4/3/80
Robert William, Rev. 13/6/58 n
Dicey,
Albert Venn, Prof. (1835–1922) 4/6/83, 18/12/85, 10/11/86, 12/11/86 L, 30/11/86, 7/2/90 n
Edward James Stephen (1832–1911), writer 8/1/62
Dick,
Colin MacKenzie, phrenologist 14/7/55
G. H. 22/11/87
M. J. 24/4/79
Dickens, Charles (1812–1870), novelist 10/10/39, 20/9/42, 13/9/43, 14/1/70, 4/9/80
Dickenson,
D. 27/7/57
Joseph, coal mine inspector 13/3/54 ?
Dickinson *see* Robartes
Dickinson,
F. J. 1/3/77
Francis Henry (–1890), Peelite M.P. 22/7/44
Goldsworthy Lowes (1862–1932) 17/6/91
Hercules Henry, Dean (–1905) 5/11/77
Lowes Cato (1819–1908), artist 14/6/71, 17/2/75
Dickson,
Miss, of Florence 31/12/87
Alexander George, Col. (1834–1889) 25/8/70
C. 1/1/67, 30/9/67
J. H., flax grower 30/1/46
J. H., miniaturist 17/3/43, 23/10/43
J. W. 15/5/78
Lothian Sheffield, Lieut. Col. 12/12/76
Samuel Auchmuty, Col. (1817–1870) 23/6/62
Thomas Alexander (1833–1909), liberal M.P. 8/9/81, 18/11/85
Thomas Miller, Rev. (–1897) 10/9/77, 12/1/87
Dickson & Davenport, auctioneers 29/4/57
Diestelkampf, Ludwig, Rev. 8/3/90
Digby,
rescue 16/6/75
George Wingfield-, of Sherborne Castle 18/4/32 n
Lucy Wingfield-, Mrs. 18/4/32
William, secretary, National Liberal Club 16/1/86
Digby & Long, Messrs. 28/8/90
Digges, W., of Merseyside 4/8/25

Dight, M. L. 25/5/89
Dignam, Thomas, solicitor 27/5/36
Dike, Rev. Dr. 6/9/88
Dilke,
Charles Wentworth, Sir (1810–1869), 1st Baronet (1862), horticulturalist 12/5/55
Charles Wentworth, Sir 15/1/70
Dill,
Samuel Mark, Rev. 5/7/37
T. H. 1/2/67
Dillon *see* Trench
Dillon,
John (1851–1927), home rule M.P. 3/2/81 n, 29/4/81, 15/5/81, 6/8/81, 1/9/81, 2/9/81, 5/9/81, 7/10/81 n, 12/10/81 c, 5/5/82, 7/5/82, 24/5/82, 29/8/82, 8/12/86, 9/12/86, 10/12/86, 4/5/87 n, 5/5/87 n, 12/8/88 n, 3/6/90, 7/3/92, 21/5/92, 21/6/92, 15/2/93
L. 28/11/88
M., consul at Newcastle 17/2/45
Dillwyn, Lewis Llewelyn (1814–1892), liberal M.P. 9/3/60
Dimsdale, Drewett, Fowler & Barnard, London bankers 15/9/58
Dinard, Mr. 22/1/87
Dinnen, A. R. 20/8/75
Dinorben *see* Hughes
Di Pietra, Salvo 2/1/86
Dirom, Mrs. 21/8/29
Disbrowe, Edward Cromwell, Sir, diplomat 11/5/43
Disney, James William King, Rev. 13/2/58
Disraeli,
Benjamin 26/8/26 n
Mary Anne, Viscountess Beaconsfield (1868), née Evans 24/2/72, 9/8/72, 19/1/73
Diss, W. 26/10/86 ?
Divett, Edward (–1864), liberal M.P. 9/2/41
Dix,
Mr., saddler of Glastonbury 28/1/77
George, of Glastonbury 28/1/77
Dixey, Albert, of Islington 28/4/79 ?
Dixie, Florence, Lady, née Douglas 15/3/90
Dixon,
Miss, nurse 8/2/56
Mr., former dissenting minister 8/6/39
Abraham (1815–1907), of Surrey 30/5/82
E. J. 30/7/34 n
George, maltster 12/1/35 ?
George (1820–1898), liberal M.P. 17/6/67 n, 10/12/70 L
Henry John, Rev. 13/3/54
J., of Old Swinford 29/3/52
James, methodist preacher 6/1/43
John, labourer of Newark 3/3/41
L. W. 3/3/76
M., child of maltster G. Dixon 12/1/35
William Hepworth (1821–1879), historian 22/7/62
William Manley Hall, Maj. Gen. (1817–1888), of B. S. A. 1/6/77
Doane, William Croswell, Bp. 19/7/78
Dobbie,
James J., secretary of Glasgow University Lib. Assoc. 6/4/74
R. W., Rev. 24/2/90
Dobbin, Orlando Thomas, Rev. Dr. (1807–1890) 1/10/68
Dobbyn, Mr. 22/1/87
Dobell,
B. 8/8/89
C. F. 1/4/78
Dobie,
Alexander, solicitor 17/3/59
John, Rev. (–1877) 28/10/59
William Murray, Dr., of Chester 1/10/77, 11/4/82, 25/9/86, 14/1/87
Dobney, H. H., Rev. 14/5/77
Dobree, Bonamy (1794–1863), banker 3/6/59
Dobson,
John Ralph, Rev. (–1874) 16/3/68
Thomas, bullion dealer of the City 13/3/33 ?
Thomas (–1885), Inland Revenue Board 27/5/53
Doby, W. A. 28/8/77
Dockerill, R., tea broker 16/2/57
Dockerill, Duchene & Dockerill, tea dealers 16/2/57
Dodd,
Edward, Rev. (–1868) 21/10/58
Joseph, Rev. (1810–1891) 23/1/33
Richard, of Toxteth 30/7/57
Dodd, Mead & Co., New York publishers 20/12/89
Dodd & Davies, tailors and drapers 23/1/41
Dodds,
Henry Luke, Rev. (1810–1886) 14/11/30
Marcus, Rev. Prof. (1834–1909) 24/10/90
Dodge,
C. B., Mrs. 12/4/78
David Low, pacifist of America 13/10/41 ?
William, Rev. (–1930) 8/5/78
Dodgson,
Edward Spencer 18/3/77 ?
Francis Vivian 18/3/77 ff, 14/2/80
Hassard Hume (1804–), at Christ Church 28/9/28
Dodshon, A. 16/5/88
Dodson,
John, Sir (1780–1858), tory M.P. 16/12/43
John George 16/12/43 n
Dodsworth, William, Rev. (1798–1861), convert to Rome 18/4/30, 3/9/93
Dodwell,
Edward (1767–1832), explorer of Greek antiquities 30/3/32

Henry John, Rev. (1825–1900) 2/6/57 ?
Doeg, Mr. 1/4/68
Doering, Emilie, Hellenist 24/5/77
Dognins,
Madame, of Cannes 21/1/83
Mons., of Cannes 21/1/83 ff, 8/2/83 ?
Doherty, Mr. 30/12/75
Doig, D. C. 22/10/91
Doiree, A. 29/4/56
Dolan, Thomas Michael, Dr., physician 14/1/78
Dolben, William Harcourt Isham Mackworth- (1806–1872) 7/11/31
Dolier, William, teacher of Liverpool 31/8/37
D'Olier, Mrs. 20/12/77
Dollfuss, Mons., of Cannes 26/2/83
Dolling, Mrs. 6/9/67
Döllinger,
Johanna, Miss 5/11/92 L
Johann Josef Ignaz von, Professor 30/9/45
Dollman, Francis, Rev., secretary of Pentonville 22/8/45
Domenighini,
Miss 9/7/78
Sig. 5/7/78
Domray, Mlle. 18/10/78
Domvile, Charles Crompton, Rev. 1/8/57
Domville,
James Graham, Sir (1812–1887), 3rd Baronet 29/5/37 n
Maria, Lady (–1863), née Solly 29/5/37
Mary Anne, Lady (–1890), née Orde 28/4/55
William, Sir (1774–1860), 2nd Baronet 29/5/37 n
Don,
Alexander, Sir (–1826), of Newton Don 8/8/28 n
Alexander Birnie 13/2/75
Donald, James, of Dorlarthers 9/9/36 ?
Donaldson,
George, art dealer 7/5/73
James, Sir (1831–1915), Knight (1907) 4/7/79 ff, 21/3/80, 6/6/83 L
John, Prof. (–1865), professor of music, Edinburgh 10/1/62
John William, Rev. (1811–1861), don 6/4/59 ?
Stuart, Sir (1815–1867), Knight (1860) 11/7/64
Donat, Mons. 5/7/82 ?
Doncaster, Miss, of Sheffield 13/6/68
Donders, Frans Cornelius, Prof. (1818–1889) 1/6/76
Donegal *see* Chichester
Donegan,
James Henry Francis, Lieut. Col. 24/4/86
W. 24/12/87
Donisthorpe, Wordsworth, Individualist author 31/7/88, 12/11/89, 21/11/89
Donkin, William Fishburn, Prof. (–1869), professor of astronomy 24/3/54
Donne, William Bodham, librarian 12/6/52
Donnelly,
Miss 9/4/32
Mr. 2/7/79
Ignatius (1831–), of U.S.A. 11/3/82 L, 10/4/82
John, Major 21/12/75
John Fretchville Dykes, Gen. Sir (1834–1902) 23/5/93
William, Capt. (1804–1879), Irish registrar general 28/2/67
Donner, John, clockmaker 7/5/47 ?
Donninghine, Miss 9/7/78
Donnithorne, Edward George, Capt. (1842–1906) 20/1/76
Donoughmore *see* Hutchinson
Doo, George Thomas (1800–1886), R. A. 9/5/77
Dopping, James Henry, Lieut. Col., Irish land agent 27/10/87, 16/11/87, 20/11/87 n
Doran, John (1807–1878), author 23/7/38 ?
Dorfuisth, Mons. 17/9/86
Dorington, John Edward (1786–), clerk of the fees at House of Commons 11/3/35, 21/2/52
Dorjeral, Mons. 14/2/68
Dormeuil, Messrs. 24/4/70 ?
Dorn, Heinrich Ludwig Egmont 3/10/75 ?
Dornbusch,
G., of London 9/2/57
K. 13/7/87
Dorr, F., Miss 8/6/55
Dorrell, Mr., printer 23/9/56, 3/12/56
Dorrien, Mr. 7/11/79
D'Orsay, A. J. 6/10/91
Dorset *see* Sackville
D'Orsey, Alex. J. D., Rev. (1812–1894) 11/7/47
Dotti, Sig., librarian in Florence 13/1/88
Doudney, David Alfred, Rev. Dr. (1811–1894) 16/8/67
Dougal, John, of Montreal 27/2/75
Dougall, W. 7/12/78
Dougherty, Prof. 28/5/92
Doughty, H. M. 19/11/90
Douglas *see* Dixie, Duncombe, Ewing, Gartshore, Stanley, Stock, Opdebeck
Douglas,
30/11/39
rescue 7/3/58, 2/2/64
Mr. & Mrs., of Fasque 15/10/51
Mrs. 23/12/69
Alexander Hamilton (1767–1852), Duke of Hamilton and Brandon (1819), whig M.P. 26/4/33

Douglas (*cont.*)
Anne Frederica Wemyss-Charteris-, née Anson, Lady Elcho, Countess of Wemyss 12/10/46 n
Archibald William, Lord (-1858), Lord Drumlanrig (1837), 7th Marquis of Queensberry (1856) 9/12/52
Charles Eurwicke, Sir (1806–1887), Knight (1859), liberal M.P. 1/5/61
David, editor of *Scott's Journal* 11/11/90
Dunbar James (1809–1895), 6th Earl of Selkirk (1820), F.R.S. 24/2/27
Frances Theodora (1798–1879), née Rose, Lady Morton 12/1/31
Francis Brown, provost of Edinburgh (1859) 1/12/59 n
Francis Richard Wemyss-Charteris- (1818–1914), 8th (known as 10th) Earl of Wemyss (1883), Lord Elcho 12/10/46, 27/2/67, 5/3/67, 5/4/73, 31/1/81 L, 22/3/86
George Sholto (1789–1858), 18th Earl of Morton (1827), diplomat 12/1/31 n
Howard, Sir (1776–1861), 3rd Baronet (1809), tory M.P. 8/12/32
John, Chester architect 10/6/92
John, journalist 26/11/79 ?
John James, Rev. 24/6/52
John Sholto (1844–1900), 8th Marquis of Queensberry (1858) 18/4/81 L, 4/2/83 n
Robert Langton, Rev. 18/10/91
R. P., Rev. 18/2/77
Sholto John (1818–1884), (styled) Lord Aberdour (1827), 19th Earl of Morton (1858) 4/11/37
Stair, Rev. (1802–1874) 14/12/31 ?
Susan Euphemia, née Beckford, Duchess of Hamilton 26/4/33
Sybil Sholto, neé Montgomery, Lady Queensberry 4/2/83
W. A. A. A. (1811–1863), 11th Duke of Hamilton 26/4/33 n
W. R. Keith, F. R. S. 26/5/33 ?
Douglas & Fordham, Messrs. 30/10/88, 10/6/92 n
Douro *see* Wellesley
Douse, W. J. 21/6/75
Douvet, P., Mons. 4/5/77, 15/8/78
Dover,
Richard, financial author 23/9/68
Thomas Birckett, Rev. 13/1/77
Doveton, F. B. 27/4/88, 14/1/90
Dow, Neal (1804–1897), temperance reformer of U.S.A. 12/4/80 ?
Dowbiggin, Thos. & Co., house agents 18/5/47
Dowdall,
Lancelot, Sir (1851–1936) 20/9/78 n
Lancelot John George Downing, Rev. 20/9/78
T., of Liverpool 17/12/56
Dowden,
B. 18/5/89
Edward, Prof. (1824–1913) 22/12/87
Dowding, William Charles, Rev., secretary of Soc. for Propagation of Gospel 16/12/51, 22/12/74
Dowell,
James Wanklyn (1809–1879) 22/5/27
Stephen (1833–1898), solicitor, historian 4/12/65
Dowlah, Jaleesood 2/3/57
Dowland, Mr. 14/1/76
Dowling,
A. J., Rev. 20/5/69, 2/6/88
L., rescue 28/5/64, 29/5/64, 26/7/64
Downe, Hugh 18/6/90
Downes,
Miss 29/10/76
John, secretary Peel Memorial Committee 12/7/50
Robert, Rev. (1795–1859) 12/4/29
Downey, J. & Co., brick merchant of London 2/12/67
Downham, George, livery stables owner 25/1/58
Downie,
Alexander Mackenzie, Sir (1811–1852), Knight (1840), court physician 4/11/36 ?
John 13/6/40, 30/6/40, 6/10/41
John Alexander, Rev., of Australia 13/6/77
William, photographer of Newcastle 7/10/62
Downing,
Mr. 17/11/81
Arthur Matthew Weld 1/5/75
Charles, barrister 8/2/48
MacCarthy (1814–1879), independent liberal M.P. 20/12/69, 13/1/70, 10/5/77
Samuel, of Birmingham 11/12/88
W. 9/1/79
Dowse, Richard, liberal M.P. (1868) 15/4/69, 15/9/72 L
Dowser, W. J. 23/1/79
Dowson,
T. D. 21/10/89
Thomas, poet 15/9/77 ?
Doyen, F. Le 1/9/65, 29/8/66
Doyle *see* Gower, North, Ridgway
Doyle,
Charles Hastings, Sir (1804–1883), Knight (1869), soldier 2/3/35
Diana Elizabeth (-1828), née Milner 17/2/28
Diana Emily Flora, Miss (1805–1879) 3/5/36, 26/3/65

Frances Mary (-1831) 25/4/31
Francis Hastings, Sir (1783-1839), Baronet (1828), major general 1/7/27
Francis Hastings Charles, Sir 15/10/25
Henry Edward (1827-1892) 6/11/77, 8/11/77
James, customs officer of Liverpool 5/6/37 ?
John B. 24/10/77 ?
Percy W., secretary of Brit. Legation in Mexico 12/6/43 ?
Sidney, né Williams-Wynn 23/5/44
D'Oyly, George, Rev. Dr., theologian 23/12/37
Drage, Geoffrey (1860-1955), secretary, Royal Commission on Labour 14/12/93 n
Drago, Raffaele, advocate 23/5/59 ?
Dragonetti, Luigi, Marquis (-1871) 30/11/50
Drake,
J. H. 27/3/80
J. P. 2/3/77
Octavius Samuel, Rev. (1809-) 7/6/29
William Henry, Sir (1812-1871), Knight (1871), controller 26/1/61 ?
William Richard, Sir (1817-1890) 17/3/74
Draper,
Mr., of Ormskirk 27/2/67
C. S. & W. H., of London 8/1/68
Francis, gilder 12/9/79 ?
Gideon, Rev. 14/5/87
John William, Prof. (1811-1882), of U.S.A. 11/2/71
Drennan, Mr. 27/4/88
Drew *see* Parish
Drew,
George Henry, solicitor 5/2/56
George Smith, Rev. (1819-1880) 22/4/68
Harry, Rev. (-1910), son-in-law 23/11/47 n, 8/1/86 ff, 2/2/86, 5/5/88, 23/12/89, 11/10/91, 29/5/93, 1/9/94
John, father of Harry Drew 31/12/85
Mary (daughter) 23/11/47
Dreyfuss & Teweles, merchants of London 20/3/79 ?
Drinkwater, George, Sir, mayor of Liverpool 18/8/29
Drisker, Mr. 19/1/86 ?
Driver, Samuel Rolles, Rev. (1846-1914), professor 4/10/82, 23/10/82, 27/11/83, 2/2/90 ff
Drohan, Matthew 13/11/90
Drought, Mr. 30/10/77
Druce,
Messrs. 10/4/77
Albert, London liberal 25/11/85
Drucker, Louis 6/2/77
Drumlanrig *see* Douglas
Drummond *see* Percy
Drummond,
Arthur Henry, Capt. (1833-1900) 13/9/76
David Thomas Kerr, Rev., episcopalian 5/9/45
Edward, Peel's p. secretary 18/10/41, 25/1/43
George (1807-1902), 14th Earl of Perth (1853) 13/6/56
Henry (1786-1860), tory M.P., Irvingite 14/6/47 n, 13/5/56
Henry Home (1783-1867), Peelite M.P., banker 17/3/52
James Robert, Sir (1812-1895), Knight (1873), R. N. 25/4/59
R. Hay-, 9th Earl of Kinoul 13/7/37 n
Robert B., Rev., of Edinburgh 15/6/76
Spencer Rodney, Rev. (-1882) 5/4/67
Thomas (1797-1840), liberal M.P., Irish undersecretary (1835) 13/7/94
T. R. Hay-, 10th Earl of Kinoul 24/5/39 n
Drury,
Edward Drury, surveyor 9/10/78 ?
Henry, Rev. (-1863) 22/6/54
W. J. J., Rev. (1792-1879), chaplain to King of the Belgians 5/2/32
Dry, Thomas, clerk at Christ Church, Oxford 27/2/33
Drybrough & Gibson, Messrs., Dalkeith photographers 19/1/86
Drysdale,
Charles Robert, Dr., physician 18/6/77
John James, Dr., doctor of Liverpool 15/4/46
Du Bled, Mr. 12/1/80
Dubray, Miss 16/10/78
Ducane, Charles, Sir (1825-1889), chairman, customs 29/12/71, 6/5/80
Du Chaillu, Paul Belloni, explorer 5/2/90
du Champ, Maxime 2/3/76
Duchatel *see* Tanneguy
Duchhayn, Mr. 30/6/80
Duchich, Nicephore, of Serbia 23/6/81
Ducie *see* Moreton
Ducie, Mr., of Fettercairn 24/8/43
Duck, Mr. 1/9/85
Ducker, Mrs., of Hawarden village 20/11/55
Duckham, Thomas (1816-1902), liberal M.P. 24/4/83 L
Duckworth,
Dyce, Sir (1840-1928), physician 12/5/86
Herbert, barrister 17/10/68
John Thomas Buller, Sir (1809-1887), 2nd Baronet, tory M.P. 17/4/46
Robinson, Rev. (1834-1911) 24/1/69, 14/3/70, 5/11/71, 21/11/71, 25/8/81
Russell (1830-1914), barrister 22/5/67
Samuel, master in Chancery 25/7/37 n
Dudderidge, G., author 22/11/87
Dudgeon,
Mr. 3/8/26
William 30/12/76

Dudley *see* Ward
Duff *see* Tennant
Duff,
Agnes Georgiana Elizabeth (-1869), née Hay, Lady Fife 7/10/64
Alexander, Rev. (1806-1878) 29/9/76, 16/5/79 n
Alexander William George (1849-1912), 6th Earl of Fife (1879), 1st Duke of Fife (1889), Viscount Macduff 22/12/71, 26/4/93 L
James (1814-1879), 5th Earl of Fife (1857), liberal M.P. 14/7/57
Mountstuart Elphinstone Grant, Sir (1829-1906), liberal M.P. (1857), Indian undersecretary (1868), colonial undersecretary (1880), governor of Madras (1881) 26/12/67, 5/3/68, 24/4/75 n, 29/5/76, 18/11/76, 17/5/79, 27/6/81, 30/6/81, 9/7/81 n, 27/7/81 n
Peter, of Edinburgh 21/3/79
Robert William (1835-1895), liberal M.P. 1/7/73
W. Pine, Rev. 25/3/78
Dufferin and Ava *see* Blackwood
Duffield,
Alexander James (1821-1890), author 30/4/78
Divie Bethune, of U.S.A. 8/10/80
Matthew Dawson, Rev. (-1866) 9/12/51
Duffy,
Charles Gavan, Sir (1816-1903), premier, Victoria, Australia 29/12/71, 5/8/85 n, 9/10/85, 2/7/86
James, publisher 29/3/48
M., Mrs., of New Zealand 11/12/86
Dufour, Jean Barthélemy Arlès-, industrialist 22/11/65, 26/8/66
Du Fresne 27/2/49
Dufton, W., ear surgeon 4/6/47 ?
Dugdale,
Alice Frances, née Trevelyan 15/4/87, 6/10/90, 19/3/92
Harriet Ella, née Portman 13/6/38 n
W. 3/7/62
William Stratford (1801-1871), conservative M.P. 13/6/38
William Stratford (1828-1882) 7/1/78 ?
W. Stratford 15/4/87 n
Duggan, Miss 9/1/78
Du Gue, Mrs., spiritualist 18/11/86
Duhaut, D., of Bruges 6/12/45
Duignan, Button & Smiles, Messrs., solicitors 10/6/74
Duke,
C., of Southwell, Notts. 6/7/42, 14/9/43
E. 2/6/34
James, Sir (1802-1873), Knight (1837), Baronet (1849), liberal M.P. 14/2/53
Thomas Oliver, surgeon 13/3/57 ?
W. 25/4/34
Dukinfield,
Henry Robert, Rev. Sir (1791-1858), 7th Baronet (1836) 9/8/35
Jane, Lady, née Cranford 24/6/61
Du Lac, S., Rev., author 22/5/88
Dulau, M. 21/5/73
Duleep Singh, Maharajah (1838-1893), Maharajah of Lahore 20/3/63, 4/10/73, 21/2/82, 28/3/82
Dumaresq,
Agnes Susan Elizabeth, great-niece 22/10/71
Edith Helen (1850-1941), née Gladstone, great-niece 20/5/50, 29/10/79, 30/5/80, 23/8/90
John Saumarez (1873-1922), relative 7/12/85 ff
William Alexander (-1880), barrister 20/5/50 n, 22/3/70, 13/7/79, 19/7/79, 25/7/79, 20/8/79, 29/10/79, 28/5/80
Du Maurier, George Louis Palmella Busson (1834-1896), artist 7/5/89 n
Dumbell, G. W. 9/4/79
Dumbell & Callister, Messrs. 20/7/53
Dumet, Miss, at Clumber 26/10/64
Dumin,
Mad. 18/12/54
Mlle., rescue 16/12/54
Dummert, Mary, Mrs., furrier 10/9/42 ?
Dumont, Henri 26/9/74
Dumreicher, A. von, Austrian legation at Naples 29/2/52
Dun,
Finlay, author on land 4/12/80
James, Rev., curate of Hawarden 4/12/80 n
T. J. C. 31/10/76
Dunbar,
Mrs. 27/6/78
C. S. 13/7/67
Henry, Dr. (-1883), physician, classicist 14/3/79
Robert Haigh 16/1/77
William, Sir (1812-1889), 7th Baronet (1841), liberal M.P. 13/12/59, 18/2/73
Duncan *see* Schwann
Duncan,
27/5/43
Mrs., spiritualist medium 18/11/84
A., of Portobello 2/4/79
Adam Haldane (-1867), 2nd Earl of Camperdown (1854), Viscount Duncan, M.P. 6/2/54
Andrew, Prof., M. D. (1794), professor of medicine at Edinburgh 21/2/35
D. L., Rev. 15/2/87
George (1791-1878), liberal M.P. 6/5/53
H., Rev. 27/2/80

James Archibald (1858–1911), liberal M.P. 30/6/90
James or William, merchant and W. S. of Edinburgh 1/5/33
John, chairman of Caledonian railway 7/3/51
Juliana Cavendish (–1898), née Philips, Lady Camperdown 24/9/69
Robert Adam Philips Haldane- (1841–1918), 3rd Earl of Camperdown (1867), Lord Duncan 14/12/65
W. & J., merchants of Liverpool 22/7/44
Duncan & Flockhart, chemists 5/5/51
Duncan & Hepburn, Messrs. 19/4/88
Duncan & Martin, Messrs. 9/11/89
Duncannon *see* Ponsonby
Duncombe,
Adolphus (1809–1830) 17/10/28
C., 2nd Baron Faversham 17/10/28 n
Harriet Christian, Lady, née Douglas 1/8/90
Martha, née Elvy 2/8/66 ?
Thomas Slingsby (1796–1861), radical M.P. 9/5/37 n, 28/2/60
Dundas *see* Lockhart
Dundas,
Mrs., in France 31/12/92
Anne (–1851) 31/12/48
Charles Amesbury Whitley Deans 23/10/69
Charles Whitley Deans (–1856), whig M.P., Flintshire 17/7/41
David, Sir (1799–1877), liberal M.P. 15/12/42, 1/12/43
George (1819–1880), tory M.P. 2/7/56
George, Rev. 25/5/50
James Whitley Deans, Sir (1785–1880), rear admiral, tory M.P. 6/7/41
Jane (–1862) 31/12/48
Lawrence (1844–1929), 3rd Earl of Zetland 16/8/80 L
Robert (–1851), 2nd Viscount Melville (1811) 31/12/48
Robert, Sir (–1835), 1st Baronet 17/11/44 n
Robert James, Rev. 18/6/76
Sophia Jane (–1865), née Williamson, Lady Zetland 18/6/52
Thomas (1795–1873), 2nd Earl of Zetland (1838), freemason, whig M.P. 28/8/35
William Pitt, lawyer 19/5/42
Dundee, Perth & London Steamshipping Co. 7/8/44 n
Dunfermline *see* Abercromby
Dungarvan *see* Boyle
Dunhan, S. Astley, historian 4/7/42
Dunington, Rev. Mr. 26/9/78
Dunkellin *see* Burgh
Dunkerley, William, Rev. 12/1/82, 24/9/86, 27/9/86 ?
Dunlop,
A. B. 21/1/89
Alexander Colquhoun-Stirling-Murray- (1798–1870), liberal M.P. 13/4/54
Alexander Graham, secretary to Loftus 29/1/59
Andrew (1810–), of Kirkcudbright 22/11/30
Henry (1799–1867), merchant of Glasgow 6/9/61
J. C. 28/10/90
Dunmore *see* Murray
Dunn *see* Grant
Dunn,
A. 28/2/68
A., liberal candidate 14/11/78
Archibald J., author 7/3/77
Henry, secretary of Brit. & Foreign School Soc. 18/3/35
John, 'Chief', 'ruler' of Zululand 23/8/82
Joseph, merchant of London 12/5/74
R., Mr. 28/1/75
William, Sir (1833–1912), 1st Baronet (1895), liberal M.P. 2/6/91
Dunne,
Francis Plunkett, Lieut. (1802–1874) 19/10/60 ?
L. 24/11/77
Dunning,
Joseph, solicitor of Leeds 30/4/49 ?
Simon, attorney 21/7/55
Dunphie, Charles J. 7/5/79
Dunphy, Henry Michael, barrister 29/8/77
Dunraven *see* Quin
Dunstan *see* Hancock
Dunstan, Mr., at Hawarden 22/9/56
Dunt, John E., lamp maker 31/3/58
Dupanloup, Félix Antoine Philibert, Bp. (1802–1878) 4/9/69
Dupin, François Pierre Charles (1784–1873), Baron Dupin, economist 22/5/51
Du Plat, George C. C. W., consul 21/10/42 n
Duplessis, rescue 18/7/62
Dupont, Mr., of Naples 18/11/50
Duport, Charles Durell, Rev. 2/3/80
Dupré *see* Blackwood
Dupree, Theodore, of U.S.A. 13/3/90
Dupressoir, Charles, French historian 25/1/67 ff, 31/1/67
Dupuch, Adolphe, Bp. (–1856), bishop of Algiers (1838) 17/12/38
Dupuis, George John (1795–1884), assistant master 14/10/25
Du Ranci, Mr. 4/7/78
Durant, rescue 5/6/63
Durasso, L. 5/12/91
D'Urban, B., Sir 26/6/46
Durell, W. J. 14/3/74
Durham *see* Lambton

Durham,
E. 30/3/91
Joseph (1814–1877), sculptor 7/7/51
Durie,
Mr., of Hawarden 26/11/57
James, distiller of Fettercairn 24/8/43
Durie & Co. 10/12/85
Durnford,
Edmund, Rev. (1809–1883) 4/11/26
Francis Edward, Rev. (1815–1881), master at Eton 28/8/63
Richard, Bp. (1802–1895) 9/1/68, 29/11/69
Walter, master at Eton 25/6/82
du Roure *see* Beaupoil
Durrell, J. C. 30/5/90
D'Urso, Pietro, Prime Minister in Naples (1851) 29/2/52
Duruy, Victor (1811–1894), French politician 15/3/65, 28/1/67
Duse, Eleonora (1858–1924), actress 31/1/89
Dusmani, Antonio Lefcochilo, Sir (–1889) 25/11/58, 13/1/59 ff, 8/2/59 ?
Duthie & Duncan 15/12/48
Duthoit, Minnie, Miss 12/7/87
Dutton *see* Pearson
Dutton,
Messrs. 20/12/79
Messrs., shoemakers 2/9/66
Mr., of Hawarden 28/12/65
H. B. 12/12/79
Ralph Heneage (1821–1892), Peelite M.P. 7/5/66
Duvergier de Hauranne, Prosper (1798–1881) 12/6/58
Duvergne, Mr. 16/5/78
Duveyrier, Charles, journalist of France 24/1/44
Duxbury, Mr. 4/8/87
Dwight, William Moss, treasury clerk 6/1/54
Dyack, Mr. 21/6/65
Dyatt, Mr. 26/5/65
Dyce,
Alexander Frederick, Rev. (1844–1898) 10/10/68
Alexander Stirling 3/11/75 ?
William (1806–1864), artist 10/6/41, 20/6/41, 23/8/41, 27/11/43, 3/5/56, 1/4/59, 30/4/59, 6/8/59, 10/8/59, 24/2/64, 30/4/64, 9/11/71, 14/6/75
Dyer,
Messrs. 28/3/79
Mr. 20/7/75
George, goldsmith 15/7/76 ?
Thomas Firminger Thiselton- 22/6/89
Dyke,
Francis Hart (–1876), Queen's proctor 1/4/54
William, Rev. (–1880), don 21/6/49
Dykes, C. P. 13/1/91
Dymoke, Henry, Sir (1801–1865), 1st Baronet (1841) 25/6/59
Dyne, John Bradley, Rev. (1809–1898), headmaster 12/3/59
Dyneley, Rev. 10/1/80
Dysart *see* Tollemache
Dyson,
A. 14/8/91
Edwin, Rev. 24/7/68
James, wine merchant of Newark 8/12/32
Joshua 23/5/90
Dyson, Hall & Parkes, parliamentary agents 7/7/45
Dyve, Rev. Mr. 14/2/87
Dzialynska, Isabella, Princess, née Czartoryski 28/1/67
Dzialynski, John, Count 28/1/67 n

Eade, Peter, Sir (1825–1915), of Norwich 1/6/85
Eads, H. L., Bp., of U.S.A. 20/4/88
Eames,
C. G. 21/9/88
R. 26/10/67
Eardley,
Culling Eardley, Sir, né Smith, 3rd Baronet 28/1/40
Sampson, 1st Baron Eardley 10/6/29 n
Eardley, Holt, solicitors 1/4/79
Earl, Edward, 'gentleman' 19/12/33
Earle,
Miss 31/3/32 ?
Hardman, Sir (1792–1879), 1st Baronet (1869), merchant of Liverpool 5/3/35 n, 6/11/62, 20/9/69
John Charles, barrister 30/3/76
Richard (1796–1848) 5/3/35 n
Thomas, I. R. clerk 11/5/53
William Hamilton Biscoe, resident in Rome, of Everton 30/3/32
Earlson, Dr. 26/10/81
Earp,
H. N., of Newark 7/4/79
Thomas 1/2/67, 4/5/76
Thomas, liberal M.P. 20/11/77
Earwaker, John Parsons (1847–1895), historian 2/4/77, 11/10/77
Eary, Patrick, victim of Irish agrarian crime 5/10/81
Eason, Mr. 2/1/86
Easson, David, factor 28/9/69
East,
rescue 21/1/64
James Buller, Sir, 2nd Baronet (1847), tory M.P. 30/1/56
Easterly, Dr. 3/12/78
Eastham, George, photographer? 3/7/60 ?

Easthope, John, Sir (1784-1865), speculator, whig M.P. 25/7/37 n
Eastlake, Charles Loch, Sir (1793-1865), president of Royal Academy 10/7/51, 7/6/54, 25/11/54, 2/5/57, 25/1/58, 4/5/61, 9/7/63
Eastnorr *see* Cocks
Eastwick, William Joseph (1808-1889) 28/2/79
Eaton,
Frederick Alexis (1838-1913), secretary of Royal Academy 27/3/79
Paul, of U.S.A. 19/6/90
Richard Jefferson (1806-), tory M.P. 18/4/45
Richard Storks, Rev. 7/10/53
Thomas, Canon (1805-1889) 2/11/75
William Ray, Rev. (1828-1915) 12/7/58
Ebden, John Bardwell, merchant of Cape Town 11/12/37
Eborall, Charles, manager of S. E. Railway 6/11/58
Ebrington *see* Fortescue
Ebsworth, Mr. 1/12/85
Ebury *see* Grosvenor
Eckenbrecher, C. Gustav von 27/7/75
Eckersall, Charles, Rev. (1797-1863) 11/5/55
Eckstaedt, Karl Friedrick Vitzthum von, Count 24/2/58
Ecole des Sciènces Politiques, Director of 24/7/75
Eddis, Arthur Shelley (1817-1893), barrister 23/3/78
Eddowes, T. S., of Birkenhead 3/4/57
Eddy,
Mr., railwayman 19/5/76
Charles Wellington, chemist 27/2/57 ?
Ede,
Miss 12/3/38
George 27/11/78
John, Mrs., of Upper Harley Street 9/3/36 ?
Eden *see* Brougham, Vansittart
Eden,
Emily, Miss (-1869), of Broadstairs 18/8/54, 5/9/54, 11/9/54, 13/9/54
Henry, Admiral (1797-1888) 30/11/63
John, attorney of Mount Pleasant 14/1/34 ?
John, solicitor of Liverpool 17/1/45
Robert, Bp., primus of Scotland, bishop of Moray 25/12/41
W., 1st Baron Auckland 2/7/33 n
William George (1829-1890), 4th Baron Auckland (1870) 17/8/69
Eden and Stanistreet, solicitors of Liverpool 24/3/42, 17/1/45
Edgar, John, Rev. Dr. (1798-1866), temperance advocate of U.S.A. 17/5/58 ?
Edgcumbe, William Henry (1833-1917), 4th Earl of Mount-Edgcumbe (1861) 8/7/89
Edge,
Frederick Milnes, writer on Anglo-American affairs 12/9/66
John Henry, Irish author 26/8/78
J. Wilcox 22/8/88 n
Edgecomb, Frederick J. S. 19/3/75 ?
Edinburgh *see* Alfred Ernest Albert, Marie Alexandrovna
Edison, Thomas, American engineer and inventor, recorder of G's voice 22/11/88
Edkins, Joseph, grammarian 27/5/74
Edmeston, James, surveyor of London 12/6/58
Edminson, Ernest Whalley 11/6/87
Edmonds, C. 29/12/73
Edmonston & Douglas, publishers 3/4/74, 23/12/76
Edmonstone,
Archibald, Sir 14/6/41
Neil Benjamin (1765-1841), director of East India Company 20/8/36
Edmunds,
George Franklin, Senator (1828-1919), of U.S.A. 19/6/85
Leonard (1802-1885), clerk 21/7/57
Edouart, Augustin Gaspard, Rev. (-1905) 19/6/51
Edward,
servant 10/7/28 ?
servant 28/10/50
Edward VII, formerly Prince of Wales 21/6/42
Edward Augustus (1767-1820), Duke of Kent 4/5/35 n
Edwardes *see* Dering
Edwardes,
William, 2nd Baron Kensington 23/11/38 n
William (1835-1896), 4th Baron Kensington (1872), liberal M.P. (1868) 24/2/75, 11/12/77
Edwards *see* Tempest
Edwards,
rescue? 22/11/53
servant 19/11/91, 5/12/91
Miss 10/12/90
Mr., servant at Hawarden 24/12/86
Amelia Ann Blanford, Egyptologist 16/5/76
A. R. 3/5/76
Arthur 9/2/77
Charles (1825-1889), liberal M.P. (1866) 9/4/58
E. A. 22/11/79
Edward (1812-1886), librarian of Manchester 14/10/53
Edward, Rev. 13/3/49
Edwin (1823-1879), solicitor 26/5/50 ?
G., villager of Hawarden 13/11/57

Edwards (*cont.*)
George T. 10/8/75
Henry, Sir (1812–1886), 1st Baronet (1866), tory M.P. 24/12/45
Henry Grey, Rev. 5/2/75
Henry Thomas, Dean (1837–1884) 6/2/67
James, Dr., physician 27/9/59
John, Sir (–1850), Baronet 22/9/53 n
John Passmore (1823–1911) 17/9/55 n
John William, barrister 14/11/78 ?
Joseph, villager of Hawarden 5/1/61
Joseph Charles, Rev. (–1896) 18/3/56
Owen, Fellow of Lincoln, Oxford 23/10/92 n
Richard Griffin, solicitor 8/3/41
Robert Clarke, architect 20/2/79 ?
Thomas, manufacturer of Birmingham 23/4/75 ?
Thomas, of Islington 3/3/75 ?
W., Rev. 6/5/78
William, of Haverfordwest 14/8/58 ?
Edwards & Ball, solicitors in Stroud 8/3/41, 30/8/56
Edwards Effendi 10/6/65
Egan, Patrick, Irish Land Leaguer 12/10/81 n, 5/5/82, 28/8/82, 28/12/92
Egerton *see* Byng, Cholmondeley, Cust, Grosvenor
Egerton,
Algernon Fulke (1826–1891), tory M.P. 2/3/65
Arthur Frederick, Capt. (1829–1866) 18/9/58
Charlotte Elizabeth, Lady (–1878), née Loftus 3/3/58
Edwin, Sir (1841–1916) 14/5/84
F. H., 8th Earl of Bridgewater 13/11/34 n
Francis (1800–1857), 1st Earl of Ellesmere (1846), né Leveson-Gower, M.P. 3/6/35, 27/9/54 ?
Francis, Adm. (1824–1895), liberal M.P., R. N. 20/12/62 n, 15/1/70, 27/4/72, 3/5/73, 26/4/80, 5/4/90 ff, 23/5/93 L
Harriet Catherine, Lady (1800–1866), née Greville 8/3/36
John Hulme Home (Cust) (1812–1851), né Cust, Viscount Alford 3/6/43, 22/7/43
Louisa, Lady, née Cavendish 20/12/62, 12/8/93
Marianne Margaret, Lady (1817–1888), née Compton, styled Lady Marion Alford, architect, author, hostess, active in Bulgarian horrors campaign 3/6/43, 22/1/67, 9/9/69, 25/6/70, 20/9/76 ff, 27/9/76, 19/9/79 ff, 1/10/79 ff, 22/11/82
Mary Margaret (–1858), née Stanley, Lady Wilton 23/6/52
Philip de Malpas Grey-, Sir (1806–1881), Baronet (1829), tory M.P. 25/1/42
Susan Isabella (–1916), Lady Wilton (1863), née Smith 23/6/52 n
Thomas (–1882), né Grosvenor, 2nd Earl of Wilton 23/6/52 n
Thomas, Rev. (–1847) 25/6/28
Thomas, Sir, 1st Earl of Wilton 23/7/40 n
William Tatton (1806–1883), 1st Baron Egerton (1859), conservative M.P. 25/6/28, 3/3/58 n
Eggers, Messrs. 24/1/87
Eggleton, L., Miss 3/4/82
Eglinton *see* Montgomerie
Eglinton, William, spiritualist and medium 29/10/84, 7/11/84
Eichthal, Gustave d' (1804–1886), French writer 25/2/65
Eiggerty, A. H. 24/11/74
Eklektikè, editor of 13/1/75 n, 9/5/75
Elam, Charles, Dr. (1824–1889) 29/7/76
Elcho *see* Douglas
Elder, Mrs. 5/5/79
Elderstreet, Mrs. 13/9/92
Eldon, T. C. 23/7/91
Eldred, J. W., liberal 27/3/80
Elfein, C. 2/11/85
Elford,
rescue 16/5/76
John, of Homerton 4/11/79
Elgin *see* Bruce
Eli, Master, servant of Hawarden 14/11/57
Eliot,
Charles William (1834–1926), president of Harvard 15/8/78
Edward Granville, Lord (1798–1877), 3rd Earl of St Germans (1845), diplomat 18/8/35
Harriot (1790–1877), née Pole-Carew, Lady St. Germans 29/11/32
Jemima, Lady, née Cornwallis, Lady St. Germans 15/8/35
John (–1823), 1st Earl St Germans 29/11/32 n
R. 23/5/56
William Gordon Cornwallis (1829–1881), Baron Eliot (1870), 4th Earl of St Germans (1877) 12/6/71 L
Elis, pauper 16/3/47 ?
Eliza, Sister 12/9/89
Elkington, Joseph James, Rev. 19/2/77
Ellaby, R. Ernest 24/4/75
Ellacombe, Henry Thomas, Rev. 26/4/48
Ellborough, Mrs. 2/5/48
Ellenborough *see* Law
Eller, Irvin, Rev. 7/7/39, 8/7/39
Ellerbeck, Mr. 5/9/85
Ellero, Pietro, of Bologna 26/1/87 ?

Ellesmere *see* Egerton
Ellice *see* Kerrison, Sinclair
Ellice,
A. C. 7/11/78
Edward (1781–1863), statesman, fur trader 23/7/34
Edward (fils) (–1880), liberal M.P. 15/4/47, 20/8/53 ff, 27/8/53 ff, 3/9/53, 14/12/61, 21/9/72 ?
Eliza Stuart (–1896), née Hagart, formerly Speirs 17/8/53 n, 18/8/53, 14/6/62
Hannah, née Grey 23/7/34 n
Harriet, née Chaplin 2/5/36
James, Rev. (1787–1856) 11/5/43 ?
Russell (1799–) 2/5/36 n
William 11/12/37 n
Ellicott, Charles John, Bp. (1819–1905), bishop of Gloucester 6/11/64
Elliot *see* Carnegie, Russell
Elliot,
Alexander James Hardy, General 24/11/85
Charles Gilbert John Brydone, Sir (1818–1895), Knight (1881), sailor 27/10/53 ?
Charlotte, Lady 11/1/79 n
E., Miss 17/10/75
E. T. 30/5/90
Frank Albert Stringer, Rev. 28/10/91
Frederick Boileau (–1880) 11/1/79
Gilbert, 2nd Earl of Minto 4/3/47 n
Henry George, Sir (1817–1907), diplomat 5/12/60, 9/5/71 L, 18/8/72 L, 4/9/72 L, 10/2/77, 22/2/77, 28/2/77, 18/3/77, 19/3/77, 27/3/77, 16/10/80
Henry Venn, Rev. 21/4/50
Hugh Frederick Hislop (1848–1932), liberal unionist M.P. 12/12/85
John Edmund (1788–1862), liberal M.P. 21/5/53
Joseph, junior 22/3/75
Robert, miner 1/7/78
Robert Henry, of India 17/2/77 ?
T. 8/1/87
William Henry, General 1/4/42
Elliot & Stock 23/12/74
Elliott,
Charles John, Rev. (1818–1881) 25/8/57
Charles Wemyss, of Boston U.S.A. Household Arts Society 16/8/72 L
Thomas Frederick, Sir (1808–1880), Knight (1869), assistant undersecretary Colonial Office 21/2/39
Ellis,
Charles Augustus (1799–1868), 6th Baron Howard de Walden, diplomat 3/10/31
E., of Board of Trade 2/5/53
G. 9/2/76
Harriet (–1914), Lady Clifden 23/8/83
Henry, Sir (1777–1855), diplomat 10/6/43
Henry, Sir (1777–1869), Knight (1833), librarian in British Museum 4/3/39
H. W. 29/11/56
J. H. 12/3/78
John Clough Williams, Rev. (1833–1913) 14/11/78 ?
John Utley, Mrs., of Hagley 4/2/61
Leopold George Frederick Agar- (1829–1899), 5th Viscount Clifden (1895), liberal conservative M.P. 28/7/71
Robert, Dr., physician 16/1/71
Robert, Rev. 18/10/76 ?
Rowland, Rev. 9/10/78
T. 28/4/76
Thomas Edward (1859–1899), liberal M.P. 16/8/92, 3/9/92, 24/11/92
William, educationalist 12/4/48 n
Wynne 9/1/35 n
Ellis & Elvey, Messrs., booksellers 7/11/89
Ellison *see* James, Vernon
Ellison,
Anne (–1847) 26/3/47 ?
Cuthbert (1783–1860) 25/12/38, 16/11/59 ?
Isabella Grace, née Ibbetson 25/12/38
Noel Thomas, Rev. (1791–1858) 26/2/31
W. 10/6/74
Ellis & White, Messrs. 30/6/79
Ellman, George, of York 1/10/60
Elmore, Alfred (1815–1881), painter 15/10/78 ?
Elouis, Charles, clerk at the Mint 24/1/42
Elphinstone,
Messrs. 30/1/80
John, 13th Baron Elphinstone, governor in India 7/4/55
Elridge,
G. H. 1/4/91
G. J., consul 24/7/78 ?
Elrington, Charles Richard, Prof. (1787–1850), regius professor of divinity in Dublin 25/4/37
Elsam, J. E. 28/12/86
Elsasser, Friedrich-August (1810–1845), painter of Germany 3/1/39
Elson, Thomas 20/8/87
Elsworth, J. 19/6/77
Elton *see* Hallam, Strachan
Elton,
Arthur Hallam, Sir (1818–1883), 7th Baronet (1853), liberal M.P. 14/7/55, 13/10/76
Charles Isaac (1839–1900), tory M.P. 14/8/86 ?
Edward, Rev. (1817–1898) 30/1/56
Elvey, George Job, Sir (1816–1894), musician 23/3/71
Elvy *see* Duncombe
Elwell, Francis Richard, photographer 25/4/76 ?

Elwin, Whitwell, Rev. (1816-1900), editor of *Quarterly Review* 19/4/55, 2/12/56, 13/12/56, 14/12/56, 20/12/56, 7/1/57 n, 17/3/57 n, 14/4/57, 18/4/57, 21/4/57, 23/4/57, 11/4/59, 12/4/59, 15/4/59, 18/4/59, 19/4/59, 14/7/59 n, 30/8/59, 5/10/62, 3/1/70
Elworth, M. S. 29/5/88
Ely *see* Loftus
Emerson *see* Tennant
Emerson, Ralph Waldo 23/4/73
Emerton, Miss 23/12/90
Emery,
George, 'gentleman' 2/5/46 ?
William, Ven. (1825-1910) 23/5/56
Emich Charles, Prince (-1814), prince of Leiningen 4/5/35 n
Emiliani, Cesare, violinist of Bologna 28/11/33
Emily, servant 28/10/50
Eminson, John, tutor 11/4/63, 1/9/64
Emly *see* Monsell
Emlyn *see* Campbell
Emma, Queen, Queen of Hawaii 20/11/65, 20/7/66
Emmanuel, Mr. 13/8/88
Emmerich, Anna Catarina (1774-1824), nun, stigmatic ecstatic 29/12/38
Emmott, Christopher Frederic, solicitor 21/3/79
Empson, William (1791-1852), editor of *Edinburgh Review* 8/11/51
Enderby, Charles, pamphleteer 19/1/44
Enfield *see* Byng
Engelbach, Lewis J., of West Bromwich 17/7/74
England,
Mrs. 26/1/43
James, Rev. Princ. 12/10/78 ?
Richard, Sir (1793-1883), soldier 16/10/55 n
William, merchant of Liverpool 27/7/74 ?
Engleheart, (John) Gardner Dillman, barrister 4/11/64
English,
Charles, Rev. (1810-1867) 24/10/32 n
John 24/10/32 ?
Thomas, surgeon dentist 24/10/32 n
Engström, Charles Robert Lloyd 31/12/75
Enley, T. 1/10/77
Ennis, E. H. 28/6/87
Enniskillen *see* Cole
Enoch, Frederick 1/2/79
Enraght, Richard William, Rev. 18/3/80
Ensell, Mr. 18/2/79
Ensor,
A. 1/10/88
G. 6/5/92
Thomas 17/3/74
Entwistle,
Mr. 20/4/78
William (-1865), tory M.P., banker 14/3/51
Epée, Charles Michel, abbé de L' (1712-1789) 18/2/32
Epinay, Prosper d' (1836-), artist 22/11/66
Erle, Peter (-1877), Queen's Counsel 18/6/53, 28/4/63
Erne *see* Crichton
Ernest,
C., journalist? 13/11/77
Charles, of York 8/5/68
Ernest Augustus (Ernest I) (1771-1851), King of Hanover (1837), Duke of Cumberland 8/4/35, 27/3/40
Errera, Alberto, economist of Italy 27/9/72
Errington,
George, Sir, British envoy to the Vatican 11/2/81 c, 17/12/81, 19/4/82, 24/10/82, 2/6/83 c, 22/5/87
George, Sir (1839-1920), 1st Baronet (1885), liberal M.P. 14/8/77
Erskine *see* Acland
Erskine,
Edward Morris (1817-1883), diplomat 18/6/70
Hay Macdowall, Rev. (1810-1896) 22/1/31
James Francis Harty St. Claire-, 5th Earl of Rosslyn 19/7/90
James St. Clair (1762-1837), 2nd Earl of Rosslyn (1805), 6th Baronet, tory whip in House of Lords, whig M.P. 8/4/36
John Francis, Earl of Mar 10/1/42 n
John Francis Erskine Goodeve (1836-1930), 29th Earl of Mar (1866) 14/4/79
Stuart R. J., liberal 24/6/92
Thomas, Hon. Rev. 10/1/42, 28/1/43
Violet Aline St. Claire-, née Vyner, Lady Rosslyn 19/7/90
Eschwege, Hermann, chemical manufacturer 22/6/65 ?
Escott,
Bickham Sweet (1800-1853), tory M.P., barrister 7/5/33
Hay Sweet, Rev. 28/3/77
Thomas Hay Sweet (-1924), journalist 17/12/78
Esdaile, David, Rev. Dr. 24/9/69 ?
Eshelby,
G., courier 30/3/55 ?
James 11/9/88
Esher *see* Brett
Eslington *see* Liddell
Esmonde,
John, Sir (1826-1876), 10th Baronet (1868), liberal M.P. 9/7/68, 18/5/69
Louisa, Lady, née Grattan 5/11/77
Españ, Mlle., rescue 2/4/56
Espin, Thomas Espinell, Rev. (-1912) 5/3/67

Espinasse, Francis, journalist 27/11/60
Essex *see* Capell
Esslemont, Peter (1834–1894), liberal M.P. 8/2/87
Esson, George A., accountant of Edinburgh 16/12/51
Estcourt,
Thomas Grimston Bucknall (1778–1853), tory M.P. 22/4/37
Thomas Henry Sutton (1801–1876), called Sotheron, Peelite M.P. 30/10/44
Estwick, Samuel, M.P. 23/3/33 n
Ethelston, Charles Wicksted (1798–1872) 19/2/52
Etty, W., R. A. 10/4/43
Etwall, R. 15/8/72
Eugen, rescue 10/3/56
Eugénie, Empress of France 7/7/72, 18/5/73, 20/2/90
Eumorfopoulo, M. 3/7/66
Evans *see* Disraeli, Hill
Evans,
Miss 28/9/66
Miss, Eton dame 7/7/78
A. E. 4/12/86
Alfred Eubule, Rev. 8/8/75
Arthur John, Sir (1851–1941), Knight (1911) 9/4/78
C. 28/7/68
David Morier (1819–1874), City journalist 24/6/67 ?
Edward, liberal chairman 28/11/91
Edward T., Rev., of Penmaenmawr 18/9/64 n
E. Rose 31/3/80
Francis Henry, Sir (1840–1905), Knight (1893), liberal M.P. 27/4/91
F. W. 15/11/77
George, Admiral 12/10/64
George de Lacy, Sir (1787–1870), soldier, liberal M.P. 7/5/33 n
George (Hampden) (1772–1842), whig M.P. 22/12/37 ?
Howard (1839–1915), journalist 1/8/78
John, of Chester 26/12/57
John, Sir (1823–1908), archaeologist 1/3/73
John Michael, Rev. 9/3/80
J. W. 9/10/78
Margaret 23/3/87
Margaret (–1893), née Freeman 9/4/78 n
Maurice J., Rev. 25/11/77
R. P., of Southwark 10/7/66
Sophia, née Parnell 22/12/37 n
T. 6/12/86
Thomas William, Sir (1821–1892), 1st Baronet (1887), liberal M.P. 1/6/66
W. 29/1/70
W. Glyn, of Chester 30/5/65, 9/11/67
William, clerk of the Admiralty 5/7/53
William, parliamentary candidate 9/1/35 n
W. T. 13/10/83
Evans & Co., haberdashers of Liverpool 6/12/67
Evarts, William Maxwell (1818–1901), of U.S.A. 17/7/63, 30/10/79
Eve, J., engineer 19/12/57
Eveleigh, John, linen draper 16/12/51 ?
Evelyn,
Mrs., rescue 18/5/60
John, 17th century diarist 23/4/43 n
L. 1/7/55
L. H., of Jamaica 18/7/40
Everard, Edward, Rev. 29/12/48
Everest,
Mary, Mrs. 9/4/45 ?
Thomas Roupell, Rev. 9/4/45 n
Everett,
R. A. 25/3/92, 15/12/93 ?
William, receiver general 23/6/43, 12/4/61
Everitt, Francis William Everitt, barrister 6/8/78 ?
Evers, Mr., of Oak Farm 5/2/48
Eversfield *see* Bligh
Eversham, Rev. Dr. 13/12/76
Eversley *see* Lefevre
Every *see* Mosley
Every, Edward, Sir 13/6/37 n
Ewart *see* Gott
Ewart,
Mrs., née Jacques 16/8/25
E. 18/8/29
John Frederick, Col. (1786–1854) 31/1/53
Joseph Christopher (1800–1868), liberal M.P. 19/8/26
Peter, Rev. (–1853) 13/1/27
William, the elder, Liverpool merchant and friend of Sir J. G, gave his name to G 16/8/25 n
William, the younger (1798–1869), radical M.P. 16/8/25 n, 16/5/46
Ewart, Myers & Co., brokers 2/1/32 n
Ewbank's Reading Room 6/2/32
Ewell, Ven. 11/12/75
Ewen, R. 19/12/87
Ewing,
Alexander, Bp., bishop of Argyll 22/4/44
Alice Louisa, Lady, née Douglas, wife of bishop 4/1/75
Humphrey Ewing Crum- (1802–1887) 10/7/63
Exell, J. S. 2/4/78
Exeter Reform Association, secretary of, 8/2/77
Exley, John Thompson 2/8/42 ?
Exmouth *see* Pellew
Eykyn, Roger, liberal M.P. (1866) 1/11/70, 29/3/71
Eyles, Edward Wells, civil servant 9/8/75

Eyre *see* Knight, Pierrepont, Vernon
Eyre,
Miss, governess 6/7/49
Charles James Phipps, Rev. (1813-1899) 30/3/78, 20/7/78
Edward John (-1901), colonial governor 31/1/46
William Thomas, Rev. (-1868) 10/3/52
Eysenhardt, F. 28/9/75
Eyston *see* Gillow
Eyton,
John Wynne, of Flintshire 3/3/57
Peter Ellis (1827-1878), liberal M.P. 30/10/57 n, 22/8/60
Robert, Rev. (1845-1908) 11/7/80, 11/11/88, 14/10/93 ff
Robert Wynne, Rev. (1787-1865), of Flintshire 13/8/56, 25/11/57
Thomas Wynne, of Flintshire 7/4/57

Faber, S. 6/2/75
Fabris,
Placido (1802-1859), historical painter & portraitist 14/1/39 n
R., Sig. 1/2/88
Faccio, B., Sig. 25/1/88
Fadella, Mr. 9/4/79
Fagan,
George, diplomat 4/1/51
George H. F., Rev. 5/10/86 ?
George Hickson Urquhart, Rev. (-1875) 6/8/52
Henry Stuart, Rev. (-1888) 30/10/76 ?, 8/1/87
Louis Alexander 7/4/79, 22/10/80 L
William Trant (1801-1859), liberal M.P. 17/4/47
Fagge, John Frederick, Rev. (-1884) 29/8/50
Fairbairn,
Andrew, Sir (1828-1901), liberal M.P. 17/12/91
Andrew Martin, Rev. (1838-1912), principal of Mansfield, Oxford 16/12/79, 1/2/85, 6/4/88, 31/1/90, 5/2/90, 15/10/93 L
Peter, flax manufacturer 5/7/43
William, Sir (1789-1874), 1st Baronet (1869), engineer 9/9/69
Fairbrother, Samuel, of Hawarden 5/2/57, 25/6/78, 13/4/81, 20/4/81
Fairchild, William, veterinary surgeon 29/7/79 ?
Fairet, M., of the Copyright Congress 19/8/58
Fairfax *see* Somerville
Fairfield,
rescue 24/3/60
Arthur Rowen 18/12/77, 4/1/79
Fairgrieve, Mr. 3/11/85
Fairhurst, Mr. 20/5/79
Fairman,
E. S. J., of Cairo 17/4/79
F. D., assistant clerk, education committee 28/4/58 ?
John N., customs 15/10/50 ?
Faithfull, Emily, Miss (1836-1895), journalist 18/7/68 ?, 15/8/78, 10/9/78 n
Fakhry Pasha, Egyptian politician 16/1/93 c, 17/1/93 c
Falbe, Christian Fredrick De, Danish minister 9/3/87
Falck, Ernest, stationer 31/3/74 ?
Falcke, David 24/3/63 ?
Falcone, Giuseppe 26/12/88
Falconer,
Mrs., 'a connection' 20/9/35
Francis A. Keith- (-1880), 8th Earl of Kintore (1844) 28/11/49
G. L., tenant of Fasque 3/12/49
G. L., Mrs., tenant 20/12/49
R., of East Mains, Balfour, Fettercairn 31/8/43
T. 25/1/56
Falconet, English resident of Naples 1/5/32
Falkender, Edward (1814-1896), architect 3/1/61
Falkland *see* Cary
Falkner,
Richard Philip, mayor of Newark (1833), attorney 21/7/35 n, 9/3/37
R. P., Mrs. 21/7/35
Thomas, Rev. (1828-1910) 25/1/56 ?
Fallati, Dr., doctor to Helen 8/10/45
Falle, Josué George (1820-1903), of Jersey 20/4/75
Fallon,
Celia, née Lynch, of Ballina House, nr. Athlone 8/4/31 ?
Simon, of Athlone 8/4/31 n
Falloon,
Daniel, Rev. (-1862) 1/12/59
William Marcus, Rev. 4/2/76 ?
Fallows, William, of Middlesbrough 5/6/68
Falmouth *see* Boscawen
Falney, E. 6/11/75
Falshaw, Mr. 6/7/74
Faluolti, Mad., of Naples 3/12/50
Falvey, T. 7/12/78
Fane *see* Villiers
Fane *see* Weigall
Fane,
Adine Eliza Anne, Lady (-1868), née Cowper 24/10/68
Arthur, Rev. (1809-1872) 10/6/62
J., 10th Earl of Westmorland 13/4/35 n
John, 11th Earl of Westmorland (1841) 14/8/44

Julian Henry Charles (1827-1870), diplomat 6/11/58, 18/3/63, 24/1/67
Priscilla Anne (-1879), née Pole, Lady Westmorland 5/10/62
Robert George Cecil, barrister, bankruptcy commissioner 14/7/47
Spencer Cecil Brabazon Ponsonby-, Sir (1824-1915) 19/5/84
Fanshawe, Frederick, Rev., fellow of Exeter, Oxford 10/12/47
Fanulla 30/4/92 n
Farabulini, David, Rev. Prof. 9/5/94
Faraday, Michael 1/12/41 n
Farbridge & Co., wine merchant 13/2/62
Farebrother, Mr. 7/8/68
Farenden, Miss, governess 29/12/25
Farinelli, Antonio 23/5/79 ?
Farini,
Domenico 12/9/76
Luigi Carlo (1812-1866) 3/3/59
Farish, James 6/10/74
Farler, John Prediger, Rev. (-1908) 16/7/79 ?
Farley, James Lewis (1823-1885) 17/10/76
Farmer, James, Sir (1823-1892) 24/3/68
Farmers' Alliance 16/6/80
Farnal, Harry, foreign office clerk 10/1/78
Farnall, H. B. 22/12/62
Farnborough *see* May
Farnfield, John Albert, solicitor 17/7/74
Farnham *see* Barry, Maxwell
Farquhar *see* Bertie, Cooper, Grey, Hook, Somerset
Farquhar,
Alice, Lady (-1925), née Brand (1862) 8/7/62
Arthur (1813-1887), W. S. 16/8/47 ?
Erica Townsend-, Lady, née Mackay 25/8/35
Henry Thomas, Sir (1838-1916), 4th Baronet (1900) 18/5/56
Horace Brand Townsend-, Sir (1844-1923) 1/3/94
James, of Laurencekirk 25/4/33
James, Mrs. 27/4/33
Mary Octavia, Lady (1814-1906), née Somerset 25/8/37 n
Sybella Martha, Lady (-1869), née Rockliff 29/11/32
Thomas Harvie, Sir (1775-1836), 2nd Baronet (1819), banker 29/11/32 n
W., Sir, 1st Baronet 30/8/35 n
Walter Minto Townsend-, Sir (1809-1866), conservative M.P. 25/8/35
Walter Rockliff, Sir 4/2/34
Farquharson,
George McBain Barnes, Col. 4/10/71 ?
James Ross, Col. 24/2/83 ff, 3/9/84 n
Robert, Rev. (1810-1881) 19/6/27
Farr,
E. 8/9/60
Thomas, Rev. 30/11/41
William, Dr. (1807-1883), statistician 9/10/65
William Wyndham (1808-1887), of Hampshire 4/2/26, 29/11/37, 30/11/37, 17/3/92
Farrant, George Binstead 21/8/56 ?
Farrar *see* Northcote
Farrar,
Adam Storey, Rev. Princ. (1826-1905) 5/12/59, 24/12/62
Frederick William, Canon (1831-1903) 25/9/82, 22/7/83, 4/8/85
John Martindale, Rev. 21/1/57 ?
Farrar & Co., solicitors 27/11/47 n
Farre, John Richard, Dr. (1775-1862), founder of Moorfields Hospital 23/11/37, 3/10/92
Farrell, E. O. 25/4/79
Farren, Nellie, actress 16/5/74
Farrer *see* Northcote
Farrer,
Henry, picture dealer 25/4/56
J., picture dealer 1/5/56
James William (1785-1863), barrister 6/7/37 ?
Thomas Henry, Sir (1818-1899), 1st Baron Farrer (1893), permanent secretary Board of Trade 3/3/36 ?, 19/7/73, 21/7/73, 17/4/86, 29/8/92
Farrer & Parkinson, solicitors 27/11/47, 1/5/56
Farrier, Mr. 17/10/86
Farrow, J., tailor? 23/1/56
Farsnet, Rev. Dr. 8/11/85
Farsyde, George James Watson, of Whitby 1/9/71
Faucit, Helena Saville (1817-1898), actress 19/11/64
Faussett,
Andrew Robert, Rev. Dr. (1821-1910) 14/7/75 ?
Godfrey, Prof. (1781-1853), professor of Divinity, canon of Christ Church, Oxford 28/2/30
L. G., Mrs. 7/12/78
Favale *see* Ulloa
Favanti, Sig., of Venice 3/10/79
Faversham *see* Duncombe
Favre,
Ferdinand, senator of France 21/7/89 ?
Jules Gabriel Claude 21/9/75
Fawcett,
Miss 12/12/69
Edgar, novelist 24/12/92, 26/12/92 L
Henry 28/3/63
John (1769-1830) 8/6/28
Millicent, Dame (1847-1929) 28/3/77
Fawcett & Preston, iron foundry of Edgehill 5/1/32

Fawens, W. 27/2/75
Fawkes, A., Rev. 1/11/92
Fawn, Messrs. 19/11/87
Fawsett, Camillus, secretary of United University Club 16/4/58
Fawsey, Mr., of Inland Revenue 12/6/65
Fayerman, Mr. 9/5/51, 4/10/56, 3/10/62
Fearn,
Mr. 13/4/80
Mrs., of Rome 31/12/66
Henry Noel, formerly Christmas 20/10/41
Fearnby, A. L. 10/11/77
Fearon,
Henry, Ven. 8/10/73
Henry B., wine merchants 9/3/60
John, Rev. 6/8/26
William Andrewes, Rev. (1841–1924) 1/11/79
Feather, E. 26/2/78
Fechner, Hermann, historian 1/8/89 ?
Fechter, Charles Albert (1824–1879), actor 29/7/61
Fedor, Russian tenor in Naples 23/12/50
Fehmi Pasha, Turkish envoy 21/1/85 c, 6/2/85 c, 10/2/85, 6/3/85, 7/3/85 c, 20/3/85 c, 25/3/85
Feilden,
Montague Joseph (1816–1898) 26/2/74
Randle Joseph, Gen. (1824–1895), tory M.P. 8/10/77
Feilding,
Mary (–1901), née Berkeley, Lady Denbigh (1865), Lady Feilding 13/12/64
Percy Robert Basil, Col. Sir (1827–1904) 11/2/71 c
Rudolph W. B., Baron Feilding (1823), 8th Earl Denbigh (1865) 4/11/44, 2/9/61
W. E. 15/6/76
William Basil Percy, 7th Earl Denbigh 20/7/44
William Henry Adelbert, Col. (1836–1895) 15/6/76 ?
Feldmann, M. F. 21/5/90
Feldnish, W. E. 4/11/89
Feldwick, William Edmund, Homerist 28/12/78
Felic[?itat]ion, M., rescue 30/5/56
Fell,
Archibald 20/2/67 ?
Edgar 12/11/91
James 5/3/80
John, Dean, dean of Christ Church 25/11/28
Fellowes *see* Gladstone, Mansfield, Walond
Fellowes,
Arthur 15/5/92 n
Edward, Maj. Gen. (–1879) 22/3/36
John, Rev. 25/1/37
M. A., Miss 12/3/36
Robert (–1869), of Shotesham Park 16/7/35 n
Susan, née Lyon 25/1/37
T. L., Rev. 21/1/47
Felton, John, coachmaker 3/6/48 ?
Fenmore, L. H., Mrs. 5/9/90
Fenn,
Mr., of Penmaenmawr 2/9/61
Mrs. 7/1/75
Fennell,
Mr. 7/9/78
Charles Augustus Maude, author 19/5/83
Fenner, F. P. 17/9/78
Fennings, P., coast guard officer 27/7/44
Fenton,
Hugh, of Hawarden 25/5/61, 12/12/62
W. H., of the Statistical Office 14/2/81 ?
William, candidate at Chester (1865) 13/4/65 n
Fenwick *see* Surtees
Fenwick,
Isabella 2/4/36
John Richard, attorney 12/3/45
W. 22/10/58
Fenzi, Cav. 24/1/88
Ferasis, Mme., dancer 9/12/50
Ferdinand,
King of Rumania 9/11/92 n, 25/11/92 ff
(1822–1855), Duke of Genoa 4/3/32
Maximilian Joseph, Archduke (1832–1914) 25/2/59
Ferdinand I, Emperor (1793–1875), Emperor of Austria 21/9/38
Ferdinand II (1810–1859), King of the Two Sicilies (known as 'Bomba') (1830) 28/4/32
Ferdinand IV and I (1751–1825), King of the Two Sicilies 15/10/38 n
Ferdinand Philippe (1810–1842), Duc d'Orléans 17/2/32
Ferel, Mons. 2/6/87
Fergolina, V., refugee? 24/5/59
Fergus,
Mr., photographer at Cannes 16/2/89
John (–1865), liberal M.P., provost of Kirkcaldy 2/5/53
Ferguson,
D., factor of Fasque 19/10/44
Emma Valentine Munro-, Miss, novelist 22/8/87 n
Fergus, Rev. 31/1/80
George, Adm. (1786–1867), conservative M.P. 3/4/37
J., home ruler 10/12/79
John, Rev. 4/1/87
J. W., Rev., episcopalian 3/1/43
Robert, M. D. 28/4/45
Robert (1817–1898), liberal M.P. 9/9/81

Ronald Craufurd Munro- (1860–1934), 1st Baron Novar (1914), liberal M.P. 2/7/86 n, 22/8/87, 23/3/89, 27/11/90, 7/5/91
Fergusson,
Mrs. 23/6/46
A. 23/11/77
James, Sir (1832–1907), tory M.P. 12/1/62
Robert Cutlar (–1838), whig M.P., East India Company director 9/6/33 n
W., Prof. Sir (1808–1877), 1st Baronet (1866), professor of surgery, King's College, London 11/6/39
Feriji, L., Sig. 14/11/78
Ferlini, Giuseppe, army doctor in Bologna, amateur archaeologist 8/1/39
Ferme, George, Mrs. 26/11/92 n
Fermoy *see* Roche
Fernand, rescue 16/2/81
Fernandez, G. 24/3/79
Fernando, Mr. 2/2/67
Ferns, George Egerton, solicitor of Cheshire 21/8/60 ?
Feroce, Gaetano 15/5/51
Ferrand *see* Surtees
Ferrand,
rescue 23/1/72
Margaret, née Moss 13/1/29
Walker (1780–1835), M.P. 13/1/29 n
William Busfield (1809–1889), tory M.P. 21/6/43
Ferrar, Michael, of Belfast 21/3/68
Ferrara, Francesco, Abbot, economist 7/10/51
Ferré, E., wrote on Ireland 2/6/87
Ferreira, Manuel, of Islington 17/6/79 ?
Ferrier *see* Grant
Ferrier, Alexander, Sir, Knight (1835), consul at Rotterdam 12/8/38
Ferrières, Charles Conrad Adolphus De, Baron (1823–1908), liberal M.P. (1880) 28/8/79, 24/7/80
Ferronays,
Albert Ferron de la 12/10/45 n
Alexandrine de la, née d'Alopens 12/10/45
Ferry,
Sgt., drill sergeant 16/7/25 n, 23/8/25, 7/12/25
Jules François Camille (1832–1907), French prime minister 28/6/84, 10/1/85, 1/4/85
Fesch, Joseph, Abp. (1763–1839), cardinal-archbishop of Lyons (1802) 11/12/38
Festing, E. R., Major 4/7/78 ?
Fetherston, F. M. 27/1/75
Fettis, Mr., surgeon of Laurencekirk 4/11/34
Feuerheerd, Mr., wine merchant 9/4/79
Few, Robert, attorney 7/8/40, 28/9/41, 21/10/65
Fewster, C. E. 29/5/78
Fewtrell, Mr. 22/6/77
Ffolkes, William B., of Bath 11/10/56
Ffolliott,
Grace C., Mrs. 21/11/77
John (1798–1868), tory M.P. 16/9/49
M. 21/11/77 n
Ffoulkes,
Major 7/12/88
Henry Powell, Rev., of Buckley 26/7/46
J., Rev. 8/12/86
J. J., of Mold 22/5/57, 19/6/57
Thomas 20/10/76
William Wynne (1821–1883), barrister 1/1/56
Ffrench, Elizabeth Mary, née O'Connell 25/4/89
Fialin, Jean Gilbert Victor (1808–1872), Duc de Persigny, French ambassador (1855) 12/3/57
Fichte, Johann Gottlieb (1762–1814), of Austria 17/12/38 n
Fiddaman, John, shoemaker of Newark 12/1/45
Field,
Mr., agent of London Soc. for protection of Young, agent of society for protection of young females 16/8/50
Cyrus West (1819–1892), of U.S.A. 24/2/62, 6/3/62, 1/8/62, 26/11/62, 27/11/62 n, 6/5/64, 12/3/68, 18/3/68, 10/2/72, 13/2/72, 4/3/72, 19/11/72, 28/11/72, 23/4/73, 3/9/74, 4/9/74, 23/8/77, 12/6/79, 26/2/80, 15/6/82
Edward, Bp. 18/3/47
Eugene, poet, of U.S.A. 22/1/90
George P., aurist 16/5/89
G. W. 29/5/57
John 18/12/41
K., Miss 22/6/78
R. C. 5/3/80
Walter, Rev. (–1876) 26/2/58
Fife *see* Duff, Louise
Fife, W. W. (1816–1867), editor, *Nottingham Daily Guardian* 17/7/58
Fifoot, Thomas 18/3/76
Figes, T. F. 3/3/76
Figgis, John Bradley, Rev. 3/5/89 ?
Filangieri, Gaetano, Prince (–1892) 1/2/89
Filder,
Herbert Wall, solicitor 22/8/60
William (–1861), Commissary general 1/4/54
Fileen,
Jonas, land owner of Demerara 26/5/36, 30/8/36, 5/10/36
Judith Susannah 26/5/36, 30/8/36, 5/10/36
Filleul, Philip, Rev. (–1875) 8/10/45

Filmer,
Edmund, Sir (1809–1857), 8th Baronet (1834), tory M.P. 21/3/53
Francis, Rev. (–1859) 23/8/52
Finch,
Capt. 19/6/81
Francis, liberal M.P. 10/7/37 n
Frederick Charles, Rev. 21/4/76
George (1790–1870), tory M.P., magnate of Rutland 18/3/33, 28/6/59 ?
John, merchant of Liverpool 25/2/48
William Stafford, Rev. 1/4/64 ?
Finchett *see* Gladstone
Finchett, James (–1825) 6/8/25
Finch Hatton *see* Turner
Finck, Herbert 20/3/78
Findlay,
Bruce 25/8/91
W. A. 9/9/78
Finelli, Carlo (1786–1853), sculptor of Italy 1/6/32
Fingall *see* Plunkett
Finlaison, Alexander Glen (–1892), national debt actuary 3/2/53
Finlason, William Francis (1818–1895), barrister 13/3/51
Finlay,
Messrs. 9/8/76
Miss 9/9/33
Alexander Struthers (1806–1886), liberal M.P. 3/11/42, 12/5/64
Charles, of Belfast 19/5/75
E. B., Rev. 24/3/91
F. D. 16/10/77
George (1799–1877), historian 20/12/58
Janet, née Struthers 4/9/33
John, gentleman of Liverpool 14/9/26
Kirkman (1772–1842), merchant of Glasgow 4/9/33
R. B., liberal unionist M.P. 23/6/86
Thomas Kirkman, merchant of Liverpool (Alston, Finlay & Co.) 12/12/26
Finlayson, 'old', cottager 3/11/33
Finlen, James, radical 18/7/68 n
Finlinson, Joshua, Rev. 15/1/47
Finn, Mrs. 5/11/74
Finne, J. F. 14/7/88
Finnie, Mrs. 22/8/75
Fioppi, jeweller? 1/6/32
Fiore, P., Prof. 8/2/89
Fioretto, G., Prof. 2/5/89
Firman, Charles George, Dr., physician 14/1/78 ?
Firth, Joseph Firth Bottomley (1842–1889), liberal M.P. 20/1/82
Fish,
Hamilton, American Secretary of State 19/5/69, 26/6/69 ff, 25/12/69, 24/1/70, 2/2/72 c, 25/2/72, 16/3/72 c, 5/4/72 c, 6/5/72 c, 13/5/72 c
L. J. 14/11/79
Fisher,
Duncan, of Montreal 11/6/40
Edward Robert, Rev. 19/6/79 ?
George, Rev. (–1873), astronomer 29/10/51 ?
J. L., of Cockermouth 12/10/60
John, of Montreal 11/6/40 n
Joseph 4/7/79
Richard, mercer 6/12/32
W. 28/3/77
W. H., manager of Oak Farm (1858) 4/6/58
William, Rev. (–1874) 21/7/68 ?
William Hayes (1853–1920), tory M.P. 31/7/93
William Webster (–1874), M. D. 8/5/49
Fisher Brothers & Co., brick manufacturers near Oak Farm 25/8/59
Fithian, Edward William, Sir (1845–1936), Knight (1905), barrister 10/2/80
Fitzclarence, Adelaide Georgiana, Lady (1820–1883) 27/9/55
Fitzgerald,
rescue 6/2/70
Augustus Frederick (1791–1874), 3rd Duke of Leinster (1804) 28/7/59, 8/11/69 L
Caroline, née Leveson-Gower, Duchess of Leinster 3/11/77
Charles William (1819–1887), Baron Kildare (1870), 4th Duke of Leinster (1874) 17/6/70, 15/2/73, 3/11/77, 5/10/81 L
Geraldine Penrose, Miss, author 20/1/91 ?
James Edward (1818–1896), Prime Minister of New Zealand 20/9/48, 22/4/58, 9/7/58, 12/11/83, 10/9/89 ?
James Gubbins (1855–), home rule M.P. 29/1/91
Jean, Lady, née Ogilvy 10/9/55
John Forster, Sir (–1877), liberal M.P. 13/6/53
Mabel, Lady 25/6/79
Maurice, Capt. 15/9/80
Michael Dillon, surgeon 13/5/48
Otho Augustus, Lord (1827–1882) 9/6/66, 2/8/69 L
Peter George, Sir (1808–1880), 1st Baronet (1880), 'Knight of Kerry' 18/10/77
William Robert Seymour Veysey-, Sir (1818–1885), Knight (1867), tory M.P. 7/6/56, 26/4/58
W. Veysey-, 1st Baron Fitzgerald and Vesey 7/7/28 n
Fitzgerald and Vesey *see* Fitzgerald
Fitzgibbon *see* Wodehouse
Fitzgibbon, Richard Hobart (1793–1865), 3rd Earl of Clare (1851), whig M.P. 18/6/35

Fitzhardinge *see* Berkeley
Fitzharry, Mr. 27/7/78
Fitzhenry, Mr. 6/1/87
Fitzherbert,
Edward Herbert (-1853), barrister 17/12/31
Mary Anne, née Smyth, formerly Weld 15/12/38 n
Thomas 15/12/38 n
Fitzmaurice,
Mrs. 19/1/41
Edmond George Petty-, Lord (1846-1935), 1st Baron Fitzmaurice (1906) 3/2/78, 26/7/81 n, 5/12/82, 24/4/84 L, 3/10/84, 30/3/85, 19/3/92, 4/5/93
Henry Charles Keith Petty- (1845-1927), 5th Marquis of Lansdowne (1866) 11/3/69, 25/4/83, 20/9/93, 2/11/93 n, 8/1/94, 10/1/94, 18/1/94, 29/1/94, 10/3/94
Henry Petty- (1780-1863), 3rd Marquis of Lansdowne (1809), whig grandee 3/10/31, 13/6/33
Henry Thomas Petty-, Sir (1816-1866), Earl of Shelburne (1836), 4th Marquis of Lansdowne (1863) 25/4/57
James, Rev. 6/6/40, 19/1/41
Louisa Emma Petty-, née Fox-Strangways, Lady Lansdowne 13/6/33
William Thomas Petty- (1811-1836), Earl of Kerry (1818), whig M.P. 20/2/33
Fitzpatrick *see* West
Fitzpatrick,
John Wilson- (1807-1883), 1st Baron Castletown (1869), liberal M.P. 4/3/70
William John (1830-1895), author 27/1/80
Fitzroy *see* Lindsay
Fitzroy,
Mrs., rescue 11/10/72, 23/2/74, 25/2/74
A. H., 3rd Duke of Grafton 16/5/26 n
A. I., Miss 20/11/91
Augustus, Rev. (1809-1869) 19/4/32
Cavendish C., Major 17/4/79
Charles Augustus, Sir, colonial governor 22/1/46
Charles Lennox, Lord (1791-1865), whig M.P. 18/3/58
George Frederick (-1810), 2nd Baron Southampton 27/2/52 n
Henry (-1863), 5th Duke of Grafton (1844) 31/5/52 n
Henry (1806-1877), squire of Northants 16/5/26
Henry (1807-1859), Peelite M.P. 7/2/52
Henry, Lord, canon of Westminster 16/5/26 n
Hugh, Lieut. Col. (1808-1879), of the Grenadiers 16/5/26
Mary Caroline (-1873), née Berkeley, Duchess of Grafton 31/5/52
Robert, Capt., Royal Navy 6/12/41
S. F., Rev. 17/4/80
Fitzwilliam,
Albreda, Lady 30/11/75
Alice Mary, Lady (1849-) 26/6/75, 9/7/75, 30/11/75
Charles William Wentworth- (1768-1857), 5th Earl Fitzwilliam (1833), whig M.P. 17/5/39
Frances Harriet Wentworth-, Lady, née Douglas, Lady Milton (1838), Countess Fitzwilliam (1857), proposed to unsuccessfully by G 7/11/37 n
George Wentworth (1817-1874), liberal M.P. 30/6/41 n
William (1839-1877), Viscount Milton, liberal M.P. 27/3/67
William Charles Wentworth- (1812-1835), Viscount Milton (1833), whig M.P. 25/9/26
William Thomas Spencer Wentworth- (1815-1902), Viscount Milton (1835), 6th Earl Fitzwilliam (1857), liberal M.P. 19/6/38, 30/11/75 n, 26/10/77 n, 27/10/77, 29/10/77, 24/6/80 L, 17/7/80 L
Fitzwilliams, Charles Home Lloyd (1843-) 30/7/78
Flaesch, Mrs., rescue 28/1/69
Flahault de la Billarderie,
Auguste, Count (1785-1870), Ambassador of France 25/10/61 n
Margaret, Comtesse, née Nairne 12/7/62
Flamburiari, Dionides, Count Sir, President of the Ionian Assembly 25/11/58 n, 23/1/59 ff, 14/2/59
Flamdy, Mr. 29/7/76 ?
Flanedy, John, of Everton, journalist? 26/4/55
Flaxman Fund, Treasurer 16/3/49
Fleetwood,
Charles, stockbroker 21/5/38 ?
Peter Hesketh-, Sir (1801-1866), Baronet (1838), liberal M.P. 21/5/34
Fleischer, Richard, editor of the *Deutsche Review* 21/9/78, 30/12/84
Fleming,
Mrs. 11/4/78
Henry (-1876), secretary to Poor Law Board, known as 'the flea' 10/5/58
James, Rev. (1832-1908) 2/7/79
Michael Anthony, bishop of Newfoundland 23/7/40 n
R. 10/9/77
W. E., Rev. 3/9/77
Flemyng,
Francis Patrick, Rev. Dr. (1823-1895) 1/5/74
William Westropp, Rev. 5/6/90

Fletcher,
Mr. 19/3/39
A. E. 20/9/89
Angus, of Board of Inland Revenue 2/2/56
Bannister (1833–1899), liberal M.P. 20/6/86
C. 12/6/76
Charles Robert Leslie (1857–1934) 31/1/90 n
George Henry, Rev. (1826–1904) 16/10/67 ?
Harriet, Lady, née Marsham 22/9/65 n
Henry Charles, Col. (1833–1879) 22/9/65
Joseph, barrister 21/2/52
Ralph (–1851), connoisseur 24/6/51
Fletcher & Co., wine merchants 18/10/71
Flockton, M. J. 12/12/77
Flood,
John, barrister of Ireland 14/5/51 ?
L. 20/12/89
W. H. Gratton 6/6/92
Floquet, Charles Thomas, politician of France 28/1/83
Florador Food Co. 26/5/88
Florance, James, parliamentary agent 19/1/35
Floriano, Fra, of Ravenna 10/6/32
Flower,
Cyril (1843–1907), 1st Baron Battersea (1892), liberal M.P. 19/10/85, 12/3/87, 24/7/87, 24/7/88, 4/5/92 n, 9/5/92
James Edward, Rev. 21/7/75
W. H. 31/12/86
William Balmber, Rev. 5/2/52 ?
Floyd *see* Peel
Floyd,
Henry, Sir (1793–1868), major general 28/5/52 ?
John, Gen. Sir, Baronet, general 20/2/35 n
Floyer,
Ernest Ayscoghe, writer 12/10/92
John (1811–1887), tory M.P. 19/6/56 ff, 9/3/70
Fludye, Mr. 18/10/78
Fluegel, M., Rabbi, of Kentucky 2/12/88
Flynn,
Dr. 10/9/88
Thomas, cheesemonger 12/4/52 ?
T. T., coalwhipper 23/5/56, 17/4/57, 21/4/57
Foecker, Rev. Herr 15/1/80
Fogarty, Mr., of Aughrim 26/10/77
Fogg,
John Barratt, of Mold 3/2/54
W. 20/1/79
Fogge,
Mr., factor 15/7/92
G. 23/8/78
Foggo, Algernon, author 22/11/87 n
Foley *see* Chabot
Foley,
Henry John Wentworth Hodgetts- (1828–1894), liberal M.P. 28/3/65
Joseph William (1821–1890), home rule M.P. 21/12/75 ?
Thomas, 3rd Baron Foley 24/9/45 n
Thomas Henry (1808–1869), 6th Baron Foley 7/6/48
Foljambe,
C. G. S., 1st Earl of Liverpool (1905) 14/11/35 n
Francis John Savile (1830–1917), liberal M.P. (1857) 21/6/72, 16/4/79 n, 31/1/85, 21/6/92
George Savile (1800–1869) 14/11/35 n
Selina Charlotte (1812–1883), née Jenkinson, formerly Wentworth-Fitzwilliam, formerly Lady Milton 14/11/35
Folkard, Mr. 4/3/90
Fölkerschamb, Baron 4/12/78
Follett,
John, vice-consul 15/4/42
William Webb, Sir (1798–1845), tory M.P., solicitor and attorney general 9/4/35
Fonblanque, Albany William (1793–1872), Board of Trade 16/7/63
Fonseca, Monteiro & Co, wine merchants 26/6/52 n
Fontanelli, Camillo (1823–1881) 30/7/59
Foot, S. C., Rev. 26/11/77
Foote,
A. R. L., Rev. 7/10/51
G. W., editor of *The Liberal* 28/3/79
John, Capt. (–1854), Royal Navy 18/10/32
John, Mrs. 18/10/32
Forbes *see* Malcolm, Montalembert, Trefusis
Forbes,
A., Mrs. 9/2/57
Alexander Penrose, Bp. 3/9/45
Archibald (1838–1900), journalist 13/11/77, 14/11/77 ff, 23/11/77, 4/12/77
Arthur K. W., barrister of Dublin 14/4/45 ?
George, of Edinburgh 24/12/35
George Arthur Hastings (1833–1889), 7th Earl of Granard (1837) 15/7/69
George Hay, Rev., episcopalian 3/9/45
Harriet Louisa Anne, Lady (–1884), née Kerr 8/10/46, 12/10/58, 1/12/76
Horatia, Lady (–1862), née Shaw 5/8/44
James David, Prof., prof. of natural philosophy and principal 9/12/33, 17/4/60
Jane (–1871) 20/9/33
John Colin (1846–), Canadian portrait painter 5/5/91, 30/7/91
John Hay (1776–1854), Lord Medwyn, Scottish judge 21/4/26
John Stuart Hepburn, Sir (1804–1866), 8th Baronet (1828) 23/8/33

Robert, of East India Company 15/5/45
the Misses 6/12/33
Walter, 18th Baron Forbes 5/8/44 n
William (-1855), tory M.P. of Callendar 11/1/37 n
William (-1891), son of Lord Medwyn 3/9/45
William, Sir, Baronet 20/9/33 n
Forcade-Laroquette, Jean de (1820-1874) 26/1/67, 14/2/72 L
Forchhammer, Peter Wilhelm, Prof. (1801-1894), of Denmark 11/6/64
Ford,
Mr., of the *Irish World* 29/6/82
Edward Onslow (1852-1901), sculptor 15/5/82 ff, 13/12/83 n
Elijah 2/4/79
Francis Clare, Sir (1830-1899), ambassador to Turkey, then to Italy 30/1/93, 1/2/93, 22/10/93 n
Frederick, mayor of Wisbech 30/8/65 n
James 8/9/76
T. 20/8/79
William (-1889), solicitor of London 31/12/51 ?
Forder, R. 24/5/78
Fordyce,
James Dingwall, lawyer of Edinburgh 10/3/79
William Dingwall (1836-1875), liberal M.P. 9/11/69 L
Fore, J. A., pamphleteer 10/8/87
Forester,
Cecil Weld-, 1st Baron Forester 16/5/43 n
George Cecil Weld- (1807-1886), 3rd Baron Forester (1874), tory M.P. 20/12/52, 14/3/70
Orlando Watkin Weld-, Rev. (1813-1894), 4th Baron Forester (1886) 6/10/77
Foresti, Typaldo, Dr., of Ionia 26/11/58
Forewood, Mr. 7/6/83
Forjelt, C. 15/2/78
Formby, H., Rev. 2/4/78
Forrest,
rescue 1/2/64, 2/2/64
J. A. 28/8/79
R. W., Rev. 29/3/68
Thomas Guest, Rev. 18/4/78
T. M. 8/5/78
Forsey, Charles Benjamin, Board of Inland Revenue 1/6/85
Forshall, Josiah, Rev. (-1863) 6/10/54
Forshaw, Thurston, Dr., physician 21/12/86, 10/8/88
Forster,
Charles, Sir (1815-1891), 1st Baronet (1874), liberal M.P., G's confidant and dining companion, often spelled 'Foster' in the *Diaries* 18/3/58, 16/4/74, 16/4/78 n, 28/3/79, 3/4/79, 13/4/83, 23/4/83, 11/6/83, 1/8/83, 8/2/84, 7/8/84, 19/11/84, 1/12/84, 16/3/85, 23/3/85, 2/4/85, 14/4/85, 14/7/85 n, 21/7/85, 27/1/86 ff, 19/3/86, 31/5/86, 24/8/86, 15/3/87, 28/4/87, 16/6/87, 22/7/87, 26/8/87, 14/6/88, 5/11/88, 19/11/88, 12/3/89, 2/8/89, 17/2/90, 28/4/90, 29/4/90, 5/8/90, 1/12/90
Charles Thornton, Rev. 15/9/87
Florence Arnold-, Miss 4/4/81 n
Francis Blake, Capt. 2/11/77
Henry (-1857), esquire bedel of divinity, Oxford 21/1/53 n
Hugh Oakeley Arnold- (1855-1909), unionist M.P. 12/4/82 n, 1/3/94 n
M. H., pay office 17/2/65
Thomas Hay, Rev. 7/6/55
William Edward 9/5/62
Forsyth,
W., Rev., presbyterian 6/7/74
William (1812-1899), tory M.P., editor of *Annual Register* 9/5/57, 6/4/77
William (1818-1879), editor of *Aberdeen Journal* 16/4/60 ?
Fort,
Richard (-1868), liberal M.P. 2/2/67
Richard, junior (1856-1918), liberal M.P. 2/11/82
Fortescue *see* Courtenay, Williams
Fortescue,
Chichester Samuel Parkinson- 24/3/54
E. B. K., Rev., of Scotland 16/1/53, 28/12/57, 29/9/69
Elizabeth, Lady, née Geale, Lady Fortescue 26/7/48
Frances Elizabeth Anne, Lady, née Braham, Lady Carlingford, known as Lady Waldegrave 27/3/49
H., 1st Earl Fortescue 4/4/38 n
Hugh, 2nd Earl Fortescue 26/7/48 n
Hugh (1818-1905), Viscount Ebrington (1841), 5th Baron Fortescue (1859), 3rd Earl Fortescue (1861), whig M.P. 16/8/43
John, Rev., canon of Worcester 21/11/51 ?
John Faithful Grover, Rev. (-1868) 9/8/54 ?
Forth Bridge Co., secretary of, 24/2/90
Fortique, Alejo, ambassador of Venezuela 22/5/44
Fortnum & Mason, grocers 7/9/43, 30/5/5, 30/4/73 L
Fortunato, Giustino (1777-1862), politician of Naples 17/11/42
Fortune, David, liberal of Glasgow 17/10/86
Forwood,
Arthur Bower (1836-1898), Liverpool political boss and tory M.P. 12/12/82 n

Forwood (*cont.*)
William Bower, Sir (1840–1928) 9/12/92
Fosbrooke, Mr. 10/11/75
Foscolo, Ugo (1778–1827) 22/5/64 n
Foster *see* Forster, Salis
Foster,
Miss 11/9/38
Mr., jnr., of Oak Farm 4/4/49
Albinia, Lady (1788–1867), née Hobart 3/3/32
Augustus John, Sir (1780–1848), Baronet (1831), diplomat 2/3/32
(Balthasar) Walter, Sir (1840–1913), physician, liberal M.P. 23/6/86, 30/12/86
B. W., Dr. 27/11/85
C. 13/2/68
C., Sir, 1st Baronet 24/5/34 n
Cavendish Hervey, Rev. (1817–1890) 3/3/32
Charles J., sec., new universities committee 4/6/52
Charles Smith (–1850), banker, tory M.P. 24/5/34
Edward and Son, auctioneers 26/4/45
Edward Ward, painter 26/12/48 ?
Frederick John (1816–1857), diplomat 3/3/32
J. J. 29/11/86
John (1787–1846), architect of Liverpool 27/4/33
John, Rev. (1807–1882) 18/3/58
John Leslie (–1842), tory M.P., judge of Ireland 11/9/38
Leslie, broker in the City? 12/2/53
Morgan Hugh (1815–1891), of the Treasury 13/8/59
N. T., Homerist 20/5/78
Peter Le Neve (1805–1879), secretary Soc. of Arts 8/6/58
Thomas Campbell (–1882), reporter, lawyer 19/10/54
William Orme (1814–1899), liberal M.P. 16/6/59, 14/5/61
W. V. L., of Oak Farm? 16/2/47
Fothergill, Ernest Henry, Rev. 21/7/79 ?
Fotheringham, L. M. 12/9/91
Fottrell, George, Sir (1849–1925), Knight (1919) 7/7/79
Fould, Achille (1800–1867), Finance Minister of France 27/5/61, 24/1/67, 25/1/67
Foulds, James L., of Edinburgh 25/11/85, 13/5/90
Foulkes,
Edmund Salisbury, Rev. 4/3/48
Henry Powell, Rev. 3/6/41, 16/12/61
Fountaine, Henry Thomas, Rev. 31/10/76 ?
Fourdrinier *see* Newman
Fourdrinier,
Eliza, Miss (–1885) 5/2/57
J. S., secretary, Electric Telegraph Co. 11/11/53
Fournet, R. 27/11/89
Foville, Alfred De, Prof. (1842–), professor in Paris 24/10/85
Fowke,
Francis, Capt. (1823–1865), architect 6/12/55
Francis, Rev. (–1902) 15/2/49
Frederick, Sir 22/7/45
Fowle, F. W., Rev., prebend of Salisbury 13/7/54
Fowler *see* Mackenzie
Fowler,
Mr. 12/4/33
Charles, architect 27/11/47 ?
Francis H. 11/1/76
Frederic Cooke, Rev. (1802–1897) 27/7/55
Henry Hartley (1830–1911), 1st Baron Wolverhampton (1908) 1/6/77 n, 10/8/82, 29/3/83, 31/5/84 n, 5/12/84, 2/3/86, 23/3/86, 10/6/86, 23/4/88, 9/5/89, 23/3/91, 23/4/91, 28/4/92, 2/5/92, 19/5/92, 16/6/92, 29/9/92, 27/10/92, 2/11/92 c, 21/11/92 c, 23/11/92 c, 1/12/92, 8/12/92 L, 21/12/92 L, 13/1/93 c, 24/7/93, 17/8/93 c, 18/8/93 c, 2/11/93, 21/11/93 c, 1/12/93 c, 14/12/93 c, 16/12/93, 28/12/93, 7/3/94 L
J. C. 13/9/88
John, Sir (1817–1898), Knight (1885), 1st Baronet (1890), engineer 17/1/60
Joseph Thomas, Rev. (1833–1924) 25/7/79
William (1828–1905), liberal M.P. (1868) 26/10/60, 8/2/67, 4/6/80 L
Fox,
Father 4/8/87
Lady 22/9/77
Mr. 24/6/86
Mrs. 15/7/87
Charles, Sir, engineer 14/10/50
Charles James 4/2/32 n
Charles Richard, Gen. (1796–1873), numismatist 17/8/66
George Lane (1816–1896) 27/2/78
Henry Elliot, Rev. (–1926) 21/11/77
H. F. 22/11/90
James Richard Thomas Lane, soldier 8/11/62 n
John, attorney of Newark 10/2/36
Lucy Frances Jane, née Mildmay 8/11/62 ?
Richard Maxwell (1816–1856), liberal M.P. 12/8/53
R. Reynolds 5/3/76
T. H. 14/7/88
Thomas Henry Lane, Rev. (–1861) 31/3/54
William, Sir (–1893), Knight (1879), politician of New Zealand 24/7/51

William Sackville Lane (-1874), tory M.P. 4/1/33 ff, 31/12/52
Foxcroft, Frank 3/9/77
Foxley, Joseph, Rev. (1827-1911) 15/7/76
Fox-Strangways *see* Fitzmaurice, Kerrison
Foxton,
George Frederick Hardman, Rev. (1825-1896), priest at Fasque 10/10/58
G. F. H., Mrs. 11/10/58
Foy,
Miss 12/9/25 ?
Louis, of Canada 12/9/25
Louis, Mrs., of Canada 12/9/25 ?
Samuel W., of Bank of England 11/9/78
Frampton, Mrs. 16/9/75
France, John F. 14/3/74
Frances, H. 7/12/78
Franceschini, Pietro 9/1/88 ?
Francesco, F., of Naples 13/7/81
Franceys, Samuel, publisher & bookseller of Liverpool 30/10/33
Franchi, Messrs., booksellers 24/1/88
Francillon, Henry James 14/7/56 ?
Francis,
Mrs. 22/6/78
George Henry, editor 9/2/47
J. D. 23/12/74
J. Deffett, of Swansea 2/8/78
Paul Charles Louis Alexander (1837-1900), Duke of Teck 19/4/66 n
S. T. 5/10/91
Francis I,
King of France 22/2/32
(1777-1830), King of the Two Sicilies 3/11/38
Francis II (1768-1835), Emperor of Austria (1804) 23/6/32
Francken, K., legal officer in Berbice 5/2/38 ?
Francoudi, D. 9/12/90
Frank, J. H. 23/12/90
Franklin,
Ellis Abraham, banker 22/10/78 ?
John, merchant in the City 8/2/48 ?
John A., of London 23/4/58
Franks *see* Norreys
Franks, Charles, of South Sea Company 16/3/53
Franqueville, Charles de 22/11/62
Franzi, Camillo, Rev. 3/10/79
Fraser,
A., diarist's godfather 16/8/25
Alexander Campbell, Rev. (1819-1914), Free Church minister & professor 26/4/52 n
Andrew (-1873), sheriff 19/3/52
Donald, Rev., presbyterian 26/12/77
Fanny C., of Leamington 31/5/43
Francis Garden (-1885), of Aberdeenshire 5/7/36 ?
G., of Jamaica 22/9/63
G. B., Lieut. Col. 29/6/46
G. & Sons, cotton merchants 20/1/43
James, of Bank of Scotland 15/4/28 n
James, Bp. (1818-1885) 16/12/61, 29/12/69 n, 3/1/70, 8/11/70 L, 23/7/81, 29/7/81, 17/8/81
James, Mrs. 15/4/28
James Baillie (-1856), explorer 23/2/54
James Chalmers Dean, Rev. 25/10/79
John, Col., of Balmakewan House, Kincardine 8/9/43 n
J. Scott, of Liverpool 13/7/78
R. D. 13/11/77
Simon, 13th Baron Lovat (1875), Master of Lovat 31/12/66
Thomas 13/7/76
Thomas Alexander, of Lovat, of Aberdour 13/5/36 ?
'three Misses' 17/4/28
William, Col., of Balmakewan House, Kincardine 1/9/37
William, Sir (1816-1898), Knight (1887), genealogist 3/11/57, 6/12/79, 25/9/84
Fraser & Tayleur, brokers of Liverpool 3/12/46
Freake, Charles James, Sir (1814-1884), 1st Baronet (1882) 25/2/70, 22/6/75, 30/5/83
Freck, H. D. 9/3/76 ?
Frederick,
Archduke 29/11/42
J. J., War Office clerk 18/6/78 ?
Prince, of Hesse 2/6/43 n
Frederick Augustus (1763-1827), Duke of York (and Albany), field marshal 5/1/27
Frederick Christian Augustus, Prince (-1880), Duke of Augustenburg, of Schleswig-Holstein 12/7/51, 15/11/60
Frederick III (1831-1888), Emperor of Germany 21/6/42 n, 19/6/56, 25/1/58, 25/7/58 n, 11/7/71, 21/7/71, 16/7/81, 30/7/84, 8/9/84, 18/6/88, 23/10/88
Frederick William IV (1795-1861), King of Prussia 2/2/39
Fredez, rescue 1/4/71
Fredin,
rescue 27/6/76
Mr. 1/7/76
Freeborn, John, consul in Rome 23/7/49
Freeland, Humphrey William (1814-1892), liberal M.P. 5/7/60, 9/7/61
Freeman *see* Evans
Freeman,
Bellingham 17/2/76 ?
Edward Augustus (-1892), historian 5/4/54, 18/8/66, 16/9/76, 18/1/77, 23/1/77, 13/2/84, 14/2/84 L, 23/9/85 L
George 15/5/89
J. 7/7/74

Freeman (*cont.*)
M., Mrs., née Horton, rescue 24/4/52
Philip, Rev. (1818–1875) 22/3/52
W. B. 7/3/78
William Peere Williams (1811–1873), high sheriff of Oxfordshire 6/6/36 ?
Freeman & Marriot, fine art dealers 25/7/89
Freeman & Son, wine merchants 29/7/56 ?
Freestun, William Lockyer, Sir (1804–1862), Knight (1860), soldier, liberal M.P. 2/5/54
Freeth, Charles or George, gentleman of London 4/12/32 ?
Freeze, Mr. 29/5/78
Freiheit, Die, editor of 26/3/81
Freis, Mr. 14/10/76
Fremantle,
Arthur James Lyon, Col. 23/5/78
Thomas Francis, Sir (1798–1890), 1st Baron Cottesloe (1874), tory M.P. 22/12/34, 5/4/53, 12/7/59 ff, 10/11/59 ff, 6/12/59, 23/1/60 ff, 10/4/61, 22/12/73, 31/12/73, 7/3/74
W. H., Rev. 5/11/80 L
William Robert, Dean, dean of Ripon (1876) 9/8/28
French,
rescue 24/5/58
rescue 4/7/88
Mme. 16/1/88
Fitzstephen (1801–1873), liberal M.P. 15/8/53, 16/3/66
H. 25/11/89
Frenchly, D. 20/1/82
Frere,
Charles, House of Commons examiner 20/12/55 ff, 19/6/56
Henry Bartle Edward, Sir (1815–1884), Knight (1859) 21/8/56, 6/3/57, 12/10/72 c, 26/4/73 c, 10/5/73 c, 1/11/73, 17/1/74 n, 27/5/79 n, 3/5/80, 12/5/80 c, 22/5/80 c, 29/5/80 c, 3/7/80 c, 24/7/80 c, 31/7/80, 15/8/81 L
John, Rev. (–1851) 7/7/26
Freshfield,
Messrs., solicitors 12/4/75 ff, 9/6/90, 17/6/90
Charles Kaye, solicitor 16/11/47
D. W. 25/11/77
Edwin 13/11/71 L, 26/5/76 ?
H. N., solicitor 12/6/73, 14/6/73 L
James William (1775–1864), tory M.P., solicitor 3/4/33, 24/3/48, 30/3/48, 1/4/48, 29/7/50, 9/7/55, 10/2/63
John Minet, Rev. 18/2/74
Frethey, Mrs. 20/6/92
Frettingham, Mr. 7/3/78
Fretwell, William, labourer 27/1/38
Freund, Max 4/1/76
Freunkel, Dr. 7/8/88
Frewen, Charles Hay (1813–1878), tory M.P. 28/2/54
Freycinet, Charles de Saulces de (1828–1923), French prime minister and foreign minister 13/4/85, 15/4/85 c
Friar,
at St. Sebastian's 12/4/32
at Venice 20/6/32
of Ireland in Rome 20/4/32
'the Frate', at Fiesole 2/10/38
Frickenhaus, August, insurance agent 22/8/77
Friedel 4/12/30
Friedlander, S. 7/12/92
Friedrich Wilhelm, Grandduke (1819–1904), Grandduke of Mecklenburg-Strelitz (1860) 28/6/43 n
Friend,
Mr. 11/9/66
Isabella 30/6/62
John Bankes (1808–1881) 30/6/62
M. K. 12/2/90
Richard, journalist? 9/11/67
Friend of Africa, editor of 8/3/41
Friesenhaben, M. 13/6/92
Frisark, Mr. 5/12/60
Frisby, William S. 11/4/77
Frist, Messrs. 25/8/60
Friswell, James Hain (1825–1878), novelist 21/3/76
Frith,
Arthur J., of Athens 10/7/58
Marishab Keith Smith, Rev. 5/7/65
William Powell (1819–1909), artist 21/11/81 L, 22/12/81, 29/12/81, 25/3/82
Frölich,
D., Count, of France 14/7/55
R., Consul 7/10/91
Froment, Mr., of France? 5/12/55
Froom 10/12/36
Frost,
Catherine 4/2/52
F. A., of Chester 15/8/76
G. D., Rev. 21/6/77
Mary, Lady, née Wood 10/5/78
Meadows, of Chester 18/11/67
Percival, Rev. 8/5/74
Robert, of Chester 18/12/62
Thomas Gibbons, Sir 19/10/71, 9/9/73, 8/8/76, 11/11/76, 3/1/79, 11/8/79
Froude,
James Anthony (1818–1894), historian, biographer and South Africanist 7/8/61, 5/2/64, 10/4/77 n, 28/1/85, 25/3/86 n, 5/7/90
U. 10/6/78
Frowde, Henry (1841–1927), O. U. P. publisher 13/2/79, 7/12/89

Fruling & Goschen, bankers 24/3/53 n
Fry,
Edward, Sir (1827-1918), judge 4/4/83
Henry, Rev. Dr., nonconformist? 18/5/68
James, Rev. 30/4/50
Joseph Storrs, Quaker 1/6/85 n
L., architect 28/12/75
Theodore, Sir (1836-1912), 1st Baronet (1894), liberal M.P. 29/6/86
W. 12/6/77
Fryer, Alfred, author of Manchester 23/2/64, 30/12/86, 12/4/87 n
Führich, Joseph von (1800-1876), painter 11/1/39 n
Fulford, Francis, Bp. (1803-1868), of Montreal 28/4/68
Fullarton, Ralph W. M., writer 29/12/92
Fuller,
Charles Francis (1830-1875), sculptor 14/1/67
F. 19/4/79
H., Col. 30/6/75
Thomas Brock, Bp. (1810-1884), bishop of Niagara 15/9/67
Fullerton,
Alexander George 29/3/45 n, 3/9/81, 3/6/92
Georgiana Charlotte, Lady, née Leveson Gower, novelist 29/3/45, 13/5/45, 14/5/45, 3/9/81 ff, 3/9/93
W. M. 13/2/90
Fullom, Stephen Watson (-1874), author 12/11/61
Fulton, T. 4/1/78
Funk & Wagnall, Messrs., publishers in U.S.A. 29/9/88, 18/1/90, 10/10/90, 6/3/91
Furbank, Thomas, Rev. (1792-1851) 23/5/39 ?
Furlong,
Charles Joseph, Rev. (1803-1874), author 14/2/34
Michael, of Dublin 5/1/87
Thomas, Bp. (1802-1875), Roman Catholic 16/4/70
Furlsham, T. H. 19/4/92
Furness,
Christopher (1852-1912), liberal M.P. 5/1/91
Horace Howard, author of U.S.A. 19/5/80, 5/8/87
John, Rev. 8/8/46 ?
Furness & Knee, auctioneers 17/3/68
Furniss, Harry (1854-1925), cartoonist 7/5/89 n
Furnivall, Frederick James (-1910), scholar, barrister 20/2/52
Furrell, James, solicitor 29/5/63 ff, 22/7/63
Furse, Charles Wellington, Ven. (1821-1900) 12/12/79 ?, 27/1/94
Fusco, Giuseppe Maria, historian of Naples 8/6/58
Fust, Herbert Jenner-, Sir (-1852) 2/4/49 n
Fyfe,
A. Gordon, sugar pamphleteer 12/5/46 n
John, of Dunoon 5/11/35 n
John, Mrs. 5/11/35 ?
T. C. 6/3/77
Fyffe, Charles Allen, barrister 26/7/78
Fysh, F. 5/7/74 ?, 30/12/74
Fytche, Albert, General (1820-1892) 4/7/71
Fyvie, Charles, Rev. 13/4/39 ?

Gaade, Mr., of Norway 20/8/85
Gabba, Carlo Francesco 1/4/77 ?
Gabbitas,
E. 7/11/67
H., messenger 22/10/53, 6/1/60 n
P. 16/2/87
Gabitas, William, of Newark 13/1/35
Gäbler, B., philologist 18/9/53
Gadaleta, O. F., of Italy 15/9/53
Gadesden, V. 1/10/90
Gadesdon, A. W. 22/1/66 ?
Gadsby, John, publisher 5/11/78
Gaekwar of Baroda 21/6/92
Gaffihin, Mr. 6/11/79
Gaffney,
George, physician 25/1/51 ?
J. P. 18/10/88
Gage,
T., 1st Viscount Gage 19/4/35 n
Thomas Wentworth, Rev. (1801-1837) 19/4/35 ?
Gähring, M., of Switzerland? 19/6/76
Gainsborough *see* Noel
Gaisford,
Alice Mary, Lady (1836-1892), née Kerr 3/11/65 ff, 15/5/79
Thomas (-1898) 3/11/65 n
Thomas, Dean (1779-1855), dean of Christ Church, regius professor of Greek, editor & publisher 24/9/31 n
Galbraith *see* Percy
Galbraith,
Henry, Rev. 29/10/77
Joseph Allen, Rev. (1819-1890), of Dublin 17/3/58 ?
Gale,
F. 1/3/78
Harrison 19/7/77
John, bookbinder of Liverpool 17/3/26
Richard, picture dealer 12/2/56
Galeotto, L., editor of Italy 18/12/50
Galiero, Sig. 13/2/90
Galindo, Samuel, writer 1/11/56
Galiotti, Sig. 29/7/62
Gall, James, publisher 27/7/48 ?
Gallagher, John, of Belfast 6/10/75

Galleano, A. L., of Italy 20/10/51
Gallenga,
Mrs. 3/1/78
Antonio Carlo Napoleone (1810–1895) 21/6/77, 31/7/78
Galletti,
Sig. 4/1/89
Guiseppe (1798–1873), liberal minister in Papal States 27/7/49
Galley, Edmund 16/8/81
Gallimore, H. 18/11/79
Gall & Inglis, publishers in Edinburgh 27/7/48 n
Gallini, Francis Cecil, Rev., Roman Catholic 4/3/76 ?
Galloway *see* Stewart
Galloway,
A., Sir (1780–1850), Knight (1848), major general 9/11/39
A. H., furniture dealer of London 15/7/68
R. 18/11/74
William, Dr., physician of Dundee 30/12/85
William Brown, Rev. 20/9/78 ?
Gallwey,
Thomas, British consul in Naples 10/11/50
William Payne-, Sir (1807–1881), Peelite M.P. 11/7/55
Galt,
Alexander Tilloch, Sir (1817–1893), Knight (1878), of Canada 17/12/59, 23/3/76, 5/5/80
William, writer on railways 8/8/43 n
Galt, Kerruish & Gent, printers 1/3/55
Galton,
Arthur, critic 27/6/87, 29/6/87
Douglas Strutt, Sir (1822–1899), Capt. R. E. 22/11/64, 1/12/65, 16/2/69 L, 18/2/69 L
Frances Anne Violetta, née Darwin 19/1/33
Francis, Sir (1822–1911), eugenist 19/5/32 n, 19/1/33 n, 14/6/90 n
Samuel Tertius (1783–1844), banker 19/5/32 ff, 19/1/33 ?
Galway *see* Arundell, Monckton
Gambart, Mr. 15/2/92
Gambetta, Léon (1838–1882) 18/10/79 n, 1/1/82, 4/1/82 n
Gamble,
David, Col., of St. Helens 5/8/68
Richard Wilson (–1887), lawyer of Ireland 2/7/53 ?
Gamgee, Arthur, Prof. 3/7/77
Gamlin,
Mr., tenant of Hawarden 19/8/79
E. 5/4/87
Hilda, Mrs. 23/12/89
Gammage, Robert George (1815–1888), chartist 28/11/55
Gammoll, G. B. 28/1/90
Gamon, Mr., Hawarden farmer 30/9/85
Gandell, W. F. 14/2/80
Ganderton, Mr. 19/8/79
Gansden, Mr.jnr 23/12/78
Garaghty, Mr. 20/5/87
Garbett,
E. R. 29/12/89
James, Prof. (1802–1879), professor of poetry 14/11/31
Garcia, Jacob & Co. 18/10/90 ?
Garden,
Francis, Rev. (1810–1884), editor 16/12/31
William Alexander, Col. 14/9/79
Gardener,
Voltaire's 14/7/32
The, at C. H. 1/2/50
Gardeners, Society of, 20/1/75
Gardenman, the, of Fasque 22/9/47
Gardiner *see* Bruce
Gardiner,
Ingram, Mrs., of London 30/6/93
Robert William, Sir, soldier 23/1/60
Samuel Rawson (1829–1902), historian 13/2/84, 16/4/91, 31/8/91 n
W. 11/6/92
Gardiners, livery stables 21/12/25
Gardiner & Son, stationers 5/12/36
Gardner,
A. 31/1/79
Dyce, Mrs. 18/12/71
Edward, of Downpatrick 12/6/75
Herbert Coulstoun (1846–1921), 1st Baron Burghclere (1895), liberal M.P. 25/6/77, 9/11/87, 10/6/90, 23/3/92, 17/12/92 L, 26/1/93
John, doctor 14/4/45 ?
Richard (1813–1856), radical M.P. 27/6/48 ?
Robert, merchant 10/6/46 ?
Samuel, cabinet maker of Chester 2/10/49
William Wells, publisher 14/6/75
Winifred, Lady, née Herbert 6/5/90
Gardson, S. 18/8/89
Garey, G. O. 9/5/76
Garfield,
James Abram, President (1831–1881) 21/7/81 n
Lucretia, Mrs. 21/7/81 L
Garibaldi, Giuseppe 10/4/64 n
Garland, F., Miss 20/10/75
Garment, W. H. 24/11/88
Garnett,
F. E., author 23/11/91
H., of York 1/9/55
William James (1818–1873), liberal M.P. 20/3/60
Garrabe, of Roanne 27/10/50
Garrard, R. & S., goldsmiths 17/6/62
Garratt, Thomas, Rev. (1796–1841) 5/3/28

Garrett,
Charles, Rev., Wesleyan 1/2/67
Charles B., Dr. 14/5/61
Garrick, E. 16/5/78
Garrick Theatre 18/3/90
Garriott, Mr., brewer 10/3/62 ?
Garrivon, Mrs., of U.S.A. 20/6/92
Garth, Evelyn, Miss 23/4/84
Gartshore,
John Murray-, soldier 22/7/48 n
Mary Murray- (-1851), née Douglas 22/7/48
Garvey, Richard, Rev., headmaster of Lincoln Grammar School, pluralist 15/12/39
Garwood, W. W. 14/11/88
Gascoigne,
Mrs., rescue 21/7/83
William Julius, Col. 15/6/91 ?
Gascoygne *see* Cecil
Gascoyne, I. 20/4/31 n
Gaskell *see* Wintour
Gaskell,
Benjamin (1781-1855), whig M.P. 8/9/29 n
Charles George Milnes- (1842-1919), liberal M.P. 5/2/73, 23/10/83 L, 1/11/83 ff, 24/6/86
Daniel 17/9/29 n
H., of Southport 18/10/68
James Milnes- 26/6/26
Mary, née Heywood 18/10/32
Mary (-1845), née Brandreth 9/9/29
Mary Milnes- (-1869), née Williams-Wynn 4/6/32 n
P. 19/3/39
Gason,
Dr., Irish physician of Rome 23/10/66
J. 22/7/75
Gasparin, A. de, Count 10/1/71
Gaspey, Thomas (-1871), author, editor 26/4/44, 29/7/50
Gasquet,
Francis Aidan, Cardinal (1846-1929) 10/10/89
Joseph, Dr. 8/11/65 ?
Gass, Matthew, pamphleteer 23/10/75
Gassiot, Charles, art dealer 14/6/75
Gasterstein, Mr. 31/7/88
Gates, Philip Chasemore, lawyer 29/3/48 ?
Gattie, William, of Brighton 30/10/67
Gattina, Ferdinando Petruccelli della (1815-1890), author of Italy, conspirator 30/7/51, 29/1/66, 19/5/77
Gatty,
Charles Tindal, antiquarian 16/9/78
William, Dr. 20/8/75 ?
Gaughran, Father 30/10/77
Gaulin, M. 7/1/88
Gaulois, Le 20/10/79
Gaunt, R. M., Rev. 10/10/78
Gausden, Mr. 1/4/79
Gaussen, François Samuel Robert Louis, Prof. (1790-1863), of systematic theology at evangelical college 15/7/32
Gausser, Frederick Charles (-1867), barrister 30/4/46 ?
Gavard, Charles, diplomat of France 24/5/71
Gavarre, Sig., opera singer 9/6/87
Gavazzi, Alessandro, Rev. (1809-1889), Roman Catholic 12/3/51, 26/3/51
Gavin, George O'Halloran, Maj. (1810-1880), liberal M.P. 11/2/65, 11/3/68
Gawne, Miss 31/1/77
Gawthern, Francis Secker, Rev. (-1855) 27/10/49 ?
Gay,
Henri, Col., of Paris 16/8/78
William, Rev. (1801-1846) 30/3/34
Gayfere, Thomas, Rev. 5/4/33
Gaylard, Thomas, dustbin inspector 19/7/77
Geale *see* Fortescue
Geale, J. Hamilton (1820-), writer of Dublin 11/12/51
Geare,
William, barrister 18/2/57 n
William, Mrs. 18/2/57
Geary,
Miss 3/7/88
C. 25/5/47 ?
Francis 12/11/68
Francis, Sir (1811-1895), 4th Baronet (1877) 3/6/35
John, Rev. 30/7/45
Joseph, whitesmith of Newark 6/8/36
Geddes,
C. 14/12/78
William Duguid, Sir (1828-1900), Knight (1892) 4/3/74
Geddis, J. W. J., poet 16/9/84
Gedge, John Wycliffe, Rev. 17/8/76 ?
Gee,
Robert, Rev. (1786-1861), wrangler 22/8/32
Thomas, Rev. (1815-1898), publisher and Methodist minister 20/6/92
Geffroy, Edmund Aimé F. (-1895), actor of France 22/10/50
Geflowski, Emanuel Edward, sculptor 9/11/74, 9/1/75, 20/4/75
Gehlsen, H. J. 14/3/87
Geikie, John Cunningham, Rev. Dr. (1824-1906) 3/7/77
Geldart,
Edmund Martin, Rev., unitarian 8/1/80
John, Dr. 15/1/33 ?
Gell,
James, Sir (1823-1905), of Isle of Man 1/10/78
J. H., of Birmingham 4/10/58

Gell (*cont.*)
John Philip, Rev. 16/11/49
Philip Lyttelton (1852–1926), imperialist and publisher 26/11/91
Gellan, William 15/6/77
Gellatly, William, of Dundee 14/8/86
Gemmall, John Alexander, Canadian author 19/4/89
Gemmell, Thomas M., of Ayr 27/2/75
Gennadios, Ioannes, Minister of Greece 16/1/77, 21/1/77
Genoa *see* Ferdinand
Gentile,
Marchese, of Naples 29/2/52
Pietro, Cardinal 24/3/79
Geohegan, Mr. 25/12/87
George I, King (1845–), of the Hellenes 20/7/76
George III, King of Great Britain 5/6/26 n
George IV, King of Great Britain 2/7/30 n
George V,
(–1878), of Hanover 28/6/53
(1865–1936) Duke of York (1892), Prince of Wales, King of Great Britain 20/3/65, 15/8/82, 6/6/85, 18/12/92, 16/2/93, 4/5/93 L, 7/6/93, 6/7/93
George,
2nd Duke of Cumberland 2/6/43 n
Messrs., booksellers 16/10/88
David Lloyd (1863–1945), liberal M.P. 29/5/90, 12/9/92 n
Henry (1839–1897), land reformer 11/11/79, 26/12/83 n, 27/12/83
J. B. 9/5/89
John, Rev. 19/7/79 ?
John Durance, dentist 17/8/48
W. H. 3/3/88
George Victor (1831–1893), Prince of Waldeck (1845) 18/8/38 n
George William Frederick Charles; Duke of Cambridge 4/12/40 n
Gerahty, Mr. 13/3/88
Gerald,
rescue 24/4/69
Mrs., rescue 12/2/77
Gerard,
G. P., a pauper? 28/4/45 ?, 4/7/48
Robert Tolver, Sir (1808–1887), 13th Baronet (1865), 1st Baron Gerard (1876) 27/4/69
Gerbel, C. N. von, poet 5/8/78
Gerdi, E. 31/12/88
Gerhard, Eduard, Prof. (1795–1867), archaeologist of Prussia 28/5/32, 22/4/61
Gerhardi, L. L. 11/4/87
Gersdorff, von, Baron, ambassador of Saxony 11/6/44
Gertig, Jul. 20/2/79
Geshov, Ivan Dimitrov 29/4/79
Gex, Edward Peter de, solicitor 13/7/55 ?
Gherardini, Madam, art collector 11/2/54
Ghica, Ioan, Prince, of Rumania 16/5/66
Ghosa, Mavernohose 1/12/91
Ghose, Lal Mohun 15/5/79, 23/5/79
Giacchetti, Francesco 21/11/79
Giallina, Sig., of Ionia 2/12/58
Gialussi, Aristide, Dr. 3/8/75
Giani, Padre 7/4/94
Gibb,
Henry Moyes, hotelier of Edinburgh 24/10/44
James, of Liverpool 18/6/60 ?
T. A. & Co., East India merchants 12/6/56 n
T. E. 24/9/87
Gibb & Bruce,
Messrs. 5/1/87
Messrs. 15/12/86
Gibbings, James, Rev., professor 12/6/43 ?
Gibbon,
Alex., pamphleteer 21/9/50
David, of Middle Temple 18/9/35 ?
Edward, historian 13/7/32, 14/7/32
Edward Howard Howard- (–1849), herald 19/10/44
Gibbons,
Alexander, of Johnstone 1/9/37
Benjamin, iron-master of Kingswinford 24/7/48
Gibbs,
Frederick Waymouth (1821–1898), tutor to Edward VII 26/6/57
Henry Hucks (1819–1907), 1st Baron Aldenham (1896), banker, tory M.P. 6/9/79, 21/10/93
John, Ven. (–1890), of Down 11/8/57
William, merchant 5/10/42
William A. 24/2/76
Gibbs, Bright & Co., of Liverpool 1/10/56 n
Gibbs & Co., bankers of Genoa 10/3/32
Gibburn, Mr., of Fasque 13/9/50
Giblin, William Robert, Prime Minister of Tasmania 9/9/84 L
Gibson,
Mr., of Aberdeenshire 28/2/87
David Cooke (–1857), artist 27/6/54
H. C. W. 4/8/88
Henry, cooper of London 30/5/64 ?
James, educational commissioner of Ireland 26/4/73
J. Burns, Dr. 12/3/80
John (1790–1866), sculptor 2/4/32, 12/11/66
John, Rev. 5/4/45
Susanna Milner- (–1885), née Cullum 13/7/58

Thomas Ellison 16/11/63, 24/8/69, 1/9/69, 2/11/76
Thomas Milner- (1806–1884), liberal M.P. 10/7/46, 26/5/59, 30/5/60, 12/4/61, 13/4/61, 14/4/61, 1/3/62, 6/3/62, 5/2/85
Giers, Nikolai Karlovich (1820–1895), minister of Russia 15/1/81, 21/9/92
Giffard,
George Markham, Sir (1813–1870), Knight (1868) 20/12/68
Hardinge Stanley (1823–1921), Earl of Halsbury, tory M.P. and lord chancellor 26/12/41 n
John Walter de Longueville (1817–1888), barrister 18/7/77 ?
Stanley Lees, editor 26/12/41
Giffen, Robert, Sir (1837–1920), Knight (1895) 22/4/79, 23/7/79, 26/12/83, 27/12/83, 14/1/86
Gifford *see* Hay
Gifford,
Edwin Hamilton, Ven. (1820–1905) 9/4/88 ?
John George, Rev. 26/4/40
Robert Francis (1817–1872), 2nd Baron Gifford 22/4/58
Stanley L., Dr. 11/8/35
Gigante, Giacinto (–1876), painter 9/12/50
Gigot, Albert 16/10/80 L
Gilbart, James William (1794–1863), banker 8/12/60
Gilbert *see* Kerr
Gilbert,
Ashurst Turner, Bp. (1786–1870), bishop of Chichester (1842) 22/1/32
Elizabeth, Miss, of Chichester 3/4/68
Elizabeth Margaretta Maria, Miss, charity worker 11/5/63, 7/5/75
George Hine, spirit dealer 6/8/74 ?
H. M. 21/12/75
Philip Parker, Rev. (1812–1886) 17/11/63
Thomas Webb 27/11/55
William Schwenck, Sir (1836–1911) 21/2/78 n
Gilbert & Fowler, Messrs. 8/10/91
Gilbertson, J. D., poet 5/5/57 ff
Gilbey, E. M., Miss 30/3/75
Gilby,
Miss, teacher of Newark 29/5/45
Mrs., of Newark 30/5/43
H. P. 19/5/76
William Robinson, Rev., wrangler 12/9/29 ff, 17/10/32
Gildea, George Robert, Rev. (1803–1887), provost of Tuam (1872) 12/2/39
Gilderson, T. 1/4/91
Giles,
C. E. 27/4/76
F. W. 10/6/68
Henry, Dr., surgeon 4/3/50
J. Alfred 3/9/76, 24/9/76, 8/10/76
J. H., Mrs. 26/2/78
John Allen, Rev. 16/2/48
John Douglas, Ven. (1812–1867) 7/6/65
Gilfillan, Mr. 27/1/79
Gilford *see* Meade
Gilkes, A. H., Rev. 12/7/87
Gill,
George Wadman, chemist 14/4/57
Henry, master mariner and captain of Liverpool 2/1/27
Henry Joseph (1836–), home rule M.P. 28/9/86
Jeremiah Cresswell, Rev. 12/2/78
John, liberal of Sheffield 21/4/89
John William (1810–), servitor 7/6/29
Paul 22/8/78
Thomas Howard, Rev. (1836–1894) 30/10/58
Gillanders,
Arbuthnot & Co., of Calcutta 20/7/76 n
George (1805–1846), merchant of Calcutta 3/7/33
Gillespie,
Charles George Knox, Rev. 17/9/85 ?
James, surgeon 13/9/79 ?
Robert 12/2/42
Robert Rollo, Col. (1830–1890) 8/8/76 ?
Gillett, J. C. & A., banker of Banbury 31/10/68
Gillgrass, Samuel, of Leeds 6/9/75
Gilliard, rescue 12/7/62
Gillies,
Adam (1760–1842), judge of Scotland 4/1/37
D. 3/4/91
H. C., Dr. 15/11/91
Robert Pearse (1788–1858) 14/7/58, 18/8/58
Gillig,
Mr. 3/7/88
C. A. 8/10/86
Gilliland, M. 11/2/91
Gillis, James, Bp. (1802–1864), vicar apostolic 27/2/43 n
Gillman,
Henry, American consul in Jerusalem 14/8/86, 9/11/86
James, Rev. (–1877) 13/8/58
Gillon, Andrew 22/3/80
Gillow,
Joseph (1850–), historian 22/10/88
Mary Anne (–1890), née Eyston 13/5/51
Richard Thomas (1806–), of Lancashire 13/5/51 n
Gillson,
Joseph, grocer of Newark 18/5/43
Thomas, merchant of Newark 8/2/38

Gill & Sons, Messrs. 13/11/77
Gilly, William Stephen, Rev. (1789–1855) 6/3/32
Gilpin, Charles (1815–1874), liberal M.P. 10/7/57
Gilston, P. 9/1/78, 9/1/79
Gilstrap, Joseph, innkeeper, mayor of Newark 19/12/34
Giltspur, C. 14/10/87
Ginsberg, Mrs. 25/7/79
Ginsburg, Christian David, Rev. Dr. (1831–1914), scholar 26/3/79, 15/7/83, 16/11/91 ff, 14/12/91 ff, 5/3/92, 11/3/92 ff, 30/3/92, 12/4/93
Ginuti, Cardinal 26/12/76
Giorgio, a horse 17/10/38
Giovanni, Michele Di, Italian advocate 6/3/75, 1/6/83
Gipps, Henry, Rev. (–1832) 17/6/32
Girard, Pierre, journalist 15/2/72
Girardin, Émile de, politician of France 28/1/67, 16/10/79
Girardot, C. E. 14/1/90
Giraud, Henry Arthur, Rev. (1818–1879) 5/5/57, 27/4/59
Girdlestone,
  Charles, Rev. (1797–1881) 18/1/29
  James, solicitor 11/10/77
Girolamo, Gaetano di, Barone, innkeeper 26/10/38
Girton College, of Cambridge 21/4/77
Girvan, Mr. 26/1/78
Gisborne, Thomas (1794–1852), radical M.P. 31/3/35
Gisdale, G. G. 24/5/90
Giudice, Signor 4/2/89
Giurlio, Luigi Prota-, Rev. 11/10/75
Giustiani, shopkeeper 22/11/38
Givan, John (1837–), liberal M.P. 10/9/81 L
Gladstone *see* Bennett, Buckley, Corry, Drew, Dumaresq, Goalen, Hardy, Lake, Larkins, Ogilvy, Wickham, Wildes
Gladstone,
  Adam Steuart, Col. (1814–1863), cousin, son of Robert G, Liverpool merchant 26/5/35, 3/7/61
  Albert Charles, Sir (1886–1967), 5th Baronet (1945) 28/10/86, 10/11/86
  Alice, niece, daughter of J. N. G 12/2/62
  Anne (mother) 17/7/25
  Anne (1839–1885), niece, daughter of T. G 30/9/50, 27/1/85
  Anne Mackenzie (sister) 18/7/27
  Annie Crosthwaite (–1931), née Wilson, daughter-in-law, wife of Stephen G 4/4/44 n, 20/12/84, 3/1/85, 29/1/85, 13/6/92
  Arthur Robertson (1841–1896), nephew, son of Robertson G 28/10/56, 13/1/58, 28/9/75, 28/1/80
  Catherine (wife) 23/7/38
  Catherine (1885–1947), grand-daughter, daughter of Stephen G 26/5/87
  Catherine Jessy (daughter) 27/7/45
  Charles Alexander (1824–1855), cousin, soldier, son of David G 5/12/54
  Charles Andrew (1888–1968), 6th Baronet, grandson, son of Stephen G 28/10/88, 4/11/88
  Charles Elsden, Capt. (1855–), cousin, son of Robert G 27/4/78
  Charlotte Louisa Alexandrina (–1884), née Kendrick, cousin's wife, wife of William G of London 30/6/58, 5/5/61, 4/8/79
  Constance Elizabeth, godchild, daughter of J. N. G 20/5/50, 30/1/77
  Constance Gertrude (1883–1963), daughter of W. H. G, grand-daughter 27/5/83
  C. W., Mrs., distant relative 27/4/62
  David (1783–1863), uncle, father's partner 14/12/25
  David Thomas, Rev. (1823–1888), cousin, son of David G 21/10/47, 1/7/65
  Elizabeth Honoria (–1862), brother John's wife 13/7/38 n, 18/1/62 ff, 2/2/62 ff
  Emily Anina, née Wynn 12/8/74
  Emmeline (–1885), née Ramsden, wife of David G 13/9/27
  Evelyn Catherine (1882–1958), daughter of W. H. G, grand-daughter 5/1/82, 8/6/82, 3/9/82, 28/4/93, 9/5/93
  Evelyn Marcella (1847–1852), daughter of T. G 30/9/50, 26/1/52
  Frances Margaret (1850–1853), daughter of T. G 30/9/50 n
  George Herbert (1860–), son of Rev. D. T. G 10/9/88, 11/3/92
  Gertrude, née Stuart, wife of W. H. G (1875), daughter-in-law 5/10/58 n, 21/7/75 ff, 30/9/75, 26/1/76, 27/4/76, 8/4/83, 22/4/83, 27/5/83 n, 25/6/85, 7/8/85, 17/5/87, 16/4/89, 8/9/90, 4/7/91, 8/7/91 ff, 1/8/91 ff, 7/9/91 ff, 1/12/91, 24/3/92, 28/4/92, 7/10/93, 20/10/93
  Helen, née Monteath, cousin's wife 28/5/57
  Helen (1810–1869), cousin 7/9/26
  Helen (daughter) 28/8/49
  Helen Jane (sister) 18/7/25
  Helen Neilson (1801–1881), cousin, daughter of Thomas G 7/9/26
  Henry Neville (son) 2/4/52
  Herbert John (son) 7/1/54
  Hugh (1777–1835), uncle, sailmaker 5/8/25
  Hugh, Mrs. 1/7/45
  Hugh Jones (1843–1874), nephew, son of Robertson G 13/1/58, 2/8/74, 5/8/74
  Hugh W., cousin 1/7/45 n
  Hugh Williamson (1851–1883), cousin, son

of John Murray G 2/9/82, 11/9/82, 18/9/82, 7/10/82 ff
Ida (1850–1874), niece, Thomas G's daughter 30/9/50, 11/5/73, 1/8/73, 10/8/73, 5/10/73, 29/3/74, 24/6/74, 30/6/74
I. N., Miss 16/1/89
James (1775–1832), uncle, Liverpool iron merchant 7/9/26 n
James (1811–1862), cousin, son of James G the elder 9/3/57, 28/5/57
James Wyld, of Biggar 19/7/58
Jane Hall (–1798), née Hall, Sir J. G's 1st wife 7/8/26 n
Janet (–1846), née Strong, aunt, wife of Thomas G 13/1/27
Janet Forest (1801–1850), cousin 13/9/27
Janet Strong (Jessie) (1829–1886), cousin, daughter of Hugh G 3/1/32, 27/11/43
John (–1852), nephew, son of Robertson G 5/5/38, 8/1/40
John, Sir (father) 16/7/25
John Eddowes, Rev. (1814–1901), cousin 21/10/39
John Evelyn, Sir (1855–1945), 4th Baronet (1926), nephew, son of J. N. G 12/9/64
John Hall, Prof. (1827–1902), not related; London liberal 25/7/68
John McAdam (1808–1835), cousin, son of Robert G (1st) 3/9/33, 7/11/35
John Murray, Rev. (1803–1869), cousin, son of Hugh G 4/1/26, 3/7/26
John Neilson, Capt. (brother) 14/9/25
John Robert, Sir (1852–1926), 3rd Baronet (1889), nephew, son of T. G 2/6/52, 25/3/89 ff, 31/10/90, 2/1/91
Louisa (–1885), niece, daughter of T. G 6/8/37, 2/12/81, 1/7/84, 7/10/84, 8/10/84
Louisa (–1901), née Fellowes, sister-in-law, wife of T. G 16/7/35, 21/7/56, 7/10/58, 10/1/80 ff, 26/3/89
Margaret (May) Neilson, Miss (1820–1871), cousin, daughter of Hugh G 29/3/55, 14/10/57
Mary Ellen (1840–1895), niece, daughter of Robertson G 1/5/40
Mary Ellen, Mrs. (–1865), née Jones, sister-in-law, unitarian wife of R. G 5/11/35, 29/9/65, 3/10/65
Mary Selina (1842–), niece, daughter of T. G 30/9/50
Maud Ernestine (–1941), née Rendel, Lady Gladstone, daughter-in-law, wife of H. N. G 18/9/89 ff, 29/1/90, 30/1/90
Montgomerie (1817–1880), cousin, son of Robert G 7/9/35
Murray (1st) (1770–1841), uncle 6/8/25
Murray (2nd) (1816–1875), cousin, son of Robert G 7/8/74, 28/8/75
Murray (3rd) (1848–1928), cousin, son of Murray G (2nd) 7/8/74, 12/8/74 n, 28/8/75
Robert (1st) (1773–1835), uncle, merchant 11/8/25
Robert (2nd) (1811–1872), cousin, Manchester merchant 23/7/26, 7/9/35
Robert (3rd) (1833–1919), cousin, son of T. S. G 1/5/40 n, 15/2/60 n
Robertson (brother) 2/8/25
Robertson (2nd) (1844–1893), nephew, son of Robertson G (1st) 13/2/54, 14/9/65, 28/9/75
Robert Steuart (1839–1909), cousin 20/6/92 ?
Samuel Steuart (1837–1909), cousin 21/4/81, 20/6/92
Stephen Edward, Rev. (son) 4/4/44
Susannah (1st) (–1833), née Finchett, aunt, wife of Murray G 6/8/25 n
Susannah (2nd) (1816–1844), cousin, daughter of James G 3/1/32
Thomas (1st) (1772–1844), uncle, ship's chandler 6/8/25
Thomas (2nd), Sir (brother) 23/8/25
Thomas Murray (1807–1877), cousin, Liverpool ironfounder 23/12/37
Thomas Steuart (1805–1882), cousin, Dumfriess-shire landowner, son of Robert G 30/4/27, 7/9/35
Walter Longueville (1846–1919), nephew, son of Robertson G 18/9/75
William (1809–1873), cousin, London merchant, son of Robert G 31/7/32, 7/9/35, 5/5/61, 10/3/73
William Glynne Charles (1885–1915), heir of Hawarden, grandson (son of W. H. G) 14/7/85, 7/8/85, 6/1/87, 27/4/87, 1/7/89, 10/7/89, 30/11/89, 9/7/91 ff, 18/8/91, 21/10/92, 27/7/96
William Henry (son) 3/6/40
Glaiser, J. W. 30/11/88
Glanville,
E. S., of Dublin 24/11/77
James, chartered accountant 16/2/75 ?
Glasgow *see* Boyle
Glasgow,
Anne 30/3/32
Robert Robertson-, the elder (–1845), né Robertson 30/3/32
Robert Robertson-, the younger (1811–1860), advocate, J. P. 23/12/33
Glass, Richard Atwood, Sir (1820–1873), Knight (1866), tory M.P. 24/8/60 n
Glass, Elliot & Co., telegraph cable manufacturers 24/8/60

Glasse, Frederick Henry Hastings, Capt. (-1884) 15/11/58, 13/3/65
Glasser, E. 16/5/78
Glass & Henderson, merchants of Liverpool 18/11/68
Gledhill, James Tidewell, merchant 12/1/76 ?
Gledstanes, John Hampden, merchant 27/5/53
Gleig, George Robert, Rev. 13/2/46
Glenalmond *see* Patton
Glencorse *see* Inglis
Glendinning,
Mrs. 25/10/88
Peter, of Dalmeny 29/3/80
Glenelg *see* Grant
Glenn, Messrs. 17/3/90
Glennie,
John David, Rev. (1795–1874) 27/4/59
John Irving, lawyer 6/11/44
John Stuart Stuart 8/7/79
Glennon, J. 14/11/89
Gliamas, Col. 19/4/52
Gloag, Archibald Robertson, Gen. 16/9/87
Gloucester *see* Mary, William Frederick
Glover,
Messrs., insurance agents 17/6/65
Frederick Robert Augustus, Rev. (1800–1881), author 28/8/39
James Grey, Dr. (-1908) 30/5/68
John Hawley, Sir (-1885) 2/8/73, 14/8/73, 30/8/73, 17/11/73, 16/12/73
S. M. 11/9/77
William, Serj. (1829–1870), serjeant-at-law 28/10/67
W. Sutton 27/1/77 ?
Gluck, James Fraser, American bibliophile 2/10/86
Gluckstein, Leopold 6/10/76
Glyn,
Carr John, Rev. (1799–1896) 4/2/65
Frederick (1861–1932), 4th Baron Wolverton (1888), banker 15/6/89, 12/4/93
George Carr (1797–1873), 1st Baron Wolverton, liberal M.P. and banker 11/3/41 n
George Grenfell 9/2/67
Georgiana Maria (-1894), née Tufnell, Lady Wolverton 26/6/68
Pascoe Charles (1833–1904), banker 6/7/86 L, 6/11/91
Richard Plumptre, Sir, 2nd Baronet 14/6/50 n
Glyn, Halifax & Co., bankers 14/6/50
Glynne *see* Gladstone, Lyttelton, Pennant
Glynne,
Catherine (-1854), daughter of Henry Glynne 12/8/50
Henry, Rev. 31/1/36
Honora (-1859) 1/1/48
Lavinia, née Lyttelton, sister-in-law 16/7/40
Mary 12/8/50, 20/8/72, 26/8/72, 6/9/75
Mary, Lady (-1854), née Neville 7/7/39, 25/7/39, 3/12/39, 4/12/39, 19/9/40, 5/1/41, 3/2/41, 19/5/41, 9/9/48, 24/3/54, 3/4/54, 19/4/54, 13/5/54, 15/5/54, 20/5/54, 3/6/54, 6/6/54, 18/7/54, 15/8/54, 20/9/54
Stephen Richard, Sir (-1815), 8th Baronet 7/7/39 n
Stephen Richard, Sir 17/10/28
Goad, John (1825–1886), marble supplier 9/12/67 ?
Goadby,
Edwin, of London 13/12/89
Joseph Jackson, Rev. (1828–1898), baptist 8/4/80
M. 6/3/90
Goalen,
Mrs., of Laurencekirk, wife of Rev. W. M. Goalen 26/9/43
Alexander, banker 23/4/28
Alexander, Rev. (-1872), don 25/3/56 n, 11/5/59 n, 17/6/66
Helen, Mrs. (-1869), née Gladstone, cousin 25/3/56, 31/5/57, 11/5/59
Robert Alexander Gladstone, godson 31/12/56
T. 19/2/70
Thomas, iron founder of Liverpool 19/9/27
Thomas, Mrs., née Gladstone, aunt (sister of Sir J. G) 19/9/27
Walter Mitchell, Rev., of Laurencekirk 26/2/29, 26/9/43 n
W. N. 21/5/59, 24/5/59
Gobat, Samuel Benoni, Rev. (-1873) 31/12/72, 2/1/73, 3/1/73, 4/1/73
Godbolt, A. 19/9/88
Goddard,
A. 1/10/86
D. F. 15/11/89
Godden, N. 25/3/76
Goddry, Mrs. 21/3/70
Goderich *see* Robinson
Godfray, Frederick, Rev. Dr. (1822–1868) 9/3/57, 17/6/57
Godfrey,
rescue 15/8/60
Edward Smith, chairman of Gladstone's election committee 31/7/32
George, cigar importer 30/6/68
J. P. 16/5/79
Thomas S., mayor of Newark 27/9/32
Thomas S., Mrs. 2/10/32
Godkin, James (1806–1879), journalist of Ireland 7/6/67

Godley,
Denis (1823–1890) 3/11/77
George, of Newark 27/12/75
John Arthur (1847–1932), 1st Baron Kilbracken (1909) 26/8/72, 11/10/72, 21/11/72, 13/12/75 ff, 10/11/76 n, 18/3/77, 10/9/77, 6/12/77, 16/8/78 ff, 12/12/78, 19/12/78, 10/1/80, 6/5/80 ff, 10/5/80 ff, 12/7/80 ff, 31/7/80, 22/11/80 ff, 28/2/81 ff, 6/1/82 ff, 15/8/82 n, 1/1/83 L, 16/4/83 L, 26/10/83, 12/11/83, 1/12/83, 9/2/84 L, 6/10/84, 22/4/85, 4/8/85, 13/9/85, 12/2/86 ff, 30/3/87, 10/11/87, 29/3/89, 3/10/89, 4/10/89, 6/10/92, 29/4/93 ff, 6/3/94 n, 3/4/94 ff
John Robert (1814–1861), colonist 9/2/49, 1/12/53 ff, 5/5/57
Sarah (–1921), née James 11/10/72
Godson, Richard (1797–1849), liberal-conservative M.P., Q. C. 11/5/33
Godwin,
John Venimore, mayor of Bradford 19/7/66
Mary (1759–1797), née Wollstonecraft, author 28/11/83, 29/11/83
W. J. 17/2/77
Gofton, Story 1/7/87
Goita, Francesco, of Spain 29/12/91, 25/9/93 L
Golding, Joseph, Rev. (1756–1848) 4/5/28 ?
Goldsmid,
Augustus, of Metropolitan Working Men's Tory Association 4/12/67 ?
F. H., Sir, lawyer, M.P. 7/2/48
Julia, Lady 26/10/82, 27/6/83, 13/7/83, 21/3/85
Julian, Sir (1838–1896), 3rd Baronet (1878), liberal M.P. 28/6/66, 22/4/72, 27/6/83
Nathaniel (1817–1860), barrister 4/7/43
Goldsmith *see* Copley
Goledu, Stephen, foreign minister of Rumania 9/8/67
Golescu, N., publicist of Rumania 4/5/58
Golia, Gaetano, Don, prisoner of Naples 12/2/51
Goltz, Robert van der 21/12/58
Gomall, James, Rev., nonconformist 13/3/74
Gomm,
Carr 23/11/93
Francis Culling Carr- 17/1/87
William Maynard, Sir, colonial governor 23/2/46
Gomme,
Mr. 14/2/78
G. L. 26/2/79
Gonache, Jules, journalist of France 4/11/64
Gondon, Jules, theologian of France 30/10/44
Gonsalez, Violet Elizabeth, Miss, author 12/8/89
Gonzadini, Giovanni, Sen. (–1887) 19/5/77
Gonzaga, Carlo Guerrieri, Marchesa 21/7/75
Gooch,
Frederick, Rev. (1804–1887) 21/10/27
John 15/2/75
Good, Augustus, cork manufacturer of London 14/10/50 ?
Goodacre, Alfred Randolph, Rev. (1839–1916) 26/10/68
Goodall,
Joseph (1760–1840), provost of Eton 21/1/27
Goodburn, E. 11/5/76
Goodday, James, Rev. (–1889) 23/6/59
Goode, William, Dean (1801–1868) 18/8/67
Goodenough, Robert William, Rev. (1809–1880) 18/10/32
Goodfellow, Stephen Jennings, Dr., physician 1/7/51
Goodford, Charles Old, Dr. (1812–1884), of Eton 1/9/48, 6/6/68
Goodhart,
Harry Chester, Prof. 15/12/91
Rose, née Rendel 15/12/91 n
Goodhew, William Stephen 30/6/79
Goodier, Mr. 13/8/74
Gooding, Mr., bailiff at Bowden 10/2/63
Goodkind, E. 21/8/89
Goodlake, Thomas William, Rev. (1811–1875) 22/10/60
Goodman,
Edward John 31/5/79
George, Sir (–1859), Knight (1852), liberal M.P. 18/12/54
Goodrich, Henry Painter, Rev. 22/7/76
Goodson, A. 25/2/78
Goodwin,
Harvey, Bp. (1818–1891) 11/7/55, 16/6/75, 8/9/81 L
John (–1869), consul at Palermo 15/10/38
Goodwyn, Henry, Gen. (–1886) 29/3/77
Gool, Mr. 5/4/80
Goold *see* Quin
Goolden, Walter 13/11/77
Goos, F., of U.S.A. 7/8/79
Gopcević, Spiridon, Montenegrin diplomat 11/9/79, 19/4/81 L
Gordon *see* Lindsay, Trotter
Gordon,
Mrs., rescue 9/3/68
Abercrombie Lockhart, Rev., educationist 2/2/39, 27/1/76
Alexander ('Bertie') Hamilton-, Gen. Sir (1817–1890), Knight (1873), soldier, equerry and M.P. 22/7/55, 12/5/56, 22/6/65, 28/11/79 n
Alex Cornewall Duff-, Sir (1811–1872), treasury clerk 5/2/49

Gordon (*cont.*)
Archibald, Gen. (1812–1886) 28/5/70
Arthur Charles Hamilton, Sir 1/7/51
A. W., of Edinburgh 3/4/80
Caroline Emelia Mary Hamilton-, née Herschell 23/2/55, 29/8/59
Charles (1847–1937), 11th Marquis of Huntly (1863) 16/7/70, 4/10/71
Charles, Col. 10/4/75
Charles George, Major General 22/1/84
Douglas 12/10/87
Douglas Hamilton-, Rev. (1824–1901) 21/12/60, 21/8/70, 24/9/87 ?
Edward Herbert, agent 1/12/32
Elizabeth, née Brodie, Duchess of Gordon 18/12/43
Fanny Duff-, Lady 20/5/74
George, 5th Duke of Gordon 18/12/43 n
George, Rev. (1764–1845) 10/12/39
George Hamilton-; Earl of Aberdeen 26/1/35
George John James Hamilton- (1816–1864), 5th Earl of Aberdeen (1860), Lord Haddo 10/6/51
George John Robert, of Ellon, diplomatist 22/5/52, 3/5/75 n
Henry William, Sir (1818–1887), brother and editor of C. G. Gordon 4/6/84, 30/7/84, 22/2/85 L, 20/3/85 L, 28/4/85 c
H. R. 7/12/86
Ishbel Maria, Lady Aberdeen 5/4/83 L, 17/12/83 n, 10/12/86, 1/12/87, 9/11/88, 17/7/89, 10/5/90, 25/2/91, 27/2/91 ff, 5/9/93 ff, 24/9/93
James Frederick Skinner, Rev. Dr. 28/5/68, 30/5/68
J. E., Lady, secretary of Protestant Association 23/6/34
John Campbell (1847–1934), 6th Earl of Aberdeen (1870), 1st Marquis of Aberdeen and Temair (1916) 12/1/70, 17/12/83, 15/9/84 ff, 10/12/86, 2/12/87 ff, 14/2/88, 10/3/88, 21/11/88 n, 19/5/89, 9/7/89, 5/12/89, 10/5/90, 26/2/91 ff, 19/3/91, 7/3/92, 21/8/92, 23/8/92, 11/3/93, 3/6/93, 5/9/93 ff
John Thomson (1813–1865), sheriff 11/7/55
Mary, née Baillie, Lady Haddo (1840) 10/6/51
Maurice Duff-, Sir 20/5/74 n
Osborne, Rev. (1813–1883), don 22/3/54, 30/1/57
Paul Joshua, solicitor of London 3/4/68
Richard, Rev. 25/3/76 ?
Robert (1787–1864), whig M.P., West Indies proprietor 18/3/33
Robert, Rear Adm. (1796–1869) 2/1/62
Robert, Rev. Dr., of Lauriston 20/4/28
Robert, Sir, diplomat 26/10/41
W. B., banker 10/5/54
William (1785–1858), captain, tory M.P. 16/1/44
William, Rev. 19/8/75 ?
William, Sir (1830–1906), 6th Baronet 3/11/85 ?
William Everard Alphonso, Capt. (1817–1906), Royal Navy 9/5/75
William Hamilton-, Vice Adm. (1755–1858), Royal Navy 3/4/37
W. J., Rev. 12/12/79
Gordon of Abergeldie 3/9/44 n
Gore *see* Underwood
Gore,
Charles, Bp. (1853–1932) 11/1/85, 12/1/85, 26/1/85, 5/7/85, 10/11/88, 12/11/88, 12/3/93 n, 20/3/93
Charles Alexander (–1897), commissioner of woods and forests 3/2/54
William Ormsby, M.P. 19/2/42
Goring, John, Rev. (–1905) 23/8/66
Gorle, J., author 27/6/55 ?
Gorloff, Gen. 24/10/76
Gorman, Thomas Murray, Rev. 25/8/76 ?, 25/3/90
Gormanston *see* Preston
Gornall, John, Rev. 13/8/74
Görres,
Guido 1/10/45
Johann Joseph von, publicist 1/10/45
Gorringe, Hugh 27/2/80 ?
Gorsham, J. 31/1/91
Gorst, John Eldon, Sir (1835–1916), tory M.P. and organisor 5/4/82, 21/7/85
Gort *see* Vereker
Gort, A. 25/4/87
Gorton, William Henry, Rev. (–1886) 7/8/52
Gortschakoff, Aleksandr Mikhailovich, Prince (1798–1883), foreign minister of Russia (1856) 8/11/70 n
Goryle, W. 27/6/55
Goschen,
George Joachim 13/2/64
Lucy, née Dalley, Lady Goschen 20/2/69
William Henry (–1866), banker 24/3/53
Gosford *see* Acheson
Goskirk 6/12/36
Gosling *see* Christie
Gosling, William Frederick, proctor 17/4/52
Goss,
Alexander, Bp. (1814–1872), bishop of Liverpool 13/3/66
John, Sir (1800–1880), Knight (1872), musician 8/3/72
Gossage, William, manufacturer of Liverpool 3/8/68

Gosse, Edmund William, Sir (1849–1928), essayist 5/11/89
Gosset, William, Sir, sergeant at arms 16/2/43
Gostwick,
Mrs. 1/8/90
Joseph 16/1/77
Got, Edmond-François-Jules (1822–1901), actor of France 11/10/79, 20/10/79
Gotley, G. H., Rev. 29/10/87
Gott,
husband of Margaret Gott 19/8/26
John, Rev. (1830–1906) 28/10/73
Joseph (1785–1860), sculptor 2/6/32
Margaret, née Ewart 19/8/26
Gough,
George Stephens, Sir (1815–1895), 2nd Viscount Gough (1869) 15/10/33 n
Hugh, Sir, 1st Viscount Gough 2/5/40 n
Jane, Lady, née Arbuthnot 15/10/33 ?
Peter 1/7/67
Thomas Bunbury, Very Rev., dean of Derry 2/5/40 ?
Gouland, Henry Godfrey, customs collector, of Port Victoria, New Zealand 15/10/51
Goulburn,
Catherine (–1865), née Montagu 24/4/35
Edward (1787–1860), judge 9/1/35 n, 28/3/37, 28/11/37
Edward, Col. (1816–1887), of Grenadier guards 29/12/38
Edward Meyrick, Rev., headmaster of Rugby 18/2/45
Frederick (1818–1878), of board of customs 21/6/59, 28/11/73
Henry, the elder (1784–1856), tory M.P., Chancellor of the Exchequer 28/3/37, 5/12/38, 11/2/40, 6/3/40, 12/2/44, 25/2/48, 29/2/48, 5/2/52, 31/3/52, 22/1/53, 31/12/53, 7/12/80
Henry, the younger (1813–1843), wrangler 24/4/35 n
Jane, née Montagu 19/5/42
Goulby, Jackson, Rev. 11/3/79
Gould,
rescue 28/2/68, 1/12/70
Henry, Rev. (1764–1839) 23/11/37
Louis Eugene, consul 17/2/81
Mrs. 1/3/71
Nathaniel 7/5/40
Sabine Baring-, Rev. (1834–1924) 1/1/79
Goulden, Alfred Benjamin Bernard, Rev. 7/2/80
Gounod, Charles (1818–1893), composer and conductor 10/7/72
Gouraud, G. E., Lieut. Col., Edison's European agent 18/12/88, 25/5/90, 25/9/90
Gourlay,
D. A., chairman, Gt. Yarmouth cttee. for the Gt. Exhibition 8/8/51
William Edmund Crawford Austin, Rev. (–1897) 23/3/54
Gourley, Edward Temperley, Sir (1828–1902), Knight (1895), liberal M.P. (1868) 10/10/71, 1/4/86 L
Gourrier, François Bonaventure, theologian of France 7/5/39
Govan,
Mr. 2/10/76
John 1/4/80
Govier, Mr. 9/12/78
Govoni, Marchese 2/2/88
Gowan,
Anthony Thomas, Rev. Princ. (1811–1884) 14/6/67
Franklin Benjamin, of U.S.A. 21/7/82
Gowdy, Mr. 22/6/93
Gowe, H. T. 9/5/90
Gower,
Albert Leveson-, Lord (1843–1874) 22/9/58, 12/8/66
Anne Leveson-, Lady (–1888), née Hay-MacKenzie, Duchess of Cromartie (1861), Lady Stafford, Duchess of Sutherland 7/5/53, 20/5/61
Castalia Rosalind Leveson- (1847–), Lady Granville 7/9/92
Cromartie Sutherland Leveson- (1851–1913), 4th Duke of Sutherland (1892) 7/10/92 L, 11/10/92 L
(Edward) Frederick Leveson- (1819–1907), liberal M.P. 3/4/62, 2/3/65, 12/7/67, 19/7/73, 24/9/73, 25/9/73, 2/4/77, 14/7/80 L, 23/8/80, 2/9/81, 6/1/83 ff, 24/3/83 ff, 14/12/83, 7/4/84, 13/1/85, 7/4/85, 26/10/85 ff, 14/6/86, 23/6/86, 4/9/86, 17/12/87, 6/6/91 ff, 13/10/92 L, 19/8/93 ff, 20/10/93 ff, 1/12/93
Emily Josephine Eliza Leveson- (1811–1872), née Doyle 17/6/34
Frederick Allen, engineer 30/4/79
George Granville Leveson- (1786–1861), 2nd Duke of Sutherland 10/2/40 n, 11/9/58 ?
George Granville Leveson- ('Mr. Leveson') (1858–1951), Gladstone's secretary 26/6/80, 8/8/85 n, 2/12/85, 10/7/86 L, 28/11/87 ff, 9/4/89, 13/4/89, 22/4/90, 15/1/91, 3/5/92, 6/5/92 ff, 21/6/92 ff, 24/9/92 ff
George Granville William Leveson- (1828–1892), 3rd Duke of Sutherland (1861), Marquis of Stafford 7/5/53 n, 8/7/80 L, 12/10/82 L
G. G. Leveson-, 1st Duke of Sutherland 3/7/39 n, 10/2/86, 10/7/86
G. Leveson-, 1st Marquis of Stafford 12/2/32 n

Gower (*cont.*)
Granville George Leveson-; Earl Granville 15/3/50
Granville Leveson-, 1st Earl Granville (1833), diplomat, tory M.P., Secretary of War 12/2/32
Granville William Gresham Leveson- (1838-) 3/5/79
Harriet Elizabeth Georgiana Sutherland-Leveson-, Lady; Duchess of Sutherland 10/2/40
Harriet Elizabeth Leveson- (1785-1862), née Cavendish 13/2/32
J. Leveson-, 1st Earl Gower 17/6/34 n
Marie Louise Pelline Leveson- (-1860), née Dalberg, Lady Granville (1840), Lady Acton 6/3/51
Ronald Charles Sutherland-Leveson-, Lord (1845-1916), liberal M.P. 2/8/45 n, 12/5/79
Victoria Alberta Leveson-, Lady (1867-) 8/4/85
William Leveson- (1806-1860), of Titsey Place 17/6/34 n
Gowing, Richard (1831-1899), editor of *The Gentleman's Magazine* 5/11/74
Gowland, George, coal merchant of London 9/3/59
Grace, Campbell 11/5/77
Graden, J. G. 16/1/91
Grady, Standish Grove (1815-1889), lawyer 4/1/49
Graf, Mr. 15/8/78
Graff, S. J. 15/8/78 ?
Grafton *see* Fitzroy
Graham *see* Campbell, Horner, Milnes
Graham,
Mrs., rescue 10/1/66, 11/1/66, 20/3/68, 21/3/68, 1/12/70, 20/1/72, 16/2/81
Charles James, barrister 20/2/75 ?
Constance Helena, Miss (-1901), Sir J's daughter 26/10/61
D., customs clerk? 21/9/60
E., rescue 27/7/63
Fanny, Lady (-1857), née Callender 13/7/53
Fortescue, Sir (1794-1880), soldier 23/3/54
George, Major (1801-1888), Registrar General 8/2/50, 19/10/54
Gerald, Lieut. Gen. (1831-1899), in Sudanese campaign 25/2/84 n, 5/3/84 c, 29/3/84, 5/5/84 c, 7/5/84, 28/3/85, 15/4/85 c
Henry John Lowndes, Sir (1842-1930) 27/7/68
James, accountant 5/11/80
James, liberal organiser in W. Scotland 6/11/85
James (-1874), 4th Duke of Montrose 16/1/74 n
James Maxtone- (1819-1901) 29/1/78
James Robert George, Sir 30/3/35
John, portrait painter 30/4/28
John, Bp. 14/9/49
John, Rev., barrister 3/6/41 ?
Malcolm Richard, Rev. (1846-1927) 25/3/75 ?
Robert Bontine Cunninghame- (1852-1936), liberal M.P. 7/2/79 ?
Robert Cunninghame Cunninghame-, Lieut. 7/2/79 ?
Thomas, Prof. (1805-1869), Master of the mint 16/3/50, 18/9/61 n
William (-1808), of Southampton 12/5/29
William (1817-1885), liberal M.P. 22/1/66, 5/12/81 L
William, Rev. (-1862) 5/9/58 n
Grahame, T. 13/6/76
Grainger,
Allerdale 13/11/75
H., of Liverpool 14/9/64
Granard *see* Forbes
Granby *see* Manners
Granby, H. 31/7/77
Grande, P., Padre 17/10/62
Grandperret, O. 16/4/62
Grandt, Mrs., rescue? 16/4/91, 21/4/91
Grane, William, solicitor 12/11/41
Granger, Farington Marsden, Dr., G's oculist in Chester 25/6/92, 22/7/92, 27/7/92, 15/10/92, 27/10/92, 24/5/93, 12/1/94, 20/2/94 L, 23/2/94 L, 19/3/94, 13/9/94
Granini, M. 4/2/89
Grant *see* McGrigor
Grant,
rescue 22/4/91
Albert (1830-1899), tory M.P., banker 16/4/66, 30/5/76
Alexander, Sir (1826-1884), principal of Edinburgh University 2/7/69
Alexander Gray, Sir (1752-1854), 6th Baronet (1825), planter in West Indies 17/1/37
Anthony, Rev. 29/6/45
Charles (1778-1866), 1st Baron Glenelg (1835), colonial secretary, whig M.P. 7/9/30
Daniel, liberal M.P. 29/3/78
David 26/4/79
Francis, Sir (1803-1878), painter 1/4/67
Francis William, Col. (1778-1853), 6th Earl of Seafield (1840), tory M.P. 31/5/37
George, G's godfather 5/8/25
George MacPherson, Sir (1839-1907), liberal (unionist) M.P. 27/11/85
Henry (-1876), butler at Christ Church 19/12/51
John (1798-1873), of Kilgraston 30/11/32 n
John W., of Edgware, London 21/2/68

J. R. 4/2/80
Julia 5/6/77
L. A., 5th Earl of Seafield 31/5/37 n
Lucy, Lady (-1881), née Bruce 30/11/32, 5/8/76, 28/6/79
Mary Anne (-1840), née Dunn 1/6/37
R. & Sons 18/11/75
Susan, Lady, née Ferrier 28/11/79
Thomas, Bp. (1816-1870), bishop of Southwark (1851), Roman Catholic 29/12/38
Ulysses Simpson, President (1822-1885) 5/6/77, 4/8/85
Grantham *see* Grey
Grantham, George (1781-1840), bursar of Magdalen 24/6/30
Grant's, inn at Dunkeld 20/8/39
Granville *see* Gower
Granville, Joseph Mortimer, Dr. (1833-1900) 20/4/78
Graser, Mr. 14/9/74
Grassi, rescue 14/5/90
Grassis, Portaz-, Abbé 5/6/75
Gratry, Auguste Joseph Alphonse, Fr. (1805-1872) 8/7/68
Grattan *see* Esmonde
Grattan, Edmund Arnout, Sir (1818-1890) 14/7/66 ?
Graves, Samuel Robert (1818-1873), mayor of Liverpool, liberal M.P. 5/10/61 n, 5/3/67
Graves & Co., print sellers 29/5/61
Gravina e Requesenz, Michele, Prince of Comitini, Neapolitan minister (1848) 29/2/52
Gray,
rescue 31/5/76
C., merchant of Liverpool 21/4/55
Charles (1782-1851), composer 26/6/48
E., also known as Leary, rescue 10/4/60, 25/4/60, 11/5/60
Edmund Archibald Stuart- (1840-1901), 15th Earl of Moray (1895) 24/9/84 n, 19/9/90
Edmund Dwyer (1845-1888), home rule M.P. 12/6/78 ff, 17/8/82, 23/8/82, 20/10/82 c, 21/10/82 c
Elizabeth Caroline (1800-1887), author 12/9/72
Francis, 14th Baron Gray 4/12/40
H. 18/11/86
H. B., Rev. Dr. 11/7/90 n
J. M. 19/12/89
John, treasury solicitor 27/2/71
John, Sir (1816-1875), Knight (1863), liberal M.P. 22/3/67, 21/9/68, 2/9/69 L, 7/9/69, 20/9/69, 28/11/69 L, 24/5/73, 5/10/81
John Edward (1800-1875), zoologist 6/12/38 ?
John Hamilton, Rev. (1800-1867), traveller 10/5/38 ?, 27/3/42, 7/1/43
J. T. 16/2/89
R., Miss, rescue 10/3/58, 10/3/59, 24/3/59
Robert, Bp. 12/4/47
Robert Alexander, Rev. (-1878), non-conformist 29/3/67 ?
Samuel O., of bank of England 11/6/79
Thomas, of board of trade 24/2/76
Train 16/7/88
Walter, Sir (1848-1918), Knight (1902), Oxford building developer and tory 4/7/85
William, Rev. (-1863) 26/7/50
Gray & Pannett, Messrs. 31/10/68
Grayson, Mrs., author 4/10/90
Grazebrook, George (1796-1877), attorney of Stourbridge 25/8/59
Grazidsi, Mr., Roman refugee 4/2/51
Greatheed, John, Rev. 4/10/74 ?
Greave, R. 19/2/77
Greaves,
A. H. 1/12/79
Henry Ley, Rev. (1846-1899) 8/2/77
Mary, of Fasque 26/9/47
Greavy, E. T. 30/12/89
Grece, Clair James, grammarian 8/7/87
Greeley, Adolphus Washington, Lieut., American explorer 17/11/85
Green,
rescue 1/2/64
Mr., of Ireland? 8/6/54
Mr., secretary to Manchester liberal association 6/11/78
Alice Sophia Amelia, Mrs. (1847-1929), historian 13/4/94, 9/5/94
Benjamin L., of Manchester liberal association 30/1/79
Bowden 14/9/79
Charles, coalwhippers commission 10/5/51
Charles Stroud, Rev., headmaster 10/3/45
Charlotte, née Symonds, widow of T. H. Green 5/2/90
C. W. 18/4/79
Duff, politician and company promoter of U.S.A. 4/10/42
George Robert, Rev. 2/1/87 ?
G. W. 22/11/77
James, Rev., chaplain of Natal 16/11/57 ?
John, Sir (-1877), Knight (1874), consul 25/1/65, 17/5/66
John Richard (1837-1883), historian 20/2/77 n, 9/6/78
Joseph 4/10/77
Joseph, of Stansted 26/12/89
Martin Johnson, junior proctor (1847) 12/6/48
Robert, maltster of Newark 12/1/35 ?

Green (*cont.*)
Sidney Faithhorn, Rev. (1841-1916) 6/9/81, 13/9/81, 23/9/81, 12/10/81, 17/10/81, 16/8/82, 2/1/83 n
T., author 30/10/75
Thomas Hill, Prof. (1836-1882), philosopher 30/1/78 n, 5/2/90 n
Thos. & Sons, brokers 28/9/46 ?
W. 26/2/56
W. H. 16/9/76
William Kirkby, Sir (1836-1891), Knight (1887), diplomat 1/1/81
William Robert 27/8/78 ?
Greenall, Peter (1796-1845), tory M.P. 9/3/46 n
Greenaway, Charles (1813-1859), whig M.P. 12/5/43 ?
Greene,
E. P. S. 21/10/89
Henrietta, née Russell 5/5/38 n
John Baker 2/1/80
John Ball, surveyor of Ireland 19/10/83
Sutherland 21/11/55 ?
Thomas (1794-1872), tory M.P. 5/5/38
Thomas Huntley, Rev., secretary of Church Penitentiary Society 6/2/52, 30/3/56 n
W. A., solicitor 27/5/87
Greenep, E. 16/4/74
Greener, T., Mr. 20/11/69, 29/1/75
Greenfield, T. 28/11/74
Greenhalg, J. S. 21/8/77
Greenhalgh, J. 21/8/77
Greenhill,
W. A. 2/9/90
William Alexander, Dr., physician 22/2/48, 10/3/65
William Ridge, Rev. 28/3/91 ?
Greenhow, A. H. 22/2/75
Greenlees, Gavin, Glasgow merchant 22/4/89
Greenock *see* Cathcart
Greenock, Provost of 17/8/65
Greenough, Mr. 7/9/79
Green's, lodging house in Oxford (in St Ebbes?) 17/1/34
Greensmith, Mr. 11/11/90
Greenway,
George Cattell, solicitor 28/11/42
S. 8/1/87
Greenwell, D. 22/6/67
Greenwood,
Frederick (-1909), journalist 29/4/80, 1/5/80 L
J. 1/1/87
J., Mrs. 1/3/71
John (-1871), assistant treasury solicitor 19/2/53, 1/3/71 n
Thomas (1851-1908), sponsor of public libraries 19/10/91 ?
W. 27/5/61
Greer,
Mr. 26/11/74
William Benjamin, Rev. 3/7/75, 4/9/78 ?
Greg,
Robert Hyde (1795-1875), antiquary 21/4/32 n
R. P. 7/8/89
William Rathbone (-1881), essayist 8/4/52
Gregg,
John Robert, Rev. 8/9/75
Robert Samuel, Abp. (1834-1896) 9/11/77
Tresham Dames, Rev. (1799-1881) 18/4/65
Gregge-Hopwood *see* Molyneux
Gregge-Hopwood, Robert 1/7/42 n
Gregorio, A. di, Marchese, of Florence 9/1/88
Gregory,
Arthur Thomas, Rev. 23/12/76
James, Rev. 11/5/28
John Bates, of Hawarden colliery 9/6/78
J. S. 6/11/59
Robert, Rev. (-1911) 25/2/48, 10/12/76
Samuel, Rev. 13/9/77
William, Dr., of Cheltenham 27/9/34 ?
William Henry, Sir (1817-1892), liberal M.P. 14/3/59, 15/6/82
Gregory XVI, Pope (1765-1846), Cappelloni, Bartolomeo Alberto 10/4/32
Gregson,
John, clerk to eccl. commissioners 16/4/63 ?
John (1806-1879), barrister 6/7/37 ?
Samuel (1795-1864), liberal M.P. 30/5/54
William, draftsman 27/1/44
Greig,
family 13/3/28
H., Miss, of Quarry Bank, Wilmslow 10/3/28
Henry Alfred, insurance 27/11/77
James, secretary of Edinburgh Chamber of Commerce 18/10/61
John James (-1881), head constable of Liverpool 7/5/52
J. S. 26/9/90
Robert, builder of London 5/5/55
Walter, merchant 31/3/74 ?
Grenfell,
Charles Pascoe (1790-1867), liberal M.P. 15/1/62
Charles William (1823-1861), liberal M.P. 21/2/55
Georgina Sebright, née Lascelles 9/9/63, 5/9/64
Henry Riversdale (1824-1902), liberal M.P. 15/1/62, 1/8/68
John Pascoe (1800-1869), consul of Brazil 11/6/42 ?
W., liberal candidate 21/3/90
Grenside, Christopher, Rev. (-1871) 2/3/57
Grenville *see* Proby

Grenville,
Anne, Lady (1772-1864), née Pitt 7/6/45, 13/5/60, 31/5/60, 20/5/61, 15/3/65
Charlotte Neville, Lady (-1877), née Legge 11/7/39, 15/6/56, 27/1/77
George 13/6/39 n
George Neville, Rev. (1789-1854), né Neville 10/7/39, 25/7/39
J. N. 12/8/43
Julia Roberta Neville (-1892), née Russell 11/7/49
Ralph Neville (1817-1886), tory M.P. 21/7/40, 13/5/41 n, 12/6/41, 24/8/41
Richard P. T. N. C., 2nd Duke of Buckingham and Chandos 17/7/44
Richard Temple-Nugent-Brydges-Chandos- (1776-1839), Duke of Buckingham and Chandos (1822) 29/3/33
R. P. C. T.-N.-B.-C.- (1823-1889), 3rd Duke of Buckingham (1861), Lord Chandos 12/5/49
Seymour Neville, Rev. (1823-1905) 3/1/47
Thomas (1755-1846), Foxite M.P., collector, C. G's uncle 10/6/39, 29/8/40, 1/9/40, 10/10/42, 12/10/42, 19/10/42, 27/10/42, 8/11/42, 25/11/43, 14/12/43, 19/12/43, 6/2/44, 13/3/44, 23/11/44, 10/6/45, 17/2/46, 24/2/46, 27/2/46, 13/7/46, 21/12/46, 13/5/48
William Wyndham, 1st Baron Grenville 7/6/45 n
Gresin, Mont, M. 20/4/27
Gresley, William, Rev. (1801-1876), writer 10/5/39
Greswell,
Joanna Julia, née Armitriding 28/8/52
Richard, Rev. 16/5/47 n
Grevel, Messrs. 2/3/92
Greville *see* Egerton, Morier, Nugent
Greville,
Algernon William Bellingham, Capt. 25/6/79
Algernon William Fulke (1841-1910) 6/8/73
Charles, Gen. Sir (1786-1836), tory M.P. 1/5/32
Charles C. F. (1794-1865), diarist 4/4/35, 26/6/35, 2/7/35
G. (-1816), 2nd Earl of Warwick 1/5/32 n
George Guy (1818-1893), 4th Earl of Warwick (1853), Lord Brooke 11/5/50
Henry Richard (1778-1816), 3rd Earl of Warwick (1816) 11/2/34
Grévy, François-Paul-Jules, President (1813-1891), of France 10/2/83, 27/2/83
Grey *see* Butler, Ellice, Lambton, Walsh, Wood
Grey,
Albert Henry George (1851-1917), 4th Earl Grey (1894) 9/6/77, 27/1/78, 29/5/86, 31/8/93 c
Alice, née Holford, Lady Grey 9/6/77
C., 1st Earl Grey 17/7/36 n
Caroline (Eliza) (-1890), née Farquhar, G's first love 11/5/35, 23/8/35 ?
Charles (1764-1845), 2nd Earl Grey (1807), Viscount Howick, Foxite whig, prime minister 3/10/31
Charles, Gen. (1804-1870), whig M.P. 11/5/35 n, 5/6/52, 25/10/53
Charles, General 26/3/52
Charles Edward, Sir (1785-1865) 20/2/63
Edward, Bp. (1782-1837), bishop of Hereford (1832) 17/7/36
Edward, Sir (1862-1933), 3rd Baronet (1882), 1st Viscount Grey of Fallodon, liberal M.P. and minister 4/6/85, 8/2/86 ff, 31/3/86, 22/7/92, 26/7/92, 26/7/93 L, 3/8/93, 24/8/93, 25/8/93, 23/9/93
Elizabeth Anne, Lady, née Howard 11/11/89
Francis Richard, Rev. (1813-1890) 18/12/31, 21/2/52, 30/9/75, 11/11/89 n
George, Sir, colonial governor 30/1/46, 29/5/70 L
George, Sir (1799-1882), 2nd Baronet (1828), whig M.P., Home Secretary 25/6/34, 24/1/55, 25/1/55, 10/6/70 L, 12/3/73 c, 27/2/83
George Harry (1765-1845), 6th Earl of Stamford (1819) 9/2/28 n
Henrietta Frances de, Lady (1784-1848), née Cole 8/6/38
Henry, Rev. 1/6/28
Henry George, Sir (1802-1894), Viscount Howick (styled) (1807), 3rd Earl Grey (1845), whig M.P., colonial secretary 14/5/33, 27/4/69 L, 28/4/69 L, 8/6/84 L, 11/6/84 L
J. C., of Greenwich 11/5/74
John, Hon. Rev. (1829-1895) 9/6/72 ?, 25/11/73
John, Rev. (1812-1895) 18/12/31
John, Sir (1780-1856), general 5/12/55
Louisa, Lady (-1830) 9/2/28
Maria, Lady (-1879), née Hamilton 21/4/49
M. G., Mrs. 8/12/75
T. 13/9/76
Thomas Philip Weddell (1781-1859), 3rd Baron Grantham (1786), 2nd Earl de Grey (1833), né Robinson 8/6/38
William, Rev. (1820-1872) 5/11/53 ?
Greyson, Mr. 15/9/77
Grice,
Joseph Hill, Rev. (1809-1867) 19/2/29
William, Rev. 4/8/77 ?
Grieg *see* Somerville
Grieg, S. (-1807) 24/2/34 n

Grier, Richard Macgregor, Rev. 2/11/72, 18/8/77
Grieve,
James Johnstone (1810–1891), provost of Greenock, liberal M.P. 17/8/65
Nathaniel, Rev. 27/11/56
Griffin *see* Tyler
Griffin,
Henry, Bp., bishop of Limerick 28/2/40
Tomkinson 7/4/94
Griffith,
Charles, Rev. (1805–1886) 27/2/31
C. Herbert 24/4/79
Edward, Chester architect 14/8/90
Griffith, Dr. 29/9/86 ?
Thomas, surgeon 25/12/42
Thomas T., Dr., physician in Wrexham 13/1/58
W., Rev. 24/12/77
Griffiths,
Mr., of Roke Farm, Hawarden 15/8/61
Mrs., of Hawarden 4/5/76
D. E., of Oak Farm 22/5/51
E. 16/9/71
G. 30/11/68
Henry James 31/10/68 ?
H. S. 3/3/80
Jane Ellen, rescue 30/4/57, 13/1/65, 13/8/65 ff, 6/5/74
John, agent of Oak Farm (1848) 11/3/48
John, Rev. (–1885), don 28/4/54
John Jnr., son of agent of Oak Farm 3/1/53 ?
L. E. 29/3/77
O. R. 7/4/80
Richard, of Hawarden 4/10/54
S., of Oak Farm 4/10/51
Tom, artist 3/9/90 ?
Grifoni, Alisse 2/1/88
Grimes, C. C., Rev. 1/7/76, 23/9/83
Grimewade, Samuel 19/10/85
Grimley, Horatio Nelson, Rev. Prof. 1/12/77
Grimshaw, Thomas Shuttleworth, Rev. (1778–1850) 6/1/39
Grimston *see* Villiers
Grimston,
Edward Harbottle (1812–1881), tory M.P. 7/6/29
James Walter (–1845), 1st Earl of Verulam 8/3/53 n
James Walter, Sir (1809–1895), 2nd Earl Verulam (1845), tory M.P. 1/2/29, 17/6/53
Grimthorpe *see* Denison
Grimwood, T. 15/12/86
Grindley, Mr. 7/6/72
Grinfield, C. J. 8/3/80
Gringer, Mrs., rescue 27/2/68, 18/3/68, 17/12/68
Grinsted, John, financial journalist 22/5/56
Grisi, Giulia (1811–1869), Italian prima donna 23/4/34, 9/1/39
Grissell, Mr. 2/4/79
Gritton (separated 1865) *see* Clinton
Grocers Company, secretary of 24/2/76
Grogan,
Edward, Sir (1802–1891), Baronet (1859), tory M.P. and barrister 13/7/53
William, house agent 26/6/54, 11/3/56, 2/4/56, 7/4/56, 7/7/74, 5/1/75, 25/2/75, 26/2/75 ff, 17/3/75 ff, 30/3/75 ff, 21/1/76, 11/7/76, 2/12/81, 22/5/85, 6/6/90
Grolley, Mr. 18/11/79
Grollo, Sig., of Ionia 11/1/59
Groom,
Miss 24/9/87
Mrs., née Wilkinson 18/3/33
A. 24/1/77
C. 14/11/79
Richard 18/3/33 n
William T. 5/2/78
Groome, F. H. 1/12/91
Grosart, Alexander Balloch, Rev. (1827–1899) 25/11/67
Groscock 2/12/41
Groser, W. H., of Banbury 12/6/75
Grossi, Pasquale, Neapolitan official 25/1/51
Grossmith,
Dr. 15/5/77
George (1847–1912), actor and author 10/8/86
Grosvenor *see* Cavendish, Egerton, Guest, Leigh, Wyndham
Grosvenor,
Caroline Susan Theodora, née Stuart Wortley 25/6/81
Charlotte Arbuthnot (–1891), née Wellesley, Lady Ebury 6/3/40
Constance Gertrude, Lady (–1880), Lady Westminster, Duchess of Westminster 20/5/61
Edwin Augustus, Prof. 1/8/89
Eleanor, Lady, née Egerton, Lady Westminster 23/7/40
Elizabeth Mary, Lady (1797–1891), née Leveson-Gower, Lady Westminster 3/7/39, 5/12/60
Hugh Lupus (1825–1899), 3rd Marquis of Westminster (1869), 1st Duke of Westminster (1874), Lord Grosvenor 4/5/57, 5/12/62, 5/11/67, 3/1/74 L, 5/11/75, 7/12/76, 8/12/76 n, 14/11/77, 3/1/78, 12/1/78, 26/9/82, 20/12/83, 29/12/83, 15/12/85, 19/12/85, 14/7/86, 26/9/92, 28/9/92 n, 13/10/92
Norman de l'Aigle (1845–1898) 25/6/81

Richard (1795-1869), Viscount Belgrave (1802), 2nd Marquis of Westminster (1845), whig M.P. 3/7/39 n, 27/7/40 n
Richard de Aquila, Lord 25/2/80
Robert, 1st Marquis of Westminster 23/7/40 n
Robert, Lord (1801-1893), 1st Baron Ebury (1857), whig M.P. 1822-57 6/3/40, 29/1/53, 12/8/71, 13/7/72, 15/7/72
Robert Wellesley (1834-1918), 2nd Baron Ebury (1893), liberal M.P. 11/7/65
Victoria Charlotte, Miss (1832-1913) 17/11/53, 28/10/83
Grote,
Arthur (1814-1886) 30/11/73 ?
George (1794-1871), radical M.P., historian 25/4/33 n, 12/9/72, 29/5/73, 2/6/73
Harriet (1792-1878), radical author 25/4/74, 26/5/75, 19/6/75, 4/7/75, 8/5/76, 4/4/77, 21/3/78
Grothin, Mr. 21/12/75
Grousset, Pascal, French author 12/12/87
Grove,
George, Rev. 1/9/77
George, Sir (1820-1900), musician, author 19/7/50
P. 29/5/77
S. 30/10/77
Thomas Fraser, Sir (1823-1897), 1st Baronet (1874), liberal M.P. 17/3/74
Thomas Newcomen Archibald (1855-1920), liberal M.P., editor, *New Review* 23/3/88
William Henry, Rev. (-1915) 1/7/79
Grover, John Septimus, Rev. (1766-1853), vice provost 29/1/26
Groves, Thomas George, barrister 16/11/64
Growcott, John, miner at Oak Farm 11/2/50
Grub, George, Prof. (1812-1892) 1/8/60
Grubb,
Sheriff 11/8/90
Isaac, baker of Oxford 21/10/57
Joseph, parliamentary agent 26/1/60 ?
Grubbe, Charles Septimus, Rev. (-1910) 21/4/79
Grueber,
Charles Stephen, Rev. (-1894) 23/1/53
Erwin, law lecturer, Balliol 4/2/90
Gruenbaum, Mr. 8/11/87
Gruggen, Frederick James, Rev. (1820-1872), schoolmaster 31/3/55
Grundy, George Docker, Rev. 15/3/77 ?
Gruner, Ludwig, artist 31/1/44
Grüninger, Mr. 18/5/87
Gualtier, Mr. 21/2/38
Guard, James, of Liverpool 2/9/66 ?
Guards' Chapel 12/12/78, 25/5/79
Guastalla, Marco, Dr. 1/1/76
Guazzaroni, Sig. 11/8/40
Gubernatis, Sig. de 22/3/92
Guccia, Sig. 25/8/91
Gudin, Charles Gabriel César, Count (1789-1874), French senator 8/9/70
Guenther, Siegmund, Dr. 13/6/77 ?
Guerault, M., French reporter 20/10/79
Gueronnière, Alfred de la, Count (1810-1884) 22/2/55
Guerra, horseman 29/5/32
Guerzoni, Giuseppe, scholar 9/6/70
Gueshoff, Ivan Estratiew (1849-1924), Bulgarian politician 15/10/85
Guest *see* Schreiber
Guest,
family, of Penryn Castle 31/8/26
J. J., Sir (-1852), 1st Baronet 1/5/55 n
Theodora, Lady, née Grosvenor 3/1/61
Thomas Hill, Rev. 19/10/91
Thomas Merthyr (-1904) 3/1/61 n
Guglielmi,
Iacopo (-1782), tenor 17/12/38
Pietro Alessandro, composer 17/12/38 n
Pietro Carlo, composer 17/12/38 n
Guglielmo, Sig. 6/10/79
Gühler, Mr. 16/5/76
Guicciardi, Enrico (1812-1895) 2/3/59 ?
Guidicini, Giuseppe de Giovanni Battista 4/3/76
Guilani, Prof. 20/12/82
Guild, Emma Marie Cadwalader, Mrs. (1843-1911), sculptor 4/3/92 ff, 24/3/92, 5/4/92
Guile, Daniel, trade unionist 20/2/78
Guillard, Mr. 4/12/76
Guiness, Arthur H., secretary of Protestant Alliance 6/11/74
Guinness,
Rev. Mr. 26/10/77
Arthur Edward, Sir (1840-1915), 1st Baron Ardilaun (1880), bought 11 Carlton House Terrace from G 25/2/75, 15/4/75
Olivia Charlotte, Lady 25/2/75, 19/7/77
Guise, William Vernon, Sir (1816-1887), 4th Baronet 23/12/68
Guistiniaius, Mr., of Rome 1/11/66
Guizot,
François Pierre Guillaume (1787-1874), French statesman 9/4/40, 4/7/40, 31/7/40, 4/7/41, 22/3/48, 29/3/48, 11/4/48, 13/4/48, 3/3/49, 9/4/51, 27/9/56, 17/3/57, 26/9/70, 10/11/70, 24/1/71, 28/1/71 c
Maurice Guillaume (1833-1892) 17/7/58
Guliemus 27/5/75
Gull, William Withey, Sir (1816-1890), 1st Baronet (1872), physician 28/10/69, 9/1/72, 30/3/85, 30/3/89
Gullick,
Thomas, bootmaker 12/6/48 ?
T. J. 23/3/92

Gullifer, Mrs. 2/6/90
Gully, James Manby, Dr. (1808–1883), physician 27/3/59
Gunn,
Mrs. 30/7/91
A. H. 16/1/89
E. 3/11/85
L. 12/10/67
Gunn, Jamieson & Co., merchants 30/7/66
Gunnill, J. A. 22/2/89
Gunston,
Henry 22/4/45 ?
William 22/4/45 ?
Guppa, Prof. 11/11/90
Gurden, William, Rev. 12/5/70
Gurdon, William Brampton, Sir 26/4/65
Gurkin, Mr. 28/5/79
Gurnell, E. 16/6/77
Gurner, William, secretary of Royal College of Physicians 11/6/74
Gurney,
rescue 31/5/59, 1/6/59
Mrs. 16/7/38
Archer Thompson, Rev. (–1887) 11/7/54, 27/1/67
Daniel, banker 20/10/58
Goldsworthy, Sir (1793–1875), inventor 19/8/51 n
H. E., banker 2/10/60, 5/10/60
Hudson (1775–1864), antiquary 8/1/38
J. 3/9/78
John, Sir 7/5/44 n
John Hampden 7/5/44, 30/11/62
Russell (1804–1878), tory M.P. 21/7/74
Samuel, banker 9/10/50
Gustavus V (1858–1950), King of Sweden (1907) 14/7/79
Gutekunst, F., of U.S.A. 12/3/90
Guthrie,
Mrs. 18/6/41
Charles John 18/4/78 ?
David K., Rev., Free Churchman 19/3/80
George, author 20/5/57
George, fiscal writer 8/9/65
J. R. 15/9/91
T., surgeon 4/11/34
Thomas, Rev. (1803–1873), presbyterian minister 31/12/49, 11/12/59, 17/4/61, 30/4/61, 10/1/62, 15/2/64, 30/9/65, 1/10/65, 9/10/71
Gutteridge,
Mr. 11/1/89
Mrs. 2/11/75
Guttery, T. 7/4/89
Guy,
Thomas, Rev. 11/4/44
William Augustus, Dr., statistician 25/10/42
Guy's Hospital, treasurer of 25/2/78 n
Gweirydd Ap Rhys *see* Pryse
Gwillim, John, Rev. (1783–1859) 24/8/32
Gwilt,
Mr. 19/2/67
Charles, solicitor 16/3/87
G. 31/1/76
Gwynne, Richard (–1865), landowner 13/5/58 ?
Gye,
Capt., of S. E. Railway 29/12/87
Frederick (1781–1869), tory M.P., tea merchant 20/3/37 ?
J. 26/6/56
Richard, Newark victualler 20/3/37 ?

Habershon, Samuel Herbert, Dr. (1857–1915), G's physician 25/6/91 ff, 26/3/94, 14/4/94, 21/4/94 ff, 21/5/94 ?
Hackman, Alfred, Rev. (1811–1874), precentor 13/8/51
Haddan,
Arthur West, Rev. 7/8/47, 25/10/52
Thomas Henry (1814–1873), barrister, member of the Engagement 23/2/45 n
Haddington *see* Hamilton
Haddo *see* Gordon
Hadfield,
George (1787–1879), liberal M.P. 29/4/53
James, attempted assassin of George III 28/7/35
S. 12/8/87
William, merchant 1/12/42
Hadin, Mrs. 2/2/78
Hadow, J. S., Rev. 28/5/55
Haed, E. A. 3/1/87
Hagart *see* Ellice, Speirs
Hagart,
Miss, of Falkirk 6/12/33
Charles (1814–1879) 16/5/28, 18/8/53
Elizabeth, née Stewart 12/5/28, 18/8/53
James McCaul (1815–1895) 16/5/28
Thomas Campbell (1774–1868), of Bantaskine, Stirling 12/5/28
Hagemeister, Julius von (1806–1878) 26/7/61
Hagen, Messrs. 13/8/89
Haggerty, Mr., American Consul and Fenian 5/6/69
Haggitt *see* Prosser
Hagopian, G., of Armenia 19/9/76, 8/12/76, 16/9/90
Haig, James Richard (1831–1896) 8/11/78, 4/12/90
Haigh *see* Lechmere
Haine, Dr. 20/6/78
Hake, Robert, Rev. 30/3/54
Hakim, M. H. 30/7/77
Halbreiter,
Miss 20/2/54
Ulrich (1812–1877), artist 13/12/53 ?

Halcomb,
J., Mrs. 21/5/46
John (1790–1852), tory M.P. 10/4/35
Halcombe, John Joseph, Rev. (1832–1910) 28/9/74
Haldane,
J. W. C. 20/9/90
Richard Burdon (1856–1928), liberal M.P. 21/6/86 n, 25/4/88, 2/8/90, 9/10/90, 13/10/90, 31/3/92, 14/5/93, 6/12/93, 14/12/93 c
Haldon *see* Palk
Hale,
Mr. 9/10/83
Horatio, American scientist 8/11/86 n, 10/11/86
Thomas 20/2/79
William Hale, Rev. (1795–1870), scholar, tory 4/2/33
Hales,
John Dixon, Rev. 20/3/56
John Wesley, Prof. (1836–1914) 2/4/89
Richard Cox, Rev. (–1906) 24/6/79
William Atherstone, Rev. (1829–1894) 10/8/68
Hales & Freeman, Messrs. 15/3/87
Haley, William, chairmaker 25/1/58 ?
Halford, Henry, Sir (1766–1844), Baronet (1809), né Vaughan, physician 19/10/26
Halifax *see* Wood
Halkett,
Mrs. 21/2/82
Hugh Colin Gustave, Baron (1861–), Baron of the Kingdom of Hanover, at Hawarden 11/6/92, 25/6/92 n
Hall *see* Gladstone, Pollen
Hall,
Mr., of Fasque 2/4/51
Augusta (–1896), Lady Llanover 20/8/60
Basil, Capt. (1788–1844), R. N., author, F. R. S. 3/1/37
Benjamin, Sir (1802–1867), 1st Baron Llanover (1859), whig M.P. 14/5/35 ?
Charles Cuthbert, author 17/12/79
Charles Henry, dean of Christ Church (1809) 8/6/30 n
Charles Radclyffe (1819–1879), physician 23/11/55 ?
Christopher Newman, Rev. 8/11/62
George 23/2/37
H. A., Rev. 10/11/88
Henry, Newark draper 27/5/37
Henry, Rev. (–1878) 11/1/53
Henry, Rev. (–1897) 28/10/78
Herbert Byng, Major (1805–1883), author 9/8/75
H. W. 4/4/76
James, Sir, Baronet 18/11/38 n
J. D. 12/4/78
John (–1895), Newcastle shipowner 8/10/62
John, Sir (1787–1860), 5th Baronet (1832), scientist 13/2/33
J. W. 28/8/79
Peter, editor of *Starchamber* 26/8/26 n
Peter, Rev. (1802–1849), divine 24/12/47
R. N. 13/9/79
Samuel Carter (1801–1889), journalist 18/1/85
Samuel Romilly, Rev. 14/7/69
S. C., secretary to Nightingale fund 16/1/56 n
Spencer (1806–1875), librarian of the Athenaeum 15/2/61
Thomas, manufacturer in Leith 3/7/86 L
Thomas B., of Truro 23/1/75
Thomas G., Rev. Prof. 30/4/47 ?
William John, Rev. (1793–1861) 10/7/57
Hallam,
Mrs. (–1826), née Roberts 5/11/26
Rev., Wesleyan at Hawarden 3/1/74
Arthur Henry 4/2/26
Eleanor (–1837) 16/6/37
Henry (1777–1859), historian 17/1/28, 23/2/33 n, 4/11/50, 28/5/56, 14/4/58, 16/10/83
Henry Fitzmaurice (1824–1850) 31/7/35
Julia Maria (1783–1840), née Elton 23/2/33
Hallé,
Charles, Sir (1819–1895), Knight (1888), musician 26/3/70 n, 8/5/88 ?
Wilma, Lady (1839–1911), née Neruda 26/3/70, 4/7/77, 19/6/83, 5/7/83
Hallett, rescue 19/5/76
Hallett & Ommaney, bankers 20/1/63
Hallewell,
Mrs. 29/4/51
John, Rev. (1795–1871) 10/12/36 ?
Halliburton, W. W., of Edinburgh Post Office 29/3/80
Halliday,
Mr. 25/12/78
Andrew, Sir 23/2/35
Maria, Mrs. 3/7/79 ?
William Halliday 3/7/79 ?
Hallifax,
Henry Crawford, soldier 4/3/26
Sydney, of Manchester 28/8/89
Hallward, John William, Rev. 3/6/59 ?
Halsbury *see* Giffard
Halsey,
Rev. Mr. 21/11/86
Thomas Plumer (–1854), tory M.P. 11/11/50 ?
Halton, G. 20/12/77, 24/12/89
Halvill, Mr. 6/8/74
Haly,
Francis, Bp. (–1855) 16/6/45

Haly (*cont.*)
John B. Standish, barrister 28/11/61, 17/12/62
William T., secretary of Southwark Fund 10/7/45 n
Ham,
printer in St. Ebbe's Oxford 25/4/31, 6/7/31
George D., editor 24/2/77
Hambleton, Mr. 19/8/77
Hamblin, Mr. 21/2/79
Hamel,
Mr. 30/7/79
Felix John, customs solicitor 16/2/54
Hamer, Mrs., rescue 12/3/88
Hamilton *see* Douglas, Grey, Howard
Hamilton,
rescue 13/3/63
rescue 9/8/71
rescue 3/3/75
Major 2/10/76
Mr., traveller in Ghent 2/2/32
Andrew, of Alliance Co. 3/3/49 n
Arthur Charles Baillie-, Rev. (1838–1910) 16/9/66 n
Arthur Philip, Adm. (–1877) 28/6/67, 18/1/68
C. E. 19/4/90
C. H., of Liverpool 18/10/76
Claud, Lord (1813–1884), tory M.P. 5/3/35, 22/2/52
Clement Edward 28/3/69
Constance Nisbet-, Miss 3/7/88
Cospatrick, Capt., R. N. 31/1/61 ff
Edward Walter, Sir 7/9/66
Edward William Terrick (1809–1898), liberal M.P. 2/6/34, 20/5/57, 2/12/93
E. K. 3/1/76
Gavin George (1872–) 17/12/88 ?
George Alexander (1802–1871), tory M.P., treasury secretary 15/3/44, 24/6/59 n
George Francis, Lord (1845–1927) 2/8/78, 26/6/83, 9/5/85 c, 30/9/85, 14/12/93 ff
George Hans, Rev. 2/10/76 n
Hamilton (1790–1873), née Campbell, Lady Belhaven 4/1/37
Isabel Elizabeth, née Lear 26/11/44, 22/1/81
James (–1829) 23/1/47
James (1811–1885), Knight (1844), 1st Duke of Abercorn (1868), Marquis of Hamilton, Viceroy of Ireland 15/5/30 n
James, Rev. (–1867), presbyterian minister 3/4/41, 5/4/41, 6/4/41, 24/9/41
James, Rev. (1813–1873) 16/9/68 ?
James Baillie, organ maker 31/7/90
John (1821–1860), editor, *Morning Star* 19/2/57
John Glencairn Carter- (1829–1900), 1st Baron Hamilton of Dalzell (1886), liberal M.P. 23/1/71, 6/12/79, 24/10/87
John McLure (1853–1936), artist 6/12/89, 3/9/90, 4/9/90, 5/9/90, 24/9/90, 1/11/92
Joseph Harriman, Rev. 22/4/49 n
L. A., Mrs. 2/8/58
Maria Baillie- (–1861), née Parker, Lady Haddington 24/11/60
Mary Ann, kept ladies' boarding school, Liverpool 8/7/29
Mary Nisbet-, Lady, née Bruce 10/11/41 n
Robert Adam Nisbet-, tory M.P. 10/11/41, 26/12/63
Robert George Crookshank, Sir (1836–1895), permanent undersecretary in Ireland (1883), Governor of Tasmania (1886) 8/5/82, 29/8/82, 22/5/83, 13/12/85 n, 24/12/85, 14/1/86, 8/2/86, 11/2/86 ff
Robert Montgomery (1793–1868), 8th Baron Belhaven and Stenton (1814), 1st Baron Hamilton (1831) 4/1/37
Sidney 30/7/89
Thomas, secretary, Manchester exhibition 24/1/57 n
Thomas (1780–1858), 9th Earl of Haddington (1828) 12/12/36, 4/1/37, 5/1/37, 6/1/37, 7/1/37
Thomas Newte, Rev. (1818–1869) 13/3/57
Walter Kerr, Bp. 11/3/27
William Alexander Baillie-, R. N. 20/11/43
William Alexander Louis Stephen Douglas- (1845–1895), 12th Duke of Hamilton (1863) 24/6/82 n, 16/8/82 n
William John, Peelite M.P. 20/5/45
William Richard (1777–1859), diplomat, antiquarian 14/1/39
W. T., of the Mint 12/8/54
Hamlet, Thomas, jeweller 18/5/41
Hamley, Edward, Rev. (1764–1835) 15/3/28
Hammond,
Edmund (1802–1890), 1st Baron Hammond (1874), permanent undersecretary, Foreign Office 20/1/55, 14/9/69 L, 17/7/70 L, 28/10/70 L, 18/9/71 L, 27/11/71 L, 17/2/72 L, 15/6/72, 20/8/72 L, 24/8/72 L, 17/9/72 L, 19/12/72, 2/1/73 L, 17/4/73 L, 4/9/73 L
Frederick, Rev. 30/11/76
G., consul 20/4/61 ?
Henry Anthony, temperance worker 18/6/77
Joseph, Rev. 25/5/89
William Oxenden (1817–1903), soldier and tory 5/9/81 n
Hamond, William Parker, Justice of the Peace 1/1/47
Hampden *see* Brand
Hampden,
Mrs., widow of the bishop 7/2/71 L

Henrietta, Miss 7/2/71
Renn Dickson, Bp. (1793–1868), professor of Moral Philosophy, Oxford, bishop of Hereford 14/11/31, 15/11/47, 9/11/56, 7/2/71, 9/9/71
Hampton *see* Pakington
Hampton,
Mrs., née Lee (or Leigh), maid 27/8/43, 29/11/44, 12/9/54, 1/1/84
Henry, Rev. 2/8/41
Henry (George), G's godson, the butler's son 15/2/52
J. S., Australian surgeon 5/5/46
William (–1870), G's butler 2/2/41, 12/9/54, 21/9/54, 31/10/70
Hamrad, Mr. 28/10/78 ?
Hanagan, J. 6/7/68
Hanbury,
Alfred, Rev. (1807–1859) 15/11/28
Francis Alfred, barrister 20/10/58
O. 17/6/46
Robert William (1845–1903), tory M.P. 10/6/78, 17/6/78
William Bateman- (1826–1901), 2nd Baron Bateman (1845) 12/7/58
Hanby, R. 16/2/56
Hancock,
Edward, of Loughborough 29/10/33 ?
E. G. 12/7/67
George, solicitor, of Rigby & Hancock 11/5/52
Thomas Henry, of Hawarden 8/8/88 n
Thomas William 22/6/75
Ursula M., née Dunstan, of Hawarden 8/8/88 n
William, solicitor, of Rigby & Hancock 20/5/52
William Neilson, Prof., Irish economist 27/2/69
Hancock, Rixon & Dunt, chandelier makers 30/3/44 ?
Hand,
Mrs. 6/6/40
Frederick James 6/6/40 n
J. 23/12/78
S. C., Miss 30/11/87
T., London solicitor 5/11/56
Handley,
John (1807–1880), liberal M.P., banker 16/10/26
Philip (1809–1884), Newark banker 31/10/25, 16/4/79
William, Rev. (1811–1873) 23/7/37
Handley, Peacock and Co., Newark bankers 31/10/25 n
Handlon, H. V. 4/8/90
Handsley, R. 12/2/76
Handyside, Peter David, Dr., physician 21/1/75
Hangar, F. H. 1/7/76
Hangen, Herr 28/2/80
Hangham, Mrs. 7/1/87
Hankey,
Henry Aitchison, Gen. (1805–1886) 17/2/85
Thompson (1805–1893), liberal M.P. 2/7/35, 3/3/65, 31/7/90
Hankin, H. A. T. 22/4/74
Hanley,
Mr., of Worksop 12/5/75
J. Laffan, journalist 10/8/76
Hanlon, Alexander Patrick, Rev. 18/6/93 ?
Hanmer,
Georgiana, Lady (–1880), née Chetwynd 4/11/63 ?
Henry H., Liverpool banker 8/10/78
John, Sir (1809–1881), 1st Baron Hanmer (1872), of Flintshire, liberal M.P. 9/3/26, 26/11/56, 4/11/62, 13/1/68, 12/9/78 ff
Watson 29/12/78
Hannah, John, the younger, Rev. (1818–1888), headmaster of Glenalmond 10/8/54, 8/7/57, 9/10/63 ff, 3/1/70
Hannan, E. H., of Liverpool 2/3/75
Hannan, R., & Co., Glasgow merchants 3/7/58
Hannay, Alexander, Rev. 15/6/78 ?
Hannen, James, Judge (1821–1894), 1st Baron Hannen (1891) 16/8/93
Hannington, Henry (1798–1870), founder of Cambridge University Cricket Club 4/10/30
Hanns, Mr. 8/3/80
Hansard,
Luke Graves (1783–1841), printer to House of Commons 7/5/38
Thomas Curson 23/2/42
Hansell, Edward Halifax, Rev. 7/2/52
Hanson,
Miss 7/1/78
Evan, Aston Hall colliery 3/6/74
J. W. 13/6/76
Hanwell,
A. W. 20/11/91
Campbell 18/7/79
Hanyon, Prof. 20/2/80
Harawitz, A., Dr. 19/12/76
Harbord *see* Boothby
Harbord,
Charles (1830–1914), 5th Baron Suffield (1853) 21/11/71
Edward (1781–1835), 3rd Baron Suffield 26/1/43 n
Harborne, H. 5/4/78
Harborough *see* Sherard
Harbour, H. 28/2/78, 9/11/91
Harcourt *see* Johnstone

Harcourt,
Anne (-1867) 11/6/39
Bernard D', Count (1821-1912), French ambassador 7/6/73, 26/6/73, 21/10/78
Catherine Julia (-1877), née Jenkinson 16/6/39 n
Edward Venables Vernon, Abp. (1757-1847), archbishop of York (1808) 24/6/37, 6/11/47
Edward William, Col. (1825-1891), tory M.P. 25/3/81
Egerton Venables (1803-1883) 25/12/41, 30/11/47
Elizabeth, Lady, née Motley, formerly Mrs. Ives 14/3/88
Francis Vernon, Col. (1801-1880), fickle suitor of Catherine Gladstone 16/6/39
George Granville Vernon- (1785-1861), whig M.P. 11/5/31 n
George Simon (1805-1871), tory M.P. 4/7/57
Lewis Vernon (1863-1922), 1st Viscount Harcourt (1917), W. V. Harcourt's secretary 3/11/83, 5/11/83, 8/8/85 n, 12/9/85, 21/9/88, 9/12/90, 12/9/93, 14/9/93
William George Granville Venables Vernon, Sir 7/12/52
Harcourt, family, of Nuneham Courtenay 28/8/28 n
Hard, C. P., Rev. 2/7/90
Hardcastle,
John, Bolton spinner 30/5/66
Joseph Alfred (1815-1899), liberal M.P. 7/4/62
Hardie, James Keir (1856-1915), labour M.P. 8/12/89 ?, 18/2/90 n
Harding,
Mr., of Hawarden 29/10/67, 6/1/68
C. S. 18/11/91
G. 16/11/90
John Dorney, Sir (-1868), Knight (1852), advocate general 24/6/47
Wyndham (1818-1885), railway company secretary 17/7/45, 21/2/49
Hardinge,
Charles Stuart, 2nd Viscount Hardinge of Lahore 21/9/42
Emily Jane, Lady (1789-1865), née Stewart 5/6/37
Frederick (1801-1875) 4/12/46 ?
Henry (1785-1856), 1st Viscount Hardinge (1844), tory M.P. and Irish secretary, Field Marshal, C. in C. 18/8/35, 5/6/37 n, 5/4/48, 12/4/48, 24/2/52, 3/7/52, 5/11/52, 18/9/54
Harding & Willby 25/6/88
Hardwick, Charles, Rev. (1798-1874) 13/3/58
Hardwicke *see* Yorke
Hardy,
Mrs. 16/5/78
Alfred Lloyd, genealogist 27/2/79 ?
Charles Atwood 18/11/75
Edward Ambrose, Rev. 23/4/77 ?
E. G. 9/4/80
Elizabeth, Miss 10/7/46
Gathorne Gathorne- (1814-1906), Viscount Cranbrook (1878), Earl of Cranbrook (1892) 7/3/61, 22/2/73 c, 17/3/73 c, 18/3/73 c, 21/3/73, 3/7/73, 10/2/77, 18/2/77
Henry John 9/10/77
John (1773-1855), tory M.P. 29/8/44
John, Sir (1809-1888), 1st Baronet (1876), tory M.P. 4/3/76
Lucy Marion (May), née Gladstone 4/3/76 n, 7/3/77, 15/8/77, 29/9/80, 14/4/83
Reginald, Sir (1848-1938), 2nd Baronet (1888) 4/3/76 n, 15/8/77
Thomas, Newark maltster 2/8/34
Thomas, prosecuted 'radical', for treason 11/7/26
Hare,
Arthur William, surgeon 25/9/91
John, Sir (1844-1921), actor 18/3/90 n, 13/1/93 n
John David, of Dublin 16/12/38
Julius Charles, Ven., Archdeacon of Lewes 29/2/44 fl, 16/12/53
Sherlock, barrister 22/7/78
Thomas, advocate of proportional representation 7/5/57, 12/3/59 n, 20/6/65
William (1833-1924), 3rd Earl of Listowel (1856), 1st Baron Hare (1869) 4/5/69, 5/7/80 L, 19/7/80 L, 16/8/80 L
Harewood *see* Lascelles
Harfeldst, Herr 21/1/79
Harfeldt, Dr. 22/1/78
Harford,
rescue 15/3/53
Mr. 13/2/68
E. 20/10/56
Hargood, Mr. 7/7/76
Hargreave, Oliver H., of London 17/3/49
Hargreaves,
Alice, Mrs., née Liddell, daughter of Dean Liddell, model for C. L. Dodgson 5/12/82 n
Thomas (1775-1846), Liverpool miniaturist 23/12/28
Harington,
Mr. 28/6/76
A., rescue 9/12/54
James Edward, Sir (-1877), 10th Baronet (1835) 23/2/52, 19/5/57
Jane Agnes, Lady, née Brownrigg 23/2/52 n

John Robert Strong, Rev., nonconformist 6/1/90
Richard, Dr., Principal of B. N. C., Oxford 14/2/48
T. C., colonial office, New Zealand 13/6/46
Harker, G., Treasurer of Victoria, Australia 14/10/61 ?
Harland, Edward James, Sir (1831–1895), 1st Baronet (1885), Belfast manufacturer and Unionist 16/1/86 L
Harley, Robert 23/4/79
Harman,
F. 5/11/75
Jeremiah, collector 14/5/44 n
P. 28/10/79
T. T., Rev. 7/8/77
Harness, Henry Dury, Sir (–1883), Knight (1873) 14/5/53
Harnett, W. 7/3/67
Harper,
A., Rev. 3/1/56
Ephraim, Rev. 10/2/45 ?
Harper, Boulton & Co., wine merchants 19/3/75
Harpur, Mrs., servant 10/12/51
Harrald, Joseph W., Spurgeon's secretary 30/10/78, 5/3/92
Harries, Gilbert Charles Frederick, Rev. (–1879) 21/10/56 ?
Harriman, Miss 14/10/90
Harrington *see* Stanhope
Harrington, E., rescue 19/7/53
Harriot, T. 22/2/76
Harris,
rescue 4/1/84
Capt. 18/12/68
Mrs., nurse 27/2/40
Andrew 30/10/75 ?
C., of Naples 22/7/49
Charles Amyand, Bp. 20/1/52 n, 24/7/53
Corisande Emma (–1876), née Bennet, Lady Malmesbury 10/3/52
Croasdaile, Rev. 20/11/90
Edward Alfred John, Sir (1808–1888) 22/7/62 n
Elizabeth F. S., author 13/2/47 n
Frederick William, Rev. 31/8/45
George, Seaforth manager 26/4/76, 31/7/80
George (1809–1890), barrister 5/2/57, 9/3/58
George Francis Robert (1810–1872), 3rd Baron Harris of Seringapatam (1845), governor of Madras 24/11/31, 15/6/46
Henry, Rev. (–1900) 21/3/54
James, Rev. (1817–1877), Headmaster, Chester Grammar School 31/12/56 fl
James Howard (–1889), 3rd Earl of Malmesbury (1841) 10/3/52
John Dove (1809–1878), liberal M.P. 13/5/65
Katharine Lucia (–1837), née O'Brien 20/1/52
Robert, Rev. (1764–1862) 9/12/32 ?
W., Rev. 20/11/78 n
William, of St. Ebbe's, Oxford 10/2/29
Harrison,
Mrs., of Hawarden 22/10/67
Amery, of Beckenham 31/8/64
Arthur (1819–1840) 10/12/38, 9/5/40
Benjamin, fils, Ven. (1808–1887) 1/2/29, 14/7/54, 19/8/54
Benjamin, père (1771–1856), Treasurer of Guy's Hospital 4/8/32
Frederic (1831–1923), lawyer, positivist and author 2/9/81, 4/1/82, 9/7/88
G. 13/12/79
George, of Hawarden 18/12/62
George, of Newark 6/4/41
George, silk merchant 5/8/26 ?
George, surgeon 13/9/42
George, Sir (1811–1885), liberal M.P. 1/1/85 n, 24/12/85, 1/1/86 n
Henry 23/12/26
Isabella, née Thornton 25/2/41 n
James Fortescue (1819–), liberal M.P. 11/12/79
John, of Penmaenmawr 3/9/55 n, 3/9/59, 30/10/60, 24/9/61
John Branfill, Rev. 16/8/69
Mary, née Le Pelly 4/2/33
Percy 23/9/90
Ralph 30/3/78
Richard, railway promotor 12/2/26
Robert (1820–1893), secretary of London Library 24/10/67 n
Smith 13/4/78
T. R., Printer to the Foreign Office 22/9/54
William, Rev. (1811–1882) 4/5/35
Harriss,
John, art dealer 23/3/58
W. 22/1/77
Harrod, H., Col. 25/10/83
Harrold, Mr. 17/12/79
Harrowby *see* Ryder
Harrower, Gordon, Rev. 8/9/90
Harshaw, R. H., Rev. 29/5/88
Hart,
A. 16/12/39
Charles Henry, American biographer 9/4/79 ?
George Augustus Frederick, Rev. (1797–1873) 8/10/49 ?
Henry Wyatt (1850–1886), barrister 3/3/68
Horace, Printer to O. U. P. 25/9/86, 1/11/90, 11/11/92 L
Jesse 27/6/78

Hart (*cont.*)
L., rescue 29/9/75
Percy M. 25/1/75
Solomon Alexander (1806–1881), artist 17/2/71
Harte, Francis Bret (1836–1902), novelist 21/11/88, 25/5/92
Harter, James Collier, Manchester merchant 12/8/53
Hartford, Mrs. 20/3/53
Hartill, John, Dudley ironfounder 9/10/47
Harting, James Vincent (–1883), solicitor 26/4/50
Hartington *see* Cavendish
Hartismere *see* Major
Hartley,
Miss 7/11/87
John 4/5/78
J. P. 4/1/87
W. 22/11/77
Hartmann,
Mr., governess's husband 13/7/56
Mrs., governess 27/10/57
Emma, Mrs., patroness of spiritualists 29/10/84, 7/11/84 L
Hartog, Marcus Manuel, Prof. (1851–1924) 15/2/78
Hartopp, Edward Bourchier (1809–1884), tory M.P. 11/3/26
Hartwell,
Edward H. B., consul in Naples 3/1/89
Robert 2/7/66 n
Harty, William, Dr. (1781–1854), protestant physician in Dublin 6/4/37
Harvard University 15/8/78
Harvest, Edward Douglas (–1895), soldier in Ionia 27/11/58
Harvey,
rescue 14/10/61
servant 3/10/53
Mrs. 4/12/32 ?
Alexander, Dr. (1811–1889) 2/7/58
Annie 30/7/87
D. 8/6/75
D., Miss 23/12/87
Daniel Whittle (1786–1863), radical M.P., police commander 6/2/33, 20/9/61
Frederick Burn, Rev. 11/8/77
George, maltster 4/12/32 ?
George Sheppard, Major 1/3/78 ?
John, Sir, colonial governor 17/6/46
Joseph 30/3/74
Richard, Rev. (1798–1889), Shelley's fag at Eton 30/3/34, 5/10/75
Robert John Harvey, Sir (1817–1870), 1st Baronet (1868) 24/5/66
Thomas, Rev. 5/3/45
Wallace, trainee barrister 6/8/48
William Wigan, Rev. (1810–1883) 2/10/43, 12/7/71 L, 26/2/72 L
Harvey Beales & Co. 21/7/91
Harwood,
Mrs. 2/9/78
Richard (1815–1887), Bolton cottonspinner 4/2/57, 26/9/64 n
Haskell, B. D., American theologian 15/1/90 ?
Haskins, Edmund Henry, Rev. 18/1/75
Haskoll, Joseph, Rev. (–1871) 16/11/51
Haslam, J. 21/7/75
Haslems, The Misses 6/11/60
Haslett, Samuel Torrens, Dr., physician 27/12/77, 11/12/79
Haslewood,
Ashby Blair, Rev. 29/7/48
Boulby, Rev. (1829–1897) 25/11/77
Hassan, Prince, Prince of Egypt 18/3/78
Hassard, A. 14/7/91
Hasslacher, Père, Jesuit 20/10/45
Hassún, Rizk Allah, publisher 28/6/77
Hastie,
Alexander (1805–1864), liberal M.P. 25/2/53 ?
Archibald (1791–1857), liberal M.P. 25/2/53 ?
W. 30/8/78
Hastings,
Edith Maud Abney- (1833–1874), Countess of Loudoun 16/9/71
Francis Theophilus Henry (1808–1875), 12th Earl of Huntingdon (1828) 6/7/70
George Woodyatt (1825–1917), liberal unionist M.P. 12/7/58, 31/3/86
H., Mrs. 6/12/64, 4/1/65, 18/1/65
Henry James, Rev. (1798–1875) 13/8/36 ?
William Warren, London solicitor 27/11/47
Haswell, George C., geologist 7/8/67 ?
Hasy, Mr. 19/6/32
Hatch, Henry John, Rev. 26/4/55 ?
Hatchard,
John (1769–1849), Piccadilly bookseller 28/7/38
John, Rev. 2/3/43
Hatchell, John (–1870), lawyer 19/6/54
Hatchett, J. 3/12/27
Hathaway, Edward Penrose, barrister 17/6/51 ?
Hatherley *see* Wood
Hatherley,
Rev. Mr., convert to Orthodox Church 2/1/72, 21/6/75
S., of Solihull 1/9/55
Hatherton *see* Littleton
Hatson, Mr. 5/3/80
Hatton,
G., of Carlton on Trent 2/10/32

George James Finch- (1815–1887), Viscount Maidstone (1826), 11th Earl of Winchilsea (1858), tory M.P. 12/12/37, 8/7/52
George William Finch- (1791–1858), 10th Earl of Winchilsea (1826), ultra tory 31/7/32
G. S. 16/2/57
Joshua, wrote as 'Guy Roslyn' 21/3/76, 24/9/78
William Robert Finch-, Rev. (1827–1909) 9/1/61 ?
Hattori, Ayawo, Japanese 6/2/91
Haug,
Karl 26/4/84
Martin, orientalist 2/7/75 ?
Haughton,
Benjamin, engineer 20/5/78 ?
William, Rev. 21/7/48 ?
Haurot, Mr. 13/7/69
Havard, Mrs. 5/6/79
Havelock, John 3/4/80
Haverfield, Thomas Tunstall, Rev. (–1866) 30/3/51 n
Haversham *see* Hayter
Haverty, Mrs. 20/8/88
Havill, Mrs. 23/6/74
Hawarden *see* Maude
Hawden, J. 21/2/78
Haweis, Hugh Reginald, Rev. (1838–1901) 24/11/72
Hawes, Benjamin, Sir, liberal M.P. 25/9/41
Hawke, J. 31/7/77
Hawker,
Mrs. 19/9/80
the Misses 3/8/46
Robert Stephen, Rev. (–1875) 25/5/49
Hawkins,
C. W. 1/1/80
Edward (–1867), of British Museum 4/5/52
Edward, Rev. 23/1/42
Ernest, Rev., secretary of S. P. G. 21/4/41, 8/5/41
F. W., of *The Theatre* 4/9/78
Henry, Judge Sir (1817–1907), 1st Baron Brampton (1899) 23/12/91
J. H., Mrs. 24/4/35 ?
John (1791–1877), solicitor and charity organiser 4/12/57
John Heywood, whig M.P. 24/4/35 n
Mary Anne, née Buckle 29/7/42 ?
Robert Samuel 29/12/77
S., of Thanet 23/6/88
William, Rev. (1776–1849), master at Cheltenham grammar school 4/9/25
W. T. 25/9/88
Hawksford, Mr. 28/9/86
Hawkshaw, John, Sir (1811–1891), Knight (1873), engineer 3/2/66
Hawksley, Thomas, Dr., physician 18/8/68
Hawley, Edward, Rev. (1829–1882) 30/10/64
Hawthorn, W. 4/4/91
Hawtrey,
Edward Craven (1789–1862), Headmaster and Provost of Eton 1/4/27, 20/1/52, 4/6/52, 22/2/75, 8/7/78, 3/1/90
Montague John Gregg, Rev. (–1886) 29/3/61
Stephen Thomas, Rev. (–1886) 11/12/54
Hay *see* Cholmondeley, Duff, Ramsay, Wellesley
Hay,
Andrew Leith, Sir (1785–1862), soldier, whig M.P., writer 5/3/35
Anne, née Bragge 22/1/30
G., 8th Marquis of Tweeddale 16/11/35 n
G. H., 7th Earl of Kinnoull 22/1/30 n
Helen Selina, née Sheridan, formerly Lady Dufferin, Lady Gifford 5/7/60
James, Rev. 26/11/89
John, of Leith 23/6/31
John, Lord (1827–), admiral, liberal M.P. 19/12/59
John Baldwin 14/11/78
John Charles Dalrymple, Adm. Sir (1821–1912), tory M.P. 18/2/64, 28/5/84
John Hay Williams-, Sir (1794–1859), 2nd Baronet (1830), formerly Williams 2/7/41 n
Louisa Burton, née Rowley, Lady Kinnoull 23/3/48
'Old Mary', cottager 12/10/34
Robert William (1786–1861), of colonial office 16/4/30
Sarah Elizabeth Hay Williams-, Lady, née Pitt 31/12/56
Thomas, Rev. Dr. (1759–1830) 22/1/30, 29/1/30
Thomas Robert, 10th Earl of Kinnoull 23/3/48
William Montagu, Lord (1827–1911), 10th Marquis of Tweeddale (1878), liberal M.P. 23/3/67
Haycraft, G. 23/9/78
Hayden,
rescue 18/4/64
Frederick William, Rev. 11/10/68
John, Rev. (–1855) 17/3/49
Hayden & Co., Guildford bankers 25/5/75
Haydn,
Joseph T., Mrs. 23/10/56
Joseph Timothy (1786–1856), historian and editor 23/10/56
Haydon,
rescue 12/5/67
Benjamin R. (–1846), artist 26/6/46 n
Hay-Drummond *see* Murray

Hayes,
Mr. 2/1/94
Edith, Mrs., rescue 18/6/62, 5/6/64, 8/8/66, 20/4/68
Edward Samuel, Sir (1806-1860), 3rd Baronet (1827) 12/5/46
George, Sir (1809-1869) 18/12/69 n
John Thomas, publisher 11/12/75 ?
Nathan 5/5/58
Thomas 17/11/86
Thomas, Rev. (-1887) 3/4/28 ?
Thomas Crawford, Dr., physician 9/8/75 ?
Thomas Travers, Lancastrian liberal 10/10/78 ff, 1/9/92 L
Hay-MacKenzie *see* Gower
Hayman,
Elizabeth, née Veysey 9/1/40 ?
Henry, Rev. 4/2/52, 21/3/74
James, author 10/8/68
John, Capt. 9/1/40 n
Richard, Fasque butler 21/9/47
Haynau, Gen. 22/1/44 n
Hayne,
Charles Hayne Seale (1833-1903), liberal M.P. 9/6/89, 5/3/91
Leighton George, Rev. (1835-1883) 20/11/61, 8/6/64
Watson Ward, solicitor 5/4/54 ?
Haynes, W. H., of New York 24/9/87
Hays, J., pamphleteer 26/1/43
Hayter,
Arthur Divett, Sir (1835-1917), 2nd Baronet (1878), 1st Baron Haversham (1906) 27/6/67, 11/10/73, 2/6/83, 8/3/84, 13/6/89, 1/12/93
George, Sir (1792-1871), Knight (1842), portrait painter 23/7/33
Henrietta, née Hope, Lady Hayter 22/10/86, 13/6/89, 1/12/93
William Goodenough, Sir (-1878), 1st Baronet (1858), liberal M.P. 1/1/53
Hayward,
rescue 12/6/88
Abraham (1801-1884), essayist 2/2/39, 13/11/71, 15/11/71, 16/11/71, 19/5/73 n, 17/3/79, 6/4/79, 6/2/84
John Curtis (1804-1874) 11/7/55 ?
R. W. G., architect in Newark 27/3/83 L
Hazard, G. 1/9/75
Hazard & Boucher, printers 1/9/75 n
Hazeldine, John Thomas, solicitor 29/7/78
Hazell, Watson & Viney, Messrs., printers in London and Aylesbury 17/4/90
Hazlehurst,
G. S. 7/10/92 L
Mary 19/8/52
Hazlitt, William (1811-1893), registrar 7/5/60
Hazzeldine, Mr., grocer 29/3/79
Hazzopulo, S. 22/12/82
Head,
Edmund Walker, Sir (1805-1868), 8th Baronet (1838), colonial governor 27/1/34, 28/2/63
F. H. 5/5/58
Francis Bond, Sir (-1875), 1st Baronet (1836) 13/6/40
Henry Erskine, Rev. (1797-1860) 8/8/57 ?
Headlam,
Arthur Charles (1862-1947) 7/2/90
Thomas 23/12/26 ?
Thomas Emerson (1813-1875), liberal M.P. 17/3/60
Heald, H. G. 19/3/77
Heale, Edmund Markham, Rev. (1825-1874) 22/8/60
Healey,
Mr. 14/2/60
Randolph Eddowed, Rev. (1847-1933) 5/10/77
Healy,
J. J. 22/11/87
John, Rev. (-1883) 28/8/57 ?
Maurice (1859-1923), home rule M.P. Cork City 15/4/91
Patrick 8/7/74 ?
R. C., Capt. 13/9/76
Timothy Michael (1855-1931), home rule M.P. 19/7/81 c, 27/7/81 n, 12/10/81, 12/4/82, 22/4/82 c, 25/4/82, 16/5/82, 10/6/82 c, 10/2/83, 15/2/83, 7/4/83 c, 31/10/84, 18/9/85, 11/10/85 n, 4/12/88, 5/12/90, 15/4/91, 12/4/93
Heap, C. 22/9/86
Heaphy, rescue 4/10/73
Heaps, J. L. 7/1/87
Heard, Mr. 9/3/75
Hearn, James, Rev. (1785-1864) 2/4/57 ?
Heartley, Charles Tebbott, Rev. (1824-1894), headmaster 31/12/56 fl
Heath,
rescue 8/2/62, 13/8/65
Mrs. 16/4/75
Charles, Rev. 20/3/76 ?
H. H. 12/1/78
John Benjamin (1790-1879), Director of Bank of England 13/1/44 n
M., Mrs., of Greenwich 30/4/65
Thomas, of Greenwich 24/1/65, 6/2/65
William, Commissioner for oaths 15/3/58
Heathcote,
Mr., the Kerrison's tutor 29/1/37
George, Rev. (1811-1895) 14/2/39
William, Sir 3/5/38
Heathfield,
Richard, published on taxation 17/6/56
W. E. 31/5/89
Heatley,
Grant H. Tod- 8/4/62

J. W. 20/8/70
Heaton,
G. 18/3/78
John Henniker (1848–1914), tory M.P. 30/10/86
William Cartledge, Rev. 2/8/78 ?
Heavyside, James William Lucas, Rev. (–1897) 17/5/52
Hebditch, S., Rev., nonconformist 22/5/75
Hebeler, Bernhard, Prussian Consul-General 2/8/43
Hebert, Charles, Rev. 17/4/45
Heckler, Isaac Thomas, Rev. (1819–1888), Roman Catholic 24/1/76 n
Heckley, Mr. 29/5/57
Hedderwick, T. C., on Eighty Club executive committee in 1890ies 10/8/76
Hedgeland, Philip, Rev. 15/8/55
Hedley, William, Rev. (–1884) 15/3/53
Hegan, Hall & Co., copper smelters 29/5/43
Hegel, George Wilhelm Friedrich (1770–1831), German philosopher 17/12/38 n
Heine, A., Dr. 4/3/80
Heinemann,
Arnold Heinrich 13/2/75 ?
Louis, shipping agent 16/3/59
William (1863–1920), publisher 24/2/90
Hel, rescue 9/7/90
Helbert,
F., Capt., organiser of Mrs Gladstone's home at Snaresbrooke 27/9/66, 21/11/67
F., Mrs. 27/9/66 n, 4/12/69
Helena Augusta Victoria, Princess, Princess of Britain and of Schleswig Holstein 25/5/46
Helena of Nassau, Princess (1831–1888) 18/8/38
Hellen, Mr. 14/2/80
Hellier, John Shaw, Rev. 30/4/79
Hellmuth, Isaac, Bp. 27/11/83
Hellyer, Thomas 2/3/76
Helmore,
R. H. 2/6/87
Thomas, Rev. (1811–1890), precentor 8/12/59
Helps, Arthur, Sir (1813–1875), Knight (1872), clerk to the Privy Council 12/11/60, 20/6/71 L
Hely, antiquarian and dealer 4/4/32
Hemer, Luke 2/4/78, 24/12/86
Heming,
Miss, model 5/8/59
Demster (1778–1874), barrister 2/11/64
H., involved in Newcastle's estate 12/2/67
Richard, of Uxbridge 20/4/35 n
Thomas (1804–1836), barrister 1/1/33, 20/4/35 n
Hemingway, F. Piercy 4/4/89
Hemstock, Richard, Newark victualler 5/8/34
Henchman, J., secretary to Metropolitan railway 16/2/65, 2/12/65
Henderson,
rescue 11/11/69
Miss, governess 5/2/50
Edmund Yeamans, Sir (1821–1896), Knight (1878), Chief Commissioner of Metropolitan Police 24/2/72
Frank (1836–1889), liberal M.P. 26/8/80
George, Adm. 25/1/47
H. D. 6/11/69 n
Henry Glass, Rev., G's chaplain 18/8/61
James, journalist 23/10/43
J. C. 12/12/77
J. D. 20/6/68
John, architect 6/10/40
John (1796–1858), collector 9/2/36 ?
W. D., of Belfast 28/8/74
William George, Rev. (–1905) 19/5/51
William James, cabinet maker 22/9/49 ?
Hendricks,
Miss 7/8/45
Frederick 27/6/67 ?
Philip Edward 7/8/45 n
Hendrie, G. 20/2/57
Hendy, Francis Paul James, Rev. (–1904) 28/3/51
Heneage,
Edward (1840–1922), 1st Baron Heneage (1896), liberal unionist M.P. 8/3/75, 9/4/86 L
George Fieschi (1800–1868), liberal M.P. 26/1/62
Hengelmuller De Hengervar, Baron 4/10/80
Hengstenberg, Ernst Wilhelm, Prof. (1802–1869), 'fundamentalist' of theology, Berlin 17/12/38 n
Henley,
rescue 4/6/83
Joseph Warner (1793–1884), tory M.P. 13/3/53
Henner, L. 1/11/75, 18/11/75
Hennessy,
Henry, Prof. 5/7/78
John Pope, Sir (1834–1891), tory M.P. 16/3/61, 7/10/91
Henniker *see* Major
Henniker, Florence, Mrs., novelist 10/5/91
Henri, T., Gladstone's oculist 17/1/86, 19/1/86, 7/5/86, 22/12/87
Henry,
Brother 29/4/75
J., of Edinburgh 5/8/78
Mitchell (1826–1910), home rule M.P. 3/3/73, 20/5/82
Pooley Shuldman (–1881), President, Queen's, Belfast 20/4/53
Stuart 2/1/34
William, of Dublin 10/8/57
W. W., of U.S.A. 10/6/92

Henry, the butler 25/6/68 n
Hens, George, policeman 31/3/80
Henslow, Mr., of Hawarden 14/10/89
Hepburn, H. P., soldier 2/1/47
Heppell, W. J. 8/8/91
Hepple, Edward 21/8/58
Heptonsball, Mr. 5/3/79
Herald, William D., Rev., Church of Scotland 1/10/76 n
Heraud, John Abraham (1799–1887), journalist 11/5/58
Herbert *see* Gardner, Hügel, Meade, Murray, Parry, Pusey, Vesey
Herbert,
rescue 11/6/61
Arthur James, Sir (1820–1897), Knight (1882) 20/1/59
Auberon Edward William Molyneux (1838–1906), radical M.P. 26/3/69, 11/3/73, 25/1/78
C., of Demerara 8/8/42
C., rescue 8/11/59
Catherine (–1856), Countess of Pembroke (1808) 21/11/56
Edward James (1818–1891), 3rd Earl of Powis (1848), Viscount Clive, tory M.P. 13/4/43, 4/10/82 L
Evelyn (–1875), née Stanhope, Lady Carnarvon (1861) 8/7/62, 25/7/68
George, clerk of Bills at Treasury 2/6/35 ?
George A., 11th Earl of Pembroke 13/4/48 n
George Edward Stanhope Molyneux (1866–1923), 5th Earl of Carnarvon (1890) 5/7/90
George Robert Charles (1850–1895), 13th Earl of Pembroke (1862) 16/6/56 n, 30/8/66, 14/9/73, 29/9/73
Gertrude (–1906), née Talbot, Lady Pembroke 16/6/56
G. S. 16/12/93 L
G. S., secretary of S.E. railway 11/4/51
Henry Arthur (–1866), liberal M.P. 26/4/53
Henry George (1772–1833), 2nd Earl of Carnarvon (1811) 3/10/31
Henry Howard Molyneux; Earl of Carnarvon 2/3/67 n
Henry John George (1800–1849), 3rd Earl of Carnarvon (1823), tory M.P. 11/12/38
John Rogers (1810–1890), painted G's portrait (1873), artist 17/6/53, 3/5/56, 2/8/60, 18/4/61, 4/7/61, 23/7/63, 24/2/64, 14/9/67, 15/9/67, 15/12/73 ff, 10/2/74, 14/7/74, 14/6/75, 21/6/75, 29/4/80, 23/11/80
K., Mrs., also known as Bailey, rescue 1/8/61, 15/5/63, 20/11/63, 19/5/64
Mary (–1866), née Balfour 10/5/53
Mary Elizabeth (1822–1911), née A'Court, Lady Herbert of Lea 4/3/47, 20/1/57, 16/3/57, 8/6/59, 1/8/61, 9/8/61, 24/10/62, 22/8/66, 25/8/66, 10/9/66, 24/9/66, 4/6/67, 6/11/70, 8/11/70, 7/6/71, 11/6/73, 15/6/73, 13/11/73, 10/12/85, 29/8/89, 31/8/89
Michael Henry, Sir (1857–1903) 17/10/79
Ottavia, née Spinelli, Lady Pembroke 16/7/50
Percy Egerton, Sir (1822–1876), soldier, tory M.P. 13/9/56
Robert George Wyndham, Sir (1831–1905), Knight (1882), G's private secretary at colonial office (1846) 3/12/54 n, 11/1/55, 4/10/81, 6/8/84 c
Robert Henry (–1862), 12th Earl of Pembroke (1827) 16/7/50 n
Sidney 12/11/30
Wilfrid Vincent, artist 9/3/68
William, Very Rev., dean of Winchester 20/7/40 n
William George, Lieut., R. N. 2/12/50 ?
William Reginald (–1870), G's godson 18/6/54
Herbert Martyne *see* Ross
Hereford *see* Devereux
Herford, E., of Macclesfield 12/9/67
Hering, E., rescue 22/7/50
Herington, Mr. 15/2/78
Heriot,
George, goldsmith, founder of Heriot's school, Edinburgh 12/12/33 n
Warner, Mrs., née Musurus 3/5/72
Herkless, John, Rev. Prof. (1855–1920) 7/11/93, 13/11/93
Herkomer, Hubert von, Sir (1849–1914), Knight (1907), artist 11/10/79, 30/3/82, 23/5/88, 25/7/88 n
Hermann,
Hugo, artist 28/4/58
J. 25/5/78
Hernbrook, Mr. 14/8/90
Heron,
Denis Caulfield (1826–1881), liberal M.P. 6/5/71
Joseph, Sir (1809–1889), Knight (1869), Manchester town clerk 11/10/53
Robert, Sir (1765–1854), 2nd Baronet (1805), whig M.P. 8/3/38
Herries,
Charles John, Sir (1815–1883), Knight (1880), chairman, Board of Inland Revenue 20/10/60, 7/5/80 L, 27/5/80 L, 6/8/80 L, 19/11/80 L, 7/12/80 L, 9/12/80 L, 21/12/80 L, 5/3/81 L, 11/3/81 L, 29/3/81 L
John Charles (1778–1855), tory M.P. 1/4/34, 7/12/80
William Lewis, Sir (–1857), Public Accounts Board 2/2/53

Herries, Farquhar, Davidson, Chapman & Co., bankers 5/2/52
Herring, Armine Styleman, Rev. (1831–1896) 29/12/76
Herrings, rescue 3/8/81
Herschell *see* Gordon
Herschell,
  Farrer, Sir 28/4/80
  John Frederick William, Sir, Baronet (1838), astronomer 22/7/53
Hertford *see* Conway, Seymour
Hertslet, Edward, Sir (1824–1902), librarian to the Foreign Office 30/10/80
Hertyka, Dr. 8/1/92
Hervey,
  Dr. 11/1/74
  Alfred, Lord (1816–1875), tory M.P. 25/2/57, 22/1/77
  Arthur Charles, Lord (1808–1894), bishop of Bath and Wells (1869) 8/10/25, 2/7/84 L, 3/7/84 L
  Charles Amelius, Rev. Lord (–1880) 5/8/54
  Frederick William (1769–1859), 1st Marquis of Bristol (1826), 5th Earl Hervey 20/6/26
  Frederick William (1800–1864), 2nd Marquis of Bristol (1859), Earl Jermyn, Peelite M.P. 26/4/38
  Frederick William John (1834–1919), Baron Jermyn (1859), 3rd Marquis of Bristol (1864), Peelite M.P. 30/12/60
  Harriet Charlotte Sophia, Lady (–1899), née Ryde 5/8/54
  Henry Arthur William (–1908) 31/7/61 n
  John William Nicholas, Lord (1841–1902) 19/5/90
  Selina Catherine, Lady (–1911), née Meade, formerly Lady Vernon, then Lady Bidwell 31/7/61
Herz *see* Rothschild
Heseltine,
  Charles, Mrs. 20/1/62
  M. Catherine, Miss 13/6/44
  William, stockbroker, antiquary 21/12/37
Hesketh, William, Rev. (1795–1858) 11/8/29
Hesketh, Bamford-,family, of Gwrych Castle 31/8/26 n
Hesp, rescue 13/7/63
Hessel, Dr. 2/2/73
Hesselby, Mr. 20/10/86
Hessey, James Augustus, Rev. Dr. (–1892), headmaster 14/3/54
Hewett,
  Edward, consul in West Africa 22/11/83 n
  Edward Balvaird, Rev. 2/11/91
  John William, Rev. (1824–1886) 27/12/56
  Prescott Gardner, Sir (1812–1891), 1st Baronet (1883), surgeon, connoisseur 9/8/61, 17/5/68, 22/3/71, 6/6/75
  William Nathan Wrighte, Adm. Sir (1834–1888) 22/11/83, 6/2/84, 12/2/84, 19/3/84, 5/5/84 c
Hewett, W.& Co., chinoiserie dealers 6/1/57, 27/2/57
Hewitt,
  E., Miss 15/5/79
  James (1811–1887), 4th Viscount Lifford (1855) 31/10/30, 21/9/71
  S. 12/1/77
Hewlett, Henry Gray (1832–1897), antiquarian 16/7/60 ?
Hewley, Sarah, Lady, née Wolrych 6/2/34
Hewson, E. 5/5/79
Hext,
  George, Rev. 15/3/53
  John Hawkins, Rev. (–1878) 17/3/54
Heygate,
  William Edward, Rev. (1816–1902) 3/7/57
  William Unwin (1825–1902), tory M.P. 17/5/65
Heys, J. 19/11/78
Heytesbury *see* A'Court
Heywood *see* Gaskell
Heywood,
  A. M., Mr.& Mrs. 4/8/54, 2/7/58, 25/5/73
  B. A. 1/4/80
  Benjamin, Sir (1793–1865), banker and M.P. 25/5/37 ?
  James (1810–1897), liberal M.P. 14/5/53
  John Pemberton (1803–1877), Liverpool and London banker, a liberal 27/10/56 n, 18/6/60, 5/4/66 n
  John Pemberton, Mrs. 21/10/52, 27/10/56 n, 18/6/60
  Sophia Ann, Lady (–1852), née Robinson 25/5/37 ?
  Thomas Percival, Sir (1823–1897), 2nd Baronet (1865) 2/1/83
  T. J. 2/11/78
Heywood, Kennards & Co., bankers 30/6/60
Heyworth, Lawrence (1786–1872), liberal M.P. 12/4/60
Hibbert,
  F., cottonspinner 10/10/78
  H. 20/9/87
  John Tomlinson, Sir (1824–1908), Knight (1893), liberal M.P. 15/3/64, 3/2/85
Hibjame, F. J. 8/4/90
Hichens *see* Tennyson
Hick,
  John (1815–1894), tory M.P. 20/11/71
  W. M. 3/5/77
Hickey, Mrs. 17/3/40
Hickie, M. 21/5/78
Hicklin, John (–1877), journalist 11/9/40
Hickling,
  Edmund L., Rev. (–1869) 24/8/68 ?
  J., Rev., Wesleyan minister 13/6/35

Hickling (*cont.*)
Robert, printer and journalist, Nottingham 1/12/32
Hicks,
rescue 16/8/58, 12/4/59
William ('Hicks Pasha'), Col. (1830–1883), commander of Khedive's army 3/11/82 n, 22/11/83, 28/6/84, 11/2/85, 30/5/85
Hickson,
Miss 24/6/79
G. 18/5/76
William Edward (1803–1870), educational philanthropist 18/5/38
Hidromenos, Andreas M., Greek author 8/5/75
Higgin, William, Bp. (1793–1867), bishop of Derry 30/5/63
Higgins,
C., Rev. 26/8/78
C. H., Dr., author in Birkenhead 26/10/86 n
Charles Longuet (1806–1885), philanthropist 17/7/35 ff
G. 14/12/87
George Gore Ouseley (1818–1874), liberal M.P. 15/8/53
J. F., Rev. 15/8/79
Matthew James (1810–1868), known as 'Jacob Omnium', journalist 10/2/49
W. C. 21/2/67
Higginson,
Mrs., G's household 2/9/51
John Macaulay, Sir, colonial governor 2/2/46
Higgs 16/8/41
Higham,
James, assistant secretary to National Debt Commissioners 22/11/53, 29/12/53
Samuel, secretary to National Debt Commissioners 24/1/48
Walter 15/11/74
Highfield, George, hatter 25/5/50 ?
Highland, T. H., of California 21/4/77
Higinbotham,
Miss 15/11/76
Newburgh, civil servant 22/3/55
Higman, W., Rev. 20/4/78
Hignett, John, Chester solicitor 27/9/49
Hildyard,
George, solicitor 3/5/50
James, Rev. (1809–1887) 13/11/56
Robert Charles (1800–1857), tory M.P. 25/11/55
Hiley, Richard William, Rev. 15/4/68
Hill *see* Cecil
Hill,
rescue 11/11/73
Annie, Miss, servant 3/12/93 n
Arthur 15/1/79
Arthur William, Lord (1846–1931), tory M.P. 31/5/88
Charles, Sabbatarian 15/2/75, 13/1/76
C. R. 28/12/85
David Octavius (1802–1870), artist 6/10/51 ?
D. D. 16/5/76
Edward, Rev. (1807–1900) 4/1/49
Edward, Rev. (1810–) 23/10/28
E. P. 3/7/79
Frederick, brother of Sir R. Hill 2/9/79
Frederick (1803–1896), Post Office clerk 16/3/60 ?
Frederick H., editor of *Daily News* 25/10/76, 11/8/77, 4/3/79, 27/9/80 L, 7/1/81 L, 25/10/84, 14/1/86 n
George, Rev. 13/10/90
George Birkbeck Norman 11/12/80
H. A. 16/12/74
H. B., Rev. 13/9/79
J., née Evans, rescue 9/6/79
J., Miss 18/7/79
James 16/1/79
James, clerk 28/2/42
Jeffrey, Rev. 17/12/74
J. M., of Burslem 7/9/63
John, Rev. (1786–1855), Vice Principal, St. Edmund Hall, Oxford 23/5/30
John Harwood, Rev. 14/9/48
J. Rowley 23/2/82
Octavia, Miss (1839–1912), philanthropist 8/5/84
Pascoe Grenfell, Rev. (1804–1882) 18/12/58 ?
R. G., Irish farmer 30/6/71
Richard, Rev. 16/3/38 ?
Rowland (1744–1833), itinerant preacher 25/3/29
Rowland, Gen. (1772–1842), 1st Viscount Hill 5/5/35
Rowland, Sir (1800–1875), 2nd Viscount Hill (1842), tory M.P. 22/5/32 n, 12/6/61, 21/3/63, 25/2/64
Rowland Clegg (1833–1895), 3rd Viscount Hill (1875), tory M.P. 21/7/59
Rowley, Bp. (1836–1887) 4/10/78
S. W., of Whitby 15/9/71
Thomas, Ven. (1790–1875), archdeacon of Derby 20/6/56
Thomas Rowley (1816–1896), liberal M.P. 10/1/84
William Noel- (1773–1842), 3rd Baron Berwick (1832), diplomat 1/5/32
Hillary, William, Sir (–1847), 1st Baronet (1805) 7/8/44
Hillebrand, Karl Arnold 5/4/75, 18/5/79
Hilliard, Ernest Stafford, Rev. 24/12/90

Hillier,
Edward John, Rev. (–1908) 21/2/80
J. 26/9/88
Hillingdon *see* Mills
Hillock, D. 11/12/75
Hillocks,
G. 11/7/67
James Inches, Rev. 27/1/77
James J., missionary 18/12/60
Hills,
Mr., of U.S.A. 5/4/67
George, Rev. 27/11/47 ?, 2/2/64 ?
Hillyard,
E. 16/12/72 n
E. A., Mrs. 16/12/72
Temple, Rev. 2/11/63
William H., Dr., physician 16/6/58
Hillyer & Fenwick, London attorneys 12/3/45 n
Hilskin, Mr. 22/7/76
Hilson,
Miss 6/4/80
William 23/12/85
Hilton,
Mrs. 28/11/78
Henry, Newark merchant 30/3/33
Henry, Rev. (1811–) 7/3/34
J. Deane 15/6/78 ?
John, of United Kingdom Alliance 28/7/79
Joseph, Rev. 17/2/53 ?
Hime, Maurice Charles, Dr., author, of Londonderry 19/11/86
Hinchinbrooke *see* Montagu
Hincks,
Francis, Sir (–1885), Canadian politician 14/6/49
Thomas, Ven. (1796–1882), of Connor 2/7/69
Hind, Charles J., property tax clerk 23/2/63
Hinde,
Messrs. 8/11/78
Francis & Sons 16/12/78
Henry Pelly, lawyer 23/7/44
John Hodgson- (1806–1869), historian, tory M.P. 4/3/51
Hindley,
Charles, carpet maker 7/4/76
Charles (–1857), liberal M.P. 24/9/46
F. W. 15/10/90
R. P. 1/12/77
Hindlip *see* Allsop
Hinds, Samuel, Bp., bishop of Norwich 14/1/50
Hine,
J. C., solicitor? 16/10/65, 2/12/67
Thomas Chambers 10/8/76
Hines,
H. C. 30/5/76
Henry 30/5/76 ?
Hinshelwood, A. Ernest, poet 29/3/93
Hinson, William, Rev. 23/3/58
Hinton,
John Howard, baptist 24/6/53 ?
'Old' 4/12/31
Zebulon Wright, Rev. 2/5/57
Hirlam, H. 29/6/77
Hiron, John, boot manufacturer 1/3/53 ?
Hirsch,
Franz, Dr. 27/6/77
Maurice, Rev. 12/5/92
Hirschfeld, French journalist 22/1/45
Hirst,
Alfred, of Huddersfield 26/1/86
Thomas Archer, Prof. (1830–1892), mathematician 18/3/68
William (1777–1858), Leeds wool manufacturer 18/1/47
William, Rev. 27/6/78
Hisborn, Mr. 26/6/77
Hitchcock,
Mr., of U.S.A. 30/3/70
Simon, brewer 27/2/68
Hitchin, W. H. 16/4/74
Hitchings, James, Rev. (1790–1850) 25/7/31 ?
Hitchman,
Mr. 4/9/78, 29/7/79
Mrs. 5/9/81
James, known as P. V. G. de Montgomery, pamphleteer 22/5/58
Hitger, Mr. 29/5/76
Hoare *see* Kinnaird
Hoare,
Messrs., bankers 5/11/75
Charles James, Archdeacon (1781–1865), Archdeacon of Winchester (1829) 31/1/38
Edward Newenham, Dean (1802–1877) 18/2/68, 7/4/68
E. N., Mrs. 20/7/68
Frances Mary, Miss (–1869) 1/10/51 ?
Henry (–1865), sheriff, synod enthusiast 2/3/52
Henry Ainslie, Sir (1824–1894), 5th Baronet (1857), liberal M.P. 30/7/67
Mary, Lady (–1871), née Marsham 2/3/52
Peter Richard (1772–1849), banker 1/10/51 n
Samuel (1783–1847), banker 2/12/37 ?
William Henry, Rev. (1809–1888) 12/5/68
Hobart *see* Foster
Hobart,
Augustus Charles, Pasha (1822–1886) 19/4/77, 10/2/85, 24/8/92
Catherine, Lady, née Carr 15/12/80 ?
Georgina Mary, Lady (–1900) 15/12/80
Robert Henry, Sir (1836–1928), 1st Baronet (1914) 27/12/77
Vere Henry (1818–1875), Baron Hobart, author 15/7/51

Hobbes, singer 13/11/25
Hobbling, W. B., Rev. 2/6/75
Hobbs, H. H. 11/4/88
Hobhouse,
Arthur, Sir (1819–1904), 1st Baron Hobhouse (1885), judge 17/4/83
Edmund, Bp. (–1904) 15/3/53
Henry (1854–1937), liberal unionist M. P 8/3/93 c
Henry William (1791–1868), liberal M.P. 23/8/36 n, 3/4/54
John Cam, Sir (1786–1869), 1st Baron Broughton (1851), whig M.P. 7/5/33 n
Hobson,
J. B. 5/3/92
William Francis, Rev. 16/1/76
Hochschild, Carl, Baron, Norway and Sweden ambassador 25/8/70
Hocker, William, Rev. 30/7/45 ?
Hockey, Miller, Mr. 1/4/88
Hockler, Messrs. 28/11/77
Hodder & Stoughton, publishers 28/11/77
Hodge,
F. R. 18/9/68
J. 25/9/78
Hodges,
J. T., Rev. 17/9/77
Thomas Law (1776–1857), liberal M.P. 22/1/53
W. 21/11/78
Hodgetts, Thomas Webb, of Hagley 14/2/50
Hodgkin, Thomas, physician and humanitarian 15/5/44
Hodgkinson,
C. G. 14/6/92
George, Newark solicitor 3/11/42
Grosvenor (1818–1881), Newark solicitor, liberal M.P. 3/11/42 n, 19/10/44, 17/4/67
Hodgson *see* Labouchere
Hodgson,
Mr. 12/5/38
Christopher 1/7/40
Edward Tucker (–1832) 31/10/27
Francis, Rev. (1781–1852), Provost of Eton 1/5/44 n
John, barrister 21/5/28 ?
Joseph (1788–1869), surgeon 19/12/42, 30/4/53 ff, 3/5/53, 3/6/53, 2/7/54 ff, 16/7/54
Kirkman Daniel (1814–1879), liberal M.P., banker 29/6/54, 23/11/65, 11/5/66, 6/4/69, 8/4/69
Richard (1812–1879), tory M.P. 29/8/62
Robert (1773–1844), dean of Carlisle (1820) 11/4/30
Robert, Rev. (1844–1917) 8/9/78
Shadworth Hollaway (1832–1912) 3/4/80 ?
W. E. 23/12/90
Hodson,
George Frederick John, Sir (1806–1888), 3rd Baronet 20/10/77 n
James Shirley (1819–1899) 6/6/77
Meriel Anne, Lady 20/10/77
Thomas E., of Lewes 23/12/46 ?
Hoey, John Baptist Cashel (1828–1892), barrister and Roman Catholic 11/9/68
Hofer, Andreas (1767–1810), Tyrolean national hero 29/6/32
Hoffay, Ernest Albert, of the Audit Office 22/2/54
Hoffgaard, J. 25/6/78
Hoffman,
19/5/32
Henry, City merchant 5/2/53 ?
Mark, of Paris 22/2/68
Hoffmann, K. 2/8/89
Hoffmeister, William Carter, Sir (1817–1890), surgeon 20/8/84
Hofgarten, shop for bronzes 28/12/38
Hofland, Mr. 30/10/75
Hofler, Prof., of Munich 1/10/45
Hog,
Harriet, Mrs. 21/3/80 n
Thomas Alexander (1835–1908), liberal of Newliston, Midlothian 21/3/80
Hogan, J. F. 7/5/89
Hogg *see* Marjoribanks
Hogg,
Annie Claudina, Miss (–1921) 3/2/80 ?
G. 27/12/56
Henry Lee, Dr., physician 9/10/78 ?
Jabez (1817–1899), eye surgeon 31/5/79
James 8/7/87
James MacNaghten McGarel, Col. Sir (1823–1890), 1st Baron Magheramorne (1887) 17/9/62, 24/6/88
James Weir, Sir (1790–1876), 1st Baronet (1846), barrister, Peelite M.P. 24/5/37
Lewis Maydwell, Rev. 26/1/76
Mary Claudina, née Swinton 15/6/46
Quintin (1845–1903), educationalist 26/3/92
Hoghton, Henry De, Sir (1821–1876), 9th Baronet (1862) 20/5/68
Hohenlohe, Louis von, Prince (1823–1866) 17/12/58 ?
Holbech *see* Mordaunt
Holborow, A. 10/6/92
Holbrook, Erastus, Dr., of U.S.A. 11/10/60
Holden,
Isaac, Sir (1807–1897), liberal M.P. 29/4/67
J. 2/9/79
James 17/5/69
Robert (–1844), Nottingham magnate 31/7/32
Holdroyd, J. 25/8/77
Hole, Samuel Reynolds, Rev. 28/3/77

Holford *see* Grey
Holford,
George Peter (-1839), penologist 10/8/35
Gwynne, Mrs. 1/7/73 ?
Mary Anne, Mrs. 12/2/90
Robert Stayner (1808-1892), tory M.P. 6/11/57, 2/7/70, 12/2/90
Holgate, William John Jennings, solicitor 22/6/67 ?
Holiday,
Henry (1839-1927), artist and liberal 8/1/80, 13/12/80, 12/5/87, 8/11/89
Mary, Miss 4/7/87
Holken, Maharajah of 13/6/87
Holker,
John, Sir (1828-1882), tory M.P. 19/5/82, 9/5/87 n
Mary Lucia, Lady Holker 5/5/83, 30/5/83, 7/2/85, 26/4/87, 9/5/87, 11/5/87, 16/5/87, 21/6/87, 25/6/87, 1/7/87, 4/7/87, 16/7/87, 30/4/90, 10/4/91
Holl,
Francis Montague (1845-1888), portrait painter 25/2/85, 2/4/87, 23/7/87, 23/9/87, 29/10/87, 31/10/87, 1/11/87, 2/11/87, 3/11/87, 4/11/87, 24/3/88, 25/7/88 n
R. D. 12/5/92
Holland,
Mr., of Hull, photographer 16/11/86
Caroline 27/2/75
Charles, Rev. 10/7/77 ?
Edward, Macinroy's agent at Fasque 15/9/51
Edward (1806-1875), liberal M.P. 6/3/60
Francis James, Rev. (1828-1907) 20/8/71 n
Frederick Whitmore, Rev. (1838-1881) 14/7/77
Henry, Sir (1788-1873), physician 14/3/55, 5/11/58
Henry Lancelot (1808-1893), banker 11/5/66 n
Henry Scott, Rev. (1847-1918) 31/10/74 ?, 9/8/76, 12/1/78, 10/9/78, 29/7/81, 27/9/81, 13/10/81, 27/9/83, 28/9/83, 18/8/84, 19/10/88, 9/12/90, 26/10/91 ff, 1/2/93
Henry Thurstan (1825-1914), 1st Baron Knutsford (1888), colonial secretary 29/5/90
Henry William 18/4/80
H. W. 18/4/80
James, Hawarden farmer 12/9/73
Samuel (1803-), liberal M.P. 19/9/92
Thomas Erskine, Sir (1835-1926), jurist 19/8/75
Holland, William & Sons, cabinet makers 13/1/54
Hollands, William Simons, architect 15/4/54 ?
Hollar, Joseph 12/2/76
Hollingsworth, Nathaniel 1/8/40
Hollingworth, A. E. 7/4/91
Hollins, Kate, Mrs., rescue 20/12/84
Hollinsed, Richard Edward, Rev. (1821-1859) 31/5/56
Hollinshed, Brook, Mrs. 14/8/91
Holloway, Thomas (1800-1883), patent medicine manufacturer 17/6/73
Holloway College 14/12/81 n
Hollowell, James Hirst, Rev., congregationalist 20/5/89
Holman,
George 5/9/87
William Henry, Rev., navy chaplain 16/4/58 ?
Holme, Samuel, master builder 15/10/36
Holmes,
rescue 30/1/74
Mrs. 9/1/86
Baptist James, Rev. 25/12/87
George John, Col. (1813-1903) 26/5/66 ?
Hugh (1840-1916), tory M.P. 11/2/80
Oliver Wendell (1809-1894), American judge and raconteur 6/3/91
Richard 12/10/90
Samuel, of Liverpool 16/12/59
Samuel, Rev. 20/4/40 ?
T. T., Rev. 28/9/86 n
W. B. 21/2/79
Holmesdale *see* Amherst
Holmgren, Frithiof 20/4/78 ?
Holms,
J. Douglas 13/6/88
John (1830-1891), liberal M.P. 21/5/70, 3/5/75
William, liberal M.P. 31/12/82 ?
Holroyd *see* Stanley
Holroyd,
George Augustus Frederick Charles (1802-1876), 2nd Earl of Sheffield (1821) 1/6/58 n
Harriet (-1889), née Lascelles, Lady Sheffield 1/6/58
Holson, C. W., Rev. 17/8/78
Holstein,
Anne Louise Germaine de Stael-, Mme., née Necker 16/6/40 n
Pedro de Sousa, Don (1781-1850), 1st Duke of Palmella, Portuguese statesman 16/8/43
Holt,
Mr. 24/6/53
Mr., of New Orleans 11/10/61
E. 17/9/78
G. 15/10/86
George (1790-1861), Liverpool broker 29/7/54

Holt (*cont.*)
Robert Durning, Liverpool liberal 7/10/78, 18/10/81 L, 12/12/82 L, 10/10/83, 27/6/86, 28/6/86, 6/10/92 L, 5/12/92 L
Thomas Littleton (1794–1879), journalist 29/12/54
Veysey Weston (1824–1881) 4/12/66
Holyoake,
Emily A., Miss 30/4/94
George Jacob (1817–1906), liberal journalist and free thinker 20/10/62, 31/8/68
M. A. 10/1/90
Malthus Questall 2/2/92
Holzmann, Maurice, Sir (1835–1901), Knight (1901), Prince of Wales' librarian 6/10/63
Home, David Milne- (1838–1901), soldier, tory M.P. 2/10/76
Home Rule Association, secretary of 29/9/90
Homing, H. 16/9/66
Hompesch, Ferdinand de, Count, Bavarian minister 28/4/69
Hone, Richard Brindley, Rev. (1805–1881) 23/1/28
Honey, Messrs., of Liverpool 24/8/71
Honeyman, Thomas 14/4/79
Hood,
Alexander Nelson, Gen. (1814–1904), 1st Viscount Bridport (1868) 28/9/64
Arthur Wellington Alexander Nelson (1839–1924), tory M.P. 5/10/76 ?
F. J. 21/12/77
Francis Grosvenor, Col. (1809–1854) 5/6/26
Peter, Dr. (1808–1890), physician 14/9/79, 30/10/79
S., 3rd Viscount Hood 5/6/26 n
Samuel, Sir, Baronet 27/8/27 n
Hook,
Anna Delicia, née Johnstone 5/1/31
Anne (–1844), née Farquhar 30/8/35 n
James (1772–1828), dean of Worcester (1825) 30/8/35 n
James, Rev. (1837–1877) 23/10/75
Robert, banker 18/11/54
Robert, of London 30/1/33
Theodore Edward (1788–1841), comic novelist 30/8/35
Walter Farquhar 5/1/31 n
Hooke, David, Rev. (–1898) 10/6/78 ?
Hooker, Joseph Dalton, Sir (1817–1911), Knight (1877), botanist 4/10/71, 7/3/78
Hoole, E., of Sheffield 10/7/65
Hooper,
E., Mrs. 13/7/77
E. W. 27/11/77
Francis John Bodfield, Rev. (–1888) 1/5/54
Richard, Rev. (1821–1894) 7/3/57
Samuel Hobbs, Rev. 18/3/68
Hope *see* Hayter, Kerr, Verney, Scott
Hope,
Miss, of Naples 10/12/50
Alexander, Gen. Sir (1769–1837), tory M.P. 1/6/35 n
Alexander James Beresford- (1820–1887), Peelite M.P. 5/3/46, 28/5/56, 10/9/59, 4/5/66, 17/5/66, 11/3/73, 15/5/82 L, 28/1/85
C. A., Rev., of Edinburgh 27/2/55
C. D. 4/6/50
Charlotte, née Lockhart 20/7/47
Ellen, née Meredith 29/11/50
Frances, Lady 29/9/46 n
Frederick William, Rev. (–1862) 29/11/50 n
George, Sir 23/9/38 n
George William (1808–1863), Peelite M.P. 14/5/40
Georgina Alicia, Lady, née Brown 24/8/35
Henry Thomas (1808–1862), Peelite M.P. 22/3/53
Hugh (1813–1876), parliamentary agent 8/6/55, 5/3/56
James Archibald, Gen. Sir (1785–1871) 31/12/53
John Adrian (1860–1908), 1st Marquis of Linlithgow (1902), 6th Earl of Hopetoun 28/11/79
Mildred Beresford-, Lady (–1881), née Cecil 1/7/57, 10/9/59, 11/9/59, 12/9/59
P. H. 26/3/77
Thomas Arthur, of Seaforth, a liberal 7/11/55, 17/7/68
Thomas C., Prof., chemist 9/5/28
Hopetoun *see* Hope
Hope-Vere *see* Loftus
Hopkey, Mr. 5/1/76
Hopkins,
John, Rev. 8/4/80
John Baker (1830–1888) 8/7/68
John Henry, Bp. (1792–1868), bishop of Vermont (1832) 10/6/39
Tighe 13/4/88
Hopkinson,
J. 12/8/68
Samuel Edmund, Rev. (1754–1831) 9/1/31
Hopper, John Robert, Rev. 8/11/45
Hopps, John Page, Rev. (1834–1911), unitarian 11/7/74, 12/4/79
Hoppus, John, Rev. Prof. (1789–1875), philosopher 20/3/70
Hopton, J. B. 25/3/78
Hopwood,
Charles Henry (1829–1904), liberal M.P. 23/6/80
Frank George, Rev. 19/9/69
G. 1/7/68
John Turner (1825–1900), liberal M.P. 13/3/68 ?

Robert 12/3/41
Horden, Bp. 20/5/82 n
Horder, W. G., Rev. 21/8/79
Hordern, Joseph, Rev. (1784-1876) 27/2/28
Horgood, Joseph Bartholomew Davey, Rev. 8/1/79
Horley, Englebert, Rev. 7/11/78 n
Horn,
Robert, Edinburgh advocate 20/12/33 ?
Thomas, Rev. (1800-1874) 12/5/54
Hornby,
Edmund Geoffrey Stanley 10/5/77 ?
Edmund Grimani, Sir 8/12/77 ?
Geoffrey Thomas Phipps, Adm. Sir (1825-1895) 21/8/67
Hugh (1792-1875), Liverpool merchant 21/8/51
James John, Rev. Dr. (1826-1909), Headmaster of Eton (1868) 14/11/69, 10/4/70, 6/7/78, 7/7/78, 31/5/79, 9/8/81 ff, 17/8/81, 25/6/82
John (-1892), tory M.P. 14/3/43 ?
Phipps, Sir (1785-1867), Comptroller General of Coast Guard 5/5/51
Thomas Dyson (1822-1889), of Liverpool 21/7/65, 1/8/68
Horne,
Donald, Edinburgh advocate 27/10/35
M. J., architect 3/5/55
Thomas, Rev. (1773-1847) 2/9/30
William, Sir (1774-1860), whig M.P., lawyer 9/6/36
Hornell, Robert, barrister 23/12/89 n
Horner,
Mr., Clerk to the Exchequer 7/11/43
Frances, née Graham 5/10/89 n
H. 31/1/61
John Francis Fortescue (1842-1927) 5/10/89
Leonard (1785-1864), geologist 21/2/61, 23/3/61, 26/3/61
Susan, Miss 27/1/88
Thomas Strangeways Fortescue (1808-1843) 14/10/28
Horniman, Mr. 20/1/91
Horsfall,
Charles, mayor of Liverpool (1832), Liverpool merchant 12/8/29
T., son of Liverpool mayor 20/7/33
T. C. 29/8/79
Thomas Berry, merchant of Everton 15/2/34
Thomas Berry (1805-1878), tory M.P. 15/2/34, 12/4/49
Horsley,
Heaneage, Rev. 25/8/47
John, china dealer 17/5/59
John Callcott (1817-1903), artist 2/11/78
Victor, opponent of anti-vivisection 10/11/92
William H. (1774-1858), musician and glee club organiser 28/3/43
Horsman, Edward (1807-1876), liberal M.P. 16/10/37, 20/4/52, 10/6/52, 17/7/54, 18/2/67
Horsnell, James, G's valet 4/3/33
Horswell, S. 4/10/56
Hort *see* Packe-Reading
Hort, Margaret, Miss 6/5/78 ?
Horton *see* Curzon, Freeman
Horton,
Francis, Rev. 1/6/78 ?
H. G., of I. R. B. 2/7/80 ?
J., rescue 27/12/53
Robert John Wilmot-, Sir (1784-1841), 3rd Baronet (1834), colonial governor 16/4/30
S. D. 28/12/89
Thomas Galland, Rev. 10/10/78
Hose,
George Frederick, Bp. (1838-1922) 13/12/79
J. W. E. 7/11/78
Hoskin, Peter Charles Mellish, Rev. (-1895) 11/5/50
Hosking, Mr. 24/12/79
Hoskins,
Anthony Hiley, Adm. Sir (1828-1900) 8/11/82
John Brownlow, barrister 11/3/59
Hoskyns, Chandos Wren- (1812-1876), liberal M.P. 18/2/73
Hosmer, Harriet, American sculptor 5/12/66, 26/7/78
Hoste, D. E., Col. 14/3/77 ?
Hotham,
Beaumont (1794-1870), 3rd Baron Hotham (1814), tory M.P. 3/1/46
Charles, Sir, R. N. 21/3/50
Frances A. J., Lady, née Rous 5/1/46
Henry, Sir 5/1/46 n
Hothfield *see* Tufton
Hotze, Henry, Confederate agent 30/7/62
Houghton *see* Milnes
Houghton & Gunn, stationers 15/4/48, 4/2/79
Houldsworth,
F. 7/1/78
Thomas (-1852), tory M.P. 19/12/32
Houlston & Wright, London publishers 25/7/68
Houlton, George, Sir 27/5/43
Housden, Mr. 25/4/79
House, G. Binning 23/2/57
Houseman, Thomas, Rev. (-1898) 10/2/76
Houson, Henry, Rev. (-1873) 17/11/65 ?
Houston,
George (1810-1843), tory M.P. 11/3/26
J. D. C., author 24/4/94

How, William Walsham, Bp. (1823–1897) 21/5/56, 17/12/73
Howan, Miss 27/12/76
Howard *see* Gower, Grey, Labouchere, Lascelles, Stuart
Howard,
rescue 11/8/82
rescue 11/6/70, 24/3/76
rescue 29/7/90
Mrs., rescue 28/6/71
Augusta Mary Minna C. Fitzalan- (–1886), née Lyons, Duchess of Norfolk, Lady Arundel 8/5/49
Cecil Frances, Lady, née Hamilton, Lady Wicklow 12/5/43
Charles Wentworth George (1814–1879), liberal M.P. 28/1/42, 22/5/64, 27/4/65, 9/4/67, 15/12/76, 16/12/76
Edward George Fitzalan-, Lord (1818–1883), 1st Baron Howard of Glossop (1869), liberal M.P. 20/6/41, 17/4/65, 1/7/70 L
Edward Granville George (1809–1880), 1st Baron Lanerton (1874) 7/6/75, 7/10/76 ff
Edward Henry, Cardinal (1829–1892) 31/7/83
E. S. 10/10/87
Frederick, 5th Earl of Carlisle 26/6/41 n
Fulke Greville Upton (1773–1846), soldier 14/6/48 n
George, 6th Earl of Carlisle 10/2/40 n
George Broadley, Rev. (1827–1913) 21/9/75
George James (1843–1911), 9th Earl of Carlisle (1889), liberal M.P. 5/6/79
George William Frederick (1802–1864), Lord Morpeth (1825), 7th Earl of Carlisle (1848), whig M.P., Irish Viceroy 13/10/32
Gerald Richard (1853–) 3/9/73 ?
Harriet, Lady 29/4/43, 7/5/43 n, 12/10/46
Henry (1802–1875), of Greystoke 17/11/66
Henry Charles, 13th Duke of Norfolk 20/6/41 n
Henry Edward John, Rev. 29/2/44 fl
Henry Fitzalan- (1847–1917), 15th Duke of Norfolk (1860) 2/4/70, 25/4/70, 30/8/70 L, 6/2/71 L, 25/3/71, 14/10/93, 26/10/93
Henry Granville Fitzalan-, Earl of Arundel and Surrey (1842), 14th Duke of Norfolk (1856) 8/5/49 n
James (1821–1889), liberal M.P. 21/4/69
James Kenneth (1814–1882), Commissioner of Woods 12/2/61
John (1753–1799), mathematician 16/12/34
John, Rev. 6/10/78
Mary Greville, née Howard 14/6/48
Philip Henry (1801–1883), whig M.P. 16/3/42, 4/9/73
William Forward, 4th Earl of Wicklow 29/4/43 n
Howard de Walden *see* Ellis
Howden *see* Caradoc
Howe,
E. R., Miss 16/8/76
Ferdinand 2/5/76
Gerald 10/6/76
Granville L. 12/4/78 ?
Joseph (1804–1873), Canadian politician 25/1/57
Richard W. P. C., 1st Earl Howe (1829) 24/7/46
W. H., publisher 10/8/87
Howel *see* Cunliffe
Howell,
A. 26/6/90
David, Rev. 5/1/70
E. 16/3/91
E., Liverpool publisher 28/9/85
George (1833–1910), liberal M.P., trade union leader 19/7/66, 1/12/71 L, 27/1/74, 31/1/74, 20/2/78
H. H. 13/9/79
Hugh, Rev. 8/12/57 ?
J. M. 30/8/79
John, Rev. 30/5/68 ?
John Aneurin, Rev. 20/2/87
Thomas, Sir (–1883), Knight (1876), contractor 17/5/52 ?
Howes,
Edward (1813–1871), tory M.P. 10/7/63
Joseph 4/1/87
Joseph, of Whitehaven 26/10/67
W. B. 28/12/77
Howick *see* Grey
Howie, Marsden 30/11/91
Howis,
William 24/5/48
William, Mrs. 14/3/49
Howlett,
Edmund 7/12/76
John Henry, Rev. (–1867) 25/9/52 n
Mary 25/9/52 ?
Howley *see* Beaumont
Howley,
William, Abp. (1766–1848), Archbishop of Canterbury (1828) 18/1/29 n
William Hamilton (1810–1833) 18/12/29
Howorth,
D. F. 13/12/90
F., Rev. 29/3/77
Henry Hoyle, Sir (1842–1923), tory M.P. 2/3/80, 14/3/90
Howson,
John Saul, Rev. Dr. (1816–1885) 8/3/50, 7/4/66, 20/1/69, 19/12/85
Mary 12/11/75
Howth *see* Saint Lawrence

Hoy, J. 19/10/85
Hoyland, rescue 8/6/64, 21/6/64
Hoyle,
Isaac (1828–1911), liberal M.P. 2/5/89
J. 4/12/78
William, criminologist 25/1/76
Hoyt, William H., of U.S.A. 3/12/86
Hozier, Henry, Sir (1838–1907), Knight (1903), soldier 16/7/70
Hubback, John, of Liverpool 26/9/43
Hubbard *see* Rendel
Hubbard,
Messrs. 30/4/94
Evelyn 5/10/89
John Gellibrand (1805–1889), 1st Baron Addington (1887), tory M.P. 19/1/42, 7/2/50, 11/11/50 ff, 14/11/50, 2/12/50, 23/1/53, 16/2/61, 19/2/61, 19/4/62, 20/11/65, 27/5/73 L, 23/7/77, 12/6/80, 11/6/81 L, 28/1/87 n
Maria Margaret (1817–1896), née Napier 28/1/51
Hubble, J., turncock 30/9/41
Huber, Victor Aimé (–1869), German author 30/1/49, 18/8/54
Hübner, Joseph Alexander, Count 20/9/76
Huckerby, Francis, Newark maltster 5/12/32
Huddlestone,
George James, Rev. 5/8/48
P., of Lincoln's Inn 6/5/33
Thomas Creswick, of Newark 14/4/41
Hudlestone,
William 6/5/33 ?
William (1826–1894), Madras civil servant 11/6/38 ?
Hudson,
rescue 27/2/64
Elizabeth, née Nicholson 9/7/46 ?
George (1800–1871), railway constructor, tory M.P. and bankrupt 10/7/44, 9/7/46, 2/11/64
James, Sir (1810–1885), diplomat in Italy 31/1/59, 2/3/59, 17/7/67, 7/6/71 L, 6/9/76
John C. 4/10/56 ?
John Thomas, optician 14/4/52
Joseph, Rev. (1793–1891) 2/8/58
J. S. 6/5/79
J. W., Dr., of Manchester 24/3/62
Robert Arundell, Sir (1864–1927), secretary, National Liberal Federation 8/9/88
Thomas B., travel writer 2/10/58
W. B. & Son, chemists 8/12/42
Huertas, E.de, Sig. 24/2/87
Huerton, rescue 3/5/64, 24/5/64
Hügel,
Friedrich von, Baron (1852–1925), author 12/11/65, 18/5/73
Mary Catherine, Lady (–1935), née Herbert 12/11/65, 28/1/66
Hugessen, Edward Hugessen Knatchbull- (1829–1893), 1st Baron Brabourne (1880), liberal M.P. 16/6/58, 28/12/72 L, 16/7/73 L
Hughan,
Jean, née Milligan 23/1/43
L. G., née Beauclerk 1/2/31 n
Thomas (1811–1879), of New Galloway 1/2/31
Hugher, Mme., opera singer 23/3/32
Hughes *see* Monk
Hughes,
Messrs., solicitors 13/11/77 n
Mrs., Hawarden nurse 11/9/56
A. J. 14/7/77
Charles, of Wrexham 27/2/75 ?
Edwin (1837–1879), Liverpool solicitor 28/8/66
Elizabeth, née Wormald 10/5/56
Gertrude, née Smyth, Lady Dinorben 4/8/69
Henry, Monsignor, Vicar Apostolic of Gibraltar (1839), bishop of Heliopolis 8/1/39
Henry, Rev. 5/6/45
Hugh Price, Rev. (1847–1902), nonconformist 29/4/92 n
Hugh Robert (1827–1911), of Kinmel, Denbigh 7/3/57, 10/3/57
J. E. 12/4/74
J. H. 16/1/91
John, Archdeacon (1787–1860), Archdeacon of Cardigan (1859), evangelical preacher 20/3/31
John Bickley, Rev. (1818–) 12/8/65
John H. 28/1/86
Joshua, Bp. (1807–1889) 16/1/70 n, 11/3/70 L, 1/9/75
Julio Henry, actor 10/8/47 ?
J. Vaughan 2/6/88
Lewis 2/3/88
Margaret (1810–), of Hawarden 3/11/89
Morgan, Rev. 10/3/75
N., Rev. 29/8/87
Robert, S. P. C. K.'s Liverpool agent 1/9/29
Robert Ball (1806–1868), sculptor 7/3/57 ?
S., Mr. 22/12/42
Thomas (1822–1896), liberal M.P., author 24/11/56, 26/3/70 c, 27/4/70 c, 6/12/76
Thomas, Rev. 13/7/68
T. J., known as 'Adfyfr' 20/4/78
W., Rev. 14/12/78
William, Rev. 15/10/88
William Bulkeley (1797–1882), Peelite M.P. 16/10/47, 3/10/72 ?
William Hughes (1792–1874), former tory M.P., author 20/6/62

Hughes (*cont.*)
William Huntley, solicitor 9/12/89
William Lewis (1767–1852), 1st Baron Dinorben (1831) 31/8/26
Hughes & Edwards, Messrs. 24/11/76
Hugo, Victor, author 21/4/41 n
Hugonin *see* Murchison
Huidekoper, Frederic 20/2/78, 26/3/78
Huish, Mark, Capt. (1808–1867), secretary of railway companies 17/7/43, 4/5/44, 13/1/57
Hulbert, Daniel Paul Meek (1816–1894), missionary 7/6/55
Hulk, Mrs. 14/12/88
Hull,
C. 12/6/78
Edward, Rev. 30/5/45
John Dawson, Rev. 11/5/45
William Wilson, Rev. 29/11/45
Hullah, J. P. (–1884), musician 21/6/47, 9/9/82
Hulland, Richard, sheriff's officer 26/6/48 ?
Hull Institution, President of 3/7/78
Hülner, Mons. 24/11/65
Hulton,
James 1/9/55
William (1787–1864), high sheriff of Lancs. 22/5/39
William Ford (1809–1879), saved G's life 22/12/31
Humble,
Henry, Rev. (–1876) 13/12/61
John Ralph, Rev. 5/10/77
Michael Maughan, Rev. (–1889) 24/8/52
Hume,
Mrs., rescue? 23/2/77
Abraham, Rev. (1814–1884) 10/9/45, 22/10/63, 28/7/65
Alexander, of Christian Emancipation League 17/10/76, 21/11/77
Charles, Rev. 16/12/51
Henry, Col., Queen's bodyguard 19/6/81
Hope 26/11/86
Joseph (1777–1855), radical M.P. 14/2/33, 28/3/51, 12/3/52
Martin, Major 4/12/91
Sharpe, Major 12/3/89
Hummelauer, M. 2/4/44 ?
Humphrey,
C. J. 4/4/91
E. 10/5/55
Francis, Rev. 21/6/75
John (1794–1863), Lord Mayor of London (1842), radical M.P. 25/10/43
Humphreys,
Miss 16/7/78
E. R., Dr. 15/4/57
George, barrister 9/1/60 ?
J., messenger 6/1/60 n
J. C., ironbuilding manufacturer 27/8/89, 2/9/89, 13/9/89 ff, 8/11/89, 12/3/90
John Hunter, Rev. (–1856) 11/7/52
Humphry, William Gibson, Rev. (1815–1886) 13/7/57
Hunloke *see* Scarisbrick
Hunn, Joan 30/12/29
Hunns, J. 12/4/78
Hunsdon *see* Cary
Hunsworth, G., Rev., congregationalist 15/4/80
Hunt,
rescue 7/9/70
E., rescue? 2/2/57
Frederick Knight (1814–1854), editor, *Daily News* 19/4/53 n
Frederick William, architect 16/1/79
George Ward (1825–1877), tory M.P. 14/5/63
H. A. 12/8/89
H. A., surveyor of public buildings 18/3/63, 28/4/63
John Francis, spiritualist 4/5/78
R. 14/12/87 n
Robert Shapland, Rev. 15/5/53 n
Thomas Newman (1806–1884), Chairman, Public Works Loan Commission 2/2/82
Thomas Newman (1808–1893), banker 11/5/66 n, 15/5/66
Thornton Leigh 26/4/60
W., Bath Liberal Association 23/1/77
William Holman (1827–1910), artist 3/5/56, 3/5/60, 27/11/73, 29/11/73, 9/5/91
William Ogle, agent 30/7/42 n
Hunter *see* Blair
Hunter,
rescue 22/7/81
Mrs. 7/6/76
Adam, Dr., physician 25/11/43
Claudius Stephen Paul, Sir (1825–1890) 28/11/58 n
Constance, Lady, née Bosanquet 28/11/58
Frederick Mercer, Consul 18/2/84
George Leslie, artist 13/2/80
James (–1869), Irish, murdered 17/10/69
J. D., Dr., physician 1/12/34
John, Rev. 17/11/57
N. W. G., Rev. 6/10/77
William Alexander, Prof. (1844–1898), liberal M.P. 23/9/76, 6/9/92, 30/11/92 L
William Wilson, Sir (1840–1900), historian 11/12/75
Huntingdon *see* Hastings
Huntingdon, Miss 2/10/58
Huntington, Mrs., Hawarden 20/1/73
Huntley,
G. 19/12/77

Henry Vere, Capt. Sir (1795–1864), 1st Baronet (1841), colonial governor 26/3/39
Huntly *see* Gordon
Huntriss, Mr. 27/6/78
Hunt & Rochell 31/1/80
Hüpeden, Dr. 25/10/42 ?
Hurlbert, William Henry (1827–1895), American journalist 29/10/85
Hurlbutt, Henry, Hawarden 16/9/75, 6/9/78
Hurley,
rescue 26/3/70
John, Mrs. 28/6/45 ?
Hurst, James (1808–1888), gamekeeper at Hawarden 13/10/73, 28/10/73, 12/5/78, 8/11/79
Hurston, rescue 10/7/63
Hurtley, J. 22/5/51
Husband,
George Radclyffe, Rev. 13/3/80 ?
John, Rev. (–1869) 26/2/58
Huskisson,
George 1/8/40
William (1770–1830), tory M.P., cabinet minister 31/3/26, 19/9/27, 18/8/29, 25/8/29, 17/9/30, 24/9/30, 7/1/61, 18/1/93
Hussey,
Ambrose (1807–1849), tory M.P. 25/11/43
Edward (1807–1894), high sheriff of Sussex 25/9/28
Henry L., author 21/7/75
Phineas Fowke, coalmine owner 20/11/41
Robert, Prof. (1801–1856), ecclesiastical historian 7/8/46 ?
Hutcheson, David & Co., steamship company 13/8/53
Hutchins,
Charles L., Rev., of U.S.A. 10/9/85
Edward John (1809–1876), liberal M.P. 7/4/68
Richard 11/8/40
W. H. B., packing case maker 24/3/75
William Horace, Rev. 24/12/51
Hutchinson,
Edward, Rev. 22/3/65
Francis, Dr., physician 10/7/77 ?
G. 10/4/73
James, Rev. (1805–1873) 9/12/38
John Dyson (1822–1882), liberal M.P. 9/5/79 ?
R. H. B. 20/1/90
Richard John Hely- (1823–1866), 4th Earl of Donoughmore (1851) 22/2/65
R. K. 3/8/76
William Nelson, Gen. (1803–1895) 5/1/80
Hutchison, Robert, Liverpool merchant and mayor 15/10/62 n, 26/8/63 n
Hutt,
D. J. 25/3/74
Fanny Anna, Lady, née Stanhope 14/11/81
George, Sir (1809–1889), soldier 25/4/32 ?
John, colonial governor 2/2/46
William, Sir (1801–1882), Knight (1865), liberal M.P. 24/2/42, 18/2/70 L, 14/11/81 n
William Wayman, Rev. (1822–1894) 13/5/78
Hüttel, John Edmund, merchant 23/11/78 ?
Huttman, J. H. 21/6/67
Hutton,
Rev. Mr., minister of Edzell 26/8/33
Arthur Wollaston, Rev. (1848–1912), editor, G's *Speeches*, librarian, National Liberal Club 21/7/88, 26/4/90 n, 1/10/90 ff, 6/10/92 L, 13/6/93 L
George, mayor of Newark (1846) 18/1/37
George Clark, Rev. Princ. (1825–1908), presbyterian controversialist 1/4/75, 29/11/81 L, 28/7/85 L, 21/5/92, 9/3/93 L
Henry, Rev. (–1863) 14/1/53
Henry D., author 27/10/77
James 1/4/78
Richard Holt (1826–1897), author and editor 16/7/66, 2/8/82, 3/8/83, 16/8/83 L, 25/7/84, 21/11/84, 16/12/84 ff, 24/7/85, 13/9/85, 21/5/86, 24/5/86 L, 2/7/86 L, 28/10/92 n
Vernon Wollaston, Rev. (1841–1887) 27/9/66
Huxley, Thomas Henry, Prof. (1825–1895), scientist 17/11/69, 30/11/70, 10/11/71, 11/3/77, 8/8/84, 5/12/85 n, 7/12/85, 8/12/85 ff, 11/12/85 ff, 16/12/85, 9/1/86 n, 28/2/86, 13/12/90, 15/12/90 ff, 18/12/90 ff, 4/5/94
Huys, Edward Drouyn de l' (1805–1881), French politician 12/7/49
Hwyl, Miss 1/4/93
Hyam,
Mr., tailor 13/10/81, 4/9/84
Mrs. 31/3/79
W. 7/8/78
Hyams, A. 6/4/78, 29/6/78
Hyason, rescue? 25/4/57
Hyatt,
G. T., Rev. 30/6/51 ?
John Carter, Rev. 23/8/77
Hyde *see* Cross
Hyde,
A. R. 18/7/70
Edward (1846–1914), 5th Earl of Clarendon (1870), Lord Hyde, liberal M.P. 30/11/68
G. 12/11/79
John Thomas, Rev. (1832–1892), professor at Addiscombe 9/6/58
Joseph, of Liverpool? 18/5/58

Hyderabad, Nizam of 15/9/88 n
Hyett, William Henry (1795–1877), whig M.P. 29/1/33
Hylton *see* Jolliffe
Hyman, Mr. 26/6/46
Hyme, J. D. O. 22/11/90
Hyndman,
Henry Mayers (1842–1920), socialist 12/7/33 n, 12/3/80, 1/10/86
John Beckles, Barbados proprietor 12/7/33
Hynes,
F., Irish prisoner 23/8/82, 29/8/82
M. 17/2/77
Hyslop, M., Miss 28/1/79

Iatrondakes, Mr. 19/5/79
Ibbetson *see* Ellison
Ibbetson, Henry John Selwin-, Sir (1826–1902), 1st Baron Rookwood (1892), 7th Baronet, tory M.P. 28/1/81
Ibbotson, Walter 20/4/80
Ibrahim, Pasha 8/7/46 n
Ibsen, Henrik (1828–1906), playwright 19/6/90 n
Iddesleigh *see* Northcote
Iggulden & Co., Neopolitan bankers 25/7/49, 13/12/50
Iglehart, Mr. 13/11/86
Ignatieff, Nikola Pavlovich, Count (1832–1908) 19/3/77, 21/3/77
Ikin, Mr. 18/5/75
Ilchester *see* Strangways
Illidge, Thomas Henry 22/6/42
Illingworth,
Alfred (1827–1907), liberal M.P. 5/12/82, 25/10/85, 23/3/86, 9/4/86, 12/5/86, 21/5/86, 2/6/86, 11/8/86, 19/11/86, 29/12/86, 18/6/88, 19/10/93 L
John Richardson, Rev. (–1915) 16/1/79
Impey, Frederick 2/10/85 ?
Imrie, A. 21/11/76
Ince,
A. 29/4/75
Henry Alexander 24/9/91 ?
William, Rev. Prof. (1825–1910) 5/3/56, 15/3/77
Inchiquin *see* O'Brien
Inderwick, Frederick Andrew (1836–1904), liberal M.P. 14/3/87
Infield, H. J. 13/11/79 ?
Ingalton, T., Eton bookseller 17/10/25
Ingersoll, Joseph Randolph, American ambassador (1853) 5/2/53
Ingestre *see* Talbot
Ingham,
Mrs. 2/8/75
Robert (1793–1875), liberal M.P. 19/2/64
Robert Wood (1846–1928), barrister 13/12/79
Ingilby,
Henry Day, Sir (1826–1911), 2nd Baronet 6/6/73 ?
William Amcotts, Sir (1783–1854), 2nd Baronet, whig M.P. 26/4/33 n
Ingle, Thomas, solicitor 16/1/77 ?
Ingledew, William, Newark maltster 17/4/41 ?
Inglefield, Edward Augustus, Sir (1820–1894), sailor 28/10/61, 5/11/61
Inglessi, Constantino 9/12/58
Inglis,
Anne, née Arbuthnot 15/10/33
Charles, Bp., 1st bishop of Nova Scotia 11/9/37 n
Hugh 15/10/33 n
J. 27/11/79
John (1810–1891), Lord Glencorse, judge 30/6/59 n
John, Bp. (1778–1850), 3rd bishop of Nova Scotia (1825) 11/9/37
Mary, Lady, née Briscoe 19/2/49
Robert Harry, Sir (1786–1855), tory M.P. 16/6/31, 3/2/33, 20/3/33, 2/11/47, 5/7/48, 2/5/49, 19/5/52, 13/7/52, 22/10/52, 19/1/54
Ingram,
Mrs. 15/10/90
Arthur John, Rev. (1840–1931) 28/3/75
C. T., Mr. 27/7/55, 4/7/56
Emily Charlotte Meynell-, née Wood 9/10/76, 20/3/77, 18/9/81, 2/10/81, 8/10/81 n, 13/7/85, 15/7/85, 28/2/92
H. F. Meynell 9/10/76 n
James, Dr. (–1850), President of Trinity, Oxford 26/1/48
Jenkyn 3/1/79
John Kells, Prof. (1823–1907), Irish economist and poet 14/12/72, 28/12/72, 16/1/73 ff, 15/2/73
Ingram-Shepherd *see* Seymour
Inman,
A. W. 3/5/76
James Williams, Rev. 23/7/56, 8/8/66
Inner Circle Club, secretary of 19/11/77
Innes,
Alexander Taylor (1833–1912), liberal 20/4/61, 7/9/67, 2/11/78, 10/11/86
Frederick Maitland 21/4/41
John Clarke, Rev. Dr. 26/2/56
William, of Raemoir 24/10/34, 8/10/49
Inskip, Wickham 11/12/79
International League of Peace and Liberty 20/9/86
International Review, editor 22/3/75
Inverclyde *see* Burns
Inverness *see* Underwood
Ionides, Alexander C., Greek consul 25/7/66

Irby,
Adeline Paulina, Miss, writer on the Balkans 16/1/77, 14/3/77, 15/3/77, 6/4/77, 7/4/77, 21/7/77 n, 24/9/78 n, 26/9/78, 27/9/78, 28/9/78, 29/2/80, 25/8/86
Frederick William (-1877), Justice of the Peace 3/5/32
Ireland,
A. 14/12/86
Alexander, journalist 2/9/89 n, 21/11/90
Alexander (1810-1894), Manchester bibliographer 14/8/68
Alexander, Mrs. 18/7/91
Thomas, Rev. 17/1/68
Thomas James (1792-1863), tory M.P. 9/1/49 ?
Irish Land Investment Co., secretary 16/6/45
Irish Monthly, editor 14/2/78
Irlam, W. 24/4/33
Irons, William Josiah, Rev. Dr. (1812-1883) 26/3/56
Ironside, Rev. 11/7/55
Irton, Samuel (1796-1866), tory M.P. 2/7/56
Irville, Mr., of Glasgow 19/9/72
Irvine,
Alexander 3/7/45
Alexander Forbes (1818-1892), advocate 12/12/59
Donald A., Rev. (-1852), tutor 24/8/46, 5/12/46
George Peters (1787-), barrister 9/7/40
I., Rev., priest at Genoa 29/7/49
J., Miss, Fasque 27/1/50
James, Rev. 2/2/49
Irving,
Alexander, Rev. Dr. 9/4/91
E., Miss 18/5/74
Edward, Rev. (1792-1834), founder of the Catholic Apostolic Church 27/1/33
H., of Ionia 18/1/59
Henry, Sir 16/4/75
James, Rev. 30/12/79 ?
J. H. 19/7/78
John (1767-1845), tory M.P., merchant 8/8/35
Thomas, civil servant 28/10/41
William, civil servant 3/1/43
Irwin,
Clarke Huston, Rev. (1858-1934) 10/10/90
James, of London 14/2/68
William, Col. (1810-1889) 5/8/78 ?
Isaac,
rescue 25/5/70
Mr. 27/5/84
David Lloyd, Rev. 12/12/67
William, house valuer 27/4/59
Isaacs,
rescue 26/5/65
A. A., editor, *The everlasting nation* 15/11/90
B. D. 3/2/79
Lewis Henry, Major (1830-1908), tory M.P. 22/7/86
Isaacson, Stephen, Rev. 28/2/45
Isard, Joseph 13/12/79
Isbister,
Messrs., publishers 18/11/91
Alexander Kennedy (1822-1883), of Hudson's Bay Co., later headmaster 6/11/47
Isham,
Charles Edmund, Sir (1819-1903), 10th Baronet (1846) 7/4/79
Emily, Lady, née Vaughan 7/4/79
Isherwood, Mr. 6/5/87
Isles, W. J. H. 8/10/91
Ismail, Khedive (1830-) 16/7/67
Ismay, Thomas H. 2/11/91
Istria, J. D' 23/10/76
Ito Hirobumi, Japanese statesman 8/3/83 n
Ivall, David, coachmaker 27/6/39
Ivall & Large, coachmakers 19/8/74
Ivanovitch, N. S. 3/8/91
Ivens, Coleman, Rev. 23/9/77, 23/9/89
Iverach, James, religous writer 5/12/59
Ives, Levi Silliman, Bp. (1797-1867), bishop of N. Carolina (1831), convert to Rome 2/11/35
Ivory,
Holmes, Edinburgh W. S. and liberal organiser 20/6/86 ff, 27/6/86, 2/7/86, 3/7/86, 10/7/86, 16/7/86, 30/6/92
Thomas (1812-1882), Advocate 20/1/78, 24/1/78

Jabat, Rafael Constantine Domingo, Portugese diplomat 30/11/25
Jacini, S. F., Count 14/1/88 ?
Jack,
Thomas C. 6/2/79
William, Prof. (1834-1924) 29/11/78
Jackins, Mr. 19/1/78
Jackman, Mr. 6/12/76
Jacks, William (1841-1907), liberal M.P., momentarily unionist 21/6/86, 2/7/86, 3/7/86, 10/7/86, 13/7/86, 8/7/92
Jackson,
rescue 30/6/90
Dr., surgeon 28/12/50
Miss 28/6/76, 11/8/79
Mrs. 26/3/32
Charles Bird, Rev. 7/12/52
Charles Robert Mitchell, Sir (1814-1874), Indian auditor 9/3/72 n
Christison S., Capt. 21/4/79
Edward, Dr. 2/9/74 ?
Francis, Innkeeper in Newark 27/1/34
G. 8/5/41

Jackson (*cont.*)
Henry Bates, treasury civil servant 21/3/53 ?
James, Rev. 17/7/45
John, Bp. (1811-1885) 4/1/68, 16/9/82 L
John Oswald, biographer 28/12/78
J. P. 31/7/75
J. R. 8/8/90
M. S. 16/10/78, 26/10/78
N. 11/8/49
Robert, fellow of New College, Oxford 11/11/49
William, Rev. Dr. (1792-1878) 2/12/74
William, Sir (1805-1876), 1st Baronet (1869), liberal M.P., railway promoter 12/2/52
Jackson & Prince, solicitors 2/3/77 n
Jacob,
rescue 9/2/71
Edwin (-1868), don 21/11/54
Philip, Ven. (1803-1884) 2/10/69
'Jacob Omnium' *see* Higgins
Jacobs,
Mrs., rescue 20/7/70, 31/7/70
Jemima, Miss, of Bath 24/3/76
Maurice 4/2/90
Jacobs and Davis, Messrs. 8/12/86
Jacobsen, Hans, shipping pilot 2/9/85
Jacobson,
Eleanor Jane, née Turner 12/10/65
William, Bp. (1803-1884), professor of divinity (1848), bishop of Chester (1865) 26/9/31, 25/1/52, 26/1/53, 28/1/53, 29/1/53, 17/1/54, 16/6/55 ff, 20/5/65, 17/6/65, 24/9/68, 15/1/69, 11/12/82 L, 12/2/84
Jacques *see* Ewart
Jaequemyns, Gustave Rolin- 3/11/76
Jaffier, Pacha, in Albania 2/2/59
Jagger, K. 21/12/75
Jagoe, William, Rev. 29/3/75
Jamblin, Mr., photographer 26/8/68
James *see* Godley
James,
footman 17/7/57
D. Prosser 6/7/68
Edward Boucher, Rev. (1819-1892), fellow of Queen's, Oxford 21/1/54
Edwin, liberal M.P. and debtor 8/4/93
Edwin John (1812-1882), barrister, liberal M.P. 26/5/56
George Payne Rainsford (1799-1860), novelist 1/12/41, 17/2/42
G. P. R., Mrs. (-1891) 24/2/59
Henry (1843-1916), novelist 28/3/77, 14/4/84, 15/4/84
Henry, Sir (1803-1877), Director of the Ordnance Survey 18/1/60
Henry, Sir (1828-1911), 1st Baron James of Hereford (1895), liberal unionist M.P. 15/9/73, 11/11/73 n, 26/11/73 n, 3/10/83 L, 19/10/83, 5/11/83 L, 23/11/83 L, 28/12/83 L, 1/1/84 L, 4/1/84 L, 10/1/84 L, 31/5/84 L, 15/8/84, 1/10/84, 31/10/84, 28/11/85, 30/12/85, 7/7/86 L, 16/7/86, 24/7/86, 27/7/86, 29/7/86 L, 5/4/87, 26/6/89, 27/2/91, 10/3/91, 17/3/92, 14/5/93 n, 16/5/93 n, 9/6/93, 10/8/93
Ivor, author 5/10/87 n
John, Rev. (-1868) 20/4/58 ?
John Kingston, Sir (1784-1869), 1st Baronet (1823), Irish banker 14/10/61
John Kingston, Sir (1815-1893), 3rd Baronet (1869) 31/1/76
R. M. 7/10/75
S. C., Lady, née Ellison, Lady Northbourne 15/1/39
Thomas, Rev. 14/10/43
Thomas Henry, author 23/7/57
W. A., liberal agent in Middlesex 11/7/65
Walter Charles, Sir; Lord Northbourne 15/1/39
Walter Henry (1846-1923), 2nd Baron Northbourne (1893), liberal M.P. 21/11/76, 9/2/93 L
W. F., Rev. 11/3/78
William, Rev. (1787-1861) 25/1/29, 2/12/56
William Hill (1834-) 30/9/92
William Milbourne, Sir (1807-1881), judge 28/6/70
William Richard, Rev. 20/4/69
James II, King of Great Britain and Ireland 17/2/32
Jameson,
Anna Brownell, née Murphy 25/6/58
Leander Starr, Dr. (1853-1917), administrator of Mashonaland 1891, henchman of Rhodes 31/8/93 c
Robert, Prof., regius professor 16/5/28
Robert William (1805-1868), journalist 22/5/67 ?
Jamieson,
G. A., Edinburgh wine merchant 3/1/53
Robert, Rev., presbyterian 22/2/47 ?
Jannasch, Robert, German author 1/2/68
Janni, Ugo, Rev. 31/3/90
Janotti, Natalie, pianist 28/10/89
Janson,
Charles Auguste Marie Joseph Forbin-, Bp. (1785-1844), bishop of Nancy and Toulouse (1824) 11/1/39
Herman D., Consul 18/8/85
Thomas Corbyn (-1863), banker 8/3/50 ?
Janssen, M. 21/11/89

Japp,
F. 28/9/44
W. N. 16/4/80
Jaques, J. W. 26/2/91
Jardine, William, merchant, chairman of Jardine, Matheson & Co. 18/5/40
Jarnac *see* Chabot
Jarrold, Messrs., publishers 10/4/79, 20/1/87
Jarvie, Alexander, Rev. 21/11/79
Jarvis, Lewis Whincop, Sir, banker 26/7/48 ?
Jaunnes, Comtesse 4/2/87
Jay,
Mr., of Snell & Co. 22/2/49
A. O., Rev., author 19/11/87, 28/11/87, 31/1/91
A. T. 9/9/78
G. O. 12/12/77
H., author 2/12/75
John (-1872), engineer 11/7/65 ?
Jeaffreson, Mr. 6/2/88
Jeans, James Stephen (1846-1913), author 27/9/88
Jebb,
John, Bp., bishop of Limerick 15/12/40
John, Rev., translator 4/2/43, 24/6/43
Joshua, Sir (-1863), prison administrator 15/2/53
Richard (1806-1884), barrister 11/2/39 ?
Richard Claverhouse, Prof. (1841-1905), regius professor of Greek, Oxford 26/2/76, 6/2/83 L
W. 29/11/77
Jebsen, Mr. 19/8/85
Jeffcott, J. M., of Isle of Man 4/10/78
Jefferson, Joseph Dunnington (-1880) 19/4/50
Jeffery,
Frederick John, numismatist 15/3/76
James Reddecliff (-1871), draper 30/1/54, 13/10/64, 6/10/65
Jefferys,
G., barrister 28/7/48
Henry Anthony, Rev. (1811-1898) 8/9/31, 9/6/37 ?
Jeffreys,
Mr. 22/1/46
John, Rev. (1771-1840) 9/6/37 ?
John Gwyn (1809-1885), barrister, conchologist 16/7/58 ?
Julius, Dr. (1801-1877), lung specialist 13/5/59
Richard, Rev. (1808-1866) 15/9/60
Jeffs, William, bookseller 9/3/39 ?
Jehanger, Sorabji 8/2/90
Jehangier,
Cowasjee, Mr. 14/6/90
Cowasjee, Mrs. 14/6/90
Jejeebhoy, Jamsetjee, Sir (1783-1859), Knight (1842), 1st Baronet (1857) 7/4/55
Jelf,
George 16/2/41
George Edward, Rev. (1834-1908) 3/4/56
William Edward (1811-1875), theologian, grammarian 2/6/27
Jellett, Morgan Woodward, Rev. 17/5/79
Jellico, George Rogers, barrister 29/2/76
Jenkins,
Mr., of Oak Farm 27/11/45
Alfred Augustus, Rev. 24/9/76 ?
B. G., Homerist 7/3/76
Edward (1838-1910), liberal M.P. 26/4/75, 28/11/79
Evan, Rev. 29/1/75
John Jones, Sir (1835-1915), liberal unionist M.P. 14/1/93
Joseph, tenant 3/12/75 ?
Leoline, Sir (1623-1685), diplomat 13/6/51 n
Robert Charles, Canon (1816-1896) 25/2/52, 4/1/75, 14/3/86
Vaughan, of Bath 20/3/79
William James, Rev. (1821-1897) 17/7/48
Jenkinson *see* Foljambe, Harcourt
Jenkinson,
Charles Cecil Cope (1784-1851), 3rd Earl of Liverpool (1828), lord steward 5/9/44
Edward George, Sir (1835-1919), Knight (1885), Spencer's private secretary; Irish civil servant 28/11/82, 27/2/83, 12/12/85, 13/12/85 n, 15/12/85, 24/12/85
John Simon, Rev. (1798-1871) 7/6/55
Robert Banks (1770-1828), 2nd Earl of Liverpool (1808), prime minister 14/4/27 n
W. C. 4/11/78
William, manufacturer 4/5/42
Jenkyns,
Henry, Prof. (1795-1878) 6/9/31
Henry, Sir (1838-1899), Knight (1877), parliamentary draftsman 15/3/86, 29/9/92 c, 16/11/92 ff, 15/6/93, 15/9/93 L
Richard (1782-1854), Master of Balliol 23/1/28 n
Jenner,
Henry Lascelles, Bp. (1820-1898) 30/9/78
William, Sir (1815-1898), 1st Baronet (1868), physician 29/9/63, 26/9/64, 11/6/69, 29/9/71, 21/11/71, 31/7/80 ff, 29/6/83, 24/11/83
Jennings,
Angus, publisher 29/4/74
Charles, agent 31/3/35
H. J., author 23/10/84
John, Rev. (1789-1883) 25/7/42
Patrick Alfred, Sir (1831-1897), of N. S. W., Australia 11/7/87

Jennyr, A. 13/10/88
Jephson,
Mrs. 21/6/31
A. W. 27/6/90
Henry, author 16/2/92
Henry, Dr., Leamington physician 27/12/30
Henry L., Irish Office 30/8/78, 4/12/78
James Saumarez, Sir (1802–1884), 3rd Baronet (1870), secretary of Carlton Club 24/7/38
Jerdan, Mr., of London 19/8/44
Jeremiah,
John, author 24/3/77 ?
John, of Clerkenwell 10/10/67
Jeremie, J., Sir 13/7/35 n
Jerichau-Baumann, Anna M. E. (1819–1881) 7/6/71
Jermyn *see* Hervey
Jermyn, Hugh Willoughby, Bp. (1820–1903) 21/4/50
Jerningham, Hubert Edward Henry, Sir (1842–1914), Knight (1893), liberal M.P. 24/6/66, 28/10/81, 25/7/84
Jerome *see* Churchill
Jerram,
Charles, Rev. 13/9/47
C. S., Homerist 20/3/78
Jerred, Mr. 12/12/76
Jerries, Mr. 5/11/87
Jerrold, William Blanchard (1826–1884), journalist 20/8/68
Jersey *see* Villiers
Jervis,
Miss 12/12/78
Mrs., rescue 6/4/59
G. W., Sheffield school teacher 29/5/74
John, Sir (1802–1856), lord chief justice (1850), liberal M.P. 25/4/50
Jervise, Andrew, antiquarian 1/1/76
Jervoise, Harry Samuel Cumming Clarke, Sir (1832–1911), diplomat 8/8/72
Jesse, Emily, née Tennyson 13/12/31 n
Jessel, George, Sir (1824–1883), judge 24/10/71 n
Jessop,
W. H. H., leased 73 Harley St. from G 1/4/82 n
William Henry Bowlestone (–1865), pamphleteer 26/11/55 ?
Jessopp, Augustus, Rev. (1823–1914) 21/5/79
Jesty, H. J. 29/4/91
Jeune, Francis, Rev. (–1868), Master of Pembroke, Oxford 15/3/53
Jevons, William Stanley (1835–1882), economist 16/3/66, 30/4/74, 10/5/74, 7/12/77, 15/8/78 n
Jewett, H. M. 18/4/90
Jewitt, Llewellynn Frederick William (1816–1886) 9/2/64
Jewson,
F. B., Mrs. 28/12/57
Frederick Bowen, Prof. (1823–1891), musician 28/12/57 n
Joachim, Joseph (1831–1907), violinist 11/2/70
'Joaquin' *see* Miller
Job, H. 2/5/79
Joberns, Charles Henry 11/4/59
Jobson, Frederick James, Rev. (1812–1881), Methodist 13/8/58 ?
Jocelyn *see* Wingfield
Jocelyn,
Frances Elizabeth, Lady, née Cowper 19/1/46
Robert (1788–1870), 3rd Earl of Roden (1820), tory M.P., protestant orangeman 13/5/33
Robert, Lord (1816–1854), Viscount Jocelyn, tory M.P. 19/1/46 n
William Nassau (1832–1892), diplomat 5/1/67
Jochmus von Cotignola, Augustus, Baron 28/6/58
Jockinson, J. W. H. 11/12/89
Jodrell *see* Stratton
Jodrell,
Francis (1776–1829) 9/2/28
John William (1808–1858), of Grenadier Guards 9/2/28
Maria, née Lemon 9/2/28
Joel, G. 29/3/90
Johann (1782–1859), Archduke of Austria, Regent of Germany 16/6/32
John,
groom 1/12/32
G., Rev. 5/4/92
Johnes, Herbert Owen 20/11/79
Johns,
W. S. 14/10/87
W. Tudor 29/7/91
Johnson,
Mr. 23/7/39
A. H. 7/5/90
B. 16/11/41
Bradley Tyler, American lawyer 1/7/83
Charles, Prof. (1791–1880), professor of Botany at Guy's 3/8/35 ?
Edward Ralph, Bp. (–1911) 15/9/76, 20/11/76
George William, Prof. (1802–1886), writer on gardening 5/10/44
H. J., Rev. 22/11/76
J. J., Prof. 2/1/91
John James (–1890), barrister 3/2/54 ?
John Samuel Willes, Capt. (–1863), Royal Navy 10/11/50
J. R., Bermondsey liberal 14/11/87

Reverdy (1796-1876), U. S. ambassador (1868) 22/10/68, 30/3/69, 6/4/69 c, 17/4/69 c, 1/5/69, 24/1/70, 24/1/72 L
Thomas, Lord mayor of London 9/10/41
William, of Broughton Hall, Hawarden 18/4/80
William, of Chester 3/11/67 n
William Henry (1810-1877) 9/5/29 n
William Moore, Judge (1828-1918), liberal M.P. 12/12/82
Johnson & Longden, stockbrokers 19/2/49
Johnston,
Alexander Keith (1804-1871), geographer 19/8/65
John Beresford 21/4/40
John C., Rev., presbyterian 1/1/87
John Octavius, Rev. 16/3/91
Robert, Bailie, of Edinburgh 3/9/64
William, Rev. 27/1/73
Johnstone *see* Hook, Napier
Johnstone,
Miss 8/7/56
Charles, Capt. (1843-1929), Royal Navy 13/11/83
Charles Hope, Major-Gen. (1835-1888) 15/10/60
E. R. 5/2/78
Harcourt Vanden-Bemp de-, Sir (1829-1916), 3rd Baronet (1869), 1st Baron Derwent (1881), liberal M.P. 11/8/73
Henry Alexander Munro-Butler- (1837-1902), Peelite M.P. 26/11/69
Henry Butler- (1809-1879), tory politician 23/12/52
John, Sir (1799-1869), 2nd Baronet (1807), whig M.P. 31/5/39 n
Louisa Augusta, Lady (1804-1869), née Harcourt 31/5/39
Rigby, rescue 19/6/58
Johnston[e], Graydon 27/8/87, 31/8/87, 5/9/87
Joissant, Jules 8/11/89
Jolivart, Léon, novelist 19/3/77
Jolliffe, William George Hylton, Sir (1800-1876), 1st Baronet (1821), 1st Baron Hylton (1866) 26/2/58
Jollivet, Thomas-Marie Adolphe (1799-1848), Breton lawyer and deputy 27/7/38
Jolly,
C. 12/9/78
John Robert, of Greenwich 14/9/73, 11/5/74, 3/2/75
Jones *see* Chisholm, Denman, Gladstone, Rio, Mayhew
Jones,
rescue 29/7/62
Mrs., lodge keeper at Hawarden 23/5/93
A., Miss 30/9/90
A., Mrs. 17/6/79
A. C. 24/8/91
A. E. 23/5/78
Ambrose, Rev. 6/3/75 ?
B., Ven. 5/1/70
Benjamin Heywood, Liverpool banker 15/10/62 ?
Bulkeley Owen, Rev. (1824-1909) 2/10/56
Charles John Graham, Rev. 10/4/40 ?
C. L. M., Rev. 13/10/77
C. W. 19/12/76
Daniel, collier 20/10/69 L
Davenport, Rev. 3/4/93
David, Rev. 27/2/45, 13/7/46
E. 7/11/81
Edward, educationalist 11/3/74
Edward Coley Burne-, Sir (1833-1898), 1st Baronet (1894), artist 15/5/79, 10/8/79, 11/8/79, 12/8/79, 13/8/79, 14/8/79, 15/8/79, 31/5/81, 3/8/81, 7/8/81, 6/1/82, 9/1/82 L, 7/6/82, 24/4/90, 18/11/93, 26/1/94 L, 4/2/94
Edward Rhys 24/4/41, 6/3/94 L
E. R., Rev. 24/8/88
Ernest Charles (1819-1869), Chartist 4/10/60
E. S. R. 29/2/68
Evan Rowland (1840-1920), liberal M.P. 6/3/94
F. 17/4/77
F. M. H., secretary, Chelsea liberal association 5/3/87
G. E. 23/4/74
Griffith Arthur, Rev. (1828-) 25/6/59
Halley, Mr. 17/4/88
Hedley 2/1/80
Henry, Rev. 8/6/40
Henry Bence, Dr. (1813-1873), physician 3/4/61
Henry Denson, Rev. 21/7/42
Henry Macnaughton, Dr., physician 1/1/75, 20/1/91
Henry O., Liverpool cornbroker 7/11/65
H. F. 25/2/76
Hugh (1777-1842), unitarian banker in Liverpool 5/11/35 n
Hugh, Rev. 3/1/50
Hugh, Rev. 5/1/70
Hugh Hughes, Rev. (-1887) 6/10/56
Hugh Lloyd 4/12/89
Hugh Lloyd 25/7/68
Inigo William, Col. 15/8/77 ?
J. B. 17/7/79
Jenkin, Rev., of Mold 31/8/57
J. J. 27/4/78
J. Morgan, Rev. 21/9/86, 8/11/89, 17/9/92 L
John 24/10/85
John, bookbinder 28/8/26

Jones (*cont.*)
John, Archdeacon (1791–1889), Archdeacon of Liverpool (1855) 16/8/25
John, Rev. (1792–1852), poet 22/11/29
John Collier, Rev. (1770–1838) 16/3/31
John Edward (1806–1862), sculptor 16/5/56
John Fowell, Rev. (1792–1877) 4/8/65
John Gregory, secretary of Liverpool Collegiate Institute 22/8/40, 2/1/43
John Herbert, Rev. (1823–1908) of Liverpool 28/1/36?21/11/68
John Rees, Rev. 30/3/41 ?
John Winter (1805–1881), librarian of British Museum 7/12/77
John Wynne, Archdeacon (1805–1888), of Penmaenmawr 17/9/64 n
J. P. 30/12/76
J. S., Rev. 3/10/87
J. Wharton 17/2/73
Lewis A., treasury civil servant 4/9/54
Llewellyn Archer Atherley- (1851–), liberal M.P. 5/3/92
M. A., Miss, rescue 5/12/84
Michael (–1851), barrister 11/7/50 ?
Morgan 24/9/87
Neville, Rev. 24/5/48
Owen, surgeon 27/4/27
Owen, Col., Boundary Commissioner 28/11/84
Peter, Rev. 20/9/74
R. A. 29/10/87
Rachel, née Albutt 17/11/28 n
R. B. 14/3/56
Richard Robert (1780–1843), Welsh philologist 28/9/26
Robert, Rev. (–1879) 21/12/52 ?
Robert Pughe, barrister 9/11/78
Roger W. 1/4/57
Ryce Wellington Lloyd, Rev. 7/1/43
Sumner S. 14/2/43
T. H. 10/6/87
Theobald, Capt., tory M.P., captain, R. N. 17/6/42
Thomas, barrister 13/6/53
Thomas, of Kinnerton 2/4/57
Thomas, poet 21/8/68
Thomas, Rev. (1800–1867) 17/7/25
Thomas Evans, Rev. (–1915), of Holywell 28/7/68
Thomas Heron (1812–1885), 7th Viscount Ranelagh (1820) 13/12/69
Thomas Hughes, Rev. 17/9/75
Thomas Mason 13/5/67
Thomas Simpson, Rev. 18/5/76
Tom, servant 1/7/40, 25/8/40, 27/12/40, 18/1/41
T. W. S., Rev., Methodist in Naples 30/1/89
William, customs comptroller 24/12/42 ff, 14/1/43 ?
William Hartwell, Rev. (–1858) 3/11/52 ?
William Henry, secretary of Social Science Association, Liverpool 11/10/61
William Morgan, Rev. 17/9/92
William West, Bp. (–1908) 25/4/78
Jones, Lloyd & Co., Liverpool accountants 22/12/76
Jones & Bonham, auctioneers 19/5/73
Jones & Campbell, Liverpool cornbrokers 7/11/65 n
Jones & Oakes, coal merchants 29/11/47
Jones & Quiggin 22/10/61
Jones & Yarrell, booksellers 24/9/46
Jopher, H., Rev. 2/5/88
Joplin,
Frederick, Rev. 23/5/45 ?
Thomas (1790–1845), author 7/2/37
Jopson,
S. B. 2/5/78
S. P. 30/9/91
Jordan,
Mr. 14/10/76
John, Rev. 9/7/50
Sylvester (1792–1861), constitutionalist 8/9/38 ?
William J., London wine merchant 8/6/55
Jorissen, Edward J. P., Dr. (1829–1912) 25/4/83
Joseph,
Abraham (–1872), china dealer 24/1/66
Edward, art dealer 20/7/74, 19/5/79
F. 22/2/89
Henry Samuel, Rev., rabbi, later anglican priest 16/1/43, 6/3/43, 7/12/63 ?
N. S., Anglo-Jewish Committee 18/7/91
Josey, Mr. 11/7/74
Joubert, J. P., Transvaal politician 15/6/80 L
Journot, M. 23/1/92
Jovanovic,
Mons. 9/9/78
Vladimir, Serbian writer 1/4/63, 28/12/75, 6/5/80
Jowett,
Benjamin, Rev. Prof. (1817–1893), regius professor of Greek, Oxford (1855), Master of Balliol (1870) 25/1/52, 25/7/53, 26/7/53, 29/7/53, 3/8/53, 20/12/53, 21/12/53, 6/1/54, 9/1/54, 7/3/54, 24/1/55, 28/1/57, 19/12/60, 6/10/61, 29/6/68, 27/9/69, 28/9/69, 13/6/70 L, 27/2/71 L, 27/6/71, 1/2/78, 10/6/81 L, 29/11/83, 25/8/84, 25/10/92
Henry 21/7/75 ?
Joy,
Miss 9/4/33
Algernon, of Bayswater 10/6/59
George 27/7/40 ?

Henry G., sculptor 10/5/81, 21/5/84
Henry Hall (1786–1840), barrister 7/8/26, 9/7/40, 28/7/40
Henry Hall, Mrs. 2/5/33
Joyce,
G. C., Rev., Warden of St. Deiniol's 1897-1916 25/3/96
James Wayland, Rev. (1812–1887), author 25/5/29, 7/5/55
L. 28/10/79
Miles (–1884), executed for Maamtrasna murders 31/10/84 n
P. W., Dr. 9/11/77
Joyner,
Miss 11/11/78
M. A., Mrs., author 16/10/78, 11/11/78
Joynes, James Leigh, Rev. (1824–1908), of Eton 14/1/64
Joynt, W. Lane, of Ireland 11/11/77
Jubb, W., Rev., independent minister 18/11/68
Jubilee Singers 14/7/73, 29/7/73, 6/12/75
Judd, John Wesley, Prof. (1840–1916) 8/10/88
Judson, Squire 15/3/80
Juglar, Joseph Clément, Dr., French economist 27/1/67
Jul, rescue 20/3/86
Julian, J. W., of Liverpool 2/5/78
Jullien, Jean Lucien Adolphe (–1932), violin prodigy 3/7/51
Jung,
Gustavus, Mrs. 27/10/79 ?
Raoul 26/7/77
Salar, Sir (1829–1883) 25/7/76
Salar, Sir (1863–1889) 2/11/87
Junor, Alexander 9/5/42, 19/6/61
Jupp, A. H. 8/6/76
Jusserand, Jean Adrien Antoine Jules (1855–1932), author, diplomat 19/6/89, 4/5/91, 27/2/92, 22/3/93
Just, Patrick, Belgian consul 27/3/44

Kaiser, E. 13/5/79
Kallaway, J., Rev. 6/11/78
Kallergis, Dimitrios, Gen. (1803–1867) 22/12/58
Kane,
Mr. (–1882), of Ireland 29/6/82
Richard Rutledge, Rev., Belfast Orangeman 20/8/87, 5/9/87
Karcher, M., translator 14/1/69
Karolyi,
A., Herr 16/1/77
Aloys, Count (1825–1889), Austro-Hungarian diplomat 20/5/79, 30/4/80, 4/5/80 L, 31/5/80, 13/7/80, 26/9/82, 4/2/84, 18/6/84
Kaspary, Joachim 2/6/76
Kaufmann, Konstantin Petrovich, Gen., Russian general 23/11/69
Kaulbach, W. von, artist in Munich 3/10/45
Kavanagh,
Arthur MacMurrough (1831–1889), tory M.P. 4/3/80 ?
D. 26/11/86
James 13/3/80 ?
James B., Rev. Dr., President of Carlow college 5/4/75, 29/10/77
James Daniel, Rev. 27/12/90
Kay,
E., and son 17/12/89
J., liberal candidate 30/3/77 n
Kaye,
John, Bp. (1783–1853), bishop of Lincoln (1827) 23/5/39
John William, Sir (1814–1876), Indian civil servant 15/3/76
Thomas, publisher of the *Liverpool Courier* 23/8/26
William Frederick John, Ven. (–1913) 16/6/66
Kayll,
Mr. 23/3/77
A., of the Isle of Man 4/10/78
Kean, Charles John (1811–1868), actor 25/4/57, 30/4/57, 12/5/57, 29/5/58, 10/6/58, 20/7/59, 22/3/62
Keane,
John, 1st Baron Keane 26/2/41
Thomas, Rev. 12/7/75
William 5/3/89
William, Rev. (1818–1873) 12/9/68, 29/8/71
Kearney, Arthur Henry, Rev. 24/6/79 ?
Kearsley, Thomas Harvey 29/10/79
Keat, George, army instrument maker 11/11/54
Keate *see* Coleridge
Keate, John, Dr. (1773–1852), headmaster of Eton 7/11/25, 30/5/26, 18/7/26, 8/11/26, 3/2/27, 20/2/27, 21/2/27, 23/2/27, 10/6/27, 3/10/27, 8/10/27, 24/10/27, 3/12/27, 24/5/34, 22/5/41
Keates, Joseph Andrew 1/2/54
Keating,
Henry Singer, Sir (1804–1888), judge 20/12/69
J. A. 15/2/76
Michael J., Dean 2/6/75
Keats,
John (1795–1821), poet 16/4/32 n
W. H., of Flintshire 27/3/57, 28/3/57
Keay, John Seymour (1839–1909), liberal M.P. 29/5/88
Keble,
John, Rev. Prof. (1792–1866), theologian and poet 15/11/29, 16/12/29, 26/6/31, 14/3/50, 24/1/56, 10/11/60, 11/11/60, 22/7/64, 23/11/64
Thomas, Rev. (1793–1875) 4/12/66

Keck, Henry Littleton Powys- (1812–1863) 27/2/28
Keeling, Mr. 3/4/80
Keen, S. 7/7/74
Keenan,
E. 24/8/91
Patrick Joseph, Sir (1826–1894), Knight (1881), educationalist 8/5/72, 1/11/77
Keene, R. R., Rev. 26/8/87
Keep,
A. P. 30/1/80
Robert Porter, Dr. (1844–1904), American classicist 26/5/77
Keet, G. J. 19/10/67
Kegan, Paul & co., publishers 29/5/79
Kehoe, Mr. 21/10/47
Keighley, T. D. 25/7/91
Keith,
Miss 16/5/78
James 27/12/89
J. M. N. 7/1/90
Patrick, of Liverpool 7/10/74
William Alexander, Rev. 16/2/56
Kekewich, Samuel Trehawke (1796–1873), tory M.P. 19/4/64
Kelher, W. A. 11/5/89
Kell, Robert John 10/2/45
Kelland, Sidney 6/1/87
Kellaway, W., editor, *Bible Echo* 18/2/76 n
Kellie,
Messrs. 31/7/88
Miss 19/2/91
Kells, J. A. 1/1/79, 26/3/79
Kelly,
rescue 26/2/67
Messrs. 24/11/86
Miss, cameo maker 2/4/69
Mr. 16/2/86
Mr., weigh house manager, Aberdeen 27/9/43
Edward Robert (–1896), publisher 29/11/51
Fitzroy, Sir (1796–1866), tory M.P., judge 29/7/40
George Fitzroy, Rev. 22/10/58
James, poet 25/5/93
John, Rev. (1801–1876), independent minister in Liverpool 6/7/35 ?, 18/3/57
W. 27/6/78
Kelly & co., William, Messrs., publishers of directories 29/11/51 n
Kelsher, W. 8/12/41
Kelso,
Archibald, Liverpool broker 28/9/75
Archibald, partner in Gladstone & co. 20/4/27
Keltie, John Scott, Sir (1840–1927), geographer 12/12/90
Kelvie, Mr. 19/3/79
Kelvin *see* Thomson
Kemble *see* Sartoris
Kemble,
Charles (1775–1854), actor 24/8/27
John Mitchell (1807–1857), philologist 3/1/42
Kemp,
George, Rev. (–1880) 25/5/57 ?
G. H. 6/5/78
Kempe,
Edward, Rev. (1778–1858) 10/3/36 ?
James Edward, Rev. (1829–1907) 14/8/58
Kempster,
Messrs. 16/5/79
J. 22/5/90
Kempt, James, Gen. Sir (1764–1854), governor of Canada 12/2/38
Kempthorne,
J., Rev. (1775–1838), mathematician 15/1/26
Sampson, colonist 21/5/41
Kendall,
Miss 19/6/90
John Robinson, Liverpool accountant 12/1/52
Kendrick *see* Gladstone
Kendrick,
Mrs., distant relative 13/9/76
J. 17/7/88
William (1831–1919), Chamberlain's brother-in-law, liberal unionist M.P. 9/4/86 c
Kenealy, Edward Vaughan Hyde (1819–1880), barrister, independent M.P. 5/1/46
Kenley, Mr. 16/3/77 fl
Kenmare *see* Browne
Kennaway *see* Newman
Kennaway, Charles Edward, Rev. 12/4/46
Kennedy *see* Kynaston, Peel
Kennedy,
Mrs. 28/1/46
Alexander Clark, geographer 6/12/87 ?
Amelia, née Briggs 13/11/38 n
Archibald, 11th Earl of Cassilis 13/11/38 n
Archibald (–1846), 1st Marquis of Ailsa 6/7/52 n
Archibald (1847–1938), 3rd Marquis of Ailsa (1870) 7/3/71
Benjamin Hall, Rev. Prof. (1804–1889), regius professor of Greek, Cambridge 27/7/75
C. J. 23/4/79
Evelyn (–1888), née Stuart, Lady Ailsa 7/3/71
John (1807–1845) 13/11/38
Thomas Francis (1788–1879), whig M.P. 6/6/53, 9/12/54, 17/12/54, 27/2/55
Kennion, George Wyndham, Bp. (1845–1922) 20/9/73

Kenny,
Miss 27/9/88
P. 5/3/78, 5/8/79
W. T., of Ireland 16/10/77
Kensington *see* Edwardes
Kensington, Paines, & Young, brokers 2/8/43 n
Kensit, John 25/10/86
Kent *see* Edward Augustus, Victoria Mary Louisa
Kent,
C. B. R. 8/5/91
Charles, Rev. (1806–1885) 30/10/67
E. A. 12/11/89
James, servant 11/2/57, 6/1/58, 21/1/58
John, Speaker, Newfoundland Assembly 23/4/57
Thomas 7/6/77
W. C. M., author 20/2/69 n
Kentish, Joseph, cabinet maker 23/2/57
Kenworthy, Mr. 24/7/79
Kenyon,
Mr., autograph hunter 15/6/77
Edward (1810–1894), landowner 14/10/28
George (1776–1855), 2nd Baron Kenyon 14/10/28 n, 5/6/38
R. W. 5/3/80
Keogh,
William, Irish Lawyer 17/1/79 ?
William Nicholas (1817–1878), barrister, liberal M.P. 15/8/53
Keppel,
George Thomas (1799–1891), 6th Earl of Albemarle (1851) 26/7/90
William Coutts (1832–1894), Viscount Bury (1851), 7th Earl of Albemarle (1891), tory M.P. 5/5/58, 1/4/80 n
Ker,
James Henry Robert Innes-, 7th Duke of Roxburghe (1879), Marquis of Bowmont, liberal M.P. 18/1/71, 18/2/73
J. H. R. Innes-, 6th Duke of Roxburghe 23/4/35 n
John, assistant secretary, customs board 23/6/43
Robert Dow, superintendant, S. M. J. railway 21/9/49
S. 12/5/69
Susanna Stephania Innes- (1814–1895), née Dalbiac, Duchess of Roxburghe (1836) 23/4/35
Kerby & Endean, publishers 5/2/80
Kerchan, M. 6/9/77
Kergoulay *see* César
Kerin, Charles, of the I. R. B. 17/1/62
Kernaghan, Adam, American journalist 8/10/77
Kernahan, Mr. 25/4/76
Kerr *see* Davy, Forbes, Gaisford
Kerr,
Cecil Chetwynd, Lady (–1877), née Talbot, Lady Lothian, admired by G 2/9/46, 21/2/74, 29/3/74, 4/4/75
Constance Harriet Mahonesa (–1901), née Talbot, Lady Lothian 31/10/63, 17/9/65, 28/3/66, 19/9/79, 16/9/86
F. H., Lord, sailor 10/11/46
Henry Francis Charles, Rev. Lord 7/10/40, 2/1/41
Herbert J. N., of Brechin 1/9/36 ?
J. 28/9/75
James 19/1/87
John W. R., 7th Marquis of Lothian 2/9/46 n
Louisa Dorothea, Lady, née Hope 7/10/40 n
R., Lady (–1861), née Gilbert 18/3/47
Robert Malcolm 26/3/80
Robert Pollok, Rev. (1850–1923) 10/11/76 ?
Schomberg Henry, Lord (1833–1900), 9th Marquis of Lothian (1870) 13/7/70
William, of Eskmount, Brechin 1/9/36 ?
William, 6th Marquis of Lothian 7/10/40, 2/1/41 n
William Schomberg (1832–1870), 8th Marquis of Lothian (1841) 31/10/63, 21/11/74
William Williamson, barrister 4/10/77
Kerr & Butcher, London tailors 28/11/62 ?
Kerrison *see* Major, Stanhope
Kerrison,
Caroline Margaret, Lady (–1895), née Fox-Strangways 29/1/37 n
Edward, Sir (1774–1853), 1st Baronet, tory M.P. 5/7/34
Edward Clarence, Sir (1821–1886), 2nd Baronet (1853), tory M.P. 29/1/37, 31/8/53, 1/9/53
Mary Martha, Lady (–1860), née Ellice 14/8/34
Kerry *see* Fitzmaurice
Kershaw, George William, Rev. 23/12/41 ?
Kersley,
Mrs. 28/3/56
Benjamin, G's carpenter 6/3/71
Kessels, Matthew (1784–1836), German sculptor 1/6/32
Kesteven *see* Trollope
Kestner,
Georg August Christian (1777–1853), art connoisseur, diplomat 10/1/39
V. Chauffour-, historian 11/7/43 ?, 8/12/45
Ketcham, Mr. 5/3/80
Ketel, Jean, artist 15/1/39 ?
Key,
Mrs. 13/2/56

Key (*cont.*)
Ashley Cooper, Sir (1821–1888), admiral 11/11/75, 8/10/80, 18/3/82, 28/5/84, 4/6/84
John, Sir (1794–1858), 1st Baronet (1831), lord mayor of London, liberal M.P. 6/8/33
Kingsmill Grove, Sir (1815–1899), 2nd Baronet 6/8/33 n
Keys, David, Mrs. 31/3/48 ?
Keyse, E. W., milliner 17/3/59
Keyworth, W. W. 7/1/90
Khalil Khaggatt 27/10/87
Khambata, Mr. 31/7/88
Khan,
Hadji Mohsin, Gen., Persian diplomat 3/4/69
Malcolm, Prince, Persian ambassador 16/7/76
Kibbin, Mr. 9/3/78
Kibblewhite, Mr. 12/12/79
Kidd,
Dr. 30/3/81
Mrs., charity worker 11/4/59
G. 5/8/70
Robert Boyd, Rev. 17/10/51
Thomas, of St. Helen's railway 15/1/50 ?
Kidson, J., Rev. 18/2/87
Kielmansegge, Adolf August Friedrich, Count, diplomat 22/6/42, 8/5/43
Kiernan,
Mr. 30/3/78
Francis, Mrs. 12/7/51
Kilbracken *see* Godley
Kilburn, William Edward, of Isle of Wight 24/7/51 ?
Kilby, Thomas, Rev. (1784–1868) 13/9/29
Kilcoursie *see* Lambart
Kildare *see* Fitzgerald
Kilgour, H., of Edinburgh 18/12/55
Kilkenny *see* Butler
Kilkenny, Mayor of 7/1/87
Killen, William Dool, historian of Ireland 20/4/75
Killey, William, of Seaforth 22/6/64
Killick, Richard Henry, Rev. 23/11/68
Killikelly,
Dr. 5/6/41
Sarah Hutchins 5/6/41 n
Kiloh, W. L. 22/2/80
Kilpatrick, Mr. 12/1/76
Kilvert, Francis, Rev. (1793–1863), antiquary 17/8/52
Kimber, S., Greenwich solicitor 17/7/75
Kimberley *see* Wodehouse
Kindersley, George Herbert, solicitor 23/1/54
King *see* Waddington
King,
Mr., Quartermaster 10/1/77
Alexander, Rev. 26/8/72 ?
Augusta Ada, née Byron, Lady Lovelace 27/3/41
Brian, Rev. 21/3/49
Charles, commission agent 22/9/54 ?
David, Rev., presbyterian minister 2/5/45 ?
E., Miss 2/10/85
Edward, Bp. (1829–1910), bishop of Lincoln (1885) 21/3/54, 3/1/70, 20/2/73, 29/9/74, 30/9/74, 3/10/74, 25/4/78, 21/1/85, 11/2/85, 21/6/88, 23/1/94
J. C. 22/8/77
J. Gould 27/1/77
John Myers, Rev. (1804–1887) 1/1/75
Joseph Berry (1804–), of Soho 2/2/32
Joshua (–1857), President of Queen's, Cambridge 29/10/51
Peter John Locke (1811–1885), liberal M.P. 19/2/57, 22/6/67, 10/7/69 c, 3/12/72 c, 5/3/73
P. T. 26/10/74
Robert Edward, Gen. (1773–1854), 1st Viscount Lorton (1806), Irish politician 5/3/36
Robert L., Hackney liberal 8/11/75
S. H. 26/4/74
S. T. 11/12/75
Stanley 9/7/79
V. 6/2/56
William, Earl Lovelace (1838) 27/3/41 n
William R., Luton liberal 17/10/78
King & Attwaters, Messrs., solicitors 29/9/49 ?
Kingdon, James Durant, Rev. (1830–1899) 31/3/68
Kinglake,
Alexander William (1809–1891), historian 24/11/27, 5/12/76, 3/12/78, 15/10/79, 18/10/79
William Chapman, Rev. (1807–1881) 16/5/26
Kingsbury, Thomas Luck, Rev. (1822–1899) 31/1/77
Kingscote,
Henry Robert (1802–1882), benefactor 19/12/43
Robert Nigel Fitzhardinge, Sir (1830–1908), liberal M.P., agriculturalist 16/3/60
Kingsdown *see* Leigh
Kingsley, Charles, Rev. (1819–1875), broadchurchman, novelist 14/11/59
Kingsmill,
Charles, Rev. 10/6/76 ?
John, Sir (–1859), of Dublin 17/2/53
Kingston, William Henry Giles, editor 25/11/48
Kinloch, Capt. 31/3/75
Kinnaird,
Mrs. 2/12/93 L

Arthur Fitzgerald 29/1/38
C., 8th Baron Kinnaird 29/1/38 n
Mary Jane, née Hoare, Lady Kinnaird (1878) 1/2/65
Kinnear,
John Boyd, barrister 11/2/57, 22/1/77
Patrick (-1848), of Longforgan near Dundee 12/12/36
Kinnersley, Rev. Mr. 21/9/83
Kinnoull *see* Hay
Kinns, Samuel, Rev., of New York 8/11/85
Kinoul *see* Drummond
Kinsman,
Richard Byrn, Rev. 19/9/69
W., of Cornwall 16/12/89
Kintore *see* Falconer
Kip, Bp. 15/2/78
Kirby,
Richard Heighway, Rev. (1817-1897) 17/5/57
Tobias, Abp., archbishop of Ephesus, Rector of the Irish College, Rome 18/1/94
Kirch & Sons, of Hamburg 10/6/73
Kiréeff, Alexander, Gen. 17/10/79
Kireyev *see* Novikoff
Kirk,
Conrad A., clerk 19/5/59 ?
Hyland C., of New York 2/1/90
John 1/11/78
John, Sir (1832-1922), consul in Zanzibar 10/5/73 c, 28/4/86
Peter, Peelite M.P. 22/5/46
Robert, Dr. 3/4/80
R. S. 10/11/88
William (1795-1870), liberal M.P. 26/5/53
Kirkby, R., rescue 9/2/57
Kirkham, John William, Rev. 28/6/77
Kirkland, John, Sir 8/5/41
Kirkpatrick,
Mrs. 24/11/81
A. F., Rev. 3/5/91
Andrew J., of Glasgow 18/11/67
Thomas, of Lancashire 1/12/68
Kirkwood,
A. 22/10/61
J. 17/6/79
Kirran, N. 7/2/79
Kirtland, C., Rev., baptist minister in Newark 10/12/44
Kirwan, Anthony Latouche, Dean (1803-1868), dean of Limerick 18/3/36 ?
Kislingbury, Emily, Miss 22/7/76
Kitchener,
Horatio Herbert (1850-1916), 1st Earl Kitchener, soldier, in Sudan 12/8/84
James, builder 8/10/67 ?
Kitchin,
D. B. 22/3/90
George William, Dean (1827-1912), educationalist 12/6/62, 9/2/74 n, 31/1/78, 27/4/83 L
Kitching and Abutt, Messrs., goldsmiths 8/8/39
Kitson,
Arthur, of U.S.A. 7/3/78 ?
James, Sir (1835-1911), 1st Baronet (1886), 1st Baron Airedale (1907), iron manufacture, liberal M.P., liberal organiser in Leeds 13/3/78, 9/4/80, 13/8/80 L, 28/9/81 L, 2/10/81 L, 9/7/86 L, 9/1/90
Kitton, John, Rev. (1815-1882), schoolmaster 7/1/48
Kitts, John, Sunderland 25/11/74
Knapp,
E. G. 13/11/77
Henry Hartopp (1782-1846), G's tutor 24/9/25 n
Knapton,
Augustus James, Rev. 2/11/78 ?
W. J., Rev. 2/11/78
Knatchbull,
Edward, Sir (1781-1849), 9th Baronet (1819), tory M.P. 21/2/34
Henry Edward, Rev. (1808-1876) 21/2/31
Knau, C. T. 17/12/89
Kneeshaw,
Henry (1839-), of Penmaenmawr 3/10/82
Richard (1797-1878), of Penmaenmawr 11/8/74
Knight *see* Caetani
Knight,
Charles, of Greenwich 18/8/76
D. 17/1/79
F. A. 7/12/89
Frederic Winn, Sir (-1897), tory M.P. 14/12/53 ?
George, auctioneer 24/1/50
H. C. 31/8/78
Henrietta, Miss, pseudonym : Henley Arden, novelist 11/1/80 n
Henrietta Gally, née Eyre 19/6/38
Henry Gally (1786-1846), tory M.P., writer and traveller 20/2/33, 19/6/38
Isabella Jane, Miss (-1871) 1/11/66
John Prescott (1803-1881), secretary of Royal Academy (1848), artist 15/1/39 ?, 22/4/57
Robert (-1890), journalist 14/6/79
Robert Skakel 18/10/76 ?
William Angus, Prof. (1836-1916) 16/11/78, 10/1/87
Knightley, Rainald Knightley, Sir (1819-1895), tory M.P. 4/4/59
Knollis, Francis Minden, Rev. Dr. (-1863) 29/6/52
Knollys,
Elizabeth, Lady (-1878), née St. Aubyn 4/10/63

Knollys (*cont.*)
Francis, Sir (1837-1924), 1st Baron Knollys (1902) 4/10/63, 16/10/78, 4/7/89, 8/3/92, 1/12/92
William Thomas, Gen. Sir (1797-1883) 4/7/63
Knott,
John M., pamphleteer 8/9/57
John William, Rev. (-1870), junior proctor (1853), fellow of B. N. C., Oxford 27/1/54
Taverner, portrait painter 1/12/79, 5/4/80
William, mayor of Oldham 8/7/65 n
Knowles *see* Putyatin
Knowles,
Miss 21/5/89
Edward 21/1/45 n
F. 18/8/71
Francis Charles, Sir (1802-1892), 3rd Baronet (1831) 4/7/76
James Sheridan (1784-1862), playwright 14/11/56
James Thomas, Sir 23/3/70
Lees, Sir (1857-1928), 1st Baronet (1903), tory M.P. 6/8/89
Walter Frank, Rev. 4/7/90
Knox,
Edmund Francis Veysey (-1921), home rule M.P. 3/10/87 ?
Fanny, Miss 22/4/68
Robert (-1859), editor, *Morning Herald* 12/5/53
Robert Bent, Abp. (1808-1893) 28/4/53
Thomas (-1858), 2nd Earl of Ranfurly (1840) 24/12/52 n
William Stuart (1826-1900), tory M.P. 24/12/52
W. M. 17/3/90
Knudtzen, Mr. 3/12/50
Knutsford *see* Holland
Knyvett,
Deborah (-1876), née Travis, musician 15/6/31
William (1779-1856) 15/6/31 n
Koch, Joseph Anton (1768-1839), artist 15/1/39
Kock, Mr., of Frankfurt 19/1/38, 31/1/38, 10/9/38, 11/9/38
Koeber, Charles, London draper 18/3/56 ?
Kohn, Miss 21/12/55
Kohut, Adolph, editor, *Berliner Zeitung* 11/10/75
Kokkinos, Emanuel C., Prof. 1/11/75, 11/11/76, 8/10/79
Kolb, F., Herr 27/5/89
Konigsmark, Madame, fortune-teller 30/3/92
Konstantinides, Georgios 21/8/79 ?
Kontostavlos, Mons., Greek foreign minister 20/1/77
Koreah, R. 4/6/58
Kornprobst, Col. 4/9/89
Korostorely, Lydia, Madame, of St. Petersburg 19/12/89
Korthi Sullogos, President of 26/5/77
Kortright, Fanny Aikin, Mrs., anti-feminist 31/1/70 L
Kösk, B., Dr. 10/6/79
Kossuth, Louis (1802-1894), Hungarian national leader 14/3/61, 15/3/61, 20/3/61, 28/10/82
Kraeger, Miss 6/1/90
Krasinski, Henry, Count (-1876) 6/8/75
Krausse, Mons.de, German diplomat 27/3/73
Kremer, John, of London 5/4/62
Kriens, Edward, author 29/1/78
Krimian, Nügherdich, Rev. 29/8/77
Krokidas, Constantine S., Greek author 5/1/60
Kruger, Paul (1825-1904), President of the Transvaal 15/6/80 L, 15/2/81 n, 2/3/81 n, 5/3/81 c, 6/3/81, 8/3/81 c
Krüger,
Herr 3/8/86
Carl Ludwig, classicist 18/12/76 ?
Carl Wilhelm (1797-1868), art collector 1/3/54
Kruse, Frederick, cabinet maker 12/11/74 ?
Kunkler, A. 29/6/52
Kuo-ta-jen, Chinese minister 19/6/78
Kusserow, Herr von 21/8/70
Kutch, Maharajah of 13/6/87
Kynaston,
Elizabeth Selina, née Kennedy 17/5/43
Herbert (1809-1878), high master of St. Paul's school 9/8/28
Herbert, Rev. (1835-1910) 12/2/79

Labalmondiere,
Douglas William Parish (1815-1893), assistant commissioner, metropolitan police 28/4/27
Joseph Julian 23/3/33 n
Joseph Julian, Mrs. 23/3/33
Labillière, Francis Peter, barrister 2/3/80
Lablache,
Frederick (1815-1887), singer 27/1/38
Luigi (1784-1858), Italian bass singer 16/2/32, 27/1/38
Labouchere *see* Stanley
Labouchere,
Henrietta, née Hodgson 28/6/89
Henry (1798-1869), whig M.P., cabinet minister 11/2/36 n, 13/8/59, 11/2/60 ?
Henry du Pré 26/5/68
Mary Matilda Georgina, Lady (-1892), née Howard, Lady Taunton 1/3/56
Lacaita,
Charles Carmichael (1853-1933), liberal

M.P., G's god-son 31/12/56 fl, 24/2/68, 31/8/77, 2/9/77, 28/11/87
James Philip, Sir 13/11/50
Lacey,
J. 27/2/78
Thomas Alexander, Rev. 31/5/88 n
W. J. 1/12/89
Lack, Mr. 20/4/65
La Claire, Mlle. 15/6/87
Lacy, Henry Charles, liberal M.P. 15/2/49 n
Ladd, Henry, temperance advocate 1/1/76 ?
Ladell,
H. R. 23/9/87
Richard, debt collector 10/7/77 ?
Ladkin, Mr. 19/7/77
Ladley, R. B. 12/11/79
Ladmore, Mr. 8/2/80
Ladner, Mr. 16/5/78
Lady Margaret Hall, Oxford 29/11/83
Lafayette, Marie Joseph Paul de, Major Gen. (1757-1834), Marquis de Lafayette, French and American revolutionary leader 11/2/32
Laffan, Thomas, of Cashel 1/11/77 ?
Laflin, Christopher 8/2/77, 10/8/77
Lagenfeld, Dr. 27/10/87
Laidlaw,
rescue 6/3/74
A. W. 21/3/87
Laine, Abbé, of Paris 20/10/50
Laing,
Frederick A., author 29/4/79
Robert, Rev. 24/4/78
Samuel (1812-1897), secretary, railway dept., Board of Trade (1842), liberal M.P., author 29/10/41, 7/7/59 ff, 22/11/59 ff, 17/3/60, 4/7/81 L
Laird, John (1805-1874), Peelite M.P. 20/12/64
Lake,
David, admirer 14/3/67
Edward, Capt. (1808-1864), sailor 25/5/52
John W., author 21/3/72 ?
Katharine (1840-), née Gladstone, niece 4/3/40, 30/3/68, 27/10/70, 2/6/81
Percy, of Rifle Association 12/9/67, 18/12/68
William Charles, Dean (1817-1897), nephew-in-law, dean of Durham 4/3/40 n, 26/10/52, 26/1/57, 29/1/57, 31/1/57, 25/9/76, 2/6/81, 26/8/83
Lalande,
Mons., of Paris 19/4/88
A., shipper 2/7/79 ?
Lalor, M.P., Mrs. 3/10/87
Lamarmora, Alfonso di, Marquis (1804-1878) 3/3/59
Lamb *see* Temple
Lamb,
Asa, of U.S.A. 25/5/77
Frederick James, Sir (1782-1853), 1st Baron Beauvale (1839), 3rd Viscount Melbourne (1848), diplomat 5/12/38
Samuel Blackman, solicitor 2/10/69
T., Irish farmer 30/6/71
W. (1779-1848), 2nd Viscount Melbourne, prime minister 18/11/34 n
Lambart, Frederick Edward Gould (1839-1905), 9th Earl of Cavan (1887), Lord Kilcoursie, liberal M.P. 16/2/84
Lambault, Mr. 15/3/80
Lambert,
rescue 18/5/85
Mr., of Canada 6/11/91
Frederick 7/5/76
John, Sir 6/12/65
Nathaniel Grace (1811-1892), whig M.P. 31/1/74 L
Richard, commission agent 16/2/57 ?
S., of Newark 27/2/44
Lambert & Rawlins, Messrs., London goldsmiths 7/12/57
Lambkin, James, mayor of Cork 3/6/52 n
Lambton *see* Ponsonby
Lambton,
George Frederick D'Arcy (1828-1879), 2nd Earl of Durham 28/9/76
John George (1792-1840), 1st Earl of Durham (1833), governor of Canada (1838), whig M.P. 21/7/32
Louisa Elizabeth, Lady, née Grey 21/7/32 n
Lamington *see* Baillie [or Baillie Cochrane]
Lamond, R., stockbroker 8/9/51
Lamond, William & Co., London stockbrokers 6/5/43
Lamonica, Luigi, G's valet 9/2/32
Lamont,
Mr., valuer 25/6/74
Mrs. 19/9/75
Serjeant 17/12/51
Lamornaix, Charles Jean Sallandrouze de (-1867), French industrialist 15/3/50
Lampard, F. 3/9/78
Lampertico, Fedele, Senator (1833-1906) 27/4/87, 6/6/90
Lamport, Charles, of Penmaenmawr 11/8/74
Lampson, Curtis Miranda, Sir (1806-1885), 1st Baronet (1866), merchant 8/11/69
Lancaster,
Benjamin, of London 16/4/58
Henry, wine merchant 24/1/53
John (1815-1884), liberal M.P. 23/10/68, 24/10/68
Lance, George, artist 18/12/82 n
Lanceley, Mr., Chester shopkeeper 21/10/52 ?
Landa, Luigi, Prof. 3/2/77, 15/3/77
Lander, John, Rev. 25/11/48
Lander & Bedells, Messrs., architects 3/6/75

Landi, Salvatore, art historian 9/11/76 ?
Landon,
L. E. L., poet 7/4/38 n
Whittington Henry, Rev. (1805-1883) 7/4/38 ?
Landreth, James, of Edinburgh 19/9/68
Landseer,
C. 2/10/73
Edwin Henry, Sir (1802-1873), artist 5/4/56, 24/5/56, 30/4/59, 22/6/61, 27/7/63, 1/8/72, 9/8/72, 7/8/73, 8/8/73, 2/10/73 n
Landzell, William, dentist 2/6/49
Lane,
Mrs. 10/10/69
Charles, Mrs. 18/5/53
Charles, Rev. (1793-1879) 18/5/53
Charles Newton, Rev. 29/10/32
Charlton George, Rev. (1836-1892) 1/1/65
C. N., Mrs. 9/4/33
Hunter (-1853), Edinburgh surgeon 31/8/46 ?
J. H. B., Col. (-1886) 31/5/79 ?
Richard James (1803-1885), commission of Irish fisheries 10/11/59
Lanerton *see* Howard
Lanfeldt, Mr. 4/4/88
Lang,
Andrew (1844-1912), author 25/6/76
Arthur Moffat 8/2/79 ?
Gabriel H., parliamentary agent 5/3/51
James Thomason, Rev. (-1923) 11/11/76 ?
John Dunmore (-1878), Australian politician 13/8/49, 29/10/68
T., Rev. 13/11/77
William, Newark glazier 2/8/34
Langbride, Frederick, Rev. (1849-1922) 16/11/87
Langbridge,
Henry Charles, Birmingham bookseller 6/4/35 n
Henry Charles, Mrs. 6/4/35 ?
Langdale, Charles (1787-1868), whig M.P. 23/7/38
Lange, Daniel Adolphus, Sir (1821-1894), engineer 17/7/57
Langel, Mons. 20/10/79
Langford *see* Rowley
Langford,
J. A. 18/3/56
Joseph Munt, publisher 11/9/66 ?
Langham, Herbert Hay 5/4/79
Langhorne,
Alexander Grant Smith, of Hawarden 16/12/61, 26/12/65, 1/1/66, 3/1/66
William Henry, Rev. (-1916) 19/12/74
Langley,
Daniel Baxter, Rev. 6/2/50
J. Baxter 26/11/68
S. 20/4/68, 25/4/68
Samuel, cab owner 1/6/52
Langsford, rescue 10/5/55
Langslow, Robert (-1853), colonial civil servant 22/2/38
Langston, James Haughton (1797-1863), tory M.P. 10/3/59
Langton,
E., Mrs., rescue 5/12/55
William Henry Gore- (1802-1875), liberal M.P. 30/4/61
Langtry, Lillie, Mrs. (1853-1929), née Le Breton, actress 26/1/82, 4/2/82 n, 25/2/82, 3/4/82, 16/2/85, 6/12/90 n
Lankester,
Mr. 23/10/77
Edwin Ray, Prof. Sir (1847-1929), zoologist 1/10/83
Lannes, Charles Louis Maurice (1836-), Comte de Montebello 30/4/67 ff
Lansbury, George (1859-1940), labour M.P. and leader 26/3/90 ?
Lansdell, Henry, Rev. 25/4/76
Lansdowne *see* Fitzmaurice
Lapasso, L., of Ionia 3/11/58
Laporte, Kroll Charles 25/7/78 ff, 4/4/80
Largie, George 10/12/51
Larios, K. 3/12/85
Larkins,
Mrs. 16/2/56, 18/12/65
A. 3/5/36 ?
C., cousin 13/5/33
John Pascall, merchant 29/12/45 ?
Mary Anne (-1866), née Gladstone 22/8/25, 3/5/36 n, 18/12/65
Nan 22/9/27 ?
• Thomas, London East India merchant 22/8/25 n
Walter Farquhar, Col., cousin 1/5/33, 26/11/55, 29/5/57, 30/12/93
W. F., Mrs. 28/7/63
Lascari, Dr., of Ionia 2/11/58
Lascelles *see* Cavendish, Grenfell, Holroyd, Lawley
Lascelles,
Arthur 11/8/41
Caroline Frances, née Brooke 11/8/41 n
Caroline Georgiana, Lady, née Howard 4/9/53
Claud (-1903) 4/9/53 ?
Edwin (-1877) 4/9/53 ?
Frank Cavendish, of foreign office 29/9/66
Gerald William 8/12/82
Henry (1767-1841), 2nd Earl of Harewood (1820), West Indian proprietor 11/5/33
James Walter, Rev. (1831-1901) 11/10/87
William Saunders Sebright (1798-1851), liberal M.P. 14/7/42
Lasseau, Prof., of Munich 1/10/45

Lataky, Mr. 14/4/57
Latey, John, novelist 9/5/77
Latham,
Alfred, banker, deputy governor, Bank of England 3/8/43 ?
J. S. 5/2/78
La Thangue, Henry Herbert, art lecturer 23/4/79
Lathbury,
Charles Edward, Rev. 26/5/88 ?
Thomas, Rev. (1798-1865) 17/6/42
Latheski, Sig. 8/2/89
Lathom *see* Wilbraham
Latimer,
J., London glover 8/10/60 ?
James 9/10/75
W. 20/11/79
Latler, Mr., librarian at Knowsley 10/10/83, 26/5/93
La Touche, John, of Harristown 22/12/68
La Trobe, Charles Joseph (1801-1875), governor of Victoria 16/2/38, 7/7/42, 5/5/46
Lattimer, W. 20/8/79
Laud, C. 28/10/79
Lauder, J. T. 7/2/91
Laugel, Auguste (1830-1914) 8/11/67, 9/11/67
Laur, E., author 27/7/75
Laurence,
D., school teacher 1/4/43
Herbert, dentist 3/7/78 ?
Percival Maitland, Sir (1854-1930) 29/10/78
Robert French, Rev. (-1885) 23/1/53
William Rogers, Rev. (1811-1843) 12/12/30
Laurens, Joseph, Abbé 18/12/79
Laurenson, Arthur, of Shetland 28/2/78
Laurie,
rescue 25/2/64
James, wine merchant 11/9/45
John Winburn, Col. 7/3/76
J. W. 11/9/89
Mary, Mrs. 20/9/54
Peter, Sir (1779-1861), London banker 2/3/38
Robert Peter, Col. (1835-1905), tory M.P. 23/6/77 ?, 28/3/78, 12/1/87
Walter, secretary, Union Bank 19/10/55 n
Lauth, Franz Joseph (1822-1892) 10/7/74
Laval *see* Lebzeltern
Lavalette, Charles Marie Félix, Marquis de (1806-1881), Marquis de Lavalette, French ambassador 6/1/69, 14/2/69, 7/7/70 L
Laveleye, Emile Louis Victor de, Belgian economist 23/7/70, 12/3/72 L, 26/5/75, 4/3/77
Lavella, Duke of, of Naples 29/2/52 fl
Lavin, M. 16/1/80
Lavis,
F. 7/6/77
H. J. J., Dr., classicist 26/12/88, 29/1/89
James, of Toxteth 5/9/56
John (1799-1867), surgeon 1/2/57
John Samuel (1824-1888), surgeon 1/2/57 ?
Lavradio, Count, Portuguese ambassador 19/10/53, 9/12/59, 14/3/60 ff, 15/11/60, 27/7/63
Law *see* Abbot, Clerk, Slade
Law,
C. 26/4/79
Charles Ewan (1792-1850), tory M.P., recorder of London 23/6/35 n
E. 29/1/77
Edward (1790-1871), 1st Earl of Ellenborough, governor of India (1841) 3/11/41, 7/8/84
Elizabeth Sophia (1789-1864), née Nightingale 23/6/35
Elizabeth Sophia, Sister (1818-1888), nun 6/10/53 ?
Francis Towry Adeane (1835-1901), soldier 9/9/81 ?
George Henry, Bp. 1/9/42 n
Hugh (1818-1883), Irish lord chancellor (1881), liberal M.P., Irish attorney general 26/2/69, 8/7/69 ff, 19/7/77, 16/10/77, 31/10/77, 18/12/78 ?, 12/6/80 c, 26/11/80 L, 20/5/81 c, 4/6/81 ?, 28/7/81 ff, 24/10/81 L, 13/5/82, 16/5/82 ff, 31/8/82
J. B. 4/2/89
John Halsey (1809-1877) 25/9/26
L. J., Miss 22/2/89
R. 1/9/76
Robert Vanbrugh, Rev. 17/12/78 ?
Thomas Graves, Rev. (1836-1904), Scottish historian 17/12/78, 2/1/79, 18/1/79, 27/3/79, 9/9/81, 20/11/85, 1/10/90 ff
William, servant 2/2/43
William, treasury civil servant 1/2/56 n
Lawes, Mrs. 8/12/77
Lawless, Richard, of Kildare 11/10/86
Lawley *see* Molyneux, Veysey, Wiel, Wortley
Lawley,
Beilby (1849-1912), 3rd Baron Wenlock (1880) 10/11/74
Beilby Richard, 2nd Baron Wenlock 27/7/40
Constance Mary, Lady, née Lascelles, Lady Wenlock 14/5/72
Francis Charles (1825-1901), G's secretary (1852), liberal M.P., gambler 10/1/47, 28/12/52 ff, 6/1/53, 16/8/53, 7/1/54, 10/6/54, 19/7/54, 22/7/54, 30/7/54,

Lawley, Francis Charles (*cont.*)
2/8/54, 3/8/54, 4/8/54, 20/9/54, 12/11/54, 10/7/56, 12/7/56, 23/7/56, 25/9/59, 14/1/61, 1/8/62, 13/2/64, 10/2/67, 23/3/67, 10/2/70 L, 22/4/72, 25/5/75 ff, 23/3/89, 29/3/89, 27/11/91 ff, 4/10/92 n
Georgiana Emily (-1891), née Somerset 9/11/52 n, 7/5/64
Henrietta, née Zaiser 24/7/77
Robert (1768-1834), 1st Baron Wenlock (1831), whig M.P. 25/3/32
Robert Neville (-1891) 9/11/52 n
Stephen Willoughby, Rev. 24/8/48
Lawn, Benjamin, bootmaker 1/6/50 ?
Lawrell, John, Rev. (-1865) 8/5/59
Lawrence *see* Boyle
Lawrence,
rescue 4/12/61, 6/5/73, 12/9/79
Alderman 19/1/81
Mrs. 12/12/90
Abbot (-1855), American minister 23/7/51
Alfred, Rev. (1791-1874) 10/3/54
Charles (-1853), mayor of Liverpool (1823) 12/2/26
Charles Washington, Rev. (1805-1861) 23/1/28
Edward, mayor of Liverpool 7/11/65
F., Rev. 24/12/77
George, solicitor 16/2/49
Henry Cripps, Dr. 15/5/78 ?
John Laird Mair, Sir (1811-1879), 1st Baronet (1858), 1st Baron Lawrence (1869), Viceroy of India (1863) 4/5/59, 5/7/79
P. M. 25/2/79
Thomas James, Rev. (1849-1919) 29/9/76 n
Lawrence & Reed, solicitors 16/2/49 n
Lawrenson, Michael, of Ireland 27/10/77
Lawrie, John Douglas, Dr., physician 19/12/76 ?
Laws, Capt., of Liverpool railway 4/3/46
Lawson,
Edward Levy- (1833-1916), 1st Baronet (1892), 1st Baron Burnham (1903), proprietor, *Daily Telegraph* 11/6/61, 1/4/71 L, 6/8/72 L, 7/8/72 L, 29/6/73, 11/1/75, 26/7/76, 8/10/76, 27/8/77, 24/9/77, 12/10/84 L
George Nicholas G., Rev. 13/11/47
James Anthony, Judge (1817-1887) 18/5/70, 23/8/82, 29/8/82, 1/9/82
J. S., Montrose printer 14/9/50
T. E. 28/5/79
Thomas Paulinus (1837-1890) 7/9/67 ?
Wilfrid, Sir (1829-1906), liberal M.P. 10/1/79, 18/11/84, 18/6/88, 8/11/88, 3/2/93, 24/4/93, 18/12/93
Lawton,
George (1808-1853), librarian 22/12/36 ?
James 13/8/79
Lay, Horatio Nelson (1898-), of China 26/1/63
Laya, M. Martin- 13/4/91
Layard,
Austen Henry, Sir (1817-1894), diplomat, liberal M.P. 3/12/41 n, 23/7/55, 16/5/68, 24/8/69, 18/10/69, 24/2/70, 30/4/80, 5/3/83 c, 8/3/83 L
Edgar Leopold (1824-1900), consul 7/6/73 n
Henry Peter John, colonial servant 3/12/41
Laycock, James Marshall, Rev. 23/11/87 n
Layman, Mr. 8/1/75
Layton,
Charles, publisher 17/7/78
G., cashier of Bank of England 12/5/68
Lazara, Senor, Spanish translator 6/12/92
Lazarus, Mrs. 16/3/91
Lazzara, Giuseppe, Sicilian guide 15/10/38
Lazzaroni, Antony, Edinburgh shop keeper 4/8/48 ?
Lea,
rescue 25/7/73
Frederick Simcox, Rev. (1823-1893) 17/4/55, 8/5/68
Job 17/7/67, 3/11/72
Simeon, Rev. 12/9/81
Thomas, Rev. 11/12/85
Thomas, Sir (1841-1902), 1st Baronet (1892), liberal M.P. 17/12/79
William, Ven. (1818-1889) 16/2/67
Leach,
Mr. 25/2/87
Henry, Rev. (1830-1921) 19/7/59
John 9/1/79
Leadbetter, Mr. 24/9/88
Leader, John Temple (1810-1903), radical M.P., G's host in Italy 23/10/29, 6/1/88, 8/1/88, 11/1/88, 13/1/88, 18/1/88, 26/1/88, 27/1/88, 3/2/88, 3/5/89
Leaf, Walter (1852-1927), classicist 16/7/92
Leahy,
James (1822-), home rule M.P. 16/6/82
Patrick, Abp. (1806-1875), Roman Catholic 9/3/73
Thomas, Rev., Roman catholic 31/10/77 ?
Leake,
Mr., of Tildesley 7/6/74
Robert (1824-1901), liberal M.P. 28/4/78
William Martin, Col., historian and classicist 25/5/57
Lear *see* Hamilton
Lear,
Edward (1812-1888), artist, poet 2/1/39
Francis, Rev. 26/11/44 n
Learmonth *see* Sinclair

Learmonth, John, Edinburgh merchant 10/12/33
Learmouth, Thomas Young, of London 8/10/58
Learoyd, Miss 21/12/78
Leary *see* Gray
Leary, John Frederick, librarian, House of Commons 17/11/57, 25/1/58
Lease, Rev. Mr., of Penmaenmawr 2/9/60
Leatham,
Edward Aldam (1828–1900), liberal M.P. 5/8/59, 16/9/81 L
William, banker 17/10/32
Leathes,
Mr. 15/2/37
Stanley, Rev. (1830–1900), Hebraist 29/6/76
Leaver, Josiah 12/2/80
Leaves, B. 16/8/77
Le Bas, H. 15/12/89
Le Beau, J. 14/3/87
Lebey, Edouard G., of Paris 20/11/79
Le Bouz, M., author 28/11/87
Le Breton *see* Langtry
Lebzeltern *see* Colloredo
Lebzeltern,
Alfred de 23/2/53 n
Ludwig Joseph de, Count (–1854), ambassador 31/1/51 n
Zenaide de, née Laval 31/1/51
Lechmere,
Edmund Anthony Harley, Sir (1826–1894), 3rd Baronet, soldier, tory M.P. 7/11/71
Louisa Katherine, Lady (–1904), née Haigh 1/8/76, 21/4/91
Lechoville, Mons. de 5/2/79
Lecky,
Elizabeth 25/11/72
John Hartpole (1805–1852) 18/6/38
Mary Anne (–1839), née Tallents 18/6/38 n
William Edward Hartpole (1838–1903), historian 18/6/38 n, 25/11/72, 2/7/86
Leconfield *see* Wyndham
Ledward, Richard Arthur, sculptor 1/8/85
Lee,
rescue 17/1/62, 3/2/74
Miss, of U.S.A. 7/2/88
Adam, of Oldham 8/2/87
A. F. 15/11/77
C. S. 10/11/91
E., rescue 7/6/52
Frederick George, Rev. (1832–1902), ritualist 12/1/60
Harry Wilmot, registrar of Charterhouse 11/2/80, 18/1/86
Hedworth, of Chester-Holyhead railway 18/9/60
J. 2/11/78
J., of Illinois 6/4/87
James Prince, Bp. (1804–1869), bishop of Manchester 30/6/57
J. B., of the Bounty Board 3/5/55
John Would, Newark attorney 2/5/33
M., Mrs. 14/2/67
Margaret, Mrs., American novelist 24/11/88
Robert, Rev. (–1868), presbyterian minister 30/4/49
Sidney, Sir (1859–1926), editor, *D. N. B.* 22/7/89, 17/10/89
Thomas Jones, Rev. (–1865), of Buckley 1/11/57
William, Ven. (1815–1883), of Dublin 20/10/77
W. S. 2/11/78
Leech,
Ann 23/6/72
John (1817–1864), cartoonist 21/4/65
John, Dr., Liverpool physician 6/5/52 ?
Leecraft, G. S. 9/8/78, 28/2/80
Leedle, Mr. 26/9/78
Leeke, William, Rev. (1798–1879) 21/10/61 ?
Leeks, Edward Frederick, solicitor 8/4/45
Leeman,
B., Miss 10/9/84
George (1809–1882), York solicitor, liberal M.P. 25/1/53, 20/10/60, 4/12/60 n, 16/6/64, 9/5/68, 11/9/77
Joseph Johnson (–1883), York solicitor, liberal M.P. 1/3/79, 28/10/80 L
William Luther, Rev. (–1905) 17/2/79, 1/3/79, 8/3/79, 1/5/87
Lee (or Leigh) *see* Hampton
Lees,
George, footman 21/2/41, 13/2/44, 8/5/44
H., Mrs., rescue 5/2/61
Henry, secretary, Edinburgh railway 8/1/50
James 2/3/41
Richard 27/3/80
Leeson, Barbara (–1874), Lady Milltown 17/3/70
Leethon, E., Dr. 20/11/89
Lefanu, William Richard (1816–1894), railway designer 31/10/77
Lefevre,
rescue 2/2/82
Mons. 21/3/78
Charles Shaw- (1794–1888), 1st Viscount Eversley (1857), Speaker (1839), liberal M.P. 27/5/39 n
G., Rev. 4/11/87
George John Shaw- 15/12/78
Henry Shaw, Messrs. 23/3/77
John George Shaw-, Sir (1797–1879), public servant 2/5/36, 20/9/41, 21/9/41
Rachel Emily Shaw- (–1885), née Wright 20/9/41 n

Leffingwell, A., Dr. 26/3/92
Lefroy,
  Anthony (1800–1890), tory M.P. 21/8/60
  Anthony Cottrell, Rev. 27/11/74
  Thomas Langlois (1776–1869), tory M.P., Irish judge 22/12/34
Legard, rescue 16/6/80
Leger,
  Louis Paul Marie, Prof. (1843–1923), historian of Austria-Hungary 30/11/85 ?
  Theodore (–1853), phrenologist 27/3/52
Léger, E. 11/3/78
Legeyt, Charles James, Rev. 22/11/76
Leggatt, T. G., translator 5/4/93
Legge *see* Grenville
Legge,
  Alfred, of Eccles 13/10/68 ?
  Alfred A. K. 6/1/75
  Edward Henry (1834–1900) 20/5/79
  Elizabeth, Lady Sherborne 21/10/77
  Frances, née Barrington, Lady Dartmouth 29/6/44 n
  James, Rev. Prof. (1815–1897) 25/4/78 n
  James Henry (1804–1883), 3rd Baron Sherborne 21/10/77 n
  William, 4th Earl Dartmouth 29/6/44
Legh,
  Misses 7/1/28
  George Cornwall (1804–1877), tory M.P. 16/4/46
  Isabella Helen 7/7/46 ?
  William Price 22/5/27
Lehmann, Rudolph 20/3/75
Leicester *see* Coke
Leicester, E. 12/10/74
Leichenstein, Dr., of Cologne 14/1/80
Leigh *see* Villiers
Leigh,
  Augustus Austen, Provost (1840–1905), Provost of King's, Cambridge 27/10/78 ?
  Caroline Amelia, née Grosvenor, Lady Leigh 14/3/61
  Chandos, of Stoneleigh Abbey 31/7/28 n
  Clement, Rev. (1786–1853) 7/8/25
  Egerton (1815–1876), soldier, tory M.P. 16/11/55 n
  Gilbert H. C (–1884), liberal M.P. 27/9/84
  Lydia Rachel (–1893), née Wright 16/11/55
  Peter, Mrs. 20/8/32
  Peter, Rev. 20/8/32 n
  Richard, Rev. 16/3/50 ?
  Thomas Pemberton, 1st Baron Kingsdown (1858) 19/3/46
  William Austen (1843–1921) 10/1/77
  William Henry (1824–1905), 2nd Baron Leigh (1850) 14/3/61 n
Leighton,
  Baldwyn, Sir (1836–1895), 8th Baronet 25/10/55 n, 6/1/82
  Francis Kuyvett, Rev., scholar 11/1/44 ?
  Frederick, Sir (1830–1896), Knight (1878), 1st Baron Leighton (1896), artist 12/11/66, 13/11/66, 29/4/80, 27/7/81, 28/3/82, 19/6/84, 25/6/84 L, 29/6/85, 2/7/85, 20/4/93 L
  James, Montrose solicitor 2/12/48, 5/12/48
Leighton, Jane, & Sons., bookbinders 21/10/43 n, 19/9/46
Leinster *see* Fitzgerald
Leishman, Matthew, Rev., presbyterian minister and Moderator, author 28/4/38
Leisk, John Lever, broker 16/4/80
Leitch, James 16/8/58, 24/8/58
Leith, John Farley (1808–1887), liberal M.P. 16/12/77
Leith Liberal Club 26/10/86
Leitner, Dr. 15/6/92
Leitrim *see* Clements
Lemarchand, John Gaspard, Sir (1803–1874), colonial governor 21/5/63 ?
Lemarchant, Denis, Sir (1795–1874), clerk to the Commons (1850), liberal M.P. 15/10/53
Lemoinne, Mons. 29/12/87
Lemon *see* Jodrell
Lemon,
  Campbell S., merchant 19/11/40 ?, 7/12/40 ?
  Charles, Sir (1784–1868), 2nd Baronet, whig M.P. 4/4/42
  Maria, Miss 9/2/28
  Thomas E., merchant 19/11/40 ?, 7/12/40 ?
Lemonnier, Charles 20/9/86 n
Lenbach, Franz, portrait painter (two portraits of G) 11/9/74 ff, 17/9/79, 11/10/79 ff, 31/8/86, 11/9/86
Lendon, Abel Seyer, Rev. (1808–) 7/6/29
Lendrum, Alexander, Rev., Scottish episcopalian 28/12/45
Lennan and Clark, Messrs. 28/9/57
Lennard, Mr. 18/12/80
Lennox,
  Arthur Gordon-, Lord (1825–1892), tory M.P. 27/6/46
  Charles Gordon- (1791–1860), 5th Duke of Richmond (1819), agricultural protectionist 4/11/54
  Charles Henry Gordon- (1818–1903), 6th Duke of Richmond (1860), conservative cabinet minister 19/5/60
  Henry George Charles Gordon-, Lord (1821–1886), tory M.P. 19/2/57
  John George, Lord (1793–1873), whig M.P. 27/2/38
Lenorègne, Mr. 30/10/77
Lenormant, François, French archaeologist 3/7/62

Lenton, G. 4/9/60
Lentry, Mr. 11/2/80
Leon,
A. 26/12/79
E. 3/11/85
Léon, Léonie, Gambetta's mistress 18/10/79 n
Leonard,
Charles H., Dr., of U.S.A. 13/1/90
Christopher William, publisher 9/2/42 ?
J. H. 23/4/90
R. M. 20/2/91
Leopardi, Giacomo (1798–1837), poet 17/1/51 n
Leopold George Duncan Albert, Prince (1853–1884), Duke of Albany (1881) 7/4/53, 18/3/82 c, 23/3/82, 27/4/82
Leopold I (1790–1865), King of the Belgians (1831) 6/2/32, 18/6/58, 24/6/58, 9/11/58, 13/6/61, 2/7/66, 6/7/66
Leopold II,
(–1909), King of the Belgians (1865), Duc de Brabant 18/6/58, 9/11/58, 17/6/65, 16/11/69, 17/11/69, 21/5/70, 27/5/70, 4/5/72, 6/5/72, 15/5/72, 8/5/73, 10/5/73, 13/5/73, 15/5/73, 19/3/79, 11/3/88, 30/9/92 L
(1797–1870), Grand Duke of Tuscany (1824) 17/5/32
Leo XII, Pope 14/1/39 n
Le Pelly *see* Harrison
Le Play, Pierre Guillaume Frédéric (1806–1882), engineer 26/3/63
Lesciotti, Sig. 12/12/79
Leslie,
rescue 23/7/57, 28/2/67
Miss 29/6/78
Charles, Bp. (–1871), bishop of Kilmore 12/3/70
George Waldegrave- (1825–1904), liberal M.P. 4/8/65
James, Dr. (1764–1858), theologian 22/11/34
John, bookseller 15/11/54
Lewis James, coachbuilder 8/2/53
Moritz von Dietrichstein-Proskau-, Count (1774–1864) 24/9/45
Robert Tronson, Rev. 2/7/75
Thomas Edward Cliffe (1826–1882), economist 9/8/67
T. J., Rev. 17/1/87
William, provost of Aberdeen 17/9/69
W. R. 7/3/76
Lessar, Mons., Russian adviser 14/4/85
Lesseps,
Charles de 30/6/83
Ferdinand de (1805–1894), canal-builder and engineer 15/8/55, 10/6/58, 4/7/70, 19/7/76, 30/6/83, 7/7/83 c, 13/7/83 c, 23/7/83 c, 18/8/83, 12/9/83, 7/11/83, 31/7/89
Lest, rescue 25/7/67
Lester,
C., rescue 11/11/62, 20/1/63
Charles Edwards (1815–1890), American author 8/8/67
John William, Rev. Dr. (1826–1876) 3/11/56 ?
W. 18/4/66
Lestrange, T., of Belfast 3/6/67
Le Strange *see* Oliphant
L'Estrange *see* Pennington
Lethaby, W., Rev. 17/3/76
Lethbridge, Roper, Sir, Knight (1890), tory M.P. 29/7/90
Letztengroschen, J. 15/7/90
Leven *see* Melville
Lever,
E. 21/2/87
Ellis, of Liverpool 25/5/85, 5/8/89
William Hesketh (1851–1925), soap manufacturer 28/11/91
Leverett & Frye, grocers 16/5/76
Leverson, Montague, of London 19/12/54
Leveson-Gower *see* Campbell, Egerton, Fitzgerald, Fullerton, Grosvenor, Gower, Morrison, Percy, Rivers, Stuart
Levi,
A. J. 7/3/90
Gerald Abraham, broker 4/9/66
Leone, Prof. (1821–1888), statistician 10/3/60
Levick, George 2/10/41
Levinge, Richard George Augustus, Sir (1811–1884), 7th Baronet (1848) 23/11/69
Levy,
Armand, of Paris 27/7/65
F. J. 21/3/74
Joseph Hiam 16/6/79
Thomas Bayley, Rev. (1812–1872) 2/11/61
Lewes, George Henry (1817–1878), biographer and partner of George Eliot 24/2/85, 21/3/85
Lewin,
Friend, Dr. 15/12/76
George Ross, Rev. (1810–1885), naval chaplain 23/2/39 ?
Jessie, Miss 19/12/78
Lewins,
Robert, Dr. 1/12/87
William, author 6/5/64, 5/6/66
Lewis,
rescue 26/1/61, 11/5/62, 5/2/64
Charles Edward, Sir (1825–1893), 1st Baronet (1887), tory M.P. 30/4/76
Edward, Rev. (–1879) 14/9/75 ?
E. Goodwyn, artist 21/3/68

Lewis (*cont.*)
E. S. 3/9/87
Evan, Rev., nonconformist 10/6/48
Francis, Rev. 7/1/46 ?
Frederick Christian (1779–1856) 3/6/32 ?
F. W. 11/7/56
George Cornewall, Sir (1806–1853), 1st Baronet (1855), liberal M.P., cabinet minister, author 25/9/35, 28/2/55, 3/3/55, 15/3/55, 20/3/55, 13/4/55, 2/5/55, 13/7/55, 31/7/55, 25/1/56, 2/3/56, 21/7/56, 13/7/58, 14/6/59, 18/6/59, 28/6/59, 1/7/60, 13/4/61, 1/5/61, 23/1/62, 30/1/62, 23/10/62, 2/3/63, 14/4/63, 18/4/63, 11/9/71, 8/1/77, 14/6/77, 22/4/80, 29/1/82
George Robert, artist 24/2/45
Gilbert Frankland, Rev. Sir (1798–1883), 3rd Baronet (1863) 4/10/45, 18/1/54, 7/3/81
Henry Owen (1842–), liberal M.P. 15/7/76
H. V. 13/11/46
James, Rev. (–1902) 1/1/67 ?
John Delaware (1828–1884) 23/3/70
John Frederick (1805–1876) 3/6/32 ?
John Harvey (1812–1888), liberal M.P. 16/7/61
John Herbert, Sir (1858–1933), liberal M.P. 9/1/87 ?
John Travers, Bp., bishop of Ontario 2/11/74
J. S. 6/11/78
Lewis, Rev. 16/12/79 ?
Maria Theresa, Lady (1803–1865), née Villiers, author 22/11/32 ?, 29/7/63
Mary Anne, Lady, née Ashton 21/2/40 n
Richard (–1883), parliamentary reporter 12/4/60 ?
Richard, Bp. (1821–1905) 18/12/82
R. Morris, Homerist 3/6/91, 29/8/92
R. T., Rev. 31/1/80
Samuel Strange, Rev. 28/10/78
Thomas, Rev., Independent minister 22/4/80 ?
Thomas Frankland, Sir (1780–1855), Baronet, chairman, poor law commission (1834), liberal M.P. 21/2/40
Walter Llewellyn, barrister 15/11/78
William, Rev. (–1870) 16/1/34
W. M., Rev. 22/11/90
Ley,
Henry, clerk to the Commons 4/3/69
Jacob, the elder 20/8/32 n
Jacob, the younger, Rev. (1804–1881) 6/9/28, 25/12/29, 20/8/32
John, Rev. (1805–1880) 25/12/29, 7/2/52
Linny, Mrs., of Southampton, supplicant 15/4/51
Leycester *see* Stanley
Leycester, Ralph Gerald (1813–1851) 1/3/27
Leyden,
Countess de 12/10/79
M. 1/7/78
Leyland, Leigh, Rev. 16/11/67
Liardet, J. E., of Greenwich 5/2/75
Libbey, Jonas M., editor, *Princeton Review* 12/7/78
Lichfield *see* Anson
Lichfield, rescue 22/2/64
Lichtenberg, George Philip, surgeon 26/12/78
Liddell *see* Hargreaves, Yorke
Liddell,
Adolphus Frederick Octavius, Sir (1818–1885), undersecretary, Home Office 7/9/83 L
Arthur Thomas (1837–1919), 5th Baron Ravensworth (1904) 18/12/70
Henry George (1821–1903), 2nd Earl of Ravensworth (1878), Baron Eslington, tory M.P. 20/2/56
Henry George, Dean 24/1/33
Henry Thomas (1797–1878), 1st Earl of Ravensworth (1855), tory M.P. 28/6/40
Robert, Rev. (–1888) 1/3/54
Lidderdale, William (1832–1902), governor of Bank of England 30/1/91
Liddle, Thomas, Edinburgh solicitor 25/11/85
Liddon, Henry Parry, Rev. (1829–1890), theologian, biographer of Pusey 8/6/57, 1/4/61, 4/9/66, 5/9/66, 27/6/68, 29/6/68, 18/6/71, 22/6/73, 8/11/74, 10/1/75, 4/7/76, 17/1/77 n, 18/1/77, 31/1/78, 19/10/82, 3/8/83, 21/1/84, 9/1/85, 12/1/85 n, 27/1/85, 14/4/85, 18/10/88 ff, 3/2/90 ff, 10/9/90
Lieto, Casimeiro di 8/11/54
Lifford *see* Hewitt, Powys
Ligertwood, Thomas, of Aberdeen University 16/2/47
Light, Henry, Sir, colonial governor 16/4/46
Lightfoot,
John Prideaux, Rev. (1803–1887), Rector of Exeter college, Oxford (1854), Vice-chancellor of Oxford (1862) 12/3/55 n, 23/2/61 n, 12/7/61, 9/5/75, 28/10/78, 28/12/82 L
Joseph Barber, Bp. (1828–1889), bishop of Durham (1879) 26/8/82, 29/8/82, 3/9/82
P., rescue 28/3/51
Lignana, Giacomo, Prof. 29/10/76, 1/11/76
Lilburne, Richard, editor, *Belfast News Letter* 8/3/75
Lilley,
E. 28/4/75
J. 25/7/77
J. P., Rev. 19/4/91
Lillicrap, Mrs. 24/1/54

Lilly,
rescue 11/12/72
William Samuel (1840–1919), journalist 29/1/82 L
Limerick, Mayor of, 3/1/87
Linardato, Sig. 25/1/59
Lincoln *see* Clinton
Lincolnshire *see* Carrington
Lind, Jenny (1820–1887), Mrs. Goldschmidt (1852), singer 28/5/47, 5/9/48, 3/7/58, 23/6/64, 14/7/73, 21/6/75, 23/6/77
Lindley, P. 10/4/77
Lindsay *see* Antrobus, Bethune
Lindsay,
rescue 16/12/65
Mrs., volunteer nurse 17/10/54
Alexander, Sir (1785–1872), general 21/5/55
Anne, née Coutts Trotter 4/1/39
Caroline Blanche Elizabeth, Lady, née Fitzroy, author 5/5/90
Colin (1819–1892), President, English Church Union (1860) 28/12/62
Coutts, Sir (1824–1913), 2nd Baronet (1837) 2/7/70, 22/6/75
Emily Florence, née Wilbraham, Lady Crawford and Balcarres 28/1/88 n
Harriet, Lady, née Gordon 8/6/75 n
Harriet Sarah Loyd-, née Loyd, Lady Wantage 22/3/67
Hugh Hamilton (1802–1881), tory M.P. 15/2/45
James (1783–1869), 7th Earl of Balcarres (1825), 1st Baron Wigan (1826), 24th Earl of Crawford and Balcarres (1848) 13/12/34 n, 20/10/49
James (1793–1855), of Balcarres 13/12/34
James, Sir (1815–1874), tory M.P. 9/3/46
James Ludovic (1847–1913), 26th Earl of Crawford and Balcarres 28/1/88 n
Maria Frances Margaret (–1850), née Pennington, Lady Lindsay 20/10/49
R. J. 23/3/80
Robert James Loyd-, Sir (1832–1901), 1st Baron Wantage (1885) 22/3/67 n
Thales 21/12/78
William (1819–1884), provost of Leith (1860) 7/1/62
William Alexander (1846–1926) 8/6/75
William Schaw (1816–1877), shipowner, liberal M.P. 8/8/54
Lindsay & Walker, Montrose bankers 29/4/51, 15/9/51
Lineham, Andrew, of Newark 14/4/41
Linell, Mr. 2/4/74
Linet, Mr. 10/8/78 ?
Linette, Miss 15/4/92
Lingen, Ralph Robert Wheeler, Sir (1819–1905), 1st Baron Lingen (1885), secretary, education office (1849), permanent secretary to treasury (1869), civil servant 11/2/62, 22/4/72, 15/8/73 L, 15/3/82, 27/1/85 L, 30/1/85 L, 23/6/85
Lingham, Gladstone 19/10/82
Link,
Mrs. 28/5/79
D. C. 5/6/75
Linkham, A. M. 19/4/92
Linklater, Robert, Rev. 19/4/79, 20/1/84
Linlithgow *see* Hope
Linnell,
Mr. 29/1/79
J. N. 23/6/68
John, senior, artist 9/5/73 n
Linney, James 1/7/68
Linning, John, accountant to Scottish excise office 20/6/36
Linnington, Adolphus Henry, merchant 4/12/78 ?
Linsell, rescue 22/6/60
Linskill, Mary (1840–1891), novelist 10/1/76
Linstott, Mr. 3/5/77
Linthwaite, Henry, Rev. (1823–1899) 14/5/61
Linton,
C. J. 6/9/60
H. 26/3/91
H. J. 2/1/86
Sydney, Rev. 26/12/69
William, Sir (1791–1876), Knight (1865), landscape artist 8/4/50, 5/4/51
Lintott, Edward 23/2/78
Linwood, rescue 27/3/78
Lion, Diodato, of Naples 6/2/91
Lipscomb, Frederick, Rev. 3/7/63 ?
Lisciotti, A. 25/5/68
Lisgar *see* Young
Lissach, M. 31/1/80
Lister *see* Russell
Lister,
Charlotte Monkton (–1911), née Tennant, Lady Ribblesdale 14/7/93
Edward 11/10/83 ?
Edward Charles, Rev. (–1895) 11/10/78 ?
George Spoforth, Justice of the Peace 12/5/75 ?
James 6/6/78
T. H. 22/11/32 n
Thomas (1790–1832), 2nd Baron Ribblesdale (1826) 26/11/32
Thomas (1854–1925), 4th Baron Ribblesdale (1876), Lords' whig whip 1880-5, 1886, Master of the Buckhounds 1892-5 14/7/93
Thomas Henry, author 22/8/40
Thomas Villiers, Sir (1832–1902), Knight (1885), of foreign office 21/4/79
W. 11/12/77

Listowel *see* Hare
Liszt, Franz (1811-1886), composer and pianist 1/1/67
Litchfield,
Charles, treasury clerk 10/2/53
E. 5/11/91
Francis, Rev. (-1876) 18/5/52
Samuel, china dealer 6/1/54
Lithgow, Mr. 18/12/79
Little,
J. Stanley 26/4/92
Michael McLean, of Newfoundland 23/7/40
Stanley 10/11/86
William John Knox, Rev. (1839-1918), theologian 17/4/74, 6/8/77, 12/10/81, 13/10/81, 17/10/81 L, 7/6/83, 19/9/87
Littleboy, John, of Brymbo, North Wales 18/9/56
Littledale,
Anthony, of Liverpool 12/8/29 ?
Henry Anthony (1810-1859), barrister 17/10/25
Richard Frederick, Rev. (1833-1890) 3/5/59
Littlehales, Thomas, Rev. (1801-1849) 26/6/43
Littlejohn, Henry D., Dr., of Edinburgh 30/8/66
Littlejohns, E. M. 2/5/91
Littler, Mr. 2/6/74
Littleton,
Edward John (1791-1863), 1st Baron Hatherton (1835), whig M.P. 29/1/33 n
E. R., 2nd Baron Hatherton 13/7/80 L
Litton,
Edward (1787-1870), Irish barrister, master in chancery 12/6/54, 20/11/63
Edward Arthur, Rev. (1813-1897) 21/3/40, 20/11/63 n
Edward Falconer (1827-1890), liberal M.P. 20/10/80
John, legal agent 23/12/52 ?
Livadas, T. 7/12/65
Liverpool *see* Foljambe, Jenkinson
Liversidge, Mr. 15/12/89
Livingston, J. L., of Liverpool 1/6/78 ?
Livingstone,
rescue 10/5/73
David, Rev. Dr. (1813-1873), explorer 29/7/64, 7/5/70, 18/11/72 c, 22/11/72 c
Llandaff *see* Matthews
Llanover *see* Hall
Lloyd *see* Thompson
Lloyd,
rescue 3/7/66, 10/5/72, 2/7/75
A. J. 12/12/79
Charles, Bp. (1784-1829), bishop of Oxford (1827) 26/5/28, 10/8/28, 16/8/28, 17/8/28, 6/9/28, 1/6/29, 20/3/82
Charles, Rev. (1809-1883) 8/6/57
Charles Dalton Clifford (1844-1891), Irish magistrate, undersecretary in Egypt 8/4/84 c, 7/5/84 c, 14/5/84 c, 24/7/84
Dorothea, of Dublin 19/10/77
Edward (-1870) 25/6/70 n
Edward, Rev. 15/8/28
Edward Owen Vaughan 5/3/88 ?
Edwards 12/7/65
Evan, of Mold 4/8/63 ?
Falkener, Eisteddfodd organiser 27/8/72
George Price 5/5/52
Humphrey, Rev. Dr. (1800-1881), Provost of Trinity, Dublin (1867) 19/6/67
Jacob, Rev. 12/9/67 ?
J. F. 22/1/75
J. H. 14/7/88
J. N., Rev. 7/12/87
John Augustus (1800-1854), engineer and surveyor 14/4/51
Julia 25/6/70
Julius, Rev. 17/11/77
L. 16/1/77
Mary Harriet, née Stapleton 22/1/31
Pennant Athelwold Lloyd Iremonger-, Capt. (1821-1909), of Flintshire 16/10/62
Sampson Samuel (1820-1889), tory M.P. 6/2/80
St. Vincent, consul in Athens 21/12/58 n
Thomas Davis, Sir (1820-1877), 1st Baronet (1863), whig M.P. 26/12/65
Thomas Henry, Rev. 14/3/79
Llwyd, Angharad (1780-1866), Welsh antiquary 19/12/63
Loader,
A., rescue 6/7/52
M., rescue 29/8/53
Lobengula (-1893), Chief of the Matabele 31/8/93 c
Loch,
Charles Stewart, Sir (1849-1923), secretary, Charity Organisation Society 30/7/87
Elizabeth, Lady 19/11/78
George (1811-1877), liberal M.P. 16/9/58
Henry Brougham, Sir (1827-1900), 1st Baron Loch (1895), colonial governor 11/10/71, 21/1/79, 23/11/92 c, 10/10/93, 28/10/93
James (1780-1855), agent to Duke of Sutherland, economist, liberal M.P. 20/9/53, 3/1/54, 13/9/58 ff, 30/10/58
Lock,
George (1832-1891), bookseller 5/4/59
John, Liverpool customs officer 6/10/29
Walter, Rev. (1846-1933) 27/11/83
Lock and Whitfield, London photographers 27/3/80

Locke,
John (1805–1880), liberal M.P. 3/8/59
John, Lieut. Gen. (–1837) 22/3/32 n
Matilda Jane, Lady (1778–1848), née Courtenay 22/3/32
R. W. 2/5/79
Locker *see* Birrell, Tennyson
Locker, Edward Hawke (1777–1849), R. N. 31/3/32
Lockhart *see* Hope
Lockhart,
Allan Elliott (1803–1878), Peelite M.P. 17/11/44 n, 1/6/53
Charlotte, née Dundas, 1883 17/11/44 ?
John Gibson (1794–1854), editor, *Quarterly Review* (1825), novelist, biographer of Scott 4/12/44, 29/11/49
Mary Jane, Mrs. 15/11/78
Robert, junior 25/11/85 ?
William, Rev. 6/2/91
William Ewart (1846–1900), artist 15/7/87, 18/6/89
Lockitt, rescue 23/5/76
Lockwood,
Mrs. 25/1/68
Crosby 2/11/78
Frank, Sir (1846–1897), liberal M.P. 9/10/93, 7/12/93
Lockyer,
Joseph Norman, Sir (1836–1920), scientist 5/11/79
Norman 5/3/73 ?
Locock,
Charles, Sir (1799–1875), 1st Baronet (1857), obstetrician to the Queen 23/11/37, 1/4/50, 2/4/50 ff, 8/4/50, 7/3/52, 1/4/52 ff, 16/1/53, 23/2/54, 8/2/56, 7/2/57, 19/8/71 L
Sidney, diplomat 17/12/58
Lodge,
Aneurin Lloyd, Rev. 10/8/65
John W. 19/7/80 ?
Loë, Carl Walther Degenhard von, Baron 27/5/77
Lofiego, Gennaro, Neapolitan shopkeeper 13/11/38
Loftus *see* Egerton
Loftus,
Anna Maria, Lady (1785–1857), née Dashwood, Lady Ely (1806) 11/3/39
Augustus William Frederick Spencer, Lord (1817–1904), diplomat 19/11/58
Jane (–1890), née Hope-Vere, Lady Ely 1/7/61
John (1770–1845), 2nd Marquis of Ely (1806) 11/3/39 n
John Henry (1814–1857), 3rd Marquis of Ely (1845) 5/6/56
Logan,
Mr. 1/6/28
Guy, mendicant 24/3/89
Henry Francis Charles, Rev. 18/8/40
John William (1845–1925), liberal M.P. 31/7/93
Robert, banker 7/4/37 ?
W. 13/4/80
William (1813–1879), temperance and prostitution reformer in Glasgow 27/12/67
Lojacomo, Padre 1/1/39
Lomas,
Mrs. 24/9/89
Holland, Rev., of Liverpool 30/8/75
Lomax,
Frederick 8/8/77
John, Rev., nonconformist 22/7/65
Thomas, barrister 14/6/55
Lombardo, Sig. 25/1/59
Lonardi, D. G., Rev. 20/11/77
Londesborough *see* Denison
Londini, E., Prof. 31/10/91
Londonderry *see* Stewart, Tempest, Vane
London Stereoscopic Co. 17/5/88
Long,
C. C. 2/11/85
C. Chaillé, Col. 11/1/90
F., Mrs. 14/3/45
Frederick Beckford 6/6/42
Harry Alfred, author 20/8/77
T., Rev. 10/12/77, 5/2/79
Walter (1793–1871), tory M.P. 18/5/38
Walter Hume (1854–1924), 1st Viscount Long (1921), tory M.P. 13/8/90
W. B., property tax clerk 14/9/48
Longbourne & Stevens, Messrs., solicitors 21/9/86
Longden, Thomas Hayter, stockbroker 19/2/49, 22/5/50
Longfellow, Henry Wadsworth (1807–1882), poet 9/7/68
Longfield, Mountifort, Judge (1802–1884) 6/11/77, 25/10/80
Longford *see* Pakenham
Longley, Charles Thomas, Abp. (1794–1868), bishop of Ripon (1836), bishop of Durham (1856), archbishop of York (1860), archbishop of Canterbury (1862) 30/4/37
Longmaid, Mr. 2/8/77
Longman,
Messrs., publishers 16/2/47
F. G. 30/1/80
William (1813–1877), publisher 16/2/47 n
Longueville, Thomas, journalist 4/3/78, 1/3/94
Lonsdale *see* Lowther

Lonsdale,
Arthur Pemberton Heywood- 16/10/72 n
John, Bp. (1788–1867), bishop of Lichfield (1843) 16/2/27
John Gylby, Canon (1818–1907), secretary, National Society 6/3/50, 23/12/90
Margaret, Miss, author 19/2/80
Loosley, G. 22/3/76
Lopes,
Henry Charles (1828–1899), 1st Baron Ludlow (1897), tory M.P. 7/5/57
Massey, Sir (1818–1908), tory M.P. with minor office 20/2/69 c, 13/4/72, 16/4/72 n, 19/4/72, 20/4/72 c, 10/7/72 n, 5/4/73 c, 22/4/73 c, 2/1/74, 12/5/85
Loraine, Nevison, Rev. 26/6/76, 18/1/85
Lord,
A. E., Rev. 27/9/78
James, barrister 8/10/41
John, Dr. 16/10/87
Loreburn *see* Reid
Lorenzi, Giovanni, Prof. 3/10/79 ?
Lorimer,
Miss 10/11/88
Rev. Mr. 6/1/87
James, Prof. (1818–1890), lawyer 16/4/58
Lorne *see* Campbell
Lorrell, Mr. 5/8/54
Lorton *see* King
Lossen, Max, Dr. (1842–1898), of Munich 13/10/75
Lothian *see* Kerr
Lothian, Maurice, of Edinburgh 10/6/56
Loudoun *see* Hastings
Lough, James Graham, sculptor 1/4/43
Louis I (1838–1889), King of Portugal (1861), Duke of Oporto 18/6/54
Louis,
Alfred Hyman, author, barrister 18/3/67, 1/11/75
N. J. 12/9/79, 5/11/79
Louis Alexander of Battenberg, later Mountbatten, Prince 24/11/83 n
Louise,
Princess, Duchess of Connaught 21/5/80
Princess (–1931), Duchess of Fife 18/1/72 ?
Princess (1848–1939), Duchess of Argyll, Victoria's daughter 10/12/59 n, 9/11/71, 29/6/72, 16/11/81, 25/3/82, 25/11/84, 24/3/86
Louis-Philippe, King (1773–1850), King of the French 13/2/32
Louisville, Mayor of 28/12/89
Lound, John, estate agent 19/5/68 ?
Lovaine *see* Percy
Lovat *see* Fraser
Loveday,
Ely (1800–1892), actor 3/7/57 ?
George Beaumont (1833–1887), actor 3/7/57 ?
Lovegrove, Edward, printer 11/6/47
Lovelace *see* King, Noel
Loveland, Henry, London bookseller 30/3/59
Lovell,
C. H. 1/1/79, 17/1/79
E., rescue 25/5/57
George Francis, Rev. 13/5/79
J. 27/12/79
Loverdo,
Mrs. 14/5/76
J. Dionysius 17/4/77, 13/12/79
S. E., Greek advocate 21/3/59, 22/12/59
Lovett,
H. W. 7/9/90
Robert, Rev., of Paris 12/2/32
William (1800–1877), Chartist 10/7/40 n
Lovinbeck, Mr. 17/11/76
Low,
Alexander, Rev. (–1873), presbyterian 25/6/52
David, Bp. 8/7/45
J. G., Rev. 31/8/91
S. L. 1/8/76
William, Brechin postmaster 5/11/51
Lowater, L., of Nottingham 10/10/77
Lowder,
Miss 2/2/60 n
Miss 2/2/60 n, 15/3/60
Charles Fuge, Rev. (1820–1880) 10/4/56
Lowe,
D. W. 16/12/79
Edward Clarke, Rev. Dr. (1823–1912) 28/4/55, 18/1/66
Georgiana, née Orred, Lady Sherbrooke 25/6/53, 1/4/90
Henry Edward, Rev. (–1895) 18/9/51, 20/4/54
J., of Stockport 7/2/80
James (–1891), editor 17/5/58 ?
Josiah Beatson, Rev. Dr., of Liverpool 18/11/75
L., Miss 10/9/76
Richard Thomas, Rev. (–1874) 6/5/52
Robert 2/3/40
Robert William, historian 13/11/90 ?
Thomas, Rev. (–1898) 3/4/78
William H., Birmingham solicitor 2/8/48 ?
William Henry, Rev. (1848–1917) 5/7/79
Lowell, James Russell (1819–1891), American ambassador and author 26/7/81 L, 3/4/82 L
Lowenthal, Emil (1835–1896), artist 18/10/66
Lowndes,
Frederick Walter, Dr. 8/3/76, 27/11/76
John James, author 21/7/40 ?
Lowne, Edward Yates 25/6/78

Lowther,
James (1840–1904), tory M.P. 3/10/73 n, 23/5/82, 18/6/82, 7/2/93, 11/2/93
William (1757–1844), 1st Earl of Lonsdale (1807) 16/11/41 n
William (1787–1872), 2nd Earl of Lonsdale (1844), Baron Lowther, tory M.P. 16/11/41
Low & Thomas, of Wrexham 12/9/71 L
Loyd *see* Lindsay
Loyd,
Harriet (–1864), née Wright, Lady Overstone 14/7/57
Samuel Jones (1796–1883), 1st Baron Overstone (1850), banker 19/1/53, 7/2/55, 12/5/63, 19/3/75
Loysdael, Mr. 4/1/87
Loyson,
Madame 20/5/76, 19/6/76, 26/7/78, 4/2/83, 8/2/83, 18/7/83
Charles Jean Marie (Hyacinthe), Father, known as 'Père Hyacinthe', maverick French priest and ecumenist 28/11/70, 24/3/76, 20/5/76, 24/5/76, 27/5/76, 17/6/76, 21/6/76, 24/6/76, 28/6/76, 11/12/78, 19/10/79, 17/6/80, 5/11/80, 18/6/82, 10/2/83
Lozzo, C., Count 18/3/89
Luard,
Col. 10/11/91
H. S. 26/12/79
Lubbock *see* Buxton
Lubbock,
John, Sir (1834–1913), 4th Baronet, 1st Baron Avebury, banker, liberal M.P. 5/2/81, 31/10/81 ff, 26/6/83, 11/10/83, 31/3/87, 22/3/90, 29/8/92 n
John William, Sir (1803–1865), 3rd Baronet (1840), astronomer 24/3/31
Nevile, Sir (1839–1914), banker 31/7/75, 29/8/92
Luca, Antonio de, Cardinal 30/4/67
Lucan *see* Bingham
Lucas,
Mrs. 11/12/67
Mrs., rescue 20/5/79
Charles, French historian 8/3/75 ?
Frederick (1812–1855), editor, *The Tablet*, secretary, Irish Tenant League, liberal M.P. 8/8/54 ?
James, Mrs. (–1849), née Beesly 18/5/38
James, the elder, West Indian merchant in Liverpool 18/5/38 n
James, the younger 18/5/38 n
John (1807–1874), artist, painted G's portrait 5/7/43, 20/7/43 n, 22/11/43, 29/11/43
Stanley 19/4/74
W. W. 11/7/90
Lucey,
C., of Oak Farm 19/8/56
Ebenezer Curling, Rev., of Dover 20/8/69
Luckock, Henry Mortimer, Canon 15/10/88
Lucy,
Charles (1814–1873), artist 5/4/69
Henry William, Sir (1843–1924), parliamentary reporter 14/5/77, 14/4/85 ?, 14/1/86 n, 30/6/86 n, 31/7/86, 7/5/89, 5/3/94 L
William, mayor of Birmingham 10/6/51
Ludlow *see* Lopes
Ludlow,
Messrs. 31/10/86
John Malcolm Forbes (1821–1911), barrister, Christian socialist 13/12/53
Ludolf, Countess, of Naples 29/2/52
Ludovic, Mr. 20/2/79
Ludovisi, Luigi Boncompagni- (1767–1841), Prince of Piombino 15/1/39
Luenze, Domenico, Sig. 24/1/88
Lugard, Frederick Dealtry (1858–1945), imperialist 23/9/92, 24/9/92, 29/9/92 c, 30/9/92 n, 3/10/92, 8/10/92, 9/11/92, 2/3/93 ff, 20/7/93 c
Luke,
Mrs. 28/9/63
George Rankine (1836–1862) 21/11/61
James, surgeon 8/7/45 ?
William Balkwill 20/11/78 ?
Lumley,
H. 11/12/74
Watkin 19/11/89
William Golden (1802–1878) 26/1/65
Lumsden, Peter Stark, Sir (1829–1918), commissioner for North West Frontier 11/4/85, 13/4/85, 21/4/85 c, 2/6/85
Lumsden & Grant, Messrs. 3/9/56
Lunalilo, King, King of the Sandwich Islands 22/2/73 n
Lund, Thomas, Rev. (–1877) 14/10/53
Lundy,
Francis James, Rev., of Canada 27/2/52 ?
John P., of U.S.A. 9/5/77 ?
Lunn,
G., Mrs., author 21/12/89
Henry Simpson, Sir (1859–1939), travel agent and ecumenist 24/4/94
John Robert, Rev. Dr. 16/1/92
Lunzi, Nicolo, Count, of Ionia 20/12/58, 17/8/59
Lupton, J. 13/2/78
Lurgan *see* Brownlow
Luscombe,
A. M., Lieut. 7/2/79
Henry Harmood 19/2/32
J. F., of Customs and Excise 18/7/77 ?
Matthew Henry Thornhill, Bp. (1776–1846), Scottish episcopal bishop to Europe (1825) 12/2/32

Lush,
Robert, Sir (1807-1881), judge 24/1/72
Samuel Clarence, solicitor 10/9/76 ?
Lushington,
Charles Manners, of the Board of Control 19/7/48
E. D., treasure of Guy's hospital 25/2/78 n, 13/11/86, 15/2/90
Henry, Sir (1775-1863), 2nd Baronet, consul in Naples 29/4/32
James Law, Sir (1779-1859), chairman, East India Company 4/9/43 n
Stephen (1782-1873), dean of Arches (1858), liberal M.P. 15/2/33
William Hurdis, Rev. (1808-1842) 8/6/30
Lusted, C. T. 2/3/89
Lutley, Edward Chorley, Rev. 16/11/77
Lutticke, George F., commission agent 21/12/76
Luttrell, George Fownes (1826-1910) 24/1/77
Lutwidge, Robert Wilfred Skeffington (1802-1873), barrister 19/6/38 n
Luxmoore,
Elizabeth Mary (-1862) 9/9/52
Frances Ann (-1879) 9/9/52
Mary (-1865) 9/9/52
W. T., manager of Albany, G's apartment 22/2/33
Lyall,
Alfred Comyn, Sir (1835-1911), Knight (1881), Indian civil servant 16/6/90, 15/7/93
Frances, Mrs., wife of G. Lyall 24/7/60
George (1819-1881), tory M.P., banker 7/4/59
John Edwardes (-1845), advocate general in Bengal 29/9/27
William Rowe, Dean (1788-1857), dean of Canterbury (1845) 18/1/29
Lycett, T. H. S. 23/2/77
Lyell,
A., of the Customs Dept. 21/12/44
Katherine M., Miss 1/3/76
Leonard, Sir (1850-1926), 1st Baronet (1894), 1st Baron Lyell (1914), liberal M.P. 8/1/86, 20/1/92
Lygon,
Catherine (-1875), Lady Beauchamp 26/6/55
Frederick (-1891), 6th Earl Beauchamp (1866) 2/1/52
John Reginald (-1850), 3rd Earl Beauchamp 26/6/55 n
Mary Catherine (-1876), née Stanhope, Lady Beauchamp 26/12/75
Lykourgos, Alexander, Abp. (-1875) 10/1/70, 29/4/70, 4/10/70 n, 5/10/70, 18/8/72 L, 4/9/72, 13/1/75, 19/9/75, 29/9/75, 30/9/75, 1/10/75, 1/11/75 n
Lyle,
William, of U.S.A. 4/8/79
William, reporter 22/4/56
Lyman, Rev. Dr., American in Rome 14/11/66
Lymington *see* Wallop
Lymington, Mr. 4/7/77
Lynch *see* Fallon
Lynch,
Mr., Fenian 6/4/69
E. 17/6/75
F. C. 25/11/89
J. F. A. 16/6/74
Stanislaus J., Irish land commisioner 17/3/86
T. T. 26/5/69
Lynchner, E. 14/8/86
Lyndhurst *see* Copley
Lyne,
Charles Richard Nunez, Rev. 9/10/78
F. 29/6/75
Joseph Leycester (1837-1908), known as Father Ignatius 11/12/68, 5/5/89
Lynes & Rivett, Messrs., architects 8/10/67
Lynian, Mr. 26/5/75
Lynn, D., Miss 21/7/87
Lyon *see* Fellowes
Lyon,
Claude Bowes- (1824-1904), 13th Earl of Strathmore (1865) 20/9/84 ff, 27/9/84
David (1794-1872), tory M.P. 10/2/37
James Wilfred, solicitor 16/6/52
J. Bowes-, 8th Earl of Strathmore 25/1/37 n
John, secretary, King's College hospital 27/6/49 n
Ralph, Rev. 8/5/41
William, mendicant 27/2/43
Lyon, Barnes & Ellis, Messrs., solicitors 16/6/52 n
Lyons *see* Howard
Lyons,
A., Mons. 21/5/90
Edmund, Adm. (1790-1858), 1st Baron Lyons (1856) 8/5/49 n
F. 29/10/86
Lewis, London liberal 6/10/87
Richard Bickerton Pemell (1817-1887), 2nd Baron Lyons (1858), 1st Earl Lyons (1887), ambassador at Constantinople (1865), ambassador at Paris (1868), diplomat 20/1/62, 12/6/69, 25/11/69, 16/7/70, 7/11/70 L, 18/11/70, 17/12/70, 17/6/71 c, 26/10/80, 3/7/82 c, 21/10/82, 27/2/83 ff, 30/6/83 L, 25/7/83, 18/2/84 c, 19/12/84 n, 21/1/85 c, 15/4/85 c
Robert Dyer, Dr. (1826-1886), liberal M.P. 30/6/80
Lysons *see* Carnegie
Lytchet Minster *see* Scott

Lyte, John Maxwell-, Rev. 4/7/76 ?
Lythbunrey, Mr. 14/2/85
Lyttelton *see* Cavendish, Glynne, Talbot
Lyttelton,
Albert Victor, Rev. 2/8/44, 5/9/91
Alfred (1857–1913), C. G's nephew, liberal unionist M.P. and cricketer 7/2/57, 9/1/77, 10/1/77, 25/7/80, 13/10/80, 14/10/80, 10/10/84, 22/2/85, 9/5/85, 21/5/85, 20/3/86, 26/2/87, 21/4/88, 8/5/89, 25/4/91, 2/3/92, 8/3/92, 3/9/92, 19/2/94, 27/2/94, 29/4/94, 24/12/94
Alfred Christopher (1886–1888) 26/2/87
Arthur Temple, Rev. (–1903), C. G's nephew 7/2/52, 12/4/77, 9/9/83 ff, 1/2/87 n, 27/9/87 ff, 28/9/88, 24/4/94
Caroline Lavinia (1816–1902), sister-in-law 23/7/39, 10/7/40
Charles George (1842–1922), 5th Baron Lyttelton, 8th Viscount Cobham 27/10/42, 29/5/68, 4/6/68, 29/4/71, 4/2/73, 6/2/73, 5/2/74 ff, 13/2/74, 24/4/76, 5/5/76, 31/12/79 ff, 3/8/93
Edith, née Balfour, niece by marriage, wife of Alfred Lyttelton 2/3/92
Edith, née Santley 29/5/84, 16/6/84, 14/7/84
George William (br.-in-law) 23/7/38 n
George William Spencer (1847–1913), cricketer and musician, G's private secretary 1871-4, 1882-5, 1892-4 28/11/83 ff, 20/3/86 ff, 22/2/88 ff, 27/4/88 ff, 25/7/88, 6/3/89 ff, 6/5/89 ff, 7/7/89 ff, 9/2/91 ff, 18/3/91 ff, 17/6/91 ff, 28/3/92 ff, 2/6/92 ff, 29/9/92 ff, 14/7/93 ff, 4/10/93 ff, 15/11/93 ff, 14/2/94 ff
Henrietta, née Cornwall 10/8/48 n
Hester Margaret (1874–) 12/1/75
Katharine Sarah, née Wortley 21/7/83
Mary (sister-in-law) 23/7/38
Mary Catherine (1850–1875) 26/5/50, 10/2/75, 19/3/75, 21/3/75
Mary Susan Caroline (–1937), née Cavendish, Lady Cobham, niece by marriage 19/10/78, 26/9/82, 15/10/89 n, 16/10/89
Neville Gerald, Gen. Sir (1845–1931), C. G's nephew 27/11/45, 15/10/73, 26/3/78, 2/11/78 ff, 13/4/80, 9/5/82, 3/8/82, 16/10/82, 8/10/90, 1/10/92
Octavia Laura (1862–1886), née Tennant, wife of Alfred Lyttelton 28/2/81 ?, 21/9/84, 22/2/85, 6/5/85, 9/5/85, 20/5/85, 21/5/85, 24/4/86, 27/4/86, 1/10/89
Robert Henry (–1939), C. G's nephew, solicitor 1/2/54, 1/7/77, 14/7/84
Sarah, Lady (1787–1870), née Spencer 23/7/39
Spencer (1818–1889), Victoria's master of ceremonies (1847) 23/12/40, 10/8/48, 29/10/77
Sybella Harriet, Lady (1836–1900), née Clive, formerly Mrs. Mildmay, 2nd wife of G. Lyttelton (1869) 29/7/61 ?, 12/12/61 ?, 14/7/69, 19/3/75, 24/4/76, 17/6/77, 1/7/77, 27/1/78, 3/3/78, 31/3/79, 24/6/79, 11/4/85, 12/5/85, 8/3/90
William Henry (1782–1837), 5th Baron Lyttelton (1828) 23/7/39 n
William Henry, Rev. (–1884) 22/12/42, 15/10/43, 8/12/44, 3/6/77, 15/4/83, 29/4/83
Lyttle, Wesley Guard 4/7/89
Lytton,
Edward George Earle Lytton Bulwer-, Sir (1803–1873), 1st Baron Lytton (1866), colonial secretary (1858), novelist, tory M.P. 23/7/55, 15/7/58, 16/7/58, 3/10/58, 27/10/58, 28/12/58, 1/1/59, 10/2/59, 25/2/59
Edward Robert Bulwer- (1831–1891), 2nd Baron Lytton (1873), 1st Earl Lytton (1880), Viceroy of India (1876) 23/1/62, 7/8/84, 28/5/89
Lyveden *see* Vernon

Mabbs, Goodeve, of Nottingham 10/4/76
Mabelan, David 20/8/86
Maberly *see* Smith
Maberly,
Thomas Astley, Rev. 11/3/51
William Leader, colonial office, post office 22/9/45
MacAdam, Mr. 10/6/76
MacAnally, David Lancaster, Rev. 30/3/87
Macanliffe, Mr. 11/4/79
MacArdy, Joseph 21/2/45 ?
Macarthur,
Edward, Gen. Sir (1789–1872), Knight (1862) 27/6/37
William, Sir, liberal M.P. 8/11/85
MacArthur,
H. 10/4/79
James, Australian 20/7/44
John (1767–1834) 27/6/37 n
Macartney,
John, Dr. (–1829), physician in Edinburgh and Liverpool 11/8/25
John, Mrs. 5/8/25
Samuel H., Dr. 19/6/77 ?
Macaulay *see* Trevelyan
Macaulay,
Charles Zachary (–1886), of Audit Office 3/3/54, 9/3/72

Macaulay (*cont.*)
Frances, sister of T. B. Macaulay 3/4/66
G., Rev., free-churchman 3/6/75
George Campbell (1852–1915) 9/5/77
John, of Canada 30/9/41 n
John, Rev. (1807–1876) 1/8/67
M., Rev. 24/9/88
Thomas Babington 6/2/33
MacBain, J. 29/6/78
MacBride,
J. J., of U.S.A. 12/4/89
John David (1778–1868), orientalist 9/3/29
MacBryde, Mr. 1/5/77
Maccabe, Edward, Cardinal (1816–1885) 18/7/82
Maccaroni Co. 29/11/77
MacCarthy,
Charles Justin, Sir (1811–1864), Knight (1857) 24/11/37
John George, Irish land commissioner 16/7/88
Maud (1884-) 6/5/93, 7/6/93
Nicholas Twite (1769–1833), known as Abbé de Levignac, Irish-born Jesuit 17/5/32 ?
MacCartney, George, tory M.P. 7/6/53
MacCaul, Alexander, Rev. Dr. (–1863) 15/12/42, 10/11/52
MacClure, Thomas, Sir (1806–1893), 1st Baronet (1874), liberal M.P. 30/3/70
MacColl,
Dugald, Rev. 6/10/77
Malcolm, Canon 29/3/58
Maccolla, Charles J., author 11/2/80
MacConville, Mr. 15/4/80
MacCorry, J. Stewart, Rev., nonconformist 13/11/74
MacCowan, A. 28/5/74
MacCree, Thomas (1797–1875), presbyterian 12/12/42
MacCrie, C. G., Rev. 3/3/79
MacCullagh, Mr. 21/11/78
MacCulloch,
David B., Liverpool broker 15/11/67 ?
John Murray, Dr. 23/9/75
Peter, pamphleteer 24/12/56 n, 14/8/58, 5/4/59
Robert, G's coachman 31/1/52
Robert, Mrs., coachman's wife 4/10/53
MacCurran, Mr., intruder 5/4/93
MacDermott, C., of Portadown 18/3/74
MacDevitt, J., Rev. 24/4/89
MacDona, John Cumming, Rev. 7/4/74
Macdonald *see* Davidson
Macdonald,
A. J., American journalist 10/10/73
G., 3rd Baron Macdonald 28/12/32 n
George, colonial governor 26/6/46 n
George (1824–1905), novelist 25/10/79 ?
J., Mrs. 3/9/63
John, Sir (–1850), Adjutant General 28/5/33 n, 26/6/46
John W., of Penmaenmawr 21/9/55
Lawrence (1799–1878), sculptor 4/12/37
T. 29/8/78
MacDonald *see* Buller
MacDonald,
Alexander (–1881), liberal M.P. 5/10/77 ?, 3/1/78, 13/2/80
D. G. F., Dr. 8/8/78
George, Rev. (1824–1905) 29/10/85 ?
James Ronald Leslie, Gen. Sir (1862–1927), wrote report on Uganda, 1892-3 30/9/92, 1/10/92, 8/10/92, 26/10/92, 1/11/92, 20/7/93 c
John (1819–1899), 6th Baron Clanranald (1873), Master of Clanranald, sailor 19/6/68
John Alexander, Sir (1815–1891), Canadian P. M. (1867) 4/4/71, 10/8/71, 12/8/71 c, 1/6/81, 25/11/84
J. W. 7/12/85
Norman Hilton (–1857), fellow of All Souls, Oxford, controller of Lord Chamberlain's department 24/5/52
Norman William (–1893), colonial governor 26/3/46
W. 9/8/77
William, Prof. (1797–1875), physician 14/12/59 ?
MacDonalt, A. 5/12/86
Macdonell, J. 12/3/79
Macdonnell,
rescue 18/6/63
Alexander (1798–1835), G's chess teacher, West Indian trader 21/5/26
G. P. 29/6/86
MacDonnell,
Alexander, Sir (1794–1875), Irish civil servant 25/8/71
Eneas, of Hampstead 9/9/44
R. 18/7/78
Richard Graves, Sir (1814–1881), Knight (1856) 24/5/64
MacDougall,
Messrs., of Canada 10/1/76
A., of Scottish N. L. F. 29/9/86
Alexander, Glasgow liberal 19/3/78, 23/8/78
William, Glasgow liberal 28/9/80
MacDowall,
Alexander B., author 5/3/88
Charles (1790–1872), London watchmaker 12/1/33 ?
Macduff *see* Duff
Mace,
C. E. 3/3/80
E. C. 3/11/85
Macedo, Sergio Teixeira de, Brazilian ambassador 8/2/53

MacElvey, Mr. 16/10/77
Macenter, Mr. 16/5/78
MacEvoy, Edward Francis (1826–1899), liberal M.P. 19/6/63
MacEwan, Alexander, broker 23/12/68
MacEwen,
Walter, Edinburgh advocate 9/5/36 ?
William C., advocate 19/3/80 ?
MacFarlane,
Donald Horne, Sir (1830–1904), liberal M.P. 28/11/80 L
James, Rev., presbyterian 12/1/46 ?
William Charles, Rev. 21/4/79 ?
Macfie,
D. J., of Borthwickhall 29/3/80
Robert Andrew (1811–1893), liberal M.P., Liverpool merchant 21/2/42, 13/10/64 n, 12/3/67, 10/1/71 L, 30/4/72 L
Macfie & Co. 21/2/42
MacGange, W. 25/6/88
MacGarel, Mr. 23/3/73
Macgeagh, Robert, Ulster Liberal Unionist 19/4/93
MacGeagh, Robert, of Belfast 16/7/77 ?
MacGettigan,
Daniel, Abp. (–1887) 29/4/81 L
MacGhee,
Richard, of Glasgow 23/1/80
Robert James, Rev. (1799–1872), protestant controversialist 20/6/35, 16/6/68
MacGill, Hamilton Montgomerie, Rev. Dr. (1807–1880), presbyterian 15/6/65
MacGillivray,
Messrs. 7/11/87
Mr. 8/9/60
Archibald, Rev. 16/11/88
William, Prof. 15/1/50
MacGitting, Mr. 9/4/80
MacGlashan, Mr. 14/9/89
MacGowan, Alexander T., Dr., physician 13/3/67
Macgregor, John (1797–1857), assistant secretary, board of trade (1840), liberal M.P., free-trader 15/9/41
MacGregor,
Donald, Edinburgh hotelier 28/10/85, 9/6/86, 17/6/86
Donald, Rev. 1/11/86
Duncan, Rev. Princ., Baptist 15/8/77
E., rescue 14/3/78, 28/5/78, 21/7/78
Evan, Sir (1842–1926), Knight (1893), admiralty 27/4/80
Francis C., consul 25/10/42, 20/10/43
Gregor (1869–1919), son of D. MacGregor, cricketer for Middlesex (wicketkeeper) 18/11/90
James, Rev. Dr. (1832–1910) 4/6/78, 28/3/80
J. S. 26/9/90
Robert, Major, poet 29/7/57, 8/7/58
MacHale, J., Bp. (1791–1881), Roman Catholic bishop of Tuam (1834) 5/5/32
Machan, J. D. 10/9/91
Macheriotti, Dr., of Ionia 25/11/58
Machin,
Messrs., bookbinders 8/9/91
Thomas, bookseller 14/4/69, 31/3/74
MacHugh, rescue 24/6/62
Macieri, D. 12/2/67
Macilwraish, Mr. 5/11/85
Macingo, Count, of Venice 8/10/79
MacInnes, Mason, Edinburgh manufacturer 22/3/80
MacInnis, John, Gen. (1779–1859), soldier in Bengal 3/4/37
Macinroy, William, Mrs. 10/4/47
Macintosh,
Miss 12/1/87
Joseph, Rev. 24/2/77
Macintyre,
Mrs., of Fasque 19/12/51
A., Rev. 22/7/78
William, Dr. (–1857), physician 23/6/51 ?
MacIver,
Mr., of Lochinver 21/9/58
Henry Ronald H. Douglas, Col. 25/10/76
Murdo, Dingwall watchmaker 12/12/44
MacIvor, James, Rev. (–1886), fellow of Trinity, Dublin 19/3/57
Mackarness,
Charles Coleridge, Rev. 26/7/92
John Fielder, Bp. (1820–1889), bishop of Oxford (1870) 18/2/64
Mackay *see* Bridgeman, Farquhar
Mackay,
Mr. 27/8/33
Mrs. 27/8/33
Mrs., rescue 1/7/57
Alexander (–1852), journalist 5/6/49
Alexander, Rev. Dr. (1815–1895) 2/9/87 ?
Charles (1814–1889), journalist 1/2/67 ?
Donald James (1839–1921), 11th Baron Reay (1877) 23/6/68, 30/3/80 ff, 22/4/80, 16/9/80 L, 20/8/83, 26/1/84, 9/5/84, 2/1/85, 1/5/91, 16/2/92, 2/5/92, 6/10/92, 28/1/93, 14/2/94
E., 7th Baron Reay 25/8/35 n
George, the elder, of Strathkyle 7/1/30 ?
George, the younger (–1868) 7/1/30 ?
John S. 19/5/88
Macintosh, Rev. 10/8/34
Mary (1855–1924), known as 'Marie Corelli', author 3/6/89 n, 4/6/89, 5/7/89, 26/7/89
R. 19/9/75
Thomas, author 24/1/91
W. 1/8/53

MacKay, the elder 7/9/33
MacKee, Henry Sheil, Prof. 14/12/77 ?
Mackenzie *see* Baring, Robertson, Sebright, Wardlaw
Mackenzie,
  A. C., Glasgow liberal 10/4/77
  Anne Watson (–1854), née Fowler 17/3/32
  Archibald Henry Plantagenet Stuart-Wortley-, Col. (1832–1890), tory M.P. and soldier 9/3/57
  Augusta (–1856) 25/4/28
  Charles, Canon (1806–1888), founder, City of London College 18/10/28
  Colin (1775–1835), of Portmore 27/1/32
  Colin, Sir, 1st Baronet (1836) 20/3/34 n
  Colin A. (–1851), diplomat 12/1/48, 30/7/51
  Colin James [Forbes] 26/11/79 ?
  C. R., secretary, London-Brighton railway 25/5/44
  Duncan, Rev. 10/8/47
  Elizabeth Caroline Mary, Lady (–1856), née Crichton, Lady Wharncliffe 15/4/54
  Evan, Sir (1816–1883), 2nd Baronet (1845) 2/9/53
  Fanny (–1826), née Mackenzie 6/11/26
  F. Humberstone (1754–1815), 1st Baron Seaforth 3/6/28 n
  F. M., Miss, of Edinburgh 27/3/76
  Francis Alexander, Sir (1798–1843), 5th Baronet, of Gairloch 25/5/33 n
  Frederick William (1816–1865), surgeon 27/2/56
  George (1810–1844) 10/7/35
  George Alexander (–1874), Liverpool merchant 10/7/35
  Georgiana Elizabeth Stuart-Wortley-, Lady, née Ryder, Lady Wharncliffe 15/5/44
  Hector, Colonel 26/6/45
  Hector, Sir, 4th Baronet 26/6/45 n
  Helen Anne 15/12/63
  Helen Anne (–1852), née Mackenzie 30/5/28 n
  Henry, Bp. (1808–1878), bishop of Nottingham (1870) 5/3/39
  James Alexander Stewart- (1784–1843), whig M.P. 27/8/27
  James Archibald Stuart-Wortley- (1776–1845), 1st Baron Wharncliffe (1826) 3/10/31
  James Dixon, Maj. 3/5/79
  James Frederick Stuart-Wortley- (1833–1870), G's private secretary (1860) 21/12/59
  James Hay, Edinburgh W. S. 5/12/55
  James Thompson, Sir (–1890) 28/11/51
  John (–1852), of Torridon 17/3/36 ?
  John Stuart-Wortley- (1801–1855), 2nd Baron Wharncliffe (1845), tory M.P. 24/8/41 n
  Joshua Henry (–1851), lord of session 30/5/28
  K. 29/8/54
  Keith William Stewart, Dingwall bailie 23/9/53
  Kenneth Augustus Muir-, Sir (1845–1930), lord chancellor's secretary 13/6/86 L
  Kythe Caroline (1811–1834), née Smith Wright 25/5/33 n
  L., Glasgow oculist 31/3/51 ?
  Mary (–1829), née Proby, Lady Seaforth 3/6/28
  Mary Stewart-, née Mackenzie 27/8/27 n
  Morell, Sir (1837–1892), physician 2/2/91
  P. 24/5/43
  S., Mrs. 4/6/28
  Sarah Anne Philomena, Lady, née Parkes 2/9/53
  Stephen, Dr., physician 1/5/94 ?
  Sutherland 24/5/28
  Thomas (1793–1856), of Applecross, tory M.P. 26/5/28
  Thomas (1797–1887), of Ord 17/3/32 n
  William Forbes, of Portmore, tory M.P. 13/1/38, 12/8/38
MacKenzie *see* Wadd
MacKenzie,
  A. C., composer 12/3/83 n
  Kenneth Smith, Sir (1832–1900), 6th Baronet (1843), liberal candidate 21/11/81
MacKew, S., Dr., of Biarritz 28/12/91 ?
Mackey, rescue 10/3/58
MacKey,
  Donald George, Rev. (–1888) 7/3/79
  Donald John, Rev. 20/8/84
  George, Rev. 10/3/87 ?
  N., chemist 7/11/85
Mackie,
  Mr. (–1848), of Fasque 8/11/48 ?
  James (1821–1867), liberal M.P. 22/8/60
  Robert Bownas (1820–1885), liberal M.P. 23/3/81
  T., of Edinburgh 13/4/78
Mackiewicz, Antony, Rev. 26/7/77
Mackingly, Mr. 2/10/74
Mackinnon, William Alexander (1789–1870), historian, tory M.P. 18/8/54
Mackintosh, C. Fraser, crofter M.P. 13/6/86 n
Mackirmal, Dr. 9/6/87 ?
Macknight, Thomas (1829–1899), editor, *Northern Whig* (1866) 15/12/54, 8/1/71 L, 26/5/87
MacKnight, Mrs., of Nottinghill, charity case 26/7/56
MacKonochie, Alexander Heriot, Rev. (1827–1887), ritualist 28/6/77
Mackworth, Digby, Sir (–1852), 4th Baronet (1838) 21/5/46

Maclagan,
rescue? 28/5/73
Andrew Douglas, Prof. Sir (1812-1900), of Edinburgh 23/10/65
MacLagan,
Peter (1823-1900), liberal M.P. 4/2/71, 25/4/88
William Dalrymple, Bp. (1826-1910) 20/7/90
Maclaren, J. W. 24/3/80
Maclauchlin, A. 21/1/78
Maclaughlin, Hubert, Rev. (-1882) 23/3/49
MacLaughlin, Alexander, Rev., of Limerick 23/6/68
Maclaurin, Archibald, Admiralty 2/5/53 ?
MacLaurin,
S., London banker 20/6/62
W. C. A., Dean 29/10/57
Maclean,
Alexander, insurance broker 19/6/51 ?
Alexander Walker, financial pamphleteer 29/11/52
Donald (1800-1874), tory M.P. 31/1/40
Hippisley, Rev. (-1895) 1/11/78 ?
John, Sir (1811-1895), Knight (1871), antiquary 21/4/76
MacLean, Thomas, art gallery proprietor 29/3/73
Maclean & Pisani, merchant 11/11/75 n
MacLeay, George, Sir (1809-1891) 27/10/70 ?
Maclehose, James J., of Glasgow 16/11/77
Macleod,
Alexander, Rev. 23/10/76
Anne, née Stephenson 14/8/32
Emily Sarah (-1896) 14/8/32
G. G. 13/10/90
Henry George, Sir, colonial governor 16/2/46
John Norman (-1835), of Dunvegan, Skye 14/8/32 n
M. D. 7/5/78
Nicholas Kenneth, Rev. 9/12/67
Norman, Rev. (1812-1872), editor, *Good Words* (1860), presbyterian 15/3/61 ?, 22/5/67
Roderick, Dr. (-1852), physician 9/3/37
Macleod of Macleod, Norman (1812-1895) 19/11/90
Maclogan, rescue 11/4/66
Maclunivan, Mr. 25/11/87
MacMahon,
Patrick (1813-1875), liberal M.P. 8/4/73 L
Thomas, Sir (1779-1860), 2nd Baronet (1817), general 11/11/57
MacMaster, Mr. 9/1/86
MacMeach, G. 27/10/88
Macmillan,
Alexander (1818-1896), publisher 28/4/68, 21/8/77, 17/8/78, 11/10/86 L, 4/11/86 L
George Augustin (1855-1936), publisher 3/4/79
J., Rev., of Dunkeld 13/11/55
Macmillan & Co., publishers 10/11/56
MacMordie, Hans 30/12/78
MacMorland, J. P., of Edinburgh 15/11/62
MacMurray, Dr. 19/7/64
MacNab,
H., of Fife 11/11/54
Thomas, of Montreal 8/7/75
Macnamara,
Dean, Roman Catholic dean of Limerick 19/4/37
Henry Tyrwhitt Jones (1820-1877), solicitor 27/2/71
Nottidge Charles, Dr. 21/8/77
William Nugent (1776-1856), Repeal M.P. 1/4/45 ?
MacNaught, John, Rev. (1826-1890) 3/1/68
Macnaughten, Daniel, assassin 18/10/41, 25/1/43 n
MacNaughton, Samuel 10/7/79 ?
MacNee, Daniel, Sir (1806-1882), portrait painter 4/4/80
Macneill, Duncan (-1874), 1st Baron Colonsay (1867), president of the court of session (1852), tory M.P., banker 18/6/44
MacNeill,
John, Sir (1795-1883), diplomat 29/3/54, 2/1/83
John Gordon Swift (1849-1926), home rule M.P. 6/11/86
MacNulty, B., supplicant 18/8/75
Maconachie, Alexander (1777-1861), Lord Meadowbank (1819), Scottish judge 24/12/34
Maconochie, Alexander, of the colonial office 9/5/46
Macphail,
Messrs. 12/9/91
A. 5/12/89
MacPhail,
Mrs., of Dingwall 9/3/70
Edmund W. St. Maur, Rev. 8/6/77 ?
William M. 15/8/77
Macpherson,
Alexander, Rev. Dr. (1781-1861) 19/1/58, 17/9/58
Geraldine (1830-1878) 23/10/66 n
Robert (-1873), artist in Rome 23/10/66
MacPhilpin, Mr., Irish journalist 12/12/79
Macqueen, John Fraser (1803-1881), official reporter of Scottish and divorce appeals 29/7/57
Macquoid, J. R. 27/2/77
MacQuoil, Mr. 22/12/87
Macrae, Mr., of Digwall 13/7/86

Macray, John, translator 30/5/45, 9/5/59
Macrea,
J. 2/9/78
James H., of Lancashire 25/1/68
Macri, Demetrio, of Paxo, Ionia 26/1/59
MacRoberts, A. 28/6/67
Macrom, Mr. 8/2/39
Macrorie, William, Bp. 7/12/65 n
Mactier, Anthony 28/10/33 n
Macunslane, Mr. 17/7/78
MacVea, E. 26/10/68
MacVeigh, Mr. 17/4/76
Madan,
Falconer (1851–1935), librarian 17/3/80 ?
George, Canon (1808–) 5/4/29
Madden,
J. W. 9/11/77
Richard Robert (1798–1886), surgeon, author 4/3/35, 16/11/65 n, 25/11/67
Maddocks,
Henry, of Hawarden 11/12/73
J. 1/5/89
Maden, John Henry, Sir (1862–1920), Knight (1915), liberal M.P. 16/1/92
Madens, rescue 12/2/56
Madhuvdas, Rugnathdas, of Bombay 25/9/90 n
Madot, Adolphus M. (–1861), artist 2/5/57
Maffei Di Boglio, Carlo Alberto Ferdinando, Count (1834–1897) 8/2/69
Magarey, Mrs. 29/1/57
Magee, William Connor, Abp. (1821–1891), priest in Ireland (1845), dean of Cork (1864), bishop of Peterborough (1868), archbishop of York (1891) 16/8/50, 5/5/90
Maggs, Uriah, bookseller 16/7/87
Maghen, Joseph 24/11/88
Magheramorne *see* Hogg
Magill, J. C. 7/9/68
Maginnis, Mr. 12/5/83
Magnay, William, Sir (1797–1871), 1st Baronet (1844), lord mayor of London (1843), stationer 15/5/44
Magniac,
Charles (1827–1891), liberal M.P. 19/3/61
H. 25/11/91
Magnus, Hugo Friedrich, Dr. 17/5/77, 19/9/80
Magorne, G. F., Rev. 23/1/77
Magoun, George F., Rev., of U. S. A. 7/5/79
Magrath, Nicholas, Surg. Lt., surgeon R. N. 22/1/35 ?
Maguire,
G. F. 6/2/79
James Rochfort (1856–1925) 31/8/93
J. F., Mrs. 20/3/69
John Francis (1815–1872), Irish author, liberal M.P. 21/2/60, 20/9/69 L
John M., Rev. 10/4/50
M., Miss 12/11/87
Thomas Miller, barrister 15/6/87 ?
Mahaffy, John Pentland, Rev. Prof. (1839–1919), fellow of Trinity, Dublin (1864), professor of ancient history, Dublin (1869) 26/10/77 ff, 28/9/78, 10/7/79, 20/12/80, 22/12/80, 12/2/81, 20/3/82 L
Mahdi, The, Islamic revolutionary leader 24/4/84 c, 1/5/84 c, 6/2/85 n, 10/2/85, 16/2/85, 7/5/85 c
Mahomet II (1785–1839), Sultan of Turkey (1808) 15/10/38
Mahon *see* Stanhope
Mahon,
Maria Elizabeth 15/5/41 ?
Ross, Sir 15/5/41 n
Thomas, Lieut. (1832–1879), Royal Artillery 28/9/50 ?
Mahony,
Pierce Charles de Lacy (1850–1930) 7/11/88
S. O., author 15/11/55
T., plumber 3/8/57
Maiden, George Augustus 9/3/55 ?
Maidstone *see* Hatton
Mailfer,
H. C. 4/5/76 n
N., of Paris 4/5/76
Main,
H. 19/5/77
Robert, Rev. (1808–1878), astronomer 19/3/63
W. 21/11/78
Maine,
Henry James Sumner, Sir (1822–1888), Knight (1871), professor of jurisprudence, Oxford (1871), author, lawyer 18/10/61, 19/2/78, 22/3/80, 17/4/86 n, 26/4/86
J. 22/9/85
J. T. 7/12/74
R. 17/5/78
Maintenon *see* D'Aubigné
Mainwaring,
Charles Kynaston (–1861), of Oteley Park, Shropshire 16/9/56
J. 5/8/91
Townshend (1807–1883), tory M.P. 27/2/56
Townshend, Mrs. 28/9/55
Mairr, J., Dr. 20/11/89
Maish & Co., print publishers 30/4/55
Maitland,
rescue 14/3/70, 15/6/77
Alexander Charles Ramsay-Gibson-, Sir (1820–1876), 3rd Baronet (1848), liberal M.P. 30/1/69
Edward Francis (1803–1870), Lord Barcaple (1862), lord of session 12/12/59

Henry, Edinburgh stockbroker 25/4/48
Horatio Lawrence Arthur Lennox, Capt., R. N. 31/3/79
John, conveyancer 1/3/48
John Gorham, barrister 10/12/52
Peregrine, Sir (1777–1854), governor of the Cape (1844) 4/2/46
Samuel Roffey (1792–1866), historian 28/8/25
Majendie,
George John, Canon (1795–1842) 14/11/30
Henry William, Rev. (1807–1869) 10/9/57 ?
Majocchi, Teodoro, cook to Princess Caroline 6/7/32
Major,
Anna Henniker- (1812–1889), née Kerrison, Lady Henniker, Lady Hartismere 15/2/37
John Henniker- (1801–1870), 4th Baron Henniker (1832), 1st Baron Hartismere (1866) 15/2/37 n, 5/3/60
P. A. 2/7/79
Makaroff, A. 6/2/77
Makin,
Charles, of Liverpool 10/4/37 ?
Thomas William, dress maker 4/4/45
Malabari, Bahramji Mehrbanji 14/7/89
Malamuso, Cav. 30/7/59
Malan, Caesar Henry Abraham (1787–1864), Swiss preacher 15/7/32
Malatesta, B., Sig. 24/1/88
Malcolm,
George Alexander, Gen. 19/10/42 n, 5/2/46
Georgiana, née Vernon-Harcourt 19/10/42
John Wingfield (1831–1902), tory M.P. 21/9/72
Mary, Lady (–1897), née Forbes 23/6/32 ?, 27/11/50
Pulteney, Adm. Sir (1768–1838) 28/8/32
William Elphinstone (1817–) 29/4/51 ?
Malcolmson,
Messrs. 18/4/70 n
Mr., of Hawarden 20/8/63
James, Rev. 24/6/76
W., merchant 18/4/70
Maldarelli, Prof. 8/2/89
Maldock, A. H. 13/3/91
Malet,
Edward Baldwin, Sir (1837–1908), consul in Egypt; ambassador in Berlin 18/11/84 L
Ermyntrude, Lady, née Russell 19/3/85
William Wyndham, Rev. 17/6/45
Malhet, M. 18/1/92
Malibran, Signora, opera singer 24/2/40
Malins,
rescue 2/7/52
Richard, Sir (1805–1882), Knight (1867), tory M.P. 11/7/64
Malinverni,
Sig. 9/1/88
Sisto Germano 10/10/77 ?
Malkom Khan, Prince, Persian minister 24/10/82 c, 30/10/82
Mallaby, Joseph, attorney in Birkenhead 22/5/53
Mallalieu, A., journalist 25/5/43 ?
Mallet, Louis, Sir (1823–1900), Knight (1868), at Board of Trade (1847), Indian civil servant (1872), free trade economist 19/2/66, 24/8/71
Mallich, Dr. 2/11/85
Malling, W. 12/4/52
Mallinsdy, Mr. 25/9/78
Mallock, John Jervis, Rev. 28/5/85
Malmesbury *see* Harris
Malomos, Mons. 17/1/78
Malone,
Silvester, Rev., Roman Catholic 11/9/67
Thomas S., London businessman 11/1/90 n
Malortie, Karl von, Baron (1838–1899), author, diplomat 14/7/66, 26/4/79
Malpas, Rev. Mr. 5/11/87
Maltby, Mrs., rescue 9/6/68, 16/6/68
Malthus, Mr. 31/3/68
Malvezin, M. 29/1/92
Malvina, Mons., artist 12/5/52
Mamiani della Rovere, Terenzio, Count (1802–1885), prime minister, Papal States (1848) 19/10/49
Mamoli, Sig. 29/9/88
Manchester *see* Cavendish, Montagu
Mancini, Pasquale Stanislao, Prof. (1817–1888), Neapolitan lawyer and Risorgimentist 8/9/51, 4/4/77 n, 10/2/83 L
Mancioni, Sig. 8/2/89
Manderfield, Charles, of Newark 30/11/41
Manderson, Thomas Claridge, Major 8/11/79
Mandeville *see* Montagu
Mandeville, Mr. 20/8/88
Mandley, Councillor 13/2/80
Manera, Father 29/2/52
Manfroni, Mario, Dr. 14/8/88
Mangan, James, Rev. Dr. 19/9/68
Manginelli, Madame 31/7/79
Mangles, Ross Donelly (1801–1877), director of East India Company, liberal M.P. 28/6/52
Mangoni, Antonio 14/2/80 ?
Manin, Daniele (1804–1857), Venetian republican leader (1848) 27/6/54, 27/9/72
Mankar, G. S. 16/6/77
Mankowane, Chief, of Bechuanaland 10/3/83 c, 22/5/83
Manley,
Orlando, Rev. 17/10/37
Richard Henry, Rev. 24/10/85

Mann,
G. H., Rev. 9/5/90
Hugh, of Lancashire 16/12/67
S. 12/8/90
W. P. 18/7/57
Manna, Giovanni, Cav., Neapolitan minister 2/1/51
Manners *see* Norman
Manners,
Charles Cecil John (1815–1888), Marquis of Granby (1815), 6th Duke of Rutland (1857), protectionist leader (1848) 12/12/48, 15/6/49
Elizabeth, Lady, née Howard, Duchess of Rutland 26/6/41 n
John James Robert, Lord (1818–1906), 7th Duke of Rutland (1888), tory M.P., cabinet minister 31/5/41, 6/3/43, 14/2/45, 31/7/46, 5/8/46, 24/5/48, 1/10/48, 3/10/48, 7/10/48, 7/5/49, 22/5/49, 3/6/51, 17/5/66, 20/6/79, 20/6/83, 21/3/84, 22/3/84, 11/11/84 n
Manners and Miller, booksellers 29/5/28
Manners-Sutton *see* Sanderson
Mannheimer, Gustav, commission agent 10/12/75
Manning,
Mrs. 26/8/76
Caroline, née Sargent 25/4/34 n
E., customs officer 26/2/45
Henry Edward, Cardinal 26/11/29 n
Manrick, Mr. 27/11/77
Mansel, Henry Longueville, Rev. Dr. (1820–1871), theologian 31/10/58
Mansfeld, Mr., portrait painter 29/3/89
Mansfield *see* Murray
Mansfield,
G. M., autograph hunter 2/12/75
John Smith (1813–1905), G's fag at Eton 30/11/25
Margaret, Lady (–1892), née Fellowes, Lady Sandhurst 25/9/63, 4/11/84, 18/11/84, 17/2/85, 6/3/88
Ralph (–1880), Australian journalist 16/3/49 ?
William Rose, Gen. Sir (1819–1876), 1st Baron Sandhurst (1871) 25/9/63
Mansfield, G. & Co., builders 13/3/51
Manson,
Alexander, Birkenhead merchant 29/1/36
Edward, auctioneer, of Christie's 3/6/47
Mant, Richard (1776–1848), biblical scholar 23/12/37 n
Manton,
Henry 4/7/86
Henry, Rev. 29/6/40
Mantrop, J. B. 29/12/79
Manvers *see* Pierrepont
Manx Times, publisher of, 8/10/78
Manzoni, Alessandro (1785–1873), Italian author and patriot 21/9/38, 24/9/38, 27/7/83
Maples, Maples & Pearse, solicitors 20/2/52
Mapleson, Marie Roze, Madame 4/4/83
Mappin, Frederick Thorpe, Sir (1821–1910), 1st Baronet (1886), liberal M.P. 12/11/90
Mar *see* Erskine
Marcello,
Andriana, Countess 25/2/59
Girolamo, Count 25/2/59 n, 3/10/79
March,
E. B., consul in Fiji 5/6/73
L. 28/11/76
Richard Alfred, accountant 18/8/68 ?
Marchant,
Joshua Le, Rev. (–1887) 23/4/67
W. T. 3/9/74 ?
Marchese, V., Rev. 1/2/89
Marchmont,
Mr. 17/11/86
A. W. 4/8/91
Marcoartu, Arturo De 17/9/75
Marcoran, Georgio, Sir 8/1/59
Marcotti, Giuseppe, of Florence; friend of J. T. Leader 9/1/88
Marcroft, William, of Manchester 16/12/67
Marcus,
A. 23/5/89
Lewis, Rev. Prof. (–1879) 19/8/67 ff, 19/6/78
Marcy, William Nichols (1810–1894), Worcestershire clerk of the peace 26/6/55, 16/8/55
Mardin, Francis, Rev. (1786–), priest in Bedlam 28/7/35
Marens, A. A. 17/1/90
Mareschalchi, Alfonso (1851–) 13/6/77 ?
Maret, Napoléon Hugues Joseph, Duc de Bassano 23/6/79
Marey, Mr. 24/6/79
Marfleet, John Isaac, Newark maltster 9/2/42
Margetson, Paul, merchant 23/5/79
Margfoy, M. 18/7/68
Marghen, Joseph 24/11/88
Margoliouth,
David Samuel, Prof. (1858–1940), Professor of Arabic, New College, Oxford 4/2/90
Moses, Rev. (1820–1881), writer on Judaism 11/5/58
Mari, Sig., Italian politician 14/1/67
Maria Anna Carolina Pia (1803–1884), Empress of Austria 21/9/38 n
Maria Isabella, née Borbona, Consort of Francis I 20/11/38
Maria Theresa,
Queen (–1867), Consort of Ferdinand II, King of the Two Sicilies 19/10/38, 21/12/50

Queen (1801-1855), Queen Consort of Charles Albert of Sardinia 2/3/32
Marie,
housemaid 16/1/46
Princess, Princess and Grand Duchess, wife of Prince Alfred (1874) 16/7/73, 5/4/83
Marie Alexandrovna, née Romduoft, Duchess of Edinburgh 9/3/74
Marie Charlotte (1840-), Archduchess 25/2/59
Marie Corelli *see* Mackay
Marino,
Prof. 23/7/88
Sig. 25/1/59
Marioni, U., Count, of Naples 25/7/51
Marjoribanks *see* Robertson
Marjoribanks,
Campbell (-1840), East India director 20/4/36 ?
Dudley Coutts (1820-1894), 1st Baronet (1866), 1st Baron Tweedmouth (1881), liberal M.P. 5/4/62, 27/9/72, 11/7/79, 27/3/86, 8/3/93, 25/7/93
Edward (1776-1868), banker 20/4/36 ?
Edward (1849-1909), 2nd Baron Tweedmouth (1894) 25/4/87, 11/7/87 ff, 4/6/88, 15/10/89, 12/3/90, 1/8/90 n, 20/10/90 ff, 25/11/90 ff, 1/3/91 ff, 5/3/91 ff, 10/5/91 ff, 18/11/91 ff, 1/7/92 ff, 10/7/92 ff, 27/7/92 ff, 20/8/92 ff, 6/9/92 L, 18/9/92 L, 1/11/92 ff, 16/12/92 ff, 25/1/93 c, 26/1/93 ff, 1/2/93 L, 4/3/93 L, 5/3/93 L, 14/5/93 ff, 22/5/93 L, 24/7/93 ff, 8/8/93 c, 11/8/93 ff, 6/9/93 L, 15/9/93 ff, 23/9/93 ff, 2/11/93 ff, 13/12/93 ff, 29/1/94 L, 10/2/94 ff, 24/2/94 ff, 21/3/94
Fanny Octavia Louisa, Lady (-1904), née Churchill, Lady Tweedmouth 1/8/90
Isabella (-1908), née Hogg, Lady Tweedmouth (1881) 21/7/63
Markham *see* Annesley, Murray
Markham, J. S. 11/8/90
Markley,
John T., author 16/10/78, 22/8/90
J. T. 16/10/78
Marks,
Edmund, architect 21/7/68
Edward, Rev., minor canon of Dublin 17/6/56 ?
Henry Stacy (1829-1898), artist 13/6/68 ?
Montague, of N. S. W., Australia 24/9/61
N. 18/4/80
Marlay, Catherine Louisa Augusta, née Tisdall 22/5/58
Marlborough *see* Churchill
Marlet, Mad. 10/3/87
Marliani, Emanuele (1799-1873), Italian senator and historian 6/4/59
Marling,
Mr. 29/9/78
Samuel Stephens, Sir (1810-1883), liberal M.P. 4/5/82
Marlow, Mr. 15/8/70
Marmora, Alessandro Ferrero de la, Count (1799-1856) 30/1/56
Marnham, Rev. 13/6/79
Marnitz, G. 26/1/78
Marochetti, Carlo (1805-1867), sculptor 12/7/55, 18/5/57, 20/5/57, 21/5/57, 22/5/57, 23/5/57, 15/8/57, 10/3/58, 18/2/62, 19/2/62, 12/3/62, 20/11/62, 1/5/63, 2/5/63, 27/7/63
Marrable,
Frederick (1818-1872), architect 3/8/52
George 6/7/68
Marrant, J., junior 27/11/76
Marratt, Charles, maths tutor at Eton 3/8/29
Marriage, Edmund 12/5/79 ?
Marriner, Mrs. 29/7/78
Marriott,
Charles, Rev. (1811-1858), tractarian 28/2/39 ?, 29/12/53
Fitzherbert Adams, Rev. 26/2/45
J. R. C. 7/1/90
Wharton Booth, Rev. (1823-1871) 1/1/58
Marris, Mr. 6/9/78
Marrow, William John, Cheshire landowner 23/12/46
Marryatt, Joseph, whig M.P., banker 8/3/34
Marsden,
A. J. 14/3/74
John Howard, Rev. Prof. (1803-1891) 22/9/63 ?
Marsh,
Catherine M., author 5/1/68, 27/7/86 L
C. J. 26/12/78
Eliza Mary Anne, wife of M. H. Marsh 4/7/55
Matthew Henry (1810-1881), liberal M.P. 4/7/55 n, 2/5/61
Thomas Coxhead Chisenhale- (1811-1875) 22/4/32
William, Rev. (-1864) 23/4/49
William Burton, Liverpool merchant 2/8/55 ?
Marshall,
Miss, applicant for post of governess 30/4/51
A. G. 17/1/89
D., Rev. 2/6/88
F., music master and organist 22/3/31, 25/3/31
George, of Chislehurst 12/5/77
George, Rev. 20/7/50
James, Rev. 19/10/41
James Garth (1802-1873), liberal M.P., linen manufacturer 18/1/47

Marsh (*cont.*)
Lambert 4/9/56
Leonard, timber merchant 20/6/49 ?
Peter, Rev. Dr. 13/10/75
Richard, Rev. 15/10/47 ?
T. D. 2/3/77
Thomas Falcon (-1878), artist 3/4/52
V., Rev. 7/1/88
William (1796-1872), liberal M.P. 19/1/65
Marshall & Edgar, Messrs., Dundee machine makers 22/1/49 ?
Marsham *see* Fletcher, Hoare
Marsham,
Charles (1808-1874), 3rd Earl of Romney (1845), Viscount Marsham, tory M.P. 23/5/27
Robert, scholar 24/6/92
Robert Bullock, Warden of Merton, Oxford (1826), G's opponent in 1852 election 13/7/52 n, 22/10/52
Marshman, Joshua Ryland (1810-) 7/6/61 ?
Marsland, George, Rev. 5/7/65
Marston,
Edward, Rev. (1818-1895) 16/8/74
R. W., Rev. 6/12/77
Martelaos, Dr., of Athens 3/11/76
Martelli, Charles Francis, solicitor 13/7/87 ?
Martens, Thedor Thedorovich, Prof. 21/7/77
Martin,
Albinus, engineer 3/12/45 ?
Benjamin, Rev. Dr. 1/1/77, 26/7/93
Charles Herbert, Rev. (-1865) 28/4/55
Charles Wykeham (1801-1870), liberal M.P. 13/8/51
Eman, fils, poet 22/9/77 n
E. R. 8/9/87
Francis (1803-1868), vice master of Trinity, Oxford 19/12/31
George, Rev. (1789-1860) 31/8/60
G. K. 23/7/78
Henry, Rev. 13/11/77 ?
H. G. 1/10/85
Hugh, Rev., presbyterian 16/11/47 ?
John Charles, Ven. (-1878) 8/10/53
Joseph 9/10/54
J. R. 29/8/78
Leopold Charles (-1889) 4/6/87
Philip Wykeham- (1829-1878), liberal M.P. 15/7/61 ff, 13/6/65, 19/10/65
R., Mrs. 15/10/37
R. A. 11/3/75
Ralph Biddulph, Sir (1838-1916), 1st Baronet (1905), liberal unionist M.P. 26/4/82
Richard, Rev. (1803-1888) 30/9/30
R. M., of Brighton 14/1/86
Robert, gamekeeper at Fasque 30/9/48
Robert, manservant 13/10/32
Robert Montgomery (1830-1868), colonial historian 30/3/35
Theodore, Sir (1816-1909), biographer of Prince Albert; poet and translator 17/2/60, 16/5/74, 11/7/76, 10/10/92
William 27/8/75 ?
William Todd, Rev. 18/7/78
Martin and Burns, Messrs. 28/11/40
Martindale,
Mrs. 13/10/77
Mrs., of Bloomsbury 31/12/37
Martine, John Melville, Rev. 2/6/58
Martineau,
Gustave, brandy merchant 15/4/80
Harriet (1802-1876), author, declined G's offer of a pension 9/6/73, 19/8/76 n
James, Rev. (1805-1900), philosopher 27/1/60, 22/9/63, 22/8/67, 2/9/67, 26/9/92
Thomas 19/8/76
Martinelli, G. 16/4/91
Martinez, Col., Italian 13/8/62
Martini, Baron 22/2/54
Martino,
L. C.de 16/10/38
René De, Chev. 5/7/75
Martyn,
Miss 12/2/90
C. 26/11/86
Charles Cecil (1809-1866), tory M.P. 8/7/34
Martyr, R. E., Board of Trade clerk 7/1/80 ?
Marum, Edward Purcell Mulhallen (1827-1890), home rule M.P. 11/5/82
Marvin, Mr. 31/7/76
Marx, M., French goods importer 24/4/49 ?
Mary, Princess (1776-1857), Duchess of Gloucester 7/5/36
Mary Adelaide Wilhelmina Elizabeth, Princess (1833-1897), Duchess of Teck 19/4/66
Mary of Teck, Princess (1867-1953), Duchess of York, Princess of Wales, Queen 4/5/93, 7/6/93, 8/6/93, 6/7/93
Marzi, E., singer 17/12/38
Marzo, Antonio Gualberto De, Prof. 13/2/83
Maskell, William, Rev. (1814-1890), Roman convert (1850), ecclesiastical historian 23/3/47
Maskelyne,
F. 16/4/74
Mervyn Herbert Nevil Story- (1823-1911), mineralogist 24/7/75
Maskew, Henry Edward, Rev. (1825-) 27/5/59
Mason,
Mr., photographer in London 8/8/61
E. A. 10/11/88
Eugene, poet 8/10/91
George, artist 14/2/73

G. W. 30/6/76
H. 6/3/83
Henry Brookland, Rev., headmaster 11/4/45 ?
Hugh (1820-1886), liberal M.P. 20/6/68
John, Rev. 28/12/75 ?
Josiah, Sir (1795-1881), Birmingham manufacturer 1/11/72
Mashfield, of Hoddesdon 12/9/60
Samuel, Hawarden 19/9/59
Massari, Giuseppi (1821-1884), Italian politician 30/1/52, 3/3/59 n
Massett, Stephen 22/6/75, 24/3/79
Massey,
Gerald 2/1/91
J. B. 8/10/91
Thomas, Rev. (1810-1888) 3/8/34
William Nathaniel (1809-1881), liberal M.P. 2/6/56
Massie,
W. W., of Edinburgh 24/4/28 n
W. W., Mrs. 24/4/28
Massimo,
Camillo Vittorio Emanuele, Prince (1803-1873) 22/11/66
Carlo, Marquis 11/1/39 n
Massingberd,
Charles John Henry Mundy- (1808-1882), Lincolnshire magnate 8/10/25
Frederick Charles, Rev. (1800-1872) 18/3/60
Massingham, Henry William (1860-1924), journalist 5/10/91, 24/3/93
Masson,
David, Prof. (1822-1907), biographer of Milton 9/5/55
George Joseph Gustave (-1888), schoolmaster 22/6/50
Victor, French publisher 13/7/53 ?
Massy,
Dawson, distressed clergyman 14/11/39 n
Hampden Hugh, Dr. 26/5/68 ?
Masterman, John (-1862), East India director, tory M.P. 8/4/36
Masters,
E. O. 23/2/77
Joseph, publisher 31/3/50
Matchwig, Mr., of the Fine Arts Club 15/7/61
Mate, rescue 4/6/56
Mather, William, Sir (1838-1910), liberal M.P. 18/3/89, 25/2/93 L, 31/8/93
Mather, William & Co. 5/2/76
Matheson,
Mr., at Fasque 30/8/44
Mr.,junior 14/4/77
Mrs. 6/5/93
F. 6/8/26 ?
Farquhar, Rev. (1808-1890), Scottish priest 3/4/55
George, Rev. Dr. (1842-1906) 25/1/78 ?, 30/8/91
J., Rev., nonconformist 24/10/75
James, Sir, 1st Baronet 25/11/70 n
Mary Jane, Lady 25/11/70
William, Edinburgh merchant 6/8/26 n
Mathesons, the young 3/7/88
Mathew,
F., of the colonial service 1/1/46
George Benevenuto (1807-), colonial governor 6/4/44
James Charles, Judge (1830-1908) 30/6/90
Murray Alexander, Rev. (1838-1880) 26/8/67
Mathews,
A. E. 27/4/78
Benjamin St. John, Mrs. 12/12/76
Charles (1803-1878), actor 16/5/74
George Fraser, Rev. 9/3/55, 23/6/68
Henry Staverton, Rev. 7/5/79 ?
J., ironmaster 5/2/48
W., Oak Farm agent 5/2/48
Mathias,
F. W., of U.S.A. 17/10/78
John, Rev. 8/8/75
Octavius, Rev. (-1864) 22/8/53
Mathieson, Charles Frederick, London merchant 7/2/56
Mathison, Gilbert Farquhar Graeme (1803-1854), educationalist 29/6/40
Matlock, C., Rev. 18/3/68
Matsey, T. 16/6/52
Matson, William Tidd, Rev. (1833-1899), Congregationalist 13/3/74
Matteoli, Sig., of Ionia 8/2/59
Matteucci, Sig. 2/2/78
Matthew,
Charles, periodical editor and publisher, reprinting G's tr. of 'Hecuba' 23/3/93
David, City merchant 27/12/36 ?
William, farmer 15/9/84 ?
Matthew & Nicoll, Messrs. 11/11/37
Matthews,
Mr., author 8/6/93
Mr., of Aberdeen 15/9/84 ?
Mrs. 28/1/69
Arnold Jerome Povoleri, Count 2/8/89, 19/1/90
Charles James 3/12/27 n
D. W. 13/12/88
Edward Walter, Rev. 14/7/77
George, Messrs., publishers 18/12/88
G. K. 8/5/74
Henry (1826-1913), 1st Baron Llandaff (1895), tory M.P., Roman Catholic, cabinet minister 7/5/79 ?
Lucia E. (1797-1856), née Bartolozzi 3/12/27
Theopholus 2/8/88

Matthews & Brookes, Messrs. 27/9/88
Matthews & Co. 30/12/89
Matthie, Hugh, Rev. (1805-1842) 21/1/28
Mattos, E. De 26/9/89
Maturin, Benjamin, Rev. 5/9/87 ?
Maubant, Fleury Polydore, actor 17/10/79
Maude *see* Monson
Maude,
Catherine Mary, Lady (-1892), née Bisshopp 20/11/54 ?
Cornwallis, 3rd Viscount Hawarden 18/6/45 n
Frederick Francis, Sir (1821-1897), soldier 20/11/54 n
R. W. 20/2/79
Maul, Richard Graham, Rev. (1820-1895) 22/7/56, 10/2/57
Maule,
G., treasury solicitor 21/6/44
William 28/5/42
Maull & Polyblank, photographers 3/8/57
Maund, Benjamin (1790-1863), botanist 15/7/56
Maunder, George, Rev. (1813-1878) 4/2/67
Maur, L., Mme. 16/6/53
Maurice,
rescue 29/4/70, 11/6/70
Mrs. 22/7/79
Elizabeth (1795-1839) 4/10/29
John Frederick, Gen. Sir (1841-1912), biographer of F. D. Maurice, soldier 19/6/77, 21/1/78
John Frederick Denison, Rev. Prof. 9/2/30
Mavrogordato, Emanuel Antonio 7/3/75, 15/3/75, 16/8/75
Mawdsley, Mr. 25/7/77
Mawer, Walter 30/4/79
Mawes, Mrs. 6/6/77
Maxfield, John, Rev. 14/2/39
Maximilian Joseph, King of Bavaria 30/6/32 n
Max Müller, Friedrich, Prof. 29/1/57
Maxse, Frederick Augustus, Admiral (1833-1900), social reformer 16/11/78
Maxted, R. G. 15/3/87
Maxwell *see* Stewart
Maxwell,
Captain 6/11/38
Dr., physician in Edinburgh 28/8/27
Miss 6/11/38
A. 17/10/90
Anne Frances Esther (1805-1868), née Stapleton, Lady Farnham 10/2/51
Caroline Elizabeth Sarah Stirling-, Lady (1808-1877), née Sheridan, formerly Mrs. Norton 13/10/58
Henry (1799-1868), 7th Baron Farnham 10/2/51 n
James Clerk-, Prof. (1831-1879), physicist 16/4/60, 10/2/83
James Morris, Rev. 25/10/68 ?
John, Sir (1791-1865), 8th Baronet (1844), liberal M.P., author 26/4/33
John Heron-, Sir (1808-1885), 6th Baronet (1844) 17/4/57
Mary, Lady 4/6/89 ?
Matilda Harriet, Lady (1802-1857), née Bruce 14/11/33
Peter Benson, Sir (1817-1893), judge 26/11/55
William Stirling-, Sir (1818-1878), 9th Baronet (took name Maxwell) (1865), art historian, tory M.P. 2/7/58
Maxwell, the younger 6/11/38
Maxwell & Keys, wine merchants 27/1/43 ?
May,
rescue 26/4/58
Mrs. 5/4/80
Edward Thompson, Rev. (-1863) 15/10/60 ?
F. 31/1/76
Frederick, royal newsagent 2/5/76 ?
George Augustus Chichester, Judge (1815-1892), Lord Chief Justice, Ireland 9/12/80
G. H. 8/4/87
H., Mrs. 14/7/76
J. Bowen 17/2/62
K., rescue 3/2/91
R. 10/1/80
Seymour 14/9/89
Thomas, Rev. (-1888) 24/9/61
Thomas Barker, magistrate 28/3/57, 26/7/61
Thomas Erskine, Sir 8/7/36
May, C.& Co., gold and silversmiths 28/5/89
May, F.& Co., booksellers 10/8/75
Mayall, John Edwin (-1867), photographer 28/4/55, 23/7/61, 6/6/84, 7/6/84
Mayer,
George, librarian, colonial office 22/12/56
Joseph (1803-1886), antiquary in Liverpool 13/10/64
Samuel, porcelain dealer 5/7/75
Mayerowitz, Brachiah, translator 28/11/79
Mayes, John 24/9/45 ?
Mayhew,
George Jeremiah, Mrs. 15/1/79
Horace (1845-), Hawarden agent, 1886-93 22/10/85, 15/11/86, 6/10/87, 22/11/87 ff, 26/11/87, 5/12/87, 10/12/87 ff, 5/3/88, 29/10/88, 28/11/88 ff, 27/2/89, 23/4/89 ff, 7/5/89 ff, 18/5/89, 14/8/89 ff, 6/10/89 ff, 16/10/89 ff, 2/11/89 ff, 26/11/89 ff, 24/12/89, 25/1/90, 27/5/90 ff, 18/8/90 ff, 18/11/90 ff, 10/7/91 ff, 2/11/91 ff
Mabel Eleanor, née Joyce 27/2/89

Thomas Rabett, Rev. 30/1/56
Maynard, William, Rev. (-1875) 9/12/40
Mayne,
Henry Blair (1813-1892), Commons clerk 5/7/56
Richard, Sir (1796-1871), chief commissioner of metropolitan police 21/4/57
Mayor,
John Eyton Bickersteth, Rev. (1825-1910), classical scholar 23/8/55
W. F. 30/6/79
W. J. 14/4/80
Mayow,
Mayow Wynell, Rev. (1810-1880) 24/12/29
S. S. W. 31/8/90
Mays, Mrs. 12/7/79
Mazzini,
Dottore, of Florence 21/1/88
Giuseppe, Italian nationalist 19/10/49, 25/2/93
Mazzola, Sig. 30/11/85
McAdam,
Robert, merchant 5/8/25 n
Robert, Mrs. 5/8/25
McAll, Samuel, Rev. (1807-1888), nonconformist 11/12/75
McAlley, Alex, London builder 1/6/47
McBurnie, Mr. 24/11/52
McCallan, John Ferguson, Rev. 31/1/77
McCalmont, James Martin (1847-1913), tory M.P. 17/9/87 ?
McCann, Nicholas (1802-1867), London surgeon 8/10/36 ?
McCarrell, R. 13/5/90
McCarthy,
Egerton Francis Mead, Rev. 1/6/77
Justin (1830-1912), author, home rule M.P. 14/11/55, 8/1/79, 22/4/82 n, 25/4/82, 24/11/90, 28/11/90, 30/11/90, 6/12/90, 10/4/91, 15/4/91, 4/3/92, 7/3/92, 21/6/92, 20/8/92, 13/1/93, 10/3/93, 10/12/93
McCaw, Messrs. 29/7/91
McCheane, Henry Dalgety, Rev. 23/5/76
McCleary, J. T. 19/11/90
McClennan, J. B., Rev., Principal of Cirencester Agricultural College 6/1/91
McClinchy, Uriah 6/9/88 n
McCloskey, Mr. 13/12/86
McClure,
A. C. 27/3/80
E. 24/12/86
McCombie, William (1809-1870), journalist 10/12/61, 20/6/64, 12/1/66
McCormick, William, Peelite M.P. 1/3/61
McCorquodale,
Messrs., printers 24/11/76
George, printer 25/11/85
George, Col. (1817-1895), of Warrington 17/10/68
McCosh, James, Rev. Prof. (1811-1894), president of Princeton (1868) 19/10/75
McCoy, Mr. 21/4/75
McCracken, James and Robert, Messrs., wine merchants 19/7/39, 28/6/67
McCraig, Duncan, Rev. 30/1/28 ?
McCrewe, G. 14/10/90
McCulloch,
A. 12/7/76
J., coachman's son 1/1/56
John Ramsay (1789-1864), comptroller of stationery office (1838), economist 16/1/47
McDevitt, James, Bp., Roman Catholic 8/3/73
McDonald, James, of Berbice 20/4/35 n
McDougall, Francis Thomas, Bp. (1817-1886), bishop of Labuan 2/8/61
McDowall, John, Edinburgh advocate 4/1/34 ?
McEnery, John, Rev., Roman Catholic 4/9/32
McFadden, Father 15/4/89 n
McGarel, Charles (-1876) 20/4/35
McGeachey, Foster Alleyne (1809-1887), tory M.P. 16/12/37, 16/3/46
McGhee, Miss 26/5/75
McGill, G. H., Rev. 19/6/47
McGlashan,
H., papermaker 1/1/56 ?
John (-1866), legal author 26/6/52
McGovern, J. B., Rev., nonconformist 18/11/79
McGowan,
Earle, Rev. 25/8/62 ?
F. 24/6/67
McGregor,
Mr., of Braemar 28/1/87
James (1808-1858), railway manager, tory M.P. 22/6/54
McGrigor,
Charles Rhoderic, Sir (1811-1890), 2nd Baronet (1858) 14/1/33, 26/8/89
James, Gen. Sir (1771-1858), 1st Baronet (1830) 1/11/25, 14/1/33 n
Mary, Lady, née Grant 28/10/26
McHardy, A. B., Lieut. Col. 19/11/89
McInroy, William, Colonel (1804-1892) 10/11/36 n, 17/10/46, 30/10/90
McIvor, E., of Lairg 21/12/82
McKay,
Nathaniel (1837-1902), of New York 10/12/88
William 25/1/27
McKean, Mr. 21/1/48
McKechnie,
A. 12/12/89
Colin G., of Darlington 16/5/67 ?, 9/6/75
McKegan, rescue 27/5/73

McKellar,
A. 24/12/55
William George, London coal merchant 26/2/53 ?
McKendrick, Mr., of Burntisland 3/7/47
McKenzie, H., Miss 15/4/91
McKenzie & Baillie, Edinburgh lawyers 19/6/55
McKeone, Edward 7/7/74
McKie, James, Sir (1838–1898), physician 23/7/66 ?
McKinnon,
Mr., of Glasgow 18/11/89
William, Sir (1823–1893), chairman of British East Africa Co. 23/6/90
McKinoch, Mr. 28/5/79
McKonky, rescue 9/7/77
McLachlan,
rescue 18/4/85, 29/3/86, 24/5/89
Mr., photographer in Manchester 14/10/64
McLaren,
Duncan (1800–1886), lord provost of Edinburgh (1851), liberal M.P. 4/5/53, 30/11/69, 22/12/81 L
John (1831–1910), Lord McLaren (1881), liberal M.P. 7/12/82
Walter Stowe (1853–1912), liberal M.P. 18/1/90
McLauchlin, Lachlan, attorney 22/8/35 ?
McLaughlin, Hubert, Rev. (1806–1882) 24/6/32
McLean, John, Dr., London physician 18/11/63 ?
McLelland, A., of Kilmarnock 8/4/73
McLennan,
A., Rev., Scottish episcopalian 9/11/54
John, instrument maker 30/11/54 ?
John Ferguson (1827–1881), advocate 11/2/65
McMahon,
Beresford Burston, Sir (1808–1873), 2nd Baronet (1837) 14/4/56 n
Maria Catherine, Lady (–1876), née Bateson 14/4/56
Patrick (1813–1875), liberal M.P. 3/6/54, 18/2/70
McManny, Mr. 9/1/78
McNair, J. R. 28/8/77, 2/7/79
McNally, George, Rev., of Ireland 8/2/68 ?
McNeile, Hugh, Dean (1795–1879), dean of Ripon (1868) 17/1/36
McNeill, Emma Augusta, Lady (–1893), née Campbell 11/12/59, 2/1/83
McNiven, Mr. 18/10/90
McOscar,
John, Dr. 22/4/78
William 22/4/78 n
McPherson, George, shopkeeper 15/10/37 ?
McPhin, William Lyon, pamphleteer 24/12/59 n
McQueen, William, Edinburgh hotelier 17/7/47
McSweeney,
Mr., radical 16/7/88
J. G., of Dublin 25/1/90
McVittie, Charles Edward (–1916) 27/11/78 ?
Meacock, Alderman 17/4/67
Meade *see* Hervey
Meade,
Elizabeth (–1858), née Herbert, Lady Clanwilliam 24/9/58
Elizabeth Henrietta, Lady Gilford, Lady Clanwilliam 24/7/78
Richard Charles Francis (1795–1879), 3rd Earl of Clanwilliam (1805) 16/6/66
Richard James, Admiral (1832–1907), 4th Earl of Clanwilliam (1879), Lord Gilford 13/2/77
Richard John, Rev. (1794–1880) 19/3/68
Robert Henry, Sir (1835–1898), Granville's secretary (1864), undersecretary, colonial office (1872) 28/1/57, 21/12/84, 24/12/84, 23/11/89 ?
Meadowbank *see* Maconachie
Meadows, Joseph Kenny, artist 16/2/49 ?
Meagher, Rev. 25/6/74
Meakins, J. 18/8/70
Meal, D. M. 2/1/80
Meale, G., of Naples 15/9/85
Meaney, Stephen J., of *Liverpool Daily Post* 28/3/57
Mearns,
Miss 13/8/90
Duncan, Rev. Dr. 6/10/43 ?
Measor, Charles Pennell, pamphleteer 4/2/67
Meath *see* Brabazon
Medd,
Arthur Octavius, Rev. 15/2/69
Peter Goldsmith, Rev. (1829–1908) 2/12/67
Medge,
Mr. 27/1/90
Eliza, Mrs., née Cole 26/1/90
Medland, Thomas, Rev. (1803–1882), chaplain to Dukes of Sutherland 7/9/34
Medley, John, Bp. 13/4/48 fl
Medlicott,
Mrs., toy shopkeeper 21/8/48
Henry Edmonstone 10/3/77 ?
Medwyn *see* Forbes
Mee, Arthur (1860–1926), journalist 2/2/89 ?
Meech 12/11/82, 11/12/82
Meehan,
Messrs., locksmiths 5/3/89
D., destitute 9/4/56, 29/4/58
Meek,
James, Sir (1778–1856), civil servant 26/10/41
James, Sir (1815–1891), banker 30/12/69

T. 18/2/76
Meekins, T. C. Mossom, barrister 19/3/57
Mehemet Ali, Khedive of Egypt 8/7/46 n
Meikle,
C. W. 12/5/76
William, poet 1/7/67 ?
Meiklejohn, John Miller Dow, Prof. (-1902), liberal candidate 6/1/77, 29/6/86
Meister, J. H. 24/7/75
Melba, Nellie, Dame (1861-1931), opera singer 15/7/89 n, 12/6/90 n
Melbourne *see* Lamb
Meldrum, Lieut. 12/1/79
Meleagros, P., of Athens 24/5/90
Meletapoulas, C. 14/5/89
Melhuish, J. J., of Salcombe Regis 4/6/64
Mellin, J. C. 9/8/77
Mellish,
George, Sir (1814-1877), Knight (1870), judge 29/11/27
William Leigh (1813-1864), G's fag at Eton 10/6/26, 29/11/27 n
Mellor,
John, Sir (1809-1887), judge 18/12/69
John William (1835-1911), liberal M.P. 11/1/87
Melly,
Charles Pierre, of Liverpool 21/4/79
George (1830-1894), liberal M.P. 20/9/58, 28/4/67, 3/10/67, 22/5/77, 30/8/78, 27/6/86
Melody, Mr., Fenian, in prison 4/12/73, 27/12/73
Melrose, Thomas, of Coldstream 27/9/76
Melvill,
Edmund, Rev. (-1857) 12/7/52
Henry, Canon (1798-1871) 30/6/33, 18/7/69
James C., secretary 29/6/42
Melville *see* Dundas
Melville,
Alexander Leslie- (1817-1889), 10th Earl of Leven (1876) 8/3/65
David, Rev. (-1904) 25/9/50
David Leslie- (-1860), 8th Earl of Leven (1820) 12/11/50
Elizabeth Anne (-1863), née Campbell, Lady Leven 12/11/50
William Rylace, Rev. (1813-1887) 26/6/67
Melvin,
James, of Ratho 29/3/80
W., of Glasgow 31/3/68
Menabrea, Luigi Federico, Count (1809-1896) 8/1/67, 12/5/76, 7/5/80, 3/7/82 c
Mence,
Miss 6/4/32
H. 10/7/79
Samuel, Rev. (1781-1860) 30/3/32 ?
Mendelsohn, Mr., photographer 1/11/84
Menken, E., bookseller 14/7/91
Menpes, Mortimer, artist 2/6/92
Mensi, Francesco, Prof. (1790-1888), Italian painter 22/9/38
Menteath,
Charles Granville Stuart- (1800-1880), 1st Baronet (1838), barrister 27/6/29 n, 16/12/31 ?
Francis Hastings Stuart-, Rev. (1807-1875) 27/6/29
Granville Wheler Stuart-, Rev. (1811-1887) 27/6/29, 18/8/74
Menu De St. Mesmin, Ernest 27/3/77 ?
Menzies,
Allan, Edinburgh lawyer 18/12/35
Frederick, Rev., don 12/7/63 ?
Meredith *see* Hope
Meredith,
Richard, Rev. (1796-1886) 12/8/47 ?
Robert Fitzgerald, Rev. 9/1/86
Thomas Edward, Rev. (1825-1892) 15/8/53
William Macdonald, Rev. 9/7/79
Meredyth, John, Rev. 20/8/41
Merell, Mr. 29/7/78
Merello, Messrs. 14/1/86 ?
Merewether,
Henry Alworth (1780-1864), serjeant-at-law 29/1/33
John, Very Rev. (1797-1850), dean of Hereford 8/5/44 n
Merighi, Pietro, poet in Palermo 5/9/51 ?
Merimée, Prosper 28/7/63, 1/8/64, 26/7/65
Merivale,
Charles, Ven. (1808-1893) 26/4/62, 9/8/69, 12/8/69
Herman (1806-1874), civil servant 24/10/35 ?
Herman Charles (1839-1906), playwright 8/2/79 n, 12/2/79
Merlo, Carlo, of Naples 29/2/52 fl
Merlot, Mme. 22/12/86
Merode, Saverio De, Count, of Rome 8/11/66
Merola, Italian singer 23/3/32
Merrifield, F. 20/8/78
Merriman,
Arthur P. 11/9/76
J. J. 11/9/76 n
John Xavier (1841-1926), South African liberal statesman 30/12/80
Nathaniel James, Bp. (1810-1882), bishop of Grahamstown (1871) 30/7/31, 14/8/77, 25/8/77
Merritos, A. 25/12/86
Merritt,
Henry (1822-1877), picture cleaner 23/3/58
William Hamilton (-1862), Canadian politician 16/2/42

Merry, William Walter, Rev. Dr. (1835–1918), rector of Lincoln, Oxford 16/1/77, 1/2/90
Merryweather, Messrs. 29/10/91
Mertel, Teodolfo, Cardinal 30/4/67
Mertens, Frederick Montgomery Dirs, Rev. 4/8/75
Merton, J. D. 1/8/79
Merz, Theodore 29/6/76
Messenger,
James A., Queen's bargemaster 10/9/63
John Alexander, imports clerk 15/1/53
Messina, Prefect of 26/1/88
Mestral, Armand de, of Vaud 25/2/44
Metastasio (1698–1782), Italian poet 21/9/38
Metaxa, B., Count 22/3/59
Metcalfe,
Mr., picture owner 11/6/50
Charles Theophilus, Sir 27/2/43
Meteyard, Eliza, Miss (1816–1879), author 2/3/65
Methuen,
Messrs., publishers 18/10/89
F. H. P., 2nd Baron Methuen 14/4/86
Methven *see* Smythe
Metlock, Mr. 19/2/45
Metz, Frédéric Auguste de (–1873), penal reformer 7/6/51
Meupes, M. 5/9/90
Meurice,
Parisian restauranteur 15/2/32
rescue 7/9/70
Meuricoffre,
Signor, Neapolitan banker; entertained G in Naples 27/12/88 ff, 15/1/89 ff, 19/7/90
Signora, Neapolitan 27/12/88 ?
Meux, Mr. 22/3/93
Mexborough *see* Savile
Meyer,
A. 13/8/90
James 9/11/77
Joseph, Liverpool jeweller 17/12/47
Meyerstein, Emil 11/10/77 ?
Meymott, John, solicitor 5/5/38 ?
Meynell,
Charles (1828–1882), Roman Catholic controversialist 8/1/79
Wilfrid (1852–1948), author 4/10/77, 11/10/78, 15/10/78 n, 29/12/89
Meyrick,
Mr., singing master 9/4/33
Frederick, Rev. (1827–1906), secretary, Anglo-Continental Society (1853), organised Bonn conferences (1874) 13/2/54, 11/12/78 n
Miall,
Arthur 8/3/80
Edward (1809–1881), liberal M.P. 18/5/55, 1/12/65, 17/2/68, 18/1/71, 25/11/71, 16/5/73
Miatchewitch, Mons. 26/7/77
Michael,
Bp., Roman Catholic bishop of Tenos 24/12/94
T., Rev. 23/8/77
Michaud, Eugène Philibert, Abbé (1839–1917), French author 26/9/66, 22/10/71
Michel, E. B. 23/5/78
Michelangioli, A. 15/1/53
Michele,
muleteer in Sicily 25/10/38
C. Eastland, editor 20/7/40
Michell, Richard (–1877), don 20/2/50
Michie, Mr. 6/9/74
Michil, W. 9/10/89
Mickiewicz, L. 28/8/88
Micklem, Thomas, solicitor 20/6/56 ?
Middlehurst,
Messrs. 11/2/80
Mr. 15/9/75
Middlemas, Mr. 6/10/76
Middleton *see* Willoughby
Middleton,
Anne, Lady, née Cust 2/7/42 n
D., schools inspector 20/2/65 ?
G., Mlle. 28/12/33 n
George, Rev., presbyterian 28/12/33 ?
W., campaigner for Plumstead Common 17/2/77, 26/7/77
William Fowle, Sir (1786–1860), 2nd Baronet (1830) 2/7/42
Midgley, R. 18/4/79
Midleton *see* Brodrick
Migliorini, R. 31/12/88
Mijatovich, C. 17/4/92
Milanesi, G., of the Accademia della Crusca 28/2/94
Milbank, Frederick Acclom, Sir (1820–1898), 1st Baronet (1882), liberal M.P. 11/10/62, 30/1/74 L
Milbanke,
John Ralph, Sir, 8th Baronet (1850) 1/10/45
Mary, née Stuart Wortley, Lady Wentworth 20/10/88
Ralph Gordon Noel (1839–1906), 13th Baron Wentworth (1862) 20/10/88
Mild, A. 19/3/90, 19/11/90
Mildert, William van, Bp. (1765–1836), bishop of Durham (1826) 8/10/38
Mildmay *see* Fox, Lyttelton
Mildmay,
Charles Arundell St. John, Rev. (1820–1904) 9/9/57
Humphrey Francis (–1866), liberal M.P. 29/7/61 n
Humphrey St. John (1794–1853), tory M.P. 13/7/37 ?
Laetitia (1803–1844) 7/6/38

Marianne Frances St. John (-1873), née Vernon 14/11/44, 29/7/61, 12/12/61
Paulet Henry St. John (1814-1858), soldier 19/1/39
Miles,
Messrs. 15/6/86
D. 3/11/85
J. B., Rev. 1/4/73
Lomas, Rev. (-1875) 1/6/47
Philip William Skinner (1816-1881), tory M.P. 14/6/44 n
S., tailor 18/6/68
William, Sir (1797-1878), 1st Baronet (1859), tory M.P. 21/6/34
W. T. 8/9/91
Miles & Edwards, upholsterers 8/4/41
Mill,
C. 10/4/76
H. T., Miss 20/9/89
John Stuart 31/7/40
William Hodge (1792-1853), orientalist 23/11/41
Millais, John Everett, Sir 25/4/77
Millan, R. M. 13/2/90
Millar,
Alexander, superintendent, Dundee railway 1/3/52
James, assist. sec., British & Foreign Schools Society 23/2/38
James, Rev., independent minister 19/7/43
Millard,
C., Miss 26/4/92
John, Prof. 8/5/68 ?
Miller,
Charles, Rev. (-1885) 30/10/31 ?, 22/3/59 ?
Cincinnatus Heine, known as 'Joaquin', American poet 3/9/73
D. A., of Hudson's Bay Co. 14/9/48
Fenwick, Mrs. 4/3/78
F. F., Miss 30/5/90
George, Rev. Dr. 26/2/42
Henry, of Frome 14/6/52
H. W. 27/8/66
James, advocate 21/11/33 ?
James, Prof. (1812-1864), professor of surgery, Edinburgh 23/10/48, 4/11/48
J. M. 17/11/77
John, bookseller 25/12/41
John Cale, Rev. (1814-1880) 1/4/51, 2/10/75, 11/11/75
Samuel, Rev. (1810-1881), presbyterian 8/12/37 ?
Samuel Christy- (-1889), took name of Miller (1862), tory M.P. 25/4/50
Taverner John, tory M.P. 22/2/60
W. H. 6/12/77
William, of Bank of England 8/10/60, 15/9/63
William, Sir (1809-), liberal M.P. 20/4/75
William E. (-1903), portrait painter 21/12/76 ?, 12/3/90 ?
Miller, J. and Sons, Edinburgh merchants 21/11/33 n
Milles, George John, 4th Baron Sondes 16/3/44
Millet, P. 5/3/92
Millett, T., French polisher 24/4/49 ?
Milligan *see* Hughan
Milligan,
Duncan 14/5/32
J., rescue 11/3/56
J. A., Glasgow agent 20/3/56
Robert, Bradford merchant, anti-corn-law leaguer, liberal M.P. 22/3/43 ?
Robert (1746-1809), West Indian merchant 14/5/32 n
S. F. 30/7/88
William, Rev. Prof. (1819-1893), of Aberdeen 24/8/68
Millikin & Lawley, instrument makers 26/1/75
Milling, Mr. 8/4/67
Millions, David T., publican 2/7/52
Mills,
rescue 21/3/70, 8/6/86
Capt. 7/1/81
Mr., villa owner 5/4/32
Arthur, secretary, Grillion's Club 5/5/90
Arthur (1816-1898), barrister, tory M.P. 17/3/47
C., rescue 27/9/70
Charles, Sir (1792-1872), 1st Baronet (1868), banker 15/5/61 ?
Charles Henry (1830-1898), 2nd Baronet (1872), 1st Baron Hillingdon (1886) 12/7/63
Charles William (1855-1919), banker, tory M.P. 2/5/87 ?
F. S. 6/3/78
James Smith, public notary 17/11/75
John Millman (-1872), barrister 3/11/58 ?
J. R., Rev. 24/8/88
L., inspector of schools 25/3/37
L. H., author 6/10/91
R., Mrs. 23/7/90
Robert Twyford, Rev. (-1874) 3/3/55
Thomas, Rev., of Dublin 27/9/90
Thomas, Rev. (1792-1879) 27/10/75
W. F. 12/5/77
William, Prof. (1793-1834) 23/2/30
William Hathorn, author 15/6/78
Millson, F. E., Rev., unitarian 28/6/76
Milltown *see* Leeson
Millwaters, H. 18/3/87
Milman,
Henry Hart, Dean (1791-1868), dean of St. Paul's (1849), historian and editor 27/2/41, 22/4/52, 29/9/65, 30/9/65, 1/10/65, 20/12/81 n

Milman (*cont.*)
Mary Ann, née Cockell 5/12/70
Milmore, M., American sculptor 15/5/70
Milne,
Miss 31/7/79
David, Adm. Sir (1763–1845) 16/5/40
George 10/8/47
George 12/11/89
Gordon, of Portobello 2/12/74
James 23/6/79
J. Gordon-, Rev. 14/12/79
W. 31/12/78
Milner *see* Doyle
Milner,
Alfred (1854–1925), 1st Viscount Milner (1902), imperialist, civil servant in Treasury 30/1/78 n, 20/8/92, 16/5/93 ff, 18/11/93
Caroline Agnes, Duchess of Montrose, later Mrs. Stirling 16/1/74
Frederick George, Sir (1849–1931), 7th Baronet (1880), tory M.P. 19/10/85, 12/7/87 ?
William Mordaunt Edward, Sir (1820–1867), 5th Baronet (1855), liberal M.P. 3/1/53
Milnes *see* Arundell
Milnes,
Annabella Hungerford (–1874), née Crewe, Lady Houghton 8/7/51
Hungerford (1812–1894), 3rd Baron Crewe (1835) 12/2/80
Margaret, née Primrose, Lady Crewe 22/1/87 n
Richard Monckton; Lord Houghton 26/11/29 n
Richard Offley Ashburton Crewe- (1858–1945), 2nd Baron Houghton (1885), Earl of Crewe (1895) 22/1/87, 19/8/92
Robert Pemberton (1784–1858), Italianophile and former M.P. 31/3/32
Sibyl, née Graham, Lady Houghton 22/1/87
Milnes Gaskell *see* Palgrave
Milroy, Gavin, medical writer 6/1/48
Milton *see* Fitzwilliam
Milton, William, Rev. 13/12/75
Milward, William (–1833) 27/3/49 n
Minchin, J. George 29/11/79
Minghetti,
Sig., of Ionia 13/1/59
Marco, Italian politician 30/7/53, 20/2/66, 4/10/79, 19/7/92
Mingley, G. W. 11/7/90 ?
Minissy, M. 3/8/91
Minnesota, Governor of 15/4/86
Minot, Miss 9/3/80
Minshull, Anne, Mrs., of Hawarden 9/8/46
Minto *see* Elliot
Minton,
Samuel, Rev. 10/4/77
T. J., of the Mint 7/12/69
Mirafiore *see* Rosina
Mirafiore, Rosina, Countess 1/2/88
Mirams, Augustus, barrister 27/1/80
Mirehouse, John, Rev. (1839–1911) 14/8/77
Mirepoix, Sigismund de Levis, Count (–1886) 10/2/51
Mirza Peer Buksh 29/7/78
Mitchell,
Miss 27/7/78
A. F., Rev. Prof. 7/11/93 n
Alexander (1831–1873), liberal M.P. 9/8/67
Alexander, Provost, Provost of Dalkeith 26/11/79, 19/3/80
Alexander F., Lord Provost of Edinburgh 14/11/85
Arthur, Sir (1826–1909), Knight (1887), archaeologist 15/11/79
C. A. 9/11/91
D., Rev. 14/5/89
George, agricultural trade unionist 11/3/76
James William, Sir (1836–1898), soldier 14/6/69 ?
John, of Bradford 18/4/65 ?
John, tory in Mossley 6/12/79
Peter (1824–1899), Canadian politician 26/1/64
Samuel, Dr. 6/12/55 ?
Thomas Alexander (–1875), liberal M.P. 26/6/45 ?, 4/12/60
W. H. 23/2/77
Mitchelson, W. G. 20/3/80
Mitchinson, Thomas, Rev. (–1862) 31/3/50
Mitchmier, Mr. 21/4/79
Mitford,
Algernon Bertram Freeman- (1837–1916), 1st Baron Redesdale (1902) 8/11/82, 14/2/85
John Reveley, Rev. (1807–1838) 14/10/29
John Thomas Freeman- (1805–1886), 1st Earl of Redesdale (1877), chairman, Lords' cttees. on private bills 16/5/26
William Townley (1817–1889), tory M.P. 16/3/60
Mivart,
James Edward, hotelier 8/12/42
Saint George Jackson (1827–1900), Roman Catholic controversialist 14/2/76
St. John J., biologist 8/12/42 n
M'Kie, T. 31/10/81
Moates, William, accountant 21/10/58 ?
Moberley, George, Bp. (1803–1885), headmaster of Winchester (1833), bishop of Salisbury (1869) 31/3/34, 1/7/72 L
Mocenigo,
Alvise 20/3/77 ?
Giovanni 20/3/77 ?

Mochizuki, Kotaro, translator of G's biography into Japanese 21/4/91
Mockler, Clara, Mrs. 25/4/76
Modena,
  Duke of 18/7/61
  C., Sig. 24/6/87
Moderna, C. 18/2/90
Moeller, P. 16/7/77, 27/7/77
Moffat,
  Mr., apothecary 13/9/42
  Hugh B., Very Rev., dean of Moray 21/4/51
Moffatt,
  Dr., in Paris 6/3/59, 30/8/59, 23/12/67, 25/12/67, 20/6/74, 27/12/74, 29/12/74, 30/10/76
  George (-1878), tea merchant, liberal M.P. 28/12/52
Moger,
  rescue 30/7/64
  George 9/2/75 ?
Mogford,
  J. 7/5/89
  Robert, lithographer 12/2/76 ?
Mohammed, Gholam, Prince 21/4/59, 16/2/60
Mohammed Hassan 20/8/91
Mohrashar, Baron 30/8/86 ?
Mohrenheim, C. 21/2/84
Moir,
  David, Bp. 20/8/44 n, 22/8/47, 27/8/47
  George (1800-1870), lawyer 14/9/51
  John, Rev. 19/8/47
  Macrae, barrister 14/3/74, 15/8/79
  William Young, Rev. 25/10/79 ?
  W. S. 25/10/79
Mole, Louis Matthieu, Comte 8/8/49
Molesworth,
  Andalusia Grant, Lady (-1888), née Carstairs 24/1/56
  George Bagot Gossett (1853-1917), barrister 1/3/80
  John Edward Nassau, Rev. Dr. (1790-1877) 14/2/41
  St Aubyn Walter, tory M.P. 13/5/79
  William, Sir (1810-1855), 8th Baronet, editor of Hobbes, radical M.P. 6/3/38 n, 3/6/41, 7/5/50, 10/4/51, 14/2/52, 5/2/53, 16/7/53, 10/11/53, 11/11/53, 21/12/53, 5/2/85
Molineux, John, music academy owner 30/12/31
Molison, Mrs. 7/9/34
Molloy, Gerald, author 15/11/77 ?
Molony,
  Mr. 5/5/79
  Patrick J., Dr., physician 26/9/74 ?
Molyn, Mrs. 21/7/80
Molyneux,
  Caroline Elizabeth, née Lawley 11/10/62 n
  Caryl Craven, Capt. (1836-1912) 11/10/62, 14/11/68
  Charles William, 3rd Earl of Sefton 1/7/42 n
  Mary Augusta, née Gregge-Hopwood, Lady Sefton 1/7/42
  William Philip (1835-1897), 4th Earl of Sefton (1855) 1/8/68 n
Momby, J. 4/11/76
Momerie, Alfred Williams, Rev. Prof. (1848-1900), theologian 31/3/89, 5/4/89, 7/4/89, 19/7/89
Monaco, D., of Naples 7/2/89 n
Monahan,
  James Henry, Judge (1804-1878) 14/8/78
  James Hunter, Canon 8/12/86
Monaldini, Sig., print and bookseller, Rome 25/5/32
Monceau, Paul, historian 8/12/91 ?
Monck *see* Cole
Monck,
  Charles Stanley (-1894), 4th Viscount Monck (1849), 1st Baron Monck (1866) 24/5/36 n, 23/11/52
  Elizabeth Louise Mary, Lady (1814-1892) 24/5/36
  H. S., 1st Earl of Rathdowne 24/5/36 n
  Julia, née Ralli 3/12/66
Monckton *see* Boyle
Monckton,
  J., 1st Viscount Galway 19/5/36 n
  J., Rev. 20/7/91
Moncreiffe, David, Sir, 6th Baronet 2/4/41 n
Moncrieff,
  Ann, Lady 15/4/28
  H., Rev., Scottish episcopalian 9/2/43
  Henry Wellwood, Rev. Sir (1809-1883), 10th Baronet (1851), Scottish freechurchman 18/4/28 n, 13/11/28, 10/10/59
  James (1811-1895), 1st Baron Moncrieff (1874), lord advocate 19/4/28, 17/2/53
  James Wellwood, Sir (1776-1851), 9th Baronet, judge 19/4/28
  James William (1845-1920), Scottish lawyer 2/10/76
Moncrieffe *see* Bridgeman, Mordaunt
Moncur, Bailie 4/12/77
Money,
  Mrs. 21/6/32
  Anne Caroline, Lady, née Taylor 6/9/41
  Charles Forbes Septimus (1818-1893) 4/9/41, 15/9/41
  James Kyrle-, Sir 6/9/41 n
  Walter, historian 29/1/77
  William Taylor (-1834), consul in Venice 15/6/32
Mongan, Mr. 31/5/79
Monk,
  Misses, relations of Waddington 29/7/84, 14/4/91, 26/1/93

Monk (*cont.*)
Mrs., rescue 12/2/73
Charles James (1824–1900), liberal M.P. 3/12/66
Jane, née Hughes 19/8/51
Monk-Bretton *see* Dodson
Monkland & Co. 25/2/50
Monkswell *see* Collier
Monro,
David, Sir (1813–1877), New Zealand politician 19/4/66
David Binning, Provost (1836–1905) 13/11/78
Edward, Rev. (1815–1866) 19/6/46
Monsell,
Charles Henry, Rev. (–1851) 26/11/50
Harriet, née O'Brien 26/11/50 n, 30/7/63
John S. B., Rev. 15/4/45
William (1812–1894), 1st Baron Emly (1874), liberal M.P., member of the Engagement 23/2/45, 26/4/53, 6/3/70, 22/4/72, 25/7/72, 11/3/73, 12/7/73 c, 12/8/73, 14/8/73
Monson,
Maria Adelaide, Lady, née Maude, Lady Oxenbridge 18/6/45
William John (1829–1898), Baron Monson, Viscount Oxenbridge, liberal M.P. 18/6/45 n
Montagu *see* Goulburn, Scott
Montagu,
rescue 20/2/66, 8/4/67
Andrew Fountain Wilson, of Doncaster 21/7/55 ?
Basil, the elder (1770–1851), author 12/12/32
Basil, the younger 25/1/33
C. 8/7/68
Edward George Henry (1839–1916), 8th Earl of Sandwich (1884), Baron Hinchinbrooke 3/5/79
E. R., 5th Baron Rokeby 24/4/35 n
George (1799–1855), 6th Duke of Manchester (1843), Viscount Mandeville, tory M.P. 24/5/34
George John, 6th Earl of Sandwich 4/4/43 n
Matthew, Baron Rokeby 19/5/42 n
Robert, Lord (1825–1902), liberal M.P. 13/3/62
Samuel, Sir (1832–1911), 1st Baronet (1894), 1st Baron Swaythling (1907), banker, liberal M.P. 31/3/86, 27/5/91
William Drogo (1823–1890), 7th Duke of Manchester (1855), Viscount Mandeville, tory M.P. 17/10/51
Montague,
Miss 22/9/82
F. W. 6/2/57
Montaguire, Mr. 21/12/85
Montalembert,
Charles Forbes René de, Comte (1810–1870), author and liberal Catholic apologist 4/3/39, 23/3/39, 7/11/52, 10/11/52, 21/6/55
Elise Rosée, née Forbes 5/3/39
Monteagle *see* Rice
Monteath *see* Gladstone
Montebello *see* Lannes
Montefiore,
Claude Goldsmid 28/3/90
Moses Haim, Sir (1784–1885), stockbroker and philanthropist 12/12/82
Monteiro, Carlos F., wine merchant 26/6/52 ?
Monteith,
Alexander H. 29/10/57
Henry (–1848), M.P. 1/5/34
Robert (Joseph Ignatius), of Carstairs, calico printer 7/7/41, 2/3/43
Montessori, Sig. 8/2/89
Monte St. Angelo, Conte di, of Naples 29/2/52 fl
Montglas,
Ernestine von, Gräffin (–1838), née von Arco 5/5/36 n
Max Josef von, Graf (1759–1838), Bavarian statesman 5/5/36 n
Montgomerie *see* Severn
Montgomerie,
A., Lord 9/1/39 n
Archibald William, 13th Earl of Eglinton (1819) 27/9/44
Montgomery,
Alberta, née Ponsonby 14/4/78
Alfred (1814–1896), commissioner of stamps 5/11/57
Edwin C., Dr. 29/2/68
Hugh de Fellenberg (1844–), Irish landowner 9/9/81 ?, 9/11/86
Robert (1807–1855), poet 16/2/31
T. 22/6/76
Monti,
Giulio, Prof. 26/1/87
Guilia (–1872), née Alberti, actress 11/11/50
P., actor 11/11/50 n
Montmorency, Miss 22/10/80
Montresor, Thomas Gage, Gen. Sir (1764–1853) 21/4/32
Montrose *see* Graham, Milner
Montshiwa, Chief, Bechuanaland chief 10/3/83 c, 23/5/83
Monty, rescue 16/10/78, 3/8/81
Moody,
Clement, Rev. (1811–1871) 26/8/62
Dwight Lyman, Rev. (1837–1899), evangelist 25/4/75, 29/6/75

James Leith, Rev. 16/9/75 ?
Nicholas James, Rev. 18/3/51
Moon,
Miss 4/3/78
Mr., of L. N. W. R. 9/4/83
Francis Graham, Sir (1796-1871), sheriff of London (1843), book and print seller 6/11/43
George Washington (1823-1909), theologian 15/7/76, 24/5/86
Richard, Liverpool merchant 18/1/63 ?
Richard, Sir (1814-1899), chairman, L. N. W. R. 5/1/72, 9/4/83
Mooney, Maurice, Rev., Roman Catholic 1/9/81 ?
Moor, James Hoare Christopher, Rev. 1/9/55 ?
Moore,
Mr., of *Illustrated London News* 28/7/51
Mrs., of Dublin 23/12/44
Aubrey Lackington, Rev. (1848-1890) 10/12/85, 22/2/88
David Christmas, Rev. 21/11/56
Dennis, of Ontario 2/2/76 ?
Edward, Rev. Dr. (-1916), Principal, St. Edmund Hall, Oxford 8/11/79, 27/12/86, 7/2/90
George (1806-1876), philanthropist 9/10/69
George Henry (1811-1870), liberal M.P. 6/4/53 ?
John, Rev., Roman Catholic 23/9/45
John Bramley, of Liverpool 29/7/46
Morris (-1885), art dealer, historian 17/7/50, 15/7/51
P. A. 5/10/44
Raffles 23/8/90
Robert J., of Isle of Man 3/10/78 n
Thomas, of Hanley 21/10/76
Thomas (1779-1852), poet 19/3/39 ?
T. T. 12/12/85
William Thomas, Rev. (1832-1926), of U.S.A., later U. K. 9/8/75
Moorhouse, James, Bp. (1826-1915) 15/1/84, 16/1/84, 17/10/87
Moorsom, Thomas, Capt., guards' officer, member of the 'Engagement' 23/2/45 n, 4/4/66
Moran,
Benjamin, American diplomat 15/5/72 ?
Patrick Francis, Cardinal (1830-1911) 9/11/77
Morandini, Giovanni (1811-1888) 3/10/79
Moray *see* Gray
Morciano and Caballino *see* Castromediano
Mordaunt *see* Smith
Mordaunt,
Charles, Sir (1836-1897), 10th Baronet, tory M.P. 10/4/69
Harriet Sarah, Lady, divorced (1875), née Moncrieffe 10/4/69
John, Sir (1808-1845), 9th Baronet (1823), tory M.P. 17/10/28
Marianne, Lady (-1842), née Holbech 14/6/34
More,
Clancy, Mr. 26/3/87
M. 1/4/69
Robert Jasper (1836-1903), liberal M.P. 17/6/68, 13/11/77
Morehead, Robert, Rev. 11/5/28
Moreira, F. I. De Carvalho, Brazilian ambassador 21/5/57 n
Morell,
Charles L., Rev., presbyterian Moderator 5/1/69
John Reynell, author 10/1/78
Morelli,
Charles Francis (1800-1882), impressario 7/6/82 ?
Luigi, Prof., of Naples 11/10/75
Moresby, John, Admiral (1830-1922) 18/8/74
Moreton,
Henry John, 3rd Earl Ducie (1853), liberal M.P. 10/12/68
Janie, née Ralli 15/7/68
Julia, Lady Ducie 5/4/76
Richard Charles, Sir (1846-1928) 15/7/68 n
Moret Y Prendergast, Sigismondo, Don 12/12/72
Morewood, R. S., Rev. 6/6/77
Morgan,
Miss, author 16/12/75
Alfred F., Rotherham liberal 22/3/79 ?
Alfred Fairfax, author 21/3/78
C., rescue 21/10/52
Campbell De, Dr., London physician 9/6/58
Charles Octavius Swinnerton (1803-1888), tory M.P. 9/1/44
David Foscue, Rev. (1807-) 29/2/60
E. C., rescue 21/10/52
Edward, maniac; involves G in court case 13/9/79
Edward, Col. (-1861), Flintshire landowner 10/4/57
George Osborne, Sir (1826-1897), liberal M.P. 24/9/68, 1/5/80, 3/7/80 c, 15/2/86 c, 14/4/86 c, 1/7/86, 10/9/87
Godfrey, Rev. 25/1/79
Harvey 11/7/92
John De 3/8/76
John Holdsworth, Rev. (-1908) 29/1/78 ?
John Parry, Rev. 9/6/76
Morgan, Rev. (-1870) 3/10/59 n
Owen (1836-1921), known as 'Morien' 31/3/75
Philip Howell, Rev. 13/1/55

Morgan (*cont.*)
Thomas, Rev. (1827-1890) 20/10/56 ?
Morgan, Martyn, George & Co., stationers 16/8/48 ?
Morghen, Raphael (-1833), engraver 5/1/88
Mori Arinori, Japanese ambassador 8/3/83 n
Moriarty, David, Bp. (1814-1877) 21/7/67
Morice, B. 4/5/79
'Morien' *see* Morgan
Morier,
Harriet, née Greville 8/2/38
James Justinian (1780-1849), diplomat, traveller and author 8/2/38 n
Robert Burnett David, Sir (1826-1893), minister in Madrid (1881), ambassador in St. Petersburg (1884), diplomat 23/6/52, 4/9/73 n, 21/4/74, 8/9/74 ff, 19/9/74, 20/9/74 ff, 9/12/74, 6/11/76, 14/10/85, 4/7/86, 17/5/92, 21/9/92
Morifalcone, M. 18/11/90
Morison,
Mrs., rescue 1/8/75
J. A. R. 10/5/76
Moritz, Emanuel 6/12/77 ?
Morlati, Sig. 12/1/89
Morley *see* Parker
Morley,
Mr. 24/6/53
Arnold (1849-1916), liberal M.P. 12/3/79, 8/8/85 n, 28/10/85, 8/1/86 n, 5/2/86, 9/4/86, 20/4/86 L, 26/4/86 L, 9/5/86 L, 12/5/86 L, 19/5/86 L, 29/5/86 ff, 23/6/86 L, 27/6/86 L, 30/6/86 L, 15/7/86 ff, 26/7/86 n, 30/7/86, 3/8/86, 11/8/86, 28/2/87 ff, 18/4/87 ff, 28/6/87 ff, 26/11/87 ff, 8/2/88 ff, 22/2/88 ff, 9/4/88 ff, 4/6/88 ff, 4/12/88 ff, 24/1/89, 6/3/89 ff, 12/4/89 ff, 2/5/89 ff, 8/7/89 ff, 8/2/90 ff, 12/6/90 ff, 24/11/90 ff, 26/1/91 ff, 1/3/91 ff, 5/3/91 ff, 13/4/91 ff, 10/5/91 ff, 28/7/91 ff, 15/10/91 ff, 28/4/92 ff, 27/5/92 ff, 13/6/92 ff, 16/8/92 ff, 16/2/93 c, 12/4/93 L
Charles (1847-1917), liberal M.P. 21/8/86 n
Daniel, Newark grocer 3/9/35
John 4/3/76
Samuel (1809-1886), liberal M.P. 18/5/58, 28/10/76
W. 29/1/78
Morne, D. 16/5/78
Morning, Mr., of Rome 13/10/66
Mornington *see* Wellesley
Moro, Prof., of Naples? 2/2/89
Morosi, Nana, of India 8/3/61
Morpeth *see* Howard
Morrah, Herbert, Rev. 30/1/90 ?
Morrall,
Cyrus, Rev. (1804-1882) 21/1/28
George, of Wolverhampton 29/8/65
Morrell,
Baker (-1854), solicitor 26/1/48
Frederick Joseph (1811-1883), solicitor 19/7/55
Morris,
Father 13/5/93
A. 19/6/68
Augustus, of Sydney, N. S. W. 24/2/82
Charles Henry, Gen. (1824-1887) 24/8/80
Evan 17/3/84
Francis Orpen, Rev. (-1893) 20/12/52
G. B., Rev., nonconformist 12/6/56
J., Miss 18/7/79
J. P. R. 22/6/75
Lewis, Sir (1833-1907), author and poet 22/2/77, 28/10/83, 17/10/92
Mowbray (1819-1874), manager of *The Times* 24/2/60
Robert, Rev. (1808-1882) 30/1/31
R. T. 4/1/77
W., Lieut. 1/9/77
William, solicitor in Chester 24/5/61 ?
William (1786-1858), Canadian merchant and politician 18/5/40
William (1811-1877), liberal M.P. 7/7/68
William (1834-1896), poet, designer, socialist 21/3/79, 17/10/92, 19/10/92
William George 12/3/38, 8/12/42
William O'Connor, Judge (1824-1904) 7/12/87
Morris & Jones, Messrs. 18/5/89
Morrison,
Alfred (1821-1897), connoisseur 10/9/66
Frederick, secretary, National Chamber of Trade 12/6/74
Hugh 16/8/92
James W., deputy Master of the Mint 4/9/41
J. R. 10/1/78
K. 22/8/51
Sophia, Lady, née Leveson-Gower 16/8/92
Walter (1836-1921), liberal unionist M.P. 5/7/69 L
W. H. 14/12/86
Morrison & Dillon, Messrs., counting house 22/1/61
Morrissey, E. 19/5/68
Morris & Sons 15/2/68
Morritt, William John Sawrey (-1874), Peelite M.P. 8/5/64
Morse,
Francis, Rev. (1819-1886) 3/12/67 n, 27/12/67
Samuel, inventor of Morse Code 20/3/39 n
Morson, W. H. 3/3/79
Morswood, Mr. 9/7/58

Mortimer, rescue 27/5/64, 26/12/68
Mortlock,
  Charles, Rev. (-1906) 11/1/76
  William, china shipper 12/2/72
Morton *see* Douglas
Morton,
  rescue 7/2/77
  Mrs. 11/8/93
  Adam, blind mat-maker, St. Ebbe's, Oxford 9/2/29
  Charles, cousin, Edinburgh lawyer 9/10/71
  Edward, Dr., physician 4/3/48
  Edward John Chalmers (1856–1902), liberal M.P. 13/9/88, 30/1/90
  G. V., Rev. 19/5/88
  Henry Thomas 25/9/76 ?
  Hugh, Dr., Newark physician 3/12/32
Moscheles,
  Mrs. 22/3/78
  Felix, artist 22/12/87
  Ignaz (1794–1870), Bohemian pianist and composer 25/5/36
Moschini, Sig. 12/7/88
Moscow, Mr. 25/4/92 ?
Moseley,
  Henry, Canon Prof. (1801–1872), mathematician 13/4/34
  William, architect 24/8/77
Moser *see* Bromley
Moses,
  John, Rev. 29/9/70 ?
  M. 22/1/77
Mosley,
  Oswald, Sir (1785–1871), 2nd Baronet (1798), liberal M.P. 5/3/36
  Sophia Anne (-1859), née Every 13/6/37
Moss *see* Ferrand
Moss,
  A. B. 9/4/90
  E. H. 6/8/89
  F. 7/1/86
  John (1782–1858), banker 11/8/25
  Samuel 30/11/85
  Thomas Edwards-, Sir (1811–1890), 1st Baronet (1868), banker 29/9/25, 30/9/56, 30/3/57, 21/2/60, 20/6/62, 23/4/72 L
Moss, James & Co. 21/9/66
Mosse, Henry Moore, Rev. 16/8/50 ?
Mossman, Thomas Wimberley, Rev. (1826–1885), controversialist, convert to Rome 19/2/57
Mostyn,
  Edward Mostyn Lloyd- (-1884), 3rd Baron Mostyn (1854), Flintshire landowner, liberal M.P. 2/7/41
  Harriet Margaret Lloyd- (-1891), née Scott, Lady Mostyn 1/9/62
  Thomas Edward Lloyd- (1830–1861), liberal M.P. 17/4/54, 6/3/57, 23/3/57 ff, 30/3/57, 7/4/57 n, 25/4/57 n
Mot, F. 11/1/78
Moth, R. 10/1/35
Motley *see* Harcourt
Motley,
  John Lothrop (1814–1877), American ambassador and historian 22/3/69, 1/4/69, 14/5/69, 1/6/69, 2/6/69, 12/6/69, 16/6/69, 15/10/69, 9/2/70, 4/9/70, 7/9/70 L, 18/9/70 L, 13/11/70 L, 20/12/70, 13/1/71, 3/9/73, 26/3/89, 27/4/89
  Mary, née Benjamin 2/9/70
Mott, John Thomas, of Barningham 29/7/68
Motte, Remi, of France 23/9/87
Mottershead, Thomas (1826–1884), trade unionist 10/10/76
Mottram,
  Charles John Macqueen, Rev. 4/2/41
  W., Rev. 18/12/79
Moulton,
  John Fletcher, Sir (1844–1921), liberal M.P., judge 31/5/86, 3/6/86, 15/11/89
  William Fiddian, Rev. Dr. (1835–1898), biblical scholar 22/6/78
Mounet-Sully, Jean (1841–1916), actor 17/10/79
Mounsey,
  E. S., Mrs. 26/5/68 ?
  Ewart Simon 26/5/68 n
Mountain,
  Armine Wale, Rev. 29/7/78 ?
  George Jehosophat, Bp. (-1863) 9/2/53
  James, Rev. 19/1/76 ?
Mount-Edgcumbe *see* Edgcumbe
Mountfield, David, Rev. (1827–1887) 26/10/75
Mountgarret *see* Butler
Mountney, George 1/10/65
Mountnorris *see* Annesley
Mount-Temple *see* Temple
Mouravieff, A. N., author 8/7/45
Mowat, Robert Anderson 23/2/91
Mowatt, Alexander Murray (1838–1869), reporter 11/4/68 ?
Mowbray,
  C. C. 24/7/74
  John Robert, Sir (1815–1899), 1st Baronet (1880), tory M.P. 29/6/52
  Robert Gray Cornish, Sir (1950–1914), 2nd Baronet (1899) 24/10/82 ?
  W. T. 17/3/74
Moxey, D. A., Dr. 23/3/80
Moxon,
  Edward (1801–1858), publisher and poet 11/10/42
  James, Rev. 6/2/77

Moylan, Denis Creagh 29/3/43 ?, 19/12/77 ?
Moyle, George, Rev. (1816–1861) 17/10/35
Mozley,
Anne, Miss (1809–1891), editor 24/1/91
James Bowling, Rev. Prof. (1813–1878), regius professor of divinity, Oxford (1871) 18/4/48, 7/11/74
Thomas, Rev. (1806–1893), historian of Tractarianism 11/6/82, 18/6/82, 22/6/82, 27/6/82
Muckleston, Edward, Rev. 4/1/53
Mudge,
William, Rev. 13/9/40
Zachary, Admiral (1770–1852) 28/7/32
Mudie,
Messrs. 25/4/79
Charles Edward (1818–1890), bookseller 25/4/79 n
Mugford,
Mr. 23/4/91
Herne, engineer 30/10/74 ?
Muggletonians, The 13/12/81, 14/1/82 n
Muir,
F., Liverpool shipbroker 4/11/68
Francis, tax surveyor 4/2/67
G. S., Rev. 28/10/90
G. W. 16/8/74
James, commission agent 5/4/52 ?
John (1810–1882), educationalist 16/4/60
Mona, Lady 21/12/85
T. H. 28/2/80
William, Dr. (–1869) 1/10/35
William, Sir (1819–1905), Principal, Edinburgh University (1884), Indian civil servant 20/1/79
Muirhead, William, Liverpool supplier 15/8/55
Mulchinoak, G. 20/5/74
Mulgrave *see* Phipps
Mulholland,
Miss 12/1/89
William 6/11/77 ?
Mull, W. 13/9/88
Mullan, Robert 2/3/75
Mullderson, Mr. 20/8/87
Muller, Daniel, sewage rate collector 21/4/59
Müller,
Herr, painted G's portrait in Rome 10/1/39
George Friedrich, Rev. (1805–1898), orphanage organiser 30/4/58
Mullins,
Mr. 11/11/62
Edward, London solicitor 7/6/53 ?
Edwin Roscoe (1848–1907), sculptor 14/12/78, 11/2/79
Mullooly, Fr., archaeologist 23/11/66 n
Mulock,
Dinah, author 28/9/79 n
Thomas Samuel, Rev., baptist 13/11/47 n
Mulvany, George F. (–1869), artist 6/8/53 ?
Mummery, Mr. 14/2/79
Muncaster *see* Pennington
Munday,
Charles F., of the Admiralty 30/11/78
Thomas, of Greenwich 21/3/79
Mundella,
Anthony John 7/2/67
M. T., Miss 19/3/77
Mundy,
Charles Godfrey (–1838) 4/5/33
Charles Godfrey, Mrs. 23/3/33
William (1801–1877), tory M.P. 19/9/61
Munich, C. J. 1/4/90
Munns, Richard, upholsterer 19/12/36 ?, 18/5/40
Munro,
Dr., of Dingwall 31/10/27
Miss 21/10/52
A. B., pamphleteer 11/10/78
Alexander (1825–1871), sculptor 18/7/51, 12/2/52, 6/11/52, 20/11/52, 13/8/53, 24/2/54, 13/10/54 ff, 25/10/54, 12/3/55, 13/7/57, 22/6/61, 9/8/61, 16/4/62, 16/5/63, 27/7/63, 26/6/82
Alexander, Mrs. 19/6/72
Alexander George, Rev. (1821–) 21/5/59
Amelia, Lady (–1849), née Browne 9/11/39
Charles, Sir (1794–1886), 9th Baronet (1848) 9/11/39 n
G. F. 5/5/91
Hugh Andrew Johnstone, Rev. Prof. (1818–1885), latinist 23/6/52, 20/10/84
Lewis 20/2/80 ?
Thomas, Sir (1761–1827), Baronet, administrator of India 21/3/38
Münster, Georg Herbert, Count, German ambassador 12/2/74, 22/2/74, 6/11/74, 13/3/75, 11/3/76, 1/10/80, 14/10/82, 4/2/84, 15/7/84, 30/7/84, 9/8/84 c, 13/3/85 c, 17/3/85, 6/7/85, 16/10/85, 16/7/86, 26/7/89, 2/8/89, 27/2/92, 27/5/92
Muntz, George Frederick (1794–1857), liberal M.P. 15/7/42, 26/4/43
Murchison,
Mrs. 20/2/90
Charlotte, Lady, née Hugonin 12/4/43
Kenneth Robert 1/11/71
Roderick Impey, Sir (1792–1871), 1st Baronet (1866), geologist 3/4/33, 5/12/62, 27/10/71
Murdoch,
Alexander Drimmie, Rev. 2/7/75
Alexander G., artisan 14/9/77
Thomas William Clinton, Sir (1809–1891), in colonial office (1839), special commissioner to Canada (1870) 16/5/46

Mure,
David (1810-1891), Peelite M.P. 12/12/59, 7/7/63
William, junior, Col. (1830-1880), liberal M.P. 20/11/78
William, senior, Col. (1799-1860), Peelite M.P. 3/3/53, 19/10/92
Murgatroyd, W. 23/11/55
Murphy *see* Jameson
Murphy,
Father 30/7/87
Mrs., rescue? 8/3/79
C. J. 4/4/91
D. F. 9/9/78
E., rescue 18/5/80
Eustace L., Rev., Roman Catholic 20/5/76
Francis Stack (1807-1860), liberal M.P. 7/3/44, 24/7/44
George Mollett (1823-1887), evangelist 23/3/65
H. H., of Sheffield 3/2/75
J., author 26/5/87, 27/5/87
Joseph John (1827-1894), author 15/8/77
Nicholas Daniel (1811-), liberal M.P. 6/4/70
Murray *see* Pakington, Smith
Murray,
Capt., in Ionia 3/1/59
Mrs., rescue 14/3/88
Mrs., rescue 24/1/60
A., 7th Lord Elibank 4/8/32 n
A. E. 18/3/90
A. Graham, Edinburgh lawyer 23/6/79
Albert Joseph, Sir (1774-1849) 25/8/38 ?
Alexander Edward (1804-1845), 6th Earl of Dunmore 13/4/48 n
A. M. 29/12/86
Archibald S. 4/12/74
Catherine, née Herbert, Lady Dunmore 13/4/48, 28/9/48
Charles Adolphus (1841-1907), 7th Earl of Dunmore (1845) 18/11/58
Charles Augustus, Sir (1806-1895), diplomat 26/8/42, 9/7/75
Charles Knight, secretary, Ecclesiastical Commission 27/1/44
David, bootmaker in Fettercairn 22/11/37, 6/11/38
David Rodney, Rev. (1791-1878) 31/7/32
David William (1777-1840), 3rd Earl of Mansfield (1796) 3/10/31
Edith, Lady 9/7/75
Eustace Clark Grenville (1824-1885) 17/9/77, 31/12/77
Francis Henry, Rev. (-1902) 19/11/73, 22/8/86
Frederica, Lady, née Markham, Lady Mansfield 3/7/46
George, Bp. (1784-1860), bishop of Rochester (1827) 13/5/33
George, Gen. Sir (1772-1846) 1/4/34
George Edward, Rev. 8/2/49
George Herbert, Sir (1849-1936), G's private secretary 1892-4 27/3/82
H. B. 16/3/87
Henry (-1845) 27/7/54 n
Henry Stormont (1812-1863), barrister 29/10/31
H. M. 2/4/78
James, civil servant 11/11/43 ?
James Augustus Henry, Sir (1837-1915), lexicographer 29/4/81 n, 31/7/81, 1/10/81, 7/2/90, 8/6/91 n
James Fitzgerald, Rev. (-1862) 8/3/52
James Francis, Chartist and Reform Leaguer 1/7/67
J. Brown 23/3/78
John, junior 1/8/38
John, senior (1778-1843), publisher 1/8/38 n, 16/4/90
John Archibald, Sir (1779-1859), Baron Murray (1839), whig M.P. 6/7/37
Patrick Aloysius, Rev. Prof. (1811-1882), professor at Maynooth 16/4/62
Richard, Dean, dean of Ardagh (1801) 28/5/37
R. J., of Nottingham 26/3/90
R. R., teller, Union bank, Edinburgh 28/9/54
Sarah Maria, Lady (-1874), née Hay-Drummond 13/7/37
Thomas Boyles, Rev. 23/2/49
William David (1806-1898), 4th Earl of Mansfield (1840), Viscount Stormont, tory M.P. 18/4/35
William Powell, barrister 27/1/79
Murtagh, J. 24/5/89
Musa, Paul Moses, Bp., Maranite bishop of Tripolis 19/12/41 ?
Muschi,
Anna, artist 9/1/39
Patrizio, of Siena, translator 9/1/39 n
Musgrave,
Edgar, of Ormskirk 22/11/67
George, Sir (1799-1872), 10th Baronet (1858) 29/1/66
Thomas, Abp. (1788-1860), archbishop of York (1847) 15/11/47 n
Musolini, Benedetto (-1885) 19/12/77 ?
Muspratt,
Edmund Knowles (1833-1923) 19/6/78 ?
Richard, of Flint 18/12/62
Mussett, Stephen 20/2/79
Mustoxidi,
Mme. 14/3/61
Andrea, Sir (-1860), of Ionia 26/11/58
Musurus *see* Heriot
Musurus, Constantine (1807-1891), Turkish ambassador 20/12/53, 2/6/58, 12/7/58,

Musurus, Constantine (*cont.*)
5/8/61, 2/1/72 L, 3/6/72, 18/8/72 n, 15/7/74, 12/3/77, 13/7/78, 14/5/80, 13/2/82, 17/6/82, 12/7/82, 13/7/82, 3/11/82, 8/11/82, 4/1/84, 22/1/84 c, 21/2/84, 7/3/84 c, 7/5/84, 18/6/84, 10/2/85, 25/3/85, 11/2/86
Muter, W. 22/5/56
Mutlow, T. A., Rev. (1776–) 8/1/26
Mutter, James, clerk, Inland Revenue 14/3/54
Mwanga,
Kabaka of Buganda 1884, deposed 1897 23/9/92
King, King of Buganda 23/9/92, 24/9/92, 26/9/92
Myer, Isaac, of U.S.A. 14/9/88
Myers,
Messrs. 7/11/79
Mrs. 20/5/85
Alfred Joseph, Rev. 4/11/78 ?
Asher Isaac (1848–1902), journalist; owned *Jewish Chronicle* 18/1/82 L, 25/1/82
Eveleen, née Tennant, photographer 25/4/90
Frederick William Henry (1843–1901), Fellow of Trinity, Cambridge, member of Psychical Society 22/8/85 n
Jacques 27/3/54
John, Rev. 24/6/28 n
M. S. 23/6/68
T. F. 16/10/90
William, broker 2/1/32 n
William, Mrs. 2/1/32 ?
Mylne, Louis George, Bp. (1843–1921) 8/11/74
Mynas, Minoide, Chevalier 4/7/57
Mynott, A. 11/2/80
Myres, George Cooper, Montrose solicitor 2/12/48
Myriantheus, Hieronymous, Archimandrite 15/3/75, 8/10/75
Mytton, Richard Herbert (1808–1869), judge 15/9/56

Nachez, violinist 5/3/90
Naden, Constance (–1889), poet 29/12/89 n
Naftel, Ernest L. 28/11/77
Naganowski, Edmond S., secretary, Friends of Poland 7/9/88
Nagle,
P. J., pamphleteer 17/3/55
William Cumming, Rev. (1810–1898) 9/7/38 ?
Nairne *see* Flahault de la Billarderie
Nairne,
Charles, Canon (–1867) 8/12/37 ?
James, secretary, N. B. R. 29/9/63
Naish,
Francis Clement, Rev. 15/6/75
John, Dublin Castle lawyer 24/5/82
S., Rev. 2/12/74
Naismith, W. 6/10/91
Namik Pasha, of Turkey 20/12/53
Nani, Giuseppi, Dr. 1/4/63
Nannini, Remigio (1521–1581), Dominican author 1/11/50
Nanson, Mr. 31/5/79
Naoroji, Dadabhai (1825–1917), President of Indian National Congress (1893), liberal M.P. 9/8/93
Napier *see* Hubbard
Napier,
Elizabeth, Lady (–1883), née Johnstone 20/9/54
Francis, diplomat 28/12/50
George Thomas, Gen. Sir (1784–1855), colonial governor 17/6/46
G. G. 8/8/89
Henry Alfred, Rev. (1797–1871) 7/3/57 ?
J., of U.S.A. 28/5/89
J. A., of Rhyl 31/3/57
John Scott, Major 8/2/88 n
Joseph, Sir (1804–1882), 1st Baronet (1867), tory M.P. 8/4/54
Robert Cornelis (1810–1890), 1st Baron Napier of Magdala (1868), soldier in India and Abyssinia 13/7/68
Robert John Milliken, Sir (1818–1884) 28/3/55
William (1821–1876) 26/1/64
Napoleon I (1769–1821), Emperor of France 13/2/32, 1/3/71
Napoleon III (1808–1873), Emperor of France (1852) 16/4/55, 18/4/55, 27/1/67, 2/1/71, 3/1/71, 1/4/71, 14/5/71, 24/1/73 c, 22/6/73, 5/7/75, 23/10/88
Nardi, Francesco, Monsignor 3/11/66, 11/9/67, 27/8/74
Nash,
Charles Barnes (1815–1892), author 13/5/58 ?
E., treasury clerk 16/5/60
John 4/2/75
Thomas Arthur, author 1/4/87
Nashe, C., Rev., nonconformist 19/2/68
Nasir-Ud-Din Haidar, King of Oudh (1827) 9/4/36
Nasmith, J. 8/8/42
Nasmyth,
Mr., of the London City Mission 4/3/45
James (1808–1890), engineer 28/9/54
Robert, Edinburgh dentist 8/1/50
Nasr-ul-Deen (1829–1896), Shah of Persia 1848, assassinated 15/2/73, 4/7/89, 5/7/89
Nassau *see* Wilhelm VII
Natali, B., shipping agent in Rome 23/7/66 ?
Nate, L., Miss 3/4/78

Nattali, Mr., of Clumber 15/4/79
Naudet, Joseph, French historian 6/4/77, 21/7/77
Naylor,
George, Rev. (1768–1854) 3/6/39
John (1813–1889), Montgomeryshire landlord 15/9/56
Nazim, Nawab 23/5/69, 27/6/71
Nealds, Mrs. 15/9/49
Neale,
C. 16/10/77
Edward Vansittart (1810–1890), barrister, Christian Socialist 21/11/28, 3/12/74
Erskine, Rev. (-1883) 9/11/52
Frederick, Rev. (1806–1872) 22/3/28 ?
Frederick Arthur, author 17/5/59
Harry Burrard, Adm. Sir (1765–1840), 2nd Baronet (1791), tory M.P. 22/8/32
John Mason, Rev. (1818–1866), hymnist 11/8/55
Neall, Mr. 13/10/75
Neate,
Charles, Prof. (1806–1879), fellow of Oriel, Oxford (1828), liberal M.P. 12/3/38, 3/4/54, 25/5/66
W. 22/2/58
Neave,
Miss, treasurer, Royal Female Philanthropic Society 6/3/50
Richard Digby (1793–1868), artist 31/12/66 ?
Neaves, Charles (1800–1876), Baron Neaves (1853), judge 12/12/59
Necker *see* Holstein
Needham,
Anne-Amelia (1819–1900), née Colville, Countess of Newry 1/11/51
Francis Jack (1815–1851), Viscount Newry (1832), tory M.P. 1/1/39
Joseph, barrister 26/2/56
Neeld,
Aubrey Dallas 28/5/86 ?
Joseph (1789–1856), tory M.P., Wiltshire landowner 8/10/38
Negreta, Sig. 14/11/64
Negri *see* Pasta
Negri, Benedetto (1784–1854), singing & piano teacher in Milan 3/8/35
Negroponte, Miss 11/8/91
Negropontis, M. J., of Constantinople 9/1/77, 22/7/77, 12/3/78 n
Neild, William, calico printer and alderman in Manchester 18/1/43, 30/6/57
Neill,
Edward Duffield, Rev. (1823–1893), of U.S.A. 31/7/75, 28/3/77
J. S. 18/5/73
Robert (1817–1899), of Manchester 28/6/66, 13/10/68
S. D. 4/11/86
W., banker in N. S. W., Australia 13/1/79
Neillson, Madame, singer 7/4/86, 1/7/86 ?
Neilson,
A., Liverpool merchant, uncle 9/7/35
Lilian Adelaide, Miss (1848–1880), actress 24/7/79, 1/7/86 ?
Robert, spirit dealer 13/8/42
Neilson, D.& J. B., Liverpool brokers 15/3/45
Neison, Francis G. P., actuary 19/6/45 ?
Nelson,
Edward Hamilton, Rev. 29/7/51
Horatio (1823–1913), 3rd Earl Nelson 26/11/47
Robert 2/6/42
Neruda *see* Hallé
Nesbit, Edith (1858–1924), author 28/8/91
Nesbitt, John, Edinburgh artist 9/4/80 ?
Nesfield, William Andrews, landscape gardener 13/8/50
Ness,
Mr., Hawarden 26/10/61
Mr., jnr., Hawarden 26/12/61
Netherby *see* Graham
Nettleship, Edward (1845–1913), ophthalmic surgeon 15/12/93, 21/3/94, 19/7/94, 27/7/94, 13/9/94
Nettleton, John Oldfield, broker 6/3/80
Neuhaus, Johann Christoph 6/3/75 ?
Neumann, Baron de, Austrian diplomat 3/12/42, 11/2/43
Neustein, Mr. 27/12/48
Neuwille, O. der 3/2/90
Nevile, Christopher, Rev. (1806–1877) 21/10/63
Nevill,
Dorothy Fanny, Lady (1826–1913), née Walpole, author 12/2/90, 2/7/93
John Henry Napier, Rev. 22/1/91
Neville *see* Glynne, Grenville, Savile, Thompson, Vavasour
Neville,
rescue 13/1/66
Catherine 19/12/41
Charles Cornwallis (1823–1902), 5th Baron Braybrooke (1861) 18/2/56
Edward, Lieut. Col. (1824–1908) 15/1/55, 16/10/55
Fanny Grace, née Blackwood, wife of W. F. Neville 4/6/51
J., née Cornwallis, Lady Braybrooke 22/7/39 n
Latimer, Rev. (1827–1904), 6th Baron Braybrooke (1902), Master of Magdalene College, Cambridge 31/10/59
Mirabel Jane, Miss (1821–1900) 31/7/59
R., 2nd Baron Braybrooke 7/7/39 n
R., 3rd Baron Braybrooke 22/7/39 n, 17/7/76

Neville (*cont.*)
Ralph (1848–1918), liberal M.P. and barrister 7/2/79, 25/4/92
Samuel Tarratt, Bp. 12/11/91
Seymour, Rev. 7/2/51, 29/5/92
William, Rev., Roman Catholic 7/11/88
William Frederick, Rev. 12/6/41 n
William Wyndham (1834–1858) 22/4/56, 25/12/58
Nevin, Robert Jenkins, Rev. Dr., of U.S.A. 24/7/78, 4/11/79, 1/10/81, 19/11/81 L
Nevins, Henry Willis Probyn-, Rev. (–1896) 22/3/75, 8/7/75, 4/11/92
New, Geoffrey, Evesham liberal 22/1/86
Newark *see* Pierrepont
Newbery, Henry James, Rev. 2/8/57 n
Newbigging, Thomas 22/6/87
Newbolt, Thomas John (–1850), East Indian director 30/6/49 ?
Newburgh *see* Bandini
Newby, George, Rev. 26/8/58 ?
Newcastle *see* Clinton
Newcombe, Richard, Rev. (1779–1857) 1/3/50, 8/4/57
Newcome, Thomas, Rev. 10/3/51
Newdegate, Charles Newdigate (1816–1887), tory M.P. 24/12/45, 5/3/75
Newell,
Mr., coalwhipper 14/5/51
Christian Frederick, Rev. 18/8/54, 13/9/54
Newick, W., Rev. 19/1/75
Newland,
Henry, Rev. (–1862), author, dean of Ferns 22/4/45
Henry Garrett, Rev. (1804–1860), high churchman 11/6/36
Newlands, Rev. 25/10/57
Newman,
Francis William, Rev. (1805–1897) 7/2/57 n, 24/9/60, 22/9/63, 15/12/92
George 7/2/75
Henry Joseph 17/5/57
H. S. 12/6/92
J., Mrs., née Fourdrinier 20/8/31 n
John B., Dr., American physician 20/12/79 ?
John Henry, Cardinal 23/8/28
Maria, née Kennaway 7/2/57
Thomas 12/7/76 ?
W. F. 27/1/92
Newmarch, William (1820–1882), statistician 19/3/55
Newnham,
N. J. 8/10/77
Obadiah Samuel, Rev. 14/5/92
W. O., Rev. 5/7/91
Newport, John, Sir (1756–1843), 1st Baronet (1789), former whig M.P. 27/2/40
Newry *see* Needham
Newton,
Charles Thomas, Sir (1816–1894), Knight (1877), archaeologist 30/7/56, 10/10/73, 13/10/73 ff, 5/9/76, 25/9/77, 24/10/87
Edward, Sir (1832–1897) 16/10/78
Henry, Rev. (1838–1921) 11/4/77
Joseph 16/4/80
P. M. 3/6/91
T., tax inspector 27/8/77
New York Herald, editor 15/10/81 L
Neymarck, Alfred 15/5/77
Niblett, Alfred N., publisher 20/6/56
Nicholas,
Braye H. W., Capt. 1/7/46
Thomas, Rev. (1820–1879), nonconformist 3/10/68 ?
Nicholas I, Tsar of Russia 7/6/44
Nicholay, Charles G., Rev. 22/4/47
Nicholl,
Andrew, artist 17/9/45 ?
G., accountant 30/4/56
Henry (1809–1845), barrister 30/9/26
John, Dr. (1797–1853), Peelite M.P. and whip 26/3/34
John Richard, Rev. (1809–1905) 30/9/26
Thomas, Rev. Dr. (1797–1867) 27/6/33, 8/2/61 ?
Nicholls,
rescue 27/1/70
H. J., barrister, of Lincoln's Inn 30/4/36
J. C. 12/12/77
Thomas, surveyor, of Holborn 18/6/38
Nichols,
S. A. 14/10/62
Thomas, liberal 10/4/80
William Luke, Rev. (1802–1889) 13/12/75
Nicholson *see* Hudson
Nicholson,
Miss 5/11/47, 15/1/61
A. 2/1/77
Arthur, Dr., G's physician in Brighton 29/3/94
Benjamin, Newark ironmonger 10/3/40
Charles, speaker of N. S. W. Council, Australia 8/10/51
Edward Williams Byron (1849–1912), Bodley's Librarian, Oxford 28/11/83 n, 25/10/92 n
George Stewart, London barrister 8/2/48 ?
James, school master 13/11/34 n
L. J. 10/4/78
W. C. 18/7/68
William Newjam, of Newark 10/2/52
William Trevor, Rev. 16/1/76
Nicol,
Dr., physician in Hanover 25/1/76
Donald Ninian 5/9/79
Henry (–1905), treasury civil servant 24/6/53

J. D. 17/9/69, 20/11/72
John, printer 11/9/89
William (1790-1879), tory M.P. 18/3/47, 21/2/65
Nicolaides, N. 30/1/89
Nicolas, Prince, Prince of Montenegro 28/11/80
Nicoll, William Robertson, Sir (1851-1923), editor, *British Weekly* (1886), liberal 19/12/89
Nicolls, Jasper Hume (1819-1877), Principal, Lennoxville, Canada 27/7/53
Nicolson,
Frederick William Erskine, Sir (1815-1899), 10th Baronet (1820) 22/9/63
James, Dean (-1889) 21/9/66
Niebuhr, Barthold Georg (1776-1831), diplomat and historian 5/4/32
Nieuwenhuis, Christian Johannes (1799-1883) 22/6/58, 9/11/58, 12/4/59
Nieuwenhuys, John, artist 6/5/33
Nightingale *see* Law
Nightingale,
Florence (1820-1910), nurse in the Crimea and campaigner for reform 19/10/54, 14/5/79
James Edward (-1892), antiquarian 7/1/84
Robert 2/6/41 ?
Robert Cubitt, Rev. 15/11/88
Nightingall, Miles, Sir 27/1/37 n
Nigra, Constantino, Cav. (1828-1907), Italian politician and diplomat 3/12/55, 29/4/85
Nihill, Daniel, Rev. (1791-1867) 1/7/37
Nikita, singer 17/3/88
Nikolaides, G., of Athens 21/4/80
Nimmo,
E. C., Mrs. 18/10/64, 23/8/80
Mary, Mrs., G's aunt 11/10/36
Thomas, G's uncle; a Glasgow pipe manufacturer 1/8/35
Nisbet,
Messrs. 3/1/77
J., of Edinburgh 5/9/87
James (1785-1854), bookseller and publisher, educationalist 17/7/38
John Marjoribanks, Canon 2/6/88
Nisbett, Hulme 18/12/89
Nisco,
Niccolo, Baron (1816-1901), Neapolitan liberal 8/7/59, 26/12/88
Nitopi, Sig. 8/2/89
Nitsch, Charles 26/4/90
Nixon,
Mrs., of London 22/5/53
A. 1/3/80
Christopher J., of Dublin 17/11/79
Francis Russell, Bp. (1803-1879), bishop of Tasmania (1842) 26/3/47
William, of the London hospital 28/6/61, 6/4/68
Nobbs, George Hunn, Rev. (-1884) 27/11/52
Nobili, Giuseppe 2/11/38
Noble,
E. 12/8/78
John (1827-1892), financial author 19/8/68
Matthew (-1876), sculptor 20/3/54, 25/7/60, 25/1/75, 2/8/75
Noddall, W. T.& S., Messrs., of Newark 27/9/77
Noel *see* Carnegie
Noel,
Augusta, Lady 19/4/80
Charles (-1866), 1st Earl of Gainsborough (1841) 4/12/49 n
Charles George Noel, Viscount Campden (1841), 2nd Earl of Gainsborough (1866) 4/7/45
Ernest (1831-), liberal M.P. 19/4/80 n, 27/11/90
Gerald James (1823-1911), tory M.P. and whip 11/3/69
James Gambie 23/7/45
Jane King, Lady Lovelace 15/2/81
Roden Berkeley Wriothesley (1834-1895), poet 20/7/74, 13/3/76, 12/11/92
Noirsain, Mons. 17/10/51
Nolan,
Father, Land Leaguer 17/12/81 L
J. 31/10/71
Thomas, Rev. 10/11/77
Noldwatt, Mr. 2/4/79 ?
Noott, Edward Henry Lane, Rev. (-1905) 22/9/77
Norchi,
Messrs., sculpture importers 27/3/79 ?, 25/5/83
C. E., of Edinburgh 19/9/90
Norfolk *see* Howard
Norman,
rescue 3/12/72
Mr., solcitor's clerk 12/4/44
Charles Boswell, soldier and author 23/1/78, 6/11/86
E. I., Lady, née Manners 3/1/35 n
Frederick J., Rev. (-1888) 23/9/46, 6/4/78
George, of Birmingham 10/1/57 ?
Henry, Sir (1858-1939), Knight (1906), 1st Baronet (1915), journalist, liberal M.P. 23/8/87, 26/7/93 n, 8/8/93, 12/8/93, 20/9/93, 10/10/93
John, Newark maltster 3/1/35 ?
John Paxton (-1871), lawyer 21/5/52
Richard, of Melton Mowbray 3/1/35 ?
Richard Whitmore, Rev., headmaster of Radley College 20/11/61
Normanby *see* Phipps
Normanton *see* Agar

Norreys *see* Bertie
Norreys,
Miss, actress 18/11/84 n, 13/1/93 n
Catherine Cecilia Jane Jephson-, Lady, née Franks 10/2/46
Charles Denham Orlando Jephson, Sir (1799–1888), liberal M.P. 1/3/43
Elizabeth Lavinia, Lady, née Vernon-Harcourt 11/5/31 n
Montague Bertie, Lord (1808–1884), 6th Earl of Abingdon (1854), tory M.P. 11/5/31, 22/4/61
Norris *see* Blair
Norris,
C. A. 26/12/76
George M., secretary, London Mechanics Institute 12/8/68
G. W. 8/10/67
Henry Handley, Rev. (1771–1850) 4/5/39
James (1796–1872), President of Corpus, Oxford 4/3/56
John Pilkington, Ven. (1823–1891) 22/2/76
John Thomas (1808–1870), liberal M.P. 1/3/60
North,
G. 11/9/28 ?
Jacob Hugo, Rev. (1812–1884) 4/3/60
James, of Newark 30/9/41
J. G. 22/6/68
John Sidney, Col. (1804–1894), né Doyle, tory M.P. 5/12/42, 10/2/65, 16/4/75
J. W., illustrator 30/11/77 ?
Northampton *see* Compton
Northbourne *see* James
Northbrook *see* Baring
Northcote,
Agnes Mary (–1840), née Cockburn 8/8/32
Cecilia Frances, Lady, née Farrer, Lady Iddesleigh 9/2/54
Henry Stafford (1792–1851) 8/8/32
Hilda, née Farrar 14/6/81
John Stafford, Rev. (1850–1920), G's godson 2/2/50, 14/6/81
Stafford Henry, Sir 30/6/42
Walter Stafford (1845–1927), 2nd Earl of Iddesleigh (1887), Baron St. Cyres 26/6/86
Northesk *see* Carnegie
Northey, Misses 21/5/90
Northeys,
Agnes, née Boreel 31/3/32
William Brook (1805–1880), guardsman 31/3/32
Northumberland *see* Percy
Northy, W. H. 9/4/74 ff, 24/5/87
Norton *see* Adderley
Norton,
Arthur Treherne, Dr., physician 11/4/78 ?
Caroline Elizabeth Stuart, Mrs. (1808–1877), née Sheridan, Lady Stirling-Maxwell (1877), campaigner and poet 25/5/35 n
Edward, author 19/10/57
Fletcher Cavendish Charles Conyers (1829–1859) 16/8/59
George Chapple (1800–1875) 25/5/35 n
John David, Sir (–1843), Knight (1842), judge in Madras 25/5/35 n
Peter, of Soho Square 12/3/53
S. W. 18/3/87
Norway, G. 19/10/89
Norwood,
Charles Morgan (1825–1891), liberal M.P. 5/12/65
J. 10/4/78
Nosotti, Charles, furniture dealer 13/7/68, 23/11/86
Notovich, Nicolai, author 29/1/92
Nottage,
Mr., photographer 25/4/73
Martha Christiana, Lady 20/5/85
Notten,
Charles van, City merchant 22/3/38 ?
Peter van, City merchant 22/3/38 ?
Noult, Mr. 17/3/68
Nourse, Henry Dalzell, barrister 11/4/78
Novar *see* Ferguson
Novello, Messrs., music publishers 18/5/94
Novikoff, Olga 14/2/73
Nubar Pasha (1825–1899), Egyptian politician 21/6/77
Nublat, M. 4/12/77
Nugée, George, Rev. (–1892) 1/3/54
Nugent,
Algernon W. F. Greville- (1841–1910), liberal M.P. 23/9/69 L
Fulke Southwell Greville- (1821–1883), 1st Baron Greville (1869) 3/8/69, 7/1/70 L
William, Rev. 15/9/68
Nunn,
Joshua 5/10/53
M., Mr. 8/10/67
M. A., Mrs. 8/10/67 n
Thomas, Rev. (1821–1877) 13/3/57 ?
Nussey, John (–1862), apothecary 25/4/50
Nuster, Mr. 17/11/53
Nüth, E. A. 15/6/76
Nutt,
D. 2/5/91, 2/3/93
J. 22/5/89
Nuttall, C. G. 11/2/78
Nye,
G. H. 5/5/94
G. H. F. 2/10/89
Nylander, Frau 30/3/91
Nys, Ernest, Prof. 3/7/79

Oakden, W. 8/1/87
Oakdew, Mr. 3/9/77
Oakeley,
Frederick, Rev. (1802–1880) 27/11/31, 20/2/45, 3/9/93
Herbert Stanley, Prof. Sir (1830–1903), musician 3/2/80
Oakes,
Charles Henry (1810–1864), barrister 2/3/31
Elijah 17/3/74
H., Sir, 2nd Baronet 12/3/31 n
John 5/9/88
Oakley,
John, Dean (1834–1891) 20/2/67, 15/3/76, 20/9/80, 8/9/81, 20/9/81
R. B. 29/8/91
Oates,
rescue 26/2/70, 17/6/70
Austin 25/2/80
Wilfred 13/12/76
O'Brien *see* Harris, Monsell
O'Brien,
Charlotte Grace, Miss (1845–1909), Irish poet and admirer of G 3/1/87
Cornelius (1782–), liberal M.P. 25/6/35
Donatus, of the railway department 13/6/44
E., Sir, 4th Baronet 6/12/37 n
Edward William, Irish landowner 18/10/75
James Thomas, Bp. (1792–1874), bishop of Ossory 13/3/64
Lucius, Sir (1800–1872), 13th Baron Inchiquin (1855), 5th Baronet, tory M.P. 21/8/48, 29/3/65
M. S. 10/12/86
Patrick, Sir (1824–1897), 2nd Baronet (1862), liberal M.P. 30/3/60
Richard Barry (1847–1918), author and biographer 7/1/80, 5/11/80 L, 4/10/83 L, 5/8/85, 7/7/86 L, 8/7/86, 22/1/91 n, 28/1/91 n
Timothy, Sir (1790–1862), 1st Baronet (1849), liberal M.P. 16/12/51
William (1825–1928), home rule M.P. 17/10/77, 19/7/90
William Smith (1803–1864), repeal M.P. 6/12/37
Obrischkoff,
Mme., Russian in Naples 18/12/50, 29/2/52 fl
O'Byrne,
Mr. 22/3/66
Mr. 23/12/86
O'Callaghan *see* Cavendish
O'Callaghan,
Mr. 16/10/87
John Cornelius (1805–1883), journalist 8/2/48
O'Carroll, J. J., Rev. 11/12/88
O'Clery,
Keyes (1845–), home rule M.P. 10/5/77
Patrick Keyes, historian 31/3/92, 1/4/92
O'Connell *see* Ffrench
O'Connell,
Daniel 17/7/28 n
Ellen Mary, Mrs. 28/1/82
F. D. F. 9/4/80
James, Sir (1786–1872), 1st Baronet (1869) 9/9/69
O'Connor,
A., assassin 29/2/72, 13/4/72, 3/12/72
Arthur, home rule M.P. 25/4/85 c
Bernard, Dr., physician 21/4/87
Feargus (1794–1855), Chartist M.P. and leader 27/5/40 n
Fitzgerald 20/7/77
Thomas Power (1848–1929), home rule M.P. and journalist 13/12/85, 3/6/86, 24/8/86, 28/4/87, 29/10/88, 10/3/93, 11/10/93 L
O'Conor, Denis (1794–1847), known as 'The O'Conor Don', liberal M.P. 18/6/45
Odell, S. E. 8/2/90
O'Dell, Stackpool Edward, phrenologist 17/2/75
Odescalchi, Carlo, Cardinal (1786–1841) 12/12/38
Odgers, H. J., Rev., unitarian 2/8/44
O'Donnell,
Mr. 24/9/76
C. V. 22/3/87
Frank Hugh O'Cahan (1848–), home rule M.P. 14/6/80, 3/7/82 c, 28/4/87 n, 6/7/88 n, 21/9/88 n
O'Donoghue, Daniel (1833–1889), liberal M.P. 25/11/65, 14/5/66, 29/7/70 L, 21/5/86
O'Dowd, James Klyne (1802–1879), Irish solicitor 17/7/69
O'Dwyer,
Father 31/10/77
Andrew Carew (–1877), pamphleteer 16/5/51
O'Ferrall, Richard More (1797–1880), liberal M.P. 21/7/64
Officer, Mr. 23/3/80
Offley *see* Wakeman
Offley,
Emma Cunliffe-, Mrs. (–1850), née Crewe 11/4/38 ?
F. Cunliffe- (–1832) 11/4/38
Offor,
George 6/3/78, 23/11/88
George (–1864), bookseller 21/2/49
O'Flaherty, Anthony (1800–), repeal M.P. 1/6/53
O'Flanagan, J. R., Rev. 3/2/79 ?
O'Flynn, J. D. 4/10/91

Ogden,
A. 3/11/86
F., of Manchester 16/9/59
H. 1/4/78
Oger, Victor, Mons., translator 13/11/74, 6/12/86
Ogilvie,
C., Miss 5/1/87
Charles Atmore, Rev. Prof. (1793-1873), regius professor of pastoral theology, Oxford (1842) 5/4/29
G., Rev. 3/12/66
Robert Annesley (1807-1879), of customs department 21/7/64, 21/9/64, 20/4/72
Ogilvy *see* Fitzgerald
Ogilvy,
David, Mrs., sister of John G. 15/4/28
David Graham Drummond (1826-1881), 7th Earl of Airlie 18/5/67 n
Donald, landowner 17/11/46
Elizabeth, née Wilson 9/8/27
Henrietta Blanche (-1921), Lady Airlie 18/5/67
John, Sir (1803-1890), liberal M.P. 18/2/60, 10/7/68
J. T. 27/6/79
Thomas, of Corrimony 27/9/72
Thomas, Capt., distant relative 23/6/63, 12/10/63
Thomas, the elder (-1826), David G's partner 18/3/26
Thomas, the elder, Mrs., née Gladstone 18/3/26 n
Thomas, the younger 7/9/26
Walter T., of the British Museum 23/9/78 ?
W. S. 23/9/78
Ogilvy, Gillanders & Co., Messrs. 3/3/82, 20/9/82
Ogle,
Miss 27/7/67
James Adey, Dr. (-1857), physician 27/4/49
John Lockhart, Rev. (-1924) 21/6/78 ?
John William, Dr. 1/7/59, 21/9/66
O'Hagan, Thomas, Judge (1812-1885), 1st Baron O'Hagan (1870), liberal M.P., lord chancellor of Ireland 19/2/63 n, 9/12/73 L, 5/3/75, 5/4/79, 25/12/80, 31/5/81 n
O'Halloran, M., Rev. 30/1/74
O'Hanlon, John, Canon, of Dublin 1/1/80
O'Hare, D. V., Rev. 21/4/79
O'Hart, John, of Dublin 18/1/76
Ohlson, Mr. 13/7/76
Oikonomides, I. N., Greek author 17/2/59 ?
O'Kane, Mr.& Mrs. 2/11/63 n
O'Keefe, Francis A., mayor of Limerick 3/1/87 n
O'Keeffe, Robert, Father (-1881) 9/7/72, 19/8/72 L, 3/9/72, 6/9/72 ff
Okes,
Mary Elizabeth, née Sibthorpe 21/9/26
Richard (1797-1888), Provost of King's, Cambridge 21/9/25, 18/1/70 L
Old,
James 17/4/92
William Watkins, of Monmouth 29/10/58
Olden, Thomas, Rev. 23/4/76
Oldfield,
Edmund (1816-1885), of the antiquities department, British Museum 30/7/56
E. O., Mrs. 24/3/55
John (-1863), soldier 18/2/50
Thomas, barrister 18/3/50, 2/4/50
Oldham,
C. H., secretary, Protestant Home Rule Association 23/10/88
J. B. 5/2/90
John Lane, Rev., chaplain to Lord Braybrooke 28/2/61
John Robert, Rev. 18/4/40
Oldrey, William, Commander, senator and Jamaican magistrate 29/6/36
Olga Nicolajevna, Princess, née Romanov, Queen of Wurtemburg 12/8/53
Oliphant,
Alice (-1887), née Le Strange 15/2/82
Laurence (1829-1888), liberal M.P., novelist and mystic 17/6/80
Margaret Oliphant, Mrs. (1828-1897), novelist 28/12/91
Olivares, d', Marquis 2/5/68
Oliveira, Benjamin (1806-1865), liberal M.P. 28/10/52
Oliver,
G., Rev. 20/8/46 ?
H. M. 26/11/89
John, Newark draper 21/1/33
Roderic, solicitor 4/12/78
Thomas, Rev. 29/10/85 ?
Oliver & Boyd, Messrs., Edinburgh publishers 2/11/65, 18/11/86
Oliverson, Richard, insurance broker 16/2/33
Olivier,
Dacres, Rev. (1831-) 1/4/61
Daniel J., Rev. 3/8/46 ?
Ollards, E. 2/11/68
Olliff, Rev. Dr. 13/2/89
Ollivier, Démosthène, French politician 3/8/46 ?
O'Loghlen, Colman Michael, Sir (1819-1877), 2nd Baronet (1842), liberal M.P. 1/5/65, 25/6/70 L, 20/4/72 L
Olózaga, Salustiano de, Senor (1805-1873), author 12/1/67
O'Malley, Joseph, Rev. 28/12/79
Ommaney *see* Scott
O'Neil,
Charles, of Newman Street 1/7/33 ?

Henry Nelson, artist 12/7/48 ?
O'Neill,
Miss 13/5/87
D. J. 6/5/89
J. J. 12/10/88
William, Rev. (1813–1883), 1st Baron O'Neill (1868) 23/10/77
Onslow,
Charles, Rev. (1810–1884) 23/4/57
Denzil Roberts, tory M.P. 12/4/78
Guildford James Hillier Mainwaring-Ellerker (1814–1882), liberal M.P. 6/2/67
Opdebeck,
Jean Alexis, Mons., Belgian courier, lover, then husband, of Lady Lincoln 4/12/32 n, 30/11/89
Susan Harriet Catherine, Lady; Lady Lincoln 4/12/32 n
Oporto *see* Louis I
Oppenheim,
Henry Maurice William (1835–1912) 5/6/88, 8/5/89, 20/5/89
Isabel, née Butler 22/7/86, 8/5/89, 23/12/93
Oppenheimer,
Charles, consul 26/8/86 n
Charles, Mrs. 26/8/86
William, art dealer 15/7/90
Oraghimian, Mr. 4/3/78
Orange,
Herr 24/9/85
James Edward Dakin, publisher 6/2/79
William, Dr., physician 1/11/79
Oranmore *see* Browne
Orban, H. J. W. Frère-, Belgian minister 17/4/69, 3/6/89
Orbanurichi, Rev. Sig. 13/2/89
Orchard, Benjamin Guiness, of Liverpool 6/8/67
Ord,
Benjamin Thomas, printer 25/8/75
John Walker (1811–1853), editor and journalist 22/2/37
William Redmond, Gen. (1792–1872) 28/11/63
Orde *see* Domville
Orde, Leonard Shafto, Rev. (1807–1895) 24/4/58
O'Reilly,
Dr. 13/11/27
Myles William Patrick (1825–1880), liberal M.P. 24/7/67
Orfew, E. 18/6/51
Orger & Meryon, London booksellers 6/6/50
Orléans,
Isabelle d', Comtesse de Paris (1865) 26/1/66
Louis Philippe Albert d' (1838–1894), Comte de Paris 28/4/59, 7/7/59, 17/10/79, 28/1/83, 9/2/83, 10/2/83 L, 11/2/83 ff
Louis Philippe Marie Léopold d' (1845–1866), Prince de Condé 6/6/59
Robert P. L. E. F. d' (1840–), Duc de Chartres 17/2/66
Orlebar, Augustus Scobell 11/7/78
Orlov, Nicholas Alexeyevitch, Prince, diplomat 13/11/65
Orlowsky, Count 7/5/32, 13/7/32
Ormathwaite *see* Walsh
Ormerod,
George Wareing (1810–1891), genealogist 24/4/77
Henry Mere (1816–1873) 8/6/59 ?
Ormond,
rescue 29/6/66, 24/7/68
H. H. 23/8/78
Ormonde, F. 8/3/78
Ormsby,
John William, Col. (–1869), artist 29/11/58
William Arthur, Rev. 23/4/56 ?
Ornsby, Robert, Prof. (1820–1889), biographer of James Hope-Scott 28/10/74, 24/11/83 L, 3/2/84
O'Roorke, J., Rev. 4/1/87
O'Rorke, Hugh Hyacinth (1834–1904), known as 'The MacDermot', lawyer 3/2/93
O'Rourke, John, Rev., of Maynooth 4/11/77
Orpen, Richard J. T., Sir, Irish solicitor 13/8/45
Orr, John Bryson 27/7/76 ?
Orred *see* Lowe
Orrock, Thomas, Edinburgh bootmaker 11/12/79 ?
Orsini, Felice (1819–1858), assassin 28/5/57, 29/5/57
Orton,
Arthur (1834–1898), the Tichborne claimant 20/3/78 ?
Frederick, Dr. 28/3/74
James 6/3/75
Thomas, Reform Leaguer in Sheffield 6/1/68
W. B. 19/8/90
Osborn,
rescue 17/11/53
Joseph 29/10/68
Montagu Francis Finch, Rev. (1824–1895) 5/5/58
Sherard, Adm. (1822–1875) 2/12/62, 26/3/74
Osborne,
Mr., E. Clifton's lover 19/8/51
A. B. 14/9/89
C. J., Mrs., of Clonmell 17/11/60, 30/6/61, 8/5/63
Conyers G. T. W., Lord (1812–1831) 16/2/31

Osborne (*cont.*)
Emily Charlotte, Lady (-1875) 12/8/54 ?
Ralph Bernal (1811-1882), né Bernal, liberal M.P. 25/3/53
Sydney Godolphin, Rev. Lord (1808-1889) 12/8/54 n
William Alexander, Rev. 4/3/41 n
Oscar II, King of Sweden 21/6/73 n, 28/5/81
Osgood,
Messrs. 3/3/92
James R., *Harper's* London agent 24/2/90
O'Shaughnessy,
C. 12/9/75
Richard, liberal M.P. 14/10/76
O'Shea *see* Parnell
O'Shea,
C. 16/10/77
William Henry, Capt. 18/9/80 L
Osler, J., Rev. 10/12/77
Osman Digna, leader of revolt in Eastern Sudan 12/2/84, 25/2/84 c, 19/8/84, 6/1/85 ff, 9/1/85 n, 10/1/85, 7/2/85 c, 10/2/85, 27/3/85 c, 30/3/85, 5/4/85, 29/5/85
Ossani, Alessandro, portrait painter 2/7/90, 4/7/90, 5/7/90
Ossington *see* Denison
Ossman Bey 18/8/93
Ossulston *see* Bennet
Ostini, Peter, Cardinal (-1849), bishop of Albano (1843), Papal Nuncio 16/5/32
Ostroff, Vasili 22/6/77
O'Sullivan,
Alice, Sister 9/9/90 ?
Daniel, mayor of Cork 30/4/69 n, 1/5/69, 4/5/69, 8/5/69, 9/5/69, 11/5/69
Mortimer, Canon (1791-1859), controversionalist 20/6/35
William Henry (1829-1887), liberal M.P. 16/8/81 L
Oswald *see* Bruce
Oswald,
Alexander Haldane (1811-1868), Peelite M.P. 12/1/50
James Townshend, of Dunnikeir 18/11/33 n
James Townshend, Mrs. 18/11/33
Otham, J. 2/6/92
Otho I (1815-1867), King of Greece (deposed 1862) 19/12/58
Ott, Chevalier 25/7/79
Otter *see* Strutt
Ottley,
Edward Bickersteth, Rev. (1853-1910), of Hawarden 20/5/77, 11/8/77 ff, 17/11/77, 26/4/78, 5/5/78, 9/9/78, 28/8/79, 7/1/80, 28/2/80, 14/5/83, 5/10/86
F. F., Exchequer clerk 26/5/59
George Philip, Rev. (1824-1891) 10/3/75
Henry Bickersteth, Rev. 17/8/77
John Bridge, Rev. 8/10/73
Lawrence, Rev. (1808-1861) 30/12/38
Otto *see* Stuart de Decies
Otto, Mr. 13/4/91
Otway *see* Pyndar
Otway, Arthur John, Sir (1822-1912), liberal M.P. 15/6/55, 6/7/66, 16/1/69 L, 30/11/70 L
Ouseley,
Frederick Arthur Gore, Rev. Sir (-1889), 2nd Baronet (1844) 26/1/53
William Gore, Sir (1797-1866), diplomat 22/3/37 ?
Outram,
Mrs., of Hawarden 13/1/71
Edmund Healy, Rev. 23/6/89
James, Gen. Sir (1803-1863) 24/6/43
Zadok Alma (-1893), G's valet; an alcoholic and suicide 24/8/83, 26/8/83, 13/8/84, 3/6/90, 14/8/91, 15/8/91, 18/11/91, 9/10/93 ff, 1/12/93 ff, 13/12/93
Ouvry, Frederic (1814-1881), Newcastle's solicitor 25/5/60, 28/10/64, 2/12/67, 27/1/73, 14/3/74, 14/5/75, 19/2/77, 25/9/77, 26/3/79, 14/4/79, 28/1/81 L, 29/3/82
Overbeck, Johann Friedrich (1789-1869), artist 8/12/38, 8/12/66
Overend, Gurney & Co., bankers 29/1/48
Overstone *see* Loyd
Overy, Henry, Rev. 15/9/77
Owen *see* Cole, Visger
Owen,
Mrs., at Eaton 22/11/55
B. 18/6/78
Edward, Rev. (1831-1883) 25/7/68 ?
Francis Philip Cunliffe, Sir (1828-1894), Knight (1878), director, South Kensington museum 9/3/75
George, of Islington 25/2/68
Horatio, bookseller 29/6/52
H. P. 19/9/76
Hugh 3/9/77
Hugh, Rev., of Llanerchymedd 28/12/55
Hugh, Sir (1835-1916), civil servant 13/11/82
Islambard, Sir (1850-1927) 20/11/91
James, Rev. 4/7/79
John, Rev. 1/9/76
John, Sir (-1861), 1st Baronet (1813), Peelite M.P. 19/5/46
Lewis Welsh, Rev. (-1884) 3/2/53
R. C., Rev. 1/5/78
Richard, Prof. Sir (1804-1892), naturalist 12/6/49, 8/4/51, 6/8/61, 21/10/61, 27/9/62, 28/9/62, 23/10/85, 11/12/85
Richard Trevor, Rev. 24/7/90

Robert (1771-1858), socialist 12/2/58
Robert, Rev. 20/11/91
Robert, Rev., don 26/6/52
William, superintendent, Somerset House 2/5/60 ?
William Hicks, Rev. (1800-1886) 8/10/67
Oxenbridge *see* Monson
Oxenbridge, E. 21/5/78
Oxenham,
Messrs., furniture dealers in Oxford Street, London 6/6/42, 6/11/43
Frank Nugent, Rev. (-1892) 24/10/75
Henry Nutcombe, Rev. (1829-1888) 15/2/75 n, 30/4/75, 20/9/79, 16/9/82 ?
Nutcombe, Rev. (-1859) 16/3/52
Oxford, Edward, attempted assassin 12/6/40 n
Oxford and Asquith *see* Asquith
Oxholm, Waldemar Tully d' (1805-1876), diplomat 11/4/56 n
Oxley,
John Swaby, Rev. 12/12/52
W. 16/11/90
Oxmantown *see* Parsons
Oxon, Mr., of Chester 23/10/55
Ozanoff, Mr., of Athens 21/12/58
Ozenne, J. E. 28/10/71

Pacifico, Monsignor 8/2/89
Pacificus, F., Rev., Roman Catholic 24/9/78
Packard, Mr. 21/12/78
Packe,
Charles William (1792-1867), tory M.P. 27/10/43
George Hussey (1796-1874), liberal M.P. 27/10/43
Packe-Reading, Kitty Jenkyn, Mrs., née Hort, married to C. W. Packe 12/5/47
Packman, Robert Collier, Rev. 20/3/41
Paden Woon, of Burma 20/9/71
Padgham, Mr. 30/8/77
Padovan, Dr., of Ionia 1/12/58
Paganini, Niccolò (1782-1840), violinist 6/1/32
Pagano, Giuseppe, innkeeper 10/5/32
Page,
Capt. 23/10/75
Mr.& Mrs., hoteliers in Palermo 15/10/38
Charles William (1806-1873) 6/9/28
James Robert, Rev. (1805-1886), historian 12/3/39
John E., journalist 15/6/78
Samuel Flood, author 21/1/78 ?
S. F. 21/1/78
William Emanuel, Dr. (1808-1868), physician 6/9/28
Pagenstecher, Hermann, German oculist 3/11/93
Pagès, Louis Antoine Garnier- 4/2/67
Paget *see* Townshend
Paget,
Alfred Henry, Lord (1816-1888) 7/5/71
Augustus Berkeley, Sir (1823-1896), diplomat 9/2/66
Charles (1799-1873), liberal M.P. 1/6/61
Clarence Edward, Lord (1811-1895), whig M.P. 1/8/59, 28/12/60, 29/12/60, 27/7/61, 9/9/61, 13/9/61, 24/10/61, 27/2/62, 11/3/63, 29/7/63, 28/1/64, 3/1/65, 2/1/66, 12/1/66, 16/1/66, 16/2/78
Edward James, Rev. (1811-1869) 17/10/28
F. E., Rev. 1/6/80 L
Francis, Dean (1851-1911), dean of Christ Church, Oxford (1892) 9/7/75 n, 18/8/81 ?, 28/8/81 ?, 2/2/90, 22/10/92
Henry William, Sir (1768-1854), Earl of Uxbridge (1812), 1st Marquis of Anglesey (1815) 31/8/26
James, Sir (1814-1899), surgeon 18/6/73, 7/8/73, 13/2/77, 20/9/79, 24/2/81 ff, 5/7/85, 15/12/93, 22/12/93, 23/12/93
Martha Stuart, Lady 4/10/71
Thomas Bradley, Rev. (-1893) 27/3/77
William, Lord (-1873), Peelite M.P. 5/6/46
Page Wood *see* Parnell
Pahlen,
Alexis von der, Count, Russian geologist 4/4/61 ?
Nicholas, Count 23/1/83
Paige, Lewis, Rev. 28/4/45
Pain,
Edward, Liverpool manufacturer 6/8/68 ?
W. H. S., of Llanover 7/6/67
Paine,
Mr. 25/3/94
Cornelius, master grocer 2/8/43
Edwin, Rev. 6/8/68 ?
W. 15/3/80
Painter, William Edward, publisher 5/6/40
Pakenham *see* Conolly
Pakenham,
Arthur (1810-) 7/5/32
Frances Julia (-1894), née Peters 10/7/50 n
John, sailor 10/7/50 n
T., 2nd Earl of Longford 8/5/33 n
Thomas, Adm. Sir 7/5/32 n
Pakes,
Charles, Rev. 2/8/77
John James, rate collector 19/7/77
Pakington,
Augusta Anne, née Murray 9/4/44 ?
John Somerset, Sir (1799-1880), 1st Baronet (1846), 1st Baron Hampton (1874), tory M.P. 9/4/44 n, 16/3/52, 23/6/52, 20/3/55, 10/1/57
Paladini, C., Prof. 16/1/89

Paley, Frederick Apthorp (1815-1888), classicist 15/11/79 ?
Palgrave,
Cecil, née Milnes Gaskell 28/9/68
Francis, Sir (1788-1861), né Cohen, historian 18/3/37
Francis Turner, Rev. (1824-1897), poet 26/6/46, 30/3/60, 16/4/62, 30/4/62, 27/11/62, 16/10/63, 22/1/64, 12/2/64, 28/9/68, 29/9/68, 30/9/68, 26/9/73, 27/9/73, 28/9/73, 22/6/75, 14/10/80, 14/10/82 ff
Robert Harry Inglis, Sir (1827-1919) 12/4/74, 17/4/86 n
William Gifford (1826-1888), consul 12/2/64, 7/6/83
Palin, William, Rev. 27/12/48
Palk,
Arthur George, Rev. (1807-1835) 4/6/29
Lawrence, Sir (1818-1883), 4th Baronet (1860), 1st Baron Haldon (1880), tory M.P. 7/2/48 n
Robert John Malet (-1878), barrister 7/2/48
Pallavicini della Priola, Emilio, Marquis (1823-1910), soldier 30/4/67
Palles, Christopher, Irish solicitor general 19/1/72 n
Pallessy, Joseph 21/4/92
Palliser *see* Philips
Palmella *see* Holstein
Palmer,
Rev. Mr., photographer 21/10/89
A. M. 13/9/88
Arthur, Ven. 3/5/78
Charles Edward, Rev. (-1889) 21/12/76 ?
Charles Mark, Sir (1822-1907), 1st Baronet (1886), Newcastle shipbuilder, liberal M.P. 8/10/62, 31/8/71
Cornelius Stocker, clockmaker 30/3/76 ?
C. S. 14/3/88
Ebenezer, poet 1/2/80
Edmund, merchant 11/3/48
Edward, Ven. (1824-1895) 28/1/53, 28/8/59, 27/7/65, 9/8/81 ff, 17/8/81, 7/12/85 L
Edward Howley, banker 20/5/76
Francis B. 12/9/85
Geoffrey, Sir 16/9/41
George (-1853), tory M.P. 11/5/40
George, Col. (1799-1883) 13/1/62
George Joseph, Sir (1811-1866), 3rd Baronet 13/7/32
G. H. 19/10/75
Henry, Rev. 25/2/45
John Hinde (1808-1884), liberal M.P. 18/3/80
John Horsley, fils 24/7/76
John Horsley, père (1779-1858), governor of Bank of England 4/7/40
Joseph William, London bookseller 17/11/56
J. R., of Cannock 1/7/76
Laura (-1885), née Waldegrave, Lady Selborne 14/11/62
Philip Hall, Rev. 10/6/48
Ray, Rev., of U.S.A. 25/9/78
Roundell; Lord Selborne 18/5/31
Sophia Matilda, Lady (-1915) 10/9/88
Thomas Witherell, Senator (1830-1913) 27/4/87
William (1824-1856), the Rugeley poisoner 26/5/56
William Jocelyn, Rev. (1778-1853) 18/10/29
William (of Magdalen), Rev. (1811-1879), theologian and convert to Rome 27/3/33
William (of Worcester), Rev. Sir (1803-1885), theologian; author of the *Treatise* 7/11/42, 19/11/66 ?, 21/11/66 ?, 9/11/82, 21/11/83 L
Palmer, Mackillop, Dent & Co., East India merchants 11/3/48 n
Palmerston *see* Temple
Palumbo, Raffaele, Prof. 7/12/77, 4/1/78
Pamphili, Giovanni Andrea Doria, Prince (1779-1838) 10/3/32
Pamphilji, Emily, née Clinton, Duchess d'Avigliano 23/7/81
Pana, Cremidi & Co., merchants 18/7/64
Panchaud,
Edouard 13/1/77 ?
Robert Augustus, china dealer 1/3/80
Panelli, Domenico, Abp., archbishop of Lydda 13/3/75
Panizzi, Anthony, Sir 4/11/42
Pankhurst,
Emmeline, Mrs. (1858-1928), suffragette 11/6/66 n
Richard Marsden, Dr. (1836-1898), barrister 11/6/66, 17/8/74
Panmure *see* Ramsay
Pano, Mr., London merchant 18/7/64
Pantaleoni, Diomede, Dr., Italian politician 21/6/51
Panter, John 15/4/74
Panterich, L.de 5/9/91
Papalettere, Simplicio, Abate (1815-1883), abbot of Monte Cassino (1858) 19/10/66, 24/10/66
Papanicolas, Georgios Dracatos, author 17/10/51
Papasso, L., of Ionia 3/11/58
Papautonopolos, S. 29/11/76
Papazian, S., Armenian delegate 2/2/78
Papengouth, M. 7/12/76
Papucci, Mr. 9/3/91
Papworth, Edgar George (1809-1866), sculptor 6/6/64

Paraden, J. H. 27/4/88
Paradice, John, bookbinder 1/3/77 ff
Parasurakis, S. A. 28/8/78
Paraviso, Benno, Birmingham agent 8/10/55 ?
Parde, A., Sig. 2/1/88
Pares, John (1833-1915) 1/8/77 ?
Pareto, Vilfredo Federico (1848-1923), Marchese di Pareto, economist 30/4/92
Parham,
C. J. 5/5/77, 16/5/78
J. 8/1/87
Parieu, E., of Paris 6/7/61, 2/3/66
Parini, George Edward, of Genoa 11/1/87, 12/1/88, 21/10/91
Paris *see* Orléans
Paris,
F. T. 8/11/75
John Ayrton, Dr. (1785-1856), President, College of Physicians 30/7/51 n
Parish,
Dorothy ['Dossie'] Mary Catherine (1890-1983), née Drew, G's grand-daughter 18/3/90, 27/6/91, 12/4/92, 5/6/92, 17/12/92, 28/9/93, 2/2/94, 23/2/94, 10/5/94
John, of Kingswinford 30/4/50 ?
Parisot, J. 6/6/59
Park,
Fletcher 18/7/79
James Alan, Sir (1763-1833) 26/4/34
J. N. 20/5/78
John, Prof. (-1913), of Belfast 1/5/79
Parke *see* Ridley
Parke,
Cecilia Arabella Frances, Lady, née Barlow, Lady Wensleydale 4/5/36
James, Judge Sir (1782-1868), 1st Baron Wensleydale (1856) 17/1/35, 4/5/36 n
John Duke, police inspector 11/5/53
Thomas Heazle (1857-1893), surgeon, explorer 23/5/92
Parker *see* Cardwell, Hamilton, Mackenzie
Parker,
Albert Edmund (1843-1905), 3rd Earl of Morley (1864), liberal 11/3/68, 10/4/86 L
Charles 17/9/27 n
Charles, Mrs. 17/9/27
Charles Stuart, fils (1829-1910), liberal M.P., editor of Peel's *Papers* 24/8/58 n, 24/1/76 ff, 7/1/84, 4/12/86, 7/4/89, 4/10/90, 23/4/91, 13/6/92
Charles Stuart, Père 24/8/58
Harriet, née Brooke 17/1/40 n
Henry, solicitor 30/7/74 ?
John (-1881), whig M.P. 14/3/43
John Henry (1806-1884), publisher in Oxford 13/6/36 ?, 12/8/62, 16/8/62, 27/8/62, 30/8/62, 8/9/62, 11/9/62, 6/11/63, 12/10/69, 6/10/70, 4/1/73, 7/1/73, 18/6/75, 2/7/75, 17/9/76, 19/9/76
John William, publisher 28/11/44 n, 1/11/60, 3/11/60, 10/10/69
Joseph, Rev. Dr. (1830-1902), Congregationalist 11/5/87, 7/7/88
Robert Townley (1793-1879), tory M.P. 17/1/40
W. G., photographer 12/10/69 ?
Parker, Hayes, Barnwell & Twisden, solicitors 2/6/52
Parkes,
Harry Smith, Sir (1828-1885), diplomat 17/4/62
Henry, Sir (1815-1896), Australian free trade politician 17/4/82
Joseph (1796-1865), radical politician and parliamentary solicitor 17/6/43 n
Parkhouse, Samuel Henry, poor rate collector 31/10/79
Parkins, William T. 1/7/74
Parkinson,
John, solicitor 27/11/47
Richard, Canon (1797-1858) 29/3/38
Parkinson & Son, dentists 4/12/27
Parks, King 9/11/83
Parmington, rescue 2/3/67
Parminter, William George, Rev. 18/4/57
Parnell *see* Evans
Parnell,
Anna, Miss 2/9/81
Charles Stewart 26/10/77 n
Henry Brooke, Sir (1776-1842), 1st Baron Congleton (1841), political economist, whig M.P. 1/8/37
J., of Southport 9/11/68
John Howard, barrister 10/6/87 ?
Katharine, Mrs. 18/9/80 n
Paronelli, Sig. 22/3/90
Parr,
J. T., Rev. 21/10/86
Thomas, Liverpool painter 6/1/29
Thomas C. (1804-), Indian civil servant 16/5/26
Parratt, Walter, Sir (1841-1924), organist 12/12/62 ff, 3/3/94
Parrish, W. G. 20/8/90
Parrott, Richard, Rev. 17/8/68
Parry,
Charles Hubert Hastings, Sir (1848-1918), composer 30/8/66
Edward, Bp. (1830-1890) 14/7/57 ?
Elizabeth Jones-, Lady 4/7/71
Elizabeth Maud, Lady (-1933), née Herbert 30/8/66, 25/6/72
F. W., Rev. 11/1/78 ?
H. A. 23/3/76

Parry (*cont.*)
Joseph Markham, Rev. 27/6/41
Neville, Rev. 23/10/68
Parton 7/9/75, 2/11/78
Samuel 27/6/79
Thomas Love Duncombe Jones-, Sir (1832–1891), 1st Baronet (1886), liberal M.P. 4/7/71 n
Parry & Co., publishers 9/7/50
Parry & Garnham 26/6/74 ?, 19/12/78
Parsons,
Miss 9/5/89
C. E. 1/12/76
Edward F., Rev. 10/7/45
Frederick Thomas, Capt. 11/11/62 ?
Henry, Rev. 3/5/77 ?
T. W. 19/8/75
William (1800–1867), Baron Oxmantown (1807), 3rd Earl of Rosse (1841), whig M.P., astronomer 21/6/33 n
Parsons & Best, wine merchants 5/8/63 ?
Partington, Henry, Rev. 7/5/68
Parton & Co., linen drapers 11/3/51
Partridge, E., rescue 13/4/62
Pascoe,
Charles E., publisher 4/11/76
Francis P. (–1893), entomologist 13/6/50
Pashley, William C., of Birkenhead 18/7/67 ?
Paskin, Charles, Commons clerk 23/12/37
Pasley, Charles William, Sir (1780–1861), of the railway department 1/4/44
Pasolini, Giuseppe, Count (1815–1876), Italian politician 28/7/63, 18/12/63
Passaglia, Carlo, Rev. 2/5/61
Passy, Hippolyte Philibert, political economist 16/9/76
Pasta, Giuditta (1798–1865), née Negri, soprano 15/6/31
Patch, John, barrister 23/3/55
Pater,
Charles Dudley, Rev. 24/9/89
Thompson 16/5/32
Walter Horatio (1839–1894), author, fellow of Brasenose, Oxford 16/5/32 n, 5/7/85
Paterson,
Messrs. 7/4/80
Miss 27/12/31 n
Mr., of U.S.A. 3/7/75
Rev. Mr., of Appin 4/2/43
A. M., of Montrose 7/12/49
George, of Castle Huntly 27/12/31 n
James (1823–1894), barrister 4/10/60 ?
John (–1855) 3/1/50
William, Edinburgh solicitor 25/11/85
Paterson & James, Messrs. 26/2/79
Paterson & Walker, involved in Oak Farm 9/12/47
Patey, J. 16/12/77
Patmore, Coventry Kersey Dighton (1823–1896), poet; mentioned for the laureatship 19/10/92 n
Paton *see* Woods
Paton,
E., Miss 24/5/28
G. 12/12/79
George, Edinburgh violinist and writing master 24/5/28 n
J. B., Rev. 15/5/79
John Brown, Rev. Dr. (1830–1911) 29/1/91
Patrick, David (1849–1914), editor, *Chambers Encyclopaedia* 30/1/90
Patten,
Anna Maria Wilson- (–1846), née Patten-Bold 16/5/34
John Wilson- (1802–1892), 1st Baron Winmarleigh (1874), tory M.P. 3/4/33, 16/5/34 n, 27/2/52, 20/9/52, 26/9/52, 27/9/52, 1/10/53, 11/6/56, 21/6/56, 30/10/56, 16/6/58, 4/10/62, 6/11/62, 24/9/67, 1/4/68, 30/9/69, 26/5/77, 13/10/84 L
Patten-Bold *see* Patten
Patterson,
C. B., of U.S.A. 8/10/83
James Laird, Bp. (1822–1902), Roman Catholic 30/11/74
John, Liverpool merchant 4/8/68 n
P. H. 16/11/90
Patteson,
Fanny, Miss 19/9/76
John, Sir (1790–1861), judge 17/1/35
Thomas, Rev. (–1874) 22/2/26
Patti, Adelina, Miss (1843–1919), opera singer 21/10/90
Pattinson, William, Rev. (1817–1891) 9/4/56
Pattison,
Frank (1834–1922) 19/7/78 ff
Mark, Rev. (1813–1884), Rector of Lincoln College, Oxford 24/5/56, 17/4/73, 8/5/75, 15/5/75, 12/3/85, 23/3/85, 29/3/85, 5/4/85
Thomas Harwood, Rev. 11/3/78
Patton,
Frederick Joseph, barrister 14/9/79 ?
George (1803–1869), Lord Glenalmond (1867), Scottish lawyer, tory M.P. 24/8/42 n, 28/9/44
Patullo, Mr. 9/9/93
Paul *see* Astor
Paul,
Charles Kegan (1828–1902), publisher and editor of Wollstonecraft 29/11/83 L
Ellen Elizabeth, Miss (–1886) 14/7/79 ?
Herbert Woodfield (1853–1935), liberal journalist and biographer of G 4/3/93
James Balfour, Sir (1846–1931) 5/6/91
William, solicitor 19/3/38

W. Y. 1/10/85
Pauliat, Louis, French historian 11/2/80 ?, 23/1/86 ?
Paulin, D., financial adviser 16/11/93
Paull,
Mrs. 12/4/90
Henry (1822-), Peelite M.P. 16/5/62
Henry John, barrister 12/4/90 n
Mary Anna, Miss 31/12/79
Paulus, Heinrich Eberhard Gottlob (1761-1851), historian 17/12/38 n
Paus, J. 30/11/74
Pawson, rescue 16/12/63
Paxton,
F., Miss 6/6/40
Joseph, Sir (1801-1865), architect 28/6/51, 31/5/60, 21/7/60, 24/7/61, 19/2/64, 22/5/65
Payen, rescue 26/4/79
Payne,
E. S. 14/10/90
H. S., Rev. 27/12/76 ?
Peter Samuel Henry (1810-1841), Fellow of Balliol College, Oxford 18/3/30
Peabody,
George (-1869), American financier 12/11/69
G. F. 18/4/89
Peace, Thomas, Bailie (1832-1892), of Kirkwall, Orkney 13/9/83
Peachey, Alfred 20/10/78 ?
Peacock,
Mr., of Hawarden 29/10/67
Anthony Taylor 8/9/37
Barnes, Sir (1810-1890), lawyer 2/6/70
John S., Middlesbrough town clerk 21/9/62
M. H., Rev., nonconformist 17/5/89
Thomas Love (1785-1866), novelist 10/12/41
Peake,
A., Miss, of Hawarden 21/2/76, 28/11/76
J. M. 3/3/79
Thomas Cross, Rev. (1817-1889) 14/4/55
Pearce,
Miss 13/12/76
George, underwriter 24/3/48
Katie, Miss 13/11/88 n
S. 28/9/75
Samuel 21/1/54
T. W. 26/1/78
W. H. 12/4/74, 13/11/88
Peard, John Whitehead, Col. (1811-1880) 8/8/61
Peare & Nashes 3/12/66
Pearman, John 21/6/41 ?
Pears,
Messrs. 13/9/81
Mr., of Whitby 3/7/68
William T., Liverpool lawyer 11/4/74
Pears, Logan and Eden, Liverpool solicitors 11/4/74 n, 3/8/74
Pearsall, Mrs., rescue 28/10/59, 3/1/60
Pearson,
Miss, the Gladstones' governess (1851) 20/3/52
Charles Henry (1830-1894), historian 13/3/58
Edward, of Wilmslow 4/7/92
Edwin, publishers 10/5/78 ?
Edwin, Sir (1802-1883) 7/11/31 ?
E. P. 31/5/78
George, Rev. (1791-1860) 6/10/56
George Charles, Canon 1/6/79
J., of Birkdale 7/5/57, 17/8/61 ?
Justly, Liverpool attorney 1/10/56
Karl (1857-1937), eugenicist 24/3/90 ?
Mary Martha, née Dutton, artist 15/7/48 ?
Thomas Hooke (-1892), soldier 3/11/49 ?
W. B. 9/7/79
Peart, Robert, Newark ropemaker 7/12/32
Pease,
Mr. 31/8/73
Alfred Edward (1857-1939), liberal M.P. 4/4/89 ?
Henry (1807-1881), liberal M.P. 15/9/57
John Whitwell, Sir (1828-1903), 1st Baronet (1882), liberal M.P. 5/1/86, 9/4/86, 15/5/86 L, 21/5/86 L, 4/6/86, 2/7/87, 22/6/93 n, 25/7/93 ff, 16/2/94 L
Joseph (1799-1872), liberal M.P. 2/4/38
Peat,
David, Adm., of Edinburgh 23/9/64 ?
John, Rev. (1809-1871) 8/6/67
Peaton, R., Rev. 1/7/76
Peccheneda, Gaetano, Chief of Police, Naples 9/2/51
Peck, Kenrick, Rev. (1769-1837) 12/1/34
Peckey, Mr. 19/7/66
Peckover, E. J. 15/3/89
Pedder, Wilson, Rev. 13/3/55
Peddie,
Euphemia L., Mrs. 1/2/78 ?
John Dick (1824-1885), liberal M.P. 1/2/78 n
R. 13/9/89
Peddle, Mr. 10/4/76
Pedro II (1825-1891), Emperor of Brazil 19/7/71, 21/7/71, 24/7/71, 27/6/77, 6/2/88
Pedro V (1837-1861), King of Portugal 18/6/54
Peek, Henry William, Sir (1825-1898), 1st Baronet (1874), tory M.P. 2/5/71
Peel *see* Barton, Brandling, Dawson, Stonor
Peel,
Alicia Jane, Lady (-1887), née Kennedy 6/7/52
Arthur George Villiers (1868-1956) 1/2/90

Peel (*cont.*)
Arthur Wellesley; (Speaker) 25/7/62
Edmund (-1850), whig M.P. 1/2/52 n
Edmund (1826-1903), of Brynypys, Flintshire 21/7/52
Frederick, Sir (1823-1906), liberal M.P. 12/7/49
John 4/5/50
Jonathan (1779-1879), tory M.P., racehorse owner 8/1/35 n, 16/7/76
Julia (-1859), née Floyd, Lady Peel, wife of the Prime Minister 20/2/35, 19/5/51
Lawrence, Sir (1799-1884) 14/11/72
Robert, Sir; (Prime Minister) 5/2/29
Robert, Sir (1822-1895), 3rd Baronet (1850), voted for home rule (1886), Peelite/tory M.P. 3/7/49, 2/8/61, 26/7/71, 19/3/75, 23/6/86 L
William Yates (1789-1858), tory M.P. 24/1/35

Peers,
Charles (-1853), sheriff 25/4/50 ?
Charles, Rev. (1811-1858) 13/6/57

Peffani, George, of Rotherhithe 3/9/74 ?

Peirce, Benjamin, Prof. (1809-1880), of U.S.A. 1/11/70

Pelham,
Charles Anderson- (1835-1875), 3rd Earl of Yarborough (1862), liberal M.P. 10/11/59
Charles Anderson Worsley Anderson- (1809-1862), 2nd Earl of Yarborough (1846), Baron Worsley, whig M.P. 12/4/42, 18/6/45 n
George, Bp. (1766-1827), bishop of Lincoln (1820), confirmed G (1827) 1/2/27
Henry Francis, Prof. (1846-1907) 31/1/90 ff
Henry Thomas (1804-1886), 3rd Earl of Chichester (1826), cavalryman 5/3/36
John Cressett, whig M.P. 22/5/32 n
John Thomas, Bp. (1811-1894) 5/6/68
Thomas Henry William, boundary commissioner 28/11/84

Pelham-Clinton *see* D'Eyncourt, Ricketts

Pellat, Fortunatus, & Co., brokers 16/5/78

Pellatt, Apsley (1791-1863), liberal M.P. 4/8/53

Pellegrini, Sig. 23/10/70

Pellet,
Mr., consul 29/6/75, 16/10/77
Gustavus, Mons. 4/6/90, 7/6/90

Pellew,
Edward (1811-1876), 3rd Viscount Exmouth (1833) 23/5/38
George, Dean (1793-1866), dean of Norwich (1828) 13/3/57

Pelliccioni, G., Prof., of Bologna 13/8/88

Pells, S. F. 10/9/91

Pelly,
John Henry, Sir, 2nd Baronet 24/6/43
John Henry, Sir (1777-1852), 1st Baronet (1840), explorer, governor of Hudson's Bay 26/11/42, 24/6/43
Lewis, Sir (1825-1892) 10/12/78 n

Pelton, W., employee of *Hansard* 8/9/55

Pemberton, Edward O., customs clerk 26/2/45 ?

Pembroke *see* Herbert

Pena, Manuel de la, Mexican politician 25/2/45 ?

Pender,
John, Sir (1815-1896), Knight (1888), liberal (unionist) M.P., telegraph promoter 27/2/65, 27/4/75, 14/3/79, 29/4/80, 12/12/80, 28/12/92, 29/12/92
Thomas, Comptroller of Taxes 26/10/48 n

Pendlebury, W. H. 1/11/78

Pendleton,
Edmund C., Canon (-1846) 22/11/39
Henrietta (1792-1875), née Benson, philanthropist 22/11/39 n

Penel, J. B. 9/6/90

Penfold,
George Saxby, Rev. Dr. 16/2/41
John Sandys, barrister 2/2/36 ?

Pengelly, William (1812-1894), geologist 24/11/64

Penistan, Joseph, Rev. (1819-1893) 9/5/79

Penleaze, John, Rev. 15/2/76

Penn,
H. 18/9/78, 20/10/89
John (1805-1878), ship engineer at Greenwich 3/2/63

Penna, Frederic 29/3/78

Pennack, W., wine merchant 9/10/78

Pennant,
Edward Gordon Douglas-, Col. (1800-1886), 1st Baron Penrhyn (1866), tory M.P. 21/9/55 n
Eleanor Frances Susan Douglas- (-1919) 16/9/61 ?
Emma Julia Sophia Douglas- (-1909) 16/9/61 ?
George Sholto Gordon Douglas- (1836-1907), 2nd Baron Penrhyn (1886), C. G's nephew-by-marriage 24/9/50 n, 13/8/75, 16/8/75, 21/10/75, 18/1/76, 19/1/76, 11/8/91, 18/8/91, 23/8/91
Gertrude Jessy Douglas- (-1940), née Glynne, Lady Penrhyn, C. G's niece 24/9/50, 21/6/74, 22/6/74 ff, 16/8/75, 19/8/75, 21/8/75, 6/9/75, 7/9/75, 8/10/75, 21/10/75, 18/1/76 n

Pennefather,
Edward (1774-1847), Irish judge 8/5/44
Richard (1808-1849), barrister, Irish undersecretary 23/6/48

Pennell, Charles Henry, Sir (1805–1898), of the admiralty 28/7/66
Pennethorne, James, Sir (1801–1877), Knight (1870), architect 9/6/47
Pennington *see* Lindsay
Pennington,
Constance, née L'Estrange, Lady Muncaster 27/4/70 n
E., actor 18/11/76
Edward, colonial office clerk 26/6/43
George James, civil list auditor 21/4/54
John (1737–1813), 1st Baron Muncaster (1783) 20/10/49 n
Josslyn Francis (1834–1917), 5th Baron Muncaster (1862) 27/4/70 n
W. H. (1831–1923), actor 23/9/70, 27/4/83
Penny,
Mrs. 26/7/92
Charles William, Rev. 1/4/76, 20/7/84
Penrhyn *see* Pennant
Penrose,
John, Rev. 15/7/76 ?
W. 2/7/80
Penruddocke, John, Rev., of Hungerford 24/4/89 ?
Pentini, Francesco, Cardinal 4/12/66
Pentney, rescue 1/7/68
Penzance *see* Wilde
Pepoli, Gioacchino Napoleone, Marquis (1825–1881), Italian politician and economist 23/11/64
Pepper, Mr. 1/8/77
Peppercorn, F. 4/3/79
Pepys,
Caroline Elizabeth (–1868), née Baker, Lady Cottenham 3/3/54
Charles Christopher (–1851), 3rd Earl of Cottenham 3/3/54 n
Perceval,
Alexander, Colonel, Sergeant at Arms 12/9/44
Arthur Philip, Rev. (1799–1853), Royal Chaplain 23/1/36
C. G., 2nd Baron Arden 23/1/36 n
Dudley Montagu, pamphleteer 3/4/45, 7/2/48
John, of Canterbury 26/2/58
Percival, E. 24/7/78
Percy,
17/8/81, 25/10/83
rescue 13/6/79
Algernon (1792–1865), 4th Duke of Northumberland (1847) 6/3/52 n
Algernon George (1810–1899), 6th Duke of Northumberland (1867), Lord Lovaine 14/6/47 n, 16/2/66, 13/5/76, 17/6/76 ff, 4/10/76
Charles Greatheed Bertie (1794–1870) 28/9/60
Charlotte F., Lady, née Clive, Duchess of Northumberland 21/5/41
Cornelius McLeod 19/3/77 ?
Edith (–1913), née Campbell, Lady Percy, Duchess of Northumberland 23/12/68 n
Eleanor, née Leveson-Gower, Duchess of Northumberland 6/3/52
Emma Barbara (–1877), née Galbraith 21/10/47 ?
George, 2nd Earl of Beverley, 5th Duke of Northumberland 17/6/43 n
Henry, Rev. (1813–1870) 21/10/47 n
Hugh (1785–1847), 3rd Duke of Northumberland 21/5/41 n
John, Prof. (1817–1889), director, School of Mines 17/6/68, 18/6/77
Josceline William (1811–1881), tory M.P. 24/6/53
Louisa (1813–1890), née Drummond, Lady Lovaine, Duchess of Northumberland 14/6/47, 13/5/56, 18/6/76 ff, 2/10/76 ?
Louisa Harcourt, née Stuart-Wortley, Lady Beverley, Duchess of Northumberland 17/6/43
William Henry, customs commissioner 27/11/44
Péreire, Isaac, French financier 16/3/65
Perfect, James, of Newark 16/4/79
Périer,
Auguste Casimir Victor Laurent 27/4/64
Casimir-Pierre (1777–1832), French premier 21/7/32
Perigal, F. 13/8/89
Perkins,
C. H. 8/1/87
Charles, Leeds solicitor 7/2/39 ?
James, customs officer in Toxteth 29/12/57
Perks,
Charles, bookseller 24/3/55
C. S. 26/10/86
Robert William, Sir (1849–1934), 1st Baronet (1908), solicitor, methodist, liberal M.P. 30/7/90, 23/6/92
Pernolet, Arthur, French deputy 8/12/77
Perowne, Edward Henry, Rev. (1826–1906) 12/9/67, 5/1/70
Perrier, Anthony George, Consul at Brest 7/8/43
Perrin,
Mr. (1814–1885), actor 16/10/79
William, of Newcastle 25/11/74
Perrins, E. H., Messrs., Liverpool brokers 16/6/45 ?
Perronnet, Amélie, née Bernoux, author 28/1/67 ?
Perrott, Frank Duerin, Rev. 21/9/91
Perry,
rescue 24/11/70
Mrs., lodging house keeper 10/3/51

Perry (*cont.*)
Charles, Bp. (1807–1891), bishop of Melbourne (1847) 20/6/43
E. C. 10/4/88
Edward Bindloss, Sir (1784–1859), 2nd Baronet (1796) 3/3/58
F. J. 17/11/75
Jevon James Muschamp, Rev. 7/12/89
Samuel Gideon Frederick, Rev. (–1881) 26/3/59
Thomas Erskine, Judge Sir (–1882), judge and liberal M.P. 12/7/53, 21/3/76
Thomas Walter, Rev. 13/8/51
William, dentist in Everton 1/9/29
W. Warring, of Tranmere 3/4/57
Persia, Grand Vizir of 9/9/92
Persigny *see* Fialin
Perth *see* Drummond
Pery *see* Russell
Pessalenti, Dr. 17/1/78
Petavel, Emmanuel, Dr. (1836–1910) 24/8/76
Peter,
D. M. 17/5/34
John Thomas Henry (1810–1883) 13/8/33 n
William (1788–1853), whig M.P. 13/8/33, 17/5/34
Peterkin, Alexander, archivist of Church of Scotland 23/3/39
Peters *see* Pakenham
Peters,
Mr. 16/2/86
Michael Nowell, Rev. (–1880) 28/3/51 ?
S. 21/6/78
S., secretary of Workmen's National Association 8/6/87
Peterson,
Mr. 27/6/62
R. E. 12/5/76
Petgrave, Ezekiel Charles, solicitor 22/11/79
Petheram, John, bookseller 25/11/43
Petherick, James, newsagent 2/11/78
Petite Marseillaise,, editor of 26/2/83
Petleybridge, Mr. 26/12/56
Peto, Samuel Morton, Sir (1809–1889), 1st Baronet (1855), liberal M.P., railway constructor 12/1/52, 26/7/62
Petre,
William Bernard (1817–1884), 12th Baron Petre (1850) 16/6/68
William H. F., 11th Baron Petre (1809) 11/5/46
Petrie,
C. S., Mrs. 12/7/75
F. 10/12/74
Francis W. H., Capt. 30/11/85 ?
James, Rev. 18/5/78
Petrocchi, P., Manzoni scholar 30/1/87
Petroni, Sig. 20/2/91
Petrovich, Georges T. 15/6/77 ?
Petrowsky, A. Roslansky, of Kharkhoff 20/8/60
Petrucci, Sig., bookseller in Rome 13/12/38
Pett, Phineas, Ven. (1756–1830), Archdeacon of Oxford 22/12/29
Petta, Sig. 17/5/62
Pettifer, H. J., pamphleteer 6/12/77
Pettigrew, Mrs. 19/7/78
Pettingell, John Hancock, American author 17/4/58 ?
Peyton, James, of Royal Exchange Assurance 17/3/58
Pezzo,
Angelia del, née Caracciolo, Duchess of Caianiello 23/12/50 n
Gaetano del, Duke of Caianiello 23/12/50
Pfeiffer,
Mrs. 23/1/82
Emily Jane, Miss (1827–1890), poet 31/12/79
Phardys, N. B. 9/1/86
Phear, John Budd, Sir (1825–1905) 18/6/89
Phelan, Patrick, Rev., Roman Catholic 20/9/77
Phelps,
Joseph Lloyd, canal clerk in Birmingham 21/4/53
Samuel (1804–1878), actor 19/11/64
Phenix, R. A., Rev. 6/11/79
Philadelphia and Reading Railway Co. 21/7/82
Philipp, Messrs. 11/8/87
Philipps, James Erasmus, Rev. Sir (1824–1912) 10/1/77 ?, 4/6/83
Philips *see* Duncan, Scourfield
Philips,
Frederick Charles, Lieut. Col. 30/1/41
George Richard, Sir (1789–1883), 2nd Baronet (1844), whig M.P. 10/3/54
Margaret Jane, née Palliser 27/12/44
Mark (1800–1873), whig M.P. 3/6/44
Robert Needham (1815–1890), liberal M.P. 13/11/65, 8/1/68
Phillimore,
Charles Bagot (–1894) 30/5/79
Charlotte Ann (–1892), née Denison, wife of R. J. Phillimore 9/10/44 n
Elizabeth (–1859), née Bagot 2/2/33
John George (1808–1865), jurist 9/8/28 ?
Joseph, Prof. (1775–1855), regius professor of civil law, Oxford 13/7/35
Lucy, nurse 6/11/95
Robert Joseph, Judge Sir 16/5/26
Walter George Frank, Sir (1845–1929), 2nd Baronet (1885), international jurist 14/7/46, 9/10/82, 18/7/86 ff, 9/10/86, 21/6/88, 22/5/89, 20/6/91, 29/11/93, 29/4/94, 12/10/95

Phillip, John (1817–1867), artist 4/12/61, 21/3/62, 28/3/62, 11/3/63
Phillipps,
Mrs. 16/4/26
James Orchard Halliwell- (1820–1889), bibliographer and archivist 11/4/65
Thomas, Sir (1792–1872), 1st Baronet (1821), bibliophile 17/6/58
Trenham W., secretary, wood and works department 5/6/47
Phillips,
rescue 17/10/59
rescue 20/7/88
Mr., pianist 12/1/33
Benjamin Samuel, Sir (1811-1889) 15/3/80
Francis Robert, Rev. (1812–1862) 6/3/39 n
Frederick, London solicitor 18/10/58
G. A. W., Prof. 13/2/58
George, Rev. (1804–1892), orientalist 13/4/34 ?
George Lort (1811–1866), tory M.P. 4/7/66
Henry (1801–1876), bass player 23/12/25
Henry Wyndham (1820–1868), artist 23/6/47
James, spiritualist 8/4/77
J. Scott, Major 28/6/79
S. R. 10/12/61
William Davies, Rev. 16/8/47
William Joseph George, Rev. (1778–1855) 6/3/39 ?
William Spencer, Rev. (–1863) 19/5/51, 13/3/52
Phillips, Richard & Co., auctioneers 19/2/67
'Phillips' and 'Barton' *see* Sinclair
Phillips and Favenc, Messrs., ale merchants 7/11/43
Phillott,
Henry Wright, Rev. 24/7/78
James Russell, Rev. (–1865) 26/2/50
Phillpotts,
Henry, Bp. (1778–1869), bishop of Exeter (1830) 22/3/33, 6/2/36, 26/3/36, 14/3/37, 16/5/37, 9/6/40, 12/5/46, 22/10/49, 7/2/50, 26/4/50, 19/3/51, 13/11/71
J. S. 16/12/74
Thomas, Canon (1807–1890) 16/5/26
Philpott, Henry, Bp. (1807–1892), bishop of Worcester (1860) 9/8/65
Phinn, Thomas (1814–1866), barrister, liberal M.P. 21/2/54
Phippen, Serjeant 25/12/75
Phipps,
Charles Beaumont, Col. Sir (1801–1866), Prince Albert's private secretary 17/10/53
Constantine Charles Henry, Rev. (1846–1932), 3rd Marquis of Normanby (1890), Baron Mulgrave 26/8/71
Constantine Henry, Sir (1797–1863), 1st Marquis of Normanby (1838), Baron Mulgrave 31/12/40
Edmund 8/2/41 ?
George Augustus Constantine, Sir (1819–1890), 2nd Marquis of Normanby (1863), Baron Mulgrave, liberal M.P. 28/2/56
Harriet Lepel, Miss, Maid of Honour 28/9/63
J. 30/7/34 n
William Hugh, Capt., R. N. 14/4/79
Phipson, E. A. 27/8/90
Phythian, A. T. 10/11/91
Piché, E., Rev. 26/8/87
Pichereau 11/6/64
Pichler, Louisa, author 19/8/91 ?
Pickard,
Lieut. 6/5/71
Benjamin (1842–1904), liberal M.P., mining trade union leader 25/3/76, 18/2/90 n, 7/6/93, 14/7/93 L, 13/11/93 c
Pickering,
Messrs. 24/9/88
Edward Hayes (1807–1852), assistant master, Eton 11/2/26
John, auctioneer in Chester 18/5/57 ?
P. A., lawyer 14/1/74
Percival André, recorder of Pontefract 29/4/26
William Percival (–1905), barrister 21/5/49
Pickersgill,
Henry William (1782–1875), artist 13/7/50
John William 3/5/76 ?
Pickford, Rev. Mr. 25/11/85
Pickles, James, of U.S.A. 29/8/89
Pickwoad, Miss, of the household 3/2/49
Picot, P., Prof. 15/7/32 ?
Picton, James Allanson, Sir (1805–1889), Knight (1881), antiquary and architect in Liverpool 1/3/65
Piddock, Mr. 5/2/70
Pierce,
E. L. 4/11/80
J. T., barrister 18/3/74
W. 28/8/79
Piercy,
B. 23/10/67
John Morpott William, Rev. (1816–1902) 28/4/38 ?
Pieritz, George Wildon, Rev. (–1884) 8/2/80
Pierrepont,
Charles Evelyn (1805–1850), Viscount Newark 28/6/36
Charles Herbert (1778–1860), 2nd Earl Manvers (1816), Viscount Newark, whig M.P. 28/6/36 n, 11/6/38
Edwards, Judge (1817–1892), American jurist and diplomat 27/7/76, 8/6/81, 13/10/87

Pierrepont (*cont.*)
Emily (-1851), née Walhouse, Lady Newark 28/6/36 n
Mary Letitia (1784-1860), née Eyre, Lady Manvers 11/6/38
Sydney William Herbert (1825-1900), 3rd Earl Manvers (1860) 27/9/72
Pierson, Arthur Tappan, Rev. Prof., of U.S.A. 6/11/86 ?
Pietro, Camille di, Cardinal 29/10/66
Pifferi, Paolo, teacher 17/3/32
Pigg, Mr. 3/8/66
Piggin, Henry, Rev. 4/10/77
Pigot, Alfred 26/1/76 ?
Pigott,
Miss 6/4/32
D. R. 23/2/77
E., Miss 31/7/91
Gillery, Sir (1813-1875), sergeant at law, liberal M.P. 17/6/61
Richard (1828-1889), forger of Parnell's letter 28/4/87 n, 20/2/89 n, 2/3/89 n
T. D. 16/7/77
Wellesley Pole, Rev. (1808-1890) 31/10/57
William Foster, Rev. Dr. (-1827) 7/5/26
Pigou, Francis, Rev. 9/2/66 ?
Pike,
E. M., Mrs. 9/2/87
G. D., Rev. 16/7/73
R. J. 23/8/76
Pilcher, T. W., of London 22/4/68 ?
Pilgrim, William, commission agent 20/12/56
Pilkington, Frederick P., architect 19/11/79 ff
Pillans,
Mr. 28/1/76
James, Prof. (1778-1864), educational reformer, professor of humanity, Edinburgh 27/4/60
Pillow, W. J. 4/5/78
Piltinger, Mr. 12/10/67
Pim, Jonathan (1806-1885), liberal M.P. 2/4/69, 21/11/71 L
Pimblett, Mr. 11/1/86, 8/8/87
Pinckard, G. H., company secretary 10/4/40 ?
Pincott, Mr. 21/6/78
Pindar, T. S. 3/1/80
Pinder,
John Hothersall, Rev. (1811-1868) 25/11/60
Thomas, of Newark 1/7/64
Pinelli, Bartolomeo (1781-1835), maker of terracotta figures, Rome 1/6/32
Pinero, Arthur Wing, Sir (1855-1934), dramatist 25/6/84
Pinfield, W. H., Liverpool accountant 30/10/55
Pink,
Mr. 20/8/79
H. 17/8/89
Pinkney, John, of Newark 11/5/41
Pinney, Charles (1793-1867), mayor of Bristol 1/11/32 n
Pinnock, William (1782-1843), educationalist, speculator 9/5/35
Pinto, D. 26/11/88
Piotrowski, Rufin, Russian exile 23/5/47 ?
Piper,
A. 5/8/76
F. 29/12/86
Frederick, reporter 25/11/79
Karl Edouard, Swedish ambassador in Turin 4/3/59 n
R. Y. 5/1/78
Pirie,
Mrs., rescue 2/3/78
John, Sir, Lord mayor of London 9/11/41
William Robson, Rev. Dr. (1804-1885), presbyterian 14/11/56
Pironneau, Armand, French lawyer 8/1/92
Pironti, Michele, judge in Naples 13/2/51
Pirouti, Count 4/2/89
Piry, Capt. 31/5/89
Pisani,
Sig., shopkeeper of alabaster 26/3/32, 2/10/38
J. 11/11/75 ?
Piselli, Sig. 8/10/75
Pistrucci,
Signora, of Rome 1/1/67
Benedetto (1784-1855), engraver and coin-designer 12/12/42, 5/6/54
Pitcairn,
J. J. 13/6/79
T., Rev. 26/8/44
Pitkethlie, Mr. 15/11/87
Pitkin, Mr. 22/1/86
Pitman,
Frederick, publisher 17/4/76 ?
Henry 17/5/78 ?
Henry Alfred, Sir (1808-1908), physician 3/7/83
John Rogers, Rev. (1782-1861), author 2/4/38
Pitra, Giovanni Batista, Cardinal 16/10/66
Pitt *see* Grenville, Hay
Pitt, A. 26/12/76
Pittis, Miss 2/10/37
Pittock, Mr., of Deal 29/10/69
Pius IX, Pope (1792-1878) 12/10/66
Pius VII, Pope (1742-1823) 22/2/32
Pixell, Charles Henry Vincent, Rev. 31/8/91
Pizzala & Co., alabaster shop 5/7/52
Place,
Francis (1771-1854), radical author 30/6/35
M. W. 13/5/67
Placidi, Miagio 23/10/76
Planché, James Robinson (1796-1880), antiquary, dramatist 26/5/74

Plant, William, auctioneer 14/11/78 ?
Planta, Joseph (1787-1847), diplomat 25/11/43
Plat, A. Du 6/8/91
Platen, Baltzar Julius Ernst von, Count (1804-1874) 26/3/60
Plater, Charles Eaton, Rev. (1798-1854), of Marlborough College 10/10/39
Platt,
 George, Rev. (1807-1883) 10/4/56
 John T. (1817-1878), Oldham engineer, liberal M.P. 22/7/65, 5/1/66, 17/12/67, 14/3/70 L
 Thomas Pell, librarian 7/8/47
Player, Horatio, London watchmaker 12/3/47 ?
Playfair,
 Elliot Minto, Gen. (1828-1899) 10/12/88
 Lyon, Prof. Sir (1818-1898), Knight (1883), 1st Baron Playfair (1892), chemist, liberal M.P. and minister 15/11/59, 23/12/61, 14/5/63, 26/9/72, 26/10/72, 18/3/73 c, 12/11/73, 25/5/81, 4/8/82 L, 12/12/84, 3/2/86 ff, 15/7/86, 14/5/87, 11/2/90 ff, 18/3/91, 11/4/91, 16/6/92
Plimsoll,
 D. 13/8/77
 Samuel (1824-1898), liberal M.P. 30/3/67, 22/2/73 n, 1/3/73 c, 18/5/73 c, 26/7/75 n, 9/4/80, 13/4/80
Plini, G. B., of Naples 11/11/89
Plowden,
 Mr. 23/11/70
 George, Mrs. 3/3/45 ?
Plowden & Chomely, Rome bankers 12/10/66
Pluggers, C. T. 14/7/68
Plumptre,
 Frederick Charles, Rev. 5/6/48
 John Francis (1781-1864) 18/9/25
 John Pemberton (1791-1864), tory M.P. 24/5/34
Plumptre & Brodrick, solicitors 9/2/48 ?
Plumridge, James Hanaway, Sir (1787-1863), whig M.P. 1/7/37 n
Plumtre *see* Ramsden
Plunket *see* Conyngham
Plunket,
 David Robert (1838-1919), 1st Baron Rathmore (1895) 23/10/77 ?
 William Conyngham (1764-1854), 1st Baron Plunket (1827), lord chancellor 8/3/27
Plunkett,
 Arthur James (1819-1881), 10th Earl of Fingall (1869) 15/4/70
 Edward, Capt. (1808-1889), 16th Baron of Dunsany (1852) 30/1/50 n, 8/5/50
 Francis Richard, Sir (1835-1907), diplomat 31/5/93
Pobyedonostsv, K. P., Russian theocratic apologist, translated *Bulgarian Atrocities* into Russian 8/9/76 n
Pochin, Mrs. 7/2/40
Pocklington *see* Campbell
Pocklington,
 Jane, née Campbell 12/1/31
 Mary 12/1/31
 Roger, Colonel (1778-1847) 12/1/31
Pocock,
 George, of Southwark 12/7/66
 Nicholas, Rev. (1814-1897), Oxford historian 29/1/49, 22/2/83
Podasta, Baron 23/1/88
Podmore,
 Mr., of Hawarden 14/1/65
 Mrs., of Hawarden 27/8/64
Poerio,
 Baron 11/1/89
 Carlo, Baron (1803-1867), Neapolitan liberal and prisoner 4/1/51, 13/2/51, 14/12/53 n, 18/12/53, 31/3/59, 11/4/59, 21/4/59, 12/1/67, 14/1/67
Pohlmann, Mrs. 13/10/88
Poisson, Jeanne Antoinette (1721-1764), Marquise de Pompadour, mistress of Louis XV 20/2/32
Pole *see* Fane
Pole,
 Edward S. Chandos, soldier 5/4/48
 William, Dr. (1814-1900), musician 21/11/76 ?
Pole-Carew *see* Eliot
Poles, Stephan (1847-1875), agitator 26/9/66 ?
Polignac, Armand de (1817-1890), Duc de Polignac 29/2/52
Polita, Antonio, of Ionia 2/12/58
Politmore *see* Bampfylde
Politti, Sig., china dealer in Rome 15/11/66
Pollard,
 Alfred William (1859-1944), historian 10/1/87, 8/11/89
 James 16/10/87, 5/11/87
 William (1815-1871), liberal M.P., economist 19/2/45
 William (1828-1893), secretary, Manchester peace society 25/11/76
Pollen,
 Elizabeth Boileau-, née Hall 18/11/38 n
 George Boileau-, Rev. (1798-1847) 18/11/38
 John, of Dublin 14/3/72 ?
 John Hungerford, Rev. (-1902) 5/6/53 ?
Pollington *see* Savile
Pollitt, Mr. 20/11/91
Pollock,
 Mrs. 5/11/67
 Frederick Montagu-, Sir (1815-1874), 2nd Baronet (1872) 10/10/72

Pollock (*cont.*)
Jonathan Frederick, Sir (1783–1870), jurist 8/1/35 n
Pollok, Robert, Rev. (–1827) 29/11/35
Polson,
Archer, legal author 2/9/56
W. G., barrister 27/4/35 ?
Polwarth *see* Scott
Polwhele, Robert, Rev. (1810–1877) 4/1/75
Pomeroy, Henry Sterling, Dr. (1848–1917), American writer on divorce 23/10/88, 4/8/90
Pommaris, Mr., author 2/12/90
Pompadour *see* Poisson
Pompeo, Niccola de, banker in Naples 4/5/52
Pond, James Burton, Major (1838–1903), of U.S.A., offers G £4000 to lecture 20/8/79
Ponsford, Mr. 27/1/75
Ponsonby *see* Montgomery
Ponsonby,
Alberta Victoria, Miss 6/10/75 ?
Barbara, Miss 26/1/82, 2/1/86, 9/3/87, 21/3/87, 9/9/89, 15/3/90, 20/3/92
Charles Frederick Ashley Cooper, 2nd Baron de Mauley (1855) 30/4/61 n
F. 27/10/77
F., 3rd Earl of Bessborough 28/11/37 n
Frances Charlotte, Lady (1812–1835), née Lambton 3/7/36 n
Frederick George Brabazon (1815–1895), 6th Earl of Bessborough (1880) 3/7/72 L, 23/8/81 L, 2/11/93 L
Frederick John, Rev. 9/11/73
Georgina Melita Maria, Miss (–1895), sister of Sir H. Ponsonby, confidant and companion of Mrs. Thistlethwayte 27/2/79, 17/6/87
Gerald Henry Brabazon (1829–1908), treasury official 20/10/60
Henry Frederick, Gen. Sir 14/4/78 n
James Henry (1807–1880), soldier 25/8/60
John George Brabazon (1809–1880), 5th Earl of Bessborough (1847), whig M.P. 3/7/36
John William (1781–1847), 1st Baron Duncannon (1793), whig minister 28/11/37
Magdalen, Miss 14/4/78
Maria Jane Elizabeth (–1897), née Ponsonby, Lady de Mauley 30/4/61
Mary Elizabeth, Lady 14/4/78
Thomas Henry (1807–1880), soldier 14/7/58 ?
William Francis Spencer (1787–1855), 1st Baron de Mauley (1838) 20/10/31
Pool, William J. 28/8/79, 27/4/88
Poole,
rescue 18/6/73
Messrs. 8/9/88
C. W. 8/12/86
John, landing waiter 8/11/43
Reginald Lane (1857–1939), historian 21/7/87
Reginald Stuart (1832–1895), archaeologist 27/2/68
Pope,
Charles, London printer 1/9/54
F. 5/8/76
Samuel, barrister 17/9/78
William Law (–1879) 23/10/25 ?
Popham, John, of Cork 2/12/65
Popoff,
Adm. 20/5/74
E., Rev. 20/7/75
Popovic, Eugène, Italian journalist 20/11/80 ?
Porcari,
Baron, Neapolitan liberal and prisoner 13/2/51
Sig., refugee 31/3/59
Porson, E., rescue 10/7/60
Portal,
Gerald Herbert, Sir (1858–1894), diplomat and East African explorer 17/9/92, 26/9/92, 29/9/92 c, 30/9/92, 13/10/92, 15/10/92, 3/11/92, 21/11/92, 23/11/92 c, 9/12/92, 11/12/92, 13/12/92, 4/2/93 ff, 20/3/93 n, 5/4/93 ff, 20/7/93 c, 15/9/93
Melville (1819–1904), tory M.P. 5/1/53
Portalis, Auguste, Baron (–1855) 2/1/54
Portarlington *see* Damer, Dawson
Portelas, Amelia 30/8/88
Porter,
rescue 7/8/61
Andrew Marshall, Sir (1837–1919), 1st Baronet (1902), liberal M.P. 3/5/82
Benjamin 8/1/57, 14/5/57, 27/8/57, 4/5/59
Edward G., Rev., of U.S.A. 31/7/75
George Richardson (1792–1851), statistician 16/10/41, 24/2/43, 31/8/43
James, Rev. 28/2/89
Jane, Miss 23/6/43
John, Rev. (–1831), Methodist 13/6/30
Robert Ker, Sir (1777–1842), artist 23/6/43 n
Sarah, Mrs., née Ricardo 16/10/41 n
William Field, merchant 12/8/29
Wilson 30/12/43
Portland *see* Bentinck
Portlock, Joseph Ellison, Maj. Gen. (1794–1864) 29/11/58
Portman *see* Dugdale
Portman,
Edward Berkeley (1799–1888), 1st Baron Portman (1837), 1st Viscount Portman (1873) 13/6/38 n, 26/3/60, 23/8/82

Fitzhardinge Berkeley, Rev. (1811–1893) 18/4/32, 22/7/75
Portsmouth *see* Wallop
Possnett, Leonard, Rev., Methodist 8/3/34
Postan, Miss 22/3/32
Poste,
Mr. 14/3/88
Edward 8/11/71
Potiquet, F. G. A., French archivist 13/3/65
Potocki, Albert 21/4/77
Pott, Joseph Holden, Canon (1759–1847), archdeacon, author 31/5/38
Potter,
Beatrix (1866–1943), author and illustrator 28/7/84 n
Benjamin, servant at Hawarden 19/9/70 n, 24/12/94
Edmund (1802–1883), liberal M.P. 3/3/65
E. G., Rev. 7/12/78
Elizabeth, of Hawarden 19/9/70, 19/11/70, 16/4/71
George (1832–1893), trade unionist 2/7/66 n
George Walpole, Rev. 22/10/78
John, Sir (–1858), Manchester merchant 29/4/54
Joseph, architect 18/8/40
J. W., Dr. 21/9/87
Philip Cipriani Hambley (1792–1871), pianist and composer 24/5/33
Rupert (1832–1914), barrister and photographer 28/7/84 n
Thomas Bayley (1817–1898), liberal M.P. 4/4/65, 14/10/72, 15/1/73 L, 31/1/81, 29/8/81 L, 22/8/84 L, 12/5/90
Thomas Henry, merchant 30/10/41 ?
W. 29/1/56
W. B. 18/5/78
William Frederick, architect 17/11/77
Pottinger, John, Colonel (1815–1877) 19/12/57
Potts,
A. W., Dr. (1834–1889), headmaster of Fettes, Edinburgh 8/10/71
George (1807–1863), Peelite M.P. 22/10/61
Poulis, H. 15/12/92 L
Poulson, George (1783–1858), antiquary 28/12/48
Poulton, G., Inland Revenue clerk 16/6/68
Pound, William, Rev. (–1881) 13/4/52
Povah, John Vigden, Canon (1803–1882) 27/3/39
Povall, G. 2/2/80
Powell,
Baden, Prof. (1796–1860), Savilian professor of geometry, Oxford 26/6/31 ?
Charles, on London Working Men's Committee 25/7/76
Edward Parry, Rev. 11/9/67 ?
George Henry Croxden, liberal agent, secretary, N. W. Lancs. Liberal Association 29/1/77, 16/8/79, 5/8/85
George Smyth Baden-, Sir (1847–1898), Knight (1888), tory M.P. 14/7/76, 1/8/90
Henry Pryor, merchant 2/3/75
John Welstead Sharp, Rev. 30/5/75
Joseph Ormsby, Rev. 28/12/51
Thomas (1797–1865) 26/6/31 ?
Walter Rice Howell (1819–1889), liberal M.P. 17/4/89
Power,
Alfred, Sir 30/1/41
James 9/10/78
John O'Connor, liberal M.P. 20/7/77, 14/6/80, 7/4/83 c, 10/4/83 n
John Talbot, liberal M.P. 25/1/69
Patrick Joseph (1850–1913), home rule M.P. 29/8/89 ?
Peter, hand-loom weaver 2/12/41
Richard (1851–1891), home rule M.P. 29/8/89 ?
Powerscourt *see* Wingfield
Powis *see* Clive, Herbert
Powis, J., J. P. 7/2/91
Powlett,
Catherine Lucy Wilhelmina (–1901), Lady Vane, Duchess of Cleveland 28/4/58
Henry George, Lord, 4th Duke of Cleveland 6/2/49
Henry William-, 3rd Baron Bayning 10/3/40 n
Pownall, Assheston, Rev. (–1886) 17/2/76
Powys *see* Colquhoun
Powys,
Atherton Legh, Rev. (1809–1886) 25/1/28 ?
Charles (1813–1897), soldier 27/2/38
Horatio, Bp. (1805–1877), bishop of Sodor and Man 3/4/43
Thomas, 2nd Baron Lilford 25/1/28 n, 14/5/40 n
Thomas Arthur, Rev. (–1871) 9/10/53
Thomas Atherton (1801–1861), 3rd Baron Lilford (1825) 1/11/30
Poynder, Clement, Rev. (1835–1929) 21/2/75 ?
Poynter,
Ambrose, architect 17/2/43, 14/12/43 n
Edward John, Sir (1836–1919), 1st Baronet (1902) 1/10/79
Pozzi, G. E. 28/10/89
Praed,
Charles Tyringham (1833–1895), tory M.P. 26/7/75 ?
Helen (–1836), née Bogle 13/6/36
Winthrop Mackworth (1802–1839), poet, tory M.P. 8/10/25, 13/6/36 n

Prance, Courtenay Connell, solicitor 4/1/69
Prandi, Fortunato, author 20/6/45
Pratt,
George Charles (1799-1866), 2nd Marquis of Camden (1840) 23/1/61
H. L. 28/5/79
Hodgson, writer on India 22/6/60
John Burnett, Rev. 28/2/57
John Jeffreys (1759-1840), 1st Marquis of Camden (1812), tory politician 3/10/31
John Tidd (1797-1870), registrar of friendly societies (1846), barrister 9/12/42, 3/4/61, 2/3/63
Lloyd 3/1/77
Pratten, William Sidney, Rev. 21/7/68
Preggin, Mrs. 17/3/88
Premi,
Sig. 19/9/89
Cornelio Benedetto 26/11/78 ?
Prendergast, Guy Lustington (1806-1887) 11/6/68
Prentice,
Mrs. 27/12/78
G. 22/12/85
Manning, Stowmarket brewer 24/5/54
Prescott,
George Frederick, Rev. (1827-1917) 14/12/75
Henry James (-1854), banker 20/6/50 ?
Oliver Sherman, Rev. 2/6/75
Prescott, Grote, Cave & Cave, Messrs., bankers 22/6/58
Preshaw, William, surgeon 16/8/37
Presland, J., Rev. 7/2/87
Pressensé, Edmond Déhault (1824-1891), author 16/5/76
Pressly, Charles, Sir (1794-1880), Knight (1866), Chairman, Board of Inland Revenue 31/12/52, 22/3/53 ff, 5/4/53 ff, 9/5/53, 24/6/53, 4/3/54, 8/4/54, 12/7/59 ff, 18/7/59 ff, 10/11/59 ff, 8/4/61, 29/11/62 ff
Preston,
rescue 22/11/63
D. U. 21/5/90
Fuller 10/10/74
Jenico William Joseph (1837-1900), 14th Viscount Gormanston 17/12/92
Matthew Morris, Rev. 11/8/57
Robert, Sir (-1847), 7th Baronet 15/11/33
Robert Berthon (-1860), Liverpool merchant 12/4/49 ?
William, mayor of Liverpool 13/9/59
William, Rev. Dr. 31/7/89
Prestwich, Joseph, Sir (1812-1896) 16/12/85, 2/1/86
Prevost, George, Rev. Sir (1804-1893) 11/4/51, 24/10/60, 30/10/60, 16/8/65 ff, 27/8/67 ff, 24/10/69, 12/11/71, 6/11/72, 13/10/73, 24/6/74, 14/11/75, 30/5/82 L, 1/1/83 L
Price,
Bartholemew, Prof. (1818-1898), fellow of Pembroke, Oxford, professor of natural philosophy 25/2/53
Bonamy, Prof. (1807-1888), political economist 10/3/29, 31/1/78
Edwin Plumer (1818-1899), Recorder 1/2/66 ?
F. L. 20/4/78
Frances Milborough Green-, Lady Price 11/3/74
George (1812-1890) 20/2/57 ?
George Edward, Capt. (1842-1926), tory M.P. 12/1/91
Grove 30/6/38
H. L. 3/7/79
James Mansel, Rev. 20/2/57
John, Mrs. 31/1/35
Joseph, stockbroker 13/11/48
Richard Green-, Sir (1803-1887), 1st Baronet (1874), liberal M.P. 12/1/66, 5/3/69
S. 22/5/56
William Philip (1817-1891), liberal M.P. 19/12/74
Price and Ball, Messrs., tailors 5/5/53 ?
Price & Sons, of Chester 13/2/58
Prichard & Collette, Messrs., solicitors 26/6/52
Prickett, Richard, Rev. 30/9/41
Pridde, W. 26/3/74
Prideaux,
Miss 6/1/87
Frederick, solicitor 22/2/40 n
Walter, solicitor 22/2/40
Priestman, John 15/8/78
Primrose *see* Milnes
Primrose,
(Albert Edward) Harry, Lord (1882-1974), 6th Earl of Rosebery (1929), Lord Dalmeny 21/2/82, 29/10/91, 20/1/93
Anne Margaret, née Anson, Lady Rosebery 27/3/41
Archibald (1809-1851), Lord Dalmeny (1814) 23/11/39 n
Archibald John (1783-1868), 4th Earl of Rosebery (1814) 23/11/39 n
Archibald Philip; 5th Earl of Rosebery 23/11/39 n
Bouverie Francis (1813-1898), secretary, board of manufactures 12/2/57
Catherine L. W., née Stanhope, Lady Dalmeny 23/11/39 n
Charles, Rev. 25/8/91
Everard Henry, Col. (1848-1885) 12/12/78
Frederica Sophia (-1867), née Anson 6/5/57

Hannah (-1890), née Rothschild, Lady Rosebery 17/4/79 n, 6/3/80, 9/1/82 n, 5/9/85, 1/12/85, 8/2/86, 10/5/88, 2/8/89, 20/10/90 n, 22/10/90, 25/11/90
Henry William, Sir (1846-1923), G's private secretary, treasury official 28/4/80, 10/9/80, 2/2/86 ff, 21/4/86 ff, 7/5/86 ff, 15/7/86 ff
Neil James Archibald (1882-1917), 5th Earl of Rosebery's son 29/10/91, 20/1/93
Prince, William Alfred, solicitor 2/3/77
Prince, A. & Co., patent office 21/2/55 ?
Pringle,
Alexander, tory M.P. 2/11/41 n
David, of Leith 4/12/79
Elizabeth Maitland Campbell, Lady (-1878) 21/8/72, 17/10/72, 19/2/73, 3/3/75, 15/3/75, 1/6/76, 5/6/76, 30/9/76 ff, 18/6/77
George, Sir (1825-1911), Knight (1882), secretary, ecclesiastical commission 15/8/65
Henry James, Rev. 15/5/45 ?
J., deputy clerk of session 28/11/33 ?
James (-1865) 31/3/45
John, Sir (1784-1869), 5th Baronet (1809) 6/6/28 n, 31/3/45 n
R. 15/8/77
Robert (-1841), whig M.P. 18/3/33
Prinsep *see* Tennyson
Prinsep, Henry Thoby (1793-1878), member of Council of India 30/8/69
Prior, T. J. 11/5/78
Prisk, Miss, housekeeper at Hawarden 13/10/71
Pritchard,
Charles, Rev. Prof. (1808-1893), astronomer 3/2/77 ?, 15/5/78
George (1796-1883), missionary and consul in Tahiti 11/3/44 n
Henry, Rev. (-1857) 20/7/54
John, tory M.P. 18/4/37 ?
Pritt, Mr. 28/5/34, 30/5/34
Pritt, Sherwood, Venables & Grubb, Messrs., parliamentary agents 28/2/50
Probart, Mr., met at Hatfield 26/11/70
Proby *see* Mackenzie, Wells
Proby,
Charlotte, Lady 23/11/42
Elizabeth (1756-1842), née Grenville, Lady Carysfort 13/6/39
Frances, Lady 21/3/44
Granville Leveson (1824-1872), 4th Earl of Carysfort (1868) 28/12/68
Granville Leveson, Adm. (1781-1868), 3rd Earl of Carysfort (1828) 22/7/29, 21/12/32
Isabella (-1836), née Howard 21/12/32
John Joshua, Sir (1751-1828), 2nd Earl of Carysfort (1789) 13/6/39 n
Probyn,
Dighton Macnaghten, Sir (1833-1924) 21/11/80
John Webb (1828-1915), author 7/7/66
Procter, Mrs. 23/11/83
Proctor,
Frederick 23/11/78
George, Rev. 27/5/68
W. H., Burnley solicitor 26/10/68
Profumo, Baron 2/2/78 ?
Prokesch-Osten, Anton, Baron (1795-1876), traveller 25/11/58
Property Defence Association 13/12/81, 16/12/81 n
Prosperi, Abate 19/4/32
Prossalendi, Stelio Doria, of Ionia 28/11/58
Prosser, Francis Richard Wegg- (-1911), took name of Wegg-Prosser (1849), né Haggitt, Peelite M.P. 31/3/48, 8/3/50
Protich, Dr. 24/9/76
Prout,
Ebenezer, Rev. (1835-1909), composer 22/10/59 n
Edward Stallybrass, Rev. 24/1/87
Thomas Jones, Rev. (1824-1909), Student of Christ Church, Oxford and reformer 27/6/59
Provand, Andrew Dryburgh (1838-1915), liberal M.P. 6/7/93
Pryce,
Edward Stisted Mostyn 19/12/77
John, Rev. 14/8/74
Pryer, Charles, cabinet maker 2/4/74
Prynne,
Miss 17/10/67
George Rundle, Rev. (1836-1903) 2/3/57
Pryor,
Arthur 28/5/78 ?
Thomas, of Greenwich 28/11/79 ?
Pryse,
Robert David, Capt. 10/4/84
Robert John (1807-1889), published as Gweirydd Ap Rhys, author 27/2/75
Psychical Research, Society for 19/10/86 n
Pugh,
Edward Stuart, merchant 7/1/78
Giles, Rev. (-1875) 10/11/50
John William, Rev. (1810-1852) 2/2/34
Pugh, E. & D. 7/10/62
Pugin,
Augustus Welby Northmore (1812-1852), architect 19/10/42 n
Edward Welby (1834-1875), architect 12/4/58, 20/12/67, 20/6/68
Louis Welby 16/5/70
Pulford, Mr., tailor 2/2/26
Pulitzer, Joseph, publisher 9/7/87 n
Pullan, H. T., of Leeds 28/12/89
Puller,
Arthur Giles 17/11/78

Puller (*cont.*)
Christopher William Giles- (1807–1864), liberal M.P. 7/8/28, 22/8/28, 8/9/28, 3/10/28
Pulliblank, Joseph, Rev. (1843–1912) 24/11/78
Pulling,
Alexander, barrister 10/10/78
Camilla Mary, Mrs. 15/11/88
F. 14/8/79
James, Rev. Dr. (1814–1879) 14/10/74
John Lenten, of Greenwich 20/11/68
Purcell,
Edmund Sheridan (–1899), biographer of Manning 12/2/80 ?, 11/6/87, 21/1/93, 29/5/93 L
Goodwin, Rev. 6/1/76
Purchas,
John, Rev. (1823–1872) 18/4/56, 26/2/71, 7/4/72
W., destitute 25/11/59, 25/3/60
Purday, Charles Henry (1799–1885), music publisher 21/2/68
Purdue, John, tax inspector 12/6/57, 24/5/58, 1/8/59
Purdy, W. 29/3/75
Purnell,
P., Inland Revenue clerk 18/5/63 ?
Thomas, exhibition organiser 3/12/63
Puseley,
Berkeley Edward, journalist 3/5/77
Daniel (1814–1882), wrote on Australasia 20/3/60, 31/1/76
Pusey,
Edward Bouverie, Rev. Prof. 28/9/28
Emily, Lady, née Herbert 25/2/43
Lucy, Lady (1768–1858), née Sherard, formerly Cave 11/5/33
Philip (1799–1855), tory M.P., writer on agriculture 11/5/33 n, 4/7/35, 8/12/42, 22/2/43, 1/3/52, 17/6/55, 20/6/55
William Bouverie, Rev. (1810–1888) 4/11/28, 18/11/42
Putenderi, Dr., of Ionia 4/12/58
Putnam,
Gertrude A. 21/1/75
G. H., American publisher 30/11/83, 3/3/91 n, 4/3/91
Puttick & Simpson, Messrs., book auctioneers, prepared sale of Acton's library 28/4/90, 14/5/90 n
Putyatin,
Young 30/12/67
Eupheme, Adm., Russian admiral 21/1/45
Mary, née Knowles 21/1/45 n
Puzzi,
Giacinta, née Toso 14/9/40 n
Giovanni, horn player 14/9/40
Pwlheli, Secretary to Library of 9/11/87
Pycock, Mrs. 21/9/77
Pycroft,
Henry T., of New Zealand 1/3/78
James, Rev. (1813–1895) 22/7/51
Pye,
C. G. 15/1/90
Emily Charlotte, née Wilberforce, Roman Catholic convert (1868) 24/10/68
Henry John (1827–1903), Roman Catholic convert (1868), barrister 13/12/55, 24/10/68
Pyke, Mr. 31/5/81
Pym,
Miss 20/6/51
Francis (1849–1927) 14/2/77 ?
Pyndar,
Catharine (–1875), née Otway, widow of H. Murray, Lady Beauchamp (1850) 27/7/54
John Reginald Lygon (–1852), 3rd Earl Beauchamp 27/7/54 n

Quail, Mr. 9/3/80
Quain, Richard, Sir (1816–1898), 1st Baronet (1891), G's physician 7/10/75, 2/5/81, 3/5/81, 1/8/83, 17/12/88
Quale, D. F. W., Rev. 9/1/86 n
Quantin, Maison, Parisian publishers 3/2/87
Quaranto, Sig., of Ionia 8/1/59
Quarati, Sig. 16/1/66 n, 9/5/66
Quaritch, Bernard Alexander Christian (1819–1899), bookseller 25/8/51, 21/1/56, 19/11/60, 20/1/61, 27/4/61, 21/5/84, 26/7/88, 16/5/89, 20/7/89
Quarry, John, Rev. Dr. 7/2/75
Quartano, Sig. 17/11/59
Quartier, W. 21/8/90
Queensberry *see* Douglas
Quekett, John Thomas (1815–1861), conservator, Hunterian museum 25/5/57
Quilliam, Mr. 27/11/77
Quillin, Mr. 5/6/62
Quilter,
Henry (1851–1907), artist and author 11/11/86, 3/6/88
William Cuthbert, Sir (1841–1911), 1st Baronet (1897), liberal unionist M.P. 5/6/86
Quin,
Augusta, née Goold, Lady Adare, Lady Dunraven 16/6/46
E. R. W. Wyndham- (1812–1871), 3rd Earl of Dunraven (1850), Lord Adare, tory M.P., member of the Engagement 3/9/41
J. H. 1/11/86, 23/8/87
John, London agent 4/10/51 ?
J. P., secretary of the Land League 12/10/81 c
Windham Thomas Wyndham (1841–1926), 4th Earl of Dunraven (1871), colonial

undersecretary 14/6/79 n, 24/6/79, 10/7/79
Quinlan, Thomas 30/5/78 ?
Quinn,
Dr. 9/11/82
C., Miss 6/5/87
J. P., Land Leaguer 12/10/81
M. J., editor, *Dublin Review* 6/5/36 n
Quirk, George, Rev. 6/3/50

Rabbinowicz, Israel Jehiel Michael, Dr., physician and scholar 17/5/79 ?
Racolins, Mr. 20/1/67
Radcliffe,
Amelia Matilda Mary Tudor (-1880), styled Countess of Derwentwater 18/9/69
James (-1836), headmaster, Kirkham grammar school 27/10/28 ?
John, Rev. (1780-1852) 25/7/31 ?
John Alexander, solicitor 16/3/49 ?
Radclyffe, Charles Edward, Rev. 20/1/48
Radford, Mrs., of Murray's, publishers 22/11/86
Radius, M. 7/3/48
Radnor *see* Bouverie
Radstock *see* Waldegrave
Rae,
John, of Hudson's Bay company 9/11/52 ?
Robert, temperance propagandist 25/5/61 ?
Robert R., Homerist 9/3/76, 15/1/86
William, Sir (1769-1842), 3rd Baronet (1815), whig M.P. 11/12/33
Rafereddin Ahmed 24/11/91
Raffalovich, A. 6/3/77
Raffalovitch, Mlle. 31/7/88
Raglan *see* Somerset
Ragouet, Mons. 12/6/88
Ragsbotham, J. 10/11/77
Raguenau, Mrs. 15/9/25
Raikes *see* Canning
Raikes,
Henry (1811-1863), registrar, diocese of Chester 30/11/41, 23/10/63
Henry Cecil (1838-1891), tory M.P. 30/11/41 n, 29/5/85
Raine, James, Rev. 26/3/52
Rainer, Mr., picture dealer 19/3/59
Rainger, William, secretary, Carlton club 7/10/49
Rainsford, Mr. 15/7/74
Rainy,
George, distant cousin, Demerara proprietor 8/8/37
Robert, Rev. Prof. (1826-1906), Scottish freechurchman 1/6/74, 2/11/78 n, 23/5/79, 29/11/81 L, 3/11/85 L, 7/11/85, 18/11/85, 6/10/92, 15/2/94
Raison, Mrs., housekeeper at Fasque 12/10/44, 18/12/46
Raith, Mr. 30/11/77
Raleigh, S. 22/1/57
Ralli *see* Monck, Moreton
Ralli,
Madame 14/6/65, 19/11/72, 30/4/73, 7/3/75, 8/5/75, 2/7/75, 7/3/76, 1/5/77, 23/6/79
Pandeli (1845-1928), liberal M.P. 8/5/71, 3/2/82, 28/3/83, 26/8/92
Pantia Stephen (-1865) 14/6/65 n
Ralph, Mr., photographer 30/1/87
Ram,
James, barrister 15/6/76
Seva 13/12/88
Rambaut, Edmund Francis, Rev. 18/10/86 ?
Ramfitt, Mr. 23/3/55
Ramke, Joseph 9/7/88
Rammingen, L. von, Princess, met G in Biarritz 28/12/92, 29/12/92
Ramsay,
rescue 15/6/69
Andrew Chrysostom, Rev. 5/1/80
Charles Fox Maule- (1885-1926), godson 12/6/85
Edward Bannerman, Dean 25/5/28
Fox Maule- (1801-1874), 11th Earl of Dalhousie (1860), Lord Panmure, whig M.P. 14/2/40
George Gilbert, Prof. (1839-1921), professor in Glasgow 7/11/79
Isabella (-1858), née Cochrane 3/1/34
James Andrew Broun, Lord (1812-1860), 1st Marquis of Dalhousie (1849), governor-general of India (1847) 16/11/35
James Henry, Sir (1832-1925), 10th Baronet (1871) 1/3/77
John (1814-1892), liberal M.P. 13/9/72
John William Maule- (1847-1887), 13th Earl of Dalhousie (1880), Scottish secretary (1886) 17/9/84 ff, 30/9/84, 24/10/84, 7/2/85, 12/6/85, 15/10/85, 23/3/86, 26/3/86 n, 27/3/86, 16/5/86, 26/5/86, 4/6/86
Robert 28/9/76
Ronald Edward Maule- (1885-1909), godson 12/6/85
Susan Georgiana, Lady (-1853), née Hay, Lady Dalhousie 16/11/35 n
Thomas, educationalist 8/6/52
William, Adm. Sir (1793-1871) 17/4/60
William Maule- (1809-1859) 7/11/37
William Mitchell, Prof. (1851-1939), classical scholar; wrote article on G's works 10/10/92, 21/9/93
Ramsbotham, Francis Henry, Dr. (1801-1868), physician 5/6/51

Ramsbottom, John (-1845), whig M.P. 12/6/26 n
Ramsden *see* Gladstone
Ramsden,
E., Miss 30/5/88
Frances Matilda (-1837), née Plumtre 8/4/38
John William, Sir (1831-1914), 5th Baronet (1839) 20/2/64
Robert 8/4/38 n
Ramsey, Septimus Fowler, Rev. 18/4/40, 13/7/40
Ramwell, Mr. 15/5/76
Rand,
Silas Tertius, Rev. 28/8/78
William, china dealer 13/3/50
Randall,
Henry Goldney, Rev. (-1881) 25/2/53 ?
James Leslie, Ven. (-1922) 1/11/79
Randell, James S., author 15/6/78 ?
Randolph,
Francis, Rev. (-1898) 10/1/77
Herbert, Rev. (-1887) 16/1/53
John James (-1899) 7/4/54
Rands, rescue 6/4/81
Ranelagh *see* Jones
Ranfurly *see* Knox
Rangabé, Alexandros Rizos, Greek politician 27/6/50
Ranken, Arthur, Rev., episcopalian 2/10/48
Rankin, James 13/12/79
Ransford, Charles, Dr., physician 6/6/49 ?
Ransoms, Messrs., bankers 17/6/44 n, 2/2/78
Raouf Pasha, Egyptian official 5/5/84
Raper, Robert William (1842-1915), fellow of Trinity College, Oxford 1871 7/2/90
Raphael, Alexander (-1850), M.P. 3/11/35
Raposardi, Sig. 21/1/89
Rashdall, Hastings, Rev. (1858-1924), theologian 6/10/92, 10/10/92 ff, 22/1/93 n
Rasponi,
Madame, of Florence 31/1/88
Mons., of Florence 31/1/88
A., Countess 23/1/88
Rassam, Christian, consul 20/2/38
Ratcliffe, Thomas, Rev. (-1892) 19/2/53 ?
Rathbone,
Philip Henry (1828-1895), Liverpool merchant and liberal 21/3/66, 25/3/73
Samuel Greg (1823-), Liverpool merchant and liberal 19/9/66
Theodore Woolman (1798-1863), Liverpool merchant 18/11/53
William (1819-1902), liberal M.P. 16/7/65, 13/1/71 L, 16/3/83, 9/6/90, 2/6/93 L, 24/8/93 L, 26/8/93 L, 30/8/93, 15/12/93, 16/12/93
Rathborne, Joseph, pamphleteer 25/4/41
Rathdowne *see* Monck
Rathmore *see* Plunket
Ratliffe & Sons, ironfounders at Hawarden 11/2/52
Ratzinger, Mr. 26/5/69
Rauch, T. J. 13/1/87
Raumer, Friedrich Ludwig Georg von (1781-1872), historian 27/5/36 n
Raven,
H., consul 9/11/58
John James, Rev. (1833-1906) 8/6/67 ?, 17/9/85
Ravensworth *see* Liddell
Rawes, Henry Augustus, Rev. (1826-1885) 8/3/55 n
Rawlings, S. T., of Frome Liberal Association 22/1/77 n
Rawlins,
Messrs. 4/8/60
Mr. 7/7/38
Mr., of Wilton 30/8/66
George, registrar of births 31/8/40, 8/12/42
J. H. 12/8/79
R. C., Glynne's political agent 24/3/57
Samuel George, solicitor 5/10/44 ?, 29/8/45
Rawlinson,
George, Rev. Prof. (1812-1902), fellow of Exeter, Oxford, professor of ancient history, Oxford 5/1/53
Henry Creswicke, Sir (1810-1895), Knight (1856), 1st Baronet (1891), liberal M.P. 2/5/57, 27/1/65
Rawnsley, Robert Drummond Burrell, Rev. (1818-1882) 25/6/77
Rawson,
Jane Eliza, Lady, née Rawson 13/7/43
Rawson William, Sir, G's private secretary at Board of Trade 6/9/41
Thomas William, of Nottingham 4/10/77
William, Mrs. 4/8/25
William, Rev. (-1870) 8/6/40
William, Rev. (1788-1872), G's first schoolmaster 4/8/25, 22/12/72
Rayleigh *see* Strutt
Rayner,
Joseph (-1883), town clerk of Liverpool 3/4/67, 1/5/68
R., Mrs. 22/2/75
Raynes, William, Rev. (1829-1894) 30/12/74
Reachman, Mr. 18/11/78
Read,
Clare Sewell (1826-1905), tory M.P. 10/2/68
G. P. 14/7/58
G. R. 24/12/90
Rudston, Capt. 28/9/68

T., Mrs., of Hawarden 3/1/55
Thomas, of Hawarden 3/1/55 n
Reade,
A. A. 6/1/87
Charles Darby, Rev. 17/7/50
John Edmund (1800–1870), poet 13/5/57
Philip, of Ireland 9/3/76
Thomas, Sir, consul 6/7/44
Reader, A. 21/5/83, 4/10/85
Readett, William Harvey, Newark maltster 30/5/43, 8/5/67
Readman, R. 9/8/50
Readwin, Thomas 14/7/87 ?
Reale, Antonio, of Naples 11/2/51
Realf, Mr., of U.S.A. 13/4/92
Rearden, Denis Joseph (1817–1885), liberal M.P. 9/6/68
Reavis, Logan Uriah (1831–1889), American author 3/3/80, 21/8/88
Reay *see* Mackay
Reb, rescue 5/7/64, 15/11/64
Rebow, John Gurdon- (1799–1870), liberal M.P. 11/4/66
Rebrey, Madame 27/6/90
Recanati, Mayor of 20/12/86
Rechten, Madame, of Naples 29/2/52
Reddell, James, Rev. (1795–1878) 28/10/32
Reddie, John, chief justice of St. Lucia 13/7/35
Redding, Cyrus (1785–1870), journalist 7/7/60
Reddish,
H. Mottram, Manchester solicitor 21/4/47
Samuel 22/11/78 ?
Redesdale *see* Mitford
Redfern,
J. 28/8/79
William, agent 10/9/78 ?
Redford,
Mrs. 12/10/48
G. 17/6/75
R. A., Rev. 26/12/74 n
Redgrave, Richard, of Department of Practical Art 21/3/54
Redhead, Thomas Fisher, Rev. 25/1/43
Redhouse, Mr. 24/7/79
Redington, Thomas Nicholas, Sir (–1862) 21/4/53
Redmond,
Alderman 8/1/86
Miss, sculptor 17/7/89
Francis, of Dublin 13/6/74 ?
John Edward (1856–1918), home rule M.P. 22/4/82 c, 26/4/82 n, 16/11/86 n, 18/11/86, 5/12/90 n, 1/10/92, 5/10/92, 26/10/92, 25/11/92, 10/6/93
Redpath,
John, Montreal merchant 11/6/40
Leopold (1813–1880), bankrupt 19/5/57
Peter, Montreal industrialist 11/6/40 n
Red Shirt, Chief, American Indian 28/4/87 n
Reed,
Mr., of Cliveden 20/8/66
A., of Greenwich 11/5/74
A. C., of Caxton Centenary Committee 29/6/77
Charles, Sir (1819–1881), liberal M.P. 4/2/74, 23/2/74, 6/1/77
C. R. 1/3/76
E., rescue 1/7/70, 7/2/74
Edward James, Sir (1830–1906), Knight (1880), liberal M.P. and naval architect 21/1/70, 6/7/89, 4/10/92 L, 23/11/93 L
G. J. 7/5/79
W. H. 2/10/77
Reed, T. S. & Co., wine merchants 1/5/68
Reekie, Mr., radical organiser in Edinburgh 1/1/86, 3/1/86
Rees,
Messrs. 8/1/79
Alan 19/3/77 ?
Charles Davies, Rev. 16/10/75 ?
Edward, Mrs. 5/6/57 n
James, Mayor of Carnarvon 30/3/74
Josiah, Sir (1821–1899), barrister 27/4/59 ?
Samuel, Rev. (–1853) 24/2/50 ?
Reeve,
Abraham Charles, Rev. (1809–1889) 4/12/57
Henry (1813–1895), editor, *Edinburgh Review* 16/4/56, 26/8/70 L, 23/9/70 L, 30/9/70 L, 3/11/70 L, 10/11/70 L, 24/1/71 L, 23/11/83
J. E. 24/3/75
Reeves,
rescue 8/6/63
John Sims (1818–1900), tenor 17/3/88
Thomas, sculptor 18/3/80
Reeves & Turner, Messrs., booksellers and publishers 19/2/73, 9/12/88 n
Regan, Mrs. 14/2/62
Rehausen, Johan Gothard de, Baron, Swedish chargé d'affaires 17/5/43
Rehbaum, W. 24/8/67, 27/7/68
Reich,
E., Dr. 26/10/92
Henry, marquetry specialist 23/4/74 ?
Lucian 23/12/85 ?
Reichel, Charles Parsons, Ven. Prof. (1816–1894) 19/10/74, 27/9/81
Reichersberg, Abbot of 26/9/86
Reid,
Alexander, Liverpool merchant 1/9/25
A. M. 4/5/78
Andrew, journalist 15/1/86
C. G., Scottish lawyer 12/9/44
Francis Neville, of Ravello 12/2/89
George Houstoun, Sir (1845–1918), Australian politician 13/7/75

Reid (*cont.*)
Henry, Rev. 12/9/45 ?
H. G. 5/12/81
H. G., Mrs., of Aston 7/12/86
H. L. 25/11/54
Hugh 19/2/90
Hugh Gilzean, Sir (1836–1911), Knight (1893), liberal M.P. 29/3/78, 2/8/78, 12/7/92
James Watson, Rev., of Glasgow 26/4/56
John James (1844–1889), lawyer 9/12/79, 16/3/80, 5/4/80
John Rae, Sir (–1867) 24/2/42
Robert Threshie (1846–1923), 1st Baron Loreburn (1906), liberal M.P. 9/6/92, 16/2/93 L
Stuart Johnson (–1927), author 21/4/79, 16/10/83 L, 23/4/92
Thomas Wemyss, Sir (1842–1905), editor, *Leeds Mercury*, biographer of G 20/5/77, 25/6/87, 11/6/88, 7/7/88 n, 28/7/88, 15/2/90, 7/11/90, 14/11/90, 27/11/90, 25/3/91, 26/2/92 n, 5/10/92
W. H. B. 9/6/90
William, Sir (1791–1858), engineer 27/7/51
Reilly, Mrs. 12/5/55
Reinach, Salomon 4/11/76 ?
Reinangle, Ramsay Richard (1775–1862), artist 28/2/57
Reinkens, Joseph Hubert, Bp. (1821–1896) 24/9/74, 17/9/81
Reisach, Charles Augustus von, Cardinal (1800–1869) 30/7/66, 17/10/66, 22/10/66
Reiss, Charles A. 4/11/79
Reith,
George, secretary, Aberdeen railway co. 9/1/50 n
John, surgeon 9/10/37 ?
Reitlinger, Frédéric, French diplomat 23/12/70, 28/12/70, 4/2/72 L
Reitzenstein, Franziska, Baroness 17/1/92
Relling, F. S., Mr. 6/2/75
Remington, Messrs. 18/10/88
Rémusat, Charles F. M. de, Comte (–1875) 26/3/52
Renald, Mr. 30/1/93
Renard, Frederick 18/4/65
Renault, Edward 22/2/76 ?
Rench, J. 3/9/79
Rendal, rescue 29/4/62
Rendel *see* Bowen, Gladstone, Goodhart
Rendel,
Ellen Sophy, née Hubbard, Lady Rendel, wife of S. Rendel, Roman Catholic? 28/1/87, 25/12/88
George 22/12/88 ff, 4/2/89 ?
James Meadows (1799–1856), engineer 31/5/53
Stuart; G's confidant 20/12/80
Rendell, William 13/3/79
Rendi, Marchesa 15/2/51
Rendlesham *see* Thellusson
Rendu, Eugène (1824–1903), French educationalist 16/5/53
Renehan, Laurence F., Rev. Dr. (–1857), President of Maynooth 10/5/52
Renham, Rev. Mr. 2/10/85
Renier, Antonio D., Dr. 26/8/87
Renishaw *see* Sitwell
Rennell, Charles John 28/8/67
Renouf, Peter Le Page, Sir (1822–1897), Knight (1896), Egyptologist 5/6/90
Renton,
C. 13/6/57
James Hall (1822–1895), broker 18/6/67
John Campbell (1814–1856), tory M.P. 2/4/49
Repington,
Charles Henry Wyndham A'Court (1819–1903), took name of Repington (1855), Peelite M.P. 23/7/54 n, 24/5/71 L
Emily A'Court, née Currie 23/7/54
Repton, Edward, Canon (1783–1860), Chaplain to the Commons 29/7/32
Restney, A. 7/2/79
Reumert, Theodore 19/3/78
Reuter, Paul Julius de, Baron (1816–1899) 31/1/60
Reventlow, Ferdinand Carl Otto, Count of Reventlow, Danish ambassador 22/6/43
Reynolds *see* Walker
Reynolds,
E., rescue 10/7/45
E. J. 19/8/78
Henry Revell (–1866), treasury solicitor 9/2/53
Henry Robert, Rev. Prof. (1825–1896) 10/6/75
S. R. 30/1/44 n
W. 14/6/77
Rhind, John (–1892), of Edinburgh, sculptor 26/11/85, 27/11/85
Rhode, R. 23/9/91
Rhodes,
Mr. 14/3/87, 8/7/89
Cecil John 14/3/87 ?
Charles, china dealer 4/3/80 ?
Frank 23/11/92 n
Henry Jackson, Rev. (1823–) 11/12/56 ?
Josiah 27/1/75
Mathew, member of the Engagement 23/2/45 n
Rhodocanakis, Demetrius, Prince 9/5/75
Rhomaides, C. B., Dr., of Athens 17/10/90
Rhys,
D. 20/2/80

Ernest 26/6/91
John, Prof. 7/9/88
Riaz Pasha, Egyptian politician 17/1/93 n, 18/1/93 c
Ribbans, Mr. 29/8/74
Ribblesdale *see* Lister
Ribeiro Saraiva, Antonio, diplomat 17/10/43
Ribetti, Sig. 27/9/87
Ribot, Alexandre Félix Joseph (1842–1923), French Prime Minister 20/10/96
Ricardo *see* Porter
Ricardo,
rescue 29/5/79, 3/8/81, 5/8/81
David (1772–1823), political economist 16/10/41 n
Osman (1795–1881), liberal M.P. 10/3/60
Ricasoli,
Bettino, Baron (1809–1880), Italian politician 22/10/66, 27/12/66 n, 7/1/67 ff, 19/7/92, 28/3/93
Vicenzo, Baron 25/1/88
Ricchetti, C., dealer in Venice 4/10/79, 6/11/79
Ricci,
Marchese 16/1/88
Francesco, Monsignor, secretary to Pius IX 27/11/66
Ricciardi, Guiseppi Napoleoni, Conte (1808–1885), Italian politician and author 19/8/51, 18/9/76
Riccio, Vedova 5/11/89
Riccioni, Sig. 5/1/91
Rice,
Charles Allen Thorndike (1851–1889), American journalist 12/9/77, 30/5/78, 1/7/78, 4/7/78, 6/7/78, 26/2/80
Charles William Thomas Spring- (1819–1870), foreign office clerk 5/6/63
Edward, Rev. Dr. 26/2/48
Edward Royd (1790–1878), liberal M.P. 1/2/66
Isaac L., of New York 19/12/79
R., coroner 26/10/87
Richard, Rev. (1793–1868) 11/7/55
Richard John Howard, Rev. 9/4/59
Stephen Edmund Spring- (1814–1865), deputy chairman, customs board 12/4/58 ff, 10/3/65
Thomas Spring- (1790–1866), 1st Baron Monteagle (1839), whig M.P. 20/1/35
Rich, Henry, Sir (–1869), 1st Baronet (1863), liberal M.P. 16/3/53
Richard, Henry (1812–1888), liberal M.P., Secretary of the Peace Society 23/10/67, 25/2/70, 28/3/70 L, 14/4/71 L, 21/6/71, 25/11/71, 8/7/73, 10/7/73 c, 12/6/80 c, 14/1/81 L, 17/2/81 L, 29/4/81, 31/8/82 L, 30/12/82 L, 25/7/83, 11/10/88 n
Richards,
Capt. 19/7/87
Messrs., gunsmiths 1/4/42
A. H. 3/12/66
E. M. 15/6/78
George, Rev. (–1884) 31/12/59 ?
G. K. 1/9/71
James Brinsley (1846–1892) 13/1/83
John, whig M.P. 29/4/35
John, Rev. 5/11/72
Joseph L., Rev. 2/8/47
Richard (1787–1860), tory M.P. 31/7/44
William Upton, Rev. (1811–1873) 2/10/42, 21/6/73
William Westley, gunmaker 22/9/42, 12/1/43
Richardson *see* Selwyn
Richardson,
Mr., farmer 15/7/41
Edward (1812–1869), sculptor 9/1/43 ff, 29/7/44
Henry Francis, solicitor 5/4/45 ?
James Nicholson (1846–), liberal M.P. 17/9/81
John F., Prof., of Rochester, U.S.A. 26/9/59
John Stewart, Sir (1797–1881) 26/4/42
Jonathan Joseph (1815–1876), tory M.P. 22/6/53
Ralph, secretary, Midlothian Liberal Association 16/3/80
Thomas, of Hawarden 6/9/48 n
Thomas, Mrs., of Hawarden 6/9/48 ?
William, solicitor 10/3/34 ?
Richbell, Mrs., lodging housekeeper 29/7/68
Richings, Frederick Hartshill, Rev. (–1888) 6/8/51 ?
Richmond *see* Lennox
Richmond,
George (1809–1896), artist, drew G's portrait 23/7/33 n, 14/1/39, 11/3/41, 13/3/41, 9/4/55, 25/4/56, 13/5/57, 24/5/57, 3/5/59, 15/5/60, 3/9/93
Irene 15/2/68 ?
Thomas (1771–1837), miniaturist 23/7/33, 14/1/39 n
William Blake, Sir (1842–1921), artist, painted G's portrait 27/12/66 n, 30/10/67, 29/3/77, 29/12/81, 16/1/82, 22/10/88, 27/10/88, 9/1/90 ff, 22/4/93, 24/10/93 ff, 16/5/94
Richson, Charles, Rev. (1806–1874), educationalist 25/4/50
Richter, Max Herman Ohnefalsch-, archaeologist 3/2/93
Rickards,
Edward James, solicitor 2/7/82
George 20/4/39 ?
George Kettilby, Prof. Sir (1812–1889), political economist 10/11/27, 20/4/39 n

Rickards (*cont.*)
G. K., Speaker's Counsel 1/9/71
Rickerby, Joseph, London printer 22/4/45 ?
Rickets, Charles, stove manufacturer 27/10/49 ?
Ricketts,
Caroline Augusta, Lady (1818–1898), née Pelham-Clinton 9/10/32
Cornwallis, Sir (1803–1885), 2nd Baronet (1842) 9/10/32 n, 26/10/64
Riddell,
Charles James Buchanan, of Canada 5/6/49
Henry Scott (1798–1870), poet 5/3/68 ?
James Milles, Sir (1787–1861), 2nd Baronet (1797), Lt. Col. 5/12/35
John Walter Buchanan, Sir (1849–1924), 11th Baronet 6/4/89
Walter Buchanan, Sir (1810–1892), 10th Baronet (1819), judge 2/2/29, 20/6/92
Ridding, George, Bp. (1828–1904), headmaster of Winchester (1866), bishop of Southwell (1884) 12/2/84, 6/7/90
Rideing, William Henry, editor, *North American Review* 22/7/87, 23/9/91, 29/12/91
Ridelle, H. 9/8/90
Ridge,
Benjamin, surgeon 14/6/47
John James, temperance advocate 30/8/79
Ridgeway, Joseph West, Sir (1844–1930), undersecretary for Ireland (1887), governed Man (1893) 30/9/92, 7/11/92 c, 23/11/92 c, 17/12/92 c, 28/12/92, 29/9/93, 7/10/93 ff, 16/10/93 ff
Ridgway,
Miss 20/2/87
James Leech (1801–1862), publisher 23/1/37
Joseph 19/10/42 n
Selina, née Doyle 19/10/42
Ridler, Mr. 7/1/84
Ridley,
Cecilia Anne, Lady, née Parke 25/6/42, 19/6/44
George (1818–1887), copyhold commissioner 12/2/61
Henry John, Canon (1788–1834) 1/12/30
Matthew White, Sir (1807–1877), 4th Baronet (1836), tory M.P. 25/6/42, 19/6/44
Matthew White, Sir (1842–1904), 5th Baronet (1877), tory M.P. 22/11/88
William Henry, Rev. (1816–1882) 11/5/56
Rietti, Sig., dealer in Venice 4/10/79
Rigaud, John, Rev. (–1888) 16/5/54
Rigby,
E., of Hawarden 6/10/59
H. L., Mrs. 30/9/42 ?
H. Lee, of Hawarden 12/7/41
John, ironfounder in Hawarden 19/9/45
John, Sir (1834–1903), liberal M.P. 9/6/93
Rigby & Hancock, Messrs., ironfounders in Hawarden 19/9/45 n
Rigdon, Mr. 11/6/74
Rigeston, Mr. 19/12/75
Rigg,
Arthur, Rev. (1812–1880), of Chester Training College 8/8/65, 11/4/68
James Harrison, Rev. Dr. (1821–1909), editor, *British Quarterly*, Methodist 25/5/68, 16/1/72 L, 10/5/79, 31/12/84 L, 25/10/85
John, Rev. (1811–1860) 14/6/34 ?
Jonathan, merchant 14/6/34 ?
Rigge, Samuel, managing clerk 5/6/34
Rignold, Mr. 19/11/79
Riland, John, Rev. 21/9/39
Riley,
Mrs. 20/11/89
A. 19/11/90
Rimbault, Edward Francis (1816–1876), musician and antiquary 13/6/42
Rimblett, Mr. 21/12/85
Rimell, Messrs. 10/3/79
Rimmel, E. 17/3/88
Rimmer, Alfred, of Broughton 31/8/75
Rines, W. 20/9/87
Rintoul, Robert Stephen (–1858), editor, *Spectator* 12/4/49
Rio,
Alexis François (1797–1874), art historian 9/6/38, 14/6/38, 16/6/38, 18/6/38, 19/6/38, 9/2/39, 26/2/39, 5/3/39, 4/6/41, 19/7/42, 5/7/45
Apollonia, née Jones, Welsh Catholic heiress 9/8/38
Riordan, James, legal author 29/5/52
Ripley,
Henry William, Sir (1813–1882), 1st Baronet (1880), liberal M.P. 27/12/60 ?
John, of Whitby 9/11/69
Ripon *see* Robinson
Rippe, J. H. 2/6/56
Rippin, H. W., liberal 20/3/80
Risk,
James George, Dr., physician 26/8/74, 19/2/87
Keats R., Dr., physician 5/9/67
Riso, Ippolito De 15/11/88
Risti, Sig., of Ionia 6/12/58
Ristori, Adelaide, Marchesa (1821–1906), actress 3/7/58, 9/7/58, 10/7/58, 2/3/59, 27/6/73, 14/7/73
Ritchie,
A. J., of Greenwich 15/3/75
David, Prof. 20/4/28 ?
John, of Fasque 8/10/58
John, Dr. 20/4/28 ?

William, Prof. 20/4/28 ?
Ritso,
rescue 10/4/88
Miss 10/4/92
Ritter, Miss 24/12/87
Rivarola, Agostino, Cardinal (1758–1842) 14/12/38 n
Rivers,
rescue 11/5/72, 27/12/84
Augustus Lane Fox Pitt-, Gen. (1827–1900), ethnological collector 12/7/80
G. Pitt-, 4th Baron Rivers 13/2/32 n
Susan Georgiana Pitt-, Lady (–1866), née Leveson-Gower 13/2/32
Riviere, William, educationalist 7/8/67
Rivington,
Charles (1754–1831), publisher 20/1/42 n
Francis, publisher 20/1/42
Rix, Herbert, librarian to Royal Society 18/9/88
Robartes,
Mary Agar-, née Dickinson, Lady Robartes 12/6/89
Thomas Charles Agar-, 2nd Baron Robartes (1882), 6th Viscount Clifden (1899), liberal M.P. 24/11/73, 12/6/89
Thomas James Agar- (1808–1882), 1st Baron Robartes (1869), liberal M.P. 24/11/73 L
Robarts,
Messrs. 9/7/69
Charles Henry, fellow of All Souls, Oxford (1865) 3/2/90
Frederick, Rev., proctor in doctors' commons 27/5/54 ?
Nathaniel, proctor in doctors' commons 27/5/54 ?
Robb,
Miss 26/12/79
W. 8/5/91
Robbins,
Alfred Farthing, Sir (1856–1931), biographer of G, journalist and editor 22/7/75 ?, 24/3/91
H. 26/11/87
John, Rev. (1832–1906) 16/11/67
Robe, Frederick Holt (1801–1871), governor of S. Australia 10/1/46
Roberts *see* Hallam
Roberts,
rescue 14/5/62, 7/3/66
Messrs., of U.S.A. 12/12/89
Mr., Chester banker 4/9/52
Mrs., midwife 16/10/42
A. B. 17/7/77
Arthur, Rev. (1801–1886), author 29/10/29 ff, 20/5/65 ?
Arthur Troughton, Capt. 3/7/41 ?
A. W. 10/8/66
C. A. 26/2/76
Charles Edward Thorney, Rev. 14/12/75
C. T. 17/2/77
C. W. 30/9/91
David (1796–1864), artist 5/5/60
Edward, Rev. 2/4/57
Elizabeth, housemaid 5/7/41, 3/5/43
F. M. 10/8/77
Frederick Sleigh, Sir (1832–1914), 1st Earl Roberts, field marshal 21/2/81, 5/3/81 c, 2/4/81 c, 15/10/81, 30/9/92 c, 1/7/93 n
G. B., Rev. 16/4/92
George Robert, Rev. (–1898) 9/5/78
Henry (1812–1874), civil servant 19/11/52
Henry Mander, Rev. 28/3/48 ?
Jane, of Hawarden 24/8/50
John, of Wellhouse Farm, Bretton 7/8/58, 6/11/60, 11/11/68, 13/9/73
John (1835–1894), liberal M.P. 30/10/79
John Bryn (1843–1931), liberal M.P. 23/8/93
J. P., of Rhyl 31/3/57
J. T., Rev., nonconformist 3/6/76
J. Varley, Dr., musician, Fellow of Magdalen, Oxford 3/2/90
L. D. 27/3/90
M. H. 14/8/90
O. E. 20/9/87
P. E. 30/12/79
R. 5/4/70
Robert Henry, Rev. (1838–1900), Baptist 20/9/66 ?
Thomas Nicolls, secretary, Liberal Registration Association 28/4/69
Thomas Quellyn, sheriff of Chester (1853) 11/1/53, 5/4/65, 23/4/65, 5/11/67, 15/8/78
W. 16/8/60
William Henry, Rev. (1795–1843) 4/12/25
William Page, Rev. (1836–1928) 2/11/76, 3/12/86
Robertson *see* Barlow, Gladstone, Glasgow, Sumner, Turner, Tyler
Robertson,
rescue 5/8/70
Miss, singer 15/3/76, 22/3/76
Mr., mineowner in Hawarden 25/3/56, 12/8/56
Mr., of Stornoway 21/5/28, 26/5/28
A. L., Mrs. 2/3/48
Andrew, G's cousin 28/9/26
Anne, née Mackenzie, G's grandmother 23/4/29
Anne, Miss 2/6/32
Charles, advocate 14/1/43
Charles, Rev. 10/4/35 ?
Chisholm 6/12/93 L
Colin (–1836), G's uncle 13/8/25 n
Colin C. F., G's cousin 13/8/25
Daniel Brooke, Sir (1810–1881), consul 18/2/71, 25/9/77 n

Robertson (*cont.*)
David (1797–1873), né Marjoribanks, 1st Baron Marjoribanks, liberal M.P. 16/5/62, 12/5/68
Divie, Mrs., G's aunt 22/9/29
Divie, fils, Rev. (–1894), G's cousin 2/2/41, 16/12/65
Divie, père, G's uncle 20/8/25 n
Edward Lovell, wine merchant, G's cousin 15/7/26
Eliza, cousin 20/8/25
Elizabeth (–1834), G's aunt 28/8/25
Ellen, Lady 25/9/77
F., Miss 22/6/73
Frances (–1851) 11/4/32 ?
George, land agent 6/6/43, 28/8/43
George, Capt., of Edinburgh 24/1/28 n
George Brown, deputy keeper of records, Edinburgh 24/9/64
George Duncan, Maj. Gen. (1766–1842) 11/4/32 n
George Samuel, Rev. (–1874) 26/1/53
H., Mrs. 15/9/41
Henry, of Kensington 17/6/43
Henry (1816–1888), liberal M.P. 15/7/73
Henry Larkins, Maj. Gen. (–1891) 30/10/54, 6/11/86, 29/4/91
Hercules James (1795–1874), Lord Benholme (1853), Scottish judge 12/9/61, 7/10/71
J., Prof. 13/1/83
James, surgeon in Fettercairn 25/11/48
James, Prof. (1803–1860), professor of divinity, Edinburgh 21/7/59
James, Rev. 16/10/51
James, Rev. Dr. (1837–1890), presbyterian 18/11/74
James Alexander, Col., antiquarian 31/1/68
James Burton, Prof. (1800–1877), history professor at R. C. university, Dublin 29/12/64
Jane Catherine, G's cousin 6/1/30
J. C. 16/3/50
J. G. 9/11/41
Johanna, G's aunt 2/8/25, 5/6/67, 10/6/67
John Anderson (1802–1862), Scottish lawyer 13/7/46
John M. G. (–1832), G's cousin 29/7/25
Johnston Forbes- (1853–1937), actor 13/1/93 n
Joseph (1810–1866), Edinburgh historian and editor 12/10/63
Lawrence, Scottish banker 16/9/64
Mary, née Chisholm 7/4/37
Mary (–1825), G's aunt 9/8/25, 14/8/25, 18/8/25
Patrick, advocate 21/11/33
S., Miss 29/9/91
Thomas Campbell (1789–1863), Indian civil servant 5/4/28
W. C., applicant 7/11/54
William 23/1/78, 30/8/78
William, G's cousin 14/10/34
William, of Ayr 4/6/88
William (1765–1844), mother's cousin 31/12/35, 7/4/37
William, Dr., physician 22/9/69 ?
William, Mrs. 21/6/44
William Archibald Scott, Rev. (–1897) 4/12/76

Robertson & Nicholson, Messrs., wine merchants 22/1/64, 18/10/83 L
Robie, T., editor, *Caledonian Mercury* 28/10/61 n, 19/11/61
Robins,
Charles Matthew, Rev. 17/7/45
Edward Cookworthy 22/10/78, 8/3/80
James, London auctioneer 6/7/67
Sanderson, Rev. (1801–1862), educationalist 8/5/37, 6/11/55
Robins, Cameron and Kemm, Messrs., London solicitors 20/11/87
Robinson *see* Grey, Heywood, Vyner
Robinson,
rescue 6/6/53
Mr., banker in Scott's, G's bank 26/3/56, 17/1/66
Mr., journalist on *Daily News* 6/4/89
Arthur Edward, Rev. 14/11/72
Colpitts 19/12/86
E., of Dukinfield; a miner? 20/9/71
E. A., translator 22/6/88 n
Frederick, barrister 23/5/45 ?
Frederick, Dr. 13/4/89
Frederick John; 1st Earl of Ripon 3/10/31
George Frederick Samuel, Lord; Earl De Grey; 1st Marquis of Ripon 10/2/53
George Richard, whig M.P. 26/3/33 n
Henrietta Ann Theodosia, née Vyner, Lady de Grey (1859), Lady Ripon (1871) 6/5/63, 25/5/71, 21/8/74, 4/9/74, 29/9/87, 15/4/88
Hercules George Robert, Sir (1824–1897), 1st Baron Rosmead, governed Cape Colony, High Commissioner of South Africa 8/3/81 c, 12/3/81 c, 25/5/81, 18/6/81, 2/10/81 ff, 19/10/81, 30/10/81, 3/11/81, 3/1/82, 12/7/82, 2/10/82, 5/10/82, 23/5/83, 29/11/83, 27/10/84, 14/3/85, 20/3/85 c, 27/3/85 c, 26/3/90, 7/11/93
James, Capt., of Edinburgh 10/12/33 n
John, clerk to the Bank of England 26/11/55
John, of Winthorpe Hall 6/10/32
John, Dr. 5/1/63 ?

John Beverley, Sir (1791–1863), Chief Justice of Upper Canada 15/12/47 ?
John Carleton, Rev. 17/5/79
John Charles, Sir (1824–1913), connoisseur 9/6/56, 16/4/62, 6/1/63, 1/5/63, 27/7/66, 17/11/66, 9/2/67
Joseph, merchant 18/4/70
Robert Spencer, Adm. Sir (1809–1889) 18/6/70 c, 17/3/71 c, 18/4/71, 26/4/71
Thomas, Sir (1827–1897), Knight (1894), liberal M.P. 25/3/92
Thomas, Ven. Dr. (1790–1873), Master of the Temple 9/4/45
William 1/3/62 ?
William Frederick, G's fag at Eton 23/9/26
William Percy, Rev. Dr. (1836–1881) 13/11/75, 30/7/77
Robison, John, Sir (1778–1843), inventor 21/7/42
Robjohns, Henry J., Rev. 5/7/76
Robson,
Mr. 25/8/66
Mr., of Natal 16/5/87
Francis, of Idle 13/4/58
J. A. 3/11/86
James Stuart, Rev. 12/6/57
J. G. 3/9/74
Thomas Frederick (1822–1864), actor and comedian 25/2/54
Roby, Henry John (1830–1915), liberal M.P. 22/10/90 n
Roche,
Edmund Burke (1815–1874), 1st Baron Fermoy (1856), liberal M.P. 6/6/53, 23/2/60, 28/1/74 L
John, grocer 27/4/69
Ralph 12/3/79
Rochussen, Charles, Dutch art historian 17/5/79 ?
Rock,
Daniel, Rev. (1799–1871), Roman Catholic 23/10/70
William Frederick, of Blackheath 30/11/68
Rocke, Mrs. 14/10/76
Rockliff *see* Farquhar
Rodber,
E., Rev. 5/10/41
William Johnson, Rev. 15/2/39, 15/6/40
Rodd, James Rennell (1858–1941), diplomat 12/12/91
Rodell, Mr. 22/1/79
Roden *see* Jocelyn
Roden,
William Sargent, Col. (1829–1882) 21/2/73
William Thomas (1817–1892), artist 11/9/77, 12/9/77
Rodler, Mr. 22/1/38
Rodriguez, J. C. 11/5/89
Rodway, O., Rev. 27/7/75
Rodwell,
John Medows, Rev. (1808–1900), orientalist 10/3/76
William, banker 20/3/60
Roe,
C. S. 26/4/77
Henry, of Dublin 20/10/77
John Erasmus, barrister 28/3/56
T. W., Rev., anglican priest in Ireland 9/3/46
Roebuck, John Arthur (1801–1879), radical M.P. 15/2/36 n, 12/1/55, 24/1/55, 9/2/55, 18/2/55 ff
Rogers,
Lieut. 29/2/60
Miss 16/1/57
A. J., Col. 10/5/79
Arnold, dentist 9/10/41
Charles, Rev. (1825–1890), antiquarian, presbyterian 16/7/56
Edmund Dawson (1823–1910), publisher, journalist and spiritualist 25/9/86, 19/2/87, 19/3/87
F., radical journalist 9/10/85
Frederic, Sir; Lord Blachford 26/5/27
James Edwin Thorold (1823–1890), economist, liberal M.P. 9/2/48, 3/4/60, 25/5/66, 29/1/78, 30/1/78, 21/2/82, 18/3/82 c, 15/8/82 L, 13/11/82, 7/7/86 L, 8/7/86
James Guinness, Rev. (1822–1911), congregationalist and liberal apologist 20/6/76, 7/7/79, 28/2/88, 7/7/88, 20/5/92
John, engraver 15/8/43 ?
John Davenport, historian 11/12/78 ?
J. W. F., author 30/11/86
R. R., Rev. 12/11/90
Samuel (1763–1855), poet 21/6/36, 22/12/37, 23/12/37, 20/10/42, 26/10/42, 28/5/51
William, Rev. (1819–1896) 23/1/56, 18/4/56, 8/5/56
William Showell, of Birmingham 5/6/77
Rogge, Friedrich Wilhelm (1808–1889) 12/3/80
Rogier, Charles Latour (1800–1885), prime minister of Belgium 14/7/62
Rokeby *see* Montagu
Rolandi,
Sig. 26/1/88
P., bookseller 19/6/55
Rolando, A. 22/6/79 ?
Roler, Dr., physician in Carlsruhe to Helen G 5/11/45
Rolfe,
E. Neville, of Naples 7/2/89
Laura, née Carr, Lady Cranworth 28/9/58

Rolfe (*cont.*)
Robert Mounsey, Sir (1790–1868), 1st Baron Cranworth (1850), lord chancellor 1/7/37 n, 23/9/46
Rolffs, Mrs. 20/7/88
Rolle, Miss 27/5/33
Rolleston,
George, Prof. (1829–1881), anatomist 26/3/68, 19/7/78
Lancelot, Col., tory M.P. 3/2/38
Rollins, Kate, of Bridlington *see* Scarsdale
Rollo, Hugh J., of Edinburgh 28/11/55, 7/12/55, 7/1/64, 11/10/71
Rolls,
Joseph Henry, customs officer 18/5/44
William, 9th Baron Rolls (1846) 14/6/45
Rolph, J. F. 24/3/79
Roma *see* Bowen
Roma, Candiano, Count 27/11/58 n
Romanes, George John (1848–1894), scientist 4/5/88, 9/9/92 L, 18/10/92 L, 22/10/92 ff
Romanov *see* Olga Nicolajevna
Romberg, Baron 13/6/77
Romilly,
Edward (–1870), of the audit board 26/5/54
John, Judge Sir (–1874), 1st Baron Romilly (1865), liberal M.P. 4/10/53
Romney *see* Marsham
Ronald, J. G. 3/1/79
Ronalds, Francis, Sir (1788–1873), Knight (1870), telegraph inventor 28/3/70
Ronayne, Charles 20/3/79, 17/4/88
Ronel, M., Miss 22/7/87
Roney, Cusack Patrick, Sir (1810–1868), Knight (1853), railway director 19/7/55
Ronge, Johannes, Rev., priest in Germany 4/10/45
Rooke, Mr., in Venice 8/10/79
Rookwood *see* Ibbetson
Room, H. 8/10/86
Roose, Dr. 18/12/89
Roostrum, Meer 24/6/43
Rootem, M. 18/2/89
Rootes, Rudge 21/4/80
Roper,
Charles Blaney Trevor- (1799–1871), Flintshire landowner, partner in Oak Farm Co.; Boydell's br.-in-law 12/7/41
R., surveyor 25/2/79
William, journalist on *The Times* 8/11/43
Roper and Drowley, Messrs., publishers 8/1/90
Rorison,
Gilbert, Rev. 10/12/56
Vincent Lewis, Rev. 30/1/80
Rorrison, James 11/12/79
Ros, Dudley Charles Fitzgerald de (1827–1907), 24th Baron de Ros (1874) 5/10/64
Rosa, Carl Augustus Nicholas (1842–1889), opera impresario 26/4/83
Roscoe *see* Sandbach
Roscoe,
rescue 12/6/80
Henry Enfield, Prof. Sir (1833–1915), liberal M.P. 1/7/84
Thomas (1791–1871), author 22/3/59
William, merchant in Liverpool 5/1/39 n, 15/2/43 n
William Caldwell 15/2/43 n
William Stanley 15/2/43
Rose *see* Douglas
Rose,
rescue 7/9/70
rescue 2/7/61, 17/7/67
Capt. 20/10/41
Miss, governess to Henry Glynne's children 20/7/59, 25/9/59, 28/8/60
Mr., coalmine owner in Hawarden 29/8/60
H. H., Rev. 14/11/39
H. St. J. 5/10/53 n
Hugh Henry (1803–1895), Baron Strathnairn, soldier 14/12/82
James Anderson (1819–1890), picture collector, solicitor 5/12/57
John, Sir (1820–1888), 1st Baronet (1872), Canadian politician and banker 28/11/70
John Nugent (1812–1867), of Inverness 28/9/25
L., rescue 20/3/60, 10/4/60
O. 8/2/78
Peter, of Demerara 12/2/34
Philip 5/10/53
Samuel, London merchant 7/3/55 ?
Rosebery *see* Primrose
Rosenberg,
A. 16/12/74 ?
William George, artist 9/3/78 ?
Rosenblatt, Mr. 20/4/78
Rosenborg, C. 4/1/83
Rosenkrone, Baron 18/8/85
Rosina, Countess of Mirafiore, mistress of Victor Emmanuel II 1/2/88
Rosinsky, Miss 7/12/88
Roskelly,
J., Dr., surgeon 7/1/51
W. 9/9/77
Rosmead *see* Robinson
Rosny, Mlle.de, rescue 4/3/70
Ross,
A., of Edinburgh 8/5/91
Alexander, surveyor general, coastguard office 10/1/44
Alexander Milton, of Canada 14/1/76

Charles (-1860), commissioner, audit board 21/3/53 ?
Charles (1800-1860), tory M.P. 20/12/34
Charles (1800-1884), journalist on *The Times* 20/2/57
David, blacksmith 13/11/34
David, of Dublin 14/4/68
David, of Montrose 23/9/52
Eric 4/1/87
F. J. (1848-1926), aide in Dublin to Spencer 8/5/82
George, of the G.P.O. 19/9/59
G. Macleod, Rev., priest in Quebec 14/2/53 ?
Henry James 3/1/88
Horatio (1801-1886), whig M.P. 10/12/34
James 31/3/50
Janet Ann, Mrs., author 3/1/88, 14/1/88, 19/1/88
J. L., Mrs. 24/9/71
John Lockhart, Rev. (1810-1891), author 24/11/29
John Stephen, Col. 5/9/77 ?
M., Lady, née Cornwallis 20/12/34 n
Patrick, Sir, retired colonial governor 31/12/45
R. 13/12/78
W. B., poet 9/10/75
W. G., alias Herbert Martyne 9/12/75
William Andrew, colonial secretary of the Gold Coast 1/5/57
William Charles, Sir (1794-1860), artist 22/6/42
W. K. 18/11/67
Rossa, Jeremiah O'Donovan, Fenian 4/2/70 c, 19/2/70 c, 26/2/70 c, 2/3/70, 17/3/83 c
Rosse *see* Parsons
Rossetti, William Michael (1829-1919), art critic 16/3/57
Rossi,
Monsignor, judge 5/11/38
Ernesto, actor 11/5/76 ?
Giovanni Battista De (1822-1894), archaeologist 24/10/66
Rosslyn *see* Erskine
Rossolino, Sig., of Zante, Ionia 24/8/60
Rostovsky, Alexis Lobanov-, Prince (1824-1896) 3/5/80
Rostron, Samuel, barrister 10/8/74
Roswag, C., of Paris 19/6/65
Roth, Henry Ling, anthropologist 24/7/78
Rothery,
H. C., Mrs. 12/12/79 ?
Henry Cadogan (1817-1888), registrar to Privy Council 1/7/62, 8/11/71
Roth family 4/4/93
Rothman, Richard Wellesley (1798-1856), registrar, University College, London 16/12/31
Rothschild *see* Primrose, Sassoon, Yorke
Rothschild,
Adelheid, née Herz 21/1/51 n
Adolph de, Baron (1823-1900), banker 30/7/64, 8/3/71
Alfred Charles, Baron (1842-1918), banker 6/7/70, 10/9/92
Alice de, Miss 1/8/85
Anthony de, Sir (1810-1876), 1st Baronet (1847), banker 21/11/62
Carl Meyer de, Baron (1788-1855), banker in Naples 21/1/51
Charlotte, Baroness (-1884) 2/3/63, 6/3/75, 18/3/75
Ferdinand James de, Baron (1839-1898), liberal unionist M.P. 1/8/85, 31/3/87, 26/4/88, 19/3/90, 17/3/93
Lionel Nathan de, Baron (1808-1879), banker 16/12/47 n, 10/5/56, 21/4/58, 16/4/59, 12/7/61, 6/3/69, 10/4/69, 19/7/73, 6/3/75, 18/3/75, 19/6/75
Louisa, Lady 31/3/88 n
Meyer, Baroness 9/3/75, 14/3/75
Meyer Carl, Baron (-1886), banker 21/1/51 n, 17/10/61, 26/6/63
Nathan Meyer de, Sir (1840-1915), 1st Baron Rothschild (1885), banker 3/3/71, 24/4/82 L, 5/8/84 c, 6/8/84 c, 29/4/85, 24/6/85 L, 3/2/86, 17/3/88, 28/2/91 ff
Rothwell,
Richard Rainshaw, Count (1809-1890) 12/10/65
Richard Rainshaw, Rev. (1772-1863) 18/5/55
R. R., Mrs. 29/7/68 ?
Rotton, Richard, chief clerk, Woods & Forests 19/6/56
Rouher, Eugène (1814-1884), French politician 21/6/62
Rouland, G., governor of Bank of France 25/1/67
Round,
Charles Gray (1797-1867), tory M.P. 8/4/42 ?
John (1783-1860), tory M.P. 30/4/42
Roundell,
Charles Saville (1827-1906), liberal M.P. 13/6/68, 10/11/69 L, 27/2/71, 25/8/71, 29/12/71, 21/8/72, 23/11/72, 28/11/72 c, 28/6/75, 9/7/80 n, 1/11/82, 26/10/83 L, 22/3/87, 1/9/90, 6/12/92, 17/12/92 c, 19/4/93, 14/3/94 L
Henry, Rev. (1825-1864) 21/3/57
Henry Dawson, Rev. (1786-1852) 30/4/39 ?
Julia, née Tollemache 20/2/81 ?
Roupell, William, liberal M.P., forger 23/5/60, 8/4/93
Rous *see* Hotham

Rous,
Augusta (-1901), Lady Stradbroke 9/12/92 L
Henry John, Adm. (1795-1877), tory M.P. and racing reformer 14/5/42, 1/6/70
Rouse,
Mr. 6/2/63
A. F. 6/5/79
Roustan, Théodore, French minister in Tunis 13/6/81
Routledge,
Edmund 10/7/87
George (1812-1888), publisher 20/6/68
Thomas, author 8/7/75
Rouzeaud,
Auguste, musician 21/11/84 n
Christine, Mad. (1843-1921), opera singer 25/5/81 ?, 21/11/84
Rovedino, Tommaso 2/8/45
Rovero, Adeodata, Mme. 23/8/51
Rowan,
Charles, Col. Sir (1782-1852), 1st chief commissioner of police 1/11/42
J. 4/12/74
Robert W., Rev., of Ballymena 12/2/78
William (1789-1879), field marshal 13/6/38
Rowbotham, Thomas Charles Leeson (1823-1875), artist 10/12/57
Rowcliffe, J. 16/5/78
Rowden,
Edward Wetherell, Rev. (1814-1870) 2/7/57
F., Rev. 19/11/87
Rowe,
George, Rev. 12/8/68 ?
George Hunter 14/1/86
R. 11/5/74
Samuel, Rev. 5/4/48 ?
W. T. 25/7/77
Rowell, Mr. 6/2/77
Rowland, W. B. 17/9/68
Rowlands,
A. 10/8/74
D., Rev. 16/4/68
F. 5/11/86
Frederick, of Hawarden 16/2/87
Jane Elizabeth, of Hawarden 16/2/87
John, Rev. (-1919) 9/7/75
William Bowden (1837-1906) 20/11/89 ?
Rowlandson, Edward, Rev. (1803-1864) 5/9/28 ?
Rowley *see* Hay
Rowley,
Misses 3/9/90
Adam Clarke, Rev. 26/4/74
C. 15/3/76
C. C., Rev. 6/10/91
Charlotte (-1871), née Shipley 19/7/33, 24/6/35
Clotworthy, 1st Baron Langford 24/6/35 n, 2/5/40 n
Frances, née Rowley, Lady Langford 2/5/40
Hercules Langford Boyle (1829-1904), landlord 5/8/57
Richard Thomas, Col. (1812-1887), tory M.P. 24/6/35 n
Rowntree, Joseph (1836-1925), manufacturer and philanthropist 4/1/53, 28/1/78 ?
Roworth, Charles, printer 18/3/57
Rowsell,
Joel (-1886), bookseller 9/7/53
Thomas James, Rev. Canon (1816-1894) 3/5/50, 27/1/56, 13/10/81, 1/7/90, 26/4/91, 25/5/92
Rowton *see* Corry
Roxburgh, W. 28/2/78
Roxburghe *see* Ker
Roy, H. E. 22/5/90
Royal College of Physicians, Edinburgh, Treasurer 7/12/86
Royal Holloway College 14/12/81 n
Royan, Baroness de 24/10/90
Royce, Mrs. 5/9/79
Royle,
John Forbes, surgeon 6/5/45
Thomas Richard Popplewell 25/5/90
Rubenstein, Mr. 8/10/77
Rubersohn, J. C. W. 1/2/44
Rubinstein, Mr. 22/12/87 n
Rudall, Francis A. 14/4/80
Rudd,
Miss 22/4/80
Eric, Rev. 1/7/46 ?
Rudini, Marquis 19/7/93
Ruff, Mrs., a bawd 10/4/50
Ruffo, Paolo, Principe di Castelcicala, Neapolitan ambassador 16/3/46
Rufford,
Francis (-1854), banker, tory M.P. 16/8/51
F. T. 27/9/72
Ruge, Arnold (1802-1880), German liberal 1/10/56
Ruggins, W. 3/11/85
Ruiz, M. F. 22/7/76, 13/10/76
Rule,
F. 4/9/78
William Harris, Rev. (1802-1890) 18/10/51
Rummals, Mr. 22/5/89
Rumney,
Peter, solicitor 11/6/74 ?
P. J. 7/5/89
Rumpf, C., Mrs., rescue 27/2/68, 25/3/68, 15/7/68, 11/2/70, 29/6/70, 20/8/70
Rumsey, Arthur, secretary, United Universities Club 25/6/67
Rundell, Bridge and Rundell, Messrs., goldsmiths 17/1/43

Rusbridge, W. 23/10/75
Rush, W. T. 24/2/77
Rushbrooke, W. G. 9/9/76
Rushe, E., clerk in army accounts 30/3/60 ?
Rusher, Mr. 31/10/75
Rushton,
Miss 25/1/42
Mrs. 13/1/38
R., of Blackpool 16/7/68
Rushworth & Jarvis, Messrs., land surveyors 14/6/62
Ruskin,
Miss, nurse 7/2/79
John 28/4/40 n
W. E. 18/3/58
Russel, Alexander (1814-1876), editor, *The Scotsman* 20/10/54
Russell *see* Greene, Grenville, Malet
Russell,
Miss, rescue 17/5/61, 12/9/70, 18/6/78
Mr., of U.S.A. 10/11/75
Mrs., of U.S.A. 24/7/86
Adelaide, Lady, née Lister, formerly Lady Ribblesdale 26/11/32 n
Adeline Marie, née Somers-Cocks, Lady Tavistock, Duchess of Bedford 23/10/78, 20/7/87
Agatha, Lady (1853-1933) 30/7/75, 15/5/79, 21/3/85, 1/7/93 n, 2/7/93
Anna Maria (-1857), née Stanhope, Duchess of Bedford 10/7/44
Arthur John Edward, Lord (1825-1892), liberal M.P. 19/7/64, 7/12/78, 14/10/85
Arthur Tozer, Rev. (1806-1874), author 27/1/38, 7/1/66, 26/6/66, 13/11/66
Bertrand Arthur William (1872-1970), 3rd Earl Russell, philosopher and reformer 20/4/78 n, 21/5/81 n
Caroline Alicia Diana, Lady (-1890), née Pery 5/5/56
Caroline Diana Rosalind 18/12/73 n
Charles Arthur, Sir (1832-1900), 1st Baron Russell of Killowen, liberal M.P. 24/8/86, 5/1/87, 18/4/87, 15/6/87, 30/6/87, 12/7/88, 20/2/89, 23/2/89, 1/4/89, 28/5/89, 27/2/90, 6/3/90, 2/12/90, 6/5/91, 22/6/92, 14/9/92 L, 9/6/93
Charles James Fox, Lord (1807-1894), sergeant-at-arms (1848) 28/6/49
Charles William (1812-1880), President of Maynooth 27/7/59
Edward Richard, Sir (1834-1920), Knight (1893), 1st Baron Russell (1920), editor, *Liverpool Daily Post* 26/2/69, 9/9/71 L, 13/1/76 n, 21/1/78, 7/10/78, 23/7/84 L, 19/4/86 L, 11/6/86, 23/8/88 ff
Elizabeth, née Sackville West, Duchess of Bedford 19/9/78 n
Elizabeth Laura Henrietta (-1886), artist 31/12/66 ?
Emily Theresa, Lady, née Villers, Lady Ampthill 22/10/66 n, 28/11/66
Frances Anna Maria (Fanny), Lady (1815-1898), née Elliot, Countess Russell, wife of Lord John Russell 4/3/47, 26/1/55, 29/5/76, 21/5/81, 1/7/93 n
Francis Albert Rollo (1849-1914) 28/4/87
Francis Charles Hastings (1819-1891), 9th Duke of Bedford (1872), whig M.P. and suicide 19/9/78, 28/8/80 L, 28/8/81 L, 27/12/83 L, 18/6/84 L, 13/12/84 L
Frederick William, Rev. 21/1/52
George Lake, Judge (1802-1878) 4/8/32, 5/5/56 n
George William Erskine (1853-1919), liberal M.P., minor office, G's religious biographer 14/6/84, 18/6/84, 13/10/84 L, 5/12/84, 13/12/84, 21/12/86, 10/3/87 ?, 6/3/94 L
George William Francis Sackville (1852-1893), 10th Duke of Bedford (1891), Lord Tavistock, liberal M.P. 23/10/78, 15/1/84 L, 10/3/87 ?, 14/7/87, 15/7/87, 8/3/91, 17/2/92, 26/2/92, 5/3/92, 2/11/92
G. J. 29/11/86
Henshaw S., barrister 18/3/68 ?
Isabel Watts 5/6/33
James, Dr., physician in Edinburgh 16/12/33
James M., farmer 23/2/87, 7/10/89
James Ward 7/2/79
Jesse David Watts (1786-1875), Peelite M.P. 5/6/33 n, 30/5/35, 4/6/35
J. H. 12/10/78
John (1766-1839), 6th Duke of Bedford (1802) 9/5/40 n, 23/4/41 n
John (1842-1876), Viscount Amberley, liberal M.P. 18/3/68, 4/7/70
John, Lord; 1st Earl Russell 26/11/32 n
John, Rev. (1787-1863) 23/5/51
John Francis Stanley (1865-1931), 2nd Earl Russell 21/5/81 n
John Fuller, Rev. 30/1/41
John Robert, of Glasgow 20/2/37 ?
John Rutherford, Dr., physician 7/7/59
John Scott (1808-1882), engineer 11/2/50
Laura, Lady, wife of Lord Arthur Russell 18/12/73, 2/7/93
Mary Agatha, Lady (-1933) 7/3/73
Michael, Bp. (1781-1848), dean of Edinburgh (1831), bishop of Glasgow (1837) 20/2/37 ?
Odo William Leopold (ambassador) 22/10/66

Russell (*cont.*)
Robert Frankland, Sir 11/7/49 n
S. D. G. 15/3/80
Sophia, née Coussmaker, Lady de Clifford 23/4/41
T. C., Rev. 21/2/80
Thomas, Rev., of Croydon 2/11/76
Thomas, Rev., presbyterian and missionary 31/12/59
Thomas Wallace, Sir (1841–1920), liberal unionist M.P. 18/9/75, 1/8/90
William 1/9/76
William, chancery accountant 19/4/53, 4/10/53
William, Lord 9/5/40
William, Sir (1822–1892), 2nd Baronet (1839), liberal M.P. 3/12/68
William Clark (1844–1911), novelist 16/3/78, 30/12/78 n
Rustum Bey, Turkish ambassador in Florence 11/1/67, 3/2/86
Ruth, H. M. B. 5/3/92
Rutherford, George Shaw, Dr., physician 21/4/57
Ruthven, Mary Elizabeth Thornton Hore- (1784–1864), Baroness Ruthven 3/4/60
Rutland *see* Manners
Rutledge, John Young, Rev. (–1872) 17/5/52 ?
Rutley, Thomas, picture dealer 17/7/50
Rutter,
D. 23/12/79
John, Dr., physician in Liverpool 3/8/29
Ruvignés, Mrs. de 31/1/77
Ryan,
Father, of Hawarden 3/8/91
Charles Lister, Sir (1831–1920), G's private secretary 1859-65, Audit Board secretary 1865, later Comptroller 24/6/59, 29/6/61, 16/7/62, 26/4/65, 12/5/65, 8/4/93
D. J. 16/10/77
Edward, Sir (1793–1875), civil service, commissioner 1/8/55
G. 7/1/78
Jane, Lady, née Shaw-Lefevre 16/7/62
Ryde *see* Hervey
Ryder *see* Mackenzie, Saurin
Ryder,
Rev. Mr. 17/7/38
Dudley (1762–1847), Viscount Sandon (1803), 1st Earl of Harrowby (1809) 3/10/31 n
Dudley (1798–1882), 2nd Earl of Harrowby (1847), Viscount Sandon 27/1/32, 3/5/41, 4/5/41
Frances (–1859), née Stuart, Lady Sandon, Lady Harrowby 6/7/33
G. A., Lady, née Somerset 19/7/37 n
George Dudley (1810–1880) 3/10/31, 25/4/34
George Lisle, treasury clerk 27/8/60
Granville Dudley, Lieut. (1799–1879) 19/7/37
Henry, Bp. (1777–1836), bishop of Gloucester (1815), bishop of Lichfield (1824) 4/6/35
Joshua Brown, Rev. 28/1/45
Sophia Lucy, née Sargent 25/4/34 n
Thomas B. 22/5/67
Ryland, George Herman, ex-clerk of Canadian executive council 22/3/49
Rylands,
J. P. 7/12/89
Peter (1820–1887), liberal M.P. 27/3/71, 9/3/72 c, 28/5/84
Ryle, John Charles, Bp. (1816–1900), bishop of Liverpool (1880) 30/9/41
Rylett, Harold, of Salford 30/3/77
Ryley,
Mrs. 21/5/89
E. 3/12/78
Ryman, J. 3/7/55
Ryumin, K. N. Bestuzhev- 8/9/76 n

Sabatelli, Felice, Neapolitan general 29/2/52
Saberton, Joseph, goldsmith 7/1/78 ?
Sabine, Edward, Gen. Sir (1788–1883) 3/7/69
Sabinjie, of Egypt 14/8/84
Sabriano,
Duchess of 19/1/51
Duke of 19/1/51
Sabuco, Gen. 18/6/87
Saburov, Peter Alexandrovitch, Count (1835–1918) 30/11/68
Sacchi, Terenzio, Italian author 14/11/54, 29/12/66
Sachs, M. 21/4/83
Sackville *see* West
Sackville, John Frederick, 3rd Duke of Dorset 22/12/41 n
Sackville West *see* Russell, Stanley
Sacré, William, Madame 24/5/58
Sadleir,
C., Mrs. 16/4/45
John (1814–1856), liberal M.P. 7/1/54
Sadler,
Mr., of Derby 27/9/77
Michael Ernest, Sir (1861–1943), educationalist 13/12/79
Michael Ferrebee, Rev. (1819–1895) 1/9/69
M. T., tory radical M.P. 28/9/29
W. E., Rev. 15/2/87
Sadler, E.& G., Messrs., tailors 29/6/52 ?
Safe, James William 21/10/49, 29/2/56
Said Pacha (–1863), Viceroy of Egypt 21/6/62, 14/7/62

Sailer, Johann Michael, Bp. (1751–1832), bishop of Regensburg (1822) 17/12/38
Sainsbury,
Henry, Dr. 30/3/59
John, bookseller and publisher 5/4/38
W. N. 5/4/38 n
Saint André, Jules, chevalier 10/12/52
Saint Ange, rescue 2/2/72
Saint Angelo,
Marchese 5/12/50
D. Niccolo, Cav., Neapolitan minister 29/2/52
Saint Aubyn,
John, Sir (1829–1908), 2nd Baronet (1872), 1st Baron St. Levan (1887), liberal M.P. 5/7/74
William John, Rev. (1814–1877) 2/7/57
Saint Clair,
Mr. 25/12/78
Charles (1768–1863), 13th Baron Sinclair (1775) 8/9/32
G. 13/6/88
Isabella Mary (–1875), née Chatto, Lady Sinclair 8/9/32
Sainte-Aulaire *see* Beaupoil
Saint George, John, Sir (1812–1891), soldier 3/3/45
Saint Hilaire, Jules Barthélemy, French politician 12/10/61
Saint Hill, Richard (1787–1869), antiquarian 9/12/51
Saint John,
Charles Orlando Henry Perkins, Lieut. 23/11/58
Frederick (–1863), surveyor general of customs 24/3/53
Spencer, diplomat 29/5/77
Spenser, Sir (1825–1910), diplomat and author 5/10/84
V. J. 1/9/66
Saint Lawrence, William Ulrick Tristram (1837–1909), 4th Earl of Howth, liberal M.P. (1868) 22/8/81
Saint Leger, William Nassau, Rev. 6/12/41
Saint Léon, Charles Victor Arthur (–1870), French violinist 21/10/50
Saint Maur,
Edward Adolphus (1775–1855), 11th Duke of Somerset 1/6/51 n
Edward Adolphus, Lord (1804–1885), Lord Seymour, 12th Duke of Somerset 9/3/40 n
Jane Georgiana, née Sheridan, Duchess of Somerset 4/7/44
Margaret (–1880), née Shaw-Stewart, Duchess of Somerset 1/6/51
Saint Oswald's College, Ellesmere 26/10/86
Saint Quentin, George Danby, Rev. (1803–1872) 8/4/32
Saintsbury, George 27/7/38
Saint-Yves, Alexandre 24/5/77
Sala, George Augustus Henry Fairfield (1828–1895), journalist 9/7/60
Salazari, Mons. 4/2/89
Salemos, Count 26/2/63
Salis,
Henrietta de (–1856), née Foster 3/4/38
Jerome Fane de, Count de Salis (1807) 3/4/38 n
Salisbury *see* Cecil, Stanley
Salisbury,
E. G., Mrs. 2/2/57
Enoch Gibbon (1819–1890), liberal M.P. 2/2/57 n
Salkeld, Joseph, bookseller 16/12/73, 14/1/82
Salmon,
S. C. 4/11/76
Thomas, poet 8/4/68 ?
Salmond,
Charles A., Rev. 24/5/79
D. S. 1/6/91
Salmonè, Mrs. 21/11/91
Salmons, Mr., messenger 9/3/53
Salomons,
Cecilia, Lady 27/7/77
D., of Ionia 25/11/58
David, Sir (1797–1873), 1st Baronet (1869), banker, liberal M.P. and G's colleague in Greenwich 12/5/52, 2/5/71 L
Salt,
R., of Birmingham 22/7/40
Samuel 28/4/52 ?
Titus, Sir (1803–1877), liberal M.P. 22/6/60
Salusbury, Philip H. B., Lieut. 12/11/76, 15/11/76, 29/5/77, 9/6/77 n
Saluse, Rosario 6/8/89
Salvadori, Sig., singer 23/3/32
Salvagnole, Vincenzo, Piedmont politician 2/11/58
Salvani, N. 31/12/88
Salvi, Marchesa, of Naples 29/2/52
Salvini, Tommaso (1829–1916), actor 7/5/75
Salvo, Rosario, author 15/1/89
Samartzidou, E., Mme., of Ionia 14/1/59
Samborne, S. S. Palmer- 21/4/79 ?
Sambourne, Edwin Linley (1844–1900), cartoonist 7/5/89 n
Sampson,
Mr. 8/1/76
Daniel Dod, Rev. (1806–1891) 16/5/26 ?
Edward Frank, Rev., Censor of Christ Church, Oxford 3/2/90
George, surgeon 16/1/46
Sampson, Low & Co., Messrs., publishers 30/7/77
Sampy, Mr. 22/7/78
Samson,
Blum, toy dealer 9/8/55

Samson (*cont.*)
Joseph Isidore (-1871), French actor 22/10/50
Samuda, Joseph D'Aguilar (1813-1885), liberal M.P. 9/3/68
Samuel,
Louis (1794-1859), of Liverpool 2/6/59 ?
Sylvester, Liverpool merchant 29/5/56
Samuelson,
Mr., of York 11/10/62
Godfrey Blundell (1863-1941), liberal M.P. 24/3/92
Henry Bernhard, Sir (1845-1937), 2nd Baronet (1905), liberal M.P. 29/8/68, 15/7/79
Joseph, Birkenhead liberal 25/1/77
Sanctuary, Thomas, Ven. (1822-1889) 17/11/77
Sandars,
George (1805-1879), tory M.P. 2/4/51, 21/7/54
Joseph, Liverpool corn merchant 23/8/26
Joseph (1821-1893), Peelite M.P. 18/7/54 n
Thomas Collett (1825-1894), barrister 30/4/56
Virginia Frances Zerlina, Lady (-1922), née Taylour 18/7/54
Sandbach,
Henry Robertson (1807-1895), of Denbighshire 5/1/39
Margaret, née Roscoe 5/1/39 n
Samuel, Liverpool merchant 16/8/25 n, 5/1/39 n
Samuel, Mrs. 16/8/25
William Robertson (-1891) 10/8/57
Sandell, R. B., merchant 5/3/77 ?
Sandeman, G. G., wine merchant 10/2/43
Sandeman, Forster & Co., wine merchants 10/2/43 n
Sanders,
Harris 1/9/87
Henry George, engineer 1/12/77
James, Rev. (-1880) 9/3/58 ?
Thomas (1809-1852), barrister 4/7/27
Sanderson,
C. E. M. (-1877) 3/12/75 n
Charlotte Matilda, née Manners-Sutton 4/1/33 n
John Scott Burdon-, Prof. Sir (1828-1905), physician 12/11/88
Richard (1783-1857), tory M.P., Quaker 4/1/33 ?
Robert, Dr., G's physician in Brighton 24/3/94
Robert Edward, Rev. Dr. (1828-1913) 31/8/75
Sanderwick, Thomas 2/4/77
Sandford,
Daniel, Bp. (1766-1830), bishop of Edinburgh (1806) 30/4/28
Daniel Fox, Rev. 10/1/62
Francis Richard John, Sir (1824-1893), educationalist 17/7/77, 28/11/84
George, Rev. (1816-1898) 14/3/48
George Montagu Warren (-1879), tory M.P. 29/3/78
John, Archdeacon (1801-1873) 15/2/35
William Robert Wills- (1770-1859) 12/9/36 ?
Sandham, James Munro, Rev. 19/12/47
Sandhurst *see* Mansfield
Sandilands,
Alan, of Buxton 22/9/75
John, Rev. 13/9/44
Percival Richard Renorden, Rev. (1826-1890) 12/12/79
Richard Samuel Butler, Rev. 29/7/41
Sandon *see* Ryder
San Donato, Duca di 13/9/92
Sandoz, Frederic (1801-1863), founder, Church Pastoral Aid Society 12/9/36
Sands,
Mr. 31/12/76
John, of Midlothian 16/9/78
M., of Jamaica 13/2/83
M., Mrs. 5/11/77
Mahlon, millionaire 2/1/85, 14/3/85 n, 24/2/87
Mary, Mrs., American hostess in London 2/1/85, 14/3/85, 26/3/85, 24/2/87, 16/2/89, 21/7/89, 11/6/90, 9/12/90, 15/6/92, 16/11/92, 2/8/93, 21/12/93, 13/5/94
Sandwich *see* Montagu
Sandwith, Humphry, Dr. (1822-1881), physician 30/1/56, 20/2/77, 28/2/77
Sandys,
Mrs. 27/7/87
R. H., barrister 27/6/76 ?
Richard 24/7/84 ?
Sanfelice, Guglielmo, Cardinal 5/2/89 n
Sanford, John Bracebridge, barrister 25/5/27, 9/6/66
San Giacomo, Prince of, Neapolitan ambassador 21/1/51
Sangster,
J. 23/11/76
William (-1888), umbrella maker 25/5/52 ?
Sanguinetti, Apollo, Prof. 8/12/77
Sankey, Ira David, Rev. (1840-1908), evangelist 25/4/75 n
Sannervanni, Dr. 9/8/89
San Severino,
Maria Antonia, Princess Bisignano 19/11/38
Pietrantonio, Prince Bisignano 19/11/38
Sanseverino di Bisignano *see* Scondito
Sansom, James, of the I. R. B. 15/4/64
Santley *see* Lyttelton

Santon, P., of London 3/2/56 ?
Santorio, Dr., of Ionia 15/2/59
Saphir, Adolph, author 1/2/58 ?
Sargeant, William, Bayswater liberal 31/1/80 ?
Sargent *see* Manning, Ryder, Tempest, Wilberforce
Sargent,
Ambrose, oil supplier 31/3/74
Charles, Sir (1821–1900), judge in Ionia 29/11/58
John, Rev. 25/4/34 n
John Neptune, Gen. 12/3/90
Thomas, secretary, I. R. B. 16/11/67
Sarnow, Gustave 5/3/80
Sarson, George, Rev. 31/8/79
Sartiges, Eugène de, Count, French ambassador in Rome 26/12/66
Sartoris,
Adelaide (–1879), née Kemble 1/6/67
Edward John (1817–1888), liberal M.P. 1/6/67 n
Sartorius, George, Col. (1840–1912), soldier in Egypt 30/5/84
Sasse, Maurice, German Liberal Party representative in London 19/7/92
Sassoon,
Albert Abdullah David, Sir (1818–1896), 1st Baronet (1890) 8/5/73, 15/7/85
Aline C., née Rothschild 25/11/93
Edward Albert 25/11/93 n
Hannah (–1895), Lady Sassoon 8/5/73
Satouroff, M. 20/2/90
Satrondattis, Mr. 3/5/79
Sauer, George, author 24/5/79
Säuger, Madame 2/8/90
Saulez, Vincent, Rev. 24/7/66
Saumarez, Arthur 8/2/87
Saunders,
A. O., coolie employer, Mauritius 29/4/36
Augustus Page, Dean (1801–1878), dean of Peterborough (1853) 2/8/28
Charles Alexander (1797–1864), secretary, G. W. Railway (1833) 4/6/48 ?
Edwin, Sir (1814–1901), Knight (1883), G's dentist 6/10/53, 7/7/85 ?
F. J. 11/5/68
George (1859–1922), journalist 1/10/77, 4/10/82
George Lemon, music teacher 24/4/38 ?
Harris 1/9/87
Herbert, of the royal household 14/3/45
James, Liverpool broker 13/10/64
James, of U.S.A. 15/6/76
R. J., Mr. 31/3/43
Robert, of Lewisham 8/9/28 n
Robert, Mrs. (–1828) 8/9/28
Samuel Walker, Rev. 23/8/29
William (1823–1895), of Central News Agency, later liberal M.P. 5/3/75, 5/1/87
Saunders, Otley & Co., publishers 17/12/60
Saurin,
Edward, Adm. (–1878) 1/4/38
Mary, Lady (1801–1900), née Ryder 1/4/38 n
William (–1839) 1/4/38 n
Savage,
James (1779–1852), architect 7/3/42 n
Thomas J. 18/11/85
Savellarides, J., of Liverpool 21/1/90
Savile,
Miss 18/3/78
Mrs. 10/4/75
Arthur, Rev. (–1870) 24/5/45
Bouchier Wrey, Rev. (1817–1888) 12/10/67, 27/5/85 L
John, 3rd Earl of Mexborough 24/5/45 n
John Charles George (1810–1899), Viscount Pollington (1830), 4th Earl of Mexborough (1860), tory M.P. 3/10/31
Lucy Georgina, née Neville 24/5/45 n
Savill, Robert (–1888), assistant secretary, L. N. W. Railway 24/7/52
Saville,
D. 17/7/68
J. A. 17/5/62
Savory & Moore, Messrs., chemists 30/9/41 ?
Savouillon, Mons., French reporter 20/10/79
Saward, E. 7/12/54
Sawer, John Lamb, solicitor 28/10/73, 20/4/77
Sawyer,
F. J. 30/3/91
John, Toxteth shipwright 21/8/56
R., barrister 22/3/77 ?
Saxe-Meiningen *see* Bernhard
Saxe-Meiningen Court Theatre 17/6/81
Saxe-Weimar-Eisenach *see* Charles
Saxton, Charles Waring, Rev., headmaster 21/7/47 ?
Say,
Frederick Richard (1826–1858), artist 23/3/52
Jean-Baptiste Léon (1826–1896), French economist and politician, ambassador in London 19/10/79, 28/2/83, 22/3/83 L, 7/9/89, 6/1/92, 26/2/92
Sayce, Archibald Henry, Rev. (1845–1933) 20/11/77
Saye and Sele *see* Twisleton
Sayer,
George 12/12/40 n
Mary, née Greenhill 12/12/40
Thomas, Dr., physician 8/5/79 ?
Sayers, R., Mr., sculptor 9/11/64
Sayle, P. 10/3/74

Sayward, Mr. 11/7/76
Sbarbaro, Pietro, Prof., professor in Macerata university 8/10/75, 14/8/76
Scalera, F., Sig. 1/2/88
Scales, Mr. 5/2/76
Scalzani, Giovanni, Dr. 15/2/59, 17/11/59, 31/7/61
Scanlan, Mrs. 21/8/71
Scardino, Sig., artist 17/11/38
Scargill,
Mrs., of Gower St. 4/7/57
E. Tudor, assistant secretary, London Library 26/2/57
Scarisbrick, Anne, Lady (-1872), formerly Hunloke 15/12/67, 9/9/68, 21/10/68
Scarlet, H. 19/11/89
Scarlett,
James (1769-1844), 1st Baron Abinger (1835), tory M.P. 17/1/35
Peter Campbell (1804-1888), diplomat 5/11/78
Robert William (1810-1832) 20/10/27
Scarr,
Henry, footman 25/8/40
Sterndale 18/11/77
Scarsdale, Mrs., also known as Miss K. Rollins, rescue 8/9/80, 20/8/81, 22/8/89, 2/9/89
Scarth,
Harry Mengden, Rev. 9/8/49
John, Rev. 19/6/79
Scase, Mr. 26/12/85
Schack, Frederick Carl Emil, Baron (1810-1859), Baron de Brockdorff, secretary, Danish legation 12/8/43
Schadow, F. W., director, painting academy, Dusseldorf 14/8/38 n
Schaeffer, Adolphe, Rev. 10/3/75
Schaeffle, Albert Eberhard Friedrich 29/3/78 ?
Schaff, Philipp, Rev. Dr. (1819-1893) 16/9/73
Scharf, George, Sir (1820-1895), secretary, National Portrait Gallery 28/6/58, 29/3/67
Schayer, Mlle. 11/2/92
Schee, Messrs. 1/7/86
Schelling, Friedrich Wilhelm Joseph (1775-1854) 17/12/38 n
Schen, rescue 24/7/63
Schenck, Robert Cumming, Gen. (1809-1890), American soldier and diplomat in London 2/2/72 c, 3/2/72, 10/2/72, 16/2/72, 17/2/72, 24/2/72, 26/2/72, 28/2/72 L, 2/3/72 c, 6/3/72, 19/3/72, 23/4/72, 24/4/72 L, 27/4/72 c, 2/5/72 c, 6/5/72 c, 8/5/72 c, 5/6/72 c, 28/11/72 L, 27/8/75, 18/2/76
Schenkhauser, Mr. 6/5/91
Schenley, Edward Wyndham Harrington (1799-1878) 23/11/61
Scherer, Henri Adolphe Edmond (1815-1889) 18/10/79
Scherr, Gregor von, Abp. (-1877) 12/9/74
Schidrowitz, Samuel, Dr. 4/10/74
Schilizzi, Baron, of Naples, author 16/1/89 n, 31/1/89, 6/2/89, 7/2/89, 11/9/92
Schleiermacher, Friedrich Daniel Ernst (1768-1834), philosopher and theologian 17/12/38 n
Schliemann, Heinrich (1822-1890), archaeologist 10/10/73, 13/10/73 ff, 9/1/74 L, 4/5/74 n, 24/6/75, 25/6/75, 22/3/77, 11/4/77, 14/4/77, 30/4/77, 8/6/77, 5/12/77
Schlüter, Auguste, Miss (-1917), the Gladstones' housekeeper 17/10/90
Schmidt,
Dr., of Cologne 14/9/79, 12/1/80
Henry 9/12/45 ?
Schmidtalz, B. J. 11/4/66
Schnadhorst,
Francis (1840-1900), liberal agent and secretary of N. L. F. 24/9/76, 21/12/77, 19/5/86, 8/6/86 n, 23/6/86, 3/6/87, 11/10/88, 10/5/89, 12/6/90, 14/12/91, 7/3/92 ff, 13/8/92, 6/10/92 L, 24/11/92
Frank 2/10/58
Schneider, Henry William (1817-1887), liberal M.P. 1/6/58
Schoeffelin, Mr. 14/7/77
Schofield,
J. W. 22/2/76
J. W., Rev. 30/4/89
S. 15/1/91
Scholefield,
James, Rev. Prof. (1789-1853), regius professor of Greek, Cambridge 13/2/48
Joshua (1744-1844), radical M.P. 1/4/43
William (1809-1867), liberal M.P. 20/5/56, 15/3/60
Schöppink, Baron von, Russian diplomat in Naples 18/12/50, 29/2/52
Schraker, Dr. 16/8/83
Schreiber,
Charles (1826-1884), tory M.P. 1/5/55 n
Charlotte Elizabeth, Lady (1812-1895), née Bertie, Lady Guest (1833), Lady Schreiber (1855), collector, antiquarian and diarist 1/5/55, 6/6/72, 20/3/73
Schreiner, Olive Emilie Albertina, Miss (1855-1920), author 1/6/89
Schridrani, Mr. 9/4/80
Schubarth, B. J., Bavarian commissioner 25/9/51
Schulte, Johann Friedrich von, Dr. 25/2/76
Schultz, Hermann A. 15/2/78 ?
Schulz, Ann Bishop, Lady (1814-1884), soprano 9/3/77
Schumbacher, Dr. 29/11/87

Schuster, E. V., Rev. 18/11/86 n
Schuyler, Eugene, American consul in Bulgaria 26/2/77, 22/1/89
Schwabe, Mrs. 16/1/66
Schwande, Mons. 8/11/90
Schwann,
Charles Ernest, Sir (1844–1929), 1st Baronet (1906), liberal M.P. 19/7/90
Elizabeth, née Duncan, Lady Schwann 19/7/90
Schwartz, C.de 27/6/62
Schwartzenberg, F. A., author 21/7/66 ?
Schwertz, Mr. 24/6/75
Scialoia, Antonio (1817–1877) 4/3/59, 7/1/67
Sclopis, Federigo, Count (1798–1878) 4/3/59
Scobelev, Gen. (–1882), Russian general 15/9/82
Scobie,
Mrs. 15/4/80
Donald Mackay, Gen. 23/9/58
Scoble, John, of Newark 22/5/38 ?
Scollock, Mr. 21/3/78
Scondito,
Livia, Duchess, née Sanseverino di Bisignano 19/11/38
Ottavio Capece-, Duke 19/11/38
Scoones, W. Baptiste, author 7/3/83
Scoresby, William, Rev. 4/1/28
Scotcher, Richard Ganney 1/12/87 ?
Scotsman, reporter of 2/9/85
Scott *see* Canning, Cracroft, Mostyn
Scott,
rescue 6/6/63, 23/4/68, 17/4/74, 19/2/76
Dr., in Paris 29/9/66
Miss 26/4/89
Mr., in Naples 18/12/50
Mr., of Central News Agency 22/4/80
Mrs., Scottish supplicant 4/11/53
Adam, engineer 28/10/74
A. J., Mrs. 7/6/66
Alexander John (1805–1866), Principal, Owen's College, Manchester 16/4/38 ?
Alfred, Rev. 7/9/79
Anne, Lady (–1849), née Ommaney 25/2/33
Benjamin (1814–1892), Chamberlain of London 1/1/75, 31/10/75 n
Charles Prestwich (1846–1932), editor, *Manchester Guardian*, liberal M.P. 3/10/91
Charlotte Anne Montagu-Douglas-, Lady (1811–1895), née Thynne, Duchess of Buccleuch 19/6/38
Cicely Susan Montagu-Douglas- (1835–1915), née Stuart-Wortley-Mackenzie, Lady Montagu of Beaulieu 14/5/57, 22/10/63
Claude Edward, Sir (1804–1874), 3rd Baronet (1849), G's banker 5/4/37, 26/4/47
Elizabeth Susan, Miss, governess 30/4/51, 16/10/90
Francis (1806–1884), tory M.P. 22/5/46
G. 10/6/76
G. A. 13/3/79
George Gilbert, Sir (1811–1878), architect 14/7/48, 11/11/57
Henrietta Cavendish-Bentinck-, née Scott 27/10/27 n
Henry John Montagu-Douglas- (1832–1905), 1st Baron Montagu of Beaulieu, tory M.P. 14/5/57 n, 4/7/76, 13/12/79
Henry Young Darracott (1822–1883), soldier and engineer 31/12/52, 22/1/53
Hugh, 4th Baron Polwarth 22/5/46 n
J., Mrs., of Brotherton, Fasque 26/10/46
James, innkeeper in Edinburgh 13/10/36 n
James, of Brotherton, Fasque 26/9/44
James Robert Hope- 19/1/29
J. H., of Brighton 13/4/72
John, surgeon 27/4/40, 11/11/42
John Haigh, Rev. 25/2/58
John Henry Reginald (1839–1891), 4th Earl of Clonmell (1866) 24/11/80, 12/12/80 L
John William Robertson (1866–1962), journalist 28/8/88
Joseph Constable Maxwell- 24/11/72 n
Lamont 26/11/88
Mary, Lady (–1844), née Buckworth 5/4/37 n
Mary Monica (Maxwell-) Hope-, Mrs., daughter of J. R. Hope-Scott 24/11/72, 12/9/73, 13/9/73, 27/7/83 L, 13/6/85 L
Peter 16/5/57
Robert, Dean (1811–1887), Master of Balliol, Oxford (1854), dean of Rochester (1870), lexicographer 16/2/30, 26/1/57, 3/1/70, 13/6/70, 13/8/72 n, 7/12/85
Robert Selkirk, Rev. 14/7/76
Roger Wakefield, Liverpool physician 20/12/44 ?
Samuel (1807–1869), banker 5/4/37
Samuel, Sir (1772–1849), 2nd Baronet of Lytchet Minster (1830), banker 25/2/33 n
T. C. 20/9/78
Thomas (1808–1878), freethinker and publisher 16/5/55, 3/10/69, 2/6/72, 16/11/73, 1/11/74, 15/8/75 n, 9/12/75, 15/12/75, 19/3/76, 5/11/76, 11/3/77
Thomas, Rev. (1831–1914) 12/11/67 ?
Walter, Rev. 12/3/78 ?
Walter, Sir 19/4/32
Walter Francis Montagu-Douglas- (1806–1884), 5th Duke of Buccleuch (1819), tory politician 16/3/44, 29/9/53
Walter Hugh (1838–1920), 8th Baron Polwarth (1867) 29/6/71

Scott (*cont.*)
William, Rev., U. P. minister 20/3/80
William, Rev. (1813–1872) 14/6/52, 31/12/56 fl, 24/6/59
Scott, J.& Co., fruit importers 19/1/43
Scourfield,
Mr. 21/6/65
John Henry Philipps, Sir (–1876), took name Scourfield (1862), né Philips 22/7/53
Scratchley, Arthur (1821–1897), actuary 30/4/60
Scribner, C., and Sons, New York publishers 17/3/80
Scrimgeour, Mr. 14/2/78
Script Phonography Co. 11/1/90
Scrivener, Frederick Henry Ambrose, Rev. (1813–1891) 18/8/45
Scrope,
George Julius Poulett, liberal M.P., political economist 27/7/46
S. T. 1/6/87
Scrumola, Senator, of Naples 31/1/89
Scudamore,
Frank Ives (1823–1884), Post Office reformer 17/12/60, 3/4/61, 25/7/72 L
William Edward, Rev. (1813–1881) 31/12/56 fl
Scull, J. E., Rev. 30/5/79
Scully,
Francis (1820–1864), liberal M.P. 24/7/54
Thomas Vincent 23/12/85
Vincent (1810–1871), liberal M.P. 3/6/53
William, Dr., physician in Torquay 1/9/32
Scunn, O., Miss 14/8/91
Scurr, W. S. 8/6/75
Seafield *see* Grant
Seaforth *see* Mackenzie
Seage, W. L. 12/3/42
Seager, Dixon, Gen. 11/10/75
Seaham *see* Tempest
Seal, William Henry, poet 31/5/78 ?
Seale, Henry Paul, Sir (1806–1897), 2nd Baronet (1844) 23/5/27
Sealy *see* Baring
Sealy, Henry Nicholas, financial author 21/10/58
Seaman & Smith, Messrs. 23/8/90
Seard, F. J. 6/10/74
Searle, Charles Edward, Rev. (1828–1902), Master of Pembroke, Cambridge 21/2/57
Sears, William, printer 17/11/75
Seath, W. 16/11/89
Seaton *see* Colborne
Seaton,
Edward Cator, Dr. (1815–1880), physician 21/11/76
E. J. 20/10/86
R., Miss 28/9/91
Sebbons, Mr., picture agent 28/4/55
Sebright,
Georgiana Mary Muir (–1874), née Mackenzie, Lady Sebright, author on the Balkans 14/3/77 n
John Gage Saunders, Sir (1843–1890), 9th Baronet (1864) 10/4/75
John Saunders, Sir, 7th Baronet, whig M.P. 9/1/39 n
Thomas Gage Saunders, Sir (1802–1864), 8th Baronet (1846) 9/1/39
Secales, Mr. 14/12/76
Seccombe, John Thomas, Dr., physician and author 6/5/76
Séché, Léon, French author 29/8/77
Sedgfield, J. 14/5/68
Sedgwick, Adam, Prof. (1785–1873), geologist, professor of geology, Cambridge 14/2/34 n, 24/11/41, 25/11/41, 2/11/59, 18/2/70
Seebohm, Frederic (1833–1912), historian 22/4/67, 4/6/80
Seeley,
John Robert, Sir (1834–1895), Knight (1894), historian 28/1/68, 27/12/83, 29/3/85
Robert Benton (1798–1886), publisher and author 20/4/39
Sefton *see* Molyneux
Segar & Tunnicliffe, Liverpool merchants 26/7/74 n
Seidenbusch, Rupert, Bp. (–1895), Roman Catholic bishop of Minnesota 17/11/88
Selborne *see* Palmer
Selby,
Charles (1802–1863), dramatist 29/5/51 ?
Henry, tenant at Hawarden 20/5/72
Walford Dakin (1845–1889), clerk in Public Record Office 15/6/68 ?
Seldon, Samuel, statistician 4/6/80
Self, William & Son, auctioneers 1/10/41
Seligman, De Witt J., of New York 18/11/90
Selim Effendi 16/12/76
Selkirk *see* Douglas
Sella, Quintino, of Italy 22/1/63, 21/9/76
Sellar,
Alexander Craig (1835–1890), liberal (unionist) M.P. 3/8/76, 23/11/83 L
D. 28/5/77
Sellwood *see* Tennyson
Selous, Henry Courtenay (1803–1893), artist 30/6/51
Selwyn,
Charles Jasper, Sir (1813–1869), tory M.P. 2/3/49
George Augustus, Bp. 3/12/25
John Richardson, Bp. (1844–1898) 5/3/79, 31/3/79
Sarah Harriet, née Richardson 10/8/54
Thomas Kynaston (–1834) 3/12/25

W., servant 26/8/55
William, Canon (1840–1914), G's godson 6/5/40, 26/8/55
William, Prof. (1806–1875) 6/7/26
Sembrey, Mr. 17/11/88
Semon, Felix, Sir (1849–1921), G's throat specialist 14/7/85 ff, 29/9/85, 29/10/85
Sen, Keshab Chandra (1838–1884), of the Brahmo Samaj sect 10/5/80
Senington, Mr. 28/9/74
Senior,
Nassau John, barrister 6/7/68
Nassau William (1790–1864), political economist 28/12/50
Serarty, Mons., Armenian Patriotic Association 29/11/88
Serena, Augusto, author and liberal activist; Eighty Club member 24/5/79
Sergeant,
Lewis (–1902), author 8/10/78
Oswald, Rev. (–1854) 22/2/50
Oswald Pattison, Rev. 14/6/78 ?
Serjeant, J. F., Rev. 24/4/79 ?
Serjeantson, Peter, T. S. G's partner 28/1/36
Sermoneta *see* Caetani
Serpell, Mr. 11/7/78
Serrano, Francisco, Marshal, Duke de la Torre 26/4/73
Serristori, Umberto, Conte (–1942) 7/10/87
Service, John, Rev. 10/12/76 n
Seton & Mackenzie, Messrs. 10/2/79
Settembrini,
Luigi 22/3/52 n
Raffaele 22/3/52
Setter, W. 19/7/77
Severn,
Elizabeth (–1862), née Montgomerie 9/1/39
Joseph (1793–1879), consul in Rome (1860), artist 16/4/32, 9/1/39, 24/10/66, 20/11/66
Seville, Fr. 9/11/66
Seward,
Frederick William (1830–1915), journalist, diplomat 15/4/91 ?
Henry Hake 4/2/41
Sewell,
Henry (1807–1879), New Zealand politician and prime minister 31/3/51
Henry Doyle, Rev. (1806–1886) 21/6/34, 17/12/40
Robert, Rev. 8/3/80
Thomas (1795–1865), of Cambridge 21/6/34
William, Rev. (1804–1874) 26/8/40, 17/12/40
William Henry, Rev. (1836–1896) 20/7/77 ?
Sexton,
George, Rev. Dr. 7/2/79
Thomas (1848–1932), home rule M.P. 27/9/81, 12/10/81 c, 14/5/86, 5/12/90 n, 15/4/91, 7/3/92, 20/5/92, 21/6/92, 2/1/93, 15/2/93 n, 16/2/93 c, 3/5/93, 8/6/93, 10/6/93, 11/7/93
Seymer *see* Denison
Seymer,
Miss 28/4/38
Harriet Ker-, née Beckford 29/9/38
Henry Ker-, fils (1807–1864), Peelite M.P. 21/10/29
Henry Ker-, père (1782–1834), naturalist 29/9/38 n
Seymour *see* Saint Maur
Seymour,
Miss, rescue 7/6/51
Mrs., rescue 10/8/70, 12/1/75
A. 9/8/76
Albert Eden, Rev. 7/11/79
Francis, Gen. Sir (1813–1890), 1st Baronet (1869) 4/10/64
Frederick Beauchamp Paget, Adm. (1821–1895) 28/4/72 n, 3/7/82 c, 8/7/82 c, 10/7/82, 15/7/82, 3/8/82 c
George H., mayor of York 14/10/50 n
George Hamilton, Sir (1797–1880), diplomat 17/3/32, 16/5/70 ?
Henry Danby (1820–1877), liberal M.P. 25/7/64, 10/4/67
Horace Alfred Damer (1843–1902), G's private secretary 19/6/80, 15/8/82 n, 20/11/83
Horatio (1810–1886), American politician 4/12/78
I. A., née Ingram-Shepherd, Marchioness of Hertford 16/9/29
John Billingsley, scholar 4/4/40
Michael, Adm. Sir (1802–1887), Knight (1855) 7/8/60, 8/11/71
Michael Hobart, Rev. 19/10/77
Munro 1/5/88
R., Rev. 28/4/49
William Digby (1805–1895), liberal M.P. 14/6/54, 22/11/69, 26/11/69, 7/12/69
Sforza, Riario, Cardinal Abp. 7/12/50
Shadforth, Thomas, Rev. 8/6/48
Shadwell,
John Aemilius, Rev. (1809–1843) 26/5/27
Lancelot, Sir (1779–1850), Vice-Chancellor of England 6/2/34
Shaen, Samuel, Surrey solicitor 4/12/57
Shaftesbury *see* Cooper
Shafto *see* Vyner
Shahamat Ali 19/1/49
Shakespear, John Davenport, Col. 6/1/64
Shakespeare,
Mr., met by G in Lowestoft 18/7/91, 20/7/91
John A., Maj. 8/5/61 ?

Shalcross, J. H. 5/4/87
Shamling, Rev. Mr. 10/5/90
Shand,
Alexander Burns, Judge (1828–1904), judge and Scottish educational commissioner 8/5/78
Charles, of Everton 2/3/33
Charles Farquhar, Sir (1812–1889), of Mauritius 25/6/60 ?
Francis, of Liverpool 14/3/57 n
George, Rev. (–1889) 31/3/52
Hans George Leslie, G's secretary as Privy Seal 18/8/92, 17/12/92, 23/12/92 ff, 7/9/93 ff, 18/9/93 ff, 4/3/94 n, 12/3/94 ff
John, Edinburgh lawyer 10/10/71 ?
Shane, rescue 28/8/93
Shank, H., Mr. 22/12/43
Shanks, James, of Toxteth 18/5/57
Shannon,
Mr. 29/4/89
George Lidwill, Rev. 27/5/58
R. Q., Rev. 18/5/28
T. M. 15/12/77
Sharland, Mr. 18/2/69
Sharman,
Rev. Mr. 23/3/80
H. R., journalist 27/9/61
J. 29/12/79
Sharp,
Joseph Budworth, author 16/5/40
Martin Richard (1819–1889), editor, *The Guardian* 29/2/60, 13/7/76
Samuel, Rev. (1773–) 12/10/32
Sharpe,
Benjamin, pamphleteer 27/11/47
C. 4/11/57
Charles Henry 12/12/90 ?
Clement Charles, Rev. (1828–1884) 22/11/60 ?
Edmund (1809–1877), railway engineer 3/10/54
F. C., of London 12/7/54
Samuel Curtis, Rev. (1814–1868) 21/8/60
William Henry Sharpe 10/6/48 ?
Sharples, Mr. 29/1/67
Sharratt, William, of Chester Training College 6/1/45
Sharrock, Henry, of Ormskirk 9/12/67
Shattery, Mrs. 24/9/67
Shaw *see* Forbes
Shaw,
Benjamin (1819–1877), barrister 24/2/58
Charles, Sir (1795–1871), retired soldier and police commissioner 9/8/51
Charles James, Rev. (1804–1878) 4/6/58 ?
Dods, Mr. 23/7/90
Ewart, of Hawarden 6/8/64, 26/9/67, 20/11/71
Frederick, Sir (1799–1876), 3rd Baronet (1869), tory M.P. 8/2/33
G. A., Rev. 22/10/83 n, 25/10/83
George, architect at Hawarden 6/8/64, 28/8/72
George Bernard (1856–1950), dramatist and socialist 28/2/88
Henry (1800–1873), artist 30/7/57 ?
John Gregory, Sir 5/8/44 n
Morton, Rev. (1817–1901) 7/12/61
Thomas George, wine merchant 24/1/53
T. W., Rev. 17/10/75
W. H., Rev. 28/4/87
William, Limerick magistrate 21/1/89
William, Newark bricklayer 21/1/35
William (1823–1895), home rule M.P. and pre-Parnell leader 6/7/80, 17/7/80, 7/12/80, 12/1/81 n, 27/1/81 L, 6/6/81, 29/7/81, 24/3/82, 4/4/82 L, 10/5/82 L, 12/5/82 L, 17/9/84, 3/9/85, 23/12/85, 14/3/86 L, 19/3/86
Wilson 24/11/86
Shawcross, Richard, Rev. 10/2/75
Shaw-Lefevre *see* Ryan
Shaw-Stewart *see* Bruce
Shaw-Stewart *see* Saint Maur
Shea,
L. U. 18/11/77
Timothy 10/6/75
Shearme, Edward 3/10/80 ?
Shears, Mrs. 30/7/78
Shedden,
Anabella Jean 26/4/58
Caroline Goodrich 1/6/52 ?
George 1/6/52 n
Shee, William, Judge Sir (1808–1868) 26/5/56
Sheehan,
Francis, Rev. 6/4/85 ?
Remy, Irish journalist 3/6/36
Sheehy, Eugene, Father, Land League sympathiser 8/9/81 n
Sheepshank, Mr. 5/12/89
Sheepshanks,
John, Bp. (1834–1912), bishop of Norwich (1893) 20/3/93, 3/4/93
John, Rev. 29/5/85 ?
Sheffield *see* Holroyd
Sheffield,
Frank, Rev. (1838–1903) 16/5/67
George (1836–1898), diplomat 2/6/57
Sheil,
B. F., supplicant 26/4/67
Richard Lalor (1791–1851), liberal M.P. 6/2/33, 28/2/33, 13/3/42, 24/12/86
Shekelton, Mr. 28/11/77
Shelburne *see* Fitzmaurice
Sheldon,
Mr. 18/11/85
D. D. 8/10/74

J. P. 23/5/78 ?
Shelley,
A. C. 26/2/78, 14/6/79 n
Frances, Lady (-1873), née Winckley 12/7/38
H. C. 21/9/91
John, Sir (-1852), 6th Baronet 12/7/38 n, 6/4/53 n
John Villiers, Sir (1808-1867), 7th Baronet (1852), liberal M.P. 30/5/54
Spencer (-1908), treasury clerk 6/4/53
Shelvey, Mr. 13/10/86
Shephard, John, Rev. 19/10/66
Shepheard, Mrs. 27/5/59
Shepherd,
George, engineer 14/5/67
William, Rev., Methodist 19/11/32
Shepherds' Friendly Society 11/6/78
Sheppard,
rescue 5/12/73
Edgar, Rev. (1845-1921) 14/2/86 n
J. D. 14/10/59
Thomas, Rev. (1763-1839) 20/11/37
William, fils, tenant at Hawarden 8/10/52
William, père, tenant at Hawarden 25/2/41
Sherard *see* Pusey
Sherard, R., 4th Earl of Harborough 11/5/33 n
Sherborne *see* Legge
Sherbourne, Charles Robert (1755-1836) 18/9/26 ?
Sherbrooke *see* Lowe
Sheridan *see* Hay, Maxwell, Norton, Saint Maur
Sheridan,
Henry Brinsley (1820-1906), liberal M.P. 18/2/64
Mathew, Dublin merchant 7/5/79 ?
Peter 29/1/77
Sherlock,
David, Serjeant (1814-1884), liberal M.P. 27/12/73
Edgar, Rev. (1820-1909) 21/10/56
Oliver 19/1/75
Randall Hopley, of *Liverpool Daily Mail* 16/12/57
William, Birmingham manufacturer 10/6/56
Sherman, William Tecumseh, Gen. (1820-1891) 7/8/72
Sherratt,
D., Messrs. 29/4/78
J., of Hawarden 4/11/56
Sherriff, H. M. 12/1/91
Sherriffs,
Anne, Mrs. 20/5/39, 28/7/45, 6/9/85
E. B. 28/7/45 n
G. 1/5/43
William 12/11/33
Sherwood,
Joseph, parliamentary agent 13/2/39 ?
Stephen, Inland Revenue messenger 18/2/73 ?
Shibley, R. A. 2/10/90
Shiells, Ross 15/12/79 ?
Shiffner, George, Rev. Sir (-1863), 3rd Baronet (1859) 30/5/54 ?
Shipley *see* Rowley
Shipley,
Charlotte, née Williams Wynn 24/6/35 n
Orby, Rev. (1832-1916) 14/5/83 L
William, Lieut. Col. 24/6/35 n
Shippard, William Henry, Capt. 17/8/59 ?
Shipper, A. F. 1/9/77
Shipton,
E. R. 14/7/88
George, Secretary, London Trades Council 29/4/92
George, Rev. 26/6/58
John Noble, Rev. (1788-1864) 13/9/56 ?
Shipwash & Co., mineral water producers 13/8/49
Shirley,
rescue 3/6/89
Evelyn Philip (1812-1882), tory M.P. 29/7/56, 13/9/64, 17/8/75
Shirlmoss, Mr. 8/12/87
Shirreff,
Francis Archibald Patullo, Rev., missionary 28/10/92
W. M., clerk in Turners' Company 24/1/76
Shirreffs, J. M., Rev. 31/10/86 n
Sholl, James 16/9/78
Shone,
Mr., geographer 29/4/90
Mr., of Penmaenmawr 8/9/62
F., Mrs., of Hawarden 17/9/56
John, of Queensferry 27/8/63
William, coachmaker in Chester 29/10/52
Shorach, R. 20/9/88
Shore,
A., Miss 15/3/87
Charles John (1796-1885), 2nd Baron Teignmouth (1834), tory M.P. 23/5/39
James, Rev. 16/4/49 n
Thomas Teignmouth, Rev. 14/4/74, 24/1/90
Short,
Augustus, Bp. (1802-1883), bishop of Adelaide (1847) 3/9/28, 14/10/28
Austin 7/8/91
Charles William, Col. (-1857) 17/3/49
Thomas Vowler, Bp. (1790-1872), taught G at Christ Church, Oxford (1828), bishop of Sodor and Man (1841), bishop of St. Asaph (1847) 14/10/28 n, 13/3/29
Shorthouse, Joseph Henry (1834-1903), author 5/12/81 L, 3/5/82, 10/10/82, 4/11/86

Shortland, Vincent, Ven. (-1880) 17/3/52
Showring, W. 2/5/88
Shreve, V., Miss, of Philadelphia 2/6/90
Shrewsbury *see* Talbot
Shrewsbury, J. V. B. 26/8/68 ?
Shrimpton,
  Messrs. 24/10/88
  Henry, Rev. 19/3/79
Shroff, A. D. 21/2/77
Shrosbery, Mr. 15/10/74
Shuldham,
  Edward Barton, Dr., physician 9/8/78 n
  John, Rev. (1794-1884) 4/10/30
Shurn, F. 8/6/93
Shury, George 25/1/45
Shutte, Albert Shadwell, Rev. (-1901) 23/11/76 ?
Shuttleworth,
  James Phillips Kay-, Sir (1804-1877), educationalist 26/2/41
  Philip Nicholas, Bp. (1782-1842), bishop of Chichester (1840), Warden, New College, Oxford 17/10/30
  Ughtred James, Sir (1844-1939), 2nd Baronet (1877), liberal M.P. 9/4/86, 11/6/87, 6/12/93, 11/1/94
Shuvalov, Petr Andreievich, Count (1827-1889), Russian ambassador in London 1874-9 8/12/76, 26/3/77, 1/5/77, 2/9/77
Sibbald, G. M. 10/8/89
Sibley, Septimus William, Dr., surgeon 9/8/87 n
Sibthorp,
  Coningsby Charles 9/5/80
  Richard Waldo, Rev. (1792-1878) 10/5/29, 27/7/79, 21/4/80, 25/4/80
Sibthorpe *see* Okes
Sibthorpe, Thomas 21/9/26 n
Sidebottom,
  E. V. 2/6/36
  Thomas Harrop (1826-1908), tory M.P. 15/11/85
  William (1841-1933), tory M.P. 19/6/78 ?
Sidgwick *see* Benson
Sidgwick,
  Arthur (-1920), classicist 11/2/88, 26/1/90
  Eleanor Mildred (1845-1936), née Balfour, Helen G's colleague at Newnham College, Cambridge, Principal of Newnham 1892 10/8/75, 4/4/76, 9/9/78, 26/10/78 n, 16/12/79 n, 18/12/79, 17/5/82, 24/9/85 ff
  Henry, Prof. (1838-1900), philosopher and political economist, President of Society for Psychical Research 9/9/78 ff, 26/10/78 n, 16/12/79 ff, 18/12/79, 27/9/81, 28/9/81, 17/5/82, 24/9/85 ff, 31/1/87
Sidmouth *see* Addington
Siemens, Karl H. von, industrialist 2/9/85
Sier, Thomas, Rev. Dr. 15/7/65
Sieveking,
  Edward, merchant 26/10/41
  Edward Henry, Sir (1816-1904), Knight (1886), physician 3/9/76, 28/5/86
  Gustavus Adolphus 30/12/77 ?
Sievewright, J. 30/12/77
Sigalis, Mons. 11/11/78
Sigerson, George, Dr. 13/12/87
Sikes,
  Charles William, Sir (1818-1889), Knight (1881), banker 10/6/56
  Francis Henry (1862-1943), photographer 12/6/92
  Frederic 20/1/86
  Thomas, Rev. (-1888) 16/5/59
Silber, A. M. 31/10/76
Silk,
  C. 8/2/79
  John Alexander, solicitor 12/4/49 ?
  R. W., coachmaker 17/4/57
Sillard, R. M. 13/9/90
Sillery, Anthony, Rev. (1788-) 9/12/38 ?
Silline, Mr., of Hawarden 27/10/58
Silverthorne, Arthur, engineer 13/6/77 ?, 8/10/78
Silvertop, George (1774-1849), Tyneside proprietor 8/1/28
Silvestri, Piero de, Cardinal 25/10/66
Sim,
  Henry, Rev. (1793-1873) 17/11/43 ?
  William, solicitor 16/6/46 ?
Simeon,
  Catherine Dorothea, Lady, née Colville 19/11/68
  Charles, Rev. (1759-1836) 18/12/31
  John, Sir (1815-1870), 3rd Baronet (1854), liberal M.P. 8/5/50, 12/6/50, 26/7/50
  S. 24/6/90
Simerberger, Mr. 16/6/77
Simkinson,
  Charles Hare, Rev. 26/4/79 ?
  H. 26/4/79
Simm, O. 23/12/81
Simmons,
  Miss 14/9/93
  A. 3/9/77
  Emily, Miss 2/11/74
  John Lintorn Arabin, Gen. Sir (1821-1903), secretary to railway commissioners 23/5/50
Simms,
  Charles Samuel (1809-1872), bookseller and poet 8/9/55
  C. S., Rev. 10/6/74
  Samuel, Rev. 23/9/77
Simnel, Abel, census clerk 22/11/60 ff, 2/3/61

Simner, Lieut. 11/8/66
Simnitt, William, Newark weaver 16/4/35
Simon,
Miss, singer 9/7/89
Collyns 18/2/76
David Worthington, Rev. 12/4/77
J., Dr., physician 13/6/86
John, Sir (1818-1897), Knight (1886), liberal M.P. 14/12/78, 3/2/82, 11/5/87
Jules François (1814-1896), French politician 26/1/67
Oswald John, novelist 15/1/90
Thomas Collins 18/2/76
Simons,
J. E. 12/3/74
M., Mrs. 11/9/79
Nicholas, Rev. (1810-1886) 2/2/39 ?
Simpkin & Marshall, publishers 8/1/73
Simpson,
rescue 23/6/80
Miss 6/3/80
Mr., Newark liberal 6/10/32
A. C. 26/3/91
Adam Lind, Rev. (1817-1893) 13/6/57 ?
Albert 26/6/68
Henry Winckworth, Rev. 26/4/50 n
James, Rev. (1787-1870) 9/9/27
James Harvey, Rev. (1825-1915) 25/2/56
James Young, Sir (1811-1870), physician 1/12/51
John, Rev. (-1899) 23/8/76 ?
John Hawkins Simpson 14/4/91
Mary E., Miss 6/7/61
R., Mrs. 2/11/40
Richard (1820-1876), journalist 4/1/75
Robert, Rev. (1795-1867), Presbyterian 6/7/35
Robert, Rev. (1796-1855) 30/9/32
Robert James, Rev. 4/4/76
R. R. 26/6/79
W. S., Rev. 9/4/81 L
Sims,
F. 21/2/56
H., housemaid 7/8/40
Simson,
A., educationalist 6/4/37
A., supplicant 21/9/60
Alexander, lawyer 9/8/55
James (-1876), Edinburgh surgeon 14/10/50 ?
Sinadino, Mr., banker in Alexandria 4/7/82
Sinapi, Mr., art dealer in Naples 28/11/50
Sinayberger, M., of Liverpool 19/10/76
Sinclair *see* Buchanan, Saint Clair
Sinclair,
A. 6/7/74
Agnes (-1876), née Learmonth 2/4/59
Andrew, Edinburgh surgeon 23/1/35 ?
Catherine (1800-1864), novelist 16/6/47, 3/4/60
George (-1871), soldier in Bengal 2/4/59 n
George, Sir (1790-1868), 2nd Baronet (1835), whig M.P. 4/1/34
George M., secretary, School of Arts library 20/12/33
Helen (-1842), née Ellice 11/12/37 n
J. 25/11/85
James (1821-1881), 14th Earl of Caithness (1855) 24/12/68
John (1791-1857), Scottish tenor 23/12/25
John, Sir (1754-1835), 1st Baronet (1786), agriculturalist and statistician 21/12/33
John, Ven. (1797-1875) 3/12/33, 9/6/44
John George Tollemache, Sir (1825-1912), 3rd Baronet (1868), liberal M.P. 24/5/43, 21/10/70 L
Julian, poet 8/8/88
L., also known as 'Phillips' and 'Barton', rescue 8/8/66, 17/1/71, 27/1/71
Thomas, essayist 12/8/79
W. 26/11/86
William 11/12/37
William Macdonald, Ven. (1850-1917) 24/2/73
Sindarn, Miss 9/5/76
Sinding, Paul C., Prof. 12/1/66
Sing, J. M. 3/6/84
Singleton,
Mrs. 15/5/89
Robert Corbett, Rev. 23/7/45
Sinisalchi, G. B. 17/1/89 ?
Sinnott, Thomas Henry, collector 21/3/59 ?
Sinthall, Dr. 4/10/74
Sismondi, Jean Charles Leonard de 16/6/40
Sisson, Mr. 7/12/64
Sissons, T., Rev., Congregationalist 1/3/76
Sitwell,
George, Sir (1797-1853), 2nd Baronet of Renishaw (1814) 13/5/35
Sitwell, Sir 25/5/33 n
Susan, Lady (-1880), née Tait 13/5/35
William Hurt (1803-1865) 23/1/36 ?
Sivewright, Charles Kane 27/2/27
Skaife, Thomas, artist 22/6/75
Skeet, Charles Joseph (1812-1892), bookseller 4/1/55, 11/9/57
Skeffington,
Mr. 30/11/88
Sydney William, Rev. 29/3/72
Skelmersdale *see* Wilbraham
Skelton, John, author 11/11/76
Skene *see* Thomson
Skene,
Felicia Mary Frances, author 20/5/76, 3/8/77
William Forbes, lawyer 25/8/46

Sketchley,
Mr. 11/9/91
Alexander, Rev. (-1874) 10/1/60
Skidmore, Joseph, of Dudley 10/7/48 ?
Skingley, Henry 10/7/34
Skinner,
Allan Maclean, Judge (1810-1885) 29/9/25, 9/10/41
Edward J., of Baltimore 25/1/76
G. 15/11/79
James, Rev. 27/3/43
J. M. 12/11/89
John, Rev. (1721-1807), correspondent of Robert Burns 9/8/92
John Edwin Hilary (1839-1894), war correspondent, *Daily News* 1/1/68, 21/6/78
William, town clerk of Edinburgh 22/11/79
William, Bp. (1778-1857), bishop of Aberdeen (1816) 28/5/41
Skirrow, Walter (1809-1890), barrister 17/5/27
Skirving, John, engraver 29/5/52
Skoines, Henry 19/8/79
Skrine, John Huntley, Warden, warden of Glenalmond 24/12/94
Skynner, Mr. 16/10/76
Slack, M., Mrs. 20/4/76
Slade,
Alfred Frederick Adolphus, Sir 28/2/77
Augusta, Mrs., née Law 1/9/42 n
James, Rev. 1/9/42, 3/3/43
Mary, Mrs., née Bolleroy 5/9/42
Slagg, John, free trader 1/11/75
Slaney, Robert Aglionby (1791-1862), liberal M.P. 14/6/54
Slater,
Edward, Rev. 3/7/56
F. W. 20/9/89
Isaac (-1883), publisher 29/11/51
Peter, sculptor 14/4/47
William (-1889), Manchester solicitor 11/10/53
Slater's Directory, publishers 29/11/51
Slatten, T. 9/9/78
Slatter,
H., coachmaker 4/4/55
John, Rev. (1817-1899) 17/7/58
Slattery, Henry Francis, mayor of Waterford 25/9/69 n
Slaughter,
Mr. 17/4/89
Mrs. 17/4/89
William Capel, Sir (1857-1917), solicitor 5/11/79
Slaughter & May, Messrs., solicitors 5/11/79 n
Sleaford, Richard 23/9/89
Sleeth, Mr. 4/11/86
Slight, Frederick, secretary, London, Brighton & S. Coast railway 9/4/58
Sligo *see* Browne
Sloan,
Maguire, Rev. 23/4/89
T. 3/11/85
Slocombe, David 18/6/78, 18/8/79
Sly, S. 19/9/88
Smail, D. 9/7/87
Small, Nellie, Miss 2/6/87
Smalley, George Washburn, American journalist 15/2/72 L, 19/11/72, 28/5/82, 20/9/84, 4/10/84 L
Smart,
Edward, Ven. (1816-1889), dean of St. Asaph 14/5/67 ?
George, of Montrose 24/2/42
Smedes, Susan Dabney, Mrs. 3/10/89
Smedley, Herbert, insurance agent 4/5/68
Smee,
J. H. 30/7/88
William (-1858), accountant, Bank of England 4/8/45
William Rae (1816-1877), clerk, Bank of England 29/12/63
Smellie, A. 26/3/77
Smiles, Samuel (1812-1904), biographer 19/4/60
Smirke, Sydney (1798-1877), architect 7/11/42 n
Smith *see* Eardley, Egerton, Stanhope, Vernon, Wynn
Smith,
Liverpool friend 28/11/25
rescue 26/3/59, 28/1/63
Miss, of Brighton 18/5/64
Mr., A. J. Balfour's agent 4/10/72
Mr., sculptor, of Aberdeen 28/7/85
Mrs., nurse 19/8/49
Mrs., of Fasque 7/5/51
Mrs., of Hawarden 28/12/63
A. E. 15/3/76
Alexander Kennedy, mechanic 24/5/53
Algernon Howell, Rev. (1845-1930) 8/8/77 ?
A. P. 2/9/79
Archibald (-1872), barrister 13/7/49
B. 3/4/51
Bernard, Rev. (1812-1892), in Rome 20/11/66
C., Miss 11/9/70
Caroline Sophia, née Murray, formerly Mordaunt 30/6/34
C. C. 29/8/74
Charles, Mrs. 5/8/25
Charles, Prof., musician 5/8/25 n
Charles Fenton, Rev. 9/8/66
Charles Joseph, of Reigate 21/3/67

Charles Roach (1807–1890), antiquarian 29/8/55
Charles Swaby, Dr., of Seaforth 22/12/72
Clement L., of Harvard, U.S.A. 15/1/79
Cook, Mr. 4/1/87
Cooke, Mrs. 17/8/87
Darby, Miss 16/7/75
E., rescue 4/7/56
Edmund James, Rev. 7/2/48
Egerton, publisher, *Liverpool Mercury* 23/8/26
E. H., Miss 4/8/79
Eleanor Elizabeth, Miss (1822–1896), of Oxford 31/1/78
E. T. 20/9/78
Eustace, Dr., physician 16/11/73
F. A. D., Miss 12/1/87
Ferdinando Dudley Lea, of Birmingham 12/2/78 ?
F. G., company secretary 28/11/40
F. R., Rev. 9/3/76
Frederick W., liberal 23/4/80
Fullner 30/4/67
George, Bp. (1815–1871) 10/7/64 n
George Barnett (1841–1909), author, biographer of G 28/12/64
George Henry 17/7/58 ?
George Robert (1793–1869), whig M.P. 13/4/39
George Sidney, author 21/7/77 ?
George Vance, Rev. Dr. 26/12/88
Gilbert, of Chester 29/12/86
Goldwin, Prof. (1823–1910), historian and controversialist; vehement unionist 19/6/52 n, 6/4/53, 26/6/54, 27/7/54, 21/4/55, 14/7/55, 1/2/56, 4/3/56, 6/3/56, 27/1/57, 14/5/57, 25/11/67, 6/3/68, 13/6/71 L, 10/2/74, 8/2/77, 20/2/77, 3/11/81 ff, 16/3/82, 27/10/92 L
G. R. 24/9/78
Gustavus, of Stratford 30/6/34 n
H., Sergeant 28/8/52
Henry, London art dealer 29/10/58 ?
Henry, Sir, Canadian politician 24/7/40 ?
Henry, Sir, sailor 28/6/45 ?
Henry J., election agent in Mold 24/3/57, 2/4/57
Henry John Stephen, Prof. (1826–1883), professor of geometry, Oxford 31/1/78
Henry Percy, Rev. 6/12/75
Henry Stooks (–1881), parliamentary officer 21/2/53
Horatio (1779–1849), essayist 18/5/64 n
Isaac Gregory, Rev. Dr. (1826–1920) 26/4/65
J., mayor of East Retford 5/10/65
J., rescue 4/4/64
J. A. 22/4/74
James (1789–1850), agricultural engineer 7/7/43
James, Ven. (–1869), archdeacon of Connor 11/12/55 ?
James Allan, Rev. 5/6/87
Jane, rescue 26/2/58
Jane (–1879), née Maberly 13/4/39 n
John, of Newark 29/1/41
John Abel (1801–1871), banker, liberal M.P. 1/7/53, 8/3/67
John Bainbridge, Rev. (–1904) 13/4/77
John Benjamin (–1879), liberal M.P. 23/12/40 n, 31/5/66
John Cotton, Rev. Dr., American 22/2/76
John Greenwood, Rev. 10/4/64
John Mark Frederick, Sir (1792–1874), soldier, tory M.P. 2/9/41
John Russell (1810–1894), bookseller 18/9/68
Joseph Newton, Rev. 25/2/77
Joshua Toulmin (1816–1869), constitutional author 5/5/49
J. Russell 3/10/90
Levi 8/5/48
M. A., Mrs. 1/1/56
Martin Seth 25/7/90
Martin Tucker (1808–1880), liberal M.P. 7/6/53, 19/5/64
Montagu Edward, Judge Sir (1809–1891) 1/11/71, 7/9/87
N. J. 13/7/78
Oswald A., poet 20/2/91
Peter, Sir, chief clerk, colonial office 23/2/46
Philip, Dr. (1817–1885), historian 30/4/77
R. E. 24/6/90
Reginald Bosworth (1839–1908), schoolmaster and author 14/5/74, 2/3/78, 31/10/85
Richard Henry, banker in Dudley 27/5/47
Roach 13/11/86
Robert, Montrose shipowner 19/7/39
Robert (1752–1838), 1st Baron Carrington (1796), banker, tory M.P. 14/8/35
Robert Frederick, Rev. 18/10/72
Robert Harvey, Rev. 17/11/79
Robert Payne, Dean (1819–1895) 11/2/70
Robert Pearsall (1827–1898), author 27/5/75
Samuel (1836–1906), liberal M.P. 12/12/82 n, 28/3/85, 27/4/88 n, 9/4/92
Samuel, Dean (1766–1841), dean of Christ Church, Oxford (1824), made G a Student of Christ Church (1829) 9/1/28, 23/1/28, 18/10/29, 14/11/29, 11/12/29, 17/11/30, 15/1/31, 17/3/31, 16/4/31, 11/6/31, 11/7/31, 24/11/31, 28/11/31
Samuel, Rev. 11/4/76 ?
S. F., Rev. 13/10/88

Smith (*cont.*)
Sidney, secretary, Liberal Registration Association 13/7/61, 13/4/71 L
Storeys-, Mr. 13/12/74
Sydney, Rev. (1771–1845), author and controversialist 7/2/35 n, 16/10/83
Theyre Townsend, Rev. 15/4/40
Thomas, sheriff of Hampshire 16/9/59 n
Thomas Berry Cusack- (1795–1866), tory M.P. and Irish attorney-general 11/6/43
Thomas Charles 10/4/75 ?
Thomas Frederick, Rev. (1821–1871) 25/6/59
Tomlinson 19/3/57
W., of Manchester 28/10/87
W., of Morley 28/10/87
Walter Chalmers, Rev. Dr. (1824–1908), Moderator of the Free Church of Scotland (1893) 22/3/80, 18/5/93 L
W. E., of the Evangelization Society 7/6/75 ?
W. F. 22/5/75
W. G. 5/12/74
William, tenant of Cop House farm, Hawarden 13/3/43, 21/10/53
William, Prof. (1808–1897) 5/7/56 ?
William, Sir (1813–1893), Knight (1892), lexicographer 24/10/67
William Bryant, bookseller 20/2/68
William Henry (1825–1891), tory M.P. 15/11/68, 26/4/73 c, 1/5/73 n, 17/3/82, 27/3/82, 4/5/82, 22/10/84 c, 4/7/87, 21/2/89, 12/7/89, 18/7/89 ff, 26/7/89, 17/2/90 ff, 14/3/90, 7/10/91
William John Bernhard, barrister 11/6/56
William Masters (1802–1861), tory M.P. 5/10/54
William Richard, auctioneer 29/2/76 ?
William Robertson, Rev. Prof. (1846–1894) 12/7/78
W. J. S., Rev. 26/10/88
W. W., Rev. 1/8/90
Smith, Daniel, & Sons, land agents 8/5/48
Smith, E., & Co., tailors 4/5/53
Smith, Payne & Smith, bankers 17/12/41
Smith & Co., Montrose booksellers 21/9/40
Smithson,
David J., elocutionist 1/8/89
William, Rev. (1816–1878) 12/1/46
Smithwick, Richard Fitzgerald, Rev. 7/12/81, 9/11/91
Smollett,
Alexander (1801–1881), tory M.P. 26/4/53
Patrick Boyle (1805–1895), Peelite M.P. 17/5/62, 24/4/74
Smyth *see* Fitzherbert, Hughes
Smyth,
Carmichael, Major 26/7/86
James Carmichael-, Gen. Sir (1780–1838), 1st Baronet (1821), colonial governor 26/12/36
Patrick James (1823–1885), home rule M.P. 25/8/71
William, Prof. (1765–1849), regius professor of modern history, Cambridge 14/9/29
William Tyler, Dr., physician 10/3/45
Smythe *see* Boyle
Smythe,
David, Lord Methven 10/12/36 n
Emily Anne (–1887), Lady Strangford, Bulgarian propagandist 7/1/75, 18/3/76, 6/7/76
George A. F. P. S. (1818–1857), 7th Viscount Strangford (1855), tory M.P. and Young Englander 14/2/39
J. F., Rev. 18/12/77
J. H., Rev. 24/2/76
Patrick Murray, Canon (1805–1872) 26/8/30
W. D. 19/3/90
William, barrister 28/7/48 ?
William (–1890), of Methven, Perthshire 30/4/54
William Barlow, Irish landowner 19/7/52
W. R., of Killnean 10/5/82 ?
Smythies, Charles Alan, Bp. (1844–1894), bishop of Zanzibar 5/9/88
Smyth & Nephew, perfumers 20/9/66
Snagge, Thomas William, Sir (1837–1914) 29/11/79
Snape, Alfred William, Rev. (–1896) 18/9/49 ?
Snell, H., house agent 23/1/56
Snell, William, Edward & Co., house agent 22/2/49, 29/5/49
Snelly, Mr. 9/7/60
Sneyd,
Lewis, warden of All Souls, Oxford 4/11/47, 1/6/57 n
Walter, Rev. (1810–1888) 17/10/28, 5/11/73
Snook, G. 6/1/87
Snow,
Albert, spiritualist 8/7/74
Arthur L. P., Rev. 15/12/74
Benjamin, Rev. 1/3/77
Henry, Rev. (1811–1874) 13/10/27 ?
Thomas, Rev. 16/3/41
William Parker (1817–1895), explorer 25/7/76
Snowball, R. 14/2/79
Snowdon, R. K., Rev. 25/11/78
Snowie, Mr. 18/8/74
Soames,
Mr. 14/2/63
A., of Newark 23/12/67

Henry, Rev. (1784-1860) 9/5/30
Soares, Theodore G. 15/11/88 n
Soden,
Mr., apothecary 4/2/63
Henry, Mr., mayor of Coventry 3/2/60, 28/9/60, 6/11/68
Sofronius, Abp. 27/5/80
Söhns, Frederick 5/4/80
Soldane, Madame 17/5/83
Soldaties, Mr., of Rome 13/11/66
Soleman, William 22/10/74
Sollohub, Leon, Count, Helen G's fiancé 6/12/38
Solly *see* Domville
Solly,
Henry, Rev. 30/10/64
Nathaniel Neal, artist 5/5/47, 27/8/62 ?
Solomé, Mons. de 29/4/86
Solomon, Mr. 15/11/82
Soltan, William Edward, banker 18/12/78
Solway, Mr. 13/6/78
Sombre, David Ochterlony Dyce- (1808-1851), whig M.P. 17/1/39
Somers *see* Cocks
Somers-Cocks *see* Russell
Somerset *see* Cholmondeley, Farquhar, Lawley, Ryder, Saint Maur
Somerset,
Charlotte Sophia (1771-1854), née Leveson-Gower, Duchess of Beaufort (1803) 2/2/38
Edward Arthur, Col. (1817-1886) 10/8/77
Emily Harriet, Lady, née Wellesley-Pole, Lady Raglan 21/10/43 n
Fitzroy James Henry, Lord (1788-1855), 1st Baron Raglan (1852), soldier 21/10/43, 9/2/55
Geraldine Harriet Anne, Lady 14/11/59
Granville Charles Henry, Lord (1792-1848), tory M.P. 31/12/34
Henry Charles (1766-1835), 6th Duke of Beaufort (1803) 2/2/38
Mary Blanche (-1916), née Farquhar, Lady Raglan 9/12/65
Somerville,
Alexander (1811-1885), journalist 21/11/55
H., rescue 4/3/67
Mary (1780-1872), née Fairfax, formerly Grieg, author and scientist 24/2/34
R. G. 14/11/78 ?
William, Dr. (1771-1860), scientist 24/2/34 n
William Meredyth, Sir (1802-1873), 1st Baron Athlumney, liberal M.P. 28/4/69
Somerville College, Oxford 29/11/83
Somes, Joseph, Peelite M.P. 15/9/41
Sommer, G. S., Dr. 21/8/91
Sommerard, Esmond Du (1817-1885), French archaeologist 4/4/71
Sondes *see* Milles
Sonera, Marchesa, of Naples 29/2/52
Soper, D. Rowley 2/12/91
Sophia,
Princess, daughter of Duke of Cumberland 2/6/43
Queen, Queen of Holland 16/3/70
Sophronius, Abp., of Cyprus 25/3/82
Sora, Duca di 7/11/66
Sorbutt, W. 3/4/55
Sordina, Mr. 24/4/77
Sorrentino, Sig. 26/12/88
Sotheby,
Charles, sailor 18/3/45
William (1757-1833), Homeric translator 20/2/33
Sothebys, Messrs., auctioneers 23/7/72
Sothern, Edward Askew (1826-1881), actor 17/11/62 n
Sott, A. 3/1/78
Soulsby, William Jameson 11/9/85
Souter,
Frank Henry, Sir (-1888), in Bombay police 6/7/75 n
Tibby, of Fasque 15/9/48, 7/5/51
W. 12/9/79
South, rescue 8/7/50
Southall, T. 12/11/68
Southampton *see* Fitzroy
Southcombe, R. 31/5/78
Southern, George, Rev., Methodist 14/12/67 ?
Southesk *see* Carnegie
Southey,
A., Rev. 25/3/78
E., Mrs., nurse? 27/10/55, 31/5/58, 5/6/58, 20/7/58
Robert (1774-1843), poet laureate (1813) 26/3/38
Southgate, Frederic, Rev. (-1885) 1/12/77
Southwark Fund for Schools and Churches 10/7/45
Southwell,
Edward James 1/12/77 ?
Thomas Arthur Joseph (1836-1878), 4th Viscount Southwell 1/8/72
Sowerby, George Brettingham (1788-1854), artist 16/12/51
Sowrey, Mr. 10/1/80
Soyer, Alexis Benoît (1809-1858), chef and author 15/4/48 n
Spackman, Mr., of Belfast 23/11/86
Spadone, Sig. 16/4/89
Spalding,
Lieut. Col. 24/9/81 n, 6/10/81
James, surgeon 27/11/37
Spark,
J., Capt. 20/8/79
R. B. 1/9/79

Sparke, J. 28/6/77
Sparkes,
John Law, secretary, G.N.E. railway 20/8/49
Samuel 19/6/77
Sparling, Philip William, Rev. (1844-1921) 12/2/76
Sparrow,
J. W. 12/10/82
W. H. 6/7/65
Spearman,
Capt. 20/2/38
Alexander Young, Sir (-1874), 1st Baronet (1840), of the National Debt Commissioners 28/12/52, 5/10/53, 7/10/53, 3/3/54, 27/3/54, 6/5/54, 10/5/54, 19/6/54, 17/7/54, 12/8/54, 18/1/55, 25/3/63, 30/4/64
Edmund Robert (1837-1918), diplomat 21/8/60
Spedding, James (1808-1881), author 16/12/31, 28/6/69
Speedy, Capt. 14/1/72 n
Speirs *see* Ellice
Speirs,
Alexander (-1844) 17/8/53 n
Archibald Alexander (1840-1868), liberal M.P. 17/8/53 n
Eliza S., Mrs., née Hagart 17/8/53 n, 19/5/57
Spence,
Henry Donald Maurice, Rev. (1836-1917) 20/4/84
James, Confederate agent, Liverpool broker 15/10/62
James, Rev. (1811-1876), Congregationalist 12/12/64
R. M., Rev. 1/8/90
Spencer *see* Lyttelton
Spencer,
Adelaide Horatia Elizabeth (-1877), Lady Spencer 15/10/63
Aubrey George, Bp. (1795-1872), bishop of Jamaica 7/1/46
Charles Robert (1857-1922), Viscount Althorp (1905), 6th Earl Spencer (1910), liberal M.P. 8/4/79, 25/7/87
Frederick (-1857), 4th Earl Spencer (1845) 3/11/49
George, of Hawarden 23/1/68
George, known as 'Father Ignatius', Roman Catholic 18/8/40
George (1799-1864) 14/4/32
George English, barrister 11/2/56
Graham 4/5/87
Herbert (1820-1903), sociologist 13/11/73, 12/1/74, 15/1/74, 20/12/76, 12/5/81, 22/6/82
James, of Greenwich 18/10/68, 24/12/68
Jeremy 20/12/52
J. M., of Hoxton 7/9/43
John Charles (1782-1845), Viscount Althorp (1783), 3rd Earl Spencer (1834), whig M.P. 21/7/32, 12/11/86
John Poyntz; 5th Earl Spencer 19/1/66
Margaret, née Baring, Lady Spencer 25/7/87
Robert Cavendish, Sir (1791-1830), sailor 20/2/26
Sarah Isabella, Lady (1838-1919) 24/1/83, 9/6/83, 7/7/83, 25/6/84, 10/3/87, 3/8/88, 25/7/94
T., Rev. 10/7/43
Spender, E. 11/3/75
Spensley, Howard (1834-1902), liberal M.P. 1/1/86
Spicer, James (1807-1888), Warden of Fishmongers' company 24/3/73 n
Spick, C. 27/1/79
Spielmann, Marion Harry Alexander (1858-1948), editor, *Magazine of Art* 31/12/77 ?, 24/10/87, 28/7/88
Spier, Miss 25/3/27 n
Spiller, Capt. 17/10/75
Spinelli *see* Herbert
Spink, Messrs., jewellers 9/8/89
Spooner *see* Tait
Spooner,
George Woodberry, Rev. 7/3/55 ?
R. B. 19/3/78
Richard (1783-1864), tory M.P. 8/6/47 n, 29/3/60
William, barrister 9/11/44 ?
William Archibald (1844-1930), Warden of New College, Oxford 9/11/44 n, 30/6/90
Spottiswode & Robertson, Messrs., parliamentary agents 2/3/48
Spottiswoode *see* Campbell
Spottiswoode,
Miss 4/8/32
John 4/8/32 n
Margaret 4/8/32
Spranger, Robert Jeffries, Rev. 20/12/47
Sprigg, Mr. 20/1/87
Spring, Mrs., army officer's wife 11/8/54
Sproule, George Thomas Paterson, Rev. 1/6/50
Spry, John Hume, Canon (1777-1854) 2/1/38
Spur, L., rescue 10/3/59
Spurgeon, Charles Haddon, Rev. (1834-1892), Baptist 21/4/68, 20/7/79, 3/1/82 L, 8/1/82, 16/1/82 L, 5/3/92 n
Squibb,
George Meyer, Rev. 22/3/92
J. 30/8/91
Squire, Edward Burnard, Rev. 27/7/57
Squires, William Westbrooke, Dr., physician 20/11/45

Staal,
Madame De 12/2/86
Mons. De 12/2/86, 4/7/86
Stack,
Dr. 4/2/81
John Herbert (-1892), journalist 1/1/62
Stacpoole, William (1830-1879), liberal M.P. 5/7/71
Stacy, W. 2/6/56
Staffetta, Marchesa della 14/1/88
Stafford *see* Gower
Stafford,
rescue 24/8/83
Augustus Stafford O'Brien (1811-1857), tory M.P. 4/5/48
James Charles, Rev. (-1873) 18/4/54
Stai, Emmanuel, of Birmingham 2/3/80
Stainer, John, Sir (1840-1901), composer 9/5/77, 29/1/82
Stainton,
Henry Tibbats (1822-1892), entomologist 31/3/55
Prosper (1813-1890), violinist 10/4/72
Stair *see* Dalrymple
Stais, V. E., Dr. 9/3/78
Staite, Mrs. 19/10/78
St. Albans *see* Beauclerk
Stalbridge *see* Grosvenor
St. Aldwyn *see* Beach
Staley,
Mrs. 8/2/79
Thomas Nettleship, Bp. (1823-1898) 4/6/68
Stalham, Henry Heathcote, Liverpool solicitor 19/2/52 ?
Stallybrass, James Steven, translator 15/5/77 ?
Stambouloff, Stephan, archaeologist 6/12/89
Stamer, Lovelace Tomlinson, Ven. Sir (1829-1908), 3rd Baronet (1860) 24/10/74
Stamford *see* Grey
Stamfordham *see* Bigge
Stampert, W. 11/12/76
Stance, Mrs. 15/1/77
Standish, Mr. 4/4/77
Stanfield,
Clarkson (1793-1867), artist 3/3/68
George Clarkson (1828-1878), artist 7/5/56
Stanford,
Maj., of Ireland 23/5/34 ?
E., London map seller 3/8/58
Edward, bookseller 9/9/91
John Frederick (1815-1880), Peelite M.P. 15/5/34, 23/5/34 n
Stanhope *see* Conyngham, Herbert, Hutt, Lygon, Primrose, Russell
Stanhope,
Alexandra, Countess, formerly Tolstoy, Lady Weardale 8/11/88 n
Catherine Lucy, Lady (-1843), née Smith 12/3/36
Charles S. S., Capt. 20/8/70
Charles Wyndham (1809-1881), 7th Earl of Harrington (1866) 5/6/26
E., tory M.P. 30/3/85, 9/4/85 c
Emily Harriet, Lady (1815-1873), née Kerrison, Lady Mahon 15/8/35
James Banks (1821-1904), tory M.P. 23/2/66
Philip Henry (1781-1855), 4th Earl Stanhope (1816) 12/3/36 n, 28/7/55 ff
Philip Henry (1805-1875), Lord Mahon (1815), 5th Earl Stanhope (1855), historian, Peelite M.P. 2/7/31 n, 28/7/55 ff, 15/5/58, 13/5/59 ff, 13/12/65, 21/6/73 n, 23/3/74, 8/3/76
Philip James (1847-1923), 1st Baron Weardale (1906), liberal M.P. 30/3/85, 30/3/87, 14/9/87, 12/6/88, 8/11/88, 6/4/92, 5/7/93, 18/10/93 L
Walter Thomas William Spencer-, Sir (1827-1911), tory M.P. 20/7/77
Staniforth,
Samuel (1769-1851), banker in Liverpool 8/8/25
Thomas, Rev. (1807-1887), oarsman 17/10/25
Staniland, Meaburn (1809-1898), liberal M.P. 25/4/61
Stanistreet,
John Frederick, solicitor in Liverpool 17/1/45 n
Thomas, of Clonmel 21/5/38 ?
Stanley *see* Cox, Egerton
Stanley,
rescue 17/6/62
Master 29/12/85
Miss 31/1/28
Arthur Penrhyn, Dean (1815-1881), dean of Westminster (1864) 31/1/28, 13/5/59, 21/11/61, 13/4/63, 16/6/63, 3/3/69, 28/11/70, 23/1/71, 18/6/75, 9/3/76, 30/3/77, 19/10/79, 5/12/80, 23/7/81, 25/7/81, 2/9/81, 20/12/81 n, 19/10/82
Augusta Frederica Elizabeth, Lady (-1876), née Bruce 18/4/63, 9/3/76
Catherine (1792-1862), née Leycester 31/1/28
Dorothy (-1926), née Tennant, Lady Stanley, advised G on reading 24/5/85, 24/6/85, 30/3/87, 14/3/89, 19/10/89 n, 25/4/90 n, 23/6/90, 12/7/90, 7/10/92 L
Edward (1790-1863), tory M.P. 4/8/37 n
Edward, Bp. (1779-1849), bishop of Norwich (1837) 29/1/28

Stanley (*cont.*)
Edward George Geoffrey Smith; 14th Earl of Derby 5/2/33
Edward Henry; 15th Earl of Derby 30/6/49
Edward James (1826–1907), tory M.P. 25/5/63 n
Edward John (Ben) (1802–1869), 2nd Baron Stanley of Alderley (1850), whig M.P. 7/5/38, 7/5/64
Edward Lyulph (1839–1925), 4th Baron Stanley of Alderley (1903), liberal M.P. 20/11/68, 10/5/82 L, 4/8/85 L
Ellin (1802–1884), née Williams 31/1/28, 19/11/54
Emma Caroline (–1876), née Bootle-Wilbraham, Lady Derby 17/3/52, 27/11/52, 1/7/53
Henry Edward John (1827–1903), 3rd Baron Stanley of Alderley (1869), in foreign office 26/9/51
Henry Morton, Sir (1841–1904), explorer 7/4/70 n, 30/7/84, 24/5/85 n, 23/6/90, 12/7/90 n, 7/10/92, 13/1/93 ?
John 20/2/41 n
John Thomas, Sir (1766–1850), 1st Baron Stanley of Alderley (1839) 31/1/28
Louisa (1799–1877) 31/1/38
Maria Josepha, Lady (1771–1863), née Holroyd, Lady Stanley of Alderley 31/1/28
Mary, née Douglas 31/7/61 n
Mary (1814–1879), charity worker 25/11/54, 6/1/56 ff, 10/2/56, 28/4/75
Mary Catherine 21/2/75
Mary Dorothy, née Labouchere 25/5/63
Rianette (1797–1882) 31/1/28
T. 24/12/89
William 31/1/28 n
William Owen (1802–1884), liberal M.P. 19/11/54 n, 18/3/68
Stanmer, G. 17/10/85
Stanmore *see* Gordon
Stanniford, C. D. 20/10/89
Stansbury,
Charles Frederick, patent agent 1/5/55
John Fortunatus (1805–1894), headmaster 19/5/58
Stansfeld, James, Sir 9/5/62
Stansmore, Mrs., G's Dame at Eton 1/12/25 n
Stanton,
George H., Rev. 19/3/74
R. 8/4/74
Walter John (1828–), liberal M.P. 6/3/80
Stanyer, William, Rev. 28/9/74 ?
Stapleton *see* Lloyd, Maxwell
Stapleton,
Augustus Granville (1800–1880), author 25/1/68
Francis George, Sir (1831–1899), 8th Baronet (1874) 9/2/80 n, 20/9/89
Mary Catherine, née Gladstone, Lady Stapleton 9/2/80, 20/9/89
Miles Thomas (–1854), 8th Baron Beaumont (1840) 23/8/52
Stapley, E. W. 11/7/79
Stapylton, rescue 16/3/58
Stark,
Alfred, Rev. 3/9/90 ?
John Mozley, book dealer 1/2/58, 9/8/77
Malcolm, journalist, G's biographer 14/7/78 n, 15/7/78, 20/11/78
Starke,
William, Lieut. Col. 4/3/79
W. J., Rev. 10/4/77
Starkie,
John Pierce Chamberlain (1830–1888), tory M.P. 19/9/68 ?
Le Gendre Nicholas, High Sheriff of Lancashire 22/11/68 n
Statham,
F. 19/12/87
Francis Reginald, journalist 6/6/76
Statter,
Miss 19/6/67
James, Rev. 19/6/67 n
St. Aubyn *see* Knollys
Staundigl, Joseph, Viennese bass 17/5/43
Staunton,
George, Gen. (1809–1880) 12/10/79
George Thomas, Sir (1781–1859), 2nd Baronet (1810), whig M.P. 26/5/46
John (1800–1879) 30/10/78 ?
William, Rev. (1806–1860) 26/4/29
Stavordale *see* Strangways
St. Cyres *see* Northcote
Stead,
J. T. 8/1/78, 30/5/92
Walter Benjamin Vere, Rev. 14/2/91 ?
William Thomas 30/9/76 n
Steade, servant 9/1/41
Stean, A. J. 23/3/78
Stear, A. 27/6/76
Stearn,
Miss 7/2/87
A. 28/6/76, 30/10/79
David De, lunacy commissioner 28/6/76 ?
Stebbing,
Henry, Rev. (1799–1883), author 15/5/43, 22/11/43
W. 26/9/61
William (–1926), author 28/1/87
Sted, A., Mrs. 17/2/75
Stedman, A. De Barton 29/8/87
Steegman, Mr. 1/3/71
Steel,
John (1786–1868), liberal M.P. 22/1/61
Thomas Henry, schoolmaster 21/6/45

Steele *see* Bowen
Steele,
Mr., of Innerleithen 4/11/90
Frederick Ferdinand Armstead, Sir (1787–1876), 5th Baronet (1872) 3/2/75
James, author 11/4/40
J. E. Marshall 17/1/90
Richard (1812–1831) 16/12/29
W. 21/12/77
Steer,
H. 16/3/68
S. 9/9/78
Steinbein, Dr., of Stuttgardt 1/11/54
Steinthal, S. Alfred, Unitarian 11/8/66, 8/2/90
Stenson, J., London bookseller 9/6/60
Stephanie Louise Adrienne (1789–1860), née Beauharnais, Grand Duchess of Baden 27/10/45
Stephen,
Alexander Condie, Sir (1850–1908), diplomat 7/5/85, 16/12/91, 18/9/93 ff, 25/10/93
James, Prof. Sir (1789–1859), undersecretary, Colonial Office 26/1/35, 5/12/81
James Fitzjames, Sir (1829–1894), lawyer and author 27/6/82 L, 6/2/83 L, 13/1/86
John, Rev., of Aberdeen 4/10/71 ?
J. T., broker 17/2/80
Margaret, Mrs. 14/6/78
S. 22/7/76
Thomas, clerk 9/12/41 ?
Stephens,
Mr., of Hawarden 20/12/61
Mr., of Ionia 10/12/58
Archibald John, barrister 17/6/45
Edward Bowring (1815–1882), sculptor 24/3/49
Margaret E., Mrs. 14/6/78
Richard, wine merchant 11/4/60 ?
Thomas, Liverpool accountant 17/10/58
Thomas (1821–1875), Welsh scholar 14/6/78 n
W. A., of Ontario 10/3/75
William Richard Wood, Ven. (1839–1902) 2/11/78
Stephenson *see* Macleod
Stephenson,
Miss, governess at Bowden 11/1/65
Alexander, Edinburgh broker 25/6/61
Benjamin Charles, treasury clerk 18/8/59
Frederick Charles Arthur, Gen. (1821–1911), commander in Egypt 23/8/84
George (1781–1848), engineer 12/6/47
Henry Frederick, Rev. 1/1/53
J., Rev., vicar of St. Thomas, Toxteth 24/9/86 n, 7/12/86
Robert (1803–1859), engineer, tory M.P. 15/4/56
William, Rev. 16/5/78 ?
William Henry, Sir (1811–1898), civil servant 24/5/46, 6/3/65, 12/8/73 L
Stepney,
Emile Algernon Arthur Keppell Cowell-, Sir (1834–1909), 2nd Baronet (1877), liberal M.P. 22/11/77 n, 26/2/91 n
John Stepney Cowell-, Sir (1791–1877), 1st Baronet (1871), liberal M.P. 4/7/68
Margaret Cowell-, Lady, née Warren, confidante of G 22/11/77, 28/2/80, 24/8/83, 5/11/83, 12/11/85, 6/9/87, 25/2/91, 26/2/91, 20/11/91 ff, 12/4/92, 3/10/92 L, 18/10/92 L
Sterling,
Edward (1773–1847), journalist on *The Times* 23/3/35 n, 25/1/43
John (1806–1844), author 23/3/35
Sterlini, Sig., customs officer in Rome 22/12/66
Stern, Sydney James (1844–1912), 1st Baron Wandsworth (1895), liberal M.P. 22/9/91
Sterry, Francis, Rev. 17/11/75
Steuart,
Andrew (1822–1905), Peelite M.P. 26/1/63
James 4/10/63
John Alexander (–1932), novelist 9/10/90
Stevens,
A.de Grasse, Miss, novelist 8/12/88
E. C., secretary, King's College Hospital 23/4/41
James, of Manchester 14/1/57, 28/5/58
John Austin (1817–1887), of U.S.A. 2/2/76 ?
Thomas, Rev. (1809–1888) 5/4/59
William A. 26/3/80
Stevenson,
C. 26/11/86
George, of Newark 19/1/35
John, Rev. 24/9/86 n, 25/10/86, 7/12/86
Joseph, Rev. 21/9/48
Stevenson & Son, carpet maker 14/9/48
Steventon, R. 28/1/79
Steward, George, Rev. (1803–1866), Congregationalist 13/3/57
Stewart *see* Cooke, Hagart, Hardinge, Vane
Stewart,
rescue 19/6/59
Miss 20/9/32
Mr. 17/10/38
A. 13/12/87
Alexander 19/8/89 ?
Alexander, Rev., rector of Liverpool 20/3/93
Alice Emma Shaw-, Lady, née Thynne 14/11/83, 30/10/90

Stewart (*cont.*)
A. M., of Glasgow 21/6/75
Catherine Shaw-, Lady, née Maxwell 23/12/36
Charles Edward, secretary, L. N. W.railway 19/8/49 n, 24/3/56
Charles Poyntz 25/7/77
David Dale, Rev. 16/12/79
E., Miss 1/10/68
Edward Richard, customs official 23/5/42, 28/5/42, 30/5/42, 3/6/43
Frederick William Robert (1805–1872), Lord Castlereagh (1822), Marquis of Londonderry (1854), tory M.P. 18/4/49
H., of St. Fist 27/9/44
Halley (1838–1937), liberal M.P. 4/12/91
Harriet Blanche, Lady (1811–1885), née Somerset, Lady Galloway 7/6/38
Houston, Adm. Sir (1791–1875) 23/1/62
James, treasury official 9/1/35
James (1827–1895), liberal M.P. 14/1/78
James Arnott, Rev. (1800–1851) 18/5/34
James Haldane, Rev. (1778–1854) 31/1/43
J. D. H., Col. (–1884) 25/1/84, 8/10/84
John, manager of the Gladstones' Demerara estates 30/7/26 n
John, mayor of Liverpool (1855) 8/10/55 n
John Archibald Shaw- (1829–1900) 19/12/65, 20/11/71
Katherine, née Wemyss Charteris 23/5/42 n
Mary Arabella (1837–1903), née Cecil, Lady Galloway 26/10/81
M. H. Shaw-, Sir, 8th Baronet (1903) 14/11/83
Michael Robert Shaw-, Sir (1826–1903), 7th Baronet (1836), tory M.P. 13/4/69
Michael Shaw-, Sir (1788–1836), 6th Baronet (1825), whig M.P. 7/1/36, 23/12/36
Morse, Mrs. 30/11/74
Patrick Maxwell (1791–1846), banker, whig M.P. 31/7/33
Randolph (1800–1873), 9th Earl of Galloway (1834), tory M.P. 5/3/36
Randolph Henry (1836–1920), 11th Earl of Galloway (1901) 14/3/77
Robert, of Torquay 20/9/32 n
Robert (1810–1866), lord provost of Glasgow 24/9/53
Thomas (–1832), G's cousin 30/7/26
William George Drummond-, Sir (1795–1871) 21/6/69
Stewart & Clapperton, Messrs. 24/12/79
Stewart & Douglas, Messrs., hatters 8/1/87
St. Germans *see* Eliot
Stibbs,
E. C. O. 27/12/89
Edward, bookseller 27/3/50 ?
Stierling,
G. S. 10/6/58 n
G. S., Mme. 10/6/58 ?
Stigant, William (1825–1915), barrister 20/4/60, 21/9/60
Stikie, Mr. 21/8/84, 26/10/86
Still, Percy 29/9/86
Stiller, Mr., of Brighton 17/4/65
Stillman, William John 15/3/75, 21/6/79, 29/9/79
Stimpson, T. A. 31/10/76
Stirling,
Fanny, Mrs. (1815–1895), actress 10/4/86 n, 11/4/86
Gordon, West Indian merchant 20/12/34 ?
James (1805–1883), of Glasgow 20/3/65
John (1811–1882), of Kippenross 25/8/42
Stirling-Maxwell *see* Norton
Stitt, J. T. 23/3/76
St. Leonards *see* Sugden
St. Levan *see* Saint Aubyn
Stobart, William James, Rev. (1840–1902) 24/5/79
Stock,
Elliot, London publisher 27/6/77, 8/11/85
Gertrude Georgina, Lady (1842–1893), née Douglas 5/1/92
John, Rev. (1817–1884), Congregationalist 4/5/68
Stockdale,
Jeremiah, Rev. 1/6/73
John Joseph (1770–1847), publisher 17/6/39 n
Stockenstrom, Andries, Sir (1792–1864), 1st Baronet (1840), colonial governor 12/2/36 n
Stocker, Charles William, Rev. Prof. (1794–1870), vice-principal, St. Alban Hall, Oxford 14/11/31
Stockwell, Thomas Henry, editor, *Baptist* 23/4/92
Stoddart, John F., advocate 29/4/28
Stoker,
Bram (1847–1912), author and Irving's manager 18/11/90
Bram, Mrs. 30/5/83 n
Stokes,
Mr., Strzelecki's servant 6/10/73
Charles, London solicitor 24/7/39 ?
C. W., of Blackheath 8/8/66, 9/8/66, 4/3/78
Edward, Rev. (–1863) 16/11/52
George Thomas, Rev. Prof. (1843–1898) 7/12/87
H. 3/3/66 ?
Henry Paine, Rev. 10/11/86
Henry Sewell (1808–1895), poet 14/7/68, 18/1/75
H. P., poet 14/6/74 ?

John, Capt., of Ionia 31/12/58 ?
John, Sir (1825-1902), engineer in Egypt 23/11/83
L., Capt. 7/11/56, 30/8/58
Louis, Rev. 1/1/86
Robert, anti-slaver 5/10/41
William, Sir (1839-1900), Irish physician 18/12/88
William Haughton (1802-1884) 19/9/76
Stokoe, John, Rev., Methodist 4/4/68 ?
Stollwerck, L. 21/8/77
Stone,
E. 22/4/68
F. F. 28/11/90
F. J. 7/2/91
H. E., Rev. 7/8/89
Henry 20/8/75
Henry Edward, Rev. 6/2/79
John Spencer (1810-) 24/10/32
R. C. 3/3/79
William, Rev. (-1877) 4/11/58
William Henry (1834-1896), liberal M.P. 10/6/59
Stoneham,
Messrs. 14/1/87
Allen, of Greenwich 17/11/68
Stonehouse,
A., Mrs. 20/5/56
Arthur, Rev. 22/3/56, 10/5/56
William 4/7/79
William Brocklehurst, Rev. 24/5/48 ?
Stonor,
Alban Charles (1817-1866), lawyer 6/4/54
Catherine, née Blundell 15/1/39
Edmund, Abp. (-1912) 30/4/67
Eliza (-1883), née Peel 18/3/52, 21/11/80
Francis (-1881), clerk of House of Lords 18/3/52 n
Thomas (-1831) 15/1/39
Thomas (-1881), 5th Baron Camoys 9/2/54
Stooks, Thomas Fraser, Rev. (1815-1874) 21/11/47
Stopford,
Edward, Bp. (1772-1850), bishop of Meath 24/12/44
Edward Adderley, Ven., archdeacon of Meath, assisted G with Irish church legislation 7/1/69, 3/3/69, 15/10/69, 14/12/72
James Thomas (1794-1858), 4th Earl of Courtown (1835), a tory 1/5/43
Storey,
A. T. 11/9/90
Samuel (1840-1925), liberal M.P. 4/11/69, 14/9/90, 18/11/93 L
Storks, Henry Knight, Sir (1811-1874), high commissioner of Ionia, succeeding G (1859) 4/11/58, 16/2/59 ff, 29/3/70, 4/7/70, 6/6/71
Stormont *see* Murray
Storr,
John S., of the ecclesiastical courts 18/2/67
John Stephens, journalist 25/11/77 ?
Richard, Newark publican 14/8/34
Storrar, John, Dr. (1811-1886) 14/7/66 ?
Story,
Robert Herbert, Rev. Prof. (1835-1907) 5/6/78
William Wetmore (1819-1895), sculptor 12/11/66 n
W. W., Mrs. 12/11/66
Stotherd *see* Clinton
Stothert, Samuel Kelson, Rev. (1826-) 19/2/58, 1/7/76
Stoughton,
Edwin Wallace (1818-1882), of U.S.A. 15/2/79
John, Rev. Dr. (1807-1897) 26/7/76
Stourton, C. P., 16th Baron Stourton 23/7/38 n
Stout, E. H. 14/6/90
Stovin *see* Wright
Stow, A. H. 1/4/91
Stowe, Harriet Elizabeth Beecher 7/5/53
Strachan,
George L., Lieut. 2/8/62
John, Bp., bishop of Toronto 20/7/40
John, Sir, of the Queen's Household 1/1/51 n
Mary Ann, Mrs., née Elton 1/1/51
Strachey,
Edward, Sir (1858-1936), liberal M.P. 18/8/93 L, 26/8/93 L
Henry Josias, Sir, 5th Baronet (1855), tory M.P. 7/3/57
William James, Rev. 4/7/77, 21/12/89
Stradbroke *see* Rous
Strafford *see* Byng
Strahan,
Alexander, publisher 10/4/71 L
George Cumine, Sir (1838-1887), Knight (1880), colonial governor 24/1/59
Samuel Alexander Kenny, Dr. 15/4/92
William, banker 13/10/27 ?
Strahan, Paul, Paul, & Bates, Messrs., bankers 30/12/53
Straker, Joseph (-1867), Newcastle ship-owner 8/10/62
Strang, John (1795-1863), author 26/8/57 ?
Strange,
E. F. 30/9/91
George Harris, Dr., physician 5/12/51
R. 25/2/78
William (1801-1871), publisher 24/2/58 ?
Strangford *see* Smythe
Strangford, Charles Stuart, of Trinity, Dublin 25/2/34

Strangways,
H. S. Fox-, 3rd Earl of Ilchester 29/1/37 n
H. T. Fox-, 2nd Earl of Ilchester 13/6/33 n
Stephen Fox- (1812–1839) 24/12/29
Stephen Fox- (1817–1848), Lord Stavordale 9/5/46, 3/8/46
Strasser, Mr. 29/7/75
Stratford, John Wingfield- (1810–1881), high sheriff 19/1/30
Stratford de Redcliffe *see* Canning
Stratheden *see* Campbell
Strathmore *see* Lyon
Strathnairn *see* Rose
Stratton,
John 9/2/28 n
Maria, née Jodrell 9/2/28
Stephen, of Birmingham 16/8/78
Strauss, David Friedrich (1808–1874), Biblical critic 17/12/38 n
Straw, E. H. 25/2/76
Streatfield, Miss 25/3/90
Street,
Arthur Joseph, Rev. (–1901) 3/3/76
C. J. 20/9/90
George Edmund (1824–1881), architect 18/12/55
Streeter, E. W. 24/12/77
Strettell,
Alfred Baker, Rev. 26/6/40 ?
John, Rev. 26/6/40 ?
Stretton, Henry 4/7/31
Strickland,
Mr. 12/11/85
Agnes (1796–1874), author 25/7/68 ?
Strike, William, customs official 9/7/42 ?
Stringfellow, Mr. 27/11/89
Strip, Mr. 7/3/78
Strong *see* Gladstone
Strong,
John, stereotyper 22/6/52 ?
Leonard (–1879) 2/2/57, 6/2/67
S., solicitor 17/12/56
Thomas, Rev. (1770–1860) 28/8/32
Strosmaier, Dr., Fribourg surgeon 7/11/45
Strossmayer, Josif Juraj, Bp. (1815–1905), bishop of Bosnia, Slavonia and Sirmium 5/11/76, 3/12/76, 3/6/77, 19/10/82, 31/8/84
Stroud,
Mrs. 18/10/69, 12/2/70
Henry F. 12/2/70 n
Struthers *see* Finlay
Strutt,
Arthur B. 23/2/49
Charles Hedley (1849–1926) 6/1/87
Edward (1801–1880), 1st Baron Belper (1856), liberal M.P. 30/3/54
Elizabeth, novelist 6/10/52
Emily (–1890), née Otter, Lady Belper 16/11/71
Henry G. (1840–1914), 2nd Baron Belper (1880) 3/2/72 n
John William (1842–1919), 3rd Baron Rayleigh (1873), physicist 20/12/71, 15/9/76
William Goodday (1762–1848), colonial governor 23/1/46
Strzelecki, Paul Edmund de, Sir (1796–1873), Knight (1869), known as 'Count', explorer of Australia 16/5/55, 30/7/61, 31/7/61, 4/8/61, 7/8/61, 23/9/61, 24/9/61, 15/10/61, 21/12/61, 16/5/62, 10/6/64, 1/12/64, 23/7/66, 20/8/66, 10/3/69 n, 26/3/69, 30/3/69, 31/3/69, 1/8/69, 21/9/70, 1/11/70, 11/7/72, 16/11/72, 3/10/73, 6/10/73, 20/4/77, 16/8/81
Stuart *see* Beresford, Canning, Gladstone, Kennedy, Ryder, White
Stuart,
rescue 15/6/69, 28/7/75
Miss 6/10/38
Alexander, Rev. (1801–1883) 19/3/57
Andrew Godfrey, Rev. (1812–1889) 28/2/79, 4/3/79
Charles (1818–1900), 12th Baron Blantyre, W. H. G's father-in-law 22/7/75, 23/7/75, 27/7/75, 28/7/75, 9/11/89
Charles, Sir (1779–1848), 1st Baron Stuart de Rothesay (1828), diplomat 24/12/34
C. W., Wolverhampton solicitor 18/5/47
Dudley Coutts, Lord (1803–1854), liberal M.P. 21/2/53
Edward, Rev. (1821–1877) 11/5/57
Evelyn (–1869), née Leveson-Gower, Lady Blantyre 5/10/58
Gwendolen Crichton- (–1932), née Howard, Lady Bute 16/4/72
Henry Villiers- (1827–1895), liberal M.P. 25/7/81, 27/4/86
J., lawyer in Demerara 7/8/38
James, Prof. (1843–1913), liberal M.P., journalist and Cambridge professor 26/10/78, 17/1/79 ff, 19/12/83, 31/7/85 L, 10/9/86, 4/1/87, 3/4/87, 10/4/87, 10/10/87 ff, 30/9/88, 21/2/89, 6/10/89, 20/5/90, 27/11/90, 29/11/90, 4/12/90 ff, 9/3/92 ff, 28/3/92, 2/6/92, 6/9/92, 11/9/92, 14/10/92, 18/10/92 n, 20/7/93 L
James Hilman, Rev. (–1885) 30/10/58
Janet, Miss 4/3/79
John (1813–1877), genealogist, lawyer 7/11/51
John, Sir (1793–1876) 21/7/71
John Patrick Crichton- (1847–1900), 3rd Marquis of Bute (1848) 16/4/72, 14/10/93 L, 26/10/93 L

John Ramsay (1811-1889), soldier 27/11/54 ?
Mary, daughter of Lord Blantyre 7/6/66
Mary, Miss 4/3/79
Patrick, Sir, colonial governor 20/2/46
Robert Leighton (1806-1882), merchant in New York 18/9/67 ?
Villiers, Lieut. Col. 12/6/72 ?
Walter (1851-1895), Master of Blantyre 30/9/75, 22/2/77
Stuart de Decies, Theresa Pauline, Lady, née Otto 20/9/55 ?
Stuart de Rothesay *see* Stuart
Stuart de Rothesay *see* Yorke
Stuart-Wortley(-Mackenzie) *see* Grosvenor, Milbanke, Percy, Scott, Talbot
Stubbings, Mr. 20/12/75
Stubbs,
Charles William, Dean (1845-1912) 22/1/94, 23/1/94
William, Bp. (1825-1901), regius professor of history, Oxford (1866), bishop of Chester (1884), bishop of Oxford (1888) 16/4/58, 9/6/75, 23/9/75, 27/12/75, 4/8/76, 20/2/77, 1/2/78, 27/11/83, 12/2/84, 13/2/84, 18/9/88 n, 16/9/89
Stucarini, L. 31/12/88
Stuckey, S. W. 21/2/89
Studart, Sig. 9/6/91
Studnitz, Arthur von 7/1/76, 25/3/76
Stuetz, Victor, historian 9/3/57 ?
Stümme, Louise, Miss/Mrs. (1820-), known as 'Mrs. Stümme', C. G's Hanoverian maid 4/7/48, 15/4/51, 6/1/75, 9/2/80, 26/10/83, 11/8/84 ff
Sturge,
E. 18/2/77, 30/7/77
Edmund 7/5/89
Joseph (1793-1859), Quaker, philanthropist and freetrader 21/6/37
Sturges, Edward, Rev. (1832-1907) 25/11/67
Stürmer, Karl, artist 4/6/48 n
Sturrah, T. 24/2/90
Sturrock,
J. F., of Edinburgh 18/10/83 L
John, shorthand writer 28/3/80 ?
Sturt,
Charles Napier (1832-1886), tory M.P. 20/4/61, 24/6/70, 16/10/72 ?
Henry Gerard (1825-1904), 1st Baron Alington (1876), tory M.P. 16/10/72 ?
Sturton, Thomas, of Deptford 10/11/75 ?
Sturtz, John James, pamphleteer 2/12/41, 15/11/43
Styles, J. 7/6/67
Suardi, Sig. 1/8/83
Suckling, Mrs. 24/1/68
Sudeley *see* Tracy
Sudlow, H., Mrs., of Liverpool 12/12/67
Suffield *see* Harbord
Suffield, Robert Rodolph, Rev. (1821-1891), Unitarian 31/12/74, 5/10/84 L
Sugden, Edward Burtenshaw, Sir (1781-1875), 1st Baron St. Leonards (1852), tory M.P. and lord chancellor 10/4/38, 26/2/57
Suleiman Pacha, Turkish diplomat 31/8/54
Sulivan, Henry William, Rev. 2/7/65
Sullivan,
Miss, of Bray 29/10/77
Mrs. 23/8/60
Arthur Seymour, Sir (1842-1900), composer 21/2/78 n, 14/9/82 n, 4/12/82, 6/12/82 L
Edward, Sir (1822-1885), liberal M.P. 22/5/66, 7/1/69 L, 29/10/69 n, 13/12/69
Edward Robert, Sir (1826-1899), 6th Baronet (1865) 13/5/58
John, Newark shopkeeper 12/1/35 ?
Robert (1854-1877) 24/10/77 n
Summerhayes *see* Dale
Summerhayes, Mr. 26/4/62
Summers,
Edgar, Rev. (1907-) 1/5/79
John, shoemaker in Newark 20/1/35 ?
Joseph, painter in Newark 20/1/35 ?
William (1853-1893), liberal M.P. 8/10/78, 9/10/84, 8/7/90
Sumner,
Miss 24/1/28
Charles, Senator (1811-1874), American senator and emancipationist 4/7/57, 6/7/57, 4/11/57, 5/11/57, 1/7/59, 22/3/69, 1/4/69, 19/5/69, 21/5/69, 23/10/69, 25/12/69
Charles Richard, Bp. (1790-1874), bishop of Llandaff (1826), bishop of Winchester (1827) 11/5/26
George Henry, Ven. (-1909), archdeacon of Winchester (1884) 30/7/51
John Bird (1780-1862), bishop of Chester (1828), archbishop of Canterbury (1848) 11/5/26 n
Marianne, née Robertson 24/1/28 n
T. 13/4/35 ?
Sunderland, Thomas (1806-1867) 26/11/29 n
Sunderland Liberal Club, Chairman 17/2/80
Sunmill, Mr. 31/12/86
Surenne, James G., Dr., physician 22/1/68
Surgeon, A. 28/2/78
Suringar, Willem Hendrik, author 5/9/51
Surr, Mr. 20/3/78 ?
Surrey, Abraham, engraver 9/7/46
Surtees,
Anne Catherine, née Ferrand 4/3/35 n
Edward, M.P. in Durham 4/3/35 ?
Elizabeth Jane, née Fenwick 18/9/57 ?

Surtees (*cont.*)
Robert Smith (1803–1864), novelist 18/9/57 n
Scott Frederick, Rev. (1813–1889) 17/3/55
Sussex *see* Augustus Frederick
Suther, Thomas George, Bp. (1814–1883) 27/9/53
Sutherland *see* Gower
Sutherland,
Mr., of Hawarden 15/8/62
Mrs. 22/6/59
Alexander John, Dr. (1811–1867), physician 21/12/29, 1/12/41, 5/3/57
David, barrister 1/12/77
George, Rev. 23/8/77
James, provost of Inverness (1853) 2/9/53
Suttaby, Capt. 23/7/77
Suttie, Francis G., Capt. 23/7/77 ?
Sutton,
Messrs. 8/12/86
Charles Manners- (1780–1845), 1st Viscount Canterbury (1835), tory M.P. 29/1/33
Charles Manners-, Abp. (1755–1828), archbishop of Canterbury (1805) 23/7/28
John Henry Manners- (1822–1877), tory M.P. and colonial governor 28/8/43
John Henry Thomas Manners- (1814–1898), 3rd Viscount Canterbury, tory M.P. 17/1/40 n
John Manners- 4/10/32
R. H. 20/8/91
Thomas Manners-, Canon (1795–1844) 31/7/32
Swabey, Henry, Rev. 3/6/50
Swain,
Mr. 21/4/60
W. E. 9/5/76
Swaine,
Edward, author 24/5/43
Leopold Victor, Col. 18/3/85 n
Swainson,
Charles Anthony, Rev. Prof. (1820–1887) 19/12/62
H. 29/1/77
Swamy,
C., Lady, née Beeby 25/4/92
Mutu Coomara, Sir (1834–1879), Knight (1874), barrister 29/12/63, 6/6/64
Swan,
Annie Shepherd (1860–1943), Scottish novelist and liberal 10/4/83, 16/4/83 L
Francis, Rev. 18/4/45 ?
John Cameron, liberal in Newcastle 5/4/80
Robert, author 14/5/34
Swan, Sonnenschein, Messrs., publishers 9/5/88
Swanhill, rescue 27/1/82
Swann,
Messrs. 24/11/87
Edward Gibbon, poet 2/12/77
Swansea *see* Vivian
Swanston, George John, of the board of trade 24/7/77 ?, 21/12/78 ?
Swanwick,
Anna, Miss (1813–1899), author 29/7/65 n, 30/5/78, 2/7/84
John, of Liverpool 29/7/65 ?
Swartnout, Dr. 23/9/86
Swayne, Robert George, Rev. 1/2/53
Swaythling *see* Montagu
Sweet, John Bradby, Rev. 6/11/47
Sweeting,
Mr., at Clumber 15/4/79
E., rescue 25/6/69
R. G., artist 16/11/75
Sweetland, E. T., of Exeter 9/8/65
Swetenham, Clement William, of Cheshire 23/10/93
Swift,
John, railway solicitor 18/3/44
M. Darwin 16/6/87
Swinburne *see* Ward
Swinburne,
Algernon Charles (1837–1909), poet; considered by G for the laureatship 18/12/72, 25/9/85 ?, 7/10/92, 10/10/92, 17/10/92 n
Constance M., Mrs. 5/7/87 ?
Helen (–1860), née Aspinall 23/9/33
J. E., Sir, 6th Baronet 5/3/34 n
M., Lieut. Col. 5/7/87 n
Thomas, Maj. Gen., of Forfar 23/9/33 n
Swindells, G. 21/5/75
Swindley,
Mr., of Hawarden 15/1/56
Mrs. (–1877), of Hawarden 3/5/77, 11/8/77
Swinfen,
Miss 14/4/31
Francis, Mrs. 10/6/53
Samuel (–1854) 14/4/31 n
Swinny,
E. A., Mrs. 18/5/63
Henry Hutchinson, Rev. (1813–1862), principal of Cuddesdon, Oxford 7/5/59
Swinston, G. S. C., autograph hunter 8/11/75
Swinton *see* Hogg
Swinton, Archibald Campbell, Prof. (1812–1890) 24/3/60
Syce, H. 10/2/75
Sydenham *see* Thompson
Sydney *see* Townshend
Syed Abdoollah,
moonshee 18/6/51
Prof., professor of Hindi, London 8/8/61
Syer, William Henry, Rev. 4/4/45 ?
Syfret, M. W. R., Miss, governess 5/11/58, 4/3/65

Sykes,
Francis William, Sir 30/6/45 n
Frederic Henry, Sir 30/6/45 n
Henrietta, née Villebois, Lady Sykes, Disraeli's mistress 30/6/45
Jessica, Lady, née Bentinck 14/2/85
John Thorley, Mr. & Mrs. 4/12/91 ?
William Henry, Col. (1790–1872), of East India Company 30/11/57, 18/1/68
Sylvester, Charles, London civil engineer 2/8/33
Symington, Alexander Macleod, Rev. 24/1/76
Symonds *see* Green
Symonds,
Alfred Radford, Rev. 7/1/53 ?
Arthur 17/2/55
Arthur G., secretary, National Reform Union 13/2/78, 5/9/81 L
John Addington, fils (1840–1893), author 27/9/73, 13/10/77 ?, 7/7/87, 7/7/88 n
John Addington, père (1807–1871) 30/8/58 ?
Thomas Edward, naval architect 22/4/79 ?
William Samuel, antiquarian 11/11/68
Symons, Benjamin Parsons (1785–1878), Warden of Wadham, Oxford 30/5/30
Synan, Edmund John (1820–1887), liberal M.P. 18/3/72
Synge,
Millington Henry, Maj. Gen. (1823–1907), engineer 15/11/53
William Webb Follett (–1891) 19/12/89
Syon, C. 20/12/87
Syre, H. S. 19/6/74
Szecsen von Temerin, Anton, Count (–1896), Count Anton 1/3/71
Szerelmey, Miklos, Hungarian author 10/5/61 ?
Szyrma, Wladislaw Somerville Lach-, Rev. 23/12/87

Taaffe, Olivia Mary, Miss (1832–1918) 29/10/77
Tabberner, John Loude, pamphleteer 17/2/48
Tabor, Robert Montagu, barrister 26/6/75 ?
Tachard, Pierre-Albert (1826–) 19/9/74, 1/7/80
Tadema, Lawrence Alma-, Sir (1836–1912), artist 10/3/74, 23/2/91
Tadolini,
Adamo (1788–1868), sculptor 24/12/66
Eugenie, soprano 9/12/50
Tafe, John, Liverpool accountant 2/6/59
Tagart,
C. 31/1/80
Francis, liberal candidate 2/10/68
J. 7/12/86
Tagore, Dwarkananth 19/7/45
Tainsh,
David, episcopalian in Glasgow 1/3/52 ?
Robert D., of the Chester railway 1/3/52 ?
Taintor, Edward C. 17/7/77
Tait *see* Davidson, Sitwell
Tait,
Mrs., rescue 9/5/84, 21/5/84, 4/12/84 n
Archibald Campbell, Abp. 24/6/36
Catherine, née Spooner 24/5/59
James (1863–1944), historian 27/5/90 ?
Lawson, liberal candidate 27/6/86
Peter Guthrie, Prof. (1860–1901) 16/4/60
Taix and Aicard, Sicilian dealers 7/11/38 n
Talbot *see* Cust, Herbert, Kerr
Talbot,
Mrs., rescue 16/11/63
Caroline Jane (–1876), née Stuart-Wortley-Mackenzie 2/2/52, 14/5/53, 6/6/53, 8/7/54, 11/7/54, 23/8/54, 16/6/56, 10/3/61, 10/6/76 ff, 12/6/76, 17/6/76
Charles, 2nd Earl Talbot 2/9/46 n
Charles John Chetwynd- (1830–1877), Viscount Ingestre (1849), 19th Earl of Shrewsbury (1868), tory M.P. 22/5/57
Christopher Rice Mansel (1803–1890), liberal M.P. 2/9/41, 29/6/83 L
Edward Stuart, Rev. (1844–1934), Warden of Keble (1870), vicar of Leeds (1889) 3/2/49 n, 13/11/72, 18/1/73, 4/1/75 ff, 28/3/75, 22/8/75, 17/1/76, 19/1/76, 14/1/77, 23/4/78 ff, 29/7/81, 18/9/81 ff, 11/5/82, 30/8/82, 31/8/82, 4/10/82, 30/9/84, 15/1/85, 3/7/85 ff, 26/7/85 ff, 20/4/88, 22/6/88, 10/11/88 ff, 25/1/89, 30/1/90 ff, 18/10/92
George, Monsignor (1816–1886), Roman Catholic priest 16/10/66, 22/10/66, 3/11/66, 7/11/66, 9/11/66
George Gustavus Chetwynd-, Rev. (1810–1896) 2/4/26
George John, Sir (1861–1938), undergraduate 29/11/83
Gerald Chetwynd- (1819–1885), director, Indian military stores 26/11/49
Henry John Chetwynd-, Viscount Ingestre (1821), 3rd Earl Talbot of Hensol (1849), 18th Earl of Shrewsbury (1856), tory M.P. 2/4/26 n, 16/5/43
James (–1883), 4th Baron Talbot of Malahide (1850) 10/10/54
James Beard (–1881), secretary, London Soc. of Protestant Young Ladies 16/8/50
James Hale, Rev. 19/9/66 ?
John (–1852), 16th Earl of Shrewsbury (1827) 2/12/50
John Chetwynd- (1806–1852), recorder 4/2/33

Talbot (*cont.*)
John Gilbert (1835–1910), tory M.P. 17/6/40 n, 7/8/52, 10/8/52, 12/9/52, 22/2/57, 24/1/58, 19/9/75, 3/10/81 L
Lavinia, née Lyttelton 3/2/49, 20/4/88, 7/5/94
Lawrence 19/4/76
Margaret, née Stuart Wortley 8/5/77 n
Maria Theresa (–1856), née Talbot, Lady Shrewsbury 2/12/50
Meriel Sarah, née Lyttelton 17/6/40
Reginald Arthur James, Gen. (1841–1929) 8/5/77
Thomas (1771–1853), colonist in Canada 10/2/49
Victoria Susan, Lady (–1856) 16/6/56
Wellington Patrick Manvers Chetwynd-, Sir (1817–1898) 9/12/52, 6/11/58, 24/1/59
William Henry Fox (1800–1877), photographer 24/1/57
Talfourd, Thomas Noon, Sir (1795–1854), liberal M.P., copyright reformer and author 1/5/39 n, 6/8/42, 5/4/82
Tallack,
T. A. 8/5/91
William, author 21/8/76, 27/12/77
Talleman, O. 15/5/78
Tallents *see* Lecky
Tallents,
Godfrey, Newark tory 14/9/40, 25/1/74 L
William Edward (1780–1837), G's agent in Newark 31/7/32, 3/10/32, 11/2/33, 2/4/34, 2/8/34
William Edward, Mrs. 9/5/38
Tallerman, Daniel 21/4/75
Talley, Mr. 29/11/76
Tallichet, E. 7/3/76 ?
Tallis, Richard, of Hawarden 24/5/61
Talmadge, John Mayow, Rev. 13/1/80
Talmadge, J. T., & Co., London tea-dealers 19/7/59
Talmage, Thomas de Witt, Rev. (1832–1902), American evangelist 23/2/90, 24/2/90
Talookdar of Majeddinpur 1/12/91
Tammage, Mr. 17/4/79
Tancred,
Thomas, Sir (–1844), 6th Baronet 29/12/36 n
Thomas Selby, Sir (1808–1880), 7th Baronet (1844) 12/11/28
William, Ven. (1818–1864), archdeacon in Tasmania 29/12/36
Tanenberg, Mr. 15/3/80
Tange, Messrs., engineers 11/2/75
Tangye,
A. 8/12/88
Richard, Sir (1833–1906), Knight (1894), industrialist, liberal and Cromwellian 11/2/75
Tanisin, M. de 25/1/66
Tankerville *see* Bennet
Tanneguy, Charles Marie (–1867), Comte de Duchatel 29/3/48
Tanner,
Charles Kearns Deane, Dr. (1849–1901), home rule M.P. 21/7/87, 12/10/87
E. 19/7/77
Tansley, Mr., Hawarden mine adviser 26/11/89
Taparelli,
Massimo (1798–1866), Marquis d'Azeglio, president, Piedmont council (1849), novelist 1/11/50, 26/2/58
Vittorio Emanuele, Marquis d'Azeglio, Piedmontese ambassador 20/9/51 n, 22/3/55, 1/6/63
Tapp, Mr., undertaker at Fasque 8/12/51
Tarbet, Mr. 2/1/75
Tarbutt, Arthur Charles, Rev. 3/3/40
Targett & Barrett, Messrs., lithographers 20/2/79 ?
Tarrine, W., Rev., Unitarian 5/5/88
Tartaglione, Mr. 24/12/86
Tarver, Charles Feral, Rev. 18/3/70
Tasker,
Miss 8/4/88
James Hunter, superintendent, S. M. J. railway 24/7/51
Tatchell, rescue 25/3/78
Tate,
Alexander, Rev. 31/5/45
James Roddam, secretary, C.of E. Scripture Readers Association 7/2/52
J. W. 21/8/77
Tatham,
Edward, Rev. (1749–1834), Rector of Lincoln, Oxford 15/2/30
F., artist 28/2/62
Tatham, Upton, Johnson, Upton & Johnson, Messrs., solicitors 13/9/49
Tatham & Proctor, Messrs., solicitors in London & Chester 9/3/40 n
Tattersall,
Mr. 8/1/87
J. F., author 23/9/91
William, of Manchester 15/8/87
Tattersall, R. & E., Messrs., auctioneers 5/5/59
Tattershall, Thomas, Rev. (1795–1846) 9/9/27
Tatton, T. W. Egerton 18/2/28 n
Tauchnitz, Christian Bernhard von, Baron, publisher; published ed. of G's pamphlets 23/7/75, 5/9/76 n, 14/10/76, 1/11/76, 7/11/76 ff, 21/1/77, 23/3/78, 7/11/78
Taunton *see* Labouchere
Taunton,
John Henry, engineer 25/5/59

Thomas Henry, wine merchant 6/10/27
Tavistock *see* Russell
Tayler, Lucy, Mrs. 10/7/57
Tayleur, Henry, Liverpool broker 3/12/46
Taylor *see* Austin, Brougham, Money
Taylor,
rescue 25/2/62, 7/7/63, 25/2/64, 6/3/68
Messrs., of Sandycroft 19/9/87
Mr., photographer at Balmoral 23/9/69
Mrs. 25/2/62
Mrs., landlady 31/10/42
B., liberal in Peterborough 30/3/80
Charles (-1894), surgeon 29/4/50 ff, 6/4/60
E. 16/5/65
E., cottager 13/12/36
Francis William, Rev. 25/1/58
Frederick Holden, solicitor 23/12/79
G., of Edinburgh 22/2/43
George, registrar 10/2/47
George Graeme Watson, owner of Monte Cristo island 13/6/62
Hannis (1851-1922), of U.S.A. 13/5/79
Henry, Sir (1800-1886), author and colonial office clerk 21/2/35, 24/3/85 L
Henry Ramsay, barrister 20/3/74, 24/3/74
Isaac (1787-1865), theologian 23/3/41
Isaac, Rev. (1829-1901), archaeologist 30/12/73
James, Rev. (1809-1898) 9/6/58 ?
James, Rev. Dr. (1813-1892) 12/9/69
James Bayard, poet 29/1/76 ?
Jesse 22/12/79
J. L. 15/7/76
John, Newark maltster 22/10/39
John, banker 8/8/57
John Daniel, china dealer 18/7/76 ?
John Fraser, Rev. (1828-1909) 11/3/61
J. Pringle, secretary of Midlothian liberal unionists 10/4/88
J. T. 15/7/76
Malcolm C., Rev. Dr., Presbyterian 2/10/71
O. 12/4/78
Peter Alfred (1819-1891), liberal M.P. 4/5/66
Pringle, Gen. (1796-1884) 12/4/75
S. B., Rev. 15/2/87
Sedley, Rev. (1834-1920) 30/12/69, 28/10/78
Simon Watson (1843-1902) 10/8/69
Thomas Edward, Col. (1811-1883), tory M.P. 5/3/57, 13/3/73, 9/12/73
Tom (1817-1880), editor, *Punch* 30/5/72
Vernon Pearce, Rev. (1809-) 8/6/30
W. 20/6/92
Weld, Mr. 2/7/75
William (1808-) 8/6/30
Taylor, Daniel & Sons, wine merchants 29/2/60
Taylour *see* Sandars
Tcheharcheff, Mme., of Florence 19/1/88
Tchernaiev, Mikhail Gregorovich, Gen. (1828-1898) 8/3/77
Tchirny, Mons. 30/5/92
Teale,
Gordon 3/9/91
Thomas Pridgin, surgeon in Oxford 6/7/85
William Henry, Rev. 5/6/42
Teall, James Eastoe 2/5/78
Teape, Charles Richard, Rev. Dr. 14/8/88
Tearle, Mrs. 28/9/78
Teasdale,
R. 25/8/77
Thomas Walmsley, Rev. (1801-) 23/5/38
Tebb, William, president, Compulsory Vaccination Abolition Soc. 2/5/87
Tebbs, S. N., Rev. 1/4/76
Teck *see* Francis, Mary Adelaide Wilhelmina Elizabeth
Teck,
Francis Paul Charles Louis Alexander, Prince, Prince of Teck 21/6/75
Mary, Princess, Princess of Teck 21/6/75
Teed,
Frederick, Mrs. 21/10/46
Frederick, Rev. 12/9/46
Teetgen, Alexander T., poet 31/1/70, 17/12/89 n
Tegeman, Mr. 19/9/86
Teignmouth *see* Shore
Télégraphe, Le 20/10/79
Teleki, Madame 23/3/68
Teleki de Széh, A., Count 6/1/67 n
Teleki de Széh, Jane Frances Harley, Countess 6/1/67
Telford, Thomas (1757-1834), engineer 31/8/26 n
Teller, J. 6/1/90
Tempest,
Adolphus Vane-, Lord (1825-1864), tory M.P. 17/8/58
Elizabeth (-1845), née Blundell 15/1/39
George H. R. C. W. Vane- (1821-1884), Viscount Seaham (1823), Earl Vane (1854), 5th Marquis of Londonderry (1872), Peelite M.P. 25/9/49
Harry Vane-, Sir 2/8/43 n
Marianne, née Sargent 24/9/66 n
Mary Cornelia Vane- (-1906), née Edwards, Lady Seaham, Lady Londonderry 22/9/53, 11/3/91
Stephen, of Broughton 15/1/39
Susan Charlotte Catherine Vane-, Lady (-1875), née Clinton 17/8/58 n, 29/1/65
Walter Joseph (1801-1868) 24/9/66
Temple,
rescue 5/7/65, 7/7/65, 3/8/74, 27/6/76
Christopher, barrister 23/1/35 n

Temple (*cont.*)
Christopher, Mrs. 23/1/35 ?
Elizabeth Cowper-, née Tollemache, Lady Mount-Temple 21/11/62
Emily Mary (1787–1870), née Lamb, Lady Cowper (1805), Lady Palmerston (1839) 22/11/52, 3/3/66, 9/3/67, 3/8/69
Frederick, Abp. (1821–1902), bishop of Exeter (1869), bishop of London (1885), archbishop of Canterbury (1896) 7/12/49, 20/8/69, 28/8/69, 22/9/69, 10/10/69, 16/10/69, 17/10/69, 20/10/69, 30/10/69, 16/11/69, 21/11/69, 3/1/70, 2/7/84 L
Henry John; Lord Palmerston 1/2/32
Isaac, Rev. (1793–1880), of Chester 14/4/65
Robert, Rev. (1829–1902) 23/9/72, 27/12/72
William, Sir (–1856), diplomat 26/7/49
William Francis Cowper- (1811–1888), Baron Mount-Temple (1880), liberal M.P. 23/7/27, 7/12/49, 17/3/59, 5/10/61, 22/7/68, 11/3/70 n, 14/6/70 n, 27/5/75
Templer, William Christopher, Rev. (–1885) 7/4/59
Templeton,
John, London baptist 22/4/68
William, of Penmaenmawr 19/9/60
Tenerani, Pietro (1789–1869), sculptor 25/10/66
Tenison,
Edward King, Lieut. Col. (1805–1878) 7/7/69
Louisa, Lady 30/1/72
Tennant *see* Asquith, Lister, Lyttelton, Myners, Stanley
Tennant,
Charles (1796–1873) 18/7/66
Charles, Sir (1823–1906), 1st Baronet (1885), liberal M.P. and industrialist, owned Millais's 1st portrait of G 19/11/79, 6/5/85, 12/2/86, 22/6/86, 16/7/86, 24/8/86, 20/3/87, 7/7/87, 28/6/88, 6/1/90 ff, 14/2/90, 3/7/90, 12/7/90, 3/11/90 ff, 2/5/92, 31/5/93
Charles Coombe (1852–1928) 6/1/90
Charles Edmund 23/1/27
Harold John (1865–1935), liberal M.P. 5/11/90
Helen (–1892), née Duff 5/11/90
James 21/12/75
James Emerson, Sir (1804–1869), 1st Baronet (1867), né Emerson, of the colonial office 11/8/35, 6/4/46
Mariquita, Mrs., Superior of Clewer House of Mercy 28/9/43, 1/8/50
Ottiwell, Rev. (1780–1863) 30/9/38
Robert John, Rev. (1809–1842) 16/12/31
William 23/1/27 ?
Tenniel, John, Sir (1820–1914), Knight (1893), cartoonist 24/5/84, 7/5/89 n, 4/10/92
Tennyson *see* D'Eyncourt
Tennyson,
Alfred; Poet Laureate 16/10/29
Audrey, née Boyle 25/6/84
Eleanor Mary Bertha, née Locker, later Mrs. Birrell 14/11/82 L
Emily (–1896), née Sellwood, wife of the poet 21/2/66, 24/7/71, 6/7/84 L
Frederick (1807–1898), poet 9/6/31
Hallam (1852–1928), 2nd Baron Tennyson (1892), biographer of the poet 24/7/71, 31/10/76, 9/9/83 ff, 26/11/83, 27/12/83 L, 25/6/84, 8/10/92 L, 27/10/92 L, 7/12/92 L
Lionel (1854–1886) 28/2/78, 3/7/84 L, 8/7/84, 26/4/86
Mary Emily, née Prinsep, formerly Hichens 7/4/72
Tensenberg, J. H. 5/1/87
Tenterden *see* Abbott
Terni, Count of 6/6/32
Terrot, Charles Hughes, Bp. (1790–1872), bishop of Edinburgh (1841) 24/11/33
Terry,
rescue 3/5/71, 12/12/71, 7/12/78
(Alice) Ellen (1847–1928), actress 20/7/78 n, 16/10/78 ?, 21/6/82 L, 8/7/82, 25/10/82, 18/6/84, 10/4/86 n, 11/4/86, 2/12/90, 29/1/91, 11/5/92, 22/11/92, 25/2/93
Eliza J., Mrs., rescue 3/7/56, 23/4/73, 7/5/76
Kate, Miss (1844–1924), actress 30/5/63, 19/6/63
Marion, actress 18/11/84
M. C. 1/5/55
Testa, Giovanni Batista, historian 15/8/53
Testard, Henri, Rev. 3/7/77 ff, 12/5/79
Teulon, Henry, printer 7/1/57
Tewfik Pasha, Khedive of Egypt 14/7/82 ff, 15/9/82, 21/10/82, 27/11/82 c, 13/12/82, 16/6/83, 19/6/83
Thackeray,
Francis St. John, Rev. 3/1/90
William Makepeace (1811–1863), author 8/6/54
Thackerby, J. D. 2/7/52
Thaddeus, Henry Jones, artist 24/1/88, 7/11/93, 10/11/93, 23/11/93
Thafer, W. R. 25/9/89
Thatcher, Thomas 23/2/87
Thayer, Eli (1819–1899) 13/4/87
Thea, Timotheus, Prof. 29/12/75, 12/11/76
Theakstone, Henry, Liverpool broker 28/6/55
Theed, William (1804–1891), sculptor 2/8/60, 16/3/65, 29/3/77, 25/6/77, 1/4/78, 21/12/87, 6/4/89

Theiner, Augustin, Rev. (1804–1874), historian 4/11/66
Thellusson,
Frederick (1798–1852), 4th Baron Rendlesham (1839), tory M.P. 17/10/44
F. W. B., 3rd Baron Rendlesham 25/9/73
Thelwall, Algernon Sydney, Rev. 12/3/40
Theobald, Robert Masters 16/5/77, 20/12/89
Theodoli, Lily, Marchesa, novelist 17/10/92, 29/12/92
Theodosius, James Henry, Rev. (1824–1893) 16/12/79
Theotokes, Ioannes Baptistes, Count (1778–1865), of Ionia 3/12/38, 28/11/58
Theresa (1822–1889), Empress of Brazil 6/2/88
Therry, Roger, Sir (1800–1874), Australian judge 17/7/48, 19/4/60
Thesiger,
Alfred Henry, Lord Justice (1838–1880) 19/6/78
Anna Maria, Lady, née Tinling, Lady Chelmsford 23/4/56
Frederick, Sir (1794–1878), 1st Baron Chelmsford, tory M.P. and lord chancellor 24/1/40
Theyne, rescue 2/4/59
Thick, J. 17/7/76 ?
Thiedemann, H. 18/6/90
Thielmann, Adolf Wilhelm von 23/2/80 ?
Thierrat, Philip, of Lyons 8/1/73
Thiers, Louis Adolphe (–1877) 4/3/52, 24/1/67, 13/9/70, 10/1/71
Thiersch, Heinrich Wilhelm Josias 17/6/76 ?
Thirlwall,
Connop, Bp. (1797–1875), bishop of St. David's (1840), historian and theologian 11/6/39, 2/7/69, 5/1/70 L, 12/1/70 L, 27/2/70, 2/12/81
Thomas James, Rev. (–1900) 10/3/77
Thirnbeck, Mr. 10/8/57
Thistlethwayte,
Augustus Frederick (1830–1887), husband of Laura Thistlethwayte 10/12/64 n, 3/7/68, 1/4/69, 7/5/69, 10/11/71, 9/12/71, 26/4/75, 14/2/78, 1/1/84, 1/1/85, 25/6/85, 9/8/87 n, 24/8/87
Laura Eliza Jane Seymour 10/12/64
Thoener, T. de 3/1/77
Tholuck, Friedrich August Gottreu, Rev. Prof. (–1877), translated G's *State and Church* into German 5/8/43
Thom,
John Hamilton, Rev. (1808–1894), unitarian 6/11/47
Sarah, tenant at Hawarden 27/8/72 ?
William, surveyor of Hawarden 30/8/45, 27/8/72 n
Thomas *see* Traherne
Thomas,
rescue 9/8/71
Alexandre Gérard (–1857), French historian 11/5/52
Ann, of Hawarden 26/10/75
C. W. 1/1/80
David, Rev., of Penmaenmawr 16/8/61, 26/8/67
D. R., Rev. 17/11/90
E. E. 27/3/74
George Fuller, Rev. 26/5/51 ?
Henry Eaton, Rev. 24/4/89 ?
J., Mrs., of Woburn 9/8/88
J. L., reporter 26/11/78
John, Canon (1811–1883) 9/5/29
John Davies, Rev. 19/8/78
L. H., Miss 3/10/87
Mesac, Bp. (1816–1892) 21/11/59 ?
N. W. 2/5/87
R. H. 27/2/80
Richard James Francis, Rev. (1813–1873) 8/9/31
S. E., journalist 5/7/78
S. Gilchrist, Mrs., wife of the engineer 19/4/91
U. K., Rev. 7/12/87
W., Rev. 2/1/87
W. H. 17/2/80
Thomatis, David, Prof., of Berlin 4/12/74
Thompson,
Rev. Mr. 3/4/44
Alfred, ballet designer 25/9/77 n
Caroline Lawley- (1792–1868), née Neville, Lady Wenlock, C. G's aunt 6/6/39 n, 2/5/68, 9/5/68
C. E. P., 1st Baron Sydenham 27/7/46 n
D. C., liberal; publisher in Dundee 22/9/86
Edward Healy, Rev. 9/6/41
Edward Maunde, Sir (1840–1929) 23/2/74 ?, 23/5/93
Elizabeth Maria, née Lloyd, author 30/8/45
F. C. 25/12/80
Francis Edward, schoolmaster 29/3/90
Frederick, consul 28/7/49
Henry Stephen Meysey-, Sir (1809–1874), 1st Baronet (1874), liberal M.P. 28/8/61 ?, 2/7/68, 3/7/68
H. Y. 20/7/65 n
J., of Brighton 31/3/66
Jacob (1810–1885), Confederate agent 8/4/65 ?
J. E. 31/12/79
John, Newark chairmaker 19/1/35 ?
John, Newark maltster 19/1/35 ?
Joseph William 14/9/76
J. T. 24/3/43
Paul Bielby Lawley- (1784–1852), 1st Baron Wenlock (1839) 6/6/39 n
Phillips 30/10/77

Thompson (*cont.*)
R., tax surveyor 22/7/35 n
Robert, Rev. 2/1/66 ?
S. E. 8/6/88
Skirving, alias J. A. Mackie, defrauder 11/3/79
Slesor, editor of *America* 30/11/88
Thomas Perronet, Gen. (1783–1869), radical M.P. 6/11/61
T. J. 3/4/91
William, mayor of Newark 2/7/35
William (1793–1854), tory M.P., shipping manufacturer 25/4/42
William, Rev., Principal, St. Edmund Hall, Oxford 7/12/53
William Hepworth, Rev. (1810–1886), Master of Trinity, Cambridge (1866) 5/9/78 ?
Thoms, William John, known as A. Merton 10/1/46 ?
Thomson,
Miss, of Edinburgh 22/2/44
Andrew M., Dr., distant relative in Edinburgh 27/4/28
C. J., distant relative in Edinburgh 4/12/79, 6/4/80
David C., Dundee publisher 14/9/89
George, town clerk 20/8/41
James, Newark maltster 19/1/35 ?
James Gibson, Edinburgh winemerchant 10/12/33
James Tertius 24/1/37, 21/9/41
John, Newark chairmaker 19/1/35 ?
J. R. C., secretary, Hyde Park College 14/5/57
William, Abp. (1819–1890), fellow and provost of Queen's, Oxford (1850), bishop of Gloucester (1861), archbishop of York (1862) 27/2/54
William, Prof. (1824–1907), 1st Baron Kelvin (1892), physicist 3/6/93
William Taylour, Sir (1813–1883) 1/3/73 ?
Zoë, née Skene 19/8/62
Thorburn, David, Rev. 17/12/63, 10/10/65
Thorn,
rescue 4/6/77
Mr., of Oakfield, Liverpool 16/7/44
Alexander, Dr., physician 11/12/51
J. L. 12/1/87
Thornber, W. H., of Rochdale 1/11/81
Thornborough, Mr. 11/1/79
Thorn & Co., bookbinders 6/10/75
Thornely,
James 25/7/78 ?
Robert 6/9/87
Thomas, liberal candidate and M.P., Liverpool merchant 13/11/32
Thornewill, Edward John, husband of Anne G 14/12/70, 19/9/71, 26/7/74
Thornhill,
Mrs. 1/7/79
Albert Frederick, Rev. 1/7/79 n
William, Rev., of Dublin 25/4/79
Thornitz, Laura 26/9/87
Thornton *see* Astell, Harrison
Thornton,
family 14/8/32
Charles, Rev. 4/3/30
Edward, translator 5/5/56
Edward, Sir (1817–1906), Knight (1870), diplomat 14/5/69, 24/1/70, 24/1/71
Henry (1760–1815), evangelical philanthropist 14/8/32 n
Henry Sykes (1800–1882), banker 16/1/49
John, Rev. 14/7/77 ?
L., rescue 1/7/75, 1/8/75
Robinson 15/2/42 n
Thomas (1786–1866), journalist on *The Times* 15/2/42
Thomas, Sir (1829–1903), liberal agent in Dundee 7/11/85
William Thomas 19/5/75
Thoroton, Charles Roos, Rev. 26/6/41
Thorp,
Charles, Ven. (1783–1862), Warden of Durham university (1833) 25/11/41
Robert, Rev. 7/2/40
Thorpe,
Mrs. 18/9/76
G. 8/1/87
James, mayor of Newark 30/9/32
William, Rev. (1778–1865) 11/6/55
Thorwaldsen, Bertel (1768–1844), sculptor 3/4/32, 10/10/38, 2/10/45
Threlfall, Thomas, barrister 26/5/79
Thring, Henry, Sir 27/3/50
Throckmorton *see* Cowper
Thrupp,
Charles Joseph 2/6/77
R. W. 25/10/79
Thum, F. 27/3/74
Thurland, W. F. 29/6/52
Thurling, Mr. 26/5/79 ?
Thurlow,
Charles Augustus, Rev. (1803–1873), Chancellor of Chester 27/11/56
Thomas Lyon (1814–1894) 3/4/77
Thursfield,
Lady 6/3/88 n
James Richard, Sir (1840–1923), Knight (1920), historian 8/3/88
Thurston, Robert Henry, Prof. (1839–1903), of U.S.A. 17/2/80
Thuyer, Mons., French Director of Posts 14/7/49
Thwaites,
Edward Nembhard, Rev. 6/4/77

George Saunders, Col. (–1866), secretary, National Gallery 3/3/53
John, Sir (1815–1870), chairman, metropolitan board of works 17/1/66
Thynne *see* Scott, Stewart
Thynne,
Alice, Lady 4/7/83
Beatrice, Lady 4/7/83
Charles J. 14/1/87
Harriet (–1892), née Baring, Lady Bath 20/4/52
Henry Frederick (–1837), 3rd Marquis of Bath (1837) 20/4/52 n
John, Rev. Lord 29/2/44
John Alexander (1831–1896), 4th Marquis of Bath (1837), Bulgarian campaigner 17/1/77 n, 31/10/80 ?
John Charles, barrister 1/3/80 ?
Katherine, Lady 4/7/83
Tibbitts, Thomas Abbott, solicitor 25/7/77
Tickell, George 5/12/74 ?
Tickle,
G. Y. 22/5/90
W. 19/12/89
Tidall, Miss 2/1/87
Tidbury, C. H., accountant 4/11/56 ?
Tidman, Arthur, Rev. 22/10/59 n
Tiedemann, H. 18/6/90
Tighe,
C. 1/12/87
Louisa Madelina, Lady 26/7/89
Tigrane Pasha, Egyptian official 13/5/84, 17/1/93 n
Tilburn, rescue 29/3/55
Tillett,
Benjamin (1860–1943), trade unionist 9/9/87 ?
Jacob Henry (1818–1892), liberal M.P. 2/6/70, 24/7/80
Tilley, John, Sir (–1898), of G.P.O. 10/12/52, 17/4/74
Tillies, D. 5/11/90
Tillnen, rescue 14/5/55
Tillotson, Rev. Mr. 10/1/78
Tilsley,
Mr., liberal chairman 13/10/85
Hugh, of I. R. B. 7/10/53
Tilston,
Margaret, servant 6/12/47
W. H. 8/5/89
Timins, John Henry, Rev. (–1894) 5/10/51
Timm, Joseph, solicitor, I. R. B. 15/2/53
Tindal,
Mr. 24/12/49
Nicholas Conyngham, Sir (1776–1846), chief justice (1829) 6/6/35
Tinling *see* Thesiger
Tinling, Edward Douglas, Rev. (1815–1897) 20/9/60
Tinworth, Mr. 30/6/83
Tipaldo,
Cav., of Venice 8/10/79
Giulio, Sig., of Ionia 8/2/59
Tippet, W. T. 2/3/75
Tipping, Mr. 5/5/79
Tirbutt, F. E. 10/5/91
Tireman, William Walter, Rev. (1807–1872) 27/2/68
Tirner, Mr. 25/12/75
Tischendorf, L. F. C. von (1815–1874), biblical scholar 15/2/65
Tisdall *see* Marlay
Tissot, Charles Joseph (1828–1884), French diplomat 16/12/70, 28/10/71
Titcomb, Jonathan Holt, Bp. (1819–1887) 22/4/68 ?
Tite, William, Sir (1798–1873), Knight (1869), liberal M.P. 21/5/60, 20/11/65, 17/1/66, 27/5/67
Titien, Mlle., opera singer 24/4/66
Titley, Edward, of Chester 7/5/44 ?
Tivoli, V. De, translator 26/8/78
Tivy, W. H., of U.S.A. 10/3/75
Tobin,
Dr., physician in Brussels 7/2/32
John, Rev. (1810–1874) 20/9/26
John, Sir (1762–1851), mayor of Liverpool (1819) 20/9/26 n
Thomas, merchant 11/1/34
Tocqueville, Alexis de (1805–1859), historian 8/8/49, 3/1/51, 6/8/58, 24/12/84
Tod, Alexander 27/6/79
Todd,
Adam Brown 8/1/87
Charles John 27/5/71 ?
Henry, of Co. Tyrone 7/6/77
Horatio, Rev. (–1868) 10/10/28
James Frederick, Rev. (1808–1863) 10/10/28
James Henthorn, Rev. Dr. (1805–1869) 26/7/44
J. H. R. 19/3/77
John Miles Rogers, solicitor 19/3/77 ?
Robert Bentley, Dr. (–1860), physician 9/11/53
Todhunter, John, Dr. (1839–1916), poet 14/6/88
Toft,
Mr. 7/7/77
Albert (1862–1949), sculptor 17/9/87
Toll, Mr. 2/1/64
Tollemache *see* Roundell, Temple
Tollemache,
Mrs. 12/12/38
Beatrix 18/12/91
Felix Thomas (–1843) 10/7/50 n
Henry James (1846–1906), tory M.P. 30/11/69 n

Tollemache (*cont.*)
John Tollemache (1805–1890), 1st Baron Tollemache (1876), tory M.P. 10/6/53, 30/11/69
Lionel Arthur (1838–1919), author, recorder of G's conversations 28/1/57, 17/8/58, 25/5/64, 11/12/64, 18/12/91 ff, 29/12/92 ff, 2/1/93 ff, 24/1/94 ff, 31/1/94 ff
Mary Stuart, Lady 29/12/81 ?
William John Manners (1859–1935), 9th Earl of Dysart (1878) 1/7/93
Tolley, W. 12/11/79
Tolmer, D. 14/4/91
Tolson, E. 12/7/76
Tolstoi, Madame 5/7/93
Tolstoy *see* Stanhope
Tolstoy, Ina, Countess 29/8/87
Tomalin, James B., of Brixton Hill 10/2/68
Tombs, John, London builder 31/10/54
Tomes,
Robert, Rev. 8/4/51 ?
T. P. 4/8/87
Tomkins, John, of Clifton 20/12/64 ?
Tomkinson,
Mr. 17/12/84
Emily, Mrs. 17/11/86
James 17/11/86
Tomlin, Alfred John, Rev. (–1901) 16/11/56 ?
Tomline, George (–1889), Peelite M.P. 28/6/48, 26/3/49
Tomlinson,
George, Bp. (1801–1863), bishop of Gibraltar (1842) 20/6/36
George Dodgson 12/10/69
H., builder 21/5/59
James (1840–1910), liberal candidate 12/4/81
Tommasini Mattiucci, Leovigildo (1824–1877), Italian liberal 17/5/59 ?
Tompson, John Edward, Rev. 16/1/68, 25/12/69
Toms, Alfred Augustus, Rev. (–1922) 2/8/77
Toncalier, S. 1/6/88 ?
Tondini, Cesario, Rev. (1839–1909) 3/9/75
Tonello, Michelangelo, Piedmontese politician 1/1/67
Tonks, J. W., of Birmingham 24/3/74
Tonkyn, J. 11/5/78
Toogood, William, journalist 14/11/49
Tooke, William (1777–1863), whig M.P. 13/2/33
Toole, John Lawrence (1830–1906), actor 14/3/78
Toomer, Joseph, stable owner 18/2/57
Toomungong, Prince, Prince of Malaya 26/7/66
Toorley, Mr. 6/3/75
Tooth, Charles, Rev. 2/1/88
Toovey, James (1813–1893), London bookseller 7/9/43
Topete, J. B., Adm. (1821–1885) 26/4/73
Topham, John, Dr. (–1887), physician 18/12/66
Torelli, Luigi (1810–1887) 4/3/59
Torey, J. L., coachmaker 8/2/48 ?
Torlonia, Prince, Duke of Bracciano, banker 5/4/32
Tornielli,
Count, Italian ambassador 12/7/93
Countess 12/7/93
Toroud, Rev. 16/11/88
Torr,
James Fenning, barrister and Eighty Club member 14/10/87
John (1813–1880), tory M.P. 22/10/75
William (1808–1874), farmer 13/6/57
Torre,
Manuel Garcia Della, sherry merchant 14/10/87
Nicholas Lee (1795–) 30/12/57
William Fox Whitbread, Rev. (1829–1912) 12/6/74
Torrens,
Robert (1780–1864), political economist, whig M.P. 22/4/41
Robert, Judge, Irish judge 25/6/46
Robert Richard, Sir (1814–1884), Knight (1884), liberal M.P. 1/3/70 n
William Torrens McCullagh (1813–1894), liberal M.P. 2/5/67, 11/3/73
Torrigiani,
Marchesa 29/9/38
Marchese, mayor of Florence 23/1/88, 28/1/88
L., author 20/7/70
Torrington *see* Byng
Torry,
John, Dean, Scottish episcopalian 7/10/46
Patrick, Bp. (1763–1852), bishop of Dunkeld (1808), bishop of St. Andrews (1844) 27/6/42
Toso *see* Puzzi
Tosti, Luigi, Rev. (–1897) 1/12/50, 27/12/66
Tottenham, Arthur Loftus, Col. (1838–1887), tory M.P. 6/6/81, 7/6/81, 13/12/81
Tottie, John William 17/3/55 ?
Toulson, James 26/12/76
Tour d'Auvergne-Lauraguais, Henri de la, Prince 29/7/64, 8/5/67
Tournay, Stewart, solicitor 28/2/48 ?
Tovey, Mr. 11/12/74
Towgood, John, barrister 13/3/50 ?
Towle, George Makepeace, author 11/7/68, 10/12/86
Towneley, Charles, tory candidate 4/8/37 n
Townley, Charles Watson (1824–1893) 28/9/69

Towns, Mr., Peel's Steward 26/1/49, 6/7/50
Townsend, George Fyler, Rev. 27/5/42
Townshend,
Edward du Pré (1806-) 31/1/37 ?
Edward Venables (1774-1845), of Cheshire 31/1/37 ?
Emily (-1893), née Paget, Viscountess Sydney 1/7/58
Henry (1813-1896) 31/1/37 ?
John Robert (-1890), 3rd Viscount Sydney (1831) 4/7/54, 18/1/71 L, 17/4/86 L, 20/2/90
Lee Porcher (1804-1871) 31/1/37 ?
Townshend & Barker, Messrs., solicitors in Chester to Gladstones and Glynnes 8/1/74, 26/10/74, 18/5/75 ff, 24/5/75, 9/12/75, 4/1/76, 10/1/76, 2/2/76
Towse, John Beckwith, lawyer 9/7/67
Towsey, T., florist? 23/1/56 ?
Toye,
E. W. 3/10/87
W. J., Rev. 1/4/76
Toynbee,
William, author 22/5/90
William, barrister 4/12/78 ?
Tozer, William George, Bp. (-1899) 23/12/74
Tracey, Matthew, of Ireland 15/3/75
Tracy,
Charles Douglas Hanbury- (1840-1922), 4th Baron Sudeley (1877) 28/1/65
Frederick Francis, Rev. (1829-1888) 9/8/78
Traherne,
John Montgomery (1788-1860), antiquary 25/7/51 ?
Morgan (1803-1867), né Thomas, tory M.P. 26/5/34 ?
Trail, William, Rev. 9/3/40
Traill,
Miss 6/1/32
L., Miss 6/1/32
Thomas Stewart, Dr., physician 18/9/26 n
Thomas Stewart, Mrs. 18/9/26
Trant, William 17/4/79, 6/5/79
Trash, S., secretary, Radcliffe hospital, Oxford 23/4/49
Travers,
John Ingham, London grocer 23/12/52
Newenham Thomas 7/11/85
S. S. 3/3/65
Travis *see* Knyvett
Trechi, Baron 19/6/45
Tredgold, Clarkson Sturge, of Cape Town 11/5/38 ?
Tree, Herbert Beerbohm (1852-1917), actor 29/3/90 n, 27/3/92
Treffry, Joseph Thomas 2/6/42
Trefusis,
Charles Henry Rolle Hepburn-Stuart-Forbes- (1834-1904), 20th Baron Clinton (1866) 11/5/55 n
Harriet Williamina Hepburn-Stuart-Forbes- (-1869), née Forbes, Lady Clinton 11/5/55
Tregaskis, D. 17/7/90, 12/9/90, 2/11/91, 8/11/92
Treherne,
J. 28/1/79
Morgan (1803-1867), tory M.P. 12/3/57
Trelawney, J., rescue 23/5/59
Trembicka, Françoise, author 24/9/41
Tremenhere, H. Seymour, inspector of mines 18/10/71
Tremlett, Francis William, Rev. Dr. 10/3/55
Tremouille, de la, Messrs. 4/2/79
Trench,
Eliza (-1869) 4/4/33 ?
Francis Chenevix, Rev. (1805-1886) 12/11/63 ?
Frederick Fitzwilliam, Rev. 23/10/68
J. Cooke 23/8/81 L
Letitia Susanna Le Poer, Lady (-1865), née Dillon 22/2/34
Richard Chenevix, Abp. (1807-1886), archbishop of Dublin (1863) 30/9/41, 5/8/54, 20/9/63, 17/6/68, 21/1/69, 5/11/77, 7/11/77, 18/7/78
Robert Le Poer, Col. Sir (1782-1824) 22/2/34 n
Thomas, Dean, dean of Kildare (1809) 4/4/33 n
William Richard, author 24/3/79
William Thomas Le Poer (1803-1872), 3rd Earl of Clancarty 28/7/51
Trenchard,
Mr. 9/5/79
Edward Penny, merchant 24/5/79
Trendell, Arthur James Richens, Sir (1836-1909), Knight (1900) 7/1/78
Trengrouse, R., liberal in Putney 7/7/79
Trequeti, di, Baron 10/5/69
Tressilian, Mrs. 18/5/47
Trevelyan *see* Dugdale
Trevelyan,
Mrs., of Whitby 27/8/71
Charles Edward, Sir (1807-1886), administrative reformer 13/6/40, 20/1/53, 26/1/53, 31/1/53 ff, 14/2/53 ff, 22/2/53, 16/3/53, 23/7/53, 12/8/53, 26/10/53, 22/11/53, 23/11/53, 23/12/53, 24/12/53, 2/1/54, 6/1/54, 9/1/54, 14/1/54, 17/1/54, 28/1/54, 21/2/54, 7/3/54, 8/4/54, 17/7/54, 21/7/54, 16/1/55 ff, 3/5/55 n, 25/11/55, 13/8/69 L, 7/3/79
Charles Philips, Sir (1870-1958), liberal (later labour) M.P. 31/3/91
George Macaulay (1876-1962), historian 31/3/91
George Otto, Sir 20/7/65

Trevelyan (*cont.*)
Hannah, Lady, née Macaulay 13/6/40 n
James Harington, Lieut. Col. (1811–1875), G's fag at Eton 26/4/26
John, Sir, 5th Baronet 26/4/26 n, 12/5/36 n
Maria, Lady (–1852), née Wilson 12/5/36
Robert Calverley (1872–1951) 31/3/91
Walter Calverley, Sir (1797–1879), 6th Baronet, naturalist 17/7/75
Trevenen, Thomas John, Rev. (–1864) 15/5/58 ?
Trevithick, F. H. 20/11/79 ?
Trevitt, James, Rev. 16/4/54
Trevor *see* West
Trevor,
Arthur Hill, Lieut. Col. (–1856) 5/3/52 ?
George, Rev. (1809–1888) 19/8/48
Thomas, Rev. Dr. 4/8/26
W. C., Maj., in Ionia 10/12/58 n
Trew,
Henry, secretary to Governor of Dominica 6/4/38
John McCannon, Rev. 8/3/41
Trewers, N. 7/11/85
Tricoupi, Spiridion (–1873), Greek ambassador 3/5/54
Trimmer,
Edward, secretary, Royal College of Surgeons 18/11/75
Robert, Rev. Dr. 19/1/87
Tringle, D. 16/10/86
Tripe, E. 24/11/91
Tripp,
Edwin H., stockbroker 29/5/56
Henry, Rev. 23/3/54
John, Rev. 5/10/87
Triscoll, Samuel, of Plymouth 30/5/55, 14/7/56
Trist,
Jane Warren, née Devonshire 9/8/48
John Fincher (1822–1890), landowner 9/8/48 n
Tristram, John William, Rev. 14/9/88
Tritton, Joseph, Rev., Baptist 6/3/75 ?
Trocke, Thomas, Rev. 26/4/46 n
Troja, Carlo, Italian politician 7/2/51
Trollope,
Anthony (1815–1882), novelist 3/5/80
John, Sir (1800–1874), 1st Baron Kesteven, tory M.P. 10/5/67
William, Rev. (–1863) 22/3/53
Troppanegar, A. 22/10/53
Tropponeger, Mr., German tutor 31/7/33
Trott, E. C. 24/3/76
Trotter,
Coutts, Sir (1767–1837), 1st Baronet (1821), partner in Coutts' bank 3/1/33
Henry, Major 9/3/81 ?
Henry Edward, Rev. (1856–1910) 25/9/92
John, tory M.P. 5/5/43
Lionel James, Capt., historian 11/6/87
Margaret Coutts, Lady (–1853), née Gordon 23/6/38
Troubetskoi,
Elizaveta Esperovna, Princess 10/2/92
Pierre, Prince (1864–1915), painted G's portrait 4/7/93, 14/7/93
Troughton, John Ellis, Rev. (–1872), of Pentrobin, Hawarden 4/1/45
Troup,
A., Rev. 23/8/77
George Elmslie, author 22/11/79
Trower,
J. 20/9/88
Walter John, Bp. (–1877), bishop of Gibraltar (1863) 26/4/31 n, 9/1/50
William Baker 26/4/31
Troy, Mr. de 13/10/56
Troyte, Arthur Henry Dyke- (1811–1857), formerly Acland, member of the Engagement 1/6/29, 23/2/45 n
Trübner, Messrs. 20/2/78, 30/10/89
Truitt,
Miss 10/11/86
Rev. Mr. 20/10/67
Trull, W. Benson, of U.S.A. 9/10/60
Trullet, Angelo Maria, Fr. (1813–1879) 3/11/66
Trumbell, H. Clay, American publisher 5/11/90
Trundell, A. J. K. 26/1/90
Truro *see* Wilde
Truscott, Thomas, of Liverpool 8/6/63
Trusted, C. J. 5/10/89
Truswell, Messrs., of Newark 22/1/45
Tsankov, Dragan, Bulgarian nationalist leader 29/8/77, 6/12/77
Tscheraz, Mons. 12/9/90
Tschirag, Mons. 6/1/90
Tseng Chilse, Marquis, Chinese ambassador 14/5/80
Tubb,
Mrs. 20/3/47
William, decorator 13/11/40
Tuccillo, Sig. 18/7/78
Tuck,
R. 10/4/80
William 31/12/74
Tucker,
A. 17/3/59
Alfred Robert, Bp. (1849–1914), Anglican bishop of Uganda 1890-1911 20/9/92 ?
Benjamin Wadham 31/10/28
C. 13/12/77
Elisabeth 2/6/77
Henry St. George (1771–1851), of East India Co. 1/5/35

Henry William, Rev., secretary, S. P. G. 18/9/76
Tuckerman, Mr., of Florence 4/1/88
Tuckwell, William, surgeon 10/8/31
Tudor, Augustus, of Ryde 19/5/55
Tudway, Robert Charles (1808–1855), tory M.P. 28/6/53
Tuer, Andrew White (1838–1900), publisher 27/4/78
Tufnell *see* Glyn
Tufnell,
Edward C., school inspector 19/12/71 ?
Edward Wyndham, Bp. (1814–1896), bishop of Brisbane 17/12/57 n, 14/1/60 n
Henry (1805–1854), whig M.P. 29/1/46
Tufo, Cesare Francesco del (1802–1886), Prince Ischitella, Neapolitan minister of war 10/2/51 n
Tufton, Henry James, Sir (1844–1926), 1st Baron Hothfield (1881) 22/8/81, 8/10/92
Tugman, James E. 17/5/76
Tugwell, George, Rev. 1/3/80
Tuke, Daniel Hack, Dr. (1827–1895), physician 3/1/79
Tulk, Charles Augustus 11/5/46
Tull, R., rescue 8/3/59
Tulloch,
Alexander Murray, Gen. Sir (1803–1864), military reformer 6/3/56
Hector, Major, Boundary Commissioner 28/11/84
John, Rev. Principal (1823–1886), Principal of St. Andrews, historian of theology 20/8/72, 2/12/79, 3/12/79, 26/6/82
Tumbini, B., of Naples 9/12/86
Tupper,
Daniel (1812–1869), of Lord Chamberlain's Office 26/4/31
Ellen (–1847), née Devis 4/3/33
Martin, Dr. (1779–1845), physician 4/3/33 n
Martin Farquhar 2/4/29
Walter Farquhar 28/11/89
William George, Rev. (–1854) 22/2/52 n
Turberville, A. C., Rev. 1/11/91
Turchi, Marino, Prof. 18/5/77
Turlls, J., Rev. 28/3/60
Turnbull,
Mrs., of Whitby 24/8/71
Alexander, consul in Marseilles 17/7/49
Robert, Bailie, of Edinburgh 18/1/86
Robert Carr, solicitor 28/9/74
William Stephenson, Rev. (–1913) 15/7/68
Turner *see* Jacobson, Williams
Turner,
rescue 20/1/60
Capt. 12/9/53
Mr., liberal in Aylesbury 19/4/79
Alexander, of Hawarden 30/9/62
Algernon 6/7/77
Augustus, Rev. 15/2/45 ?
Caroline, Lady, née Finch Hatton 26/8/41 n
Charles (1803–1875), G's election opponent in S. Lancs. 20/7/65
E. L. 10/4/79
F. H. 23/12/79
Freeman, Col. 21/4/88 n
George James, Judge Sir (1798–1867) 30/8/65
G. F. 11/1/77
Gladstone 11/11/86
J., alias A. Walter, rescue 26/11/63, 4/12/63
James Aspinall (1797–1867), liberal M.P. 3/11/59
J. H. 22/4/58, 1/9/66
John Matthias, Bp. (1785–1831), bishop of Calcutta (1829) 7/12/27
John Matthias, Mrs., née Robertson 24/1/28
Llewelyn, Sir (1823–1903), Knight (1870) 1/5/77
Sydney, Rev. 19/5/48
Thomas, equity draftsman 27/3/48 ?
Thomas (1804–1883), treasurer of Guy's Hospital, London 25/4/63
Turner, Turner and Morris, Messrs., bankers in Gloucester 17/12/25
Turnerelli, Edward Tracy, anti-Russian propagandist 7/1/74, 1/5/76, 11/6/77
Turners' Company, G a member 16/2/76, 13/10/81
Turney, Alderman, of Nottingham 18/10/87 n
Turnor, Christopher (1810–1886), tory M.P. 26/8/41
Turquand, Paul James, Rev. 18/5/78 ?
Türr,
Adeline, née Wyse 18/12/58
Estevan, Gen. 18/12/58 n
Turriffs, Gavin 24/2/74
Turton,
E. 1/11/92
Edmund Henry, Capt. 25/8/71 n
Thomas, Dean (1780–1864), dean of Westminster (1842) 26/6/45
Turville, Francis Charles Fortescue, Sir (1831–1889), Knight (1875) 21/1/59
Tuscany *see* Leopold II
Tuturgi, Athanasius, Bp., bishop of Tripolis 19/12/41
Tweddell,
John 5/8/39 n
Robert, Rev. (1772–) 5/8/39
Tweed, James Peers, Rev. (–1890) 5/6/52
Tweeddale *see* Hay
Tweedie, James 6/7/78

Tweedmouth *see* Marjoribanks
Twells, Edward, Bp. (1828–1898) 22/2/61
Twemlow, Elizabeth 8/7/29
Twining, Thomas (1806–1895), charitable donor 17/4/62
Twisleton,
Edward Turner Boyd (1809–1874) 17/2/33, 29/6/66, 23/11/69
F., 13th Baron Saye and Sele 17/2/33 n
Twiss,
Mrs. 20/2/79
Travers, Prof. Sir (1809–1897), lawyer 18/5/44
Twist,
Joseph Wilding, Rev. (–1865) 31/3/50
Thomas Kenyon, Liverpool merchant 30/6/48
Tyler,
Elizabeth Ann (–1830), née Griffin 18/10/34 n
Flora 18/10/34
George Griffith, distant relative 27/12/51
Henry, Capt., royal engineers 30/7/66
James Endell, Canon (1789–1851), G's cousin by marriage 31/10/30, 23/1/34
Jane, née Robertson, G's cousin 23/1/34
Mary Jane (1834–), G's god-daughter and cousin 8/12/34, 3/2/35, 10/7/73
Roper Trevor, Rev. 29/11/52 ?
William, London stationer 27/3/53
William Robertson, Capt. (–1863), relative 17/11/63
Tylor,
Alfred (1824–1884) 26/3/77
Edward Burnett, Sir (1832–1917), anthropologist 4/2/90
Tyndal, Charles, of Bank of England 14/8/58 n
Tyndale,
Henry Annesley, Rev. 9/9/90
John William Warre, barrister and bank manager 17/2/27
Tyndall, John, Prof. (1820–1893), physicist 19/1/66
Tyner, William, Rev. 6/3/50
Tyrell, John Tyssen, Sir (1795–1877), 2nd Baronet (1832), tory M.P. 21/1/35, 10/10/42
Tyreman, Mr. 5/2/90
Tyrer, James, treasurer, Liverpool Sailors Home 31/7/46 n
Tyrrell,
Edward, Remembrancer 24/10/46
John, Liverpool merchant 9/9/33 ?
William, Bp. 13/4/48
Tyrwitt, Robert Philip (1798–1886), magistrate 6/3/71
Tytler,
James, Edinburgh lawyer 30/11/33 ?
Patrick Fraser (1791–1849), historian 30/11/33 ?
Tywett, Mr. 28/5/77
Tzikco, Pericles 17/2/80
Tzwiet, Mons. 6/1/77

Uexküll, Jakob Johannes von, Baron (1823–1885), Russian in Naples 29/2/52
Ulloa,
Girolamo, Gen. 19/10/66
Pietro Cala, Marchese di Favale, Duca di Lauria 25/1/64
Umberto I (1844–1900), King of Italy (1878) 20/7/75
Underhill,
Charles, surgeon 4/12/79
Edward Bean, Rev. Dr. 16/6/88
Underwood, Celia L. G., Lady, née Gore, Duchess of Inverness (1840) 3/8/53
Unghara,
Sig., Neapolitan hotelier 25/7/49
Signora 25/7/49
Unsell, James W. 9/8/78
Unsworth, Messrs., china dealers 21/1/54
Unwin,
Messrs., printers and publishers 27/11/77, 24/6/79
Edward, printer 27/11/77, 24/6/79 n
Thomas Fisher (1848–1935), publisher 8/2/87
Upperton, Charles Stuart, Rev. (1829–1916) 3/9/74
Uppington,
Caroline, nurse 26/2/46, 2/2/47, 6/9/47, 10/9/47, 20/5/53, 31/8/53
Charles 11/2/50
E., Miss 6/9/49
F., Miss 8/8/50
Upton, William J. 20/6/77
Upward, A. 20/8/91
Uranga, Nemesio 14/3/80
Urban Club 23/4/77
Urquhart,
Adam, Edinburgh lawyer 3/9/45
David (1805–1877), radical-tory M.P. 18/3/33
Usborne, Thomas (1810–1869), historian 22/3/48
Usibeba, Chief, Zulu chief 19/12/83
Ussher,
John (–1907), of co. Waterford 18/12/76 ?
Mary, née Warburton 18/12/76
Utterton, John Sutton, Ven. (1814–1879) 3/11/72
Uwins,
Mrs. 9/3/55
Thomas (1782–1857), artist 5/4/51
Uxbridge *see* Paget

Vaccaj, Nicola (1790–1848), composer and singer 13/12/33
Vadura, V. 31/12/88
Vakeels, The 9/4/45
Valaorite, Aristos, of Ionia 1/2/59
Valaoriti, Spiridione, Sir, of Ionia 3/12/58
Valaviti, Cav., of Ionia 18/1/59
Valentine,
Mrs. 4/3/92
James, English merchant in Palermo 6/12/51
William, Rev. 29/11/47
Valentine, young 22/1/79
Valerio, Lorenzo, Italian politician 3/8/61
Valery, Sig. 4/10/89
Valetta, S. J., of Genoa 23/2/75
Valettas, Ionnes N., Prof. 8/2/64
Valin, Claude Marie, Abbé 15/9/77
Valisma, Eustachio, of Ionia 29/11/58
Vallance, James, solicitor 6/10/42
Vallati, Sig., artist in Rome 16/1/39, 12/11/66
Valletoy, H. 29/4/63
Vallombrosa, Duke of 30/1/83
Valpy,
Francis Edward, Rev. (–1882) 16/3/50 ?
Leonard Rowe, barrister 10/4/66
Richard, in statistical department, Board of Trade 2/1/68 n
Valsamachi, Demetrio, Sir, of Ionia 11/10/41
Valucri, Sig. 13/3/67
Valussi, Pacifico, author 13/12/75
Van Campen, Samuel Richard 15/7/91
Vance, John (–1875), tory M.P. 13/7/53
Van Den Driesche, D., manufacturer 29/6/87 ?
Vandenhoff,
Mrs., actress 5/10/75 n
Henry J., actor 14/6/79
Vanderbyl, Mr. 15/12/87 ?
Van Der Fan, Bartout 18/7/76
Vandervelde, A., of Belgian legation 14/6/79
Van de Weyer,
Madame 11/3/52
Sylvain (1802–1874), Belgian minister in London 11/3/52 n
Vandyck & Brown, Messrs., photographers in Liverpool 29/1/75
Vane *see* Powlett, Tempest
Vane,
rescue 4/10/73
Charles William, Sir, né Stewart, 3rd Marquis of Londonderry 2/8/43
Frances Anne Emily, née Vane-Tempest, Lady Londonderry 2/8/43 n
William Henry (1766–1842), 1st Duke of Cleveland (1833) 6/2/49 n
Vane-Tempest *see* Churchill, Vane
Vanlennep, Henry J., in Athens 21/12/58
Vanlerberghe, Mr. 25/4/38
Van Oss, S. F. 27/9/90
Vansittart,
Caroline (1782–1851), née Eden 2/7/33
C. Arthur 14/6/73
Nicholas (1766–1851), 1st Baron Bexley (1823), tory M.P. and cabinet minister 13/5/33
Vanstorm, Mr. 17/9/66
Van Zandt, Ferdinand S. (–1892) 27/11/85
Vardon, Thomas, librarian, House of Commons 12/1/53
Varnish, Henry, silk manufacturer 10/4/75
Varvogli, President, President of Greece 29/3/54
Vasey, Mr. 27/7/77
Vassilachi, Elia, of Ionia 26/11/58
Vaughan *see* Halford, Isham
Vaughan,
Mrs. 8/4/78
Charles John, Rev. Dr. (1816–1897) 15/4/58, 8/7/60
Charles Richard, Sir (1774–1849), diplomat 11/4/33 ?
David James, Rev. (1825–1905) 26/8/68
Edward Prothero, Rev. 30/3/38
Henry Halford, Prof. (1811–1885), regius professor of modern history, Oxford (1848) 12/4/31, 7/4/79
Herbert Alfred, Cardinal Abp. (1832–1903), bishop of Salford (1870), archbishop of Westminster (1892) 5/8/61, 25/11/70, 10/11/92
James, Rev. (1806–1886) 25/4/31
Kate (1852–1903), dancer 1/12/73
Robert, Rev. Dr. (1795–1868) 10/1/42, 15/11/64
Thomas, of Middlesbrough 9/10/62
Vaux, S. H., Mrs. 25/10/79
Vavasour,
Henry Mervyn, Sir 22/11/41 n
Louisa Anne, Lady, née Neville 22/11/41
Vavassour, Mr. 8/9/76
Vearey, T. 20/7/91
Vedana, G., Sig. 8/8/88
Veitch, William, of Edinburgh 26/7/76
Veith, Philip (1793–1877), artist 11/1/39 n
Veja, Dr., of Ionia 26/1/59
Vela, Vicenzo (1820–1891), sculptor 4/3/59
Velli, Luigi, of Rome 21/6/78
Velluti, Sig., of Venice 4/10/79
Venables,
Miss 5/5/59
Mr. 3/4/77
Edmund, Rev. (1819–1895), antiquary 20/8/64, 8/10/70, 15/1/72, 16/1/94
George, Rev. (1821–1908) 8/4/56
George Stovin (1810–1888), barrister, journalist 18/12/52

Venables (*cont.*)
Richard, Ven. (1775–1859) 18/2/42, 16/4/45
Venn, Henry (1796–1873), secretary, C. M. S. (1841) 15/4/49
Venning, Edward John, Rev. 25/3/68 ?
Ventura,
Giacchino (1792–1861), advocate 13/12/38
Teodoro, of Ionia 4/12/58
Vera, Leon Galindo y de 21/2/57 ?
Verbeck, Mr., conjuror 6/5/85
Verdon, Thomas K. de, author 17/8/77
Vere, Aubrey Thomas de, poet 4/8/42
Vereker, Standish Prendergast (1819–1900), 4th Viscount Gort, (1865) 20/5/69
Verhaegen, Pierre T., Belgian politician 6/11/56 ?
Verindor,
F. 16/6/90, 16/8/90
Verne, rescue 18/4/91
Verner,
James Edward, Lieut. Col. (1804–1865) 27/1/39
Thomas, Lieut. Col. (1774–1853), courtier 26/12/38
William, Col. Sir (1782–1871), tory M.P., Orange Master 20/7/42 n
Vernet, Horace (1789–1863), artist 20/2/32
Verney,
Edward Hope, Capt. Sir (1838–1910) 10/6/78
Eliza, Lady (–1857), née Hope 23/9/38
Frederick William (1846–1913) 22/11/78
Harry, Sir (1801–1894), né Calvert, 2nd Baronet, liberal M.P. 5/12/33, 23/9/38
Henry Peyto- (1773–1852), 16th Baron Willoughby de Broke (1820) 10/7/38 n, 5/7/52 n
Margaret Peyto-, Lady (1800–1880), née Williams, Lady Willoughby de Broke 10/7/38, 5/7/52
Vernon *see* Mildmay
Vernon,
Miss 7/3/76
Mrs., rescue 30/4/70, 5/8/70
Augustus Henry (1829–1883), 6th Baron Vernon (1866) 29/4/69
Catherine (–1867) 19/5/53 ?
Frances Julia Harcourt- (–1844), née Eyre 2/12/39 n
Frances Margaret, Lady Vernon 20/10/87
George John Venables- (1803–1866), 5th Baron Vernon (1835), whig M.P. 15/2/39
George William Henry Venables- (1854–1898), 7th Baron Vernon (1883), whig peer 13/7/87, 20/10/87
Granville Edward Harcourt- (1816–1861), Peelite M.P. 24/5/39, 22/11/52, 28/12/52
Granville Harcourt- (1792–1879), Peelite M.P. 2/12/39, 10/6/40, 11/12/61, 28/7/65
Henry George, Rev., of Liverpool 22/4/63 ?
Isabella Caroline, Lady (–1853), née Ellison 22/3/49
John E., Irish land commissioner 17/3/86
John Richard, Rev. 30/8/67 ?
Pyne Jesse Brand, Mrs. (–1872), wife of Granville Vernon 20/5/61, 11/12/61
Robert (1774–1849), art collector 20/5/48
Robert Vernon (1800–1873), 1st Baron Lyveden (1859), né Smith 15/2/40, 11/8/71 L
Thomas Bowater 28/9/74, 17/5/76
Vernon-Harcourt *see* Malcolm, Norreys
Verrschagen, Herr 1/11/87
Verschoyle, Hamilton, Rev., of Dublin 11/1/56
Verulam *see* Grimston
Vesey,
Constance Mary (1851–1886), née Lawley 19/6/77
Emma (–1884), née Herbert, Lady de Vesci 4/7/61, 28/7/61 ?
Eustace (1851–1886) 19/6/77
John Robert William (1844–1903), 4th Viscount De Vesci (1875), Irish landowner; G's host in Ireland 7/11/77 ff, 23/11/83, 23/9/85, 8/11/85, 12/2/86 L, 19/2/86 L
Thomas (1803–1875), 3rd Viscount De Vesci (1855) 4/7/61 n
Vestris, A. A. (–1825) 3/12/27 n
Vevey & Co. 14/3/87
Veysey *see* Hayman
Veysie, Daniel, Rev. (1799–1866), Oxford proctor 23/8/28
Viale, N., Sig. 16/4/62
Viarol, Mons. 3/12/91
Vicheli, Count 12/5/77
Vicini, Gustiniano 14/1/89
Vickers, J. S., agent of Hawarden estate (1874) 2/5/64, 9/12/73, 16/12/73, 8/1/74, 4/4/74, 6/4/74, 5/6/74, 26/10/74, 6/1/76 ff, 30/5/77, 31/7/77 ff, 8/8/77, 11/5/78, 29/8/79, 24/9/80, 27/8/88
Victor Emmanuel I, King of Savoy 29/2/32 n
Victor Emmanuel II (1820–1878), King of Sardinia, King of Italy 4/3/32
Victoria, Queen 28/5/34 n
Victoria Adelaide Mary Louise, Princess (1840–1901), Princess Royal, Empress of Germany 21/6/42, 25/1/58 n, 15/7/74, 20/5/79, 16/7/81, 30/7/84, 8/9/84, 15/3/91
Victoria Mary Louisa, Princess (1786–1861), Duchess of Kent 4/5/35 n

Victoria of Hesse, Princess 24/11/83
Vidal, Francis, Rev. (1805–1884) 4/4/57, 27/1/59
Vightoller, Mr. 7/12/75
Villadicani, Francisco di Paola, Cardinal Abp. (1780–1861), Cardinal Abp. of Messina (1843) 2/11/38
Villari,
  Mad. 20/7/90
  Pasquale, Prof., historian 11/7/65, 2/1/88, 25/1/88, 31/1/88, 1/2/88, 20/7/90
Villars, Mons. 3/12/86
Villebois *see* Sykes
Villiers *see* Lewis, Brandling
Villiers,
  Catherine (1810–1874), née Grimston, Lady Clarendon 8/3/53, 20/4/53, 11/5/53, 7/6/53
  Charles Pelham (1802–1898), liberal M.P., friend of Laura Thistlethwayte 15/3/38, 11/7/42 n, 13/11/52, 1/8/82, 20/10/82, 21/10/82, 22/5/85, 5/1/86, 20/3/86, 21/3/87, 6/2/94
  Edward Hyde, 5th Earl of Clarendon (1870) 30/11/73
  George Augustus Frederick (1808–1859), 6th Earl of Jersey (1859), Viscount Villiers, Peelite M.P., Peel's son-in-law 20/1/36
  George Child-, 5th Earl of Jersey (1805), racehorse owner 13/4/35 n
  George William Frederick; Earl of Clarendon 19/8/31 n
  Henry Montagu, Bp. (1813–1861), bishop of Carlisle (1856), bishop of Durham (1860) 19/8/31
  L., rescue 19/1/61
  Margaret Elizabeth Leigh, née Leigh, Lady Jersey 17/7/90
  Sarah Sophia (1785–1867), née Fane 13/4/35
Vincent,
  Miss, of Hawarden 1/5/78
  Mr. 11/1/74
  Mrs., rescue 16/3/60
  Charles Edward Howard, Col. Sir (1849–1908), tory M.P. 24/1/90, 17/2/93 L
  C. Howard 24/1/83
  Edgar Vincent (1857–1941), financier 10/11/79, 5/12/80
  James Vincent, Dean (1793–1876) 10/9/61
  May, Miss 1/5/78
  William Thomas, registrar 21/12/75 ff, 14/2/76, 21/9/78
Vineis, Nicolo, advocate, author 29/2/88, 1/3/88
Viner, George Barber Peregrine, Rev. 27/9/75 ?
Vircis, Cav. 21/1/88
Virtue, J. S. & Co., booksellers 16/11/91
Vischering, Clemens August Droste von, Abp. (1773–1845), archbishop of Cologne (1835) 15/8/38
Visconti, Countess 10/8/86
Visger, Jean A., Mrs., née Owen 15/11/89
Vistahermosa, de, Count, Spanish ambassador 18/2/67
Vita, V. M., poet 6/3/79
Vitali,
  Egidio, wine shipper 29/6/78
  M., of Ionia 1/12/58
Vitalis, Georgios, Greek sculptor; carved statue of G for Athens 23/10/83, 26/10/83, 19/7/88 n
Vitelleschi,
  Amy Nobili-, née Cochrane-Baillie 3/7/75
  Francesco Nobili-, Marchese 3/7/75, 8/10/85, 24/6/89
Vitzthum von Eckstaedt, Karl Friedrich, Count, diplomat 30/1/56, 24/2/58
Vivian,
  A. B., Rev. 21/6/78
  Averil, Lady Swansea 12/7/93
  Beatrice 2/4/77 ?
  Edward 1/10/76 ?
  Henry Hussey, Sir (1821–1894), 1st Baronet (1882), 1st Baron Swansea (1893), liberal M.P. 13/3/60, 27/6/80 L, 7/6/85, 9/4/86, 13/5/87, 2/6/87, 3/6/87
  Hussey Crespigny (1834–1893), 3rd Baron Vivian (1886), diplomat 16/9/83, 7/6/85
  I. H. 10/5/39
  John Cranch Walker (1818–1879), financial secretary, War Office 2/2/70
  Richard Hussey, Brigadier (1775–1842), 1st Baron Vivian (1841) 12/6/26 n, 10/5/39
  W. C. 24/8/89
Vivien, Miss, rescue 13/11/60
Vizetelly, Henry Richard (1820–1894), engraver and editor, *Illustrated Times* (1855), published Zola 25/6/52, 12/3/57 n, 27/4/88 n
Vladimir, Grand Duke 14/6/71
Voeux, Mons. de 16/5/62
Voight, J., opera singer 14/7/73
Voivodas, Mid Wilanovich, governor of Moldavia, 21/5/78 ?
Volkaerslake, Baron de 26/10/91
Voller, Mr., horsedealer 8/8/56
Volpi, Anna 3/6/32
Volta, Escaud 4/11/76
Volti, Signor 16/4/80
von Alten *see* Cavendish
von Arco *see* Montglas
Von Neergaard, Mrs. 14/7/90
Vores, Thomas, Rev. (–1875) 1/11/62
Voules,
  H. 19/5/77

Voules (*cont.*)
Ian Arthur, Rev. 19/2/67 ?
J. P., Rev. (1800–1834), chaplain in Rome
1/4/32
Voûte, Jan Reiner, Dutch author 19/7/66 ?
Voysey, Charles, Rev. (1828–1912),
controversialist 19/3/76 ?
Vulliamy, Benjamin Lewis (1780–1854), clock
maker 1/4/43
Vyner *see* Compton, Erskine, Robinson
Vyner,
Eleanor Margaret, Mrs. (–1913), née Shafto,
confidante of G 30/1/83 ff, 11/2/83 ff,
24/6/83, 12/7/83, 28/6/84, 5/2/88,
17/2/89 ff, 19/7/90, 9/2/92
Mary, Lady (1809–1892), née Robinson
24/6/83
Robert C. de G. 30/1/83 n
Vyse,
George Howard, Col. 18/12/77
Richard Henry Richard Howard, Col.
(1813–1872), tory M.P. 16/7/63
Vyvyan,
Edward R., liberal candidate 23/3/80
Richard Rawlinson, Sir (1800–1879), 8th
Baronet (1820), tory M.P. 14/6/33

Waagen, Gustav Friedrich (1794–1868), art
historian 26/5/57, 13/11/58
Wace, Henry, Rev. Dr. (1836–1924), professor
of church history, London (1875), leader
writer for *The Times* 24/4/89
Wachtmeister, H., Count, Swedish diplomat in
Naples 29/2/52
Wacksell, P. 21/1/90
Wadd,
Caroline, Miss (1810–) 29/7/29
Caroline, Mrs., née MacKenzie 29/7/29
William 29/7/29
Waddell,
Peter Hately, Rev. 27/9/75
William Wardlaw 24/11/71
Waddie, Charles, secretary, Scottish Home
Rule Association 9/12/88, 24/8/90,
13/10/90
Waddilove,
R. D. 8/12/37 n
William James Darley, Canon (1783–1859)
8/12/37
Waddington *see* Bunsen
Waddington,
David, tory M.P. 18/8/54
Horatio (1799–1867), Home Office civil
servant 11/12/65
Mary, Mrs. (–1923), née King 19/10/79
T. F. 12/11/90
William Henry (1826–1894), French foreign
minister and ambassador in London
18/12/77, 19/10/79, 28/2/83, 25/7/83,

15/8/83, 21/2/84, 14/5/84 c, 24/5/84 c,
10/6/84 c, 14/6/84, 19/11/84, 7/3/85 c,
14/3/85, 25/3/85 c, 28/4/85 c, 24/6/85,
15/3/86, 1/11/92 ff, 4/11/92 ff,
20/1/93 ff, 30/1/93 ff, 1/3/93, 17/3/93,
4/5/93, 14/7/93 ff, 18/12/93
Waddy,
H. T., lawyer and Eighty Club member
9/9/78
Samuel Danks (1830–1902), liberal M.P.
4/2/74, 26/4/77, 28/10/79, 1/5/80 L,
19/7/80, 12/3/81 L, 14/5/81
Wade,
Frederick Tobias, Rev. (–1884) 12/3/56
Nugent, Rev. 26/5/47 n, 4/9/67 ?
Thomas, Lieut. Col. 18/2/36
Thomas Francis, Sir (1818–1895),
ambassador to Pekin 21/3/77
Wadham, John Charles 8/5/79 ?
Wager, Thomas 11/7/90
Waggett, John Francis, barrister 12/6/79 ?
Waghorn, Thomas (1800–1850), pioneered
land route to India 30/7/40
Wagne, Mrs. 2/6/76
Wagner,
Arthur Douglas, Rev. (1825–1902)
3/4/58 n, 19/4/65
Richard (1813–1883), composer 8/5/75 n
Wagner & Huret, Messrs., milliners 3/3/63 ?
Wagstaff, Messrs. 3/1/80
Wainewright, Reader, barrister 28/7/35 ?
Wainham, E., Rev., methodist at Hawarden
29/12/85
Wainwright,
Edward Harper, Rev. (1799–1864) 16/8/47
W., Liverpool agent 9/8/57
Wait,
J. F. 29/6/88
William Killigrew (1826–), tory M.P.
20/12/77
Waite,
Joseph, Rev. (1824–1908) 16/6/67
Nellie, Miss, autograph hunter 30/11/85
Wakefield,
Edward, subaltern 25/3/33
Edward Gibbon (1796–1862), radical
imperialist 23/6/36 n, 22/1/46 ff
Joseph C., printer 2/1/79 ?
Wakeford, William, Rev. 31/3/93
Wakeham,
C. T., Rev., of Edinburgh 25/1/78
Maurice, of Southport 9/8/66
Wakeman,
Henry Offley (1852–1899), historian
1/11/87
Offley Penbury, Sir (1799–1868), 2nd
Baronet 18/5/38 n
Sarah, née Offley 18/5/38 n
Walcot, Charles, Rev. (–1875) 18/9/52

Walcott,
John Edward, Adm. (1790–1868), tory M.P. 16/5/55
Mackenzie Edward Charles, Rev. (1821–1880) 25/4/54
Waldegrave *see* Palmer
Waldegrave,
Frances Elizabeth Anne, Lady (1821–1879), née Braham, Lady Waldegrave, political hostess; married C. S. P. Fortescue 1863 10/2/55, 8/5/58, 17/6/59, 24/6/59, 25/2/60, 17/11/60, 8/5/61, 19/6/61, 3/6/63, 22/7/63, 2/3/64, 8/2/65, 6/7/67, 7/7/67, 15/2/68, 14/3/68, 25/4/68, 5/7/68, 26/3/69, 26/2/70, 22/7/70, 3/8/71, 30/10/71, 6/12/72, 8/3/73, 3/12/73, 13/3/74, 10/2/76, 15/7/76, 17/2/77, 10/6/77, 14/6/77, 29/3/79
George Granville (1786–1857), 2nd Baron Radstock (1825) 25/5/42
Granville Augustus William (1833–1913), 3rd Baron Radstock (1857) 27/11/62
Susan Charlotte, née Calcraft, Lady Radstock 27/11/62
William (–1859), 8th Earl Waldegrave (1846) 21/1/50
Waldie,
Mr. 2/1/86
S. 10/10/40
Waldron,
rescue 21/1/64, 12/11/64
Lawrence (1811–1865), liberal M.P. 23/8/60
Waldstein, Charles, Sir (1856–1927), archaeologist 14/7/91
Waldy, Richard, Canon (1795–1868) 7/9/32 ?
Wale, H. 20/6/77
Wales, J. 15/1/78
Walesby, Francis Pearson, recorder 7/6/48
Walewska, Marie Anne, Countess, née de Ricci 4/2/51, 17/6/52
Walewski, André-Florian-Joseph-Colonna, Count, French diplomat 4/2/51 n
Walford,
Messrs. 26/7/78
Edward (1823–1897), genealogist 26/5/57, 1/1/90
Ernest Leopard 23/9/90
Henry, Rev. 10/6/78
Walhouse *see* Pierrepont
Walk, S. 15/7/78
Walker *see* Childers
Walker,
Mrs., of Edinburgh 26/2/42
Charles Edward, Rev. 16/5/57
C. J. 2/5/79
C. M. 12/6/76
Elizabeth (1800–1876), née Reynolds, engraver and artist 30/1/44
Frederick William Edward Forestier, General (1844–1910), commander of British troops in Egypt 1889-95 21/1/93, 22/1/93
G., of U.S.A. 21/9/78
George J. 20/3/74
George Townshend, Gen. Sir (1764–1842) 29/9/38
G. M. 22/8/76
J. A. 10/5/76
James, Bp. (1770–1841), bishop of Edinburgh (1830) 2/11/35
J. E., Rev. 27/9/78
Joseph Need (1790–1865), landowner in Worcestershire 21/8/51
Josiah, Rev. (–1882) 17/8/67
Lawrence, solicitor 13/7/46
L. G. 28/7/58
M. E., Mrs. 10/6/59
N., Rev. 22/10/74
Oliver Ormerod, Capt. (1833–1914) 22/12/76
Richard (1791–1870), schoolteacher in Oxford 9/2/34
Robert, Rev. Prof. (1801–1865) 9/12/31 n, 30/1/60
Robert John (1801–1869), of U.S.A. 16/7/63, 26/5/65
S., Mrs. 13/10/52
Samuel Abraham, Rev. (–1879) 6/3/45 ?
Samuel Alexander, photographer; photographed G 28/7/62, 26/7/64, 3/9/93 ?
Thomas (1822–1898), editor, *Daily News* (1858) 5/2/69, 13/7/69
Thomas Larkins (–1860), architect 19/6/46
William (1791–1867), engraver 30/1/44
Wiltstone Flint, Newark baker 11/4/45 ?
Walkerston, Mr. 26/7/76
Walkey, Charles Eliot, Rev. 16/8/48
Walkinshaw, E., merchant 4/8/42
Wall,
Charles Baring (1795–1853), tory M.P. 3/6/34
George, chairman, Hoylake liberal association 12/8/87
Henry, Rev. Prof. (–1873) 24/1/53
James, Rev., nonconformist 6/3/75, 11/4/80
Richard, Rev. (1820–1899) 8/10/58
Rudolf, Swedish editor 1/12/87 n
T. S. 4/11/87
Wallace,
rescue 5/3/86
Miss 23/12/91
E. 2/6/75
Johnstone 13/3/78
Richard, Sir (1818–1890), 1st Baronet (1871), tory M.P. 5/8/71

Wallace (*cont.*)
Robert (-1855), radical M.P. 3/11/43, 4/1/45
Robert, Rev. Dr. (1831-1899), liberal M.P. 19/9/69
William Baillie, Rev. 18/8/75
Wallen, Mr., of the N. B.railway 27/1/68
Wallenstein, H. L. 23/8/89
Wallentine, Mr. 16/7/88
Waller,
A. R. 18/12/85
C. B., Rev. 2/11/85
Daniel, Rev. 1/1/47
G. E. 18/11/91
William, engraver 11/11/68
Wallerstein, Henry L. 31/8/78
Walley, Christopher 9/10/86
Wallich, George Charles, Dr., physician 6/1/86
Wallis,
Messrs. 28/9/86
Miss 8/12/90
Mrs. 15/2/56
Mrs., G's housekeeper in Albany, London 25/3/33
C. Woodward, barrister 24/2/76 ?
George (1811-1891), keeper, S. Kensington museum 23/7/66
Henry (1805-1890), picture dealer 31/10/79
H. M. 20/11/90
Wallop,
Eveline (-1906), née Herbert, Lady Portsmouth 31/10/79
Isaac Newton (1825-1891), 5th Earl of Portsmouth (1854) 19/6/68
Newton (1856-1917), 6th Earl of Portsmouth (1891), Lord Lymington, liberal M.P. 6/9/77
Walmsley,
James Vickers 2/10/77 ?
Joshua, Sir (1794-1871), Knight (1840), liberal M.P. 6/11/52, 18/11/65
P. 15/2/76
T. 21/10/62, 22/12/62
Walond, Mrs., née Fellowes 24/5/53
Walpole *see* Nevill
Walpole,
J. 13/11/77
Joseph Kidd, Rev. (-1869), navy chaplain 28/7/58
Spencer Horatio (1806-1898), tory M.P. 2/5/49, 18/8/80, 22/12/80, 18/4/81 L
Walrond, Theodore (1824-1887) 11/1/70 n
Walsh,
J., of Flint 19/10/68
Jane, Lady (-1877), née Grey 25/5/58
John, American ambassador in London 25/4/78
John Benn, Sir (1798-1881), 2nd Baronet (1825), 1st Baron Ormathwaite (1868), Peelite M.P. 15/1/72 L
L., Miss 1/1/83
Michael Henry H. (1820-) 25/5/37 ?
Peter, Fr. 12/9/86 n, 13/9/86
William, Cardinal (1885-1921) 20/2/86 L, 20/5/86, 30/10/86 L
Walter,
E., Capt. 18/5/65
Edward, Sir (1823-1904), soldier 1/6/85
H., Liverpool solicitor 31/8/65
John (1818-1894), proprietor of *The Times* 24/2/48 ?
Odiarne Coates, Dr., physician in Broadstairs 24/8/54
Walterer, Mme. 3/8/76
Walters,
rescue 26/1/84
rescue 9/5/51
Charles, Rev. (1785-) 23/1/31
Henry Littlejohn Master, Rev. (1819-1898) 28/9/69 ?
John Vodin, Rev. 19/9/78 ?
Thomas, Rev. 17/6/79 ?
W. C., Rev. 18/4/78
Walther, David, theologian 3/8/37 ?
Walthew, Richard, solicitor 28/5/59
Walton,
James (1802-1883), cotton manufacturer 13/10/53
T., of Newark 20/1/45
Walton & Bushell, Messrs., East Indian merchants 3/8/60
Wandsworth *see* Stern
Wantage *see* Lindsay
Waras, Mr. 10/8/78 ?
Warburton *see* Ussher
Warburton,
Maj. 22/6/33 n
Mrs. 22/6/33
Henry (1784-1858), liberal M.P. 1/5/39 n
Joseph William 8/10/67
Mary, née Brooke 19/10/42
Piers Egerton- (1839-1914), tory M.P. 4/8/46
Rowland Eyles Egerton- (1804-1891), blind poet 3/9/42, 29/5/76, 1/12/76, 4/12/76, 18/12/76 ff, 8/9/79 ff
Thomas Acton, Rev. (1813-1894) 22/5/67
William, Dean (1806-1900) 19/8/65, 12/4/69 L
Ward,
Mr., of Hawarden 12/12/73
Adolphus, Sir (1837-1924), historian 12/11/78 ?
Alfred, solicitor 16/3/47
Anne Maria, Mrs., of Eton 5/4/40 ?
E. C. 12/9/79

Edward Langton, Rev. (1809–1881) 9/3/29
Edward Matthew (1816–1879), artist 31/1/65
Elizabeth, landlady 1/12/32
Ellen, Mrs., of Liverpool 23/7/47
Emily Elizabeth (–1882), née Swinburne 5/3/34 ?
G. M., of Ebbw Vale 29/4/75
Henry George, Sir (1797–1860), Lord High Commissioner in Ionia (1849), liberal M.P. 30/5/33, 5/3/34 n
James, author 24/12/67
John Gifford, Dean (1779–1860), dean of Lincoln (1845) 4/4/30
Mary Augusta (1851–1920), née Arnold, known as 'Mrs. Humphry Ward', novelist 29/4/76 ?, 16/3/88 n, 8/4/88, 11/9/88, 30/1/90, 9/4/92
Robert (–1843), of Norfolk 13/2/33
Robert Plumer 18/5/42
Samuel, American author 28/11/79 ff, 15/11/83
Thomas, of St. Ebbe's, Oxford 17/3/31 ?
Thomas Humphry, *Times* leader-writer 29/4/76 n, 11/9/88
Thomas Ogier, surgeon 12/1/53
T. Poole, statistician, Board of Trade 4/8/43 ?
Wilfrid Philip (1856–1916), Roman Catholic, biographer 21/11/90, 10/12/90, 16/3/94
William, Newark labourer 2/2/39
William (1817–1885), 11th Baron Ward (1835), 1st Earl of Dudley (1860), chief creditor of the Oak Farm Co., Peelite politician 8/2/48, 21/4/54, 24/4/54, 15/6/71 L
William Craig, Rev. 9/1/41
William George, Rev. (1812–1882), theologian and convert to Rome 24/2/43, 23/11/43, 22/9/44, 26/11/44, 13/2/45
William Harry Perceval, Rev. (1811–1875) 21/6/42, 28/1/75
Wardale, Charles Bradford, Rev. (–1903) 30/11/76
Wardell,
E., Mrs., of Broughton 23/4/51
Edward, servant 11/3/49
John R., Dr., physician 13/11/76
William, of Broughton 23/4/51 n
Wardlaw,
A. Clarke 11/9/41
James (–1867) 20/3/34 n
Jane, née Mackenzie 20/3/34
Wardleworth, Mr. 16/4/89
Ward & Lock, publishers and booksellers 5/4/59 n, 22/10/81
Wardrop, James, Rev. 2/4/80
Ware,
George, music hall singer 4/3/80
John 25/5/77
Waring,
C. B., of New York 9/2/76
John Burley (1823–1875), architect 4/6/67
Waring Bros., bankers 7/2/85
Wark, Andrew, stockbroker 12/9/77, 21/6/79
Warleigh, Henry Smith, Rev. 17/5/75
Warmisham, Elizabeth, Mrs., author 24/3/88
Warne,
Frederick, publisher 11/8/91
T. 26/6/78
Warner,
Charles, lawyer 25/4/45 ?
Charles (1846–1909), actor 1/10/80
Charles, Rev. (1818–1900) 2/6/55, 14/5/65
Edward (1818–1875), liberal M.P. 25/7/60, 30/3/65, 2/6/70 L
Elizabeth, Mrs. 3/4/66
Henry James Lee- (1809–1886) 30/7/27
Maria, Mrs. 24/4/75
Samuel Alfred, Capt. (–1853), inventor 13/7/46
Thomas (–1883), of Brighton 14/5/64, 3/4/66 n, 16/2/78
Thomas, Mrs., of Brighton 16/2/78
Warre,
Edmond, Rev. (1837–1920) 6/7/79, 11/6/90
John Ashley (1787–1860), whig M.P. 21/5/60
Warren *see* Bulkeley, Stepney
Warren,
Catharina Barbara, née de Salis-Soglio, Lady de Tabley 25/9/41
Charles, Gen. Sir (1840–1927), soldier in Southern Africa 31/10/84, 28/1/85, 20/3/85 c, 27/3/85
Eleanor Leicester Leighton-, Lady (1841–1914), née Warren, formerly Lady Leighton 25/10/55
Frederick Edward, Rev. 4/11/76
George Fleming (1811–1887), 2nd Baron De Tabley (1827), a liberal, poet 6/6/40
George Washington 25/7/77 n
Henry George, lodginghouse keeper, London 21/10/58
John Byrne Leicester (1835–1895), 3rd Baron De Tabley (1887) 5/4/60, 26/12/71
Richard Peter, Rev. 16/7/77
Samuel (1807–1877), tory M.P. 25/2/57
Thomas Herbert (1853–1930), President of Magdalen college, Oxford (1885) 13/10/91 n
William Fairfield, Prof. 20/9/81
William J., hotel keeper 25/1/40
Warring, Charles B., Principal 24/6/88 n

Warrington,
Thornhill, Col. 27/8/58
William (-1866), stained-glass maker 5/5/49 ?
Wartegg, De, Mr. 17/7/88
Warter, John Wood, Rev. (1806-1878) 2/2/29, 14/6/47
Warwick *see* Greville
Warwick, rescue 25/4/55
Wash, A. 12/8/76
Washburn, George, Rev. Dr. (1833-1915), congregationalist 22/5/80
Wason, Peter Rigby (1798-1875), liberal M.P. 25/3/34, 18/1/60
Wassilieff,
Mme. 29/8/77
J., Rev., Orthodox priest in Paris 15/2/65
Wastall, E. 15/6/88
Waterfield,
O., publisher 30/1/71
Thomas Nelson (1799-1862), civil servant 26/4/58
Waterford *see* Beresford
Waterhouse,
Alfred (1830-1905), architect 14/10/64
Edwin (1841-1917), accountant; handling Granville's debts 29/9/92, 15/10/92
Nicholas, archivist in Liverpool 21/5/59 ?
Waterlow, Sydney Hedley, Sir (1822-1906), liberal M.P., lord mayor of London 12/7/66, 22/10/72
Waterman, T. T. 31/5/78
Waters,
Edward, Dr., physician in Hawarden 5/8/72, 19/5/83
Ernest E. 14/10/76, 25/7/77
E. W., of Hawarden 4/5/76
George, Irish distiller 20/1/55
Jane, Mrs., rescue case, Hawarden 2/4/57, 9/10/59, 1/11/60, 20/4/67, 16/4/68, 6/10/69
Lizzie, of Hawarden 7/1/76
Richard George, of Dublin 11/12/74
Thomas Houghton, Dr. 24/9/75
Waterston, Messrs. 20/12/77, 29/7/79
Waterworth, James, Rev. 26/6/41
Wathen, George H., author 12/3/55
Watherley, Mr. 26/3/74
Watherston, E. J. 12/12/77
Watkin,
Absalom, Manchester merchant 6/3/58 ?
Edward William, Sir (1819-1901), 1st Baronet (1880), liberal M.P. and railway proprietor, proponent of Channel Tunnel 24/5/65, 26/7/83 L, 17/10/87, 8/3/88, 11/9/88 n, 18/2/89, 22/5/89, 3/8/89, 23/8/89, 3/9/89 n, 10/9/89, 23/11/89, 11/1/90, 23/3/91, 12/9/92 ff, 26/9/92 L, 1/10/92 L, 26/10/92 L, 21/2/94
H. G. B. 8/1/90
John William Spiller, Rev. (-1908) 29/10/53
R. 14/2/77
Watkins,
Anne, Mrs., at Hawarden 10/6/51, 12/1/80
E., Mr., involved with Helen G 24/4/72
Frederick B., author 25/1/75
Watkinson, James, labourer 11/3/78
Watrin, Abbé, of Paris 20/10/50
Watson,
A. G., Rev. 7/8/89
Albert, Rev. 18/1/75 ?
Alexander, Rev. 24/4/42
C. Knight, secretary, Society of Antiquaries 29/4/74
E., rescue 7/3/51
E. H., of Boston 23/4/78
Forbes 19/7/79
H. B. M. 13/5/90
James, Newark shopkeeper 22/7/37
James, Sir (1801-1889), Knight (1874), G's stockbroker, lord provost of Glasgow 31/8/50, 3/3/51, 12/6/51, 19/9/72, 22/2/73 L, 18/2/74 n, 23/5/76, 25/11/79, 4/12/79, 27/3/83 L
James Jonathan, Dr. 23/8/73 ?
Joshua (1771-1855), philanthropist 18/3/35
Joshua, Bp., bishop of St. Asaph 3/11/75
Marion, Miss 22/12/59, 18/5/65, 29/3/69, 16/3/77, 25/4/79
P. F. 28/5/77
Ralph, lawyer 7/3/55 ?
Robert Grant (-1892), diplomat 11/11/70
Robert Spence, Dr. (1837-1911), secretary, National Liberal Federation 2/10/91
S. J., poet 28/1/76
Thomas, mastermariner, Liverpool 2/1/27
Thomas, Dr., surgeon 5/12/64 ?
W. H. 4/11/79
William (1858-1935), poet 28/10/92, 16/11/92, 25/11/92
W. L. 12/3/80 n
W. M. 27/12/77
Watson & Smith, Messrs., G's stockbrokers in Glasgow 28/1/56
Watt,
Mrs. 7/8/78
Basil H. 5/1/77 ?
Hugh (1848-1921) 24/5/79, 1/4/90
Isaac, land agent 15/9/41
James Henry (1799-1867), engraver 29/8/55 ?
John 23/3/74
John, Laurencekirk postmaster 3/11/51
R., of Hawarden 16/3/77
Watton, Alfred, secretary, Mariners' Society 3/5/79 n

Watts,
rescue 4/2/62, 19/6/78
Alaric Alexander (1797–1864), poet and journalist 13/7/54
Charles A., editor, *Agnostic Annual* 14/8/88
David Pike 30/5/35 n
George Frederick (1817–1904), artist; painted G's portrait twice 25/3/59, 1/5/68 n, 7/4/72, 16/5/76, 13/6/76, 1/6/78, 29/12/81, 28/3/82, 24/6/85, 29/6/85, 9/8/93, 26/1/94 L, 4/2/94
James, Rev. 29/3/75 ?
James, Sir (1804–1878), Knight (1857) 26/3/62
J. C., Rev., Methodist 20/6/79
Margaret Anne, Lady (–1892), née Buckley 13/5/62
R. D., poet 11/1/68
Wauchope, Robert, Adm. (–1862) 8/1/36
Wauchope, Moody & Hope, Messrs., Edinburgh wine merchants 24/2/63
Waugh,
Arthur Thornhill, Rev. (1842–1922) 17/10/76
F. G., of Rugby 20/10/64
Francis Gledstones 14/5/77
John George, solicitor 26/10/67
Waugh & Sons, carpetfitters 23/3/59
Waveney *see* Adair
Wawn, John Twizell (1801–1859), liberal M.P. 23/7/44
Way, A. 26/2/80
Wayland, H. L., of U.S.A. 11/1/80
Waylen, Edward, Rev. 5/1/46
Wayte, Samuel William, Rev. (–1898) 24/2/50
Weaden, J. W. 28/11/74
Weale,
Charlotte, Miss, known as Sister Doratea, of the House of Mercy, Clewer 21/1/52
Robert Morey, Rev. 23/12/89 n
Wear, E., Miss 25/7/67
Weardale *see* Stanhope
Weare, Thomas William, Rev. (–1871) 29/12/60
Weatherby, F., linen supplier 3/8/57
Weaver,
Mr. 13/5/82
A. E. 4/4/88
B. W. 27/10/77, 18/5/78, 18/12/78
Richard, revivalist preacher 3/12/65
Webb,
Miss 6/6/66
A'Court, Mrs. 8/5/67
Alfred, secretary, Irish National League 26/10/83
Alfred John (1834–1908), home rule M.P. 6/5/91
Allan Beecher, Bp. (1839–1907) 30/10/78
Benjamin, Rev. (1819–1885) 4/7/57, 17/9/71, 15/8/76, 16/8/76, 18/8/76
C. J., of Antrim 2/3/88
Edward Brainerd, engineer 12/4/77
G. 7/9/77
H. C. 9/10/78
James (–1889), artist 24/7/63
John, Canon (1776–1869) 21/8/25
Sidney (1858–1943), colonial office clerk, Fabian and historian, on Executive Committee of Eighty Club 14/12/87 ?, 31/8/88, 3/9/88
T. H. 12/1/78
Thomas Henry, editor, *North and South* 16/2/87 n
William, Rev. (1775–1856), of Cambridge 20/1/49
W. T. 22/2/80
Webber,
Edward Alexander, Rev. (–1872) 13/3/51
Vivian A. 1/9/79
William Thomas Thornhill, Rev. 16/8/79 ?
Weber, F. 4/11/91
Webley, E., Miss, charity worker 22/3/48
Webster,
rescue 2/2/65
George, Rev. Dr. 4/11/77 n
James C., secretary, the Athenaeum 22/3/59
John (1810–1891), of Aberdeen 14/7/58 n
O., Dr. 30/3/76
Sarah Johanna, Lady 19/4/66 ?
Thomas, barrister 5/12/45 ?
Thomas (1800–1886), artist 26/6/39 ?
Thomas, Rev. (–1840) 18/12/31
Wentworth, Rev. 5/1/92, 30/12/92, 4/1/93, 21/2/93 ff, 25/9/93, 30/1/94
Wed, B. 15/7/76
Weddell, William 21/4/60
Wedderburn,
David, Sir (1835–1882), 3rd Baronet (1862), liberal M.P. 30/3/80
William, Sir (1838–1918), 4th Baronet (1882), liberal M.P. and judge in India 8/6/93 L
Wedgwood,
Aaron 27/10/63
Godfrey (1833–1905), potter 20/4/76
Hensleigh (1803–1891), philologist, registrar of carriages 6/2/41
Weedall, Henry (1788–1859), president, St. Mary's, Oscott 1/7/51
Weeks,
A. M., of U.S.A. 5/6/76
G. W. 16/4/74 ?
Wegg-Prosser *see* Prosser
Weguelin, Thomas Mathias (1809–1885), liberal M.P. 29/3/54 n
Weigall,
Henry, sponsor, the Newport refuge 24/3/74

Weigall (*cont.*)
Henry (1829–1925), artist; painted C. G's portrait 27/7/88
Rose Sophia Mary (–1921), née Fane 5/10/62
Weigh, T., porter 10/1/45
Weightman,
John, of Newark 8/2/40 ?
William, chemist in Newark 8/2/40 ?
Weil, S. 30/4/87
Weill, Mr., of U.S.A. 18/8/76
Weinmann, Frederick L., author 28/2/80
Weir,
rescue 22/6/67
Mrs., cook 3/3/43
Alexander McC., of Notts. 5/4/78, 16/10/86
D. H., Rev. Prof., of Glasgow 21/9/72 ?
James Galloway (1839–1911), liberal M.P. 2/8/88
Weis, Ludwig, author 7/4/56 ?
Weisenfeld, Mr. 29/5/78
Weisse, Z. A., Dr., of U.S.A. 18/4/79
Weissmann, Mr. 11/11/86
Welburck, Mr. 5/2/68
Welby,
John Earle, Rev. (1786–1867) 5/3/33
Reginald Earle, Sir (1832–1915), 1st Baron Welby (1894), treasury civil servant; permanent secretary, treasury (1885) 5/3/33 n, 23/11/75 ff, 6/12/77, 11/8/80 L, 6/11/80, 30/9/81 ff, 17/11/81 L, 17/3/82 L, 27/3/82 L, 6/4/82 L, 22/6/82 L, 11/9/82, 14/9/82, 5/11/83, 12/7/84, 18/5/85, 13/6/85, 23/6/85 L, 18/2/86, 20/2/86 ff, 30/3/86, 3/4/86 ff, 22/4/86 L, 8/8/86, 19/3/87, 25/4/87, 7/11/87 ff, 12/4/88, 24/4/88, 16/10/88, 19/7/89, 3/5/92, 20/8/92 n, 19/1/93 ff, 11/2/93 ff, 23/3/93 ff, 16/5/93 ff, 7/6/93, 13/6/93 ff, 29/8/93, 16/10/93, 27/10/93 ff, 5/12/93, 3/2/94 L, 14/2/94 ff
Thomas Earle, Bp. (1810–1899), bishop of St. Helena (1861) 27/2/33, 5/3/33 n
Weld *see* Fitzherbert
Weld, Thomas, Cardinal (1773–1837) 15/12/38
Weldon,
Mrs. 29/6/78
Mrs., singer 13/7/63, 7/1/94
George Warburton, Rev. (1825–1889) 4/2/87 ?
Georgina, Mrs., litigant 5/10/71, 11/12/76
James W., banker 17/3/68
Thomas, Newark accountant 2/2/39
Welford, Richard Griffiths, Judge 23/3/43, 24/3/43
Welkins, J. S. 6/12/77
Welland, George, engraver 2/7/79
Welland Vale Co. 6/9/77
Welldon, James Edward Cowell, Rev. (1854–1937) 3/4/87
Weller, Theodore (1802–1880), artist 1/6/32
Wellesley *see* Grosvenor
Wellesley,
Arthur; Duke of Wellington 3/10/31
Arthur Richard (1807–1884), Lord Douro (1814), 2nd Duke of Wellington (1852), 6th Earl of Mornington (1863), tory M.P. 15/7/35, 12/7/58 n
Elizabeth (–1904), née Hay, Duchess of Wellington 12/7/58
Gerald Valerian, Dean 18/2/26
Henry (1773–1847), 1st Baron Cowley (1828), diplomat 26/9/45
Henry, Rev. 13/6/48
William Henry George, Capt. (1806–1815) 3/1/34
Wellesley-Pole *see* Somerset
Wellhausen, Julius, Prof. (1844–1918) 23/1/94
Wellington *see* Wellesley
Wellman, W. G. 29/5/88
Wellnall, F., journalist 5/2/67
Wells *see* Bowyer
Wells,
David Ames (1828–1898), economist 24/6/67, 5/1/70 L
Elizabeth, Lady, née Proby 19/2/42
George 14/3/76
Giffard (1802–1876), headmaster 4/11/32 ?
Henry Tanworth (1828–1903), artist 21/3/83, 7/3/87
J. B. 1/10/77
Joseph 1/2/38 ?
M. 23/12/89
P. C. 4/11/86
Thomas Spencer, Sir (1818–1897), 1st Baronet (1883), surgeon 20/4/83
William, author 27/1/79
William, Capt. 19/2/42 n
Wells and Lambe, Messrs. 8/8/39
Wellwood, Mr. 10/3/77
Welsh,
John, Rev. 3/6/47 ?
J. R., printer 20/5/79
Welton, Thomas Abercrombie, statistician 7/9/77
Wemyss *see* Douglas
Wemyss, Mrs. 11/6/78
Wemyss Charteris *see* Stewart
Wendt, Dr. 27/1/92
Wenham, John George, Rev. (–1895), Roman Catholic 9/6/52 ?
Wenkirten, Mr. 2/9/76
Wenlock *see* Lawley, Thompson
Wensleydale *see* Parke
Wentworth *see* Milbanke

Wentworth, William Charles, of Sydney, Australia 3/9/42
Wentworth-Fitzwilliam *see* Foljambe
Werner, Hildegard, Miss, Swedish journalist in Newcastle 1/12/87
Werninck, Henry 6/1/76 ?
Werth, J. W. 17/7/79
Wertheimer, Julius (-1924) 20/6/87 ?
Wesford, Mr. 11/7/62
Wesley,
W. 30/8/79
W., Messrs., booksellers 31/12/86
West *see* Cecil
West,
rescue 29/5/79
Algernon Edward, Sir 23/12/68
August William 31/7/90
Constance, Miss 15/11/83
D. M. 19/9/76
Edith M., née Trevor 31/7/90
Elizabeth Sackville-, Lady, née Sackville, Lady Delawarr 22/12/41 n
George, of Hawarden 4/1/68
George John Sackville- (1791-1869), 5th Earl Delawarr 22/12/41
Henry Wyndham (1823-1893), barrister, liberal M.P. 3/6/92
John, Dean (1806-1890), of Dublin 22/10/77 n
John Beatty (1793-1841), barrister, repeal M.P. 17/2/37
J. W., Rev., nonconformist 18/4/54
Lionel Sackville Sackville (1827-1908), 2nd Baron Sackville (1888), diplomat 25/7/49
Mary, Lady, née Barrington, wife of Sir A. E. West 11/5/69, 9/10/90
Mary Cornwallis, née Fitzpatrick 21/4/80
Moses Ebenezer 2/7/77
Richard Temple, Rev. (1825-1893) 29/9/70, 17/2/89
T. R., Rev. 25/7/76
Washbourne, Rev. (1811-1897), fellow of Lincoln, Oxford, record plural voter 14/6/53
William, Rev., curate at Hawarden 30/8/60
William Cornwallis Cornwallis- (1835-1917), liberal (unionist) M.P. 3/5/72
Westall,
Mrs. 9/4/44
Samuel Thomas Maling 9/4/44 n
Westbury *see* Bethell
Westcombe, A., Rev. 3/7/78
Westcott,
Brooke Foss, Bp. (1825-1901) 26/10/78
Philip (1815-1878), artist, painted G's portrait 25/11/54, 27/11/54
Westell, W. 9/1/77
Westell's, Messrs., London booksellers 29/1/56, 1/8/56, 17/1/58, 11/11/59
Western, Thomas Sutton, Sir (1821-1877), 2nd Baronet (1873), liberal M.P. 21/3/61
Westgarth, William (1815-1889) 28/5/89
Westhead, Joshua Proctor Brown- (1807-1877), liberal M.P. 17/7/51
Westlake, John, barrister 24/4/79 ?
Westmacott,
Horatio, Rev. 30/1/56
Richard, Sir (1775-1856), sculptor 3/6/44
Westminster *see* Grosvenor
Westmorland *see* Fane
Weston,
Mr. 4/2/32, 6/2/32
Edward 23/5/43 ?
Westpark *see* Cavendish
Westropp, Hodder Michael 24/7/75, 17/6/79
Wetherall,
Edward Robert, Sir (1815-1869), soldier 27/2/69
George Augustus, Sir (1788-1868), soldier 12/4/59 n
Wetherby, Arthur, stockbroker 9/7/55 ?
Wethered, Florence James, Rev. (1807-1867) 27/2/27
Wetherell,
Nathaniel Thomas (1800-1869), antiquarian 10/2/57
Thomas Frederick (1830-1908), editor 16/10/69 L
Wette, Wilhelm Martin Leberechte de (1780-1843), philosopher 17/12/38 n
Weyland, Richard, Maj., whig M.P. 11/5/31 n
Weymouth,
John Francis, solicitor 27/2/75
Richard Francis, Rev. Dr. 9/10/78, 11/6/79 n
Whale,
C. F. 17/12/75
George, liberal in Woolwich 4/6/75, 3/9/76, 25/1/77
Whalley,
George Hampden (1813-1878), liberal M.P. 18/9/56, 17/2/60, 27/7/65
John Master, Rev. (-1861) 25/3/52 ?
Sykes 12/7/78
Wharlow, John Robert, parliamentary agent 11/3/87
Wharncliffe *see* Mackenzie
Wharton, Joseph Crane, Rev. 21/5/82
Whately,
E. J., Miss, daughter and biographer of Abp. Whately 7/1/70
Richard, Abp. (1787-1863), broadchurch theologian; archbishop of Dublin 1831 15/11/28
Whatham, John, Liverpool shoemaker 11/7/39 ?
Whatman, James (1813-1887), liberal M.P. 7/11/54

Wheatley,
Messrs. 11/12/89
L. A. 20/8/91
Wheatstone, Charles, Sir (1802–1875), physicist 4/7/40
Wheeler,
Mr., of Hawarden 20/12/61
A. W., of Abbeyliex 10/11/77
George Domville, Rev. 15/10/78 ?
James Luff, bootmaker 26/3/29
Wheeler's, Messrs., stationers and publishers 23/1/33
Wheelwright, H. 16/7/66
Wheen, Thomas 23/6/79
Whelan, Robert W., Rev. 4/11/77
Whewell, William, Prof. (1794–1866), Master of Trinity, Cambridge 16/12/31, 11/8/40, 14/8/40, 2/11/59
Whibley,
Capt. 15/8/78
D., Mr. 15/12/75
Whidelington, Mr. 5/5/75
Whiffin, John, accountant 11/2/62
Whigham, James 4/10/76 ?
Whiley, H. 25/8/77
Whipple, Henry B., Bp., episcopalian bishop of Minnesota 1859-1901 22/7/88
Whitaker,
George Herbert, Rev. (1847–1930) 26/2/80
Joseph (1820–1895), publisher 22/7/56
Robert, Liverpool commission agent 27/3/55
Samuel, railway secretary 27/12/48 ?
Whitbourn, W. 27/1/77
Whitbread,
Samuel (1830–1915), liberal M.P. 6/7/68, 28/2/85 L, 15/2/86 L, 23/3/86, 21/4/86, 28/4/86, 1/5/86, 11/5/86, 12/5/86 ff, 19/5/86 ff, 11/8/86, 23/5/87, 20/7/93
Samuel Howard (1858–1944) 22/10/85 ?
Whitburn, T. 26/3/90
Whitcombe, Robert Henry, solicitor in Bewdley 20/2/55, 16/8/55
White,
Miss, rescue 8/6/67, 5/4/70, 5/8/70
Mrs. 2/8/85
Arnold (1848–1925), journalist and liberal imperialist 5/6/86 ?, 21/2/88
Arnold William, Sir (–1893), solicitor 16/11/54 ?
Campbell, Mr. 21/4/87
Charles, Rev. 1/1/26 ?
Charles William, Capt. (1838–1890), liberal M.P. 22/6/68
D. 28/3/77
E. D. 18/2/80
Edward, Rev. (1819–1898), congregationalist 23/8/76
Edward M. 26/4/45 ?
Emily, née Stuart, Lady Annaly 28/4/80
F. A. 11/9/91
Francis Gilbert, Rev. 4/2/52
Frederick Anthony 11/12/78
George Cosby, Rev. 11/5/47 n
George Preston, barrister 30/4/67
H., Mrs. 11/2/78
Henry (1789–1873), 1st Baron Annaly (1863), liberal M.P. 22/2/61
Henry (1850–1927), Americal diplomat 7/8/85
Henry, Rev. (1836–1890) 15/3/68
Henry Master, Ven. (1821–1892) 16/8/65, 12/7/67
H. Vere, Rev. 24/5/90
James (1809–1883), liberal M.P. 23/12/65
Jesse 18/6/78
J. H. 21/7/79
John Alexander, Rev., of Leith 10/1/62
John Meadows, solicitor 21/2/49 n
John Tahourdin (1809–1893), schoolmaster 25/4/31
Joseph Blanco, Rev. (1775–1841), né Blanco, Roman Catholic, Anglican and Unitarian 22/5/31, 22/5/45 ff
Joseph Neville, Rev. 20/7/91
J. S., Rev. 9/5/92
Luke (1829–1888), 2nd Baron Annaly (1873) 28/4/80
Robert Dennis, Maj. 7/6/50 ?
Samuel George Booth, Rev. (1812–1880) 29/11/27
T. A. 7/12/86
William (1806–1893), doorkeeper, House of Commons 13/4/74
William Arthur, consul 22/2/75 ?
William Hale (1831–1913), novelist 10/10/78 ?
White & Borrett, Messrs., solicitors 21/2/49
Whitehead,
George, Rev. 4/12/77 ?
Thomas, Rev. 7/5/55
Whitehouse,
Frederick Cope, archaeologist 22/7/85
H. 19/1/69 ?
Whitehurst, Edward Capel 27/1/67
Whitelaw, John, of Dunfermline 13/4/68
Whiteside,
James, Chief Justice (1804–1876), tory M.P. 8/5/56
John William, Rev. Dr. (1808–1864) 22/7/57
Whiteway, William Vallence, Sir (1828–1908), Newfoundland politician 26/4/93
Whitfield *see* Carnegie
Whitfield,
Miss 23/2/75
Mr., photographer 12/3/80
E. E. 9/12/89

Frederick, Rev. 15/7/68
Whitford, Robert Wells, Rev. (-1879) 26/4/52
Whiting,
Charles Goodrich (1842-1922), American journalist 24/9/78 ?
J. E., of Leeds 11/3/78
Whitley,
D. 1/8/76
John, Dr. (-1855) 24/5/54
Whitling,
H. J. 6/4/74
Robert Charles Storrs, Rev. 17/9/78
Whitlock, George Stewart, Rev. 13/7/55
Whitmore, Charles Shapland, Judge (1806-1877) 28/6/69
Whitnall, rescue 16/11/53
Whittaker,
J., of Accrington 14/11/79
John William, Rev. 16/12/44
Thomas Palmer, Sir (1850-1919), liberal M.P. 7/11/79
Whittaker & Co., booksellers 17/3/48
Whittall, A. 1/3/78
Whittam, George, clerk to House of Commons 4/4/48
Whittard, Thomas Middlemore, Rev. (1829-1920) 9/7/68
Whittegg, Mr. 2/1/80
Whitten, Henry 8/2/77, 16/6/79, 5/11/86
Whittingham,
Thomas, of Hawarden 9/8/46 n
Thomas, Mrs., of Hawarden 9/8/46
W. B., Messrs. 3/9/87
Whittington, Richard, Rev. 1/6/78 ?
Whittle, J. Lowry 6/12/74
Whitton, Henry 30/8/77
Whitty,
Edward Michael (1827-1860), journalist 21/7/56, 15/1/57
James, Liverpool merchant 17/11/68 ?
Robert, Rev. (1817-1895), Jesuit 24/7/85, 4/10/89 n
Whitwell,
M. 29/9/74
S. 23/11/67
Whitworth,
Joseph, Sir (1803-1887), 1st Baronet (1869), armament manufacturer 11/10/53, 23/2/66, 10/7/69, 9/9/69
William Allen, Rev. 27/8/93 n, 3/9/93 L
Whyte,
Mrs. 9/9/33
A., Rev. Dr. 10/12/83
Alexander, Rev. 27/8/33
J. 8/2/56
R. D. 3/4/91
William John 14/2/67
Whytock, A. 27/3/43
Wichart, Messrs. 25/4/87
Wickens, John, Sir (1815-1873), Knight (1871), lawyer 11/3/59
Wicker, H. B. 9/8/90
Wickes, John Floyer, Rev. 23/6/51 ?
Wickham,
Agnes (daughter) 18/10/42
Catherine Mary Lavinia, grand-daughter 8/6/75
Edward Charles, Dean (1834-1910), G's son-in-law (1873), dean of Lincoln (1894) 18/10/42 n, 18/8/73, 8/9/73, 19/10/73, 12/7/74, 26/12/74, 1/1/75, 4/1/75 ff, 2/1/76 ff, 17/1/76, 1/4/76 ff, 29/7/76, 31/7/77 ff, 1/9/78 ff, 9/1/79, 31/10/79 ff, 18/12/80, 11/8/81, 26/12/81 ff, 30/8/82 ff, 19/7/84 ff, 8/1/85 ff, 22/12/86, 2/1/87 ff, 18/9/87, 22/9/87, 21/4/88, 31/5/89, 16/9/89, 2/9/90 ff, 19/1/91 ff, 12/7/91, 3/3/92, 16/4/93, 9/1/94 L, 23/1/94 L, 7/4/94 ff
F. G. 9/4/80
Henry Wickham (1800-1867), liberal M.P. 14/7/62
John, of Batcombe 5/2/53
Lucy Christian, grand-daughter 1/1/80
Robert, Ven., archdeacon of St. Asaph 31/3/57
Thomas Vowler, Rev. (-1892) 9/1/68
William, of the Ballot Society 8/2/56
William Gladstone (1877-), grandson; known as 'William of Wickham', later trade commissioner in South Africa 31/10/79, 26/11/91, 12/4/93, 9/1/94
Wicklow *see* Howard
Widal, Auguste, Dr., Homerist 8/10/63
Wiebe, Edward, Prof. 11/2/80 ?
Wiel, Alethea Jane, née Lawley 23/1/88
Wieler, William Julius, author 17/2/77, 23/12/77 ?
Wiese, Ludwig Adolf, historian 30/7/50
Wiesenlanger, T. 3/12/74
Wigan *see* Lindsay
Wigan, Alfred Sydney (1814-1878), actor 25/2/54, 11/2/61
Wigglesworth, Alderman 28/8/78
Wight,
L. H. 18/5/78
Thomas, solicitor 20/8/36 ?
Wigley, Mr. 27/11/78
Wigner, J. T., Rev., nonconformist 25/2/82
Wigram,
Joseph Cotton, Bp. (1778-1867), bishop of Rochester (1860) 8/5/34, 1/4/67
Money (1790-1873), shipowner 25/7/50
Wilberforce *see* Pye
Wilberforce,
Albert Basil Orme, Rev. 23/8/74
Emily, née Sargent 25/4/34 n

Wilberforce (*cont.*)
Ernest Roland, Bp. (1840–1907) 11/8/73, 1/11/77 ff, 30/5/82
Henry William, Rev. (1807–1873), convert to Rome and Catholic journalist 21/11/29, 25/4/34, 2/7/40
Mary, née Sargent 25/4/34 n
Reginald Garton (1838–1914) 30/8/75, 22/11/80 L, 6/7/82 L
Robert Isaac, Ven. (1802–1857), convert to Rome 25/6/35, 18/2/41, 12/1/52, 13/1/52, 19/7/52, 15/10/53 ff, 23/10/53, 2/9/54, 4/10/54, 7/10/54 ff, 19/10/54, 21/10/54
Samuel, Bp. 2/9/30
William (1759–1833), philanthropist 25/7/33, 25/6/35
Wilbraham *see* Lindsay
Wilbraham,
Charles Philip, Rev. (1810–1879) 9/11/55
Edward Bootle- (–1898), 2nd Baron Skelmersdale (1853), 1st Earl of Lathom (1880) 14/10/52 n
Edward Bootle- (1771–1853), 1st Baron Skelmersdale (1828), tory M.P. 7/8/38
Jessy, née Brooke 13/9/45
Richard, Gen. Sir (1811–1900), Knight (1873) 21/12/70
Richard Bootle- (1801–1844), tory M.P. 4/8/37 n, 7/8/38 n
Roger William (–1897), treasury clerk 20/9/53
Wilcockson, Henry 15/4/80
Wild,
rescue 21/4/63
Miss 3/2/90
Henry, customs clerk 10/2/65 ?
James William (1814–1892), architect 7/2/67 ?
Wilde,
Augusta Emma (–1866), née D'Este, Lady Truro 19/2/52
Edward Archer (1826–1889), solicitor 30/11/67 ?
Frederick George Stanley, Dr. 4/11/79
James Plaisted (1816–1899), 1st Baron Penzance (1869) 30/5/82, 17/5/86
Jane Francesca, Lady 29/10/77
Oscar Fingall O'Flahertie Wills 15/5/77
Ralph, Rev. 3/7/41
S. De 30/5/77
Thomas (1782–1855), 1st Baron Truro (1850), lord chancellor 1/11/32 n
Wilder, Charles (1808–1838), schoolmaster at Eton 25/9/26
Wildes,
Evelyn Charlotte, née Gladstone, niece 2/3/67
George Henry (–1888), G's relative by marriage 2/3/67 n
Wilding, F. 15/5/79
Wildridge, T. 17/4/89
Wilhelm VII (1792–1836), Grand-Duke of Nassau (1816) 27/8/38
Wilkes,
C. 15/7/76
John A. 31/12/40
Wilkie, J. 10/6/75
Wilkins,
Messrs. 7/1/78
Augustus Stanley, Prof. 1/11/71
George, Rev. 17/1/46
John William (1829–), lawyer 19/5/55
L. H. 15/7/90
Nathaniel George, Rev. 25/4/75
William Henry, novelist; wrote as W. H. de Winton 1/3/91 fl
Wilkinson *see* Denison, Groom
Wilkinson,
Mrs. 5/5/57
Abraham, Dr., physician 18/3/33 n
C. N. 15/9/77
Edmund, lawyer in Liverpool 4/10/36
Edward, Rev. 7/5/79
E. H. 13/3/90
F. C., solicitor 10/5/71
George Howard, Bp. (1833–1907) 6/6/59, 28/12/82, 16/1/83, 10/3/83, 6/2/94
Henry Spenser (1853–1937), journalist and defence specialist 1/3/94 n
John, Rev. (1817–1876) 27/5/52
Mary (–1885), née Crump 9/11/52
Samuel, Rev. (–1907) 5/11/79
Thomas Edward, Bp. (1837–1914) 20/9/75
T. Lewis, Dr., physician 9/11/52 n
William Arthur (1795–1865), liberal M.P. 25/1/56 ?
Wilks,
John, fils (–1846), swindler 5/3/36 ?
John, père (1765–1854), radical M.P. 5/3/36 ?
S. 30/8/78
Samuel Charles, Rev. (–1872) 8/8/65
William, Rev. (1843–1923) 6/7/77, 21/7/77
Willcock, Henry, Sir (1788–1858), of the East India Co. 9/2/36
Willdridge, T. T. 31/5/88
Willes,
James Shaw, Judge Sir (1814–1872) 4/2/52 n, 21/10/71
James Shaw, Mrs. 4/2/52 ?
William I,
(1772–1843), King of the Netherlands 2/2/32 n
(1797–1888), King of Prussia, Emperor of Germany 19/6/56, 23/1/58 n

William II,
(1792–1849), King of the Netherlands (1843) 2/2/32
(1859–1941), Crown Prince, Emperor of Germany 3/10/63, 5/10/63
William III, King of Holland 16/3/70 n
William IV (1765–1837), King of Great Britain and Ireland (1830) 2/7/30 n, 16/10/93
William Frederick, Prince (1776–1834), Duke of Gloucester (1805) 7/5/36 n
Williams *see* Cobden, Hay, Stanley, Verney
Williams,
rescue 21/6/69
Adin, robe-maker, Oxford 16/1/33
A. G., of Worksop 13/11/75
A. L., Mrs. 16/12/77
Alfred, Rev. (–1877) 5/1/52 ?
Alfred Henry, Rev. (–1907) 31/7/64 ?
Benjamin, of Oak Farm 16/3/50 ?
Benjamin Bacon (–1870), stockbroker 8/5/54
Cadogan, pamphleteer 14/2/48
Charles, Rev., nonconformist 3/10/32
Charles, Rev. (1807–1877), principal of Jesus, Oxford 10/5/59
Charles H. 28/10/79
Charles James Watkin, Sir (1828–1884), liberal M.P. 16/4/68
David (–1860), warden of New College, Oxford 11/6/52
David, Rev. 29/12/82
David, Rev. (–1882) 6/8/56, 17/4/63, 11/5/63
Edmund Sydney, bookseller 9/8/47 ?
Edmund Turberville, Rev. (1817–1885) 18/7/54
Erasmus Henry Griffies-, Rev. Sir (–1870), 2nd Baronet (1843) 31/3/52
Frances (–1841), née Turner 23/3/33
Frederick Sims (1811–1863), barrister 3/5/57
F. S. 7/12/77
G., rescue 5/10/53, 26/10/53
George, Rev. (1814–1878), topographer 21/12/39, 4/10/70
G. F., of New York 24/12/74
H. R., secretary to Shaftesbury memorial 8/8/91
Hugh, Rev. 2/8/45 ?
James Hamlyn, Sir (1790–1866), 3rd Baronet (1829), whig M.P. 4/4/38 n
James Reynold, Rev. (1828–1900) 13/5/60, 16/2/62
John, Capt., engineer 17/5/52
John, Rev. (1798–1873) 23/8/28
John, Ven., archdeacon 5/3/42
John Carvell (1821–1907), liberal M.P.; secretary of the Liberation Society 14/5/68, 5/7/70 L, 22/5/71 L, 31/8/89
John Deakin, Chester builder 26/6/54 ?
Joseph, Dr. (1814–1882), physician 19/7/57
Joseph William, auctioneer 28/12/55 ?
Leigh 29/6/63
Mary, of Hawarden 11/11/56
Mary, Lady (–1874), née Fortescue 4/4/38
Maysmore 15/12/62
Michael (1785–1858), liberal M.P. 23/3/54 ?
Monier Monier-, Prof. Sir (1819–1899), Sanskrit scholar 1/9/75
M. R. 10/5/88
Obadiah, pamphleteer 8/1/68 ?
O. O. 4/4/91
Penry, fils (1807–1886), landowner 6/12/29
Penry, père (1798–1885), artist 1/6/32
Peter Mostyn 9/10/78
R. B. 11/9/66
R. D. 2/12/80
Richard Vaughan, Judge 28/9/74
Robert, Rev. 11/11/92
Robert, fils (1811–1890), tory M.P. 19/2/35, 29/3/46, 24/5/46, 3/8/93
Robert, père (1767–1847), banker, tory M.P. 20/3/33
Robert Wynne 23/9/59
Rowland, fils, Rev. 12/3/49
Rowland, père, Rev. 12/3/49
R. P. 17/4/80
S. N. 15/4/89
Stephen Frederick, Rev. (1825–1897) 30/7/57 ?
Thomas, Rev. 1/4/88
Thomas, Rev. 7/6/48 ?
Thomas Peers (1795–1875), tory M.P. 25/6/63 ?
T. R., photographer 22/7/61
Watkin, liberal M.P. 28/4/80
Watkin Lewis Griffies-, Sir (1800–1877), 3rd Baronet 14/7/66
William (–1865), liberal M.P. 28/4/53
William Fenwick, Gen. Sir (1800–1883), 1st Baronet (1856) 21/6/58
W. J. 7/5/78, 16/5/78
Williams, Deacon & Co., bankers 29/4/48
Williams, Granville & Co. 19/3/45
Williams, John & Co., stationers 8/1/47 ?
Williams & Norgate, Messrs., London booksellers 26/11/55
Williamson *see* Dundas
Williamson,
Mrs., rescue 5/12/59, 5/1/60, 15/1/60, 19/1/60
Benjamin, Dr., physician in Aberdeen 19/8/47
D. R., Rev., poet 13/11/90, 22/9/91
Edward Walter, lawyer 10/10/68 ?
James (1842–1930), 1st Baron Ashton (1895), liberal M.P. 16/7/90

Williamson (*cont.*)
R., Rev. Dr. (1802–1865), headmaster 28/4/39
Stephen, liberal M.P. 7/11/86 n, 9/6/88
Williams-Wynn *see* Doyle, Gaskell, Shipley
Willink, William W., secretary, public works loan board 25/10/62, 5/7/73
Willis,
rescue 9/3/73
George, London bookseller 5/12/54
John Walpole, Judge (1793–1877) 12/5/37
Robert, Prof. 24/11/41
Thomas, Rev. (1801–1857) 23/12/32 ?
William (1835–1911), liberal M.P. 12/11/89
Willmer,
Charles (1819–1897) 4/8/79
Henry 10/1/35 ?
Willmott, Robert Aris, Rev. 15/5/41
Willock, William Alexander, author 10/7/56
Willoughby,
Henry (1761–1835), 6th Baron Middleton (1800), a tory 31/7/32
Henry Pollard, Sir (1796–1865), 3rd Baronet (1813), tory M.P. 23/3/54
Willoughby de Broke *see* Verney
Willox, John, of Edzell 7/10/51, 25/9/53
Wills,
Frederick, Sir (1838–1909), 1st Baronet (1897), tobacco magnate 23/12/90 ?
George Alfred, Sir (1854–1928), 1st Baronet (1923), tobacco magnate 10/10/78 ?
G. F. 3/1/77
John, lawyer 12/9/36 ?
John, Rev. (–1873) 27/6/59
Joseph, mayor of Plymouth 17/7/77 n
William Gorman (1828–1891), dramatist 10/4/86 n
William Henry (1830–1911), liberal M.P., tobacco merchant 28/4/81 L, 7/3/82 L
Willson,
Anthony (1812–1866), of Lincolnshire 18/12/31
Samuel, dealer 4/4/59
Willyams, Sarah Brydges, Mrs. (1780–1863), friend and correspondent of Disraeli 17/3/88, 28/2/91
Wilmer, David (1804–1870) 10/1/35 ?
Wilmot,
rescue 13/4/75
Charles Octavius Eardley- (1824–1886), soldier 29/11/51
John Eardley-, Sir (1783–1847), 1st Baronet, tory M.P. (1832), governed Van Dieman's Land (1842) 29/4/46
John Eardley Eardley-, Judge Sir (1810–1892), 2nd Baronet (1847), tory M.P. 17/6/29 n, 4/5/46
Wilshere, Charles Willes (1814–1906) 8/3/75
Wilson *see* Bagehot, Bromley, Gladstone, Ogilvy, Trevelyan
Wilson,
Dr., of Toronto 29/10/87
Rev. Mr., presbyterian 9/11/48
A., rescue 28/3/67, 17/5/70
A., Miss 15/12/79
Alexander Stephen 27/8/76
Ambrose John, Rev. (1853–1929) 6/2/79
Andrew (1780–1848), artist 11/4/32
Arthur Charles, Rev. (–1880) 21/2/54
Benjamin, Rev. 19/7/51
Charles Bowman, Dr., physician 4/4/44 n
Charles Heath (1809–1882), art critic 3/6/32
Charles Henry (1833–1907), liberal M.P. 24/5/89, 25/6/93 L
Charles Rivers, Sir (1831–1916), civil servant and financier 17/2/73, 21/8/73 L, 30/6/81 L, 29/8/92, 10/9/92, 20/9/92 L
Charles Thomas, Rev. 11/8/41
Charles Townshend, Capt. (1823–1887) 20/7/60
Daniel, Rev. (–1886) 5/11/49
Donald Mackenzie, of Ross-shire 23/9/46
E., Rev. 24/3/43
George 2/5/79
George (1808–1870), Manchester merchant and free-trader 4/10/55, 17/7/65, 18/7/65
George, Rev. 13/3/57
George Grant 30/11/85
Giffin, Sir, Master in Chancery 4/11/43
Harry 3/9/76
Henry Bristow, Rev. Prof. (1803–1888) 16/2/42
Henry Joseph (1833–1914), liberal M.P. 24/12/77
Hill Wilson, Rev. 24/5/90
Horace Hayman, Prof. (1786–1860), professor of Sanskrit, Oxford 28/6/52
Isabella, Mrs., lodging-housekeeper 27/9/53
J., Sir J. G's partner 16/8/25 n
J., Mrs. 16/8/25
James 4/11/81
James (1805–1860), founder of *The Economist*, liberal M.P. 28/2/45, 9/7/49, 6/10/53, 7/10/53, 17/1/54, 18/1/54, 8/5/54
James Arthur, Dr., physician 26/3/77
James Grant, American author 14/2/80
James Maurice, Rev. 10/7/87
J. J. 19/4/79
John, secretary, Newark savings bank 1/1/33
John Matthias, Rev. Prof. (1813–1881), philosopher 21/2/54

Joseph Havelock (1858–1929), labour M.P. 20/7/93
Joshua (1795–1874), barrister and author 13/6/44
J. W. 29/12/77
Mackenzie 23/9/46
Mathew, Sir (1802–1891), 1st Baronet (1874), liberal M.P. 19/8/35, 18/2/74
Nathaniel, Rev. 10/2/75
Robert Francis, Canon (1809–1888) 11/2/30, 22/3/75
Robert Thomas, Sir (1777–1849), governor of Gibraltar (1842) 9/4/46
Robert W. R., barrister 10/1/80
Roger Carus-, Rev. (1792–1839) 6/8/39
Stephen Lea, Rev. (1818–1899) 2/2/57
T. Alderson, poet 24/11/67 ?
Thomas, Glasgow liberal 22/10/88
Thomas, Liverpool shipbuilder 9/12/41
Thomas, of Newark 5/6/39
Walter F. 21/10/78
William, attempted to blackmail G 10/5/53
William Carus-, Rev. 7/9/77
Wilson, Casey & Phillips, Messrs., silk merchants 26/6/48 n
Wilson-Patten *see* Buller
Wilton *see* Egerton
Wilton,
rescue 26/6/65
John, Dr., physician 25/3/80 ?
Wimberley, Charles Irvine, Rev. 16/5/59
Wimbush, Miss 8/1/88
Wimperis, Edmund Morison (1835–1900), artist 9/1/68
Wimpole, Mrs. 7/4/53
Winans,
Mrs. 15/8/74
William Louis 11/7/74
Winchilsea *see* Hatton
Winckley *see* Shelley
Windeatt, E. 10/9/77
Winder, Mr., photographer 14/6/64
Windle, Mr., at Clumber 15/4/79
Window, Mr., involved with telegraphy 22/8/59
Windsor *see* Clive
Windus, Ansley, solicitor 6/8/59 ?
Winens, Mrs. 14/12/82
Wing,
Louisa, of Windsor 24/3/75
William, Newark bookkeeper 19/1/35
William (1810–1882), antiquarian 23/7/57 ?
Wingfield,
Elizabeth Frances Charlotte (1813–1884), née Jocelyn, Lady Powerscourt 6/10/38
John Harry Lee 30/5/78 ?
Mervyn (1836–1904), 7th Viscount Powerscourt (1844) 31/12/71
Richard (1815–1844), 6th Viscount Powerscourt 6/10/38 n
Winks, A. F. 8/1/90
Winmarleigh *see* Patten
Winn *see* Cross
Winn,
Mrs. 2/9/77
James Michell, Dr. 2/6/76, 31/12/85
Rowland (1820–1893), tory M.P. 3/10/73 n
William Nelson, Rev. 26/3/79 ?
Winnerz, Mr. 4/7/78
Winnington, Thomas Edward, Sir (1811–1872), 4th Baronet, liberal M.P. 10/3/40 n
Winsall, J., hatter 21/6/74
Winslow,
Charles de Blois, Rev. 30/6/74
Forbes Benignus (1810–1874), psychologist 9/8/49
Irving, Mrs., of Boston, Mass., actress 19/6/90
John Lyndhurst, Rev. 1/11/78 n, 1/12/78, 6/12/78, 7/12/78
Winsor, J. B. 21/12/75
Winspear, Mr. 20/8/77
Winstanley, Clement (1775–1855), chairman, Leicester railway 1/7/45
Winston,
Robert, of Chelsea radical association 27/12/79
T. 8/11/75
Winter,
rescue 15/4/58
Mr. 6/10/65
Allenson 23/2/88
C. T. 9/4/79
D. L., Rotherham liberal 21/10/87
John, treasury messenger 5/12/64
Winterbotham,
Henry Selfe Page (1837–1873), liberal M.P. 14/7/68, 31/5/70, 10/6/70, 25/11/71, 19/3/73, 20/3/73, 29/12/73
L. W. 23/12/73
Rayner, Rev. (1843–1926) 30/12/78
Winters, Mr. 8/1/68
Winthrop, Robert C. (1809–1894), of U.S.A. 9/7/68
Wintle,
R. W. 22/2/70
W. J., Rev. 16/4/91
Wintour,
Fitzgerald Thomas, Rev. (1829–1898) 1/6/33 n
Isabel Milnes (1833–), née Gaskell 1/6/33
Wirz, G. E., hymnist 3/1/76
Wise,
Clement, author 15/11/90
J. 30/4/29
John Ayshford (1813–1870), liberal M.P. 15/2/60

Wiseman,
G., Rev. 5/8/76
Nicholas Patrick Stephen, Cardinal Abp. (1806–1865), archbishop of Westminster (1850) 14/4/32, 28/7/36, 6/12/38, 12/12/38, 24/12/38, 7/1/39, 15/1/39, 18/8/40, 11/6/42, 23/9/45, 18/10/45, 5/8/61, 6/8/61, 18/1/80 n
Wishas, D. 13/3/52
Wishlade,
James Emanuel, cottager 4/2/30, 29/7/33 n
Mary Ann, Mrs. 29/7/33
Wiszniewski, Adam, Prince, Polish economist 6/5/65
Witburn, P. 15/1/91
Witham, P. 26/6/90
Wither, Lovelace B., Rev. 17/4/69
Witherby, Robert Hale, Rev., of Glenalmond 21/10/59
Withers,
Mr. 31/3/34
W. Stanley, Homerist 20/1/87
Witherspoon, Joseph 24/1/75
Withington, J. S., Rev., Leeds methodist 9/8/75
Withrow, Rev. Mr. 26/2/77
Witney, rescue 16/10/78
Wittelsbach, Charles Theodore (1839–1888), Duke of Bavaria 19/9/79
Wittgenstein,
Caroline Louise Leontine Sayn-, Countess 24/9/79
Elenore Casimire Ludovic Sayn-, Countess 24/9/79
Witton, H., clerk in war office 18/7/66 ?
Witts, W., of Westminster 1/12/54
Witty, John Francis, Rev. 19/3/57
Wix, Horatio Nelson, furniture manufacturer 27/4/59 ?
Wixley, W. M. 19/7/90
Wizbroo, Mr. 7/3/79
Wodehouse,
Algernon, Rev. (1814–1882) 22/4/57, 21/8/57
Berkeley (1806–1877), resident of Zante, Ionia 15/12/58 n
Edmond, tory M.P. 14/12/41, 10/3/42, 28/3/43
Florence, née Fitzgibbon, Lady Kimberley 10/1/71
John (1771–1846), 2nd Baron Wodehouse (1834) 23/3/46
John; Earl of Kimberley 9/6/53
Philip Edmund, Sir (1811–1887), colonial governor 14/12/42
Thomas, Rev. 17/11/76
Wolf, E. H. 8/2/79
Wolfe, Arthur, Rev. (–1892) 21/7/75
Wolff,
rescue 26/6/54
Emil (1802–1879), German sculptor 1/6/32
Henry Drummond Charles, Sir (1830–1908), secretary to high commissioner, Ionia (1859), tory M.P. and diplomat (1880) 3/11/58, 15/5/66, 28/2/75, 19/7/76, 24/3/77, 27/3/77, 28/6/82 L, 28/10/82 L, 10/2/86, 16/2/86 c, 22/2/86 c, 25/2/86 c, 1/11/92, 18/4/93, 18/7/93
Henry W., Reform and Eighty Club member 4/3/75
Joseph, Rev. Dr. (–1862) 3/5/52
Wolffers, Fr. von, Baron 2/11/75
Wolffsohn, Julius, Mrs. 30/1/80, 27/12/88
Wolfosclea, Mad. 11/1/88 ?
Wollaston, William Munro, Rev., of Cannes 22/1/83
Wollstonecraft *see* Godwin
Wolowski, Louis François Michel Raymond, French economist 2/11/71
Wolrych *see* Hewley
Wolseley,
Charles, Sir (1769–1846), 7th Baronet (1817), radical reformer 12/12/38
Garnet Joseph, Sir 2/8/73
John, Dean 21/8/60
Louisa, Lady 25/3/74
W., Sir, 6th Baronet 27/1/35 n
William Bertie (1797–1881), colonial civil servant 27/1/35
Wolverhampton *see* Fowler
Wolverson, F. 3/4/78
Wolverton *see* Glyn
Womack, M. W. 1/1/75
Womersley, Robert, chemical manufacturer 2/1/80 ?
Wood *see* Frost, Ingram
Wood,
rescue 31/1/56
Miss 20/4/71
Agnes Elizabeth (–1919), née Courtenay, Lady Halifax 22/4/69
Alexander, Scottish lawyer 27/2/40, 9/11/43
Alexander, Dr. (1817–1884), Edinburgh physician 1/10/64
Andrew, Rev. (1834–1917) 12/7/61
Charles, Sir; 1st Viscount Halifax 9/3/33 ?
Charles Alexander, Sir (1810–1890), emigration commissioner 24/1/28, 19/6/38 n, 23/10/83, 31/10/83
Charles Lindley (1839–1934), 2nd Viscount Halifax (1885) 17/12/64
Charles Robert, Rev. 6/5/79 ?
Christopher, of Edinburgh 23/6/31
E. A. 29/12/79

Francis Derwent (1871–1926), sculptor 23/2/94 ?
Frederick John, Rev. 8/9/81, 20/9/81
George William (1781–1843), liberal M.P. 23/2/43
Henry Evelyn, Gen. Sir (1838–1919) 2/3/81, 5/3/81 c, 6/3/81, 8/3/81 c, 12/3/81, 17/3/81 c, 22/3/81, 14/4/81, 15/5/81, 17/5/81, 25/5/81, 9/6/81, 18/6/81, 26/9/81 ff, 8/11/82, 1/12/82 c, 4/12/82 c, 4/3/84, 8/3/84
Henry Hayton, Rev. (–1882) 17/7/80
Hugh 19/2/67
I. J. 28/5/68
James Alexander, Rev. (1819–1893) 1/12/67 ?
J. H., Rev., nonconformist 8/8/75
Jimie, shopkeeper and banker 20/12/25
John, Edinburgh schoolmaster 19/5/28, 16/12/34
John, of Birkenhead 2/7/76, 28/5/77
John George, Rev. (1827–1889) 20/3/78
John Page, Rev. Sir (1796–1866) 26/4/50
John Ryle, Rev., royal chaplain 4/12/40
John W., poet 18/8/77 ?
Joshua, Rev. (–1878) 13/7/50 ?
M., Mrs. 2/1/79
Mary, Lady, née Grey, Lady Halifax 9/3/33 n, 26/4/43
Peter Almeric Leheup, Canon (1816–1897) 3/3/36
Richard, Rev. (–1880) 25/5/57, 1/6/59
Robert B., Lieut. Col. 22/8/46
Samuel Francis (1809–1843), barrister 9/6/27 ?
Sheridan 11/4/89
Sophia (–1906), née Brownrigg 25/6/38 n
Thomas (1777–1860), tory M.P. 19/6/38
Thomas, Rev. (–1894) 18/12/76
Walter, solicitor 4/7/76
Western (1804–1863), liberal M.P. 5/2/62
William Page, Sir 23/2/49
William Rayner (1811–1884), Manchester merchant 23/12/65
W. S., Rev. 10/12/89
Woodall,
Edward Harrison, Rev. 30/12/53
W. 30/12/79 ?
William (1832–1901), liberal M.P. 10/6/84 L, 20/8/88
Woodard,
Luke, American evangelist 20/4/57
Nathaniel, Rev. 1/1/47
Woodburn, Samuel (–1853), art collector 22/6/53
Woodcock,
Charles, Canon 21/12/29
Henry, colonial judge 7/3/53 ?
W. H., of Wigan 9/3/46
Woodd, Basil 5/6/31
Woode,
J. M., Mrs. 15/1/27 ?
J. M., Rev. 15/1/27 n
Woodfin, Mr. 28/2/77
Woodford, James Russell, Bp. (1820–1885) 28/9/62, 21/8/72
Woodgate,
H. A., Mrs. 25/9/52
Henry Arthur, Canon (1801–1874) 14/3/30
Thomas, London antique dealer 7/12/60 ?
William, solicitor 22/6/55
Woodhead, J. 3/9/77
Woodhouse,
Harriet Emmeline (1821–1905), née Gladstone 13/9/27 n
William 13/9/27 n
Woodifield, Robert Denby, of the import department 15/1/53
Woodlock, Bartholomew, Bp. (–1890) 21/2/66, 13/3/68
Woodmason,
John Matthias, Rev. 25/10/57 n
Mathias, of Littlemore, Oxford 20/3/44
Woodroffe, Nathaniel George, Rev. (1765–1851) 22/8/32
Woodrow, T. J. 23/7/91
Woodruff, C. S. 18/4/92
Woods,
rescue 2/6/80
Henry (1822–1882), liberal M.P. 7/12/67
J. W. 14/11/89
Mary Anne, née Paton, soprano 23/12/25
Samuel (1846–1915), liberal/labour M.P. 7/6/93, 10/7/93 L, 14/7/93 L, 11/8/93 L, 18/8/93 L, 4/11/93 L
Virna, Miss, dramatist 8/12/92
Woodward,
Henry, Rev. 2/4/44
J. Henry, Rev. 4/4/48
Thomas, Dean (1814–1875) 16/5/59
Thomas Best 28/7/74
Woolacott, Hugh 26/8/87 ?
Woolard, Mr. 12/2/78
Woolat, Mr. 20/9/78
Woolfe, rescue 11/8/54
Woolfit,
Miss 22/7/37 ?
Joseph, Newark fishmonger 22/7/37 n
Joseph, Mrs. 22/7/37 ?
Woollam, Mr. 17/11/77
Woollcombe,
Edward Cooper, Rev. (1816–1880), fellow of Balliol, Oxford 2/11/47
Thomas (1800–1876), of Devonport 12/3/56
William Wyatt, Rev. (1813–1884), fellow of Exeter, Oxford 25/2/53, 15/3/53

Woolley, John (1816–1866), principal of Sydney University 22/8/53
Woollright, Chidson & Wait,, Messrs., Liverpool merchants 16/10/52 ?
Woolner, Thomas (1825–1892), sculptor; carved G's bust twice 16/4/62, 30/4/62, 19/8/63 ff, 27/6/64, 8/12/65, 14/1/67, 26/5/68, 24/9/70, 2/4/73, 20/4/75, 2/12/81, 22/12/81 L, 29/12/81 L, 2/2/82, 23/2/82, 30/10/82, 5/5/83, 26/10/83
Woolrych, Humphrey William, Serjeant (1795–1871) 23/4/60
Woosnam, Richard 23/4/74 ?
Wooster, D. 1/12/67
Wootton, J. 31/12/78, 16/4/79
Wordsworth,
Charles, Bp. (1806–1892), warden of Glenalmond (1846), bishop of St. Andrews (1852) 7/10/30, 30/4/51, 1/5/51, 29/9/61
Christopher, fils, Bp. (1807–1885), bishop of Lincoln (1868) 15/12/31 n, 3/2/41, 28/8/47, 9/5/70 L, 10/5/70 L, 6/9/72, 31/10/72, 23/12/83 L, 12/2/84 L
Christopher, père, Rev. (1774–1846), Master of Trinity, Cambridge 15/12/31
William; poet 14/10/29
Work,
Mrs. 12/8/53
P. 3/5/51
Worke, P. Leslie 9/9/64
Working Men's Lord's Day Rest Association 15/2/75 n
Workmen's National Association 8/6/87 n
Workmen's Neutrality Committee 19/2/78 n
Wormald *see* Hughes
Wornum, Ralph Nicholson (1812–1877), keeper, National Gallery (1854) 7/2/57
Woronzov-Dachekow, J. J., Count 7/4/81
Worrall, T. H. 27/12/78
Worsley *see* Pelham
Worsley,
Maj. 17/7/72
F., author 26/4/62 n
Henry, Rev. 9/8/91
Philip Stanhope (1835–1866), poet 8/11/65, 9/11/65
Thomas (–1885), Master of Downing, Cambridge 23/12/45
Worth, W. H. 27/8/75
Worthington, James William 8/6/42
Wortley *see* Lyttelton, Stuart-Wortley
Wortley,
Archibald James Stuart- (1849–1905), artist 1/4/89
James Archibald Stuart- (1805–1881), Peelite M.P. and manic depressive 13/11/32, 18/4/53, 23/1/54, 2/8/54, 3/8/54, 24/5/56, 5/3/57, 9/3/57, 11/3/57, 25/4/57, 2/5/57, 5/8/57, 2/4/58, 12/4/58, 11/6/58, 30/7/58, 2/8/58, 20/5/59, 23/11/59, 21/8/60, 31/8/60, 17/5/61, 1/7/65 n, 13/12/67, 26/4/68, 3/8/69, 8/11/69, 18/3/73, 8/9/73, 9/9/73, 21/1/74, 27/2/74, 16/7/74, 24/7/74, 14/1/75, 21/2/75, 31/3/75, 21/1/76, 10/3/76, 7/5/76, 29/3/77, 28/2/78
Jane Stuart-, née Lawley 24/7/39, 15/3/57, 25/4/57, 2/5/57, 21/6/68, 3/8/69, 12/8/82
William Talbot Stuart- (–1863) 26/2/53
Wouldridge, Harry, of Islington 28/2/68
Wradieff, Mr. 20/2/78
Wrangham,
Digby Cayley, barrister 15/12/41
Francis, Ven. (1769–1842) 15/12/41 n
Wratislaw, Albert Henry 29/5/77 ?
Wray,
Mr., architect 15/6/57
Cecil, Rev. (–1878) 21/5/52 ?
Cecil Daniel, Rev. (–1866) 21/5/52 ?
John, police officer 10/5/42 ?
M., wharfinger 12/8/48
William Mark, Rev. (–1886) 12/6/60
Wreford, Henry (1806–1892), Neapolitan correspondent of *The Times* 6/5/57
Wren,
Mrs. 1/10/87
Abraham, of Liverpool 4/11/68
Walter (1834–1898), liberal candidate 18/9/78
Wrench,
T. W., Rev. 25/1/63 n
V. C. 8/7/78
Wrenfordsley, Henry Thomas, Judge Sir (–1908) 11/2/56 ?, 11/3/59
Wrick, Mr. 23/12/78
Wright *see* Lefevre, Leigh, Loyd
Wright,
Miss, rescue 21/11/53
Mr., of Hull 29/8/71
Arthur, Rev. (1836–1909) 18/11/75
Charles Tylden, of Woodlands, Shireoaks 30/10/64, 15/3/74
E., of Hawarden 30/9/52
E. D. 27/6/78
G. F. 29/1/86
Henry, of Newark 2/10/40
Henry Press, Rev. (1814–1892) 19/1/60
Hornsby 18/6/78
Ichabod Charles (1795–1871), translator 18/7/64
James, of Oxford University Press 1/10/57
James Camper, Rev. (1774–1838) 30/10/25
J. B. 28/4/68
J. E. 16/10/86

J. M. 23/3/80
John, clerk in Port of London 3/6/45 ?
John P., of Bridgnorth 22/10/88
John Smith (1773-1851), of Nottinghamshire 25/5/33
Macer 4/4/91
Philip, of the Bishop of London's Fund 10/1/74
Robert Patrick, Sir (1857-1938) 2/8/79
Sarah Caroline (-1860), née Stovin 25/5/33
S. J. 23/4/74
Thomas (-1827) 8/6/26
V. C., assistant land commissioner 6/7/46 ?
William N., bookseller 28/2/45
Wright, J.& P., Messrs., linen drapers in Edinburgh 27/11/39, 9/1/40
Wrightson,
Arthur Bland, Rev. 17/6/79
William Battie (1789-1879), liberal M.P. 4/1/68 ?
Wrigley, Frank, music teacher in Hawarden 1/11/61, 9/11/61, 21/12/65
Wrottesley,
Arthur (1824-1910), 3rd Baron Wrottesley (1867) 18/12/69
John, Sir (1771-1841), 1st Baron Wrottesley (1838), whig M.P. 13/9/30 n, 15/7/33
Walter (1810-1872), barrister 13/9/30 n
Wulff, S. 29/12/75
Wurtele, J. S. C., Speaker, Quebec Legislative Assembly 1/6/87
Wyatt,
E. 7/11/67
Matthew Digby, Sir (1820-1877), architect 7/2/62
Richard James (1795-1850), sculptor 23/4/32
T. M. 27/3/75
Walter James, Capt. 22/7/67
Wybrov, Mr. 22/11/76
Wyckoff, Dr. 24/2/77
Wyke, Charles Lennox, Sir (1815-1897), diplomat 9/6/63
Wyld,
James (1838-1887), liberal M.P. 4/11/68 n
P. 4/11/68, 17/3/74
Wylde, P., of Bollington 23/12/86, 31/12/86
Wylie,
Mr., of Ransom's, London 17/6/44
A. H., Liverpool merchant 21/1/46
D. G., Rev. 27/8/91
James, of Mid-Calder 3/10/33 n
James Allan, Rev. Dr. (-1894) 11/1/78
J. H. 24/1/87
Jonathan C., schoolmaster 16/3/75
Wyllie, James, Liverpool merchant 23/1/71 n, 25/11/75
Wylrow, Mr. 4/3/80
Wylson, G. J. 29/1/78
Wyman, Messrs. 25/7/79
Wyndham *see* Burrell
Wyndham,
E., rescue 18/1/61
George, 1st Baron Leconfield 5/7/45 n
George (1863-1913), tory M.P.; Balfour's secretary 1887, lived near Hawarden 5/11/87, 14/9/88 ?, 27/10/88
Madeleine 5/7/93
Percy Scawen (1835-1911), tory M.P. 5/6/72 c, 5/7/93 n
Sibell Mary, Lady Grosvenor 9/10/82, 29/12/96
Thomas Heathcote, Rev. 7/2/80 ?
Wynen, W. G.& Sons, merchants 14/11/46 ?
Wynford *see* Best
Wynn *see* Gladstone
Wynn,
Charles Watkin Williams- (1775-1850), tory M.P. 17/5/34 n
Charlotte Williams- (1807-1869), diarist 24/5/52, 3/6/52, 14/9/63
Harriet Antonia Williams-, Lady, née Clive 1/3/38 n
Henry Watkin Williams-, Sir (1783-1856), diplomat 24/6/35 n
Herbert Watkin Williams- (1822-1862), tory M.P. 15/9/56
Hester Frances Williams-, Lady (-1854), née Smith 24/6/35
Mary Williams- (-1838), née Cunliffe 17/5/34
Watkin Williams-, Sir (1772-1840), 5th Baronet (1789) 1/3/38
Watkin Williams-, Sir (1820-1885), 6th Baronet (1840), tory M.P. 15/9/56
Wynne,
E. E. 6/7/67
Robert, Rev. (1828-1881) 11/3/57 ?
Thomas 6/1/87
William Watkin Edward (1801-1880), tory M.P. 31/3/54
Wynter, Philip, Rev., vice-chancellor of Oxford 17/3/42
Wyon,
A. 8/12/87
Leonard Charles (1826-1891), engraver 9/7/46
William (1795-1851), engraver 8/12/41
Wyse *see* Türr
Wyse,
Thomas, Sir (1791-1862), Knight (1857), diplomat and M.P. 15/1/39, 30/10/60
Winifrede Mary, author 18/12/58, 10/5/69
Wyvill, Marmaduke (1791-1872), liberal M.P. 20/12/38 ?

Xenos, Aristides, Greek consul 17/5/59, 19/3/78

Xidian, Anastasio T., Sir, of Ionia 10/1/59

Yancolov, Mr. 29/4/79
Yarborough *see* Pelham
Yarnall, Ellis, of Philadelphia 17/10/65
Yates,
Miss 21/4/79
Arthur C., journalist 7/9/77
George Parry, of Liverpool 17/11/68 ?
James, Rev. (1822–1868) 15/5/56 ?
William, Rev. 3/12/76
William Holt, Dr. (1802–1874), physician 19/12/39
Yeaman, James (1816–1886), liberal M.P. 27/2/78 ?
Yeates,
Benjamin 9/8/90
George, bedstead maker 3/4/52 ?
Yeaton, rescue 20/5/68
Yeats,
John Sebastian, stockbroker 25/6/52 ?
W. 31/10/87
W. E. 26/4/79
William, Dr., physician 8/9/77
Yelverton, Hastings Reginald, Adm. Sir (1808–1878) 4/9/73, 4/10/73
Yerbury, Frank 17/1/79
Yolland, William, Col. (1810–1885), railway inspector, board of trade 18/12/63
Yonge,
Charles (1781–1830), schoolmaster 3/12/25
John Eyre, Rev. (1818–1890), of Eton 22/1/61
Reginald, Rev. (–1889), of Toxteth 22/12/72
Richard, Rev. (–1878) 3/9/67
William Wellington, Rev. (–1878) 29/5/60
Yool, William Alexander (–1883), actuary 21/9/50
York *see* Mary of Teck
York (and Albany) *see* Frederick Augustus
Yorke *see* Cocks
Yorke,
Mr., musician 10/8/50
Alexander 16/1/84
Charles Philip (1799–1873), 4th Earl of Hardwicke (1834) 20/3/56
Eliot C.(Annie), Mrs., née Rothschild 8/6/89 n
Eliot Thomas (1805–1885), tory M.P. 23/4/52
Elizabeth Margaret, Lady (1789–1867), Lady Stuart de Rothesay 15/10/41
Susan (–1886), née Liddell, Lady Hardwicke 13/5/57
Yorston, C. H., of Edinburgh 26/10/79
Young,
A., Mr. 9/5/61
Adam (1817–1897), of Board of Inland Revenue 11/11/81
Adelaide, Lady, née Dalton, Lady Lisgar 25/11/58, 30/11/58
B. C. 29/1/75
C. C. 14/3/79
Charles Mayne (1777–1856), comedian 3/12/27
Edward, Rev. 15/12/42
Edward P., Dr., physician 16/6/59
E. R., Rev. 13/2/90
George (1819–1907), Lord Young, liberal M.P. and Scottish judge 27/7/68 ?, 7/10/71, 20/4/72 L, 9/2/74 L
George, Sir (1837–1930), 3rd Baronet (1848) 7/3/77
George Frederick (1791–1870), Peelite M.P. 11/5/41, 23/4/58
Henry Edward Fox, Sir (1808–1870), colonial governor 21/3/64
J., Rev. 21/10/86
J. Lewis, phonograph operator 7/3/90
John, Prof. (1835–1902), of Glasgow 26/5/79
John, Rev. Dr. (1805–1881), Albion Scottish church minister 1/1/61
John, Sir (1807–1876), 1st Baron Lisgar (1870), Peelite M.P. and colonial governor, lord high commissioner of Ionia 1855-9 16/5/26, 7/12/47, 12/12/48, 31/3/52, 13/12/52, 25/11/58, 26/11/58, 7/12/58, 25/12/58, 9/1/59, 22/1/59, 18/1/61, 26/10/69 c, 10/11/69 c, 10/8/71, 8/11/71 c, 2/3/72 c, 14/10/72 n
R. Calder 19/9/78
Richard (1809–1871), liberal M.P. 27/7/68 ?
Robert 24/5/39 n
T. 27/11/74
T. E. 17/11/90
Thomas, receiver-general, G.P.O. 10/8/54
Thomas Charles, lawyer 5/3/89
W. H., London chemist 10/9/59 ?
William, silversmith 4/1/45
William Laurence, Sir (1806–1842), 3rd Baronet (1815), tory M.P. 22/11/37
William T., secretary, tithe trust 27/6/49
W. P. 20/3/52
Yriarte, Charles E., journalist 4/3/78 ?

Zaba, N. F., Polish exile 23/11/33
Zaccharini, Sig. 6/2/89
Zafiropulo, Stephanos 21/12/78
Zähnsdorff, F., bookbinder 9/10/90
Zaimes, Dr. 25/9/77 ?
Zaiser *see* Lawley
Zambarla, Dr., of Ionia 8/12/58

Zambelli, N. Temistoc, Ionian judge 29/11/58, 13/1/59 ?
Zamoyski, André, Count (1800–1874) 8/7/63 ?
Zanini, Demetrio, of Barcelona 3/12/90
Zankof, Dragan Kiryak, Bulgarian emissary 10/10/76, 23/10/76, 26/10/76, 26/5/81 L
Zapropoulos, M. 14/7/80
Zavo, Georgio, Dr. 8/1/61
Zaza, M. 26/6/77
Zazel, performer 2/7/77 n
Zea, Señor, Spanish foreign affairs minister 5/11/25
Zeitter, Mr., piano maker 14/2/43
Zeozel, performer 2/7/77
Zerreh, Mr. 1/3/77
Zervos, Sig. 8/10/79
Zetland *see* Dundas
Zicaliotti, Alexander, Liverpool tobacco merchant 11/10/78
Ziemann, Dr. 2/12/77
Zillah, Sister 28/5/90
Zincke,
  Foster Barham, Rev. (1817–1893), antiquary 25/1/38, 12/5/52, 6/5/83, 27/12/83
  Frederick Burt, of Jamaica 25/1/38
Zinn, Mr. 6/4/51 ?
Zino, L., Neapolitan banker 29/2/52
Znechinelli, Consul 19/6/90
Zobeir Pasha, Sudanese slave trader 21/2/84, 29/2/84 c, 5/3/84 c, 15/3/84 c, 8/6/84, 30/7/84, 12/8/84, 19/8/84, 12/3/85 c, 20/3/85 c, 20/9/92
Zohrab,
  Conrad, G's valet 25/6/80
  James, consul at Erzerum 2/8/78 ?
Zorn, John C. L. 14/7/68
Zouche *see* Curzon
Zoupolides, Dr. 4/2/87
Zucchi, Carlo, Comte, Neapolitan general 15/4/52
Zumbini, Bonaventura, Prof., historian; published study of G and Italy 18/5/77, 14/8/88 n
Zurla, Giacinta Placido, Cardinal (1769–1843), cardinal vicar of Rome, author 3/6/32
Zwinckenbart, Mr., visitor to Hawarden 30/4/76

GLADSTONE'S READING

Information on certain aspects of this index will be found in 'Using the Indexes' at the start of this volume. A bibliography of Gladstone's own writings will be found in the 'Subject Index' under 'publications by Gladstone' and 'letters and articles for the press'.

A.
'How shall we supply our cotton market? A letter to T. M. Gibson' 1862 (1862) 28/10/62

A. A. I.
From darkness to life. 1872 5/3/93

Abbadie, Jacques
'Chemical change in the Eucharist. In four letters showing the relations of faith to sense, etc.' 1867 17/9/71

Abbey, Charles John, and Overton, John Henry
The English Church in the eighteenth century. 1878 (2v. 1878) 27/11/82

Abbot, Francis Ellingwood
The genius of Christianity and free religion. 1875 28/5/77

Abbot, George Abp. of Canterbury
A treatise of the perpetuall visibilitie and succession of the true church in all ages. 15/10/82

Abbott, Edwin Abbott
'The latest theory about Bacon. A reply to ... Spedding', *C.R.*, xxviii. 141 (June). 1876 5/6/76
'The signs of the Church' from *Cambridge Sermons preached before the university.* 1875 6/5/75 ?
Onesimus. Memoirs of a disciple of St. Paul. 1882 26/3/82
Philochristus. Memoirs of a disciple of the Lord. 1878 24/2/78
The way out of agnosticism. 1890 21/9/90 ?

Abbott, Jacob
The teacher; or, moral influences employed in the instruction and government of the young. 1833 16/5/35
The young Christian; or, a familiar illustration of the principles of Christian duty. 1833 7/7/33

Abbott, John Stevens Cabot
The mother at home; or, the principles of maternal duty. 1830 14/8/41

Abbott, Lyman
The epistle of Paul to the Romans. 1888 14/4/89

A'Beckett, Gilbert Abbott, and Lemon, Mark
Sardanapalus; or the 'Fast' King of Assyria. 1853 24/4/89

Abeken, Heinrich
'A letter to ... Pusey ... in reference to certain charges against the German Church, etc.' 1842 28/3/42
Geschichtliche Darlegung. 1842 27/8/43

Abel, Sir Frederick Augustus Bart.
'On explosive agents applicable to naval and military uses, as substitutes for gunpowder, etc.' 1872 29/7/72

Abelard, Peter
History of Abelard, ed. J. Delacour. 1725 28/3/58

Abercrombie, John M.D.
'Address delivered in ... Aberdeen ... on occasion of his installation as Lord Rector of the university' 1835 3/2/36
The harmony of Christian faith and Christian character. 1835 24/6/38

A Bishop's Chaplain
A few words on the Athanasian creed. 1841 12/2/43

Abolition of the Navigation laws. 25/3/47

About, Edmond François Valentin
La question romaine. 1859 7/5/59
Le roi des montagnes. 1857 4/5/65, 30/5/65
Tolla; a tale of modern Rome. 1855 17/3/56

Abraham, Charles John Bishop of Wellington, New Zealand
'The divine principles of Christian missions to the heathens. A sermon, etc.' 1869 6/6/69
'The Episcopal conference of 1867. An address, etc.' 1867 8/12/67
Sermon on Job. 10/7/81

A brief exposition of the established principles and regulations of the United Society of Believers called Shakers. 1851 30/10/80

A British merchant
Review of the Neapolitan sulpher question. 1840 4/5/40

Abu Talib Ibn Muhammad Khan
The travels of Mirza Abu Taleb Khan in Asia, Africa and Europe ... tr. Charles Stewart. 1810 (2v. 1810) 7/3/42

Account of Busbrook model settlement. 20/10/77

Account of great distress at St. Ninian's. 1748 20/11/51

'Account of insurrection in St. Domingo' 9/5/33 ?

Account of the life, death and writings of the Revd Dr. Dodd. 1777 18/3/88

Account of the Sociétés Évangéliques. 18/12/41

Achelis, Ernst
D. R. Rothe. 1869 11/2/77 ?
Ackland, Joseph
The spirit of reverence. 1870 15/4/70
Acland, Sir Henry Wentworth Bart.
'A letter from a medical student on some moral difficulties in his studies . . . to the Rev. J. H. North' 1841 4/12/41
'A letter to . . . Gladstone on the formation of the Initiative Board in the university of Oxford' 1854 3/2/54
'Feigned insanity, how most usually simulated and how best detected. An essay, etc.' 1844 11/3/45
'Ground-work of culture. Address, etc.' 1883 29/10/83
'Oxford and modern medicine. A letter to Dr. James Andrew, etc.' 1890 5/2/90
'Remarks on the extension of education at the university of Oxford, in a letter to Rev. W. Jacobson' 1848 30/12/48
'The Harveian Oration, 1865' 1865 27/6/65
'The inaugural Robert Boyle lecture' 1892 17/9/92
'The public health. An address, etc.' 1880 21/11/80
Biographical sketch of Sir Benjamin Brodie. 1864 3/11/63
National health. 1871 15/7/71
The plains of Troy. 1839 6/11/55
Acland, Hugh Dyke
'A brief sketch of the history and present situation of the Valdenses in Piedmont, etc.' 1825 19/11/37 ?
Acland, Sir Thomas Dyke 11th Bart.
'National education. The present state of the question elucidated' 1839 11/2/39
'On cathedrals' 1839 26/2/39
'Speech . . . at the nomination of candidates for the representation of . . . Birmingham . . . 28th of April' 1859 3/5/59
'The discouragement of elementary mathematics in general education at Oxford, etc.' 1867 25/5/67
Meat, milk and wheat: an elementary introduction to the chemistry of farming. 1857 15/8/55
Acland, later Troyte, Arthur Henry Dyke
'A letter . . . On the present state of religious societies, and the mode of obtaining contributions etc.' 1840 21/2/40
Daily steps towards heaven; or, practical thoughts on the gospel history. 1849 13/4/50
Liturgia domestica; or, services . . . from the Book of Common Prayer. 1840 27/2/40
A common-sense radical
The lackeys of the Turk; an indictment, a protest and a warning. 1878 6/2/78
A critical examination of the 'Essays and Reviews', by an American layman. 1861 13/10/61
Acton, John Emerich Edward Dalberg Baron Acton
'Sendschreiben an einen deutschen Bischof des Vaticanischen Concils . . . September 1870' 1870 13/11/70
'The War of 1870: a lecture, etc.' 1871 8/6/71
On Eliot, *N.C.*, xvi. 464 (March). 1885 2/3/85
On German historians, *E.H.R.*, i. 7 (January). 1886 1/9/86
On Talleyrand, *N.C.*, xxix. 685 (April). 1891 11/4/91
A. D.
The accomplished hypocrite; or brass glitters more than gold. A moral tale, founded on facts. 1822 (2v. 1822) 22/10/25
Adair, Robert Alexander Shafto Baron Waveney
Forty years since; or, Italy and Rome. A sketch. 1876 18/12/76
The Established Church of Ireland, past and future. 1869 (2v. 1869) 25/2/69
Adam, Alexander LL.D.
A summary of geography and history both ancient and modern. 1794 23/5/29
Roman antiquities; or, a description of the manners and customs of the Romans. 1791 18/1/31, 4/2/33
Adam, Robert M.A.
The religious world displayed. 1809 (3v. 1809) 11/4/86
Adam, William Patrick
Thoughts on the policy of retaliation, and its probable effect on the consumer, producer . . . ship-owner. 1852 13/5/52
Adam of St. Victor
Elucidatorium ecclesiasticum, ed. L. Gautier. 1858 (2v. 1858–59) 30/10/59
Adams, C. C.
The Bible: a scientific revelation. 1882 24/6/83
Adams, Charles Francis the Younger
Richard Henry Dana. A biography. 1890 (2v. 1890) 18/6/91
Adams, Henry Brooks
Democracy. An American novel. 1880 22/6/82
Adams, Myron
Creation of the Bible. 1892 21/6/91 ?
Adams, Walter Marsham
The drama of empire. 1891 5/2/91
Adams, William M.A., Fellow of Merton College, Oxford
The old man's home. 1847 2/5/47
Adams, later Laffan, Bertha Jane Leith
Louis Draycott. The story of his life. A novel. 1889 (2v. 1889–90) 31/12/89
Adderley, Charles Bowyer Baron Norton
'Statement of the present Cape case. Addressed to the Society for Reform of Colonial Government' 1851 5/4/52

'The Australian Colonies Government Bill discussed' 1849 7/2/50
A few thoughts on national education and punishments. 1874 30/7/74, 18/11/77
Essay on human happiness. 1849 (2v. 1849–60) 20/1/61
High and Low Church. 1892 8/10/93
Some reflections on the speech of the Rt. Hon.... Lord John Russell on colonial policy. 1850 15/3/50
Adderley, Hon. James Granville
Stephen Remarx. The story of a venture in ethics. 1893 1/5/93, 10/9/93
Addington, Rev. Henry
'Some account of the abbey church of St. Peter and St. Paul at Dorchester, Oxfordshire' 1845 17/9/45
Addis, William Edward
Christianity and the Roman empire. 1893 30/4/93, 14/1/94
Addison, Rev. Canon Berkeley
'An earnest and solemn remonstrance, addressed to the Rev. D. T. K. Drummond ... By a Presbyter' 1843 15/5/52 ?
Addison, Charles Greenstreet
The history of the Knights Templars, the Temple Church, and the Temple. 1842 18/11/42
Addison, Right Hon. Joseph
Remarks on several parts of Italy. 1705 18/9/47
Addison, Lancelot Dean of Lichfield
The present state of the Jews—more particularly related to those in Barbary. 26/3/84
Addresses presented to H. R. H. the Prince of Wales during his state visit to British North America. 1860 4/2/65
'Address for the anniversary festival of the Literary Fund Society', 13 May 1840. 21/5/40
Address to conservative members. 1845 22/1/45
A dictionary of musicians, published by Sainsbury. 1825 10/4/38
Adler, H.
'Jews and Judaism. A reply', *N.C.*, iv. 133 (July). 1878 4/8/78
Adler, Hermann Nathan
'Is it well with thee?' A sermon. 1893 6/8/93
Sanitation as taught by the Mosaic law. 1893 26/1/94 ?
Adler, Nathan Marcus
'The Jewish faith. A sermon, etc.' 1848 10/2/48
Adolphus, John Barrister-at-Law
The history of England, from the accession to the decease of King George the Third. 1840 (7v. 1840–45) 14/8/86, 26/9/87
Adorni, Saint Catherine of Genoa
'Treatise on purgatory' from Vita e dottrina. 1858 14/12/79 ?
Advent lessons. 12/12/46 ?
Adventures of a young rifleman in the French and English armies... from 1806 to 1816. 1826 25/3/26
Advice to clergy. 27/7/52
Adye, Sir John Miller G. C. B.
'The British army', *N.C.*, vi. 344 (August). 1879 1/8/79
Aeschylus
Agamemnon. 18/7/31
Opera. 7/7/27, 10/4/30, 8/10/30
Persae. 10/2/30
Prometheus vinctus. 30/11/27, 6/2/30, 23/10/30, 31/10/31
Prometheus vinctus, ed. H. M. Stephenson. 1885 9/7/85
Septem contra Thebas. 8/2/30, 4/11/31
A. F.
Confirmation according to scripture. 1857 5/6/57
A few words on the corn laws, by a landowner. 1846 3/2/46
A few words on the monitorial system at Harrow, by one who was a monitor. 1854 14/1/54
'A few words to [Newman] ... by an Anglican priest' 1846 12/6/47
Afranius, Lucius
Reliquae, ed. Otto Ribbeck. 1852 1/7/76
Agar, William
The holy, catholic, apostolic Church of Ireland truly represented. 1853 15/3/68
Aggression on Tahiti. (not found) 8/4/43
[A glance at the Irish Question]. 1866 (not found) 31/1/66
Agnew, E. C.
The young communicants. 1840 21/3/41
Agnostic Faith. Enlarged from a paper on 'Ethical Theism', in the National Review, of February 1884. 1889 7/4/89
Agrarian endowment. 19/1/46 ?
Agresti, Michele
Il Senato conservatore delle leggi. 1845 14/1/51 ?
A history of the Brooklyn bridge. 1883 29/6/84
Aïdé, Charles Hamilton
Songs without music. Rhymes and recitations. 1889 20/11/89 n
Aids to the study of German theology. 21/2/75 ?
Aiken, Peter Freeland
A comparative view of the constitutions of Great Britain and the United States... in six lectures. 1843 4/3/43
Aikin, Lucy
Memoirs of the court of King Charles the First. 1833 (2v. 1833) 7/7/40
Ainsworth, William Harrison
Jack Sheppard. A romance. 1839 31/8/61
John Law, the projector. 1864 (3v. 1864) 6/4/66

Airy, Sir George Biddell K. C. B.
'Essays on the invasion of Britain by Julius Caesar; etc.' 1865 16/11/65
Aitchison, David
'Strictures on the duke of Argyll's essay on the ecclesiastical history of Scotland' 1849 29/4/49
'The truth with boldness; in two parts' 1841 19/2/41
Aitchison, James Alexander
The chronicle of mites, etc. 1887 25/11/87 ?
Aitken, Robert Incumbent of Pendeen
'Church reform spiritually considered. A letter to the Rt. Hon. W. E. Gladstone' 1871 11/6/71
The prayer book unveiled in the light of Christ: or, unity without liturgical revision. 1863 2/8/63
Aitken, William Hay Macdowall Hunter
The school of grace. Expository thoughts on Titus II. 1880 29/10/82
Akenside, Mark
'The pleasures of imagination', a poem in three books. 1744 30/12/40
Akerman, J. W.
'Native government in Natal' 1877 6/8/77
A knight of faith. 3/9/90
Aksakov, Ivan Sergeevich
'Condensed speech of ... Aksakov, vice-president of the Slavonic Committee of Moscow, October 1876' 1876 30/12/76
Albarella, Vincenzo
'L'Italiano Vincenzo Albarella ... a ... Gladstone' 1851 26/9/51
Albemarle, The. 1. 1/1892 22/12/1891
Albert, Prince Consort
The life of His Royal Highness the Prince Consort, by Sir T. Martin. 1875 21/12/74, 6/11/76, 29/4/79
The principal speeches and addresses of ... the Prince Consort, ed. Sir A. Helps. 1862 22/1/63
Alberti, C.
Gustav Freytag. 1886 24/10/90
Alcock, Sir Rutherford
The capital of the tycoon: a narrative of a three years' residence in Japan. 1863 (2v. 1863) 30/6/63, 1/7/63, 2/2/64
Alcoforado, Marianna
The letters of a Portuguese nun ... tr. Edgar Prestage. 1893 7/9/93
Alcott, Louisa May
Little Women and Good Wives. 1871 26/10/71 ?
Alden, H. M.
God in his world. 1890 14/12/90
Alderson, Sir Edward Hall Baron Alderson
A letter to the Bishop of Exeter. 1850 3/6/50
Selections from the Charges and other detached papers of Baron Alderson. 1858 6/8/65
Two letters to Henry Phillpotts, Bishop of Exeter. 1851 11/5/51
Aldrich, Henry D.D., Dean of Christ Church
Artis logicae compendium. 17/10/31
Aldrich, John Cobbold
'Church decoration not popery but piety.' A sermon. 1843 2/1/44
Aldrich, Thomas Bailey
Prudence Palfrey. A novel [serialised]. 1886 10/4/84
Aldworth, John
'The Estatica of Youghal, compared with ... the Tyrol; in a letter to the earl of Shrewsbury' 1843 6/8/43
Alembert, Jean Le Rond D'
Dialogues. 1847 26/9/75
'A letter of remonstrance, addressed to an undergraduate ... the tenets of Dr. Pusey and Mr. Newman' 1840 26/3/40
A letter to ... Brougham ... respecting episcopacy in Scotland. 1849 26/4/60
A letter to Lord Brougham on divine philosophy. 1840 26/4/60
A letter to ... the bishop of Glasgow. By a Scotch presbyter. 1850 3/10/50
A letter to the bishops of the Church of England. 1843 28/8/43
A letter to the Lord Bishop of Lincoln, occasioned by some recent lay addresses to his grace the Archbishop of Canterbury by an incumbent. 1842 22/3/42
A letter to the members of the General Assembly of the ... Church of Scotland. By a ... vestryman. 1857 26/5/57
Alexander, Mrs. C. F.
Hymns for little children. 1848 30/4/76
Alexander, George Gardiner
Confucius, the great teacher. A study. 1890 16/11/90, 17/7/91
Alexander, James wine merchant of Edinburgh
Suggestions for a simple system of decimal notation and currency, after the Portuguese model. 1854 20/12/54
Alexander, Sir James Edward
An expedition of discovery into the interior of Africa. 1838 (2v. 1838) 22/3/38
Alexander, John Incumbent of St. Columba's, Edinburgh
A letter to ... William Skinner ... Bishop of Aberdeen ... on the eucharistic doctrine. 1857 17/5/57
Alexander, Robert Major-General, East India Company
The rise and progress of British opium smuggling, and its effects upon India, China, etc. 1856 20/12/56, 8/5/90

Alexander, W.
Notes and sketches of northern rural life in the eighteenth century. 1877 17/10/77
Alexander, William Archbishop
'The great question,' and other sermons. 1885 24/1/86
Leading Ideas of the Gospels. 1872 17/11/72 ?
Royalty and loyalty . . . A sermon. 1886 30/8/87
Sensationalism, a sermon. 1873 19/1/73
St. Augustine's holiday and other poems. 1886 12/12/86
The witness of the Psalms to Christ and Christianity. 1877 11/4/79, 23/3/90
Alexander, William M.D., of Edinburgh, the younger
The history of women, from the earliest antiquity to the present time. 1779 (2v. 1779) 30/7/58
Alexander, William of the Aberdeen Free Press
Johnny Gibb of Gushetneuk in the parish of Pyketillim; with glimpses of the parish politics about A.D. 1843. 1871 28/9/71
Sketches of life among my ain folk. By the author of 'Johnny Gibb of Gushetneuk'. 1875 5/10/75
The making of Aberdeenshire. A paper. 1888 30/8/88
Alexander, William Lindsay
'The good man. A sermon occasioned by the death of . . . E. B. Ramsay' 1873 19/1/73
Anglo-Catholicism not apostolical. 1843 5/5/43
Switzerland and the Swiss churches: being notes of a short tour. 1846 8/10/47
The incarnation. 1871 9/10/71
Alexander, W. L.
The Good Man. 1873 19/1/73
Alfieri, Count Vittorio
Agamemnon. 1828 23/8/33
Della tirannide. 1801 (2v. 1801) 23/9/37
Il Misogallo. Prose e rime. 1799 29/12/54
Opere, ix. lxxxvii. 1807 28/9/33
Oreste. 1815 4/9/33
Satire di Vittorio Alfieri da Asti. 1806 26/8/59
Alford, Daniel Pring
The retreat, and other poems. 1874 2/7/75
Alford, Henry Dean of Canterbury
'The compacted body. A sermon . . . With an appendix on post-Reformation suffragan bishops' 1870 24/4/70
'The idylls of the King', *C.R.*, xiii. 104 (January). 1870 19/1/70
How to study the New Testament. 1867 (3v. 1867) 30/10/67
Quebec chapel sermons, preached in . . . 1854–57. 1857 (7v. 1854–57) 24/1/69
The Greek testament; with a critically revised text. 1849 17/2/50, 11/7/60
Alger, William Rounseville
A critical history of the doctrine of a future life. 1864 5/8/71, 7/7/78
Alison, Sir Archibald 1st Bart.
'Free trade and protection' 1844 21/8/44
History of Europe during the French Revolution. 1833 (10v. 1833–42) 13/11/35, 1/7/39, 14/8/66
Lives of Lord Castlereagh and Sir Charles Stewart. 1861 23/12/61
Practice of the criminal law of Scotland. 1833 10/4/90
The principles of population, and their connection with human happiness. 1840 (2v. 1840) 5/9/40
Alison, Sir Archibald 2nd Bart.
On army organisation. 1869 24/9/70
A Liverpool merchant on free trade. 30/4/46
All about the Salvation Army. 1884 11/7/86
Alla Civiltà Cattòlica: riposta de un prelato romano. 6/12/50
Allah, Habeeb Risk
Thistles and Cedars of Lebanon. 1853 31/12/53
Allardice, Robert Barclay
Agricultural Tour in the United States and Upper Canada. 1842 15/8/42
Allen, John Master of Dulwich College
Inquiry in the rise and growth of the Royal Prerogative in England 1830. 1844 (2nd edn) 20/5/50
Allen, John of Liskeard
State Churches and the Kingdom of Christ. 1853 31/7/53
Allen, Joseph
A charge delivered to the clergy of the diocese of Ely. 1841 28/11/41
Allen, Captain William
A plan for the immediate extinction of the slave trade. 1849 11/5/49
Allen, William F.R. S.
A plan for diminishing the poor's rate in agricultural districts. 1833 28/6/34
All'Europa. 1851 20/11/51
Alley, Jerome
Vindicae Christianae. 1826 25/4/58
Allies, Thomas William
A Life's Decision. 1880 30/9/83
Formation of Christendom. 1875 (pt. 3) 24/10/75
Journal in France . . . with letters from Italy. 1849 14/1/49
On the Influence of Practical Piety on the temporal and eternal interests of mankind. 1838 21/6/38
See of St. Peter. 1850 4/10/50
See of St. Peter. 1866 (3rd edn) 11/2/66, 11/6/71
Sermons on the Epistle to the Romans. 1844 21/4/44
The Church of England cleared from the charge of schism. 1846 21/6/46

Allies, Thomas William (*cont.*)
The Church of England cleared from the charge of schism. 1848 (2nd edn) 12/11/48
The Royal Supremacy. 1850 19/4/50
Allingham, William
Laurence Bloomfield in Ireland. A modern poem. 1864 17/5/64
Allix, Pierre
Remarks on the ecclesiastical history of the antient church of the Albigenses. 8/6/45
Allnatt, Charles F. B.
Cathedra Petri. 1878 11/8/91
Which is the True Church?. 1879 13/6/80
Allocutions. 1867 19/1/75
Allocuzione della Santita di nostro Signore Pio IX. 1855 11/11/55
Allon, Henry
Christ, the Book and the Church. Address. 1864 15/5/64
Land and the Puritans. 1882 9/6/88
Memorial to T. Binney. 1874 26/11/76
Vision of God and other sermons. 1876 29/10/76
Allport, Josiah
Sermon preached by A. Sall, ed. J. Allport. 21/12/42
True Catholic and Apostolic Faith maintained in the Church of England by A. Sall, ed. J. Allport. (1840 edn) 21/12/42
Allsopp, Thomas
Letters, conversations and recollections of S. T. Coleridge, ed. T. Allsopp. 1836 (2v.) 24/2/36
Almack, John
Character, Motives and Proceedings of the Anti-Corn Law League. 1843 25/2/43
Almon, John
The correspondence of the late John Wilkes, ed. J. Almon. 1805 (5v.) 11/1/49
Aloe, Stanislas d'
Guide pour la galerie des tableaux du Musée Bourbon. 1842 (2v. 1842–43) 17/12/50
Alsop, James Wilcox
'Home Rule. An Address' 1880 18/10/80
Altar of the Church of England in New Zealand. 1867 24/11/67
Alvary, W. C. [William Erkine]
Gilbert Freethorne's Heritage. 1888 13/10/88
Ambrogini, Angelus
Poesie italiane. 1825 22/1/51
A medical man's plea for a winter garden in the Crystal Palace. 1851 25/7/51
A Member of the University of Oxford
Strictures on no. 90 of 'the tracts for the times'. 1841 (2v. 1841) 19/4/41
A memoir of Lord Liverpool. 28/12/29
American tracts. 28/5/46 ?
Ames, Joseph
Typographical Antiquities: being an historical account of printing in England. 1749 19/12/79
Amicis, Edmondo de
Romance of a schoolmaster. 1893 (3v.) 15/3/93
Amiel, Henri Frédéric
Journal in Time. 1885 (2v.) 6/6/85
Journal, tr. Mrs. Humphry Ward. 1885 5/4/88
A modern heretic . . . a novel with a purpose. 1894 25/2/94
Amos, Sheldon
Existing laws of Demerara for the regulation of coolie immigration. 1871 2/2/76
Lectures on International Law. 1874 11/4/74
Primer of the English constitution and government. 1873 4/2/80
Purchase of Suez Canal Shares and international law. 1876 2/2/76
Ampère, Jean Jacques
L'Empire romain à Rome. 1867 (2v.) 18/5/72
Voyage dantesque. 1850 17/12/66
An account of the life, transactions and death of Rob Roy M'gregor. 1810 10/4/76
An account of the siege and destruction of Jerusalem, with some observations on . . . state of the Jews. 1822 25/12/36, 28/9/90
'An address to operatives' 1841 27/9/42
'An address to . . . the archbishops and bishops of the Church of England . . . by a low churchman' 1835 3/2/36
'An address to the protestant electors of Great Britain and Ireland' 1839 27/2/40
An aged curate. 3/8/51
'An answer to the Archbishop of York on the subject of eternal torments. By a Bachelor of Divinity' 1865 5/2/65
'An appeal to patrons on their solemn responsibility before God and man for . . . of their sacred trust' 1836 24/2/41
An appeal to the public in behalf of the Jews. 1834 3/3/35
Anarchie Française. 1892 20/6/92
Anderdon, John Lavicount
Life of Thomas Ken, Bishop of Bath and Wells. 1851 15/5/59, 3/3/61
Anderson, Adam
An historical and chronological deduction on the origin of commerce. 1764 (2v.) 20/11/48
Anderson, Arthur
Communications with India, China &c. 1843 18/11/43
Anderson, B. R.
Broken lights; poems and reminiscences. 1888 20/9/88
Anderson, Caroline Dorothea
Practical Religion Exemplified, by letters and passages from . . . Rev. Robert Anderson. 1845 10/8/45

Anderson, Charles Henry John
Ancient Models: containing some remarks on church building. 1840 26/7/40
Anderson, Christopher
Annals of the English Bible. 1845 (2v.) 6/1/61
Anderson, David
'Scenes' in the Commons. 1884 9/11/86
Anderson, J.
The Union of the British North American provinces. 1859 29/3/60
Anderson, James Maitland
University of St. Andrews. A historical sketch. 1878 16/9/82
Anderson, James Stuart Murray
Memoir of the Chisholm, late M.P. for Inverness-shire. 1842 27/6/42
Newfoundland and British North America School Society. A sermon. 1844 2/5/45
Sermons on various subjects. 1837 1/5/50 ?
The dead yet speaking. A sermon . . . after the death of Sir Robert Peel. 1850 31/7/50
The Present Crisis. Four sermons. 1851 25/5/51
The trials of the Church . . . two sermons on the Gorham case. 1850 1/5/50 ?
Anderson, John government agent
Acheen, and the ports of the north and east coasts of Sumatra. 1840 30/1/74
Anderson, John of Glenside, Mauritius
Descriptive account of Mauritius. (n.d.) 27/5/40
Anderson, Joseph
Scotland in Early Christian Times. 1881 3/7/81
Anderson, Mr.
Letter to the Duke of Richmond. 1844 11/7/44
Timely Hints. 25/3/43
Anderson, Robert headmaster
History of Scotland. 1874 19/4/79
Anderson, Robert perpetual curate, Brighton
Lord's Prayer. 1840 8/11/40
The Book of Common Prayer. 1839 26/4/40
Anderson, Sir Robert
A Doubter's Doubts about Science and Religion. 1889 15/12/89
Anderson, Robert Patrick
Commentary on the First Chapter of Genesis. 1889 1/11/85
Anderson, William LL.D.
Discourses. 1859 (2nd edn) 30/12/60
Anderson, William Minister
The Latest of Questions answered in the Earliest of Books. 1881 25/11/81
Andocides
Opera. 8/5/29
Andrea, Cardinal
La Curia Romana e i Gesiuti. 1866 14/10/66
Andrew, John
The practice of inoculation impartially considered. 1765 4/10/93
Andrew, Sir William Patrick
Indian railways and their probable results. 1848 4/1/61
Memoir on the Euphrates Valley route to India. 1857 24/2/57
Our scientific frontier. 1880 (3v.) 21/6/80
The Euphrates Valley route to India. A paper. 1873 19/2/73
Andrewes, Lancelot
The Greek devotions, ed. P. G. Medd. 1892 6/11/92
Andrews, Alexander
History of British Journalism. 1859 (2v.) 27/12/68 ?
Andrews, Thomas
Studium generale. A chapter of contemporary history. 1867 25/12/67
Andrews, William
Bygone England. Social studies in its historic byways and highways. 1892 9/10/93
Curious Epitaphs collected from the graveyards of Great Britain and Ireland. 1883 24/10/83 ?
Old Church Lore. 1891 12/8/91
Old-Time Punishments. 1890 2/3/91
An enquiry into the affairs of Ireland. 1731 18/3/86
A new analogy between religion and nature. 1881 18/9/81
A new world of being. 4/1/74
An exposition of the church [of Rome], *in view of recent difficulties and controversies, and the present needs of the age.* 1875 9/3/75
Anglican Church Magazine xi. 1891 17/12/91
Anglo-Continental Report. 1867 26/1/68
Anglo-Continental Society
Report of the Proceedings of Dr. Camilleri in Italy. 1861 18/9/61
Anglo-Maderensis
Letter to the Bishop of London on . . . foreign chaplaincies. 1853 30/10/53
Angus, Joseph
An Analysis of Butler's Analogy of Religion. 1882 8/8/86
Christ our Life. 1853 27/3/59
Egypt and the Bible. 1863 18/6/65
Four lectures on the advantages of a classical education. 1846 3/2/79
The Voluntary System. 1839 1/1/40
An interior. 1876 (?) 1/12/75
An introduction to vegetable physiology. 1845 1/9/53
Anne d'Autriche
Amours. 10/11/83
Annuaire des Deux Mondes 1852–1853. 1853 7/10/53
Annual Register. (n.d.) 2/6/86
Annual Register. 1774 3/1/40
Annual Register. 1791 9/1/40

Annual Register. 1800 10/4/82, 3/9/85
Annual Register. 1816 15/7/82
Annual Register. 1819 31/3/63
Annual Register. 1845 28/11/63
Annual report of the philanthropic society's farm school for the reformation of criminal boys. 1848 19/5/48
anon.
Baptism and Registration. 1837 20/5/39
Diary of an artist. 1875 23/5/75
Five years in a protestant sisterhood and ten years in a catholic convent. An autobiography. 1869 9/5/69
Gospel in the book of Joshua. 1872 (not found) 2/6/72
Anonymous journalism. 1855 21/2/55
Anquetil Duperron, Abraham Hyacinthe
Dignité du commerce. 1789 8/1/55 ?
Anselm, St.
Cur Deus Homo, tr. E. S. Prout. 1886 20/2/87
Meditations. (1859 edn) 23/3/73
Opera. 17/9/60
Anson, Sir William Reynell
Law and Custom of the Constitution. 1892 (2v. 1886–92) 3/2/90, 25/7/92
Ansted, David Thomas
Gold Seekers' Manual. 1849 9/2/49
Anstey, F. [Thomas Anstey Guthrie]
Vice Versa, or a lesson to fathers. 1882 23/11/82
Anstey, Thomas Chisholm
Guide to the history of the laws and constitution of England, consisting of six lectures. 1845 26/6/45
Anstice, Joseph
Hymns. 1836 20/7/36
Influence of the Roman Conquests upon literature and the arts in Rome. 1834 16/6/34
'Answer to a letter addressed to the Lord Chancellor on the case of the dissenters . . . by a Clergyman' 1834 10/12/34
Answer to the auditors' reports. 19/2/34
Answer to View of Internal Evidences. 24/8/56
Ante-Nicene Christian History. 1869 5/12/69
Antenori, G.
Studii sociali. 1885 28/1/89
Anti-Jacobin; or Weekly Examiner. 1798 8/7/89
Antitractarian Barrister
The morality of tractarianism. 1850 11/4/50 ?
A plain letter to Joseph Cowen. 1882 22/7/82
Apochrypha. 21/6/26
Apostolic Christians and the Catholics of Germany. 1845 5/7/45
'Appeal to the members of the S.P.C.K., on doctrinal charges lately introduced into the series, etc' 1844 2/2/44
'Appeal to the members of the S.P.C.K., on doctrinal charges lately introduced into the series of tracts circulated under their authority' 1844 2/2/44
Appeal to the people of England. 1870 29/11/70 ?
Appeal to wisdom and piety of our ancestors on Church reform. 1835 6/10/39
Appleyard, Ernest Silvanus
Claims of the Church of Rome. 1848 23/2/48
Eastern Churches. 1850 29/3/50
Proposals for Christian Union. By a member of the Church of England. 1845 12/5/47
Sure Hope of Reconciliation. 1847 12/3/48
Appuzi, Canon
Catechismo filosofico. 1850 23/2/51
A Protestant
'The "pith and marrow" of the present controversy in the Church of Scotland', sec. xi. 1841 19/5/41
Apthorp, East, and Mayhew, Jonathan
Observations on the charter and conduct of the society for the propagation of the gospel. 1856 24/8/56
Apuleius, Lucius
The metamorphosis, or golden ass, tr. T. Taylor. 30/8/42
Aquila
Excerpta ex reliquiis versionum. (1859 edn) 9/12/60
Aquinas, St. Thomas
Summa Theologica. (1762 edn) 17/9/43
Arabian Nights Entertainment. 1785 27/1/30 ?, 15/9/85 ?
Arbuthnot, Archibald
Memoirs of the remarkable life and surprising adventures of Miss Jenny Cameron. 1746 9/8/26
Arbuthnot, George
Pamphlet on the 1844 Bank Act. 1856 (priv. pr.) 28/7/56
Archaeological Review. 3. 297, 376. 7/1889. Cecil Smith 12/8/1889
Archer, Ann
Memoirs. 1787 (4v.) 5/6/45
Archer, Thomas
A Plan for Relieving Pressure on the Poor Rates. 1832 26/2/68
Arden, William Lord Alvanley
The State of Ireland Considered. 1841 16/11/41
Arduini, Carlo
La primogenitá di Galileo Galilei rivelata dalle sue lettere. 1864 18/1/67
Aredichian, P. G.
Liturgia Armena. 1832 9/6/33
Arelius, M. Antonius
Reflections, ed. G. Long. 1874 12/9/81
Areopagitica Secunda: or Speech of the Shade of John Milton on . . . Talfourd's Copyright . . . Bill. 1838 30/5/38

A report of the Hopwood wills case. 1855 12/7/55
Aretino, Pietro
Cortigiana. 7/11/61
Il Marescalco, commedia. 5/11/83
La prima (seconda) parte de Ragionamenti. 27/12/43, 25/11/61, 9/1/65, 25/10/78
La puttana errante. 11/5/59 ?
Aretius, Benedictus
A Short History of Valentinus Gentilis, the tritheist. 25/7/52
Arfwedson, Carl David
United States and Canada. 1834 19/3/35
Argument in Defense of Colonial Taxation. 1774 10/2/46
Ariosto, Ludovico
Orlando furioso, ed. A. Panizzi. 1834 (4v.) 1/11/55
Orlando furioso, ed. R. Zotti. 1822 19/8/58
Orlando furioso, tr. H. Crocker. 1755 14/7/49
Aristides
The apology of Aristides on behalf of Christians, from a Syriac ms., ed. J. R. Harris. 1891 20/8/93
Ariston: a Tragedy. 1870 20/12/75
Aristophanes
Archarneses. 30/9/73, 10/10/73, 24/1/89
Batrachoi. 11/12/73
Birds. 9/1/73, 28/10/73, 16/2/89
Ecclesiazusae. 24/12/73
Eirene. 3/11/73
Equites. 21/1/30, 25/1/89
Hippes. 13/10/73
Nephelai. 20/10/73
Nubes. 24/9/29, 19/3/30, 16/9/31
Plutus. 8/12/73
Sphekes. 23/10/73
The Frogs. 13/2/89
The Knights, tr. Thomas Mitchell. 1820 3/2/30
Thesmophoriazusae. 8/12/73
Aristotle
Aristotle on the constitution of Athens, ed. F. G. Kenyon. 1891 31/1/91
Ethics. 1/2/30, 9/5/30, 10/5/30, 1/10/30, 25/7/31, 2/11/31
Opera. 23/8/26
Poetics. 22/2/31, 7/11/55
Politics. 19/2/31, 6/2/34, 10/2/34, 15/8/34, 13/12/34, 3/10/35, 27/10/35, 10/11/35, 21/11/35, 14/8/56, 3/9/60, 28/9/60, 16/8/61
Rhetoric. 29/6/29, 24/10/29, 21/1/30, 17/11/31, 16/9/52
Arlincourt, Charles Victor Prévôt d'
L'Italie rouge. 1850 8/1/51
Armand, M.
Histoire des amours... d'Abélard et d'Eloise. 1724 (2v.) 14/1/82
Armenian litury. 17/3/33, 9/6/33
Armeniense en Turquie. 1880 6/11/77
Armit, Robert Henry
The history of New Guinea and the origin of the negro race. 1876 10/8/77
Armitage, Robert
Primitive Church in its Episcopacy. 1844 30/1/44
Armitstead, J.
Letter to Lord John Russell on the Rights and Property of the Church. 1850 4/12/56
Sabbath Day Cheese Making. 1841 5/12/56
Armstrong, Mrs. D. pseud. E. Lake
Longleat. 1870 (3v.) 12/8/70
Armstrong, Edmund John
Poems by the late Edmund J. Armstrong. 1865 4/1/66
Poetical Works of Edmund J. Armstrong, ed. G. F. Armstrong. 1877 14/11/79
Armstrong, Francis
Trumpet of Armageddon. 1820 14/1/32
Armstrong, George
Abuse of Power in the State: the cause and support of corrupt power in the Church. 1838 3/2/39
The Duke [funeral oration]. 1852 5/12/52
Armstrong, George Francis
Stories of Wicklow. 1886 13/5/86
Tragedy of Israel. 1872 (3v. 1872–6) 6/4/73, 30/1/76
Armstrong, John Bishop of Grahamstown
Sermons on the Festivals. 1845 23/1/53
Parochial Sermons. 1854 16/5/57
Armstrong, John Physician and Poet
Poetical Works. 1781 28/12/65, 27/4/69, 10/4/82
Armstrong, Nicholas
A Funeral Address... Rev. W. Wilks. 1832 26/2/68 ?
Sermons on Various Subjects. 1854 14/2/69
Army Purchase Question... evidence of Royal Commission. 1858 27/2/60
Arnando, Giovanni Battista
Il Nihilism. 1879 27/12/79
Arnason, Jón
Icelandic legends, tr. G. E. J. Powell & E. Magnusson, 2nd series. 1866 26/3/66
Arnaud, Abbé Martial Marcet de la Roche
Mémoires d'un jeune Jésuite. 1828 14/1/55
Arnauld, Agnès
Lettres publiées sur les textes authentiques avec une introduction par M.P. Fangère. 1858 (2v. 1858) 21/2/58, 21/3/58
Arnauld, Antoine
La perpétuité de la foy de l'église catholique touchant l'eucharistie. 16/4/48
Arnobius
Adversus Gentes. 19/11/75

Arnold, Sir Edwin
Adzuma; or, the Japanese wife. A play. 1893 12/3/93
Education in India. A Letter. 1860 25/6/62
Indian Song of Songs. 1875 8/8/76
Pearls of the Faith. 1883 19/12/82
The Song Celestial. 1885 3/6/85
Arnold, Frederick
Our Bishops and Deans. 1875 (2v.) 4/8/75
The Public Life of Lord Macaulay. 1862 29/3/62, 27/8/62
Arnold, Matthew
A French Eton; or, middle class education and the State. 1864 10/6/64
Culture and Anarchy. 1869 30/3/69
England and the Italian Question. 1859 2/8/59
Essays in Criticism. 1865 15/9/65 ?
Irish essays and others. 1882 5/4/82, 19/1/86
Last essays. 1877 20/5/77
Literature and Dogma. 1873 7/6/73
Merope, a tragedy. 1858 1/1/58
On Christmas, *C.R.* xlvii.457, 517 (April). 1885 1/4/85
On Translating Homer. 1860 2/2/61, 9/1/63
On Translating Homer. Last Words. 1862 29/3/62
Poems. 1856 2/5/57
Sohrab and Rustum. 1853 9/3/55
St. Paul and Protestantism. 1870 14/11/69, 5/4/76
Study of Celtic Literature. 1867 14/6/67
The Letters, Speeches and Tracts of Edmund Burke on Irish Affairs. 1881 8/7/81
The Poetry of Byron. 1881 8/7/81
The Popular Education of France. 1861 11/6/61
Arnold, Sir Robert Arthur
English drunkenness and Swedish licensing. 1877 7/2/77
Free Trade in Land. 1871 7/7/71
From the Levant, the Black Sea, and the Danube. 1868 (2v.) 8/5/78 ?
History of the Cotton Famine. 1864 26/7/64, 31/7/65
Arnold, Thomas
Christian duty of conceding the Roman Catholic claims. 1829 4/4/29
Fragment on the Church. 1844 17/12/45
History of Rome. 1839 (3v. 1839–43) 19/2/45, 29/11/56
History of the Peloponnesian war [by Thucydides], ed. T. Arnold. 1830 (3v. 1830–5) 21/1/31
Introductory lectures on modern history. 1842 22/10/42
Man Created. (n.d.) 15/2/35
Postscript to Principles of Church Reform. 1833 24/5/33
Principles of Church Reform. 1833 30/1/33
Sermons. 1829 (3v. 1829–34) 1/5/30, 10/6/30, 25/12/30, 1/1/32, 4/11/32, 7/4/33, 23/6/33, 20/10/33, 25/5/34, 1/6/34, 22/6/34, 27/7/34, 21/9/34, 28/9/34, 26/10/34, 11/1/35, 18/1/35, 8/2/35, 22/3/35, 29/3/35, 26/4/35, 10/5/35, 7/6/35, 14/6/35, 28/6/35, 19/7/35, 2/8/35, 9/8/35, 27/9/35, 29/5/36, 5/6/36, 28/6/40, 5/7/40
Sermons on Scripture. 1845 6/4/49
Thirteen letters on our social condition, addressed to the editor of the Sheffield Courant. 1832 16/12/32
Arnoldt, Johann Friedrich Julius
Timoleon. 1850 5/5/80
Aroux, Eugène
Dante Hérétique, révolutionnaire et socialiste. 1854 2/9/78
Arrivabene, Carlo
Urgency of the Venetian Question. 1864 14/6/64
Arthur, William
Count Campello. An autobiography. 1881 19/11/81
Italy in Transition. 1860 8/7/60
Modern Jove. 1873 22/5/73
The Pope, the Kings and the People. 1877 23/2/77, 20/1/78
A Saxon's remedy for Irish discontent. 1868 21/3/68
Ascham, Roger
The Schoolmaster. 21/8/37
A second letter to Councillor Blackburn. 1836 22/10/36
Asgill, John
Defence upon his expulsion from the Commons. 1712 24/4/83 ?
Ashcroft, T.
Turko-Servian War. A Lecture. 1876 9/11/76
Ashe, Isaac
Divine origin of Christianity. 1875 27/6/75
Ashley, Anthony Evelyn Melbourne
Life of Palmerston. 1876 (2v.) 17/2/76
Ashton, John
Social Life in the Reign of Queen Anne. 1882 (2v.) 15/8/82, 18/11/82
Ashton, Samuel Elkanah
Commercial Depression. 1879 1/2/79 ?
Ashworth, Henry
Pamphlet on the factory bill. 1833 24/4/33
The Preston Strike. 1854 18/10/54
Ashworth, James George
Imperial Ben. 1879 23/1/79
Asiatic Quarterly Review. 6. 60. 7/1893. Siam 24/7/1893
Aspinall, James
Address . . . at free trade meeting. 1844 12/4/44
Parish Sermons. 1854 13/8/54

A statement by the society of apothecaries, on... the Apothecaries' Act. 1844 20/12/44
A Statement of Facts. 1837 2/2/37
A statement of facts relative to the island of Jamaica. 1852 18/6/52
Atcheson, N.
Collection of reports on British trade. 1807 12/10/47
Athanasius
Festal Letters... ed. W. Cureton. 1848 22/4/48
Athenaeus
Deipnosophistai. (3v. tr) 29/6/55, 10/6/78
Atherton, John
The Case of John Atherton. 1710 10/12/81
Atkins, Thomas
Reminiscences of twelve years' residence in Tasmania. 1869 27/8/71
Atkinson, A.
Ireland exhibited to England. 1823 (2v.) 5/2/58 ?
Atkinson, Henry George
Letters on the laws of man's nature and development. 1851 6/8/90
Atkinson, John Christopher
Forty years in a moorland parish. 1891 14/4/92, 4/9/92
Atkinson, Lucy
Recollections of Tartar Steppes and their inhabitants. 1863 21/7/63
Atkinson, Miles
Practical sermons. 1812 (2v.) 28/10/49
Atkinson, Thomas Witlam
Travels in the regions of the upper and lower Amoor. 1860 30/7/60
Atkinson, William
Principles of political economy. 1840 23/6/40
Spirit of Magna Carta. 1841 21/5/41
A treatise on political reform, or vote by lot the only way to obtain a pure election, by 'Mentor'. 1837 25/3/59
Attention aux Balkans!. 1876 23/11/76
Atterbury, Francis
Power of charity to cover sin. 1708 4/8/39
Auber, Peter
China. An outline of its government, laws, and policy. 1834 15/5/40
Aubertin, Charles
Étude critique sur les rapports supposés entre Sénèque et Saint Paul. 1857 29/10/85
Aubin, Penelope
Life of Carlotta Du Pont. 1739 8/10/82
Auchmuty, Arthur Compton
Dives and Pauper, and other sermons. 1887 18/8/89
Audin, Jean Marie Vincent
Histoire... de M. Luther. 1839 (3v. 1839–46) 11/10/74
Life of Luther. 1841 7/11/44
Audisio, G.
Idea storica e razionale della diplomazia ecclesiastica. 1864 25/11/66
Augier, Guillaume Victor Émile
Le Fils de Giboyer. Comédie en cinq actes. 1861 6/9/86
Les Effrontés. Comédie en cinq actes. 1861 1/9/86
Augustine, St.
Ad Catholicos... (de unitate ecclesiae). 15/10/37
Confessions. 3/6/32, 31/8/34, 5/10/34, 26/11/34
De Civitate Dei. 11/10/35, 21/8/36, 6/11/36, 20/12/36
De Haeresibus. 11/10/37
De Nuptiis. 7/10/37
De Ordinine. 9/8/63
De Peccatorum. 5/10/37, 16/6/39
De sancta virginitate. 21/10/37
De Utilitate Credendi. 1/10/35, 24/10/37
In Psalmos. 9/10/49
Tractatus contra quinque Haereses. 13/10/37
Augustine, Sister
Sister Augustine, Superior of the Sisters of Charity. 1880 13/2/81
Aungervyle Society
Aungervyle Society reprints, ed. E. M. Goldsmid. 1881 (4 series 1881–7) 27/4/84
Aurelius, Marcus Antonius
Reflections, ed. G. Long. 1874 12/9/81
Austen, Jane
A memoir of, by J. E. A. Leigh. 1870 24/6/71
Emma. 1816 7/10/72
Mansfield Park. 1814 7/8/50, 10/7/69
Northanger Abbey. 1818 25/7/90
Pride and Prejudice. 1813 28/11/53, 7/8/69
Austin, Alfred
Savonarola. 1881 7/12/81
The human tragedy. 1876 23/5/76
The Tower of Babel. 1874 9/2/75
Tory Horrors or the question of the hour... A letter to Gladstone. 1876 15/9/76, 11/12/76
Austin, John
A plea for the Constitution. 1859 19/3/59
The province of jurisprudence determined. 1832 (2nd edn 1861) 2/3/63
Austin, Sarah
Characteristics of Goethe. From the German of Falk, von Müller. 1833 (3v.) 23/1/93 ?
On National Education. 1839 28/5/39
Austin, William barrister
On the imminent depreciation of gold. 1853 25/7/53
Austin, William of Boston, Mass.
Letters from London: written during the years 1802 and 1803. 1804 1/1/81

Austin, William Piercy
A Charge delivered to the clergy . . . of Guiana. 1852 7/3/52
Austrian Red Book. 1868 16/3/68
Author of 'Milly Clifford'
Galveston. 1868 30/7/72
Autobiography of a 'man' of Kent. 1867 22/6/67
Autobiography of a working man. 1862 27/5/72
Automathes [R. Griffith]
Something New. Essays. 1772 29/8/78
Aveling, Frederick Wilkins
Who was Jesus Christ?. 1878 24/7/87
Aveling, Thomas William Baxter
'Why we keep the Sabbath' 1876 19/11/76
Avesani, Gian Francecso
La Pace di Villafranca. 1859 3/8/59
Avilla, Count d'
Lectures on the origin and growth of the conception of God. 1892 29/5/92
A voice for China to my countrymen, the government and my church. By a minister of the established church. 1840 14/4/40
Avrillon, Jean Baptiste Élie
Guide for . . . advent, tr. E. B. Pusey. 1844 15/12/44
Guide for . . . Lent. 1844 23/2/45
Year of Affections. 1845 20/3/45
Awdry, John Wither, and Patteson, John
Suggestions with regard to certain proposed alterations in the University and colleges of Oxford. 1854 15/3/54
A word for truth, by an English seaman. 1860 26/4/60
Aylward, A.
Transvaal of today. 1878 5/8/78 ?
Aylward, Alfred
The Transvaal of today. 1878 5/8/78
Aylwin, D. C.
A series of letters on the Navigation Laws. 1849 24/3/49
Aytoun, James
Railways and currency. 1847 18/11/47
To the independent electors of Edinburgh. 1832 2/3/52 ?
Aytoun, William Edmondstoune
Lays of the Scottish cavaliers. 1848 20/9/50, 8/11/65
Twenty-second book of Iliad, tr. W. E. Aytoun. 1839 11/1/62
Azzurri, Fr.
La nuova sala amici. 1865 29/11/66

B., R. N.
Corn and wages, or a few propositions and remarks on variations in the price of corn and . . . wages. 1841 17/6/41
Babbage, Charles
Opera. 29/7/38 ?
Passages from the life of a philosopher. 1864 9/6/64
Reflections on the decline of science in England. 1830 24/12/47, 14/4/67
Sketch of the philosophical characters of Dr. Wollaston and Sir H. Davy. 1830 14/4/67
The Exposition of 1851. 1851 25/1/52
Babington, Churchill
Mr. Macaulay's Character of the Clergy. 1849 1/1/76
Bachaumont, [J. B. Lever]
Scènes de la vie parisienne. 1878 8/11/79
Bachelor
[on] *Ecclesiastical Courts Bill.* 8/7/45
Backhouse, James
Lecture on French Protestantism. 1884 9/6/84
Bacon, Francis
Advancement of Learning. 15/12/29, 28/10/34
Advertisement . . . touching the controversies of the Church of England. 3/11/40, 16/11/40
Certain considerations touching the better pacification and edification of the Church of England. 3/11/40
Confession of faith. 16/11/40
Essays, ed. R. Whately. 1856 12/6/61
Novum Organum. 5/9/34
Bacon, Nathaniel
A relation of the fearefull Estate of Francis Spira in the year 1548. 10/12/81 ?
Bacon, Thomas Scott
The reign of God not 'the reign of law'. 1878 27/7/79
Bacon Society, Journal of the. 1. 3. 6/1887 24/5/1887
Bad Company, or the Magpye. 1796 15/9/92
Baddeley, Thomas
Sure Way to find out the true religion. 1820 9/12/38
Badeley, Edward Lowth
Considerations on divorce a vinculo. 1857 5/6/57
Badely, Edward Lowth
Privilege of religious confessions in English courts of justice considered. 1865 5/8/65
Speech [on deceased wife's sister]. 1847 27/1/48
Baden-Powell, George Smith
Protection and Bad Times. 1880 12/4/80
Badger, George Percy
History of the Imams and Seyyids of Oman. 1871 2/10/77
The Government in its relations with education and Christianity in India. 1858 9/10/59
Visit to the Isthmus of Suez Canal works. 1862 16/5/62
Badnall, Hopkins
Pamphlet on the Colonial Church. 15/12/52 ?
Baedeker, Carl
Southern Italy and Sicily. 1880 24/12/88

Baffi, V.
I poeti della patria. 1863 22/8/66 ?
Bagdon, James Oscar
A brief comparison of the . . . Anglican and Greek churches. 1869 22/5/70
Bagehot, Walter
Biographical Studies [with essay on Gladstone]. 1881 13/4/81
Economic Studies, ed. R. H. Hutton. 1880 5/2/80
Essays on parliamentary reform. 1883 26/11/83
Estimates of some Englishmen and Scotchmen. 1858 5/3/58, 11/1/65
Literary Studies. 1879 (2v.) 2/6/79
Lombard Street. 1873 7/10/73
Parliamentary Reform; an essay. 1859 8/3/59, 24/11/65
Physics and Politics. 1872 27/12/72
Practical Plan for Assimilating the English and American money. 1869 11/2/69
The English Constitution. 1867 18/2/67
Bagenal, Philip Henry Dudley
The American Irish and their influence on Irish politics. 1882 21/7/82
The priest in politics. 1893 11/6/93
Baggs, Charles Michael
Funeral Oration delivered at the solemn obsequies of the Lady Gwendoline Talbot, Princess Borghese. 1841 22/8/41
Bagot, Daniel
A letter to . . . the vestry of St. James Chapel, in reference to the Scottish communion service. 1842 11/12/42
Art of Poetry by Horace, tr. D. Bagot. 1863 11/12/63
Inspiration of the Holy Scriptures. 1878 7/4/78
Letter to a friend. 1845 14/6/45
Sermon preached . . . on . . . the day after the death of Prince Albert. 1861 12/1/62
The Atonement. 1860 25/12/60
Bagot, John
Observations on the present law affecting home made spirits in bond. 1853 30/3/53
Bagot, Richard
Charge delivered to the clergy of the diocese of Bath and Wells, at the primary visitation. 1847 22/6/47
Charge delivered to the clergy of the diocese of Oxford. 1838 13/2/39
Bagshaw, Edward
Two arguments in parliament. 2/12/49
Bagshawe, John B.
Credentials of the Catholic Church. 1879 31/8/79
Bagwell, Richard
A plea for national education. 1875 3/8/75
Bailey, Philip James
The Age; a colloquial satire. 1829 11/6/50
Baillie, Joanna
Alienated Manor. 1836 14/7/41
Orra: a tragedy. 1851 25/10/75
The second marriage. 1828 1/8/28
Bain, Alexander
James Mill. A biography. 1882 21/9/84
Bain, Donald
Egregious and dangerous fallacies of the anti-corn law league. 1843 18/5/43
Ireland, its wants and capabilities. 1836 17/8/43
Substance of two letters . . . on Ireland. 1837 24/7/43
Tithes, their origin and now proper use. 1832 31/1/34 ?
Bain, Ebenezer
Merchant and craft guilds. 1887 30/11/87
Baines, Edward
History of Cotton Manufacture in Great Britain. 1835 19/10/41, 21/9/61
National education. 1856 9/4/56
Speech on Borough Franchise. 1861 19/4/61
Baines, Thomas
A History of the Commerce and Town of Liverpool. 1852 6/8/51
Baker, C.
Livy's History of Rome, tr. C. Baker. 1814 21/9/30
Baker, Harriet Newell
Stopping the Leak. 1865 31/8/73
Baker, James chaplain
The three personal authorities by divine right, God's remedy against lawlessness. 1874 20/1/75
Baker, Lt. Col. James
Turkey in Europe. 1877 9/5/77
Baker, James of Clifton
A forgotten Englishman . . . Peter Payne, the Wycliffite. 1890 25/8/90
Our foreign competitors: their life and labour. 1892 27/2/93
Baker, Sir R.
Theatrum redivivum, or the theatre vindicated. 23/11/62
Baker, Samuel White
Cyprus as I saw it in 1879. 1879 12/11/79
Explorations of the Nile. 1866 (2v.) 11/6/66
Nile tributaries of Abyssinia. 1867 28/12/67
Baker, T.
Letters to and from Lord Lyttelton on vaccination. 1877 15/1/77
Baker, T. H.
Records of seasons, prices of produce. 1883 19/1/84
Bakewell, Frederick Collier
Natural evidence of a future life. 1835 29/7/36
Balbo, Cesare
Della storia d'Italia. 1846 20/9/51

Balch, E.
An author's love: being the unpublished letters of P. Mérimée's Inconnue, by D. T. S. [E. Balch]. 1889 (2v.) 6/4/89, 21/8/90
Balderwood, R. G.
Robbery under arms. 1888 (3v.) 4/6/88, 1/9/88, 6/1/89
Baldwin, John Denison
Pre-historic nations. 1869 16/8/91
Baldwin, L.
The story of a marriage. 1892 (3v.) 27/3/92
Bale, George Gilley Pritchett
The elements of the anatomy and physiology of man. 1879 16/6/79
Balfour, Arthur James
A fragment on progress. 1892 23/4/94 ?
The religion of humanity. 1888 6/1/89
Balfour, Elizabeth
The red manor. 1883 9/4/84
Balgarnie, Robert
Arkite worship. 1881 3/10/81
Ball, John
What is to be done for Ireland?. 1849 17/2/49
Ball, John Thomas
Historical Review of Legislative Systems Operative in Ireland. 1888 4/6/88
Ball, Robert Stawell
Starland. 1889 21/8/90
Story of the Heavens. 1885 (2v. 1885–8) 9/5/89, 29/6/89, 19/12/89
Ball, Thomas Hanly
Vindication of the established Church of England & Ireland. 1868 1/8/69
Ballantyne, John
Comparison of English and dissenting churches. 1830 25/12/31
Ballantyne, Robert Michael
Hudson's Bay. 1848 5/7/49
Ballerinius, Petrus
De vi ac ratione primatûs romanorum pontificum. 1845 (1845–7) 18/4/51
Balleydier, Alphonse
Histoire de la révolution de Rome. 1851 2/10/51
Ballou, M. M.
Summer journey to Alaska. 1891 25/3/91 ?
Balmes, Jaime Luciano
Protestantism and Catholicity compared. 1849 29/2/52
Balzac, Honoré de
Séraphita. 1885 29/6/89
The Comédie Humaine and its author, by H. H. Walker. 1879 13/1/79 ?
Bamford, Samuel
Passages in the Life of a Radical. 1841 (2v. 1841–3) 4/5/49
Bancroft, George
History of the American Revolution. 1852 (3v. 1852–4) 24/7/55
History of the Constitution of the United States. 1882 (2v.) 11/8/82
History of the United States of America. 1848 15/7/48, 14/10/61, 14/2/75, 21/6/87
Bandello, Matteo
Novella. 13/10/42, 11/9/45
Banerjea, Krishna-Mohana
Rig-Veda Sanhita. 1875 8/1/82
Banfield, Thomas E.
Six Letters to... Peel. 1843 3/2/43
Banim, Michael
Tales by the O'Hara family. 1825 4/1/27
Bankes, George Nugent
A day of my life, by an Eton boy. 1877 23/2/77
Banks, John
The Destruction of Troy. 26/12/82
Bannatyne, Dugald J.
Handbook of Republican institutions in the United States of America. 1887 15/12/87
Bannister, Saxe
The control of the Privy Council. 1844 30/4/46
Bannister, T.
The Suffrage nationalized. 1853 28/11/53
Barbara di Gravellona, Francesco
Leo XIII... Verses. 1888 11/2/89
Barbarin, Antoine
Ordonnance... portant à la défence de lire... 14/10/51
Barbauld, Anna Letitia
Collection of essays and tracts in theology, ed. J. Sparks. 1823 30/1/48
Barbazan, Étienne
L'Ordre de Chevalerie avec dissertation... 1759 18/9/61
Barber, Joseph
Sermon on 'Party Spirit' in Sermons. 1809 24/2/33
Barber, Thomas Walter
Scientific Theology. 1884 14/9/90
Barber, William Cambridge
The religious difficulty in national education. 1875 6/1/76
Barberini, Francesco
Collectio Romana bipartita... historiae ecclesiasticae monumentorium. 5/12/51
Barclay, Alexander of Jamaica
Practical View of Slavery. 1826 31/12/32, 1/1/33
Remarks on Emigration to Jamaica. 1840 27/2/40
Barclay, Alexander Priest
The Shyp of Folys. (1874 edn) 22/6/76
Barclay, Hugh
The justice's digest of the law of Scotland. 1894 25/2/94 ?
Barclay, Robert
Apology for the true Christian divinity. 19/10/73

Bardsley, Joseph
The Irish Church: should it be disestablished? A few plain reasons why it should not. 1868 22/8/68
Baretti, Guiseppe Marc' Antonio pseud. A. Scannabue
Opere. 1838 (4v. 1838–9) 21/11/66
Barham, Richard Harris Dalton
*Ingolds*by Legends. 1840 (3v. 1840–7) 7/6/62
The Life and remains of Theodore Edward Hook. 1849 18/2/49, 15/10/64
Baring, Alexander Lord Ashburton
Financial and Commercial Crisis considered. 1847 24/5/47
Baring, Francis Thornhill Lord Northbrook
Memorandum by the earl of Northbrook, on Viscount Cranbrook's Despatch to Lord Lytton of Nov. 18th. 1878 27/11/78 ?
Barker, Charles
The Character and Anecdotes of Charles II. 1853 26/12/86
Barker, Henry Ross
Looking Back. 1891 3/5/91, 9/11/91
Barker, H. J.
Original English. 1889 23/12/88, 27/7/89, 30/5/90
Barker, Thomas
Plain Sermons. 1858 29/12/67
Barkley, Henry C.
Between Danube and Black Sea. 1876 23/11/76
Barlow, Adela F.
Convent Experience. 1875 30/7/75
Barlow, James William
Eternal punishment and eternal death; an essay. 1865 28/9/65
History of Ireland during the period of Parliamentary experience. 1875 13/10/86
Barlow, Jane
Irish idylls. 1893 11/7/93
Barnard, James
Life of... Richard Challoner. 1784 6/3/81
Barnes, John monk
Catholico-Romanus Pacificus. 11/7/52
Select discourses concerning councils, the pope, schism. 23/6/56
Barnes, Ralph
An Appeal to the People of England. 1834 14/5/34
Letter to Russell. 1849 18/2/47
Letter to Sir J. Campbell. 1837 16/3/37
On episcopal revenues. 1850 11/7/50
Papal brief considered. 1850 20/3/51
Remarks... bishop of Natal. 1866 4/2/66
Thoughts on William Ewart Gladstone's Chapter of Autobiography. 1869 12/3/69
Barnes, Richard William
Public opinion considered in letters. 1855 11/1/56, 28/1/90 ?
Repentance of Judas. Sermon. 1865 14/2/69
Tracts on Oxford seat. 1865 7/2/65
Barnes, William
Poems of rural life in Dorset dialect. 1844 1/2/63, 15/8/66
Tiw; or... roots and stems of the English as a Teutonic tongue. 1862 27/7/69
Barnum, Phineas Taylor
The Life of P. T. Barnum written by himself. 1855 28/1/90
Baron, John pseud. Vignorniensis
Historical view of the nature and results of vaccination. 1838 15/4/40
Baronial and ecclesiastical antiquities of Scotland. 1845 (1st v.) 15/5/46
Barr, James
Anglican church architecture. 1842 3/4/42
Barr, Matthias
Poems. 1872 (2 pt.) 8/6/72
Barrett, George Slatyer
Religion in daily life. 1893 13/5/94 ?
The influence of... Dr. Pusey, and of the Oxford movement. 1882 13/10/82
Barrett, Jonathan Tyers
Temptation of Christ in the wilderness. 1821 9/6/83
Barrett, William Garland
Veiled gospels from 'New Sketches'. 1859 27/9/68
Barri, Comptesse Du
Mémoires. 1829 (4v.) 9/10/48, 7/7/61, 30/5/85
Barrie, James Matthew
A window in Thrums. 1889 30/5/90
Auld licht idylls. 1888 1/11/88
The little minister. 1891 (3v.) 9/11/91
Barrington, John Shute
An essay on the teaching and witness of the holy spirit. 1785 18/3/88, 16/6/89
Barrington, Jonah
Personal sketches of his own times. 1827 (3v. 1827–32) 30/10/77
Barrington, Matthew
Letter to Peel. 1848 20/7/48
Barrister, A
Orthodox theories of prayer. 1874 23/8/74
Barrister of Lincoln's Inn, A
King's College and Mr. Maurice. 1854 7/1/74
Barron, Henry Winston
Queen Victoria and Italy. 1859 4/12/67
Barrot, Camille Hyacinthe Odilon
De la centralisation et de ses effets. 1861 25/10/71
Barrow, Isaac
Sermon upon the passion of our blessed Saviour. 13/12/29
Barrow, John D.D.
The case of Queen's college. 1854 18/2/54

Barrow, John F.R.S.
The life... of Sir Francis Drake. 1843 5/1/84 ?
Barrow, Sir John
A voyage to Cochin China. 1806 24/6/44
Barrow, John Croker
Mary of Nazareth. 1889 (3v. 1889–90) 23/12/88
Towards the truth. 1885 25/10/85
Barrow, William
Familiar sermons. 1819 19/10/28
Barruel, Augustin
Storia del clero di Francia in tempo della rivoluzione tr. di Farfa. 1795 (3v.) 6/10/38
Barry, Alfred
Church questions of the day. 1868 14/1/72 ?
Clergy and laity in the church. Sermon. 1877 15/7/77
Manifold witness for Christ. 1880 14/11/80
Barry, Henry Boothby
Few words on Oxford institutions. 1854 21/2/54
Remarks on the three proposals for reforming the construction of the university of Oxford. 1854 13/1/54
Thoughts on renovation of cathedral institutions. 1852 19/11/52
Barry, Michael Joseph
The pope and the Romagna. 1860 3/3/60
Barry, M. J.
Ireland as she was, as she is, and as she shall be. 1845 7/9/89
Barry, William Francis
The new Antigone. 1887 (3v.) 18/11/87
Barter, William Brudfnell
English church not in schism. 1845 19/4/46
Gainsaying of Core. 1846 3/10/47
Letter to the Hebdomadal Board. 1845 31/1/45
Postscript to 'English Church not in schism'. 1846 19/4/46
Remarks made by Lord Morpeth. 1841 7/4/41
Barthélemy, Comte de
Marie Antoinette. 1882 11/11/82
Bartholmess, Christian Jean Guillaume
Huet, évêque d'Avranches. 1850 8/3/74, 18/2/83 ?
Bartholomew, Christopher Churchill
Address to clergy... of Plympton. 1867 13/10/67
Bartholony, François
Quelques idées financières. 1860 23/2/60
Bartle, George W.
Jesus of Nazareth. 1877 29/8/77
Scriptural doctrine of Hades. 1869 11/1/74, 20/8/76
Bartlett, D. W.
Life of Joan of Arc. 1855 14/3/71
Bartlett, Thomas
Memoirs of the life... of Joseph Butler. 1839 3/10/58, 6/9/63
Bartoli, Daniello
Dell'istoria della compagnia di Giesu l'Asia. 17/11/61
Bartoli, Daniello, and Maffei, G. P.
The life of St. Francis Xavier with a preface by Dr. Faber. 1858 8/8/58
Barton, John
The reality, but not the duration of future punishment, is revealed. 1865 23/6/72
Bartrum, Edward
Promotion by merit. 1866 24/7/66
Baruchson, Arnold
Address. 1861 28/11/61
Baruffaldi, Girolamo
Il grillo. 1738 25/9/61
Barville, John
An account of the late conversion of Mr. John Barville alias Barton from popery to the reformed Church of England. 1710 12/9/58
Barzellotti, Giacomo
David Lazzaretti di Arcidosso detto il santo. 1885 18/3/88
Bashkirtseff, Marie
Journal de Marie Bashkirtseff. 1877 (2v.) 20/7/89
Journal, translated by M. Blind. 1890 13/3/90 ?
Lettres. 1891 25/6/91
Basire, Isaac
The ancient liberty of the Brittanick church. 22/6/56
Bassanio, [John Arthur Coupland]
Edward the Confessor. 1886 9/12/92
Bassett, Francis Tilney
Catholic epistle of St. James. 1876 20/11/81
Bastard, Thomas Horlock
Scepticism and social justice. 1872 26/1/73
Batacchi, Domenico
Il Zibaldone. 1805 21/10/87 ?
Bate, John
Influence of mind on mind. 1883 13/5/83
Perils of ritualism in the Churches. 1881 18/9/81, 19/1/90
Bate, S. Stringer pseud. Walter S. Raleigh
Cardinal Wolsey and the love of the poets. 1874 28/11/75 ?
Bateman, Frederic
On aphasia, or loss of speech. 1890 16/5/90
Bateman, Josiah
La Martinière. 1839 3/2/40
Life of Henry Venn Elliott. 1868 8/7/83
Bates, Ely
A Chinese fragment. 1786 11/6/74
Bather, Lucy Elizabeth
Footprints in the sands of time. Biographies for young people. 1860 12/9/61

Bath Guide, the original. 1811 3/8/68
Bathurst, Henry
Memoirs of the late Dr. H. Bathurst. 1857 17/4/59
Bathurst, S.
Memoirs of M. J. de Staal. 1877 25/6/76
Battle of Mordalloc; or, how we lost Australia. 1888 24/11/92
Battle of the faith. 2/1/87
Batty, Beatrice
An English girl's account of a Moravian settlement in the Black Forest. 1858 18/7/58
Bauer, Caroline
Posthumous memoirs. 1884 (4v. 1884–5) 11/10/84, 18/10/84
Baumgarten, Michael
Letter to the earl of Shaftesbury on the oppression of the Christian . . . by the Danish government. 1857 9/5/57
Baup, Charles
Précis des faits . . . Canton de Vaud. 1846 4/10/46
Baur, Ferdinand Christian
Die Christliche Lehre. 1841 (3v. 1841–43) 2/11/45
Erwiederung auf . . . Möhler. 1836 31/10/45
Geschichte der christlichen Kirche. 1863 (5v. 1863–77) 17/1/75 ?
Baur, Wilhelm
Religious life in Germany during the wars of independence. 1870 (2v.) 8/11/83
Baxendell, Joseph
On changes in the rates of mortality from different diseases. 1876 14/1/77
Baxter, Richard
Life of Richard Baxter, by J. H. Davies. 1887 20/5/88
Practical works . . . with a life of the author . . . by the Rev. W. Orme. 1830 2/6/44
Reliquae Baxterianae. (3v.) 22/9/89
Baxter, Robert Dudley
[Pamphlet to R. M. Milnes, who replied 1852]. 1852 6/4/52
English parties and Conservatism. 1870 1/2/70
Narrative of facts. 1833 12/3/33
National debts. 1871 22/9/70
Panic of 1866 with its lessons on the Currency Act. 1866 22/6/67
Re-distribution of seats and the counties. 1866 12/5/66
Reform Bill. The franchise returns critically examined. 1866 14/4/66
Taxation of the United Kingdom. 1869 22/1/69
Baxter, William Edward
Free Italy. Lecture. 1874 16/12/74
Bayford, Augustus Frederick
Gorham, clerk, against the Bishop of Exeter, the argument . . . on behalf of Rev. G. C. Gorham. 1849 4/3/50
Bayle, Pierre
Critique . . . Calvinisme de Maimbourg. 1714 29/1/47
Dictionnaire historique. (2v.) 27/2/49, 19/9/61, 27/9/61
Bayley, John Robert Laurie Emilius
Sermons on the person and work of the Holy Spirit. 1860 27/4/90
Bayley, Peter
Orestes in Argos. 1825 21/5/61 ?
Bayliss, Sir Wyke
The witness of art. 1876 18/2/78
Bayly, Ada Ellen pseud. Edna Lyell
Donovan. 1882 (3v.) 20/3/83, 27/4/83
We two. A novel. 1885 9/3/86
Bayly, Anselm
Alliance of musick poetry & oratory. 1789 22/6/57, 7/12/89, 18/7/90
Bayly, Elisabeth Boyd
Jonathan Merle. 1889 7/12/89, 18/7/90
Baynes, Robert Hall
'Man, being in honour, abideth not.' Sermon. 1865 19/3/76
Bazancourt, César de
The Crimean Expedition, to the capture of Sebastopol, tr. R. H. Gould. 1856 (2v.) 28/3/56
Bazely, Henry
Henry Bazely: the Oxford evangelist. By E. L. Hicks. 1886 23/4/86
Beale, Anne
Country courtships, a novel. 1870 (3v.) 20/8/70
Beale, Lionel Smith
Disease germs. 1870 13/1/71
Beamish, Charles
[pamphlet against superannuation]. 1833 29/3/33
Beamish, Richard
Memoir of the life of Sir Marc Isambard Brunel. 1862 24/3/62
Bean, James
Zeal without innovation. 1808 27/10/54, 3/8/79
Beard, Arthur
Bar-Jonah, the son of the Resurrection. 1887 3/7/87
Beard, Charles
Martin Luther and the reformation in Germany. 1889 15/12/89
The Reformation of the sixteenth century. 1883 16/8/84
The soul's way to God. 1875 13/4/75 ?
The universal Christ and other sermons. 1888 27/2/89, 29/9/89
Beard, John Relly
Manual of Christian evidence. 1868 16/8/68
Progress of religious thought. 1861 26/3/71

Beardsley, Eben Edwards
Life . . . of the Right Reverend Samuel Seabury. 1881 10/7/81
Beattie, William
Portraits of eminent conservatives. 1846 31/12/40
Beatty, Pakenham
Spretae carmina Musae. 1893 3/11/93
Beauclerk, Caroline Frederica and Henrietta Mary
Tales of fashion and reality. 1836 27/6/36
Beauclerk, Lady Diana de Vere
A summer and winter in Norway. 1868 25/3/69
Beauclerk, William Nelthorpe
Rural Italy. 1888 27/2/89
Beaujoint, Jules
Secret memoirs of Madame de Pompadour. 1886 27/9/86
Beaulieu, Luke de
Reformed monastery. (2 pt.) 1/10/65
Beaumont, Francis, and Fletcher, John
King and no king. 2/8/27, 3/8/91
The custom of the country. 7/11/61, 9/11/61
The maid's tragedy. 9/11/61
The tragedy of Valentian. 3/8/91
Beaumont, Gustave Auguste de la Bonninière de
Ireland, Social, Political and Religious. 1840 (2v. tr.) 4/2/40
L'Irlande, sociale, politique, et religieuse. 1839 (2v.) 25/2/70
Marie, ou l'Esclavage aux États-Unis. 1835 25/5/35
Memoir . . . Alexis de Tocqueville. 1861 18/10/61
Beaumont du Repaire, Christophe de
Mandement . . . portant condamnation d'un livre qui a pour titre: Emile, ou de l'éducation, par J. J. Rousseau. 1762 29/8/58
Beauvoir, Ludovic de
Voyage round the world. 1869 (3v. 1869–72) 18/9/73
Beaven, James
On intercourse between the Church of England and the churches of the East. 1840 26/9/41
Recreations of a long vacation. 1846 30/5/46
Beavis, L. U.
National capital is movable. 1871 22/11/79 ?
Beccadelli, Ludovico
Vita del cardinale Gasparo Contarini. 1746 2/9/77
Becher, John Thomas
Anti-pauper system. 1828 2/5/34
Becker, Victor
L'auteur de l'Imitation. 1882 9/5/86, 18/7/86
Beckers, Dr.
Onania. 13/7/29
Beckford, William Thomas
Italy, Spain and Portugal. 1840 11/8/46
Beckmann, Johann
Des Herrn Sagens Chemische Untersuchung verschiedener Mineralien. 1775 4/2/58 ?
History of inventions and discoveries. 1797 (4v. 1797–1814) 6/4/47
Becon, Thomas
Works. (3v. 1560–64) 19/7/45
Beddoe, John
Address to Anthropological society. 1870 16/4/70
Bedell, William
Life of Bishop Bedell, ed. Mayor. 1871 17/12/71
Bedford, James
The great comet. 1857 29/5/57
Beecham, John
Colonization . . . of New Zealand. 1838 8/2/38, 4/6/38
Remarks upon the latest official documents relating to New Zealand. 1838 4/6/38
Beechey, Henry William
The literary works of Sir J. Reynolds. 1835 (2v.) 29/5/35
Beeston, William
Hieronymian Hebrew. 1843 8/5/64
Beeton, Samuel Orchart
Illustrated dictionary of religion, philosophy, politics and law. 1886 1/1/91
Behn, Aphra
Feign'd Curtizans. 17/8/37
Histories and novels. 2/9/58
Oroonoko. 24/8/87
The Widow Ranter. 16/9/51
Behr, François Jean Désiré
Recherches sur l'histoire des temps héroïques de la Grèce. 1856 4/8/77
Beith, Alexander
Memories of disruption times. 1847 24/6/77
Beitmann, Hans
Hans Beitmann's party. 1868 18/6/89
Beke, Charles Tilstone
Jesus the Messiah. 1872 5/5/72
Belaney, Robert
Mr. Gladstone himself reviewed and analysed. 1876 19/2/76
Belcher, Thomas Waugh
Our Lord's miracles of healing considered in relation to some modern objections and to medical science. 1872 2/6/72, 6/9/91
Robert Brett of Stoke Newington. His life and work. 1889 6/3/92
Beldam, Joseph
A letter to the Right Hon. Lord John Nelson . . . on national education. 1850 11/7/50
On sugar duties. 24/9/41
Bell, Alexander Graham
The voice by wire and postcard . . . containing

descriptions of Bell's and Dolbear's telephones. 1878 15/3/78
Bell, Alexander Melville
Visible speech, every language universally legible, exactly as spoken. 1864 30/9/64
Bell, Andrew
Experiment in Education made at the Male Asylum of Madras. 1797 17/4/41
Bell, Arthur John
Why does man exist?. 1890 25/1/91
Bell, James
Ancient History, tr. C. Rollin. 1828 1/3/30
Bell, Robert
Early ballads illustrative of history, traditions and customs, ed. R. Bell. 1856 18/9/82 ?
Life of Canning. 1846 15/7/46
Bellairs, Blanche
Transvaal War 1880–81. 1885 8/5/85
Bellairs, Henry Walford
Traditions of Nuneaton and its neighborhood. 1860 5/11/75 ?
Work. The law of God, the lot of man. Sermon. 1852 25/7/52
Bellamy, Edward
Looking backward, 2000–1887. 1888 6/10/89
Bellamy, George Anne
Apology for life . . . written by herself. 1785 (5v.) 28/1/48
Memoirs . . . by a gentleman. 1785 11/7/85
Bellarmi, V.
Del prim. art. dello Statuto in relatione colla questione romana. 1888 19/2/88
Bellarmino, St. Robert
De arte bene moriendi libri duo. 29/1/88
Die Selbstbiographie. 1887 10/4/87
Dottrina cristiana. 1831 24/3/33
Bellet, Charles Félix
Le manuel de M. Paul Bert. 1882 29/12/84
Belleysan, D. Bugistre-
Les intrigues moscovites en Turquie. 1877 26/3/77
Belly, Félix
Déchéance et liberté. 1870 2/9/70
Beloe, William
History of Herodotus. 1799 9/11/29
Belot, Adolphe
*La bouche de Madame X***.* 1882 17/11/88
Mademoiselle Girard, ma femme. 1870 6/6/88
Belsham, Thomas
Letters to the . . . bishop of London, in vindication of the Unitarians. 1815 11/6/29
Memoirs of the late revd. Theophilus Lindsey. 1812 27/5/55
New testament. 1808 4/8/29
Belsham, William
Memoirs of the reign of George III. 1795 (4v.) 6/1/38
Bemis, George
American neutrality. 1867 11/2/67
Benham, William
Catherine and Crawford Tait, wife and son of Archibald Campbell . . . memoir. 1879 26/10/79
Benisch, Abraham
Bishop Colenso's objections to the historical character of the Pentateuch and the Book of Joshua. 1863 18/8/78 ?
Benison, Henry Worsley Seymour Worsley-
Nature's fairyland. 1888 15/5/88
Bennett, Anne Ramsden
[On Leopardi]. 18/6/54
Iphigenia in Tauris, with original poems. 1851 3/9/51
Lucrezia Borgia [in *Weldon's Register*]. 1862 6/12/62
Our Lady of good counsel in Genazzano. 1888 4/11/88
Passing away. 1878 17/11/78
Bennett, Hugh
A plain statement . . . that marriage within the prohibited degrees is forbidden in Scripture. 1849 21/2/49
Bennett, James
Lectures on the history of Jesus Christ. 1825 (3v.) 1/6/45
Memoirs of the life of Rev. David Bogue. 1827 26/6/53
Sermon. 7/12/45
Bennett, William Cox
Narrative poems and ballads. 1875 4/4/84
Bennett, William James Early
A farewell letter to his parishioners. 1851 8/6/51
A pastoral letter to the parishioners of Frome. 1852 16/4/52
Apostasy. A sermon in reference to the late event at St. Paul's, Knightsbridge. 1847 16/11/47
Defence of the Catholic faith. 1873 22/2/74
First letter to . . . Russell, on the present persecution of a certain portion of the English Church. 1850 15/12/50
Letters to my children on Church subjects. 1843 (2v. 1843–50) 29/12/50
Plea for toleration in the Church of England. Letter to Pusey. 1867 25/7/67
Some results of the tractarian movement of 1833. 1867 3/4/86
The Church, the Crown and the State, their junction or their separation. 1850 26/2/50
The old church porch. 1867 (5v. 1867–8) 30/6/67
Why church rates should be abolished. 1861 24/3/61
Benrath, Carl
Bernardino Ochino of Sienna. 1876 31/12/76

Benson, Arthur Christopher
Poems. 1893 31/10/93
William Laud, sometime Archbishop of Canterbury. A study. 1887 11/12/87
Benson, Christopher
Certain and sufficient maintenance, the right of Christ's ministers. 1834 23/2/34
Congé d'élire, or the present mode of making English bishops. 1848 12/2/48
Discourses on tradition and episcopy. 1839 15/9/39
On the proceedings of the ecclesiastical commission. Letter. 1837 31/5/38
Rubrics and the canons of the Church of England considered. 1845 20/2/45
Sermon. 10/3/33
Benson, Edward Frederic
Dodo, a detail of the day. 1893 (2v.) 14/9/93, 16/9/93
Benson, Edward White
Christ and his times. 1889 19/1/90
Benson, Mary Eleanor
At sundry times and in divers manners. 1891 (2v.) 29/11/91, 4/3/92, 3/4/92
Bentinck, George
Address to King's Lynn electors. 1847 27/7/47
Lord George Bentinck: a political biography, by B. Disraeli. 1852 5/2/52
Racing life of Lord George Bentinck, by F. C. Lawley and J. Kent. 1892 4/10/92
Bentley, George C. T.
'Conservatives on themselves' in *Fortnightly Review*, xliii.611. 1885 (May 1885) 4/5/85
Bentley, Richard
A confutation of atheism. 16/12/55
A sermon upon popery. 1715 16/12/55
Richard Bentley, by R. C. Jebb. 1876 20/5/82
Bentley, Samuel
Sermons on prayer. 1871 (1871 edn) 1/2/74 ?
Benvenuti, Bice
Fantasia e realtà. Novelle. 1886 14/3/91
Béranger, Pierre Jean de
Chanson inédite. 1828 11/5/75
Oeuvres complètes. 1834 (4v.) 26/10/48
Berens, Edward
Christmas stories (poacher's tale). 1823 18/5/30
Beresford, John George
Charge, delivered at his annual visitation. 1845 8/3/46
Correspondences... illustrative of the last thirty years of the Irish parliament. 1854 16/8/93
Letter to the... bishop of Exeter on... church discipline bill. 1856 20/3/56
Beresford, Marcus Gervais
Charge... addressed to... Diocese of Armagh and Cloghere, at the annual visitation, 1864. 1865 2/4/65
Berington, Joseph
Faith of Catholics. 1813 27/10/61
History of the lives of Abeillard and Heloisa. 1787 11/11/55
Literary history of the middle ages. 1814 19/1/56
Berington, Simon
Memoirs of Signor G. di Lucca. 1737 6/9/36
Berkeley, George
Alciphron. 1732 (2v.) 25/8/45, 3/8/63
Passive obedience. 11/9/41
Principles of human knowledge. 1770 14/9/41, 13/8/63
The Querist. 1735 (3v. 1735–7) 15/8/63
Works... with an account of his life. 1784 (2v. 1784) 10/8/63
Berkeley, John
Memoirs. 18/9/32
Berlioux, Étiennes Félix
Slave trade in Africa in 1872. 1872 25/3/72
Bernard, Montague
A historical account of the neutrality of Great Britain during the American civil war. 1870 6/4/70, 15/3/71
Introductory lecture on international law. 1859 22/12/59
Lecture on alleged violations of neutrality by England in the present war. 1863 10/7/63
On the principle of non-intervention. 1860 22/12/60
Schleswig-Holstein question considered. 1864 30/5/64
Two lectures on the present American war. 1861 15/11/61
Bernard, Nicholas
Life of James Usher. 1837 21/3/56
Bernard, Thomas Delaney
Progress of doctrine in the new testament. 1864 4/3/77, 30/10/81
The rites of sepultre and memorials of the dead. 1854 28/2/76 ?
Bernard of Clairvaux, St.
Canticles. 25/2/47
De Consideratione. 5/12/48
Epistolae. 1/8/47
Quattro epistolae. (1848 edn) 17/3/61
Sermones de tempore, de sanctis, de diversis. 18/8/44
Bernays, Adolphus
Lectures. 25/4/44 ?
Berni, Francesco
Opere burlesche. 1726 (3v.) 17/1/52, 11/1/88, 26/9/88
Orlando innamorato. 27/10/55, 23/10/65
Béroalde de Verville, François
Le moyen de parvenir. Oeuvre [usually attributed to F. Béroalde de Verville]. 26/6/65

Berry, Mary
Extracts of the journals and correspondence, ed. Lady Lewis. 1865 (3v.) 28/10/65
Bert, Pierre
Le livre de famille. 1830 7/3/32
Bertolotti, Antonino
Francesco Cenci e sua famiglia. 1879 21/6/84
Bertrand, Alexandre Louis Joseph
Essai sur les dieux protecteurs des héros grecs et troyens dans l'Iliade. 1858 11/2/60, 22/9/66
Bertrand, Alexis
La psychologie de l'effort et les doctrines contemporaines. 1889 14/4/89
Besant, Annie
An autobiography. 1893 7/2/94
On eternal torture. 1874 18/10/74
Besant, Walter
For faith and freedom. 1889 (3v.) 21/3/89
Best, John Richard
Modern society in Rome, a novel. 1856 (3v.) 21/5/56
Best, Samuel
Reasons why we should not revise the liturgy. 1845 3/3/45
Bethell, Christopher
Charge to the clergy of the diocese of Bangor. 1843 10/12/43
Remarks on a petition . . . to withhold . . . the divorce and matrimonial clauses act. 1858 28/1/58
Bethune, Alexander Neil
The clergy reserve question in Canada. 1853 14/2/53
Bethune, Chevalier de
Lettres à l'éditeur des lettres de Clement XIV. 1776 15/5/45
Bethune, George Washington
The claims of our country on literary men. 1849 15/2/52
Bettridge, William
A brief history of the church in upper Canada. 1838 3/9/38
Beugnot, Arthur Auguste
Histoire de la destruction du paganisme en Occident. 1835 (2v.) 8/1/88
Beust, Friedrich Ferdinand von
Memoirs . . . written by himself, ed. Baron de Worms. 1887 (2v.) 4/7/87, 10/4/93
Bevan, William Latham
Historical note on the episcopate in Wales. 1879 13/5/83
Beveridge, William
Private thoughts upon religion. 1709 1/8/30
The great necessity and advantage of public prayer and frequent communion. 1840 (edn Manning) 20/9/40
The paschal lamb. 1707 17/8/56
Beverley, Robert Mackenzie
A letter . . . on the present corrupt state of the Church of England. 1831 2/6/31
Tombs of the prophets. Sermon. 1831 26/8/31
Beving, C. A.
La comédie de Nuées d'Aristophane. 1844 30/5/64
Bewick, Thomas
A Memoir. 1862 27/10/70
Bianchi, Luigi
Incidents in the life of an Italian. 1860 15/6/60
Bianchi-Giovini, Aurelio
Biografia di frà Paolo Sarpi. 1836 (2v.) 21/3/39
Critica degli Evangeli. 1853 (2v.) 14/10/66
Bianconi, F.
La question d'Orient dévoilée. 1876 16/3/77
Biber, George Edward
Catholicity v. Sibthorp. 1842 13/2/42
The kingdom and church of Hawaii. 1865 19/11/71
The seven voices of the spirit: being the promises given by Christ through the spirit to the church. Sermons. 1857 23/8/57
Bible. 25/9/25, 11/11/25, 22/1/26, 12/2/26, 14/5/26, 11/6/26, 10/9/26, 31/1/27, 4/4/27, 9/9/27, 25/11/27, 2/12/27, 13/1/28, 16/3/28, 27/4/28, 23/6/28, 9/7/28, 15/12/28, 2/7/29, 4/8/29, 18/10/29, 24/12/29, 13/4/30, 14/7/30, 26/12/30, 17/7/31, 24/7/31, 1/4/32, 27/8/32, 3/9/32, 29/10/32, 2/6/33, 29/8/33, 27/4/34, 12/9/34, 24/12/34, 7/8/36, 26/11/37
Bibliographie clèrico-galante, par L'Apôtre bibliographe. 1884 (2v. 1884–6) 22/2/88
Bibliotheca Sacra and Theological Review. 19/8/1888
Bickersteth, Edward Dean of Lichfield
A charge . . . delivered to the archdeanery of Buckingham. 1867 14/7/67
Bickersteth, Edward Rector of Walton
Divine warning to the church. 1842 26/11/42
Permanence and progress of divine truth. 1842 1/6/42
Testimony of the reformers. 1836 8/3/36
The national fast of 1847. 1847 24/3/47
Bickersteth, Edward Henry
Evangelical churchmanship and evangelical eclecticism. 1883 13/1/83
Milton's 'Paradise Lost'. 1876 31/10/75
Opening address at the Exeter diocesan conference. 1889 3/11/89
Some words of counsel addressed to the clergy and laity of his diocese. 1888 1/7/88
The master's home-call. 1872 12/1/73
The reef and other parables. 1873 28/12/73
Yesterday, today and forever. Poem. 1866 28/7/67, 9/2/68

Bickersteth, Robert
A charge delivered to the clergy of the diocese of Ripon. 1870 13/8/71
Life of R. Bickersteth, by M. C. Bickersteth. 1887 17/4/87
Bickford, James
Christian work in Australasia. 1878 2/3/79
James Bickford: an autobiography of Christian labour. 1890 23/1/91
Biddle, John
The apostolical and true opinion concerning the Holy Trinity. 1/1/60
Biden, James
Plain and practical sermons. 1853 25/12/53
Biese, Carl Julius Adolph Alfred
Die Entwicklung des Naturgefühls. 1882 8/11/87
Bigelow, John
Molinos the Quietist. 1882 23/7/82
Bigg, Charles
The Christian Platonists of Alexandria. 1886 19/11/93, 26/11/93
Biggs, William
Never go to war about Turkey. 1847 8/3/48
Bigotry and progress. A metaphysical romance. 1888 12/11/92
Bigsby, Robert
Tribute to the memory of Scanderbeg the Great. 1866 17/10/76
Bikelas, Demetrios
Loukis Laras. Reminiscences of a Chiote merchant during the War of Independence, translated with an account of the author by J. Gennadius. 1881 5/2/81
Seven essays on Christian Greece. 1890 4/12/90
Biley, Edward
On the miracle recorded in the tenth chapter of the book of Joshua. 1873 30/11/73
Billington, Elizabeth
Memoirs. 1792 16/7/85
Bineau, J. M.
Rapport . . . sur le projet de budget rectifié. 1848 10/2/53
Bingham, Denis Arthur
Inside Paris during the seige. 1871 28/6/71
Bingham, John Elliot
Narrative of the expedition to China. 1842 (2v.) 16/3/46
Bingham, Joseph
Origines ecclesiastiae. 1708 (10v. 1708–22) 23/5/41
Bingham, W. P. S.
A few words on the divorce bill. 1857 16/6/57
Binney, Hibbert
Letter to the archbishop of Canterbury. 1878 26/1/79
Binney, Thomas
An argument in relation to the Levitical marriage law. 1850 10/7/50 ?
Conscientious clerical nonconformity. 1839 14/5/48
Lights and shadows of church-life in Australia. 1860 15/4/60
Money: a popular exposition in rough note. 1865 1/1/65
Sermon. 1869 4/4/69
The words of Jesus, with what underlies them. 1863 1/3/68
Binns, Richard William
Century of potting in the city of Worcester. 1865 21/4/66
Binterim, Anton Joseph
Kirche und den Staatem. 1845 (2v. 1845–6) 28/1/47
Biographical Sketch of Alice, Grand Duchess of Hesse. 1884 9/12/83
Bionne, Henry
La question du percement de l'isthme de Panama. 1864 30/12/64
Birch, J.
The reverend C. Dodgson's new tests of orthodoxy. 1853 22/10/53
Birch, Samuel
[Egyptian texts in vol. VI of] *Records of the past.* 1876 (12v. 1873–81) 27/10/76
Records of the past . . . vol. 1 Assyrian texts. 1874 28/7/74
Birch, Scholes Butler
On the therapeutic action of oxygen. 1857 5/3/58
Birch, T.
The unreasonableness of revenge. 1720 31/8/73
Birch, Thomas
The wisdom and goodness of God proved from the frame and constitution of man. 1749 7/1/72
Birch, William John
An inquiry in the philosophy and religion of Shakespeare. 1848 2/8/73
The real and the ideal. 1840 (2v.) 9/8/42
Bird, C. S.
[pamphlet on church economy]. 1833 2/2/33
Birkbeck, John
The present position of the Eastern question. 1878 21/1/78
Birks, Thomas Rawson
A letter to . . . Russell . . . on the admission of Jews to Parliament. 1848 9/2/48
A memoir of the reverend Edward Bickersteth. 1852 (3rd edn 2v.) 6/8/54
First Elements of sacred prophecy. 1843 22/6/47 ?
Modern physical fatalism and the doctrine of evolution. 17/3/78
Revised code and the report of the Royal Commission on education. 1862 17/1/62
The Pentateuch and its anatomists. 1869 28/8/81

True prerogative and glory of the Jews. 1877 6/1/78
Bischoff, James
Foreign tariffs. 1843 17/4/43
Bishop, Sir Henry Rowley
The law of Java. 1822 22/5/44
Bishop, Joel Prentiss
Commentaries on the law of marriage and divorce. 27/3/81 ?
Bishop, Maria Catherine
A memoir of Mrs. Augustus Craven. 1894 17/12/94, 24/12/94
Bishop's chaplain
A few words on the Athanasian creed. 1841 2/3/41
Bismarck versus Christ. 1872 13/11/73
Bismark's deeds and aims. 1889 11/10/89
Bisset, Andrew
'Sir Walter Scott', in *Essays on historical truth*. 1871 9/12/71
Bisset, Robert
Life of Edmund Burke. 1798 27/4/58
Bisset, Thomas
Suggestions on university reform. 1850 25/5/50
Bithell, Richard
Creed of a modern agnostic. 1883 11/6/84
Bitzius, Albert pseud. J. Gotthelf
The soul and money. 1872 18/1/80 ?
Bjornson, Bjornstjerne Martinus
Heritage of the Kurts. 1892 21/9/92, 10/10/92
In God's way. 1891 28/5/91
Björnstjerna, Magnus Frederik Ferdinand
British empire in the east. 1840 11/6/40
Black, A. and E.
Biographies of Lord Macaulay in the Encyclopedia Britannica. 1860 16/3/60
Black, Charles Ingram
Confession. A letter to his parishioners. 1858 7/7/64
The proselytes of Ishmael. 1881 25/8/89 ?
Black, Clementina
Orlando. 1879 5/3/81 ?
Black, J. W.
Colonel Ingersoll's reply to W. E. Gladstone briefly considered. 1889 24/2/89
Blackburn, Henry George
Travelling in Spain in the present day. 1866 20/7/67
Blackburn, John
Evidence of the truth of Christianity. 1840 25/12/61
Popular biblical educator. 1854 (2v. 1854–5) 1/4/60
Blackburn, Peter
The doctrine of the New Testament law concerning divorce and separation. 1857 12/7/57
Blackburn, Thomas
Visions of the king. 1881 9/10/81
Blackburne, Francis
The confessional. 1766 11/1/40
Blackburne, Gertrude Mary Ireland
In opposition. A novel. 1888 (3v.) 31/7/88
Blackburne, Jonathan
A brief historical inquiry into the introduction of stone altars into the Christian church. 1844 14/7/44
Blacket, John
Divine truth in the light of reason and revelation. 1893 6/8/93
Blackie, John Stuart
'On ... Greek mythology' in *Horae Hellenicae*. 1874 1/6/74
Faust. 1834 6/10/80
Gaelic language. 1864 16/11/64
Gaelic societies, highland depopulation and land law reform. 1880 28/6/82 ?
Lay sermons. 1881 31/7/81
Lecture on Plato. 1867 3/5/67
Letter to the people of Scotland on the reform of their academical institutions. 1888 24/7/88
On the living language of the Greeks. 1853 27/5/72, 2/11/72
Scottish highlanders and the land laws. 1885 26/12/84
The union of 1707 and its results; a plea for Scottish home rule. 1892 6/7/92
The wisdom of Goethe. 1883 10/7/83
University reform. Eight articles. 1848 12/12/59
War songs of the Germans. 1870 30/5/70
Blackley, William
Apostolical loosing and binding ... the keys ... as given to St. Peter. 1846 12/12/47
Blackmore, Richard Doddridge
Lorna Doone. 1869 (3v.) 25/6/90
Blackmore, Richard White
Mouravieff's history of the Russian church, tr. R. W. Blackmore. 1842 22/10/42
Blackstone, William
Commentaries. 1765 (4v.) 27/8/32, 24/10/37, 18/3/39, 30/4/50
Blackwell, Elizabeth
Purchase of women: the great economic blunder. 1887 6/1/87
Blackwell, Thomas
An enquiry into the life and writings of Homer. 1735 25/7/55
Blackwood, Frederick Temple Hamilton Temple Lord Dufferin
Contributions to an inquiry on ... Ireland. 1866 14/5/66
Letters from high latitudes. 1857 30/7/57
Mr. Mill's plan for the pacification of Ireland examined. 1868 25/2/68
Blackwood's Edinburgh Review.
23. 445, 431. 4/1828. Bhurtpore 9/5/1828
23. 520, 504. 4/1828. Public men; changes in ministry 8/5/1828

Blackwood's Edinburgh Review (cont.)
36. 542, 530. 10/1834. on Coleridge, & Italy 8/10/1834
53. 143. 8/1842. Ministry 23/8/1842
57. 595. 5/1845. Spain 6/6/1845
60. 645. 12/1846. Denmark 19/12/1846
60. 740, 754. 12/1846. Game 21/12/1846
61. 243. 2/1847. Taxation 16/2/1847
61. 93. 1/1847. on Peel 22/1/1847
63. 219. 2/1848. West Indies 1/5/1848
64. 632. 11/1848. Tories 3/5/1848
67. 34, 94. 1/1850. California, & on Gladstone 22/1/1850
75. 507. 5/1854. Oxford Reform Bill 6/6/1854
79. 20. 1/1856. War 24/1/1856
84. 127. 8/1858. Gladstone's Homer 12/8/1858
89. 1. 1/1861. Finance 21/1/1861
90. 115. 7/1861. Budget 1/7/1861
93. 133, 245. 2/1863. politics 13/2/1863
98. 459. 10/1865. Leopardi 3/11/1865
100. 9/1866 17/9/1866
103. 367. 3/1868. Gleig on Opposition 4/3/1868
103. 383. 4/1868. on Horace 31/3/1868
104. 129. 8/1868. on Disraeli 14/8/1868
116. 8/1874. Tales 22/8/1874
136. 737, 817. 12/1884. on Wiclif; Croker; the Crisis 3/12/1884
142. 443. 10/1887. Brabourne 30/9/1887
142. 753. 12/1887. Hugessen 13/10/1890
150. 461. 10/1891. Foreign policy 26/9/1891
152. 293. 8/1892. Ministry 27/8/1892
331. 673. 5/1843. Commerce, Spain 4/5/1843

Blades, William
Books in chains. 1892 3/11/92
The enemies of books. 1880 17/6/90

Blagdon, Francis William
Paris as it was, and as it is. 1803 (2v.) 9/1/27 ?

Blaikie, William Gordon
Better days for working people. 1863 26/8/64
The preachers of Scotland. 1888 21/10/88

Blaine, Delabere Roberton
Artistic copyright. Report. 1858 8/3/58

Blair, Hugh
A critical dissertation on the poems of Ossian, the son of Fingal. 1763 18/10/26
Lectures on rhetoric and belles lettres. 1783 (2v.) 31/1/26, 3/2/26, 21/2/26
Sermons. 1777 (5v. 1777–1801) 23/10/25, 13/11/25, 5/2/26, 12/2/26, 23/4/26, 4/5/26, 7/5/26, 14/5/26, 21/5/26, 25/6/26, 9/7/26, 1/10/26, 8/10/26, 24/10/26, 21/1/27, 4/2/27, 18/2/27

Blair, William Thomas
Lecture on ritualism. 1873 28/4/75

Blake, Henry Arthur [pseud. T. MacGrath]
Pictures from Ireland. 1880 13/12/80

Blake, William artist
Songs of Innocence. 1888 (new edn) 6/8/89

Blake, William F.R.S.
Observations on the principles which regulate the course of exchange. 1810 11/3/61

Blakemore, Richard
Letter to . . . Bathurst, on the subject of poor laws. 1819 1/8/43

Blakesley, Joseph William
Conciones academicae. 1843 28/7/44
English Catholics and English ultramontanism. 1874 21/12/74
Herodotus with a commentary. 1854 9/1/57
Thoughts on the recommendations of the ecclesiastical commission. 1837 5/2/37, 11/3/37
Where does the evil lie?. 1845 17/3/45

Blakey, Robert
Memoirs, ed. H. Miller. 1879 6/12/81

Blanc, Jean Joseph Louis
Historical revelations inscribed to Lord Normanby. 1858 1/7/58
Organisation du travail. 1841 1/4/48

Bland, Miles
Algebraic problems. 1812 20/9/28, 22/7/29
Elements of hydrostatics. 1824 21/10/30

Blatch, William
Memoir of the right reverend D. Low. 1855 30/3/56

Blavatsky, Helena Petrovna
Isis unveiled. 1877 (2v.) 4/2/79

Blaze de Bury, Henri
Les salons de Vienne et Berlin. 1861 12/3/84 ?

Blenkinsopp, Edwin Clennell Leaton
Doctrine of development in the Bible and the Church. 1869 22/5/70

Blennerhassett, Sir Rowland
Peasant proprietors in Ireland. 1884 19/4/84

Blessington, Lady Marguerite
Confessions of an elderly lady. 1838 12/8/39
Desultory thoughts. 1839 31/8/39
Victims of society. 1837 (3v.) 25/4/37

Blew, William John
Church restoration. 1869 6/6/69
Letter to the bishop of Nottingham. 1870 28/8/70
Medea. 1887 6/12/87

Bligh, Edward Vesey
Letters on church reform. 1871 27/10/72
Prophetical signs of the second coming. 1891 15/3/91

Blignières, Célestin de
Du progrès des idées politiques. 1864 5/8/82

Blind, Mathilde
George Eliot. 1883 12/12/89
Madame Roland. 1886 14/10/89
Selected poems. 1892 21/11/91

The ascent of man. 1889 21/10/89
The journal of Marie Bashkirtseff, tr. M. Blind. 1890 13/3/90

Bliss, Laurence
A modern romance. 1892 30/9/92

Blomfield, Charles James
Charge delivered to the clergy of the diocese of London. 1834 15/7/40
Charge delivered to the clergy of the diocese of London. 1838 3/2/39
Charge delivered to the clergy of the diocese of London. 1842 5/11/42
Charge delivered to the clergy of the diocese of London. 1846 13/3/47
Charge delivered to the clergy of the diocese of London. 1850 4/4/51
Charge delivered to the clergy of the diocese of London. 1854 12/11/54
God's ancient people not cast away. 1843 25/6/43
Manual of family prayers. 1831 4/9/32
National education. Sermon. 1838 11/3/38
Sermons. 1829 5/12/44
Speech of the Lord Bishop of London . . . on education. 1839 27/7/39
Speech on marriage [reprinted as a pamphlet]. 1841 1/6/41
The light of the world. Sermon. 1842 20/2/42
Three sermons on the church. 1842 24/4/42

Bloomfield, Georgiana
Reminiscences of court and diplomatic life. 1883 (2v.) 13/2/83

Blosius, Franciscus Ludovicus
A mirrour for monkes. (1871 edn) 14/5/71

Blount, Charles
The oracles of reason . . . letters [by Blount, Gildon and others]. 3/8/62

Blundell, William
A cavalier's note book. 1880 23/10/89

Blunt, Anne Isabella Noel
Pilgrimage to Nej, the cradle of the Arab race. 1881 (2v.) 2/3/81

Blunt, Henry
Discourses upon some of the doctrinal articles of the Church of England. 1835 3/5/35
The Lord's day. Sermon. 1832 5/2/32
Twelve lectures on the history of Abraham. 1831 14/10/32
Two discourses upon the sacrament of the Lord's supper. 1825 6/4/34
Zeal of Jehu not Christian zeal. 1833 17/2/33

Blunt, John Henry
Christian view of Christian history. 1866 7/10/66
Condition and prospects of the Church of England. 1871 26/3/71
Household theology. 1865 28/1/66
Plain account of the English Bible. 1870 14/8/70
Reformation of the Church of England 1514–1662. 1882 (2v. 1882) 11/3/83, 19/8/83, 29/11/85, 28/5/88

Blunt, John James
History of the Christian Church during the first three centuries. 1856 20/9/57
Sketch of the Reformation in England. 1832 23/9/40

Blunt, Walter
Dissenters' baptisms and church burials. 1840 10/2/41
Ecclesiastical restoration and reform. 1847 20/3/47

Blunt, Wilfrid Scawen
A new pilgrimage, and other poems. 1889 8/11/93
Future of Islam. 1882 22/7/82

Bluntschli, Johann Caspar
'Die organisation des europäischen Staatenvereins' in *Die Gegenwart*. 1878 18/7/79
Der staat Rumänien und das Rechtverhältniss der Juden in Rumänien. 1879 14/8/79

Blyden, Edward Wilmot
A voice from bleeding Africa, on behalf of her exiled children. 1856 22/9/60
Christianity, Islam and the negro race. 1887 18/9/87
From West Africa to Palestine. 1873 27/6/73
Hope for Africa. 1861 28/9/61 ?, 24/6/66 ?
The Negro in ancient history. 1869 3/6/69 ?

Boaden, James
An inquiry into the authenticity of . . . portraits of Shakespeare. 1824 30/9/59

Boase, Charles William
Oxford. 1887 31/5/92

Boccaccio, Giovanni
Amorosa visione. 12/4/44
Decamerone. (1812 edn) 3/10/34, 20/10/34, 22/10/35, 14/7/60, 24/5/72
Tale of Griselda. 7/10/35
Vita di Dante Alighieri. (various edns) 25/3/88

Bochart, Samuel
Sermons. 1714 (3v.) 1/11/88

Bodin, Jean
Les six livres de la république. 13/4/41

Bodley, John Edward Courtenay
Roman Catholicism in America. 1890 16/10/90

Bodley, Sir Thomas
Reliquiae Bodleianae. 1703 30/9/85

Boehmer, Eduard
Lives of the twin brothers Juan and Alfonso de Valdés. 1883 21/5/83

Boehmer, George Rudolf Wilhelm
Ist der Geist oder die Schrift für die Regel des Christlichen Glaubens zu halten?. 1845 17/10/45

Boero, Giuseppe
Istoria della conversione all chiesa cattolica di Carlo II. 1863 20/9/80 ?
Boethius
Opera. 3/1/26
Boetticher, Carl Gottlieb Wilhelm
Der Baumkultus der hellenen. 1856 23/12/75
Bogan, Zachary
Homerus. 11/9/65
Bogue, David, and Bennett, James
History of dissenters. 1808 (4v. 1808–12) 1/6/44
Bohn, Henry George
Guide to the knowledge of pottery, porcelain, and other objects of vertu. 1857 22/6/57, 10/3/59
Origin and progress of printing. 1854 5/9/73
Boiardo, Matteo Maria
Orlando Innamorato. 4/1/50
Boileau, Alexander Henry Edmondstone
Memorandum for reorganising the Indian army. 1858 14/11/68 ?
Boissard, Ferjus
Dante révolutionnaire et socialiste mais non hérétique. 1858 19/4/70
Boissard, Louis
L'Eglise de Russie. 1867 (2v.) 11/8/67
Boissevain, Gideon Maria
The money question. 1891 11/2/91
Boissier, Marie Louis Antoine Gaston
La religion romaine d'Auguste aux Antonins. 1874 (2v.) 30/9/77
Bolling, Edward James
Religious zeal foolishness to the world. A sermon. 1870 5/2/71
Bolton, Sidney
Lord Wastwater. 1892 (2v.) 23/11/92
Bomba, Domenico
La chiesa cristiana nella sua origine. 1874 21/12/74
Bompas, M.
'The argument for belief', *New Review*, xxi. 632 (July). 1893 9/7/93
Bonaparte, Louis-Lucien
On the dialects of eleven . . . countries. 1877 16/11/91
Bonaparte, Napoléon-Louis
[Correspondence with his brother Joseph]. 1855 (2v.) 1/2/55
Des idées Napoléoniennes. 1838 9/6/58
Bonaventura, St.
Life of Christ, tr. Oakeley. 1844 16/6/44
Psalter of the blessed virgin Mary illustrated. 1840 14/12/51
Boncompagni, Carlo
L'Italie et la question romaine. 1862 27/11/62
La rinunzia del ministero Rattazzi ed il Parlamento. 1862 18/12/62
Pouvoir temporel du Pape. Introduction by A. Levy. 1864 22/12/63
Boner, Charles
Forest creatures. 1861 24/10/62
Bonet-Maury, Amy Gaston Charles Auguste
Des origines du christianisme. 1881 19/8/81, 2/11/84
Bonghi, Ruggero
On W. E. Gladstone's Church and State and on finance. [reprinted in his 'Opere', iv, 1935]. 1880 27/2/80
Bonhomme, Jean François Honoré
Madame de Pompadour. 1880 12/4/84 ?
Bonilla, Jean de
Traité de la paix de l'âme. 1865 24/2/56
Bonnot de Mably, Gabriel
Observations sur les romains. 1751 25/5/36
Bonnycastle, Richard Henry
The Canadas in 1841. 1841 14/5/41
Bonwick, James
Egyptian belief and modern thought. 1878 14/7/78, 18/11/81
Mormons and the silver mines. 1872 25/1/72
Boos, Martin
Life and persecutions. 1836 26/12/47
Booth, Catherine
Salvation Army. 1883 17/6/83
Booth, Henry
Carrying question in reference to railways and canals. 1841 5/3/41
Considerations on licensing. 1862 30/1/62
Taxation, direct and indirect. 1860 5/1/60, 28/1/61
Booth, James C. B.
Problem of the world. 1879 26/7/79
Booth, James F.R.S.
Education. 1846 9/8/46
Examination the province of the state. 1847 23/10/47
The Lord's supper. 1870 1/5/70
Booth, Thomas C.
Our meat supply. 1878 7/3/78
Booth, General William
The future of missions and the missions of the future. 1889 21/7/89
Booth, William
In darkest England and the way out. 1890 26/10/90, 16/11/90
Bopp, Franz
A comparative grammar. 1845 (1845–50) 16/12/56
Borgianelli, Enrico
Discorso sull'antica e moderna Gesuitofobia . . . 1850 (2v. 1850) 22/11/50
Borlase, Edmund
History of the execrable Irish rebellion 1641. 22/7/86
History of the Irish Confederation . . . 1641–3, ed. J. T. Gilbert [contains reprint of essays]. 1882 11/1/82, 17/5/82

The reduction of Ireland to the Crown of England. 13/1/91
Borlase, William
Observations on the ancient and present state of the Islands of Scilly. 1756 15/1/84
Borlase, William Copeland
Age of the saints. 1878 24/11/78
Borrow, George Henry
The bible in Spain. 1843 (3v.) 19/9/43
Borthwick, Algernon
Address on the eastern question. 1878 26/2/78
Borthwick, Jane, and Findlater, Sarah
Hymns from the land of Luther. 1854 (4v. 1854–62) 5/8/83
Bory de Saint Vincent, Jean Baptiste Geneviève Marcellin
Histoire et description des îles Ioniennes. 1823 23/12/58
Bosanquet, James Whatman
Metallic, paper and credit currency. 1842 17/10/43
Bosanquet, Samuel Richard
Principia. Essays. 1843 18/4/60
The poor law amendment acts. 1839 4/8/43
The Romanists, the established church and the dissenters. 1851 9/3/51
Boscawen, William St. Chad
[on Assyrian inscriptions]. 6/12/75
Bose, Shib Chunder [Siva-Chandra Vasu]
The Hindoos as they are. 1881 4/6/81
Bossuet, Jacques Bénigne
Conférence avec M. Claude. 20/2/81
Histoire . . . des églises protestantes. (2v.) 21/1/36, 17/4/36
Oraisons funèbres. 25/3/32 ?
Boswell, James
Letters to Temple, ed. Sir P. Francis. 1856 11/2/57, 15/6/58
Life of Samuel Johnson. 1791 (3v.) 8/12/25, 24/4/26, 22/5/26
Life of Samuel Johnson, ed. J. Murray. 1831 11/12/60, 2/9/63, 26/10/63, 26/9/64, 3/10/64, 1/11/64
The life of Samuel Johnson, ed. Birkbeck Hill. (6v. 1887) 25/9/87
Bosworth, Thomas
On 'rattening' in the book trade. 1868 27/2/68
Botta, Carlo Giuseppe Guglielmo
History of Italy. 1828 (2v.) 28/3/33
Boucharlat, Jean Louis
Mort d'Abel; le sacrifice d'Abraham. 1827 17/10/28
Boucher, J. S.
Doctrine. 1891 23/10/91 ?
Pamphlet on North Wales training college. 1867 25/4/67
Boucherett, Ayscoghe
A few observations on corn and currency. 1840 16/10/41
Boufflers, Stanislas Jean de
Oeuvres. 1792 22/8/66
Bouhours, Dominique
The life of St. Francis Xavier, trans. Dryden. 1/2/48
Bouillé du Chariol, François Claude Amour de
Memoirs relating to the French revolution. 1797 26/8/89
Boulgaris, Nickolaos Timoleon
Les sept îles ioniennes et les traits qui les concernent. 1859 26/3/59
Boult, Joseph
On the alleged submarine forests in the shores of Liverpool bay. 1865 16/6/65
Boulter, Hugh
Letters written . . . to several ministers of state. 1769 (2v. 1769–70) 8/9/87
Boulton, William Biggs
The history of White's [club]. 1892 (2v.) 12/1/93
Bourget, Paul Charles Joseph
André Cornélis. 1887 26/2/87, 5/4/87
Cosmopolis. 1893 6/3/93
Le disciple. 1889 27/8/90, 2/9/90
Bourienne, Louis Antoine Fauvelet de
Mémoire sur Napoléon. 1829 25/2/32, 15/11/32
Bourinot, Sir John George
Federal government in Canada. 1889 14/4/93
The intellectual development of the Canadian people: an historical review. 1881 29/9/81
Bourke, Ulick J.
The Aryan origin of the Gaelic race. 1875 19/11/77
Bourn, Samuel
Discourses on the principles and evidences of natural religion. 1760 (2v.) 1/11/63
Bourne, Henry Richard Fox
Memoir of Sir Philip Sidney. 1862 11/10/62
Bourne, John
Railways in India. 1848 7/6/48
Bouterwek, Friedrich
Geschichte der Poesie. 1801 (12v. 1801–50) 6/10/59
Boutmy, Émile Gaston
Etudes du droit constitutionnel. 1885 19/10/89
Bouvier, A.
Le divin d'après les apôtres. 1882 23/3/84 ?
Bouvier, Jean Baptiste
A dogmatical and practical treatise, or indulgences. 1839 25/10/45
Bowden, John William
A few remarks on pews. 1843 4/6/43
The life pontificate of Gregory VII. 1840 (2v.) 30/4/41
Thoughts on the work of the six days of creation. 1845 22/6/45, 3/12/91
Bowdler, Thomas
Quid Romae Faciam?. 1841 23/1/42

Bowen, C. E.
[On East Indian rail and steam]. 25/11/51
Bowen, Charles Synge Christopher
Alabama claims and arbitration. 1868 25/2/68
Bowen, Edward Ernest
Harrow songs. 1886 12/4/86
Bowen, George Ferguson
Ithaca in 1850. 1850 17/7/51, 21/8/77
Mount Athos, Thessaly and Epirus. 1850 5/7/51
Bower, Alexander
History of the University of Edinburgh. 1817 (2v.) 4/4/60
Bowles, J. L.
Keramic Art of Japan. 1875 3/1/89
Bowles, William
Pamphlets on naval subjects. 1854 13/2/56
Bowman, William
Address in surgery, read at . . . the meeting of the British Medical Association. 1866 25/9/66
Bowring, Edgar Alfred
Poems of Goethe, tr. E. A. Bowring. 1853 26/6/79
Bowring, Sir John
Adelbert von Chamisso's 'Peter Schlemihl's wundersame Geschichte'. 1814 5/1/31 ?
Autobiographical recollections. 1877 1/4/78
Kingdom and people of Siam. 1857 (2v.) 17/4/57
Political and commercial importance of peace. 1846 5/2/56
Report on statistics of Tuscany, Lucca, the Pontifical and the Lombardo-Venetian states. 1837 19/1/63
Servian popular poetry, tr. J. Bowring. 1827 7/4/76
Bowyer, Sir George
Differences between the holy see and the Spanish government. 1856 2/4/56
Observations on the Arguments of Dr. Twiss respecting the new Catholic hierarchy. 1851 30/3/51
Readings delivered before the Honourable Society of the Middle Temple. 1850 17/7/50
Roman documents relating to the new hierarchy. 1851 21/3/51
The Cardinal Archbishop of Westminster and the new hierarchy. 1851 3/4/51
The English constitution: a popular commentary on the constitutional law of England. 1841 26/10/42
Boxer, Edward Mourrier
Remarks on the system proposed by the royal Commissioners for the defence of the country. 1862 20/6/62
Boxhorn, Marcus Zuerius
Opera. 11/9/65
Boyce, John Cox
Nigh unto the end. 1880 20/11/81
Boyd, Archibald
Episcopacy, ordination, lay-eldership, and liturgies, considered in five letters. 1839 21/1/40
Boyd, S. H.
Select poems of Synesius and Gregory Nazianzen. 1814 8/8/86 ?
Boydell, James
Letter to Sir Stephen Glynne on the suspension of the Oak Farm works written in consequence of remarks made by . . . W. E. Gladstone. 1848 8/9/48
Treatise on landed property. 1849 13/2/50
Boyer, Abel
The political state of Great Britain. 1732 8/9/69
Boyer d'Agen, Auguste Jean
Le clergé de France devant la République. 1892 7/2/92
Boyle, A.
The sympathy and action of England in the late eastern crisis. 1878 5/2/79
Boyle, Ann Lady Cork
Memoirs and thoughts. 1886 19/2/86
Boyle, Robert
Some motives and incentives to the love of God. 8/1/43
B. R.
The dissenter's catechism. 1703 11/11/49
Brabazon, Reginald
Social arrows. 1887 (2nd edn) 2/3/88
Brace, Charles Loring
Dangerous classes of New York. 1872 18/12/73
Bracebridge, Charles Holte
A letter . . . on the affairs of Greece. 1850 25/6/50
Authentic details of the Valdenses in Piedmont and other countries. 1827 19/2/60
Braddon, Mary Elizabeth
Dead men's shoes. 1876 (3v.) 25/2/81
Eleanor's victory. 1863 (3v.) 18/11/63
Gerard. 1891 (3v. 1891) 22/10/91
The Doctor's wife. 1864 29/3/66
The Venetians. A novel. 1892 (3v.) 13/6/92, 22/8/92
Bradford, Samuel
Discourse concerning baptismal and spiritual regeneration. 1709 13/7/28
Bradford, Samuel Dexter
Letters to W. M. Meredith on Treasury. 1850 20/4/50
Bradlaugh, Charles
Genesis. Its authorship and authenticity. 1882 21/10/88
Life of, by H. Bradlaugh. 1894 17/12/94
The Irish question: what it has been, what it is, and how to deal with it. 1868 17/7/68
The land, the people, and the coming struggle. 1871 27/1/71

Bradlaugh, Hypatia
Charles Bradlaugh. A record of his life and work. 1894 17/12/94
Bradley, George Granville Dean of Westminster
Recollections of Arthur Penrhyn Stanley . . . Three lectures. 1883 4/3/83, 1/6/89
Bradley, Katharine Harris pseud. Arran Leigh
The new Minnesinger and other poems. 1875 21/5/76
Brady, William Maziere
'Vice-regal speeches' from *Essays on the English state church in Ireland.* 1869 8/4/69
Alleged conversion of the Irish bishops. 1866 2/9/66
Anglo-Roman papers. 1890 22/12/90
Essays on the English state church in Ireland. 1869 10/6/69
Facts or fictions? Seven letters on 'the facts concerning the Irish Church'. 1867 2/6/67
Remarks on the Irish church temporalities. 1865 7/11/65
Some remarks on the Irish church bill. 1869 26/4/69
State papers concerning the Irish church. 1868 15/5/68, 24/1/86
Two letters . . . concerning Irish church revenues. 1868 7/1/68
Brahmo, Somaj
Year Book. 1881 25/12/76 n, 20/5/83
Year Book. 1882 20/5/83
Braim, Thomas Henry
The history of New South Wales. 1846 (2v. 1846) 19/1/47
Bramhall, John
Castigations of Mr. Hobbes. 8/7/45
Vindication of himself and the episcopal clergy. 29/12/40
Brand, Wilhelm Ferdinand
London life seen with German eyes. 1887 28/1/87, 8/6/87
Brande, William Thomas
Outlines of geology. 1817 7/8/50
Brandes, G. M. C.
Beaconsfield. 1880 17/5/80
Brandis, J.
Die Bedeutung der sieben Thore Thebens. 1867 1/2/68
Branięki, Xavier Ksawery-
Les nationalités slaves, lettres au R. P. Gagarin. 1879 20/8/79, 25/6/85
Brassey, Sir Thomas Earl Brassey
A colonial naval volunteer force. Lecture. 1878 9/9/78
A voyage in the 'Sunbeam'. 1883 12/8/85
Wages in 1873. 1873 16/12/73
Work and wages practically illustrated. 1872 18/11/72
Braund, James H.
History and revelation. 1870 (3v. 1870–5) 19/9/75
Bray, Charles
Illusion and delusion. 1873 14/9/73
Manual of anthropology. 1871 17/3/74
Toleration. 1875 3/5/75
Breach of privilege . . . the evidence of John Bull [at] *the secret committee on national distress.* 1848 12/1/49
Bredenbachius, Mathias
De dissidiis Ecclesiae. 2/4/47
Bree, Charles Robert
An exposition of the fallacies in the hypothesis of Mr. Darwin. 1872 5/1/73
Brehm, Alfred Edmund
Bird-life. 1874 8/11/81
Bremer, Fredrika
The neighbours. 1842 (2v. 1842) 27/3/45
Brenon, Edward St. John
The tribune reflects. 1881 9/4/81
Brent, Daniel
Proposed permissive variations in the use of the church services. 1863 3/1/64
Brentano, Lujo
On the history and development of gilds. 1870 26/2/73
Brète, J. de la
Le roman d'une croyante. 1892 27/2/92
Breton, M.
China; its costume, arts, manufactures. 1813 (4th edn) 10/1/26
Brett, Reginald Baliol
Footprints of statesmen during the eighteenth century in England. 1892 23/12/92
Brett, Robert
Devotions for the sick room and for times of trouble. 1743 22/11/46
Brett, Thomas
A collection of the principal liturgies used . . . in the celebration of the holy eucharist. 1720 27/12/40, 18/11/60
Brevint, Daniel
Depth and mystery of the Roman mass. 19/11/54
Brevi riposte alle lettere di Sir W. E. Gladstone indiritte al conte Aberdeen . . . al . . . popolo Napoletano. 1851 23/1/52
Brewer, John Sherrin
Athanasian creed vindicated. 1871 12/11/71
Athanasian origin . . . of the Athanasian creed. 1872 21/4/72
Endowments and establishment of the Church of England. 1885 15/9/88
Reign of Henry VIII. 1884 (2v.) 30/4/84, 26/11/88
Brewster, Sir David
Introductory address. 1859 22/11/59

Brewster, John
A secular essay. 1802 23/9/83, 13/1/84
Brialmont, Alexis Henri
Histoire du duc de Wellington. 1856 (3v. 1856–7) 3/8/60
Briano, Giorgio
La politique française en Italie. 1856 28/5/56 ?
Bricknell, William Simcox
Oxford: Tract no. 90. 1844 5/12/44
Bridges, Charles
Life of Martin Boos, Roman Catholic priest in Bavaria. 1855 17/12/82
Memoir of Miss Mary Jane Graham. 1823 21/7/35
Bridges, John Henry
Two centuries of Irish history 1691–1870. 1888 27/6/88
Bridges, Robert Seymour
Prometheus the fire giver. 1883 5/11/92
Shorter poems. 1893 30/10/93
Bridgett, Thomas Edward
Life of Blessed John Fisher. 1888 22/7/88
Bridle, J.
Letter to the Reverend Dr. Lowth. 1758 20/7/58
Briefe einer reisenden Dame aus der Schweitz 1786. 1787 12/10/72
Brierley, Benjamin
Tales and sketches of Lancashire Life. 1862 (4v. 1862–3) 16/1/63
Briffault, Frédéric T.
The prisoner of Ham. 1846 17/11/64
Briggs, Charles Augustus
Messianic prophecy. 1887 12/6/87
Whither? A theological question for the times. 1889 10/11/89
Briggs, Mary
In loving memory of Mary Briggs, wife of Sir E. W. Watkin. 1888 25/3/88 ?
Bright, John
La question Irlandaise [speech in Dublin, 30 October 1866, tr. C. de Nettancourt]. 1867 10/12/67
Speech on legislation and policy for India. 1858 13/8/58
Bright, William
Hymns and other poems. 1866 28/11/75
Roman claims tested by antiquity. 1877 13/5/77
Brimley, George
Essays... ed. by W. G. Clark. 1858 12/8/58
Brindley, T. H.
Definitio Fidei apud Concilium Chalcedonense. 1887 14/11/86
Brine, Lindesay
Taeping rebellion in China. 1862 4/12/62
Brinkman, A.
The controversial methods of Romanisation. 1888 25/3/88
Brinsley-Richards, James
Seven years at Eton 1857–1864. 1883 12/5/83
Brinstead, Henry
Leaves from the diary of an extinguished clergyman. 1886 19/1/87
Bristow, Amelia
Sophia de Lissau. 1828 26/3/26
British and Foreign Anti-Slavery Society. Annual Report 17/11/1842
British and Foreign Review.
1. 102. 7/1835. Russia; Quadruple Treaty 29/7/1835
1. 190. 7/1835. English literature 24/7/1835
9. 433. 10/1839. Christ; Gladstone on State & Church 28/1/1840
10. 322. 1/1840. Cracow 10/7/1840
12. 1. 5/1841. Russian manufacturers 8/11/1841
12. 462. 9/1841. Corn laws 19/1/1842
16. 1. 10/1843. Anglocatholicism 19/10/1843
16. 363. 1/1844. on Arnold 18/1/1844
16. 397. 1/1844. Cathedrals 4/6/1848
17. 136. 4/1844. Anglocatholicism 8/4/1844
British Critic.
1. 482. Copleston's sermons 24/4/1830
3. 452. Van Mildert's sermons 24/4/1830
6. 130. Soul 7/11/1830
6. 194. Wilson's sermons 24/4/1830
7. 374. on Milman 13/5/1830
9. 206. Blomfield 17/1/1831
13. 465. 4/1833. Church 12/5/1834
15. 1. 7/1830. Locke 21/7/1831
17. 390–425. Religious parties 18/5/1835
21. 427–42. on R. Burgess 5/4/1837
22. 261. 10/1837. Les Affaires de Rome 18/7/1840
25. 143. 1/1839. Jesuitism 4/5/1839
26. 101. on Stephen 1/12/1839
26. 152. 7/1839. on Soames 1/12/1839
26. 228. on T. Chalmers 1/12/1839
27. 355. 4/1840. Hope on Magdalen statutes 20/3/1840
27. 40. 1/1840. Non-jurors 12/1/1840
28. 263. 10/1840. on Countess of Huntingdon 10/4/1841
28. 391. 10/1840. Todd's Discourses 13/4/1841
28. 471, 371. New Churches, & Chanting 11/4/1841
29. 280. 4/1841. Bowden's Gregory VII 30/4/1841
29. 388, 249. 4/1841. West Indies 5/4/1841
30. 214. 7/1841. on Faussit 20/8/1841
31. 1. 7/1834. Memoirs of R. Watson 22/1/1835

31. 36. 1/1842. on Buddicom 15/1/1842
31. 428. 4/1842. on C. A. Heurtley 5/4/1842
32. 1. 7/1842. Psalms & Hymns 2/8/1842
32. 300. 10/1842. 17th Century 15/10/1842
32. 428, 436. 10/1842. Hampden, & Pews 27/10/1842
33. 1. 1/1843. St Anselm 21/1/1843
33. 10. Dante 22/1/1843
33. 110. on Drummond 17/1/1843
33. 163. 1/1843. on Williams 26/1/1843
33. 202. Church Authority, & Welsh Sees 19/1/1843
33. 282. 1/1843. Notices, & on Bishop's Charges 16/1/1843
33. 295. 4/1843. Auricular confession 7/4/1843
33. 68. Monuments 25/1/1843
34. 129, 170. 7/1843. Ancient Music, & Jerusalem Bpric. 14/7/1843
34. 195. 7/1843. Pusey's sermon 3/8/1843
34. 466, 515. 10/1843. Pusey books 15/10/1843

British Magazine.
17. 90. 1/1840. Liverpool Collegiate Institution 9/1/1840
19. 246–7. Church Societies 6/1/1841
25. 1. 1/1844. on Cyril Lucar 7/1/1844
26. 283. 9/1844. Hierurgia Anglicana 7/1/1844
28. 555. 5/1845. Maynooth 11/5/1845
31. 49. 1/1847. St Bernard 10/1/1847
7/12/1839

British Quarterly Review.
1. 175. 7/1869. Gladstone & House of Lords 19/7/1869
1. 582. 5/1845. Ireland 2/6/1845
16. 289, 544. 11/1852. Univ. Comm.; Convocation 6/2/1853
17. 317, 420. 5/1853. Guyon ; Mortmain 22/5/1853
21. 182. 1/1855. The war 17/1/1855
23. 219. 1/1856. War 24/1/1856
39. 291. 1/1864. Finance 4/5/1864
41. 290. 4/1865. Translating Homer 1/4/1865
41. 325. 4/1865. Church & Atonement 2/4/1865
44. 59, 90. 7/1866. on Comte 8/7/1866
45. 4/1867 21/5/1867
46. 125. 7/1867. Rogers 6/7/1867
46. 97, 143. 7/1867. Keble and Herbert; Dr Simpson 30/6/1867
48. 465. 10/1868. Bunsen 4/10/1868
51. 362. 4/1870. Plantagenets 22/6/1870
52. 7/1870 10/7/1870
57. 1. 1/1873. Curtis's B. L. 5/1/1873
58. 189, 1. 7/1873. Ministry, & French Reformation 5/7/1873
58. 60. 7/1873. Catholicism 6/7/1873
59. 470. 4/1874. on Gladstone 17/4/1874
60. 171. 7/1874. Politics 27/7/1874
61. 168. 1/1875. Bismarck 3/1/1875
67. 321, 482, 506. 1/1878. Mycenae; the war; Eastern Question 15/4/1878
67. 379, 462. 4/1878. on F. Harrison, & Disestablishment 14/4/1878
70. 177. 7/1879. Greece 21/7/1879

British trade
Collection of reports on British trade, ed N. Atcheson. 1807 12/10/47

Britten, Barkley
Our effective artillery. 1870 7/9/70

Britton, John
History and antiquities of the metropolitical church of York. 1819 9/1/47

Britton, T. H.
On the thirty-nine articles. 1857 24/5/57

Broadhouse, John
Facts about fiddles. 1879 9/8/79

Broca, Pierre Paul
On the phenomena of hybridity in the genus homo. 1864 13/8/84

Brock, William
Mr. Gladstone the betrayer of the religion and liberties of the country. 1869 21/8/69

Brodie, Benjamin Colliss
Psychological inquiries. 1854 (pt. 1) 30/7/54

Brodie, Peter Bellinger
Tax on succession and burdens of land. 1850 27/4/53

Brodrick, Alan
Forest poems. 1869 19/12/81

Brodrick, George Charles
Abolition of tests. 1866 17/2/66, 30/12/75
English land and English landlords. 1881 8/12/80
Irish land question. 1874 23/7/74
Irish land question. Past and present. 1881 30/12/81
Memorials of Merton College. 1885 25/5/92 ?
Promotion by merit in relation to government and education. 1858 15/3/59, 30/3/59

Brodrick, George Charles, and Fremantle, W. H.
Collection of judgements . . . of the privy council. 1865 29/1/65

Brogden, James
Illustration of liturgy and ritual. 1842 (3v. 1842) 18/9/42

Broglie, Achille Léonce Victor Charles de
Rapport presenté [on education]. 1844 4/2/45

Broken Troth. 1861 (2v.) 27/3/67

Brome, Richard
Dramatic works. 1873 (3v.) 26/11/77

Brongniart, Alexandre
Traité des arts céramiques. 1854 9/3/59
Brontë, Anne
Agnes Grey. 1847 13/10/58
Brontë, Charlotte
Jane Eyre. 1847 14/9/54, 19/9/54
Life and works of Charlotte Brontë and her sisters. 1875 (7v.) 30/12/89
Shirley. 1849 26/12/54
Villette. 1853 29/7/57
Brontë, Emily
Wuthering Heights. 1847 6/10/58
Brooke, Henry
History of a reprobate. 1784 29/4/82
Brooke, James Mark Saurin, and Hadden, A. W. C.
Transcript of registers of St. Mary Woolnoth. 1886 28/3/86
Brooke, Richard
Liverpool as it was during the last quarter of the eigtheenth century. 1854 (8v.) 18/4/59
Brooke, Stopford Augustus
Freedom in the Church of England. Six Sermons. 1871 24/3/72, 1/4/72
Sermons preached in St. James chapel. 1869 8/8/69
Sermons preached in St. James chapel... second series. 1875 2/5/75
The need and use of getting Irish literature into the English tongue. 1893 27/6/93
Brookes, Henry
The Bank Act of 1844. 1861 30/5/61
Brookes, Warwick
[untraced memoirs of Warwick Brookes]. 27/9/82
Warwick Brookes's pencil pictures by T. Leatherbrow. 1889 23/8/90
Brooks, Phillips
Sermons preached in English churches. 1883 21/6/85
Brosses, Charles de
L'Italie il y a cent ans. 1836 (2v.) 14/8/66
Brougham, Henry Peter Lord Brougham
A discourse on the objects, advantages and pleasures of science. 1827 30/4/28
Discourse of natural theology. 1835 28/7/36
Historical sketches of statesmen who flourished in the time of George III. 1839 (3v. 1839–43) 4/9/43, 2/9/58
Inquiry into the colonial policy of the European powers. 1803 (2v.) 16/8/34
Installation address... at the University of Edinburgh. 1860 11/5/60
Letter to the marquess of Landsdowne... on the late revolution in France. 1848 28/8/58
Letter, on national education, to the duke of Bedford. 1839 22/6/40
Letters to William Forsyth. 1872 12/1/72
Life and time of Henry, Lord Brougham, written by himself. 1871 (3v.) 31/3/71
Lives of men of letters and science who flourished in the time of George III. 1845 (2v.) 2/9/58
Political philosophy. 1843 (3v.) 21/2/56
Reply to... Russell... on the... Reform Act. 1839 14/5/39
Speech on parliamentary reform. 1857 24/8/57
Speeches... relating to public rights, duties, and interests. 1838 (4v.) 6/2/39
Broughton, Rhoda
Belinda. 1882 (3v. 1882–4) 25/3/85
Second thoughts. 1880 (2v.) 7/6/81
Broughton, William Grant
Correspondence. 1849 27/4/50
Brouwer, Pieter van Limburg
Histoire de la civilisation... des Grecs. 1833 (8v. 1833–42) 9/11/74, 29/11/86
Brown, Andrew Morton
The leader of the Lollards. 1848 25/6/54, 2/6/77 ?
Brown, Charles John
Church establishments defended. 1833 15/6/34
Brown, Henry
Sonnets of Shakespeare solved. 1870 4/6/70
Brown, James Baldwin the elder
Historical account of the laws enacted against the Catholics. 1813 3/11/69
Brown, James Baldwin the younger
First principles. Essays of ecclesiastical truth. 1871 22/1/71
Our morals and manners. 1878 28/8/78
Our theology in relation to the intellectual movement of our time. 1878 18/9/78
Religious equality in the light of history. 1872 21/4/72
The higher life. Sermons. 6/6/75
Brown, John D.D.
Exposition of the Epistle of the Apostle Paul to the Hebrews. 1862 (2v.) 29/1/63, 19/4/63
Exposition of the Epistle... of the Apostle Paul to the Galatians. 1853 4/12/59
Memories of the past. 1863 31/5/63
What ought dissenters of Scotland to do in the present crisis?. 1840 19/5/41
Brown, John M.D.
'John Leech' from *'Horae Subsecivae'* 1862 3/3/65
Essay on Dr. Chalmers from *'Horae Subsecivae'.* 1861 17/3/61
Letter to Dr. Cairns. 1860 17/3/61
Marjorie Fleming; a sketch. 1863 24/12/63
Memoir of A. H. Hallam from *'Horae Subsecivae'.* 1858 7/11/59
Rab and his friends. 1859 8/11/59
Brown, John Minister at Bunyan meeting
John Bunyan, his life. 1885 27/12/85
Brown, John Minister at Haddington
Life of Reverend J. Hervey. 1832 11/5/34

The posthumous works of the late Rev. Mr. John Brown. 1797 11/6/93 ?
Brown, Sir John
[Pamphlet on naval reserve]. 12/8/63
Brown, John Joseph
The vision of Barabbas. 1891 7/11/91
Brown, John William
The life of Leonardo da Vinci. 1828 8/7/58 ?
Brown, Joseph
The Norwood hymnbook. 1843 28/1/43
Brown, R.
Four years at the court of Henry VIII. 1854 (2v.) 12/5/88 ?
The Wearmouth abbots. 1862 21/12/62 ?
Brown, Robert author
John Wesley's theology. A lecture. 1865 2/11/62
Philosophy of evangelicalism. 1857 12/8/60
Rationale of Justification by Faith. 1856 10/4/57
Brown, Robert F. S. A.
A trilogy of the life to come. 1887 2/5/87
Great Dionysiak myth. 1877 (2v. 1877–8) 24/3/77, 8/2/87
Poseidon. 1872 11/5/72
The myth of Kirkê. 1883 5/11/83, 21/6/87
The unicorn. 1881 23/10/81, 3/2/85
Brown, Robert of Barton-upon-Humber
Babylonianism. 1868 12/11/82
Brown, Robert solicitor
Lecture on the social unity of humanity. 1862 2/11/62
Brown, Samuel Borton
Fire-baptism of all flesh. 1882 29/4/83
Brown, Thomas M.D.
The poetical works of the late Thomas Brown. 1820 (4v.) 15/10/58
Brown, Thomas of Edinburgh
Reminiscences of an old traveller throughout different parts of Europe. 1843 7/7/57
Brown, Thomas of Shifnal
Works of M. Voiture, tr. J. Dryden. 1705 27/3/81 ?
Brown, Thomas Kenworthy
The Madeira chaplaincy treated of... in a letter to R. T. Lowe. 1848 9/8/48
Brown, William
New Zealand and its aborigines. 1845 6/5/46
Browne, Edward Harold
[Note on Genesis i.5. 'Later Gleanings', 50]. 27/12/85
An exposition of the thirty-nine articles. 1850 28/10/60
Antichrist. A sermon. 1883 2/12/83
Charge. 1869 5/12/69
Charge delivered to... the diocese of Ely. 1884 27/4/84
Convocation... a letter to S. H. Walpole. 1852 12/9/52
Position and parties of the English Church. Letter. 1875 12/12/75
Sacrifice—altar—priest. Six letters. 1866 27/5/66
The Old Catholic movement on the continent of Europe. 1875 23/5/75
Three sermons. 1872 31/1/75
Browne, Felicia Dorothea afterw. Hemans
Tales and historic scenes, in verse. 1819 16/10/25
Browne, George Forrest
The venerable Bede. 1879 5/9/86
Browne, H. R. F.
Life of John Locke. 1876 (2v.) 7/4/82 ?
Browne, Hugh Junor
The grand reality, being experiences of spirit life. 1888 21/9/91
Browne, Isaac Hawkin
Poems upon various subjects. 1768 6/4/27
Browne, John Cave
Lambeth Palace and its associations. 1883 17/8/83
Browne, Robert Henry Nisbett
Christ in Genesis. 1870 10/8/90 ?
Browne, Robert William
History of Roman classical literature. 1853 9/10/57
Browne, Thomas
Religio Medici. 14/1/82
Browne, Thomas Alexander pseud. Rolf Boldrewood
The miner's right. 1890 (3v.) 7/5/90
Browne, William
The whole works, ed. W. C. Hazlitt. 1868 3/12/70
Browne, William Alexander Francis
Sisterhoods in Asylums. 1866 20/5/66
Brownell, Charles
A letter to... Earl of Clarendon... in reply to Sir C. Lemon. 1847 27/5/47
Brownell, Henry Howard
Ephemeron. 1855 12/12/55
Brownfield, Arthur
What England owes to Ireland. 1887 12/1/87
Browning, Colin Arrott
The convict ship, and England's exiles. 1844 3/9/48
Browning, Elizabeth Barrett
Letters to R. H. Horne. 1877 (2v.) 1/6/85
Browning, Oscar
Despatches of Earl Gower 1790–92, ed. O. Browning. 1885 30/11/85, 8/6/88
England and Napoleon in 1803. 1887 21/5/88
Modern France, 1814–1879. 1880 8/7/80
Browning, Robert
Agamemnon of Aeschylus. 1877 27/10/77
Aristophanes' apology. 1875 5/8/75
Browning as a philosophical and religious teacher, by H. Jones. 1891 21/8/92

Browning, Robert (*cont.*)
Fifine at the fair. 1872 21/11/73
Life of Robert Browning, by W. Sharp. 1891 8/9/91
Paracelsus. 1835 11/6/36
Poetical works. 1863 (3v.) 22/8/63
Bruce, Charles Alexander
Report on the manufacture of tea . . . in Assam. 1839 24/11/40
Bruce, James 8th Earl of Elgin
Letters and journals. 1872 15/11/72
Bruce, Robert, and Knox, John
Biographical sketches. 1873 30/1/73
Bruce, William
State of society in the age of Homer. 1827 30/11/57
Bruce, William Napier
Life of General Sir C. Napier. 1885 15/5/88
Bruce, Wyndham Knight
The story of an African chief: Khama. 1893 20/12/93
Brugsch, Heinrich
A history of Egypt under the Pharaohs. 1879 (2v.) 3/1/79, 30/5/84, 15/11/86
Brumm, Carl
Bismarck: his aims and his deeds. 1889 14/3/89 ?
Brunn, Heinrich von
Die Kunst bei Homer. 1868 16/6/74
Brunner, P. H. von
Gebetbuch für aufgeklärte katholische Christen. 1845 19/10/45
Brunswik, Benoît
La succession au trône de Turquie. 1872 5/1/78
La verité sur Midhat Pacha. 1877 15/2/77
Brunton, Thomas Lauder
Bible and science. 1881 3/7/81
Bruun, Malthe Conrad afterw. Malte-Brun
Précis de géographie universelle. 1810 (5v. 1810–17) 28/4/30
Bry, Theodor de
Grands voyages. (25pts 1590–1634) 19/4/38
Bryant, Jacob
A dissertation concerning the war of Troy. 1796 1/3/47
A new system or an analysis of ancient mythology. 1774 (3v. 1774–76) 9/8/62
Expostulation [in reply to attack on 'the war of Troy']. 1799 10/3/47
Observations on a treatise . . . by Chevalier. 1795 1/3/47
Some observations on the vindication of Homer . . . by J. B. S. Morritt. 1799 10/3/47
The sentiments of Philo Judeus. 1797 25/11/93
Bryant, Sophie
Celtic Ireland. 1889 24/6/89
Bryant, William Cullen
Picturesque America, or the land we live in. 1872 (2v. 1872–3) 9/9/72 ?
Bryce, James D.D.
Public education in its relation to Scotland and its parish schools. A letter to . . . Aberdeen. 1845 23/2/54 ?
Bryce, James Viscount Bryce
[on Theodora] in *'Contemporary Review'*, xlvii.153, 266. 1885 (February 1885) 4/2/85
Academical study of the civil law. 1871 25/3/71
England and Ireland. 1884 20/1/87
Handbook of home rule, ed. J. Bryce [incl. Gladstone]. 1887 24/9/87
The American commonwealth. 1888 (3v.) 27/12/88, 30/9/89
The Holy Roman Empire. 1864 30/3/66, 20/3/76
Transcaucasia and Ararat. 1877 1/11/77
Brydone, Patrick
Tour through Sicily and Malta. 1773 (2v.) 8/8/38
Bryson, J.
Preacher and pulpit orator. 1875 15/8/75
Brzoska, Heinrich Gustav
De geographia mythica. 1831 27/12/75
Buchanan, David
The heresy and sham of all the leading so-called Christian sects. 1875 9/3/75
Buchanan, George
History of Scotland. 2/2/50
Latin poetry. 15/11/25 ?
Psalmorum Davidicorum. 21/5/26, 18/6/26, 22/10/26, 12/11/26, 2/12/26, 4/2/27, 18/2/27, 25/3/27
Buchanan, James
Facts . . . on state prisons in England. 1834 23/3/35
Buchanan, Robert
On the relation of the law . . . to the mission and work of Christ. 1866 5/8/66
Support of the Christian ministry. Address. 1864 26/6/64
The ten years conflict. 1849 (2v.) 10/3/50
Buchanan, Robert Williams
Drama of Kings. 1871 11/12/71
London poems. 1866 8/1/70
Napoleon fallen. 1870 22/7/71
New Abelard. 1884 31/3/84
On descending into hell, a letter concerning the proposed suppression of literature. 1889 29/9/89
Teuton monologue [from Poetical Works]. 1874 (3v.) 16/4/71
The Wandering Jew. A Christmas Carol. 1893 12/1/93 ?
Buchanan, William
Memoirs of painting. 1824 (2v.) 26/5/52
Buchheim, Carl Adolf
German grammar. 1863 13/1/64

Buchholz, Eduard
Die Homerischen Realien. 1871 (3v. 1871–85) 27/4/74, 15/10/88
Büchner, Friedrich Carl Christian Ludwig
Der Gottes-Begriff. 1874 28/3/75
Buckham, Philip Wentworth
Theatre of the Greeks. 1825 7/11/28
Buckingham, James Silk
'New plan of National colonization' from his *Canada* 1843 6/4/43
America, historical, statistic, and descriptive. 1841 25/5/41
Buckland, Anna
Record of Ellen Watson. 1884 27/12/84
Buckland, Francis Trevelyan
Curiosities of natural history. 1858 6/9/58
Notes and jottings from animal life. 1882 28/6/85
Buckland, William
Addresses to London Geological Society. 1841 24/3/42
Geology and minerology considered. 1836 28/10/36
Sermon... on reopening of choir. 1848 25/6/48
Buckle, Henry Thomas
Common place books. [vol II of Miscellaneous Works]. 1872 1/2/73
History of civilisation in England. 1857 (2v.) 25/1/58
The life and writings of H. T. Buckle, by A. H. Huth. 1880 (2v.) 17/4/81
Buckley, Arabella B.
Moral teachings of science. 1891 3/11/91
Buckley, James Monroe
Faith-healing, Christian science and kindred phenomena. 1892 26/3/93
Buckley, Michael Bernard
Life of the Rev. Arthur O'Leary. 1868 16/12/68
Buckmaster, John Charles
Substance of a paper on the nature and amount of aid... promoting... science. 1863 31/8/67
Budd, William
Siberian cattle-plague. 1865 14/12/65
Buddicom, Robert Pedder
Friendship with God. 1839 15/1/42
Two sermons on the death of his late Majesty [George III]. 1820 27/9/40
Budge, Ernest Alfred Thompson Wallis
Book of governors. Historia monastica of Thomas, Bishop of Magra. 1893 10/9/93
Nebuchadnezzar, king of Babylon. 1884 2/3/84
Budinszky, Alexander
Die Universität Paris und die Fremden an der selben im Mittelalter. 1876 19/9/92
Bugg, Francis
The pilgrim's progress from Quakerism to Christianity. 25/8/78
Bukharov, Dmitry Nikolaevich
La Russie et la Turquie. 1877 12/11/76
Bull, Charles
Soho in olden time... lecture. 1849 5/8/85
Bull, George
Vindication of the Church of England. 1719 18/4/41
Works, ed. R. Nelson. 1827 (7v.) 26/1/62
Bull, Henry
Christian praiers and holy meditations. 13/11/42
Bull, John, and Brother Jonathan
Dialogues. 1852 12/3/68
Bull, Patrick
A wolf in sheep's clothing. 1775 15/6/45
Bullen, Arthur Henry
Carols and poems from the fifteenth century to the present time. 1886 2/11/86
Buller, Charles
Responsible government for colonies. 1840 12/2/49
Systematic colonisation [speech in the Commons]. 1843 19/3/51 ?
Bullingbrook, E.
Duty and authority of Justices of the Peace... for Ireland. 1766 12/10/87
Bullitt, John Christian
A review of Mr. Binney's pamphlet on 'the privilege of the writ of habeas corpus'. 1862 19/4/62
Bullock, Charles
What church?. 1868 9/1/81
Bullock, T. H.
The Chinese vindicated. 1840 9/5/40
Bulmer, John
Elegiacs. 1881 28/9/81
Bülow-Cummerow, Ernst Gottfried Georg von
Der Zollverein, sein System und dessen Gegner. 1844 8/5/45
Bulstrode, Whitelocke, and Dr. Wood
Letters. 1717 2/1/44
Bulteel, Henry Bellenden
Reply to Dr. Burton's remarks upon a sermon preached at St. Mary's. 1831 1/3/31
Sermon on I Corinthians ii. 12. 1831 15/2/31
Bulwer, Edward George Earle Lytton Baron Lytton
England and the English. 1833 22/7/33
Eugene Aram. 1832 8/4/84
Horace, Odes and Epodes. 1893 10/10/93
Kenelm Chillingly. His adventures and opinions. 1873 27/3/73, 9/4/73
Leila. 1838 30/8/38
Lost tales of Milebus. 1866 22/1/66
My novel; or, varieties in English life. 1851 (1851–52) 9/9/53, 10/9/53
Poetical works. 1852 (5v. 1852–54) 30/1/68
Rienzi. 1835 (3v.) 4/4/36, 21/2/87

Bulwer, Edward George Earle Lytton (*cont.*)
Speeches of Edward, Lord Lytton. 1874 31/10/87
St. Stephen's. A poem. 1860 24/3/66
The Caxtons. 1849 (3v.) 19/11/75
The duchess de la Vallière. 1836 8/9/73
The lady of Lyons, or love and pride. 1838 29/8/38
The new Timon. 1846 20/11/46
The Parisians. 1873 (4v.) 22/11/73
The student. 1835 24/8/35
Bulwer, Rosina Doyle afterw. Bulwer Lytton, Baroness Lytton
Shells from the sands of time. 1876 15/1/80
Bulwer, William Henry Lytton Earle
Despatch . . . on Turkish convention. 1843 11/1/64
France, social, literary, political. 1834 (2v.) 14/10/34, 23/10/34
Life and correspondence of Henry John Temple, Lord Palmerston. 1870 (3v. 1870–4) 12/11/70
Sir Robert Peel. An historical sketch. 1874 29/10/74
Speeches of Mr. Webster at Capon Springs, Virginia. 1851 1/8/64
Bunbury, Edward Herbert
History of ancient geography among the Greeks and Romans. 1879 (2v.) 23/12/79
Bunhill fields, inscriptions on tombs in. 1867 3/3/67
Bunkley, Josephine M.
Miss Bunkley's book. The testimony of an escaped novice. 1857 22/1/82
Bunsen, Christian Carl Josias von
Beschreibung der Stadt Rom. 1842 5/1/45
Die Verfassung der Kirche der Zukunft. 1845 2/9/43
Die Zeichen der Zeit. Briefe an Freunde. 1855 (2v.) 27/1/56
Egypt's place in universal history. 1848 (5v. 1848–67) 26/12/57, 1/9/77
God in history. 1868 (3v. 1868–70) 2/3/68
Hyppolytus and his age. 1852 24/10/52
Le forum Romanum expliqué selon l'état des fouilles. 1835 29/12/38
Memorandum . . . Schleswig Holstein. 1848 19/4/48
Signs of the times. 1856 23/8/74
Bunsen, Frances von
Memoir of Baron Bunsen. 1868 29/4/68
Bunting, Jabez
Memorials of the late Rev. Richard Watson. 1833 29/12/54
Bunyan, John
Life of John Bunyan, by E. Venables. 1888 22/9/89
The pilgrim's progress. 16/8/46, 3/1/64, 6/4/90, 26/6/91
Buonarrotti, Michel Angelo
Rime. 14/6/38
Burder, Henry Forster
Memoir of the Reverend George Burder. 1833 9/9/55
Burge, William
Letters to Lord Glenelg. (not found) 15/4/36
Observations on the supreme appellate jurisdiction of Great Britain. 1841 22/2/41
On the choral service of the Anglo-Catholic church. 1844 22/1/44
The Temple Church. An account of its restoration and repairs. 1843 6/2/43
Burges, George
Address . . . to the bishop of Norwich. 1838 16/5/43
Commentary on the Act for the commutation of tithes in England and Wales. 1838 12/6/53
Reflections on the . . . present spirit of the times. 1819 12/6/53
Burges, Sir James Bland afterw. Lamb
Richard the First: a poem. 1800 25/11/78
Burgess, Henry
Disestablishment and disendowment. 1875 3/2/76
Burgess, James John Haldane
Shetland sketches and poems. 1886 23/2/91
Burgess, Richard
A city for the Pope. 1860 12/12/60
An enquiry into the State of the Church of England congregations [abroad]. 1850 21/2/50
Educational statistics. 1838 12/4/38
National education by rates or taxes. 1855 26/4/55
National education question practically considered. 1842 21/11/42
Sermons for the times. 1851 9/3/51
What may this system of National Education be?. 1838 6/5/38
Burgess, Thomas
First principles of Christian knowledge. 1804 17/8/28
Burgess, William Penington
Wesleyan hymnology. 1845 24/8/74
Burgh, James
Political disquisitions. 1774 (3v. 1774–5) 18/6/32
The dignity of human nature. 1754 2/11/90
Burgon, John William
A plain commentary on the four holy gospels. 1855 18/11/55
Disestablishment of religion in Oxford. 1881 31/12/80
Disestablishment. Sermon. 1868 4/11/68
Inspiration and interpretation. Seven sermons. 1861 7/7/61
Letters from Rome to friends in England. 1862 19/1/62, 16/11/66

Oxford reformers. 1854 22/2/54
Plea for a fifth Final School. A letter. 1868 22/2/68
Plea for the study of divinity in Oxford. 1875 7/2/75
Some remarks on art. 1846 26/10/47
The last twelve verses of the gospel according to S. Mark. 1871 20/2/76
The portrait of the Christian gentleman [P. F. Tytler]. 1859 2/4/59
Treatise on the pastoral office. 1864 1/5/64

Burke, Edmund
A letter from Edmund Burke ... to the sheriffs [of Bristol] ... *on the affairs of America*. 1777 28/3/45
A letter from ... Edmund Burke to a noble lord, on the attacks made upon him and his pension. 1796 10/6/42
A philosophical enquiry into the origin of our ideas of the sublime and beautiful. 1756 21/6/31
A short account of a late short administration. 1766 24/3/45
A vindication of natural society. 1756 20/6/31, 24/3/45
An appeal, from the old to the new whigs. 1791 22/9/26, 23/5/31 ?
Epistolary correspondence of Edmund Burke and Dr. French Laurence. 1827 30/4/37, 9/1/86
Gladstone and Burke, by H. de Fellenberg. 1886 9/11/86
History of the life and times of Edmund Burke, by T. Macknight. 1858 (3v. 1858–60) 17/2/58, 20/12/60, 23/1/61
Letter to a Peer of Ireland on the penal laws against Irish Catholics. 1782 3/4/45, 9/4/45
Letter to ... Henry Dundas ... with the sketch of a negro code. 1792 8/4/45
Letters, speeches and tracts on Irish affairs, ed. Matthew Arnold. 1881 8/11/81, 19/7/86
Life of, by W. Willis. 1889 15/11/89
Mr. Edmund Burke's Speeches at his arrival at Bristol, and at the conclusion of the poll. 1774 27/3/45
Observations on a late state of the nation. 1769 24/3/45
Opera. 13/7/26, 12/11/55, 27/3/57, 31/7/67, 14/12/85, 29/12/85, 9/1/86
Reflections on the revolution in France and on the proceedings in certain societies in London. 1790 1/6/31, 30/7/69, 7/8/69, 4/12/84
Scotsman's answer to Burke in 1779 [on Roman Catholics]. (not found) 23/10/44
Speech of Edmund Burke on moving his resolutions for conciliation with the colonies. 1775 27/3/45
Speech on the motion ... for charging the Nawab of Arcot's private debts to Europeans, on the revenues of the Carnatic. 1785 26/9/26
Speech on ... American taxation, April 19, 1774. 1775 25/9/26, 16/1/38, 27/3/45, 8/12/85
Speech on ... Mr. Fox's East India Bill. 1784 25/9/26, 1/4/45, 21/4/45
Speech on ... the oeconomical reformation of the civil and other establishments. 1780 28/3/45
Substance of the speech of ... Edmund Burke ... on the army estimates ... Comprehending a discussion of the present situation of affairs in France. 1790 21/2/40
The speeches of ... Edmund Burke in the House of Commons and in Westminster Hall. 1816 (4v.) 25/9/26, 27/3/33
The works of Edmund Burke, ed. W. King and F. Laurence. 1803 (16v. 1803–27) 24/3/45
The works of Edmund Burke, ed. with a preface by G. Croly. 1840 (2v.) 16/4/45
Thoughts on the cause of the present discontents. 1770 26/3/45, 5/5/86
Two letters ... to gentlemen in the City of Bristol on the Bills relative to the trade in Ireland. 1778 2/5/42, 16/3/82

Burke, Oliver Joseph
South isles of Aran, County Galway. 1887 17/11/87

Burke, S. Hubert
Historical portraits of the Tudor dynasty and the reformation period. 1879 (4v. 1879–83) 15/3/79, 24/7/80, 28/7/80, 17/12/82, 11/7/83

Burn, James Dawson
Autobiography of a beggar boy. 1855 15/5/56
Three years among the working classes in the United States during the war. 1865 13/1/66

Burn, Richard
Ecclesiastical law. 1763 (2v. 1763–5) 31/7/38, 20/8/52

Burnaby, E. H. V.
A ride to Khiva. 1876 13/12/76

Burnet, Gilbert
Bishop Burnet's History of his own time, ed. M. J. Routh. 1823 (6v.) 20/11/40
Exposition of the thirty-nine articles. 24/1/30, 4/4/30
History of the reformation of the Church of England. (3v. 1679–1715) 28/2/33, 25/12/61, 1/6/88
History of the rights of princes ... relating chiefly to the pretensions of the Crown of France. (2v.) 25/12/46
Life ... of Sir Matthew Hale. 16/11/62
Some passages of the life and death of ... Rochester. 6/11/59

Burnet, James
Of the origin and progress of language. 1773 (6v. 1773–92) 28/12/64

Burnet, Thomas
De statu mortuorum. 1727 24/1/47
Telluris theoria sacra. 27/11/26 ?
Burnett, A.
Tillage, a substitute for manure . . . illustrated by . . . Jethro Tull. 1859 31/8/59
Burnett, Frances Eliza Hodgson
Editha's burglar. 1888 23/7/88
Little Lord Fauntleroy. 1886 12/11/87, 16/11/87, 19/1/88
Little Saint Elizabeth. 1890 27/3/90
Sarah Crewe. 1887 24/7/88
Surly Tim's troubles. 1877 28/12/87
Burney, Frances [afterw. d'Arblay]
Diary and Letters of Madame d'Arblay [Fanny Burney] *edited by C. F. Barrett*. 1842 (5v.) 27/12/43, 22/9/85
Evelina. 1778 (3v.) 6/4/66, 14/11/68
The wanderer. 1814 (5v.) 23/6/86
Burnley, William Hardin
Opinions on slavery and emancipation in 1823. 1833 13/5/33, 12/7/33
Burns, Robert
Book of anecdotes. 1841 14/5/41
Burns and the Kirk, by A. Webster. 1888 9/11/90
Reliques of Robert Burns, ed. R. H. Cromek. 1808 6/11/54
Songs and ballads. 1823 17/10/45 ?
The complete works . . . with introduction by A. Cunningham. 1887 (new edn) 4/7/87
The works of Robert Burns, ed. C. Annandale. 1888 (7v. 1888) 9/8/92
Burr, Enoch Fitch
The doctrine of evolution. 1873 26/10/73
Burritt, Elihu
A journal of . . . three days in Skibbereen. 1847 5/4/47
Chips from many blocks. 1878 2/5/78
Elihu Burritt; a memorial volume containing a sketch of his life and labours. 1879 29/6/80 ?
Burrows, Montagu
Collectanea. 1890 6/6/90
Pass and class. An Oxford guidebook. 1860 24/12/60
Burt, John Thomas
Results of the system of separate confinement. 1852 3/5/53
Burton, Charles Henry
The royal supremacy. Sermon. 1850 2/3/51
Burton, Edward
A description of the antiquities of Rome. 1831 3/4/32, 28/7/32
Introduction to the metres of Greek tragedians. 1814 20/1/29
Remarks upon a sermon [by Bulteel]. 1831 18/2/31
Sequel to remarks on church reform. 1832 26/1/33
Testimonies of the Ante-Nicene fathers to the . . . Trinity. 1831 30/9/49
Thoughts on the separation of church and state. 1834 19/2/34
Thoughts upon the demand for church reform. 1831 26/8/31
Burton, John
A presbyterian clergyman looking for the church. 1855 24/1/58
Burton, John Hill
History of Scotland. 1867 (7v. 1867–70) 19/4/86, 2/4/88
History of Scotland [chapter 24]. 1853 (2v.) 17/1/85
Life and correspondence of David Hume. 1846 21/7/58
Burton, Robert
Anatomy of melancholy. 15/8/29
Burton, William Westbrooke
State of religion and education in New South Wales. 1840 13/5/40
Bury, John Bagnell
A history of the later Roman Empire. 1889 (2v.) 16/11/89
Busby, James
The federation of colonies. 1858 3/5/59
Buselli, P.
Assunzione corporea di Maria. 1863 28/10/66
Bush, George
Notes, critical and practical . . . on the Book of Leviticus. 1861 19/2/65
Bushe, Gervase Parker
Some considerations on the income tax. 1845 1/2/45
Busk, Rachel Harriette
The folk songs of Italy. 1887 29/6/87
Bussy, Charles de [Charles Marchal]
Les courtisanes devenues saintes. 1859 12/6/59
Butcher, Samuel Henry
Some aspects of the Greek genius. 1891 16/12/91
Butler, Alexander Hume
Poems written in barracks. 1868 22/6/68
Butler, Annie Robina
Little Kathleen; or sunny memories of a child-worker. 1890 12/9/88 ?
Butler, A. R.
Stepping stones to bible history. 1889 28/7/89 ?
Butler, Charles Barrister
Account of the life of . . . Rev. Alban Butler. 1799 8/9/78 ?
Book of the Roman Catholic church. 1825 17/9/33
Historical memoirs respecting the English, Irish, and Scottish catholics. 1819 (4v. 1819–21) 26/1/38, 26/11/74, 7/2/91
Memoir of the life of Henry Francis d'Agnesseau, chancellor of France. 1830 3/1/55
Reminiscences. 1822 (2v. 1822, 27) 18/10/42

The life of Hugo Grotius. 1826 29/10/42, 11/8/65
Butler, Charles of Philadelphia
The American lady. 1849 1/10/87 ?
Butler, Clement Moore
Inner Rome, political, religious, social. 1866 21/1/66
Butler, Frances Anne
Journal... on a Georgian plantation. 1863 23/7/63
Butler, George
Sermons preached in Cheltenham College chapel. 1862 15/10/82
Butler, Henry Montague
'Crossing the Bar' and a few other translations. 1890 6/1/91
Six translations from the Old and New testaments in homeric verse. 1876 5/5/76
Butler, Joseph
A Charge. 1751 31/3/29
An introduction to Bishop Butler's 'Analogy', by Joseph Wilson. 1810 10/1/91 ?
Analogy of religion. 1736 27/4/30, 28/4/30, 10/5/30, 4/7/30, 19/7/30, 8/10/31, 24/10/31, 29/1/38, 21/8/76, 1/1/88
Fifteen sermons preached at the Rolls chapel. 1726 19/7/31, 2/9/60, 14/3/94
Sermon [on education]. 1745 9/3/40
Works of Bishop Butler, ed. S. Halifax. 1807 (2v. new edn) 26/6/45, 4/3/94, 18/3/94
Works of Joseph Butler, ed. S. Halifax. 1804 (2v.) 18/3/94
Butler, Josephine Elizabeth
[on C. Booth] *Contemporary Review*, lviii. 639. 1890 (November 1890) 2/11/90
Apology for Rebecca Janett. 1885 13/12/85
Catharine of Siena. Biography. 1878 13/10/78
Life of Jean Frederic Oberlin, pastor of the Ban de la Roche. 1882 9/1/83
Memoir of John Grey of Dilston. 1869 7/2/91
Some thoughts on the crusade against the state regulation of vice. 1874 10/5/74
Sursum corda. Annual address to the Ladies National Association. 1871 12/8/71
Butler, Pierce Somerset
Butler against Mountgarret. Comment upon the judgement of the House of Lords. 1859 30/1/61
Butler, Samuel philosophical writer
The Fair Haven. 1873 1/6/73
Butler, Samuel poet
Hudibras. 5/8/40, 15/1/61, 18/10/64
Butler, W. Archer
Christ sought and found in the Old Testament. 1857 7/4/87 ?
Butler, William John
What is our present danger? A sermon. 1891 4/1/91
Butt, Isaac
Fixity of tenure; heads of a suggested legislative enactment. 1866 9/7/66 ?
History of Italy. 1860 (2v.) 25/6/60
Home government for Ireland. 1874 6/1/76
Irish Corporation Bill. Speech... in the House of Lords. 1840 5/6/40
Land tenure in Ireland. 1870 22/3/70 ?
Land tenure in Ireland, a plea for the Celtic race. 1866 9/7/66
The liberty of teaching vindicated. 1865 26/11/65
Two lectures on protection. 1846 25/3/46
Buxton, Charles
A survey of the system of national education in Ireland. 1853 27/3/53
Ideas of the day on policy. 1866 3/1/66
Buxton, Sydney Charles
Finance and politics: an historical study. 1888 (2v.) 19/5/88, 20/8/88
Buxton, Thomas Fowell
Memoirs, ed. by his son, C. Buxton. 1848 28/11/49
The African slave trade and its remedy. 1839 (2v. 1839–40) 8/3/39, 30/5/40
The remedy, being a sequel to the African slave trade. 1839 2/5/39
Buzantios, Gregorios
Hellenic spirit. Address. 1868 30/12/68
By a parent
Some remarks on the present studies and management of Eton School. 1834 13/3/34
By E (Epsilon)
Photograms of an eastern tour. 1859 23/7/59
Byles, John Barnard
Foundations of religion in the mind and heart of man. 1875 23/1/76
Byng, Frederick
Smithfield and Newgate markets. 1851 17/5/51
Byng, George
Speech... on the affairs of Ceylon in the House of Lords. 1851 24/4/51
Byng, John
A collection of several pamphlets... relative to the case of Admiral Byng. 1756 23/8/66
Byrne, James
Letter on the Irish Church question... to Gladstone. 1867 2/2/67
Byron, George Gordon Noel
Beppo. 1818 25/6/61
Byron painted by his compeers. 1869 21/5/75
Childe Harold's Pilgrimage. 1812 3/12/35, 8/12/35, 13/1/36, 30/9/37, 27/10/54, 20/10/59, 27/6/61, 5/5/66
Don Juan. 1819 (14 cantos, 1819–24) 24/8/37, 7/9/37, 21/5/72, 4/1/78, 4/12/91

Byron, George Gordon Noel (*cont.*)
English bards and Scotch reviewers. 1809 21/12/26, 4/4/84
Heaven and earth. 1823 17/4/89
Hours of idleness. 1807 15/9/37
Les maîtresses authentiques de Lord Byron, by F. Rabbe. 1890 22/3/92
Manfred. 23/11/29
Marino Faliero, Doge of Venice. 1821 17/4/33
Mazeppa. 25/11/29
Observations on an article in Blackwood's Edinburgh Magazine. 1820 26/8/37
Parisina. 1816 31/5/38
The Corsair. 1814 30/10/28
The prisoner of Chillon. 1816 25/11/29, 6/11/37, 25/6/61
Works of Lord Byron, ed. T. Moore. 1832 (17v. 1832–3) 23/10/67
Bystander, The. 1. 1 10/2/1880

Cabet, Etienne
Eau sur feu, ou réponse à Timon. 1845 27/10/45
Cadet de Gassicourt, Charles Louis
Essai sur la vie privée d'Honoré Gabriel Riquetti de Mirabeau. 1820 5/8/58
Cadogan, William Bromley
Life of Reverend William Romaine. 1827 1/3/57 ?
Cadorna, Carlo
Il potere temporale dei papi. 1884 6/10/84 ?
Le relazioni internazionali dell'Italia e la questione dell'Egitto. 1882 11/10/82
Caetani, Michelangelo Duke di Sermoneta
Tre chiose . . . nella Divina Commedia di Dante Alighieri. 1876 25/9/84
Caine, Thomas Henry Hall
Richard III and Macbeth: the spirit of the romantic play. 1877 28/12/77 ?
The little Manx nation. 1891 30/6/91
The scapegoat. A romance. 1891 (2v.) 14/10/91
Caird, Sir James
High farming under liberal convenants the best substitute for protection. 1849 17/12/49
Irish land question. 1869 29/10/69
Landed interest and the supply of food. 1878 15/10/78
The British land question. 1881 18/11/81
Caird, John
Introduction to the philosophy of religion. 1880 18/4/80
Religion in the common life, a sermon. 1855 17/2/56
Sermons. 1858 12/9/58, 23/5/80
Cairnes, John Elliot
'Political economy and land', *Fortnightly Review*, xiii.41. 1870 (January 1870) 4/1/70
The character and logical method of political economy. 1857 19/11/57
The slave power . . . the real issues involved in the American contest. 1862 1/12/62, 5/2/72, 28/11/72
University education in Ireland. A letter to J. S. Mill. 1866 29/10/72
Calamy, Edmund fils
Abridgement of Mr. Baxter's history of his life and times. 1782 25/5/41
An historical account of my own life . . . ed. J. T. Rutt. 1829 28/1/33, 3/4/43
Calcraft, John William [John William Cole]
Defence of the stage. 1839 3/2/84
Caldecott, John
A practical guide . . . to bookkeeping by double entry. 1851 17/11/55
Caldicott, John William
Religious education and religious freedom . . . a letter to W. E. Gladstone. 1872 25/3/72
Calendar of state papers. 16/10/88, 24/9/89
Calhoun, John Caldwell
Eulogies delivered in the Senate and House of Representatives . . . on the life and character of J. C. Calhoun. 1853 17/10/53
John C. Calhoun: disquisition on government . . . ed. C. Gordon Post. 1850 8/10/52
Life of J. C. Calhoun, presenting a condensed history with speeches. 1843 1/12/43
Callard, Thomas Karr
The geological evidences of the antiquity of man reconsidered. 1875 3/6/75
Callender, James Thompson
Political progress of Britain. 1792 22/2/66
Calmon, Marc Antoine
William Pitt, étude financière et parlementaire. 1865 13/7/65, 1/1/86
Calmour, A. C.
The amber heart and other plays. 1888 19/6/87 ?
Calthorpe, Somerset John Gough
Letters from head-quarters, or the realities of the war in Crimea. 1856 21/3/57
Calvert, Frederick Baron Baltimore
Trial of Frederick Calvert, Esq., Baron of Baltimore. 1768 4/8/52
Calvert, Frederick barrister
Denominationalists and secularists. 1876 14/3/76
Letter to the Rt. Hon. the Speaker, upon private bill legislation. 1863 24/12/63
Remarks upon the jurisdiction of the Inns of Court. 1874 5/3/74
Wrongs and remedies. 1877 24/2/77
Cambridge
A few brief remarks on reform. 1870 18/12/73
Cambridge Camden Society
Report. 1841 25/11/41
Transactions. 1841 22/11/41

Camden Society
Letters of Queen Elizabeth and James VI. 1849 19/9/82
Cameron, Charles Hay, and Ryan, Sir Edward
A letter to . . . the court of directors of the East India company. 1850 13/5/53
Cameron, Charles Richard
The mystical sense of the binding of Satan. 1850 10/10/90 ?
The revolutions of 1848. A recommencement of the judgements upon the papacy. 1848 10/6/48
Cameron, Ebenezer
Auld Reekie's fair and the grand old man. 18/1/87
Cameron, Jane
Memoirs of Jane Cameron, female convict. 1864 (2v.) 24/9/91
Campan, Jeanne Louise Henriette
The private life of . . . Marie Antoinette. 1887 (new edn) 7/3/88
Campanella, Giuseppe Maria
Life in the cloister, in the Papal Court, and in exile. An autobiography. 1877 23/3/77
My life and what I learnt in it. An autobiography. 1874 20/3/77
Campbell, Arabella Georgina
Life of Fra Paulo Sarpi. 1869 21/4/70, 10/5/89
Campbell, Augustus
Convocation: a letter to the clergy of the archdeaconery of Liverpool. 1852 21/11/52
Campbell, Colin architect
Vitruvius Britannicus, or the British architect. 1717 (3v. 1717–25) 9/10/76
Campbell, Diana Anne Geraldine
Miss Sellon and the sisters of mercy. 1852 11/4/52
Campbell, Douglas
The puritan in Holland, England and America. 1892 (2v.) 16/10/92
Campbell, Dugald
Speech on the case of Prof. Marcus Dods. 1890 7/4/90
Campbell, George Professor
Philosophy of rhetoric. 1776 3/11/31
Campbell, Sir George
A handy book on the Eastern Question. 1876 7/12/76
Fortnightly Review, xxxv.552 [Irish land]. 1881 (May 1881) 24/12/83 ?
Irish land. 1869 11/8/69, 27/11/69
Campbell, George Douglas Duke of Argyll
'Diplomatic history of the eastern question' in *Edinburgh Review*, c. 1. 1854 (July 1854) 3/3/63
'Flint drift and human remains' in *Edinburgh New Philosophical Journal*, xiii. 145. 1861 7/4/61
'Iona' from *Good Words.* 1870 12/1/71
'On animal instinct' *Contemporary Review, 352.* 1875 (July 1875) 2/9/75
'Professor Huxley and the Duke of Argyll' in *Nineteenth Century*, xxix. 670. 1891 (April 1891) 11/4/91
'Professor Huxley on Canon Liddon' in *Nineteenth Century*, xxi. 321. 1887 (March 1887) 27/2/87, 17/12/90
Address to the national committee of British freed-man's associated societies. 1865 29/12/65
Address to the royal society of Edinburgh. 1864 11/10/67
Address . . . on fossils. 1852 28/5/52
Anthropomorphism in theology. 1875 18/4/75
Continuity and catastrophes in geology. 1883 20/11/83
Correspondence with the Rev. Andrew Gray on 'Presbytery examined'. 1849 15/2/49
Eastern question. Speech. 1876 20/9/76
Geology: its past and present. 1859 4/6/59
Inaugural address . . . on his installation as Lord Rector of . . . University of Glasgow. 1856 22/12/56
Letter to the peers . . . on . . . the Church of Scotland. 1842 3/2/42
Presbytery examined: an essay. 1848 3/10/48
Primeval man. 1869 21/3/69
Recent speculations on primeval man. Good words. 1868 2/3/68, 1/11/68
Reign of law. 1867 23/2/67
Some words of warning to the Presbyterians of Ireland. 1890 4/3/91
Speech on . . . Patronage Act of 1874. 1874 20/11/74
Speech . . . on the motion of Lord Panmure. 1858 25/3/58
The burdens of belief, and other poems. 1894 13/3/94
The eastern question from . . . 1856. 1879 (2v.) 4/6/78, 14/10/78, 20/2/79, 13/3/79
The twofold protest . . . letter . . . to the bishop of Oxford. 1851 7/3/52
The unity of nature. 1884 3/2/84
The unseen foundations of society. An examination of the fallacies and failures of economic science. 1893 3/5/93
Campbell, James Colquhoun
A charge . . . to the clergy of the diocese of Bangor. 1872 27/10/72
Campbell, John Baron
Letter to . . . Lord Stanley . . . on the law of Church Rates. 1837 13/6/37
Life of John, Lord Campbell . . . ed. by his daughter. 1881 9/3/81, 21/3/81
Lives of the Lord Chancellors. 1845 (7v. 1845–7) 15/8/46, 23/9/48, 13/10/48, 25/10/48, 2/11/48

Campbell, John Baron (*cont.*)
Shakespeare's legal acquirements considered. 1859 30/8/59
Campbell, John D.D.
Conquest of England. Letters to the Prince Consort. 1861 28/11/68
Campbell, John Professor
The Hittites, their inscriptions and their history. 1891 6/9/91
Campbell, John Douglas Sutherland Marquis of Lorne
A trip to the tropics and home through America. 1867 23/3/67
Imperial federation. 1885 19/5/85
Viscount Palmerston, K. G. 1892 2/9/92
Campbell, John MacLeod
Responsibility for the gift of eternal life. 1873 23/3/73 ?
Thoughts on revelation, with special reference to the present time. 1862 11/10/63
Campbell, Lewis, and Garnett, William
The life of James Clerk Maxwell. 1882 27/1/83
Campbell, Sir Neil
Napoleon at Fontainebleau and Elba. 1869 24/3/69
Campbell, Robert James Roy
The Indian mutiny: its causes and remedies. A letter to ... Palmerston. 1857 12/8/57
Campbell, Thomas poet
Essay on English poetry. 1848 28/6/55
Gertrude of Wyoming; a Pennsylvania tale; and other poems. 1809 21/1/26
Letters from the south. 1837 (2v.) 8/4/56
Campbell, Lord William Frederick Baron Stratheden and Campbell
The Ministerial Position and its dangers. 1883 27/7/83
Campello, Enrico di
Cenni autobiografici. 1881 29/10/81
Count Campello and Catholic reform in Italy, by A. Robertson. 1891 10/5/91
Campion, Edmund
Decem Rationes propositae in Causa Fidei et Opuscula eius selecta. 22/12/39
History of Ireland. 15/1/70
Camus, Jean Pierre
Beauties of St Francis de Sales. 1829 28/5/43
Canada, Hints on case of. 1838 17/1/38
Canada report [probably Durham's]. 3/1/40
Candlish, Robert Smith
A Letter to the Marquis of Normanby. 1841 19/3/41
Friendly address to the dissenters of Scotland. 1840 18/9/46
Remarks on ... the Dean of Faculty's letter to the Lord Chancellor. 1839 27/11/39
Candy, Thomas Henry
Antediluviana, or an answer to Dr. Colenso's doubts respecting the flood. 1864 20/7/90
Canestrini, Giovanni
Origine dell'uomo. 1866 18/11/66
Canning, Albert Stratford George
Lord Macaulay, essayist and historian. 1882 6/4/82
Thoughts on religious history. 1891 17/11/91
Canning, George
Speeches, ed. R. Therry. 1828 30/3/35
Substance of the speech ... on Lord Morpeth's motion for a committee on the state of Ireland. 1812 15/7/86 ?
Canning, Lady
A brief exposition of the foreign policy of Mr. Canning as contrasted with that of the existing administration. 1830 28/10/30
Canning, Stratford Lord Stratford de Redcliffe
Exile of Calauria; or the last day of Demosthenes. 1872 15/1/72
Life of ... Viscount Stratford de Redcliffe, by Stanley Lane Poole. 1888 8/10/88
On Turkey in *Nineteenth Century*, v.1:707. 1877 (June 1877) 31/5/77
On Turkey in *Nineteenth Century*, v.2. 1879 (January 1879) 2/1/79
Shadows of the past. In verse. 1866 24/3/68
The Eastern question. 1881 11/2/81
Canones et decreta ... concilii Tridentini. 1/3/46
Canons, code of ... of the Church of Scotland. 1838 19/12/38
Canons for the government of the Protestant episcopal church in the U.S.A. ... constitution. 1832 30/7/48
Cant, the world of. 1881 21/10/86
Cantab.
Apostolic succession not a doctrine of the Church of England. 1870 22/10/82
Canterbury Association papers. 1850 (1850–52) 4/1/52
Cantini, Lorenzo
Vita di Cosimo de' Medici primo Gran-Duca di Toscana. 1805 13/8/75
Canton, W.
A lost epic and other poems. 1887 24/1/90
Cantù, Cesare
La Letteratura italiana esposta alla gioventù per via d'esempi. 1851 24/12/66
Capecelatro, Cardinal Alfonso
Gladstone e gli effetti de' Decreti Vaticani. 1875 8/4/75
Capefigue, Jean Baptiste Honoré Raymond
Diplomatists of Europe. 1845 9/7/45, 28/3/55
La duchesse de Portsmouth et la cour galante des Stuarts. 1861 8/8/81
Louis XIV, son gouvernement et ses relations diplomatiques. 1837 (6v. 1837–38) 18/8/69
Richelieu, Mazarine, la Fronde et le règne de Louis XIV. 1835 (8v. 1835–36) 20/9/70

Capel, Thomas John
Reply to... Gladstone's 'Political expostulation'. 1874 25/12/74
Capes, John Moore
'Prospects of a new German reformation' in *Contemporary Review*, xviii. 376. 1871 (October 1871) 23/10/71
Reasons for returning to the Church of England. 1871 1/4/71
To Rome and back. 1873 15/2/74
What can be certainly known of God and Jesus of Nazareth?. 1880 29/2/80
Capital and labour [possibly the National Federation of Associated Employers' newspaper]. 3/8/75
Capodistria, V.
Analisi del Trattato di Parigi. 1/1/59
Capper, Samuel James
Shores and cities of the Boden See. 1881 4/1/81
Wanderings in wartime. 1871 27/11/71
Capps, Edward
The national debt financially considered. 1859 22/2/60
Capron, F. H.
The antiquity of man. 1892 4/10/92
Caraccioli, Louis Antoine de Marquis
Life of Pope Clement XIV. 1776 30/8/63
Caracciolo, Enrichetta
Memoirs of Henrietta Caracciolo. 1864 5/1/65
Caracciolo de Brienza, M.
Omaggio a Dante Alighieri, ed. Duke M. Caracciolo di Brienza. 1865 4/11/66
Caractacus
Opera. 8/4/31
Cardon, Raffaele
Svolgimento storico della costituzione inglese. 1883 (2v.) 30/1/83
Cardwell, Edward
History of conferences... connected with the revision of the Book of Common Prayer. 1840 9/10/40
Reformatio legum ecclesiasticarum. 1850 15/6/57
Synodalia, ed. E. Cardwell. 1842 6/8/42
The two Books of Common Prayer. 1838 22/3/40
Carellis, Edward
The great problem solved. 1885 3/4/85
Carey, Henry Charles
International copyright question considered. 1872 9/8/79
Carey, Peter Stafford
Epistle to the Galatians. 1867 22/3/68
Cargill, William
The currency, showing how a fixed gold standard places England at a permanent disadvantage. 1845 5/10/54
Caritat, Marie Jean Antoine Nicholas Marquis de Condorcet
Influence de la révolution de l'Amérique... 1788 22/10/60
Carleton, Hiram
Treatise on meaning of Greek roots. 1875 28/2/76
Carleton, William
Fardorougha the miser. 1839 23/4/47
The black prophet. 1847 3/4/47
Carlile, James
System of Irish education explained and defended. 1832 1/5/37
Carlisle, Arthur Drummond
Round the world in 1870. 1871 5/9/71 ?
Carlisle, Nicholas
'Correspondence on the Mint' in *Memoir of William Wyon... Chief Engraver of the Royal Mint*. 1837 17/4/43
Carlisle, William
Essay on evil spirits. 1825 23/4/82, 27/9/85
Carlon, Cecil Baylis
*England's sin. Honour sold. Truth betray*ed. Sermon. 1884 23/4/86
Carlyle, Alexander
Autobiography of Dr. Alexander Carlyle. 1860 28/1/61
Carlyle, Gavin
Moses and the prophets. 1890 7/7/90
The light of all ages. 1873 18/5/73
Carlyle, Jane Welsh
Life of Jane Welsh Carlyle, by Anne E. Ireland. 1891 20/7/91
Carlyle, Thomas essayist
'Walter Scott' from *Critical Essays*. 1840 7/2/68
Biographical essays II. Burns. 1854 27/8/57
Critical and miscellaneous essays. 1839 (4v.) 5/2/39
Early letters, ed. C. E. Norton. 1886 (2v.) 12/12/87
French revolution: a history. 1837 (3v.) 15/3/39
History of Frederick the Great. 1858 (6v. 1858–65) 9/7/62
Latter day pamphlets, ed. T. Carlyle. 1850 (8pt.) 18/2/50
Letters addressed to Mrs. Basil Montagu and B. W. Porter. 1881 10/4/84
Oliver Cromwell's letters and speeches. 1845 (2v. 1845–6) 22/12/62
On heroes, hero-worship, and the heroic in history. 1841 6/9/41
Past and present. 1843 26/6/43
Reminiscences of my Irish journey in 1849. 1887 23/11/87
Reminiscences, ed. J. A. Froude. 1881 (2v.) 11/3/81
Sartor Resartus. 1834 28/12/42
T. Carlyle and R. W. Emerson. Correspondence 1834–1872., ed. C. E. Norton. 1883 (2v.) 3/5/83
The life of John Sterling. 1851 17/8/53

Carlyle, Thomas of the Scottish Bar
On symbols in worship. 1853 3/1/76 ?
Carmen Sylva, or, Elizabeth Queen of Roumania. 1885 20/12/84
Carmichael, Mrs. A. C.
Domestic manners and social conditions ... in the West Indies. 1833 (2v.) 27/5/36
Carmichael, James
Corn laws. Remarks on Mr. McCulloch's statement. 1842 24/1/42
Carmichael, John pseud. Veritas
Romanism and Scottish episcopacy. 1858 14/3/58
Carné, Louis Joseph Marie de
Les fondateurs de l'unité française. 1856 (2v.) 1/3/93
Carne, Robert Harkness
Sermons. 1810 30/3/29 ?
Carnegie, Andrew
'On poverty' in *Nineteenth Century, xxix:367*. 1891 (March 1891) 18/3/91
'The library as a field for philanthropy', in *Library Journal*. 1890 25/12/89 ?
Address to college students. 28/1/85
Some facts about the American republic. 1890 7/9/90
Carnegie, James Lord Southesk
Jonas Fisher. Poem. 1875 19/2/75
Paradise, or notes on some pictures in the Royal Gallery. 1871 31/7/71
The burial of Isis, and other poems. 1884 19/9/84
Carnegie, William Hartley
Through conversion to the creed. 1893 28/5/93
Carpenter, Alfred
Preventive medicine in relation to the public health. 1877 8/10/77
Some points in the physiological and medical aspect of sewage irrigation. 1870 2/4/70
Carpenter, Joseph Estlin
The first three gospels, their origin and relations. 1890 12/10/90
Carpenter, Lant
Brief notes on the Rev. Dr. Arnold's 'Principles of church reform'. 1833 8/9/33
Carpenter, Mary
Address ... at conference on ragged schools. 1861 21/8/69
Carpenter, William Benjamin
'On ... inland seas', *Contemporary Review*, xxii. 372. 1873 (August 1873) 13/1/73
Nature and man. Essays scientific and philosophical. 1888 11/11/88
Principles of mental physiology. 1874 7/6/74
Temperature and life of the deep sea. Lecture. 1866 12/11/74
Temperature of the sea. Lecture. 1871 4/3/80 ?
The truth about vaccination and smallpox. 1881 28/10/81
Carpenter, William Boyd
Permanent elements of religion. 1889 12/1/90
Carpmael, William
The law of patents for inventions, familiarly explained. 1842 (3rd edn) 10/6/43
Carr, John
First three sections of Newton's Principia. 1821 21/1/29
Carr, Ralph
Penalty of death retained for cruel atrocities. 1841 20/2/41
Carrias, Victoriano
Gibraltar to Bourbonless Spain; or, England and Spain in the Mediterranean. 1869 9/3/69
Carrière, Philipp Moriz
Die philosophische Weltanschauung der Reformationszeit. 1847 26/3/88
Carroll, William George
Collapse of the faith. 1871 10/9/71
Carson, James M.D.
Essays on digestion. 1863 4/10/67
Carson, James Crawford Ledlie
Miscellaneous papers. 1883 1/3/85
Carter, Anna Maria
Selections from the letters of the late Miss Carter, ed. W. Palmer. 1793 12/1/48
Carter, James Gordon
Letters to ... Prescott on the free schools of New England. 1824 3/8/64
Carter, Thomas Thellusson
'Crisis of the Church of England', *Nineteenth Century*, i. 417. 1877 (May 1877) 24/4/77
'Thoughts for the hours' from *Manual of Devotion for Sisters of Mercy*. 1868 (2v.) 7/5/76
Harriet Monsell. A memoir. 1884 10/8/84
Objections to sisterhoods considered. 1853 13/2/53
Rome Catholic and Rome papal. 1850 7/12/51
Royal commission and the eucharistic vestments. A letter to Gladstone. 1867 28/7/67
The first five years of the House of Mercy, Clewer. 1855 27/4/56
The passion and temptation of our Lord. 1863 27/12/63
Cartwright, Thomas
Diary of Thomas Cartwright, Bishop of Chester. 1843 3/10/86
Carus, P.
The soul of man. 1891 29/11/91
Carwithen, John Bayley Somers
History of the Church of England. 1829 (3v. 1829–33) 21/1/34, 25/2/35
Cary, Edward
Catechist catechiz'd concerning the oath of allegiance. 9/1/65 ?
Cary, Henry Francis
The early French poets. 1846 19/5/48
Cary, Lucius Lord Falkland
Speech ... concerning episcopacy. 4/9/71

Casaubon, Isaac
Ad Frontonem Ducaeum S. J. theologum epistola. 5/9/46
Ephemerides. 1850 (2v.) 14/3/52
Epistolae. 1709 (4 pt.) 13/8/46
Case of Irish Church curates. 9/1/72
Case of the British West Indies stated by the West India Association of Glasgow. 1852 22/7/54
Cassan, Stephen Hyde
Lives of the bishops of Winchester. 1827 (2v.) 26/7/46
Cassander, Georgius
De communione sub atraque specie dialogus [preface by Calixtus]. 10/12/54
Opera. 25/1/85
Castelvetro, Lodovico
Sposizione . . . a xxix canti dell'Inferno dantesco. 1886 (1886 edn) 15/5/86 ?
Casti, Giovanni Battista
Gli animali parlanti. 1802 (3v.) 23/1/43, 21/9/61
Il Poema tartaro di Giambattista Casti. 1803 (2v.) 9/8/49
Novelle. 1804 18/9/61
Castille, H.
Saint Arnauld et Canrobert. 1856 27/11/56
Castille, Hippolyte
'Le marquis Delcanetto' in 'Portraits politiques au dix-neuvième siècle' 1856 (1856–9) 9/8/56
Castle, Egerton
Consequences. A novel. 1891 29/1/91
Caswall, Alfred
Treatise on copyholds. 1840 11/8/45
Caswall, Henry
A brief account of the method of synodal action in the American church. 1851 19/10/51
A pilgrimage to Canterbury in 1852. 1852 12/9/52
America and the American church. 1839 8/9/41
City of the Mormons. 1842 24/8/42
Prophet of the nineteenth century. 1843 4/3/43
Scotland and the Scottish church. 1853 20/11/53, 31/5/88
Synodal action necessary to the church. A letter to . . . Gladstone. 1852 4/4/52
The Jerusalem chamber. 1852 31/10/52
The Jubilee [of the S. P. G.]. 1852 4/7/52
The western world revisited. 1854 9/7/54
Catéchisme de l'église catholique Orthodoxe d'Orient. 1851 22/8/86
Cater, William, and Hudson, James
An expostulatory letter to . . . Alston. 1843 14/1/66
Cathédral Les Bas Souhaits. (untraced) 10/3/90
Cathena
Cathena, seu explicatio locorum qui in Pentateucho subobscuriones occurrunt. 18/3/49
Catherine II
Histoire secrète des amours et des principaux amans. 1799 10/8/87 ?
Memoirs . . . written by herself. 1859 10/8/69, 30/3/85
Catherine of Genoa, St.
'Treatise on purgatory' from *Vita e dottrina.* 14/12/79
Catholicism without popery. 19/8/55
Catholic layman
A short letter . . . by a Catholic of the Anglican church to Bagot. 1841 13/5/41
Catholic Presbyterian.
2. 401. 12/1879. Religion in Holland 30/11/1879
3. 3/1880. Early British Church 7/3/1880
3. 321. 5/1880. Presbyterian history 2/5/1880
4. 8/1880 15/8/1880
Catholic revival, by a Working Man. 1877 22/9/78
Catullus, Caius Valerius
Atys, Peleus et Thetis. 24/5/61
Opera. 19/12/26, 27/9/90
Poems, tr. by Sir T. Martin. 1861 24/5/61, 27/9/90
Caulfield, James
Portraits, memoirs and characters of remarkable persons. 1819 (4v. 1819–20) 19/8/34
Caulfield, Richard
Annals of the cathedral of St. Coleman, Cloyne. 1882 16/4/82
Caulfield, Sophia Frances Anne
Avenele, and other poems. 1870 8/4/71
Caumont, Charlotte Rose de
Histoire de Marguerite de Valois, reine de Navarre. 1749 7/6/53
Causes célèbres étrangères publiées en France pour la première fois. 1827 (5v. 1827–8) 27/6/48
Causes of contempt of the clergy . . . 1796 26/10/62
Cautus
A letter to . . . William Skinner. 1852 11/3/52
Cave, Alfred
The battle of the standpoints. 1890 3/5/91
The inspiration of the old testament, inductively considered. 1888 16/9/88
Cave, William
Primitive Christianity. (2v.) 18/2/38
Cavendish, Elizabeth Christiana Duchess of Devonshire
Anecdotes and biographical sketches. 1863 4/7/65
Cavendish, Richard
A letter . . . on the actual relations between Church and state. 1849 17/4/49
Letter . . . on the judgement in the Gorham case. 1850 11/5/50

Cavendish, Spencer Compton Lord Hartington
Speech on disestablishment of Irish church (28 April 1868). 1868 24/8/68
Cavendish, William George Spencer 6th Duke Devonshire
Handbook of Chatsworth and Hardwick. 1845 18/11/61
Cavour, Count Camillo B. di Benso
Diario inedito, ed. D. Berti. 1888 29/6/88
Oeuvre parlementaire. 1862 29/10/62
Speech on annexation bill: 11 October 1860. 1860 5/11/60
Thoughts on Ireland, its present and future. 1868 26/12/68, 15/4/93, 28/4/93
Cawdrey, Daniel
Diatribe triplex. 27/4/50
Cayley, Charles Bagot
English hexameters. 1863 25/4/63
Cayley, Edward Stillingfleet the elder
Corn laws. Speech. 1839 11/1/42
Reasons for the formation of the Agricultural Protection Society. 1844 20/8/44
Cazalet, Edward
Bimetallism and its connection with commerce. 1879 5/9/79
Cazenove, John Gibson
Inconsistency real and apparent. Sermon. 1866 6/5/66
Modern theism. 1872 24/11/72
On certain characteristics of Holy Scripture [with reference to Jowett's interpretation of scripture]. 1861 24/3/61
Some aspects of the Reformation. 1869 18/7/69, 16/5/75
Cecil, Richard
A friendly visit. 1792 9/2/34
Memoirs of John Bacon. 1801 11/8/78
Memoirs of Rev. John Newton. 1808 11/8/78
Cecil, William Baron Burleigh
Memoirs, ed. Ralph Courteville. 1738 23/7/92
Cellini, Benvenuto
Due trattati, uno intorno alle otto principale arti dell'oreficeria. 1/11/61
Vita de Benvenuto Cellini. 1831 28/9/61 ?
Centenary of Methodism. 1839 25/6/39
Centlivre, Susanna
Bold stroke for a wife. 1718 24/10/25
Cent nouvelles nouvelles. 13/7/48, 29/3/69
Century Magazine. 17. 871. 4/1890. Putnam 18/4/1890
Cerati, Abbé
Du célibat. 1829 6/3/39
Cervantes, Miguel de
'La Gitanilla' from *Novelas Ejemplares*. 9/12/35
Don Quixote. 5/4/27, 11/12/27, 21/9/81, 7/11/81
Life of Miguel de Cervantes Saavedra, by J. F. Kelly. 1892 9/12/92
Novelas Ejemplares. 7/12/35
Cesaresco, Evelyn Martinengo-
Italian characters in the epoch of unification. 1890 17/4/90
Chabas, François Joseph
Études sur l'antiquité. 1872 27/4/74
Chadwick, Sir Edwin
Address on railway reform. 1865 14/2/65
Report . . . on inquiry into the sanitary conditions of the labouring classes. 1842 (2v. 1842–3) 3/8/58
The financial value of sanitary science. 1887 10/9/88
Chadwick, John M.D.
Christianity versus Paganism. Seven letters. 1870 11/12/70
Chadwick, John White
The man Jesus: a course of lectures. 1881 28/12/81
Chalkiopulos, P., and Gennadius, P.
Orations on Sir R. Church. 1873 13/9/73
Challemel-Lacour, P.
Revue des Deux Mondes, lxxxviii.809 [on Sir G. C. Lewis]. 1870 (July 1870) 24/8/70
Challis, Thomas M.
Smithfield and Newgate markets, as they should and might be. 1851 3/6/51
Challoner, Richard
Martyrs to the Catholic faith. 1878 10/8/79
Chalmers, George
An estimate of the comparative strength of Britain during the present and four preceding reigns. 1782 18/8/88
Political annals of the present united colonies. 1780 4/3/46
Chalmers, Thomas D.D.
Christian and civic economy of large towns. 1821 (3v. 1821–3) 24/2/41
Discourses on Christian revelation viewed in connexion with the modern astronomy. 1817 10/12/26, 25/12/26
Five lectures on predestination. 1837 23/12/49
Memoirs of the life and writings of Thomas Chalmers, D.D., by W. Hanna. 1849 (4v. 1849–52) 18/12/49
On political economy in connexion with the moral states and moral prospects of society. 1832 30/3/42
On the adaption of external nature. 1833 (2v.) 28/9/35
On the evangelical alliance. 1846 26/9/46
On the evils which the church . . . in Edinburgh has suffered. Ecclesiastical destitution of Scotland. 1835 14/6/35
On the use and abuse of literary and ecclesiastical endowments. 1827 23/1/38
Remarks on the present position of the Church of Scotland. 1839 20/1/40

Remarks on the right exercise of church patronage. 1836 13/7/39
Reply to the attempt to connect the cause of church accommodation with party politics. 1835 21/4/38
Speech on the proceedings of the church deputation in London. 1835 24/12/35
Speeches and tracts. 1823 14/12/33
Substance of a speech [on the Auchterarder case]. 1839 30/4/43
The evidence and authority of Christian revelation. 1814 27/11/31
Works. 1848 (vol vi) 10/4/49

Chamberlain, Joseph
Speeches, ed. H. W. Lucy. 1885 27/11/85
The Radical Programme; with a preface by . . . Chamberlain. 1885 20/10/85, 4/11/85, 6/11/85

Chamberlain, Walter
The case against the Burials Bill. 1875 13/1/76

Chamberlayne, Edward
Angliae Notitia, or the present state of England. (5th edn 1671) 5/10/58

Chambers, A. B.
Proceedings of the St. Louis chamber of commerce, in relation to the improvement of the navigation of the Mississippi river . . . with a statement 1842 20/1/43

Chambers, John David
Review of the Gorham case. 1850 5/5/50
Strictures legal and historical on judgement . . . on Martin vs. Mackonochie. 1869 30/5/69

Chambers, Robert publisher, the elder
Ancient sea margins, as memorials of changes in relative level of sea and land. 1848 1/10/58
Traditions of Edinburgh. (1869 edn) 17/1/76
Vestiges of the natural history of creation. 1844 12/7/47

Chambers, William publisher
Exploits and anecdotes of Scottish gypsies. 1886 5/7/86

Chambrun, Comte de
Ses études politiques et littéraires. 1889 2/7/89

Chamerovzow, Louis Alexis
Borneo facts versus Borneo fallacies. 1851 25/5/77
The New Zealand question and the rights of aborigines. 1848 7/8/48

Chamfort, Sébastian Roch Nicolas
Oeuvres complètes. 1824 (5v.) 22/4/45

Chandler, George
Inaugural address [to Literary and Philosophical Society]. 1831 8/2/39
Sermon [on receiving a convert]. 1843 17/11/44

Chandler, John
Horae Sacrae. 1848 15/6/48

Chandler, Samuel
Great Britain's memorial against the Pretender and popery. 1745 31/12/74

Chandless, William
A visit to Salt Lake . . . and residence in the Mormon settlement. 1857 27/5/58

Channing, William Ellery
Lectures on the elevation of the labouring portion of the community. 1840 26/8/42
Letter to . . . Henry Clay, on the annexation of Texas. 1837 3/2/38
Memoir of William Ellery Channing, with extracts from his correspondence and mss. 1848 21/3/52
Remarks on the character and writings of Fénelon. 1829 14/10/29
Self culture. An address introductory to the Franklin lectures. 1838 26/8/42
The Church. A discourse delivered in . . . Philadelphia. 1841 4/6/42 ?

Channing, William Henry
Lessons from the life of Theodore Parker. 1860 22/12/69 ?

Chantal, Jeanne Saint
Lettres inédites de la Saint mère Jeanne Françoise Frémyot. 1860 17/3/61

Chantreau, P. N.
Lettres de Barcelonne. 1792 15/10/66

Chapman, Charles
Pre-organic evolution and the Biblical idea of God. 1891 9/4/93

Chapman, Elizabeth Rachel
Why we should oppose divorce. 1890 8/1/90, 8/12/90

Chapman, James Bishop
Charge . . . to the clergy of his diocese. 1847 6/8/48

Chapt de Rastignac, Armand Anne Auguste Antoine Sicaire de
Accord de la révélation et de la raison, contre le divorce. 1790 3/5/85

Chapter in the life of a poor man. 3/8/42

Characteristics of old church architecture in the mainland and western islands of Scotland. 1867 20/10/61

Charles, Elizabeth afterw. Mrs. Rundle
Early Christian missions of Ireland, Scotland and England. 1893 18/6/93, 2/7/93

Charles, I., and Henderson, Alexander
The papers which passed at New-castle . . . concerning the change of Church government. 13/4/41

Charles Louis de Baron de Montesquieu
'Dissertation sur la politique des romains dans la religion' in 'Considérations . . . des romains' 1834 10/11/40

Charlesworth, Maria Louisa
Female visitor to the poor. 1846 13/6/47

Charrière, Ernest
St Hélène, ou souvenir d'un voyage aux Grandes Indes. 1826 21/6/34

Chase, Salmon Portland
Financial report. 1863 31/12/63
Financial report before Congress. 1861 30/12/62
Chasles, Victor Euphémion Philarète
Études politiques. 1846 21/11/50 ?
Études sur la littérature et les moeurs . . . de l'Angleterre. 1850 5/9/54
Chastel, Étienne Louis
Histoire de la destruction du paganisme dans l'empire d'Orient. 1850 12/10/92
Chastenet, H. Bourgeois du
Nouvelle histoire du concile de Constance. 1718 (2v.) 24/1/75
Chaster, Albert William
Powers, duties, and liabilities of executive officers. 1886 16/11/87
Chateaubriand, François René de
Essai sur la littérature anglaise. 1836 (2v.) 27/1/37
Génie du christianisme. 1802 4/11/35
Vie de Rancé. 1844 12/3/54
Chatfield, Allen William
Songs and hymns of earliest Greek Christian poets. 1876 27/1/78
Chatterton, Thomas
The works of Thomas Chatterton. 1803 (3v.) 9/12/53
Chaucer, Geoffrey
Troilus and Criseyde. 22/11/56
Chauncy, Charles
Letter to the Rev. Mr. George Whitefield. 1745 22/2/63
Chaussard, Pierre Jean Baptiste
Fêtes et courtisanes de la Grèce. 1801 (4v.) 22/5/72
Chautauqua, U.S.A.
Chautauqua literary and scientific circle. 1885 19/9/86
Chavannes, François Louis Frédéric
Alexandre Vinet considéré comme apologiste et moraliste chrétien. 1883 29/7/83
Chepmell, Edward Charles
A domestic homoeopathy restricted to its legitimate sphere of practice. 1848 30/12/56
Chermside, Mrs. Henry Lowther
The Thorntons of Thornbury. 1874 (3v.) 22/12/74
Chesney, Charles Cornwallis, and Reeve, Henry
Military resources of Prussia . . . and France. 1870 4/10/70
Chesney, Sir George Tomkyns
'Value of India', in *Nineteenth Century*, iii. 227. 1878 (February 1870) 30/3/78
A true reformer. 1873 (3v.) 25/6/73
The battle of Dorking. Reminiscences of a volunteer. 1871 18/5/71
Chesson, Frederick William
Turkey and the slave trade. A statement of facts. 1877 20/3/77
Chester, Bishop of
Churches consecrated in 1839. 1839 24/12/39
Chester, Historical sketches of nonconformity in. 1864 5/4/64
Chevalier, Jean Baptiste le
Description of the Plain of Troy. 1791 1/3/47
Chevalier, Michel
De la baisse probable de l'or, des conséquences . . . sociales. 1859 (2v.) 28/3/59
Exposition universelle . . . Rapports. 1862 10/2/64
La Guerre et la crise. 1866 26/9/66
Lettres sur l'organisation du travail. 1848 16/11/59
Mexico, ancient and modern. 1864 14/7/64
Mexico, before and after conquest. 1846 21/5/62
Remarks on the production of the precious metals, tr. D. Forbes Campbell. 1853 16/1/53
Cheyne, Patrick
Answers . . . to the appeal of the Reverend Gilbert Rorison. 1858 6/11/59
Letter to . . . St. John's, Aberdeen. 1852 24/2/52
Reasons of appeal. 1859 16/10/59
Cheyne, Thomas Kelly
Life through Christ and for Christ. 1880 25/9/82
Prophecies of Isaiah. 1882 25/9/82
Cheynell, Francis
Chillingworthi novissima. 18/4/86, 9/11/91
Chikhachev, Petr Aleksandrovich
Chances de paix et de guerre. 1875 7/8/76
Child, F. J.
English and Scottish ballads. 1882 (5v. 1882–98) 11/9/82
Child, Gilbert William
Church and state under the Tudors. 1890 9/6/90
Child, Sir Josiah
Brief observations concerning trade and interest of money. 10/12/53
Child, Lydia Maria née Francis
History of the condition of women in various ages and nations. 1835 (2v.) 28/9/55
Childers, Hugh Culling Eardley
On some impending financial questions. 1887 23/2/87
Childs, George William
Recollections. 1890 11/8/90
Chili, Le, et l'Espagne. 1865 14/12/65
Chillingworth, William
Religion of Protestants a safe way to salvation. 13/9/35, 18/8/40
Works. 1742 (10th edn) 5/5/76
Works. 1838 (3v. Oxf. edn) 10/8/40

Chilton, Henry Herman
Woman unsexed. A novel. 1892 5/3/92
[Chimney sweep]
Chimney sweeping described. 1816 1/2/41
China
Anti-foreign riots in China in 1891. 1892 17/3/92
China, the new quarrell in. 1859 22/11/59
China famine. Illustrations. 1878 16/8/78
Chinese in California. 1880 27/4/90
Chisholm, Caroline
The story of the life of Mrs. Caroline Chisholm, the emigrants' friend. 1852 13/7/90
Chishull, Edmund
Charge of heresy, maintained against Mr. Dodwell's . . . discourse. 1706 23/8/76
Chorier, Nicholas
Satyra sotadica. 13/4/52
Chorley, Henry Fothergill
Autobiography, memoir, and letters. Compiled by Henry G. Hewlett. 1873 (2v.) 11/3/74
Memorials of Mrs. Hemans. 1836 27/10/36
Chretien, Charles Peter
A letter to Rev. F. D. Maurice. 1859 30/10/59
Christ, the perfect way; or the finding of Christ. 1882 18/3/83
Christ and the fathers. 1887 13/2/87
Christian Apologist. 2. 10/1876. Mr Nevins 29/10/1876
Christian confession from a modern point of view. 28/11/86
Christianity, the human origin. 1831 12/1/82
Christian Observer.
30. 697-708. 11/1830. Drummond & Codrington estates 31/12/1830
34. 1, 26. 1/1834. Cholera 16/1/1834
39. 285. 5/1839. Gladstone's book 1/5/1839
41. 677. 11/1841 14/11/1841
45. 5/1866 6/5/1866
45. 411. 6/1866. on Newman 10/6/1866
64 5/2/1865
65. 4/1866 8/4/1866
349 4/8/1867, 13/10/1867
362. 2/1868 9/2/1868
370. 10/1868. on Thorold 25/10/1868
Christian Remembrancer.
1. 1. 1/1851 23/3/1851
1. 393. 6/1841. Patristic and Anglican churches 4/7/1841
7. 1. 7/1841 14/7/1841
9. 133, 86. 1/1845. Wynter; Jerusalem Bishopric 4/1/1845
9. 145. 1/1845. Hermesianism 12/1/1845
9. 188. 1/1845. Oxford 3/1/1841
9. 201. 1/1845. on Laud 15/1/1845
9. 517. 4/1845. Oxford and Ward 1/4/1845
10. 144. 7/1845. on B. White 3/7/1845
11. 113, 167. 1/1846. on W. H. Mill; Schism 4/1/1846
11. 465. 4/1846. Pusey's Sermon 2/4/1846
12. 222. 7/1846. Jerusalem Bishopric 1/7/1846
12. 325. 10/1846. Sugar Duties 10/10/1846
12. 377, 411. 10/1846. Allies; Hook & Education 11/10/1846
13. 366, 436. 4/1847. Animal Magnetism; Louis XIV 19/4/1847
13. 392, 273, 484. 4/1847. Swedish Church 18/4/1847
14. 113, 143, 178,. 7/1847. School Trusts 1/7/1847
14. 379. 10/1847. Simeon 23/10/1847
14. 419. 10/1847. Colonial Bishops 24/10/1847
15. 214. 1/1848. Hampden 2/4/1848
15. 56. 1/1848. Hampden 2/1/1848
16. 27. 7/1848. Ecclesiology 2/7/1848
16. 456. 10/1848. Gorham 25/12/1848
17. 129, 1. 1/1849. Marriage; Penitentiaries 11/2/1849
17. 265. 4/1849. Grote 4/4/1849
18. 151, 226. 7/1849. Allies; Geology 2/7/1849
18. 302, 373, 404. 10/1849. Hymnology; Cathedrals; Palestrina 4/11/1849
19. 164, 1. 1/1850. Cholera; Gorham 3/3/1850
19. 187. 1/1850. Dante; on Carlyle 1/2/1850
19. 331. 3/1850. Eusebius 31/3/1850
19. 471. 3/1850. Church & State 30/3/1850
20. 203. 7/1850. Synods 21/7/1850
20. 488. 10/1850. Missions 6/10/1850
21. 4/1851 6/4/1851
22. 7/1851. on Chalmers 6/7/1851
22. 319. 10/1851. Quakerism 19/10/1851
23. 1. 1/1852. on Coplestone 6/1/1852
23. 249. 4/1852. on Huc 4/4/1852
23. 89. 1/1852. Jansenism 4/1/1852
25. 140, 213. 1/1853. on Bunsen 2/1/1853
25. 289. 4/1853. St Paul 3/4/1853
26. 1. 7/1853. Metaphysics 3/7/1853
26. 263. 10/1853. Wilberforce's Eucharist 20/11/1853
27. 84. 4/1854. Census 2/4/1854
29. 1. 4/1855 8/4/1855
30. 7/1855 15/7/1855
30. 101. 7/1855. Dogmatic theology 29/7/1855
30. 241. 6/1851. on C. Merivale 22/6/1851
31. 1. 1/1856 13/1/1856, 6/4/1856
31. 84. 1/1856. Dulwich College 20/1/1856
32. 7/1857. Religious biography 27/7/1856
32. 423. 12/1856. Church in France 14/12/1856

Christian Remembrancer (*cont.*)
33. 200. 1/1857. Pitzipios 18/1/1857
33. 257. 6/1857. Mormonism 5/4/1857
34. 233, 87. 7/1857. on Theiner; Charlotte Brontë 26/7/1857
35. 1/1858 31/1/1858, 2/4/1858
35. 330. 4/1858. on Buckle 6/5/1858
36. 331. 10/1858. Gladstone's Homer 21/10/1858
36. 431. 10/1858. Scots Ecclesiastical Affairs 31/10/1858
38. 10/1859 10/7/1859, 16/10/1859
38. 401. 10/1854. on Liguori 12/11/1854
39. 1. 1/1860. Quakers 8/1/1860
39. 80. 1/1860. Church cause 9/1/1860
40. 215. 7/1860. Sardinia 12/8/1860
40. 303. 10/1860. Oxford 14/10/1860, 23/12/1860
41. 224. 1/1861. Tischendorf 10/3/1861
43. 257. 7/1862. Italy 20/4/1862
44. 200. 7/1862. Scottish Office 19/10/1862
45. 328. 4/1863. Finance 18/4/1863
47. 1/1864 7/2/1864
47. 189. 1/1864. on Renan 31/1/1864
48. 1. 7/1864 10/7/1864
49. 1. 4/1865 9/4/1865
49. 78, 204. 1/1865. Church politics 23/1/1865
50. 10/1865 29/10/1865
51. 1/1866 14/1/1866
51. 214. 1/1866. on Lecky 18/2/1866
51. 397. 1/1866. Spencer 15/4/1866
52. 130. 7/1866. Ecce Homo 15/7/1866
52. 88. 7/1866. Grossteste 8/7/1866
53. 406. 4/1867. Scots Office 19/4/1867
54. 10/1867 27/10/1867
55. 1/1868 12/1/1868, 5/4/1868
56. 7/1868 12/7/1868
56. 271. 7/1868. on Greg 1/11/1868
103. 168. 1/1859. Cheyne case 20/3/1859
Christian Year. 13/1/1833
Christie, Albany James
Luther's jubilee. 1883 14/1/84
Martyrdom of St. Cecily. 1865 21/1/72
On holy virginity; with a brief account of the life of St. Ambrose. 1843 24/11/44
The end of man. 1886 11/4/86
Union with Rome. 1869 11/7/69
Christie, James M.A.
The oblation and invocation in the Scottish communion offices vindicated. 1844 22/6/90
Vindication of the Church of Scotland. 1847 28/3/47
Christie, James Reverend
Men and things Russian. 1879 13/12/78
Christie, Thomas William
A reply to Gladstone's 'Ritual and ritualism'. 1875 2/5/75, 5/5/78
Christie, William Dougal
Explanation of the scheme of the London Library, in a letter to the Earl of Clarendon. 1841 11/2/41
Life of Anthony Ashley Cooper, First Earl of Shaftesbury. 1871 (2v.) 4/3/72
Notes on Brazilian questions. 1865 26/1/65
The ballot and corruption and expenditures at elections. Essays. 1872 4/3/72
Christison, Sir Robert
The life of Sir Robert Christison, bart... ed. by his sons. 1885 (2v. 1885-86) 8/10/86
Christmas at Greycastle. 18/2/85
Christoffel, Raget
Zwingli: or, the rise of the Reformation in Switzerland, tr. J. Cochran. 1858 7/6/58
Christopher, Alfred Millard William
A few thoughts on... Popery. 1868 2/2/79 ?
Christ our ideal. 1882 26/3/82
Christ's College, Brecon, its past history and present capabilities considered, with reference to a bill now before parliament. 1853 15/5/53
Christ the pupil of Buddha. 1890 22/6/90
Chrysostom, St. John
De Sacerdotio. 24/12/40
On priesthood. 9/2/35
Church, Alfred John
The legend of St. Vitalis and other poems. 1887 28/4/87
Church, Frederick John
The trial and death of Socrates. 1880 18/7/80
Church, Richard William
Dante. An essay. 1878 5/10/79
Essays and reviews. 1854 4/1/57
Life and letters of Dean Church. Edited by his daughter, M. C. Church. 1894 17/12/94
On some influences of Christianity upon national character. 1873 28/6/79 ?
On the relations between Church and State. 1881 23/1/81
St. Anselm. 1870 28/8/70
The Oxford movement. Twelve years 1833–1845. 1891 27/3/91, 5/4/91
Times of refreshment. Sermon. 1868 17/5/68
Twofold debt of the clergy. 1869 14/11/69
Church, present crisis in. Letter from a country priest ... 1867 3/8/67
Church and People. 4. 109. 1/1890. on Gladstone 21/12/1889
Church comprehension. A letter to Gladstone. 1868 7/6/68
Church defence... by the author of 'the Banner'. 1885 4/12/85
Church establishment in Ceylon. Three letters. 1850 27/1/80
Church Hymn Book. 1835 13/9/40
Churchill, Charles Henry
Mount Lebanon, a ten years' residence. 1853 (3v. 1853) 8/3/62

The Druses and Maronites under Turkish rule 1840–60. 1862 8/3/62
Churchill, John Winston Spencer- Lord Blandford
Letter to Sir George Grey. 1856 11/2/56
Church in Scotland: the recent schisms. 1845 23/11/45, 22/3/46
Churchman, an English. Keble's tract on marriage. 1849 26/4/49
Churchman, The
5. 649 10/1841. On the cabinet 29/9/41
5. 662 10/1841. On church poverty 1/10/41
6. 354 4/1892 15/5/92
Churchman's family magazine. 1865 31/1/65
Churchman's monthly review i. (Jan 1841). 1841 15/1/41
Churchmen's protest against national society. 22/5/40
Church Missionary Society
Annual report. 1848 14/8/48
Jubilee papers. 1848 25/2/49
Church of Christ in the Middle Ages. 1845 31/10/47
Church of England, by a member of the Carlton. 1873 6/7/73
Church of England, Justice to. 1838 15/2/38
Church of England. Is it the church of God?. 1871 20/8/71
Church of England monthly review in *'Church of England Monthly Magazine', ii 385 (June 1857)*. 1857 5/6/57
Church of England Quarterly Review.
1. 426. 4/1837. American Episcopalian Church 22/6/1837
10. 365, 387. 10/1841. Oxford Theology 29/9/1841
10. 431. 10/1841. Christianity; Corn Laws 1/10/1841
10. 447. 10/1841. Conservative Ministry 2/10/1841
11. 157. 1/1842. Church in Ireland 1/1/1842
14. 1. 7/1843. Church extension 6/7/1843
14. 1. 7/1843. Reply to Quarterly 2/7/1843
14. 184, 161. 7/1843. Factory Bill 29/6/1843
16. 1. 7/1844. Symbolism 4/7/1844
17. 290. 4/1845. Jesuits 17/4/1845
Church of England. Reform or disestablishment, which? By one of her Presbyters. 1873 21/12/73
Church of Rome under Protestant governments. 1866 10/4/69
Church of Scotland magazine. 1834 24/8/34
Church Quarterly Review.
1. 115. 10/1875. Theodore of Mopsuestia 21/11/1875
5. 347. 1/1878. Culture abroad 22/1/1878
6. 117. 4/1878. Arnold & Clough 18/4/1878
6. 123. 10/1878. Development 27/10/1878
6. 503. 7/1878. Cathedrals 28/7/1878
15. 301, 368. 1/1883. Ecclesiastical courts 11/3/1883
27. 316, 425. 1/1889 21/4/89
28. 112. 4/1889. Old Testament 13/8/1889
30. 4/1890. on Gladstone's review of *Ellen Middleton* 17/4/1890
32. 29. 4/1891. Neo-paganism 20/5/1891
Church reform, by a Member of the Church of England. 1846 24/3/46
Church Review (American).
10. 497. 1/1858. Bishops 30/5/1858
11. 369. 10/1858. State of the Church 2/1/1859
12. 7/1859 18/9/1859
56. 1. 1/1890. Old Catholics 9/3/1890
Church's claim on the loyalty of her children. 24/11/45
Churchwardens, a few words to. 1841 15/4/41
Churton, Edward
Church's claim to self-government. 1851 30/7/51
Early English Church. 1840 17/5/40
Góngora: a historical and critical essay on the times of Philip III and IV of Spain. 1862 (2v.) 24/11/62
Memoir of Joshua Watson. 1861 (2v.) 2/6/61
The gifts of God to the good: sermon. 1855 21/3/55
Churton, Ralph
Lives of William Smyth . . . and Sir Richard Sutton. 1800 4/9/87
Churton, William Ralph
Influence of the Septuagint Version of the Old Testament upon the progress of Christianity. 1861 26/5/61
Uncanonical and apocryphal scriptures. 1884 26/10/84
Ciampi, Ignazio
Innocenzo X Pamfili e la sua corte. 1878 28/7/84
Ciangulo, Nicolo
Aventures singulières de Nicolo Ciangulo. 1724 24/8/66
Cibber, Colley
The comedy call'd the Non-Juror. 1718 13/7/41
Cicero
Academia. 20/9/36
De claris oratoribus. 15/8/36, 3/4/73
De finibus. 27/9/36, 8/11/36
De inventione. 26/9/62
De legibus. 4/2/33, 5/2/33
De natura deorum. 7/12/36, 23/11/57, 3/10/70

Cicero (*cont.*)
De officiis. 17/12/36, 16/7/91
De oratore. 16/12/29, 13/10/31, 8/8/64, 24/8/64
De republica. 28/5/55
Epistles. 15/10/31
Opera. 3/8/26, 31/8/26, 2/9/26, 30/9/26, 7/10/26, 9/6/27, 31/1/28, 1/1/31, 19/8/59
Tusculanae disputationes. 2/4/29, 13/4/29, 30/4/29, 17/6/29, 19/11/36
Ciocci, Raffaele
A narrative of iniquities and barbarities practised at Rome. 1844 5/11/44
Ciriani, Filippo
Del presente e futuro Stato politico d'Europa. 1871 28/3/72
Citizen of Westminster
The land tax. 1837 23/7/53 ?
Clancy, John Joseph
Six months of 'Unionist' rule. 1887 9/9/87
Tracts on the Irish question. 1886 8/7/89
Clancy, William
Catholic church in British Guiana . . . a letter to the Archbishop of Vienna. 1841 22/9/41
Clapperton, Hugh, Denham, Dixon, and Oudney, W.
Narrative of travels and discoveries in northern and central Africa. 1826 4/1/30
Claricio, Geronimo
Apologia . . . contro detrattori della poesia di . . . Boccaccio. 12/4/44
Clark, Francis Foreman
Plain sermons for country congregations. 1839 26/11/54 ?
Clark, Sir James
Influence of climate in the prevention and cure of chronic diseases. 1829 29/7/50
Memoir of John Conolly, M.D., comprising a sketch of the treatment of the insane in Europe and North America. 1869 18/9/69
Clark, John M.A., Ph. D.
Church as established in its relations with dissent. 1866 23/5/69
Clark, John Willis and Hughes, Thomas McKenny
The life and letters of the Rev. Adam Sedgwick. 1890 (2v.) 3/7/90
Clark, William George
Few words on Irish questions. 1868 17/10/68
Peloponnesus: notes of study and travel. 1858 22/6/58
Present dangers of the Church of England. 1870 6/3/70
Clarke, Edward Daniel
Travels in various countries of Europe, Asia and Africa. 1810 (6v. 1810–23) 15/3/27, 1/11/54, 11/12/76
Clarke, George Rochfort
Images in the windows of churches . . . letters. 1868 12/8/68
Clarke, James Freeman
Christian doctrine of prayer. Essay. 1854 8/8/76
Clarke, John Erskine
Common-life sermons. 1872 15/7/77
Clarke, Joseph Butterworth Bulmer
Three letters . . . on the revival of convocation. 1854 17/2/54
Clarke, Marcus Andrew Hislop
For the term of his natural life. 1870 (3v. 1870–72) 13/5/85
Clarke, Mary Anne
Biographical memoirs and anecdotes of the celebrated Mary Anne Clarke. 1809 17/7/89
Clarke, Samuel of St. James, Westminster
Fourth defense of an argument made use of in a letter to Mr. Dodwell. 1708 15/8/76
Clarkson, Edward
The Suez navigable canal for accelerated communication with India. 1843 16/11/43
Clarkson, Thomas philanthropist
Not a labourer wanted for Jamaica. 1842 21/7/42
The history of the . . . abolition of the African slave trade. 1808 (2v.) 18/5/49
Clason, Patrick
Two sermons preached . . . after the funeral of . . . Robert Gordon. 1853 20/11/64
Claud
From cloister to altar. 1890 28/2/90
Claude, Jean
Catholick doctrine of the eucharist in all ages, in answer to . . . M. Arnaud. 2/1/81
Claudianus, Claudius
De raptu Proserpinae. (1874 edn?) 10/8/78
Claughton, P., Rev. Prof. Cairns, and others
The Jews in relation to the church and the world. A course of lectures . . . with a preface by . . . Claughton. 1877 20/10/78
Claughton, Thomas Legh
A charge . . . delivered to the clergy . . . of the diocese of Rochester. 1873 21/12/73
Duty of preparing ourselves to receive the Lord's supper. 1856 4/10/57
Our present duties in regard of Holy baptism. 1850 25/3/50
Clay, Walter Lowe
'Church and the working classes' from *Essays on church policy.* 1868 31/5/68
Clay, Sir William
Remarks on the experiences of restricting the issue of promissory notes to a single issuing body. 1844 25/4/44
Clay, William Keatinge
Liturgical services. Liturgies and occasional forms of prayer set forth in the reign of Queen Elizabeth, ed. Rev. W. K. Clay. 1847 27/2/48
Clayden, Arthur
The revolt of the field . . . the rise and progress of

the National Agricultural Labourers' Union. 1874 13/4/74
Clayden, Peter William
England under Lord Beaconsfield. The political history of . . . 1873 to . . . 1880. 1880 23/2/80
England under the coalition . . . 1885 . . . to 1892. 1892 13/6/92
Five years of liberal and six years of conservative government. A lecture. 1880 13/6/92 ?
Proposed electoral divisions of London. 1884 26/1/85
Clayton, C.
Only a girl. 1883 29/9/83
Clegg, James nonconformist
Extracts from the diary and autobiography of James Clegg, ed. Kirke. 1899 17/8/79 ?
Clemens, Friedrich
Geschichte der Jesuiten. 1845 14/11/45
Clement of Alexandria
[exortation]. 13/8/63, 12/9/65
Clements, Jacob
The farmers' case with regard to education . . . in a letter . . . to the farmers of Upton St. Leonards. 1851 5/1/52
Clements, Robert Bermingham
Present poverty of Ireland convertible into the means of her improvement under a well-administered Poor Law. 1838 21/8/47
Clement XIV, Ganganell, G. V. A.
Lettere. 1823 (2v.) 29/10/44
Clergyman
Clergyman's apology for favouring the removal of Jewish disabilities. 1847 27/11/47
Fundamental reform of the church establishment. In the remarks upon Lord Morpeth's Irish Church Bill. 1835 30/3/36
Reply to His Grace the Lord Archbishop of York's pastoral letter. 1864 16/7/64
Why should we petition against the new divorce bill?. 1857 10/8/57
Clergyman's Magazine. 11. 240. 4/1876. Ryle 27/4/1876
Clericus
Answer to Dr. Philpott's letter. 1828 16/4/28
Clericus anglicanus
Ecclesiastical legislation. Three letters. 1836 22/7/36
Clericus cantabrigiensis
Primitive doctrine of eucharistic doctrine. 1876 14/4/78
Clericus Kensingtonensis
Letter to the bishop of London. 1834 6/4/34
Cleron, Joseph Othenin Bernard de Count d'Haussonville
Switzerland. A history of French and English diplomacy in that country. 1850 22/6/50
Clewer, Community of
Tentative rules of the Community of Clewer. 1863 (finalised 1863) 22/1/54
Clews, Henry the elder
Twenty-eight years in Wall Street. 1888 26/5/89
Clifford, Edward of the Church Army
Broadlands as it was. 1890 20/8/90
Father Damien. A journey from Cashmere to his home in Hawaii. 1889 28/7/89
Clifford, Lucy
Love letters of a worldly woman. 1891 26/11/91
Clifford, William Joseph Hugh
Catholic allegiance. A pastoral letter. 1874 6/12/74
Clifton, Robert Cox
Manchester church. A pamphlet. (not found) 21/2/50
Clinch, George
Antiquarian jottings relating to Bromley. 1889 25/2/90
Clinton, Henry Fynes
Fasti Hellenici. The civil and literary chronicle of Greece from the earliest accounts to the death of Augustus. 1824 (3v. 1824–34) 23/10/28, 26/1/47
Literary remains of H. F. Clinton. 1854 22/1/55
Clinton, Henry Pelham Duke of Newcastle
Thoughts in times past tested by subsequent events. 1837 10/3/37
Clissold, Augustus
Transition; or, the passing away of ages or dispensations . . . being an illustration of the doctrine of development. 1868 31/1/69 ?
Clive, Caroline Archer
Paul Ferroll. 1855 11/3/56
Poems by V., by the author of 'Paul Ferroll'. 1840 20/3/41, 10/7/74, 31/12/89
Clodd, Edward
Childhood of the world. A simple account of man in early times. 1873 25/1/76
Story of creation. A plain account of evolution. 1888 13/9/91
Clode, Charles Mathew
Military forces of the Crown, their administration and government. 1869 (2v.) 19/3/69, 15/2/70
Close, Francis
A Christian's duty in the present crisis. 1829 31/3/29
A course of nine sermons . . . to illustrate . . . the liturgy of the Church of England. 1825 18/2/38
A few more words on education bills. 1856 9/4/56
An Indian restrospect, or what has Christian England done for heathen India?. 1858 11/7/58
Christian education. A lecture. 1854 4/3/56
Church architecture scripturally considered from the earliest ages to the present time. 1844 28/4/44

Close, Francis (*cont.*)
Miscellaneous sermons preached in the parish church of Cheltenham. 1829 18/3/30
Protestant faith or the way called heresy: a sermon. 1835 29/1/43
Sermons for the times . . . especially with reference to the education of children of the working classes. 1837 20/3/38
Spiritual Republicanism inconsistent with the genius of monarchical institutions. 1841 23/2/41
The restoration of churches is the restoration of Popery. 1844 28/11/44
Clough, Arthur Hugh
Poems . . . with a memoir by F. T. Palgrave. 1862 4/8/62
Poems . . . with a memoir by F. T. Palgrave. 1888 (revised edn) 10/5/90
Clyde, James
Romaic and modern Greek compared with one another, and with ancient Greek. 1855 7/12/58
Coates, Dandeson
Present state of the New Zealand question considered. 1838 24/2/38
Principles . . . of the New Zealand Association examined in a letter to Lord Glenelg. 1837 20/12/37
The New Zealanders and their lands. Report of the select committee of the House of Commons. 1844 29/11/44
Cobb, Gerard Francis
Separation not schism. A plea for the position of Anglican reunionists. 1869 31/10/69
The kiss of peace, or England and Rome at one on the Doctrine of the Holy eucharist. 1867 6/12/68
Cobbam, James Maclaren
Cure of souls. A novel. 1879 21/8/79
Cobban, James Maclaren
The red sultan. The remarkable adventures in Western Barbary of Sir Cosmo MacLaurin Bart. 1893 (3v.) 8/8/93, 12/8/93
Cobbe, Frances Power
'Agnostic morality' in *Contemporary Review*, xxxiii. 783. 1883 (June 1883) 3/6/83
Contemporary Review, xlvi.795 [faithless world]. 1884 (December 1884) 30/11/84
Moral aspects of vivisection. 1875 29/2/76
Cobbett, William
Cobbett's Weekly Political Register. (1802–1835) 10/9/27, 19/1/32
History of the Protestant Reformation in England and Ireland. 1824 (1824–26) 4/3/39, 26/3/69, 27/11/87
Parliamentary History of England. 1806 (1806–20) 11/5/40
Cobbold, George Augustus
Religion in Japan: Shintoism, Buddhism, Christianity. 1894 29/4/94
Cobden, Richard
How wars are got up in India. The origin of the Burmese war. 1853 18/8/53
Life of Richard Cobden, by John Morley. 1881 (2v.) 24/10/81
Mr. Cobden and 'The Times'. Correspondence between Delane and Hunt. 1864 5/2/64
Richard Cobden, Roi des Belges, by S. van der Weyer. 1862 21/1/63
Richard Cobden; philanthropist and statesman, by J. Sibree. 1865 28/5/65
Russia, Turkey and England. 1876 24/1/77
Speeches on questions of public policy. 1878 (2v. 1878 edn) 7/3/78
The political writings of R. Cobden. 1867 (2v.) 1/6/66, 24/1/77
The three panics: an historical episode. 1862 25/4/62
What next and next?. 1856 12/1/56
Cobden Club essays. Local government and taxation. 1875 4/3/77
Cochrane, Alexander Dundas Ross
Exeter Hall; or church polemics. 1841 29/11/41
Kingdom of Greece. 1862 6/1/63
The map of Italy. 1856 22/7/56
The state of Greece. 1847 15/3/47
Who are the Liberals?. 1852 13/11/52
Young Italy. 1850 30/7/50
Cochut, A.
'La politique du libre échange' in *Revue des Deux Mondes*, xxxiii. 672. 1861 (March–April 1861) 26/4/61
Cockburn, Sir Alexander James Edmund
Charge . . . to the Grand Jury at the Central Criminal Courts, in the case of the Queen against Nelson and Brand. 1867 27/5/67
Letter to . . . Lord Penzance . . . on his judgement in the case of Combe v. Edwards. 1878 20/7/79
Cockburn, Henry Thomas Lord Cockburn
Examination of the trials for sedition which have hitherto occurred in Scotland. 1888 (2v.) 4/5/88
Journal of Henry Cockburn. 1874 1/8/74
Memorials of his time. 1856 1/3/61
Cockle, Mrs. Rita Francis Moss
The golden quest and other poems. 1890 12/12/90
Cocquelin, C.
Les comédiens par un comédien: réponse à Octave Mirabeau. 1882 5/1/89
Codd, Edward Thornton
Diocesan theological colleges preferable to departmental. Letter. 1853 25/12/53
Coddington, Henry
A treatise on the reflexion and refraction of light, being part I of a system of optics. 1829 (2v. 1829–30) 18/4/31

Codrington College report. 1831 16/5/47
Coffey, G.
Home rule. 1888 22/5/88
Coffignon, A.
Paris vivant. La corruption à Paris. 1889 3/9/89
Coffin, Charles Carleton
Our new way round the world. 1882 16/1/82
Cognel, François
La vie Parisienne sous Louis XVI. 1882 5/8/88
Cogniard, Hyppolyte
Byron à l'école de Harrow. 1834 22/6/47
Cohen, Sir Francis afterw. Palgrave
[Murray's] *Hand-book for travellers in northern Italy.* 1842 15/1/67
Observations on the principles to be adopted in the establishment of new municipal corporations. 1832 18/1/34
Remarks ... to Lord Melbourne ... on 'Observations on the state of historical literature'. 1832 27/4/35
Truths and fictions of the middle ages. The merchant and the friar. 1837 6/12/41
Coke, Sir Edward
Institutions of the lawes of England [second part]. (4v. 1642–44) 2/5/50
Colan, P.
La belle Gabrielle, ou les amours de Henry IV. 1814 13/9/82
Colart, L. S.
Histoire de France. 1825 29/2/52
Colborne, John
With Hicks Pasha in the Sudan. An account of the Senaar campaign in 1883. 1883 3/12/83 ?
Coldstream, John Phillips
On the increase of divorce in Scotland. 1881 13/12/88
Cole, Henry of Clare Hall, Cambridge
A manual of practical observations on our public schools. 1848 3/7/48
Cole, John William
Russia and the Russians, comprising an account of the Czar Nicholas and the House of Romanoff. 1854 16/2/56
Cole, N.
Meditations on the song of songs. 6/9/74
Cole, Cardinal Reginald
Reformatio Angliae, tr. H. Raikes (Chester, 1839). 23/7/39
Colebrooke, George
Six lessons on intolerance including ancient and modern nations and different religions and sects. 1791 21/2/57
Colebrooke, Henry Thomas
Essays on the religion and philosophy of the Hindus. 1858 7/3/80
Coleman, Charles Handley
The Irish Church. A lecture. 1868 22/8/68
Coleman, John Noble
Memoir of the Reverend R. Davis ... a missionary in New Zealand. 1865 1/10/71
Colenso, Frances Ellen pseud. Zandile
Faithful unto death. 1872 10/10/80
Ruin of Zululand; an account of British doings in Zululand since the invasion of 1879. 1884 (2v. 1884–85) 26/7/84
Colenso, John William
Argument of the Bishop of Natal before the Supreme Court of Natal. 1867 3/5/74 ?
Digest upon Zulu affairs, preceded by correspondence with ... Frere. 1879 9/3/79
Letter to the laity of the diocese of Natal. 1864 22/5/64
Natal sermons. Second series. 1868 1/3/68
St. Paul's epistle to Romans. 1861 29/5/81
Ten weeks in Natal. 1855 11/4/73
The historic character of the pentateuch vindicated. A reply to ... Colenso ... by a layman. 1863 8/3/63
The new Bible commentary by the Bishop of Natal and other clergy of the Anglican Church. 1871 (6v. 1871–74) 9/1/87
The pentateuch and book of Joshua critically examined. 1862 (7v. 1862–79) 7/12/62, 7/8/64, 25/12/72
What doth the Lord require of us? Sermon. 1879 22/4/79
Coleridge, Bernard John Seymour
Judgment of the Court of Appeal in ... Queen v. *Hertford College.* 1878 31/8/79
Coleridge, Derwent
Compulsory education and rate payment. Speech. 1867 11/5/67
Education of the people. Letter to Sir John Coleridge. 1861 7/12/61
Coleridge, Edith
Memoir and letters of Sara Coleridge. 1873 (2v.) 13/11/73
Coleridge, Hartley
Lives of illustrious worthies of Yorkshire. 1835 21/10/35
Coleridge, Henry James
Giving glory to God. Sermon. 1873 2/12/74
Coleridge, Henry Nelson
Greek poets. 1834 20/11/53
Introduction to Homer. 1830 14/9/31
Table talk of S. T. Coleridge, ed. H. N. Coleridge. 1835 (2v.) 23/9/37
The literary remains of S. T. Coleridge, ed. H. N. Coleridge. 1836 (2v.) 26/2/36
Coleridge, John Duke Baron Coleridge
Address delivered to the Glasgow Juridical Society 25th May 1887. 1887 8/7/87
Inaugural address delivered to the members of the Philosophical Institution, Edinburgh. 1870 6/12/70

Coleridge, John Duke Baron Coleridge (*cont.*)
Memorials of Oxford. Poems. 1844 6/5/79, 8/11/91
Speeches delivered in the Court of the Queen's bench in the case of Suarin v. *Starr & another.* 1869 25/6/69
Coleridge, Sir John Taylor
Memoir of the Rev. John Keble. 1869 7/2/69
Notes on the Reform Bill. By a barrister. 1831 20/4/31
Public school education. A lecture delivered at the Athenaeum, Tiverton. 1860 16/10/60
Remarks on ... report of the judicial committee in the case of Elphinstone against Purchas ... letter to Rev. Canon Liddon. 1871 26/3/71
Coleridge, Samuel Taylor
[Schiller's] *The Death of Wallenstein*, tr. S. T. Coleridge. 1800 30/8/33, 25/9/33
A lay sermon. 1839 25/3/64
Aids to reflection. 1825 21/2/30, 21/3/30
Christabel. 1816 12/10/33, 6/11/34
Confessions of an inquiring spirit, ed. H. N. Coleridge. 1840 31/1/41, 26/1/90
France: an ode. 1798 1/1/69
Letters to ... Daniel Stuart. 1889 8/7/92
Letters, conversations and recollections of S. T. Coleridge, ed. Thomas Allsop. 1836 (2v.) 8/2/39, 18/2/40
On the constitution of the Church and State according to the Idea of Each. 1830 20/8/37, 30/10/37, 31/10/37
On the Prometheus of Aeschylus: an essay. 1825 3/5/47
Osario; a tragedy. 1797 15/3/74
Poetical works. 1878 5/6/79
Seven lectures on Shakespeare and Milton. Preface by Collier. 1856 4/8/64
The friend: a literary, moral and political weekly paper. 1809 (1809–10) 30/11/29
The rime of the ancient mariner. 1798 17/3/30
The three graves. 1818 23/4/30
Coleridge, Sara the younger
Memoir and letters of Sara Coleridge. 1873 (2v.) 4/1/74
Coleridge, Stephen William Buchanan
The sanctity of confession. A romance. 1890 1/4/90
Coleridge, William Hart
A charge delivered in the cathedral church of Barbados. 1838 30/12/39
Charge delivered to the Church of England in British Guiana. 1837 14/6/37
Charges delivered to the clergy of Barbados and the Leeward Islands. 1835 18/2/35
Sermon ... at the consecration of ... bishop of Barbados. 1842 25/9/42
Coles, Abraham
Wine in the word. An inquiry concerning the wine Christ made, the wine of the Supper. 1878 19/1/79 ?
Coles, Cowper Phipps
Spithead forts. A reply to the royal commissioners' second report on our national defences. 1861 10/6/61
Colet, Louise Révoil
L'Italie des Italiens. 1862 (4v. 1862–64) 10/8/68
Les derniers abbés. 1868 11/8/68
Collalto, Massimo di
La donna nella famiglia e nella società. 1888 19/7/88
Collections of the Dorchester antiquarian and historical society. 1844 (1844–50) 7/6/52
Colles, William Morris
Sisters of mercy; sisters of misery; or Miss Sellon in the family. 1852 11/4/52
Collet, Sophia Dobson
Indian theism, and its relation to Christianity. 1870 17/4/70
Theistic devotions. 1876 25/12/76 n
Colletta, Pietro
Storia del reame di Napoli. 1832 (2v.) 12/11/50
Collette, Charles Hastings
Queen Elizabeth and the penal laws, with an introduction on Mr. Cobbett's history of the protestant reformation. 1890 23/9/90
The Rev. S. Baring Gould on 'Luther and justification'. A reply. 1873 25/10/74
Collier, Jeremy the Nonjuror
An ecclesiastical history of Great Britain, from the first starting of Christianity to the end of the reign of King Charles II. 1708 (2v. 1708–14) 4/2/75, 25/5/88
Collier, John Payne
History of English dramatic poetry to the time of Shakespeare: and annals of the stage to the Restoration. 1831 (3v.) 2/7/41
Collier, William Francis
The central figures of Irish history from 400 A. D. to 1603 A. D. 1891 7/9/92
Collier's Water, Croydon. 1862 13/8/63
Collinet, Paul and Arbois de Joubainville, M. H. d'
Essais d'un catalogue de la littérature épique d'Irlande. 1883 3/12/87 ?
Collingwood, Cuthbert naturalist
Bible and the age: or an elucidation of the principles of ... interpretation of the scripture. 1886 25/12/86
Vision of creation. A poem. 1872 21/12/81
Collins, Antony
Priestcraft in perfection. 1710 22/4/47
Collins, Charles Allston
Cruise upon wheels: a chronicle of some autumn wanderings in ... France. 1863 28/11/63
Collins, Elisabeth
Metrical translations from the works of Lamartine ... Delavigne ... Hugo and Béranger. 1850 12/2/82

Collins, Frederick Howard
An epitome of the synthetic philosophy... with a preface by Herbert Spencer. 1889 (2v. 1889–94) 3/10/89
Collins, Henry F.R. A. S.
A treatise on nature as exhibiting the works and goodness of God. 1886 17/10/86
Collins, John Churton
Study of English literature... at the universities. 1891 23/11/91
Collins, William Lucas
Thucydides. 1878 25/3/78
Collins, William Wilkie
Dead secret. 1857 (2v.) 20/1/63
Hide and seek. 1854 4/7/54
Jezebel's daughter. 1880 (3v.) 18/2/82
Collisson, Marcus
South Australia in 1844–45. 1845 3/4/46
Colls, John Flowerdew
Utilitarianism unmasked. A letter to the Rev. M. A. Gathercole. 1844 24/1/44
Collyer, Mary
The Messiah, by F. G. Klopstock, tr. M. Collyer. 1749 5/2/26
Colman, George the younger
Broad grins. My nightgown and slippers and other humorous works. 1815 16/2/28
Colmondley, M.
Diana Tempest. 1893 (3v. 1893–4) 26/1/94
Colonial bishoprics
Proceeding at a meeting. 1841 27/4/41
Colonial Church Chronicle.
1. 10/1847 29/7/1847, 24/10/1847
1. 225. New Zealand 2/1/1848
1. 369. New Zealand 30/4/1848
3. 321. 3/1850. Missions 4/3/1850
3. 361. 4/1850. Tinnevelly 31/3/1850
4. 41. 8/1850. Natal 11/8/1850
9. 121 4/2/1857
Colonial society
Report... on the causes and consequences of the missionary operations in China. 1843 27/7/43
Colonna, Vittoria
Le rime di Vittoria Colonna. 1840 (edn 1840) 28/12/66
Colquhoun, John Campbell M.P.
Hints on the questions now affecting the Church of Scotland addressed to members of the Church of England. 1840 6/2/41
Ministerial policy in Ireland; its affect on Church and state. 1845 13/6/45
Plan of church extension and reform. 1849 (2nd edn) 15/1/49
Remarks on Sir John Pakington's Education Bill. In a letter to... Walpole. 1855 22/4/55
System of national education in Ireland: its principle and practice. 1838 19/1/38
Two letters addressed to the deputation from Glasgow and the ministers and elders... of the Church of Scotland. 1843 22/3/43
William Wilberforce, his friends and his times. 1866 1/11/91
Colquhoun, Patrick
Treatise on wealth, power and resources of the British empire. 1815 (2nd edn) 7/3/36
Colquhoun, Sir Patrick MacChombaich de
Dismissal of the Ionian judges. A letter to... Storks. 1864 20/8/64
Colt, Samuel
On the application of machinery to the manufacture of... fire-arms. 1853 28/10/53
Colton, Calvin
Genius and mission of the Protestant Episcopal church in the United States. 1853 24/11/53
Columba, St.
Life of and work of St. Columba, by Edward A. Cooke. 1888 28/8/92
Colvin, Sir Sidney
Landor. 1881 13/7/81
Combe, Andrew
Physiology of digestion considered with relation to the principles of dietetics. 1836 (2nd edn) 2/1/45
Combe, George phrenologist
Currency question considered in relation to... the Bank Restriction Act. 1856 24/4/56
Life and correspondence of Andrew Combe, M.D. 1850 3/8/62
Secular instruction, or the extension of church endowments?. 1852 13/6/52
Combe, T. [Adèle Huguenin]
Jonquille; or, the Swiss smuggler. 1891 22/1/92
Comber, Thomas Dean of Durham
Friendly and seasonal advice to the Roman Catholics of England, ed. W. F. Hook. 1829 17/1/47
Memoirs of the life... of Thomas Comber. 1799 21/10/55
The plausible arguments of a Romish priest from anitiquity answered. 1/8/52
Commercial traveller. 1856 29/7/79
Companion to the Prayer Book. 1845 29/5/47
Comparetti, Domenico Pietro Antonio
Saggi dei dialetti greci. 1866 17/10/67
Compte rendu. 1876 7/11/76
Compton, Theodore
Life and correspondence of the Rev. John Clowes. 1874 7/4/89
Comte, Isidore Auguste Marie François Xavier
Appeal to conservatives. 1889 6/11/89
Catechism of positive religion. 1858 7/7/67, 16/12/72
Comyn, Tomás de
State of the Philippine Islands. 1821 1/7/44

Conant, John D.D.
Life of... John Conant, by his son. 1823 22/11/81
Concile ecumenique et les droits de l'état. (1869?) 25/5/69
Concilium Tridentium [session vii]. 6/7/34
Condemnation of spiritualism. 23/9/91
Conder, Alfred
Discontent of Ireland: its origin and cause. 1886 14/8/86
Conder, Eustace Rogers
Basis of faith. A critical survey of the grounds of Christian theism. 1875 24/2/78
Conder, Francis Roubiliac
Fraser's Magazine, cii.185 [on London's water supply]. 1880 (August 1880) 6/3/80
Railway transit. A letter. 1841 16/2/42
Conder, Josiah editor
Designs of the dissenters. A letter to the King. By a protestant dissenter. 1834 20/3/34
Italy. 1831 (3v.) 19/9/38
Confession, a general, of Christian churches. 3/1/36
Confessional unmasked. 1867 20/12/67
Confession of Augsburg. 14/11/41
Confessions d'un jeune anglais. 17/6/92
Confucius
Confucius, the great teacher, by George G. Alexander. 1890 16/11/90, 17/7/91
Congregational Review. Fairbairn 8/5/1887
17. 321 1875. On Vaticanism 6/3/75
Congregazione... del sinodo di Pistoja. 1786 11/7/47
Congreve, Richard
'The west'; Part I of International Policy Essays. 1866 12/9/66
Human Catholicism. Two sermons. 1876 16/7/76
Roman empire of the west. Lectures. 1855 5/9/60
Coningsby, pseud.
The present crisis, or the Russo-Turkish war and its consequences. 1853 24/11/53
Conington, John
Horace. Satires, Epistles and Poetica. (new edn 1892) 23/10/93, 12/12/93
Miscellaneous writings... ed. J. A. Symonds. 1872 (2v.) 6/12/72
Odes of Horace, the Latin text with Conington's translation. 1863 10/8/63
Connelly, Pierce pseud. Pascal
Cases of conscience. 1851 28/9/51
Petition of Pierce Connelly, clerk [on suppression of convents]. 1851 23/11/51
Reasons for abjuring allegiance to the see of Rome. A letter to the Earl of Shrewsbury. 1852 4/2/52
The coming struggle with Rome not religious but political. 1852 16/10/53
Connie
Edith Coppleston. 1886 21/4/86
Connor, Marie Flora Barbara afterw. Leighton
The lady of Balmerino. A romance of the Grampians. 1891 (3v.) 16/11/91
Conrad, Johannes
German universities for the last fifty years. 1885 23/5/85
Consalvi, Ercole
Mémoires du Cardinal Consalvi. 1864 (2v.) 24/11/64
Consecrations versus desecration. An appeal to thebp of London against the bill for the destruction of the city churches and the sale of burial ground. 1854 13/1/56
Conseil Presbyteral, Eglise communicator [re: A. Coquerel fils]. 1864 13/3/64
Conservative peers and the reform ministry. 1837 18/11/37
Conservative-Radical
The future capital of the British empire. 1883 18/9/83
Consett, Thomas
The present state and regulation of the Church of Russia, tr. T. Consett. 1729 29/3/57
Considerations on the state of Scotch Roman Catholics. 1779 12/2/47
Considerations sur la question des principautés. 1858 16/3/58
Constable, Henry chaplain
Hades; or the intermediate state of man. 1873 6/8/76
Constable, Henry Strickland pseud. Henry Strickland
Fashions of the day in medicine and science. 1879 13/2/79
Travel thoughts and travel fancies. 1854 3/4/55
Constable, Thomas
Archibald Constable and his literary correspondents. 1873 (3v.) 30/3/91
Constant de Rebecque, Benjamin Henri
Commentaire sur l'ouvrage de Filangieri. 1822 2/7/55
Constitution of... Sardinia. 1851 19/9/51
Contarella, Salvatore
Federico III il saggio. La politica europea: auguri e speranze. 1888 9/1/89
L'equilibrio europeo. Considerazione di diritto pubblico internazionale. 1887 9/1/89
Contemporary Review.
1. 524. 10/1886. Bp. of Carlisle 25/12/1886
7. 429. 3/1868. Magee on Maurice 24/3/1868
10. 321. 3/1869. Two religions 26/3/1869
12. 50. 9/1869. Homer 4/9/1869
14. 495, 540, 597. 7/1870. Pusey 3/7/1870

15. 440. 10/1870. Helps 28/10/1870
15. 524, 567. 11/1870. Stanley 6/11/1870
15. 630. 11/1870. on Gladstone 20/10/1870
16. 486, 519, 555. 2/1871. Stanley; Capes; Bavarian Catholics 30/4/1871
16. 537. 3/1871. Native Races 2/3/1871
18. 248. 9/1871. on George Mackenzie 11/10/1871
21. 283. 1/1873. Creeds 12/1/1873
21. 616. 3/1873. on Greg 27/7/1873
22. 7/1873 16/7/1873
22. 37. 6/1873. Froschammer 27/7/1873
23. 20, 53. 12/1873. J. S. Mill 25/1/1874
24. 23. 6/1874. Maurice 31/5/1874
24. 339, 360. 8/1874. Greg; Mivart 4/8/1874
24. 374, 397. 8/1874. Ellenborough 15/8/1874
24. 516, 503. 9/1874. Heat & living matter; teaching of Christ 5/9/1874
25. 623, 610. 3/1875. Life at high pressure; Satan 7/3/1875
31. 365, 217. 1/1878. Freeman; Duke of Argyll 16/1/1878
32. 364. 6/1878. Punishment 2/6/1878
33. 458. 10/1878. American competition 15/10/1878
34. 717. 3/1879. George Cowell 23/3/1879
35. 404. 6/1879. The week 6/6/1879
35. 422. 6/1879. Russia 4/6/1879
37. 1. 1/1880. England in the 18th century 6/1/1880
37. 392. 3/1880. Cassels on parliaments 28/2/1880
37. 601. 12/1879. Turkey 30/1/1880
38. 544. 10/1880. Why Keep India 4/10/1880
38. 716. 11/1880. Irish land 4/11/1880
38. 981. 12/1880. Irish land 2/12/1880
39. 31, 45. 1/1881. Jews in Germany; Christianity 26/12/1880
43. 204. 2/1883. Lilly 18/2/1883
43. 357. 3/1883. Highlands 5/3/1883
43. 373. 3/1883. Craven 3/3/1883
43. 439. 3/1883. Paris 6/3/1883
43. 685, 732. 5/1883. Haweis on J. R. Green 6/5/1883
44. 1, 19. 7/1883. on Luther 1/7/1883
44. 203. 8/1883. Lilly 1/3/1885
44. 609. 11/1888. Frederick William I 30/10/1888
44. 695. 11/1888. Puritanism 11/11/1888
45. 354. 3/1884. Fairbairn 1/6/1884
45. 642. 5/1884. on Newman 4/5/1884
45. 857. 6/1884. Princess Alice's letters 1/6/1884
46. 635, 617, 488. 11/1884. Laveleye; Seeley; Reed 3/11/1884
46. 795. 12/1884. Frances Power Cobbe 30/11/1884
47. 164, 233. 2/1885. Fairbairn; Myers 1/2/1885
47. 392. 3/1885. Himalayan 3/3/1885
47. 517, 536. 4/1885. Fowler on prices 3/4/1885
48. 1, 10. 7/1885. on Victor Hugo 30/6/1885
48. 188, 249. 8/1885. Gold; Scotch Disestablishment 1/8/1885
48. 352, 439. 9/1885. Goodwin; Fairbairn 20/9/1885
48. 457, 503. 10/1885. Newman; Powell 1/10/1885
48. 470. 10/1885. Argyll 1/12/1887
48. 693. 11/1885. Dougal 4/12/1885
48. 723. 11/1885. Healy 1/12/1885
51. 153. 2/1887. Fitzmaurice on Ireland 2/2/1887
51. 305, 347. 3/1887. Thring; Selborne 12/3/1887
51. 577. 4/1887. Ireland 20/4/1887
51. 794. 6/1887. Frances Power Cobbe 29/5/1887
51. 84. 1/1887. MacColl on Dicey 3/1/1887
52. 523. 11/1887. D. Wells 29/10/1887
52. 867. 12/1887. Scottish Church 30/11/1887
53. 358. 5/1888. Playfair 28/5/1888
53. 537. 4/1888. MacColl on Islam 6/5/1888
53. 537, 748. 5/1888. T. P. Goll and W. Wright 7/5/1888
53. 773. 6/1888. France; Robert Elsmere 30/5/1888
54. 447. 9/1888. Ireland 31/8/1888
55. 157. 2/1889. Bismarck 2/2/1889
55. 637. 5/1889. Dale on Bright 29/4/1889
55. 692. 5/1889. Huxley 14/5/1889
55. 888. 6/1889. Johnson 3/6/1889
55. 900, 910. 6/1889. Genesis; Boulanger 4/6/1889
56. 274. 8/1889. Peer Gynt 13/8/1889
56. 622. 10/1889. J. McCarthy 29/9/1889
57. 215, 187, 290. 2/1890. Driver; Hill; Greenwood 29/1/1890
57. 240. 2/1890. R. B. Haldane on Eight hours 13/10/1890
57. 325, 421. 3/1890. Döllinger; Church rates 2/4/1890
57. 537. 4/1890. Cave 4/5/1890
57. 769, 900. 6/1890. Manning 30/5/1890
57. 797. 6/1890. J. D. Coleridge 14/7/1890
58. 473. 10/1890. Holland on Liddell 7/10/1890
58. 639. 11/1890. Butler on Booth 2/11/1890
58. 673. 11/1890. McCarthy 30/10/1890

Contemporary Review (*cont.*)
59. 465. 4/1891. Italy 19/3/1891
59. 750. 5/1891. Presbyterian church 1/5/1891
59. 777. 6/1891. Crispi on France 27/5/1891
59. 803. 6/1891. Stephen 30/5/1891
60. 760, 729. 11/1891. Ireland 31/10/1891
60. 840. 12/1891. A. G. Tait 29/11/1891
61. 1. 1/1893. Tsarist persecutions 6/11/1892
61. 1, 106. 1/1892. Stundists 27/1/1892
61. 153, 197. 2/1892. Italy; labour 13/2/1892
61. 172, 262. 2/1892. Manning 14/2/1892
62. 1. 8/1892. Irish Protestantism 30/8/1892
62. 336. 9/1892. on Huxley 14/12/1892
62. 609. 11/1892. Mather on labour hours 4/6/1892
63. 305. 3/1893. Harrison on Home Rule Bill 25/2/1893
63. 761. 6/1893. Colclough on Ulster 31/5/1893

Continho, J. J. da Cunbra
Essay on commerce of Portuguese colonies. 1807 1/9/71

Convers, Duncan
Marriage and divorce in the United States. 1889 24/5/91 ?

Conversations on the corn laws. 20/5/46

Conversazione delle fanciulle: dialoghi famigliari. 1865 29/7/66

Convict treatment and national defences. 1847 29/10/47

Convocation: opinions of Sir Frederick Thesiger. 1853 27/2/53

Conway, Moncure Daniel
'Gladstone' in *North American Review*, cxxxvi. 223. 1883 (March 1883) 6/10/83
[on the war question]. 10/4/78
David Friedrich Strauss. Commemorative services. 1874 21/4/74
Emerson at home and abroad. 1882 3/6/82
Idols and ideals with an essay on Christianity. 1877 (2 pt.) 25/3/77
Thomas Carlyle. 1881 16/4/83

Conybeare, Charles Augustus Vansittart
The place of Iceland in the history of European institutions. 1877 30/7/81

Conybeare, John Bishop of Bristol
A defence of revealed religion. 1732 27/8/76

Conybeare, John Josias
The Bampton lecture for 1824. Attempt to trace the history and ascertain the limits of the . . . interpretation of the scriptures. 1824 8/8/39

Cook, Charles Henry pseud. John Bickerdyke
Irish Midsummernight's Dream. 1889 12/10/89

Cook, Frederick Charles
The book of psalms. 1880 17/1/90

Cook, George D.D.
A few plain observations on the enactment of the General Assembly, 1834, relating to patronage and calls. 1834 8/12/34, 25/8/38
History of the Church of Scotland from the . . . Reformation to the Revolution. 1815 (3v.) 7/3/34

Cook, John Minister of Haddington
Statement of facts regarding the parochial schools of Scotland. 1854 24/2/54

Cook, Rose Terry
Steadfast, the story of a saint and a sinner. 1889 8/6/89

Cooke, Charles Walwyn Radcliffe
Four years in parliament with hard labour. 1890 7/6/90

Cooke, Edward Sec. at War in Ireland
Arguments for and against our union between Great Britain and Ireland. 1798 8/6/86, 27/5/89

Cooke, Edward Alexander
Life and work of St. Columba. 1888 28/8/92

Cooke, George Willis
George Eliot: a critical study of her life, writings and philosophy. 1883 4/2/84

Cooke, George Wingrove
History of party: from the rise of Whig and Tory factions . . . to the passing of the Reform Bill. 1836 (3v. 1836–37) 6/5/47

Cooke, Layton
Practical observations on the importation of foreign corn. 1826 17/1/42

Cooke, William barrister
Life of Samuel Johnson. 1785 7/7/79
Memoirs of S. Foote, Esq. 1805 (3v.) 14/7/29

Cooke, William Smith
The Ottoman Empire and its tributary states-excepting Egypt. 1876 15/10/78 ?

Cookesley, William Gifford
Letter to the archbishop of Dublin [on the Sisters of Mercy]. 1853 13/2/53
Sermons. 1843 (2v.) 11/8/44

Cookson, M.
'The nation before party' in *Nineteenth Century*, v. 755. 1879 (May 1879) 30/3/79

Cooper, Alfred of Brighton
Eucharist not a true and proper propitiary sacrifice . . . a sermon. 1875 24/5/85

Cooper, Antony Ashley 1st Earl of Shaftesbury
Memoirs, letters and speeches, ed. W. D. Christie. 1859 21/8/63

Cooper, Antony Ashley 7th earl of Shaftesbury
Life and work of the seventh earl of Shaftesbury, by E. Hodder. 1887 (3v.) 24/2/87, 27/2/87, 19/3/87
Moral and religious education of the working classes. 1843 16/3/43

Cooper, Basil Henry
The hieroglyphical date of the exodus in the annals of Thothmes. 1860 22/11/60
Cooper, Charles Henry
Memorials of Cambridge. 1880 (3v.) 1/10/80
Cooper, Charles Purton
A letter to the Solicitor-General upon the bill to simplify and improve the proceedings of the High Court of Chancery in Ireland. 1850 27/9/87
Substance of speech . . . respecting Lady Hewley's foundations. 1834 4/6/44
The act of settlement and the Pope's apostolic letters. 1851 19/3/51
The government and the Roman Catholic members of Parliament. 1851 25/3/51
Cooper, Edward Rector
The crisis, or an attempt to shew from prophecy . . . the prospects and the duties of the Church of Christ. 1825 14/3/26
Cooper, James Fenimore
The bravo. A Venetian story. 1831 (3v.) 1/10/34
The headsman . . . a tale. 1833 20/9/60
Cooper, John Dunning
Prometheus bound, from . . . Aeschylus. 1890 4/7/90
Cooper, Thomas Bishop of Lincoln, Winchester
Answer to Apology of Private Mass. 1850 22/6/51
Cooper, Thomas the Chartist
Evolution, the stone book, and the mosaic record of creation. 1878 25/9/78
Life of Thomas Cooper, written by himself. 1872 5/5/81
The poetical works of Thomas Cooper. 1877 10/5/81
Cooper, William Ricketts
The Horus myth in its relation to Christianity. A paper [to the Victorian Institute]. 1877 6/6/76
Coote, Charles LL.D.
History of the union of Great Britain and Ireland. 1802 27/9/89
[Cope on sex], in *The Monist*, i.38. 1890 (October 1890) 8/11/90
Copland, James Rev.
Reasons why we believe the Bible. 1878 5/1/79
Copleston, Edward
Charge delivered to the clergy of the diocese of Llandaff . . . 1842. 1842 2/12/42
False liberality and the power of the keys. 1841 6/5/41
Reply to the calumnies of the Edinburgh Review. 1810 4/8/40, 5/4/71
Copleston, Reginald Stephen
Aeschylus. 1870 11/1/71
Buddhism, primitive and present, in Magadha and in Ceylon. 1892 14/1/93
Copleston, William James
Memoir of Edward Copleston, D.D., Bishop of Llandaff. 1851 24/2/61
Copner, James
Sketches of celibate worthies. 1885 7/8/86
Coquelin, C.
Les comédiens par un comédien. 1882 5/1/89
Corbet, William Joseph
What is Home Rule?. 1882 22/7/84 ?
Corbett, Elizabeth Burgoyne
Mrs. Grundy's victims. 1893 23/6/93
New Amazonia. 1889 28/11/89
Corbin, Diana Fontaine Maury
Life of Matthew Fontaine Maury [of the Confederate navy]. 1889 14/1/90
Corbould, Dorothea Mary
Loyal hearts. A novel. 1883 30/12/89 ?
Cordery, John Graham
Iliad of Homer. A translation, with Greek text. 1871 (2v.) 12/1/71
Cordner, J.
Unitarianism. 1846 13/6/69
Corelli, Marie i.e. Mary Mackay
A romance of two worlds. 1886 31/5/89
Ardath, story of a dead self. 1889 6/8/89, 10/8/89
Cormenin, Louis-Marie de la Haye Viscount
Feu, feu. 1845 15/10/45
Oui et non. 1845 15/10/45
Corneille, Pierre
Horace, tragédie. 31/7/45
Le Cid, tragi-comédie. 25/7/45, 8/1/78
Polyeucte martyr, tragédie. 16/4/26, 23/4/26, 30/4/26
The Chronicle of the Cid, ed. H. Morley. 1883 26/1/85
Cornelio, Giuseppe Vittorio Pilati de
La rincarnazione, ovvero il mistero della vita futura. 1882 25/2/83
Cornhill Magazine. 33. 563. 6/1876. Macaulay 7/6/1876
Cornish Jeux. 1/8/91
Cornutus, Lucius Annaeus
Phornuti speculatio de deorum natura. 10/2/58
Cornwallis, Charles 1st Marquis Cornwallis
Correspondence of Charles, first Marquis Cornwallis. 1859 (3v.) 6/1/87
Corrie, G. L.
Brief historical notices of the interference of the crown with the affairs of the English universities. 1839 14/5/50
Corrigan, Sir Dominic John
University education in Ireland. 1865 27/9/65
Corry, J. P.
Competition and its influence in producing distress. 1842 1/2/42
Corsini, Bartolomeo
Il torracchione desolato di Bartolomeo Corsini. 1768 (2v.) 15/8/51

Cortes, D. J. Donoso
Colecció. 1848 (2v.) 6/6/50
Cory, William Johnson
Ionica. 1891 10/3/91
Cosin, John
Bishop Cozens's argument proving that adultery works a dissolution of marriage [in Works vol iv p. 489 ff.]. 6/6/57
Coster, George Thomas
Poems and hymns. 1882 3/12/82
Costituzione dommatica. 1871 30/4/70
Costituzione politica del Regno di Napoli. 1849 21/2/51
Cotterill, Charles Foster
Agricultural distress, its cause and remedy. 1850 2/9/50
The past, present, and future position of... railway companys. 1849 7/2/49
Cotterill, Henry
Charge delivered June 19th, 1867. 1867 8/12/67
Does science aid faith in regard to creation?. 1883 16/9/83
Funeral sermon on E. B. Ramsay. 1873 24/2/73
Cotton, Charles
Poems. 11/7/29, 2/10/34
Voyage to Ireland in burlesque. 4/10/59
Coubertin, Pierre de Baron
L'éducation en Angleterre. 1888 3/12/88
Council on Education
School in relation to the church. 1847 26/4/47
Counter plea for the poor. 1841 15/10/41
Counter theory, the. 27/3/53
Country clergyman
A few words to Lord Ashley. 1843 25/3/43
Courayer, P. F. Le
Défence de la dissertation sur la validité des ordinations des Anglois. 1723 (2v.) 29/12/42, 3/1/43
Defence of English ordinations. 1844 3/11/44
Last sentiments. 1787 13/7/45
Courier and Evening Gazette. 12/2/41
Courier de la Méré, Paul Louis
Pamphlets politiques. 1832 (2v.) 3/6/79 ?
Court, Major Henry M. R. A. S.
A review of the income tax in its relation to the national debt. 1853 10/6/53
Digest of the realities of the Great Western Railway. 1848 14/9/48
Illustration of theory and facts, giving a solution of the intricacies of the corn question. 1826 19/7/43 ?
Courtenay, Charles Lesley
God's work and God's glory. A sermon. 1873 31/8/73
Courtenay, Reginald
The future states, their evidences and nature considered... showing the value of a gospel revelation. 1843 19/12/86
Courtenay, William 10th Earl of Devon
Letter from an Irish proprietor to the ministers of religion of the district. 1847 24/2/48
Courteney, John pseud. Clericus Surriensis
Protest against the pamphlet of B. W. Noel. 1837 27/5/38
Courthope, William John
Paradise of birds: an old extravaganza in a modern dress. 1870 6/8/85
Courtin, Antione de
The rules of civility, or certain ways of deportment observed in France. 5/10/58 ?
The rules of civility; or, the maxims of genteel behaviour, tr. of 'Nouveau traité de la civilité'. 1703 3/11/64 ?
Courtney, Leonard Henry
Contemporary Review, xlix.457. 1886 (April 1886) 1/3/86
Two articles of 1880. 1880 17/12/85
Courtney, William Leonard
Life of John Stuart Mill. 1889 13/4/89
Courtney, William Prideaux
Parliamentary representation of Cornwall to 1832. 1889 16/5/89
Cousin, Victor philosopher
Madame de Longueville. Études sur les femmes illustres de la société du XVII siècle. 1855 17/2/64
On the state of education in Holland as regards schools for the working classes and for the poor, tr. Leonard Horner. 1838 9/2/39
Ouvrages inédits d'Abelard... publiés par M. V. Cousin. 1836 6/10/58
Rapport sur l'état de l'instruction en... Prusse. 1833 20/5/38
Report on the state of public eduction in Prussia, tr. Sarah Austin. 1834 26/6/34
Covel, John
Some account of the present Greek church with reflections on their present doctrine and discipline. 1722 3/1/58
Cowell, John Welsford
Letters to F. T. Baring on the institution of a safe and profitable paper currency. 1843 26/11/62
Letters to F. T. Baring on the institution of a safe and profitable paper currency. 1858 19/1/44
Southern secession. A letter addressed to Capt. M. T. Maury, Confederate Navy. 1862 25/1/62
Cowen, Joseph
[speeches on the eastern question]. 1880 16/3/80
Cowie, Robert
Shetland, descriptive and historical. 1871 2/6/74
Cowley, Abraham
Poems... with Life, by Dr. Johnson in A. Chambers, *Works of the English Poets* 1810, vol vii. 1810 8/1/52

Cowley, Charles
Our divorce courts: their origin, and history. 1879 12/12/92
Cowley, Hannah
The belle's stratagem. 1782 17/5/26
Cowper, Mary Countess
Diary of Mary, Countess Cowper. 1864 26/6/83
Cowper, William poet
Poems translated from the French of Madame de la Motte Guion. 1801 1/1/37, 13/2/74
The life of William Cowper, by R. B. Seeley. 1855 30/10/70
The task, a poem in six books . . . to which are added . . . Tirocinium. 1785 4/6/26, 23/9/48, 2/2/80, 11/2/80, 23/9/89
Cowtan, Robert
Biographical sketch of Sir Anthony Panizzi. 1873 20/6/74
Cox, Anne pseud. A. Gray
Jerome, a novel. 1891 (3v.) 10/5/91
Cox, George Valentine
Recollections of Oxford. 1868 9/10/68
Cox, George William
Mythology of Aryan nations. 1870 (2v.) 7/10/85
Tales of Thebes and Argos. 1864 24/10/67
Cox, Homersham pere
Antient parliamentary elections. A history. 1868 17/1/68
British Commonwealth: or a commentary on the institutions and principles of British government. 1854 15/12/54
First century of Christianity. 1886 24/1/86, 17/11/89
History of reform bills of 1866 and 1867. 1868 21/2/68
Is the Church of England Protestant?. 1874 30/9/74
Cox, John Charles Rector
Minute book of the Wirksworth [presbyterian] *classis.* 1880 24/9/82
Cox, John Edmund
The right training of children. A sermon. 1850 27/3/53
Cox, Robert Curate
Secession considered: in a letter to the Rev. J. L. Harris. 1832 24/2/33 ?
Cox, Samuel D.D.
Commentary on the Book of Job. 1880 15/5/81, 25/12/85
Quest of the chief good. Expository lectures on the Book of Ecclesiastes. 1868 10/1/69
Coxe, Arthur Cleveland
Athanasion: an ode. 1842 12/2/43, 7/8/43
The criterion: a means of distinguishing truth from error . . . with four letters to . . . Pusey. 1866 5/5/67
The Vatican Council. A letter to Pius IX. 1870 4/8/78
Coxe, William
Memoirs of the life and administration of Sir Robert Walpole. 1798 (3v.) 5/2/27
Coxhead, John James
Science the handmaid of religion. An address. 1877 11/3/77
Crabbe, George poet
Life of G. Crabbe, by his son. 1834 10/5/35, 19/12/64
News-paper: a paper. 1785 11/1/65
Parish Register; a poem. 1829 14/1/65
Poems [Sir Eustace Grey, Justice Hall, The Borough]. 1807 26/12/36, 14/8/37
Tales. 1812 13/12/36, 25/4/71
Cracroft, Bernard
Essays political and miscellaneous. 1868 (2v.) 23/4/68
Craig, Edward
On the important discrepancy between the Church of England and the Scottish episcopal community. 1842 7/2/43
On the important discrepancy between the Church of England and the Scottish episcopal community . . . a supplement. 1843 12/3/43
Respectful remonstrance. 24/4/28
Craig, Edward Thomas
The Irish land and labour question. 1882 7/4/86 ?
Craik, George Lillie
Romance of the peerage: or curiosities of family history. 1848 (4v. 1848–50) 18/5/86
Cramer, John Antony
Catenae in Acta SS Apostolorum. 1838 25/2/38
Geographical and historical description of Ancient Greece. 1828 (3v.) 11/3/30, 20/12/55
Inaugural lecture on the study of modern history [at Oxford]. 1843 9/5/43
Crampton, Josiah
The three heavens. 1879 27/2/81, 9/2/82
Cranbrook, James
On responsibility. 1874 16/8/74
Cranmer, Thomas
Defence of the true and catholike doctrine of the . . . sacrament. 28/3/41
Cranz, David
Alte und Neue Brüder-Historie. 1771 23/8/74
Craven, James Brown
History of the episcopal church in Orkney. 1883 14/12/83 ?
Craven, Keppel Richard
Tour thro' the southern provinces of the Kingdom of Naples. 1821 1/12/38
Craven, Pauline Marie Armande Aglaé
Deux incidents de la question catholique en Angleterre . . . Gladstone et les catholiques anglais. 1875 19/4/75 ?
Life of Lady Georgiana Fullerton, tr. H. J. Coleridge. 1888 7/7/88

Craven, Pauline Marie Armande Aglaé (*cont.*)
Memoir of, by M. C. Bishop. 1894 17/12/94, 24/12/94
Craven, William
The Jewish and Christian dispensations compared. 1813 28/12/63
Crawford, Francis Marion
Dr. Claudius. A true story. 1883 25/8/83
Mr. Isaacs: a tale of modern India. 1883 13/1/83
Zoroaster. 1885 26/5/85
Crawford, John Marshall
Mosby and his men: a record of the adventures of that renowned partisan ranger, John S. Mosby. 1867 4/12/67
Crawford, William
Report on penitentiaries of the United States of America [xlvi. 349]. 1834 18/7/35
Crawford, William Sharman
Correspondence between William Sharman Crawford and Rev. Dr. Molesworth on papal aggression. 1851 23/3/51
Defence of small farmers of Ireland. 1839 25/7/42, 29/6/70
Review of circumstances connected with the past and present state of the protestant and catholic interests in Ireland. 1833 9/7/92 ?
Trade of Ireland and the Repeal of the Union. 1833 9/7/92 ?
Creagh, James
Armenians, Koords and Turks. 1880 (2v.) 4/2/80 ?
Over the borders of Christendom and Eslamiah. 1876 (2v.) 8/11/76
Creasy, Sir Edward Shepherd
History of the Ottoman Turks from the beginning of their empire to the present time. 1854 (vol i) 5/12/54
Imperial and colonial constitutions of the Britannic Empire, including Indian institutions. 1872 10/7/72
Sub rege sacerdos. Comments on Bishop Hampden's case. 1848 18/4/48
The text book of the constitution, Magna Carta, the Petition of Right and the Bill of Rights. 1848 9/11/53
Crébillon, Claude Prosper Jolyot de
La nuit et le moment. 1762 2/4/72
Creighton, Mandell
Memoir of Sir George Grey, bart. 1884 11/4/84
Crepaz, Adele
Die Gefahren der Frauen-Emancipation. 1892 1/10/92, 3/10/92
Crétineau-Joly, Jacques Augustin Marie
[letters from Joly to Père Theiner on Clement XIV, Dec. 1852, Jan. 1853, reprinted in] *Bonaparte, le Concordat de 1801 et le Cardinal Consalvi*. 1869 24/7/59
Histoire religieuse, politique et littéraire de la Compagnie de Jésus. 1844 (5v. 1844–45) 10/7/45
Creuzé de Lesser, Baron Auguste François
Les chevaliers de la table ronde. Poème en vingt chants, tiré des vieux romanciers. 1812 29/8/59
Creuzer, George Friedrich
Symbolik und Mythologie der alten Völker. 1810 (6v. 1810–23) 10/8/62
Crevier, Jean Baptiste Louis
History of Roman emperors from Augustus to Constantine. 1814 4/10/25
Crisp, Tobias
Christ alone exalted, being the complete works of Tobias Crisp, D.D. 9/10/59
Christ under sin. 29/3/50
Crispi, Francesco
Francesco Crispi, by F. Narjoux. 1890 23/4/90
Crockett, Samuel Rutherford
Dulce cor. Being the poems of Ford Beréton (S. R. Crockett). 1886 7/9/91
Croesius, Gerardus
Sive historia Hebraeorum ab Homero. 1704 21/3/58
Croesus, a tragedy. 1871 21/11/71
Croft, Sir Herbert
The abbey of Kilkhampton. 1780 25/3/64 ?
Croiset, Jean
A spiritual retreat for one day in every month. By a priest of the Society of Jesus. 1710 12/4/57
Croker, John Wilson pseud. E. B. Waverley
Quarterly Review, lxxix. 202 [on French agriculture]. 1846 (December 1846) 22/10/79
Sketch of the state of Ireland, past and present. 1885 (new ed.) 14/3/85
Two letters to Malachi Malagrowther. 1826 4/12/63
Croll, James
What determines molecular motion?. 1872 11/1/73
Croly, David O.
Essay, religious and political on ecclesiastical finance. 1834 29/8/35
Croly, George
Divine origin and obligation of marriage. 1836 13/5/36
Marriage with the sister of a deceased wife, injurious to morals and unauthorised by Holy Scripture. 1849 12/8/49
Crombie, Alexander
Letter to . . . Tancred . . . on the ballot. 1837 21/2/37
Crompton, J.
The lost ring. 1889 17/12/89
Crompton, Joseph William
Comprehension of dissenters. A letter. 1868 16/5/69

Cromwell, Oliver
Monarchy asserted to be the best, most ancient and legall form of government, in a conference ... with Oliver, late Lord Protector. 29/9/88
Oliver Cromwell's letters and speeches, ed. Thomas Carlyle. 1845 (2v.) 22/12/62
Some particulars concerning law [on Quakers]. 14/9/80 ?
Cromwell, Thomas Kitson
Excursions thro' Ireland. 1820 (2v.) 11/9/45
Crookes, Sir William
Researches in the phenomena of spiritualism. 1874 4/3/74
Cropper, James of Liverpool
Vindication of a loan ... to West Indian planters. 1833 16/5/33
Crosby Hall lectures on education. 1848 8/1/49
Crosland, Camilla née Toulmin
Light in the valley. My experiences of spiritualism. 1857 2/9/58
Croslegh, Charles
Christianity judged by its fruits. 1884 25/5/84
Cross, Joseph translator
Daughter of the gods. Ballads from the first, second, and third books of the Iliad. 1891 7/11/91
Crosthwaite, Charles
What profit is there of baptism? A letter. 1866 1/4/66
Crosthwaite, John Clarke
'On Maynooth' in *British Magazine*, xviii. 555. 1845 (May 1845) 11/5/45
Communio Fidelium. An historical inquiry into the mode of distributing the Holy Communion. 1841 28/3/41
Modern hagiology. 1846 (2v.) 25/1/46
Sermons on practical subjects. 1840 12/4/40
The Christian ministry, and the establishment of Christianity. 1835 23/2/40
The remembrance of Christ. A sermon on the Holy Communion. 1843 30/7/43
Crotty, Michael
Letter ... to Rev. Dr. Murray. 1836 22/4/36 ?, 21/12/44
Crowe, John William
Our army; or, penny wise and pound foolish. 1856 29/4/56
Shadows of the war. 1856 29/4/56
Crozier, John Beattie
Lord Randolph Churchill. A study of English democracy. 1887 4/3/87
Cruikshank, Alexander P. J.
Life ... of Louis Mary Grignon de Montfort. 1870 4/8/89 ?
Cruttwell, Clement
Works of Bishop Wilson ... with his life. 1782 30/9/55
Cruttwell, Wilson Clement
A churchman's letter to the parishioners of Frome. 1852 18/4/52
Crystal Palace. 1851 28/9/51
Cubitt, George
Strictures on Mr. O'Connell's Letters to the Wesleyan methodists. 1840 16/6/40
Cudworth, Ralph
The true intellectual system of the universe. (1731) 22/8/31
Cumberland, Duke of
Historical memoirs. 1767 21/1/76
Cumberland, Stuart C.
The Queen's highway from ocean to ocean. 1887 25/6/87
Cumming, John Minister of Scottish Nat'l Church
Apology for the church of Scotland. 1837 26/5/38
Present state of the Church of Scotland; a letter to ... Cholmondeley. 1843 17/12/43
The Christian nursery. A sermon. 1852 7/11/52
Cundall, Joseph
On bookbinding ancient and modern. 1881 21/9/87
Cunegundis, St.
Vita. 1865 19/7/83
Cunningham, Sir Henry Stewart
Is 'good news from Ireland' true?. 1864 25/3/65
The Heriots. 1890 (3v.) 28/3/90
Cunningham, Peter F. S. A.
London in 1857. 1857 17/6/58
Story of Nell Gwyn. 1852 8/8/65
Cunningham, William Archdeacon
The path towards knowledge. 1891 15/3/91 ?
Cunningham, William principal
Letter to John Hope. 1839 27/11/39
Strictures on Rev. James Robertson's ... observations upon the Veto Act. 1840 26/2/41
Cunningham, William pseud. Eta
Virgil's first pastoral. 1884 27/8/92
Cunynghame, Sir Henry Harding Samuel
Travels in the Eastern Caucasus. 1872 30/11/72
Curate of Riggs; a sketch of clerical life. 1890 24/12/92
Curci, Carlo Maria
Il Vaticano regio tarlo superstite della chiesa cattolica. 1883 30/12/83
Italien und die Kirche. 1879 3/10/79
La nuova Italia ed i vecchi zelanti. 1881 25/8/81
Ragione dell'opera. 1874 5/9/75
Una divinazione sulle tre ultime opere di Vinc. Gioberti. 1848 (2v.) 8/12/50
Vaticanism. Preface by Plumptre. 1884 30/11/84

Cureton, William
The doctrine of the Holy Trinity not speculative but practical. A sermon. 1858 4/1/63
Three sermons preached at the Chapel Royal, St. James. 1848 23/4/48
Vindiciae Ignatianae. 1846 10/4/46
Curll, Edmund
Memoirs of the life and writings of Matthew Tindall. 1733 18/4/92
Curran, John Philpot
Speeches. 1809 (2v.) 10/8/87
Currie, James
Life of Robert Burns. 1826 (1826 edn) 24/1/84, 30/1/84
Works of Robert Burns. 1800 20/2/72
Curry, John priest
Catholicity, liberty, allegiance: a disquisition on Mr. Gladstone's 'Expostulation'. 1875 7/1/75
Curteis, George Herbert
Dealing with difficulties of belief. 1884 15/3/85
Dissent in its relation to the Church of England. 1871 16/6/72
Evangelization of India. Sermon. 1857 9/7/65
Spiritual progress. Four sermons. 1855 18/4/86
Curtis, George Ticknor
Constitutional power of Congress over the territories [argument in Dred Scott case]. 1857 6/11/62
Curtius, Ernst
Die Ionier vor der ionischen Wanderung. 1855 9/12/57
History of Greece, tr. A. W. Wood. 1868 (5v. 1868–73) 4/8/76
Curtius, Julius S.
Das Kunstgesetz. 31/7/88
Curwen, Henry
History of booksellers. 1873 14/1/79
Curzon, George Nathaniel
National Review, iii.515 [on Oxford politics]. 1884 (June 1884) 3/6/84
Curzon, Robert Baron Zouche
Armenia. 1854 18/3/56
Visits to monasteries in Levant. 1849 12/5/49
Cusack, Mary Frances
Life inside the Church of Rome. 1889 19/3/90, 29/11/92
The liberator. 1877 (1877 edn) 22/11/77, 26/11/88
The nun of Kenmare. 1889 14/5/89
Cusani, Francesco
La Dalmazia, le isole Ionie e la Grecia visitate nel 1840. 1847 (2v.) 26/2/59
Cushing, Caleb
Treaty of Washington. 1873 23/5/73
Cust, Sir Edward
Colonies and colonial government. 1845 30/6/45
Custine, Astolphe de
A Russian's reply to M. de Custine's 'Russia in 1839'. 1844 22/3/44
The empire of the Czar. 1843 (3v. tr) 11/12/43
Cutting, Sewall Sylvestre
Discourse. 1843 20/8/76 ?
Cutts, Edward Lewes
Christians under the Crescent in Asia. 1877 6/11/83
Turning points of English church history. 1874 28/5/85
Cuvier, Georges L. C. F. Dagobert de
Essay on the theory of the earth. 1813 8/8/50, 17/5/69, 10/10/85
Cyprian, St.
De oratione. 18/12/45
De unitate ecclesiae. 11/4/41
Epistles. 1844 2/9/45
Cyril, St. of Jerusalem
Catechetical lectures [trans. R. W. Church]. 1838 (2v.) 20/9/46

Dacosta, John
Facts and fallacies regarding irrigation as a prevention of famine in India. 1878 22/7/78
The Indian budget for 1877–78. Remarks on the financial position of the government of India. 1877 21/8/79
Dageus Nyheten. 1/12/87
Dahlgren, Sarah Madeleine Vinton
Divorced. A novel. 1887 6/7/89
Daillé, Jean
A treatise concerning the right use of the Fathers, in the decision of the controversies that are at this day in religion. 25/12/47
Daily devotions for young persons. 1844 18/1/52
Dairnvaell, Georges Marie Mathieu-
Code des Jésuites. 1845 15/11/45
Dakeyne, John Osmond
Baptismal regeneration. A notice of 'An examination of the charge of the bishop of London, Oct. 1822', which appeared in the 'Record' newspaper. 1843 19/2/43
Dale, Darley [Francesca Maria Steele]
Noah's ark: a tale of the Norfolk Broads . . . illustrated by Paul Hardy. 1890 20/5/90
Dale, Robert William
Christ and the controversies of Christendom. 1869 23/5/69
The atonement. 1875 20/5/75
The doctrine of the real presence and of the Lord's supper. 1870 1/1/71
The Evangelical Revival, and other sermons. With an address on the work of the Christian ministry in a period of theological decay and transition. 1880 27/10/80
The mutual relations of physical science and faith. Sermon. 1865 25/3/66

Dalgairns, Bernard [John Dobrée Dalgairns]
'Is God knowable' in *Contemporary Review*, xx. 615. 1872 (October 1872) 24/11/72
Life of St. Stephen Harding, Abbot of Citeaux. 1844 3/12/43

Dalgleish, Walter Scott
The cruise of the royal mail steamer Dunottar Castle round Scotland on her trial trip. 1890 5/3/91

Dall, Caroline Wells Healey
What we really know about Shakespeare. 1886 5/1/86

Dallaway, James
Observations on English architecture. 1806 13/5/94

Dallinger, William Henry
The Creator, and what we may know of the method of creation. 1887 4/4/88

Dalloz, Charles Paul Alexis
L'Épargne par la Dépense. 1867 7/3/67

Dalmedico, Angelo
Prose e versi. (Per le nozze di Cesare Parenzo con Estella Dalmedico.). 1870 6/10/79

Dalrymple, John 2nd Earl of Stair
Some passages in the life of John, second Earl of Stair. 1835 24/12/78 ?

Daly, David Bingham
Handy book of practice in the Lord Mayor's Court, in ordinary actions and in foreign attachment, under the new statute and rules of Court. 1861 10/2/62

Daly, John Bowles
Ireland in 1798. ed. J. B. Daly. 1888 9/5/88
Ireland in the days of Dean Swift. 1887 21/7/87 ?

Daly, Robert
A correspondence which arose out of the discussion at Carlow between a Protestant and a Roman Catholic clergyman. 1825 28/4/49
Lectures on a few portions of Scripture. 1850 20/3/53

Damant, Mary
Peggy: a tale of the Irish rebellion. 1888 (new edn) 6/8/88

Damen, Arnold
Father Damen's lecture . . . The Catholic church the only true church of God . . . a verbatim report by H. W. Waller. 1875 23/1/76

Damer, W.
The vicar of Ellismond. 1892 16/4/93

Dana, Dr.
Creation. 1885 25/1/90

Dana, Richard Henry author
Richard Henry Dana, a biography by Charles Francis Adams, the younger. 1890 18/6/91
Two years before the mast. 1841 19/12/70, 13/1/71

Danby, Frank [Julia Frankau]
A babe in Bohemia. 1889 30/11/89

Dandolo, Emilio
The Italian volunteers and Lombard Rifle Brigade, being an authentic narrative of . . . 1848–9 . . . Translated from the edition published at Turin in 1849. 1851 6/2/52

Dandolos, Antonios
Des îles Ioniennes sous la protection britannique, pour servir de réponse au livre . . . écrit en anglais . . . sous un titre égal. 1851 19/1/59
Le protectorat anglais aux îles Ioniennes. Lettre respectueuse . . . à Mgr le Marquis de Normanby. 1861 1/4/63
Lettre . . . á son excellence le Ministre des affaires étrangères de sa Majesté Britannique la reine Victoria. 1864 15/4/64

Danger of democratic re-action. 1864 16/5/77
Danger of the Church of England. 2/12/49
Dangers de la question d'Orient. 1865 4/9/65
Dangers of English Protestantism. 12/11/79

Daniel, Gabriel
Réponse aux Lettres Provinciales de L. Montalte, ou Entretiens de Cléandre et d'Eudoxe. 31/5/46

Danielson, John Richard
Finland's union with the Russian empire. With reference to M. K. Ordin's work 'Finland's subjugation' . . . translated from the third Swedish edition. 1891 2/11/91

Dannreuther, Edward George
Richard Wagner: his tendencies and theories. 1873 16/11/74

Danson, John Towne
A contribution towards an investigation of the changes which have taken place in the condition of the people of the United Kingdom. 1848 2/5/48

Dante Alighieri
'Pater Noster' in Professione de Fede. 19/11/37
'Purgatorio' from The Divine Comedy of Dante, tr. H. W. Longfellow. 1864 18/2/64
Dante Alighieri, by G. A. Scartazzini. 1879 15/12/87
Dante and Swedenborg, by F. Sewall. 1893 24/1/93 ?
Dante e la libertà moderna. 1865 30/12/75 ?
Dante's Divina Commedia, by F. L. Hettinger. 1887 11/2/88
De monarchia. 5/1/61, 16/1/61, 23/6/87
De vulgari eloquentia. 2/1/61
Divina Commedia. 16/9/34, 20/9/34, 4/10/34, 11/11/36, 13/6/38, 15/6/41, 28/2/44, 5/3/44, 14/8/46, 30/10/46, 9/10/59, 20/1/67, 26/12/85
Handbook of Dante, by G. A. Scartazzini. 1887 15/12/87
Inferno. 5/5/35, 14/11/36, 28/7/41, 18/10/66, 26/10/66, 29/10/66, 21/9/76, 25/9/76, 25/8/86
L'Opere di Dante, by G. A. G. Carducci. 1888 29/1/88

Dante Alighieri (*cont.*)
La Divina Commedia, ed. G. M. Cornoldi. 1887 16/12/87
La Divina Commedia . . . con comento analitico di G. P. R. Rossetti. 1826 16/11/36
Paradiso. 23/1/36, 27/2/36, 24/3/36, 24/3/37, 28/6/39, 29/6/39, 25/3/53, 17/4/53, 1/6/53, 8/9/74, 15/9/79, 22/10/79, 3/9/82
Purgatorio. 6/11/35, 25/11/35, 4/12/35, 10/8/41, 21/12/66, 18/6/76
The Commedia and Canzoniere, tr. E. H. Plumptre. 1886 3/5/92
The Divina Commedia . . . Samples of a new translation by E. H. Plumptre. 1883 2/1/83
The Purgatory, tr. W. Shadwell, introduction by W. Pater. 1892 (2v. 1892–9) 12/2/93
Vita di Dante Alighieri, by G. Boccaccio. (many edns) 25/3/88
Vita Nuova. 25/12/55
Danvers, Alicia
Academia: or the humours of . . . Oxford. 1/6/55
Darby, John Nelson
An analysis of Dr. Newman's Apologia Pro Vita Sua: with a glance at the history of popes, councils and the church. 1866 10/9/82
Synopsis of the books of the Bible. 1857 (5v. 1857–67) 9/8/68
Dardanelles for England. 1876 11/11/76
Daremberg, Charles Victor
Collection des médecins grecs et latins. 1851 (7v. 1851–79) 2/9/94 ?
La médecine dans Homère: ou, Etudes d'archéologie sur les médecins, l'anatomie, la physiologie . . . médecine dans les poèmes homériques. 1865 19/12/65
D'Argout, M. de
Java, Singapore and Manilla. 1842 26/6/44
Dark through to light. 1886 (3rd edn 1886?) 3/12/86
Darling, H. G.
Electrical psychology . . . from J. B. Dods, ed. H. G. Darling. 1851 21/11/55
Darling, Sir Ralph
Remarks on the libel published by Mr. R. Robison . . . against Lieut.-General Ralph Darling. 1835 21/8/35
Dart, Joseph Henry
The Iliad of Homer in English hexameter verse. 1862 14/1/62
Daru, Pierre Antoine Noel Bruno Count
Histoire de la république de Venise. 1821 (8v.) 23/10/58
Darwin, Charles Robert
Darwin and after Darwin, by G. J. Romanes. 1892 28/5/92
Life and letters of Charles Darwin, by F. Darwin. 1887 (3v.) 27/2/88
On the origin of species by means of natural selection. 1859 10/12/59
The descent of man. 1871 (2v.) 7/7/71
Darwin, Erasmus
The botanic garden; a poem, in two parts. 1792 15/4/26
The temple of nature; or, the origin of society: a poem, with philosophical notes. 1803 24/4/26
Das Anglopreusische Bisthum zu St. Jacob in Jerusalem. 1842 15/10/42
Das Anglopreussische Bisthum zu St. Jacob in Jerusalem. 1842 15/10/42
Dasent, Sir George Webbe
Annals of an eventful life. 1870 (3v.) 4/6/70
Popular tales from the Norse. 1859 11/11/72
Daubeny, Charles Giles Bridle
Address on . . . Fielding Herbarium. 1853 20/6/54
Can physical science obtain a home in an English university? An inquiry, suggested by some remarks . . . in a late number of the Quarterly Review. 1853 21/12/53
D'Aubigné, Jean Henri Merle-
Geneva and Oxford, a discourse. Translated from the French. With an introduction by E. Bickersteth. 1843 17/6/43, 30/3/77
Histoire de la Réformation. 1835 (5v. 1835–53) 22/7/38
Daudet, Alphonse
Jack. Moeurs contemporains. 1876 (2v.) 17/8/80
L'Evangéliste. Roman parisien. 1883 27/10/89
Lettres de mon moulin. 1869 15/9/86
Daumas, Melchior Joseph Eugène
The horses of the Sahara, and the manners of the desert . . . with commentaries by the Emir Abd-el-Kader. Translated . . . by James Hutton. 1863 7/5/81
Daunt, William Joseph O'Neill
Eighty-five years of Irish history, 1800–1885. 1886 (2v.) 30/6/86, 7/7/86, 21/3/93
Essays on Ireland. 1886 21/4/86
Davanzati Bostichi, Bernardo
Scisma d'Inghilterra sino alla morte della reina Maria, ristretto in lingua propria fiorentina. 22/1/44
Davenport, Christopher pseud. Franciscus a Santa Clara
Paraphrastica expositio Articulorum. 1865 18/2/66
Davenport, John Sidney
The dispensation of the Parousia: or the personal presence of Christ with his church. 1876 22/10/76
Davey, Horace Baron Davey
The law of public meeting. A speech delivered at a . . . meeting of the Home Rule Union. 1887 21/11/87

Davidson, Charles barrister at law
Common forms in conveyancing; including recitals. 1846 31/5/64
Concise precedents in conveyancing; adapted to the act for simplifying the transfer of property. 1845 27/6/68
Davidson, John Morrison
The book of Erin, or, Ireland's story told to the new democracy. 1888 27/11/88
Davidson, Randall Thomas
Life of Archibald Campbell Tait, Archbishop of Canterbury. 1891 (2v.) 6/6/91
Davidson, Samuel
The doctrine of Last Things contained in the New Testament, compared with the notions of the Jews and the statements of church creeds. 1882 10/10/82
Davies, Charles Greenall
Educational difficulties; how are they to be met?. 1857 14/3/57, 20/2/68
Davies, Charles Maurice
Unorthodox London: or phases of religious life in the metropolis. 1873 8/5/73
Davies, David Christopher
A treatise on slate and slate quarrying, scientific, practical, and commercial. 1878 4/11/78
Davies, George Christopher
On Dutch waterways. The cruise of the S. S. Atlanta on the rivers and canals of Holland and the north of Belgium. 1887 10/1/87
Davies, Sir John
A discovery of the true causes why Ireland was never entirely subdued. 4/12/69
A poem on the immortality of the soul. 1733 17/6/86
Historical Tracts, ed. George Chalmers. 1786 14/8/45
Davies, John Fletcher
The Eumenides of Aeschylus. 1885 11/9/85
Davies, John Llewelyn
The work of Christ; or the world reconciled to God. Sermons . . . with a preface on the atonement controversy. 1860 18/3/60
Davies, Lady Lucy Clementina
Recollections of society in France and England. 1872 (2v.) 28/10/73
Davies, Mercer
The bishops and their religion: two letters addressed to the lord bishop of Ripon. 1886 21/11/86
Davies, R. Rice
The Cambrian sketch-book. Tales, scenes, and legends of Wild Wales. 1876 3/9/78 ?
Davies, Thomas bookseller
Dramatic miscellanies: consisting of critical observations on several plays of Shakespeare. 1784 20/10/40
Memoirs of the life of David Garrick, Esq. 1780 (2v.) 28/7/33, 21/4/68
Some account of the life of Philip Massinger. 1779 26/6/30
Davis, Charles Augustus
Letters of J. Downing, Major . . . to his old friend, Mr. Dwight, of the New-York Daily Advertiser, ed. C. A. Davis. 1835 (2nd English) 19/10/43
Davis, Charles Henry
Liturgical revision illustrated and vindicated on orthodox principles . . . with an introduction by Lord Ebury. 1859 16/2/62
Davis, Henry George
The memorials of the hamlet of Knightsbridge. With notices of its immediate neighbourhood, ed. Charles Davis. 1859 2/12/67
Davis, Jefferson
Life of Jefferson Davis, by R. J. Walker. 1863 13/7/63
Life of Jefferson Davis, with a secret history of the Southern Confederacy, by E. A. Pollard. 1869 23/3/73 ?
President's message and accompanying documents. To the Senate and House of Representatives of the Confederate states. 1863 8/2/64
Davis, Sir John Francis
The Chinese: a general description of the Empire of China and its inhabitants. 1836 (2v. 1836–40) 28/4/40
Davis, Nathan
Carthage and her remains: being an account of the excavations and researches on the site of the Phoenician metropolis in Africa. 1861 9/1/65, 26/10/67
Davis, R.
Garibaldi; or the rival patriots; a dramatic operetta in two acts. 1860 14/4/74 ?
Davis, Richard Harding
Gallagher and other stories. 1891 15/6/91
Davis, Thomas Vicar of Roundhay
Annus sanctus; or, aids to holiness in verse, for every day in the year. 1877 6/1/78
Davis, Thomas Osborne
Thomas Davis: the memoirs of an Irish patriot, 1840–1846, by Sir Charles Gavan Duffy. 1890 3/12/90
Davis, William
An olio of bibliographical and literary anecdotes and memoranda original and selected. 1814 18/9/47
Davison, John B. D.
An inquiry into the origin and intent of primitive sacrifice, and the scripture evidence respecting it [with] *reflections on the Unitarian controversy.* 1825 31/7/31, 15/9/67
Remains and occasional publications. 1841 3/9/48
Davitt, Michael
The 'Times'-Parnell Commission. Speech delivered . . . in defence of the Land League. Carefully revised. 1890 3/3/90

Davy, Sir Humphry Bart.
Salmonia: or days of fly fishing. In a series of conversations. With some account of the habits of fishes belonging to the genus Salmo. By an angler. 1828 8/1/44
Davys, George Bishop of Peterborough
Village conversations on the liturgy of the Church of England. 1820 (1824) 25/8/29
Dawbarn, William
Government, conduct and example. 1867 25/1/73
Dawe, William Carlton
Mount Desolation. An Australian romance. 1892 1/6/92
Dawes, Richard Dean of Hereford
Manual of educational requirements necessary for the civil service. Report of the commissioners [and] *preface on its educational value and importance.* 1856 16/5/54 ?
Observations on the working of the government scheme of education, and on school inspection, suggesting... extended inspection for [church schools]. 1849 23/2/49
Dawkins, Sir William Boyd
Early man in Britain and his place in the tertiary period. 1880 25/7/90
Dawson, Alfred
English landscape art in... 1877. 1877 6/8/77
Dawson, Sir John William
Modern ideas of evolution as related to revelation and science. 1890 21/11/90
Modern science in Bible lands. 1888 26/7/90
Points of contact between revelation and natural science. 1885 21/11/86
The origin of the world according to revelation and science. 1877 1/12/89
Dawson, Samuel Edward
Copyright in books. An enquiry into the origin, and an account of the present state of the law in Canada. A lecture. 1882 29/11/87
Dawson, William James
The redemption of Edward Strahan. A social story. 1891 5/12/91
Day, George Game
A letter to Richard Cobden, Esq., M.P., in reply to remarks contained in his speech, delivered at Covent-Garden Theatre, on Wednesday, March 20, 1844. 1844 22/8/44 ?
Day, Robert
Free thoughts in defence of a future state. 20/9/91
Day, Samuel Phillips
Down South; or, an Englishman's experience at the seat of the American war. 1862 (2v.) 6/4/66
Day, William Ansell
Russia and the Eastern Question. 1877 (not found) 14/1/77
Day census of the city of London. 1881 18/2/82
d'Azeglio, Massimo Tapparelli
Dell' emancipazione civile degl' Israeliti. 1848 23/5/48
Diario dell'assedio di Navarino Memore di G. Collegrio. 1857 25/7/57
Ettore Fieramosea. 1833 2/3/35
La politique et le droit chrétien... 1860 6/1/60
Niccolo de' Lapi. 1841 4/7/48
Deacon, Edward Erastus
Another letter to the right hon. Lord Stanley, M.P. on the law of church rates; being an answer to the letter of the Attorney General [John Campbell]. 1837 16/6/37
Deale
Crockford's; or, life in the West. 1828 (2nd edn) 21/8/34
Dealtry, William Archdeacon of Surrey
Obligations of the national church. A charge delivered at the visitation in Hampshire, September, 1838. 1838 22/2/39
On the importance of caution in the use of certain familiar words. A charge delivered in the autumn of 1843, at the visitation in Hampshire. 1843 19/11/43
Religious establishments tried by the word of God: a sermon preached in St. John's chapel, Bedford Row... May 1, 1833. 1833 (1835 edn) 8/5/36, 23/7/37
The excellence of the liturgy. A sermon preached at All Saints' church, Southampton... April 22, 1829. 1829 5/7/29
The national church a national blessing... a charge delivered at the visitation in Hampshire in the autumn of 1834. 1835 24/4/36
Dean, George Alfred
A treatise on the land tenure of Ireland, and influences which retard Irish progress. 1869 28/1/70
Deane, Christopher Page
A short history of Ireland. 1886 26/7/86
Deane, John Bathurst
The worship of the serpent traced throughout the world, and its traditions referred to the events in Paradise: proving the temptation and fall of man. 1830 22/12/75
Deane, William John [Spence-Jones, H. D. M.]
The pulpit commentary, etc., by Henry D. M. Spence (Ecclesiastes. Exposition by Rev. W. J. Deane). 1880 19/3/82
De Bary, R. B.
Thoughts upon certain leading points of difference between the Catholic and Anglican churches. 1843 23/4/43
Debary, Thomas
Notes of a residence in the Canary islands, the south of Spain, and Algiers; illustrative of religion in those countries. 1851 7/1/52

Our sectaries, how we shall meet them? A letter to a bishop. 1875 5/12/75
Debates on ritualism in the provincial synod. 1868 1/1/69
Debidour, Antonin
Histoire diplomatique de l'Europe depuis l'ouverture du congrès de Vienne jusqu'à la clôture du congrès de Berlin, 1814–1878. 1891 29/6/91
De Bow's Southern and Western Review. 1881 5/2/81
De Burgh, Ulrick John Lord Clanricarde
Inquiry into the truth of accusations against . . . Clanricarde in . . . Hancock vs. Delacour. 1855 5/3/58
De Caux, John William
The herring and the herring fishery, with chapters on fishes and fishing, and our sea fisheries in the future. 1881 18/11/81, 16/8/90
Dechamps, Adolphe
Le prince de Bismarck et l'entrevue des trois empereurs. M. Thiers et la France. 1872 (2nd edn) 27/11/72
Decimal coinage. A short and easy method. 1854 31/7/55
Declaration by the committee of the constitutional party in the Church of Scotland. 1843 7/3/43
De Crespigny, Caroline
A vision of great men, with other poems: and translations from the poetesses of Germany. 1848 5/3/93
Defoe, Daniel
A friendly rebuke to one Parson Benjamin; particularly relating to his quarrelling with his own church. 1719 5/10/82
A voice from the South. 1707 7/4/93
An historical account of the bitter sufferings . . . of the episcopal church in Scotland under . . . the presbyterian church government. 1707 22/8/44, 3/1/86
Journal of the plague year. 1722 4/7/38, 6/11/83
Memoirs of a cavalier. 1720 23/10/89
The adventures of Robinson Crusoe. 1719 16/12/61
The fortunate mistress, or a history of the life of Lady Roxana. 1724 3/10/83, 17/1/84
The fortunes and misfortunes of the famous Moll Flanders. 1722 11/1/84, 17/1/84
The history and remarkable life of Colonal Jack. 1723 20/10/83
Dekker, Eduard Douwes pseud. Multatuli
Max Havelaar; or, the coffee auctions of the Dutch trading company. 1868 14/2/68
de la Bruyère, J.
Les caractères ou les moeurs du siècle. 2/3/57
Delacour, Rev. James
History of Abelard, ed. J. Delacour. 1725 (?) 28/3/58
Deland, Margaret Wade
John Ward, preacher. 1888 3/7/88
Delany, Mary
The autobiography and correspondence of Mary Granville, Mrs. Delany, ed. Rt. Hon. Lady Llanover. 1861 (3v.) 9/6/83
Delany, Patrick pseud. Philoleutherus Dubliniensis
Reflections upon polygamy and the encouragement given to that practice in the scriptures of the old testament. 1737 9/12/60
Delarive, William
La question de Savoie. 1860 (2v.) 16/5/60
Le droit de la Suisse. 1860 16/5/60
Delavigne, Casimir
Louis XI, tragédie en cinq actes et en vers. 1832 11/2/32
Delbert, Philip
Social evolution . . . edited by Frederick Wingfield. 1891 10/5/91
Delbos, Léon
Les deux rivales. L'Angleterre et la France. 1890 (2nd edn) 4/5/92
De Leon, Thomas Cooper
Four years in rebel capitals: an inside view of life in the Southern Confederacy, from birth to death. 1890 10/9/90
De Lesseps, F. M.
The isthmus of Suez question. 1855 14/8/55
Delessert, Eugène
Souvenirs d'un voyage à Sydney, Nouvelle-Hollande, fait pendant l'année 1845. 1847 31/5/47 ?
Delille, John Douglas
Canon Lucifer. A novel on an English social aspect. 1887 7/8/87
De Lisle, Edwin Joseph Lisle March Phillipps
A comparison between the history of the church and the prophecies of the apocalypse . . . from the German. 1874 24/12/76
Delitzsch, Franz Julius
Iris: studies in colour and talks about flowers . . . . Translated . . . by the Rev. A. Cusin. 1889 2/10/89
Old Testament history of redemption. Lectures . . . . translated from manuscript notes by Samuel Ives Curtiss. 1881 6/10/89
Delitzsch, Johannes
Das Lehrsystem der römischen Kirche dargestellt und beleuchtet. 1875 22/5/75
Della supremazia papale; argomento fondato sulla s. Scrittura e sull'antichità ecclesiastica. 1864 15/5/64
De Maistre, J.
Du pape. 1819 (2v.) 23/3/45
Deman, E. F.
Flax; its cultivation and management: with instructions in various Belgian methods of growing and preparing it for market. 1851 24/3/52

Demaus, Robert
Introduction to the history of English literature. 1860 1/10/64
William Tyndale. A biography. A contribution to the early history of the English bible. 1871 17/3/72
De Merlin, M.
Memoirs of Madame of Malibran. 1840 24/2/40
Demidov, Paul Pavlovich
The Jewish question in Russia... Translated by J. Michell. 1884 (2nd edn) 6/6/91
Demmin, Auguste Frédéric
Guide de l'amateur de faïences et porcelaines, poteries. 1863 17/10/63
Demoiselle de bonne famille. 2/12/88
Demosthenes
Opera. 24/2/27, 9/7/27, 23/7/27, 11/11/27, 7/3/31, 27/12/33
Denarius, [Sir Henry Cole]
Shall we keep the Crystal Palace, and have riding and walking in all weathers among flowers, fountains, and sculpture?. 1851 26/6/51
Denifle, Heinrich Suso
Die Universitäten des Mittelalters bis 1400... Erster Band. Die Entstehung der Universitäten des Mittelalters bis 1400. 1885 20/4/92, 2/9/92
Denison, Edmund Beckett Baron Grimthorpe
A reply to Dr. Farrar's answer to Sir Edmund Beckett's 'Should the revised New Testament be authorized?'. 1882 8/1/82
Against the sceptics. 10/4/81
Letter... on the clause relating to the clergy in the bill for allowing marriages with a deceased wife's sister or niece. 1849 16/5/49
The life of John Lonsdale, bishop of Lichfield; with some of his writings. 1868 15/11/68
Denison, Edward Bishop of Salisbury
A charge delivered to the clergy of the diocese of Salisbury, at his third visitation, in April and May, 1845, by Edward Denison. 1845 11/5/45
A charge delivered to the clergy of the diocese of Salisbury, at the primary visitation of Edward, Lord Bishop of Salisbury, in 1839. 1839 31/12/39
A charge delivered to the clergy of the diocese of Salisbury, by Edward Denison, D.D., Bishop of Salisbury, at his second visitation, September 1842. 1842 5/10/42, 6/8/43
A charge delivered to the clergy of the diocese of Salisbury... July and August, 1848. 1848 29/10/48
A charge delivered to the clergy of the diocese of Salisbury... September and October, 1851. 1851 30/11/51
A review of the state of the question respecting the admission of dissenters to the universities. 1835 4/2/35
Difficulties in the church. A sermon, preached at the re-opening of the church of Longbridge Deverell, December 23, 1852. 1853 23/1/53
Letters by and to, ed. J. Owen. 1845 17/6/47
Sermons preached before the university of Oxford. 1836 29/10/37
Sorrow and consolation: a sermon preached... Easter-day, 1850, being the day after the funeral of the Very Rev. Francis Lear. 1850 28/4/50
The church the teacher of her children. A sermon, preached at St. Margaret's, Westminster. 1839 4/6/39
The obligations of the clergy in preaching the word of God: a charge, delivered to the candidates for holy orders, at his ordination, in Lent 1842. 1842 9/4/42
Denison, Edward M.P.
Letters and other writings of the late Edward Denison... Edited by Sir Baldwyn Leighton, Bart. 1872 28/1/72, 3/6/77
Denison, George Anthony
1. The schools of Christendom. 2. The decay of Greek and Latin... 3. The science of flogging, its natural, efficient, and salutary application ... 1886 17/11/86
An appeal to the clergy and laity of the Church of England, to combine for the defence of the church, and for the recovery of her rights & liberties. 1850 3/4/50
Church education. The present state of the management clause question. 1849 11/2/49
Church rate a national trust. 1861 7/4/61
Church rate. What ought Parliament to do?. 1861 8/9/61
Church schools and state interference. A letter... to the Rt. Hon. William Ewart Gladstone. 1847 23/11/47
Concio Archidiaconi de Taunton in sistendo prolocutore Cantuarensi habita. 1869 24/3/69
Notes of my life, 1805–1878. 1878 25/7/78, 16/4/93
Paper delivered to the registry of the diocese of Bath and Wells, September 30, 1856, by G. A. Denison. 1856 15/6/56
Saravia on the Holy Eucharist, the original Latin from the MS... tr. G. Denison. 1855 17/2/56
Statement, letters and memorials addressed to... the Incorporated Society for Promoting the Education of the Poor. 1848 13/7/48
Supplement to Notes of My Life, 1879, and Mr. Gladstone, 1886. 1893 16/4/93
The archbishop's bill. Speeches of the archdeacon

of Taunton, with prefatory note and amendment. 1874 9/5/74
The catechism of the Church of England the basis of all teaching in parish schools. A charge. 1853 8/5/53
The charge of the archdeacon of Taunton, April 1860. 1860 2/5/60
The charge of the archdeacon of Taunton, April 21, 1868. 1868 29/4/68
The charge of the archdeacon of Taunton. April 27, 1875. 1875 30/5/75
The church and the school. Two sermons preached in St. Peter's Church, Derby. 1851 5/10/51
The church and the world. The law divine. The world's law. The charge of the archdeacon of Taunton April, 1883. 1883 10/6/83
The churches of England and Ireland one church by identity of divine trust: a paper read at a special meeting of the Irish Church Society, Dublin. 1868 23/10/68
The three policies. A letter to the Lord Bishop of Gloucester and Bristol. 1871 13/8/71

Denison, Stephen Charles
Is the ballot a mistake?. 1838 10/2/38, 11/4/38

Denison, Sir William Thomas
A church a social institution. A lecture . . . to the Young Men's Christian Association. 1858 14/9/58
National elementary education. A letter addressed to the members of the Church of Christ in England and her colonies. 1868 12/7/68

Denman, George
The first book of Pope's Homer's Iliad translated into Latin elegiacs. 1873 26/12/72

Denman, James Lemoine
The vine and its fruit, more especially in its relation to the production of wine: embracing an historical and descriptive account of the grape. 1864 21/1/64

Denman, Thomas Baron Denman
A letter from Lord Denman to Lord Brougham, on the final extinction of the slave-trade. 1848 (2nd edn) 16/6/48
Reasons for legalising marriage with a deceased wife's sister. 1852 16/11/52

Dennie, William Henry
Personal narrative of the campaigns in Affghanistan, Sinde, Beloochistan, etc. Detailed in a series of letters of the late Colonel W. H. Dennie. 1843 8/2/43

Dens, Petrus
Theologia moralis et dogmatica. 1832 5/9/41

Dent, Robert Kirkup
Old and new Birmingham. A history of the town and its people. 1878 26/5/78

Denton, William
Montenegro. Its people and their history. 1877 9/8/77
Servia and the Servians. 1862 4/5/63
The ancient church in Egypt. The substance of a paper read on . . . May 30, 1883 at the Victoria Hall, Norwich. 1883 19/8/83
The Christians in Turkey. 1863 30/10/76

Denvir, John
The Irish in Britain, from the earliest times to the fall and death of Parnell. 1892 2/7/92

De Quincey, Thomas
'Homer and the Homeridae', in *Selections grave and gay.* 1854 21/9/59
'On murder, considered as one of the fine arts' in *Selections grave and gay.* 1854 7/11/61
'Whiggism in its relations to literature', *Selections grave and gay.* (14v. 1853–61) 23/9/59
Autobiographic sketches. 1853 (2v. 1853–4) 20/10/54
Collected writings, ed. D. Masson. 1889 (14v. 1889–90) 19/3/90
Confessions of an English Opium-Eater. 1821 20/4/35
Life of, by A. H. Japp. 1890 23/7/90
Selections grave and gay, from writings published and unpublished. 1853 (14v. 1853–60) 20/10/54, 14/8/67

Deramey, J. P.
Précis du mouvement catholique-libéral dans le Jura bernois 1873–1874. 1875 18/11/75

[Derby]
Psalms and hymns. 1835 13/9/40

Derbyshire, George
Dunstable: a poem; and Graves of the poor. To which is subjoined a History of Dunstable; with some account of Dun the robber. 1830 14/5/69 ?

D'Eremas, J. P. Val
The serpent of Eden. 1888 18/5/88

Dering, Edward Heneage
Memoirs of Georgiana, Lady Chatterton. With some passages from her diary. 1878 16/5/78

Dering, Ross George
Coraldi; or, the curse of love. 1889 (2v.) 18/6/89

Der-Mikelian, Arshag
Die Armenische Kirche in ihren Beziehungen zur byzantinischen vom iv. bis zum xiii. Jahrhundert. 1892 22/5/92

Dermot the unbaptised. 28/9/49

De Ros, William Lennox Lascelles Fitzgerald Baron De Ros
Journal of a tour in the principalities, Crimea, and countries adjacent to the Black Sea in the years 1835–36. 1855 5/12/55

Deroulède, Paul
Chants patriotiques. 1882 6/2/83 ?

Der Reliquien über die Verehrung. Eine Stimme aus der evangeliche Kirche. 1845 3/11/45

Deschamps de Saucourt, M.
Les premiers amours, ou Zémire et Zilas. 1784 28/5/52

Des Maizeaux, Pierre
An historical and critical account of the life and writings of William Chillingworth. 1725 28/3/75
An historical and critical account of the life and writings of... Mr. John Hales. 1719 20/9/45
Religion of Protestants. 28/3/75
Desnoiresterres, Gustave le Brisoys
Iconographie Voltairienne. 1879 6/9/86
Voltaire aux Délices. 1871 (1871-73) 13/11/73
Desprez, Philip Charles Soulbieu
Daniel and John, or the apocalypse of the Old and ... New Testament. 1878 8/12/78
Daniel, or the apocalypse of the Old Testament... with an introduction by Rowland Williams. 1865 1/12/78
Deutsch, Emanuel Oscar Menahem
'"Talmud" ... Ur tidskriften' in *Quarterly Review*, cxxiii. 41. 1868 (October 1867) 16/2/68
Deux mots sur les finances de la Grèce. 1856 11/2/57, 28/11/57, 28/11/58
de Valois, Marguérite
Comtes et nouvelles. 31/5/47, 15/9/58
Deverell, William Trapnell
The Norman conquest; or, the land question regarded from an historical standpoint. 1870 7/2/87 ?
The pilgrims and the anglican church. 1871 19/4/78
Devereux, James Edward
On Lord Wharncliffe's Catholic bequest bill, and other Catholic matters... Part the first. 1844 30/10/44
Devereux, Walter Bourchier
Lives and letters of the Devereux, Earls of Sussex in the reigns of Elizabeth, James I, and Charles I, 1540-1646. 1853 15/3/88
Devey, Joseph
The life of Joseph Locke, civil engineer. 1862 17/2/64
Devine, Fr. Pius a Spirito Sancto
Life of Fr. Ignatius Spencer, ..., ed. Fr. Pius a Spirito Sancto. 1866 2/9/66, 21/2/86
The Life of St. Paul of the Cross. 1867 22/12/67 ?
Devine, Fr. Pius
Life of Father Ignatius of St. Paul's, Passionist, ..., ed. Fr. Pius, Passionist. 1866 2/9/66, 21/2/86
Devizes, History of. 1857 31/1/77
Dewar, Daniel Rev.
Observations on the characters, customs and superstitions of the Irish. 1812 (2v.) 31/10/88
The glories of Christ's kingdom. A sermon, preached... at the twenty-sixth general meeting of the London Missionary Society. 1820 13/9/46 ?
Dewar, Edward Henry
A letter to Dr. A. Neander... on his review of... 'German Protestantism, and the right of private judgment in the interpretation of Holy Scripture'. 1845 6/7/45
German Protestantism, and the right of private judgment in the interpretation of Holy Scripture. A brief history of German theology. 1844 31/10/44
Dewees, Francis Percival
The Molly Maguires. The origin, growth, and character of the organization. 1877 11/7/82
De Winton, W. H.
St. Michael's eve. 1892 1/3/91
Dexter, John Thomas
The government of London. 1875 14/8/75
Diary of an artist. 1875 23/5/75
Dibdin, Thomas Frognall
Reminiscences of a literary life. 1836 (2v.) 3/1/57
The old paths: being two sermons preached on the first and second Sundays of Advent, in the district church of St Mary, Bryanston Square. 1844 5/6/45
Dicey, Albert Venn
'Home Rule Movement' in *The Nation*, xlii. 444. 1886 (June 1886) 10/7/86 ?
England's case against Home Rule. 1886 10/11/86, 12/11/86, 30/11/86
Lectures introductory to the study of the law of the Constitution. 1885 2/11/85, 18/12/85, 24/12/85
Letters on Unionist delusions... Republished from 'The Spectator'. 1887 30/9/87
The privy council. The Arnold prize essay, 1860. 1887 23/4/91
Dicey, Sir Edward
'Mr. Gladstone and our empire', in *Nineteenth Century*, ii. 292. 1877 (September 1877) 31/8/77
'Nubar Pasha and Armenia', in *Nineteenth Century*, iv. 548. 1878 (September 1878) 31/8/78
'The Unionist campaign', in *Nineteenth Century*, xx. 294. 1886 (August 1886) 4/8/86
'The Unionist vote', in *Nineteenth Century*, xx. 1. 1886 (July 1886) 6/7/86
[on an Egyptian Protectorate], in *Nineteenth Century*, vii. 333. 1880 (February 1880) 2/2/80
Cavour. A memoir. 1861 5/9/61
England and Egypt. 1881 9/5/82
Nineteenth Century, xvi. 156 [on Egypt]. 1884 (July 1884) 2/7/84
Six months in the federal states. 1863 (2v.) 30/4/63, 20/5/63

Dick, Andrew Coventry
Dissertation on church polity. 1835 24/11/39
Dickens, Charles
A tale of two cities. 1859 12/8/91
American notes for general circulation. 1842 (2v. 1842) 8/11/42
Change for the American Notes: in letters from London to New York. By an American Lady. 1843 13/9/43
David Copperfield. 1850 26/8/80, 4/9/80
Mugby junction. 1866 1/2/67
Oliver Twist. 1838 30/5/39
The letters of Charles Dickens. Edited by his sister-in-law (Georgina Hogarth) and his eldest daughter (Mamie Dickens). 1879 (3v. 1879–81) 15/1/80
The life and adventures of Nicholas Nickleby. 1838 (1838–39) 7/9/39
The old curiosity shop. 1841 19/8/82
The posthumous papers of the Pickwick Club. 1836 (1836–37) 22/10/47
Dickinson, Evelyn
A vicar's wife. 1892 18/3/92
Dickinson, Francis Henry
Convocation and the laity. A letter to the Ven. Archdeacon Grant. 1857 12/7/57
Dickinson, Francis Henry, and Freeman, Edward A.
Suggestions with regard to certain proposed alterations in the universities and colleges of Oxford. 1854 2/4/54
Dickinson, Goldsworthy Lowes
From king to king. 1891 16/6/91
Revolution and reaction in modern France. 1892 8/11/92
Dickinson, Reginald
Summary of the rules and procedure of foreign parliaments. 1882 2/3/82
Dickinson, William
History and antiquities of the city of Newark. 1819 24/6/41
Dickinson's Q[?uarterly] *R*[?eview] *11. 228 'Luke's gospel' (April 1876)*. 1876 23/4/76
Dickson, Thomas Alexander
An Irish policy for a Liberal government. 1885 18/11/85
Dictionary of National Biography. 1885 ff. 13/11/89 n
Diderot, Denis
Le fils naturel. 1758 24/9/81
Les bijoux indiscrets. 1748 (2v. 1881 edn) 22/8/66, 24/1/85
Didon, Henri Louis
Indissolubilité et divorce. Conférences de Saint-Philippe de Roule, avec préface et épilogue. 1880 4/9/86
Jésus Christ. 1891 (2v.) 20/12/91
Science without God... Translated from the French by Rosa Corder. 1882 12/2/82
Die Morgenröthe. 1862 4/7/86
Diepenbrock, Melchior von
Hirtenbrief des... Fürstbischofes von Breslau, Melchior Freiherrn von Diepenbrock an den gesammten ehrwürdigen Clerus. 1845 16/10/45
Diezel, Gustav
Russia, Germany and the eastern question... Translated... by Frederica Rowan. 1854 31/8/54
The formation of a national party in Germany, a necessity of the present crisis in Europe. Translated... by Frederica Rowan. 1855 26/1/56
Difendiamo la famiglia. 31/3/93
Digby, Sir Everard
Papers or letters of Sir Everard Digby, chiefly relating to the Gunpowder-Plot, and written by him during his imprisonment in the Tower. 24/3/89
Digby, Sir Kenelm
Private memoirs of Sir Kenelm Digby, Gentleman of the Bedchamber to King Charles the first. Written by himself. 1827 5/9/78
Digby, Kenelm Henry
Ouranogaia. 1872 28/1/73
Digby, Lord George, and Sir Kenelm
Letters between the Lord George Digby, and Sir Kenelm Digby Kt., concerning religion. 7/9/56
Digest of patents of the United States of America. 1840 12/7/44
Digest of the canons for the government of the Protestant Episcopal Church in the U.S.A. 1866 16/6/67
Dignitary of the church
Letter on the ecclesiastical commission. 1839 18/2/39
Dilke, Charles Wentworth
Mr. Pope's literary correspondence. 1735 (1735–37) 30/12/61
Dilke, Sir Charles Wentworth 2nd Bart.
Greater Britain: a record of travel in English-speaking countries during 1866 and 1867. 1868 (2v.) 11/11/68, 23/11/69, 23/12/69, 15/1/70
The fall of Prince Florestan of Monaco. By himself. 1874 27/3/74
Dill, Edward Marcus
The mystery solved: or, Ireland's miseries: the grand cause, and cure. 1852 19/12/52
Dillon, George F.
The virgin mother of good counsel. A history of the ancient sanctuary in Genazzano. 1884 28/9/84
Dillon, J. J.
Observations in explanation of the provident institutions. 1817 21/9/89

Dillon, P.
The murder of John Kinsella. 1888 5/11/88 ?
Dillon, Robert Crawford
The Lord Mayor's visit to Oxford, in the month of July, 1826. Written at the desire of the party, by the Chaplain to the Mayoralty. 1826 19/12/76
Dilthey, Wilhelm
Life of Schleiermacher. 1870 22/9/73
Dilworth, W. H.
The royal assassins containing... trial and execution of F. Ravaillac for the murder of Henry IV... R. F. Damiens for stabbing Lewis XV. 1759 19/9/81, 23/5/84
Di Menna, Giovanni Battista
Authentic correspondence of J. B. Di Menna with two Roman Catholic priests in Malta. 1841 28/4/41
Diocese of London
Diocesan Board of Education report. 1840 4/7/40
Dio e l'uomo. 26/3/89
Diplomatie et la question d'Orient. 1878 23/4/78
Dircks, Henry
The life, times, and scientific labours of the second Marquis of Worcester. 1865 11/3/65
Dirks, F. Servais
Life of St Antony of Padua, of the Order of Friars-Minor... Translated from the French. 1865 23/8/68
Disney, John
Memoirs of the life and writings of Arthur Ashley Sykes. 1785 1/11/43
Disraeli, Benjamin Earl of Beaconsfield
'Church and Queen.' Five speeches delivered by the Rt. Hon. B. Disraeli, M.P., 1860–1864. Edited... by a member of the University of Oxford. 1865 28/5/65
Beaconsfield, by G. Brandes. 1880 17/5/80
Beaconsfield: a mock-heroic poem, and political satire. 1878 9/8/78
Coningsby. 1844 (3v. 3rd edn) 4/6/44
England and France; or, a cure for the ministerial Gallomania. 1832 11/10/32, 20/10/32
Home letters. Written by Lord Beaconsfield, 1830–1852, ed. Ralph Disraeli. 1885 9/1/86, 12/6/86
Inaugural address delivered to the University of Glasgow, November 19, 1873. 1873 (2nd edn) 28/1/74
La jeunesse de Lord Beaconsfield, by V. Valmont. 1878 16/10/79
Lord Beaconsfield, by James A. Froude. 1890 5/7/90, 25/10/90
Lord Beaconsfield. A biography, by T. P. O'Connor. 1877 12/4/77
Lord Beaconsfield. A political sketch, by C. J. 1878 21/12/78
Lord George Bentinck: a political biography. 1852 31/1/40 n, 5/2/52
Lothair. 1870 18/5/70
Mr. Gladstone's finance, from his accession to office in 1853 to his budget of 1862. 1862 28/1/63
Parliamentary reform. A series of speeches on that subject delivered in the House... by the Right Hon. B. Disraeli (1848–1866). 1867 13/2/67
Parliamentary reform. Speech of the chancellor of the exchequer, delivered in the House of Commons Feb. 28, 1859, on... Bill to amend ... representation. 1859 16/3/59
Sybil; or, the two nations. 1845 (3v.) 20/2/84
Tancred: or, the new crusade. 1847 (3v.) 15/5/48 ?
The crisis examined. By Disraeli the younger. 1834 27/12/34
The premier's defence of his administration. An appeal to the justice of the British nation. 1879 11/2/79
The Runnymede letters. With an introduction and notes by Francis Hitchman. 1885 9/3/85
The voyage of Captain Popanilla. By the author of 'Vivian Grey'. 1828 27/1/58, 16/2/58
Vivian Grey. 1826 (5v.) 27/2/74
D'Israeli, Isaac
Curiosities of literature... With a view of the life and writings of the author. By his son [Benjamin Disraeli]. 1849 (3v. 4th edn) 11/7/54, 16/5/77
Quarrels of authors; or, some memoirs for our literary history, including specimens of controversy to the reign of Elizabeth. 1814 24/3/62
The genius of Judaism. 1833 2/4/58, 4/6/67
Dissenters
[Scottish dissenters remarks]. (not found) 4/5/37
Distant hills, the. 1844 14/4/44
Divizio, Bernardo da Bibbiena Cardinal
La calandra. 7/11/61
Divorce for desertion. 20/10/69
Divorce satirique. 5/8/83
Dix, William Giles
The university of the South. An address delivered at Beersheba Springs, Tennessee. 1859 10/11/59 ?
Dixon, Charles naturalist
Annals of bird life: a year-book of British ornithology. 1890 6/5/90
Dixon, James Wesleyan minister
Annual address of the Conference of Methodist Societies. 1841 12/9/41
The pain of the present and the happiness of the future life. A sermon. 1859 5/12/86
Two discourses. [MS]. 6/1/43
Dixon, Richard Watson
History of the Church of England from the

abolition of the Roman jurisdiction. 1878 (1877–80) 22/12/78, 19/1/83
Mano, or a poetical history: of the time of the close of the tenth century: concerning the adventures of a Norman knight. 1883 (4v.) 1/2/84
Dixon, William Hepworth pseud. Onslow Yorke
New America... With illustrations from original photographs. 1867 (2v.) 20/2/67
Proof private. Lord Bacon's confession: a statement of the facts. 1861 22/6/61
Secret history of 'the International' Working Men's Association. 1872 12/4/72
Spiritual wives. 1868 (2v.) 14/2/68
The story of Lord Bacon's life. 1862 16/2/62, 23/5/63
Doane, George Washington
A brief examination of the proofs by... Boardman ... to sustain his charge that... the Church of England have returned to... errors of popery. 1841 29/8/41
A word for the church: consisting of... 'the Churchman' and 'the High Churchman vindicated'; two episcopal charges by... J. H. Hobart. 1832 23/1/34
Episcopal address, delivered at the Convention of the Protestant Episcopal Church in the diocese of New Jersey. 1833 29/1/34
Looking unto Jesus: the sermon... next after the decease of... B. D. Winslow. 1842 15/4/43
Sermon from seven sermons preached at the consecration... of the parish church of Leeds. 1841 5/12/41
Sermons on various occasions: with three charges. 1842 4/4/49
The gospel in the church. A sermon before the annual convention of the Diocese of Massachusetts. 1832 23/1/34
The remains of the Rev. C. H. Wharton, with a memoir of his life by George Washington Doane. 1834 (2v.) 10/1/57
The reply of the Bishops of New Jersey in reply to the paper, read before the Court of Bishops... by the Bishops of Ohio and Maine. 1852 11/4/52
Doane, William Croswell
The life and writings of G. W. Doane, bishop of New Jersey. 1860 19/1/34
Dobbin, Orlando T.
A plea for tolerance toward our fellow-subjects in Ireland who profess the Roman Catholic religion. With a prefatory letter addressed to... Kimberley. 1866 27/9/66
The sabbath of heaven. A sermon [on Heb. iv. 9] *delivered in Albion Chapel Hall... during the prevalence of cholera*. 1849 20/8/54
Dobbs, Archibald Edward the elder
General representation on a complete readjustment and modification of Mr. Hare's plan. 1871 23/11/71
Dobell, Horace Benge
On diet and regimen in sickness and health. 1882 (7th edn) 30/12/82 ?
Dobell, Sydney Thompson
Of parliamentary reform: a letter to a politician. 1865 16/11/65
Dobney, Henry Hamlet
A letter... to the archbishop of Canterbury, on that portion of his recent pastoral which affirms 'the everlasting suffering of the lost'. 1864 21/8/64
Judas, or a brother's inquiry concerning the betrayer. A dream. 1872 6/5/77
Dobson, Susannah Mrs.
The life of Petrarch. 1775 (2v.) 14/8/34
Document pour servir à l'histoire de l'application de l'article 24 du traité de Paris en Moldavia. 1857 14/8/57
Dodd, Charles pseud. Hugh Tootell
The church history of England... chiefly with regard to Catholics. 1737 8/9/78, 25/9/89
Dodd, E.
Reform your arches. The course of law ecclesiastical illustrated. 1853 23/5/53
Dodd, George
The land we live in. 1854 24/5/75
The textile manufactures of Great Britain. 1844 (6v. 1844–46) 23/10/48
Dodd, George William
Boscobel. A narrative of the adventures of Charles II after the battle of Worcester. 1859 6/2/80 ?
Dodd, Philip Stanhope
The address of the Revd. P. D. to the Camberwell Volunteers, on their enrolment; September 27th, 1803. 1803 22/9/72 ?
Dodd, Thomas dealer in prints
Memoirs of Thomas Dodd, William Upcott and George Stubbs, R. A. 1879 25/5/81
Dodd, William LL.D.
The beauties of Shakespeare... selected from each play. 1752 19/8/33
Doddridge, Sir John
The history of the ancient and moderne estate of the principality of Wales, Dutchy of Cornwall, and Earldome of Chester. 14/5/89
Doddridge, Philip
Family expositor, or a paraphrase and version of the New Testament. 1760 (6v. 1760–62) 2/10/31 ?
Life of Col. James Gardiner. 1832 12/3/82
The correspondence and diary of Philip Doddridge, ed. J. D. Humphreys. 1829 (5v. 1829–31) 3/9/40
The rise and progress of religion in the soul, illustrated in a course of serious and practical addresses. 1745 26/6/31
Dodgson, Charles Rector of Croft
Preach the Gospel. A sermon. 1839 13/10/39

Dodington, Bartholomew
Diary of B. Dodington, ed. Wyndham. 1784 1/9/84
Dods, John Bovee
The philosophy of electro-biology, ed. G. W. Stone. 1852 26/12/55
Dods, Marcus the younger
Mohammed, Buddha, and Christ. Four lectures on natural and revealed religion. 1877 20/6/77
Dodsworth, William Rev.
A letter to the Rev. E. B. Pusey on the position which he has taken in the present crisis. 1850 17/6/50
Discourses on the Lord's supper. 1835 5/3/36, 1/4/38
Remarks on the second letter of... R. W. Sibthorp ... entitled 'A further answer to the inquiry, why have you become a Catholic?'. 1842 17/4/42
Sermon on the national fast. 1847 4/4/47
Why have you become a Romanist? A letter to Rev. R. W. Sibthorp. 1842 9/2/42
Dodwell, Henry the elder
A preliminary defence of the epistolary discourse, concerning the distinction between the soul and spirit. 1706 18/8/76
Dodwell, William
The Athanasian creed vindicated and explained. 1802 14/10/27
Three charges on the Athanasian creed. 1802 18/10/29
Doederlein, Johann Ludwig Christoph Wilhelm von
Homerisches Glossarium. 1850 17/10/57 ?
Doetsch, P. pseud. D. J. Juvenalis
Juvenal ein Sittenrichter seiner Zeit. 1874 20/9/74
Döllinger, Johann Joseph Ignaz von
'The British Empire in India', in *Contemporary Review*, xxxv. 385. 1879 (June 1879) 19/4/79
Akademische Vorträge. 1888 (3v.) 7/6/88, 22/7/88
Briefe und Erklärungen ... über die vaticanischen Decrete 1869–1887. 1890 10/8/90
Der Papst und das Concil. Von Janus. 1869 9/10/69
Der Protestantismus in Bayern und die Kniebeugung. 1843 3/10/45
Die einflussereichste Frau der französischen Geschichte. 1886 22/5/88
Die Papst-Fabeln des Mittelalters ... Zweite Auflage. 1863 6/9/63, 27/9/63
Die Universitäten sonst und jetzt. 1867 3/6/73, 10/9/73
Die Vergangenheit und Gegenwart der katholischen Theologie. 1864 6/10/74
Einige Worte über die Unfehlbarkeitsadresse. 1870 25/6/70
Heidenthum und Judenthum. Vorhalle zur Geschichte des Christenthums. 1857 30/8/57, 6/6/88
Hippolytus and Callistus: or, the church of Rome in the first half of the third century. 1876 29/10/76
Hippolytus und Kallistus: oder die Römische Kirche in der ersten Hälfte des dritten Jahrhunderts. 1853 29/1/54
Ignaz von Döllinger, by E. Michael. 1892 13/9/92
Ignaz von Döllinger. Erinnerungen by L. von Kobell. 1892 27/10/92
Irrthum, Zweifel und Wahrheit. Eine Rede an die Studierenden. 1845 12/10/45
Kirche und Kirchen, Papstthum und Kirchenstaat. Historisch-politische Betrachtungen ... Zweiter unveränderter Abdruck. 1861 9/2/62, 3/1/75
Lectures on the reunion of the churches. 1872 27/3/72, 30/8/74
Lehrbuch der Kirchengeschichte. Zweite, verbesserte Auflage. 1843 25/10/46
Luther. 1851 3/8/51
Studies in European history ... translated by M. Warre. 1890 23/11/90
Studizkeiten. 23/12/88
Umrisse zu Dante's Paradies, von P. von Cornelius ... mit erklären dem Texte von Dr. J. D. 1830 3/6/88
Domaine autour de Rome. (not found) 17/11/62
Doman, Henry
'The Cathedral' and other poems. 1864 8/1/73
Domestic tyranny, or woman in chains. 1842 (not found) 8/3/42
Donaldson, J.
'Women in Greece', in *Contemporary Review*, xxxiv. 700. 1879 (March 1879) 3/3/79
Donaldson, John William
The new Cratylus, or contributions towards a more accurate knowledge of the Greek language. 1839 16/8/55
The theatre of the Greeks, a series of papers relating to the history and criticism of the Greek drama. 1860 (7th edn) 13/8/76
Donaldson, Walter
Recollections of an actor. 1865 9/12/65
Donisthorpe, Wordsworth
The claims of labour; or, serfdom, wagedom, and freedom. 1880 28/9/80
Donkin, William Fishburn
A defence of voting against the propositions to be submitted to Convocation on Feb 13, 1845. 1845 19/2/45
Donnelly, Ignatius
Atlantis: the antediluvian world. 1882 7/3/82

The golden bottle. 1892 19/3/93
The great cryptogram: Francis Bacon's cipher in the so-called Shakespeare plays. 1888 (2v.) 16/5/88
Dor, Henri
De l'évolution historique du sens des couleurs: réfutation des théories de Gladstone et de Magnus. 1879 8/5/79
Doran, John
Habits and men. 1855 14/5/56
London in Jacobite times. 1877 (2v.) 15/2/78
Dore, John Read
Old bibles, or an account of the various versions of the English bible. 1876 28/4/89
Dorschaeus, Petrus
Christum divinitatis suae per omnes homilias suas assertorem dissertatione theologica Judaeis et Judaizantibus opposita exhibet J. Steenbuchius. 1718 7/8/64
Dorscheus, Johannes Georgius
J. G. Dorschei Thomas Aquinas exhibitus Confessor Veritatis Evangelicae Augustana Confessione repetite, juxta seriem Controversarium. 3/11/61
Dostoevsky, Fédor Mikhailovich
Le crime et le châtiment. 1884 (2v.) 9/9/89
Dotti, Giovanni
Canzona d'un piagnone, ed. G. Dotti. 1864 4/3/88
Douay Catechism, Abstract of. 1718 11/7/35
Doucoudray Holstein, H. L. V.
Memoirs of Simon Bolivar. 1830 (2v.) 26/10/42
Douglas, David publisher
The journal of Sir Walter Scott. 1890 (2v.) 10/11/90
Douglas, Lady Gertrude Georgina afterw. Stock
A wasted life and marr'd. 1891 (3v. 1891) 25/12/91
Douglas, Henry Alexander
Charge delivered... 12th January, 1875. 1875 4/6/75
Douglas, James teacher
An introductory geography... intended as an introduction to the text-book of geography. 1867 7/12/85
Douglas, Janet Mary
The life and selections from the correspondence of William Whewell. 1882 14/2/82
Douglas, Robert Vicar of Bredgar
Irish church question. A paper. 1868 23/8/68
Douglas, Thomas Lord Selkirk
A narrative of occurrences in the Indian countries of North America, since the connexion of... Selkirk with the Hudson's Bay Company. 1817 11/8/48
Observations on the present state of the Highlands of Scotland, with a view of the causes and probable consequences of emigration. 1805 17/1/85
Douthwaite, William Ralph
Gray's Inn. 1886 21/1/93
Dowd, James
Limerick and its sieges... Illustrated. 1890 26/5/90
Dowden, Edward
Shakespeare: a critical study of his mind and art. 1875 3/12/77, 10/8/78
Dowden, John Bishop of Edinburgh
Religion in relation to the social and political life of England. A sermon preached... at the opening of the Church Congress. 1886 14/11/86
The annotated Scottish communion office. An historical account. 1884 11/11/84
The saints in the Calendar and the Irish synod. A sermon. 1873 3/8/73
Dowden, John
Thirty-four letters written to James Sharp... by the Duke and Duchess of Lauderdale. 1893 21/2/94
Dowding, William Charles
German theology during the Thirty Years' War. The life and correspondence of G. Calixtus. 1863 28/11/63
Religious partizanship and other papers. 1854 4/6/54
The coming of the Church of England: with a glance at Scarborough. 1875 5/9/75
Dowell, Stephen
A sketch of the history of taxes in England from the earliest times to the present day. 1876 12/5/80
Dowling, H.
The Western Railway: the cost, working expenses, and traffic returns. A paper read at the Mechanics' Institute, Launceston. 1863 25/11/64
Downe, Hugh
Innocent victims: a story of London's life and labour. 1890 12/7/90
Downe, Thomas
The first principles of the oracles of God. 22/2/74 ?
Downey, Edmund pseud. F. M. Allen
Through green glasses. 1887 17/10/87
Downie, M. M.
A girl in the Carpathians. 1891 10/5/91
Dowson, John M.D.
Erasmus Darwin: philosopher, poet and physician, a lecture to the Literary and Philosophical Society of Whitby. 1861 24/3/86
Doyen, F. le
Projet de reconstitution de la Banque de France. 1865 1/9/65
Doyle, Sir Francis Hastings Charles
'Doncaster of Leger', *N. Sport Magazine.* 1838 (November 1838) 1/8/39

Doyle, Sir Francis (*cont.*)
'James Hope Scott', in *Macmillans Magazine*, xl. 321. 1884 (March 1884) 6/3/84
Lectures delivered before the University of Oxford. 1868 30/1/69
Lectures on poetry, delivered at Oxford . . . second series. 1877 26/8/79
Miscellaneous verses. 1834 1/4/34
Miscellaneous verses. 1840 22/1/41
Reminiscences and opinions . . . 1813–1885. 1886 15/10/86, 23/1/88
Robin Hood's Bay, an ode. 1878 7/9/78
The Return of the Guards, and other poems. 1866 31/1/67
The two destinies. A poem. 1844 12/7/44
Yorkshire heiress, a comedy [early version]. 1885 1/8/82 ?

Doyle, James
An essay on the Catholic claims, addressed to the Rt. Hon. the Earl of Liverpool. 1826 20/12/70, 31/10/74, 16/3/84

D'Oyley, E.
Letter to Earl Grey [on church rates]. 1834 2/4/34
Life of William Sancroft. 1821 (2v.) 16/5/41

Drach, David Paul Louis Bernard
De l'harmonie entre l'Eglise et la synagogue. 1844 (2v. 1844) 4/11/66

Drage, Geoffrey
Eton and the empire: an address. 1890 27/6/91

Drake, Charles Frederick Tyrnliff
Literary remains of C. F. T. Drake. 1877 25/2/78

Drane, Augusta Theodosia [Mother Francis Raphael]
Morality of tractarianism. 1850 23/5/50

Draper, John William M.D., LL. D
History of the American civil war. 1871 (3v.) 11/2/71, 17/2/71
History of the conflict between religion and science. 1872 25/12/74
History of the intellectual development of Europe. 1864 (2v.) 5/7/63

Drayton, Michael
The first part of the true . . . historie, of the life of Sir John Old-Castle. 15/9/36

Drew, Count Francis Bickerstaff
How Ben behaved himself [a satire on Lord Beaconsfield's parliament]. 1880 29/3/80

Drew, George Smith
Contemporary Review, xxxv.815 [on Dr. Rushwell]. 1879 (August 1879) 3/8/79
Nazareth, its life and lessons. 1872 3/8/72
Reasons of faith, or the the order of the Christian argument developed and explained. 1862 2/11/62

Drexelius, Hieremias
The heliotropium, or conformity of the human will to the divine, ed. R. N. Shute. 1881 23/9/83
Driven to Rome. 1877 24/8/79

Driver, Samuel Rolles
'Cosmology of Genesis', in *The Expositor.* 1886 (January 1886) 3/1/86
Biblical commentary on the prophecies of Isaiah by F. Delitzsch, with introduction by S. R. Driver. 1890 20/10/89
The book of Daniel, with introduction and notes. 1877 19/9/91

Droop, Henry Richmond
The Edwardian vestments. An investigation into the history and construction of the Ornaments-Rubric. 1875 6/6/75

Druitt, Robert
Report on the cheap wines from France, Italy, Austria, Greece and Hungary; their quality, wholesomeness, and price. 1865 11/5/65

Drummond, David Thomas Kerr
A sermon for the times . . . with an introduction and copious appendix. 1842 8/5/42
Correspondence between C. H. Terrot . . . and D. T. K. D. 1842 14/11/42
Historical sketch of the episcopy in Scotland from 1688 to the present time. 1845 5/9/45
Reasons for withdrawing from the Scottish Episcopal Church, and for accepting an invitation to continue . . . as a clergyman of the Church of England. 1842 21/11/45
The Scottish Communion Office examined, and proved to be repugnant to scripture. 1842 21/11/45

Drummond, Henry F.R. S. E.
Natural law in the spiritual world. 1883 16/12/86

Drummond, Henry M.P.
Abstract principles of revealed religion. 1845 13/3/45, 8/10/76
Discourses on the true definition of the Church, one, holy, catholic, and apostolic, and kindred subjects. 1858 (1860 edn) 30/12/60 ?
Letter on the payment of the Roman Catholic clergy, to Sir R. H. Inglis, Bart. 1845 22/5/45
Letter to Thomas Phillips, Esqre. R. A., on the connection between the fine arts and religion, and the means of their revival. 1840 12/6/47
On government by the Queen and attempted government by the people. 1842 12/5/42
On the condition of the agricultural classes of Great Britain and Ireland . . . With a preface by H. Drummond. 1842 (2v.) 29/7/42
On the future destinies of the celestial bodies. 1855 8/5/59
Reasons wherefore a Clergyman of the Church of England should not become a Roman Catholic. In reply to the Rev. R. W. Sibthorp. 1842 27/2/42

Remarks on the Churches of Rome and England, respectfully addressed to . . . Dr. Wiseman and W. Palmer. 1841 14/10/60
Reply to the Rev. R. Wilberforce's Principles of Church authority. 1855 22/4/55
Social duties on Christian principles. 1830 24/10/30
Speeches in Parliament. 1860 (2v.) 16/11/83
The fate of Christendom. 1854 (3rd edn) 16/5/55

Drummond, Robert Blackley
Erasmus, his life and character, as shown in his correspondence and works. 1873 (2v.) 26/8/81

Drummond, William
Poems: by William Drummond, of Hawthorne-deane. The second impression. 29/8/60

Drury, Henry
Arundines Cami, sive Musarum Cantabrigiensium Lusus canori: collegit atque edidit H. D. 1841 22/11/41

Dryden, John
All for love, or, the world well lost. A tragedy . . . written in imitation of Shakespeare's stile. 16/9/42
Amboyna, a tragedy. 15/9/42
Aurengzebe: a tragedy. 15/9/42
Epistles, elegies and epitaphs from The miscellaneous works of John Dryden . . . with . . . notes . . . and an account of his life. 1760 (4v.) 14/1/64
Essay of dramatick poesie. 1/12/92
Fables ancient and modern; translated into verse, from Homer, Ovid, Boccace & Chaucer: with original poems. 5/12/26 ?, 9/4/31 ?, 23/11/36, 24/1/62
Religio Laici. Written in a letter to John Dryden, Esq. 4/11/61, 7/5/70
Secret love, or the Maiden-Queen. 14/9/42
The Hind and the Panther. A poem, in three parts. 7/5/70, 15/8/90
The poetical works of John Dryden. With life, critical dissertation, and explanatory notes by . . . G. Gilfillan. 1855 (2v.) 4/2/75
The rival ladies. A tragi-comedy. 10/9/42
The state of innocence, and fall of man. 12/7/41
The wild gallant: a comedy. 7/9/42, 30/11/92
The works of John Dryden, ed. Sir Walter Scott. 1828 (18v.) 15/8/90
The works of Virgil. Translated into English verse by J. Dryden. 14/9/46
Troilus and Cressida. 11/11/56

Drysdale, George
The Irish land question. 1867 22/6/68

Duberly, Frances Isabella
Journal kept during the Russian war: from the departure of the army from England in April 1854 to the fall of Sebastopol. 1855 1/2/56

Dublin Magazine. 1. 1. Ireland 19/1/1844

Dublin Review.
1. 5/1836. Pusey's appendix 6/5/1836
2. 168. 12/1836. Pusey 14/5/1838
2. 493, 329. 4/1837. Church of England; No Popery 21/6/1837
3. 325. 10/1837. Vaudois 13/12/1837
4. 1. 7/1834. Protestant emigration 30/7/1834
5. 285. 10/1838. Apostolic succession 29/12/1838
6. 416. 5/1839. Froude 1/7/1839
8. 240. 2/1840. Catholicity 23/3/1840
8. 334. 5/1840. Lingard 19/6/1888
10. 131. 1/1868. Education 19/1/1868
10. 498. 4/1868. Ireland 23/4/1868
12. 221. 2/1842. Anglicanism 6/3/1842
12. 525. 5/1842. Protestantism 10/6/1842
14. 1. 2/1843. Recent charges 21/3/1843
14. 243. 10/1885. Chichester on Ireland 14/2/1887
14. 430. 4/1870. Education Bill 23/4/1870
14. 451, 341. 4/1870. Ireland; Sarpi 20/4/1870
15. 103. 9/1843. Oxford movement 30/10/1843
17. 236, 252. 9/1844. Cooper's Lectures; Italian Apostates 28/10/1844
18. 233. 3/1845. Mazzini 6/4/1845
18. 370. 6/1845. Spain 7/7/1845
18. 555. 6/1845. Nicene Fathers 5/7/1845
19. 522. 12/1845. Oxford Movement 16/1/1845
20. 243. 10/1888. J. Morris on Gladstone 25/8/1889
20. 243. 10/1888. on Gladstone 28/10/1888
20. 357. 4/1873. M. Arnold 13/5/1873
20. 448. 4/1873. University Bill 9/5/1873
20. 83. 3/1846. Conversions 23/4/1846
23. 132. 9/1847. Bunsen 22/10/1847
24. 7/1890 11/7/1890
24. 170. 1/1875. Ward on Expostulation 3/2/1875
24. 454. 4/1875. on Gladstone 28/5/1875
25. 342. 10/1875. Anglicanism 16/12/1875
26. 152. 3/1849. India 11/4/1849
28. 469. 6/1850. G. Achilli 9/7/1850
30. 3/1851. Catholic Hierarchy 19/4/1851
38. 234. 3/1850. Gorham 3/5/1850
44. 336. 6/1858. Party 10/7/1858
82. 300. 9/1873. Socrates 26/9/1873
84. 129, 108, 205. 7/1874 12/8/1874

Dubois, Jean Antoine
Description of the character, manners and customs of the people of India. 1805 15/9/33

Dubois de Saint-Gelais, Louis François
Remarques sur l'Angleterre faites en 1713. 1717 22/11/89

Du Bois-Reymond, Emil Heinrich
Uber den deutschen Krieg. Rede... Dritter unveränderter Abdruck. 1870 21/12/70
Du Boulay, John
Evidences of rational evangelism. 1875 22/8/75
Du Cambout de Pont-Château, Sébastien Joseph
La morale pratique des Jésuites. 23/1/76
Ducane, Sir Edmund Frederick
The punishment and prevention of crime. 1881 31/10/85
Ducarel, Andrew Coltée
The history of the royal hospital & collegiate church of St. Katharine, near the tower of London, from 1273. 1780 (vol 2) 30/4/65
Du Chaillu, Paul Belloni
Explorations and adventures in Equatorial Africa. 1861 15/5/61
The Viking Age. 1889 (2v.) 29/8/91
Duchâtel
Nos désastres et leur origine. 16/1/92
Du Châtelet, Alexandre Jean Baptiste Parent
De la prostitution dans la ville de Paris considérée sous le rapport de l'hygiène publique, de la morale et de l'administration. 1836 (2v.) 9/7/45, 23/4/67
Duentzer, Heinrich
Die homerischen Fragen. 1874 7/4/74
Duff, Alexander D.D.
The Church of Scotland's India Mission; or a brief exposition of the principles on which that Mission has been conducted in Calcutta... address. 1835 18/6/35
Duff, Sir Mountstuart Elphinstone Grant
Inaugural address delivered to the University of Aberdeen, on his installation as Rector. 1867 18/12/72
Studies in European Politics. 1866 26/12/67
The Eastern question. A lecture. 1876 18/11/76
Duff Gordon, Lady
The amber witch, ed., tr. W. Meinhold. 1844 10/8/44, 6/11/82
Duffield, Alexander James
The ingenious knight Don Quixote de la Mancha ... A new translation... by A. J. Duffield. 1881 8/12/80
Duffy, Sir Charles Gavan K. C. M. G.
'Mr. Gladstone's Irish constitution' in *Contemporary Review*, xl. 609. 1886 (May 1886) 26/6/86
A bird's-eye view of Irish history. 1882 27/9/87
The price of peace in Ireland. A letter to... the Earl of Carnarvon. 1885 9/10/85
Thomas Davis: the memoirs of an Irish patriot, 1840–1846. 1890 3/12/90
Young Ireland. 1880 (2v. 1880–83) 6/11/80
Dugdale, Henry Geast
The life and character of Edmund Geste, the principal compiler of the Liturgy of the Church of England. 1840 6/10/82
Du Haussay, Nicolle
The private memoirs of Madame Du Hasset, lady's maid to Madame de Pompadour. 1825 26/10/81
Duigenan, Patrick
The nature and extent of the demands of the Irish Roman Catholics fully explained. 1810 24/3/40 ?
Dukinfield, Sir Henry Robert
A letter to the inhabitants of the parish of St. Martin-in-the-Fields. 1847 22/7/47
A memoir, by Mrs. Dukinfield. 1861 23/6/61
Dulaure, Jacques Antoine
Des divinités génératrices, ou du culte du phallus chez les anciens et les modernes... ed. J. A. Dulaure. 1885 12/7/85, 26/7/85
Histoire abrégée de différents cultes. 1825 (2v. 2nd edn) 17/8/85
Duller, Eduard
Die Jesuiten wie sie waren und wie sie sind. Zweite... stark vermehrte Auflage der 'Geschichte der Jesuiten'. 1845 27/7/47
Dumas, Alexandre the elder
Count of Monte Cristo. 1846 (2v.) 18/9/46
Duchess de Berri, tr. A. Dumas. 1833 16/11/33
Dumas, Alexandre the younger
L'ami des femmes. Comédie en cinq actes... Nouvelle édition. 1864 9/9/86
Les idées de Mme. Aubray. 1867 10/6/67
Dumont, Pierre Etienne Louis
Recollections of Mirabeau. 1832 (2nd edn) 17/10/32
Dunbar, Edward Dunbar
Social life in former days, chiefly in the province of Moray. 1865 17/3/66
Dunbar, William the poet
The poems of W. D. now first collected. With notes, and a memoir of his life, by D. Laing. 1834 11/5/64
Dunblane, Synod of
Register of the diocesan synod of Dunblane 1662–1688. 1877 11/9/92
Duncan, George John C.
Memoir of the Rev. Henry Duncan, Minister of Ruthwell. 1848 12/6/53
Duncan, Mrs. George John C.
Pre-Adamite man; or the story of our old planet. 1860 15/12/60, 5/10/65
Duncan, John LL.D.
Colloquia Peripatetica: deep-sea soundings. Being notes of conversations with the late John Duncan... By William Knight. 1870 12/6/70

Duncan, Jonathan B.A.
The principles of money demonstrated, and bullionist fallacies refuted. 1849 12/5/57
Duncan, William Professor
The elements of logick. 1748 21/10/31
Duncker, Maximillian Wolfgang
History of Greece, from the earliest times to the end of the Persian war; translated from the German . . . by S. F. Alleyne. 1883 19/9/91
The history of antiquity. From the German, . . . by E. Abbott. 1877 6/1/78
Duncombe, Thomas Slingsby
The Life and Correspondence of T. S. Duncombe . . . edited by his son, T. H. Duncombe. 1868 (2v.) 26/11/67
Dunlop, Alexander afterw. Murray Dunlop
A letter to the Earl of Aberdeen on the correspondence recently published by his Lordship. 1840 29/7/40
An answer to the Dean of Faculty's . . . 'Letter to the Lord Chancellor,' on the claims of the Church of Scotland in regard to its jurisdiction. 1839 28/11/39
Tracts upon tracts on the intrusion of ministers. New Series. 1839 8/12/39
Dunlop, Alison Hay
Anent Old Edinburgh and some of the worthies who walked its streets, with other papers by A. H. D. Edited by her brothers, with biographical notes. 1889 16/12/90
Dunlop, John Colin
History of Roman Literature, from its earliest period to the Augustan age. 1823 (3v. 1823–28) 21/11/57
Dunlop, Robert
Life of Henry Grattan. 1888 24/5/89
Dunlop, Dr. William
The uses of creeds and confessions of faith . . . edited, with a preface and notes, by J. Buchanan. 1857 24/5/57
Dunn, Andrew
The conversion and edifying death of A. D.: or a guide to truth and happiness. 1826 (3rd edn) 9/12/38
Dunn, Archibald J.
The rise and decay of the rule of Islam. 1877 8/3/77
Dunn, Henry
Liber Librorum: its structure, limitations and purpose. A friendly communication to a reluctant sceptic. 1867 24/7/67
National education, the question of questions, being an apology for the Bible in schools for the nation. 1838 24/2/38, 19/5/38
Dunn, John of the Hudson's Bay Company
History of the Oregon Territory and British North-American fur trade; with an account of the habits and customs of the principal native tribes. 1844 1/8/44
Dupanloup, Félix Antoine Philibert
La Convention du 15 septembre et l'Encyclique du 8 décembre. 1865 12/3/65
Lettre de Mgr. l'Evêque d'Orléans au clergé de son diocèse, relativement à la définition de l'infaillibilité au prochain concile. 1869 28/11/69
Lettre . . . sur les prophéties contemporaines, avec l'opinion de plusieurs Conciles. 1874 24/5/74
Premières (nouvelles, dernières) lettres à M. M. les membres du conseil municipal de Paris sur le centenaire de Voltaire. 1878 (3v.) 19/5/78
Second letter . . . to M. Minghetti, on the new Italian military law, and its consequences with regard to the clergy, with a brief note from Pope Pius IX. 1876 26/3/76
Duperron, V. Hébert-
Essai sur la polémique et la philosophie de Saint Clément d'Alexandrie. 1855 15/3/74
Dupin, Baron François Pierre Charles
Canal maritime de Suez. Institut Impérial de France. Second rapport à l'Académie des Sciences. 1858 3/6/58
Du Plessis, Armand Jean Cardinal, Duc de Richelieu
L'histoire du ministère de . . . Richelieu. (4v. 1649) 10/11/83 ?
Mémoires du Cardinal Richelieu, ed. C. B. Petitot. 1819 17/10/85 ?
Testament politique d'A. Du P. Cardinal duc de Richelieu. 4/2/48 ?
Duplomb, Charles
L'hôtel de la reine Marguerite, première femme de Henri IV. Précédé d'une étude sur le palais des Thermes, l'abbaye de Saint-Germain-des-Prés. 1881 22/8/83
Du Pontet, René Louis Alphonse
Alaricus. Carmen latinum Cancellarii praemio donatum. 1890 22/8/90
Dupont-White, Charles Brook
Le progrès politique en France. 1868 27/7/70
Duppa, Richard
The life and literary works of Michael Angelo Buonarotti. 1806 13/1/50
Duprat, Pascal
Essai historique sur les races anciennes et modernes de l'Afrique septentrionale. 1845 18/10/75
Durand, M.
Helen Trevelyan; or, the ruling race. 1893 17/9/93
Durgesa Nandini, or the chieftain's daughter. A Bengali romance. 1880 27/12/93
Dusautoy, Frederic
The great apostacy of the last sixteen centuries. 1873 30/11/73
Dusmani, A. L.
La missione di W. E. Gladstone nelle isole Ionie. 1869 (1869–71) 31/12/72

Dutens, Joseph Michel
Mémoires sur les travaux publics de l'Angleterre, suivis d'un mémoire de l'esprit d'association et sur les différentes modes de concession. 1819 19/9/50
Dutens, Louis
Mémoires d'un voyageur. 1806 (3v.) 26/3/89 ?
Dutton, Amy
The streets and lanes of a city: being the reminiscences of Amy Dutton. With a preface by the Bishop of Salisbury. 1871 24/9/71
Dutton, W. E.
History of crusades. 1877 15/8/77
Duvergier de Hauranne, Prosper
Des principes du gouvernement représentatif et de leur application. 1838 23/8/58
Histoire du Gouvernement Parlementaire en France, 1814–48. 1857 (10v. 1857–72) 7/6/65
Duveyrier, Charles
L'Empereur François-Joseph I et l'Europe. 1860 19/12/60
Lettres politiques. Par l'auteur de La Pairie envisagée dans ses rapports avec la situation politique. 1843 11/1/44
Dwight, Sereno Edwards
The Hebrew wife: or, the law of marriage examined in relation to the lawfulness of polygamy and to the extent of the law of incest. 1836 11/5/49
Dwinelle, John W.
American opinions on the 'Alabama,' and other political questions. 1870 25/1/70
Dwyer, Philip
Work and its reward in the Irish church. 1866 8/4/66
Dyce, William R. A.
Notes on shepherds and sheep. A letter to J. Ruskin. 1851 21/5/51
The National Gallery its formation and management considered in a letter... to Prince Albert. 1853 14/2/53
Theory of the fine arts. 1844 13/7/44, 25/7/44
Dyer, J. F. T.
Great men at play. 1889 (2v.) 20/6/89
Dyer, Oliver historical writer
Great senators of the United States forty years ago, 1848 and 1849. With personal recollections... of Calhoun, Benton, Clay. 1889 12/2/90
Dykes, James Oswald
The beatitudes of the kingdom. 1872 21/9/73
Dykes, John Bacchus
Eucharistic truth and ritual. A letter to... the Lord Bishop of Durham occasioned by his... reply to an address from certain laymen in the diocese. 1874 25/10/74
Dymond, Jonathan
The church and the clergy: showing that religious establishments derive no countenance from the nature of Christianity. 1834 2/7/35
Dyson, Mrs. Charles
Memorials of a departed friend. 1836 (new edn) 23/10/36

E., J. O.
Is Ireland to obtain home rule?. 1887 24/6/87 ?
Eadie, John LL.D.
Lectures on the bible to the young. 1848 30/5/86
Eales, Samuel John
Via crucis: fourteen sermons on the passion of... Jesus Christ, forming a series of meditations for Lent. 1880 19/12/80
Earl, George Windsor
Enterprise in tropical Australia. 1846 14/3/46
Earl and the Doctor
South Sea bubbles. By the Earl [of Pembroke] and the Doctor [G. H. Kingsley]. 1872 5/2/72
Earle, John
Psalter of the great Bible of 1539. 1894 13/2/94
Earle, John Charles
Light leading unto light; a series of sonnets and poems. 1875 18/6/76
The spiritual body. An essay in prose and verse. 1876 30/3/76
Eastern Church Association
Report of the committee of the Eastern Church Association [on Catholic congress in Cologne]. 1872 10/11/72
Eastlake, Lady Elizabeth née Rigby
Life of John Gibson.... Edited by Lady Eastlake. 1870 26/10/70
Eastwick, Edward Backhouse
Dry leaves from young Egypt. By an Ex-political. 1851 23/2/52
Eastwick, William Joseph
Lord Lytton and the Afghan war. 1879 22/2/79
Speech... on the case of the Ameers of Sinde. 1844 8/4/45
Eaton, Thomas Ray
Shakespeare and the Bible. 1858 16/10/65
Ebel, Johann Gottfried
The traveller's guide through Germany. 1818 28/7/32
The traveller's guide through Switzerland. 1818 7/7/32, 28/7/32
Ebers, Georg
Uarda. Roman aus dem alten Aegypten. 1877 12/8/84
'Ecce Agnus Dei!' Or, Christianity without mystery. 1868 18/10/68
Ecce Episcopus. 28/1/72
Ecce Homo: a survey of the life and work of Jesus Christ [by J. R. Seeley]. 1866 25/12/65 ?

Ecce Homo! or a critical inquiry into the history of Jesus Christ. 1799 18/10/63
Ecclesia Dei; the place and functions of the church in the divine order of the universe. 1866 23/9/66
Ecclesiastic and Theologian Review. 14. 133, 165. 7/1852. Reviews 3/10/1852
Ecclesiologist, The.
7. 47. 2/1847. Oxford cathedral 30/12/1847
10. 361. 4/1850 31/3/1850
11. 73. 8/1850. Prayer book 11/8/1850
2/9/1842
Ecilaw, Ary pseud.
Le roi de Thessalie. 1886 9/2/86
Eckenbrecher, C. Gustav von
Die Lage des Homerischen Troja. 1875 25/9/75
Eckermann, Johann Peter
Conversations with Goethe in the last years of his life [American translation]. 27/5/37
Eckstaedt, Carl Friedrich Vitzthum von
Maurice, Conte de Saxe, et Marie-Josèphe de Saxe ... lettres et documents inédits. 1867 19/11/67
Eclectic Review. 5. 365–85. 4/1839. New series 2/4/1839
Economist, The.
3. 31 2/8/1845, 8/8/1845
3. 669. Gladstone's Spanish policy 19/7/1845
23/7/1845
Eden, Eleanor
Easton and its inhabitants. 1858 9/9/58
The semi-detached house. Edited by Lady T. Lewis. 1859 22/9/59
Eden, Robert Bishop
Charge. 1858 (2v. 1858–61) 7/7/64
Charge delivered... August 28, 1877. 1877 7/10/77
The sin and danger of faithlessness and impatience in the present crisis of the church. A sermon. 1850 25/3/51
Eden, Robert Henley 2nd Baron Henley
A plan of church reform. 1832 (2v.) 18/8/32
Eden, William Baron Auckland
The journal and correspondence of William, Lord Auckland. With a preface and introduction by the Bishop of Bath and Wells. 1860 (4v.) 5/3/61
Edersheim, Alfred
Prophecy and history in relation to the Messiah. The Warburton lectures for 1880–1884. 1885 17/5/85
The life and times of Jesus the Messiah. 1883 (2v.) 16/1/91
Edge, Frederick Milnes
Slavery doomed: or, the contest between free and slave labour in the United States. 1860 31/5/64
The destruction of the American carrying trade. A letter to Earl Russell. 1863 5/2/64
Edgeworth, Maria
'Absentee' in *Tales of fashionable life.* 1809 (6v. 1809–12) 7/7/41, 9/4/90
'Emilie de Coulanges' in *Tales of fashionable life.* 1812 (6v. 1809–12) 12/4/90
'Love and law' in *Comic dramas in three acts.* 1817 18/8/27
Castle Rackrent. 1800 14/4/90
Comic dramas in three acts. 1817 (2nd edn) 21/8/27
Garry Owen, or the snow-woman: and poor Bob, the chimney-sweeper. 1832 20/7/61
Helen, a tale. 1834 (3v.) 31/3/34
Lame Jervas. The story of Tarlton and poor Loveit. 1861 16/8/73
Orlandino. 1848 31/5/55
Patronage. 1814 (4v.) 25/6/74
Vivian and Almeria... Tales of fashionable life. 1856 2/3/90
Édib, Effendi
Traduction du rapport présenté par... Édib Effendi. 1876 18/8/76
Edinburgh Review.
14. 423, 513. 3/1827. on Catholics 9/5/1827
14. 446. 3/1827. on Shipping Interest 28/5/1827
26. 107. 2/1816. on Culloden Papers 15/2/1827
28. 125. 3/1817. Annual Parliaments 22/12/1848
30. 120. 6/1818. Birkbeck on America 16/2/1827
30. 503. 9/1818. on Burgh Reform 19/2/1827
42. 304. 8/1826. Macaulay on Milton 13/10/1826
47. 118–131. 1/1828. Pestalozzi 25/9/1829
47. 242, 100. 1/1828. on Moncreiff, and Parties 15/4/1828
49. 159. 3/1829. Utilitarians 3/10/1829
49. 218–272. 3/1829. Catholics 26/9/1829
49. 300. 6/1829. Sadler on Ireland 5/10/1829
49. 317. 6/1829. Drama 7/10/1829
49. 439. 6/1829. Signs of Times 2/10/1829
54. 100–114. 8/1831. Evangelical Party 4/4/1832
61. 1. 7/1835. Macaulay on Mackintosh 6/7/1847
66. 477–522. 1/1838. Negroes 22/1/1838
67. 1. 4/1838. Brougham on Press 27/4/1838
72. 227. 10/1840. Ranke 8/12/1840
72. 340. 1/1841. E. I. commerce 16/2/1841
73. 271. 4/1841. Tract Ninety 21/4/1841
73. 560. 7/1841. Macaulay on Holland 16/7/1841

Edinburgh Review (*cont.*)
74. 359, 506. 1/1842. State Duties 24/1/1842
75. 187. 4/1842. Budget 22/4/1842
75. 515. 7/1842. F. List on political economy 16/7/1842
76. 241. 10/1842. on the Session 13/10/1842
76. 382. 1/1843. Private Judgement 27/1/1843
76. 464. 1/1843. Sewell 15/1/1843
77. 190. 2/1843. Distress of the nation 22/2/1843
77. 501. 4/1843. Puseyism 24/4/1843
78. 517. 10/1843. on the late Session 26/10/1843
79. 1/1844. Ireland 7/2/1844
79. 105. 1/1844. Zöllverein 24/9/1844
79. 189. 1/1844. Ireland 1/2/1844
79. 351. 4/1844. Milnes on Chatham 18/4/1844
79. 476. 4/1844. on Scinde 16/4/1844
80. 309. 10/1844. Puseyism 25/10/1844
80. 474. 10/1844. Tory rule 29/10/1844
80. 517. 10/1844. Young England 30/10/1844
80. 526. 10/1844. Chatham 2/11/1844
81. 385. 4/1845. Oxford 22/4/1845
81. 399. 4/1845. Jesuits 19/4/1845
83. 275. 4/1846. on Campbell 29/4/1846
86. 397. 10/1847. Christian evidence 19/1/1848
87. 138. 1/1838. State of the Nation 4/1/1848
87. 170. 1/1848. Kosmos 5/1/1848
88. 402. 4/1849. on Mrs Gaskell 15/5/1849
88. 435. 4/1849. on Strickland 10/4/1849
88. 499, 462. 4/1849. on Union & on Argyll 8/4/1849
88. 94, 163. 7/1848. Strauss 4/7/1848
90. 249. 7/1849. on Macaulay 1/10/1849
90. 293. 10/1849. Reason and Faith 12/11/1849
90. 357, 525. 10/1849. Agriculture, & Coal 13/11/1849
90. 473. 10/1849. Schools of Design 22/11/1849
91. 62. 1/1850. Mining 9/2/1850
91. 87. 1/1850. Orangemen 18/2/1850
94. 213. 10/1851. Greg on reform bill 27/4/1852
95. 213. 1/1852. Reform 6/4/1852
95. 321, 453. 4/1852. on education, & on J. Knox 16/5/1852
95. 59. 1/1852. on Phillpotts 24/1/1852
97. 240. 1/1853. Income tax 29/3/1853
97. 342, 420. 4/1853. Church, & on Disraeli 3/4/1853
98. 273. 10/1853. Church Parties 8/11/1853
98. 488. 10/1853. Newspaper stamps 25/3/1854
100. 305. 10/1854. Church rates 4/11/1854
100. 420, 490, 534. 10/1854. on Macaulay's speeches; army; railway policy 3/11/1854
100. 43. 7/1854. Teetotalism 29/9/1854
101. 261. 1/1855. The war 17/1/1855
101. 537. 4/1855. Army reform 3/5/1855
102. 1. 8/1855. on Dryden 1/8/1855
105. 266. 1/1857. Persia 20/1/1857
105. 517, 522. 4/1857. China, & Dissolution 15/4/1857
106. 322. 10/1857. on Napier 2/11/1857
106. 432. 10/1857. on Campbell 4/11/1857
107. 358. 4/1858. on Thiers 27/4/1858
107. 443, 465. 4/1858. on Brougham, & on Buckle 7/9/1858
108. 502. 10/1858. Gladstone's Homer 21/10/1858
109. 247, 264. 7/1859. Tennyson, & Government 11/8/1859
109. 264. 1/1859. Reform 18/2/1859
111. 236. 1/1860. Greg on taxation 24/3/1866
111. 32. 7/1874. Speaker's Bible 22/11/1874
113. 387. 4/1861. Eton 26/4/1861
113. 461. 4/1861. Essays & Reviews 5/5/1861
114. 145, 233. 7/1861. Church in Italy 21/7/1861
115. 104. 1/1862. Military expenditure 25/1/1862
115. 185. 1/1862. Salt Lake 26/1/1862
115. 376. 10/1859. on Carlyle 4/11/1859
116. 549. 10/1862. Hops, & American struggle 18/10/1862
117. 1. 1/1863. on Dalhousie 11/4/1863
117. 444. 4/1863. on Canning 10/4/1863
117. 498. 4/1863. Inspiration 12/4/1863
117. 498. 4/1863. Supernatural 14/6/1863
121. 223. 1/1865. "7 per cent" 28/1/1865
125. 439. 4/1867. Ritualism 5/5/1867
125. 578. 4/1867. Situation 18/5/1867
126. 376. 10/1867. Madagascar 27/10/1867
126. 499. 10/1867. Rubric 20/10/1867
127. 42. 1/1863. on Gentz 9/3/1863
128. 251. 7/1868. Church 18/7/1868
130. 417. 10/1869. Bismarck 23/9/1870
131. 256. 1/1870. Irish land 6/1/1870
132. 154. 7/1870. Cox's Angevins 17/10/1870
133. 1. 1/1871. France 24/1/1871
133. 207. 1/1871. Military forces 26/1/1871

133. 287. 4/1871. on Lord Broughton 13/5/1871
133. 358. 4/1871. Chorizontes 17/6/1871
152. 281, 258. 7/1880. Ministry 19/7/1880
155. 60, 155, 279. 1/1882. Whigs; Ireland; on Cobden 24/1/1882
158. 547. 10/1883. Aberdeen 17/10/1883
159. 41. 1/1884. on Spencer 24/2/1884
162. 286. 7/1885. Waters 17/8/1885
168. 271. 10/1888. Grenville 22/3/1889
176. 557. 10/1892. Government 22/10/1892
222. 558. 4/1859. Italy 14/4/1859
Edmonds, Cyrus R.
The life and times of General Washington. 1835 (2v. 1835–6) 6/1/38
Edmonds, Elizabeth Mayhew
Fair Athens. 1881 28/1/82
Hesperas: rhythm and rhyme. 1883 2/12/83
Edmonstone, Sir Archibald
A letter to the Bishop of Glasgow and Galloway, on the present aspect of church matters. 1850 1/9/50
Leonora: a tragedy. 1832 21/9/32
Remarks on the state of the established church in Ireland. 1836 25/5/36
Edmunds, Leonard
The history of the Edmunds scandal. 1869 20/12/62
Education Magazine.
1. 334. 5/1840 30/3/1840
5 9/1/1840, 2/5/1840
Education Review. 1. 1. 11/1891 6/11/1891
Edwards, Amelia Blandford
A thousand miles up the Nile. 1876 29/12/76
Edwards, Bryan
The history, civil and commercial, of the British colonies in the West Indies. 1793 (3v. 1793–1801) 2/1/36 ?, 5/8/48
Thoughts on the late proceedings of government respecting the trade of the West India islands with the United States of North America. 1784 5/8/48
Edwards, Edward
Free Town Libraries, their formation, management, and history; in Britain, France, Germany and America. 1869 5/4/79 ?
Libraries and founders of libraries. 1865 14/3/65
The life of Sir W. Ralegh. Based on contemporary documents preserved in the Rolls House, the Privy Council Office. 1868 (2v.) 14/12/69
Edwards, Mrs. Henry Sutherland
The secret of the princess, a tale of... life in Russia. 1891 (2v.) 12/12/90
Edwards, Henry Thomas Dean of Bangor
Church of the Cymry. A letter to the Right Hon. W. E. Gladstone. 1869 30/1/70
The Babel of the sects and the unity of Pentecost. 1872 13/10/72
Wales and the Welsh church. 1889 22/9/88
Edwards, John Passmore
The war a blunder and a crime. 1855 17/9/55
Edwards, Jonathan the elder
The works of President Edwards. By S. E. Dwight. 1830 (10v.) 26/8/39
Edwards, William Bengal Civil Service
Personal adventures during the Indian Rebellion in Rohilound, Futtehghur, and Oude. 1858 30/8/58
Egan, Pierce the elder
Sporting anecdotes; original and select... by an amateur sportsman. 1807 1/7/83
Egerton, John Coker
Sussex folk and Sussex ways... Reprinted from 'The Leisure Hour' and 'The Sussex Advertiser'. 1884 3/10/87
Egglestone, William Morley
Stanhope and its neighbourhood. 1882 12/12/84
Stanhope memorials of Bishop Butler. 1878 13/12/84
Egidy, Christoph Moritz von
Serious thoughts. Translated from the German by the Bibliographical Bureau, Berlin. 1891 27/6/91
Eichthal, Adolphe d'
De la monnaie de papier et des banques d'émission. 1864 28/3/64
Liberté des échanges et protectionnisme: leur effet sur le sort des ouvriers. 1890 14/1/91
Eichthal, Gustave d'
[Essay on the Pentateuch] *in Mélanges de critique biblique.* 1886 17/1/76 n, 30/1/87
Les trois grands peuples méditerranéens et le Christianisme. 1865 20/1/66
Notice sur les services rendus à la Grèce et aux études grecques par... G. d'E. 1877 3/10/77
Socrate et notre temps. 1881 22/9/81
Elam, Charles
Winds of doctrine: being an examination of the modern theories of automatism and evolution. 1876 23/12/76, 10/1/86
Elector
Defects in election committees and in the courts of revising barristers, with a plan for improving them. Addressed to the members of the H. of Commons. 1838 24/1/38
Electoral abuses considered, and a novel remedy suggested. By a defeated candidate. 1859 3/12/59
Elements of taxation, by X and Y. 1852 22/3/53
Eliot, Edward Archdeacon of Barbadoes
Christianity and slavery; in a course of lectures preached at the cathedral and parish church of St. Michael, Barbadoes. 1833 19/5/33
Eliot, Edward Granville Earl St. Germans
Papers relating to Lord Eliot's mission to Spain in the spring of 1835. 1871 1/12/71

Eliot, Edward Granville Earl St. Germans (*cont.*)
Reasons for not signing an Address on . . . papal aggression. 1850 4/3/51
Eliot, George [Marian Evans, aft Cross]
Adam Bede. 1859 16/4/59, 16/5/59, 25/5/59
Agatha. 1869 2/10/80
Essays and leaves from a notebook, ed. C. T. Lewes. 1884 12/11/89
Felix Holt. 1866 12/7/66, 7/8/66
George Eliot, by M. Blind. 1883 12/12/89
Middlemarch. 1871 (3v.) 17/11/74, 30/12/74
Mill on the Floss. 1860 (3v.) 20/3/84
Romola. 1863 26/8/69
Scenes of clerical life. 1858 (2v.) 14/6/81
Silas Marner. 1861 11/5/61, 5/4/84, 24/4/84
The legend of Jubal, and other poems. 1874 1/10/80
Eliot, Sir John
De jure maiestatis, or, political treatise of government (1628–30), and the letter-book of Sir J. Elliot. 1882 (2v.) 16/5/82
The monarchie of man. 1879 5/8/79
Elizabeth I
The secret history of the most renowned Queen Elizabeth, and her great favourite, the Earl of Essex. (2v.) 30/11/83
Elizabeth of Bohemia, Queen Consort of Frederick I
Memoirs relating to the Queen of Bohemia. By Lady Frances Erskine. 1770 11/8/87
Elizabeth of Roumania, Consort of Charles I, King of Roumania
Les pensées d'une reine. 1882 16/4/84
Eller, Irvin
A few plain words to plain people on the duty of Christian unity: and on the proper exercise of the right of private judgement. 1839 7/7/39
The history of Belvoir Castle from the Norman conquest to the nineteenth century. 1841 24/6/41
Ellicott, Charles John
[Diocesan progress]. (not found) 16/5/86 ?
Are we to modify fundamental doctrine? Being five addresses. 1885 17/1/86
Church prospects, church reform, and church parties; being three addresses delivered to . . . the diocese of Gloucester and Bristol. 1872 15/11/74
Church work and church prospects. A charge . . . at his primary visitation. 1864 6/11/64
Considerations on the revision of the English version of the New Testament. 1870 12/6/70
Some present dangers of the Church of England. Seven addresses. 1878 21/12/78
What is the real distinction between England and Rome?. 1876 17/10/75
Elliot, Lady Charlotte
Mary Magdalene, and other poems. 1880 1/1/82
Medusa, and other poems. 1878 9/1/79
Elliot, Gilbert Dean of Bristol
A letter to J. S. Harford [in reference to a Bill occasioned by the Papal Aggression of 1850]. 1851 3/4/53
Bristol Cathedral. Letter to the subscribers for building a new nave. 1876 4/5/76
Letter to Viscount Palmerston . . . on the address voted by Convocation on June 29th, 1855. 1855 11/12/55
Ornaments, rubrics, &c. A letter. 1874 20/12/74
The Reformation and the Counter-Reformation. Which shall it be? Address. 1874 20/4/75 ?
Three letters to the Archbishop of Canterbury, on the repeal of the twenty-ninth canon. 1860 4/11/60
Elliot, John Lettsom
A letter to the electors of Westminster. From a conservative. 1848 23/3/47
A letter to the electors of Westminster. From an aristocrat. 1850 18/4/50
Three to one: a comedy. 1850 3/7/79
Elliott, Charles D.D.
A vindication of the Mosaic authorship of the Pentateuch. 1884 10/1/86
Elliott, Ebenezer
Corn-law rhymes. 1831 (3rd edn) 3/7/43 ?
Life of Ebenezer Elliott, the Corn Law rhymer, by J. Watkins. 1850 22/11/51
Elliott, Edward Vicar of Tuxford
Pastoral address on the institution of a prayer meeting, in connexion with the established church, with rules and regulations. 1834 17/1/38
Elliott, Mrs. Grace Dalrymple
Journal of my life during the French revolution. 1859 6/4/59
Ellis, Clement
The Gentile sinner, or, England's brave gentlemen: characterized in a letter to a friend, both as he is, and as he should be. 29/8/52
Ellis, George F.R.S.
Specimens of the early English poets, ed. G. Ellis. 1790 6/10/59
Ellis, Grace Atkinson afterw. Oliver
Arthur Penrhyn Stanley. His life, work, and teachings. 1885 30/6/85
Ellis, Henry F.R.S.
A voyage to Hudson's-Bay . . . in . . . 1746 and 1747, for discovering a North West passage; with . . . a short natural history of the country. 1748 12/8/48
Ellis, Joseph of Balcombe
Caesar in Egypt, Costanza, and other poems. 1876 30/6/76

Ellis, Robert B. D.
Contributions to the ethnography of Italy and Greece. 1858 10/2/58
Ellis, Rowland
Some aspects of woman's life. Five Lenten addresses. 1881 27/11/81
Ellis, Sir Samuel Burdon
Memoirs and services of... Sir S. B. Ellis from his own memoranda. 1866 27/8/70
Ellis, Thomas Flower
Outlines of general history. 1828 10/10/28 ?
Ellis, William author
A few questions on secular education. 1848 12/4/48
Outlines of social economy. 1846 16/3/47
Three letters from a London merchant. 1866 30/3/77
Ellis, William missionary
The American missionary in the Sandwich islands: a vindication and an appeal. 1866 22/10/71
Ellison, Noel Thomas
Protestant errors and Roman Catholic truths. 1829 31/1/36
Elmsley, Peter
[on Socrates and Euripides]. 8/3/31
Euripis Medea... recensuit et illustravit P. Elmsley. 1818 11/3/30
Elmslie, William Gray
Professor W. G. Elmslie... Memoir and sermons. Edited by W. R. Nicoll... and A. N. Macnicoll. 1890 27/5/91
Elphin, Lucian
Passages in the life of Sir L. Elphin. 1889 (2v.) 12/10/89 ?
Elphinstone, Mountstuart
The history of India. 1841 (2v.) 15/6/58
Elrington, Charles Richard
A few suggestions in reply to the Rev. C.R. E. on national education in Ireland. 1847 2/7/47
Subscription to the xxxix Articles. A sermon. 1842 14/5/45
The whole works of... J. Usher... with a life of the author, and an account of his writings. 1847 4/9/64
Elsdale, Henry
Studies in the Idylls. An essay on Mr. Tennyson's 'Idylls of the King'. 1878 14/10/78
Elton, Sir Arthur Hallam
The ballot a conservative measure. 1856 24/12/56, 21/2/60
The case against the Ministry plainly stated. 1858 9/3/58
Where are we drifting? or, a plain question for the British people on the war with Russia. 1855 7/6/55
Elton, Sir Charles Abraham
The Brothers, a monody; and other poems. 1820 5/2/26
Elwin, Whitwell
The works of A. Pope... With introduction and notes by W. Whitwell. 1871 26/11/70
Ely Cathedral Church
Hand-book to the Cathedral Church of Ely. With engravings. 1852 29/9/54
Elze, Carl Friedrich
Lord Byron: a biography. With a critical essay on his place in literature. Translated... and edited with notes. 1872 5/2/72
Emeritus
Colonial ex-governors and their claims. A letter addressed to the Right Hon. W. E. Gladstone. By one who has served. 1864 21/1/64
Emerson, George Rose
London: how the great city grew. 1862 5/7/67
William Ewart Gladstone, Prime Minister of England. A political and literary biography. 1881 21/10/81
Emerson, Ralph Waldo
An oration delivered before the literary societies of Dartmouth College. 1838 18/2/39
English traits. 1856 31/10/56
Essays. 1841 24/1/49
Representative men. 1850 2/3/50
Emerson, Richard
An address to the clergy and parishioners of St. Leonard, Shoreditch, and through them to the whole kingdom... What has the Vicar done? Come and see!. 1843 7/3/80 ?
Emerton, James Alexander D.D.
A letter to... Lord John Russell on University Reform. 1854 4/5/54
England and France. La France et l'Angleterre. 1859 6/11/60
Emigration from India. The export of coolies and other labourers to Mauritius. 1842 12/4/42
Endean, James Russell
What is the eternal hope of Canon Farrar? Also a correspondence with the Canon. 1878 15/6/78
Enderby, Charles
Our money laws the cause of national distress. 1847 29/11/47
The Auckland islands: a short account of their climate, soil and productions. 1849 15/3/49
The distress of the nation; its causes and remedies. 1844 29/12/43
England, George Rector of Woolterton
An enquiry into the morals of the ancients. 1737 1/7/92
Engleheart, Gardner D.
Journal of the progress of H. R. H. the pr ce of Wales through British North America; and his visit to the United States. 1860 13/2/65
English Catholic
Criticism of monsignor Capel. 1875 13/1/75
Papal infallibility. 1870 8/1/75

English Churchman.
3 8/12/1845
3. Trinity College, Glenalmond 4/12/1845
3. 507 14/8/1845, 22/8/1845
3. 532 9/9/1845, 14/9/1845
3. 715 13/11/1845, 19/11/1845
Oakeley's letter 27/12/1844
English Churchwomen of the Seventeenth Century. 1845 13/7/45
English Historical Review. 1. 105. Greville papers 31/8/1886
Englishman
England in Egypt, the highway to India. 1877 4/7/77
English Review.
1. 157, 179. 3/1845. Rome; Simony 2/4/1845
1. 305. 7/1844. Newman 29/6/1844
1. 336. 7/1844. Gladstone's review of Ellen Middleton 24/5/1844
1. 362. 7/1844. Dark Ages 30/6/1844
2. 1. 10/1844. Anglocatholicism 27/10/1844
2. 1. 10/1844. Symbolism 27/11/1844
2. 179. 10/1844. Ward 28/10/1844
2. 295, 460. 12/1844. France, on Jelf 3/1/1845
2. 424. 12/1844. Monasteries 12/1/1845
3. 192. 3/1845. German liturgy 6/4/1845
3. 328. 6/1845. Maynooth 2/7/1845
3. 441. 6/1845. Pearson 4/7/1845
4. 173. 10/1845. Ireland 24/11/1845
4. 24. 10/1845. Intelligence 27/11/1845
4. 309. 12/1846. Ignatius 12/1/1846
4. 386. 12/1845. Newman 4/1/1846
4. 434. 12/1845. Parties 2/1/1846
4. 501. 12/1845. Foreign Intelligence 3/1/1846
5. 161. 3/1846. Music 2/4/1846
6. 127. 9/1846. Hook 18/10/1846
6. 489. 12/1846. Development 29/1/1847
7. 378, 483. 6/1847. Roman Catholic schools 1/7/1847
8. 289, 430, 489. 12/1847. Convocation 2/1/1848
8. 354. 12/1847. Unity theories 3/1/1848
9. 157. 3/1848. Church & State 2/4/1848
9. 255. 6/1848. Papacy 2/7/1848
9. 298. 6/1848. Madeira 9/7/1848
10. 257–500. 12/1848 4/2/1849
11. 255–500. 6/1849 7/7/1849
12. 107. 9/1849. Kneller Hall 21/11/1849
12. 288. 12/1849. on Palmer 10/2/1850
12. 30. 9/1849. Seymour 25/11/1849
13. 257. 6/1850 13/8/1850
14. 1. 9/1850. Hungary 9/10/1850
17. 337. 7/1852. Attack on Gladstone 1/7/1852

Engström, Charles Robert Lloyd
Christianity and evolution; or, the spiritual life the supreme court of judgment. A sermon. 1883 25/11/83
The claim and the claimant; or, Christianity the religion of fact and common sense. 1875 9/1/76
Enraght, Richard William
My ordination oaths and other declarations: am I keeping them?. 1880 15/12/80
Ensor, Thomas
The case decided: protectionists and free traders reconciled: a letter addressed to the electors of Somerset. 1849 11/7/49
Entwistle, William
On railways. 15/3/47
Eon de Beaumont, Charles Geneviève L. A. A. T. d' Chevalier
Loisirs de Chevalier d'E. de B. . . . sur divers sujets importans d'administration. 1774 (13v.) 8/4/86
Epictetus
The works of Epictetus . . . A translation from the Greek based on that of E. Carter, by T. W. Higginson. 1865 26/9/71
Epinay, Louise F. P. de la Live d'
Mémoires et correspondance de Madame d'Epinay, ed. J. P. A. Parison; preface by J.-C. Brunet. 1818 14/10/58, 21/4/66, 14/1/82
Episcopal church in Scotland in full communion with the Church of England. 1849 7/3/49
Erasmus, Desiderius
Familiarium colloquiorum opus multis nominibus vtilissimu, nuc postrema cura ab authore . . . recognitum, magnaq accessione auctum. 2/6/55
Life of, by J. Jortin. 1758 (2v. 1758–60) 9/12/53
Peregrinatio Apostoloru Petri & Pauli, cum ratione temporu. 28/9/74
Pilgrimages to St. Mary of Walsingham and St. Thomas of Canterbury, ed. J. G. Nichols. 1849 6/10/84
The prayers of Erasmus, ed. Coldswell. 1872 15/9/72
Erastus
The theses of Erastus touching excommunication; translated from the Latin, with a preface, by R. Lee. 1844 31/8/44
Erckmann, Emile, and Chatrian, Pierre A.
Histoire d'un conscrit de 1813. 1864 26/4/65
Histoire d'un homme du peuple. 1865 (5th edn) 9/12/65
Histoire d'un paysan, 1789 (1792–1815). 1868 (4v.) 25/5/68
Histoire d'un sous-maître. 1871 19/6/71
L'ami Fritz. 1864 13/7/65

La guerre. 1866 11/8/66
Le blocus. 1867 12/6/67
Le fou Yégof. Episode de l'invasion. 1862 2/10/66
Waterloo; suite du Conscrit de 1813. 1865 11/5/65
Ernest II, Duke of Saxe-Coburg
'Russia' [pamphlet]. 1859 16/8/59
Erskine, Lady Frances
Memoirs relating to the queen of Bohemia. By one of her ladies. 1770 11/8/87
Erskine, Thomas Baron Erskine
A view of the causes and consequences of the present war with France. 1797 10/4/82
Erskine, Thomas of Linlathen
Memoirs of Thomas Erskine, ed. W. Hannah. 1877 (2v.) 23/12/90
Remarks on the internal evidence for the truth of revealed religion. 1820 29/11/29
The brazen serpent; or, life coming through death. 1831 30/1/31
The unconditional freeness of the gospel: in three essays. 1828 24/11/29
Escande, Georges
Hoche en Irlande 1795–1798. 1888 9/1/93 ?
Escott, Bickham S.
A letter... on the present state of the reform question. 1831 25/3/31
Escott, Hay Sweet
Papers on emotion in religion: and preaching to the uneducated. 1876 13/4/79 ?
Escott, Thomas Hay Sweet
England: its people, polity and pursuits. 1879 (2v.) 7/11/79
Esdaile, James of Perth
Civil and religious institutions... inseperably connected. 1833 14/11/33 ?
Espen, Zegerus Bernardus van
Jus ecclesiasticum universum hodiernae disciplinae praesertim Belgii, Galliae, et vicinarum provinciarum accommodatum. 1753 (2v.) 27/6/40
Espin, Thomas Espinelle
Clerical subscription and the act of uniformity. A sermon [on 2 Tim. i.13] preached before the university of Oxford... with notes. 1864 14/2/64
Sermon. The benefits to be expected by the devout communicant. 1865 4/2/66
Espinasse, Francis
Life and times of François-Marie Arouet, calling himself Voltaire. 1866 (vol i) 29/3/67
What reading and writing have become. 1850 17/4/55
Essay on the extent of man... agency in... saving faith. 1827 (not found) 24/1/34
Essays and Reviews [By F. Temple, R. Williams, B. Powell, H. B. Wilson, C. W. Goodwin, M. Pattison and B. Jowett. Edited by J. Parker]. 1860 10/5/60
Essays on reform. 1867 10/4/67
Essays on the church. 1833 2/5/34
Essays on the Irish church. 1866 (not found) 3/6/66
Estcourt, Edgar E.
The question of anglican ordinations discussed... With an appendix of original documents and facsimiles. 1873 24/9/82
Estourmel, Joseph D' Count
Souvenirs de France et d'Italie dans les années 1830, 1831 et 1832. 1848 29/9/92, 22/10/92
Estramberg, L. d'
La Russie et ses accusateurs. 1854 5/6/54
Estwicke, Nicholas
Dialogue of a conformist and a nonconformist. 27/12/46
Eton College
Speech of counsel... on behalf of the... masters at Eton against the Great Western Railway extension. 1848 21/6/48
Etoniana, ancient and modern. 1865 20/8/73
Eucharistic Month, The. 6/4/1851
Euclid
Opera. 21/7/26, 9/9/26, 7/10/26, 6/11/26, 18/11/26, 26/1/27, 10/8/27, 26/1/28, 21/6/28
Euphron, pseud.
Remarks on the proposed bill... [the Jew bill]. 1848 9/2/48
Euripides
Alcestis. 26/2/27
Bacchae. 31/10/28
Cyclops. 23/5/91
Euripidis opera omnia;... eruditorum [R. Porson, etc.] *observationibus illustrata.* 1821 9/3/27
Hecuba. 25/10/26, 31/1/27, 21/2/27, 14/11/55
Helena. 25/5/91
Heracleidae. 27/5/91
Iphigenia in Aulis. 7/11/55
Medea. 28/1/26, 27/5/26, 17/6/26, 7/7/26
The Iphigeneia at Aulis of Euripides, with introduction and notes by C. E. S. Headlam. 1875 14/3/78
Troades. 6/11/55, 24/11/56
European remodellings: a plan with a variation. 1848 20/4/48
Eusebius
Opera. 16/12/90
Evangelical Alliance
Report to the 18th conference of the Evangelical Alliance. 1864 18/12/64
Evans, Alfred Bowen
India. Two discourses delivered in the church of St. Andrew, Wells street. 1857 12/1/80
Evans, Arthur Benoni
'The phylactery', a poem on 'national religious declension' 1836 28/5/42

Evans, Sir Arthur John
Illyrian letters: a revised selection of correspondence from the Illyrian Provinces of Bosnia, Herzegovina, Montenegro, Albania, Dalmatia, Croatia. 1878 16/4/78
Through Bosnia and the Herzegóvina on foot, during the insurrection, August and September 1875, with an historical review of Bosnia. 1876 20/10/76
Evans, Caleb
Sermons [published posthumously]. 1822 30/7/32
Evans, Charles M.D.
An examen of parts relating to the Society of Friends in a recent work by R. Barclay. 1878 22/11/91
Evans, Eyre
Evils affecting Ireland. 5/2/33
Evans, Sir George de Lacy G. C. B.
A letter to the electors of Westminster. 1833 13/12/61
Evans, Henry Bentall
Our West Indian colonies. Jamaica a source of national wealth and honour. 1855 6/11/55
Evans, Howard Heber
St. Paul the author of the Acts of the Apostles, and of the third gospel. 1884 7/12/84
St. Paul the author of the last twelve verses of the second gospel. 1886 30/10/87
Evans, James Cook
Letter to Lord Lyndhurst . . . on the proposed alteration of the law of charitable trusts. 1844 31/5/44
Translation of the act of accusation, and of the sentence pronounced . . . upon F. and R. Madiai . . . with an introduction. 1852 20/11/52
Evans, John LL.D.
Brief sketch of the several denominations into which the Christian world is divided. 1795 20/8/26
Evans, Maurice J.
The cross of Christ by Zoeckler, tr. M. J. Evans. 1877 25/11/77
Evans, Robert Wilson
An appeal against the union of the dioceses of Bangor and St. Asaph. 1842 31/12/42
Scripture biography. 1834 21/12/34
The church of God, in a series of sermons. 1832 10/3/33, 28/12/34
Evans, William Washington
The blood of the holy one, the lord Jesus, and sparks of light on health. 1865 8/11/68
Evanson, Edward
The dissonance of the four generally received evangelists, and the evidence of their respective authenticity examined. 1792 2/11/62
Evarts, William Maxwell
Speech of Mr. Evarts, a delegate of the United States, at the International Monetary Conference at Paris, on the 19th day of May, 1881. 1881 21/6/81
Evelyn, John F.R. S.
A character of England . . . presented to a nobleman of France. 6/5/60
The life of Mrs. Godolphin, ed. S. Wilberforce. 1843 23/4/43
Everard, Edward of Bishop's Hull
A letter setting forth that baptismal regeneration . . . is the cause for controversy. 1849 20/1/50
Everett, Edward
Academical education. An address delivered . . . at the inauguration of Washington university. 1857 6/6/60
An oration delivered at Charlestown, on the seventy-fifth anniversary of the battle of Bunker Hill, June 17, 1850. 1850 24/2/63
Speech . . . on American institutions, in reply to the discussion in the British House of Lords. 1860 27/8/60
Every day occurences. 1825 (2v.) 11/8/28
Ewald, Alexander Charles
Sir Robert Walpole: a political biography. 1676–1745. 1878 25/2/88
The life and times of the Hon. Algernon Sydney, 1622–1683. 1873 27/3/85
Ewald, Georg Heinrich August von
Geschichte des Volkes Israel bis Christus. 1843 (3v. 1843–52) 23/5/80
Ewing, Alexander Bishop
'Che til ma twille'. Sermon [on emigration]. 1852 12/9/52
A charge delivered to the clergy of Argyll and the isles, by the bishop . . . 12th September, 1860. 1860 1/10/60
A letter to . . . E. B. Ramsay . . . on the co-operation of the Church Society with the Committee of Council on Education. 1853 19/6/53
A plea for the Highland and non-juring congregations of 1688–1745, &c. of Scotland. 1869 (2nd edn) 26/5/69
An address to the younger clergy and laity on the present state of religion. Being some contribution towards a defence of the Church of England. 1865 4/6/65
An explanation of the position of the twenty-first canon of the Scottish Episcopal Church. 1844 (2nd edn) 22/4/44
Episcopacy in Scotland. 1845 20/11/45
Introduction to 'The atonement by law' in Present day papers. 1870 14/11/69
On materialism in Christianity: being a caution against gross conceptions of the sacraments. The substance of a Charge. 1867 14/2/69
The lamb of God. A sermon preached Aug. 10, 1848. 1849 15/6/51

Ewing, Juliana Horatia
Jackanapes . . . with illustrations by R. Caldecott. 1883 16/3/84
Ewing, Thomas J.
The distribution of Parliamentary borough constituencies compared with the actual distribution of towns . . . in northern, midland and southern England. 1867 18/4/70
Ewing, T. J.
A collapsed programme, and the platform chief's reflections on past errors and plans for a new start [satirical verses on W. E. Gladstone]. 1878 22/8/78
Examen rapide des questions communes. 1844 (not found) 13/7/44
Examination of Canon Liddon's B. L. By a Church of England clergyman. 1871 (not found) 27/4/73
Ex-Dissenter
My life: by an ex-dissenter. 1841 28/8/42
Ex-Fellow, An [of Jesus College, Oxford]
Thoughts on the proposed Reform at Oxford, as far as it affects Jesus College . . . By an ex-Fellow. 1854 15/5/54
Ex-Jockey, An
Horse racing. 1867 10/10/67 ?
Experiences of a 'vert'. 1864 12/6/64
Exposé . . . des cures opérées en France par le magnétisme animal, par M. S. 1826 12/2/63 ?
Exquemelin, Alexander Olivier
The history of the Bucaniers of America. 21/8/37
'Extempore prayer' 1837 2/4/38
Extracts from the Presbytery book of Strathbogie, A. D. MDCXXI-MDCLIV. 1843 28/9/44
Extra physics. 1878 25/12/78
Eylert, Rulemann Friedrich
The religious life and opinions of Frederick William III, King of Prussia . . . Translated from the German by J. Birch. 1844 2/2/45
Eyre, Charles R. C. bp of Glasgow
The history of St. Cuthbert; or, an account of his life, decease, and miracles. 1849 13/12/49
Eyre, Edward John
Journals of expeditions of discovery into Central Australia, and overland from Adelaide to King George's Sound, in 1840–1. 1845 (2v.) 3/1/46
Eyre, John R.
Justice or coercion? Some leading English opinions upon Home Rule in Ireland and elsewhere. 1886 3/4/90
Eyre, Selwyn
Sketches of Russian life and customs, made during a visit in 1876–7. 1878 13/4/78
Eyre, Sir Vincent
The military operations at Cabul, which ended in the retreat and destruction of the British army, January 1842. 1843 9/2/43
Eyton, John Vicar of Wellington
Sermons on various subjects. 1815 (2v.) 9/12/27
Eyton, Robert
The kingdom of Christ in its relation to the world. A sermon. 1877 27/11/81

F., A.
Confirmation according to scripture. 1857 5/6/57
F., T. B.
Reunion of Christendom. 1887 26/6/87
Faber, Frederick William
All for Jesus. 1853 12/2/54
Hymns for the use of the schools and congregation of St. Wilfrid's, Staffordshire. 14/1/83
Questions for self-examination; designed primarily for the use of young persons. 1843 3/11/44
Sights and thoughts in foreign churches and among foreign people. 1842 11/9/45
The Cherwell water-lily, and other poems. 1840 10/12/40
Faber, George Stanley
A dissertation on the prophecies that have been fulfilled, are now fulfilling, or will hereafter be fulfilled relative to the . . . period of 1260 years. 1807 (2v.) 31/3/33 ?
A general and connected view of the prophecies relative to the conversion . . . and future glory of the houses of Judah and Israel. 1808 (2v.) 31/3/33 ?
A treatise on the origin of expiatory sacrifice. 1827 17/3/33
Christ's discourse at Capernaum fatal to the doctrine of transubstantiation on the very principle of exposition adopted by the . . . Roman church. 1840 21/9/45
Facts and assertions: or a brief and plain exhibition of the incongruity of the peculiar doctrines of the Church of Rome. 1833 29/4/33
Sermons on the Romans iii. 23–6 and I Thessalonians, v. 21. 1816 17/11/33
Sermons on various subjects and occasions. 1816 (2v. 1816–20) 26/8/27
The primitive doctrine of justification, investigated; relatively to the several definitions of the Church of Rome and the Church of England. 1837 20/4/38
Fabliaux et contes des poètes français des xi-xve siècles, publiés par Barbazon. 1808 (4v.) 13/5/48
Fabre, Ferdinand
L'Abbé Tigrane, candidat à la Papauté. 1873 21/3/85
Facts and observations with reference to Masters, R. N. With a plan for the removal of their disabilities. 1845 12/3/57

Facts and thoughts for the additional curates' aid society. 1849 21/1/50

Fairbairn, Andrew Martin
Christ in the centuries and other sermons. 1893 31/3/93 ?
Studies in the life of Christ. 1880 12/2/80
The churches and the colleges: their work for religion and the nation. Address. 1878 9/9/78, 28/12/79
The place of Christ in modern theology. 1893 15/10/93
The reformation and the revolution of 1688. 1889 3/4/90

Fairbairn, Sir William
The life of Sir W. Fairbairn, Bart... Partly written by himself. Edited and completed by W. Pole... With portrait. 1877 28/5/77

Fairholme, George
A general view of the geology of scripture, in which the unerring truth of the inspired narrative... is exhibited and distinctly proved. 1833 17/9/47

Fairley, William F. S. S.
Epitaphiana: or the curiosities of churchyard literature... with an introduction... by W. F. 1873 13/3/92

Fairplay, F.
Repeal of the Union. 1831 4/11/86

Faithfull, J. G.
Wayside thoughts. 1860 (1860–63) 22/9/65

Falconer, Lanoe
Cecilia de Noel. 1891 7/11/91

Falconer, William
The poetical works of W. F. With a life by J. Mitford. 1854 6/5/88

Falding, Frederick John
The Christian ministry and modern thought. 1892 13/11/92

Falkener, Edward
Daedalus; or, the causes and principles of the excellence of Greek sculpture. 1860 28/12/60
Ephesus, and the temple of Diana. 1863 21/5/72
On the Hypaethron of Greek temples; a paper read before the Archaeological Society of Berlin. 1861 18/9/61

Falk Laws, Victim of. 1879 4/5/79

Falloux, Frédéric Alfred Pierre de
A. Cochin... Translated from the French by A. Craven. 1877 12/8/77
Discours et mélanges politiques. 1882 (2v.) 12/2/83
Memoirs of the Count de Falloux. From the French. Edited by C. B. Pitman. 1888 (2v.) 9/11/88

Family of St. Richard the Saxon. 1844 (2v.) 26/5/44

Famous parks and gardens. 1880 20/1/87

Fane, Julian C. Henry, and Lytton, R. Bulwer pseud. Neville Temple and Edward Trevor
Tannhäuser; or, the battle of the bards. A poem. 1861 11/6/61

Fane, Robert George Cecil
Ministry of Justice; its necessity as an instrument of law reform. 1848 26/6/48
Tenant-Right; its necessity as a means of promoting good farming. No. ii. (reprinted from the *Law Review*). 1849 14/4/49

Fardella, Vincenzo Marquis di Torrearsa
Ricordi su la rivoluzione siciliana degli anni 1848 e 1849. 1887 18/7/88

Fardorollgha the miser. 23/4/47 ?

Farini, Luigi Carlo
Il conte Buol ed il Piemonte: lettera... a Lord J. Russell. 1859 21/3/59
La diplomazia e la quistione Italiana; lettera... al Signor G. Gladstone. 1856 20/1/58
Lo Stato Romano dall'anno 1815 all'anno 1850. 1851 (3v. 1850–1) 27/11/50, 30/5/59
The Roman State from 1815 to 1850, tr. W. E. Gladstone, assisted by Mrs. A. R. Bennett. 1851 (4v. 1851–4) 27/11/50, 21/12/50, 3/6/51

Farini, Pellegrino
Opere. Vol. X. Lettere. 1853 27/2/53 ?, 1/12/66

Farley, James Lewis
Egypt, Cyprus, and Asiatic Turkey. 1878 4/12/78
The decline of Turkey, financially and politically... With portrait of the late Fuad Pasha. 1875 (2nd edn) 18/11/75
Turks and Christians. A solution to the Eastern Question. 1876 24/10/76

Farquhar, Barbara H.
The pearl of days. 1848 8/11/48

Farquhar, George
The stage-coach, a comedy. 1705 23/4/67

Farr, Edward
[Tribute to Sidney Herbert]. (not found) 27/11/61 ?

Farr, Thomas
A remedy for the distresses of the nation. 1840 23/12/41

Farr, William C. B.
A system of life insurance which may be carried out under the control of the Government. 1861 21/3/64
Remarks on a proposed scheme for the conversion of the assessments levied on public salaries... into a 'Provident Fund' for the support of orphans. 1849 3/8/57

Farrar, Adam Storey
A critical history of free thought in reference to the Christian religion. Eight lectures preached

before the University of Oxford. 1862 25/1/63
Science in theology; sermons preached in St. Mary's, Oxford, before the university. 1859 4/12/59
Farrar, Frederic William
Eternal hope. 1878 3/3/78
Righteousness exalteth a nation! A sermon. 1870 7/8/70
The conquest over temptation. A farewell sermon. 1871 24/9/71
The life of Christ. 1874 (2v.) 27/10/77
Farrer, Henrietta Louisa afterw. Lear
'Willie's grave' in *Tales of Kirkbeck* 1869 1/8/69
Bossuet and his contemporaries. By the author of 'A Dominican artist'. 1874 28/1/75
Life of Robert Gray, bishop of Cape Town . . . Edited by . . . Charles Gray . . . With portrait and map. 1876 (2v.) 17/1/76
The life of Madame Louise de France, daughter of Louis XV; also known as the Mother Thérèse de St. Augustin. 1869 15/8/69
Farrer, James
Notice of Runic inscriptions discovered during recent excavations in the Orkneys. 1862 16/7/62
Farrer, Richard Ridley
A tour in Greece, 1880. . . . With . . . illustrations, by Lord Windsor. 1882 17/4/84
Farrer, Thomas Henry Baron Farrer
The sugar convention. [Letters reprinted from 'The Times']. 1889 11/3/89
Fass Schonk, a tale. 24/8/78
Father Oswald; a Genuine Catholic Story. 1842 26/2/43
Faucher, Léon
Dictionnaire de l'économie politique. 1855 12/1/55
Histoire financière. De la situation financière et du budget. 1850 18/4/50 ?
Faudel, Henry
A few words on the Jewish disabilities addressed to Sir R. H. Inglis. 1848 24/2/48
Fauriel, Claude Charles
Chants populaires de la Grèce moderne. 1824 (2v.) 19/2/59
Dante et les origines de la langue et de la littérature italiennes. 1854 (2v.) 9/6/69
Histoire de la poésie Provençale. 1846 4/10/59
Songs of Greece, tr. C. B. Sheridan. 1825 16/8/59
The last days of the Consulate. 1885 6/5/93
Faussett, Godfrey
The revival of popery. A sermon. 1838 20/2/39
The thirty-nine articles considered as the standard and test of the doctrine of the Church of England [on Tract 90]. 1841 5/9/41
Fausti, Lodovico
Difesa per il Cav. Lodovico Fausti fatta innanzi il tribunale supremo della Sacra Consulta. 1863 30/11/66
Faustine. 16/10/45
Faut-il une Pologne?. 10/10/54
Favre, Jules Gabriel Claude
Rome et la république française. 1871 16/11/71
Fawcett, Edgar
An heir to millions. 1892 (2v.) 20/12/92, 26/12/92
Fawcett, Henry
'The House of Lords' in *Fortnightly Review*, xvi.491. 1871 (October 1871) 27/10/71
Essays and lectures on social and political subjects. By H. Fawcett and M. G. Fawcett. 1872 19/4/72
Indian finance. Three essays. Republished from the 'Nineteenth Century'. 1880 2/3/80
Manual of political economy. 1863 22/1/64, 22/2/65
Pauperism: its causes and remedies. 1871 10/6/71
State socialism and the nationalisation of the land. Reprinted from 'Macmillan's Magazine'. 1883 31/1/84
The economic position of the British labourer. 1865 10/11/65
F. C.
Free trade. 1852 24/9/52
Featherstonehaugh, George William
Observations on the Treaty of Washington, signed 9th August, 1842, with the Treaty annexed. 1842 4/2/43
Feis, Jacob
Shakspere and Montaigne: an endeavour to explain the tendency of 'Hamlet' from allusions in contemporary works. 1884 10/11/84
Fell, Margaret
Testimony of Margaret Fell concerning . . . George Fox. 31/10/90
Fell, R.
Memoirs of the public life of the late . . . Charles James Fox. 1808 9/11/54
Fellowes, A.
What is the truth?. 1892 15/5/92
Fellowes, Robert LL.D.
Religion without cant; or, a preservative against lukewarmness and intolerance; fanaticism, superstition and impiety. 1801 19/4/41
Fellowes, William Dorset
A visit to the monastery of La Trappe, in 1817; with notes taken during a tour through Le Perche, Normandy, . . . and the environs of Paris. 1818 17/4/38
Fénelon, François de la Mothe
Lettre sur la lecture. 1709 10/3/39

Fenn, Charles
A compendium of the English and foreign funds, and the principal joint stock companies. 1837 9/10/54
Fennell, Charles Augustus Maude
Pindar. 1879 15/5/83
Fenton, Elijah
The Odyssey . . . translated from the Greek by A. Pope and E. Fenton. 1750 28/8/63
Ferguson, William Dwyer
The Common Law Procedure Amendment Act (Ireland) the general orders, appendix of forms and statutes, and general index. 1857 (2nd edn) 15/11/69
Ferguson, William Dwyer, and Vance, Andrew
The tenure and improvement of land in Ireland, considered with reference to the relation of landlord and tenant, and tenant-right. 1851 16/11/69, 25/11/69
Fergusson, Alexander
The religious establishment in Scotland examined . . . a tract occasioned by the late persecution against A. Fergusson. 1771 4/9/59
Fergusson, James architect
Rude stone monuments in all countries; their age and uses. 1872 24/9/72
The peril of Portsmouth; or, French fleets and English ports. With a plan. 1852 4/2/53
Tree and serpent worship; or, illustrations of mythology and art in India in the first and fourth centuries. 1868 24/11/75
Ferme, Mrs. George pseud. George Douglas
Tib. 1892 26/11/92
Fermoy, Philip Roche pseud. Robert Johnson
A commentary on the memoirs of T. Wolfe Tone, in which the moral and physical force of Ireland, to support national independence, is . . . examined. 1828 24/9/86
Ferrar, Nicholas
Nicholas Ferrar. Two lives by his brother John and by Dr. Jebb, now first edited with illustrations by J. E. B. Mayor. 1855 2/4/55
Ferrari, Giuseppe
La Fédération Italienne. Deux discours . . . prononcés au Parlement de Turin, dans les séances des 8 et 11 Octobre 1860. 1860 15/12/66
Ferré, Emmanuel
L'Irlande. La crise agraire et politique, ses causes, ses dangers, sa solution. 1887 24/5/87
Ferrier, James Frederick
Observations on church and state, suggested by the Duke of Argyll's Essay on the ecclesiastical history of Scotland. 1848 26/1/49
Ferrier, J. P.
Caravan journeys and wanderings in Persia, Afghanistan, Turkistan, and Beloochistan: with historical notices of the countries . . . between Russia & India. 1856 6/1/57
Ferrier, Susan Edmonstone
Marriage, a novel. 1818 8/10/83
The inheritance. 1824 (3v.) 9/9/29
Ferri-Pisani, Camille
[Religioni e stati]. (not found) 22/12/75 ?
Fessler, Joseph
The true and false infallibility of the Popes. A controversial reply to . . . Dr. Schulte . . . translated from the German by A. St. John. 1875 2/1/75
Feuillet, Octave
La morte. 1886 24/6/86
Le roman d'un jeune homme pauvre. 1858 16/9/86
Monsieur de Camors. 1867 6/3/90
Few words about Ireland. 1865 31/10/88
Few words to churchwardens. 1841 16/4/41
Feydeau, Ernest Aimé
Fanny. 1858 16/4/89
Fezensac, Raymond Emery Philippe Joseph
Souvenirs militaires de 1814 à 1864. 1863 29/6/65
Ffoulkes, Edmund Salusbury
[on the Council] in *Quarterly Review,* cxxviii. 162. 1870 (January 1870) 23/1/70
A manual of ecclesiastical history. 1851 4/1/52
An historical account of the addition of the words 'filioque' to the Creed of the West. 1866 6/10/67
Christendom's divisions. Being a philosophical sketch of the divisions of the Christian family in east and west. 1865 4/3/66
Dogma distinguished from doctrine. A sermon. 1879 21/12/79
One more return from captivity; or my submission to the Catholic church vindicated and explained. 1855 4/3/55
Primitive consecration of the Eucharistic oblation, with an earnest appeal for its revival. 1885 8/3/85
The Athanasian Creed reconsidered; being an Appendix to 'The Athanasian Creed; by whom written'. 1872 7/1/72
The Athanasian Creed: by whom written and by whom published; with other enquiries on creeds in general. 1871 3/12/71
The Roman index and its late proceedings. A second letter to Archbishop Manning. 1869 5/1/69
Three letters, addressed to the Bishop of Oxford, on marriage with the deceased wife's sister. 1849 26/1/49
Union at home first. A sermon. 1871 24/9/71
Fichte, Johann Gottlieb
The destination of man. Translated from the German by Mrs. P. Sinnett. 1846 2/11/84
Ficquelmont, Carl Ludwig von Count
Pensées et réflexions morales et politiques du Comte de Ficquelmont . . . précédées d'une notice sur sa

vie par M. le Baron de Barante. 1859 28/9/63
Field, Cyrus West
The Atlantic telegraph. 1856 23/3/93
Field, Edwin Wilkins
Correspondence [between E. W. Field and C. G. Loring] *on the present relations between Great Britain and the United States of America*. 1862 1/1/63
Field, F.
Vetus testamentum Graece LXX Interpretes. 1859 18/12/59 ?
Field, Henry Martyn
From Egypt to Japan. 1877 10/1/78
History of the Atlantic telegraph. 1866 26/6/67
The Irish Confederates and the Rebellion of 1798. 1851 2/10/89
Field, Horace
The ultimate triumph of Christianity. 1879 27/7/79
Field, John chaplain
A report presented to the magistrates of Berkshire [on Reading gaol]. 1848 16/2/49
Prison discipline. The advantages of the separate system of imprisonment, as established in the county gaol of Reading. 1846 19/6/48
Field, Richard Dean of Gloucester
Of the church. Five bookes (an Appendix containing a defense of such partes . . . as have bene either excepted against, or wrested to . . . Romish errours). (5v. 1606–10) 25/6/48
Fielden, John
The curse of the factory system; or, a short account of the origin of factory cruelties. 1836 21/5/36
Fielding, Henry
A clear state of the case of Elizabeth Canning, who hath sworn that she was robbed and almost starved to death by a gang of gipsies and other villains. 1753 28/7/77
Amelia. 1752 (4v.) 6/9/42, 27/9/71
The history of the adventures of Joseph Andrews. 1742 (2v.) 7/1/48
Tom Jones. 1749 29/4/26, 8/8/87
Fielding, John
Fielding's new peerage of England, Scotland and Ireland. 1784 (2v.) 12/8/73
Fielding, Sir John
A plan for preventing robberies within twenty miles of London. With an account of the rise and establishment of the real thieftakers. 1755 17/8/63
Fienhaber, C. G.
Euripides. Iphigenia in Aulis. 1841 7/11/55
Filangieri, Gaetano Cav.
La scienza della legislazione (Elogio storico del Cavaliere G. F. scritto dall' avvocato D. Tommasi). 1804 (2v.) 2/6/55
Filaret, Vasily Mikhailovich Drozdov
Sermon by Filaret, Metropolitan of Moscow, in A. P. Stanley's *Essays*. 1870 18/6/71
Filder, William
The commissariat in the Crimea; being remarks on those parts of the Report of the Commission of Inquiry into the supplies of the British army. 1856 18/3/56
Filicaja, Vincenzio da
Poesie toscane. 1827 (2v.) 17/7/37
Filon, Augustin
Profils anglais. Randolph Churchill.—Joseph Chamberlain.—John Morley.—Parnell. 1893 20/1/92
Filon, Charles Auguste Désiré
Histoire comparée de France et d'Angleterre. 1832 26/3/84
Finance and trade of the United Kingdom. 1852 11/2/52
Finland, The law of. 24/4/89
Finlason, William Francis
The Catholic hierarchy vindicated by the law of England. 1851 21/3/51
The history of the law of tenures of land in England and Ireland: with particular reference to Inheritable Tenancy. 1870 7/1/70
Finlay, Alexander Struthers
Letters on a journey to Bombay, through Syria and Arabia in 1834–35. 1837 4/8/37
Our monetary system. Some remarks on the influence of bullion in the Bank of England on commercial credit and on the rate of interest. 1864 6/2/64
Finlay, George
Greece under the Romans; a historical view of the condition of the Greek nation, from . . . its conquest . . . until the extinction of the Roman Empire. 1844 25/10/58
History of the Byzantine and Greek empires, from 716 to 1453. 1854 (2v.) 10/7/54, 22/8/54, 18/9/76
The history of Greece from its conquest by the Crusaders to its conquest by the Turks, and of the empire of Trebizond 1204–1461. 1851 21/5/72
Finlay, Kirkman
Letter to . . . Lord Ashley, on the cotton factory system, and the ten hours' factory bill. 1833 16/3/33
Finlayson, Thomas Campbell
Biological religion. An essay in criticism of . . . H. Drummond's 'Natural law in the spiritual world'. 1885 27/9/85, 11/7/86
The meditations and maxims of Koheleth. A practical exposition. 1881 3/1/91
Finlen, James
Mr. J. Finlen's defence of himself against the attacks made upon him by the parliament and press of England. 1868 20/8/68

Fiorentino, G.
Il Pecorone. 12/2/58
Firenzuola, Agnolo
Ragionamenti di M.A. F. . . .et il discacciamento delle nuove lettere, inutilmente aggiunte nella lingua Toscana. Nuovamente stampati. (2v.) 4/10/59
Firmin, Thomas
The life of Mr. F. T., late citizen of London: written by one of his most intimate acquaintance . . . with an account of his religion. (2v.) 29/5/44
Firth, Joseph Firth Bottomley
London government, and how to reform it. 1882 15/3/83
Fisher, George Park
The beginnings of Christianity. With a view of the state of the Roman world at the birth of Christ. 1877 7/6/79
The grounds of theistic and Christian belief. 1883 11/8/89
The nature and method of revelation. 1890 29/6/90
Fisher, Henry
A sermon preached . . . at the ordination held by the . . . Bishop of Calcutta, 1835. 1835 17/4/43
Fisher, John
Life of blessed John Fisher, by T. E. Bridgett. 1888 22/7/88, 25/9/89
Life of John Fisher, by J. Lewis. 1855 (2v.) 30/8/91
Fisher, John Cowley
Liturgical purity, our rightful inheritance [A treatise advocating a new revision to the Book of Common Prayer]. 1857 6/6/57, 25/10/63
Fisher, Richard Swainson
A new and complete statistical gazetteer of the United States of America, founded on and compiled from official federal and state returns. 1853 25/4/63
Fiske, John asst. librarian, Harvard
Darwinism and other essays. 1879 26/10/84
The beginnings of New England; or, the Puritan theocracy in its relations to civil and religious liberty. 1889 8/2/90, 7/5/93
The critical period of American history, 1783–1789. 1888 5/12/88
The destiny of man viewed in the light of his origin. 1884 12/12/87
The idea of God as affected by modern knowledge. 1885 28/9/90, 28/12/90
Fitch, Sir Joshua Girling
Charity schools and the endowed schools commission. 1873 14/9/89
Fitzgerald, James Edward
Address of his honour the superintendent at the opening of the first legislative council of the province of Canterbury, New Zealand. 1853 11/3/54
An examination of the charter and proceedings of the Hudson's Bay Company with reference to the grant of Vancouver's Island. 1849 14/9/48
Fitzgerald, J. F. the Knight of Kerry
A letter to Sir R. Peel on the endowment of the Roman Catholic Church of Ireland. 1845 7/7/45
Fitzgerald, John F. G. Purcell
A letter of earnest remonstrance to the Right Hon. W. E. Gladstone . . . upon his appointment of a co-writer with infidels [i.e. Temple] to a . . . bishopric. 1870 29/1/70
Fitzgerald, Penelope F.
A protest against agnosticism: the rationale of philosophy of belief. 1890 5/4/91
Fitzgerald, Percy Hetherington
A new history of the English stage, from the Restoration to the liberty of the theatre in connection with the Patent Houses. 1882 (2v.) 4/8/85
Charles Townsend, wit and statesman. 1866 5/4/67
Croker's Boswell and Boswell. Studies in 'The life of Johnson'. 1880 27/5/80
The entertainer. 1892 26/5/92 ?
The great canal at Suez: its political, engineering, and financial history. With an account of the struggles of its projector, F. de Lesseps. 1876 (2v.) 2/8/76
The life of George the fourth, including his letters and opinions; with a view of the men, manners and politics of his reign. 1881 (2v.) 4/6/81
The life of William IV. 1884 (2v.) 11/9/84
The royal dukes and duchesses of the family of George III. A view of their life and manners for seventy years, 1760–1830. 1882 (2v.) 24/1/84
Fitzgerald, William Bishop of Cork
Cautions for the times. Addressed to the parishioners of a parish in England by their former rector, ed. Richard Whately. 1851 8/8/60
The revival of synods in the United Church of England and Ireland. A charge delivered in September 1861. 1861 24/11/61
Fitzgibbon, Gerald Q. C.
A banded ministry and the Upas tree. 1873 27/3/73, 27/11/73
The land difficulty of Ireland, with an effort to solve it. 1869 13/9/69 ?
Fitzgibbon, John Earl of Clare
The speech of J., Lord Baron F. . . .on the reading of the Bill for the relief of His Majesty's Roman Catholic subjects, March 13, 1793. 1798 3/4/45

The speech of... John Earl of Clare... in the House of Lords of Ireland, on a motion made by him on Monday, February 10, 1800. 1800 19/5/86

Fitzhugh, George
Sociology for the South, or the failure of a free society. 1854 12/11/63

Fitzmaurice, Lord E. G. P.
Life of William, Earl of Shelburne. 1875 (3v. 1875–6) 1/3/75

Fitzpatrick, William John
'The Sham Squire;' and the informers of 1798. With a view of their contemporaries. To which are added jottings about Ireland seventy years ago. 1866 1/9/87
Correspondence of Daniel O'Connell... Edited ... by W. J. Fitzpatrick. 1888 (2v.) 26/10/88
Memoirs of R. Whately, Archbishop of Dublin. With a glance at his contemporaries and times. 1864 (2v.) 24/1/80
The life, times and correspondence of Dr. Doyle, Bishop of Kildare and Leighlin. 1880 (2v. enlarged edn) 13/11/80
Who wrote the Waverley novels? Being an investigation into certain mysterious circumstances attending their production. 1856 18/8/58

Fitzroy, A. I.
Dogma and the Church of England. 1891 19/11/91

Fitzroy, Lord Charles
Ionian islands. Letters by Lord C. Fitzroy and documents from other sources, on past and recent events in the Ionian islands. 1850 25/11/58

Fitzroy, Robert Admiral
Remarks on New Zealand, in February 1846. 1846 20/8/46

Flanagan, Thomas Professor
A history of the church in England, from the earliest period to the re-establishment of the hierarchy in 1850. 1857 (2v.) 17/4/59, 27/1/75

Flassan, Gaëtan de Raxis de
History of the Congress of Vienna. 1829 (3v.) 4/4/78

Flaubert, Gustave
Salammbô. 1862 19/4/86

Flaxman, John
Lectures on sculpture... as delivered before the president and members of the Royal Academy. With a brief memoir of the author. 1829 31/5/42, 24/12/88

Fleetwood, William Bishop of St. Asaph
The judgement of the Church of England in the case of lay-baptism and of Dissenters' baptism. 1712 12/4/57
The works of... W. Fleetwood. 1854 (3v. vol i) 13/6/57

Fletcher, Carteret John Halford
Woman's equality with man in Christ. A sermon. 1871 16/7/71

Fletcher, Mrs. Eliza
Autobiography of Mrs. Fletcher, of Edinburgh, with selections from her letters and other family memorials. Compiled and arranged by... Lady Richardson. 1874 7/9/84

Fletcher, John dramatist
The tamer tamed, a comedy. 19/12/56
The two noble kinsmen... written by the memorable worthies of their time, Mr. J. F. and Mr. W. Shakespeare. 12/12/63

Fletcher, Joseph of Hanley
The select works and memoirs of... J. Fletcher. Edited by J. F., Junr. 1846 (3v.) 9/4/48

Fletcher, William Justice
An Irish judge on an Irish question: reprint of Mr. Baron Fletcher's Charge to the co. Wexford Grand Jury in 1814, with introduction by J. J. Clancy. 1886 9/9/87

Fleury, Claude
Historia Ecclesiastica Latine reddita, et notis illustrata. 1758 (87v. 1758–94) 26/1/75

Flint, Robert
A sermon preached in St. Giles' Church, Edinburgh. 1881 24/7/81
The duties of the people of Scotland to the Church of Scotland. A lecture. 1882 22/11/85 ?

Florian, Jean Pierre Claris de Florian
La bonne mère. 1/6/26
Le bon ménage, ou la suite de la Bonne mère, comédie en un acte et en prose. 1786 29/5/26
Le bon père. Comédie en un acte et en prose. 29/5/26
Les jumeaux de Bergame. 30/5/26, 31/5/26
Oeuvres inédites... recueillies par R. C. G. de Pixerécourt [vol 4, entitled 'Théâtre']. 1824 (4v.) 27/5/26

Florine; ou, la belle Italienne [Cabinet des fées, vol. 1]. 1785 (1785–6) 16/7/58, 20/6/91

Flower, James Edward
Sacerdotalism... an address. 1875 (1875) 20/7/75

Flower, John Wickham
A layman's reasons for discontinuing the use of the Athanasian creed. Letter to the Dean of Norwich in answer to his pamphlet. 1872 24/11/72

Flower, William Balmbro'
Choral services and ritual observances. Two sermons. To which is prefixed an address... on the present troubles with the church. 1856 23/3/56

Flower, Sir William Henry K. C. B.
The horse: a study in natural history. 1891 17/3/92

Floyd, Isobel Henderson
Stolen America. 1890 1/8/90

Fluegel, Maurice
Gedanken über religiöse Bräuche und Anschauungen. 1889 24/1/89
Fogazzaro, Antonio
Daniele Cortis. Romanzo. 1887 (3rd edn) 10/8/88
Folengo, Teofilo pseud. Pitocco Limerno
Orlandino. 19/11/77
Foley, H. J.
Our lanes and meadow paths; or, rambles in rural Middlesex. With illustrations and a map. 1887 4/7/87
Folk tales of the Magyars. 1889 7/11/89
Fonblanque, Albany
England under seven administrations. 1837 (3v.) 3/4/37
The life and labours of Albany Fonblanque. Edited by his nephew E. B. de Fonblanque. 1874 21/11/74
Fonseca, Christoval de
Tratado del amor de Dios. 4/9/87
Fontaine, Jean de la
Contes et nouvelles en vers. (2v.) 20/9/61
Fonvielle, Wilfrid de
Les miracles devant la science. 1880 12/4/85
Foot, Arthur Wynne
Symptoms and treatment of the cattle plague, with a sketch of its history and progress. 1866 16/2/66
Foote, Henry Wilder the elder
Wilder's address in Sermons preached in Boston on the death of Abraham Lincoln. 1865 15/3/65
Foote, Samuel
A trip to Calais; a comedy in three acts as originally written, and intended for representation. 1778 27/3/88
The maid of Bath; a comedy in three acts. 1778 29/3/88
Forbes, Alexander Penrose Bishop of Brechin
A charge delivered to the clergy of the diocese of Brechin in synod assembled... on the 27th of August, 1862. 1862 7/9/62
A commentary on the Te Deum. 1850 4/1/52
A plea for sisterhoods. 1849 29/4/49
A primary charge delivered to the clergy of his diocese at the annual synod. 1857 13/10/57
A primary charge delivered to the clergy of his diocese at the annual synod. 1858 (2nd edn w/additions) 28/2/58
A sermon preached... before the Church Penitentiary Association. 1864 10/7/64
A short commentary on seven penitential psalms. 1847 9/5/47
A short explanation of the Nicene creed. 1852 5/12/52
An explanation of the thirty-nine articles. 1867 31/12/71, 1/9/78
Deepening of the spiritual life. 1873 18/5/73
Introduction to the thirty-nine articles. 1867 19/11/71 ?
Jesus our worship; a sermon preached at the consecration of St. Columba's church, Edinburgh. 1848 20/2/48
Pastoral letters on foreign missions. 1873 15/10/73
Reply to the pleadings in the case of Henderson and others versus the Bishop of Brechin, before the Episcopal Synod of the Scottish Episcopal Church. 1860 12/1/60
Sermon on Mr. Morse. 16/10/48
The body is for the Lord. The substance of a sermon. 1871 23/7/71
The Church of England and the doctrine of papal infallibility. 1871 15/10/71
The claims of the laity to vote as constituent members of synod practically considered: a charge. 1873 15/10/73
The Scottish communion office done into Greek. 1865 25/4/67
The waning of opportunities, and other sermons practical and doctrinal. 1860 2/5/60
Forbes, Archibald
[on Russia, Turkey and Bulgaria], *Nineteenth Century*, ii.561. 1877 (November 1877) 13/11/77, 23/11/77
The war correspondence of the Daily News, 1870. 1871 4/12/77
Forbes, Duncan Lord President of the Court of Session
Some thoughts concerning religion, natural and revealed. With reflexions on the sources of incredulity with regard to religion. 1750 21/6/74
Forbes, G. H.
Christian sacrifice in the Eucharist... by a layman. 1844 8/9/44
Forbes, James F.R. S.
Oriental memoirs: selected and abridged from a series of familiar letters written during seventeen years' residence in India. 1813 (4v. 1813–15) 26/4/31
Forbes, John of Corse
Instructiones historico-theologicae de Doctrina Christiana et vario rerum statu. 24/9/43
Forbes, William Advocate
A treatise of church lands and tithes. 1705 7/8/45 ?
Some considerations on the Scottish poor-law question: in a letter to a friend. 1845 7/8/45
Forbes, William Bishop of Edinburgh
Considerationes modestae et pacificae controversiarum de justificatione, purgatorio, invocatione sanctorum et Christo Mediatore, [et] *Eucharistia*. 29/3/50, 18/10/68
Ford, John dramatist
'Tis pitty shees a whore. 6/7/27
The broken heart. 7/7/27

The lover's melancholy. 5/7/27
Ford, Richard of Exeter
Hand-book for travellers in Spain. 1845 31/7/47
Fore, J. A.
Coercion without crime. 1887 10/8/87 ?
Foreign and Colonial Quarterly Review. 11. 211, 250. 7/1843. Gioberti on Italy; India 15/7/1843
Foreign Church Chronicle.
3. 3/1879 23/3/1879
4 6/2/1880
11. 12/1887. Old Catholics 4/12/1887
Foreign Church Review. 14. 9/1890 4/9/1890
Foreign Quarterly Review.
2. 437. 10/1828. Carlyle on Heeren's Heyne 15/7/1840
10. 297. 10/1832. on Chateaubriand 9/11/1832
10. 411. 10/1832. on Gouverneur Morris 12/11/1832
10. 508. 10/1832. Milton 8/11/1832
10. 514. 10/1832. on Louis Philippe 10/11/1832
14. 1. 8/1834. Madame de Stael 13/8/1834
14. 298. 12/1834. Italy 9/12/1834
20. 378–402. 1/1838. Hanoverian constitution 13/1/1838
27. 184. 4/1841. Guizot 3/4/1841
Foresta, Marquis J. de
Lettres sur la Sicile, écrites pendant l'été de 1805. 1821 (2v.) 7/12/60 ?
Forester, Baron Orlando
Letter to Dr. Sewell. 1859 8/5/59
On Hampden. 1847 22/2/48
Forester, Thomas
The island of Sardinia: with remarks on its resources, and its relation to British interests in the Mediterranean. 1861 23/2/61
Formby, Henry
Monotheism... the primitive religion of the city of Rome. An historical investigation. 1877 23/6/77, 14/4/78
Sacrum Septenarium; or, the seven gifts of the holy ghost, as exemplified in the life and person of the blessed virgin. 1874 7/1/76
The little book of the martyrs of the city of Rome. With... illustrations. 1876 16/1/76
Fornari, Vito
Della vita di Gesù Cristo. 1869 (3v. 1869–93) 15/4/70
Fornelli, Nicola
Il libro del Padre Curci e i partiti politici in Italia. 1878 18/3/78
Forneron, Henri
Louise de Kérouaille, Duchesse de Portsmouth. Avec un portrait. 1886 14/6/86, 17/6/93
Forrow, Alexander
The Thames and its docks: a lecture. 1877 24/8/77
Forshall, Josiah
The first twelve chapters of the Gospel according to St. Matthew, in the received Greek text; with various readings, and notes... By... J. F. 1864 29/5/64
Forster, Anthony
South Australia; its progress and its prosperity... With a map. 1866 17/3/68
Forster, Charles
Mahometanism unveiled; an inquiry, in which that arch-heresy, its diffusion and continuance, are examined... tending to confirm the Christian faith. 1829 3/4/30
Thirty years' correspondence between J. Jebb,... and A. Knox... Edited by... C. Forster. 1834 (2v.) 10/1/36
Forster, Henry Rumsey
The Stowe catalogue. 1848 6/5/57
Forster, Hugh Oakeley Arnold
The citizen reader. 1886 26/4/94
The truth about the Land League, its leaders, and its teaching. 1882 (2nd edn) 8/4/82, 12/4/82
Forster, John barrister
The life of Charles Dickens. 1872 (3v. 1872–74) 24/3/74
Forster, William Edward
Life of W. E. Forster, by T. Wemyss Reid. 1888 (2v.) 7/7/88, 1/8/88, 6/8/88
William Penn and T. B. Macaulay; being brief observations on the charges made in Mr. Macaulay's History of England against the character of W. Penn. 1849 25/5/76
Forsyth, Joseph of Elgin
Remarks on antiquities, arts, and letters during an excursion in Italy in... 1802 and 1803. 1813 24/4/27, 1/5/32
Forsyth, Robert Advocate
Remarks on the Church of Scotland: its history, constitution, and recent proceedings; its present peril; and a suggestion of remedies. 1843 24/8/44
Forsyth, William Q. C., LL.D.
History of ancient manuscripts. A lecture. 1872 15/6/72
History of the captivity of Napoleon at St. Helena, from the letters and journals of the late Lieut.-Gen. Sir H. Lowe, and official documents ... 1853 (3v.) 26/5/59
Life of Cicero... With illustrations. 1864 (2v.) 6/2/67
The law relating to simony considered, with a view to its revision. 1844 3/3/44
The Slavonic provinces south of the Danube: a sketch of their history and present state in relation to the Ottoman porte. With a map. 1876 19/7/76
Forteguerri, Niccolò Bishop of Ancyra
Ricciardetto, poema. 1766 (2v.) 2/1/88

Fortescue, Chichester Samuel Parkinson Baron Carlingford
Christian profession not the test of citizenship. An essay for the day. 1849 4/5/49
Fortescue, Robert Henry
The Tudor supremacy in jurisdiction unlimited. A sermon. 1850 21/7/50
Fortier, Alcée
Bits of Louisiana folk-lore. 1888 22/3/90 ?
Louisiana folk-tales. 1895 22/3/90 ?
Fortin d'Ivry, T.
Question d'Irlande. O'Connell. 1843 27/12/90
Fortnightly Review.
7. 161. 2/1867. Hayward on Lady Herbert 3/2/1867
12. 241. 9/1869. Cox on Gladstone and Homer 4/9/1869
15. 580. 5/1871. Agrarianism 12/5/1871
20. 7/1873 21/7/1873
29. 153, 207. 2/1878. Eastern Question; on Melbourne 7/2/1878
29. 387. 7/1878. Indian thought 6/9/1878
29. 477. 4/1878. on Disraeli 15/4/1878
29. 691. 5/1878. on Beaconsfield 18/5/1878
29. 805. 6/1878. Dislike of science 25/6/1878
29. 867. 6/1878. on Beaconsfield 12/6/1878
30. 250. 8/1878. on Beaconsfield 1/8/1878
30. 26. 7/1878. Ireland 4/7/1878
30. 616. 11/1878. Berlin Treaty 28/12/1878
30. 726. 5/1880. State of affairs 29/4/1880
31. 647. 5/1879. Morley 12/6/1879
31. 667, 718. 5/1879. on Clifford; on Phillip II 13/6/1879
31. 894. 6/1879. Music 5/6/1879
32. 767. 12/1879. Kabul 30/1/1880
34. 1, 8. 7/1880. Religious Liberty; French land 6/8/1880
34. 147. 8/1880. Separation of American Colonies 6/8/1880
34. 556. 11/1880. Greece 27/11/1880
39. 2/1883 15/2/1883
39. 822, 841. 6/1883. Church of England 3/6/1883
40. 1. 7/1883. Radicalism 5/7/1883
40. 457, 521. 10/1883. France; Barrére 2/10/1883
40. 466. 10/1883. Westbury Russell on Irving 8/10/1883
40. 50. 7/1883. Wordsworth 4/7/1883
40. 713, 728, 737. Poetry; Ireland; Suez 1/11/1883
42. 126. 7/1884. MacColl 7/7/1884
42. 313, 414. 9/1884 3/9/1884
42. 557. 11/1884. on Gladstone 3/11/1884
44. 1, 102. 7/1885. Ireland; Oxford Professorship 11/7/1885
44. 149, 178. 8/1885. Paris press; on Pasteur 13/8/1885
44. 203. 8/1885. on Lord Peterborough 14/8/1885
44. 218. 8/1885. Arnold 7/8/1885
44. 240, 277. 8/1885. Lilly; Scotch Church 6/9/1885
46. 617, 488. 11/1886. Müller 4/11/1884
46. 98. 7/1886. Ireland 2/7/1886
47. 442. 3/1887. Freemantle on theology 21/8/1887
50. 313. 9/1888. The session 20/10/1888
51. 732. 5/1889. Manning on education 9/5/1889
52. 293. 9/1889. Freeman on home rule 14/1/1890
52. 789. 12/1889. K. Blind 15/12/1889
54. 481. 10/1890. Dillon on Russia 30/11/1890
57. 272. 2/1892. Marriage 19/2/1892
57. 313. 3/1892. Kelvin on energy 19/6/1892
57. 465. 4/1892. Moulton on Pensions 4/4/1892
59. 145. 2/1893. Dilke on Uganda 13/1/1893
Fort Pillow Massacre. Report. 1864 15/9/64
Fortune, Robert
A residence among the Chinese: . . . from 1853 to 1856 . . . With suggestions on the present war. 1857 22/7/57
Foscolo, Niccolò Ugo
Decamerone. 1825 16/9/78
I sepolcri. Epistole in versi. 1809 13/4/64
Ultime lettere di Jacopo Ortis. 1802 28/8/33, 6/9/58
Foster, Charles
The story of the Bible, from Genesis to Revelation . . . Told in simple language, and adapted for all ages, but especially for the young. 1882 27/1/85 ?
Foster, J.
Essays. 1805 3/1/30
Four great teachers. 1890 21/9/90
Fothergill, J. M.
[on pain]. (not found) 4/5/84
Fothergill, S. F.
Essays on popular subjects. 1888 18/10/91
Fottrell, Sir George K. C. B.
Inaugural address delivered before the Literary and Historical Society of the Catholic University of Ireland . . . 2nd December, 1870. 1871 6/4/71
Letter containing a scheme of Irish University Reform, addressed to . . . the Marquis of Hartington. 1873 18/1/73

Fould, A.
[speech of 24 Feb 62]. 29/3/62
Foundation of faith assisted. 1835 18/5/35
Fournet, Jules
Madame Henriette Grote. Notice biographique. 1879 31/5/79 ?
Fournier de Flaix, E.
L'indépendance politique et agraire de l'Irlande. 1886 24/9/86
Fourth Report of Commissioners of National Education in Ireland, P. P., xvii. 49. 1838 29/1/38
Foville, Alfred de
Etudes économiques:... le Morcellement. 1885 24/10/85, 26/10/85
Fowle, Fulwar William
Aholah and Aholibah. A sermon, having reference to recent immoral legislation by the British parliament. 1871 16/7/71
Fowle, Thomas Welbanke pseud. Cellarius
An essay on the right translation... regarded as exhibiting the silence of the New Testament as to the conditions of the future life. 1877 11/3/77
An essay on the right translation... regarded as exhibiting the silence of the New Testament as to the conditions of the future life... A new analogy. 1881 26/3/82
Fowler, Edward Bishop of Gloucester
The design of Christianity; or, a plain demonstration... that the enduing men with inward real righteousness or true holiness, was the ultimate end. 31/12/54
Fowler, John head master
R. W. Sibthorp. A biography. 1880 20/4/80
Fowler, John Coke
Ancient laws... of Wales attributed to Howel the Good. 1887 13/9/88 ?
Fowler, Lorenzo Niles
Temperaments: their classification and importance. A lecture. 1864 6/6/80 ?
Fowler, William LL. B.
The crisis of 1866: a financial essay. 1866 7/2/67
Thoughts on 'Free trade in land'. 1869 16/2/69
Fowler, William Chauncy
The cultivation of taste, An address delivered at the... anniversary of the Mount Holyoke female seminary, South Hadley, Mass. 1850 18/1/66
Fox, Lady Caroline Baroness Holland
Memoirs of old friends. 1882 (2v.) 24/3/82
Fox, Charles James
A history of the early part of the reign of James the second, with an introductory chapter. 1808 5/10/35
A letter to the electors of Westminster. 1793 13/12/67
Correspondence of... G. Wakefield with... C. J. F... chiefly on subjects of Classical literature. 1813 12/12/67
Memorials of... C. J. Fox, ed. Lord John Russell. 1853 (4v. 1853–57) 19/1/55
The speeches of the Rt. Hon. C. J. Fox, in the House of Commons. 1815 (6v.) 28/6/32, 4/7/55
Fox, G.
Iconoclastes. 16/12/26
Fox, Henry Richard afterw. Vassall, Baron Holland
Foreign reminiscences... edited by his son, H. E. Lord Holland. 1850 25/3/51
Letter to the Rev. Dr. Shuttleworth [on Roman Catholic Emancipation]. 1827 29/11/30
Some account of the life... of L. F. de Vega Carpio. 1806 11/12/65
Fox, J. A.
A key to the Irish question. Mainly compiled from the speeches of eminent British statesmen and publicists. 1890 28/11/89
Why Ireland wants Home Rule. 1887 28/1/87
Fox, Samuel
Monks and monasteries: being an account of English Monachism. 1840 11/1/45
Fox, Sir William
The six colonies of New Zealand. 1851 4/8/51
The war in New Zealand. 1860 12/1/61
Foxe, John
The Book of Martyrs. 14/4/32
Foxton, Frederick J.
Popular Christianity, its transition and probable development. 1844 15/4/60, 28/8/64, 20/2/80
Frampton, Robert Bishop of Gloucester
The life of R. F., Bishop of Gloucester, deprived as a Non-Juror 1689. Edited by T. S. Evans ? 1876 5/3/77
France, l'Ancienne. 1887 14/9/86
Franceson, Charles Frédéric
Essai sur la question, si Homère a connu l'usage de l'écriture, et si les deux poèmes de l'Iliade et de l'Odysée sont en entier de lui. 1818 3/11/65
Franciosi, Giovanni
Dante e Raffaello [Extracted from the 'Memorie' of the Reale Accademia di Scienze, Lettere ed Arti of Modena]. 1882 21/1/83 ?
Francis, Francis the Elder
The diplomatic history of the Greek war, from the foundation of the Hetairia to the Treaty of Adrianople. 1878 15/11/77
Francis, John of the Bank of England
History of the Bank of England, its times and traditions. 1847 (2v.) 19/11/47
Francis, Sir Philip G. C. B., pseud. Junius
Letters of Junius. 1769 (1769–72) 9/1/38

Francis, Sir Philip G. C. B., pseud. Junius (*cont.*)
Memoirs of Sir Philip Francis, edited by Merivale. 1867 (2v.) 7/3/68
Mr. F.'s speech in the House of Commons... 28 May, 1806, against the exemption of foreign property in the funds from the duty on income. 1806 26/9/62 ?
Political satires. 1768 1/3/41
Francklin, J. F.
The indivisibility of Christ's church. 1857 16/10/59 ?
Frank, Constantin
Philosophismus und Christenthum. 1875 25/3/75
Franklin, Benjamin LL.D.
A collection of the familiar letters and miscellaneous papers of B. Franklin. Now for the first time published. 1833 26/12/37 ?
The autobiography of Benjamin Franklin. 1818 26/12/37
Franqueville, Alfred Charles Ernest Franquet de
Le gouvernement et le parlement britannique. 1887 (3v.) 5/7/87
Les institutions politiques, judiciaires et administratives de l'Angleterre. 1863 11/5/64
Franzos, Carl Emil
Die Juden von Barnow. Novellen. 1878 27/5/88
For the Right. Given in English by J. Sutter. With a preface by G. MacDonald. 1887 27/2/89
Fraser, David
The divine afflatus; a force in history. 1875 15/8/75
Fraser, James Bishop of Manchester
A charge delivered at the third visitation of his diocese... 1880. 1880 28/11/80
Charge delivered at his primary visitation, at the Cathedral, Manchester... Dec 3rd and 4th, 1872. 1872 12/1/73
Charge delivered at his second visitation. 1876 26/11/76
The revised code of the Committee of Council on Education, its principles, tendencies, and details, considered in a letter to... Bishop of Salisbury. 1861 16/12/61
Fraser, Major James
Major F.'s manuscript: his adventures in Scotland and England:... 1696–1737. Ed. A. Fergusson. 1889 (2v.) 2/4/89
Fraser, Sir William K. C. B.
Registrum Monasterii S. Marie de Cambuskenneth. 1872 12/2/73
Fraser's Magazine.
8. 663. 12/1873. Mill 29/11/1873
9. 1, 364. 1/1834. Toryism 1/8/1834
13. 707. 6/1835. Art of Pluck 18/7/1836
15. 146. 2/1837. Church rates 25/2/1837
19. 1. 1/1839. on W. F. Hook 18/2/1839
28. 729. 12/1843. Ireland 19/1/1844
30. 253. 9/1844. Fiction 21/9/1844
38. 275. 9/1848. Steamships 5/9/1848
40. 449. 10/1859. West Riding 24/10/1859
44. 237. 9/1851. Review of Farini 17/10/1851
45. 711. 6/1852. Book trade 5/7/1852
50. 9/1854. Ministry; Persia; The war 2/9/1854
51. 1. 1/1855. Spain 18/1/1855
54. 398, 486. 10/1856. Perrone; Naples 8/10/1856
55. 5/1857 2/5/1857
59. 489. 4/1859. Mill on Reform 30/3/1859
59. 50. 1/1859. Gladstone's Homer 22/1/1859
59. 509. 5/1859. Buckle 20/5/1859
60. 11/1859 7/11/1859, 3/12/1859
60. 643. 12/1859. Defence 2/12/1859
61. 301. 3/1860. on P. B. Shelley 1/3/1860
61. 447. 4/1860. Thomas Love Peacock 29/4/1860
62. 438. 10/1860. Macaulay 4/10/1860
65. 198, 258. 2/1862. Mill on American War 3/2/1862
66. 337. 9/1862. Buckle 6/9/1862
72. 9/1865 14/9/1865
72. 537, 665. 11/1865. on Palmerston; on Lecky 11/11/1865
73. 1. 1/1866. Government of London 13/12/1865
73. 477. 4/1866. Reform 2/4/1866
73. 683. 6/1866. Reform 9/6/1866
73. 746. 6/1866. Ecce Homo 10/6/1866
74. 243. 8/1866. Ministry 9/8/1866
74. 277. 9/1866. Church of England 16/8/1866
74. 327. 9/1866. Washington 15/8/1866
76. 135. 8/1867. Buckle 13/8/1867
76. 169. 8/1867. Marriage 23/8/1867
76. 541. 11/1867. Voltaire 17/11/1867
76. 679. 12/1867. Belgium 6/12/1867
77. 407. 3/1868. Ministry 30/3/1868
79. 113. 1/1869. Ministry 17/5/1869
79. 651. 5/1869. Dante 29/5/1869
80. 257. 8/1869. Irish Church 12/8/1869
81. 86. 1/1870. Robert Lee 4/1/1870
97. 548. 5/1878. Origen & Celsus 19/5/1878
100. 1. 7/1879. Government 22/7/1879
101. 421. 3/1880. Elections 3/3/1880
101. 837. 6/1880. Government 29/6/1880
Fraticelli, Pietro J.
Storia della vita di Dante Alighieri, compilata... sui documenti in parte raccolti da G. Pelli in parte inediti. 1861 11/1/88
Frederick William, Prince later William I
Glaubensbekenntniss. 1858 9/1/59

Frederick William I
The emperor's diary. 1888 23/10/88
Free Church of Scotland Assembly Address. 1845 17/7/45
Freeland, Humphry William
Lectures and miscellanies. 1857 1/8/63
On the reduction of the Continental armies... Translated... by H. W. Freeland. 1875 7/12/75
Freeman, Edward Augustus
Comparative politics. Six lectures... With The Unity of History, the Rede Lecture read before the University of Cambridge, May 29, 1872. 1874 5/6/74, 25/9/76
Historical essays. 1871 (4v. 1871–92) 28/5/92 ?
History of the cathedral church of Wells, as illustrating the history of the cathedral churches of the old foundation. 1870 28/1/77
Sketches from the subject and neighbour lands of Venice... With illustrations. 1881 23/11/81
The growth of the English Constitution from the earliest times. 1872 26/4/72
The Ottoman power in Europe, its nature, its growth, and its decline. 1877 23/11/77
Freeman, Joseph John
The Kaffir War; a letter addressed to the Rt. Hon. Earl Grey... Secretary of State for the Colonies, containing remarks on the present war. 1851 27/3/51
Freeman, Philip
A plea for the education of the clergy, in a letter to the... Bishop of Exeter, and the clergy of the Diocese, lately assembled in Synod. 1851 21/3/52
The principles of divine service. An inquiry concerning... the Order for Morning and Evening Prayer, and... administration of the Holy Communion. 1855 (2v. 1855–62) 20/1/56, 24/8/62
Thoughts on the proposed Dissolution... By a member of the Committee. 1845 29/5/45
Freeman, Strickland
The art of horsemanship, altered and abbreviated, according to the principles of the late Sir S. Medows. 1806 19/1/77
Freer, Martha Walker
The life of Marguerite d'Angoulême, Queen of Navarre... from numerous unpublished sources. 1854 (2v.) 26/6/57
Free thoughts on the Ministry. A letter. 1838 11/5/38
Fremantle, Sir Arthur James Lyon G. C. M. G.
Three months in the Southern States, April-June 1863. 1863 2/1/64
Fremantle, William Henry Dean of Ripon
Lay power in the parishes, the most needed Church Reform. 1869 15/8/69
The world as the subject of redemption.... Eight lectures delivered... on the foundation of... J. Bampton. 1885 8/2/85
French, Gilbert J.
The life and times of Samuel Crompton, inventor of the spinning machine called the Mule. 1859 4/10/59
French, J. W.
Practical ethics. 1865 22/1/65
French, R. C.
Genoveva. A poem. 1843 2/9/44 ?
French, William Master of Jesus College, Cambridge
A new translation of the Book of Psalms... by W. French and G. Skinner. 1842 (2nd edn) 30/10/43
French Protestant Pastor
The Anglican bishopric at Jerusalem. 1843 11/4/43
Frere, Sir Henry Bartle Edward
Indian missions. The church and the age. 1870 24/9/76
Frere, John
The docrine of imposition of lands. 1845 6/4/45
Frere, John Hookham
Aristophanes. A metrical version of the Acharnians, the Knights, and the Birds. 1840 8/1/73
The works of J. H. F. in verse and prose, now first collected; with a prefatory memoir by... W. E. and Sir B. Frere. 1872 (2v.) 15/12/71
Freytag, Gustav
Debit and credit. A novel... tr. from the original ... by Mrs. Malcolm. 1857 (2v.) 13/3/58
Gustav Freytag. Sein Leben und Schaffen von C. Alberti. 1886 24/10/90
Pictures of German life in the xvth, xvith, and xviith centuries.... Translated fromthe original by Mrs. Malcolm. 1862 (2v.) 13/8/73
Friedlieb, Joseph Heinrich
Oracula Sibyllina... recensuit,... illustravit... J. H. F. 1852 14/5/59
Friedrich, J. B.
Die realien der Iliade und Odyssee. 1851 10/6/57
Friedrich, Johann Professor
Documenta ad illustrandum Concilium Vaticanum anni 1870. 1871 (2v.) 27/11/74
Gott meine eingige Hoffnung. 1873 30/9/74
Friese, Philip C.
Semitic philosophy. 1890 28/8/92
Frilley, G., and Vlahoviće, Jovan
Le Monténégro contemporain. 1870 10/4/77
Frohschammer, Jakob
Das neue Wissen und der neue Glaube. Mit besonderer Berücksichtung von D. F. Strauss' neuester Schrift: 'Der alte und der neue Glaube'. 1873 4/9/73

Frohschammer, Jakob (*cont.*)
Der Fels Petri in Rom. Beleuchtung des Fundamentes der römischen Papstherrschaft. 1873 23/11/73
The Romance of Romanism. A discovery and a criticism ... A translation of 'Der Fels Petri', 'Der Primat Petri'. 1878 7/8/78
Frölich, Count David
Sketch of a plan for the reform of the laws and regulations respecting money and currency. 1855 21/9/55
Frost, Thomas
Forty years' recollections: literary and political. 1880 30/9/80
The life of Thomas, Lord Lyttelton. 1876 3/10/76
Froude, James Anthony
History of England from the fall of Wolsey to the death of Elizabeth. 1856 (12v. 1856–70) 23/5/56, 20/9/58, 14/5/60, 10/11/63, 23/1/64, 21/9/66, 8/12/69, 12/5/93
Inaugural address delivered to the University of St. Andrews, March 19, 1869. 1869 30/3/69
Letters and memorials of Jane Welsh Carlyle, edited by J. A. Froude. 1883 (3v.) 3/4/83
Lord Beaconsfield. 1890 5/7/90, 25/10/90
Short studies on great subjects. 1867 (2v.) 22/9/67
The divorce of Catherine of Aragon. 1891 12/5/93
The English in Ireland in the eighteenth century. 1872 (3v. 1872–74) 25/11/72, 25/3/86, 29/3/86, 23/3/87
The English in the West Indies; or, the Bow of Ulysses ... With illustrations ... by the author. 1888 27/8/88
The nemesis of faith. 1849 11/4/49
The science of history. Lecture. (not found) 5/2/64
Thomas Carlyle: a history of the first forty years of his life. 1882 (2v.) 2/4/82, 27/5/82, 3/6/82, 22/10/84
Froude, Richard Hurrell
Remains of the late Rev. R. H. Froude, ed. J. H. Newman and J. Keble. 1838 (2v. 1838–39) 15/3/38, 28/3/40
State interference in matters spiritual. A reprint from a work entitled: 'Remains of R. H. F.' With a preface by W. J. E. Bennett. 1869 19/10/69
Fry, Alfred Augustus
A lecture on Lord Macaulay ... delivered at Constantinople. 1861 9/11/64
Fry, Caroline afterw. Wilson
The Listener in Oxford. 1840 18/2/44
Fry, Mrs. Elizabeth
Observations on the visiting, superintendence and government of female prisoners. 1827 9/1/31
Fry, Henry Phibbs
An appeal to the ... bishop of Sydney ... against the condemnation pronounced upon Dr. Fry and other clergymen. 1856 22/3/68 ?
Fry, Herbert editor
Our schools and colleges. Containing the principal particulars respecting endowed Grammar Schools, ... as also ... respecting colleges and universities. 1867 22/6/68 ?
Fry, Thomas Charles
A social policy for Churchmen. 1892 11/12/92
Fryer, Alfred of Manchester
The sugar duties. An examination of the letter addressed by E. Potter to the Rt. Hon. W. E. Gladstone. 1864 16/2/64
Fugger-Gloett, Count Hermann Joseph von
Warum sind wir Römisch-Katholisch?. 1874 23/9/74
Fulcher, George Williams
Life of Thomas Gainsborough ... by G. W. Fulcher, edited by his son. 1856 10/6/70
Fullarton, Ralph W. Macleod
Tannhäuser. 1893 29/12/92
Fuller, Francis
Plan for opening and developing the Alexandra Park and Palace, and employing their resources and capabilities for the benefit of the public. 1870 13/1/77
Shall we spend £100,000 on a Winter-Garden for London, or in endowing schools of design in Birmingham, Manchester. A letter. 1851 20/5/69
Fuller, John Mee
The student's commentary on the Holy Bible. Founded on the Speaker's Commentary. 1879 7/4/82
Fuller, Morris Joseph
Pan-Anglicanism: what is it? or, the Church of the Reconciliation. 1889 23/6/89
The Court of Final Appeal: or, the appellate jurisdiction of the Crown in ecclesiastical cases. 1865 28/5/65
The Lord's day; or, Christian Sunday: its unity, history, philosophy, and perpetual obligation. 1883 11/5/84
Throne of Canterbury, or the archibishop's jurisdiction. 1891 28/6/91
Fuller, Thomas D.D.
A comment on the eleven first verses of the fourth chapter of S. Matthews Gospel, concerning Christ's temptations. Delivered in XII sermons. 31/10/80
Good thoughts in bad times, consisting of personall meditations; Scripture observations, Historicall applications; Mixt contemplations. 17/7/70
The church-history of Britain; from the birth of Jesus Christ, untill the year 1648. 19/3/39
Fullerton, Lady Georgiana Charlotte
A will and a way. 1881 (3v.) 6/9/81

Ellen Middleton, a tale. 1844 (3v.) 8/5/44, 7/7/88, 29/12/89
Grantley Manor. A tale. 1847 (3v.) 26/6/47
La Comtesse de Bonneval, histoire du temps de Louis XIV... Précédée d'une introduction par P. Douhaire. 1857 16/8/57
Life of Lady Georgiana Fullerton, by P. M.A. A. Craven. 1888 7/7/88
Life of Marchessa Guilia Falletti di Barolo. 1866 9/9/66
The Gold-Digger and other verses. 1872 5/1/72
The life of Luisa de Carvajal. 1873 (2nd edn 1881) 6/11/81, 22/1/82

Fullom, Stephen Watson
The mystery of the soul: a search into man's origin, nature, and destiny. 1865 24/12/65

'Fundamental reform of the Church Establishment' 1836 21/2/36

Furness, William Henry D.D.
The Declaration of Independence. A discourse. 1862 25/1/62

Fustel de Coulanges, Numa Denis
La cité antique. 1871 16/6/92

Fyfe, Alexander Gordon
Suggestions for separating the culture of sugar from the process of manufacture; with a plan for establishing a central sugar factory at Annotto Bay. 1846 12/5/46

G., C. W.
Two decades and a lustrum. [Reflections on historical events, 1850–75, in verse and prose]. 1875 8/8/78

Gabell, I. H. L.
The accordance of religion with nature. 1842 10/1/64

Gage, Henry Hall Viscount Gage
The question of marriage with sister of a deceased wife. 1860 24/2/61

Gagneur, L.
Une dévote fin de siècle. 1891 10/9/92

Gairdner, Sir William Tennant K. C. B.
On medicine and medical education. Three lectures, with notes and an appendix. 1858 4/5/60

Galbraith, T.
New monetary theory the absolute depreciation of gold demonstrated to the extent of fifty percent. 1863 11/11/63

Gale, Charles James
A letter to the earl of Dalhousie on railway legislation. 1844 21/3/44

Gall, James the younger
Immediate salvation for the chief of sinners: or, a practical guide for anxious inquirers. 1864 15/4/92
Instant salvation by the instant acceptance of a mediator and surety. 1864 26/6/70

Gallenga, Antonio Carlo Napoleone pseud. L. Mariotti
A historical memoir of Fra Doliuno. 1853 15/1/54, 27/3/59
Italy in 1848. 1851 12/5/52
Italy revisited. 1875 (2v.) 15/1/76

Gallwey, Peter
Apostolic succession. A handbook. 1889 (2nd edn) 25/12/89

Gallwey, Thomas
Short essays on the Irish Established Church. 1869 16/1/69

Galt, Sir Alexander Tilloch
Canada: 1849 to 1859. 1860 17/1/60

Galt, William
Railway reform: its expediency and practicability considered. 1843 8/8/43
Railway reform: its importance and practicability considered as affecting the nation, the shareholders, and the government. 1865 8/9/64, 13/1/65

Galton, Arthur
The character and times of Thomas Cromwell: a sixteenth century criticism. 1887 27/6/87

Gambardella, Spiridione
What shall we do with the glass palace? A letter addressed to the Commissioners of the Great Exhibition. 1851 8/7/51

Gamber, Eli
Le moribond de l'Europe. Ancienne complainte. 1865 10/10/77

Games, Joshua Hughes né Jones
The one book. 1892 25/9/92

Gammon, Frederic T.
Cyprus: its history and prospects. 1878 8/6/80 ?

Gamon, John
The consistory court of Chester, its practice, fees, etc., with some remarks on ecclesiastical courts. 1877 3/4/77

Gandy, Henry
Old England, or the government of England proved to be monarchical and hereditary. 1705 20/2/80

Garanties du Sainte-Siège. 26/9/61

Garbett, James Archdeacon of Chichester
A charge delivered... at Chichester, and... at Storrington. 1854 4/12/54
A review of Dr. Pusey's sermon; and the doctrine of the eucharist according to the Church of England. 1843 29/10/43
De re critica praelectiones Oxonii habitae. 1847 1/2/48
Diocesan synods and convocation. A charge, delivered to the clergy... of the Archdeaconry of Chichester. 1852 8/2/52
Dr. Pusey and the University of Oxford. A letter to the Vice Chancellor of the university. 1843 14/9/43

Garbett, James Archdeacon of Chichester (*cont.*)
Is unauthorized teaching always schismatical? A sermon preached before the University of Oxford. 1844 31/5/44
Popery and infidelity in the last times. A sermon. 1847 23/11/47
The church and the age. A sermon preached before the Diocesan Association. 1851 15/2/52
The offices of the holy spirit. A sermon. 1846 12/7/46
The sense, the mind, and the spirit. A sermon. 1844 23/6/44
The temple better than the gold. A sermon. 1844 18/2/44
The university, the church, and the new test. With remarks on Mr. Oakeley's and Mr. Gresley's pamphlets. A letter to the Bishop of Chichester. 1845 28/1/45
What kind of synod does the Church of England require? A letter to the Lord Bishop of Chichester. 1853 29/5/53

Garden, Francis Lord Gardenstone
Travelling Memorandums made in a tour upon the continent of Europe in the years 1786, 87, 88. 1791 (3v. 1791–95) 20/9/44

Garden, Rev. Francis
[Scottish communion office]. (not found) 4/1/46
Can an ordained man become a layman? Some remarks on Mr. Hibbert's bill, now before the House of Commons. 1870 8/5/70
Vindication of the Scottish Episcopate and those adhering thereto. 1847 5/4/47

Gardiner, Sir Robert William G. C. B.
Military analysis of the remote and proximate causes of the Indian Rebellion, drawn from official papers on the government of India. 1858 29/3/58
Political and legislative considerations on national defence: addressed to the people of England. 1860 23/1/60
Question of legislative military responsibility. 1857 (2nd edn) 4/5/57
Report on the numerical deficiency, want of instruction, and inefficient equipment of the Artillery of the British Army. 1848 24/6/48

Gardiner, S. R.
Address at Bangor. 1891 31/8/91 ?

Gardner, John Dunn
The Ionian Islands in relation to Greece, with suggestions for advancing our trade with the Turkish countries of the Adriatic and the Danube. 1859 12/2/77

Garfit, Arthur
The conscience clause and the extension of education in the neglected districts. 1868 28/2/68

Garibaldi, Gen. Giuseppe
Clelia. Il Governo del Monaco. Roma nel secolo XIX. Romanzo storico politico. 1870 4/5/70

Garnerius, Joannes
De causa Honorii Summi Pontificis et VI Synodi. 28/10/55

Garnett, F. E.
In Afrikanderland. 1891 23/11/91

Garrick, David
The life of David Garrick, by P. H. Fitzgerald. 1868 (2v.) 17/9/87

Gartshore, Mrs. Murray
Cleveland, a tale of the Catholic church. 1847 24/7/47, 12/12/83

Gaskell, Elizabeth Cleghorn
Cranford. 1853 4/1/75
Mary Barton: a tale of Manchester life. 1848 (2v.) 28/4/49
North and South. 1855 11/11/63
The life of Charlotte Brontë. 1857 (2v.) 27/4/57

Gaskell, J. Milnes
Records of an Eton schoolboy. 1883 23/10/83, 26/11/83

Gaskell, P.
Artisans and machinery: the moral and physical condition of the manufacturing population considered with reference to mechanical substitutes. 1836 13/4/37

Gaskell, William
Strong points of Unitarian Christianity: a lecture. 1873 29/12/72

Gasparin, Count Agénor Étienne de
Après la paix: considérations sur le libéralisme et la guerre d'Orient. 1856 27/3/56
La république neutre d'Alsace. 1870 11/8/70 ?
The uprising of a great people. The United States in 1861 . . . From the French . . . By M. L. Booth. 1861 7/8/61

Gasquet, Francis Aidan Cardinal
Edward VI and the Book of Common Prayer. 1890 6/11/90, 1/2/91, 12/7/91, 2/8/91
Henry VIII and the English Monasteries. An attempt to illustrate the history of their suppression. 1888 (2v. 1888–89) 11/3/88

Gass, W.
Symbolik der griechischen Kirche. 1872 5/3/76

Gassiot, John P.
Monetary panics and their remedy, with opinions of the highest authorities on the Bank Charter Act. 1867 (2nd edn) 4/2/67
Second letter to J. A. Roebuck . . . With an analysis of the divisions in the House of Commons during the last session of parliament. 1856 8/4/56

Gattina, Petruccelli della
Histoire diplomatique. 1864 (4v. 1864–66) 26/3/77

Gatty, Alfred
Church and state. A sermon [on Matth. ii. 11]. 1869 21/2/69
Gaume, Jean Joseph
Life of the good thief. From the French... Done into English by M. de Lisle. 1882 21/5/82
Où en sommes-nous? Études sur les évènements actuels 1870 et 1871. 1871 28/10/71
Gauntlett, Anne
Dissolving views. 1849 28/6/84
Gaussen, Samuel Robert Louis
Théopneustie, ou inspiration plénière des Saintes Écritures. 1842 (2nd edn) 2/1/81
Gay, John poet
Poems on several occasions. 1720 24/2/62 ?
Gayarré, Charles
Louisiana; its colonial history and romance. 1851 5/6/85 ?
Geale, Hamilton
Ernesto di Ripalta: a tale of the Italian Revolution. 1849 (3v.) 5/9/51
Gee, Richard Vicar
'From Sunday to Sunday.' An attempt to consider familiarly the weekday life and labours of a country clergyman. 1865 10/12/70
Geffcken, Friedrich Heinrich
Church and State: their relations historically developed... Translated and edited with the assistance of the author by E. F. Taylor. 1876 (2v.) 13/3/77
The British empire, with essays on Prince Albert, Lord Palmerston, Lord Beaconsfield, Mr. Gladstone, and reform of the House of Lords. 1889 15/4/93
Geikie, John Cunningham
Hours with the Bible; or, the Scriptures in the light of modern discovery and knowledge... With illustrations. 1881 18/12/81, 11/6/82
Gell, John Philip
Church ministry in Kensington. 1867 24/11/67
Gell, Sir William
Itinerary of Greece... and an account of Argolis. 1810 27/12/55
The geography and antiquities of Ithaca. 1807 15/10/88
The topography of Troy and its vicinity, illustrated and explained by drawings and descriptions. 1804 10/8/55
Gemariah, Amos
Vampires of the Church of England. 1890 19/10/90
Gems from the poets, illustrated. The designs by F. A. Lydon. Printed in colours from wood blocks. 1858 (1858-60) 28/9/60
Gemuenden, G. P. von
Die Weltgeschichte chronologisch-synchronistisch dargestellt. 1806 12/7/84
Genealogist. 9. 153. 1/1893. Gledstanes of Coklaw 31/10/1893
General description of the Britannia and Conway Tubular bridges on the Chester and Holyhead Railway. 1849 14/9/49
Génin, François
Les Jésuites et l'université. 1844 24/10/45 ?
Lettres de Marguerite d'Angoulême. 1841 13/6/50
Genlis, Stéphanie Félicité Brulant de
Vie pénitente de Madame de la Vallière. 1807 17/7/53
Gentleman's Magazine. 23. 278, 291, 351, 467-81. on Jews 16/1/1841
Geoffrey of Monmouth
Historia regum Britanniae, ed. J. A. Giles. (new edn 1844) 23/8/59
George, Henry
Progress and poverty: an inquiry into the cause of industrial depressions and of increase of want with increase of wealth. 1880 11/11/79, 4/10/83, 13/12/83, 27/12/83
Georgini, G. B.
Sui dominio temporale dei Papi. Considerazione. 1865 21/5/65 ?
Gerard, Dorothea afterw. Longard de Longgarde
Orthodox. 1888 14/3/89, 25/2/93
Gerard, G. poet
Grace and remembrance: poems. 1856 23/4/57
Géraud, P.
l'Unitéisme, religion universelle. 1882 11/2/83
Gerbet, Olympe Philippe Bishop of Perpignan
Considération sur le dogme générateur. 1829 27/10/50
Consideration on the eucharist. 1839 9/2/45
Gerhard, Eduard
Griechische mythologie. 1854 (4v.) 20/11/67
Germs of Romanism. 1874 3/5/74
Gerson, J. Charlier de
De potestate ecclesiae. 3/2/75
Sermon inédit... sur le retour des Grecs à l'unité. 1859 13/11/59
Gervinus, Georg Gottfried
Die Mission der Deutsch-Katholiken. 1845 8/12/45
Gesner, Johann Matthias
Socrate et l'amour grec. Dissertation... Traduite en français pour la première fois. Texte latin en regard, par A. Bonneau. 1877 15/10/79
Gesner, Salomon
Life of Salomon Gesner. 3/10/25
Giannone, Pietro
Professione di fede. 1730 27/6/53
Gibbings, Richard
Report of the trial... of P. Carnesecchi... Edited, with an English translation. 1856 30/11/56

Gibbings, Richard (*cont.*)
Roman forgeries and falsifications: or, an examination of counterfeit and corrupt records: with especial reference to Popery. 1842 22/10/43
Gibbins, Henry de Beltgens
The industrial history of England . . . with maps. 1890 23/9/90
Gibbon, Alexander
Taxation: its nature and properties. With remarks on the incidence and the expediency of the Repeal of the Income Tax. 1851 1/9/51
Gibbon, Edward
A vindication of some passages in the fifteenth and sixteenth chapters of the History of the Decline and Fall of the Roman Empire. 1779 13/7/63
Memoirs composed by himself. 1827 (2v.) 11/9/65
The decline and fall of the Roman empire, ed. H. H. Milman. (12v. 1838–9) 19/7/41
The history of the decline and fall of the Roman empire. 1821 (12v. 1821–27) 14/10/25, 26/10/25, 26/11/25, 5/12/25, 12/3/27, 7/5/27, 26/5/27, 14/6/27, 19/5/29, 17/1/34, 12/5/34, 11/4/88
The history of the decline and fall of the Roman empire, abridged by J. Adams. 1789 (2v.) 21/1/31
The life of E. Gibbon, esq. With selections from his correspondence and illustrations by H. H. Milman. 1839 6/6/90
Gibbs, Edward J.
Parliamentary reform, considered as a question of principle and not of party. 1867 11/5/67
The County Franchise and rural municipalities. 1876 1/6/76
Gibbs, Frederick Waymouth
English law and Irish tenure. 1870 7/2/70
Recognition: a chapter from the history of the North American and South American states. 1863 27/6/63
The foreign enlistment act. 1863 17/11/63
Gibbs, W. A.
Harold Erle. A biography. 1871 27/2/71
Gibson, Edmund Bishop of Lincoln
Codex juris ecclesiastici Anglicani. 1713 28/12/39, 3/6/50
Synodus Anglicana: or the constitution and proceedings of an English Convocation shown . . . to be agreeable to the principles of an episcopal church. 1702 25/12/39, 17/10/52
The Bishop of London's pastoral letter to the people of his diocese . . . occasion'd by our present dangers . . . With a postscript. 1745 1/8/52 ?
Gibson, James Professor
Some brief conclusions, historical, scriptural, legal, and moral, against the marriage of a man with the sister of a deceased wife. 1855 15/4/55
Gibson, Thomas Ellison
Crosby records; a cavalier's notebook: being notes . . . of William Blundell, ed. T. E. Gibson. 1880 15/3/82
Lydiate Hall and its associations. 1876 2/11/76
Gibson, W.
Poems of many places. 1881 18/11/81
Gibson, William Sidney
'The renaissance at Alnwick' in *Lectures and essays on various subjects, historical, topographical, and artistic*. 1858 25/2/72
Gideon; 'The mighty man of valour'. 1839 2/6/39
Giffen, Sir Robert K. C. B.
[articles on Ireland] *in Nineteenth Century*, xix.329. 1886 (March 1886) 27/2/86
Essays in finance. 1880 (2nd series) 10/1/80, 13/12/88
Gladstone's work in finance. 1869 8/1/69
Recent changes in prices and incomes compared. 1888 2/3/88
The growth of capital. 1889 13/5/90
Gifford, John [John Richards Green]
A history of the political life of W. Pitt; including some account of the times in which he lived. 1809 (3v.) 27/3/68
Political life of W. Pitt, the younger. 1809 (6v.) 21/8/33
Gifford, Richard Rector
Outlines of an answer to Dr. Priestley's disquisitions relating to matter and spirit. 1781 28/8/76
Gifford, William editor
The Baviad and Maeviad. 1794 25/1/27, 6/12/62
The satires of A. Persius Flaccus translated into English verse by W. G. 1821 13/11/28
The satires of D. J. Juvenalis translated into English verse by W. G . . . with notes and illustrations. 1802 7/11/28
Gilbart, James William
The elements of banking. 1852 30/3/54, 10/12/60
The history and principles of banking. 1834 4/2/56, 19/11/63
The history of banking in America: with an inquiry how far the banking institutions of America are adapted to this country. 1837 16/2/61
Gilbart, Thomas
The Reformation from Popery, the work of God. A sermon [on Exod. viii. 19], preached . . . December 28, 1817. 1818 24/6/66
Gilbert, Ashhurst Turner Bishop of Chichester
A pastoral letter . . . to the clergy and laity of the diocese of Chichester. 1843 13/11/43
Charge. (not found) 20/7/45

Gilbert, Sir John Thomas
A Jacobite narrative of the war in Ireland, 1688–1691 with contemporary letters and papers, ed. Sir J. T. Gilbert. 1892 11/6/92
Documents relating to Ireland 1795–1804. 1893 18/1/93
History of the Irish confederation and the war in Ireland... Edited by J. T. Gilbert. 1882 (7v. 1882–91) 11/1/81

Gilbert, Joseph Congregational divine
The Christian atonement, its basis, nature, and bearings... With notes and illustrations. 1834 22/10/53

Gilbert, William novelist
Contrasts. Dedicated to the ratepayers of London. 1873 28/6/73
Disestablishment from a church point of view. 1875 10/11/75

Gilchrist, Mrs. Anne
Mary Lamb. 1883 27/1/89

Gilderdale, John Smith
Disciplina Rediviva: or, hints and helps for youths leaving school. 1856 25/12/56

Gilfillan, George
Alpha and omega; or, a series of scripture studies. 1860 (2v.) 14/4/67
The bards of the bible. 1852 11/9/90

Gill, Henry Galloway
The pretensions of ultramontanism. 1873 28/9/73

Gill, Lady Isobel
Six months in Ascension. An unscientific account of a scientific expedition. 1878 23/11/78

Gill, Thomas Hornblower
A letter... touching ritualism. 1878 21/4/78
The anniversaries. Poems in commemoration of great men and great events. 1858 22/10/58

Gillane, John
The life of... J. Sage. 1714 7/10/48

Gillies, Hugh Cameron
The meaning of pain. 1891 15/11/91 ?

Gillies, John LL.D.
Aristotle's Ethics and Politics... translated... Illustrated by introductions and notes... By J. G. 1797 3/10/35

Gilliland, Mary S.
The future of morality as affected by the decay of prevalent religious beliefs. 1887 1/7/88 ?

Gillis, James Bishop of Limyra
A discourse [on Matt. xvi. 13] on the mission and influence of the Popes. 1850 21/3/51
A letter to... D. Maclaren, Lord Provost of Edinburgh, on the proposed 'Voluntary' amendment of the Lord Advocate's Educational Bill for Scotland. 1854 4/4/54
Report of foundation of Edinburgh Holy Guild of St. Joseph Friendly Society. (not found) 27/2/43

Gillmor, William
The Public Worship Regulation Act. Two sermons [on Titus i. 5]. 1875 26/3/75

Gillow, Joseph
A literary and biographical history, or bibliographical dictionary of the English Catholics; from the breach with Rome in 1534 to the present time. 1885 (4v. 1885–95) 14/5/88
The Haydock papers: a glimpse into English Catholic life under the shade of persecution and in the dawn of freedom. 1888 24/10/88 ?

Gilman, A.
The story of the nations. 1885 7/12/87

Gilmore, James R. pseud. Edmund Kirke
Among the pines; or, South in Secession-time. 1865 (1862?) 28/11/62
My Southern friends. 1863 1/8/63

Gilpin, William Prebendary of Salisbury
The life of B. Gilpin, collected from his life, written by G. Carleton. 1753 (2nd edn) 16/8/29, 4/10/85

Ginsburg, Christian David
The Essenes; their history and doctrines. An essay, reprinted from the Transactions of the Literary and Philosophical Society of Liverpool. 1864 25/1/91

Gioanetti, Victor Aimé
Discorso sulla fabbrica di porcellana stabilita in Vinovo. 1859 14/7/59

Gioberti, Vincenzo
Il Gesuita moderno. 1846 (5v. 1846–47) 4/5/48, 28/1/50
Opere. 1856 16/11/56, 23/11/56

Girard, Jean Baptiste
The case of M. K. Cadière against... J. B. G. 1731 17/11/61

Girard, Jules Augustin
Le sentiment religieux en Grèce, d'Homère à Eschyle, étudié dans son développement moral, et dans son caractère dramatique. 1869 9/11/74

Girard, L. Dominique
Hydraulique appliquée. Chemin de fer glissant, nouveau système de locomotion. 1864 14/11/64

Girardin, Emile de
L'Empereur Napoléon III et l'Europe. 1859 12/8/59
La question du moment... la republique, est-elle audessus du suffrage universel?. 1850 19/5/64

Giraud, Pierre
Manuel de principales dévotions et confréries auxquelles sont attachées des indulgences. 1844 16/11/47

Girdlestone, Charles
'Dissenting Churches', from The questions of the day by the creature of an hour. 1857 20/12/63

Girdlestone, Charles (*cont.*)
A course of sermons for the year. 1834 (2v.) 29/6/34
A letter on church reform addressed to the Regius Professor of Divinity in the University of Oxford, with one remark on the plan of Lord Henley. 1832 16/1/33
A second letter on church reform, in justification of church reformers; with a proposal for the abolition of pluralities. 1833 18/1/33
Affection between the church and the dissenters. A sermon, on Luke ix.49, 50. 1833 7/2/33
God's word and ministers. A sermon [on 2 Tim. iii. 16, 17] preached... at the... visitation of the... Bishop of Chester. 1838 17/2/39
Number: a link between divine intelligence and human. An argument. 1875 10/8/77
Seven sermons on the course of the Christian life. 1823 27/1/33
Seven sermons on the Lord's supper: with appropriate devotions. 1833 19/1/34
The increase of mankind a blessing. A sermon preached... on the occasion of the present disturbances in the manufacturing districts. 1842 25/9/42
The judgment of Solomon, applied to the question of educating the children employed in factories and mines. A sermon [on 1 Kings iii.27]. 1843 8/5/43
The questions of the day by the creature of an hour; or social subjects discussed on scripture principles. 1859 (new edn) 28/2/69 ?
Twenty parochial sermons, with an appendix containing parochial papers. 1832 23/4/31
Girdlestone, Edward
The Committee of Council on Education: an imaginary enemy, a real friend. 1850 16/3/50
The education question. 1852 12/3/52
Girdlestone, Robert Baker
The foundations of the Bible: studies in Old Testament criticism. 1891 (2nd edn) 8/2/91
Gisborne, Thomas the elder
A familiar survey of the Christian religion, and of history as connected with the introduction of Christianity, and with its progress to the present. 1799 27/1/28
The principles of moral philosophy investigated, and applied to the constitution of civil society. 1789 2/9/31
Gisborne, Thomas the younger
Essays on agriculture. 1854 10/7/54
On the present crisis. Mr. G.'s address to the electors of North Derbyshire. 1834 27/12/34
Gissing, George Robert
The unclassed. A novel. 1884 (3v.) 3/9/87
Thyrza. 1887 (3v.) 17/10/87
Giusti, Giuseppe
Poesie... Illustrate con vignette da A. Matarelli e commentate da un condiscepolo dell'autore. 1868 (1868–78) 14/9/68
Gladstone, Florence M.
'The Gledstanes of Gledstanes and Coklaw, 1296–1741' *The Genealogist.* 1893 31/10/93
Gladstone, George F.R.G.S.
The Irish church bill: considered in a series of letters. 1869 31/5/69
Gladstone, Sir John
A statement of facts connected with the present state of slavery in the British sugar and coffee colonies, and in the United States of America. 1830 12/12/30, 18/12/30
Plain facts intimately connected with the intended repeal of the Corn Laws: or probable effects on the public revenue and the prosperity of [England]. 1846 22/2/46 n
The repeal of the Corn Laws... considered. 1839 1/2/39
Gladstone, John Neilson
A sermon and a short memoir of J. N. Gladstone, by H. A. Merewether. 1863 29/3/63
GLADSTONE, William Ewart
See Subject Index, 'publications', for Gladstone's books and periodical articles, and 'letters and articles for the press' for his journalism.
Gladstone, William Henry
A selection of hymns and tunes made and arranged by W. H. Gladstone. 1882 9/12/88
On purity in musical art, by A. F. J. Thibaut, tr. W. H. Gladstone. 1877 14/9/84
Glascock, William Nugent
Naval sketch-book.... By an officer of rank. 1826 4/4/26
Glass, Charles E.
Advance thought. 1876 5/11/76
Glassford, James
Lyrical compositions selected from the Italian poets: with translations. 1846 (2nd edn) 12/9/62
Glasson, Ernest Désiré
Histoire du droit et des institutions politiques, civiles et judiciaires de l'Angleterre comparés au droit et aux institutions de la France. 1881 (6v. 1881–83) 13/2/83
Gleig, George Robert
A narrative of the campaigns of the British army at Washington, and New Orleans, under Generals Ross, Pakenham and Lambert, in the years 1814 and 1815. 1821 8/11/47
Directions for the study of theology. 1827 11/4/58 ?
Story of the battle of Waterloo. 1847 6/10/47
The constitution of the Scotch Episcopal Church, precisely stated, in a charge. 1829 29/8/44
The history of the British Empire in India. 1830 (4v. 1830–35) 2/12/57

The life of Major-General Sir T. Munro, Bart... late Governor of Madras. With extracts from his correspondence and private papers. 1830 (3v.) 8/5/58
The subaltern. 1825 13/1/92
Glennie, John Stuart Stuart
Europe and Asia. Discussions of the Eastern Question in travels through independent, Turkish, and Austrian Illyria. 1879 8/7/79
Gloag, Paton James
Closing address of Rev. P. J. Gloag, D.D., Moderator of the General Assembly of the Church of Scotland, 1889. 1889 6/4/90
Introduction to the Pauline Epistles. 1874 9/2/75
Glover, Frederick Robert Augustus
Ecclesia et Synodus: or, the church's claim for self-deliberation; being a series of letters on this subject. 1837 18/4/38
Queen Anne's bounty. What is Queen Anne's bounty?... With reference to the acts and neglects of the Ecclesiastical Commission. 1839 14/2/40
Reduction of prebendaries, being portion of a series of papers entitled, What will the church say to the suggestions of the Ecclesiastical Commission?. 1837 11/2/40
Gneist, Heinrich Rudolph von
Englische Verfassungsgeschichte. 1882 13/2/83
Goalen, Alexander
Four sermons on the 'Comfortable words' in the office for the holy communion. 1860 5/8/60
Goalen, Walter
Gideon, a poem. 1868 18/4/69
Goblet, Eugène Count d'Alviella
L'évolution religieuse. 1844 12/10/84
Godard, John George
Poverty, its genesis and exodus. An inquiry into the causes and the method of their removal. 1891 25/11/91
Godconton, R.
[Remarks ... on narrative ... of ... hordes]. 1835 (not found) 19/2/36
Goddard, Charles Archdeacon of Lincoln
The ordination service, in reference to candidates for orders, explained and defended. 1846 4/4/46
Goddard, Julia Bachope
Psychologus: the story of a soul. 1887 21/4/87
Godkin, James
A guide from the Church of Rome to the church of Christ. 1836 26/12/42 ?
Ireland and her churches. 1867 6/6/67, 23/3/68
Godley, John Robert
A selection from the writings and speeches of J. R. G., collected and edited by J. E. Fitzgerald. 1863 28/3/63
Extracts from Letters of John Robert Godley to C. B. Adderley [Edited by C. B. Adderley. With a portrait]. 1863 25/3/64
Letters from America. 1844 (2v.) 19/3/44
Observations on an Irish Poor Law. 1847 26/3/47
Godwin, George Editor of 'The Builder'
On the desirability of obtaining a National Theatre not wholly controlled by the prevailing popular taste. 1878 7/11/78
Godwin, William the Elder
Mandeville. A tale of the seventeenth century in England. 1817 (3v.) 12/12/92
Things as they are; or, the Adventures of Caleb Williams. 1794 (3v.) 1/11/44
Thoughts on man, his nature, productions and discoveries; interspersed with some particulars respecting the author. 1831 8/6/74
Goebel, C. C. T. F.
Handbuch der pharmaceutischen Chemie. 1840 26/6/68
Goethe, Johann Wolfgang von
Aus meinem Leben. 1811 (1811–22) 11/8/63
Bride of Corinth. (n.d.) 12/10/33, 10/12/45, 16/11/77
Characteristics of Goethe, by S. Austin. 1833 (3v.) 23/1/93 ?
Der fünfte Mai. Ode... in der italischen Urschrift nebst Uebersetzungen von Goethe, Fouqué, etc. [tr. of Manzoni's 'In morte di Napoleone ...']. 1828 6/2/88
Die Leiden des jungen Werthers. 1774 1/10/72, 7/10/72
Egmont, a tragedy [German Classics, edited by C. A. Buchheim, vol. 1]. 1869 27/4/69
Faust. 1808 (2 part 1808–32) 17/1/56, 27/10/58, 8/8/63, 25/8/63
Faust, tr. J. Anster. 1835 9/6/36
Faust, tr. J. Lee. 1887 2/2/87
Goetz of Berlichingen by J. W. von Goethe, translated by Walter Scott. 1799 3/11/68
Iphigenie auf Tauris. 1787 22/9/36
Opera. 19/8/33
Theilnahme an Manzoni. 1827 13/2/38
Wilhelm Meisters Lehrjahre. 1777 5/11/36, 10/11/36
Gogol, Nikolai Vasil'evich
The Inspector-General... A comedy... translated ... with introduction and notes, by A. A. Sykes. 1892 9/11/92
Goita, F.
Cuestión de Irlanda. 1891 (not found) 29/12/91
Goldbeck, Johann Christian
The metaphysics of man. 1806 14/4/91 ?
Goldoni, Carlo
La Bottega del caffè. 1755 (not found) 18/7/49
La Locandiera. Commedia. 1751 (not found) 23/10/60

Goldsmid, Sir Francis Henry Bart.
Reply to the arguments advanced against the removal of the remaining disabilities of the Jews. 1848 10/2/48
Goldsmith, Oliver the poet
The works of Oliver Goldsmith, ed. P. Cunningham. (4v. 1854) 6/1/55
A history of the earth and animated nature, etc. Preceded by a memoir of the author by J. F. Waller. 1876 25/1/76
An history of England, in a series of letters from a nobleman to his son [on Richard]. 1771 (2v. 1764) 5/4/28
Poems. 1786 13/9/80
She stoops to conquer: or, the mistakes of a night. A comedy. As it is acted at the Theatre-Royal in Covent-Garden. 1773 16/1/82
The life of Oliver Goldsmith, by T. Percy. 1801 30/11/57
The traveller, or a prospect of society. 1764 15/6/26
The Vicar of Wakefield. 1766 5/9/50, 4/11/67, 6/1/68
Goldziher, I.
Mythology among the Hebrews, tr. Russell Martineau. 1877 8/5/79
Golightly, Charles Portales
Brief remarks upon No. 90 [Tracts for the Times by J. H. Newman]. 1841 13/3/42
Golitsuin, Prince Nikolai Borisovich Prince Galitzin
Lettres à un ami sur l'office divin de l'église Catholique Orthodoxe d'Orient... Traduites du Russe par le Prince Nicolas Galitzin [by A. N. Murav'ev]. 1850 14/4/61
Gomme, Sir George Laurence ed.
The Gentleman's Magazine library. 1883 20/2/85
Goncourt, Edmond L. A. de, and Jules A. de
Gavarni. L'homme et l'oeuvre. 1873 19/12/73
Journal des Goncourts. Mémoires de la vie littéraire. 1887 (9v. 1887–96) 10/5/92
Gondon, Jules
A letter to the Rt. Hon. W. E. Gladstone, in answer to his two letters to the Earl of Aberdeen on the state prosecutions of the Neapolitan Government. 1851 1/10/51
Conversion de soixante ministres anglicans ou membres des Universités Anglaises et de cinquante personnes de distinction... Newman, Ward et Oakeley. 1847 (2nd edn) 29/4/47
De l'état des choses à Naples en Italie. 1855 18/2/56
De la réunion de l'église d'Angleterre-Protestante à l'église Catholique, par J. G... avec une introduction par Mgr Manning. 1867 21/6/57
Du mouvement religieux en Angleterre. 1844 5/10/44, 21/6/57
La terreur dans le royaume de Naples. Lettre au Rt. Hon. W. E. Gladstone... en réponse à ses deux lettres à Lord Aberdeen. 1851 27/1/52
Situation et affaires du royaume de Naples... nouvelle édition. 1857 4/7/57
Gooch, Mrs. Elizabeth Sarah
The life of Mrs. Gooch, written by herself. 1792 (3v.) 17/7/85
Goodchild, John Arthur
Somnia medici. In verse. 1884 (2v. 1884–87) 4/7/87
Goode, William Dean of Ripon
A defence of the thirty-nine articles as the legal and canonical test of doctrine in the Church of England... a reply to the Bishop of Exeter's remarks. 1848 12/5/48, 25/2/49
A letter to the Bishop of Exeter; containing an examination of his letter to the Archbishop of Canterbury. 1850 2/5/50
A supplement to his work on the eucharist; containing two letters of Bishop Geste... together with a reply to Dr. Pusey's Answer, and a few remarks. 1858 6/10/82
Altars prohibited by the Church of England. 1844 (2v.) 7/7/44
Review of the judgment of Sir H. J. Fust, kt., in the case of Gorham v. the Bishop of Exeter. 1850 25/2/50
Rome's tactics; or, a lesson for England from the past,... with a brief note of Rome's allies in the Church of England. 1867 17/3/67
The case as it is; or, a reply to the letter of Dr. Pusey to... the archbishop of Canterbury, including a... statement of the... views of the Tractators. 1842 13/12/42
Tract XC historically refuted; or, a reply to a work by the Rev. F. Oakeley, entitled 'The subject of Tract XC historically examined'. 1845 11/11/48
Goodhart, Charles Joseph
The lawfulness of marriage with a deceased wife's sister examined by scripture. In a letter to a friend. 1848 15/2/49
Goodman, Godfrey Bishop of Gloucester
The court of king James the first... To which are added letters illustrative of the personal history of the most distinguished characters in the court. 1839 (2v.) 2/7/45
Goodsir, Joseph Taylor
Seven homilies on ethnic inspiration; or on the evidence supplied by the pagan religions of both primaeval and later guidance and inspiration. 1871 29/1/71
Goodwin, Harvey Bishop of Carlisle
[on apparitions] in *Contemporary Review*, xlvi. 423. 1884 (September 1884) 4/9/84

A charge delivered... July, 1872. 1872 25/8/72
Essays on the Pentateuch. 1867 1/12/78
My second year. A pastoral letter to the clergy of the diocese of Carlisle. 1871 15/1/82
The first year of my episcopate. A pastoral letter. 1870 25/12/70
The foundations of the creed. 1889 3/11/89
Walks in the regions of science and faith. 1883 20/5/83

Gordon, Abercromby Lockhart
Sermon [on education]. 1839 17/2/39
The system of national education in Scotland... a report of a committee of the synod of Aberdeen. 1839 18/3/42

Gordon, Adam Lindsay
Ashtaroth; a dramatic lyric. By the author of 'Sea spray and smoke drift'. 1867 16/12/88

Gordon, Alexander author of 'Fish catching on the Dogger'
The folks o'Carglen: or, life in the north. 1891 1/8/91

Gordon, Alexander civil engineer
Observations addressed to those interested in either rail-ways or turnpike-roads. 1837 4/9/40

Gordon, Alexander writer on imperial federation
The future of the Empire; or, a brief statement of the case against imperial federation. 1889 30/4/89

Gordon, Arthur Hamilton Baron Stanmore
Fiji. An address before the Aberdeen Philosophical Society. 1878 17/3/79
The Aberdeen correspondence. [Letters and papers of Lord Aberdeen privately printed by A. H. Gordon]. (9v. 1846 ff.) 11/2/61
The Earl of Aberdeen. 1893 17/2/93
Wilderness journeys in New Brunswick. 1864 28/7/65

Gordon, Charles George Major-General
[on the Sudan] *in Pall Mall Gazette Extra N. 7.* 1884 (February 1884) 19/2/84
Letters of General C. G. Gordon to his sister M.A. Gordon. 1885 (2nd edn 1888) 25/3/88
Reflections in Palestine. 1883. 1884 27/4/84
The journals of Major-Gen. C. G. Gordon... at Kartoum. 1885 20/3/85

Gordon, George 1st Duke of Gordon
An account of the besieging of Edinburgh. 25/11/85

Gordon, George John James Hamilton 5th Earl of Aberdeen
Correspondence with Thomas Chalmers. 1840 27/6/40
Memoir of Lord Haddo, in his latter years fifth earl of Aberdeen. Edited by E. B. Elliott. 1867 (2nd edn) 13/12/65
The Aberdeen correspondence. [Letters and papers of Lord Aberdeen privately printed by A. H. Gordon]. (9v. 1846ff.) 11/2/61

Gordon, George John Robert
A new cathedral for Aberdeen. A letter to the... bishop of Aberdeen. 1861 8/9/61

Gordon, Hunter
The present state of controversy between the Protestant and Roman Catholic churches. 1837 19/5/39
The question of the Irish colleges shortly stated; with some observations on the validity of the rescripts relative to these institutions. 1849 2/6/49

Gordon, James Bentley
History of the Rebellion in Ireland... in 1798... with an appendix. 1801 6/5/89

Gordon, Osborne
Considerations on the improvement of the present examination statute, and the admission of poor scholars to the university. 1847 23/7/47

Gordon, Pryse Lockhart
Personal memoirs, or reminiscences of men and manners, at home and abroad, during the last half century. 1830 (2v.) 1/3/40

Gordon, Robert D.D.
Christ as made known to the ancient church; an exposition. 1854 (4v.) 5/4/68
Memorial addressed to the members of Her Majesty's Government by R. Gordon... and others, Commissioners. 1841 23/9/41

Gordon, Robert Augustus
The Church's claim and Archdeacon Denison's resolution compared. A letter to the Bishop of Oxford. 1852 8/6/52

Gordon, Thomas Major-General in the Greek army
History of the Greek revolution. 1832 (2v.) 13/11/76

Gordon, Thomas of Kirkcudbright
The character of an independent Whig. 1719 26/4/63

Gore, Catherine Grace Francis
Mothers and daughters, a tale of the year 1830. 1831 (3v.) 9/1/83

Gore, Charles
The clergy and the creeds. A sermon preached before the university of Oxford... 1887. 1887 21/8/87
The ministry of the Christian church. 1888 11/11/88
The mission of the church. 1892 12/3/93, 20/3/93

Gorham, George Cornelius
Examination before admission to benefice by the Bishop of Exeter. 1848 16/7/48

Gorman, Thomas Murray
Christian psychology:... a new translation of Swedenborg's Tractate De Commercio Animae et Corporis. 1875 23/8/76
The Athanasian creed and modern thought. 1870 20/2/70

Gorman, William James Gordon
Converts to Rome. A list of over three thousand protestants who have become Roman Catholics since the commencement of the nineteenth century. 1884 5/10/84
Gorres, Johann Joseph von
Athanasius. 1838 14/9/47
Gospel of nature. Being proofs of a creator. 1875 (not found) 9/6/90
Gosse, Sir Edmund William
Gray [a biography]. 1878 (1882 edn) 21/6/90
Gosselin, Jean Edme Auguste
The power of the pope during the middle ages... origin of the temporal power of the holy see. 1853 15/12/61
Gossner, Johannes Evangelist
The life and persecutions of Martin Boos... edited by J. G. 1836 26/6/36
Gostwick, Joseph afterw. Gostick
German culture and Christianity: their controversy in the time 1770–1880. 1882 18/4/82
Gostwick, Joseph, and Harrison, Robert afterw. Gostick
Outlines of German literature. 1873 26/4/73
Gother, John
Nubes Testium; or, a collection of the primitive fathers, giving testimony to the faith. 26/8/77 ?
Gough, E.
Defence and definition of verbal inspiration. 1890 11/1/91
Gouland, Henry Godfrey
Plan of a proposed new colony, to be called Britannia. 1851 8/10/51
Goulburn, Edward Meyrick
A reply to some parts of Mr. Ward's defence. 1845 18/2/45
Short devotional forms for morning and night... compiled and adapted from Bishop Andrews. 1851 22/8/52
The confession of a reticent Dean. A letter... to the Bishop of Lincoln, on... ritual conformity. 1881 14/11/81
The education of the world. Replies to 'Essays and Reviews'. 1862 12/1/62
The life, letters and sermons of bishop Herbert de Losinga... edited... by E. M. G... and H. Symonds. 1878 (2v.) 27/6/80
Thoughts on personal religion, being a treatise on the Christian life, in its two chief elements, devotion and practice. 1862 28/5/65, 15/1/71
Goulburn, Henry
Financial statement... May 29, 1846. 1846 4/7/46
Gould, Frederick James
The agnostic island. 1891 5/7/91
Gould, George
*On the refusal of Christian burial to the unbaptis*ed. A letter. 1861 10/2/61
Gould, Sabine Baring
Curious myths of the Middle Ages. 1866 7/9/69
Historic oddities and strange events. 1889 (2v. 1889–91) 7/1/90
Iceland: its scenes and sagas... With numerous illustrations and a map. 1863 30/12/72
Mehalah: a story of the salt marshes. 1880 (3v.) 6/12/86
Richard Cable the lightshipman. 1888 (3v.) 8/2/93
Some modern difficulties: nine lectures. 1875 19/9/75
The death and resurrection of Jesus. Ten lectures for Holy Week and Easter. 1888 27/11/88
The lives of the saints. 1872 (17v. 1872–89) 8/4/77
The mystery of suffering. Six lectures. 1877 (1877–80) 20/5/77
The origin and development of religious belief. 1869 (2v. 1869–70) 12/12/69
Yorkshire oddities, incidents and strange events. 1874 (2v.) 26/9/75 ?
Gouraud, Charles
Histoire des causes de la grandeur de l'Angleterre despuis les origines jusqu'à la paix de 1763. 1856 20/3/84
Gourrier, François Bonaventure
Letter to the Lord Bishop of London on the state of religion in France. 1836 30/7/38
National catholicity or the prospects of the Christian Church in south-western Europe considered. 1844 27/1/44
What is the church? The questions answered in an essay, shewing that the church of Christ is one, holy, apostolic. 1843 19/11/43
Gover, William
The Church of England. Reform or disestablishment, which?. 1874 19/7/74
Gowen, Franklin B.
Argument... in the case of P&E Railroad Co. vs. the Catawiosa Railroad. 1866 10/9/75
Gower, Lord Francis Leveson afterw. Egerton, Earl of Ellesmere
Address to the Royal Geographical Society in London. 1854 27/9/54
Faust, a drama, tr. Lord F. Leveson Gower. 1823 3/3/57
History of the War of Sicilian Vespers by M. Amari, tr. Earl of Ellesmere. 1850 19/4/51
The Paria, by M. Beer, tr. Earl of Ellesmere. 1829 3/6/36
Gower, Lady Harriet Catherine Leveson afterw. Egerton, Countess of Ellesmere
Journal of a tour of the Holy Land. 1841 20/8/41

Gower, Henrietta Elizabeth Leveson Countess Granville
Letters, ed. F. Leveson-Gower. 1894 (2v.) 10/4/94
Gower, Lord Ronald Charles Sutherland Leveson
Last days of Marie Antoinette. An historical sketch. 1885 23/1/85
My reminiscences. 1883 (2v.) 5/6/83
G. R.
The three barriers: notes on Mr. Darwin's 'Origin of Species'. 1861 19/1/62 ?
Graetz, Hirsch
History of the Jews. 1891 (5v. 1891–5) 24/5/91
Graham, Miss Clementina Stirling
Mystifications. 1869 28/9/69
Graham, Douglas Cunninghame
Glimpses of Abyssinia; or, extracts from letters written ... to the King of Abyssinia in ... 1841. 1867 2/12/67
Graham, Mrs. Isabella
The life of Mrs. Isabella Graham, of New York. 1832 10/8/34
Graham, Sir James Robert George
Corn and currency; in an address to land owners. 1826 13/12/41
Free trade in corn the real interest of the landlord, and the true policy of the state. By a Cumberland landowner. 1828 8/1/42
The life of ... Sir J. R. G. Graham, by W. T. MacCullagh Torrens. 1863 23/3/63, 15/5/63
The speech delivered by Sir J. Graham ... at a dinner given ... in Carlisle, by the Conservatives of East Cumberland. 1838 16/2/38
Graham, John W.
Neaera. A tale of ancient Rome. 1886 (2v.) 2/11/86, 4/11/86
Graham, Mary Jane
The freeness and sovereignty of God's justifying and electing grace. 1833 19/7/35
The test of truth. 1831 19/7/35
Graham, Richard Lord Preston
Angliae Speculum Morale; the moral state of England, with the several aspects it beareth to virtue and vice. 17/8/79
Graham, Thomas Master of the Mint
Report made to the Board of Trade on the loss of the Amazon. 1852 2/7/52
Graham, Thomas John M.D.
Sure methods of improving health, and prolonging life ... by a physician. 1828 (3rd edn) 24/12/27 ?
Graham, William
The creed of science, religious, moral and social. 1881 4/12/81
Grahame, James
The Sabbath, a poem. 1804 12/4/63
Gramont, Count Philibert de
Memoirs of the life of Count de Grammont ... amorous intrigues of the court of England in the reign of ... Charles II. Translated from the French. 1714 25/9/43
Grancey, Baron de Maudat-
Chez Paddy. 1887 15/8/87
Grand canal. Statement. 1844 13/7/44
Grand Vizier unmasked, by a protestant tory. 1827 23/6/27
Grant, Sir Alexander
Oxford. A lecture. 1864 19/7/64
Grant, Mrs. Anne
Essays on the superstitions of the highlanders of Scotland. 1811 31/8/64
Grant, Anthony
An historical sketch of the Crimea. 1855 9/6/55
Sermon [on John iii. 19]. The powers of darkness prevailing over the disobedient. 1866 5/3/68
The Ramsden sermon on the extension of the Church in the colonies and dependencies of the ... Empire. 1852 27/6/52
Grant, Brewin
'Mr. Gladstone's missing link.' Lecture. (The Irish Church; an English Dissenter's view of it). 1868 23/1/73
Grant, Daniel
Home politics, or the growth of trade considered in its relation to labour, pauperism and emigration. 1870 14/11/70
On the policy of liberalism. 1875 13/2/75
Grant, George Monro
Religions of the world in relation to Christianity. 1890 17/1/92
Grant, James
Random recollections of the House of Commons. By one of no party. 1836 20/11/35
St. Stephen's, or pencillings of politicians, by Mask. 1839 21/4/40 ?
Grant, Ulysses Simpson
Personal memoirs. 1885 (2v. 1885–86) 25/3/89 ?
Grapel, William
The church's holy-days the only safe-guard against the desecration of the Lord's day. 1848 16/4/48
Gratry, Auguste Joseph Alphonse
Henri Perreyve. 1866 13/5/66
Jesus Christ. A reply to M. Renan. Translated from the French. 1868 31/5/68 ?
Petit manuel de critique. 1866 19/5/66
Grattan, Henry
Life of H. Grattan, by R. Dunlop. 1889 24/5/89
Memoirs of Henry Grattan. 1846 (5v.) 18/9/85

Grattan, Henry (*cont.*)
Mr. Grattan's address to his fellow-citizens [on resigning his seat in Parliament]. 1797 23/8/86
Mr. Grattan's celebrated speech on the motion of Mr. Fox... 1805, for the Irish Catholics. 1805 11/6/34
Speeches... comprising a brief review of the most important events in the history of Ireland. 1811 (vol 1) 18/10/80
Graves, Charles Bishop of Limerick
Charge. 1864 (not found) 1/12/67
Graves, Richard
The spiritual Quixote. 1783 (3v.) 27/8/45
Graves, Samuel Robert
Railway amalgamations... speech... delivered ... Liverpool Chamber of Commerce. 24th January, 1872. 1872 20/2/72
Gray, Andrew Minister
Catechism on the principles and constitution of the Free Church of Scotland. 1882 25/10/46
Oxford Tractarianism, the Scottish Episcopal College, and the Scottish Episcopal Church... speech. 1842 1/9/44
Gray, Asa
Natural science and religion. Two lectures. 1880 20/12/85
Gray, David
The Luggie and other poems... With a memoir by J. Hedderwick, and a prefatory notice by R. M. Milnes. 1862 8/5/62
Gray, Elizabeth Caroline
The Empire and the Church, from Constantine to Charlemagne. 1857 22/11/71 ?
The history of Etruria... Translated from the German of K. O. Müller. 1843 (3v. 1843–68) 11/9/72
Gray, John Lecturer on political economy, Edinburgh
An efficient remedy for the distress of nations. 1842 10/5/43
Gray, Sir John
The Irish church establishment. The statements of Sir J. Gray... examined. 1866 20/3/68
Gray, John Hamilton Vicar of Bolsover
Letter to the bishop of London, on the state of the Anglican congregations in Germany. 1843 12/2/43
Remarks, addressed to R. M. Beverley... on his letter to... the Archbishop of York. 1831 27/6/31
Gray, John Henry Archdeacon of Hong Kong
China: a history of the laws, manners and customs of the people... edited by W. G. Gregor. 1878 (2v.) 22/7/78
Gray, Robert Bishop of Bristol
A serious address to seceders and sectarists of every description. 1812 17/8/28
Gray, Robert Bishop of Cape Town
A statement relating to... the consecration, trial, and excommunication of... Dr. Colenso. 1867 16/3/67
Gray, S. Brownlow
The revival of Bp. Berkeley's Bermuda College: a letter to... the Archbishop of Canterbury. 1853 19/6/53
Gray, Thomas poet
Elegy in a country churchyard. 1750 4/3/94
Letters of Thomas Gray. 1814 23/9/28, 18/9/87
Poems. 1775 13/4/65, 26/3/84
Works of Thomas Gray, with memoirs of his life and writings, by W. Mason. 1814 20/1/26
Gray, William
Chorographia; or, a survey of Newcastle upon Tine. 10/10/91
Great Britain and New South Wales. An appeal... against... charges for police and gaols. 1841 23/3/41
Great Exhibition
The theology and morality of the Great Exhibition as set forth in certain leading articles. 1851 20/7/51
Grecs, Dette nationale des. 27/2/66
Greeley, Horace
Alcohol. 1857 9/8/87
The American conflict: a history of the Great Rebellion in the United States... 1860–'65. 1864 (2v. 1864–66) 20/3/65
Greely, Adolphus Washington
Three years of Arctic service. An account of the Lady Franklin Bay expedition of 1881–84. 1886 (2v.) 14/12/87
Green, Alice Stopford
Henry the second. 1888 5/7/88
Town life in the fifteenth century. 1894 (2v.) 13/4/94
Green, John Richard
A short history of the English people. 1874 1/12/75
History of the English people. 1877 (1877–80) 19/2/78, 15/8/80, 1/7/83, 14/8/84, 2/9/87
The making of England. 1881 15/2/82
Green, Samuel
The life of Mahomet, founder of the religion of Islam, and of the empire of the Saracens. 1840 7/2/73 ?
Green, Thomas Bowden
Fragments of thought; being wayside notes and fireside scraps. 1875 30/10/75
Green, Thomas Hill
Witness of God, and faith. Two lay sermons [on 1 Cor. v. 7, 8, and 2 Cor. v. 7] ed. by A. Toynbee. 1883 7/10/83, 22/4/88
Greene, John Baker
The Hebrew Migration from Egypt. 1879 2/1/80

Greene, Robert
Orlando Furioso. 7/8/65
The dramatic works of R. G., to which are added his poems. With... account of the author... by A. Dyce. 1831 (2v.) 28/7/58
Greenhill, Alfred
Is it so? or, the logic of the Pope in his claim to infallibility. 1871 21/9/75 ?
Greenhill, William Alexander
Life of... Sir J. Stonhouse, Bart., M.D. With extracts from his tracts and correspondence. 1844 7/9/56
Greenlees, Gavin
Gifford lectures and Max Müller: their religion considered in the light of philology and history. 1889 28/4/89
Greenwood, George Colonel
Hints on horsemanship. 1839 8/6/39
Greenwood, George Wright
A manual of the practice of conveyancing... To which are added concise common forms and precedents. 1856 5/9/56 ?
Greenwood, James
A night in a workhouse. Reprinted from the 'Pall Mall Gazette'. 1866 5/2/66
Greenwood, Thomas
Cathedra Petri. A political history of the Great Latin Patriarchate. 1856 (1858–65) 25/9/58, 18/8/61, 21/10/74, 1/1/75, 24/11/78
Greer, J. R.
Orange flags on churches. A plea for the sanctity of the house of God. 1866 2/4/68
Greer, Mrs. Sarah D.
Quakerism; or the story of my life. By a lady. 1851 8/7/55
Greer, Tom
A modern Daedalus. 1885 3/5/86
Greg, Robert Hyde
Scotch farming in England. 1842 1/11/42
Scotch farming in Lothian. 1842 1/11/42
The factory question, considered in relation to its effects on... health and morals. 1837 25/4/37
Greg, William Rathbone
'Foreign policy of Great Britain', in *Nineteenth Century*, iv. 393. 1878 (September 1878) 31/8/78
'The American republic', in *North British Review*, xxx. vi. 233. 1862 (February 1862) 8/2/62
Enigmas of life. 1872 23/11/73
Not over-production, but deficient consumption, the source of our sufferings. 1841 30/12/41 ?
Past and present efforts for the extinction of the African slave trade. 1840 18/2/41
Political problems for our age and country. 1870 19/2/70
The creed of Christendom; its foundations and superstructure. 1851 30/3/73, 22/2/74
The German schism and the Irish priests... a critique of Laing's Notes. 1845 28/12/45
The one thing needful. 1855 24/2/55
The way out [in advocacy of administrative reform]. 1855 6/3/55
Gregg, Tresham Dames
The apostacy of the Roman Catholic church clearly demonstrated... a lecture. 1845 30/4/65
Grégoire, Louis
Dictionnaire encyclopédique des sciences. (various edns.) 3/5/85
Gregory, Alexander
Discourses on the Book of Revelation, with an introduction. 1875 17/10/80
Gregory, Charles Hutton
Address of C. H. Gregory, Esq. on his election as president of the Institution of civil engineers. 1868 14/8/68
Gregory, Robert, and Liddon, Henry Parry
The Purchas judgment. A letter to the... bishop of London by the two senior canons of St. Paul's. 1871 13/6/71
Gregory, William
Letters to a candid enquirer on animal magnetism. 1851 25/4/51
Gregory the Great
Liber regulae pastoralis. 18/10/40
Gregory XVI
Encyclical letter. 1832 10/5/33
Gregson, Samuel
Royal North Lancashire Agricultural Society. The speech... at the meeting... August 30, 1855. 1855 14/1/76 ?
Gregson, Thomas George
Speech... on the state of public education in Van Dieman's land. 1850 13/6/54 ?
Grellet du Mabillier, Étienne de
Memoirs of the life and Gospel labours of S. G., edited by B. Seebohm. 1860 (2v. 1860) 19/12/90, 4/1/91
Grellier, J. J.
The history of the national debt from 1688 to the beginning of 1810. 1810 15/4/54 ?
Grenville, George Nugent Temple Baron Nugent
Remarks on the office of Lord High Commissioner in the Ionian islands, in reply to... 'Morning Chronicle'. 1835 1/12/58
The ballot discussed in a letter to the Earl of Durham. 1837 28/11/37
Grenville, Ralph Neville
Cathedrals. A letter to the... bishop of Bath and Wells. 1871 26/11/71
Grenville, Richard Plantagenet T. N. B. C. Duke of Buckingham and Chandos
Memoirs of the Court and Cabinet of George the third from original family documents. 1853 (2v.) 11/2/53, 17/3/53

Grenville, Richard Plantagenet T. N. B. C. (*cont.*)
Memoirs of the court of England, during the Regency, 1811–1820. From original family documents. 1856 (2v.) 27/3/84
Memoirs of the court of George IV . . . from original family documents. 1859 (2v.) 14/3/59

Grenville, Richard Temple Earl Temple
The Grenville papers . . . the correspondence of Richard Grenville . . . and George Grenville . . . ed. W. J. Smith. 1852 (4v. 1852–53) 14/5/52

Grenville, William Wyndham Baron Grenville
Essay on the supposed advantage of a sinking fund. 1828 21/8/43, 6/8/66
Letter from . . . Lord Grenville to the Earl of Fingall. 1810 3/4/45
Nugae Metricae (Addenda). 1824 25/1/58
Oxford and Locke. 1829 10/3/41

Gresley, William
A second statement of the real danger of the Church of England . . . answers to . . . objections. 1846 12/7/46
Anglo-Catholicism. A short treatise on the theory of the English church. 1844 18/1/44
Charles Lever. 1841 7/4/41
Clement Walton; or the English citizen. 1840 12/9/40
Portrait of an English churchman. 1838 7/3/39
Priests and philosophers. 1873 14/12/73
Remarks on the necessity of attempting a restoration of the national church. 1841 22/8/41
Sermons on some of the social and political duties of a Christian. 1836 25/8/39
Suggestions on the new statute to be proposed in the University of Oxford. 1845 16/1/45
The necessity of zeal and moderation in the present circumstances of the Church . . . in five sermons. 1839 17/3/39, 8/9/39
The prayer book as it is. 1865 3/12/65
The real danger of the Church of England. 1846 11/3/46

Greswell, Edward
[untraced letter by E. or R. Greswell on the proposed Initiative Board for Oxford University]. 1852 (not found) 29/10/52
A letter to . . . the Duke of Wellington, Chancellor of the University of Oxford. 1837 23/10/52

Greswell, Richard
On education in the principles of art. 1844 1/7/44

Greswell, William Parr
Memoirs of Angelus Politanus, A. S. Sanazarius, Pelrus Bembus, Hieronymus Fracastorius . . . etc. 1801 3/6/53

Greville, Charles Cavendish Fulke
Past and present policy of England towards Ireland. 1845 9/4/45
The Greville memoirs. A journal of the reigns of King George IV and King William IV . . . . Edited by H. Reeve. 1874 (8v. 1874–87) 10/11/74, 8/1/75, 29/10/85, 20/1/87, 22/1/87, 5/2/87

Greville, Henry William
Leaves from the diary of H. G. Edited by the Viscountess Enfield. 1883 (1883–1905) 14/7/83

Grey, Charles 2nd Earl Grey
Correspondence of Princess Lieven and Earl Grey. 1890 (3v.) 29/1/90, 19/2/90
Some account of the life and opinions of Charles, second Earl Grey. 1861 20/5/61
The Reform Act, 1832. The correspondence of the late Earl Grey with . . . William IV and with Sir H. Taylor. 1867 6/3/67

Grey, Charles Lieutenant-General
The early years of . . . the Prince Consort [Albert], compiled under the direction of . . . [Victoria]. 1867 13/7/67

Grey, Henry George 3rd Earl Grey
[On colonies] *in Nineteenth Century*, v.935. 1879 (June 1879) 31/5/79
Parliamentary government considered with reference to a reform of parliament. An essay. 1858 1/3/58
Speeches . . . on the second reading of the Corn Law Bill . . . March 9th, 1842 . . . 1842 7/4/60

Grey, John
A sermon, preached . . . in behalf of the special fund for providing national schools for manufacturing. 1843 15/10/43

Grey, Simeon
True churchmen: their position and duties in the present day. 1853 6/3/53 ?

Grey, Theresa
Idols of society; or gentility and femininity . . . republished from Fraser's Magazine. 1874 7/6/81

Gribble, Thomas
Judged by his words. An attempt to weigh a certain kind of evidence respecting Christ. 1870 20/3/70
Scriptural studies; our church and our times. 1867 16/2/68

Grierson, Miss
Pierre and his family; or, a story of the Waldenses. 1823 18/3/26

Griffin, Gerald
'Holland-Tide'; or, Munster popular tales. 1827 13/2/28

Griffin, Sir Lepel Henry
The great republic. 1884 2/7/84

Griffith, Charles
The present state and prospects of the Port Philip district of New South Wales. 1845 21/4/46
Griffith, Thomas
Farewell sermons; preached in Ram's Episcopal Chapel, Homerton. 1872 28/4/72 ?
Fundamentals; or bases of belief concerning man, God, and the correlation of God and men. A handbook. 1871 19/1/73
The gospel of the divine life. A study. 1881 10/9/81
Grimm, Baron Friedrich Melchior von
Correspondance littéraire, philosophique et critique . . . par le baron de Grimm et par Diderot. 1813 (17v.) 16/8/37
Grimm, Jacob Ludwig Carl and Wilhelm Carl
German popular stories and fairy tales, as told by Grammer Grethel . . . Revised translation by E. Taylor. 1849 1/1/27
Grimshawe, Thomas Shuttleworth
A memoir of the rev. Legh Richmond. 1828 21/12/28
Grindle, Edmund Samuel
This church and realm; or, the rights of the church and the royal supremacy. 1871 25/6/71
Grinfield, Edward William
An apology for the septuagint . . . its claims to biblical and canonical authority . . . stated and vindicated. 1850 2/3/62
An expostulatory letter to the rt. rev. N. Wiseman . . . on the interpolated curse in the Vatican septuagint. 1850 11/5/50
The Christian cosmos. The son of God the revealed creator. 1856 22/2/57
Grinfield, Thomas
The history of preaching. . . . With a preface by R. Eden. 1880 25/7/80
Griselini, Francesco
Del genio di F. P. Sarpi in ogni facoltà scientifica. 1785 (2v.) 10/9/48 ?
Griswold, Rufus Wilmot
The poets and poetry of America. 1842 23/4/44
Groome, Francis Hindes
In gipsy tents. 1880 11/4/81
Gross, Gustav
Karl Marx. Eine studie. 1885 14/1/85 ?
Grossi, Tommaso
I Lombardi alla Prima Crociata, canti quindici. 1826 15/11/38
Ildegonda. Dramma in due atti. 1820 (1859) 6/9/36, 17/11/58
Marco Visconti, storia del trecento, cavata dalle cronache di quel secolo, e raccontata da T. G. 1834 13/10/36
Ulrico e Lida. Novella. 1837 7/12/38
Grossman, L.
Maimonides. 1890 14/8/90
Grosvenor, Lady Elizabeth Mary Marchioness of Westminster
Narrative of a yacht voyage in the Mediterranean during the years 1840, 1841. 1842 (2v.) 1/1/44
Grosvenor, Lord Robert Baron Ebury
Leaves from my journal. . . . By a member of the late parliament. 1852 25/2/52
The laity and church reform. 1886 24/6/86
Grote, Augustus Radcliffe
The new infidelity. 1881 6/4/90
Grote, George
A history of Greece. 1846 (12v. 1846–56) 19/3/47, 16/7/56, 9/11/57, 8/8/59, 5/11/64, 27/10/75, 21/1/87
Fragments on ethical subjects by the late G. Grote. 1876 15/1/76
Plato, and the other companions of Sokrates. 1865 (3v.) 8/2/68, 13/9/94
Seven letters on the recent politics of Switzerland. 1847 12/4/48, 3/6/76
Speech . . . delivered . . . in the House of Commons on . . . the vote by ballot at elections. 1833 22/6/71
The personal life of George Grote, by Harriet Grote. 1873 29/5/73
Grote, Harriet
A brief retrospect of the political events of 1831–1832, as illustrated by the Greville and Althorp memoirs. 1878 7/11/78
Collected papers (original and reprinted) in prose and verse. 1842–1862. 1862 16/4/67
Some account of the hamlet of East Burnham. 1858 31/5/67
The personal life of George Grote. 1873 29/5/73
Grote, John
Essays and reviews. An examination of some portions of Dr. Lushington's judgment. 1862 15/11/63
Ground, William David
An examination of the structural principles of . . . H. Spencer's philosophy: intended as a proof [for theism]. 1883 20/4/84
Ecce Christianus. 1879 23/11/79
Grousset, Paschal pseud. Philippe Daryl
Ireland's disease. Notes and impressions . . . author's English version. 1888 3/12/87
Grove, Joseph
The lives of all the earls and dukes of Devonshire, descended from Sir W. Cavendish. 1764 5/11/82
Grub, George the elder
An ecclesiastical history of Scotland, from the introduction of Christianity to the present time. 1861 (4v.) 14/11/61
Grueber, Charles Stephen
Article xxix. Considered in reference to the three sermons of the archdeacon of Taunton. 1854 (1855) 10/8/56
Three recent decisions [on matters of ritual by the Judicial Committee of the Privy Council]. A letter. 1875 30/6/75

Gruner, Ludwig
Scripture points from the frescoes of Raphael in the Vatican... Edited by L. Gruner. 1866 31/1/44
Guadagnoli, Antonio
Poesie giocose... del Guadagnoli Giusti. 1872 5/11/73
Guadagnoli, Pietro
Sonetti... Centuria prima. 1785 23/7/49
Guadet, Joseph
De la Représentation Nationale en France. 1863 27/7/64
Gualdi, Abbate [Gregorio Leti]
The life of Donna Olimpia Maldachini... Faithfully rendered into English [by Henry Compton, later bishop of London]. 9/9/45
Gualterio, Marquis Filippo Antonio
Gli ultimi rivolgimenti Italiani... seconda edizione, riveduta ed arricchita di nuovi documenti. 1852 (4v.) 8/4/51
Guarini, Giovanni Battista
Il Pastor Fido: tragicomedia pastorale. 17/10/37
Gubernatis, Count Angelo de
Zoological mythology; or the legends of animals. 1872 (2v.) 19/5/78
Guer, Jean Antoine
Moeurs et usages des Turcs, leur religion, leur gouvernement civil, militaire et politique; avec un abrégé de l'histoire Ottomane. 1746 (2v. 1746–47) 5/8/50
Guerrazzi, Francesco Domenico
Discorsi politici. Un serto all'Italia. 1849 13/8/49
Isabella Orsini, Duchessa di Bracciano. 1844 4/2/87
L'assedio di Firenze. 1836 (5v.) 13/9/51
La battaglia di Benevento. Storia del secolo xiii. 1829 (4v.) 13/11/49
Guerrieri-Gonzaga, Cardinal Cesare
I parroci eletti. 1875 27/6/75
Guest, Lady Charlotte Elizabeth afterw. Schreiber
The Mabinogion: from the Llyfr Coch o Hergest, and other ancient Welsh manuscripts: with an English translation and notes. 1838 (3v. 1838–49) 1/11/59
Guettée, François René afterw. Vladimir
Exposition de la doctrine de l'église Catholique orthodoxe. 1866 2/7/93
La Papauté moderne condamnée par le Pape Saint Grégoire le Grand... Extraits des ouvrages de Saint Grégoire. 1863 12/4/74
Lettre à M. Dupanloup, Evêque d'Orléans, à propos de sa pastorale... à l'occasion des fêtes de Rome. 1868 17/5/68
Guibord, Joseph
History of the Guibord Case. 1875 8/1/76
Guicciardini, Francesco
The temporal and spiritual power of the Pope. Translated from the Italian of... Guicciardini... by J. Fowle. 1860 2/5/75
Guiccioli, Countess Teresa afterw. Rouillé de Boissy
Lord Byron jugé par les témoins de sa vie. 1868 23/12/68
Guidara di Rivarolo, Francesco la
An echo from the Vatican: or the Pope the cruel leader of the blind. 1844 12/7/44
Guides pittoresque du voyageur en France. 1838 (6v.) 28/10/50
Guignard, Alexis Count de Saint-Priest
Histoire de la chute des Jésuites au XVIII siècle, 1750–1782. 1844 5/11/45
Guilhaud de Lavergne, Louis Gabriel Léonce
Economie rurale de la France depuis 1789. 1861 25/5/63
La banque de France et les banques départementales. 1865 25/3/65
Guilhem de Clermont-Lodève, Guillaume Emmanuel Joseph Baron de Sainte-Croix
Recherches historiques et critiques sur les mystères du Paganisme. Seconde édition; corrigée par le baron Silvestre de Sacy. 1817 (3v.) 12/11/83
Guillon, Edouard
La France et l'Irlande pendant la révolution. Hoche et Humbert. D'après les documents inédits des archives de France et d'Irlande. 1888 16/6/88
Guilty or not guilty? Being an inquest on the Conservative government and ministry. 1842 31/10/42
Guinnard, A.
Three years' slavery among the Patagonians... From the third French edition, by C. S. Cheltnam. 1871 21/6/71
Guinness, Henry Grattan the elder
The week and its origin: a rejoinder to the article by the bishop of Carlisle [H. Goodwin] in the 'Contemporary Review', October, 1886. 1886 25/12/86
Guiron, James J.
The sacred heart: a correspondence between... [J. J. G., Assistant Secretary to] *Archbishop Manning:... and A. Nicholson.* 1873 16/11/73
Guizot, François Pierre Guillaume
[Unsigned editorial on L'Université Catholique] *Revue Française* v.5. 1838 13/6/38
Christianity reviewed in its relation to society. 1871 6/4/72
Democracy in France. January, 1849. 1849 6/2/49
Du catholicisme, du protestantisme et de la philosophie en France. M. Guizot's Theory of

Syncretism and Coalition. Translated [by F. F. Barham]. 1839 22/5/41
Etudes sur les beaux arts en général. 1852 25/3/57
Histoire de la révolution d'Angleterre depuis l'avènement de Charles 1er jusqu'à la restauration de Charles II. 1826 (1826–27) 17/6/34
L'Eglise et la société chrétienne. 1861 22/10/61
La France et la Prusse responsables devant l'Europe. 1868 26/10/68
Le duc de Broglie. 1872 22/12/71, 12/1/72
Le prince Albert, son caractère.... Précedé d'une préface par M. G. 1863 4/10/63
Memoires pour servir à l'histoire de mon temps. 1858 (8v. 1858–67) 26/10/58, 22/3/64
Sir Robert Peel: étude d'histoire contemporaine. 1856 27/9/56
Speech on Pritchard affair in Tahiti. 1844 (not found) 11/3/44
Washington. 1841 18/4/48

Gunn, William
Cartonensia: or, an historical and critical account of the tapestries in the palace of the Vatican... with notes and illustrations. 1831 26/5/38

Gurney, Archer Thompson
A letter of entreaty and remonstrance... to... Dr. Pusey. 1864 1/1/65
Faust. Part II. rendered by A. Gurney. 1842 23/5/74
On certain recent propositions, and the prospect of reunion: a letter to... the Lord Bishop of Oxford, with an appendix. 1866 15/4/66

Gurney, Joseph John
A winter in the West Indies, described in familiar letters to H. Clay, of Kentucky. 1840 4/11/40
Observations on divine worship as practised by the... Society of Friends. 1824 11/9/29
Puseyism traced to its roots. 1845 5/6/45
Reconciliation, respectfully recommended to all parties in the Colony of Jamaica. A letter addressed to the planters. 1840 7/7/40

Gutch, John
Collectanea curiosa; or, miscellaneous tracts, relating to the history and antiquities of England and Ireland, the Universities, etc. 1781 (2v.) 26/1/47

Guthrie, Malcolm
On Mr. Spencer's formula of evolution as an exhaustive statement of the changes of the universe... [and]... criticisms of Spencer's 'First Principles'. 1882 29/5/84

Guthrie, Thomas
Studies of character from the Old Testament. Reprinted from the Sunday Magazine. 1867 (1867–70) 17/5/74
The city: its sins and sorrows. Being a series of sermons from Luke xix. 41. 1857 16/8/57

Guthrie, William of Brechin
A general history of Scotland, from the earliest accounts to the present time. 1767 (10v.) 4/9/44

Gutteridge, Joseph
Lights and shadows in the life of an artisan. 1893 15/10/93

Gutteridge, Thomas
Church rates: means proposed for surmounting the obstacles to the granting and collecting of them. 1842 27/12/42

Guttmann, Augustus
De Hymnorum Homericorum historia critica particulae quattuor. 1869 9/10/75

Guy, John
School geography. 1869 3/12/70

Guy, William Augustus
'Introductory lecture delivered at King's College ...' reprinted from Provincial Medical Journal and Retrospect of the Medical Sciences, n.s. i. 23. 1842 1/10/42
John Howard's winter's journey. 1882 12/3/82

Guyau, Jean Marie
L'irréligion de l'avenir. Etude sociologique. 1887 10/6/88

Guyon, A. H.
The earth and the moon. 1850 17/3/90

Guyon, Jeanne Marie
La vie de Madame J. M. B. de la M.-G., écrite par elle même. 1791 (3v. 1792) 13/2/87
Poésies et cantiques spirituels [collected and edited by P. Poiret]. 1722 (4v.) 13/2/87

Guyot, Arnold Henri
Creation, or, the Biblical cosmogony in the light of modern science. 1884 7/2/86

Habberton, John
Helen's babies. 1876 (1878) 7/5/78
The Bowsham puzzle and my friend Moses. 1884 23/8/89

Habershon, Matthew
A dissertation on the prophetic scriptures, chiefly those of a chronological character. 1834 28/2/41

Haddan, Arthur West
Apostolical succession in the Church of England. 1869 15/8/69
The church patient in her mode of dealing with controversies. A sermon [on Psal. xxxvii. 1–3]. 1851 2/3/51
The training of Samuel, and the training of King Jehoash. A sermon [on 2 Kings xii. 2]. 1862 30/11/62

Haeckel, Ernst Heinrich Philipp August
Anthropogenie, oder Entwickelungsgeschichte des Menschen. 1874 24/9/74
The history of creation: or the development of the earth and its inhabitants by the action of natural causes. 1876 21/5/82, 13/12/91

Hagenbach, Carl Rudolph
A textbook of the history of doctrines, tr. C. W. Buch. 1871 (2v.) 19/8/76
German rationalism, in its rise, progress, and decline, in relation to theologians, scholars, poets, philosophers, and the people. 1865 8/1/65
Haggard, Sir Henry Rider K. B. E.
King Solomon's mines. 1885 22/12/85
Hague, William
Ralph Waldo Emerson. (Life and Philosophy.) A paper read... Dec. 14, 1883. With afterthoughts by W. H. 1884 4/4/85
Hahn, Johann Georg von
Albänesische Studien... Nebst einer Karte und andern artistischen Beilagen. 1854 8/8/62, 29/12/76
Hahn-Hahn, Countess Ida Maria Luise Sophie Frederica Gustave
Jenseits der Berge. 1840 (2v.) 11/10/45
Halcombe, John
Letters on unfulfilled prophecy. 1845 29/6/45
Halcombe, John Joseph
The fourfold gospel. 1890 24/4/92
Haldane, Richard Burdon Viscount Haldane
'Eight Hours' in *Contemporary Review*, lvii.240. 1890 (February 1890) 13/10/90
Life of Adam Smith. 1887 3/10/87
Hale, Charles Reuben
Innocent of Moscow, the apostle of Kamchatka and Alaska. 1877 7/10/77
Hale, Horatio
The origin of languages, and the antiquity of speaking man. An address. 1886 8/11/86
Hale, Sir Matthew
Contemplations moral and divine. 20/8/43
Hale, William Hale
A charge delivered to the clergy of the archdeaconry of London. 1849 27/6/49
A method of preparation for confirmation, containing forms of self-examination and devotion. 1827 2/7/28
An essay on the supposed existence of a quadripartite and tripartite division of tithes in England. 1832 (2v. 1832–33) 28/3/33
Clerical subscription considered: in a letter to H. Hoare, Esq. 1864 15/2/64
Remarks on the two bills now before parliament, a bill for registering births, deaths and marriages ... and a bill for marriages. 1836 30/3/36
Some remarks on the probable consequences of... a general registry of births, and legalising... Dissenters' baptisms. 1834 23/4/36
Suggestions for the extension of the ministry by the revival of the lesser orders of ministers: in a charge... 1853. 1853 19/6/53
The abolition of church rates a measure preparative to the overthrow of the established church as the national religion. A charge. 1859 20/11/59
The antiquity of the church rate system considered. 1837 17/6/37
The case of obedience to rules in things indifferent; and the power of the offertory... a charge. 1843 7/6/43
The doctrine and government of the Anglican church under the supremacy of Henry the Eighth considered. 1869 3/6/69
The duties of deacons and priests in the Church of England compared with suggestions for... sub-deacons. 1850 24/2/50
The queen's supremacy the constitutional bond of union between the Church of England and her branches in the colonies. 1867 21/7/67
Hales, Francis
'Tell it to the church.' An appeal from the bishop [of Melbourne, C. Perry] *to the church*. 1853 20/3/56
Hales, John Canon of Windsor
Golden remains of the ever memorable Mr. J. Hales (Dr. Balcanqual's letters from the synod of Dort...). (3v.) 22/10/82
The works of the ever memorable... J. Hales of Eaton. Now first collected together. 1765 (3v.) 19/8/77
Hales, John Wesley
Longer English poems, with notes, philological and explanatory, and an Introduction on the teaching of English. 1872 2/4/89
Hales, William
Abridgment of a correspondence between the courts of Rome and Baden... respecting... Baron Wessenberg. 1819 4/1/80 ?
Half hours with our metropolitan ministers. 1857 (1857–58) 15/1/58
Haliburton, Robert Grant
Intercolonial trade our only safeguard against disunion. 1868 31/7/68 ?
The dwarfs of Mount Atlas. Statements... as to the existence of a dwarf race south of the Great Atlas. 1891 15/12/91
Haliburton, Thomas Chandler pseud. Sam Slick
An historical and statistical account of Nova-Scotia. 1829 (2v.) 13/5/46 ?
The bubbles of Canada. 1839 13/5/46
The clockmaker; or the sayings... of Samuel Slick, of Slicksville. 1837 (2v. 1837–38) 1/4/39
Hall, Anna Maria
The Whiteboy: a story of Ireland in 1822. 1845 (2v.) 23/6/87
Hall, Christopher Newman
Address delivered at the Autumnal Meeting of the Congregational Union of England and Wales ... 1866. 1866 26/9/66
Atonement the fundamental fact about Christianity. 1893 21/5/93
Christian victory; or, the hidden manna and the white stone. 1856 13/12/74 ?

Congregationalism for Christ. 1855 27/11/64
Death in the palace. [A funeral sermon on Jer. ix. 21 preached on . . . the death of the prince consort]. 1862 29/12/61
Divine brotherhood. Jubilee gleanings, 1842–1892. 1892 18/9/92
From Liverpool to St. Louis. [Reprint of paper which appeared in The Broadway Magazine]. 1870 30/5/69
Prayer: its reasonableness and efficacy. 1875 28/2/75
Richard Cobden, M.P. A lecture. 1865 14/5/65
The American war. A lecture delivered in London, Oct. 20, 1862. 1862 7/11/62
The cardinal and the encyclical [of 8 Dec. 1864]. *A lecture to young men.* 1865 2/4/65
The holy Catholic faith. 1862 18/5/62
The Lord's prayer: practical meditation. 1883 9/12/83 ?

Hall, Mrs. Christopher Newman
Through the Tyrol to Venice. 1860 16/8/64

Hall, Hubert
Society in the Elizabethan age. 1891 26/10/91

Hall, John iron merchant
The iron trade, with remarks pointing out the true cause and cure for its existing state of depression. 1843 2/5/43

Hall, John poet
Balm of Gilead. 19/2/32

Hall, Joseph
Observations of some specialities of divine providence in the life of Joseph Hall, Bishop of Norwich. 7/8/31 ?

Hall, Peter
Fragmenta liturgica, ed. P. Hall. 1848 7/3/49

Hall, Robert Pastor, Broadmead
Modern infidelity considered. 1800 17/2/28
On the work of the holy spirit. The circular letter from . . . Baptist Churches of the Northamptonshire Association, assembled . . . May . . . 1809. 1809 27/4/34
Reviews of . . . Foster's Essays. 1825 30/3/30
The works of Robert Hall . . . With a brief memoir of his life by Dr. Gregory, and observations . . . by John Foster. 1832 (6v. 1831–32) 2/6/44

Hall, Samuel Carter
[On Maynooth]. (not found) 3/4/45
A book of memories of great men and women of the age, from personal acquaintance. 1871 25/4/73
The use of spiritualism?. 1884 18/1/85

Hall, Spencer
Documents . . . relating to the reign of Elizabeth . . . translated from the Spanish . . . by S. H. 1865 26/6/65

Hall, S. W.
The law of impersonation as applied to abstract ideas and religious dogmas. 1861 17/6/63

Hall, William Henry Bullock
Gleanings in Ireland after the land acts. 1883 12/1/84

Hall, William John
The doctrine of purgatory and the practice of praying for the dead as maintained by the Romish church, examined. 1843 22/1/43

Hallam, Arthur Henry
Essay on Cicero. 1832 16/3/32
On the influence of Italian works of imagination on the same class of composition in England. 1832 4/4/32
Poems. 1830 19/5/30, 4/6/30, 15/6/30, 22/6/30
Remains in verse and prose . . . With a preface and memoir. 1862 9/1/62, 2/12/92
Remains in verse and prose . . . With a preface and memoir [by Henry Hallam]. 1834 5/2/34, 18/6/34, 3/8/34
'Remarks on Rossetti's Dante' in *Remains in verse and prose.* 1834 24/6/34
The poems of A. H. Hallam, by R. Le Gallienne. 1893 24/11/93
'Theodicaea Novissima' in *Remains in verse and prose.* 1834 3/8/34

Hallam, Henry
View of the state of Europe during the Middle Ages. 1818 15/7/31, 20/9/31, 10/10/31, 24/10/31, 7/10/92

Halliday, Sir Frederick James K. C. B.
Minute of the honourable F. J. Halliday, Lieut.-Governor of Bengal, on the state of the police, and of criminal justice in . . . Bengal. 1857 10/6/57

Halliwell, James Orchard afterw. Halliwell-Phillipps
A brief account of the life, writings and inventions of Sir S. Morland. 1838 13/12/73

Halsted, Edward Pellew
Iron-cased ships. A series of lectures delivered before the Royal United Service Institution . . . 1861. 1861 31/7/61

Haly, William Taylor
The opinions of Sir R. Peel, expressed in parliament and in public. 1843 13/3/57

Hamilton, Alexander
Alexander Hamilton, an historical study, by G. Shea. 1877 14/3/77
The federalist, or the new constitution. 1788 (2v.) 18/4/50

Hamilton, Alexander Henry Abercromby
Quarter sessions from Queen Elizabeth to Queen Anne . . . Translated and edited, with a memoir. 1878 8/8/80

Hamilton, Edward T.
A second letter to the editors of the Sydney Morning Herald on the augmentation of the licence fees. 1844 21/11/44

Hamilton, Edward T. (*cont.*)
Letter to the editors of the Sydney Morning Herald, on the augmentation of the licence fees. 1844 21/11/44
Hamilton, Lady Emma
Memoirs of Emma, Lady Hamilton... New edition, edited and annotated by W. H. Long ... With portraits. 1891 29/4/91
Hamilton, Gavin
Scottish and English scholarship. 1883 7/9/83
Hamilton, Henry Blackburne
The Privy Council and the National Society. The question concerning... Church of England schools. 1850 2/2/50
Hamilton, Henry Parr
[letter to Hook]. (not found) 19/4/47
Hamilton, James Minister of the National Scotch Church
Moses the man of God; a course of lectures. 1871 29/1/71
The harp on the willows: or, the captivity of the church in Scotland. Addressed to the people of England. 1843 26/2/43 ?
Hamilton, James Traveller in Africa
Wanderings in North Africa. 1856 18/2/68
Hamilton, John advocate
A remonstrance respectfully addressed to the members of the legislature... in relation to the Scottish Church question. 1841 27/2/41
Letter to Sir George Sinclair, Bart.... in reference to the 'Scotch Church question'. 1842 27/4/42
The present position of the Church of Scotland explained and vindicated. By a lay member of the church. 1839 6/12/39
Hamilton, John Bishop of Dunkeld
The catechism set forth by Bishop Hamilton... Together with the two-penny faith. 1882 27/8/82
Hamilton, Richard Winter
Sermons. 1846 (2nd edn) 8/7/49
Hamilton, Robert LL.D., F.R.S.E.
An inquiry concerning the rise and progress, the redemption... and management of the national debt of Great Britain. 1813 25/2/53
Hamilton, Thomas Captain
Men and manners in America. By the author of Cyril Thornton. 1833 (2v.) 7/9/33
Hamilton, Walter F.R.G.S.
The poets laureate of England. Being a history. 1879 1/11/92
Hamilton, Walter Kerr Bishop of Salisbury
A charge to the clergy and churchwardens of the diocese of Salisbury, at his triennial visitation in August, 1858. 1858 24/10/58
A charge to the clergy of the diocese of Salisbury at his primary visitation in August, 1855. 1855 9/9/55
A charge... at his triennial visitation in August, 1864. 1864 16/10/64
A charge... at his triennial visitation, in May, 1867. 1867 23/6/67
In the midst of life we are in death. A sermon [on James iv.14] preached... after the death of... E. Denison... Bishop of Salisbury. 1854 19/3/54
Morning and evening services for every day in the week, and other prayers arranged for the use of families. 1842 15/5/53
Our founder's purpose. A sermon [on Job xxiii. 3] preached... in the chapel of Merton College, Oxford. 1864 25/12/64
The cathedral commission. A letter to... the Dean of Salisbury. 1853 15/5/53
Hamilton, Sir William
Campi Phlegraei. Observations on the volcanos of the two Sicilies. 1776 8/9/88
Hamilton, William Gerard
Parliamentary logick. To which are subjoined two speeches delivered in the house of commons in Ireland. 1808 25/4/45, 6/9/82
Hamilton, William Richard
Address to the Royal Geographical Society of London... 22nd May, 1843. 1843 15/7/43
Memorandum on the subject of the Earl of Elgin's pursuits in Greece. 1811 2/10/64
Hamilton, William Tighe
The Irish land bills of the late government considered. 1853 21/2/70
Hamley, Sir Edward Bruce K. C. B.
The war in the Crimea... With portraits and plans. 1891 16/4/91, 28/4/91
Hammer-Purgstall, Baron Joseph von
Geschichte des Osmanischen Reiches. 1827 (10v. 1827–35) 23/2/77
Hammond, Henry D.D.
A paraenesis: or seasonable exhortatory to all true sons of the Church of England. (1841) 16/5/41
Hammond, Joseph
Church or chapel? An eirenicon. 1889 19/1/90
Hampden, Renn Dickson
A course of lectures introductory to the study of moral philosophy. 1835 18/7/45
A lecture on tradition, read before the university, in the Divinity School, Oxford... March 7th, 1839. 1839 2/6/39
An attempt to justify the agitation against the appointment of Dr. Hampden... a letter to Archdeacon Hare; by a tutor of a college. 1848 8/2/48
Bampton lectures of the year 1832... second edition. 1837 11/2/49, 2/10/59
Four sermons, preached in the Cathedral of Christ Church, before the University of Oxford. 1842 20/5/43

Observations on religious dissent. 1834 16/2/36
Sermons to Oxford university 1836–47. 1848 4/3/49
Some memorials of R. D. Hampden... edited by his daughter H. Hampden. 1871 11/2/71
The case of Dr. Hampden. The official and legal proceedings connected with the appointment of Dr. Hampden to the See of Hereford. 1848 9/1/49
The charge delivered at the fourth triennial visitation of the... Bishop of Hereford. 1859 9/10/59
The charge delivered at the third visitation of the diocese. 1856 18/1/57
The church not in danger. 1848 10/2/48
The fathers of Greek philosophy. 1862 4/2/62
The Hampden controversy: the whole of the correspondence... between the bishops... and Lord John Russell. 1847 18/12/47
The Lord our righteousness. A sermon [on Jer. xxiii. 5, 6]. 1839 24/5/40

Hampson, John
Memoirs of John Wesley. With a review of his life and writings, and a history of Methodism. 1791 (3v.) 2/5/58

Hampson, R. T.
Medii Aevi Kalendarium, or dates, charters, and customs of the Middle Ages. 1841 (3v.) 27/7/42

Hancock, George
The pew question. A case, decided at Yeovil, in the diocese of Bath and Wells. 1851 13/3/53

Hancock, John M.D.
Observations on the climate, soil, and productions of British Guiana, and on the advantages of emigration to... that country. 1835 11/5/70

Hancock, Thomas
A bishop must have the good report of those who are without the church. A sermon preached... after the confirmation of Dr. Temple. 1870 30/1/70
Christ and the people. Sermons chiefly on the obligations of the church to the state and to humanity. 1875 25/12/75
The return to the father. Sermons on a part of the parable of the Prodigal Son. 1873 2/11/73

Hancock, William Neilson
Local government and taxation in Ireland. 1875 12/8/86
Report on the supposed progressive decline of Irish prosperity. 1863 17/10/64

Handbook of elements of oil-painting. 1842 5/1/44

Handbook to the places of public worship in London. 1851 14/6/52

Hanger, George Baron Colraine
The life, adventures, and opinions of Col. G. Hanger. Written by himself. 1801 (2v.) 24/10/49

Hankey, Thomson
Banking: its utility and economy. A lecture... with... the working and management of the Bank of England. 1860 16/1/64
The principles of banking, its utility and economy; with remarks on... the Bank of England. 1867 2/1/67

Hanmer, Sir John Baron Hanmer
Fra Cipolla, and other poems. 1839 21/5/39
Notes and papers to serve for a memorial of the parish of Hanmer in Flintshire. 1872 28/12/71
Proteus, and other poems. 1833 11/7/34

Hann, William
Chapel and other trust debts. Letters shewing the means of management and certain liquidation. 1864 29/8/65

Hanna, William
Letters of T. Erskine... from 1800 till 1840, ed. W. Hanna. 1877 23/12/90 ?
Memoirs of the life and writings of Thomas Chalmers, D.D. 1849 (4v. 1849–52) 18/12/49

Hannah, John
Discourses on the fall and its results. 1857 2/8/57, 4/9/59
The annual address of the conference to the Methodist societies. 1841 12/9/41
The relation between the divine and human elements in holy scripture. Eight lectures preached before the University of Oxford. 1863 29/11/63

Hannington, James Bishop of the C. of E. in Africa
Life of James Hannington, first bishop of Eastern Equatorial Africa. 1887 3/4/87

Hanson, John H.
The lost prince: facts tending to prove the identity of Louis the seventeenth of France and the Rev. Eleazer Williams, Missionary. 1854 21/10/54

Hanson, William
Maynooth endowment and nunneries bills. Letters to Lord Alfred Hervey. 1853 1/11/57

Harcourt, Edward Vernon afterw. Vernon
A sermon preached at the coronation of King George IV. 1821 23/4/43

Harcourt, Edward William
The Harcourt papers. Edited by E. W. Harcourt. 1880 (14v. 1880–1905) 3/9/81, 5/12/83, 6/6/89

Harcourt, Leveson Vernon
The doctrine of the deluge; vindicating the scriptural account from the doubts recently cast upon it by geological speculations. 1838 (2v.) 31/3/39

Harcourt, Sir William George Granville Venables Vernon
A speech addressed to his constituents... at Oxford, on December 21, 1874. 1875 13/1/75

Harcourt, Sir William George Granvile Venables Vernon (*cont.*)
Letters by Historicus on some questions of international law. 1863 27/6/63
Plan for the amendment of the law. 1871 15/11/71
The morality of public men . . . by an Englishman. 1852 4/12/52, 26/5/53

Harcourt, William Vernon Canon of York
Letter . . . on the proposed disendowment of the Church in Ireland. 1868 22/8/68
What is truth? A poetical dialogue on the philosophy of natural and revealed religion. 1869 28/11/69

Harden, William Dearing
An inquiry into the truth of dogmatic Christianity. 1893 8/10/93

Hardenberg, Baron Friedrich Leopold von
Novalis Schriften. Herausgegeben von L. Tieck und F. Schlegel. 1805 (2v.) 25/3/89

Harding, Wyndham
Railways. The gauge question. Evils of a diversity of gauge, and a remedy. 1845 16/7/45

Hardinge, Charles Stewart 2nd Viscount Hardinge
Viscount Hardinge. [A biography] *By his son . . . Charles Viscount Hardinge.* 1890 10/5/91

Hardinge, Thomas
An answere to Maister Iuelles chalenge, . . . augmented with certain quotations and additions. 29/3/46, 28/11/68

Hardwick, Charles Archdeacon of Ely
A history of the articles of religion. 1851 10/10/88
A history of the Christian church. Middle age, with four maps constructed . . . by A. K. Johnston. 1853 27/11/53
Christ and other masters: an historical inquiry into some of the chief parallelisms and contrasts. 1855 (4v. 1855–59) 19/1/57
Universities and the Church of England. 1854 20/7/54

Hardwicke, William M.D.
Life and health assurance for the working classes. An answer to the question how the government may best acquit itself. 1864 12/7/64

Hardy, Robert Spence
The legends and theories of the Buddhists, compared with history and science. 1866 27/5/66

Hardy, Thomas
'The Dorsetshire labourers' in *Longman's Magazine*, ii. 252. 1883 (July 1883) 6/11/83
Tess of the D'Urbervilles. 1891 (3v.) 30/4/92
The return of the native. 1878 (3v.) 20/8/89

Hare, Augustus John Cuthbert
The story of two noble lives. 1893 (3v.) 22/12/93, 12/2/94
Wanderings in Spain. 1873 23/4/73

Hare, Augustus William
Sermons to a country congregation. 1836 (2v.) 5/8/38, 22/11/40, 3/9/43

Hare, Francis
The difficulties and discouragements which attend the study of the scriptures. 1714 17/10/69

Hare, Julius Charles
A letter to the dean of Chichester, on the agitation excited by the appointment of Dr. Hampden to the see of Hereford. 1848 4/2/48
A letter to the hon. R. Cavendish, on the recent judgement of the Court of Appeal, as affecting the doctrine of the church. 1850 19/4/50
Better prospects of the church: a charge to the clergy of the archdeaconry of Lewes. 1840 5/2/41
The History of Rome . . . translated by J. C. Hare and Connop Thirlwall. 1828 29/9/29
The unity of the church. A sermon [on Ephes. iv.4–6] preacht . . . December 10, 1840. 1845 12/2/45

Hare, Thomas
A treatise on the election of representatives, parliamentary and municipal. 1859 12/3/59
The development of the wealth of India. Reprinted from Macmillan's Magazine. 1861 22/6/61

Hargreaves, William
Revelations from Printing-House Square. Is the anonymous system a security for the purity and independence of the press? A question for The Times. 1864 17/6/64

Harington, Edward Charles
Brief notes on the Church of Scotland, from 1555 to 1842. 1843 13/8/43
The reformers of the Anglican church, and Mr. Macaulay's History of England. 1849 28/4/49

Harland, John
Lancashire lyrics: modern songs and ballads of the County Palatine. 1866 20/11/79

Harle, William Lockey
The total repeal of the navigation laws, discussed and enforced, in a letter to Earl Grey. 1848 29/6/48

Harley, Timothy
Christian poems. 1865 7/5/65

Harness, William
Visiting societies and lay readers. A letter to the lord bishop of London. By Presbyter Catholicus. 1844 14/7/44
Welcome and farewell. 1837 16/5/38

Harper, Francis Whaley
Dialogues on national church and national church rate. 1861 23/5/75

Harper, Samuel Brown
A voice from the North. An appeal to the people of England on behalf of their church. By an English priest. 1850 3/4/50

Harraden, Beatrice
Ships that pass in the night. 1893 24/5/93
Harris, Elizabeth Furlong Shipton
From Oxford to Rome: and how it fared with some who lately made the journey. By a companion traveller. 1847 13/2/47
Rest in the church. 1848 11/2/48
Harris, George
Civilization considered as a science, in relation to its essence, its elements, and its end. 1861 25/7/62
Harris, George Collyer
Lessons from St. Peter's life. 1865 16/2/89 ?
Harris, Henry
An essay on priesthood. Intended chiefly as an answer to the theory of the church as advanced by Dr. Arnold. 1849 15/4/49
Historical religion and biblical revelation. 1867 21/7/67
The church and the priesthood. A review of Dr. Mowbray's Bampton lectures for 1868. 1869 24/5/74
Harris, James
Philosophical inquiries. 1780 (3v. 1780–89) 8/2/30
Three treatises. The first concerning art. The second concerning music, painting and poetry. The third concerning happiness. 1744 21/5/31
Harris, James Howard 3rd Earl of Malmesbury
A series of letters of the first Earl of Malmesbury ... edited by his grandson. 1870 7/10/70
Diaries and correspondence of James Harris, first earl of Malmesbury ... edited by his grandson, the third earl. 1844 (4v.) 21/4/45
Memoirs of an ex-minister. An autobiography. 1884 (2v.) 6/10/84, 15/11/84
Harris, John miner
The strange preacher, John the Baptist. 1881 13/4/90 ?
Harris, John Principal of New College, London
Mammon; or, covetousness the sin of the Christian church. 1836 17/7/36
Harris, John pseud. Kuklos
The Church of England, the British Empire, and the Chinese. 1876 13/6/76
Harris, Stanley
Old coaching days ... illustrated by John Sturgess. 1882 11/1/83
Harrison, Alexander James
Problems of Christianity and scepticism. 1891 29/1/93
Harrison, Benjamin Archdeacon of Maidstone
A charge delivered to the clergy of the archdeaconry of Maidstone. 1846 24/5/46
An historical inquiry into the true interpretation of the rubrics of the Book of Common Prayer respecting the sermon and the communion service. 1845 27/7/45
Charity never failing. A sermon preached in Canterbury Cathedral, on occasion of the death of William Rowe Lyall, D.D., Dean of Canterbury. 1857 9/2/68
Church rate abolition, in its latest form. 1855 6/6/58
Disestablishment and disendowment by instalment, and piecemeal. A charge ... 1882. 1883 1/7/83
Prospects of peace for the church in the prayer book and its rules. A charge ... April 1875. 1875 31/10/75
The church in its divine constitution and office, and in its relations with the civil power. A charge. 1877 8/7/77
The church rate question, and the principles involved in it. A charge. 1854 18/6/54
The church the guardian of her children: her guide the oracles of God. A charge. 1850 10/6/50
The church's works and wants at the present time. A charge. 1881 24/7/81
The continuity of the church, and its present position, in England. A charge. 1886 23/4/86
The more excellent way of unity in the church of Christ. A charge. 1878 13/10/78
The present position of the Church of England, and the consequent duties of her ministers. A charge. 1851 3/6/51
The remembrance of a departed guide and ruler in the church of God. A charge. 1848 25/6/48
The study of different languages, as it relates to the philosophy of the human mind: a prize essay. 1832 14/9/32
Harrison, Constance Cary
Flower De Hundred. The story of a Virginia plantation. 1890 24/2/91
Harrison, Frederic
Oliver Cromwell. 1888 9/8/88
Order and progress. Part I. Thoughts on government. Part II. Studies of political crises. 1875 11/5/76
Harrison, James
The Catholic Apostolic Church—Irvingism—its pretensions and claims considered ... By a late member. 1872 13/9/72
The fathers versus Dr. Pusey ... doctrine of the real presence. 1873 5/1/73
The last days of Irvingism; or, ritualism, Romanism, and the Catholic Apostolic Church. 1873 12/10/73
Harrison, Samuel Bealey
An analytical digest of all the reported cases determined in the House of Lords and the several courts of Common Law. 1856 (2v. 4th edn) 13/2/65
Harrison, Mrs. St. L. pseud. L. Malet
The wages of sin. 1892 17/2/91, 26/2/91
Harrison, William Henry
Spirits before our eyes. 1879 18/8/78

Harshal, David Addison
Life of the Rev. George Whitefield. 1866 15/8/69
Hart, Mrs. Elizabeth Anna
Freda. A novel. 1878 (3v.) 2/10/93
Mrs. Jerningham's journal. 1869 26/8/70, 10/2/76
The runaway: a story for the young. 1872 9/2/80
Hart, William Henry
A memorial of Nell Gwynne ... and T. Otway. Ed. W. H. Hart. 1868 27/7/85
Hart, William R.
Eternal purpose. A study of the scripture doctrine of immortality. 1881 14/5/81
Harte, Francis Bret
The heathen Chinee ... and other poems. 1871 15/5/71
The luck of Roaring Camp, and other sketches. 1870 24/1/79
Hartley, Charles
The Serpent of Cos. 1878 16/12/78
Hartley, David M.P.
Letters on the American War. 1718 5/7/52
Observations on man. 1749 (2v.) 3/9/63
Hartley, John Wesleyan minister
Hid treasures and the search for them: being the substance of lectures delivered to Bible classes. 1859 11/10/68
Hartmann, Carl Robert Eduard von
Die Selbstzersetzung des Christenthums und die Religion der Zukunft. 1874 29/9/75
The religion of the future ... translated from the German ... by E. Dare. 1886 5/6/88
Hartsen, Fr. A. von
Der Katholicismus und seine Bedeutung in der Gegenwart. 1874 13/1/75
Hartshorne, Albert
Hanging in chains. 1891 5/10/91
Hartshorne, Charles Henry
Extracts from the register of Sir T. Butler. 1861 27/10/61
Hartshorne, Emily Sophia
Enshrined hearts of warriors and illustrious people. 1861 25/10/61
Hartwig, Georg M.D.
The sea and its living wonders. Translated from the fourth German edition and partly rewritten. 1860 8/12/60
Harty, William
Failure of the Reformation in Ireland: its true causes developed in a petition, addressed to the House of Lords. By a Protestant layman. 1837 1/4/37
Harvey, A. C.
The Book of Chronicles in relation to the Pentateuch. 1892 1/10/93
Harvey, Alexander M.D.
Man's place unique in nature ... by a University professor. 1865 6/1/67
Harvey, Thomas Curate of Thaxted
Correspondence between ... T. Harvey and the bishop of London's chaplain ... on ... Mr. Harvey's licence to the curacy of Margaretting. 1845 14/3/45
Letters addressed to the bishop of London [C. J. Blomfield] *in reference to ... Mr. Harvey's dismissal ...* 1845 30/10/53
Harvey, William Wigan
The history and theology of the three creeds. 1854 (2v.) 18/2/55
Harvey, William Woodis
The love of the church of God and of his earthly sanctuary [A consecration sermon on Ps. xxvi. 8]. 1845 7/7/50
Harwood, George
Disestablishment: or, a defence of the principle of a national church. 1876 5/7/77
The coming democracy. 1882 5/8/82
Harwood, Philip
History of the Irish rebellion of 1798. 1844 19/9/89
Haslett, William
The Queen's University of Ireland. The supplemental Charter considered. 1867 6/1/68
Hassencamp, Robert
History of Ireland from the Reformation to the Union. 1888 8/7/93
Hastings, Lady Flora Elizabeth Rawdon
The Lady Flora Hastings: her life and death. 1839 18/9/39
Hastings, Henry James
Reasons for not signing the proposed address to the bishop of Worcester, and remarks on ... Gorham v. Bishop of Exeter; in a letter. 1850 21/5/50
Hastings, Warren
The history of the trial of Warren Hastings ... or an impeachment by the Commons ... for high crimes and misdemeanors. 1796 15/1/58
Hatch, Edwin
'Canonical obedience' in *Contemporary Review*, xliii. 289. 1883 (February 1883) 12/2/83
Progress in theology. An address. 1885 14/12/84
The organization of the early Christian churches. Eight lectures. 1881 25/12/81
Hatchard, Thomas Goodwin
'The workmen, they are of men.' A sermon [on Isa. xliv. 11] in behalf of the Lancashire distress. 1862 30/11/62
Hathaway, W. S.
The speeches of the Rt. Hon. W. Pitt. Ed. W. S. Hathaway. 1806 (4v.) 19/10/80
Hatsell, John
Precedents of proceedings in the House of Commons under separate titles; with

with observations. 1818 (vol 3 new edn) 24/2/54

Hatton, Joseph

By order of the Czar. The tragic story of Anna Klosstock, Queen of the Ghetto. 1890 (3v.) 12/9/91

The new Ceylon. Being a sketch of British North Borneo, or Sabah... With... maps. 1881 2/1/82

Hatton, Joseph, and Harvey, M.

Newfoundland... its history,... present condition, and... prospects. 1883 2/5/91

Haug, Martin

Essays on the sacred languages, writings and religion of the Parsees. 1862 (1890 edn) 15/9/91

Haughton, John

The depression of agriculture, with a proposal for its remedy. 1879 3/3/79

Haughton, Samuel

University education in Ireland. 1868 25/2/68

Haughton, S. M.

The precious name! or, Jesus only. 1881 2/10/81

Havergal, Frances Ridley

Coming to the king. Hymns by F. R. Havergal and others. 1886 23/5/86

Havergal, Maria Vernon Graham

Memorials of F. R. Havergal. 1880 19/6/80

Haviland, Alfred

Abstracts of two papers [on heart disease and dropsy and on the geographical distribution of cancer]. 1869 24/5/69

Haweis, Hugh Reginald

'Old violins', in *Contemporary Review*, xxi.85. 1872 (December 1872) 7/12/72

Music and morals. 1871 13/12/71

The third and last voyage of Captain Cook, ed. H. R. Haweis. 1886 18/9/86

Haweis, John Oliver Willyams

Sketches of the Reformation and Elizabethan age taken from the contemporary pulpit. 1844 5/6/59

Hawker, Mary Elizabeth

Mademoiselle Ixe. 1891 1/1/91

Hawker, Robert Stephen pseud. Reuben

Memorials of R. S. Hawker... Collected, arranged, and edited by F. G. Lee. 1876 16/9/77, 16/11/79

Prose works. 1893 25/6/93

Hawkes, Joseph Henry

A liberal's appeal to liberals for the toleration of the Christian morality and religion in some of the schools of the state. 1892 14/8/92

Hawkins, Edward

A letter to the principal of Magdalen Hall upon the future representation of the University of Oxford. 1853 12/2/53

Additional notes on subscription, academical and clerical, with reference to the Clerical Subscription Act of 1865. 1866 21/3/66

An inaugural lecture upon the foundation of Dean Ireland's Professorship, read before the University of Oxford. 1848 21/2/48

Book of psalms... with... explanatory notes. 1857 28/3/58

Christ our example. A sermon [on Luke ix. 23, etc.]. 1853 12/2/54

Considerations upon the Athanasian creed and the proposed synodical declaration. 1874 8/6/73

Historical notices of the missions of the Church of England in the North American colonies. 1845 12/4/46

Our debts to Caesar and to God. A sermon [on Matth. xxii. 21]. 1868 3/1/69

Recent expansion of the Church of England. Ramsden sermon for 1864. 1864 21/8/64

Sermons on scriptural types and sacraments. 1851 25/5/51

Sermons on the church, preached before the University of Oxford. 1847 21/8/81

The apostolical succession. A sermon [on 2 Tim. i. 6, 7] *preached in the chapel of Lambeth Palace.* 1842 9/4/42

The duty of private judgment. A sermon [on 1 Thess. v. 21]. 1838 26/5/61

The duty of weighing the relative importance of questions, specially of religious questions. A sermon. 1871 23/4/71

The liberty of private judgment within the Church of England. A sermon [on Matth. ix. 36-38]. 1863 22/3/63

The nature and obligation of apostolic order. A sermon [on Acts xi. 41, 42, 47]. 1842 13/2/42

Hawkins, Francis Bisset

Germany: the spirit of her history, literature, social condition and national economy. 1838 28/9/56 ?

Hawkins, Sir John

The life of Samuel Johnson, LL.D. 1787 22/8/72

Hawkshaw, Sir John

Rapport... sur les travaux du canal de Suez, suivi des observations de M. Voisin... Documents publiés par M. F. de Lesseps. 1863 24/7/63

Hawley, Richard

An essay on free trade. 1878 1/1/79

Hawthorne, Nathaniel

The house of seven gables. 1851 23/6/51

The scarlet letter. 1850 18/6/51

Hawtrey, Edward Craven

Chapel lectures [read in ms.]. 1848 16/5/47

Il Trifoglio; ovvero Scherzi metrici d'un Inglese. 1839 14/8/43

Lectures on church catechism delivered in Eton College chapel. 1846 7/6/46

Hawtrey, Montague
Sponsors for the poor. 1840 21/6/40
Hawtrey, Montague John Gregg
Justice to New Zealand, honour to England. 1861 28/3/61
Hawtrey, Stephen Thomas
A letter containing an account of St. Mark's School, Windsor. 1857 3/6/57
Haxthausen, Baron August von
Transcaucasia. Sketches of the nations and races between the Black Sea and the Caspian [Tr. from the German by J. E. Taylor]. 1854 28/9/76
Hay, John Barras
Inaugural addresses by Lords Rectors of the University of Glasgow. 1839 31/3/60
Hay, Sir John Charles Dalrymple
Memorandum. Rear-Admiral Sir J. C. D. Hay's compulsory retirement from the British navy. 1870 5/5/70
Hay, Sir John Hay Drummond G. C. M. G.
Western Barbary: or its wild tribes and savage animals. 1844 30/11/44
Hayden, J.
Observations on the national system of education in Ireland. 1838 17/3/49
Haydon, Benjamin Robert
Some enquiry into the causes which have obstructed the advance of historical painting for the last seventy years in England. 1829 12/1/49 ?
The life of B. R. Haydon . . . from his autobiography and journals. Edited and compiled by Tom Taylor. 1853 (3v.) 23/3/55
Hayes, T. T.
Lord Beaconsfield. A paper read . . . before the members of the Leigh Liberal Club. 1878 21/6/79 ?
Hayley, William
A tribute to the memory of William Cowper . . . occasioned by the perusal of his works, and the memoirs of his life. 1808 9/4/74
Hayman, Henry
Dialogues of the early church. 1851 20/6/52
The Odyssey of Homer, ed. H. Hayman. 1866 (3v.) 25/1/73, 1/12/86
Why do we suffer? and other essays. 1889 22/12/89
Hays, J.
Pamphlet on the corn laws. 1843 (not found) 26/1/43
Hayward, Abraham
'Ireland and the land question', in *Fraser's Magazine*, lxxxi. 121. 1870 (January 1870) 5/1/70
'Lothair', in *Macmillan's Magazine*, xxii. 142. 1870 (June 1870) 30/5/70
[on Cavour] in *Quarterly Review*, cxlviii. 99. 1879 (July 1879) 21/8/79
[on Greville journals] in *Quarterly Review*, cxxxviii. 1. 1875 (January 1875) 16/1/75
[on Holland House] in *Quarterly Review*, cxxxv. 405. 1873 (October 1873) 20/10/73
A selection from the correspondence of A. Hayward . . . from 1834 to 1884. With an account of his early life. Edited by H. E. Carlisle. 1886 28/1/85 n, 11/10/86 n, 9/12/86, 4/1/87
Biographical and critical essays. Reprinted from reviews, with additions and corrections. 1858 (5v. 1858–74) 23/4/58, 28/2/74
Dr. Johnson's Mrs. Thrale's Autobiography . . . edited by A. Hayward. 1861 20/5/61
Faust: a dramatic poem, translated into English prose . . . by the translator of Savigny. 1833 18/1/36, 9/5/78
More about Junius. The Franciscan theory unsound. Reprinted from Fraser's Magazine. 1868 29/1/68
Verses of other days. 1847 21/7/47
Hazlehurst, G. S.
The reunion of Christendom. 1892 7/10/92
Hazlitt, William Carew
History of the Venetian republic: her rise, her greatness, and her civilization. 1860 28/6/60
Head, Sir Edmund Walker
Essays on the administration of Great Britain from 1783 to 1830 . . . edited by Sir E. Head. 1864 7/4/64
Report on the law of bastardy: with a supplementary report on a cheap civil remedy for seduction. 1840 5/5/40
Head, Sir Francis Bond
A narrative. By Sir F. B. Head. Supplemental chapter. [A vindication of his government of Upper Canada]. 1839 25/2/39
An address to the House of Lords against the bill before Parliament for the union of the Canadas. 1840 25/5/40
Bubbles from the Brunnens of Nassau [By an old man]. 1834 25/4/34
Rough notes taken during some rapid journeys across the Pampas and among the Andes. 1826 4/11/47
Stokers and pokers . . . By the author of 'Bubbles from the Brunnens of Nassau'. 1849 12/3/49
The defenceless state of Great Britain. 1850 11/2/56
The emigrant. 1846 2/1/47 ?
Three letters to Lord Brougham on the execution of . . . Lount and Matthews. 1838 11/8/38
Words on defence. 1846 19/1/46 ?

Head, Sir George
A home tour through the manufacturing districts of England in the summer of 1835. 1836 (2nd edn) 24/10/43
Head, Henry Erskine
Observations on early rising and on early prayer. 1828 (1829) 6/2/29
The ultimate and proximate results of redemption: chiefly deduced from the oath sworn unto Abraham. 1854 9/8/57
Head, Richard Gent.
The life and death of the English rogue. 12/8/90
Headlam, Clinton Edward Sowerby
The Iphigeneia at Aulis of Euripides, with introduction and notes by C. E. S. Headlam. 1875 14/3/78
Headlam, James Wycliffe afterw. Headlam-Morley
Election by lot at Athens. 1891 11/11/91
Headlam, Stewart Duckworth
Priestcraft and progress; being sermons and lectures. 1878 16/2/79
Headley, Phineas Camp
The life and campaigns of... U. S. Grant, from his boyhood to the surrender of Lee... [with] *official reports of Sheridan, Meade, Sherman and Grant.* 1866 10/6/67
Healy, Timothy Michael
A word for Ireland. 1886 16/10/86
Why there is an Irish land question and an Irish Land League. 1881 12/1/81
Heard, John Bickford
National Christianity; or, Caesarism and clericalism. 1877 9/10/87
Heartiness in public worship. By a London Churchwarden. 1860 18/11/60
Heartley, Charles Tebbott
Our cathedrals and their mission. 1855 29/4/55
Heath, Francis George
Peasant life in the west of England. 1880 (new edn) 23/11/80
Heath, George
The poems of G. Heath.... With an introduction by... J. Badnall... Memoir by F. Redfern... Memorial edition. 1880 30/1/84
Heath, Richard
Edgar Quintet, his early life and writings. 1877 (1881 edn) 9/5/81
The English via dolorosa; or, glimpses of the history of the agricultural labourer. 1884 2/11/84
Heath, Richard Ford
Life of Titian, in Illustrated biographies of the great artists. 1879 18/9/79
Heathcote, William Beadon
Documentary illustrations of the principles to be kept in view in the interpretation of the thirty-nine articles. 1841 22/8/41
Of the practical doctrine of the incarnation. A sermon. 1846 10/5/46
Heathcote, William Selfe
My salvation army experience. 1891 22/2/91
Heathfield, Richard
Contributions to the 'Postulates and Data' and other essays... inclusive of suggestions for a future budget... [and] *liquidation of the public debt.* 1853 14/11/53
Heber, Reginald
Hymns, written and adapted to the weekly church service of the year. Ed. Amelia Heber. 1827 17/8/28
Narrative of a journey through the Upper Provinces of India from Calcutta to Bombay in 1824–25. 1828 (2v.) 21/6/28, 15/9/33
The whole works of... Jeremy Taylor... With a life of the author, and a critical examination of his writings by R. Heber. 1822 22/11/29
Thirty sermons. 1829 18/7/29
Hebert, Charles
A reply to the pamphlet of W. G. Clark... entitled The Dangers of the Church of England. 1870 15/4/70
Hechler, William Henry
The Jerusalem bishopric. Documents, with translations... from 'Das Evangelische Bisthum in Jerusalem'... arranged and supplemented by W. H. Hechler. 1883 (2v.) 26/8/83, 5/4/85
Hecker, Willem
Die Israeliten und der Monotheismus... Aus dem Holländischen übersetzt. 1879 30/3/79
Hedley, John Cuthbert
A sermon [on 1 Cor. xv. 54, 55] preached at the funeral of... Thomas Joseph Brown, O.S.B., bishop of Newport. 1880 29/4/88
Heeren, Arnold Hermann Ludwig
A manual of ancient history.... Translated from the German. 1829 9/3/31
A sketch of the political history of ancient Greece. Translated from the German. 1829 27/2/30
Ideen über die Politik, den Verkehr und den Handel der vornehmsten Völker der alten Welt. 1793 (3v. 1793–1812) 11/2/68
Hegel, Georg Wilhelm Friedrich
The ethics of Hegel, by J. M. Sterrett. 1893 3/9/93
Hehn, Victor
The wanderings of plants and animals from their first home.... Edited by J. S. Stallybrass. 1885 20/10/85
Heimweh, Jean
Le régime des passeports en Alsace-Lorraine. 1890 5/3/90
Questions du temps présent. Triple alliance et Alsace-Lorraine. 1892 23/8/92
Heine, Heinrich
Poems and ballads... Done into English verse by Theodore Martin. 1878 (1881 edn) 6/1/82

Heine, Heinrich (*cont.*)
Poesie und Prosa, ed. A. Lévy. 1891 16/12/91, 13/1/92
The poems of Heine complete, translated in the original metres, with a sketch of Heine's life. By E. A. Bowring. 1846 (1861 edn) 8/1/64
Hélie, Augustin
La Rome des Papes. 1861 5/8/76
Helping Hand, B.
Band of Hope enterprise, by B. Helping Hand. 1866 17/6/66
Helps, Sir Arthur K. C. B.
Friends in council; a series of readings and discourses thereon. 1847 7/11/59
Life and labours of Mr. Brassey. 1805–1870. 1872 12/8/72
Organization in daily life. An essay. 1862 11/12/60
Realmah. By the author of 'Friends in Council'. 1868 31/12/69
The life of Hernando Cortes. 1871 5/4/71
The life of Las Casas, 'The apostle of the Indies'. 1868 17/1/68
The principal speeches and addresses of His Royal Highness the Prince Consort. Ed. Sir A. Helps. 1862 21/1/62
Hemming, George Wirgman
A just income tax, how possible. 1852 18/1/53
Henderson, Ebenezer
Directions to the awakened sinner. [A sermon on Micah. iv. 6–8]. 1831 21/3/58 ?
The Vaudois; comprising observations made during a tour to the valleys of Piedmont, in . . . 1814. 1845 20/1/84
Henderson, Fred
By the sea, and other poems. 1890 20/1/90
Henderson, James consul
A review of the commercial code and tariffs of Spain, with reference to their influence on the general interests, credit and finances. 1842 7/2/43
State and prospects of Spain. 1841 10/12/41 ?
Henderson, William
Clues: or leaves from a chief constable's note book. 1889 (1891 edn) 3/11/90
Hengstenberg, Ernst Wilhelm
Christologie des Alten Testaments und Commentar über die Messianischen Weissagungen der Propheten. 1829 (3v. 1829–35) 26/7/63
Dissertations on the genuineness of Daniel and the integrity of Zachariah . . . . Translated by . . . B. P. Pratten. 1848 30/4/54
Dissertations on the genuineness of the Pentateuch . . . Translated from the German by J. E. Ryland. 1847 (3v.) 10/3/89
Henley, John
Mr. Henley's letters and advertisements which concern Mr. Whiston. Published by Mr. Whiston, with a few notes. 1727 5/11/82
Hennell, Charles Christian
An inquiry concerning the origin of Christianity. 1838 4/10/85
Hennell, Sara Sophia
Essay on the sceptical tendency of Butler's 'Analogy'. 1859 23/12/60, 31/5/93
On the need of dogmas in religion. A letter to T. Scott. 1874 16/8/74
Hennessy, Sir John Pope
Sir Walter Raleigh in Ireland. 1883 19/5/83
Henniker, Mrs. Florence Ellen Hungerford
Sir George. A novel. 1891 (2v. 1891–93) 10/5/91
Henningsen, Charles Frederick
Scenes from the Belgian revolution. 1832 16/3/36
Henry, Matthew
The family bible, or, complete commentary . . . by the Rev. M. Henry. 1838 27/6/91
Henry, Patrick
Patrick Henry. Life, correspondence and speeches, by W. W. Henry. 1891 (3v.) 10/6/92 n
Henry, Walter
Events of a military life; being recollections after service in the Peninsular war, invasion of France, the East Indies, St. Helena, Canada, etc. 1843 (2v.) 18/6/43
Henry, William Wirt
Patrick Henry. Life, correspondence and speeches. 1891 (3v.) 10/6/92
Henslow, George
The theory of evolution of living things and the application of the principles of evolution to religion considered. 1873 18/1/74
Heraclides, Ponticus
Opera. 15/11/57
Heraud, John Abraham
Shakespere, his inner life as intimated in his works. 1865 8/2/65
The judgement of the flood. 1834 11/11/83
Herbert, Algernon
Nimrod. A discourse upon certain passages of history and fable. 1826 5/5/57
Herbert, Edward Earl of Powis
Speech . . . in the House of Lords . . . a bill for preventing the union of the sees of St. Asaph and Bangor. 1843 20/6/43
Herbert, George poet
Herbert's poems and the country parson. A new edition; with the life of the author; from Isaak Walton. 1824 25/3/27
Poems. 29/4/29
The Temple, ed. J. H. Shorthouse. 1882 25/6/82
Works of George Herbert, ed. W. Pichering. 1835 (2v. 1835–36) 8/2/63
Herbert, Henry Howard Molyneux Earl of Carnarvon
Letters of Philip Dormer, fourth earl of

Chesterfield to his godson . . . Now first edited . . . by the Earl of Carnarvon. 1890 4/8/90

Herbert, Henry John George Earl of Carnarvon
Reminiscences of Athens and the Morea: extracts from a journal of travels in Greece in 1839. By the late Earl of Carnarvon . . . Edited by his son. 1869 29/3/69

Herbert, Mary Elizabeth Baroness Herbert of Lea
Impressions of Spain in 1866 . . . With . . . illustrations. 1867 31/1/67
The passion play at Ammergau. 1890 23/11/71

Herbert, Sidney Baron Herbert
Proposals for the better application of Cathedral Institutions to their intended uses; in a letter to the Dean of Salisbury. 1849 4/2/49

Herbert, William
Musae Etonenses; seu carminum delectus nunc primum in lucem editus. 1795 30/12/69

Herdman, William Gawin
Pictoral relics of ancient Liverpool. Accompanied with descriptions of the antique buildings. 1843 16/10/72

Herford, Brooke
The story of religion in England. A book for young folk. 1878 29/9/78

Hergenroether, Joseph Adam Gustav
Anti-Janus. Eine historisch-theologische Kritik der Schrift 'Der Papst und das Concil' von Janus. 1870 8/1/71

Hermann, Carl Friedrich
Lehrbuch der griechischen Staatsalterthümer. 1831 22/10/57

Hermann, Johann Gottfried Jacob
Homeri hymni et epigrammata. 1806 17/8/72

Hermes, Trismegistus
The Hermetic works. The virgin of the world . . . Now first rendered into English . . . by Dr. Anna Kingsford and E. Maitland. 1885 15/9/85 ?

Herodotus
History, tr. T. Gaisford, ed. P. E. Laurent. 1827 (2v.) 15/8/28
Historiae. 4/10/25, 7/10/26, 6/11/26, 22/1/27, 27/1/27, 29/3/27, 7/5/27, 28/9/27, 13/8/28, 26/8/28, 15/5/30, 2/6/30, 22/6/30, 30/7/30, 1/2/31, 19/10/31, 16/11/55, 21/7/75, 9/8/75, 16/12/92

Heron, Denis Caulfield
The constitutional history of the university of Dublin; with some account of its present condition. 1847 26/12/71

Heron, Robert Matthews afterw. Heron-Fermor
The Suez canal question. A letter. 1875 13/1/76

Herpin, Luce pseud. Lucien Perey
Histoire d'une grande dame au XVIIIe siècle. La princesse Hélène de Ligne. 1887 (2v. 1887–90) 20/3/93, 27/3/93

Herries, Edward
A letter to the editor of 'The Edinburgh Review' in reply to an article on a 'Memoir of the public life of the Right Hon. J. C. Herries'. 1881 4/6/81

Herries, John Charles
Memoir of the public life of the Right Hon. J. C. Herries . . . With an introduction by Sir C. Herries. 1880 (2v.) 3/12/80

Herring, Thomas Archbishop
Letters . . . to William Duncombe . . . from the year 1728 to 1757; with notes, and an appendix. 1777 29/7/58

Herschel, John Frederick William
A preliminary discourse on the study of natural philosophy. 1831 1/12/35, 30/12/48
The Iliad of Homer, translated into English accentuated hexameters, by Sir J. F. W. Herschel. 1866 15/2/62, 3/10/68
Two letters to the editor of the Athenaeum, on a British modular standard of length. 1863 13/1/64

Hershon, Paul Isaac
Treasures of the Talmud . . . translated by P. I. Hershon . . . with notes. 1881 19/11/81

Hervé, Edouard
La crise Irlandaise depuis la fin du dix-huitième siècle, jusqu'à nos jours. 1885 27/8/86

Hervey, Lord Arthur Charles
A charge delivered . . . in April, 1866. 1866 17/9/69
A few hints on infant baptism. 1838 13/4/38
A letter to the Rev. Christopher Wordsworth, D. D . . . on the declaration of the clergy on marriage and divorce. 1857 10/8/57
A sermon against the errors of popery. 1838 13/4/38
A suggestion for supplying the literary, scientific and mechanics' Institutes . . . with lecturers from the universities. 1855 12/7/55
Charge delivered to the clergy and churchwardens of the diocese of Bath and Wells at the general visitation held in April and May, 1873. 1873 20/7/73
Metaphysics, a lecture. 1854 27/11/54 ?
The Book of Chronicles in relation to the Pentateuch and the 'Higher Criticism'. 1892 3/12/93
The genealogies of our lord and saviour Jesus Christ as contained in the gospels of Matthew and Luke, reconciled. 1853 13/11/53
The inspiration of holy scripture. Five sermons. 1856 13/4/56

Hervey, Elizabeth Countess of Bristol
An authentic detail of particulars relative to the Duchess of Kingston. 1788 18/5/93

Hervey, Elizabeth Countess of Bristol (*cont.*)
The life and memoirs of Elizabeth Chudleigh . . . Duchess of Kingston. 1788 4/8/72, 5/1/82
Hervey, James
Eleven letters . . . to . . . John Wesley. 1765 3/5/57
Remarks on Lord Bolingbroke's Letters on the study and use of history. 1752 (1756) 3/2/56
Theron and Aspasio. 1755 (3v.) 28/11/92 ?
Hervey, Lord John
Memoirs of the reign of king George II . . . Edited . . . by J. W. Croker. 1848 (2v.) 22/7/48
Hervey, Maurice H.
The trade policy of imperial federation from an economic point of view. 1892 (?) 9/10/89
Heseltine, William
A tenant's statement of the conduct recently pursued . . . by the dean and chapter of Canterbury. 1838 29/1/38
Hesiod
Opera. 14/1/56
Theogony. 11/8/62, 19/8/91
Hessey, James Augustus
A scripture argument against permitting marriage with a wife's sister. 1855 (3rd edn) 15/4/55
Church and state questions in 1876. A charge. 1876 5/8/77
Sunday, its origin, history and present obligation, considered in eight lectures . . . [Bampton lectures]. 1860 25/11/60
The public-school boy: being an address . . . July 18, 1864, in the chapel of the Forest School, Walthamstow. 1864 22/9/66
The revision of the lectionary . . . With remarks on the subject of . . . the translation of the bible. 1868 27/12/68
Hetherington, Helen F., and Burton, Henry Darwin
Paul Nugent—materialist. 1890 (2v.) 5/7/90
Heugh, Hugh
Notices of the state of religion in Geneva and Belgium. 1844 14/12/44
Heurtley, Charles Abel
Justification. Eight sermons preached before the university of Oxford in 1845 . . . [Bampton lectures]. 1846 5/7/46
The union between Christ and his people. Four sermons preached before the university of Oxford. 1842 5/4/42
Hewitt, Ethel May
The effacement of Oriel Penhaligon. 1892 12/10/92
Hewitt, James Viscount Lifford
A plea for Irish landlords. A letter to Isaac Butt, Esq. on his 'Plea for the Celtic race'. 1867 20/2/67
Ireland, and the Irish church. 1842 31/7/42
Hewlett, John B. D.
Sermons on different subjects. 1805 (4v. 1805–25) 21/3/30
Hey, Samuel
Some account of the religion of Margaret Gray 1808–26. 16/12/27
Heydenreich, Eduard
Fabius Pictor und Livius. 1878 14/10/58 ?
Heygate, William Edward
Care of the soul; or sermons on some points of Christian prudence. 1851 9/5/52
Catholic antidotes. 1858 13/8/65
Consider the consequences . . . entreaty not to make any change in the Prayer Book without the consent of the church. 1867 28/7/67
Memoir of the Rev. J. Aubone Cook . . . vicar of South Benfleet. 1860 11/3/60
Sudden death, and other stories. 1880 19/12/81
The doctrines of original sin and the trinity . . . correspondence between a clergyman and a layman of Boston, U.S. 1859 22/4/60
The good shepherd; or, meditations for the clergy upon the example and teaching of Christ. 1860 6/9/63
What churchmen should do at this time. A paper. 1878 29/9/78
Why I am a Christian, or, a few reasons for our faith. 1876 14/4/76
Heylli, Georges d' pseud. Antoine Edmond Poinsot
Delaunay. Sociétaire de la Comédie-Française. 1883 21/5/84
Heylyn, Peter
Ecclesia restaurata; or, the history of the reformation of the Church of England. 9/12/40
Heyne, Christian Gottlob
[work on philology]. 26/6/56
C. G. Heynii excursus in Homerum. 1822 2/1/47
Heywood, James M.P.
Collection of statutes for the university and colleges of Cambridge, ed. J. Heywood. 1850 11/7/50
The recommendations of the Oxford University commissioners. 1853 9/12/53
Heyworth, Lawrence
Glimpses at the origin, mission, and destiny of man . . . taxation, peace, war, etc. 1866 10/2/67
On economic fiscal legislation. 1845 6/6/51 ?
Hibbert, Frank
Bad trade and how to avoid it. By a cotton spinner. 1878 11/10/78
Hibernia pacata. 1887 13/1/87
Hickes, George
Devotions in the ancient way of offices. 1701 5/11/54

Hicklin, John
The 'Ladies of Llangollen', as sketched by many hands. 1847 6/2/92
Hicks, Edward Lee
Henry Bazely: the Oxford evangelist. A memoir. 1886 23/4/86
Hicks, Henry
On the Cae Gwyn cave, North Wales... (From the Quarterly Journal of the Geological Society). 1888 25/9/88
Hickson, William Edward
The use of singing as a part of the moral discipline of schools. A lecture. 1838 18/5/38
Hierurgia Anglicana. 1848 1/9/44
Higginbotham, J. J.
Men whom India has known. 1874 (2nd edn) 28/10/83
Higgins, C. H.
[Lectures on Shakespeare and Bacon]. 26/10/86 ?
Higgins, Matthew James pseud. Jacob Omnium
Cheap sugar. 1847 6/11/47
Cheap sugar... third letter. 1848 6/11/47
Three letters to the editor of 'the Cornhill Magazine' on public school education. By Paterfamilias. 1861 9/7/61
Higgins, William Mullinger
The mosaical and mineral geologies, illustrated and compared. 1832 9/10/85, 12/8/91
High Church Man
Address to Protestant Episcopalians on the subject of a tract called 'Origin of the terms High and Low Churchmen'. 1827 9/5/60
Highton, Henry
Dean Stanley and Saint Socrates. The ethics of the philosopher and the philosophy of the divine. 1873 16/10/73
Hilaire, Jules Barthélemy Saint
Le Christianisme. Trois lettres. 1880 28/3/80
Hildreth, Richard
The white slave: or Memoirs of a fugitive. 1852 16/10/52 ?
Hildyard, James
A revision of the liturgy urged with a view chiefly to the abridgement of the Morning Service. 1856 14/11/56
Hilhouse, William
Indian notices: or, sketches of the habits, characters, languages... of the several nations [of British Guiana]. 1825 12/5/35
Hill, Abraham
Some account of the life of Dr. Isaac Barrow. 4/5/28
Hill, Charles
Continental Sunday labour. A warning to the English nation. 1877 26/8/77
Hill, Edwin
Principles of currency. Means of ensuring uniformity of value and adequacy of supply. 1856 15/1/56
Hill, Frank Harrison
Questions for a reformed parliament. 1867 20/11/69
Hill, Frederic
National force. Economical defence of the country from internal tumult and foreign aggression. 1848 6/3/48
Parliamentary reform. How the representation may be amended safely, gradually and efficiently. 1858 12/7/65
The county franchise difficulty, how removable. 1878 23/2/78
Hill, George Birkbeck Norman
Dr. Johnson, his friends and his critics. 1878 24/7/78
The life of Sir Rowland Hill... and the history of the penny postage. 1880 (2v.) 23/11/80
Hill, George William
Memoir of Sir B. Halliburton. 1864 7/1/65
Hill, James Hamlyn
The earliest life of Christ. 1893 24/12/93
Hill, Matthew Davenport
Public education plans for the government and liberal instruction of boys in large numbers: as practised at Hazelwood School. 1825 26/5/38
Hill, Octavia
Homes of the London poor. 1875 21/9/91
Hill, Pascoe Grenfell
Fifty days on board a slave-vessel in the Mozambique Channel, in... 1843. 1844 27/4/49
Hill, Sir Richard
Goliath slain, being a reply to... Nowell's answer to Pietas Oxoniensis. 1768 22/12/46
Pietas Oxoniensis, or... account of the expulsion of six students from St. Edmund Hall, Oxford. 1768 8/4/48
Hill, Sir Rowland K. C. B.
Memorandum... on the net revenue of the Post Office. 1862 22/1/63
Hillebrand, Carl
Six lectures on the history of German thought, from the Seven Years' War to Goethe's death. 1880 29/10/80
Hillern, Wilhelmine von
The vulture maiden. 1867 25/9/79
Hillocks, James Inches
Hard battles for life and usefulness. 1884 10/8/84
Life story. A prize autobiography. 1860 13/12/60
Life struggles: an autobiographical record of the earlier trials and later triumphs of... J. I. H. Edited... by G. Gilfillan. 1876 27/1/77
Hime, Maurice Charles
Morality. An essay addressed to young men. 1884 (8th edn) 19/11/86
Unbelief: an essay addressed to young men. 1885 14/11/86

Hincks, Sir Francis
Canada: its financial position and resources. 1849 27/6/49
Reply to the speech of the Hon. J. Howe . . . on the union of the North American provinces. 1855 27/7/55
Hinds, Samuel
A charge delivered to the clergy of the diocese of Norwich . . . primary visitation. 1852 9/9/52
Free discussion of religious topics. 1868 (2v. 1868–69) 16/8/68
The latest official documents relating to New Zealand, with introductory observations. 1838 23/2/38
Hine, Edward
The English nation identified with lost Israel. 1872 22/9/72
Hinshelwood, A. Ernest
Through starlight to dawn. 1893 29/3/93 ?
Hinton, James
The mystery of pain: a book for the sorrowful. 1866 6/5/66
Hinton, John Howard the elder
A plea for the liberty of education. A second letter to . . . James Graham, on the educational clauses of the Factories Bill. 1843 8/4/43
The case of the Manchester educationalists. A review of the evidence taken before a committee. 1852 (2v. 1852–54) 12/3/52
The test of experience: or, the Voluntary Principle in the United States. 1851 10/5/68
Hippolytus
Opera. 13/2/27
Hipsley, William
Undine: the spirit of the waters. A poem containing a version of the narrative by Baron de la Motte Fouqué. 1886 26/10/86
Hird, W. G.
Scripture names and their relation to ancient history. 1875 19/11/76
Hiron, Samuel Franklin
Things new and old. A sermon. 1881 27/11/81
Hirscher, G. B.
Lo stato attuale della chiesa. 1862 14/9/62
Hirscher, Johann Baptist von
Sympathies of the Continent, or proposals for a new reformation . . . translated and edited . . . by A. C. Coxe. 1852 7/6/52
Hislop, Alexander
The two Babylons: their identity, and the present Antichrist also the last. 1853 27/12/74
Historical and critical remarks upon the tariff. 1787 24/6/53
Historical notices of the Society of Dilettants. 1855 4/10/58
History of Torcello. (not found) 7/10/79
Hitchens, James Hiles
The penalty; or, the eternity of future punishment. 1878 2/1/82
Hitchman, James pseud. P. V. G. de Montgomery
[on land tenures]. 21/5/58
Hoadly, Benjamin
An answer to Dr. Snape's second letter. 1717 4/1/40
Defence of episcopal ordination. 1707 30/12/39
Several discourses concerning the terms of acceptance with God. 1711 5/1/40
Hoare, A. H.
The church in England from William III to Victoria. 1886 (2v.) 4/8/89
Hoare, Charles James
A charge delivered in October 1851 to the clergy of Surrey. 1851 20/2/53
A charge delivered to the clergy of the archdeaconry of Winchester in April, 1837. 1837 19/2/38
A charge . . . 1838 6/6/39
A letter to the . . . Bishop of London [on the Cathedral Question]. 1840 15/5/40
Hoare, Edward Newenham
A letter to T. F. Buxton, Esq., M.P., in reply to his speech on the Irish tithe bill. 1836 5/7/36
Letter to the Rt. Hon. Lord Stanley, M.P. on the present state of the question of national education in Ireland. 1842 21/7/48
Hoare, Richard Colt
Journal of a tour in Ireland A. D. 1806. 1807 20/11/86
Hoare, William Henry
Present position of the church. The baptismal and educational questions. Three letters to . . . Sir G. Grey. 1850 (3v.) 5/6/50
Hobart, Vere Henry Baron Hobart
'Parliamentary Reform' in *Political Essays.* 1866 12/2/66
Essays and miscellaneous writings . . . . With a biographical sketch. Edited by Mary Lady Hobart. 1885 (2v.) 20/1/88
On capital punishment for murder. An essay. 1861 11/1/61
Political essays . . . with short biographical sketch. 1877 (new edn) 27/8/77
The 'Mission' of Richard Cobden . . . Reprinted . . . from Macmillan's Magazine. 1867 18/6/73
Hobbes, Thomas
Behemoth. The history of the civil wars of England from the year 1640 to 1660. (1681 edn) 11/9/32
Eight bookes of the Peloponnesian Warre by Thucydides . . . interpreted and tr. Thomas Hobbes. 24/11/28
Hobhouse, Arthur Baron Hobhouse
'Native Indian judges in Mr. Ilbert's bill', in *Contemporary Review*, xliii. 795. 1883 1/6/83
A lecture on the characteristics of Charitable Foundations in England. 1868 31/12/68

Hobhouse, John Cam Baron Broughton
A journey through Albania and other provinces of Turkey in Europe and Asia . . . 1809 and 1810. 1813 (2v.) 14/6/48, 25/9/62, 8/11/76
Historical illustrations of the fourth canto of Childe Harold . . . the ruins of Rome; and an essay on Italian literature. 1818 9/7/55

Hocking, Joseph
Jabez Easterbrook; a religious novel. 1890 2/12/91 ?

Hocking, Silas Kitto
Crookleigh. A village story. 1888 8/9/89

Hocking, William John
Mors Janna vitae: a contribution to the problem of immortality. 1891 26/7/91

Hodder, Edwin
The life and work of the seventh earl of Shaftesbury. 1887 (3v.) 24/2/87, 27/2/87, 19/3/87

Hodge, Charles
A commentary on the Epistles to the Romans. 1835 12/11/37

Hodgkin, Thomas D. C. L.
Claudian; the last of the Roman poets. Two lectures. 1875 8/6/75, 9/8/78

Hodgkin, Thomas M.D.
A letter to Richard Cobden . . . on free trade and slave labour. 1848 17/4/48
On the importance of studying and preserving the languages spoken by uncivilised nations. 1835 11/5/36

Hodgson, Joseph
The Hunterian Oration, delivered at the Royal College of Surgeons of England . . . 1855. 1855 23/12/56

Hodgson, Richard
The constitution . . . of Wesleyan Methodism. 1841 25/9/41

Hodgson, William Ballantyne
Turgot: his life, times, and opinions. 1870 1/12/79

Hodgson, William Earl
Unrest; or, the newer Republic. 1887 16/9/90

Hoeck, Carl
Kreta. Ein Versuch zur Aufhellung der Mythologie und Geschichte . . . 1823 (3v. 1823–29) 7/11/57

Hoey, Mrs. Frances Cashel
A selection from the letters of Madame de Rémusat . . . from the French. 1881 12/10/81

Hoey, John Cashel
[on Irish land] in *Dublin Review*, xiii.443. 1869 (October 1869) 16/10/69

Hoffman, Franz
Franz von Baader, als Begründer der Philosophie der Zukunft. 1856 10/11/74

Hoffmann, Karl Friedrich
Katechismus der Christlichen Lehre. 1843 3/11/45 ?

Hoffmann, Murray
A treatise on the law of the Protestant Episcopal Church in the United States. 1850 23/5/52

Hofman, H. F.
Katherina von Bora. 1845 24/1/90

Hogan, James Francis
Robert Lowe, Viscount Sherbrooke. 1893 7/11/93, 9/1/94
The lost explorer, an Australian story. 1890 13/10/90

Hogarth, William
The analysis of beauty, with a view of fixing the fluctuating ideas of taste. 1753 12/5/75

Hogg, James
The poetical works of J. Hogg. 1822 (4v.) 25/5/26, 11/9/82

Hogg, Sir James Weir
Addresses delivered . . . to the students at the East-India College, at Haileybury. 1846 6/5/47

Hogg, Lewis Maydwell
What is doing in furtherance of church reformation in Italy? A letter to the bishop of Pennsylvania. 1867 14/4/67

Hogg, Lewis Maydwell, and Woodcock, T. Parry
A letter to the . . . bishop of London, on the subject of the present religious movement in Italy. 1861 18/9/61

Hole, Richard
An essay on the character of Ulysses as delineated by Homer. 1807 13/9/77

Hole, Samuel Reynolds
A little tour in Ireland. By an Oxonian. 1859 14/1/61

Holford, T. G.
Short vindication of . . . Millbank. 1825 (3v.) 29/7/35

Holland, Francis James
The constraint of Christ. A sermon [on 2 Cor. v. 14]. 1878 27/10/78

Holland, George Calvert
An exposition of Corn-law repealing fallacies and inconsistencies. 1840 21/1/41
Letter to J. R. M'Culloch . . . in answer to his statements on the Corn Laws. 1841 27/8/41
Suggestions towards improving the present system of Corn-Laws. 1841 4/10/41
The physiology of the foetus, liver, and spleen. 1831 27/10/55

Holland, Sir Henry
Chapters on mental physiology. 1852 25/10/59
Essays on scientific and other subjects. 1862 8/7/68 ?
Recollections of past life. 1872 4/3/72

Holland, Henry Richard Lord Holland
Memoirs of the Whig party. 1852 (1852–54) 9/3/52, 14/7/90

Holland, Henry Scott
God's city and the coming of the kingdom. 1894 1/4/94
In memoriam. A sermon [on Tim. iv. 6, 7] *preached . . . for the Pusey Memorial Fund.* 1883 4/2/83
Logic and life, with other sermons. 1882 19/2/82
Memoir of Madame Jenny Lind-Goldschmidt. 1891 (2v.) 27/5/91
Holland, Sir Thomas Erskine
A lecture on the treaty relations of Russia and Turkey from 1774 to 1853, delivered at Oxford. 1877 13/5/77
An inaugural lecture on Albericus Gentilis delivered at All Souls College November 7, 1874. 1874 19/8/75
Holles, Denzil Baron Holles
Memoirs of Denzil Lord Holles . . . from . . . 1641 to 1648. 24/8/32
Hollings, James Francis
Lord Macaulay. A lecture. 1860 28/7/60
Hollingsworth, Arthur George Harper
The folly of going to Rome for a religion. In two letters to a friend. 1846 24/2/46
The holy land restored; or, an examination of the prophetic evidence for the restitution of Palestine to the Jews. 1849 24/2/50
Holloway, James Thomas
Eucharista, or, a vindication of the Lord's supper from the superstition and idolatry of modern innovations . . . sermons. 1845 4/5/45
The reply. Baptismal regeneration and sacramental justification not the doctrine of the English church. 1842 1/12/42
Holmes, Oliver Wendell
The autocrat of the breakfast-table. 1858 16/9/69
Holt, Emily Sarah
Sister Rose; or, Saint Bartholomew's Eve. 1870 11/10/81
Holtzmann, Heinrich Julius
Über Fortschritte und Rückschritte der Theologie. 1878 7/1/78
Holyoake, George Jacob
[on political gambling], *in Contemporary Review*, xxiii.638. 1874 (March 1874) 10/3/74
A new defence of the ballot in consequence of Mr. Mill's objections to it. 1868 26/9/73
Deliberate liberalism. Four instances of it. 1886 3/4/86
John Stuart Mill, as some of the working classes knew him. 1873 4/7/73 ?
Life of Joseph Rayner Stephens . . . with an introductory chapter by J. S. Storr. 1881 16/11/81
Self-help by the people. History of co-operation in Rochdale. 1858 10/8/78
Sixty years of an agitator's life. 1893 (2v.) 18/10/93
The good of going to Paris to see the Exhibition; a letter to Willis Chater. 1867 27/10/70
The logic of co-operation. 1873 2/7/75 ?
The provincial mind. 1878 10/8/78
Holyoake, Malthus Questell
Memoirs of Charles Dickens. 2/2/92 n
Home, Henry Lord Kames
Sketches of the history of man. 1774 (4v.) 28/12/64
Home and Foreign Review.
1. 1. 7/1862. Acton on Wiseman 2/7/1862
4. 1. 1/1864. Munich 6/1/1864
4. 209. 1/1864. Conference 24/1/1864
4. 667, 623. 4/1864. Rome; Smith's Dictionary 10/4/1864
Homeford, Caleb
Matrimonial union considered. 1871 3/12/71
Homer, Henry Sacheverell
An enquiry into the means of preserving and improving the public roads of this kingdom. 1767 15/9/52
Homer
First Book of the Iliad, tr. C. S. Simms. 1866 9/6/74
Homer's Iliad, ed. by Ludwig Preller. 1879 12/3/91
Hymn to Mercury, tr. P. B. Shelley? 9/7/36
Hymns. 22/4/35, 9/7/36, 23/12/46, 1/2/68
Iliad. 29/1/28, 26/7/30, 14/9/30, 15/9/30, 30/9/30, 24/8/31, 1/10/31, 17/11/31, 13/1/38, 1/10/46, 21/11/46, 29/1/47, 25/2/47, 6/8/55, 22/10/55, 10/7/56, 6/9/56, 19/11/56, 14/12/57, 4/3/58, 2/11/67, 10/8/69, 1/1/74, 2/8/77, 18/8/77, 13/9/78, 3/11/82, 17/2/83, 18/8/85, 24/10/85, 25/9/91, 5/10/91
Iliad, ed. T. S. Brandeth. 1/12/40
Index Homericus, ed. A. Gehring. 1891 (2v. 1891–95) 7/12/92
New readings of Homer. 1860 12/10/60
Odyssey. 18/6/28, 18/7/28, 21/7/28, 6/8/28, 12/9/28, 6/7/30, 6/9/30, 13/9/30, 8/10/30, 20/12/30, 5/1/31, 15/8/31, 21/6/41, 2/12/46, 23/12/46, 14/8/55, 5/10/55, 22/10/55, 26/6/56, 1/7/56, 14/7/56, 7/8/56, 22/12/56, 30/10/58, 1/11/67, 15/11/67, 4/1/68, 16/4/73, 1/1/74, 7/8/77, 18/8/77, 10/1/83, 17/1/83, 14/2/83, 18/11/86, 15/2/87, 24/4/93
Odyssey, Books i–xii, translated into English verse by the Earl of Carnarvon. 1886 4/11/86
Opera. 19/9/25, 21/1/26, 26/9/26, 21/2/27, 26/6/27, 23/12/29, 9/9/31, 1/2/68
Sens de couleur chez Homer. 9/2/86

The Iliad of Homer rendered into English blank verse. By Edward Earl of Derby. 1864 (2v.) 5/12/64
The Iliad of Homer, done into English prose by [Walter Leaf]. 1883 (1886 edn) 11/5/86
The Iliad of Homer, tr. Alexander Pope. 1715 (6v. 1715–20) 26/12/64, 1/1/74, 8/11/76
The Iliad . . . rendered in Homeric verse by L. Shadwell. 1844 26/4/62
The Iliad . . . The first three books . . . translated into English hexameters . . . by F. H. J. Ritso. 1861 14/5/61
The Odyssey of Homer, tr. Alexander Pope. 1725 (5v. 1725–26) 30/1/58

Home Rule for Wales. 1888 5/10/88
Home Rule step by step. By an Unionist Home Ruler. 1889 16/12/89

Honan, M. B.
The court and camp of D. Carlos. 1836 23/7/36

Hone, Richard Brindley
Archbishop Usher, in Lives on eminent Christians. 1833 18/1/35
H. Hammond, in Lives on eminent Christians. 1833 1/2/35
John Evelyn, in Lives on eminent Christians. 1833 1/3/35

Honey, W. E. Archdeacon of Sarum
Church rates . . . an enquiry. 1859 26/7/59

Hook, James
[pamphlets on church pluralities]. 1802 21/1/33
A sermon [on 2 Chron. xvii. 8, 9] preached in . . . St. Paul's . . . children educated in the Charity Schools. 1819 6/1/33
A sermon [on Eph. iv. 3] as preached at St. George's, Hanover Square . . . and at St. James' . . . 1812. 1812 6/1/33

Hook, Theodore Edward
The choice humorous works, ludicrous adventures, Bon Mots, puns and hoaxes of T. Hook, with a new Life. 1873 27/8/74

Hook, Walter Farquhar
A call to the union on the principles of the English Reformation. A sermon [on Acts vii. 26]. 1838 8/2/39
A letter to his parishioners on the use of the Athanasian creed. 1838 13/4/38
An ecclesiastical biography . . . lives of ancient fathers and modern divines. 1841 (8v. 1841–51) 6/11/37, 3/1/47
An inaugural discourse [on Acts xx. 27] preached in the parish church of Leeds. 1837 6/7/37
Auricular confession: a sermon [on 1 John i. 9] preached Oct. 29th, 1848. 1848 18/2/49
Gorham v. the Bishop of Exeter. A letter . . . on the present crisis of the church. 1850 23/3/50
Helps to self-examination. A new edition, revised and corrected. 1846 6/12/46
Letter to the bishop of Ripon, on the state of parties in the Church of England. 1841 11/4/41
Life of W. F. Hook, by W. R. W. Stephens. 1878 (2v.) 22/12/78
Lives of the Archbishops of Canterbury. 1860 (12v. 1860–84) 23/12/60, 8/11/63, 28/9/88
Lives of the Archbishops of Canterbury [intro. to vols. vi and vii]. 1860 (1868) 28/6/68
Lives of the Archbishops of Canterbury [vol. ix]. 1860 24/3/72
Lives of the Archbishops of Canterbury [vol. v]. 1860 21/2/75
On the means of rendering more efficient the education of the people. 1846 9/7/46, 14/4/70
Peril of idolatry. A sermon [on 1 John v. 21]. 1842 24/7/42
Presbyterian rights asserted. By a Presbyter of the Church of England. 1839 28/12/39
Reasons for contributing towards the support of our English bishop at Jerusalem . . . letter to a friend. 1842 19/1/42
Sermon [on Acts vii. 28] at Longley's visitation. 1838 16/12/38
Take heed what ye hear. A sermon [Mark iv. 24] With a preface on . . . existing controversies in the Church. 1844 15/12/44
The cross of Christ; or, meditations on the death and passion of our blessed Lord and Saviour. 1844 20/3/45
The disestablished church in the republic of the United States of America. A lecture. 1869 8/6/69, 13/2/70
The disestablishment of the theocracy. A sermon [on 1 Sam. xii. 23]. 1868 12/7/68
The duty of English churchmen, and the progress of the church in Leeds. A sermon [on Matt. v. 16]. 1851 30/11/51
The eucharist a sacrament and a sacrifice. A sermon [on Pet. ii. 5] preached . . . 5th of July, 1846. 1847 21/2/47
The gospel and the gospel only, the basis of education. A sermon [on Mark xvi. 15, 16]. 1839 29/8/39
The last days of our Lord's ministry. A course of lectures. 1832 30/12/32
The novelties of Romanism; or, Popery refuted by tradition. A sermon [on 1 Cor. xi. 16]. 1839 29/12/39
The three Reformations: Lutheran—Roman—Anglican. 1847 31/1/47
Two sermons. 1846 9/7/46

Hooke, Nathaniel
An account of the conduct of the Dowager Duchess of Marlborough. 1742 3/10/83
The Roman history from the building of Rome to the ruin of the commonwealth. 1738 (4v. 1738–71) 11/10/25

Hooker, Richard
Discourse on justification. 27/9/29
Life of Richard Hooker, by I. Walton. 7/12/28
Of the Lawes of Ecclesiasticall Politie. (1594–97) 12/7/29, 6/9/29, 29/9/29, 27/12/31, 25/8/33, 13/10/33, 25/10/35, 26/3/37, 8/7/38, 10/11/39
The works of Richard Hooker . . . arranged by . . . J. Keble. 1836 5/9/44
Hoole, John
Jerusalem delivered by T. Tasso, tr. J. Hoole. 1763 22/12/64
Hooper, George
A fair and methodical discussion of the first and great controversy . . . concerning the infallible guide. 17/12/76
Hooper, James John
The establishment of a school of jurisprudence in the University of Oxford . . . advocated in a letter. 1854 20/2/54
Hooper, S.
Speech of 3 Feb. 1862, on Treasury Note Bill. 1862 5/6/62
Hope, Alexander James Beresford-
A popular view of the American civil war. 1861 13/12/61
Letters on church matters, by D. C. L. 1851 2/7/52 ?
The Irish church and its formularies. A letter. 1870 11/1/71
The place and influence in the Church movement of Church Congresses. 1874 8/3/74
Worship in the Church of England. 1874 16/4/75
Hope, G., Morse, A., and Grey. W. R.
The three prize essays on agriculture and the corn-law. 1842 22/2/43
Hope, J.
An historical essay on architecture. 1835 (2v.) 7/1/43
Hope-Scott, James Robert
Memoirs of J. R. Hope Scott, by R. Ornsby. 1884 (2v.) 13/10/83, 14/11/83, 24/11/83
The bishopric of the United Church of England and Ireland at Jerusalem, considered in a letter to a friend. 1841 15/12/41
Hopgood, James
'A scheme for the disestablishment of the Church of England' in *Contemporary Review*, xxiii. 966. 1874 (May 1874) 2/10/74
Disestablishment and disendowment of the Church of England. 1875 11/7/75
Hopkins, Evan Henry
The walk that pleases God. 1887 20/1/87
Hopkins, Jane Ellice
Active service; or [Miss Sarah Robinson's] *work among our soldiers.* 1872 24/3/72
Hopkins, John Baker
The English Revolution. 1868 11/5/68
Hopkins, John Henry
The Church of Rome in her primitive purity compared with the Church of Rome at the present day. 1837 17/1/47
The law of ritualism examined in its relation to the word of God, to the primitive church. 1866 10/2/67
Hopps, John Page
The truth seeker. 1878 10/11/78
Hoppus, John
Recollection of student-life, and thoughts on our times: an address . . . Rotherham College. 1868 20/3/70
Hoppus, Mary A. M. afterw. Marks
Masters of the world. 1889 (3v.) 25/1/89
Miss Montizambart. 1885 (2v.) 22/9/90
Hopwood, Frank George
An address on the principles and practice of Christian alms-giving. 1839 29/3/40
Hopwood, Henry
Principles of national education. 1840 31/1/41
Horace
Ars poetica. 28/11/28
Carmen saeculare. 18/10/93
Epistles and satires. 24/2/90
Horace: with notes by . . . C. Girdlestone . . . and W. A. Osborne. 1848 27/4/48
Odes. 16/6/26, 21/7/26, 16/2/28, 18/3/29, 29/6/31, 16/12/93
Odes, tr. by Sir Theodore Martin. 1860 13/2/60
Opera. 19/9/25, 2/11/25, 6/5/26, 2/6/26, 27/9/26, 16/3/27, 25/5/27, 12/8/28, 2/3/32, 14/5/32, 21/5/32, 24/5/32
Studies . . . in the Odes of Horace, by A. W. Verrall. 1884 26/1/94
The Odes of Horace . . . translated . . . by Henry George Robinson. 1844 13/2/60
Horbery, Matthew
An enquiry into the scripture-doctrine concerning the duration of future punishment. 1744 1/9/72, 22/8/75, 20/8/76
Horder, William Garrett
The hymn lover. An account of the rise and growth of English hymnody. 1889 31/7/90
Hore, Alexander Hugh
Eighteen centuries of the church in England. 1881 14/1/83
Horn, J. Edouard
Des finances de l'Autriche. 1860 25/9/60
Hornby, James John
Remains of A. Knox. 1834 (4v. 1834–37) 5/2/83 ?
Horne, George
A commentary on the Book of Psalms. 1776 (2v.) 9/10/49

Horne, Richard Hengist
A new spirit of the age, ed R. Hengist. 1844 (2v.) 15/4/44
John Ferncliff. 1868 19/9/73
Orion. An epic poem, in three books. 1843 14/10/58
Horneck, Anthony
Sirenes. 7/9/51
The happy ascetick: or, the best exercise. To which is added a letter. 27/5/49
Horner, Jonah
On health: what preserves, what destroys, and what restores it. 1857 16/9/57
Horner, Leonard
Address delivered at the anniversary meeting of the Geological Society of London . . . 1861. 1861 23/3/61
Memoirs of Francis Horner. With selections from his correspondence. 1843 (2v.) 23/10/41, 24/3/43
On the employment of children, in factories . . . in the United Kingdom, and in some foreign countries. 1840 10/5/43
Horsfall, Thomas Coghlan
The study of beauty in and art in large towns. Two papers, . . . with an introduction by John Ruskin. 1883 20/1/91
Horsley, Samuel
An apology for the liturgy and clergy of the Church of England. 1790 22/4/44
Dissertation on prophecies. 1815 31/8/31
Nine sermons on the nature of the evidence by which the fact of our Lord's resurrection is established. 1815 30/8/57
Sermons. 1812 (3v.) 18/8/50
Sermons, ed. H. Horsley. 1810 (2v.) 4/12/31, 24/4/59, 10/9/65, 29/9/72, 15/10/76
Speeches. 1813 (2v.) 11/8/42, 12/8/79
Tracts in controversy with Dr. Priestley. 1789 3/6/83
Horst, Georg Conrad
Siona. Ein Beitrag zur Apologetik des Christenthums. 1826 14/5/90
Hort, Dora
Tahiti, the garden of the Pacific. 1891 10/5/91
Horton, George
The municipal government of the metropolis. 1865 30/8/65
Horton, Sir Robert John Wilmot
Protestant securities suggested, in an appeal to the clerical members of the University of Oxford. 1828 15/7/28
Hosack, John
Mary Queen of Scots and her accusers. 1869 29/6/85
Hosken, James Dryden
Phaon and Sappho, a play . . . with a selection of poems. 1891 24/5/92
Verses by the way. 1893 2/8/93
Hoskin, W.
Introductory lectures . . . on architecture. 1842 24/1/43
Hoskyns, Chandos Wren
A short inquiry into the history of agriculture in ancient, mediaeval and modern times. 1849 19/12/49
Land in England, land in Ireland, and land in other lands. 1869 17/2/73
Hotten, John Camden
Abyssinia and its people: or, life in the land of Prester John, ed. J. C. Hotten. 1868 7/1/68
Houldey, William Ephraim
Auricular confession and the Church of England. A sermon. 1873 12/10/73
Hour of trial; stages in the trial of Queen Caroline. 1820 7/6/78
Household Words vi. 145. 1852 (October 1852) 7/11/52
Houston, James D. Craig
Daughter of Leontius: Byzantine life. 1894 24/4/94
Houston, Thomas
The judgment of the papacy and the reign of righteousness. 1851 4/11/77
Howard, George Broadley
An old legend of St. Paul's. 1874 19/10/74
The future supply of clergy for the service of the Church of England considered in a letter . . . [to W. E. G.]. 1875 7/10/75
Howard, George William Frederick 7th Earl of Carlisle
Diary in Turkish and Greek waters. 1854 23/10/54
Lectures and addresses, in aid of public education; including a lecture on the poetry of Pope. 1852 28/10/54
Howard, Lady Harriet
Josiah. 1842 7/5/43
The birthday. 1844 14/7/44
Howard, Henry Granville Fitzalan 14th Duke of Norfolk
A few remarks on the social and political condition of British Catholics. 1847 5/1/48
The lives of Philip Howard Earl of Arundel and of Anne Dacres, his wife. Edited from the original mss. 1857 7/7/57
Howard, John
The astrologer of Leeds. 1881 23/12/81
Howard, Richard Baron
An enquiry into the morbid effects of deficiency of food . . . their occurrence amongst the destitute poor. 1839 21/8/42
Howarth, Sir Henry Hoyle
Glacial nightmare and the flood. A second appeal to common sense from the extravagance of some recent geology. 1893 (2v.) 3/6/93

Howe, John of Magdalen College, Oxford
The living temple . . . a good man is the temple of God. (1845) 13/12/46
True religion. (1813) 5/5/44 ?
Howe, Joseph Lieut. Governor of Nova Scotia
Confederation considered in relation to the interests of the Empire. 1866 24/9/66
Letter to . . . Gladstone . . . review of the debate on the foreign enlistment bill and our relations with the United States. 1856 25/1/57
Speech . . . on the union of the North American provinces. 1855 11/7/55
Howe, P. B. Lord Sligo
Jamaica under the apprenticeship system. 1838 4/4/38
Howe, Thomas
A farewell address [on 2 Cor. vi. 11–13] delivered . . . at Walpole. 1767 13/4/72 ?
Howell, David
Welsh nationality. 1892 2/9/92
Howell, George
Waste lands and surplus labour. 1871 1/12/71
Howell, H. S.
An island paradise and reminiscences of travel. 1892 29/4/93
Howell, James
Instructions for forreine travell, 1642. Collated with the second edition 1650 . . . by Edward Arber. 1869 21/9/76
Howell, Thomas Bayly, and Howell, T. J.
State trials, xxv.891. 1816 15/8/43 ?
Howells, William Dean
A foregone conclusion. 1875 11/8/85
The undiscovered country. 1882 (2v.) 27/8/86
Howley, Edward
Competitive endowment, and Trinity College Dublin. 1872 21/1/73
Howley, William
A charge delivered at his ordinary visitation in September, 1840. 1840 23/10/42
A charge delivered at his ordinary visitation, 1844. 1844 27/9/44
A letter addressed to the clergy and laity of his province. 1845 14/1/45
Howorth, Sir Henry Hoyle
The Columban clergy of North Britain, and their harrying by the Norsemen. 1879 30/8/91
The Irish monks and the Norsemen. 1880 2/2/80
The mammoth and the flood: an attempt to confront the theory of uniformity with . . . recent geology. 1887 6/8/90
Howson, John Saul
'Before the table.' An enquiry . . . into the true meaning of the consecration rubric in the . . . Church of England. 1875 12/12/75
'Dean Milman and St. Paul's' in *Quarterly Review*, cxxvi.218. 1869 (January 1869) 26/12/69
Deaconesses; or the official help of women in parochial work and in charitable institutions. 1862 6/7/62
Samuel among them that call upon his name, an inaugural sermon [on Ps. xcix. 6]. 1867 13/10/67
The history of the Mediterranean; a lecture. 1849 19/10/70 ?
The Lord's table, vestments, and the eastward position. A letter to a layman. 1875 21/1/77
The metaphors of St. Paul. 1868 31/1/69
Hoyle, William
Crime in England and Wales in the nineteenth century. An historical and critical retrospect. 1876 29/1/76
Our national resources; and how they are wasted. An omitted chapter in political economy. 1871 13/10/71
Hubbard, John Gellibrand
A census of religion. Denominational worship. The national church. Three essays. 1882 6/4/82
How should income tax be levied? Considered in a letter to . . . D'Israeli. 1852 12/11/52
National finance. Two letters—reprinted from the Times—upon public income and the national debt. 1880 26/2/80
Reform or reject the income tax. Objections to a reform of the income tax considered, in two letters to . . . the Times. 1853 30/12/52
Ritual revision. A letter to E. Bickersteth [on his speech at the Brighton Church Congress]. 1874 23/12/74
The conscience clause of the Education Department. Illustrated from the evidence . . . [by] the Select Committee on Education. 1865 3/1/65
The currency and the country. 1843 23/1/44
Vindication of a fixed duty on corn: to which are added remarks . . . [on] the speech of R. A. Christopher . . . at Lincoln. 1842 6/1/42
Huber, Johannes Nepomuk
Der Alte und der Neue Glaube. Ein Bekenntniss von D. F. Strauss. 1873 21/1/73
Huber, Marie
Letters concerning the religion essential to man . . . translated from the French. 1738 3/11/90
Huber, Victor Aimé
The English universities . . . an abridged translation, edited by F. W. Newman. 1843 (2v.) 23/5/44
Huberto
The ghost of Dunboy Castle. 1889 31/10/88
Huc, Evariste Régis
Travels in Tartary, Thibet and China, 1844–1846. Translated by William Hazlitt. 1852 (2v.) 16/12/52
Hudleston, John
A brief account of particulars occurring at the happy death of our late sovereign Lord King Charles II in regard to religion. 7/11/64

Hudson, C. F.
Debt and grace, as related to the doctrine of a future life. 1861 13/11/64
Hudson, Frank
The last hurdle. A story of sporting and courting. 1888 17/10/88
Huebner, Count Joseph Alexander von
Ein Jahr meines Lebens, 1848–1849. 1891 8/6/91
Hugessen, Edward Hugessen Knatchbull Baron Brabourne
'Facts and fictions in Irish history' in *Blackwood's Magazine*, cxl.419. 1886 (October 1886) 29/9/86, 29/10/86
[On Gladstone] in *Nineteenth Century*, xxi. 397. 1887 (March 1887) 26/2/87
[On politics] in *Blackwood's Magazine*, cxlii. 753. 1887 (December 1887) 13/10/90
Mr. Knatchbull-Hugessen's speech upon education, spoken at Sandwich . . . January 26, 1872. 1872 22/10/73
Protectionist parodies. 1850 16/10/65 ?
The life, times, and character of Oliver Cromwell. A lecture. 1877 3/3/77
Hughes, Eilian
Some aspects of humanity. 1888 29/9/89
Hughes, Henry
A letter to the dean and chapter of St. Paul's, on . . . church accommodation, the education of the children of the poor, and . . . condition of the people. 1845 30/5/45 ?
Hughes, John poet
Letters of Abelard and Heloise. To which is prefix'd a particular account of their lives. 1765 30/7/55
Hughes, Joshua Bishop of St. Asaph
A charge delivered to the clergy of the diocese of St. Asaph . . . September and October 1874. 1874 20/12/74
Hughes, Joshua pseud. Veritas
The university of Brecknock. 1853 27/2/70, 9/7/76
Hughes, Thomas author of 'Tom Brown's School Days'
James Fraser, second bishop of Manchester. A memoir 1818–1885. 1887 6/3/87
Memoir of Daniel Macmillan. 1882 30/7/82
The old church. What shall we do with it?. 1878 27/6/78
Hughes, Thomas of Market Rasen
The human will: its functions and freedom. 1867 28/6/68
Hughes, Thomas Patrick
Notes on Muhammadanism. 1875 (1875–78) 3/2/78
Hughes, William F.R.G.S.
The geography of Scotland and Ireland. 1852 28/1/70 ?
Hughes, William Vicar of Llanuwchllyn
The Welsh bible and its editions: a lecture on the translation of Bishop Morgan. 1888 15/10/88
Hughes, William R.
Constance Naden: a memoir. 1890 5/4/90
Hugo, Victor Marie
Histoire d'un crime. 1877 11/9/86
Les misérables. 1862 16/2/63, 15/7/63
Napoléon-le-petit. 1852 22/11/52
Shakespeare. 1864 5/3/72
Huidekoper, Frederic
Judaism at Rome B. C. 76 to A. D. 140. 1876 9/6/78
The belief of the first three centuries concerning Christ's mission to the underworld. 1854 28/4/78
Huish, Robert
Memoirs of George the Fourth. 1830 (2v. 1830–31) 15/1/48
Hull, Edmund C. P.
England and the Suez canal. 1883 29/5/83
Hull, Edward F. G. S.
The coal-fields of Great Britain: their history, structure, and duration. 1861 22/10/61
Hull, Rev. Edward of Liverpool
The institution and abuse of ecclesiastical property. 1831 16/1/36
Hull, John Dawson
A letter . . . to the Bishop of Exeter [Phillpotts]. 1845 31/5/45
Hull, William Winstanley
MDCCCXLV. The month of January, Oxford. 1845 25/1/45
Thoughts on church reform. 1832 26/1/33
Hullah, John Pyke
Grammar of vocal music, for the use of public schools and adults . . . method of Wilhelm . . . adapted to English use. 1843 15/1/57
The history of modern music. A course of lectures delivered at the Royal Institution of Great Britain. 1861 23/12/61
The whole book of psalms . . . set to appropriate chants for four voices. 1844 4/4/45
Hulton, Samuel Fletcher
Rixae Oxonienses . . . Illustrated with views of demolished buildings of Oxford taken from Skelton. 1892 28/1/92
Human priesthood and clergy unknown to Christianity, ed. by 'S. H.'. 1860 22/2/77
Humboldt, Friedrich Heinrich Alexander von
Kosmos. Entwurf einer physischen Waltbeschreibung. 1845 (5v. 1845–62) 29/5/49
Hume, Abraham LL.D.
Christian hour. 1875 25/7/75
Ecclesiastical history of Liverpool. 1881 13/1/82
Results of the Irish census of 1861, with a special reference to the condition of the church in Ireland. 1864 31/5/64

Hume, David
A concise and genuine account of the dispute between Mr. Hume and Mr. Rousseau. 1766 1/4/72
An enquiry concerning human understanding. 1758 22/10/34
Essays. 1741 (2v. 1741–42) 22/8/29, 5/2/79
Essays and treatises. 1758 5/2/79
The history of England. 1754 (6v. 1754–62) 16/4/25, 15/12/26, 18/12/26, 30/12/26, 13/1/27, 12/3/27, 28/4/27, 10/7/27, 29/8/27, 13/9/27, 12/10/27, 28/10/27, 11/10/31, 7/5/35, 6/10/35, 19/11/89, 10/9/92
The philosophical works. 1826 (4v.) 2/6/45, 5/2/79
Hume, James Deacon
The laws of the customs. 1833 (3v. 1833–36) 2/7/38
Humphreys, Edward Rupert
England's educational crisis: a letter to . . . Palmerston . . . By the head master of an English Grammar school. 1856 15/2/56
In and out. 1857 30/4/57 ?
The dangers and duties of the present time: being the substance of two lectures. 1853 20/2/53
The warnings of the war: a letter to the Rt. Hon. Lord Palmerston . . . By 'a British Commoner'. 1855 27/3/55
Humphreys, Henry Noel
A history of the art of printing, from its invention to . . . the middle of the sixteenth century. 1867 31/5/72
Humphry, William Gilson
A commentary on the revised version of the New Testament. 1882 31/7/81
The new table of lessons explained, with . . . a tabular comparison of the Old and New Proper Lessons for Sundays and holy-days. 1871 24/12/71
Hungarian, An
The emperor of Austria versus Louis Kossuth: a few words of common sense, based on . . . facts. 1861 23/12/61
Hunt, James Henry Leigh
Lord Byron and some of his contemporaries; with recollections of the author's life and of his visit to Italy. 1828 22/9/62
The autobiography . . . with reminiscences of friends and contemporaries . . . new edition, revised by the author . . . introduction by his eldest son [T. Hunt]. 1860 24/10/63
Hunt, John D.D.
[On J. H. Newman] in *Contemporary Review*, xxvii. 168. 1876 (June 1876) 1/4/76
[the P. M. G. on dogmatic extremes], in *Contemporary Review*, xxiii. 437. 1874 (February 1874) 1/2/74
Religious thought in England from the reformation to the end of the last century . . . history of theology. 1870 (3v. 1870–73) 21/8/70
Hunt, Thornton Leigh
The rationale of railway administration . . . the greatest possible . . . accommodation, cheapness and safety. 1846 8/4/46
Hunt, William Holman
Jerusalem. Bishop Gobat in re Hanna Hadoub. 1858 23/5/58
Hunter, Sir William Wilson
A life of the earl of Mayo, fourth Viceroy of India. 1875 (2v.) 11/12/75
England's work in India. 1881 7/6/81
The Indian Musalmans: are they bound in conscience to rebel against the Queen?. 1871 (1872) 26/2/78
The marquess of Dalhousie. 1890 19/4/90
Huntington, George
The church's work in our large towns. 1864 18/9/64, 24/9/71
Huntington, Jedediah Vincent
Lady Alice, or the new Una. A novel. 1849 12/4/49
Huntington, William
The Arminian skeleton: or, the Arminian dissected and anatomized. 1787 19/10/28
Huntington, William Reed
The church-idea. An essay towards unity. 1870 19/4/70
Hurd, Richard
Memoirs of Richard Hurd, by F. Kilvert. 1860 21/8/64
Hurnall, J.
Epochs of the church of Lyons, ed. J. Hurnall. 1843 28/3/45
Hus, Jan
Liber egregius. 1/9/78 ?
Husenbeth, Frederick Charles
Our blessed lady of Lourdes: a faithful narrative of the apparitions . . . near Lourdes, in the year 1858. 1870 11/11/77
Huskisson, William
Biographical memoir of William Huskisson, by J. Wright. 1831 26/4/33
Free trade. Speech . . . in the House of Commons . . . February, 1826. 1826 31/3/26
The question concerning the depreciation of our currency stated and examined. 1810 27/3/56, 9/3/61
The speeches . . . with a biographical memoir. 1831 (3v.) 18/5/48, 7/3/56
Hussey, James MacConnell
Nehemiah's example an incitement to all Christians to contend for the Sabbath. A sermon [on Neh. xiii. 17]. 1849 19/8/66
Hussey, Robert
Reasons for voting upon the third question to be

proposed in convocation... [on Tract XC by Newman]. 1845 12/2/45
Remarks on some proposed changes in the public examinations. 1848 29/1/49
Sermons, mostly academical. 1849 (1850) 24/3/50
The church from the beginning until now. A sermon [on 1 Tim. iii. 15]. 1847 28/11/47
The rise of papal power, traced in three lectures. 1851 30/3/51, 3/9/71

Husson, Jules François Félix pseud. Champfleury
Histoire de la caricature antique. 1865 14/7/65
The cat, past and present. From the French... by Mrs. Cashel Hoey. 1885 12/4/92

Hutchins, George
The Church of England identified with the primitive church of Jerusalem. A sermon [on Acts xvi.31]. 1845 1/10/54

Hutchins, John
The history and antiquities of the county of Dorset. 1861 (4v. 1861–73) 13/12/69 ?

Hutchinson, John
A new account of the confusion of tongues. 1731 30/11/62

Hutchinson, Peter Orlando
The diary and letters of... T. Hutchinson... Compiled. 1883 (2v. 1883–6) 3/5/84

Huth, Alfred Henry
The life and writings of H. T. Buckle. 1880 (2v.) 17/4/81

Hutt, Sir William
The state duties considered. 1839 (1842) 20/7/42

Hutton, Annie
The embassy in Ireland of Monsignor G. B. Rinuccini, tr. A. Hutton. 1873 1/12/88

Hutton, Arthur Wollaston
Our position as Catholics in the Church of England. 1872 7/8/92
Principle and politics. A lecture. 1891 5/2/93 ?
Sir Thomas More and his utopia; the 'new learning' of the 16th c. in relation to social reform. 1885 30/6/88
The Anglican ministry, its nature and value in relation to the Catholic priesthood. An essay, preface by Newman. 1879 22/6/88, 9/9/88

Hutton, Catherine
Reminiscences of a gentlewoman of the last century: letters... edited by her cousin, Mrs. C. H. Beale. 1891 16/10/91

Hutton, George Clark
The word and the book: the question of Holy Writ. 1891 22/3/91

Hutton, Henry Dix
Modern warfare: its positive theory, and true policy. With an application to the Russian War. 1855 22/1/56
Proposals for the gradual creation of a farmer-proprietary in Ireland. 1868 14/9/69
The Prussian land-tenure reforms and a farmer-proprietary for Ireland. 1867 8/11/67, 28/2/68

Hutton, Richard Holt
[On Bagehot] in *Fortnightly Review*, xxviii. 453. 1877 (September 1877) 4/10/77
[Review of G. Eliot's life] in *Contemporary Review*, xlvii. 372. 1885 (March 1885) 2/3/85
Cardinal Newman. 1891 14/9/90, 3/10/90
Criticisms of contemporary thought and thinkers. 1894 (2v.) 2/5/94
Essays on some of the modern guides of English thought in matters of faith. 1887 10/11/87
Essays; theological and literary. 1871 (2v. 1877 edn) 23/5/77
Sir Walter Scott. 1878 6/7/78

Hutton, Vernon Wollaston
[Untraced pamphlet]. 22/9/78
Church authority, its mode of expression and its limits. 1875 17/12/76

Hutton, William
The life of William Hutton. 1816 13/10/80

Huxley, Thomas Henry
'Science and pseudo-science', in *Nineteenth Century*, xxi. 481. 1887 (April 1887) 4/4/87
'Scientific and pseudo-scientific realism', in *Nineteenth Century*, xxi. 191. 1887 (February 1887) 20/2/87
'The keepers of the herd of swine' [on Gladstone's biblical criticism], in *Nineteenth Century*, xxviii. 976. 1890 (December 1890) 13/12/90
[Evolution of theology] in *Fortnightly Review*, xix. 346. 1886 (March 1886) 28/2/86
[On Réville] in *Nineteenth Century*, xxviii. 849. 1885 (December 1885) 2/12/85
American addresses, with a lecture on the study of biology. 1877 16/2/79
Evidence as to man's place in nature. 1863 13/1/82
Evolution and ethics. 1893 16/7/93
Huxley and Swedenborg, by R. L. Tafel. 1889 6/10/89
Lay sermons, addresses and reviews. 1870 5/6/71
Physiography. 1877 25/5/85

Hyde, Edward Lord Clarendon
Religion and policy and the countenance and assistance each should give to the other. 1811 (2v.) 26/11/40
The true historical narrative of the rebellion and civil wars in England. 1702 (3v. 1702–4) 20/11/26, 24/1/27, 1/2/27

Hymns ancient and modern. 1861 (2nd edn 1875) 13/8/93, 8/4/94

Hymns for the Church of England. 1859 2/2/62
Hyndman, Henry Mayers
'The bankrupcy of India' in *Nineteenth Century*, v. 443. 1879 (March 1879) 27/2/79
The text-book of democracy. England for all. 1881 30/11/82

Igiene del'Occhi. 29/5/39
Ignatius, Saint Bishop of Antioch
Syriac version of the Epistles, ed. W. Cureton. 1845 5/8/45
Iliowizi, Henry
Jewish dreams and realities contrasted with Islamitic and Christian claims. 1890 18/4/90
Illingworth, John Richardson
Sermons preached in a college chapel. 1881 13/3/81
Sermons preached in the chapel of Keble College. 1878 25/11/77
Imaginary history of the next thirty years. 1857 13/4/57
Imbert de Saint-Amand, Baron Arthur Léon
Les femmes de Versailles. 1885 (4v. 1885–95) 14/10/86
Imlay, Gilbert
A topographical description of the Western Territory of North America . . . letters to a friend in England. 1792 3/12/83
Immortality. A clerical symposium. 1885 23/4/86
Imperial and Asiatic Quarterly Review. 5. 55. 1/1893. Uganda 5/1/1893
Imposteurs, les trois. 30/3/84 ?
'Inaugural addresses, delivered on the occasion of the opening of the University of Sydney' 1852 15/9/53, 16/9/53, 17/9/53
Ince, William
The Luther commemoration of the Church of England. A sermon [on Pet. ii. 16]. 1883 24/11/83
Inchbald, Elizabeth
A simple story. 1791 (4v.) 7/8/51
Inchbald, John
The Bank Act: what it is, and what it does, and the laws which regulate the price of money, briefly explained. 1858 19/2/61
Increase of faith [treatise]. 1867 22/12/67
Indian Church Quarterly Review.
4. 127. 4/1891. Cheyne on the bible 21/6/1891, 20/8/1891
4. 139. 4/1891. Indian philosophies 22/6/1891
Ingelow, Jean
Mopsa the fairy. 1869 20/8/84
Off the skelligs. 1872 (4v.) 6/5/72
Poems. 1863 25/10/63
Ingersoll, Robert Green
Liberty in literature. Testimonial to Walt Whitman . . . An address. 1890 31/8/91
Inghirami, Francesco
Galleria Omerica, raccolta di monumenti antichi . . . per servire allo studio dell'Iliade e dell'Odissa. 1831 (3v. 1831–36) 1/1/47
Ingle, John
'Such a time as this'. A sermon . . . at the anniversary of the English Church Union, Exeter Branch . . . 1864. 1865 19/11/65, 7/3/69
The Roman meeting-house in the Mint. A letter. 1873 12/10/73
Ingleby, Clement Mansfield
Shakespeare—the man and the book: being a collection of occasional papers on the bard and his writings. 1877 (2v. 1877–81) 3/7/80
Inglis, Henry David
The Tyrol, with a glance at Bavaria. 1833 17/9/34
Inglis, John
A vindication of ecclesiastical establishments. 1833 25/12/33
Inglis, Sir Robert Harry
The Jew bill. Substance of a speech delivered in the House of Commons 16th December 1847. 1848 9/2/48
The universities and the Dissenters. Substance of a speech delivered in the House of Commons. 1834 9/4/34
Ingoldsby Letters. 1862 (vol i) 7/6/63
Ingraham, Joseph Holt
The prince of the house of David. 1856 (1890 edn) 20/4/90
Ingram, John Kells
Considerations on the state of Ireland: being the substance of an address. 1864 8/3/64, 14/12/68
Essays in political economy. By T. E. C. Leslie, ed. J. K. Ingram. 1878 29/8/78
Ingram, Thomas Dunbar
A history of the legislative union of Great Britain and Ireland. 1887 30/6/87, 2/9/87, 8/12/87
Innes, Alexander Taylor
The law of the creeds in Scotland: a treatise on the legal relation of churches in Scotland. 1867 23/6/67
Innes, John
Letter to the Lord Glenelg, secretary of state for the colonies . . . on negro apprenticeship. 1838 29/3/38
Thoughts on the present state of the British West India Colonies, and . . . the African slave trade. 1840 31/7/40
Innes, William
Letter addressed to an approving but undecided hearer. 1843 28/7/46
The church in the army. 1838 4/3/68
Innocent III, Pope
Mysterorum Evangelicae legis. 1860 24/8/90

Inventories of Jarrow, ed. Raine. 1855 29/10/82
Investigator
Revelation of science in scripture, three lectures... by Investigator. 1875 2/6/75
Reverend Dr. Cumming. 1860 13/1/61
Irby, Adeline Paulina, and Mackenzie, G. M. M.
Travels in the Slavonic provinces of Turkey-in-Europe. 1877 (2v.) 14/12/76 n, 15/3/77
Ireland, Alexander
William Hazlitt... Selections... With a memoir. 1889 2/9/89
Ireland, Mrs. Annie Elizabeth
Life of Jane Welsh Carlyle. 1891 20/7/91
Ireland, Samuel William Henry
The confessions of W. H. Ireland containing the particulars of his fabrication of the Shakespeare manuscripts. 1805 7/12/26
Ireland as a kingdom and a colony. 1843 30/7/68
Ireland her Church and People, by a tory. 1841 29/11/41
Ireland's true daughter. 1881 3/3/81
Ireland under British rule. 1868 21/12/68
Irish Ecclesiastical Journal.
2. 9/1843. Pusey 23/10/1843
2. 1. 2/1843. Romish miracles 2/3/1843
3. 257. 11/1845. Irish reformation 6/12/1845
3. 29. 9/1844 29/9/1844
Irish Liberal, An
Irish issues. 1888 17/10/88
Irishman
A letter addressed to... Russell on the idea of establishing a republic in Ireland. 1848 5/12/61
Irish poor law: past, present, future. 1849 24/2/49
Irish stew. 1886 1/9/87
Irons, William Josiah
'Apologia pro vita' ecclesiae Anglicanae. In reply to John Henry Newman, D.D. 1864 3/8/64
'My words shall not pass away.' A sermon. 1864 21/2/64
Athanasius contra mundum... letter to... Convocation assembled. 1872 25/2/72
Considerations on taking holy orders in the Church of England. 1872 23/6/72
First hundred years of Christianity... times of St. Paul to St. Justin M. 1877 29/9/78
New legislation for the church. Is it needed? A letter to... the archbishop of Canterbury. 1874 3/5/74
Notes of the church: a sermon [on Isa. lxii. 12]. 1845 7/12/45
On miracles and prophecy: being a sequel to the arguments of the 'Bible and its interpreters', with... notes. 1867 19/1/68
Professor Tyndall's 'Fragments of science for unscientific people' in relation to theology and religion. 1872 23/6/72
Proposed surrender of the prayer-book and articles of the Church of England. A letter. 1863 7/6/63
Sequel to a pamphlet on the Royal Supremacy, entitled the 'Present crisis in the Church of England'. 1850 30/4/50
The Bible and its interpreters. The popular theory: the Roman theory: the literary theory: the truth. 1865 20/8/65
The idea of a national church. 1862 31/8/62
The judgments on baptismal regeneration. 1850 17/3/50
The theory of development examined, with reference... to Mr. Newman's Essay, and... Rule of St. Vincent of Lerins. 1846 22/2/46
Irvine, Andrew
Romanism, as represented by... Newman, briefly considered. 1846 3/4/46
Irvine, J. T.
Historical sketches of the church of St. Lawrence, in Ludlow; and its restoration by G. G. Scott, architect, by his clerk of the works. 1860 9/9/60
Irvine, William Fergusson
A letter to the Edinburgh University Council. 1863 31/12/63
Irving, Edward
[Introductory essay to W. Gilpin's Life of Bernard Gilpin]. 1824 23/8/29
Edward Irving, by W. Wilks. 1854 13/4/81 ?
For the oracles of God, four orations. For judgment to come, an argument, in nine parts. 1823 10/6/60
The prophetical works... Edited by... G. Carlyle. 1867 (2v. 1867–70) 12/6/70
The signs of the times. 1829 25/3/47
Irving, John Henry Brodribb
The stage. Address delivered... at the Perry Barr Institute. 1878 22/3/78
Irving, Joseph
The drowned women of Wigton, a romance of the Covenant, suggested by Mr. Napier's 'Memoirs of Dundee'. 1862 19/11/62
Irving, Washington
Tales of a traveller. 1825 27/8/44
The life and voyages of Christopher Columbus. 1828 (4v.) 12/12/48
The life of Oliver Goldsmith. 1844 (2v.) 3/10/78
Isham, Thomas
The journal of Thomas Isham, of Lamport... 1671 to... 1673... in Latin... Tr. by the Rev. R. Isham. 1875 12/8/79
Isocrates
Helenae encomium. 6/10/55
Israel in Britain. 27/9/76
Ives, Levi Silliman
Trials of a mind in its progress to Catholicism; a letter to his old friends. 1854 5/1/61

Ivimey, Joseph
Triumph of the Bible in Ireland: or, extracts from three months' correspondence of the . . . Baptist Irish Society. 1832 22/8/32 ?

Jacini, Count Stefano Francesco
L'Italia ed il Papato. Posizione del problema. 1887 24/12/87
La proprietà fondiaria e le popolazioni agricole in Lombardia. Studj Economici. 1854 1/3/59
Pensieri sulla politica italiana. 1889 4/7/89
Sulle condizioni economiche della Provincia di Sondrio. 1858 11/4/59

Jack, M.
The religious difficulty in Ireland. 1870 12/12/89 ?

Jackman, Isaac
The divorce, a farce. 1790 19/10/79

Jackson, Edward Dudley
The crucifixion, and other poems. 1834 26/1/68

Jackson, Sir George
The Bath archives. A further selection from the diaries and letters of Sir G. J. ed. by Lady Jackson. 1873 (2v.) 7/5/73

Jackson, H. M.
Glimpses of three coasts. 1886 27/11/86

Jackson, John actor
History of the Scottish stage. 1793 25/12/63

Jackson, John Bishop of Lincoln, then London
A charge delivered to the clergy . . . of the diocese of Lincoln . . . October, 1867. 1867 8/12/67
On national education, with remarks on education in general. 1838 21/7/45
Positivism. A lecture. 1871 1/10/71
The parochial system. A charge delivered to the clergy of the diocese of London . . . November 1871. 1871 17/12/71

Jackson, T. B.
Exodus and other poems. 1830 19/12/30

Jackson, Thomas Dean of Peterborough
Treatise on the holy Catholic church. (book 1) 17/1/64

Jackson, Thomas Prebend. of St. Paul's
The substance of two inaugural addresses, delivered . . . [at commercial schools in Mile End & Bermondsey]. 1842 25/9/42

Jackson, Thomas Wesleyan minister
The life of J. Goodwin . . . vicar of St. Stephen's, Coleman Street, London . . . civil war and interregnum. 1872 10/10/82

Jackson, William
Right and wrong. A sermon [on Rom. i. 20 and ii. 15] upon the question . . . is a science of natural theology possible?. 1870 9/10/70
The doctrine of retribution. Eight lectures preached . . . on the foundation of the late J. Bampton. 1875 24/12/75

Jacob, Sir George LeGrand
English government of India . . . A letter . . . Reprinted from 'The Daily News'. 1860 8/10/89 ?
The Rajah of Sarawak. 1876 (2v.) 4/6/77

Jacob, General John
The views and opinions of . . . J. Jacob . . . Collected and edited by . . . L. Pelly. 1858 9/3/58

Jacob, P. I.
Curiosités des sciences occultes. 1885 3/11/87 ?

Jacob, Thomas Evan
The life and times of Bishop Morgan, the translator of the Bible into Welsh. 1890 14/11/90

Jacobs, Joseph
The persecution of the Jews in Russia. 1890 30/11/90

Jacobson, William
A charge delivered to the clergy of the diocese. 1871 5/11/71
A charge delivered to the clergy of the diocese [of Chester] *at his primary visitation, October, 1868.* 1868 15/11/68
Clerical duties. A sermon. 1836 14/4/36
On the Athanasian creed. A speech . . . in the Convocation of York, February 21st, 1872. 1872 7/4/72
S. Clementis Romani, S. Ignatii, S. Polycarpi . . . quae supersunt . . . recensuit . . . et illustravit. 1838 3/3/39
Sixteen sermons preached in the parish church of Iffley, Oxon. 1840 7/2/41

Jacobus, Melancthon Williams
Notes . . . on the book of Genesis. 1865 12/2/65

Jacolliot, Louis
La bible dans l'Inde. Vie de Iezeus Christna. 1869 18/4/69

Jager, Abbé Jean Nicholas
Histoire de Photius, patriarche de Constantinople . . . d'après les monuments originaux . . . inconnus. 1844 21/12/56

Jamaica enslaved and free. 1846 30/11/77

James, George Payne Rainsford
Agincourt. A romance. 1844 (3v.) 22/11/44
Forest days: a romance of old times. 1843 (3v.) 11/3/43
Mary of Burgundy. 1833 (3v.) 31/1/45
Morley Ernstein; or, the tenants of the heart. 1842 (3v.) 17/5/42
Some remarks on the corn laws, with suggestions for an alternative . . . in a letter . . . Charles Wyndham, M.P. 1841 4/12/41
The false heir. 1843 (3v.) 1/6/43

James, Henry novelist
Daisy Miller. A comedy in three acts. 1883 14/4/84
The Madonna of the Future, and other tales. 1879 (2v.) 23/8/81

James, Henry of New York
The social significance of our institutions: an oration. 1861 4/2/76
James, Ivor
The Welsh language in the 16th and 17th centuries . . . Reprinted from the Red Dragon. 1887 5/10/87
James, Sir John Kingston
The Jerusalem delivered . . . Translated into English verse. 1865 22/12/64
James, John Thomas
The Italian schools of painting, with observations on the present state of the art. 1820 6/8/50
James, W.
*Mistakes and misstatements in the book of Rug*by School. 1859 23/11/64
James, Walter Charles Baron Northbourne
A vindication of the usage of closing the morning service with a sermon. 1846 27/4/45
The birth-place of Bede. 1866 31/3/67
James, William historical writer
The naval history of Great Britain . . . 1793, to . . . 1820. 1822 (5v. 1822–24) 10/9/51
James, William Unitarian minister
The leading doctrines of Unitarian Christianity: a sermon. 1837 17/6/38
James, William Henry
The two James's and the two Stephensons; or, the earliest history of passenger transit on railways. 1861 2/6/62
James I
A remonstrance of . . . King James I for the right of kings . . . Against . . . Cardinal of Perron, etc. 20/8/44
Triplici nodo triplex cuneus; or, an apologie for the oath of allegiance. 16/8/44
James II
Attempt of King James II to force a Dissenter [A. Francis] *upon Magdalen College, Oxford, February 1687.* 1834 21/5/34
Attempt of King James II to force a Dissenter [J. Hough] upon Magdalen College, Oxford, April 1687. 1834 21/5/34
Jameson, Anna Brownell
Legends of the monastic orders, as represented in the fine arts . . . second series of sacred and legendary art. 1850 14/8/59
Sisters of Charity and the communion of labour. Two lectures . . . with a . . . letter to Lord John Russell. 1859 24/7/59
Jamieson, Jane H.
The Laird's secret. 1882 (2v.) 1/9/83
Jamieson, John
An etymological dictionary of the Scottish language . . . [with] dissertation on the origin of the language. 1808 (2v.) 28/9/71
Sermons on the heart. 1789 (2v. 1789–90) 30/9/88
Jamieson, Robert
A further appeal . . . against the proposed Niger expedition; a letter addressed to . . . Lord John Russell. 1841 5/2/41
An appeal . . . against the proposed Niger expedition. A letter to . . . Lord John Russell. 1840 5/2/41
Jamieson, Thomas Hill
Notice of the life and writings of A. Barclay. 1874 25/6/76
Janet, Paul Alexandre René
Les problèmes du XIXe siècle. La politique—la littérature—la science—la philosophie—la religion. 1872 28/7/73
Saint-Simon et le Saint-Simonisme . . . Cours professé à l'école des sciences politiques. 1878 26/8/78
Janina, Countess Olga pseud. R. Franz
Souvenirs d'un pianiste. Réponse aux Souvenirs d'une Cosaque. 1874 10/10/84
Jannet, Claudio
Les Etats-Unis contemporains . . . précédé d'une lettre de M. Le Play. 1889 (2v. 4th edn) 18/7/89
Janson, Charles William
A view of the present condition of the States of Barbary. 1816 2/10/67
Janssen, Johann
Geschichte des deutschen Volkes seit dem Ausgang des Mittelalters. 1890 27/8/90
Janssen, Jules
L'Age des étoiles. 1887 20/11/89
Japp, Alexander Hay
Industrial curiosities. Glances here and there in the world of labour. 1880 22/12/80
Thomas de Quincey: his life and writings. 1890 23/7/90
Jardine, John
Christian sacerdotalism, viewed from a layman's standpoint, or tried by holy scripture. 1871 22/9/72
Jarvis, Samuel Farmar
Worldly and Christian education compared. A sermon [on 1 Cor. viii. 1]. 1844 9/6/44
Jay, Harriett
The priest's blessing; or poor Patrick's progress from this world to a better. 1881 8/9/81, 9/4/83
The queen of Connaught. 1875 (3v.) 3/11/75
Jay, John
The rise and fall of the pro-slavery democracy, and the rise and duties of the Republican party. An address. 1861 18/11/62
Jebb, Henry Gladwyn
Out of the depths; the story of a woman's life. 1859 24/11/59
Jebb, John
A speech . . . in the House of Peers . . . June 10, 1824 . . . Irish tithe composition amendment bill. 1824 15/12/40
Dialogue on the choral service. 1842 25/3/42 ?

Jebb, John (*cont.*)
Practical theology, comprising discourses on the liturgy and principles of the United Church of England and Ireland. 1830 (2v.) 12/1/40
The choral service of the United Church of England and Ireland. 1843 25/6/43
Jebb, Richard Claverhouse
[on progress on Greece] *in Macmillan's Magazine*, xxxix.419. 1879 (March 1879) 4/3/79
A primer of Greek literature. 24/9/77, 4/5/78
Homer: an introduction to the Iliad and the Odyssey. 1887 9/3/87
Modern Greece; two lectures ... With papers on 'The progress of Greece' and 'Byron in Greece'. 1880 24/8/80
Richard Bentley. 1876 20/5/82
The work of universities for the nation, past and present. 1893 26/8/93
Jeffcott, John M.
Mann, its names and their origins. 1859 (1878 edn) 11/10/78
Jefferson, Joseph Dunnington
A sermon ... upon the occasion of the deaths of two infants. 1850 18/4/50
Jefferson, Thomas
Life of, by H. S. Randall. 1858 (3v.) 30/11/61 ?
Memoirs of the Hon. T. Jefferson, president of the United States ... edited by S. C. Carpenter. 1809 (2v.) 16/1/38, 27/3/50
Jeffreys, Henry
Sentiments of the late Archdeacon Jeffreys with a brief memoir by J. Jeffreys. 1854 1/5/55
Jeffreys, Julius
The British army in India: its preservation by an appropriate clothing, housing ... encouragement. 1858 8/7/58
Jelf, Richard William
An inquiry into the means of grace ... in eight sermons preached before the University of Oxford. 1844 10/11/44
Sermon iv from 'An inquiry into the means of grace ... in eight sermons ... ' etc. [Bampton lectures]. 1844 17/3/72
Sermons, doctrinal and practical, preached abroad. 1835 27/1/49
Specific evidence of unsoundness in the volume entitled 'Essays and Reviews'. 1861 24/3/61
Via Media; or the Church of England our providential path between Romanism and Dissent. A sermon. 1842 13/2/42
Jelf, William Edward
Quousque? ... Considerations on ritualism ... By a high churchman of the old school. 1873 25/8/73
Secession to Rome. 1873 17/8/79
Jelly, Thomas
A brief enquiry into the condition of Jamaica ... her perilous state of political ... and agricultural embarrassment. 1847 22/6/48
A cursory glance at the past and present condition of Great Britain ... a beacon to the British sugar colonies. 1848 23/6/48
Jenkins, David Judge
Pacis consultum. 26/6/87 ?
Jenkins, John Edward
Barney Geoghegan, M.P. and Home Rule at St. Stephens. 1877 22/10/77
Glances at inner England. A lecture delivered in the United States and Canada. 1874 19/4/74
Lutchmee and Dilloo: a study of West Indian life. 1877 (3v.) 6/3/78
The blot on the Queen's head; or, how little Ben ... changed the sign of the 'Queen's Inn'. 1876 27/3/76
The church and the law. A speech ... in the House of Commons on Romanising practices. 1878 26/6/78
The Russo-Turkish war. Janus; or the double-faced ministry. 1877 2/5/77
Jenkins, Robert Charles
A few words on the creed of Pius IV as justifying separation from the Roman church. 1842 8/2/74
Bullam 'Ineffabilis' ad veterum Romanorum Pontificum judicium revocavit R. C. J. 1867 7/4/67
Ignatian difficulties and historic doubts: a letter to ... the Dean of Peterborough. 1890 20/7/90
Romanism: a doctrinal and historical examination of the creed of Pope Pius IV. 1882 12/11/82
The last gleanings of a Christian life. An outline of the life of Thomas Park ... briefly sketched. 1885 22/2/85
The life of Valentin Alberti. 1889 20/10/89
The papal infallibility in the light of the Council of Basle. 1872 2/1/75
The privilege of Peter, and the claims of the Roman church confronted with the Scriptures. 1874 25/7/80
The true apostolic succession. A brief commentary on a passage from ... St. Gregory Nazianzene. 1890 16/2/90
Jenkinson, Charles Earl of Liverpool
A collection of all the treaties of peace, alliance and commerce ... 1648 to ... 1783. 1785 (3v.) 21/6/61
A treatise on the coins of the realm, in a letter to the king. 1805 28/11/59, 13/2/62
Life and administration of ... Lord Liverpool, by C. D. Yonge. 1868 (3v.) 10/12/68
Jenkinson, John Simon
Marriage with a wife's sister not forbidden by the word of God ... [Keble's tract] proved to be unscriptural ... in a letter to the Rev. C. B. Dalton. 1849 27/4/49

Jenner, Sir William
The practical medicine of to-day: two addresses. 1869 23/9/69
Jennings, Henry James
Cardinal Newman: the story of his life. 1882 6/12/81
Lord Tennyson, a biographical sketch. 1884 21/10/84
Jennings, Louis John
Mr. Gladstone: a study. 1887 25/6/87 ?
The Croker papers. 1884 (3v.) 25/10/84
Jenny's room. 1877 9/3/79
Jephson, Henry
The platform, its rise and progress. 1892 (2v.) 16/2/92
Jeremie, John
Four essays on colonial slavery. 1831 2/2/33
Letter to Buxton... on Negro emancipation and African civilization. 1840 2/7/40
Recent events at Mauritius. 1835 7/7/35
Jeremy, Walter D.
The Presbyterian fund and Mr. Daniel William's Trust: with biographical notes of the trustees. 1885 9/1/87
Jerningham, Sir Hubert Edward Henry K.C.M.G.
Life in a French chateau. 1867 29/7/67
Norham castle. 1883 1/11/84
To and from Constantinople. 1873 16/3/73 ?
Jerram, Charles
A sermon [on 2 Tim. i. 12] occasioned by the death of J. M. Good. 1827 16/1/31
Conversations on infant baptism, and some popular objections against the Church of the United Kingdom. 1819 10/5/29, 26/1/34
Jerrold, Douglas William
The schoolfellows: a comedy. In two acts. 1835 13/4/39
Jerrold, William Blanchard
Egypt under Ismail Pacha. Being some chapters of contemporary history. 1879 20/5/82, 4/8/84
Jervis, Henry Jervis White
History of the island of Corfu, and of the republic of the Ionian islands. 1852 15/11/58
Jervis, William George
The poor condition of the clergy and the causes considered, with suggestions for remedying the same. 1856 17/3/56
Jervise, Andrew
Epitaphs and inscriptions from burial grounds and old buildings... of Scotland, with... notes. 1875 (2v. 1875–9) 24/1/76
Jesse, John Heneage
London and its celebrities: a second series of literary and historical memorials of London. 1850 (2v.) 22/4/70
London: its celebrated characters and remarkable places. 1871 (3v.) 11/3/71
Jesse, William
The life of George Brummell... commonly called Beau Brummell. 1844 (2v.) 24/5/44, 27/6/85
The life of George Brummell... commonly called Beau Brummell. 1844 (new edn 2v. 1886) 5/12/85
Jessopp, Augustus
Norwich... with map. 1880 31/10/84
One generation of a Norfolk house. A contribution to Elizabethan history. 1878 11/5/79
Jeune, Francis
The Epistles written by the spirit of the living God. A sermon... at the consecration of John [Kaye]. 1853 15/5/53
Was Paul crucified for you? A sermon... on the satisfaction of the Lord Jesus Christ. 1863 10/1/64
Jevons, Thomas
The prosperity of the landholders not dependent on the corn laws. 1840 23/9/41
Jevons, William Stanley
A serious fall in the value of gold ascertained, and its social effects set forth. 1863 15/5/63
The coal question. 1865 1/2/66
The match tax: a problem in finance. 1871 29/6/71
The principles of science: a treatise on logic and scientific method. 1874 (2v.) 30/4/74 ?
Jewel, John
A defence of the apologie of the Churche of Englande. 9/10/70
Apologia ecclesiae Anglicanae. 1/7/38, 28/11/68
Sacraments. (1840 edn) 29/3/46
Jewitt, Llewellynn Frederick William
Grave-mounds and their contents: a manual of archaeology... Celtic... Romano-British, and ... Anglo-Saxon periods. 1870 15/6/70
The Wedgwoods: being a life of Josiah Wedgwood ... and a history of the early potteries of Staffordshire. 1865 4/5/65
Jewsbury, Maria Jane afterw. Fletcher
Letters to the young. 1828 26/12/30
Joannes de Fordun
Scoti-Chronicon, sive Scotorum historia. 2/10/72
Job, Miss Mortimer Jane
Can it cure? A treatise on the healing power of animal magnetism, or electricity. 1867 1/5/70
Jocelyn, Robert 3rd Earl of Roden
Observations on Lord Alvanley's pamphlet on the state of Ireland and proposed measures for restoring tranquillity to that country. 1841 8/12/41
Jocelyn, Robert Viscount Jocelyn
Six months with the Chinese expedition; or, leaves from a soldier's notebook. 1841 3/3/41

Joel, Moritz
Die letzten Lebenstunden des Kaisers Nicolaus des Ersten . . . aus dem Russischen übertragen. 1855 20/10/55
Johnes, Arthur James
Preface to a reprint of an essay on the Causes of Dissent in Wales. 1870 2/1/70
Johnson, Bradley Tyler
The foundation of Maryland, and the origin of the Act concerning Religion of April 21, 1649. 1867 (1883) 1/7/83
Johnson, D. M.
Lethe and other poems. 1882 7/5/90
Johnson, George B.
Poems and sonnets. 1874 24/10/73
Johnson, George Henry Sacheverell
Sermons preached in Wells cathedral. 1857 14/6/57, 6/9/57
Statement of the Dean of Wells . . . his acceptance of the living of St. Cuthbert . . . and . . . resignation. 1872 28/5/72
Johnson, H. P.
The campaign of 1776. 1878 25/3/80 ?
Johnson, James
A tour in Ireland; with meditations and reflections. 1844 27/5/46
Johnson, R.
A reply to a recent speech of Sir R. Palmer on the Washington Treaty and the Alabama claims. 1871 24/10/71
Commentary on the memoirs of T. Wolfe Tone. 1828 30/11/39
Johnson, Richard Locke
Brilliant prospects. 1870 8/7/71
Johnson, Samuel LL.D.
'Milton' in *Lives of the English poets.* 1779 (3v.) 17/11/55
Irene; a tragedy. 1749 30/9/26
Johnsoniana. 1884 (new edn) 30/12/84
Life of Johnson, by Boswell. 1791 (2v.) 8/12/25, 24/4/26, 22/5/26
Life of Johnson, by Boswell, ed. J. Murray. 1831 (2v.) 11/12/60, 2/9/63, 26/10/63, 26/9/64, 3/10/64, 1/11/64
Lives of the English poets. 1779 19/9/25
Memoirs of the life and writings of Samuel Johnson, by W. Shaw. 1785 7/11/86 ?
Prayers and Meditations. 1785 1/10/26
Taxation no tyranny. 1774 27/5/26, 6/2/47
The Idler. 1761 (2v.) 3/8/68
Thoughts on the late transactions respecting the Falkland Islands. 1771 1/5/56
Witticisms, ed. J. Merry. 1791 4/1/48
Johnson, Samuel Rector of Corringham
Julian the Apostate: being a short account of his life. 1682 11/12/70
Johnston, James
Our educational policy in India. 1879 28/7/79
Johnstone, Catherine Laura pseud. C. Joyneville
The historical families of Dumfriesshire. 1889 24/6/92
The life and times of Alexander I, Emperor of all the Russias. 1875 (3v.) 16/11/76
Johnstone, Henry Alexander Munro Butler
Ireland. Letters reprinted from the 'Morning Post' . . . to the Rt. Hon. W. E. Gladstone. 1868 17/2/68
The Eastern question . . . Reprinted from the 'Pall Mall Gazette'. 1875 14/9/75
Johnstone, James of Edinburgh
A few days on the Continent . . . a reply to [Gladstone's] . . . 'Vaticanism'. 1875 9/4/75
Johnstone, James de Chevalier
Memoirs of the Chevalier de Johnstone . . . translated . . . by C. Winchester. 1870 (3v. 1870–71) 23/1/72
Johnstone, John
The works of S. Parr . . . with memoirs of his life and writings. 1828 16/9/29
Johnstone, R. W.
The telegraph and its proposed acquisition by the government. 1867 16/7/67
Johnstone, William Henry
Sunday and the sabbath: or, reasons for identifying the Lord's day of the apostles with the sabbath of Moses. 1853 15/4/55
Joinville, Francis Ferdinand Philip L. M. d'Orleans
La guerre d'Amérique. 1862 20/12/64
Jolly, Alexander
Observations upon the several Sunday services prescribed by the liturgy throughout the year. 1828 26/12/41
Observations upon the several Sunday services prescribed by the liturgy . . . memoir by . . . J. Walker. 1840 (3rd edn) 31/10/41
Some plain instructions concerning the nature and constitution of the Christia 30/12/48
Joly, Aristide
Antoine de Montchrétien, poète et économiste normand. 1865 15/2/73
Joly, Vincent pseud. M. Jacob
Le Juif errant. 1834 25/10/45
Jomard, Edmé François
Voyage à l'oasis de Syonah. 1823 4/4/49 ?
Jones, Agnes Elizabeth
Memorials . . . By her sister. 1871 24/2/84
Jones, Alfred Barron
Observations on the diseases and loss of the teeth. 1853 24/4/53
Jones, Ernest Charles
Corayda; a tale of faith and chivalry, and other poems. 1860 6/10/60
Labour and capital: a lecture. 1867 21/2/67

Jones, Evan
A vindication of the educational and moral condition of Wales, in reply to W. Williams, Esq. 1848 15/3/48
Jones, Frederick Robert
The Huddersfield tenant-right system. 1860 6/8/64
Jones, Griffith Hartwell
Barbaric Greece and Italy. 1891 21/10/91
Jones, Harry
The perfect man, or Jesus an example of godly life. 1869 25/9/69
Jones, H. D.
God's providence the Queen's inheritance. 1842 21/7/42
Jones, Sir Henry
Browning as a philosophical and religious teacher. 1891 21/8/92, 25/9/92
Jones, Henry
Wales and its prospects. 1890 28/5/90
Jones, Henry Bence
The life and letters of Faraday. 1870 2/6/70
Jones, Henry Macnaughton
The study of life. 1874 2/1/75
Jones, J.
A token of Christian love. 8/1/87 ?
Jones, John Congregational Minister
Spiritualism the work of demons. 1871 27/4/74
Jones, John Perpetual Curate of Cradley, Worcs.
Bishop Hall, his life and times; or, memoirs of the life... of... Joseph Hall... Bishop of Exeter. 1826 21/3/41
Classical studies. 1866 3/2/66
Jones, John Precentor of Christ Church, Oxford
A reply to the Rev. W. B. Knight's 'Remarks' on Welsh orthography. 1831 18/2/70 ?
Jones, John writer on astronomy
The sun a magnet. 1880 17/4/93
Jones, Owen
An apology for the colouring of the Greek Court in the Crystal Palace. 1854 25/10/54
Jones, Richard
A few remarks on the proposed commutation of tithes. With suggestions of some additional facilities. 1833 25/4/36
A letter to... Sir R. Peel... on the bill introduced into Parliament... Parochial Rates. 1840 6/7/40
Jones, T.
Uriel, and other poems. 1857 29/8/57
Jones, Thomas W. S.
Inni sacri per uso delle chiese. 1881 27/1/89 ?
Jones, T. Wharton
A true relation of the life and death of... William Bedell. 1872 16/2/73
Jones, William of Nayland
The Catholic doctrine of the Trinity proved. 1756 10/9/29, 4/8/31
Jones, William Basil Tickell Bishop of St. David's
The peace of God: sermons on the reconciliation of God and man. 1869 6/2/70
Jones, William Basil Tickell, and E. A. Freeman
The history and antiquities of St. David's. 1856 11/7/52
Jones, William Bence
[On Irish land]. 16/4/70
The Irish church from the point of view of one of its laymen. 1868 19/5/68
Jones, William Henry Vicar of Mottram
A letter... on the question of 'Church Rates', chiefly as it concerns our populous parishes. 1859 25/11/59
The temple of pleasure and the Lord's Day: a sermon. 1852 17/10/52
Jonson, Ben
Poetaster, or the arraignment. 7/6/26, 24/6/26
The Alchemist. A comedy. 1732 6/7/26, 7/7/26
The silent woman. 24/6/26
Volpone, or the fox. A comedy. 22/6/26
Joplin, Thomas
An examination of Sir Robert Peel's Currency Bill of 1844. In a letter to the bankers of the [U.K.]. 1844 22/2/44
An examination of the Report of the Joint Stock Bank Committee. 1836 22/2/37
Jordan, John
An appeal to the evangelical clergy against their ... use of the baptismal and confirmation services. 1850 19/6/50
The crisis come, being remarks on... Newman's letter to Dr. Jelf, and on 'Tracts for the Times' no. 90. 1841 19/4/41
Jorgenson, J.
The convict king. 1881 17/11/91
Jortin, John
Remarks on ecclesiastical history. 1751 (3v. 1751–4) 24/8/45
Six dissertations upon different subjects. 1755 31/7/45 ?
The life of Erasmus. 1758 (2v. 1758–60) 9/12/53
Joseph, Henry Samuel
Memoirs of convicted prisoners; accompanied by remarks on the causes and prevention of crime. 1853 3/11/53
Josephus
Opera. 15/12/90
Joubert, Léo
Essais de critique et d'histoire. 1863 10/8/64
Jourdan, W. L.
The ocean, its tides. 1873 13/3/81
Journal des débats 27, 28, 30. 1851 (September 1851) 13/10/51
Journal des Economistes. 43. 9/1888 22/9/1888
Journal d'un voyage à Paris. 1862 22/6/67

Journal of the Alabama Senate 1863 14/11/63 ?
Journal of the Bacon Society (June). 1887 (i no. 3) 24/5/87
Journey to Scotland. 26/9/73
Jowett, Benjamin
On the interpretation of scripture. 1860 2/12/60
Statements of Christian doctrine and practice, extracted from . . . [his] published writings. 1861 3/3/61
The dialogues of Plato, tr. with analyses and introduction by B. Jowett. 1871 22/2/71, 27/2/71
The epistles of St. Paul to the Thessalonians, Galatians, Romans: with . . . notes and dissertations. 1855 17/6/55
Jowett, Benjamin, and Stanley, A. P.
Examination statute improvement. 1848 25/3/48
Joyce, Arthur J.
Last glimpses of Convocation . . . the latest incidents and results of synodical action in the church. 1853 1/5/53, 7/3/69
Joyce, James Wayland
Acts of the church, 1531–1885. The Church of England her own reformer. 1886 19/4/86
Ecclesia Vindicata. A treatise on appeals in matters spiritual. 1862 7/9/62
England's sacred synods. A constitutional history of the convocations of the clergy. 1855 6/5/55
The duty of the civil power to promote the faith of the national church. An assize sermon. 1857 3/5/57
The kingdom not of this world . . . a letter to . . . Canon Seymour. 1867 9/6/67
The national church. An answer to an essay on 'The National Church' by H. B. Wilson [in Essays & Reviews]. 1861 7/7/61
Joyce, Patrick Weston
The origin and history of Irish names of places. 1875 (3v.) 9/11/77
Joyner, Mrs. Mary Anne
Cyprus, historical and descriptive. Adapted from the German. 1878 9/11/78
Jubilee Memorial of the Scottish Congregational Churches. 1849 1/6/84
Jukes, Andrew Henry
'Catholic Eschatology' examined. A reply to . . . H. N. Oxenham's recent papers in the 'Contemporary Review'. 1876 26/8/76
Jukes, Andrew John
The second death and the restitution of all things . . . A letter to a friend. 1867 20/5/75
Jusserand, Jean Adrien Antoine Jules
A French ambassador at the court of Charles the Second. Le comte de Cominges, from his unpublished correspondence. 1892 2/6/92
Piers Plowman. A contribution to the history of English mysticism. 1894 26/4/94
The English novel in the time of Shakespeare . . . translated from the French by E. Lee. 1890 8/5/91
Justin, Saint martyr
Works. 1861 13/9/65
Justinian I, Emperor of the East
Institutiones, from Digest of Roman law. 1/3/54
Juvenal
Opera. 24/9/25, 23/5/26, 13/11/26, 13/3/28, 29/3/28, 9/3/29, 17/5/30, 18/1/31, 28/5/91

K., K.
Wales and its people. 1869 9/11/69
Kalisch, Mauritius
A historical and critical commentary on the Old Testament. 1858 24/8/73
Theology of the past and the future. 1871 16/7/71
Karapanos, Konstantinos
Dodone et ses ruines. 1878 12/4/78
Karcher, Théodore
Etudes sur les institutions politiques et sociales de l'Angleterre. 1867 9/1/69
Katakazes, Constantine
Politique anglaise en Orient. 1877 19/1/78
Kate Trevelyan. (not found) 24/8/81
Katholische Kirchenzeitung. 10/9/38
Katholisches Gebethbuch. 1854 9/11/56
Kavanagh, Arthur Macmorrough
The cruise of the R. Y. S. Eva. 1865 29/10/77
Kavanagh, Julia
Nathalie; a tale. 1850 (3v.) 27/4/74
Women in France during the eighteenth century. 1850 (2v.) 19/6/68
Kay, Alexander
Florine, a dramatic poem. 1858 26/4/93 ?
Kay, David
Austria-Hungary . . . With maps. 1880 28/10/80
Kay, William
Crisis Hupfeldiana; being an examination of Hupfeld's Criticism on Genesis. 1865 22/4/66
The influence of Christianity on the position and character of women. 1859 12/2/60
Kaye, John
A charge to the clergy of the diocese of Lincoln, delivered at the triennial visitation. 1840 28/11/41
A charge to the clergy of the diocese of Lincoln . . . triennial visitation. 1843 23/10/43
A letter to . . . the Archbishop of Canterbury on the recommendations of the Ecclesiastical Commission. 1838 11/5/38
A sermon preached at the consecration of Woolsthorpe Church, March 4th, 1847. 1847 4/3/47

An address after confirmation, delivered at Eton College... May 26 1842. 1842 12/6/42
Some account of the writings and opinions of Justin Martyr. 1829 14/9/65, 29/7/77
The ecclesiastical history of the second and third centuries, illustrated from... Tertullian. 1826 28/2/30

Kaye, Sir John William K. C. S. I.
Christianity in India: an historical narrative. 1859 24/3/59
History of the war in Afghanistan. 1851 24/2/52
Jerningham; or, the inconsistent man. 1836 (3v.) 24/7/67
Selections from the papers of Charles, Lord Metcalfe. Ed. Sir J. W. Kaye. 1855 14/12/57
The administration of the East India Company. 1853 10/5/58

Keane, John F.
My journey to Medinah: describing a pilgrimage ... performed by the author disguised as a Mohammedan. 1881 30/1/82
Six months in Meccah... Pilgrimage to Meccah ... by an Englishman professing Mohammedanism. 1881 20/1/82

Keary, Annie
Castle Daly: the story of an Irish home thirty years ago. 1875 (3v.) 14/7/75
The nations around Palestine. 1870 16/10/71

Keay, J. Seymour
The landlord, the tenant and the taxpayer... the Irish land purchase bill. 1890 23/4/90

Kebbel, Thomas Edward
'The political novels of Lord Beaconsfield' in *Nineteenth Century*, vi.604. 1879 (September 1879) 22/9/79
[on personal government] *in Nineteenth Century*, iv.1137. 1878 (December 1878) 28/11/78
Essays upon history and politics. 1864 28/11/78

Keble, John
[Review of Gladstone's State and Church] *in The British Critic*, xxvi. 355. 1839 (October 1839) 8/10/39
A few very plain thoughts on the proposed admission of dissenters to the university of Oxford. 1854 12/7/54
A postscript to the third edition of the sermon entitled 'Primitive tradition... in Holy Scripture'. 1837 19/11/37
Against profane dealing with holy matrimony in regard of a man and his wife's sister. 1849 3/4/49
An argument for not proceeding immediately to repeal the laws which treat the nuptial bonds as indissoluble. 1857 6/3/57
Church matters in 1850. 1850 26/2/50
Church matters in 1850. No. 2. 1850 17/10/50
De poeticae vi medica; praelectiones academicae Oxonii habitae. 1844 (2v.) 1/6/57
Heads of consideration on the case of Mr. Ward. 1845 25/1/45
Letters of spiritual counsel and guidance, by the late J. K... edited by R. F. Wilson. 1870 28/8/70
Letters of spiritual counsel and guidance... third edition, much enlarged. 1875 21/3/75
Life of Keble, by W. Lock. 1893 7/5/93
Lyra Innocentium. Thoughts in verse on Christian children. 1846 24/5/46
Miscellaneous poems [with preface by G. Moberly]. 1869 30/7/87
National apostasy considered. 1833 27/10/33
Primitive tradition in Holy Scripture. A sermon. 1836 5/3/37, 11/2/38
Sequel of the argument against immediately repealing the laws which treat the nuptial bond as indissoluble. 1857 4/7/57
Studia sacra. Commentaries on the introductory verses of St. John's gospel... Epistle to the Romans. 1877 16/3/90, 8/6/90
The case of Catholic subscription to the thirty-nine articles considered... the present crisis. 1841 4/5/41
The Christian year. 1827 31/5/29, 8/4/32, 23/9/32, 30/9/32, 18/11/32, 16/12/32, 13/1/33, 14/4/33
The duty of hoping against hope: a sermon; preached at Harrow Weald chapel. 1846 13/12/46
The life of... T. Wilson... Bishop of Sodor and Man. 1863 8/6/63

Keble, John, and Newman, John Henry
Remains of the late Rev. R. H. F[roude], ed. J. Keble and J. H. Newman. 1838 28/3/40

Kehoe, T.
Some considerations in favour of forming a settlement at the confluence of the Niger and Tchadda. 1847 29/2/48

Keightley, Thomas
The mythology of ancient Greece and Italy: for the use of schools. 1832 13/12/60

Keith, Alexander
Sketch of the evidence from prophecy... foretold, and which have been clearly or literally fulfilled. 1823 14/8/36
The signs of the times as denoted by the fulfilment of historical predictions... to the present day. 1832 9/2/33

Keith, Sir Robert Murray
Memoirs and correspondence (official and familiar)... edited by Mrs. G. Smyth. 1849 (2v.) 9/11/49

Keller, Otto
Die Entdeckung Ilions zu Hissarlik. 1875 24/9/75

Kelly, Sir Fitzroy
A letter to Lord Lyndhurst on the late debate upon China. 1857 10/3/57
A letter to the Lord High Chancellor upon the late Order in Council. 1878 8/12/78
Kelly, William F.R.G.S.
A letter stating and reviewing 'the Irish difficulty' and suggesting a few simple expedients. 1868 20/2/68
Kelly, William of Guernsey
The collected writings of J. N. Darby. 1867 (34v. 1867–1900) 1/11/68
Keltie, Sir John Scott
Applied geography . . . with maps and diagrams. 1890 12/12/90
Kemble, Frances Anne afterw. Butler
Journal of F. A. Butler. 1835 (2v.) 26/9/35
Record of a girlhood. An autobiography. 1878 4/1/79
Kemble, John Philip
Macbeth and King Richard the third: an essay, in answer to Remarks [by Whately] on . . . Shakespeare. 1817 6/5/74
Kemp, Daniel William
The Sutherland democracy. 1890 24/2/90
Kempen, Martin von
Opus polyhistoricum, dissertationibus xxv. de osculis . . . 11/5/59
Kempis, Thomas à
De Imitatione Christi. 1/6/30, 30/6/30, 4/11/38, 1/4/47, 12/4/50, 26/1/51, 2/2/51, 25/10/57, 16/9/60, 21/4/61, 6/2/63, 30/3/66, 14/10/66, 4/11/66, 25/12/66, 21/6/68, 26/3/69, 27/6/69, 19/9/69, 27/8/71, 29/3/72, 29/9/72, 8/2/74, 10/2/74, 16/2/74, 17/2/74, 22/4/77, 6/5/77, 13/4/79, 20/4/79, 14/12/79, 12/1/80, 21/3/80, 23/10/87, 19/12/88, 13/1/89, 7/7/89, 22/10/89, 22/3/91, 2/5/92, 11/6/93, 30/7/93
Ken, Thomas
The life of . . . by E. H. Plumtre. 1888 (2v.) 6/10/88
The practice of divine love. An exposition upon the church catechism. 13/9/40
The works of . . . T. K . . . published from original manuscripts, by W. Hawkins. 1721 (4v.) 1/4/60
Kendall, James
Miscellaneous and free strictures on the . . . Wesleyan connexion towards the Church of England. 1836 10/3/37
Kendrick, Tertius T. C.
The Ionian islands. 1822 29/1/59
Kenealy, Edward Vaughan Hyde
Goethe; a new pantomime (poems). 1850 2/6/80
Poems and translations. 1864 30/9/77
Kennan, George
Siberia and the exile system. 1891 (2v.) 21/1/92
Tent life in Siberia, and adventures among the Koraks and other tribes in Kamtchatka and Northern Asia. 1870 13/5/92
Kennaway, Charles Edward
Thoughts for the Lent season of 1848. 1848 26/3/48
Kennedy, Benjamin Hall
A letter to the Bishop of Lichfield . . . on public school discipline in general. 1842 13/3/42
The divinity of Christ. A sermon. 1883 4/2/83
Kennedy, Grace
Father Clement. A Roman Catholic story. 1823 18/12/25, 14/7/33
Kennedy, James Houghton
Natural theology and modern thought. 1891 1/3/91
Kennedy, James Shaw
Notes on the defences of Great Britain and Ireland. 1859 23/7/59
Kennedy, John M.A.
A popular argument for the unity of Isaiah. With an examination of the opinions of . . . Cheyne . . . and others. 1891 17/6/91, 21/6/91
Our place in Christendom and in the Catholic Church . . . inaugural address . . . Congregational Union of England and Wales. 1872 2/6/72
Kennedy, Patrick
Legendary fictions of the Irish Celts. Collected and narrated by P. K. 1866 10/11/69
Kennedy, Thomas Francis
Letter to Lord John Russell . . . relative to his removal from the office of Commissioner of Woods. 1854 21/6/54
Kennion, Thomas
Letter to . . . W. F. Hook . . . with observations upon his letter [attacking the Pastoral Aid Society]. 1841 29/4/41, 13/3/42
Kenny, Thomas
The life and genius of Shakespeare. 1864 11/2/64
Kenrick, John
Phoenicia. 1855 16/6/63, 13/4/70, 12/9/75
Kenrick, Peter Richard
The validity of Anglican ordinations examined . . . the consecration of Matthew Parker . . . Archbishop. 1841 19/1/75
Kenrick, William
A review of Dr. Johnson's new edition of Shakespeare . . . the poet defended from the persecution of his commentators. 1765 17/12/73
Kent, James
Commentaries on American law. 1826 (4v. 1826–30) 16/7/40

Kent, William Charles Mark
The Gladstone government ... by a Templar. 1869 25/5/77 ?
Kenyon, Sir Frederic George
Aristotle on the constitution of Athens. 1891 31/1/91
Keogh, Edward Stephen
A few specimens of 'Scientific History' from ['The Pope and the Council' by] Janus. 1870 13/1/70
Keogh, William Nicholas
A record of traitorism; or, the political life of Mr. Justice Keogh ... reprinted from the 'Nation'. 1872 19/7/72
Keppel, George Thomas Earl of Albemarle
Fifty years of my life. 1876 (2v.) 8/5/76
Memoirs of the Marquis of Rockingham and his contemporaries; with original letters and documents. 1852 (2v.) 13/6/61
Keppel, Sir Henry
The expedition to Borneo of H. M. S. Dido. 1846 (2v.) 3/2/46
Ker, John
Sermons. 1886 (2nd edn) 19/12/86
Sermons. 2 series. 1869 (1869–86) 1/8/69
The psalms in history and biography. 1886 12/12/86, 29/12/89
Kergorlay, Louis Gabriel César de Viscount
Corps législatif. Session 1860. Discours prononcé ... loi concernant le tarif des laines, des cotons. 1860 30/5/60
Kernahan, John Coulson
A book of strange sins. 1893 10/2/94
Kerr, Walter Montague
The far interior: a narrative of travel and adventure from the Cape of Good Hope ... to ... Central Africa. 1886 (2v.) 20/6/87
Kerr, William Schomberg Robert Marquis of Lothian
Fragment of a parallel between the history, literature, and art of Italy in the middle ages. 1863 30/10/63
The Confederate secession. 1864 4/1/65
Kershaw, Samuel Wayland
Protestants from France, in their English home. 1885 1/8/86
Keshan, Daniel
Ireland; an enquiry into the social condition of the country, with suggestions for its improvement. 1853 29/10/53
Ketley, Joseph
The two liturgies A. D. 1549 and A. D. 1552, with other documents, ed. J. Ketley for the Parker Society. 1844 29/10/54
Kettlewell, John
A companion for the penitent, and for persons troubled in mind. 14/12/45
Kettlewell, Samuel
The authorship of the De Imitatione Christi with many interesting particulars about the book. 1877 11/8/78
Keyser, Henry
The law relating to transactions on the stock exchange. 1850 19/6/50
Keys of the Creeds, by anon. 1875 13/9/75
Khama, Chief
The story of an African chief: Khama, by W. Knight-Bruce. 1893 20/12/93
Khedives and Pashas. Sketches of contemporary Egyptian rulers and statesmen. By one who knows them well. 1884 15/4/84
Khmerkin, M.
Les Juifs en Russie. 1893 7/7/93
Khomyakov, Alexsyei Stepanovich pseud. Ignotus
L'église Latine et le Protestantisme, au point de vue de l'église d'Orient. Recueil d'articles. 1872 20/8/73
Quelques mots par un Chrétien Orthodoxe sur les communions Occidentales. 1855 29/2/56, 19/12/58
Kidd, Benjamin
Social evolution. 1894 2/4/94
Kidd, Thomas
Tracts and miscellaneous criticisms [of R. Porson], ed. T. Kidd. 1815 7/3/31
Killen, William Dool
The Bible versus the board. 1835 27/3/37
The board unmeshed. 1836 12/4/37
Kilvert, Francis
Memoirs of the life and writings of Richard Hurd ... correspondence and other unpublished papers. 1860 21/8/64
Kimbolton, Lord
[Papers on Lord Kimbolton, probably in 'Harleian Miscellany', v]. 1744 19/2/64 ?
King, Mr. of Canton
Opium crisis, a letter addressed to Charles Elliot, Chief Superintendent of the British Trade with China. 1839 19/3/40 ?
King, Alexander
Protestantism and the church of Rome ... Discussion between ... G. Spencer ... and A. K. 1876 11/6/76
King, Bryan
Sacrilege and its encouragement ... an account of the St. George's riots ... letter ... to ... bishop of London. 1860 11/4/60
King, Charles William
The natural history of precious stones and of precious metals. 1867 24/11/75
King, David LL.D.
The principles of geology explained ... notes and appendix by J. Scouler. 1850 (4th edn) 31/8/53
The ruling eldership of the Christian church. 1845 2/6/45 ?

King, David LL.D. (*cont.*)
Two lectures, in reply to . . . Chalmers, on church extension, delivered in Greyfriars Church . . . 1838. 1839 27/5/39
King, Edward
Practical reflections upon every verse in the Book of Genesis. 1892 28/5/93
King, Harriet Eleanor Hamilton
The disciples. 1873 7/12/73
King, John Glen
The rites and ceremonies of the Greek church, in Russia . . . account of its doctrine, worship and discipline. 1772 19/11/54
King, Peter 1st Baron King
An enquiry into the constitution, discipline, unity and worship . . . of the primitive church. 14/5/48
King, Peter 7th Baron King
The life of John Locke, with extracts from his correspondence, journals, etc. 1829 (1830 edn) 15/3/39
King, Peter John Locke
Injustice of the law of succession to the real property of intestates. 1855 (3rd edn) 17/6/61
King, Robert diocesan curate, Armagh
A primer on the history of the . . . Catholic church in Ireland from the introduction of Christianity to the . . . modern Irish branch of the church of Rome. 1845 (3v. 1845–51) 27/6/45 ?
Kingdom, William
Suggestions for improving the value of railway property and for the eventual liquidation of the national debt. 1850 22/2/53
Kinglake, Alexander William
The invasion of the Crimea: its origin, and an account of its progress down to the death of Lord Raglan. 1863 (8v. 1863–87) 24/1/63, 11/2/63, 13/7/66, 5/1/77
Eothen, or traces of travel, etc. brought home from the East. 1844 15/8/45
King's College, London. Report presented by the Council to the General Court. 1836 8/5/36
Kingscote, Henry
A letter to . . . the archbishop of Canterbury on the present wants of the church. 1846 27/9/46
Sir John Pakington's plan. A reply to the 'Remarks' of C. J. Colquhoun. 1855 27/4/55
Kingsford, Anna
Clothed with the sun. Being the book of the illuminations of . . . Kingsford, ed. by E. Maitland. 1889 2/7/89
Kingsford, Anna, and E. Maitland
A letter addressed to the Fellows of the London Lodge of the Theosophical Society. 1883 21/12/83
Kingsley, Charles
Alton Locke. 1850 17/3/51
Discipline and other sermons. 1868 20/12/68
Hypatia. A romance. 1863 11/12/75
Letters and memories. 1877 28/10/77
Plays and Puritans, and other historical essays. 1873 24/2/89
The saint's tragedy; or the true story of Elisabeth of Hungary, Landgravine of Thuringia. 1848 31/5/48
What, then, does Dr. Newman mean? A reply to a pamphlet lately published by Dr. Newman. 1864 2/4/64
Why should we pray for fair weather? A sermon. 1860 22/2/60
Kingsley, Henry
The recollections of Geoffrey Hamlyn. 1859 (3v.) 23/8/78
Kingsley, John
Irish nationalism; its origin, growth, and destiny. 1887 4/10/87, 25/9/88
Kingsmill, Sir John
Taxation in Ireland in connexion with the extension of the property and income tax acts to that kingdom. 1853 7/3/53
Kinloch, Sir Archibald Gordon
The trial of Sir A. G. K. . . Bart. for the murder of Sir F. Kinloch . . . his brother German. 1795 15/8/43
Kinnaird, George William Fox Baron Kinnaird
Profitable investment of capital, or 11 years practical experience in farming . . . letter . . . to his tenantry. 1849 15/12/49 n
Kinnear, John Boyd
The mind of England on the Eastern Question. 1877 (2nd) 16/5/77
Kinnear, John G.
The crisis and the currency: with a comparison between the English and Scotch systems of banking. 1847 13/7/47
Kinns, Samuel
Graven in the rock; or, the historical accuracy of the Bible confirmed. 1891 15/7/91
Moses and geology; or the harmony of the Bible with science. 1882 15/12/85
Kiörning, Olaus
Commentatio historico-theologica qua . . . controversia de Consecrationibus Episcoporum Anglorum. 1739 20/4/45
Kip, William Ingraham
The history, object, and proper observance of the holy season of Lent. 1844 11/3/49
Kipling, Rudyard
The light that failed. 1890 3/6/91
The Naulahka: a tale of west and east. 1892 5/9/92
Kirk, E.
A daughter of Eve. 1889 2/5/89
Kirk, John Foster
History of Charles the Bold, Duke of Burgundy. 1863 (3v. 1863–68) 24/11/63

Kirkman, Thomas Penyngton
Church cursing and atheism. 1869 22/8/69, 8/6/84
Kirkpatrick, Alexander Francis
The divine library of the Old Testament. Its origin, preservation, inspiration and permanent value. 1891 3/5/91
Kirkwood, Anderson
The union question: its status quo, and the present duty of its promoters. An address. 1868 3/5/68
Kitchin, George William
On a right judgment. A sermon preached before the University of Oxford. 1864 15/1/65
Kitchiner, William
The art of invigorating and prolonging life by food, clothes... sleep. 1821 17/4/28
Klaczko, Julian
The two chancellors, Prince Gortchakof and Prince Bismarck... tr. by Mrs. Tait. 1876 1/2/77
Knapp, Henry Hartopp
Tempora Subseciva. Verses, serious and comic. 1835 30/1/36
Knight, Charles
The old printer and the modern press. 1854 7/7/83
The struggles of a book against excessive taxation. 1850 6/2/50
Knight, Henry Gally
A letter to the Earl of Aberdeen, Secretary... for foreign affairs [on his official policy, etc.]. 1829 29/11/30
Poems. 1815 15/7/42
The Normans in Sicily: being a sequel to 'An architectural tour in Normandy'. 1838 29/8/38
Knight, Richard Payne
Prolegomena in 'Carmina Homerica, Ilias et Odyssea'. 1808 15/12/55
Knight, Samuel
Forms of prayer, for the use of Christian families. 1791 27/4/28
The life of Dr. J. Colet... founder of St. Paul's School. 1724 21/11/41
The life of Erasmus: more particularly that part of it, which he spent in England. 1726 31/10/63
Knight, William Angus
The philosophy of the beautiful. 1891 29/10/91
Knight's Penny Magazine. 1. 225. Campbell 21/10/1846
Knight's Quarterly Review.
1. 17 26/6/1827
2. 369. 4/1824. Long Parliament 31/5/1826
3. 17-33. 8/1824. Milton 17/7/1827
Knobel, August
Die Völkertafel der Genesis. Ethnographische Untersuchungen. 1850 15/6/90, 11/8/90
Knocker, Edward
An account of the Grand Court of Shepway... installation of... H. J. Temple, Viscount Palmerston... Keeper of H. M. Cinque Ports. 1862 24/8/69
Knollis, Francis Minden
The sling and the stone; or, what is Christian education? A sermon. 1842 15/1/43
Knott, John W.
A letter to the parishioners of St. Saviour's, Leeds. 1851 4/1/52
Knowles, Francis
Observations and reflections on the Athanasian Creed, in three letters to a Society. 1819 3/9/71 ?
The balance of scriptural evidence on trinitarianism and unitarianism. 1835 (3v.) 4/8/79
Knowles, James Sheridan
The beggar of Bethnal Green. 1834 12/10/59
The hunchback, a play in five acts. 1832 11/10/59
Knox, Alexander
Essays on the political circumstances of Ireland, written during the administration of Earl Camden. 1799 14/9/87
On the doctrine of baptism in the Church of England. 1820 19/1/35
Remains of Alexander Knox, ed. J. J. Hornby. 1834 (4v. 1834-7) 15/3/34, 10/9/37, 2/11/37, 13/12/37, 24/3/40
The doctrine of the sacraments, as exhibited in several treatises. 1838 18/11/77
Thirty years' correspondence between J. Jebb... and A. K. 1834 14/6/35
Knox, John
History of the reformation. 2/11/56
Knox, Robert D.D.
The crisis. Plain truths and stern facts for earnest men. 1868 17/10/68
Knox, Robert M.D.
The races of men: a fragment. 1850 (1850-62) 12/6/67
Knox, Robert Bent Bishop of Down, then Armagh
A charge. 1867 14/11/75
The Irish church. 1867 17/8/69
Knox, Thomas Francis
The letters and memorials of William Cardinal Allen 1532-1594. 1878 (1882) 19/2/83
Kohl, Johann Georg
Reisen in Irland. 1843 (2v.) 22/2/44
Travels in Scotland: translated from the German. With notes by the translator [John Kesson]. 1844 19/8/44
Kohut, Adolph
Was lehrt die Bibel über den Gehorsam gegen Staat und Obrigkeit?. 1875 1/8/75

Konstantinides, Georgios pseud. G. Skleros
Homerike theologia. 1876 3/9/79
Koran, tr. G. Sale. 1734 13/1/77
Korf, Count Modest Andreevich
The accession of Nicholas I... translated from the original Russian. 1857 9/12/57, 2/10/58
Kortright, Fanny Aikin
A little lower than the angels. 1874 2/5/74
He that overcometh. A novel. 1876 (2v.) 30/4/76
Pro aris et focis. 1869 31/1/70
The dean; or, the popular preacher. 1859 (3v.) 11/2/70
Kossovo: Serbian national song. 1881 22/8/81
Kossuth, L.
'Russian aggression' in *Contemporary Review*, xxxi. 1. 1877 (December 1877) 1/12/77
Kotzebue, August Friedrich Ferdinand von
Der Wirrwar. 1788 (1803) 17/12/33
Little German towns. 1803 26/8/33
Koulouriotes, A. J.
Greece: her past condition under King Otho, her present requirements... and her future prospects. 1863 24/4/63
Krasinski, Count Walerian Skorobohaty
Historical sketch of the rise, progress, and decline of the Reformation in Poland. 1838 (2v. 1838–40) 13/3/38
Kraszewski, J. I.
The Jew. 1890 9/7/91
Krause, Ernst
Erasmus Darwin und seine Stellung in der Geschichte der Descendenz-Theorie. 1880 2/3/80
Kuenen, Abraham
Three notices of the 'Speaker's Commentary' from the Dutch..., tr. J. Muir. 1873 30/11/73
Kugler, Franz Theodor
A hand-book of the history of painting... tr. from the German by Mrs. M. Hutton, ed. C. L. Eastlake. 1842 28/8/45, 10/1/67
Künzel, Heinrich also Kuenzel
Leben und Reden Sir R. Peel's. 1851 (2v.) 7/9/52
Kurth, G.
Les origines de la civilization moderne. 1886 21/12/89
Kurtz, Johann Heinrich
Sacrificial worship of the Old Testament. 1859 20/12/63
Kynaston, Herbert
Church extension. A sermon. 1840 16/2/40
Strena poetica. 1849 9/5/50

Labadie, Jean de
Déclaration... devant prestre... raisons qui l'ont obligé à quitter... l'église Romaine. 23/2/68
Labaro. 1. 1. Vesuvius 31/3/1890
Labitte, Jules
Le renversement temporel de la papauté. 1861 21/10/81
Lachmann, Carl Conrad Friedrich Wilhelm
Fernere Betrachtungen über die Ilias. 1843 29/1/47
Uber die ersten zehn Bücher der Ilias. 1839 29/1/47
Lach-Szyrma, Wladyslaw Somerville
'True relations of science to religion' in Pleas for the Faith. Especially designed for the use of missionaries. 1873 7/12/73
La Civiltà Cattolica no. 35, 36. 23/11/51
Lackington, James
Memoirs of the first forty-five years of the life of J. Lackington... written by himself, in... letters to a friend. 1791 12/6/61
[La] *Coalition*. 1860 19/4/60
Lacordaire, Jean Baptiste Henri
Conférences de Notre-Dame de Paris. Années 1835 (–1851). 1844 (4v. 1844–51) 14/6/68
Der Heilige Stuhl. Eine zeitgemässe historisch-philosophische Betrachtung. 1838 2/9/43
Mémoire pour le rétablissement en France de l'ordre des Frères Prêcheurs. 1839 27/3/39
Vie de Saint Dominique. 1841 17/8/62
Lacretelle, Jean Charles Dominique de
Histoire de France pendant le dix-huitième siècle. 1808 (4v. 1808–26) 22/4/59
La Croix De Ravignan, Gustave François Xavier de
On the Jesuits, their Institute, doctrines, etc., tr. W. C. Atchison. 1844 8/6/45
Lactantius, Lucius Coelius Firmianus
Lactantii Firmiani de divinis institutionibus adversus gentes rubrice primi libri incipiunt. 13/9/65
L'Affaire Mortara. 1858 26/5/59
Laffan, May later Hartley
Ismay's children. 1887 (3v.) 4/10/87
Lagrange, Charles
The great pyramid... an independent witness to the literary chronology of the Hebrew Bible, and British-Israel identity. 1894 7/8/93 ?
La Gueronnière, Alfred Dubreuil Hélion de
Aux électeurs de France. 1870 12/12/70
Le pape et le congrès. 1859 28/12/59
Les hommes d'état de l'Angleterre au xixe siècle ... un coup d'oeuil sur la Russie et son politique. 1855 8/1/55, 22/2/55
Politique extérieure. Speech. 1862 23/12/63
Laicus
Psycothen, or Reflections in verse on some of the graver aspects of human life. 1892 24/6/92
Laing, David
Sermons, chiefly resulting from daily experience. 1847 24/2/49, 17/5/74

Laing, Francis Henry
The two evolutions: the real and the mock. 1888 1/7/88, 26/8/88
Laing, Joseph
Observations on the . . . grievances inflicted upon merchant seamen, by the maritime laws . . . of England. 1841 8/1/64
Laing, Samuel the elder
Notes on the rise, progress, and prospects of the schism from the Church of Rome . . . instituted by J. Ronge and J. Czerski. 1845 22/8/46
Laing, Samuel the younger
'A month in Connemara' in *Fortnightly Review*, xl. 674. 1883 (November 1883) 7/11/83
A modern Zoroastrian. 1887 20/7/87
Atlas prize essay. National distress; its causes and remedies. 1844 20/7/44
Coercion in Ireland. 1888 22/10/88
Lecture on the Indo-European languages and races. 1862 25/7/62
Pre-historic remains of Caithness . . . with notes on the human remains by T. H. Huxley. 1866 3/8/76
The poor man's income tax. 1861 27/6/61
Laird, Mrs. E.
The true solution of the present religious difficulties . . . address to . . . Pope Pius IX, and the Père Hyacinthe. 1875 1/11/74
Laird, Macgregor
Narrative of an expedition . . . by the river Niger, in the steam-vessels Quorra and Alburkah in 1832–4. 1837 (2v.) 20/9/37
The effect of an alteration in the sugar duties on the . . . people of England and the Negro race. 1844 2/4/44
Lake, William Charles
Christ the life of the world. A sermon. 1859 2/2/62
Humility and love, the law and life of Christianity. A sermon. 1856 24/5/57
Preface on the 'Oxford Declaration' and on Mr. Maurice's 'Letter to the Bishop of London'. 1864 16/1/65
The inspiration of scripture . . . sermons . . . With a preface on the 'Oxford Declaration'. 1864 6/11/64
The two religious movements of our time. A sermon. 1882 19/1/90
L'Allemagne et la Belgique. 1870 18/12/70
L'Alliance franco-allemande. Par un Alsacien. 1888 2/6/88
Lamartine de Prat, Marie Louis Alphonse de
L'Italia e Pio Nono, discorso, recato in Italiano. 1847 14/11/50
Souvenirs, impressions, pensées et paysages, pendant un voyage en Orient (1832, 33). 1835 30/7/35
Lamb, Andrew Simon
The church and the franchise. 1886 13/11/89
Lamb, Charles
A tale of Rosamund Gray and old blind Margaret. 1798 17/3/41
Elia. Essays. 1823 17/3/41
Final memorials, ed. T. N. Tatfourd. 1848 14/9/48
The last essays of Elia. 1833 21/6/37
The works of Charles Lamb. 1818 (2v.) 15/8/62
Lamb, John
An historical account of the thirty-nine articles . . . With . . . copies of the Latin and English manuscripts. 1829 29/9/88
Lamb, Mary Ann
Mary and Charles Lamb: poems, letters, and remains . . . with reminiscences and notes by W. C. Hazlitt. 1874 10/4/75
Lamb, William Viscount Melbourne
Lord Melbourne's papers. Edited by L. C. Sanders. With a preface by the Earl Cowper. 1889 23/11/89
Lord Melbourne, by Henry Dunckley. 1890 9/1/91
Memoirs of . . . Viscount Melbourne, ed. W. T. M. Torrens. 1878 (2v.) 26/11/89
Lambert, Benjamin
A lecture on wit, humour, and pathos. 1861 30/5/68
Lambert, Frederick
The church's cause: being an appeal to churchmen to realise and uphold the claims of the church. 1886 21/11/86
Lambert, Joseph
Agricultural suggestions to the proprietors and peasantry of Ireland. 1845 25/9/69
Lambeth Review. 1. 3/1872 11/4/1872
Lamennais, Hugues Félicité Robert de
De la société première. 5/6/87
Essai sur l'indifférence. 1817 (1817–23) 23/1/53
Paroles d'un croyant. 1899 13/8/93 ?
Lämmer, H., ed.
Monumenta Vaticana. 1861 16/9/89
La Motte Fouqué, Baron Friedrich Heinrich Carl de
Undine. A romance, translated from the German. 1818 16/7/44
Lancaster, Joseph
System of education of the poor. 1821 11/1/49
Lancaster, Thomas William
The harmony of the law and the gospel with regard to the doctrine of a future state. 1825 17/11/30, 18/11/30, 19/11/30
Lander, G.
The anatomie of the Roman clergy. 24/1/85
Landoni, Teodorico, and Vanzolini, G. eds
Lettere scritte a Pietro Aretino, ed. T. Landoni, G. Vanzolini. 1873 (4v. 1873–5) 5/4/88
Landor, Sir Thomas Dick
Highland legends. 1880 2/8/81 ?

Landor, Walter Savage
Imaginary conversations of literary men and statesmen. 1824 (5v 1824–29; 1868 edn) 6/8/39, 16/1/68, 23/7/85
Popery: British and foreign. 1851 13/9/85
The letters of a conservative: in which are shown the only means of saving what is left of the English church. 1836 9/6/93

Landseer, John
A descriptive, explanatory, and critical catalogue of fifty... pictures... in the National Gallery. 1834 26/10/42

Lane, Laura M.
Life of Laura Lane, by A. Viner. 1890 31/8/90

Lanfrey, Pierre
Etudes et portraits politiques. 1864 19/9/70, 28/4/71

Lanfrey, Pièrre
Histoire de Napoléon Ier. 1867 (5v. 1867–75) 20/3/67, 1/7/71

Lang, Andrew
Custom and myth. 1884 16/11/84
Helen of Troy. 1882 7/10/82
Homer and the epic. 1893 12/5/93
Oxford. Brief historical and descriptive notes. 1882 26/1/91
The library... With a chapter on modern English illustrated books by Austin Dobson. 1876 7/7/83
The life of Stafford Northcote. 1890 (2v.) 25/2/90, 25/10/90, 31/10/90
The Odyssey of Homer, done into English prose by S. H. Butcher... and A. Lang. 1879 23/1/79

Lang, Gabriel H.
Letter to... H. Goulburn... Chancellor of the Exchequer... on the unequal pressure of the railway passenger tax. 1842 18/7/42
Letter to... W. E. Gladstone... on the importance in a national point of view of railway extension. 1844 19/1/44
Reasons for the repeal of the railway passenger tax. 1851 29/11/51

Lang, John Dunmore
Historical account of the separation of Victoria from New South Wales. 1837 (2v. 2nd edn) 6/6/37
Letter to Lord Stanley... on proroguing the legislative council of New South Wales. 1845 11/6/49

Lang, Robert Hamilton
Cyprus: its history, its present recourse and future prospects. 1878 22/10/78

Langbridge, Frederick
Love-knots and bridal bands: poems and rhymes of wooing and wedding, and valentine verses. 1883 11/5/86 ?
Poor folks' lives: ballads and stories in verse. 1887 16/11/87

Langdale, Charles
Memoirs of Mrs. Fitzherbert; with an account of her marriage with H. R. H. the Prince of Wales. 1856 25/3/56, 8/11/83

Langdon, William Chauncy
Some account of the Catholic Reform Movement in the Italian church. 1868 31/10/69

Lange, Daniel Adolphus
Lord Palmerston and the isthmus of Suez canal. Two letters... to... the Times. 1857 18/7/57
The isthmus of Suez canal question viewed in its political bearings. 1859 21/9/59

Langen, Joseph
Geschichte der Römischen Kirche bis zum Pontifikate Leo's I. 1881 (4v. 1881–93) 16/10/81, 17/7/91, 11/8/91, 17/7/92
Geschichte der Römischen Kirche von Gregor VII. bis Innocenz III. 1893 9/7/93, 23/7/93
Johannes von Damaskus. Eine patristische Monographie. 1879 (1885 edn) 5/9/86

Langford, John Alfred
A century of Birmingham life: or, a chronicle of local events, from 1741 to 1841. 1868 (2v.) 19/8/68

Langham Magazine. 1. 6/1876 12/6/1876

Langland, William
Piers Plowman, by J. A. A. J. Insserand. 1894 26/4/94

L'Angleterre jugée. 23/9/64

Langley, Batty
A sure method of improving estates by plantations of oak, elm, ash, beech, and other timber trees. 1728 28/8/63

Lanigan, Stephen M.
Home rule: a study in social science. 1879 14/10/87

Lansdell, Henry
Through Siberia... with illustrations and maps. 1882 (2v.) 25/1/82, 17/3/84

Lantsheere, Léon de
De la race et de la langue des Hittites. 1891 20/11/92

Lanzi, Luigi Antonio
The history of painting in Italy, from the period of the revival... to the end of the eighteenth century. Tr. T. Roscoe. 1828 (6v.) 6/8/38

La politique Anglaise. 1860 18/7/60
La question Bulgare. 1888 9/11/87
La question d'Orient comme conséquence inévitable du partage de la Pologne. 1877 28/9/77
La question d'Orient. Un homme et une solution. 1860 3/4/60
La question Irlandaise. 1860 23/7/60
La rappresentazione dell'Anima Dannata. 16/11/66

Larchier, Claude
Physiologie de l'amour moderne, ed. P. Bourget. 1891 15/1/92

Lardner, Dionysius
A rudimentary treatise on the steam engine. 1848 22/9/49
Mechanics. 1830 17/11/31
Mechanics. Introduction to geometry. 1823 27/6/31
Mechanics. Treatise on calculus. 1825 2/7/31
Outlines of history. 1831 22/1/33
The Cabinet Cyclopaedia. 1829 (133v. 1829–44) 3/10/35
La Règle du tier-ordre des pénitens, instituée . . . père S. François pour . . . personnes seculières. 17/9/48, 7/1/55
Laroche, Michel de
Mémoires littéraires de la Grande Bretagne. 1720 (16v. 1720–24) 19/2/82
La Russia. Studio Storico. 1887 9/11/87
Lasserre, Henri
Les saints évangiles. 1888 20/5/88
Lasteyrie du Saillant, Count Charles Phillbert de
Histoire de la confession sous ses rapports religieux, moraux et politiques, chez les . . . anciens et modernes. 1846 13/2/48
Last words of an English Catholic. 1857 1/2/57
Latham, Robert Gordon
Descriptive ethnology. 1859 (2v.) 1/11/61
Man and his migrations. 1851 11/3/52, 1/11/57
The English language. 1841 27/9/61
The nationalities of Europe. 1863 (2v.) 23/7/63
Lathbury, Thomas
'A letter to . . . Peel . . . on the restoration of suffragan bishoprics' in *British Magazine*, xxv. 309 (March). 1844 24/1/44
A history of the convocation of the Church of England . . . from the earliest period. 1842 21/3/45
A history of the nonjurors, their controversies and writings; with remarks on . . . rubrics in the Book of Common Prayer. 1845 11/3/45
Latimer, Hugh
Sermons. 1788 29/11/85
The works of H. Latimer . . . Edited for the Parker Society by . . . George Elwes Corrie. 1844 (2v. 1844–45) 8/2/46
La torture en Sicile. 1860 1/5/60
La Turquie Mirées. 4/2/61
Laud, William
A relation of the conference between William Laud . . . and Mr. Fisher the Jesuit, ed. Cardwell. 1839 5/2/40
A relation of the conference between William Laud . . . and Mr. Fisher, the Jesuit. 27/10/61, 27/1/84
Life and times of William Laud, by J. P. Lawson. 1829 (2v.) 11/4/35
Life of Archbishop Laud, by C. W. Le Bas. 1832 31/3/36
The autobiography of Laud . . . collected from his remains. 1839 24/12/42
The private devotions of William Laud, ed. Faber. 1838 2/2/40
The works of . . . William Laud. 1847 (7v. 1847–60) 23/8/57
Lauder, William
An essay on Milton's use and imitation of the moderns in his Paradise Lost [preface by Dr. Johnson]. 1750 7/1/57
King Charles I vindicated from the charge of plagiarism . . . and Milton himself convicted of forgery. 1754 4/8/63
Laudor, Edward Wilson
The bushmen, or life in a new country. 1847 6/11/47
Lauer, Julius Franz
Quaestiones Homericae. 1843 25/8/91
Laugel, Auguste
L'Angleterre politique et sociale. 1873 17/5/73
Laur, E. of Heidelberg
Bossuet und die Unfehlbarkeit. 1875 4/7/75
Laurence, Rev. John
Christian prudence; or, Christianity a gospel of peace. 1720 28/8/90 ?
Laurence, Richard Archbishop of Cashel
The doctrine of the Church of England upon the efficacy of baptism vindicated from misrepresentation. 1816 (2v. 1816–18) 18/10/29
Laurence, Robert French
An inquiry into the . . . condemnation of Dr. Hampden. 1848 16/2/48
The churchman's assistant at Holy Communion . . . With additions and directions for the use of communicants. 1860 11/5/60
Laurence, Roger
Lay-baptism invalid: or, an essay to prove that such baptism is null and void. 1710 20/7/29
Laurens, Abbé
Le cas d'un curé Gallican; ou explication de l'infallibilité du Pape et de l'église ultramontaine. 1875 4/11/79 ?
Laurent, Peter Edmund
Introduction to the nine books of the history of Herodotus, tr. P. E. Laurent. 1827 15/8/28
Laurie, James
Decimal coinage. A practical analysis of the comparative merits of . . . a decimal currency for the United Kingdom. 1854 16/9/54
Laurie, Sir Peter
Prison discipline and secondary punishments. 1837 2/3/38
Laurie, William Ferguson Beatson
Ashé Pyee, the superior country; or, the great attractions of Burma to British enterprise and commerce. 1882 3/1/82
Lauth, Franz Joseph
Homer und Aegypten. 1867 22/8/73

L'Autriche dans le royaume Lombardo-Vénetien. 1859 2/5/59
La Vallée, Joseph
Cécile, fille d'Achmet III. 1787 28/1/52
Lavater, Johann Caspar
Werke. 1834 (6v. 1834–38) 17/9/50
Laveleye, Baron Emile Louis Victor de
'The future of France', in *Fortnightly Review,* xiv. 615. 1870 (December 1870) 22/12/70
Des causes actuelles de guerre en Europe et de l'arbitrage. 1873 30/6/73
Etudes et essais. 1869 29/7/70
L'avenir religieux des peuples civilisés. 1876 22/3/76
L'instruction du peuple. 1872 8/5/72
La péninsule des Balkans. 1886 (2v.) 21/1/87
La Prusse et l'Autriche. 1870 23/8/70
Protestantism and Catholicism ... bearing upon the liberty and prosperity of nations ... [introductory letter by Gladstone]. 1875 14/4/75
Regulated vice in relation to morality. An Address, tr. from the French. 1884 3/2/84
Lavelle, Patrick
The Irish landlord since the revolution. 1870 5/2/70
Lavie, Germain
Letter to Baron Rothschild, on the proposed alteration to the law relative to sales and pledges, etc. 1857 8/8/57
Lavington, George
The enthusiasms of Methodists and Papists compared. 1749 1/9/40
The Moravians compared and detected. 1755 23/8/74
Lavis, Henry James Johnston
Monograph of the earthquakes of Ischia ... 1881 and 1883 ... And some calculations by ... S. Haughton. 1885 7/1/89
Law, Edward Earl of Ellenborough
A political diary, 1828–1830 ... Edited by Lord Colchester. 1881 (2v.) 18/6/81, 4/3/87, 14/4/87, 28/7/87
Law, George Henry
Reflections upon tithes, with a plan for a general commutation of the same. 1832 1/12/32
Law, John pseud.
Captain Lobe. 1889 29/11/89
Law, Thomas Graves
A historical sketch of the conflicts between Jesuits and Seculars in the reign of Queen Elizabeth. 1889 2/12/89
Edinburgh Review, clviii.354. 1883 (October 1883) 26/8/84
Introductory memoir of [John Craig] including a reprint of his catechism. 1883 31/3/83
The catechism of John Hamilton ... 1552, ed. T. G. Law. 1884 27/9/84
Law, William
A serious call to a devout and holy life, adapted to the state and condition of all orders of Christians. 1729 13/10/29, 16/8/68
The grounds and reasons of Christian regeneration, or, the new birth. Offer'd to ... Christians and Deists. 1750 (1845 edn) 24/8/45
Three letters to the bishop of Bangor. 1717 18/7/39, 20/12/57
William Law's defence of church principles, ed. J. O. Nash and C. Gore. 1893 31/12/93
Lawes, Sir John Bennet, and Gilbert, Sir Joseph H.
On the home produce, imports, and consumption of wheat. 1868 4/1/69
Lawless, Emily
Grania: the story of an island. 1892 (2v. 1892–4) 16/4/94
Hurrish. A study. 1886 (2v.) 23/12/86, 1/1/87
With Essex in Ireland. 1890 2/6/90
Lawless, Valentine Browne 2nd Baron Cloncurry
Personal recollections of the life and times ... of Valentine, Lord Cloncurry. 1849 28/5/86, 3/6/86
Lawley, F.R.
Ropes for drowning Conservatives. 1866 2/4/66
Lawley, Francis Charles
'Sir Banastre Tarleton' in *Blackwood's Edinburgh Magazine,* cxvi.432. 1874 (October 1874) 2/10/74
Racing life of Lord George Cavendish Bentinck. 1892 4/10/92
The bench and the Jockey Club. 1889 29/5/89
Law Magazine. 11. 94. 2/1834 23/5/1834
Lawrence, Arthur Evelyn Barnes
Churchmen to churchmen: matters of controversy. 1893 6/8/93
Lawrence, Charles
A letter on agricultural education, addressed to a youth. 1851 23/3/51
Lawrence, George Guerard
Three months in America, in the summer of 1863. Two lectures. 1864 19/1/66
Lawrence, James Henry
A picture of Verdun, or the English detained in France. 1810 8/9/71
L'Empire des Nairs, ou le paradis de l'amour. 1814 (4v.) 21/6/52
The Etonian out of bounds; or poetry and prose. 1828 (3v.) 4/6/28 ?
Lawrence, Sir Thomas
Life and correspondence of Sir T. Lawrence, by D. E. Williams. 1831 20/5/46
Lawson, John
Lectures concerning oratory. 1758 11/1/91

Lawson, John Parker
History of the Scottish episcopal church from the revolution to the present time. 1843 19/3/43
The life and times of William Laud... Archbishop of Canterbury. 1829 (2v.) 11/4/35
Layard, Austen Henry
Contemporary Review, xlvii.609. 1885 (May 1885) 13/5/85
Nineveh and its remains. 1849 (2v.) 24/4/52
The Turkish question. Speeches delivered in the House of Commons... 1853, and... 1854. 1854 10/5/77
Layland, Lady Frances afterw. Layland-Barratt
Doubts are traitors: the story of a Cornish family. 1889 6/5/93 ?
Lay patron
Some thoughts on the present and future of the Irish church. By an Irish lay patron. 1868 30/12/68
Lay preachers in the Church of England. 1877 26/11/76
'Lays of Poland' 1836 4/2/36
Lea, Henry Charles
A history of auricular confession and indulgences in the Latin church. 1896 (3v.) 5/10/90
Superstition and force. Essays on the wager of law—the wager of battle—the ordeal—torture. 1866 27/12/85
Lea, John Walter
The bishops' 'Oath of homage'. 1875 9/1/76
Leader, John Daniel
Mary, Queen of Scots, in captivity. A narrative of events. 1880 11/12/80
Leader, John Temple
La Parrocchia di S. Martino a Majano. Cenni storici. 1875 17/1/88 ?
Life of Sir Robert Dudley, Earl of Warwick and Duke of Northumberland. 1895 17/12/94
Philological pastimes of an Englishman in Tuscany, with some letters of W. E. Gladstone to J. T. Leader. 1898 6/1/88 n
Vita di Roberto Dudley, Duca di Northumbria. 1895 17/12/94
Leading doctrines of the Gospels. 1870 13/10/72
Leaf, Walter
The Iliad of Homer, done into English prose. 1883 (1886 edn) 11/5/86
Leahy, David
The judgment of Lord Denman in the case of O'Connell and others. 1844 23/8/89
Leake, William Martin
On some disputed questions of ancient geography. 1857 14/4/57
Travels in Northern Greece. 1835 (4v.) 1/10/67
Travels in the Morea. 1830 (3v.) 22/7/50
Lean, William Scarnell
Essay on faith. 1865 2/6/67
Lear, Edward
Journals of a landscape painter in Southern Calabria. 1852 23/12/70
Leatham, William
Letters on the currency, addressed to C. Wood. 1840 14/7/40
Leatherbrow, T.
Warwick Brooke's pencil pictures. 1889 23/8/90
Leathes, Stanley
Characteristics of Christianity. 1884 25/12/83
Old Testament prophecy, its witness as a record of divine foreknowledge... Warburton lectures. 1880 13/6/80
Le Bas, Charles Webb
Life of bishop Jewel. 1835 27/9/35
Life of Wiclif. 1832 30/7/32
Sermons on various occasions. 1828 (2nd edn) 14/6/29
The life of archbishop Laud. 1832 31/3/36
Le Bouthillier de Rancé, Armand Jean
Maximes chrétiennes et morales... Nouvelle édition. 1699 16/7/54 ?
Lechler, Gotthard Victor
Geschichte des englischen Deismus. 1841 7/4/50
Johann von Wiclif und die Vorgeschichte der Reformation. 1873 (1884 edn) 23/5/85
John Wiclif and his English precursors... tr. from the German... by P. Lorimer. 1878 2/6/85
Lechmere, Joscelyne
Synopsis, or a synoptical collection of the daily prayers... of the Greek Orthodox, tr. Katherine Lady Lechmere. 1891 19/4/91
Leckie, Charles
Church question... Report of the discussion... on the question 'Whether the magistrate... has any authority... to establish Christianity'. 1838 6/7/79
Leckie, William
A letter to the Rt. Hon. Sir Robert Peel, on the Bank Charter Bill. 1847 18/11/47
Lecky, William Edward Hartpole
[On Ireland] *in North American Review*, clii.11. 1891 (January 1891) 10/1/91
A history of England in the eighteenth century. 1878 (8v. 1878–90) 17/4/78, 26/7/82, 27/4/86, 4/5/87, 16/5/87, 3/3/91
History of European morals from Augustus to Charlemagne. 1869 (2v.) 25/4/69
History of the rise and influence of the spirit of rationalism in Europe. 1865 (3v.) 3/6/65
Leaders of public opinion in Ireland. 1861 6/2/72, 15/11/87
Lectures on the holy Catholic church. 1852 19/9/52
Lectures on the miracles at Bremen. 6/8/71
Lee, Frederick George
Historical sketches of the Reformation. 1879 (1878–79) 12/1/79

Lee, Frederick George (*cont.*)
Memorials of . . . R. S. Hawker . . . Collected, arranged, and edited by F. G. Lee. 1876 16/9/77, 16/11/79
More glimpses of the world unseen, ed. by F. G. Lee. 1878 19/9/80
The repeal of the Public Worship Regulation Act. 1875 4/4/75, 21/4/78
The S. George's riots, a plea for justice and toleration. A letter to the Rt. Hon. W. E. Gladstone. 1860 26/4/60
The validity of the holy orders of the Church of England maintained and vindicated. 1869 10/10/74
Lee, Margaret
Divorce. A novel. 1882 24/11/88
Lee, Robert D.D.
Prayers for public worship. 1858 28/1/58
Reform of the Church of Scotland. 1864 12/1/79
Lee, Robert Edward
Vindication from the Northern standpoint of General R. E. Lee, by Thomas Sweeney. 1890 28/8/90 ?
Lee, Samuel
Six sermons on the study of the Holy Scriptures. 1830 28/8/59
Lee, William Archdeacon of Dublin
A sermon preached . . . at the consecration of . . . Richard Chenevix, Lord Archbishop of Dublin. 1864 (?) 10/1/64
Some strictures on Dr. Brady's pamphlet in which he denies the descent of the hierarchy. 1866 25/3/65
The inspiration of Holy Scripture: its nature and proof. Eight discourses. 1854 14/4/76
The position and prospects of the Church of Ireland touched upon in two sermons. 1867 31/10/67
Lee, William Professor
Recent forms of unbelief: some account of Renan's 'Vie de Jésus'. 1864 24/1/64
Leech, A. S.
Nine fortunes; an autobiography. 1872 31/12/72
Leech, H. J.
The Irish roll call: a record of the government of Ireland, from 1685 to 1885. 1886 5/3/88
Leeds, Josiah W.
A history of the United States of America. 1877 4/12/85
Leeke, William
A few suggestions for increasing the incomes of many of the smaller livings. 1838 17/4/38
Lees, William Nassau
The drain of silver to the East, and the currency of India. 1863 25/11/63
Lefault, Guillaume
Petite traicte contre l'abominable vice de paillardise et adultère qui est aujourd'huy en coustume, etc., ed. L. L. 1868 12/4/85
Lefèvre, André Paul Emile
Essais de critique générale. 1871 18/10/86
Lefevre, George John Shaw Baron Eversley
'Home Rule' in *Nineteenth Century*, xix. 424. 1886 (March 1886) 26/5/87
A decade of inflation and depression . . . The opening address of the President of the Statistical Society. 1878 30/12/78
Combination and coercion in Ireland. 1890 18/2/90
English and Irish land questions. Collected essays. 1881 1/6/81
English commons and forests. 1894 17/2/94
Irish members and English gaolers. The treatment of political offenders. 1889 10/8/89, 26/8/89 n
Peel and O'Connell. A review of the Irish policy of parliament from the Act of Union. 1887 26/5/87
The game laws. 1874 16/6/74, 18/3/80
The personal payment of rates and the Reform Act of 1867. 1868 9/3/68
Lefevre, George John Shaw
'Greece at the Congress of Berlin' in *Fortnightly Review*, xxx. 271. 1878 (August 1878) 2/8/78
Leffingwell, Albert
Illegitimacy; and the influence of seasons upon conduct. Two studies in demography. 1892 29/3/92
Lefroy, T. E. P.
The Christian ministry. 1890 25/4/90
Le Gallienne, Richard
The poems of A. H. Hallam. 1893 24/11/93
The religion of a literary man. 1893 3/12/93
Legard, Francis Digby
More about farm lads, ed. F. D. Legard. 1865 14/10/65
Leger, Louis Paul Marie
A history of Austro-Hungary from the earliest time to the year 1889 . . . tr. Mrs. Birkbeck Hill. 1889 16/11/89
Legge, Alfred Owen
Pius IX, the story of his life to the restoration in 1850. With glimpses of the national movement in Italy. 1850 (2v.) 18/12/74
Legge, James
The life of Confucius. 1867 26/7/74
The religions of China. Confucianism and Taoism . . . compared with Christianity. 1880 9/9/86
Leggo, William
The history of the administration of . . . Frederick Temple, Earl of Dufferin . . . late Governor General of Canada. 1878 18/12/88
Lehec, Henri
Généalogie des Bourbons de France, d'Espagne, de

Naples et de Palme . . . jusqu'à nos jours. 1880 15/4/85 ?
Leibnitz, Baron Gottfried Wilhelm von
A system of theology . . . Translated, with . . . notes, by Charles William Russell. 1850 31/8/51
Leibnitz, Gottfried Wilhelm von
Correspondence with Bossuet and Molan. 1815 (1815 edn) 26/4/35
Essais de héodicé. 1710 8/6/34
Lettres et opuscules inédits. 1854 11/9/87
Systema theologicum. (1819 edn) 19/4/35
Leigh, James Edward Austen
A memoir of Jane Austen. 1870 24/6/71
Leigh, T. Pemberton
Letter to Langdale on privilege. 1837 29/2/40
Leighton, Sir Baldwin
Recollections of Theodore Mansel Talbot and his time. 1889 12/5/89
Leighton, Robert
A practical commentary upon the two first chapters of the First Epistle of St. Peter. 25/12/31, 2/11/34, 22/11/35
Eighteen sermons . . . first published in 1692 . . . with an account of his life. 1745 1/6/45
Praelectiones Theologicae, in auditorio publico Academiae Edinburgenae. 6/3/31
Sermons. 14/3/69
Leighton, William
Poems. 1870 1/1/71
Leland, Thomas
The history of Ireland, from the invasion of Henry II. 1773 (3v.) 7/9/37
Lelièvre, Matthieu
John Wesley, sa vie, et son oeuvre. 1868 (new edn 1891) 17/1/92
Le Marchant, Sir Denis
The reform ministry, and the reformed parliament, ed. Sir D. Le Marchant. 1833 2/11/33
Le Marchant, Sir Henry Denis
Memoir of John Charles Viscount Althorp, third Earl Spencer, ed. Sir D. H. Le Marchant. 1876 22/5/76
Lemercher de Longpré, Charles Baron d'Haussez
Great Britain in 1833. 1833 (2v.) 6/8/33
Lemon, Sir Charles
A letter to the . . . Earl of Clarendon on the copper ore duties. 1847 17/5/47
On the proposed tariff as it affects tin, copper, and timber, used in mines. 1842 7/4/42
Lempriere, John
Universal biography. 1808 22/3/30
Lemprière
Oxford university election. Dr. Lemprière's letter. 1853 8/1/53
Lenclos, Ninon de
Lettres de Ninon de Lenclos. 1750 11/4/85, 18/8/90
Lennard, H.
Follies and fancies. 1881 10/6/81
Lennius, A.
Der Kampf der Geschlechter und der Volkspartei zu Athen: ein historischer Versuch. 1829 5/1/92
Lennox, Charles 3rd Duke of Richmond
Letter from the Committee of Ulster Volunteers to the Duke of Richmond . . . with his Bill [for Reform]. 1783 6/6/64
Letter from the Committee of Ulster Volunteers to the Duke of Richmond . . . with his Bill [for Reform]. 1783 (1793 edn) 10/6/92
Lennox, Lord William Pitt
Memoir of Charles Gordon Lennox, fifth Duke of Richmond, K. G. 1862 8/8/64
Lenormant, Charles
Commentaire sur le Cratyle de Platon. 1861 26/8/62
De la divinité du Christianisme, dans ses rapports avec l'histoire. 1869 24/8/79
The book of Genesis. 1886 8/5/87
Lenormant, François
Essai sur la propagation de l'alphabet phénicien dans l'ancien monde. 1872 (1872–73) 4/9/72
Introduction à un mémoire sur la propagation de l'alphabet phénicien dans l'ancien monde. 1866 8/9/68
La monnaie dans l'antiquité. 1878 (3v.) 13/2/78
Les origines de l'histoire d'après la bible et les traditions des peuples orientaux. 1880 (1880–84) 28/12/84, 4/1/85, 8/8/90
Les premières civilisations: études d'histoire et d'archéologie. 1874 (2v.) 2/5/74
Les sciences occultes en Asie. 1874 (2v. 1874–75) 5/8/75
Manuel d'histoire ancienne de l'Orient jusqu'aux guerres médiques. 1868 (2v.) 4/9/68
Monographie de la voie sacrée Eleusinienne. 1864 (vol i) 5/1/80, 6/1/86
Leo I, Pope
'Sermones' in Migne *P.L.*, lvi. 31/12/54
Leo XIII, Pope
Poesie Latine di sua santità papa Leone XIII. 1881 27/5/84
Leonard, Daniel
Massachusettensis. 1776 8/2/47
Léonard, J.
Souvenirs. 18/7/86
Leone, Abate
The Jesuit conspiracy. The secret plan of the order. 1848 15/3/49
Leopardi, Giacomo
La poésie. (1886 edn) 17/12/86
Opere. 1845 (6v. 1845–49) 28/7/49, 6/10/49
Leopardi, Monaldo
La santa casa di Loreto. 1841 7/10/49

Leopardi, Pietro Silvestro
Narrazioni storiche . . . con molti documenti inediti relativi alla guerra dell'indipendenza d'Italia. 1856 18/9/56
Le Pape et l'Irlande. 1888 30/7/88
Le Play, Pierre Guillaume Frédéric
La constitution de l'Angleterre considérée dans ses rapports avec la loi de Dieu. 1875 21/9/85
La réforme sociale en France déduite de l'observation comparée des peuples européens. 1864 (2v.) 1/7/85, 29/7/85
Leriche, Abbé
Etudes sur les possessions en général et sur celle de Loudun en particulier. 1859 12/4/85
Les Abyssiniennes et les femmes du Soudan oriental d'après les relations de Bruce, Browne, etc. 1876 19/5/85
Lesage, Alain René
Gil Blas. 1715 (4v. 1715–35) 18/10/72
Le Sage, Alain René
Histoire de Gil Blas de Santillane. 1715 (4v. 1715–35) 14/11/26
Leslie, Charles M.A.
A short and easie method with the Deists. 7/5/26
A short method with the Romanists. 1835 22/7/38
The case of the Regale and of the Pontificat stated . . . the Church, as to her purely spiritual power. 21/2/38
The charge of Socinianism against Dr. Tillotson considered. 5/4/50
The rehearsal. 1708 (4v. 1708–09) 20/7/46
Leslie, Charles Robert
A hand-book for young painters. 1855 22/1/55
Leslie, Robert Joshua
The life and times of . . . John Leslie . . . Bishop of the Isles, Scotland, and . . . Raphoe and Clogher. 1885 (1887) 17/4/87, 3/7/87
Leslie, Thomas Edward Cliffe
The military systems of Europe economically considered. 1856 1/5/60
Les principautés Roumaines et l'empire Ottoman. 1858 22/11/75
Lesseps, Ferdinand Marie de
History of the Suez canal. 1870 6/9/71
The history of the Suez canal. A personal narrative, tr. Sir H. D. Wolff. 1876 1/1/76
Lessing, Gotthold Ephraim
'Leibnitz von den ewigen Strafen' in *Works.* 1839 (ix) 5/9/58
Laocoon. 1766 23/6/49
Nathan the wise. 1779 11/4/82, 14/8/87
Nathan the wise, tr. W. Taylor. 1791 5/8/58
Lester, Charles Edwards
The glory and shame of England. 1841 (2v.) 18/2/67
The Mexican republic. An historic study. 1878 11/10/78
Lester, Elizabeth B.
The Quakers; a tale. 1817 28/2/38 ?
L'Estrange, Alfred Guy Kingham
The literary life of . . . W. Harness. 1871 11/12/71
L'Estrange, Henry
Platonia. A tale. 1893 11/9/93
Leti, Gregorio
The life of Donna Olimpia Maidalchini Pamfili. 24/10/66
Leti, Pomponius
Otto Mesi a Roma. 1873 23/4/75
Letter on R. Baxter's Narrative. 1833 18/8/33
Letter on the present wants of the church. 1846 8/5/47
Letters from an Armenian. 1757 5/8/79
Letters from an Irish student. 1809 (2v.) 30/7/32
Letters from heaven. 1886 3/12/91
Letters from the archbishop of Canterbury . . . and the bishop of Natal. 1866 1/4/66
Letter to Earl Grey, by a dissenting minister. 1834 4/4/34
Letter to the E. of Chichester M. N. L. Missim, by a clergyman. 20/3/40
Letter to the Prince of Wales. 1795 17/7/89
Letter to the Queen. 1841 15/1/42
Lettres d'une bourgeoise. 1/7/81
Le turban et la tiare. (not found) 2/9/65
Leupold, H.
Hans Sachs aus Nürnberg. 1876 10/1/76
Lever, Charles James
A day's ride: a life's romance. 1864 (1878 edn) 9/9/79
A rent in the cloud and St. Patrick's eve. 1871 23/11/77
Lord Kilgobbin: a tale of Ireland in our own time. 1872 (3v.) 27/3/72
Levi, Leone
[on sugar duties]. (not found) 5/4/64
On Richard Cobden. An introductory lecture delivered in King's College, London. 1865 3/1/66
On taxation; how it is raised and how it is expended. 1860 21/6/60
Wages and earnings of the working classes . . . in a report to Sir Arthur Bass, M.P. 1867 22/7/67
Lévy, Armand
L'empereur, Rome et le roi d'Italie. 1861 12/9/61
Lewes, Charles Lee
Memoirs of . . ., containing anecdotes . . . of the English and Scottish stages, during a period of forty years. 1805 (4v.) 7/5/80
Lewes, George Henry
Aristotle: a chapter from the history of science. 1864 18/1/65
The life and works of Goethe. 1855 (2v.) 21/12/63
Lewin, George Harrison Ross
Father Gilpin: the most conscientious priest in the North. 1891 25/9/92

The continuity of the English church. 1880 5/6/81, 2/10/92
Lewin, Hermann
Poema morale. 1881 21/10/89 ?
Lewin, Malcolm
Torture in Madras. 1855 22/3/56
Lewin, Walter
Clarke Aspinall. A biography. 1892 2/12/92
Lewins, Robert
Life and mind: their unity and materiality. 1873 1/6/73, 2/9/77
Lewins, William
A history of banks for savings in Great Britain and Ireland... account of Mr. Gladstone's financial measures. 1866 5/6/66
Her Majesty's mails: an historical and descriptive account of the British post office. 1864 2/5/64
Lewis
['Dioceses of St. Asaph and Bangor', in Add MS 44732, f.1, anon. pamphlet]. 3/1/43 ?
Lewis, Sir George Cornewall
'The amber trade of antiquity' in *Notes and Queries, vi.* 1858 (July 1858) 6/7/58
A dialogue on the best form of government. 1863 3/3/63
An essay on the government of dependencies. 1841 18/11/41, 3/3/63
An essay on the origin and formation of the Romance languages... examination of M. Raynouard's theory. 1839 20/12/62
An historical survey of the astronomy of the ancients. 1862 21/1/62
An inquiry into the credibility of the early Roman history. 1855 27/6/57, 26/10/58
Essays on the administrations of Great Britain from 1783 to 1830... Edited by Sir E. Head, Bart. 1864 7/4/64
Letters of the Rt. Hon. Sir G. C. Lewis to various friends. Edited by... Sir Gilbert F. Lewis. 1870 14/5/70
On local disturbances in Ireland; and on the Irish Church question. 1836 25/8/45, 20/11/69
Remarks on the third report of the Irish Poor Enquiry Commissioners. 1837 22/6/37
Remarks on the use and abuse of some political terms. 1832 5/2/42
The influence of authority on matters of opinion. 1849 11/9/71, 8/1/77
Lewis, James Rev. of Leith
Defence of ecclesiastical establishment; in reply to the Rev. A. Marshall's letter to... Thomson. 1830 4/5/50
Lewis, J. D.
The dean of Canterbury. A letter. 1871 13/8/71
Lewis, John Vicar of Minster
An essay towards an account of bishops suffragan in England. 1738 2/10/62
The life of John Fisher, Bishop of Rochester... With an introduction by T. Hudson Turner. 1855 (2v.) 9/12/55, 30/8/91
Lewis, John Travers Bishop of Ontario
The holy eucharist: a visitation charge... October 28th, 1879. 1881 15/10/81
Lewis, Matthew Gregory
Journal of a West Indian proprietor, kept during a residence in... Jamaica. 1834 5/11/36
Lewis, Rhys
Rhys Lewis, ed. D. Owen. 1888 2/9/88
Lewis, T. D.
Causes célèbres d'Angleterre. 1883 11/4/85
Liaño, Enrique Sant' A. de
Die Kirche Gottes und die Bischöfe. Denkschrift ... 1869 31/7/70
Lias, John James
The atonement viewed in the light of certain modern difficulties... Hulsean lectures for 1883, 1884. 1884 27/7/84
Liberal, A
Limits of free trade, etc. 1889 6/5/89
Liberal, The. 1. 145. 4/1879. on Gleanings 28/3/1879
Libri Carrucci dalla Sommaia, Count Guglielmo Bruto Icilio Timoleone
Histoire des sciences mathématiques en Italie. 1838 (4v. 1838–41) 26/5/48 ?
Lichnowsky, Prince Eduard Marie
Geschichte des Hauses Habsburg. 1836 (8v.) 30/11/37
Liddell, Henry George
A commemoration sermon preached... on the Sunday after St. Frideswide's Day, 1880. 1880 5/12/80
A history of Rome. 1855 (2v.) 9/12/81
Liddell, Henry Thomas Earl of Ravensworth
Carmina Latina, partim nova, partim e lingua Britannica expressa. 1865 18/3/65
Liddell, Robert
A letter to the lord bishop of London, on confession and absolution, with... reference to... A. Poole. 1858 31/10/58
On the daily celebration of holy communion: a sermon. 1868 9/2/68
Liddon, Henry Parry
Apostolic labours an evidence of Christian truth: a sermon... at the consecration of the... bishop of Nassau. 1864 13/3/64
Christ and human law: a sermon. 1869 4/4/69
Edward Bouverie Pusey. A sermon. 1884 2/3/84
Life of Edward Bouverie Pusey... ed... by the Rev. J. O. Johnston... and the Rev. R. J. Wilson. 1893 (4v. 1893–7) 16/3/91 n, 7/1/94
Noah. A sermon. 1872 1/12/72
Preface to 'Practical reflections on every verse of the Psalter'. 1890 30/3/90

Liddon, Henry Parry (*cont.*)
The day of work: a sermon preached . . . the morrow of the funeral of . . . H. L. Mansel. 1871 3/9/71
The power of Christ's resurrection: a sermon. 1869 8/8/69
The Purchas judgment. A letter of acknowledgment to the Rt. Hon. Sir J. T. Coleridge. 1871 30/4/71
The secret of clerical power: a sermon. 1865 31/12/65
The victor, in the times of preparation. Sermon. 1868 19/7/68
The worth of the Old Testament: a sermon preached in St. Paul's cathedral . . . December 8, 1889. 1890 9/2/90
Thoughts on present church troubles, occurring in four sermons, preached . . . in December, 1880. 1881 6/2/81

Lieber, Franz
Manual of political ethics. 1838 (2v. 1838–39) 16/6/41

Liebig, Justus von
An address to the agriculturalists of Great Britain . . . principles and use of artificial manures. 1845 4/8/45

Liechtenstein, Princess Marie
Holland House. 1873 (2v.) 19/11/73

Lieven, Princess Doroteya Khristoforovna
Correspondence of Princess Lieven and Earl Grey. Edited and translated by G. Le Strange. 1890 (3v.) 29/1/90

Life and scenery in Missouri. By a missionary priest. 1890 9/10/91

Life beyond the grave, described by a spirit, through a writing medium. 1876 10/4/79

Life in Paris; a drama in three acts, in 'Hodgson's Juvenile Drama'. 1822 (2v.) 28/10/59

Life in Paris. A play [Hodgson's Juvenile Drama]. 1822 (2v.) 28/10/59

Life's greatest possibility. An essay in spiritual realism. 1892 8/6/92

Lightfoot, John D.D.
Collected works. (2v.) 14/3/30
Horae Hebraicae et Talmudicae. 1658 (2v.) 28/12/56

Lightfoot, Joseph Barber
Bishop Lightfoot. A sketch of his life and works. 1894 25/2/94
On a fresh revision of the English New Testament. 1871 (1871, 1872) 30/4/71, 18/2/72
Primary charge. Two addresses delivered to the Clergy of the Diocese of Durham . . . 1882. 1884 28/9/84
Strength made perfect in weakness: a sermon. 1873 23/3/73
The apostolic fathers. S. Clement of Rome. A revised text, with introduction, notes and translations. 1877 13/5/77
The Epistles of St. Paul. 1865 30/5/75

Liguori, Saint Alphonso Maria de
La gloire de Maria [English translation]. (1852) 23/11/51

Lilley, James Philip
The Sabbath. 1891 19/4/91 ?

Lilly, William astrologer
Several observations upon the life and death of Charles I, late King of England. 20/8/32

Lilly, William Samuel
'The Christian revolution' in *Contemporary Review*, xlv. 241. 1884 (February 1884) 10/2/84
Ancient religion and modern thought. 1884 15/6/84
The great enigma. 1892 4/12/92

Linares, Vincenzo
Cholera in Palermo. 1838 16/9/38

Lind, Jenny
Memoirs of Jenny Lind-Goldschmitt, by H. Scott Holland. 1891 (2v.) 27/5/91

Lindenschmit, Heinrich
Schliemann's Ausgrabungen in Troja und Mykenae. 1878 16/2/78

Lindesay, Sir David
The monarche and other poems of Sir D. Lindesay, ed. J. Small. 1883 25/2/83

Lindley, William
A reply to the bishop of Lincoln's Pastoral to the Wesleyan Methodists in the diocese of Lincoln. 1873 10/8/73

Lindsay, Lord Alexander William Crawford 25th Earl of Crawford
A brief analysis of . . . the case of Gorham v. *the bishop of Exeter.* 1850 15/6/50
Argo; or the quest of the golden fleece. A metrical tale, in ten books. 1876 1/5/76
Conservatism; its principle, policy, and practice. A reply to Mr. Gladstone's speech at Wigan, etc. 1868 7/12/68
Etruscan inscriptions analysed, translated and commented upon. 1872 8/12/73 ?
On the theory of the English hexameter, and its applicability to the translation of Homer. A letter. 1862 24/4/62
Progression by antagonism: a theory, involving . . . the present position, duties and destiny of Great Britain. 1846 1/10/46
Scepticism a retrogressive movement in theology and philosophy, as contrasted with the Church of England. 1861 4/8/61, 30/8/63
The creed of Japhet, that is, of the race popularly surnamed Indo-Germanic, etc., ed. the Countess of Crawford. 1891 30/11/91

Lindsay, Lady Caroline Blanche Elizabeth
About robins. Songs, facts, and legends, collected and illustrated. 1889 7/5/90

Bertha's earl. A novel. 1891 (3v.) 6/5/91
Caroline. 1888 3/5/90
Lyrics, and other poems. 1890 18/12/90
Lindsay, Colin
Magna Charta, A. D. 1865; or, Declaration of the liberties of the Colonial Church. 1865 16/4/65
Union and unity. An address to the members of the English Church Union and others. 1860 23/9/60
Lindsay, Hugh Hamilton
Letter to . . . Viscount Palmerston on British relations with China. 1836 16/3/36
Lindsay, James
The progressiveness of modern Christian thought. 1892 2/11/93
Lindsay, William Schaw
Letters on the navigation laws (reprinted from the Morning Herald): addressed to Lord J. Russell. 1849 27/2/52
Our merchant shipping: its present state considered. 1860 24/1/60
Lindsey, Theophilus
Conversations on Christian idolatry. 1792 7/1/55
Lingard, John
A vindication of certain passages in the fourth and fifth volume of the History of England. 1826 (1827) 13/6/88
Observations on the laws and ordinances . . . in foreign states, relative to . . . Roman Catholic subjects. 1817 (1851) 25/3/51 ?
On Lingard, in *Dublin Review.* 1888 (June 1888) 13/6/88
The history of England. 1823 (8v.) 11/1/34, 13/1/34, 19/1/36, 29/9/40, 29/5/88, 20/9/88
Linklater, Robert
A sermon preached . . . before the boys of Wellington College. 1879 10/8/79
Linskill, Mary pseud. Stephen Yorke
In exchange for a soul. 1889 2/8/90
Tales of the North Riding. 1871 30/8/71
Linton, Charles Robert
The revised version of the New Testament. What is to be said for and against it? An address. 1881 26/3/82
Linton, Eliza Lynn formerly Lynn
The lake country. 1864 1/3/64
Linton, William
Colossal vestiges of the older nations. With a diagram. 1862 6/7/62
Linwood, William
Four sermons on the Catholic church. 1841 23/1/42
Two sermons on baptismal regeneration, and on receiving the body and blood of Christ. 1842 10/4/42
Lion, D.
The philosophy of right. 1891 6/2/91 ?
List, Georg Friedrich
The national system of political economy. 1841 16/7/42
Lister, Thomas Henry
Granby. 1826 (3v. third edn) 23/4/29
Life and administration of Edward, first earl of Clarendon, with original correspondence. 1837 (3v. 1837–38) 12/11/40
Literary celebrities. 1887 6/1/87
Literary Churchman. 20/9/1857
Literary fund address. 1840 21/5/40
Littell's Living Age. 175. 668, 695. Vincigliata, Carteret 5/1/1888
Little, Andrew George
The Grey Friars in Oxford. 1892 18/6/92
Little, William John Knox
Sacerdotalism. 1893 27/10/93
Sermons preached for the most part in Manchester. 1880 27/6/80, 2/10/87
The broken vow. A story of here and hereafter. 1887 12/6/87
The light of life: sermons. 1888 6/11/88
The mystery of the passion of our most holy redeemer. 1881 24/6/83
The waif from the waves; a story of three lives. 1894 18/5/94
Littledale, Richard Frederick
'Relation of clergy to politics' in *Contemporary Review,* xxiii. 92. 1873 (December 1873) 12/4/74
'Why ritualists do not become Catholics' in *Contemporary Review,* xxxiii. 792. 1878 (November 1878) 3/11/78
Additional services. A second letter to Charles Thomas . . . Archbishop of Canterbury. 1868 23/2/68
Catholic revision. A letter to Charles Thomas . . . Archbishop of Canterbury. 1867 12/7/67
Incense. A liturgical essay. 1866 30/3/66
Plain reasons against joining the Church of Rome. 1880 26/9/80
Preface to 'The holy eastern church: a popular outline of its history'. 1870 13/3/70
The north-side of the altar. A liturgical essay. 1865 16/7/65
Tradition: a lecture. 1870 25/12/70
Unity and the rescript. A reply to Bishop Ullathorne's Pastoral against the A. P. U. C. 1864 9/7/65
Littlehales, Thomas
A letter on the education of the middle classes. 1840 26/6/43
How can the church evangelise the world? A sermon. 1844 13/4/45
Little Mary. 1840 5/4/41
Litton, Edward Arthur
The church of Christ. 1851 24/12/54
The connection of the church and state, with a particular reference to the Irish church. An address. 1868 27/12/68

Liverani, Francesco
Il Papato, l'Impero e il Regno d'Italia: memorie. 1861 17/10/61
Livermore, George
An historical research respecting the opinions of the founders of the republic on Negroes. 1862 27/4/63
Liverpool and slavery by a genuine 'Dicky Sam'. 1884 22/12/84
Liverpool East India and China Association Report. 1842 10/3/42
Liverpool East India and China Association Report. 1843 (not found) 9/2/43
Liverpool East India and China Association Report. 1844 2/3/44
Liverpool East India and China Association Report. 1845 11/3/45
Liverpool Financial Reform Association
Tract III [on taxation]. 1848 7/9/52
Lives of Russian saints. 29/3/57
Livingston, William
Examen du gouvernement d'Angleterre, comparé aux constitutions des Etats-Unis. 1789 19/9/78
Livingstone, David
Cambridge lectures, together with a prefatory letter by Professor Sedgwick. 1858 31/10/59
Missionary travels and researches in South Africa. 1857 14/3/57
Livius, Thomas
St. Peter, bishop of Rome. 1888 15/4/88
Livland und Irland. 1883 6/4/87
Livy, Titus
Opera. 13/5/29, 21/7/29, 2/9/29, 7/7/30, 25/7/31
Llandaff Memoir. First Annual report of the society for providing additional pastoral superintendence. 1852 25/3/52
Llewelyn, William Henry
Vivisection: shall it be regulated or suppressed?. 1876 19/6/78
Lloyd, Charles barrister
A calm inquiry into all the objections . . . to the educational provision of the Factory Bill. 1843 16/5/43
Lloyd, Clifford
Ireland under the Land League. 1892 26/3/92
Lloyd, Humphrey
The university of Dublin, in its relation to the several religious communions. 1868 18/5/68
Lloyd, William
Papists no Catholicks. 15/8/75
Lloyd, William Watkiss
On the Homeric design of the shield of Achilles. 1854 5/11/63
Pindar and Themistocles. 1862 7/8/62
The age of Pericles: a history of the politics and arts of Greece from the Persian to the Peloponnesian war. 1875 (2v.) 11/11/75
The history of Sicily to the Athenian war; with elucidations of the Sicilian odes of Pindar. 1872 30/12/72
Lobley, James Logan
Geology for all. 1888 21/5/88
Loch, John D.
An account of . . . the system of general religious education established in Van Diemen's Land in 1839. 1843 4/2/46
Lock, Walter
John Keble. 1893 7/5/93
Locke, John
An essay concerning human understanding. 11/12/34, 25/2/36, 31/3/36
'Letters on toleration' in *Works.* (1812 edn) 13/5/27, 27/5/27
Life of Lohn Locke, by Peter, Lord King. 1830 15/3/39
Some thoughts concerning reading and study for a gentleman. 1720 20/3/39
The reasonableness of Christianity, as delivered in the scriptures. 3/6/27, 17/6/27, 24/6/27, 1/7/27, 19/8/76
Locke, Joseph, and Stephenson, G.
[pamphlet on the Guages]. 15/7/48
Lockhart, John Gibson
Ancient Spanish ballads. 1823 29/12/41
Ancient Spanish ballads. 1841 (new edn) 29/12/41
Life of Robert Burns. 1828 11/10/59
Memoirs of the life of Sir Walter Scott. 1837 (7v. 1837–38) 9/5/37, 3/2/68
Reginald Dalton. 1823 (3v.) 25/4/48
Remarks on the novel of Reginald Dalton. 1824 30/9/61
Valerius, a Roman story. 1821 29/4/69
Lockhart, John Gibson, and Wilson, J.
Peter's letters to his kinsfolk. 1819 24/8/43
Lockhart, William
Cardinal Newman: reminiscences of fifty years since. 1891 1/10/90, 23/8/91
Lodge, Rev. John
A sermon preached . . . before the . . . Justices of Assize. 1799 18/12/64
Lodvill, Philip
The orthodox confession . . . from the version of P. Mogila. Faithfully translated into English. 1762 25/7/58
Loeher, Franz von
Ueber Deutschlands Weltstellung. 1874 3/10/74
Lofft, Capel
Ernest, or political regeneration. 1839 1/1/40 ?
Logan, William
The great social evil: its causes, extent, results, and remedies. 1871 17/6/88
The moral statistics of Glasgow. 1849 15/12/64
Loiseleur, Jules
Les points obscurs de la vie de Molière. 1877 12/9/87

Lolme, Jean Louis De
The constitution of England. 1775 27/7/31, 10/8/31, 18/8/31, 20/6/78, 25/6/78
Lombard, Jean
Byzance. 1890 27/5/92
L'agonie. 1891 6/5/92
London and Westminster Review.
29. 308. 8/1838. on Milnes 3/8/1838
33. 10/1839 4/2/1840
London as it is today. 1851 9/2/91
London clergyman, A
Remonstrance to Quarterly Review. 1843 28/6/43
London Magazine.
5. 335. 7/1825. Loss of Kent 8/3/1828
6. 450, 464. 12/1826. Black Book 26/2/1828
10. 14. 1/1828. Charity schools 27/2/1828
10. 84. 1/1828 26/2/1828
London Quarterly Review.
1. 233–51. 2/1829. Pollock 18/3/1829
1. 44–85. 2/1829. Reform 14/3/1829
3. 197, 240. 1/1885. on Hope Scott; on Prince Bismarck 31/12/1884
9. 1. 10/1857. London university 10/10/1857
9. 208. 10/1857. Indian mutiny 7/10/1857
18. 229. 10/1817. Bishop Watson 11/3/1829
20. 1. 4/1863 1/6/1863
20. 493–546. 4/1863. Books 7/6/1863
37. 100. 1/1828. Heber 27/8/1829
39. 429. 1/1873. Education 4/1/1873
57. 345. 1/1882. Defoe; Curci; Darwinism 4/1/1882
London Review. 2. 533. D'Israeli & Aristocracy 5/2/1836
Longfellow, Henry Wadsworth
'Purgatorio' from *The Divine Comedy of Dante*, tr. Longfellow. 1864 18/2/64
Arran. 1873 4/6/78
Evangeline, a tale of Acadie. 1848 27/1/49
Final memorials, ed. S. Longfellow. 1887 9/6/87
Kéramos, and other poems. 1878 12/6/78
Kavanagh, a tale. 1849 16/11/49
King Robert of Sicily. 1863 15/11/63
Poems. 1848 18/12/48 ?, 9/4/70
Tales of a wayside inn. 1863 16/12/63
The belfry of Bruges and other poems. 1848 18/12/48 ?
The building of the ship. 1880 11/12/69 ?
The courtship of Miles Standish. 1858 15/2/67
The seaside and the fireside. 1849 12/9/50
Longfellow, Samuel
The life of Henry Wadsworth Longfellow, with extracts from his journals and correspondence. 1886 (2v.) 11/4/86
Longfield, Mountifort
'Land tenure in Ireland', in *Fortnightly Review*, xxxiv. 137. 1880 (August 1880) 7/11/80, 14/12/80, 19/2/81
Tenure of land in Ireland. 1870 10/3/70
Longinus
[on the sublime]. (not found) 17/9/52
Fragments. (1724) 18/9/52 ?
Longley, Charles Thomas
A charge. 1841 17/10/41
A charge. 1844 21/11/44
A charge addressed to the clergy of the diocese of Ripon, at the triennial visitation. 1847 24/10/47
A letter to the parishioners of St. Saviour's, Leeds. 1851 13/7/51
A pastoral letter to the clergy of the diocese of Ripon. 1850 18/6/50
A primary charge addressed to the clergy of his diocese. 1864 4/12/64
Sermon. 1841 28/11/41
Longman
[on Scottish disabilities]. (not found) 20/4/62
Longman, C. J.
'A publisher's view of international copyright' in *Fraser's Magazine*, ciii.372. 1881 (March 1881) 28/2/81
Longman, William President of the Alpine Club
Church rate legislation. Letter. 1868 14/12/79
Lonsdale, Margaret
Sister Dora. 1880 15/2/80, 6/5/82, 22/5/86
Lopes, Sir Lopes Massey
Speech on local taxation. 1871 11/4/71
Lorain, Paul
Mémoire de l'université d'Oxford. 1850 19/2/56
Loraine, Nevison
The battle of belief. 1891 1/1/93
The sceptic's creed: can it reasonably be held? Is it worth the holding?. 1885 18/1/85
Lord, A. E.
The shock of corn . . . A sermon on the death of Mrs. Mary Scott, Hersham. 1878 29/9/78
Lord, David N.
Visions of paradise. An epic. Vol. I. 1867 25/12/70
Lord, James
Maynooth college; or, the law affecting the grant to Maynooth. 1841 4/3/41
The Protestant character of the British Constitution. 1847 26/11/75
Lord John Manners. A political and literary sketch . . . the Young England party and . . . the factory acts, by a non-elector. 1872 28/8/72
Lorimer, James
Constitutionalism of the future; or, Parliament the mirror of the nation. 1865 22/12/65

Lorimer, James (*cont.*)
Of the denationalisation of Constantinople, and its devotion to international purposes. Lecture, etc. 1876 7/11/76
Lorimer, John Gordon
The Christian's voice of devotion, a manual of prayer for family and private worship. 1858 3/11/67
The past and present condition of religion and morality in the United States . . . argument for established churches. 1834 7/4/34
Loserth, Johann
Huss und Wiclif. 1884 30/10/87
Lossing, Benson J.
Our country. A household history from the discovery of America [to 1876]. 1875 (3v. 1875–8) 26/7/88 ?
Lott, Emmeline
The Grand Pacha's cruise on the Nile to the viceroy of Egypt's yacht. 1869 (2v.) 4/3/69
Lotze, H.
Geschichte der deutschen Philosophie seit Kant. 1882 19/9/92
Lotze, Rudolf Hermann
Microcosmus: an essay concerning man and his relation to the world . . . tr. E. Hamilton and E. E. C. Jones. 1885 12/11/85
Louis Napoleon . . . the anti-Christ, the beast, etc. 1863 26/11/65
Love, Benjamin
Records of Wesleyan life. 1843 (1845) 10/6/47 ?
Love and unbelief. 7/1/90
Lover, Samuel
Legends and stories of Ireland. 1834 19/9/36
Lover of peace, A
The Irish establishment and Irish discontent. 1868 4/3/68
Love too is vanity. 26/4/86
Love v. marriage [concerned with the Phalanstère]. 1848 20/1/54
Low, David
On landed property, and the economy of estates. 1844 3/6/45 ?
Low, James G.
Memorials of the church of St. John the Evangelist. 1891 31/8/91
Lowder, Charles Fuge
Twenty-one years in S. George's Mission. An account of its origin, progress, and works of charity. 1881 22/2/82
Lowe, Helen
The prophecy of Balaam, the Queen's choice, and other poems. 1841 31/12/41
Lowe, Richard Thomas
The Madeira chaplaincy treated of . . . in a letter [from T. K. Brown]. 1848 9/8/48
Lowe, Robert Viscount Sherbrooke
'Imperialism' in *Fortnightly Review*, xxx.453. 1878 (October 1878) 9/10/78
'The docility of an imperial parliament' in *Nineteenth Century*, vii. 557. 1880 (April 1880) 26/3/80
Life of Robert Lowe, by A. P. Martin. 1893 22/5/93
Life of Robert Lowe, by J. F. Hogan. 1893 7/11/93
Speech [on coinage]. 1869 21/8/69
Speeches and letters on reform; with a preface. 1867 22/2/67
The national debt. Speech, etc. 1871 22/6/71
Lowell, James Russell
Among my books. 1870 (1870–76) 18/10/90
The Biglow papers . . . second series. 1862 4/2/62
Lowell, R.
The new priest in Conception Bay. 1889 24/11/89
Lowndes, John James
An historical sketch of the right of copyright. 1840 13/2/40
Loyd, Samuel Jones
Decimal association. Answers to the questions . . . by Lord Overstone to the Decimal Coinage Commissioners. 1857 22/4/57
Reflections suggested by . . . Palmer's pamphlet on the 'Causes and consequences of the pressure on the money-market'. 1837 7/3/37
Speech delivered by Lord Overstone . . . 15th March 1860 . . . on the treaty of commerce with France. 1860 29/3/60
Thoughts on the separation of the departments of the Bank of England. 1844 10/2/57
Tracts and other publications on metallic and paper currency, ed. J. R. MacCulloch. 1858 1/2/60
Loyson, Charles Jean Marie Père Hyacinthe
Catholic reform [with preface by A. P. Stanley]. 1874 7/12/74
Catholic reform and the anglican church. Correspondence . . . tr. Lady Durand. 1879 10/11/78
Catholic reform. Letters, fragments, discours by Father Hyacinthe. 1874 1/4/94
De la réforme Catholique. 1872 7/7/72
France et Allemagne; discours prononcé le 20 décembre, 1870. 1871 5/2/71
Lubbock, John Baron Avebury
Address. 1879 15/5/80
Pre-historic times, as illustrated by ancient remains, and the manners and customs of modern savages. 1865 6/7/66, 27/3/68, 25/9/75, 19/3/90
The origin of civilisation and the primitive condition of man. 1870 27/5/71
Lubbock, Sir John William Bart.
'On the imperial policy of Great Britain', *Nineteenth Century*, i. 37. 1877 (March 1877) 3/4/77

'Our national balance sheet', *Nineteenth Century*, xiii. 561. 1883 (April 1883) 6/4/83

Lubbock, Sir John William
On the clearing of the London bankers. 1860 19/10/60

Lucas, Edward
The life of Frederick Lucas, M.P. 1886 (2v.) 21/7/86

Lucas, Frederick
Reasons for becoming a Roman Catholic; addressed to the Society of Friends. 1839 30/8/41

Lucas, Joseph F. G. S.
Horizontal wells. A a new application of geological principles to effect the solution of the problem of supplying London with pure water. 1874 23/6/74

Lucas, Samuel M.A.
Charters of the old English colonies in America. 1850 5/3/50
The causes and consequences of national revolutions among the ancients and moderns compared. A prize essay. 1845 7/6/45

Lucas, Rev. Samuel F. G. S.
The Noaic deluge; its probable physical effects and present evidences. 1873 12/8/73

Lucian
Dialogi Deorum. 19/10/71 ?
Opera. 19/4/43

Luckock, Herbert Mortimer
After death. An examination of the testimony of primitive times respecting the . . . faithful dead. 1879 17/12/79, 15/10/88 n
Footprints of the son of man as traced by St. Mark. 1884 21/12/84
John Wesley's churchmanship as interpreted by . . . and E. T. Carrier, Wesleyan Minister. 1891 11/10/91
Studies in the history of the Book of Common Prayer. 1881 11/12/81
The divine liturgy, being the order for holy communion historically, doctrinally and devotionally. 1889 31/3/89
The intermediate state between death and judgment, being a sequel to After Death. 1890 12/4/91

Luckock, Hubert Mortimer
The church in Scotland. 1892 9/4/93, 31/12/93

Lucretius
Opera. 28/12/29, 25/10/30, 14/5/32, 21/3/38, 15/7/85, 29/7/85

Lucy, Ernest W.
The Molly Maguires of Pennsylvania, or Ireland in America; a true narrative. 1882 6/12/82

Ludlow, John Malcolm
Christian socialism and its opponents: a lecture. 1851 12/10/51
King's College and Mr. Maurice. 1854 9/4/54

Ludlow, Walter Robert
Zululand and Cetewayo, containing an account of Zulu customs, manners and habits. 1882 22/8/82, 23/8/82

Luke, Jemima née Thompson
Sketches of the life of T. Thompson. 1868 23/8/68

Lukis, William Collings
On the class of rude stone monuments, which are . . . called in England, Cromlechs, etc. 1875 5/2/77

Lumby, Joseph Rawson
Early dissent, modern dissent, and the Church of England. 1870 31/7/70

Lundie, Robert Henry
The late Mr. Bryce Allan. In memoriam. 1874 9/8/74

Lunn, Mrs. G.
Shamrock and rose. 1888 (2v.) 21/12/89

Lunzi, Count Ermanno
Della condizione politica delle Isole Ionie sotto il dominio Veneto. 1858 21/12/58
Storia delle Isole Ionie sotto il reggimento dei Repubblicani Francesi. 1860 27/11/60

Lupton, Joseph Hirst
St. John of Damascus. 1882 29/8/86

Lushington, Franklin
Dismissal of the Ionian judges. A letter to . . . Lord Stanley. 1863 19/6/63

Lushington, Henry
A detailed exposure of the Apology put forward by the Neapolitan government. 1851 1/1/52
A great country's little wars, or England, Affghanistan, and Sinde. 1844 31/7/44
La Nation Boutiquière and other poems, chiefly political. 1855 16/7/55
The broad and narrow gauge; or, remarks on the report of the gauge commissioners. 1846 23/3/46

Lushington, Henry, and Lushington, F.
Two battle-pieces. 1855 1/2/55

Lushington, Stephen
The judgment . . . delivered . . . in the cases of Westerton against Liddell (Clerk) Horne and others, etc., ed. A. F. Bayford. 1855 10/12/55

Lushington, Vernon
How shall the strong man use his strength? or, the right and duty of war, with application to the present crisis. 1855 10/6/55

Luthardt, Christoph Ernst
De compositione Evangelii Joannei. 1852 10/10/75

Luther, Martin
Table talk. (1832) 7/11/44 ?
The way to prayer, tr. Singer. 1846 17/9/48

Lux Mundi. 1889 31/1/90, 14/9/90

Lyall, Sir Alfred Comyns
The rise and expansion of the British dominion in India. 1893 8/4/93, 21/6/93

Lyall, Edna
To right the wrong. 1893 (3v.) 24/10/93
Lyall, William Rowe
Propaedia Prophetica: a view of the use and design of the old testament; followed by two dissertations. 1840 15/11/40
The nature and true value of church property examined, in a charge delivered to . . . Colchester. 1831 6/8/31
Lycurgus
Travels of Lycurgus the Spartan. 1809 14/3/43
Lyell, Sir Charles
Elements of geology. 1838 27/12/49
Mount Etna. 1859 16/5/59
Principles of geology . . . to explain the former changes of the earth's surface. 1830 (3v. 1830–33) 9/6/61 ?
Lynch, Hannah
Daughters of men. 1892 6/5/92
The prince of the glades. 1891 (2v.) 27/2/91
Lynch, Helen
Daughters of men. 1892 18/4/93
Lynch, Thomas Toke
Gatherings from notes of discourses by the late T. T. Lynch. 1885 (1st series) 19/4/85
Sermons. 1871 3/12/87 ?
Lynd, R. J.
Present crisis in Ireland. 1886 18/1/86
Lyne, Joseph Leycester Father Ignatius
Brother Placidus; and why he became a monk. A tale for the young men of the times. 1870 12/11/71
Leonard Morris; or, the Benedictine novice. 1871 1/11/71
Mission sermons and orations . . . Ed. J. V. Smedley. 1886 15/5/87, 12/6/87, 5/5/89
Modern infidelity. A sermon. 1870 14/7/72
Lyon, Charles Jobson
History of St. Andrews, episcopal, monastic, academic, and civil . . . ecclesiastical history of Scotland. 1843 (2v.) 26/12/43
Three letters on the Duke of Argyll's work, entitled 'Presbytery examined'. 1849 29/4/49
Lyon, William P.
Homo versus Darwin: a judicial examination of statements recently published by Mr. Darwin. 1872 13/10/72
Lyons, Daniel
Christianity and infallibility, both or neither. 1891 12/6/92
Lysias
Oratio in Eratosthenem. (1835) 27/12/76
Lysons, Daniel
The environs of London, being an historical account of the towns, villages and hamlets. 1792 (4v. 1892–96) 14/4/87
Lyte, Sir Henry Churchill Maxwell
A history of Eton College. 1440–1875. 1875 27/12/75
A history of the University of Oxford from the earliest times to the year 1530. 1886 8/6/92
Lyttelton, Arthur Temple
Dogmatic religion. 1886 4/5/86 ?
Lyttelton, Edward
'Athletics in public schools' in *Nineteenth Century*, vii. 43. 1880 (January 1880) 13/2/80
Lyttelton, George Baron Lyttelton
Dialogues of the dead. 1760 27/7/39
Memoirs and correspondence, ed. Phillimore. 1845 (2v.) 18/7/45
Lyttelton, George William Baron Lyttelton
Address to young men read at the Wordsley Institute, November, 1875. 1875 17/1/76
Contributions towards a glossary of the Glynne language. By a student. 1851 4/8/51
Ephemera. 1865 27/3/57, 17/12/64, 21/1/72
The colonial empire of Great Britain, especially in its religious aspect. 1850 6/2/50
The four gospels . . . with explanatory notes. 1856 10/8/56
Thoughts on national education. 1855 13/6/55
Tracts: I. On infant baptism. II. On the Athanasian Creed. 1857 15/3/57
Lyttelton, Lady Sarah Spencer
Correspondence of Sarah Spencer, Lady Lyttelton . . . 1787–1870, ed. Mrs. H. Wyndham and intro. by Lady F. Cavendish. 1912 14/10/89
Lyttelton, William Henry 3rd Baron Lyttelton
Some account of Napoleon. 1836 18/5/54
Lyttelton, William Henry
Address on holy communion. 1844 8/12/44 ?
Church establishments: their advantages, social and religious. A lecture. 1861 29/1/63, 31/12/71
Dangers to truth from controversy and agitation. A visitation sermon. 1850 12/8/50
Holy scripture, the witness to the revelation of God in all facts. A sermon. 1866 11/2/66
Scripture revelations of the life after death . . . with remarks upon cremation. 1875 30/1/76
Sins of trade and business. A sermon. 1874 30/8/74
Some reasons for want of success in the Christian ministry. An ordination sermon. 1851 10/8/51
The leaven of the kingdom of God, or, Christianity leavening common life and conversation. A sermon. 1852 15/2/52
The testimony of scripture to the authority of conscience and of reason. 1861 5/11/71
Lyttle, W. G.
Betsy Gray; or, Hearts of Down: a tale of ninety-eight. 1894 2/7/89
Lytton, Edward Robert Bulwer Earl of Lytton
Julian Fane. A memoir. 1871 1/7/72

Life of Edward Bulwer, Lord Lytton. 1885 15/9/86
Speeches of Edward Lord Lytton... With... a prefatory memoir by his son. 1874 2/11/74
Lytton, Rosina
Life of Rosina, Lady Lytton, by L. Devey. 1887 6/10/87

M. A.
Ward and the new test. 1844 9/1/45
Mabelan, David
Home rule and imperial unity. An argument for the Gladstone-Morley scheme. 1886 20/8/86
Maberly, Thomas Astley
A letter to the Rev. H. Wellesley. 1850 2/3/51
Macalister, Alexander
Evolution in church history. 1882 31/12/82
Macarthur, Sir Edward
Colonial policy of 1840 and 1841... proceedings of the Legislative Council of New South Wales. 1841 9/6/41
Macarthur, James
New South-Wales, its present state and future prospects: being a statement. 1837 3/10/37, 12/6/41
Macartney, Hussey Burgh
Experiment of three hundred years... the efforts made by the English government to make known the gospel to the Irish nation. 1847 14/11/80 ?
Macaulay, James
Ireland in 1872; a tour of observation. With remarks on Irish public questions. 1873 7/3/73, 12/10/87 ?
Macaulay, Kenneth
Voyage to St. Kilda. 1763 24/8/81
Macaulay, Thomas Babington
'Lord Bacon' in *Essays*. 1843 15/9/71, 11/4/76
'Milton' and 'Machiavelli' in *Essays*. 1868 14/4/76
'Warren Hastings' in *Essays*. 11/1/86
[article on John Milton] in *Edinburgh Review*, xlii. 304. 1826 (August 1826) 13/10/26
[Review of Croker's ed. of Boswell's 'Life of Johnson'], *Edinburgh Review*, liv. 1. 1831 (September 1831) 24/6/52
[Review of Gladstone's *The State in its relations with the Church*], *Edinburgh Review*, lxix. 231 (April 1839) 9/4/39, 15/4/39, 3/1/40
Biographies... contributed to the Encyclopaedia Britannica. 1860 5/2/63
Historical essays. 1850 (4v.) 27/5/56, 1/1/86, 11/1/86, 12/1/86
John Dryden. An essay. 1828 17/6/61
Speech... on the repeal of the union with Ireland, 6 February 1833. 1833 4/6/86, 16/12/87
The history of England, from the accession of James II. 1849 (5v. 1849–61) 2/2/49, 23/3/61
The lays of ancient Rome. 1842 3/11/42, 30/5/72, 15/9/82
Macbride, John David
Observations on the last supper. 1832 17/8/56
The Mohammedan religion explained: with an introductory sketch of its progress. 1857 15/5/59
MacCabe, William Bernard
Florine, princess of Burgundy. 1855 26/4/93 ?
MacCalmont, Robert
Some remarks on the contract packet system, and on ocean penny postage. 1851 26/2/53
MacCarthy, Daniel Bishop of Kerry
Dissertations chiefly on Irish church history. 1864 9/2/70
MacCarthy, Denis Florence
Poems. 1882 18/9/82
Shelley's early life from original sources. With incidents, letters and writings. 1873 14/8/73
The two lovers of heaven... From the Spanish of Calderon. 1870 27/3/70
MacCarthy, Egerton Francis Mead
The government code: its injurious effect upon national education. A paper. 1879 5/2/79
MacCarthy, John George
A plea for the home government of Ireland. 1871 20/1/72, 18/10/77
Henry Grattan. A historical study. 1886 11/10/87
MacCarthy, Justin M.P.
'Dublin Castle' in *Contemporary Review*, xlvii. 153, 266. 1885 (February 1885) 4/2/85
[On Lecky], in *Contemporary Review*, lviii. 673. 1890 (November 1890) 30/10/90
A history of our own times. 1879 (4v.) 6/1/79
Miss Misanthrope. 1878 (2v.) 25/1/81
Sir Robert Peel. 1890 10/1/91
MacCarthy, Justin Huntly
Ireland since the union. 1887 1/3/87
The thousand and one days. 1892 (2v.) 8/6/92
MacCaul, Alexander
A sermon preached... at the consecration of the... bishop of the United Church of England and Ireland in Jerusalem. 1841 2/12/41
Aids to faith. 9/10/85
An examination of Bp. Colenso's difficulties with regard to the pentateuch. 1864 (pt. 2 1864) 27/3/64
Remarks on Dr. McCaul's plea, from Lev. xviii. 18, for marrying a deceased wife's sister. 1859 20/11/59
The Jerusalem bishopric. 1845 8/4/45, 10/5/57
MacCaul, Joseph Benjamin
Dark sayings of old. Being an attempt to elucidate certain difficult passages of Holy Scripture. 1873 7/9/73

MacCausland, Dominick
Adam and the Adamite: or, the harmony of scripture and ethnology. 1864 6/2/65
The builders of Babel. 1871 17/8/71
MacCay, John
A general view of the history and objects of the Bank of England. 1822 17/11/63
MacClellan, John Brown
The new testament... a new translation. 1875 (2v.) 14/2/75
MacCoan, James Carlile
Consular jurisdiction in Turkey and Egypt. 1873 17/6/73
Egypt as it is. 1877 11/7/77
MacColl, Hugh
Ednor Whitlock. 1891 13/12/91
MacColl, Malcolm
'Islam and civilization' in *Contemporary Review*, liii. 537. 1888 (April 1888) 6/5/88
'Some current fallacies about Turks, Bulgarians, and Russians', in *Nineteenth Century*, ii. 831. 1877 (December 1877) 12/10/78
Christianity in relation to science and morals. 1889 18/8/89, 1/6/90
Eternity of punishment. An article reprinted from the 'Ecclesiastic'. 1864 11/9/64
Is there not a cause? A letter to Colonel Greville-Nugent, on the disestablishment of the Irish church. With a vindication of Mr. Gladstone, etc. 1868 16/10/68
Lawlessness, sacerdotalism, and ritualism discussed in six letters... to... Lord Selborne. 1875 11/4/75, 10/10/81
Mr. Cheyne and the bishop of Brechin. A letter to ... W. E. Gladstone. 1860 17/6/60
My reviewers reviewed, in a preface to the third edition of 'Lawlessness, Sacerdotalism, etc.'. 1875 22/6/75
Papal infallibility. 1873 24/12/74
The 'Damnatory clauses' of the Athanasian creed rationally explained in a letter to... Gladstone. 1872 21/7/72, 13/2/76
The Eastern question: its facts and fallacies. 1877 28/3/77
The Ober-Ammergau passion play. 1870 5/2/70
Three years of the Eastern question. 1878 (chapter 1) 22/4/78
MacCosh, James
The duty of Irish Presbyterians to their church at the present crisis... of the gospel ministry. 1868 6/6/68
MacCrie, Thomas the elder
History of the progress and suppression of the reformation in Italy in the sixteenth century. 1827 29/9/33
On church establishments. 1833 23/12/33
The life of John Knox. 1812 18/12/36, 26/10/56
MacCrie, Thomas the younger
Sketches of Scottish church history... from the reformation to the revolution. 1841 2/9/47
The life of Mr. Robert Blair. 1848 23/3/56
MacCullagh, William Torrens
Reform of procedure in parliament to clear the block of public business. 1881 3/12/81
MacCulloch, John
Proofs and illustrations of the attributes of God, from the facts and laws of the physical universe. 1837 (3v.) 20/5/41
MacCulloch, John Ramsay
'Life of Adam Smith' prefixed to *Wealth of Nations* 1828 11/7/55
A dictionary of commerce. 1869 (1869–71 edn) 20/4/69
A dictionary, geographical, statistical, and historical, of... the world. 1841 14/5/44
A treatise on the principles and practical influence of taxation and the funding system. 1845 26/1/53, 29/2/64
A treatise on the succession to property vacant by death. 1848 7/3/48
An essay on the circumstances which determine the rate of wages, and the condition of the labouring classes. 1826 10/3/54
Considerations on partnerships with limited liability. 1856 2/4/56
Memorandums on the proposed importation of foreign beef and live stock, addressed to A. Murray. 1842 28/4/42
Russia and Turkey. From the geographical dictionary. 1854 30/9/54
Statements illustrative of the policy and probable consequences of the proposed repeal [of corn laws]. 1841 12/10/41
The principles of political economy. 1830 (2nd edn) 17/11/41
MacDevitt, John
Introduction to the Sacred Scriptures. 1889 28/4/89
University education in Ireland and 'Ultramontanism'. Being an examination of arguments... by J. L. Whittle. 1866 5/4/66
MacDonald, Alexander solicitor
Love, law, and theology, or the outs and ins of the veto case: an ecclesiastical legal-romance. 1869 25/12/71, 3/1/72
MacDonald, Alexander war correspondent
The land of Ararat; or, up on the roof of the world. 1893 28/3/93
MacDonald, Donald
Introduction to the pentateuch: an inquiry, critical and doctrinal, into the... Mosaic writings. 1861 (2v.) 23/11/62
MacDonald, George
Alec Forbes of Howglen. 1865 14/5/66

Letters from hell. 1884 7/10/85
Unspoken sermons. 1865 21/7/67
MacDonald, James
Religion and myth. 1893 14/1/94
MacDonald, Lieut. Col. James Horsburgh
The errors and evils of the Bank Charter Act of 1844. 1855 17/2/57
MacDonald, Robert
From day to day; or, helpful words for Christian life. Daily readings for a year. 1879 26/9/80
Macdonell, Agnes
Quaker cousins. A novel. 1879 (3v.) 14/9/80
Macdonell, James
France since the first empire, ed. by his wife, A. H. Macdonell. 1879 15/5/80
Macdonell, John
The land question, with particular reference to England and Scotland. 1873 12/3/87
Macdonell, W. J.
Reminiscences of the late Alexander Macdonell, first Catholic bishop of upper Canada. 1888 14/1/90
Macdonnell, Alexander
A letter to T. F. Buxton... in refutation of allegations respecting... slaves in the British West India Colonies. 1833 7/3/33
Macdonnell, Eneas
[on Gorham]. (not found) 3/2/50
A short reply to a long speech upon the Maynooth question. 1845 23/6/45
An appeal to the opponents of the Maynooth grant. 1845 7/1/45
Catholic question. Practical views of the principles and conduct of the Catholic clergy and laity of Ireland. 1827 11/2/45
Letter to... Gladstone, respecting the Maynooth grant. 1845 18/3/45
My first speech; and my latest advice to my countrymen. A fragment. 1849 17/3/49
Shrewsbury sentiments for Whig festivals. 1844 18/3/44
The Roman Catholic oath considered. 1835 8/5/35, 6/7/35
Macdonnell, Robert
Irish nationality in 1870. By a Protestant Celt. 1870 23/12/85 ?
MacDougall, James
The ascension of Christ, and other sermons. 1884 31/5/85
MacDowall, Alexander B.
Facts about Ireland. A curve-history of recent years. 1888 3/3/88
MacDowall, William
Among the old Scotch minstrels, studying their ballads of war, love, social life, folk-lore and fairyland. 1888 16/7/88
MacDowell, Cameron Joseph Francis Stuart
Parisiana... or, the volunteer with the besieged armies, 1870–71. 1871 24/5/71
MacDuff, John Ross
Memories of Olivet. 1868 8/1/71
Saint Paul in Rome. 1871 26/11/71
MacEvoy, John
A free enquiry into the Irish education question. 1866 28/2/66
MacEwan, Charles M.
Dangerous divinity in high places; a review of a lecture by... Caird. 1882 20/8/84
MacFarlan, W. L.
Behind the scenes in Norway. 1884 10/9/85
MacFarlane, Alexander
Sailm Dhaibhidh ann dan Gaoidhealach. 1753 11/1/63
MacFarlane, Charles
A glance at revolutionized Italy: a visit to Messina, and a tour... in... 1848. 1849 26/4/49
The Neapolitan government and Mr. Gladstone. A letter to the Earl of Aberdeen; being a reply to [Gladstone]. 1851 19/8/51
Macfarlane, Sir Donald Horne
Ireland versus England. 1880 28/2/80, 28/11/80
MacFarlane, James D.D.
The late secession from the Church of Scotland. 1846 2/9/47
MacFarlane, Rev. James of Aberchirder
Remarks on the tracts lately published, on the intrusion of ministers on reclaiming congregations. 1839 (3v.) 9/12/39
Macfarlane, John LL.D.
Pulpit echoes; or, passages from discourses and expositions. 1868 26/6/81
Macfarren, C.
Oberon. 1826 14/9/92 ?
MacGahan, Januarius Aloysius
Campaigning on the Oxus, and the fall of Khiva. 1874 24/10/76
MacGeoghegan, James
Histoire d'Irlande, ancienne et moderne. 1758 (3v.) 1/8/45
MacGhee, Robert James
A letter to the Protestants of the United Kingdom [on]... *the real principles of the Roman Catholic bishops and priests in Ireland.* 1835 25/6/35
A sermon on the death of... J. H. North. 1831 3/6/35
Rome and England: the two churches, the two reformations, and the two creeds. Lectures. 1852 8/10/74 ?
MacGhee, Robert James and Daly, R.
On the... non-scriptural education of the poor of Ireland... letters... to the archbishop of Dublin. 1831 26/11/43
MacGilchrist, John
The life of W. E. Gladstone. 1868 17/5/69
Macgillivray, William
The natural history of Dee side and Braemar... ed. by E. Lankester. 1855 6/10/71 ?

Macgregor, Duncan
Mariner Newman; a voyage in the good ship 'Glad Tidings' to the promised land. 1877 19/8/77
Macgregor, John M.A.
The voyage alone in the yawl 'Rob Roy', from London to Paris, and back by Havre, the Isle of Wight. 1867 9/4/68
MacGregor, John Secretary to the Board of Trade
'Account of Dutch East India Colonies' in 'Commercial Statistics' 1843 (5v. 1843–50) 9/1/43
Financial reform: a letter to the citizens of Glasgow. 1849 3/2/49
The commercial and financial legislation of Europe and America; with a pro-forma revision of... taxation. 1841 15/9/41
MacGregor, Patrick
Introduction to 'The genuine remains of Ossian... translated into a preliminary dissertation' by J. Macpherson. 1841 16/9/58
MacHale, John R. C. Archbishop of Tuam
[Sermons]. (not found) 10/3/39
Five sermons. 1832 15/12/39
The letters of... under their respective signatures. 1847 (1888 edn) 8/9/89
Machiavelli, Niccolò
'Ritratti delle cose della Francia, & dell' Alamagna', *Opere.* 4/11/61
Canti Carnascialeschi. 27/7/58, 18/9/61
Discorsi. 28/4/36, 24/5/36, 12/10/71
I legaz alla corte di Roma. 25/9/61
Il Principe. 9/3/33, 25/9/34, 7/10/34, 30/10/34, 6/11/64, 11/8/91
Il Principe, with introduction by Acton. (1891) 11/8/91
Istorie Fiorentine. 13/10/71
La clizia. 6/11/61
Mandragola. 1887 21/11/87
Machyn, Henry
The diary of H. Machyn, citizen... of London. 1840 25/5/85
MacIlvraine, Charles Pettit
Oxford divinity compared with that of the Romish and Anglican churches. 1841 26/4/41
Righteousness by faith... comparison of the doctrine of the Oxford Tracts with... Romish and Anglican. 1868 17/5/68
The chief danger of the Church in these times. A charge... to... the diocese of Ohio... Sept. 8th. 1843. 1843 9/6/44
Macintosh, Duncan
Brethrenism, or, the special teachings, ecclesiastical and doctinal of... Plymouth Brethren. 1875 20/5/75
MacIvor, James
A letter to the... bishop of Derry and Raphoe, on the present state of the education question. 1857 19/3/57
Some papers on intermediate education in Ireland. 1869 9/6/69
Mackail, John William
Thermopolae. 1881 6/1/92 ?
Mackarness, John Fielder
A charge... diocese of Oxford at his primary visitation, April 16, 1872. 1872 5/5/72
A few words to the country parsons touching the election for the University of Oxford. 1847 1/7/47
Memorials of the episcopate of J. F. Mackarness, by C. C. Mackarness. 1892 7/8/92
Mackay, A.
'Locksley Hall' in *Notes and Queries.* 1875 (October 1875) 29/10/86
Mackay, Alexander
Analysis of the Australian colonies' Government Bill. 1850 22/3/50
The crisis in Canada; or vindication of Lord Elgin ... in reference to the Rebellion Losses Bill. 1849 26/5/49
Mackay, Charles
Memoirs of extraordinary popular delusions. 1841 (3v.) 4/3/74
The liberal party, its present position and future work. 1880 2/1/91 ?
The poetry and humour of the Scottish language. 1882 15/1/83
Mackay, Eric
Nero and Actea. 1891 13/7/91
Mackay, James
Molochology not theology: Penang sermons. 1870 6/2/70
Mackay, Robert William
The progress of the intellect, as exemplified in the religious development of the Greeks and Hebrews. 1850 (2v.) 13/7/62
Mackenzie, Alexander
The history of the Highland clearances. 1883 27/2/83
Mackenzie, Charles F.R.S.
Notes on Hayti, made during a residence in that republic. 1830 (2v.) 20/5/33
Mackenzie, Charles Prebendary of St. Paul's
Individual responsibility. 1850 2/3/51
Mackenzie, Charles Frederick Bishop of Central Africa
In Zululand. The story of the Mackenzie Memorial Mission. 1872 25/5/84
Mackenzie, Sir George
Vindication of His Majesty's government and judicatures in Scotland. 26/9/44
Mackenzie, Georgina Mary
Travels in the Slavonic provinces of Turkey-in-Europe... With a preface by... W. E. Gladstone. 1867 (2nd edn 2v) 13/6/67, 7/4/77
Mackenzie, Georgina Mary, and A. P. Irby
The Turks, the Greeks and the Slavons. Travels in

the Slavonic provinces of Turkey-in-Europe. 1867 14/3/67, 14/12/76
Mackenzie, Henry author
Julia de Roubigné, a tale. 1777 (2v.) 26/8/43
Mackenzie, Henry Bishop of Nottingham
Commerce a divine missionary. 1845 25/5/45
Essay on the life and institutions of Offa, King of Mercia, A.D. 755–794. 1840 14/4/40
On ... the removal of Jewish disabilities. A letter to the parishioners of Great Yarmouth. 1847 8/12/47
Ordination sermon. 1845 25/5/45
Pastoral letter to the parishioners of St. Martin in the Fields. 1849 25/1/49
The mission of the Scottish Episcopal Church. A sermon. 1854 22/10/54
Mackenzie, Holt
Address [on corn laws]. 1841 18/9/41
Mackenzie, James Rev.
The history of Scotland. 1867 8/8/87
Mackenzie, James S. S. C.
The general grievances and oppression of the isles of Orkney and Shetland ... ed. by A. G. Groat and H. Cheyne. 1836 20/11/71
Mackenzie, James Thompson
The best means of defraying the expenses of the Afghan war. 1878 3/12/78
Mackenzie, Mary Jane
Private life; or, varieties of character and opinion. 1829 20/8/36
Mackenzie, William Bell
Saul of Tarsus: his life and its lessons. 1864 30/3/72
Mackie, John
A harbour of refuge in Wick Bay. Letter to ... W. E. Gladstone. 1860 12/1/61
Mackie, T.
The politics of the future. 1881 31/10/81 ?
Mackinnon, William Alexander
History of civilization. 1846 (2v.) 18/8/54
Mackintosh, Charles Henry
Notes on the book of Exodus. 1858 5/3/65
Mackintosh, Sir James
Dissertation on the progress of ethical philosophy, chiefly during the seventeenth and eighteenth centuries. 1830 13/9/31
Dissertation on ... ethical philosophy ... with a preface by W. Whewell. 1836 5/5/36
Memoirs, ed. R. J. Mackintosh. 1835 21/9/35
Vindiciae Gallicae. Defence of the French revolution ... against the accusations of ... Burke. 1791 14/10/28, 14/7/43
Mackintosh, John LL.D.
History of civilization in Scotland. 1878 (3v. 1878–83) 24/11/83
Mackintosh, Robert James
Memoirs of the life of ... Sir James Mackintosh. Edited by his son. 1835 21/9/35
Macknight, James LL.D.
The Ulster tenant's claim of right: or, land ownership a state trust. 1848 20/10/69
Macknight, Thomas
History of the life and times of Edmund Burke. 1858 (3v. 1858–60) 17/2/58, 20/12/60, 23/1/61
The life of H. St. John, Viscount Bolingbroke. 1863 14/3/63, 15/4/73
The right hon. Benjamin Disraeli: a literary and political biography. 1854 30/12/53
Thirty years of foreign policy. A history of the secretaryships of ... Aberdeen and ... Palmerston. 1855 12/12/54
Mackonochie, Alexander Heriot
Judgment of the Lord Chief Justice. 1878 20/7/79
Mackworth, Sir Humphrey
Peace at home; or a vindication of the ... bill for preventing danger from occasional conformity. 1703 18/3/88
MacLagan, Peter
Land culture and land tenure in Ireland. 1869 8/12/69
Maclagan, William Dalrymple
The church and the age: essays ... Edited by A. Weir and W. D. M. 1870 (2v.) 30/8/91 ?
The threefold work of the threefold ministry; being a sermon. 1875 19/12/75 ?
Maclaren, Alexander
'Time for thee to work'. The annual sermon for the National Bible Society of Scotland. 1874 22/10/76
The God of the Amen, and other sermons. 1891 13/9/91
Maclaren, Charles
A dissertation on the topography of the plain of Troy. 1822 5/9/55
Select writings, political, scientific, topographical, and miscellaneous, etc. Ed. R. Cox and J. Nicol. 1869 (2v.) 16/4/69
MacLaren, James
Sketch of the history of the currency. 1858 8/12/63
MacLaughlin, J.
Les voyageurs, historiens et économistes anglais. 1892 10/1/92 ?
MacLaurin, Colin
A treatise of algebra. 1748 17/7/29
Maclear, George Frederick
'St. Boniface' in *Apostles of Mediaeval Europe.* 1868 12/9/69
Maclennan, Isaac
Hymns. 1834 31/7/87
MacLennan, John Ferguson
Memoir of Thomas Drummond. 1867 24/6/67, 29/3/88
Primitive marriage. An enquiry into the origin of the form of capture in marriage ceremonies. 1865 31/1/65

Macleod, Alexander
Christian worship: its development, and the true purpose of ritual. A sermon. 1873 6/7/73
Macleod, Norman
The concluding address to the general assembly of the Church of Scotland, May 1869. 1869 7/11/69
Maclevy, James
Curiosities of crime in Edinburgh. 1861 30/3/61
Macmahon, John Henry
Church and state in England; its origin and use. 1873 26/5/77
MacMahon, Thomas O'Brien
Remarks on the English and Irish nations. 1792 5/8/63
MacMasters, S. Y.
A Methodist in search of the Church. 1862 29/12/89
Macmeadow, Mr.
[on turf question]. (not found) 22/11/73
Macmechan, William
To disestablish the church is to discrown the Queen. The church and the common law. 1868 28/10/73
Macmillan, Hugh
Bible teachings in nature. 1867 10/5/67
The Riviera. 1892 3/3/92
Macmillan's Magazine.
1. 161. 1/1860. on Louis Napoleon 7/1/1860
3. 179. 1/1861. Diamonds 5/1/1861
5. 441. 3/1862. Royal deaths 21/1/1862
6. 177. 7/1862. West 8/7/1862
6. 345. 8/1862. Montenegro 13/9/1862
10. 554. 10/1891. Russia 13/10/1891
22. 292. 8/1870. on Clarendon 12/8/1870
28. 222. 5/1873. O'Connell 13/7/1873
30. 559. 10/1874. Prussia 9/10/1874
33. 275. 1/1876. Montenegro 22/3/1877
37. 171, 161. 3/1878. Heligoland; Russia 20/3/1878
38. 385. 9/1878. Two sides to a saint 1/9/1878
39. 390. 3/1879. Haberdashers' Hall 7/3/1879
40. 471. 4/1884. Colonies 15/4/1884
41. 125. 12/1879. Colour-sense 13/12/1879
48. 26, 59. 5/1883. Huxley; Bryce 30/4/1883
51. 241. 2/1885. Morley on G. Eliot 16/3/1885
51. 446. 4/1885. Morley on Pattison 6/4/1885
58. 247, 285. 8/1888. Doyle; Coleridge 28/8/1888
58. 417. 10/1892. Harrison on Huxley 5/10/1892
58. 545. 10/1892. Indian finance 5/10/1892
58. 689. 11/1892. Lugard 8/11/1892
58. 74. 7/1892. Tollemache 29/12/1892
58. 834. 12/1892. Momerie 14/12/1892
132. 439. 10/1870. on Lubbock 23/11/1870
Macmullen, Richard Gell
Two exercises for the degree of B. D., read in the Divinity School, Oxford, 18th and 19th April, 1844. 1844 27/4/44
Macnaught, John
Coena domini: an essay on the Lord's supper. 1878 2/6/78, 19/3/82
The doctrine of inspiration: being an inquiry concerning the . . . authority of Holy Writ. 1856 23/10/59
MacNaughten, Stephen
The gospel in Great Britain. 1884 25/12/84
MacNeill, Sir John
Progress and present position of Russia in the East. 1836 22/5/43
MacNeill, John Gordon Swift
How the Union was carried. 1887 8/2/87
The Irish parliament: what it was, and what it did. 1885 18/11/85
MacNevin, Thomas
The history of the Volunteers of 1782. 1845 18/2/88
MacNish, Robert
'The Metempsychosis' in *Tales from Blackwood, ii.* 1859 21/9/60
Macpherson, Antoine
De verklaring van Paulus aan die van Rome, de lust en het verlangen . . . van het Evangelie. 1857 18/4/58 ?
MacPherson, Florence
Poetry of modern Greece: specimens and extracts, tr. F. MacPherson. 1884 2/6/84
Macpherson, Hector Carsewell
W. E. Gladstone: political career. 1892 23/6/92
MacPherson, Robert
Vatican sculptures. 1863 29/10/66
Macqueary, Thomas Howard
Evolution of man and Christianity. 1890 8/6/90
MacQueen, Kenneth
Who is to blame for the Indian mutinies?. 1857 9/6/58
Macquoid, Katharine Sarah
A faithful lover. 1882 (3v.) 27/6/82
Doris Barugh. A Yorkshire story. 1878 (3v.) 5/12/81
Macrae, David
Diogenes among the D.D.'s: a book of burlesques. 1883 16/10/71 ?
George Gilfillan. Anecdotes and reminiscences. 1891 15/11/91
Macrobius, Ambrosius Theodosius
Somnium Scipionis ex Ciceronis libro de republica exerptum. 25/4/50

Madan, Martin
Letters to J. Priestley . . . occasioned by his late controversial writings. 1786 13/8/55
Thelyphthora, or a treatise on female ruin. 1780 14/2/56, 16/6/57
Madden, Daniel Owen pseud. D. North
Chiefs of parties, past and present, with original anecdotes. 1859 (2v.) 21/4/59
Ireland and its rulers, since 1829. 1843 (3v. 1843–44) 28/3/56
Madden, Richard Robert
A twelvemonth's residence in the West Indies, during the transition from slavery to apprenticeship. 1835 (2v.) 18/8/35
Reminiscences from 1798 to 1886. 1891 11/1/94 ?
The history of Irish periodical literature . . . 17th to the middle of the 19th century. 1867 (2v.) 27/12/67
The life and martyrdom of Savonarola, illustrative of the history of church and state connexion. 1853 (2v.) 14/8/53
The literary life and correspondence of the Countess of Blessington. 1855 (3v.) 30/6/83
The memoirs—chiefly autobiographical,—from 1798 to 1886 . . . Edited by his son T. M. Madden. 1891 10/11/91
Travels in Turkey, Egypt, Nubia, and Palestine in 1824–27. 1829 (2v.) 2/7/30
Madelaine's Fault. A story of French life, tr. M. Neale. 1882 19/3/82
Madhuvdas Rugnathas
Story of a widow remarriage. 1890 25/9/90
Maffei, Marquis Francesco Scipione
Merope, a tragedy. Tr. Mr. Ayre. 1740 25/10/33, 26/11/33
Magee, William Bishop of Raphoe
A charge delivered at his triennial and metropolitan visitation . . . 10th of October, 1826. 1827 24/3/68
Discourses on the scriptural doctrines of atonement and sacrifice. 1801 1/7/55, 3/8/62
Magee, William Connor Bishop of Peterborough
The voluntary system: can it supply the place of the established church? With recent facts and statistics from America. 1860 22/4/60
Magician, the. 29/6/76
Magnanini, V.
Armonia della religione colle scienze e collo stato. 1877 6/12/77
Maguire, John Francis
Father Mathew: a biography. 1863 19/12/63
Letters in vindication of the Church of Ireland. 1850 12/4/50
Pontificate of Pius the Ninth. 1870 27/11/70
Rome: its ruler [Pius IX] and its institutions. 1857 (1859 edn) 14/2/60, 13/3/60
The Irish in America. 1868 18/1/68
The next generation. 1871 (3v.) 27/4/71
Maguire, Justin
Alastor; an Irish story of to-day. 1888 19/4/89 ?
Mahaffy, Sir John Pentland
Rambles and studies in Greece. 1876 (1878 edn) 28/9/78
Contemporary Review, xli.160. 1882 (January 1882) 30/12/81
Prolegomena to ancient history. 1871 12/12/72
Social life in Greece from Homer to Menander. 1874 13/11/86
The decay of modern preaching. An essay. 1882 8/3/82
Mahan, Alfred Thayer
The influence of sea power upon history. 1889 13/12/90
Mahoney, R. J.
Credo Experto. Address. 1880 1/12/80
Mahony, J. W.
Hamlet's mission: a critical enquiry into . . . his mode of carrying out the command of the ghost. 1875 21/1/77
Mahony, Peirce
The truth about Glenbeigh. 1887 14/2/87
Mailfer, Henri Charles
De la démocratie en Europe. Questions religieuses et juridiques. Droit public interne. 1874 29/1/75
Maimbourg, Louis
L'Histoire véritable du Calvinisme, ou Mémoires historiques touchant la Réformation. 21/1/47
Maimon, Salomon
An autobiography. Tr. from the German by J. C. Murray. 1888 14/5/88
Main, Robert
A sermon preached . . . during the meeting of the British Association for the Advancement of Science. 1875 28/11/75
Replies to 'Essays and Reviews'. With . . . letters from the Radcliffe Observer. 1862 9/2/62
Maine, Sir Henry James Sumner
Ancient law. 1861 27/6/61, 6/8/66, 4/7/80
Popular government. Four essays. 1885 12/1/86, 26/4/86
The early history of the property of married women, as collected from Roman and Hindoo law. A lecture. 1873 16/6/73
Maine, J. P. L. de la Roche du Marquis de Luchet
Mémoires authentiques pour servir à l'histoire du Comte de Cagliostro. 1786 29/4/67
Maistre, Count Joseph Marie de
Considérations sur la France. 1796 21/5/50
Examen de la philosophie de Bacon, où l'on traite . . . questions de philosophie rationelle. 1836 (2v.) 29/4/76

Maitland, Brownlow
The argument from prophecy. 1877 28/2/78
Theism or agnosticism: an essay on the grounds of belief in God. 1878 3/3/78
Maitland, James 8th Earl of Lauderdale
An inquiry into the nature and origin of public wealth, and . . . the means and causes of its increase. 1819 28/1/33
Substance of . . . speech in the House of Lords, on . . . the Ionian Islands. 1820 27/11/58
Maitland, John Gorham
Property and income tax. The present state of the question. 1853 8/12/52, 15/2/53
Maitland, Samuel Roffey
A letter to a friend, on the Tract for the Times No. 89. 1841 26/4/41
Convocation. Remarks on the charge recently delivered by the . . . bishop of Oxford. 1855 24/1/55
Eruvin; or, miscellaneous essays on subjects concerned with the nature, history, and destiny of man. 1831 9/5/58
Essays on subjects connected with the Reformation in England. Reprinted, with additions, from the 'British Magazine'. 1849 18/7/52
The dark ages: a series of essays. 1844 11/2/44
Maitland, Sir Thomas
Address . . . to the Primary Council, February 3, 1817: Le Tre Costituzioni. 1849 31/12/58
Substance of the Earl of Lauderdale's speech . . . explanatory of . . . conduct as Lord High Commissioner of the Ionian Islands. 1822 30/11/58
Major, Johannes
A history of Greater Britain . . . Tr. from the original Latin and edited . . . by A. Constable. 1892 21/3/92
Major, Richard Henry
The voyages of the Venetian brothers, N. and A. Zeno, to the Northern seas. 1873 6/2/74
Malan, César Henri Abraham
Témoignage rendu à l'Evangile. Par un ministre de Dieu. 1813 28/10/32
Malan, S. C.
A short summary of the Armenian church and people. 1868 29/8/80 ?
Malcolm, James Peller
Anecdotes of the manners and customs of London, from the Roman invasion to the year 1700. 1811 16/10/67
Malcolm, Sir John
A memoir of central India. 1823 (2v.) 7/12/42
The history of Persia, from the most early period to the present time. 1815 (2v.) 6/11/57
Malden, Henry
On the origin of universities and academical degrees. 1835 20/5/48, 17/10/71
Maldonatus, Joannes
A commentary on the holy gospels, tr. and ed. by G. J. Davie. 1888 (2v.) 27/10/89
Malet, William Wyndham
On church extension. 1840 21/1/43
The olive leaf: a pilgrimage to Rome, Jerusalem, and Constantinople, in 1867, for the reunion of the faithful. 1868 26/7/68
The tithe redemption trust. A letter to Lord Lyttelton. 1849 18/5/49
Malleson, George Bruce
The mutiny of the Bengal army. 1857 (2v.) 13/10/57
Mallet, David
The life of Francis Bacon. 1740 12/12/29
Malleus Ritualistarum; or, 'The Ritual Reason Why Not'. 1872 8/11/74
Mallock, William Hurrell
'Positivism on an island' in *Contemporary Review*, xxxii. 1. 1878 (April 1878) 29/3/78
'The logic of toleration' in *Nineteenth Century*, v. 64. 1879 (January 1879) 23/2/79
Is life worth living?. 1878 (1879 edn) 10/8/79
The new republic. 1877 (2v.) 11/6/77
Malone, Sylvester
Tenant wrong illustrated in a nutshell; or a history of Kilkee . . . during the last seven years . . . letter to . . . Gladstone. 1867 27/6/67
Malortie, Baron Carl von
Diplomatic sketches [on Gladstone]. By an outsider. 1878 (vol 3 1878–79) 21/7/79
Egypt: native rulers and foreign interference. 1882 8/12/82
Malory, Sir Thomas
The byrth, lyf and actes of King Arthur, ed. R. Southey. 1817 (2v.) 14/8/59
Malta, Correspondence and remarks on the constitution. 1887 22/11/87
Maltby, Edward
A charge delivered to the clergy of . . . Durham, at the visitation in July, August and September, 1845. 1845 8/1/54
A charge delivered to the clergy of . . . Durham, at the visitation, in July and August, mdcccxli. 1841 12/10/41
Mamiani della Rovere, Count Terenzio
Sul papato. 1851 3/5/52
Man, history of the isle of. 1821 28/4/76
Manchester
A counter-plea for the poor, showing that the cause of their distress is not attributed to the corn laws. 1839 16/10/41
Manchester Church Question plainly stated. 1850 24/2/50
Manchester Socinian controversy. 1825 10/8/62
Report of the directors to a special . . . meeting of the Chamber of Commerce and Manufactures at Manchester, on . . . restrictions on trade. 1841 15/12/41
Manchester Cathedral letters. 5/5/74

Mancini, Marie Thérèse Barbon Mazarini Duchess de Nivernois
Pensées diverses. 1870 24/2/84
Mancini, P. B.
[On Machiavelli]. 15/9/53
Mandat-Grancey, Baron Edmond de
Chez Paddy. 1887 15/8/87
Mandeville, Bernard de
A modest defence of public stews: or, an essay on whoring, as it is now practis'd in these kingdoms. 1724 28/11/64
Enquiry into the original of moral virtue, wherein it is shown that virtue is founded in the nature of things. 1728 9/9/43
The fable of the bees; or, private vices publick benefits. 1714 (2nd edn 1723) 15/8/29, 13/9/43, 21/8/59
Manfredi, Fulgenzio
Were 'heretics' ever burned alive at Rome? A report of... the Roman inquisition against F. Manfredi, ed. R. Gibbings. 1852 7/8/53
Manfrin, Pietro
Gli Ebrei sotto la dominazione romana. 1888 (4v. 1888–97) 16/1/89
Manin, Daniele
La Vénétie devant l'Europe. Correspondance diplomatique de Manin. 1859 3/8/59
Mann, Horace barrister
Civil service competitions, considered as a means of promoting popular education. 1857 12/11/57
Mann, Mrs. Horace
Juanita. 1887 19/5/88
Manners, Lord John James Robert 7th Duke of Rutland
[On the Spanish match] in *Oxford and Cambridge Review*, i.639. 1845 (December 1845) 9/12/45
English ballads and other poems. 1850 17/5/50
Lord John Manners... by a non-elector. 1872 28/8/72
Notes of an Irish tour. 1849 27/4/89
The speech of Lord John Manners on the laws of Mortmain in the... Commons... August 1st. 1843. 1843 27/10/43
The monastic and manufacturing systems. 1843 23/11/43
Manning, Henry Edward
'How shall Catholics vote?', *Dublin Review*, xiv. 403. 1885 (October 1885) 6/11/85
A charge delivered at the ordinary visitation of the archdeaconry of Chichester in July, 1841. 1841 22/8/41
A charge delivered at the ordinary visitation of the Archdeaconry of Chichester in July 1842. 1842 24/8/42
A charge delivered at the ordinary visitation of the archdeaconry of Chichester in July, 1843. 1843 31/7/43
A charge delivered at the ordinary visitation of the archdeaconry of Chichester in July, 1845. 1845 20/7/45
A charge delivered at the ordinary visitation of the archdeaconry of Chichester in July 1846. 1846 27/9/46
A charge delivered at the ordinary visitation of the archdeaconry of Chichester in July 1848. 1848 12/8/48
A letter to the... Archbishop of Armagh. 1873 21/9/73
A pastoral letter... Quinquagesima Sunday. 1868 22/2/68
Appendix to 'Sermon on rule of faith'. 1838 29/3/39
Caesarism and ultramontanism. 1874 25/1/74
Christ and Antichrist: a sermon at the Mass of Requiem for those who fell in defence of Rome. 1867 31/5/74
Essays on religion and literature. By various writers, ed. H. E. Manning. 1867 (2nd series) 22/5/67
Ireland. A letter to Earl Grey. 1868 14/3/68
Is the Education Act of 1870 a just law?. 1886 12/11/87 ?
Leo XIII and the condition of labour. 1891 2/8/91
Miscellanies. 1877 (3v. 1877–8) 9/12/88
Modern society: a pastoral for Lent. 1871 19/2/71
National education and parental rights. 1872 21/4/72
National education, a sermon preached... in behalf of the Chichester Central Schools. 1838 21/4/39
Omnia pro Christo. Oración fúnebre... de su Eminencia... N. Wiseman... traducido... por M. Dupont. 1865 5/3/65
Paris and London in Catholic union. A sermon. 1861 3/11/61
Penitents and saints. A sermon preached on behalf of the Magdalen Hospital. 1844 23/6/44 ?
Preface to new ed. of W. Beveridge, 'The great necessity and advantage of publick prayer and frequent communion'. 1840 20/9/40
Rome the capital of Christendom: a sermon. 1870 9/10/70
Sermon on rule of faith. 1838 24/3/39
Sermon preached at the funeral of the Countess of Gainsborough... 1867. 1867 1/12/67
Sermons. 1842 15/10/42
Sermons. 1843 (4v. 2nd edn) 12/3/43, 4/10/57, 29/9/72
Sermons on ecclesiastical subjects. 1863 22/11/63
Sermons preached before the University of Oxford. 1844 24/11/44
Sin and its consequences. 1874 1/3/74

Manning, Henry Edward (*cont.*)
Temporal sovereignty of the popes. Three lectures. 1860 28/4/61
That legitimate authority is an evidence of truth. A paper. 1872 16/5/72
The appellate jurisdiction of the Crown in matters spiritual. A letter to the . . . Bishop of Chichester. 1850 9/7/50
The blessed sacrament the centre of immutable truth: a sermon. 1864 30/6/64
The centenary of Saint Peter and the General Council: a pastoral letter to the clergy. 1867 29/9/67
The Convocation and the Crown in council: a second letter to an Anglican friend. 1864 21/8/64
The Crown in council on the Essays and Reviews: a letter to an Anglican friend. 1864 9/4/64
The daemon of Socrates. A paper. 1872 2/3/72
The dignity and rights of labour. A lecture. 1874 28/7/74
The divine glory of the sacred heart. 1873 30/11/73
The English Church, its succession and witness for Christ. A sermon . . . at the visitation. 1835 3/8/35
The fourfold sovereignty of God. 1871 10/9/71
The glory of the righteous. 1844 (1845) 28/12/45
The grounds of faith. Four lectures delivered in St. George's church, Southwark. 1852 19/12/52
The internal mission of the holy ghost. 1875 20/6/75
The last glories of the Holy See grander than the first. Three lectures, with a preface. 1861 15/9/61
The mind of Christ the perfection and bond of the Church. A sermon. 1841 25/12/41
The mission of St. Alphonsus: a sermon preached on his feast . . . at St. Mary's, Clapham. 1864 23/10/64
The moral design of the apostolic ministry. A sermon preached . . . at an ordination held by . . . bishop of Chichester. 1841 19/9/41
The objective certainty of the immaterial world. A paper read before the Metaphysical Society. 1879 9/1/81
The present crisis of the Holy See tested by prophecy. Four lectures. 1861 8/9/61
The preservation of unendowed Canonries. A letter to William . . . Bishop of Chichester. 1840 12/7/40
The principle of the Ecclesiastical Commission examined in a letter to the . . . Bishop of Chichester. 1838 28/9/37, 17/2/38
The reunion of Christendom. A pastoral letter to the clergy. 1866 25/2/66
The temporal mission of the holy ghost; or, reason and salvation. 1865 3/12/65
The temporal power of the pope in its political aspect. 1866 10/9/66
The temporal power of the vicar of Jesus Christ. 1862 24/7/64
The unity of the church. 1842 27/2/42, 21/7/78, 27/9/91
The Vatican Council and its definitions: a pastoral letter. 1870 27/11/70
The Vatican decrees in their bearing on civil allegiance. 1875 2/2/75
The working of the Education Act. 1886 12/11/87 ?
The workings of the holy spirit in the Church of England. A letter to . . . E. B. Pusey. 1864 29/12/64
Towards evening. 1889 28/12/89
Truth before peace; a sermon. 1865 1/1/65
What one work of mercy shall I do this Lent? A letter to a friend. 1847 7/3/47

Manning, Henry Edward and F. Meyrick
Moral theology of the Church of Rome. 1855 9/9/55

Manning, Robert
England's conversion and reformation compared. 1725 12/6/59

Manry, Sarah M.
The statesmen of America in 1846. 1847 29/7/47

Mansel, Henry Longueville
Man's conception of eternity: an examination of Mr. Maurice's theory of a fixed state out of time. 1854 23/4/54
Scenes from an unfinished drama, entitled Phrontisterion. 1852 (4th edn) 22/10/52
The limits of religious thought examined in eight lectures preached before the University of Oxford. 1858 24/10/58

Mansfield, Richard
Don Juan. 1891 31/8/92

Mansfield, William Rose
On the introduction of a gold currency into India. 1864 8/7/64

Manson, Richard Taylor
The synod of Streonshall, or Council of Whitby: a parenthesis of Anglican church history. 1888 15/7/88

Mant, Richard
A letter to . . . H. H. Milman . . . reputed author of A History of the Jews. 1830 8/5/64 ?
An appeal to the Gospel, etc . . . in a series of discourses [Bampton lectures]. 1812 25/10/29
History of the Church of Ireland, from the Reformation to [1801]. 1840 (2v.) 29/4/40, 14/3/69
Religio quotidiana: daily prayer the law of God's church. 1846 30/6/46
The Holy Bible, ed. R. Mant. 1814 (3v.) 14/1/26, 27/5/27, 24/6/27, 1/7/27,

29/7/27, 12/8/27, 7/10/27, 21/10/27, 27/10/27, 11/11/27, 25/11/27, 27/4/29, 21/6/29, 18/10/29, 8/11/29, 1/4/30, 4/4/30, 17/7/31
The laws of the church; the churchman's guard against Romanism and Puritanism. Two charges. 1842 17/4/43
Two tracts intended to convey correct notions of regeneration and conversion. 1817 20/7/28
Manual of the system of primary instruction pursued in the model schools of the British and Foreign School Society. 1831 29/5/38
Manuel des frères et soeurs du Tiers-Ordre de . . . St. Dominique, ed. H. D. Lacordaire. 1844 28/10/45
Manzoni, Alessandro
Adelchi. 1822 24/7/54
Adelchi. 1823 13/2/38
I promessi sposi. 1825 (1825–7) 12/8/34, 18/9/63
Il cinque maggio. 1840 6/2/88, 24/1/92
Inni sacri ed Odi. 1824 4/2/38
Osservazioni. 1834 2/5/35
Preface to 'Carmagnola'. 1820 5/2/38
Storia della colonna infame. 1842 23/11/43
Marbeau, Edouard
La Bosnie depuis l'occupation Austro-Hongroise. 1880 28/9/80
Slaves et Teutons. Notes et impressions de voyage. 1882 19/12/82
Marbot, Jean Baptiste Antoine Marcellin de
Mémoires. 1891 (3v.) 21/12/91
Marcellina
From foam of the sea, by S. Farina, tr. Marcellina. 1880 5/1/80
Marcet, Jane
Conversations on natural philosophy. 1824 7/5/28
Marcus Aurelius
Opera. 24/7/80, 22/9/81, 24/9/81
Maret, Henri Louis Charles
Le pape et les evêques, défense du livre sur le concile général et la paix religieuse. 1869 30/7/71
Margoliouth, Moses
The bane of a parasite ritual, a sermon on . . . the real presence and the recent judgment of the Privy Council. 1872 25/8/72
Mariage, Nouvelle physiologie du. 1866 14/9/81
Maria Harcourt. Novel. 1788 8/6/36
Maria Theresa and Marie Antoinette. 1865 9/9/79
Marie Louise, Empress
Correspondence of Marie Louise, wife of Napoleon I. 1887 24/3/87
Marii, Luigi
Dante e la libertà moderna. 1865 30/12/75 ?
Marini, Giovani Battista
Adone. 12/12/53, 21/9/78, 23/7/80
Markham, Sir Clements Robert
The threshold of the unknown region. 1873 26/1/74
Markham, Gervase
The famous whore, or noble curtizan. 1609 2/12/92
Markland, James Heywood
On the reverence due to holy places. 1845 14/1/47
Remarks on the sepulchral memorials of past and present times. 1840 17/12/46
Markley, John T.
Songs of humanity and progress; a collection of lyrics contributed to various publications. 1882 22/8/90
Markoras, Georgios
All'articolo del Drs. G. B. Scandella, su l'enciclica di Pio IX. 1853 23/1/59
Chrysostom's liturgy, tr. G. Markoras. 6/2/59
Risposta all'articolo della Civiltà Cattolica. 1854 23/1/59
Marlowe, Christopher
Opera. 15/11/55, 27/1/90
The tragicall history of the life and death of Doctor Faustus. 11/1/49
Marnan, B.
The resident magistrate. 1889 1/11/89
Maroncelli, Pietro
Addizioni alle mie prigioni. 1833 19/3/34
Marr, Wilhelm
Der Sieg des Judenthums über das Germanenthum, etc. 1879 10/3/79
Marriage of near kin. 1773 (not found) 16/9/61
Marriage with a deceased wife's sister, etc. By a member of the University of Oxford. 1858 16/9/64
Marriott, Charles Vicar
A lecture delivered at the diocesan college, Chichester, at the opening of Lent Term. 1840 1/3/40
Five sermons on the principles of faith and church authority. 1850 18/12/64
Marriott, Fitzherbert Adams
Is a penal colony reconcilable with God's constitution of human society and the laws of Christ's kingdom? A letter to Sir W. T. Denison. 1847 14/3/48
Marriott, Wharton Booth
The testimony of the catacombs and of other monuments of Christian art, from the 2nd to the 18th century. 1870 5/6/70
Vestiarium Christianum. The origin and gradual development of the dress of the holy ministry. 1868 28/6/68
Marriott, William Thackeray
The Liberal Party and Mr. Chamberlain. 1883 24/12/83
Marryat, Florence
Diary in America. 1839 8/7/39

Marryat, Florence (*cont.*)
Jacob Faithful. 1834 26/10/64
Newton Forster. 1832 10/12/32 ?
Marryat, Joseph of Swansea
A history of pottery and porcelain, medieval and modern. 1857 2/7/57
Collections toward a history of pottery. 1850 18/11/59
Marsden, John Buxton
Influence of the Mosaic code. 1862 11/9/88
The history of the early Puritans: from the Reformation to the opening of the Civil War in 1642. 1850 10/12/54
The history of the later Puritans: from the opening of the Civil War in 1642 to ... 1662. 1852 10/12/54
Marsden, John Howard
Two introductory lectures upon archaeology, delivered in the University of Cambridge. 1852 18/6/72
Marsh, Catherine M.
From dark to dawn, or the story of W. Roland. 1873 12/1/73
Memorials of Captain Hedley Vicars. 1856 18/4/58
Shining light. 1869 23/5/69
The life of the Rev. W. Marsh. 1867 5/1/68
The rift in the clouds. 1871 8/11/91
Marsh, Edward Garrard
The Christian doctrine of sanctification, in eight sermons ... [Bampton lectures 1848]. 1848 27/8/48
Marsh, George Perkins
The origin and history of the English language and of the early literature it embodies. 1862 18/7/70
Marsh, Herbert
A comparative view of the churches of England and Rome. 1814 27/10/61
Horae Pelasgicae ... inquiry into the origin and language of the Pelasgi, or ancient inhabitants of Greece. 1815 23/6/56
Marsh, John B.
Hops and hopping. 1892 5/8/93
Marsh, Leonard
The shadow of Christianity, or the genesis of the Christian state. 1866 22/7/66 ?
Marsh, William Nathaniel Tilson
The church and state; or, a brief apology for the Church of England, in her connexion with the state. 1849 24/4/49
Marshall, Arthur F. pseud. Archdeacon Chasuble
The comedy of convocation. 1867 15/5/69
Marshall, Charles
The Latin prayer-book of Charles II. 1882 14/10/83
Marshall, James M.A.
Memoir of the Rev. J. Marshall, by his son, J. Marshall. 1856 30/10/56
Marshall, John Chief Justice
The life of George Washington. 1804 (5v. 1804–7) 15/9/48, 11/8/82
Marshall, Thomas William M.
Notes on the episcopal policy of the holy Catholic church ... development of the modern religious systems. 1844 25/9/59
Marshall, William
The art of reading church music ... the practice of choral psalmody. 1842 12/9/45
Marston, Charles Dallas
The position of the laity in the church. 1868 25/12/68
Martel, Michel
Martel's Elements, containing new essays on education. 1796 23/9/61 ?
Martens, Carl von Baron
Guide diplomatique. 1832 6/2/56
Martens, Thedor Thedorovich
Das Consularwesen und die Consularjurisdiction im Orient. 1874 27/7/77
La question égyptienne et le droit international. 1882 1/1/83
Martensen, Hans Lassen
Christian dogmatics. A compendium of the doctrines of Christianity, tr. W. Urwick. 1865 13/2/76
Martial
Opera. 2/11/25
Martin, Arthur Patchett
Life and letters of Robert Lowe, Viscount Sherbrooke. 1893 (2v.) 22/5/93
Martin, Bon Louis Henri
Daniel Manin, and Venice in 1848–49 ... [tr. from French with an introduction by L. Butt]. 1862 (2v.) 9/12/62, 3/2/73
Martin, Edward Sandford
A little brother of the rich and other poems. 1888 7/9/91 ?
Martin, Félix
Les cimetières et crémation; étude historique et critique. 1881 19/6/84
Martin, Frances
Angelique Arnauld, Abbess of Port Royal. 1873 27/4/73
Elizabeth Gilbert and her work for the blind. 1887 8/11/87
Martin, Lady Helena
On Ophelia and Portia. 1880 1/4/81
Martin, J.
Prüfet die Geister. Predigte. 1845 19/10/45
Martin, Jean Pierre Paulin
'What hinders the ritualists from becoming Roman Catholics?' in *Contemporary Review*, xxxiii. 113. 1878 (August 1878) 4/8/78
'What hinders the ritualists ... a rejoinder' in *Contemporary Review*, xxxiv. 77. 1878 (December 1878) 8/12/78

Anglican-Ritualism as seen by a Catholic and foreigner. A series of essays . . . on the present position of the church in France. 1880 30/11/80

Martin, Leopold Charles
Swansea and Gower, with the Mumbles and adjacent bays: a guidebook and handbook. 1879 3/6/87

Martin, Robert Montgomery
Ireland before and after the union with Great Britain. 1843 13/11/43
Railways—past, present, and prospective. 1849 9/2/49
The British Colonial Library. 1836 (10v. 1836–7) 6/5/37
The Hudson's Bay territories and Vancouver's island; with an exposition of . . . rights, conduct and policy. 1849 27/12/48
The sugar question in relation to free trade and protection. 1848 1/7/48

Martin, Sir Theodore
A life of Lord Lyndhurst, from letters and papers in possession of his family. 1883 31/8/83, 4/12/83, 9/12/83, 2/1/84
Essays on the drama. 1874 (2v.) 1/5/75
Goethe's Faust, translated into English verse. 1865 8/8/63
Notes on the present system of private bill legislation. 1872 7/6/72
The life of His Royal Highness the Prince Consort . . . With portraits and views. 1875 (5v. 1875–80) 21/12/74, 6/11/76, 29/4/79
The Odes of Horace. 1860 13/2/60
The poems of Catullus . . . translated into English verse. 1861 24/5/61, 6/1/76

Martin, Thomas of Dublin
The true solution of the Irish question by measures which are shown to be indispensable. 1868 24/6/68

Martin, William
Memorandum on the reconstruction of the Bengal army. 1857 8/10/57 ?

Martin, William Todd
The doctrine of an impersonal God in its effects on morality and religion. 1875 26/3/75

Martineau, Arthur
No need of a living infallible guide. 1851 16/3/51

Martineau, Harriet
'Demerara' from *Illustrations of Political economy* 1832 14/1/48
'For each and for all' from *Illustrations of political economy* 13/1/48
Autobiography. With memorials by M. W. Chapman. 1877 13/3/77, 7/4/77, 1/11/85
Deerbrook. A novel. 1839 (3v.) 13/8/42
Eastern life, present and past. 1848 (3v.) 23/11/49
Illustrations of political economy no. 1. 1832 2/2/33
Illustrations of political economy no. 9. 1832 4/2/33
Retrospect of western travel. 1838 (3v.) 18/8/42
Society in America. 1837 (3v.) 23/5/37

Martineau, Harriet, and Atkinson, H. G.
Letters on the laws of man's nature and development. 1851 6/8/90

Martineau, James
'Expansion of the Church of England' in *Contemporary Review,* i. 6. 1886 (July 1886) 18/7/86
A word for scientific theology in appeal from the men of science and the theologians. An address. 1868 7/6/74
Church life? or sect life? The Unitarian position. A letter addressed to the Rev. S. F. Macdonald. 1859 16/6/67
Endeavours after the Christian life. 1843 (2v. 1843–7) 12/1/79
Modern materialism: its attitude towards theology. A critique and defence . . . From the Contemporary Review. 1876 18/5/76
Religion as affected by modern materialism: an address. 1874 6/12/74
The God of the living. 1864 8/1/65
The national church as a federal union. 1887 8/4/87
The pretensions of the Roman Catholic church . . . reprinted from 'Old and New'. 1872 12/2/75 ?
The transient and the permanent in theology. An address. 1862 18/12/62

Martinez, Col.
[On Italian unity]. (not found) 13/8/62

Martyn, Henry
Controversial tracts on Christianity and Mohammedanism. 1824 11/7/60
Memoir [by J. Sargent]. 1819 8/4/27

Martyn, John
P. Virgilii Maronis Bucolicorum Eclogae decem. The Bucolicks of Virgil, with an English tr. and notes. 1749 28/1/26 ?
P. Virgilii Maronis Georgicorum libri quatuor. The Georgicks of Virgil, with an English tr. and notes. 1741 16/2/26

Marum, Edward Purcell Mulhallen
A vindication of the pope and the Catholic religion: being a reply to . . . W. E. Gladstone [Vatican Decrees]. 1874 11/12/74

Marx, Jacob
Histoire de la robe de Jésus-Christ conservée dans la cathédrale de Trèves. 1844 (2v.) 18/10/47

Marx, Karl
Karl Marx. Eine Studie, by G. Gross. 1885 14/1/85 ?

Marzo, Antonio Gualberto de
La croce bianca in campo rosso vaticinata nella Divina Commedia pel risorgimento d'Italia. 1885 25/1/88

Masers de Latude, Jean Henri
Memoirs . . . during a confinement of thirty-five years in the state prisons of France. 1787 17/2/88

Masheder, Richard
The right honourable W. E. Gladstone: a political review. 1865 19/1/66, 21/6/66 ?

Maskell, William
A dissertation upon the ancient service books of the Church of England. 1846 25/10/46
A first letter on the present position of the High Church party. 1850 23/2/50
Sermons. 1849 7/10/49
The ancient liturgy of the Church of England . . . uses of Sarum, Bangor, York and Hereford, and the modern Roman liturgy. 1844 20/9/46
The outward means of grace. A sermon. 1849 29/10/48

Mason, Arthur James
The faith of the gospel: a manual of Christian doctrine. 1892 12/6/92

Mason, Ernest
Womanhood in the God-man. 1891 18/10/91

Mason, Thomas Monck
Creation by the immediate agency of God, as opposed to . . . natural law . . . a refutation of [Chambers' 'Vestiges of the Natural History of Creation']. 1845 6/6/80

Mason, William
Elfrida, a dramatic poem, written on the model of antient Greek tragedy. 1772 4/3/80

Massari, Giuseppe
Garanzie per la libertà della chiesa. 1871 2/4/71
I casi di Napoli dal 29 gennaio 1848 in poi. Lettere politiche. 1849 21/2/51
Il conte di Cavour. 1873 12/12/73
Il signor Gladstone ed il governo Napolitano; raccolta di scritti intorno alla questione Napolitana. 1851 9/10/51
La vita ed il regno di Vittorio Emanuele II di Savoia, primo re d'Italia. 1878 (2v.) 28/7/78

Massey, Gerald
In memory of John William Spencer, Earl Brownlow. 1869 26/6/70
The Hebrew and other creations fundamentally explained. A lecture . . . With a reply to . . . A. H. Sayce, etc. 1887 8/11/87

Massey, William Nathaniel
A history of England during the reign of George the third. 1855 (4v. 1855–63) 23/7/55, 11/3/64, 20/4/90

Massillon, M.
Pensées. 1749 10/4/41

Massingberd, Francis Charles
The English reformation. 1842 18/8/50
The law of the church and the law of the state. 1859 14/7/59

Massinger, Philip
The city madam. 17/7/26
The Duke of Millaine. A tragaedie. 11/7/27
The excellent comedy called the Old law, or a new way to please you. 17/7/26, 29/5/27
The fatall dowry: a tragedy. 1/7/26
The great duke of Florence. A comicall historie. 16/6/27
The maid of honour. 5/7/26
The parliament of love. 18/6/27
The plays of Philip Massinger . . . with notes . . . by W. Gifford. 1813 19/7/27
The Renegado, a tragaecomedie. 21/6/27
The Roman actor; a tragaedie. 23/6/27
The unnaturall combat. A tragedie. 18/7/27

Massinger, Philip, and Decker, Thomas
The virgin martyr. 17/7/27, 22/8/33

Massini, Carlo
Vita della santissima vergine Maria, madre di Dio. 1788 7/9/51

Masson, David
The life of John Milton; narrated in connexion with the political, ecclesiastical, and literary history of his time. 1859 19/5/71

Masson, Edward
An apology for the Greek church; or hints . . . promoting the religious improvement of the Greek nation, ed. J. S. Howson. 1844 28/11/44

Masson, Frédéric
Napoleon at home. 1894 (2v.) 13/1/94
Napoleon: lover and husband. 1894 8/2/94

Master of Arts
The fiscal discrimination of the sugar duties condemned on the principles of free trade. 1864 3/2/64

Mather, James
Ships and railways. 1846 26/3/47

Matheson, George
Growth of the spirit of Christianity from the first century to the dawn of the Lutheran era. 1877 (2v.) 16/11/77

Matheson, G. F.
[on the mint]. (not found) 24/2/49
How can the church educate the people?. 1844 20/5/44

Matheson, James D.D.
A narrative of the visit to the American churches. 1835 (2v.) 1/5/36
Voluntary churches the true churches of Christ . . . discourse delivered at the ordination of . . . S. Binks. 1829 12/4/37

Matheson, Sir James
The present position and prospects of the British trade with China . . . an outline of . . . its past history. 1836 28/3/36

Mathews, S.
Men, places and things. 1887 26/6/87
Mathews, Sir William
The great conversers, and other essays. 1874 7/8/74
Mathias, F. W.
The conquest of the world by the Jews. An... essay, revised and tr. 1878 17/10/78 n, 20/10/78
Mathias, G. H. D.
English B.A.'s and Prussian Freshmen. A comparison of the matriculation examinations of the universities of the two countries. 1868 21/2/68
Mathias, Thomas James
The pursuits of literature, or What you will: a satirical poem, in dialogue. 1794 24/1/27
Mativet, M.
La nouvelle Cythère. 1888 30/4/88
Matson, Henry James
Remarks on the slave trade and African squadron. 1848 21/7/48
Matthews, Henry
The diary of an invalid; being the journal of a tour ... in Portugal, Italy, Switzerland and France ... 1817-1819. 1820 9/3/32
Maud, John
The doctrine of endless torments... debated. 1755 22/6/74
Maude, Thomas
The invitation, or urbanity: a poem. For the benefit of a Sunday-school. 1791 20/6/69
Maule, Sir William Henry
Memoir of the early life... etc., ed. E. Leathley. 1872 19/6/72
Maundrell, Henry
A journey from Aleppo to Jerusalem. 1703 22/4/30
Maupassant, Guy de
Pierre et Jean. 1888 28/9/90
Maurel, Jules
Le duc de Wellington. 1853 18/5/53
Maurette, Jean Jacques
Farewell to the pope! or motives of separation from the church of Rome, tr. by P. Fraser. 1846 10/10/46
Mauri, Achille
Opere del Cardinale S. Pallavicino. 1834 4/12/49
Maurice, Sir John Frederick K. C. B.
The balance of military power in Europe. An examination of the war resources of Great Britain. 1888 30/4/88
The life of F. D. Maurice... chiefly told in his own letters. 1884 19/3/84, 2/4/84
Maurice, John Frederick Denison
[ms. on state religion]. 1838 3/2/38
Educational Magazine, n.s., ed. J. F. D. Maurice. 1840 (4v. 1840-1) 9/1/40
Eustace Conway: or, the brother and sister. A novel. 1834 1/5/34, 4/6/35
Has the church, or the state, the power to educate the nation? A course of lectures. 1839 5/5/39, 22/1/40
Letter on the attempt to defeat the nomination of Dr. Hampden. 1847 11/12/47
Reasons for not joining a party in the church. A letter to... S. Wilberforce. 1841 28/4/41
Sermons on the Sabbath-day; on the character of the warrior; and on the interpretation of history. 1853 9/1/53
The claims of the bible and of science. Correspondence... on... controversy respecting the Pentateuch. 1863 11/10/63
The Kingdom of Christ; or, hints on the principles, ordinances, and constitution of the Catholic church... in letters to... the Society of Friends. 1837 5/3/37
The kingdom of Christ; or, hints on the principles, ordinances, and constitution of the Catholic church... in letters to... the Society of Friends. 1842 (2nd edn) 16/4/43
The new statute and Mr. Ward. A letter to a non-resident member of Convocation. 1845 26/1/45
The religions of the world, and their relation to Christianity... in eight [Boyle] lectures. 1847 22/9/67
The responsibilities of medical students. A sermon. 1838 29/4/38
Theological essays. 1853 17/9/76
Thoughts on the duty of a Protestant in the present Oxford election. 1847 26/7/47
Three letters to the Rev. W. Palmer... on the name 'Protestant'. 1842 (2nd edn) 16/1/40, 17/8/43
What is revelation? A series of sermons on the epiphany. 1859 4/12/59
Maurice, Thomas
A dissertation on the Oriental Trinities, extracted from... 'Indian Antiquities'. 1800 21/12/36
Indian antiquities: or, dissertations relative to the ancient geographical divisions. 1793 (7v. 1793-1800) 25/12/84
Maury, Louis Ferdinand Alfred
Croyances et légendes de l'antiquité. Essais de critique. 1863 28/6/63, 28/9/92
Histoire des religions de la Grèce antique depuis leur origine jusqu'à leur complète constitution. 1857 (3v.) 13/3/58
Maxwell, David
The vision of the world: a forecast of the future. 1890 7/4/90
Maxwell, E. B.
Bishop's conversion. 1892 27/11/92
Maxwell, Sir Herbert Eustace
Life and times of W. H. Smith. 1893 (2v.) 8/9/93

Maxwell, Sir P. B.
Malay conquests. 1878 4/9/78
Maxwell, Perriton
Whom shall we hang? The Sebastopol inquiry. 1855 18/7/55
May, Thomas
A breviary of the history of the parliament of England. 21/8/32, 21/6/80
Solar-life, the desire of all; or, How to live a happy life for ever. 13/11/87
May, Thomas Erskine Baron Farnborough
A treatise upon the law, privileges, proceedings and usage of parliament. 1844 2/11/71
Democracy in Europe: a history. 1877 (2v.) 14/11/77
Remarks and suggestions with a view to facilitate the dispatch of public business in Parliament. 1849 15/2/49
The constitutional history of England. 1861 (2v.) 26/1/61, 27/2/63
Mayer, Isaac
Source of inspiration. 1879 17/9/88 ?
Mayer, Joseph
Address to the members of the Historic Society of Lancashire and Cheshire. 1867 10/5/67
Mayhew, Henry
London labour and the London poor. 1851 (2v.) 6/12/51
Maynard, Michel Ulysse
Voltaire, sa vie et ses oeuvres. 1867 (2v.) 6/6/68
Maynooth
Maynooth, endowment vindicated. 1845 20/5/45
Maynooth, pamphlet on. 1836 20/1/36
Maynooth, the crown and the country. 1845 5/4/45
Mayor, Joseph B.
'The restitution of all things' in *Contemporary Review*, xxvi. 886. 1876 (May 1876) 16/5/76
Mayow, Joannes
A tract of the disease rhachitis, commonly called the rickets, etc... Together with a method of cure. 13/8/54
Mayow, Mayow Wynell
A reply to a memorial on the subject of ritual. 1872 25/12/72
A second letter to... W. Maskell... Some thoughts on the position of the Church of England. 1850 28/8/50
Eight sermons on the priesthood, altar and sacrifice. 1867 31/3/67
Mazzini, Giuseppe
A Pio IX... lettera. 1847 22/7/49
Italy, Austria and the pope. A letter to Sir James Graham, Bart. 1845 14/7/48 ?
Scritti politici. 1848 (1848–9) 21/8/51
To Louis Napoleon. 1858 8/4/58
Mazzuchelli, G. M.
Vita di Pietro Aretino. 1830 12/3/88
M. C.
Light on the path. 1885 3/4/87
McCombie, W.
The Irish land question... in a letter to... Gladstone. 1869 22/9/69
McComb's Presbyterian Almanac. Irish taxation 12/6/1883
McGuire, Judith White
Diary of a Southern refugee, during the war. By a lady of Virginia. 1868 5/4/90
McKay, Nathaniel
Free-trade toilers. 1888 10/12/88 ?
Starvation wages for men and women. 1888 10/12/88 ?
McLaren, Duncan
One year's experience of the new public-house act in Edinburgh. 1855 30/3/60
The life and works of D. McLaren, by J. B. Mackie. 1888 (2v.) 1/5/89
McLean, John
Twenty-five years in Hudson's Bay. 1849 (2v.) 14/6/50
McNeil, John
Sermons. 1890 (3v. 1890–91) 15/2/91
McNeile, Hugh
Discrimination in doctrine. 1834 18/2/34
Lectures on the Church of England. 1840 10/3/40
Letters to a friend, who has felt it his duty to secede from the Church of England. 1834 9/5/34
Popery theological. Another challenge! Reply... to the Rev. J. Siddon. 1829 21/3/30
Mead, Henry
The Sepoy revolt: its causes and its consequences. 1857 24/4/58
Meade, Herbert
A ride through... New Zealand... selections from... journals and letters. 1870 7/7/75
Meade, Joseph Fulton
The Athanasian Creed and legislation... Synod of the Church of Ireland. 1875 23/5/75
Meade, Lillie Thomas afterw. Smith
The medicine lady. 1892 (3v. 1892–3) 2/1/93
Meale, G.
Moderna Inghilterra. 1888 23/7/88
Mearns, Andrew
The bitter cry of outcast London. An inquiry into the condition of the abject poor. 1883 3/11/83
Meason, Malcolm Ronald Laing
The bubbles of finance: joint-stock companies... modern commerce, money lending, and life insuring. 1865 29/9/66
The profits of panics: showing how financial storms arise. 1866 29/9/66
Medd, Peter Goldsmith
Diligence in prayer. A sermon. 1878 25/9/81
The one mediator: the operation of the son of God in nature and in grace. Eight lectures. 1884 17/2/84

Medici, Lorenzo de' the elder
Poesie del magnifico Lorenzo de' Medici, ed. L. Nardini and S. Buonajuti. 1801 (2v. 1801) 22/9/57
Poesie . . . tratte da testi a penna della libreria Mediceo-Laurenziana, ed. W. Roscoe. 1791 8/5/94 ?
Medina-Pomar, Duke de
Fashion and passion; or, life in Mayfair. 1876 (3v. 1876) 30/9/76
The heir to the crown. A drama. 1877 18/5/77
Medley, John Bishop of Fredericton
A charge delivered to the clergy of the diocese of Fredericton . . . July 3, 1877. 1877 18/11/77
A charge to the clergy of the diocese . . . delivered . . . June 30, 1868. 1868 27/9/68
A charge to the clergy of the diocese . . . with the sermon. 1854 22/1/54
A sermon preached before the provincial synod of Canada. 1877 18/11/77
Sermons. 1845 29/3/46
Medlycott, J. T.
The church and her assailants. A lecture. 1868 16/2/68
Meek, Robert
Reasons for attachment and conformity to the Church of England. 1831 19/8/32
Meester De Ravestein, Émile de
À propos de certaines classifications préhistoriques. 1875 5/4/79
Meiklejohn, John Miller Dow
Life and letters of W. B. Hodgson, ed. J. M. D. Meiklejohn. 1883 21/1/86
Melancthon, Philipp
The confession of Augsburg. 14/11/41
Mélito, Count André François Miot de
Mémoires. 1880 (3v.) 19/8/80
Mellor, Enoch
Priesthood in the light of the New Testament . . . Lecture for 1876. The Congregational Union lecture. 1876 14/5/76
The searcher searched: or, H. Carpenter confronted with the truth. 1862 29/7/62
Melly, George
Lecture to the working class. 1865 13/1/65
Melmoth, William the elder
The great importance of a religious life considered. 1711 (1812 edn) 14/3/92
Melvill, Henry
A selection from the lectures delivered at St. Margaret's, Lothbury. 1853 26/11/54
Protestantism and popery. 1839 14/4/39
Melville, David
A practical question about Oxford, considered in a letter to . . . Gladstone. 1850 22/9/50
Religious instruction in School Board schools. 1871 13/11/71
Melville, Herman
Narrative of a four months' residence among the natives of a valley of the Marquesas islands, or a peep at Polynesian life. 1846 2/3/46
Omoo: a narrative of adventures in the South Seas. 1847 4/10/47
Melville, Montagu Robert
Reform, not subversion! A proposed Book of Common Prayer. 1834 12/4/57
Member of the British legislature, A
The interest of Europe in the conditions of peace. 1870 5/11/70
Memnon, pseud.
The 'Edinburgh Review' and the Suez canal. 1876 28/2/76
Mémoires historiques sur la Corse . . . 1774–1777. 1889 22/1/77
Memoirs of the City of Salisbury. 1851 30/1/62
Memorandum on the Danish-German question. 1864 13/2/64
Memorial of a meeting of the elders . . . to Sir Robert Peel. 1843 7/3/43
Memorial . . . to Sir Robert Peel, by Ministers of the Church of Scotland. 1842 7/3/43
Menander
Menander fragments. 3/8/63
Ménant, Joachim
Rapport . . . sur les inscriptions Assyriennes du British Museum. 1862 24/3/74
Mence, Richard
The mutual rights of husband and wife . . . draft of a bill. 1838 1/5/39
Menken, Gottfried
Selections from the Discourses of, tr. from the German by T. Jackson. 1834 12/10/72 ?
Menzies, Allan
Report to the trustees of the bequest of . . . J. Dick . . . for the benefit of . . . Schoolmasters. 1835 26/12/35
Mercer, L. P.
The little ones. The Lord's care for them here and hereafter. 1882 18/8/82
Mercy-Argenteau, Count Florimond Claude de
Correspondance secrète du Comte . . . avec l'Empereur Joseph II et le Prince de Kaunitz. 1835 (1874 edn) 23/4/83, 4/7/83, 21/8/83
Meredith, George
Diana of the crossways. 1885 18/8/91, 20/8/91
Merewether, Francis
The ministerial succession. A sermon preached at Broadstairs . . . October 7th, 1838. 1839 25/12/39
Merewether, Henry Alworth
A sermon . . . and a short memoir of John Neilson Gladstone. 1863 29/3/63
Merewether, Henry Alworth, and Stephens, Archibald J.
The history of the boroughs and municipal corporations of the United Kingdom. 1835 (3v.) 9/2/35

Merewether, John
A charge. 1844 9/6/44
Mérimée, Prosper
An author's love . . . the unpublished letters of . . . 'Inconnue'. 1889 (2v.) 6/4/89
Lettres à M. Panizzi, 1850–1870. Publiées par M. Louis Fagan. 1880 (3v.) 2/3/81
Lettres à une inconnue . . . Précédées d'une Etude . . . par H. Taine. 1874 (2v.) 8/4/89
Merit v. patronage: or the present position of the question of civil service competitions. 1858 17/5/58
Merivale, Charles
A history of the Romans under the Empire. 1850 (8v. 1850–62) 4/7/61, 20/2/63
Merivale, Herman
'Joseph the Second' in *Historical Studies*. 1865 10/3/65
Lectures on colonization and colonies delivered before the university of Oxford in 1839, 1840 . . . 1841. 1841 (2v.) 9/11/42, 6/4/43
The character of Socrates, as drawn by Xenophon and Plato . . . a prize essay, read . . . June 23, 1830. 1830 12/12/30, 18/12/30
Merlin, Countess Mercédès
Memoirs of Madame Malibran by the Countess . . . and other intimate friends. 1840 (2v.) 24/2/40
Merriman, Nathaniel James
The Kafir, the Hottentot, and the frontier farmer. 1854 25/12/53
Merritt, Henry pseud. R. Dalby
Dirt and pictures separated in the works of the old masters. 1854 30/3/58
Robert Dalby and his world of troubles. 1865 8/1/66
Merry England. 14. 159, 235. 1/1890. Gladstone on *Ellen Middleton* 29/12/1889
Merryweather, F. Somner
Bibliomania in the middle ages. 1849 17/11/87
Meschin, Thomas de
The Lord Chancellor and the Edmunds enquiry. 1865 20/12/65
Meslier, Jean
Le bon sens du curé J. Meslier. 1822 24/12/94
Meteyard, Eliza
A group of Englishmen . . . being records of the younger Wedgwoods and their friends. 1871 26/10/71
The life of Josiah Wedgwood from his private correspondence and family papers. 1865 (2v.) 21/4/65, 25/7/65
Methodism as it is. 21/10/46
Metropolitan Churches Fund report. 1854 22/1/54
Metropolitan Police Court jottings. By a magistrate. 1882 1/4/82
Metropolitan Visiting Association Report. 1844 18/12/44
Metropolitan Visiting Association Report. 1845 19/12/45
Metternich, Prince Clemens Wenzeslaus Nepomuk Lothar von
Memoirs. 1880 (1880–82) 5/5/80
Meves, William Augustus
The 'Prisoner of the temple', an introductory account of the life of Louis Charles de Bourbon. 1860 17/6/60
Meynell, H.
Canon Woodard's scheme for the education of the middle classes. 5/1/68
Meynell, William pseud. J. Oldcastle
Cardinal Newman: a monograph. 1883 13/10/85
The cardinal archbishop of Westminster. 1886 27/5/86
Meyrick, Frederick
Baptism; regeneration; conversion, ed. F. Meyrick. 1884 27/6/84
Correspondence between members of the Anglo-Continental Society and Old Catholics, ed. F. Meyrick. 1874 (1874–77) 11/10/74
Correspondence between the . . . Friends of Spiritual Enlightenment and the Anglo-Continental Society . . . on . . . Anglican orders, ed. F. Meyrick. 1875 2/8/75
Isaaci Casauboni ad epistolam . . . Cardinalis Perronij responsio, ed. F. Meyrick. 1875 16/9/75
Jehovah or Baal? A sermon preached before the university of Oxford. 1865 27/12/65
On Dr. Newman's rejection of Liguori's doctrine of equivocation. 1864 7/4/64
The outcast and the poor of London . . . sermons preached at the Chapel Royal, Whitehall. 1858 27/6/58
The practical working of the church of Spain. 1851 20/1/52
Two sermons preached before the university of Oxford. 1854 4/12/54
What is the working of the church of Spain? What is implied in submitting to Rome?. 1851 18/5/51
Meyrick, Frederick and Manning, H. E.
Moral and devotional theology of the church of Rome, according to . . . S. Alfonso de' Liguori. 1855 9/9/55
Miall, Edward
The church and state question. 1848 6/4/48
The church property question . . . two lectures delivered in . . . Bristol, February 8th and 10th, 1860. 1868 12/4/68
Michael, Emil
Ignaz von Döllinger. Eine Characteristik . . . 1892 13/9/92, 19/9/92
Michaelis, Johann David
Raisonnement über die protestantischen Universitäten in Deutschland. 1768 (4v. 1768–76) 10/1/73

Michaud, Eugène
Comment l'église romaine n'est pas l'église catholique. 1872 7/4/72
De l'état présent de l'Eglise Catholique-Romaine en France. 1875 21/4/75
La théologie et le temps présent. 1893 3/1/93
Programme de réforme de l'église d'Occident proposé aux anciens Catholiques et aux autres communions chrétiennes. 1872 25/2/72
Michaud, Louis Gabriel
Biographie universelle ancienne et moderne. 1843 (1843–65) 6/12/62
Michel, Francisque
Les Ecossais en France. Les Français en Ecosse. 1862 17/7/62, 6/7/92
Michelet, Jules
Du prêtre, de la femme, de la famille. 1845 16/4/45
Guerres de religion 1547–72. (various edns.) 24/8/84 ?
Histoire de France. 1833 (15v. 1833–65) 23/6/66
Michell, Richard
The nature and comparative value of the Christian evidences considered generally, in eight sermons. 1849 17/2/50
Michelsen, Edward Henry
The Ottoman empire and its resources. 1853 16/9/58
Michiels, Joseph Alfred Xavier
Secret history of the Austrian government and of its systematic persecutions of Protestants. 1859 20/10/59
Michon, Jean Hippolyte
Le Maudit. 1864 (3v.) 24/8/65
Mickiewicz, Ladislas
Adam Mickiewicz. 1888 28/8/88 ?
Middleton, Conyers
Cicero. 1741 11/8/25, 26/3/29
Middleton, Thomas Fanshaw
The doctrine of the Greek article; applied to the criticism and the illustration of the new testament. 1808 28/6/57
Midnight thoughts. 1862 31/8/79
Mignet, François Auguste Marie
Charles Quint: son abdication, son séjour et sa mort au monastère de Yuste. 1854 30/9/54
Histoire de Marie Stuart. 1851 (2v.) 20/9/53
History of the French revolution from 1789 to 1814. 1824 (2v.) 29/5/34
Notice historique sur la vie et les travaux de M. Hallam. 1861 18/2/62
Mijatovic, Count Cedomilj
Constantine, the last emperor of the Greeks. 1892 18/4/92
Miles, Charles Popham
An address to the members of St. Jude's congregation, Glasgow. 1844 21/1/45
Further disclosures of Scottish episcopacy: a third address to the members of St. Jude's... Glasgow. 1844 22/1/45
Memoir of F. L. MacKenzie. 1857 13/12/63
Reply to Bishop Russell: a second address to the members of St. Jude's congregation, Glasgow. 1844 22/1/45
Miles, Ellen E.
Our home beyond the tide, and kindred poems. 1878 21/6/90
Miles, Pliny
The social, political, and commercial advantages of direct steam navigation... via Galway, Ireland. 1858 25/6/59
Military officer, A
The crisis of India. 1857 10/11/57
Mill, J.
Apology of Socrates. 1775 22/11/30, 28/11/30
Mill, James
Elements of political economy. 1821 27/6/42
James Mill, by A. Bain. 1882 21/9/84
The history of British India. 1818 (4v.) 29/4/58
Mill, John M.D.
The Ottomans in Europe; or, Turkey in the present crisis with the Secret Societies' maps. 1876 18/2/77
Mill, John Stuart
Autobiography. 1873 4/7/73
Chapters and speeches on the Irish land question. 1870 17/5/71
Considerations on representative government. 1861 16/4/61, 25/6/61, 26/4/86
Dissertations and discussions. 1859 (4v. 1859–75) 5/7/59, 22/5/67, 3/10/67, 4/2/68
Inaugural address delivered to the University of St. Andrew's, Feb. 1st, 1867. 1867 4/2/67
J. S. Mill, as some of the working classes knew him, by G. J. Holyoake. 1873 4/7/73
On liberty. 1859 10/3/59, 15/5/59, 28/5/59, 5/8/65, 19/4/66
On the autobiography of J. S. Mill, by E.R. Russell. 1874 25/5/74
Personal representation. Speech... delivered in the House of Commons. 1867 23/5/67
Principles of political economy. 1848 7/1/53, 10/12/59, 19/4/66, 11/8/66, 13/8/66
Principles of toleration. 1837 10/12/39
The life of J. S. Mill, by W. L. Courtney. 1889 13/4/89
The subjection of women. 1869 2/6/69
Thoughts on parliamentary reform. 1859 22/3/59
Mill, William Hodge
A letter to a clergyman in London on... Hampden's Bampton lectures. 1848 12/2/48

Human policy and divine truth. A sermon, preached... before the university of Cambridge. 1850 21/4/50
The priest's commission for remitting and retaining sins. A sermon. 1843 7/5/43

Millar, Alexander Hastie
The story of Rob Roy. 1883 27/9/83

Miller, Charles
The duty of a Conservative government towards the clergy... considered, in a letter to... Gladstone. 1841 30/9/41

Miller, Edward of New College, Oxford
The church in relation to the state. 1880 30/5/80
The future effects of the Folkestone judgment [Risdale v. Clifton & others]: a letter. 1877 5/8/77
Unscientific criticism... new teaching concerning the books of the old testament: a letter to... Liddon. 1890 22/3/90

Miller, George D.D.
A letter to... E. B. Pusey... in reference to his letter to the Lord Bishop of Oxford. 1840 1/2/41
The present crisis of the Church of England considered. 1845 9/1/45, 17/1/79
The Queen v. Millis. Writ of error. Notes on the opinions of... Lord Brougham and Vaux and Lord Campbell. 1844 23/1/44

Miller, Hugh the elder
First impressions of England and its people. 1847 9/7/47
Letter from one of the Scotch people to... Lord Brougham and Vaux, on the... Auchterarder case. 1839 9/7/40
My schools and schoolmasters. 1854 23/2/56
Sutherland as it was and is; or, how a country may be ruined. 1843 15/10/43
The testimony of the rocks; or, Geology in its bearings on the two theologies, natural and revealed. 1857 29/9/72

Miller, James Professor of surgery
Nephalism the true temperance of scripture, science and experience. 1861 24/12/60

Miller, James Rector
Humours of Oxford, a comedy. 1730 4/6/84

Miller, Joaquin
A ship in the desert. 1875 19/6/75
Life amongst the Modocs: unwritten history. 1873 23/7/73

Miller, John M.A., Fellow of Worcester Coll.
Things after death. Three chapters on the intermediate state; with thoughts on family burying places. 1848 21/4/48

Miller, John of Princeton, NJ
A commentary on Romans. 1887 6/5/88 ?

Miller, John pseud. Justitia
Peculiarities of the Scottish episcopal church. 1847 7/6/57

Miller, John Cale
Disestablishment: a sermon. 1871 16/7/71

Miller, Joseph
A history of the witches of Renfrewshire. 1809 (1877 edn) 4/6/88 ?

Miller, William solicitor
The heavenly bodies, their nature and habitability. 1883 9/12/83, 30/6/92
Wintering in the Riviera. 1879 (1880 2nd edn) 22/1/83

Miller, William Haig
The mirage of a life. 1850 (1883 edn) 15/9/90

Milligan, William
'Last Supper', in *Contemporary Review*, viii. 481. 1868 (August 1868) 18/6/82 ?
Religion of ancient Greece. 1882 18/6/82
The present position and duty of the Church of Scotland... Address. 1882 28/3/83

Millin de Grandmaison, Aubin Louis
Minéralogie Homérique. 1790 2/2/58

Millingen, Julius
Arbitrary detention by the Inquisition at Rome of three Protestant children. 1842 14/10/42

Millingen, Julius R. van
Ancient unedited monuments (painted Greek vases). 1822 (3v. 1822–26) 26/1/57

Millington, Ellen I.
Heraldry in history, poetry and romance. 1858 7/12/61

Mills, Arthur
Colonial constitutions: an outline of the constitutional history... of the British dependencies. 1856 25/4/56
Systematic colonisation. 1847 20/4/47

Mills, Benjamin
The nature, extent and right imrovement of Christian liberty: a sermon. 1741 13/7/35

Mills, Charles
The history of the crusades for the recovery and possession of the holy land. 1820 (2v.) 22/3/28

Mills, Lawrence Heyworth
Avesta. 1880 6/10/91

Mills, William B. D.
Lecture on the theory of moral obligation... lectures delivered before the university of Oxford. 1830 17/9/60
The belief of the Jewish people and of the most eminent Gentile philosophers... in a future state. 1828 9/9/60

Milman, Henry Hart
A memoir of Lord Macaulay. 1862 28/11/61
Annals of St. Paul's cathedral. 1868 10/1/69, 26/2/72
Belshazzar. 1822 25/10/25
Church extension in the British colonies and dependencies: a sermon preached at St. Mary's, Oxford. 1860 19/2/60

History of Latin Christianity; including that of the Popes. 1854 (6v. 1854–55) 27/8/54, 30/10/74, 26/1/75
The Bacchanals of Euripides, tr. H. H. Milman. 1865 13/9/66
The fall of Jerusalem. 1820 22/1/26
The history of Christianity from the birth of Jesus to the abolition of paganism in the Roman empire. 1840 (3v.) 26/2/40
The history of the Jews. 1829 13/5/30, 22/9/78, 28/5/90, 14/12/90, 30/5/91
The life of E. Gibbon, Esq. 1839 6/6/90
Milman, Robert Bishop of Calcutta
Convalescence. Thoughts for those who are recovering from sickness. 1865 15/8/80
The life of Torquato Tasso. 1850 29/11/55
The love of the atonement: a devotional exposition of the fifty-third chapter of Isaiah. 1853 24/9/54
Milne, David
On the parallel roads of Lochaber. 1847 19/8/47
Milne, Robert Matthew
Clerical oaths and their equivalents a hindrance to unity. 1858 21/10/58
Milner, John chaplain, Royal Navy
Remarks on the new doctrine of the real objective presence as propounded by the ritualists. 1874 8/4/77
Milner, Joseph
Gibbon's account of Christianity considered: together with some strictures on Hume's Dialogues concerning natural religion. 1781 3/4/84
The history of the church of Christ. 1794 (5v. 1810 edn) 17/8/34, 14/8/36
Milner, Joseph Thorpe
Lectures on important subjects in Christian theology . . . for young . . . in the Wesleyan communion. 1835 12/4/35
Milner, Thomas Hughes
The present and future state of Jamaica considered. 1839 19/3/39
Milnes, Richard Monckton Baron Houghton
Address . . . on social economy. 1862 17/10/73
Answer . . . to R. Baxter on the South Yorkshire Isle of Axholme Bill. 1852 6/4/52
Life of Monckton Milnes, by T. Wemyss Reid. 1890 (2v.) 7/11/90
Life, letters, and literary remains of John Keats. 1848 (2v.) 23/8/73
Memorials of a tour in some parts of Greece: chiefly poetical. 1833 1/7/35
Monographs, personal and social . . . with portraits. 1873 24/6/73, 2/6/77
On the apologies for the massacre of St. Bartholomew. 1856 28/6/58 ?
One tract more, or, the system illustrated by 'The Tracts for the Times', externally regarded. 1841 31/5/41
Palm leaves. 1844 30/3/44
Poems of many years. 1838 6/4/38
Poems, legendary and historical. 1844 25/4/44
Poetry for the people, and other poems. 1840 13/8/40
Real union of England and Ireland. 1845 21/5/45
Selections, ed. H. J. Gibbs. 1891 10/5/91
The events of 1848, especially in their relation to Great Britain. A letter to . . . Marquis of Lansdowne. 1849 12/2/49
Milnes, Robert Offley Ashburton Marquis of Crewe
Gleanings from Béranger. 1889 9/10/89
Milroy, Gavin
The cholera not to be arrested by quarantine: a brief historical sketch. 1847 5/1/48
Milton, John
Areopagitica. 30/3/74
Epitaphium Damonis. 20/5/26 ?
Lycidas. 7/7/56
Paradise Lost. 6/2/26, 26/2/26, 4/3/26, 12/3/26, 16/4/26, 28/5/26, 4/9/30, 31/10/30, 14/11/30, 8/6/34, 6/12/35, 27/12/35, 13/1/36, 27/11/36, 4/12/36, 20/8/37, 27/1/38, 2/12/41, 18/11/55, 25/12/55, 15/8/58, 19/1/62, 1/2/63, 11/6/65, 25/3/66, 23/5/69, 27/8/71, 5/9/81, 12/2/82, 30/9/90
Paradise Regained. 17/2/26, 28/11/30, 4/12/30, 25/12/32, 11/11/55, 6/7/56
Samson Agonistes. 6/10/27, 9/7/56, 14/5/93
The doctrine and discipline of divorce. 14/6/57
The life of John Milton; narrated in connexion with the political, ecclesiastical, and literary history of his time, by D. Masson. 1859 19/5/71
Milton, William
Fancies and fallacies of the opponents of the Purchas judgment examined. 1875 8/12/75
Mr. Parker's fallacies refuted. A letter to . . . Lord Selborne . . . on the advertisements and ornaments rubric. 1880 29/2/80
Milward, A.
The decimal coinage. A letter to . . . the chancellor of the exchequer. 1853 5/12/53
Minchin, James George Cotton
The growth of freedom in the Balkan peninsula. Notes of a traveller. 1886 9/2/87
Mind. 3. 129. 1/1878. Colour-sense 27/2/1878
Mines of Ireland. 2/7/58
Minghetti, Marco
Della riforma delle leggi frumentarie in Inghilterra. 1846 15/9/53
Della riforma delle leggi frumentarie in Inghilterra. 1846 (1854 edn) 14/11/59
Discorsi . . . 7 ed 8 maggio 1875. 1875 29/6/75
Saggio di provvedimenti di Finanza. 1866 13/2/66

Minghetti, Marco (*cont.*)
Stato e chiesa. 1878 9/12/77
Ministers of Lincoln
The abolishing of the Book of Common Prayer by reason of above fifty grosse corruptions. 28/9/44
Minto, W.
[On the Afghan question], *in Nineteenth Century*, v. 132. 1879 (January 1879) 2/1/79
Minton, Samuel afterw. Minton-Senhouse
Letters to the 'Christian World'. 1877 17/2/78
The evangelicals and 'The Edinburgh'. A reply. 1853 2/1/54
Minut, Gabriel de
De la beauté. Discours divers. (new edn 1865) 4/4/88
Mir Hasan Ali, Mrs.
Observations on the Mussulmanns of India. 1832 (2v.) 3/10/77
Misgivings. 1876 (2v.) 23/1/76
Mismer, Charles
Souvenirs du monde musulman. 1892 24/12/92
Missionaires Muscovites. 21/12/76
Missionary bishoprics. 1860 8/4/60
Mitchel, John
The history of Ireland, from the Treaty of Limerick to the present time. 1868 24/9/86
Mitchell, Alexander of Dalkeith
Political and social movements in Dalkeith. 1882 5/6/82
Mitchell, Sir Arthur
The past in the present. 1880 2/1/83
Mitchell, Charles
[On newspaper stamps]. (not found) 25/2/54
Mitchell, George
Letters . . . to Earl Russell, respecting the late events at Warsaw, and in Poland. 1862 13/2/62
Mitchell, Joseph
Plan for lessening the taxation . . . improved administration of the railways of Great Britain and Ireland by the state. 1865 2/2/65
Mitchell, Samuel Augustus
A general view of the United States. 1846 11/6/60
Mitchell, Silas Weir
Characteristics. 1892 24/1/93 ?
Mitchell, Thomas
Aristophanes' 'The Knights', tr. T. Mitchell. 1820 3/2/30
Aristophanis Comoediae. 1794 30/9/73
Mitchell, W.
Is Scotland to be sold again? Home Rule for Scotland . . . with a retrospect of 1891 and 1892. 1893 26/1/93
Mitchell, Walter
Bryan Maurice or the seeker. 1868 23/6/89
Mitchell, William
The story of the crucifixion, the resurrection, the forty days and the ascension. 1890 4/1/91
Mitford, John
The life of Thomas Gray. 1814 4/10/28
Mitford, John Thomas Freeman Earl of Redesdale
Lord Macaulay on the Coronation oath. 1869 9/6/69, 9/12/73 ?
Observations on the judgment in the Gorham case: and the way to unity. 1850 1/5/50
Reasonings on some disputed points of doctrine. 1874 29/11/74
Reflections on the doctrine of regeneration, and its connexion with both sacraments. 1849 15/1/50
The infallible church and the holy communion of Christ's body and blood. Correspondence [with Manning]. 1875 (2v.) 5/12/75
Thoughts on English prosody and translations from Horace. 1859 28/10/59
Mitford, Mary Russell
Rienzi. A tragedy, in five acts. 1828 16/5/38
Mitford, William
The history of Greece. 1784 (5v 1784–1818) 2/12/28, 4/11/31, 17/12/55
Mivart, Saint George Jackson
'Contemporary evolution', in *Contemporary Review*, xxii. 595. 1873 (September 1873) 28/9/73
'What is the good of truth?' [Metaphysical Society paper]. 1876 13/6/76
[on animals and plants] in *Contemporary Review*, xxxvi. 13. 1879 (September 1879) 1/9/79
[on conversion in England] in *Dublin Review*, xii. 65. 1884 (July 1884) 26/9/84
[on evolution] in *Nineteenth Century*, xxi. 263. 1884 (August 1884) 3/8/84
[on organic nature] in *Fortnightly Review*, xliii. 323. 1885 (March 1885) 31/3/85
Contemporary evolution. An essay on some recent social changes. 1876 14/5/76, 16/5/86
Man and apes, an exposition of structural resemblances bearing upon questions of affinity and origin. 1873 29/1/74
Nature and thought: an introduction to a natural philosophy. 1882 4/11/83
On the genesis of species. 1871 25/7/71
Moberly, George
A few remarks on the proposed admission of Dissenters into the university of Oxford. 1834 5/5/34
Charge delivered to the clergy and churchwardens of the diocese of Salisbury. 1882 1/10/82
Five short letters to Sir W. Heathcote . . . on the studies and discipline of public schools. 1861 30/11/61

He that believeth and is baptised shall be saved [sermon with appendix on the Athanasian Creed]. 1872 15/9/72
Introduction to logic. 1838 17/10/31
Practical sermons. 1838 29/12/39
Primary charge to the clergy and churchwardens of the diocese of Salisbury. 1870 2/10/70
Sermons preached at Winchester College. 1844 28/4/67
Some remarks on 'Essays and Reviews'... revised preface to... second edition of 'Sermons on the beatitudes'. 1861 3/2/61
The administration of the holy spirit in the body of Christ. Eight lectures. 1888 25/12/91, 24/1/92, 21/2/92
The proposed degradation and declaration... a letter... to the Master of Balliol College [on W. G. Ward]. 1845 27/1/45
The sayings of the great forty days, between the resurrection and the ascension... in five sermons. 1844 7/4/44

Moberly, George Herbert
The odes of Pindar. Translated into English metre. 1876 31/1/76

Mocatta, Frederic David
The Jews of Spain and Portugal and the inquisition. 1877 6/6/77

Mochnacki, Maurycy
Faut-il une Pologne? tr. and ed. by H. Lebrun. 1854 10/10/54

Modena documenti. 1859 30/8/59
Modern hagiology. 1845 20/7/45
Modern Methodism. 1844 6/4/44
Modern Review.
1. 1, 51. 1/1880. Reviewing; St Thomas Aquinas 3/1/1880
4. 494. 7/1883. Revenue 29/7/1883
5. 617–762. 10/1884 5/10/1884

Modern Wesleyism compared with... Wesley. 1844 29/2/44 ?

Moehler, Johann Adam
Neue Untersuchungen der Lehrgegensätze zwischen den Katholiken und Protestanten. 1835 12/8/47, 1/9/78
Symbolik, oder Darstellung der dogmatischen Gegensätze der Katholiken und Protestanten ... 1832 (1832–1843) 18/10/45 ?, 27/9/74

Moeran, Edward Busteed
Ritualism and Romanism. A paper. 1879 28/7/79

Moffat, John Smith
The lives of Robert and Mary Moffat. By their son. 1885 22/11/85, 4/7/86

Moffatt, George
On the bankruptcy law of England. 1865 4/1/66

Mogila, Petr
The orthodox confession... Faithfully translated into English [by Philip Lodvill]. 1762 25/7/58

Molbech, Christian Knud Frederik
Ambrosius. A play. From the Danish by A. Berry. 1879 15/9/83

Molesworth, John Edward Nassau
An answer to... John Davison's inquiry into the origin and intent of primitive sacrifice. 1826 7/8/31
Remarks on church rates and the Rochdale contest. 1841 13/2/41
The Berean Scripture Reader. A sermon preached on the baptism of G. W. Philip. 1843 19/2/43
The domestic chaplain; or, sermons on family duties for every day in the year. 1838 (2v.) 10/7/57

Molesworth, Sir William
Materials for a speech in defence of the policy of abandoning the Orange River Territory, May 1854. 1854 31/5/54
Report from the select committee... on transportation... with notes. 1838 30/3/38

Molesworth, William Nassau
History of the Church of England from 1660. 1882 27/12/81, 7/9/82
The history of England from the year 1830. 1871 (3v.) 27/2/72, 26/9/87
The history of the Reform Bill of 1832. 1865 31/12/64

Moleville, Bertrand de
Histoire de la révolution de France. 1801 (14v. 1801–03) 11/4/88

Molière, Jean Baptiste de
George Dandin. 16/2/26, 6/12/61, 19/5/83
L'École des Femmes. 29/5/26
L'École des Maris. 4/5/26
L'Étourdi. 13/2/26, 19/9/61
L'Amour Médecin. 17/2/26
L'Avare. 24/2/26, 28/10/61, 8/8/65, 21/5/83, 9/8/90
L'Impromptu de Versailles. 13/6/26
La Comtesse d'Escarbagnas. 18/8/59
Le Bourgeois Gentilhomme. 3/10/25, 30/10/61, 12/5/83, 12/8/90
Le Festin de Pierre. 3/2/26
Le Médecin Malgré Lui. 7/11/25, 1/11/53, 29/1/75
Le Malade Imaginaire. 30/9/25, 1/10/61, 17/5/83
Le Mariage Forcé. 22/7/46
Le Misanthrope. 11/3/26, 23/7/46, 9/9/90, 18/9/90
Les Femmes Savantes. 17/4/26, 15/5/83
Les Fourberies de Scapin. 7/10/61, 14/8/90
Les Précieuses Ridicules. 24/1/26, 17/7/46, 18/7/46
Monsieur de Pourceaugnac. 7/8/90
Tartuffe. 18/2/26, 5/8/63, 30/1/75, 19/9/90, 20/9/90

Molinos, Miguel
On daily communion. 15/1/43
The spiritual guide which disintangles the soul, tr. from the Italian. 25/12/42
Moll, Herman
New description of England and Wales. 1724 28/4/86
Moller, Georg
An essay on the origin and progress of Gothic architecture. 1824 24/12/44
Molloy, Gerald
Geology and revelation. 1870 13/4/73
Molloy, Joseph Fitzgerald
Royalty restored, or London under Charles II. 1885 (2v.) 18/6/86
The life and adventures of Peg Woffington. 1884 (2v.) 17/4/88, 5/9/90
Molmenti, Pompeo Gherardo
La Dogaressa di Venezia. 1884 31/8/86
Moltke, Count Helmuth Carl Bernhard von
The Russians in Bulgaria and Rumelia in 1828 and 1829 . . . From the German. 1854 3/6/54, 16/12/76
Molyneux, Capel
Baptismal regeneration . . . reply to C. Molyneux. 1842 16/12/42
Is it expedient? or, the Sabbath question. 1852 20/2/53 ?
Molyneux, William
The case of Ireland's being bound by Acts of Parliament in England, stated. (1770 edn) 14/12/86
Momerie, Alfred Williams
Inspiration and other sermons. 1889 28/3/89
The origin of evil. 1881 21/12/90
Mommsen, Theodor
Römerische Geschichte. 1854 (1854–55) 5/12/57
Monahan, John
Records relating to the dioceses of Ardagh and Clonmacnoise. 1886 12/12/86
Monarchy asserted, to be the best, the most ancient and legall form of government. 29/9/88
Moncreiff, Henry
Letter to Lord Melbourne . . . Church of Scotland. 1840 8/5/41
Moncreiff, Sir Henry Wellwood
Creeds and churches in Scotland. 1869 21/2/69
The Free Church principle: its character and history . . . Chalmers lectures. 1883 29/4/83
The identity of the Free Church Claim from 1838 to 1875. A letter to . . . the Duke of Argyll. 1875 4/4/75
Money, Edward
A letter on the cultivation of cotton . . . addressed to Sir H. Verney. 1852 16/6/52
Money, Walter
The first and second battles of Newbury and the siege of Donnington Castle during the Civil War. 1884 19/7/84
Monfalcone, Pierre
Monte-Carlo intime. 1891 14/2/92
Mongredien, Augustus
Trade depression, recent and past. 1885 26/8/85
Monk, James Henry
A charge delivered to the clergy of the diocese of Gloucester and Bristol. 1841 8/12/41
A charge delivered to the clergy of the diocese of Gloucester and Bristol. 1844 26/12/44
A charge delivered to the clergy of the diocese of Gloucester and Bristol. 1854 12/11/54
The life of Richard Bentley. 1830 14/12/55
Monk, William
Dr. Livingstone's Cambridge lectures. 1858 28/10/59
Monmouth; a drama. 1880 1/4/80
Monnier, Marc
La Camorra. 1863 9/3/63
Monod, Adolphe Louis Frédéric Théodore
La femme. Deux discours. 1848 10/11/58
Monro, David Binning
'The Iliad' book I. (1885 edn) 19/10/85
Monro, Edward
A few words on the spirit in which men are meeting in the present crisis in the church. A letter. 1850 8/4/50
Leonard and Dennis; or, the soldier's life. A tale . . . of the present war. 1855 21/1/55
Parochial work. 1850 7/7/50
Purity of life. A sermon. 1850 24/2/50
Reasons for feeling secure in the Church of England. 1850 14/10/50
The fulfilment of the ministry. A sermon. 1848 3/2/50
The parish. 1853 1/5/53
Monselet, Pierre Charles
Le petit Paris. Tableaux et figures de ce temps. 1879 28/11/81 ?
Monsell, John Samuel Bewley
English sisterhoods. An address. 1863 28/6/63
Hymns of love and praise for the church's year. 1863 7/4/71
Our new vicar, or, Plain words on ritual and parish work. 1867 26/5/67
The rector and his friends; dialogues on some of the leading questions of the day. 1869 13/12/68
Monsey, Messenger
A sketch of the life and character of the late Dr. Monsey. 1789 4/9/83
Montagu, Anne Paule Dominique de
Memoirs of A. P. D. de Noailles, Marquise de Montagu. 1866 1/7/66
Montagu, Auguste Louis César de
Etudes sociales d'après la révélation. Réponse à M. Donoso Cortés. 1851 4/6/52

Montagu, Basil
Some thoughts upon liberty and the rights of Englishmen. By a lover of order. 1819 8/2/33 ?
The private tutor: or thoughts upon the love of excelling. 1820 8/2/33
Montagu, Charles Earl of Halifax
The works and life of Charles, Earl of Halifax. 1715 (2v.) 9/1/57
Montagu, Mrs. Elizabeth
An essay on the writings and genius of Shakespeare, compared with the Greek and French dramatic poets. 1769 19/10/70
Montagu, Lady Mary Wortley
Letters and works. 1887 4/8/88
Works. 1837 14/7/45
Montagu, Lord Robert
Arbitration instead of war, and a defence of the commune. 1872 15/5/72
Civilization and the See of Rome. 1874 29/10/74
England and the Eastern Question. 1877 15/7/77
Expostulation in extremis: or, remarks on Mr. Gladstone's 'Political Expostulation on the Vatican Decrees'. 1874 27/11/74
Montague, Philip
The West Indian: or, the happy effects of diligence and self-control, exemplified. 1827 28/1/49
Montaigne, Michel de
Essais. 1820 (6v. 1820–22) 23/4/45
Montalembert, Count Charles Forbes René de
Des Intérêts catholiques. 1852 7/11/52
Discours. 1845 14/10/45, 22/10/45
Histoire de Sainte Elisabeth de Hongrie, Duchesse de Thuringe. 1836 10/9/38
La victoire du nord aux Etats-Unis. 1865 9/6/65
Le testament du P. Lacordaire publié. 1870 16/4/70
Les moînes d'Occident depuis Saint Benoît jusqu'à Saint Bernard. 1860 (7v. 1860–77) 24/2/67
Lettre à M. le Comte de Cavour. 1860 10/5/61
Memoir of Montalembert, by M. O. Oliphant. 1872 23/11/73, 17/12/73
The political future of England... revised by J. W. Croker. 1856 4/1/56
Un débat sur l'Inde au parlement anglais. 1858 3/12/58
Montefiore, Claude Goldsmid
Lectures on the origin and growth of religion as illustrated by the... ancient Hebrews. 1892 22/1/93, 12/2/93
Montez, Lola
Autobiography and lectures, ed. C. C. Burr. 1858 18/6/92
Montgomery, Florence
Thrown together: a story. 1872 10/6/72
Montgomery, Henry
Speech delivered at the meeting of the remonstrant synod of Ulster. 1843 1/3/44
Montgomery, Hugh de Fellenberg
Gladstone and Burke. 1886 9/11/86
Irish land and Irish rights. 1881 18/1/81
Montgomery, James
Greenland, and other poems. 1819 29/1/26, 29/4/26
Montgomery, Robert
The gospel before the age; or, Christ with Nicodemus. An exposition for the times. 1844 12/5/44
The ominpresence of the deity. A poem. 1828 23/3/29
The Scottish church and the English schismatics ... letters on the recent schism in Scotland. 1847 12/12/47
Month, The.
3. 7/1865 5/12/1865
8. 129. 6/1876. Macaulay 7/6/1876
17. 374, 396. 6/1879. Probabilism; on Cobbett 27/7/1879
22. 393. 12/1874. Coleridge 26/12/1874
Monthly record of eminent men. 1890 11/4/90
Monthly Review. 3. 608–9. 12/1830 12/12/1830
Monti, Giulio
Studi critici. 1887 12/10/87
Monti, Vincenzo
Aristodemo; tragedia. 1786 30/12/54
Galeotto Manfredi. 1788 1/1/55
Iliade, tr. V. Monti. 1812 2/8/58, 23/12/64
La Basvilliana. 1793 (1824) 26/12/54
Poesie. 1800 (2v.) 29/12/54
Montrond, Clément Melchior Justin M. Fourcheux de
Le curé d'Ars. 1865 23/9/67
Moodey, Martha Livingstone
Alan Thorne. A novel. 1889 27/6/89
Moodie, John
Principles and observations on many... subjects, for the health of nations and individuals. 1848 2/2/49
Moody, Dwight Lyman
The London discourses. 1875 17/11/75 ?
Moon, George Washington
The revisers' English. 1882 (2v.) 11/1/82
With all my worldly goods... a novel. 1889 27/12/89
Moore, Aubrey Lackington
Evolution and Christianity. 1883 2/12/83, 26/2/88
Lectures and papers on the history of the Reformation in England and on the continent. 1890 30/11/90, 21/12/90, 25/1/91
Science and faith. Essays on apologetic subjects, with an introduction. 1889 12/5/89, 13/10/89

Moore, Aubrey Lackington (*cont.*)
Science and the land. 1892 10/8/93 ?
Moore, Courtenay
Some practical instances of the weakness of contemporary agnosticism. 1890 10/4/90
Moore, Daniel
Our Sabbaths in danger. A sermon. 1852 7/11/52
The divine authority of the Pentateuch vindicated. 1863 19/7/63
Moore, George
The power of the soul over the body considered in relation to health and morals. 1845 24/10/58
The use of the body in relation to the mind. 1846 25/9/59
Moore, John M.D.
A journal during a residence in France from . . . August to . . . December 1792. 1793 (2v.) 14/1/40
Moore, Thomas poet
A selection of Irish melodies. 1808 (10v. 1808–34) 23/12/61
Lalla Rookh. 1817 29/7/39, 5/12/53
Memoirs of Captain Rock, the celebrated Irish chieftain. 1824 20/4/68, 1/4/89
Memoirs of the life of the Right Hon. R. B. Sheridan. 1825 15/1/35
The Epicurean. 1827 28/1/30
The Fudge family in Paris. 1818 10/10/35, 13/10/71
The life and death of Lord Edward Fitzgerald. 1831 (2v.) 19/4/36
The poetical works. (1878 edn) 27/1/79
Travels of an Irish gentleman in search of a religion. 1833 (2v.) 29/4/33
Works. 1833 (2v.) 12/10/71
Moore, Thomas Rector of All Hallows the Great
The case for establishment stated. 1885 15/9/85 ?
Moore, Thomas Separatist preacher, the elder
A brief discourse about baptism. 8/2/29 ?
Moore, William Thomas
The life of Timothy Coop. 1889 5/5/89
Moraïtines, Petros Aristides
La Grèce telle qu'elle est. 1877 19/3/78
Morale Catholica. 21/6/35
More, Mrs. Hannah
'Tis all for the best. 1820 8/6/28
An essay on the character and practical writings of Saint Paul. 1815 14/12/28, 3/4/31
An estimate of the religion of the fashionable world. By one of the laity. 1791 7/1/38
Hints towards forming the character of a young princess. 1840 30/10/40
Practical piety. 1811 14/12/34
Sacred dramas: chiefly intended for young persons. 1782 2/10/25
Strictures on the modern system of female education. 1799 (2v.) 7/12/34
Tales. 1819 30/1/30
The spirit of prayer. 1825 17/4/31
More, Robert Jasper
Under the Balkans. Notes of a visit to the district of Philippopolis in 1876. 1877 17/10/77
More, Thomas
A letter . . . impugnynge the erronyouse wrytyng of John Frith. 20/11/75
Sir Thomas More and his new utopia, by A. W. Hutton. 1885 30/6/88
The apologye of syr Thomas More knyght. 21/11/75
The life of Sir Thomas More, by Cresacre More . . . ed. J. Hunter. 1828 12/8/55
Moreau, Jacques Louis
Histoire naturelle de la femme, suivie d'un traité d'hygiène. 1803 (2v.) 8/3/82
Morehead, Robert
Poetical epistles and specimens of poetical translation, particularly from Petrarch and Dante. 1864 10/1/76
Sermons. 1816 25/1/29
Morehouse, Frederic Cook
Some American churchmen. 1892 10/4/92 ?
Morell, Thomas
Lexicon Graeco-Prosodaicum, ed. E. Maltby. 1824 (2v.) 9/11/25
Moret, Eugène
La grande dévote. 1879 2/11/79
Moreton, Julian
A letter to the Rev. H. Bailey in reply to recent strictures upon missionary societies, and the missionaries. 1864 26/3/64
Morgan, Arthur, and Brown, Charles H.
The disintegrator. A romance of modern science. 1892 5/6/92
Morgan, David Thomas
Hymns and other poetry of the Latin church, tr. D. T. Morgan. 1870 7/4/71 ?, 8/8/80
Morgan, Godfrey
British church service and prayer book. 1878 25/1/79 n
Morgan, Hector Davies
The doctrine and law of marriage, adultery and divorce. 1826 (2v.) 7/2/50
Morgan, Henry Arthur
The tenure of fellowships considered especially with reference to college tutors and lecturers. 1871 26/5/71
Morgan, James Appleton
Macaronic poetry, collected with an introduction. 1872 14/2/79 ?
Morgan, John Edward
The danger of deterioration of race from the too rapid increase of great cities. 1866 26/3/66
Town life among the poorest: the air they breathe and the houses they inhabit. 1869 2/3/69

Morgan, John Minter
Religion and crime; or, the condition of the people. 1840 25/3/41
Morgan, William
Life of W. Morgan, by T. E. Jacob. 1890 14/11/90
Life of W. Morgan, by W. Hughes. 1891 10/7/92
Moriarty, David R. C. Bishop of Kerry
On the Christian Brothers' schools. A sermon. 1866 2/6/72 ?
Moriarty, James J.
All for love; or, From the manger to the cross. 1883 30/5/86
Morier, David Richard
Turkey and the Christian powers. 1876 6/11/76
Morier, James Justinian
Ayesha, the maid of Kars. 1834 (3v.) 12/9/35
Morier, Robert Burnet David
The policy of Denmark toward the duchies of Schleswig Holstein, tr. R. B. D. Morier. 17/2/51 ?
Moritz, Carl Philipp
Travels through various parts of England, in 1782. 1798 (4v.) 23/5/87
Morley, Henry
El Cid, tr. H. Morley. (1883 edn) 26/1/85
Morley, John Viscount Morley of Blackburn
[on the House of Lords], *Macmillan's Magazine*, i. 230. 1884 (July 1884) 17/7/84
[on the month], *Macmillan's Magazine*, i. 147. 1884 (June 1884) 5/6/84
Aspects of modern study. 1894 20/4/94
Burke. 1867 29/2/68, 12/8/79
Diderot and the encyclopaedists. 1878 (2v.) 24/10/78
English men of letters, ed. J. Morley. 1878 (67v. 1878–1919) 22/12/81
On the study of literature. 1887 9/6/87 ?
Rousseau. 1873 (2v.) 12/10/74
Studies in literature. 1891 26/1/91
The life of Richard Cobden. 1881 (2v.) 24/10/81
Voltaire. 1872 16/1/72
Voltaire. 1872 (1886 edn) 14/7/86
Walpole. 1888 8/11/89
Morren, Nathaniel
My church politics: in letters to my people. 1842 22/10/44
Morris, Caleb
The servant of the age. A discourse. 1843 9/7/43
Morris, Francis Orpen
All the articles of the Darwin faith. 1877 15/4/77
Morris, Herbert William
Work-days of God; or, science and the Bible. 1888 4/2/90
Morris, John
Catholic England in modern times. 1892 31/3/93, 14/5/93
Morris, John Brande
Jesus the son of Mary. 1851 (2v.) 31/1/64
Morris, John Webster
Observations on the marriage laws, particularly in reference to the case of desertion. 1815 3/12/40
Morris, Sir Lewis
Gycia. A tragedy in five acts. 1886 18/10/86
Songs unsung. 1883 28/10/83
The ode of life. 1880 27/1/84
Morris, M.
Il Falcone. 5/8/76
Morris, William
The Earthly Paradise. 1868 (3v. 1868–70) 26/3/70, 4/5/74, 14/10/92
The life and death of Jason. Poem. 1867 11/8/68
Morris, William Bullen
The life of Saint Patrick, Apostle of Ireland. 1878 23/6/78 ?
Morris, William O' Connor
The land systems of Ireland. 1888 8/12/87, 14/10/90
Morrison, Alexander
The fate of Fred Lavers: a tale of a lonely life. 1893 4/2/93
Morrison, Mrs. Eliza
Memoirs of the life and labours of Robert Morrison . . . compiled by his widow. 1839 26/9/73
Morrison, James
Observations illustrative of the defects of the English system of railway legislation. 1846 25/3/46
The influence of English railway legislation on trade and industry. With an appendix of . . . documents. 1848 27/6/48
Morritt, John Bacon Sawrey
A vindication of Homer and of the ancient poets and historians. 1798 8/3/47
Morton, J. and Trimmer, J. *An attempt to estimate the effects of protecting duties on . . . agriculture.* 1845 22/12/45
Moses Ben Maimūn
Maimonides' Kiddusch Hachodesch. 1889 15/9/89
Mosheim, Johann Lorenz von
An ecclesiastical history, tr. A. Maclaine. (6v. 1811 edn) 21/4/41
Institutionum historiae ecclesiasticae. 1726 (4v.) 5/5/33
Moss, Arthur B.
The Bible and evolution. 1890 4/12/92
The old faith and the new. 1885 4/5/90
The source of 'The ancient mariner'. 1890 9/4/90

Mossman, Thomas Wimberley
A history of the Catholic church of Jesus Christ from the death of Saint John to . . . second century. 1873 11/4/73
Sermons. 1857 14/12/79
The relations which at present exist between church and state in England. A letter to . . . Gladstone. 1882 17/9/82

Motley, John Lothrop
Causes of the civil war in America. 1861 22/10/61
History of the United Netherlands. 1860 (4v. 1860–67) 27/11/63
The correspondence of J. L. Motley, ed. G. W. Curtis. 1889 12/3/89
The rise of the Dutch republic. 1855 (3v.) 20/3/60

Motte, Standish
Outline of a system of legislation for securing protection to the aboriginal inhabitants. 1840 31/3/41

Moullet, C.
De l'être en général et de l'être en particulier. 1845 23/7/48

Moultrie, John
Poems. 1837 29/5/37

Mountain, George Jehoshaphat
A circular letter from the bishop of Montreal to his clergy on church vestments. 1845 12/9/45
Journal of the visitation of the diocese of Montreal. 1841 20/7/45 ?
Songs of the wilderness. 1846 4/7/46
The journal of the bishop of Montreal, during a visit to the . . . North-West America Mission. 1849 1/12/52

Mountfield, David
The church and nonconformists of 1662. 1861 7/4/61

Mountford, William
Miracles, past and present. 1870 17/6/77

Mouravieff, Andrei Nikolavich
A history of the church of Russia, tr. R. W. Blackmore. 1842 22/10/42

Moustoxudes, Andreas
Illustrazioni Corciresi. 1811 (2v. 1811–4) 28/1/59

Moy de Sons, Baron Ernst von
Sendschreiben. 1845 20/10/45

Mozley, Anne
Letters and correspondence of J. H. Newman. 1891 (2v.) 18/1/91

Mozley, James Bowling
'Blanco White' in *Christian Remembrancer.* 1845 (November 1845) 9/11/78
A review of the baptismal controversy. 1862 9/11/62, 17/1/69
Essays, historical and theological. 1878 (2v.) 12/2/79, 31/12/82
Letters of J. B. Mozley . . . edited by his sister [Anne Mozley]. 1884 19/10/84
Observations on the colonial church question. 1867 5/5/67
Observations on the propositions to be submitted to Convocation on February 13. 1845 16/1/45
Oxford university sermons. 1879 9/11/79, 11/3/88
Ruling ideas in early ages and their relation to Old Testament faith: lectures. 1877 21/1/77
Sermons preached before the university of Oxford and on various occasions. 1876 14/5/76, 9/7/76
Subscription to the articles. A letter to Professor Stanley. 1863 3/6/63
The primitive doctrine of baptismal regeneration. 1856 16/5/56
The Roman council. A sermon. 1869 28/11/69
The theory of development. A criticism of Dr. Newman's essay on the development of Christian doctrine. 1845 12/8/47

Mozley, Thomas
Letters from Rome on the occasion of the Oecumenical Council 1869–1870. 1891 (2v.) 30/6/91
Reminiscences, chiefly of Oriel College and the Oxford Movement. 1882 (2v.) 12/6/82, 18/6/82, 27/6/82
The church committee, or an incident in the life of John Wilful. 1841 1/9/41

M.P.
Letter to Peel. 1846 17/1/46

Muggeridge, Richard M.
Notes on the Irish difficulty: with remedial suggestions. 1849 6/2/49

Muggletonian Hymn Book. (n.d.) 13/12/81

Muir, William D.D.
A letter to the congregation of St. Stephen's, Edinburgh, on the present church question. 1839 28/2/40

Muir, Sir William
Caliphate: its rise, decline and fall. 1891 19/2/93

Muir, Sir William K. C. S. I.
Life of, by R. Smiles. 1888 7/8/89
The life of Mahomet and history of Islam, to the era of the Hegira. 1858 (4v. 1858–61) 19/1/79
The Lord's supper an abiding witness to the death of Christ. 1882 7/4/85

Mulhall, Michael G.
Balance-sheet of the world for ten years, 1870–1880. 1881 2/11/81
Fifty years of national progress. 1837–1887. 1887 16/4/87
Mulhall's dictionary of statistics. 1883 29/5/84
The progress of the world in arts, agriculture . . . and public wealth. 1880 1/9/80

Mulholland, Rosa
Gianetta: a girl's story of herself. 1889 15/2/89
Marcella Grace. An Irish novel. 1886 7/12/88
Mullaly, John
The laying of the cable, or the ocean telegraph. 1858 23/4/71
Mullens, Joseph
The religious aspects of Hindu philosophy stated and discussed. A prize essay. 1860 23/4/60
Müller, Carl Otfried
'Orchomenos und die Minyer' in *'Hellenischer Stämme und Städte', vol i.* 1820 (3v. 1820–24) 4/8/56, 14/11/57
A history of the literature of ancient Greece, tr. G. C. Lewis. 1840 (1840–42) 10/10/55
Introduction to a scientific system of mythology, tr. J. Leitch. 1844 18/10/67
Müller, Friedrich Max
'Bunsen 1868' in *Chips from a German workshop.* 1870 20/11/70
'Comparative mythology' in *Oxford Essays.* 1856 22/11/56
'Lectures of Darwin' in *Fraser's Magazine,* lxxxviii. 1. 1873 (July 1873) 19/7/73
'Lessons of Jupiter' in *Nineteenth Century*, xvii. 626. 1885 (October 1885) 23/10/85
'Philosophy of Mythology' in *Chips from a German workshop, vol ii.* 1867 30/11/71
[Lectures on the Vedas]. 1854 29/5/63
Anthropological religion: the Gifford lectures. 1892 9/1/92
Biographical essays. 1884 13/12/84
Chips from a German workshop. 1867 (3v. 1867–75) 19/10/68
Contemporary Review, xlix. 772. 1886 (June 1886) 11/6/86
Goethe and Carlyle. 1886 14/9/92 ?
India, what can it teach us? A course of lectures delivered at the university of Cambridge. 1883 20/1/83
Introduction to the science of religion. 1870 3/10/70
Lectures on the origin and growth of religion. 1891 9/9/91
Lectures on the origin and growth of religion as illustrated by the religions of India. 1878 18/8/79
Lectures on the science of language. 1861 (1861–64) 18/2/62
Memoirs of Baron Stockmar, ed. F. M. Müller. 1872 (2v.) 19/12/89
On Missions. A lecture delivered in Westminster Abbey, on December 3, 1873. 1873 1/2/74
Physical religion. 1891 12/11/93
Preface to 'Chips from a German workshop'. 1867 (vols 1 & 2) 6/10/68
Rig-Veda-Samhitâ, ed. F. M. Müller. 1849 (6v. 1849–74) 25/9/59, 13/2/76
Vorlesung. 1872 28/12/72
Müller, Joseph
Erinnerungen der heiligen katholischen Kirche. 1845 11/10/45
Müller, Wilhelm of Dessau
Homerische Vorschule. 1836 13/7/47
Mullinger, James Bass
A history of the University of Cambridge. 1888 8/9/92
Mulock, Dinah
A legacy, being the life of John Martin. 1878 (2v.) 28/9/79
Mulock, Thomas S.
Two letters. 1820 4/12/47
Munchausen, Baron pseud.
Baron Munchausen's narrative of his marvellous travels and campaigns in Russia. 1785 2/6/87
The travels and surprising adventures of Baron Munchausen. 1868 9/6/76
Mundy, Harriet Georgiana
The journal of Mary Frampton, ed. H. G. Mundy. 1885 27/9/86
Munro, Hugh Andrew Johnstone
Elegy written in a country churchyard, by Thomas Gray, tr. into Latin by Munro. 1880 6/1/74
T. Lucreti Cari De rerum natura libri sex, ed. Munro. 1860 15/7/85
Munro, Joseph Edwin Crawford
The constitution of Canada. 1889 12/10/89
Muntz, George Frederick
Letter upon corn and currency. 1841 8/5/41
Mura, Bonfiglio
Il clero e la società moderna. 1860 8/12/66
Murat, Charles Louis Napoléon Achille
Exposition des principes du gouvernement républicain . . . en Amérique. 1833 21/6/33
Murchison, Sir Roderick Impey
Address delivered at the anniversary meeting of the Geological Society of London. 1842 24/3/42
Address to the Royal Geographical Society of London: delivered at the anniversary meeting. 1844 5/7/44
Address to the Royal Geographical Society of London: delivered at the anniversary meeting. 1867 10/7/67
Murdoch, Alexander G.
Lilts on the Doric Lyre: a collection of humerous poems and versified sketches of Scottish manners and character. 1873 18/2/80
Mure, David
Reply to the Quarterly Review. 1847 4/12/47
The commercial policy of Pitt and Peel. 1847 19/6/47
Mure, William
A critical history of the language and literature of antient Greece. 1850 (5v. 1850–57) 1/9/55, 3/8/68

Mure, William (*cont.*)
Remarks on two appendices to the second volume, third edition, of Mr. Grote's History of Greece. 1851 2/8/51
Muriel, or social letters. A novel. 1873 (3rd edn) 23/3/71
Murphy, J.
Convict no. 25; or, the clearances of Westmeath. 1886 26/5/87
Murphy, J. L.
An essay towards a science of consciousness. 1838 17/10/60
Murphy, John Nicholas
Ireland industrial, political, and social. 1870 4/2/70
Murphy, Joseph John
An Irishman's view of Irish politics. 1869 28/1/69
Habit and intelligence, in their connexion with the laws of matter and force . . . scientific essays. 1879 9/11/79
The scientific bases of faith. 1873 19/8/77, 4/8/78
Murphy, William
The case of the confessional unmasked. 1868 5/6/68 ?
The confessional unmasked. 1868 20/12/67 ?
Murray, Alexander Stuart
'On Homer' in *Contemporary Review*, xxiii. 218. 1874 (January 1874) 17/6/76
Handbook of Greek archaeology. 1892 14/3/92
Manual of mythology . . . With notes, revisions and additions by William H. Klapp. 1872 (1872–74) 17/6/76
Murray, Andrew
Love made perfect. 1894 13/5/94 ?
Murray, Charles Augustus
Travels in North America during the years 1834, 1835 and 1836. 1839 (2v.) 25/11/39
Murray, Charlotte
Abiding in thee. A collection of poems. 1887 28/9/84 ?
Murray, Eustace Clare Grenville
The coming to. 1870 7/1/73
Turkey; being sketches from life. 1877 6/7/77
Murray, George
A charge delivered . . . at the triennial visitation . . . in October, 1843. 1843 12/11/43
Murray, James
Murray's Oxford English dictionary. 8/6/91
Murray, John
Life of John Murray, by S. Smiles. 1891 23/3/91
Murray, John publisher, the younger
Scepticism in geology and the reasons for it . . . By Verifier. 1877 16/2/78
Murray, John publishing firm
Handbook to the Ionian isles. 1840 24/12/46
Handbook for travellers in Central Italy. 1843 23/7/49
Handbook for travellers in Denmark, Norway, Sweden and Russia. 1839 11/8/85 ?
Handbook for travellers to France. 1849 25/10/50
Murray, Patrick Aloysius
The divine origin of the supremacy of the Roman See . . . A lecture. 1861 20/4/62
Murray, Richard
A history of the church in Ireland. 1840 22/5/42
Murray, Thomas
The life of R. Leighton, D.D., Archbishop of Glasgow. 1828 17/8/34
Murray, Thomas Boyles
Jubilee tract: great success from small beginnings . . . Society for promoting Christian Knowledge in 1698–9. 1849 23/2/49
Pitcairn: the island, the people and the pastor; with a short account of the Mutiny of the Bounty. 1853 24/4/53
Murray's Magazine.
1. 1/1887. G. Russell 21/12/1887
1. 161. 1/1860. on Louis Napoleon 7/1/1860
1. 173, 200. 2/1887. on Shaftesbury 30/1/1887
1. 721. 6/1887. on Sydney Smith 30/5/1887
3. 179. 1/1861. Diamonds 5/1/1861
5. 441. 3/1862. Royal deaths 21/1/1862
6. 177. 7/1862. West 8/7/1862
6. 345. 8/1862. Montenegro 13/9/1862
10. 554. 10/1891. Russia 13/10/1891
22. 292. 8/1870. on Clarendon 12/8/1870
28. 222. 5/1873. O'Connell 13/7/1873
30. 559. 10/1874. Prussia 9/10/1874
33. 275. 1/1876. Montenegro 22/3/1877
37. 171, 161. 3/1878. Heligoland; Russia 20/3/1878
38. 385. 9/1878. Two sides to a saint 1/9/1878
39. 390. 3/1879. Haberdashers' Hall 7/3/1879
40. 471. 4/1884. Colonies 15/4/1884
41. 125. 12/1879. Colour-sense 13/12/1879
48. 26, 59. 5/1883. Huxley; Bryce 30/4/1883
51. 241. 2/1885. Morley on G. Eliot 16/3/1885
51. 446. 4/1885. Morley on Pattison 6/4/1885
58. 247, 285. 8/1888. Doyle; Coleridge 28/8/1888
58. 417. 10/1892. Harrison on Huxley 5/10/1892
58. 545. 10/1892. Indian finance 5/10/1892
58. 689. 11/1892. Lugard 8/11/1892
58. 74. 7/1892. Tollemache 29/12/1892
58. 834. 12/1892. Momerie 14/12/1892
132. 439. 10/1870. on Lubbock 23/11/1870

Musaeus
'Hero and Leander', tr. E. Arnold. 1873 31/7/73
Musgrave, George
Dante's Divine Comedy. 1893 7/11/93
Musgrave, George Musgrave
Ten days in a French parsonage in the summer of 1863. 1864 (2v.) 16/10/64
Musgrave, Sir Richard
Memoirs of the different rebellions in Ireland from the arrival of the English. 1801 26/3/68
Musgrave, Thomas
A charge delivered to the clergy of the diocese of Hereford. 1845 24/8/45
A charge delivered to the clergy of the diocese of York. 1849 5/2/50
Musset, Louis Charles Alfred de
Poésies nouvelles. 1860 19/8/69
Musset Pathay, Victor Donatien de
Oeuvres inédites de J. J. Rousseau suivies d'un supplément. 1825 28/8/58
Muttirolo, G.
Un Desiderio sulla predicazione. 20/1/39 ?
Mutu Coomara Swamy
Arichandra: the Martyr of Truth: a Tamil Drama. 1863 22/12/63
Myers, Frederick
Catholic thoughts on the church of Christ. 1838 22/8/69, 27/12/74
Myers, Frederic William Henry
Saint Paul. 1867 18/11/92
Wordsworth. 1880 5/5/88
My experiences in a lunatic asylum. By a sane patient. 1879 7/2/79
My rectors, by a ... curate. 1890 11/1/90
Mystagogus, Cleidophorus pseud.
Mercury's Caducean rod; or, the great and wonderful office of the Universal Mercury ... displayed. 1704 (2v.) 6/12/50
Mysteries of London. 1849 19/12/48

Naden, Constance Caroline Woodhill
A modern apostle ... and other poems. 1887 21/1/90
Complete poetical works. 1894 7/5/94
Further reliques, ed. G. M. McCrie. 1891 16/1/91, 25/10/91
Songs and sonnets. 1881 31/5/81
Naegelsbach, Carl Friedrich von
Die homerische Theologie in ihrem Zusammenhange dargestellt. 1840 5/1/57, 1/9/79, 3/9/91
Die nachhomerische Theologie des griechischen Volksglaubens bis auf Alexander. 1857 14/11/67
Nairne, Baroness Carolina
Life and songs of the Baroness ... memoir and poems of Caroline Oliphant the younger, ed. C. Rogers. 1869 9/1/72
Naldi, Michele Angelo
La Chiesa e il Papato: ragionamento sull' attuale quistione. 1861 23/2/62
Nani, Giovanni
Il credito fondiario ed il credito agricolo. 1863 1/4/63 n
Nansen, Fridtjof
The first crossing of Greenland. 1890 (2v.) 3/3/91
Naper, James L. W.
Observations on fixity of tenure. 1843 24/8/47
Napier, Sir Charles
Lights and shadows of military life, ed. Vigny. 1840 15/3/52
The colonies: treating of their value generally—of the Ionian islands in particular. 1833 12/1/58
Napier, Sir Joseph
Lectures on Butler's Analogy of Religion to the constitution and course of nature. 1864 21/2/64
Richard Baxter and his times. A lecture. 1855 16/12/55
The college and the university. 1871 30/1/73
Napier, Macvey the younger
Selections from the correspondence of ... Macvey Napier ... edited by his son, M. Napier. 1879 13/9/80, 17/6/86
Napier, Mrs. Robina
Johnsoniana: anecdotes of ... Samuel Johnson ... by Mrs. Piozzi ... and others ... edited by R Napier. 1884 30/12/84
Napier, William Francis Patrick
History of the war in the Peninsula and in the South of France, from ... 1807 to ... 1814. 1828 (6v. 1828–40) 11/5/41
The conquest of the Scinde, with some introductory passages in the life of Major-General Sir Charles James Napier. 1845 (2v.) 27/1/45
The life and opinions of General Sir C. J. Napier. 1857 (4v.) 16/3/57
Napoleon III
L'attentat du 14 Janvier 1858 [on Napoleon III]. 1858 15/3/58
L'empereur Napoléon III et l'Italie. 1859 17/3/59
Les titres de la dynastie napoléonienne. 1868 25/3/68 ?
Napoléon-le-petit, by Victor Hugo. 1852 22/11/52
Napoleon III, and Italy. What will be done? And why? By a man in Manchester. 1859 3/8/59
Napoli e la costituzione. 1848 6/2/51
Napper, William
An exposition of the doctrine of the United Church of England and Ireland concerning ... baptism. 1843 5/1/76
Nardi, Francesco
[On Ireland]. (not found) 18/8/68

Nardi, Francesco (*cont.*)
Il concilio ecumenico e i diritti dello stato... Risposta all' opuscolo 'Le Concile... et... l'état'. 1869 8/6/69
Sul tentativo anti-cattolico in Inghilterra e l'opuscolo dell'... Gladstone. 1875 16/1/75
Nares, Edward
Memoirs of the life and administration of William Cecil, Lord Burghley. 1828 26/10/84
Narjoux, Félix
Francesco Crispi. L'homme publique—l'homme privé. 1890 23/4/90
Narration of proceedings in the bill of 1792. 1792 30/8/44
Narrow and wide guages considered. 1845 16/7/45
Nash, Francis Herbert
The divine education of the church, and modern experiments. 1857 27/10/61 ?
Nash, James Okey, and Gore, C.
William Law's defence of Christian principles. 1893 31/12/93
Nash, Richard West
Stray suggestions on colonization. 1849 9/2/49
Nash, Thomas Arthur
The life of Richard Lord Westbury. 1888 (2v.) 1/4/87 n
Nasmyth, James
James Nasmyth. An autobiography, ed. S. Smiles. 1883 10/2/83
National Club Addresses
[on papal bull, 2nd series iii. II]. 1847 10/2/48
[viii-xii on Irish church]. 2/6/49
National Review.
1. 107. 11/1864. Todleben 14/12/1864
1. 411. 10/1855. British Statesman 13/10/1855
1. 438. 10/1855. St Paul 14/10/1855
2. 468, 357. 4/1856. Peace; Macaulay 17/4/1856
4. 84. 1/1857. Spurgeon 6/2/1857
5. 230. 7/1857. Newport 19/7/1857
7. 137, 184. 7/1858. Gladstone's book 4/7/1858
7. 40. 7/1858. Gladstone's book 2/7/1858
10. 1. 1/1860. Architecture 12/1/1860
10. 215. 1/1860. Reform 11/1/1860
11. 219, 110. 7/1860. on Gladstone 20/7/1860
13. 241, 451. 10/1861. Cotton; Foreign policy 14/10/1861
15. 327. 10/1862. Louis Napoleon 24/11/1862
15. 452. 6/1890. Blind on Gladstone 10/7/1890
16. 1. 4/1863 17/4/1863
16. 389. 4/1863. Bolingbroke 22/5/1863
16. 488. 4/1859. Italy 10/4/1859
16. 734. 2/1891. Blind on Schliemann 3/6/1891
18. 273. 10/1859. Canning 20/10/1859
18. 368. 10/1859. Tennyson 15/10/1859
20. 301. 11/1892. Hutton on Renan 18/12/1892
National society annual report. 1847 20/4/46, 1/6/47
National society for promoting the education of the poor in the principles of the established church. 29/7/35
Naville, Ernest
The Christ. Seven lectures, tr. T. J. Després. 1880 10/6/81
The heavenly father. Lectures on modern atheism ... tr. H. Downton. 1865 29/12/82
Naysmith, J. and Carpenter, J.
The moon. 1887 30/7/87
Neal, Daniel
The history of the Puritans. 1837 29/9/40 ?
Neale, E. D.
Maryland not a Roman Catholic colony. 1875 8/4/75
Neale, Erskine
Reasons for supporting the Society for the Propagation of the Gospel in foreign parts. 1830 23/1/31
Neale, E. St. J.
[Report from Foreign Office on Japan]. 2/1/63
Neale, John Mason
'John Mason Neale' from *The Guardian* [obit. by Littledale]. 1866 (August 15, 1866) 10/11/67
A few words of hope on the present crisis of the English church. 1850 17/3/50
A history of the Holy Eastern Church. 1850 (5v. 1850 edn) 11/7/80, 23/1/81
A history of the so-called Jansenist church in Holland. 1858 6/6/58
Aytoun Priory; or the restored monastery. 1843 28/8/43
Commentary on the psalms. 1860 29/4/60
Essays on liturgiology and church history. 1863 15/2/63
Hierologus; or, the church tourists. 1843 21/1/44
Lectures principally on the church difficulties of the present time. 1852 22/8/52
Notes, ecclesiological and picturesque, on Dalmatia, Croatia, Istria, Styria... Montenegro. 1861 16/3/62, 12/1/77
Songs and ballads for the people. 1843 11/9/45
The Holy Eastern Church; a popular outline. 1870 11/9/70
The life and times of Patrick Torry. 1856 18/4/56
The liturgies of St. Mark, St. James, St. Clement, St. Chrysostom, St. Basil. 1859 11/8/61

The place where prayer was wont to be made; the re-introduction of private devotion in churches. 1844 5/11/44
The triumphs of the cross . . . tales and sketches of Christian heroism. 1845 27/7/45
Voices from the East. 1859 11/11/60
Neale, William Johnson
History of the mutiny at Spithead and the Nore. 1842 23/5/81
Neander, Johann August Wilhelm
Das Leben Jesu. 1845 7/4/49
History of the Christian religion and Church during the first three centuries, tr. Henry J. Rose. 1831 (2v. 1831–41) 12/5/34
Predigten. 1826 7/2/47
Ueber den Kayser Julianus und sein Zeitalter. Ein historisches Gemälde. 1812 10/9/67
Neate, Charles
Considerations on the punishment of death. 1857 27/4/57
Objections to the government scheme for the present subjection and future management of . . . Oxford. 1854 3/4/54
The history and uses of the law of entail and settlement. 1865 11/1/70
Three lectures on taxation, especially that of land, delivered at Oxford . . . 1860. 1861 1/3/65
Neate, J.
A statement of the arguments against reform. 1831 28/2/42
Necker, Jacques
De l'importance des opinions religieuses. 1788 23/5/47
Necklace of liberty. 13/4/89
Needell, Mrs. John Hodder
Stephen Ellicott's daughter. 1891 19/8/91
Needham, R. W.
The church and the synod; a letter to the . . . bishop of Exeter. 1851 3/8/51
Neele, Henry
The literary remains of . . . Consisting of lectures on English poetry, tales. 1829 8/10/30, 14/10/30
Neil, James
Palestine explored, with a view to its present natural features . . . which throw light on . . . the Bible. 1882 22/11/92
Nelson, Horatio 3rd Earl Nelson
Present position of the High Church party. A few words from a layman. 1874 15/11/74
Nelson, Robert
A companion for the festivals and fasts of the Church of England: with collects and prayers. 1704 4/4/47
An address to persons of quality and estate. 1715 (2v.) 4/9/87
Memoirs of the life and times of the pious Robert Nelson by C. F. Secretan. 1860 1/7/60
The great duty of frequenting the Christian sacrifice . . . With suitable devotions . . . from the ancient liturgies. 1707 29/1/27, 14/12/45
The life of . . . George Bull . . . Bishop of St. David's . . . history of . . . controversies in which he was engaged. 1713 19/7/41
Nelson, Thomas surgeon
Remarks on the slavery and slave trade of the Brazils. 1847 20/4/47
Nemo
A few words on the new Irish colleges. 1845 19/6/45
What is truth? A consideration of the doubts as to the efficacy of prayer raised by evolutionists, materialists, and others. 1890 3/5/91
Nesbit, Edith
Life's sunny side. 1890 17/1/90
Nesbit, John Collis
On agricultural chemistry, and the nature and properties of Peruvian Guano. 1856 (7th edn 1860) 4/11/60
Nesbitt, John
The happy effects of the outpouring of the holy spirit. 1802 11/12/64
Nestorides
[Letters to *The Times*]. 25/7/40
Nestorius
[Sermons and letters]. 25/7/40
Neville, Christopher
A letter to Lord Ebury on the present state of the church. 1861 3/3/61
A letter to the Right Hon. W. E. Gladstone . . . on the present state of the church question. 1863 21/10/62
Corn and currency, in a letter to A. Alison. 1846 7/3/46
Defence of free trade in corn. 1841 28/12/41
The Irish difficulty. A letter to the Right Hon. W. E. Gladstone. 1868 30/6/68
The new tariff. 1842 19/7/42
Neville, Henry
A few comments on . . . Gladstone's Expostulation. 1875 25/2/75
Nevin, William Wilberforce
Vignettes of travel. Some comparative sketches in England and Italy. 1881 17/3/85
Nevins, John Birkbeck
Picture of Wales during the Tudor period. 1893 22/10/93
Nevins, Willis Probyn
Development versus fossilized Christianity. 1881 11/9/81
Ireland and the Holy See in the Middle Ages. 1879 23/2/79
The Jesuits, and other essays. 1874 19/10/75
Why I left the church of Rome. 1870 7/9/79
New, Alfred Henry
The coronet and the cross: or, memorials of . . . Selina, Countess of Huntingdon, compiled from . . . documents. 1857 9/11/62

Newbery House Magazine.
4. 129, 181. 2/1891. Old Testament 1/2/1891
8. 4/1893 7/4/1893
Newbigging, Thomas
History of the forest of Rossendale. 1868 3/8/67
Speeches and addresses, political, social, literary. 1887 22/6/87
Newcome, Richard
A memoir of Gabriel Goodman... With some account of Ruthin School... Also, of Godfrey Goodman. 1825 19/9/40
Newdegate, Charles Newdigate
A letter to the Right Hon. H. Labouchere on the balance of trade... during the last four years. 1849 24/3/49
Newland, Henry
Observations on the past and present condition of the education of the poor in Ireland. 1845 21/4/45
Remarks addressed to W. H. Bellamy... on the state of education in Ireland. 1849 9/5/49
The life and contemporaneous church history of Antonio de Dominis, Archbishop of Spalatro. 1859 22/5/59, 27/9/74
Newland, Henry Garrett
[Pamphlet on tithes in Ireland]. 1832 30/3/33
An examination of the scripture lessons, as translated and published by H.M. Commissioners of Education in Ireland. 1836 3/7/36, 29/4/39
Forest scenes in Norway and Sweden. 1854 5/1/55
South Church Union lectures. Three lectures on Tractarianism, delivered in the Town Hall, Brighton. 1852 26/12/52
Newman, Francis William
A Christian commonwealth. 1883 1/11/84
An Homeric translation. A reply to Arnold. 1861 6/6/61, 8/1/63
Contributions chiefly to the early history of Cardinal Newman. 1891 27/1/91
James and Paul. A tract. 1869 8/10/93
Secret hymns. 1892 11/12/93, 31/12/93
The corruption now called neo-Malthusianism. 1889 8/9/90
The cure of the great social evil, with special reference to... Contagious Diseases' Acts. 1869 30/3/70
The Iliad, tr. F. W. Newman. 1856 15/2/62
The soul, her sorrows and her aspirations. An essay... the natural history of the soul... true basis of theology. 1849 29/6/49
Newman, Henry Stanley
Days of grace in India; a record of visits to Indian missions. 1882 3/9/82
Newman, John Henry
'Postscript' [with preface, to article on inspiration of scripture]. 1884 31/8/84
'Reverence due to the Virgin Mary' in *Parochial Sermons ii.* 1842 9/4/37, 26/1/90 ?
'Via Media' from Tracts for the Times. 1877 10/10/86
[on the formula] in *The Atlantis*, i. 330. 1858 22/4/66
[on the inspiration of scripture] in *Nineteenth Century*, xv. 185. 1884 (February 1884) 17/2/84
A letter addressed to... R. W. Jelf in explanation of no. 90 in the series called the Tracts for the Times. 1841 17/3/41
A letter addressed to... the Duke of Norfolk on occasion of Mr. Gladstone's recent expostulation. 1875 14/1/75
A letter to the Rev. E. B. Pusey, D.D., on his recent Eirenicon. 1876 4/1/80
A letter to the Rev. Godfrey Faussett... on certain points of faith and practice. 1838 20/2/39
A letter to the... Bishop of Oxford, on occasion of no. 90, in the series called the Tracts for the Times. 1841 8/4/41
A letter to... E. B. Pusey. 1866 4/2/66
A rationale or practical exposition of the Book of Common Prayer, by A. Sparrow, ed. J. H. Newman. 1839 22/3/40 n
An analysis of Dr. Newman's Apologia Pro Vita Sua: with a glance at the history of popes, councils and the church, by J. N. Darby. 1866 10/9/82
An essay in aid of a grammar of assent. 1870 27/3/70, 28/9/73, 25/8/78, 12/3/79, 9/12/83, 1/1/88
An essay on the development of Christian doctrine. 1845 28/11/45
Apologia pro vita sua. 1864 24/4/64 n, 22/5/64, 27/5/64, 13/6/64
Cardinal Newman, by R. H. Hutton. 1891 14/9/90, 3/10/90
Cardinal Newman, reminscences of fifty years since, by W. Lockhart. 1891 1/10/90
Cardinal Newman, the story of his life, by H. J. Jennings. 1882 6/12/81
Characteristics from the writings of... Newman, arranged by W. S. Lilly. 1880 (5th edn) 2/10/80
Discourses on the scope and nature of university education. 1852 9/4/52
Elucidations of Dr. Hampden's theological statements. 1836 18/2/36
Essay on the miracles... of the early ages. 1843 21/1/44
Essays. 1872 (2v.) 22/12/71
Lectures on justification. 1839 15/4/38, 25/4/41
Lectures on the history of the Turks in its relation to Christianity. 1854 16/9/76

Lectures on the present position of Catholics in England: addressed to the Brothers of the Oratory. 1851 17/8/51
Lectures on the prophetical office of the church, viewed relatively to Romanism and popular Protestantism. 1837 7/5/37, 1/12/45
Letter to... Ullathorne. 1870 1/3/70
Letters and correspondence, ed. A. Mozley. 1891 (2v.) 18/1/91
Letters on Anglican difficulties. 1850 14/7/50
Loss and gain. 1848 5/5/48
Lyra Apostolica. 1836 16/1/48, 18/3/66
Mr. Kingsley and Dr. Newman. 1864 16/2/64
Notes of a visit to the Russian Church in the years 1840, 1841 [by W. Palmer], ed. J. H. Newman. 1882 9/11/82
Parochial sermons. 1834 (6v. 1834–42) 23/8/35, 5/2/37, 13/3/42, 24/7/42, 23/1/48
Sermon preached... at the Requiem Mass for the repose of the soul of J. R. Hope Scott. 1873 6/9/73
Sermons preached on various occasions. 1857 16/5/75
Sermons, bearing on subjects of the day. 1843 10/12/43
Sermons, chiefly on the theory of religious belief, preached before the University of Oxford. 1843 26/3/43
The Arians of the fourth century. 1833 (2v. 1834–42) 9/3/34, 24/1/75
The church of the fathers. 1840 7/3/41
The devotions of bishop Andrewes, translated from the Greek and arranged anew. 1842 27/11/42, 25/2/66
The dream of Gerontius. 1865 18/3/66, 28/7/66, 11/8/67
The ecclesiastical history of M. l'Abbé Fleury... to the end of the fourth century, tr. J. H. Newman. 1842 6/11/42
The idea of a university. 1873 26/5/92, 19/10/92
The lives of the English saints. 1844 (1844–45) 3/12/43 n
The office and work of the universities. 1856 20/1/73
The pope and the revolution. 1866 6/12/66
The restoration of suffragan bishops recommended as a means of... more equal distribution of episcopal duties. 1835 17/3/35
Tract XC. 1841 12/3/41, 23/3/41, 15/4/41
Tracts for the Times [1–3 only]. 1833 27/10/33, 10/11/33
Tracts, theological and ecclesiastical. 1874 5/4/74, 25/7/75
Verses on various occasions. 1868 12/1/68

Newman, John Henry, and Keble, J.
Remains of Hurrell Froude, ed. J. H. Newman and J. Keble. 1838 (2v. 1838–9) 15/3/38, 28/3/40

Newmarch, William
The new supplies of gold: facts and statements, relative to their actual amount; and... effects. 1853 29/3/54

New Monthly Magazine. 114. 300. 11/1858. On Gladstone's *Homer* 4/11/1858

Newnham, Philip Hankinson
Thy heart with my heart. Four simple letters on the holy communion. 1888 18/8/89

Newnham, William Orde
Alresford essays for the times. 1891 5/7/91

New Quarterly Review.
1. 1. 3/1852. on books 13/3/1852
1. 143. 4/1853. Gold 31/3/1853
5. 279, 403, 484. 4/1845. Russia 1/4/1845
5. 59. 1/1845. Young England 2/1/1845
6. 207. 7/1845. Lords of the soil 9/7/1845

New reform bill: leading clauses. 1852 15/12/52

New Review.
1. 201, 217. 8/1889. Russia; Arnold 24/8/1889
1. 3. 7/1889. Boulanger 31/8/1889
1. 532, 561. 11/1889. Italy; Elections 1/11/1889
2. 1. 2/1890 10/2/1890
3. 208. 9/1890. Kegan Paul on Newman 30/8/1890
5. 12/1891 2/12/1891
5. 443. 11/1891. Hamilton on the Private Secretary 4/12/1891
8. 439. 4/1893. Novikoff on Russia and Rome 7/5/1893
21. 632. 7/1893. Bompas on belief 9/7/1893

Newton, Benjamin Wills
Regeneration in its connexion with the cross... lecture delivered in Duke Street chapel, St. James's Park. 1860 4/6/60

Newton, Sir Isaac
Observations upon the prophecies of Daniel and the Apocalypse of St. John. 1733 26/4/30
Principia Mathematica. 23/1/29, 18/2/29, 9/3/29, 6/8/31

Newton, John
An authentic narrative of some... particulars in the life of... in a series of letters to... Haweis. 1764 10/8/34

Newton, John, and Cowper, William
Olney hymns in three books. 1779 13/4/28

New Zealand
Handbook. 1848 1/10/53

'Nibelungenlied', ed. F. H. von der Hagen. 1820 5/9/59

'Nibelungenlied', tr. A. G. F. Barham. 1887 28/5/87

Nichol, John
Fragments of criticism. 1860 27/4/60
Inaugural lecture to the course of English language and literature in the University of Glasgow. 1862 9/12/62

Nicholas, Thomas
The pedigree of the English people. 1868 23/3/68
Nicholl, John
Recollections. 1822 7/9/26
Nicholls, Sir George
On the conditions of the agricultural labourer; with suggestions for its improvement. 1846 19/9/46
Nichols, A.
Chapters from the physical history of the earth. 1880 13/2/80
Nicholson, George Incumbent of Little Budworth
A dictionary of correspondences . . . from the writings of E. Swedenborg. 1841 14/5/44
Nicholson, George of Cape Town
The Cape and its colonists; with hints to settlers in 1848. 1848 5/8/48
Nicholson, John Aldwell
'The living voice of the Church'—what it is not, and what it is . . . Reprinted from the 'Church Times' 1877 10/8/79
A reply to Cardinal Manning's . . . Essay entitled 'Dr. Nicholson's Accusation of the Archbishop of Westminster'. 1878 18/2/78
The mass in Bayswater. Lectures on the false doctrines of the Romish altar. 1859 11/1/63
Nicholson, William
The purity of the ministry the strength of the church. 1838 28/4/39
Nickel, Joseph
Predigten. 1841 9/11/45
Nicol, A.
Acclimatisation of the Salmonidae at the antipodes. 1882 25/4/84
Nicol, David
The political life of our time. 1889 (2v.) 24/6/90
Nicolay, Charles Grenfell
A proposal to establish a missionary college on the North-West coast of British America . . . letter to . . . Gladstone. 1853 10/7/53
Nicole, Pierre
Essais de morale, contenus en divers traités sur plusieurs devoirs importants. 1781 (14v. 1781–2) 14/8/36, 12/1/39, 27/8/43, 21/4/61, 9/10/64, 23/12/66, 20/1/67
Les prétendus réformés convaincus de schisme. 16/7/36, 9/9/83 ?
Préjugez légitimes contre les Calvinistes. 5/6/36
Traité de la prière. 1866 5/9/58
Niebuhr, Barthold Georg
A dissertation on the geography of Herodotus, tr. from the German. 1830 25/1/31
A letter upon the Roman Catholic emancipation question, and the state of Ireland in 1829. 1887 8/6/87
Niewenhuys, Christianus Johannes
A review of the lives and works of some of the most eminent painters. 1834 24/1/61
Niger, Radulphus
Radulphi Nigri Chronica. The Chronicles . . . now first edited by R. Anstruther. 1844 18/8/48
Nightingale, Florence
How many people may live and not die in India. 1863 (2nd edn 1864) 12/11/64
Observations . . . on the evidence . . . on the sanitary state of the army in India. 1862 (1863) 23/9/63
The institution of Kaiserwerth on the Rhine, for the practical training of deaconesses. 1851 9/5/52
Nightingale, Joseph
A portraiture of Methodism . . . an impartial view of the rise, progress, doctrines, discipline and manners of the Wesleyan Methodists . . . letters. 1807 13/5/49
Nihill, Daniel
Prison discipline in its relations to society and individuals, as . . . conducive to personal reformation. 1839 25/3/39
Suggestions on the revival of ecclesiastical assemblies in the Church of England. 1834 2/5/36
Nikolaides, G.
Topographie et plan stratégique de l'Iliade, avec une carte topographique et stratégique, ed. G. d'Eichthal. 1867 26/1/67, 21/9/75, 9/4/83
Nilsson, Sven
The primitive inhabitants of Scandinavia . . . ed., with an introduction by Sir J. Lubbock. 1868 21/3/68
Nineteenth Century.
2. 561. 11/1877. Forbes on Russia, Bulgaria and the war 13/11/1877
2. 586, 621. 11/1877. Perry on Comte; sun spots 16/11/1877
3. 1052. 6/1878. on Voltaire & Du Chatelet 16/9/1878
3. 1052, 1033. 6/1878. on Voltaire; Greek religion and Inscriptions 2/6/1878
3. 136, 183. 1/1878. Ruskin's lecture; Stanley on absolution 30/12/1877
3. 567, 571. 3/1878. The situation 27/2/1878
3. 71. 1/1878. Midhat Pacha 25/12/1877
3. 712, 687. 4/1878. Clifford; Elam 31/3/1878
4. 858. 11/1878. Lowe on political economy 2/11/1878
4. 932. 11/1878. Stratford Canning 1/11/1878
6. 66. 7/1879. Church of England 13/7/1879
6. 953. 12/1879. Irish land 28/11/1879
7. 256, 318, 361. 2/1880. The Gospel 1/2/1880
7. 27, 107. 1/1880. Essex & Queen Elizabeth; on Canning 9/1/1880

7. 389, 493. 3/1880. Navy; Home rule 1/3/1880
7. 593, 567, 583. 4/1880. Deep sea; Home rule 10/4/1880
7. 685. 4/1880. Native armies of India 13/4/1880
8. 119, 19. 7/1880. Mallock; Martin 11/7/1880
8. 177, 305. 8/1880. Manning; Justin MacCarthy 10/8/1880
8. 182. 8/1880. Tuke of Ireland 13/8/1880
8. 481, 501. 9/1880. on Villon; Burials bill 5/9/1880
8. 513, 646. 10/1880. Obstruction or clôture; India 5/10/1880
8. 672. 10/1880. Lymington 12/10/1880
8. 861. 12/1880. Justin MacCarthy 1/12/1880
8. 876. 12/1880. Irish land 2/12/1880
13. 14. 1/1883. Dalgleish; Scotland 1/1/1883
13. 173. 2/1883. G. D. Campbell 9/2/1883
13. 314. 2/1883. Manning 1/4/1883
13. 729. 5/1883. Whigs 1/5/1883
14. 262. 8/1883. Death 12/8/1883
14. 339. 8/1883. Italy 11/8/1883
14. 753. 11/1883. Jews 3/11/1883
15. 100. 1/1884. Medieval convent life 9/1/1884
15. 71, 1, 167, 49. 1/1884. Ireland; Religion; Mormons; Melbourne 8/1/1884
15. 721. 5/1884. Keay 5/5/1884
15. 849. 5/1884. on Maurice 4/5/1884
16. 451, 460. 9/1884. Lords; Highland Crofters; Federation 3/9/1884
16. 530, 663. 10/1884. Monastery; Irish Emigration; Beaconsfield 1/10/1884
16. 68. 7/1884. Manifestations 7/7/1884
16. 935. 12/1884. Proportional representation 4/12/1884
17. 1072. 6/1885. Crimes Act 1/6/1885
17. 827. 5/1885. Death 3/5/1885
18. 1, 14. 7/1885. Swinburne 4/7/1885
18. 249. 8/1885. Reforming Jesuit; Ireland 2/8/1885
18. 30. 7/1885. Mivart 5/7/1885
18. 432. 9/1885. Taking Orders 10/9/1885
18. 900, 978. 12/1885. Max Müller; on Leopardi 1/12/1885
19. 22–65. 1/1886. Federation articles 31/12/1885
19. 8, 26. 12/1885 30/12/1885
20. 581. 10/1887. J. F. Stephen 4/10/1887
20. 766. 12/1887. Ingram on Gladstone 1/12/1887
21. 165. 2/1887. Gladstone on Ireland 6/1/1887
21. 180. 2/1887 1/1/1887
21. 191. 2/1887. Huxley on realism 20/2/1887
21. 321. 3/1887. Argyll on Huxley 27/2/1887
21. 397. 3/1887. Brabourne on Gladstone 26/2/1887
21. 481. 4/1887. on Huxley 4/4/1887
22. 552. 10/1887. F. Hill 30/9/1887
22. 602. 11/1887. Copyright 31/10/1887
22. 625. 11/1887. Irish land 6/11/1887
22. 850. 12/1887. Mivart; Goodwin 4/12/1887
23. 1, 54. 1/1888. Norway; Cremation 6/1/1888
23. 115. 1/1888. Stephenson 8/1/1888
23. 468. 3/1888. Morley on France 25/7/1888
23. 716, 734. 5/1888. Lords; Church of England 28/4/1888
23. 817, 838. 6/1888. Kropotkin; Pasteur 28/8/1888
24. 262. 8/1888. America 29/8/1888
24. 360. 9/1888. Scottish miners 31/8/1888
24. 465. 10/1888. France 29/9/1899
24. 617. 11/1888. Examinations 30/10/1888
24. 785, 799. 12/1888. Playfair; Greenwood 10/12/1888
25. 140. 1/1889. F. Harrison on Bryce 11/1/1889
25. 351. 3/1889. H. Wace 10/3/1889
25. 409, 415. 3/1889. Westminster Abbey 18/3/1889
25. 552. 4/1889. Monte Carlo 11/4/1889
25. 558, 582. 4/1889. Ionia; O'Connell 10/4/1889
26. 160. 7/1889. The Shah 5/7/1889
26. 257. 8/1889. Brabourne on Gladstone 30/7/1889
26. 476, 500. 9/1889. Lilly; High churchmen 1/9/1889
26. 65. 7/1889. Kidd on Beaconsfield 29/6/1889
26. 801. 11/1889. Rome 31/10/1889
26. 825. 11/1889. Jessop 30/10/1889
26. 912. 12/1889. Russia 1/12/1889
27. 150. 1/1890. Tithes 2/1/1890
27. 424. 3/1890. Teagne 3/3/1890
27. 651, 688. 4/1890. Mrs Ward; Bismarck 1/4/1890
28. 369. 9/1890. Senior on politics 1/9/1890
28. 5. 7/1890. Huxley 29/6/1890
28. 660. 10/1890. Rees on Hindus 25/9/1890
28. 694, 854. 11/1890. Grey; Davitt 6/11/1890
28. 876. 12/1890. Manning 20/11/1890
28. 967. 12/1890. Huxley on Swine 13/12/1890
29. 267. 2/1891. Japan 23/4/1891

Nineteenth Century (*cont.*)
29. 363. 3/1891. Carnegie on poverty 18/3/1891
29. 415. 3/1891. Vernon on mortgages 7/3/1891
29. 455. 3/1891. Huxley on Gladstone 4/3/1891
29. 477. 3/1891. Hughes on Wesley 19/6/1892
29. 495, 507. 3/1891. Knowles; Dunraven on tariffs 9/3/1891
29. 670, 685. 4/1891. on Huxley; on Talleyrand 11/4/1891
29. 904. 6/1891. on Huxley 1/6/1891
29. 96. 1/1891. Schloss on Jews 1/1/1891
30. 699, 712, 764. 11/1891. Pepys; Psychical Society 30/10/1891
30. 872. 12/1891. De Vesci 4/12/1891
30. 933, 939. 12/1891. Norway; Women 3/12/1891
30. 951. 12/1891. Cheyne on Gladstone 29/11/1891
31. 280. 2/1892. Manning 16/2/1892
31. 293. 2/1892. Panama Canal 15/2/1892
31. 586. 4/1892. Keats 30/3/1892
31. 899. 6/1892. H. J. Gladstone on Ireland 5/5/1892
31. 950. 6/1892. Crime 26/10/1892
31. 950. 6/1892. Morrison on crime 5/6/1892
31. 964, 950. 6/1892. Jessop and Rees 8/6/1892
32. 177. 8/1892. Why I voted for Gladstone 31/8/1892
32. 285. 8/1892. Forbes on Eugenie 11/8/1892
32. 711. 11/1892. Pollock on Renan 18/12/1892
32. 831. 11/1892. Tennyson's death 2/11/1892
32. 899, 930, 952. 12/1892. Tennyson 14/12/1892
33. 1710. 4/1893. Sweden 3/4/1893
33. 189. 2/1893. Jephson on Gladstone 1/2/1893
33. 273. 3/1893. Lambert on Tennyson 2/3/1893
33. 480, 525. 3/1893. Crime; on Alfred de Musset 28/2/1893
33. 545. 4/1893. J. Chamberlain on home rule 30/3/1893
33. 559. 4/1893. Redmond on home rule 28/4/1893
33. 637. 4/1893. Mivart on retribution 2/4/1893
33. 927. 6/1893. Ulster 1/6/1893
33. 93. 1/1893. Myers on modern poets 5/1/1893
34. 34. 7/1893. Mrs H. Ward on the creed 29/6/1893
34. 36. 7/1893. Curzon on Siam 17/7/1893
34. 489. 9/1893. on Mivart 13/9/1893

Nippold, Friedrich
Richard Rothe... Ein Christliches Lebensbild auf Grund der Briefe Rothe's entworfen von... Nippold. 1873 (2v. 1873–74) 25/7/86, 26/8/88

Nisard, Marie Léonard Charles
Histoire des livres populaires... depuis le 15e siècle jusqu'à l'etablissement de la Commission d'examen. 1854 28/2/56

Nisco, Niccola
Costituto di N. Nisco, accusato di riato di maestà. 1850 5/2/51
Ferdinando II ed il suo regno. 1884 25/12/88

Nitzsch, C. I.
Babylon and Jerusalem: a letter addressed to Ida, countess of Hahn-Hahn. 1851 10/10/52
Eine protestantische Beantwortung... 1835 1/8/47
System der christlichen Lehre für academische Vorlesungen. 1831 7/1/55

Nitzsch, Gregor Wilhelm
'Des Odysseus Erzählung von Alkinoos' from Erklärende Anmerkungen zu Homer's Odyssee. 1826 (3v. 1826–40) 3/11/57

Nixon, Brinsley
Theism. An address. 1875 9/2/75

Nixon, Francis Russell
A charge delivered... at the visitation held in... May 1851. 1851 8/2/52
Lectures, historical, doctrinal, and practical, on the catechism of the Church of England. 1843 30/5/47

Noble, Pierre le
Histoire du père la Chaize. 23/8/66

Noel, Lady Augusta
Hithersea Mere. 1887 (3v.) 16/11/87

Noel, Baptist Wriothesley
A defence of a tract entitled 'The Unity of the Church'... letter to Clericus Surriensis. 1837 1/6/38
A plea for the poor. 1841 13/10/41
Essay on the union of church and state. 1848 30/12/48
The Catholic claims. A letter to the Lord Bishop of Cashel. 1845 6/8/45
The state of the metropolis considered, in a letter to... bishop of London. 1835 25/4/35
The unity of the church, another Tract for the Times, addressed to... members of the establishment. 1836 13/5/37

Noel, Caroline M.
The name of Jesus, and other poems for the sick and lonely. 1873 3/5/74

Noel, Charles George Lord Gainsborough
The British chaplaincy in Madeira. 1847 18/12/47

Noel, Eugène
Rabelais. 1850 26/12/84
Noel, Roden Berkeley Wriothesley
A little child's monument. 1881 9/4/81
A modern Faust, and other poems. 1888 25/3/90
A philosophy of immortality. 1882 26/2/82
Beatrice and other poems. 1868 25/8/69
Essays on poetry and poets. 1886 29/4/86, 15/2/93
Livingstone in Africa. 1874 17/3/75
The house of Ravensburg. 1877 21/9/77
The red flag, and other poems. 1872 24/12/72
Nohl, Ludwig
Liszt. 1882 19/9/86 ?
Norman, Charles Boswell
Armenia, and the campaign of 1877. 1878 19/1/78
Tonkin; or France in the Far East. 1885 26/2/85
Norman, George Warde
An examination of some prevailing opinions as to the pressure of taxation in this and other countries. 1850 20/10/62
An examination of some prevailing opinions as to the pressure of taxation in this and other countries. 1850 (4th edn 1864) 1/2/64
Norris, John
A philosophical discourse concerning the natural immortality of the soul. 1708 (2v.) 6/7/90
Norris, John Pilkington
Lectures on Butler's Analogy. 1887 2/1/87
Rudiments of theology. A first book for students. 1876 20/2/76
North, Brownlow
'Yes! or No!' Genesis xxiv. 1–58. 1867 18/7/69
North, Jacob Hugo
Two sermons. 1877 25/9/81
North American Review.
86. 487. 4/1858. Indian Revolt 22/4/1858
94. 408. 4/1862. English and French opinion 22/6/1862
110. 260. 4/1870. Travel 19/7/1870
120. 84. 1/1875. Currency 12/3/1875
126. 466. 5/1878. Human depravity 19/5/1878
129. 342. 10/1879. Aldis on Napoleon 30/10/1879
136. 1. 1/1883. Ward Beecher 9/3/1884
145. 616. 12/1887. Field/Ingersoll controversy 18/12/1887
146. 31. 1/1888. Ingersoll 18/1/1888
148. 687, 711. 6/1889. Shipping; Religion 21/6/1889
150. 547. 5/1890. Goldwin Smith 6/5/1890
152. 11. 1/1891. Lecky on Ireland 10/1/1891
154. 603. 5/1892. London society 5/10/1892
156. 685. 6/1893. A. Carnegie 13/6/1893
Carnegie on wealth (proof) 19/6/1889
North British Review.
9. 365. 6/1868. St Louis 14/6/1868
9. 429. 6/1868. on Bunsen 7/6/1868
14. 319–49. 2/1851. Italy 16/7/1851
15. 254. 5/1851. Supremacy 11/5/1851
16. 49. 11/1851. on Mill 8/4/1852
17. 1. 5/1852. on Roebuck 1/5/1852
17. 205. 5/1852. Review of Hanna's Chalmers 2/5/1852
17. 559. 8/1852. Review of J. Moseley 13/10/1852
18. 1. 11/1852. Oxford Commission 6/11/1852
21. 505, 544. 8/1854. on Harcourt; on Murchison 31/7/1854
23. 137. 5/1855. Civil Service 30/4/1855
23. 266. 5/1855. War 5/5/1855
24. 11/1855. Greg on cabinets 12/11/1855
25. 399. 8/1856. Rogers 5/8/1856
25. 493. 8/1856. Crimean campaign 31/7/1856
25. 515. 8/1856. Oude 2/8/1856
27. 277. 11/1857. Allison's History 10/11/1857
29. 25. 8/1858. Gladstone's *Homer* 12/8/1858
33. 428. 11/1860. Macaulay 26/11/1860
34. 255. 2/1861. Palmerston 19/4/1861
35. 1. 8/1861. Universities 3/8/1861
36. 233. 2/1862. Greg on American Republic 8/2/1862
36. 345. 5/1862. Homer 12/5/1862
41. 253. 6/1864. Philanthropy 15/12/1864
41. 338. 7/1864. Liturgical Revision 1/12/1864
41. 463. 6/1864. Richardson 8/12/1864
42. 107. 3/1865. University tests 23/5/1865
48. 1. 3/1868. Trade unions 15/2/1868
53. 183. 10/1870. Vatican Council 20/11/1870
101. 435, 1. 10/1869. Irish land; *Juventus Mundi* 15/10/1869
Northcote, James
The Life of Sir Joshua Reynolds. 1813 (2v. 1813–15) 18/7/90
Northcote, Stafford Henry Earl of Iddesleigh
A short review of the history of the navigation laws of England. 1849 1/7/48
A statement of facts connected with the election of ... Gladstone as member for the university of Oxford in 1847, and ... re-election in 1852 and 1853. 1853 22/2/53
Lectures and essays. 1887 12/7/87
Life, letters and diaries of Sir Stafford Northcote, by A. Lang. 1890 (2v.) 25/2/90, 25/10/90

Northcote, Stafford Henry Earl of Iddesleigh (*cont.*)
Probate . . . duties. Speeches by Mr. J. Dodds . . . S. Northcote. 1879 23/12/79
Scraps, odds and ends. 1888 27/6/88
Twenty years of financial policy. A summary of the chief financial measures passed between 1842 and 1861. 1862 2/8/62, 22/4/79
Norton, Andrews
A statement of reasons for not believing the doctrine of Trinitarians concerning the nature of God. 1819 26/9/53 ?
Norton, Caroline Elizabeth Sarah
A letter to the Queen on Lord Chancellor Cranworth's marriage and divorce bill. 1855 24/10/55
A plain letter to the Lord Chancellor on the Infant Custody Bill. 1839 29/4/39
English laws for women in the nineteenth century. 1854 21/3/54
Lost and saved. 1863 (3v.) 27/6/63
Stuart of Dunleath. 1853 10/2/52 ?
The Dream, and other poems. 1840 3/12/40
The lady of La Garaye. Poem. 1862 6/1/62
The separation of mother and child by the law of 'Custody of Infants', considered. 1838 7/6/38
Norton, Edward
National finance and currency with the operation of gain or loss of gold in peace and war. 1860 12/11/57
The Bank Charter Act of 1844 truthfully considered. 1857 (2nd edn) 12/11/57
Nossoff, Serge
La Russie comique. 1891 13/3/92 ?
Notes on Ecce Homo [Anon. pamphlet]. 1866 23/2/68
Notice sur la vie de la Révérande Mère Sainte-Justine. 1865 14/4/75
Notizia dei protestanti. 1834 23/9/38
Nott, Eliphalet
Lectures on temperance. 1847 10/3/52
Nott, Josiah Clark, and Gliddon, R. G.
Types of mankind: or Ethnological researches illustrated by . . . papers of S. G. Morton. 1854 9/9/77
Nouet, Jacques
Homo orationis, exercitia spiritualia secundum normam S. Ignatii de Loyola. 1845 16/8/46
Nouvelle Revue. 1. 5, 56. Introduction; Türr's article 15/10/1879
Novikov, Olga
'Russia, Rome and the Old Catholics' in *New Review*, viii. 439. 1893 (April 1893) 7/5/93
[Review by Gladstone of 'Russia and England from 1876 to 1880', with preface by J. A. Froude] in *Nineteenth Century*, vii. 538. 1880 (March 1880) 14/2/80
Fraser's Magazine, ciii. 30. 1881 (January 1881) 30/1/81 ?
Novra, Henry
Spirit-rapping, explained and exposed. A lecture. 1860 17/9/61
Nowakowski, A. von, and Flechner, H.
Brasilien unter Dom Pedro II. 1877 29/5/77 ?
Now and then [untraced]. 29/4/48
Nowell, Alexander
Catechismus . . . with a Life, ed. W. Jacobson. 1835 12/1/45
Nowlan, P. J.
An Irish primer for English statesmen: being a reply to a letter of Mr. Goldwin Smith. 1867 6/1/68
Nox Praecessit. 10/11/67
Nugée, George
The necessity for Christian education to elevate the native character in India. An essay. 1846 8/3/57
Nugent, George Thomas John
A reply to the 'Narrative of the case of the Marchioness of Westmeath'. 1857 13/7/57
Nugent, Paul
Life of Nugent, by H. F. Hetherington. 1890 (2v.) 5/7/90
Nulty, Thomas
Letter . . . to Joseph Cowen, Esq., M.P., on the state of public affairs in Ireland. 1881 5/10/88 ?
[Nursing Sisters' Institute Report]. 1848 20/8/48
Nutt, George
Gaisford prize. Greek comic iambics. 1866 7/2/90 ?
Nye, George Henry Frederick
The story of the Church in Wales. 1890 11/5/90
Nye, Stephen
A brief history of the Unitarians. 24/6/55

Oakeley, Frederick
A few words to those churchmen, being members of Convocation, who purpose taking no part in Mr. Ward's case. 1845 5/1/45
A letter on submitting to the Catholic Church. Addressed to a friend. 1845 18/11/45
A letter to . . . the bishop of London, on a subject connected with the recent proceedings at Oxford. 1845 20/2/45
A letter to . . . the bishop of London, on a subject connected with the recent proceedings at Oxford. 1845 (2nd letter) 24/3/45
A letter to . . . the Duke of Wellington upon the principle and tendency of . . . 'Bill abolishing subscription to Articles of Religion in certain cases'. 1835 29/6/35
Explanation of a passage in an article on certain works of Bishop Jewel . . . letter to . . . C. S. Bird. 1842 19/6/42

Historical notes on the Tractarian movement. 1865 16/12/64
Lyra liturgica. Reflections in verse for Holy Days and seasons. 1865 16/7/65
Manual of devotion for the Holy Communion. 1843 7/9/45
Prayers for a blessing on the work of building a new church. 1841 3/10/42
Preface to 'Sermons, preached chiefly in the Chapel Royal, at Whitehall'. 1839 26/3/39
Remarks upon Aristotelian and Platonic ethics, as a branch of the studies pursued in . . . Oxford. 1837 10/5/37
Sermons, preached chiefly in the Chapel Royal, at Whitehall. 1837 12/5/39
The Athanasian Creed: four lectures suggested by the present controversy. 1872 29/12/72
The claim to 'hold, as distinct from teaching,' explained, in a letter to a friend. 1845 6/7/45
The leading topics of Dr. Pusey's recent work [Eirenicon] *reviewed in a letter to . . . Manning.* 1866 4/3/66
The priest on the mission. A course of lectures on missionary and parochial duties. 1871 5/3/71
The question of university education for English Catholics . . . its moral and religious bearings. 1864 3/3/72
The subject of Tract XC examined in connection with the history of the thirty-nine articles. 1841 29/4/41
The voice of creation as a witness to the mind of its divine author. Five lectures. 1876 2/4/76
Things dispensable and things indispensable: the importance of distinguishing between them. 1844 22/12/44
Oakley, John
'The Conscience Clause.' Its history, terms, effect and principle. A reply to . . . Denison. 1866 27/2/66
Oastler, Richard
A letter to the Archbishop of York. 1836 10/2/36
'Objects and principles of the Systematic Beneficence Society' 8/1/65
O'Brien, Charlotte Grace
Lyrics. 1886 3/1/87 ?
O'Brien, Edward
The lawyer, his character and rule of holy life, after the manner of . . . Herbert's Country Parson. 1842 3/8/42
O'Brien, Henry
The round towers of Ireland: or, the mysteries of Freemasonry, of Sabaism, and of Budhism . . . unveiled. 1834 3/5/84
O'Brien, James Thomas Bishop of Ossory
A charge delivered . . . in October, 1863. 1864 6/3/64
A charge delivered . . . in September 1842. 1843 29/10/43
A charge delivered . . . in September 1845. 1846 13/5/47
A charge delivered . . . in September 1851. 1852 25/4/52
Speech to the church education society for Ireland. 1850 7/6/50 ?
The case of the established church in Ireland. 1867 4/8/67, 17/9/69
The disestablishment and disendowment of the Irish branch of the United Church, considered. 1869 (2v.) 7/3/69
The expediency of restoring at this time to the Church her synodical powers, considered. 1843 27/10/43
O'Brien, Lucius Baron Inchiquin
Ireland. The late famine, and the poor laws. 1848 21/8/48
O'Brien, Richard Barry
'Irish wrongs and English remedies' in *Nineteenth Century*, xviii. 707. 1885 (November 1885) 1/11/85
Articles on Ireland 1886. 1886 7/7/86
Fifty years of concessions to Ireland. 1831–1881. 1883 (2v.) 9/10/83, 12/10/85, 7/7/86 n
Irish wrongs and English remedies. 1887 22/4/87
The autobiography of Theobald Wolfe Tone, 1763–1798, ed. R. B. O'Brien. 1893 12/10/93, 19/11/93
The Irish land question and English public opinion. With a supplement on Griffith's valuation. 1881 11/5/81
The parliamentary history of the Irish land question, from 1829 to 1869. 1880 4/11/80
Thomas Drummond, Under-Secretary in Ireland, 1835–40. Life and letters, by R. B. O'Brien. 1889 22/2/89
O'Brien, Thomas
A glance at parties. 1844 22/8/44 ?, 6/12/44
Observateur Catholique.
5 3/1/1858
8/3/1857
Observations on a friendly adviser. 30/7/31
Observations on army administration. By a general officer. 1868 1/2/68
Observations on factory labour. 1844 4/5/44
Observations on Irish laws of real property. 1847 26/11/47
Observations on the marriage laws. 1815 12/6/57
Observations on the working of the Emancipation Act [British and Foreign Anti-Slavery Soc. pamphlet]. 21/3/36
O'Callaghan, A.
Observations on the state of political and religious feeling in Ireland. 1827 12/10/87
O'Clery, Patrick Keyes The O'Clery
The making of Italy. 1892 1/4/92

O'Connell, Daniel
A memoir on Ireland, native and Saxon. 1843 (3rd edn 1885 vol 1) 20/10/86, 12/11/86
Centenary life of O'Connell, by J. O'Rourke [with Gladstone's letter in reprints]. 1875 17/11/77, 26/11/88
Correspondence of O'Connell, ed. W. J. Fitzpatrick. 1888 (2v.) 26/10/88
Letters to the reformers of England, on the Reform Bill for Ireland. 1832 13/4/69
Report to the Repeal Association. 1840 13/4/87 ?
The Liberator, Daniel O'Connell, his life and times, by M. F. Cusack. 1872 26/11/88
O'Connor, Feargus
A series of letters . . . to Daniel O'Connell . . . conduct during the agitation of . . . Catholic emancipation. 1836 3/1/37
O'Connor, Roger
Chronicles of Eri; being the history of the Gaal Sciot Iber, or Irish people. 1822 (2v.) 15/1/83, 20/4/86
O'Connor, Thomas Power
Benjamin Disraeli. 1879 (2v. 1879–81) 30/7/81
Benjamin Disraeli, Earl of Beaconsfield. A biography. 1877 12/4/77
Charles Stuart Parnell. A memory. 1891 21/10/91
Gladstone's House of Commons. 1885 29/5/85
The Parnell movement, with a sketch of Irish parties from 1843. 1886 15/11/87 ?, 1/11/88
O'Conor, Charles
Columbanus ad Hibernos. 1810 13/8/45
O'Conor, Matthew
Military history of the Irish nation, comprising a memoir of the Irish brigade in the service of France. 1845 9/11/92 ?
O'Dell, Stackpool Edward
Merciful or merciless. A novel. 1886 31/7/86
Odger, G.
'The land question' in *Contemporary Review*, xviii. 23. 1871 (August 1871) 2/8/71
O'Donnell, Charles James
The black pamphlet of Calcutta. The famine of 1874. 1876 28/2/76
O'Donnell, Frank Hugh
'Fenianism, past and present' in *Contemporary Review*, xliii. 747. 1883 (May 1883) 2/5/83
Public education: its necessity, and the ideas involved in it. 1867 1/3/73 ?
O'Dwyer, Carew
The Catholic question of 1851 considered. 1851 21/3/51
Oesterreich und die orientalische Frage. 1875 9/12/76
Oetker, Friedrich
Helgoland. Schilderungen und Erörterungen. 1855 (2nd edn 1878) 30/10/78
Office, the divine. 1878 15/9/78
O'Flanagan, James Roderick
The Munster circuit. Tale, trials and traditions. 1879 16/9/80
Ogilvie, Charles Atmore
Considerations on subscription to the thirty-nine articles . . . to the serious attention of candidates for holy orders. 1845 6/8/48
Ogilvy, Thomas
Statistical evidence affecting the question of the Navigation Laws. 1849 5/5/49
O'Grady, Standish James
Early bardic literature, Ireland. 1879 30/5/82, 27/7/85
Red Hugh's captivity. A picture of Ireland, social and political, in the reign of Queen Elizabeth. 1889 20/3/89
O'Hagan, John
The poetry of Sir Samuel Ferguson. 1887 4/2/87
O'Hagan, Thomas
Occasional papers and addresses. 1884 19/3/84
Speech of 18th June, 1863. 1863 27/6/63
The study of jurisprudence, Roman, English and Celtic. An address. 1867 15/7/68
O'Hart, John
Irish pedigrees; or, the origin and stem of the Irish nation. 1876 (1876–78) 29/1/76
Ohnet, Georges
Le maître de Forges. 1884 26/1/89
Serge Panine. 1881 14/1/89
O'Keeffe, Robert
[Judgment of L. C. Justice]. 1873 27/3/73
Ultramontanism versus civil and religious liberty. 1875 21/1/75
Okely, William
A letter to Robert Southey . . . on his Life of the late Mr. John Wesley. 1820 16/8/76 ?
Okes, Richard
Musae Etonenses: sive Carminum Etonae conditorum delectus. Series nova. 1856 (1856–69) 2/10/27
Oldham, Richard Samuel
The eve of a campaign a time for self searching . . . A sermon. 1855 10/3/58
Old New Zealand. 1876 26/12/76
Old Whig. 1735 (1735–38) 3/3/48
Oliari, Alcide
Dei volghi Pelasgici. Armonie nella storia. 1870 2/1/71
Oliphant, Laurence
The Russian shores of the Black Sea in the autumn of 1853. 1853 20/5/53
Oliphant, Margaret Oliphant
'Mrs. Carlyle' in *Contemporary Review*, xlxii, 609. 1883 (May 1883) 5/5/83

A beleaguered city, being a narrative of certain recent events in the city of Semur. 1880 13/7/83

Caleb Field; a tale of the Puritans. 1851 30/9/51

Francis of Assisi. 1868 15/1/71

Innocenta. 1892 9/1/92

Jerusalem, its city and hope. 1891 21/12/91

Memoir of Count de Montalembert... A chapter of recent French history. 1872 23/11/73

Miss Marjoribanks. 1866 (3v.) 22/9/82

Salem chapel. 1863 (2v.) 8/5/81

The life of Edward Irving, Minister of the National Scotch Church, London. 1862 (2v.) 11/5/62

The makers of Florence: Dante, Giotto, Savonarola; and their city. 1876 28/12/87

The makers of Venice: Doges, conquerors, painters, and men of letters. 1887 16/12/87

Oliveira, Benjamin

A few observations upon the work of the Isthmus of Suez canal, made... in April, 1863. 1863 22/8/63

Oliver, George

Collections towards illustrating the biography of the... [British] members of the Society of Jesus. 1845 8/12/61

Oliver, Robert

Unnoticed apologies. A talk on the Irish question. 1888 29/8/90

Ollivier, Olivier Émile

L'église et l'état au concile du Vatican. 1879 (2v.) 11/8/89 ?

Olmsted, Frederick Law

Journeys and explorations in the Cotton Kingdom. 1861 (2v.) 17/2/62

O'Mahony, Denis Patrick Michael

Rome, semper eadem. 1875 29/4/75, 10/11/77

O'Malley, Thaddeus

Harmony in religion. 1872 28/2/75

Home rule on the basis of federalism. 1873 9/7/73, 19/9/85

O'Meara, Kathleen pseud. G. Ramsay

Thomas Grant, first bishop of Southwark. 1886 13/5/88

Omega, pseud.

Public education. Why is a new code wanted?. 1861 5/12/61

Ommanney, George Druce Wynne

The Athanasian creed; its use in the services of the church. A paper. 1872 24/3/72

O'Neill, Mrs.

The Bondman: a story of the times of Wat Tyler. 1833 31/1/90

O'Neill, T. Warren

The refutation of Darwinism; and the converse theory of development: based exclusively upon Darwin's facts. 1880 2/1/81, 5/2/82

Onslow, Guildford

'Tichborne.' Reasons why he should have had the benefit of the doubt. 1874 11/5/74

On the present and future of Ireland, by a merchant. 1865 18/2/65

Oort, Henricus

Evangelie en Talmud uit het oogpunt der zedelijkheid vergeleken. 1881 29/7/83

Operatives, address to. 1841 27/9/42

Opie, John

Lectures on painting delivered at the Royal Academy of Arts. 1809 19/1/49

Opium: some pros and cons of the Opium Question. 1840 11/2/40

Order of the administration of the Lord's Supper... for the use of the Church of Scotland. 1881 17/12/94

Oregon, two tracts on. 1846 27/3/46

O'Reilly, Edmund Joseph

The relations of the church to society. Theological essays. 1892 13/3/92

Orkney, Trials for witchcraft. 1837 8/9/82

Orléans, Comte de Paris

Les associations ouvrières. 1869 25/5/69

Orléans, F. D'

Duc d'Orléans. Lettres 1825–1842. 1889 3/9/89

Orléans, H. E. P. L. Duke d'Aumale

Discours... à l'académie française. 1873 3/5/73

Lettre sur l'histoire de la France. 1861 19/4/61

Séance de l'académie française. 1881 17/5/81

Orme, William

The practical works of... R Baxter. 1830 9/11/62

Ormerod, Thomas Johnson

A charge at the... visitation of... Archdeacon of Suffolk. 1850 (1867) 12/5/67 ?

Ornsby, Robert

Memoirs of James Robert Hope-Scott. 1884 (2v.) 13/10/83, 14/11/83, 23/11/83, 24/11/83, 10/12/83, 2/1/84, 3/2/84

O'Rourke, John

The centenary life of O'Connell. 1875 17/11/77, 26/11/88

Orr, James

The Christian view of God and the world as centring in the Incarnation. Being the Kerr lectures for 1890–91. 1893 2/4/93

Orsini, Felice

Memorie e documenti intorno al governo della repubblica Romana. 1850 5/11/50

Orsini, Mathieu

The history of the Blessed Virgin Mary. 1872 19/8/77

Orthodoxie et papisme. 1859 13/11/59

Osborn, R. D.

'India under Lord Lytton' in *Contemporary Review,* xxxvi. 553. 1879 (December 1879) 2/12/79

Osborn, Sherard
On the impressment of British seamen and the necessity for a Naval Militia Bill. 1874 26/11/74
Osborne, William Alexander
[speciman notes for school classical textbooks]. 4/3/41 ?
Osgood, Samuel
Bryant among his countrymen; the poet, the patriot, the man. An ovation. 1879 2/2/79
Osgood's rebellion and what became of it; or, Days at Westbrook College. 1877 6/4/90
O'Shaughnessy, Arthur William Edgar
An epic of women, and other poems. 1870 1/6/71
O'Sullivan, Mortimer
A guide to an Irish gentleman in his search for a religion. 1833 24/11/33
Theory of developments on Christian Doctrine. 1846 10/5/46
Otter, William
[unpublished circular to rural deans]. 15/4/40 ?
Ottley, Edward Bickersteth
Rational aspects of some revealed truths. 1887 15/5/87
Ottley, Henry
The challenge to the church of God: 'Give us a reason of your hope?' A sermon. 1882 18/5/84
The great dilemma: Christ his own witness or his own accuser. 1881 16/10/81
Ottoman, l'Empire. 1877 23/11/77
Otway, Thomas
Caius Marius. 20/10/28
Friendship in fashion. A comedy. 17/10/28
The atheist: or the second part of the Souldier's Fortune. 27/10/28
The orphan. 22/10/28
The souldier's fortune: a comedy. 24/10/28
Venice Preserv'd, or, the plot discovered. A tragedy. 18/10/28
Ouchterlony, John
The Chinese war. 1844 29/4/44
Our coal and our coal pits. 1854 25/7/57
Our country, an essay. 1855 4/12/86
Our foreign relations [pamphlet]. 1869 2/4/69
Our Lady's Tumbler. A twelfth century legend. 1894 1/4/94
Our tent in the Crimea and wanderings in Sebastopol. 1856 8/3/56
Outline of ancient history. 1830 18/9/76
Outram, George
Lyrics, legal and miscellaneous, ed. H. G. Bell. 1874 23/12/81
Outram, James
Memoir on Egypt. 1849 21/3/60
Rough notes of the campaign in Sinde and Affghanistan, in 1838–39. 1840 6/9/57
The conquest of Scinde, a commentary. 1846 9/12/46
Ouvry, Henry Aimé
Stein and his reforms in Prussia, with reference to the land question in England. 1873 7/8/78
Oven, B. van
Ought Baron de Rothschild to sit in parliament? An imaginary conversation. 1847 16/12/47
Overall, John
The Convocation book of 1606 [printed for W. Sancroft (1690) and republished]. 1844 5/11/44
Overbeck, Frederick
Account of the picture. 1843 29/5/45
Overbeck, J. Joseph
Catholic orthodoxy and Anglo-Catholicism, a word about intercommunion between the English and the Orthodox churches. 1866 9/9/66
Overton, John Rector of St. Crux
The true churchmen ascertained: or, an Apology for . . . Evangelical ministers. 1801 29/10/54, 3/8/79
Overton, John Henry
John Hannah. A clerical study. 1890 23/1/90
Life in the English church 1660–1714. 1885 20/12/85
William Law, nonjuror and mystic . . . A sketch of his life, character and opinions. 1881 5/6/81
Ovid
Fasti and Epistolae. 16/12/45, 31/12/70
Metamorphoses. 16/7/25, 6/8/31, 28/3/57, 26/4/67, 21/5/90
Opera. 16/7/25, 5/3/27, 28/3/27, 8/8/33
Tristia. 11/6/55
Owen, Henry
Gerald the Welshman. 1889 2/8/90
Owen, Isabel Burnard
Poems. 1858 16/1/64
Owen, Sir Richard K. C. B.
Antiquity of man as deduced from the discovery of a human skeleton during the excavations. 1884 20/10/85
Palaeontology, or a systematic summary of extinct animals and their geological relations. 1860 (2nd edn 1861) 7/12/61, 7/12/85
Owen, Robert B. D.
An apology for the 'High Church' movement. 1851 18/3/51
An introduction to the study of dogmatic theology. 1858 27/12/63
The Kymry, their origin, history, and international relations. 1891 20/11/91
Owen, Robert socialist
Synopsis of four lectures. 1838 27/2/41 ?
The life of Robert Owen. Written by himself. 1857 27/4/58
Owen, Robert Dale
The debatable land between this world and the next. 1871 10/12/71

Owen, Sidney James
India on the eve of the British conquest. A historical sketch. 1872 28/2/73
Owenson, Lady Sydney afterw. Morgan
Absenteeism. 1825 5/11/88
Diary and correspondence. 1859 12/3/59
The life and times of Salvator Rosa. 1824 (2v.) 15/10/32
Oxenden, Ashton
Plain sermons. 1893 5/11/93
Oxenham, Henry Nutcombe
'Jukes' defence of universalism', *Christian Apologist*, i. 87. 1876 (October 1876) 17/12/76
Catholic eschatology and universalism. An essay on the doctrine of future retribution. 1876 2/7/76
Dr. Pusey's 'Eirenicon' considered. 1866 29/4/66
Preface to 2nd edn of *'Catholic eschatology'.* 1878 15/12/78
Short studies in ecclesiastical history and biography. 1884 15/6/84
The Catholic doctrine of atonement: an historical inquiry into its development in the church. 1865 14/5/71, 17/12/74
Oxford, Member of Convocation of
Concensus omnium. 1838 19/7/38
Oxford and Cambridge Review.
1. 45. 7/1845. on Smythe 2/8/1845
1. 639. 12/1845. The Spanish Match 9/12/1845
2. 51. 1/1846. Manners on the Crisis 9/1/1846
5. 495. 10/1847. Poll Book 21/10/1847
Oxford Essays [H. B. Wilson on schemes of Christian comprension]. 1857 5/4/57
Oxford Essays [J. Conington on Pope's poetry]. 1858 8/7/58
Oxford Essays [R. J. King on Carolingian romance]. 1856 16/12/56
Oxford prize poems. 1826 (7th edn) 11/3/28
Oxford Tutors' Association
On professorial and tutorial system (no. 3). 1853 6/12/53
On University extension (no. 1). 1853 15/12/52
Oxford University
Delegacy of non-collegiate students Report. 1875 25/12/75
Six letters on the subject of an address presented ... to the heads of colleges in November 1845. 1846 25/2/46
Oxford University Magazine. 1. 3. 1834. On Shelley 4/4/1834
Oxley, William
Modern messiahs and wonder workers. 1889 16/11/90

P., A. B.
Greece and Turkey. The indisputable rights of Greece. An appeal to the Christian world. 1878 6/2/78
Pacca, Bartolomeo
Historical memoirs, tr. G. Head. 1850 24/4/51
Pacification Européenne. 19/3/1886
Packe, Charles
The spirit of travel. 1856 23/1/57
Padelletti, Guido
[on Italian Church policy]. 1/9/75
Page, Cyril William
A letter to the bishop of London. 1846 3/4/46
Page, David
Handbook of geological terms and geology. 1859 17/11/62
Page, Richard pseud. D. Hardcastle
Action of the corn laws. 1841 22/9/41
Page, Thomas C. E.
Report on the eligibility of Milford Haven for ocean steam ships, and for a Naval arsenal. 1859 26/12/59
Page, Thomas Incumbent of St. Matthew's
An earnest appeal to the nation at large, on the mischievous effects of beer houses. 1846 17/3/47
Paget, Francis Edward
A student penitent of 1695. 1875 17/1/75
Milford Malvoisin; or, pews and pewholders. 1842 4/3/42
St. Antholin's; or, old churches and new. A tale for the times. 1841 1/8/41
Sursum corda: aids to private devotion. 1859 16/1/76
Tales of the village. 1840 24/10/41
The curate of Cumberworth: and the vicar of Roost. 1859 3/3/60, 27/12/67
The pageant; or, pleasure and its price. 1843 30/6/88
Paget, Lord George
A letter to ... Russell containing suggestions for raising a reserve force. 1852 3/7/52
Paget, John Barrister-at-law
An inquiry into the evidence relating to the charges brought by Lord Macaulay against William Penn. 1858 2/6/76
Ecclesiastical courts ... the case of Talbot v. *Talbot.* 1854 12/2/56
Paradoxes and puzzles, historical, judicial, and literary. 1874 14/6/76
Paget, Violet pseud. Vernon Lee
The Countess of Albany. 1883 30/7/85
Paglia, Antonio Dalla pseud. A. Paleario
The benefit of Christ's death, intro. C. Babington. 1843 (1855 edn) 14/9/56, 3/3/63
Pailleron, Edouard
Le monde, où l'on s'ennuie. 1881 8/9/86

Paine, Thomas
Age of reason. 1794 8/12/48
The American crisis. 1792 13/12/48 ?
The rights of man. 1790 (2 parts, 1790–92) 16/2/35

Pakington, John Somerset
National education. Address . . . to . . . the Manchester Athenaeum, November 18th, 1856. 1856 26/12/56

Paladin, pseud.
Glances at great and little men. 1890 18/11/90

Paladini, Carlo
Gladstone e Dufferin in Italia. 1889 16/1/89 n

Palestine, Our work in. Exploration fund report. 1872 8/6/72

Paley, Frederick Apthorp
'Iliad' of Homer, books 1–12. 1867 28/5/73
Quintus Smyrnaeus and the 'Homer' of the tragic poets. 1876 4/9/77
The church restorers: a tale treating of ancient and modern architecture and church decorations. 1844 8/12/44

Paley, William
Horae Paulinae: or the truth of the scripture history of St. Paul evinced. 1790 15/3/29
Natural theology: or, evidences of the existence and attributes of the deity, collected from the appearances of nature. 1802 10/9/28
Principles of moral and political philosophy. 1785 4/11/27, 25/11/27, 2/12/27, 6/1/28, 27/7/30, 11/8/30, 23/10/31, 3/11/40
The complete works of William Paley . . . and a life of the author by . . . R. Lynam. 1825 8/3/29
View of the evidences of Christianity. 1794 30/9/27

Palgrave, Francis Turner
Handbook to the fine art collection in the international Exhibition of 1862. 1862 17/5/62
Hymns. 1867 23/6/57
Lyrical poems. 1871 19/5/71
The golden treasury. 1861 20/7/61

Palgrave, Sir Reginald Francis Douce
The House of Commons. Illustrations of its history and practice. A course of three lectures. 1868 27/3/69

Palgrave, William Gifford
Hermann Agha: an Eastern narrative. 1872 (2v.) 12/6/83

Palin, William
The history of the Church of England, from the revolution to the last acts of Convocation . . . 1688–1717. 1851 29/6/51

Pallavicino, Sforza
Istoria del Concilio di Trento. (2v. 1656, 57) 5/2/80

Palmer, Alfred Neorard
The town, fields and folk of Wrexham in the time of James the first. 1884 27/12/83

Palmer, Ebenezer
Tendrils in verse. 1880 (3rd edn) 1/2/80

Palmer, Ebenezer Reeves
The development of revelation: an attempt to elucidate the nature and meaning of Old Testament studies. 1892 12/4/92

Palmer, John Horsley
Reply to the reflections of Mr. S. Jones Loyd, on . . . 'Causes . . . of the pressure upon the money-market'. 1837 7/3/37
The causes and consequences of the pressure upon the money-market. 1837 7/3/37, 25/7/76

Palmer, R.
[Missionary instructions]. (not found) 4/12/37

Palmer, Roundell Earl of Selborne
[on radicalism] in *Contemporary Review*, li. 347. 1887 (March 1887) 12/3/87
A defence of the Church of England against disestablishment . . . letter to . . . W. E. Gladstone. 1886 5/12/86
Notes on some passages in the liturgical history of the reformed English church. 1878 17/2/78
Speech . . . on a motion for the abolition of patents for inventions [28 May, 1868]. 1869 1/10/68
Speech . . . on the 'Alabama' question. 1863 12/2/72
The book of praise. 1862 21/12/62
The connection of poetry with history. A lecture. 1852 21/2/57

Palmer, T. pseud.
A letter to . . . Campbell. 1856 11/6/56

Palmer, Thomas H.
On the evils of the present system of primary instruction. 1837 22/6/40 ?

Palmer, William of Magdalen College
A letter to a Protestant-Catholic. 1842 23/9/42
A letter to . . . Dr. Hampden. 1842 12/9/45
Aids to reflection on the seemingly double character of the established church. 1841 12/12/41, 4/1/42
An appeal to . . . the Scottish bishops and clergy. 1849 18/3/49
Dissertations on subjects relating to the 'Orthodox' or 'Eastern Catholic' communion. 1853 13/2/53
Harmony of Anglican doctrine with the doctrine of the Eastern church. 1846 28/6/46
Notes of a visit to the Russian Church in the years 1840, 1841, ed. J. H. Newman. 1882 9/11/82
Remarks on . . . the Turkish question. 1853 27/9/53

Palmer, William of Worcester College
[on the Oxford Movement] in *Contemporary Review*, xliii. 636. 1883 (May 1883) 2/5/83
A compendious ecclesiastical history, from the earliest period to the present time. 1840 24/5/40

A fifth letter to N. Wiseman, D.D.... proofs of the idolatry and superstition of Romanism. 1841 3/10/41
A letter to N. Wiseman. 1841 14/4/41
A second letter to N. Wiseman. 1841 3/5/41
A seventh letter to N. Wiseman. 1842 1/5/42
A sixth letter to N. Wiseman, D.D. on the doctrine of purgatory. 1841 12/12/41
A speech read at... meeting of the Society for Promoting Christian Knowledge. 1840 24/7/40
A third letter to N. Wiseman. 1841 3/5/41
A treatise on the church of Christ; designed chiefly for the use of students in theology. 1838 (2v.) 28/7/38, 15/8/38, 16/8/38, 19/3/39, 25/12/61, 20/3/81, 27/3/81, 11/11/83, 25/5/88
An eighth letter to N. Wiseman. 1842 1/5/42
An examination of... R. W. Sibthorp's reasons for his secession from the church. 1842 4/2/42
An inquiry into the possibility of obtaining means for church extension without parliamentary grants. 1841 24/11/47
Letters to Wiseman. 1842 10/3/45, 9/2/90
Narrative of events connected with the publication of the Tracts for the Times. 1843 13/10/43, 11/4/84
Origines Liturgicae, or antiquities of the English ritual, and a dissertation on primitive liturgies. 1832 (2v.) 17/3/33, 5/7/40
Remarks on... Arnold's 'Principles of church reform'. 1833 15/3/33
The apostolical jurisdiction and succession of the episcopacy in the British Churches vindicated against... objections of... Wiseman in... Dublin Review. 1840 21/7/40, 20/12/76
The doctrine of development and conscience, considered in relation to... Catholic system. 1846 3/1/47

Palmer, Sir William
Results of the 'Expostulation' in their relation to the unity of Roman Catholicism. 1875 30/3/75 ?

Palumbo, Raffaele
Carteggio... con Lady Emma Hamilton... con un sommario storico. 1877 1/1/78

Pamphili, Eusebius
Evangelica Praeparatio. 24/6/65, 9/7/65, 6/8/65

Panam, Pauline Adelaïde Alexandre
Memoirs of a young Greek lady... against... the reigning Prince of Saxe-Cobourg, tr. W. H. Ireland. 1823 10/4/73

Panizzi, Anthony
[review of Rossetti] in *The Foreign Review and Continental Miscellany*, ii. 175. 1828 5/11/42
On the supply of printed books from the library to the reading room of the British Museum. 1846 13/6/46
Orlando furioso di Ariosto. 1834 (4v.) 1/11/55
Orlando innamorato di Bojardo... with an essay on the romantic narrative poetry of the Italians. 1830 5/4/50

Pantaleoni, Diomede
Del presente e dell'Avvenire del Cattolicismo a proposito del Concilio Ecumenico. 1870 15/1/70

Panzani, Gregorio
The memoirs of G. Panzani... tr. J. Bevington. 1793 (1813 edn) 15/3/51

Papanikolas, Georgios Drakatos
Ionian islands. 1851 15/11/51 ?
Usque adeo? or, What may be said for the Ionian people. 1853 12/11/58

Paparrhegopoulos, Konstantinos
Histoire de la civilisation hellénique. 1878 27/1/78

Pape, le orgia e diletti de. 1/2/72
Papers for the times, ed. Lewin. 1879 29/9/78, 26/1/79
Paradisus animae. 25/2/46, 12/7/91

Pardoe, Julia S. H.
Louis the Fourteenth, and the court of France in the seventeenth century. 1847 (3v.) 13/1/86

Pareto, Vilfredo Federigo Damaso
Il protezionismo in Italia. 1891 27/4/92 ?

Paris, Gaston Bruno Paulin
Etude sur le rôle de l'accent latin dans la langue française. 1862 22/9/65

Parish registers. 1867 26/5/77

Parisis, Pierre Louis
Démonstration de l'Immaculée Conception de la bienheureuse Vierge Marie. 1849 7/10/60

Parker, James
Memorandum respecting the connection between Oxford university and the family of... Parker of Oxford. 1863 4/8/63

Parker, John Henry C. B.
An introduction to the study of Gothic architecture. 1849 14/8/50
Roman exploration fund. 1871 14/9/71

Parker, Joseph Independent minister
Church questions: historical and moral reviews. 1863 10/12/62
Ecce Deus. Essays on the life and doctrine of Jesus Christ. 1867 18/8/67
Job's comforters: scientific sympathy. 1874 28/11/77
Nonconformity in relation to the book of Common Prayer [a lecture]. 1863 28/12/62
The Paraclete: an essay on the personality and ministry of the holy ghost. 1874 21/2/75
Tyne Chylde: my life and teaching. 1886 1/5/87
Weaver Stephen: odds and evens in English religion. 1885 14/12/87 ?

Parker, J. W.
A prospectus for the publishing association. 15/5/52

Parker, Matthew
Correspondence of M. Parker, ed. J. Bruce and T. J. Perowne. 1853 13/1/56
De antiquitate Britannicae ecclesiae et privilegiis ecclesiae Cantuariensis. 12/11/49
Parker, Reginald A.
Observations on the remuneration of attorneys and solicitors. 1853 6/3/54
Parker, Theodore
A sermon of merchants preached... Nov. 22, 1846. 1847 10/10/51
Sermons. 1853 6/11/59, 8/6/73
The public education of the people. An oration. 1850 6/3/68
Parkes, Sir Henry
Speeches on various occasions connected with the public affairs of New South Wales, 1848–1874. 1876 17/8/76, 4/11/78
Parkes, Joseph
Memoirs of Sir Philip Francis... with correspondence and journals. 1867 (2v.) 28/11/67
Parkinson, James
The fire's continued at Oxford: or, the Decree of Convocation for burning the 'Naked Gospel'. 16/5/77 ?
Parkinson, Joseph Charles
The ocean telegraph to India. A narrative and a diary. 1870 1/7/70
Parkinson, Richard
The Church of England and five of her societies. A sermon. 1842 20/3/42
The constitution of the visible church of Christ considered... in eight discourses. 1839 14/5/65
The true equality of mankind. An assize sermon. 1843 25/6/43
Parkman, Francis the younger
Montcalm and Wolfe. 1884 (2v.) 5/1/85
'Parliamentary history', xxviii. 351. 21/2/40
Parnell, Charles Stewart
Charles Stewart Parnell. A memory, by T. P. O'Connor. 1891 20/10/91
Parnell, Henry Brooke Baron Congleton
On financial reform. 1830 (4th edn 1832) 31/5/33, 21/3/34
Parnell, William
An inquiry into the causes of popular discontents in Ireland. By an Irish country gentleman. 1804 26/9/88
Parnellism unmasked. By an Irish nationalist. 1885 10/11/85
Parochial letters from beneficed clergymen. 1829 3/12/30
Parousia, the critical enquiry into. 1878 23/6/78
Parr, Harriet
Echoes of a famous year. 1872 10/8/72
Parr, Samuel
A letter to... Dr. Milner, occasioned by... his book, entitled 'The end of religious controversy'. 1825 3/12/41
Parry, Ellen Webley
An epitome of Anglican church history, from the earliest ages to the present time. 1879 28/9/92
Parry, William
Remarks on the present aspect of the Turkish question. 1853 19/2/53 ?
Parry, William Edward
[One of several accounts of Arctic expedition in 1827]. 28/2/28
Parsloe, Edmund pseud. Vox
Astronomy and the bible reconciled. 1890 29/5/90
Parsons, Charles Edward
Clerks; their position and advancement. 1876 20/12/76
Parsons, Thomas William
The first canticle, Inferno, of the Divine Comedy, tr. 1867 31/5/68
Parsons, William Earl of Rosse
A few words on the relation of landlord and tenant in Ireland, and in other parts of the United Kingdom. 1867 20/2/67
Parton, James
Life of Voltaire. 1881 (2v.) 29/7/81
Partridge, J. Arthur
Citizenship versus secularists and sacerdotalists, in the matter of national teaching. 1873 4/7/76 ?
The making of the Irish nation: and the first fruits of federation. 1886 10/8/86
Pascal, Blaise
Pensées. 18/7/30
Pensées, ed. P. Fangère. (1844 edn) 13/9/63, 25/8/78, 16/2/89
Pasini, Valentino
Sulla necessità... di accordare al regno Lombardo-Veneto la Perequazione della sua imposta. 1858 11/4/59
Paskevich, Ivan Feodorovich Prince of Warsaw
La Russie dans l'Asie-Mineure. 1840 21/3/77
Pasley, Charles William
Essay on the military policy and institutions of the British Empire. 1810 30/11/59
Passaglia, Carlo
A plea for the Italian cause. Addressed to Catholic bishops. 1861 2/4/61
De Immaculato Deiparae semper Virginis Conceptu. 1854 (3v. 1854–55) 9/10/59
Della Scomunica: avvertenze d'un Prete Cattolico. 1861 13/12/61
La questione della indipendenza ed unità d'Italia dinanzi al clero. 1861 26/9/62, 8/12/66
Pro causa Italica ad Episcopos Catholicos. 1861 14/10/61
Risposta di Monsignor Nardi. 1861 2/12/61
Sugli articoli dell'Armonia e della Civiltà Cattolica. 1861 8/12/61

Past, present and future [a pamphlet]. 1844 10/1/44
Pastorale sur l'instruction de l'Eglise. 1710 8/5/36
Pastoral letter [to the Protestant Episcopal Church, from the American bishops]. 19/1/34
Pastoral letter from the bishops of the Protestant Episcopal church in the confederated states. 1862 22/2/63
Pater, Walter Horatio
Marius the epicurean. 1885 (2v.) 4/7/85, 15/12/92
Studies in the history of the Renaissance. 1873 3/8/73, 19/9/75
Paterson, Daniel
Paterson's British itinerary . . . direct and principal cross roads of Great Britain. 1785 (2v.) 25/11/85
Paterson, David James
The Lord's day, or Christian Sabbath: why it must be kept holy, and how. 1853 19/1/61 ?
Paterson, William
England's glory; or the great improvement of trade in general, by a royal bank . . . to be erected. 9/1/65
Patmore, Coventry Kersey Dighton
The angel in the house. 1858 (2v.) 31/7/59
Paton, James
British history and papal claims from the Norman conquest to the present day. 1893 (2v.) 4/6/93
Paton, John Brown
The origin of the priesthood in the Christian church. 1877 2/10/77
Patrick, Simon Bishop of Chichester, then Ely
A treatise of repentance, and of fasting, especially of the Lent-fast. 4/7/40
Autobiography. 1839 14/1/49
The parable of the pilgrim. 25/12/46
Patrick, St.
The writings of St. Patrick, ed. G. Y. Stokes and C. H. H. Wright. 1887 19/8/88
Patronage, Law of, in Scotland. 1869 21/9/69
Patrons, appeal to. 1836 24/2/41
Patten, Thomas
A letter to . . . Lord North . . . concerning subscription to the 39 articles. 1773 24/7/61
Patterson, Henry Sheridan
The Imâm Mahdi; or, the Moslem millennium, from the Koran and authentic traditions. 1884 5/3/85
Patterson, James Laird
Rome and Italy. A letter to . . . Duke of Norfolk. 1876 15/7/76
Patterson, John Brown
On the national character of the Athenians . . . Edinburgh prize essay. 1828 19/4/28, 24/4/60
Patterson, Robert Hogarth
Railway finance. 1867 11/1/68
The economy of capital; or, gold and trade. 1865 16/9/64
Patteson, John Coleridge
Life of J. C. Patteson, missionary bishop of the Melanesian Islands, by C. M. Yonge. 1872 20/10/72, 2/7/74, 14/11/78
Pattison, Mark
Isaac Casaubon. 1875 1/3/75
Memoirs, ed. Mrs. Pattison. 1885 12/3/85, 27/7/90
Recollections of Pattison, by L. A. Tollemache. 1885 9/11/85, 13/12/85
Suggestions on academical organisation, with especial reference to Oxford. 1868 10/4/73, 17/4/73
Paul, Alexander
Short parliaments, a history of the national demand for frequent general elections. 1883 12/8/84
The history of reform. A record of the struggle for the representation of the people in Parliament. 1884 14/8/84
Paul, Charles Kegan
Biographical sketches. 1883 26/6/83
Letters to Imlay, by Mary Wollstonecraft, ed. C. K. Paul. 1879 28/11/83, 30/7/87
Maria Drummond: a sketch. 1891 28/8/92
William Godwin: his friends and contemporaries. 1876 (2v.) 12/11/83, 23/1/84
Paul, Robert Bateman pseud. J. H. Tregenna
The autobiography of a Cornish rector. 1872 (2v.) 23/11/72
Paul, William
Past and present of Aberdeenshire; or, reminiscences of seventy years. 1881 1/7/82
Paulding, James Kirke
A sketch of Old-England, by a New-England man. 1822 20/4/29
Pausanias, the traveller
Pausaniae Graeciae descriptio. 1829 (3v.) 11/8/63, 31/8/64
Pausaniae Graeciae descriptio, tr. A. R. Shilleto. (new edn 1886) 20/4/86
Payne, Peter
A forgotten Englishman . . . Peter Payne, the Wycliffite, by James Baker. 1890 25/8/90
Peace, John
A descant on the penny postage. 1841 17/9/70
Peace, William
The reformed Church of England—What is she?—Where is she? . . . the Knightsbridge Church Cases. 1857 23/8/63
Peacock, George
A treatise on algebra. 1830 15/7/30
Peacock, Reginald
The repressor over much blaming of the clergy, ed. C. Babington. 1860 (2v.) 15/7/60

Pearce, Joseph Henry
Inconsequent lives: a village chronicle. 1891 27/11/91
Pearce, Zachary
The dean of Winchester his character of the English clergy. Being a translation of a Latin sermon. 1742 9/1/76
Pearson, Charles Buchanan
'Hymns and hymn writers' in *Oxford Essays.* 1858 30/5/58
Pearson, Carles Henry
Letter... on a scheme for making Oxford education more accessible to medical students. 1858 13/3/58
National life and character: a forecast. 1893 20/1/93, 3/3/93
Pearson, George
The danger of abrogating the religious tests... letter to... the Duke of Gloucester. 1834 30/5/47
Pearson, Hugh Nicholas Dean of Salisbury
Memoirs of the life and correspondence of... C. F. Swartz. 1834 (2v.) 17/8/34
Pearson, John Bishop of Chester
An exposition of the Creed. 26/6/31, 3/3/32, 27/6/45
Prefatio paraenetica ad Vetus Testamentum Graecum ex versione Septuaginta. 24/7/31, 30/3/34
Pearson, John Batteridge
How to amend the law on church-rates. 1867 18/4/67
The observance of Sunday in England. 1867 14/11/86
Pearson, Karl
The ethic of free thought. A lecture. 1888 27/4/90
Pearson, Samuel
Conscience and the church in their relations to Christ and Caesar. 1875 3/5/75
Pearson, William Henley afterw. Jervis
The student's France. 1862 23/4/67
Pecchio, Giuseppe
Osservazioni semi-serie di un Esule sull'Inghilterra. 1831 9/2/33
Peck, Francis
Desiderata Curiosa... Memoirs, letters, wills and epitaphs. 1732 (1732–35) 18/11/44
Peck, Nathaniel, and Price, T. S.
Report of... meeting of the Free Colored People of Baltimore... delegates to visit British Guiana and... Trinidad. 1840 25/6/40
Peckover, E. Josephine
Foreshadowings of Christianity. 1888 15/3/89
Pedder, Henry C.
Issues of the age: or, consequences involved in modern thought. 1874 4/12/88
Pedrelli, G.
Il giansenismo di un secolo. 1835 8/12/38 ?
Peel, Sir Lawrence
A sketch of the life and character of Sir Robert Peel. 1860 26/7/60
Peel, Sir Robert
[Speech on Irish railways] in *Hansard's Parliamentary Debates*, xc. 65. 1847 (February 16, 1847) 18/2/47
Inaugural address at the establishment of a library and reading room at Tamworth. 1841 10/2/41
Letter... to the electors for the borough of Tamworth. 1847 21/7/47
Life, political career, and death of Sir Robert Peel. 1850 2/8/50
Memoirs [in ms.], ed. Lord Mahon and E. Cardwell. 1856 3/10/51
Peel, by J. R. Thursfield. 1891 21/4/91
Reflections suggested by the career of the late Premier. 1847 20/8/58
Sir Robert Peel and his era. 1843 28/1/43
Sir Robert Peel, by C. S. Parker. 1891 (3v.) 23/4/91
Sir Robert Peel, by J. McCarthy. 1890 10/1/91
Speech on repeal of malt tax. 1835 13/5/80
Speech on the financial condition of the country. 1842 14/11/88
The speech of... 5th March 1829, on... the disabilities affecting... Roman Catholic subjects. 1829 5/4/45
Peel, and the corn law crisis. 1846 7/3/46
Pegge, Samuel
Some account of the species of prelates formerly existing... called 'Bishops in partibus infidelium'. 1780 2/10/62
Peile, Thomas Williamson
The Christian temple and its representative priesthood. 1849 20/1/50
The Church of England not high, not low, but broad as the commandment of God. 1850 25/5/51
Pélage
L'Abbé Junqua et l'archevêque de Bordeaux. 1872 26/5/72
Pelham, John Thomas
The charge... at his primary visitation. 1858 24/10/58
Pellew, George
[Sermon on Heb. viii. 1] in *Sermons.* 1848 21/4/39
A letter to... Peel... on the means of 'rendering Cathedral Churches most conducive to... efficiency'. 1837 6/1/38
Pelliccia, Alessio Aurelio
The polity of the Christian church of early, mediaeval, and modern times, tr. J. C. Bellett. 1883 13/5/83
Pellico, Silvio
Eufemia di Messina. 1822 16/7/34

Francesca da Rimini. 1818 12/7/34
Le mie prigioni. Memorie. 1832 3/6/33, 18/3/34
The life of the Marchesa Giulia Falletti di Barolo, tr. Lady G. Fullerton. 1866 9/9/66
Pellissier, Pierre Augustin
Les grandes leçons de l'antiquité. 1880 28/12/84
Pember, George Hawkins
Earth's earliest ages, and their lessons for us: including a treatise on spiritualism. 1884 21/12/84, 11/1/85
Pemberton, H.
The history of Monaco, past and present. 1867 10/9/69
Penn, Granville
A comparative estimate of the mineral and Mosaical geologies. 1822 10/9/47
An examination of the primary argument of the Iliad. 1821 26/9/57
Penna, Frederic
Production of voice. 1886 22/12/86
Pennant, Thomas
A tour in Scotland. 1769 (1771 edn) 25/9/37, 19/9/53, 9/9/72, 24/10/83
History of quadrupeds. 1781 (2v.) 8/6/86
Pennell, Joseph
Our journey to the Hebrides. 1889 22/11/89
Pennington, Arthur Robert
John Wiclif: his life, times and teaching. 1884 2/6/84
Pennington, James
A letter to K. Finlay... on the importation of foreign corn, and... precious metals in different countries. 1840 30/12/41
Penrose, John
Happy ignorance: or, church and state. 1847 5/7/47
Penton, Stephen
The guardian's instruction. 29/7/52
Pepys, Henry
A charge, delivered to the clergy of the diocese of Worcester. 1842 23/10/42
Pepys, Samuel
The diary of Samuel Pepys. 1828 (5v.) 25/6/49, 6/4/78
Perceval, Arthur Philip
A claim for relief on behalf of the Church of England... in the appointment of her bishops. 1836 20/11/47
A collection of papers connected with the theological movement of 1833. 1842 22/5/42
A letter to the members of both houses of parliament, on the Dissenters' Petitions, and on Church grievances. 1834 5/2/34
A letter to... John Bird, Lord Bishop of Chester, with remarks on his late charge. 1841 21/12/41
A letter to... Sir Robert Peel... on the present state of the Church of England. 1835 24/1/36
A vindication of the principles of the authors of the 'Tracts for the Times'. 1841 18/4/41
A vindication of the proceedings relative to the mission of Bishop Alexander to Jerusalem. 1843 7/5/43
An apology for the doctrine of apostolical succession; with an appendix on the English orders. 1839 19/1/40
On the episcopacy of the Moravians. 1841 12/12/41
Results of an ecclesiastical tour in Holland and Northern Germany. 1846 26/4/46
Sermons preached chiefly at the chapel royal, St. James's. 1839 15/8/75
The amelioration of Ireland contemplated, in a series of papers. 1844 20/7/45
The Roman schism illustrated from the records of the Catholic church. 1836 28/12/37
Two plain sermons on fasting. 1844 28/4/44
Two sermons: i. on Christian duty in time of danger or anxiety. ii. on the means of... religious education. 1843 30/7/43
Perceval, G. C.
Plain sermons preached in a village church. 1831 (3v.) 11/10/50
Perceval, Spencer
Life of Spencer Perceval, by Spencer Walpole. 1874 (2v.) 26/1/74
The church question in Ireland. 1844 26/4/44
The substance of a speech delivered... 1809... on the inquiry into the conduct of... the Duke of York. 1845 18/4/45
Percival, John
The connection of the universities and the great towns. 1873 16/6/73
Percy, Elizabeth
Meditations and prayers... before, at, and after the receiving of the Holy Sacrament of the Lord's Supper. 26/12/80
Percy, John
Metallurgy. The art of extracting metals from their ores, and adapting them to various purposes. 1861 (vol 1–3, 5 1861–80) 16/4/68
Treatise on metallurgy. 1864 (2v.) 17/6/68
Pereira, Antonio afterw. Pereira de Figueiredo
Tentativa theologica. 1847 25/4/47
Pereire, Isaac
La banque de France et l'organisation du crédit en France. 1864 18/4/65
Perfetti, Filippo
Il clero e la società, ossia della riforma della chiesa. 1862 25/9/64, 14/10/66
L'uomo, studi morali. 1863 21/10/66
Périer, Auguste Casimir Victor Laurent
[on finance] in *Revue des Deux Mondes,* xxi. 679. 1861 (February 1861) 5/2/61
Les sociétés de Coopération. 1864 26/4/64

Perling, P.
Un nonce du Pape. 1884 11/6/84
Perowne, Edward Henry
The godhead of Jesus: four sermons. 1867 21/4/67
Perowne, John James Stewart
Confession in the Church of England. 1877 29/7/77
The book of psalms. (1870 edn) 1/5/70, 23/7/71
Perowne, Thomas Thomason
The essential coherence of the old and new testaments. 1858 8/1/88 ?
Perraud, Adolphe Louis Albert
Etudes sur l'Irlande contemporaine. 1862 20/12/86, 10/2/87
Perrault, Charles
Parallèle des anciens et des modernes, en ce qui regarde les arts et les sciences. Dialogues. (4v. 1688–96) 26/9/56
Perreau, Daniel
An explicit account of the lives of... D. and R. Perreau... likewise the remarkable case of Mrs. Rudd. 1776 26/3/84
Perrein, J. A.
A Frenchman to his new countrymen of England. A pestilence... of drunkenness. 1865 27/12/65
Perrens, François Tommy
Jérôme Savonarole, sa vie... ses écrits... avec des pièces justificatives. 1854 9/11/58
Perricone, Corrado
Su Niccolò Machiavelli. 1871 12/10/71
Perrin, Raymond St. James
The religion of philosophy, or the unification of knowledge. 1885 10/7/87 ?
Perrinchief, Richard
The royal martyr; or, the life and death of King Charles I. 5/11/82
Perrone, Giovanni
Praelectiones theologicae. 1840 (8v. 1840–43) 18/7/52
Studi teologici spettanti al Cattolicesimo e al Protestantesimo. 1858 (2v.) 21/10/66
Perrot, Clement
Report on the persecutions of the French protestants. 1816 26/8/78
Perry, Arthur Latham
Elements of political economy. 1866 13/8/68
Perry, Charles
A letter... to the hon. secretary of the Special Committee for... [the] diocese [of Melbourne]. 1849 14/7/50
Clerical education, considered with an especial reference to the universities... letter. 1841 3/3/41
Five sermons preached before the university of Cambridge in... 1855. 1856 1/2/63
The Christian's light shining to God's glory, a sermon. 1847 29/8/47
Perry, Frederick
The fruits of the spirit; together with fragments of Christian ethics. 1863 11/8/67
Perry, George Gresley
The history of the Church of England. From the death of Elizabeth to the present time. 1861 (3v. 1861–64) 26/3/65
Perry, Richard
Proceedings of the first Church of England synod for the Diocese of Melbourne, ed. R. Perry. 1857 31/5/57
Perry, William Stevens
Anglo-American sympathy with continental reform. A sermon. 1875 14/11/75
Persecution and death of the baroness von Beck. 1852 2/7/52
Persecution of Dr. Welton and family. 1718 16/10/82 ?
Persecution of Jews in Russia. 1881 18/1/82
Persecution of Protestants in the year 1845. 1845 19/8/52
Persius Flaccus
Opera. 14/2/27, 28/5/30
Peruzzi, Ubaldino
Discorsi detti alla Camera dei Deputati. 1863 15/7/63
Perverter in high life. 1851 11/12/74
Pétavel-Olliff, Emmanuel
Lettre à S. M. le roi de Prusse. 1870 11/12/70
Peter, Robert Godolphin
A letter to churchmen and to dissenters. 1870 9/10/70
Peter, St.
Leaves from the life of the apostle Peter. 1892 25/12/92
Peterkin, Alexander
Records of the kirk of Scotland. 1843 4/6/43
Peters, Hugh
Tales and jests. 8/4/48
Peterson, William
C. Taciti Dialogus de Oratoribus... revised text, with introductory essays. 1893 20/9/93
Petheram, John
Reasons for establishing an authors' society. 1843 25/11/43
Petit de Bachaumont, Louis
Anecdotes piquantes. 1881 10/10/85
Petition of the nine hundred priests. 14/11/62
Peto, Samuel Morton
Observations on the report of the Defence Commissioners, with an analysis of the evidence. 1862 18/6/62
Supplement to... pamphlet on national defences. Rejoinder to the semi-official pamphlet. 1862 21/7/62
Taxation: its levy and expenditure, past and future; being an enquiry into our financial policy. 1863 22/1/63

The resources and prospects of America, ascertained during a visit to the States in . . . 1865. 1866 17/4/66
Petrarch
Sonnets. (1777 edn) 31/12/47 ?
Petrie, George
The ecclesiastical architecture of Ireland, anterior to the Anglo-Norman invasion . . . an essay. 1845 11/12/46
Petritzopoulos, Demetrios
Saggio storico sulle prime età dell'Isola di Leucadia nell' Jonio. 1814 12/11/58
Petronius
Opera. 22/1/36
Petruccelli della Gattina, Ferdinando
Histoire diplomatique des Conclaves. 1864 (4v. 1864–66) 22/1/65
La rivoluzione di Napoli nel 1848. 1850 1/8/51
Petty, Sir William
Political anatomy of Ireland. (2v.) 4/7/34, 23/7/47, 11/12/69
Reflections upon some persons and things in Ireland. 30/11/87
Petty-Fitzmaurice, E.
'English land question' in *Contemporary Review*, xix. 419. 1872 (March 1872) 26/1/72
Peyrat, Eugénie
Le synode Protestant et le schisme Catholique. 1872 9/6/72
Peyrère, Isaac de la
Men before Adam. 26/8/66
Pfeiffer, Emily Jane
Under the Aspens: lyrical and dramatic. 1881 19/11/81, 21/1/82
Pfleiderer, Otto
The Hibbert lectures, 1885 . . . on the influence of . . . Paul on the development of Christianity. Tr. J. F. Smith. 1885 20/9/85
Pflug, Ferdinand
Unter dem Doppeladler. 1855 25/1/56
Phallic worship, a description of the mysteries of the sex worship of the ancients with the history of the masculine cross. 1886 22/4/89
Phallism: a description of the worship of lingam-yoni. 1889 22/5/90 ?
Phelan, Charlotte Elizabeth afterw. Tonna
The System: a tale of the West Indies. 1827 5/5/28
Phelan, James of Memphis, Tennessee
The New South. The Democratic position on the tariff. Speech. 1886 29/11/86
Phelan, Rev. William
History of the policy of the Church of Rome in Ireland. 1827 21/6/40 ?
Phelps, Elizabeth Stuart afterw. Ward
Jack the fisherman. 1887 7/5/88
The struggle for immortality. 1889 24/8/90
Phenomena of industrial life. 1854 17/5/54
Philae; or, the throne of the priest. A drama of ancient Egypt, in three acts. 1882 20/12/80
Philip, Robert
The life and times of the Reverend George Whitefield. 1837 18/2/38
Philips, Ambrose
The life of John Williams, lord keeper of the Great Seal . . . and archbishop of York. 24/1/41
Philips, Francis Charles
As in a looking glass. 1889 (2v. 1889) 14/8/89
Philips, Francis Charles, and Wills, Charles Jame
The fatal phryne. 1889 (2v. 1889) 27/6/89
Phillimore, Catherine Mary
'Dante's Paradise' in *St. Paul's Magazine*, viii. 63. 1871 (April 1871) 16/4/71
'Manzoni' in *Macmillan's Magazine*, xxviii. 270. 1873 (July 1873) 13/7/73
Princess Opportunity, and the Lady Remorse. 1882 21/1/84
The warrior Medici. 1887 5/10/87
Phillimore, Greville
Uncle Z. 1881 15/11/81
Phillimore, John George
A letter on the article . . . 'Robert Phillimore's Lyttelton' . . . to the Rt. Hon. J. W. Croker. 1846 27/8/46
History of England during the reign of George the Third. vol. 1. 1863 21/7/63
Phillimore, Lucy
Sir Christopher Wren, his family and his times. 1881 12/11/81
Phillimore, Sir Robert Joseph
A letter to . . . Lord Ashburton, suggested by the questions of international law. 1842 15/1/42
A report of the proceedings in the visitatorial court . . . against the dean of York. 1841 27/4/41
Clergy discipline. A letter to . . . the Archbishop of Canterbury. 1872 11/2/72
Commentaries upon international law. 1854 (4v. 1854–61) 21/12/52, 5/1/57
Judgement delivered . . . in the cases of Martin v. Mackonochie and Flamank v. Simpson. 1868 22/3/68
Judgment . . . in the case of the office of the judge promoted by Sheppard v. Bennett. 1871 26/8/74 ?
Russia and Turkey. Armed intervention on the ground of religion . . . a question of international law. 1853 25/7/53
The Cagliari. Dr. Phillimore's opinion. 1858 8/3/58
The case of the creole considered, in a second letter to . . . Lord Ashburton. 1842 16/5/42
The Constitution as it is, or Democracy?. 1837 20/4/37
The practice and courts of civil and ecclesiastical law, . . . examined . . . in a letter to . . . Gladstone. 1848 12/6/48, 10/11/61

Phillimore, Sir Robert Joseph (*cont.*)
The study of the civil and canon law in its relation to the state, the church, and the universities. 1843 10/4/43
Thoughts on the law of divorce. 1844 16/4/44
Phillipps, Ambrose Lisle March afterw. Phillipps de Lisle
Mahometanism in its relation to prophecy. 1857 21/12/73
On the future unity of Christendom. 1857 7/11/74 ?
Remarks on Newman's Letter to Jelf. 1841 2/4/41
Phillipps, Edward Thomas March
The ordinances of spiritual worship:... edited by his daughter. 1863 28/11/68
Phillips, Charles Commissioner, Insolvent Debtors' Court
Recollections of Curran and some of his contemporaries. 1818 19/3/58
Phillips, Edmund
Bank of England charter, currency, limited liability companies, and free trade. 1856 14/2/56
Phillips, John F.R.S.
Life on the earth, its origin and succession. 1860 15/12/85
Phillips, Montagu Lyon
Worlds beyond the earth. 1855 20/4/55
Phillips, Richard F.R.S.
A letter to Dr. D. B. Reid... in answer to his pamphlet. 1831 10/2/48 ?
Phillips, Sir Thomas Q. C.
Wales: the language, social condition, moral character. 1849 20/2/70
Phillpotts, Henry Bishop of Exeter
[letter to Bishop of Exeter]. (not found) 16/1/45
A charge delivered to the clergy of the diocese of Exeter, at the triennial visitation. 1842 14/9/42, 2/10/42
A charge delivered... at his triennial visitation. 1845 16/9/45
A charge delivered... at the triennial visitation. 1848 17/9/48
A letter to Sir R. Inglis... on... an article in the Edinburgh Review, No. 193... 'Bishop Phillpotts'. 1852 3/2/52
A letter to the Abp. of Canterbury. 1850 25/3/50
A letter to the archdeacon of Totnes... on the necessity of episcopal ordination. 1852 22/1/52
A letter to the clergy of the diocese of Exeter, on the use of the offertory. 1843 27/10/43
A letter to... Lushington, on his judgement in the case of Westerton v. Liddell. 1856 16/1/56
A pastoral letter to the clergy of his diocese, April 1854. 1854 23/4/54
A pastoral letter to the clergy of the diocese. 1857 26/4/57
A pastoral letter... on the present state of the church. 1851 16/4/51
A reply to... Russell's letter to the remonstrance of the bishops. 1847 15/12/47
Address... to the clergy of his diocese on the conduct of the Rev. Henry E. Head. 1838 10/9/38
An ordination sermon. 1843 12/11/43
Charge delivered to the clergy of the diocese of Exeter,... at his primary visitation. 1833 14/3/34
Charge delivered to the clergy of the diocese of Exeter... at his triennial visitation. 1836 2/2/37
Correspondence between the Bp. of Exeter and... Macaulay. 1860 9/5/60, 10/1/61
Letter on the bill for legalising marriage with the sister of a deceased wife. 1860 29/1/60
Letter to the archdeacons... of Exeter, on the proposed office of scripture-readers. 1847 24/10/47
Life, times and writings of Dr. H. Phillpotts, by R. N. Shulte. 1863 14/7/64
Speech... on the Church Discipline Bill. 1856 11/5/56
The Bishop of Exeter's charge to the clergy of his diocese. 1839 26/1/40
The case of the Revd. Mr. Shore... A letter to the Archbishop of Canterbury. 1849 16/4/49
Philoctetes
Opera. 31/12/30
Philomneste, pseud.
La Papesse Jeanne. 1862 19/10/62
Philosophus
Amy Clarefort. A romance of the year 1900. By Philosophus. 1893 1/7/93
Philosophy of Puseyism. 1843 12/12/43
Philosophy of the plan of salvation. 1883 5/8/83
Philp, G. W.
'Reasons for renouncing unitarianism... with prefatory remarks... by J. E. N. Molesworth' 1843 19/2/43
Philpott, Henry Bishop of Worcester
[pamphlet opposing catholic relief]. 1827 1/5/28 ?
A Charge. 1871 9/7/71
A charge delivered... in June 1865. 1865 20/8/65
A charge... in June 1868. 1868 26/7/68
Philpotts, William John Archdeacon of Cornwall
An answer to the infidels; in a charge to the clergy of Cornwall. 1864 10/7/64
Phippen, Francis
Authentic memoirs of Edmund Kean, containing a specimen of his talent at composition. 1814 7/5/75

Phipps, Constantine Henry Marquis of Normanby
A vindication of the Duke of Modena from the charges of Mr. Gladstone. 1861 16/10/61
Speech delivered in the House of Lords... June 7th, 1859... with an appendix on Italian affairs. 1859 21/6/59
Phipps, Joseph
Brief remarks on... ecclesiastical impositions in this nation,... as they relate to Dissenters. 1769 8/7/35
Phlipon, Jeanne Marie afterw. Roland de la Platère
The works of J. M. Phlipon Roland... ed. L. A. Champagneaux. 1800 11/10/47
Photographs of the Norfolk Broads. 1890 20/5/90
Phythian, J. C.
Scenes of travel in Norway. 1877 12/9/85
Piard, P. A. J.
Le conservateur de la santé, ou médecine des familles. 1852 15/3/58 ?
Piave, Francesco Maria
La Traviata. 1856 4/5/57
Picard, Eugène Ernest
Essai exégétique sur Rom. v. 12–21. Thèse. 1861 17/11/61
Pichler, Aloys
Die Theologie des Leibnitz. 1869 (2v. 1869–70) 12/10/74
Geschichte der kirchlichen Trennung zwischen dem Orient und Occident. 1864 (2v. 1864–5) 20/9/74, 10/11/76
Pickens, Francis W.
Speech... on the tariff and the restrictive policy: delivered in the House of Representatives. 1842 13/10/42
Pickering, Anna Maria Diana Wilhelmina pseud. Percival Pickering
A life awry. 1893 (3v.) 14/10/93
Pickering, Charles M.D.
The races of man; and their geographical distribution. 1844 10/7/53
Pickering, John F.R.G.S.
Anti-vaccination..., in a letter to the Leeds Board of Guardians. 1876 10/1/77
Pickering, Joseph M.A.
Practical sermons selected from the manuscripts of ... J. Pickering. 1821 (2v. 1821) 19/1/34
Pickering, Octavius
The life of Timothy Pickering. By his son, O. Pickering. 1867 (4v. 1867–73) 7/12/87
Pickering, Percival Andree
An essay on friendship. 1875 19/1/75
Remarks on treating..., relating to the election of Members of Parliament. 1849 21/2/49
Picton, Sir James Allanson
City of Liverpool. Selections from the municipal archives and records. 1883 (2v. 1883–6) 16/5/83
Memorials of Liverpool, historical and topographical. 1872 5/12/72
Philological papers. 1864 27/8/64
The architectural history of Liverpool. 1858 2/12/72
Picton, James Allanson
'Christian pantheism' from *The mystery of matter and other essays.* 1873 26/3/73
Sir James A. Picton. A biography. 1891 3/11/91
The conflict of oligarchy and democracy. Six lectures. 1885 17/11/86
The mystery of matter, and other essays. 1873 30/3/73
Pidansat de Mairobert, Mathieu François
Anecdotes sur Madame la Comtesse Dubarri. 1776 8/9/69
Piggin, Henry
The ministerial gift. An ordination charge... at the Methodist New Connexion Conference, Leeds, 1877. 1877 7/10/77
Pigot, David Richard
A letter on the removal of R. O'Keeffe from the office of manager of the Callan schools. 1873 15/5/73 ?
Pike, Godfrey Holden
Ancient meeting-houses; or, memorial pictures of nonconformity in Old London. 1870 11/2/72
Pike, Luke Owen
A history of crime in England,... the changes of the laws in the progress of civilization. 1873 (2v. 1873–76) 10/10/87
Pike, Richard of Nottingham
Quaker anecdotes, ed. R. Pike. 1883 4/3/83
Pilkington, George
The unknown tongues discovered to be English, Spanish and Latin. 1831 16/1/32
Pilkington, James Bishop of Durham
The works of James Pilkington, ed. J. Scholefield. 1842 8/9/78
Pillans, James
Eclogae Ciceronianae, ed. by J. Pillans. 1845 5/5/60
Pillersdorff, Baron Franz Xaver von
Austria in 1848 and 1849, tr. G. Gaskell. 1850 29/2/52 ?
Pim, Jonathan
Ireland and the imperial parliament. 1871 21/11/71
The condition and prospects of Ireland. 1848 28/4/48
The land question in Ireland. 1867 27/12/76 ?, 21/12/80
Pindar
Nemean odes. 3/6/84 ?
Opera. 9/6/26, 6/9/26, 5/11/29, 24/11/29

Pinder, John Hothersall Principal of Wells theological college
The candidate for the ministry. A course of... lectures on the First Epistle of Paul... to Timothy. 1837 25/11/60
Pinkerton, Allen
The spy of the rebellion. 1883 7/2/83
Piozzi, Mrs. Hester Lynch Thrale
Anecdotes of the late Samuel Johnson. 1786 23/7/52, 19/8/72
Love letters of Mrs. Piozzi, written when she was eighty, to W. A. Conway. 1843 3/10/92
Unpublished letters by Mrs. Piozzi to the Williams family. 28/9/55
Pirie, William Robinson Minister of the West Church of Perth
The philosophy of Christianity. 1872 29/6/79
Pironneau, Armand
Discours de rentrée... L'Irlande et son législateur M. Gladstone. 1886 5/1/92
Pitman, Emma Raymond
Vestina's martyrdom; a story of the catacombs. 1869 21/12/69
Pitt, Thomas Lord Camelford
Narrative and proof. Pamphlets. 1785 8/1/57
Pitt, William Lord Chatham
Authentic memoirs... of the late Earl of Chatham. 1778 23/9/34
Letters written by... Earl of Chatham to his nephew, Thomas Pitt. 1804 1/2/26
Speeches. 1848 13/6/78
The Earl of Chatham at Chevening in 1769, privately printed by Stanhope. 1855 28/7/55
Pitt, William the Younger
Correspondence between William Pitt and the Duke of Rutland. 1890 20/3/90, 11/10/90
Speech... [on] the resolutions which he proposed... [as] the basis of an union between Great Britain and Ireland. 1799 11/6/34
The Speech of... W. Pitt... on... an additional sum for the reduction of the public debt. 1792 21/5/66
The speeches of... William Pitt in the House of Commons. 1806 (4v. 1806) 15/6/32, 15/3/52, 19/9/85, 2/2/93
Pitt, William, and Manners, C. the Younger
Correspondence between Mr Pitt and the Duke of Rutland, Lord-Lieutenant of Ireland, 1771–87. 1842 13/10/42
Pitts, Joseph the Elder
The Holy Spirit the author of immortality. 1708 24/8/76
Pitzipios, Prince Jakobos Georgios
The Eastern question solved, in a letter to Lord Palmerston. 1860 26/6/60
Pius IV, Pope
Translation of the creed of Pope Pius IV, with explanatory remarks. 1843 27/4/43 ?
Pius IX, Pope
Encyclical letter of Pope Pius IX, dated 9 November 1846. 1846 19/12/46
Litterae Apostolicae SS. Domini Nostri quibus hierarchia episcopalis in Anglia restituitur. 1850 12/11/50
Place, Francis Political reformer
Pamphlets for the people. 1835 23/6/35
Plain Facts. An answer to Lord George Bentinck's address to the electors of Kings Lynn. 1847 17/11/47
Plain sermons by contributors to the 'Tracts for the Times'. 1839 (10v. 1839–48) 30/8/40
'Plain words to plain people on the present dissensions in the church' 1842 4/8/42
Planché, James Robinson
The recollections and reflections of J. R. Planché... A professional autobiography. 1872 (2v. 1872) 9/7/72
Planché, Matilda Anne afterw. Mackarness
A trap to catch a sunbeam. 1850 19/1/51
Old Joliffe; not a goblin story. 1845 27/2/45
Plan of campaign... extracts from the speeches and writings of the Parnellite party and press. 1887 (1887–89) 3/12/87 ?
Platner, Ernst Zacharias, C. Bunsen and others
Beschreibung der Stadt Rom. 1830 (3v. 1830–37) 5/1/39
Plato
Commentaire, by C. Lenormant. 1861 26/8/62
Crito. 15/9/37 ?
Dialogues. 10/4/28
Laws. 18/8/37, 6/10/37
Opera. 25/2/28, 4/6/32, 30/7/33, 27/8/64
Phaedo. 7/7/30, 6/10/30, 8/11/30, 24/12/30
Plato, and the other companions of Sokrates, by G. Grote. 1865 (3v.) 8/2/65
Plato, by J. S. Blackie. 1867 3/5/67
Platonic dialogues for English readers, ed. W. Whewell. 1845 (3v. 1845–52) 2/11/59
The dialogues of Plato, tr. B. Jowett. 1871 22/2/71
The Republic. 23/8/32, 16/8/33, 24/9/33, 16/12/33, 7/8/65, 12/9/65
Timaeus. 29/9/37
Platon, Petr Georgievich Levshin Abp. of Tver, and Metropolitan of Moscow
The present state of the Greek church in Russia, etc., tr. R. Pinkerton. 1814 21/3/56
Platt, Thomas Pell
A letter to... E. B. Pusey. 1840 26/4/40
Facts respecting certain versions of Holy Scripture... reply to an article in the... Quarterly Review. 1827 9/12/27
Plautus
Bacchides. 20/9/52

Playfair, Lyon Baron Playfair
On teaching universities and examining boards. 1872 25/10/72
On teaching universities . . . With reference to Irish university education. 1873 8/2/73
Subjects of social welfare. 1889 29/4/89
The inosculation of the arts and sciences. Address delivered . . . 29th September, 1870. 1870 22/2/71
Playfair, William
France as it is, not Lady Morgan's France. 1819 (2v. 1819–20) 18/11/88
Plimsoll, Samuel
Our seamen. An appeal. 1873 18/6/73
Plowden, Francis LL.D.
[On the French revolution]. (not found) 17/9/45
An historical review of the state of Ireland. 1809 (2v.) 18/8/45, 29/12/85
The history of Ireland, from its union with Great Britain in January 1801 to October 1810. 1811 (3v. 1811) 18/8/87
Plumptre, Charles John
The religion and morality of Shakespeare's works; being a lecture. 1873 5/3/76
Plumptre, Edward Hayes Dean of Wells
Calmness in times of trouble: a sermon. 1868 16/5/69
Confession and absolution; a sermon preached . . . Advent Sunday, 1873. 1874 8/3/74
King's College Sermons. 1859 23/10/64
Movements in religious thought, . . . Three sermons. 1879 4/5/79
Peace or War? A sermon. 1878 24/11/78
Perversions to Rome. A sermon. 1877 5/8/77
Respice, aspice, prospice, and the law of progress in theology. Two sermons. 1876 15/4/76
The ideal of cathedral life. A sermon. 1882 29/12/81
The life of Thomas Ken . . . Bishop of Bath and Wells. 1888 (2v. 1888) 6/10/88
The spirits in prison, and other studies on the life after death. 1884 16/11/84
The spirits in prison. A sermon. 1871 9/7/71
Plumptre, Henry Western
A plain statement of facts relative to the proposed new church in Nottingham. 1838 16/1/38
Plunket, William Conyngham 4th Baron Plunket, Bishop of Meath etc.
Commutation considered specially with a view to compensation for diminished security. 1869 29/6/69
Plunkett, George Noble Count
The early life of Henry Grattan. 1878 10/10/78
Plutarch
'De mulierum virtutibus', one of Plutarch's *Moralia.* 8/4/71
De audiendis poetis. 11/8/55
De Iside et Osiride. 7/9/88, 14/9/88
De sera numinis vindicta. 30/8/83, 6/9/83
Pocock, Nicholas
'Troubles connected with the Prayer Book of 1549', *Camden Society, 2nd series,* xxxvii. 1885 10/10/86 ?
Church congresses: a paper read before the Bristol Church Union. 1864 8/5/64
Records of the Reformation; the divorce 1527–1533. 1870 (2v. 1870) 11/9/88
The principles of the Reformation shewn to be in contradiction to the Book of Common Prayer. 1875 20/4/81
The recovery from the principles of the Reformation. 1877 14/4/81
Troubles connected with the Prayer Book of 1549 . . . Edited by N. P. 1884 19/10/85
Poerio, Carlo
Atti e difesa della causa di C. Poerio ed altri. Ed. G. Tofano. 1850 29/1/51 ?
Costituto di C. Poerio, ex-ministro e deputato, al parlamento di Napoli. 1830 22/2/51
Speech of C. Poerio, late minister of public instruction. 1851 26/9/51
Poirson, Auguste
Histoire du règne de Henri IV. 1856 (2v. 1856) 7/1/87 ?
Polano, Pietro Soave Fra Paolo
The history of the council of Trent, tr. Sir Nathaniel Brent. 9/1/43
Polhausen, A.
Vaticanism; or, 'papal floundering and blundering'. 1875 22/12/75 ?
Poli, Oscar de Viscunt
Vaudouan (Chroniques du Bas-Berry). 1865 10/3/65 ?
Political catechism; a treatise in four parts, on organic reform. 1858 24/3/79
Political perils in 1859. 1859 27/4/59
Pollard, Albert Frederick
The Jesuits in Poland. The Lothian essay, 1892. 1892 22/10/93
Pollard, Edward Albert
Life of Jefferson Davis, with a secret history of the Southern Confederacy. 1869 23/3/73 ?
Pollen, John Hungerford the elder
Narrative of five years at St. Saviour's, Leeds. 1851 3/8/51
Pollock, Sir Frederick 3rd Bart.
'On ecclesiastical courts' in *Hansard's Parliamentary Debates,* lxviii. 1040. 1843 (April 28, 1843) 15/2/44 ?
Pollok, Robert Probationer of the United Session Church
The course of time: a poem, in ten books. 1827 (2v. 1827) 6/6/30, 25/10/35
Polson, John
Monaco, and its gaming tables. 1881 1/4/82

Polybius
Histories. 22/10/29, 24/11/29, 10/9/31, 20/6/33
Pomeroy, Henry Sterling
Is man too prolific... with a letter from... Gladstone. 1891 23/12/91
The ethics of marriage... With a prefatory note by T. A. Emmet... introduction by... J. T. Duryea. 1888 23/10/88
Pomery, E. de
La morale naturelle. 1891 9/12/90
Pomo, Percy
Percy Pomo; or, the autobiography of a South Sea Islander. 1881 24/1/82
Pompeii (anon., 1831-2, 2nd ed. 1846 under name of William Clarke). 1831 (1831-2) 21/11/38
Ponet, John Bishop of Rochester and then Winchester
An apologie. 8/6/45
Poole, Braithwaite
A report to the... directors of the London and North Western Railway Company on coal traffic. 1849 7/11/49
Poole, George Ayliffe
On the present state of parties in the Church of England. 1841 21/12/41
The appropriate character of Church architecture. 1842 20/3/42
The divinity of Christ asserted; and the doctrine of the atonement vindicated, in two sermons. 1835 15/5/36
The life and times of Saint Cyprian. 1840 24/3/44
Poole, Matthew
Annotations upon the Holy Bible... vol. 1 by M. Poole. 1852 6/4/88
Poole, Reginald Stuart
Horae Aegyptiacae: or, the chronology of ancient Egypt. 1851 15/5/74
Poole, Stanley Lane
The life of the Right Hon. Stratford Canning, Viscount Stratford de Redcliffe. 1888 (2v. 1888) 8/10/88
The people of Turkey. By a consul's daughter and wife, ed. S. L. Poole. 1878 (2v. 1878) 12/7/78
Poole, William H.
Anglo-Israel, or the Saxon race proved to be the lost tribes of Israel. 1879 5/11/80
Pope, Alexander
'Pastorals' in J. Tonson, ed., *Poetic Miscellanies.* 1709 28/7/52
An essay on criticism. 1711 5/1/78
Poem of Eloisa to Abaelardus. 1765 18/8/37, 30/7/55, 2/10/69
Preface to his translation of the Iliad. 1715 3/11/55, 4/1/62
The Dunciad, ed. W. Roscoe. 1824 (10v. 1824) 13/12/62, 20/11/79
The Rape of the Lock. 1714 1/11/28, 23/7/33, 1/1/62
The Rape of the Lock, in W. W. Elwin's ed. of his *Works.* 1871 (10v. 1871-89) 11/2/71
The Works of Alexander Pope... With introduction and notes by W. W. Elwin. 1871 (10v. 1871-89) 13/2/71
Works, ed. W. Roscoe. 1824 (10v. 1824) 11/8/25
Pope, Walter
The life of... Seth, Lord Bishop of Salisbury. 25/9/64
Popery in the Scotch Episcopal Church. An examination of a sermon... by the Revd. P. Cheyne. 1844 21/12/44
Popery not the old religion by a member of the Church of England. 1845 20/4/45
Popery weighed in the balances and found wanting. 1840 23/1/76
Popovitski, Aleksandr Ivanovich
La question religieuse d'Orient and d'Occident. 1853 26/12/58
Porson, Richard
Tracts and miscellaneous criticisms, ed. Thomas Kidd. 1815 7/3/31
Porter, George Richardson
The effect of restrictions on the importation of corn, ... with reference to landowners. 1839 13/12/41
The progress of the nation. 1843 (3v. 1843) 24/2/43
Porter, Jane
Sir Edward Seaward's narrative of his shipwreck. 1831 (3v. 1831) 4/4/33
Thaddeus of Warsaw. 1803 18/8/32
Porter, John Scott
Is the 'national' or the 'denominational' system of education... best suited to... Ireland. 1868 25/2/68
Porter, Whitworth
Life in the trenches before Sebastopol. 1856 4/5/55
Porteus, Beilby Bishop of Chester, then of London
A summary of the principal evidences for the truth and divine origin of the Christian revelation. 1800 18/5/30
Life of Secker. 1770 6/7/28
The beneficial effects of Christianity on the temporal concerns of mankind. 1804 3/3/32 ?
The works of... B. Porteus... with his life by... R. Hodgson. 1811 (6v. 1811) 16/8/46
Portfolio. 3.1. on Concordat 9/4/1844 ?
Postlethwayt, Matthew
The necessity of understanding the grounds and principles of religion briefly represented. 1715 26/9/68
Poston, Charles D.
The Parsees: a lecture. 1870 20/8/72 ?

Potapenko, Ignaty Nikolaevich
A Russian priest. 1891 24/7/91
Pott, Joseph Holden Archdeacon of London
Elementary discourses, designed for the use of a young person after confirmation. 1792 6/7/28
The rule of faith considered, a charge delivered by archdeacon J. H. Pott. 1839 13/10/39
Potter, Edmund
A picture of a manufacturing district. A lecture. 1856 20/2/56
The sugar duties. A letter to the Rt. Hon. W. E. Gladstone. 1864 15/1/64
Potter, Elisha R.
Considerations on . . . the adoption of a constitution and extension of suffrage in Rhode Island. 1842 21/10/58
Potter, Henry Codman Bishop of New York
Shams in Lent; or, the real and the false in Lenten duties. 1875 7/3/75
Potter, John Bishop of Oxford then Abp of Canterbury
Archaeologia Graeca. (1697–8) 9/3/27, 25/11/28
Potter, Samuel George
Of what religion is Mr. Gladstone? Important revelations of a conspiracy. 1873 4/2/73
Potter, William Simpson
Letters from India during H. R. H. the Prince of Wales' visit in 1875–6. 1876 10/12/80 ?
Potts, Mrs. Henry
Did Francis Bacon write 'Shakespeare'? Thirty-two reasons for thinking that he did. 1885 30/7/85 ?
Pouget, François Aimé
Institutiones Catholicae in modum catecheseos (English tr. 1851). 1725 7/6/57
Powell, A. M.
Town and forest. 1860 8/5/60
Powell, Baden
A short treatise on the principles of the differential and integral calculus. 1829 25/11/31
Essays on the spirit of the inductive philosophy, the unity of worlds. 1855 14/7/55
The elements of curves. 1828 18/11/31
The State-Church. A sermon preached before the university of Oxford. 1850 2/3/51
Powell, F. G. M.
Four addresses to the clergy of Coventry. 1881 4/12/81
Powell, George Smith Baden-
New Homes for the Old Country. 1872 13/5/72
Powell, Harcourt
Ewart Conroy. 1882 29/7/82
Powell, Harry Townsend
Tithe commutation in 1969, or the working of the Tithe Act illustrated by an example of commutation in 1705. 1837 18/1/38
Powell, T.
Marguerite: a tragedy. 1844 1/10/62 ?
Power, Frank
Letters from Khartoum, written during the siege. 1885 8/4/85
Power, John O'Connor
The Anglo-Irish quarrel, a plea for peace. 1886 6/2/86
Powys, Atherton Legh
Liturgical revision and church reform . . . In a letter to Lord . . . Palmerston. 1856 20/5/56
Powys, Horatio Bishop of Sodor and Man
A pastoral letter to his congregation. 1848 31/10/58
Charge. 1857 31/10/58
The believer's support in 'times' of trouble. 1840 25/1/44 ?
Powys, Littleton
The claims of the British and Foreign Bible Society on the Church of England. 1830 8/10/30, 9/10/30, 10/10/30, 11/10/30, 12/10/30, 13/10/30, 14/10/30
Poynder, John
A history of the Jesuits. 1815 26/3/32
Poynet, John Bishop of Rochester, then of Winchester
Catechism, etc. 25/10/63, 14/4/65
Poynter, Ambrose
Lecture on Arabesques in Vatican. 1840 17/2/43
Pozzo, Count Ferdinando dal
Catholicism in Austria. 1827 6/2/36
Practical information for emigrants. 1832 25/3/35
Praed, Mrs. Rosa Caroline Murray
The romance of a station. 1890 (2v. 1890) 14/4/90
Praed, Winthrop Mackworth
The poems of W. M. Praed. Revised and complete edition. 1885 (2v. 1885) 10/12/89
The poems of W. M. Praed. With a memoir by . . . Derwent Coleridge. 1864 (2v. 1864) 16/2/65
Prange, Francis
Germany versus Denmark . . . By a Liverpool merchant. 1864 3/2/64
Prantl, Carl von
Aristoteles über die Farben . . . Erläutert . . . von C. Prantl. 1849 4/2/58
Pratt, Hodgson
University education in England for natives of India. 1860 21/6/60
Pratt, John Burnett
Four sermons preached in St. Paul's episcopal church, Dundee, in 1841 and 1842. 1842 2/7/43
Pratt, Josiah, and Henry, John the younger
Memoir of the Rev. Josiah Pratt. 1849 27/12/57
Prayerbook weighed in the balance. 8/10/71

Prayers for the young. 1851 25/4/52
Preller, Ludwig of Weimar
Griechische mythologie. 1854 (2v. 1854) 22/11/67, 8/4/71
Homer's Iliad, ed. L. Preller. 1879 12/3/91
Prendergast, John Patrick
Ireland from the Restoration to the revolution, 1660–1690. 1887 29/8/87
The Cromwellian settlement of Ireland. 1865 11/7/67, 7/12/69, 31/1/70, 8/8/79, 29/7/87
Presbyter Anglicanus
Eternal punishment. 1864 16/6/72
Presbyterian Review and Religious Journal.
9. 46. 11/1836. on Dodsworth 17/12/1836
14. 615, 685. 1/1842. Church of England; reforms 4/12/1842
Prescot, Kenrick
Letters concerning Homer the sleeper in Horace: with additional classic amusements. 1773 19/6/58
Prescott, Peter
Methodism in relation to popery: a letter to the Rev. W. Arthur. 1880 3/1/82
Prescott, Thomas Oliver afterw. Hiller (Oliver Prescott)
God manifest: a treatise on the goodness, wisdom, and power of God. 1858 12/11/65
Prescott, William Hickling
History of the reign of Philip the second, king of Spain. 1855 (3v. 1855–9) 19/3/56, 2/9/79
Present Attack on Subscription. 1771 (& 1835) 7/5/35
Present forms of scepticism and Romanism viewed and contrasted as conflicting yet cognate systems. 1851 23/2/68
Pressensé, Edmond de
The Church and the French Revolution . . . translated from the French by J. Stroyan. 1869 16/4/69
Pressensé, Francis de
L'Irlande et l'Angleterre depuis l'acte d'union jusqu'à nos jours, 1800–1888. 1889 29/12/88
Preston, Thomas F.R.H.S.
The jubilee of George III. 25 October, 1809. 1887 24/6/87
Pretyman, John Radclyff
Relations of church and state. 1848 14/5/48
The Church of England and Erastianism since the Reformation. 1854 9/8/57
Pretyman, Richard
'A review of no. 90 of "The Tracts for the Times": with observations upon the articles' 1841 17/10/41
Prevost, Sir George 2nd Bart.
A charge delivered at the primary visitation of the archdeaconry of Gloucester. 1865 27/8/65
Prévost-Paradol, Lucien Anatole
Discours de réception prononcé à l'Académie française. 1866 15/12/66 ? ?
La France nouvelle. 1868 7/12/70
Priaulx, Osmond de Beauvoir
Questiones Mosaicae, or the Book of Genesis compared with the remains of ancient religions. 1842 28/2/58, 28/12/85
Price, Bartholomew
The presence of God in the creation. A sermon preached before the university of Oxford. 1855 6/1/56
Price, T. C.
Faith in the son of God. 1845 12/2/47
Price, Uvedale M.A. of Christ Church, Oxford
An essay on the picturesque as compared with the sublime and beautiful. 1794 (2v. 1794–8) 20/8/63
Prichard, Iltudus Thomas
The chronicles of Budgepore: life in Upper India. 1870 (2v. 1870) 29/11/78
Prichard, James Cowles M.D., F.R.S.
Researches into the physical history of mankind. 1826 (2v. 1826) 22/8/58, 20/8/61
The eastern origin of the celtic nations proved. 1831 28/1/58
Prideaux, Humphrey Dean of Norwich
The Old and New Testament connected in the history of the Jews and neighbouring nations. 1716 (2v. 1716–18) 14/6/30
The original and right of tithes. 1710 31/3/34
Priestley, Joseph LL.D.
Discourses on the evidence of revealed religion. 1794 15/9/78
Letters to the Jews; inviting them to an amicable discussion of the evidences of Christianity. 1786 23/3/90
Three tracts. 1791 1/7/55
Primitive Christianity and modern spiritualism. 1890 26/9/90
Primrose, Archibald Philip 5th Earl of Rosebery
A rectorial address delivered before the students of Aberdeen university. 1880 17/11/80
Pitt. 1891 19/3/91, 24/11/91
Prince Maurice of Statland. 1890 27/5/90 ?
Princeton Review.
5. 34. 1/1862. England and America 24/2/1862
54. 1/1878. Eastern problem 9/2/1878
54. 150. 1/1878. Evolution 10/2/1878
54. 361, 451. 3/1878. Bible & the public school; preaching to the dead 14/4/1878
Pringle, John Watson
Remarks on the state and prospects of the West Indian colonies. 1839 19/4/39
Prior, Matthew
Solomon on the vanity of the world. 1719 3/5/31

Pritchard, Charles
Occasional thoughts of an astronomer on nature and revelation. 1890 23/3/90 ?
The continuity of the schemes of nature and of revelation. A sermon. 1866 14/1/77 ?
Pritchard, George Baptist minister
Remains of James Smith. 1840 13/8/72
Pritchard, William Tarn
Reform of the ecclesiastical courts: an analysis of the present state of the question. 1853 29/5/53
Probyn, John Webb
Italy: from the fall of Napoleon I., in 1815, to the death of Victor Emmanuel, in 1878. 1884 8/3/89
Probyn, May
A ballad of the road, and other poems. 1883 25/10/83
Proceedings of the Statistical Society of London. 1835 27/7/35
Procter, Bryan Waller pseud. Barry Cornwall
An autobiographical fragment and biographical notes. 1877 1/1/79, 13/1/80
Charles Lamb: a memoir. 1866 9/8/66
Proctor, Richard Anthony
'On the pyramid' in *Contemporary Review*, xxxvi. 93. 1879 (September 1879) 1/9/79
Astronomy. 1888 15/9/90 ?
Lessons in elementary astronomy. 1871 4/6/71
Light science for leisure hours. A series of familiar essays on scientific subjects. 1871 11/10/71 ?
Profeta, Il
Riduzione dal poema di Moore di Italo Robin. 1897 30/1/89 ?
Prokopovich, Emile de
The black book of Russia. 1876 24/12/76
Prompt, Pierre Inés
Le Jeu public et Monaco. 1882 3/4/82
Propertius, Sextus
Sexti Aurelii Propertii elegiarum libri quattuor, ed. W. A. B. Hertzberg. 1843 (3v. 1843–5) 25/8/45 ?
'Property tax versus income tax, in a letter ... to the representatives of the United Kingdom' 1848 6/3/48
Proposal for uniting the kingdoms of Great Britain and Ireland. 1751 6/11/91 ?
Prota-Giurleo, Luigi
Leone XIII e S. Tommaso d'Aquino. Osservazioni critiche sull'Enciclica del 4 agosto 1879. 1880 11/4/80
Pensieri di un credente. 1887 23/10/87
Statuto dogmatico-organico-disciplinare della Chiesa cattolica nazionale italiana. 1875 6/10/75
Protest against Puseyism. 4/5/43
Protestant ascendancy and Catholic emancipation reconciled by a legislative union. 1800 27/2/68
'Protestantism and churches in the east' (a tract of the Catholic Institute). 1842 25/1/42 ?
Protéstation du pueple des deux Siciles, tr. G. N. Ricciardi. 1848 8/12/51
Prothero, George Walter
Life of Simon de Montfort. 1877 12/3/72 n, 19/2/78, 12/3/78
Prothero, Rowland Edmund Baron Ernle
The life and correspondence of Arthur Penrhyn Stanley, D.D., late Dean of Westminster. 1893 (2v. 1893) 21/1/94
Proto Pallavicino, Francesco Duke di Maddaloni
The motion of inquiry on the state of the two Sicilies. 1862 31/3/62
Proverbs of Aphobis. 1858 19/11/76
Prowett, Charles Gipps
Religious equality in Ireland ... A letter to the Right Hon. B. Disraeli, M.P. 1868 27/9/68
Prudentius
Translations from Prudentius, by F. St. John Thackeray. 1890 22/3/91
Prudenzano, Francesco
Francesco d'Assisi e il suo secolo considerato in relazione con la politica. 1857 5/2/93
Prussia in relation to the foreign policy of England. 1875 7/1/75
Pryce, John
A history of the early Church. A manual. 1869 21/11/69
Lay agency as an auxiliary to the Christian ministry in Wales. 1864 9/6/72
The ancient British Church. A historical essay. 1878 26/1/79
pseud. An Anglo Levantine
Our Consuls in the East: a parliamentary enquiry into their proceedings imperative. 1855 25/4/55
pseud. A Peer
'Revise the liturgy' 1845 14/2/45
pseud. F. Airplay
'Prince Albert; why is he unpopular?' 1856 5/2/57
pseud. Monius
[On free trade]. 22/6/49
Psychical Research, Journal of Society for.
2. 408. 10/1886. Proceedings of Psychical Society 19/10/1886
2. 449. 7/1885. Psychical Transactions 22/8/1885
Psychosis
Our modern philosophers: Darwin, Bain and Spencer [in verse]. 1887 7/11/86, 4/9/87
Public documents on various subjects connected with the interests of Prince Edward Island. 1841 23/4/58
'Publius'
'Thoughts on finance and colonies, by Publius' 1846 28/4/48

Pueckler-Muskau, Prince Hermann Ludwig Heinrich von
Tutti Frutti from the papers of the departed. 1834 (2v.) 19/7/34
Pugin, Augustus Welby Northmore
An apology for the revival of Christian architecture in England. 1843 22/9/43
An earnest address, on the establishment of the hierarchy. 1851 1/3/51
Pulci, Luigi
Morgante maggiore. 9/2/50
Pullen, Henry William
The fight at Dame Europa's school. 1870 7/12/70
Puller, Frederick William
The duties and rights of parish priests and the limits of obedience . . . a letter. 1877 14/10/77
Pulliblank, Joseph Curate of Walton, Liverpool
Lectures on the Sermon on the Mount. 1877 24/11/78
Pulling, Alexander the elder
The City of London Corporation inquiry. 1854 6/3/54
Pulling, Frederic Sanders
The life and speeches of the marquis of Salisbury. 1885 (2v. 1885) 26/6/85
Pulteney, William
Considerations on the present state of public affairs, and the means of raising the . . . supplies. 1779 26/2/47
Thoughts on the present state of affairs with America and the means of conciliation. 1778 26/2/47
Purcell, Edmund Sheridan
On church and state. 1867 20/2/75
Purcell, Goodwin
Stone upon stone, and church management in the present day. By a country clergyman. 1874 7/1/76
Puseley, Daniel pseud. Frank Foster
Number one; or the way of the world. 1863 16/5/64
The rise and progress of Australia, Tasmania, and New Zealand . . . By an Englishman. 1857 19/3/64
Pusey, Edward Bouverie
'Churches in London', reprinted from *British Magazine*, viii. 581. 1835 (November 1835) 9/5/36
'Scriptural views of Holy Baptism', in *Tracts for the Times, 67–69.* 1835 (1835, 1836) 13/3/36
A letter to the bishop of London in explanation . . . statements . . . a letter by the Rev. W. Dodsworth. 1851 18/4/51
A letter . . . on some circumstances connected with the present crisis in the English Church. 1842 25/3/60
All faith the gift of God. Real faith entire. Two sermons. 1855 6/1/56
An earnest remonstrance to the author of the 'Pope's pastoral letter to . . . the university of Oxford'. 1836 4/5/36
An Eirenicon. Part 3. 1870 22/10/71
Case as to the legal force of the judgment of the privy council. 1864 21/8/64
Catena Patrum, Tracts for the Times, no. 81. 1837 14/12/40
Chastisements neglected forerunners of greater. 1847 20/6/47
Christ, the source and rule of Christian love. A sermon. 1841 21/2/41
Collegiate and professional teaching and discipline, in answer to Professor Vaughan's strictures. 1854 22/4/54
Daniel the prophet. Nine lectures delivered in the . . . university of Oxford. 1864 26/3/65, 27/1/85
Dr. Hampden's past and present statements compared. 1836 26/3/36
Dr. Hampden's theological statements compared. 1836 18/3/36
Entire absolution of the penitent. A sermon. 1846 8/3/46
Eve. A sermon. 1872 8/12/72
God is love . . . two sermons preached in . . . Ilfracombe. 1844 1/12/44
Life of E. B. Pusey . . . ed . . . by the Rev. J. O. Johnston . . . and the Rev. R. J. Wilson. 1893 (4v. 1893–7) 16/3/91 n, 7/1/94
Marriage with a deceased wife's sister prohibited by holy scripture. 1849 10/3/49
Nine sermons, preached before the university of Oxford. 1859 4/9/64
Our Pharisaism. A sermon. 1868 26/4/68
[Pamphlet]. 30/1/33
Parochial sermons. 1852 (2v. 1852–3) 29/1/54
Patience and confidence. The strength of the Church. 1836 (2v. 1836–7) 19/11/37
Preface to the fourth edition of the 'Letter to . . . Richard, Lord Bishop of Oxford . . . '. 1840 4/2/41
Review of A. P. Perceval, *British Critic*, xxvii. 40 [actually by J. H. Newman]. 1840 (January 1840) 12/1/40 ?
Sermons preached before the university of Oxford, 1859–1872. 1872 2/2/73
Subscription to the 39 Articles. 1835 1/7/35
The articles treated on in Tract 90 reconsidered . . . in a letter to R. W. Jelf. 1841 10/6/41
The Church of England a portion of Christ's one Holy Catholic Church. An Eirenicon. 1865 22/10/65, 18/2/66
The conflict: in a superficial age. Sermon. 1865 5/2/65
The doctrine of the Real Presence. 1855 13/5/55

The holy eucharist a comfort to the penitent . . . with an appendix by Revd. W. J. Copeland. 1843 30/6/43
The responsibility of intellect in matters of faith. 1873 2/2/73, 14/8/92
The royal supremacy not an arbitrary authority but limited by the laws of the church. 1850 5/5/50
This is my body. A sermon. 1871 18/6/71
Thoughts on the benefits of the system, of fasting enjoined by our Church, Tracts for the Times, No. 18. 1834 16/3/34
Unlaw in judgements of the Judicial Committee, and its remedies. A letter. 1881 13/2/81
What is of faith as to everlasting punishment. 1880 15/9/80
Pusey, Philip
'On the progress of agricultural knowledge', *Journal of the Royal Ag. Soc. of England*, iii. 169. 1842 2/2/42
'The poor in Scotland'; reprinted from the Christian Observer. 1844 2/11/44
The improvement of farming. What ought landlords and farmers to do?. 1851 3/3/52
The new constitution: remarks by P. Pusey. 1831 25/4/31
'Puseyism in London'. Reprinted from The Morning Post. 1843 21/8/43
Puseyism the school of the infidels . . . by a layman of the established church. 1865 31/10/65
Pushkin, Aleksandr Sergeevich Russian writer
Eugene Onéguine; a romance of Russian life, in verse . . . Translated . . . by Lieut.-Col. Spalding. 1881 23/9/81 ?
Pycroft, James
A course of English reading . . . with anecdotes of men of genius. 1844 20/11/55
Oxford memories, a retrospect after fifty years. 1886 (2v. 1886) 28/3/87
Pycroft, James Wallis
The Oxford University Commission: a letter addressed to Sir R. H. Inglis. 1851 18/7/55
Pye, G.
Education. 1872 3/3/72
Pye, Henry John
Convocation. A sermon on the late synodical condemnation of the 'Essays and Reviews'. 1864 24/1/64
Pym, William Wollaston
The Jew an important member of the Body of Christ. The substance of a sermon. 1843 13/7/50
Pyne, J. B.
Windsor with its surrounding scenery . . . a series of lithographed plates. 1840 25/4/64 ?

Quarterly Journal of Psychological Medicine, founded 1848 by Forbes Benignus Winslow. 9/8/49
Quarterly Journal of Science. 1. 1. 1/1864 8/1/1864
Quarterly Review.
8. 1, 355. 5/1809. Persians 6/3/1827
8. 215. 9/1812. Euripides 27/2/1827
11. 144. 4/1814. on Lacretelle 8/3/1829
14. 283. 1/1816. Culloden 30/6/1826
14. 39. 10/1816. on Alison 6/7/1828
15. 475. 7/1816. Regeneration 30/6/1828
16. 129. 10/1816. Selkirk 9/3/1829
16. 144. 10/1816. Pacific 12/3/1829
16. 27. 10/1816. on Phillips 30/6/1829
16. 37. 10/1816. Sumner 7/3/1829
18. 229. 10/1817. Bishop Watson 12/3/1829
25. 95. 4/1821. Etonian 10/6/1826
30. 79. 10/1823. Belsham 12/6/1829
30. 79. 10/1823. New Testament 29/7/1827
31. 111. 4/1824. Biddulph 17/7/1827
31. 229. 12/1824. Dissent 15/7/1827
31. 26. 12/1824. Memoirs 22/7/1827
33. 1. 12/1825. Catholics 7/2/1826
33. 1. 12/1825. Reformation 22/7/1827
33. 260. 1/1826. London University 14/11/1827
33. 356. 3/1826. Revelation 22/7/1827
33. 37. 1/1826. Burma 18/11/1827
33. 375. 3/1826. Popery 29/7/1827
33. 410–29. 3/1826. Slavery 24/4/1826
33. 491. 3/1826. Church in Ireland 15/7/1827
34. 305. 9/1826. Cathedrals 8/4/1829
34. 35. 6/1826. Industry 9/8/1826
34. 378. 9/1826. Parry 28/3/1829
36. 1–28. 6/1827. Bible 2/8/1827
36. 285. 6/1827. Catholics 14/6/1827
36. 305. 10/1827. Popery 12/1/1828
36. 391. 10/1827. Agriculture 14/1/1828
37. 194. 1/1828. Hallam 16/1/1828
37. 523. 3/1828. N. Pole 26/3/1829
38. 114–45. 7/1828. Jews 19/7/1828
38. 305. 10/1828. Paley 17/4/1829
38. 335. 10/1828. Ireland 17/4/1829
39. 99. 1/1829. Paley 16/4/1829
44. 511. 2/1831. Scrope on Irish poor law 25/3/1847
45. 97. 12/1839. Gladstone's State and Church 29/12/1839
48. 320. 12/1832. Poor Laws 19/4/1833
48. 542. 12/1832. Church reform 7/1/1833
48. 570. 10/1885. Strawfield 2/10/1885
49. 136, 1. 4/1833. Martineau; on Shirley 27/8/1833
49. 29. 4/1833. Le Vasseur 29/8/1833
49. 464, 485. 7/1833. French Revolution, Port Admiral 22/8/1833
49. 47. 4/1833. Memoir of Neff 30/8/1833

Quarterly Review (*cont.*)
49. 522. 7/1833. Domestic & foreign policy 21/8/1833
50. 218. 10/1833. Novels; Reformed Parliament 26/8/1833
51. 117. 3/1834. Life of Adam Clarke 27/3/1834
53. 1. 2/1835. Bennett's New South Wales 14/2/1835
53. 229. 2/1835. Turkey 13/2/1835
53. 261. 2/1835. Peel's address 11/2/1835
53. 289. 4/1835. Beaumont 25/4/1835
53. 548. 4/1835. Fisher Ames 24/4/1835
53. 79, 174. 2/1835. Coleridge's Table Talk; Church & voluntary system 12/2/1835
55. 234. 12/1835. Lieber 8/1/1836
55. 35. 12/1835. Poor Law 1/5/1835
57. 182. Brewster & Keith 1/11/1836
57. 182. Last session 10/10/1836
59. 395. 10/1837. Etiquette 2/11/1837
59. 439. 10/1837. Universities 3/11/1837
59. 484. 10/1837. Pickwick 6/11/1837
62. 131. 6/1838. Art 21/6/1838
62. 232. 5/1843. Croker on Rubrics 31/5/1843
62. 390. 4/1838. Pusey on Tyler 9/5/1838
62. 53. 5/1843. on Hook's Peregrine Bunce 2/6/1843
63. 591. 1/1839. Head 1/4/1839
65. 283, 153. 12/1839. Review of Lofft's Ernest 1/1/1840
65. 642. 3/1840. China 15/4/1840
66. 446. 9/1840. on Carlyle 13/10/1840
67. 203, 117. 12/1840. Scottish Church 25/12/1840
68. 145. 6/1841. on Swinburne 6/7/1841
69. 419. 3/1842. on Loch; Church of England 14/4/1842
70. 289. 9/1842. Pitt's correspondence 29/9/1842
70. 385. 9/1842. Tennyson 28/9/1842
71. 244. 12/1842. on A. C. C. L. 24/12/1842
72. 553. 9/1843. Croker on policy of ministers 8/9/1843
73. 1. 12/1843. Inglis on Vaudois Church 29/12/1843
73. 224. 6/1844. Railways 6/7/1844
73. 467. 10/1844. Arnold 18/10/1844
73. 508. 10/1844. Malmesbury 19/10/1844
73. 87. 12/1843. T. Jones' review article 28/12/1843
75. 149. 12/1844. Gladstone's review of Ward 22/9/1844
75. 201. 12/1844. Colonial religion 31/12/1844
75. 222. 12/1844. Repeal 1/1/1845
75. 403. 3/1845. Malmesbury 1/5/1845
75. 403, 485, 519. 3/1845. Malmesbury; Miss Berry; Whigs 5/5/1845
75. 532. 3/1845. Mediterranean 10/7/1845
75. 54. 12/1844. on Eothen 11/1/1845
75. 805. 3/1845. Convocation 30/3/1845
76. 137. 6/1845. Spain 3/7/1845
76. 204. 6/1845. Marmont 4/7/1845
76. 247. 6/1845. Ireland 30/6/1845
76. 299. 9/1845. on Michelet 25/11/1845
76. 354. 9/1845. Round towers 8/10/1846
76. 62. 6/1845. Brougham 1/7/1845
77. 298. 12/1845. The Crisis 22/12/1845
77. 323. 3/1846. Commerce 7/6/1846
77. 404. 3/1846. Newman 10/4/1846
78. 216. 6/1846. Lyttelton 1/7/1846
78. 377. 9/1846. Education 24/10/1846
78. 425. 9/1846. Cologne 27/10/1846
78. 463. 9/1846. Peel 23/10/1846
79. 1. 12/1846. Montrose 12/3/1847
79. 127. 12/1846. Ragged schools 20/2/1847
79. 238. 12/1846. Ireland 12/1/1847
79. 336, 399. 3/1847. Gallus; Utrecht 8/4/1847
79. 484, 463. 3/1847. Sidmouth; Out-door relief 7/4/1847
81. 230. 6/1847. Finance 9/7/1847
81. 274. 6/1847. Peel 2/7/1847
81. 440. 9/1847. Edward Lear 8/11/1847
81. 526. 9/1847. Jews 21/10/1847
81. 541. 9/1847. Parliament 22/10/1847
81. 571. 6/1847. Stuarts; Lindsay 10/7/1847
82. 142. 12/1847. Lodging houses 17/1/1848
82. 261. 12/1847. Ministers 15/1/1848
82. 453, 541. 3/1848. Army 11/4/1848
83. 110. 6/1848. Countess Ossory 8/7/1848
83. 165. 6/1848. Cabet 11/7/1848
83. 199. 6/1848. France 12/7/1848
83. 359. 9/1848. Penitentiaries 12/10/1848
83. 552. 9/1848. Italy 11/10/1848
83. 70. 6/1848. C. Joly 13/7/1848
84. 1. 12/1848. Railways 3/1/1849
84. 153. 12/1848. Thackeray 4/1/1849
84. 185. 12/1848. Austria 9/1/1869
84. 222. 12/1848. Italy 10/1/1849
84. 238. 12/1848. France 5/1/1849
84. 264. 12/1848. Castlereagh 6/1/1849
84. 501–48. 3/1849. on MacFarlane and Italy 18/7/1851
85. 103. 6/1849. Scottish Church 21/8/1849
85. 156. 6/1849. Democracy 5/7/1849
85. 225–59. 6/1849. Beaumont on Foreign Policy 18/7/1851
85. 313. 9/1849. Welsh Methodism 28/10/1849

85. 346. 9/1849. Fontenelle 9/11/1849
85. 399. 9/1849. Bridge 22/10/1849
85. 452. 9/1849. Agitators 26/10/1849
85. 563. 9/1849. Rome 25/10/1849
85. 563–616. 9/1849. Rome 19/7/1851
85. 82. 6/1849. Chess 26/9/1849
86. 384. 3/1850. Grote 2/4/1850
86. 480. 3/1850. Ireland 28/3/1850
87. 274. 6/1850. Cochrane; Louis Philippe 23/7/1851
87. 395. 9/1850. California 4/10/1850
87. 533–557. 9/1850. Cochrane's, Young Italy 22/7/1851
88. 100. 12/1850. Mysteries of Ceylon 22/4/1851
88. 247. 12/1850. Ministers and Pope 18/4/1851
88. 564. 3/1851. John Russell 3/5/1851
89. 203–56. 6/1851. Rubric versus Usage 17/8/1851
89. 307–32. 9/1851. on Ruskin 19/10/1851
89. 451, 491. 9/1851. Papal Pretensions 18/10/1851
90. 226. 12/1851. Farini 3/1/1852
90. 567. 3/1852. Ministries 7/4/1852
91. 37. 6/1852. Ireland 18/7/1852
91. 402. 9/1852. Croker on Hanna 17/10/1852
91. 461. 9/1852. Langdale 16/10/1852
91. 541. 9/1852. Croker 9/10/1852
92. 1. 12/1852. J. Armstrong 14/1/1853
92. 157. 12/1852. Croker on British Museum 12/1/1853
92. 236. 12/1852. Croker on Disraeli's budget 11/1/1853
93. 192. 6/1853. Oxford Commission 5/12/1853
93. 349, 387. 9/1853. Beckett's murder 21/10/1853
94. 105. 6/1856. Guizot's Charles I 17/7/1856
94. 171–195. 12/1853. Relief of Chinese rebels 22/1/1854
94. 60, 160. 6/1856. Greece; Police 16/7/1856
96. 200. 12/1854. War 15/1/1855
96. 277. 12/1854. Conduct of War 13/1/1855
97. 1. 6/1855. Archdeacon Hare 14/7/1855
97. 245. 6/1855. War 13/7/1855
97. 291. 9/1855. Huet 25/11/1855
97. 513. 9/1855. Pitt & Fox 8/11/1855
98. 249. 12/1855. War 25/1/1856
98. 502, 535. 3/1856. Eastern Question 14/5/1856
99. 1. 6/1856. Savonarola 3/8/1856
99. 235. 6/1856. America 31/7/1856
99. 396. 9/1856. Montaigne 14/10/1856
99. 489, 371. 9/1856. Port Royal; Church building 12/10/1856
101. 123. 1/1857. Rats 3/2/1856
101. 168. 1/1857. Raglan 31/1/1856
101. 304, 501. 4/1857. Political Squibs; Persia 25/4/1857
101. 324. 4/1857. U. S. Slavery & Lord Overstone 24/4/1857
102. 165. 7/1857. Manchester Exhibition 20/7/1857
102. 289, 354. 10/1857. Cornwall; Euphrates Route 13/11/1857
102. 453. 10/1857. Parish priest 18/10/1857
102. 88. 7/1857. Ritualism 19/7/1857
103. 139. 1/1858. Church Extension 16/2/1858
103. 279. 3/1858. Boswell 20/4/1858
103. 483, 505. 3/1858. Public Speaking; Lucknow 16/4/1858
103. 526. 3/1858. 1857 Political Committee 16/3/1858
104. 106, 151. 7/1858. Wiclif; Blunt 18/7/1858
104. 325. 10/1858. Horace 21/10/1858
104. 475. 10/1858. India 13/8/1858
105. 255. 1/1859. Reform 18/2/1859
106. 174. 7/1859. Pacific island 16/7/1859
106. 245. 7/1859. Invasion 15/7/1859
107. 1. 1/1860. Gold 19/1/1860
107. 514. 4/1860. Budget 23/4/1860
108. 265. 7/1860. Conservatives 18/7/1860
109. 212, 248. 1/1861. Essays & Reviews 22/1/1861
110. 1. 7/1861. De Quincey 21/8/1861
110. 139. 7/1861. Scottish Character 22/8/1861
110. 329. 10/1861. Coal Mines 6/11/1861
110. 544. 10/1861. Church Rates 5/11/1861
111. 400. 4/1862. Clergy training 27/4/1862
112. 535. 10/1862. America 31/1/1862
113. 253. 1/1863. Government 20/1/1863
114. 368. 10/1863. Lyell's Man 29/10/1863
114. 480. 10/1863. Italy 28/10/1863
115. 236, 242. 1/1864. Duchies 21/1/1864
115. 289. 4/1864. Confederates 22/4/1864
116. 176. 7/1864. Public Schools 22/7/1864
116. 212. 7/1864. Travel in England 23/7/1864
116. 245. 7/1864. House of Commons 20/7/1864
116. 439. 10/1864. Lockhart 31/10/1864
116. 528. 10/1864. Newman 4/11/1864
117. 4/1865 11/4/1865
117. 1. 1/1865. Blake 21/1/1865
117. 93. 1/1865. Derby's travels 18/1/1865

Quarterly Review (*cont.*)
118. 193, 280. 7/1865. Church; Election 2/7/1865
118. 280. 7/1865. Six year old Parliament 12/6/1865
118. 371. 10/1865. Italy 24/10/1865
119. 435. 4/1866. Coal & Smoke 25/4/1866
119. 515. 4/1866. Ecce Homo 15/4/1866
119. 530. 4/1866. Cranbourne on Reform 13/4/1866
120. 259. 7/1866. Reform 17/7/1866
123. 173. 7/1867. Agricultural Gangs 17/7/1867
123. 244, 35. 7/1867. Reform; Cornwall 15/7/1867
123. 306. 10/1867. Moscow 7/12/1867
123. 533. 10/1867. Ministry 19/10/1867
123. 93. 7/1867. Law Courts 18/7/1867
124. 1. 1/1868. on Scott 22/1/1868
124. 147. 1/1868. British Museum 24/1/1868
124. 255, 225. 1/1868. Lowe; Ireland 21/1/1868
124. 287. 4/1868. Macaulay 22/4/1868, 27/5/1876
124. 357. 4/1868. Dr South 26/4/1868
124. 385. 4/1868. Universities 1/5/1868
124. 537. 4/1868. Irish Church 21/4/1868
125. 254. 7/1868. Ireland 14/7/1868
125. 78. 7/1868. Coleridge 17/7/1868
126. 394. 4/1869. Party Government 14/4/1869
126. 559. 4/1869. Irish Church 15/4/1869
127. 493. 10/1869. Convocaton 18/10/1869
128. 218, 251. 1/1870. Irish Cauldron 24/1/1870
128. 342. 4/1870. Napoleon 14/4/1870
128. 386, 560. 4/1870. Wales, Ireland 12/4/1870
128. 432. 4/1870. Non-historic Times 16/4/1870
129. 10/1870 19/10/1870
129. 182. 7/1870. Rig Veda 23/1/1871
129. 244. 7/1870. Army 16/7/1870
129. 327, 369. 10/1870. Palmerston 21/10/1870
129. 392, 540. 10/1870. Peace 22/10/1870
129. 485. 10/1870. German songs 9/11/1870
129. 63. 7/1870. Lothair 15/7/1870
130. 256, 122. 1/1871. The War; Invasion of France 3/2/1871
130. 407. 4/1871. Civil Pensions 19/4/1871
130. 432. 4/1871. Church & Nonconformity 1/5/1871
130. 71, 164. 1/1871. on Bismarck; Irish Chancellors 4/2/1871
134. 169, 1. 1/1873. Froude; Princess Charlotte 23/1/1873
134. 255. 1/1873. Irish University 18/1/1873
134. 457, 552. 4/1873. Greek; Irish University 22/4/1873
135. 1. 7/1873. English Poetry 18/7/1873
135. 539. 10/1873. Political article 23/10/1873
135. 98. 7/1873. Grote 11/8/1873
136. 103, 251, 74, 150. 1/1874. Sacerdotalism; Liberal party; Mrs Somerville; on Mill 19/1/1874
136. 289. 4/1874. German Church 29/4/1874
136. 332. 4/1874. on Bishop Wilberforce 26/4/1874
136. 526. 4/1874. on Schliemann 21/4/1874
136. 566. 4/1874. on Schliemann; Liberal party 24/4/1874
137. 416. 10/1874. Venice 25/11/1874
137. 542, 283. 10/1874. Jesuits 17/10/1874
138. 107. 1/1875. Life of Albert 18/1/1875
138. 459. 4/1875. Vatican controversy 17/4/1875
140. 385. 6/1842. Tennyson 23/8/1859
141. 285. 4/1876. on Green's History 13/4/1876
145. 188. 1/1878. on Melbourne 23/2/1878
146. 141. 7/1878. on Madame Du Deffaud 27/7/1878
146. 232. 7/1878. Crown and Army 18/7/1878
146. 289. 10/1878. Dryden 28/10/1878
146. 331. 10/1878. British Empire 30/10/1878
146. 443. 10/1878. Cyprus 23/10/1878
146. 519. 10/1878. Protestantism 20/10/1878
147. 277. 1/1879. Party government 17/1/1879
147. 49. 1/1879. Aggressive nonconformism 26/1/1879
147. 552. 4/1879. African war 21/4/1879
148. 1. 7/1879. Prince Consort 17/7/1879
148. 255, 289. 7/1879. Scotch politics 16/7/1879
149. 125. 1/1880. Hellenism 3/2/1880
149. 230. 1/1880. on Duke of Somerset 31/1/1880
150. 141. 7/1880. Marie Antoinette 29/7/1880
155. 459. 4/1883. France in 1883 18/4/1883
156. 270. 7/1883. Politics 6/8/1883
156. 305. 10/1883. Hawkins 17/10/1883
156. 452. 10/1883. Bugeard 18/10/1883
157. 249. 7/1888. Local government 17/7/1888

157. 272. 1/1884. The Session 15/1/1884
157. 289, 473. 4/1884. Hope-Scott 20/4/1884
157. 387. 4/1884. Vatican 19/4/1884
158. 229. 7/1884. Foreign policy 24/7/1884
158. 495. 10/1884. Masillon 26/10/1884
158. 518. 10/1884. Croker 24/10/1884
159. 147. 1/1885. Chatterton 19/2/1885
159. 220. 1/1885. Salisbury on Redistribution 19/1/1885, 20/1/1885
159. 267. 4/1885. on Samuel Johnson 22/4/1885
161. 281. 10/1885. Old Testament 21/10/1885
163. 116, 180. 7/1886. Missions; Eastern Sacred Books 11/7/1886
163. 363, 460. 10/1886. American poetry; New Testament 17/10/1886
164. 322, 507. 4/1887. Non-jurors 20/4/1887
165. 1. 7/1887. on Lecky 22/7/1887
165. 273. 10/1887. Reformation 23/10/1887
165. 327. 10/1887. Dairy produce 28/10/1887
165. 535. 10/1887. Conservatism 21/10/1887
166. 112. 1/1888. Mammoths 14/2/1888
166. 31. 1/1888. Catholics in England 12/2/1888
167. 273. 10/1888. Robert Elsmere; M. Arnold 24/10/1888
167. 303, 504. 10/1888. O'Connell; S. Rogers 25/10/1888
168. 136. 1/1889. Gambling 11/3/1889
168. 167. 1/1889. Russell on Burgon 12/3/1889
168. 297. 4/1889. Motley 26/4/1889
168. 332. 4/1889. Goethe 27/4/1889
169. 42. 7/1889. Old age 16/7/1889
170. 112. 1/1890. Welsh church 24/1/1890
170. 80. 1/1890. Poland 25/1/1890
171. 1, 172. 7/1890. Walpole; Eton 15/7/1890
171. 287. 10/1890. Chesterfield 19/11/1890
171. 386. 10/1890. Scott 17/11/1890
173. 1, 173. 7/1891. Peel; J. Murray 16/7/1891
173. 211. 7/1891. Seche 19/7/1891
175. 1. 7/1892. on E. A. Freeman 3/9/1892
175. 538. 10/1892. The government 21/10/1892
176. 549. 4/1893. Reaction 19/4/1893
176. 73. 1/1893. Bishop Lightfoot 29/1/1893
177. 178. 7/1893. Bookbinding 22/7/1893
Church & Landlords 28/8/1833
on Dr Haussez & Dermoncourt 20/11/1833
Sarrans 19/1/1833

Quatrefages de Bréau, Jean Louis Armand de
The Prussian race ethnologically considered, tr. Isabella Innes. 1872 3/11/73

Queen Elizabeth's opinion concerning Transubstantiation, ed. 1688. 7/1/76 ?

'Quelques mots sur la lettre du czar . . . question d'orient au point de vue de sa popularité en France' 1854 19/4/54 ?

Quesnel, Pasquier
Le Nouveau Testament en Français avec des réflexions morales. 25/3/32

'Question des sucres. Aux gens embarrassés pour faire une loi' 1864 9/1/64

Quételet, Lambert Adolphe Jacques
Du système social et des lois qui le régissent. 1848 2/2/54 ?
Sur l'homme et le développement de ses facultés, ou essai de physique sociale. 1835 (2v. 1835) 26/6/55

Quin, Edwin Richard Wyndham 3rd Earl of Dunraven
Notes on Irish architecture, ed. M. Stokes. 1875 (2v. 1875–77) 4/11/77

Quin, Windham Thomas Wyndham 4th Earl of Dunraven
The Irish question examined in a letter to the 'New York Herald', a speech in parliament. 1880 25/5/90

Quinet, Edgar
Du génie des religions. 1842 6/4/84
L'Ultramontanisme ou l'église Romaine et la société moderne. 1844 14/7/47
La révolution religieuse au dix-neuvième siècle. 1851 6/2/81 ?

Quintilian
Opera. 8/8/64

Rabbe, Félix
Jeanne d'Arc en Angleterre. 1891 1/5/92
Les Maîtresses authentiques de Lord Byron. 1890 22/3/92
Shelley, sa vie et ses oeuvres. 1887 12/4/92

Rabelais, François
The works of F. Rabelais, ed. P. A. Motteux. (3v. 1693–4) 17/8/37, 15/2/48

Rabutin, Roger de Count de Bussy
Histoire amoureuse des Gaules. 29/9/83
Lettres de Madame . . . de Sévigné. 1726 23/5/86

Raccolta di Novellieri Italiani. 1833 (2v. 1833) 6/10/59 ?

Racine, Jean
Alexandre. 29/10/33
Andromaque. 1/11/33, 22/11/56
Athalie. 26/2/26
Esther. 12/2/26, 26/2/26, 12/5/26
Iphigénie. 25/6/27

Racine, Jean (*cont.*)
Les Frères Ennemis. 21/10/33
Works. 1/9/25
Radcliff, Ebenezer
Two letters addressed to the right rev. prelates, who a second time rejected the Dissenters bill. 1773 24/8/56
Radcliffe, Charles Bland
A new chapter in the story of nature. 1886 17/10/86
Proteus, or unity in nature. 1878 26/3/78
Radcliffe, Richard of Queen's College, Oxford
Letters of Richard Radcliffe and John James... ed. Margaret Evans. 1888 6/4/88
Radford, Daniel
The theology of Christian ordinances. An eirenicon. A letter to... Bishop Perry. 1884 30/3/84
Rae, Matthew John
The ornaments' rubric, and its relation to ritualism. A paper. 1881 9/10/81
Rae, William Fraser
'American claims on England' in *Westminster Review*, xxxvii. 211. 1870 (January 1870) 14/1/70
Maygrove. A family history. 1889 (3v. 1889) 21/11/89
The business of travel: a fifty years' record of progress. 1891 5/8/91
Wilkes, Sheridan, Fox: the opposition under George the Third. 1874 13/2/74
Raikes, Henry Barrister-at-Law
Observations on the Ecclesiastical Courts bill, brought in this session. 1843 7/3/43
Raikes, Henry Chancellor of the Diocese of Chester
A charge addressed to the churchwardens of the diocese of Chester. 1844 7/7/44
A popular sketch of the origin and development of the English constitution. 1851 (2v. 1851–54) 17/8/52
Remarks on clerical education. 1831 28/3/34 ?
Raikes, Thomas
A portion of the journal kept by T. Raikes, Esq., from 1831 to 1847. 1856 (4v. 1856–57) 15/8/57
France, since 1830. 1841 (2v. 1841) 4/5/41
Railton, George Scott
Heathen England, and what to do for it. 1877 6/1/78
Railways in Egypt. Communication with India. 1857 2/11/57
Raine, John
The origin, progress and evils of alienation of tithes from the Church. A sermon. 1852 1/8/52
Rainoldes, John
The summe of the conference betwene John Rainoldes and John Hart. 5/3/82, 19/3/82
Rainy, Alexander
On transfer of property by public auction and private contract. 1845 4/4/46
Rainy, Robert
Church and State, chiefly in relation to Scotland. 1878 19/5/78
The Epistle to the Philippians. 1893 5/11/93
Three lectures on the Church of Scotland. 1872 18/2/72
Raleigh, Mary
Alexander Raleigh. Records of his life. 1881 16/4/82
Raleigh, Sir Thomas K. C. S. I.
Irish politics. 18/10/89 ?
Raleigh, Sir Walter
Observations touching trade and commerce with the Hollander and other nations, ed. J. R. MacCulloch. (1653, new ed. 1859) 29/3/59
The cabinet-council: containing the chief arts of empire, and mysteries of state. 15/9/53, 16/9/53, 17/9/53
The poems of Sir Walter Raleigh: now first collected,... introduction by Sir Egerton Brydges. 1813 23/8/37
Ram, James Military tutor
The philosophy of war. 1878 29/6/78
Rambaud, Alfred Nicolas
Français et Russes. Moscou et Sévastopol, 1821–1854. 1877 21/2/77
The history of Russia from the earliest times to 1877, tr. L. B. Lang. 1879 (2v. 1879) 6/3/79
Rambler, The (later *Home and Foreign Review*).
1. 501. 10/1862. Wiseman 26/10/1862
5. 17. 5/1861. U. S. 8/5/1861, 8/2/1866 4/5/1861
Ramée, Marie Louise de la
In a winter city; a sketch. 1876 29/4/90
Ramsay, Edward Bannerman Dean of Edinburgh
A letter to the... Lord Provost of Edinburgh,... of providing the city with an efficient peal of bells. 1863 2/8/63
An earnest appeal to members of the Scottish Episcopal Church on... its financial institutions. 1863 27/9/63
Christian responsibility considered in its application to the events and circumstances of human life. 1864 2/10/64
Memoir of the late Bishop Terrot. 1872 26/5/72 ?
Memoir of Thomas Chalmers. 1849 15/5/49 ?
On the genius of Handel. Lecture to the Edinburgh Philosophical Institution, 6 Jan. 1862. 1862 11/1/62
Pastoral letters on various practical subjects. 1861 22/6/62

Preaching the gospel to the poor. 1867 16/8/68
Reminiscences of Scottish life and character. 1858 10/9/59, 12/7/73, 4/4/74
Sermons on various subjects and occasions. 1843 12/3/43
The art of reading and preaching distinctly: a letter to a young clergyman. 1869 10/10/71
Two lectures on some changes in social life and habits. 1857 24/6/57

Ramsay, Thomas
The shortcomings of our public education: a letter to... the Earl of Lonsdale. 1852 3/3/65

Ramsay, Sir William Mitchell
The Church in the Roman Empire before A. D. 170... With maps. 1893 27/8/93

Randall, Henry Stephens
The life of Thomas Jefferson. 1858 (3v. 1858) 30/11/61 ?

Randall, James Archdeacon of Berks.
A letter to... Ven. E. Berens... constitution of the ultimate court of appeal in causes ecclesiastical. 1850 28/5/50
Charge delivered... in June, 1861. 1861 11/8/61
Charge delivered... in June, 1865. 1865 12/11/65
The Judicial Committee of the Privy Council. 1878 8/12/78, 13/11/79

Randles, Marshall
For Ever: an essay on eternal punishment. 1871 27/4/79

Randolph, Francis
A sermon preached in the morning... the fast day, Oct. 19, 1803... Cathedral Church of Bristol. 1803 12/2/54 ?

Randolph, John Bishop of Oxford, Bangor, and of London
Praelectiones academicae in Homerum, Oxonii habitae annis 1776–1783. 1870 3/10/70

Rankabes, I. G. Rizos
The Greeks. 1853 (3v. 1853–5) 2/8/53

Ranke, Leopold von
'Ferdinand I', first published in *Historisch-politische Zeitschrift.* 1832 3/2/53
A history of England, principally in the seventeenth century. 1875 (6v. 1875) 14/8/84
Aus dem Briefwechsel Friedrich Wilhelms IV. mit Bunsen. 1873 13/9/74
Deutsche Geschichte im Zeitalter der Reformation, tr. S. Austin. 1845 18/4/52
The ecclesiastical and political history of the popes of Rome... tr. from the German by S. Austin. 1840 (3v. 1840) 14/7/40, 29/10/66

Ranyard, Mrs. Ellen pseud. L. N. R.
The book and its story: a narrative for the young. 1854 16/1/55
The missing link; or Bible women in the homes of the London poor. 1859 8/5/60

Raoul-Rochette, Désiré
Lectures on ancient art. 1854 10/7/77 ?

Rathborne, Joseph
Are the Puseyites sincere? A letter... to a... Catholic Lord Bishop on the Oxford Movement. 1841 17/5/41
The Church in its relations with truth and the state; a reply to the work by W. E. Gladstone. 1841 21/4/41

Rational Quarterly, ed. Robert Owen. 1853 23/7/53

Ratramnus, Monk of Corbey
Bertrami Presbyteri de corpore et sanguine Domine liber, etc., ed. H. W. and W. C. C. 1838 25/10/63
La perpétuité de la foy de l'Église Catholique touchant L'Eucharistie défendue, ed. A. Arnauld. 11/10/68

Ratzinger, Georg
Geschichte der kirchlichen Armenpflege. 1868 26/5/69

Raumer, Friedrich Ludwig Georg von
England im Jahre 1835. 1836 (3v. 1836–42) 6/4/36

Rawdon, John Dawson
Letter to the trustees of the National Gallery. 1851 24/7/51

Rawlins, C. A.
The famine in Ireland. A poem. 1847 14/6/87

Rawlinson, George Professor of Ancient History in Oxford
A manual of ancient history from the earliest times to the fall of the western empire. 1869 30/8/75 ?
History of Phoenicia. 1889 22/3/90, 11/7/90
On the genuineness and authenticity of the Pentateuch. 1861 9/2/62
The alleged historical difficulties of the Old and New Testaments. 1871 18/6/71, 20/10/72
The antiquity of man historically considered. 1883 24/12/82
The contrasts of Christianity with heathen and Jewish systems; or, nine sermons. 1861 10/2/61
The five great monarchies of the ancient Eastern world. 1862 (4v. 1862–7) 30/11/62
The historical evidence of the truth of the Scripture Records stated anew. 1859 27/11/59
The history of Herodotus. A new English version, edited... by G. Rawlinson. 1858 3/3/58, 13/11/67
The kings of Israel and Judah. 1889 25/8/89
The origin of nations. 1877 26/4/78
The religions of the ancient world. 1882 2/9/91
Thoughts on the closing year. A sermon. 1855 25/1/55

Rawdon, John Dawson (*cont.*)
Thoughts on the closing year. A sermon . . . With an appendix on the examination of Dissenters. 1855 25/1/55
Rawlinson, Sir Henry Creswicke
A selection from the miscellaneous inscriptions of Assyria. 1866 27/1/65 ?
'The Russian advance in Central Asia' in *Nineteenth Century*, xvii. 557. 1885 (April 1885) 31/3/85
[On Afghanistan] in *Nineteenth Century*, vii. 197. 1880 (February 1880) 2/2/80
'The results of the Afghan War' in *Nineteenth Century*, vi. 377. 1879 (August 1879) 10/11/79
Raynal, Guillaume Thomas François
A philosophical and political history of the British settlements and trade in North America. 1779 6/12/48
A philosophical and political history of the settlements of the Europeans in the West Indies. 1782 (6v. 1782) 31/12/33
Read, Clare Sewell M.P.
The education and wages of the agricultural labourer; an address. 1867 10/2/68
Reade, Amye
Ruby. 1889 18/6/90
Reade, Charles
It is never too late to mend. A matter of fact romance. 1856 (3v. 1856) 20/1/57
Peg Woffington. A novel. 1857 12/9/90 ?
The cloister and the hearth. A tale of the Middle Ages. 1861 (4v. 1861) 22/11/61
The double marriage; or white lies. 1882 13/11/87
Reade, Compton
Pictura picturae; a poem. 1871 8/5/71
The 'Golden Crowns' series. 1872 28/12/72
Reade, John Edmund
The poetical works of John Edmund Reade. 1852 (2v. 1852) 21/1/56
Reade, William Winwood pseud. Francesco Abati
The martyrdom of man. 1872 4/12/72
Reasons for Christianity; and the hope therein founded. 1833 8/5/33
Reasons on behalf of country bankers. 16/4/44
Reasons why the clergy should adopt the national plan of education, by a Presbyter. 1840 10/7/40
Récamier, Jeanne Françoise Julie Adelaïde
Souvenirs et correspondance tirés des papiers de Madame Récamier. 1860 (2v. 1860) 6/2/62
Recanati, Giovanni Battista
Poesie. 1717 5/8/49
Recantation; or, the confessions of a convert to romanism; a tale. 1845 13/5/45
Receuil de plusieurs pièces pour servir à l'histoire de Port Royal. 1740 20/10/39
Reclus, Élisée
Évolution et révolution. Conférence faite à Genève, le 5 mars 1880. 1880 4/5/84
The ocean, atmosphere and life. 1873 (2v. 1873) 30/1/73
Recollections of old Liverpool. 1863 18/8/87
Recollections of . . . service . . . in . . . Venezuela and Colombia by an officer of the Colombian navy. 1828 (2v. 1828) 27/4/42
Records of the English Catholics under the penal laws. 1878 (2v. 1878–82) 18/1/83
Recueil des documents pour la plupart secrets et inédits. 1853 26/12/53
Redman, M.
The aspect of the times, to the end of this age. 1876 26/9/80
Redmond, John Edward
'Readjustment of the Union: a nationalist plan' in *Nineteenth Century*, xxxii. 509. 1892 (October 1892) 5/10/92, 17/10/92
[On Home Rule] in *Nineteenth Century*, xxxiii. 559. 1893 (April 1893) 28/4/93
Irish protestants and Home Rule: a lecture delivered . . . 29 November, 1886. 1887 9/9/87
Red-tapeism: its cause; by one behind the scenes. 1855 5/5/55
Reed, Andrew the elder
Memoirs of life. 1863 10/12/71
Reed, Charles Edward Baines
Memoir of Sir Charles Reed. 1883 6/5/83
Reed, Rebecca Theresa
Narrative of a six months' residence in a convent. 1835 24/10/35
Rees, Thomas D.D.
History of Protestant Nonconformity in Wales, from its rise to the present time. 1861 27/4/76, 27/12/83, 13/1/84
Rees, William Lee
From poverty to plenty; or, the labour question solved. 1888 24/9/88
Reeve, Henry C. B.
Petrarch. 1877 21/3/78
Reflections on the public worship act by a Looker on. 1875 3/7/75
Reformatio legum ecclesiasticarum, etc., ed. John Fox. 4/8/38
'Reform in the ecclesiastical provision for the parish of Manchester' 1847 24/2/48
Refutation of a statement, etc. 1833 4/7/33
Regaldi, Guiseppe
L'Egitto antico e moderno. 1882 4/1/77
Reghellini de Schio, M.
Examen du Mosaïsme et du Christianisme. 1834 (3v. 1834) 5/8/83
Regle du tiers-ordre de St. Francois d'Assise. 1845 7/1/55
Regnard, Jean François
Le distrait. (n.d.) 19/6/26
Le joueur. (n.d.) 10/7/26

Regnault, Élias Georges Soulange Oliva
Histoire politique et sociale des principautés Danubiennes. 1855 3/12/57 ?
Regnier, Jacques Auguste Adolphe
Traité de la formation des mots dans la langue grecque. 1850 17/1/51 ?
Reichel, Charles Parsons Bishop of Meath
Necessary limits of Christian evidences. A sermon. 1874 18/10/74
The earliest missionary organisation of the Christian Church. A sermon. 1890 1/6/90
The Irish university question. 1867 7/1/68
The nature and origin of episcopacy. A sermon. 1877 7/1/77
Reichel, Charles Parsons, and Anderson, W. Bishop of Meath
Trinity college, Dublin and university reform. 1858 16/6/58
Reid, Daniel
The divine footsteps in human history. 1862 20/7/62 ?
Reid, Sir Hugh Gilzean
Past and present; or social and religious life in the North. 1871 29/10/71
Reid, Rev. John
Voices of the soul answered in God. 1866 28/2/69 ?
Reid, Robert of Glasgow
Glasgow past and present: illustrated in . . . the reminiscences . . . of Senex. 1851 8/11/65
Reid, Stuart Johnson
A sketch of the life and times of . . . Sydney Smith. 1884 16/10/83, 9/10/84
Reid, Sir Thomas Wemyss
Charlotte Brontë. A monograph . . . with illustrations. 1877 11/6/77
Life of the Right Hon. W. E. Forster. 1888 (2v. 1888) 7/7/88, 1/8/88, 6/8/88
The life, letters, and friendships of Richard Monckton Milnes, first Lord Houghton. 1890 (2v. 1890) 7/11/90
Reid, William political economist
The life and adventures of the Old Lady of Threadneedle Street. 1832 24/1/56
Reid, W. S.
The enhancing value of gold and the industrial crisis. 1883 10/4/83
Reinach, Joseph
La Serbie et le Monténégro. 1876 12/1/77
Reinkens, Joseph Hubert Bishop of the Old Catholics
Louise Hensel und ihre Lieder. 1877 21/1/80
Relation contenant les lettres que les religieusesde Port-Royal ont écrites. 24/9/65
Religious systems of the world: addresses at Smith Place Institute. 1890 5/1/90
'Religious worship, England and Wales', *Parliamentary Papers 1852–3*, lxxxix. 1. 1852 (1852–3) 3/1/54
'Remarks on a late tract by . . . Keble' 1849 18/4/49
'Remarks on fasting, and on the discipline of the body; in a letter to a clergyman, by a physician' 1848 4/8/48
'Remarks on Ireland' 1867 6/1/68
'Remarks on Paley's Evidences. By an old graduate' 1873 18/5/73
'Remarks on the actual state of the University of Cambridge' 1830 8/5/31
Remi, C.
Mon Oisiveté. 1779 14/10/82
Rémusat, Charles François Marie de Count
Abélard. 1845 (2v. 1845) 20/4/57
Channing, sa vie et ses oeuvres, avec une préface de C. de Rémusat. 1857 30/4/61
De la philosophie allemande. 1845 25/8/71
Des controverses au sein du Protestantisme. 1829 16/11/54
Saint Anselme. 1853 23/9/60
Rémusat, Claire Élisabeth Jeanne de Countess
Mémoires de Madame de Rémusat, 1802–1808. 1880 (3v. 1880, 1881) 2/7/80
Remy, Jules, and Brenchley, J.
A journey to the Great-Salt-Lake-City. 1861 (2v. 1861) 16/10/61
Renan, Joseph Ernest
Études d'histoire religieuse. 1858 30/1/58
An essay on the age and antiquity of the Book of Nabathaean Agriculture. 1862 14/9/72, 4/11/75
De la part des peuples Sémitiques dans l'histoire de la civilization. 1862 7/9/72
Histoire des origines du Christianisme. 1863 (8v. 1863–83) 14/4/75, 8/4/83
Histoire générale et système comparé des langues sémitiques. 1855 21/11/71
L'Antechrist. 1873 9/8/74
Le Judaïsme et le Christianisme, identité originelle et séparation graduelle. 1883 26/10/91
Les Apôtres. 1866 3/4/74
Mission de Phénicie dirigée par M. E. Renan. 1864 (3v. 1864–67) 6/9/67, 11/11/67
Nouvelles considérations sur le caractère général des peuples sémitiques. 1859 16/8/79
Souvenirs d'enfance et de jeunesse. 1883 1/5/83
Vie de Jésus. 1863 2/8/63, 25/12/65
Renaud, George
A few words on the divorce bill, in its relation to Scripture and the Church services. 1857 11/8/57
Rendall, Frederic
School leaving examinations . . . university inspection. 1872 4/11/91 ?
Rendall, Magnus C.
Gladstone's foreign and colonial policy; an address delivered . . . 1884. 1884 15/12/92 ?
Rendell, Elias de la Roche
The antediluvian history, and narrative of the Flood. 1850 12/11/65

Rendu, Eugène
De l'instruction primaire à Londres dans ses rapports avec l'état social. 1853 15/5/53
Rennell, James
Observations on the topography of the Plain of Troy. 1814 30/8/55
Remarks on the topography of ancient Babylon. 1816 12/4/73
The geographical system of Herodotus examined and explained. 1800 23/6/30
Renouf, Sir Peter Le Page
Lectures on the origin and growth of religion, as illustrated by the religion of ancient Egypt. 1880 16/11/84, 15/11/86, 31/5/90
The character of the Rev. William Palmer... as a controversialist. 1843 12/11/43
The condemnation of Pope Honorius. 1868 19/7/68
Reorganisation du Système de Banques. 1863 19/12/63
'Repertory of inventors patents' 1843 16/8/43
Reply to 'A few words on the monitorial system at Harrow'. 1854 14/1/54
Reply to Mr. Gladstone, by a monk of St Augustine's, Ramsgate. 1874 11/12/74
Report by the committee of negotiation... Caledonian Railway Company to confer with ... interests. 1851 27/8/53
Report... for inquiring into the state of the university of Oxford. 1853 11/12/53
Report of a Commission appointed for a revision of the revenue system by the Congress of the United States of America. 1866 14/2/66
Report of addresses at a missionary meeting at Toronto. 1866 5/8/66
Report of inspectors of mines... for the year 1872. 1873 26/2/74
Report... of the Chamber of Commerce and manufacturers at Manchester, etc. 1841 11/10/65
Report... of the conference of the clergy of the united diocese of Down and Connor and Dromore. 1862 (3v. 1862–64) 12/3/65
Report of the deputation to English bishops from Scottish schismatics using the English prayer book. 1847 5/4/47
Report of the diocesan synod of Sarawak. 1866 23/4/67
Report of the Melanesian mission for 1858. With a statement of accounts. 1858 22/8/58
Report of the Melanesian mission for 1861. 1861 28/7/61
Report of the Temperance Association. (not found) 29/4/34
Report on commerce and navigation in the United States of America. 1842 29/10/42
[Report on the Mettray colony]. 1839 25/9/46
[Report on the Mettray colony]. 1846 25/9/46
Report on the state of Ireland, P. P., i. 751. 1863 31/3/63 ?
Reports of the Society for Promoting the Education of the Poor in Ireland. 1813 (1813–33) 6/4/35
Report... the present state of records in the United Kingdom, P. P., xvi. 1. 1836 28/2/37
'Representation as introduced into the lower house of the convocation of... Canterbury, etc.' 1852 14/11/52
Reresby, Sir John 2nd Bart.
The Memoirs of... Sir John Reresby. 1734 23/11/81
Restoration of the church of St. Mary Redcliffe, Bristol: an appeal. 1842 24/1/43
Results of the synod of the Protestant church of the United Brethren or Unitas fratrum 1858 11/4/58
Retablissement du pouvoir temporel du pope par... Bismarck. 1885 8/5/87
Retallack, D. C.
The great apostacy demonstrated in an exposé of anti-Christian doctrines. 1865 19/1/68
Reusch, Franz Heinrich
'Galileo and the Roman Inquisition' in *Contemporary Review*, xxxvii. 665. 1880 (October 1880) 7/1/86
Bibel und Natur. 1862 14/12/84, 27/1/85, 1/2/85
Nature and the Bible, tr. Kathleen Lyttelton. 1886 (2v. 1886) 4/4/86
Reuss, Eduard Wilhelm Eugen
Die Geschichte der heiligen Schriften alten Testaments. 1881 9/12/84, 27/1/85
Review of Reviews.
1. 255. 4/1890. Vesuvius 31/3/1890
4. 9. 7/1891. Prince of Wales 26/6/1891
Review of the banking system of Britain. 1821 25/6/33
Review of the conduct of the Prince of Wales. 1797 31/1/93
Réville, Albert
Essais de critique religieuse. 1860 7/4/71
Prolégomènes de l'histoire des religions. 1883 19/7/85
Prolegomena of the History of Religions, tr. by A. S. Squire ... intro ... F. M. Müller. 1884 13/9/85
Revue Contemporaine.
1. J. Ferry 25/2/1885
6. 809. Homer 3/2/1859
13. 614. 1/1860. French Navy 10/1/1860
Revue des Deux Mondes.
1. 103. 1/1856. Rémusat on Fox 14/2/1856
18. 792. Banking 14/12/1854
31. 657. 2/1861. Finance 5/2/1861
32. 4/1861 8/4/1861
34. 721. 8/1879. on Merimée 20/9/1879
55. 535. 2/1883 15/8/1885

56. 725. 4/1865. Palmerston 17/12/1865
62. 150. 3/1866. Forçade 9/8/1866
70. 275. 8/1885. Perrot 23/7/1885
77. 9/1886. on Voltaire & Rousseau 4/9/1886
85. 43. 1/1888. St. Augustine 20/1/1888
85. 70. 1/1888. Diplomacy 23/1/1888
87. 872. 6/1888. Foreign policy 18/7/1888
88. 7/1870. Gladstone 6/7/1870

Revue Independante. 1. 1 14/10/1859

Reybaud, Marie Roch Louis
Jérôme Paturot à la recherche d'une position sociale. 1842 23/10/50 ?
Jérôme Paturot à la recherche de la meilleure des républiques. 1848 (3v. 1848) 23/10/50 ?

Reynald, Hermile
Histoire de l'Angleterre depuis la mort de la Reine Anne jusqu'à nos jours. 1875 23/2/75
Mirabeau et la Constituante. 1872 25/7/74

Reynolds, Edward Bishop of Norwich
The sinfulness of sin. 18/5/34

Reynolds, Frederic Mansel
Miserrimus. 1833 8/12/81

Reynolds, George Archdeacon of Lincoln
A letter to... Dr. Lisle... upon a refusal to receive... a paper concerning ecclesiastical courts. 1742 13/4/43

Reynolds, Henry Robert
John the Baptist. 1874 28/2/75

Reynolds, Joseph William
The natural history of immortality. 1891 18/6/93
The supernatural in nature. A verification by free use of science. 1878 9/1/81

Rhind, Thomas
An apology for... T. Rhind; or... the... reasons for which he separated from the presbyterian party. 1712 21/10/49

Rhodes, M. J.
The visible unity of the Catholic Church. 1870 (2v. 1870) 19/4/78

Rhys, Sir John
Lectures on the origin and growth of religion as illustrated by Celtic heathendom. 1886 11/3/88

Ricardo, David economist
Plan for the establishment of a national bank. 1824 9/3/37

Ricardo, John Lewis
The anatomy of the navigation laws. 1847 29/5/48

Ricci, Abbé Lorenzo General of the Jesuits
La vie de l'Abbé L. Ricci, dernier Général des Jésuites,... traduite de l'Italien. 1776 9/5/45

Ricciardetto
Richardet, Poëme, tr. A. F. Duperrier Dumouriez. 1781 (2v. 1781) 31/10/55

Ricciardi, Count Giuseppe Napoleone
Histoire de la révolution d'Italie en 1848. 1849 23/10/51
The autobiography of an Italian rebel. Translated from the Italian. 1860 8/7/60

Rice, R.
Irish Intermediate Education Act: suggestions for the practical working of it. 1878 20/9/78

Rice-Jones, D.
In the slums. 1884 22/5/84

Rich, Sir Henry
What will the Lords do?. 1831 24/9/31
Yes or No? A political pamphlet. 1852 3/6/59

Richard, Charles Louis
Préservatif nécessaire à toutes les personnes. 1776 15/5/45

Richard, Henry M.P.
History of the origin of the war with Russia. 1876 25/11/76
Letters on the social and political condition of the principality of Wales. 1866 21/10/67 ?
On standing armies. 1868 9/7/68
The present and future of India under British rule. 1858 29/4/58

Richards, A. B.
Oxford unmasked. 1842 27/9/42

Richards, James D.D.
Lectures on mental philosophy and theology. 1846 17/7/55

Richards, Thomas of Coychurch
Antiquae linguae Britannicae Thesaurus; being a British or Welsh-English dictionary. 1753 29/10/60

Richards, Westley gunmaker
Loading at breech and loading at muzzle, for military weapons. 1863 12/7/64

Richards, William LL.D.
The perpetuity of Christian baptism. 1806 9/7/65

Richards, William Upton
Familiar instructions on mental prayer. 1852 5/9/52

Richardson, Alfred S.
The revival of superstition: and how shall we meet it?. 1874 27/7/74

Richardson, Sir Benjamin Ward
On alcohol: a course of six Cantor Lectures delivered before the Society of Arts. 1875 11/2/75

Richardson, James African traveller
The cruisers: being a letter... in defence of armed coercion for the extinction of the slave trade. 1849 5/2/50

Richardson, John F. Professor of Latin, Univ. of Rochester
Roman Orthoëpy; a plea for the restoration of the true system of Latin pronunciation. 1859 28/9/59

Richardson, Joseph barrister
Criticisms on the Rolliad. 1784 3/8/50
Richardson, Ralph M.D.
The simplicity of life; an introductory chapter to pathology. 1873 7/4/74
Richardson, Samuel novelist
Clarissa Harlowe. 1747 (7v. 1747–8) 11/9/51, 14/11/51
Pamela. 1741 4/1/32
The history of Sir Charles Grandison. 1754 (7v. 1754) 9/7/47
Richmond, Legh
The dairyman's daughter. 1819 18/4/30
Richmond, Wilfrid John
Christian economics. 1888 2/9/88
Richson, Charles
A sketch of some of the causes... abandonment of the voluntary system in the support of schools. 1851 15/12/51
Richter, Jean Paul F.
Life of Jean Paul F. Richter, tr. C. B. Lee. 1845 16/9/73
Richter, Max Hermann Ohnefalsch
Kypros, die Bibel und Homer. 1893 (2v. 1893) 3/2/93
Rickards, Sir George Kettilby K. C. B.
Remarks on the laws relating to attempts against the person of the Sovereign. 1842 28/7/42
The House of Commons: its struggles and triumphs. A lecture. 1856 23/3/73
Three lectures delivered before the university of Oxford in Michaelmas term, 1852. 1852 30/3/53, 9/2/55
Riddell, Charles James Buchanan
Remarks on the organization of the British Royal Artillery. 1852 7/12/52
Riddell, James Fellow of Balliol College, Oxford
Reliquiae Metricae. 1867 26/9/67
Ridding, George Bishop of Southwell
The primary charge of George Ridding... Bishop of Southwell... October 11th, 1887. 1887 4/12/87
Ridgeway, Robert Joseph
Innovations in the settled order of divine worship of the Church of England. 1868 16/2/68
Ridley, Nicholas Bishop of Rochester and then of London
De Coena Dominica assertio contra sceleratam illam Transubstatiationis haeresim. 1556 25/10/63
Praefatio et protestatio N. Ridleii. 1555 20/12/40 ?
The works of Nicholas Ridley... edited, for the Parker Society, by... Henry Christmas. 1841 16/1/42
Ridolfi, Cosimo Marquis
Breve nota a una storia. 1859 3/6/59
Toscana ed Austria. 1859 14/4/59
Ridout, Thomas
Ten years of Upper Canada in peace and war, 1805–1815; being the Ridout letters. 1891 22/6/91, 16/7/91
Rienzi, Niccolò Gabrino di
La vita di Cola di Rienzo Tribuno del Popolo Romano. 1828 18/12/38
Rifts in the veil; a collection of inspirational poems and essays, ed. W. H. Harrison. 1878 12/1/79
Rigaud, Stephen Jordan Bishop of Antigua
The inspiration of holy scripture, with reference to the Epistles of St. Paul. 1856 27/10/89
Rigby, Lady Elizabeth afterw. Eastlake
Letters from the shores of the Baltic. 1844 17/10/44
Livonian tales. 1846 15/6/46
Rigg, James Harrison
Discourses and addresses on leading truths of religion and philosophy. 1880 30/5/80
Essays for the times on ecclesiastical and social subjects. 1866 31/5/68, 5/7/68
The character and life-work of Dr. Pusey. A sketch and study. 1883 7/12/84
The churchmanship of John Wesley, and the relations of Wesleyan Methodism to the Church of England. 1879 18/5/79
The natural development of national education in England. An inaugural address. 1875 17/7/75
The relations of... Wesleyan Methodism to the Church of England, investigated and determined. 1868 15/11/68
Riis, Jacob August
How the other half lives: studies among the poor. 1890 29/12/90
Riland, John Hon. Chaplain to the Magdalen Asylum
Ecclesiae Decus et Tutamen. 1830 18/9/39
Rimius, Heinrich
A candid narrative of... the Herrnhuters, commonly called Moravians or Unitas Fratrum. 1753 2/8/74
Rinck, Wilhelm Friedrich
Die Religion der Hellenen. 1855 (2v. 1855) 13/8/91
Rinuccini, Giovanni Battista Archbishop of Fermo
The embassy in Ireland of... G. B. Rinuccini, tr. A. Hutton. 1873 1/12/88
Rio, Alexis François
Épilogue à l'Art chrétien. 1870 (2v. 1870) 3/7/70
De l'Art chrétien. 1836 (2v. 1836–41) 18/6/38
De l'Art chrétien... nouvelle édition. 1861 (4v. 1861–67) 28/5/61
De la Poésie chrétienne. 1836 12/8/38
La petite Chouannerie ou histoire d'un collège breton sous l'Empire. 1842 6/6/42

The four martyrs ... Translated from the French. 1856 28/3/58
Ripa, Father Matteo
Memoirs ... during thirteen years of residence at the court of Peking ... translated ... by F. Prandi. 1844 7/12/44
'Riposta di un Italiano a due lettere del signor Gladstone a Lord Aberdeen' 1851 6/3/52
Riquetti, Honoré Gabriel Count de Mirabeau
Choix des lettres de Mirabeau à Sophie. 1818 5/8/58
Mirabeau's letters during his residence in England 1784–85. 1832 23/8/75
Ritchie, James Ewing
The London pulpit. 1854 14/5/58
Ritchie, John D.D.
Speech ... the injustice and immoral tendency of the corn and provision laws. 1842 26/4/45
Ritchie, Robert civil engineer
Observations on the sanatory arrangements of factories. 1844 30/7/44
Ritschl, Albrecht
Die christliche Lehre von der Rechtfertigung und Versöhnung. 1870 (3v. 1870–74) 4/2/83
'Ritualism in its treatment of the Divine Word: bya member ... General Council ... Univ. of Edinburgh' 1873 24/10/75
Rive, T. de la
Le péril social et le devoir actuel. 1889 6/12/89
Rive, William de la
Reminiscences of the life and character of Count Cavour ... translated ... by E. Romilly. 1862 6/11/62
Rivett, Alfred William Lovely
Ten years' church work in Natal ... with an introduction by ... E. M. Goulburn. 1890 12/4/91
Rivington, William
Church extension in the diocese of London. 1853 4/12/59
Rizos Rankabes, Alexandros I.
Précis d'une histoire de la littérature néo-hellénique. 1877 (2v. 1877) 14/2/78
R. N. B
Corn and Wages. 1841 17/6/41 ?
Robbins, Sir Alfred Farthing pseud. Nemesis
Five years of Tory rule. 1879 11/7/79
Roberti, G.
Petit traité sur les petites vertus, traduit de l'italien. 1840 16/11/45
Roberts, Alexander D.D.
Discussions on the Gospels. 1862 (2v. 1862) 1/2/64
Inquiry into the original language of St. Matthew's Gospel. 1859 29/1/60
The Bible of Christ and his Apostles. 1879 26/9/80
Roberts, George Bayfield
The Doctrine of the Apostolical Succession as set forth in the Prayer Book, the ancient fathers and the New Testament. 1877 12/5/78
Roberts, John Askew
Wynnstay and the Wynns. 1876 23/1/82
Roberts, Miss Margaret novelist
Mademoiselle Mori: a tale of modern Rome. 1860 (2v. 1860) 13/8/65 n, 12/10/66
Roberts, Margaret Anne
In Memoriam. Charles Edward Stuart, Count d'Albanie. 1881 15/3/91 ?
Roberts, Miss R.
The Peruvian letters, translated from the French. 1774 (2v. 1774) 27/10/86 ?
Roberts, Samuel of Sheffield
The wickedness of the new Poor Law, addressed to serious Christians of all denominations. 1839 4/4/43
Roberts, William M.A., Barrister-at-law, of Lincoln's Inn
Church memorials and characteristics. 1874 22/10/77
Memoirs of the life and correspondence of Mrs. Hannah More. 1834 (4v. 1834) 17/7/64
The portraiture of a Christian gentleman. By a barrister. 1829 18/6/31
Roberts, William, and Nicholson, W. M.A., Barrister-at-law, of Lincoln's Inn
The call upon the Church considered in two essays. 1838 5/2/39, 18/2/40
Roberts, William Page Dean of Salisbury
Law and God. 1874 5/12/74
Robertson, Alexander Barrister-at-law
Lectures ... John Graham of Claverhouse, ... and his times. 1889 17/10/89
Robertson, Rev. Alexander of San Remo
Count Campello and Catholic reform in Italy. 1891 10/5/91
Robertson, C. F. Bishop of Missouri
The Louisiana Purchase in its influence upon the American system. 1885 11/9/90
Robertson, C. Gordon
Report of the proceedings ... in the Lethendy case. 1839 6/12/39
Robertson, Charles Advocate
Report of the Auchterarder case, the earl of Kinnoull, ... against the presbytery of Auchterarder. 1838 (2v. 1838) 3/7/43
Robertson, Divie
Let all things be done decently and in order. A sermon. 1857 17/5/57
Robertson, Frederick William
An address delivered at the opening of the working men's institute. 1849 11/1/52
Lectures on the influence of poetry on the working classes. 1852 11/1/52 ?
Life and letters of F. W. Robertson, ... edited by Stopford A. Brooke. 1865 (2v. 1865) 15/1/66

Robertson, Frederick William (*cont.*)
Scotland under her early kings. 1862 (2v. 1862) 2/7/79 ?
The Israelite's grave in a foreign land. A sermon. 1850 11/1/52
Robertson, James Professor, Oriental Languages, Glasgow
The early religion of Israel. 1892 1/1/93, 16/4/93
Robertson, James Craigie
Becket, Archbishop of Canterbury. A biography. 1859 12/1/60
How shall we 'conform to the liturgy of the Church of England?'. 1843 22/10/43
The bearings of the Gorham case: a letter to a friend. 1850 21/6/50
Robertson, J. M.
Puritanism in power. 1890 25/1/91
Robertson, John D.D.
Pastoral counsels: being papers on practical and devotional subjects. 1867 24/5/68
Robertson, William D.D. the historian
The history of America. 1777 (2v. 1777) 30/12/35, 2/4/55
The history of Scotland during the reigns of Queen Mary and of King James VI. 1759 16/12/35
The history of the reign of the Emperor Charles V. 1769 (3v. 1769) 3/12/33
Robertson, William Minister of Sprouston
Essays and sermons. 1891 27/10/91
Robertson, William of Rochdale
The life and times of Right Hon. John Bright. 1877 24/1/78
Robins, Rev. Arthur
The present position of the 'Liberal' Party. 1862 19/7/62
Robins, Sanderson
A defence of the faith. 1862 1/12/61
A letter to the Rev. G. A. Denison. 1851 31/8/51, 22/2/52
A sermon preached in the Church of the Holy Trinity, Shaftesbury. 1842 15/5/42
A speech delivered... at the meeting of the National Society, June 4, 1851. 1851 30/6/51
An argument for the royal supremacy. 1851 1/3/51
On party spirit in the English Church. 1860 13/1/61
Shibboleth. A sermon. 1858 30/5/58
Some reasons against the revival of convocation. 1850 1/9/50
The building of beautiful churches, a privilege and a duty. A sermon. 1843 13/4/45
Twenty reasons for accepting the Revised Educational Code. 1862 14/2/62
Robinson, Christopher
Church questions. Practical methods for the arrangement of an abridged morning service. 1859 4/12/59
Robinson, E.
The revolt of Flanders. 1848 10/8/86
Robinson, E. G.
Baccalaureate sermons. 1890 7/4/90
Robinson, Frank of Southport
A descriptive history of Southport, ... on the western coast of Lancashire. 1848 2/1/62 ?
Robinson, Frederick M.D.
The new Religio Medici. Chapters on present-day subjects. 1887 13/4/89
Robinson, Frederick John Earl of Ripon
The influence of taxation on the price of corn considered. 1815 20/1/41
Robinson, George Richard
Facts versus theory..., a retrospect of our past policy, with hints for future improvement. 1843 27/1/43
Robinson, Hastings
The Zurich letters. Translated and edited by H. Robinson. 1842 (2v. 1842–45) 8/2/46
Robinson, Heaton Bowstead
Memoirs of... Sir Thomas Picton, including his correspondence. 1835 (2v. 1835) 11/11/35
Robinson, Henry George
The Gospel of Christ... with special reference to the teachings of the 'Essays and Reviews'. 1861 7/12/62
Robinson, John chief clerk issue dept., pseud. Rusticus
The world on the Thames. 1855 26/11/55 ?, 27/11/55 ?
Robinson, John D.D., Rector of Clifton, Westmoreland
Archaeologia Graeca. 1807 1/10/31
Robinson, John Treasury Secretary
Letter to Sir J. Sinclair, bart. 1794 26/3/47
Robinson, Sir John Beverley
Canada and the Canada Bill... the proposed measure for the future government of Canada. 1840 23/4/40
Robinson, Sir John Charles
A critical account of the drawings by Michel Angelo and Raffaello in the University Galleries Oxford. 1870 22/6/70
Catalogue of the various works of art forming the collection of Mathew Uzielli. 1860 2/6/60
Inventory of the objects forming the collections of the Museum of Ornamental Art. 1856 25/5/59
Memoranda on fifty pictures, selected from a collection of works of the ancient masters. 1868 29/1/68
The National Gallery. 1867 7/6/67
Robinson, Mary
Vancenza, or the dangers of credulity. 1792 10/10/87
Robinson, Matthew Vicar of Burneston, Yorkshire
Autobiography of Matthew Robinson. 1855 5/8/55

Robinson, W. C.
Pilgrim's Jerusalem. 1890 20/12/90
Robinson, William Baptist Minister
Expositions of the Book of Revelation. 1875 25/12/75
The first chapter of the Bible, and the last chapter of astronomical science viewed in conjunction. 1856 15/11/85
Robson, J. Lothian
Till death us sever... A novel. 1888 9/5/89
Robson, Joseph
An account of six years residence in Hudson's Bay from 1733 to 1736 and 1744 to 1747. 1752 (2v. 1852) 12/8/48
Roche, Antonin
Les poètes français. Recueil de morceaux choisis. 1844 4/8/58
Rochechouart, Louis Victor Léon de Comte
Souvenirs sur la Révolution, l'Empire et la Restauration. 1889 25/3/92
Rochejaquelein, Henri Auguste Georges du Vergier de la Marquis
Sénat. Séance du 18 Mars, 1863. Discours sur les affaires de Pologne. 1863 11/4/63
Rochford, Mrs. Anne
The velvet coffee-woman, or, the life, ... and amours of the late famous Mrs. Anne Rochford. 1728 24/5/84 ?
Rock, Daniel
The Church of our fathers. 1849 (3v. 1849–53) 10/8/62
Rodd, James Rennell Baron Rennell
The customs and lore of modern Greece. 1892 7/12/91 ?
Rodriguez, Alonso Jesuit, of Valladolid
The practice of Christian perfection. 1861 (3v. 1861) 7/8/87
Rodwell, John Medows
The Koran: translated from the Arabic... by J. M. R. 1876 13/1/77
Rodwell, William
On the Bank-Notes Issues Bill, its alterations, amendments, and withdrawal. 1865 29/7/65
Roe, Azel Stevens
I've been thinking; or, the secret of success... Edited by C. B. Tayler. 1853 29/8/88
Roebuck, Right Hon. John Arthur
History of the Whig Ministry of 1830 to the passing of the Reform Bill. 1852 (2v. 1852) 9/2/52
The colonies of England. 1849 23/5/49
Roese, Ferdinand
Über die scenische Darstellung des Goethe'schen Faust. 1838 30/4/89
Rogers, Benjamin Bickley
A free enquiry into the difficulties suggested by Dr. Colenso... veracity of the Pentateuch. 1863 21/6/63
Rogers, Charles D.D.
Genealogical memoirs of the families of Colt and Coutts. 1879 4/3/82
Rogers, Frederic Lord Blachford
A short appeal to members of convocation upon the proposed censure of No. 90. 1845 9/2/45
Some account of legal development of the colonial episcopate. 1883 7/3/83
Rogers, Henry
The eclipse of faith; or, a visit to a religious sceptic. 1852 29/5/53
Rogers, James Edwin Thorold
A sermon. 1865 14/5/65
Cobden and modern political opinion. 1873 5/2/74
Historical gleanings. A series of sketches. 1870 26/8/78, 4/5/81
The economic interpretation of history. Lectures. 1888 1/10/88
The first nine years of the Bank of England. 1887 6/4/87
Rogers, James Guinness
'The union of the liberal party' in *Nineteenth Century*, vi. 361. 1879 (August 1879) 7/7/79 ?, 1/8/79 ?
Nineteenth Century, xvi. 396. 1884 (September 1884) 28/8/84
Present-day religion and theology. 1888 9/9/88 ?
The age and our work in it. An address. 1874 15/3/75 ?
The Ulster Problem. 1886 19/6/86 ?
Rogers, Samuel poet
Italy. 1822 29/12/31
Poems. 1845 (2v. 1845) 16/7/45
Recollections of the table talk of Samuel Rogers, etc., ed. A. Dyce. 1856 1/3/56
The pleasures of memory. 1792 5/3/34
Rogers, Thomas A. M., Chaplain to Archbishop Bancroft
The catholic doctrine of the Church of England, an exposition of the thirty nine articles. 1854 29/10/54
Rogers, Walter Thomas
A manual of bibliography. 1890 8/6/93 ?
Rogers, William Rector of St. Botolph's, Bishopsgate
In perils in the sea. A sermon. 1877 1/7/77
Reminiscences of William Rogers... Compiled by R. H. Hadden. 1888 13/3/88, 25/1/92
The educational prospects of St. Thomas Charterhouse. A letter to the Right Hon. Lord J. Russell. 1854 27/11/54
Roh, Peter
Was ist Christus?. 1887 7/10/90
Rolle, Pierre Nicolas
Recherches sur le culte de Baccus. 1824 (3v.) 5/9/92 ?

Rolph, Dr. John, and Hagerman, Christopher A.
Speeches . . . on the bill for appropriating the proceeds of the clergy reserves to . . . general education. 1837 21/7/40
Roman Catholicism. 1851 12/6/92 ?
Roman Catholic Prayer Book. (n.d.) 24/9/26
Roman de Violette, Le. Oeuvre posthume d'une célébrité masquée. 1870 24/1/88 ?
Romanes, George John
Darwin and after Darwin. 1892 28/5/92, 12/6/92
Poems: 1879–1889. 1889 4/10/91
Romanoff, H. C.
Sketches of the rites and customs of the Greco-Russian Church. 1868 20/9/68
Rome et ses provinces. 1860 14/2/60
Romilly, Henry
Public responsibility and vote by ballot. 1867 12/3/69
Romilly, Lord
Judgement for Colenso in Colenso v. Gladstone. 1866 18/11/66
Romilly, Sir Samuel
Memoirs of the life of Sir Samuel Romilly. 1840 (3v. 1840) 26/9/87
The speeches of Sir Samuel Romilly in the House of Commons. 1820 (2v. 1820) 24/6/78
Ronge, Johannes
Katholische Dichtungen. 1845 9/10/45
Roose, Edward Charles Robson
Leprosy and its prevention, as illustrated by Norwegian experience. 1889 30/11/89
Roots, a plea for tolerance. 1873 29/6/73
Rorison, Gilbert
Notes on 'Scottish Episcopacy, past and present: by Alexander Thomson, esq. of Banchory'. 1860 19/8/60
Report of the speech . . . in opening the case for the presentment of P. Cheyne before the bishop. 1858 25/7/58
The depression of the clergy the danger of the Church. A sermon. 1856 7/12/56, 8/8/57
The three barriers: notes on Mr. Darwin's 'Origin of Species'. 1861 19/1/62
'Rosas, and some of the atrocities of his dictatorship . . . By a British gentleman' 1844 19/12/44
Roscher, Wilhelm Heinrich
Hermes der Windgott. 1886 23/2/87 ?
Studien zur griechischen Mythologie und Kulturgeschichte. 1878 (4v. 1878–95) 10/1/87, 6/4/91
Roscoe, William
Letter to Henry Brougham . . . the subject of reform in the representation of the people in Parliament. 1811 29/8/33
On the origin and vicissitudes of literature, science and art . . . a discourse. 1817 14/2/43
The life and pontificate of Leo the Tenth. 1805 (4v. 1805) 10/10/34
The life of Lorenzo de' Medici, called the Magnificent. 1795 (2v. 1795) 10/9/34
Rose, George
The diaries and correspondence of the Right Hon. George Rose . . . Edited by . . . L. V. Harcourt. 1860 (2v. 1860) 14/1/60, 13/11/65, 7/12/82
Rose, H.
Three sheiks: an Oriental narration in verse. 1884 24/4/84
Rose, Henry Rector of Brington
Three lectures on architecture in England from the earliest to the present time. 1843 18/12/44
Rose, Henry John Archdeacon of Bedford
The English liturgy a protest against Romish corruptions. Two sermons. 1850 28/2/58 ?
Rose, Hugh James B. D.
An apology for the study of divinity: being, the Terminal Divinity Lecture. 1834 6/4/34
An appendix to 'The state of the Protestant Religion in Germany; etc.'. 1828 22/12/39
Brief remarks on the dispositions towards Christianity generated by prevailing opinions. 1830 28/4/33, 17/5/34
Christianity always progressive, being the Christian Advocate's publication for the year 1829. 1829 15/12/72
The gospel an abiding system. With some remarks on the 'New Christianity' of the St. Simonians. 1832 22/5/34
The state of the protestant religion in Germany; in a series of discourses. 1825 3/10/30
The tendency of prevalent opinions about knowledge considered. A sermon. 1826 16/4/34
Rose, William Stewart
Letters from the north of Italy. 1819 2/8/45, 21/7/79
Rosini, Giovanni
Luisa Strozzi, storia del secolo xvi. 1832 (4v. 1832–33) 17/4/38
Rosmini Serbati, Antonio
A short sketch of modern philosophies, and of his own system. 1882 20/6/88
Delle Cinque Piaghe della Santa Chiesa. 1849 5/1/51
Life of A. Rosmini Serbati . . . Edited by W. Lockhart. 1886 (2v. 1886) 11/1/87 ?
Rosny, J. H.
Nell Horn de l'Armée de Salut. Roman de moeurs londoniennes. 1886 11/4/92
Ross, Alexander of the 'Pacific Fur Company'
Adventures of the first settlers on the Oregon or Columbia river. 1849 18/6/49

Ross, Alexander Milton
Recollections and experiences of an abolitionist; from 1855 to 1865. 1875 11/1/76
Ross, Donald Minister of Loth
Pictures of pauperism. The condition of the poor described by themselves. 1847 9/7/47 ?
Ross, H. J.
Thoughts on the objectionable system of labour for wages in the West India colonies. 1742 14/2/42
Ross, Janet Ann
Italian sketches. 1887 3/1/88 n
Ross, John Lockhart
Letters on diocesan theological colleges, in connexion with proposed cathedral alterations. 1848 26/2/48
Reciprocal obligations of the church and the civil power. 1848 26/2/48
Traces of primitive truth in the principal nations of the world. 1858 29/1/82
Ross, Ronald novelist
The child of ocean. A romance. 1889 28/12/89
Ross, Thomas Farmer, in the Carse of Gowrie
Lord Kinnaird's letter to his tenantry 'on profitable investment of capital'. 1849 15/12/49
Ross, Walter Bullar
Occasional verses. 1875 9/10/75
Ross, William Tait
Poems. 1881 30/8/82
Ross, William Tait pseud. Herbert Martyne
Poems. 1876 31/12/75
Ross, W. S.
The bottomless pit. 1894 17/12/94
Rossetti, Christina Georgina
Goblin Market and other poems... With two designs by D. G. Rossetti. 1862 28/8/66
The Prince's Progress, and other poems. With two designs by D. G. Rossetti. 1866 22/7/66
Verses. 1893 22/4/94
Rossetti, Dante Gabriel
Notes on the Vita Nuova and minor poems of Dante. 1866 12/5/83
Rossetti, Gabriele Pasquale Giuseppe
Sullo spirito antipapale che produsse la riforma. 1832 15/11/36
Rossetti, Maria Francesca
A shadow of Dante. Being an essay towards studying himself, his world, and his pilgrimage. 1871 4/2/72
Rossi, Giovanni Battista de Cavaliere
Angelica Kauffmann. 1866 21/9/92
Inscriptiones Christianae urbis Romae septimo saeculo antiquiores. Edidit I. B. de Rossi. 1861 2/12/66 ?
La Roma sotterranea cristiana descritta ed illustrata. 1864 (4v. 1864–97) 2/12/66 ?
Rossignol, Jean Pierre
Les métaux dans l'antiquité. 1863 17/11/70

Roth, Henry Ling anthropologist
Agriculture and peasantry of Eastern Russia. 1878 24/7/78
Roth, Mathias M.D.
The fever-dens in the West-Central and North-Western districts of London. 1879 1/2/79
Rothe, Richard
Die Anfänge der Christlichen Kirche. 1837 11/10/39
Dogmatik. 1870 (2v. 1870) 15/8/88
Rothschild, Clementina de
Letters to a Christian friend on the fundamental truths of Judaism... Translated from the German. 1869 10/12/91
Rothschild, Constance de afterw. Baroness Battersea
The history and literature of the Israelites, according to the Old Testament and the Apocrypha. 1870 (2v. 1870) 29/3/72 ?
Rougé, Vicomte Olivier Charles Camille Emmanuel de
Extraits d'un mémoire sur... attaques dirigées contre l'Egypte par les peuples de la Méditerranée. 1867 31/1/68
Mémoire sur l'origine égyptienne de l'Alphabet Phénicien. 1874 1/4/74 ?
Roumanian question in Transylvania and in Hungary. 1891 15/4/91
Roundell, Charles Savile
The progress of the working classes during the reign of the Queen: 'a goodly record'. 1890 22/8/90
Roundell, Mrs. Julia Anne Elizabeth
A visit to the Azores. With a chapter on Madeira. 1889 19/8/89
Cowdray: the history of a great English house. 1884 26/2/84
Rous, William John Lieutenant-Colonel
Glauké. 1883 19/7/83
Rousseau, Jean Jacques
Émile, ou de l'éducation. 1762 (4v. 1762) 8/8/58, 23/9/61
A letter from M. Rousseau... to M. D'Alembert ... theatrical entertainments on the manners of mankind. 1759 26/10/58
Du Contrat Social; ou, principes du droit politique. 1762 13/8/31
Les Confessions. 1781 (1781–1788) 23/6/35, 5/8/58
Oeuvres poétiques. 1823 (2v. 1823) 19/9/81
Roussel, Napoléon
Différence entre Catholicisme et Protestantisme. 1845 3/7/75
Routh, Charles Henry Felix
On overwork and premature mental decay: its treatment... Read before the Medical Society of London. 1873 21/6/74

Routledge, James
English rule and native opinion in India. From notes taken 1870–74. 1878 2/8/78
Routledge, Thomas
Bamboo considered as a paper-making material. With remarks on its cultivation and treatment. 1875 13/7/75
Row, Charles Adolphus
Christian evidences viewed in relation to modern thought. Eight lectures. 1877 6/10/78
Letter to Sir R. H. Inglis Bart., in reply to his speech on university reform. 1850 24/5/50
Letter to . . . Russell . . . on the constitutional defects of the university and colleges of Oxford. 1850 7/3/50
The historical evidence of the resurrection of Jesus Christ. A lecture. 1873 6/12/85
The moral teaching of the New Testament viewed as evidential to its historical truth. 1872 6/10/72
The nature and extent of divine inspiration, as stated by the writers . . . of the New Testament. 1864 26/1/73, 16/2/73
Row, John and Row, William
The history of the Kirk of Scotland. 1842 28/3/43
Rowcroft, Charles
Tales of the colonies; or, the adventures of an emigrant. Edited by a late colonial magistrate. 1843 14/2/46, 30/12/85
Rowe, Nicholas
Jane Shore. 1714 25/8/59
Rowe, W. H. barrister
The ballot: its utility and efficacy proved. 1833 26/2/33
Rowell, George Augustus
An essay on the beneficent distribution of the sense of pain. 1857 21/11/86
On the storm in the Isle of Wight, Sept. 28, 1876, and on the cause of storms. 1876 17/5/77
Rowland, David solicitor
Laws of nature, the foundation of morals. 1863 16/1/64
Rowsell, Thomas James
The English universities and the English poor . . . sermons preached before the University of Cambridge. 1859 22/1/60
Rowton, Walter
God's trial by fire; or, wood, hay, and stubble. A review, . . . of condemned work. 1870 20/9/75
Science's quarrel with the Bible. Two lectures. 1876 23/1/76
Royal Agricultural Society, Journal of the. 4. 23. Pusey on Drainage 3/7/1843
Royer, Alfred
The English prisoners in Russia: a personal narrative of the First Lieutenant of H. M. S. Tiger. 1854 2/11/54
Rucellai, Giovanni Francesco
Il giubileo dell'anno 1450. 1887 10/1/88
Un'Ambasciata. Diario dell'Abate G. F. Rucellai. 1884 11/3/85, 2/2/88
Rudall, Edward
The complaints of the manufacturers against the corn laws, considered . . . in a lecture. 1840 18/10/41
Rudd, Mrs. Margaret Caroline
Authentic anecdotes of the life and transactions of Mrs. Margaret Rudd. 1776 (2v. 1776) 25/12/86
Rudelbach, Andreas Gottlob
Hieronymus Savonarola und seine Zeit. 1835 28/11/47
Ruffini, Giovanni Domenico
Doctor Antonio; a tale. 1855 10/10/55
Rugnathdar, Madhurdas
Story of a widow remarriage. 1890 (1890?) 25/9/90
Rugnathdas, Madhurdas
Story of a widow's remarriage. 25/9/90
'Rules for holy living; with questions for self-examination' 1842 4/4/47
Rumer, Alexander
Political causes of commercial depression and distress. 1879 7/2/79
Ruminations on railways. 1845 (11 parts) 14/2/45
Rundle, Thomas Bishop of Derry
Memoirs. 1789 21/10/83 ?
Rupp, Julius
Reason and religion . . . Tr. from the German, with a . . . sketch of the author, by Mme A. C. Rasche. 1881 16/1/81
Rusden, George William
The great refusal. By Vindex. 1890 29/1/91
Rush, Richard
Memoranda of a residence at the Court of London. 1833 2/9/33
Occasional productions, political, diplomatic and miscellaneous. 1860 29/10/63
Ruskin, John
'Salsette and Elephanta'; a prize poem recited in the theatre, Oxford. 1839 28/4/40 n
A disciple of Plato. A critical study of John Ruskin, by W. Smart. 1883 26/10/80 ?
Fors Clavigera. Letters to the workmen and labourers of Great Britain. 1871 (9v. 1871–87) 15/3/78
Modern painters, volume III. 1856 20/3/56
Notes on some of the principal pictures exhibited in the rooms of the Royal Academy. 1858 20/5/58
On the present state of modern art; lecture at the British Institution. 1867 7/6/67
Praeterita. Outlines of scenes and thoughts perhaps worthy of memory in my past life. 1885 (3v. 1885–1900) 21/6/85, 1/10/86

Pre-Raphaelitism. 1851 9/6/54
The opening of the Crystal Palace considered in some of its relations to the prospects of art. 1854 24/8/54
The political economy of art: being the substance . . . of two lectures delivered at Manchester, 1857. 1857 27/1/58
The seven lamps of architecture. 1849 15/2/50
The stones of Venice. 1851 (3v. 1851–53) 29/7/51
The study of beauty in and art in large towns. Two papers, by T. C. Horsfall, intro. J. Ruskin. 1883 20/1/91
Russel, Annie
The alien Transvaal. A moral review. 1885 9/8/87
Russel, William Augustus
A new and authentic history of England. 1777 5/6/26
Russell, Charles Baron Russell of Killowen
Letter to the electors of Dundalk on the condition of Ireland. 1882 8/4/82
New views of Ireland. Or, Irish land: grievances: remedies. 1880 20/12/80
Russell, Charles William
The life of Cardinal Mezzofanti, with an introductory memoir of eminent linguists. 1858 13/5/58
Russell, David D.D.
A catechism on the first principles of the holy scriptures. 1831 25/3/45 ?
Russell, Edward Richard Baron Russell of Liverpool
On the autobiography of John Stuart Mill. 1874 25/5/74
The autobiography and memorials of Miss Harriet Martineau. A paper. 1877 16/6/77
The true Macbeth. A paper read before the Literary and Philosophical Society of Liverpool. 1875 4/1/76
Russell, George of His Majesty's Office of Works
A tour through Sicily in the year 1815. 1819 2/8/39
Russell, James Secretary to the M. L. A. S.
Sugar duties. Digest and summary of evidence taken by the Select Committee, etc. 1862 1/12/63
Russell, John 4th Duke of Bedford
Correspondence of John, fourth Duke of Bedford . . . with an introduction by Lord John Russell. 1842 (3v. 1842–46) 15/2/65
Russell, John Advocate
A tour in Germany, and some of the southern provinces of the Austrian Empire. 1824 (2v. 1824) 24/6/61
Russell, Lord John Earl Russell
A letter to Lord John Russell . . . on the misgovernment of Ireland . . . by a friend to British connexion. 1847 20/3/47
A third letter to the Right Hon. Chichester Fortescue on the state of Ireland. 1869 26/1/69
An essay on the history of the English government and constitution. 1821 29/4/35
Corrected report of the speech of Earl Russell on the Irish Church, on the 24th of June 1867. 1867 24/3/68
Don Carlos; or, persecution. A tragedy, in five acts. 1822 4/9/90
Essays on the rise and progress of the Christian religion in the west of Europe. 1873 2/4/73
Letter to the electors of Stroud, on the principles of the Reform Act. 1839 16/3/82
Life of Lord John Russell, by Spencer Walpole. 1889 (2v.) 24/5/89 n, 22/10/89, 6/11/89
Memorials . . . of C. J. Fox, ed. Lord John Russell. 1853 (4v. 1853–57) 19/1/55
Recollections and suggestions. 1813–1873. 1875 17/2/75
Selections from speeches of Earl Russell 1817 to 1841, and from despatches 1859 to 1865. 1870 (2v. 1870) 21/1/70
Strike, but hear. A new view of the Eastern Question . . . a second letter to . . . Lord John Russell, by the author of 'Russian Turkey'. 1856 24/1/56
The foreign policy of England, 1570:1870. A historical essay. 1871 4/8/76
Russell, John Viscount Amberley
An analysis of religious belief. 1876 (2v. 1876) 17/7/76
Russell, John Abraham Archdeacon of Clogher
Remains of Charles Wolfe. 1825 (2v. 1825) 16/2/34
Russell, John Scott
The fleet of the future: iron or wood? . . . a reply to some conclusions of General Sir H. Douglas. 1861 16/2/61
Russell, Michael Bishop of the Scotch Episcopal Church
An affectionate address to the managers and congregation of St. Jude's, Glasgow. 1844 1/2/45
History of the Church in Scotland. 1834 (2v. 1834) 6/11/56
The historical evidence for the apostolical institution of episcopacy. 1830 9/2/40
The liturgy a bond of brotherhood. A sermon. 1843 22/10/43
The position of the Scottish Episcopal Church with regard to . . . the United Church of England. 1845 22/11/45
Russell, Robert of Pilmuir, Leven
Ulster tenant-right for Ireland; or notes upon notes taken during a visit to Ireland in 1868. 1870 20/12/80 ?

Russell, William LL.D., Historical writer
The history of America. 1778 (2v. 1778) 3/1/38
The history of modern Europe. 1779 (5v. 1779–84) 27/11/34

Russell-Killough, Henry Count
L'Angleterre et la France. 1871 29/2/72

Russia, Europe and the East. By a foreigner. 1885 8/9/85

Russia and the Jews. A brief sketch of Russian history and the condition of its Jewish subjects. By a Reader. 1890 20/9/91

Rustoff, Michael
What will Mrs. Grundy say?; or, a calamity on two legs. 1891 4/4/91

Ruxton, George Augustus Frederick
Adventures in Mexico and the Rocky Mountains. 1847 22/12/47
The Oregon question. A glance at the respective claims of Great Britain and the United States. 1846 26/3/46

Ryan, John M. R. S. L.
Personal narrative. Sir Robert Peel's claims to the confidence of protestant conservatives. 1841 14/1/42

Ryan, William P.
The heart of Tipperary. A romance of the land league. With an introduction by W. O'Brien. 1893 26/6/93

Ryder, Arthur Gore D.D.
The baptismal regeneration of infants. A scriptural study. 1873 16/11/73

Ryder, George Dudley
Subscription to the articles. 1845 19/4/45

Ryder, Henry Bishop of Gloucester, then Lichfield
A charge addressed to the clergy of the diocese of Lichfield and Coventry, ... August, 1832. 1832 14/7/33

Ryle, John Charles Bishop of Liverpool
A charge delivered to the clergy of the diocese. 1884 26/10/84
Is all scripture inspired? An attempt to answer the question. 1890 13/5/90 ?
The charges delivered at his primary visitation. 1881 13/11/81
What is ritualism? and, why ought it to be opposed?. 1866 31/5/85

Ryley, E. actuary
Decimal coinage. A brief comparison of the existing system ... the decimal coinage ... another system. 1853 6/1/54

Rymer, Richard
Memoirs of the life, ministry and character of ... W. Jones, late Wesleyan minister. 1842 1/1/60

Ryn, J. G. van
Disestablishment a duty: an appeal to the conscience. 1875 14/3/75

S., T.
A yoke for the Roman-Bulls. 1866 30/1/84

Saalschuetz, Joseph Levin
Das Mosaische Recht. 1846 (2v. 1846–8) 27/1/89

Saavedra, Angel de
Insurrection de Naples en 1647 ... tr ... baron L. d'Hervey de Saint-Denys. 1849 (2v.) 22/6/52 ?

Saburov, P. A.
La Banque d'Etat et le papier-monnaie. 1867 10/9/68

Sacheverell, Henry
Proceedings against Henry Sacheverell. 1710 31/1/48

Sack, Carl Heinrich
Die Kirche von Schottland. 1844 (2v. 1844–5) 9/12/59

Sack, Israel
Die Religion Altisraels. 1885 30/1/90, 1/5/90

Sacram memoriam Regis Friderici Guilemi III. 1845 23/6/45

Sacred poetry ... for the use of the Irish National Schools. 1835 10/5/46

Sacro Annale. (not found) 28/11/66

Sadleir, Franc
National Schools of Ireland defended ... a letter. 1837 6/4/37

Sadleir, Michael Ferrebee
Address ... manifestation of the Incarnation. 1867 26/12/69
An argument for the Athanasian Creed. 1872 3/11/72
Church doctrine, Bible truth. 1865 15/3/68
Scripture truths. 1874 26/9/75

Saffi, Aurelio
Sul Canto XXVI dell'Inferno. 1882 18/3/84

Saint Alban, Guild of. (not found) 24/7/59

Saint Alban's, Holborn. By a layman. 1871 12/2/71

Saint-Arnaud, Maréchal de
Lettres. 1855 3/3/56

Sainte-Beuve, Charles Augustin
Port-Royal. 1840 (5v. 1840–61) 8/2/91, 10/5/91, 28/6/91

Saint-Hilaire, Jules Barthélemy
Iliad. 1868 (2v.) 3/6/74

Saint James's vestry. (not found) 27/1/43

Saint John, Charles William George
Short sketches of the wild sports and natural history of the Highlands. 1846 (2v.) 18/12/46

Saint John, Henry Viscount Bolingbroke
Letters on the spirit of patriotism; on the idea of a patriot king; and on the state of parties at the accession of King George the first. 1752 16/8/79
Letters on the study and use of history. 1752 (2v.) 23/11/35

Works [memoirs]. 1809 (8v.) 21/3/63
Works [on authority]. 1754 (7v. 1754–98) 16/6/47
Saint John, James Augustus
History of the four conquests of England. 1861 (2v.) 26/5/62
Life of Sir Walter Raleigh. 1868 (2v.) 4/3/68
Saint John, R. C.
Church and wife. 1872 3/3/72
Saint John, Sir Spenser Buckingham
Hayti; or, the Black Republic. 1884 30/9/84, 5/10/84 n
Saint John, Theophilus J.
Fifty two original sermons. 1790 3/3/27
Saint Leger, William Nassau
Discourse upon the condition and prospects of the nation. 1841 5/12/41
The profession of the true faith. 1841 5/12/41
Saint Maur, Edward Adolphus Duke of Somerset
Alternate circles and the connexion with the ellipse. 1851 4/2/67
Saint Paul's school
Apposition. 1844 7/6/44
Saintsbury, George Edward Bateman
The Earl of Derby. 1892 3/9/92
Saint-Simon, Henri Jean Victor de Duc de Saint-Simon
Mémoires. 1829 (7v.) 25/10/70
Saint Victor, Adam de
Elucidatorium Ecclesiasticum. 1858 (2v. 1858–9) 29/10/59
Sale, Lady Florentia
Journal of the disasters in Affghanistan, 1841–2. 1843 18/4/43
Sale, George
The Koran. 1734 13/1/77
Sales, Saint Francis de
Introduction to a devout life. 22/10/45
Life of St. Francis de Sales [Christian biographies], by Henrietta L. Farrer. 1871 17/4/87
Sall, Andrew
The catholic and apostolic faith maintained in the Church of England, ed. J. Allport. (new edn 1840) 21/12/42
Salmon, George
A historical introduction to the study of the books of the New Testament. 1885 (2v. 1885–6) 26/7/85, 9/1/87, 11/3/88
The infallibility of the Church. 1888 15/11/88, 14/4/89
Thoughts on the present crisis of the Church of Ireland. 1870 10/3/86
Salmon, Thomas
An impartial examination of Bishop Burnet's History of his own Times. 1724 3/9/44
Salmond, Charles Adamson
Exposition and defence of Prince Bismarck's Anti-Ultra-Montane policy. 1876 30/1/76
Salomons, Sir David
[on oaths]. (not found) 25/4/50
The case of D. Salomons, Esq. 1844 18/7/51 ?
The Corn Laws; their effect on the trade of the country considered, with suggestions for a compromise. 1841 11/12/41
Salusbury, Philip H. B.
Two months with Tchernaieff in Servia. 1877 9/6/77
Salvador, Joseph
Histoire des institutions de Moïse et du peuple Hébreu. 1829 (4v. 1829–30) 21/9/88
Salvagnoli, Vincenzo
Della indipendenza d'Italia. 1859 2/4/59
The independence of Italy. 1860 18/10/60
Salvation: what it is. 1875 27/8/76
Salvo di Pietraganzili, Rosario
I Siculi. Ricerca di una civiltà italiana anteriore dalla greca. 1884 (2v. 1884–7) 14/1/89
Samuelson, Sir Bernhard
The Agricultural Holdings Act, 1875. A speech. 1879 2/7/79
Sancroft, William
A sermon preached at the consecration [of seven bishops]. 6/6/41
Sand, George
Consuelo. 1843 6/7/47
La Mare au Diable. 1846 13/9/86
La petite Fadette. 1848 26/12/88
Sanday, William
The authorship and historical character of the fourth gospel. 1872 9/9/77
The Oracles of God. 1891 2/10/92
Sandeman, Robert
The honour of marriage opposed to all impurities. 1777 1/3/63
Sander, Nicholas
Rise and growth of the Anglican schism, ed. D. Lewis. 1877 10/10/80, 29/9/89
Sanders, E. S. G.
Spiritualism. What is it?. 1880 26/12/80
Sanders, Lloyd Charles
Lord Melbourne's papers. 1889 23/11/89
Sanderson, James
The Irish land question. 1870 2/2/70
Sanderson, Robert
Fragmentary illustrations of the history of the Book of Common Prayer from . . . Bishop Wren, ed. W. Jacobson. 1874 1/10/74
Sandford, Charles Waldegrave
Duties of the clergy. A sermon. 1875 7/10/75
Pastoral letter. 1876 7/1/77
Pastoral letter. 1878 22/9/78
Pastoral letter. 1882 11/2/83
Pastoral letter. 1889 3/3/89
Works of counsel to English churchmen abroad. 1892 5/11/93
Sandford, Bishop Daniel
Remains of . . . Daniel Sandford, ed. J. Sandford. 1830 (2v.) 17/8/32

Sandford, John Archdeacon of Coventry
A charge... to the clergy... of Coventry. 1852 1/8/52, 1/8/53
Church rates and the census. A charge. 1860 19/8/60
Church topics of the day. A charge. 1864 7/8/64
Eight lectures on fellowship with God. 1835 1/3/35
Middle class education; or, our endowed and commercial schools. A sermon. 1864 18/9/64
Parochalia, or Church, school, and parish. 1845 6/1/45
The Irish Church Establishment. A speech. 1868 15/8/68
The mission and extension of the Church at home. Bampton Lectures. 1862 20/7/62

Sands, David
Journal of the life and gospel labours of David Sands. 1848 22/4/83

Sands, J. of Tranent
Out of the world; or, Life in St. Kilda. 1876 21/9/78

Sandvoss, Franz [pseud. Xanthippus]
Kalypso, von Xanthippus. 1886 3/12/86

Sandwith, Humphry
A narrative of the siege of Kars. 1856 7/2/56

Sandys, Charles
The memorial and case of the Clerici-Laici [of Canterbury Cathedral]. 1848 11/12/48

Sandys, Bishop Edwin
Sermons, ed. J. Ayre. 1841 2/1/42

Sandys, George William
A letter to Sir James Graham [on national education]. 1843 29/5/43

Saphir, Adolph
Christ and the scriptures. 1867 26/11/71
The divine unity of Scripture. 1892 16/4/93, 25/6/93, 23/7/93

Sapho
Opera. 16/9/86

Sarasvati, Ramabai
The high-caste Hindu woman. 3/8/85

Sardou, Victorien
Daniel Rochat. Comédie. 1880 3/9/86
La Famille Benoîton. Comédie. 1866 19/5/66
La Tosca. 1887 27/3/89 ?

Sargant, William Lucas
Essays of a Birmingham manufacturer [Ireland and land tenure; Princess and dowry; Comparative morality]. 1869 (4v. 1869–72) 14/12/69, 13/11/71, 15/11/71

Sargent, John
Memoir of... Henry Martyn. 1819 8/4/27

Sarpi, Pietro
A treatise of ecclesiastical benefices and revenues, tr. T. Jenkins. 1736 26/8/40

Sarrans, Bernard
Memoirs of General Lafayette and of the French Revolution of 1830. 1832 (2v.) 6/11/32

Saturday Review, matrimony. 27 September 1862. 1/3/1863

Saunders, Emily Susan Goulding
Spiritualism. What is it?. 1864 25/2/75

Saunders, John
Hirell. A novel. 1869 (3v.) 22/7/69
Love's martyrdom. A play. 1882 (2nd edn) 26/10/83

Saunders, William
Through the Light Continent. 1879 26/7/79

Savarese, Giovanni Battista
Introduzione alla storia critica della filosofia dei santi padri. 1856 21/11/81

Savile, Bouchier Wrey
Anglo-Israelism and the Great Pyramid; an examination of the alleged claims of Queen Victoria to the Throne of David. 1880 27/12/80
Letter to W. J. E. Bennett. 1868 28/5/69
The Great Secret. 1855 22/8/80
The Neanderthal skull on evolution, in an Address supposed to be delivered A. D. 2085. 1883 27/5/85

Saxon's remedy for Irish discontent. 1868 21/3/68

Sayce, Archibald Henry
Fresh light from the ancient monuments. 1883 29/10/93, 3/12/93
Preface to Schliemann's Troja. 1884 27/11/83
The Hibbert Lectures... on the origin and growth of religion [in Babylon]. 1887 11/2/87, 12/2/88, 1/12/89

Sayer, John
The law of costs. 1768 21/2/62 ?

Scamperdale
The evils of Ireland considered. In a letter to... Fortescue... with the draft of a Bill... By Scamperdale. 1866 12/3/66

Scandret, J.
Sacrifice the Divine Service, from the covenant of Grace to the mystery of Man's redemption. 1707 (new edn 1840) 20/8/48

Scargill, William Pitt
Autobiography of a dissenting minister. 1834 29/11/34

Scarisbrike, Edward
The life of the Lady Warner... in religion called Sister Clare of Jesus. 8/5/84

Scarpa, G. B.
Cenni sull'estratto del dispaccio indirizzato a Sua Eccellenza il Lord Altro Commissionario. 1858 3/1/59

Scarron, Paul
Le Roman comique. 1752 21/4/54

Scartazzini, Giovanni Andrea
Dante Alighieri. 1879 15/12/87
Handbook to Dante. 1887 15/12/87, 11/1/88
Zur Dante-Bibliographie, vom Anfang des Jahres 1869–70. 1871 2/2/88

Scarth, John
Twelve years in China. The people, the rebels, and the Mandarins. 1860 15/10/60
Schaeffer, Adolphe
Non Possumus. 1869 20/2/75
Schaff, Philipp
Church and state in the United States. 1888 10/1/90
Scheme of the Otago Free Church colony. 1845 3/1/46
Scherer, Edmond Henri Adolphe
Alexandre Vinet. 1853 14/2/83
De l'état actuel de l'église réformée. 1845 10/1/45
Etudes critiques. 1865 (10v. 1863–95) 22/10/79
Mélanges de critique religieuse. 1860 28/1/83
Scherer, Wilhelm
History of German literature. 1886 (2v.) 9/9/86 ?
Schiller, Johann Christoph Friedrich von
Das Lied von der Glocke. 1828 22/6/37
Die Braut von Messina. 1803 19/11/33
Die Jungfrau von Orleans. 1802 1/11/33
Die Piccolomini. 1800 30/9/64
Die Räuber. 1781 13/10/34, 21/10/34, 1/11/34
Die Verschwörung des Fiesko zu Genua. 1783 14/11/34
Don Carlos. 1787 6/10/34
History of the Thirty Year's War in Germany, tr. Capt. Blanquière. 1799 (2v.) 19/9/72, 23/9/72, 31/10/72
Maria Stuart. 1801 17/10/33
Wallenstein. Ein dramatisches Gedicht. 1800 13/6/32, 5/10/63, 28/9/64
Schink, Johann Friedrich
Prinz Hamlet von Dännemark. Marionnettenspiel. 1799 8/9/79
Schlegel, August Wilhelm von
A course of lectures on dramatic art, tr. J. Black. 1815 27/9/27
Der Sturm [tr. of The Tempest]. 5/4/34
Schleiermacher, Friedrich Daniel Ernst
A critical essay on the gospel of St. Luke, tr. C. Thirlwall. 1825 20/8/48
Life... as unfolded in his autobiography and letters, tr. F. Rowan. 1860 (2v.) 22/9/73, 12/10/73
Schley, Winfield Scott
Report [on the] *Greely Relief Expedition of 1884.* 1887 26/12/87
Schliemann, Heinrich
Ilios, Stadt und Land der Trojaner. 1881 22/2/81
Ithaka, der Peloponnes und Troja. 1869 7/1/74
Orchomenos. 1881 6/6/84
Troja... mit Vorrede von A. H. Sayce. 1884 27/11/83, 15/1/84, 28/5/91
Trojanische Alterthümer. 1874 9/3/74, 25/9/75
Troy and its remains, ed. P. Smith. 1875 25/9/75
Schmakowsky, Wilhelm Julius von
Die päpstliche Würde in legitimer Form. 1845 4/11/45
Schmidt, Charles Guillaume Adolphe
Social results of early Christianity. 1885 25/10/85
Schmidt, Leopold Valentin
Die Ethik der alten Griechen. 1882 (2v.) 22/1/83
Schmidt, Wilhelm Adolf
Elsass und Lothringen. 1870 31/10/70
Schneegans, Wilhelm, and Schneegans, Julius
Die Stellung der protestantischen und katholischen Kirche zum Staate, der Cultus, die Kirchenzucht und die Sonntagsfeier. 1845 7/11/45
Schnitzler, Johann Heinrich
Secret history of the governemnt and court of Russia under the Emperor Alexander and Nicholas. 1847 (2v.) 12/11/47
Schoemann, Georgius F. C.
Commentatio Macrobiana. 1871 5/1/71 ?
Schoenemann, Carl Traugott Gottlob
De geographia Homeri. 1787 23/4/47
Schoenhof, Jacob
The industrial situation and the question of wages. 1885 28/6/90
Scholefield, James
[Lecture]. (not found) 20/5/46
The golden pipes: the Word of the Lord to England. 1848 11/2/48
Schomburgk, Richard
A description of British Guiana, geographical and statistical. 1840 6/6/40
Schrader, Eberhard
The cuneiform inscriptions and the Old Testament. 1885 (2v. 1885–8) 24/11/89, 27/1/90
Schreiber, Aloys Wilhelm
The traveller's guide to the Rhine. 1836 (new edn) 13/8/38
Schreiber, Carl Christian Ernst
Ithaca. 1829 14/9/77
Schreiner, Olive Emilie Albertina pseud. Ralph Iron
Dreams. 1891 1/1/91, 30/10/93
The story of an African farm. 1883 (2v.) 17/4/85, 1/6/89 n
Schuerer, Emil
Geschichte des Jüdischen Volkes. 1890 (2v.) 28/12/90
Schulte, Johann Friedrich von
Contemporary Review, xxxv. 773. 1879 (August 1879) 3/8/79
Der Cölibatszwang und dessen Aufhebung. 1876 23/2/76

Schulte, Johann Friedrich von (*cont.*)
Die Altkatholicismus. 1887 17/4/90
Die Macht der römischen Päpste über Fürsten. 1871 13/12/74
Schultz, Heinrich Hermann
Old Testament theology. 1892 24/3/89
Schulz, Albert
An essay on the influence of Welsh tradition upon the literature of France, Germany and Scandinavia. 1841 9/10/89
Schuster, Albert
W. E. Gladstone's Homerische Studien, frei bearbeitet von Dr. A. Schuster. 1863 2/1/64
Schuyler, Eugene
Mr. Baring's and Mr. Schuyler's Report (on the atrocities committed upon the Christians in Bulgaria). 1876 22/1/77
Peter the Great, Emperor of Russia. 1884 (2v.) 9/2/84, 28/4/84
Turkistan. Notes of a journey in Russian Turkistan, Khokand, Bukara, and Kuldja . . . with maps and illustrations. 1876 (2v.) 10/10/76
Schwartz, A.
'On Dies Irae', *Macmillan's Magazine*, xxx. 455. 1874 (September 1874) 14/9/74
Schwartz, Joost Marius Willem van der Poorten pseud. M. Maartens
The sins of Janet Avelingh. 1889 (2v.) 20/6/93
Schwickert, Johann Joseph
De l'Allemagne littéraire et philologique et des travaux de critique et d'interprétation des anciens, en particulier de Pindar. 1879 26/10/78
Science without religion. (not found) 3/8/84
Sclopis, Count Federigo
Delle relazioni politiche tra la dinastia di Savoia ed il governo britannico (1240–1815). 1853 19/9/53
La domination française en Italie, 1800–1814. 1861 2/3/58, 8/10/61
Scobell, Edward
A few thoughts on church subjects; viz. uniformity, daily service, gown and surplice, private dress, pews, preaching. 1843 21/5/43
Scobell, J.
A reply to the postscript of the Rev. J. M. Neale. 1858 28/1/58
Scoble, John
Hill Coolies. A brief exposition of the deplorable conditions of the hill coolies in British Guiana and Mauritius. 1840 10/3/40
Texas; its claims to be recognised as an independent power by Great Britain. 1839 6/2/40
The working of the negro apprenticeship system. 1838 7/5/38
Scone
Liber Ecclesiae of Scone. 1843 23/9/84 ?
Scoones, William Baptiste
Four centuries of English letters, edited and arranged by W. B. Scoones. 1880 (3rd edn 1883) 7/3/83
Scoresby, William the younger
Journal of a voyage to the Northern whale-fishery. 1823 17/1/32
[Scotch mixtures]. (not found) 3/8/87
Scotch Sermons. 1880 6/7/80
Scots families in Scandinavia. (not found) 20/6/84
Scotsman's answer to Burke. 1779 (?) 23/10/44
Scott, Abraham
Three sermons on the evidences of the Scriptures. 1832 (new edn 1879) 7/9/79
Scott, Alexander John
Discourses [to the Y.M.C.A.]. 1866 10/6/66
Notes of four lectures on the literature and philosophy of the Middle Ages. 1857 10/6/66
Scott, George Gilbert
A plea for the faithful restoration of our ancient churches. 1850 25/8/50
Remarks on secular and domestic architecture, present and future. 1857 23/7/58
The revival of gothic architecture . . . Two lectures. 1857 28/3/58
Scott, John bookseller
Letter to the Chancellor of the Exchequer on his proposed sale of the land tax. 1798 12/6/48 ?
Scott, John M.A., of North Ferriby
The history of the Church of Christ, particularly in its Lutheran branch. 1826 (3v. 1826–31) 18/7/41
Scott, Robert Dean of Rochester
Sermons preached before the University of Oxford. 1860 9/12/60, 13/8/65
The Church's path, the Christian's responsibility. Two sermons. 1845 23/11/45
Scott, Thomas of Ramsgate
An address to the friends of free inquiry and free expression. 1865 2/6/65
Conversations, edited by a woman for women, by F. J., published by T. Scott. 1872 14/7/72
Ramsgate tracts. 1872 4/8/72
Spiritual pantheism, by F. H. J., published by T. Scott. 1872 14/7/72
The English life of Jesus. 1871 6/7/73
Scott, Thomas Rector of Aston Sandford
The rights of God. 1793 22/5/31
Scott, Sir Walter
A collection of scarce and valuable tracts [the Somers tracts], edited by Walter Scott. 1809 (13v. 1809–15) 10/12/40
A Legend of Montrose. 1819 12/8/26, 20/2/29, 6/10/82
A letter to the Editor of the Edinburgh Weekly

Journal, from Malachi Malagrowther, on the proposed change of currency. 1826 20/11/63
Anne of Geierstein. 1829 (3v.) 10/7/29, 8/9/68
Aunt Margaret's Mirror. 1829 12/9/60
Castle Dangerous. 1831 22/12/31
Goetz of Berlichingen by J. W. von Goethe, translated by Walter Scott. 1799 3/11/68
Guy Mannering. 1815 (3v.) 5/12/48, 9/4/80, 13/10/80, 17/12/90
Ivanhoe; a romance. 1819 (3v.) 14/7/34, 6/9/71
Kenilworth; a romance. 1821 (3v.) 18/7/39, 31/8/52, 18/4/94
Letters of Sir Walter Scott; addressed to the Rev. R Polwele; D. Gilbert, Esq.; F. Douce, Esq.;[with] *an autobiographical memoir of Sir Hussey Vivian*. 1832 6/5/32
Life of Jonathan Swift. 1814 28/10/68
Lord of the Isles. A poem. 1815 26/2/27, 30/6/40
Marmion; a tale of Flodden Field. 1808 25/7/39, 26/7/39, 5/10/47
Memoirs of the life of Sir Walter Scott, by J. G. Lockhart. 1837 (7v. 1837-8) 30/7/68
Old Mortality. 1816 (3v.) 16/8/27, 13/1/73
Opera. 1/9/94
Paul's Letters to his Kinsfolk. 1816 18/9/35
Peveril of the Peak. 1822 (4v.) 1/10/60, 13/4/89
Quentin Durward. 1823 (3v.) 13/9/52
Rob Roy. 1818 (3v.) 23/8/27, 23/9/57, 22/12/76, 15/1/91
Rokeby; a poem. 1813 17/6/40
St. Ronan's Well. 1823 (3v.) 3/4/57, 15/9/79
Tales of a Grandfather; being stories taken from Scottish history. 1827 (4 series 1827-9) 13/1/29, 2/4/30, 31/10/33, 30/1/85
Tales of the Crusaders. 1825 (4v.) 13/3/28, 15/9/60
The Abbot. 1820 (3v.) 28/7/33, 18/8/52, 18/9/75, 15/10/75, 22/7/92
The Antiquary. 1816 (3v.) 20/7/27, 2/5/37, 15/12/48, 30/7/68, 3/1/83
The Black Dwarf. 1816 21/8/27, 8/8/33, 2/10/57
The Bride of Lammermoor. 1819 (3v.) 8/8/26, 15/10/30, 2/8/33, 6/8/33, 5/2/68, 25/9/82, 4/10/82, 26/11/90, 1/12/90, 2/12/90
The Chronicles of the Canongate. 1827 (2v.) 8/12/27, 27/5/28
The Doom of Devergoil, a melo-drama. Auchindrane, or the Ayrshire tragedy. 1830 27/10/68
The Fair Maid of Perth. 1828 14/6/28
The Fortunes of Nigel. 1822 (3v.) 15/9/57
The Heart of Midlothian. 1818 (3v.) 15/11/27, 9/10/57, 12/1/85
The Highland Widow. 1827 8/12/27, 11/9/60
The history of Scotland. 1830 (2v.) 31/10/33, 19/4/86
The Journal of Sir Walter Scott, from the original manuscript at Abbotsford, edited by David Douglas. 1890 (2v.) 10/11/90
The Lady of the Lake; a poem. 1810 1/8/39, 9/4/59, 9/11/75, 22/1/84, 31/1/84
The Lay of the Last Minstrel, a poem. 1805 26/2/27, 21/3/34, 15/6/57
The life of Dryden. 1808 24/7/46, 12/10/72, 16/8/90 n
The life of Napoleon Buonaparte, Emperor of the French. With a preliminary view of the French Revolution. 1827 (9v.) 16/11/32, 4/12/32, 29/12/32, 19/1/33
The Monastery. A romance. 1820 (3v.) 4/8/52, 28/8/75
The Pirate. 1822 (3v.) 13/9/94
The poetical works of . . . Scott . . . with all his introductions, notes . . . edited by J. G. Lockhart. 1857 17/10/71
The Talisman. 1825 13/3/28, 14/9/60
The two drovers. 1827 8/12/27, 13/9/60
The works of John Dryden, ed. Sir Walter Scott. 1828 (18v.) 15/8/90
Waverley novels. 29/9/93, 1/9/94
Waverley; or, 'Tis sixty years since. 1814 (3v.) 14/8/26, 21/11/48, 7/9/71, 29/8/76, 11/12/76, 21/12/76, 1/9/92, 5/10/92
Woodstock; or, the Cavalier. 1826 (3v.) 2/8/26

Scott, William of Christ Church, Hoxton
A letter to the Rev. Daniel Wilson, occasioned by his recent 'Appeal to the Evangelical Members of the Church of England'. 1850 16/10/50

Scott, Sir William Baron Stowell
Substance of a speech of Sir W. Scott . . . relative to the non-residence of the clergy, and other affairs of the Church. 1802 6/12/72

Scott, William Anderson
The Christ of the Apostles' Creed. 1867 16/9/66, 23/6/72

Scott, General Winfield
Memoirs of Lieut.-General Scott, written by himself. 1864 (2v.) 20/3/65

Scotti, Angelo Antonio
Teoremi di Politica Cristiana. 1831 (2v.) 13/8/46

Scottish Church Review. 7/1/1884
Scottish Episcopal Church's Synodal proceedings. 1859 9/10/59
Scottish Episcopal Magazine. 16/12/1848
Scottish Guardian.
1. 2/1864
3. 132. 3/1866. R. Gray's letter 19/8/1866
Scottish Magazine and Churchman's Review.
1. 461. 10/1851. Daily prayer 19/10/1851
2. 160. 4/1852. Ritualism 18/4/1852

Scottish Magazine and Churchman's Review (*cont.*)
2. 265. 6/1852. G & synods 6/6/1852
2. 329. 7/1852. Laity & synods 4/7/1852
2. 471. 10/1849. Synods 11/11/1849
2. 520. 11/1852. Bishop Torry's obituary 14/11/1852
3. 105. 3/1853. Kingsley 20/3/1853
Scottish Review.
1 3/12/1882
1. 236. 2/1883. on Tait 25/2/1883
1. 52. 11/1882. Dr Smith's poems 9/1/1883
4. 1. 7/1884. on Abp. Sharp 31/8/1884
8. 1. 7/1886. Scottish home rule 13/8/1886
8. 61. 7/1886. Turgeniev 15/8/1886
10. 213. 10/1887. The union 7/11/1887
14. 399. 10/1889. Bate on Scottish parliament 17/10/1889
Scougal, Henry
Few to be saved [sermon on Luke xiii. 23]. 3/2/33
The life of God in the soul of man. 13/4/34
The works of Mr. Henry Scougal... and a sermon preached at his funeral. 1759 (2v.) 27/9/63
Scratchley, Arthur
A practical treatise on Savings Banks, containing a review of their past history and present condition, and of legislation on the subject. 1860 28/4/60, 15/1/61
Scriblerus, Martin pseud.
An heroic epistle to the Rev. Richard Watson. 1780 11/8/29 ?
Scribner's Monthly Magazine.
6. 633. 11/1889. Bashkirtseff 7/12/1889
21. 28. 11/1880. on the Bonapartes 2/11/1880
Scriptural education in Ireland. 1832 12/4/37
Scriven, J. E.
An Irish farmer on the land difficulty. 1870 9/2/70
Scrope, George Poulett
A plea for the rights of industry in Ireland. 1848 14/4/48
Extracts of the evidence taken by the late Commission of Inquiry into the occupation of land in Ireland, on the subject of waste lands reclamation. 1847 8/5/47
How is Ireland to be governed?. 1834 20/4/46
Letters to Lord John Russell on the expediency of enlarging the Irish Poor Law to the full extent of the Poor Law in England. 1846 23/7/46
Memoir of... Charles Lord Sydenham, with a narrative of his administration in Canada. 1843 17/7/44
No Vote, No Rate; or, Household Suffrage made at once safe and popular. A proposal made in 1850 and renewed in 1867. 1867 28/3/67
Principles of political economy, deduced from the natural laws of social welfare, applied to the present state of Britain. 1833 7/7/36
Scrymgour, Edward Phillips
The doctrine of the Cross. 1882 14/5/82
Scudamore, Frank Ives
Life insurance by small payments; a few plain words concerning it. 1861 6/3/64
Scudamore, William Edward
England and Rome. 1855 24/3/55
Letters to a seceder from the Church of England to the Church of Rome. 1851 7/3/52
Scudder, Horace Elisha
Noah Webster. 1881 12/3/93 ?
Scull, S. A.
Greek mythology systematised. 1880 2/10/80
Scullard, Herbert Hayes
Martin of Tours, Apostle of Gaul. 1891 16/8/91
Seabury, Samuel
[on the Scots Prayer Book] in *The Guardian.* 1862 (September 24, 1862) 28/9/62
Seager, Charles
Auricular confession. 1842 23/4/43
The Female Jesuit abroad; a true and romantic narrative of real life. 1853 10/4/55, 24/9/63, 30/11/63
Seal, Horace Samuel
On the nature of state interference. 1893 30/7/93
Searle, Frederick Charles
To a boy leaving school for university. With a preface by J. F. C. Welldon. 1892 5/9/93
Seaver, Jonathan
The authority of Christ. 1891 25/10/91
Seccombe, John Thomas
Science, theism and revelation, considered in relation to Mr. Mill's Essay on Nature, Religion and Atheism. 1875 30/4/76
Séché, Léon
Les derniers Jansénistes, 1710–1870. 1891 (3v.) 6/1/91 n, 17/1/92
Secker, Thomas
Eight charges delivered to the clergy... of Oxford and Canterbury. 1769 6/9/40
Lectures on the catechism of the Church of England. 1769 25/2/27
Oratio Synodalis. 1761 20/9/40
The works of Thomas Secker. 1775 (3v.) 24/3/67
Secolo. 3/7/88
Secondat, Charles Louis de Baron de Montesquieu
Défence de l'esprit des lois. 1750 9/11/40
De l'esprit des lois. 1748 9/11/40
Lettres persanes. 1721 (2v.) 9/4/49, 15/9/58
Reflections on the causes of the grandeur and declension of the Romans. 1734 2/9/31
Second coming of the Lord. 1834 9/11/58
Second reformation. (not found) 5/8/51

Secretan, Charles Frederick
Memoirs of the life and times of the pious Robert Nelson. 1860 1/7/60
Sedgwick, Professor Adam
A discourse on the studies of the University [of Cambridge]. 1833 11/3/42
A memorial by the Trustees of Cowgill Chapel, with a preface and appendix, on the climate, history and dialects of Dent. 1868 3/2/69
Dr. Livingstone's Cambridge Lectures, together with a prefatory letter by Professor Sedgwick. 1858 31/10/59
Life of Adam Sedgwick, by Clark and Hughes. 1890 (2v.) 3/7/90
Sedgwick, John M.A.
Hints on the establishment of public industrial schools for the working classes. 1853 19/6/53
Sedley, Sir Charles
The works of Sir Charles Sedley in verse and prose. 1722 (2v.) 8/1/52
Seebohm, Benjamin
Memoirs of the life and gospel labours of Stephen Grellet [of the Society of Friends]. 1860 (2v.) 19/12/90
Seebohm, Frederic
'The land question' in *Fortnightly Review*, xiii. 89. 1870 (January 1870) 5/1/70
The Oxford Reformers of 1498. 1867 18/4/67
The spirit of Christianity: an essay on the Christian hypothesis. 23/12/76
Seeley, Sir John Robert
'Milton's poetry' in *Macmillan's Magazine*, xix. 407. 1869 (March 1869) 14/8/69
'Roman imperialism' in *Macmillan's Magazine*, xx. 281. 1869 (August 1869) 14/8/69
Ecce Homo: a survey of the life and work of Jesus Christ. 1866 21/12/65, 22/7/66, 19/8/66, 20/10/67
Life and times of Stein; or Germany and Prussia in the Napoleonic Age. 1878 1/1/79
Natural religion. By the author of Ecce Homo. 1882 15/7/82, 13/8/82
The expansion of England. 1883 27/12/83, 30/5/84
Seeley, Leonard Benton
Horace Walpole and his world. 1884 1/1/84
Seeley, Mary
The later Evangelical Fathers. 1879 21/4/81
Seeley, Robert Benton
Essays on the Church. By a layman. 1834 6/3/38, 26/5/40
Remedies suggested for some of the evils which constitute 'the Perils of the Nation'. 1844 1/2/45
The Church of Christ in the Middle Ages. An historical sketch. 1845 11/1/46
The life of William Cowper. 1855 30/10/70
Segneri, Paolo the elder
Concordia tra la fatica e la quieta nell'orazione. 21/4/59
Quaresimale. 27/12/57, 13/3/59
Ségur, Alexandre Joseph Pierre de
Les femmes, leur condition et leur influence dans l'ordre sociale chez différents peuples anciens et modernes. 1803 (3v.) 20/11/69
Seilhac, Victor de
L'Abbé Dubois, premier ministre de Louis XV. 1862 (2v.) 19/9/81
Selden, John
The historie of tithes. That is, The practice of payment of them. The positive laws made for them. The opinions touching the right of them. 11/4/34
Selfe, H. S.
The United Kingdom Mutual Annuity Society. 1861 16/3/64
Sell, Carl
Alice, Grand Duchess of Hesse. 1884 8/1/84
Sellar, William Young
The Roman poets of the Republic. 1863 16/6/63
Sellon, Edward
Annotations on the sacred writings of the Hindus; being an epitome of some of the most remarkable and leading tenets in the faith of that people. 1865 13/8/84
Sellon, Priscilla Lydia
Reply to a tract by the Rev. J. Spurrell... containing certain charges concerning the Society of the Sisters of Mercy of Devonport and Plymouth. 1852 19/3/52
Sellon, William R. B.
Miss Sellon and the Sisters of Mercy. A contradiction of alleged acts of cruelty exercised by Miss Sellon. 1852 12/10/52
Selwyn, George Augustus
[Reply to Fitzroy]. 1846 (not found) 21/8/46
A charge. 1848 1/4/49
An idea of a colonial college. 1848 25/6/48
Are cathedral institutions useless? A practical answer to this question, addressed to W. E. Gladstone. 1838 1/3/38, 8/4/40
How shall we sing the Lord's song in a strange land? A sermon. 1842 20/3/42
New Zealand. Part II. Journal of the Bishop's visitation tour from August to December 1843. 1847 17/3/49
Sermons preached chiefly in the Church of St. John Baptist, New Windsor. 1842 14/4/44
Thanksgiving sermon... preached by the Bishop of New Zealand on his arrival. 1842 30/4/43
Vox Ecclesiae. (not found) 25/2/39
Selwyn, Gulielmus
Origenes contra Celsum, ed. G. Selwyn. 1860 17/10/86

Selwyn, William Canon of Ely
[On cathedrals]. (not found) 27/4/39
Pastoral colloquies on the South Downs. 1875 11/4/76
The Creeds of Nicaea, Constantinople, and Athanasius. 1873 6/4/73
The doctrine of types, and its influence on the interpretation of the New Testament. 1829 21/11/30
The substance of an argument... against those clauses of the Benefices Bill which confer additional powers on the Ecclesiastical Commissioners. 1838 7/6/38
Senato di Roma ed il Papa. 1865 (2nd edn) 15/11/66
Seneca
Ad Helviam Matrem. 12/8/64
Senestrey, Bishop Ignatius
Hirtenworte des Hochwürdigsten Herrn Bischofs Ignatius... über die Beschlüsse des vaticanischen Concils. 1870 13/11/70
Senex Rusticus
Truth and candour vindicated from the assaults, and Christian ministers from the compliments of Dr. Parker... in his recent defences of Mr. Beecher. 1875 3/9/75
Senior, Nassau William
A letter to Lord Howick, on a legal provision for the Irish poor, commutation of tithes, and a provision for the Irish Roman Catholic clergy. 1831 6/6/37
Biographical sketches. 1863 1/1/72
Conversations and journals in Egypt and Malta. Edited by M. C. M. Simpson. 1882 (2v.) 14/6/56, 5/7/60, 17/4/62
Conversations with distinguished persons during the Second Empire. Edited by M. C. M. Simpson. 1880 (2v.) 3/11/60, 28/5/61
Conversations with M. Thiers, M. Guizot, and other distinguished persons, during the Second Empire. 1878 (2v.) 21/2/53
Journals kept in France and Italy from 1848 to 1852. With a sketch of the revolution of 1848. Edited by M. C. M. Simpson. 1871 (2v.) 28/12/50 n, 12/6/52 n, 26/6/72, 4/7/75
Journals, conversations and essays relating to Ireland. 1868 (2v.) 21/7/68
Letters on the Factory Act, as it affects the cotton manufacture. 1837 3/3/38, 18/3/44
On national property, and the propects of the present administration. 1835 2/2/35
Remarks on the opposition to the Poor Law Amendment Bill. By a Guardian. 1841 5/6/41
Sephton, John
The lenten element in life. 1884 24/8/84
Septenville, Baron Edouard de
L'intention de l'Angleterre en 1863. 1863 5/3/63
Septuagenarius
Britain's wreck; or, breakers ahead. 1853 19/6/53
Serao, Mathilde
Farewell love! A novel. 1894 23/3/94
Sergeant, Lewis
[On ritualism]. (not found) 24/4/79
John Wyclif. 1893 26/2/93
New Greece. 1878 30/9/78
Sermons in glass. (untraced) 9/7/54
Servia: her aim and story. 1884 17/5/84 ?
Sestini, Bartolommeo
La Pia de'Tolomei. 1822 13/3/37
Seton, George
Memoir of Alexander Seton, Earl of Dunfermline. 1882 17/12/94
The past and the present. 1878 8/8/78
Settembrini, Luigi
Difesa di Luigi Settembrini. 1850 28/3/51
In morte di Carlo Poerio. Discorso. 1867 23/7/67
Sévigné, Marchioness Marie de
Lettres. 1726 26/5/55, 1/9/60
Lettres choisies. 1810 (3v.) 4/9/84
Memoirs, ed. P. E. de Coulanges. 1820 8/9/83
Sewall, F.
Dante and Swedenborg. 1893 24/1/93
Seward, William F.R.S.
Anecdotes of some distinguished persons. 1795 (4v.) 19/12/61, 25/3/89
Seward, William Wenman
Collectanea Politica; or the political transactions of Ireland, from the accession of George III. 1801 (3v. 1801–4) 27/10/86, 13/5/89
Sewell, Elizabeth Missing
Amy Herbert. By a Lady. 1844 (2v.) 17/9/45
Gertrude. 1845 (2v.) 11/8/46
Laneton Parsonage; a tale for children on the practical use of a portion of the Church catechism. 1846 19/7/46
Margaret Percival. 1847 16/2/47
Sewell, Mary
Our Father's Care. A ballad. 1870 3/10/70
Sewell, William
[inaugural lecture]. 3/5/37
[on church discipline]. (not found) 5/8/39
A year's sermons to boys. 1854 30/4/54
Address to a Christian congregation on the approach of the Cholera Morbus. 1831 13/12/31
Christian communism. 1848 25/2/49 ?
Christian morals. 1840 3/8/40
Christian politics. 1844 28/6/44, 19/12/80
Collegiate reform; a sermon [on John iv. 19]. 1853 16/1/54
Hawkstone; a tale of and for England in 184–. 1845 (2v.) 25/4/45
Journal of a residence at the College of St. Columba, in Ireland. 1847 18/7/47

Letter to . . . E. B. Pusey on the publication of No. 90 of Tracts for the Times. 1841 22/3/41
Second letter to a dissenter on the opposition of the University of Oxford to the Charter of the London College. 1834 2/4/34
The duty of young men in time of controversy. 1843 21/6/43
The nation, the Church, and the University of Oxford. 1849 20/1/50
The plea of conscience for seceding from the Catholic Church to the Roman schism in England. 1845 7/12/45
The University Commission; or, Lord John Russell's postbag of April 27, 1850. 1850 30/4/50
Thoughts on the admission of dissenters to the University of Oxford; and on the establishment of a state religion; in a letter to a dissenter. 1834 26/3/34
Sexby, Edward
Killing no murder. 6/3/38
Sexton, George
A portraiture of Mormonism. 1849 23/8/51
Scientific materialism calmly considered. 1874 7/2/79
Seyd, Ernest
Reform of the Bank of England note issue. 1873 (2v.) 11/2/73
Seymour, Aaron Crossley Hobart
Life and times of Selina, Countess of Huntingdon. 1839 (2v. 1839–40) 23/1/40
Seymour, Henry Danby
Russia on the Black Sea and the Sea of Azof. 1855 13/5/56
Seymour, Horatio
'The government of the U.S.A.' in *North American Review*, xii. 359. 1878 27/11/78
Address before the New York State Agricultural Society. 1880 12/11/80
Seymour, Michael Hobart
[Christ Church, Dublin]. (not found) 18/5/69
Letters . . . to the Bishop of London, . . . conclusive evidence that the doctrines of the Church of Rome . . . are fearfully in force at this day in Ireland. 1835 (2nd edn) 12/3/43
The nature of Romanism, as exhibited in the Missions of the Jesuits and other orders. 1849 8/6/49
Seymour, Richard Canon of Worcester
Diocesan synods. A letter. 1867 4/1/69
Shadows from the Cross. 1879 1/6/79
Shadows of a sick room. 1873 25/1/74
Shadwell, Charles
The Purgatory of Dante . . . introduced by W. Pater. 1892 (2v. 1892–9) 12/2/93
Shadwell, Lancelot of St. John's, Cambridge
The Iliad of Homer faithfully rendered in Homeric verse. 1844 26/4/62
Shadwell, Lancelot Vice-Chancellor of England
The Unitarians defeated . . . substance of the judgement in Attorney General v. Shore. 1834 6/2/34
Shaffner, Taliaferro Preston
The war in America . . . showing the origin and cause of the present secession war. 1862 15/5/62
Shahamat Ali
The Sikhs and Afghans, in connexion with India and Persia . . . from the journal of an expedition to Kabul. 1847 17/1/49
Shakespeare, William; [s = seen]
A Midsummer Night's Dream. 30/5/55, 6/8/59 s, 3/11/70 s
A Winter's Tale. 13/11/37, 3/7/56 s, 17/6/81 s
Antony and Cleopatra. 21/4/70, 1/12/73 , 2/12/73, 6/12/90 s, 20/1/94, 29/1/94, 6/2/94
As You Like It. 11/6/55, 5/3/66, 19/3/66, 19/2/74
Coriolanus. 10/10/56, 24/6/69, 1/7/69
Cymbeline. 17/6/80, 6/6/93, 12/2/94, 12/11/94
Hamlet, Prince of Denmark. 24/8/27 s, 29/7/61, 12/8/61 s, 22/2/68, 16/4/75 s, 4/3/76, 8/5/76, 13/5/76, 17/11/76 s, 18/11/76, 19/2/79 s, 24/3/79 s, 25/3/79
Henry IV, Part I. 17/9/27, 22/11/33, 14/6/55, 22/6/55, 21/8/57, 9/6/61, 27/10/62, 2/1/63, 22/4/64 s, 30/5/71, 21/10/81, 29/3/94
Henry IV, Part II. 19/9/27, 19/10/27, 25/11/33, 21/6/55, 31/5/71, 30/12/87, 2/4/94
Henry V. 2/12/33, 10/11/53 s, 25/6/55, 5/5/59 s, 3/11/62, 31/5/71, 31/12/87, 6/4/94
Henry VI, Part I. 11/12/33, 29/6/55, 28/12/64, 1/6/71, 19/5/82, 2/3/94
Henry VI, Part II. 13/12/33, 2/6/71, 26/5/82, 13/3/94
Henry VI, Part III. 14/12/33, 6/7/55, 2/6/71, 16/3/94
Henry VIII. 26/12/61, 20/4/65, 18/3/69, 5/3/78, 23/7/80, 24/7/80, 11/5/92 s, 12/5/92, 24/5/93
Introduction to the philosophy of Shakespeare's sonnets, by R. Simpson. 1868 4/6/68
Julius Caesar. 15/5/69, 21/4/93, 4/11/93, 11/11/93, 15/11/93
King John. 29/3/31, 4/8/55, 31/5/64, 17/7/67, 31/10/71 s, 28/4/77, 9/4/94
King Lear. 18/5/26, 20/6/33, 29/10/35, 19/10/52, 29/5/58 s, 10/6/58 s, 9/10/65, 25/10/65 s, 29/6/80, 26/6/88, 21/11/92 s, 22/11/92, 5/6/93
Love's Labour Lost. 13/6/55, 15/7/80

Shakespeare, William (*cont.*)
Macbeth. 31/1/26, 10/7/27, 4/6/33, 10/11/37, 10/2/64, 19/10/64 s, 26/2/76, 28/6/89, 25/6/93
Measure for Measure. 14/3/27, 8/7/80
Much Ado About Nothing. 26/3/27, 13/7/80, 25/10/82 s, 29/1/91 s
Othello. 10/11/28, 5/12/29, 14/12/29, 8/8/55, 4/11/65, 7/11/65, 19/2/76 s, 20/9/76 s, 1/10/80 s, 15/6/81 s, 17/6/81, 29/12/93, 4/1/94, 18/1/94
Pericles, Prince of Tyre. 6/2/28, 19/4/70, 18/12/93
Richard II. 19/10/27, 7/7/55, 22/4/57 s, 16/5/57 s, 20/8/57, 22/3/94
Richard III. 15/11/26, 8/9/31, 5/8/62, 3/6/71, 4/5/77 s, 22/2/94
Romeo and Juliet. 21/1/29, 30/3/31, 21/10/37, 7/8/63, 28/11/71, 20/5/76, 24/7/79 s, 8/7/82 s, 8/11/84 s
The Comedy of Errors. 22/3/31, 8/11/37, 28/4/77
The Merchant of Venice. 27/10/47, 1/6/55, 13/7/58 s, 10/2/74, 12/2/74, 13/2/74 s, 25/7/77, 28/2/80 s
The Merry Wives of Windsor. 31/3/57, 2/4/57, 24/4/68, 1/9/88, 21/5/94
The Taming of the Shrew. 1/2/26, 15/7/33, 18/2/81, 30/3/81
The Tempest. 22/3/27, 8/10/33, 5/4/34, 18/10/56, 8/8/57 s, 31/7/79, 22/5/94
The Two Gentlemen of Verona. 2/8/28, 8/4/31, 8/8/45, 18/4/70
Timon of Athens. 2/2/93
Titus Andronicus. 18/4/70
Troilus and Cressida. 2/2/28, 27/6/33, 11/12/55, 12/11/56
Twelfth Night, or what you will. 12/8/45
Shakspeare, Charles
St. Paul at Athens. 1878 9/2/79
Shall Gothic architecture be denied fair play?. 1860 4/5/60
Shand, Mr.
[Letter to Stanley]. (untraced) 24/4/33
Sharman, Henry Risborough
The Fire Duty. The duty on fire insurance: reasons for its abolition or reduction. 1861 11/1/61
Sharp, Sir Cuthbert
Memorials of the rebellion of 1569. 1840 15/1/47
Sharp, Elizabeth Amelia
Songs and poems of the sea. 1888 26/3/90
Sharp, Major Jelf
Correspondence between Major Jelf Sharp and the Warden of Trinity College, Glenalmond. 1848 28/2/48
Sharp, Sarah
Idolatry. 1891 12/4/91
Sharp, William poet
Life of P. B. Shelley. 1887 5/6/89
Life of Robert Browning. 1891 8/9/91
Sharpe, Benjamin
Plan for an extension of the currency. 1847 26/11/47
Sharpe, Edmund
A letter on branch railways. 1857 13/3/58
Sharpe, Henry Edward
On the abolition of the negro apprenticeship. 1838 29/3/38
Sharpe, William M.D., writer of verse
Man a splendid creation. 1873 21/1/74
The conqueror's dream, and other poems. 1878 21/5/78
Shaw, Sir Charles
The abuses of the Irish Church. 1866 30/3/69
Shaw, George Bernard
Cashel Byron's profession. 1886 28/2/88
Shaw, Morton
National Education and the Conscience Clause. A letter to the Bishop of Ely. 1870 23/1/70
The burial question. 1879 14/4/79
The position of the Holy Table considered with regard to the position of the celebrant. 1874 31/3/75
Shaw, Thomas George
Wine, the vine, and the cellar. 1863 4/11/63
Shaw, William M.A.
Memoirs of the life and writings of Samuel Johnson. 1785 7/11/86 ?
Shaw, William of Limerick
Irish trade. 1889 21/1/89
Shaw, William Rector of Chelvy
A sermon [on John xviii. 37]. 1810 2/9/55
Shea, George
Alexander Hamilton. 1877 14/3/77
Shee, Sir Martin Archer
Alasco; a tragedy . . . excluded from the stage by the Lord Chamberlain. 1824 28/10/85
Letter to Lord John Russell . . . on the alleged claim of the public to be admitted gratis to the exhibition of the Royal Academy. 1837 21/8/37
Shee, Sir William
Papers, letters and speeches in the House of Commons on the Irish land question, with a summary of its parliamentary history. 1863 23/10/69
Shelley, Mary Wollstonecraft
Frankenstein, or the Modern Prometheus. 1818 12/1/35, 13/1/35
Shelley, Percy Bysshe
Alastor; or the spirit of solitude. 1816 9/11/29, 3/11/30, 9/11/30, 29/3/31
An address to the Irish people. 1812 17/7/86
Essays, letters from abroad, translations and fragments, ed. Mary Shelley. 1840 (2v.) 10/2/40

Life of Shelley, by W. Sharp. 1887 5/6/89
Posthumous poems, ed. Mary Shelley. 1824 9/11/29, 30/6/32, 8/10/33
Prometheus Unbound. 1820 10/11/29
Queen Mab: a philosophical poem; with notes. 1813 2/2/30
Relics of P. B. Shelley, ed. R. Garnett. 1862 16/6/72
Shelley: sa vie et ses oeuvres, by F. Rabbe. 1887 12/4/92
The Cenci. 1819 13/11/29, 9/10/33
The revolt of Islam. 1818 16/3/32

Shepherd, Henry
Cursory remarks on the inefficiency of the ecclesiastical establishment in India. 1827 28/8/28

Shepherd, John C.
The Anti-Game Law prize essay. 1847 24/2/48

Shepherd, William
Life of Poggio Bracciolini. 1802 15/11/34

Sheppard, John of Frome
An autumn dream: thoughts in verse on the intermediate state of happy spirits. 1837 26/2/37
Essays designed to afford Christian encouragement. 1833 16/9/90

Sheppard, John George
The Christian obligations of citizenship. 1847 8/12/47

Sheridan, Charles Brinsley
Songs of Greece from the Romaic text, by C. C. Fauriel, tr. C. B. Sheridan. 1825 16/8/59

Sheridan, Richard Brinsley Butler
A Trip to Scarborough. 1781 16/9/72
Sheridaniana. 1826 3/4/27
Speech ... in reply to Mr. Pitt's speech on the Union with Ireland. 1799 19/9/85
The Camp. 1778 26/5/55
The Critic. 1781 26/5/55, 27/8/60
The Rivals. 1775 29/8/60
The School for Scandal. 1781 28/8/60

Sheridan, Thomas Jacobite
A discourse on the rise and power of Parliaments. 22/11/86

Sheridan, Thomas M.A.
Life of Jonathan Swift. 1784 17/7/46

Sherlock, William Canon of Kildare
An essay on future punishment. 1865 5/10/65

Sherlock, William Dean of St. Paul's
A practical discourse of religious assemblies, ed. H. Melville. 1840 27/9/40

Shimmin, Hugh
The courts and alleys of Liverpool, described from personal inspection. 1864 26/3/64

Shipley, Orby
A specimen of recent Anglican controversy with Rome. 1880 13/6/80
Invocation of saints and angels. 1869 4/7/69
Secular judgements in spiritual matters. 1871 30/4/71
Six short sermons on sin. 1867 1/9/67
The Church and the World. Essays on questions of the day, ed. O. Shipley. 1866 13/5/66
The daily sacrifice and divine liturgy. 1868 13/2/70
The four cardinal virtues considered in relation to the public and private life of Catholics. 1867 18/12/70
The liturgies of 1549 and 1662. 1866 20/5/66

Shirley, Evelyn Philip
Some account of English deer parks. 1867 20/9/67

Shirley, James
Poems. 12/1/49
The contention of Ajax and Ulysses, for the armor of Achilles. 25/11/56

Shirley, John
Evenings with Homer. 1869 12/4/69

Shirley, Walter Waddington
Some account of the Church in the Apostolic Age. 1867 23/8/68
Undogmatic Christianity. A sermon. 1863 15/11/63

Shoberl, Frederick
Persecutions of popery; historical narratives of the most remarkable persecutions occasioned by the intolerance of the Church of Rome. 1844 (2v.) 19/7/44

Shooter, Joseph
The Kafirs of Natal and the Zulu country. 1857 26/12/73

Shore, Charles John Baron Teignmouth
Reminiscences of many years. 1878 (2v.) 11/3/79

Shore, Emily
Journal of Emily Shore, ed. M. E. Shore. 1891 26/4/91

Shore, Frederick John
Notes on Indian affairs. 1837 (2v.) 17/1/49

Shore, James
The case of the Rev. Mr. Shore [in answer to Phillpotts]. 1849 25/5/49

Shore, Thomas Teignmouth
Some difficulties of belief. 1877 30/3/77

Short, Thomas Vowler
A sketch of the history of the Church of England to the Revolution, 1688. 1832 (2v.) 21/1/34
Charge. 1853 27/11/53
Charge. 1856 12/10/56
Charge. 1865 10/12/65, 19/11/71
Letter to the Dean of Christ Church on the state of the public examinations in the University of Oxford. 1822 12/2/29
National education, and the means of improving it. 1835 3/2/36
Sermons on some of the fundamental truths of Christianity. 1829 10/1/30

Shorthouse, John Henry
Blanche Lady Falaise: a tale. 1891 1/12/92
John Inglesant; a romance. 1880 14/7/81, 10/10/82
Little schoolmaster Mark. 1883 5/1/85
Sir Percival. A story of the past and the present. 1886 2/11/86, 4/11/86
The Temple, by George Herbert, with an introductory essay by J. H. Shorthouse. 1882 25/6/82
Shrewsbury, John Vincent Brainerd
Memorials of W. J. Shrewsbury. 1868 27/9/68
Shulte, R. N.
Life, times and writings of Dr. H. Phillpotts, Lord Bishop of Exeter. 1863 14/7/64
Shurdham, Edward Barton
Clergyman's sore throat, or, follicular disease of the pharynx. 1878 9/8/78
Shutte, Reginald Neale
A memoir of the late Rev. H. Newland. 1861 23/6/61
The life, times, and writings of Dr. H. Phillpotts, Lord Bishop of Exeter. 1863 14/7/64
Shuttleworth, Sir John Phillips Kay
A scheme for the local and general administration of endowments, especially those of middle-class education. 1866 21/2/67
Letter to Earl Granville on the Revised Code of regulations . . . on education. 1861 11/11/61
Public education, as affected by the Minutes of the Committee of the Privy Council. 1853 13/2/53
Recent measures for the promotion of education in England. 1839 12/10/39
Report on the training of pauper children. 1839 9/2/41
Shuttleworth, Philip Nicholas Bishop of Chester
Not tradition but revelation. 1838 9/9/38
Sermons on some of the leading principles of Christianity. 1827 5/4/29
Sibree, James
Richard Cobden; philanthropist and statesman. 1865 28/5/65
Sibree, Marie
The credentials of conscience. A few reasons for the popularity of Ecce Homo. 1868 19/4/68
Sibree, Peter
Memoir of Joseph Sturge. 1862 29/5/64
Sibthorp, Sir Christopher
A friendly advertisement to the pretended Catholics of Ireland. (2v.) 27/11/87
Sibthorp, Richard Waldo
A further answer to the enquiry: Why are you become a Catholic?. 1842 27/4/42
Some answer to the enquiry: Why are you become a Catholic?. 1842 20/1/42
The claims of the Catholic Church. 1841 25/11/41
Sicherer, Hermann von
Ueber Eherecht und Ehegerichtsbarkeit in Bayern. 1875 17/2/75
Sidgwick, Cecily pseud. Mrs. Andrew Dean
Isaac Eller's money. 1889 28/1/93
Sidgwick, H.
'Idle Fellowships' in *Contemporary Review*, xxvii. 679. 1876 (April 1876) 1/4/76
Sidney, Edwin
Life of Sir Richard Hill, bart., M.P. 1839 2/3/56
Life of the Rev. Rowland Hill. 1833 10/1/38, 6/1/50, 10/10/58
The life, ministry, and selections from the remains of the Rev. Samuel Walker. 1835 2/8/68
Sidney, Samuel
Australian handbook. 1848 7/4/49
Sigerson, George
Modern Ireland: its vital questions, secret societies . . . by an Ulsterman. 1868 17/11/68
Political prisoners at home and abroad. 1890 21/1/90
Sikes, Charles William
Good times; or, the savings bank and the fire-side. 1854 24/12/56
Post Office Savings Bank. A letter to . . . W. E. Gladstone. 1859 29/11/59
Siljeström, Pehr Adam
Vaccinationsfragan. 1874 8/12/76
Sillard, P. A.
Life and letters of John Martin . . . and other 'Young Irelanders'. 1893 24/6/93
Silver domino, The. 1892 (3rd. edn) 8/10/92
Silver whistle, The. 1889 (2v.) 26/12/89
Simcox, E.
'On the influence of J. S. Mill' in *Contemporary Review*, xxii. 297. 1873 (July 1873) 13/7/73
Simcox, George Augustus
A letter to G. A. Simcox . . . from a friend . . . lately received into the Catholic Church. 1866 2/12/66
Simeon, Charles
Memoirs of the life of the Rev. Charles Simeon, ed. W. Carus. 1847 17/5/47
Simmonds, Peter Lund
Waste products and undeveloped substances: or, hints for enterprise in neglected fields. 1862 8/6/63
Simms, Charles S.
The first Book of the Iliad, tr. C. S. Simms. 1866 9/6/74
Simms, Samuel
The oath of allegiance; what it imports. 1877 23/9/77
Simon, David Worthington
The Bible an outgrowth of theocratic life. 1886 26/6/91
Simon, G. Eugène
La Cité chinoise. 1885 26/2/86

Simon, Sir John
Report on the Contagious Diseases Act, showing the expense, impolicy, and general inutility of its proposed extension to the civilian population. 1871 2/6/69
Simon, Jules F.
La Religion naturelle. 1856 3/2/67
Le gouvernement de M. Thiers . . . 1873. 1879 6/2/79
Simon, Oswald John
The world and the cloister. 1890 (2v.) 15/1/90
Simon, Richard
Critical history of the Old Testament. (4v.) 8/3/91
Simon, St.
Historical works, ed. J Stevenson. 1855 1/5/57
Simon, Thomas Collins
The mission and martyrdom of St. Peter. 1852 20/2/76
Simond, Louis
A tour in Italy and Sicily. 1828 13/4/29
Simpson, Alexander
The Oregon Territory. Claims thereupon by England and America considered. 1846 18/6/57
Simpson, Forster George
Lectures on the typical character of the Jewish Tabernacle, priesthood and sacrifices. 1852 30/4/60
Simpson, James advocate
The philosophy of education, with its practical application to a system of popular education as a national objective. 1834 26/3/41
Simpson, Sir James Young
Anaesthesia, or, the employment of chloroform and ether in surgery, midwifery. 1849 16/1/60
Antiquarian notices of syphilis in Scotland in the 15th and 16th centuries. 1862 22/5/62 ?
Hospitalism. 1869 30/7/69
Simpson, Margaret Eleanor Barbour afterw. Root
Building for God, or houses not made with hands. 1887 16/10/87
Simpson, Mary E.
Ploughing and sowing; or, annals of an evening school in a Yorkshire village. 1861 23/1/61
Simpson, Richard
Introduction to the philosophy of Shakespeare's sonnets. 1868 4/6/68
Simpson, Robert
Remarks on a pamphlet [on anti-Popery]. 1835 4/1/35
Sermons, doctrinal, experimental, and practical. 1836 26/7/36
Simpson, Thomas
Life and travels of Thomas Simpson. 1845 11/8/48
Narrative of the discoveries on the North Coast of America, effected by the officers of the Hudson's Bay Company 1836–39. 1843 10/8/44
Simpson, William
A private journal kept during the Niger expedition, from May 1841, until June 1842. 1843 9/2/44 ?
Sims, Thomas
Brief memorials of J. F. Oberlin . . . with an introductory sketch of the history of Christianity in France. 1830 25/8/33
Sinclair, Catherine
Modern accomplishments, or the march of intellect. 1836 11/8/36
Scotland and the Scotch, or the Western Circuit . . . Shetland and the Shetlanders. 1840 8/12/87 ?
The journey of life. 1847 27/2/66
Sinclair, Sir George
Selection from the correspondence carried on . . . for the adjustment of the Scottish church question. 1842 5/12/42
Sinclair, John Archdeacon of Middlesex
[tract]. 28/1/34
Carthaginian and British mercenaries compared; a sermon. 1857 6/9/57
Charge. 1844 9/6/44
Charge. 1865 21/5/65
Charge. 1867 9/6/67
Charge. 1873 1/6/73
Church questions of 1853. 1853 15/5/53
Church rates . . . a charge. 1860 5/8/60, 21/7/62
Dissertations vindicating the Church of England. 1833 5/10/34, 5/4/43
Essay on church patronage. 1835 6/11/41
Great Britain and America. A farewell sermon preached in . . . New York. 1853 25/12/53
How to find out God. A charge. 1863 15/5/64
Remarks on the Common School system of the U.S. 1857 9/3/57
Two charges . . . in 1861 and 1862. 1863 17/5/63
Sinclair, John M.P.
Scenes and stories of the North of Scotland. 1890 (2v. 1890–1) 29/7/90
Sinclair, John poet
Nakiketas, and other poems. 1887 8/8/88
Sinclair, Sir John
Observations on the Scottish dialect. 1782 9/10/58, 2/9/85
Statistical account of Scotland; drawn up from the communications of the ministers of the various parishes. 1791 (21v. 1791–9) 26/1/76, 3/9/85
The history of the public revenue of the British Empire. 1784 (3v. 1784–90) 2/12/52
Sinclair, Sir John George Tollemache
A defence of Russia and the Christians of Turkey; including a sketch of the Eastern Question, from 1686 to September 1877. 1877 21/11/77

Sinclair, Thomas
The Mount; speech from its English heights. 1878 12/8/79
Sinclair, William
Sermon. (not found) 12/12/37
Uniomachia. 18/12/33
Sinding, Paul C.
History of Scandinavia. 1866 20/3/66
Singer, Samuel Weller
Researches into the history of playing cards. 1816 19/1/77
Sinnett, Alfred Percy
Esoteric Buddhism. 1883 26/8/83
'Sir William Dunbar and the Scottish schism: a letter to [Blomfield], etc.' by a Presyter of Aberdeen. 1845 23/6/45
Sismondi, Jean Charles Léonard Simonde de
Etudes sur l'économie politique. 1837 (2v. 1837–8) 18/3/37
Sismondi, Jean Charles Leonard Simonde de
Etudes sur les sciences sociales. 1836 (2v. 1836–8) 4/1/54, 22/6/54, 23/9/54
Histoire de la renaissance de la liberté en Italie. 1832 (2v.) 13/8/67
Histoire des Français. 1821 (31v. 1821–44) 25/10/70
Histoire des Républiques italiennes du moyen age. 1807 (16v. 1807–18) 6/4/33, 15/7/34
History of the fall of the Roman Empire. 1834 (2v.) 18/3/37 ?
Sittenfeld, Conrad pseud. Conrad Alberti
Gustav Freytag... Ein Festblatt zur Feier seines siebzigsten Geburtstags. 1886 24/10/90
Six sermons preached at the consecration of the church of St. John... Jedburgh. 1845 31/8/45
Six years travels in Russia. By an English lady. 1859 (2v.) 18/2/63
Skeffington, Sydney W.
The sinless sufferer. Six sermons. 1872 29/3/72
Skeleton at the plough. 10/5/75
Skelton, Sir John
The great Lord Bolingbroke, Henry St. John. 1868 27/11/76
The impeachment of Mary Stuart, sometime Queen of Scots. 1876 29/11/76
Skene, William Forbes
Celtic Scotland. 1876 (3v. 1876) 28/6/76
Sketches of Ultramontane action. 1873 29/10/73
Sketchley, R. F.
Notes on Newark. A lecture. 1860 13/1/60
Skey, Robert S.
Birmingham and Liverpool Junction Canal. Report to the Committee. 1841 11/1/42
Skinner, James Vicar of Newland
An act of spiritual communion. 1880 10/4/81
The revelation of the Anti-Christ: and how to receive it. 1861 1/12/61
Skinner, John Bishop
Primitive truth and order vindicated from modern misrepresentation: with a defence of episcopacy, particularly that of Scotland. 1803 14/8/42
Skinner, John Dean
An ecclesiastical history of Scotland. 1788 (2v.) 22/10/44
Songs and poems... with a sketch of his life by H. G. Reid. 1859 25/5/85
Skinner, John Edwin Hilary
Roughing it in Crete in 1867. 1868 8/1/68
Slack, Henry James
The philosophy of progress in human affairs. 1860 20/11/60
Slade, Sir Adolphus
Maritime states and military navies. 1859 3/12/59
Slade, James
An explanation of the Psalms. 1832 16/3/34, 27/7/34
Slater, Edward
Letters on Roman Catholic tenets... and on the supposed connexion of Catholicism with the late rebellion in Ireland. 1813 24/11/74
Slater, Thomas Ebenezer
The philosophy of missions, a present day plea. 1882 31/8/83
Slatter, John
Church endowments. 1868 20/12/68
Slaughter, Mihill
Railway intelligence. 1849 16/10/52
Sleeman, William Henry
A journey to the Kingdom of Oude in 1849, 1850. 1858 2/4/58
Slight, Henry Spencer
A letter to the Bishop of Oxford... suggestive of means for supplying the present want of colonial clergy and missionaries. 1848 30/12/48
Sloan, J. McGavin
New aids to reflection. 1889 11/8/89
Small, Annie Hunter
Light and shade in Zenana missionary life. 1890 4/1/91
Small, John M.A.
The monarche and other poems of Sir D. Lindsay. 1883 25/2/83
Small, John of Fetter Lane
Caution!!! to the Brighton shareholders and the public at large, against the Crystal Palace removal to Sydenham. 1852 3/7/52
Smart, Christopher
The poems of the late Christopher Smart. 1791 (2v.) 20/11/81 ?
Smart, Newton
The Ecclesiastical Commission considered: and suggestions offered for increasing the efficiency of the Church. 1839 25/4/39
Smart, William
A disciple of Plato. A critical study of John Ruskin. 1883 26/10/80 ?

Smedes, Susan Dabney
Memorials of a Southern Planter. 1887 7/10/89, 4/11/89
Smedley, Edward
History of the Reformed Religion in France. 1832 (3v. 1832–4) 30/12/32
Smee, Alfred
Principles of the human mind. 1849 22/4/52
Smee, William Ray
Three letters to [Gladstone]. 1. the gold discoveries, silver and gold; 2.the gold discoveries, paper and credit; 3.the civil service. 1861 3/1/61
Smellie, Alexander
The romances of King Arthur. 1877 30/8/77
Smiles, Robert
Brief memoir of W. Muir. 1888 7/8/89
Smiles, Samuel
A publisher and his friends. Memoir... of John Murray. 1891 23/3/91
George Moore, merchant and philanthropist. 1878 26/5/78
Industrial biography; ironworkers and toolmakers. 1863 5/11/63
James Nasmyth. An autobiography, ed. S. Smiles. 1883 10/2/83
Lives of the engineers, with an account of their principal works. 1861 (3v. 1861–2) 23/1/62
Robert Dick, baker, of Thurso, geologist and botanist. 1878 21/11/78
Self-Help; with illustrations of character and conduct. 1859 9/1/60, 10/10/61
The Hugenots; their settlements, churches, industries in England and Ireland. 1867 1/4/68
Workmen's earnings, strikes and savings. 1861 26/6/61
Smith, Adam
An enquiry into the nature and causes of the wealth of nations [further eds. by D. Buchanan, 4v. 1814, by J. R. MacCulloch, 4v. 1828]. 1776 (3v.) 12/3/41, 30/9/41, 1/11/41, 9/5/43, 15/8/46, 18/8/46, 29/10/46, 12/12/63, 31/5/76
Life of Adam Smith, by R. B. Haldane. 1887 3/10/87
Smith, Albert Richard
The adventures of Mr. Ledbury, and his friend Jack Johnson. 1844 (3v.) 3/12/57
Smith, Alexander
A summer in Skye. 1866 11/1/73
Poems. 1853 26/9/53
Smith, Benjamin
The power of the tongue; or, chapters for talkers. 1863 3/8/64 ?
Smith, C.
The repentance of Paul Wentworth. A novel. 1889 (3v.) 9/12/90
Smith, Catherine Barnard
Poems. 1869 11/12/69
Smith, Charles Rector of Newton
An inquiry into the Catholic truths hidden under certain articles of the creed of the Church of Rome. 1844 (4v. 1844–56) 27/4/62
Truths hidden by the false witness of Convocation. 1834 24/4/38
Smith, Charles Edward
The world lighted; a study of the Apocalypse. 1890 23/11/90
Smith, Charles Hamilton
The natural history of horses. 1841 3/1/82
Smith, Sir Culling Eardley afterw. Eardley
Christianity in Turkey. Correspondence of the governments of Christendom relating to executions in Turkey for apostacy from Islamism. 1855 26/4/56
The Book of Common Prayer... slightly altered. 1854 10/12/54
The rights of the laity in the universities. A letter to Lord Monteagle, and correspondence with the Rev. Dr. Hawkins. 1856 8/3/56
Smith, E. B.
An appeal to the General Assembly of the Presbyterian Church. 1875 5/12/75
Smith, Edmund James
Two letters... on the origin and progress of the Ecclesiastical Commission. 1863 4/11/63
Smith, Eliza
Five years a Catholic: with indictments of foreign convent life. 1850 20/7/51
The progress of beguilement to Romanism. A personal narrative. 1850 20/7/51
Smith, F.R.
Old Testament in the Jewish church. 1881 24/4/81
Smith, George Bishop of Victoria
A narrative of an explanatory visit to... China, and to the islands of Hong Kong and Chusan, in behalf of the C. M. S. 1847 27/7/50
Our national relations with China. 1857 10/6/57
Smith, George F. A. S.
Life and reign of King David. 1867 4/2/77
The Cassiterdes: an inquiry into the commercial operations of the Phoenicians in Western Europe, with particular reference to the British coal trade. 1863 19/10/65
Smith, George Minister of Birse
Truth as revealed, of Voluntaryism and Free Churchism opposed to the Word of God. 1847 19/11/48
Smith, George Minister of Trinity, Poplar
The right of private judgement. 1851 2/4/51 ?
Smith, George of Coalville
Our canal population. The sad condition of the women and children. 1875 25/1/76
The cry of the children from the brickyards of England; a statement and an appeal, with remedy. 1871 9/9/71

Smith, George of the British Museum
Assyrian discoveries... on the site of Nineveh. 1875 12/1/90
Notes on the early history of Assyria and Babylonia. 1872 15/8/85
The Chaldean account of Genesis. 1876 4/12/76, 24/7/85, 14/1/90
Smith, Sir George Adam
The Book of Isaiah. 1889 (2v. 1889–90) 3/1/92
Smith, George Barnett
Sir Robert Peel. 1881 9/7/81
Smith, George Vance
Christians and Christians. 1883 6/5/88
The bible and its theology. 1892 22/5/92
The bible and popular theology; a restatement of truths... with special reference to recent works by... W. E. Gladstone and others. 1871 4/6/71
The spirit and word of Christ. 1874 28/6/74
Smith, Goldwin
[On Canada] in *Nineteenth Century*, xx. 14. 1886 (July 1886) 12/7/86
[On the election] in *Nineteenth Century*, xx. 305. 1886 (September 1886) 29/9/86
A plea for the abolition of tests in the university of Oxford. 1864 11/3/68
Canada and the Canadian question... with map. 1891 7/5/91
Essays on questions of the day. 1894 22/4/94
Irish history and Irish character. 1861 25/10/61
The civil war in America: an address... at... Manchester union and emancipation society. 1866 23/3/66
The foundation of the American colonies. A lecture. 1861 23/12/61
The Irish question. Three letters to the editor of the Daily News. 1868 24/1/68
The relations between America and England. A reply to the late speech of Mr. Sumner. 1869 29/6/69
The study of history. A lecture. 1859 2/8/59
Three English statesmen (Pym, Cromwell, Pitt), a course of lectures on the political history of England. 1867 6/8/67, 9/7/86
Smith, Henry Minister of St. Clement Danes
The sermons of Mr. Henry Smith... with a memoir... by Thomas Fuller... 1866 (2v. 1866) 1/3/85
Smith, Horatio
Brambletye House; or cavaliers and roundheads, a novel. 1826 (3v. 1826) 7/12/26
Smith, Isaac Gregory
Anarchy: an appeal to members of the Church of England. 1867 23/10/67
Characteristics of Christian morality. Considered in eight lectures. 1873 10/8/73
Smith, James Baptist minister
Food for the Soul. 1873 17/12/76
Smith, James, and Smith, Horatio solicitor to the ordnance
Rejected addresses, or the new theatrum poetarum. 1812 19/11/41, 20/2/61, 21/4/70
Smith, John A. civil engineer
A treatise on land surveying in theory and practice. 1869 4/1/69
Smith, John Benjamin
An enquiry into the causes of money panics... letter to M. Ross. 1866 28/3/73
Smith, John Cotton
[work on Gladstone's 'Homer']. (not found) 21/2/76
Evolution and a personal creator. 1874 7/9/79
Smith, John Pye
The necessity of religion to the well-being of a nation. 1834 26/6/38
Smith, John Stores
Social Aspects. 1850 21/11/52
Smith, John Thomas Keeper of Prints in the British Museum
Nollekens and his times, from... Roubiliac... to ... Blake. 1828 (2v. 1828) 11/8/86
Smith, Joshua Toulmin
Local self-government and centralization: the characteristics of each, and its practical tendencies. 1851 13/8/87 ?
Parallels between the constitution and constitutional history of England and Hungary. 1849 26/4/49
Smith, Mary Rebecca Darby
Recollections of... La Marquise de Boissy and the Count de Waldeck. 1878 2/11/80
Smith, Oswald A.
Auburnia. 1891 25/2/91
Smith, Philip B.A.
A smaller ancient history of the East. 1871 26/8/72
Smith, Protheroe
Scriptural authority for the mitigation of the pains of labour by chloroform. 1848 12/12/69 ?
Smith, Reginald Bosworth
Carthage and the Carthaginians. 1878 15/5/78
Life of Lord Lawrence... with portraits and maps. 1883 (2v. 1883) 26/9/83
Mohammed and Mohammedism. 1874 13/5/74
Smith, Richard Travers
Doctrinal revision: a sermon. 1872 19/1/73
Smith, Robert Pearsall
International copyright by an American. 1886 8/1/86
Smith, Samuel M.P.
The credibility of the Christian religion. 1872 25/12/72
Smith, Samuel Vicar of Lois-Weedon
A word in season... addressed to the stout British farmer. 1849 16/9/54

Smith, Sydney Canon of St. Paul's
'On Mrs. Trimmer of Lancaster's plan of education' in *Edinburgh Review*, ix. 177. 1806 (October 1806) 19/3/35
A letter to Archdeacon Singleton, on the Ecclesiastical Commission. 1837 4/2/37
Ballot. 1839 18/2/39, 24/5/49
Catholic claims. 1825 5/4/45
Elementary sketches of moral philosophy, delivered ... in ... 1804, 1805 and 1806. 1850 6/5/55
Letters on the subject of the Catholics to my brother Abraham, by Peter Plymley [Sidney Smith]. 1808 6/8/40
Second letter to Archdeacon Singleton, being the third of the cathedral letters. 1838 30/5/38
Selections from the letters of Sydney Smith. 1854 (2v. 1854) 13/2/55
The wit and wisdom of the Rev. Sydney Smith. 1860 13/6/67
Third letter to Archdeacon Singleton. 1839 25/2/39
Two volumes of sermons. 1809 (2v. 1809) 30/11/39, 13/1/45

Smith, Sydney Fenn
The alleged antiquity of Anglicanism. A reply to Lord Selborne. 1888 14/10/88

Smith, Theyre Townsend Vicar of Wymondham
Remarks on the influence of Tractarianism ... in promoting secessions to the Church of Rome. 1851 10/8/51

Smith, Thomas fellow of Magdalen College, Oxford
'Enautikon'; sive de causis remediisque dissidiorum ... 13/1/43
An account of the Greek Church ... under Cyrillus Lucaris. 13/1/43

Smith, Walter Chalmers
Kildrostan. A dramatic poem. 1884 28/5/84
Olrig Grange. 1872 18/3/72
Raban: or, life-splinters. 1880 9/12/80

Smith, William D.D., Provost of College of Philadelphia
Discourses on several public occasions during the war in America. 1759 24/9/37

Smith, Sir William LL.D.
A classical dictionary of Greek and Roman biography, mythology and geography. 1842 10/10/56 n, 3/10/63
A dictionary of Greek and Roman antiquities. 1842 7/11/61
A dictionary of the Bible, ed. W. Smith. 3/3/91

Smith, William Frank verse writer
Poems. 1864 25/9/75

Smith, William Henry
Life and times of W. H. Smith, by H. E. Maxwell. 1893 (2v.) 8/9/93

Smith, William Robertson
Lectures on the religion of the Semites. 1889 18/4/90, 1/6/90
The prophets of Israel and their place in history to the close of the eighth century B.C. 1882 7/5/82

Smith-Neill, James George
Historical record of the ... East India Company's 1st Madras European regiment ... by a staff officer. 1843 14/4/57 ?

Smithson, David J.
Elocution and the dramatic art. 1887 1/8/89

Smollett, Tobias George
The history of England ... designed as a continuation of Mr. Hume's. 1790 5/6/26

Smyth, Charles Piazzi
Life and work at the great pyramid ... during ... 1865. 1867 (3v. 1867) 30/7/71
Our inheritance in the Great Pyramid. 1880 (4th edn) 18/6/84

Smyth, Sir James Carmichael
Precis of the wars in Canada, from 1755 to the Treaty of Ghent in 1814. 1826 6/5/62

Smyth, John Paterson
How God inspired the Bible. Thoughts for the present disquiet. 1892 30/10/92
How we got our Bible: an answer to questions suggested by the new revision. 1885 24/11/89, 1/4/90, 9/4/90

Smyth, Newman
Old faiths in new light. 1879 19/7/85

Smyth, Robert Carmichael
[on B. N. A. railway]. (not found) 13/3/49
Memorandum on the necessity of a secretary of state for our defence and war establishment. 1852 20/2/52

Smyth, William Professor of modern history in Cambridge
English lyricks. 1797 21/5/65
Lectures on modern history. Second ... series. On the French Revolution. 1840 (3v. 1840) 6/3/41 ?
Memoir of Mr. Sheridan. 1840 2/7/41

Smyth, William Woods
An examination of Mr. H. Drummond's work, 'Natural law in the spiritual world'. 1884 14/12/84 ?
The government of God: embracing agnosticism, evolution, and Christianity. 1882 10/9/82

Smythe, Lady Emily Anne née Beaufort, Viscountess Strangford
The eastern shores of the Adriatic in 1863. 1864 10/4/77

Smythe, George Augustus Frederick Percy Sydney 7th Viscount Strangford
Angela Pisani: a novel ... with a brief memoir of the author [Viscountess Strangford]. 1875 (3v. 1875) 30/3/75
Historic fancies. 1844 15/11/44

Smythe, Percy Ellen Frederick William 8th Viscount Strangford
Original letters and papers . . . upon philological and kindred subjects, ed. Viscountess Strangford. 1878 22/3/78
Snow, Rev. George D'Oyly
'Post tenebras lux'; or the gospel message to him who desires to believe . . . introduction by F. D. Maurice. 1864 25/4/64
Snyder, A. E.
The civil war from a Southern standpoint. 1890 28/1/91
Soames, Henry
An inquiry into the doctrines of the Anglo-Saxon Church . . . At the lecture founded by . . . John Bampton. 1830 9/5/30
The history of the reformation of the Church of England. 1826 (4v. 1826–8) 26/8/60, 25/9/89
Soans, Richard Gilbert
Sermons for the young. 1891 11/3/94 ?
Soave, Giovanni Francesco
Novelle morali. Edizione . . . accresciuta. 1788 21/4/35
Sociétés Evangéliques' Report. 1836 18/12/41
Society in London. By a foreign resident. 1885 28/4/85
Sollen sich die Christen beschneiden. 1800 4/4/84
Solling, Gustav
L'Alsace et la Lorraine. 1871 9/2/71
Solly, Henry
Charles Dayrell: a modern Bacchanal. 1883 3/3/85
Solomon, Henry of London
Daniel Deronda, [by 'George Eliot'] from a Jewish point of view. 1877 18/4/77
Solon, Louis Mark Emanuel
The art of the old English potter . . . illustrated with fifty etchings by the author. 1883 22/8/88
Some account of St. Mary's home at Wantage . . . by the chaplain. 1851 11/4/52
Some considerations on . . . on the West India colonies. 1823 22/7/54
'Some pros and cons of the opium question; with a few suggestions . . . British claims on China' 1840 11/2/40
Some queries relative to the Jews, occasioned by a late sermon: with some other papers [Orig. published in the Norwich Mercury]. 1753 5/8/63
Somerville, Alexander
Letters of one who has whistled at the plough. 1842 28/1/43 n
Whistler at the plough. 1852 28/1/43
Somerville, Alexander Neil
The Churches in Asia. Extracts from the home letters of A. N. Somerville . . . [ed. W. F. Somerville]. 1885 27/6/86
Somerville, Mary
Physical geography. 1848 (2v. 1848) 22/9/54
Somerville, Thomas D.D.
My own life and times 1741–1814 [ed. W. L.]. 1861 4/6/61
Somerville, William the poet
The poetical works of William Somerville. 1766 (2v. 1766) 7/1/61
Sophie-Adélaide. Histoire contemporaine. 1886 1/11/87
Sophocles
Ajax. 16/2/29, 7/5/29
Antigone. 24/1/29
Electra. 26/10/26, 6/11/26, 21/5/29
Oedipus Coloneus. 14/1/28, 9/9/28
Oedipus Tyrannus. 1/3/26, 30/9/26, 22/10/30
The tragedies of Sophocles. A new translation, . . . by Edward Hayes Plumptre. 1865 1/1/66
Trachiniae. 11/11/26, 13/11/30, 15/8/31
Sopwith, Thomas
Account of the museum of economic geology, and mining records office, etc. 1843 23/11/44
Sorbière, Samuel de
A voyage to England . . . done into English from the French original. 1708 (2v. 1708–9) 10/9/44, 28/4/89
Sorelli, Guido
My confessions to Silvio Pellico. The autobiography of G. Sorelli. 1836 10/8/36
Sortain, Joseph
Romanism and Anglo-Catholicism: lectures. 1841 3/7/42 ?
Soury, Jules
Jésus et les Évangiles. 1878 7/3/79
South, Robert D.D.
Posthumous works of Robert South, containing . . . memoirs of his life and writings. 1717 30/8/40
Sermons preached upon several occasions (1737–44, new ed. 1843). 1843 11/1/57
Southall, James C.
The recent origin of man, as illustrated by geology and . . . prehistoric archaeology. 1875 20/2/78
Southall, Mrs. M.
A Companion to the Book of Common Prayer. 1832 7/11/47 ?
Southcott, Joanna
Collected Tracts. 1801 (7v. 1801–10) 10/2/61
Southey, Robert
A Tale of Paraguay. 1825 20/3/26
Sir Thomas More: or, colloquies on the progress and prospects of society. 1829 (2v. 1829) 30/1/36, 14/9/42
Southey's Common place book, ed. by his son-in-law J. W. Warter. 1849 (4v. 1849–51) 10/2/50
Specimens of the later English poets, with preliminary notices. 1807 (3v. 1807) 2/12/37

Thalaba the destroyer (a metrical romance). 1801 (2v. 1801) 14/4/70
The Book of the Church. 1824 (2v. 1824) 13/5/38
The doctor. 1847 (7v. 1834–47) 9/11/47
The life of Nelson. 1813 (2v. 1813) 7/5/55
The life of the Rev. Andrew Bell. 1844 (3v. 1844) 24/6/45
The life of Wesley; and the rise and progress of Methodism. 1820 (2v. 1820) 20/7/29, 25/3/49, 6/3/81
The poetical works of Robert Southey. 1840 (10v. 1838–40) 16/1/62
The remains of Henry Kirke White... with an account of his life, by R. Southey. 1807 13/11/25
The works of William Cowper... with a life of the author by the editor, Robert Southey. 1835 2/9/82
Southgate, Bishop Horatio
Narrative of a tour through Armenia, Kurdistan, Persia and Mesopotamia. 1840 (2v. 1840) 11/3/56
Southwell, Rev. Robert
Marie Magdalens funerall teares. 9/10/42
Souvenirs d'une Cosaque. 2/8/83
Soyres, John de
Montanism and the primitive Church. 1878 29/6/79
Spackman, William Frederick
The commercial barometer from 1845 to 1853, showing the operation of the present system of currency. 1853 10/12/53
Spalding, Martin John R. C. Archbishop of Baltimore
Pastoral letter... on the Papal infallibility. 1870 30/5/75
Spanheim, Friedrich the younger
De papa foemina inter Leonem IV et Benedictum III. Disquisitio historica. 18/9/45
Sparrow, Anthony Bishop of Exeter then Norwich
A rationale or practical exposition of the book of Common Prayer... [new ed. J. H. Newman 1839]. 22/3/40
S. P. C. K.'s annual report, with sermon by Longley prefixed. 1842 7/11/42
Spear, William pseud. U. S. E.
Emanuel Swedenborg, the spiritual Columbus. A sketchby U. S. E. 1876 27/8/78 ?
Spectateur de l'Orient. on C. Lucar; Chillon 23/9/1855
Spectator.
16. 4/1843. Sugar 15/4/1843, 21/4/1843
4/1867. The division; Gladstone & Disraeli 20/4/1867
Spedding, James
[On Bacon] in *Contemporary Review,* xxvii. 653. 1876 (April 1876) 1/4/76
[On Bacon] in *Contemporary Review,* xxviii. 821. 1876 (May 1876) 16/5/76
Evenings with a reviewer... examination of Mr. Macaulay's articles on Lord Bacon. 1881 (2v. 1881) 28/6/82
Publishers and authors. 1867 12/2/67
Reviews and discussions, literary, political and historical, not relating to Bacon. 1879 8/4/90
Spence, James of Liverpool
On the recognition of the Southern Confederation. 1862 12/8/62
The American union; its effect on national character and policy. 1861 23/11/61
Spencer, Aubrey George Bishop of Newfoundland then Jamaica
[pamphlet]. (not found) 9/10/53
A charge delivered at... the Archdeaconry of Jamaica... 1844. 1845 11/12/45
Spencer, Frank Ernest
Did Moses write the Pentateuch after all?. 1892 27/11/92
Spencer, George John Trevor Bishop of Madras
A charge... at the second triennial visitation in ... Madras... and... Colombo. 1843 9/7/43
A visitation charge addressed to the missionary clergy... in Tinnevelly and Travancoor. 1841 12/12/41
Journal of a visitation-tour in 1843–4. 1845 8/8/45
Journal of a visitation... in the diocese of Madras, 1840–41. 1842 25/7/42
Spencer, Herbert
'The coming slavery' in *Contemporary Review,* xlv. 461. 1884 (April 1884) 1/4/84
First principles. 1862 21/11/72
The morals of trade. 1874 30/8/74
The principles of sociology, vol. 1. 1876 (3v. 1876–96) 20/12/76, 3/4/77
Spencer, John Dean of Ely
De legibus Hebraeorum ritualibus, et earum rationibus. (3v. 1685) 28/10/88
Spencer, John Charles Lord Althorp
Copy of the correspondence between the chancellor of the exchequer and the Bank of England. 1833 4/2/80 ?
Spencer, Oliph Leigh
The life of Henry Chichelé, Archbishop of Canterbury. 1783 16/4/54
Spencer, Thomas Perpetual curate of Hinton charterhouse
Practical suggestions on Church reform... fourth thousand. 1840 24/12/40
Remarks on national education... fifth thousand. 1840 2/1/41
What David did: a reply to the Queen's letter. 1843 10/7/43

Spenser, Edmund
A view of the state of Ireland. 13/6/45, 20/1/70
The Faerie Queene. (2v. 1590–96) 29/9/35, 4/10/47, 26/1/50
[S. P. G. Appeal]. 1843 12/4/43
S. P. G. pamphlet
'Rise and progress of the missions of Tinnevelly' 21/4/45
Spicer, Henry
Church and stage. 1881 13/2/81
Spineto, Marquis
Lectures on the elements of hieroglyphics and Egyptian antiquities. 1829 13/9/30
Spinoza, Benedictus de
A letter . . . to . . . a convert. 1869 7/3/69
Spiritual phenomena or invisibles. 1867 12/1/73, 26/4/74
Spirit World. 1 8/4/1879
Spottiswoode, John Archbishop of St. Andrews
The history of the Church of Scotland. 18/3/39
Spottiswoode Miscellany
The Spottiswoode Miscellany. 1844 (2v. 1844–5) 7/10/48, 5/1/62
Spranger, Robert Jefferies
Report on the Catholic mode of electing bishops, tr. R. J. Spranger. 1869 3/10/69
Spring-Rice, Thomas 1st Baron Monteagle
Corn laws. The consequences of the sliding scale. 1843 8/5/43
Letter to . . . the archbishop of Dublin, on . . . the Ecclesiastical Titles Act. 1851 26/9/51
Spry, John Hume
[An address]. 19/3/44
Some observations . . . the future regulation of cathedral and collegiate bodies. 1838 19/2/38
Spurgeon, Charles Haddon
A double knock at the door of the young. 1875 25/4/75
Be of good cheer: the Saviour's comforting exhortation enlarged upon. 1881 27/11/81
Fear not, or comfort for the comfortless. 1861 4/1/63 ?
My sermon-notes. A selection from outlines of discourses. 1884 (4v. 1884–95) 24/5/91
Sermons. 1856 (2v. 1856–8) 29/12/61, 24/5/68, 22/3/74
The metropolitan tabernacle: its history and work. 1876 26/5/78
Spurrell, James
A rejoinder to the reply of the Superior of the Society of the Sisters of Mercy. 1852 11/4/52
Miss Sellon and the 'Sisters of Mercy'. 1852 20/2/52
Stack, John Herbert
The inner life of the Civil Service. 1861 (2v. 1861) 1/12/62
Stackhouse, Thomas Vicar of Beenham
The miseries . . . of the inferior clergy in and about London. 1722 26/10/62
Staël-Holstein, Anne Louise Germaine de Baroness
A treatise on ancient and modern literature. 1803 (2v. 1803) 30/3/83
Allemagne. 1810 (2v. 1810–13) 19/6/33 ?
Corinne; ou l'Italie. 1807 20/8/32, 4/11/56
Delphine. 1802 28/8/80, 11/9/80
Dix années de mon exil. 1821 19/2/34
Eloge de M. Guibert. 1790 13/3/34
Essais dramatiques. 1821 3/3/34
Jane Gray. 1787 10/3/34
Stahl, Friedrich Julius
Die Kirchenverfassung nach Lehre und Recht der Protestanten. 1840 10/11/40
Stahr, Adolf Wilhelm Theodor
Tiberius. 1873 7/6/81
Stalker, James
Imago Christi: the example of Jesus Christ. 1889 12/1/90
Stanford, Edward publisher, the elder
Ethnography of Turkey. 1877 19/12/76
Stanhope, Eugenia
The deportment of a married life. 1790 14/1/60
Stanhope, George Dean of Canterbury
Pious meditations. 1701 10/11/33
The common obstructions to faith, and a good life considered. 1727 30/8/68 ?
Stanhope, Lady Hester Lucy
Memoirs of the Lady Hester Stanhope. 1845 (3v. 1845) 21/10/46
Stanhope, Philip Dormer 4th Earl of Chesterfield
Letters to his son. 1774 (2v.) 18/10/34
Letters, ed. Carnarvon. 1890 4/8/90
Stanhope, Philip Henry 5th Earl Stanhope, Lord Mahon
A letter to Jared Sparks. 1852 3/11/52
Correspondence between . . . Pitt and . . . Duke of Rutland, Lord Lieutenant of Ireland, 1781–1787. 1842 28/4/86
Essai sur la vie du Grand Condé. 1842 6/12/42
History of England. 1836 (7v. 1836–54) 29/10/36
History of England comprising the Reign of Queen Anne until the Peace of Utrecht. 1701–1713. 1870 21/3/70, 27/3/84
History of England from the Peace of Utrecht. 1836 (7v. 1836–54) 12/2/52
History of the war of the succession in Spain. 1832 (2v. 1832–3) 8/6/44
Life of the Right Honourable William Pitt. 1861 (4v. 1861–2) 2/4/61, 11/3/62, 23/9/85, 3/9/87
Miscellanies, ed. Lord Stanhope. 1863 12/1/63, 6/2/68

Notes of conversation with King Louis-Philippe, at Claremont, March 30, 1848. 1873 26/2/73
Secret correspondence connected with Mr. Pitt's return to office in 1804, ed. Stanhope. 1852 18/3/52
Spain under Charles the second; or extracts from the correspondence of the Hon. A. Stanhope... 1690–1700. 1840 8/2/40
Were human sacrifices in use among the Romans?, ed. Lord Stanhope. 1860 26/3/60

Stanley, Arthur Penrhyn Dean of Westminster
A letter to the lord bishop of London on the state of subscription in the Church of England. 1863 17/5/63
An address on the connection of Church and State delivered at Sion College on February 15, 1868. 1868 18/3/68
Charles Kingsley: a sermon preached in Westminster Abbey on January 31, 1875. 1875 5/9/75
Dedication of Westminster Abbey. A sermon. 1866 21/1/66
Do states, like individuals, inevitably tend, after a certain period of maturity, to decay?. 1840 4/7/40
Great opportunities. A farewell sermon. 1863 24/1/64
Historical Memorials of Canterbury. 1855 25/8/54 ?
Historical Memorials of Westminster Abbey. 1868 30/10/68
How are the mighty fallen. 1873 21/9/73
Lectures on the history of the Church of Scotland delivered in Edinburgh in 1872. 1872 18/2/72
Lectures on the history of the Eastern Church. 1861 23/4/61
Life and correspondence, by R. E. Prothero. 1893 (2v.) 21/1/94
Sermons and essays on the apostolical age. 1847 6/2/48
The Athanasian Creed, with a preface on the general recommendations of the Ritual Commission. 1871 18/8/72
The Bible: its form and its substance. Three sermons. 1863 22/3/63
The Gypsies; a prize poem, recited in the theatre, Oxford. 1837 7/8/37
The life and correspondence of Thomas Arnold, D.D., late head master of Rugby School. 1844 (2v. 1844) 4/7/44, 24/8/44
The South African controversy in its relations to the Church of England. A speech. 1867 6/10/67
The three Irish Churches; an historical address delivered at Sion College on Jan. 28, 1869. 1869 6/2/69
Three introductory lectures on the study of ecclesiastical history. 1857 5/2/65

Stanley, Edward Bishop of Norwich
A few observations on religion and education in Ireland. 1835 3/6/37
A sermon preached before the Society for the propagation of the Gospel in foreign parts. 1843 24/5/43

Stanley, Edward George Geoffrey Smith 14th Earl of Derby
Farther facts connected with the West Indies: a second letter to W. E. Gladstone. 1851 26/7/51
Report of the proceedings at the laying of the foundation stone of the Liverpool College Institute. 1841 2/1/43
The Iliad of Homer rendered into English blank verse. By Edward Earl of Derby. 1864 (2v.) 5/12/64
Translations of poems, ancient and modern. 1862 24/6/62

Stanley, Edward Henry Smith 15th Earl of Derby
[Speech on the disestablishment of the Irish Church, April 1868]. 1868 16/11/68 ?
Claims and resources of the West Indian colonies. A letter to... W. E. Gladstone. 1850 28/5/50
Six weeks in South America. 1850 19/8/50
The Eastern atrocities. Lord Derby's defence. 1876 12/9/76

Stanley, Edward Lyulph 4th Baron Sheffield
Oxford University reform. 1869 17/12/69
Three letters on Oxford University reform. 1876 26/2/76

Stanley, Mary
Hospitals and sisterhoods. 1854 17/12/54

Stanley, Thomas the elder
Anacreon, Bion, Moschus, ed. T. Stanley. (new edn 1815) 19/10/49

Stanley, William 6th Earl of Derby
Sir William Stanley's Garland. 1800 3/10/92 ?

Stanley, William Dean of Saint Asaph
The faith and practice of a Church of England-Man,..., ed. R. Eden. 1848 13/7/56

Stanley, William Owen
The union of the sees of St. Asaph and Bangor: and the nature of the episcopal revenues. 1843 27/4/43

Stansfeld, Hamer
A letter to Richard Cobden... on our protective and restrictive currency laws. 1850 6/10/54
The currency act of 1844, the cause of the panic of October 1847. 1854 5/10/54

Stansfeld, Sir James G. C. B.
Substance of the speeches of the Rt. Hon. J. Stansfeld, M.P. 1875 22/6/75
The Italian movement and Italian parties. Two lectures. 1862 17/3/62

Staples, Robert Jr.
Agitation in Ireland, from a landlord's point of view. 1880 17/4/82 ?
Stapleton, Augustus Granville
George Canning and his times. 1859 22/7/59, 28/5/60
Ireland. The origin of Fenianism. 1868 29/1/68
The political life of the Right Honourable G. Canning from . . . Sept. 1822, to his death. 1831 6/2/36
The real monster evil of Ireland. 1843 10/7/43
Stapleton, Miles Thomas Baron Beaumont
France and Austria in central Italy. 1852 21/8/52
Stark, James M.D.
The Westminster Confession of Faith critically compared with the holy scriptures. 1863 23/8/63
Stark, Malcolm
Life of the Right Honourable William E. Gladstone, M.P., by a London Journalist. 1878 20/11/78
Life of the Right Honourable William E. Gladstone, M.P., by a London Journalist [expanded ed.]. 1879 20/11/78
Stark, Robert of Torquay
What is truth? A reply to the reply of the Rev. J. Walker to . . . the Rev. J. C. Hume. 1853 10/12/89 ?
Starke, C. N.
The primitive family. 1889 13/9/90 ?
Starke, Mrs. Mariana
Information and directions for travellers on the Continent. 17/5/32, 10/7/32, 28/7/32, 17/10/38
The beauties of Carlo Maria Maggi paraphrased. To which are added sonnets by M. Starke. 1811 4/7/32
Starr, Henry Wellington
Remains of . . . H. W. Starr . . . with a memoir of his life by his sister [E. C. Starr]. 1847 21/11/47
Stateman's theology, A. 31/5/63
Stateman's Year Book. 1889 13/3/89 ?
Statement and correspondence . . . concerning a proposed new church at Tonbridge. 1875 28/2/76, 26/11/76
Statement . . . by the committee of the General Assembly on the act . . . calling of the ministers. 1839 20/12/41
Statement explanatory of the ordinance passed to create the Roman Catholic priests of St. Sulpice a corporate body. 1840 11/6/40
Statement of proceedings relating to the establishment of a bishopric . . . in Jerusalem. 1841 4/1/42
Statement respecting the non-intrusion principle of the Church of Scotland. 1841 28/4/44 ?
State secret, A. 2/8/77
Statham, Francis F.
Our Protestant faith . . . a course of lectures upon the distinctive errors of Romanism. 1851 3/4/56
Statham, Francis Reginald
Blacks, Boers and British, a three-cornered problem. 1881 25/4/81
Free-thought and True-thought: a contribution to an existing argument. 1884 25/5/84, 22/1/85
From old to new. A sketch of the present religious position. In eight lectures. 1872 14/11/72
The social growths of the nineteenth century . . . the substance of four lectures. 1872 1/12/72
Statham, William Mann
The abiding Christ, and other sermons. 1885 5/7/85
Statistical Journal and Record. ;26/2/1849
Statius, Pope Publius Papinius
The First Book of Statius, his Thebais, tr. A. Pope. 27/6/37, 1/7/37
Statutes of the colleges of Oxford. 1853 20/4/54
Statut organique de la Roumélie orientale. 1879 28/6/79 ?
Staunton, Sir George Leonard
An authentic account of an embassy from the king of Great Britain to the Emperor of China. 1797 (2v. 1797) 16/1/41
Staunton, Sir George Thomas
Corrected report of the speech . . . on the opium trade, in the House of Commons. 1843 29/5/43
Staunton, Howard
The chess-player's handbook. 1847 12/8/50
Staunton, Michael
A reply to M. Martin's 'Ireland before and after the Union'. 1844 5/2/44
Stead, William Thomas
The discrowned king of Ireland. (1890?) 26/3/90 ?
Steane, Edward
The evangelical alliance and religious liberty. 1864 20/12/70
The reciprocal duties of Church members. 1835 4/3/39
Stebbing, Henry D.D., F.R.S.
A sermon, preached on the fifth of November. 1839 16/6/44
Stebbing, Thomas Roscoe Rede
Essays on Darwinism. 1871 30/12/73 ?
Stebbing, William
Peterborough. 1889 7/2/90
Sir Walter Ralegh. A biography . . . With a frontispiece. 1891 22/12/91, 1/2/92
Some verdicts of history reviewed. 1887 26/1/87
Stedman, Sir Algernon Methuen Marshall
Oxford: its life and schools. 1887 5/9/87, 25/9/87

Steele, James of Edinburgh
The philosophy of the evidence of Christianity. 1834 7/7/39
Steele, Joshua
An essay towards establishing the melody and measure of speech. 1775 12/5/75
Steele, Sir Richard
The Christian hero. 1701 11/1/57
The Romish Ecclesiastical history of late years. 1714 17/3/36
The Spectator. 22/5/26
Steen, Cornelis van den called Cornelius A Lapide
St. Luke's gospel. 1887 8/4/87
Steere, Edward Missionary Bishop of Central Africa
An historical sketch of the English brotherhoods . . . at the beginning of the eighteenth century. 1856 17/5/57
Steinbach, Henry
The Punjaub, being a brief account of the country of the Sikhs. 1845 14/12/46
Steinmetz, Andrew
The Novitiate; or a year among the English Jesuits. 1846 11/4/46
Stephen, Sir Alfred Chief Justice of New South Wales
Thoughts on the constitution of a second legislative chamber for New South Wales. 1853 17/5/53
Stephen, Caroline Emelia
Quaker Strongholds. 1890 31/12/90
Stephen, Sir George Secretary to . . . Board of Education.
A Letter to . . . Lord John Russell, on the probable increase of rural crime. 1836 13/3/37
The adventures of a gentleman in search of a horse. 1835 2/11/36
The Jesuit at Cambridge. 1847 (2v. 1847) 26/6/47
Stephen, Sir James K.C.B.
Essays in ecclesiastical biography. 1849 (2v. 1849) 12/12/52, 17/5/79, 23/5/79
Stephen, Sir James Fitzjames
'Caesarism and ultramontanism' in *Contemporary Review*, xxiii. 497. 1874 (March 1874) 22/3/74
'On parliamentary government' in *Contemporary Review*, xxiii. 165. 1874 (January 1874) 2/1/74
A digest of the law of evidence. 1876 13/6/77
Authority in matters of opinion. 1877 20/5/77
Liberty, equality, fraternity. 1873 13/7/73
Remarks on the proof of miracles. 1875 9/11/75
Stephen, Sir Leslie K.C.B.
History of English thought in the eighteenth century. 1876 (2v. 1876) 18/4/84
Samuel Johnson. 1878 1/10/78
The uniformity of nature. 1879 6/4/79
Stephen, Sarah
Passages from the life of a daughter at home. 1845 30/12/49
Stephen, Thomas Medical librarian, King's College London
The history of the Church of Scotland from the Reformation to the present time. 1843 (4v. 1843–5) 11/8/44
The life and times of Archbishop Sharp. 1839 11/1/41
Stephens, Alexander
Memoir of J. Horne Tooke. 1813 (2v. 1813) 17/8/29
Stephens, Archibald John Q.C.
A letter to . . . Baron Cranworth . . . on the constitution of the ecclesiastical courts. 1853 29/4/53
A treatise on the Corporation Act. 1835 25/7/35
Adelaide diocesan constitutions. 1854 17/6/55 ?
The statutes . . . the ecclesiastical and eleemosynary institutions of England, Wales . . . 1845 (2v. 1845) 5/5/50
Stephens, William Richard Wood Dean of Winchester
A memoir of the Right Hon. William Page Wood, Baron Hatherley. 1883 (2v. 1883) 18/3/83
Christianity and Islam. The Bible and the Koran. 1877 10/7/81
Memorials of the South Saxon See and cathedral church of Chichester. 1876 14/1/77
Saint Chrysostom; his life and times. 1872 19/5/72
The life and letters of W. F. Hook. 1878 (2v. 1878) 22/12/78
Stephenson, Robert civil engineer
Address . . . on his election as president of the Institution of Civil Engineers. 1856 16/4/56
Steps towards heaven. 1862 31/5/85
Sterling, Sir Anthony Coningham
Russia under Nicholas the First, tr. A. Sterling. 1841 17/5/41
Sterling, John M.A.
Essays and Tales, collected and edited with a memoir by J. C. Hare. 1848 (2v. 1848) 23/3/48
Poems. 1839 21/8/40
Twelve Letters by J. S. 1851 12/3/76
Sterne, Laurence
A sentimental journey through France and Italy. 1768 6/1/73 ?
The life and opinions of Tristram Shandy, gentleman. 1760 (9v. 1760–67) 26/3/57
The sermons of William Yorick. 1760 (7v. 1760–9) 29/3/57
The works of Laurence Sterne. 1872 9/12/80
Works. 1769 2/9/50

Sterrett, James Macbride
The ethics of Hegel. 1893 3/9/93
Steuart, J.
Bogota in 1836–7. 1838 8/11/42
Steuart, John Alexander
Kilgroom. A story of Ireland. 1890 9/10/90
Letters to living authors . . . with portraits. 1890 21/8/91
Stevens, A. de Grasse
Miss Hildreth. A novel. 1888 (3v. 1888) 8/12/88
Stevens, Charles Abbott
Remarks on the rating of tithe commutation rent-charge. 1856 26/5/56 ?
Stevens, William poet
The truce of God and other poems. 1879 16/11/79
Stevenson, Francis Seymour
Historic personality. 1893 31/5/93
Stevenson, John D.D., of the Scotch Mission, Bombay
Hindoo caste. 1858 5/12/57
Stevenson, John Hall
Crazy Tales. 1762 18/8/37
Fables for grown gentlemen. 1761 5/9/71 ?
Stevenson, Robert Louis
Footnote to history. Eight years of trouble in Samoa. 1892 19/5/93
Island nights' entertainments. 1893 25/5/93
Kidnapped: being memoirs of the adventures of David Balfour, in the year 1751. 1886 29/7/86
New Arabian Nights. 1882 (2v. 1882) 16/4/84
Strange case of Dr. Jekyll and Mr. Hyde. 1886 13/2/86
The Wrecker. 1892 2/8/92
Treasure Island. 1883 14/4/84
Stevenson, William G.
Thirteen months in the rebel army; being a narrative of personal adventures . . . by an impressed New Yorker. 1862 26/11/62
Steward, George Independent minister
Memoir of George Steward. 1868 25/9/69
Stewart, Alexander of Egremont
Reminiscences of Dunfermline and neighbourhood . . . with chronological appendix, 1064–1880. 1886 13/12/87
Stewart, Archibald Minister of Glasserton
History vindicated in the case of the Wigtown martyrs. 1867 11/11/78 ?
Stewart, Balfour
Lessons in elementary physics. 1870 5/6/73
Stewart, Charles Poyntz
Vatican influence under Pius V and Gregory XIII. 1877 5/8/77
Stewart, David Dale
Evangelical opinion in the nineteenth century. 1879 29/2/80
Stewart, Dugald
The philosophy of the active and moral powers of man. 1828 (2v. 1828) 19/7/30
Stewart, Duncan Minister of Dornoch
A concise hebrew grammar. 1872 15/11/85
Stewart, James Haldane
Invitation to united prayer for the outpouring of the Holy Spirit. 1842 29/1/43
Stewart, General William
Outline of a plan for the general reform of the British land forces. 1806 9/10/61
Stigand, William
'French Unity' in *Contemporary Review*, xvi. 321. 1871 (January 1871) 10/1/71
A vision of Barbarossa, and other poems. 1859 6/11/60
Athenäis; or, the First Crusade. 1866 15/4/67
The life, work, and opinions of Heinrich Heine. 1875 (2v. 1875) 27/3/77
Stillingfleet, Edward Bishop of Worcester
A rational account of the grounds of Protestant religion. 7/2/40, 9/12/40
Origines sacrae, or a rational account of the grounds of Christian faith. 17/9/65
Stillman, William James
Herzegovina and the late uprising. 1877 7/2/77
Stirling, James of Glasgow
Letters from the slave states. 1857 13/1/62
Unionism: with remarks on the report of the Commissioners on Trades Unions. 1869 20/12/69
Stirling, Sir William afterw. Stirling Maxwell
The cloister life of the Emperor Charles the Fifth. 1852 24/10/52
St. Ninian's Report. 1748 20/11/51
Stockdale, James
Annales Caermoelenses; or, annals of Cartmel. 1872 3/5/73
Stockmar, Baron Christian Friedrich von
Denkwürdigkeiten aus den Papieren . . . ed. E. Freiherr v. Stockmar. 1872 4/11/72
Memoirs of Baron Stockmar . . . ed. F. Max Müller. 1872 (2v. 1872) 19/12/89
Stoddart, George Henry
The history of the Prayer Book. 1864 25/6/65, 21/5/71
Stoker, Bram
The Snake's Pass. 1890 18/11/90
Stokes, Henry Sewell
Poems of later years. 1874 2/6/74
Scattered leaves. 1862 6/12/62
Stokes, John Lort
Discoveries in Australia. 1846 (2v. 1846) 15/5/46
Stone, Elizabeth
God's Acre; or, historical notions relating to churchyards. 1858 6/2/81

Stone, Ella
Ring in the true. A story of transition times in village life. 1892 26/4/92
Stone, Henry Edward
David; the man after God's own heart. 1888 21/8/92
Stoney, G. Johnstone
Four memoranda on university reform in Ireland. 1872 7/2/73 ?
Stonhouse, Sir James
Admonitions against swearing. 1773 25/10/29
Stonor Report
Minutes of evidence given before the Committee of Privileges. 1854 7/6/54 ?
Stopes, Charlotte Carmichael
The Bacon-Shakspere question. 1888 8/8/88
Stopford, Edward Adderley Archdeacon of Meath
A report to the Lord Bishop of Meath on the state of elementary schools in the diocese. 1844 21/12/44
A report... with a correspondence. 1845 30/5/45
Notes of preparation for the General Convention of the Church of Ireland. 1870 6/3/70
To clergy and laity. 1868 10/1/69
Stoppani, Antonio
Sulla Cosmogonia Mosaica. 1887 13/1/91
Stories selected from the History of England. 9/1/47
Story, Joseph U. S. Supreme Court Justice
Commentaries on the constitution of the United States. 1833 (3v. 1833) 11/5/50
Story, Robert Herbert
Life and remains of R. Lee, D.D. 1870 (2v. 1870) 7/1/72
Memoir of the life of Robert Story. 1862 29/6/62
Story of a penitent soul. 1892 11/9/92
Story of David and Bathsheba. (2v. 1622) 29/11/87
Stothard, Mrs. Anna Eliza afterw. Bray
Life of T. Stothard. With personal reminiscences. 1851 17/5/73
Stothert, James Augustine
Justorum Semita... A history of the saints and holydays. 1843 21/4/44
Stoughton, Rev. John of Kensington
Church and state two hundred years ago. 1862 20/3/81
Ecclesiastical history of England. The Church of the Restoration. 1870 (2v. 1870) 6/2/87
Ecclesiastical history of England. The Church of the revolution. 1874 5/4/74, 2/1/76
Lights and shadows of primitive Christendom. 1891 30/6/91
Religion in England under Queen Anne and the Georges. 1702–1800. 1878 (2v. 1878) 2/3/79
Stowe, Charles Edward
Life of Harriet Beecher Stowe, compiled from her letters and journals. By her son C. E. Stowe. 1889 28/11/92
Stowe, Mrs. Harriet Elizabeth Beecher
Oldtown folks. 1869 (3v. 1869) 19/5/84
Poganuc people, their loves and lives. 1878 26/9/89
Sunny memories of foreign lands. 1854 22/8/54
The key to Uncle Tom's Cabin. 1853 5/9/53
The minister's wooing. 1859 18/2/84
Uncle Tom's Cabin. 1852 (2v. 1852) 23/9/52, 12/10/52, 15/10/52, 14/3/87
Stowell, Hugh Canon of Chester
First annual report of the Church Pastoral Aid Society. 1836 11/9/36
St Paul's Magazine.
1. 148. 10/1867. The session 27/9/1867
1. 531. 10/1867. Leader 21/2/1868
Strachan, James Morgan
Juggernaut: its present state under British patronage and support. 1843 10/3/43
The connexion of the East India Company... 1840 6/2/41
Strahan, Samuel Alexander Kenny
Marriage and disease. A study of heredity. 1892 15/4/92
Strang, John LL.D., City Chamberlain of Glasgow
Glasgow and its clubs. 1864 31/10/65
Report on the mortality bills of the city of Glasgow and suburbs, for 1851. 1852 16/3/52
Strange, Sir Robert
An inquiry into the rise and establishment of the Royal Academy of Arts. 1775 30/7/59
Stratton, Charles Sherwood
An account of the life... of C. S. S., the American dwarf known as General Tom Thumb. 1844 17/3/55
Strauss, David Friedrich
Das Leben Jesu für das Deutsche Volk bearbeitet. 1864 22/4/66
Das Leben Jesu... zweite verbesserte Auflage. 1837 (2v. 1837) 15/2/48
Der alte und der neue Glaube. Ein Bekenntniss. 1872 1/12/72
Streitschriften... über das Leben Jesu. 1838 24/3/47
Ulrich von Hutten. 1858 (2v. 1858) 25/9/74
Strauss und Torney, Victor Friedrich von
Essays zur allgemeinen Religionswissenschaft. 1879 8/9/86, 25/5/90
Street, George Edmund Rector of Upton, Scudamore
Some account of Gothic architecture in Spain. 1865 28/2/65
Street, James Christopher
The nature and character of Jesus. 1889 20/9/90 ?

Strickland, Agnes
Lives of the Queens of England. 1840 (12v. 1840–8) 22/8/80
Lives of the Tudor princesses. 1868 28/3/86
Strode, Sir George of Westerham
. . . , a discourse of Holy Love . . . done into English . . . by Sir G. Strode, Knt. 9/8/68, 22/12/72
Stronbuy, or Hanks of Highland yarn. By the author of 'Tobersnorey'. 1881 4/8/81
Struggles for life; or, the autobiography of a dissenting minister. 1854 30/5/86
Struthers, John M.D. Minister, Free Church, Old Aberdeen
How to improve the teaching in the Scottish universities. 1859 8/12/59
Strutt, Elizabeth
Articles on Rome. 6/10/52
Strutt, Percy
The inductive method of Christian inquiry. An essay. 1877 3/1/83
Strype, John
Annals of the Reformation and establishment of religion. 1824 (4v. 1824) 15/9/88, 15/9/89
Annals of the reign of Queen Mary. 1706 (2v. 1706) 22/5/88
Memorials of . . . Thomas Cranmer, Archbishop of Canterbury. (2v. 1694) 22/1/32, 24/3/33, 5/5/33
The history of the life and acts of . . . Edmund Grindal . . . Archbishop of . . . Canterbury. 1710 3/6/50
Strzelecki, Count Paul Edmund de K. C. M. G.
Physical description of New South Wales and Van Diemen's land. 1845 27/3/46 ?
Stuart, Alexander Moody
Life and letters of Elizabeth, last Duchess of Gordon. 1865 5/3/65
The Bible true to itself: a treatise on the historical truth of the Old Testament. 1884 9/10/87
Stuart, Edward M.A.
Fair play for Brother Ignatius. A letter to . . . the Lord Bishop of London. 1864 5/2/65
Some thoughts on low Masses. Addressed to members of Convocation. 1863 2/8/63
Stuart, Henry Lord Darnley
Ballad on the murder of Lord Darnley. 25/10/64
Stuart, Henry Windsor Villiers
Egypt after the war: being the narrative of a tour of inspection. 1883 14/1/84
The funeral tent of an Egyptian Queen. 1882 4/7/82
Stuart, James
A chapter of science, or, what is a law of nature? Six lectures. 1883 3/8/84
Stuart, J. S.
America and the Americans versus the Papacy and the Catholics: a lecture. 1853 29/12/72 ?
Stuart, Roberto M.
Fiesole. 1871 16/6/75 ?
Notti insonni. Memorie della contessa Elisa d'Alloro raccolte da Roberto Stuart. 1878 27/6/78
Stubbs, Charles William Bishop of Truro
Christ and Free-thought. An address to secularists. 1883 19/8/83
Christianity and democracy. Socialism and social reform. Two sermons. 1881 29/12/81
The land and the labourers. 1885 10/11/85
The mythe of life. Four sermons, with an introduction on the social mission of the Church. 1880 12/1/81, 27/9/85
Stubbs, E. T.
In Memoriam. H. M. M. S[tubbs]. 1877 13/7/81
Stubbs, William successively Bishop of Chester, Oxford
A charge delivered . . . October, 1886. 1886 2/1/87
An address delivered by way of a last statutory public lecture. 1884 22/8/84
An address delivered by way of inaugural lecture . . . Revised. 1867 27/2/67
The apostolical succession in the Church of England. A letter. 1866 25/3/66
The constitutional history of England in its origin and development. 1866 (3v. 1866) 22/11/75, 14/8/84
Stuckey, John
A compleat history of Somersetshire. 1742 26/1/77 ?
Sturge, Joseph
Memoir of Joseph Sturge, by P. Sibree. 1862 29/5/64
Sturge, Joseph the elder, philanthropist
Memoirs. 1864 30/3/44 n
Sturgis, Howard Overing
Tim. 1891 3/11/91
Sturgis, J.
'Wanted: a leader' in *Nineteenth Century*, xx. 183. 1886 (August 1886) 4/8/86
Suckling, Rev. Alfred Inigo
Selections from the works of Sir J. Suckling. 1836 17/1/86 ?
Suckling, Sir John
Fragmenta aurea. (4v. 1646) 24/7/46, 28/10/55
Poems, ed., with intro. by W. C. Hazlitt. 1874 19/11/79 ?
Suckling, Rev. Robert Alfred
Sermons, plain and practical . . . Ed. by I. Williams. 1853 21/12/56
Suffield, Mark Oliver
Five letters on a conversion to Roman Catholicism. 1873 5/10/73
Is Jesus God? A sermon. 1873 2/11/73
Life of Robert Rodolph Suffield. 1893 24/9/93

The Vatican decrees and the 'expostulation' [of the Rt. Hon. W. E. Gladstone]. 1874 16/12/74
Suffield, Robert Rodolph
A Croydon episode. 1876 27/2/76
Life of, by M. O. Suffield. 1893 24/9/93
Suffolk county enrollment list. 1863 13/11/65
Sugden, Edward Burtenshaw Baron St. Leonards
A letter to ... Viscount Melbourne, on ... the appellate jurisdiction of the Court of Chancery. 1835 21/1/36
Suggestions for a revision of the Prayer Book. 1859 8/7/59
Sullivan, Alexander Martin the elder
New Ireland. 1877 (2v. 1877) 3/11/77, 15/8/82, 5/9/90
Sullivan, Mrs. Arabella Jane
Recollections of a chaperon, ed. Lady Dacre. 1833 (3v. 1833) 19/9/33
Sullivan, Sir Edward Robert
Letters on India ... to J. Tremayne Esq. 1858 12/5/58
Sullivan, William Kirby
On the manners and customs of the ancient Irish ... ed, with an intro. by W. K. S. 1873 23/1/74
University education in Ireland. A letter to Sir J. D. Acton, Bart., M.P. 1866 27/3/66
Sumner, Charles United States Senator
[Report favouring termination of the Canadian reciprocity treaty, 20 Dec. 1864]. 1864 4/4/65 ?
On the crime against Kansas. Speech ... in the Senate of the United States. 1856 9/10/56
Our claims on England. Speech delivered ... on the Johnson-Clarendon treaty. 1869 12/5/69
Slavery and the American war. Speech ... Nov. 5, 1864. 1864 10/1/65
Speech of Charles Sumner on the Bill for the admission of Kansas as a free state. 1860 23/6/60
The national security and the national faith, speech at the Republican convention. 1865 3/10/65 ?
The Sumner Outrage. A full report of the speeches at the meeting of citizens in Cambridge. 1856 8/10/56
Sumner, Charles Richard Bishop of Llandaff and then Winchester
A charge delivered to the clergy of the diocese of Winchester, October, 1845. 1845 7/12/45
A charge delivered to the clergy of the diocese of Winchester, September, 1841. 1841 9/12/41
A charge delivered to the clergy of the diocese of Winchester, ... October 1837. 1837 22/3/38
Sumner, George Henry Bishop of Guildford
Peace, Christ's legacy to his Church: a sermon ... at the consecration of the Rev. A. Oxenden. 1869 19/9/69
Sumner, John Bird Bishop of Chester
A charge addressed to the clergy of the diocese of Chester, ... in May and June, 1844. 1844 10/11/44
A charge delivered to the clergy of the diocese of Chester. 1832 14/7/33
A charge delivered to the clergy of the diocese of Chester, at the primary visitation. 1829 12/1/30
A practical exposition of the Gospel according to St. John. 1835 7/2/36
A practical exposition of the Gospel of St. Luke. 1832 11/12/35
A series of sermons on the Christian faith and character. 1821 20/8/37, 23/8/46
A treatise on the records of the creation, and on the moral attributes of the Creator. 1816 (2v. 1816) 1/1/31, 5/1/31
Apostolical preaching considered, in an examination of St. Paul's Epistles. 1815 22/2/29
Sermons on the principal festivals of the Christian Church. 1827 12/4/29
The doctrine of justification briefly stated. 1843 18/6/43
The evidence of Christianity, derived from its nature and reception. 1824 25/9/25
Sundry homilies. 17/1/47
Supernatural religion, an enquiry [anon.]. 1874 (2v. 1874) 16/5/74
Surin, Jean Joseph
The foundations of the spiritual life, tr. E. B. Pusey. 1844 12/1/45
Suringar, Willem Hendrik
My visit to Mettray in 1845 ... translated from the Dutch. 1851 17/12/51
Surtees, Scott Frederick
Church abuses and church reform. Four letters to E. Horsman Esq. 1849 13/3/49
Surtees, William Edward
A sketch of the stock of Nevill, Earls of Northumberland in the Saxon times. 1843 12/10/47
Sutcliffe, Rev. James
A letter to the ... Bishop of London. 1843 16/6/43
Sutcliffe, Thomas Governor of the island of Juan Fernandez
An exposition of the facts relating to the rise and progress of the woollen ... manufactures. 1843 13/1/43
Suter, James
The Ordinance of Levites. 1867 10/11/67
Sutherland, James Middleton
William Wordsworth: the story of his life. With critical remarks on his writings. 1887 27/10/91

Sutton, Christopher
Disce vivere. Learne to live. (new edn 1839) 16/2/40 ?
Swaine, Edward
Law and conscience: or, the duty of dissenters on church taxes. 1844 18/1/44
The shield of Dissent; or, dissent in its bearings on legislation. 1839 11/3/40
Swainson, Charles Anthony
Further investigations as to the origin and object of the 'Athanasian Creed'. 1871 18/2/72
The Parliamentary history of the Act of Uniformity, 13 and 14 Charles II. Cap. 4. 1875 18/7/75
The rubrical question of 1874. A brief historical enquiry. 1874 11/6/75
Swainson, William Attorney General of New Zealand
New Zealand. The substance of lectures on the colonization of New Zealand. 1856 1/5/56
Swan, Annie Shepherd afterw. Burnett-Smith
Aldersyde, a Border story of seventy years ago. 1883 10/4/83 n, 16/4/83
Swan, Robert
The principle of church rates. 1837 14/4/37
Swann, Edward Gibbon
The bread question; or where the shoe pinches. 1855 (2v. 1855) 15/1/56
Swanwick, Miss Anna
An utopian dream, and how it may be realized. 1888 15/7/88
Egmont. A tragedy in five acts. 1846 23/6/79
The Agamemnon, Choephori, and Eumenides of Aeschylus translated into English verse. 1865 29/7/65
Swayne, Robert George
The voice of the Good Shepherd to his lost sheep ... the parable of the Prodigal Son. 1868 20/10/72 ?
Swedenborg, Emanuel
What, and how of the eternal worker: the work and the plan?. 1862 25/1/63
Sweeney, Talbot
A vindication from a northern standpoint of Gen. R. E. Lee and his fellow-officers. 1890 28/8/90 ?
Sweet, James Bradby
Religious liberty, and the Church in chains. 1847 29/10/47
Sweetman, Walter
A few thoughts on the infallibility of the Pope. 1870 29/5/70, 29/7/76
Swift, Deane
An essay upon the life, writings, and character of Dr. Jonathan Swift. 1755 10/11/68, 23/10/85
Swift, Edmund the elder
Spiritual law in the natural world. 1890 9/11/90
Swift, Jonathan Dean of St. Patrick's
A letter to the whole people of Ireland, by M. B. Drapier. 1724 8/11/61, 11/12/61, 31/1/81
An account of a battel between the ancient and modern books in St. James's library. 1704 15/12/55
Directions to servants in general. 1745 14/2/26
Life of the Rev. Dr. Jonathan Swift, by T. Sheridan. 1784 17/7/46
Saint Patrick's purgatory. 1716 15/10/64
The poetical works of J. Swift. 1736 18/4/70
Works, vols. iv, vi–x, ed., with a biography by Walter Scott, Esq. 1814 29/10/68
Swifte, Edmund Lewes Lenthal
Homeric Studies. 1868 27/3/69 ?
Swinburne, Algernon Charles
'Charles Reade' in *Nineteenth Century*, xvi. 550. 1884 (October 1884) 2/10/84
Atalanta in Calydon. A tragedy. 1865 6/3/73
Bothwell: a tragedy. 1874 29/9/76
Marino Faliero. A tragedy. 1885 25/6/85
Poems and ballads. 1866 2/1/73, 7/10/92, 10/10/92, 17/10/92 n
Queen Yseult: a poem in six cantos. 1858 18/6/73
The Heptalogia. 1881 6/6/81
The Queen-Mother. Rosamond. Two plays. 1860 17/12/72
Swinburne, Henry Vendue master at Trinidad
'Courts of Europe' in *Quarterly Review*, lxviii. 684. 1841 (June 1841) 6/7/41
Travels in the two Sicilies, in the years 1777, 1778, 1779, and 1780. 1783 (2v. 1783–5) 2/8/82
Swinny, Henry Hutchinson
Sermons on several occasions, ... with a preface by the Lord Bishop of Oxford. 1865 28/3/69
Sybel, Heinrich Carl Ludolf von
Kleine historische Schriften. 1863 6/2/88
Klerikale Politik im neunzehnten Jahrhundert. 1874 10/9/74
Les droits de l'Allemagne sur l'Alsace et la Lorraine. 1871 8/3/71
Sybel, L. von
Die Mythologie der Ilias. 1877 22/8/91
Sybert, A.
Statistical annals of the United States. 1898 6/11/87
Sydow, Carl Leopold Adolph
Aktenstücke. 1873 2/2/73
The Scottish church question. 1845 17/9/48, 5/1/75 ?
Sykes, Arthur Ashley
The eternal peace of the Church only obtainable by a zeal for scripture in its just latitude. 1716 21/11/91
Syme, David
On the modification of organisms. 1891 25/12/90, 18/1/91

Symeon
De Sacra Liturgia, ed. Migne, *PG* clv. 253. 12/10/47
Symes, Joseph
The Methodist conference and eternal punishment: do its defenders believe the doctrine?. 1877 25/11/77
Symington, Andrew James
The reasonableness of faith. 1870 10/7/70
Symmons, Charles D.D.
The prose works of J. Milton; with a life of the author. 1806 17/6/57
Symonds, Arthur
Papers relative to the obstruction of public business and the organisation of the Civil Service. 1853 2/2/54
Symonds, John Addington The younger
Renaissance in Italy. 1877 (7v. 1875–86) 8/11/77, 11/10/83
Sketches in Italy and Greece. 1874 30/1/77
Studies of the Greek poets. 1873 (2v. 1873–6) 29/9/73
Symons, Benjamin Parsons
The claims of the Church of England upon her members. A sermon. 1843 23/4/43
Symons, Jelinger Cookson
A scheme of direct taxation for 1853. 1853 11/2/53
Sir Robert Peel as a type of statemanship. 1856 17/5/58
Sympneumata. 15/8/86
Synge, Edward Bishop of Raphoe
'An answer to all the excuses, etc.' S. P. C. K. tract. 1744 25/12/29
Synge, Millington Henry
Canada in 1848: being an examination of the existing resources of British North America. 1848 2/4/49
Synodal action in the Church of England seasonable and safe... by a presbyter. 1852 27/3/59

Tabaraud, Mathieu Matherin
Histoire critique des projets... pour la réunion des communions chrétiennes. 1824 12/6/72
Tabberner, John Loude
Direct taxation and parliamentary representation. 1860 25/11/59
Tabor, J. A.
Supreme law illustrated in answer to the question, What is truth?. 1879 17/10/80
Tacitus
Annals. 4/4/36, 7/5/36, 3/9/60
Dialogus de Oratoribus... revised text, with introductory essays... by W. Peterson. 1893 20/9/93
Germania. 16/2/26, 17/8/57, 11/3/72
Opera. 6/10/25, 3/11/25, 2/2/26, 28/9/26, 2/4/31, 14/4/88
Tafel, Rudolf Leonhard
Huxley and Swedenborg. 1889 6/10/89
Tahity, Aggression on. (not found) 8/4/43
Taine, Hippolyte Adolphe
La Philosophie de l'art en Italie. 1866 9/1/67
Les origines de la France contemporaine. 1876 (6v. 1876–94) 10/4/84, 17/2/92, 23/1/94
Notes sur l'Angleterre. 1872 30/3/72
Voyage en Italie. 1866 (2v.) 28/8/66
Taisey-Chatenoy, Irène de
À la court de Napoléon III. 1891 28/5/92
Tait, A. C.
The mission of the Church of England. 1866 18/3/66
Tait, Archibald Campbell
Charge... delivered to the clergy of the diocese of London. 1858 5/12/58
Charge... delivered to the clergy of the diocese of London. 1862 14/12/62
Charge... delivered to the clergy of the diocese of London. 1866 23/12/66
Harmony of revelation and the sciences. 1864 1/1/65
Letter to the Vice-Chancellor of the University of Oxford. 1845 28/1/45
Life of... Tait, Archbishop of Canterbury, by R. T. Davidson. 1891 (2v.) 6/6/91
The Church and the Law. 1877 29/3/77
The word of God. Sermons. 1863 (2 pt.) 17/4/64
Tait, Peter Guthrie, and Stewart, Balfour
Unseen Universe. 1875 28/11/75
Tait's Edinburgh Magazine.
9. 528. 8/1842. Moffat 17/8/1842
11. 294. 5/1844. Scottish Episcopacy 21/10/1844
16. 525. 8/1849. Oxford 14/8/1849
Talbot, Edward Stuart
Preparation in history for Christ. 1889 29/12/89
Talbot, John 16th Earl of Shrewsbury
Hints towards the pacification of Ireland. 1844 27/4/44
Letter to Lord John Russell. 1851 8/8/51
Letter... descriptive of the Estatica of Caldero. 1841 15/11/41
Reply to MacHale. 1848 10/2/48
Talbot, Thomas
Greece and the Greeks, or, a historic sketch of Attic life and manners. 1880 12/10/80
Talbot, William Henry Fox
Records of the past: being English translations of the Assyrian and Egyptian monuments. 1873 (vol 1) 21/12/73
Talbot versus Talbot. 1854 7/8/54
Talfourd, Thomas Noon
Athenian captive: a tragedy. 1838 1/5/38
Glencoe, or the fate of the MacDonalds. 1840 12/6/40

Talfourd, Thomas Noon (*cont.*)
Ion: a tragedy in five acts. 1836 13/6/35
Speech for the defendant in R. v. Moxton. 1841 21/12/48
Three speeches on copyright. 1840 30/1/40
Tallack, William
Peter Bedford, the Spitalfields philanthropist. 1865 18/6/65
Tallemant, Gédéon
Historiettes de Tallemant des Reaux. 1834 (2v. 1834–5) 15/4/65, 6/11/79
Talleyrand-Perigord, Count Charles Maurice de
Correspondance diplomatique, ed. G. Pallain. 1891 5/5/92
Tallis, Thomas
Order of Service. 1843 9/12/45
Talmadge, William
Letters from Florence on the religious reform movements in Italy. 1866 26/4/66
Tamburini, Pietro
Vera Idea della Santa Sede. 1818 10/11/50
Tangye, Sir Richard
The growth of a great industry. 1890 3/6/90
Tasca, Count Ottavio
Ode a Torino. 1860 28/9/61
Tasso, Torquato
Aminta. 28/1/33, 28/6/55
Jerusalem Destroyed. 28/5/28
La Gerusalemme Liberata. 1768 9/8/33, 28/3/36, 18/4/36, 28/5/53
Tassoni, Count Alessandro
La secchia rapita. 26/1/50
Tatam, William Kellock
Letter to ... Peel on the endowment of the Papacy. 1844 15/12/44
Tattersall, J. F.
Memories of Hurstwood. 1889 19/9/91
The baptism of the Viking. 1890 21/9/91
Tauler, Johann
History and life of J. Tauler, preface by C. Kingsley. 1857 20/10/61
Taverner, Richard
Epistles and Gospels. 1/11/57
Tayler, John James
A retrospect of the religious life of England. 1845 (2nd edn 1853) 21/8/53
Tayler, William of the Middle Temple
History of the taxation of England. 1853 21/7/54
Taylor, Algernon
Convent life in Italy. 1862 22/11/63
Scenes in French monasteries. 1866 14/4/67
Taylor, Charles of St. John's College, Cambridge
Teaching of the Twelve Apostles. 1886 27/6/86
Taylor, Charles Benjamin
The Lord's Day. 1830 2/4/34
Taylor, Edgar
Suffolk Bartholomeans. A memoir of the ministerial and domestic history of John Meadows. 1840 6/7/75
Taylor, E. E. L.
The Christian sanctuary in its relation to human interest and the Divine Glory. 1853 20/2/53 ?
Taylor, Frederick
Telfer's system of horse-taming. 1858 15/10/61
Taylor, George Writer to the Signet
Treatise on the Joint Stock Act 1847. 1847 12/10/47
Taylor, George Ledwell
Autobiography of an octogenarian architect. 1870 (2v. 1870–2) 28/9/74 ?
Taylor, H.
Digest of dispatches on China ... with a connecting narrative and comments. 1840 7/4/40
Taylor, Sir Henry
'Remarks' in reply to the Edinburgh Review, April 1838. 1838 5/9/38
Autobiography. 1874 (2v. priv. pr.) 15/5/83
Autobiography. 1885 (2v.) 24/3/85
Correspondence, ed. E. Dowden. 1888 3/4/88
Edwin the Fair. 1842 12/8/42
Isaac Comnenus. 1828 23/5/35
Notes from books. 1847 31/12/47
Philip van Artevelde. 1834 24/7/34
St. Clement's Eve. A verse play. 1862 24/4/62
The Virgin Widow. 1850 11/5/50
Taylor, Isaac
Natural history of enthusiasm. 1829 27/6/30
Saturday evening. 1832 3/2/33
Spiritual Christianity. 1841 23/3/41
Taylor, James headmaster
Appeal to the Archbishop of York on the uncondemned heresies of Wilberforce's Eucharist. 1854 26/3/54
Taylor, James of Bakewell
A view of the money system. 1828 16/11/59
Taylor, James of Glasgow
Scottish covenanters. 1881 31/5/82
Taylor, Jeffreys
Aesop in rhyme. 1820 4/12/47 ?
Taylor, Jeremy
Discourse of the liberty of prophesying. 13/1/41
Holy dying. 3/4/36
Holy living. 27/12/29
The Great Exemplar. 9/4/49
The marriage ring; or, the mysteriousness and duties of marriage. 1842 30/4/49
Taylor, John
A catechism of the currency. 1835 25/3/56
Essay on money. 1830 25/4/64
Taylor, John Elloe
The sagacity and morality of plants. 1884 18/5/84

Taylor, Malcolm Campbell
Historical account of the union between church and state in Scotland. 1886 13/7/87
Taylor, Robert West
[Review of a 'Chapter of Autobiography']. (not found) 31/12/68
Taylor, Sedley
On clerical subscription. 1869 30/12/69
The conduct of Her Majesty's Ministers on the Eastern Question. 1877 1/5/77
Taylor, Tom
Life of Benjamin Robert Haydon. 1853 (3v.) 23/3/55
Taylor, Una Ashworth
City of Sarras. 1887 31/10/89, 19/11/89
Taylor, William of Norwich
Historic survey of German poetry. 1828 (3v. 1828–30) 27/7/58
Nathan the Wise, by G. E. Lessing, tr. W. Taylor. 1791 5/8/58
Taylor, William Cooke
Factories and the factory system. 1844 26/3/44
Memoirs of the House of Orleans. 1849 (3v.) 3/4/86
[Tcherkess]
The Tcherkess and his victim: sketches illustrative of the... life in Constantinople. 1880 15/11/80
Teale, William Henry
Lives of English laymen, Lord Falkland, Izaak Walton, R Nelson. 1842 30/5/42
Seven sermons... in Leeds. 1841 17/8/43, 11/8/67
Tebb, William Scott
Recrudescence of leprosy and its causation by vaccination. 1893 3/6/93
Tebbs, Henry Virtue
Essay on adultery and divorce. 1822 5/9/60
Teeling, Charles Hamilton
Personal narrative of the 'Irish Rebellion' of 1798. 1828 22/10/88
Teetgen, Alexander T.
Blessed hope. 1889 17/12/89
Fruit from Devon. Poem. 1870 31/1/70
Tegg, William
Wills of their own, curious, eccentric and benevolent. 1876 28/7/77
Tegoborski, Conte Ludwik
De la politique anglo-française. 1854 8/4/54
The productive force of Russia. 1855 (2v.) 6/12/55
Temple, Frederick
'Education of the World', in *Essays and Reviews.* 1860 8/5/60
On God's spiritual revelations to man. 1870 30/12/69
Sermons in Rugby Chapel. 1862 (2v. 1862–9) 6/10/61, 7/5/65, 17/10/69
The relations between religion and science. Bampton Lectures. 1884 25/12/84
Temple, Henry
Catholic faith. Six lectures on the Athanasian creed. 1873 31/8/73
Temple, Henry John Viscount Palmerston
Opinions and policy of... Viscount Palmerston... memoir by G. H. Francis. 1852 21/5/59, 21/3/77
Temple, Sir John
The Irish rebellion 1641. 7/8/89
Temple, Sir Richard
'Canning' in *Men and events of my time in India.* 1882 14/9/82
Contemporary Review, xlvii. 305. 1885 (March 1885) 2/3/85
Temple, Solomon
What does she [Victoria] do with it?. 1871 9/9/71
Temple Bar Magazine.
22. 349. 2/1868. Epitaphs 9/2/1868
56. 355. 7/1879. Tallemant des Reaux 7/7/1879
88. 270. 2/1890. Stage fright 25/4/1890
Temptation of our Lord. 1840 8/3/68
Tenax
National education. 1843 (?) 8/4/43
Tennant, Robert John
Sermons, preached to the British congregation at Florence. 1844 1/9/44
Tennent, James Emerson
Treatise on copyright. 1841 9/2/41
Wine, its use and taxation. 1855 3/3/53
Tennyson, Alfred
'Last Tournament' in *Contemporary Revew.* 1871 (December 1871) 30/11/71, 1/11/72
Aylmer's Field. 1864 2/9/64, 27/11/67
Ballads and other poems. 1880 27/11/80
Becket. 1884 10/12/84, 25/2/93
Death of Oenone. 1892 2/11/92
Enoch Arden. 1864 30/4/62, 2/9/64
Gareth and Lynette. 1872 25/10/72
Idylls of the King. 1859 17/6/59, 14/7/59, 24/8/63, 7/7/77, 28/6/92
In Memoriam. 1850 23/6/50, 30/8/50, 14/7/59, 8/9/79
Life of Tennyson, by H. J. Jennings. 1884 21/10/84
Locksley Hall, Sixty Years After. 1886 11/12/86
Maud, and other poems. 1855 14/7/59, 26/8/63, 15/5/70
Ode on the death of the Duke of Wellington. 1852 25/11/52
Poems. 1842 (2v.) 15/10/42, 14/7/59
Poems by two brothers. 1893 9/5/93
Poems, chiefly lyrical. 1830 14/7/30, 23/7/30, 12/2/33, 16/9/33
Queen May. 1875 24/6/75
The Foresters. 1892 23/4/92

Tennyson, Alfred (*cont.*)
The Lover's Tale. 1870 2/6/79
The Princess; a Medley. 1847 14/7/59, 12/8/59
The Throstle. 1889 13/12/89
Vivien. 1869 25/8/71
Tennyson, Charles
Speech on reform. 1828 8/3/34
Tennyson, Frederick
Daphne and other poems. 1891 18/9/91
Terence
Eunuchus. 30/1/29
Hecyra. 6/3/29, 27/3/29
Opera. 28/11/28, 20/2/29
Phormio. 5/2/29
Terpstra, Jacobus
Antiquitas Homerica. 1831 20/11/56
Terrel des Chênes, E.
Paix ou guerre. 1871 15/2/71 ?
Terrell, H.
Was Shakespeare a lawyer?. 1871 3/2/71
Terrot, Charles Hughes
Correspondence between . . . C. H. Terrot and the Rev. D. T. K. Drummond. 1842 14/11/42
Primary charge . . . in Edinburgh. 1842 17/5/42
Reasons for avoiding controversy. 1839 19/2/39
Sermon. (not found) 12/4/36
Testa, G. B.
Storia della Guerra di Federigo Primo. 1853 (2v.) 16/6/53
Thackeray, Lady Anne Isabella afterw. Ritchie
Records of Tennyson, Ruskin, Browning. 1892 4/12/83 n
Thackeray, Francis
History of William Pitt, Earl of Chatham. 1827 (2v.) 5/1/38, 13/7/60, 10/5/77
Thackeray, William Makepeace
English humourists of the eighteenth century. 1853 22/8/53
The history of Henry Esmond. 1852 3/12/52, 22/7/93
The history of Samuel Titmarsh and the Great Hoggarty Diamond. 1841 24/1/50
Vanity Fair. 1848 11/1/49, 23/1/49, 16/8/64, 17/9/64
Thaumas de la Thaumassière, Gaspard
Histoire de Berry. 1865 (4v. 1865–71) 30/4/67
Thayer, William Roscoe
Hesper: an American drama. 1888 16/9/89
The 'Alabama': a statement of facts. 1863 14/11/63
'The Anti-Climax in Midlothian: a review of Mr. Gladstone's campaign in 1884, by an eyewitness' 1884 22/9/84
The apostolical Christians and Catholics of Germany . . . a narrative of the present movement. 1845 5/7/45
The appeal of five fellows of St. John's College to the Visitor. 1869 14/1/70
Theatre de Madame. (not found) 25/5/52
The Balham mystery, or the Bravo poisoning case. 1876 21/11/76
The Bay of Gold. 1881 15/10/87
The Bible (revised version). 12/2/93
The book of Benjamin. Appointed to be read in households [satire on B. Disraeli]. 21/12/78
The book of private prayer. Presented to the convocation . . . by a committee of the lower house. 1879 30/3/79
The Brahmo year-book for 1879 [on Indian theism]. 1879 25/12/79
The carrier's case considered in reference to railways. 1841 9/3/41
The case of the parish of Alhallows the wall. 12/7/68
The Catechist or light from a crowd of witnesses. 1830 (2 no.) 11/1/65
The Christian pioneer. 1826 (1826–45) 19/4/34
The church, the state and the bible: a trinity in unity. 1852 20/2/52
The church and her doctrines. 1/11/91
The churchman's year-book for 1852, or the ecclesiastical annual register. 1852 25/4/52
The constitution of the Guild of St. Alban. 1854 20/1/56
The converted Unitarian. 1852 10/8/90
The cost price of producing foreign corn, by a merchant. 1841 16/10/41
The cross and the crescent. 1853 17/5/53
The crown or the tiara? Considerations on the present condition of the Waldenses. Addressed to the statesmen of civilized Europe. 1842 25/1/42
The Devil at Oxford. 1847 22/11/81
The Devil demonstrated. By a Physiologist. 1878 23/6/78
The diplomatic service. 1869 5/1/70
The dying priest and the cleansing note. With a prefatory note by . . . J. H. Wilson. 1875 2/3/75
The Euchologion [part of the liturgy according to the Greek rite]. 30/1/59
The faithful friend; or, two conversations on worldly intercourse and family duties. With a memoir of the writer, by a brother. 1834 8/4/38
The famous whore. (1868 edn) 14/9/71 ?
The farmers and the clergy. 1831 (?) 9/9/31
The financial exigencies of Ireland. 1864 (2v.) 18/1/64
The four Georges and the English humourists of the eighteenth century. 10/12/81
The Franchise: Freemen: Free Trade . . . By the author of the People's Blue Book. 1867 6/3/67
The Franchise. What shall we do to it?. 1858 22/3/59

The French convert. 1790 (1790) 10/10/75
The friend of Africa. (not found) 8/3/41
The General's daughter. By the author of 'A Russian Priest'. 1892 16/9/92
The Gladstone government, by a Templar. 1869 18/2/69
The great problem of Christianity. 1881 2/11/84
The Greek Testament, with the readings adopted by the Revisers. 1881 14/5/82
The green bag: a new farce. 1807 31/7/89
The Grosvenor papers. An answer to J. S. Mill's 'Subjection of Women'. 1869 (3v. 1869–70) 17/5/70
The guildhalls of Plymouth. Their history, past and present. 1874 14/7/77
The history and antiquities of Rochester cathedral. 1800 26/1/62
The House of Argyll. 1871 22/11/71
The House of Charity at St. Raphael's, Bristol. 1878 2/6/78
The impressment of seamen. 1834 3/3/34
The independence of the universities and colleges of Oxford and Cambridge. By a layman. 1838 29/4/50
The Indian spectator. 1889 14/7/89
Theiner, Augustin
Church and State. (not found) 28/4/78
Dell'introduzione del Protestantismo. 1850 12/1/51
Theiner, Johann Anton
Merkweurdiges Umlaufschreiben. 1827 7/3/39 ?
The Irish problem and how to solve it. 1881 11/5/81
The Italian cause, its history and hopes. 1859 27/7/59
The Kottabos. A college miscellany. 29/10/77
The lady of the rock; a rhyme. 1884 26/8/84
The land question. An outline of social history. 1870 1/2/70
The left leg or the right (pamphlet). 1831 18/7/31
The liberal party and the Catholics (with reference to 'The Vatican Decrees'). 1874 17/12/74
The life, political and official, of John, Earl of Eldon, anecdotal and critical. 1827 9/7/27
Thelwall, Algernon Sydney
The iniquities of the opium trade with China. 1839 3/3/40
The merchant's bane, or the antagonism between gold law and the Bank of England. 1861 19/2/61
The ministry and the sugar duties. 1844 14/2/45
The naturalist. 1875 (10v. 1875–85) 21/11/78
The Nene in danger. Considerations on the present aspect of the Nene Valley drainage and navigation improvement scheme. 1862 7/1/62
The new Godiva, a dialogue. 1883 28/1/84
The new Tory guide; lampoons. 1819 5/3/64
The new whole duty of man, containing the faith as well as the practice of a Christian. 1744 14/4/65
'The 'No Popery' premier [i.e. Disraeli] and the Irish people. By an Irish Catholic' 1868 7/11/68
The Norman people. 1874 18/3/74
Theocritus
Idylls. 24/9/25, 17/6/26, 12/11/56
Theodoli, Lily
Scenes from Roman life. Under Pressure. 1892 (2v.) 17/10/92, 29/12/92
Theologia Germanica, ed. F. Pfeiffer. 1854 18/6/54
Theologian, The.
1. 7/1844 2/8/1845
3. 310. 5/1847. Scotch Schism 4/5/1847
Theological Review. 1. 1. 3/1864. Introduction 6/3/1864
Theology and morality of the Great Exhibition. 1851 20/7/51
Theories of History. 1862 30/1/62
Theory of money: being an attempt to give a popular explanation of it. 1844 8/6/44
The Penny Magazine. 1833 8/4/33
The permanent laws of the emancipated colonies. 1838 11/8/38
The poll for two burgesses to serve in parliament for the university of Oxford. 1852 22/10/52
The Pope, his rights and duties. A letter to . . . Wiseman. By a Catholic layman. 1860 11/1/60
'The position of curates of the Church of England: a letter to Edward Horsman by a curate' 1852 17/6/52
The preacher, containing sermons by eminent living divines; (a weekly paper). 1831 (1831–5) 2/3/34
The prebendary . . . ; Being the substance of letters to the Morning Herald in 1836 and 1837. 1838 (2v. 1838) 13/5/38
The Protestant movement in Italy. 1860 18/9/61
'The questioner questioned: or, a few inquiries . . . by a member of convocation' 1850 1/6/50
'The question of compensation to the owners of slaves calmly considered' 8/4/36
Therapeutes [pseud. D. Brodie]
The healing art. 1859 1/4/60
'The real character and tendency of the proposed reform' 1831 30/3/31
The Record (the evangelical newspaper). 20/5/60
The reformation reformed, by a nomad. 1871 23/4/71
The reign of George VI. [An imaginary history of England at the beginning of the twentieth century]. 1763 23/8/78
The religion of Rome described by a Roman. 1873 29/8/75

'The remorse of Orestes' 1841 24/8/41
The Reviews Reviewed. 1860 26/4/60
The ritualistic conspiracy. 1877 7/10/77
'The Royal Exchange and the palace of industry, or, the possible future of Europe and the world' 1851 9/11/51
Therry, Roger
Comparison of the oratory of the House of Commons thirty years ago, and the present time. 1856 14/3/57
'The rule of faith . . . A letter to the . . . Bishop of Oxford by a priest in the Oxford diocese' 1867 26/1/68
The Russian catechism . . . published by order of the czar, tr. J. T. Philipps. 1723 9/12/45
The secret policy of the Jansenists and the present state of the Sorbon . . . translated out of the French copie. 8/7/55
The Sister of Mercy; a tale for the times we live in. 1854 24/1/58
The soldier's manual, compiled for the use of infantry, in the Nagri and English characters, etc. 1827 17/11/29
'The spirit of the nation' 1843 3/7/43
The state of the clergy in Virginia, before the American revolution [n.d., c. 1800]. 19/9/52
The supremacy of man. A suggestive inquiry respecting the philosophy and theology of the future. 1876 12/11/76
The Survival. With an apology for scepticism. 1877 16/9/77
'The Vestments' illegal, or the rubric: its history and meaning. By a layman. 1867 27/8/75
Thibaut, A. F. T.
On purity of musical art, tr. W. H. Gladstone. 1877 4/6/84
Thicknesse, Francis Henry
Self-help the help of all. 1885 31/5/85
Thiers, Louis Adolphe
Histoire de la révolution française. 1843 (10v.) 13/3/43, 16/8/86
History of the Consulate and the Empire, tr. D. F. Campbell. 1845 (20v. 1845–62) 28/5/60, 11/12/62, 15/12/62
Speech on the commercial policy of France, tr. St. Felix. 1852 19/4/53
Thiersch, Heinrich Wilhelm Josias
Griechenlands Schicksale. 1863 14/6/88
On Christian Commonwealth. 1876 31/12/76
Things to come. 1891 13/11/92
Thirlwall, Connop
A History of Greece. 1835 (8v. 1835–47) 5/1/47, 6/4/71
Charge. 1842 29/12/42
Charge. 1845 21/11/45
Charge. 1851 22/2/52
Charge. 1857 6/12/57
Charge. 1866 17/2/67
Charge. 1869 30/11/69
Charge. 1872 8/12/72
Contemporary Review, xxvi. 703. 1875 (October 1875) 6/10/75
Diocesan synods. A letter. 1867 7/4/67
John Yonge Akerman. 1874 13/12/74 ?
Letter to J. Bowstead concerning education in South Wales. 1861 12/10/61
Letters to a friend, ed. A. P. Stanley. 1881 12/12/81 ?
Letters, literary and theological, ed. Perowne and Stokes. 1881 2/12/81 ?
Missionary duties, difficulties and prospects. 1872 14/4/72
Present state of relations between science and religion. 1867 15/2/67
Remains. 1877 (3v. 1877–8) 21/1/87
Speech in the House of Lords [on Jewish disabilities]. 1848 13/6/48
Submersion of ancient cities. 1860 6/4/60
This troublesome world. By the authors of 'The medicine lady'. 1893 17/1/94
Tholuck, Friedrich August Gottgetreu
Der Staat in seinem Verhältnisse zur Kirche [translation of Gladstone's book]. 1843 5/8/43
Die Lehre von der Sünde. 1823 25/5/36, 19/6/36
Thom, David
Liverpool churches and chapels. 1854 16/2/90
Thom, W.
The happiness of dead clergymen, provided they die in the Lord. 1769 25/12/84
Thomas, Charles W.
Adventures on the West Coast of Africa. 1864 29/5/66 ?
Thomas, David Richard
History of St. Asaph. 1874 28/1/70 ?
Thomas, Joseph Neville Houghton
Real and National Church Reform. 1843 13/4/43
Thomas, Josiah
An address . . . with a protest. 14/7/28
Thomas, Sidney Gilchrist
Memoir and letters of S. G. Thomas, by R. W. Burnie. 1891 17/4/91
Thomas, W. of Whitland
The disestablishment campaign in its bearings on established churches and unestablished Nonconformity. 1886 2/1/87
Thomas, William Clerk of Council to Edward VI
The Pilgrim . . . a dialogue on Henry VIII, ed. J. A. Froude. 1861 8/1/61
Thomas, William of Denton
Observations on canals and railways. 1825 27/11/67 ?
Thomas, William Cave
Holiness of beauty. 1863 12/7/63

Thompson, Benjamin
Deaf and Dumb, or the orphan. 1801 21/10/25
Thompson, D'Arcy Wentworth
Daydreams of a schoolmaster. 1864 13/4/64
Thompson, Edward D.D.
Triumph of Christianity. 1841 26/4/41
Thompson, G.
Speech on the Corn Laws. 1842 28/1/42
Thompson, H.
Elephanta. 1839 28/4/40
Thompson, Sir Henry F.R.G.S.
Cremation; the treatment of the body after death. 1884 25/3/89
Thompson, H. S.
Ireland in 1839 and 1869. 1870 29/1/70
Thompson, Mrs. Jemima afterw. Luke
Sequel to the female Jesuit. 1852 16/10/63
Thompson, Joseph Parrish
Church and State in the United States. 1873 27/12/74
Contest with Ultramontanism in Germany... A speech. 1874 3/5/74
Thompson, P.
Healthy moral homes for agricultural labourers. 1863 12/1/65
Thompson, Robert Anchor
The Oxford Declaration. A letter to W. R. Fremantle. 1864 17/5/64
Thompson, W. D.
Christian miracles. 1888 16/9/88
Thoms, William John
Hannah Lightfoot. 1867 22/12/73
Nineteenth Century, iv. 88. 1878 (July 1878) 12/11/78
Three notelets of Shakespeare. 1865 24/12/73
Thomsen, Grímur
Garanties anglo-françaises. 1848 17/1/79
Thomson, Andrew D.D.
Life of Principal Harper. 1881 6/11/81
Thomson, C.
Letters of S. Rutherford. 1836 (2v.) 24/2/39
Thomson, Henry Byerley
Military forces and institutions of Great Britain. 1855 16/2/56
Thomson, J.
Sermon on the nature of theism. 1870 17/9/71
Thomson, James poet
Works. 1757 (4v.) 11/8/60
Thomson, John
Tables of interest... showing the exchange on bills. 1768 12/7/54 ?
Thomson, Katherine
Cardinal Wolsey. 1824 2/5/28
Thomson, William Archbishop
An open college best for all. 1854 9/3/54
An outline of the necessary laws of thought. 1849 12/1/53
Charge. 1865 19/11/65
Pastoral letter to the laity of York. 1864 6/5/64
Seven years. A charge. 1870 13/11/70
The atoning work of Christ. 1853 30/10/53
The power of atonement. 1860 10/6/60
Thomson, William Thomas
Decimal numeration and... coinage. 1854 17/7/54
Tables of interest. 1853 12/7/54
Thorburn, David
The divine origin... of tithes. 1841 17/12/63
Thorburn, Grant
Men and manners in Britain. 1834 3/12/35
Thornbury, George Walter
Life of J. M. W. Turner. 1862 (2v.) 7/6/62
Thorneycroft, G. B.
[Pamphlet on corn]. (not found) 20/1/41
[Speeches]. (not found) 14/1/42
Thornhill, W. J.
The passion of Dido. 1878 25/4/79
Thornissen, J. J.
Quelques considérations sur la théorie du progrès indéfini. 1860 12/9/86
Thornton, Edward of East India House
Chapters on the modern history of British India. 1840 2/7/42
Summary of the history of the East India Company. 1833 29/3/76
The history of the British Empire in India. 1841 (6v. 1841–5) 29/4/58
Thornton, Henry
An enquiry into the nature and effects of the paper credit of Great Britain. 1802 30/3/54
Thornton, John Wingate
The historical relation of New England to the English Commonwealth. 1874 17/7/75
Thornton, William Thomas
Old-fashioned ethics and common-sense metaphysics. 1873 16/5/75 ?
Over-population and its remedy. 1846 19/2/46
Plea for peasant proprietors. 1848 25/2/48
Thorold, Anthony Wilson
'Evangelical clergy of 1868' in *Contemporary Review*, viii. 569. 1868 (August 1868) 23/8/68
Pastoral letter. 1878 29/12/78
Thorp, Charles
Charge to the clergy of the archdeaconry of Durham. 1844 12/9/51 ?
Thorp, Robert barrister
Church extension. 1841 27/8/41
Practical conservatism. 1840 5/2/40
Thorp, Thomas
Charge. 1843 1/10/54, 26/4/60
Church rates and endowed schools. 1860 29/4/60
Restoration of the Round Church. 1845 7/7/45
Thorpe, William D.D.
Letter on Sewell's Christian Morals. 1841 3/6/41

Thorpe, William D. D. (*cont.*)
The Christian Sabbath. 1856 20/2/56
Thoughts on academic education in Ireland. (not found) 30/3/45
Thoughts on reform. 1859 2/2/65
Thoughts on the Athanasian Creed... By a layman. 1886 2/5/86
Thoughts on the present threatening aspect. (not found) 17/7/33
Thoughts on traits of the ministerial policy. 1843 18/7/43
Thouvend, L.
Le secret de l'Empereur. 1889 11/12/89
Thring, Edward
Memory of Edward Thring, by J. H. Skrine. 1889 31/5/91
Thring, Henry
[On home rule] in *Contemporary Review,* li. 305. 1887 (March 1887) 12/3/87
Suggestions for colonial reform. 1865 31/1/65
The supremacy of Great Britain. 1851 29/3/53
Thucydides
Eight books of the Peloponnesian war, tr. Thomas Hobbes. 24/11/28
History of the Peloponnesian War. 14/10/28, 12/3/29, 12/6/30, 7/7/30, 7/8/30, 1/9/30, 17/9/31, 25/1/47, 19/12/54, 21/4/59, 3/10/59, 4/10/59, 9/1/71
Thurlow, Charles Augustus
The Church established as the guardian and witness of the truth. 1837 21/7/38
Thursfield, Emily
England and Ireland. 1884 27/8/85
Thursfield, Sir James Richard
Peel. 1891 22/4/91
Thynne, John Alexander Lord Bath
Observations on Bulgarian affairs. 1880 29/3/80
Tichborne romance; the trial of Tichborne v. Lushington. 1871 23/1/72
Ticknor, George
History of Spanish literature. 1849 (3v.) 29/9/57, 5/10/59
Life, letters and journals. 1876 (2v.) 7/9/76
Ticozzi, Stefano
Vita di Gesù. 1826 23/2/41 ?
Tiele, Cornelis Petrus
Die Assyriologie und ihre Ergebnisse für die vergleichende Religionsgeschichte. 1877 6/3/87 ?
Tierney, Mark Aloysius
Letter to... Chandler. 1844 21/11/44
Tillotson, John
Form of prayers used by William III. 1704 16/11/62
Works, ed. R. Baker. 1717 (2v.) 19/10/56
Times Best Blessing. (not found) 23/6/50
Times of trouble in the Church. (not found) 3/2/45
Timins, Charles
Testimony of Jesus. 1862 22/3/68 ?
Timpson, Thomas
Memoirs of Mrs. Elizabeth Fry. 1847 31/7/59
Tindall, Matthew
Memoirs of the life and writings of Matthew Tindall, ed. E. Curll. 1733 18/4/92
Tipaldo-Foresti, P.
Biografia di G. K. Tipaldo. 1878 7/10/79
Tiptaft, William
Sermon. 1830 21/3/30
Tiraboschi, Girolano
Compendium on the literary history of Italy until the formation of the modern Italian language. 1835 31/10/55 ?
Life of Petrarch. 1804 28/12/47
Tischendorf, Lobegott Friedrich Constantin
Are our Gospels genuine?. 1869 29/8/69
Synopsis Evangelica. 1851 5/12/58
Titcomb, Jonathan Holt
The Church of England in Northern and Central Europe. 1885 13/9/85
Tittmann, Carl Christian
Meletemata Sacra. 1816 20/4/57
Tocnaye, De La
Rambles through Ireland. 1799 (2v.) 30/10/88
Tocqueville, Alexis de
Democracy in America, tr. H. Reeve. 1840 (2v.) 23/4/40
L'Ancien Régime et la Révolution. 1856 28/10/61
Memoirs, letters and remains. 1861 (2v.) 8/12/84, 24/12/84
Tod, Isabella M. S.
Women and the Franchise Bill. 1884 13/3/84
Todd, Adam Brown
Homes, haunts and battlefields of the Covenanters. 1886 (2v.) 9/1/87
Poetical Works [on Gladstone]. 1906 8/1/87
Todd, Charles Hawkes
The Irish Church, its disestablishment and disendowment. 1869 28/2/69
Todd, Henry John
A defence of the true and catholick doctrine... by the most Revd. Thomas Cranmer. 1825 31/3/43
Todd, James Henthorn
Books of the Vaudois. 1865 13/8/65
University of Dublin. Remarks... on T. Wyse. 1844 21/12/44, 1/2/73
Todd, Tweedy John
Book of analysis. 1831 27/8/42
Todd, William Gowan
Church of St. Patrick: a historical inquiry into the independence of the ancient Church of Ireland. 1844 11/6/44

Todhunter, Isaac
Life of William Whewell. 1876 24/4/76
Todhunter, John
The Banshee. 1888 14/6/88
Toland, John
An account of the courts of Prussia and Hanover. 1705 18/3/93
Hypatia. 1753 24/8/90
Tollemache, Beatrix
Engleberg, and other verses. 1890 18/12/91
Tollemache, Lionel Arthur
Recollections of Pattison. 1885 9/11/85, 13/12/85
Safe studies. 1884 17/1/84
Stones of stumbling. 1891 20/12/91
Tolstoi, Aleksei Konstantinovich
La Mort d'Ivan le Terrible. 1879 10/5/92
Prince Serebryani. An historical novel of the times of Ivan the Terrible. 1892 25/1/93
Tolstoi, Jacques
La Vérité sur la question de l'Orient. 1855 28/10/53
Tolstoi, Lev Nikolaevich
Christ's Christianity. 1885 13/12/85
La Sonate à Kreutzer. 1890 21/5/90
La Vie, tr. E. Jardetzky. 1888 4/7/88
The kingdom of God is with you, tr. A. Delano. 1894 23/3/94
Tomkins, Frederick, and Jencken, H. D.
Compendium of Roman law. 1870 3/12/70
Tomkins, Jacob
A sketch of aristocracy. 1835 22/4/35
Epistle to... I. Tomkins. 1835 27/7/35
Tomkinson, William
The diary of a cavalry officer. 1894 14/4/94
Tomline, George Pretyman
Elements of Christian theology. 1799 (2v.) 31/12/26
Life of William Pitt. 1821 (2v.) 2/12/52, 29/4/68, 26/3/90
Memoir of William Pitt. 1787 28/8/26
Tomlins, Richard
Reply to a circular forwarded by the Committee of Weston v. Liddell. 1857 4/10/57
Tomlinson, George
Charge, delivered to the clergy of... Gibraltar. 1845 2/3/45
Report of a journey to the Levant. 1841 4/6/41
Tomlinson, John Tomlinson
The 'historical' grounds of the Lambeth Judgement examined. 1891 15/3/91
The legal history of Canon Stubbs. 1884 6/3/84
Tondini, Caesarius
The future of the Russian Church. 1876 10/4/92
The primacy of St. Peter. 1879 27/12/79
Two sermons on the death of Ambrose de Lisle. 1878 7/7/78
Tone, Theobald Wolfe
Autobiography, ed. R. Barry O'Brien. 1893 12/10/93, 19/11/93
Commentary on the memoirs of T. Wolfe Tone, by P. R. Fermoy. 1828 17/8/87
Life... written by himself. 1826 (2v.) 23/5/65
Tonna, Charlotte Elizabeth
Derry, a tale. 1886 8/8/86
Letters from Ireland. 1838 15/7/41
The wrongs of woman. 1843 (4v. 1843–4) 11/1/45
Tonson, Jacob
Poetic miscellanies. 1709 27/7/52
Tooke, John Horne
Diversions of Purley. 1786 2/11/55
Letter to Dunning [on the conjunction 'that']. 1778 29/10/60
Proceedings in action for debt. 1792 6/4/62
Tooke, Thomas
History of prices and of the state of circulation. 1838 (6v.) 19/8/42, 14/11/46
Inquiry into the currency principle. 1844 2/5/44
On the Bank Charter Act of 1844, its principles and operation. 1856 8/1/56
Topham, Edward major
Letters from Edinburgh. 1776 24/2/88
Topinard, Paul
L'Anthropologie. 1876 22/12/84
Toplady, Augustus
Scheme of Christian necessity. 1775 30/10/31
Works. 1794 (vol 6) 9/3/45
Topp, St. John
'The marriage and divorce laws' in *Melbourne Review*, iv. 429. 1879 12/2/80
Torcy, Marquis De
Memoirs. 1757 (2v.) 28/10/70
Torelli, G. [pseud. d'Arco]
Massimo d'Azeglio. 1873 13/2/66 ?
Torelli, Count Luigi
La questione del potere temporale del Papa. 1870 8/3/75
Tories, whigs, and radicals. (not found) 24/12/34
Torquemada the Younger
Letter to the Vice-Chancellor of... Oxford. 1843 5/8/43
Torre, Federico
Memorie storiche sull'intervento francese. 1851 14/11/51
Torrens, Robert
Colonization of South Australia. 1835 18/6/36
Essay on the external corn trade. 1815 30/3/46
Letter to Sir R. Peel... on the condition of England. 1843 1/2/43
Paper intended to have been given to the Committee on the affairs of South Australia. 1841 21/4/41, 30/8/41, 2/11/41, 29/11/41

Torrens, Robert (*cont.*)
Systematic colonisation. 1849 19/4/49
The budget. First letter. 1841 30/8/41
The budget. Third letter. 1841 2/11/41
Torrens, William Torrens MacCullagh
Memoirs of... Melbourne. 1878 (new edn 1890) 26/11/89
Torrente, Mariano
Slavery in the island of Cuba. 1853 15/10/53
Torry, Patrick
Pastoral letter. 1845 8/3/46
Tory, A new-fashioned. 1877 2/4/77
Toscane, La, et ses grand-ducs autrichiens. 1859 17/9/59
Toscanelli, Giuseppe
Religione e Patria. 1890 17/9/90
Tosti, Luigi
'Della donna considerata nell'arte', *Scritti vari.* (n.d.) 25/9/66
Storia del Concilio di Costanza. 1853 (2v.) 28/8/60, 24/1/75
Storia della Lega Lombarda. 1848 18/2/51
Storia di' Abelardo. 1851 2/9/60
Totleben, Count Eduard Ivanovich
Défense de Sébastopol. 1863 (2v. 1863–4) 25/7/64
Touchard-Lafosse, G.
Chronique de l'Oeil-De-Boeuf. 1829 (8v. 1829–33, 4 edn 2v. 1878–80) 19/4/82
Toulmin, Joshua
Four discourses on baptism. 1811 26/1/34
Historical view of the state of the Dissenters in England. 1814 1/6/44
Life of John Biddle. 1789 26/5/44
Series of letters [on Socinianism] to the Revd. J. Freeston. 1812 27/1/84
Tourzel, Duchess of
Mémoires. 1883 (2v.) 17/7/88, 26/7/88
Towgood, Micaiah
A dissent from the Church of England fully justified. 1753 13/1/56
Towle, Eleanor A.
Virginia Tennant. 1888 (2v.) 10/7/89 ?
Towle, George Makepeace
Young people's History of Ireland. 1886 10/12/86
Townsend, George Canon of Durham
Baptismal Regeneration. 1850 20/2/50
Sermons on miscellaneous subjects. 1849 25/2/49
Sermons on some of the most interesting subjects of theology. 1830 21/6/30
The doctrine of Atonement. A sermon. 1838 30/3/39
Townsend, George Alfred
The entailed hat. 1884 14/6/84
Townsend, George Fyler
The Churchman's Year. 1842 (2v.) 26/5/42
Townsend, Thomas Stewart
Facts and circumstances relating to the condition of the Irish clergy of the Established Church. 1832 11/2/32
Policy of a separate grant for education in Ireland, considered. 1849 19/5/49
Townsend, William Charles
History of the House of Commons. 1843 (2v. 1843–4) 14/3/54
Townsend, William John
Great Schoolmen of the Middle Ages. 1881 27/8/82, 21/3/86
Townshend, Chauncy Hare
Facts in Mesmerism. 1840 23/8/48
Toynbee, Joseph
Benificence in disease. 1865 17/6/65
Toynbee, William
Lays of common life. 1890 30/5/90
Tozer, Mr.
[On coinage]. (not found) 27/10/59
Trabucco, Giacomo
Sulla vera posizione dei terreni terziari del bacino piemontese. 1875 24/12/75
Tracts for the Times, no. 24. 'The scriptural view of the Apostolic Commission'. 2/2/34
Tracts for the Times, no. 75. 12/12/38, 16/12/38
Tracts for the Times, no. 88. 'The Greek devotions of Bishop Andrewes'. 31/12/38
Trades' unions and strikes. 1834 (not found) 4/4/34
Traill, Mrs. Catherine Parr née Strickland
The backwoods of Canada. 1836 8/3/37
Traill, John Christie
Letter to the Marquis of Blandford, on the management of church property. 1856 23/4/56
Traité de Paillardise. 4/7/86
Trapassi, P.
La Clemenza di Tito. 25/11/33
Travers, John
Letter... upon the tea duties. 1834 30/3/34, 30/3/53 ?
Tredgold, Thomas
The steam engine: its invention and progressive improvement. 1838 (2v. 1838–9) 26/6/40 ?
Tregelles, Arthur E.
James I. A drama. 1890 12/12/90
Queen Elizabeth. A drama. 1890 12/12/90
Tregelles, Samuel Prideaux
Remarks on... the Book of Daniel. 1852 22/9/91
Trelawney, Edward John
Records of Shelley, Byron, and the Author. 1878 (2v.) 26/10/78
Tremblicka, F.
Mémoires d'une Polonaise. 1841 5/11/41
Trench, Francis
Diary of travels in France and Spain. 1845 27/5/45

Trench, Maria
James Skinner. 1883 16/10/83, 9/8/85
Trench, Melesina
Remains of the late Mrs. Richard Trench. 1862 19/9/62
Thoughts of a parent on education. 1837 16/3/37
Trench, Richard Chenevix
Charge. 1865 26/11/65
Charge. 1868 1/11/68
Charge. 1871 5/11/71
Gustavus Adolphus. Two lectures. 1865 20/6/65
Letters and memorials. 1888 (2v.) 11/7/88, 25/11/88
Notes on parables. 1841 5/11/41, 19/6/70
On some deficiencies in our English dictionaries. 1857 11/2/58
On the Authorized Version of the New Testament: in connexion with some recent proposals for its revision. 1858 14/9/62
On the study of words. 1851 11/12/52
Poems. 1865 15/1/65
Sacred Latin poetry. 1849 (2nd edn 1864) 16/8/63, 11/9/64
Sermons . . . preached in Westminster Abbey. 1860 22/7/60
Star of the Wise Men. 1850 17/2/50
The story of Justin Martyr and other poems. 1835 31/8/35, 14/2/36, 4/10/38
Trench, Thomas Richard Frederick Cooke
Reconstruction of the Church in Ireland and the uses of commutation. 1869 23/1/69
Trench, William Richard
Ierne, a tale. 1871 (2v.) 13/3/90
Realities of Irish life. 1868 25/1/69
Trench, William Thomas Le Poer Lord Clancarty
Ireland, her present condition and what it might be. 1864 7/9/65
Trenck, Baron Friedrich von der
Memoirs. 1878 26/10/78, 22/9/86
Trent, Council of
Canones et Decreta. (new edn 1848) 1/3/46, 28/6/85
Trevelyan, Sir Charles Edward
From Pesth to Brindisi. 1870 29/7/76
Letters on the mutiny of Vellore. 1857 19/4/58 ?, 14/9/62
Statement . . . on recall from Madras. 1860 22/7/60, 22/12/60
Trevelyan, Sir George Otto
Early history of Charles James Fox. 1880 18/11/80
Life and letters of Lord Macaulay. 1876 (2v.) 23/3/76
Pope and his patron. 1862 16/6/62, 19/9/62
Speeches on army reform. 1870 4/1/71
The ladies in Parliament. 1869 23/1/69, 16/11/69
Trevor, Arthur Hill 3rd Viscount Dungannon
Life and times of William III. 1835 (2v. 1835–6) 9/3/55
Trevor, George
On disputed rubrics and the Public Worship Regulation Act. 1875 27/4/75
On ecclesiastical courts. 1882 4/1/85
Party spirit. 1851 23/8/51, 11/12/52
Sermons. 1844 27/3/47
The Athanasian creed: the damnatory clauses. 1873 27/7/73
The convocation of the two provinces. 1852 6/3/53
Triad of essays on Holy Scripture. 1865 19/11/65
Trial of occasional conformity. (not found) 25/11/49
Tribunalis Christi. (not found) 2/11/56
Tricoupis, S.
Historia tes Hellenikes Epanastaseos. 1853 (4v. 1853–7) 16/11/76
Trinitate, G. P. da Sancta
True state of the case considered . . . the Oxford Tracts. 1839 1/6/39
Tristram, W. O.
Lounsta. 1890 6/8/91
Triumph of moral good. 1870 (not found) 11/9/70
Troil, Uno von
Letters on Iceland. 1780 27/2/58
Trollope, Anthony
'Iceland' in *Fortnightly Review*, xxiv. 175. 1878 (July 1878) 18/12/78
An autobiography. 1883 8/11/83
Barchester Towers. 1858 (3v.) 8/4/58
Framley Parsonage. 1861 (3v.) 28/8/61
The Eustace diamonds. 1873 (3v.) 5/3/73
Trollope, Frances
Domestic manners of the Americans. 1832 12/10/32
The Vicar of Wrexhill. 1837 (3v.) 18/11/37
Town and Country. 1848 (3v.) 16/11/50 ?
Trollope, Thomas Adolphus
A peep behind the scenes at Rome. 1877 11/3/78
Tuscany in 1849 and 1859. 1859 18/9/59
Tromholt, Sophus
Under the rays of the Aurora Borealis. 1885 (2v.) 8/8/85
Trotter, John Bernard
Walks through Ireland in 1812, 1814 and 1817. 1819 22/8/93
Trower, Walter John
[Two letters on the Gorham case]. 1850 2/7/50
An address. 1849 20/1/50
Charge. 1855 6/1/56
Defence of the City of God. 1852 27/6/52, 23/1/53
Letter to . . . Russell [on convocation]. 1847 13/12/47
Pastoral letter. 1851 30/6/51

Trueba y Cosió, Joaquín Telesforo de
Paris and London. 1831 (3v.) 19/4/34
Trussardi, Giacinto
Gallofobia e monumento mania. 1888 14/10/89
Lettera aperta a SS Leone XIII. 1888 14/10/89
Trustees address [at Burlington College, New Jersey]. 1846 2/2/48
Truth, what is it, and opinion, what is it not?. 1840 19/6/40
Truth about opium smoking. 1882 12/5/83
Truthseeker, ed. J. P. Hopps. 1886 7/11/86
Tucker, Charlotte Maria
Exiles in Babylon. 1864 27/9/68
War and Peace; a tale. 1862 29/1/63
Tucker, George
Progress in the United States. 1843 30/1/45
Tucker, Henry St. George acct. gen. for Bengal
Review of the financial situation of the East India Co. in 1824. 1825 22/6/58
Tucker, Henry William
Memoir of Bishop Selwyn. 1879 (2v.) 22/3/79, 3/4/81
Memoir of Edward Field. 1876 3/12/76
Tucker, Josiah
A series of answers [on American independence]. 1776 10/2/47
Brief and dispassionate view of... the Trinitarian, Arian and Socinian systems. 1774 28/2/47
Cui Bono? What benefits can arise from the war?. 1781 10/5/49
Four tracts and two sermons, on political and commercial subjects. 1774 (2v.) 20/2/47, 1/1/60
Humble address and appeal [on American independence]. 1775 9/2/47
Letter to... Burke [on America]. 1775 11/2/47, 25/10/62
Letters to... Dr. Kippis [on dissent]. 1773 9/4/49
Tucker, William of Chard
Predestination calmly considered from principles of reason. 1821 30/10/36
Tucker, William Hill
Eton of old; or, eighty years since 1811–22. 1892 24/2/93, 13/3/93
Tuckerman, Henry Thomas
A sheaf of verse bound for the fair. 1864 29/7/64
Tuckwell, William
The ancient ways. Winchester fifty years ago. 1893 13/7/93
Tudor, John R.
The Orkneys and Shetland. 1883 11/6/84
Tufnell, Edward Carleton, and Shuttleworth, J. K.
Report on the training of pauper children. 1839 9/2/41
Tuke, James Hack
A visit to Connaught... 1847. 1848 20/4/48
Achill and the west of Ireland. 1886 7/4/87
Irish distress and its remedies. The land question. 1880 11/8/80
Tulloch, John
Position and prospects of the Church of Scotland. 1878 16/6/78
Religion and theology. A sermon for the times. 1875 8/10/75
Tupper, Henry
Primogeniture and entail. 1864 15/6/68
Tupper, Martin Farquhar
A modern pyramid. 1839 17/2/40
A third series of Proverbial Philosophy. 1867 17/5/67
Coronation Ode. 1838 16/7/38
Dozen ballads... about church abuses. 1854 8/1/54
Geraldine. 1838 25/10/37, 13/5/59
Hactennus. 1848 28/12/47
Probabilities. 1847 17/3/47
Proverbial philosophy. 1838 11/2/38
Raleigh... a play. 1866 26/1/66
The antiritualist satire. Tupper's Directorium. 1867 9/7/67
The crock of gold. A rural novel. 1844 6/4/44
The twins. A domestic novel. 1844 11/4/44
Turberville, Arthur C.
Types of the saintly life. 1891 1/11/91
Turchia e la Civilta. (not found) 18/12/77
Turgenieff, Ivan
Fathers and children. 1863 2/3/80
Terres vierges. 1877 16/3/80
Turgot, Anne Robert Jacques
Oeuvres, ed. Daire & Dussard. 1844 (2v.) 17/8/48
Turkey in 1860. By R. J. C. 1860 4/9/60
Turkish dog. (not found) 13/10/76
Turnbull, David
Travels in the West. Cuba, with notices of... the slave trade. 1840 4/6/40
Turnbull, William Barclay David Donald
Parochial disorganisation. (not found) 10/1/45
Turner, Charles Tennyson
Collected sonnets. 1880 28/10/80
Turner, Francis
Brief memoirs of N. Ferrar, ed. T. M. MacDonogh. 1837 24/12/43
Turner, John D.D.
Justice done to human souls, in a short view of Mr. Dodwell's book. 1706 14/8/76
Turner, John musician
Manual of introduction in vocal music. 1833 3/3/38
Turner, Joseph Mallord William
Life of J. M. W. Turner, by G. W. Thornbury. 1862 7/6/62

Turner, Sharon
History of England. 1799 (9v. 1799–1823) 27/3/35, 28/2/39
Turner, Thomas
Letter on the collegiate parish church of Manchester. 1850 13/3/50
Turnerelli, Edward Tracy
The 'Sacred Mission' of the Russian wolf among the Christian sheep of Turkey. 1877 20/6/77
Türr, Stefan
La solution pacifique de la question d'Orient. 1877 3/1/78
Remarks on a new Congress of Vienna. 1864 14/6/64
Turriffs, G.
[On Aberdeen]. (not found) 26/2/74
Turton, Thomas
Roman Catholic doctrine of the Eucharist. 1837 31/1/47
Statement. (not found) 23/2/38
Text of the English Bible . . . considered. 1833 22/6/34 ?
Thoughts [on admitting dissenters to degrees]. 1834 29/5/34
Vindication of the literary character of Professor Porson. 1827 24/5/61
[Tuscan persecutions, dedicated to Gladstone; not found]. 1853 25/9/53
Tuttle, Hudson
Scenes in the spirit world. 1855 25/8/72
Twamley, Louisa Anne afterw. Meredith
Notes and sketches of New South Wales . . . 1839 to 1844. 1844 9/3/46
Twamley, W.
The cause of the Dublin poor. 1886 15/2/87 ?
Tweed, Henry Earle
The apostles and the offertory. 1860 4/11/60
Tweed, James Peers
The Oxford Commission . . . Three letters to W. E. Gladstone. 1852 23/10/52
Tweedie, Ethel B.
A writer's jaunt to Norway. 1894 13/3/94
Twiss, Horace
Public and private life of . . . Lord Eldon. 1844 (3v.) 30/9/44
Twiss, Travers
Letter . . . on the law studies of the University [of Oxford]. 1856 30/1/56
Tests of a thriving population. 1845 8/7/45
The duchies of Schleswig-Holstein. 1848 13/1/49
The Letters Apostolic of Pope Pius IX. 1851 1/3/51
The Oregon question examined. 1846 6/3/46
Two lectures on machinery. 1844 16/5/44
Twistleton, E. T. B.
Evidence on Common Schools in Massachusetts. 1854 14/4/49, 30/11/54
Two letters to Sir Robert Peel on his proposed banking measures; by an ex M.P. 1844 8/7/44, 25/4/53
Two months in the Confederate States, by an English merchant. 1863 12/5/63
Two Unions: their effects in England and Scotland. 1844 17/2/44
Tyler, James Endell
Henry of Monmouth. 1838 26/11/40
Image worship of the Church of Rome. 1847 24/10/47
Meditations on Common Prayer. 1849 (2v.) 22/4/49
Oaths: their origin, nature and history. 1834 19/3/35
Primitive Christian worship. 1840 3/5/40
Worship of the Blessed Virgin Mary. 1844 5/5/44
Tyler, R. E.
Questions of the day: Indian revenue from Indian opium. 1857 10/6/57
Tyler, Thomas
Christ the Lord [reply to Colenso]. 1863 23/2/68
Tyler, William Seymour
Theology of Greek poets. 1867 2/10/86
Tylor, Edward Burnett
Anthropology. 1881 3/5/81
Primitive culture. 1871 (2v.) 8/12/71, 24/5/72
Winged figures of the Assyrian and other ancient monuments. 1890 17/9/90
Tyndale, William
An answer to . . . More's Dialogue The Supper of the Lord, ed. H. Walter. 1848 18/5/56
Brief declaration of the Sacraments. 7/2/36, 18/5/56
Tyndall, John
Faraday as a discoverer. 1868 27/1/69
Sound. Eight lectures. 1867 7/3/68
Tyng, S. H.
[Pamphlet on Gladstone]. (not found) 26/4/68
Tyrwhitt, Richard St. John
Contemporary Review, xxxiii. 81. 1878 (August 1878) 4/8/78
Tytler, Alexander Fraser
Elements of history. 1855 24/9/72
Life of Petrarch. 1810 27/11/80
Tytler, Patrick Fraser
England under the reign of Edward VI and Mary. 1839 30/9/40
Tytler, Sarah [Henrietta Keddie]
Marie Antoinette. 1883 9/4/84

Ubaldini, Petruccio
Descrittione del Regno di Scotia. 18/10/37
Ubicini, Jean Henri Abdolonyme
Letters on Turkey, tr. Lady Easthope. 1856 (2v.) 3/5/58

Uda, M.
Il cuore di una beghina. 1862 3/11/66
Uffizia della Settimana Santa. 1806 31/3/33
Uffizio della Domenica delli Palmi. 23/3/34
Ugolinus, Bartholomaeus
Tractatus de Officio et Potestate Episcopi. 17/9/65
Uhden, Hermann Ferdinand
The Anglican Church in the nineteenth century, tr. W. C. C. Humphreys. 1844 12/1/44
Ullathorne, William Bernard
A plea for rights and liberties of religious women. 1851 2/4/51
History of the restoration of the Catholic hierarchy in England. 1871 11/6/71
Mr. Gladstone's Expostulation unravelled. 1875 16/1/75
Remarks on the proposed Education Bill. 1850 11/7/50
Synodal discourse. 1875 4/6/75
The Döllingerites, Mr. Gladstone and apostates from the faith. 1874 23/11/74
Ullmann, Carl
Reformers before the Reformation. 1854 (2v.) 27/7/56
Zukunft der Evangelische Kirche Deutschlands. 1845 13/11/45
Ulloa, Pietro Calá Duca di Lauria
Lettres Napolitaines. 1864 25/1/64, 15/11/66
Ulrici, Hermann
Shakespeare's dramatische Kunst. 1847 (2v.) 19/12/59
Ultimate principle of religious liberty. 1860 8/8/60
Ultramontane action, Sketches of. 1873 29/10/73
Umfreville, Edward
Present state of Hudson's Bay. 1790 12/8/48
Underhill, Edward Benn
Letter to . . . E. Cardwell, with illustrative documents on Jamaica. 1865 7/1/66
Union Chapel sermons. 1878 27/4/79
Union Review.
1. 27, 123. 5/1888. on Zola; Martial 3/6/1888
2. 233. 8/1859. on Gladstone 12/8/1859
2. 598. 1/1864. Celibacy 25/12/1864
3. 1. 1/1865. Doctrinal developments 8/1/1865
4. 1/1866 14/1/1866, 11/3/1866, 6/5/1866, 1/7/1866, 2/9/1866
5. 1/1867 3/3/1867, 12/5/1867, 7/7/1867, 27/10/1867
6. 1/1868 12/1/1868, 10/4/1868, 5/7/1868
6. 398. 9/1868. Cardinal York 27/9/1868
6. 481. 1/1868. Dr Newman 8/11/1868
7. 1/1869 3/1/1869, 7/11/1869
7. 193. 1/1869. Women 2/5/1869
7. 323, 432. Eastern Church 21/11/1869
8. 1/1870 2/1/1870, 10/7/1870, 6/11/1870
9. 1/1871 15/1/1871, 5/3/1871
Buddhism 6/7/1873
Union without communion. (not found) 26/5/68
United Kingdom and disunited Church. (not found) 29/12/68
United Service Magazine. 515. on Raglan 19/9/1855
Unité Romaine. (not found) 13/10/45
Universal Review.
1. 27, 123. 5/1888. on Zola; Martial 3/6/1888
2. 233. 8/1859. on Gladstone 12/8/1859
2. 598. 1/1864. Celibacy 25/12/1864
3. 1. 1/1865. Doctrinal developments 8/1/1865
4. 1/1866 14/1/1866, 11/3/1866, 6/5/1866, 1/7/1866, 2/9/1866
5. 1/1867 3/3/1867, 12/5/1867, 7/7/1867, 27/10/1867
6. 1/1868 12/1/1868, 10/4/1868, 5/7/1868
6. 398. 9/1868. Cardinal York 27/9/1868
6. 481. 1/1868. Dr Newman 8/11/1868
7. 1/1869 3/1/1869, 7/11/1869
7. 193. 1/1869. Women 2/5/1869
7. 323, 432. Eastern Church 21/11/1869
8. 1/1870 2/1/1870, 10/7/1870, 6/11/1870
9. 1/1871 15/1/1871, 5/3/1871
Buddhism 6/7/1873
University education in Ireland in . . . 1860. 1861 2/7/61
University of Durham. What shall we do with it? By a Quondam Fellow. 1863 5/3/63
Un mot sur les affaires d'Orient. (not found) 18/7/54
Unwin, William Jordan
Education the work of the people. A letter to . . . Russell. 1856 3/4/56
Prussian primary education, its organisation and results. 1857 28/2/57
Upham, Charles Wentworth
Life of General Washington. 1852 (2v.) 1/7/52
Upham, Thomas Cogswell
Life, religious opinions and experience of Madame de la Mothe Guyon. 1847 3/6/53
Upton, John prebendary of Rochester
Critical observations on Shakespeare. 1746 4/8/55
Uranga, Nemesio
Jésus et la religion naturelle. 1880 14/3/80, 9/5/80
Urfey, Thomas d'
Wit and mirth. 1719 (5v.) 15/2/76
Urlin, Richard Denny
John Wesley's place in Church history. 1870 3/4/70

Urlin, Richard Denny, and Key, Thomas
The transfer of land and declaration of title acts. 1863 4/5/64
Urquhart, David
An appeal against faction. 1843 15/8/43
Diplomacy and Commerce. 1840 20/4/40
Diplomatic transactions in Central Asia from 1834 to 1839. 1841 6/6/43
England, France, Russia, and Turkey. 1834 17/8/35
Reflections on thoughts and things. 1844 11/3/45
The Edinburgh Review and the Afghan war. 1843 5/7/43
The French in Africa, Algiers, and Morocco. 1844 7/6/45
Wealth and want. 1845 14/6/45
Urquhart, William Pollard
Essays on subjects on political economy. 1850 15/2/56
Urwick, William the younger
The servant of Jehovah. 1877 20/7/90
Usurpations of England the chief source of the miseries of Ireland. 1780 15/3/90

V. [Mrs. Archer Clive]
Poems. 1872 17/10/85
Poems. 1890 (new edn) 21/12/90
V., W. F.
Letter . . . to H. MacNeile on the Maynooth Grant. 1845 19/5/45
V., W. T.
Angels and their ministry. 1869 4/9/70
Vaccari Diotallevi, Costanza
Le rivelazione impunitarie nella causa Venanzi-Fausti. 1863 19/9/66
Vacher, Thomas Brittain
Parliamentary Companion. 1844 11/6/44
Valbezen, E. de
Les Anglais et l'Inde. 1857 25/1/58
Valdès, Juan de Spanish reformer
XVII Opuscules, ed. J. T. Betts. 1882 20/5/83 ?
Valentini, Baron de
Description of the seat of war in European Turkey, tr. M. Gore. 1854 14/5/55
Valeria [Eleanor Lloyd]
[Marriage law opinions]. (not found) 26/4/84
Valetta, J. N.
Life of Homer. 1867 10/6/67
Valin, Claude Marie
De l'Ultramontanisme et du Gallicanisme. 1877 15/9/77
Valla, Laurentius
Elegantiae. 12/5/59
Vallée, J. La
Cécile. 1787 (2v.) 28/1/52
Valmont, Victor
La jeunesse de Lord Beaconsfield. 1878 16/10/79
Valpy, E.
The Greek testament with English notes. 1826 20/4/28
Valussi, Pacifico
La Parte dello Stato. 1875 9/12/75
Vambéry, A.
'England and Russia' in *Nineteenth Century*, vii. 917. 1880 (June 1880) 8/6/80
Vandam, Albert Dresden
An Englishman in Paris. 1892 (2v.) 13/8/92
Vane, Charles William Stewart
Letter to Lord Ashley on . . . mines. 1842 26/11/42
Vane, Thomas
Lost sheep returned home, or the motives of the conversion to the Catholike Faith of F. V. 25/6/65
Van Mildert, William
A charge delivered to the clergy of the diocese of Durham. 1831 11/12/31
An inquiry into the general principles of Scripture-interpretation [Bampton lectures 1814]. 1815 14/1/55
Enquiry into the general principle of scriptural interpretation. 1815 14/1/55
Sermons. 1831 (2v.) 26/1/40
Sermons on several occasions, and charges. 1838 1/5/53
Sermons preached before the honourable society of Lincoln's Inn, from . . . 1812 to . . . 1819. 1831 26/1/46
Works. 1823 (11v. 1823–8) 14/2/41
Works of D. Waterland. 1822 11/10/68
Vannutelli, Vincenzo
Studio comparativo fra l'Oriente e l'Occidente. 1892 15/1/93
Van Praet, J.
Essais. 1867 (3v. 1867–84) 12/8/70, 17/3/74
Van Ryn, J. G.
Disestablishment, a duty: an appeal to the conscience. 1875 12/8/76
Vansittart, Nicholas
Outline of a plan of finance. 1813 7/2/56
Varese, Carlo
Sibilla Odaleta. 1828 19/9/37
Varin, Charles Victor
Théophile, ou, Ma Vocation. 1834 26/5/89, 14/7/89
Varley, Henry the elder
Priesthood: the true and the false. 1887 5/5/87
Varley, Isabella
God's providence house. 1865 (3v.) 3/5/66
Varnier Miritello, Michele J. J. Father Felix
Why I left the communion of the church of Rome. 1860 29/7/60

Varthema, Ludovico de
Travels, ed. J. W. Jones. 1863 29/1/64
Vasari, Giorgio
Life of Fra Angelico, tr. G. A. Bezzi. 1850 4/3/60 ?
Vasey, George pseud. Index
Individual liberty, legal, moral, and licentious, in which the political fallacies of . . . Mill's essay 'On Liberty' are pointed out. 1867 10/1/68
Vasili, Paul [Juliette Adam]
La société de Londres. 1885 13/6/85, 29/6/85
Vates Secundus, [G. A. Sala]
The Great Exhibition 'wot is to be'. 1850 7/9/51
Vátsyáyana
Kama Sutra, ed. R. F. Burton and F. F. Arbuthnot. 1883 2/5/84
Vattel, Emerich de
Droit des gens. 1758 29/4/40
Vaudoncourt, G. de
Memoirs of the Ionian Islands. 1816 9/12/46
Vaughan, Charles John
A few words on the Crystal Palace question. 1852 11/11/52
Authorised and revised sermons. 1882 27/4/84
Father of light. Sermon. 1873 10/8/73 ?
Indian sorrow and its lessons. 1857 4/10/57
Lectures on Revelation. 1863 (2v.) 27/11/64
Revision of the liturgy. 1860 24/6/60, 29/12/67
Sermon on the death of Prince Albert. 1861 12/1/62
St. Paul's Epistle to the Philippians. 1883 10/5/85
The personality of the tempter. 1851 26/2/54 ?
The revised code . . . considered. 1861 29/11/61
Three sermons preached at Cambridge. 1865 4/6/65
Vaughan, David James
Thoughts on the Irish Church question. 1868 18/9/68
Vaughan, Edward Thomas Rector of Harpenden
Some reasons of our Christian hope. 1876 16/8/91
Vaughan, Henry poet
Poems. 22/2/63
Poems. 1884 (new edn) 28/11/86
Works. 1871 (new edn) 9/11/72, 30/6/74
Vaughan, Henry Vicar of Crickhowell
Nine sermons. 1837 7/11/47, 12/12/47
Vaughan, Henry Halford
Oxford reform and Oxford professors. 1854 5/2/54
Vaughan, Herbert Alfred
A pastoral letter. 1875 4/1/75 ?
The Roman question international and British. 1889 16/3/89
The sufferings of Pope Leo XIII. 1888 22/2/88
True basis of Catholic politics. 1883 4/4/86
Vaughan, James
Sermons preached at Christ Church, Brighton, 1863–1868. 1865 (4v. 1865–8) 18/6/65
Vaughan, Robert
Congregationalism. 1841 7/1/42
Revolutions in English history. 1859 (3v. 1859–63) 20/11/64
The age and Christianity. 1849 10/2/50
The Christian Warfare. 1832 (8v.) 25/6/36
The way to rest. 1866 29/7/66
Vaughan, Roger Bede
Hidden springs. 1876 14/1/76
Vaughan, Virginia
The new era. 1880 23/11/80
Vaux, Laurence
A catechism or Christian doctrine necessarie for chyldren and the ignorant people. (new edn 1885) 14/2/86
Vauzelles, Jean Baptiste de
Histoire de . . . Francis Bacon. 1833 (2v.) 23/10/34 ?
Vehse, Carl Eduard
Shakespeare als Protestant, Politiker, Psycholog und Dichter. 1851 2/10/78
Venetti, pseud.
Tableau d'amour conjugal. 1751 12/5/59 ?
Veneziann in Morea. (not found) 11/11/58
Venn, Henry B. D.
Colonial church legislation. 1850 18/5/50
Venn, Henry evangelical
Sermons. 1759 14/8/36 ?
Ventura da Raulica, R.
Oraisons funèbres. 1848 24/11/50
Venus la populaire. 1727 16/6/90
Verax [Abbé Thomas]
La verité, toute la verité, rien que la verité sur la chasteté . . . dans le clergé catholique. 1881 10/4/85
Verax [H. Dunckley]
The Crown and the Cabinet. 1878 26/1/78
Vere, Aubrey Thomas de
Alexander the Great. 1874 15/6/74
Antar and Zara. 1877 18/11/77
English misrule, Irish misdeeds. 1848 8/3/48
Ireland's church property. 1867 2/2/67
Legends of Saxon Saints. 1879 29/6/79
Legends of St. Patrick. 1872 16/8/72
Mary Tudor. 1875 (new edn) 16/9/75
May carols. 1857 7/10/57
Poems. 1855 20/7/61
St. Thomas of Canterbury. 1876 12/7/76
The song of faith and other sonnets. 1842 10/11/42
Verga, Giovanni
Novelle Rusticane. 1883 6/3/91
Véricour, Raymond de
Historical analysis of Christian civilization. 1850 11/3/71

Milton et la poésie épique. 1838 28/11/38
Verney, Eliza
Practical thoughts on Isaiah. 1858 30/8/57
Verney, Frances Parthenope
Cottier owners, little takes and peasant proprietors. 1885 28/12/81 n
The grey pool and other stories. 1891 1/9/91
Verney, Harry
[on Ireland]. (not found) 20/5/45
Letters... of the Verney family. 1853 8/1/47
Verrall, Arthur Woollgar
Studies literary and historical in the Odes of Horace. 1884 26/1/94
Verro, Pietro
Osservazione sulla tortura. 1777 29/11/43
Versöhnende Gedanken über Religions-Differenzen in Form eines offenen Sendschreibens. 1845 21/10/45
Vesey Fitzgerald, William Foster
Egypt, India, and the colonies. 1870 23/1/73
The Suez canal. 1867 26/10/70
Veuillot, Louis François
Le droit du Seigneur au moyen-âge. 1871 20/5/93
Via Catholica. 1873 9/2/73
Viaggio dei missionari Lombardi. 1852 21/6/53
Vicini, Gioacchino
La rivoluzione dell'anno 1831 nello Stato Romano. 1887 10/1/89
Vickers, John author
The real Jesus... from a Jewish standpoint. 1891 22/5/92
Victoria, Queen
Leaves from the journal of our life in the Highlands, from 1848 to 1861. 1867 (new edn 1868) 3/2/67, 10/1/68
More leaves from the journal of a life in the Highlands, from 1862 to 1882. 1884 2/2/84, 13/2/84
Victorian hymns. 1887 26/6/87
Victorian Magazine. 2. 11/1863 4/2/1864, 17/2/1864
Vidal, Mary Theresa
Cabramatta, and Woodleigh farm. 1850 15/8/50
Vie d'une Parisienne. (not found) 1/4/88
Viesse de Marmont, Auguste Frédéric Louis
State of the Turkish empire, tr. J. M. F. Smith. 1839 4/7/53
Vila y Pons, José
Le traité de paix. 1871 28/1/71
Village conversations. 1873 6/2/86
Village tragedy, The. 1800 9/11/87
Villari, Pasquale
Discorso del deputato Villari sulle relazioni dello stato colla Chiesa. 1875 27/6/75
La Storia di Girolamo Savonarola. 1859 (2v. 1859–61 new edn 1887) 20/5/61, 5/2/87, 12/6/87, 2/4/89
Le lettere meridionali. 1878 12/1/88
Ville, François de
Phantome de Jansénisme. 4/12/64
Villehardouin, Geoffroy de
La conquête de Constantinople, ed. F. Bouchet. 1891 (2v.) 8/3/93
Villemain, Abel François
Histoire de Cromwell. 1819 (2v.) 21/12/72
Villemain
'Essais sur... Pindar', Journal des savants. 1859 10/5/59
Villiers, George Bussey
The correspondence between the Earl and the Countess of Jersey and Dr. Randolph. 1796 31/1/93
Vince, Samuel F.R.S.
Complete system of astronomy. 1797 (3v. 1797–1808) 7/6/30
Principles of hydrostatics. 1796 9/3/29
Vincent de Lerins, St.
Commonitorium. 4/9/64
Vincenzi, Luigi
De Hebraeorum et Christianorum. 1875 12/8/88
Vinci, Leonardo da
Trattato della Pittura. (many edns.) 25/7/38
Vindication of the bardic accounts of the early invasions of Ireland. 1850 8/8/68
Vindication of the conduct of the Irish Catholics during the late administration. 1807 6/11/93 ?
Vinet, Alexandre Rodolphe
Essai sur la manifestation des convictions. 1842 24/12/43
Lettres. 1882 (2v.) 22/1/83
Life of Vinet, by L. M. Lane. 1890 31/8/90
Studies on Pascal. 1859 7/4/89
Vie de Vinet, par E. H. A. Scherer. 1853 14/2/83
Virgil
Aeneid. 13/4/29, 4/5/29, 15/5/29, 9/6/29, 23/6/29, 6/7/29, 7/5/30, 20/12/30, 31/12/30, 15/1/31, 21/4/31, 1/10/31, 17/11/31, 1/5/32, 10/5/32, 1/6/32, 18/6/33, 10/7/34, 30/12/37, 4/11/38, 31/7/46, 12/9/46, 28/8/52, 6/8/55, 10/9/56, 12/1/58, 19/5/73, 19/3/78, 5/7/78, 30/8/81, 18/5/82, 19/2/89
Eclogues. 30/1/26, 15/2/26, 6/3/28
Georgics. 16/2/26, 2/10/27, 26/1/29, 4/1/31, 2/3/32, 4/11/38
Opera. 2/11/25, 21/3/27, 21/11/27, 23/12/29, 19/4/30, 27/5/30, 25/8/30, 1/10/31, 29/12/37, 8/1/40, 28/5/84
Vlasto, E. A.
Les derniers jours de Constantinople. 1883 16/2/83
Vogan, Thomas Stewart Lyle
Doctrine of the Apostolical Succession developed and proved. 1838 3/3/39

Vogel, Adolf Bernhard
Franz Liszt als Lyriker. 1887 6/5/87
Vogel, E. F.
Historisch-kritische Betrachtungen... 1842 11/6/45
Vogel, Sir Julius K.C.M.G.
Great Britain and her colonies. 1865 30/6/65
Voice from Ireland. (not found) 11/5/37
Voice from the Motherland. (not found) 14/4/63
Volkmann, Richard
Geschichte und Kritik der Wolfschen Prolegomena zu Homer. 1874 27/12/84
Volney, Constantin François de
Les Ruines, ou Méditations sur les Révolutions des Empires. 1791 3/7/32
Voltaire, François-Marie Arouet de
'Dialogues' in *Miscellanies, philosophical, literary, historical*. 1779 25/9/61
Candide. 1759 28/4/35
Histoire de Charles XII roi de Suède. 1731 27/9/26
Iconographie Voltairienne, by G. le Brisoys Desnoiresterres. 1879 6/9/86
L'Ecossaise. 1760 22/7/45
La Pucelle d'Orléans. 1755 7/7/45
Le siècle de Louis XIV. 1751 (2v.) 8/10/70, 18/5/72
Letters on the English nation. 1733 4/9/43
Lettres à son Altesse sur Rabelais et sur d'autres. 1768 27/3/81
Lettres de Mlle. de Ninon de Lenclos au Marquis de Sévigné... aumenteés de notes... trouvées dans les papiers de M. de Voltaire. 1782 18/5/72
Life of Voltaire, by J. Parton. 1881 (2v.) 29/7/81
Samson. 1760 22/7/45
Zayre. 1733 25/7/45
Vos, Geerhardus
The Mosaic origin of the Pentateuchal Codes. 1886 27/3/87
Vossius, G. J.
De theologia gentili. 28/8/59
Vox Clamantis. 21/8/92 ?
Voye, M. J. G. de la
The word!. 1868 23/8/76
Voysey, Charles
Mr. Gladstone on the course of religious thought. 1876 20/5/77, 7/2/86
Orthodoxy and pantheism. A sermon. 1872 19/1/72
The gospel of adversity. 1875 8/8/75
The influence of dogma upon religion. 1872 10/3/76 ?
The liberal clergy. 1868 5/7/68
The mystery of pain. 1878 2/7/76, 16/7/76, 8/8/80 ?
The Revised Prayerbook. 1871 24/6/80
Vyvyan, Richard Rawlinson
Letter... upon the commercial and financial policy of Sir Robert Peel's administration. 1842 19/7/42

W., W. F.
Prayers for the dead, for the use of members of the Church of England. 1845 1/6/45
Waagen, Gustov Friedrich
Works of art and artists in England, tr. H. E. Lloyd. 1838 (3v.) 26/5/38
Wachsmuth, Ernst Wilhelm Gottlieb
Historical antiquities of the Greeks with reference to their political institutions, tr. E. Woolrych. 1837 (2v.) 21/12/55
Wackerbath, Francis Diederich
The Egyptian bondage, or a second call to union, on the principles of the holy Catholic Church. 1842 21/1/42
Wadd, William
Cursory remarks on corpulence. 1816 25/10/86
Waddell, Peter Hateley the elder
Ossian and the Clyde. 1875 24/9/75
Waddie, Charles
How Scotland lost her Parliament and what came of it. 1891 10/2/91
Waddilove, William James Darley
Canadian church robbery, being a brief series of letters and papers. 1840 15/4/40
Waddington, George
Present condition and prospects of the Greek or Oriental Church. 1829 (new edn 1854) 9/2/41, 11/11/76
Three lectures on national education. 1845 28/5/45
Waddington, Julian Rattray
Janet, or glance at human nature. 1839 (3v.) 27/2/39
Waddy, Samuel Danks
Liberal and conservative finance from 1857 to 1880. 1879 6/11/79
Wade, John
New parliament. An appendix to the Black Book. 1826 20/11/26
The Black Book; or, corruption unmasked: being an account of persons, places, and sinecures. 1820 (2v. 1820–3) 9/2/34
Wade, W. M.
Truth spoken in love. 1840 19/2/41
Waghorn, Thomas of the Royal Navy
Letter to... W. E. Gladstone on the extension of steam navigation from Singapore to Port Jackson. 1846 28/5/46
Wagner, Arthur Douglas
Christ or Caesar? A letter to the archbishop of Canterbury. 1774 (2v. 1874–7) 25/2/77
Wagner, Richard
Richard Wagner: his tendencies and theories, by E. G. Dannreuther. 1873 16/11/74

The music of the future. 1873 20/11/74
Waifs and strays. 1886 14/12/86
Wainwright, Jonathan Howard
Gold currency and funded debt. 1864 12/7/64
Wake, Charles Staniland
Serpent-Worship. 1888 26/4/89
Wakefield, Edward
An account of Ireland, statistical and political. 1812 (2v.) 6/6/88
Wakefield, Edward Gibbon
A statement of the principles and objects for a proposed national society for the cure and prevention of pauperism by means of systematic colonisation. 1830 1/2/49
A view of the art of colonisation. 1849 28/3/51
Facts relating to the punishment of death in the metropolis. 1831 8/7/36
Mr. Coates and the New Zealand Association. 1837 6/6/38
The British colonisation of New Zealand. 1837 24/11/37
Wakefield, Edward Jerningham
Adventure in New Zealand. 1845 (2v.) 17/3/46
Wakeman, Henry Offley
History of religion in England. 1884 19/7/85
The Church and the Puritans. 1887 30/10/87
Walcott, Mackenzie Edward Charles
William of Wykeham and his Colleges. 1852 27/4/54
Waldeck-Rousseau, Pierre Marie René
Discours. 1888 13/12/88
Waldegrave, Samuel
New Testament millenarianism. 1855 28/10/55
Walford, Edward M.A., of Balliol College, Oxford
William Pitt: a biography. 1890 1/1/90
Walker, Archibald Dunbar
Egypt as a health resort. 1873 24/1/76
Walker, Charles
Pax super Israel. 1867 3/1/69
Three months in an English monastery. 1864 11/6/64
Walker, Clement
The mysterie of the Two Iunto's, Presbyterian and Independent. 11/9/32
Walker, Francis Amasa
Ninth census [of the U.S.A.]. 1872 (3v.) 6/12/73
Walker, George
La dette Américaine, et les moyens de l'acquitter. 1865 13/9/65
Walker, George Albert
Internment and disendowment. 1843 13/2/43
Walker, H. H.
The Comédie Humaine and its author, with a translation from the French of Balzac. 1879 13/1/79 ?
Walker, James
A serious expostulation with the Revd. Edward Craig. 1826 29/6/28
Walker, James Barr
Philosophy of salvation. 1845 4/5/79
Walker, James Edward
Titles of Psalms. 1879 24/11/78
Walker, James Thomas
The reasonableness of Christianity. 1888 20/1/89
Walker, John antiquary
Oxoniana. 1809 (4v.) 5/11/59
Walker, John of Dublin
Letters on primitive Christianity. 1874 19/9/75
Walker, John philologist
The academic speaker; or a selection of parliamentary debates . . . odes, scenes, and speeches. 1797 23/2/27, 3/10/93
Walker, John Rector
An attempt towards recovering an account of the numbers [of clergy] . . . sequester'd, harrass'd &c. in the late times of the Grand Rebellion. 1714 28/12/39
Walker, Norman Lockhart
Robert Buchanan, D.D., an ecclesiastical biography. 1877 10/6/77
Walker, Philip Francis
Afghanistan: a short account. 1881 28/5/81
Walker, R.
The two threes. 1883 22/4/84
Walker, Robert James
Jefferson Davis. Repudiation, recognition and slavery. 1863 13/7/63
Walker, Samuel Abraham
How long will the laity bear it? A question for the sheep against the shepherds. 1864 9/10/74
Walker, Thomas
The Quaker's opera. 1728 17/3/73
Walker, William Dean of Aberdeen and Orkney
Life of G. Gleig, bishop of Brechin. 1878 6/5/83
Walkey, Charles E.
One hundred queries . . . about Convocation. 1852 20/2/53
Wall, Charles William
Examination of the ancient orthography of the Jews. 1835 30/5/73
Wall, Joseph
The trial of Governor Wall, executed at the Old Bailey [1802]. 1867 5/9/71
Wallace, Alfred Russel
Contributions to the theory of natural selection. 1870 20/6/74
Forty-five years of registration statistics. 1885 23/1/85
The 'why' and 'how' of land nationalization. 1883 8/10/89

Wallace, Charles J.
The analogy of existence and Christianity. 1892 7/2/92
Wallace, Donald Mackenzie
Egypt and the Egyptian question. 1883 1/1/84, 9/6/84
Russia. 1877 12/1/77
Wallace, Dr.
Dr. Wallace on the state of Greenock. (not found) 3/5/60
Wallace, Henry
Prayer... in relation to natural law. 1875 7/3/75
Representative responsibility, a law of divine procedure. 1867 24/5/68
Wallace, Lewis
Ben-Hur. 1880 23/9/83, 26/7/84
Wallace, Robert
Study of ecclesiastical history in its relation to theology. 1873 1/7/77
Waller, Charles Blackmore
Apocalypse viewed under the light of the doctrines of the unfolding ages. 1878 29/6/79
Waller, John Francis
Report of the proceedings at a visitation... at Trinity College, Dublin. 1858 15/6/58
Walpole, Charles George
A short history of the Kingdom of Ireland. 1882 2/3/87
Walpole, Horace Earl of Orford
A catalogue of the royal and noble authors of England. 1806 (5v.) 22/12/26
Anecdotes of painting in England. 1762 (3v. 1762–3) 25/6/61
Historic doubts on the life and reign of King Richard III. 1770 26/11/69
Horace Walpole and his world, by L. B. Seeley. 1884 1/1/84
Letters, ed. J. Wright. 1840 (6v.) 11/3/85
Letters... to Sir H. Mann. 1833 6/1/37, 25/11/53
Memoirs of the reign of King George II. 1846 31/1/56, 28/6/80, 14/3/85
Memoirs of the reign of King George III. 1859 (2v.) 31/5/59, 14/5/85
The Castle of Otranto, a story. 1765 10/5/84
The mysterious mother, a tragedy. 1791 5/9/71
Walpole, Robert
Life of Walpole, by John Morley. 1888 8/11/89
Walpole, Spencer
History of England from the conclusion of the Great War in 1815. 1878 (5v. 1878–86) 7/10/86, 6/6/89
Life of Lord John Russell. 1889 (2v.) 24/5/89 n, 22/10/89, 6/11/89
Life of Spencer Perceval. 1874 (2v.) 26/1/74
The land of Home Rule. An essay on the history and constitution of the Isle of Man. 1893 8/2/93
Walpole, Spencer Horatio
Speech on... Jewish Disabilities Bill. 1848 24/3/48
Walsh, John Benn Lord Ormathwaite
Astronomy and geology compared. 1872 29/12/71, 13/1/72
Chapters of contemporary history. 1836 8/2/36
Lessons of the French Revolution. 1873 22/1/73
Popular opinions on parliamentary reform. 1831 16/4/31, 15/7/45 ?
Walsh, John Edward
Sketches of Ireland sixty years ago. 1847 5/11/47
Walsh, Peter
Four letters on several subjects. 12/9/86
Walsh, William John Archbishop
Reply to the Earl of Meath's attack on the priests and people of... Wicklow. With an appendix containing Mr. Parnell's speech. 1885 22/12/85
Walter, James
Shakespeare's true life. 1889 5/2/90
Walter, Richard
A voyage round the world [by G. Anson] compiled by R. Walter. 1748 26/5/40
Walter, Weever
Letters from the Continent. 1828 18/1/32
Walters, Henry Beauchamp
Odysseus and Kirke on a Boetius vase. 1893 9/8/93
Walters, John Thomas
Tory or Liberal: for which shall I vote?. 1880 12/1/80
Walton, Izaak
Life of Dr. Sanderson, late bishop of Lincoln. 21/9/28
Life of Richard Hooker. 7/12/28
The compleat angler or the contemplative man's recreation. 24/8/27
War, unlawfulness of. (not found) 24/12/39
Warburton, Eliot
The Crescent and the Cross. 1845 (2v.) 21/8/45
Warburton, J., Whitelaw, J., and Walsh, R.
History of the City of Dublin. 1818 6/1/73
Warburton, Rowland Eyles Egerton
Hunting songs and ballads. 1834 9/12/45, 16/8/62
Poems, epigrams, and sonnets. 1877 1/3/77
Warburton, William Bishop
A rational account... of the Lord's Supper. 1761 28/11/68
Letters from a late eminent prelate to one of his friends. 1808 11/5/39
The alliance between Church and State. 1736 20/6/37, 1/5/38
The divine legation of Moses demonstrated. 1737 (2v. 1737–41) 25/7/31

Ward, Aylmer
Rationalism and its relation to Mr. Gladstone's Expostulation. 1875 6/9/75
Ward, George Robert Michael
The statutes of Magdalen College, Oxford. 1840 4/12/47
Ward, Harriet
Five years in Kaffirland. 1848 (2v.) 12/7/50
Ward, Henry George
The first step to a poor law for Ireland. 1837 9/3/37
Ward, James pampleteer
Railways for the many and not for the few; or, how to make them profitable to all. 1846 15/3/47
Ward, James
Zenobia. A drama. 1833 20/1/34
Ward, John
The fall of Lucifer. 1836 1/12/36
Ward, J. W. Earl of Dudley
Letters of the Earl of Dudley to the Bishop of Llandaff. 1840 18/4/40
Ward, Mary Augusta [Mrs. Humphry Ward]
'The apostle's creed', *N.C.* xxxiv. 34 (July). 1893 29/6/93
Amiel's Journal. 1885 5/4/88
David Grieve. 1892 (3v.) 26/1/92
Marcella. 1894 (3v.) 26/4/94
Robert Elsmere. 1888 (3v.) 17/3/88, 6/4/88
Ward, Wilfrid Philip
The wish to believe. 1884 28/12/84
W. G. Ward and the Oxford Movement. 1889 8/6/89, 16/2/90
William George Ward and the Catholic revival. 1893 1/10/93, 9/12/93
Ward, William Bishop
A statement with reference to the proposed suppression of the bishopric of Sodor and Man. 1837 1/3/37
Ward, William George
A few more words in support of No. 90 of Tracts for the Times. 1841 26/5/41
An address to members of Convocation in protest against the proposed statute. 1845 23/1/45
Strictures on Mr. F[oulkes]'s letter to Archbishop Manning. 1869 18/4/69
The Anglican establishment contrasted to . . . the Catholic Church of every age [two letters]. 1850 18/8/50, 16/10/50
The Ideal of a Christian Church considered in comparison with existing practice. 1844 15/9/44
W. G. Ward and the Catholic revival, by W. P. Ward. 1893 1/10/93, 9/12/93
W. G. Ward and the Oxford Movement, by W. P. Ward. 1889 8/6/89, 16/2/90
Ward, William Harry Percival
Divine service. 1855 21/10/55
Union of the spiritual and temporal. 1864 (new edn) 5/6/64
Warden, H. F.
The theatre's unrehearsed tragedy. 1882 15/1/83
Wardlaw, Ralph
Christian ethics. 1834 13/2/34
National church establishments explained. 1839 6/6/39
The importance of the voluntary church controversy. 1839 30/5/39
Wardle, Gwyllym Lloyd
A circumstantial report of the . . . charges preferred against the Duke of York. 1809 3/12/59
Wardle, Thomas
An address on art culture. 1882 14/10/82
Waring, Charles
Some things in America, set forth in thirteen letters. 1880 9/2/80
Waring, Robert
Amoris Effigies. 20/6/52
Warleigh, Henry Smith
Hear the Church of England. 1872 2/6/72
Warren, Sir Charles
Underground Jerusalem. 1876 29/5/77
Warren, Elizabeth
Savonarola, the Florentine martyr. A reformer before the reformation. 1880 3/11/81 ?
Warren, George John Lord Vernon
Dante. 1844 23/4/45
Warren, John Byrne Leicester 3rd Baron de Tabley
A guide to the study of book-plates. 1880 21/10/80
Orpheus in Thrace and other poems. 1901 22/11/93 ?
Poems, dramatic and lyrical, 2nd series. 1893 22/4/93
Rehearsals: a book of verses. 1870 7/1/73
The soldier of fortune. A tragedy in five acts. 1876 4/3/76
Warren, Samuel barrister
Ten Thousand a Year. 1841 (3v.) 19/9/42
The opium question. 1840 10/2/40
Warren, Thomas Alston
An address . . . on the subject of the cow-pox. 1803 22/3/37
Warren, W. F.
The true key to ancient cosmology. 1882 13/11/82
Warring, Charles B.
Strike but hear me. The Mosaic account of the creation. 1875 11/12/75, 15/1/77, 24/6/88, 8/5/92
Warter, John Wood
Clerical synods. 1852 4/7/52
Holy matrimony; a sermon. 1837 26/3/37
The highchurchman of the old school, and the good dissenter of the old school. 1852 5/12/52
The teaching of the prayer book. 1845 11/7/52

Warton, John [William Wood]
Death-Bed scenes and pastoral conversations. 1827 (3v. 1827–8) 23/3/28, 30/5/41
Warton, Joseph
Essay on the writing and genius of Pope. 1756 29/8/83
Warton, Thomas
The history of English poetry. 1774 (3v. 1774–81) 25/8/59
Washington, George
Histoire de Washington, by C. H. de Witt. 1855 20/12/65
Life and times of George Washington, by C.R. Edmonds. 1835 (2v. 1835–6) 6/1/38
Life of George Washington, by C. W. Upham. 1852 (2v.) 1/7/52
Life of George Washington, by John Marshall. 1804 (5v. 1804–7) 15/9/48, 11/8/82
The writings of George Washington . . . correspondence, addresses . . . and other papers, ed. J. Sparks. 1833 (3v. 1833–37) 4/1/38
Wassa, Effendi
The truth on Albania and the Albanians. 1879 24/5/79
Waterhouse, Charles Henry
Insignia Vitae; or, Broad principles and practical conclusions. 1890 13/7/90
Waterland, Daniel
Critical history of the Athanasian creed. 1724 24/9/26
Review of the doctrine of the Eucharist. 1737 11/10/68
The case of Arian subscription considered. 1721 25/12/61, 28/4/67
Works. 1823 (11v. 1823–8) 14/2/41
Waters, Robert
William Shakespeare portrayed by himself. 1888 8/12/88
Waters, Robert Edmund Chester
Genealogical memoirs of the kindred families of Thomas Cranmer and Thomas Wood. 1877 7/7/77
Parish registers in England. 1883 7/9/83, 12/9/83
Waterton, Charles
Essays on natural history, with an autobiography of the author. 1838 13/9/44
Wathen, George Henry
The golden colony; or, Victoria in 1854. 1855 11/3/55
Watherston, James Henry
Trial of the Pix. 1860 27/11/60
Watkins, Henry William
Modern criticism considered in its relationship for the fourth gospel. 1890 16/6/90
The church in Northumbria. 1881 5/2/82
Watkins, John author
Life of Ebenezer Elliott, the Corn Law rhymer. 1850 22/11/51
Watson, Aaron
For lust of gold. 1892 10/5/92
Watson, Alexander town clerk
The anti-jacobin: a hudibrastic poem. 1794 27/11/51
Watson, Alexander Vicar of Marychurch
A lenten address to the congregation of St. John's, Cheltenham. 1843 19/3/43
A letter to the laity of the Church of England. 1842 23/4/42
An apology for the plain sense of the doctrine of the Prayer Book on holy baptism. 1850 20/6/50, 12/9/58
Christian loyalty. 1841 18/7/41
Sermons on doctrine, discipline and practice. 1843 5/3/43
The church's own action . . . against Romish aggression. 1850 9/3/51
Watson, George
Watson redivivus. Four discourses, ed. J. M. Gutch. 1860 2/12/60
Watson, George W.
A practical and theoretical essay on oblique bridges. 1839 1/11/92 ?
Watson, J. H.
[on railways]. (not found) 6/4/46
Watson, John of Montrose
Esther, an epic poem. 1845 17/8/44
Watson, John Selby
Life of Richard Porson. 1861 8/5/61, 12/8/67
Life of William Warburton. 1863 6/4/68
Watson, Lily
Vicar of Langthwaite. 1894 13/9/94
Watson, Richard
An apology for the bible; in a series of letters to T. Paine. 1796 15/7/66
Chemical essays. 1781 (5v. 1781–7) 3/11/57
Observations on Southey's Life of Wesley. 1820 4/3/49
Substance of a speech intended to have been spoken in the House of Lords. 1803 10/9/70
Watson, Robert Addison
Gospels of yesterday. 1888 15/7/88
Watson, William conspirator
Important considerations; or, a vindication of Queen Elizabeth. Edited by . . . J. Mendham. 1831 21/10/73, 13/9/75
Watson, William poet
Poems. 1892 28/10/92, 16/11/92
Watts, A. A., and Howitt, A. M.
Aurora. 1875 5/1/75
Watts, John
The working man; a problem. 1875 24/12/75
Watts, Robert
The doctrine of eternal punishment vindicated. 1873 4/6/93
The newer criticism and the analogy of the faith. 1881 26/12/81

Watts, T.
'The truth about Rossetti' in *Nineteenth Century*, xiii. 404. 1883 (March 1883) 10/3/83
Waugh, Edwin
Besom Ben. 1865 5/5/82
Lancashire sketches. 1869 15/5/82
Lancashire songs. 1863 11/6/70
Wayside Cross. (not found) 16/1/49
W. B.
The comparative merits of direct and indirect taxation. 1846 20/3/47
Weatherly, Frederick Edward
Muriel, the Sea-King's daughter, and other poems. 1870 23/3/71
Weatherly, Lionel Alexander
The supernatural. 1891 3/12/91
Webb, Alfred
The opinions of some protestants regarding their Irish catholic fellow-countrymen. 1886 19/11/86
Webb, Allan Becher
Notes of six addresses. 1879 27/1/84
Webb, Benjamin
Sketches of Continental Ecclesiology. 1848 5/9/52
Webb, William John Wesley
England's inheritance in her Church. 1878 24/11/78
Weber, Friedrich
A popular history of music from earliest times. 1891 6/11/91
Weber, Georg Professor
Geschichte der akatholischen Kirchen und Secten von Grossbritannien. 1845 11/2/55
Weber, Wilhelm Ernst
Die elegischen Dichter. 1826 5/2/87 ?
Webster, Alexander unitarian
Burns and the Kirk. 1888 9/11/90
Webster, Augusta
Disguises; a drama. 1879 15/1/80 ?
Webster, Daniel
Speech on slavery. 1850 1/5/50
Speech on the constitution. 1833 (new edn 1861) 19/4/62
Webster, Edward
The public and private business of the House of Commons considered in relation to the economization of the time of the House and its members. 1868 30/4/70
Webster, Grace
Memoir of Dr. C. Webster. 1853 24/12/60 ?
Webster, John
The Duchess of Malfi, ed. Hazlitt. 1856 9/11/81
Webster, William Bullock
Ireland considered as a field for investment or residence. 1852 2/12/52
Wedgwood, Frances Julia
John Wesley. 1870 11/8/72
Wedgwood, Josiah the elder
A catalogue of cameos. 1773 19/10/63
Address to the workmen in the pottery. 1783 18/5/77
Weekes, Henry
The Prize Treatise on the Fine Arts Section of the Great Exhibition. 1851 1/1/53
Wegele, Franz Xaver von
Dante's Leben und Werke. 1852 9/3/76 ?
Wegg-Prosser, Francis Richard
The Branch-Church theory; a dialogue. 1852 10/4/51, 14/11/52
Weill, Alexandre
Mystères de la création. 1856 29/4/83
Weingarten, Hermann
Die Revolutionskirchen Englands. 1868 26/2/76, 25/3/83
Pascal als Apologet des Christenthums. 1863 24/3/83
Weisener, L.
Marie Stuart et le Comte de Bothwell. 1863 15/11/92
Welcker, Friedrich Gottlieb
Der epische Cyclus oder die Homerischen Dichter. 1865 (2v. 1865–82) 1/11/67, 12/3/91
Griechische Götterlehre. 1857 (3v. 1857–63) 25/2/58, 3/9/63
Weldon, Anthony
The court and character of King James. 29/8/91
Welford, Richard Griffiths
[On tobacco]. 1847 (not found) 6/1/48
How far will Free Trade in corn affect the farmer?. 1843 23/3/43
Wellesley, Arthur Duke of Wellington
Despatches, correspondence, and memoranda 1819–1832. 1877 (6v. 1867–80) 8/4/78
The Eastern Question. Extracted from the correspondence of the Duke of Wellington. 1877 12/3/77
Wellesley, Gerald
A sermon preached . . . in Windsor Castle [on the Duchess of Kent]. 1861 23/6/61
Wellhausen, Julius
Die Composition des Hexateuchs. 1889 8/5/90
Geschichte Israels. 1878 25/8/8 ?9
Prolegomena zur Geschichte Israels. 1883 8/5/90
Wellington College and the Horse Guards. 1878 1/4/79
Wells, David Ames
Report on taxation [of the U.S.A.]. 1869 4/1/70
Wells, James Moderator
Christ and the heroes of heathendom. 1886 3/10/86, 28/8/87
Wellwood, Arthur
Snatches of world-song. 1891 21/9/91
Wellwood, Sir Henry Moncrieff
Account of the life and writings of J. Erskine. 1818 24/2/39

Wellwood, Sir Henry Moncrieff (*cont.*)
Brief account of the constitution of the Established Church of Scotland. 1833 8/12/39
Welschinger, Henri
Le divorce de Napoléon. 1889 15/3/89
Welsford, H.
On the origin and ramifications of the English language. 1845 15/12/57
Welsh, Mr.
[On convict labour]. (not found) 20/7/47
Wesley, Charles
Sermons. 1816 2/4/82
Wesley, John
'Duty of constant communion', *Works.* 1829 (14v. 1829–31) 5/7/41
Journal of John Wesley. 1827 (4v.) 20/6/58
Life of John Wesley, by F. J. Wedgwood. 1870 11/8/72
Life of John Wesley, by Lelièvre. 1891 17/1/92
Life of John Wesley, by Luckock. 1891 11/10/91
Life of John Wesley, by Southey. 1820 (2v.) 12/7/29, 10/8/29
The homes . . . of John Wesley. 1891 26/7/91
Wesley's place in church history, by R. D. Urlin. 1870 3/4/70
Wesleyan Methodist Magazine.
16 30/1/1870
21. 433. 5/1875. Vatican controversy 21/5/1875
Wesleyan Preacher's letter to Mr. King. (not found) 14/9/49
West, Algernon Edward
Sir Charles Wood's administration of Indian affairs from 1859 to 1866. 1867 19/8/72
West, John
Journal during a residence at the Red River colony, British North America. 1824 16/9/48
Westall, William B.
A queer race: the story of a strange people. 1887 4/3/90
Westcott, Brooke Foss
Address to the University Church Society. 1872 17/8/73
An introduction to the study of the gospels. 1860 25/12/79
Cathedral foundations in relation to religious thought. 1872 11/2/72
Essays in the history of religious thought. 1891 4/9/92
General survey of the history of the canon of the New Testament. 1855 5/10/62
The gospel of life. 1892 15/1/93, 26/3/93
The gospel of the resurrection. 1866 21/10/66
The historic faith. 1883 8/7/83
Westermayer, Anton
Predigt. 1843 30/10/45
Western, Charles Callis
Letter to the Earl of Liverpool on the cause of our present distress. 1826 1/9/41
Western Bank of Scotland
How to mismanage a bank. 1859 13/1/60
Westerton, Charles
Popish practices at St. Paul's, Knightsbridge. 1854 17/12/54
Westgarth, William
Australia Felix. 1847 21/12/53
Half a century of Australian progress. 1889 21/5/89
Westhead, Joshua Proctor Brown
[On colonial baronage]. (not found) 16/6/52
The XVIIIth chapter of Leviticus not the marriage code of Israel. 1850 15/7/50
Westmeath, Marchioness of
Narrative of the case of the Marchioness of Westmeath. 1857 5/5/57
Westminster Review.
6. 502. 1/1838. J. S. Mill on Canada 2/2/1838
12. 1. 1/1830. Coleridge 12/12/1830
12. 269, 355, 472. 4/1830. Moore's Byron; Montgomery's Satan; Channing 12/4/1830
12. 386. 4/1830. Random records 14/4/1830
14. 210, 103, 232. 1/1831. Tennyson; on George IV; Wellington 5/1/1831
14. 269. 4/1827. Education 9/6/1827
14. 341. 4/1827. Truth 8/6/1827
14. 42. 1/1831. Hannibal 11/1/1831
14. 440. 4/1831. Reform 16/4/1831
15. 149. 7/1831. Reform bill 29/12/1831
16. 1. 1/1832. Oxford 3/1/1832
18. 493. 4/1833. Radical policy 3/7/1833
34. 127. 6/1840. Buxton's remedy 17/6/1840
36. 167. 7/1841. Dissolution 31/8/1841
37. 265, 394. 4/1842. Bentham; Political Retrospect 11/5/1842
41. 319. 6/1844. on Sir J. Graham 3/6/1844
42. 491. 12/1844. City administration 29/1/1845
47. 136. 4/1847. Strauss 24/4/1847
50. 1. 10/1848. Russell 20/12/1848
50. 436. 1/1849. Ireland 17/2/1849
53. 165. 4/1850. Anglican church 3/5/1850
53. 448. 7/1850. Prostitution 8/7/1850
1. 551. 4/1852. Book trade 2/4/1852
2. 205. 7/1852. Taylor on Peel 19/7/1852
9. 91. 1/1856. War 24/1/1856
13. 478. 4/1858. Medical Reform 2/4/1858, 1/6/1858
15. 444. 4/1859. Italy 10/4/1859
16. 7/1859 12/7/1859
16. 112. 7/1859. India 21/7/1859
16. 41. 7/1859. Jowett 17/7/1859

16. 503. 10/1859. Tennyson 15/10/1859
20. 272. 7/1861. Tocqueville 25/10/1861
21. 150. 1/1862. Homer 29/1/1862
22. 489. 10/1862. Slave power 28/10/1862
23. 57. 1/1863. Colenso 20/1/1863
25. 30. 1/1864. Mont Cenis Tunnel 29/2/1864
30. 7/1866 17/9/1866
36. 415. 10/1869. Theology 7/11/1869
43. 208. 1/1873. Ministry 7/2/1873
43. 3. 1/1873. Religion & the school boards 19/2/1873
86. 147. 7/1866. Probyn on Italian affairs 7/7/1866
92. 179, 556. 7/1869. Prostitution 6/11/1869
128. 1136. 12/1887. Darwin 2/12/1887
128. 793. 10/1887. Ireland 1/10/1887
128. 929. 11/1887. Hartington 3/10/1887
129. 12. 1/1888. Dr Johnson 10/1/1888
129. 29. 1/1888. Isle of Man 13/1/1888
129. 405. 4/1888. Copyright 25/7/1888
129. 600. 5/1888. Drunkards 24/7/1888
130. 186. 8/1888. Caird on marriage 25/8/1888
130. 310. 9/1888. Forster 2/9/1888
131. 522. 5/1889. Shakespeare 18/5/1889
131. 545. 5/1889. The future 19/5/1889
132. 1. 10/1889 3/10/1889
133. 417. 4/1890. Divorce 3/4/1890
135. 648. 6/1891. Gambling 17/6/1891
136. 476, 497. 11/1891. Canada; Ireland 12/11/1891
138. 483. 11/1892. Tom Paine 6/12/1892
138. 8. 7/1892. Mohammedanism 4/9/1892
139. 386. 4/1893. Disestablishment 22/4/1893
140. 1. 7/1893. Canadian finance 12/7/1893

Weston, Jessie
Ko Meri... a story of New Zealand life. 1890 7/10/90 n

Westropp, Hodder Michael
On the Fanaux de cimitières in France, and the Round Towers in Ireland. 1863 19/1/78
Pre-historic phases. 1872 10/8/75
The cycle of development. 1881 13/6/81

West Somerset
A new-fashioned tory. 1877 2/4/77

Wetenhall, Edward
Enter into thy closet. 15/8/52

Wetherell, Charles
Substance of the speech... on incorporating London University. 1834 14/7/34

Weyer, Sylvain van der
Richard Cobden, Roi des Belges. 1862 21/1/63

Weymouth, Richard Francis
[On Obrinus]. (not found) 30/9/78
The resultant Greek testament. 1886 12/5/87

Wharton, Charles Henry
A letter to the Roman Catholics of the City of Westminster... [on] the motives which induced him to relinquish their communion. 1784 29/10/26

Wharton, Henry
A specimen of some errors and defects in the History of the Reformation... by Gilbert Burnet. 9/8/63

Whately, Elizabeth Jane
Life of Richard Whately. 1866 (2v.) 23/8/68

Whately, Richard
A charge delivered. 1843 26/11/43
Cautions for the times. 1853 25/11/55
Elements of logic. 1826 14/2/29
Elements of rhetoric. 1828 14/7/31
Essays on some of the difficulties in the writings of St. Paul. 1829 19/3/29
Historic doubts relative to Napoleon Buonaparte. 1819 24/3/30
Introductory lectures on political economy. 1831 (2v. 1831–2) 19/1/48
Introductory lessons on Christian evidences. 1843 10/7/53
Letters on the Church. By an Episcopalian. 1826 22/3/29, 3/4/35
Life of Richard Whately, by E. J. Whately. 1866 (2v.) 23/8/68
Protective measures in behalf of the established church. 1851 7/3/52
Speech in the House of Lords [on Jewish disabilities], *August 1833.* 1848 9/2/48
Statements and reflections respecting the church and the universities... the appointment of the bishop of Hereford. 1848 16/1/48
Substance of a speech on transportation. 1840 14/1/46
The kingdom of Christ delineated. 1841 10/3/44
The proposed evangelical alliance. 1846 9/10/46
Thoughts on secondary punishment. 1832 15/1/46

Whately, Thomas
Remarks on some of the characters of Shakespeare. 1785 4/7/63

What is faith? A reply to Dr. Baylee's challenge to Dr. Colenso. 1863 24/5/63

Wheatley, J. H.
The legend of Ravensholm. 1874 18/7/74

Wheaton, Henry
Elements of international law. 1836 (2v.) 8/10/53

Wheeler, James Talboys
An abridgement of Old Testament history. 1867 8/3/67

Whewell, William
Astronomy and general physics considered with reference to natural theology; 3rd. Bridgewater Treatise. 1833 13/11/34, 1/9/79, 11/10/85, 4/2/90, 5/8/90

Whewell, William (*cont.*)
English hexameter translations from Schiller, Goethe, Homer, Callinus and Meleager. 1847 16/6/47
History of the inductive sciences. 1837 (3v.) 25/4/76
Of a liberal education in general. 1845 (3v. 1845–52) 13/1/48
Of the plurality of worlds. 1853 15/5/54, 21/5/54
On the foundations of morals. 1838 31/3/39
On the principles of English university education. 1840 3/8/40
Platonic dialogues for English readers. 1845 (3v. 1845–52) 2/11/59
Six lectures on political economy. 1863 19/1/63
The life and selections from the correspondence of William Whewell, by Janet Douglas. 1882 14/2/82
The life of William Whewell, by I. Todhunter. 1876 24/4/76
Whigs and Tories both wrong. 1835 12/3/44
Whiston, Robert
Cathedral trusts and their fulfilment. 1849 6/6/49
Whiston, William
An account of the Convocation's proceedings against Mr. W. 1711 18/12/46
Memoir of Samuel Clarke. 1730 30/7/65
Several hundred texts of holy scripture. 1807 3/5/50
The genuine works of Flavius Josephus. 1737 28/12/56
Whitaker, Charles
Remarks on Lord Derby's Reform Bill. 1867 6/5/67
Whitaker, Evelyn
Miss Toosey's mission. 1878 8/2/80, 1/6/90
Whitaker, Samuel
The Church—the ark of salvation. 1841 25/3/42
Whitby, Daniel
Reflections on some assertions and opinions of Mr. Dodwell. 1707 16/8/76
White, Edward
Life in Christ. 1846 3/8/50, 17/10/75, 6/8/76, 2/5/86
The mystery of growth. 1863 31/10/73
White, George Cecil
The discipline of suffering. 1880 11/9/81
White, Gilbert
The natural history of Selborne. 1849 7/8/66
White, John Meadows
Suggestions for the rating of the Tithe Commutation Act. 1845 24/2/49
White, Joseph Blanco
Letters from Spain. 1822 30/8/42
Life of Blanco White, by J. H. Thom. 1845 (3v.) 6/5/45
Observations on heresy and orthodoxy. 1835 16/5/45
Practical and internal evidence against catholicism. 1825 14/5/45
White, pseud. Martingale
Sporting scenes and country characters. 1840 21/6/41
White, William Bishop
Memoirs of the Protestant Episcopal Church in the United States of America. 1820 28/6/48
White, William Swedenborgian
Life of Swedenborg. 1867 (2v.) 8/4/68
White, William Hale 'Mark Rutherford'
An argument for the extension of the franchise. 1866 6/3/66
Mark Rutherford's deliverance. 1885 17/12/85
The revolution in Tanner's Lane. 1887 21/9/87
White, William Henry
Architecture and public buildings. 1884 16/7/84
Whitefield, George
Six sermons. 1750 30/5/80
Whitehead, Charles
Market gardening. 1880 6/10/80
Profitable fruit growing. 1884 24/12/83, 19/8/89
Whitehurst, Edward Capel
The ballot. A reply to Sidney Smith and... Russell. 1853 14/5/53 ?
Whiteley, Henry
Three months in Jamaica, in 1832. 1833 18/4/33
Whitley, John D.D.
Life everlasting. 1846 30/6/46
Whitmore, Charles James
The bible in the workshop [on Colenso]. 1863 24/5/63
Whitmore, William Wolryche
A letter on the Corn Laws, to the Manchester Chamber of Commerce. 1839 22/12/41
A second letter on the present state and future prospects of agriculture. 1841 17/12/41
Letter to Lord John Russell on railways. 1847 8/11/47
Plain thoughts on Free Trade. 1849 17/12/49
The wine duties. 1853 19/9/53
Whittaker, Sir Thomas Palmer
Free trade, reciprocity, and foreign competition. 1879 7/11/79
Whittier, John Greenleaf
Poems. 1857 27/2/65
Whittingham, Ferdinand
Bermuda, a colony, a fortress and a prison. 1857 20/5/61
Whittle, James Lowry
Catholicism and the Vatican. 1872 9/6/72, 30/11/74

Whittmore, W. M.
The Seventh Head, or Louis Napoleon foreshadowed. 1853 22/11/54
Whitty, Edward Michael
History of the Session 1852–3. 1854 19/12/53
Whitty, Irwine
A selection of letters and meditations, ed. W. Palmer. 1833 13/1/33
Whitty, Michael James
Tales of Irish life. 1824 (2v.) 13/11/77
Whitworth, Richard
The advantages of inland navigation. 1766 16/9/52
Whitworth, William Allen
Quam Dilecta: a description of All Saints', Margaret Street, with historic notes of the Margaret Chapel. 1891 27/8/93
Who am I?. (not found) 10/6/66
Who is to blame for the war between Denmark and Germany?. 1849 24/3/49
Whyte, Alexander D.D.
A commentary on the Shorter Catechism. 1883 9/12/83
Whyte, Alexander of Fettercairn
The duty of prayer. 1834 12/1/34, 6/7/34
The heritage of God's people. 1837 21/5/37
The Lord's Supper. 1839 3/8/42 ?
Whytehead, Thomas
College life. Letters to an Under Graduate. 1845 31/5/46
Wickham, Edward Charles
The works of Horace, with a commentary. 1874 4/4/74
Wiclif, John
Christ's Real Body not in the Eucharist. 1857 5/10/82
Huss und Wiclif, by J. Loserth. 1884 30/10/84
Life of, by A. R. Pennant. 1884 2/6/84
Life of, by C. W. Le Bas. 1832 30/7/32
Life of, by G. V. Lechler. 1878 2/6/85
Memorial works in Latin, ed. R. Buddensieg. 1883 (2v.) 25/12/83
Tractatus de officio regis, ed. Pollard and Sayle. 1887 4/8/89
Widal, Auguste
Etudes littéraires et morales sur Homère. 1860 8/10/63 n
Wiesener, Louis
La jeunesse d'Elizabeth d'Angleterre. 1878 8/3/79
Wight, John
Sunday in London. 1833 27/6/35
Wightman, Julia Bainbridge
Haste to the rescue, or work while it is day. 1859 1/4/60
Wigram, Joseph Cotton
A Charge. 1864 5/12/69
Practical hints on Sunday Schools. 1833 25/1/35
Wikoff, Henry
A New Yorker in the Foreign Office. 1858 20/9/58
Wilberforce, Henry William
[Statement, in proof]. 11/2/45
Christian Unity. 1842 23/3/42
On the danger of State interference with the trust deeds of Church schools. 1847 20/7/47
The building of the house of God... St. Laurence church rebuilt. 1839 27/9/40
The Church and the Empires. 1874 23/11/87
The parochial system; an appeal to English churchmen. 1838 3/2/39
Wilberforce, Robert Isaac
A charge. 1841 22/8/41
A charge. 1842 17/12/42
A charge. 1844 23/9/44
A charge. 1845 20/7/45
A charge. 1846 28/7/46
A charge. 1847 4/7/47
A charge. 1848 2/7/48
A charge. 1850 23/6/50
A letter to the Marquis of Lansdowne on the establishment of a Board of National Education. 1839 18/5/39
A second letter to... Lansdowne on the system of inspection best adapted for national education. 1840 1/2/40
A sketch of the history of Erastianism. 1851 11/6/51
An inquiry into the principles of church-authority. 1854 15/10/54
Church courts and church discipline. 1843 22/3/43
Family Prayers, by William Wilberforce, ed. R. I. Wilberforce. 1834 1/6/34
Life of William Wilberforce. 1838 (5v.) 24/4/38, 6/6/40
Rutilius and Lucius; or, stories of the third age. 1840 16/1/42
Sermons on the Holy Communion. 1854 16/7/54
Sermons on the new birth of man's nature. 1850 12/5/50
The doctrine of Holy Baptism. 1849 10/2/50
The doctrine of the Holy Eucharist. 1853 22/5/53
The doctrine of the Incarnation. 1848 4/3/49
The Evangelical and Tractarian movements. 1851 6/7/51
The five empires. 1840 5/1/41
The sacramental system. 1850 25/4/50
Wilberforce, Samuel
A charge. 1867 10/3/67
A charge [on discipline]. 1863 25/12/63
Address delivered at the confirmation at Eton College. 1847 13/6/47
Address delivered at the confirmation at Eton College. 1851 6/4/51

Wilberforce, Samuel (*cont.*)
Charge at the triennial visitation [at Oxford]. 1857 13/12/57
Charge to the clergy of Oxford. 1848 29/12/48
Charge to the clergy of Oxford. 1851 1/2/52
Charge to the clergy of Oxford. 1860 20/1/61
Charge to the clergy of Surrey. 1840 1/11/40
Charge to the clergy of Surrey. 1841 22/8/41
Charge to the clergy of Surrey. 1842 2/12/42
Charge to the clergy of Surrey. 1843 26/11/43
Charge to the clergy of Surrey. 1844 22/12/44
Charge to the clergy of Surrey. 1845 25/5/45
Charge to the diocese of Oxford. 1854 3/12/54
Charge, delivered to the candidates for ordination. 1846 10/1/46
Four sermons... preached before Queen Victoria. 1842 15/5/42
Heroes of Hebrew history. 1870 20/3/70, 17/1/90
History of the Protestant Episcopal Church in America. 1840 28/10/44
Letter to... Lord Brougham on the government plan of education. 1840 1/2/40
Life of Samuel Wilberforce, by A. R. Ashwell and R. G. Wilberforce. 1879 (3v. 1879–82) 6/8/79, 3/9/79, 21/12/79, 22/11/80, 2/4/81, 6/7/82, 17/12/82, 25/12/82
Life of William Wilberforce. 1838 (5v. 1838) 24/4/38, 6/6/40
Poems, ed. R. G. Wilberforce. 1884 26/4/85
Pride a hindrance to true knowledge. 1847 25/7/47
Rome: her new dogma and our duties. 1855 8/4/55, 13/2/61
Sermons. 1844 19/1/45
Sermons preached before the University of Oxford. 1839 23/6/39, 9/7/39
The deceitfulness of sin. 1853 25/12/53
The ministry of reconciliation. 1840 11/10/40
The planting of nations a great responsibility. 1852 18/7/52
The power of God's word needful for national education. 1838 18/2/39
The principles of the English Reformation [sermon for 5 November]. 1855 2/12/55
Two sermons [by S. Wilberforce and C. Wordsworth] preached in connexion with the consecration of St. Andrew's chapel, Fasque. 1847 28/8/47
Union with Christ. 1848 18/2/49
Wilberforce, William philanthropist
A practical view of the prevailing religious system of professed Christians [with an introductory essay by Daniel Wilson]. 1797 5/4/29, 8/1/38
Family prayers, ed. R. I. Wilberforce. 1834 1/6/34
Life of Wilberforce, by J. C. Colquhoun. 1866 1/11/91
Life of William Wilberforce, by R. I. and S. Wilberforce. 1838 (5v.) 24/4/38, 6/6/40
Wilberforce, William the younger
Law and practice of election committees. 1839 8/2/39
Wild, George John
The Revised Version: the oracles of God. 1879 15/1/82
Wild, John James
Thalassa. An essay on the depth, temperature and currents of the ocean. 1878 11/11/78
Wild, William Taylor
A letter to R. M. Beverley... being an examination of his lay-sermons. 1831 26/8/31
Wilde, Frederick George Stanley
Brainfag from mental worry and overwork. 1877 4/11/78
Wilde, Oscar
[unpublished sonnet]. 15/5/77
Poems. 1881 1/8/81
The Happy Prince. 1888 14/7/88 n
Wilde, Sir William Robert Wills
Lough Corrib: its shores and islands. 1867 27/11/77
Wildered, A. B.
The Ritualist's Progress. 1875 27/5/82
Wildman, Richard
What is Convocation?. 1853 23/2/54
Wilkes, Anna
Ireland: Ur of the Chaldees. 1873 23/12/73
Wilkes, Charles
Narrative of the United States exploring expedition during 1838–1842. 1844 (5v.) 17/8/48
Wilkes, George
Shakespeare, from an American point of view. 1877 11/4/82
Wilkie, William
Poetical works. 1794 21/12/81
Wilkins, Augustus Samuel
Phoenicia and Israel. An historical essay. 1871 18/11/71
Wilkins, David
Concilia magnae Britannicae et Hibernicae. 1737 (4v.) 30/5/88, 28/9/88
Wilkins, George Archdeacon
Letter to Lord J. Russell, on church rates. 1837 15/3/37
Letter... to Rev. H. W. Plumptre on his projected church at Nottingham. 1838 27/6/38
Wilkins, George of Dublin
The growth of the Homeric poems. 1885 24/10/85
Wilkins, John headmaster
Notes on the church catechism. 1877 31/10/80 ?

Wilkins, John William
Letter to Lord Palmerston . . . on Cambridge University reform. 1855 18/5/55, 15/10/56
The Second Congress and the Russian claim to the Isle of Serpents and Bolgrad. 1857 6/1/57
Wilkins, Mary Eleanor afterw. Freeman
A humble romance and other stories. 1890 21/1/91
Jane Field. 1892 18/10/93
New England nun. 1891 22/6/91 ?
Wilkins, Nathaniel George
Errors and terrors of blind guides. The popular doctrine of everlasting pain refuted. 1875 21/4/75
Wilkins, William Henry pseud. W. H. de Winton
St. Michael's eve. 1892 (2v.) 1/3/91, 20/5/92
Wilkinson, George Blakiston
South Australia, its advantages and resources. 1848 27/7/48
Wilkinson, George Howard
Absolution. A sermon. 1874 25/10/74
Confession. A sermon. 1874 9/8/74
Instructions in devotional life. 1871 24/9/71
The Broken Covenant. The substance of a sermon. 1878 19/7/78
Wilkinson, Henry Spenser
The eve of Home Rule: impressions of Ireland in 1886. 1886 22/6/86
Wilkinson, James John Garth
On human science. 1876 10/12/76
Wilkinson, John friend of Israel
Israel my glory, or Israel's mission and missions to Israel. 1889 6/9/91
Wilkinson, John of Merton
Popular education. 1852 26/11/52
School boards in country parishes. 1874 22/2/74
Wilkinson, John Bourdieu
Aids to mental prayer. 1871 12/1/73
Instructions on the parables. 1870 18/6/71
Wilkinson, John Gardner
Dalmatia and Montenegro. 1848 (2v.) 14/2/77
Manners of the ancient Egyptians. 1837 (3v. 1837–41) 15/9/91
Three letters on the policy of England towards the Porte and Mohammed Ali. 1840 8/5/40
Wilkinson, Matthew
Schools sermons preached in the chapel of Marlborough College. 1852 6/3/53 ?
Wilkinson, William Cleaver
Edwin Arnold as poetizer and as paganist. 1884 27/10/89
Wilkinson, William Francis
A plea for the study of Hebrew in preparation for Holy Orders in the Church of England. 1870 9/6/70
Modern materialism. 1878 8/9/78

Wilkinson, William George
The Burial Service vindicated against the charge of the Dissenters. 1879 26/1/79
Wilks, Samuel Charles
Correlative claims and duties; or, an essay on the necessity of a church establishment in a Christian country. 1821 3/9/32
Essay on the influence of a moral life on our judgement in matters of faith. 1822 17/9/65
Essay on the signs of conversion and unconversion in Ministers of the Church. 1814 3/8/28
Wilks, Washington
Edward Irving: an ecclesiastical and literary biography. 1854 17/2/56, 13/4/81 ?
Willett, Richard
A memoir of Hawarden Parish, Flintshire. 1822 11/9/40
Williams, Charles
The Armenian campaign; diary of the campaign of 1877. 1878 30/4/78
Williams, Charles James Blasius
Authentic narrative of the case of the late Earl St. Maur. 1870 29/3/70
Williams, David
Lessons to a young prince. 1791 15/3/48
Williams, D. E.
Life and correspondence of Sir Thomas Lawrence. 1831 (2v.) 7/6/38
Williams, Frederick Sims
Thoughts on the doctrine of eternal punishment. 1857 3/5/57
Williams, George of King's
Christ's gifts to men. 1842 23/10/42
The Orthodox Church of the East in the eighteenth century. 1868 24/1/69
Williams, Isaac
A few remarks on the charge of the bishop of Gloucester . . . on the subject of reserve . . . as taught in the Tracts for the Times. 1841 8/12/41
Autobiography, ed. Sir G. Prevost. 1892 24/5/92
Devotional commentary on the gospel narrative. 1842 22/3/42
Williams, Isaac Fellow of Trinity College, Oxford
A short memoir of the Revd R. A. Suckling. 1859 9/11/56
Williams, Isaac
Our Lord's nativity. 1851 6/3/59
The Baptistry, or the way of eternal life. 1842 31/12/43, 22/10/71
The gospel narrative of the Holy Week harmonised. 1843 9/4/43
Thoughts on the study of the holy gospels. 1842 5/9/58
Williams, James apprentice
Narrative of events since 1 August 1834 [on slavery]. 1837 2/6/37

Williams, Jane
History of Wales, derived from authentic sources. 1869 13/4/70
Williams, John Archdeacon
Essays . . . on prehistoric records. 1858 15/12/62
Homerus. 1842 26/1/57
Life and actions of Alexander the Great. 1829 8/9/29
Primitive tradition: a letter to the . . . Edinburgh Review. 1843 28/8/57
Williams, John author
A defence of the Welsh people against the misrepresentations of their English critics. 1869 23/9/75
Williams, John
Disappointment. 1814 11/8/26
Williams, John educationalist
A discourse at the opening of the Welsh Educational Institution. 1849 26/2/49
Williams, John Carvell
Religious liberty in the church-yard; or the case for the Burials Bill restated. 1876 1/3/76
Williams, Sir Monier Monier
Buddhism in its connection with Brahmanism and Hinduism and in its contrast with Christianity. 1889 7/4/89, 11/8/89
Indian epic poetry. 1863 26/9/75 ?
Williams, Montagu Stephen
Later leaves. 1891 2/2/91
Leaves of a life, being the reminiscences of Montagu Williams, Q. C. 1890 21/2/90
Williams, Rowland
An earnestly respectful letter . . . on the difficulty of bringing theological questions to an issue. 1860 29/7/60
Psalms and litanies. 1872 10/4/81
Rational godliness. 1855 3/2/56
Williams, Watkin Lady
Even such is life. 1888 (3v.) 9/2/89
Williams, William M.P.
Letter to . . . Russell on . . . education in Wales. 1848 9/2/48
Williamson, David R.
Poems of nature. 1888 13/11/90, 22/9/91
Williamson, Stephen
The relations between church and state and the tithing system. 1886 7/11/86
Willinck, Arthur
The world of the unseen. 1893 26/5/93
Willis, Browne
A survey of the catherdral church of St. David's. 1717 11/7/52
Willis, Edward Cooper
The law and practice of bankruptcy. 1884 9/11/85 ?
Willis, Nathaniel Parker
Inklings of adventure. 1836 (3v.) 12/9/36
Life, here and there; or, sketches of society and adventure at far-apart times and places. 1850 4/3/50
Willis, Richard Bishop
An address to those of the Roman communion in England. 8/12/39
Willis, Robert physician
Benedict de Spinoza; his life, correspondence and ethics. 1870 4/10/72
Servetus and Calvin. 1877 6/4/78
The Pentateuch. 1875 8/5/81
Willis, Robert Professor
The architectural history of Canterbury Cathedral. 1845 31/10/54
The architectural history of Glastonbury Abbey. 1866 18/8/66
Willis, W.
John Milton. 2/10/87
Willis, William
Edmund Burke; the story of his life. 1889 15/11/89
Willis, William Downes
Outline of proposals for the adjustment of the education question between the Church and the Education Committee of the Privy Council. 1848 13/3/48
Willmore, Graham
Is trial by jury worth keeping?. 1850 20/2/50
Wills, Charles
Baptismal regeneration. A letter to C. H. Spurgeon. 1864 14/8/64
Willson, Thomas Edgar
It is the law; a story of marriage and divorce in New York. 1888 6/7/89
Wilmot, Barbarina Baroness Dacre
Dramas, translations and occasional poems. 1821 (2v.) 31/7/35
Tales of the peerage and the peasantry, ed. Baroness Dacre. 1835 (3v.) 8/7/35
Wilmot, John Earl of Rochester
Sodom, or the quintessence of debauchery. 21/8/66 ?
The works of the Earls of Rochester, Roscommon, Dorset, the Duke of Devonshire. 1721 15/8/82
Wilmot, John Eardley Eardley
Lord Brougham's law reforms. 1860 17/10/61
Parliamentary reform. 1854 21/12/53
Wilson, A.
England's policy in China. A pamphlet. 1860 31/8/60
Wilson, Alexander Johnstone
Banking reform. An essay on prominent banking dangers and the remedies they demand. 1879 27/3/79
Reciprocity, bimetallism and land-tenure reform. 1880 2/2/80
The resources of modern countries. 1878 (2v.) 6/3/78
Wilson, Alexander Stephen
A creed of tomorrow. 1872 27/8/76

Wilson, Andrew printer
Arbitration between the University of Cambridge and Andrew Wilson. 1806 5/5/69
Wilson, Benjamin
Letter to . . . W. E. Gladstone . . . on the new bill for the removal of Jewish disabilities. 1853 24/8/53
Plain sermons. 1850 (2v. 1850–3) 27/7/51
Twenty-one reasons for the re-election of Mr. Gladstone respectfully addressed to the members of Convocation. 1852 17/7/52
Wilson, Carus
[Letter to J. Wilson Patten]. (not found) 23/5/36
Wilson, C. H.
A sketch of Swift's life and a collection of anecdotes about him. 1804 (2v. 1804) 27/1/47
Wilson, Charles Thomas
Illustrations of the doctrine and discipline of the church, illustrated from the apostolical fathers. 1845 23/5/47
Inquiry into the doctrines of the Tracts for the Times. A farewell sermon. 1842 16/7/42
Wilson, Charles William
The strategic importance of the Euphrates Valley railway. 1873 17/6/73
Wilson, Claude
Sonnets to the Queen and other poems. 1880 28/11/92
Wilson, C. T.
Russian lyrics in English verse. 1887 13/6/87
Wilson, Daniel antiquary
Caliban: the Missing Link. 1873 29/7/79
Prehistoric annals of Scotland. 1862 (2v.) 12/12/62, 26/9/67
Prehistoric man; researches into the origin of civilization in the old and new world. 1862 3/8/63
The lost Atlantis; and other ethnographical studies. 1892 8/11/92
Wilson, Daniel Bishop
A defence of the Church Missionary Society. 1818 14/7/28, 25/9/36 ?
Charge . . . to the clergy of the diocese of Calcutta. 1838 29/3/40
Charge . . . to the clergy of the diocese of Calcutta. 1843 18/6/43
Introductory essay to W. Wilberforce's Practical View. 1797 5/4/29
Letters from an absent brother. 1825 (2v.) 12/7/32, 28/7/32
Sermons and tracts. 1825 (2v.) 22/1/60
The divine authority and perpetual obligation of the Lord's Day. 1831 30/1/31
Wilson, Daniel Vicar of Islington
A revival of spiritual religion the effectual remedy. 1851 3/8/51
Appeal to the evangelical members of the Church of England. 1850 16/10/50
Holy scripture, the only infallible guide. 1835 10/5/85
The inspired scriptures. 1861 19/8/83
Wilson, E.
The theory of foreign exchanges. 1861 3/10/61
Wilson, Edward Rector
Prayer for the dead. 1870 17/5/74
The pleas of the church. Five essays, addressed to . . . W. E. Gladstone. 1869 4/4/69
Wilson, Francis
A letter to the Rev. W. Gresley. 1850 7/5/50
Wilson, George
The five gateways of knowledge. 1856 6/11/56
The grievance of the university tests, as applied to the professors of physical science in Scotland. 1852 24/9/52
Wilson, H.
'Indian budgets and Indian deficits' in *Fraser's Magazine*, xciv. 667. 1879 (June 1879) 11/6/79
Wilson, Harriette
Memoirs. 1825 (4v.) 30/10/28, 17/10/72
Wilson, Harry Bristow
A letter to . . . T. T. Churton [condemning the Tracts]. 1841 30/3/41
Wilson, Henry Bristow
A brief examination of prevalent opinions on the inspiration of the holy scriptures. 1861 14/6/63
The communion of saints. 1851 11/12/53, 1/1/54
Wilson, Henry Schütz
Poets as theologians. 1888 29/1/90
Wilson, Horace Hayman
Works. 1862 (12v. 1862–77) 20/9/63
Wilson, James editor
The government of India in relation to famines and commerce. 1877 26/11/77
Wilson, James of *The Economist*
Capital, currency and banking; being a collection [from] The Economist. 1847 29/11/54
Financial measures for India. 1860 28/3/60
Fluctuations of currency, commerce and manufactures referable to the Corn Laws. 1840 21/12/41
Influences of the Corn Laws, as affecting all classes of the community, and particularly the landed interest. 1839 17/12/41
Wilson, James Maurice
Essays and addresses; an attempt to treat some religious questions in a scientific spirit. 1887 10/7/87
Wilson, James Spottiswoode
The creation story and nebular theory [in the Impregnable Rock] by W. E. Gladstone, investigated. 1890 15/10/90
Wilson, J. H.
Zalmoxin. 1891 18/10/91 ?
Wilson, John inspector of hospitals
Medical notes on China. 1846 21/3/46

Wilson, John Professor
Essays critical and imaginative. 1857 (4v.) 20/7/57
Wilson, Joseph
Letters on the truth and certainty of natural and revealed religion . . . an introduction to Bishop Butler's 'Analogy of Religion'. 1810 10/1/91 ?
Wilson, Joshua barrister
English presbyterian chapels proved to have been orthodox foundations. 1844 12/6/44
Memoir of the life and character of Thomas Wilson. 1846 16/9/48
Wilson, Matthew pseud. Edward Knott
Mercy and truth. 18/8/40
Wilson, Robert of S. Bantaskine
The Franco-German war. With supplement and history of the Commune by his father. 1881 12/10/82
Wilson, R. W. of New York
Florida, U.S.A. 1880 3/2/80
Wilson, R. W.
The rectory of Valehead. 1830 9/4/31
Wilson, Thomas Bishop
A short and plain instruction for the better understanding of the Lord's Supper. 1736 27/7/28
Sacra Privata, ed. W. Denton. 1853 2/4/55
The true Christian method of educating children. 1729 (new edn 1833) 23/7/37
Wilson, Thomas of Cambridge
Catholicity spiritual and intellectual. 1850 28/11/52
Wilson, Thomas M.
Local option in Norway. 1891 29/8/92
Wilson, William Samuel
The ocean as a health resort. 1880 27/12/81 ?
Wilson, William Wilson Carus
Christ revealed. 1851 8/8/52
Winchell, Alexander
Science and religion. 1882 29/1/82 ?
Windeatt, Edward
The parish church of St. Mary, Totnes. 1876 10/9/77
Windham, William
The diary of the Right Hon. William Windham, 1784–1810, ed. Mrs. H. Baring. 1866 29/5/66
Windt, H. de
Siberia as it is. 1892 30/3/92
Wingard, Carl Frederik
Review of the latest events and present state of the Church of Christ. 1845 8/6/45
Wingfield, Lewis S.
Lady Grizel. An impression of a momentous epoch. 1878 (3v.) 13/3/84
Winn, James Michell
Darwin. 1883 11/2/83
Mind and living particles. 1878 (2v.) 5/6/79
Winslow, Benjamin Davis
The sermons and poetical remains of B. D. Winslow, ed. G. W. Doane. 1842 15/4/43
Winslow, Forbes Benignus
Obscure diseases of the brain and disorders of the mind. 1860 29/7/60
Physic and physicians. 1842 22/4/52
Winslow, Lyttelton Stewart Forbes
Spiritualistic madness. 1876 21/11/76
Winter, C. T.
Becket . . . dramatised from the old chroniclers. 1879 25/2/79
Winter, James W.
'Gigantic Inhumanity'. South African note on Woman Slavery Convention and the diamond and gold fields. 1877 3/7/77
Winter, John Spearman
French treaty rights in Newfoundland. The case for the colony. 1890 24/6/90
Winter, John Strange i.e. Henrietta E. V. Stannard
Soul of the bishop. 1893 (2v. 1893–5) 22/9/93
Winterbotham, Rayner
On the real character of the early records of Genesis. 1878 30/12/78
Sermons and expositions. 1874 18/10/74
Winthrop, Robert Charles
Address at the unveiling of the statue of Col. W. Prescott. 1881 9/12/81
Eulogy pronounced at the funeral of G. Peabody. 1870 9/3/70
Wise, Clement
Puritanism in power. 1890 15/11/90 ?
Wiseman, Nicholas Patrick Stephen
'Italian tourists' in *Dublin Review*, vi. 1. 1839 (January 1839) 20/3/39
A letter respectfully addressed to the Revd. J. H. Newman upon some passages in his letter to the Revd. Dr. Jelf. 1841 12/4/41
A reply to Dr. Turton's 'Roman Catholic doctrine of the Eucharist considered'. 1839 21/3/47
An appeal to the reason and good feeling of the English people on . . . the catholic hierarchy. 1850 5/12/50
Convents. A review of two lectures by M. H. Seymour. 1852 26/6/53
Conversion. A letter to Mr. Alexander Chirol and his family on their happy admission to the communion of the holy catholic church. 1847 14/4/48
Fabiola, or the Church of the Catacombs. 1854 15/6/56, 25/7/58
Four advent lectures on Concordats. 1855 7/9/58
Inaugural discourse . . . at the first meeting of the Academy of the Christian Religion. 1861 6/8/61
Judging from the past and the present, what are the prospects for good architecture in London?. 1864 3/6/64

Lectures on the principle doctrines and practices of the Catholic Church. 1836 12/7/36, 26/4/40
Lectures on the Real Presence. 1836 23/5/86, 25/7/86
Letter on catholic unity, addressed to the Earl of Shrewsbury. 1841 11/10/41
Pastoral letter . . . for the building of churches and schools. 1864 26/6/64
Recollections of the last four Popes and of Rome in their times. 1858 2/4/58
Remarks on a letter . . . from W. Palmer . . . of Worcester College. 1841 19/5/41
The final appeal in matters of faith. 1850 3/4/50
The religious and social position of Catholics in England. 1864 13/3/64
Three lectures on the catholic hierarchy. 1850 9/3/51
Twelve lectures on the connexion between science and revealed religion. 1836 17/1/86
Wislicenus, Adolph Timotheus
Beitrag zur Beantwortung der Frage: Ob Schrift? Ob Geist?. 1845 15/10/45
Wislicenus und seine Gegen. Eine Erflärund der protestantischen Freunde. 1845 17/10/45
Wit and Wisdom. 1889 7/11/89
Witherow, Thomas
Derry and Enniskillen in . . . 1689. 1873 6/1/74
Withers, Philip
Alfred's apology. 1789 12/1/46 ?
Witt, Cornelis Henri de
Histoire de Washington. 1855 20/12/65
Thomas Jefferson. 1861 19/12/65
Witt, Henriette de
Monsieur Guizot in private life. 1880 28/2/81 ?
Wittgenstein, Emil zu Sayn-
Der Schutz der Christen im Orient. 1860 21/9/79
Wix, Samuel
Christian union without the abuses of Popery. 1820 20/2/42
Reflections concerning the expediency of a council of the Church of England and the Church of Rome being holden. 1818 6/1/42
Wlastoff, Georges
Prometheus and Pandora. 1883 29/10/83
Wodrow, Robert
Life of James Wodrow, ed. J. Campbell. 1828 19/11/82
The history of the sufferings of the Church of Scotland, from the Restoration to the Revolution. 1721 (2v. 1721–2) 25/4/39
Woffington, Margaret
Life of Peg Woffington, by C. Reade. 1857 12/9/90
Life of Peg Woffington, by J. F. Molloy. 1884 (2v.) 17/4/88, 5/9/90
Wolf, Christian Wilhelm Friedrich August
Prolegomena ad Homerum. 1759 26/3/47
Wolfe, Charles
Remains, ed. J. A. Russell. 1829 17/5/40
Wolff, Henry Drummond
Some notes of the past, 1870–1891. 1893 7/12/92, 3/3/93
Wolff, Joseph
Journal . . . of Joseph Wolff in a series of letters to Sir T. Baring. 1839 10/4/41, 27/1/61
Travel and adventures. 1860 (2v. 1860–1) 27/5/60, 27/1/61
Wolffers, Fr. von
Turkey's fall the decline of England. A suggestion and a warning to Turkish bondholders and Russian money-lenders. 1875 1/12/75
Wollstonecraft, Mary
A vindication of the rights of men, in a letter to . . . E. Burke. 1790 3/12/83
A vindication of the rights of woman. 1792 11/5/49, 7/1/64
An historical and moral view of the origin . . . of the French Revolution. 1794 4/12/83
Letters to Imlay, ed. C. K. Paul. 1879 28/11/83, 30/7/87
Wolowski, Ludwik Franciszek Michel Rajmond
Réponse à la lettre de M. Chevalier . . . sur la Question des Bankes. 1867 24/12/66
Un chapitre de l'histoire financière de l'Angleterre. 1865 22/9/66
Women, The social and political dependence of. 1867 6/5/67
Wood, Anthony à
Athenae Oxonienses, edited by Philip Bliss. 1813 (4v. 1813–20) 7/10/92
The history of the visitation of the University of Oxford by a Parliamentary Commission . . . 1647–1648, abridged from the annals of Anthony à Wood. 1837 11/7/50
Wood, Edward J.
The Royalist's Daughter. A poem. 1856 11/7/67
Wood, Henry
Natural law in the business world. 1887 14/8/87
Wood, James Dean
Elements of optics. 1799 11/5/29
Principles of mechanics. 1796 2/9/28
Wood, John of Edinburgh
Account of the Edinburgh Sessional School. 1829 1/1/35
Wood, John writer
Ancient astronomy. 1882 2/9/82
Wood, John George
Petland revisited. 1890 26/6/91
Wood, J. R.
Devotional readings. 1885 27/9/85
Wood, Robert
An essay on the original genius and writings of Homer. 1769 21/1/47

Wood, Thomas Lett
London health and London traffic. 1859 12/12/60
Wood, Thomas Winter
The Bedouin, and other poems. 1852 23/7/67 ?
Wood, William physician
Insanity and the lunacy law. 1879 1/3/79
Wood, William Converse
Five problems of state and religion. 1877 6/1/84
Wood, William Dyson
Hamlet; from a psychological point of view. 1870 23/1/71
Wood, William Page 1st Baron Hatherley
A vindication of the law prohibiting marriage with a deceased wife's sister. 1861 24/2/61
Life of Lord Hatherley, by T. A. Nash. 1888 1/4/87 n
The continuity of scripture. 1867 25/12/73
Woodard, Nathaniel
A plea for the middle classes. 1848 24/6/48
Woodbury, Levi
Speech on the tariff: delivered in the Senate. 1844 15/3/44
Woodford, J. R.
The great commission, ed. H. M. Luckock. 1886 2/5/86
Woodgate, Henry Arthur
'Essays and Reviews' considered. 1861 15/9/61
A commonsense view of the Athanasian Creed. 1872 29/9/72
An earnest appeal to members of the Oxford Convocation on the proposed assumption of ecclesiastical powers by the University. 1845 30/6/45
Anomalies in the English Church no grounds for seceding. 1857 5/7/57
Considerations on the position and duty of the University of Oxford. 1843 31/10/43
Sermons on the Sunday historical lessons. 1854 14/12/56
The authoritative teaching of the church shown to be in conformity with scripture. 1839 29/9/39, 6/10/39
The scribe instructed . . . A sermon. 1867 30/6/67
University reform. National faith considered in reference to endowments. 1854 2/4/54
Woodgate, Walter Bradford
A modern layman's faith. 1893 30/4/93, 12/11/93
Woodhouse, Robert
Treatise on isoperimetrical problems. 1810 9/8/31
Woodhouse, S.
The Queen of the Humber. 1884 9/8/84
Woodrooffe, Sophia
Lethè, and other poems. 1844 15/2/45
Woodruff, Hiram Washington
The trotting horse of America. 1868 11/6/81
Woods, K. P.
Metzerott, shoemaker. 1889 7/11/89
Woods, Margaret Louise
Esther Vanhomrigh. 1891 (3v. 1891–2) 9/6/92
Woods, Nicholas Augustus
The past campaign: a sketch of the war in the East. 1855 (2v.) 9/2/56
Woods, Virna
The Amazons. 1891 8/12/92
Woodward, Francis Blake
Christ risen the foundation of the faith. 1861 30/6/61
Remarks on a petition . . . for a revision of the liturgy. 1860 12/2/60
Sermons. 1850 8/10/54
Woodward, Henry
Essays; thoughts and reflections; and sermons. 1864 (5th edn) 15/1/65
The expediency of preaching against the amusements of the world. 1841 12/9/41
Thoughts on the points at issue between the Established Church and the National Board of Education in Ireland. 1844 14/6/44
Woodward, Matthew
The past and present of the parish church of Folkstone. 1892 18/9/92
Woodward, Richard
The present state of the Church of Ireland. 1787 22/2/63, 7/10/87
Woodward, Thomas Best
Treatise on the nature of man regarded as triune. 1874 19/8/74
Woollcombe, Edward Cooper
University extension and the poor scholar. 1848 1/7/48
Woolman, John Quaker
Journal of . . . John Woolman. 1776 26/10/90
Woolmer, Charles Edward Shirley
The shadow and the very image. 1874 29/11/74
Woolner, Thomas
Pygmalion. 1881 20/12/81
Woolson, Constance Fenimore
Jupiter lights. 1889 8/9/90
The front yard, and other Italian stories. 1889 4/1/89
Worboise, Emma Jane
Husbands and wives. 1873 7/10/74
Word in season, A. 1849 16/9/54
Word of warning to all . . . in these perilous days, A. 1834 26/3/47
Wordsworth, Charles of St. Andrews
Charge. 1862 9/11/62
Christian boyhood at a public school. 1846 8/7/46
Commission on prayer. 1843 5/2/43
Evangelical repentance. 1841 30/1/42, 5/6/42

Letter to . . . W. E. Gladstone on the doctrine of Religious Liberty as propounded in his letter to the Bishop of Aberdeen. 1852 16/3/52
Man's excellency a cause of praise and thankfulness. 1864 10/7/64
National Christianity. 1851 21/9/51
On Shakespeare's knowledge and use of the bible. 1864 11/5/64
Opinion on the appeal of the Rev. P. Cheyne. 1858 1/7/60
Wordsworth, Christopher Master of Trinity
The Ecclestiastical Commission and the Universities. 1837 28/3/37
Wordsworth, Christopher of Lincoln
A plea for the diocese of Maritzburg. 1871 25/6/71
Academic unity. 1847 29/8/47
Athens and Attica. 1836 20/6/36
Beautiful scenery: with what feelings to be contemplated. 1850 25/3/50
Charge. 1870 7/1/72
Church extension. 1843 18/6/43
Conjectural emendations of passages in ancient authors. 1883 25/6/89
Defence of the Queen's Supremacy, against Romish aggressions. 1846 3/5/46
Diary in France, mainly on topics concerning education and the church. 1845 2/3/45
Heathen and Christian philanthropy. 1838 3/6/38
Inscriptiones Pompeianae. 1837 14/4/38
Is Rome Babylon?. 1850 11/9/50
Lectures on the Apocalypse. 1849 12/9/51, 26/12/76
Letter to Lord John Manners [on Maynooth]. 1845 1/6/45
Letter to the members of Lincoln College, Oxford [on proposed changes]. 1880 27/11/80
Letters to M. Gondon, on the destructive character of the Church of Rome. 1847 21/3/47
Mohammedan woe. A sermon. 1876 26/11/76
Occasional sermons. 1851 1/6/51
Old Catholic Congress. 1872 18/8/72
On a proposed subdivision of dioceses. 1860 13/1/61
On divorce. 1857 28/6/57
On the admission of dissenters to graduate in the University of Cambridge. 1834 17/4/34
On the Athanasian Creed. 1872 7/4/72
On the Court of Final Appeal. 1884 13/1/84
On the inspiration of holy scripture. 1851 9/3/51
On the state of church patronage. 1874 5/3/74
Righteousness exalteth. 1848 29/12/48
Sequel to Letters to M. Gondon. 1848 21/5/48
St. Hippolytus. 1853 2/2/62
The General Synod. A speech. 1875 5/12/75
The history of the Church of Ireland. 1869 21/2/69
The inspiration of the bible. 1861 6/10/61
The Maccabees and the church. 1871 3/12/71
The new testament. 1859 11/5/84
Theophilus Anglicanus. 1843 21/1/44, 10/11/61
Tour in Italy. 1863 14/2/63, 12/12/63
Twelve addresses. 1873 27/7/74
Wordsworth, Christopher of Peterhouse
Scholae Academicae . . . the English universities in the 18th century. 1877 22/2/78
Wordsworth, Dorothy
Recollections of a tour in Scotland, ed. J. C. Shairp. 1874 25/7/74
Wordsworth, John
The one religion. 1881 4/10/91
Wordsworth, William
Ecclesiastical sonnets. 1822 3/8/34
Kendal and Windermere railway. Two letters reprinted. 1845 29/1/44
Life of William Wordsworth, by J. M. Sutherland. 1887 27/10/91
Opera. 12/5/32, 26/10/32, 27/10/32
Peter Bell, a tale in verse. 1819 9/6/36
The Excursion. 1814 15/11/33, 8/5/34, 26/12/34, 22/1/35, 17/8/40, 11/12/44, 27/1/91
The poetical works of William Wordsworth. With a life of the author. 1865 28/8/79
The Prelude; or, growth of a poet's mind. 1850 7/2/53
The White Doe of Rylstone; or the fate of the Nortons. 1815 24/6/36
Yarrow revisited, and other poems. 1835 29/4/35, 9/6/36
Word to the wise, A. 1847 15/9/51
Worgan, John Hartland
Speculum Ecclesiae Anglicanae. 1843 26/7/45
World at war. (not found) 9/3/73
Worms, Henry de Lord Purbright
England's policy in the East. 1877 29/3/77
Wormstall, Joseph
Hesperien. 1878 4/11/78
Wornum, Ralph Nicholson
Lectures on painting, ed. R. N. Wornum. 1848 8/12/48
Worsley, Francis
The last Thane. 1843 21/4/62
Worsley, Henry
The dawn of the English reformation. 1890 9/8/91
Worsley, Philip Stanhope
The Iliad of Homer. 1865 8/11/65
The Odyssey of Homer. 1861 28/12/61
Worsley, Thomas
Christian drift of Cambridge work. Eight lectures. 1865 24/12/65
Worth, Thomas
A second letter to . . . Gladstone [on contagious diseases]. 1870 30/3/70

Worthley, Mrs.
The New Continent. 1890 (2v.) 22/1/90
Wortley, Emmeline Charlotte Elizabeth Stuart
Fragments and fancies. 1837 27/10/37
Wortley, James Archibald Stuart
Law of marriage. 1849 30/4/49
Wortley, Victoria Stuart
Links and clues. 1881 28/8/81
Wrangham, Francis
[Speech]. 29/3/45
Wratislaw, Albert Henry
John Hus. The commencement of resistance to papal authority on behalf of the inferior clergy. 1878 30/12/83
Wraxall, Nathaniel William
Posthumous memoirs of his own time. 1836 (3v.) 1/9/36
Wray, Cecil
A sermon . . . in Liverpool. 1843 30/4/43
The bishops' call to conformity. 1869 3/1/69
Wray, George
The sound policy of the existing law of marriage [on deceased wife's sister]. 1849 20/3/49
Wrigglesworth, Edmund
Illustrated guide to Hull. 1889 28/8/90
Wright, Carroll Davidson
A report on marriage and divorce in the United States, 1867 to 1886. 1889 5/5/89
Wright, Charles Henry Hamilton
Biblical essays . . . on Job. 1886 30/5/86, 8/11/91
The Divinity School of Trinity College, Dublin, and its proposed improvement. 1879 27/4/79, 27/4/84
The University of Dublin: a scheme of reform. 1873 12/3/74, 9/7/76
Wright, Ichabod Charles
The Iliad . . . translated into blank verse. 1859 19/3/59
Thoughts on the currency. 1841 28/12/41
Wright, J. H.
Confessions of an almsgiver. 1881 20/1/84 ?
Wright, John editor
Biographical memoir of . . . William Huskisson. 1831 26/4/33
Wright, John horticulturalist
Mushrooms for the million. 1884 (2v. 1884–7) 11/1/87
Wright, John Martin Frederick
Alma Mater; or, seven years at the University of Cambridge. 1827 (2v.) 11/8/65
Wright, Richard unitarian
An apology for Dr. Martin Servetus. 1806 3/2/50
Wright, Thomas
History of caricature and grotesque. 1865 27/10/65
Political poems and songs relating to English history . . . from the accession of Edward III to that of Richard III. 1859 (2v. 1859–61) 26/2/60
Political songs of England, from the reign of John to that of Edward II. 1839 12/3/72
Womankind in Western Europe, from the earliest times to the seventeenth century. 1869 8/11/72
Wright, Thomas Preston
Letter to Charles Wordsworth . . . on the difficulties of his synodal theory. 1851 1/6/51
Urgent reasons for reviving the synodical functions of the Church. 1849 10/2/49
Wright, W.
Yayin; or the Bible wine question, by Professors Watts, Wallace and Murphy . . . and the Revd. W. Wright. 1875 29/8/75
Wright, William D.D.
The Empire of the Hittites. 1884 10/10/84
Wrigley, Thomas
Look before you leap. Railway accidents, their cause and cure. 1871 28/3/71
W. S.
True chronicle . . . of the life . . . of Thomas Lord Cromwell. 21/12/52
Wyatt, Matthew Digby
On the influence exercised upon ceramic manufactures by the late Mr. Herbert Minton. 1863 4/11/63
Wyatt, William Edward
The Christian altar. 1846 18/9/70
Wycherley, William
Miscellany poems: as satyrs, epistles, love-verses, songs, sonnets. 1704 5/8/46
Wycliff, John
Life of, by L. Sergeant. 1893 26/2/93
Wyld, George
[on clairvoyance etc.]. (not found) 8/3/85
Wylde, Katharine
Mr. Bryant's mistake. 1890 (3v.) 23/8/90
Wylie, A. H.
American corn and British manufactures. 1845 25/1/45
Wylie, James Aitken
Rome and civil liberty; or, the Papal aggression in relation to the sovereignty of the Queen. 1864 15/3/68
The history of protestantism. 1874 (3v. 1874–7) 21/3/80
Which sovereign? Queen Victoria or the Pope?. 1888 1/3/90
Wylie, William Howie
Thomas Carlyle. 1881 12/4/81
Wyllie, John William Shaw
Essays on the external policy of India. Edited, with a brief life, by W. W. Hunter. 1875 24/9/78
Wynn, Charlotte Williams
Extracts from letters and diaries of Charlotte Williams Wynn. 1871 17/3/71

Wynne, E.
The Old Bible, or the martyr's gift. 1875 14/1/76
Wynne, John Huddlestone
A general history of Ireland, from the earliest accounts to the present time. 1773 8/12/75
Wynne, Richard
Essays on education, by Milton, Locke, and the authors of *The Spectator.* 1761 22/6/49
Wynter, Andrew
The borderlands of insanity and other allied papers. 1875 18/6/75
Wyse, John
The spectre of the Vatican. 1875 11/6/82
Wyse, Thomas
An excursion in the Peloponnesus in the year 1858. By the late Sir T. Wyse, edited by his niece, W. M. Wyse. 1865 (2v.) 23/10/65, 10/5/69
Impressions of Greece. 1871 3/3/71
Wyss, Johann David
The Swiss Family Robinson. 1818 (2v.) 7/12/61

X
Monnaie et métaux précieux. 1857 19/10/60
Xenophon
Hellenica. 17/2/27, 12/3/29, 8/9/30
Xenos, Stephanos Theodoros
East and West, a diplomatic history of the annexation of the Ionian Islands to the Kingdom of Greece. 1865 23/3/65
Yates, James
Narrative of the origins and formation of the international association for obtaining a uniform decimal system of measures, weights and coins. 1856 (draft) 30/12/54
On the irregularities in the versification of Homer. 1856 27/11/56
Yates, John Ashton
Colonial slavery. Letters to ... Huskisson. 1824 8/7/63
Yeadon, James Edward
Nonconformity vindicated. 1866 2/9/66
Yelverton, Maria Theresa Lady Avonmore
Martyrs to circumstance. 1861 (2v.) 26/9/82
Yonge, Charles Duke
The life and administration of ... Lord Liverpool. 1868 (3v.) 10/12/68
The life of Marie Antoinette. 1876 (2v.) 3/7/76
Yonge, Charlotte Mary
Biographies of good women ... edited by the author of 'The Heir of Redclyffe'. 5/11/65
History of Christian names. 1863 6/4/68
Journal of the Lady Beatrix Graham. 1871 21/5/71 ?
Kenneth; or, the rearguard of the Grand Army. 1850 4/12/53
Life of J. C. Patteson, missionary bishop of the Melanesian Islands. 1872 (2v.) 20/10/72, 2/7/74, 14/11/78
Musings over the Christian Year and Lyra Innocentium ... together with a few gleanings of recollections of the Rev. J. Keble. 1871 9/9/83
The Heir of Redclyffe. 1853 (2v.) 16/5/53
Yorke, Charles Isaac
A respectful address to the Bishop of London. 1842 14/5/43
Yorke, Grantham Munton
The school and the workshop. 1856 19/10/56
Youard, Henry George
Disestablishment viewed in the light of history. 1877 6/4/84
Youatt, William
The horse. 1831 9/2/76
Young, Arthur
A tour in Ireland. 1780 (2v.) 28/9/86, 13/6/87
An enquiry into the legality and expediency of increasing the Royal Navy by subscriptions for building county ships. 1783 12/4/48
The example of France, a warning to Britain. 1793 17/3/57
Travels in France, 1787–1789. 1889 1/2/92
Young, Benjamin Charles
Modern discoveries of science anticipated by the Bible account of the Creation. 1886 19/9/86
Young, Edward
Night thoughts on life, death, and immortality. 1777 (2v.) 25/9/25, 18/2/27, 8/7/27
Young, Sir Frederick
An address on imperial federation. 1876 24/7/76
Young, George Frederick
Free-trade and the Navigation Laws. 1849 5/3/49
Young, John
The Christ of history. 1855 26/8/66
The light and life of men. 1866 13/5/66
The province of reason. 1860 6/5/60, 1/1/61
Young, Thomas Charles
Lectures on Scots law. 1889 5/3/89

Zahn, Theodor
Das apostolische Symbolum. 1893 23/4/93 ?
Zamberti, Bartolommeo
Isolario. 24/9/53
Zamoyski, Wladyslaw
Poland. A letter to the ... Earl of Ellenborough. 1861 11/11/61, 8/9/88 ?
Zanelli, Domenico
Roma e S. Pietro. 1867 8/10/79
Zangwill, Israel
Children of the ghetto. 1892 (3v. 1892–3) 22/10/92

Zart, Gustav
Einfluss der englischen Philosophen. 1881 9/9/92, 19/9/92
Zeno, A., and N.
The voyages of the Venetian brothers, A. and N. Zeno, to the Northern Seas, by J. Major. 1892 21/3/92
Zerffi, Gustavus George
The Irish question in history. 1886 7/10/86
Zeta
Reply to a pamphlet, entitled 'India and Lord Ellenborough'. 1845 9/1/45
Zimmern, Heinrich
Die Assyriologie. 1889 18/12/89
Zincke, Foster Barham
'On the Limagne' in *Fortnightly Review*, xxx. 821. 1878 (December 1878) 27/12/78
A month in Switzerland. 1873 (3v. 1873–5) 11/6/73
Egypt of the Pharaohs and of the Khedive. 1871 29/12/71, 27/8/75, 8/10/90
Some thoughts about the school of the future. 1852 18/4/52
The plough and the dollar, or the Englishry of a century hence. 1883 6/5/83, 27/12/83
Why must we educate the whole people?. 1850 15/6/51
Zippe, Franz Xaver Maximilian
Geschichte der Metalle. 1857 27/6/68
Zola, Emile
La Bête humaine. 1890 11/2/92
La Terre. 1887 27/4/88, 2/5/88
Nana. 1880 27/6/89, 2/7/89
Piping hot!. 1885 29/6/88
Zöllvereinsblatt. 38. 9/1843. British commercial policy 26/10/1843
Zubof, Count Roman I.
The nationalists. 1890 11/9/90
Zumbini, Bonaventura
Saggi critici. 1876 19/5/77
Studi sul Petrarca. 1878 7/6/79

SUBJECT INDEX

Information on certain aspects of this index will be found in 'Using the Indexes' at the start of this volume.

Aachen 24/7/32 ff
  cathedral of 24/7/32
Abbeyleix, Queen's County (De Vesci)
abbreviations
  G's use of for numbers 27/8/90 n
Aberdeen 17/9/84, 13/7/92
  G Freeman of 26/9/71
  King's College 6/10/58
Aberdeen, Earl of *See* Gordon
Aberdeen, University of
  G declines invitation to stand for Rectorship of 13/2/75
Aberdovey 9/9/56
Abergeldie Castle 1/10/44, 25/9/63, 29/9/71
  Victoria offers to let to G 27/8/64
Aberystwyth 10/9/56
  Belle Vue hotel excellent 10/9/56
Abney Hall, Cheshire (Watts) 21/4/62
Aboyne Castle (Huntly) 4/10/71
abstinence
  as remedy for sin 26/10/45
abstract resolutions
  G's dislike of 27/6/54
Abyssinia 21/11/67, 25/11/67, 26/11/67, 23/4/68 n, 6/3/69 c, 20/3/69 c, 4/5/69 c, 17/3/71 c, 10/12/72, 7/3/84 c
  Prince Alamayu case 14/1/72 n, 22/1/72 c
Académie des Sciences *See* France
accidents 11/2/33, 16/2/33, 11/11/33, 14/2/34, 29/7/42, 21/9/42
  boy falls off ship 17/12/58
  cab nearly overturned 24/10/76
  Captain, H.M.S
    capsizing of 9/9/70, 18/4/71 n
  C. G's bad fall 8/6/49
  C. G's carriage accident 1/5/67
  climbing, to W. H. G and S. E. G 17/9/70
  eye damaged by hard gingerbread thrown in Chester 25/6/92 ff
  falling brick, dropped or thrown 3/5/82
  fall over drawer of writing table 24/12/94
  fall through failing sight 2/7/93
  finger bruised in course of treefelling 29/1/68
  fire at Hawarden Castle 22/1/79
  G falls from horse in Rotten Row 4/4/63
  G shoots off his lefthand forefinger 13/9/42 ff
  gun cotton experiment shatters Downing Street windows 1/8/72
  head wound from a fall 23/2/81 ff
  heifer, G knocked down by 29/8/92, 8/9/92
  Helen G falls from carriage 28/8/52
  hurt heel 12/1/53, 22/1/53 ff
  Irish mail 21/8/68
  lightning kills Henry Glynne 30/7/72 n
  Megaera, H.M.S
    beached 5/8/71 c, 7/8/71, 3/11/71 c, 8/11/71 c
  on railway 15/8/61
  Peel's fall 1/7/50
  pin-shot cartridge thrown at G (unexploded) 13/6/89
  to children 6/11/40
    H. N. G burns hand at snapdragon 29/12/62
  treefelling
    splinter in G's eye 23/12/67
    tree felled onto estate worker 31/12/70
    tree felled with H. N. G in it 27/12/67
  Wilberforce's, on fall from horse 21/7/73
  See also Drew (Mary), Gladstone (Sir John)
accounts 31/12/33, 30/12/34, 31/12/35, 1/7/36, 31/12/36, 31/10/37, 30/11/37, 2/3/38, 6/12/39, 10/3/40, 11/1/41, 10/2/41, 1/11/42, 4/11/42, 26/12/46, 22/3/47, 13/3/48, 8/2/49, 13/2/49, 18/5/50, 4/3/51, 16/2/52, 5/12/53, 26/12/53, 4/2/56 ff, 6/3/58, 10/10/59, 23/12/59 ff, 31/8/60, 1/10/61, 7/7/62, 5/8/62 ff, 14/1/64, 29/12/64, 12/1/65 ff, 18/9/65, 12/12/65, 14/12/65, 9/8/67, 5/1/69, 1/1/72, 2/1/73, 15/4/73, 1/1/75, 31/12/75, 1/1/77, 29/12/77, 31/12/77, 23/12/79, 7/2/80, 27/12/80, 31/12/81, 29/12/82, 14/1/84, 4/1/86, 1/1/87, 17/1/91, 12/10/92
  £43,000 to be distributed among G's children 1/1/90, 4/1/90
  bonfire of papers to 1866 inclusive 6/9/67
  charitable, to be kept separately 6/12/39, 5/12/41, 4/11/42, 30/6/44, 16/3/55, 2/4/55
  Egyptian Tribute Loan held by G
    £45,000 12/10/76, 13/12/76, 16/8/77
  estimate of G's future income 20/12/65
  G rather flush 23/6/82
  G's earnings from literature
    to 1890: £14, 862 20/3/91

accounts (*cont.*)
G's finances pinched: explanation to C. G 2/9/72
G's property and pending arrangements 12/12/87
G thriving in midst of distress 31/12/78
Hampton assisting with 23/5/59
Hawarden reversion and 20/12/65
Metropolitan line losses 5/4/71, 3/10/84
private locked account book 29/8/60
retrenchment of consumption in G's houses 2/2/47
satisfactory nature of 19/3/40
since 1831 4/11/42
statement of G's income and property 26/12/56, 11/1/61, 19/7/71, 30/5/74, 1/6/74, 1/1/79
See also railways
Accrington Liberal Club 12/7/78 n
Achilli case 30/6/52
Achnanalt 9/10/72
Acland, Henry Wentworth, Sir (1815–1900), regius professor of medicine, Oxford (1858) 4/5/48, 20/1/52, 29/1/53, 20/1/54, 16/6/55, 26/1/57 ff, 21/11/61, 22/11/61, 29/4/64, 18/5/67, 24/2/73, 13/7/77, 31/1/78, 26/7/78, 20/11/80 ff, 26/4/81, 5/7/85, 13/11/88, 5/2/90
as Radcliffe trustee 26/1/57, 30/1/57
at Hawarden 23/7/58, 17/1/73, 11/1/74
G attends Ruskin's lecture with 7/6/67
G visits University Museum with 9/5/59
holds meeting for G 19/6/55
letters from G to, printed 2/8/81, 29/10/83, 11/12/85, 16/12/85, 10/10/92, 17/10/92, 15/8/93
treating W. H. G's Asiatic cholera 24/8/54 ff
Acland, Thomas Dyke, Sir (1809–1898), 11th Baronet (1871), liberal M.P., member of the Engagement 22/9/28, 22/10/29 ff, 29/8/30 ff, 19/5/31, 4/6/31, 15/5/33 ff, 4/2/37 ff, 10/12/37, 1/5/38, 17/5/38, 4/2/39, 20/2/39, 9/5/39, 21/7/40, 1/4/41, 27/11/52, 23/6/66, 20/2/67 ff, 8/7/75, 20/7/75, 29/5/76, 25/1/77 ff, 1/3/77, 22/2/78, 11/6/79, 16/6/80, 18/8/83, 6/7/85, 5/1/86, 7/1/86, 14/6/89
at Hawarden 10/12/85 ff
deplores G's excessive references to class 15/6/86
discusses his future with G 15/8/55, 16/8/55 ff
education and 21/7/40
G and home rule, notes on 14/7/85 n, 12/12/85 n
G's retirement as Prime Minister and 5/3/94
letters from G to, printed 28/8/69, 24/7/71, 6/5/73, 13/1/82, 28/3/82, 7/8/82, 13/11/84, 15/6/86, 20/7/86, 23/8/86, 3/12/93, 5/3/94, 7/3/94
qualities of 7/8/82
State and Church and 2/8/38
Temple's appointment to Exeter and 28/8/69
the Engagement and 24/11/44, 4/7/45, 14/3/47, 11/6/49
true model of English gentleman 16/12/85
Act of Uniformity Bill 3/6/72, 5/6/72, 9/7/72
Acton, John Emerich Edward Dalberg, Sir (1834–1902), 8th Baronet (1837), 1st Baron Acton (1869), historian, lord-in-waiting 1892–5 9/4/59, 4/5/59, 2/5/61, 6/3/63, 12/3/63, 4/6/63, 26/7/63 n, 14/6/65, 27/4/68, 13/7/71, 22/11/72 n, 19/2/74, 17/5/74, 11/3/76, 6/6/76, 21/6/76, 8/7/76, 3/4/77, 19/4/77, 12/12/80, 9/1/81, 10/8/82, 7/2/83, 4/7/84, 22/11/84 ff, 20/2/85, 6/3/85, 13/6/85, 12/7/85, 14/6/86, 11/8/86, 15/8/86, 18/8/86, 18/6/87, 27/6/87, 24/7/89, 16/6/90, 11/8/91, 18/6/92, 23/6/92 ff, 30/6/92 ff, 6/10/92, 30/10/92 ff, 23/11/92, 25/11/92, 16/12/92 ff, 4/3/93 ff, 28/3/93 n, 3/4/93 ff, 14/5/93, 11/6/93, 12/9/93 ff, 29/9/93, 1/12/93 ff, 11/12/93 ff, 28/12/93 ff, 11/1/94, 19/2/94 ff, 11/5/94
American civil war and 8/2/66
a most satisfactory mind 12/2/83
at Dalmeny 30/6/92 ff
at Hawarden 18/1/69 ff, 2/11/76 ff, 12/1/77 n, 14/1/78, 31/12/81 ff, 30/5/87 ff, 27/8/87 ff, 13/9/87 ff, 23/10/87, 17/10/88 ff, 23/11/89 ff, 16/11/91 ff
Captaincy for 23/8/92
discourages G from retiring as prime-minister 20/2/84
Döllinger and 10/10/69
G at Aldenham 9/11/74 ff
Goethe and 6/2/88
G proposes as British Museum trustee 26/7/71
G's autobiography and 8/7/92
G's final retirement and 2/3/94
G's Romanes lecture and 19/9/92 ff
G with in Cannes 4/2/88 ff
home rule and 1/6/87
honorary fellowship at All Souls, G's part in arranging 10/6/90 n
in opinion goes beyond Döllinger, in action stops short 2/11/76

in Rome 5/12/66 ff, 19/12/66
Ireland and 1/7/85
letters from G to, printed 1/12/69, 8/1/70, 1/3/70, 8/11/71, 22/8/72, 10/9/73, 19/9/80, 14/12/81, 26/12/81, 3/2/84, 31/8/84, 27/1/85, 11/2/85, 24/8/92, 19/9/92, 26/9/92, 5/10/92, 7/10/92, 10/10/92, 17/10/92, 6/2/94, 8/2/94
library of 14/5/90 ff, 17/6/90
G's memorandum on, printed 9/6/90
G's role in saving 14/5/90, 9/6/90 ff
Lordship-in-Waiting for 19/9/92, 25/11/92
navy estimates crisis and
letter to G on 2/2/94
peerage for 3/8/69
plan for G's autobiography and 16/8/87 n, 27/8/87
Poet Laureateship and 7/10/92 ff
Pope, election of 22/8/72
ranks George Eliot above Scott 11/2/85
the more he sees the more G likes 4/4/64
The Vatican Decrees(1874)
Acton comments on at Hawarden 29/10/74, 30/10/74
Ultramontanism and 1/12/69, 8/1/70, 22/8/72
Vatican Council and 13/1/70, 1/3/70, 24/3/70, 25/3/70, 3/4/70, 8/11/71
expects Pope to prevail 29/12/69
Janus letters 1/12/69
letter of to be sent to the Queen 1/12/69
Vaticanism, corrects proofs of 15/2/75
visits of, a daily treat 23/9/93
with G at Braemar 15/7/92 ff
with G at Dalmeny 30/6/92 ff
with G in Biarritz 18/1/94 ff
with G in Brighton 15/3/94 ff
with G in Cannes 18/1/83 ff, 15/2/89 ff
with G in Munich/Tegernsee 16/9/79 ff, 27/8/86 ff
with G in Venice 5/10/79
wonderful learning of 6/9/86
See also Carnegie, Döllinger, Gower, Herbert, Scott
Adderbury House (Baring) 24/6/31
Adderley, Charles Bowyer, Sir (1814–1905), 1st Baron Norton (1878), Peelite M.P. 8/3/43, 5/2/52 ff, 13/7/89
G gives a gentle tap to 6/4/78
letters from G to, printed 24/10/84, 10/9/93
most improper speech of 6/4/78
Reform Bill 1884 and 24/10/84 ff
Addiscombe
East India Military College
G examining at 11/6/58
Additional Curates Society 31/1/38, 3/2/38, 17/3/38, 20/7/47, 18/11/56, 15/4/59, 19/5/79, 21/12/89 n
G's speech at Chester on 18/11/56
Aden
Turkish aggression at 15/11/73
administrations *See* governments
administrative reform 15/6/55 n, 18/6/55, 10/7/55, 19/3/56, 19/9/56
Administrative Reform Association 26/1/56 n
Admiralty
Peel suggests post for G in 31/8/41
Adullamites
G's attack on 5/4/66 n, 10/2/67 n, 18/2/67 n
reconciliation attempted 27/2/67, 5/3/67
adultery
G committing adultery in the heart 22/4/49
advertisement tax 13/5/53, 10/6/53, 18/6/53, 1/7/53 ff
advowson of Liverpool, G's purchase of *See* Liverpool
Affirmation Bill 5/3/83 c, 24/3/83, 2/4/83, 5/4/83, 7/4/83 c, 16/4/83, 24/4/83, 3/5/83
clergy's memorial on 6/4/83
G's long and *bergeistert* speech on 26/4/83
Afghanistan 3/6/43, 4/5/69 c, 4/10/73 c, 28/11/78, 6/12/78, 10/1/80, 12/3/80, 29/5/80 c, 9/6/80, 16/6/80, 19/6/80 c, 10/7/80, 24/7/80 c, 31/7/80 n, 25/8/80, 6/9/80 c, 7/9/80, 8/2/81, 21/4/81, 15/8/81, 24/11/81, 1/2/82 c, 18/2/82 c, 8/8/83 c, 1/7/85, 7/8/85, 20/12/85, 4/7/86, 30/8/92, 7/9/92, 30/9/92 c, 15/7/93, 26/7/93
Afghan Committee, G unable to join 15/11/78 n, 18/11/78 n
border disputes with Russia 10/12/72 c, 28/2/85 c, 12/3/85 ff, 4/4/85 c, 6/4/85 ff
Merv 18/2/84 c, 22/2/84
Oxus boundary 10/12/72 c
frontier commission 4/3/85 ff, 4/4/85 c, 5/4/85 ff, 9/5/85 c, 2/6/85, 8/6/85 c, 11/6/85, 20/7/86 c
Herat agreement 3/5/80 c
Herat incident 12/3/85 cf, 20/3/85 c, 24/3/85 c, 27/3/85 c
amicably settled 2/5/85 c
Kandahar, withdrawal from 6/9/80 c, 7/9/80, 9/9/80, 10/9/80, 25/10/80, 12/11/80 c, 8/3/81 c, 10/3/81, 12/3/81 c, 19/3/81 c, 25/3/81
Queen's Speech and Queen's objections 7/1/81, 10/1/81
Penjdeh incident 13/3/85 n, 8/4/85 ff
amicably settled 2/5/85 c
Pishin 25/10/80
See also India, memoranda (printed), Russia (Central Asia)

Africa
Africa Association 18/3/53
Berlin Conference on 8/10/84 c, 20/11/84 c, 20/1/85 c, 21/1/85 c
neutralisation of Congo 20/11/84 c
Cameroons and 7/3/85 c
Dahomey 4/9/73
discussed with Leopold II 14/5/90
G addresses missionary meeting at Cambridge 1/11/59
human sacrifices in
not crimes under African moral law 4/9/73
Italian aggression and 7/6/71
Kilimanjaro region
G opposes forward movement in 14/12/84
lecture by Smithies on at Hawarden 5/9/88
Livingstone in
arms in kind not to be given to expedition of 18/11/72 c, 22/11/72 c
limited guarantee to 7/5/70 c
meeting on 23/4/39 ff, 8/7/39
Niger Company
charter for? 21/1/85 c
Niger delta
oil trade in 30/1/72 c
Nyassa Anti-Slavery and Defence Fund 22/9/88
Porto Nuovo 8/8/83 c
protectorates in
definition of duties of 20/1/85 c
West African territorial proceedings 25/10/83 c, 17/11/83 c
See also Congo, Dahomey, deputations, Egypt, Liberia, Madagascar, South Africa, Sudan, Uganda
age
decline in power of reading 6/9/93
G rebels against old age 29/12/60, 29/12/61
G's memorandum on his physical decline, printed 13/9/94
old age and politics 19/2/74, 25/2/74, 30/6/85
old age appointed for snapping of threads 29/12/96
pity for old age 23/2/93
responsibilites of old age 29/12/92, 31/12/92
ripeness of old age 28/1/77
sleeplessness in old age
a weakness, unfitting G for Parliament 18/12/93
Zadok Outram's help to G in old age 3/12/93
agnostics
Bradlaugh case and toleration of 11/6/81
Agricultural Employment Institution 23/3/33
Agricultural Society (Royal) of England
G proposes toast to in Chester 22/7/58
agriculture 21/8/83 c, 26/1/86 n, 25/11/92
Agricultural Labourers' Union 4/12/73 n
Carlingford and 15/3/83
committee of Council for 15/3/83, 17/3/83 c, 27/3/83
distress in 30/6/79 n, 4/7/79 n, 9/12/92, 17/12/92 c, 26/1/93, 27/8/93
Richmond commission 19/6/80 c, 9/12/80, 18/1/81, 21/1/81, 28/4/81
fruitfarming, G's speech on 9/1/84
hiring fairs 7/2/79 n
machinery the one legitimate and wholesome check on 23/8/73
Royal Commission on 20/7/93 c
See also cabinet, corn laws, free trade, harvests, haymaking
Alabama claims *See* cabinet, Palmer, United States, Wodehouse
Albania 5/3/77, 27/9/80
G visits 2/2/59
impression most saddening: indolence, decay, stagnation 2/2/59
Albany *See* houses
Albert, Prince (1819–1861), Prince Consort (1840) 27/1/40, 11/3/40, 16/8/43, 30/7/46, 31/7/46, 16/2/53, 4/6/53, 3/8/53, 5/1/54, 3/4/54, 29/4/54, 14/11/59
1851 Exhibition and 19/8/51, 2/6/52, 5/6/52, 24/10/53, 25/10/53, 24/4/58
agriculture and 1/3/52
Albert Hall
opening of 29/3/71
Albert Memorial
G alone in criticising 23/3/63
American civil war and
anti-Northern 28/11/61
conversation but no politics 1/12/60, 2/12/60
death of 14/12/61, 15/12/61
discussing Italy with G 4/1/60
funeral of 23/12/61
G arranges royal marriage settlements with 13/2/61
G defends in letter to *Morning Chronicle* 15/1/54
G discusses finance and universities with 12/1/53
G discusses peace terms with 25/2/56
G discusses Roebuck committee with 18/2/55, 21/2/55
G explains 1853 budget to 9/4/53
G's Address on 23/4/62
G's audiences of 8/6/54
G's conversation on improvement with 31/8/54
G sends copy of Farini to 17/6/51

G's memoir of 27/12/61 ff
G speaks to on the Commons 30/4/58
G's verses on death of 27/12/61 n
G wins money at cards from 9/1/45
like a new Evangel 21/3/50
Marochetti's monument to 20/11/62
plays part in G becoming Chancellor 22/12/52 n
shows minute on Turkish question to G 25/10/53
the Eastern question and 25/10/53, 9/11/53, 11/11/53
thinks Russell's letter shameful 30/11/54
See also Crimean war, Exhibition (Great), Victoria
Albert Hall *See* London
Albery, J. *See* plays seen
Albury (Drummond/Percy) 13/5/56 ff, 17/6/76
Aldenham Park, Shropshire (Acton) 9/11/74
Alderley rectory, dinner at 18/2/28
Alderney *See* memoranda
Aldworth, Haslemere (Tennyson) 22/7/71
Alessandria 8/3/32
Alexandra, Princess (1844–1925) 10/3/63, 19/4/63, 27/4/63, 20/3/65, 3/3/68, 5/4/73, 14/7/73, 15/5/74, 13/7/78, 5/5/80, 12/6/81, 28/3/82, 3/5/85, 5/1/86, 30/1/87, 27/7/89, 21/7/90, 12/12/91, 15/8/92
at tea with the Gladstones 27/3/71
charm of 9/5/63
G staying at Sandringham 30/11/72 ff
service for recovery of Prince of Wales and 21/12/71
unmistakeable liberalism of 4/3/82
Alexandria *See* Egypt
Alfieri's plays, comments on 10/10/33
Algiers
bombardment of, 1816 15/7/82
alien immigration 11/2/93
G's memorandum on 7/2/93
See also Mundella
Aliens Act, Ireland
extension to England 17/6/82 n, 19/6/82 c, 20/6/82
allowance, G's, fixed at own request 19/3/40
All Saints
reflections on 1/11/55
All Saints, Margaret Street (Margaret Chapel) 6/4/34, 4/4/41, 7/4/41 ff, 17/10/41, 24/3/42, 5/8/42 ff, 7/11/43 ff, 14/1/44, 24/2/44 ff, 7/4/44, 19/1/45 ff, 6/12/45, 11/1/46 ff, 21/5/46 ff, 17/4/47 ff, 5/12/47 ff, 24/4/48 ff, 24/3/49 ff, 24/2/52, 23/3/56, 23/11/62, 21/6/73, 12/5/89
beauty of services 7/4/44
decline of services at 20/4/78
G composed by worship at 8/2/45
G's recollections of history of 3/9/93
G's visit to with Butterfield and Dyce 1/4/59
rebuilding of 4/7/45 ff, 13/4/54
All Souls, Oxford 12/11/88
Acton's honorary fellowship, G's part in arranging 10/6/90 n
G as Hon. Fellow of 11/5/59
induction 11/5/59
G dining in 4/11/47, 11/5/59, 12/5/59, 31/1/90 ff
G lunching in 25/10/52, 20/6/55
G's visit to 31/1/90 ff
plans for 25/12/89
reredos of 9/11/74
W. H. G unsuccessful candidate at 23/9/63, 4/11/63
Alma, battle of *See* Crimean war
Alnwick Castle (Northumberland) 2/10/76
Alps
crossing 8/2/32 ff, 28/10/50 ff
tunnels under 28/2/32
views of 27/2/32, 28/10/50
Alsace-Lorraine
annexation of 21/10/70, 7/11/70, 10/11/70, 16/11/70, 23/11/70
G fails to persuade cabinet to object to 30/9/70 c
G's memorandum on, printed 25/9/70, 23/11/70
not to be taken by Germany against inhabitants' will 12/9/70
See also Bismarck, cabinet, France, Franco-Prussian war, Germany, Max Müller, memoranda
Althorp (Spencer) 12/10/52, 7/11/73, 4/4/79, 7/12/91
liberal leadership meeting at 7/12/91 ff
library of 8/11/73
Alton Towers (Shrewsbury)
vast outlay and poor result of 31/10/63
Amalfi 9/5/32, 9/2/89
ambition
to make an Estate for my children 23/10/69
trifling compared with inward sin 21/2/41
Wilberforce tells G he should follow Palmerston
G says 'no' 20/10/63
ambition, G's 3/5/41, 16/9/41
America
G declines to write on George Washington for 30/11/88 n
Amiens
cathedral of 9/8/49
Ampthill Park 24/10/78
anarchism
G's comments on 10/12/93

Anatolikes Omospondiae 14/5/89 n, 24/8/89
Ancient Music *See* Music (Ancient)
ancient right franchises *See* Reform Bills
Ancona 7/6/32, 10/10/66
Anglo-Indians *See* India
Angra Pequeña *See* South Africa
animal magnetism 29/12/38
annuities 8/5/33, 10/1/69, 20/9/92
  G's government-backed plan 1/3/64 n, 5/3/64, 7/3/64, 17/3/64, 21/4/64, 25/4/64 ff
    passed 20/6/64
Anstice, Joseph, (1808–1836), professor of classics, King's, London 10/11/28, 16/11/28, 22/10/29, 20/11/29, 16/12/29, 10/1/30, 23/5/30, 5/6/30, 18/7/30, 24/7/30, 12/9/30, 24/10/31, 25/1/33 ff, 16/5/33, 6/2/34 ff, 21/6/35
  assists G in decision about profession 8/8/30
  death of 2/3/36
anticlericalism 23/4/40
Anti-Corn-Law League 16/3/44
  danger of Chartist/A. C. L. L. combination 11/6/43
  Walsall by-election and 19/1/41
Anti-Papal League of Edinburgh 31/12/72
Anti-Slavery Committee
  G denounced by 30/7/32
apostolical succession 27/5/37, 8/12/37, 19/1/38, 29/1/38, 7/11/39, 13/11/39
Appellate Jurisdiction Bill 10/7/56
Apsley House (Wellington) 25/5/35, 25/5/67
Arabi Pasha *See* Egypt
Arbroath 7/10/46
Arbuthnott Farmers' Club
  G's speech on free trade to 1/12/49
Archaeological Society 2/7/75
archery 26/8/26 ff, 17/5/28, 5/8/29, 17/9/34, 22/8/36, 28/8/60, 31/8/60
Ardrossan 6/7/47
Arezzo 3/10/38
Argyll, Duke of *See* Campbell
Argyll House 14/2/57, 21/5/73, 26/3/74, 27/6/80
Argyll Rooms
  G attempting rescue work outside of 22/7/50
Ariosto
  G's digest of 14/7/49, 7/12/49 ff
  tomb of 14/6/32
aristocracy
  corrupted by 'ploutocracy' 13/9/71
  G's defence of hereditary wealth 19/9/90 n
Aristotle
  abstract of *Ethics* 2/11/31
  discussed with Macaulay 8/2/45
  epitome of *Rhetoric* 29/6/29 ff, 4/12/29 ff, 24/3/30, 30/3/30
  immense value to public men of his *Politics* 20/11/35
  Politics
    analysis of 1/9/34, 3/10/35, 25/11/35
    G's translation of 10/9/60 ff, 28/8/61 ff
  Politics studied with W. H. G 3/9/60 ff, 16/8/61 ff
Arley Hall (Warburton) 9/9/45, 24/10/55, 1/12/76, 8/9/79
Armenia 25/5/83, 3/8/93, 20/10/96
  Armenian Patriotic Association 29/11/88 n
  census of 24/7/80 c
  liturgy of 17/3/33, 9/6/33, 16/6/33
  liturgy of, G studying 17/3/33
  Turkish atrocities in 12/8/93
    G's letter to *Daily News* on 25/8/89
    See also Bryce
Armitstead, George (1824–1915), 1st Baron Armitstead (1906), manufacturer and G's companion 20/12/80, 15/3/88, 30/4/88, 20/11/88, 24/3/91, 9/4/91, 30/7/91 ff, 15/2/92, 27/4/92 ff, 29/10/92 ff, 17/12/92 ff, 9/2/93 ff, 15/6/93 ff, 3/7/93 ff, 5/9/93 ff, 22/12/93 ff, 5/1/94 ff, 12/3/94 ff
  at Hawarden 29/10/89, 11/9/91 ff, 27/6/92, 22/8/92, 19/10/93 ff
  G's host in Biarritz 16/9/91 n, 15/12/91 ff
  G's host in Hastings 25/3/91 ff
  introduces G to labour M.P.s 26/4/87
  qualities of
    rare modesty, courtesy, generosity 26/3/91
army
  artfully constructed monopoly of professional classes in 14/8/82
  augmentation of forces
    G's battle with Herbert over 2/4/60, 13/4/60
  Battle of Dorking and
    mischievous as well as mad 24/5/71
  buildings for 19/2/70 c
  commissariat and 23/11/54 ff, 20/1/55
  espionage and 21/7/82
  estimates 27/11/59, 30/11/59, 5/12/59, 23/1/62, 30/1/62 ff, 7/10/64, 12/2/69 c, 20/2/69 c, 10/12/69 c, 17/12/69 c, 30/8/71, 11/12/71, 12/12/71, 14/12/71 c, 18/12/71 c, 29/1/72, 10/2/72 c, 15/2/72 c, 6/12/72 ff, 22/1/73 c, 29/1/73 c, 15/10/73, 1/12/73, 19/1/74, 22/1/74, 31/5/80, 15/12/80, 1/2/81, 17/11/81, 26/12/81, 10/1/82, 21/11/82, 14/1/84, 19/1/84, 21/1/84, 26/1/84 c, 9/7/84 c, 25/7/84 c, 11/11/84 c, 2/12/84 c, 16/12/84, 2/2/85, 9/2/85 c, 16/2/85 c, 17/2/85 c, 12/2/86, 13/2/86, 15/2/86 c,

19/2/86 ff, 22/2/86 ff, 25/12/86, 7/1/93 ff, 16/2/93, 22/2/93, 23/2/93 c
1874's of special significance 15/10/73
cabinet committee on 29/11/62
effect of Indian silver question on 28/5/86
Egypt and 21/11/82
G gives in to cabinet on for two years 9/11/72
G reluctantly but quietly consents to 30/1/61
G's memorandum on, printed 12/12/71
G very lonely in cabinet on 30/11/59
prospects of agreement with navy bad 17/1/74
Queen's intervention over 14/12/93 c
reduced 29/1/73 c
retrenchment and 30/8/71, 9/9/71, 12/9/71, 16/9/71
supplementary, for Sudan 2/2/85, 9/2/85 c, 17/2/85 c, 7/3/85 c
unsatisfactory talk with Cardwell on 7/12/72
flogging in 21/3/67, 8/7/79 n, 15/7/79, 17/7/79, 14/5/80
G votes against abolition 2/4/33
fortifications plan 16/12/59 ff, 23/5/60 ff, 4/7/60, 13/7/60, 16/7/60
distinct basis settled 25/7/60
Franco-Prussian war and 23/7/70 c, 25/7/70 c, 30/7/70 c
G at Cobhame review 21/6/53
G's evidence to Ridley Royal Commission on establishments 21/7/88, 25/7/88, 23/11/88
G's memorandum on widows' army pensions 21/11/59
Guards, the
band of to go to U.S.A. 5/6/72 c
Cardwell's plan to abolish/reform 14/12/71 c, 18/12/71 c, 23/1/72 c
nursing in 25/11/54 n
officers of
G's memorandum on 25/9/71, 5/10/71
Prussian system offers lessons for, G thinks 21/9/70, 23/9/70, 8/10/70, 2/5/71
parade on return from Egypt 18/11/82
Life Guards 22/10/82
purchase abolition 12/3/70 c, 21/9/70 n, 4/10/70, 8/10/70, 13/10/70 ff, 26/10/70, 20/1/71 c, 25/1/71 c, 28/1/71 c, 11/2/71 c, 15/2/71 c, 18/2/71 c
bill in Commons 12/6/71 ff, 3/7/71
commission on effects of 19/7/73 c, 29/8/73, 3/9/73, 15/9/73, 17/9/73
cost of 8/3/71, 18/3/71
G opposes funding by special fund from land tax 3/1/71
G's assessment of the case for 27/5/71
liberal party and 8/3/71
loan to pay for outrages G 19/1/71
Lords' obstruction to 10/7/71, 12/7/71 c, 14/7/71 c, 20/7/71 c, 22/7/71 c, 29/7/71
obstructed in Commons 16/3/71
royal warrant, threat of cancelling 12/7/71 c, 15/7/71 c, 20/7/71
rations of 22/12/53
recruitment through the Post Office 10/10/83
reform of 11/1/69, 12/1/69, 21/1/70 c, 29/3/70, 25/6/70 c, 16/3/71, 18/12/73, 1/7/80, 16/12/80 c, 22/1/81 c, 4/3/82 c, 2/11/92
cadets should start in ranks 13/10/70
leisured class and 13/10/70
memorandum on, printed 11/11/79
officers 21/9/70
report on Prussian military system for cabinet ordered by G 21/9/70
results seen at Tel-el-Kebir 15/9/82
reserves called out 24/7/82
for Sudan 9/2/85 c
standing army, moral conditions of 23/8/64
troops used for harvesting at Woodstock 3/9/72, 27/10/72, 5/11/72
United Service Institution
G suggests government help for 20/1/72, 22/1/72
use of under civil authority 15/7/82
War Office plans Ashantee war without G's knowledge 2/8/73 n, 30/8/73, 5/9/73, 15/9/73, 21/9/73, 23/9/73, 26/9/73, 28/9/73, 3/10/73 c, 4/10/73 c, 10/10/73
See also Cardwell, Cavendish, Childers, colonies, estimates, fortifications plan, Gordon, Herbert (Sidney), India, memoranda, memoranda (printed), Militia, navy, Temple, Volunteers, Wolseley
arnica *See* medicines
Arnisdale 25/8/53
Arrears Bill *See* Ireland, memoranda (printed)
arson
destroys Hawarden church 29/10/57
art 4/4/32
conversation of artists delightful 16/5/63
G attends Ruskin's lecture on state of modern art 7/6/67
G wanting in higher poetic sense, distinguishing the true artist 25/11/78
See also artists under individual names, busts of G, Christie's, Cobden, coins, Disraeli, galleries visited, Gladstone (Catherine), Gower, Homer, individual artists, Liverpool, Manchester, Millais, Naples,

art (*cont.*)
Peel, photographs of G, pictures, portraits of G, Pre-Raphaelites, Primrose, rescue work, Rome (studios visited), Royal Academy, sculpture, statues of G
Artemis
G's lecture at Eton and article on 21/2/91 ff, 6/3/91 ff, 14/3/91
Arthurianism, G's study of 14/8/59 ff, 7/9/59 ff
Artists' General Benevolent Institution
G speaks at 31/3/60
Ashantee *See* Gold Coast
Ashbourne Act *See* Ireland
Ashridge, Berkhamstead 9/6/83, 26/8/93
Asia, Central
Khiva, Russian expedition to 28/11/73 c
Merv 28/11/73 c
railway through
Afghans worried about 19/12/73
railway through: nothing to be done by U.K. 17/5/73
Russian encroachment in 22/1/73 c, 5/12/78, 17/5/80 c, 21/8/80 c
spheres of influence in 21/9/92
Asquith, Herbert Henry (1852–1928), 1st Earl of Oxford and Asquith; barrister; liberal M.P. and journalist, home secretary 1892–5, prime minister 1906–16 2/4/87 ?, 16/4/87, 19/4/87 n, 4/4/89, 7/3/90, 12/12/91, 22/7/92, 26/7/92, 2/8/92, 8/8/92 n, 14/8/92 ff, 16/11/92 n, 22/1/93, 9/2/93, 15/7/93, 16/11/93 ff, 5/1/94 n
alien immigration and 7/2/93
at Hawarden 28/10/93
coal lock-out and 10/11/93
Ecclesiastical Commission and 7/10/92
Featherstone incident and 26/9/93 n, 7/10/93, 14/12/93 c
Glasgow Lord Rectorship and 19/9/93
G's retirement as Prime Minister and 5/3/94
home rule and 13/1/93 c, 7/10/93
India and 15/7/93
letters from G to, printed 19/9/92, 23/9/92, 7/10/92, 14/10/92, 1/12/92, 23/2/93, 26/2/93, 15/9/93, 7/10/93, 10/11/93, 5/3/94
marriage to Margot of 19/2/94, 10/5/94
nonconformity and 7/10/92 n
religious disabilities
annotating G's memorandum on 2/2/91
Trafalgar Square, meetings in 14/10/92
Uganda and 23/9/92
unemployment and 18/8/93 c
Welsh disestablishment and 10/11/93
will rise, G thinks 28/10/93
assassinations 13/3/81 ff, 13/6/81 c, 21/7/81
threat of death on G 13/6/81 c
Assessed Rates Bill 10/4/69 c
assizes 29/3/26
Assynt mountains 21/9/58
Assyriology
G's lecture to Oxford Union on 1/2/90, 5/2/90
Aston Clinton (Lord Rothschild) 31/3/88, 8/4/90
a very edifying house 15/4/90
not overdone like many Rothschild houses 1/4/88
Aston colliery *See* Hawarden Castle (estate of)
Astronomical Society 14/11/62
asylums visited
Bedlam 28/7/35
Middlesex lunatic asylum 2/4/36
Athanasian creed 21/4/54, 23/1/71, 20/5/71, 5/11/71, 11/3/72
atheism
Bradlaugh case and toleration of 11/6/81
forces in the world for 26/8/72
Athenaeum *See* clubs
Athens
Acropolis
G's visit to 20/12/58
English School [of Classical Studies] in, proposal for 6/2/83, 18/5/83, 25/6/83
G attends Russian church in 19/12/58
G's visit to 18/12/58
statue of G in University of 23/10/83, 26/10/83, 19/7/88 n
University Library
G visits 20/12/58
Atlantis 11/3/82
atonement 29/12/29, 30/1/31, 8/7/32, 9/2/36, 27/7/84, 18/2/94 ff.
attornies' certificate duty
G's opposition to abolition of defeated 19/5/65
Auber *See* operas
audiences of the Queen *See* Victoria
Audit Board 2/2/53, 1/2/54, 26/7/54, 23/1/55, 8/7/59, 23/1/60, 1/2/61, 24/10/61
G's financial plan and 16/2/56
Audit Commission 28/1/64, 18/7/64, 4/7/65
irregular appointments to 18/2/73 n
Audley End (Braybrooke) 15/11/41 ff, 22/9/54 ff, 19/3/58, 3/11/59, 28/2/61
extraordinary psalter at 24/9/54
Augsburgh 29/9/45
Augustine, St.
commentary on, compiled by G 9/10/49
comments on 20/11/39
Confessions, reflections on 26/11/34
G quotes to the Pope 22/10/66

Auronzo 29/9/79
Aurora Borealis 21/9/58
Australia 4/6/49, 26/1/58
  Australia Bill 22/3/50, 7/5/50, 13/5/50, 1/8/50
  case of J. W. Willis 24/6/46
  church in 4/1/46, 7/5/46
  Colonial Union of colonies of, G favours 19/5/83
  federal council for 9/9/84, 23/10/84
  G's memorandum on imperial veto 20/12/54
  G's phonograph recording for 6/3/90 n, 8/3/90
  intercolonial conference in
    New Guinea and 8/12/83
  mint of 4/2/53
  New South Wales 27/6/37, 12/2/94 c
    bishoprics in 24/3/46
    criminals in 23/4/46
    National League of Sydney, President of 10/2/88
  postal contract with 26/4/73 c
  Queensland
    New Guinea and 10/3/83 c, 21/4/83 c, 19/5/83, 13/6/83 c, 27/6/84 c
  religion in 7/6/37
  rescue cases going to 7/6/52 ff, 16/6/52, 24/6/52, 29/6/52, 10/1/53
  South Australia 15/2/41, 2/3/41, 16/6/49, 14/10/93
  tariffs and 29/12/71, 25/1/72, 26/1/72, 27/1/72 c, 9/2/72, 10/2/72 c, 2/3/72 c, 15/3/72, 13/4/72 c, 22/3/73 c
    agreed to, obligations of treaty being saved 1/3/73 c
  telegraph to 27/2/63
  transportation 7/2/46 ff, 28/2/46 ff
  Van Diemen's Land
    criminals in 20/3/46 n
    Eardley-Wilmot recalled 29/4/46
    education in 21/2/46
    female prisoners in 27/4/46 n
  Western Australia
    convicts' families to be sent out 19/6/69 c
    See also memoranda (printed), New Guinea
Austria 27/6/32 ff, 17/9/38 ff, 24/9/79, 18/11/84, 23/9/85, 11/9/86 ff
  churches in 17/9/38
  Gmunden 15/9/86
  good roads of 5/7/32
  G's aim to end Italian occupation by 30/6/59
  G's memorandum on commercial treaty with, printed 13/2/65
  G's policy towards 4/5/80, 14/5/80, 26/9/82
  home rule memorial to 22/1/81 c
  loan to 4/3/93
  Smyrna and 9/10/80, 14/10/80
  St. Martin (Arco-Valley) 11/9/86 ff
    monastery of 13/9/86
  trade treaty with 20/11/72 c
  troops in Italy liked 12/6/32, 14/6/32
  troops in Italy marching 28/2/59
  See also home rule, memoranda (printed)
authors *See* journals (G's)
Authors' Association 26/2/39
autobiography, G's
  Carnegie's involvement in 21/4/92 n
    suggests G dictate 3/3/91 n
  Cassell's offer £5000 for copyright of 25/6/87
  Century Co., New York, offers £250,000 3/3/91
  plans for 15/8/87 n, 16/8/87 n, 27/8/87
  writing of 8/7/92 ff, 10/8/92 ff, 22/2/93, 4/7/93, 17/12/93
    on Hallam 25/11/93
Autun 23/2/32
Auxerre 22/2/32
Aviemore 5/9/39, 9/10/72
Avignon 25/1/39
Aylesbury
  liberal deputation from 21/4/79

backgammon 28/12/26 ff, 10/4/27, 18/1/28, 26/12/28 ff, 3/8/29, 18/1/33, 5/9/33 ff, 8/9/34 ff, 13/8/36, 31/3/37, 28/12/37, 29/4/67 ff, 14/8/69, 15/8/74 ff, 3/5/86, 7/7/86 ff, 20/10/86 ff, 18/1/87 ff, 26/5/87 ff, 27/5/87, 10/12/87, 18/1/88 ff, 22/5/88 ff, 27/12/88 ff, 2/1/89 ff, 20/5/90, 26/9/90, 22/12/90 ff, 2/1/91, 22/5/91 ff, 13/7/91 ff, 5/8/91 ff, 16/9/91 ff, 17/12/91 ff, 31/12/91 ff, 26/1/92 ff, 13/4/92 ff, 2/6/92 ff, 22/7/92 ff, 4/8/92 ff, 26/9/92 ff, 29/11/92 ff, 26/12/92 ff, 7/1/93 ff, 9/2/93 ff, 4/3/93 ff, 16/3/93, 25/4/93, 11/7/93 ff, 6/9/93 ff, 27/10/93 ff, 4/11/93 ff, 22/12/93 ff, 5/1/94 ff, 12/3/94 ff
Bacon's *Novum Organum*, analysis of 22/9/34, 1/1/36
Baden
  G's visit to Helen G 8/10/45 ff
  memorandum on temptations undergone at 19/7/48
Baden, Duchy of 15/9/38
Bala 7/9/56
Balaam *See* memoranda (printed)
Balfour, Arthur James (1848–1930), 1st Earl of Balfour (1922), family friend of the Gladstones; tory M.P.; Irish secretary

Balfour, Arthur James (*cont.*)
1887-92 11/7/72, 21/3/74, 1/8/74, 28/2/75, 25/3/75, 8/5/75, 3/3/76, 24/6/76, 7/5/77 n, 17/6/79, 16/6/85 ff, 28/6/89, 18/2/91, 27/5/92, 31/7/92, 31/7/92 ff, 26/9/92, 24/3/93 c, 11/8/93, 7/9/93, 10/12/93, 2/5/94
accommodating G in Carlton Gardens 29/9/75
all members of his family interesting 15/9/78
at Hawarden 18/11/71, 11/7/72, 11/1/74, 31/5/74, 20/10/83 ff
attack on G by 6/11/87
death of May Lyttelton and 25/3/75
'del miglior luto', G thinks 20/11/74
friendships with the Gladstone/Glynne girls 2/6/74
G at Whittinghame 14/11/74 ff
G invites to join his Irish visit 8/10/77 n
given over to the almost raving licence of an unbridled tongue 17/5/82
G's retirement and 2/3/94
G staying at shooting lodge of 3/10/72
home rule and
G's conversation on at Eaton 15/12/85, 16/12/85, 20/12/85, 23/12/85, 24/12/85, 5/1/86, 3/7/86
Irish secretary
Coercion Bill 28/3/87 ff, 18/4/87, 29/4/87 ff
G's criticism of 3/12/88
letters from G to, printed 20/12/85, 23/12/85, 5/1/86, 3/7/86, 1/8/93, 2/3/94
Local Government Bill and 29/12/93 c
Mary G and 18/11/74, 20/11/74
navy and 14/12/93
person of great charm, G thinks 7/10/72, 31/5/74
qualities of
exhibitionism 17/5/82
See also Ireland, Whittinghame
Balkans *See* Austria, Bosnia, Bulgaria, Eastern question, Greece, memoranda (printed), Moldavia, Montenegro, publications, Rumania, Russia, Serbia, Turkey, Wallachia
Ballater 6/9/36, 2/9/39
absence of tourists in 6/9/39
ballet
ad nauseam in Venice 24/2/59
G deplores 31/7/50
G hopes never to see another 14/11/38
G's better opinion of, in Paris 21/10/50
Balliol College, Oxford 11/5/31, 26/10/52, 27/1/53, 27/11/83, 4/2/90
G dining in 2/11/47, 26/1/57
G discussing university reform in 2/11/47
G lunching in 10/5/59
balloons, ascents of 2/7/33
ballot 16/1/33, 4/2/33 ff, 4/3/69 n, 28/9/83
Ballot Bill (Leatham) 16/3/70 c, 25/6/70 c
bill for 1870 5/11/69
bill for 1871 2/11/70 c, 7/11/70 c, 25/1/71 c, 18/2/71 c, 6/5/71 c, 5/7/71 c, 6/7/71 n, 15/7/71 c, 24/7/71 c, 5/8/71 c
G votes for with mind satisfied & as to feeling a lingering reluctance 29/6/71
bill for 1872 21/10/71 c, 22/1/72 c, 25/1/72 c, 30/1/72, 18/4/72, 18/6/72
Cardwell offers resignation over 18/4/72 n
dissolution on? 6/7/72 c
Lords' amendments to 18/6/72, 22/6/72 c, 26/6/72 c, 1/7/72, 3/7/72, 6/7/72 c, 10/7/72 c
cabinet committee on 2/11/70 c
conservative party and 11/8/71
G's articles on 17/1/33, 4/2/33
G votes against 7/3/37, 15/2/38, 8/8/48, 30/3/52
select committee on 6/3/69 c, 12/2/70 c
See also cabinet (committees of)
balls
Catherine Gladstone 10/5/60, 15/5/60, 3/7/61, 2/6/65, 28/6/65, 28/4/69, 11/5/69
Children's Ball (Catherine G) 25/4/57
Children's Ball (Queen) 1/5/55, 25/4/56, 7/3/59, 11/5/60
Colonel Pennant 26/6/66
Countess De Pérsigny 20/6/59
Duchess of Sutherland 16/6/47
Duchess of Wellington 12/7/58
Duke of Devonshire 24/5/48
fancy dress
G as Sir Leoline Jenkins 13/6/51, 18/6/51
Guards' 26/6/63
Lady Ashburton 18/6/51
Lady Charlotte Denison 24/5/52
Lady Clarendon 11/5/53
Lady Derby 3/6/59
Lady Fitzwilliam 29/5/61
Lady Lansdowne 13/6/33
Lady Ripon 24/6/75
Lady Salisbury 18/6/52
Lady Waldegrave 22/6/70
Lady Wilton 23/6/52, 18/6/67
Lord Camden 15/6/58
Louisa Gladstone 19/6/63
Madame Bernstorff 9/2/66
Madame Brunnow 14/7/58, 15/6/69
Marlborough House 4/7/64, 17/7/72, 10/3/75

Mrs Goschen 30/1/73
Oxford (Oriel) 18/6/55
Prince of Wales 3/6/68, 20/7/76
Stafford House (Anne Sutherland) 7/7/63, 15/5/74
Swinfen 14/1/33
the Queen 10/5/38, 10/5/39, 3/6/41, 15/4/42, 12/5/42, 25/4/45, 14/5/47, 11/6/47, 16/5/49, 13/6/49, 15/6/53, 1/5/54, 8/5/56, 8/6/59, 29/6/59, 25/6/73, 19/5/74
worries about 5/3/32
Balmakewan House (Fraser) 8/9/43
Balmoral Castle (The Queen) 25/9/63, 25/9/64, 10/9/69, 26/9/71, 20/8/73, 5/9/84, 8/9/84
Albert's memorial obelisk, G drinks whisky at 26/8/73
Brown's grave (and alack! *six* obelisks) 10/9/84
Crathie church, G attending 25/9/64, 1/10/71
G holds prayers in camera 12/9/69
G minister in attendance at 25/9/63 ff, 25/9/64 ff, 10/9/69 ff, 26/9/71 ff, 20/8/73 ff
G not attending presbyterian services at 27/9/63 ff
omnibus games on the billiard table 17/9/69 ff
pleasantest part of G's Court experience 7/9/92
Banavie 19/8/53, 10/9/58, 20/9/72
Bangor 18/9/60
Bank Charter Act 13/1/44, 6/5/44, 27/5/73
amendment of
discussed at Political Economy Club 2/2/66
G argues for modification of 11/12/57, 10/1/69
genesis of 13/1/44
G's memorandum on reform of, printed 31/3/73
Peel and
a baptismal creed 18/5/83
provision for relaxation of 14/5/73 c, 17/5/73 c
Childers and Goschen unhappy with 17/5/73 c
Bank Hall, Warrington (Wilson-Patten) 1/10/53, 24/9/67, 30/9/69
banking
G's memorandum on banks and discount houses 17/10/60
G's memorandum on country bank notes 3/3/64
Royal Bank of Scotland London branch
granted 24/5/73 c, 5/7/73 c
refused 1/3/73 c
See also Rothschild's, Savings Banks, Scotland
banking crises 16/12/25 ff, 11/5/66 ff, 7/10/78
absence of governmental responsibility, G asserts 18/4/70 n
Bank Notes Issue Bill 16/3/65 ff, 10/4/65, 1/5/65 ff, 11/5/65 n, 23/11/65
Bank of England 6/4/54, 18/4/54, 12/10/60, 19/12/60, 21/11/62
1866 panic and 11/5/66
deficiency bills and 6/4/54, 12/4/54 ff, 19/9/54
G's meeting with on reduction of profits 3/12/60, 30/1/61
G's memorandum and 16/2/56, 20/2/56
G's memorandum on the Bank's profits 27/11/60
G's Resolutions on 7/2/61
Overend & Gurney's putsch 18/4/60 n, 19/4/60 n
private issues and 21/11/63
bankruptcy
G examined in Court of Bankruptcy 17/5/48
See also Birmingham, Oak Farm
Bankruptcy Bill 5/5/80 c, 13/5/80 c, 8/6/81, 4/12/82, 2/8/83, 8/8/83 c, 10/8/83
Bantaskine, Falkirk (Hagart) 4/12/33, 9/1/37
baptism
G's views and writings on 13/7/28, 27/7/28, 24/8/28, 21/12/28, 6/1/29, 8/2/29, 24/2/29 ff, 29/3/29, 28/4/29, 29/12/29, 16/9/32, 23/12/32, 3/1/34, 29/9/38, 2/2/48, 7/2/52
of G's children 15/7/40, 16/7/40, 24/11/42, 1/5/44, 19/8/45, 21/12/47, 21/9/49, 28/4/52, 18/2/54
of G's grandchildren 8/6/75, 4/11/88, 8/4/90
of royal infants 28/6/53
Baptist Chapel, visited 24/10/30, 23/12/32
Barclay & Perkins brewery 22/1/44
Barfreston church 16/9/54
Baring, Thomas George (1826–1904), 2nd Baron Northbrook (1866), 1st Earl Northbrook (1876), liberal M.P., Governor-General of India 1872–6, First Lord of the Admiralty 1880–5, unionist free-trader 22/7/76, 27/11/78, 7/12/78, 6/3/79, 3/5/80 c, 9/6/80, 27/6/80, 8/10/80, 9/7/81 c, 5/6/82 ff, 10/7/82, 24/10/82 c, 31/12/82, 16/3/83, 21/8/83, 13/11/83 c, 23/2/84, 30/9/84, 16/12/84, 10/1/85, 20/1/85, 25/6/85, 2/3/88
at Hawarden 9/10/82
Egypt and 25/8/82 ff, 31/8/82, 29/4/84

Baring, Thomas George (*cont.*)
Egypt and (*cont.*)
mission to 2/8/84 c, 4/8/84, 5/8/84 c, 6/8/84 c, 12/8/84, 14/8/84, 19/8/84, 27/8/84
report of mission 7/11/84, 15/11/84, 19/11/84 c, 22/11/84 cn, 19/12/84, 24/12/84, 2/1/85 cn, 3/1/85
G at Stratton Park 17/11/83 ff
home rule and 21/1/86
India, Viceroy of 13/2/72
Argyll opposed to appointment of 13/2/72 n
letters from G to, printed 15/10/72, 25/10/80, 15/12/80, 3/5/82, 5/7/82, 13/7/82, 15/12/83, 24/1/84, 10/2/84, 11/2/84, 12/2/84, 4/3/84, 24/4/84, 28/5/84, 2/6/84, 4/6/84, 4/8/84, 12/8/84, 14/8/84, 12/11/84, 14/11/84, 20/11/84, 19/12/84, 24/12/84, 6/1/85
resignation, threat of 16/5/85
Sudan and 24/4/84 ff, 2/6/84 ff, 29/4/85 ff
See also Adderbury, admiralty, Egypt, Gordon, Sudan
Barmouth 13/9/55, 15/9/92 ff
Barnard Castle 7/9/69
Barrow-in-Furness
G speaks in 19/9/67, 8/9/83
Bartholomew Bouverie, G's pen-name 4/6/27, 28/6/27, 22/11/27
See also Eton Miscellany
Basilicata 10/11/38
few signs of poverty in 10/11/38
Basle 18/7/32
Basques *See* Spain
Basutoland *See* South Africa
Bath 2/5/27 ff, 23/5/63
bathing 6/6/26, 14/6/26, 21/6/26, 6/7/26, 10/8/26, 10/7/27, 24/6/28 ff, 8/8/29, 30/7/31, 4/8/41 ff, 24/4/46, 6/7/47, 24/6/49 ff, 21/8/50 ff, 10/9/52 ff, 14/8/54 ff, 6/9/54, 5/9/55 ff, 5/9/59 ff, 27/9/59 ff, 3/9/60 ff, 15/8/61 ff, 15/8/62 ff, 3/9/63 ff, 16/5/64 ff, 31/8/64 ff, 18/4/65 ff, 11/8/67 ff, 11/8/68, 23/8/71, 7/8/74 ff, 11/8/74, 17/8/74 ff
a very powerful agent, G finds 8/9/59
water over-warm at Brighton 16/5/64
Batley drops *See* medicines
Baveno 3/8/49
Bayonne 8/1/92, 28/12/92, 25/1/94, 8/2/94
cathedral of 31/12/91
Beaconsfield, Earl of *See* Disraeli
Beaconsfield club 5/3/80 n
Beaumaris 17/9/61
beauty
female 4/1/40, 15/2/40, 21/4/40
in rescue cases 30/7/59
Beazley, S. *See* plays seen
Bechuanaland *See* South Africa
Bed-Chamber crisis 7/5/39 ff
Beddgelert 14/9/55, 12/9/92
Beddgelert Chalet (Watkin) 12/9/92 ff
Bedfordbury chapel of ease
G assisting with 8/3/49 ff, 1/4/49, 13/5/49 ff, 23/6/50, 6/4/51 ff, 12/2/52, 22/2/52, 13/6/52 ff
G Precentor at 22/4/49
Bedlam, visit to 28/7/35, 29/7/35
beer duty 1/4/82, 20/5/85, 9/6/85 c
See also malt tax
Beeslack, Penicuick (J. Cowan) 25/10/90
Belfast
deputation from declined 16/1/86
Queen's college 20/4/53
See also Ireland
Belgium
Antwerp 3/2/32
Bruges and Ghent 2/2/32, 26/7/32 ff
Brussels 4/2/32, 26/7/32, 15/11/45, 8/11/58, 25/8/86, 18/9/86
Franco-Prussian war and
British treaties with France and Prussia 30/7/70 c, 1/8/70 ff, 11/8/70
tribute to G from Leopold II 14/5/90
Ostende 26/7/32 ff
peace protocols and 6/5/56
threatened by Germany and France 30/1/69, 18/2/69, 28/4/69
trade tolls of 1/3/62, 6/3/62
war of 1831 5/8/31
Waterloo, field of
patriotic sensations at 8/2/32
Bellinzona 5/10/66
bellringing 6/11/46, 24/11/46
at Penmaenmawr
G delighted with his bell 20/2/87
G teaching 24/11/46
looked down on in Scotland 22/11/46
bells
at Hawarden
churchwarden's meeting, G at 23/10/74
bellringers in Newark 27/12/75
passing of time and 31/12/54, 31/12/65
rung for British successes in Egypt 16/9/82
symbols of new birth 31/12/41
Belvoir Castle (Rutland) 25/6/41, 26/6/41, 3/3/47 ff
fulfills idea of noble's position 5/3/47
Ben Macdhui, ascended 9/9/36, 11/9/84
Ben na Buird, Cairngorms 4/9/39
Bentham, Jeremy
theological MSS, G's inspection of 25/4/74
Berber *See* Sudan
Berchtesgarten, Bavaria 18/9/74
Berkeley Square *See* houses

Berkhampstead (Lady S. Spencer) 9/6/83, 7/7/83, 3/8/88
Berlin
china factory visited 12/11/58
G's visit to 11/11/58, 12/11/58
Berlin, Congress of
Protocols 23/7/78, 30/7/78
G's speech on 30/7/78
reading of disturbs G's sleep 30/7/78
Berlin, Treaty of 30/4/80, 14/5/80
Berlin Conference *See* Africa, cabinet
Berlin Conference on Africa *See* Africa
Bermondsey Gladstone Club 14/11/87 n
Bernard, St.
quoted in journal 15/1/47
studied 21/6/47, 17/1/49
translation of sermon by G 29/3/61 ff
Bernini 22/12/38
Berwick, Sir J. G's candidacy 13/6/26 ff
Berwick-on-Tweed 2/10/76
Besançon 6/8/49
besetting sins *See* sin
Bessborough Commission *See* Ireland (land question)
Bestwood colliery, G's visit to 28/9/77
Bestwood Park, Nottingham (St Albans) 26/9/77
Betchworth (Goulburn) 28/3/37 ff
Bethesda 15/9/55
Bethnal Green *See* London
Betteshanger (James) 15/7/54, 14/9/54 ff, 8/6/61, 19/5/66, 21/10/79
Bettisfield (Hanmer) 17/9/56, 12/9/78
Bettys-y-Coed 11/9/55
Biarritz
British Club in
initially declines to elect G to membership 17/12/91 n
decision G should convalesce in 11/12/92
Grand Hotel, G staying at 16/12/91 ff, 21/12/92 ff, 14/1/94 ff
Russian church of 19/12/91
See also Armitstead
Bible
biblical criticism 3/11/48
consolation from 16/7/65, 1/12/68, 1/2/89 ff, 23/2/90 ff
continuous reading of intended 16/4/47
copying from 10/4/31
Gadara case and G's dispute with Huxley 13/12/90, 15/12/90 ff
Gladstone family Bible
G enters child's name in 23/9/49
G plans edition with lessons noted 3/9/47
G's articles on for *Good Words* 6/1/90
memorising of 27/3/31
notation by G for private reading 3/9/47
notations in 13/1/28 ff
reading with C. G 26/7/39, 31/8/39, 15/8/44
Revised Version of 7/5/70 c, 14/6/70, 24/4/71, 17/7/81, 23/1/82, 26/1/82
See also childrearing, Gladstone (Catherine), God, prayer, Psalms, scripture
bigot, G described as a 1/2/40
billiards 1/1/27, 10/1/28, 9/9/29, 12/10/32, 17/10/32, 3/9/33, 21/8/34 ff, 10/9/35 ff, 18/8/36 ff, 28/10/36, 31/3/37, 7/9/37 ff, 25/11/37, 26/7/39, 24/1/40, 18/8/46 ff, 9/4/49
Billingbear 17/4/41, 27/12/41
bills abandoned *See* cabinet, Commons (House of)
bimetallism 8/6/81 n, 25/6/81 c, 27/6/81, 3/6/89, 4/6/89, 29/8/92, 2/9/92, 28/2/93
Dante and 2/12/92
Java and 10/9/92
silver question and 28/5/86
See also cabinet, India
biographies of G's friends and contemporaries
letters lent for
A. C. Tait 22/7/90
Cobden 20/6/77
Harriet Martineau 19/8/76 n
Hook 18/7/78 n, 2/11/78 n, 10/2/79 n
Hope 13/9/73, 27/7/83
Houghton 7/11/90
Lyndhurst 31/8/83
Maurice 19/6/77 n
Panizzi 22/10/80
Peel (Parker) 4/12/86
R. W. Sibthorp 27/7/79
Sidney Herbert 14/10/92
Stratford de Redcliffe 18/8/88 n
Tennyson 7/12/92
Wilberforce 30/8/75 n, 3/9/79, 22/11/80, 19/12/80, 6/7/82
letters used in
W. E. Forster 11/6/88 n
Biograph's biographical sketch of G 28/1/79
Birkenhead
G visits Laird's works 7/10/65
liberal excursion to Hawarden from 4/8/79
Birkhall 4/10/63
Birk Hall, Deeside 3/10/44
Birmingham 1/8/25, 17/8/25, 19/7/26, 24/10/32, 23/9/45, 5/2/48, 16/5/48 ff, 24/8/48, 31/5/77 ff
G at concert by Jenny Lind 5/9/48
G examined in Court of Bankruptcy 17/5/48
G's speeches in 31/5/77 ff, 5/11/88, 7/11/88
new gun factory in 5/3/84 c
St. Chad's (R. C.) church 24/9/42, 23/9/45
See also Newman
Birmingham Post 22/5/85

birth control
Bradlaugh's trial and 18/6/77 n
G and Pomeroy's campaign against 23/10/88, 4/8/90
G appalled by Mill's views on 19/5/73
Mary Drew's memorandum of G's views on the 'most saddening and sickening' of subjects 28/10/88
See also Bradlaugh, Mill
Biscoe, Robert, Rev. (1802–1870), one of G's tutors at Christ Church
advice as G's Tutor 22/1/28 ff, 18/10/28, 19/10/28, 26/1/29, 13/3/29, 11/5/29, 16/10/29, 11/11/29, 23/11/29, 25/11/29, 16/1/30, 19/3/30, 25/5/30, 14/9/30, 18/10/30, 9/11/30, 30/11/30, 15/1/31, 5/2/31, 16/4/31, 25/1/32
suggests G teach at Christ Church 23/11/29
Bishops Resignations Bill 6/6/71, 8/7/71 c, 18/7/71, 9/7/72, 1/1/84
G opposes 23/7/56 ff
Bishopthorpe (Abp. of York) 2/12/39
Bismarck, Otto Eduard Leopold von, Prince (1815–1898), chancellor of Prussia 1862, of Germany 1871–90 18/8/70, 20/10/70 c, 21/10/70, 24/2/71, 25/2/71, 4/3/71, 1/4/71, 24/9/78, 18/11/84, 30/12/84, 5/3/85, 7/3/85 c, 9/6/85 cn, 7/11/85, 28/4/86, 19/1/89, 2/2/89, 18/3/90 n, 1/4/90, 30/8/92
Africa and 14/6/84 c, 21/6/84 c, 27/6/84 cn
Berlin Conference and 20/11/84 c
Alsace-Lorraine, annexation of
G's memorandum on, printed 25/9/70
disarmament and 18/2/70
Egypt and 2/12/84 c, 13/3/85 c
G's assessment of 18/3/90 n
Heligoland and 2/1/85 n
ideas and methods of, not ours 3/3/74
insolent threat by 28/2/85 c
interfering in Bavaria 16/2/70, 1/3/70
Lenbach's portrait of 17/9/79
Luxembourg and 15/12/70 c, 17/12/70 c, 29/12/70
Napoleon and Bismarck of equal trustworthiness 20/7/70
New Guinea and 27/6/84 c
Paris, siege of 18/11/70
Vaticanism, G sends copy of 5/3/75 n
bismuth *See* medicines
Blachford, Lord *See* Rogers
Black Craig, Perthshire 5/9/93
Blackheath *See* Greenwich constituency, speeches
Blackheath House (Aberdeen) 19/7/53
blackmail
Wilson's attempt on G, for rescue work 10/5/53 ff, 14/6/53, 15/6/53
Black Sea clauses *See* Russia
Blairgowrie 20/8/39, 8/9/46, 10/9/93
Blenheim Palace (Marlborough) 23/11/61
Blind, Institute for
G speaking at 10/5/63, 11/5/63
blind, meeting for
G addresses 14/5/68
Blind, Royal Commission on
G encourages 28/8/83
boating/sculling
at Cliveden 29/7/54, 23/4/64, 6/6/65
at Fasque 27/9/34, 18/8/36, 21/9/39
on Lake Geneva 16/7/32
on Thames 19/8/31, 17/4/43 ff
See also Eton College
Bodelwyddan (Williams Hay) 27/9/55
bodily wants *See* memoranda (printed)
Bodmin
G's speech at 12/6/89
Boer war *See* South Africa
Boiardo, digest of 3/1/50 ff, 17/1/50 ff
Bologna 11/6/32 ff, 26/9/38, 9/10/66
churches of 12/6/32, 10/10/66
University and Library of 13/6/32
Bologna, University of
University and Library of
G's hon. degree *in absentia* 13/8/88
Bolton 11/10/64
Bolton Republican Club 5/8/71 c
bombs, manufacture and sale of 17/3/81
bookbuyers
an intelligent class 2/11/50
bookbuying 3/9/25, 17/10/25, 17/1/26, 29/5/26, 23/8/26, 28/4/28 ff, 30/5/28, 7/10/29 ff, 27/10/29 ff, 11/7/37, 29/3/43, 1/2/44, 30/5/49, 19/1/54, 15/11/54, 18/7/55, 21/1/56, 2/11/71, 10/2/90
in Athens 22/12/58
in Cologne 23/7/32
in Florence 10/1/88 ff, 26/1/88 ff
in Milan 9/7/32, 7/10/66, 8/10/66
in Naples 27/11/50 ff
books bound 24/12/50
in Paris 29/1/39
in Rome 5/1/39, 8/1/39
in Turin
means of intercourse with an intelligent class 2/11/50
bookcases 28/4/40
installed in Temple of Peace 3/10/54
books
G's article on housing of 17/12/89
G's London collection
sold to Wolverton 24/3/75

valued at £150 for *Hansard*, £670 the rest 24/3/75
books, G's catalogues of 9/9/26, 19/12/27, 26/7/45, 28/7/45 ff, 7/3/49 ff, 22/8/65
700 volumes of English poetry 23/8/78
Bibliotheca Homerica 16/8/65
dictionaries and reference 24/8/65
G making a set of his printed works 30/7/77
index of pamphlet volumes 6/4/37
index of 'Tracts' to 1853 15/3/55
privately printed books 23/8/65
Shakespeare 18/10/70
theology 16/9/77
See also reading (lists of)
booksellers
monopoly of 23/1/52, 12/5/52
Bootle 9/10/83
G's speech at 13/11/68
Borneo 10/7/51, 5/6/69 c, 25/5/77 n, 26/5/77
Charter of 28/10/92
G's article on Brooke 26/5/77
Boscastle
G's speech at 13/6/89
Bosnia/Herzegovina 4/5/80, 14/5/80, 31/5/80
meeting on 16/7/77
Bouchicault *See* plays seen
Boulogne 30/1/39, 18/10/50
Boulogne negotiations *See* Ireland
Boveridge, Dorset (Mrs. Thistlethwayte) 11/12/69
Bowden Park (J. N. G) 23/1/57 ff, 19/2/62, 6/6/62, 3/2/63, 13/8/66, 26/10/70, 29/1/77
bowel complaints *See* illnesses
Bowes Museum, Barnard Castle
strange edifice 21/9/76
bowls, G playing 7/8/27, 11/3/28
Bowmen, Society of Royal British 7/8/46, 30/8/48, 5/8/62, 4/8/63
Bradfield College
G on Council of 11/7/90 n
Bradford
G unable to visit 19/10/93
Bradlaugh, Charles (1833–1891), liberal M.P. and secularist 1/9/71, 18/5/83, 16/7/89
birth-control trial and 18/6/77 n
case of 2/5/80 n, 21/5/80, 24/5/80 ff, 29/5/80 c, 1/6/80, 19/6/80 c, 21/6/80 ff, 26/6/80 c, 27/6/80, 1/7/80, 10/7/80, 12/3/81 c, 18/4/81, 21/4/81, 22/4/81, 26/4/81 ff, 13/5/81 c, 11/6/81, 2/7/81, 3/7/81, 19/7/81 c, 1/8/81 ff, 6/8/81 c, 6/1/82 c, 25/1/82 c, 1/2/82 c, 7/2/82 c, 11/2/82 c, 18/2/82, 22/2/82 c, 4/3/82 c, 28/3/82, 17/10/82, 13/11/82 c, 5/3/83 c, 24/3/83, 16/4/83, 11/2/84 c
atheism and 2/5/81
G a Hot Kerite on 19/6/80
G declines to support expulsion 22/2/82 c
gross error of presenting himself for the oath 11/6/81
Resolution of 1880 expunged from Commons' Journals 27/1/91
consummate speaker 23/6/80
G prefers dealings by letter 20/6/81
letters from G to, printed 20/6/81, 2/7/81, 18/2/82
republicanism of 1/9/71
seat of 20/6/81
See also Affirmation Bill
Braemar 3/9/39, 9/9/46
episcopalian chapel in 7/9/84
Fife Arms 14/7/92 ff
Highland Games at, G attends: a very pretty sight 28/8/73, 4/9/84
Invercauld Arms 6/9/36
Roman Catholic chapel at 9/9/46
Brahmo sect *See* India
brain
G's brain has in evening a feminine susceptibility 14/11/71
sameness of tug on 1/2/81
Brand, Henry Bouverie William, Sir (1814–1892), 1st Viscount Hampden (1884), 23rd Baron Dacre (1890), liberal M.P., Speaker of the Commons 1872–84 21/11/53, 22/6/59 n, 8/7/61, 15/5/62, 20/4/63, 11/1/66 ff, 24/5/66 ff, 7/1/67 n, 2/5/67 ff, 14/6/75, 4/7/77, 2/8/77, 23/10/80, 1/3/82, 1/1/84, 9/12/85, 14/3/94
1867 Reform Bill and 14/2/67 ff
advises G to stand again in Oxford 12/7/61
attending cabinet 30/1/82 c, 1/2/82 c
G discusses party prospects with 25/7/63, 3/2/64
G's assessment of 14/3/94
letters from G to, printed 20/7/70, 12/8/73, 3/10/73, 30/10/73, 29/12/73, 23/2/74, 24/5/80, 1/6/80, 26/6/80, 25/11/80, 15/12/80, 18/12/80, 19/12/80, 20/1/81, 7/6/81, 3/7/81, 23/8/81, 18/1/82, 31/1/82, 1/4/82, 7/5/82, 3/7/82, 12/8/82, 17/10/82, 3/12/83, 3/1/84, 24/1/84, 11/4/84, 14/5/86
memorial service for 22/3/92
O'Kelly case and 31/5/83
Speaker of the House 25/1/72, 23/2/74, 22/2/84, 25/2/84

Brand, Henry Bouverie William, Sir
Speaker of the House (*cont.*)
controversially adjourns 41 hour sitting 2/2/81
G's plans for 8/11/71
testimonial to 12/2/67, 3/7/67, 25/11/67, 17/2/68, 28/3/68
brandy *See* medicines
brandy duties 18/9/41 ff
Brasenose College, Oxford 30/6/31, 24/1/34
Brazenose Hall, Oxford 23/1/28, 10/6/31
Brazil
treaty with 5/10/41 ff, 5/11/41 ff, 27/1/42 ff, 21/10/43, 17/11/43, 20/11/43, 22/12/43, 7/3/44
breakfasts, G's 26/10/49, 20/7/50, 15/5/51 ff, 22/4/52 ff, 29/4/52 ff, 10/5/52 ff, 27/5/52 ff, 21/4/53 ff, 26/5/53 ff, 7/7/53, 11/5/54 ff, 7/5/57, 14/5/57, 15/4/58 ff, 17/6/58, 31/3/59, 14/4/59, 19/5/59 ff, 14/7/59, 9/5/61 ff, 25/7/61 ff, 21/2/62, 15/5/62, 5/6/62 ff, 25/6/63 ff, 23/7/63, 12/5/64 ff, 11/5/65 ff, 1/6/65 ff, 19/4/66 ff, 21/6/66 ff, 9/5/67 ff, 30/4/68 ff, 18/6/68 ff, 25/6/68, 16/7/68, 15/4/69 ff, 1/7/69 ff, 21/5/70 ff, 8/6/71 ff, 22/6/71 ff, 1/5/72 ff, 11/7/72 ff, 12/6/73, 25/6/73, 13/3/74 ff, 1/8/74, 4/3/75 ff, 29/4/75 ff, 8/7/75 ff, 17/2/76 ff, 30/3/76 ff, 1/6/76 ff, 13/7/76, 28/10/76, 19/4/77 ff, 14/6/77 ff, 5/7/77 ff, 16/5/78 ff, 13/6/78 ff, 24/4/79 ff, 12/6/79 ff, 3/6/80 ff, 12/2/81, 28/3/81, 28/4/81 ff, 10/6/81, 25/5/82 ff, 2/11/82, 19/4/83, 7/6/83 ff, 5/7/83, 26/6/84, 23/4/85, 17/7/86
becoming a fatigue 10/7/79
plans for 26/10/49
really notable 4/4/78
Brechin 22/8/44, 17/9/84
Brechin Castle, Brechin (Dalhousie) 17/9/84
Brenner pass 28/6/32, 2/7/32, 25/9/79
bribery, G's article on 26/12/32
Bribery Bill 18/7/68
Bridgewater House (Ellesmere) 16/5/55
Bridgnorth 10/11/74 ff
Bright, John (1811-1889), freetrader, liberal M.P. and cabinet minister, president of board of trade 1868-70, chancellor of the duchy 1873-4, 1880-2, unionist 21/10/42 n, 15/12/52, 1/5/55, 1/10/56, 2/5/61, 23/6/66, 25/6/66, 22/3/69, 8/11/69, 12/3/70 c, 3/2/74, 14/1/75, 15/2/75 n, 24/2/75, 15/4/75, 23/4/75, 17/7/76 ff, 2/8/76, 5/10/76, 14/12/76, 19/3/77, 19/4/77, 25/1/78, 22/2/78, 2/5/78, 19/6/79, 21/7/79, 26/2/80, 2/3/80, 5/3/80, 27/4/80, 5/5/80, 16/8/80, 14/1/81, 3/3/81, 5/8/81, 13/10/81, 7/1/82 c, 9/1/82 c, 10/2/82, 11/3/82, 2/5/82 c, 5/6/82, 7/7/82, 13/11/82, 22/3/84, 27/2/85, 14/3/85, 24/4/85, 1/12/85, 12/1/86, 23/3/86, 3/4/86, 8/7/86, 25/12/86, 24/2/87
Alabama and 1/9/69
at Cobden's funeral 7/4/65
at Hawarden 13/11/71, 13/9/73, 29/1/79 ff, 1/2/79, 16/4/80, 1/11/83 ff, 15/10/85
attack on tories by a breach of privilege? 18/6/83, 22/6/83
bad spirit shown by 17/7/54
breach of privilege, accused of by Northcote 18/6/83
'Bright party'
G tipped to lead 19/6/61
Burials Bill and Convocation 16/8/80, 19/8/80, 9/9/80
cabinet, G persuades to rejoin 14/11/71 ff
Cobden Treaty and 1/11/71
Crimean speeches of 6/7/76 n
death of 27/3/89
dissolution in January 1874, seems to approve 18/1/74
Duchy, Chancellor of
accepts conditionally 4/8/73 ff
accepts finally 14/8/73 n
G tries to persuade him to accept 26/7/72
education and 25/11/71, 29/11/71, 10/5/73, 14/8/73, 30/10/73
Egypt and 27/10/69
resignation over invasion of 10/7/82 ff
Fenians and 16/10/69
Franco-Prussian war and
resignation of, initially prevented by G 1/8/70, 4/8/70, 8/8/70, 10/8/70, 12/9/70, 19/11/70, 11/12/70, 16/12/70
G consults on possible nonconformist peers 4/8/69
G discusses Danubian Principalities with 22/4/58
G discusses India with 22/4/58
G persuades to join cabinet 4/12/68
G's Birmingham visit and 1/6/77
G's memorandum on 30/8/78
G's tribute to 29/3/89
health of 16/3/70, 12/9/70, 28/5/84
diabetes diagnosed 19/6/88
Herculean efforts of 31/7/69
home rule and 25/11/71, 19/3/86, 20/3/86, 12/5/86, 14/5/86, 5/4/87
crass ignorance of 7/7/86

letter opposing read to Chamberlain's meeting 31/5/86 n
row with G over 2/7/86
income tax and 9/3/64
Ireland and 30/11/67
Irish coercion
may resign over 2/3/70
Irish land and 27/10/69, 30/11/69, 5/12/69, 30/12/69, 13/1/70, 29/3/81 c
G covers for 30/4/69
G critical of his views on 22/5/69
land purchase clauses 26/1/70 c, 28/1/70 c, 1/2/70 c, 2/2/70 c, 27/6/70, 8/5/80, 14/5/80 c, 9/12/80, 15/12/80, 1/1/81, 27/3/82, 5/3/83 c
proposes foreign inquiry 31/7/69, 31/7/69 c
seven propositions of 4/12/69
letters from G to, printed 3/2/69, 15/2/69, 22/5/69, 31/7/69, 4/8/69, 1/9/69, 13/10/69, 16/10/69, 25/11/69, 30/11/69, 4/12/69, 30/12/69, 13/1/70, 16/3/70, 27/6/70, 1/8/70, 4/8/70, 8/8/70, 10/8/70, 12/9/70, 1/10/70, 16/11/70, 19/11/70, 28/11/70, 11/12/70, 16/12/70, 24/10/71, 1/11/71, 25/11/71, 29/11/71, 25/1/72, 10/5/73, 14/8/73, 27/8/73, 26/9/73, 10/10/73, 30/10/73, 10/1/74, 27/1/74, 5/2/74, 9/2/74, 1/7/80, 19/8/80, 20/8/80, 5/12/80, 23/12/80, 29/9/81, 22/10/81, 10/7/82, 12/7/82, 13/7/82, 14/7/82, 23/5/84, 25/11/84, 1/6/85, 19/3/86, 12/5/86, 14/5/86, 2/7/86
makes a mess of a speech 11/2/69
Midlothian and 29/1/79, 30/1/79
president of board of trade 5/12/68 ff
public career feared over 19/6/88
qualities of
a loyal friend: a most pure politician 27/3/89
radicalism in cabinet and 5/2/85
raises competence of ambassadors 14/5/69 c
Reform League deputation and 11/2/67 n
resignation of the government and 12/3/73
resignations of 1/8/70, 4/8/70, 8/8/70, 10/8/70, 12/9/70, 19/11/70, 11/12/70 ff, 10/7/82 ff
speech of on foreign policy
powerful and one-sided 1/11/58
trade union law reform and 27/9/73
See also Ireland, liberal party, Reform Bills
Brighton 30/3/42 ff, 25/5/44 ff, 11/4/46 ff, 24/4/46 ff, 17/4/50 ff, 24/4/52, 3/4/58, 3/3/60, 3/4/60, 8/3/61, 16/3/61, 14/5/64, 15/4/65, 29/3/66, 6/4/72, 16/2/78, 19/2/81, 30/3/85 ff, 4/4/91, 12/11/92, 3/3/93, 30/3/93, 7/4/93, 9/6/93, 24/11/93, 9/12/93, 22/12/93, 5/1/94, 12/3/94, 22/3/94
aquarium of 2/4/85
Devil's Dyke 8/4/91, 26/12/93
Metropole Hotel, G staying at 4/4/91 ff
sea air makes G another man 18/3/61
water over-warm at 16/5/64
Bristol
liberals of visit Hawarden 27/5/90
Britannia Bridge 18/9/60
British Critic
change of tone in 8/9/42
British East Africa Company 20/9/92 ff, 30/9/92 ff, 11/11/92 c, 11/12/92
See also Uganda
British Honduras *See* Mexico
British Institution 7/6/56, 8/6/61, 25/6/63, 4/6/64, 3/2/66, 18/5/67
G attends Ruskin's lecture at 7/6/67
British Medical Association
G praises 7/8/73
British Museum 13/6/46, 15/7/51, 7/6/56, 6/8/75, 13/8/83, 10/4/88, 6/2/91
Castellani collection 12/6/71, 2/9/73 n
government purchase of 16/8/71 c
Cesnola collection 15/11/72, 19/11/72, 21/11/72, 28/11/72
Cyrenian sculptures 15/10/61
Elgin marbles 11/2/35, 21/10/61
G as trustee of 8/4/53, 17/4/54, 22/3/56, 5/4/56, 4/2/57, 23/5/57, 27/5/57, 9/12/57, 27/3/58, 29/5/58, 12/6/58, 12/3/59, 9/4/59, 28/5/59, 24/4/61, 10/2/62, 1/6/64, 25/5/67, 9/7/67, 16/5/68, 17/3/69, 30/4/72, 18/2/78, 18/4/81, 22/4/81, 2/5/81 ff, 22/2/93
and Panizzi's reading room 8/4/53, 2/5/57
Disraeli chosen as trustee 25/3/63
movement of natural history collections 8/7/61, 2/12/61 ff, 19/5/62
proposes Acton 26/7/71
resignation as a personal trustee 2/5/81
G proposes Rosebery as trustee
Rosebery prevaricates, then accepts 19/3/83, 27/3/83
G working at 30/7/56, 1/4/74, 1/6/83, 19/5/87, 26/8/87, 14/5/90, 14/12/91 ff, 30/3/92, 12/6/95
natural history department 21/10/61
Shapira MSS 13/8/83
state purchasing policy towards 16/8/82
Sunday opening of 7/2/85 c
See also Darwin, Disraeli, memoranda, Milnes
British Quarterly Review *See* publications
British South Africa Company 31/8/93 c, 10/10/93, 28/10/93
See also South Africa

Broadlands (Lady Palmerston) 22/7/68, 7/6/89
Broadstairs
  holiday at 12/8/54
bronchitis *See* illnesses
Brookes's club *See* clubs
Brougham, Henry Peter (1778-1868), 1st Baron Brougham and Vaux, Lord Chancellor (1830), liberal M.P.; friend of G in later life 2/4/54, 17/2/58, 29/11/59, 9/11/60, 17/10/61, 14/11/62, 11/10/63, 20/7/64, 7/12/65, 29/6/68, 31/3/71, 18/4/71, 15/2/83, 31/8/83, 25/9/83, 21/2/93
  Canada and 8/6/49
  Colonial policy, G's analysis of 19/9/34
  G agrees with over clergy discipline 23/10/57
  G at church with 16/11/62
  G's mother and 11/10/64
  G visits Brougham Hall 22/10/57 ff, 1/9/58 ff, 4/10/62 ff, 10/10/64
  monument for, no precedent for 4/11/69
Brougham Hall (Brougham) 22/10/57, 1/9/58, 4/10/62, 10/10/64
Bruce, Henry Austin (1815-1895), 1st Baron Aberdare (1873), liberal M.P.; home secretary 1868-73 4/3/74, 3/5/80, 26/6/82, 9/3/93
  Burials Bill and 17/4/70
  chairs Royal Commission on Poor Law 2/11/92 cn
  Fenians and 19/10/69
  gas stokers' case
    cabinet recommends reduction of sentences 15/1/73, 22/1/73 c
  G's visit to Swansea and 3/6/87, 5/6/87
  home secretary 5/12/68 n
  hours of labour and 15/11/72
  letters from G to, printed 6/1/69, 21/1/69, 11/6/69, 30/6/69, 19/10/69, 2/12/69, 1/1/70, 24/1/70, 3/3/70, 20/3/70, 17/4/70, 8/6/70, 3/12/70, 19/7/71, 1/9/71, 28/2/72, 1/3/72, 2/11/72
  licensing and 9/12/69 c
  Mundella's factory bill: disapproves 7/6/73 c
  Niger Charter and 21/1/85 cn
  republicanism and 1/9/71 n
Brunswick 10/11/58
Bryce, James, Prof. (1838-1922), 1st Viscount Bryce (1914), regius professor of civil law, Oxford (1870), liberal M.P.; chancellor of duchy 1892-4, president of board of trade 1894 4/7/70, 20/2/77, 12/7/78, 17/5/79, 12/3/80, 23/7/84, 19/6/85, 10/3/87, 6/7/87, 19/7/87, 22/6/88, 9/7/88, 28/6/89, 4/12/90, 4/4/92, 17/6/92, 21/11/92 c, 21/1/93, 22/11/93 ff, 3/3/94
  a rising man 18/12/82
  Armenia and 12/8/93
  articles on Ireland by 5/8/85
  at Hawarden 16/1/84
  chancellor of the duchy 15/8/92 ff
    laments smallness of work in 2/9/92
  home rule and
    G's plan for *Hand-Book of Home Rule* 8/7/86, 17/7/86, 30/11/86, 28/12/86, 24/9/87
  letters from G to, printed 31/5/80, 23/10/82, 8/10/85, 8/7/86, 17/7/86, 26/7/86, 30/11/86, 28/12/86, 15/8/92, 1/10/92, 19/10/92, 6/12/92, 27/2/93, 16/6/93, 1/9/93, 21/9/93
  meets G in Amalfi 11/2/89
  Ulster and 2/12/85
  young and rising 18/3/70
  See also Ireland, secret service money
Bryn-y-auchyn
  climbed 20/8/58
Buckingham palace
  bad taste of 1/7/35
Buckley
  G electioneering in 25/3/57, 30/11/85
  infant school at 5/9/40
Buckley Institute
  G fundraising for 11/11/78
budgets (other than G's)
  1842 11/3/42, 13/3/42 ff, 14/11/88
    G's assistance on excise clauses of 8/1/42 ff
  1848
    defects of 18/2/48, 25/2/48, 29/2/48, 13/3/48
    G's speech on, gratifies Peel 10/3/48
  1851 5/4/51
  1852 (1st) 30/4/52
  1852 (2nd) 16/12/52
  1856
    G's speech on 22/2/56
  1857 11/2/57, 13/2/57, 14/2/57, 20/2/57, 6/3/57
    G apologises for personal remarks in speech on 23/2/57 n
  1858
    G supports 19/4/58
  1869 3/4/69, 6/4/69 c, 8/4/69
  1870 9/4/70, 11/4/70 n
  1871 31/3/71, 3/4/71, 11/4/71, 17/4/71 c, 19/4/71 c, 20/4/71, 22/4/71 c, 24/4/71, 6/5/71 c
    death duties and 11/4/71, 19/4/71 c, 20/4/71
    Lords' and 24/4/71, 26/4/71
    match tax and 11/4/71, 19/4/71 c, 24/4/71, 27/4/71 n
  1873 29/3/73 c, 2/4/73, 5/4/73 c, 7/4/73
    G's preliminary comments on 19/12/72

real forward step in the Session 7/4/73
1875
very guilty Budget 7/5/75, 8/6/75
1877
G decides not to speak on 23/4/77
1880 11/3/80
1883 3/4/83 c, 5/4/83 ff
1884 22/4/84 c
1885 19/3/85, 20/3/85 c, 1/4/85, 5/4/85, 20/4/85 c, 21/4/85 c, 30/4/85 n, 7/5/85, 9/5/85 c, 15/5/85 c, 16/5/85 c, 20/5/85, 30/5/85, 31/5/85, 5/6/85 c, 7/6/85, 8/6/85, 10/6/85, 23/7/85
death duties and 21/4/85 c
direct taxation and 2/2/85, 21/4/85 c
government defeated on 8/6/85
indirect taxation and 2/2/85, 21/4/85 c, 7/5/85, 10/6/85, 23/7/85
likely to raise political question of the first order 2/2/85
1886 7/4/86, 8/4/86, 9/4/86 c
1887 25/4/87
1888 26/3/88, 9/4/88
1891 23/4/91 n
1892 11/4/92
1893 16/2/93, 24/3/93 c, 24/4/93
1894
most Radical of G's lifetime 25/7/94
annual reckoning not to be disturbed 9/7/72
details of best not disclosed to cabinet till imminent 3/3/55
G's list of 'remnants' sent to Lowe 10/1/69
to maintain steady surplus of income over expenditure 14/2/57
See also Cardwell, Churchill, Disraeli, Goschen, Government of Ireland Bill, Lowe, memoranda (printed), Peel, Wood
budgets prepared by G
1853 21/3/53 ff, 28/3/53 ff
budget speech (4. 75 hours) 18/4/53, 19/4/53
explained to cabinet 9/4/53, 11/4/53, 12/4/53
financial plan of 7/4/53 ff
1854 28/2/54 ff, 6/3/54
debate on 13/3/54 ff
1854 (supplementary) 3/5/54, 6/5/54, 8/5/54, 22/5/54
1859 16/7/59, 18/7/59, 21/7/59
navy scare of 1893 and 5/2/94 ff
simple passage through cabinet 16/7/59
1860
budget speech (4 hours) 10/2/60
in cabinet 28/1/60, 31/1/60, 3/2/60
navy scare of 1893 and 10/1/94 ff
plans for 9/11/59, 22/11/59
Victoria tells G to prepare large budget 14/11/59
wine licence scheme 20/2/60
1860 (supplementary) 16/7/60
1861 10/2/61, 19/3/61 n, 26/3/61, 29/4/61
and paper duties repeal 12/4/61
budget speech (3 hours) 15/4/61
explained to Palmerston 10/4/61, 12/4/61
sudden late demands on 10/4/61
1862 1/2/62, 13/2/62, 29/3/62, 31/3/62, 3/4/62, 7/4/62
1863 15/11/62, 22/11/62, 3/3/63, 28/3/63, 31/3/63, 15/4/63, 16/4/63
abolition of charities' tax privileges 24/4/63, 4/5/63
budget speech (3 hours) 16/4/63
sketch of, printed 1/1/63
winds up a chapter in finance & of G's life 16/4/63
1864 22/3/64, 29/3/64, 4/4/64 ff, 21/4/64
budget speech (3 hours) 7/4/64
1865
budget speech (2 hours 35 minutes) 27/4/65
leak to *The Times* 29/4/65
sketched at Hawarden 9/1/65
worked on in bed 8/3/65
worked on in Brighton 17/4/65
1866
budget speech (2 hours 30 minutes) 3/5/66
sketched 26/3/66
sketched in April 1865 29/4/65
1874
memorandum summarising, printed 19/1/74
plan to abolish income tax and sugar duties, partly paid from death and spirit duties 11/8/73
preparations for 12/8/73
rough mem. & computation for: 8 million needed 29/9/73
1880 5/6/80 c, 10/6/80 ff
mistake in 11/6/80
1881 25/2/81, 29/3/81, 2/4/81, 4/4/81
probably G's last 4/4/81 n
1882 7/3/82, 18/3/82 c, 31/3/82, 6/4/82, 20/4/82 ff, 24/4/82
army estimates and 30/1/62 ff
details released to newspapers 1/4/62
buggery
S. Glynne accused of 3/6/41
Buildwas Abbey 3/1/57
Builth Wells 14/7/52
Bulgaria 13/8/76 ff, 1/9/76 ff, 5/9/76 ff, 26/5/81, 2/7/81 c, 17/9/82, 22/2/86 c, 1/4/86 c, 28/4/86, 7/11/86, 24/8/92

Bulgaria (*cont.*)
Bulgarian schism 13/11/71 n, 27/11/71, 18/8/72, 4/9/72
union with E. Roumelia
time not yet ripe 22/5/80
See also Eastern question, Orthodox churches, Turkey
Bulgarian horrors
Comitato di Soccorso per la Causa Slava(Rome) 23/10/76
extent of public feeling on 2/10/76 ff
G's extra-Parliamentary speeches on 9/9/76, 25/9/76 ff, 8/12/76, 16/1/77, 1/9/77
City Temple conference 22/3/77
lecture on Forbes' article 23/11/77
Staindrop 23/9/76
tour of South-West 17/1/77 ff
Philippolis committee on 23/10/76 n
St. James's Hall conference 5/12/76 ff, 8/12/76
The Bulgarian Horrors and the Question of the East (1876) 28/8/76 ff, 5/9/76
Workmen's Hyde Park Demonstration Committee
'fountain' of G's Bulgarian pamphlet 23/8/76 n
See also letters, publications
bullets
dum-dum 24/4/69 c
Burials Act Amendment Bill
G opposes 22/7/57
Burials Bill 17/4/70, 27/4/70 c, 12/12/72 c, 26/11/73 c, 5/5/80 c, 10/5/80, 12/5/80 c, 1/6/80, 3/7/80, 4/8/80 ff, 5/5/85, 15/2/86 c, 14/4/86 c
cabinet unable to undertake 12/12/72 c
G supports 7/6/50, 26/3/73
See also nonconformists
Burke, Edmund
G learning by heart 16/10/32
G's dispute with Montgomery over 9/11/86 n
G's veneration for 13/10/84, 27/5/86
Ireland and America
immortal wisdom on 18/12/85, 20/4/86
perhaps made the revolutionary war 13/10/84
religion and 17/9/81
right to government and 6/7/84
sometimes almost divine 9/1/86
See also Mundella
Burlington Fine Arts Club 14/2/73
Burlington House
G's role in national purchase of 23/3/54
See also memoranda
Burma 20/1/81, 15/2/86 c, 1/11/92
annexation of 15/2/86 c, 16/2/86 c
G given gifts by deputation from 25/3/71
route through 15/6/72 c
Burnham Beeches 31/7/54, 20/5/61
Burntisland ferry 25/10/44, 6/7/47, 18/10/47
Burslem 26/10/63
business, G's lack of knowledge of 2/12/44
busts of G
Adams-Acton 9/11/64, 11/11/64, 12/11/64, 16/11/64, 17/11/64, 18/11/64, 19/11/64, 21/11/64, 7/12/78 ?, 31/1/84, 22/9/91, 31/3/92, 16/5/92, 12/8/92, 12/1/93
G wild with sitting to 21/11/64
statue done in Rome (for Liverpool) 18/10/66 ff, 5/12/66, 24/12/66
Boehm, J. E. 25/11/79, 27/11/79, 10/5/81
Burnand 17/7/68, 24/7/68, 25/7/68
Crittendon, J. D. 25/1/72, 25/6/72, 26/6/72, 28/6/72
Ford, E. O. (National Liberal Club) 15/5/82, 16/5/82
Geflowski 9/1/75
Guild, E. M. C.- 4/3/92, 5/3/92, 7/3/92, 8/3/92, 10/3/92, 24/3/92, 5/4/92
Joy, Henry 10/5/81
Ledward, R. A. 1/8/85, 3/8/85, 4/8/85
Marochetti 18/5/57, 20/5/57, 21/5/57, 22/5/57, 23/5/57, 2/7/57, 3/7/57, 4/7/57, 7/7/57, 11/7/57, 16/7/57, 20/7/57, 23/7/57, 10/3/58
product of extraordinary power 10/3/58
Morton Edwards 25/5/67
Mullins, E.R. 14/12/78 ?, 16/12/78 ?, 22/2/79, 21/7/79, 22/7/79
Munro, A. 13/10/54, 14/10/54, 16/10/54, 21/10/54, 23/10/54, 24/10/54, 25/10/54, 12/3/55
Noble, M. 2/8/75
Redmond, Miss 17/7/89, 19/7/89
Rhind, J. 26/11/85, 27/11/85
Smith, Mr., of Aberdeen 28/7/85, 29/7/85
Theed, W. 6/4/89, 8/4/89
Thistlethwayte, Laura 9/1/75
Toft, A. 17/9/87, 19/9/87
Woolner, T.(Guildhall) 2/12/81, 22/12/81, 29/12/81, 10/1/82, 26/1/82, 28/1/82, 2/2/82, 23/2/82
Woolner, T.(Oxford University) 19/8/63, 20/8/63, 21/8/63, 22/8/63, 24/8/63, 25/8/63, 26/8/63, 27/8/63, 28/8/63, 4/6/67, 26/5/68
Homeric plinth of 4/6/67, 26/5/68
Butleigh (Neville-Grenville) 18/8/66
Butler, Joseph 17/12/84
analysis of his *Analogy* 3/5/30 ff, 10/7/30, 19/7/30, 2/11/31
Darwinian question
Joseph Butler supplies the method for handling 24/12/72
discussed by Graham 10/7/46

excellence of 9/3/40, 10/3/40
G's 'Pope' 23/5/72
G working on 26/6/45 ff, 5/9/47 ff, 4/3/94, 11/3/94 ff, 2/4/94 ff, 12/6/95
labours finished 29/12/96
Hindustani translation of 28/10/92 n
influence on G from 1830 16/11/69, 15/2/80
miracles and 15/2/76
the *Vestiges* and 17/7/47
See also Darwin, publications
Buttermere 25/10/57
bye-elections *See* elections (general/bye)
Byron's *Childe Harold*
notes on 13/1/36, 10/10/37

cabinet
1853 budget and 9/4/53 ff
army
G resists forces' augmentation 3/4/60
attended by chief whip 8/8/93 c
bills abandoned 25/6/70 c, 2/7/70 c, 16/7/70 c, 22/7/71 c, 15/7/72, 17/7/72 c, 28/6/73 c, 5/7/73 c, 10/7/73 c, 2/7/81 c, 19/7/81 c, 11/7/82 c, 7/7/83 c, 28/9/83, 9/7/84 c, 15/5/85 c
bills before
procedure for checking drafting 21/8/72
bills planned for coming Session 28/1/61 c, 22/12/68 c, 5/11/69 c, 2/11/70 c, 21/1/71, 25/1/71 c, 21/10/71 c, 8/11/71 c, 25/1/72 c, 30/1/72 c, 17/7/72 c, 15/11/72 c, 24/1/73 c, 21/11/73 c, 1/12/73 c, 5/5/80 cf, 6/5/80, 17/5/80, 12/11/80 c, 25/11/80 c, 4/12/82 c, 20/11/83 c
circulation of memoranda on, no precedent for 6/5/80
budget details to be withheld from till last moment 3/3/55
bye-elections and 25/1/93 c, 1/2/93
cabinet dinners 10/1/44, 17/1/44, 24/4/44, 19/11/44, 18/2/46, 4/3/46, 18/3/46, 25/3/46, 29/4/46, 13/5/46, 29/12/52, 30/12/52, 23/2/53, 6/4/53, 20/4/53, 20/7/53, 1/2/54, 8/3/54, 31/5/54, 28/6/54, 26/7/54, 11/8/54, 21/11/60, 28/11/60, 30/4/80, 15/1/81, 1/2/82
1st given by G 6/5/46
G expected to announce retirement but says nothing 17/2/94
on resignation 16/2/74
cabinet of the 'four Egypts' 16/7/84 c
chaired by Granville in G's absence 24/7/69 c
church patronage responsibility of 27/10/43
committee of
exemptions 18/3/73
committees of
Alderney breakwater 2/7/70 c
army estimates 29/11/62
ballot 2/11/70 c, 7/11/70 c, 16/12/80
bank issues 27/1/64, 27/4/64, 29/4/64
Berlin Conference 8/10/84 c
cattle plague 7/2/66
civil service 31/7/69 c, 8/12/69
corn (attended as Vice-President) 9/12/41, 19/1/42, 20/1/42
corrupt practices 12/11/80 c, 16/12/80 c
county government 13/11/83 c
Crimes Act 28/4/85 c
Dover House 24/4/69 c
education 11/11/59, 28/11/59, 2/12/59, 17/5/73 c
Egypt 20/11/84 c
estimates 27/1/64 ff, 18/3/64
extradition 24/4/69
franchise 13/1/66, 18/1/66, 22/1/66, 2/2/66, 10/2/66, 12/2/66, 13/2/66, 15/2/66, 20/2/66
government committee on redistribution 8/8/84, 9/8/84 c, 15/8/84, 29/9/84
Government of Ireland Bill 21/11/92
Government of Ireland Bill financial clauses 31/3/86, 1/4/86 c
hours of polling 9/3/72 c
income tax 18/12/52, 29/12/52, 16/2/53
Indian army 27/1/60, 2/5/60
Indian currency 5/6/93
Irish land purchase 28/4/84 c
Irish universities 4/12/65
law courts 15/11/60
leaks from cabinet 6/1/82 c, 25/2/82 c
licensing 6/7/72 c
local government 10/11/81 c, 30/1/82
Local Government Bill 12/2/94 c
local taxation 5/11/69 c, 15/2/73 c
local veto 21/11/92 c
London County Council 21/11/92
London government 6/1/82 c
Matabeleland 13/11/93 c
navy estimates 1/12/62, 20/1/65
one man, one vote 21/11/92 c
park accommodations 1/7/71 c
railway amalgamations 10/2/72 c
real estate intestasy 9/12/69 c
redistribution 27/3/66, 4/4/66, 9/4/66
Red Sea telegraph 26/1/61
reform 12/11/59
registration 31/10/92 c, 21/11/92 c
Scottish education 20/1/71
Suez canal in wartime 21/5/70 c, 28/5/70 c
suffragan for Exeter 6/4/64

cabinet (*cont.*)
committees of (*cont.*)
superannuation 11/11/59
Swaziland 27/10/92 c, 23/11/92 c
telegraph funds' misappropriation 7/6/73 c, 25/7/73 c
Treasury 24/6/59
Uganda and Macdonald's report 20/7/93 c
West African territories 25/10/83 c, 22/11/83 c
Wolseley's expedition 12/2/85
compromise needed in 13/5/43
deemed inquorate with 10 24/1/73
dinner cabinet at Palmerston's 21/11/60
directorships and membership of: not to coincide 19/8/92 c, 27/10/92 c, 31/10/92, 14/8/93
discussion of G's continuation as leader in 20/7/86 c
Duke of Cambridge attends 6/3/60
estimates only adopted on exact figures 3/1/94
G joins for 1st time 13/5/43, 15/5/43
G's final cabinet: 'a really moving scene' 1/3/94
G's list of colleagues in (69) 10/3/93
G's reports to the Queen
much business unsuitable for report to her 24/6/82
Spencer to get copies of, though not a cabinet member 24/6/82
G's resignation *all but* settled 2/6/60
informal cabinet 22/2/81
Kaleidoscopic character of 30/5/60
leaks from 29/4/65, 29/12/69, 30/12/69, 15/11/80 c, 17/12/80, 8/4/81 c, 6/1/82, 29/4/82, 30/4/82, 12/10/84, 22/10/84 c, 13/11/84, 22/5/85, 30/5/85, 29/3/86 c
committee on 6/1/82 c, 25/2/82 c
limitations on speeches by members of 2/7/83
limits to freedom as a cabinet minister 28/7/83
meeting at Coombe Warren (B. Currie's house) 29/3/84
meeting in 11 Carlton House Terrace 26/4/73, 26/7/73
meeting in railway carriage on *Alabama* 21/3/71
ministers no title to consultation on membership of 18/4/81
minutes of
1843–66 15/5/43, 20/5/43, 27/5/43, 3/6/43, 8/6/43, 11/6/43, 15/6/43, 19/8/43, 17/11/43, 20/11/43, 11/1/44, 12/1/44, 13/1/44, 12/2/44, 13/2/44, 2/3/44, 16/3/44, 23/3/44, 25/3/44, 2/4/44, 16/5/44, 15/6/44, 16/6/44, 17/6/44, 25/11/44, 9/1/45, 9/2/55, 17/2/55, 18/2/55, 21/2/55, 17/9/59, 1/12/59, 21/1/60, 26/11/60, 28/1/61, 9/2/61, 16/2/61, 13/4/61, 3/8/61, 31/1/62, 29/3/62, 10/4/62, 24/6/64, 25/6/64, 29/1/66, 2/2/66, 28/4/66
1868–74 22/12/68, 26/1/69, 2/2/69, 8/2/69, 12/2/69, 20/2/69, 27/2/69, 6/3/69, 13/3/69, 20/3/69, 6/4/69, 10/4/69, 17/4/69, 24/4/69, 30/4/69, 1/5/69, 4/5/69, 8/5/69, 9/5/69, 14/5/69, 29/5/69, 5/6/69, 12/6/69, 19/6/69, 26/6/69, 3/7/69, 10/7/69, 17/7/69, 21/7/69, 24/7/69, 31/7/69, 6/8/69, 9/8/69, 26/10/69, 30/10/69, 3/11/69, 5/11/69, 10/11/69, 7/12/69, 9/12/69, 10/12/69, 14/12/69, 17/12/69, 21/1/70, 22/1/70, 25/1/70, 26/1/70, 28/1/70, 1/2/70, 2/2/70, 4/2/70, 12/2/70, 19/2/70, 26/2/70, 5/3/70, 12/3/70, 16/3/70, 19/3/70, 26/3/70, 2/4/70, 9/4/70, 27/4/70, 7/5/70, 14/5/70, 21/5/70, 28/5/70, 14/6/70, 18/6/70, 23/6/70, 24/6/70, 2/7/70, 9/7/70, 14/7/70, 16/7/70, 23/7/70, 25/7/70, 30/7/70, 6/8/70, 10/8/70, 30/9/70, 20/10/70, 2/11/70, 4/11/70, 7/11/70, 10/11/70, 11/11/70, 25/11/70, 28/11/70, 30/11/70, 15/12/70, 17/12/70, 19/1/71, 20/1/71, 25/1/71, 28/1/71, 1/2/71, 6/2/71, 11/2/71, 15/2/71, 18/2/71, 24/2/71, 25/2/71, 4/3/71, 11/3/71, 16/3/71, 17/3/71, 25/3/71, 27/3/71, 1/4/71, 17/4/71, 18/4/71, 19/4/71, 22/4/71, 6/5/71, 13/5/71, 20/5/71, 10/6/71, 17/6/71, 24/6/71, 1/7/71, 5/7/71, 8/7/71, 12/7/71, 15/7/71, 20/7/71, 22/7/71, 24/7/71, 29/7/71, 5/8/71, 9/8/71, 12/8/71, 16/8/71, 21/10/71, 24/10/71, 25/10/71, 27/10/71, 31/10/71, 3/11/71, 6/11/71, 8/11/71, 11/12/71, 14/12/71, 15/12/71, 18/12/71, 19/12/71, 19/1/72, 22/1/72, 23/1/72, 25/1/72, 27/1/72, 30/1/72, 2/2/72, 3/2/72, 10/2/72, 15/2/72, 17/2/72, 24/2/72, 2/3/72, 9/3/72, 16/3/72, 19/3/72, 5/4/72, 9/4/72, 13/4/72, 20/4/72, 27/4/72, 2/5/72, 6/5/72, 8/5/72, 10/5/72, 13/5/72, 27/5/72, 28/5/72, 30/5/72, 5/6/72, 8/6/72, 10/6/72, 11/6/72, 12/6/72, 15/6/72, 16/6/72, 22/6/72, 26/6/72, 29/6/72, 6/7/72, 10/7/72, 17/7/72, 24/7/72, 31/7/72, 8/8/72, 10/10/72, 11/10/72, 12/10/72, 14/10/72, 15/11/72,

18/11/72, 20/11/72, 22/11/72, 26/11/72, 28/11/72, 3/12/72, 5/12/72, 7/12/72, 10/12/72, 12/12/72, 22/1/73, 24/1/73, 27/1/73, 29/1/73, 31/1/73, 4/2/73, 8/2/73, 15/2/73, 22/2/73, 1/3/73, 8/3/73, 12/3/73, 13/3/73, 22/3/73, 29/3/73, 5/4/73, 22/4/73, 26/4/73, 3/5/73, 10/5/73, 14/5/73, 17/5/73, 24/5/73, 7/6/73, 14/6/73, 21/6/73, 28/6/73, 5/7/73, 10/7/73, 12/7/73, 19/7/73, 24/7/73, 25/7/73, 26/7/73, 30/7/73, 2/8/73, 6/8/73, 3/10/73, 4/10/73, 10/11/73, 12/11/73, 15/11/73, 17/11/73, 21/11/73, 26/11/73, 28/11/73, 1/12/73, 23/1/74

1880–85 3/5/80, 5/5/80, 12/5/80, 14/5/80, 17/5/80, 22/5/80, 29/5/80, 5/6/80, 12/6/80, 19/6/80, 26/6/80, 3/7/80, 10/7/80, 17/7/80, 24/7/80, 21/8/80, 4/9/80, 6/9/80, 30/9/80, 10/11/80, 12/11/80, 15/11/80, 17/11/80, 19/11/80, 25/11/80, 13/12/80, 14/12/80, 16/12/80, 30/12/80, 31/12/80, 4/1/81, 15/1/81, 22/1/81, 29/1/81, 12/2/81, 15/2/81, 19/2/81, 22/2/81, 5/3/81, 8/3/81, 12/3/81, 17/3/81, 19/3/81, 26/3/81, 28/3/81, 2/4/81, 8/4/81, 29/4/81, 4/5/81, 13/5/81, 20/5/81, 28/5/81, 2/6/81, 13/6/81, 15/6/81, 25/6/81, 2/7/81, 9/7/81, 19/7/81, 23/7/81, 6/8/81, 13/8/81, 20/8/81, 12/10/81, 10/11/81, 6/1/82, 7/1/82, 9/1/82, 25/1/82, 27/1/82, 30/1/82, 1/2/82, 3/2/82, 7/2/82, 11/2/82, 18/2/82, 25/2/82, 4/3/82, 18/3/82, 31/3/82, 22/4/82, 22/4/82 n, 25/4/82, 27/4/82, 1/5/82, 2/5/82, 4/5/82, 6/5/82, 8/5/82, 10/5/82, 13/5/82, 23/5/82, 31/5/82, 10/6/82, 19/6/82, 21/6/82, 3/7/82, 8/7/82, 13/7/82, 18/7/82, 20/7/82, 24/7/82, 29/7/82, 31/7/82, 3/8/82, 5/8/82, 12/8/82, 13/9/82, 20/10/82, 21/10/82, 24/10/82, 3/11/82, 8/11/82, 13/11/82, 16/11/82, 27/11/82, 1/12/82, 4/12/82, 5/3/83, 10/3/83, 17/3/83, 3/4/83, 7/4/83, 14/4/83, 20/4/83, 28/4/83, 5/5/83, 7/5/83, 26/5/83, 2/6/83, 13/6/83, 23/6/83, 7/7/83, 13/7/83, 19/7/83, 23/7/83, 25/7/83, 8/8/83, 21/8/83, 22/8/83, 25/10/83, 10/11/83, 13/11/83, 17/11/83, 20/11/83, 22/11/83, 3/1/84, 4/1/84, 22/1/84, 24/1/84, 26/1/84, 31/1/84, 6/2/84, 8/2/84, 11/2/84, 12/2/84, 18/2/84, 21/2/84, 25/2/84, 29/2/84, 5/3/84, 7/3/84, 29/3/84, 2/4/84, 8/4/84, 21/4/84, 22/4/84, 23/4/84, 28/4/84, 1/5/84, 5/5/84, 7/5/84, 14/5/84, 17/5/84, 24/5/84, 27/5/84, 9/6/84, 10/6/84, 14/6/84, 21/6/84, 24/6/84, 27/6/84, 5/7/84, 9/7/84, 14/7/84, 16/7/84, 18/7/84, 25/7/84, 2/8/84, 5/8/84, 6/8/84, 9/8/84, 6/10/84, 8/10/84, 22/10/84, 31/10/84, 7/11/84, 11/11/84, 15/11/84, 19/11/84, 20/11/84, 22/11/84, 27/11/84, 2/12/84, 2/1/85, 3/1/85, 20/1/85, 21/1/85, 6/2/85, 7/2/85, 9/2/85, 11/2/85, 16/2/85, 17/2/85, 20/2/85, 28/2/85, 7/3/85, 12/3/85, 13/3/85, 20/3/85, 24/3/85, 27/3/85, 4/4/85, 9/4/85, 11/4/85, 13/4/85, 14/4/85, 15/4/85, 20/4/85, 21/4/85, 25/4/85, 28/4/85, 2/5/85, 7/5/85, 9/5/85, 15/5/85, 16/5/85, 5/6/85, 8/6/85, 9/6/85

1886 15/2/86, 16/2/86, 22/2/86, 25/2/86, 13/3/86, 26/3/86, 29/3/86, 1/4/86, 6/4/86, 9/4/86, 14/4/86, 4/5/86, 8/5/86, 25/5/86, 8/6/86, 20/7/86

1892–4 19/8/92, 29/9/92, 30/9/92, 27/10/92, 31/10/92, 2/11/92, 4/11/92, 7/11/92, 11/11/92, 21/11/92, 23/11/92, 17/12/92, 11/1/93, 13/1/93, 16/1/93, 17/1/93, 18/1/93, 20/1/93, 23/1/93, 25/1/93, 27/1/93, 14/2/93, 16/2/93, 23/2/93, 8/3/93, 24/3/93, 5/5/93, 6/6/93, 19/6/93, 5/7/93, 20/7/93, 8/8/93, 17/8/93, 18/8/93, 31/8/93, 3/11/93, 13/11/93, 21/11/93, 1/12/93, 14/12/93, 29/12/93, 9/1/94, 12/2/94, 23/2/94, 26/2/94, 1/3/94

correspondence on nature of 8/6/84, 11/6/84

on Uganda 30/9/92

shown to Spencer and Dufferin 13/11/69, 7/12/69 c

signing of, inquiry into 8/6/84, 11/6/84

minutes of missing 28/6/82, 1/7/82, 5/7/82, 27/7/82

nonconformists in 30/12/82

now sometimes just a talking-shop 6/8/59

paper duties in

Palmerston opposes repeal 5/5/60, 22/5/60

portrait of by Lowes Dickinson 14/6/71

pro-cabinet 7/5/82

quasi-cabinets 4/4/71, 29/4/72, 9/5/72, 10/6/72, 23/6/73, 7/9/80, 15/6/82, 20/6/82, 28/6/82, 1/7/82, 23/10/82, 19/5/84, 20/6/85

bye-cabinet 6/7/80

cabinet (*cont.*)
relations of Foreign Secretary and First Lord towards 25/9/92, 27/9/92, 4/3/94
reshuffles of 27/6/70 n, 1/7/70, 2/8/70 ff, 17/12/70 ff, 1/12/82 c, 12/12/82
resignation of 13/3/73
votes in 8/8/83 c, 17/5/84 n
See also ex-cabinet, Victoria
cabinets
character of, and radicalism 5/2/85
cab licences 27/7/53
cabs
accidents 11/2/33, 16/2/33, 8/3/38
cabhunting 4/2/37 ff
Cader Idris
clouds prevent complete ascent of 12/9/55
Caernarvon 31/8/26, 15/9/62
Cairngorms, walks in 9/9/36 ff, 4/9/39 ff
Cairn o'Mount 6/9/34, 29/9/36, 30/9/37, 26/8/39, 5/9/43 ff, 13/9/44, 10/9/46, 23/8/47, 20/1/49, 20/10/49, 6/9/51, 25/9/69
Caithness
boat trip from Dunrobin to 14/9/58
Calabria 8/11/38
list of places visited in 11/11/38
sport in 11/11/38
calculus 14/11/28, 3/10/29, 2/7/31 ff
Calcutta *See* India
Caledonian Asylum, London 2/3/41
Caledonian canal
G sails through 28/9/53, 10/9/58
G shareholder in 26/4/60, 25/3/62
Caledonian railway *See* railways (G shareholder in)
Callander, curling at 11/1/37
Calvin 3/9/38
Cambridge
visits to 15/12/31, 22/11/41, 31/10/59, 26/10/78
staying with the Sidgwicks 26/10/78 ff
Cambridge, Duke of *See* George
Cambridge, University of
constituency and redistribution 26/11/84 ff
Corpus Christi College 28/10/78
Fitzwilliam Museum 3/11/59, 28/10/78
Girton College fundraising 21/4/77 n
G receives LL.D from 1/11/59
inaccurate moral considerations in 14/11/40
King's College 23/11/41, 24/11/41, 27/10/78, 31/1/87
lionising in 16/12/31
Magdalene College 22/11/41
Gs staying at 31/10/59 ff
Pepys' library visited 27/11/41, 3/11/59, 29/10/78
Newnham College 31/1/87, 18/12/93
G presents copies of his Homeric works to 11/10/86
G's visit to 31/1/87
Helen G in right place at 31/1/87
Helen G's appointment at 27/4/78
much pleased with the structure and all I saw 29/10/78
unsettled state of belief at 27/4/78
Peterhouse chapel 3/11/59
regius history chair 2/7/69 n
accepted by Seeley 2/9/69
declined by Merivale 9/8/69, 12/8/69
revenues of, inquiry into 17/6/71 c, 20/6/71
Selwyn College
G speaks to students of at luncheon 1/2/87
St. John's College 29/10/78
Trinity College 15/12/31 ff, 25/11/41, 2/11/59, 27/10/78
G declines invitation to join Claypipe Society 4/11/79 n
petition supporting G's Eastern question Resolutions 9/5/77
Trinity Hall 28/11/41
University Library 3/11/59
See also Gladstone (Helen)
Cambridge House (Palmerston) 14/6/59, 15/6/59
Camden Society, G at meeting of 22/11/41
Campbell, George Douglas, Lord (1823–1900), Marquis of Lorne (1837), 8th Duke of Argyll (1847), lord privy seal 1853–5, 1859–66, 1880–1, Indian secretary 1868–74, unionist; resigned over Irish land 30/4/45, 30/9/48, 15/1/53, 11/6/53, 5/4/54, 28/6/54, 23/3/55, 8/3/56, 21/3/57, 4/7/57, 13/5/59 ff, 29/10/59, 10/12/59, 15/12/59, 7/3/60, 30/5/60, 23/6/60 ff, 16/11/60 ff, 17/4/61, 2/5/61, 3/7/61, 3/8/61, 17/1/62, 20/1/62, 29/1/63, 14/6/63, 10/1/66 ff, 15/2/66, 5/5/66, 9/6/66 ff, 30/3/67, 4/5/67, 25/2/68 ff, 27/4/68 ff, 16/5/68 ff, 1/7/68, 18/7/68, 3/11/68, 23/12/68, 20/2/69 c, 22/3/69, 4/8/69, 3/4/70 n, 11/6/70, 16/1/71 ff, 24/5/71, 23/10/71, 16/6/72, 18/11/72, 23/11/72, 15/3/73, 22/3/73 c, 23/4/73, 21/5/73, 21/6/73 c, 29/6/73, 21/11/73, 25/11/73 ff, 9/2/74, 14/1/75, 30/4/75, 30/6/75, 7/4/76, 13/5/76, 16/5/76, 9/2/77, 10/2/77, 31/3/77, 5/6/77, 2/2/78, 18/3/78, 17/4/78, 25/4/79, 5/5/79, 12/5/79, 21/4/80 ff, 22/5/80, 27/6/80, 12/9/80, 1/1/81, 21/4/81, 9/3/82, 21/6/82, 1/1/83, 22/1/83, 1/2/83, 17/5/83, 18/8/83, 10/5/84, 18/4/85, 9/5/85, 30/7/87, 5/7/88, 4/4/91,

5/7/91, 14/6/92, 3/6/93, 10/9/93, 9/5/94
1853 budget and 14/4/53 ff
1866 Reform Bill and 19/6/66
advises G on treatment of the Queen 16/3/62
at Hawarden 22/12/55, 5/11/67, 6/11/67, 12/1/78 n, 10/10/78 ff
death of Duchess of Argyll while sitting next to G 24/5/78
discusses Mrs. Thistlethwayte with G 2/7/66
episcopacy versus presbytery, discussed with G 1/7/66
free from all gall and guile, G thinks 14/5/59
G argues with over Crimean peace 27/4/55
G at Inveraray 25/9/65 ff
G at Roseneath: funeral of the Duchess 4/6/78
G enjoys discussing future punishment with 2/4/64
G's article on 27/7/92 ff
G's relations with Motley and 1/4/69
G's retirement as liberal leader
of G's mind on 5/3/74
home rule and 31/12/85, 27/1/86, 28/12/86
income tax and 15/1/53 ff
India, Viceroy of
opposed to appointment of Northbrook 13/2/72
Indian secretary 5/12/68 ff, 24/12/68, 30/9/70 c, 7/11/70 c, 22/11/71
in Florence 6/1/67
in Rome 2/12/66 ff, 17/12/66 ff, 25/12/66 ff
discussing Dante with G 7/12/66
Irish land and 11/10/69, 29/11/69, 4/12/69, 5/1/70, 26/1/70 c, 10/6/80, 3/12/80, 25/12/80, 31/12/80 c, 29/1/81 ff, 9/3/81, 28/3/81, 21/4/81, 30/11/81
resignation threats on 12/6/80 c, 14/6/80 ff, 28/3/81 ff
kindness of 14/6/59
learnt little as a minister 15/4/81
letters from G to, printed 31/8/59, 6/6/60, 14/1/69, 1/4/69, 30/8/69, 11/10/69, 29/11/69, 4/12/69, 9/12/69, 5/1/70, 8/1/70, 16/2/70, 6/9/70, 20/4/71, 22/11/71, 13/2/72, 19/3/72, 28/9/73, 1/11/73, 19/12/73, 17/1/74, 14/6/80, 15/6/80, 18/6/80, 6/7/80, 10/7/80, 9/10/80, 14/10/80, 26/10/80, 1/11/80, 23/11/80, 3/12/80, 25/12/80, 18/1/81, 29/1/81, 11/2/81, 9/3/81, 28/3/81, 11/4/81, 14/4/81, 22/4/81, 28/4/81, 18/5/81, 30/11/81, 3/10/83, 30/7/84, 22/8/84, 31/8/84, 10/9/84, 11/9/84, 28/9/84, 1/11/84, 30/9/85, 27/1/86, 20/4/86
never thoroughly gave himself to politics 15/4/81
'Primitive Man' and 21/3/69
Punjab Tenancy Act and 30/8/69
rationalism discussed with 30/9/65
reading Tennyson aloud at Cliveden 4/6/59
In Memoriam 30/7/54
Reform Bill 1884 and 18/7/84 n, 30/7/84, 22/8/84, 31/8/84, 10/9/84 ff, 28/9/84, 1/11/84
resignation of 28/3/81 n, 7/4/81, 8/4/81 c, 11/4/81, 14/4/81
ritualism and 17/5/68
Roman Catholic schools and 15/6/70 n
Savings Banks Bill and Lords and 15/8/60 n
Scottish Education Bill and 10/4/69 c
the Thistlethwaytes and 1/4/69
U.S.A. and 31/5/56, 21/2/63
with G to Liverpool reform meeting 5/4/66
See also Egypt, Florence, India, Inverary, Ireland, publications, Rome
Camperdown, Forfarshire (Camperdown) 27/9/69
Canada 27/2/37, 4/3/37 ff, 28/11/37, 22/12/37, 5/1/38, 20/1/38, 22/1/38, 23/1/38, 7/3/38, 1/5/38, 18/5/38, 10/8/38, 14/12/38, 5/6/39, 30/5/40, 16/5/49, 30/5/49 ff, 5/12/92
Canada Act 14/6/49, 15/6/49
Canada University meeting 13/6/50
clergy reserves 16/3/40, 24/3/40, 9/4/40, 9/6/40, 15/6/40, 3/7/40, 6/7/40, 20/7/40, 4/3/53, 12/3/53, 18/3/53
confederation of 6/12/64, 8/12/64, 9/5/65 ff, 10/6/65
conferences in London on 19/5/65 ff, 25/5/65 ff
corn and flour 27/4/43, 29/4/43, 19/5/43
defence and withdrawal of British troops, memorandum printed 19/1/70
defences of 2/3/46 ff, 23/7/64, 24/5/65, 29/8/70, 9/4/72 c
G's memorandum on 11/7/64 ff
guarantee of £3,600,000 granted 28/11/72 c
guarantee of £4million for requested 15/10/72, 28/11/72 c
Montreal's fortifications 14/5/69 c, 15/10/72
Quebec garrison 17/12/70 c, 4/7/71, 5/7/71 c
emigration to 5/6/69 c
Fenians in 26/10/69 c, 10/11/69 c, 16/7/70 c, 10/8/71
compensation for 25/3/71 c, 12/8/71 c, 18/12/71 c

Canada (*cont.*)
finances of
G's memorandum on 14/12/61, 10/4/62
fisheries and 1/4/71 c, 3/4/71, 4/4/71, 10/6/71 c, 5/4/72 c, 27/4/72 c, 1/3/73 c, 28/6/73 c, 3/10/73 c
Governor Generalship of 3/1/46, 25/4/83, 11/5/83, 19/5/83
G's mem. on Address 1/6/46, 3/6/46
G's memorandum on Canadian confederation and defences 19/1/65
Hudson's Bay Co. 28/4/46, 10/8/48, 30/5/49, 5/7/49, 20/7/58
G on select cttee. on 18/2/57 ff
indefensible frontier of 30/3/69
nation, gradual education into 15/10/72
Newfoundland 12/2/38, 20/2/38, 25/6/38, 6/8/38, 13/4/39, 26/6/39, 2/4/41, 12/2/81 c, 25/4/91, 12/10/92
delegates from meeting G 2/5/91
Saint Pierre, proposed sale of by France to U.S.A. 21/10/71 c
Saint Pierre/Miquelon 10/7/72 c
Nova Scotia 25/5/38, 12/6/68
Prince Edward Island
G's Resolutions on 23/4/58, 5/5/58
railways of
G's memoranda on 14/12/61, 10/4/62, 2/12/62
rebellion in 5/6/49
Red River rebellion 5/3/70 c, 16/3/70 c, 19/3/70 c, 7/5/70 c, 15/5/70, 25/6/70 c, 6/8/70 c
amnesty, except for murderers 12/7/73 c
responsible government in 28/12/58
speech on 8/3/37, 29/5/40
state religion, desirability of 9/6/40
Sudan and
offer of help for 17/2/85 c
tariffs of
differential tariffs not an articulus of separation 14/10/72
tea bill not to be disallowed 3/12/72
union in 13/6/40
United States proposes union with 24/1/70, 25/1/70 c, 28/1/70 c
U.S.A. proposes cession of as Alabama indemnity 26/6/69 c
Vancouver Island 18/4/49 ff, 30/5/49, 19/6/49 n, 18/2/57 n
Vaticanism and 10/3/75
See also Cardwell, memoranda, memoranda (printed), United States
Canaletto 4/5/32
Cannes 18/1/83 ff, 4/2/88 ff, 15/2/89 ff, 8/1/95, 9/1/95, 29/12/95, 2/1/96 ff
beneficial effects of stay at 31/12/83
G's recuperation from insomnia in 18/1/83
another visit in the air 2/1/85
G staying at Hotel Montfleury 4/2/88 ff
Canning, Charles John (1812-1862), 1st Earl Canning (1859), governor of India (1856), Viceroy of India (1859), Peelite M.P. 11/10/27, 27/11/27, 15/12/29 ff, 26/12/29 ff, 20/1/30, 25/2/30, 1/5/30, 4/6/31, 11/10/31, 21/3/35, 14/7/35, 18/10/36, 11/11/36, 27/1/42, 28/1/42, 26/2/51, 8/11/52, 29/12/52, 10/10/53, 1/8/55, 24/11/55
Brock's statue of 20/6/76
death of 16/6/62, 17/6/62
formation of Palmerston's government and 6/2/55 ff
funeral of 21/6/62
G's defence of 21/5/58
Indian mutiny and 11/5/58 ff, 21/5/58
Oxford University bill and 5/7/54, 11/7/54 ff
return from India 5/5/62
Canterbury 14/7/54, 18/9/54
Canterbury cathedral 14/7/54, 18/9/54
St. Augustine's 18/9/54
canvassing *See* elections (general/bye)
Cape Colony *See* South Africa
Cape Wrath 1/9/80
capital punishment
G votes against abolition of 29/7/40
Cap Martin 27/2/95
Capri 10/5/32 ff
Tiberius' villa 11/5/32
Captain, H.M.S *See* accidents, ships
Capua 23/5/32, 24/7/49
Caracci 4/5/32
Carcassonne 13/1/92
card games
beggar my neighbour 24/12/29
commerce 27/8/30, 5/9/68
dummy 1/11/34, 2/12/36 ff
écarté 13/10/32
G losing money at Court on 6/4/46
picquet 1/4/39, 9/7/39, 12/9/39 ff, 29/10/40, 3/2/41, 29/3/42, 26/1/43, 4/4/44, 17/7/45, 26/9/48 ff
snapdragon 6/1/52, 29/12/62
vingt et un (pontoon, black jack)
watched 6/8/46
whist 24/3/31, 11/10/32, 17/10/32 ff, 3/12/32, 17/12/32 ff, 7/1/33, 2/11/33, 13/1/34, 30/8/34 ff, 6/11/35, 13/9/36 ff, 30/11/36, 2/12/36, 25/10/37, 22/3/39 ff, 13/5/39 ff, 7/9/39, 1/9/40 ff, 12/8/42 ff, 29/8/43 ff, 11/4/44, 10/8/44 ff, 23/11/44, 25/9/48, 28/4/59, 1/11/60, 7/8/61, 26/8/61, 21/8/62, 9/8/64, 7/8/65, 15/10/67 ff, 3/10/68, 19/8/69, 3/6/70, 5/9/70,

6/10/70, 26/9/72, 8/4/73, 4/4/77, 21/8/80, 7/3/83, 16/4/84, 10/9/84 ff, 18/12/84, 3/2/85 ff, 7/4/85, 3/9/85 ff, 27/1/86, 12/8/86, 28/10/86 ff, 28/9/91, 17/11/91, 6/12/92
32/- lost to Grenville 27/11/44
at Cannes 23/1/83 ff
G playing with Prince of Wales 29/9/71
prevents sleep 27/11/44
Cardiff
Freedom of 6/7/89
G's speech at 7/6/87
cards, G playing 24/11/27, 29/11/27, 18/9/30, 21/12/30, 25/12/30 ff, 5/1/31 ff, 29/12/31 ff
See also card games
Cardwell, Edward (1813–1886), 1st Viscount Cardwell (1874), Peelite M.P., Oxford City (1852), colonial secretary (1864), war secretary (1868) 20/3/43, 31/7/44, 25/2/48, 17/6/48, 20/7/50, 17/1/52 ff, 20/1/52, 24/2/52, 6/11/52, 9/11/52, 15/1/54, 24/3/55, 28/7/55, 13/6/56, 10/3/58, 10/8/59, 13/7/63, 15/7/63, 16/2/64 n, 12/6/66, 19/3/68 ff, 15/6/68 ff, 14/1/71, 25/3/73, 26/7/73, 1/8/73, 2/8/73, 3/2/74, 5/2/74, 22/2/74, 25/4/74, 9/1/75, 18/6/75, 18/3/76, 11/2/77, 9/6/77, 3/7/78, 9/7/79, 17/5/80
1866 panic and 11/5/66
Alabama arbitration and 9/4/72 n, 13/6/72
army estimates and 6/12/72, 7/12/72, 9/12/72, 12/12/72 c, 15/10/73, 1/12/73, 19/1/74, 22/1/74
1874's of special significance 15/10/73
army reform and 17/11/69, 21/1/70 c, 29/3/70, 2/4/70 c, 21/9/70 ff, 2/11/70, 30/11/70 c, 21/12/70, 16/3/71, 2/5/71, 18/12/73
greater than any since 1815 21/8/72
need for a tract on his period at War Office 21/8/72, 3/9/72
purchase abolition 21/9/70 n, 23/9/70, 4/10/70, 8/10/70, 14/10/70, 22/10/70, 17/1/71, 20/1/71 c, 25/1/71 cf, 16/2/71, 27/5/71 ff, 11/7/71 ff
retrenchment essential in 9/9/71, 11/12/71 ff
at Hawarden 7/9/67 ff
ballot, offers resignation over 18/4/72 n
breakup of Aberdeen's ministry and 1/2/55
budget of 1853
alternative plan for 12/4/53, 13/4/53, 14/4/53
budget of 1874: G's plan for
abolish income tax and sugar duties, partly paid from death and spirit duties 11/8/73
Canadian confederation and 9/5/65, 15/10/72
conferences in London on 19/5/65 ff
Eyre's case and 1/12/65
Franco-Prussian war and 16/7/70, 24/7/70, 26/7/70 ff, 14/8/70
funeral of 23/2/86
G discusses banking with 15/12/60
G gives sharp warning on motion to 11/5/58
G's Oxford University seat and 13/5/47
G's resignation as liberal party leader and opposes it 10/1/75
in Florence 6/1/67
in Rome 4/11/66 ff, 22/12/66 ff
Irish disestablishment and 19/7/69
Irish land and 21/9/69
letters from G to, printed 11/1/69, 12/1/69, 19/7/69, 21/9/69, 17/11/69, 8/4/70, 29/6/70, 16/7/70, 24/7/70, 26/7/70, 27/7/70, 21/9/70, 23/9/70, 4/10/70, 8/10/70, 14/10/70, 22/10/70, 26/10/70, 2/11/70, 18/11/70, 23/12/70, 19/1/71, 11/2/71, 16/3/71, 2/5/71, 11/5/71, 22/5/71, 27/5/71, 10/7/71, 11/7/71, 9/9/71, 12/9/71, 6/11/71, 8/11/71, 20/11/71, 11/12/71, 20/1/72, 22/1/72, 21/8/72, 3/9/72, 27/10/72, 5/11/72, 6/12/72, 29/8/73, 3/9/73, 5/9/73, 15/9/73, 17/9/73, 18/9/73, 23/9/73, 15/10/73, 1/12/73, 18/12/73, 4/1/74, 15/9/82
political promise of 1/6/44
sad spectacle of, monitory of our lot 22/2/83
Speakership and 27/10/71 c, 6/11/71, 8/11/71
supports Palmerston against paper duty repeal 5/5/60
tells Lowe he must resign as chancellor 2/8/73
war secretary 5/12/68
withdraws as candidate for Oxford University 22/6/47 ff
career, G's *See* Gladstone (Sir John), offices held, Peel, politics, profession, public life
Carlingford, Lord *See* Fortescue
Carlisle 28/1/50, 1/10/53, 29/9/69
Carlow election 22/4/36
Carlsruhe 28/9/45
Carlton Club *See* clubs, clubs (G member of)
Carlton Gardens *See* houses
Carlton House Terrace *See* houses
Carlyle, Thomas
intolerant conversation of 21/6/49
See also Dramatis Personae, memoranda (printed)
Carmarthen 13/7/52

carnal sin *See* sin
Carnarvon, Earl of *See* Herbert
Carnarvon Burgh
G's speeches at 12/9/92
Carnegie, Andrew (1835–1919), steel manufacturer and philanthopist 18/6/87, 20/6/87, 18/6/89, 22/7/90, 30/7/91, 15/6/93
Acton's library and 14/5/90 n, 9/6/90 ff
a giant millionaire 22/4/92
article on 'Wealth' by
G republishing in U. K. 20/6/89 n
G's views on 25/12/89
at Hawarden 19/9/90, 21/4/92 ff
democracy and 7/9/90
donations to liberal party 21/4/92
G's article on 19/9/90
G's autobiography and
invites G to write 3/3/91 n, 10/4/91
suggests G dictate it 3/3/91 n
Homestead strike and 19/9/92
income of £370000 p.a. 13/6/87
offers G loan for life of 'any sum' without interest 13/6/87
Carrara marble quarries 14/3/32
carriage duty 6/4/82, 31/5/82
carriages
bought in Frankfurt 11/9/38, 22/11/38
Carton, Maynooth (Leinster)
Carton, R. C. *See* plays seen
Carvarvon liberals
visit to Hawarden (including Lloyd George) 29/5/90
Caserta 22/5/32
Cassiobury Park, Hertfordshire (Ebury) 18/6/70, 12/8/71, 13/7/72, 3/8/88
Castellamare 10/5/32
Castle Howard (Lanerton) 7/10/76
Castle Line ships *See* ships
castor oil *See* medicines
catalogues 27/11/69 *See also* books, Homer, papers
catechism 14/2/39, 20/2/39 ff
Caterline Church, Aberdeenshire 28/9/48
cathedrals 28/11/37, 10/12/37, 19/12/37, 28/1/38, 31/1/38, 13/6/38, 23/2/39, 25/2/39, 5/3/39, 8/3/39 ff, 11/2/40, 7/3/40 ff, 4/5/40, 13/6/40, 25/2/82 c, 13/3/83, 24/3/86
Blomfield twisted on 14/3/40
constituent element of the nation's life 9/4/81
emoluments in 17/3/56
low-churchmen mostly unsuitable as Deans 16/4/83
speech on 29/6/40
See also memoranda
Cathedral Schemes Bill
G drafts 22/2/56 ff
Catholic Apostolic Church (Irving's) 19/6/76
Gordon Square church
G at with Duchess of Sutherland 4/4/54
Liverpool church
G attends 27/1/33, 15/5/75
Catholic emancipation 12/9/26, 2/10/26, 7/3/27 ff, 14/6/27, 16/6/27, 7/3/28, 1/5/28, 12/5/28, 15/5/28, 5/2/29, 4/4/29, 17/9/29, 16/2/31, 23/10/32
G always in favour of 22/10/81 n
cattle plague 14/12/65, 25/12/65, 5/1/66, 8/1/66, 7/1/68, 20/2/69 c, 8/5/83, 31/1/84 *See also* foot and mouth
caucus *See* liberal party
Cavendish, Frederick Charles, Lord (1836–1882), financial secretary, liberal M.P., Irish secretary (1882), murdered in Phoenix Park (1882), 27/7/2 ff, 18/12/61, 20/12/62, 11/12/63, 5/2/64, 14/2/64, 3/2/66, 4/5/66, 29/5/66, 25/6/66, 20/2/68 ff, 23/4/68, 22/7/70, 16/5/71, 12/5/72, 23/10/72, 26/10/72, 6/2/73 ff, 12/6/73 ff, 5/7/73 ff, 5/10/73, 19/11/73, 20/2/74 ff, 5/7/74, 21/12/74, 24/12/74, 25/12/74, 28/12/74, 20/3/75, 9/5/75, 12/7/75, 26/7/75, 24/10/75, 2/3/76, 21/4/76, 15/5/76, 8/10/76, 12/12/76, 19/3/77, 3/6/77 ff, 26/7/77, 2/2/78, 1/3/78, 16/5/78 ff, 24/5/78 ff, 24/6/78, 15/7/78, 23/7/78, 18/12/78, 29/1/79 ff, 21/2/79, 28/3/79, 24/4/79, 26/6/79, 4/7/79, 21/7/79, 10/12/79 ff, 11/3/80 ff, 20/4/80 ff, 8/5/80, 29/5/80, 4/7/80, 18/8/80 ff, 30/10/80, 8/11/80, 4/1/81, 28/5/81, 9/6/81, 22/10/81, 31/10/81 ff, 6/2/82 ff, 14/3/82, 1/1/84
assassination of 6/5/82 ff, 15/5/82
engagement of 21/4/64 ff
funeral of 11/5/82
G's verses on 12/5/82, 17/5/82, 20/5/82 ff, 29/5/82, 6/6/82
G's private secretary 23/7/72 ff, 27/2/73
Irish secretary 3/5/82 ff
land purchase and 12/4/82
letters from G to, printed 4/2/81, 22/6/81, 18/11/81, 21/1/82, 12/4/82
marriage of 7/6/64
qualities of 23/4/76
Woolner's bust of 5/5/83
Cavendish, Lucy Caroline, Lady Frederick Cavendish (1841–1925), née Lyttelton, diarist, Mrs G's niece, wife and widow of Lord F. Cavendish 5/9/41, 28/4/56, 2/5/56, 8/11/62, 11/12/63, 10/6/71, 30/7/72, 19/11/73, 20/2/74 ff, 5/7/74, 26/7/75, 2/3/76, 21/4/76,

12/12/76, 23/7/78, 21/2/79, 4/7/80, 31/10/81 n, 4/11/81 n, 17/5/82, 20/5/82 ff, 6/6/82 ff, 29/6/82, 10/8/82, 10/11/82, 25/11/82, 23/12/82 ff, 16/1/83, 11/3/83, 29/4/83, 20/10/83, 5/1/84, 9/8/84 ff, 19/10/84, 6/1/85, 2/2/85, 24/3/85, 28/4/85, 28/7/85, 10/2/86, 14/5/86, 15/7/86, 19/11/86, 8/3/87, 11/6/87, 24/6/87, 23/12/87, 23/2/88, 24/5/88 ff, 7/3/89, 25/5/89 ff, 4/10/89 ff, 3/8/90, 14/6/91, 25/3/92, 6/6/92 ff, 14/6/92 ff, 16/10/92 ff, 11/10/93 ff, 27/3/94
courting 11/12/63, 12/12/63, 5/2/64, 13/2/64
engagement of 21/4/64
future punishment, discusses with G 24/10/72
G discusses his retirement with 1/6/86
G discusses political futures of Hartington and F. Cavendish with 24/12/73
gives *imprimatur* for G's review of Reid's *Forster* 9/8/88
G staying with at Penmaenmawr 28/9/82 ff
her judgment is worth having 8/8/88
marriage of 7/6/64
one of us 24/12/83
Phoenix Park murders and 6/5/82 ff, 27/2/83
sermons and 19/6/87
sound, Christian, heroic 14/6/82
Cavendish, Spencer Compton (1833–1908), Marquis of Hartington (1858), 8th Duke of Devonshire (1891), postmaster general 1868–70, Irish secretary 1870–4, Indian secretary 1880–2, war secretary 1882–5, unionist leader of the whigs 15/5/64, 19/6/66, 17/7/66, 9/6/68, 20/11/68, 9/12/69, 12/9/70, 4/3/75 ff, 30/6/75, 20/7/75, 19/11/75 ff, 21/6/76, 17/7/76, 24/1/80, 5/3/80, 20/4/80 ff, 4/8/80 ff, 23/8/80, 25/10/80, 8/11/80, 25/2/81, 28/5/81, 4/6/81, 9/10/81, 15/10/81, 3/2/82, 1/5/82 ff, 13/5/82 ff, 23/5/82 c, 16/12/82, 2/3/83, 28/4/83, 2/7/83 ff, 27/7/83, 31/7/83, 19/2/84, 23/2/84, 27/3/84 ff, 3/11/84 ff, 31/1/85, 16/2/85 c, 14/4/85, 5/5/85, 3/7/85, 28/7/85, 2/9/85, 12/1/86, 21/1/86 ff, 18/2/86, 7/5/86, 24/12/86 ff, 5/4/87, 6/7/87, 23/4/88, 14/5/88, 12/6/88, 21/2/89, 14/5/92, 23/9/92, 8/10/92, 6/9/93
absurd caricature of G's views by 14/1/86
at Hawarden 29/12/70
ballot and 6/3/69 c
developing 6/8/75
Duchess of Manchester and
Queen refuses to receive her 6/12/68
Eastern question and
vote of credit on: attempts to bolt 29/1/78
Egypt and 31/5/82 ff, 20/1/85
fails to speak as promised in Commons 27/7/82
stiff on 31/5/82
G and Mrs. O'Shea
alarm at communications between 15/10/82
general election 1885 and 7/8/85, 22/8/85
Granville's debts and 7/5/91
G's offer of Exchequer when he retires 5/5/82
G's retirement and
opposed to 13/11/82 n
G's uneasy relations with 23/1/80 n
G with at Holker Hall 19/9/67, 30/1/85 ff
home rule and 25/1/74, 1/2/74, 15/12/85, 17/12/85 ff, 30/12/85 ff, 2/1/86, 12/1/86 ff, 21/1/86, 7/4/86, 17/8/86
conciliation with fails 19/5/86
extent of support for: 66 25/5/86
G's sketch of plan to 17/12/85
in a state of morbid sensibility over 22/12/85
Resolution and 19/5/86 ff, 23/5/86
Indian secretary 1880–2 23/4/80 ff, 10/11/81 c
good speech by 25/3/81
Ireland
G regrets Hartington's early clashing with Parnell 3/9/85
Ireland and
courted the hostility of Parnell 10/11/85
Irish land and 9/12/69, 23/12/69, 6/4/70, 27/11/75 ff, 31/12/80 c, 25/2/81, 16/3/86
Irish local government and 22/1/83, 3/2/83, 10/2/83
Irish secretary 1870–4 28/9/71, 15/6/72 c, 8/7/73
accepts under G's pressure 23/12/70, 28/12/70, 30/12/70
Granard case 19/7/72
Keogh case 19/7/72, 23/7/72
local government and 1/5/72
national schools and 17/7/72 c, 31/7/72, 19/8/72
railways purchase 22/1/72, 10/12/72 c, 15/2/73
railways purchase: threatens resignation on, as supports 10/2/73
university bill and 20/4/72 c, 6/10/72, 26/10/72, 31/10/72, 15/11/72 c, 20/11/72, 22/11/72 c, 28/11/72 c, 3/2/73

Cavendish, Spencer Compton (*cont.*)
Irish secretary 1870–4 (*cont.*)
university bill: threatens resignation over 1/12/72
Westmeath inquiry 25/2/71 c, 4/3/71 c, 25/3/71 c, 17/4/71 c, 19/4/71 c, 22/4/71 c, 17/11/80 c, 19/11/80 c
leader of liberal party in Commons 7/2/76, 16/3/76, 26/2/77, 23/3/77, 7/6/77, 27/6/77, 19/7/77, 16/1/78, 6/12/78 ff, 20/2/79 ff, 5/3/79, 28/3/79, 10/5/79, 20/5/79, 4/7/79, 10/4/80 ff
Eastern question and 28/6/76, 23/3/77, 5/5/77, 25/1/78, 2/8/78
excellent speech by 8/2/77
G disgusted with liberals' treatment of 18/2/75
position as in temporary abeyance 3/12/83
letters from G to, printed 6/4/70, 28/9/71, 22/1/72, 1/5/72, 21/8/72, 6/10/72, 26/10/72, 31/10/72, 1/12/72, 14/12/72, 28/12/72, 3/2/73, 10/2/73, 8/7/73, 12/8/73, 25/1/74, 6/5/80, 8/5/80, 12/5/80, 14/5/80, 9/6/80, 16/6/80, 25/6/80, 14/8/80, 25/8/80, 8/9/80, 9/9/80, 23/10/80, 12/11/80, 20/12/80, 7/1/81, 14/1/81, 21/1/81, 26/1/81, 8/2/81, 10/2/81, 25/2/81, 10/3/81, 7/4/81, 21/4/81, 5/5/81, 21/5/81, 27/6/81, 4/10/81, 13/12/81, 8/5/82, 28/8/82, 9/10/82, 15/10/82, 13/11/82, 30/11/82, 19/12/82, 15/1/83, 3/2/83, 10/2/83, 10/10/83, 22/10/83, 7/11/83, 23/11/83, 3/12/83, 6/12/83, 7/12/83, 18/12/83, 29/12/83, 3/1/84, 16/2/84, 27/2/84, 1/3/84, 6/3/84, 10/3/84, 19/3/84, 21/3/84, 22/3/84, 13/4/84, 13/5/84, 16/5/84, 28/6/84, 2/7/84, 19/8/84, 20/8/84, 21/8/84, 23/8/84, 13/9/84, 1/10/84, 13/10/84, 29/10/84, 18/11/84, 19/11/84, 6/1/85, 9/1/85, 10/1/85, 14/1/85, 20/1/85, 7/2/85, 12/2/85, 16/2/85, 27/2/85, 5/3/85, 21/3/85, 22/3/85, 28/3/85, 1/4/85, 2/4/85, 8/4/85, 10/4/85, 29/4/85, 30/4/85, 11/5/85, 14/5/85, 30/5/85, 10/6/85, 18/7/85, 3/9/85, 4/9/85, 8/9/85, 11/9/85, 13/9/85, 10/11/85, 18/11/85, 1/12/85, 15/12/85, 17/12/85, 19/12/85, 20/12/85, 23/12/85, 2/1/86, 14/1/86, 30/1/86, 5/2/86, 16/3/86, 7/4/86, 23/5/86, 3/8/86, 17/8/86
liberal unionists and 16/7/86 ff
G tells his mind to 21/9/86
like a bull in a china shop 9/12/86
Manchester, Duchess of and 30/12/83
Phoenix Park murders and 6/5/82 ff
Plan of Campaign and 8/12/86
political anxiety of 9/10/82
Post Office
refuses to return to 12/8/73
premiership and
advises the Queen to send for G 23/4/80
report of audience of the Queen, printed 22/4/80
purchase abolition
wants to accept defeat 15/7/71 c
reduces postage on newspapers 4/2/70 c
reform and 13/5/64
Reform Bill 1884 and 22/10/83 ff, 7/11/83, 23/11/83, 3/12/83, 6/12/83 ff, 18/12/83, 29/12/83, 27/2/84, 18/7/84
conferences with tories on 7/11/84 c, 13/11/84 ff
conversations with Beach 31/10/84 c
G's interview with to dissuade from resignation on 31/12/83, 1/1/84, 3/1/84
prepossessions of 29/12/83
should not have said 'compromise' 6/10/84
resignation, threats of 16/5/85
Irish railways 10/2/73
Irish university bill 1/12/72
resignation of the government and 13/3/73 ff
Sudan and 8/2/84 ff, 23/4/84 c, 13/5/84 ff, 28/6/84 ff, 2/7/84 ff, 6/8/84 c, 19/8/84, 23/9/84, 27/2/85 n, 21/3/85 ff, 2/4/85, 10/4/85, 14/4/85, 15/4/85 c, 29/4/85, 30/4/85
instructions to Wolseley not a well-balanced statement of cabinet's view 9/1/85
ominously anxious for cabinet on 31/7/84
threatens resignation on 1/8/84
trapped by Disraeli 4/4/76
unlikely to join tories 16/7/86
War Secretary 1/12/82 ff, 15/12/82 ff
See also Daily Telegraph, Afghanistan, army, Bulgarian horrors, Chatsworth, Eastern question, Ireland, slavery, Sudan, Zanzibar
Cavendish College, Cambridge 29/9/76
Caxton Exhibition
G's speech at 6/6/77, 30/6/77
Cecil, Robert Arthur Talbot Gascoyne-, Lord (1830–1903), Viscount Cranborne (1865), 3rd Marquis of Salisbury (1868), journalist, Indian secretary 1874–8, foreign secretary 1878–80, 1885, 1886–92, 1895–1900, Prime Minister

1885, 1886–92, 1895–1902, tory M.P. 4/2/56, 4/3/68, 11/12/68 ff, 12/6/69, 9/6/70, 12/6/70, 13/6/70, 10/3/72, 30/7/73, 23/10/73 n, 22/3/74, 21/5/79, 31/5/79, 3/5/80 c, 16/6/80, 24/11/81, 5/5/84 c, 3/12/84, 13/1/85, 4/8/87 n, 6/2/88, 17/12/89, 27/11/91, 26/8/92 ff, 23/9/92, 20/1/93 c, 4/2/93, 19/5/93, 20/7/93, 23/2/94 c
attack on G in *Quarterly* 2/8/61 n
Balkan policy of
G delighted by 1/12/85 ff, 20/12/85
Chancellor of University of Oxford 17/6/70
character of
sensible decline of 13/4/81
Cleveland commission and 30/6/71
conversations with G 22/3/67
Franco-Prussian war and 4/3/71 c
G argues with on Jewish disabilities 14/3/60 n
G at Hatfield 11/12/68 ff, 26/11/70, 15/7/71, 7/12/72, 12/7/73, 27/2/75 ff, 17/7/75
G feels sharply severed from 21/4/81
Gordon's letters and 25/3/88 n
government of 1885–6
beaten, G thinks wisely, on Collings' amendment 26/1/86
coercion in Ireland would have led to Parliamentary breakdown 13/2/86
duty to formulate Irish policy 3/9/85, 12/12/85 ff, 20/12/85
government of 1886–92
defeated on Asquith's amendment 8/8/92 ff
Irish policy of 9/12/86, 10/12/86, 27/12/86
strange proposals of 19/8/86, 23/8/86
G's confidence in honour of 4/12/70
G shocked by diplomatic language of 4/7/86
home rule and 15/12/85 ff, 23/12/85
Hottentot speech!! 16/5/86, 17/5/86
interesting dinner party given by 29/6/75
Ireland and
complains about boundary commission 24/12/84
Irish disestablishment and 22/6/69
letters from G to, printed 30/6/71, 27/11/84, 1/12/84, 5/12/84, 19/6/85, 1/8/86
misstatements by 8/4/78 n
model of political integrity, G thinks 17/6/70
Parnell and
avoids antagonising 10/11/85
personal denigration of G 9/2/88 n
pessimism of 30/9/84
prime minister 1885 9/6/85, 13/6/85, 16/6/85, 20/6/85 ff
ill to deal with, requiring incessant watching 24/6/85
prime minister 1886–92 20/7/86 n
redistribution and 30/9/84, 6/11/85
Reform Bill 1884 19/8/84
conferences with liberals on 7/11/84, 13/11/84 ff, 26/11/84 ff
does not want an accommodation, G thinks 13/10/84
mad behaviour of 6/7/84
rejection of by Lords 2/7/84, 13/7/84 n
university seats and 26/11/84, 28/11/84, 29/11/84, 1/12/84
unrestrained character of 31/8/84
resigns on reform 2/3/67 n
socialism, leader of 27/10/85
succession to Beaconsfield
G regrets reputation for untruthfulness will exclude 21/4/81
supports G's bill abolishing compulsory church rates 19/2/68
Tunis and 13/5/81 c
Uganda and 28/10/92
university tests, Resolutions on 22/4/71 c, 25/4/71
university tests and 1/12/70 n, 4/12/70, 6/5/71 c
See also Commons (House of), Hatfield, Ireland, redistribution
census of religion 3/1/54, 24/1/54, 7/7/60, 9/7/60, 3/7/80 c
for Ireland only 14/5/80 c
G supports for 1861 9/7/60
G supports for 1871 8/6/70, 2/7/70 c
Central Asia *See* Asia (Central)
Ceylon 20/2/49 ff, 26/1/84 c
G's speech on 29/5/51
Chalmers, Thomas, Rev. Prof. (1780–1847), preacher and professor of morals & divinity
lectures on established churches 27/4/38, 1/5/38 ff, 4/7/38
Chamberlain, Joseph (1836–1914), mayor of Birmingham (1873), president, board of trade 1880–85, president, local government board (1886), radical liberal (unionist) leader (1886), 15/8/73 n, 3/5/80, 1/11/80, 3/3/81, 17/12/82, 6/6/83, 30/10/84, 27/11/84 c, 18/1/85 n, 16/2/85 c, 19/6/85, 7/7/85, 13/7/85, 8/8/85, 30/9/85, 14/11/85, 22/1/86, 16/2/86 c, 8/5/86 c, 19/5/86, 24/12/86 ff, 15/3/87, 2/4/87, 3/4/87, 14/7/87 n, 8/2/90 n, 30/6/90, 8/4/92 n, 12/1/93 ff, 18/1/93, 23/5/93, 6/9/93, 14/9/93, 10/12/93
Afghanistan and 20/3/85
American missionaries indignant with 16/6/88

Chamberlain, Joseph (*cont.*)
at Hawarden 7/10/85 ff
attack by 25/7/93
attack on Hartington 8/7/79 n
Bankruptcy Bill and 10/8/83
Bright celebrations and
speech annoys the Queen 22/6/83, 26/6/83
Chamberlainism rather in the dust 7/5/86
channel tunnel and 19/7/83 c, 26/7/83
Cobden Club speech of 22/6/83, 2/7/83
Collings' salary and 8/2/86
Devonshire Club meeting with 21/2/87
disestablishment and 6/11/85, 9/3/86
Eastern question and 1/5/77 n
supports G 7/5/77 n
Egypt and 10/10/82, 21/10/82, 24/10/82 c, 19/11/84 c
federal scheme of
G abstains from criticising 24/4/86
French treaty and 4/10/81
G cannot write 'Kootooing' letters to 20/4/86
G does not mean to be sat on by 13/12/85
G paying harmless compliment to 27/12/86
Grillion's club and
blackballed for despite G's support 11/2/88
G visits in Birmingham 31/5/77 ff
G will save for cabinet if he can 18/12/82
home rule and 12/1/86 ff, 21/1/86
Ireland and 23/12/80, 5/3/81 c, 15/12/81, 10/1/82, 1/5/82 ff, 16/3/85, 30/3/85, 28/4/85 ff, 4/5/85, 18/7/85, 23/5/93
anti-Spencerian 9/5/85 c
central board plan 24/4/85, 5/5/85, 6/5/85, 9/5/85 c, 11/5/85, 21/5/85, 1/6/85, 5/6/85 c, 8/6/85 c, 17/7/85, 20/7/85 n, 1/8/85, 4/8/85, 7/8/85, 11/9/85, 25/2/86 n
coercion, opposes 17/11/80 c
conciliation with hopeless 8/5/86
extent of support for: 8 25/5/86
has tried G rather hard over land purchase 19/4/86
land purchase and 20/5/85, 21/5/85, 1/6/85, 13/2/86 n, 25/2/86, 20/3/86, 22/3/86, 23/3/86 n, 11/4/86, 15/4/86, 19/4/86, 22/4/86, 24/4/86
negotiations with Parnell and O'Shea by 19/4/82 ff, 22/4/82 c, 25/4/82 ff, 13/5/82, 8/6/82, 10/6/82 c, 27/6/85 n, 24/1/86 n
objections to as possible Irish secretary 3/5/82
resignation of 15/3/86 ff, 26/3/86 c, 27/3/86, 4/4/86, 11/4/86, 15/4/86
successful meeting on home rule bill 31/5/86
Judas and 27/7/93 n
leads education deputation to meet G 9/3/70 n
letters from G to, printed 27/4/80, 21/5/80, 17/11/80, 23/12/80, 8/6/81, 2/7/81, 4/10/81, 15/12/81, 10/1/82, 10/2/82, 10/3/82, 19/4/82, 3/5/82, 6/5/82, 13/5/82, 8/6/82, 19/10/82, 21/10/82, 14/12/82, 15/12/82, 2/7/83, 2/8/83, 10/8/83, 3/12/83, 6/12/83, 19/12/83, 22/12/83, 26/7/84, 6/10/84, 8/10/84, 28/10/84, 31/10/84, 31/1/85, 5/2/85, 25/2/85, 6/5/85, 20/5/85, 22/5/85, 1/8/85, 9/9/85, 11/9/85, 14/9/85, 26/9/85, 25/10/85, 6/11/85, 18/12/85, 29/12/85, 8/2/86, 25/2/86, 15/3/86, 16/3/86, 27/3/86, 4/4/86, 11/4/86, 15/4/86, 5/2/93
liberal unionists and liberal party
accommodation between? 2/8/86, 13/8/87
contemptuous as usual 9/12/86
G's meeting with on Ireland and reconciliation 5/4/87
Lords and 26/7/84
G in substantial concurrence on 22/12/83
Manchester Ship Canal and 13/6/87
measures power of doing good by capacity to do harm 29/12/86
party unity and 9/9/85
President of L. G. B.
circular on temporary public works 16/2/86 n
President of the Board of Trade 1880–5 27/4/80 ff
qualities of
gift of repulsive power 21/4/86
radicalism under-represented in cabinet, complains of 5/2/85
radical programme of, G reading 20/10/85, 4/11/85, 6/11/85
radical views of
beyond general measure of the government 27/4/80
reform and 10/11/81 cn, 3/12/83, 7/12/83, 22/12/83 ff, 4/1/84 c, 30/7/84, 6/10/84, 8/10/84
resignation of
threat of 16/5/85
willing to retire 10/6/82
rising in the distance 31/12/83
Round Table conferences and 27/12/86 ff, 21/2/87, 26/2/87
South Africa and 3/5/80 c, 29/5/80 c, 24/12/80, 6/3/81, 3/6/81, 8/6/81, 23/7/81 c, 24/11/82, 28/10/84
taxation and 23/4/85, 24/4/85, 25/4/85 c

temperate behaviour of 22/6/83
treats concessions as acknowledging his superiority 20/4/86
Uganda and 5/2/93
unauthorised programme of 31/1/85, 11/7/85
See also cabinet, deputations, education, Ireland, liberal party, memoranda, Radical Programme
Chambéry 28/2/32, 29/10/50, 5/3/59
Chancellor of the Exchequer *See* Exchequer, offices
change
opening but not alarming 31/12/68
Channel Islands
Alderney
harbour of 17/3/53, 29/3/73 c, 10/7/73 c
Jersey 20/4/75
channel tunnel 19/6/69 c, 12/10/81 c, 11/2/82 c, 18/2/82 c, 29/7/82 c, 5/8/82 c, 12/8/82 c, 19/7/83 c, 13/3/86 c, 5/6/90, 26/9/92, 1/10/92, 26/10/92, 23/11/92 c, 2/1/93, 18/2/93
cabinet divided over 11/2/82 c
Chamberlain and 19/7/83 c
French report on 22/3/83
government not party to further bills for 19/7/83 c
G's inspection of preliminary works of 11/3/82
home rule to have precedence over 27/6/88
Tennyson and 1/5/83
works on to be halted? 4/3/82 c, 31/3/82 c
Chapel of Ease, Bedfordbury *See* Bedfordbury chapel of ease
character
W. H. G's fundamentally excellent 20/10/48
charades
played at Fasque 29/12/48, 12/1/50
played at Hawarden Castle 29/12/65, 12/12/92
played at Hawarden orphanage 2/1/83
played at Hawarden Rectory 8/10/59
played at Mrs. Talbot's 9/5/56
played at Savernake 1/2/77
charitable donations 22/10/28 fl, 30/9/39, 10/3/40, 30/9/41, 31/10/60 n, 1/6/74
accounts to be separate 6/12/39
G paying students' fees 26/2/78 n
proportion too small 4/11/42
reduced by financial crisis 29/12/47
sixth of income to be earmarked for 12/3/40
charitable subscriptions 1/3/38, 8/2/67
Christian Knowledge Society 24/4/30
Jewish Conversion Society 24/4/30
Liverpool Mariners Church Society 24/4/30
Oxford Benevolent Society 24/4/30
S. P. C. K. 24/4/30
charitable visiting 21/2/28, 13/9/29, 22/1/30, 4/11/31, 27/8/33, 2/11/34, 13/2/36, 29/12/36, 10/11/37, 14/11/37, 27/1/42 ff, 28/8/46 ff, 7/5/51, 18/1/63, 27/8/64
Fetter Lane refuge 23/3/62
Newport Market refuge 3/2/65
G's speech at 25/3/74
prayers during, comments on 29/10/37
Sally Clark, 106 23/1/68
waking hours of one day to be spent on 28/8/46
with C. G 8/9/44, 11/10/48, 11/8/77
See also rescue work
charities
abolition of income tax exemption of 1/1/63, 21/3/63
G's memorandum on 24/4/63
proposals withdrawn 4/5/63
tax on 5/3/81
Charity, House of
planned by G, James, Acland etc. 3/5/46, 4/5/46 ff
Rose Street 14/3/47, 11/5/47, 26/11/47, 22/5/49, 11/6/50, 19/2/52 n, 22/2/52, 26/6/62
G as Visitor of 26/5/47 ff, 18/5/48
See also House of Mercy
charity, private, importance of 13/2/36
Charity Voting Reform Association 11/7/78
Charles I 21/7/27
prayerbook of 5/1/37
Charterhouse
eating at 31/1/33, 4/2/33, 13/5/51
G governor of 20/4/36, 21/4/36, 20/7/67, 29/11/67, 16/7/68, 17/1/71, 15/5/74, 16/6/75, 26/6/75, 6/12/77, 12/12/78, 6/3/79 n
moving the school 12/7/66
chartism 16/3/40, 9/4/48, 10/4/48, 19/11/89 n
caused by want of employment 3/2/45
danger of Chartist/A.C.L.L. combination 11/6/43
G drafts anti-chartist declaration of loyalty 21/4/48
G's assistance to Ernest Jones 4/10/60
G sworn as Special Constable 11/3/48, 10/4/48, 12/6/48
Château Scott, Cannes (Wolverton) 18/1/83 ff
Chatham 15/10/61
Chatsworth House (Devonshire) 14/11/61, 29/5/73, 22/11/73, 18/11/75, 11/5/82

Chatsworth House (*cont.*)
library of 31/5/73, 3/6/73 ff
Chedworth Roman Villa 4/10/75
Cheltenham 3/9/25
Chequers, Buckinghamshire (Astley)
G's visit to 9/4/90
chess, G playing 2/9/25, 25/2/26, 9/3/26, 17/3/26 ff, 26/4/26, 9/6/26, 14/7/26, 5/4/27 ff, 23/11/27, 29/11/27, 10/12/27, 8/5/28, 30/12/28 ff, 13/4/29 ff, 15/9/29, 29/8/38 ff, 23/8/39 ff, 27/12/39 ff, 6/1/40 ff, 5/8/40, 29/9/40, 18/7/46, 15/2/47 ff, 3/1/48 ff, 22/8/48, 2/8/51, 1/10/52, 23/10/56
soundly beaten by S. Glynne 1/10/49
with C. G 27/8/39 ff, 13/1/40 ff, 9/10/40 ff, 2/1/41, 27/9/42 ff, 13/4/43, 26/10/43 ff, 30/1/44, 31/12/44, 17/7/46 ff, 12/9/49
Chester 1/2/36, 2/10/49, 24/9/50, 9/8/52, 10/8/52, 27/8/52, 26/10/52, 5/11/60, 23/5/61, 10/10/61, 4/11/64, 31/5/65, 14/10/69, 14/1/79, 26/7/79, 27/10/88
agricultural show at 8/9/73 ff, 12/9/73
Cathedral 1/9/42, 6/1/44
reopening of 8/8/76
Chester show 21/7/58
G electioneering in 31/3/57, 31/5/65, 12/7/65 ff
G's eye damaged by hard gingerbread thrown in 25/6/92
G speaking in 12/10/57, 14/1/79, 22/1/90, 29/5/93
infirmary 24/9/67, 30/9/67
King's School
G's speech at foundation stone laying 8/9/75
liberal politics in 19/8/79, 19/7/80
G attempts and fails to arbitrate 12/11/68, 13/11/68
G declines offer of a Chester seat 9/9/73
Prince of Wales' visit to 14/10/69 ff
torchlight procession in 8/12/79
Training School 1/9/42, 4/9/83
Volunteer review, G attends 5/11/60
Westminster Park
G walks in opening procession 5/11/67
W. H. G candidate/M.P. for 12/4/65 ff, 24/4/65, 24/5/65, 31/5/65, 12/7/65 ff
See also constituencies
Chevening (Stanhope) 30/3/37, 28/7/55
Chiavari 12/3/32
chibouk
G smokes in Albania 2/2/59
childbirth 3/6/40, 17/10/42 ff, 4/4/44
notes on 3/6/40
Childers, Hugh Culling Eardley (1827–1896), in Australia (1851), liberal M.P. (1860), 1st lord of admiralty (1868), chancellor of the duchy (1872), war secretary (1880), chancellor of the exchequer (1882) 2/12/65, 12/12/65, 10/5/66 ff, 31/3/68 ff, 24/5/68 ff, 5/2/73, 15/2/73 c, 21/9/73, 19/4/75, 18/3/79, 3/4/79, 21/4/80 ff, 17/9/81, 13/9/82, 1/1/83, 5/3/85, 28/4/85 c, 19/6/85, 24/12/85, 19/2/86, 22/2/86, 11/5/86, 20/7/86 c, 20/9/86 ff, 30/11/86, 4/3/87 ff, 28/6/87, 24/8/87, 27/1/88, 24/2/88 ff, 9/4/88, 8/5/88, 13/11/88 ff, 13/3/89, 9/7/89, 5/12/90, 30/7/91, 21/1/92 ff, 14/11/92
Admiralty first lord 5/12/68
army reform and 16/12/80 c
at Hawarden 19/12/83
discouraged 3/2/69
disestablishment and 9/3/86
Duchy, Chancellor of 1/8/72
Egypt and 15/6/82 ff, 25/8/82 ff, 24/10/82 c, 19/11/84 c, 20/11/84, 19/12/84 ff, 2/2/85
Exchequer and 31/5/82 ff, 1/12/82 ff, 5/4/83 ff, 14/1/84 ff, 9/1/85 ff, 30/1/85
fails as a retrencher? 16/12/84
Franco-Prussian war and 23/7/70 c, 6/8/70 c, 19/8/70
health of 16/1/71 n, 1/3/71, 26/4/71
resignation through ill-health 1/3/71
income tax abolition
bold plan of 2/4/73
Irish finance and 11/1/94
Irish land and 9/12/80 ff, 12/4/82, 13/5/84 n, 30/3/85, 13/5/85, 23/7/85, 25/7/85
letters from G to, printed 20/12/70, 26/4/71, 2/4/73, 12/2/74, 31/5/80, 18/9/80, 10/12/80, 16/12/80, 18/12/80, 31/1/81, 1/2/81, 31/8/81, 6/9/81, 14/9/81, 15/10/81, 26/12/81, 10/1/82, 15/1/82, 15/7/82, 31/8/82, 7/9/82, 10/9/82, 12/9/82, 15/9/82, 16/9/82, 22/9/82, 2/11/82, 21/11/82, 1/12/82, 15/2/83, 7/3/83, 5/7/83, 18/8/83, 10/9/83, 12/9/83, 15/9/83, 25/9/83, 7/11/83, 14/1/84, 19/1/84, 21/1/84, 25/1/84, 8/3/84, 20/3/84, 28/4/84, 30/5/84, 6/6/84, 8/6/84, 16/6/84, 23/9/84, 2/10/84, 3/10/84, 8/11/84, 16/12/84, 21/12/84, 31/12/84, 9/1/85, 29/1/85, 2/2/85, 16/2/85, 5/4/85, 7/5/85, 14/5/85, 20/5/85, 31/5/85, 23/7/85, 25/7/85, 28/9/85, 10/2/86, 13/2/86, 20/2/86, 9/3/86, 18/3/86, 19/3/86, 24/4/86, 4/6/86

resignation, threat of 16/5/85
Treasury establishment and 2/1/66
war secretary 1880–2 23/4/80
Queen's doubts about 23/4/80
childhood
recollections of 9/7/40, 17/11/78, 15/10/93, 30/12/93 n
nothing but selfishness and sin 6/11/53
childrearing
arithmetic usually taught by C. G 13/2/47
taught by G 13/2/47
asses milk used 22/12/42
beauty of children in illness 22/9/47
book too stimulating for children 28/9/49
breastfeeding difficulties 21/11/40, 4/11/42, 16/11/42 ff, 4/4/52 ff
C. G gives children's ball 25/4/57
children in church 28/10/42
children thieves of time 5/7/40, 6/7/40
children to be kept from Roman Catholic proselytising 4/5/43
encouragement of banking 17/4/68
G bathing with children 14/8/54 ff
G dealing with children's bad language 10/4/63
geography taught by G 23/8/45
G gives history lecture 18/12/49
G gives religious instruction 5/11/43 ff, 10/8/45 ff, 25/8/46 ff, 20/11/46 ff, 28/11/46 ff, 2/2/47 ff, 16/12/55, 22/6/56, 11/4/58, 19/6/59 ff, 2/11/62
G giving lessons 21/11/45, 23/7/46 ff
G giving picture lessons 22/4/59
G helping with baby 1/8/41 ff, 26/4/42, 28/4/44
G organises children's congregation 28/2/47
G playing charades with children 29/12/48
G playing cricket with children 26/8/50, 12/9/51 ff, 28/9/51
G playing whist with children 27/8/61, 21/8/62
G preparing children for Confirmation 21/8/54 ff, 30/11/56, 17/4/59
grandchildren, G gives money presents to 13 15/12/93
G sets examinations to his children 8/11/62
G singing with children 15/8/52 ff
G's reflections on his children's qualities 1/1/48
G studying Aristotle's *Politics* with W. H. G 3/9/60 ff
G studying Homer with sons 6/8/55 ff, 6/1/58 ff
G's whips Willy for inattention 28/9/47
G takes children to colonial office dinner 9/6/46
G takes children to Diorama 29/7/48
G taking children on seaside picnics 2/1/51
G taking children to Great Exhibition 21/6/51 ff
G teaching chanting 23/8/46
G teaching geography 28/8/46, 16/9/46 ff, 20/11/46 ff, 17/7/56 ff
G teaching Greek 8/8/51 ff, 2/1/56 ff
G teaching Italian 31/10/50 ff, 28/11/53 ff, 10/12/53 ff, 12/1/55 ff, 10/9/55 ff, 5/1/57 ff, 19/10/57 ff, 23/10/60 ff, 26/12/60, 18/8/62
G teaching Latin 23/1/47, 15/1/49, 24/7/52, 29/11/53 ff, 6/8/55 ff, 3/1/56 ff, 6/1/57 ff, 17/8/57 ff, 19/8/59 ff, 11/8/64 ff
a means to knowing children 3/10/52
G teaching music 27/9/46 ff
G teaching reading 12/12/44
G teaching to ride 14/8/44, 20/11/45, 26/10/54 ff
G uses Hamiltonian (conversational) method 23/1/47
illnesses of children
erysipelas 18/9/47 ff
music and 12/12/40, 15/8/52
nursing, G helping with 23/8/45
parties for children 8/8/46
politics causes neglect of 9/4/53
reflections on 29/10/40, 29/12/40
snowballing 10/2/47
taking children abroad 18/10/50
teething 22/11/40, 10/1/41, 14/3/41
walks with children 15/2/46 ff, 19/4/46, 1/7/46, 25/1/47 ff
family walk 27/5/49
See also governesses, James, nurses
children
almost all G's children help as private secretary, never with a failure 3/7/86
G's financial dispositions for 26/12/56, 1/6/74, 12/12/92, 4/9/96
details of extent of 4/9/96
G's wondrous absence of sorrow or anxiety about his children 14/1/64
See also G's sons and daughters
China 17/3/40, 21/6/77, 20/11/83 c, 6/10/84 c, 27/11/84 c, 1/11/92
Annam and 7/5/83
audience question in 27/1/73 c
bombardment of Canton 23/2/57, 26/2/57 n, 27/2/57, 3/3/57
British relations with 15/1/69
China mail contract 5/7/61
compensation for 24/8/41 ff
G's memorandum 2/8/61
England's national iniquity towards 14/5/40
financial statement on 16/7/60
G's memorandum on 22/9/59

China (*cont.*)
G's memorandum on faults of British policy, printed 17/2/63
G speaks against war & opium trade 8/4/40
mediation on 22/10/84 c
missionaries in 18/2/71
mission of to London 30/5/66
overland route to 15/6/72
relations with Russia 3/7/80 c
renegotiation of treaty of Tein-tsin 19/6/69 c
Resolution on 24/3/40
Tientsin incident 15/9/59, 17/9/59
war with European powers a disgrace 18/2/71
See also memoranda, opium, Russia, Temple (Henry), Wellesley
Chislehurst, Kent (Lord R. Cavendish) 11/6/64, 2/7/64, 20/5/65, 5/5/66, 9/6/66, 13/6/68, 24/7/69, 9/7/70, 13/5/71, 17/6/71, 1/7/71, 29/7/71, 8/6/72, 6/7/72, 17/5/73, 21/6/73, 5/7/73, 26/7/73, 2/8/73
Chiswick (Duchess of Sutherland) 16/5/63, 27/6/63, 23/7/63, 21/5/64, 22/4/65, 27/4/65, 24/6/65, 1/6/66, 5/6/66, 13/7/66, 28/7/66, 3/2/67, 6/2/67, 13/2/67, 23/2/67, 26/2/67, 9/3/67, 23/3/67, 16/4/67, 4/5/67, 18/5/67, 22/6/67, 23/7/67, 27/7/67, 1/12/67, 16/5/68, 18/7/68 *See also* Gower
chloroform *See* medicines
cholera
C. G susceptible to during pregnancy 19/8/49
in Sicily 28/10/38, 29/10/38
blamed on monarchy 29/10/38
See also illnesses
cholera, epidemic of
1832 21/3/32, 27/4/32, 2/5/32, 22/7/32, 29/7/32, 22/8/32, 1/1/33, 16/1/33 n, 14/4/33 n
in Torquay 13/9/32, 20/9/32
Cholmeley School, Highgate 7/6/65
Chorley 16/10/72
Christ 19/3/26, 27/4/28, 30/5/29, 29/12/29, 2/2/32, 8/7/32, 6/10/33, 29/12/34, 29/12/35, 16/7/40, 29/12/40, 29/12/41, 29/12/42, 19/7/48, 29/12/49, 29/12/52, 20/5/54, 26/12/54, 1/1/55, 7/5/57, 31/12/76, 14/8/82, 31/12/83, 20/4/85, 31/12/93
blood of 17/1/31, 17/4/31, 3/9/38, 22/10/38
corpse of in Naples 17/5/32
death of 22/4/48
Ecce Homo
depictions of dissatisfying 12/1/39
G exceeds his age 29/12/44
G's memorandum on life of 16/10/59
life of with Dyce's prints, planned 27/11/43, 19/12/43
Christ Church, Broadway 14/12/43
Christ Church, Oxford 9/1/28, 10/10/28 ff, 17/1/34 ff, 9/6/75, 11/11/88, 2/2/90 ff
Bible clerk at 19/6/30
Cathedral (and Chapel)
G's dissatisfaction with 24/7/31
poor (sometimes better) attendance at 5/4/29, 7/6/29, 5/7/29, 1/11/29, 7/3/30, 7/8/31
Christ Church Ordinance, 1858 30/1/57, 16/4/57
Collections 12/12/28, 10/4/29, 6/7/29, 11/12/29, 1/4/30, 12/12/30
Common Room of 23/1/34, 30/1/34, 9/2/34, 24/10/52, 27/1/53
G speaking in 3/6/57
condition of religion at 25/4/30
Dean Gaisford's installation 15/10/31
disturbances in cathedral 23/3/30
Dr. Lee's Gallery 3/6/57
drunken death at 16/2/31 ff
Fell's exhibition(G successful) 29/10/29 ff
Gaudy at 27/6/29, 2/11/29, 19/6/30, 1/11/30, 1/11/47, 8/6/53
G speaking at 9/6/75
G beaten up 24/3/30
G dines with the Dean 20/6/30, 17/11/30, 11/6/31, 23/10/52, 4/2/90
G missing chapel at 5/6/31 ff, 30/10/31
imposition for, written 7/6/31
G staying at Deanery 18/11/61 ff, 9/6/75, 22/10/92
G taking tea at the Deanery 2/2/90
horse kept by G at 2/5/31, 6/7/31, 24/8/31, 20/10/31, 18/1/34
idleness at 22/5/30, 1/6/30
Library
G given key of 11/7/31
G working in 12/7/31 ff
portraits of G commissioned
Richmond, W. B.(rejected by the College) 29/12/81, 16/1/82 ff
Watts, G. F. 19/5/74 ff, 16/5/76, 9/6/77 n, 1/6/78, 29/12/81
Watts, G. F.: deemed unacceptable when shown at the Gaudy 1/6/78 n
prickbill, G as 23/1/30 ff, 3/2/30 ff, 2/5/30 ff, 16/10/30 ff, 7/11/30, 11/12/30
private tuition at 30/11/30
rooms at 14/10/28 ff, 16/10/29
Canterbury II. 7 15/1/30
S. E. G at 7/10/61 n
servitors at 1/2/29

Student of, G as 25/11/29, 1/12/29, 11/12/29, 24/12/29, 15/10/31
teaching, G asked to assist in 23/11/29
visit of Prince and Princess of Wales 16/6/63
visits to 21/1/32 ff
W. H. G at
G advises immense importance of steady work 27/5/58
wins Slade exhibition 27/5/58
See also idleness, Liddell, Oxford (University of), WEG Essay Club
Christendom
Vatican Council and 19/11/72
Christian Art, Institution of
planned 3/9/42, 9/9/42
Christianity
declining to pre-Constantine position 10/11/71
evolution and 27/5/85
G seeks reconciliation of modernity with 16/11/69
human sacrifices and
part in abolishing 4/9/73
industry and 31/8/46
priesthood and 30/8/40
retrocession of 13/11/56
Christian Knowledge Society 6/2/38
Christie's auction rooms 18/2/33, 19/2/33, 21/2/33, 6/5/33, 22/5/35, 3/6/35, 22/4/45, 4/6/45, 8/6/47, 24/2/53, 22/6/53, 23/6/53, 15/3/54, 8/3/56, 25/4/56, 31/5/56, 6/6/56, 6/5/57, 15/5/57, 16/5/57, 25/2/58, 16/3/58, 18/3/58, 20/3/58, 23/3/59, 24/3/59, 9/4/59, 11/4/59, 12/4/59, 26/5/59, 15/11/59, 6/3/61, 19/3/61, 22/3/61, 30/4/61, 28/5/61, 29/5/61, 22/6/61 ff, 4/7/61, 26/3/62, 9/4/62 ff, 18/7/62 ff, 8/5/63, 10/2/65 ff, 1/3/65, 6/2/67, 9/2/67 ff, 22/5/67 ff, 29/2/68, 20/5/68, 23/5/68, 10/6/68, 20/6/68, 27/1/69, 13/4/69, 8/7/69, 23/2/70, 7/3/71, 8/5/71, 23/10/71, 30/1/72, 4/3/72, 12/3/72, 19/4/72, 6/5/72, 14/5/72 ff, 7/6/72, 6/2/73, 20/3/73, 6/6/73, 15/6/73, 24/2/74 ff, 25/4/74, 20/5/74, 11/3/75, 10/4/77, 30/4/79, 19/5/79, 12/5/81, 3/6/82, 3/4/83, 12/6/84, 23/3/86, 30/3/86, 1/3/87, 6/7/87, 8/3/88, 28/4/88, 2/5/89, 25/5/89, 17/3/90, 6/6/90, 13/6/93
Addington's sale 26/2/58
Ashburnham sale 16/7/50, 20/7/50
Baillie sale 14/5/58
Beckford library sale 24/6/82, 16/8/82 n
Bernal sale 12/3/55
Cadogan sale 30/3/65
Cunningham sale 9/6/49, 24/6/51
Eardley's sale 28/6/60
Exeter sale 5/6/88
Falcke sale 13/4/58 ff
G buys 2 Giorgione's 15/3/56
G buys Biard's 'Madame du Barry' (61 guineas) 3/5/61
G buys Bonifazio 2/6/56
G buys Clarkson for £100 3/3/68
G buys Linnell's portrait of Peel 9/5/73
G buys Vivarini 13/6/63
Hamilton sale 24/6/82, 16/8/82
handling valuation and sale of contents of 11 Carlton House Terrace and of G's china and art collection 24/3/75 ff, 5/4/75 ff, 12/4/75, 21/6/75, 23/6/75
Joly de Bammeville's collection
G's part in purchase for nation of 6/6/54, 7/6/54, 8/6/54
Leech sale 21/4/65
M'Callum sale 30/5/67
Redpath sale 19/5/57
sale of G's china at 21/4/63 ff
Solly's pictures 5/5/47
to see the Giorgione 23/6/53
Woodburn's pictures 22/6/53
Christmas
Christmas tree at Hawarden 6/1/58, 1/1/90
Christy minstrels 10/9/70
church
character of 30/5/80
church, late for 21/2/41
church and state principles 24/6/41, 23/9/41, 27/3/42, 25/7/43, 19/6/45, 20/2/48, 2/5/49, 1/5/51, 6/3/64, 16/11/69, 10/5/80, 6/2/83
classical authors used for 11/12/40
clergy of established church will always be a tory corps d'armée 3/7/85
difficulty of implementation 23/7/38, 14/12/38
idolatry of 2/12/83
voluntary system the way forward 30/3/69
See also Church of England, Church of Scotland, disestablishment, Ireland, Maynooth, nonconformists, Peel
church attendance
prevented 12/4/43
Church Building Society 2/7/38, 15/3/47, 7/5/47, 17/5/52, 30/5/56
Church Defence Association
a piece of Tory machinery 8/9/81
G advises Hugessen not to join 28/12/72
Church Defence Institution 10/12/71
churches attended regularly
St. James's, Piccadilly 31/1/41 ff
St. Martin's 31/1/41 ff
parish meeting of 26/2/50
Visiting Association planned 23/5/50

churches attended regularly (*cont.*)
St. Paul's, Knightsbridge 24/6/43 ff
proposed engagement of 31/5/50
church extension 23/2/36, 29/3/36, 7/4/36 ff, 2/7/38, 20/4/39, 25/4/39, 4/5/40
Churchill, Randolph Henry Spencer, Lord (1849–1898), tory M.P. and cabinet minister 1/1/78, 29/7/81, 16/7/85, 21/7/85, 8/9/85, 10/9/85, 12/5/86 n, 17/5/86, 31/7/86 n, 11/8/86, 16/11/86, 8/12/86, 9/12/86, 30/12/86, 5/4/87, 12/7/87, 4/12/88, 11/3/89, 27/2/90, 21/7/90, 6/4/91, 24/11/92, 6/3/94
chancellor of the exchequer 17/6/85
Egypt and 16/6/83
'Elijah's mantle' and
moral bathos of 14/5/83
excellent speech on budget by 25/4/87
foul language of 11/7/84 n
G cannot enter counter-bidding for Irish vote by 8/8/85
governing spirit of tory party 30/9/85
G's assessment of 11/3/89 n
home rule and 15/12/85, 5/1/86 n
Orangemen and 20/5/86 n, 6/9/86
Randolph-Healy concordat on 7/1/86
seditious speeches on Ulster 20/5/86
letters from G to, printed 16/6/83, 26/6/83, 18/12/86
meeting with G 13/7/87
resignation of 23/12/86 ff
G's provisional sympathy for reasons for 31/12/86 n
strong brutal element within? 18/11/85
tricks of 3/9/85
Church Missionary Society
Uganda and 24/9/92, 26/9/92
Church of England
17th century and 30/3/41
articles of 16/4/26, 11/6/26, 28/5/32, 13/11/38
G's memorandum on, printed 31/12/93
authority in 1/2/85
bishops of
G tries to increase 17/5/50
increase in numbers 26/10/69 c, 3/11/69
career in for G considered 23/11/29, 3/8/30, 8/8/30, 12/8/30
catholicism of 25/11/38, 24/10/43, 28/10/43, 21/4/74
choirs of 7/1/94
churching of women 25/6/40, 24/11/42, 4/2/54
church parties in 14/6/83
clergy of
attending balls 26/11/38
Sydney Smith on badness of 16/10/83
unmitigated Toryism of bulk of 8/9/81
clerical incomes in 25/4/93
Compline, G reads daily 16/5/77
conversions to Rome 15/1/39, 25/2/41, 11/6/42, 20/2/45, 10/3/45 n, 1/4/45, 14/2/47, 7/4/51, 2/9/54
rending and sapping the church 31/12/51
Convocation of 19/10/34, 20/11/37, 20/4/44, 26/4/44, 12/5/44, 7/11/52 n, 11/8/80, 16/8/80, 17/8/80, 19/8/80, 20/8/80
assists decline of Erastianism 6/9/72
Denison affair 13/8/56, 23/8/56, 24/8/56, 26/8/56, 1/9/56, 5/11/56
education grants and 21/7/40, 15/6/43 ff, 25/7/43
free conference in 1/9/67, 15/9/67, 20/10/67, 8/12/67, 22/12/67, 29/12/67, 5/1/68, 12/1/68, 19/1/68, 26/1/68, 2/2/68, 9/2/68
G's confirmation 25/1/27, 28/1/27, 1/2/27
G uprooted from 19/8/51
in Amalfi 10/2/89
in Biarritz 20/12/91 ff
in Florence 2/1/88
in Genoa 11/3/32
in Lyons 26/2/32
in Naples 29/4/32, 6/5/32, 20/5/32, 18/11/38, 2/12/38, 10/11/50 ff
in Paris 12/2/32, 19/2/32
in Rome 1/4/32, 8/4/32, 15/4/32, 20/4/32, 22/4/32, 7/10/38, 9/12/38, 25/12/38, 30/12/38
in Rotterdam 12/8/38
in Venice 17/6/32
laity's parochial power 15/8/69
Lambeth conference 22/6/76
localist character of 27/10/80
low church service in 16/5/75
missions of
G at lodging house service 21/1/72
music of, G's memorandum on, printed 7/1/94
Offertory integral part of service 4/2/44
on the Continent 14/10/38
orders of 24/9/38
Papacy and 20/10/96
patronage and
G's attitude to church parties 14/6/83
poor music of 8/12/39, 13/9/40
Prayer Book 13/5/32
arranged by G for family use 17/4/42, 22/12/44, 16/2/45
lectionary reform 7/5/70 c, 9/5/70, 10/5/70, 25/6/70 c, 2/7/70 c, 3/5/71, 6/5/71 c, 20/5/71, 6/6/71, 24/6/71, 24/6/71 c, 29/4/72
Puseyite clergy in 20/6/42

Queen Anne's Bounty
G on Board of 19/7/76
reform of 23/1/33, 10/1/84, 11/1/84
article by G 30/11/32, 10/1/33
remiss in commemoration of saints 1/4/32
Royal Supremacy and 28/4/50, 29/4/72
schism with Rome 7/10/38, 31/7/42
pain of 31/3/32
state of a crushing care 29/12/50
Synod of 20/11/37, 5/2/43
system of 13/5/32, 4/5/34
the Gorham case and 13/1/50 ff
true basis of unity in 30/3/41
visible corporation spiritually endowed 20/2/48
See also Church Defence Association, church extension, Church Missionary Society, Church Pastoral Aid Society, Church Penitentiary Society, church rates, Liberal Churchmen's Union, Metropolitan Visiting Association, National Society, nonconformists, Papacy, patronage, Public Worship Regulation Bill, ritualism, Supremacy (Royal), Wales
Church of England Working Men's Protestant Union 14/1/87 n
Church of Scotland 22/5/28
Auchterarder case 24/5/39, 27/5/39
colonial committee of 25/6/40
communion service of
comments on 18/8/39
deputation from 18/6/69, 19/6/69 c
disestablishment of
establishment has not another decade to live, G thinks 18/6/78
tests for desirability of 2/11/78, 23/5/79 n
disruption of 8/3/43, 18/5/93
funeral service of 7/9/33
General Assembly of 22/5/28, 26/5/28
laity in 20/7/52, 22/7/52
non-intrusion committee of 27/6/40
patronage question in 5/4/41, 7/4/41, 15/3/42, 3/7/74, 6/7/74, 3/11/74, 16/2/75, 12/3/86
proposed end of government grant to 6/8/69 c
services attended by G 30/11/79, 7/12/79
a dismal business 6/10/72
Argyll marriage: service a mingle-mangle 12/5/79
coldness of services in 1/10/43
G likes older Presbyterian way 7/12/79
See also Church of England, Free Church of Scotland, Scotland
church parties
Canterbury regards G as party man 7/12/43
G's abhorrence of 15/2/40
Church Pastoral Aid Society 9/2/37, 16/2/37, 21/12/89 n
church patronage 14/1/43 *See also* patronage (church)
Church Penitentiary Association 23/4/57
church principles 8/1/40
feared by Roman Catholics 15/12/38
Church Principles considered in their results(1840) 18/10/41, 20/10/41
dedicated to Lyttelton 16/8/40
dedication, problematic writing of 20/8/40
Manning assisting with 16/2/40 ff, 17/7/40
plan for American reprint 5/6/41
proofs of 9/9/40 ff, 5/10/40
reviews of
Cambridge University Magazine 21/4/42
Churchman's Review 15/1/41
writing of 1/10/39 ff, 13/12/39 ff, 17/7/40 ff, 6/8/40 ff
finished 15/7/40
Church Quarterly Review
G's review of Martin, fails to publish 26/4/75, 8/5/75
Church Rate Abolition Bill
G introduces and passes 8/5/66, 18/7/66, 11/3/68 ff, 24/3/68, 24/7/68
church rates 15/3/37, 23/5/37, 30/4/38, 25/5/53 ff, 9/5/54, 1/3/56, 25/9/56, 9/3/59, 11/8/65, 4/3/66, 30/4/66
abolition of
G suggests an accommodation on 7/3/66
association to support, G discourages 14/2/41
G argues for compromise solution 8/6/58
G opposes abolition of 15/3/37, 23/5/37, 12/6/37, 21/6/54, 13/7/59, 14/5/62
G's memorandum on, printed 7/6/61, 4/5/66
G's memorandum on reform of 26/7/59, 25/4/63
G's plan for 27/11/53
Hawarden parish and 17/1/61, 24/1/61 n
See also Hawarden, Heathcote, memoranda, memoranda (printed), nonconformists
Church Rates (Compulsory) Abolition Bill
sponsored by G 19/2/68 ff
supported by Cranborne 19/2/68
Church Temporalities Bill *See* Ireland
Churchwarden, G as at Fasque 8/11/46
Cicero, house of 24/5/32
Ciprano 24/5/32
circus, G at 3/9/70, 23/2/89
Barnum's 30/1/90
Cirencester
Agricultural College 2/10/75
civil list
pensions 12/6/69 c
See also Court

civil service
common library for 5/6/69 c
competitive examinations in 5/6/69 c, 31/7/69 c, 10/11/69 c, 23/11/69, 8/12/69, 25/2/70 n
cabinet committee would insulate Clarendon and Bright 23/11/69
effect on chief whip's patronage 8/12/69
foreign office's notorious exemption from 6/12/70
Lowe's contribution to 23/11/69
Order in Council for 28/5/70 c
to be considered departmentally 9/8/69 c, 7/12/69 c, 31/12/69
treasury minute on 16/5/70
expenditure in, committee on 15/2/73 c, 18/2/73, 10/5/73 c, 24/5/73 c, 21/6/73 c
expenditure on 10/5/73 c, 21/6/73 c
G's evidence to Ridley Royal Commission on establishments 21/7/88, 23/11/88
not to stand for Parliament 31/10/84
reform of 23/1/54, 26/1/54, 10/7/55
salary increases demanded by 3/12/72 c, 9/12/72 c
Trevelyan's MS book on 26/1/53
writers in public offices 24/5/73 c, 7/6/73 c
See also memoranda, Northcote/Trevelyan report
Civita Vecchia 19/1/39, 22/7/49, 27/7/49, 8/11/50 ff, 19/2/51
Clarence House (Edinburgh) 5/4/83
Clarendon, Earl of *See* Villiers
Clarendon Press *See* Oxford University Press
Clarendon Trust
G trustee of 16/7/58, 13/6/65, 23/6/65, 3/5/67, 22/11/67
wound up 26/4/71
Clark, Andrew, Sir (1826–1893), 1st Baronet (1883), G's physician 19/11/59, 26/7/69 ff, 7/8/69, 30/12/69, 29/5/71 ff, 18/6/71, 22/8/71, 23/9/71, 23/7/73 ff, 7/8/73, 1/11/73, 19/1/74, 4/8/75, 29/3/76, 10/3/78, 16/3/79, 15/6/79 ff, 29/2/80, 31/7/80 ff, 5/10/80, 13/1/81 ff, 23/2/81 ff, 5/5/81 ff, 14/8/81, 20/4/82, 24/2/84, 11/3/84 ff, 6/4/84, 2/1/85, 7/9/85, 29/10/85, 9/3/86, 10/3/86 ff, 7/4/86 ff, 2/10/86, 14/1/87 ff, 1/8/87 ff, 9/3/89, 21/2/90, 14/4/90, 13/2/91, 10/5/91 ff, 22/6/91 ff, 6/3/92, 22/5/92, 30/7/92 ff, 18/10/92, 31/10/92 c, 15/12/92, 8/2/93, 13/3/93 ff, 23/4/93 ff, 3/7/93 ff, 23/2/94
at Hawarden 17/12/75 ff, 31/12/81 ff, 28/9/85 ff, 6/11/87, 14/9/91 ff
at Penmaenmawr 17/8/74 ff
attending Granville 30/3/91 ff
attending W. H. G 2/3/89 ff, 27/4/89, 21/9/90 ff, 5/7/91 ff
death of 3/11/93, 6/11/93
a heavy loss 29/12/93
declines permission for G's Midlothian visit 7/1/83
finances of 16/11/93 n
G at memorial service for 11/11/93
G's resignation as liberal party leader and opposes it 10/1/75
G's retirement from politics and 13/3/73, 26/11/82, 1/6/86
G staying with in Perthshire 22/9/84
health of 30/10/93
letters from G to, printed 22/10/81, 20/1/83, 27/10/92, 12/1/93
memorial to 21/12/93, 3/5/94
on ship with G 31/8/80
treatment of G's throat and 16/7/85 ff
class
Acland deplores G's excessive references to 15/6/86
cattle plague voting a class question 10/7/83
classes' opposition to reforms 12/11/86
G a thoroughgoing inequalitarian but dislikes growing spirit of class 24/5/86
G warped by the spirit of anti-class? 24/5/86
leisured and wealthy 13/10/70, 14/8/82
Lords' willingness to act as class encourages socialism 23/4/86
middle class
persecuted in Naples 13/2/51
opposition to public interest by professional classes 14/8/82
professional classes, monopoly, and the tories; memorandum printed 14/8/82
Unionists warped by the spirit of 24/5/86
union of classes 16/9/80
upper classes
ill-qualified to guide the community 10/5/80
See also working class
Cleeve, St. Mary's Abbey 25/1/77
Cleopatra's Needle *See* Egypt, London
clergy
artfully constructed monopoly of professional classes in 14/8/82
clergy of established church will always be a tory corps d'armée 3/7/85
Clergy Relief Bill 23/4/49, 2/5/49, 6/5/49, 18/6/62, 9/7/62
Cleveland Commission *See* Oxford (University of)
Clewer
House of Mercy at
G doing accounts of 5/12/53

G sending rescue cases to 4/3/51, 4/7/51, 31/7/63
G visits 5/6/54
Clifton, Emma *See* rescue work (significant cases)
Clinton, Henry Pelham Fiennes Pelham- (1785–1851), 4th Duke of Newcastle (1795), protectionist tory; G's patron for his Newark seat 6/7/32, 15/7/32, 30/7/32, 9/9/32, 9/10/32, 25/10/32, 9/6/33, 22/6/33, 11/10/33, 6/2/34, 3/4/34, 4/8/34, 15/12/34, 30/12/34, 28/11/37, 11/7/39, 2/12/39, 10/4/42, 22/12/45 n
ruin of 18/11/42
Clinton, Henry Pelham Fiennes Pelham- (1811–1864), Earl of Lincoln, divorced Lady Lincoln 1850, 5th Duke of Newcastle 1851, G's friend and patron, Peelite M.P., secretary for war 1852–2, for colonies 1859–64 8/6/30, 23/4/31, 13/5/31 ff, 21/5/31 ff, 22/10/31, 6/7/32, 7/10/32, 4/12/32, 15/12/32 ff, 26/4/33, 2/8/34, 11/3/35, 21/3/35, 20/1/36, 11/3/38, 30/3/40, 29/6/41, 21/10/41, 18/11/42, 3/5/45, 30/12/46, 15/3/49, 28/9/49, 16/5/51, 15/1/52 ff, 9/2/52, 27/2/52, 31/3/52, 28/4/52, 29/11/52, 12/2/53, 29/7/53, 13/8/53, 6/10/53, 17/12/53, 31/5/54, 21/11/54, 10/8/59, 30/5/60, 5/8/61, 12/4/62, 17/2/93
1853 budget and 14/4/53
at Coblenz 24/8/38
at Hawarden 7/9/49 ff
corn laws and 6/12/45, 20/12/45
death of 19/10/64
last of G's contemporaries who were also political friends 19/10/64
divorce of 26/2/50
G examined as witness in 1/4/50, 28/5/50
G's personal statement to Commons on 14/8/57
funeral of 27/10/64
G as trustee and executor of 1/7/56, 26/10/64 ff, 8/12/64, 5/1/65, 16/10/65 ff, 2/12/67, 12/6/68, 8/9/70, 25/1/74, 14/3/74, 15/3/74, 10/5/75, 28/9/77, 6/6/78 ff, 25/6/78
chaotic condition of estate 28/10/64 ff
deed demitting G's trusteeship 9/8/78
resigns as 9/7/78, 28/1/81
G guardian of his children 26/5/43, 31/8/53, 27/10/71, 27/1/73, 6/6/75, 12/6/75
governmental crisis and 26/2/51
G reports on Lady Lincoln to, from Italy 31/7/49 ff
G's warm conversation with in Carlton 27/2/52
ill-health of 25/11/63, 10/2/64, 24/3/64, 18/4/64, 29/5/64
in Rome 5/12/38 ff
last illness of 5/10/64 ff
marital problems of 26/5/43, 29/6/43 ff, 31/10/44, 14/11/47, 2/8/48, 20/6/49 ff, 16/8/49 ff, 1/8/53
opposes Derby's government from first 24/2/52
outbreak of war and 22/2/54
Roebuck committee and
refuses to answer on cabinet & outbreak of war 28/4/55
Roebuck's motion and 24/1/55, 18/2/55
stands nearly alone among Peelites 26/3/52
supports G over 1861 budget 13/4/61
the Peelites and 9/12/47
thinks Hardinge shabby 24/2/52
See also Clumber, Crimean war, Opdebeck, Peelites, Thistlethwayte
Clio 29/11/76 n
Cliveden (Sutherland) 15/6/48, 29/7/54, 4/6/57, 4/7/57, 4/6/59, 13/8/59, 10/3/60, 12/5/60, 2/6/60, 23/6/60, 21/7/60, 23/4/61, 11/5/61, 18/5/61, 15/6/61, 13/1/62, 20/1/62, 15/2/62, 15/3/62, 2/5/62, 31/5/62, 14/2/63, 21/2/63, 14/3/63, 21/3/63, 10/4/63, 13/6/63, 11/7/63, 2/4/64, 23/4/64, 17/1/65, 6/5/65, 3/6/65, 8/7/65, 21/4/66, 30/6/66, 11/8/66, 21/9/66, 1/3/68, 21/3/68, 15/3/73, 1/11/84
Argyll reading Tennyson aloud at 4/6/59
delightful evening discussing future punishment 2/4/64
Garibaldi at 23/4/64
glees sung at on a Sunday 5/6/59
G's conversation with Garibaldi at 24/4/64
G sculling at 23/4/64
See also Campbell, Gower
clôture *See* cabinet, Commons (House of)
Club, The *See* clubs
clubs, G guest at
Athenaeum 4/3/91
library of 5/10/92, 7/10/92
Brooks's 27/1/82, 7/10/84, 28/9/92, 6/3/94
with private secretaries 6/3/94
Devonshire 14/5/81, 2/8/82, 21/11/84, 21/2/87
Eighty club 11/7/84
Garrick 19/4/71, 24/9/77, 14/9/82
Reform 7/9/81, 14/8/82, 18/7/89, 19/7/93
Savage
too long and clouds of tobacco fearful 14/6/79
The Club, Oxford 6/2/90

clubs, G member of
Biarritz club 17/12/91 n, 29/12/91
Carlton 7/3/33, 8/3/33, 25/3/33, 18/4/33, 26/4/33, 3/6/33, 1/7/33, 22/7/33, 26/2/34, 18/4/34, 23/4/34, 28/5/34, 12/7/34, 29/7/34, 20/12/34, 23/5/35, 12/6/35, 25/6/35, 2/2/36, 22/2/36, 12/7/37, 27/5/38, 30/5/38, 28/6/38, 27/6/40, 12/4/48, 20/10/54, 9/4/55, 30/4/59, 1/5/59
billiards at 13/12/37
Disraeli vilipended in 25/7/56
excessive optimism about general election 30/4/59
G in lion's den at 20/12/52
G's warm talk with Newcastle on sofa 27/2/52
library cttee., G on 30/5/37, 14/6/37, 9/2/39, 12/2/39, 20/2/40, 16/5/40, 1/2/41 ff
resigns from 15/3/60, 29/3/60
tea at 13/6/42
Fine Arts 15/7/61 n, 17/7/61
Glee club 22/3/34
Grillion's 31/1/40, 5/2/40, 10/2/41, 1/9/41 ff, 29/6/42 ff, 5/6/44, 7/5/45, 21/4/47 ff, 12/7/48, 4/5/50, 23/7/50, 16/7/51, 21/4/52, 30/6/52, 2/4/56, 3/5/56, 2/7/56, 29/6/59, 15/2/60, 25/4/60, 9/2/61, 24/4/61, 14/5/62, 29/4/63, 7/5/64, 9/7/64, 10/2/66, 27/6/66, 9/2/67, 29/4/68, 10/6/68, 4/5/70, 20/7/70, 3/5/71, 6/7/72, 18/2/78, 11/3/78, 9/5/79, 3/5/80, 25/6/81, 1/8/81, 2/4/83, 23/7/83, 3/5/84, 14/7/84, 11/5/85, 15/2/86, 22/3/86, 2/5/87, 27/6/87, 11/2/88, 9/4/88, 25/2/89, 3/5/89, 13/5/89, 24/6/89, 21/4/90, 5/5/90, 16/6/90, 4/8/90, 3/12/90, 31/1/91, 2/2/91, 13/4/91, 9/5/92, 20/2/93, 27/2/93, 10/4/93, 24/4/93, 25/4/93, 31/7/93, 10/9/93
Chamberlain blackballed for despite G's support 11/2/88
G dines alone at 13/4/85
National Liberal
39 Club dinner in 4/4/89
golden wedding reception and speech at 26/7/89
library of 17/11/88
library of, G's speech on 2/5/88
President of 21/11/82, 9/3/83, 3/5/83, 4/11/84, 24/6/87
Oxford and Cambridge 28/2/33, 4/3/33, 9/3/33, 1/6/35, 30/5/37, 29/6/37, 23/11/37, 4/12/37 ff, 12/3/38, 24/9/59, 29/5/78
G chairman of 29/5/40
Reform 17/5/69
reluctance to join 17/5/69 n
The Club 21/4/57, 23/2/58, 17/5/59, 15/5/60, 2/7/61, 8/4/62, 12/5/63, 15/12/68, 14/2/71, 27/2/72, 20/5/73, 28/5/78, 22/4/79, 28/6/81, 28/2/82, 22/1/86, 10/5/87, 13/5/90
Clumber(Newcastle) 9/10/32, 7/1/35, 20/1/37, 20/12/39, 15/1/52 ff, 26/10/64, 7/12/64, 17/10/65, 11/5/75, 6/6/78
fire at 26/3/79, 14/4/79 ff
See also Clinton (G as trustee), Peelites
Clydesdale Junction railway *See* railways (G shareholder in)
Clyffe, Corton, Lowestoft (J. J. Colman) 17/5/90 ff, 26/6/91 ff, 16/7/91 ff
coach journeys
abroad 2/2/32 ff, 22/2/32 ff, 8/3/32, 26/4/32 ff, 5/6/32 ff, 10/7/32 ff, 12/9/38 ff, 11/10/38 ff, 25/1/39 ff, 25/9/45 ff, 12/11/45 ff, 15/6/49, 23/7/49 ff, 26/10/50, 21/2/51 ff, 4/3/59, 10/10/66
costs of horses and coach 29/10/50
accidents 14/2/34, 7/1/35, 3/6/55
in Britain 15/9/25, 15/12/25, 19/1/26, 13/3/26, 13/4/26, 19/7/26, 20/9/26, 5/12/26, 18/1/27, 2/4/27, 2/5/27, 22/9/27, 3/12/27, 22/1/28 ff, 11/4/28 ff, 6/6/28, 29/7/28 ff, 21/2/29, 6/7/29, 1/4/30, 20/12/31, 28/7/32, 16/8/32, 23/9/32 ff, 24/10/32, 10/2/34, 7/8/34 ff, 18/12/34 ff, 14/1/36, 15/10/36, 13/1/37 ff, 25/7/37 ff, 27/11/39 ff, 23/12/39, 24/9/40 ff, 30/11/40, 26/8/42, 11/10/43, 12/8/46, 29/12/46, 31/3/47, 7/7/47, 18/7/47, 18/10/47, 2/1/57, 24/9/63
coal
lock-out of 1893 6/10/93, 11/10/93, 5/12/93, 6/12/93
cabinet's conciliation measures for 10/11/93, 13/11/93 c
G's letter of conciliation 13/11/93
Rosebery as conciliator 13/11/93 c
See also Hawarden Castle (estate of), Mundella, national debt, Primrose, Stansfeld
coal duty
speech on 12/6/43
coal famine
favours coal owners 22/2/73
great public calamity 22/2/73
no governmental remedy possible 22/2/73
coalition
conditions for 18/12/52

coalwhippers
G at meeting of 14/5/51
G on select ctte. for 6/6/51 ff
Lords committee on
G gives evidence to 23/7/57
Coalwhippers Bill 17/7/43 ff, 1/8/43 ff, 19/6/56 n
Cobden, Richard (1804–1865), free-trader and radical M.P. 23/1/41, 26/11/52, 7/1/55, 12/1/56, 16/6/57 ff, 12/11/59, 10/6/61, 4/3/62, 1/4/68, 8/7/86, 25/2/94
almost reckless in aversion to Palmerston, Morley thinks 24/10/81 n
at Hawarden 12/9/59
a worrying man on corn? 25/8/41
Burnard's bust of 7/7/65
death of
G shocked by 3/4/65
finances of 13/10/92
French treaty and 12/9/59, 13/9/59, 19/1/60
G writes Instructions for 10/1/60, 11/1/60, 15/1/60
funeral of, G attends 7/4/65
Morley's biography of, G's involvement in 20/6/77 n, 29/1/78 n, 24/10/81
motion opposing Palmerston's China policy does honour to the Commons 3/3/57
name is great: & will be greater 7/4/65
Peel's panegyric on 30/6/46, 10/7/46
portrait of 2/4/69
Walsall by-election and 23/1/41
See also France, free trade, Herbert (Sidney), Morley, radicalism
Cobden Club 31/1/81
G addresses on Franco-Prussian war 23/7/70
inaugural dinner of
G's speech at crudely executed 21/7/66
publications of 31/1/81, 29/8/81
Cobden Treaty 12/9/59, 11/1/60, 21/1/60, 23/1/60 n, 25/1/60, 3/2/60, 8/3/60, 9/3/60, 6/10/62, 5/7/71 c, 29/7/71 c, 5/8/71 c, 30/6/81, 24/10/81
expectations of fully sustained 24/1/72
G receives deputations on 3/2/60
not beginning new system of tariff treaties 4/1/82
prosperous ending to 9/3/60
renegotiation of 16/1/69, 25/11/69, 29/11/69, 16/1/70, 27/1/70, 24/8/71, 21/10/71 c, 24/10/71 c, 27/10/71 c, 31/10/71 c, 1/11/71, 8/11/71 c, 11/12/71 c, 14/12/71 c, 19/1/72 c, 24/1/72, 27/1/72 c, 10/2/72 c, 14/2/72, 15/2/72 c, 9/4/72 c, 24/8/72, 17/9/72, 10/10/72 c, 12/10/72 c, 14/10/72 c, 5/12/72 c, 19/12/72, 24/1/73 c, 27/1/73, 10/7/73 c
See also Cobden (Richard), France
Cobhame military review
G attends 21/6/53
Coblenz 16/8/38 ff
cockamaroo (Russian bagatelle) 21/10/53, 1/11/53
coercion *See* Ireland
coffee
causing G's insomnia? 28/3/48
Coggeshall, visit to with O'Connell 10/7/34
coinage 21/8/62
coins, G's collection of 2/8/79
Coldstream 26/9/76 ff
Collection of Taxes Bill
defeated 20/6/64
Collections, book of, kept by G 18/5/28 ff
collections, G's *See* books, coins, pictures, porcelaine
colliers
wages of 20/10/69
Collins, E. *See* rescue work (significant cases)
Cologne 23/7/32, 14/8/38 ff, 14/11/45, 10/11/58, 15/9/79, 25/8/86, 18/9/86
cathedral, building of 23/7/32, 15/8/38, 10/11/58, 15/9/79
Cologne Choral Union, tour of U.K. 19/6/53
Cologne singers 27/5/54
Colonial Bishopric Fund (G trustee) 27/4/41, 10/6/41, 12/6/41, 18/6/42, 16/5/45, 17/6/47, 30/6/47, 23/6/48, 14/5/49, 7/7/52, 6/6/56, 19/6/91
Colenso and 30/3/65 n, 12/5/65, 20/6/65, 19/7/68, 10/8/68
Colenso sues and wins 20/6/65, 26/6/65, 27/6/65, 21/11/65, 22/11/65, 7/12/65
G's speech at meeting of 19/6/91
colonial bishoprics 24/4/41 ff, 7/5/46, 9/6/53
colonial church 22/2/38, 16/3/46, 13/1/50 ff, 6/5/50
episcopal patents not to be issued to colonies with representative governments 6/8/69 c
G's Colonial Church Bill 16/2/52, 28/4/52, 18/5/52, 19/5/52 ff, 24/5/52, 22/6/52, 23/6/52, 18/5/53, 18/7/53, 19/7/53, 2/8/53, 28/3/54 ff, 10/4/54, 29/6/54, 23/1/55
G purposely mute during debate 20/3/54
Colonial Office 11/5/35, 20/7/38, 27/6/39, 23/12/45 ff
farewell to 4/7/46
G as Secretary of State 22/12/45 ff
G as undersecretary 26/1/35 ff, 18/4/35, 27/6/82
G reorganising 9/4/46, 16/5/46 ff
official dinner 9/6/46

Colonial Reform Association 20/2/50
Colonial Society 27/2/43, 10/3/69
colonial system, paper on 27/10/35
colonies 10/5/37, 24/11/37, 25/11/37, 16/2/49, 16/3/49, 12/4/49, 26/6/49, 27/1/72 c
chartered companies and 18/10/93
essentially bad, Ripon thinks 4/11/93 n
colonial alarmism 24/12/84
Colonial Committee planned 19/3/41
Colonial Conference 14/4/87 n, 14/5/87
concurrent endowment and, G expects a speech uncorked on from Disraeli 16/7/73
copyright in 24/1/73
corn bills and 29/4/43
defence of
G's arguments to select committee 6/6/61
G's memorandum on, printed 19/1/70, 13/10/70
make war at U. K.'s expense 25/11/69
troop withdrawals 28/1/70 c, 29/8/70, 4/7/71, 5/7/71 c
unnecessary by U. K. if colonies control own foreign policy 29/12/71
differential duties for 18/3/42 ff
emigration to 19/3/70 c
Fenianism and
G fears may be formidable in 22/10/66
finances of
G's memorandum on 14/12/61
foreign policy and 5/4/93
G's lectures on 7/1/52, 12/10/55, 12/11/55, 12/10/57, 3/9/67
G's memorandum on colonial trade 8/2/62
G's need to speak truths on 13/5/50
G's writings on 1/12/48 ff
intercolonial duties
regret recorded 17/6/71 c
joint imperial representation, difficulties of 30/4/72
military expenditure in 28/1/60
missions, chiefly colonial, G's lecture on 7/1/52
Pius IX discusses Roman Catholicism in with G 22/10/66
political processes in
nationalisation of Canada one of the most interesting 15/10/72
protectorate: definition of 20/1/85 c
responsible government in 28/12/58
and Ionia 28/12/58
now fixed policy of British government 28/12/58
restrict action of home govt. in on religion 15/6/40
right action on religion in 15/6/40
royal commission on defence of British possessions and commerce abroad 12/6/80, 15/6/80, 10/3/84, 5/5/84 c
Royal Commission on health exhibition declined 9/7/84 c
royal commission on imperial security, proposed by Russell 18/6/70 c
state religion, desirability of 9/6/40
tariffs of
control by colonies of 16/5/71, 22/5/71, 29/12/71, 25/1/72, 6/7/72 c, 3/12/72
differential tariffs not an articulus of separation 14/10/72
trade with 8/12/41, 18/3/42 ff
See also Africa, Australia, Bechuanaland, British East Africa Company, British Honduras, British South Africa Company, Burma, Canada, Cape Colony, Ceylon, Colonial Bishopric's Fund, colonial church, Demerara, Dilke, emigration, Empire, Eyre case, Fiji, France, Germany, Gibraltar, Gold Coast, Gower, Grinqualand West, Heligoland, Imperial Federation League, Jamaica, Leeward Islands, Mauritius, memoranda, memoranda (printed), missions, Na
New Hebrides, Orange Free State, Singapore, slavery, Solomon Islands, South Africa, Swaziland, Transvaal, Uganda, West Indies, Wodehouse, Zanzibar, Zululand
Colonsay 30/8/80
colour *See* Homer
Columbus, curious account of 19/4/38
Colwood Park, Sussex (Mr. Justice Bowen) 25/7/90
Combe *See* Coombe
Comédie Française
performing in private houses in London 23/6/79, 2/7/79, 1/7/93
commerce, minister of
G declines request for 20/3/71, 25/10/83 c
commercial treaties
conditions for Foreign Office negotiation of 5/3/83 c
committees
distracting and dissipating effect of 16/2/39
See also select committees
committees of cabinet *See* cabinet
Commons, House of 7/4/30, 22/9/31
abstract resolutions, G deplores 18/2/73 n
Address and 17/2/86
bill for shorter parliaments considered by G 5/12/88
Bradlaugh case and
House acted *ultra vires* 11/6/81
budget of 1860
G's most arduous operation 10/2/60

burning of 20/10/34, 14/1/35
business of 14/7/43
calm in means progress 15/3/81
C. G attending 22/3/41, 14/2/42
Chiltern Hundreds and
G's attempt to change 8/4/93
class interests in 3/1/71
clôture in 8/11/71 c, 15/11/80 c, 15/12/80, 20/1/81, 22/1/81 c, 29/1/81 c, 9/1/82 c, 7/4/82
American solution to 7/1/82 c
Gibson's amendment on 29/7/82 c, 12/8/82 c, 9/10/82, 17/10/82, 20/10/82 c, 31/10/82, 2/11/82
committees of
membership of 8/5/80, 22/5/80 c, 29/5/80 c, 1/6/80
devolution of power from 23/10/80
dissolution considered 19/6/66, 25/6/66, 26/6/66, 13/3/73 c, 17/3/73, 18/1/74, 20/1/74, 23/1/74 c, 15/5/86, 2/6/86 ff
decided on 21/1/74
G's memorandum on, printed 20/1/74
division on Cobden's motion does honour to 3/3/57
division on Tests missed: a sin 30/4/44
establishment of 25/11/80
expedition of business in 13/3/69 c
family taken to 16/5/39
first attendance as M.P. at 29/1/33
Front Bench, G continues to sit on after retirement as party leader 15/2/75
G abstaining deliberately 19/2/52
G has no intention of quitting 23/2/74
G Leader of
1865 28/10/65 ff
Goulburn encourages G to speak more 6/3/40
Grand Committees of 8/11/71 c, 23/10/80, 11/11/80, 1/2/82 c, 19/6/82 c, 30/12/82, 5/3/83 c, 17/4/83, 7/7/83 c, 10/8/83, 24/1/84 c, 31/10/92
G's behaviour in
Duchess of Sutherland gives excellent advice on 14/5/60
G's last speech, and last appearance in 1/3/94
G's parliamentary jubilee 13/12/82
G's petition on reform presented 2/7/31
G troubled before start of Session of 30/1/93
G uses egg and wine during budget speech 10/2/60
home rule and 5/5/86
hooting incident in 12/4/78
keeps G excessively from home 5/2/40
land bill 1881
G in House 24-36 hours per week 28/6/81
legislative timetabling difficulties in 24/3/70, 12/4/70
bills abandoned 25/6/70 c, 2/7/70 c, 16/7/70 c, 28/6/73 c, 10/7/73 c
liberal party and liberal unionists' seats in 3/8/86
liberty, special guardian of 19/7/82
library of, G working in 6/11/74, 15/6/88
lighting in 16/5/39
maiden speech 3/6/33, 8/6/33
first remarks, on Newark petition 30/4/33
intended 6/3/33, 2/4/33, 28/5/33, 30/5/33, 31/5/33
second remarks, on Edinburgh petition 21/5/33
ministerial confidence of the root principle of our institutions 6/12/85
morning sittings 2/4/70 c, 5/6/71
moved like an army for Irish disestablishment 3/6/69
night work in disruptive 15/4/43
number of divisions voted in 26/7/42
number of M. Ps., conclave on 27/11/67, 2/12/67, 14/2/68
obstruction and blockage in 1/4/78, 23/10/80, 11/1/81 ff, 17/1/81, 21/1/81 ff, 1/2/81 ff, 7/6/81, 10/11/81 c, 6/1/82 c, 18/1/82, 13/3/82, 1/4/82, 1/5/82, 12/6/82, 16/6/82, 23/6/82, 30/6/82, 8/7/82 c, 12/8/82, 17/8/82, 20/10/82 c, 21/10/82 c, 27/2/83, 17/5/83, 31/7/83, 20/3/84, 22/3/84, 6/2/86, 15/2/86 c, 4/3/93 ff, 31/5/93 ff, 6/7/93
41 hour sitting adjourned by the Speaker 2/2/81
by tories 8/6/82
G's Resolution for a quasi Dictatorship 3/2/81
G's share of sitting, 19 hours 1/7/82
informal cabinet on 1/2/81
Resolutions on 30/1/82 c, 1/2/82 c, 3/2/82, 7/2/82 c, 11/2/82 c, 18/2/82 c, 20/2/82, 24/10/82 c, 10/11/82, 28/11/82, 30/11/82, 1/12/82
sad scene never to be forgotten 27/7/93 ff, 31/7/93
tory procedural proposals 21/2/87 ff, 4/3/87, 1/4/87, 5/4/87
obstruction and devolution in, memorandum printed 23/10/80, 11/11/80
opposition bench
G on for first time for 15 years 6/7/66
payment of members 29/5/86 n, 31/12/91, 20/7/92, 22/7/92, 31/1/93, 9/2/93, 24/3/93 c

Commons, House of (*cont.*)
opposition bench (*cont.*)
Carnegie's offer 21/4/92 n
G devises scheme for 2/7/88, 6/7/88 n
G's memorandum on, printed 22/7/92
G to take no part in debate 24/3/93 c
to be opposed 2/4/70 c, 5/4/70
poor attendance by official members in 2/8/69
private bills in 15/11/73 c, 1/2/82 c, 7/7/83 c
questions in
interlocutory/consequential questions an impediment to public business 31/1/82
resignation, explanation of 4/2/45
sarcastic questions in, not to be answered 19/6/80 c
shorter parliaments, G supports 15/5/34, 21/11/92 c
Speakership of 18/1/71, 27/10/71 c, 31/10/71 c, 6/11/71, 8/11/71, 11/12/71 c, 18/12/71 c, 10/11/83 ff, 13/11/83 c, 17/11/83 c, 23/11/83 c, 3/12/83, 11/12/83
strangers in 26/5/70
thought-reading demonstration in, G attends 19/6/84
votes of confidence 1/5/41 ff, 6/7/49, 27/6/84 c
fearful character of 16/1/40
Irish University Bill to be regarded as 3/3/73 n
See also Bradlaugh (case of), Brand, Denison, May, Peel, speeches
Commons Protection League 3/8/76 n
communism 2/12/83
community of goods 3/7/39
Como, Lake 5/7/32, 20/9/38, 31/7/49 ff, 3/10/66
Lady Lincoln found at 31/7/49 ff
site shown to C. G 6/10/66
company
as channel of sin 26/10/45
Compensation for Disturbance Bill *See* Ireland
compositions by G *See* music
Concert of Europe *See* Europe (Concert of)
concurrent endowment *See* Ireland
Confederacy *See* United States
confession
not made freely, even on paper 17/1/47
voluntary and periodic 25/12/40
Congo 24/10/82 c, 3/4/83
neutralisation of 20/11/84 c
Portugal and 26/5/83 c
conic sections 28/6/31 ff
conscience
liberation of 27/7/40
conservatism
depends largely on inflaming public passion 28/2/85
G prejudiced in views on? 28/2/85
G's 6/7/84, 9/7/84 n
history of G's relationship to 10/5/80, 25/4/88 n, 26/10/92
religion and 4/3/38, 9/5/41
unqualified to resist dangerous innovation 28/2/85
See also memoranda (printed)
Conservative association of City of London 9/2/36, 19/3/36, 13/4/36
conservative party
ballot and 11/8/71
Beaconsfield's finance and 30/9/85
Canning the Exemplar of G and Gaskell 9/9/71
causes assisting the success of, memorandum printed 14/8/82
class interest dominates in 10/12/85
country members, regrettable decline of 24/7/71
dangerous and demoralised condition of 9/9/85
decline of reverence in
G's memorandum on, printed 15/8/90
deeply wounded by sugar crisis 17/6/44
Derby's view of reunion of 4/2/57
deviance from conservatism by 10/5/80
disunity in 22/7/44
end of Peel's government and 2/7/46 ff, 9/7/46, 10/7/46, 13/7/46
expectations that G will lead 10/7/46
future of 1/2/40, 3/5/41, 5/8/44, 20/12/45
G denies all obstructive 27/2/52
G hopes for liberal policy from 24/2/52
G of different turn of mind to 25/3/44
G resents comparisons of Peel's party with present day's 11/8/71
G's early conservatism 11/8/71
G's row with Bentinck 24/8/46
G thinks tory govt. with Bentinck leader in Commons strange 5/8/46
home rule party, cooperation with
appeal for 10/6/85, 15/12/85 ff, 2/1/86 ff
indirect taxation and 10/6/85
in power, removes tendency of opposition to economy 13/3/56
Ireland and 30/6/85
dependence on Irish vote 3/9/85
Irish land and 23/11/80
Irish settlement by, preferred by G 8/12/85 n, 9/12/85, 12/12/85 ff, 16/12/85 ff, 20/12/85 ff, 24/12/85 ff
overture to Balfour on 20/12/85, 23/12/85

jingoism of 30/9/85
lacks sufficient conviction to split 27/10/85
may soon think of another advent to power 16/9/72
national religion and 9/5/41
navy and 19/12/93 ff, 9/1/94 c
Northcote's feeble leadership of 13/1/85
Peelites and 19/2/50 ff, 27/2/50 ff, 24/2/52
Peel represented respectable conservatism 30/9/85
plays into hands of extreme liberals 30/9/85
policies Peelites agree with 31/3/57
Reform Bill 1884 and 19/8/84 ff, 25/8/84 ff
reverence forgotten by 10/12/85
strength of under new franchise 6/11/85
succession to Beaconsfield: G expects Richmond 21/4/81
taxation and 16/7/85
to be supported in complete scheme for Ireland 8/12/85
tory democracy 30/9/85
a miserable imposture 30/6/85
'tory democracy' and
demagogic nature of 11/2/85
foreign to true conservatism 11/2/85
toryism's two legs 10/12/85
Toryism that breaks up Empires 23/6/86
weakness of 4/2/57, 31/3/57
will never resume its natural position until Disraeli retires 21/3/73
See also Cecil, Disraeli, Ireland, jingoism, memoranda (printed), Parnell, Peel, Peelites, Reform Bills, Stanley
Conspiracy to Murder Bill 10/3/58
G votes against 19/2/58
Constance, Lake 15/9/38
constituencies
considered with Wolverton
Chester 31/12/73, 3/1/74
Newark 31/12/73
contested but not won
S. W. Lancashire 3/8/68 n
discussed with James: Oxford vs. S. Lancs. 9/6/61
G's parliamentary jubilee 13/12/82, 15/12/82
held
Greenwich 1868–80 18/11/68 n, 3/2/74
Leeds 1880 11/3/78 n, 13/3/78 n, 28/3/78, 12/3/79 n, 12/3/80 n, 7/4/80
Leith 1886 2/7/86
Midlothian/Edinburghshire 1880–95 16/5/78, 17/5/78, 12/3/80 n, 5/4/80, 28/11/85, 2/7/86, 13/7/92, 24/8/92 n
Newark 1832–46 30/11/32 ff
Oxford University 1847–65 5/8/47 ff
South Lancashire 1865–8 16/7/65, 18/7/65 ff
offered but not accepted
Brighton 18/3/73
Chester 9/9/73
Kincardineshire 20/11/72
Middlesex 4/2/37, 6/2/37
Newark 9/1/72 n, 25/1/74
South Lancashire 5/6/39, 9/5/44, 19/3/61 n, 18/7/61, 19/7/61
Southwark 3/12/78
West Riding? 7/2/61
suggested but not finalised
Chester? 22/7/46
City of London 13/6/61 ff, 12/7/61
Flint Boroughs 19/6/78
Liverpool 21/1/46, 2/2/46, 3/2/46
Montrose? 28/7/47, 29/7/47
Oxford City 10/5/46 n
Scarborough 17/4/47, 30/4/47, 3/5/47
S. W. Lancashire 9/7/68
Wigan 28/2/46 n, 9/3/46, 17/3/46 n, 6/4/46, 8/4/46, 30/1/47
See also Edinburghshire/Midlothian, Greenwich, Leeds, Manchester, Newark, Oxford University, South Lancashire
constitution
balanced character of
ministers to recognise and defend 2/7/83
monarchy and 16/10/93
Constitutional Defence Committee
deputation to G 17/7/60
contagious diseases
G's memorandum on, printed 18/2/63
Contagious Diseases Acts 25/7/68, 24/4/69 c, 3/12/70, 1/7/71 c, 5/7/71 c, 8/7/71 c, 19/7/71, 3/2/72 c, 26/11/72 c, 17/5/73 c, 5/2/74, 9/1/83, 21/4/83 c, 28/4/83, 29/4/92 n
Anglican petition against 24/5/73 c
cabinet nearly all ready to abandon compulsory examination 27/10/71 c, 3/11/71 c
G pairs on with Stansfeld 20/4/83
G regrets delay in inquiry 3/12/70
G's memorandum on, printed 15/7/71
Josephine Butler and 26/6/82
no cabinet support for repeal 8/7/71 c
open question in cabinet 14/4/83 c
repeal of, cabinet decides on 19/12/71 c
royal commission on 21/5/70 c, 2/5/71
See also cabinet, India, memoranda (printed)
Contemporary Review *See* publications
contract
Irish land and 2/9/69, 20/9/69
Convention Act, not to be repealed 20/4/72 c, 2/5/72

convents
  inquiry into
    agreed to 2/4/70 c, 3/4/70, 27/4/70 c
  Newdegate's bill 9/3/72 c
  See also Roman Catholic Church
converation
  as channel of sin 26/10/45
conversion, G's concern and writings 10/1/30, 11/1/30, 23/5/30
converts to Rome 1/4/45, 10/8/45, 12/1/52, 31/1/52, 16/11/69, 5/10/84
  Anne Bennett (cousin) 8/6/71
  Duchess of Buccleuch 24/9/65
  F. Oakeley 20/2/45, 10/3/45, 10/3/45 n
  G deletes Hope as executor 8/4/51
  Helen Gladstone 30/5/42 ff
  H. E. Manning 2/3/51, 6/3/51, 9/3/51, 16/3/51, 30/3/51, 6/4/51, 7/4/51
  J. Hope 6/3/51 ff, 30/3/51, 6/4/51, 7/4/51, 8/4/51
  Lady Herbert 19/3/65, 22/8/66, 13/11/73
  list of 15/10/78 n
  Miss Stuart 28/2/79, 4/3/79
  religious trials beyond G's grasp 29/12/51
  Ripon, Lord 21/8/74
  R. I. Wilberforce 2/9/54
Conway 3/9/55, 2/9/60
cookery
  G's speech on 1/5/78, 26/2/79 n
Coolattin Park, Co. Wicklow (Fitzwilliam) 26/10/77
Coombe Hurst (Mrs. Vyner) 23/6/83, 28/6/84, 13/6/85
Coombe Warren, Kingston (Currie) 19/3/84, 2/4/84, 24/7/84
  meeting of cabinet at 29/3/84
Coombe Wood, Kingston (Wolverton) 21/6/84, 12/7/84, 11/7/85, 18/7/85, 24/3/86, 3/4/86, 8/5/86, 15/5/86, 31/7/86, 1/6/89
Coopers, Chislehurst (C. Morley) 21/8/86
Copenhagen
  G's visit to 16/9/83 ff
Cop House farm *See* Hawarden Castle
Coppice, Henley (Phillimore) 11/8/60, 28/11/63, 6/8/66, 30/9/75, 9/9/79, 21/9/82, 14/7/88
copyright 16/5/36, 21/6/36, 12/4/38, 9/5/38, 20/6/38, 10/4/39, 1/5/39, 4/2/40, 19/2/40, 5/2/41, 6/4/42, 9/5/42, 2/8/42 ff, 6/8/42, 22/2/44, 18/10/44, 2/1/45, 5/4/82, 15/8/87
  in colonies 24/1/73 c
Cork Constitution
  libels G 3/6/61 n
cork cutters 1/3/60
Cormutzie, Linn of 7/9/36
corn laws 3/4/28, 17/5/33, 7/3/34, 16/3/37, 15/3/38, 19/2/39, 18/3/39, 3/4/40, 26/5/40 n, 3/5/41, 4/6/41, 23/8/41, 7/9/41, 7/10/41 ff, 23/10/41 ff, 20/1/42 ff, 10/2/43 ff, 13/3/43, 10/1/69, 3/12/85
  Cobden and 25/8/41
  corn returns 16/11/41
  crisis over 6/12/45, 16/12/45, 20/12/45
    G puzzled by its timing 16/12/45
  discussed with Young England 11/2/46
  euthanasia of 7/3/42
  government's measure unsatisfactory 1/2/42 ff
  grain substitution 13/1/42 ff
  G's conversation with Lincoln on 6/12/45, 17/12/45, 20/12/45
  G's view of repeal 6/12/45, 20/12/45
  in their nature mutable 8/12/42
  new scale 2/2/42 ff
  Peel's mem. on 17/12/41
  repeal of 30/6/46, 10/7/46, 13/7/46, 19/10/49, 22/4/80
  ruminated on 8/9/41
  slippery position of G on 10/3/43
  speech on 13/2/43, 10/3/43, 9/5/43, 13/6/43, 25/6/44
  stringent and severe 21/1/42
  the old law a delusion 6/12/45
  Walsall by-election and 19/1/41 ff
  See also Anti-Corn Law League, Peel
corporation tax 21/5/53
Corpus Christi College, Oxford 28/1/57
  G's visit to library and Ruskin's rooms 24/4/78
Correggio 18/4/32, 4/5/32
correspondence
  dictated, not written 14/1/83
  size of 5/5/53, 17/5/53, 3/3/74, 11/10/76 ff, 30/7/77 ff, 8/8/77, 8/7/78, 9/8/78, 25/6/79, 28/8/79, 23/2/80, 29/12/83
    itemised list of for one day 8/7/78
correspondence, G's *See* letters, letters from G listed under individual recipients, private secretariat, private secretaries
Corrimony (Ogilvy) 27/9/72
corrupt boroughs, abolition of 7/2/82 c, 11/2/82 c
corrupt practices 12/11/80 c
Corrupt Practices Bills
  1872 21/10/71 c, 22/1/72 c, 10/7/72 c, 15/7/72 c, 17/7/72 c
  1881 30/12/80 c, 28/5/81 c
  1883 4/12/82
Corstorphine
  G's speech at 6/7/92
Cortina 27/9/79
Corwen 6/9/56
Cosenza 9/11/38

cost of living index, G proposes 20/12/72
cotton
distress in 21/4/62, 27/12/62 n
See also Lancashire
cotton famine *See* Lancashire
coughs *See* illnesses
County Councils *See* local government
Court
back-stairs pressure by
more than there ought to be, G thinks 3/9/73
card games at
G losing money 6/4/46
civil list
Dilke's inquiry into 9/3/72 c, 11/3/72, 16/3/72, 19/3/72
G arranging 13/2/61 ff
home rule and 28/12/85
concerts at 3/5/47, 12/5/51, 6/7/53, 8/5/54, 2/6/54, 30/4/56, 2/7/56, 25/1/58, 18/6/58, 1/6/59, 22/6/59, 11/5/70, 6/7/70, 5/6/72, 26/6/72, 28/6/76, 16/7/79
Jenny Lind exquisite 28/5/47
divorced women at, position of 31/3/81
Drawing Room 21/3/33, 28/5/34, 5/3/35, 28/5/35, 18/5/37, 28/4/42, 26/2/46, 19/5/49, 27/4/54, 29/3/55, 29/5/56, 18/5/60, 27/6/61, 16/5/63, 3/5/64, 4/5/64, 14/6/64, 18/5/65, 9/3/66, 13/5/80, 6/3/83, 4/3/86
Agnes G presented at 24/3/60
really a rush 9/3/66
Eastern question and
Cambridge, black as thunder, declines to offer hand 11/3/78
G dining at 9/4/42, 30/1/46, 6/4/46, 27/3/52, 3/8/53, 20/2/61
probably for last time 7/3/50
Household peers and 1/9/92
humanity not smothered in 28/6/43
levée 26/2/34, 17/5/37, 19/2/40, 18/3/40, 12/5/41, 16/3/42, 29/3/43, 5/3/45, 18/2/46, 1/3/48, 26/2/51, 2/3/53, 20/4/53, 7/3/55, 20/2/56, 18/2/58, 6/4/59, 23/2/60, 25/2/63, 2/5/66, 12/5/66, 30/5/68, 27/2/69 c, 25/2/71, 22/3/71, 26/4/71, 14/3/72, 11/3/74, 6/3/76, 12/3/77, 11/3/78, 10/3/80, 31/5/80, 5/4/81, 23/5/81, 9/3/82, 17/6/82, 12/3/83, 23/4/83, 14/3/85, 11/5/85, 1/3/87, 2/4/89, 9/3/91, 24/4/93
G's first 20/3/33
ministerial attendance at 25/6/81 c
Mistress of the Robes
Duchess of Bedford's attempts to resign as 28/8/81
G's difficulty in filling 23/8/92, 7/9/92, 8/10/92
presentation of Address at 16/2/53
Queen's garden party 29/6/87
royal finances 27/1/40, 19/6/89 ff
Edinburgh's settlement 31/8/93 c, 8/9/93 ff, 14/9/93 ff, 18/9/93 ff, 25/10/93, 3/11/93 c, 5/11/93
impact of Radicalism on 4/7/89
'What does she do with it?', circulated to cabinet 9/9/71, 21/9/71 n
royal marriage settlements
Act of Settlement and Ferdinand of Rumania 18/10/92 ff, 9/11/92 ff
G arranges 13/2/61 ff, 13/2/71, 31/7/71, 6/1/82 c, 23/3/82
State Ball 10/5/38, 10/5/39, 3/6/41, 15/4/42, 12/5/42, 6/6/45, 13/6/49, 15/6/53, 1/5/54, 9/5/55, 25/4/56, 8/5/56
fancy dress 13/6/51
court dress, G buys 16/3/33
Court Hey (R. Gladstone) 3/8/41, 6/1/43, 27/10/44, 25/11/45, 29/7/46, 24/9/50, 19/10/52, 5/11/53, 14/6/55, 6/10/55 ff, 29/9/56, 25/10/56, 9/9/59, 10/10/61, 14/10/62, 25/8/64, 12/10/64, 18/7/65, 2/10/65, 13/10/65, 4/11/65, 18/9/67, 13/10/68, 20/10/68, 18/9/72, 21/12/72, 5/9/73, 9/4/74, 25/7/74, 23/11/74, 14/5/75, 23/9/75, 17/11/76, 23/8/79, 22/11/79, 28/1/80, 26/6/86, 18/10/90, 5/12/91
G's welcome not so warm 25/7/74
hymn singing at 27/6/86
Coutts, Angela Georgina Burdett-, Lady (1814–1906), hostess and Anglican philanthropist 26/6/61, 2/7/62, 6/5/64, 5/12/64 ff, 15/10/72, 16/5/74, 4/3/76, 13/3/76, 29/1/94
at Hawarden 25/9/62, 22/8/64
fish, wants a commission on 2/5/72 c
letters from G to, printed 6/9/80
marriage of
gross error of 11/6/81
G's attempts to prevent 6/9/80, 8/9/80, 10/9/80, 14/9/80, 19/9/80
the Gs staying with in London 17/11/64
cow, G knocked down by wild 29/8/92, 8/9/92
Cowley, Oxford 8/9/28
Cowper, E. *See* rescue work (significant cases)
Craven scholarship *See* Oxford (University of)
credit *See* Government of Ireland Bill, Ireland
credit, votes of 21/7/54, 24/7/54, 25/7/54, 30/7/70, 31/7/70, 21/6/77, 29/6/77, 25/1/78 n, 20/7/82 ff

credit, votes of (*cont.*)
Daily News and 22/6/77
Egypt 20/7/82 c, 27/7/82 ff, 21/11/82
on Eastern question
liberals oppose 26/1/78, 29/1/78, 4/2/78, 8/2/78
Sudan 1/8/84, 2/8/84 c, 5/8/84 c, 16/2/85, 17/2/85 c, 20/3/85 c, 1/4/85
to be for Sudan and military preparations 11/4/85 c, 20/4/85 c, 21/4/85 c, 25/4/85 c, 27/4/85, 11/5/85, 31/5/85
Crewe Hall, Cheshire (Crewe) 10/11/74
cricket
played 8/6/26, 23/6/26, 31/5/27, 7/6/27, 26/6/27, 5/7/27, 10/7/30 ff, 24/7/30 ff, 11/9/30, 9/8/51
played with children 26/8/50, 28/8/51
round the hat 4/9/67, 25/8/69
G plays with his four sons 24/8/69
watched 27/5/29, 12/6/29, 24/6/39, 29/6/50, 7/8/54, 16/8/56, 24/6/82
Crimean war 15/2/54, 22/6/54, 10/11/54 n
Alma, victory of 2/10/54, 11/10/54
commissariat and 23/11/54 ff
deficit caused by 3/2/55
destroys financial equilibrium 13/3/56
dislocated G's frame of mind 25/11/78 n
financing of 11/4/54, 2/5/54, 3/5/54 ff, 8/5/54 ff, 22/5/54 ff, 3/3/55, 20/4/55
role of loans 3/3/55, 13/4/55
Swedish subsidies 23/5/54
vote of credit of £3 million 21/7/54, 24/7/54
G's memorandum on sending troops for Sebastopol 22/6/54
G's review of Greville on 3/2/87 ff
G's review of Martin really an article on 26/12/77
G's speech 'in the sense of peace' 24/5/55
Kars, siege of 17/4/56, 22/4/56, 23/4/56, 26/4/56
insolent speech by Palmerston on 29/4/56
nursing in 25/11/54 n
peace protocols 29/4/56 ff, 6/5/56
periodicals on
G regards as 'all mad' 24/1/56
Roebuck's motion and 24/1/55 ff, 29/1/55, 18/2/55 ff
Sebastopol 9/2/55
Sebastopol committee 17/4/55 ff, 14/5/55, 15/5/55, 21/5/55, 20/6/55, 29/2/56 n
victory of 27/9/55
Vienna protocols 10/5/55, 14/5/55, 21/5/55, 3/8/55
See also Eastern question, France, Gordon, Phillimore, Roebuck Committee, Russell, Russia, Temple (Henry), Turkey
Crimes Bills *See* Ireland
Criminal Law Amendment Bill 31/7/85
Crinan canal 19/8/53
crises
three running together: Egypt, Gordon, franchise 2/8/84
Cromwell, Oliver 24/11/27
Crown Private Estates Bill 14/6/73 c, 5/7/73 c, 19/7/73 c, 21/7/73 n
Crystal Palace
at Sydenham 10/6/54, 8/6/55, 27/7/76, 20/3/82, 20/6/83, 26/6/85
Blondin performing at 24/7/61
'Moses in Egypt' at 29/6/88
opening of 10/6/54
Hyde Park
erection of 14/10/51
G votes to take down 29/4/52
visited 15/4/51
Cuba 24/4/69 c, 10/7/69 c
cuckoo of spring, first 30/4/94
Cuddesdon, G living at, and visits to 7/8/28, 21/6/30, 5/7/30 ff, 4/6/31, 30/7/31, 30/8/31, 8/9/31, 25/11/31, 20/1/52, 8/6/57 ff, 6/5/59
S. G confirmed there 8/5/59
Cuffnell's, Lyndhurst (Harcourt) 5/12/82
Cumbrian wrestling 5/9/73
cupping, used for treatment 2/2/40, 7/4/42, 18/10/45
curiosity
as cause of sin 26/10/45
curling 11/1/37
currency 2/1/33, 25/1/33, 22/4/33 ff, 1/7/33, 3/7/33, 9/8/33, 24/3/34, 22/2/38
G's memorandum on reform of Bank Charter Act, printed 31/3/73
notes on 1/1/34
customs
amalgamation with inland revenue planned 28/11/73 c
duties 11/3/53, 12/5/53, 13/5/53 ff, 9/6/53
reform of 12/3/53, 26/3/53, 28/3/53, 10/11/81, 12/11/81
Cyprus 4/3/79, 14/4/81, 18/4/81, 3/2/83
free institutions for, G encourages 14/4/81, 4/10/81
sickening case of 20/6/79

Dahomey 23/6/63
Fort Whydah and Portugal 26/5/83 c
Daily News 18/1/69, 5/2/69, 19/5/75, 6/4/77 n, 23/4/80, 27/9/80, 2/5/85, 19/6/85, 7/11/85, 10/12/85, 14/1/86, 18/3/86, 30/6/86, 31/7/86, 25/12/86, 5/3/94
Bulgarian horrors and 1/9/76

reveals authorship of G's Franco-Prussian war article 3/11/70
Daily Telegraph
contemptible leader in 30/8/82
G's contacts with 11/6/61, 20/3/70, 1/4/71
Hunt arranges for W. H. G to report on Ireland 2/8/66, 6/1/68, 16/1/68
Negropontis affair and 27/8/77, 19/9/77, 24/9/77, 20/11/77 n, 12/3/78 n, 30/8/82
See also Gladstone (W. H.), Hunt, Ireland
Dalkeith
G's speeches at 26/11/79, 19/3/80, 1/4/80, 21/11/85, 25/10/90, 5/7/92
Dalkeith (Buccleuch) 30/12/48 ff, 1/4/80
Dalmahoy (Morton) 1/11/37, 25/11/39
Dalmeny(Rosebery) 13/11/39, 24/11/79, 16/3/80, 28/3/80, 1/4/80, 27/8/84, 24/9/84, 9/11/85, 29/6/92
Barnbougle Castle 28/8/84
Dalzell, Motherwell (Carter-Hamilton) 6/12/79
Dante
abstract of cycle of punishments in 8/12/36
bimetallism and 2/12/92
Bunyan reminds G of 6/4/90
discussions of 11/5/54
Divina Commedia
each reading an event in life 20/1/67
G makes 'notabiliora' of 29/10/66 ff
G quotes at Monte Cassino 28/12/66 n
G's article on 16/4/92 ff
G's 'conspectus' of 3/9/86
G's speech on 6/4/89
merits of
G's letter on displayed in Dante's house in Florence 20/12/82 n
quoted in G's Journal 9/6/39, 9/5/40, 29/12/40, 27/3/42, 28/12/44, 1/11/50
studied in Florence 22/1/88
tomb of 19/3/32, 11/6/32
translation of 28/11/36, 16/6/37, 26/11/37, 9/10/38, 10/1/76, 7/8/79 ff
Virgil and 1/9/93
Danube
conference on navigation on 19/1/71 c
source of 14/9/38
Darmstadt 12/9/38
Dartmouth 27/8/80, 8/6/89
Dartmouth, Royal Naval College
G's visit to 12/7/77
Darwin, Charles Robert (1809-1882), scientist 6/12/41 n, 11/3/77, 23/10/77, 24/7/79, 9/1/86 n
Darwinian question
G lacks physical knowledge to deal with 24/12/72
Joseph Butler supplies the method for handling 24/12/72
'Darwinism and Dogma', poem on fly-leaf of journal 16/3/77
G calls on 11/3/77
G little acquainted with his works 15/1/72
G's memorandum on Darwinism, printed 17/12/81
G's offer of British Museum trusteeship declined 30/4/81
letters from G to, printed 30/4/81
survival of the fittest and Simon de Montfort 12/3/78
the age leapt to unwarranted conclusions about 15/1/72
See also Butler (Joseph), memoranda (printed)
dead, prayers for 10/9/42
Deaf and Dumb Association
G speaks at 20/5/59
Deal 22/5/66
Deal Castle (Sydney) 4/6/70, 13/8/70, 24/8/81
death
arrangements for G's funeral discussed with C. G 28/3/94
childhood and 20/9/47
G feels ten years older from death of Duchess of Sutherland 28/10/68
Newcastle's
last of G's contemporaries who were also political friends 19/10/64
of Catherine Jessy G 2/4/50 ff
of Robertson G 23/9/75
of Sir J. G 29/11/51 ff, 7/12/51
retirement from liberal leadership and
G has passed through into better life 16/1/75
very busy around G 2/2/73
Wilberforce's, on fall from horse 19/7/73
death, consideration of 29/12/28, 6/10/33 ff, 21/10/33, 11/2/34 ff, 18/6/34, 3/9/35, 22/9/35 ff, 2/10/35, 7/11/35, 14/11/35, 29/4/40, 9/5/40, 9/7/40, 21/12/46, 9/4/50 ff, 4/10/50 ff, 11/2/54, 16/6/56, 16/8/57 ff, 21/6/62, 6/2/63, 29/9/65 ff, 31/10/70, 31/12/74, 21/3/75, 19/4/76, 23/4/76, 29/12/76, 28/12/79, 29/12/86, 31/12/93
ballrooms and 3/5/36
death of Lady Beaconsfield 19/1/73
Declaration on absence of infidelity by G to the marriage bed, to be opened after G's death 7/12/96
to die in church a great euthanasia 28/12/79
verses on, printed 13/7/94
See also assassinations

death duties 26/11/80, 1/12/80, 7/12/80, 2/3/81, 5/3/81, 11/3/81, 29/3/81, 10/1/82, 13/3/82, 21/4/85 c, 27/3/88, 9/4/88, 21/4/88 ff, 23/4/88, 20/7/92, 16/2/93
 1894 budget and 25/7/94
 memorandum on, printed 2/10/80
 See also succession (legacy and probate duties)
debt *See* Hawarden, national debt, Oak Farm
Deceased Wife's Sister Bill 30/5/82, 1/1/83, 17/8/92
 G abstains on 7/2/50
 G supports 27/4/70
 no government action on 17/4/69 c
Deddington, Oxon. 19/3/31
Dee, Linn of 7/9/36, 5/9/39 ff
Dee, river
 finest in Scotland 6/9/39
Dee Bridge
 G's speeches at 16/8/87, 3/8/89
Deepdene, Dorking(Hope) 4/5/79
deer, red 6/9/39
defects
 Lady Waldegrave points out G's errors and defects to him 7/7/67
defence 2/2/53, 5/2/53
De Grey, Earl *See* Robinson
Delavigne *See* plays seen
Demerara *See* West Indies
Denbigh 9/9/52
Denison, John Evelyn (1800–1873), 1st Viscount Ossington (1872), Eton and Christ Church with G, whig M.P.; Speaker of the Commons 1857–72 20/12/30 n, 3/6/31, 28/6/31, 26/12/67, 10/7/71
 Commons business and 18/1/71
 letters from G to, printed 12/8/69, 26/5/70, 18/1/71
 resignation of 27/10/71 c
Denmark 27/1/64, 4/2/64, 5/5/64, 11/6/64, 22/6/64
 debate on an epoch in foreign policy 8/7/64
 Franco-Prussian war and 30/7/70 c, 6/8/70 c
 Fredensborg 17/9/83
 G opposes sending navy to Copenhagen 24/2/64 n, 30/4/64
 G's reply to Disraeli on 4/7/64
 G's visit to 16/9/83 ff
 non-interference in, G supports 24/6/64, 25/6/64, 3/7/64, 4/7/64
 Rosenborg Castle 17/9/83
 Victoria and 16/6/64
 See also Copenhagen, memoranda (printed)
dentist 11/10/42
 Saunders 7/10/53, 15/1/55, 25/10/62, 29/5/66, 1/6/66, 10/7/66, 7/5/67, 12/5/68, 2/5/72, 22/4/73, 29/4/73, 7/5/73, 6/6/73, 9/6/73, 3/6/75, 2/7/78 ff, 9/7/78, 12/7/78 ff, 22/7/78, 20/4/80, 24/8/82
 See also teeth
depression 4/6/38, 5/6/38 n, 6/1/39, 5/1/93
 Lady Glynne's 25/7/39, 6/8/39
deputations 21/2/42
 administrative reform 19/3/56
 advertisment tax 18/6/53
 Africa Association 18/3/53
 amalgamated engineers 10/5/64
 Anti-Income Tax League 24/4/73
 Anti-Maynooth (Newark) 1/5/45
 architects 13/5/70
 Australian Mint 28/7/59
 Aylesbury liberals 21/4/79
 bankers 12/1/53, 8/4/65, 20/4/65, 8/5/65, 11/5/65, 12/5/65
 Bank of Ireland 29/6/53
 beersellers 7/1/60, 13/3/60
 Belfast Festival 10/4/72
 B. N. A. 23/11/61
 Bulgarian horrors 7/9/76
 Burma 25/3/71
 Cambridge university tests 8/12/69
 Canada 22/5/65 ff, 16/6/65
 Canadian church 9/4/38
 cattle 8/4/42
 cattle plague 30/11/65, 8/5/83
 cattle plague in Cheshire 4/3/69
 chambers of commerce 3/2/60, 20/3/71
 charities 4/5/63
 chicory 25/1/53, 17/2/53
 China mail contract 5/7/61
 City conservancy 22/1/55
 City of London 20/5/64, 29/11/72
 civil service administration 26/1/56
 coachmakers 5/2/53
 coalwhippers 13/7/49, 7/3/52, 27/2/56, 28/4/56, 19/6/56, 5/2/57
 consolidated annuities 22/2/53
 Constitutional Defence Committee 17/7/60
 constitutional deputation to G in Florence 14/1/88
 conveyancing 24/4/65
 coopers 23/4/60
 corn trade 30/3/60
 county suffrage 21/1/74
 customs reform 11/3/53, 12/3/53
 distillers 27/2/60, 31/3/62
 doctors 10/12/44
 Dublin Chamber of Commerce 29/6/53
 Eastern question, at Hawarden 8/5/78
 Edinburgh workmen 21/6/86
 education 2/2/53
 eight hours question 16/6/92
 employers' liability 2/6/80, 3/6/80 ?
 factories 10/3/37

Farmers' Alliance 16/6/80, 21/6/82
fine arts 30/11/60
fire insurance 28/7/59
franchise 25/10/83, 31/1/84
Franchise Bill 20/3/66
friendly societies 5/3/64
from Cornwall 27/5/42
Galway contract 4/7/59, 15/7/59, 16/5/61, 17/11/62
Garibaldi 10/5/64
glass 28/4/53
glove trade 3/2/60
Greece 12/6/79
Greenwich clergy 10/4/72
Hawarden church yard gates 20/10/76
hop duty 25/6/59
hops 5/2/53, 17/2/53, 5/3/62, 30/4/62
Hyde liberals 23/9/89
Imperial federation
  G's notes for 12/4/93
income tax 9/2/57
income tax commissioners 18/7/61
income tax in Brighton 23/2/63
Irish curates 21/5/79
Irish distillers 9/6/54
Irish education 24/7/71
Irish government 28/3/93
Irish land and the 3Fs. 12/1/81
Irish mail 13/4/83
Irish presbyterians 19/12/53, 6/2/69, 17/6/69
Irish railways 7/3/65, 9/3/69
Irish schoolmasters 31/1/71
Irish stock certificates 30/4/63
Killin 2/12/79
labour M.P.s 23/2/93
Labour Representation League
  on French republic 27/9/70
law education 1/2/72
Leith 28/11/79
licensing 9/3/69
life assurance
  G's notes on 27/2/64
Limerick Harbour 2/5/65
Liverpool 29/12/79, 21/10/81, 27/10/81
Liverpool magistrates 11/4/62, 13/3/63
Liverpool shipping 18/2/56
local government 7/11/93
local taxation 12/2/69
malt credit 24/2/63
maltsters 1/4/62
Manchester Education Bill 17/2/54
Manchester liberals 23/11/89
Manchester shipping 26/2/56
millers on flour 25/1/42
miners on eight hours 3/3/93
miners on eight hours question 18/2/90
miners opposing eight hours limitation 19/4/93
Mining Association 1/5/93
National Education League 9/3/70
National Education Union 11/3/70
Nelson Memorial Fund 9/6/54
newspapers anti-stamp 28/11/54
Nottingham Irish 20/10/87
omnibuses 20/11/54
Oude, King of 4/7/59
Oxford professors 1/4/54
paper hangers 2/3/60
pawnbrokers 17/6/67
penny bank charges 21/3/61
publicans 22/4/61
Quakers on education 13/5/70
railway
  Croydon 5/10/42
railways 30/4/39, 1/7/44
raisins 23/5/53
Reform League 11/2/67
Rochdale 3/11/81
Roman Catholic Liverpudlians 21/1/68
savings banks 24/5/53
Scottish church 27/3/51
Scottish disestablishment 29/11/81, 29/8/84
Scottish education 16/4/69
Scottish episcopalians 10/5/55, 11/5/55
Scottish Free Church 2/5/90
Scottish malt spirits 21/3/54
Scottish national library 23/3/65
Scottish nonconformists on Eastern question 23/5/78
Scottish savings banks 1/7/53
Scottish temperance 29/6/60
Scottish Universities Bill 14/5/58
silk trade 3/2/60
silk weavers 13/3/60
soap 22/2/53
spirit duties 23/5/65
stage carriages 16/3/66
stamp duties 7/2/53, 20/11/54
stamps 18/3/54
Stroud Green church 2/7/85
sugar importers 25/5/54, 21/3/62
sugar refinering workmen 18/5/81
sugar refiners 21/12/53, 25/5/54, 20/5/73
Sunday openings, for and against 16/3/69
tea 23/5/53, 2/5/65
temperance 20/1/68
tobacco duties 17/2/63, 6/3/63, 18/3/63
Transvaal 3/3/81, 12/11/83
unemployment (London) 28/12/93
Unitarians 1/6/44
University of London 16/2/53
university tests 15/12/69
vestries of London 10/6/67
Water Colour Society 21/2/73
Waterford estate 17/2/70
Western bank 18/2/64

deputations (*cont.*)
wine duties 7/2/53
wine fortification 18/5/63
wine traders 27/2/60
working men's assurance 5/3/64
workmen on franchise 4/11/84
Derby, City of 19/1/47
G's visit to 20/10/87 ff
Derby, Earls of *See* Stanley
Derby, the 25/5/26
G attends with Granville
race gives G a tremor 1/6/70
G does not attend, on chief whip's advice 24/5/71
Design, School of 10/6/41, 11/10/41
G gives prizes at 24/7/44
destitution 25/11/43
Devises 31/1/77
devolution 28/1/74
Devonshire, Duke of *See* Cavendish
Devonshire Club *See* clubs
Devonshire House (Devonshire) 13/5/64, 24/6/68, 25/5/70, 24/5/71, 17/5/74, 2/6/75, 7/2/76, 8/6/77, 6/8/78, 10/5/79, 27/6/79, 30/6/79, 7/7/79, 22/7/79, 10/3/80, 22/6/81
diaries, G's *See* journals (G's)
dictionaries *See* Murray
Dictionary of National Biography
G assisting in writing entries
E. C. Hawtrey 3/1/90 n
Sir J. Gladstone 22/7/89 n, 13/11/89 n
Sir S. Glynne 17/10/89 n, 13/11/89 n
Didcot
meeting on platform of 8/7/52
diet 10/3/47, 8/3/48
Dijon 1/10/66
Dilke, Charles Wentworth, Sir (1843–1911), 2nd Baronet (1869), author and authority on imperialism; liberal M.P., foreign office under-secretary 1880–2, president of local government board 1882–5, assisted in redistribution conferences 1884, co-respondent in divorce suit 1885–6 11/11/68, 23/11/69, 3/5/73 c, 12/6/79, 8/7/79, 27/4/80 ff, 13/6/80, 4/9/80, 8/6/81, 22/7/81, 29/7/81, 6/2/82, 26/5/82, 3/8/82 c, 24/10/82 c, 4/11/82, 11/12/82 n, 14/12/82, 17/12/82, 18/12/82, 19/12/82, 31/7/83, 1/12/83, 14/7/84 ff, 17/2/85 c, 27/2/85, 3/3/85, 14/3/85, 23/3/85, 5/5/85, 6/7/85, 13/7/85, 18/7/85, 1/8/85, 9/9/85, 11/9/85, 6/11/85, 14/11/85, 10/12/85, 13/12/85, 8/8/93 c
cabinet and
caution about confidentiality 5/3/83 n
candidacy for Forest of Dean 1/7/89, 10/8/89, 5/3/91 n, 12/3/91, 4/5/92
G's memorandum on, printed 13/3/91
civil list, inquiry into 9/3/72 c, 11/3/72, 16/3/72 c, 19/3/72
Crawford divorce case and 18/9/85 n, 10/12/85 n, 2/2/86, 14/2/86, 7/7/86, 18/7/86 n, 27/7/86, 2/1/87
deplorable report of 21/7/86
Dilke's Privy Councillorship and 24/7/86, 28/7/86, 1/8/86
terrible cant of verdict in 23/7/86
Egypt and 15/4/93, 17/4/93, 18/4/93 ff, 24/4/93, 1/5/93
Franco-Prussian war and 4/3/71 c
G does not mean to be sat on by 13/12/85
Greater Britain recommended by G 5/1/70
great Parliamentary loss of 7/7/86
G's regret at having had to pass him by on certain occasions 7/7/86
home rule and 21/1/86
indirect taxation and 21/4/85
Ireland and
declines chief secretaryship 8/5/82 cf
land purchase and 20/5/85, 21/5/85
local government and 20/5/85 ff, 5/6/85 c, 21/7/85
visit to 5/6/85 c
letters from G to, printed 15/1/70, 11/3/72, 11/5/80, 18/6/80, 5/9/80, 1/1/81, 28/7/81, 2/11/81, 1/1/82, 4/1/82, 31/5/82, 28/12/82, 31/12/82, 11/4/83, 2/8/83, 28/9/83, 6/11/83, 8/12/83, 13/12/83, 15/4/84, 13/5/84, 30/5/84, 8/8/84, 15/8/84, 29/9/84, 26/10/84, 13/11/84, 23/11/84, 26/11/84, 28/11/84, 14/12/84, 13/1/85, 21/4/85, 24/4/85, 21/5/85, 21/7/85, 18/9/85, 28/9/85, 2/2/86, 1/3/94
local government and 10/9/83
curious speech on 10/12/85
marriage of 18/9/85
naval defence and 1/3/94
plaguy speech by 4/5/92
Queen and the Duchy and 12/12/82 ff, 19/12/82
redistribution inquiry and 8/8/84, 9/8/84 cn, 15/8/84, 29/9/84, 6/10/84, 26/10/84, 24/12/84
Reform Bill 1884 and
conferences with tories on 7/11/84 c, 13/11/84 ff
supplying data for 6/11/83, 9/11/83 ff, 8/12/83, 13/12/83
republicanism of
mad to prosecute, G thinks 17/11/71 n, 4/12/71

magistrate presided at meeting for 29/3/73 c
Queen expects apology 3/5/80, 28/12/82 n
Queen's income tax, speech and inquiry 11/12/71 c, 25/1/72 c
resignation, threat of 16/5/85
Stead's article on 8/2/92
Straits conference, moves motion of censure on 27/3/71 c, 30/3/71
ends as egregious fiasco 3/4/71
See also Egypt, Ireland, local government, memoranda (printed), Parnell, redistribution, Reform Bills
Dingwall 2/9/53, 11/9/58
entirely metamorphosed 27/9/58
G Freeman of 2/9/53, 27/9/53
journey to abandoned 19/8/36
dinner
at 4 p.m. 15/12/49
dioramas 26/6/35, 2/7/35
directorships with cabinet office
liberals to avoid 19/8/92, 27/10/92 c, 31/10/92
Dirleton 6/9/45
disarmament 12/6/80 c
discipline
blessing of 19/4/51
destroyed by Hope and Manning's conversions to Rome 19/4/51, 11/5/51
Diseases Prevention Bill 2/8/83
disestablishment 15/2/69, 16/2/75, 17/10/84, 31/10/85 n, 3/11/85 ff, 7/11/93
Church of Scotland
has not another decade to live, G thinks 18/6/78
Dillwyn's Resolution on 9/3/86
Miall's motion on, G opposes 16/5/73, 5/7/73
presbyterians and 15/2/69, 8/4/69
principle of not yet accepted by the English people 6/11/85
See also Church of England, Church of Scotland, Ireland, liberal party, Liberation Society, Lords (House of), nonconformists, Palmer, Wales
Disraeli, Benjamin (1804–1881), 1st Earl of Beaconsfield (1876), author, wit and tory radical, chancellor of the exchequer 1852, 1858–9, 1866–8, Prime Minister 1868, 1874–80 27/12/34, 23/1/46 n, 11/2/46 ?, 10/3/48, 15/5/48, 15/3/49, 6/7/49, 19/2/50, 24/2/52, 1/5/52, 17/5/52, 11/11/52 n, 26/11/52, 21/3/54, 23/3/54 ff, 11/7/54, 24/3/57, 16/2/58, 18/6/59, 22/6/59, 23/3/61, 7/4/62, 28/1/63, 28/6/64 n, 16/2/66, 5/7/66, 22/5/67, 16/3/68, 18/3/68, 6/12/68, 11/12/68, 18/2/69, 4/4/70, 8/4/70, 22/4/70, 18/5/70, 13/6/70, 9/8/71, 14/8/71, 6/2/72, 1/4/72 n, 27/2/73, 20/3/73, 21/3/73, 6/5/73, 9/12/73, 6/1/74, 28/1/74, 16/3/76 n, 4/4/76, 9/6/76 n, 17/7/76 n, 27/7/76, 27/8/76 n, 12/4/77, 5/12/77 n, 12/12/78, 21/12/78, 23/1/79, 11/2/79, 4/5/79 n, 29/3/80, 3/5/80 c, 17/5/80, 7/12/80, 9/12/80, 28/3/81, 30/7/81, 17/11/81, 22/3/82, 28/12/82, 10/10/83, 20/2/84, 10/10/84, 9/3/85, 30/9/85, 28/12/86, 19/3/87, 9/5/87 n, 5/7/90, 28/2/91, 6/10/92, 17/3/93, 12/8/93, 14/10/93, 18/10/93
1852 budget and 16/12/52
Palmerston thought good but impracticable 12/4/53
1857 budget and 14/2/57
1866 Reform Bill and 27/4/66
1869 budget and 12/4/69
agricultural distress and
G opposed to 11/4/51
American revolution centenary and 28/5/89
anticipates defeat 1880 2/4/80 n
assails G on Navigation Acts 23/3/49
astonishing error on malt tax by 9/5/54
astounding announcment of the new Asiatic Empire 8/7/78
as trustee of British Museum 25/3/63
at dinner at G's 18/3/68
at odds with his own side on Irish disestablishment 29/3/69, 14/10/93
bad tact of 22/2/58
Beaconsfield, Lady
death of: G's letter of consolation 19/1/73
G visits to inquire after her health 9/8/72
below his mark but in earnest 28/6/50
British government's purchase of shares in Suez Canal
G expects grave consequences from 26/11/75
cannot be bargained out of the saddle 26/4/56
cannot be thrown away like a sucked orange 14/2/57
civil talk with 16/3/74
Cobden Treaty and 20/2/60
complains at G's absence from Commons 15/5/74
concurrent endowment and the colonies, G expects a speech uncorked on 16/7/73
crown private estates and 5/7/73, 7/7/73

Disraeli, Benjamin (*cont.*)
death of 29/3/81, 19/4/81
G inquires after 29/3/81, 30/3/81
no more extraordinary man surviving him 19/4/81
touching circumstances of 22/4/81
declines to form a ministry 13/3/73 ff
disposition of Peelites to vote with 19/2/50, 27/2/50, 1/3/50
does good service 1/4/56
Eastern question and 30/1/78 ff, 18/7/78
easy and agreeable at dinner 4/5/50
finance in 1866
makes most useful declarations 23/7/66
Franco-Prussian war and 1/8/70
funeral of
adjournment of the House for 22/4/81
G offers public funeral 19/4/81
G unable to attend: heavy engagements 24/4/81
G ascribes book of to Croker 20/10/32
G careful to restrain expression of feelings about 26/1/78 n
G discusses with Carnarvon 26/1/78, 14/2/78
G dreaming his answer to 3/7/64
G might with advantage pair off with and retire 21/3/73
G never his rival, by will or intention 21/4/81
good in his kind 6/8/75
Gortschakoff note
accusations against G on 25/2/71
government of 1868
liberals decide on immediate dissolution 1/5/68, 4/5/68
two heavy defeats 18/5/68
government of 1874
defeat of certain 31/3/80 ff
dissention in cabinet of 17/1/78
G reading his *Life of Bentinck* 23/3/54 ff, 15/4/54
G reading Macknight's *Life* of 30/12/53, 10/1/54, 13/1/54
G reading *Vivian Grey* 27/3/74 ff
first quarter extremely clever, the rest trash 20/3/74
G's attack on 1852 budget of 16/12/52
G's relations with
all right between us 21/5/79
G's row with over Chancellor's robe etc. 6/3/53
G supports 30/6/51, 23/2/57
G's view of his political position 26/4/56
G votes with 19/2/50, 21/2/50
G watching Review from his roof 28/5/64
habit of systematically speaking in the small hours 15/3/69
health of 24/3/70
in cahoots with Delane 12/3/52
Ireland, speech on murder in
G asks Fortescue to check 25/2/71
Judicature Bill and 3/7/73, 4/7/73
letters from G to, printed 1/8/70, 19/4/71, 9/5/71, 21/5/71, 18/3/72, 4/4/72, 19/1/73, 5/7/73
makes a mess of speech 25/7/56
married in same year as G 19/1/73
metallic mind of 29/5/80
Millais' portrait of 30/4/81 n
mischievous speech on the Queen's incapacity 1/10/71
motion of no confidence moved by 26/4/71
motion on poor laws 27/2/50
outdone by Bright 23/4/75
overture from on Irish church 18/7/69 ff
party, G attends 25/3/68
passage of arms with over 1854 budget 6/3/54
plot of, foiled by silence 15/7/73
poorly received at Royal Academy dinner 3/5/79
Prime Minister 25/2/68 ff
resignation of 29/11/68 ff
protection in 1852 and 9/12/80
public monument to 24/4/81
G's anxieties about proposing 22/4/81, 9/5/81
G's proposal of an irony of fortune 22/4/81
Reform Bill 1867 and 11/2/67, 13/2/67, 14/2/67, 25/2/67, 6/3/67, 4/4/67, 6/4/67, 9/5/67 n, 28/5/67
astounding declaration of consistency by 28/5/67
relations with Salisbury
G makes helpful suggetsions 21/5/79
Resolutions on reform by 11/2/67, 12/2/67
Rothschild reads G his letters to Mrs. Williams 17/3/88, 28/2/91
sound and manly judgment of 9/8/92 n
Straits question and 25/2/71, 4/3/71
strange escapade of 6/5/75
tipsy when speaking on Irish disestablishment 3/4/68
trick of, baffled 3/3/53
vilipended in Carlton Club 25/7/56
Washington, Treaty of 19/4/71, 9/5/71, 21/5/71
Westmeath motion and 27/2/71 n
wizard of Hughenden Manor 19/10/71
See also Times, budgets, colonies, conservative party, Eastern question, Peelites
Dissenters Chapel Bill 18/5/44 ff
Lady Hewley's case 4/6/44 ff
speech on 6/6/44
dissolution *See* Commons (House of), memoranda (printed), Victoria

distress, law of 15/1/82
district councils *See* local government
divorce 7/9/49
divorced women at Court, position of 31/3/81
G said to have bribed to avoid call as co-respondent 3/6/61 n
G's article on 28/10/89
G's study of literature on 12/6/57 ff, 3/7/57 ff, 8/1/90, 8/12/90, 30/5/91, 12/12/92, 12/5/93 ff
legal divorce not in G's view complete 7/9/49
O'Kane divorce suit citing Palmerston 2/11/63 ff
Royal Commission on
G discourages 17/8/82
See also Clinton, Dilke, marriage, memoranda, O'Shea, Opdebeck, Parnell, publications, Stead, Temple (Henry)
Divorce and Matrimonial Causes Bill 20/5/57, 10/6/57, 24/7/57 ff, 13/10/57
G's filibuster against 4/8/57 ff
docklands *See* navy
Dodson, John George (1825-1897), 1st Baron Monk-Bretton (1884), liberal M.P., deputy Speaker and cabinet minister 6/9/70, 4/4/72, 3/10/77, 27/7/81, 17/12/82 ff, 23/12/82, 26/11/84
1884 Reform Bill and 28/4/84 n
Irish University Bill 1873, motion on 5/3/73
letters from G to, printed 9/5/80, 19/7/80, 19/1/81, 4/11/81, 21/11/81, 24/11/81, 10/1/82, 30/1/82, 11/3/82, 14/3/82, 13/11/82, 23/12/82, 4/4/84, 15/10/84
dogma
scripture and 9/10/59
dogs *See* Pincher
Dolgelly 11/9/55, 17/9/92
Döllinger, Johann Josef Ignaz von, Professor (1799-1890), theologian and liberal catholic 30/9/45 ff, 10/10/69, 26/4/71, 19/11/72, 10/1/73, 10/9/73, 30/12/74, 6/1/75, 29/8/75, 8/2/76, 24/5/76 n, 4/8/76 n, 2/11/76, 23/5/79, 19/9/80, 30/1/88, 19/9/92, 27/10/92, 5/11/92
assurance to G on Roman jurisdiction 22/11/50
church establishments and 19/10/82
deafness of 19/9/79
Egypt and 19/10/82
G's articles on 13/1/90 ff, 25/8/90
G's attempt to invite to Britain 17/9/81
G's visits to 30/9/45 ff, 8/9/74 ff, 17/9/79 ff, 11/10/79 ff
account of 1845 visit thought lost 30/8/74
at Tegernsee 17/9/79 ff, 27/8/86 ff
recalled 25/3/70, 21/4/74
Hebrew studies of 7/9/86
influence on G's Homeric writings 6/9/57 n
in London 15/5/51 ff
letters from G to, printed 10/10/69, 25/3/70, 21/7/71, 29/4/72, 6/9/72, 21/4/74, 19/10/82
O'Keeffe case in Ireland and 6/9/72
Old Catholics and 30/9/74, 2/10/74, 7/3/75
Palmer's *Treatise* and 19/10/82
Vatican Council and 25/3/70 ff, 21/7/71, 19/11/72
expects too much from British government 24/3/70
Vaticanism, comments on 19/2/75
Dollis Hill (Aberdeen) 20/5/82, 10/6/82, 17/6/82, 1/7/82, 8/7/82, 22/7/82, 5/8/82, 16/6/83, 14/7/83, 29/7/83, 5/7/84, 20/6/85, 27/6/85, 21/7/85, 27/7/85, 3/8/85, 5/6/86, 5/3/87, 10/3/87, 16/3/87, 14/4/87, 7/5/87, 23/5/87, 8/6/87, 10/6/87, 21/6/87, 27/3/88, 5/5/88, 12/5/88, 16/6/88, 7/7/88, 22/2/89, 18/5/89, 22/6/89, 20/7/89, 10/5/90, 27/6/90, 31/1/91, 7/2/91, 11/2/91, 2/3/91, 6/3/91, 20/6/91, 29/4/92, 3/5/92, 16/6/93, 7/7/93, 21/7/93, 13/4/94
garden parties at 7/5/87, 18/6/87, 25/6/87, 9/7/87, 7/7/88, 28/6/90
G's use of as alternative to arranging a London house 5/3/87
missionary gathering at 16/6/88
Dolomites 18/9/79, 22/9/79, 25/9/79 ff
Domodossola 3/8/49
Donizetti *See* operas
donkeys 10/5/32
Dorchester House 1/7/58
Dover 27/10/76, 12/11/80 c
Dover Harbour Bill 29/3/73 c, 10/5/73 c, 4/7/73, 5/7/73 c
G at the races 24/8/70
harbour fortification and improvement 7/7/83 c
snowballs thrown at the Gladstones by angry tories in Dover 27/12/87 n
See also memoranda
Dover Castle 21/8/69, 16/8/70
Dover House *See* London
Dover's powder *See* medicines
Downing, Flintshire (Denbigh) 27/8/67
Downing Street
gun cotton experiments shatters Downing Street windows 1/8/72
See also houses

Doyle, Francis Hastings Charles, Sir (1810–1888), 2nd Baronet (1839), at Eton and Christ Church with G, G's 'best man', poet and receiver-general of customs 20/5/26, 3/6/26, 17/6/26, 20/6/27, 23/7/27, 17/11/27, 27/12/27, 17/2/28, 17/1/29 ff, 8/3/29, 25/3/29, 3/4/29, 9/5/29, 17/10/29, 25/3/30, 30/8/30, 12/9/30, 25/4/31, 30/6/32, 2/3/33, 14/10/33, 6/2/34, 13/2/34, 13/7/35, 8/2/36, 10/8/37 ff, 24/3/38, 11/11/41, 4/12/41, 4/5/42, 10/11/52, 14/6/56, 7/8/66, 8/8/66, 26/3/69, 2/4/72, 14/1/75, 23/11/75, 25/11/78, 29/11/78, 22/5/79, 7/9/80, 20/11/82
  at Fasque 3/9/34 ff
  at Hawarden 30/12/70 ff, 17/8/79 ff, 31/12/81 ff
  criticism of G's review of *Maud* 25/11/78
  death of 12/6/88
  G's oldest friend alive 30/12/70
  idleness of 4/2/31
  letters from G to, printed 10/5/80, 22/10/81
  Reminiscences of 15/10/86, 23/1/88 ff
    silly parts of 1/2/88
  verses of 15/9/37
draughts, G playing 4/8/27, 17/9/27 ff, 23/8/28 ff, 27/12/37, 29/9/40 ff
drawing/sketching 25/7/26 ff
Drayton manor (Peel) 18/1/36
dreams 19/7/34, 25/8/34
  at Monte Cassino 27/12/66
  G dreaming his answer to Disraeli 3/7/64
  G dreams of next estimates 10/8/64
  of Parliament, the Court and breakfast with the Queen 2/1/96
Dresden 13/11/58
  china shopping in 13/11/58 ff
  gallery of
    shown round by Waagen 13/11/58
  G doing rescue work in 14/11/58
Drew, Mary (1847–1927), née Gladstone, daughter, author and G's secretary as needed 23/11/47 ff, 28/10/69, 2/12/70, 18/6/74 ff, 23/11/74, 30/9/76, 28/10/80, 5/11/80, 24/8/82, 6/1/83, 5/6/83, 24/8/83, 22/2/84, 14/6/84, 4/5/85, 24/9/85, 11/12/85, 16/12/85, 12/11/86, 23/11/86, 5/5/88, 4/10/89, 15/11/90, 14/6/91, 26/9/91, 26/4/92, 30/10/93, 7/1/94 ff, 6/3/94
  Acton and 11/2/85
  all-sufficing in point of society 5/1/77
  as G's secretary 18/3/79, 14/1/90 ff
  at Whittinghame 18/11/74
  birth of daughter 18/3/90
  confirmation of 22/3/63, 29/3/63
  consulted on G's article on Döllinger 14/1/90
  eyesight of 5/8/50, 15/10/50 ff
  G consults on article on Lecky 11/7/87
  G discusses Tennyson review with 21/12/86
  health of 27/4/50 ff, 2/1/51, 1/6/51 ff, 29/9/51, 14/1/55, 13/10/80, 14/2/87, 26/5/87, 12/4/92, 22/2/93 ff
    dangerous illness of 25/9/86 ff, 22/10/86, 27/10/86
  in Rome 12/10/66 ff
  marriage of 28/12/85, 31/12/85, 8/1/86, 2/2/86, 12/2/86
  piano-playing 22/10/78
    excellent promise of 21/4/59
  publications of 1/6/84
  qualities of 1/1/48, 23/11/66
    most womanish of the daughters 23/11/57
  quickest of the children 22/11/48
  ranks George Eliot above Scott 11/2/85
  riding with G 6/3/61 ff
  scarlet fever of 22/3/56 ff
  tract for mothers by 25/11/87
  treefelling with G 2/10/83
  with G in Norway 8/8/85 ff
  See also childrearing, Drew
drink
  whisky, G drinks to Albert's memory 26/8/73
Dropmore House (Grenville) 7/6/45, 13/6/48 ff, 11/11/53, 14/6/56, 13/5/60, 20/5/61, 31/5/62, 13/7/63, 3/8/66, 13/8/66
drugs *See* laudanum, medicines, opium
Drumguish 1/9/73 n
Drumlanrig (Buccleuch) 29/9/53, 6/9/58, 22/9/65
Drumnadrochit 27/9/72
Drumtochtie 10/9/34, 28/10/51, 9/10/58, 3/9/85, 1/11/90
drunkenness
  first seen abroad
    an English drunk 10/11/50
dual monarchy *See* Ireland
Dublin 5/11/77
Dudbrook, Essex (Carlingford) 9/6/77
duelling, G against 13/7/26
Dufferin Lodge, Highgate (G. G. Glyn) 12/6/69, 3/7/69
Dufferin Lodge, Highgate (Herbert) 4/5/61
Dulcigno 19/9/80, 27/9/80 ff, 16/10/80, 27/10/80
Dumas *See* plays seen
Dumas' *Montecristo*
  in Christian view frightful 16/10/46
Dunblane
  cathedral at 13/10/58

Dundee 26/7/37 ff, 15/11/37, 11/10/43
G Freeman of 29/10/90
Dundee Advertiser 15/9/93
Dun Echt (Lindsay) 20/10/49
Dunkeld 19/8/39
Dunottar castle 15/9/34, 15/9/43
Dunrobin Castle (Sutherland) 3/9/53 ff, 11/9/58
family prayers at 12/9/58
G ill at 4/9/53 ff
See also Gower
Duns 1/10/76
Dunster Castle (Fownes-Luttrell) 24/1/77
Durdans, Epsom (Rosebery) 19/3/81, 7/5/81, 3/6/81, 1/4/82, 22/4/82, 27/5/82, 3/6/82, 30/6/82, 8/4/84, 8/11/84, 28/3/85, 18/2/88, 24/2/88, 6/7/89, 19/4/90, 18/3/93
Durer, Albert 31/12/38
Durham 28/11/39, 25/9/76
duty
difficulties of 25/3/41
to father 27/10/48
G finds irksome 15/4/40, 21/9/43, 28/2/44

earliest recollection 21/12/25
ears
deafness a great difficulty 29/12/93
decline of hearing measured by audibility of Hawarden church services 27/5/87
less than half of Commons' proceedings audible to G 31/1/94
problems with 10/8/31, 12/7/93
treatment by Field 16/5/89
singing noise in G's good ear 10/1/87
earthliness, danger of 11/6/39
Eastbourne
holiday at 23/6/49 ff
Eastern church 30/12/55 *See also* Orthodox churches
Eastern Churches Association 4/10/70 n
Eastern question 7/10/53, 9/11/53, 11/11/53, 16/12/53, 17/12/53, 19/2/54 ff, 30/7/56, 28/10/70, 14/9/75, 23/11/75, 6/5/76, 22/6/76 n, 28/6/76, 11/7/76 ff, 14/7/76, 24/7/76, 25/7/76 ff, 31/7/76, 28/10/76, 5/12/76, 17/1/77 ff, 4/2/77, 26/6/77, 6/7/77, 1/9/77, 14/11/77, 31/12/77, 11/2/78, 14/2/78, 16/2/78, 20/3/78, 20/5/78, 31/10/78, 2/1/79, 17/2/79, 30/4/80, 14/5/80, 21/5/80, 3/7/80 c, 24/7/80 c, 4/9/80, 10/9/80, 19/9/80, 23/9/80, 1/10/80, 2/10/80, 3/10/80, 9/10/80, 12/10/80, 27/10/80, 10/11/80 c, 28/11/80, 5/12/80, 15/1/81 c, 19/4/81, 4/9/82, 6/9/82, 24/10/82, 15/11/83, 31/8/84, 23/9/85, 8/10/85, 7/11/85, 2/12/85, 20/12/85, 22/2/86 c, 14/4/86 c, 6/9/86
astounding announcment of the new Asiatic Empire 8/7/78
Austria and 4/5/80
bears cardinally on our race 29/12/76
Berlin, Congress of 28/3/78 n, 5/4/78
Besika Bay, British fleet to 4/7/77
Bulgarian schism and 4/9/72
coercion of Turkey by British fleet planned 27/9/80, 30/9/80 c
deep hold of popular mind taken by 7/10/78
fleet to Constaninople 24/1/78 n
G discusses with Albert and Victoria 9/11/53, 11/11/53
great sabbath dawning in the East 10/2/78
G's article on Montenegro 14/4/77, 19/4/77
a holy work 15/4/77
G's Resolutions on 30/4/77 ff, 5/5/77, 7/5/77, 14/5/77
decision to move 26/4/77 ff
defeated 14/5/77
solitary struggle for 7/5/77
G's speech in Seven Dials
some cheer, some markedly silent and obtuse 9/4/78
G's time never better spent 16/5/77
Ignatiev letters and 19/3/77, 21/3/77
Judaic sympathies and 6/10/76 n
medical students and 19/2/78 n, 25/2/78 n
Negropontis affair 9/1/77, 27/8/77 n, 19/9/77, 24/9/77, 20/11/77 n, 12/3/78 n
notes on Granville's speech on, printed 1/9/77
outbreak of war and 22/2/54
not fighting for Turks but warning off Russia, G thinks 22/2/54
part assigned to G great and good beyond his measure 31/12/77
recall of Elliot 18/3/77 ff, 27/3/77
reserves called out 28/3/78 n, 8/4/78
San Stephano, peace of 4/3/78
Smyrna to be held as guarantee 4/10/80
varied European support 9/10/80, 12/10/80, 27/10/80
speech avoiding the *main* issue 23/3/77
Turkish fascination! 27/6/77
See also Bulgaria, Cavendish, Cyprus, Disraeli, Goschen, liberal party, memoranda, memoranda (printed), nonconformists, publications, Suez Canal, Turkey
East India Club 13/7/68
East India Company *See* India

Eaton Hall (Grosvenor/Westminster) 11/1/40, 18/1/41, 26/12/43 ff, 5/1/44, 6/1/45, 27/9/52, 22/11/55, 28/10/61, 10/12/61, 24/12/62, 9/1/65, 15/10/69, 3/9/72, 11/10/82, 20/12/83
hosts seem bored at 10/1/65
shooting at 24/12/44, 27/12/44, 1/1/45
vast works in progress at 2/9/72, 12/12/76
Ebbe's Fleet (Augustine's landing place) 26/8/54, 6/9/54
Eboli 10/11/38
Ecce Homo
G's review of 20/11/67 ff, 8/12/67
read/discussed 21/12/65 ff, 26/12/65, 5/8/66, 19/8/66, 19/11/67
Ecclesiastical Commission
Ecclesiastical Commission Bill
G tries to amend 17/5/50 ff, 15/7/50
G as commissioner 22/11/60
G assisting 27/6/48
Ecclesiastical Courts Bill 15/2/43, 27/2/43 ff, 30/5/82
Ecclesiastical Courts Commission 22/1/81 c, 10/1/84, 11/1/84
Ecclesiastical Titles Bill 27/2/51, 7/3/51, 21/3/51, 24/3/51, 25/3/51, 19/5/51, 4/7/51, 20/2/55
repeal of 9/12/69 c, 23/1/70, 27/4/70 c, 7/5/70 c, 2/7/70 c, 6/8/70 c, 2/11/70 c, 6/5/71 c
Vatican Council, effect on 16/4/70
Echo 19/5/69, 25/5/69
eclipse
of the moon 23/8/77
economics *See* memoranda (printed), political economy
ecumenism 11/5/38, 24/9/38, 8/11/41, 24/4/94 n
Anglican orders and 11/6/38
Old Catholics and Orthodox churches and 30/9/74
Papal supremacy and 30/9/74
thoughts on promoted by St. Peter's 31/3/32, 22/4/32, 8/10/38
Edinburgh 12/4/28 ff, 7/12/33 ff, 12/8/34, 28/11/34, 20/10/35 ff, 31/12/36, 7/1/37, 26/7/37, 12/8/37, 27/11/39, 1/12/40, 2/9/45, 9/12/46, 14/4/47, 19/7/47, 28/7/47, 8/1/50 ff, 16/4/50, 23/9/50, 10/12/59, 15/4/60 ff, 9/1/62, 10/10/63, 23/9/64, 7/10/71, 14/11/74, 17/11/74, 24/11/79 ff, 16/3/80 ff, 24/3/80, 31/3/80, 17/6/86, 20/10/90, 27/10/90, 27/9/93
Arthur's Seat 28/10/35, 31/10/35, 7/11/35, 21/6/86, 24/10/90
Episcopal Church Society 1/12/40
Fettes College, G's visit to 8/10/71
Free Kirk Hall 14/12/59
G Freeman of 4/10/53, 9/10/53
Gladstone family living at 12/4/28 ff
G's speeches in 25/11/79 ff, 17/3/80 ff, 30/8/84 ff, 9/11/85 ff, 17/6/86 ff, 21/10/90 ff, 27/10/90 ff, 30/6/92 ff, 27/9/93
G staying at 1 Rothesay Terrace (J. B. Balfour) 20/10/90
Holyrood Palace 13/12/59
Liberal Club 22/3/80, 31/3/80
Mackay's hotel 8/1/50
Mercat Cross of
G's restoration of 3/2/85 n, 13/6/85, 23/11/85
National Gallery 13/12/59
Philosophical Association of
G declines hon. membership if disruptive 1/4/81
Philosophical Society of
G President of 16/4/88 n
Rosebery Club of 28/11/85
Royal College of Physicians
G dining with 12/10/63
Royal Society of 16/12/33
St. Giles' cathedral 30/12/79, 24/10/90
St. Margaret's chapel, the Castle
G's plan to restore 30/9/84
St. Mary's cathedral 30/12/79, 21/3/80 ff, 28/3/80, 20/6/86
Water of Leith 24/12/35
See also constituencies, Dalmeny House, Leith, Marseilles, Midlothian
Edinburgh, Perth, Dundee railway *See* railways (G shareholder in)
Edinburgh, University of
Chancellorship of
G stands and is defeated 16/5/68 n, 21/11/68 n, 17/2/69 n
G Lord Rector of 12/12/59 ff, 15/4/60 ff, 10/1/62 ff, 24/9/64 ff, 2/11/65 ff
Addresses as 20/11/59, 4/12/59, 7/4/60 ff, 16/4/60, 11/9/65 ff, 3/11/65
choosing Curators of Patronage 12/12/59
re-elected 15/11/62
G's honorary doctorate from 15/4/60
professorial salaries at 17/12/35 ff
Rectorship of 18/10/83
G declines to stand again for 30/12/92 n
Symposium Academicum
G singing at 10/1/62
See also Trevelyan
Edinburgh Academy
latin pronunciation in 11/1/62
Edinburgh Annuity Tax Bill 21/4/69 n
Edinburgh Evening News
good workman's paper 21/6/86 n, 27/6/86

Edinburgh Review *See* publications
Edison, Thomas *See* phonograph, recordings
Edmunds' case 14/2/65, 21/3/65, 25/3/65, 27/3/65, 1/7/65, 3/7/65, 5/7/65
Edmunds v. Gladstone, Lowe and Stansfeld 22/6/72, 6/8/72, 7/8/72
G at court for 22/7/72, 7/8/72
education 18/10/32, 18/3/35, 8/3/36, 8/12/37, 16/2/38, 24/2/38, 1/3/38, 8/3/38, 9/3/38, 14/4/38, 27/4/38 ff, 14/6/38, 15/1/39, 14/2/39 ff, 30/4/39, 10/6/39, 19/6/39, 20/6/39, 26/3/62, 26/6/80 c, 15/3/83
aspect of public policy lying within reach 31/3/57
block grant for proposed by Lingen 27/1/85, 30/1/85
conservative party and 1/2/40
department of proposed 26/6/83, 29/6/83
Education Bill 1873 17/5/73 c, 10/7/73 c, 12/7/73 c
education code 1871 12/8/71 c
changes to 10/7/72 c
education committee 24/1/53
education minute 14/11/61
education vote
G's memorandum on 2/1/60
enormous costs of 27/4/80
Factory Bill 1843 and 17/3/43, 25/3/43, 31/3/43, 15/6/43, 17/6/43
G arranging compromise with Northcote on 27/3/62
Golden Lane schools
G lays foundation stone of 8/5/56
grant for 21/7/40, 19/12/43
gratuitous 11/9/85, 14/9/85
G's schedule 13/2/53
higher education
G enquires into German endowments 10/1/73
government funding for declined 24/4/69 c, 14/4/71
Kay's training school, Battersea 5/4/41
liberal party and 12/3/73, 5/7/73, 14/8/73, 29/8/73
minister for
G alarmed at prospect of 7/9/84, 16/9/84
may be desirable 3/10/84
National Technical University, proposal for 10/10/71 n
Owen's college
government money for declined 24/4/69 c, 14/4/71
people sponsored by G
G. Christie 7/2/39
plan for a law school/university
objectionable for two universities to give law degrees 8/7/71 c
public schools
discussed at Balmoral 15/9/69
pupil teachers 2/1/60
revised code 16/12/61
tory minute on cancelled 20/1/53, 25/1/53
ultramontanism, effect on 1/12/69
See also Bradfield, cabinet (committees of), Charterhouse, childrearing, Elementary Education Bill, Endowed Schools Bill, Forster, Geddington, Germany, Gladstone (Helen), governesses, Harrow, Harrow Weald, Hawarden, Ireland, Lancing College, liberal party, Liverpool, Man (Isle of, King william's College), Manchester, Manning (H. E.), memoranda (printed), National Education League, National Education Union, National Society, nonconformists, Privy Council, public schools, Ripon, Scotland, secularism, St. Paul's, Wellington, Westminster, Woodard schools
education, G's *See* Christ Church (Oxford), Eton College, Oxford (University of), Wilmslow
Educational Magazine 2/4/41, 3/4/41
Edward VII (1841–1910), Prince of Wales, King of Great Britain and Ireland, Emperor of India 3/4/54, 10/12/62, 2/5/63, 23/6/64, 8/7/64, 12/3/67, 3/6/68, 23/5/70, 29/9/71, 5/6/72, 26/6/72, 29/6/72, 6/7/72 c, 18/11/72 c, 19/2/73, 21/2/73, 5/4/73, 14/7/73, 23/7/75, 20/7/76, 6/7/78 n, 24/4/80, 5/5/80, 29/5/80, 6/6/80, 24/6/80, 22/4/81, 28/5/81, 12/6/81, 19/6/81, 21/2/82, 2/3/82, 3/6/82, 23/8/82, 23/9/82, 7/5/83, 26/5/83, 13/8/83, 29/12/83 n, 26/10/84, 25/2/85, 3/5/85, 6/6/85, 24/6/85, 5/1/86, 2/2/86, 4/7/89, 27/7/89, 20/2/90, 21/7/90, 9/2/91, 12/12/91, 8/3/92, 15/8/92, 1/12/92, 18/12/92, 3/6/93, 5/7/93, 27/7/96
awareness of Queen's deficiencies? 27/7/96
brings his children to Downing St. 15/8/82
cabinet information and 7/11/92 c
dissuaded from attending Napoleon III's funeral 24/1/73 n
Eastern question and
good relations restored with 3/5/79
Egypt, not allowed to accompany the invasion 29/7/82 c
employment for to be found 19/1/72 c, 9/3/72, 11/3/72, 28/8/72
on Indian Council? 28/8/72, 8/9/72
rejects G's Irish plan 30/11/72 n
worthy and manly mode of life needed for 9/3/72

Edward VII (*cont.*)
finances of 19/6/89 ff, 29/6/89
G meets at the Derby 1/6/70
G meets in Norway 28/8/85
G playing cards with 29/9/71
Greece and 6/3/65
G staying at Sandringham 30/11/72 ff, 20/11/80 ff, 30/3/83, 29/1/87 ff
G with on the Riviera 28/1/83, 30/1/83
illness of 8/12/71 ff
Thanksgiving service for recovery of 19/12/71 c, 10/1/72, 19/1/72 c, 22/1/72 c, 2/2/72 c, 24/2/72 c, 27/2/72
in Chester 14/10/69 ff
G discusses Fenians with 16/10/69
India, visit to 10/4/75
Ireland and
G's proposals to Victoria rejected 25/6/71, 2/7/72 ff
Parnell and 29/4/85
visit to 7/2/85 c, 29/4/85
kisses C. G's hand 27/7/96
land bill, G explains to 7/2/70
meets G in Cannes 17/2/89
mislead by comrades 21/12/61
Mordaunt divorce scandal
critical time for 23/2/70
G's conclave on 10/4/69, 11/4/69, 12/4/69
Queen asks G to speak seriously to Prince on 22/1/70
much reduced, G thinks 17/11/93
natural intelligence of 7/2/70
Pope and 5/4/72 c
Reform Bill 1884
desires passing of 4/9/84
shirking saying a word to G 9/6/77, 27/6/77
Tranby Croft affair and 4/6/91 ff, 19/6/91
visit to Oxford 16/6/63 ff
wedding of
most gorgeous sight ever witnessed by G 10/3/62
W. H. G with in Germany 16/8/57
See also India, Ireland, Marlborough House, memoranda, memoranda (printed), Sandringham, Victoria
Edzell castle 10/9/33, 12/11/36, 24/9/46, 18/9/84
egotism, G accused of by Doyle 10/5/80
Egypt 1/6/58, 2/6/58, 10/12/72 c, 13/9/81, 18/9/81, 12/10/81 c, 4/1/82 n, 7/1/82 cn, 25/1/82 c, 1/2/82 c, 3/2/82 c, 4/3/82 c, 22/4/82, 26/5/82, 31/5/82, 10/6/82 c, 19/6/82 c, 20/6/82 c, 21/6/82 c, 28/6/82, 1/7/82 c, 3/7/82 c, 16/8/82, 23/8/82, 20/10/82 c, 6/11/82, 19/11/83, 18/1/84, 4/2/84, 25/2/84 c, 6/3/84, 22/3/84, 2/4/84 c, 3/4/84, 17/4/84 ff, 5/6/84, 23/6/84, 5/7/84 c, 11/8/84, 12/12/84, 18/12/84 ff, 13/2/85, 17/2/85, 30/5/85, 7/8/85, 24/8/92 ff, 13/9/92, 10/10/92, 1/11/92, 7/11/92 c, 19/5/93 ff, 22/9/93 ff, 18/10/93, 18/12/93, 11/1/94, 20/10/96
a holy subject 8/6/84
Alexandria
avoid further destruction of 13/7/82
bombardment of 3/7/82 c, 10/7/82, 11/7/82 n, 12/7/82, 13/7/82 c, 14/7/82
reconstruction of 13/7/82
water supply of 20/7/82 c
Arabi
expected to be crushed with little fighting 23/7/82
one of the greatest villains alive 23/7/82
trial and exile of 13/11/82 c, 16/11/82 c, 4/12/82 c
violence of 14/7/82
Blunt refused admission to 25/2/84 c
Blunt's contacts with G on 20/1/82, 22/3/82
bondholders and 7/5/84 c, 18/12/84, 20/1/85 c, 7/2/85 c
Bosphore Egyptienne
suppression of 13/4/85, 15/4/85 c, 25/4/85 c
Britain's one really vulnerable point 24/12/84
cabinet of the 'four Egypts' 16/7/84
Caisse de la Dette and 21/10/82, 5/3/84 c, 25/7/84 c, 24/3/85 c
Englishman to head 24/5/84 c, 27/5/84 c
cholera in 7/7/83 c, 22/8/83 c
Cleopatra's needle
no government money for bringing to U.K. 15/2/73 c
conference on 31/5/82, 19/6/82, 21/6/82 c, 23/6/82, 3/7/82 c, 20/7/82 c, 29/7/82 c
consular arrangements in 19/6/82 c
Control and 20/10/82 c, 21/10/82 c, 8/11/82 c, 1/12/82 c
Egyptian Tribute Loan held by G £45,000 12/10/76, 13/12/76, 16/8/77
finance of 20/3/84 ff, 16/6/84 ff, 21/6/84 c, 24/6/84 c, 27/6/84 c, 11/11/84 c, 20/11/84 cf, 2/12/84 c, 18/12/84, 2/1/85 c, 20/1/85 c, 29/1/85, 2/2/85, 4/2/85, 7/3/85 c, 13/3/85 c, 20/3/85 c, 24/3/85 c
British contribution to come from accruing value of Canal shares 20/3/84

conference on 2/4/84 c, 8/4/84 c, 1/5/84 c, 5/5/84 c, 14/5/84 c, 17/5/84 c, 27/5/84 c, 23/6/84, 16/7/84 c, 18/7/84, 24/7/84, 25/7/84 c, 1/8/84, 2/8/84 c, 6/8/84 c
need for equitable taxation system in 18/12/84, 19/12/84
force against might serve the cause of peace 12/7/82
France would control if independent 5/11/69
intervention in
groundwork for 19/6/82 c, 21/6/82
invasion of
bondholders and 17/9/82
Britain discharging single-handed a European duty 6/9/82
British churchbells to be rung for success of 16/9/82
decision for 31/7/82 c
G apprehensive about fate of Cairo 7/9/82
no state of war with a recognised power 16/9/82
popularity of 9/11/82
Tel-el-Kebir, battle of 13/9/82 n, 14/9/82, 15/9/82, 16/9/82
unwarranted by any other interest than the canal 6/9/82
Wolseley to put down Arabi and establish Khedive's power 31/7/82
jingoism and 8/8/83
Khedive of 13/7/82 c
Khedive's coup d'état 16/1/93 c, 17/1/93 c, 18/1/93 c, 20/1/93 c, 23/1/93 c
G's memorandum on, printed 17/1/93
loan to 4/11/69 ff, 23/11/69, 25/11/69, 7/12/69 c, 9/12/69 c, 22/1/84 c, 7/5/84 c, 4/2/85
neutralisation of 24/5/84 c
occupation of
costs of 15/9/82
Egyptians' view of 15/4/93
length of 28/6/84, 19/11/84 c, 18/4/93, 20/4/93
political arrangements for 15/9/82, 3/8/83
railways in
Sutherland's proposal for purchase impossible 12/10/82, 20/10/82 c
relations with Turkey and 6/10/69, 8/10/69, 26/10/69 c, 17/11/69, 20/11/69, 5/1/70, 21/6/82 ff, 21/1/85
Sultan cedes rights over Egyptian budget 8/10/69
riots in Alexandria 11/6/82 n
Rothschild and 5/8/84 c, 6/8/84 c, 11/4/85 c
Said, Viceroy of Egypt
entertainment by in mixed taste 16/7/62
G entertains 26/6/62
G meets 21/6/62, 28/6/62, 25/6/69
visit of planned 25/5/69
self-government for the present impossible 17/9/82
settlement of 21/10/82
G's memorandum, printed 15/9/82
slavery in
convention for abolition of 10/7/73 c
Sultan's power in 18/9/81, 15/6/82 n, 21/6/82 c, 25/7/82, 31/7/82 c, 3/8/82 c, 31/8/82, 15/9/82, 22/1/84 c, 7/3/84 c
troops for 15/6/82 n, 21/6/82 c, 5/7/82 n, 22/9/82, 8/3/84, 20/1/93 ff, 17/7/93
cost of 12/9/82, 22/9/82, 24/10/82 c, 21/11/82, 27/11/82 c, 15/1/83, 10/11/83 c
partial withdrawal of 22/9/82, 13/6/83 c, 8/8/83 c, 22/8/83 c, 23/10/83, 25/10/83 c, 4/3/84, 4/2/93
partial withdrawal of: Queen's intolerable interference over 4/10/82
Turkey and
severance of Egypt from Turkey our future policy 24/3/85 c
withdrawal from
G's memorandum on, printed 20/4/93
navy expansion and 11/1/94
Wolff mission to 16/2/86 c, 22/2/86 c, 25/2/86 c, 28/2/86
See also Baring, cabinet (committees of), France, Germany, God, India, Italy, memoranda, memoranda (printed), Primrose, Stanley, Sudan, Suez canal, Turkey, Wolseley
eight hours question 8/12/89 n, 18/2/90, 29/4/92 n, 1/7/92, 20/7/92, 1/8/92, 25/2/93, 1/5/93, 3/5/93, 10/7/93, 14/7/93, 11/8/93, 18/8/93, 3/11/93 c, 4/11/93
Admiralty and War Office and 9/12/93, 12/12/93
miners opposing eight hours limitation 19/4/93
stiff deputation to G on 16/6/92
Eighty Club
G's speech to 19/4/87
See also clubs
eirenic writers, G plan for series of books on 7/11/74 ff
Eisteddfodd *See* Wales
Elderslie (A. A. Spiers) 17/8/53 ff
election petitions
elections, general/bye
1826 9/6/26 ff

elections, general/bye (*cont.*)
1831
G's broadsheet on 23/4/31
1832 9/9/32, 13/9/32 ff, 24/9/32 ff, 11/12/32
Address for 4/10/32 ff, 6/12/32 ff, 14/12/32
analysis of 8/1/33
expenses 28/9/32
1834 15/12/34 ff, 10/1/35, 23/1/35
Address for 22/12/34
1835 31/1/35 ff
1837 20/6/37 ff
Address for 23/6/37, 3/7/37
1841 20/6/41 ff, 3/7/41 ff
Address for 8/6/41
1841 (bye, on office) 8/9/41 ff
Address for 3/9/41
1847 11/7/47 ff
1852 1/6/52, 5/6/52 ff, 8/7/52, 10/7/52, 13/7/52
Address for 9/6/52, 10/6/52
poll book of 22/10/52
1853 (bye, on office) 3/1/53, 5/1/53, 20/1/53
Address for 2/1/53
1857 5/3/57, 6/3/57 ff, 7/4/57, 16/4/57 n
G unopposed in 30/4/57
1859 4/4/59, 19/4/59, 30/4/59
on taking office in Ionia 12/2/59 n
1859 (bye, on office) 20/6/59 ff, 30/6/59 n
G sore and demoralised by 20/6/59
1865 13/7/65 ff
G defeated in Oxford; a dear dream dispelled 17/7/65
1868 1/8/68 ff, 8/9/68 n, 12/10/68 ff, 20/10/68 ff, 13/11/68 ff, 21/11/68, 24/11/68, 1/12/68, 2/12/68
Address for 16/9/68, 25/9/68, 5/10/68, 8/10/68
brilliant prospects of 1/8/68
1868 (bye, on office) 10/12/68 n, 21/12/68
1874 18/1/74, 20/1/74, 23/1/74 ff, 6/2/74 ff
Address for: almost a pamphlet 20/1/74 ff
Address for: ultramontane criticisms deleted by cabinet 23/1/74
causes of defeat 6/2/74
general prospects far from clear 28/1/74
swept away by a torrent of gin and beer 6/2/74
1880 8/3/80 ff
Address for 9/3/80, 11/3/80
1880 (bye, on office) 29/4/80
1885
Address for 22/8/85, 27/8/85 ff, 2/9/85, 5/9/85 ff, 8/9/85, 11/9/85 ff, 14/9/85 ff, 17/9/85, 3/12/85, 24/4/86
disestablishment and tory success in English boroughs 26/11/85, 27/11/85, 3/12/85
expectations of very sanguine 17/9/85
fair trade and 26/11/85, 27/11/85, 3/12/85
Grosvenor's forecast 18/11/85
Ireland and 7/8/85, 22/8/85, 3/12/85
Parnell & National League's attack on liberal party as perfidious etc. 21/11/85 n, 3/12/85
plans for 30/6/85, 11/7/85, 20/7/85 n, 23/9/85
results of 26/11/85 ff, 1/12/85 ff
tory/Parnell alliance and 10/11/85, 18/11/85, 27/11/85, 1/12/85, 3/12/85, 8/12/85 n, 9/12/85, 12/12/85, 13/12/85, 16/12/85 ff, 19/12/85, 20/12/85, 22/12/85 ff, 26/12/85, 29/12/85 ff
1886 8/6/86 ff
defeat, memorandum on causes of, printed 10/7/86
defeat a great relief, especially for G's relations with Victoria 8/7/86
defeat a smash 8/7/86
G's rescue work and London constituencies 16/7/86 n
parliamentary tactics following 8/7/86 ff
peers and 27/6/86
Queen objects to G electioneering beyond his constituency 27/6/86
result of 27/6/86, 3/7/86, 8/7/86, 9/7/86
shortage of liberal candidates for 1/7/86
1892 27/5/92 ff, 9/7/92 ff
'church' effect and 13/7/92
gain of 80 seats in Britain expected 4/7/92
good results expected 4/6/92
small liberal majority the heaviest burden for G 6/7/92
by-election required in Greenwich on G's acceptance of the Chancellorship? 9/8/73, 3/10/73 c, 1/12/73 c, 29/12/73, 10/1/74, 21/1/74, 2/2/74
canvassing 25/9/32 ff, 1/12/32, 7/5/33 ff, 29/12/34 ff, 17/7/37 ff, 24/12/40, 20/1/41 ff, 15/6/41 ff
in Dundee (pelted) 31/7/37
in flesh G desires defeat and ease 2/7/86
S. Lancashire 4/8/37 ff, 18/7/65 ff
contested by G, list of, printed 15/2/92
G hopes to avoid tory/Peelite clashes in 6/3/57
G requests table on liberal party's record 16/1/74
G's articles on electoral facts 16/8/87 ff, 5/11/89 ff

much bothered with the figures 19/11/89
liberal candidates and
Bassetlaw, G speaking for 11/12/90
Bath and Gloucester 10/5/73 c
Bridgwater 26/2/70 c
Dover, heavily lost 23/9/73
Glasgow 23/9/76
Hartlepool 5/1/91, 22/1/91
High Wycombe 11/9/76
Longford 7/1/70
Newark 29/3/70
electoral districts *See* Reform Bills
electricity
Big Ben illuminated by 6/5/73
Elementary Education Bill 1870
amendments to
very grave 13/5/70, 16/5/70, 21/5/70
Bible and 29/5/70, 10/6/70
clause 25 of 7/12/72 c, 11/12/72, 12/12/72 c
changes to meet objections to 7/12/72 c, 12/12/72 c, 24/1/73 c, 27/1/73 c, 5/4/73 c
changes to meet objections to: not introduced 4/2/73 cn
magistrates refusing to pay rates because of 15/2/73 c
nonconformist objections to 12/6/71, 25/11/71, 19/3/73, 20/3/73
critical measure of the government 24/3/70
deputations on 25/5/70
exchequer building grants discontinued 15/6/70
exchequer (rather than rate) grant to voluntary schools 15/6/70
Forster's rating proposal will not do 4/11/69
G's imagined ultimatum on 30/4/70
G's interview with Winterbotham on 20/3/73
in cabinet 10/11/69 c, 4/2/70 c, 12/3/70 c, 16/3/70 c, 26/3/70 c
in Commons
Cowper-Temple amendment 14/6/70 n, 16/6/70
Dixon's amendment 14/3/70, 18/3/70 n
Jacob Bright's amendment 30/6/70, 1/7/70, 5/7/70
Richard's amendment 24/6/70
planned 1/9/69, 2/10/69, 4/11/69, 5/11/69
state should provide secular teaching, G thinks 4/11/69
with Forster and de Grey 5/11/69
rate-provided schools, G's memorandum on, printed 29/5/70, 25/11/71
rate schools and 16/3/70, 29/5/70, 5/7/70, 12/8/71 c
religious difficulties with 24/3/70, 26/3/70, 28/3/70, 25/11/71
Roman Catholic schools and 16/4/70 ff, 15/6/70 n, 22/6/70, 29/6/70, 1/7/70
school boards, powers of 16/5/70, 29/5/70
Vatican Council, effect on 16/4/70
See also deputations
Ellesmere 17/9/56
eloquence, G writing on 1/10/27, 10/10/27
Ely
Ely cathedral 26/9/54
Emanuel Hospital 1/7/71 c, 8/3/73 c, 12/3/73 c, 10/5/73 c, 13/5/73
emigration 5/3/70, 3/8/83
loan for, declined 9/4/70 c
Empire
G opposes additions to
Fiji & all that lies beyond it 26/2/73
Ireland may have all compatible with unity of 11/9/85
unity of 3/9/85, 17/12/85, 19/12/85
See also Colonial Office, colonies, Foreign Office, Imperial Federation League
Employers Liabilities Bill 9/5/80, 12/5/80 c, 2/6/80, 3/6/80, 3/7/80 c, 19/7/80, 24/7/80 c
Employers Liability Bill 20/2/94
Lords' amendments to 12/4/94 c
plans for 1/8/92, 2/11/92 c, 5/5/93 c, 31/8/93 c
Endowed Schools Bill 26/1/69 c, 9/2/69 c
G votes against Bright on 6/7/59
Endowed Schools Commission 10/12/72 c
Engagement, The 23/2/45, 4/7/45, 3/8/45, 11/6/46, 14/3/47, 11/6/48, 11/6/49
early plans for 27/3/42, 6/11/43, 7/2/44, 24/11/44
G's review of his life in reference to it 11/6/48
House of Charity unsuitable for him 11/6/48
list of persons to be prayed for 13/4/48
members of 23/2/45
Ornsby's biography of Hope-Scott and 24/11/83
rules of 23/2/45
See also Lay Union
engagement to marry *See* proposals of marriage
Englemere House, Ascot 14/7/93
English Historical Review
Creighton appeals to G to assist by contributing 3/2/87 n
G declines Gardiner's invitation to write on Peel 16/4/91
G's review of Greville for 3/2/87 ff, 21/7/87 n
English Review
G's view of 1/4/44
See also publications

En route for Cannes 8/1/95
entertaining
dinner parties
1st given in 13 Carlton House Terrace 9/2/41
invitations for 1/3/41
epics, reflections on 3/9/34
Episcopal Church of Scotland 13/4/28 ff, 28/4/38, 30/7/40, 23/10/48, 7/11/56
bishops' incomes augmentation 16/9/45 ff
Endowment Association
G speaks for 11/1/62
fund to aid Scottish bishoprics 26/8/45
Scottish Office 2/9/45, 29/9/47, 1/5/62
synods in 1/11/51, 2/11/51 n
See also Fasque, Ramsay
Epping Forest
government defeated on 28/4/71
preservation of and access to 12/2/70 c, 2/5/72 c
Epsom salts 25/4/28 *See also* medicines
Erasmus
on Oxford 13/11/38
statue of 12/8/38
Erastianism
G's anti-Erastianism 24/6/71 n, 22/1/74
loss of ground by, G thinks, since 1830s 6/9/72
errors
Lady Waldegrave points out G's errors and defects to him 7/7/67
most gigantic frequently the most excusable and least gratuitous 1/3/71
Erskine (Blantyre) 31/10/65
erysipelas *See* illnesses
Escrick (Wenlock) 29/11/39, 30/12/46, 11/10/62, 8/5/68
essays and papers by G, unpublished
African mission 26/4/39
Anglicanism 25/1/83
annexation of Scinde 20/6/43
apostolical succession 10/3/37, 22/3/37, 15/10/37
Ariosto 7/12/49, 31/12/49
article on Austrian occupation of Modena rejected by the *Quarterly* 30/8/59, 2/9/59
Bacon 11/9/34
baptism 13/7/28
Bed-Chamber crisis 15/5/39, 16/5/39
Boiardo, digest of 3/1/50
Caroline Farquhar 22/8/35
causation 1/11/34
church and state 4/7/39
church extension 29/3/36
Church of Scotland 14/8/44, 14/9/44
church patronage 14/1/43
church property 9/6/34
church rates 4/4/34
Clerk-Maxwell's life 10/2/83
colonies 17/11/35
commercial policy 17/3/43
concordance of psalms 12/8/49 ff
conscience 27/10/33
conscience in governments 9/4/37
conversion 10/1/30, 11/1/30
current theological controversies 29/12/42, 29/12/44
later scrutiny of 13/8/88
cycle of psalmody 5/9/47 ff, 30/9/47, 1/10/47 ff
Dante 28/2/44, 27/10/46
death 5/1/62
depression 5/6/38 n
development 11/11/46 ff
dialogues 21/9/45
disqualification of Scottish clergy 8/3/52
dramatic unities 25/5/37
Dutch war 10/11/32
Ecclesiastical Titles Bill 20/7/51
economics 6/5/43
education 7/11/35, 21/11/35 ff, 5/5/38
egotism 29/6/36
Ethics 24/5/31, 24/11/33, 23/2/34, 3/4/39, 4/4/39
eucharistic devotions 25/4/41, 10/10/41, 6/3/42, 8/5/42, 10/12/93, 17/12/93
exemptions 12/6/38
experience 8/3/35, 19/4/35
family prayers 23/2/40, 22/12/44
fasting 21/3/47
Foreign Enlistment Act (rejected by *Q.R. N*) 21/6/56
free will 16/11/46
fullness of time 11/9/31, 18/9/31, 23/9/31
fund to aid Scottish bishoprics 26/8/45
G. C. Lewis 11/9/71
Gorham case 19/4/50
government of Ireland 20/4/39
Greek words 13/8/72
guilt 20/10/33
Heligoland 15/4/43
hereditary aristocracy 11/4/33
Hermes 7/11/85
history 2/12/35
holy communion 29/3/40
Homeric geography 10/12/46
Homer's ethics 23/1/83
horse in Homer 9/9/72 ff
Hume's *Enquiry* 22/10/34
ideas of writing and speaking 11/4/36 n
Irish church prospects 15/9/34 ff
Irish education 13/4/37 ff, 25/4/37, 1/5/37, 22/5/37 ff
Jerusalem bishopric 30/8/43
justification by faith 24/9/37
Lachmann vs. Homer 4/1/47 ff
La Fanatica 11/4/35

lecture on missions, chiefly colonial 7/1/52
Leopardi 6/10/49
Lessons from Homer 7/11/85
Locke 3/12/35
Lord's Supper 26/3/34, 12/4/40
love of neighbour 12/1/45
Machiavelli's *Discorsi* 29/4/36
Manning's conversion 30/3/51
miracles 26/6/59
miracles, Stephen's paper on 13/2/76
morality of religion 6/12/35
morals 26/11/35, 25/12/35
Naaman 26/11/48
necessitarianism 14/10/46
necessity 26/6/45 ff, 25/8/45 ff
notes on Courayeur 13/1/43
Odyssey 22/1/83
of keeping books and papers 25/11/37
on *Church Principles* 18/10/41
on Newman's *Essay on development* 1/12/45
on vanity 7/11/42
our colonial system 27/10/35
Oxford question 1/7/35
pamphlet on the Reform Bill 21/6/31, 1/7/31, 9/7/31, 13/7/31, 17/7/31
Papal aggression 24/3/51
'Party as it was and is. A sketch of the political history of twenty years' 30/3/55 ff
Pattison, Mark 12/3/85, 23/3/85
Pattison's 'Life of Casaubon' 15/5/75
peculiarities in religion 26/10/35
Plato 16/6/30
poetry 12/2/34
political concession 30/11/35
political economy 21/2/43, 31/8/46
political tract 21/11/34
politics 10/11/35, 28/11/35
poor laws 13/7/37
prayer 29/2/44
predestination 26/7/35
preparations for the sacrament 29/6/34
prevalent theories of government 17/12/35
Principle of Government 24/5/31
principles of social intercourse 17/4/31
private judgement 16/12/37, 24/6/38
Prospectus of Liverpool 2/11/32
protest on church affairs 14/1/43
public speaking 1/3/36
Pulci 12/2/50 ff
Racine 12/11/33
rationalism 14/12/37
R. D. Hampden 20/2/36
reformation, the 25/1/83
religion 1/7/38
religion and policy 11/5/45
Remarks on the present state 9/12/32
resurrection 19/4/40
revenues of Welsh sees 14/1/43
review of Benrath's *Bernardino Ochino* 3/1/77
review of C. Bauer, *Posthumous memoirs*, 4v.(1884) 11/10/84
review of S. Gopcević, *Montenegro und Die Montenegriner*(1877) 15/3/77, 17/3/77
rules of construction for 39 articles 11/8/47
Sabbath 3/7/31 ff
sacraments 24/12/37
saving faith 24/1/34
schoolmasters 25/5/38, 26/5/38
Scottish bishops' incomes augmentation 16/9/45
Scottish synods 4/7/52
Secreta Eucharistica 6/3/42, 8/5/42, 27/11/42, 21/12/42, 24/12/42, 2/2/45, 9/2/45, 30/4/48
social intercourse 13/7/34
social obligation 8/12/35 n
state of the church 13/8/43, 2/9/43
sugar duties 24/6/44
ten talents 17/12/48
Test Acts 29/2/28, 21/3/28
the fall 17/11/33
theology 27/8/43, 9/5/47
the will 11/10/36
Thy will be done 24/2/56
tithes 31/1/34
treating in Newark 6/8/34
union of the will 28/5/43
Visit to Clumber 28/11/32
Visit to Newark 17/10/32, 31/10/32, 26/11/32
West Indian education 21/3/35, 1/5/35
See also baptism, letters, memoranda, publications, theological writings, WEG Essay Society

Essays and Reviews 1/4/61 n, 10/11/63, 9/3/64, 15/3/64, 25/3/64 ff, 21/11/69
G attends Privy Council for judgment on 8/2/64
G signs petition on 10/7/64
no formal editorship of, G tells Pusey 10/10/69
Temple's essay unbalanced but not heretical 21/11/69
See also memoranda

estimates 8/2/53 ff, 24/1/84 c, 26/1/84 c
always settled at dagger's point 28/1/65
G dreams of next estimates 10/8/64
means of calculating 4/1/94
navy 8/2/53, 3/1/65 ff
ordnance 9/2/53
sky not clear for 1/12/63
See also army, navy

eternal punishment 23/1/34 *See also* punishment (eternal)

ethics, comments on 4/1/43 *See also* memoranda (printed)

Etna, Mount, ascended 29/10/38 ff
Eton College 15/9/25 ff, 19/1/26 ff, 13/4/26, 27/7/26, 21/9/26 ff, 18/1/27, 6/5/27, 22/9/27, 18/4/49, 27/2/69 c, 13/6/84
a better Eton 26/7/84
atonement, discussion with masters on 27/7/84
dinners in London, G attending 24/5/34, 22/5/41, 22/4/91
epitomes written at 14/10/25, 8/11/25, 24/4/26, 30/4/26, 14/5/26, 4/6/26
Eton Society 7/10/25 ff, 14/10/25, 22/10/25, 27/10/25, 5/11/25, 3/12/25, 4/2/26, 11/2/26, 4/3/26, 29/4/26, 6/5/26, 20/5/26, 27/5/26, 1/7/26, 15/7/26, 11/10/26, 4/11/26, 11/11/26, 18/11/26, 2/12/26, 27/1/27, 3/2/27, 12/2/27, 24/2/27, 3/3/27, 19/5/27, 26/5/27, 28/9/27, 13/10/27, 24/11/27
G Chairman of 2/12/26 ff, 24/3/27
G returns to speak to 4/4/40
G speaking at 29/10/25, 19/11/25, 28/1/26, 25/2/26, 11/3/26, 22/4/26, 6/5/26, 13/5/26, 17/6/26, 24/6/26, 4/7/26, 7/7/26, 25/9/26, 30/9/26, 7/10/26, 14/10/26, 28/10/26, 17/2/27, 12/5/27, 2/6/27, 16/6/27, 23/6/27, 30/6/27, 7/7/27, 14/7/27, 21/7/27, 23/7/27, 6/10/27, 20/10/27, 27/10/27, 29/10/27, 3/11/27, 10/11/27, 1/12/27
G's visit to, 1878 7/7/78
G Vice-president of 21/1/26 ff, 22/2/26, 13/5/26, 20/5/26, 3/6/26, 10/6/26, 18/10/26
vote of thanks to G at 1/12/27
fagging at 26/4/26
feelings on leaving 2/12/27 ff
French lessons at 23/9/25 ff, 25/1/26 ff, 4/5/26 ff, 22/7/26
G called up 21/2/27, 26/2/27, 10/3/27, 12/3/27, 14/3/27 ff, 8/5/27 ff, 25/5/27, 16/6/27 ff, 6/10/27
G captain of Fifth 31/10/26
G's criticisms of at Marlborough 3/2/77, 21/2/77 n, 1/7/77
G's delight in returning to 31/3/40
G's memoir of E. C. Hawtrey 3/1/90
improved religious behaviour in 30/7/43
Keate's punishments 3/10/26, 25/5/27
lectures by G at 6/7/78, 5/7/79, 14/3/91
length of holiday at 16/12/93
London dinners 18/5/33
messing at 18/10/25, 19/11/26
Montem 20/4/26, 16/5/26 ff
Newcastle scholarship, G examining 18/1/40, 25/1/40, 2/3/40 ff, 27/3/40, 28/3/40, 30/3/40 ff
new grammar of
scandalous errors in 11/11/58
playing fields of 19/5/85
plays at 3/2/26, 8/2/26, 3/3/26, 28/10/26
recollections of 16/9/28, 13/1/83 n, 13/5/83, 23/10/83
rowing/sculling at 19/9/25 ff, 1/3/26, 15/4/26, 29/4/26, 1/6/26 ff, 11/6/27, 23/6/27
scriptores at 16/2/27, 9/6/27, 24/9/27, 22/10/27
spoilt by plutocracy 3/2/77 n
visits to 5/3/34, 22/6/39, 30/3/40 ff, 30/10/41, 29/7/43, 10/1/45, 9/6/45, 29/5/47 ff, 29/6/50, 19/1/52, 4/6/52, 14/1/53, 8/6/53 ff, 23/7/53, 4/6/54, 30/7/54, 4/6/57, 21/5/61, 7/5/65, 3/12/68 n, 12/12/68, 10/4/70, 19/3/71, 4/6/72, 27/6/75, 15/4/78, 6/7/78, 31/5/79, 5/7/79, 24/6/82, 24/6/82 ff, 26/7/84, 19/5/85, 14/3/91 ff
G's lecture, organized by Curzon 6/7/78
wall game 2/12/25, 29/11/27
See also Eton Miscellany, Gaskell, Hallam, publications, Salt Hill
Eton Miscellany (ed. G as Bartholomew Bouverie) 15/5/27, 22/5/27, 26/5/27, 3/6/27, 26/6/27, 2/7/27, 13/7/27, 28/7/27, 30/8/27 ff, 25/9/27, 23/10/27 ff, 12/11/27, 17/11/27, 27/1/29, 2/7/30, 6/5/35
Hallam and 2/12/92
eucharist, particular comments on 4/3/27, 13/4/27, 10/6/27, 21/7/27 ff, 4/5/28, 2/6/28, 6/7/28, 21/9/28, 1/2/29, 3/5/29, 6/12/29, 9/4/30, 22/5/31, 2/9/32, 25/12/32, 5/5/33, 2/6/33, 1/6/34, 14/12/34, 28/5/35, 25/12/36, 27/5/37, 5/8/38, 7/4/39, 17/10/41, 25/12/42, 14/1/44, 7/12/45, 8/11/46, 13/5/47, 19/7/48, 1/1/49, 7/4/49, 25/12/49, 14/4/54, 18/5/56, 13/8/56, 4/10/68, 11/10/68, 18/10/68, 25/10/68, 25/12/72, 13/4/73, 7/9/73, 24/6/74, 5/2/80, 23/5/93, 10/12/93, 2/2/94
assuages G's brute passions 25/12/54
G abstains, from sense of sin 22/4/49, 12/5/50
G addresses Hawarden household on 8/11/68
G's engagement to C. G and 26/5/39, 8/6/39, 16/6/39
Oxford seat and 13/5/47
peculiar shame at 4/2/49
Scottish office 14/9/34, 25/8/39
Vaticanism and 21/2/75
W. H. G and 25/12/54

See also Christ Church (Oxford), essays and papers
eucharistic devotions 25/4/41, 10/10/41, 24/7/92
Europe
arbitration and 12/3/72
authority of combined opinion of 30/6/59
Concert of 11/2/71 n, 17/2/71, 6/9/80 c, 16/9/80, 30/9/80 c, 1/10/80, 1/2/82 c, 22/4/86, 18/7/93
Egypt and 14/7/82 ff
joint invasion of Egypt by? 25/7/82 ff
ought to be a cable, sometimes seems a thread 27/10/80
represents the civilised world 14/7/82
consent of against ultramontanism desired 7/6/71
huge armaments in 23/2/70
ill, unless France is well 4/1/72
Italian unification will contribute to stability of 26/3/61
public international law of 23/11/70
evangelicalism
Church music and 7/1/94
G once in very close connection with 15/10/93
little political philanthropy of 15/10/93
now so barren 16/1/84
See also Chalmers, Church of England, Church of Scotland, Gorham case
Evelyn, John, MSS of 23/4/43, 16/5/45
evil
courted by G 19/7/48
G's reflections on 30/11/56
evolution
birds and 11/12/85
Christianity and 7/12/85
Darwin and 9/1/86 n, 8/12/92
Neanderthal man and 27/5/85
the age leapt to unwarranted conclusions about Darwin 15/1/72
Ewell, Surrey 1/8/36
Ewelme 28/7/58
Ewelme, rectory of 19/3/71, 12/7/71, 26/2/72, 8/3/72
Ewloe school 14/8/77, 15/1/79
examinations *See* Oxford (University of)
ex-cabinet 14/7/66, 12/2/67, 16/2/67, 20/2/67, 26/2/67, 20/3/67, 14/1/75, 18/6/85, 5/7/87
18 attending 29/3/78
home rule and 8/2/90 n
meeting on Ireland 21/1/86
discussions about 31/1/85, 3/1/86, 5/1/86, 12/1/86
minutes of 12/2/67
excema *See* illnesses
Exchequer
Chancellor of
ought to be unpopular 13/8/73
Chancellorship of 31/8/41
most invidious office in the cabinet 21/12/84
Court of 25/2/53, 12/11/59, 12/11/60, 12/11/61, 12/11/63
G sitting as Judge in 7/6/53
G as Chancellor of 23/12/52 ff, 13/6/59 ff, 9/8/73 ff, 23/4/80 ff, 31/1/86 n
advice to Lewis as successor 28/2/55, 1/3/55, 3/3/55
entertainments: petty but rigid necessity 2/4/53
intent on gaining 13/6/59 n
plans for leaving 5/5/82, 8/5/82, 17/5/82, 31/5/82
resignation from 22/2/55, 23/2/55, 28/2/55
G's memorandum and 16/2/56, 20/2/56
G's resignation *all but* settled 2/6/60
Argyll mediates 4/6/60
Exchequer bills 5/10/53, 2/5/54, 4/3/61
Exchequer Bills Bill
draft of 21/11/60
See also memoranda (printed)
excommunication 10/9/42
Exeter 13/7/77
speech and weird procession at 13/7/77
Exeter College, Oxford 26/9/31, 30/1/49, 25/1/52, 29/1/53, 28/1/57
G dining in 2/6/57
G staying in 1/11/47 ff
G visits library of 1/6/57
Exeter Hall 1/6/40, 20/10/41, 9/8/57
meetings at 20/6/35
Exhibition, Great, 1851 31/1/50
G a Commissioner 31/1/50 n, 28/2/50, 15/6/50 ff, 5/3/51 ff, 10/5/51, 30/5/51 ff, 19/8/51, 1/3/52, 2/6/52, 5/6/52, 16/3/53, 8/4/56, 12/4/56, 1/5/56, 1/5/58, 14/6/58, 10/6/59, 19/1/61, 19/1/63, 23/3/63, 23/5/65, 12/5/70, 3/4/71
Inscription Committee 13/7/50 ff, 21/5/51
S. Kensington buildings 2/6/52, 5/6/52, 17/10/53, 24/10/53, 25/10/53, 22/7/57, 27/3/58, 15/8/59, 14/3/62, 10/6/63, 12/6/63, 15/6/63, 9/4/70 c, 2/7/70 c, 28/6/73 c, 17/7/80 c, 1/1/84
G donates part of porcelain collection to 23/7/66, 1/6/67
G loans ivories for exhibition in 9/7/83
G receives Queen at 14/4/58, 12/6/63

Exhibition, Great (*cont.*)
visited 15/4/51, 16/5/51, 21/5/51, 22/5/51, 6/6/51, 7/6/51, 21/6/51, 23/6/51, 24/6/51, 25/6/51, 28/6/51, 5/7/51, 11/7/51, 12/7/51, 18/7/51, 19/7/51, 21/7/51, 22/7/51, 26/7/51, 30/7/51
G takes C. G's Bedfordbury party to 7/7/51
See also Crystal Palace
Exhibition, International (1862)
G on pottery jury of 29/4/62, 7/5/62, 10/5/62, 19/5/62, 21/5/62, 23/5/62, 26/5/62, 28/5/62, 4/6/62, 13/6/62, 14/6/62, 28/6/62
opening of 16/4/62, 2/5/62
exhibitions
American plants 2/6/56
Battle of Waterloo 18/6/45
Burford's Panorama 21/6/51
cartoons 1/7/43
Colosseum lantern show
exemplification of 19th century 22/7/36
Diorama 29/7/48
French exhibition 25/7/55
health
G's reception at 8/5/84
of frescos (Dyce) 28/6/44
Sebastopol panorama 12/7/55
Somerset House 15/7/36, 18/7/36
watercolours 25/4/57, 26/4/84
women watercolourists 30/5/57
Wyld's Globe 23/6/51
explosions 16/3/83, 17/3/83 c
eyes
almost useless for reading notes for speeches 4/3/93
bad from influenza 26/3/41
better, strangely against G's desires 24/5/93
burning in left 5/6/63
cataract in
early signs of 2/7/92, 22/7/92
G's memorandum of history of consequences of, printed 13/9/94
operation on G's right eye 21/3/94, 23/5/94, 19/7/94 ff
eye damaged by hard gingerbread thrown in Chester 25/6/92
eyeglass forgotten for speech on Eastern question Resolutions 7/5/77 n
G fitted with pince-nez with 'Pure Periscopic' pebbles 17/1/86 n, 19/1/86
Granger's interview on state of G's eyes 20/2/94, 23/2/94
green spectacles disliked 8/10/38
G's retirement from politics and 23/9/93, 8/2/94, 12/2/94
family discussion about 29/9/93
G tells Cowan of situation 28/9/93
G's show arcus senilis 8/12/57
G's spectacles' specifications 15/3/77 fl
G stung on eyelid by wasp 23/10/86
improvement of 8/2/39
left eye
decline in 15/10/92
declining effectiveness of 2/7/92
left eye damaged and used with dark spectacles 25/6/92 ff, 29/6/92 ff
list of maxims for improvement of 21/8/40
problems with 16/8/31, 23/8/31, 25/2/32, 29/1/34, 27/4/35, 2/2/36, 22/5/36, 28/8/36, 26/11/36, 11/12/36, 18/1/37, 24/1/37 ff, 1/2/37, 31/5/37, 24/6/37, 27/10/37, 13/11/37, 23/12/37, 28/12/37, 5/3/38, 10/3/38, 20/4/38, 12/5/38, 1/7/38, 18/7/38, 8/2/39, 7/5/39, 3/4/40, 10/7/40 ff, 25/7/40, 9/11/44, 10/3/45 ff, 17/5/46, 16/8/49 ff, 16/11/49 ff, 29/4/65, 25/6/92 ff
candlelight reading almost impossible 14/12/93, 4/1/94, 27/1/94
'Il Male Occhio' 24/12/94
in Italy 3/10/38
use of eyes much impeded 30/7/92, 23/4/93
writing no difficulty 25/10/93
reading impaired by decline of effectiveness of 22/6/83, 15/9/93
splinter in from treefelling 23/12/67
indentation near the pupil 25/12/67
stronger than before 5/6/55
treatment of 10/2/37 ff, 23/11/37, 9/10/38, 3/10/92
type-writing
G's difficulties with 15/7/94
vinegar used to treat 3/4/40
See also age, blind, Drew (Mary)
Eyre case
G's notes on 1/12/65
no pension for Eyre 25/1/72 c
payment of expenses unavoidable 2/3/72 c, 15/6/72 c, 29/6/72 c

Fabliaux, read by G as pornography 13/5/48, 19/7/48, 22/2/49
factories
hours of labour and 15/11/72 c, 18/11/72 c
factories visited 18/1/47
Allsopp's brewery, Burton 16/10/65
Anchor works, Saltney 12/9/90
Barrow works 19/9/67
Bass's brewery, Burton 16/10/65
Bridgnorth carpets 11/11/74
Cooperation Mill, Oldham 18/12/67
Delarue's 5/4/56

Enfield's, Birmingham 1/6/77
Gossage's soap works, Widnes 16/11/68
in Manchester 11/10/53 ff, 22/4/62
Laird's works, Birkenhead 7/10/65
Nottingham lace 11/5/75
paper factory, Amalfi 11/2/89
Platt's works, Oldham 18/12/67
Plumpherston shale works 28/10/90
Ransome's 2/2/78
Factory Bill
1843 25/3/43 ff, 15/6/43, 17/6/43
1844
G favours compromise on 25/3/44
need for compromise on 22/3/44 ff
probable defeat of govt. on 16/3/44 ff
See also education
factory reform 18/5/36, 20/7/38
faggot voting 9/7/41, 6/12/79 n
G makes S. Glynne one in Flintshire 16/1/65
failures
G's first defeat on a financial measure 20/7/60
fair trade 6/11/85, 3/12/85
imposture of 18/9/81, 22/9/81, 29/9/81
Falconhurst (Talbot) 14/5/53, 8/7/54, 26/3/64, 25/3/65
G convalescing at 8/7/54 ff
Falmouth 28/8/80
G's speech at 11/6/89
family life
blessings of 29/12/96
Farini's *Lo Stato Romano*
read by G 27/11/50 ff
translated by G 27/11/50 ff, 21/12/50 ff, 1/2/51 ff, 9/9/51 ff, 9/10/51 ff, 6/11/51 ff, 1/3/52
Farmers' Alliance 16/6/80, 21/6/82
Farnborough (Farquhar) 4/7/46
Farnham Castle, (Bishop of Winchester) 29/7/82
Farquhar, Walter Rockliff, Sir (1810–1900), 3rd Baronet (1836), at Eton and Christ Church with G 4/2/34, 15/2/35, 10/12/35, 13/2/36, 18/2/36, 4/3/37, 4/12/43, 14/1/44, 4/7/46, 30/1/52, 16/11/52, 14/1/54, 5/8/54 ff, 17/5/56, 1/3/62, 21/1/63, 28/1/64, 20/2/64, 17/12/65, 28/7/66, 2/1/68, 19/1/71, 22/2/72, 16/5/72, 27/3/73, 5/3/75, 18/2/76, 9/7/76, 29/6/79, 4/3/83, 4/5/90, 6/3/92, 30/10/92
consulted about Wilberforce 8/5/59
letters from G to, printed 26/10/92, 15/2/93
Welsh church and 15/2/93
See also Polsden Lacy
Fasque 20/8/33, 13/8/34, 7/9/35, 11/8/36, 10/9/36, 31/10/36, 14/8/37, 25/9/37, 8/11/37, 20/8/39 ff, 6/9/39, 26/9/40 ff, 11/8/42 ff, 23/8/43, 9/8/44, 4/10/44 ff, 12/8/46 ff, 31/3/47 ff, 7/7/47, 28/7/47, 13/9/48 ff, 3/10/49 ff, 20/10/49, 9/1/50 ff, 13/4/50, 1/9/50, 17/4/51, 2/5/51, 29/8/51, 1/11/51, 6/10/58 ff, 8/10/64, 25/9/69, 29/6/74, 24/1/80, 18/9/84, 1/9/85, 25/2/89, 29/10/90 ff, 25/9/91
Anne G's coffin brought to 6/10/48
Damrong, Prince of Siam at 25/9/91
G bids adieu to as a home 26/12/51
Guy Faux celebrations at 5/11/49
last sight of? 27/3/89
Lord J. Manners at 1/10/48 ff
Mrs. Gladstone ill at 15/8/31
no grouse shot 1847 12/8/47
plan for chapel at 21/9/40, 20/10/44
problems with poachers at 3/11/51
servants' ball at 1/1/50
St. Andrew's Chapel 12/8/46, 16/8/46 ff, 17/10/46, 8/11/46, 8/10/58, 27/1/80
consecration of 6/8/47, 28/8/47
difficulties of keeping open in winter 2/12/46 ff
funeral of C. J. G in 13/4/50
G discourages use of surplice in 26/9/47
G's delight in 8/11/46
G's inscription marking Agnes' recovery 28/9/47
G taking service in 20/1/50
internment of Gladstone bodies from Seaforth 2/11/48
numbers at services 11/4/47
opening of 18/10/46
plans for 15/8/44, 19/8/44, 22/8/44, 20/10/44, 1/3/46
rows about conduct of services 5/10/49 ff, 25/10/49
vault of, G visiting 13/9/50 ff, 3/5/51, 4/5/51, 13/9/51, 11/12/51 ff, 30/6/74
times of walks at 17/12/51
winecellar of 26/11/40
See also memoranda
Fast Days 21/9/32
Public Fast (for the famine) 24/3/47
Fast Days, merits of 21/3/32
fasting 16/3/34, 13/4/38, 13/2/39, 30/3/39, 10/4/41, 20/2/47, 10/3/47, 24/3/47, 3/4/47
fasting at night 3/1/31
Fawcett, Henry (1833–1884), liberal M.P. and cabinet minister 1/4/70, 3/4/70, 11/3/73, 19/3/73, 2/3/75, 30/4/75, 22/3/77, 4/7/78, 15/8/78 n, 22/5/79, 12/3/80 n, 22/6/81, 17/12/82, 13/10/83, 5/3/84 c, 7/11/84 n

Fawcett, Henry (*cont.*)
India and 23/10/80, 16/8/82, 28/7/83
Irish university bills and 28/7/71, 29/7/71 c, 25/8/71, 3/9/71, 28/9/71, 27/10/71 c, 20/3/72, 5/4/72 c, 13/4/72 c, 24/4/72 ff, 21/8/72, 29/3/73 c, 26/4/73 c
government defeat on 25/4/72
inadmissable 18/3/73 c
letters from G to, printed 19/4/72, 28/3/81, 16/9/82, 8/5/83, 28/7/83
limits to freedom as a cabinet minister 28/7/83
local taxation and 19/4/72
post office and 28/3/81, 22/6/81, 2/6/83 c, 10/10/83, 13/11/83 c, 14/1/84
women's suffrage and 15/4/84 n, 13/6/84 n
Featherstone incident 26/9/93, 7/10/93, 6/12/93, 14/12/93 c
federalism
Rosebery's interest in 8/2/90 n
Feldkirch 3/7/32
femininity
G struck by Josephine Butler's 21/12/72 n
femininity, characteristics of 4/1/40
Fenians *See* Ireland
Ferrara 14/6/32
Fettercairn House (Forbes) 15/8/42, 12/10/46, 18/8/47, 21/4/51 ff, 4/7/74
psalm-singing at 12/10/46, 21/10/46 ff
Fiji
annexation of by U. K.
G delays action on 25/2/73, 24/5/73 c, 5/6/73, 7/6/73, 13/6/73
G refuses to be a party to 26/2/73, 4/8/74
German claims on 7/2/85 c
incorporation into New South Wales favoured by cabinet 29/7/71, 27/10/71 c, 31/10/71 c
no basis for movement on, G thinks 8/5/73, 24/1/74
protectorate for opposed 22/6/72 c, 25/6/72
Rotumah/Grenville island annexed to 24/7/80 c
slavery in 22/1/72
Fileen property 30/8/36
Finale 18/1/67
finance
basis of G's mind in finance and philanthropy 29/12/96
critical in 1873 9/11/72
deficit forecast 11/1/93 c, 16/2/93 n
financial statement on China 16/7/60
G expects high prices to slacken in 1873 9/11/72
G meditates on future of 19/7/59
G's attack on Northcote's 28/4/79
G's list of 'remnants' sent to Lowe 10/1/69
G's memoranda on 16/2/56, 20/2/56, 14/2/57
G's memorandum on cabinet differences over 30/5/60
hinge of the general election, probably 30/10/73
indirect taxes and 1871 budget 11/4/71 ff
local government
dramatic plan for reform of 2/1/74
may provide driving force for liberal party 14/8/73
onward men on 30/5/60
panic of 1866 11/5/66
principle of consolidating measures in one Bill 1/7/60
prospective budget plan the best chance of election success 9/2/74
sinking fund 21/5/66
stationary men on 30/5/60
tory management of 30/1/79
See also army estimates, budgets, colonies, Government of Ireland Bill (1886, 1893), India, Ireland, local government, Lowe, memoranda, memoranda (printed), money, national debt, navy estimates, Peel, taxation
Finance, Ministry of
planned by G 16/2/56, 20/2/56
finances, G's personal
£12000 to six of G's children 12/12/92
£43,000 to be distributed among his children 1/1/90, 4/1/90
account of given to H. N. G 23/4/94
G makes over £40,000 to St. Deiniol's 6/11/95
See also accounts, railways (G shareholder in), will (G's)
Financial Reform Almanack 1885
disestablishment and 30/10/85, 4/11/85
Fine Arts Club 15/7/61 n, 17/7/61, 2/7/62, 9/7/67 *See also* clubs
finger
G shoots off his lefthand forefinger 13/9/42
Forbes' portrait and 5/5/91 n
Finland *See* home rule
fire insurance 22/4/65, 10/1/69
defeat on 21/3/65
fireworks 5/6/26, 4/6/27, 28/6/38, 19/7/39, 24/5/53, 29/5/56, 21/10/75, 27/7/76
Fish Dinners *See* Greenwich
fisheries
exhibition 5/7/83
North Atlantic disputes 12/2/81 c, 8/3/81 c
Scottish trawling 26/5/83 c
Fisher's auction rooms 7/3/71, 9/3/71
fishing 28/7/27, 9/8/28 ff, 22/8/53
on Loch Fyne 28/9/65

Fishmongers Company 11/2/69
flagellation 25/9/38 *See also* scourge
Fleetwood 5/7/47, 11/9/48
Flint
G electioneering in 25/3/57
Flintshire
bye-election in 24/5/61 ff
G pairs with H. Glynne 25/5/61
politics of 30/12/56, 5/3/57, 6/3/57, 9/3/80, 30/11/85 ff, 10/12/85
Peelites smashed in 7/4/57
register of 29/8/72
Flodden, field of 27/9/76
flogging in the army
G opposes abolition of 14/3/34, 13/4/36, 7/4/37
See also navy (flogging in)
Florence 16/3/32 ff, 27/9/38 ff, 4/1/67 ff, 31/12/87 ff
Accademia Reale 23/3/32, 11/1/67
Castagnole 19/1/88
Cathedral 17/3/32, 28/9/38, 15/1/67, 31/12/87
Certosa di Val d'Ema 27/1/88
constitutional deputation to G 14/1/88
Dante's house in 12/1/88
Fiesole 24/3/32, 2/10/38, 13/1/88
G's speech to admirers 1/1/88
Italian parliament in
G visits 10/1/67
Laurentian library 22/3/32
Majano, Leader's villa 11/1/88, 18/1/88
marble manufacturing in 24/3/32
Palazzo Torriguiani 29/9/38, 24/1/88
Palazzo Vecchio 23/1/88
Pitti palace 20/3/32, 29/9/38, 2/10/38, 8/1/67, 20/1/88
San Marco 21/1/88
San Miniato 30/1/88
San Salvatore 30/1/88
Santa Croce 19/3/32, 7/1/88 ff
Santa Maria Novella 12/1/88
studios visited
Connelly's 10/1/67
Fuller's 14/1/67
Hildebrand's 30/1/88
Orsi's 25/1/88
Uffizi 17/3/32 ff, 28/9/38 ff, 5/1/67 ff, 7/1/88 ff
Venus de Medici, admiration for 20/3/32, 4/9/34
Villa Bello Sguardo 9/1/88
Villa Palmieri (Crawford and Balcarres) 28/1/88
Villa Petraia 1/2/88
Villa Rondinelli 16/1/88
Villa Stibbort 17/1/88
See also galleries visited
Flushing 14/9/79
Folkestone 20/12/92, 27/12/95
Fontainbleau, Palace of 21/2/32 ff
food
retrenchment of consumption in G's houses 2/2/47
foot and mouth disease
a class question 10/7/83
bill in Lords on 6/2/84 c, 11/2/84 c
live animal importation not to be prohibited 14/4/83 c, 10/5/83
See also cattle plague
Forbes, Alexander Penrose, Bp. (1817–1875), bishop of Brechin (1848), known as 'the Scottish Pusey' 13/10/57, 2/11/59, 29/4/72
at Hawarden 2/10/74
G's appreciation of 10/10/75 n
letters from G to, printed 16/10/71
Old Catholics and 2/10/74
trial of for heresy 11/12/59 n
Ford Bank, Didsbury (T. Ashton) 26/10/89
Ford Castle, Coldstream (Waterford) 26/9/76
Fordoun, St. Palladius' Chapel 8/10/46, 30/8/47, 3/9/85
Foreign and Colonial Review *See* publications
Foreign Enlistment Bill 20/4/34, 19/12/54, 22/12/54, 30/6/56
Franco-Prussian war and 25/7/70 c, 2/8/70, 6/8/70 c
G doubtful of his vote on 19/12/54
G votes with government on 1/7/56
Foreign Office
honours and 11/1/94
need for retrenchment at 21/10/69
foreign policy
aspect of public policy lying within reach 31/3/57
Britain views 'domination' of any power with dissatisfaction 14/9/70
G's narrowness of capacity and knowledge of 11/1/69
need for absence of controversy on 23/4/80, 4/5/80
silence in Commons on 10/2/70
foreign secretaryship *See* Cecil, Gower, Primrose, Russell, Stanley, Temple
forestry *See* India, treefelling, treeplanting
Forster, William Edward (1818–1886), educated as Quaker; liberal M.P., educationalist; vice-president council 1868–74, Irish secretary 1880–2; resigned over Kilmainham, supported imperial integration 12/2/67, 15/2/67, 11/3/67 ff, 4/7/67, 17/4/72, 31/10/72, 2/12/72, 25/3/73, 12/7/73 c, 27/8/73, 3/2/74, 26/6/76, 28/6/76, 10/7/76 n, 2/8/76, 7/2/77, 19/3/77, 21/4/80 ff, 26/4/80, 18/6/80 ff, 22/7/80 ff, 4/9/80,

Forster, William Edward (*cont.*)
30/9/80 c, 12/5/82, 24/5/82, 7/8/82, 3/2/83, 23/8/83, 22/12/83, 3/5/84, 28/5/84, 20/2/85 c, 25/2/85, 1/12/85
at Hawarden 19/4/81 ff, 15/9/81 ff
ballot bill and 1/2/71 c, 18/2/71 c
death of 5/4/86 n, 9/4/86
Education Bill 1870 and 2/10/69, 4/11/69, 5/11/69, 16/3/70 ff, 8/6/70, 27/6/70, 12/8/71 c, 29/11/71, 7/12/72 c, 12/12/72 c, 24/1/73 c, 27/1/73 c, 4/2/73 c, 20/3/73, 21/3/73, 22/3/73 c, 15/9/73
memorandum on read by G 4/11/69
Friends and 27/8/81, 10/10/82
G reviewing his relations with 7/7/88 n
G's review of Reid's *Life* of 6/8/88 ff
controversy with Selborne over 21/9/88 ff
Household Franchise Bill 1873 and 23/7/73
Irish coercion and 7/10/80 ff, 25/11/80 c, 13/12/80 c
advocates arrest of national and local Land League leaders 3/10/81
disastrous consequences of 1/6/82
release of suspects and 17/9/81, 21/9/81
Irish secretary 8/5/80 ff, 25/10/80 ff, 31/12/80 c
discussion with on core of Irish question 17/3/82
intended move to in 1873 2/8/73, 15/9/73
resignation as 1/5/82 ff, 20/5/82
suggests Spencer replace Cowper as Viceroy 17/5/81, 31/5/81, 3/4/82
wishes to become Lord Lieutenant Deputy 3/4/82
Land Bill 1881 and 25/10/80 ff, 3/12/80 ff, 14/12/80 c, 15/12/80 ff, 31/12/80 c, 1/1/81 ff, 5/3/81 ff
letters from G to, printed 8/6/70, 12/6/71, 31/1/72, 20/3/73, 23/7/73, 15/9/73, 30/10/73, 8/5/80, 22/5/80, 7/6/80, 10/6/80, 21/6/80, 24/6/80, 25/6/80, 10/7/80, 12/7/80, 14/7/80, 15/7/80, 7/10/80, 9/10/80, 25/10/80, 26/10/80, 4/11/80, 7/11/80, 11/11/80, 16/11/80, 17/11/80, 24/11/80, 29/11/80, 3/12/80, 4/12/80, 7/12/80, 9/12/80, 15/12/80, 17/12/80, 25/12/80, 1/1/81, 10/1/81, 5/3/81, 6/3/81, 29/3/81, 4/4/81, 22/4/81, 15/5/81, 17/5/81, 31/5/81, 6/6/81, 27/8/81, 5/9/81, 8/9/81, 21/9/81, 27/9/81, 3/10/81, 4/10/81, 5/10/81, 9/10/81, 13/10/81, 21/10/81, 22/10/81, 27/2/82, 24/3/82, 5/4/82, 12/4/82, 15/4/82, 29/4/82, 30/4/82, 10/10/82, 28/5/83
Lords and 4/9/80
Parnell and 22/2/81 c, 21/9/81 ff, 3/10/81 ff
position of excellent 24/3/70
Reid's *Life* of and G's letters 11/6/88 n
throws G over *nominatim* on Eastern question 9/10/76
See also Elementary Education Bill, Ireland
Fort Augustus 11/9/58
Fortescue, Chichester Samuel Parkinson- (1823–1898), 1st Baron Carlingford (1874), liberal M.P.; Irish secretary 1865–6, 1868–70, married Lady Waldegrave; president of board of trade 1870–4; privy seal 1881–5; president of council 1883–5; unionist 23/3/54, 24/3/54, 1/8/60, 19/11/60, 13/2/61, 3/6/63 n, 2/3/64, 27/3/67, 23/11/67, 21/2/68, 23/5/68, 3/11/69, 15/8/70, 6/5/72, 18/11/72 c, 6/12/72, 10/5/73 c, 3/2/74, 13/3/74, 5/3/75, 10/2/76, 15/7/76, 17/2/77, 10/6/77, 11/6/77, 5/7/78, 18/4/79, 29/11/80, 4/12/80, 9/12/80, 18/1/81, 8/4/81 c, 20/5/81 n, 29/3/82, 5/4/82 n, 25/4/82 n, 13/5/82, 10/6/82, 2/12/82, 5/3/83 c, 8/2/84, 27/6/84 ff, 28/2/85
abstains from voting for government 19/4/71
Fenians and 9/10/69, 5/11/70
fobbed off with lord lieutenancy 2/8/73
formation of 1886 ministry and 7/2/86
G meets Delane with 22/2/68
great gentleman, G thinks 4/8/66
Ireland and 3/2/64, 30/11/67
Irish disestablishment and 22/2/69 ff
Irish Land Bill 1870 and 15/9/69 ff, 26/11/69 ff, 13/12/69 ff, 10/1/70 ff, 29/1/70 ff
G's memorandum of differences with 3/12/69
Irish Land Bill 1881
G requests help with 23/3/81, 6/4/81
thinks G confused over 25/3/81 n
Irish secretary 5/12/68 ff
Irish university bill and 26/2/73
letters from G to, printed 23/1/69, 22/2/69, 15/3/69, 29/3/69, 3/8/69, 4/8/69, 15/9/69, 17/9/69, 1/10/69, 9/10/69, 14/10/69, 16/10/69, 18/10/69, 21/10/69, 27/10/69, 22/11/69, 25/11/69, 26/11/69, 2/12/69, 3/12/69, 5/12/69, 7/12/69, 8/12/69, 9/12/69, 17/12/69, 23/12/69, 10/1/70, 12/1/70, 2/3/70, 6/4/70, 15/8/70, 19/8/70, 7/9/70, 11/10/70, 5/11/70, 26/11/70, 28/11/70, 25/2/71, 19/4/71, 24/8/71, 26/2/73, 23/3/81, 6/4/81, 8/4/81,

25/5/81, 28/7/81, 15/3/83, 17/4/83, 26/6/83, 1/7/84, 7/9/84, 11/9/84, 16/9/84, 7/2/86
lord president 15/3/83 ff
complications over duties of 17/4/83
G's impatience with 17/4/83
lord privy seal 8/4/81 ff, 15/3/83 ff
G's attempts to move him from 7/9/84, 11/9/84, 16/9/84, 17/9/84, 25/9/84, 27/9/84, 7/10/84, 10/10/84
president of the board of trade 17/12/70
See also agriculture, Ireland
Forth Bridge
G supplies books for workmen on 8/10/84
G's visit to 28/8/84
marvellous, not ugly structure 22/10/90
fortifications plan 16/12/59 ff, 23/5/60 ff, 13/7/60, 16/7/60, 31/3/62, 4/4/62, 6/5/63, 27/3/80 n, 24/10/81
distinct basis settled 25/7/60
G gives great blow to 31/3/62
G's last shot in the locker 16/7/60
See also army, resignation
Fortnightly Review *See* publications
fortune, irony of 6/3/85
fortune-telling
G's fortune told 1/4/92 n
fossils, G's interest in 3/9/32 ff, 19/9/32
Fountain's Abbey 26/10/87
Fox, Charles James 3/5/41
G disappointed in 16/10/35
France 9/2/32 ff, 22/1/39 ff, 14/7/49 ff, 8/8/49, 18/10/50, 6/9/80 c
absence of drunkenness in 28/2/32
Académie des sciences morales et politiques, G member of 9/3/65
attends 24/1/67, 26/1/67
Africa, West, forts and 10/11/73, 8/8/83 c, 21/4/84 c
alliance with 19/2/55
American civil war and 23/10/62 n, 12/11/62
atheism in 14/6/38
attitude to Bourbons 15/2/32
bomb in Chamber of 10/12/93
British relations with
G's reflections on 6/9/70
Canada and
Saint Pierre/Miquelon 21/10/71 c, 10/7/72 c
China and 7/5/83 c, 6/10/84 c, 22/10/84 c, 27/11/84 c
Cobden treaty with 12/9/59, 13/9/59, 17/9/59, 5/7/71 c, 29/7/71 c, 5/8/71 c, 11/5/80
G writes Instructions for 10/1/60, 11/1/60, 15/1/60
renegotiation of 16/1/69, 24/8/71 ff, 18/6/80 ff
commercial treaty with 23/7/81 c, 28/7/81, 6/8/81 c, 20/8/81 c, 12/10/81 c, 2/11/81, 1/1/82, 4/1/82, 6/1/82 c, 21/1/82
demon of ambition in 18/2/69
Egypt and 26/10/69 c, 5/11/69, 17/11/69, 1/2/82 c, 3/2/82 c, 13/5/82 c, 31/5/82 c, 21/6/82 c, 8/7/82 c, 13/7/82, 16/11/82 c, 4/12/82 c, 29/12/82, 7/3/84 c, 4/5/84 ff, 14/5/84 ff, 9/6/84 c, 10/6/84 c, 14/6/84 c, 16/6/84, 28/6/84, 16/7/84 c, 2/1/85 c, 20/1/85, 21/1/85 c, 2/2/85, 10/3/86, 15/3/86, 1/11/92, 16/1/93 ff, 19/5/93 ff, 25/5/93 ff, 14/7/93 ff
invited to join invasion of 24/7/82 c
elections in 5/6/69 c
Floquet's bill to expel Bourbon and Bonapartist princes 28/1/83, 10/2/83
free trade and
unlearning the elementary lessons 24/1/72
free trade in 29/11/69
French embassy in London
tone of theatricals bad 28/7/60
G's interviews with French newspapers 20/10/79, 22/10/79, 23/10/79
G's interview with President Carnot
G's Vatican pamphlets banned from sale at railway stations 10/11/75
Italian unification and 30/6/59, 26/3/61
land tenure in compared with Ireland 1/9/69, 13/9/69, 29/11/69
militarism in 20/1/94
Moroccan loan and 26/9/61
Napoleon and Bismarck of equal trustworthiness 20/7/70
navy of 2/12/84 c, 10/1/94 c
G's inspection of ironclads 16/2/83
need for strong neighbours to curb 18/2/69
new constitution of a sham 28/4/70
'patriotism' and 20/1/69
Political Economy Society
G addresses 26/1/67
politics of 11/2/32
Pondicherry
possible British annexation of 6/2/71, 11/2/71, 16/2/71
railways in
inferior branch lines 2/10/66
republic in
British recognition of 27/9/70 n, 30/9/70 c, 10/1/71, 19/1/71 c, 15/2/71 c
difficulty of preventing it becoming ridiculous 14/9/70
roads of 25/1/39
Spain, throne of, and 7/7/70

freedom of cities granted to G
Aberdeen 13/9/71 n, 17/9/71, 26/9/71
Cardiff 6/7/89
Dingwall 2/9/53, 27/9/53
Dublin 7/11/77
Dundee 29/10/90
Edinburgh 4/10/53, 9/10/53
Hamilton 6/12/79
Inverness 27/9/53
Kirkwall 13/9/83
Liverpool 6/10/92, 3/12/92
Newcastle 3/10/91
Perth 1/12/79
free trade 17/11/30 n, 14/2/33, 9/3/33, 4/6/41, 6/12/45, 24/2/52 ff, 11/11/52 ff, 13/7/75 n, 7/11/79 n, 13/11/79, 8/10/81, 29/10/90 n, 26/9/92
Britain so strong in world market as to be free of huckstering 2/11/81
formation of Derby's government and 24/2/52, 25/2/52, 27/2/52
France and 29/11/69
unlearning the elementary lessons 24/1/72
G's little faith in tariff treaties 30/6/81
G thinks great controversy over, ended 26/11/52
opponents of Cobden Treaty agree to principle of 3/2/60
U.S.A. and 5/1/70, 7/12/88 n
G's article on 7/12/88 ff
See also Cobden, Cobden Treaty, corn laws, fair trade, France, Gladstone (Sir John), Peel, tariffs
Freiheit, Die
prosecution of 26/3/81 c
French
G teaching 7/11/34, 12/11/34
French revolution 15/12/38, 19/12/38
Burke wrong on 8/7/81
centenary of
G attends Paris celebrations of 3/9/89 ff
tory boycott of 28/5/89
G's ignorance of 16/11/32
See also Pitt
friendly societies 7/6/69
G declines to receive deputation from 7/6/69, 9/6/69 n
G's government annuities plan and 1/3/64, 5/3/64, 7/3/64
Loyal Order of Ancient Shepherds
G chairing meeting of and admitted member of 10/6/78, 11/6/78, 12/6/78
Frogmore
royal mausoleum at 16/1/62
Frognall, Foot's Cray, Kent (Sydney) 9/9/76
Frome 22/1/77
Frome affair 4/4/52, 16/4/52 ff, 7/6/52, 8/6/52 ff, 18/6/52
Fuentarabia 26/12/91
Fulham, G engaged in marriage at 8/6/39
funerals 22/2/29 ff, 7/9/33, 15/2/34, 30/9/35, 23/3/37, 8/7/37, 4/6/38, 17/6/48, 8/11/48, 13/4/50, 21/5/50, 11/10/50, 19/10/52, 26/1/54, 20/5/54, 24/8/57, 19/3/58, 21/12/60, 28/2/61, 9/8/61, 23/12/61, 3/1/62, 21/6/62, 12/2/63, 2/5/63, 17/11/63, 3/10/65, 27/10/65, 9/5/68, 3/11/68, 12/11/69, 19/4/70, 27/10/71, 25/1/73, 10/3/73, 21/6/73, 25/11/73, 15/1/74, 24/6/74, 30/6/74, 5/9/74, 19/10/74, 25/3/75, 28/8/75, 9/3/76, 22/4/76, 17/6/76, 16/4/78, 5/6/78, 5/7/79, 11/5/82, 21/9/82, 23/9/82, 6/2/84, 27/1/85, 27/5/85, 19/12/85, 23/2/86, 24/5/86, 11/11/87, 12/6/88, 26/3/89, 20/2/90, 16/10/90, 25/11/90, 29/4/91, 23/4/92
arrangements for G's funeral discussed with C. G 28/3/94
presbyterian, comments on 14/8/47
Fushie Bridge 6/6/28
old whig landlady of 12/6/69
future
G's mixed feelings about 3/12/93

Gaglignani's Messenger 25/5/32, 16/6/32, 19/7/32
Gairloch 12/9/83
Galashiels (Reay) 30/3/80
galleries visited
Accademia, Bologna 12/6/32, 26/9/38
Accademia, Florence 23/3/32 ff
Accademia, Venice 19/6/32 ff, 2/10/79 ff
Agnew's 24/6/81
Antwerp 3/2/32
Apsley house 25/5/35
Atherstone's 24/7/38
Bartolozzi 31/7/83
Bold Street, Liverpool 10/9/59, 11/10/61
Borghese, Rome 23/11/66
Bowes museum, Barnard Castle 21/9/76
Brera, Milan 9/7/32, 22/9/38
Brignola, Genoa 7/11/50
British Artists 3/4/75
British Institution 10/4/34
Campidoglio, Rome 1/6/32 ff
Capo di Monte, Naples 23/11/50 ff
Cardinal Fesch's 11/12/38
Carelli's, Naples 9/12/50
Doré 13/6/72
Dragonetti's, Naples 30/11/50
Dresden 13/11/58
Duc de Berri 26/5/34
Dudley's 25/7/51

galleries visited (*cont.*)
Dulwich 2/7/63, 23/6/65, 5/6/75
Farrer's 30/4/56
Fine Arts Society 3/6/82
Forbes's 21/5/41
Frankfurt 11/9/38
French gallery 29/3/73
Gallarini, Rome 7/11/66, 9/11/66
Gassiot's 14/6/75
Grosvenor Gallery 9/5/77, 30/4/79, 30/4/80, 30/4/81, 2/3/82, 29/4/82, 14/7/85, 30/4/87
Grosvenor House (Westminster's) 23/7/40
Hine's 28/4/83
Holford's 2/7/70
Hope's 23/6/36
Jerichau's 7/6/71
Leuchtenberg, Munich 6/10/45
Louvre 14/2/32 ff, 26/9/45, 14/7/49, 8/8/49, 23/10/50, 16/10/79 ff, 1/3/83, 27/2/92
Maclean's 4/5/71, 29/3/73, 3/4/75
Marine 22/4/75
Meyer's, Liverpool 13/10/64
Miss Clarke's china 10/12/57
Modena 26/9/38
Museo Gregoriano 16/1/39
museum, Lyons 27/2/32
National Gallery 7/5/33, 4/6/33, 15/6/35, 9/6/36, 20/4/37, 7/6/37, 16/4/38, 7/5/39, 1/6/43, 3/3/53, 21/7/53, 12/3/56, 21/5/56, 7/6/62, 9/7/63, 27/7/71, 5/2/91
G shown round by Eastlake 9/7/63
G trustee of 7/1/54, 24/4/69
Kruger collection, G helps in purchasing 1/3/54, 20/6/54
Peel collection 5/5/71
New Gallery 1/5/89, 30/4/90, 11/4/91
Nuremberg 21/9/74
Palais des Arts, Lyons 25/2/32
Palazzo Barberini 31/12/38
Palazzo Borghese, Rome 18/4/32 ff, 9/1/39
Palazzo Colonna 14/12/38
Palazzo Corsini 12/1/39
Palazzo Doria 7/4/32 ff, 30/5/32, 5/1/39
Palazzo Farnese, Rome 11/12/38
Palazzo Madama, Turin 2/11/50
Palazzo Mareschalchi, Bologna 12/6/32
Palazzo Palagonia, Palermo 15/10/38
Pall Mall 3/4/75, 30/3/78
Perugia 4/10/38
Pinakothek, Munich 1/10/45, 10/9/74, 13/10/79
Pitti Palace, Florence 20/3/32 ff, 29/9/38, 2/10/38
Portrait Gallery 19/6/58
Quirinal (Rome) 17/1/39
Regent gallery
Okey's exhibition 3/5/56
Rogers' 21/4/56, 2/5/56
Rosa Bonheur's 'The horse fair' 30/4/57
Rothschild's 13/4/72
Royal Pictures 22/4/47
R. Vernon's 20/5/48
Society of British Artists' 26/3/42, 28/3/46
St. Angelo's, Naples 5/12/50
Studio, Naples 2/5/32 ff, 14/5/32 ff, 14/11/38 ff, 17/11/38 ff, 23/11/38 ff, 27/11/50
Suffolk Street 27/3/74
Temple's, Naples 5/12/50
T. Hamlet's 18/5/41
T. V. Barker's 21/7/57
Uffizi, Florence 17/3/32 ff, 28/9/38, 1/10/38, 5/1/67 ff, 7/1/88 ff
Universita, Palermo 16/10/38
Vatican museum 4/4/32 ff, 20/12/38, 3/1/39, 10/1/39, 17/1/39
poor opening hours of 10/1/39
Vernon's 1/8/50
Villa Ludovisi 15/1/39
Villa Massimi (Rome) 11/1/39
Walker, Liverpool 11/10/83
Ward's 15/3/56, 25/3/56
Westminster's 18/6/47
Woodburn's (at Christies) 22/6/53, 17/4/54
Zambeccari, Bologna 12/6/32
See also National Portrait Gallery
Galuppi *See* operas
Galvanism *See* medicines
Galway
Queen's college 20/4/53
Galway contract 13/9/59, 3/8/61 *See also* deputations
gambling
Tranby Croft affair 4/6/91, 10/6/91 ff, 19/6/91
game laws 4/3/71 c, 17/3/71 c, 6/5/71 c, 25/1/72 c, 2/3/72 c, 5/5/80 cf, 19/6/80 c, 10/7/80 c
games and sports *See* backgammon, billiards, boating, bowls, card games, chess, cricket, Cumbrian wrestling, curling, Derby (the), draughts, fishing, golf, horse racing, otter hunting, riding, rowing, running, sculling, secretaire, shooting, walks (long)
gaols 15/8/25
gardening 30/6/28
cottage gardening
G's speech on 21/8/90
G's speech on 17/8/76, 28/8/79
Garendon Park, Leicestershire (Phillips de Lisle)
G's visit to de Lisle's monastery 7/10/73, 8/10/73

Garibaldi, Giuseppe (1807–1882)
at Palmerston's 16/4/64
at Stafford House 13/4/64
deputation on 10/5/64
G persuades to abandon provincial tour 17/4/64
G quite satisfied with 12/4/64
G's conversation with at Cliveden 24/4/64
G's farewell to 25/4/64
G's party for 20/4/64
reception at Chiswick 12/4/64
See also Italy, Temple (Henry)
Garrawalt, Lynn of 3/9/39
Garrick Club *See* clubs
Garsington 19/8/28
Garter *See* patronage
Gaskell, James Milnes- (1810–1873), G's schoolfriend, Lord of the Treasury, tory M.P. 26/6/26 ff, 7/7/26, 5/10/26, 15/5/27, 23/7/27 ff, 27/7/27, 17/1/29 ff, 19/5/29, 8/9/29 ff, 17/10/29, 26/3/30, 9/8/31, 19/10/31, 14/10/32, 29/1/33, 3/2/33, 22/6/36, 28/2/38, 9/4/40, 23/3/41, 4/9/41, 4/6/42, 29/4/43, 14/11/43, 17/7/54, 7/5/55, 19/5/55, 4/3/68, 29/6/68, 4/9/71 ff, 31/10/83
Canning the Exemplar of G and Gaskell 9/9/71
deathbed of, G visits 2/2/73
G meets Guizot with 3/3/49
Maynooth grant and 20/1/44 ff
memoirs of Eton life of 23/10/83
religion and 1/3/31
secretary of WEG society 23/10/29, 19/3/30
See also Eton College
gas stokers, case of *See* Bruce, cabinet, trade unions
Geddington preparatory school
W. H. G at 30/1/50 ff
general elections *See* elections (general/bye)
Geneva 13/7/32 ff
Geneva, Lake 12/7/32
Genoa 9/3/32, 20/7/49, 29/7/49, 4/11/50, 21/2/51, 17/1/67
Hotel Feder 4/11/50, 21/2/51
monstrous carriage charges in 7/11/50
radical posters in 20/7/49
Geographical Society 24/5/58, 11/4/59, 23/5/59, 26/5/62, 8/12/62, 23/5/64
geography *See* Homer
Geological Society
G dining with 15/2/62
George III *See* Pitt
George William Frederick Charles (1819–1904), Duke of Cambridge, commander-in-chief of the army (1856) 12/1/53, 2/4/59, 16/11/59, 6/3/60, 22/5/61, 10/3/66, 2/5/66, 12/6/66, 25/6/69, 21/1/71, 5/6/71, 20/12/71, 26/6/72, 19/3/73, 14/7/73, 3/9/73, 27/2/74, 20/3/75, 18/3/76, 16/6/80, 21/5/81, 1/4/83, 9/2/92, 22/1/93
army reform and 16/12/80
back-stairs pressure by 3/9/73
Eastern question and
black as thunder, declines to offer hand 11/3/78
highly embarrassing language of 14/9/81
purchase abolition and 3/6/71
his vote on the bill 8/7/71 c, 10/7/71, 12/7/71 c, 15/7/71 c
German
G learning 27/6/32 ff, 5/11/32, 23/5/33 ff, 1/8/33 ff, 7/7/36, 17/8/38, 29/8/38 ff
Germans
far from egotistic while abounding in nationality 18/8/38
Germany
Africa, East, and 30/12/84, 28/4/86
Africa, South, and
G glad to see as neighbours in 21/12/84
Africa and
Angra Pequeña 14/6/84 c, 21/6/84 c
proposes Berlin Conference 8/10/84
Alsace-Lorraine and
plebiscite and 23/11/70
Anglo-German Agreement 1890 19/6/90, 8/7/90, 24/7/90
anti-toryism in 21/7/32
Britain views 'domination' of with dissatisfaction 14/9/70
Cameroons and 7/3/85 c
church controversy in 15/11/73 c
colonising by welcomed by G 21/12/84, 12/3/85
condition of labour in 1/9/38
Delagoa Bay and
an idle fear 30/12/84
Egypt and 2/12/84 c, 2/1/85 c, 13/3/85 c
emigrant ship of 27/1/73 c, 28/1/73, 29/1/73 c
feudalism in 26/8/38
Fiji and 7/2/85 c
intellectual life of
reason established in, G thinks 30/9/74
vigorous 30/9/74
Jews in 20/8/38
Krupp guns used by Mahdi 24/4/84
lacks the sympathies of Europe 24/2/71
militarism in 20/1/94
mind of
Döllinger's Universitäten the best description of 10/9/73
New Guinea and 27/6/84 c, 6/8/84 c, 9/8/84 c, 6/10/84 cn, 3/1/85 c, 7/3/85 c

Germany (*cont.*)
philosophy of, has added little to knowledge of mind and men 16/2/73
Pole, the, and 7/3/85 c
Pope, election of 22/8/72
principles of free polity, British differences with Germany on 26/2/71
Prussia
religious education equated with nationality in 4/11/69
sack-races in 18/8/38
Smyrna and 9/10/80
St. Lucia and 7/3/85 c
threatening annexation of Belgium 30/1/69
Transvaal and 17/11/84
troops of 21/7/32
ultramontanism and
support for the rational party in the church 22/8/72
universities of
G enquires into their endowments 10/1/73
'War in Sight' crisis in 5/3/75
war with France
possibility of 30/1/69
See also Alsace-Lorraine, Berlin, Bismarck, cabinet, Franco-Prussian war, Max Müller, memoranda (printed), Prussia, Rhine, Turkey
getting up, G's regulations for 12/12/25 ff
Gherardini collection
purchased for nation by G 11/2/54, 20/3/54
ghost stories 1/5/30
Giacommetti, P. *See* plays seen
Gibbon, Edward
Decline and fall
epitome of 2/11/25 ff, 25/11/25 ff, 23/2/26
Milman's edition's deficiencies 27/7/41
Robert Elsmere and 11/4/88
G votes against 3/3/27
house of, in Lausanne 13/7/32, 16/7/32
See also Hume
Gibraltar 10/4/69 c, 24/2/70, 26/2/70 c
Gillingham
G's speech at 17/6/89
Gilside, Gateshead (W. Hutt) 6/10/62
giraffe (piano) 3/8/28 ff
Gladstone, Agnes *See* Wickham
Gladstone, Anne (1773–1835), née Robertson, mother 17/7/25, 27/4/35
body brought to Fasque 2/11/48
Brougham and 11/10/64
death of 17/9/35 ff, 23/9/35 ff, 2/10/35, 23/9/36, 20/9/47, 23/9/47, 23/9/51, 2/9/85
G believes from erysipelas 20/9/47
G reads bible to 17/5/35 ff
illnesses of 19/11/25, 8/1/26, 5/9/27 ff, 26/5/28, 15/8/31, 29/12/31, 21/11/32 ff, 31/8/33, 16/11/33, 9/12/33, 15/8/34, 1/5/35, 2/5/35 ff, 14/5/35, 20/5/35, 11/7/35 ff, 7/9/35 ff
Gladstone, Anne Mackenzie (1802–1829), sister and godmother 18/7/25, 11/2/27, 24/12/27, 20/1/28, 19/4/28, 24/12/41, 19/2/49, 24/12/49
coffin of
brought to Fasque 1848 6/10/48
death and funeral of 19/2/29 ff, 31/12/29, 18/2/30 ff, 24/12/30, 19/2/33, 20/2/34, 24/12/36, 19/2/40, 19/2/48, 24/12/60, 24/12/65, 24/12/78
deathbed attendant 7/2/79 n
happy anniversary of 19/2/43
illnesses of 29/8/25, 24/12/25, 8/1/26, 18/7/26 ff, 8/9/26 ff, 13/12/28, 9/2/29 ff
letters of 17/4/31
Gladstone, Catherine (1812–1900), née Glynne, wife 23/7/38, 3/1/39 n, 6/1/51, 6/1/55, 31/12/56, 6/1/57, 6/1/61, 4/8/72, 15/8/72, 6/1/73, 5/3/73, 14/6/73, 10/10/73, 3/11/73, 15/2/74, 12/4/74, 29/4/74, 13/6/74, 26/6/74, 29/7/74, 6/1/75, 16/3/75, 30/7/75, 15/9/75, 8/10/75, 1/9/76, 28/11/76, 26/12/76, 6/1/77, 2/8/77, 27/8/77, 26/11/77, 29/4/78, 3/8/78, 6/1/79, 7/2/79, 7/5/79, 19/5/79, 20/7/79, 2/8/79, 8/11/79, 29/12/79, 6/1/80, 8/2/80, 12/8/80, 20/8/80, 17/9/80 ff, 31/12/80, 28/6/81, 21/9/81, 11/11/81, 18/11/81, 6/1/82, 31/1/82, 14/4/82, 5/6/82, 5/10/82, 6/1/83, 29/6/83, 26/9/83 ff, 1/10/83, 26/11/83, 6/1/84, 4/4/84, 10/5/84 ff, 1/7/84, 8/8/84, 9/12/84, 6/1/85, 7/1/85 ff, 14/3/85, 22/4/85, 30/4/85, 10/8/85 ff, 18/9/85, 11/12/85, 5/2/86, 6/3/86 ff, 23/3/86 ff, 18/4/86 ff, 26/4/86 ff, 27/5/86 ff, 23/6/86 ff, 14/10/86, 13/1/87, 7/2/87 ff, 8/8/87 ff, 15/10/87, 15/3/88, 16/5/88, 6/1/89, 16/3/89, 30/9/89, 13/12/89 ff, 4/5/90, 18/7/90 ff, 6/1/91, 6/1/92 ff, 8/6/92 ff, 26/6/92 ff, 25/7/92 ff, 28/11/92 ff, 6/1/93 ff, 20/5/93 ff, 2/8/93 ff, 6/1/94 ff, 12/2/94 ff
1857 a year of tears for 6/1/58
1874 election and
G startles by mention of probable consequences 7/2/74
absences from G 25/4/42, 11/4/49 ff, 20/6/50 ff, 16/7/50 ff, 13/2/52,

22/5/52, 1/7/52, 1/7/53, 11/3/54 ff, 1/8/54, 26/1/57, 23/6/57, 9/7/59, 10/7/59, 13/8/60, 1/8/61, 7/12/63, 27/5/65, 6/9/69, 24/3/70, 8/9/70, 15/6/74, 2/7/75, 12/4/90, 3/11/90 ff, 24/2/91, 21/3/91, 30/6/91, 27/1/92 ff, 1/4/92 ff
accepts G's proposal of marriage 8/6/39 ff
accident to 9/9/62
accompanies G on visit to Oxford 5/2/90 ff
admirable qualities of 6/2/39, 26/7/39 ff
alarm about a novelty to G 28/7/47
amanuensis for translation of Farini 20/12/50 ff
as G's secretary 5/9/53 ff, 13/4/80 n
assists with St. Andrew's, Fasque 2/12/46 ff
at All Saints, Margaret St. 16/10/42
at Osborne 24/1/69
at Stafford House 11/3/58
at the Commons 22/3/41
at Windsor 19/4/63
birthday of
  forgotten by G in prayers 6/1/50
Bow Street, evidence against trickster given at 11/3/79
Bradley's portrait of 28/5/42
breastfeeding
  3 month old baby brought in 31/8/49
  difficulties of 21/11/40 ff, 10/1/41, 4/11/42, 7/11/42 ff, 28/11/42, 4/4/44, 6/4/44, 8/4/44, 10/4/44, 25/4/44, 28/7/45 ff, 24/11/47 ff, 29/8/49 ff, 4/4/52
  G rubbing breasts 25/11/47 ff, 30/8/49 ff, 4/4/52 ff, 9/1/54 ff
  weaning 19/12/42 ff, 20/8/52, 21/8/52
bust of by Adams-Acton 26/1/84
chaplain to G, acting as 25/7/94
chessplaying with G 27/8/39, 9/10/40 ff, 27/9/42 ff, 30/1/44 ff
children's romances and 22/6/75 ff, 26/6/75, 1/7/75
churching of 25/6/40, 24/11/42, 19/8/45, 21/12/47, 21/9/49, 28/4/52, 4/2/54
constitution of 4/9/40
conversation on religion with Hope 5/10/46
cotton famine and
  assisting in Blackburn 31/12/62
cousin of, strange, incredible horror 1/7/65
Crawford divorce case and 21/7/86
cuts sod of Wrexham, Mold, Connah's Quay railway 22/10/62
death of Stephen Glynne and 18/6/74, 20/6/74 ff
  future seemed to clear a little before her 26/6/74
death of W. H. G and 30/6/91, 5/7/91 ff
experiments with ear-trumpet 9/6/93
freshness and vigour of 6/1/76
garden party of 22/7/70
Garibaldi's visit and 20/4/64, 25/4/64
G consults on Ionian decision 23/10/58 ff
G consults on publication of *Chapter of autobiography* 23/9/68
G discusses Mrs. Thistlethwayte with 19/12/69
G discusses party organisation with 20/10/51
G enjoys nursing 7/3/47
G explains plans for St. Deiniol's to 15/8/88
given lead as medicine in error 8/2/56
giving musical parties 19/5/57
G leaves in Naples 18/2/51
G leaves with fever cases 18/5/61
G nursing 7/2/51, 13/2/51
golden wedding of 25/7/89
G playing billiards with 30/7/39
G reading Bible with 26/7/39 ff, 31/8/39, 12/12/39, 11/9/40, 8/10/40, 10/12/40, 15/8/44, 27/12/74
G reading with 18/7/39 ff, 2/1/70
G's letter proposing marriage 19/1/39 n
G speaking for 14/8/84
G spending time with 15/4/44, 17/4/44
G's plan of reading with 9/9/39
G's rescue work and
  warns him of credulity 14/6/73
G's responsibilities to 15/7/39
G's retirement from liberal leadership, reluctant to accept 4/3/74, 7/1/75, 18/11/81, 21/11/81
  low as a result 14/1/75 ff
G's treasure 15/12/93
G's walks with, now rare 5/7/63
G's will and 31/1/76, 1/1/79, 4/1/79
  approves family arrangements 4/1/79
G urges self-denial to 21/1/44
Hampstead smallpox hospital and 7/9/71 n
Hawarden bazaar and 14/8/76
Hawarden estate and
  administratrix of 28/8/74
Hawarden estate's future and 1/9/65
Hawarden Horticultural Society, dispute with 29/5/87
health of 13/7/39, 3/6/40 ff, 26/6/40, 16/8/40 ff, 15/11/40, 10/4/41, 31/5/41, 4/5/42, 25/10/48 ff, 7/1/51 ff, 16/1/53, 7/4/55, 14/11/57, 24/2/58, 3/4/58, 25/8/59, 30/8/59, 2/9/59, 6/1/61, 28/6/61, 19/3/79, 10/12/79, 13/10/80 ff, 23/7/81, 5/12/81, 6/1/82, 15/7/83, 26/11/83, 2/12/83, 23/3/84, 12/12/86, 15/10/88 ff, 23/10/89, 8/11/90 ff, 30/11/90, 30/12/90, 9/7/91 ff, 11/1/92, 2/2/92 ff, 11/2/92, 22/2/93 ff, 15/5/93, 29/11/93, 4/12/93, 14/3/94 ff, 25/4/94, 5/11/95, 25/3/96, 29/12/96
  deafness 27/9/91

Gladstone, Catherine (*cont.*)
health of (*cont.*)
erisypelas 25/12/69, 26/12/69, 3/8/75, 14/8/81, 3/3/82
erythema, suffering from 27/12/74, 20/12/93 ff
heart trouble 19/11/39, 18/12/39
ill at Valsecure 2/2/92 ff
ill from excessive charitable work 6/12/64, 27/7/65, 3/8/66 n
neuralgia, suffering from 18/8/67
height: 5ft. 7. 75ins.(in stockings or slippers) 26/12/59
her adoptive family and 20/8/39
hero-woman, G thinks 6/1/62
her sister's death and 16/8/57 ff
holds 'Assembly' 18/5/46
in Ionia 24/11/58 ff
gives ball 31/1/59
holds reception for the ladies 13/12/58
in Rome 16/12/38, 20/12/38, 21/12/38, 12/10/66 ff
insomnia of 23/8/52 ff, 7/9/52, 16/1/83
introduced to Laura Thistlethwayte 18/5/87, 8/5/88
involved with G's rescue work 2/8/50
Jubilee 1887 and 15/2/87
lays foundation stone 26/6/62
laziness prevents G writing to on wedding anniversary 25/7/86
letters from G to, printed 23/7/81, 29/7/81, 30/7/81, 1/8/81, 2/12/81, 24/8/82, 25/8/82, 26/8/82, 28/8/82, 21/10/82, 26/3/83, 24/8/83, 26/10/83, 1/1/84, 8/10/84, 2/1/85, 17/2/85, 8/4/85, 2/5/85, 1/7/86, 3/7/86, 15/8/92, 29/9/92, 17/12/92, 11/3/93, 18/11/93, 2/12/93, 19/12/93, 23/12/93, 21/3/94
list of her suitors 15/6/39
London home, G reluctant to contemplate
C. G regards sale of house with reluctance & discomfort 30/3/75
discussed with C. G 18/3/75
love and service of remain wonderful 29/12/93
lunching with Laura Thistlethwayte 23/7/87, 20/7/89
menopause of 25/8/59, 30/8/95
Midlothian campaigns and 26/11/79
neglect of 30/3/40
Newport Market refuge and 3/2/65
nobility of 6/1/68, 6/1/91
normally teaches arithmetic 13/2/47
nurse, incomparable 20/1/47, 29/5/71, 31/3/80 ff, 25/2/81
patronage, church, discussed with 25/9/73
peerage for: offer rejected on G's advice 21/3/94
piano playing
pupil of Liszt 1/1/67
playing backgammon with G 23/5/91 ff
playing the organ 11/7/47
political conversations with 3/8/64
political negotiations by 18/5/82 n
with the Roseberys 10/1/83 ff
portraits of
Herkomer (Hawarden) 23/5/88, 25/7/88 n
Weigall 27/7/88
pregnancies of 18/9/39 ff, 26/10/39 ff, 1/5/40, 3/5/40, 23/5/40, 13/9/42, 3/4/44, 25/7/45, 5/7/47, 15/7/47, 18/7/47, 26/7/47, 28/7/47, 8/6/49, 19/8/49, 7/1/51, 18/11/51, 7/3/52
bad fall while pregnant 8/6/49
enthusiasm for 18/10/42
in childbirth 3/6/40, 17/10/42, 18/10/42, 4/4/44, 27/7/45, 22/11/47, 23/11/47, 27/8/49, 28/8/49, 1/4/52, 2/4/52, 7/1/54
miscarriage of 7/1/51
near miscarriage 1/10/47
prevents visit to Windsor 4/1/54
susceptibility to cholera during 19/8/49
Queen and
advises softening G's memorandum for 17/7/72
C. G at Windsor alone 12/3/84
reaction to G's shooting accident 13/9/42
reading Scott to G 10/10/92 ff
reading sermons to G 19/11/93
reads G all the Psalms 30/7/92
received by the Queen 28/4/42
return from Naples 9/4/51
Riviera, thrives on 11/2/92
Russian famine, G drafts letter for her on 11/2/92
Scarlet Fever Home of 21/3/82
sees Palmerston on ecclesiastical patronage 9/3/60
selfish behaviour of G to 18/5/61
sensitivity of 8/8/39
Shadwell home and 22/5/78
singing duet 11/12/62
sleeping badly 11/1/58, 13/1/58, 3/2/58, 7/2/58, 8/2/58, 10/2/58, 16/1/83
Snaresbrook refuge and home and 21/11/67
spitting blood 25/4/47
Stephen Glynne's death and 18/6/74 ff
strength of, increased 5/9/64
system of much deranged 13/1/58
Tennyson and 4/7/90
the Herberts at Wilton and 30/8/66
views on luxury 6/2/39
Windsor, visits alone 11/7/93
Women's Liberal Federation and 22/5/89 n

Gladstone, Helen Jane (*cont.*)
in Cologne
alarming accounts of 10/1/80
visited by G 7/9/74, 22/9/74 ff, 15/9/79
in Germany 6/7/45 n, 21/7/45, 13/9/45
journeys abroad 5/8/38
living at Castle hotel, Richmond 18/9/66
living at St. Helen's Priory, Isle of Wight 12/8/59
G visits at 12/8/59, 5/8/61, 17/2/64, 30/1/65
mental condition of 12/10/44 ff
mind broken 8/9/47
mind restored 13/11/47
need to be with Roman Catholics 12/10/44
opium addiction of 12/10/44, 8/10/45 ff, 6/8/47, 20/8/47 ff, 6/10/47, 14/10/47, 6/8/48, 19/1/80
disliking opium 5/10/47
prematurely aged 20/2/58
reading bible with 23/8/33
recovers speech 13/11/45
refuse to be touched by G 16/10/45
religion in the balance 13/11/47
religious position of
G able to sympathise with 22/9/74
religious profession, G's memorandum on 8/2/80, 21/9/80
Roman catholicism
conversion to 30/5/42, 31/5/42 ff
deathbed views of 12/1/80 ff, 2/9/82 n
G accused of causing 28/5/47
Roman Catholicism and 31/10/37, 26/6/38 ff, 9/1/41 ff, 27/1/41 ff, 10/2/41, 23/2/41, 1/3/41 ff, 26/5/42 ff, 11/6/42 ff, 29/12/42, 4/5/43
sent abroad 24/10/41, 27/10/41
servants of, intoxicated 9/1/41
strange behaviour to guests 9/10/44
to be denied laudanum 6/10/47
to be kept from G's children 4/5/43
will of 6/7/45, 21/7/45, 7/2/81
will seems broken 5/10/47
withdraws H. J. G from Eton: very inconvenient mistake 19/10/66
Gladstone, Henry Neville (1852–1935), 1st Baron Gladstone of Hawarden (1932), son; businessman in India; G's secretary as needed 2/4/52, 3/1/62, 15/1/65, 16/1/68, 2/4/71, 21/8/71, 22/1/73, 23/1/73, 13/6/74, 18/6/74 ff, 1/11/74, 17/4/76, 22/4/76, 6/5/76, 26/7/76, 22/10/76, 1/1/79, 17/7/80, 22/9/80, 6/6/84, 2/5/85, 19/7/85, 15/12/85, 17/7/87, 30/10/87, 1/6/89, 7/10/89, 10/12/90, 15/6/91 ff, 23/11/91, 1/10/92, 17/12/92, 28/3/93, 17/10/93, 2/12/93 ff, 15/2/94 ff, 13/4/94 ff, 27/7/96
accidentally felled in tree 27/12/67
allowance for
loan of £12000 at 2 per cent. p.a. 27/4/76
at Eton 20/9/64, 21/9/64
bad language of 10/4/63
Chandernagore monopoly negotiated by H. N. G with French government 3/2/91, 5/3/91
'Commander-in-Chief' 28/6/92
commerce, starts in 23/1/71
finds rather severe 30/1/71
commercial position of 9/6/87
further difficulties with Wyllie 29/11/89
in difficulties with his firm 19/11/89
confirmation of 1/3/68, 28/3/68
death of W. H. G and 7/7/91 ff
engagement (abortive) to Evelyn Garth of 23/4/84, 25/4/84, 27/4/84
engagement of to Maud Rendel 27/9/89, 30/9/89
finances of 3/3/82, 1/6/85
good, acute, affectionate 2/3/58
Hampstead cottage of 4/2/93, 11/3/93 ff, 8/7/93
Hawarden estate and 21/11/87, 23/11/87
Ilbert bill and 17/4/83, 1/6/83
illnesses of
possible meningitis 23/2/54
in India 18/8/74, 1/12/74, 2/12/74, 27/10/76, 19/10/80, 21/4/81, 1/6/82, 3/4/84, 23/9/85, 15/1/86, 20/5/89
chief reward: a great Education 15/6/87
ill-used by J. Wyllie 25/11/75, 18/12/75, 23/12/75 ff, 25/3/76 ff, 20/7/76
returned quite unchanged 7/6/87
in Italy with parents 7/1/88 ff
in Rome 15/12/66 ff
intelligence awakening 6/11/62
letters from G to, printed 21/4/81, 2/12/81, 3/3/82, 23/6/82, 1/6/83, 12/2/86, 16/7/86, 25/12/89 n, 20/1/92, 24/7/93, 31/1/94
marriage of 30/1/90
private secretary, acting as 4/7/92 ff
profession of 21/4/67, 29/8/69, 31/10/69, 30/12/69, 1/10/84
merchant, declares intention to become 17/8/64
qualities of
great merchant with spirit at once bold and cautious 23/9/87
sad business of 30/11/67, 7/12/67
Seaforth estate and 19/4/74
See also childrearing
Gladstone, Herbert John (1854–1930), 1st Viscount Gladstone, son; liberal M.P.; G's secretary as needed 8/8/6, 7/1/54, 7/1/61, 17/12/61, 8/9/64, 25/1/65,

3/1/66, 16/1/68, 19/12/70, 14/1/71, 26/3/71, 6/4/71, 13/9/72, 19/12/73, 26/12/73, 12/1/74, 13/4/74, 23/5/74, 18/6/74 ff, 11/9/74, 12/4/76, 15/4/76, 22/4/76, 26/8/76 ff, 19/9/76, 8/12/76 n, 5/1/77, 7/1/77, 15/3/77, 9/8/77, 1/1/79, 14/8/79, 29/12/79, 7/4/80 ff, 12/6/80, 30/6/80, 13/8/80, 12/10/80, 23/11/80 ff, 21/4/81, 22/4/81, 3/10/81, 9/10/81, 15/12/81, 16/12/81, 18/10/82, 3/2/83, 2/3/83 ff, 3/10/83, 6/11/83, 11/1/84 ff, 14/6/84, 8/8/84, 5/10/84, 30/11/84, 17/1/85, 26/1/85, 8/7/85 ff, 13/9/85, 14/9/85, 8/1/86, 14/1/86, 24/1/86 n, 25/1/86 ff, 11/5/86 ff, 7/1/87, 27/3/87 ff, 7/4/87, 17/7/87, 12/4/88, 3/10/88 ff, 3/12/88 ff, 3/2/89, 20/3/89, 24/9/89, 7/1/90 ff, 4/5/90 ff, 8/11/90 ff, 21/7/92, 23/8/92, 11/1/93 ff, 2/6/93, 2/12/93 ff, 15/4/94 ff

£4000 of his portion from G to be lent to W. H. G 27/12/82
allowance for
  £5000 more than brothers 3/3/82
  loan of £12000 at 2 per cent. p.a. 27/4/76
a remarkable child 7/1/57
article on labour and liberals, capital 30/1/92, 1/2/92
as G's Private Secretary (unofficial) 4/2/80, 16/3/80 ff, 13/1/90
at Eton 18/4/66, 4/6/72
bad language of 10/4/63
breadth and depth of 7/1/62
confirmation of
  delayed by illness 13/2/70, 27/2/70
constituencies held
  Leeds 8/4/80 ff, 9/3/94
death of W. H. G and 7/7/91 ff
financial secretary for war 12/2/86 ff
fright about 15/7/58
good answer to G by 16/5/59
G's autobiography and 25/6/87 n
G's polemical talk with 23/1/94
G's resignation and 9/1/94
G's visit to Leeds and 8/10/81
G teaches backgammon to 14/8/69
Hawarden Kite and 14/12/85 n, 17/12/85 ff, 31/12/85
health of
  asthma 21/9/78
home undersecretary 17/8/92 ff
India, visit to 9/11/86
  lecture on 13/1/90
Ireland and 9/10/81, 21/10/81, 15/12/81, 24/2/82, 4/8/85, 11/10/85 ff, 6/8/89, 7/8/91, 21/11/91
  excellent article on 5/5/92
  G discusses basis of home rule measure with 14/11/85
  G suggests as assistant to Spencer 9/5/82, 12/5/82
  Hawarden Kite and 15/12/85 n, 17/12/85 ff, 31/12/85 n
  negotiation with F. H. O'Donnell 22/4/82, 21/9/88 n
  urges G to declare position on 14/11/85
letters from G to, printed 13/10/83, 18/10/85, 14/11/85
Montenegro, proposed visit to 19/4/81
Privy Councillor 10/3/94
profession of 26/2/71, 13/9/71, 7/1/72, 14/1/72 ff, 25/12/75, 24/3/76, 19/11/76, 21/4/81
  discussed in the Dolomites 29/9/79
  leaning towards politics 29/9/79
  sailor, declares intention to become 17/8/64
public speaker, promise as 4/6/72
qualities of 13/9/71, 7/1/72
  fine fellow, most lovable 7/1/76
  such good company 13/9/77
seats contested but lost
  Middlesex 18/3/80
seats held
  Leeds 7/4/80 n, 8/4/80, 9/4/80, 3/5/86
South Africa, visit to 20/3/77
speaks on behalf of G 3/8/85
University college, Oxford 21/4/72, 17/4/73
  changes from classics to history 19/10/73 n
  first in modern history 19/6/76
  G's paper of suggestions for 7/10/72
  retakes divinity; third in Mods. 17/10/74
will hardly be an ordinary man 7/1/62
withdrawn by Helen G from Eton: very inconvenient mistake 19/10/66
See also childrearing

Gladstone, John, Sir (1764–1851), 1st Baronet (1846), father, merchant: grain and sugar trader, tory M.P., West Indian proprietor 16/7/25, 7/3/29, 18/6/31, 13/7/31, 27/4/35, 25/9/35, 11/7/43, 11/12/50, 7/10/58, 19/1/85, 2/5/88
  accident to 8/3/38
  aged 2/9/50 ff
  anger with T. G over G's Oxford candidacy 9/7/47 ff, 30/7/47, 1/8/47, 2/8/47
  articles by 25/1/33
  as M.P./candidate 4/10/25, 12/11/25, 2/6/26, 15/6/26 ff, 3/8/26, 20/3/27, 24/9/30, 29/9/30, 6/5/34, 27/7/37
  biography of, planned by S. Smiles 19/4/60
  bounty of 8/11/46
  Bradley's portrait of 16/5/42

Gladstone, John, Sir (*cont.*)
brain, failure of 12/9/50
church views of 24/3/39
complains at G's lack of attendance on 25/3/41
corn laws and 2/2/42, 10/2/43 ff
deafness of 12/9/51
death of 7/12/51, 7/12/52, 2/9/85
G enchained re-reading account of 25/10/85
declining frequency of visits to 12/2/46
defended in Commons by G 14/5/41 n, 16/5/41
D.N.B. entry on, G checking 22/7/89 n, 13/11/89 n
excitable on occasion 27/10/48
fever of 27/1/50
final illness of 29/11/51 ff
financial dispositions of 16/9/36, 30/8/39, 20/9/39, 14/1/40, 8/2/40, 17/11/40, 2/11/46, 14/9/48, 18/9/48, 21/9/48, 22/9/48, 28/9/48, 21/11/48, 24/10/49, 25/10/49, 12/11/49, 28/12/49
details of for G 28/9/48
free trade and 5/5/49, 10/10/49, 8/11/49, 20/11/49, 5/12/49, 17/12/49
fires two batteries at G on 14/9/48, 4/10/49
repetitive views of 9/10/49
tries to change G's views on 20/11/49
funeral service of
family disputes over 8/12/51 ff
games with 18/1/27, 7/11/34, 14/2/37
G arranges rota of attendance on 15/3/50, 31/8/51
G assisting in writing *D.N.B* entry of 22/7/89, 13/11/89 n
G drawn unwillingly into freetrade conversation with 16/1/49
G kisses before and after death 13/12/51
G opposes about ferry 30/10/48
G playing cards with 26/3/39, 1/4/39, 13/5/39 ff, 8/7/39, 7/9/39, 17/10/39, 4/11/40 ff, 1/1/41, 22/10/41 ff, 29/3/42, 26/1/43, 16/2/46, 17/8/46 ff, 5/4/47 ff, 25/9/48
those days gone 4/8/50
time taken up by 11/10/44
G reading sermons to 21/1/49, 8/9/50, 20/4/51 ff
G reading to 2/12/33, 18/2/40 ff, 29/11/49 ff
G's finances and 7/5/38
G's marriage and 5/6/39
G's memoir of his last days 9/12/51
G's mem. on his affairs 8/9/50 ff
G thinks himself worthless to 28/3/39
G thinks mentally ill 15/4/50, 27/4/50
health of 12/12/35, 18/4/36, 28/1/40, 2/2/40, 20/2/40 ff, 23/4/40, 23/8/43, 11/12/43, 25/1/47, 1/6/48, 11/12/48, 29/11/49 ff, 11/12/49, 17/4/51, 29/8/51
declining 7/2/51
suffers mild stroke? 25/1/47
influence on G's career 4/8/30, 12/8/30, 24/2/31, 17/1/32, 30/7/32, 11/3/35, 19/4/38, 23/4/39, 5/6/39, 26/8/41 ff
at formation of 1841 government 26/8/41 ff
inheritance left by 13/12/51
lacks composure 11/12/47
Leith church 9/3/39, 28/9/40, 1/12/40
letters of 20/12/51
all before 1812 destroyed 20/12/51
Liverpool church 8/4/41
Maynooth, satisfied with G's explanation 4/2/45
needs G's conversation often 27/10/48
notes on his early days 16/9/37
Oak Farm and 28/9/40, 31/12/40, 27/3/41, 22/10/44, 26/11/45, 22/8/46 ff, 28/11/46, 12/4/47, 20/11/47 ff, 10/1/48 ff, 13/3/48
trusts Boydell 29/10/46
on slavery 14/2/33, 8/9/35, 16/9/35
operation on 4/3/41
pays for church in Newark 17/9/40
Peel offers baronetcy to 20/6/46
pictures partitioned 12/6/47
political advice 28/11/34 ff
politics of 2/1/33, 9/3/33, 11/9/33, 30/9/33, 11/10/33, 4/3/38, 1/2/39
portraits of 5/7/39, 9/3/68 n, 30/10/90
prayers written by 16/11/48
property of 22/2/41
proposes G as his biographer 10/8/26
rejects G's offer to go to West Indies 19/4/38, 26/4/38
relations with Helen G 18/11/39, 27/1/41 ff, 4/5/43, 5/9/44, 12/10/44
gives way to 20/6/42
residuary estate of 9/6/52, 11/6/52 ff, 17/6/52
Seaforth church and
G arranges provision for in father's memory 18/8/70
secretary, G acting as 8/10/30, 1/6/33, 17/10/33 ff, 12/4/36 ff, 13/8/36 ff, 8/11/39, 17/2/40, 27/4/40, 11/12/49
impatience caused by 15/4/40
St. Andrew's, Fasque and 19/8/44 ff, 15/9/44 ff, 20/10/44, 20/7/45, 16/2/46, 10/4/46, 17/11/46
tells G to study direct taxation 16/2/47
thinks has treated G unjustly for election expenses 30/10/48

time spent with by G 5/10/49
Trinity College, Glenalmond and 1/10/40, 13/10/40, 17/11/40, 30/11/40, 19/9/41 ff, 16/2/46
unwilling surrender of will to 21/9/43
vigour of 7/7/47 ff, 3/10/49
will of 30/9/48, 8/11/48 ff
execution of 13/12/51, 16/12/51, 20/12/51 ff, 15/1/52
G suggests alterations to 21/11/48 ff
youthful appearance of 31/1/39
See also corn laws, Fasque, free trade, Leith, Oak Farm, Trinity College (Glenalmond), West Indies
Gladstone, John Neilson, Capt. (1807–1863), brother, tory M.P., Wiltshire landowner 10/11/25, 23/11/25, 9/12/25, 2/2/26, 25/7/26, 12/7/28, 18/1/31, 3/4/34, 17/6/36, 26/2/37, 20/7/38, 17/2/40, 4/3/40, 19/1/41, 4/2/41, 20/6/42, 18/1/44, 6/3/48, 13/9/48, 14/9/48, 24/9/48, 20/5/50, 31/8/50 ff, 31/5/51, 9/6/51, 2/12/51 ff, 19/4/60, 23/5/62, 28/1/63, 24/9/63
at Hawarden 7/8/62, 1/10/62
beaten at Ipswich 1/8/47
candidate in Walsall against S. Lyttelton 23/12/40
death of 1/2/63, 6/2/63, 29/3/63
funeral of 12/2/63
G tidying affairs of 9/2/63 ff
G visits at Bowden 23/1/57 ff, 6/6/62
marriage of 7/2/39, 18/2/39
wife's death 18/1/62 ff, 2/2/62 ff
on Sebastopol committee 25/4/55
row with 27/6/49, 16/9/49
travelling on Continent with G 2/2/32 ff, 3/7/32
Gladstone, Robertson (1805–1875), brother, Liverpool merchant and radical, mayor of Liverpool 7/6/29, 30/7/29, 15/11/29, 1/10/34, 4/5/40, 27/10/44, 15/11/46, 30/9/47, 24/9/50, 2/12/51, 5/2/52, 14/10/52, 19/10/52, 12/7/53, 5/11/53, 27/12/54, 14/6/55, 11/7/56, 25/10/56 ff, 29/6/57, 15/10/58, 4/9/61, 10/10/61, 11/10/61, 15/10/62, 12/2/63, 12/10/64 ff, 20/9/65, 13/10/65, 4/11/65 ff, 13/10/68, 18/11/68, 25/5/69, 28/8/69, 10/10/70, 29/5/71, 25/9/71, 18/10/72, 22/12/72 ff, 9/4/74, 25/7/74, 5/9/74, 12/10/74, 23/11/74, 14/5/75, 17/11/76 n
death of 18/9/75, 23/9/75
death of his son Hugh 2/9/74
death of his wife 29/9/65, 2/10/65 ff
failing powers of 7/10/65 n
funeral of 28/9/75
G in religious argument with 5/10/47
G's welcome from not so warm 25/7/74
helping in G's S. Lancashire campaign 17/7/65 ff
letters from G to, printed 8/2/73, 22/2/73, 21/3/73
Liverpool shipping and 18/2/56 n
Manchester Education Bill and 5/2/52, 11/2/52
marriage to unitarian of 5/11/35, 15/11/35, 16/11/35, 18/11/35, 30/12/35, 9/1/36, 28/1/36
mayor of Liverpool 6/1/43
physical and mental decline of 14/5/75, 16/5/75
portrait of 12/3/90
Seaforth estate and 9/4/74
G cancels letter on for fear of wounding 14/4/73
G loses £6000 through R. G.'s mismanagement 18/4/74, 1/6/74
sugar duties and 21/3/62 n
will of, faulty, G thinks 28/9/75
Gladstone, Stephen Edward, Rev. (1844–1920), son; Rector of Hawarden 4/4/44, 25/4/44, 1/5/44, 3/10/62, 12/11/67, 3/8/69, 30/8/69, 6/2/70, 4/11/70, 14/12/70, 22/9/71 ff, 16/12/71, 25/12/71, 24/11/72, 9/4/73, 11/4/73, 16/4/73, 21/4/73, 7/4/74, 18/6/74 ff, 24/2/75, 18/5/75, 29/6/75, 30/9/75, 14/11/75, 1/2/76, 18/10/76, 25/12/76, 15/3/77, 26/11/77, 4/1/78, 6/5/78, 8/5/78, 10/6/78, 8/9/78 n, 10/11/78, 1/1/79, 15/1/79, 28/1/79, 17/2/79, 8/4/79, 19/8/79, 2/9/79, 12/2/80, 16/2/80 ff, 23/10/80, 25/10/80, 11/4/81, 27/5/81, 24/10/81, 8/12/81 ff, 27/12/81 ff, 2/9/82, 24/9/82, 18/12/82, 26/3/83, 18/1/84, 13/1/85, 16/12/85, 17/4/86, 27/4/86, 3/5/86, 5/7/86, 28/10/86, 12/11/86, 27/5/87, 8/10/87, 10/12/87, 19/12/87 ff, 26/3/89, 21/4/89 ff, 17/9/89, 3/10/90, 16/11/90 ff, 12/12/90 ff, 22/5/91 ff, 3/12/91, 26/4/92 ff, 13/6/92, 29/11/92 ff, 22/4/93 ff, 17/9/93, 14/12/93
at Christ Church, Oxford 17/10/62, 16/10/63
at Cliveden 16/6/61
at Eton 16/4/56, 10/12/56, 20/9/60
Calcutta, intention of working in 10/9/82
climbing accident in Switzerland 17/9/70 n
confirmation of 17/4/59
confirmed by Wilberforce 8/5/59

Gladstone, Stephen Edward (*cont.*)
Declaration on absence of infidelity by G to the marriage bed, to be opened after G's death, recorded with S. E. G 7/12/96
declares wish to be a clergyman 13/1/56
diocesan proctorship and 19/11/79, 21/11/79
disestablishment and 8/11/85
engagement of 14/12/84, 20/12/84
eucharist and 4/10/68
financial settlement for 20/12/84, 26/12/84, 1/6/85
G discusses retirement with 25/5/85
G's pastor 7/12/96
G teaching latin to 24/7/52 ff, 12/2/53
heirs of, and Hawarden estate 9/7/91
in Florence with parents 14/1/88 ff
in Rome 15/12/66 ff
Jubilee 1887 and 15/2/87
leaving Eton 8/1/62
letters from G to, printed 22/1/93, 20/3/93, 3/4/93, 8/4/93
marriage of 29/1/85
marriage of, G encourages 11/1/77
operations to his eye 26/7/56, 28/7/56
ordination of 20/12/68, 31/12/68, 13/3/70
overstudying 14/1/64
patronage, church, discussed with 25/9/73, 18/12/82 ff, 9/1/83 ff
qualities of 1/1/48, 3/10/52, 20/2/53, 4/4/56, 7/8/56, 23/12/72, 14/10/80
Rector of Hawarden 5/8/72, 15/8/72, 17/11/72, 3/10/90
conducts Agnes G's wedding 27/12/73
dissatisfied with his work there 10/9/82, 3/4/93 ff, 20/5/93, 26/5/93 ff, 17/6/93
hopes to cease being 3/4/93, 8/4/93
murmurs in the parish against liturgical innovations by 27/10/72, 1/11/72
religious disposition of 6/4/55, 19/4/57
romances of 1/11/81, 11/11/81 ff, 2/12/81, 24/8/82, 10/9/82
sent to prep. school at Torquay 20/1/54, 21/1/54
sermons, notable, of 13/2/87
South Africa, visit to 20/3/77
spitting blood 11/4/82
tells a lie 3/9/52
United States, visit to: plans for 30/4/76
will of 5/8/91
See also childrearing, Christ Church (Oxford)
Gladstone, Thomas (2nd), Sir (1804–1889), 2nd Baronet (1851), brother; tory M.P.; Kincardinshire landowner 6/8/25, 5/8/26, 16/1/27, 3/5/27, 26/6/29 ff, 29/10/31, 17/10/32, 7/4/33 ff, 16/7/35, 8/12/35, 16/10/40, 29/7/42, 22/8/42, 18/2/43, 29/8/46, 2/9/46, 3/9/46, 23/11/48, 24/11/49, 30/9/50 ff, 2/12/51 ff, 26/1/52, 11/1/54, 16/5/61, 10/7/63, 21/6/64, 5/10/65, 22/6/66, 19/7/66, 6/7/67, 7/7/68, 26/9/69, 25/7/71, 10/3/73, 11/5/73, 1/8/73, 10/8/73, 5/10/73, 28/2/74, 29/3/74 ff, 28/9/75, 29/9/75, 25/7/76, 14/6/77, 18/3/78, 20/3/78, 2/7/78, 21/7/78, 25/7/78, 24/5/79, 8/3/80, 16/6/80, 10/12/81, 25/4/82, 24/7/82, 14/8/82, 8/3/83, 16/7/83, 25/7/84, 16/11/84, 3/12/84, 28/3/85, 1/9/85 ff
an edifying sight 2/9/85
as his father's secretary 27/2/40
at Hawarden
with his family 18/7/56, 21/7/56, 27/10/80
death and funeral of his daughter Ida 24/6/74, 30/6/74
death of 20/3/89
death of Helen Gladstone 10/1/80 ff
declines to support G at Oxford 17/5/47
escapades of 4/8/32
fatal illness of 2/3/89 ff
financial affairs of 31/5/51, 9/6/51, 21/6/51
funeral of 26/3/89
G informs him he is declining offer of Kincardineshire constituency 20/11/72
G objects to his marriage 10/7/35 ff
G's religious differences with 17/5/47, 9/7/47, 10/7/47, 30/7/47, 2/8/47
G visits at Fasque 8/10/64 ff, 25/9/69, 29/6/74, 24/1/80, 18/9/84, 1/9/85 ff
inheritance of Fasque and 3/9/46
letters from G to, printed 3/4/72, 20/11/72, 23/2/74, 23/7/82, 25/7/82, 19/6/85
marriage of 27/8/35, 10/9/35
military opinion gleaned from dinner at 24/5/79
political career of 17/7/30, 30/7/32, 21/2/33, 28/3/33, 15/12/34, 1/4/35, 5/2/39 n, 12/2/41, 30/6/41, 30/7/42, 20/4/65 n, 6/6/65
makes a mess of it 28/7/65
religious failings of 1/9/32
votes against G at Oxford 1/8/47
will of 27/3/89
Gladstone, towns named 15/6/81
Gladstone, William Henry (1840–1891), son; liberal M.P.; musicologist; owner of Hawarden 3/6/40 ff, 5/8/40 ff, 23/10/40, 11/4/41, 1/8/41 ff, 29/8/42, 28/10/42, 5/10/43, 4/4/44, 6/8/45, 3/6/47, 3/6/48, 3/6/49,

17/6/49, 22/3/50, 3/6/53, 3/12/54, 3/6/56, 29/8/69, 6/9/69, 7/7/71, 7/11/71, 25/12/71, 14/8/73, 26/12/73, 18/3/74, 4/4/74, 2/6/74, 19/7/74, 11/9/74, 15/10/74 ff, 30/7/75, 3/8/75, 21/10/75, 20/12/75, 17/2/76, 3/6/76, 23/6/76, 16/10/76, 7/5/77, 3/6/77, 29/4/78, 20/8/78, 12/2/79, 18/3/79, 3/5/79, 30/6/79, 31/10/79, 6/11/79, 9/12/79, 3/1/80 ff, 18/12/80, 18/4/81, 15/11/81, 25/11/81 ff, 5/1/82, 29/1/82, 16/5/82, 25/9/82, 20/12/82 ff, 6/11/83, 6/12/83, 17/1/84, 20/10/84, 30/11/84, 14/12/84, 27/4/86, 19/6/86, 23/6/86 ff, 29/9/86 ff, 20/11/86 ff, 1/1/87, 3/2/87 ff, 6/4/87 ff, 30/5/87, 12/6/87, 7/10/87, 21/12/87, 5/3/88, 28/3/88 ff, 3/6/88, 15/9/88, 27/11/88, 9/12/88 ff, 24/9/89 ff, 5/10/89, 13/11/89, 16/1/90, 19/8/90, 12/12/90
5ft. 11ins. (in stockings or slippers) 26/12/59
admitted to Oxford 1/6/57, 3/6/57
allowance of 9/1/54, 4/1/55 ff
as heir of Hawarden
  subject not to be thought of 8/9/40
assisting G's private secretary 9/7/59 ff, 5/10/81
at Christ Church
  G lunches in his rooms in Peckwater 9/5/59
at Dollis Hill 11/5/90, 15/2/91
at Eton 26/4/52, 4/6/52, 19/11/52, 8/6/53, 13/9/53, 25/10/53, 3/6/54, 10/12/56
  G given delightful account of 30/7/54
  well described as centripetal 25/10/53
at Geddington prep. school 30/1/50 ff, 12/4/50 ff
at Lincoln's Inn 14/5/63, 12/1/64
baptism of 15/7/40, 16/7/40
birth of 3/6/40
breaks down at Eton interview 20/1/52
candidacy at Blackburn? 29/2/64
character fundamentally excellent 20/10/48
classical abilities improving 6/1/52, 7/1/52
climbing accident in Switzerland 17/9/70
confirmation of 9/12/54
constituencies contested/held
  Chester 12/4/65 ff, 24/4/65 ff
  E. Worcestershire 30/11/77 n, 9/3/80 ff, 14/4/80
  Whitby 18/6/68 n, 3/7/68, 4/7/68, 18/11/68, 22/8/71 ff, 30/11/77 n, 17/9/78
Continental 'grand tour' of 13/1/63 ff
Daily Telegraph and
  Hunt arranges for W. H. G to report on Ireland 2/8/66
  reports on Ireland 6/1/68, 16/1/68
death of 4/7/91
delight in Sabbath 8/11/46
Eastern question and
  G urges to handle 6/11/76
energy not equal to virtue of 12/12/62
engagement of, to Gertrude Stuart 21/7/75 ff
examination to enter Eton 29/7/51, 30/7/51
excellent cricketer 7/8/54
excellent intelligence of 28/9/60
fatal illness of 2/7/91 ff
  news kept from G 3/7/91
finished at Eton 26/3/58
funeral of 8/7/91
G discusses his future with him 10/10/60
G gives history lecture to 18/12/49
G gives religious lessons to 5/11/43 ff, 10/8/45, 25/8/46 ff
G helping with revision for Oxford examinations 4/10/59
G riding with 3/8/53
G's church appointments and 12/5/69
G's letter on his going to Oxford 10/10/58 ff
G's memoir of 8/7/91
G's private secretary 5/9/53, 26/4/65 ff, 13/5/65 ff, 4/12/68 ff, 7/9/73 ff, 18/10/73, 24/4/74, 30/1/80
  editing G's election speeches 8/7/86
G studying Aristotle with 3/9/60 ff, 16/8/61 ff
G's will and
  left all G's landed property 1/1/79
G takes to Margaret chapel 6/6/47
G teaches psalm-chanting to 4/12/46 ff
G teaches to ride 14/8/44
G teaching Greek to 8/8/51 ff, 3/1/52 ff
G teaching Latin to 23/1/47 ff, 11/12/47 ff, 15/1/49 ff, 21/5/49 ff, 23/8/50, 3/1/52 ff, 21/12/55
G tells him of Sir J. G 26/9/89
Guy Faux and 5/11/49
G warns of his sister's death 7/4/50
G writes set of prayers for 29/8/47
Hawarden estate 25/8/65, 23/2/89 n
  arrangements consequent on W. H. G's death 9/7/91 ff
  deed constituting W. H. G owner 28/9/75
  G's letter on duties of a landowner 4/4/75
  owner of 18/6/74, 14/12/74, 6/1/80, 24/9/80, 17/4/82
  residence on 12/4/76, 13/4/76, 25/4/76, 27/4/76, 3/9/78, 8/10/78, 1/11/78 ff

Gladstone, William Henry (*cont.*)
health of 23/6/89, 11/9/89 ff, 9/11/89, 1/12/89, 29/12/89, 20/1/90, 3/6/90, 21/9/90, 11/10/90, 4/6/91 ff, 30/6/91 ff
distant hope of absolute recovery 3/3/89
improving 29/4/89 ff
piteous condition of 16/4/89 ff
seizure 2/3/89
hymns by published 9/12/88
ill from not chewing 4/9/49
improving character of 13/1/54
in Rome 15/12/66 ff
interest in music 11/4/41
Ireland and
disagreement with his father's policies 13/4/81
friendship with Cullen 6/11/77
reporter in 16/1/68, 13/3/68
reporting on for *Daily Telegraph* 2/8/66, 6/1/68, 16/1/68
lack of interest in reading 12/12/44
lack of solidity of scholarship of 28/9/60
Latin verses of 22/12/51
Law and History School, studying for 9/6/62
3rd class in 12/12/62
Leeswood, living at 29/8/77, 3/1/78
letters from G to, printed 2/8/84, 14/9/84, 8/7/86
listlessness of 20/10/48, 3/1/49 ff
Literae Humaniores, studying
2nd class in 7/6/62
loss of ground by, in race of learning 13/12/57
maiden speech of 25/2/68, 13/3/68, 16/3/68
makes speech at dinner 27/7/48
marriage of 30/9/75
marriage settlement of at least £2000p.a. 22/7/75
memorial to 10/6/92
G writes inscription for 26/6/92
most satisfactory as helper 14/1/65
music and 14/9/84
naughtiness better than G's goodness 13/1/49
naughtiness of 13/9/47
needs more uniform strength of will 20/10/48
offices held
junior treasury lord 26/10/69
on G's accident 14/9/42
operation on 2/6/91
plan for 4/6/91
Penmaenmawr, thinking of living in 12/4/76
playing whist with adults 29/9/48
politics and 18/4/81, 23/4/81, 2/8/84
disinclination for removed 6/9/64
opposition to home rule of 24/6/86, 30/6/86, 3/7/86
retirement from 23/9/85, 10/10/85
prepared for confirmation 5/9/47
prepared for confirmation by G 21/8/54 ff, 22/4/55
progress of his mind 29/5/42
qualities of 1/1/48
relationship with Gertrude Glynne 21/6/74 ff
religious views of 10/12/49
romances of 7/6/66, 14/7/66, 21/6/74, 16/8/74, 22/6/75 ff, 26/6/75 ff
seats of
considered for Denbigh 7/7/64
shown Eton 9/6/45
singing lessons arranged for 2/2/47
suffers Asiatic cholera 24/8/54
sweet temper of 4/6/40
taciturnity of 9/9/65
taken to King's, Cambridge, music 24/11/41
taking final exams.
first crisis of his life 3/6/62
placed in 2nd. class: news was chill 7/6/62
tomb of 25/8/91
treefelling with W. E. G 4/12/67 ff, 21/12/67 ff
tutored by Jelf for Oxford 16/4/58
unsuccessful candidate at All Souls 23/9/63, 4/11/63
urges amnesty for Fenians 13/10/69
visits to Königswinter 30/6/57
weight of 29/12/40
whipped for inattention by G 28/9/47
will of 23/4/89
wins Slade exhibition 27/5/58
with G at Dunrobin 4/9/53 ff
W. M. H. Church as tutor of 21/12/47 ff
See also childrearing, Christ Church, Hawarden Castle
Gladstone, Wyllie & Co.
H. N. G working for 23/1/71
Gladstone Almanack 1885
G protests against 31/12/84
Gladstone children
list of maternal ancestors of 28/2/59
Gladstone family
religious state of 31/8/32 ff, 22/1/33, 29/9/33, 25/12/33
Glamis Castle 20/9/84
Glan Conway 16/9/62
Glasgow 25/10/36, 13/1/37, 1/8/37, 24/9/40, 2/12/40, 11/8/46, 12/9/48, 3/10/49, 31/8/50, 9/9/58, 30/10/65, 5/6/78
deputation to G on constituency boundaries 6/6/68

Glasgow Municipal Bill 17/2/72 c
G's speeches in 1/11/65, 5/12/79, 2/7/92
Wellington hotel 22/8/43
Glasgow, University of
G Lord Rector of 11/4/76 n, 19/5/76 n, 10/4/77 n, 15/10/77 n, 15/11/77 n, 17/11/77 n
Rectorial Address 7/11/79 n, 13/11/79 ff, 5/12/79
torchlight procession for 4/11/79
Rectorship of
Asquith's candidacy (unsuccessful) 19/9/93
Glasgow Home Rule Association 10/12/79 n
Glasgow Liberal Club 19/11/77
Glastonbury Abbey 18/8/66
Gleanings of Past Years *See* publications
Glen, Innerleithen (Sir C. Tennant) 1/11/90
Glenalmond *See* Trinity College (Glenalmond)
Glen Clova 6/10/71
Glencree *See* Ireland
Glendalough *See* Ireland
Glen Dye Lodge (Sir T. Gladstone) 18/9/84
Glenquoich Lodge (E. Ellice) 20/8/53
Glenshee 9/9/46
Globe, The
describes G as bigot 1/2/40
Gloucester 16/7/25, 18/8/25, 6/12/25, 14/3/26, 5/10/75
G's speech at 7/6/87
gloves
flesh gloves used by G 21/12/44
glove trade 3/2/60
Glyn, George Grenfell (1824–1887), 2nd Baron Wolverton (1873), G's political confidant, liberal M.P.; chief whip 1868–74 16/7/66, 13/3/67 ff, 2/5/67 ff, 1/7/67 ff, 13/6/69, 10/7/69, 26/10/69, 31/10/69, 3/11/69, 8/12/69, 20/1/70 ff, 6/4/70, 29/3/71, 4/4/71, 21/10/71 ff, 13/12/72, 23/3/73, 25/3/73, 14/5/73, 13/6/73, 16/6/73, 4/7/73, 29/7/73 ff, 8/8/73 ff, 31/12/73, 1/2/74, 5/2/74, 5/7/74, 14/1/75, 2/6/75 ff, 20/7/75, 29/9/75, 18/5/76, 31/7/76, 7/2/77, 26/4/77, 5/5/77, 8/7/77, 26/7/77, 2/2/78, 11/12/78, 27/3/79, 14/6/79, 19/4/80, 26/4/80, 8/5/80, 2/7/80, 23/8/81, 5/9/81, 30/6/82, 9/7/82, 10/12/82, 2/7/83, 10/2/84, 22/2/84, 21/6/84, 28/6/84, 12/7/84, 10/3/85, 3/7/85, 11/7/85, 18/7/85, 28/1/86 ff, 24/3/86, 27/3/86, 31/7/86 ff, 21/9/86 ff, 20/6/87, 28/6/87
at Hawarden 7/10/67 ff, 24/12/70, 13/9/73, 1/9/74, 9/12/76, 18/9/77 ff, 12/12/79, 10/4/80 ff, 29/5/85 ff, 16/9/85 ff, 10/12/85 ff, 12/10/87
chief whip 3/7/67 n, 18/11/67 ff, 20/2/68 ff, 2/4/68 ff, 3/12/68 ff, 26/1/69 ff, 22/1/70 ff, 2/6/70, 17/8/70, 29/12/70, 8/3/71, 26/4/71, 30/1/72, 27/4/72 c, 26/7/72
and patronage 30/8/69 ff, 4/7/70, 5/11/72
and press management 18/1/69
attends cabinet on ballot 24/7/71
attends cabinet on defeat of government 12/3/73 c
bye-elections and 23/8/71
Derby(race), advises G not to attend 24/5/71
dissolution calculations 6/7/72
effect of civil service reform on his patronage 8/12/69
estimates and 22/1/73 ff
Irish University Bill and defeat of the government 4/3/73 ff
persuades G to join Reform Club 17/5/69 n
death of 7/11/87, 11/11/87
declines a viscountcy 15/7/86
dissolution in January 1874, seems to approve 18/1/74
excellence of 8/10/67
G discusses Mrs. Thistlethwayte with 20/12/69
G on his yacht 19/8/82 ff
G recuperating from insomnia in his Cannes villa 18/1/83 ff
G's resignation as liberal party leader and 14/2/74, 11/3/74
letters from G to, printed 11/3/69, 19/5/69, 28/8/70, 21/1/71, 31/5/71, 23/8/71, 4/9/71, 1/10/71, 19/10/71, 30/1/72, 1/4/72, 3/7/72, 16/9/72, 5/11/72, 22/1/73, 30/12/73, 13/4/80, 30/8/82, 22/3/84, 17/6/85, 31/1/86, 7/6/86, 15/7/86
situation of the government, discussed with 1/6/85
Glynllivon Castle (Newborough) 15/9/62
Glynne, Henry, Rev. (1810–1872), whig M.P. (1831), Rector of Hawarden (1834), G's brother-in-law (1839) 16/7/40, 7/8/43, 2/1/48, 3/1/48, 19/5/48, 20/5/48, 14/10/48, 5/1/52, 7/1/53, 14/2/54, 31/8/59, 10/3/60, 13/3/60, 15/3/60, 10/9/65 n, 22/10/67, 23/9/77
death of 30/7/72
caused by lightning 30/7/72 n
funeral of 5/8/72
marital plans of
Miss Lowder 2/2/60, 5/2/60 ff, 13/2/60, 14/2/60, 18/3/60, 21/3/60 ff, 1/11/60

Glynne, Henry (*cont.*)
marital plans of (*cont.*)
Miss Rose 28/8/60, 29/8/60, 3/9/60, 6/9/60, 24/10/60, 21/11/60, 26/11/60, 27/11/60, 3/12/60, 5/12/60, 10/12/60, 11/12/60, 20/12/60, 3/1/61, 17/1/61, 4/2/61, 8/7/62
pairs with G in Flintshire bye-election 25/5/61
S. Glynne's affairs and 29/8/64
See also Phillimore
Glynne, Mary *See* Lyttelton
Glynne, Stephen Richard, Sir (1810–1874), 9th Baronet (1815), G's brother-in-law; whig M.P.; owner of Hawarden 17/10/28 ff, 18/11/28, 16/7/36, 21/7/36, 21/3/37, 9/5/38, 1/8/38, 17/2/39, 21/2/39, 13/7/52, 19/7/52, 3/3/70, 4/8/72, 13/12/73, 4/4/74, 5/1/75, 25/1/75, 15/8/76, 23/1/94
abroad with G 10/9/38, 15/11/38 ff, 19/1/39 ff
accused of buggery 3/6/41
allowance of £500 p.a. for 27/8/50
candidate in Flintshire 3/7/41 ff, 23/3/57 ff, 7/4/57
death of, in Shoreditch High Street 17/6/74, 31/12/74
makes G briefly owner of Hawarden 17/6/74
debts of 8/1/64, 20/12/65
D. N. B. entry on checked by G 13/11/89 n
funeral of 24/6/74
G and C. G encourage to marry 4/3/49
G arranges his affairs 3/1/48 ff, 14/3/48 ff, 31/12/48, 14/1/49 ff, 9/9/50, 7/1/53, 3/12/56, 24/12/56, 11/1/58 ff, 26/7/58, 31/8/58, 27/12/59, 28/8/60, 19/8/64
dark but not hopeless 14/3/48, 26/8/50
grave but not menacing 31/8/63
G writes election addresses for 26/3/57, 8/4/57, 9/4/57
Hawarden Castle and
at once host and guest in 19/4/74
illness of 18/6/73
in Italy with G 15/11/38 ff, 6/12/38 ff, 19/12/38, 7/2/51, 1/11/66 ff
in Naples 7/2/51 ff
let down electorally by Lord Westminster 7/4/57 n
letters from G to, printed 24/10/70, 1/4/72
memorial to 6/10/74
qualities of 17/6/74
testamentary arrangements of
estate to pass to C. G's male children 27/6/55, 3/7/55, 9/7/55
of very deep interest to G 27/6/55
See also Christ Church
Glynnese, glossary of 4/8/51 ff
God
accumulation of stock and 31/8/46
agency of 2/12/33
defends from disease 11/4/42
discernment of numbed by sin 31/12/43
Eastern question and 31/12/77
Egypt and 23/6/84
employment of G for His purposes 20/5/80
final salutation in journal to 29/12/96
general election and 30/3/80, 3/4/80, 5/4/80, 6/7/86
G prays He be near Beaconsfield's pillow while dying 29/3/81
great and high election of 28/12/79
G's forgetfulness of 31/12/68
G's true standing with 29/12/85
G upheld in Commons by a strength not his own 11/5/93
immovable dispensations of 17/2/33, 31/10/38
intention of, in G's accident 13/9/42 ff
invasion of Egypt and 15/9/82
judged and ordered G's marriage wisely 26/11/39
judgements on England
China policy 14/5/40
just retribution of on Oak Farm 16/11/47
mercies of unrecordable 30/11/43
monument to Beaconsfield and 9/5/81
navy estimates crisis and 3/1/94
no sign of Divine abandonment 29/12/61
political economy and 31/8/46
prayer and, printed 9/12/75, 15/12/75
primary purposes of 29/12/78
providential dispositions of 29/12/33, 17/12/34, 29/12/34, 29/12/35, 14/10/38, 14/5/43, 1/10/47, 9/10/59, 13/1/78, 30/11/78, 29/12/78, 5/12/79, 5/4/80, 6/4/80, 3/12/93
and G's Oxford candidacy 22/6/47
G aware of dangers of fanatical language about 29/12/78
G's retirement and 5/1/83
Majuba, British defeat at: the Hand of Judgment? 28/2/81
triable by tests 29/12/78
retribution of 23/5/38
signs of divine care 29/12/44
split in home rule party and 17/12/90
temporal mercies of 29/12/40
unbounded goodness of 29/12/60
visitation in the form of sickness 7/11/32
weather and 9/11/88
will hold the mind of Britain steady 27/6/41
See also memoranda (printed), Providence, Psalms

godchildren, G's
  C. C. Lacaita 31/12/56
  C. F. Maule 12/6/85
  Constance E. G 20/5/50
  Gertrude Glynne 24/9/50, 29/9/50
  Henry Hampton 15/2/52
  J. S. Northcote 2/2/50
  list of 31/12/56
  Mary Ellen G 1/5/40
  Mary Tyler 3/2/35
  Mr.[?] Neville 31/12/56
  N. G. Lyttelton 27/11/45
  R. A. Goalen 31/12/56
  R. E. Maule 12/6/85
  W. Goalen 13/4/48
  William Henry Goschen 17/7/70
  William Reginald Herbert 18/6/54
  William T. Stuart-Wortley 26/2/53
  W. R. Farquhar 13/4/48, 18/5/56
  W. Selwyn 6/5/40, 3/12/54, 26/8/55
Goethe, J. W. von
  discussion of 19/1/38
  G translating 19/8/33 ff, 3/9/33, 22/1/34, 8/4/34, 5/7/34, 9/9/34, 17/9/34, 17/6/36, 13/6/37
  Iphigenia, notes on 20/9/36
gold
  price of
    G denies diminution of 13/11/69
Gold Coast
  Ashantee war 14/8/73, 30/8/73 ff, 5/9/73, 21/9/73, 3/10/73 c, 17/11/73 c, 21/11/73 c, 1/12/73 c, 16/12/73, 3/2/74, 22/2/74
    Coomassie, expedition to, further than expected 17/11/73 c
    Coomassie, expedition to: objective of 4/10/73
    Coomassie, expedition to unnecessary, G argues 14/8/73, 30/8/73, 4/9/73, 5/9/73, 15/9/73, 17/9/73, 21/9/73, 23/9/73, 26/9/73, 28/9/73, 3/10/73 c, 4/10/73 c, 10/10/73
    Glover sent as commissioner 2/8/73 c, 14/8/73
    Glover's use of slaves in, deplored 16/12/73
    partial prohibition of arms 24/5/73 c
    withdrawal of marines from 28/6/73 c
  Dutch and 16/10/70, 30/1/72 c
Goldsmiths' Co. 22/6/42, 15/3/43, 20/3/44, 7/12/54, 22/1/66, 14/7/80
gold standard
  change of value in the sovereign proposed 6/7/72 c
  See also bimetallism, memoranda (printed)
golf 12/9/61, 31/1/94
Golspie
  Homer in school at 22/9/53
gomma d'oliva 13/11/38
Gordon, Arthur Charles Hamilton, Sir (1829–1912), Knight (1873), 1st Baron Stanmore (1893), Aberdeen's son; G's secretary in Ionia, colonial governor 1/7/51, 28/12/59, 5/12/71, 21/5/79, 13/6/79, 12/8/83, 31/7/90, 4/10/90, 16/7/93
  at Hawarden 30/10/74, 31/10/74, 25/9/78, 28/9/78, 23/11/78 ff, 2/10/85 ff, 4/10/90 ff, 15/10/91 ff, 11/9/92, 14/10/92
  Fiji, Governor of 22/3/75
  in Ionia
    displeases G by poor work 22/1/59, 26/2/59
  in Ionia with G 17/11/58 ff, 1/12/58
    unwell 9/12/58
  letters from G to, printed 17/2/93, 21/2/93, 25/2/93
  Life of Sidney Herbert, agrees to write 31/8/89 n, 14/10/92
  on voyage to Norway with G on *Pembroke Castle* 9/9/83 ff
  Tennyson's peerage and 18/9/83
  The Vatican Decrees(1874)
    comments on at Hawarden 29/10/74
  uneasy conversation with 2/9/93
  wishes to marry Agnes G 4/10/61
Gordon, Charles George, Major General (1833–1885); in China and Africa; led mission to Sudan 1884–5, killed in Khartoum after failing to evacuate 22/1/84 c, 16/5/84, 26/10/92
  Berber and
    wild telegrams from Gordon on 18/9/84 ff
  Commons debate on 12/5/84 ff
  death of 5/2/85, 6/2/85 c, 7/2/85 c, 10/2/85 n, 11/2/85 ff, 22/2/85
    prayed for by Wolseley 5/2/85
  family of 22/2/85 n, 28/2/85 c
  G not personally acquainted with 22/2/85
  grave error in choice of 30/5/85
  journal of 20/3/85 c, 21/3/85, 22/3/85 ff, 28/4/85 c
    poisoned stuff in 22/3/85
  letters of, and the Queen 25/3/88
  qualities of 22/2/85
  relief of 22/4/84 cf, 2/6/84 ff, 5/7/84 ff, 16/7/84 c
    Benson's proposal for public prayers for 12/5/84
    cost of 24/5/84 c, 8/6/84 ff
    expedition not presently warranted 27/5/84
    expedition to Dongola/Khartoum 30/7/84, 31/7/84, 1/8/84 ff, 19/8/84, 23/9/84

Gordon, Charles George (*cont.*)
relief of (*cont.*)
from the south? 6/10/84 c
G disappointed by cabinet on 16/7/84 c
Gordon by own account not in danger 12/5/84
G's memorandum opposing an expedition, printed 31/7/84
G's summary of position 30/7/84
military plans for 13/5/84, 16/5/84, 24/5/84 c, 27/5/84 c, 28/5/84, 30/5/84, 2/6/84 ff, 10/6/84 c, 5/7/84 c, 16/7/84 c
military reverse to be avoided 2/6/84
much difficulty felt 5/7/84 c
Nile, use of 24/4/84 ff, 13/5/84, 16/5/84, 28/5/84, 30/5/84, 18/7/84 c, 9/1/85 n
Nile, use of: G warns of difficulties 13/5/84
small expedition insufficiently considered 30/5/84
volunteer expedition: offer declined 28/4/84 c, 1/5/84 c
Wolseley's expedition 23/8/84 ff, 23/9/84
rescue of 13/4/84
Sudan mission of 22/1/84 ff, 29/3/84 c, 21/4/84 c, 21/9/92 ff
Baring's instructions to 22/1/84 c
chooses not to answer messages from London 19/8/84
Gordon's rebellious ideas 19/8/84
has full discretion to remain 2/4/84 c
nothing heard from 14/8/84
no troops for 23/4/84 c
placed under Baring by cabinet 22/1/84 c
reasonable hope of much good from 24/1/84
telegram requesting opinion of 8/2/84 c, 9/2/84, 10/2/84
terrible and instructive experience of 21/9/92
to report 22/1/84 c
telegrams to
appears to ignore 13/4/84
withdrawal of 13/3/84 n, 15/3/84
See also cabinet, memoranda (printed), Sudan, Victoria, Wolseley
Gordon, George Hamilton- (1784–1860), 4th Earl of Aberdeen (1801), colonial secretary (G's superior) 1834–5, foreign secretary 1841–6, prime minister 1852–5 17/8/33, 26/1/35, 2/4/35 ff, 27/10/36 ff, 31/10/36, 24/3/40, 22/8/41, 23/8/41, 21/10/42, 3/12/42, 22/3/48, 14/3/49, 15/3/49, 30/6/49, 26/2/51, 5/4/51, 13/4/51, 4/6/51, 10/6/51, 17/1/52, 24/2/52, 16/3/52, 31/3/52, 11/11/52, 4/12/52, 14/12/52, 15/12/52, 10/1/53, 5/2/53, 4/10/53, 8/10/53, 9/10/53, 26/10/53, 16/11/53, 19/12/53, 16/1/54, 17/6/54, 25/6/54, 15/7/54, 25/11/54, 8/1/55 ff, 2/5/55, 6/5/55, 7/6/55, 10/7/55, 31/1/56, 4/5/56, 6/6/56, 13/6/56, 6/8/56, 16/2/58, 17/2/58 ff, 8/5/58, 14/5/58, 26/5/58, 28/9/58 ff, 6/5/59, 18/5/59 ff, 24/7/59, 28/6/60, 20/2/69 c, 4/10/90, 19/3/94
1853 budget and 11/4/53 ff
1854 Reform Bill and 22/2/54
advises G to join Palmerston's government 6/2/55
at Wilton 20/1/57
biography of, by A. Gordon 16/6/91, 17/2/93, 21/2/93
bust of 3/6/72, 12/7/73
character of, G writing on 7/4/61
correspondence of, printed by A. Gordon 7/10/68, 16/1/71, 20/1/71, 11/9/83 ff
G encourages publication of 30/1/71 n
deeply wounded by G's lack of support 25/7/54
evidence to Sebastopol committee 14/5/55
forming his government 21/12/52 ff
funeral of
no common occasion 12/12/60
G changes pamphlet at his request 13/4/51, 10/7/51
government of 21/12/52, 25/11/54, 28/11/54
attempted resignation 24/1/55 ff
beaten three times in week 14/4/53
chaotic meeting of M. Ps. 17/7/54
disintegrating 25/11/54 ff, 6/12/54 ff
dissolution considered 14/4/53, 15/4/53
G's memorandum on reasons for continuing it 4/2/55
Kennedy affair 9/12/54 ff, 17/12/54, 21/1/55, 28/2/55
Roebuck's motion and 24/1/55 ff
G's conversations with
on Neapolitan prisons 30/11/51, 17/1/52
on Peel's position 19/10/49
on the Queen's rationalism 17/10/49
on the Roman question and Italy 19/10/49
G's notes on discussions of consequences of letter to 17/4/56
G's report of negotiations with Heathcote 26/4/56
judges Lawley scandal not a cabinet matter 2/8/54
last illness of 25/11/60 ff
G's final visit to 5/12/60

letters from G to, printed
on future of Peelism 31/3/57
on position of parties and government 13/3/56
outbreak of war and 22/2/54
Peel's panegyric on Cobden and 10/7/46
qualities of 27/9/52
recovery from illness 6/12/57, 29/9/58 ff
reflections on start of Crimean war 9/2/55
resigns 6/2/55
Roebuck's motion and 24/1/55 ff
See also Crimean War, Haddo House, Herbert (Sidney), Italy
Gore Bridge
G's speech at 4/7/92
Gorham case 11/1/50, 7/2/50, 8/3/50 ff, 19/6/50 ff, 11/3/51 ff, 9/5/54, 5/11/56, 16/11/69
a crisis of the Church of England 13/1/50
Declaration on
G refuses to sign 18/3/50
disastrous division in Lords on 3/6/50
G overestimated scope of 16/11/69
G's Address to Bishop of London 16/3/50
G's proposed engagement on 19/5/50 ff
G's resolutions on 10/3/50 ff
Hope and 11/1/50, 8/3/50 ff
Phillpotts and 7/2/50
Goschen, George Joachim (1831–1907), 1st Viscount Goschen, liberal M.P.; president, poor law board 1868–71, lord of the Admiralty 1871–4, negotiated with Sultan 1880–1, unionist chancellor of the exchequer 1887–92 23/11/65, 10/1/66 n, 17/7/66 ff, 5/7/67, 20/2/69, 5/11/69 c, 1/12/70, 1/3/71 n, 15/9/73, 10/7/74, 8/7/76, 1/5/77, 21/6/77 n, 30/4/80 n, 14/5/80, 3/7/80 c, 24/7/80 c, 4/11/81, 8/5/82 c, 12/5/82, 21/3/84, 8/4/84, 22/11/84, 27/2/85, 15/11/85, 22/11/85, 1/12/85, 22/12/85, 30/1/86, 26/4/86, 1/5/86, 27/6/86, 25/12/86, 9/3/88, 18/3/91, 30/5/92, 29/8/92, 14/1/93, 26/6/93
1866 panic and 11/5/66
1866 Reform Bill and 19/6/66
1867 Reform Bill and 14/2/67 ff
at Admiralty
navy estimates 8/12/73, 19/1/74, 22/1/74
supplemental estimate unnecessary, G thinks 9/7/72
Chamberlain and National Councils, discussions on 11/7/85, 14/7/85
Chancellor
G intends to make in 1874 23/1/74
declines India 24/4/80 n
declines War Office because of franchise views 31/5/82, 1/6/82
discredit of 1/3/93
Eastern question and 24/7/80 c, 3/10/80, 27/10/80, 28/3/81 c
G his son's godfather 17/7/70
letters from G to, printed 17/1/69, 16/9/71, 17/6/72, 9/7/72, 18/9/72, 9/11/72, 21/9/73, 1/1/74, 17/1/74, 3/10/80, 27/10/80, 1/6/82, 17/11/83, 30/11/83, 11/7/85, 26/11/85
local taxation and 5/11/69, 17/9/72, 18/9/72, 24/9/72
sound on, G thinks 25/1/73
not a rigid economist 15/12/80
offer of Speakership to, declined 17/11/83 ff, 22/11/83 c
Queen's request to form administration 29/1/86
shipbuilding program and
G asks for costs 24/11/73, 1/1/74
something of a pillar 3/10/80
See also admiralty, budgets, Ireland, liberal party, local government, navy, poor law
Gounod *See* operas
gout *See* illnesses
governesses
F. Brown 30/10/47, 15/11/47, 3/11/48, 13/1/49 ff
difficulties with 12/5/49, 30/5/49
dismissed 30/5/49
hardness of 6/2/49
teaching Latin 11/12/47 ff
Madame Bourgeau 5/8/56, 6/8/56
Miss Bishop (singing) 9/1/64
Miss Eyre 24/8/49 ff
Miss Scott 3/8/52
Miss Stephenson 11/1/65
Miss Syfret 5/11/58, 1/1/62, 3/1/62, 26/2/63, 4/3/65
Mrs. Hartmann 27/10/57
government
art and science of
G's memorandum on, printed 11/6/88
boundless extravagance of
G opposes 3/2/57
G's resolutions on 6/2/57 ff, 14/2/57, 6/3/57
monarchy nearest to divine intentions 29/8/40
precedent for not calling for leader of the Opposition 22/4/80
government, local *See* local government
Government of Ireland Bill 1886
a battle between the nation and the classes 28/4/86
American states and 14/11/85
changes to 8/4/86 c
conclave on 17/2/86, 6/3/86, 15/3/86, 23/3/86, 2/4/86, 12/4/86, 15/4/86
conservative character of 20/4/86, 26/4/86, 27/4/86

Government of Ireland Bill 1886 (*cont.*)
customs and excise and 22/3/86, 29/3/86 c, 31/3/86 c, 1/4/86 c, 3/4/86, 5/4/86 n, 6/4/86 n
debt and 14/11/85, 28/12/85, 18/3/86 ff, 19/4/86
defence and 14/11/85
derivative Chamber acting under Imperial authority 18/11/85
desirability of one decisive measure 18/11/85
dissolution on
cabinet decides for nem. con. 8/6/86 c
favoured by G 15/5/86, 2/6/86, 4/6/86, 7/6/86, 8/6/86, 10/7/86
drafted by Thring 2/3/86 ff, 2/4/86
draft of heads of 14/11/85, 28/12/85
economy, promotion of 19/4/86
financial clauses of 6/3/86 ff, 18/3/86, 5/5/86
cabinet committee on 31/3/86, 1/4/86 c
G's summary of proposed pecuniary relations 19/4/86
plans 1 and 2 29/3/86 c
proportion of Imperial and Irish contributions 29/3/86 c, 31/3/86, 1/4/86 c, 3/4/86, 5/4/86, 6/4/86 c
foreign policy and 29/3/86 c
given precedence over Land Purchase Bill 23/3/86
in cabinet 29/3/86 c, 1/4/86 c, 6/4/86 c, 14/4/86 c
in Commons 8/4/86, 13/4/86
2nd. Reading of 10/5/86 ff, 7/6/86
2nd. Reading of: heavy defeat on 7/6/86
replace by Resolution? 14/5/86 ff, 21/5/86 ff, 9/7/86
Irish credit must be like Caesar's wife 19/4/86
Irish members and 14/11/85, 28/12/85, 14/4/86 c, 20/4/86, 29/4/86, 4/5/86 c, 9/5/86, 25/5/86 ff, 11/5/96 ff
G's mind open on 31/12/85, 2/2/86
memoranda on, printed 5/5/86, 9/5/86, 11/5/86
Standing Committee/Joint Commission to demarcate actions of? 5/5/86, 11/5/86 ff
tide running strongly on 21/4/86
judiciary and 29/3/86 c, 1/4/86 c, 4/4/86
meeting with Scottish M.P.s on 5/6/86
memorandum on 2nd Reading, printed for cabinet 5/5/86
memorandum on read to potential members of cabinet 30/1/86
not a 'Parliament' 29/3/86 c, 1/4/86 c
opponents of encourage separatism 20/4/86
plan for 8/2/86 ff, 13/2/86, 5/3/86
precedence over Land Purchase Bill a matter of policy 18/3/86
preparation of analogous to a budget 7/4/86
proposed delay till autumn 12/5/86 ff
public enthusiasm for 8/4/86, 4/5/86, 26/5/86, 6/6/86
Receiver General and 23/3/86, 29/3/86 c, 19/4/86
religious establishments and 6/4/86 c
Resolution on? 22/3/86
strain of work on leaves G stunned 27/6/86
the biggest question of our time 3/1/86
Two Orders of
2nd. Order by election with property qualification 6/4/86 c
likely tory representation in 22/3/86
Ulster and 18/11/85, 22/3/86, 29/3/86 c
veto and 29/4/86
Dicey's theory important for 18/12/85
war taxation and 19/3/86, 30/12/86
See also Balfour, cabinet, Cecil, Chamberlain, Commons (House of), Hamilton (E. W.), Ireland, liberal party, memoranda (printed), Morley, Parnell
Government of Ireland Bill 1893 1/8/92 ff, 9/11/92, 15/9/93
accompanied by Land Act? 18/1/93 c, 14/2/93 c
cabinet committee on 21/11/92 c, 23/11/92, 24/11/92, 25/11/92
drafted by Jenkyns 15/9/93
financial clauses of 11/11/92, 24/11/92, 5/12/92, 2/1/93, 16/1/93 c, 18/1/93 c, 20/1/93, 14/2/93 c, 16/2/93 c, 5/5/93 cf, 25/5/93 ff, 6/6/93 c, 25/7/93 n
errors in calculations for by A. Milner 16/5/93 ff
G's memoranda on, printed 24/11/92, 14/1/93, 18/1/93, 20/1/93, 3/5/93, 16/5/93, 25/5/93
G's position seems peculiar 30/5/93
G's Propositions on, printed 11/11/92
in cabinet 31/10/92 n, 11/11/92 c, 11/1/93 c, 13/1/93 c, 16/1/93 c, 18/1/93 c, 23/1/93 c, 5/5/93 c
in Commons
2nd. Reading 6/4/93 ff
3rd. Reading 30/8/93, 1/9/93
character of opposition unknown to G, so detached from merits and rule 8/5/93
guillotined 30/6/93 n, 13/7/93 ff, 20/7/93 ff, 17/8/93 c, 18/8/93 c
G upheld by strength not his own 11/5/93
in Committee 8/5/93 ff
introduced by G 13/2/93, 17/2/93

Irish members in Commons and 11/11/92, 12/11/92, 15/11/92, 18/11/92, 19/11/92, 21/11/92 c, 23/11/92 ff, 9/12/92, 5/7/93 c, 24/8/93, 26/8/93
 exclude from voting on British questions 13/1/93 c
 G's memoranda on 15/11/92, 22/11/92
 retention of difficult, but no choice 13/1/93
Irish peers and 1/10/92
Irish presbyterian Address supporting 12/8/93
plans for 1/8/92 ff
Receiver General and 11/11/92, 15/11/92, 16/11/92
rejected by Lords 2/9/93, 9/9/93
'Supremacy' clause of 24/11/92, 5/12/92, 10/5/93, 14/5/93, 16/5/93
Victoria demands changes in wording of Queen's Speech on 29/1/93
See also cabinet, finance, Hamilton (E. W.), Harcourt, Ireland, Lords (House of), memoranda (printed), Morley, Victoria

Government of Ireland Bill 1894
 G's plans for 15/9/93, 7/10/93

governments, G's
 1868–74
 abolish income tax and sugar duties, partly paid from death and spirit duties: might give a chance 11/8/73
 cabinet reshuffle 27/6/70 n, 1/7/70, 17/12/70 ff, 2/8/73 ff
 defeat of on Callan schools 22/5/73
 defeat of on Epping Forest 28/4/71
 defeat of on Fawcett's Irish University Bill 25/4/72
 defeat of on Irish University Bill 3/3/73, 11/3/73 ff
 defeat of on local taxation 16/4/72 n
 defeat of on Richard's motion for international arbitration 8/7/73
 defeat of on Scottish education 6/5/72 n
 dissolution on Lords amendments to ballot bill? 6/7/72 c
 fading popularity of 3/1/71
 formation of 3/12/68 ff
 G an old hack in 24/3/70
 general censure abroad against, G thinks 23/8/71
 general loss of vital power of 21/3/73
 has not redeemed election pledges on retrenchment 9/11/72
 marjority hard to maintain on Irish land 12/8/69
 most laborious G has seen 24/3/70
 need to promote radicals 6/1/71
 poor attendance of members of in Commons 2/8/69, 25/6/70, 19/4/71, 12/8/71 c, 23/7/72, 8/7/73 n
 progress of its legislation 24/3/70
 resignation of on general election defeat 9/2/74, 12/2/74, 14/2/74, 17/2/74
 resignation of on Irish University Bill's defeat 12/3/73 ff
 resignation of over Lords amendments to ballot bill considered 6/7/72 c
 resignations actual or attempted 11/3/69 n, 4/8/70 ff, 30/11/70, 4/12/70, 11/12/70, 16/1/71, 1/3/71, 18/4/72 n, 12/7/72 n, 1/12/72
 1880–5
 defeated on the budget 8/6/85
 formation of 23/4/80 ff
 general position of, G's assessments 21/4/81, 24/11/81, 2/12/81, 3/3/82, 13/3/82, 16/3/82, 23/6/82, 1/12/82, 3/2/83, 17/4/83, 15/11/83, 31/12/83, 28/5/84, 31/8/84, 7/9/84, 29/1/85, 30/5/85
 may end through death of Gordon 5/2/85
 membership of planned 12/4/80
 no sign of decrepitude 18/1/84
 plans for changes in 15/11/81
 premiership question 10/4/80 ff, 13/4/80 ff
 resignation of 9/6/85 ff, 24/6/85
 resignation of mooted 25/9/84, 27/9/84, 30/9/84
 resignation over Sudan contemplated 5/2/85, 24/2/85, 26/2/85 n, 27/2/85, 28/2/85 c
 resignations actual or attempted 12/6/80 ff, 14/6/80, 10/7/80, 17/11/80, 24/11/80, 19/12/80, 2/5/82, 10/6/82, 10/7/82 ff, 28/4/83 n, 22/10/83 ff, 3/1/84, 1/8/84, 25/9/84, 1/12/84, 24/12/84, 31/1/85 n, 24/2/85, 21/4/85, 24/4/85, 8/5/85, 14/5/85, 16/5/85 c
 resignations: only three today 16/5/85 c
 winding up of 2/5/85
 1886
 formation of 27/1/86 ff, 12/2/86
 general position of, G's assessments 12/2/86, 16/7/86
 perhaps less radical than that of 1880–5 12/2/86
 plans in event of defeat of Government of Ireland Bill 7/5/86
 resignation of 20/7/86 c
 resignations actual or attempted 15/3/86 ff, 26/3/86, 5/4/86, 9/4/86, 10/4/86, 11/4/86, 14/4/86, 17/4/86
 1892–4
 autumn sittings to be held 8/8/93 c
 cabinet lists 14/8/92 ff
 extent of disappointment of would-be members of 6/9/92

governments, G's (*cont.*)
1892-4 (*cont.*)
G expects dissolution before 1894 22/7/92
home rule's priority in 31/10/92
plans for 1893 Session, printed 20/7/92
preference to concisely treatable subjects, save home rule 19/8/92 c
programme not to be limited to home rule 29/10/92
resignations actual or attempted 12/4/93
Gower, Granville George Leveson- (1815-1891), 2nd Earl Granville (1846), G's friend and confidant, foreign secretary 1851-2, 1870-4, 1880-5, colonial secretary 1868-70, 1886, warden of the Cinque Ports 15/3/50, 21/3/50, 28/12/52, 5/2/53, 5/3/53, 6/4/53, 20/4/53, 28/1/54, 15/7/54, 8/3/55, 7/6/55, 12/3/57, 18/6/59, 12/8/59, 23/1/60, 30/5/60, 10/10/61, 14/3/62, 13/7/62, 19/1/63, 30/1/63, 27/3/63, 2/2/64, 22/6/64, 20/7/64, 23/2/65, 1/6/66, 29/1/67 ff, 21/7/67 ff, 6/3/68, 26/5/68 ff, 10/12/68, 20/2/69 c, 12/8/69, 4/9/69, 2/11/69, 20/1/70 ff, 11/8/70 ff, 10/11/70 ff, 14/12/70, 14/1/71, 9/5/71, 2/4/72 ff, 5/5/72, 3/2/73, 21/2/73, 19/6/73, 24/6/73, 1/8/73, 18/5/74, 5/3/75, 28/4/75, 30/4/75, 21/6/75, 30/6/75, 4/2/76, 25/5/76, 26/6/76 ff, 17/7/76, 1/8/76, 27/10/76, 9/6/77, 27/7/77, 16/7/78, 25/7/78, 14/6/79, 29/6/79, 22/10/79 ff, 22/1/80, 24/2/80 ff, 8/3/80 ff, 19/4/80 ff, 31/7/80 ff, 4/9/80 ff, 19/9/80, 6/10/80, 8/10/80, 8/11/80, 1/1/81, 24/2/81, 12/3/81, 18/4/81, 2/5/81 ff, 4/6/81, 20/7/81, 25/8/81 ff, 15/10/81, 15/11/81, 5/1/82, 1/5/82 ff, 13/5/82 ff, 5/6/82 ff, 16/6/82 ff, 20/6/82 ff, 24/6/82 ff, 7/7/82 ff, 8/7/82 c, 24/7/82, 21/10/82 ff, 24/10/82 c, 4/12/82 ff, 2/3/83 ff, 8/3/83, 16/3/83, 2/7/83 ff, 9/7/83 ff, 24/8/83, 25/9/83 ff, 1/1/84 ff, 27/3/84 ff, 8/4/84 ff, 17/4/84 ff, 3/11/84, 13/11/84 ff, 24/3/85 c, 7/4/85, 30/4/85, 2/6/85, 22/6/85, 23/6/85, 7/8/85, 21/1/86 ff, 3/2/86, 4/2/86, 15/3/86 ff, 15/7/86 ff, 31/7/86, 19/9/86 ff, 26/1/87 ff, 21/2/87 ff, 19/3/87 ff, 18/4/87 ff, 23/5/87, 25/6/87, 26/7/87, 26/12/87, 8/2/88 ff, 3/5/88 ff, 20/2/89 ff, 24/7/89, 7/3/90 ff, 24/4/90 ff, 3/8/90 ff, 1/9/92, 28/10/92, 7/2/94, 4/3/94, 19/3/94
1866 Reform Bill and
ministers' meeting to discuss resignation/dissolution 25/6/66
Acton's library and 9/6/90 n, 17/6/90
as Staffordshire man 15/6/71
at Hawarden 18/1/69 ff, 13/9/73, 26/12/78 ff, 22/9/80, 18/12/84 ff, 31/10/85 ff, 5/12/85 ff, 30/10/86 ff, 2/11/87 ff, 18/10/89 ff
attempts to form government 1859 11/6/59, 22/4/80
chairs cabinet in G's absence 24/7/69 c, 26/7/73
civil service reform and foreign office exemption 6/12/70
colonial secretary 1868-70 5/12/68
conversation on possible ministerial arrangements 10/7/68
death and memorial service of 31/3/91, 4/4/91
debts of estate of 20/4/91, 4/5/91 ff, 14/10/91, 6/5/92, 12/5/92 ff, 30/5/92 ff, 24/9/92 ff, 8/10/92, 13/10/92, 15/10/92
declines G's offer of a marquisate 22/7/86
dissolution in January 1874, seems to approve 18/1/74
Egypt and 27/10/69, 25/1/82 ff, 10/6/82 ff, 29/7/82 ff, 18/12/84 ff, 7/3/85 c, 16/1/93
fatal illness of 30/3/91 ff
fire at house of 10/3/79
foreign secretary
too old to be 30/1/86
foreign secretary 1870-4 27/6/70 ff, 14/2/72, 12/5/72, 27/1/73 c
Alabama arbitration and 20/4/72 c, 6/5/72 c, 13/6/72, 15/6/72
foreign secretary 1880-5 23/4/80 ff, 12/6/80 c, 12/10/80 ff, 27/10/80 ff, 8/3/81 c, 18/8/83, 24/3/85 c, 26/3/85 ff, 4/4/85 cf
G consults with on coming days and events 19/3/68
G discusses education with 16/11/64
G discusses party prospects with 3/2/64, 12/8/69 ff
G greatly likes 21/3/50
G's Golden Wedding and 25/7/88
G's infinite loss from death of 5/11/92
G's relationship with as foreign secretary, as man and wife 28/2/71
G's resignation as liberal party leader and 14/2/74 ff, 16/2/74, 5/3/74 ff, 11/3/74, 27/12/74, 31/12/74, 9/1/75, 10/1/75, 14/1/75
opposes it 10/1/75
G's retirement as prime minister and 25/11/82, 31/1/83

G staying with while researching for *The Bulgarian Horrors* 4/9/76 ff
G's views on his education policy 2/1/60
home rule and 1/11/85 ff, 23/12/85 ff, 30/12/85, 12/1/86 ff, 21/1/86 ff, 23/3/86 ff, 4/4/86 ff, 9/5/86
promising harmony on 6/12/85
Irish disestablishment and
and Lords' clash with Commons over amendments 22/7/69 ff
letters from G to, printed 22/12/85, 26/12/85, 31/12/85
liberal leader in the Lords 23/4/74, 4/2/76, 7/2/76, 11/2/76, 23/2/76, 8/3/76, 5/4/76, 22/6/76, 7/2/77, 26/2/77, 7/6/77, 26/6/77, 2/7/77, 26/7/77, 16/1/78, 29/1/78, 1/3/78, 27/6/78, 1/12/78, 2/12/78, 3/12/78, 28/3/79, 10/4/80 ff, 23/8/80
Eastern question and 24/7/76, 28/7/76, 5/9/76, 11/9/76, 7/4/77, 9/4/77, 5/5/77, 1/9/77, 10/7/78
G urges to lead party on Bulgarian campaign 11/9/76
premiership in 1880 and 22/4/80
mental force and initiative
water-drinking not favourable to, G thinks 26/12/78
most delightful of colleagues 13/8/69
navy retrenchment and, Goschen to consult on 1/1/74
non-interference in Denmark 24/6/64, 25/6/64
out hunting 24/1/70
paper duties and 21/5/60
Parnell and the O'Shea divorce and 24/11/90 ff
political situation, G's long letter on 8/9/74
protests against G's resignation of premiership 11/11/81
qualities of 26/12/78
a great feud composer 22/12/85
dear and fast friend 31/3/91
gentle, considerate as well acute and cautious 31/12/83
Reform Bill 1884 and 11/7/84 n, 8/7/85 n
resignation of the government and 12/3/73 ff, 15/3/73 ff
serene temper of 10/3/79
Sudan and
death of Gordon and 5/2/85 ff, 25/2/85
supports G over 1861 budget 13/4/61
takes G racing
Dover races 25/8/70
the Derby 1/6/70
The Bulgarian Horrors and the Question of the East (1876)
G discusses text with 5/9/76
timidity of, Harcourt's view 15/6/85 n
Wilberforce's death and 19/7/73 ff
See also memoranda, Walmer Castle
Gower, Harriet Elizabeth Georgiana Sutherland-Leveson-, Lady (1806–1868), née Howard, Duchess of Sutherland, G's confidant, Mistress of the Robes for liberal govts. 1837–61 10/2/40, 2/8/45, 3/9/53 ff, 18/9/53 ff, 26/12/53, 8/6/55, 12/7/55, 21/6/56, 2/4/57, 30/5/57, 26/1/58, 27/1/58, 21/4/58, 24/4/58, 29/4/60, 23/10/61, 18/4/62, 1/5/62, 13/11/62, 28/11/62, 16/4/63, 25/6/63, 7/6/64, 13/1/66, 15/1/66, 1/6/66, 30/6/66, 13/7/66, 11/8/66, 21/9/66, 1/12/67, 1/1/68 ff, 16/5/68, 30/9/75 n, 4/11/77, 1/11/84
at Chiswick, G with 16/5/63
at Hawarden 22/12/55, 24/12/55, 15/9/65
at Penmaenmawr 9/9/62 ff
bust of by Noble 7/12/68
death of 19/10/68, 20/10/68, 24/10/68, 28/10/68
discusses Mrs. Thistlethwayte with G 2/7/66
funeral of 3/11/68
G alone with at Cliveden 23/4/61
G at Dunrobin 11/9/58 ff
G at State Ball of 16/6/47
G at Trentham 8/12/59
G discusses prayers for the dead with 11/3/60
G meets at Commons 21/4/58
grandmother of G's daughter-in-law 30/9/75
G reads 'Dream of Gerontius' to 28/7/66
G visits Dunrobin 3/9/53 ff
health of 13/8/59, 13/1/62, 17/1/65, 11/3/66, 12/3/66, 20/3/66, 4/5/67, 22/6/67, 2/3/68, 21/6/68, 18/7/68
her mind healthy and good 23/4/61
in Somerset, G with 23/5/63
marvellous quickness of 11/7/61
monument to, G writes inscription for 11/4/71
none will fill her place for G 28/10/68
remarkable power of appropriating grief 14/2/63
remarkable reception for in Assynt 21/9/58
statue of, by Noble 9/6/70
tells G about the Queen 14/1/62
troubled 25/7/66
Victoria's seclusion and 18/1/65
visits Irvingite church with G 4/4/54
warmest and dearest friend that man ever had 28/10/68
See also Cliveden, Court, death, Dunrobin Castle, Stafford House, Victoria

Graham, James Robert George, Sir (1792–1861), 2nd Baronet of Nertherby (1824), cabinet minister and whig/Peelite M.P., home secretary 1841–6, first lord of the Admiralty 1852–5 30/3/35, 9/3/38, 25/2/39, 30/1/40, 26/2/40, 24/2/41, 3/11/41, 29/2/48, 19/3/49, 27/6/49, 27/2/50, 1/3/50, 27/2/51, 26/3/52, 13/11/52, 25/11/52, 28/11/52, 6/4/53, 20/7/53, 16/12/53, 15/7/54, 6/12/54, 15/12/54, 17/12/54, 8/1/55 ff, 2/5/55, 26/4/56, 13/6/56, 31/3/57, 16/2/58, 17/2/58 ff, 26/5/58, 8/3/59, 31/5/59, 24/7/59, 30/9/85, 18/9/92, 21/2/93, 15/9/93, 19/3/94
- at Admiralty 8/2/53, 16/12/53
- attack on Canning's proclamation 20/5/58, 23/5/58 n
- Carlisle speech of 31/3/52
- Cobden Treaty and 16/1/60
- comments on G's plan of finance 16/2/56
- corn laws and 21/1/42 ff, 7/3/42, 10/3/43, 21/2/46
- death of 26/10/61
- death of Lady Graham 27/10/57
- factory education clauses and 25/3/43 ff, 15/6/43, 17/6/43 ff
- favours joining with liberals 24/2/52
- fortifications question and 20/7/60, 21/7/60 n
- G at Netherby 3/9/58 ff
- G discusses with Brougham 23/10/57
- G dissatisfied with speech of 10/5/50
- G's *Q.R.* paper on finance and 15/12/56
- G's rows with Palmerston and 19/7/61
- income tax exemption and 11/4/53 ff
- makes no comment on *State and Church* 9/2/39
- Maynooth and 13/2/44
- negotiates with Russell 12/3/52
- Peelites and Palmerston and 17/4/56
- reform and 14/3/59
  - G does not understand his position 6/9/58
- rigidity of 23/3/44
- Roebuck's motion and 24/1/55 ff, 5/2/55 ff, 18/2/55 ff
- the church and 22/4/38
- tory split and 8/7/46, 10/7/46, 13/7/46, 5/4/51, 24/2/52, 12/3/52

Granard case *See* Ireland
Grantown-on-Spey 9/10/72
Granville, Earl *See* Gower
Graphic Society 10/5/48, 13/3/50, 8/5/50
Grasse 5/2/83, 23/2/83, 12/2/92
Gray's Inn
- G dining at 25/1/93

Great Exhibition *See* Crystal Palace, Exhibition (Great, 1851)

Greece 17/6/50 ff, 24/8/69, 7/6/70, 12/6/79, 30/6/79, 22/7/79, 6/9/80 c, 30/12/80 c, 8/3/81 c, 26/3/81 c, 28/3/81 c, 10/2/86, 15/2/86 c, 16/2/86 c, 22/2/86 c, 10/3/86, 1/4/86 c, 14/4/86
- Anatolikes Omospondiae 14/5/89 n, 24/8/89
- brigands in
  - Dilessi murders 27/4/70 c, 7/5/70 c, 14/5/70 c, 20/5/70, 22/5/70 c, 23/5/70, 25/6/70 c, 30/7/70 c, 10/8/70 c
- Chamber of Deputies
  - G visits 22/12/58
- Concert of Europe used against 22/4/86, 28/4/86, 4/5/86
- Corinth
  - G visits 23/12/58
- Don Pacifico affair 17/6/50
  - G's speech on 27/6/50
  - Palmerston's speech on 25/6/50
- finances of 30/1/69, 7/9/92, 11/9/92
- G attends Russian church in 19/12/58
- G greeted as Phil-Hellenic in Zante 15/12/58 n
- Greek request for British officers for army 7/2/82 c
- G's article 'Greece and the Treaty of Berlin', *N.C.*, v. 1121(June 1879) 20/5/79
- G sees demonstration in Cephalonia for 'enosis' with 10/12/58 n
- G's visit to 17/12/58 ff
- Ionian Islands' annexation to Greece 7/7/63
- King of
  - G considered as 10/6/62 n
  - Gen. Peel considered 10/6/62
- Lutraki 17/12/58
- Piraeus
  - G's visit to 18/12/58
- royal palace
  - G dines at 21/12/58
- Senate of
  - G attends 20/12/58
- Turkey and 22/12/68 c, 6/1/69, 11/1/69
- Unionism and 26/8/92
- *See also* Athens, Turkey

greed, G's
- not satisfied with the last 22 years, or the last 35! 26/6/74

Greek alphabet
- extract of 21/6/58

Greek anapaestics, G not up to 9/11/25, 12/5/26
Greek architecture 8/5/32
Greek tragedy, superiority of 3/10/33
Greenock 9/8/34, 23/9/40, 3/12/40, 3/10/49, 30/8/80

Greenwich
Fish Dinners at 20/6/40, 13/8/53, 10/8/59, 25/7/63, 17/8/81, 16/8/82
G proposes Palmerston's health at 10/8/59
Shrewsbury fête at 26/6/58
Greenwich constituency 18/11/68 ff, 20/11/72, 31/12/73, 3/1/74, 11/5/74, 30/11/78
Blackheath speeches
too long yet not long enough for full development 27/10/71 c, 28/10/71
bye-election required on G's acceptance of the Chancellorship? 9/8/73, 3/10/73 c, 1/12/73 c, 29/12/73, 10/1/74, 21/1/74, 2/2/74
law officers find not 3/10/73
demands for G's resignation from 11/1/71 n
deputation on Bulgarian horrors 7/9/76
election more like a defeat than a victory 3/2/74
G giving school prizes in 11/11/75
Greenwich Advanced Liberal Association 1/12/71
G's speeches in
G abstaining from speaking 30/12/69
G unlikely to stand for at next election 11/10/73
G visits 21/12/68
radicalism in 6/5/72
visits to, postponed 11/1/71
Grey, Charles, General (1804–1870), secretary to Albert 1849–61, to the Queen 1861–70 29/11/68 ff, 5/3/94
G's premiership and 1/12/68 ff
at Hawarden with Queen's commission 2/12/68
telegram from leads G to say 'my mission is to pacify Ireland' 1/12/68 n
letters from G to, printed 28/3/69
politics of 3/12/68, 11/1/69
Grey's government, fall of 11/7/34
Griffith's valuation *See* Ireland (land question)
Grillion's Club *See* clubs
Grinqualand *See* South Africa
Grittleton House 9/6/62
Grosvenor, Richard de Aquila, Lord (1837–1912), 1st Baron Stalbridge (1886), whig M.P. Flintshire 1861–86; chief whip 1880–5 5/11/67, 21/6/68, 1/2/80, 10/3/80 ff, 10/6/80 ff, 31/7/80, 6/1/81 ff, 24/3/81, 21/4/81 ff, 22/7/81 ff, 27/7/81 ff, 25/1/82 c, 24/3/82, 10/6/82, 24/7/82 ff, 8/11/82, 31/7/83, 25/10/83, 8/4/84 ff, 9/5/84 ff, 11/8/84, 6/9/84, 31/1/85, 5/3/85 ff, 4/4/85 ff, 18/6/85, 2/7/85, 4/8/85,7/8/85, 1/12/85, 3/12/85, 2/1/86, 8/1/86 n, 12/1/86, 23/1/86 ff, 2/2/86, 10/2/86
at Hawarden 8/9/85 ff, 14/9/85, 5/10/85, 21/12/85
attends cabinet 7/5/85 c
candidate for Flintshire 30/11/85 ff
difference with G 21/12/85
election 1885 and 22/8/85, 8/9/85 ff
home rule and 3/11/85 ff, 21/12/85, 23/12/85, 26/12/85
letters from G to, printed 29/8/72, 23/8/81, 25/8/81, 17/9/81, 14/11/81, 24/2/82, 3/5/82, 29/8/82, 5/12/82, 20/1/83, 27/3/83, 3/8/83, 21/8/83, 23/11/83, 27/11/83, 18/1/84, 31/1/84, 20/3/84, 27/9/84, 18/6/85, 6/7/85, 22/8/85, 2/9/85, 17/9/85, 23/9/85, 9/10/85, 24/10/85, 6/11/85, 8/11/85, 18/11/85, 27/11/85, 6/12/85, 10/12/85, 30/12/85, 5/1/86, 7/1/86
silly pamphlet by 24/6/86
grouse
none shot at Fasque 1847 12/8/47
Grove Park, Warwick (T. G) 30/9/50 ff
Grove Park, Watford (Clarendon) 6/11/69
Guardian, *The* *See* publications
Guatemala
Guatemala road 24/10/61, 5/6/63, 20/7/91
Guido 18/4/32, 2/6/32, 9/6/32, 11/6/32, 12/6/32, 13/6/32, 9/7/32, 26/9/38, 1/10/38, 11/12/38, 31/12/38
Guisachan, Inverness-shire (Sir D. Marjoribanks) 27/9/72
very Conservative party at, but genial and cordial 3/10/72
Gunpowder Plot, got up by Cecil 15/12/38
Guy Faux
G betrayed into excess by 5/11/49
Guy's Hospital
G governor of 13/5/35, 15/3/37, 15/5/78
jingoism against 25/2/78 n
opens new Medical College of 26/3/90 n
visited 4/8/32, 12/5/41, 9/5/60, 14/11/60, 12/11/62, 11/11/63

Habeas Corpus *See* Ireland
Haddington 7/9/45, 15/11/74
Haddo House (Aberdeen) 27/10/36, 19/9/37, 17/10/49, 29/10/51, 28/9/58 ff, 15/9/84
Haddon Hall (Rutland) 16/11/61, 23/11/75
Hagley
village dinner, G speaks at 28/10/63

Hagley (Lyttelton) 22/1/40 ff, 3/8/40, 22/1/41, 17/12/42 ff, 11/11/44, 11/12/44, 19/11/45 ff, 6/3/47 ff, 44/2/48 ff, 22/8/48 ff, 3/4/49 ff, 9/2/50, 1/3/50 ff, 2/8/50, 1/8/51, 11/12/52, 8/12/53, 19/4/54, 16/5/54, 3/1/57 ff, 16/8/57 ff, 18/8/57, 2/2/61, 24/1/62, 28/3/63, 27/10/63, 29/12/68, 1/1/69, 15/1/70, 21/12/71, 24/3/75, 17/1/76, 22/4/76, 4/5/76, 1/6/77, 6/11/88
plays at 7/1/57
Haileybury
G examining at 28/6/52
haircuts 24/9/28, 2/8/30
Halifax, Viscount *See* Wood
Hall, Christopher Newman, Rev. (1816–1902), congregationalist; G's link with nonconformity 23/3/64, 21/7/64, 8/11/71, 6/9/76, 28/10/76, 2/6/78, 5/5/79, 16/6/88
arranges meeting of dissenting ministers with G 15/11/64, 25/1/66, 13/2/68, 12/7/76, 6/7/77
church rates and Alabama incident discussed 13/2/68
on Vaticanism; disestablishment; Moody & Sankey; Scottish patronage 16/2/75
teeth and claws not very terrible 25/1/66
brings working men to tea with G 31/3/64
letters from G to, printed 23/11/71
See also nonconformists
Hallam, Arthur Henry (1811–1833), G's Eton schoolfriend; at Trinity, Cambridge, the subject of *In Memoriam* 4/2/26, 7/5/26, 13/5/26, 25/5/26, 9/6/26, 19/6/26, 5/7/26 ff, 7/8/26, 24/9/26, 29/9/26 ff, 5/11/26, 3/1/27, 24/3/27 ff, 23/7/27, 30/7/27, 9/10/27, 14/11/27, 3/9/28, 11/11/28, 8/5/29, 12/9/29, 16/9/29, 23/9/29, 22/6/30, 2/2/33, 7/2/33 ff, 23/2/33, 19/3/33, 18/5/33, 31/7/33, 9/1/62, 26/4/86, 2/12/92
Chantrey's bust of 22/7/34
death of 6/10/33 ff, 14/10/33, 29/10/33, 18/6/34 ff, 15/9/35, 14/11/35, 23/9/36, 10/5/40
engagement of 13/12/31
G's intimacy with 24/9/26
G's recollections of 25/11/93
G visits in Cambridge 15/12/31 ff
Le Gallienne's edition of his *Poems* 24/11/93 ff
letters of 6/2/34, 18/2/34
G reading: astonishing 13/1/78
memorial to 29/5/63, 30/5/63, 2/6/63
messing with G 19/11/26 ff, 6/5/27
suggests renewal of correspondence 19/12/31
summary of G's relations with 14/9/29
visits to Oxford 13/10/29, 15/10/29 ff, 9/6/31 ff
See also Eton College, Tennyson
Hallam's *Middle Ages*
analysis of 23/10/33 ff, 2/12/33
Hallingbury (Canning) 26/12/29
Hambledon 7/8/66
Ham House 25/5/64, 1/7/93
Hamilton, Edward Walter, Sir (1847–1908), Knight (1894), G's private secretary 1873–4, 1880–5, treasury official from 1885 1/8/69, 2/8/69, 11/8/73, 5/3/74, 9/3/74, 23/5/80, 31/7/80 n, 11/8/80, 19/4/81, 27/1/82, 7/4/82 n, 15/8/82 ff, 6/1/83, 8/2/83, 5/3/83 ff, 12/11/83 ff, 2/1/84 ff, 5/4/84, 11/4/84, 7/10/84, 8/3/85 ff, 12/4/85, 20/5/85, 7/6/85, 27/6/85, 31/1/86, 19/3/87, 14/3/88, 24/3/88, 14/12/88, 12/3/89, 8/4/89, 27/6/89, 1/8/89, 13/5/90, 25/11/90 ff, 30/3/91, 6/4/91, 10/12/91, 31/3/92, 6/10/92, 19/1/93 ff, 18/3/93 ff, 11/5/94
at Hawarden 22/11/81 ff, 7/11/87, 18/10/88
at the Treasury 30/6/85 ff
dissolution on home rule, opposes 2/6/86
entertains G at the Reform 7/9/81
G's private secretary 11/8/73 ff, 5/3/74, 2/8/80 ff, 30/6/85
G's tribute to 30/6/85
Irish finance and 18/2/86 ff, 10/3/86 ff, 27/3/86 ff, 16/11/92, 11/2/93 ff, 16/5/93 ff, 13/6/93 ff, 24/7/93 ff
letters from G to, printed 18/5/83, 30/6/85, 16/12/85, 23/12/85, 31/12/85, 2/6/86, 16/7/86, 24/7/93, 13/2/94
navy estimates crisis and 13/2/94 ff
See also Ireland, Primrose, private secretaries, rescue work, Treasury
Hamilton, Walter Kerr, Bp. (1808–1869), G's friend at Eton and Christ Church, tractarian bishop of Salisbury 1854 27/9/27, 18/7/30 ff, 17/4/33, 20/1/34 ff, 30/1/34, 25/8/35, 19/3/38, 17/5/39, 12/4/41 ff, 26/11/44, 20/2/49, 31/3/53, 21/11/54, 13/3/55, 17/1/57, 19/1/57, 30/3/61, 7/2/64, 24/8/66, 17/6/68, 4/4/69, 13/3/70, 3/4/70, 6/7/82
at Hawarden 1/10/55 ff, 31/10/61
confirms Agnes G 6/6/57
G's role in his bishopric 19/3/54
G stays with at Salisbury 5/6/57 ff, 3/9/66 ff

G tries to make Warden of T. C. Glenalmond 4/9/45
health of 24/3/69
saintliness of 11/2/85
war prayer of, used by G 17/11/54
Hampton, William *See* servants
Hampton Court
Raphael cartoons in 31/5/47
Hampton Court Palace 19/5/56
Handel's *Messiah* 1/7/34
Hanover Chapel 23/4/48 ff
Hansard 15/8/42, 24/4/57, 10/8/66, 20/11/68, 28/11/72, 6/7/76
G's speech on official reporting 20/4/77
parliamentary printing inquiry 18/7/54
Harcourt, William George Granville Venables Vernon, Sir (1827–1904), Knight (1873), barrister and liberal M.P., home secretary 1880–5, chancellor of the exchequer 1886, 1892–5 15/2/73, 28/6/73 c, 8/3/75, 29/2/76, 19/7/77, 25/1/78, 6/4/78, 6/4/79, 25/2/80, 3/5/80 c, 5/3/81 c, 15/2/82, 4/6/82, 8/6/82, 10/6/82 c, 8/7/82 c, 1/12/82 cn, 17/1/83, 2/7/83 ff, 7/11/83, 25/1/84, 18/2/84, 27/6/84, 1/7/84, 28/3/85, 4/4/85, 28/4/85, 21/5/85, 27/6/85, 7/7/85, 18/7/85, 31/12/85, 14/1/86, 24/3/86, 1/4/86 c, 25/5/86 ff, 20/7/86 c, 20/8/86, 19/9/86 ff, 21/2/87 ff, 18/4/87 ff, 9/6/87, 21/7/87, 24/8/87, 9/4/88, 13/7/88, 13/11/88 ff, 15/3/89 ff, 10/2/91 ff, 4/4/91, 15/4/91, 9/6/91 ff, 26/2/92, 28/4/92 ff, 26/5/92 ff, 13/6/92 ff, 27/7/92 ff, 23/11/92 ff, 11/1/93 ff, 16/3/93 ff, 19/6/93 c, 17/7/93 ff, 8/8/93 c, 13/12/93 ff, 21/2/94 ff
1867 Reform Bill and 8/3/67
as 'Historicus' 27/6/63
at Althorp 7/12/91
at Hawarden 3/11/81 ff, 19/12/83, 22/10/85, 1/11/86 ff, 11/10/88 ff, 15/10/89
Chancellor of the Exchequer 6/2/86 ff
neglecting details 22/2/86
crofters and 25/9/84, 12/12/84, 15/1/85, 19/1/85, 14/2/85, 16/2/85 c
death duties and 14/7/92
disestablishment and 9/3/86
dispute with G over control of police 27/2/83, 20/3/83, 26/3/83 ff, 4/4/83 ff, 11/5/83, 14/5/83, 18/5/83, 23/5/83
disquieting conversation with 21/7/93
Egypt and 6/8/84 c, 20/1/93 c
elections and 14/7/92
eyesight of 22/7/92
future of
G's memorandum on, printed 17/6/92
G at Cuffnell's 5/12/82 ff
G at Malwood 5/6/89
G's final cabinet and
Harcourt's speech of farewell 1/3/94 c
G's short breeze with 9/6/82
Heligoland and 19/6/90
home rule and 12/1/86 ff, 21/1/86, 31/1/86 ff, 23/3/86 ff, 14/4/86 c, 1/5/86, 11/5/86, 15/10/89, 11/11/92, 13/1/93 c, 16/1/93 ff, 25/5/93 ff
financial clauses and 16/1/93 ff, 16/2/93 ff
McCarthy's impossible proposition 30/11/90
restive on 8/2/90
Home Secretary 28/4/80 ff
Judicature Bill and 18/3/75
law reform and 21/11/71
letters from G to, printed 6/12/80, 7/12/80, 12/12/80, 8/1/81, 5/2/81, 6/3/81, 17/3/81, 13/4/81, 18/4/81, 31/5/81, 27/7/81, 1/8/81, 5/8/81, 16/8/81, 18/8/81, 6/9/81, 13/9/81, 23/9/81, 25/10/81, 16/12/81, 18/12/81, 19/12/81, 15/1/82, 16/1/82, 30/1/82, 20/2/82, 3/5/82, 6/5/82, 16/5/82, 17/5/82, 8/6/82, 10/6/82, 16/6/82, 17/6/82, 20/6/82, 10/7/82, 21/7/82, 4/8/82, 20/8/82, 31/8/82, 1/9/82, 17/9/82, 18/11/82, 25/11/82, 17/12/82, 18/12/82, 28/12/82, 11/2/83, 27/2/83, 15/3/83, 20/3/83, 24/3/83, 26/3/83, 27/3/83, 30/3/83, 4/4/83, 5/4/83, 25/4/83, 27/4/83, 5/5/83, 14/5/83, 18/5/83, 23/5/83, 24/5/83, 16/7/83, 28/8/83, 7/9/83, 18/10/83, 5/11/83, 23/12/83, 26/12/83, 29/12/83, 10/1/84, 1/2/84, 29/2/84, 5/4/84, 4/5/84, 27/6/84, 28/6/84, 10/7/84, 4/8/84, 6/8/84, 26/8/84, 17/9/84, 25/9/84, 31/10/84, 5/12/84, 12/12/84, 18/12/84, 15/1/85, 19/1/85, 20/1/85, 14/2/85, 24/2/85, 30/3/85, 14/4/85, 15/4/85, 16/4/85, 25/4/85, 27/4/85, 5/5/85, 8/5/85, 13/6/85, 15/6/85, 20/6/85, 3/7/85, 21/7/85, 12/9/85, 31/12/85, 3/1/86, 31/1/86, 6/2/86, 8/2/86, 12/2/86, 13/2/86, 14/2/86, 16/2/86, 17/2/86, 19/2/86, 20/2/86, 22/2/86, 20/3/86, 25/3/86, 8/4/86, 10/4/86, 12/4/86, 1/5/86, 12/5/86, 28/5/86, 29/5/86, 8/7/86, 2/8/86, 7/8/86, 11/8/86, 6/9/86, 7/9/86, 10/9/86, 13/9/86, 21/9/86, 27/10/86, 16/11/86, 18/12/86, 24/12/86, 27/12/86, 29/12/86, 30/12/86,

Harcourt, William George Granville Venables Vernon, Sir (*cont.*)
letters from G to, printed (*cont.*) 14/7/92, 18/7/92, 22/7/92, 26/7/92, 31/7/92, 2/8/92, 29/8/92, 10/9/92, 21/9/92, 23/9/92, 24/9/92, 25/9/92, 26/9/92, 8/10/92, 13/10/92, 22/10/92, 28/10/92, 5/11/92, 8/11/92, 9/11/92, 17/11/92, 18/11/92, 22/11/92, 24/11/92, 11/12/92, 16/12/92, 1/1/93, 5/1/93, 7/1/93, 10/1/93, 11/1/93, 13/1/93, 16/1/93, 18/1/93, 19/1/93, 21/1/93, 22/1/93, 26/1/93, 27/1/93, 31/1/93, 5/2/93, 9/2/93, 13/2/93, 16/2/93, 18/2/93, 22/2/93, 1/3/93, 8/3/93, 14/3/93, 28/5/93, 5/6/93, 7/6/93, 22/6/93, 18/7/93, 19/7/93, 6/9/93, 7/9/93, 9/9/93, 12/9/93, 14/9/93, 15/9/93, 16/9/93, 19/9/93, 21/9/93, 29/9/93, 16/10/93, 25/10/93, 7/11/93, 13/11/93, 5/12/93, 9/12/93, 10/12/93, 12/12/93, 16/12/93, 28/12/93, 30/12/93, 5/2/94, 7/2/94, 25/2/94, 2/3/94, 4/3/94
navy estimates crisis and 27/12/93 ff, 2/1/94 ff, 5/2/94 ff, 25/2/94
G's dispute over 1860 figures with 10/1/94 ff
G's memorandum on, printed 9/1/94
Parnell and the O'Shea divorce and 24/11/90 ff
Public Worship Regulation Bill and 5/8/74
qualities of
another outburst from 19/5/87
an uneasy political travelling companion 15/6/87
ill-use of G 14/8/92
ranting complaints of 6/4/86
worse than ever in cabinet 6/4/86
resignation, threat of 16/5/85
resignation of intended 25/7/94
secret service money and 12/6/82
Sudan and 21/8/84
suggests his son for an appointment 12/9/93, 14/9/93
Uganda and 20/9/92 ff, 29/9/92 c, 22/10/92 ff, 18/11/92 ff, 5/1/93
Victoria and
Harcourt to write nightly report on Commons for 27/1/93
See also budgets, cabinet, Ireland, Uganda
Hardwicke Hall 3/6/73
Hardy's *Tess of the D'Urbervilles*
gives image of a world without a Gospel 8/5/92
G's profound disgust at 30/4/92 n
hares
200 white hares seen 2/10/44
Harlech 13/9/55
Harley Street *See* houses
Harper's Magazine *See* publications
Harrow School
G speaks at 4/7/67, 25/3/82
statutes of 1/7/71 c
visited 7/6/43, 3/4/87
Harrow Weald
St. Andrew's College 11/7/48, 9/7/51, 23/1/53
Hartington, Lord *See* Cavendish
Harvard University
Phi Beta Kappa at
G declines invitation to speak to 15/1/79
harvests 2/8/25, 17/8/25, 2/7/32, 14/10/36, 10/9/38, 14/10/54 n, 8/8/55, 10/8/63, 11/8/79 ff, 14/6/80, 25/8/81, 18/8/82, 30/8/82, 1/9/82, 15/7/83, 27/8/83, 12/8/84, 18/8/85 ff
better in Germany 15/9/79
harvest service 7/10/74, 3/7/87, 16/9/90
mechanised reaper at Hawarden 10/8/63
spoilt by rain 27/8/77, 7/9/77, 5/9/79, 9/9/79
troops used for harvesting at Woodstock 3/9/72, 27/10/72, 5/11/72
Hastings 25/3/91
G's speech at 17/3/91
Hatchett's Inn, Piccadilly 3/12/27
Hatchford, Surrey (Sir W. M. Townsend-Farquhar) 20/2/64
Hatchlands, Guildford 8/6/91, 28/5/92, 4/8/92, 9/8/92, 29/4/93, 23/6/93, 29/7/93
Hatfield (Salisbury) 13/6/67, 11/12/68, 13/12/68, 26/11/70, 15/7/71, 20/7/72, 7/12/72, 12/7/73, 27/2/75, 17/7/75
chapel of
careful and seemly service 27/11/70
great sight, for the trees alone 13/6/67
Hatherley, Lord *See* Wood
Haverfordwest 12/7/52
Hawarden
Anchor works, Saltney
G's speech at 12/9/90
church 9/10/54 ff, 7/11/54
churchwarden's meeting on bells, G at 23/10/74
destroyed by fire 29/10/57 ff
funeral of Sir S. Glynne in 24/6/74
G attends vestry meeting 21/8/56, 19/11/57
occupied by excursionists 28/5/90
restoration of by G. G. Scott 5/11/57 ff, 11/11/57, 19/11/57, 19/8/59
rood loft and gates of 9/6/92
church rate 17/1/61
poll 29/10/58, 30/10/58

clergy retreat at 1/10/74 ff
collieries near 19/7/39
Gladstone Memorial Fountain 14/8/90, 29/12/90
Glynne Arms
G dines in 25/11/69
wild heifer's head in 29/8/92 n
Hawarden Church Union 6/1/41
Hawarden Institute 18/6/57, 13/9/75, 14/9/75
new Institute opened by G 22/5/93
Jubilee 1887
arrangements for 15/2/87
Lady Glynne's funeral 20/5/54
mission to 16/12/79, 29/1/80 ff, 5/2/80, 3/2/87, 7/2/87 ff
Monad Library (early name for St. Deiniol's) 31/10/89 ff, 20/11/89
potters of 1/12/86
schools in 17/7/39
G gives evidence to commissioners on 3/6/90
School Board controversially avoided 15/8/73
St. Deiniol's Library 6/12/92 ff
damaged in storm 14/11/90 n
decision to name it 'St. Deiniol's' 5/12/89
discussed with C. Gore 10/11/88, 12/11/88
early plans for 12/7/86, 15/9/87, 15/8/88 ff, 15/9/88 ff, 8/8/89, 19/8/89, 21/8/89 ff, 20/11/89
first books delivered 21/12/89
G makes over £40,000 to 2/11/95
ground floor for theology, 25000 volumes 21/8/89
G's memorandum on heads of purposes of, printed 12/11/88
G sorting books in 23/12/89 ff, 11/1/90 ff, 28/1/90, 22/5/90 ff, 8/8/90 ff, 22/8/90 ff, 6/10/90 ff, 19/11/90 ff, 5/1/91, 4/8/91 ff, 1/9/91 ff, 6/10/91 ff, 3/11/91, 20/4/92 ff, 7/6/92 ff, 2/9/92, 4/10/92 ff, 20/5/93 ff, 6/10/93 ff
Harry Drew in temporary charge of 1/9/94
named 'Monad' 31/10/89 ff
temporary galvanised iron plan for 23/8/89, 24/8/89 ff, 27/8/89 ff, 2/9/89, 11/9/89 ff, 8/11/89, 8/8/90 ff, 6/10/90
trust for 12/11/88, 11/1/91, 8/4/93, 2/11/95 ff, 29/12/96
Wardenship of 25/3/96
Volunteers
G's speech to 4/12/91
reviewed 11/10/60, 4/6/92
Wigan choir singing at 6/9/88
See also Gladstone (Stephen), memoranda, memoranda (printed)
Hawarden Castle
bazaar at 12/8/76, 4/8/79
questionable experiment, not to be repeated 14/8/76, 5/8/79
Christmas tree at 6/1/58
cipher telegram to, G decoding 12/10/70
dinner for over 400 at 26/10/75, 27/10/75
estate of 2/9/42, 2/1/44, 20/12/44, 1/1/52, 15/4/52, 8/1/74, 10/1/74, 13/1/74, 25/2/74, 4/4/74, 15/10/74, 15/9/80, 3/10/83, 23/9/85
arrangements consequent on W. H. G's death 9/7/91 ff
Ashworth's farm purchase 12/10/55, 23/10/55
Aston colliery, strike at 8/6/74, 9/6/74, 10/6/74, 12/6/74
Aston Hall (Dundas) property bought by G for £57000 23/10/69, 11/11/69, 20/4/70 ff, 1/7/70, 16/11/70, 4/4/83
Aston tenantry 6/1/71, 12/4/71, 5/1/72, 13/8/72
Aston works 11/9/71
Bateman's errors about 8/12/80
briefly owned by G 17/6/74
cattle plague in 25/12/65, 5/1/66, 8/1/66
Chester block bought by G 21/8/49, 25/8/49, 14/9/49, 27/8/52
circumstances of 10/12/87
coal famine, benefiting from 22/2/73
coalfield ends anxieties of 15 years 8/8/62
coalfield of 25/3/56, 28/3/56, 18/9/56, 25/9/56, 3/10/56, 4/10/56 ff, 21/10/56 ff, 31/10/56 ff, 20/11/56, 4/12/56 ff, 23/12/56 ff, 11/6/57 ff, 9/9/57, 19/12/57, 26/12/57, 26/7/58, 11/8/58, 27/8/58, 19/8/59 ff, 6/10/59 ff, 20/12/59 ff, 28/8/60 ff, 9/10/60 ff, 22/10/60 ff, 10/12/60 ff, 27/9/61, 7/12/61 ff, 25/4/62, 4/8/62 ff, 8/8/62, 4/11/62 ff, 6/12/62 ff, 13/8/63 ff, 4/8/64 ff, 19/8/64, 28/8/65 ff, 1/10/67, 25/1/68 ff, 6/4/68 ff, 31/12/70, 2/9/74, 25/11/74, 7/1/76, 17/3/77, 22/12/79, 9/3/80, 4/4/83, 29/8/83 ff, 24/9/86, 21/11/87 ff, 30/9/89, 11/3/91, 18/4/91, 16/6/91, 25/8/92, 12/10/92
coalfield of: strike in 9/6/74 ff, 12/6/74
Cop House Farm 7/9/49, 25/9/49, 21/10/53
deed constituting W. H. G owner 28/9/75

Hawarden Castle (*cont.*)
estate of (*cont.*)
difficulties of in agricultural depression 21/12/82, 27/12/82
excellent propects of 8/8/62
fee-simple of G's land transferred to W. H. G 9/9/82 ff, 20/10/82, 22/10/82
finances of prove romantic for G 31/12/56
financial history of 3/10/85
financial history of, G's memorandum on 18/6/74
flowershow of 3/9/74, 15/8/78
foundry of 23/9/62
G becomes owner of land in 10/1/48 ff, 6/11/48, 4/5/49, 21/8/49
G digging on 15/7/56, 17/7/56 ff
Gladstone walk 26/6/56
Glynne cottage 26/8/72
G rides boundaries of his property on 6/7/55
G's memorandum on debt reduction 24/9/80
G's memorandum on the succession to 23/6/74, 5/10/74, 6/10/74
G's plan for development of 6/1/80
G's purchase of reversion of, from the Glynnes 17/7/65, 7/8/65, 25/8/65, 20/12/65, 18/4/67, 30/9/67, 13/4/68, 1/6/74
Hawarden House (the Red House) 1/11/78, 27/9/84
Lancastrians employed to improve 19/9/62 ff
mechanised reaper introduced 10/8/63
mineral prospects of clouded 15/1/64
Moor Farm, sale of 8/1/52 ff
mortgages on 9/10/50, 5/5/52, 31/12/79
owned by W. H. G 18/6/74, 6/1/80
poachers on 28/10/73, 7/6/74
Prescott estate 13/8/72
reaping machine introduced 13/8/52
Rent dinner 6/1/53, 2/1/55, 7/1/56, 5/1/58, 2/1/60, 8/1/61, 7/1/62, 1/1/63, 5/1/64, 3/1/65, 8/1/66, 7/1/68, 9/1/72, 10/1/73, 5/1/75, 4/1/76, 9/1/77, 6/1/80, 12/1/82, 9/1/90, 15/1/91
rent reduction of 15 per cent 5/11/79
reversion to G on W. H. G's death (to exclude Gertrude Glynne) 11/8/91 ff, 12/3/92
Saltney separation 19/9/73
Shordley property 2/11/53
steam plough introduced 14/9/65
succession to 2/1/48, 27/6/55, 9/7/55
The Cottage (Glynne Cottage) 26/8/72, 5/9/72
to pass to C. G's male issue 27/6/55, 9/7/55
Townshend & Barker agents of 26/10/74
tramways built on 15/4/52, 31/7/52, 2/9/52
walks in 28/11/55
feast for 900 children at 25/10/75
fire at 22/1/79
French play at 20/10/55
G at
1836–1858 30/1/36, 13/7/39 ff, 6/8/39, 24/12/39 ff, 11/9/40, 17/9/40, 8/12/40 ff, 1/7/41, 14/8/41, 27/8/42, 23/12/42, 7/1/43, 19/8/43, 22/12/43, 28/12/43, 16/12/44, 21/8/45, 15/9/45 ff, 8/12/45, 25/12/45, 14/7/46 ff, 31/7/46 ff, 22/12/47 ff, 20/8/49 ff, 25/9/49, 12/8/50 ff, 24/9/50, 7/10/50, 17/7/52 ff, 11/9/52, 26/10/52, 25/12/52 ff, 1/1/53, 1/10/53 ff, 14/10/53 ff, 28/10/53, 24/11/53, 19/5/54 ff, 21/10/54, 23/12/54, 26/5/55 ff, 9/6/55, 21/6/55, 29/9/55, 9/10/55, 29/10/55, 26/11/55, 7/12/55, 21/6/56, 13/7/56 ff, 31/7/56 ff, 18/9/56, 1/10/56 ff, 29/11/56, 10/6/57 ff, 28/8/57 ff, 27/10/57 ff, 27/1/58 ff, 20/7/58, 16/8/58, 22/10/58 ff
1859–1868 18/8/59, 30/8/59, 10/9/59, 10/9/59 ff, 3/10/59 ff, 15/12/59, 17/12/59, 27/8/60, 29/9/60, 20/10/60, 21/12/60, 24/5/61, 10/8/61, 17/9/61, 11/10/61, 25/10/61, 6/12/61, 11/12/61, 24/12/61, 24/4/62, 2/8/62, 17/9/62, 15/10/62, 27/10/62, 3/12/62, 11/12/62, 31/7/63, 15/10/63, 2/11/63, 8/12/63, 18/12/63, 4/1/64, 2/8/64, 26/8/64, 17/10/64, 31/10/64, 10/12/64, 6/1/65, 11/1/65, 12/4/65, 12/7/65, 20/7/65, 27/7/65, 20/9/65, 11/10/65, 9/12/65, 18/12/65, 18/4/67, 27/8/67, 5/9/67, 24/9/67, 3/12/67, 20/12/67, 4/1/68, 4/4/68, 29/7/68, 5/8/68, 15/9/68, 17/10/68, 24/10/68, 4/11/68, 28/11/68
1869–1874 2/1/69, 30/9/69, 16/10/69, 19/11/69, 21/12/69, 12/4/70, 17/9/70, 1/10/70, 12/11/70, 2/12/70, 19/12/70, 4/4/71, 6/9/71, 11/10/71, 11/11/71, 23/12/71, 17/5/72, 3/8/72, 10/8/72, 18/10/72, 14/12/72, 23/12/72, 9/4/73, 11/8/73, 6/9/73, 9/10/73, 6/12/73, 3/4/74, 11/4/74, 25/4/74, 22/5/74, 27/7/74, 28/8/74, 26/9/74, 12/11/74, 23/11/74

1875–1880 1/1/75, 15/1/75, 17/5/75, 7/8/75, 2/9/75, 24/9/75, 5/10/75, 12/11/75, 30/11/75, 22/1/76, 8/4/76, 24/4/76, 2/8/76, 12/9/76, 11/10/76, 28/10/76, 18/11/76, 9/12/76, 15/5/77, 28/7/77, 29/9/77, 12/11/77, 8/12/77, 18/1/78, 26/4/78, 8/6/78, 7/8/78, 14/9/78, 7/10/78, 30/10/78, 20/12/78, 8/4/79, 26/7/79, 25/8/79, 3/11/79, 8/12/79, 29/1/80, 7/4/80, 13/9/80, 12/10/80, 27/11/80, 17/12/80
1881–1886 9/4/81, 10/9/81, 14/10/81, 29/10/81, 14/11/81, 3/12/81, 10/1/82, 4/4/82, 29/8/82, 16/9/82, 23/9/82, 3/10/82, 16/12/82, 12/5/83, 25/8/83, 22/9/83, 12/10/83, 27/10/83, 4/12/83, 18/12/83, 5/1/84, 27/5/84, 12/8/84, 26/9/84, 9/10/84, 6/12/84, 3/1/85, 22/1/85, 16/2/85, 22/5/85, 7/9/85, 30/10/85, 28/11/85, 17/4/86, 22/6/86, 28/6/86, 22/9/86
1887–1896 1/1/87, 2/2/87, 26/5/87, 6/8/87, 13/8/87, 27/8/87, 13/9/87, 28/10/87, 11/11/87, 18/5/88, 6/8/88, 13/11/88, 5/12/88, 13/4/89, 3/8/89, 10/9/89, 25/10/89, 4/12/89, 20/5/90, 6/8/90, 6/11/90, 11/12/90, 22/5/91, 7/7/91, 31/7/91, 3/10/91, 12/4/92, 2/6/92, 25/6/92, 21/7/92, 20/8/92, 22/9/92, 30/9/92, 26/11/92, 18/5/93, 28/9/93, 13/3/95, 2/4/95, 30/9/95
Golden Wedding celebrations at 3/8/89 ff, 26/8/89
G's new (old age) dressing room on first floor 20/11/69
horticultural fête at 17/8/76
house feuds in 13/10/71 ff, 17/10/71
inheritance of 8/9/40
joint residence in planned 5/1/52
letting of discussed 30/12/47, 24/1/48, 20/8/50
liberal pilgrimages to 26/5/77, 26/4/86, 4/10/86, 30/5/87 ff, 4/10/87
Bacup 20/8/77
Birkenhead 4/8/79
Bolton 4/8/77
Bristol 27/5/90
Derby 22/12/83
Hull 28/5/88
Leeds 22/5/88
Leigh and Rossendale 1/9/77
Newcastle 30/8/78
Rochdale 26/5/88
Salford and Over Darwen 18/8/77
marriage celebrations at 25/10/75 ff
music at 7/8/39, 25/12/39, 23/7/58 ff, 23/10/60 ff, 31/10/61, 13/12/67 ff, 4/1/72
ordinarily song or dance after dinner 24/8/58
Octagon (for G's MSS)
plans, construction and working in 15/8/87, 30/8/87, 1/10/87, 6/10/87 ff, 29/10/87, 21/11/87, 16/12/87, 24/5/88, 1/6/88, 4/6/88, 7/8/88, 11/8/88, 1/5/89, 15/8/89, 9/11/89, 6/9/90 ff, 23/10/93
stowage of papers in 17/9/88 ff
plays at 5/1/56, 5/9/56, 18/12/56
servants' balls 8/8/39, 29/12/85, 6/1/87
Temple of Peace 15/10/53, 3/10/54, 26/12/54 ff, 22/10/60, 27/10/60, 28/9/61, 3/8/64, 17/10/64 ff, 22/10/64, 20/4/67, 18/5/69, 10/8/72, 18/5/75, 21/5/75, 30/8/76
extension of shelving in 17/4/74 ff
G's political correspondence stored in 22/10/64
total of books in: 5185 3/1/55
See also servants
Hawarden Embankment Trust 15/10/57, 23/12/57, 5/8/62, 24/10/64
See also Dee trust
Hawarden Kite 17/12/85 ff
See also Gladstone (Herbert John), Ireland (home rule for)
Hawarden Rectory 3/9/40 ff
Hawkins, Edward, Rev. (1789–1882), Provost of Oriel, Oxford 1828–74 23/1/42, 5/7/48, 22/1/52, 23/1/52, 22/10/52, 13/1/53, 27/1/53 ff, 16/6/55 ff, 27/1/57 ff, 31/5/57, 17/6/59, 28/4/70
inaugural lecture of 2/11/47
letters from G to, printed 17/6/70
superintends G's Oxford constituency visit 1/6/57
university tests and 17/6/70
Hawthornden Castle 14/5/28
Hay, R. W., case of 30/5/36
haymaking 26/6/28 ff, 11/8/36, 28/6/85
head
G's head measured at S. Kensington 14/6/90
Headington *See* Oxford
health
G examined by Paget 15/12/93
G's digestive organs starting to fail 29/12/93
G's good health 21/3/41, 29/12/53, 29/12/78, 16/6/82 n, 22/5/92, 6/3/93, 2/1/96
contingent on freedom of position 28/12/79
inconvenienced by old age but not enough to stop work 29/12/91
physical conservation noteworthy 29/12/89

health (*cont.*)
G's good health (*cont.*)
stronger than for some years 16/6/82 n
See also illnesses
hearing, G's *See* ears
hearing, problems with
aureoniphone used? 21/3/86
See also ears
Heathcote, William, Sir (1801-1881), 5th Baronet (1825), tory M.P.; G's colleague as Oxford university M.P. 3/5/38, 30/5/40, 7/3/54, 26/6/54, 8/3/55, 19/2/56, 5/3/56, 6/3/56, 5/6/56, 31/5/57, 1/6/57, 12/3/59, 12/3/67, 8/7/67, 9/7/80
at Hawarden 22/9/56 ff
church rates and 20/3/66
G explains behaviour since 1853 to 4/5/61
G's encomium of 23/8/81
G's negotiations with on Peelites' future 17/4/56, 26/4/56, 6/6/56
G's Oxford seat and 22/3/60
G visits at Hursley
G composes resignation Address with 11/11/60
Irish Church Bill sent to 3/3/69
letters from G to, printed 3/3/69, 9/7/80
MS on reunion with Rome 18/3/55, 27/3/55
serious illness of 27/3/59, 29/3/59, 17/4/59
heatwaves 17/7/25 ff, 26/6/26, 26/7/30, 23/5/47, 6/7/52 ff, 31/7/56 ff, 15/7/66, 22/7/72, 23/7/73, 9/7/74 ff, 15/7/76, 15/7/81, 26/7/85, 19/6/93, 7/7/93, 17/8/93
88 in shade with draft 16/6/58
umbrellas used in Piccadilly 20/4/57
Hegel *See* Oxford (University of)
Heidelberg castle 12/9/38
height, G's
5ft. 10. 75ins.(in stockings or slippers) 26/12/59
5ft. 11ins. (in shoes) 15/9/61
Heligoland 15/4/43, 2/1/85 n, 19/6/90, 8/7/90
Hendon *See* London
Henley regatta 10/6/29
Herbert, Henry Howard Molyneux (1831-1890), 4th Earl of Carnarvon (1849), Christ Church, Oxford, colonial secretary 1866-7, 1874-80, Irish lord lieutenant 1885-6 25/4/68, 17/7/69 c, 17/7/75, 24/6/77 n, 24/1/78 n, 25/1/78, 26/1/78, 10/4/78, 3/5/79, 28/6/79, 12/7/79, 27/12/80, 10/3/84 n, 9/10/85, 22/12/85
Acton's library and 14/5/90
G's memorandum of conversation on tory cabinet with, printed 26/5/78
Homeric scholarship of 4/11/86
home rule and 15/12/85 ff, 5/7/86
memorial service for 3/7/90
Parnell and 12/12/85
Reform Bill 1884 and
offer of 'men of weight' compromise 22/10/84 ff
requests interview with G 30/7/89
resignation of 14/1/86
See also Ireland, memoranda (printed)
Herbert, Sidney (1810-1861), 1st Baron Herbert of Lea (1861), Admiralty secretary 1841-5, war secretary 1845-6, 1852-5, 1859-60 12/11/30, 26/5/31, 18/6/31, 20/6/34, 4/3/47, 5/3/47, 7/6/49, 27/2/50, 8/6/50, 17/1/52, 9/2/52, 11/2/52, 9/3/52, 4/5/52, 23/6/52, 14/11/52, 29/11/52, 2/2/53, 5/3/53, 31/3/53, 18/4/53, 30/7/53, 10/8/53, 6/10/53, 8/11/53, 29/12/53, 10/2/54, 15/3/54, 23/3/54, 31/3/54, 4/8/54, 14/11/54 ff, 13/12/54 ff, 30/3/55, 2/5/55, 7/6/55, 2/5/56, 31/5/56, 17/1/57, 14/2/57, 31/3/57, 27/7/57, 8/3/59, 14/3/59, 16/11/60, 22/3/61, 4/5/61, 4/10/90
angry at G's acceptance of Ionian office 11/1/59 n
as Radcliffe trustee 22/1/57, 5/4/59
as war secretary 26/11/59, 28/11/59, 30/11/59, 16/12/59, 17/6/60
G's battle with over forces' augmentation 2/4/60, 13/4/60
at Hawarden 17/9/52 ff, 25/9/52 ff, 20/10/55 ff, 24/9/56 ff
church legislation and 29/3/46, 18/5/50
corn laws and 25/3/46
death of 2/8/61
discusses parties with G 31/5/50
education and 25/1/53
funeral of 9/8/61
gloomy about the future 18/5/59
Gordon's *Life* of 31/8/89
Gorham case and 18/5/50, 5/6/50 ff
grandson of 16/12/93
G's difference over Vienna protocols 22/5/55, 22/10/55
G's fervent wish never to part with in public life 21/2/58
G's view of his conduct in 1857 election 19/3/57
health of 17/4/56
illness of 31/3/61, 2/4/61, 22/6/61, 10/7/61, 31/7/61
memorial to 18/10/61, 28/11/61, 6/12/61, 17/3/62, 4/7/62, 23/6/63, 18/7/64, 1/6/67
Peelite tactical meeting with 27/2/52
Peel's panegyric on Cobden and 10/7/46

resignation through ill-health of 8/6/61
speech on vote of credit cheers Aberdeen 25/7/54
Vienna protocols and 21/5/55
Herculaneum 14/5/32 ff
heredity 17/12/81
Hereford 15/7/52
Herodotus, analysis of 22/6/30, 21/9/30
Herschell, Farrer, Sir (1837–1899), 1st Baron Herschell (1886), liberal M.P.; lord chancellor 1886, 1892–5 24/12/85, 6/4/86 c, 8/5/86 c, 11/5/86, 26/5/86, 11/2/88, 5/3/91, 4/4/92, 18/10/92, 15/11/92, 9/3/93 c, 17/5/93
in Biarritz with G 30/12/91 ff
letters from G to, printed 4/4/86, 5/4/86, 24/7/86, 27/8/92, 10/9/92, 9/11/92, 18/11/92, 14/3/94
need to appoint liberal magistrates and 18/11/93
Hertford House (Hertford)
pictures and porcelain at 24/6/67
Highcliffe Castle 27/7/89
High Elms, Farnborough (Sir J. Lubbock) 10/3/77, 5/2/81
highlanders, disarming of 17/6/26
Highland Games, G attending 28/8/73, 4/9/84
Hillfoot House, Glasgow (Sir J. Watson) 19/9/72
Hillingdon 20/4/35, 17/8/35
Hillingdon Court (C. H. Mills) 11/7/63
Himley Hall (Ward) 2/9/48, 9/11/88
Historic Society of Lancashire and Cheshire
G president of 22/10/63
history 3/12/33
golden moments of 1/5/82, 7/6/86 n
home rule and
vital to understanding of 3/7/86
Scottish crofters and
G's historicist analysis of position of 19/1/85
value of plays to illuminate 6/11/33
hoaxes
planned by G 10/1/49
Holker Hall (Devonshire) 19/9/67, 30/1/85
Holland
Java, bimetallism and 2/9/92, 10/9/92
Penang and Acheen and 5/4/73 c, 10/5/73 c, 30/8/73
Holland House 6/7/53, 9/7/53, 20/7/70, 22/8/83, 23/8/83
Holmbury (E. F. Leveson-Gower) 19/7/73, 28/5/75, 2/4/77, 2/6/79, 14/8/80, 2/10/80, 24/3/83, 15/4/84, 4/4/85, 12/6/86, 28/7/88, 6/6/91, 18/8/93
death of Wilberforce at 19/7/73
G's closing visit to 18/8/93
Holnicote (Acland) 26/1/77
Holwood, Kent (Lord Cranworth) 23/7/64, 7/7/66
Holyhead 12/11/77
G visits *Great Eastern* at 19/10/59
Holywell
G electioneering at 27/3/57
attacked for speech on Palmerston at 16/4/57 n
homeless, refuge for
G and Hope planning 4/12/43, 13/12/43, 19/1/44
Homer
Buchholz's achievement 30/12/81
colour in 4/2/58 ff
geography in 27/11/57, 19/1/58, 1/9/65
defies G 12/2/47
G's catalogue, Bibliotheca Homericana (now in Bodleian) 16/8/65
G sends copies of to E. W. Blyden of Liberia 16/6/60
G's writings on translated into Italian 7/12/77 n
Homeric plinth to bust of G 4/6/67
Homeric prayers 9/9/88
horses in 9/9/72
Hymn to Apollo 12/10/74, 21/8/75, 18/2/76
Iliad
35th time of reading? 3/11/86
digest of 2/9/57 ff
inaccuracies of, about Ionia 24/11/58 ff
Shield of Achilles translated 14/12/64 ff, 11/10/67 ff, 11/1/71 ff, 16/8/72 ff, 20/12/73 ff, 9/4/74, 24/4/74
study of 18/7/28 ff, 12/9/28, 29/1/47 ff, 7/9/47 ff, 10/9/47, 7/7/55, 6/8/55 ff, 12/10/55 ff, 19/11/55 ff, 8/12/55, 11/2/56, 25/6/56 ff, 4/8/56 ff, 22/6/57 ff, 20/8/57 ff, 19/11/57, 2/11/61, 11/7/67 ff, 12/8/67 ff, 6/4/68 ff, 1/1/69 ff, 14/10/69, 11/1/71 ff, 10/4/71 ff, 23/8/71, 30/11/71 ff, 23/8/72 ff, 16/9/72, 4/4/74, 28/4/76 ff, 2/8/77 ff, 17/1/83 ff, 30/4/83 ff, 1/9/83 ff, 7/11/85 ff, 27/9/86 ff, 1/11/86 ff, 10/1/87 ff, 21/4/87, 10/5/87, 10/6/87, 10/8/88 ff, 27/8/88 ff, 11/1/89, 29/10/89 ff, 16/11/89 ff, 2/1/90 ff, 26/5/90 ff, 10/6/90 ff, 11/10/90, 6/10/91 ff, 25/7/92 ff, 19/10/92
as work for G's retirement 30/3/75
for Ionian visit 30/10/58
G doubts his ability 20/10/57
G sound in conscience about 31/12/57
in Norway 18/8/85
interrupted by labour dispute at Hawarden 3/9/56

Homer (*cont.*)
Shield of Achilles translated (*cont.*)
metals in 2/6/68 ff, 25/6/68
Nekuia 12/10/75 ff
Schliemann's discoveries 10/10/73 n, 13/10/73 ff, 9/1/74, 5/11/75
service to religion as well as literature 10/2/58
written 3 or 4 times over 19/11/57
theology and 22/11/57
theomythology and 28/11/57 ff
thesaurus of made by G 13/9/67 ff, 31/10/67 ff, 5/11/67 ff, 4/2/68, 10/2/68 ff, 10/8/69 ff, 11/4/74, 13/4/74 ff, 21/4/74, 25/5/74 ff, 4/12/75 n, 10/1/76, 13/8/77 ff, 18/9/78 ff, 11/2/79 ff, 17/2/79, 8/3/79, 27/9/86
translations by G 26/12/59
trochaic translation of 17/12/61 ff, 13/1/62 ff, 22/1/62, 23/1/62, 27/1/62, 16/8/62, 19/12/62 ff, 13/1/63, 14/1/63
read by Tennyson 30/7/62
restlessness drives G to work on 30/1/62
threatens to become a dissipation 31/12/61
worked on in Crewe waiting room 9/1/62
well construed in Golspie school 22/9/53
See also bibliographical index, Ionian Islands, Italy, journal (G's), Olympian religion, publications
home rule 14/10/71, 26/10/71 n, 21/11/71, 25/11/71, 28/1/74, 1/2/74, 30/6/76, 10/12/79 n, 23/10/80, 29/1/85 n, 13/11/85, 20/7/93
a battle between the nation and the classes 28/4/86
absence of clear definition of 28/1/74
Austria-Hungary and 17/7/85, 8/9/85, 30/11/85 n
Basques and local self-government and 25/9/93
can only be proposed by government of the day 12/12/85
colonial precedents for 17/7/85, 9/10/85, 1/4/86 n, 1/7/86, 2/7/86, 5/12/92
G reading Canada Acts 9/10/85, 1/4/86 n
have solved problem of the veto 29/4/86
European experiences of 2/7/86
federal home rule
Childers' plan 28/9/85
final triumph of certain 9/7/86
Finnish experience of 8/9/85
for Basutoland, Derby suggests 24/4/83
G's conversation on with Balfour 13/12/85, 20/12/85 ff
G's declaration on to Derby 1/10/85 n
Norwegian experience of 8/9/85
not dangerous to the Empire 24/4/86
not to be equal treatment throughout for the three countries 30/11/86
overwhelmingly supported in Ireland 24/4/86
Parnell's 'Proposed Constitution for Ireland' 3/11/85
precedence of over other measures 27/6/88
Protestant Home Rule Association 16/2/87 n, 23/10/88 n
Scandinavian precedents for 21/4/86
support of the civilized world for 9/7/86
the people do not know the case 8/7/86
Unionists warped by the spirit of class 24/5/86
See also Chamberlain, Commons (House of), Government of Ireland Bills (1886, 1893, 1894), Ireland (home rule for), letters, memoranda (printed), Parnell, Scotland, suzerainty, Victoria, Wales
honours system *See* patronage (honours), Peel, peerage
Hook, Walter Farquhar (1798–1875), church historian; vicar of Leeds 1837–59, dean of Chichester 1859–75 5/1/31 n, 21/3/45, 18/1/47, 3/1/70, 8/6/73
astonishing labours of 18/1/47
at Hawarden 27/8/67, 28/8/67
G's memorial lecture on 10/2/79
letters from G to, printed 8/3/69, 8/6/69
Life of, G's letters used for 2/11/78 n
memorial to 11/11/75
Hooker's *Ecclesiastical Polity*, analysis of 29/9/29, 5/10/29 ff
hope
preponderates over fear 29/12/44
Hopetoun House, East Lothian 28/11/79
Hope-Scott *See* Scott
horizon
G's horizon enlarges 29/12/60
horse racing
Derby, G attends with Granville
race gives G a tremor 1/6/70
Derby, G does not attend, on chief whip's advice 24/5/71
encourages sin 29/12/32
G at Dover races with Granville 24/8/70
G reluctant to allow servants to attend 25/8/40
horses
in Homer 9/9/72
national supply of 15/2/73 c
Niger 1/5/67
origin of, and W. S. Blunt 14/9/80
See also accidents, Christ Church
Horsley, West (H. Currie) 22/7/54
Horticultural Society, Royal 5/5/49

hospitals *See* Guy's, Middlesex
Hotel Bedford, Paris 14/10/79
Houghton, Lord *See* Milnes
Houghton Hall, Norfolk
  stately but woe-begone 31/3/83
Houghton-le-Spring 25/9/76
House of Charity
  unsuitable for G's charity works 11/6/48
House of Mercy
  G drafts plan for 14/2/45
houses
  rules for 1/2/41, 4/2/41
houses occupied by G
  Albany L2, Piccadilly 4/2/33 ff, 2/3/33 ff, 11/2/34 ff, 28/8/35, 2/2/36
    dinners given in 4/3/34
  29 Berkeley Square 5/7/56
  1 Carlton Gardens (S. Rendel) 29/2/92 ff
  4 Carlton Gardens (A. J. Balfour) 29/9/75, 22/1/76, 2/2/76 ff, 31/3/76
  6 Carlton Gardens
    bookcases for 3/6/47
    garden of 23/2/49
    G arranging clothes in 10/2/49
    inspected 17/4/47 ff, 26/5/47
    let to Vernon 19/1/53
    moved into 6/11/47 ff
    party for schoolgirls in 10/7/50
    wine cellar of 23/5/49
  4 Carlton House Terrace 26/7/55 n, 25/1/56
    let 22/4/56
  11 Carlton House Terrace 27/3/56, 28/3/56, 7/4/56, 10/4/56, 12/4/56 ff, 10/5/56, 28/7/56 ff, 2/2/57, 18/4/60, 27/2/65, 15/12/68 n, 28/6/69, 14/1/71, 19/1/72, 29/7/72, 10/10/72, 21/1/73, 19/5/73, 10/11/73, 16/1/74, 5/9/74
    bought from Arundel 7/4/56
    cabinet meeting in 26/4/73, 26/7/73
    informal cabinet meeting at 18/3/73
    let at 100 guineas per week 15/5/57
    moved into 27/2/58
    picture gallery of 23/4/57, 11/5/57, 13/5/57, 25/5/57, 26/5/57, 25/3/58, 2/4/58
    Prince of Wales at ball 28/6/65
    sale of, to Sir A. E. Guinness 1/6/74, 7/7/74, 5/1/75, 25/2/75, 12/4/75, 15/4/75
    tenure of must end with office 20/12/65
    to be given up at end of present government 13/12/73
  13 Carlton House Terrace 14/1/40, 8/2/40, 11/2/40 ff
    Bunsen and sale of 15/5/47
    humanised by books
    musical party at 26/5/42, 5/7/43
    sale of fails 29/5/49
    sold to Lord Grey for wretched price 11/7/49, 23/3/50
  18 Carlton House Terrace (Granville) 4/9/76
  21 Carlton House Terrace (Lord F. Cavendish) 22/4/74, 25/4/74, 6/5/76 ff
  23 Carlton House Terrace
    taken for the summer 17/3/75, 18/3/75, 17/4/75
  10 Downing Street 6/5/80 ff, 1/2/86 ff, 15/7/86, 25/10/92
    as office (not lived in) 22/12/68 ff, 21/2/74, 3/3/74
    moving out of 25/6/85 ff
  11 Downing Street (as Chancellor) 29/12/52, 17/1/53, 19/1/53, 3/2/53, 9/8/59, 16/4/61, 3/2/62
    Queen's birthday dinner at 24/5/53
  73 Harley Street 21/1/76, 4/2/76, 8/2/76, 9/5/76, 13/5/76 ff, 11/7/76, 25/1/78, 22/4/78, 14/5/78 ff, 27/11/78
    Jenny Lind singing in 23/6/77
    leased for 30 years 8/2/76
    leased to W. H. H. Jessop 1/4/82 n
    windows broken by jingo mob 24/2/78
  1 Richmond Terrace (B. W. Currie) 24/6/85, 29/6/85 ff, 8/8/85
  10 St. James's Square (later Chatham House) 13/12/89, 29/1/90
  16 St. James's Street 8/2/88 ff, 4/6/88 ff
  G too timid at 77 to begin a new London house 5/3/87
  London home, G reluctant to contemplate 18/3/75
    C. G's opposition to G on 30/3/75
Houses of Mercy 8/1/44, 14/2/45, 24/5/48, 17/5/51, 26/1/64 *See also* Charity (House of), Clewer, rescue work
house tax 19/11/41, 5/4/51, 6/8/64, 19/4/71 c, 6/4/82
  G's financial plan and 16/2/56
  local government taxation reform and 2/1/74
  plan to increase 17/11/54
housing
  costs of 15/1/40
  problem caused by want of motive power 12/11/83
  Royal Commission on 8/5/84 n
    agreed to 8/2/84 n
    rejected by G 2/7/83
Howick(Grey) 3/10/76
Hoylake
  G staying at Royal Hotel 11/8/87 ff
  reminiscent of Paestum 26/7/41

Hudson's Bay *See* Canada
Hugo *See* plays seen
Hume, David
analysis of *Enquiry* 22/10/34
discussed with Liddell 27/7/58
epitome of his *History* 19/12/26 ff
greater historian than Gibbon 12/3/27, 14/6/27
humour *See* mirth
Hunt, Thornton Leigh (1810–1873), journalist on *Daily Telegraph* 1855–72, regular link between G and liberal press 26/4/60, 5/12/61, 24/12/61, 3/2/62, 1/4/62, 16/5/62, 24/10/62, 18/3/63, 26/3/63, 7/5/63, 22/6/63, 14/10/63, 1/2/64, 21/4/64, 2/5/64 ff, 21/6/64, 5/7/64 ff, 11/11/64 ff, 4/2/65, 21/6/65 ff, 11/7/65 ff, 24/10/65 ff, 3/2/66 ff, 21/3/66 ff, 19/4/66 ff, 19/7/66 ff, 26/9/66, 31/1/67 ff, 13/4/67 ff, 31/7/67, 19/11/67 ff, 25/2/68 ff, 14/3/68, 5/2/69 ff, 9/12/69, 16/6/70, 22/8/70
at Hawarden 7/9/65
Daily Telegraph and
arranges for W. H. G to report on Ireland 2/8/66
Huntercombe (Lady E. Wells) 18/6/42
Hunterian Museum 17/4/52, 25/5/57, 14/2/65, 13/2/77
Hursley Park (Heathcote) 10/11/60
hustings, G on 11/12/32 ff, 5/1/35 ff, 24/7/37 ff, 23/3/57 ff, 4/4/57 ff
Hyde Park *See* london
Hyères 28/1/92
hymns composed by G 2/9/29

icecream
bought in Italy 24/7/49
Iddesleigh, Earl of *See* Northcote
idleness
as cause of sin 26/10/45
idleness, concern over and attempts to avoid 14/12/27, 29/12/27, 28/4/28, 15/6/28, 15/7/28, 26/9/28, 23/10/29, 11/11/29, 5/2/30, 22/2/30, 27/3/30, 10/4/30, 15/11/30 ff, 29/12/30, 13/1/31, 15/4/31, 10/9/31, 29/1/34, 1/10/64
See also Christ Church (Oxford)
Ilbert Bill *See* Gladstone (Henry Neville), India, Robinson
Iliad *See* Homer
illnesses in household
fever 15/5/61 ff, 17/5/61
scarlet fever in Rome 23/12/66
illnesses of children 19/1/47 ff
Asiatic cholera 24/8/54
croup 2/1/51, 1/6/51 ff, 29/10/53, 14/1/55, 16/1/63
erysipelas 18/9/47 ff
eye operation of Stephen G 26/7/56, 28/7/56
fever 18/9/47 ff
measles 20/8/51, 7/1/56
meningitis 29/3/50 ff
scarlet fever 2/4/42, 22/3/56, 11/7/69
smallpox 17/8/51
whooping cough 29/4/50
See also cholera
illnesses of G 15/11/27, 2/1/29, 27/4/29, 24/1/30 ff, 23/12/33, 8/7/34
at times of political crisis 23/7/69 ff, 16/12/69, 7/5/70, 19/7/70, 19/1/74 ff, 3/5/81 ff, 12/2/85 ff
biliousness 7/12/93
blood, poverty of 7/1/70
bowel complaint 7/7/56, 23/9/57, 4/3/63, 10/5/67, 10/4/69, 19/11/69, 28/5/71, 14/6/76, 6/4/79, 14/1/80, 12/2/85 ff, 4/2/86, 25/3/86, 11/4/90 ff, 15/2/91 ff
caused by frost 17/1/79
caused by linen sheets? 6/4/79
bronchitis 22/2/72 ff, 4/4/73
chicken pox 4/7/54 ff
colds 5/12/40 ff, 21/12/53, 1/10/59, 2/10/59, 16/12/59, 14/1/61, 10/12/62, 7/6/69, 10/9/69, 1/2/71 ff, 26/5/72, 18/10/72, 22/5/74, 12/3/75, 5/12/75, 22/2/78, 14/3/79 ff, 9/5/79, 7/8/79, 26/8/79, 24/10/79 ff, 4/10/80 ff, 30/3/81, 15/2/82 ff, 17/9/82, 15/3/83, 2/3/84, 8/3/84 ff, 31/8/84, 2/3/85, 7/3/86 ff, 10/10/86 ff, 26/3/87 ff, 20/5/87 ff, 18/8/87 ff, 15/10/87 ff, 26/1/88, 31/1/88, 5/3/89 ff, 29/9/89, 20/2/90 ff, 5/10/90, 11/11/90, 7/12/90, 13/12/90 ff, 11/6/91 ff, 28/7/92 ff, 6/1/93 ff, 13/3/93 ff
consciousness in left leg 26/4/70
constipation 2/1/85
cough 20/1/47, 29/3/47 ff, 24/2/48, 27/7/50 ff, 3/8/50 ff, 18/3/56, 16/12/59, 1/1/60, 25/11/64, 15/12/69 ff, 24/12/69 ff, 10/1/70 ff, 20/11/70, 24/3/75, 17/10/81 ff, 18/4/82, 2/8/87 ff, 8/3/89 ff, 10/5/91 ff, 20/6/91 ff, 7/3/94 ff, 23/3/94 ff
derangement 7/7/87
diarrhoea 7/10/54 ff, 11/9/56, 12/9/56, 11/7/60, 4/11/61, 30/5/64, 1/9/64, 2/9/68, 28/10/68, 25/8/69, 21/8/73, 24/9/74, 20/10/74, 6/11/74, 17/11/75, 27/7/76, 11/4/77, 24/9/77,

12/10/77, 29/10/77, 22/2/78, 3/6/78, 6/1/79 ff, 3/5/81, 30/9/82 ff, 29/11/82, 11/7/85, 31/12/88, 23/1/89 ff, 10/7/89, 21/12/91, 10/1/92
dysentery 19/5/71
earache 22/3/70
English cholera 25/5/48
erysipelas 4/10/47 ff, 13/10/48 ff, 18/9/49, 4/6/53, 3/11/53
bad attack at Dunrobin 4/9/53 ff
both arms affected 13/10/47 ff
prevents G speaking 29/5/48
resurgence of 25/5/48 ff
worse 27/10/47
excema 23/2/91, 7/3/91
in the eye 12/3/92 n
faceache 5/11/48, 30/8/63, 30/4/72, 15/4/73, 23/1/78, 25/1/78, 3/1/80, 6/2/80, 8/10/89 ff
fever 1/7/54 ff
fever, depression of 23/7/73 ff
fever/liver
in Rome 11/12/66 ff
from electioneering 4/5/31 ff
giddyness in head from ears 10/1/87 ff
gout 6/8/75
in left hand 21/3/93
gumboil 30/1/57, 31/1/57, 1/2/57, 26/7/78 ff, 11/8/78, 2/8/85, 18/1/89 ff
headaches 19/11/25, 25/11/25, 29/11/25, 15/10/26, 27/6/28, 19/3/29 ff, 26/4/29, 24/1/30 ff, 2/8/30, 31/12/30, 3/8/31, 15/4/33, 13/9/36, 7/1/37, 19/8/38, 27/7/50, 1/7/54 ff, 18/3/56, 28/9/72 ff
head wound from a fall 23/2/81 ff
hurt heel
made worse by doctor 12/1/53, 22/1/53 ff, 1/6/53 ff
in Belgium 5/2/32
influenza 15/3/40, 22/4/40, 26/3/41, 15/5/46, 8/5/48, 18/4/58, 29/9/66, 7/3/77, 24/7/77, 31/7/80 ff, 10/5/91 ff
attack of causes interruption of journal 10/5/91 ff
in Paris 29/9/66
irritation of hands 18/2/85
liver deranged 9/7/56, 15/6/79
lumbago 27/2/62, 14/12/75, 23/8/76 ff, 14/11/77 ff, 28/12/77, 30/12/80, 6/10/81 ff, 27/12/82 ff, 27/8/83, 30/6/84 ff, 2/1/85 ff, 9/9/85, 22/12/92
nausea 5/11/70, 26/7/71, 4/8/71, 2/9/71, 22/2/78, 3/6/78, 30/7/80 ff
nettle-rash 7/9/54 ff
neuralgia 27/7/51, 31/7/51 ff, 4/8/51 ff, 7/8/51, 13/8/55, 24/11/56, 14/9/57, 15/9/57 ff, 22/9/62, 24/9/62, 1/10/62, 14/10/62 ff, 22/10/62, 19/9/65, 25/9/65, 16/9/76 ff, 11/8/77, 5/7/79, 3/3/80, 14/9/80, 26/5/83 ff, 15/12/83, 4/2/84, 12/9/85 ff, 1/8/86
diminished by coffee 19/12/56
nosebleeding 20/10/64
pain in right hand 29/1/91
relaxation of chest 2/5/47
rheumatism 30/12/71, 9/2/86, 16/1/90, 31/3/91
scarlet fever in 1818–19 14/9/53
seasickness 18/8/33, 5/11/38, 22/1/39, 21/8/43, 8/8/44, 25/9/45, 17/11/45, 8/11/58, 20/2/59, 12/11/77, 28/8/80, 19/8/82 ff, 9/8/85 ff
lessons of 8/8/44
singing in the ears 10/1/87
sore throat 30/3/33, 30/11/34, 30/4/35, 1/10/36 ff, 14/1/47 ff, 21/2/47 ff, 3/4/47, 20/8/50, 22/1/51 ff, 15/10/52 ff, 31/10/58 ff, 8/3/65, 7/1/68, 12/1/76 ff, 15/10/81 ff, 6/7/85 ff, 30/7/87 ff, 21/10/87
causes severe loss of voice 16/6/85, 6/7/85 ff
diagnosed as 'chronic laryngeal catarrh' 20/7/85
necessitates sea voyage 8/8/85 ff
treatment by electronisis for 16/7/85, 17/7/85 ff, 7/8/85
sound in jugular vein 7/1/70
sprained ankle 23/9/58 ff
stomach upset 29/11/65, 24/3/80 ff, 29/1/84, 15/4/93
tightness of chest 8/12/63 ff, 19/10/72 ff, 19/1/74, 28/3/76 ff, 6/8/76, 6/2/78
tonsils 11/1/81 ff
vertigo 5/2/83
while revising for Schools 25/8/31 ff
See also Clark, Gladstone (Catherine), medicines, voice (loss of)
imagination, function of 31/10/86
Imperial Federation League
deputation to G
G's notes for 12/4/93
membership of 12/4/93 n
Imperial Institute 30/1/87, 12/2/87
impurity
new rules for avoiding 31/5/50
incarnation, doctrine of 25/10/38, 29/12/40
Ince Blundell, Lancashire (C. J. Weld-Blundell) 19/9/65, 8/9/68, 22/10/89

income tax 17/3/42, 17/8/43, 16/2/47, 25/2/48, 3/3/48, 5/4/51, 12/3/52, 2/12/52 ff, 28/12/52 ff, 3/1/53 ff, 1/3/53 ff, 31/3/53, 20/5/53 ff, 6/6/53, 9/2/57, 11/2/57, 14/2/57, 9/3/57, 21/7/59 n, 23/3/60, 20/2/61, 13/4/61, 1/1/63, 21/12/70, 11/4/71, 19/4/71 c, 30/8/71, 15/10/72, 19/12/72, 6/4/76, 5/6/80 c, 15/2/83, 25/4/84, 11/11/84 c, 21/4/85 c, 24/2/91
abolition of 1/7/60, 12/2/62
abolish income tax and sugar duties, partly paid from death and spirit duties 11/8/73
cannot be paid for out of new indirect taxation 2/4/73
Childers' bold plan 2/4/73
highly attractive to G 2/4/73
memorandum summarising means of, printed 19/1/74
Anti-Income Tax League deputation
G's desires in same direction 24/4/73
aspect of public policy lying within reach 31/3/57
differentiation of 18/12/52, 15/4/53, 16/2/61, 19/2/61 ff, 24/3/63 n
G advises Piedmontese government on 3/3/59 n
G objects to select cttee. on 8/5/51
G reduces exemption line to £100 11/4/53 ff
G's dispute with Lecky over 8/7/87 ff
G's financial plan and 16/2/56, 20/2/56
G threatens 13d. tax if no army retrenchment 13/4/60
India and 15/10/72
Peel wants extension of 17/8/43
public revulsion against 18/12/52
support for to be conciliated 14/2/57
threat of increase a strong physic 1/2/62
See also memoranda
Income Tax Association 24/1/57
Incorporated Church Building Society
G speaking at 12/5/63
India 13/6/40, 21/5/53, 25/5/53, 30/6/53, 29/1/79, 28/2/79, 12/3/80, 9/1/82 c, 24/7/84, 15/2/86 c, 26/3/86, 25/2/94
adds nothing to actual strength of the Empire 24/11/81
annexation of Scinde 27/5/43, 3/6/43 ff, 24/6/43, 27/6/43, 1/7/43, 4/7/43, 3/8/43
as precedent for 1880 23/4/80
Outram's book on 9/12/46, 11/12/46
Outram's paper on 24/6/43, 1/7/43, 4/7/43
Arms Act 16/6/80, 23/10/80, 26/1/81
army of 6/7/58, 2/5/60, 13/10/70, 26/10/70
G's memorandum on 27/1/60, 2/5/60
native army, reduction of expenditure 25/2/71
reform of, G's memorandum, printed 13/10/70
bimetallism and 2/9/92 n, 28/3/93, 6/6/93 c
silver question and 28/5/86, 20/11/92
Brahmo sect, G's interest in 25/12/76, 6/1/78, 25/12/79, 26/12/80, 20/5/83
Britain's pledge to 24/11/81
British severance of sudden, violent or discreditable nature undesirable 15/10/72
Calcutta, Oxford Mission to
S. E. G's wish to join 10/9/82
Chandernagore monopoly negotiated by H. N. G with French government 3/2/91, 5/3/91
civil service of
open competition in? 2/6/93 ff, 6/6/93 c
Contagious Diseases Acts and 24/3/93 c, 25/3/93
cotton duties and 20/2/94 n, 21/2/94, 23/2/94 c
East India Act 21/5/86
committee of inquiry favoured by G 5/5/80, 23/10/80
East India Military College
G examining at 11/6/58
Egypt and 8/7/82 c
costs of army in 12/8/82 c, 28/8/82, 6/9/82, 15/9/82, 30/11/82, 1/12/82 c, 15/1/83, 27/7/83, 28/7/83
engineering college for 7/11/70 c
famine and distress in 26/11/73 c, 17/1/74
G speaks at Mansion House meeting on 28/3/61
finance of 20/7/59 ff, 22/7/59 n, 18/3/79, 10/5/79, 13/5/79 n, 22/5/79, 3/5/80 c, 8/5/80, 12/5/80, 14/5/80, 9/6/80, 11/8/80, 14/8/80, 8/9/80, 23/10/80, 8/2/81, 10/2/81, 5/3/81 c, 16/3/81, 5/5/83 c, 8/5/83, 13/7/83 c, 12/9/92, 8/6/93, 19/6/93 c, 8/8/93 c, 17/8/93 c, 23/2/94 c
forestry and the N. W. frontier of 4/3/93
G at reception in London for Indian residents in Britain 14/6/90
G denounced by Anglo-Indians 15/12/83
Gladstone, Wyllie & co., Calcutta 18/8/74 n
gold standard and
G's memorandum on, printed 2/9/92
G opposes nominated Council for 14/6/58
G's ignorance of 24/6/43
G's Resolutions on E. I. government 4/6/58, 7/6/58
H. J. G's lecture on 13/1/90

H. N. G in 18/8/74
Ilbert bill and 17/4/83, 22/5/83, 25/9/83, 21/10/83, 22/10/83, 25/10/83 c, 15/12/83 n, 18/1/84, 4/3/84
cannot be given up 26/5/83 c
G's feeling on strong and unequivocal 1/6/83
G's feelings on, strongly with Ripon 22/5/83
not to be postponed 10/10/83, 11/10/83, 21/10/83, 25/10/83 c
income tax in 19/3/61, 15/10/72
Indian mutiny 9/5/58 n, 11/5/58, 19/5/58, 21/5/58
India Office
less economical than the government generally 10/12/73
India stock, payments of 21/8/73
land tenure in compared with Ireland 1/9/69
London-Bombay railway proposal
government not the proper judge of, but capitalists and engineers 12/9/71
Mayo, assassination of 13/2/71
pension for Lady Mayo 18/3/72, 19/3/72, 5/4/72 c, 13/4/72 c, 27/4/72 c
memorandum on Indian government 12/4/58
opium trade and 4/6/80, 27/10/92, 15/6/93, 22/6/93
Royal Commission on 22/6/93, 30/6/93, 24/7/93, 3/8/93
payments by for military expenditure 12/2/70 c
political training of our fellow-subjects to be promoted 15/10/72
Pondicherry
possible British annexation of 6/2/71, 11/2/71, 16/2/71
Press Act 16/6/80, 24/11/81, 13/3/82
press of 27/6/78
G's attack on India Press Act 23/7/78
Punjab Tenancy Act 30/8/69
purchase abolition, financial contribution to 28/1/71 c, 11/2/71 c
railways in 5/6/69 c
gauge controversy 3/10/73, 1/11/73, 17/11/73 c
recall of Ellenborough 3/6/43, 24/6/43 ff, 2/4/44
Royal Commission on health exhibition declined 9/7/84 c
sages of 7/12/85
salt tax of 24/12/68
Scinde, Vakeels from, met 12/4/45
Sikhs
defeat of at Moodkee and Ferozeshuhur 23/2/46
Somnauth question 9/3/43
Sudan and
troops for? 7/2/85 c
Suez canal
material interest in 6/9/82
Tonk, Nawab of 24/6/71 c
Treasury control of finance of 22/11/71
ultimate power in 17/4/83
Viceroy of, problem of finding 26/7/93, 8/8/93 c, 20/9/93, 23/9/93 ff, 29/9/93
Elgin appointed 3/10/93
See also army, Asia (Central), Baring, Egypt, essays, Gladstone (Herbert), Gladstone (Stephen), income tax, memoranda, memoranda (printed), Robinson(Ripon), Russia
India Council Bill 20/2/69 c, 13/3/69 c
indirect taxes 11/2/57, 14/2/57, 30/7/69
provide excessively large proportion of taxation 16/7/85
to be levied on a few well-chosen articles 14/2/57
See also budgets, corn laws, tariffs, taxation
industry
not at variance with principles of the gospel 31/8/46
inequalitarian, G thoroughgoingly 24/5/86
infallibility 7/8/63
influenza *See* illnesses
Ingestre (Shrewsbury) 30/10/63
Innerleithen
G's speech at 30/3/80
Inner Temple
G speaks at 3/6/68
Innsbruck 29/6/32, 24/9/79
insomnia 28/3/48
after speaking 23/3/36
See also Gladstone (Catherine), sleep
Institution for Religious Retirement
proposed by Manners 7/2/44
insurance *See* fire insurance
insurance duty 8/3/61
International, First
meeting in London
information on to be given to other governments 1/7/71 c
inventions, G's interest in
American Devil 24/10/79
Ansell's fire damp apparatus 19/3/66
Austin & Quick's contrivance 5/6/46
Big Ben illuminated by electricity 6/5/73
Capt. Warner's invention 13/7/46, 21/5/47
Edison's phonograph 22/11/88
gun cotton experiment shatters Downing Street windows 1/8/72
Leger's Magnetoscope
results from appear mostly very true to G 27/3/52
linotype 26/6/89

inventions, G's interest in (*cont.*)
Maxim gun 2/5/85
phonograph, demonstration of 18/3/78
reaping machine at Hawarden 13/8/52
telegraph 20/3/39, 4/7/40
telephone, demonstration of 18/3/78, 30/4/79
Inveraray 17/8/39
Inveraray Castle (Argyll) 25/9/65
G fishing at 28/9/65
Rob Roy's cottage visited 27/9/65
Inverate (Kerrison) 31/8/53
Invercauld 30/8/73, 3/9/84
Invergarry House, Inverness-shire (E. Ellice) 21/9/72
Inverness 11/9/58
G attends court in 28/9/58
G china-hunting in 28/9/58
G Freeman of 27/9/53
home rule and 13/6/86, 23/6/86
Inversnaid 16/8/39
investments, G's *See* accounts, finance (G's personal), railways (G shareholder in)
Ionian Islands
annexation to Greece 7/7/63, 23/11/70
G's memorandum on, printed 7/7/63
Assembly of
G's dealings with 28/1/59 ff, 5/2/59
G's speech to 5/2/59
petition for union with Greece rejected by G 31/1/59, 5/2/59 n
cabinet decides to surrender 8/12/62
cabinet discusses 23/3/61
Cephalonia 10/12/58 ff
Crani, ruins of 14/12/58
demonstration for 'enosis' in 10/12/58 n
G holds Levee in 13/12/58
G's report on events of 1849 in 15/1/59, 25/1/59
Mr. Stephen's mill 14/12/58
Peloponnesus seen from 13/12/58
constitutional changes proposed by G for 28/12/58
constitution of 1/12/58 ff, 28/12/58, 4/1/59, 8/1/59, 10/1/59, 11/1/59, 5/2/59 n
G's draft on proposed Senate 19/1/59
G's draft on the Presidency 21/1/59
Corfu 24/11/58 ff, 24/12/58 ff
balls attended 29/11/58 ff
Casino of, G visits 28/1/59, 31/1/59
Castellanos, drive to 18/1/59
cathedral of 28/11/58
Coracchiana, G visits 9/2/59
expedition to Manduchio 2/12/58
G addresses Senate of 26/11/58
G and family depart from 19/2/59
Garuna 11/2/59
G dancing quadrilles 29/11/58
Homer's inaccuracies about 24/11/58 ff
Pantaleone, expedition to 19/1/59
Platutera church 2/12/58
San Salvador 12/2/59
'Ship of Ulysses', G visits 12/2/59, 14/2/59
Dusmani's 'clever but dishonest' attack on G's mission 31/12/72
G as absorbed in their affairs as in any Parliamentary business 31/12/58
G as Commissioner Extraordinary (later Lord High Commissioner) of 24/11/58 ff
G's Report on 1/12/58 ff, 28/12/58
Hellenism in 28/12/58
Ithaca 9/12/58
G makes speech in Italian in 9/12/58
Lytton's suggestion G should go to 3/10/58, 4/10/58, 19/10/58, 23/10/58 ff
G decides to accept 27/10/58
G disinclined to refuse 26/10/58
Paxo 12/1/59
race and 28/12/58
Santa Maura 7/12/58, 9/12/58
suitability of population for popular institutions
G ambivalent about 28/12/58
Zante 15/12/58
G greeted as Phil-Hellenic 15/12/58
See also Disraeli, Homer, Oxford (University of)
ipecacuanha *See* medicines
Ireland
Act of Union with
a gigantic though excusable mistake 19/9/85
long suspected by G 19/9/85
repeal of 17/7/85
agricultural improvement plans 22/5/83
Arms Bill 12/2/81 c, 6/3/81, 19/3/81 c, 25/3/81, 14/4/86 c, 12/5/86
Arrears Bill 25/4/82, 2/5/82 c, 4/5/82 c, 10/5/82 ff, 13/5/82 c, 15/5/82 ff, 20/5/82, 23/5/82 c, 8/6/82, 13/6/82, 29/6/82, 5/7/82, 6/7/82, 8/7/82 c, 11/7/82 c, 18/7/82 c, 19/7/82, 29/7/82 c, 3/8/82 c, 5/8/82 c, 7/8/82, 8/8/82
Belfast
invitation of G to, declined 14/10/71, 21/10/71 c
Orangemen in 8/3/93 c
riots in 21/8/72, 27/8/72
Bolton's case 23/7/84
Burke a magazine of wisdom on 18/12/85
Callan schools 26/4/73 c, 22/5/73 n, 24/5/73 c, 14/6/73 c, 28/6/73 c, 5/7/73 c

Catholic university for 12/5/65
church fund in 7/3/83
Church of England in 22/7/27, 12/2/33, 31/3/35, 23/7/35, 12/8/35, 4/7/36, 4/3/44, 2/3/65, 28/11/80
  Church Temporalities Bill 14/3/33, 1/4/33 ff, 21/6/33, 8/7/33, 4/7/34
  Convocation of 7/1/69, 23/1/69, 26/1/69 c
  disestablishment of 2/2/65 n, 28/3/65
  G's letter to Hannah on disestablishment 9/6/65, 31/3/68 n, 20/4/68, 21/4/68
  G's Resolutions on disestablishment 19/3/68 n, 23/3/68, 30/3/68, 3/4/68, 30/4/68, 7/5/68
  justified by truth 3/5/45
  like a nightmare to G 25/4/45
  recognition of 9/5/41
  Suspensory Bill 1/5/68, 14/5/68, 22/5/68, 5/6/68, 16/6/68, 18/7/68 n
  tithes 1/6/36
clemency, act of, needed 9/9/81
coercion in 27/2/33 ff, 18/7/34, 2/3/70, 12/3/70 c, 12/1/71
  Arrears Bill: whig defections on 7/7/82
  Balfour's bill 28/3/87 ff, 18/4/87, 29/4/87 ff
  conservative policy and 24/10/81
  Crimes Act: renewal of 18/3/85, 30/3/85, 28/4/85 c, 5/5/85, 6/5/85, 9/5/85, 11/5/85 n, 15/5/85 c, 30/5/85, 1/6/85, 5/6/85 c, 8/6/85 c
  Crimes Bill 8/5/82, 10/5/82 cf, 13/5/82 c, 16/5/82, 20/5/82, 24/5/82, 8/6/82, 10/6/82 c, 12/6/82 ff, 16/6/82, 18/6/82, 19/6/82 c, 20/6/82 c, 23/6/82, 24/6/82, 29/6/82, 29/12/83, 29/1/85 n
  Crimes Bill: we have asked overmuch 1/6/82
  criminal legislation not the way to solve Ireland's evils 13/2/86
  G's appetite for less than the average liberal's 8/6/82
  G seeks alternative to suspending Habeas Corpus 9/10/80 ff, 22/10/80, 25/10/80, 2/11/80, 4/11/80, 7/11/80, 11/11/80, 14/11/80, 16/11/80, 17/11/80 c, 19/11/80, 24/11/80, 25/11/80 c, 5/4/82
  Habeas Corpus suspension 7/2/71 ff, 9/10/80 ff, 13/12/80 c, 16/12/80 c, 4/1/81 c, 22/1/81 c
  liberal Resolution on 21/6/88 ff
  local suspension of Habeas Corpus 1/5/69 c, 26/11/69, 2/2/70 c, 5/3/70
  Peace Preservation Bill 16/3/70 c, 24/3/70, 14/5/80 c
  renewal of legislation for 26/4/73 c
  weakness of case for 7/2/71 ff
Compensation for Disturbance Bill 5/6/80, 12/6/80 c, 18/6/80, 24/6/80, 3/7/80 c, 5/7/80, 8/7/80, 10/7/80 c, 14/7/80, 15/7/80, 16/7/80 c, 19/7/80, 26/7/80, 1/11/80, 9/12/80
  Argyll's threat of resignation on 12/6/80 c, 14/6/80, 15/6/80
  evictions and 14/7/80
  harmful consequences of rejection of 14/10/80
compensation for improvement 22/5/69
concurrent endowment in 12/2/44 ff, 4/3/44, 8/7/44
conquered by England 5/5/64
constabulary of 5/10/81, 12/10/81, 13/10/81
  cost of 17/9/69, 5/7/73 c, 8/7/73, 25/10/80, 29/8/82
Convocation in
  G's memorandum, printed 20/2/64
Cowper's inexperience as Viceroy 18/12/80
crimes in 7/12/69, 7/2/71, 9/2/71 ff, 4/11/80, 17/11/80 c, 13/12/80 c, 29/6/82, 13/2/86, 2/11/88 n, 8/3/93 c
  Freeman/Kinsella affair 15/5/89
  G's memorandum, printed 24/1/70
  Hunter murder 17/10/69, 26/10/69 c
  Limerick amnesty appeal 22/11/73
  Maamtrasna murders 23/8/82, 24/12/82 n, 8/10/84 c, 31/10/84, 30/6/85, 18/7/85, 21/7/85
  Ribbonmen, evidence on in cabinet 18/2/71 c
  Westmeath inquiry and bill 25/2/71 c, 2/3/71, 4/3/71 c, 25/3/71 c, 17/4/71 c, 19/4/71 c, 22/4/71 c, 6/5/71 c, 31/5/71, 2/6/71, 26/4/73 c
Daily Telegraph and
  Hunt arranges for W. H. G to report on Ireland 2/8/66
dark and dreary cloud on horizon 12/12/80
day of humiliation in 20/11/46
distress in 1/12/82 c, 1/1/83, 7/3/83
dual monarchy with 17/7/85
Dublin
  explosion in 28/12/92, 2/1/93
  French republicans in, scandalous reception of 25/8/71
  G Freeman of 7/11/77
  G's visit to 22/10/77, 5/11/77 ff, 29/8/80
  Phoenix Park meeting 12/8/71 c, 25/8/71
  riot in 9/8/71 c, 16/8/71 c, 17/8/71 ff
Dublin packet 28/3/54
Dublin university
  university reform and 26/10/72, 28/11/72 c

Ireland (*cont.*)
ecclesiastical policy
lies within reach 31/3/57
educational grant to
G votes for 12/6/40
education in 8/8/33, 11/4/37, 15/6/72 c, 4/11/92 c
of the higher class 17/12/40
emergency in overshadows all else 12/2/86
emigration from 18/2/70, 15/1/81, 1/6/81, 9/7/81 c, 14/7/81 n, 18/7/82, 19/7/82, 5/5/83 c, 25/7/83 c, 3/8/83
famine in 20/12/45 ff
G laments loan for 24/2/47
Fenians 23/2/66, 27/4/68 n, 18/7/68 n, 20/8/68, 20/10/68 n, 23/1/69, 28/3/69, 27/4/69, 13/10/69, 16/12/69, 26/9/70, 5/11/70, 11/11/70 c, 19/7/77, 20/7/77, 28/11/80, 12/6/82, 29/6/82, 19/7/82
aim at giving to resistance the noble form of public war 26/11/69
amnesty for 2/2/69 c, 4/8/69, 23/9/69, 13/10/69, 5/11/69 c, 3/9/70 ff, 14/9/70
amnesty for: G fails to persuade cabinet 30/9/70
amnesty not granted 18/10/69, 19/10/69, 5/11/69 c, 7/6/72 n
and mayor of Cork 30/4/69 c, 1/5/69 c, 4/5/69 c, 9/5/69 c
attack on the Queen 29/2/72, 13/4/72 c, 3/12/72 c
bad laws make bad men 21/6/72
G assures Pope not formidable in Ireland 22/10/66
inquiry into prisoners 16/3/70 c
like Satan in the Apocalypse, furious to be ending 2/12/69
means of stopping manufacture of 28/3/69
need for Irish bishops to support land bill against 1/3/70
need to break up the remedial process 1/3/70, 3/3/70
O'Donovan Rossa case 4/2/70 c, 19/2/70 c, 26/2/70 c, 2/3/70
Papacy to condemn 28/1/70 c
political disease of 26/11/69
release of 9/12/70, 15/12/70 c, 4/12/73, 27/12/73, 22/8/81
represent 'irreconciliables' of France 26/11/69
rooted in bad laws 3/9/70
self-love and pride of 28/3/69
statues blown up by 21/6/72
wholly altered public mind in England and Scotland 28/4/69
finances of, Childers' Royal Commission on 11/1/94, 29/1/94
Fortescue and 3/2/64
franchise of 1/3/50, 8/5/50 ff, 10/5/50, 11/5/50 ff, 1/6/50, 8/4/73, 7/6/80, 12/11/80 c, 11/10/82, 3/2/83, 3/10/83 ff, 22/10/83, 23/10/83 ff
a quarter of voting power Roman Catholic 9/9/81
future of 4/5/82
Galway college
university reform and 14/12/72
Galway election prosecutions 6/7/72 c, 17/7/72 c, 24/7/72 c, 25/7/72, 1/8/72
no more to be carried forward 22/2/73 c
general election 1885 and
an epoch, possibly a crisis 7/8/85
general state of, G by no means disappointed with 9/12/73
government of 17/4/39
need for reform of 23/8/83
working Viceroy impossible if Secretary in cabinet 23/8/83
Granard case 19/7/72
Grattan's parliament 17/12/85
green flag of
has distinct and higher footing than the orange 27/8/72
G requests office in 31/8/41, 16/9/41
G suggests series of articles on 5/8/85
G's visit to 24/7/72, 1/8/72, 17/10/77 ff
Abbeyleix 7/11/77 ff
Balfour invited to join 8/10/77 n
Bray Head 18/10/77
Bray: least Irish part of Ireland 18/10/77
Carton, Maynooth 3/11/77 ff
Consilla 10/11/77 ff
conversation with Cullen 6/11/77
Coolattin, Co. Wicklow 26/10/77 ff
Dargle Fall 31/10/77
Dublin 20/10/77, 22/10/77, 5/11/77 ff, 12/11/77
Dublin: Dublin Castle 6/11/77
Dublin: Freedom of 7/11/77
Dublin: Marlborough Street Schools 6/11/77
Dublin: National Gallery 3/11/77
Dublin: Port of 6/11/77
Dublin: Royal Dublin Society 3/11/77
Dublin: Trinity College 22/10/77
Glasnevin 3/11/77
Glencree Reformatory 30/10/77
Glendalough: nothing seen equal to 25/10/77
interview with W. O'Brien on 17/10/77
Kilkenny 9/11/77
Killiney Hill 24/10/77
Kilruddery 17/10/77 ff

larger parts of fade from view 18/10/77
Maynooth College: a saddening impression: what havock have we made of the vineyard of the Lord 5/11/77
McClure judges time still unripe 1/8/72
not enough of *Ireland*: but no choice 20/10/77
O'Connell tomb and tower 3/11/77
Powerscourt 29/10/77 ff
Rathdrum 25/10/77
stays with De Vesci: rare people, difficult not to love 8/11/77
Ulster visit intended but not possible 16/10/77 n
visits farm on Parnell's estate 26/10/77
G's visit to 1880 29/8/80
higher education
G's memorandum, printed 8/6/65
higher education in 28/7/71, 3/9/71, 28/9/71, 29/11/71
Roman hierarchy and 19/8/70
home rule for 5/9/85 n, 13/11/85, 14/11/85, 12/12/85 ff, 30/12/85 ff, 30/10/86, 28/7/92 ff, 2/8/92 ff
Aberdeen speech and 26/10/71 n, 21/11/71, 25/11/71
American Union as base for 8/3/88
a mighty heave in the body politic 13/11/85
basis of the plan 3/11/85, 14/11/85, 12/12/85 ff
believed necessary by permanent officials 13/12/85, 15/12/85, 24/12/85
colonial precedents for 17/7/85, 4/8/85 n, 9/10/85
consequences of not granting 23/6/86
conservative character of 20/4/86, 26/4/86, 27/4/86, 28/10/92
defensive provisions for landowners required 28/9/85
discussed with Spencer 14/10/71
examination of 30/1/86, 2/2/86, 4/2/86 n, 12/2/86, 18/2/86, 20/2/86, 24/2/86, 5/3/86, 12/3/86, 13/3/86 c, 14/3/86 ff
final triumph of certain 9/7/86
financial clauses 1886, revision of 18/12/89, 23/12/89
financing of 28/9/85, 3/11/85
first essential: clear and independent liberal majority 13/11/85
G deliberately silent on 18/2/86
G disposed towards more than most, subject to non-exclusivity & imperial safeguards 25/11/71
G's articles on 26/7/86, 6/1/87, 2/9/87, 24/9/87, 30/1/88, 6/8/88, 23/5/89, 23/8/90, 21/6/92, 27/7/92
G's attack on Dicey's a-historicism 12/11/86
G's memorandum on, printed 28/10/92
Hawarden Kite 15/12/85 n, 17/12/85 ff, 31/12/85 n
historical study of encouraged by G 3/7/86, 7/7/86, 17/7/86, 26/7/86
Irish members and Westminster (after 1886) 24/5/87, 26/5/87, 4/6/87 n, 18/12/89, 17/5/92
Irish presbyterian Address supporting 12/8/93
land purchase and 19/12/85, 9/1/86 n, 14/1/86, 30/1/86, 2/2/86
memorandum on, printed 23/12/85
memorandum on prime points of difficulty, printed 8/8/89
memorandum on read to potential members of cabinet 30/1/86
national petition considered by G 5/12/88
not a request to repeal the Union 1/7/86
nothing but clear liberal majority can carry 18/10/85
Parnell and the O'Shea divorce case 21/11/90 ff
perfect political equality should be basis of 12/12/85
plan for *Hand-Book of Home Rule* 7/7/86, 8/7/86, 17/7/86, 26/7/86, 30/11/86, 28/12/86, 24/9/87 ff
plan for *Hand-Book of Home Rule*: secret service money used for 26/7/86
postponed for 5 or 6 years? 29/12/90
prayer for 27/7/86
priority for, G's memorandum on 31/10/92
protection of landlords, not of Protestants, the greatest difficulty 18/10/85
question that affects millions 29/12/90
Rosebery suggests committee to reconsider 1886 bill 7/7/89 n
Rosebery's very imprudent declaration on 15/3/94
selfGovernment was stolen by fraud and force 23/8/86
Shaw's speech 1880 14/3/86, 19/3/86 n
source of strength rather than of danger 24/4/86
subject probably has a future 10/2/82
sub-legislation for 10/10/73
Ulster and 28/9/85, 2/12/85
Ulster and, G's speech on 18/6/92
home rule party
Boulogne negotations, Parnell and 22/1/91 n, 28/1/91
cooperation with conservative party by 10/6/85 ff

Ireland (*cont.*)
home rule party (*cont.*)
difficulty of placing confidence in 28/9/85
expulsion from Commons and separate assembly in Dublin? 17/7/86
G little faith in any plan for breaking up 23/12/80
G's meetings with leaders of 7/3/92
G's meeting with whips of on Parnell's assertions 5/12/90
G uncertain of programme of 8/8/85
less likely to disintegrate 3/9/85
local government and 5/12/82
meetings in Committee Room 15 5/12/90 ff
memorial to Austria 22/1/81 c
place of seating in the Commons 12/6/93
proposed delay of home rule bill and 7/5/86 ff, 20/5/86
reduced from 65 to 40 3/2/83
represents the Irish nation 2/7/86
should settle with tories before election 18/10/85
size of sections in 6/7/80
split in 6/12/90, 15/12/90, 17/12/90, 22/1/91 n, 28/1/91, 15/4/91, 26/11/92, 10/6/93
splitting of a vital objective achieved 3/2/83
tory/Parnell alliance 8/6/85, 17/7/85, 10/9/85, 30/9/85, 27/10/85, 13/11/85, 14/11/85, 21/11/85 n, 1/12/85, 3/12/85, 6/12/85, 12/12/85 ff, 19/12/85 ff, 24/12/85 ff, 7/1/86 ff
will shift centre of gravity between the two countries 30/6/85
withdrawal from Commons and separate assembly in Dublin rumoured 7/1/86
income tax in
G imposes 11/4/53 ff, 28/4/53, 27/6/53
G supports 20/4/49
industry in 3/11/82, 21/2/85
Irish Church Commission 1/4/69 c, 7/5/69 n
Irish exhibition at Olympia, financial failure of 7/8/91
Irish government
G's concern about narrowness of 7/9/70
Irish Loyal and Patriotic Union 12/2/86 n, 19/2/86 n
Irish nation 10/9/85
danger of conflict with 10/9/85
Irish question
only liberal party can deal with 9/9/85
Irish question: G much oppressed in nerve by bigness of 27/4/68
Irish security and secret service money 9/6/82
Keogh case 6/7/72 c, 15/7/72 c, 17/7/72 c, 24/7/72 c, 8/8/72 c
Kilkenny bye-election 15/12/90 n
'Kilmainham treaty' 1/5/82 cf
a golden moment 1/5/82 c
not a negotiation 1/5/82 c
labouring class of, rumination on 16/12/67
Land Act 1881
Dillon's encouraging speech on 5/9/81
land bill
church is enough for today 28/4/69
land bill 1870
amendments to 16/7/70 c, 23/7/70 c, 25/7/70 c
amendments to, sharp crisis over 4/4/70, 6/4/70, 7/4/70 ff
a sort of Land Charter 25/6/80
Bright land purchase clauses 28/1/70 c, 1/2/70 c, 2/2/70 ff, 27/6/70, 5/3/83 c
Cairns' bill amending 24/6/71 c
Christian's judgment on 22/6/71 n, 24/6/71 c
compensation for disturbance, full of difficulties 15/9/69
compensation for improvement 21/9/69 ff
drafted by Thring 18/12/69 ff
drafting of 17/12/69, 10/1/70, 13/1/70
Dublin press and 7/9/69
G expects labour but no other form of difficulty 24/3/70
G presents at Altar 17/4/70
Gray's 1873 amendment of declined 24/5/73 c
ground broken very satisfactorily on 30/10/69
G's letter to English bishops on 20/6/70
in cabinet 30/10/69 c, 3/11/69 c, 10/11/69 c, 14/12/69 c, 17/12/69 c, 21/1/70 c, 22/1/70 c, 25/1/70 c, 26/1/70 c, 28/1/70 c, 1/2/70 c, 4/2/70 c, 26/3/70 c, 2/4/70 c, 27/4/70 c, 7/5/70 c, 21/5/70 c, 28/5/70 c, 18/6/70 c, 23/6/70 c, 9/7/70 c, 23/7/70 c, 25/7/70 c
in Commons 15/2/70, 7/3/70 ff
influence of Campbell's pamphlet on 11/8/69, 13/8/69, 24/8/69, 1/12/69, 2/12/69, 29/4/70
in Lords 20/6/70 ff
Lifford committee on 29/6/72 c
may drive Fenians to some mad attempt, G fears 17/2/70
neither requires nor admits of great amendment 9/12/73
planned 1/9/69, 2/9/69, 15/9/69, 17/9/69, 20/9/69, 21/9/69, 1/10/69,

9/10/69, 13/10/69, 14/10/69, 16/10/69, 18/10/69, 21/10/69, 30/10/69 c, 3/11/69 c, 4/11/69, 5/11/69 c, 6/11/69, 10/11/69, 25/11/69, 26/11/69, 28/11/69, 29/11/69, 2/12/69, 3/12/69, 4/12/69, 5/12/69, 7/12/69, 8/12/69, 9/12/69, 10/12/69, 10/2/70
political complications of 15/9/69
reception so favourable G trembles 16/2/70
to be basis of 1881 bill 9/12/80, 14/12/80, 31/12/80 c
Ulster tenant right and 2/9/69, 7/9/69, 15/9/69, 17/9/69, 20/9/69, 1/10/69, 14/10/69, 16/10/69, 3/11/69, 4/11/69, 22/11/69, 25/11/69, 28/11/69, 29/11/69, 9/12/69, 14/12/69, 17/12/69, 8/1/70, 10/1/70, 11/1/70, 1/3/70, 22/3/70, 12/6/80 c, 10/7/80
vital principle of 4/12/80
will radically change English/Irish relative positions 22/4/70

land bill 1881 7/11/80 ff, 11/12/80 ff, 9/2/81 ff, 5/3/81 ff
3 F's and 19/11/80 c, 3/12/80, 4/12/80, 16/12/80 n, 27/12/80, 31/12/80 ff, 10/1/81 ff, 12/1/81 n
3 F's and: G opposed to as in 1870 28/4/81
amendments to 25/5/81, 28/5/81 c, 2/6/81 c, 25/6/81 c, 26/7/81, 27/7/81, 6/8/81 c
big in purpose more than bulk 7/4/81
Childers' paper 9/12/80 ff
Court, role of 21/1/81, 19/2/81, 5/3/81, 6/4/81, 7/4/81, 2/6/81 c, 25/6/81 c, 24/11/81
division into temporary and permanent provisions, G's doubts about 19/2/81
Dowse's paper and 4/12/80, 7/12/80
emigration and 15/1/81, 1/6/81, 9/7/81 c, 14/7/81 n, 7/3/83
excellent reception of 11/4/81, 13/4/81, 15/4/81
fair rent and 9/12/80, 14/12/80, 10/1/81, 5/3/81, 7/4/81, 22/4/81, 27/4/81, 20/5/81 c, 28/5/81 c, 6/6/81, 15/6/81 c
free sale and 3/12/80, 9/12/80, 12/12/80, 14/12/80, 31/12/80 c, 10/1/81, 29/1/81
G cautious about introducing 7/11/80
G pledged heads and heels to passing 14/4/81
in cabinet 31/12/80 c, 15/1/81 c, 29/1/81 c, 19/2/81, 22/2/81 c, 5/3/81 c, 19/3/81 c, 26/3/81 c, 28/3/81 c, 2/4/81 c
in Commons 7/4/81, 28/4/81 ff, 13/5/81 c, 16/5/81, 19/5/81 ff, 27/5/81 ff, 25/6/81 c, 5/7/81 ff, 19/7/81 ff, 22/7/81, 27/7/81, 29/7/81, 30/7/81
in Lords 11/8/81 n, 13/8/81 c, 15/8/81, 16/8/81 ff
instrument for giving contentment to Ireland 4/5/82
Irish public opinion and 10/1/81
Land League and 5/7/81 n
landlords' remedies and 6/3/81
Longfield's plan, influence of 25/10/80, 7/11/80, 29/11/80, 3/12/80, 14/12/80 c, 19/2/81
Lords' committee on 11/2/82 c, 18/2/82 c, 24/2/82, 25/2/82 c, 27/2/82, 23/5/82 c, 21/6/82 c, 23/4/86
memoranda for, printed 9/12/80, 14/12/80
O'Connor Don's paper 7/12/80
peasant proprietary and 5/12/80, 9/12/80, 12/12/80, 14/12/80 c, 15/12/80, 16/12/80 c, 22/12/80, 23/12/80, 29/12/80
preparation of 29/11/80 ff
press and 7/1/81
really a landlords' bill 5/7/81 n
Redmond/Healy amendment of, 1882 19/4/82, 22/4/82 c
remodelling of 8/1/81
rent arrears and 3/12/80 ff, 9/12/80, 14/12/80 ff, 2/7/81 c
Resolutions on 1/12/80 n, 14/12/80 c
role in confronting and beating the Land League 1/6/81
Roman catholic clergy and 29/4/81
state as money advancer 15/12/80 ff
tenant right and 9/12/80, 14/12/80 ff, 28/5/81 c
to balance coercion 24/11/80, 12/12/80 c, 20/12/80, 23/12/80
to follow coercion 25/11/80 c
Ulster custom and 3/12/80, 9/12/80, 14/12/80, 27/12/80, 21/1/81

land bill 1887 12/7/87 ff, 25/7/87, 28/7/87 n

Land League 30/9/80 c, 2/10/80, 7/10/80, 9/10/80, 21/10/80, 1/11/80, 7/11/80, 14/4/81, 6/6/81, 7/6/81, 14/6/81, 30/7/81, 22/8/81, 12/10/81 c, 13/10/81, 26/12/81
abandonment of meetings by 22/10/81
American money for 13/2/81 n
arrest and imprisonment of Parnell and others 12/10/81 c
arrest of Dillon 29/4/81 c

Ireland (*cont.*)
Land League (*cont.*)
counter-association against needed 9/12/80, 12/12/80
illegality in England of, in question 22/10/81
kind of collapse of 22/10/81
need to split followers from leaders by Land Act 5/9/81
proscription of 7/11/80, 10/11/80 c, 17/11/80 c, 19/11/80 c, 25/11/80, 12/10/81 c, 21/10/81
prosecution of leading members of 21/10/80, 25/10/80 ff, 20/12/80 ff
suspension of, inquiry into 30/9/80 c, 7/10/80, 9/10/80, 25/10/80, 26/10/80, 27/10/80, 2/11/80, 7/11/80
timidity of Irish in opposing 9/12/80, 12/12/80, 20/12/80, 22/12/80, 27/9/81, 13/10/81
will be beaten by the Land Act 3/3/82
will do everything to obstruct Land Act 5/9/81
Land League, Ladies 29/8/82
Land League and
Tyrone by-election 8/9/81 ff
landlords 18/10/69 ff, 28/11/69
debt of honour due to 23/3/86
directly associated with State Policy all along 23/3/86
not to be converted into stipendiaries 28/11/69
land purchase 10/7/69 c, 5/5/80 c, 8/5/80, 14/5/80 c, 5/12/80, 9/12/80, 10/12/80, 14/12/80, 15/12/80, 22/12/80, 23/12/80, 27/12/80, 1/1/81 ff, 12/4/82, 30/4/82 ff, 5/3/83 c, 13/5/84, 17/5/84 c, 30/3/85, 13/5/85, 15/5/85 c, 16/5/85, 21/5/85, 30/5/85, 23/7/85, 25/7/85, 1/8/85, 23/12/85, 9/1/86, 14/1/86, 30/1/86, 5/4/87, 13/7/88, 19/11/88, 24/4/90, 1/5/90
Ashbourne Act 1885 23/4/86
cabinet committee on 28/4/84 c
Cavendish's plan 12/4/82
contemporaneous with home rule, G proposes 19/12/85, 23/12/85
difficulties of 13/5/84
logical priority of 2/2/86
misunderstanding with Chamberlain and Dilke over 20/5/85, 21/5/85
Treasury help to W. H. Smith 17/3/82, 27/3/82
land question 8/7/66, 9/7/66 ff, 25/7/66, 5/11/75, 20/11/75, 2/5/79 n, 18/9/80, 7/11/80 ff, 11/12/80 ff, 12/2/86, 19/2/86, 5/8/90, 29/11/90, 19/3/91
and political economy 5/12/69
Bessborough commission 19/6/80 c, 25/6/80, 26/6/80 c, 17/7/80 c, 24/7/80 c, 25/10/80, 19/11/80 c, 29/11/80, 3/12/80 ff, 9/12/80 ff, 21/1/81, 15/4/81, 30/11/81
conspiracy against property has taken root 3/12/80
evictions 10/6/80 ff, 16/9/92, 28/7/93
Griffith's valuation 21/10/81
history as influence on 5/1/70, 8/1/70
history of 9/12/80, 12/11/86
land valuation 24/5/73 c
nationalization no solution 25/10/80, 4/11/80
new valuation needed 29/11/80
O'Brien on 4/10/83
O'Brien's book on 5/11/80
O'Shea's paper on 18/9/80
Parnell's bill 1886 7/9/86, 10/9/86, 13/9/86, 21/9/86
sheer panic over 9/12/80
Tipperary and Cashel evictions 5/6/90, 9/6/90
Tipperary and Cashel evictions: Dillon's visit to Hawarden on 3/6/90
to be dealt with straight after the church 22/5/69
wild agitation for destruction of landlord/tenant relationship 21/9/69
land reformers, sober class of 21/9/69
land tenure
G's memorandum on 17/9/69
legality the key to progress 23/6/82
legislative plans for 5/5/80 c
liberal party in 3/2/83, 19/10/83
local government bill 1882
plan for 10/11/81 c
local government for 10/12/80 ff, 15/12/80, 31/12/80 c, 30/12/82, 7/4/83 c, 17/5/83, 18/3/85, 30/3/85, 4/5/85 ff, 15/5/85 c, 21/5/92, 24/5/92
central board plan 5/5/85, 9/5/85 c, 15/5/85 c, 21/5/85, 30/5/85, 1/6/85, 5/6/85 c, 10/9/85, 11/9/85, 15/9/85, 3/11/85
G's assessment of needs 12/4/82
needed to give Ireland a political system 5/12/82
prime importance of 30/12/82
self-government, advance in 1/5/72
to balance renewal of Crimes Act 18/3/85
lord lieutenancy of
abolition of planned 4/5/85, 15/5/85 cn
bill to abolish protestant exclusiveness of 8/4/84 c
G's plan to replace with Prince of Wales 25/6/71

Mitchelstown incident 12/9/87, 7/6/88 n
Molly Maguires and 11/7/82, 19/7/82, 21/7/82, 5/12/82, 27/2/83
nationalism and
effect of franchise reform on ultra-nationalism 19/10/83
National League
attack on liberal party as perfidious etc. 21/11/85
nestling imperceptibly in G's mind 2/9/41
nonconformists and 11/5/87
O'Keeffe case 9/7/72, 10/7/72 c, 17/7/72 c, 31/7/72 c, 14/8/72, 19/8/72, 10/9/72, 26/4/73 c, 3/5/73 c, 10/5/73 c, 14/5/73 c, 24/5/73 c, 14/6/73 c, 21/6/73 c, 10/7/73 c, 6/8/73 c, 12/8/73
G's meeting with O'Keeffe 3/9/72
Orangemen 29/5/69 c, 28/4/71, 13/10/81, 20/2/84, 8/3/93 c
inquiry into 25/2/84 c
Orange Tory, G accused of having been 11/8/71
Parnellism and 10/9/81
Parnell's 'Proposed Constitution for Ireland' 8/8/85, 24/10/85, 3/11/85
Party Processions Act 16/3/72 c, 22/8/72, 27/8/72
Peace Preservation Bill 24/1/81 ff
peasant proprietary in
a very Conservative measure 22/5/69
Peel's policy towards clergy of 28/3/69
peers of
deservedly unpopular 1/10/92
natural heads of Irish society 1/10/92
Phoenix Park murders 6/5/82 ff, 1/6/82
Daily News and 9/5/82
G hopes for a conviction on 9/5/82
Irish and English reaction to 1/6/82
'Parnellism and crime' and 28/4/87 n
trial of murderers 20/2/83
police bill 7/7/83 c, 31/7/83
power to vex but not to wound the Empire 3/12/83
prayed for by G 10/4/87
presbyterian marriages in 21/7/43
press in
power of executive to sieze publications 12/3/70
priesthood in
Cullen's tyranny over 3/12/77 n
Property Defence Association 13/12/81, 16/12/81 n
Protection of Person and Property Bill 30/12/80 c, 24/1/81 ff, 30/4/82
renewal of 24/3/82
public expenditure in
profligacy of 8/5/80
Queen's colleges
university reform and 21/8/72
railways in 7/3/65, 18/5/66
state aid/purchase 16/2/69, 18/2/69, 24/4/69 c, 26/6/69 c, 3/7/69 c, 17/9/69, 13/10/69, 25/11/69, 21/12/70, 22/1/72, 27/4/72 c, 10/12/72 c, 4/2/73 c, 8/2/73 c, 15/2/73, 15/2/73 c, 26/4/73 c
state aid/purchase: Hartington threatens resignation on 10/2/73
state aid/purchase: not to be undertaken 8/2/73 c
rebellion of 1798 4/6/41
Reform Bill 1868 1/5/68 n, 5/5/68, 20/7/68, 8/4/73
Reform Bill 1884
G's reluctance to reduce number of Irish M. Ps. 29/10/84
registration in 11/1/44, 12/1/44
Regium Donum 22/7/43
religious census of 14/5/80 c
rent arrears in 15/6/81 c, 27/1/93
No Rent campaign 5/4/82, 8/4/82, 15/4/82, 22/4/82 c, 1/5/82, 4/5/82 c, 5/5/82, 19/7/82
repeal meetings in 15/5/43, 20/5/43, 8/6/43
G urges caution towards 8/6/43, 11/6/43
repeal of the union
G opposes 29/4/34
resident magistrates in 10/5/82, 12/5/82, 17/5/82
Ribbonmen 18/2/71 c
Roman Catholic church and 17/12/81, 1/6/82
a quarter of voting power Roman Catholic 9/9/81
Roman Catholic education 14/4/44, 6/5/44
Roman Catholic University in Dublin
undesirability of G-Manning correspondence on 22/6/70
royal residence in
audience of Queen on 25/6/71
confrontation with Queen on 2/7/72 ff, 5/7/72, 17/7/72
plan for 22/12/68 c, 21/6/71, 24/6/71 c, 25/6/71, 1/7/71 c, 5/7/71 c, 20/4/72 c, 17/7/72, 27/8/72, 28/8/72, 12/10/72 c, 22/2/73 n
Schleswig comparison and 5/5/64
secret societies
use of secret service money against 8/5/82 n, 9/6/82, 12/6/82, 18/6/82, 22/6/82
select committee on land tenure
Palmerston persuaded to accept 31/3/65

Ireland (*cont.*)
separation from U.K.
election under Ballot Act will test desire for 26/8/72
no evidence of popular desire for 26/8/72
social revolution in 4/5/82
speaking in
Parnell & Co.'s monopoly of 21/9/81
spirit duties 20/6/43
Sunday closing in 13/7/83 c, 16/7/83 ?
tenant right
deputation on 26/2/66
tithe abolition in 26/11/69
tobacco duties and 19/2/63
tramways in
state assistance for 23/6/83 c, 8/8/83 c
trilogy of land, social order and autonomy 2/2/86
Trinity College, Dublin 29/3/69
G's visit to, and speech to clamorous students 22/10/77
university reform and 21/8/72, 26/9/72, 26/10/72, 28/11/72 c, 14/12/72
Ulster
pretensions to rebel of 12/4/93
Ulster and 16/10/77 n, 13/11/83 c
glebe lands 19/7/69, 22/7/69
G's speech on 18/6/92
Union Rating Bill: no government help for 15/2/73 c
union with
G's speech on repeal 9/2/82
Unitarians in 21/7/43
United Irishmen and separatism 7/7/86
University Bill 1873 6/10/72, 15/10/72 c, 20/11/72 c, 22/11/72 c, 28/11/72 c, 3/12/72 c, 5/12/72 c, 10/12/72 c, 12/12/72 c, 14/12/72, 28/12/72, 31/1/73 c, 8/2/73 c, 15/2/73, 16/2/73, 22/3/73 c, 1/4/73
amendments to 22/2/73 c, 1/3/73 c
defeat of 8/3/73 n, 11/3/73, 12/3/73 c, 13/3/73 ff
defeat of: G unsurprised by 11/3/73
difficulties more formidable than expected 14/12/72
Dodson's motion on 5/3/73
favourable reception of 22/2/73
G's draft agreed to 22/1/73 c
G's memorandum on 18/1/73
G writes Heads of 20/11/72, 29/11/72
Henry's motion on 3/3/73
Ingram assisting with 16/1/73 ff
introduced by G 13/2/73
Roman Catholic bishops and 15/2/73, 26/2/73, 27/2/73, 1/3/73 c, 3/3/73, 8/3/73
seems likely to pass 22/2/73
university question 8/6/65, 20/6/65, 3/9/71, 28/9/71, 21/10/71 c, 27/10/71 c, 29/11/71, 16/1/72, 20/4/72 c, 24/4/72 ff, 17/7/72 c, 26/9/72, 6/10/72, 11/10/72 c, 26/10/72, 31/10/72, 15/11/72 c, 20/5/79, 24/7/79, 5/5/80 c
bill to take priority in 1873 6/10/72, 12/11/72
examining universities and 26/9/72, 26/10/72, 31/10/72
nonconformity and 16/1/72
presbyterian university suggested 4/6/81
Trinity, Dublin and 21/8/72
warning and judgment for our sins as a nation 31/12/80
Washington, Treaty of
Fenians and 10/6/71 c
Westmeath 7/2/71 ff, 17/11/80 c
W. H. G and
friendship with Cullen 6/11/77
reporting on for *Daily Telegraph* 2/8/66, 6/1/68, 16/1/68
Whiteboyism in 26/11/69
See also Cork Constitution, Abbeylieux, Belfast, Bright, cabinet (committees of), Chamberlain, Church of England, Churchill, Commons (House of), conservative party, Coolatin Park, Disraeli, Dublin, Fawcett, Fortescue, France, Galway, Gladstone (Herbert), Gladstone (William Henry), Government of Ireland Bill 1886, Government of Ireland Bill 1893, Government of Ireland Bills, Hamilton, Harcourt, home rule, Irish church disestablishment, jingoism, Lords (House of), Lowe, Maynooth, memoranda, memoranda (printed), O'Connell, O'Shea, Parnell (C. S.), Parnell (Katharine), politics, Powerscourt, publications, Reform Bills 1884, Russell, Spencer, Temple (Henry), Thistlethwayte, United States, Victoria, Wilberforce
Irish church disestablishment
bill in cabinet 8/2/69 c, 9/2/69, 15/2/69 c, 20/2/69 c, 22/2/69, 27/2/69 c, 29/5/69 c
bill in the Commons 1/3/69 ff, 16/4/69, 21/4/69 ff, 6/5/69
notable and historic division on 23/3/69
bill in the Lords
amendments to it 3/6/69, 12/6/69, 19/6/69 c, 26/6/69 c, 3/7/69 c, 8/7/69, 13/7/69, 14/7/69, 17/7/69, 18/7/69, 19/7/69 c, 21/7/69 c, 23/7/69
concurrent endowment and 13/7/69 ff

G denies brought forward by Fenianism 27/4/69, 28/4/69
G drafts the bill 24/12/68 ff
glebe lands and 26/6/69 c, 13/7/69, 17/7/69 c, 19/7/69, 22/7/69
Ulster and 22/7/69
Irish bishops and 6/1/69, 7/1/69, 6/2/69
Palmer's clause 8/5/69 c, 9/5/69 c, 13/5/69
plans for 1/12/68, 18/12/68, 19/1/69 ff
outline 28/11/68
will sooth Irish sentiment 28/4/69
See also Ireland
ironclads *See* navy
Irving, Henry, Sir (1838–1905), actor; manager of the Lyceum from 1878 16/4/75, 19/6/79 n, 29/6/82, 8/7/82, 25/10/82, 21/4/83, 1/7/88
as Becket 25/2/93
as Benedict 29/1/91
as Faust 10/4/86
as Hamlet
food for thought 19/2/79
performance shows growth 24/3/79
private reading, G attends 8/5/76
work of ability but not good 16/4/75
as Henry VIII 11/5/92
as Lear 22/11/92
as Othello
remarkable study 19/2/76
as Richard III
a great performance 4/5/77
as Shylock
his best part, G thinks 28/2/80
Bram Stoker as stage manager 18/11/90 n
in 'The Lyons Mail' 5/3/78
letters from G to, printed 11/4/86
Irvingites 22/1/33, 27/1/33, 12/3/33 n
G's visits to Albury 13/5/56 ff
G thinks Irving's judgment noble but shipwrecked 22/6/62
Ischia 11/5/32, 29/1/89
Islam
G visits mosque in Albania 2/2/59
Isle of Man *See* Man (Isle of)
Italian
lessons in 2/4/32 ff, 16/4/32
See also childrearing
Italy 2/3/32 ff, 19/9/38 ff, 21/7/49 ff, 29/10/50 ff, 6/10/66 ff, 31/12/87 ff, 28/10/93
Africa and 7/6/71
alliance with Germany
G's proposed speech in Naples on 19/1/89 n
article by G on Austrian occupation of Modena
rejected by the *Quarterly* 30/8/59 n, 2/9/59
Austrian occupation of 21/9/38
Bossoli's cartoons of war, shown in London 2/8/60
Carlists in 23/3/32
castles in 11/11/38
Congress for 9/12/59
cabinet supports 28/10/59
currency of, strange state of 12/10/66
Egypt and 20/7/82 c
ferries of 14/6/32
finance of
deficit a danger to Europe 18/2/69
G advises in Florence on Italian budget 7/1/67, 11/1/67, 14/1/67
G discusses with Hudson 17/7/67
Franco-Prussian war
British understanding with 10/8/70 c
free church in a free state 15/9/70
Garibaldi's visit to Britain 12/4/64 ff
G entertained by Italian deputies in Florence 14/1/67
government of sends good wishes to G 10/2/83
G's articles on 11/4/59, 18/4/89
G's best off-hand speech given on 8/8/59
G's conversation with Aberdeen on 19/10/49
G's conversation with Derby on 4/2/57
G's letter to Russell on
causes sleepless night 3/1/60
G's memorandum on cabinet differences over 30/5/60
G's objectives for
cessation of direct Austrian dominion 30/6/59
change in Pope's temporal power 30/6/59
G speaks for 11/4/62
G's writings on Homer translated into Italian 7/12/77 n
Mediterranean and 26/8/92
militarism in 19/3/94
nationalism in 28/10/93
politics of 2/11/50
poor clothing of peasantry 11/10/38
Pope, election of 22/8/72
quarantine regulations of 6/11/50 ff
richness of the countryside 24/9/38
roads in 26/6/32
Russell's dispatch on unification and 31/8/59
Savoy
cabinet on 21/3/60
Russell's questionable language on 26/3/60
scenery compared with England 14/6/32
scenery of the south 11/11/38
size of towns in 11/11/38
Sudan and 9/2/85 c

Italy (*cont.*)
theology faculties abolished in? 2/9/92
traditionalism of regions in 22/10/66
trains not on time in 9/10/66
Turin, bad pronunciation in 2/11/50
ultramontanism and 22/8/72
unification of
G finds Pope not objecting in principle 22/10/66
G's memorandum on quasi-unification, printed 30/6/59
G's memorandum on unification, printed 26/3/61
will contribute to European stability 26/3/61
Unita Italiana 13/2/51
unsurpassable beauty of 10/5/32
Vatican and
G suggests settlement 15/9/70
Venetia
G's memorandum on 20/12/60
war in 1/5/59
See also Bologna, Capri, Capua, Dante, Florence, Garibaldi, Genoa, Gordon, Lacaita, Milan, Monte Cassino, Naples, Padua, Palermo, Panizzi, Pompeii, publications, Rome, Russell, Salerno, Sicily, Temple (Henry), Turin, Vaudois, Venice, Vesuvius, Vicenza
ivories
G's collection of
loaned to exhibition in S. Kensington 9/7/83
Iwerne Minster (Wolverton) 22/8/82, 15/6/89

Jamaica 13/2/33, 25/3/39, 9/4/39, 3/5/39, 6/5/39, 5/6/39, 10/6/39, 10/11/69 c
Eyre case
G's notes on 1/12/65, 13/12/65
Florence affair and 2/10/83, 10/11/83 c
Jamaica Duties Act 31/5/43
See also Eyre case, West Indies
James, Walter Charles, Sir (1816–1893), 2nd Baronet (1829), 1st Baron Northbourne (1884), tory M.P. and confidant of G 15/1/39, 18/3/47, 17/4/47, 18/4/47, 26/3/48, 11/2/49, 13/3/50, 24/3/50, 12/2/52, 22/2/52, 21/1/53, 26/3/54, 16/3/55 n, 2/4/55, 11/3/59, 4/5/59, 26/2/61, 17/8/64, 9/3/66, 7/2/67, 24/11/67, 16/3/68, 1/3/69, 22/3/69, 19/4/69, 13/8/69, 21/3/70, 3/6/70, 21/2/71, 12/3/71, 3/4/71, 9/6/71, 19/6/71, 11/3/72, 15/4/72, 13/5/72, 29/7/72, 31/1/73, 17/2/73, 13/3/73, 10/6/73, 12/6/73, 21/2/74, 1/3/74, 19/3/74, 25/8/74, 17/2/75, 19/3/75, 5/6/75, 17/3/76, 16/5/76, 24/6/76, 27/10/76, 7/2/77, 7/5/77, 17/5/78, 1/7/78, 28/2/79, 30/3/79, 21/10/79 ff, 14/3/80, 18/6/80, 11/7/80, 4/2/81, 11/2/81, 27/5/81, 7/3/82, 9/5/82, 4/11/82, 29/5/83, 15/6/83, 11/5/84, 20/3/85, 27/6/85, 7/7/85, 16/5/86, 7/3/87, 25/3/87, 30/4/87, 23/5/87, 12/4/88, 16/7/88, 20/3/90, 25/3/90, 19/6/90, 12/3/91, 28/4/91, 13/5/92, 26/2/94, 11/3/94
at Hawarden 17/9/90 ff
death of 9/2/93
G discusses Oxford constituency with 9/6/61
G guardian of his children 10/5/52, 31/8/53
G's recollections of 9/2/93
G staying with 15/7/54, 14/9/54, 19/5/66, 26/12/87
quality of conversation of 19/8/64
See also Bettishanger
James's powder pills *See* medicines
Jansenism 15/12/38
Japan 9/2/64, 13/9/69
admiration for G among Japanese 6/1/91 n
biography of G translated into Japanese 21/4/91, 23/4/91
British troops in
to be friendly but circumspect 5/12/72 c
G favours inviting intelligent Japanese to Britain 14/9/69
G's memorandum on 9/12/62
importance of friendly intercourse with 14/9/69
Japanese Fine Art Exhibition, London 27/7/87
Mikado of, health of proposed by G 7/12/72
Java
bimetallism and 2/9/92, 10/9/92
jealousy, G's, of Sandon 3/5/41
Jedburgh 22/11/74
Jerusalem
panorama of 2/7/35
Jerusalem bishopric 15/10/41 ff, 23/11/41 ff, 15/12/41 ff, 27/9/83
G proposed as trustee of 30/10/41, 5/11/41, 7/11/41, 8/11/41, 11/11/41, 27/9/83
See also Church of England, letters
Jervaux Abbey (Ailesbury) 5/10/76
Jesuits 3/3/32, 27/3/81, 2/4/83 n
closed against the access of truth 3/12/50
hardened offenders 23/11/69
Jewish disabilities 27/8/26, 23/8/29, 20/5/30, 18/4/33, 22/5/33, 26/6/33, 24/4/34, 11/6/34, 31/3/41, 18/4/45, 4/5/46, 4/11/47, 15/11/47, 12/12/47, 16/12/47, 17/12/47, 3/4/48, 4/5/52

G argues with Salisbury on 14/3/60 n
G committed to end 11/12/47 n, 12/12/47, 16/12/47, 11/2/48, 24/2/53 n
raises doubts about continuing in Commons 16/12/47
G's clear conscience on 4/5/48
G's vote on his first step towards liberalism 26/9/92
opposition to G's hon degree for his stand on 5/7/48
Jews
Chief Rabbi, G's meeting with 21/11/93
condition of 4/2/90 n
Eastern question and 6/10/76 n
future state among
G's article on 12/9/91
in Roumania 1/12/79 n
British will intervene for with circumspection 15/6/72 c
Jewish burial service 25/11/90
Platonic montheism and
G's memorandum on, printed 15/6/88
pogroms and
G's letter to the press on 15/10/90
priesthood of 30/8/40
Russian persecution of 9/1/82, 18/1/82, 22/1/82, 25/1/82, 27/5/91 n
Russo-Jewish committee 18/7/91 n
jingoism 7/2/78 ff, 10/3/78 ff, 26/9/82, 8/8/83, 11/2/85, 1/6/85, 30/9/85, 5/2/94
calling for repression in Ireland 23/12/80
colonial alarmism 24/12/84
G's windows smashed
not very sabbatical 24/2/78
medical students and 19/2/78 n, 25/2/78 n
meeting abandoned 19/2/78
Uganda and 26/9/92
journal, G's 22/7/26, 5/8/26, 19/8/26, 8/9/26, 14/4/27, 14/12/27, 13/6/28, 8/1/29, 15/7/29, 17/10/29, 11/9/31, 17/11/31, 1/2/32, 12/2/32, 10/3/32, 17/4/32, 25/5/32, 17/9/32, 22/9/32, 12/10/32, 30/1/35, 21/2/35, 23/4/36, 16/8/38, 6/2/39, 28/10/44, 23/4/47, 11/8/49, 1/2/50
allowed to lag 5/7/51, 11/7/51, 12/7/51
'arranged and put by' 28/8/89
at Colonial Office 30/1/35, 21/2/35
attempted use of for confession 15/1/47, 17/1/47
attempt to maintain notation of books and certain dates
'No: I *cannot* do it' 24/12/94
authors quoted at start/finish of volume
Aeschylus (Prometheus Vinctus) 1/1/84
Ampère 13/8/65
Ariosto 23/4/48
Aristophanes (Wasps) 16/6/72 fl
Bible (Apochrypha) 1/1/79
Bible (Job) 8/9/85
Bible (Matthew) 1/7/93
Bible (Paul) 1/7/93
Bible (Psalms) 1/7/93
Bunsen 1/5/67
B. W. Proctor 1/1/79
Capefigue/Richelieu 20/9/70
Coleridge 1/1/69
Cowper (Madame de la Mothe Guyon) 13/2/74
Dante 10/4/82
Dante (Paradiso) 12/6/87
Ecclesiasticus 12/6/87
Eumenides 8/9/85
Euripides (Hecuba) 25/2/55
Euripides (Troades) 16/3/77 fl
Gardiner, Bishop 24/7/80
Goethe 1/1/64
Herodotus 21/7/75 fl
Homer (Odyssey) 8/9/85
Longinus 1/3/52
Marcus Aurelius 24/7/80
Marino 24/7/80
Menander 1/5/62, 21/9/70
Ovid (Metamorphoses) 16/6/72 fl
Philemon 1/5/62
Pindar 10/4/82
Plutarch 10/4/82
Propertius 1/3/52
Quintilian 31/12/63, 1/1/64
Rémusat 1/3/91
Savonarola 12/6/87
Shakespeare (Henry VIII) 24/7/80
Shakespeare (King John) 1/5/67, 29/12/96
Shakespeare (King Lear) 29/12/96
Shakespeare (Merchant of Venice) 13/2/74
Shakespeare (Richard III) 1/7/93
Shakespeare (The Tempest) 1/1/79
Shelley 16/6/72 fl
Stahr, A. 24/7/80
St. Gregory 23/4/48
Suetonius 1/3/52
The Echo 16/3/77
W. H. de Winton 1/3/91
William Law 1/3/91
changed conventions for recording sin 31/5/50
commonly dry 25/7/94
Commons, G sometimes forgets to record attendance at 4/3/75
Davidson's custody of, 1928 9/5/83 n
end of continuous entries in 23/5/94
but books and certain dates to be noted 17/12/94

journal (*cont.*)
foreign languages used in 14/11/33, 8/7/35, 24/8/35, 28/8/35 ff, 25/9/35, 18/11/35, 30/12/35, 9/1/36, 15/1/36, 20/1/36, 13/2/36, 24/5/36, 4/7/36, 8/1/38, 17/1/38, 4/3/38, 13/4/38, 28/4/38, 8/10/38, 16/12/38, 18/12/38, 15/6/39, 16/6/39, 2/7/39, 15/7/39, 20/9/39, 4/10/39, 16/11/39, 18/11/39, 19/11/39, 20/11/39, 3/5/40, 8/9/40, 17/11/40, 10/4/41, 9/8/42, 28/12/44, 21/1/45, 3/11/45, 18/10/46, 26/10/46, 20/12/46, 23/4/48, 13/5/48, 15/5/48, 18/5/48, 3/6/49, 22/11/50, 19/8/51, 7/1/52, 1/7/52, 4/11/52, 29/6/53, 6/8/53, 12/8/53, 18/2/54, 14/4/54, 14/1/55, 20/8/55, 1/6/56, 25/7/56, 16/8/56, 21/2/58, 27/4/62, 31/12/63, 6/6/67, 12/5/69, 20/11/74, 29/12/75, 5/6/76, 5/7/79, 7/10/79, 16/1/80, 3/10/81, 5/1/84, 31/12/86, 9/1/88, 7/11/88, 29/12/89, 30/12/89, 31/12/92, 24/12/94
Glynnese in 22/4/88
hours spent in devotion, work etc., recorded 23/8/45 ff, 31/8/45 ff
hours spent in recreation etc., recorded 24/2/45
interrupted by influenza 10/5/91 ff
kept in table drawer 5/11/73 n
last entry of 29/12/96
left behind: pages tipped in 5/11/73 ff
likely to assume epigrammatical form 13/12/38
mislaid 20/1/30
mutilation of 25/8/93 n
newspaper cutting pasted into 30/6/85, 1/3/91
reduced by time spent with father 5/10/49
relief from the small grind of 17/12/94
so easy to write, but to write honestly nearly impossible 29/12/96
travel journals 1/2/32 ff, 11/8/38 ff, 13/10/38 ff, 12/11/38, 31/1/39, 2/3/39, 25/10/50 ff, 17/10/77 ff, 15/9/79 ff
later reading of 3/1/63
verses in 10/1/34, 28/12/79, 24/2/82
written on train 4/11/74
written up late 19/10/87
X used in diary heading to mark sinful encounters
1852–1858 30/12/52 ff, 24/5/53, 8/6/53, 9/6/53, 23/6/53, 24/6/53, 25/6/53, 26/6/53, 27/6/53, 28/6/53, 29/6/53, 19/7/53, 23/7/53, 27/7/53, 4/8/53, 6/8/53, 15/8/53, 30/12/53, 2/1/54, 13/1/54, 17/1/54, 18/1/54, 25/1/54, 28/1/54, 8/2/54, 21/2/54, 11/3/54, 14/3/54, 22/3/54, 1/4/54, 6/4/54, 24/4/54, 31/5/54, 14/6/54, 23/6/54, 28/6/54, 1/8/54, 2/8/54, 11/8/54, 29/8/54, 16/10/54, 12/11/54, 16/11/54, 9/12/54, 16/12/54, 18/12/54, 28/1/55, 5/2/55, 8/2/55, 16/2/55, 12/3/55, 11/4/55, 12/4/55, 25/4/55, 5/5/55, 14/5/55, 6/6/55, 18/7/55, 19/7/55, 21/7/55, 5/12/55, 4/3/56, 10/3/56, 11/3/56, 12/3/56, 24/3/56, 26/3/56, 15/4/56, 23/5/56, 26/5/56, 30/5/56, 2/6/56, 3/6/56, 4/6/56, 4/7/56, 5/7/56, 22/7/56, 31/1/57, 5/2/57, 6/2/57, 7/2/57, 9/2/57, 16/2/57, 28/2/57, 11/3/57, 12/3/57, 13/3/57, 16/3/57, 15/4/57, 2/5/57, 5/5/57, 7/5/57, 13/5/57, 15/5/57, 25/5/57, 26/5/57, 29/5/57, 1/7/57, 2/7/57, 3/7/57, 6/7/57, 11/7/57, 15/7/57, 16/7/57, 17/7/57, 19/7/57, 21/7/57, 22/7/57, 23/7/57, 25/7/57, 28/7/57, 2/8/57, 8/8/57, 11/8/57, 12/8/57, 8/12/57, 24/1/58, 26/1/58, 22/2/58, 23/2/58, 26/2/58, 10/3/58, 24/3/58, 14/4/58, 16/4/58, 20/4/58, 22/4/58, 26/4/58, 27/4/58, 28/4/58, 12/5/58, 21/5/58, 27/5/58, 28/5/58, 3/6/58, 16/6/58, 22/6/58, 26/6/58, 9/7/58, 13/7/58, 12/8/58, 13/8/58, 14/8/58, 15/8/58, 15/10/58, 19/10/58, 20/10/58, 21/10/58, 4/11/58, 5/11/58, 14/11/58
1859–1863 8/3/59, 29/3/59, 2/4/59, 6/4/59, 8/4/59, 26/4/59, 19/5/59, 25/5/59, 1/6/59, 19/6/59, 20/6/59, 23/6/59, 28/6/59, 29/6/59, 6/7/59, 9/7/59, 12/7/59, 26/7/59, 15/8/59, 14/10/59, 15/10/59, 16/10/59, 17/10/59, 9/11/59, 5/12/59, 8/12/59, 9/1/60, 14/1/60, 15/1/60, 16/1/60, 17/1/60, 20/1/60, 16/2/60, 22/2/60, 29/2/60, 19/3/60, 28/3/60, 9/4/60, 25/4/60, 21/5/60, 12/6/60, 14/6/60, 22/6/60, 27/6/60, 7/7/60, 16/7/60, 4/8/60, 7/8/60, 17/8/60, 18/8/60, 12/10/60, 12/11/60, 13/11/60, 26/11/60, 30/11/60, 4/12/60, 15/12/60, 18/12/60, 31/1/61, 5/2/61, 12/2/61, 10/4/61, 14/5/61, 16/5/61, 17/5/61, 14/10/61, 17/10/61, 18/10/61, 23/10/61, 12/11/61, 13/11/61, 14/10/63, 27/10/63
after rescue work in Corfu 4/1/59, 7/1/59, 8/1/59, 10/1/59, 17/1/59, 18/1/59, 28/1/59, 29/1/59, 10/2/59
but unconnected with rescue work 11/1/57, 12/1/57, 13/1/57, 4/8/58, 6/8/58, 14/1/61

when reading pornography 15/9/58, 11/5/59, 12/5/59, 13/5/59, 18/9/61, 19/9/61, 20/9/61, 21/9/61, 23/9/61, 24/9/61, 25/11/61
See also Thistlethwayte (Laura)
journeys *See* coach journeys, railways, ships, travels abroad, voyages
journeys abroad *See* travels
Jubilee 1887
at Hawarden
G's speech on 30/8/87
Queen will dislike his speech, G thinks 10/9/87
G at service for 22/5/87, 21/6/87
too courtly, G thinks 21/6/87
Jubilee Singers 14/7/73, 29/7/73, 6/12/75
Judaism 12/8/79 ff
Judicature Bill 15/11/72 c, 24/1/73 c, 29/1/73 c, 10/5/73 c, 24/5/73 c, 7/6/73 c, 21/6/73 c, 23/6/73, 28/6/73 c, 2/7/73, 3/7/73, 5/7/73 c, 10/7/73 c, 12/7/73 c, 14/7/73, 24/7/73 c
consequences for law officers 10/11/73 c
G's memorandum for cabinet on Hardy's amendment to 3/7/73
tory attempt to amend 18/3/75
Judicial Committee of the Privy Council *See* Privy Council
Judicial Reform Bill 19/12/71 c
Jura pass 2/10/66

Kandahar *See* Afghanistan
Kars, siege of *See* Crimean war
Keble College, Oxford 17/4/70, 14/5/70, 21/5/70, 13/11/72, 7/11/74, 3/5/76, 31/1/78, 23/4/78, 26/11/83, 3/7/85, 4/4/88, 10/11/88
charter of 17/4/70, 14/5/70 c, 21/5/70 c, 25/4/78
consecration of 3/4/76
G's speech at opening of 25/4/78
Keele Hall, Staffordshire (W. Sneyd) 5/11/73
Keir (Stirling-Maxwell) 13/10/58 ff
Kenilworth castle 1/8/28, 31/10/32
Kensington palace 4/5/35
Keogh case *See* Ireland
Keswick 24/10/57
Kew Gardens 26/3/37, 3/7/72, 22/7/72
Khartoum *See* Sudan
kidnapping
in South Seas 30/1/72 c
Killin 17/8/39
deputation from 2/12/79
'Kilmainham Treaty' *See* Forster, Gladstone (Herbert), Ireland, Parnell
Kilruddery, Bray (Meath) 17/10/77
Kimberley, Earl of *See* Wodehouse
Kincardineshire
constituency of, offered to G but declined 20/11/72
King's College, London 31/7/28, 3/10/31, 28/4/38, 1/7/40, 14/10/42, 13/3/45, 25/7/45, 6/5/48, 13/11/62, 29/7/64, 6/7/76, 8/7/78
Council of, G on 28/4/38, 6/7/38, 28/2/40, 10/4/40, 12/6/40, 11/6/41, 25/6/75
G launches financial appeal of 14/5/72
the Maurice affair 27/10/53, 7/1/54
King's College Hospital 14/6/58, 27/2/74
Momerie case in 31/3/89, 5/4/89, 7/4/89, 19/7/89
Kingussie
good hotel, sadly disturbed by the rats 1/9/73
King William's College *See* Man (Isle of)
Kinlochewe 1/9/53
Kinnaird, Arthur Fitzgerald (1814–1887), 10th Baron Kinnaird (1878), banker and confidant of G and Mrs. Thistlethwayte, liberal M.P., philanthropist 29/1/38, 8/7/39, 27/2/40, 14/3/40, 12/5/41, 22/5/41, 28/11/44, 19/7/53, 7/11/64, 26/1/65, 23/5/66, 19/11/67, 1/1/68 ff, 11/10/69, 8/11/69, 18/1/71, 19/1/71 c, 17/8/71, 1/11/73, 3/3/75, 23/9/84, 3/8/85
abroad with G 8/9/38, 10/9/38, 5/10/38, 25/10/38 ff, 5/11/38, 6/11/38, 13/11/38, 15/11/38
accompanies G on visit to Mrs. Thistlethwayte at Boveridge 11/12/69 ff
ascending Etna 29/10/38 ff
criticisms of G 6/2/39
liberalism of 13/11/38
organising Moody-Sankey meetings 25/4/75
with G at religious service in theatre 23/3/62
Kinnaird Castle (Sir J. Carnegie) 29/11/48, 4/12/49
Kinross 14/11/33
Kinsella affair *See* Ireland
Kirkmichael
G's speech at 20/7/92
Kirkwall, Orkney
G's visit to 13/9/83 ff
Kirriemuir
the most Gladstonian town in Scotland 1/11/88 n
Knole (Sackville-West) 30/7/55, 14/5/59
Knowles, James Thomas, Sir (1831–1908), architect and publisher, editor of *C.R.* (1870–7) and *N.C.* (from 1877), founded Metaphysical Society 1869, published many of G's periodical articles 15/5/74, 16/7/75, 8/2/76,

Knowles, James Thomas, Sir (*cont.*)
2/4/76, 8/1/77 n, 28/2/77, 21/7/77, 5/11/77, 4/12/77, 13/4/78, 25/5/78, 15/6/78, 16/10/78, 22/12/78, 21/3/79, 1/4/79, 4/1/80, 6/9/80 n, 8/9/80, 25/12/80, 3/1/81, 30/5/81, 27/10/81, 19/11/81, 14/8/82, 16/8/83, 26/11/83, 8/8/84, 24/4/85, 29/10/85, 12/1/86, 15/1/86, 22/2/87, 3/3/87, 16/5/87, 15/8/87, 4/5/88, 16/5/89, 27/2/90, 30/6/90, 5/8/91 n, 11/11/92, 21/7/93, 21/11/93, 6/3/94
as architect 30/5/76
at Hawarden 12/10/76 ff
consults G on political articles 7/7/79
Edison records G after dinner at 22/11/88
letters from G to, printed 14/9/80, 2/9/81, 31/10/83, 5/8/85, 9/10/92
Knowles, S. *See* plays seen
Knowsley Park (Derby) 26/10/81, 8/10/83
Korea
Port Hamilton 11/4/85 c

Labouchere, Henry du Pré (1831-1912), liberal M.P., anti-imperialist and editor of *Truth* 9/5/81 n, 3/7/81, 8/6/82, 10/6/82, 29/3/84 c, 20/11/84 n, 11/10/85, 16/12/85, 19/12/85, 31/12/85, 14/1/86, 24/1/86 n, 18/3/86, 19/5/86, 2/8/88 n, 12/3/89, 28/6/89, 3/3/90, 18/3/90, 20/11/91, 21/5/92, 19/7/92, 23/11/92, 3/7/93
exclusion from 1892 government of 27/7/92 ff, 3/8/92, 11/8/92 ff, 15/8/92 n, 22/8/92, 25/8/92, 1/9/92, 6/9/92, 10/9/92, 26/9/92, 5/10/92, 15/10/92, 11/11/92 c
intermediary with Chamberlain
memorandum on, printed 9/5/86
Ireland and 20/11/85
G's draft Address for 11/10/85
letters from G to, printed 13/7/86, 29/12/86, 22/8/92, 25/8/92
Lords and 21/11/84, 20/11/85
Matabele and 6/11/93, 9/11/93 n
Parnell and the O'Shea divorce and 24/11/90 n
Uganda and 17/10/92, 11/1/93 ff, 3/2/93 n, 4/2/93, 20/3/93 n
labour, division of
enables accumulation of stock 31/8/46
Labour Department 1/8/92
labour disputes
conciliation in 9/5/90, 13/11/93
labour M.P.s *See* working classes
Labour Representation Committee
Eastern question and 19/2/78
Labour Representation League 23/11/76
deputation on French republic 27/9/70
Labuan
G opposes occupation of 18/6/46, 21/8/48
Lacaita, James Philip, Sir (1813-1895), author, Italian politician 13/11/50, 11/5/54, 11/1/55, 10/3/59, 25/6/59, 11/8/59, 19/3/60 ff, 24/8/60, 5/4/61, 18/9/61, 22/11/61, 20/2/62, 29/7/62, 21/3/63, 20/5/65, 15/3/68, 24/3/68, 28/6/71, 12/11/73, 22/11/73, 6/11/74, 3/7/75, 21/6/76, 24/6/80, 10/9/80, 8/10/80, 30/9/81, 5/8/82, 16/10/82, 13/8/83 ff, 23/10/83, 7/8/85, 5/9/85, 21/8/86, 10/7/89, 18/7/90, 31/7/91, 20/6/92, 31/7/94
advising G on antiquarian books 20/6/88
arrested in Naples
G wild at inability to help 3/1/51, 4/1/51
released 12/1/51
at Hawarden 26/9/61 ff, 16/10/67 ff, 21/10/73, 17/9/85, 24/8/91
cataloguing Chatsworth library 3/6/73, 19/11/75, 20/12/80
constitutional monarchy and 16/10/93
fine intelligence of 15/11/58
G's secretary in Ionia 15/11/58 ff, 9/12/58 ff, 28/12/58 ff, 20/7/59
G staying in his flat in Florence 31/12/87 ff
informs G about Neapolitan politics 16/11/50, 26/9/61
introduces G to Neapolitan ecclesiastics 28/11/50 ff, 7/12/50
lecture by 7/6/54, 28/6/54, 10/6/58, 24/6/58
letters from G to, printed 28/3/92, 2/9/92, 16/10/93
temporal power of Pope and 7/6/71
Lady Margaret Hall, Oxford
G's visit to 29/11/83
Laggan 20/8/53
Lairg 20/9/58
Lake District
G's tour of 24/10/57
Lambert, John, Sir (1815-1892), secretary, local government board 1871-82 10/3/66, 12/3/66, 7/5/66, 28/5/66, 18/6/66, 25/9/66
advising G on 1867 Reform Bill 14/2/67
Irish land and 24/8/69, 3/12/69 ff, 22/12/69
Lambeth Palace 16/5/35, 14/4/38, 25/7/38, 14/5/85
G dining at 1/7/40, 13/6/60, 18/6/64, 17/4/69, 1/5/72, 16/7/73, 13/5/85, 25/5/89, 11/6/90
Lampeter. St. David's College 11/6/69
Lamport Hall(Sir C. E. Isham) 7/4/79
Lancashire
cotton famine in 6/11/62, 15/11/62, 17/11/62, 19/11/62 n

C. G assisting in Blackburn 31/12/62
G's speech in Chester on 27/12/62
G's speech on at Hawarden 1/1/63
men from employed at Hawarden 19/9/62 ff, 28/11/62 ff
redistribution and 13/10/84
See also constituencies
Lancaster 9/6/28, 26/12/51
Lancaster, Duchy of
G's proposed reform of 27/5/72 c
Lancing College
G governor of 31/8/75 n
land
bad effects of 1894 budget on 25/7/94
concentration of ownership of, and tory success 14/8/82
G's speech on rural population 11/12/91
land transfer bill 16/3/70 c, 15/11/72 c, 29/1/73 c
reform of 22/12/70, 3/1/71, 3/12/72 c, 22/4/73 c, 7/8/85, 14/9/85, 26/1/86 n, 27/2/91
G's speech on London unearned increment 26/7/87, 29/7/87
not to be undertaken in 1874 21/11/73
primogeniture 8/3/93 c
recovery of waste land by state would fail, G thinks 1/12/71
Scottish crofters and English implications 19/1/85
unused waste lands 16/12/73
rural labourers
G's article on 4/1/92
tenure in England 17/9/69, 19/3/81 c, 18/11/81
Bateman's errors about Hawarden estate and G 8/12/80
See also Ireland, land purchase, Scotland
Land League *See* Ireland
Land Purchase Bill 1886
bait of for landlords 21/4/86
Bright's accusation against G on 2/7/86
credit and
limitation to £60 millions 20/3/86, 14/4/86 c, 19/4/86
damaged by Hartington and Irish landlords 12/6/86
drafted by Thring 5/3/86, 24/3/86
everyone dancing on grave of 4/7/86
financing of 12/2/86 ff, 23/3/86 ff
future of cloudy 12/6/86 ff
in cabinet 13/3/86 c, 29/3/86 c, 14/4/86 c
in Commons 16/4/86
landlord rejection of would liberate government 26/3/86
plan for framed 12/2/86 ff, 3/3/86 ff, 7/4/86
precedence over Government of Ireland Bill a matter of policy 18/3/86
press and 30/6/86
Receiver General and 23/3/86
to follow Government of Ireland Bill 23/3/86, 7/4/86
West Indian precedent 19/4/86
Landro 25/9/79
land tax 13/8/53, 22/12/70, 3/1/71
languages *See* childrearing, French, German, Greek, Ionian Islands, Italian, Latin, Norway (Norwegian), Paris, Spain (Spanish)
Lanhydrock House, Bodmin (Lord Robartes) 12/6/89
Lansdowne House 19/3/53
Lanslebourg 1/3/32, 30/10/50
Larpool, Whitby (E. H. Turton) 25/8/71
Later Gleanings *See* publications
Latimer, Buckinghamshire (Chesham) 25/2/65, 17/3/66, 14/7/66, 13/4/67, 20/3/69, 28/3/72, 23/3/78, 19/10/78
Latin
G teaches by Hamiltonian method 23/1/47 ff
Scottish pronunciation of 11/1/62
See also childrearing
Laud, Abp.
Life of, too 'Laudish' 7/4/36
trial of 5/8/31
laudanum
used for toothache 25/8/39
Launceston
G's speech at 14/6/89
Laurencekirk 23/8/33, 11/8/44 ff
Lausanne 12/7/32 ff, 16/7/32, 5/8/49
Laverno 2/8/49
Lavington 7/4/65
law
artfully constructed monopoly of professional classes in 14/8/82
good lawyer may be a bad historian 4/6/83
judges being made P. C. on retirement 26/1/73
judges' pensions 27/1/73
judges' salaries 27/1/73, 28/1/73, 29/1/73 c
Public Prosecutor Bill 10/5/73
Scottish and Irish appeals 27/1/73
strict review of legal expenditure proposed by G 28/1/73
See also Inner Temple, Lincoln's Inn, Middle Temple
law, international 23/11/70, 16/3/71, 4/9/73
arbitration and 24/1/72, 21/10/73
law courts 5/2/66, 19/2/66, 7/2/67, 29/5/67, 19/7/67, 22/11/67, 6/3/69 c, 29/5/69, 19/6/69 c, 31/7/69 c, 27/7/82, 4/12/82
Ayrton-Street controversy 23/6/73, 28/6/73 c

law courts (*cont.*)
decision on Street and Barry 29/7/67
G's memorandum on 5/12/60, 9/3/69
law officers
not to practise privately 14/8/93
salaries of 27/10/92 c
law reform
aspect of public policy lying within reach 31/3/57
Harcourt's tract on 21/11/71
juries
unanimity of 16/3/70 c
Palmer's plan for a law school/university 8/7/71 c, 1/2/72, 1/12/73 c
laws
bad laws & policy make bad men 21/6/72
laxity
measured by tension of Oxford 13/4/41
Laycock Abbey (Fox Talbot) 24/1/57
Lay Union, meeting to form 16/5/37
laziness
prevents G writing to C. G on wedding anniversary 25/7/86
lead *See* medicines
leadership
public-speaking and 1/5/62
Leamington Spa
Clarendon hotel 6/4/33
Gladstone family at 13/9/32, 25/10/32, 20/12/32 ff, 4/4/33 ff, 29/5/35
G on holiday with 30/7/28, 11/4/29, 12/1/30, 9/6/30, 26/6/30, 8/10/30, 17/12/30, 21/3/31 ff, 18/6/31 ff
Leaswood (Wynn Eaton) 30/8/58
Lecco 6/7/32
lectures given by G
colonies 7/1/52, 12/10/55, 12/11/55, 12/10/57, 3/9/67
Homer (at Eton) 5/7/79
Mount Etna 5/1/63
Romanes Lecture, Oxford 24/10/92
Sir Walter Scott 3/2/68
thrift 4/1/64
leeches, used for treatment 2/2/40
Leeds
a wonderful community 9/10/81
exhibition in
G lends china to 13/3/68
G elected for 7/4/80 n, 10/5/80
G's visit to 6/10/81 ff, 25/10/87
plans for 10/5/80, 13/8/80, 13/9/81, 28/9/81, 29/9/81, 2/10/81
H. J. G member for 7/4/80 n, 10/5/80
offer of constituency from Leeds' liberals 11/3/78, 13/3/78 n, 28/3/78, 12/3/79
Leeward Islands *See* West Indies
Lefevre, George John Shaw- (1831–1928), 1st Baron Eversley (1906), liberal M.P. and cabinet minister 5/3/79, 25/5/81, 7/5/82 n, 27/6/83, 9/2/85 c, 28/4/85, 8/6/85 c, 14/1/86, 3/12/88, 24/5/89, 7/5/90, 9/3/92, 14/8/92
home rule and
G's plan for *Hand-Book of Home Rule* 8/7/86
letters from G to, printed 22/12/80, 27/12/80, 25/5/81, 12/11/83, 10/10/84, 9/12/92
resignation, threat of 16/5/85
legacy duties 1/3/53, 10/1/69
Legacy Duty Bill 11/5/53, 12/5/53 ff
Leghorn 21/1/39, 28/7/49, 8/11/50, 20/2/51
Leith 27/12/33, 6/5/34, 27/1/80
demand for increased armaments from 16/2/94
G's ship anchored at 2/9/80
Sir J. G's St. James's church in 9/3/39, 15/3/40, 11/1/62
Leith constituency
G elected for 1886 2/7/86, 3/7/86, 10/7/86, 13/7/86, 22/8/87 n
Lenbach, F. *See* portraits of G
Lent, observation of 8/2/37, 13/2/39, 30/3/39, 4/3/40, 2/4/41, 10/4/41, 22/3/42, 8/3/48, 10/4/52, 9/2/53, 21/3/55, 6/4/60
better observance of 17/2/47
deficiency in 27/3/42, 15/4/43, 9/4/46, 10/3/47, 19/4/51, 18/4/78
in Paris 29/1/39
Leonardo da Vinci 7/7/32, 9/7/32, 22/9/38, 1/10/38
Leopardi
G visits tomb of 17/1/51
letters *See* correspondence
letters and articles for the press
Albion 6/1/32
Baptist
Welsh disestablishment 23/2/87
Colonial Church Chronicle 4/3/50
Daily Chronicle
home rule not dangerous to the Empire 24/4/86
Daily News
Bulgarian horrors 14/9/76
Turkish atrocities in Armenia 25/8/89
Daily Review (Edinburgh)
home rule 30/4/86 n
Daily Telegraph 8/10/76
elections 6/7/68
Evening Standard 29/5/47, 30/5/47
Guardian
G and the Jerusalem bishopric 1841 27/9/83
on the harvest, by 'Ruricola' 13/10/54
S. Lancs. seat offer 19/3/61
Liverpool Courier 11/8/26, 23/8/26, 13/9/26, 31/7/28

Liverpool Mercury 22/12/28, 11/11/68
Liverpool Standard 16/11/30, 4/12/30, 5/4/31, 8/4/31, 20/5/31, 22/8/31, 23/9/31, 5/11/32, 19/11/32, 24/11/32, 30/11/32, 21/12/32 ff, 24/12/32, 26/12/32, 27/12/32, 29/12/32, 31/12/32, 2/1/33, 3/1/33, 4/1/33, 5/1/33, 7/1/33, 8/1/33, 10/1/33, 11/1/33, 14/1/33, 15/1/33, 16/1/33, 17/1/33, 26/1/33, 27/1/33, 29/1/33, 30/1/33, 1/2/33, 4/2/33, 6/2/33, 9/2/33, 13/2/33, 14/2/33, 16/2/33, 19/2/33, 26/2/33, 2/3/33, 17/6/35
Montrose Standard 17/12/49
Morning Chronicle
defending Albert on Eastern question 15/1/54
on fall of Derby's government 20/12/52
on Oxford reform ('Academicus') 16/2/49, 17/2/49
oppression in Rome 6/10/51
Peel's obituary 4/7/50
Morning Herald
denying he caused Helen G's conversion to Rome 28/5/47
Morning Post 12/7/34, 19/9/34, 27/9/34, 10/12/36, 9/2/47, 24/3/50
Morning Star
church rates 24/1/61
New York Herald (not sent) 16/10/81
Scotsman 9/12/79, 23/12/79, 5/3/80
Scottish Leader 31/12/86
The Times 10/1/42, 30/1/42, 31/1/42, 17/10/62, 5/8/64, 23/2/77, 5/3/77, 27/6/77, 2/7/77, 11/10/77, 2/5/78
Bulgarian horrors 14/9/76
disestablishment 17/10/84
Hawarden estate 23/2/89
Washington's greatness 4/10/84
letters and papers, cataloguing and storing of 1/3/34
letters by G to Farr
attempted sale of by Sotheby's 17/3/92
liberal Catholics 8/5/32
Liberal Churchmen's Union 22/1/93
liberalism 7/4/32, 13/11/38, 1/2/85, 26/10/92
centralisation, accused of 31/12/82
constructionist tendencies of 11/2/85
especially hard for liberal government to rule despotically 14/4/81
G's progress towards 26/9/92
role of peerage in leading liberal movements 17/9/85
See also Bright, Commons (House of), Ireland, liberal party, liberty, Mill
liberal party 18/12/52, 13/7/53, 31/3/57, 30/5/85, 11/10/85, 18/10/85, 20/10/96
1874 election and
poor organisation not the cause of defeat 9/2/74
swept away by a torrent of gin and beer 6/2/74
victory as likely soon as late 20/1/74
1880 election and 8/3/80 ff, 1/4/80 ff
1885 election and 7/8/85, 2/9/85, 3/9/85, 8/9/85 ff, 17/9/85, 30/9/85, 11/10/85 ff, 30/10/85, 11/11/85 ff, 3/12/85, 6/12/85 ff
achievements in 19th century of 1/7/86
adoption of a measure ensures probability of success 19/8/84
advanced party in, G will never lead 12/3/73
army purchase abolition, hesitant support for 8/3/71
better respecter of property than the tories 27/10/85
bye-elections and 23/8/71, 16/9/72, 10/5/73 c, 23/9/73, 1/7/80, 21/4/81, 5/9/81, 8/9/81, 5/12/82, 12/12/82, 22/3/84, 27/9/84, 11/2/87, 3/8/87, 4/6/88 n, 30/6/88, 13/3/89 n, 30/6/90 n, 22/10/90, 11/12/90, 16/12/90, 2/6/91 n, 16/7/91 n, 3/10/91, 24/1/92, 25/1/93 c
drink and no-popery affecting 23/8/71
hold on constituencies weakened 16/9/72
ill-advised for prime minister to be involved in, G thinks 6/10/92
cabinets of, and radicalism 5/2/85
caucus in 20/7/78 n
centralisation, accused of 31/12/82
Churchmen in 29/11/93
condition of 14/8/73, 24/12/74, 30/6/85
must pass through period of trial and reflection 23/2/74
suffering for its virtues 24/11/73
constituencies cannot dictate course of Parliamentary business 13/10/83
crotchety or egotistical behaviour in 5/2/74
defeat of 1866 Reform Bill and 19/6/66 ff
disestablishment and 3/11/85 ff, 14/11/85 ff
divisions in 30/1/79, 26/10/85, 10/11/85
G's sympathies with advanced section on: education, economy, factious spirit, land laws, reform 12/3/73
home rule and 7/8/85, 3/9/85 ff, 9/9/85 ff, 30/9/85, 26/12/85, 2/1/86 ff, 15/3/86 ff, 26/3/86, 1/5/86 ff, 7/6/86 ff
less in opposition than in government 12/7/86
no cause or great public object on which to combine 12/3/73, 7/3/74, 14/1/75

liberal party (*cont.*)
divisions in (*cont.*)
opposition to bulk of party in 7/3/74
press and 23/3/88 n
suspended by a dissolution? 20/1/74
dominant tendencies of
G cannot concur with 14/1/75
Eastern question and
deputations to G at Hawarden 8/5/78
education bill and 25/11/71, 30/10/73, 14/1/75
Egypt and
party meeting on? 19/7/82
Granville liberal leader in the Lords
G urges to lead party on Bulgarian campaign 11/9/76
G's differences with on education 12/3/73, 7/3/74
G's leadership of 7/7/79, 13/12/79, 20/7/86 c, 17/8/86
cabinet supports continuation of 20/7/86 c
discussed with Rosebery 28/11/79
resignation from 16/2/74, 19/2/74, 25/2/74, 5/3/74, 7/3/74, 11/3/74, 27/12/74, 31/12/74, 7/1/75, 9/1/75, 11/1/75, 14/1/75
resignation from: but still sits on Front Bench 15/2/75 n
G's leadership of weakening 29/4/71 n
G's Resolutions on Eastern question
attempted compromise on 5/5/77
moved without support in *Upper* official circle 27/4/77, 30/4/77 ff
solitary struggle for 7/5/77
G unable to lead for ordinary purposes of opposition 14/1/75
home rule and 12/12/85, 16/12/85, 26/12/85, 28/12/85, 2/1/86, 5/1/86, 7/1/86, 14/1/86 ff
difficulty of uniting on 13/11/85, 23/3/86
dissolution on 8/6/86
force for would be broken up by Parnell's continuance 23/11/90
G's memorandum on, printed 28/10/92
McCarthy's impossible proposition 30/11/90
party meeting desirable but not yet 1/4/86
in Wales 1/4/72
Irish disestablishment and 19/3/68 n
Irish Land Bill and
danger of repeat of 1866 22/4/70
Irish local government and
divided on 7/6/85
Irish University Bill and defeat of the government 4/3/73, 11/3/73 ff
jealousy among local leaders of 16/9/72 n
labour M.P.s and 26/4/87
leadership in Lords of 13/4/91
legislative achievements of 19/8/84
liberal unionists 17/3/87 n, 14/6/87 n, 29/7/87 n, 5/8/87 n, 13/8/87 n, 12/6/88 n, 11/9/88, 28/10/92, 26/4/93, 23/5/93
cooperation with on liberal grounds 20/7/86 c, 6/9/86
hostility to coercion of 12/7/86
memorandum on, printed 12/7/86
place of sitting in Commons 12/1/93 ff
toryism of the worst type 23/6/86
London
disputes in 8/7/78
Lords' reform and 19/8/84
meetings of 26/2/67, 21/3/67, 5/4/67, 31/5/67, 6/7/71, 29/5/83, 9/7/84 c, 10/7/84, 27/11/84 c, 1/12/84, 27/3/93
G always hates, Rosebery thinks 8/12/85 n
Government of Ireland Bill 25/5/86 c, 27/5/86
not practicable to hold meeting on home rule 4/5/86 c
Willis's Rooms meeting: G not attending 6/6/59 n
minorities and
may split on 6/12/83
moderate section of 30/9/85
more healthy than of late 8/8/67
most effective economists when in opposition 13/3/56
multiplication of candidates of 5/2/74
navy estimates crisis and 19/12/93, 9/1/94, 5/2/94
need for pamphlets defending 4/3/93
nonconformists and 5/7/73
will probably use power to put liberals in a minority 29/8/73
organization of
G's speech on 30/11/78
Parnell and the O'Shea divorce case and
G's memoranda on, printed 21/11/90 ff
Parnell's continued leadership means end of common action 28/11/90
peerage of
ludicrous daily splutterings of 17/4/86
rapid disintegration regretted by G 14/4/86
personnel of considered by G 'with a view to contingencies' 28/2/68
positive force to carry forward needed 14/8/73
finance may provide 14/8/73
possibility of great schism in 5/7/73
radicals and 1/1/86, 28/10/92
home rule withdraws factious support from 27/4/86

role in course of Victorian legislation 19/8/84
Round Table conferences and 27/12/86 ff, 21/2/87, 23/2/87 ff, 26/2/87
G's memorandum on, printed 26/2/87
Scottish liberal M.P.s 31/1/81
socialism and 28/10/85
strength of
on dissolution in 1872 on Lords' amendments to ballot bill 6/7/72
thought to fare better at general than bye-elections 16/1/74
Ulster and 22/1/86 n
weakness of in 'the classes' 28/4/86
whigs and radicals should be able to combine in 13/11/82
Women's Liberal Federation 10/5/88
G's speech to 22/5/89
See also Cavendish, Chamberlain, clubs (Eighty Club), Commons (House of), constituencies, deputations, elections, Glyn, Grosvenor, Hawarden Castle, Ireland, liberty, Lords (House of), National Liberal Club, National Liberal Federation, National Liberal League, patronage, radicalism, Scotland, Wales
liberal policy
public economy and 29/11/71
Liberal Registration Association 21/1/75
liberal unionists *See* Bright, Cavendish, Chamberlain, Goschen, liberal party
Liberation Society 4/5/66 n, 5/7/70 n, 22/5/71, 29/8/73 n, 1/5/77 n, 22/10/85, 8/11/85
poor affair; its causes remote and for the present feeble 28/12/72
Liberia *See* Homer
liberty
believed in by few men 2/7/86
representation believed in by even fewer 2/7/86
cause of links Egypt and U.K. franchise 28/5/84
Commons and 19/7/82
not taught G by Eton or Oxford 10/5/80
libraries
G's speech on free libraries 12/2/91
library, G's 9/9/26, 19/12/27, 6/4/37, 26/7/45 ff, 7/3/49 ff, 3/3/52, 31/5/52 ff
books sent for binding 28/2/52, 3/3/52 ff
G's article on housing of books 17/12/89
weeding of 3/3/52
Licensing Bills
1870 9/12/69 ff
1871 2/11/70, 4/11/70 c, 8/11/70 c, 10/11/70 c, 25/3/71 c, 6/5/71 c
1872 17/7/2 c, 6/11/71 c, 13/4/72 c, 2/5/72 c, 10/7/72 c, 15/7/72
Lichfield 16/4/78
Liddell, Henry George, Dean (1811–1898), dean of Christ Church, Oxford 1855–91, lexicographer 24/1/33, 27/7/58, 23/5/65, 31/12/67, 8/11/74, 21/9/82, 5/12/82 n, 27/11/83, 11/11/88, 2/2/90 ff
at Hawarden 27/7/58, 5/10/61
at Penmaenmawr 20/8/61, 23/8/61, 8/9/68
British museum trusteeship and 2/5/81
Cleveland commission and 20/6/71, 30/6/71
Deanery of Durham, declines 26/8/83
Deanery of Westminster, declines 23/7/81 ff, 29/7/81, 2/8/81, 8/8/81
declines invitation to join Selborne commission 7/10/80
G makes suggestions for the *Lexicon* 5/10/61
G staying with 18/11/61 ff, 9/6/75, 30/1/78
letters from G to, printed 3/2/70, 24/3/70, 20/6/71, 28/3/72, 7/10/80, 5/12/80, 2/5/81, 4/10/82, 26/8/83, 13/2/84
returns portrait of G to Watts 16/5/76 n
rumour he wishes to quit Christ Church 2/8/81
university tests and 23/6/64, 3/2/70, 24/3/70, 24/4/71
See also Christ Church (Oxford)
Liège
fortifications against Germany of 25/7/32
life
downhill of 29/12/44
G failing to prepare for crisis of 31/12/57
onward steps in 31/3/76
purpose of
still unclear 29/12/57
swimming for his life, a man does not see the country through which the river winds 31/12/68
unwinding the coil of 29/12/75
Lifford committee *See* Ireland
Limehouse *See* London
Limericks by G 10/9/62
Lincoln, Lord *See* Clinton
Lincoln, town of 29/3/95
G's speech at 20/5/90
Lincoln cathedral 3/12/39 ff
Lincoln's Inn
dinners at 25/1/33, 26/1/33, 28/1/33, 30/1/33, 19/4/33, 22/4/33 ff, 3/5/33, 26/5/33, 27/5/33, 4/6/33, 19/4/34, 20/4/34, 23/5/34, 25/5/34, 29/5/34, 4/6/34, 19/4/35, 21/4/35, 26/4/35, 22/4/36, 26/4/36 ff, 28/5/36 ff, 26/5/37, 17/11/37 ff, 25/1/38 ff, 21/6/76, 12/6/77, 25/6/89, 17/11/93

Lincoln's Inn (*cont.*)
G looks over 7/12/60
Manning's candidacy as Preacher 4/11/43
petition for dismissal 23/4/39
Linlithgow 6/4/80
Literary Fund
G speaks at dinner of 22/6/59
literature
gains increasing hold on G 31/12/56
G's earnings from
to 1890: £14, 862 20/3/91
Littleburys, Mill Hill (Aberdeen) 19/6/80, 3/7/80, 17/7/80, 24/7/80, 25/6/81, 2/7/81, 23/7/81, 30/7/81, 6/8/81
Littlemore *See* Oxford
Liverpool 2/8/25, 7/7/29 ff, 11/1/34, 14/1/36, 25/1/36, 15/10/36, 3/8/37, 13/8/39, 3/12/40, 8/1/41, 29/7/46 ff, 2/10/49, 30/8/50, 24/9/50, 27/12/51, 19/10/52 ff, 5/11/53, 14/6/55, 24/10/56, 22/10/57, 26/10/57, 15/10/58, 10/10/61, 5/4/66, 4/8/68, 14/5/75, 22/12/75, 7/10/78, 10/10/83
advowson of purchased by G for £7200 23/12/89, 31/12/89
Athenaeum library 18/9/26
Bold Street gallery 10/9/59, 11/10/61
bye-election in 17/8/61
cattle show 23/7/41
Chamber of Commerce of
G honorary member of 14/9/64
Eastern question and
G's excellent reception 17/11/76
exhibition at 25/10/56, 31/10/56
Free Public Library Museum
G's porcelain collection displayed 13/3/67, 24/5/67, 18/9/67, 15/11/67, 25/7/74
G electioneering in 3/4/57, 28/6/86
'masses and classes' speech at Hengler's Circus 28/6/86
G Freeman of 6/10/92, 3/12/92, 5/12/92
Knotty Ash
Gladstone vault at 19/10/52
Lord Mayorality for 6/6/93 c
Mariners Charity Soc. 4/1/28
Mersey tunnel, G involved in construction of 28/10/75 ff, 11/10/83
Naval and Military Bible Society 18/12/28
New Brighton 28/10/56
new docks
G visits with Bright 1/10/56
Roman Catholic Liverpudlians
deputation to G 21/1/68
School for the Indigent Blind 4/12/40, 9/1/41
School of Science
G speaks at opening of 10/10/61
shipping deputation from 18/2/56
St. Andrew's, Renshaw st. 23/12/27
St. Thomas's, Seaforth 13/1/52
St. Thomas's, Toxteth 28/12/51, 13/1/52, 7/10/55, 20/9/81, 12/12/81, 26/12/81, 6/6/92, 9/6/92
advowson inherited by G 28/12/51
candidates for incumbency of 24/9/86, 25/10/86
dismal spectacle at 22/12/72, 24/8/79
happily changed 19/10/90
promising work at 6/12/91
Unitarian chapel, Hope Street 7/11/53
University College of
G assists in endowing Italian Chair in 31/10/91
Walker art gallery 11/10/83
wards of, inquiry into working of 23/7/84
See also constituencies, Court Hey, Gladstone (Robertson), Seaforth
Liverpool Collegiate Institution 24/8/39, 21/11/39, 2/1/43, 6/1/43, 22/10/57
G's speech at opening 29/9/56
Lowes Dickinson's portrait of G for 14/6/71
Liverpool Post 19/4/86
Llandudno 23/8/61
Llangwm church 8/9/56
Llanidloes 12/9/56
Llanrwst 10/9/55, 28/9/60
Lloyd's Weekly Newspaper *See* publications
local government 15/10/81, 3/2/83, 27/1/85, 7/8/85 ff, 14/9/85, 14/4/86 c, 20/7/92, 1/12/93 c
County Boards 17/1/69, 9/2/69 c, 10/4/69 c, 19/6/69 c, 12/2/70 c
County Councils and 4/11/81, 21/11/81, 27/1/82 c
women's eligibility for 18/3/91
County Councils Bill 27/1/82, 30/1/82 ff
district councils and
slight savour of dualism 19/12/81
finances of
dramatic plan for reform of 2/1/74
free and large decentralisation needed 24/11/81
grants in aid and 19/1/81, 4/11/81 ff
G's survey of its future development 4/11/81, 24/11/81
Local Government Bill 1882 10/1/82, 11/3/82, 14/3/82
Local Government Bill 1893-4 1/12/93 c, 14/12/93 c, 29/12/93 ff, 12/2/94 c, 23/2/94 c, 26/2/94 c, 1/3/94 c
London 1/1/70, 10/11/81
means of improving Commons 23/10/80
parish councils and 20/7/92, 1/8/92, 19/8/92 c

police and
G determined police should come under local control 19/12/81, 30/1/82, 20/7/92, 1/8/92
Provincial Assemblies the ulterior development 3/2/83
Stansfeld's bill 1/7/71 c, 5/7/71 c
Stansfeld's memorandum 28/11/73 c
to be G's task for 1883 1/6/82
to be on agenda for 1871 1/1/70
to be on agenda for 1883 10/9/83
See also Ireland, London, Scotland
Local Government Board
reform of 13/11/82
Local Rating Bill 11/3/71 c
Loch Avon
Highland women at 5/9/39
Loch Avon, Cairngorms 5/9/39
Lochinver 21/9/58
Loch Lomond 15/8/39
Lochnagar, ascended 8/9/36, 3/9/39, 6/10/63
Locke, John
annihilates half creation 13/1/36
denied toleration to atheists 11/6/81
discussed 28/12/91, 19/9/92
Human understanding, overrated but useful 9/4/36
lodger franchise *See* Reform Bills
logarithms 7/4/28 ff
London
absence from needed for growth, work, reflection 29/12/75
Albany 3/10/31, 28/8/35
Albert Hall
G at Gounod's concert in 10/7/72
G at 'Messiah' in 26/2/73, 23/3/83
Irish concert attended by G 17/3/90
opening of 29/3/71
St. Patrick's Day concert at 17/3/88
Albert Memorial 26/3/74
G alone in criticising 23/3/63
Alleyn's School, Dulwich
G gives prizes at 20/6/67
Bermondsey Gladstone Club 14/11/87 n
Berner's hotel 6/1/30
Bethnal Green museum 4/3/71 c
Wallace collection in 28/3/74
Central Committee of Metropolitan Unemployed 18/8/93 n
Chelsea Coffee Tavern, G opens 3/4/79
Claridge's hotel 8/12/76 n
Cleopatra's needle
no government money for bringing to U.K. 15/2/73 c
coal tax
G opposes 4/12/86
Cockpit of 30/10/93
Constitution Hill 17/6/71 c
Cremorne Gardens
G sees Leotard at 6/8/61
rescue work in 30/7/62
docks of 3/7/76
Dover House, use of 7/3/85, 12/3/85 c
Dulwich picture gallery 2/7/63, 23/6/65, 5/6/75
East End museum, government support for 12/8/71 c
evangelising of
G unable to assist Wilberforce in 9/1/73
G in: 1827–1858 22/9/27, 3/12/27, 2/4/30 ff, 3/10/31 ff, 29/7/32 ff, 24/1/33, 18/4/33 ff, 3/2/34, 11/2/34 ff, 17/2/34, 20/12/34, 8/1/35 ff, 30/5/35, 1/8/35, 2/1/36, 30/1/37, 1/4/37, 17/11/37, 15/1/38, 30/1/39 ff, 14/1/40, 6/4/40, 25/1/41, 29/11/41, 4/4/42, 24/9/42, 16/1/43, 13/10/43, 10/1/44, 30/5/44, 28/10/44, 19/11/44, 8/1/45, 14/2/45, 29/3/45, 24/9/45, 4/12/45, 17/4/46, 28/4/46, 15/4/47 ff, 31/5/47, 29/10/47, 7/2/48, 25/1/49, 11/4/49, 25/6/49 ff, 9/8/49, 22/9/49, 30/1/50, 18/2/50, 2/10/50, 14/10/50, 26/2/51, 8/5/51, 19/1/52, 26/1/52, 12/10/52, 21/10/52, 4/11/52, 13/12/52, 31/1/53, 2/4/53, 9/5/53, 19/5/53, 4/10/53, 21/5/54, 15/7/54, 7/8/54, 19/9/54, 16/10/54 ff, 9/11/54, 26/3/55, 15/6/55, 22/11/55, 5/12/55 ff, 19/1/56, 19/5/56, 30/6/56, 6/1/57, 16/1/57, 9/4/57 ff, 1/7/57, 17/8/57, 2/12/57, 23/1/58, 16/2/58 ff, 5/4/58 ff, 12/8/58 ff, 19/10/58
G in: 1859–1868 8/3/59, 17/5/59, 6/6/59, 27/8/59, 16/9/59, 14/10/59, 20/10/59, 27/10/59, 7/11/59, 15/11/59, 16/12/59, 2/1/60 ff, 5/3/60, 12/3/60, 10/4/60, 25/6/60, 23/7/60, 13/8/60, 12/10/60, 8/11/60, 12/11/60, 15/12/60, 18/1/61, 4/2/61, 12/3/61, 18/3/61, 2/4/61, 24/4/61, 6/5/61, 13/5/61, 22/5/61, 27/5/61, 10/6/61, 17/6/61, 6/8/61, 14/10/61, 16/10/61, 11/11/61, 22/11/61, 27/11/61, 30/11/61, 23/12/61, 12/1/62, 17/1/62, 21/1/62, 27/1/62, 17/2/62, 20/2/62, 17/3/62, 20/3/62, 31/3/62, 28/4/62, 5/5/62, 2/6/62, 11/6/62, 22/10/62, 10/11/62, 8/12/62, 19/1/63, 13/2/63, 16/2/63, 23/2/63, 9/3/63, 16/3/63, 23/3/63, 30/3/63, 14/4/63, 20/4/63, 18/5/63, 28/5/63, 15/6/63, 18/6/63, 29/6/63, 13/7/63, 10/11/63, 30/11/63, 7/12/63, 16/12/63, 2/1/64, 20/1/64,

London (*cont.*)
G in: 1859–1868 (*cont.*)
18/2/64, 22/2/64, 21/3/64, 29/3/64, 4/4/64, 25/4/64, 19/5/64, 23/5/64, 13/6/64, 4/7/64, 25/7/64, 28/7/64, 7/11/64, 4/1/65, 18/1/65, 31/1/65, 27/2/65, 27/3/65, 14/4/65, 20/4/65, 24/4/65, 28/4/65, 8/5/65, 22/5/65, 1/6/65, 7/6/65, 26/6/65, 10/7/65, 24/7/65, 26/7/65, 21/10/65, 8/11/65, 22/11/65, 15/12/65, 9/1/66, 26/2/66, 19/3/66, 4/4/66, 7/4/66, 23/4/66, 7/5/66, 23/5/66, 11/6/66, 2/7/66, 9/7/66, 16/7/66, 8/8/66, 27/8/66, 11/9/66, 17/9/66, 24/9/66, 29/1/67, 25/2/67, 11/3/67, 25/3/67, 17/4/67, 1/5/67, 6/5/67, 20/5/67, 14/6/67, 24/6/67, 8/7/67, 15/7/67, 29/7/67, 18/11/67, 31/12/67, 13/2/68, 3/3/68, 23/3/68, 21/4/68, 11/5/68, 18/5/68, 3/6/68, 15/6/68, 21/6/68, 29/6/68, 6/7/68, 20/7/68, 23/7/68, 3/12/68, 15/12/68
G in: 1869–1874 22/1/69, 25/1/69, 1/2/69, 22/3/69, 1/4/69, 14/6/69, 28/6/69, 5/7/69, 30/7/69, 4/9/69, 26/10/69, 8/11/69, 15/11/69, 17/11/69, 6/12/69, 13/12/69, 20/1/70, 11/4/70, 25/4/70, 8/6/70, 20/6/70, 23/6/70, 27/6/70, 11/7/70, 8/8/70, 19/8/70, 6/9/70, 9/9/70, 20/9/70, 26/9/70, 19/10/70, 27/10/70, 24/11/70, 28/11/70, 30/11/70, 14/12/70, 14/1/71, 13/2/71, 20/3/71, 17/4/71, 8/5/71, 15/5/71, 5/6/71, 19/6/71, 26/6/71, 3/7/71, 10/7/71, 17/7/71, 24/7/71, 31/7/71, 7/8/71, 14/8/71, 20/10/71, 9/12/71, 15/1/72, 19/1/72, 3/4/72, 8/4/72, 15/4/72, 29/4/72, 27/5/72, 10/6/72, 24/6/72, 8/7/72, 15/7/72, 21/7/72, 29/7/72, 5/8/72, 10/10/72, 14/11/72, 2/12/72, 10/12/72, 21/1/73, 17/3/73, 21/4/73, 5/5/73, 19/5/73, 5/6/73, 23/6/73, 7/7/73, 10/7/73, 14/7/73, 21/7/73, 29/7/73, 4/8/73, 2/10/73, 10/11/73, 25/11/73, 3/12/73, 16/1/74, 10/3/74, 16/3/74, 22/4/74, 13/5/74, 4/7/74, 13/7/74, 30/7/74, 5/9/74, 25/9/74, 4/11/74
G in: 1875–1880 7/1/75, 12/2/75, 1/3/75, 29/3/75, 3/5/75, 24/5/75, 31/5/75, 10/6/75, 28/6/75, 10/7/75, 19/7/75, 29/9/75, 9/11/75, 20/1/76, 2/2/76, 4/4/76, 6/5/76, 20/6/76, 17/7/76, 4/9/76, 24/10/76, 5/12/76, 5/2/77, 12/3/77, 9/4/77, 4/6/77, 11/6/77, 14/7/77, 24/9/77, 3/12/77, 16/1/78, 25/1/78, 1/2/78, 18/2/78, 25/3/78, 17/4/78, 14/5/78, 12/6/78, 8/7/78, 15/10/78, 27/11/78, 18/2/79, 21/4/79, 19/5/79, 9/6/79, 7/7/79, 20/8/79, 11/9/79, 25/10/79, 11/1/80, 22/1/80, 23/2/80, 19/4/80, 12/5/80, 17/5/80, 20/6/80, 5/7/80, 19/7/80, 26/7/80, 24/8/80, 4/9/80, 29/9/80, 4/10/80, 8/11/80, 22/11/80, 13/12/80, 29/12/80
G in: 1881–1886 1/1/81, 7/2/81, 21/2/81, 7/3/81, 21/3/81, 25/4/81, 9/5/81, 23/5/81, 20/6/81, 27/6/81, 4/7/81, 11/7/81, 18/7/81, 25/7/81, 1/8/81, 8/8/81, 15/8/81, 7/9/81, 11/10/81, 8/11/81, 5/1/82, 24/1/82, 9/3/82, 17/4/82, 24/4/82, 28/4/82, 1/5/82, 12/5/82, 22/5/82, 1/6/82, 5/6/82, 12/6/82, 19/6/82, 26/6/82, 3/7/82, 10/7/82, 17/7/82, 24/7/82, 31/7/82, 7/8/82, 25/8/82, 13/9/82, 20/10/82, 9/12/82, 16/1/83, 2/3/83, 29/3/83, 2/4/83, 23/5/83, 11/6/83, 18/6/83, 25/6/83, 2/7/83, 9/7/83, 12/7/83, 16/7/83, 30/7/83, 6/8/83, 21/9/83, 24/10/83, 8/11/83, 20/11/83, 30/11/83, 22/1/84, 2/2/84, 31/3/84, 7/4/84, 21/4/84, 9/6/84, 16/6/84, 23/6/84, 30/6/84, 7/7/84, 14/7/84, 21/7/84, 28/7/84, 6/10/84, 21/10/84, 3/11/84, 10/11/84, 24/11/84, 26/11/84, 1/1/85, 20/1/85, 5/2/85, 12/3/85, 9/4/85, 20/5/85, 4/6/85, 15/6/85, 22/6/85, 6/7/85, 13/7/85, 20/7/85, 25/7/85, 30/7/85, 7/8/85, 29/10/85, 11/1/86, 10/2/86, 25/3/86, 5/4/86, 4/5/86, 10/5/86, 16/5/86, 7/6/86, 16/6/86, 14/7/86, 13/8/86, 23/8/86, 19/9/86
G in: 1887–1896 25/1/87, 21/2/87, 14/3/87, 13/4/87, 6/5/87, 21/5/87, 7/6/87, 9/6/87, 20/6/87, 24/8/87, 12/9/87, 10/11/87, 8/2/88, 20/2/88, 27/2/88, 9/4/88, 8/5/88, 14/5/88, 4/6/88, 18/6/88, 9/7/88, 16/7/88, 30/7/88, 3/12/88, 14/12/88, 20/2/89, 28/2/89, 1/5/89, 20/5/89, 2/6/89, 17/6/89, 24/6/89, 1/7/89, 8/7/89, 22/7/89, 29/7/89, 2/9/89, 9/9/89, 29/1/90, 8/2/90, 15/4/90, 21/4/90, 12/5/90, 4/6/90, 28/6/90, 28/7/90, 24/11/90, 26/1/91, 2/2/91, 9/2/91, 3/3/91, 10/3/91, 16/3/91, 9/4/91, 9/6/91, 4/7/91, 28/7/91, 11/12/91, 29/2/92, 27/4/92, 2/5/92, 23/5/92, 30/5/92, 13/6/92, 27/7/92, 8/8/92, 11/8/92, 16/8/92, 28/9/92, 25/10/92, 14/11/92, 16/12/92, 10/1/93, 22/2/93, 8/3/93, 20/3/93, 6/4/93, 10/4/93, 1/5/93, 15/5/93, 29/5/93,

12/6/93, 19/6/93, 26/6/93, 3/7/93, 10/7/93, 17/7/93, 24/7/93, 31/7/93, 14/8/93, 21/8/93, 28/8/93, 1/11/93, 4/12/93, 13/12/93, 27/12/93, 8/1/94, 10/2/94, 3/3/94, 21/3/94, 7/1/95, 10/3/95, 23/3/95, 25/6/95
Golden Lane schools
G lays foundation stone of 8/5/56
Greenwich Hospital
navy education, to be used for 30/1/72 c
G returns to for rescue work 15/8/50
G's bodily condition sensibly improved by escape from 29/3/85
Guards' Chapel
G's inscriptions for 12/12/78, 25/5/79
Hendon
G opens sewage works at 23/4/87
Hendon Hall 27/4/87
Hyde Park
G visits 'field of battle' after reform demonstration in 24/7/66
socialist heard lecturing in 17/4/42
Volunteer review in, G attends 23/6/60
Kew Gardens 23/2/72, 13/4/72 c
Leicester Square
G plans church in 4/5/46, 21/5/46, 16/3/48, 26/3/48, 4/2/49, 11/2/49, 5/5/50, 16/3/55 n, 2/4/55
Liberal and Radical Union
G's speech to 31/5/92
liberal party in
disputes in 8/7/78
G meets London liberal M. Ps. 24/3/90
Limehouse, G's speech in 15/12/88, 18/12/88 n
local government bill 1882
plan for 10/11/81 c
local government in 1/1/70, 12/11/80 c, 31/1/83 n, 11/2/83 n, 24/3/83, 25/4/83, 5/5/83 c, 23/5/83, 24/5/83, 26/5/83 c, 18/12/88 n, 20/7/92, 27/10/92 c, 31/10/92 c, 23/11/92 c, 17/12/92 c, 23/1/93
1884 bill 4/1/84 c
cabinet committee on 6/1/82 c
control of police and 27/2/83, 20/3/83, 26/3/83, 30/3/83, 4/4/83, 5/4/83, 11/4/83, 28/4/83 c, 11/5/83, 14/5/83, 18/5/83, 23/5/83
Harcourt's plan 16/12/81, 18/12/81, 19/12/81, 6/1/82 c
Metropolitan Government Bill 10/7/80 c
municipal government measure 25/1/72 c, 17/7/72 c
no bill in 1871 11/11/70 c
no bill in 1872 31/10/71 c
no bill in 1873 3/12/72 c
no bill in 1884 10/9/83
withdrawal of bill a serious mischief 11/4/83
London Bridge
Cole's picture of 15/1/94
London County Council
G's visit to 24/6/90
London home, G reluctant to contemplate 18/3/75
London Tavern
G dining at 8/5/52
Marylebone liberal association 19/7/87
Marylebone Women's Liberal Association
G's speech to 16/4/88
metropolitan police 3/5/73
North London Industrial Exhibition
G presides at 7/11/64
Parliament Street, plan for 20/8/83, 25/10/83 c, 31/10/83, 13/11/83 c
Piccadilly
Eros fountain, G writes inscription for 8/8/91
poor rate in 28/4/93
Rates Equalisation Bill 23/11/92 c, 23/1/93 c
rating of government property in 2/1/74
Regent's Park
improvement of woods in 27/7/78
Regent's Park, expansion of 13/3/83
Royal Exchange, opening of 28/10/44
Serpentine
frozen 2/1/54
sewers of
G inspects 12/7/62, 18/7/63
St. James's park, road in 14/5/70 c, 28/5/70 c, 14/6/70 c
St. Pancras workhouse, G's speech to inmates of 21/8/79
Temple Bar 2/2/81
Thames embankment 25/1/72 c, 18/11/72 c
Tower of London
of very mournful interest 27/6/83
Trafalgar Square
meetings in 20/3/69 c, 14/10/92
Trafalgar Square riots 8/2/86 n, 10/2/86 n, 13/2/86, 16/2/86 n, 14/10/92 n
tory promotion of? 16/2/86 c
unemployment in
deputation to G on 28/12/93
Warren's Hotel 27/1/40, 11/2/40
water supply of 7/11/70 c
See also Dollis Hill, houses, Hyde Park
London, City of
beauty of 3/7/76
constituency of
G considers standing for 13/6/61 ff, 12/7/61
G invited to meet notabilities 23/4/53

London, City of (*cont.*)
G visits 24/3/48, 30/3/48, 17/8/48, 19/2/49, 31/3/49, 19/5/49, 22/5/50, 29/7/50, 7/10/50, 15/10/50, 10/2/52, 24/3/52, 16/6/52, 24/4/55, 1/4/58, 13/10/81
G visits as Chancellor 12/1/53, 31/12/53, 15/11/54, 21/11/62
G visits on B. of T. business 30/3/44
jingoism in 13/10/81
livery companies
inquiry into 5/5/80 c
Royal Commission on 23/1/93
Turners' Company 13/10/81
Freeman of London through 17/3/76
G admitted to 16/2/76
London, University of 9/5/49, 16/2/53, 11/5/70
London County Council *See* deputations, London
London Diocesan Board
G's speech to 22/6/47
London Library 8/10/42, 12/4/49, 6/5/57, 22/2/58, 17/4/62, 27/10/65, 20/2/75, 14/8/82, 31/3/87, 22/6/87, 18/2/88, 15/6/88, 5/5/90, 5/3/91, 28/10/92
committee of, G on 25/7/40, 3/2/41, 20/2/41, 27/2/41, 16/6/49, 13/3/52, 29/5/52, 12/6/52, 12/7/75, 29/5/79
G selecting church history books for 7/1/41, 20/2/41
G takes chair at, *vice* Tennyson 29/5/89
Homeric books in 2/7/79
inaugural meeting of 18/7/40
London Tavern *See* London
Longford (Bouverie) 21/1/57
Longford (Radnor) 1/9/66
Longleat, Wiltshire (Bath) 31/8/66, 17/1/77
Lords, House of
attacks on G in 10/9/93
bishops in
discussed with Wilberforce 26/10/68
need to consider removal of 21/3/84, 22/3/84
committee on coalwhippers
G gives evidence to 23/7/57
committee on North British railway
G examined by 28/7/62, 25/7/67
G attending 3/10/31, 19/3/33, 25/6/33, 18/7/33, 19/7/33, 30/7/33, 18/1/38, 7/5/39, 12/5/40, 24/7/40, 6/9/41, 18/2/50, 25/2/50, 7/2/56, 22/2/56, 30/5/62, 15/6/69, 6/12/84
G declines a peerage 23/2/74
urged to take one by O'Gorman Mahon 24/8/81
G drafts objections to Lords' amendments to Oxford bill 28/7/54
G's memorandum, 'paper duty and taxing power of the two Houses' 30/6/60
G's Religious Disabilities Bill and 14/10/93
home rule and 18/10/85, 28/10/92, 4/7/93
problem weighs little with G 13/11/85
institution opposed to liberalism 19/8/84, 25/8/84
Irish disestablishment and
clash with Commons over amendments 15/7/69 ff
possibility it may reject the bill 7/1/69
judicial powers of
Selborne's proposals 27/1/73
liberal leadership in 13/4/91, 18/8/92, 13/12/92, 5/1/93
liberal peers in
need to appoint to high office 3/3/94
life peerages 16/3/69, 10/4/69 c, 24/4/69 c
makes beautiful job of Oxford Bill 7/7/54
only irresponsible power known to our constitution 6/7/84
organic change in 19/8/84
G's strenuous attempts to avert 19/8/84, 26/8/84, 31/8/84, 13/12/84
passes paper duties repeal
a great event for G 7/6/61
privileges of 10/7/73, 12/7/73 c
purchase abolition and 10/7/71 ff
recent legislative career on the whole bad 10/9/84
Reform Bill 1832 29/9/31, 3/10/31 ff, 24/4/32, 26/4/32, 25/5/32, 31/5/32
Reform Bill 1884 30/1/84
bishops and 2/7/84
rejection a suicidal act 8/7/84
rejection of 2/7/84 ff, 8/7/84
Royal Assent given 6/12/84
reform of 16/3/69, 19/8/84, 25/8/84, 7/8/85
rejection of liberal bills
leading to a crisis 13/2/94, 23/2/94, 23/2/94 c, 26/2/94 c, 1/3/94 c, 1/3/94 n
rejects betterment 9/12/93
rejects Compensation for Disturbance Bill 16/8/80, 21/8/80 c, 1/11/80, 9/12/80
rejects Government of Ireland Bill 2/9/93, 9/9/93
Roman Catholic peers and 7/10/93, 10/10/93
rejects Irish Registration Bill 21/8/83, 22/8/83 c
rejects Paper Duties Bill 15/5/60, 21/5/60 n
G's speech on Resolutions on 5/7/60
meditated aggression of 15/5/60

rejects Reform Bill 1884
a suicidal act 8/7/84
thus endangers the monarchy 25/8/84
Savings Banks Bill and
Palmerston settles with Derby 15/8/60, 16/8/60
Scottish peerage 13/3/69 c, 16/3/69, 17/4/69 c
Sunday trains and 27/7/44, 28/7/44, 2/8/44, 3/8/44
See also Cecil, Chamberlain, Commons (House of), liberal party, University Tests Bill
Loretto, church at 7/6/32
Losely House, Guildford 28/3/83
Lourdes
G's visit to 12/1/92
Louvre, Paris *See* galleries visited, Paris
love of self *See* selflove
Lowe, Robert (1811–1892), 1st Viscount Sherbrooke (1880); Adullamite 1866–7; liberal M.P., chancellor of the exchequer 1868–73, home secretary 1873–4 16/12/61 n, 14/3/62, 14/5/63, 1/6/64, 5/4/66 n, 22/3/67, 28/2/70, 22/3/71, 28/6/73, 31/7/73, 22/1/74, 17/2/76, 3/10/77, 29/11/77, 20/4/80, 8/8/81, 31/3/82, 7/8/84, 16/11/84, 12/11/86, 8/6/87
1870 budget 2/4/70 c, 9/4/70 c
1871 budget 3/4/71, 11/4/71 ff, 17/4/71 c, 19/4/71 c, 20/4/71 ff
match tax and 11/4/71, 19/4/71 c, 24/4/71
1873 budget
G's preliminary comments on 19/12/72
at Hawarden 2/12/71 ff
a wreck, very touching 1/4/90
biography of 22/5/93 ff, 10/1/94 ff
chancellor of the exchequer 5/12/68 ff, 30/7/69, 11/2/70, 30/8/71, 14/3/72 ff, 24/7/72
1869 budget 3/4/69, 6/4/69 c, 8/4/69 ff, 12/4/69
and government stock management 4/3/70, 17/3/72
G sends list of 'remnants' to 10/1/69
local taxation and 24/9/72
suggests exchequer grants to schools 15/6/70
told to resign, via Cardwell 2/8/73
civil service reform and 23/11/69, 8/12/69
currency plan of 21/12/70, 22/12/70, 31/3/71, 26/11/72 c
deficiencies of, devastatingly spelt out by G 13/8/73
Dover harbour 4/7/73
drill in assisted schools, favours 21/12/70
G's article on, 'The county franchise, and Mr. Lowe thereon', *N.C.*, ii. 537(November 1877) 9/10/77 ff
G's epitaph for 29/6/73, 18/7/73
home secretary 1873–4 2/8/73 ff
Fenians, release of 4/12/73, 27/12/73, 19/1/74
letters from G to, printed 10/1/69, 12/4/69, 30/7/69, 21/10/69, 23/11/69, 8/12/69, 11/12/69, 4/3/70, 15/6/70, 9/7/70, 6/12/70, 21/12/70, 22/12/70, 3/1/71, 18/3/71, 31/3/71, 3/4/71, 11/4/71, 24/4/71, 10/8/71, 30/8/71, 21/11/71, 29/1/72, 14/3/72, 17/3/72, 20/4/72, 22/4/72, 26/6/72, 28/6/72, 25/7/72, 13/8/72, 24/9/72, 26/10/72, 7/11/72, 19/12/72, 20/12/72, 31/1/73, 25/3/73, 17/4/73, 11/6/73, 4/7/73, 28/7/73, 13/8/73, 3/9/73, 27/9/73, 22/11/73, 4/12/73, 16/12/73
local taxation and
sound on, G thinks 25/1/73
peerage for 29/4/80
physical incapacity of 28/3/79
quarrel with Ayrton 20/11/71
retrenchment and
fails to speak for 14/12/71
retrenchment at the foreign office and 21/10/69
review of G's *Financial statements* 6/1/64 n
sad escapade of 6/8/73
sugar duties and 14/3/72, 20/4/72
trade union law reform and
G requests to undertake 3/9/73, 27/9/73, 26/11/73 c, 1/12/73 c
Zanzibar mail contact 'scandal' and 28/7/73
See also budgets, finance, reform, taxation
Lowestoft
G's speech at 17/5/90
Lowther Castle (Lonsdale) 23/10/57
Lucerne 2/10/66, 20/12/88
Ludlow Castle 16/7/52
Luffness (G. W. Hope) 5/9/45
Lugano 6/10/66
lumbago *See* illnesses
lunatics, repatriation of 8/11/71 c
Luther 3/9/38, 10/9/38, 15/12/38, 17/9/48, 6/4/49, 12/11/83
Lutheran Church
attended in Coblenz 19/8/38
demands of sense in 3/9/38
prayers of 3/9/38
sermons in 9/9/38
Luxembourg
Franco-Prussian war and 16/7/70 c, 21/8/70, 13/12/70, 15/12/70 c, 29/12/70, 30/1/71

luxury
relative term 6/5/43
Lyons 25/2/32, 28/10/50
factory at 27/2/32
Lysways, Lichfield (Forster) 16/4/78
Lyttelton, George William (1817–1876), 4th Baron Lyttelton (1837), C. G's brother-in-law, scholar, co-translator with G; manic depressive 23/7/38 n, 6/10/52, 3/1/54, 18/1/54, 30/11/55, 11/12/55, 25/6/56, 14/6/66, 1/12/67, 30/12/68, 28/1/71, 7/3/71, 4/11/71, 31/7/72, 23/11/72, 22/1/73, 15/2/73, 18/7/73, 18/3/74, 22/3/74, 24/4/74, 23/6/74, 1/10/74, 8/1/75 ?, 24/3/75, 25/3/75, 14/4/75, 21/10/75, 17/1/76 ff, 31/3/76, 23/6/76 n, 28/1/81, 31/12/81, 6/7/82, 9/6/83
10th child of 18/2/54
anxiety about 13/6/60
as colonial undersecretary
bewildered 9/1/46 ff, 17/1/46 ff
death of 19/4/76 ff
causes of: suicide? 19/4/76, 7/5/76, 14/5/76
engagement and marriage of 11/6/39 ff, 17/6/39 ff
funeral of 22/4/76
G assists rehabilitation of 2/10/57, 28/10/60 ff
G composes *Translations* with 2/10/57, 2/11/60 ff
G dissuades from selling Oak Farm 26/8/40
G helps put in order his business affairs 9/10/52 ff
G makes colonial undersecretary 30/12/45, 6/1/46
G's obituary of, *The Guardian*, 26 April 1876 23/4/76
letters from G to, printed 29/4/71, 26/7/71, 29/7/71
Mary's death and 16/8/57 ff
not elected as High Steward at Cambridge 30/10/40, 14/11/40
remarriage of
G and C. G's plans for 28/10/60, 29/10/60
See also Hagley, Lyttelton, (Mary), Oak Farm, publications
Lyttelton, Mary (1813–1857), née Glynne, G's sister-in-law; wife of G. W. Lyttelton 23/7/38, 17/6/40, 16/7/40, 19/7/40, 3/1/54, 1/2/54, 25/6/56
bears her 12th child 7/2/57
death of 16/8/57 ff, 2/2/61
account by G. W. Lyttelton of 1/10/57
engagement and marriage of 11/6/39 ff, 17/6/39 ff
funeral of 24/8/57
illnesses of 9/7/42

Maamtrasna murders *See* Ireland
Macaulay, Thomas Babington (1800–1859), 1st Baron Macaulay (1857), historian; reviewer of G's *State and Church*, whig M.P. 5/4/48, 23/11/52, 4/4/54, 18/5/55, 11/8/71, 23/1/77, 29/1/82, 25/9/83
copyright and 5/2/41
discussion of Aristotle with 8/2/45
dispute with Croker 9/5/76
G attends his funeral 9/1/60
G's review of Trevelyan's *Life* of 23/3/76, 3/4/76 ff
History by
equal to England's expectation 18/12/55
met in St. Peter's, Rome 24/12/38
Oxford and 8/2/45
review of *State and Church* 9/4/39 ff, 15/4/39, 3/1/40
'Warren Hastings' perhaps his most brilliant piece 12/1/86
See also publications, Trevelyan
Macclesfield
G first contemplates free trade during visit to 29/10/90 n
power looms at 28/1/28, 27/2/32
MacColl, Malcolm, Canon (1831–1907), high church and liberal controversialist, preferred by G 19/11/63, 27/6/71, 21/7/71, 9/5/75, 12/11/76, 31/7/78, 21/4/80 ff, 30/10/80, 14/4/81, 16/4/81, 26/1/82, 4/6/82, 18/11/82, 4/3/83, 3/8/83, 7/11/83, 12/11/83, 21/1/84, 27/4/86, 8/7/86, 9/3/87, 27/7/87, 3/7/88, 29/7/90, 10/5/91, 18/10/92, 23/8/93
at Hawarden 11/11/76, 10/12/81, 30/12/82, 2/6/84 ff, 4/10/85, 13/12/85, 1/1/87 ff, 22/5/88, 27/4/89 ff, 16/8/89, 29/5/90 ff, 20/1/91
Dilke divorce case and 2/1/87
'intellectual' lunch with, to meet Olive Schreiner 1/6/89
letters from G to, printed 27/3/81, 16/5/83, 4/6/83, 30/1/84, 2/7/84, 13/7/84
meeting with Salisbury unauthorised 23/12/85
misunderstanding with Palmer 21/11/83
Scrutator, writes as 30/1/71
Machiavelli
notes on *Discorsi* 29/4/36
tomb of 19/3/32
machinery, export of 29/12/41, 21/5/42, 23/5/43, 17/6/43, 10/8/43

Macintosh coat 6/11/38
Mackenzie, A. C. *See* operas
Macmillan's Magazine *See* publications
Madagascar 24/10/82 c, 27/11/82 c, 4/12/82 c, 8/8/83 c, 22/8/83 cn, 24/8/83, 22/10/83 ff, 25/10/83 c, 13/11/83 c, 15/11/83, 1/11/92
  no British title to interfere 10/3/83 c
  postal contract and 31/12/84
Madrigal Society 19/6/34
Magdalen College, Oxford 28/1/49, 20/6/55, 24/4/78, 5/4/88, 12/11/88, 13/10/91
  G breakfasts in: a gigantic dissipation 6/2/90
  Holman Hunt's 'May Morning' 9/5/91
Magdeburg 11/11/58
Maggiore, Lake 10/7/32
magistrates
  in Lancashire 12/6/69 c, 23/2/93 c, 27/2/93
  need to appoint liberal magistrates 18/11/93
Mahdi, The *See* Sudan
Mahometans 4/10/81, 15/11/83
  in Uganda 20/9/92 ff
Maida, battle of 9/11/38
Maidenhead 12/6/45
maiden speech
  intended 6/3/33
maiden speech, G's *See* Commons (House of)
Malacca Straits 28/1/74
Mallwyd 8/9/56
Malta 10/3/84
  G's speech on 30/7/90
malt tax 13/3/43, 5/7/53, 12/7/53, 7/3/65, 2/4/73 n, 4/5/80, 7/5/80, 11/5/80, 5/6/80 c, 8/6/80, 21/6/80, 24/6/80, 26/6/80, 6/7/80, 17/8/81
  G misses division on 26/4/33, 30/4/33
Malvern, meeting with Hallam at 13/10/29
Malwood, Lyndhurst (Sir W. Harcourt) 5/6/89
Man, Isle of
  bishop's stipend 5/4/84
  Douglas
    G's speech in 3/10/78
  Falcon's Nest, Port Erin 2/10/78
  Government House 3/10/78
  G's visit to 1/10/78 ff
  King William's College
    G's speech at 2/10/78
  Laxley 4/10/78
  Peel 3/10/78
  Peveril hotel, Douglas 1/10/78
Manchester 7/9/29, 14/2/34 ff, 15/1/52, 10/10/53 ff, 27/9/54, 29/6/57, 17/10/87
  Commercial Association
    supports 1853 budget 28/4/53
  deputation on shipping from 26/2/56
  Eastern question and 8/5/78
  Education Bill of 5/2/52, 11/2/52
  education deputation 2/2/53
  exhibition in
    G lends sculptures to 29/6/57
  Free Trade Hall
    cordial auditory of 23/4/62
    speech in 23/4/62
  G's speeches in 12/3/53, 13/3/53, 23/4/62, 24/4/62, 18/7/65, 25/6/86, 26/6/86, 2/12/89 ff
  Jubilee exhibition 17/10/87
  Lord Mayorality for 6/6/93 c
  Owen's college 8/4/69, 24/4/69
    government money for declined 24/4/69 c, 14/4/71
  ship canal of 4/12/89
  statue of G by Theed for 25/6/77
Manchester constituency, G defeated in 19/7/37 ff
Manchester Guardian
  Uganda and 26/9/92
Manchester School 22/2/55
  trade unions and 5/7/69
Manchester Ship Canal *See* Manchester
mankind
  destinies of affected more by good or evil than by Parliament 30/3/75
Mannheim 21/7/32
Manning, Henry Edward, Cardinal (1808–1892), archbishop of Westminster 1865; G's Anglican friend and confidant, archdeacon of Chichester 1840, convert to Rome over Gorham case 1851, cardinal 1875, 26/11/29 n, 17/3/31, 5/4/35, 10/4/35, 29/3/37 ff, 23/4/37, 28/9/37, 22/11/37, 28/11/37, 19/12/37, 10/2/38, 18/2/38, 21/2/38, 2/5/38, 26/6/39, 20/5/40, 2/7/40, 12/7/40, 23/3/41, 17/5/41, 26/1/42, 19/11/42, 17/1/43, 3/11/43, 29/11/44, 11/2/45, 24/5/45, 11/1/46, 16/3/46, 2/2/49, 22/9/49, 9/6/50, 21/7/50, 2/10/50, 21/11/52, 28/11/52, 7/8/53, 16/9/55, 20/3/61, 28/4/61, 21/10/63, 11/9/66, 21/5/67, 7/8/67, 20/5/68, 21/6/68, 26/7/68, 25/10/69, 27/10/69, 12/3/70 c, 11/3/74, 21/4/74, 20/6/75, 3/3/83, 2/12/83, 30/5/85, 14/7/90, 2/6/92 n
  appears to confirm his Anglicanism 10/7/48
  assisting with *Church Principles* 16/2/40 ff, 25/5/40, 17/7/40
    gives *imprimatur* to 16/8/40
  candidacy as Preacher, Lincoln's Inn 4/11/43

Manning, Henry Edward, Cardinal (*cont.*)
chill indescribable underlays external smoothness of 20/3/61
consulted on G's joining Cabinet 13/5/43, 15/5/43
conversion to Rome 6/3/51, 9/3/51, 16/3/51, 30/3/51, 5/4/51, 6/4/51, 7/4/51
G unmanned by 19/4/51, 11/5/51
darkening prospects for 3/10/50
death of 13/1/92, 14/1/92
differences with G, G's account of 16/11/69
education bill and 27/10/69, 1/3/70
education donation scheme and 10/5/89
G discusses temporal power of Pope with 23/7/64
godfather to W. H. G 16/7/40
Gorham case and 8/3/50 ff, 2/5/50 ff, 16/11/69
G reading proofs of 12/7/40, 27/2/42, 14/11/49
G's recollections of 4/3/93, 17/10/94
G working on MS letters of (216) 13/6/55, 26/10/61
his relations with Newman and 11/11/69
infallibility, sends nine propositions of 23/5/72
in Rome with G 12/12/38, 13/12/38, 18/12/38, 19/12/38, 25/12/38, 26/12/38, 27/12/38, 29/12/38, 1/1/39
Mass in English College 29/12/38
intense conversation with 20/3/46
Irish disestablishment and 12/7/69 ff
Irish Land Bill, G sends copy of 16/2/70
Irish University Bill and 23/12/72, 16/2/73, 3/3/73, 8/3/73, 13/3/73
letters from G to, printed 3/6/69, 12/7/69, 13/7/69, 24/7/69, 25/10/69, 11/11/69, 16/11/69, 23/1/70, 16/2/70, 1/3/70, 26/3/70, 16/4/70, 22/6/70, 2/8/70, 14/8/70, 15/9/70, 12/10/70, 18/10/70, 28/7/71, 10/11/71, 20/2/72, 23/5/72, 13/7/72, 26/8/72, 16/2/73, 1/3/73, 3/3/73, 8/3/73, 13/3/73, 22/1/74, 14/1/82, 19/4/83, 21/2/84, 9/1/86
letters to G to 1851, thought lost 29/5/93
local option and 14/1/82
long talk with G 26/6/64
Maynooth and 8/4/45
Newman and 24/10/43, 28/10/43
on church matters 30/3/41
on Convocation 12/5/44
preaching
G impressed by 25/5/45, 29/4/49
proposed as seeker of Lady Lincoln 7/7/49
Purcell's *Life* of
G assisting in composition of 11/6/87, 29/5/93
sad air of unreality of 21/9/73
sermons read to C. G 23/10/42, 30/10/42, 6/11/42
terrorism in Ireland and 1/3/70
need for Irish bishops to act 1/3/70
thought himself dying, 1847 21/4/74
Tract 90 and 23/3/41
Vatican Council and
ultramontanism of 1/12/69, 16/4/70
Ultra of Ultras 20/12/69
Vaticanism and
devious ways of 2/2/75
G looks black at 5/7/75
Ward's degradation and 9/1/45
See also converts, Ireland, Rome
Mansfield College, Oxford
G dines in 5/2/90 n
Mansion House 23/12/34, 9/4/35
Manzoni, Alessandro
Ode on Napoleon (Cinque Maggio) 4/1/61, 29/7/62, 6/8/62 ff, 22/12/62, 13/1/63, 8/2/88, 24/1/92, 21/2/92, 24/2/92
learned 9/2/38
transcribed for Duchess of Sutherland 8/7/61
Marcus Aurelius
bought in Rome 4/6/32
Margaret Street chapel *See* All Saints (Margaret Street)
Margate 21/8/54
Marksburg castle 4/9/38
Marlborough College
speech to boys at 3/2/77
Marlborough House (Prince of Wales) 20/3/54, 23/6/64, 17/7/72, 19/2/73, 15/5/74, 10/3/75, 23/7/75, 13/7/78, 5/5/80, 6/6/80, 23/2/81, 4/3/82, 28/4/82, 20/11/82, 26/10/84, 3/2/86, 21/7/86, 27/7/89, 14/7/90, 5/7/93, 23/2/94
unSundaylike 3/5/85
Marlborough trust
G trustee of 24/6/68
Mar Lodge 10/9/84
marmalade, G making 19/4/27
marriage
anniversary of 25/7/40, 25/7/41
forgotten 26/7/43
banns not used 29/6/39
divorced women at Court, position of 31/3/81
financial arrangements of 19/6/39, 24/7/39
G and C. G encourage S. Glynne to marry 4/3/49
G's 'deathbed' declaration on fidelity to the marriage bed 7/12/96

ideal of above the ordinary married state 22/4/49
Marriage Bill 3/5/49, 10/5/49, 4/7/49
of G and Catherine Glynne 25/7/39
Golden Wedding celebrations 25/7/88, 25/7/89
warning voice on marriage day 25/7/39
proposals of by G
Caroline Farquhar 3/9/35 ff, 8/6/39, 9/6/39, 13/6/39, 26/11/39
Catherine Glynne 18/1/39 n, 6/2/39, 6/6/39, 8/6/39, 9/6/39 ff
Frances Douglas 7/11/37, 14/11/37, 20/11/37, 17/1/38, 31/1/38, 4/6/38, 19/6/38, 23/6/38, 30/6/38, 13/6/39, 26/11/39
reflections on 6/3/34, 17/6/34, 4/6/35, 16/7/35, 12/2/36, 28/6/36, 4/8/36, 17/12/39, 29/12/41, 28/6/43, 10/8/48, 21/7/58, 22/7/58 n, 23/10/88, 4/8/90
sin formally enhanced during 19/7/48
See also romances
Marriage Bill 25/4/55, 9/5/55 *See also* divorce
Marseilles 22/1/39, 16/7/49 ff, 22/2/51
Cannabière 24/1/39
compared with Edinburgh 24/1/39
Hotel Beauveau 23/1/39
marriage notices in 24/1/39
sales of Scott in 24/1/39
Mary, Queens of Scots, G's view of 14/7/27
Mary, Virgin 2/2/32, 22/9/38, 22/10/38, 2/12/38
Marylebone *See* London
Mass *See* Roman Catholic Church
masses 11/9/61
Jack Sheppard a dangerous book for 11/9/61
See also working classes
Master of the Mint, G as *See* Mint (The)
masturbation? 13/7/29, 17/11/29, 19/2/30, 8/4/30, 12/1/31, 1/4/31
match tax 11/4/71 ff
mathematics
difficulties with 7/12/29, 29/9/30, 2/11/30, 9/11/30 ff, 30/6/31 ff, 20/7/31, 26/11/31
G coached in 3/8/27, 17/8/27, 24/1/28 ff, 6/7/30 ff, 25/11/31
G working 3 hours at Porson's equation 19/8/67
Maurice, John Frederick Denison, Rev. Prof. (1805–1872), broadchurch theologian; member of WEG club, professor in London 1840, in Cambridge 1866 9/2/30, 22/1/31, 27/10/53, 29/10/53, 19/6/77 n
Mauritius
coolie immigration to 5/5/46, 6/5/46, 11/6/46
fortifications of 19/4/71 c
young children in 26/10/71
Maxim gun
G at demonstration of 2/5/85
Max Müller, Friedrich, Prof. (1823–1900), German philologist & orientalist, in Oxford from 1850; professor from 1868 30/1/57, 31/12/67, 31/1/78
Alsace-Lorraine and 8/10/70
at Hawarden 18/12/84, 7/12/92 ff
lecture by 29/5/63
letters from G to, printed 9/10/70, 29/12/70, 30/1/71, 24/2/71, 26/2/71, 28/2/71, 1/3/71, 24/12/72, 10/1/73, 12/2/81
reads G's paper to Oriental Congress 7/9/92 n
May, Thomas Erskine, Sir (1815–1886), 1st Baron Farnborough (1886), Clerk to House of Commons 1871–86 6/2/61, 27/10/71 c, 2/2/74, 10/2/74 n, 27/3/76, 4/7/78, 26/7/80, 23/10/80, 15/11/80 c, 2/2/81, 8/6/81, 2/12/81, 31/1/82, 24/4/82, 3/7/82, 26/10/82, 24/1/84, 30/1/84, 5/2/84, 24/2/85, 23/6/85, 13/7/85, 18/1/86, 22/1/86, 5/4/86, 15/4/86, 6/3/90
1867 Reform Bill and 1/4/67
attending cabinet 30/1/82 c, 1/2/82 c
Franco-Prussian war and Parliament 22/7/70
funeral of 24/5/86
letters from G to, printed 22/7/70, 19/6/80, 18/4/86
liberal influence of 30/1/84
peerage for 18/4/86
retirement of 16/4/86, 17/4/86
Mayence
troops in 21/7/32
Maynòoth College
disestablishment and 22/2/69, 29/3/69
G's visit to
a saddening impression: what havock have we made of the vineyard of the Lord 5/11/77
statutes and debates, summary of 18/7/40
Maynooth grant 20/1/44, 12/2/44, 13/2/44, 28/2/44, 8/7/44, 23/11/44, 25/11/44, 9/1/45, 28/1/45, 3/4/45, 11/4/45, 21/5/45, 10/5/52, 11/5/52, 23/2/53, 18/11/68 n
a Trojan horse 21/5/45
ended 6/5/69 n
G's comments on in cabinet 12/2/44 ff
G votes for 20/7/42, 18/4/45 n

Maynooth grant (*cont.*)
like a nightmare to G 25/4/45
possible destruction of government by 20/1/44
reflections and speech on 11/4/45, 29/4/45
G rereads 26/3/68
speech displeases govt. 29/4/45
votes on 26/6/37, 20/7/42
See also Gaskell, Ireland, memoranda, Peel, resignation considered
Mechanics' Institute, secretary of 28/10/62
Medical Act (1858) Amendment Bill 17/5/73 c
medical students *See* Guy's Hospital, jingoism, Middlesex Hospital
medicines
arnica 2/7/93
arrowroot 24/8/54, 25/1/89, 12/4/94
atrophine 16/4/94
barley water 22/10/81
Batley drops 4/10/47
bismuth 14/4/94, 17/4/94, 1/9/94
blistering liquid 27/8/49, 6/4/50
blue pill 9/10/48, 3/9/49, 18/9/49, 28/4/53, 29/4/53, 11/7/54, 7/10/56
brandy 24/8/54
calomel 2/10/36, 22/2/47, 3/8/47, 4/9/49, 6/4/50, 1/1/51, 1/6/51, 30/11/51, 11/1/87
castor oil 25/10/48, 6/11/74, 16/6/79, 26/9/79, 1/10/82, 13/4/84, 6/8/85, 15/2/91
chloroform 14/8/55, 26/7/56, 13/9/85
croton oil 30/11/51
Dover's powder 6/4/50
Epsom salts 25/4/28
fomenting 23/9/47
Galvanism (used on R. Cavendish) 19/11/73
ice 15/9/53
ipecacuanha 22/10/87
James's powder pills 4/2/60
laudanum 14/8/55
lead (given in error) 8/2/56
mustard emetic 24/8/54
mustard plaister 2/10/36, 4/2/60
peppermint water 25/10/48
poultices 23/9/47, 5/9/53 ff, 16/9/73, 31/7/80
linseed 22/10/87
quinine 26/9/65, 30/4/72, 14/9/80, 28/5/83, 15/12/83, 13/9/85, 1/8/86 ff
Salicine 6/1/93
sal-volatile 12/9/56
scammony pill 30/11/51
Seidlitz powder 3/8/47
Senna 29/8/49
sleeping draught 2/1/85
snow (as anaesthetic) 7/1/51
terebine 1/4/94
vaccination 19/7/52
Melbourne government
dismissal of 18/11/34 ff
fall of 3/5/41 ff, 9/5/41, 4/6/41, 21/8/41 ff, 27/8/41
memoranda
1853–4 tax reductions 9/4/53
Alderney harbour 17/3/53
amendment of Toleration Act 13/8/48
Athanasian Creed 8/6/73
Atlantic telegraph 1/8/62 ff
Australia Bill 22/8/49
Australian mint 4/3/53
Austrian treaty 13/2/65
bank profits 27/11/60, 28/11/60
banks and discount houses 17/10/60
bastard sugars 20/2/44
Biblical exaggeration 13/7/90
British Museum 13/11/61
burials bill 11/8/80
Burlington House 23/3/54
Burlington House, plans for 21/10/59
business of B. of T. 1/2/45
Canada Address 1/6/46, 3/6/46
Canadian defences 22/1/46, 3/3/46
Canadian duties 20/1/46, 20/2/46
cathedral emoluments 17/3/56
chancery funds 27/12/60
China 22/9/59
China compensation 2/8/61
church rate reform 26/7/59
church rates 27/11/53, 25/4/63, 11/8/65
Circassians' transport 3/6/64
civil service exchanges 20/6/65
civil service reform 23/1/54
Clergy Relief Bill 6/5/49, 22/8/49
Clydesdale Junction railway 30/4/50
coinage 21/8/62
colonial church 13/1/50, 23/1/55
colonial governors' superannuation 22/2/64
colonial policy 1/12/48
commending European intervention in American civil war 7/7/62
conversion of funds 19/2/53, 9/3/53
coolie immigration to Mauritius 6/5/46
copper ores 23/3/46
copyright 22/2/44, 2/1/45
cotton loan 7/12/71
customs duties 11/3/53
Dee minerals 30/7/67
defence against Layard's attack 23/7/55
defence of Canada 11/7/64 ff
Dover harbour 3/7/73, 4/7/73
Eastern question 11/11/53
Edmunds' case 14/2/65, 16/2/65
education schedule 13/2/53
Egyptian finance 15/7/84, 29/12/84

Essays and Reviews 26/3/64 ff
estimates for gross expenditure 2/2/53
European intervention in American civil war 23/10/62 ff
Exchequer Bills 19/2/53, 17/5/61
expenditure 19/4/60 ff
export of machinery 23/5/43
Fasque chapel 1/3/46
finance 16/2/56, 20/2/56
foreign and colonial duties 8/2/45
fortifications 14/1/60, 22/1/60, 23/5/60, 16/7/60
framework knitters 5/12/43
franchise and redistribution 21/11/83
French treaty 9/10/71, 2/11/71
future punishment 13/11/64
government property 7/6/73 n
G prevents division of New Zealand 14/5/46
Granville's debts 6/5/92, 8/6/92
Greek mythology and Symonds 27/9/73
Greek question 23/3/54
Harrison's case 13/2/65
Hawarden estate 8/8/51
Hawarden estate affairs 10/1/48, 27/1/48
Hawarden estate: male succession to 4/11/89
Hawarden estate residue 1/1/52
Hawarden reversion and trust scheme 29/8/65, 24/9/80 ff
Helen G's religious profession 8/2/80
Heligoland 15/4/43
H. J. G's will 7/2/81
house tax 17/11/54, 6/8/64
house tax and 1851 budget 8/4/51
Hudson's Bay Co. 28/4/46
imperial veto 20/12/54
income tax 3/1/53 ff, 18/1/53, 9/2/53, 31/3/53, 15/4/53
  abolition of 12/2/62
India (for cabinet) 10/6/53
Indian government 12/4/58
international arbitration and the three rules 21/10/73
Ionian constitution 1/1/59, 11/1/59, 19/1/59, 21/1/59
Ionian finances 27/2/64
Irish Authority 24/2/86, 1/3/86
Irish land purchase finance 11/3/86
Irish railways 13/9/69
Irish tithe rent charges 3/6/72
Irish universities 5/12/72
iron-clads 7/10/63
Japan 9/12/62
Java duties 4/7/44
Jewish disabilities 18/4/45
Kennedy affair 21/1/55
Kensington estate 17/10/53
law courts 5/12/60, 27/4/61
legacy & probate duties 7/3/53
life of Christ 16/10/59
Malta 15/6/46 n
Maynooth and Church of Ireland 19/6/45, 2/7/45
Moravians at the Cape 6/6/46
Mysore 16/4/44
National Debt Commission 24/11/54
naval force 18/12/60
New Zealand land claims 20/3/46
nomination of bishops 31/1/48
nonconformists, Roman and otherwise 10/6/88
Oak Farm & S. Glynne's affairs 3/10/48, 5/10/48
Olympian religion 24/2/71
opium 29/1/44
opposing occupation of Labuan 18/6/46
Oxford reform 10/6/45, 21/6/45, 27/12/53
Palmerston and paper duties 3/8/60
Pantonian Trust 9/2/48, 10/2/48
paper duty and taxing power of the two Houses 30/6/60
papermakers 20/4/61
Peel's memoirs 4/10/51
Portuguese duty 27/2/44
Post Office 17/10/59
Prince of Wales' income 19/2/63
private issues 21/11/63
private secretariat 8/7/85
property and debts, G's 11/1/61
Railway Dept. of B. of T. 25/7/44
railways 3/2/44, 18/5/44, 22/5/44
railways, redemption of 6/8/64
redistribution and franchise 21/11/83
reform of Oxford University 2/4/53
religious disabilities 2/2/91
retrenchment 29/8/43
R. I. Wilberforce's conversion 4/10/54
Roman Catholic Irish education 14/4/44, 6/5/44
Roman question 27/3/63
Rome, renewal of relations with 18/4/44 ff
  Peel's view of 22/4/44
royal grants 18/7/89
royal marriage settlements 14/2/61, 11/12/65, 29/6/89
Russia and Afghanistan 13/4/85
Scheldt tolls 6/3/62, 10/12/62
Schleswig-Holstein 4/12/63
Seaforth church 24/5/57, 25/1/71
Seaforth estate 30/10/56
Shaftesbury's life 19/3/87
Sir J. G's last days 9/12/51 ff
slave trade 9/5/49
South Sea Company 9/8/53
St. Deiniol's library 12/11/88
St. Deiniol's trust 14/9/89
subscription at Oxford 6/7/63

memoranda (*cont.*)
succession duty and insurance 9/11/61 n
Sudan, military position in 8/4/85
suffragan bishops 19/7/64
sugar duties 29/8/43, 4/9/43, 10/10/43, 19/6/44 ff
Sunday trains 29/7/44
superannuation 12/1/55
tea duties 26/12/46
testamentary dispositions of S. Glynne 3/7/55, 9/7/55
the Bath 2/4/46
transportation 7/2/46
treasury bonds 13/3/53
Treaty of Washington and the indirect claims 19/2/72
troops for Sebastopol 22/6/54
Turkey 8/3/44
Turkish budget 12/12/63
Turkish loan 22/2/64
Van Diemen's Land education 21/2/46
Venetia 20/12/60
vote of credit 21/7/54
Wakefield's New Zealand proposals 27/3/46
West Indies immigration 25/2/46
widows' army pensions 21/11/59
Wolseley and the Sudan 1/3/85
wood duties 12/9/65
Zollverein 2/7/44, 18/10/44, 19/10/44, 30/10/44
See also essays and papers
memoranda (printed in *Diaries*)
Afghanistan and Russia 20/3/85
Alabama arbitration 1/4/71
Alsace and German Lorraine 23/11/70
annexation of Alsace-Lorraine 25/9/70
army estimates 12/12/71
army purchase abolition 13/10/70
army purchase abolition and liberal support 8/3/71
army reform 11/11/79
Arrears Bill 10/5/82
Atlantic telegraph 2/4/62
Australian tariffs 26/1/72
Austria, commercial treaty with 13/2/65, 13/11/65
Balaam 7/5/57
Balkans and Turkish policy 14/5/80, 21/5/80
Bank Charter Act, reform of 31/3/73
Beach and redistribution 5/11/84
being, constituent parts of 31/10/86
bodily wants 30/11/56
'Box and Cox' verses 21/11/88
budget of 1863 3/3/63, 12/3/63, 21/3/63, 8/4/63
budget of 1874 19/1/74
building tax 23/4/65
cabinet and Italy, retrenchment and reform 30/5/60
Canadian confederation and defences 19/1/65
Canadian defence and withdrawal of British troops 19/1/70
Canadian railways and finance 14/12/61
Carlyle's qualities 3/6/82
Carnarvon, conversation on cabinet with 26/5/78
causes assisting conservatism 14/8/82
Cetewayo and Zululand 22/6/83
charities and income tax exemption 24/4/63
China and faults of British policy 17/2/63
Christianity 1/7/55
church, character of 30/5/80
Church music 7/1/94
church rates, proposals to end compulsory powers for 4/2/66
church rates and Cross's Bill 7/6/61
commercial treaty with Austria 13/2/65, 13/11/65
Confederacy and sovereignty 28/4/71
Confederate agent's view of civil war 31/7/62
conservatism, decay of 10/12/85
Conservatives, decline of reverence among 15/8/90
Contagious Diseases Acts 15/7/71
contagious diseases in the forces 18/2/63
country bank notes 3/3/64, 1/4/64
Creation 22/6/94
dangers of the age 26/9/81
Darwinism 17/12/81
death duties 26/11/80
death duties, reform of 2/10/80
Declaration on absence of infidelity by G to the marriage bed 7/12/96
Decline of reverence among conservatives 15/8/90
Denmark, non-interference in 24/6/64, 25/6/64
Dilke, the liberal party and home rule 13/3/91
Dilke's motion on Egypt 18/4/93
dissenters and church rates 4/5/66
dissolution 1868 1/5/68, 6/5/68
dissolution and the Queen 17/5/86, 18/5/86
dissolution in January 1874 20/1/74
Eastern question 27/9/80, 1/10/80
Eastern question: the Ignatiev letters 21/3/77
economics 6/5/43
education bill: rate provided schools 29/5/70
education vote 2/1/60
Egypt, settlement of 15/9/82

Egypt, troops for 21/6/82
Egypt and the British occupation 18/4/93, 20/4/93
Egypt and the crisis of 1893 17/1/93
ejaculatory prayer 12/10/56
election defeat 1886, causes and consequences of 10/7/86
elections contested by G, list of 15/2/92
establishments eccesiastical 6/3/64
ethics 4/1/43
Exchequer Bills Bill 21/11/60
Franchise and Seats Bill settlement 28/11/84
Franchise Bill and the present situation (for the Queen) 13/8/84, 19/8/84
  abstract of 25/8/84
franchise reform 22/1/66, 29/1/66, 2/2/66, 15/2/66
French government's appeal to neutral powers 30/9/70
general election 1885, plans for 7/8/85
God and the Psalms 20/5/94
Gold standard and India 2/9/92
Gordon's relief 31/7/84
government annuities plan 5/3/64
Government as an art and science in ancient times 11/6/88
Government of Ireland Bill 1886
  2nd. Reading 5/5/86
  Irish members and the Commons 11/5/86
Government of Ireland Bill 1893 11/11/92
Government of Ireland Bill and Morley's report 5/12/92
Government of Ireland Bill to be reintroduced amended 26/5/86
government purchase of railways 19/12/64
Grammar of Assent 6/12/81, 14/8/82
G's audience of the Pope 22/10/66
G's position during tory minority government 16/6/85
Harcourt and the coming government 17/6/92
Harcourt's Irish finance proposals 18/1/93
Hartington's position 18/2/86
Hawarden estate reversion 20/12/65
heredity 17/12/81
Herodotus 26/12/92
higher education in Ireland 8/6/65
history and home rule 17/7/86
Hodder's *Life* of Shaftesbury 19/3/87
Home Rule and British politics 28/10/92
Home Rule and the Cabinet 30/1/86
Home Rule and the Session 31/10/92
Home Rule: prime points of difficulty 8/8/89
Home Rulers' place of seating in the Commons 12/6/93
hours of trial, sorrow, care and evil 30/11/56
house tax 23/4/65
Idola Templi 19/12/81
Ignatiev's letters and the Eastern question 21/3/77
Incidental to resignation 2/1/96
India and the gold standard 2/9/92
Indian army 27/1/60
individuality in literature 3/6/82
infallibility 7/8/63
insomnia 7/1/83
interview with Aristarchi on Balkans 21/5/80
interview with Capt. O'Shea 5/5/82
interview with Musurus on Balkans 14/5/80
Ionian Islands' annexation to Greece 7/7/63
Ionian Islands Report 28/12/58
Ireland and the future 4/5/82
Ireland and the government 5/3/86
Irish church disestablishment 18/12/68
Irish Convocation 20/2/64
Irish crime levels 24/1/70
Irish deputation and Parnell's assertions 5/12/90
Irish disestablishment and the Lords 14/7/69, 17/7/69, 18/7/69, 19/7/69, 20/7/69, 21/7/69, 22/7/69
Irish disestablishment and the poor 1/12/68
Irish Government 1886 (in vol. xi, Appendix II) 20/3/86
Irish Government Finance 1886 (in vol. xi, Appendix II) 31/3/86
Irish Government finance 1893 24/11/92, 14/1/93, 18/1/93, 20/1/93, 3/5/93, 16/5/93, 25/5/93
Irish Government. Points prepared for conversation with Parnell 18/12/89
Irish Home Rule 23/12/85
Irish Home Rule and the political situation 26/12/85
Irish land 3/12/69, 14/12/69, 10/3/70, 22/3/70
Irish land and Irish government 14/3/86
Irish Land Bill 1881, provisions of 14/12/80
Irish land (in vol.xi, Appendix II) 20/2/86
Irish land law 9/12/80
Irish law and order 30/4/82
Irish members and liberal reunion 26/5/87
Irish nationalism; its growth and character 4/6/88
Irish question and the government 12/12/85
Irish representation at Westminster 15/11/92, 22/11/92
Irish security and secret service money 9/6/82
Irish tactics 5/12/88

memoranda (printed in *Diaries*) (*cont.*)
Irish University Bill 18/1/73
Irish whips and Parnell's leadership 4/12/90, 5/12/90
Italian policy 7/1/60
Italy
quasi-unification of 30/6/59
unification of 26/3/61
justice 12/3/57
Land Purchase Bill, retention of 23/3/86
land tenures in England 17/9/69
land tenures in Ireland 17/9/69
law and order in Ireland 30/4/82
lay power in the church 15/8/69
life assurance 27/2/64
local autonomy in Turkey 24/7/80
London Municipal Bill and the police 11/5/83
Lords and the Reform Bill (for the Queen) 13/8/84, 19/8/84
abstract of 25/8/84
malt duty 7/3/65
meeting with Chamberlain on Ireland and reconciliation 5/4/87
method, in disposal of time and money 22/8/58
military organisation and army purchase 13/10/70
monarchy 29/8/40
Moroccan loan 26/9/61
Munster, interview with 30/9/80
national freedom 24/9/81
nationality and the Greeks 7/9/63
navy estimates 1893–4 1/1/94, 4/1/94, 9/1/94, 20/1/94
negotiations with incoming conservative government, 1885 16/6/85
Newman's theology 1/2/85
obstruction and devolution in the Commons 18/10/80 ff, 23/10/80, 11/11/80, 23/8/81
obstruction in the Commons 8/7/82
old age and physical decline 13/9/94
Old Catholics and Rome 30/9/74
original sin 6/12/48
Palmerston and paper duties repeal 26/5/60
paper duties and the Lords 1/7/60
Parnell and the O'Shea divorce case 21/11/90, 22/11/90, 28/11/90, 30/11/90, 4/12/90, 5/12/90, 29/12/90
Parnell and the Tory Government 31/12/85
Parnell interview and the future Home Rule Bill 23/12/89
Parnell's visit to Hawarden 18/12/89, 23/12/89
Payment of M.P.s 22/7/92
Peel and the Peelites 12/12/48
Platonic monotheism and the Jews 15/6/88
politics 29/8/40, 6/12/48, 14/8/82, 11/6/88, 5/12/88, 15/8/90, 19/3/94
powers of the Treasury 2/12/62
procedures for releasing budget details 1/4/62
Programme for Session of 1893 20/7/92, 1/8/93
propositions on prayer 9/12/75, 15/12/75
rate provided schools (three parts) 29/5/70
rate schools and elective boards 25/11/71
reasons for maintaining Aberdeen's government 4/2/55
rebellion and the Confederacy 28/4/71
redistribution 29/1/66, 5/11/84
Reformation and the Church of England 16/8/88
Reform Bill 1867 and the franchises 16/5/67
Reform Bill conferences 13/11/84, 22/11/84, 26/11/84, 28/11/84
relief of Gordon 31/7/84
religion 21/12/48, 31/5/88, 26/12/92
Report on constitution of the Ionian Islands 28/12/58, 6/1/59, 15/2/59, 23/4/59 ff
resignation following 1886 election defeat 12/7/86
resignation of leadership of the liberal party 14/1/75
resignation of the Premiership 21/2/94, 22/2/94, 24/2/94, 28/2/94, 3/3/94, 10/3/94, 19/3/94
retirement, reflections on 25/7/94
Round Table conference 26/2/87
Rousseau 24/9/81
Royal grants 9/7/89
Russell and paper duties repeal 26/5/60
Russell government's breakup over Reform Bill 26/6/66
Russia and the Pendjeh incident 21/4/85
Schleswig-Holstein 5/5/64
secret service money and Ireland 9/6/82
Session of 1893 31/10/92
settlement of Egypt 15/9/82
Shaftesbury's *Life* 19/3/87
Simon de Montford 12/3/72
sin 26/10/45
sleeplessness 7/1/83
Smash of 1886 10/7/86
state and religion 19/6/45
statement of assets and liabilities 1/6/74
St. Deiniol's Library: heads of purposes 12/11/88
Sudan and Wolseley's expedition 11/4/85
sugar refiners and Convention of 1863 14/3/72
testamentary memorandum 1/1/79

theology 30/8/40, 20/2/48, 1/1/55, 9/9/55, 7/5/57, 9/10/59, 2/11/60, 7/8/63, 12/3/72, 6/12/81, 19/12/81, 14/8/82, 1/2/85, 31/5/88, 15/6/88, 2/11/90, 31/12/93, 20/5/94
Thirty Nine Articles 31/12/93
tobacco duties 31/1/63
toryism's two legs 10/12/85
Transvaal, suzerainty over 12/3/81
Turkey, local autonomy in 24/7/80
Uganda 20/9/92, 24/9/92, 30/9/92
Verses on death 13/7/94
Vincentius 12/3/72
Whitbread's plan for a Resolution on home rule 19/5/86
will and self-determination 2/3/91
withdrawal from Egypt 20/4/93
women's suffrage and the 1884 Reform Bill 9/5/84
work for next session
1866 31/8/65
memory
book and life memory go ill together 8/8/64
weakness of 6/11/86
Mentmore Towers (Rothschild/Rosebery) 19/3/64, 17/4/79, 7/5/80, 10/9/80, 13/8/81, 6/2/86, 4/8/88, 9/12/91
G plants tree at 21/4/79
unsabbatical 20/3/64
Mentone 21/1/67
Mercers' Company 27/5/57
Mersey Tunnel *See* Liverpool
Merton College, Oxford 20/1/34, 22/1/34, 24/1/34, 8/2/34, 12/2/45
mesmerism
Leger's results seem mostly very true to G 27/3/52
mesmerism, G's interest in 23/8/48, 9/9/48
to be tried on Lady Glynne? 9/9/48
Messina, Straits of 5/11/38
Metaphysical Society
discussion led by Huxley 17/11/69
discussion on miracles 9/11/75, 15/2/76
discussion on Newman and mysteries 12/1/75
G President of 12/1/75, 9/3/75, 9/11/75, 9/4/78
Lord A. Russell on persistence of religious feeling 9/5/76
Methodists 25/9/32, 17/5/41, 18/6/41, 19/12/43
educational grants to 17/6/43
See also Burials Bill, disestablishment, Elementary Education Bill (religious difficulties), nonconformists
Metropolitan line
G a shareholder in 1/2/61, 18/11/62
G on opening train of 24/5/62
Metropolitan Loans Bill 6/8/69 c
Metropolitan Schools Committee 8/2/41
Metropolitan Visiting Association
planned by G 2/12/43 ff, 8/12/43 ff
Mexico
protest against Indian invasion of Honduras from 28/11/72 c
Meyerbeer *See* operas
Michelangelo 4/4/32, 15/4/32, 19/4/32, 5/5/32, 1/10/38, 2/10/38, 9/10/38, 22/12/38, 9/1/39, 18/1/39
microscopes, exhibition of 12/6/33
Middlesbrough
G at iron works of 9/10/62
G's visit to 25/8/62 n, 9/10/82
speeches at 9/10/62
Middlesex Hospital
G's Address to students at 24/6/58
Middle Temple 18/5/70, 14/11/72, 4/12/82, 14/11/83
G looks over 7/12/60, 8/11/64
Midlothian campaign, 1st
plan and preparations for 14/11/79 ff
reflections on 28/12/79
speeches of
Aberfeldy 1/12/79
Dalkeith 26/11/79
Dunfermline 1/12/79
Edinburgh, Music Hall 25/11/79
Edinburgh, Waverley Market 29/11/79
from train 24/11/79, 8/12/79
Glasgow 4/12/79
Hamilton 6/12/79
Inverkeithing 1/12/79
list of speeches and size of audiences, printed 11/12/79
Motherwell 6/12/79
Perth 1/12/79
publication of 9/12/79 ff, 20/12/79, 7/1/80
West Calder 27/11/79
triumphant procession at start of 24/11/79
undertaken at Granville's request 23/1/80 n
Midlothian campaign, 2nd
1880 election campaign 16/3/80 ff, 2/4/80
Midlothian campaign, 3rd
1885 election campaign 9/11/85 ff
Address, printed 3/12/85
G good for two or three speeches in 29/9/85
Midlothian campaign, 4th
1886 election campaign 17/6/86 ff
Address for 9/6/86, 10/6/86 ff
speeches edited by W. H. G 8/7/86
Midlothian campaign, 5th
1892 election campaign 29/6/92 ff
Address 22/6/92
Midlothian result much below expectation 13/7/92

Midlothian constituency
G paying own expenses 1886 8/6/86
G's retirement from 29/1/94
home rule and 30/4/86 ff, 4/7/93
Liberal Unionist Association of 10/4/88 n
negotiations about 16/5/78, 17/5/78, 24/6/78, 8/1/79 n, 29/1/79, 27/6/85
Granville's express sanction 24/10/82
G will never sit for another seat 27/6/85
invitation accepted 30/1/79
speeches on Reform Bill 1884 in 30/8/84 ff
visits to 29/8/84 ff, 9/11/85 ff, 27/9/93
plans for 19/8/82, 9/9/82, 30/12/82, 5/1/83, 7/1/83, 8/1/83, 24/8/83, 11/7/84, 22/7/84, 16/8/84 ff, 6/9/93, 9/9/93
See also Edinburgh, Primrose
Milan 6/7/32 ff, 21/9/38 ff, 30/7/49, 28/2/59, 6/10/66, 21/12/88
Cathedral 22/9/38, 1/3/59, 7/10/66
china shopping in 1/3/59
land tenure in 21/9/38
protestants in 8/7/32
S. Maria delle Grazie ('Last Supper') 22/9/38
Milbank penitentiary
committee of 7/10/42, 17/3/43
militarism in Europe 20/1/94
G declines to see England set the world in arms 20/1/94
G warns cabinet of 9/1/94
Morley and 4/1/94, 7/1/94
See also Germany, Italy
military reviews
Hyde Park, G moved to tears by 17/5/33
Militia 6/3/69 c, 30/11/70 c, 23/5/82 c
embodiment of 20/7/82, 26/3/85 n, 27/3/85 c
Local Militia Bill 20/2/52 n, 26/4/52
reform of
G's memorandum on, printed 13/10/70
See also army
Mill, John Stuart (1806–1873), liberal M.P. (1865), philosopher and economist 31/7/40, 11/7/65, 21/7/66, 20/5/67, 12/6/68, 23/10/68, 13/11/73, 5/9/88, 20/9/92, 18/10/92
death of discussed with the Queen 13/5/73
eternal punishment and 16/11/73 n
G and Courtney's *Life* of 5/9/88
letters from G to, printed 3/6/69
memorial meeting for
birth control question and 19/5/73
G declines to attend, but ready to serve on committee 16/5/73
most open mind of his generation 3/10/92
toleration of atheists and 11/6/81
Millais, John Everett, Sir (1829–1896), artist; painted G's portrait four times 25/4/77, 30/5/81, 10/2/85, 25/2/85, 26/9/87, 17/5/89 n, 3/5/92
at Hawarden 13/10/84 ff
baronetcy for 24/6/85
letters from G to, printed 24/6/85
studio of, visited by G 13/3/73
G meets Lillie Langtry at 26/1/82 n
See also portraits of G (Millais)
Mill Hill School
G speaks and presents prizes at 11/6/79
Milnes, Richard Monckton (1809–1885), 1st Baron Houghton (1863), G's schoolfriend; author, wit and poet, Peelite M.P. 26/11/29, 28/11/29 ff, 14/4/32 ff, 19/4/32, 29/4/32, 5/5/32, 15/5/32, 4/7/56, 16/7/58, 17/3/59, 20/4/61, 4/6/64, 2/7/67, 13/3/73 c, 3/5/73, 10/6/75, 28/3/77, 18/4/81, 8/8/81, 3/12/82, 21/5/85, 11/9/88 n
at Hawarden 19/10/55, 18/1/73, 15/10/82, 22/9/88 ff
attack on G's Whitby speech on London press 13/9/71
Crimean war and 19/10/55
Demon, not of Demagogism but of Demophilism, thinks G possessed by 13/9/71 n
letters from G to, printed 13/9/71, 4/5/81
mismanagement of assists G and government 28/2/60
pornographic library of 6/7/83 n
Reid's biography of 7/11/90 ff
G's review of 14/11/90 ff
Milton, John
G deplores political conduct of 14/10/26
Paradise Lost
notes on 13/1/36
See also divorce (G's article on)
mind
basis of G's political mind in finance and philanthropy 29/12/96
character of 20/7/33
decline of leading to revival? 19/8/79
ministries *See* governments
Minley Manor, Farnborough 12/5/93
Mint, The
G as Master of 6/9/41, 29/9/41, 19/7/42, 18/10/43
Pyx, trial of 22/6/42, 9/2/44
new coinage of 5/11/92
minutes of cabinets *See* cabinet
miracles *See* Gladstone (Helen Jane), Naples, Newman, Roman Catholic Church
mirth
G's reflections on 30/11/56
miscarriages 9/7/42
missions overseas 6/12/29
Mitchelstown *See* Ireland
Modane 29/2/32, 30/10/50, 30/12/87

Modena 26/9/38
Moel Famma 22/8/55
Mold 27/10/52, 29/9/56, 2/9/87
agricultural show at 20/9/71
Agricultural Show at
G addresses 24/9/62, 19/8/73
election riot in 8/7/41
floods and legal action against railway at 15/10/73, 27/11/73
G electioneering in 23/3/57 ff, 26/3/57, 28/3/57, 30/3/57, 7/4/57
library of
G presents books to 15/11/91
Moldavia 4/5/58, 23/11/70
Molière *See* plays seen
Molly Maguires *See* Ireland
Monad *See* Hawarden
monarchy 28/5/35
compared to King of Kings 10/4/42
danger to unless Prince of Wales employed 9/3/72
isolated and endangered by Lords' rejection of Reform Bill 25/8/84
Old Testament and 29/8/40
poor reputation of 25/6/71
power to dismiss ministers of 16/10/93
stronger than under William IV 10/5/80
Mona's Herald, publisher of 8/10/78
monasteries *See* Roman Catholic Church
Monckton Milnes *See* Milnes
money
currency in circulation 28/11/72 c
G denies fall in value of 28/1/73
G's memorandum on reform of Bank Charter Act, printed 31/3/73
G's worries about
prayer for 29/12/49
Lowe's plan to reform currency 21/12/70, 22/12/70, 31/3/71, 26/11/72 c, 28/11/72 c
theology, G's reflections on and 1/1/55
See also bimetallism
Monk Bretton *See* Dodson
Monte Carlo
'wicked': observed from yacht 24/2/83
Monte Cassino 22/5/32, 23/5/32, 3/12/38, 19/10/66 n, 18/2/69, 21/2/84
abbot Papalettere of 19/10/66 n, 24/10/66
G discusses with Italian ministers in Florence 5/1/67, 7/1/67, 14/1/67
G dreaming at 27/12/66
G's speech on 31/7/66
visit to 27/12/66, 28/12/66
delayed 11/12/66 n
Montenegro 17/7/80 c, 25/9/80, 27/9/80, 30/9/80 c, 27/10/80, 19/4/81, 8/10/85
G's article on Montenegro
a holy work 14/4/77, 15/4/77, 19/4/77
keeps him warm, even hot, while writing 19/4/77
See also Gladstone (Herbert), publications
Montrose 17/10/44
representation of 28/7/47, 29/7/47
Montrose, Duke of, G votes for 26/5/27
Montrose Standard 14/9/37
Moody-Sankey meetings
G at 25/4/75, 29/4/75, 16/5/75
moon
and preparation for death 23/9/47
Moor Farm *See* Hawarden Castle
Moor Park (Lord R. Grosvenor) 29/1/53, 2/4/72
Moral Reform Union 8/12/90 n
Moravian missionaries 15/1/34
Mordaunt divorce *See* Edward VII
Morley, John (1838–1923), 1st Viscount Morley of Blackburn, editor, *Fortnightly Review* 1867–82, editor, *Pall Mall Gazette* 1880–2, liberal M.P. 1883; Irish secretary 1886, 1892–5 29/2/68, 17/5/79, 18/5/79, 13/4/80 n, 21/4/80 ff, 28/9/80, 5/4/82, 31/7/85, 11/10/85, 16/2/86 c, 20/3/86 ff, 16/7/86 ff, 20/8/86, 16/11/86 ff, 30/12/86, 1/3/87 ff, 20/5/87, 23/5/87, 9/6/87, 8/5/88, 25/6/88, 10/7/88 ff, 13/11/88 ff, 3/12/88 ff, 15/3/89 ff, 25/6/89, 10/7/89 ff, 18/3/90 ff, 16/6/90 ff, 11/12/90, 28/1/91 ff, 4/5/91 ff, 6/6/91 ff, 30/6/91, 27/7/91 ff, 3/3/92 ff, 28/4/92 ff, 13/6/92, 17/6/92 ff, 27/7/92 ff, 11/11/92 ff, 11/1/93 ff, 16/1/93 ff, 4/3/93 ff, 15/3/93 ff, 16/5/93, 10/6/93 ff, 19/6/93 ff, 11/8/93, 5/11/93, 27/2/94 ff, 31/3/94, 25/7/94
Acton's library and 9/6/90 n
at Althorp 7/12/91 ff
at Hawarden 17/12/70, 1/11/86, 28/11/86 ff, 13/8/87 ff, 11/10/87, 13/9/88 ff, 18/10/89 ff, 30/9/90 ff, 7/9/92, 9/12/92 ff
Chamberlain and 26/4/86, 13/8/87
Church of England and 27/10/80
coming government and offices in 3/7/92
Declaration on absence of infidelity by G to the marriage bed, opened for Morley 1900 7/12/96 n
diary of, extracts from 15/1/86 n, 22/3/86 n, 23/3/86 n, 27/3/86 n, 31/3/86 n, 5/4/86 n, 14/4/86 n, 11/5/86 n, 14/5/86 n, 18/5/86 n, 27/5/86 n, 8/6/86 n
disestablishment and 9/3/86
G cannot help liking 10/3/77

Morley, John (*cont.*)
Government of Ireland Bill and 12/3/86 ff, 26/5/86 ff
negotiations with Parnell on 31/3/86, 3/4/86, 5/4/86 n, 9/7/86 n
Government of Ireland Bill and Morley's report, G's memorandum on, printed 5/12/92
G's appraisal of his *Life of Cobden* 24/10/81
G's best stay 6/11/92, 9/12/92
G selfishly talks down 22/2/91
G's envoy to Rosebery 6/11/92
has sold his soul for Ireland 11/2/94
home rule and 15/1/86 ff, 22/3/86, 23/3/86 ff
G's plan for *Hand-Book of Home Rule* 8/7/86, 30/11/86
home rule party and 8/12/86, 15/11/92
in Biarritz with G 17/12/91 ff
Irish secretary 1886 31/1/86 ff, 12/3/86 ff, 10/4/86 ff
Irish secretary 1892–5 19/8/92 ff, 26/9/92 ff
letters from G to, printed 27/10/80, 16/10/81, 24/10/81, 17/8/82, 26/9/82, 25/10/83, 2/2/86, 22/3/86, 3/4/86, 19/4/86, 20/4/86, 21/4/86, 8/5/86, 12/5/86, 14/5/86, 3/6/86, 9/7/86, 8/12/86, 25/12/86, 26/8/92, 16/9/92, 26/9/92, 10/10/92, 15/10/92, 17/10/92, 9/11/92, 11/11/92, 12/11/92, 15/11/92, 16/11/92, 26/11/92, 13/12/92, 28/12/92, 2/1/93, 12/1/93, 17/1/93, 22/1/93, 15/2/93, 10/5/93, 14/5/93, 25/5/93, 30/5/93, 9/6/93, 10/6/93, 15/9/93, 29/9/93, 14/10/93, 14/12/93, 28/12/93, 5/1/94, 7/1/94, 11/1/94, 29/1/94
navy estimates crisis and 14/12/93 ff, 28/12/93 ff
arranges G's withdrawal to Biarritz 10/1/94
seems sympathetic to G's position 3/1/94
Parnell and the O'Shea divorce
G's published letter to on 24/11/90
'Parnellism and crime' and 6/7/88
Parnell's land bill and 7/9/86, 10/9/86, 13/9/86
qualities of
always upright and calm 17/6/87
a prop 10/4/89, 17/1/93
morale 13/8/87
radical programme and
G dismayed to find him author of disestablishment plan in 8/11/85
reads proofs of G's *Impregnable Rock* 20/4/92
Rosebery and foreign secretaryship and 4/8/92 ff
Sudan and 20/2/85 c, 23/2/85 n
thinks G old and weary 8/2/90 n
Uganda and 9/12/92 ff
will resign with G over navy estimates 11/2/94
See also Acton, cabinet, Cobden, Ireland, Parnell
Mormons 21/4/77 n
Morning Post
reports of séance attended by G 7/11/84
Morocco 24/5/84 c
loan to
G's memorandum on, printed 26/9/61
mosque
G visits in Albania 2/2/59
Moulins 27/1/39, 26/10/50, 24/2/51
Mount Cenis pass 1/3/32, 31/10/50
Mount Teviot (Lothian) 21/11/74
Mozart *See* operas
Muggletonians
G reading Hymn Book of 13/12/81
mules 17/10/38 ff, 25/10/38 ff, 31/10/38
Mulgrave Castle (Normanby) 26/8/71
Müller, F. Max *See* Max Müller
Mundella, Anthony John (1825–1897), manufacturer and liberal M.P., President, Board of Trade 1886, 1892–4 15/9/68, 17/3/71 c, 2/3/77, 26/6/83, 27/6/84, 12/1/86, 8/2/86, 9/3/86, 26/5/86, 25/12/86, 20/7/87, 3/5/88, 26/3/90, 10/3/91, 28/3/91, 14/8/92, 13/11/93 c, 27/11/93 ff, 28/12/93, 10/2/94
alien immigration and 7/2/93
at Hawarden 13/12/86
at Political Economy Club, G impressed by 7/12/77
Burke and 13/12/86 n
disestablishment and 9/3/86
education and 27/4/80 ff
warned about costs by G 27/4/80
factory bill of 7/6/73 c
home rule and 4/4/86
hours of labour and 18/11/72 c
letters from G to, printed 22/3/71, 27/4/80, 13/7/86, 5/2/94
trade union legislation and 3/7/69 cn, 5/7/69
Munich 30/9/45 ff, 8/9/74 ff, 18/9/74 ff, 16/9/79, 10/10/79 ff, 27/8/86
Leuchtenberg gallery 6/10/45
Nymphenburg Palace 2/10/45
Pinakothek 1/10/45, 10/9/74, 13/10/79, 27/8/86
Munich, University of
Honorary Diploma for G from 6/9/72

murders
Dilessi, Greece 27/4/70, 7/5/70 ff
Lord W. Russell 9/5/40
Phoenix Park 6/5/82 ff
Murray, John, junior (1808–1892), publisher
Handbooks
France 25/10/50
S. Germany, G corrects proofs of 22/9/38
Sicily, G's journal used for 29/10/38, 1/11/38, 2/11/38, 6/11/38, 11/11/38
publishing *State and Church* 1/8/38, 2/8/38 ff, 7/8/38, 17/12/38
Murray's English Dictionary
G arranges civil list pension for Murray 1/10/81 n
Scriptorium of, G visits 7/2/90
Murray's Magazine *See* publications
music
Bach's *Passion* 22/3/78
most beautiful, but wrong for Good Friday 19/4/78
Palestrina, beauty of 30/4/46
See also singing
Music, Ancient 17/3/34, 23/4/34, 7/5/34, 7/3/36, 9/3/36, 25/5/36, 17/5/37, 28/3/38, 30/5/38, 8/5/39, 24/3/40, 24/3/41, 24/5/41, 2/5/42, 16/5/42, 29/3/43
music, G composing 20/10/36
He hath not despised 10/10/49
Nil in manu 24/10/44
Psalm lxxxi 7/10/49, 14/10/49
Psalm xlii 23/9/49, 27/9/49, 28/9/49
The day of wrath 24/10/44
Und ob die wolke 6/10/48
musical parties 15/3/33, 18/3/33, 16/5/34
Music Hall (New), Long Acre 21/6/47
Musicians, Society of 20/1/75
mustard *See* medicines

Naples 28/4/32 ff, 11/5/32 ff, 21/5/32, 11/10/38, 11/11/38, 24/7/49 ff, 10/11/50, 22/1/88 ff
Academia Reale di Canto e Ballo 30/12/50
Albergo de'Poveri 23/11/38
Armstrong works at Pozzuoli, G's visit to 22/1/89
arrests of liberals in 3/1/51, 4/1/51, 12/1/51, 4/2/51 ff
G's insomnia caused by 4/2/51
bad weather of 15/11/50 ff
Barone's art shop 30/11/50, 2/12/50 ff
Berice 7/1/89
Camaldolite convent 16/5/32, 13/11/38
Capo di Monte 23/11/50 ff, 15/1/89
carriage costs in 11/11/50
cathedral of 16/12/50
characteristics of Neapolitans 21/5/32
Chiaja Gardens
rescue work in? 12/1/89
churches in 30/11/38
Crocelle hotel 13/11/38
de' Gerolomini church 16/12/50
English grocery shop in 14/11/50
errors committed in 26/9/61
Filangieri museum 1/2/89 n, 6/2/89
G's speech at 7/2/89
G meets Cardinal Archbishop of 7/12/50
government of relies on tory party 13/2/51
G's clean breast about government of 29/1/51
G's rooms at 5 Chiatamone 12/11/50, 13/11/50 ff
G watched by spies in 11/2/51
Hotel des Etrangers 10/11/50 ff
ladies' school in 20/11/38
La Trinità monastery 14/12/50
liquefaction of St. Gennaro 5/5/32, 22/12/50
lists of Neapolitans met by G in 29/2/52
lottery of
draw attended by G 21/12/50
MSS sent by Neapolitan priests 12/10/51
Museo Nazionale 7/2/89
Neapolitan exiles in London
assisted by G 13/3/59, 15/3/59, 18/3/59, 19/3/59, 23/3/59, 31/3/59 n, 11/4/59
negotiation with 14/7/43
Nisida prison
condition of prisoners in 13/2/51
G visits 13/2/51
no good map of 21/11/50
Operaji, G's speech at 6/2/89
popularity of British in 24/11/38
Pozzuoli 1/5/32, 9/1/89
prisons visited 12/2/51, 13/2/51
G prays for in Litany at Fasque 26/10/51
problems with police 22/11/38
prohibited books in 16/11/38
rock slide in 31/12/88
Russian community in, visited by G 18/12/50
Santa Chiara 5/5/32, 26/11/50, 22/12/88
S. Severo 5/12/50
St. Martino 25/11/50, 4/1/89
Studio of 2/5/32 ff, 14/5/32 ff, 17/5/32, 14/11/38, 27/11/50, 6/12/50, 11/1/89
Swiss Chapel, G attending 1/1/51
Teatro de' Fiorentini 11/11/50
Toledo 28/4/32
Trinita Maggiore 22/11/50
Vicaria prison and courts 3/1/51, 4/1/51
G visits prison 12/2/51
Villa Rocca Bella (Rendel)
G staying at 22/12/88 ff

Napoleon I 15/2/32, 19/1/33, 15/12/38, 15/8/53
G's sensations on reading Scott's account of death of 19/1/33
Natal *See* South Africa
National Association for the Promotion of Social Science
G addresses 16/10/58
national debt 1/1/53 ff, 25/5/66, 14/1/93
coal stock and 1/2/66 n
conversion of
into terminable annuities 20/4/66
National Debt, Commissioners of 1/1/53, 4/4/53, 4/4/54, 24/11/54, 8/7/59, 10/4/60, 12/10/60, 7/4/63, 9/2/65, 22/5/65, 10/7/65, 20/9/92
good plan for 12/8/54
National Education League 9/3/70
National Education Union 11/3/70
nationalism
in Ionia 28/12/58
in Ireland 3/2/83
nationality
abstract sentiment for 28/12/58
greatest strength of the Irish demand 23/8/86
Irish nation 10/9/85, 13/11/85
national followed by individual freedom 24/9/81
religious education equated with in Prussia 4/11/69
Scotland and 7/12/80
G's speech on 30/5/89
See also Ireland, jingoism, Scotland
National Liberal Club *See* clubs (G member of)
National Liberal Federation
G's speeches to
Birmingham 31/5/77, 7/11/88
London 11/4/88
Newcastle, plans for 14/9/91
National Liberal League 21/3/79 n
National Portrait Gallery
for G a meeting of the dead 11/7/68
G trustee of 28/6/60, 29/11/60, 20/3/62, 27/3/63, 7/6/64, 7/2/67, 22/11/67, 29/11/67, 29/5/68, 12/3/69, 9/5/71, 16/5/72, 27/11/73, 13/7/75, 8/3/76, 22/3/76, 17/7/78, 6/2/82, 6/11/82, 18/7/85, 24/3/86
National Society 28/4/38, 5/5/38, 15/5/38 ff, 15/2/39, 16/2/39, 29/6/40, 2/6/47, 7/6/48, 27/11/52, 30/11/52, 11/5/70
National Thrift Society 5/5/88 n, 19/10/88
nature
admonition from 1/11/55
force of 31/10/38
nausea *See* illnesses
Naval Defence Act 1/4/94 ff
Navigation Acts 3/4/48, 18/4/48, 11/5/48, 2/6/48, 9/6/48, 13/2/49, 6/3/49, 9/3/49, 12/3/49, 15/3/49 ff, 20/3/49 ff, 23/3/49 ff, 28/3/49, 23/4/49, 26/2/51
G's view of reciprocity 11/5/48
Peelite negotiations with government on 21/3/49, 22/3/49
Peelites and
G astounded at suggestion of open question 13/2/49
reciprocity and 22/3/49
navy
Admiralty Bill 6/7/72
battleships and 15/12/93
Captain disaster 9/9/70, 2/11/70 c
coaling stations 2/12/84 c
disarmament and 9/4/70
dockyards 21/1/70 c
Dover Harbour Bill 29/3/73 c, 4/7/73, 5/7/73 c
estimates 8/2/53 ff, 10/4/61, 12/4/61, 3/1/65, 19/1/65 ff, 2/1/66, 13/3/67, 26/1/69 c, 2/2/69 c, 20/2/69 c, 10/12/69 c, 15/12/70 c, 18/12/71 c, 29/1/72, 6/12/72 ff, 8/12/73, 1/1/74, 17/1/74, 19/1/74, 22/1/74, 15/12/80, 16/12/80 c, 15/2/83, 24/1/84, 25/1/84, 26/1/84 c, 11/11/84 c, 12/11/84, 2/12/84 c, 21/12/84, 29/1/85, 2/2/85, 9/2/85 c, 12/2/86, 13/2/86, 15/2/86 c, 19/2/86 ff, 22/2/86 ff, 7/1/93 ff, 23/2/93 c, 8/8/93 c
Admirals' threat of resignation over 9/1/94 c
cabinet committee on 1/12/62
cabinet mad and drunk over 17/2/94, 19/3/94
crisis of 1893–4 over 14/12/93 c, 15/12/93 ff, 27/12/93 ff, 1/1/94 ff, 11/1/94 ff, 2/2/94 ff, 23/2/94 ff
G alone over 3/1/94
G gives in to cabinet on for two years 9/11/72
G in absolute isolation over 5/1/94
G's memoranda on, printed 1/1/94, 4/1/94, 9/1/94, 10/1/94, 14/1/94, 20/1/94
increased 29/1/73 c
list of G's interviews on 23/1/94
mad and mischievous scheme 9/1/94, 10/1/94
Palmerston's wild proposal on 25/2/61, 27/2/61
prospects of agreement with army bad 17/1/74
Queen's intervention over 14/12/93 c

supplemental estimate unnecessary, G thinks 9/7/72
those of 1894 the most Radical measure of G's lifetime 25/7/94
flogging in
abolition to follow army 22/5/80 c
government's intention to end 5/7/71 c, 28/7/71 n
fortifications plan 8/1/60 ff, 23/12/70
Franco-Prussian war and 23/7/70 c
British officers sent to French Baltic fleet 16/7/70 c
marines ready for Antwerp 24/7/70, 26/7/70
Greenwich Hospital
navy education, to be used for 30/1/72 c
G's memorandum on naval force 18/12/60
Hamilton's motion on 14/12/93 ff
poor government majority over 19/12/93
H.M.S. *Britannia*, Dartmouth
G's visit to 12/7/77
improved ships of 28/8/32
iron-clad inquiry 2/11/70 c, 4/11/70 c
iron-clad programme 25/9/63, 30/9/63, 5/10/63, 2/11/70 c
G's doubts about 5/7/83
need for review of 5/7/83
shift away from, G welcomes 20/12/70
merchant navy
Plimsoll's Commission and Bill 22/2/73 n, 1/3/73 c, 10/5/73 c, 26/7/75, 9/4/80, 14/5/80 c, 24/7/80 c
Royal Commission on loss of life at sea 5/7/84 c, 31/10/84 c
mobilisation of Channel Fleet: mischievous rumour 6/1/85
naval review, G at 11/8/53
numbers of ranks of officers in 5/7/73 c
postal contacts to Africa and 31/12/84
recruitment of cadets to 5/7/73 c
retrenchment in, difficulties of 1/1/74
scare of 1884 30/9/84, 20/11/84 c, 2/12/84 c, 16/12/84, 5/2/94
Stead's astounding proceedings on 30/9/84
shipbuilding program
G asks for costs of 24/11/73, 1/1/74
shipbuilding programmes 28/12/60 n, 29/12/60
two-power standard 2/12/84 c
Victoria disaster 25/6/93 ff, 23/11/93
wages in docklands 4/2/73 c, 8/2/73 c
See also accidents, army, Baring, cabinet, estimates, fortifications, France, Germany, God, Naval Defence Act, navy (merchant), Pacific, politics (retirement from), Primrose, ships, Spencer
navy, merchant
manning of 5/3/53
Naworth Castle, Brampton (Lord Carlisle) 2/9/73
Negropontis affair *See* Eastern Question
Nelson Memorial Fund 9/6/54
Netherby (Graham) 3/9/58
Neue Freie Presse 19/4/80 n
Neufchatel 2/10/66
neuralgia *See* illnesses
Nevers 25/10/50
Newark 24/9/32, 1/12/32, 2/8/34, 17/1/37, 21/1/37, 17/7/37, 17/12/39, 12/9/40, 14/6/41, 17/10/65, 16/4/79
workhouse of 19/1/37
See also constituencies
Newark constituency 15/7/32, 30/7/32, 9/9/32, 25/10/32, 2/11/32, 30/11/32 ff, 12/12/32 ff, 14/1/33, 15/12/34, 29/12/34 ff, 8/6/35, 28/12/36, 17/1/37, 17/7/37, 7/2/38 ff, 7/4/38, 14/2/39, 17/12/39, 12/9/40, 15/6/41 ff, 8/9/41 ff, 22/4/78 n, 13/8/78, 16/4/79
Address to Prince Albert, presented by G 11/3/40
Address to Queen, presented by G 18/3/40
Anti-Maynooth deputation 1/5/45
dissenters in 18/12/39, 16/9/40, 18/6/41
education in 16/9/40 ff
G's speech on 17/9/40
G pays for organ in 17/9/40
G's father pays for church in 17/9/40
Manners as G's colleague 31/5/41, 11/6/41, 13/6/41 ff
move from considered 3/5/45
petition on house & window tax 30/4/33
plan for church and education board in 21/9/40
poor law guardians 13/9/41
recollection of campaigns in 27/12/75 n
Red Lion Club 8/10/32, 4/12/32, 14/12/32
scot and lot voters in
jubilee dinner for G 27/3/83
treating in 7/6/33 ff, 17/6/33, 17/7/33, 11/10/33, 29/10/33 ff, 17/12/33, 2/8/34, 28/11/34, 31/5/41, 2/6/41, 4/6/41
vacated by G by holding office 22/12/45 n
Newbattle, Edinburgh (Lothian) 2/11/65
New Brighton, the Wirral
holiday in 19/7/41
Newcastle 6/10/62 ff, 1/10/91
daring works for transformation of the Tyne 8/10/62
diocese of 17/2/82
G Freeman of 3/10/91

Newcastle (*cont.*)
National Liberal Federation meeting at
G's speech to ('Newcastle Programme') 2/10/91, 5/7/93
Newcastle, Dukes of *See* Clinton
New College, Oxford 7/11/29, 11/11/29, 14/12/29, 5/7/48
chapel of 3/6/57
Newdigate poetry prize *See* Oxford (University of)
New Forest
G's visit to 5/6/89 ff
Newfoundland *See* Canada
New Guinea
protectorate for 8/12/83, 27/6/84, 5/7/84 c, 6/8/84 c, 9/8/84 c, 6/10/84 c, 3/1/85 c, 17/2/85 c, 28/2/85 c
native policy in 21/1/85 c
Queensland's wish to appropriate 10/3/83 c, 21/4/83 c, 23/4/83, 19/5/83, 13/6/83 c, 8/12/83
annexation nullified 13/6/83 c
New Hebrides 27/6/84 n
Newman, John Henry, Cardinal (1801-1890), theologian and poet; convert to Rome 1845; Cardinal 1879 23/8/28, 21/6/29, 28/6/29, 2/9/30, 6/3/31, 30/3/41, 15/4/41, 17/5/41, 7/12/43, 2/9/44, 16/8/65, 1/3/70, 11/7/72, 14/1/75, 24/1/75, 13/10/75, 1/7/76, 4/8/76 n, 16/9/76, 28/4/78, 18/6/82, 2/5/85
Achilli case 30/6/52
at G's breakfast 21/6/66
attack on Peel unjust 19/8/41, 20/8/41
discussed at the Metaphysical Society 12/1/75
doubts Catholicity of Church of England 24/10/43, 28/10/43
Eastern question and 2/12/76
Essay on development 28/11/45 ff
essays on miracles stumbling 21/1/44
G prays for as in spiritual danger 13/4/48
greater name than Keble or Pusey 25/4/78 n
G send proofs to 15/6/45
G visits at the Oratory, Birmingham 1/6/77
infirm philosophy of 16/5/47
'Lead, kindly light' quoted in journal 15/7/92
letters from G to, printed 12/12/81, 17/12/81, 18/12/81, 9/11/82
liberalism and 1/2/85
low churchmanship of 9/9/71
meetings with 20/8/31, 6/9/31, 29/1/34, 17/4/43
reconciliation requested by G & others 17/6/45
Roman Catholicism and 15/1/39, 31/7/42
sermon has chinks of scepticism 16/5/47
sermons a great gift which he cannot remove 23/1/48
sermons alone basis of high reputation 24/7/42
theology of
memorandum on, printed 1/2/85
Tract 90 and 12/3/41, 30/3/41, 15/4/41, 24/10/43
proposed censure of 6/2/45 ff, 11/2/45, 13/2/45
Vatican Council and
latent defect and peculiarity penetrates the effect of all his gifts 25/3/70
See also Ireland, Manning, Oxford (University of), publications, Rome, sermons
Newport
G's speech at 7/6/87
worst atmosphere known since Black Hole 7/6/87
New Review 23/3/88 n
newspaper reporters
contacts with
The Times 15/2/42
newspapers
anti-stamp deputation 28/11/54
G encourages Glyn to buy *Echo* 19/5/69
G hurt by tone of 28/7/63
G's necessity of reading 23/8/49
home rule and 21/6/86
included in G's proposed cost of living index 20/12/72
interviews by G 15/2/72 n, 17/10/77, 20/10/79
leaks to 18/1/54 n
London press's hostility to liberal government 6/5/73
P. M. G. bought by liberals 29/4/80 n, 1/5/80
London press up to the mark on Bulgarian horrors 15/9/76
Newspaper Press Fund
G addresses 29/6/67
procedures for budget release 1/4/62
reduction of postage on 4/2/70 c
speech attacking London press 2/9/71 n, 4/9/71
reply to Houghton's criticisms 13/9/71
tory character of 3/12/85
war-press and Eastern question 7/2/78
See also Daily News, Daily Telegraph, Freiheit, Morning Post, Pall Mall Gazette, Scotsman, Times, Egypt, France, letters and articles, paper duties
Newspaper Stamp Bill 17/1/55 n, 19/1/55, 3/3/55, 19/3/55, 20/3/55, 27/3/55, 23/4/55

New York *See* United States
New Zealand 9/2/38, 11/6/38, 27/5/40, 12/2/48, 21/8/48, 24/7/51, 28/7/51, 30/7/51, 9/2/52, 15/5/61
  Auckland legislative council 25/6/62
  British troops withdrawn from 20/5/69, 29/5/69 c
  Canterbury settlement 12/10/52, 15/10/52, 4/1/53, 19/1/53, 5/11/53
  defence of
    troop withdrawals 28/1/70 c
  delegates to U.K. from 27/2/70
  emigration to
    loan for declined 9/4/70 c
  expedition to, allowed no more advances 26/7/65
  G on select cttee. on 13/7/40
  G prevents division of 14/5/46
  land claims in 20/3/46
  letter to G from legislative houses of 26/10/83
  loan to 7/5/70 c, 14/5/70 c
  New Zealand Bill 16/1/52
    G's resolutions on 31/1/52
  plan for church colony in 21/5/41, 21/9/41
  testimony to G from lady admirers in 11/12/86 n
  Treaty of Waitangi
    G's alarm at 1/1/47
  votes for women in 18/10/92
  Wakefield's proposals for 27/3/46
  See also memoranda, Selwyn
Niagara Falls 27/10/32
Nice 22/1/67, 6/2/83, 24/2/83
nihilism
  conference on, U.K. not participating in 4/5/81 c
Nîmes 13/1/92 ff
  Roman buildings in 14/1/92
Nineteenth Century
  G suggests series of articles on Ireland for 5/8/85
  See also publications
Nineteenth Century Art Society 11/5/89, 13/5/89
Nineveh
  Layard's discoveries 5/3/49
Nisero incident 3/7/84, 5/7/84 c
nonconformists
  1874 election and 27/1/74
  angry with 'liberal' church people 30/12/85
  Burials Bill and 10/5/80
  cabinet and 30/12/82
  church rates and
    deputation on 17/2/68
  Commons, increase of numbers in 1/5/80
  deputation on education 17/5/71, 22/4/72
  dinner for 17/5/89
  Eastern question and 1/5/77
  education and
    undecided between secular and unsectarian religous teaching, G thinks 27/1/74
  education bill and 29/5/70, 31/5/70 n, 10/6/70, 25/11/71, 29/11/71
  Elementary Education Bill and 24/3/70, 20/3/73
  G attends opening of Allon's Independent Chapel 5/12/77
  G dining with Perks and the Wesleyans 30/7/90
  G's debt to 11/5/87
  G seeks to appoint nonconformist peers 4/8/69
  G's speech on Eastern question to 18/4/78
  Hall arranges meeting of dissenting ministers with G 15/11/64, 25/1/66, 13/2/68, 12/7/76, 6/7/77
    on Vaticanism; disestablishment; Moody & Sankey; Scottish patronage 16/2/75
    teeth and claws not very terrible 25/1/66
  incapacity for understanding full share of British history 30/3/69
  indulgence to G shown by 5/7/73
  liberal party and 5/7/73, 29/12/73, 28/3/81
    will probably use power to put liberals in a minority 29/8/73
  met at Mrs. Birks' 22/3/78
  modern nonconformity learnt about from C. Berry 8/11/88
  not in best humour 10/1/72
  Parker arranges meeting of dissenting ministers with G 11/5/87
  patronage and 30/12/82
  pray for G and Irish disestablishment 15/7/69
  reform of Church of England and 10/1/84
  religious census and 9/7/60
  thanksgiving service for Prince of Wales and
    difficulties anticipated 21/12/71, 10/1/72
    Queen to attend nonconformist service for 17/1/72
  Wales and 13/5/83
  See also liberal party, Newark constituency, patronage
Norfolk House 4/5/53
Norman conquest, G favours 22/4/26
Norris Green (Heywood) 27/10/56, 13/11/68, 28/1/85
North American Review *See* publications
Northbourne, Lord *See* James
Northbrook, Lord *See* Baring
Northcote, Stafford Henry, Sir (1818–1887), 1st Earl of Iddesleigh (1885), G's private secretary at Board of Trade 1842–5, tory M.P. and Cabinet

Northcote, Stafford Henry, Sir (*cont.*)
Minister 30/6/42, 21/10/42, 6/12/44, 15/11/47, 27/6/48, 23/4/49, 9/1/53, 21/11/53, 22/11/53, 14/1/54, 16/1/55, 2/8/62 n, 4/3/68, 19/7/76, 10/4/77 n, 17/1/78, 24/1/78, 23/12/79, 7/1/80, 8/5/80, 31/5/80, 6/1/81, 11/1/81, 17/9/81, 5/10/81, 7/2/82 c, 5/4/82, 6/5/82 c, 24/6/82, 8/11/82 c, 20/6/83, 19/7/83, 2/8/83, 21/8/83, 18/10/83, 3/1/84, 3/4/84, 4/4/84, 23/9/84, 20/2/85 c, 23/2/85 n, 13/6/85, 17/6/85, 19/6/85, 28/10/93, 29/1/94
as G's private secretary 30/6/42 ff
assisting G in Oxford seat 20/3/47 ff, 13/5/47, 19/5/47 ff, 7/4/59, 18/6/59
at Hawarden 10/8/65
chancellor of the exchequer, G expects him to be 13/6/85
clôture and 20/1/81 ff
death of 12/1/87, 27/1/87, 8/2/87 n
declines to serve on G's election committee 22/6/59 n
excellence of 3/4/71
finance of
G's attack on 28/4/79
truly ignoble 6/8/78
flabby weakness of 31/8/84
foreign secretary
G suggests as 12/7/86
G arranging compromise on education with 27/3/62
Glasgow Rectorship: defeated by G 15/11/77 n
G deeply resents Northcote's standing 3/12/77 n
G makes better known to Aberdeen 19/1/54
handsome in acknowledgment 9/5/81
India, Viceroy of, unsuitable for? 13/2/72
Leader of the House
not up to his work 8/2/77
letters from G to, printed 3/4/71, 20/1/81, 11/3/81, 22/4/81, 3/2/82, 3/3/82, 4/3/82, 6/5/82, 11/8/82, 11/12/83, 14/11/84, 29/11/84, 12/6/85, 15/6/85, 25/6/85
little weight or influence 13/1/85
nasty work of 28/5/80
Reform Bill 1884
conferences on 13/11/84 ff
retirement of expected 24/8/83
Ripon to try to attract 3/4/71
shabby feebleness of 10/7/80
unwilling to assume responsibility 13/1/85
Washington, Treaty of
commissioner for 3/4/71 ff
weaker than water 1/2/81
See also budgets, Commons (House of), conservative party, finance
Northcote-Trevelyan Report 12/8/53 ff, 22/11/53, 30/11/53
North East
G's tour of 6/10/62 ff
Norton Priory(Brooke)
G's wedding night spent at 25/7/39
Norway
Aalesund 26/8/85 ff
Bergen 18/8/85
bread prices in 12/8/85
character of church services in 16/8/85
coronation of Oscar II 21/6/73 c
fishing in 12/8/85, 22/8/85
G known by sight in 14/8/85
G learning Norwegian 11/8/85 ff
G's visits to 15/9/83 ff, 11/8/85 ff
Gudvangen 21/8/85
Hardanger fiord 12/11/85
Molde 26/8/85
Odde 14/8/85
Stalheim 22/8/85
stalking in 22/8/85
Stavanger 11/8/85
Norwich 23/1/37
cathedral 7/1/38, 8/1/38, 17/5/90
G's speech at 16/5/90
Norwood (Talbot) 3/7/58, 15/8/58
nosebleeds *See* illnesses
Notes and Queries 7/10/92
Nottingham 19/12/32, 16/10/65, 2/12/67, 8/9/70, 15/3/74, 10/5/75, 18/10/87
Nottingham, College (later University) of
G's speech at foundation of 27/9/77
Nova Scotia *See* Canada
Novikoff, Olga (1841–1908), née Kireyev, campaigned with G on Bulgaria in 1870s, known as 'M.P. for Russia'; 24/2/73, 13/10/76, 27/10/76, 5/12/76, 8/12/76, 8/5/77, 3/12/77, 16/10/78, 3/12/78, 17/10/79, 18/10/79, 14/2/80, 15/3/81, 11/11/82, 28/7/83, 12/6/84, 29/10/85, 28/1/86, 23/2/88, 10/2/91, 19/3/91, 14/3/92, 6/11/92 n, 29/11/93
G's review of her *Russia and England* 14/2/80, 16/2/80 ff
letters from G to, printed 14/2/73, 4/5/80, 25/9/80, 16/10/80, 28/11/80, 18/1/82, 22/1/82, 8/8/83, 1/7/85, 16/11/86
Nuneham Courtney (Harcourt) 10/4/41 ff, 15/4/43 ff, 27/3/45 ff, 4/7/48 ff
Nuremberg 20/9/74 ff
strong individuality of its buildings 21/9/74
nurses
Caroline Uppington 26/2/46, 2/2/47, 6/9/49, 10/9/49, 20/5/53, 31/8/53

Dixon
administers lead in error 8/2/56
Mrs. Baker 10/9/49
Mrs. Clark 4/6/40, 6/7/40
Mrs. Harris 27/2/40
Mrs. Roberts 8/11/42
wetnurses 4/11/42 ff, 19/12/42 ff
mortality of children nursed by 16/11/42

Oak Farm 7/10/40, 19/3/41, 23/8/41, 26/8/41 ff, 16/2/43 ff, 22/8/46 ff, 15/2/47 ff, 23/3/47, 8/8/48 n, 24/8/48 ff, 6/11/48, 31/3/49, 11/2/50, 21/8/51 ff, 12/6/52, 20/8/52, 7/9/55, 22/1/56 n, 17/3/56, 25/9/60, 21/1/62, 6/8/63, 26/11/87
1845 Agreement on 6/12/44 ff
accounts of 31/12/40
affairs looking well 22/1/41
bankruptcy of 27/8/47, 28/8/47 ff, 16/11/47, 20/11/47, 22/11/47, 23/11/47 ff
just retribution of 16/11/47
true dishonour of 23/11/47
Boydell's book on profitable management! 13/2/50
declining viability of 2/6/42
distracts G from parliamentary work 21/2/48
G dissuades Lyttelton from selling 26/8/40
G distrusts Boydell 29/10/46
Goulburn consulted on 1/9/41
G's solution for 6/1/48 ff, 10/1/48 ff
immense liabilities 2/12/44
lessons for G from 2/12/44
mem. of agreement on 10/4/47
no more aid without inquiry 28/11/46
plan for chapel at 21/9/40, 26/12/40, 30/4/41
plan for release from 2/12/44
reduces money for charity 4/11/42
sale of by G 5/4/49, 30/4/49, 5/5/49
seems a good concern 22/8/40
Sir J. Gladstone and 28/9/40, 31/12/40, 19/5/42, 21/5/42, 6/2/44 ff, 22/10/44 ff, 22/10/49
visited 14/11/44, 26/11/45, 4/2/48
Oakley (Kerrison) 26/1/37, 26/12/37
Oaths Bill 29/4/81 c, 2/5/81 ff, 2/7/81
Oatlands (Egerton) 26/5/36
Oban 19/8/53, 28/9/53, 10/9/83
obligations and duties to parents 15/4/40
Observer, The 23/5/86
obstruction *See* Commons (House of)
Occasional Sermons Bill 14/5/73
O'Connell, Daniel (1775–1845), Irish M.P.; prosecuted for treason 1843; the 'Liberator' 5/2/33, 18/2/33, 5/3/33, 2/7/34, 10/7/34, 19/7/34, 21/7/34, 3/11/35, 22/4/36 n, 15/1/39, 26/2/39, 20/6/40, 4/6/41, 14/7/43, 22/11/77, 26/10/80, 18/11/80, 5/10/81, 7/10/81 n, 17/12/81, 3/7/82, 12/11/86, 28/12/86, 29/11/90, 12/1/93
a man regardless of laws human & divine 4/6/41
deep impression on G of dictum on religion by 6/2/83
defended by Rio 4/6/41
G's recollections of published in O'Rourke's *Life* 17/11/77 n
G's review of his *Correspondence* 26/11/88 ff
G visits tomb of 3/11/77
memorial to 21/1/89 n
trial of 22/10/80
Octagon *See* Hawarden Castle
Odd Fellows Friendly Society 22/7/37
office
as affecting G's duty 30/9/41
offer from Derby of colonial office/board of control to G
rejected after discussion with Aberdeen 22/5/58, 23/5/58, 26/5/58
tenure raises G's spirits 23/12/45
offices (political) held by G
Chancellor of the Exchequer 1852 23/12/52, 28/12/52
resignation from 22/2/55, 23/2/55, 28/2/55
Chancellor of the Exchequer 1859–66 13/6/59 ff
resignation from 19/6/66 ff, 5/7/66, 6/7/66
Chancellor of the Exchequer 1873–4 9/8/73 ff
Chancellor of the Exchequer 1880–2 23/4/80 ff, 1/12/82
Commissioner Extraordinary to the Ionian Islands 5/11/58 ff
First Lord of the Treasury 1868–74 3/12/68 ff
resignation from 13/3/73, 17/2/74
resignation from unsuccessful 16/3/73
First Lord of the Treasury 1880–5 23/4/80 ff
First Lord of the Treasury 1886 29/1/86, 1/2/86
First Lord of the Treasury 1892–4 15/8/92 ff
length of time in office 1/1/83
Lord High Commissioner to the Ionian Islands 25/1/59
resignation from 1/2/59 n
Lord Privy Seal 1892–4 15/8/92 ff, 5/3/94
Master of the Mint 1841 6/9/41 ff, 29/9/41 ff

offices (political) held by G (*cont.*)
President, Board of Trade 1843–5 13/5/43, 15/5/43
Secretary of State for War and the Colonies 1845–6 22/12/45 ff
Treasury Board 1834 20/12/34
Under-Secretary for the Colonies 1835 26/1/35 ff
Vice-President, Board of Trade 1841–3 31/8/41 ff
Old Bailey
J. R. Herbert v. E. W. Pugin
G gives evidence for Herbert 14/7/74
trial of E. Roberts (servant) 3/5/43, 11/5/43, 12/5/43
trial of Wilson, blackmailer
G attends but remains mute 14/6/53, 15/6/53
trial of W. Law(servant) 2/2/43
trial of W. Palmer, the Rugeley poisoner
G attends 26/5/56
Old Catholics and their Congress 6/9/72, 31/10/72, 10/11/72 n, 14/2/73, 20/9/74 n, 31/5/75, 29/8/75, 30/10/75 n, 6/8/76
G's memorandum on them and their relations with Rome, printed 30/9/74
Olympian religion
abbreviated 'O. R.' in journal 12/2/91 ff
G's articles on 10/10/91 ff, 5/11/91 ff
G's work on 24/2/71, 8/1/80 ff, 4/9/86, 10/1/87 ff, 12/2/91 ff, 21/3/91 ff, 11/8/91 ff, 8/9/91 ff, 13/4/92 ff, 4/6/92 ff, 27/12/92 ff, 29/12/96
now to be done or never 4/11/86
On train 19/12/88, 21/12/88, 14/2/89, 19/2/89, 24/2/89, 27/2/89
Opdebeck, Susan Harriet Catherine, Lady (1814–1889), née Douglas-Hamilton, formerly Lady Lincoln, divorced by Lincoln 1850; married her lover; friend of the Gladstones & of Mrs. Thistlethwayte 23/2/33, 20/1/37, 5/6/37, 21/12/39, 26/5/43, 12/7/43, 30/12/46, 19/5/47, 7/3/52, 16/4/54, 5/10/64, 2/11/64, 31/12/80 n, 3/1/81, 8/3/81, 21/7/81, 11/11/81
death of 30/11/89 n
divorce of 26/2/50, 1/4/50, 7/5/50, 28/5/50
alimony of, dispute over 29/5/50
effect of opium on 6/8/48
flees abroad with lover 2/8/48
adultery and pregnancy of 20/6/49
Manning & G proposed as searchers 7/7/49
G's mission to find 7/7/49 ff, 13/7/49 ff
found at Como 31/7/49 ff
once the dream of dreams 5/8/49
See also Opdebeck
opera
avoided so as not to see ballet 14/11/38
operas seen
Anna Bolena (Donizetti) 23/3/32
Barbiere di Seviglia, Il (Rossini) 3/6/61
in Corfu 12/2/59
in Rome 25/10/66
Bianca (Balfe) 28/1/61
Box and Cox (Sullivan) 5/8/69
Colomba (A. C. Mackenzie) 12/4/83
Der Freischütz (Weber) 24/4/66
Don Giovanni(Mozart) 3/12/27, 29/10/45
Faust (Gounod) 4/7/63, 9/6/87
Fra Diavolo (Auber) 15/6/58
Il Protettore dell'Orfana(Galuppi) 19/5/32
Il Trovatore (Verdi) 30/10/66
I Masnadieri (Verdi) 30/7/49
Iolanthe (Gilbert and Sullivan) 4/12/82
I Puritani (Donizetti) 30/6/87
La Figlia del Reggimento (Donizetti) 21/4/57
La Gazza Ladra (Rossini) 16/6/60
La Schiava in Bagdad (Pacini, in Naples) 10/12/50
Les Huguenots (Meyerbeer) 17/6/58, 24/6/70
Linda di Chamounix (Donizetti, in Genoa) 5/11/50
L'Italiana in Algieri (Rossini) 30/11/37
Lohengrin (Wagner) 8/5/75, 23/6/88
Lucia di Lammermoor (Donizetti) 18/7/49, 21/10/50, 14/5/57
Lucrezia Borgia (Donizetti) 10/5/53
Nozze di Figaro, Le (Mozart) 27/1/38
Patience (Gilbert and Sullivan) 14/9/82
Romeo and Juliet (Gounod) 15/7/89, 12/6/90
The Flying Dutchman (Wagner) 10/3/82
The Mikado (Gilbert and Sullivan) 29/7/85
The Scorcerer(Gilbert and Sullivan) 21/2/78
Un Ballo in Maschera (Verdi) 30/7/61
opium 19/3/40, 2/5/40, 12/5/40, 14/5/40, 4/7/40, 6/7/40, 17/8/41, 24/8/41 ff, 26/8/41 ff, 16/9/41, 13/5/43, 15/11/43, 10/4/81, 21/4/81
corrupting influence of 6/8/48
G persuaded not to move motion on 13/5/40, 14/5/40
G's speech on 27/7/40
meeting on 24/4/40
Peel's speech only partly acceptable 4/4/43
See also China, Gladstone (Helen), India
opposition
G unable to lead liberal party for ordinary purposes of 14/1/75
no private secretary in 3/3/74, 5/3/74
optimism, G's 7/5/82 n

Orange Free State *See* South Africa
Orange movement 22/2/36
Murphy: refer to magistrates 29/5/69 c
See also Ireland
Orchard Neville (Lady Grenville) 17/8/66, 27/1/77
Order of Merit *See* patronage (honours)
ordnance survey 23/12/53, 24/12/53
Oriel College, Oxford 31/10/28 ff, 29/1/34, 5/7/48, 22/1/52, 27/1/53, 3/2/90
G staying at 22/10/52 ff, 16/6/55 ff
Oriental Bank Corporation Bill 14/5/73 c
Oriental Congress
G's paper for 22/8/92 ff, 7/9/92 n
See also Max Müller, publications
Orleans 25/10/50
Orleans House (Aumale) 10/5/58, 12/5/58, 31/5/59, 16/7/64, 28/7/66, 20/6/68
Orme's Head *See* Penmaenmawr
Orthodox churches
Bulgarian schism 13/11/71 n, 27/11/71, 18/8/72, 4/9/72
G attends Russian church in Athens 19/12/58
Greek church proselytising in Wolverhampton
mischievous character of 2/1/72
Greek Sullogoi of Constantinople 18/6/78, 19/6/78 n
G's comments on to Victoria 19/3/62
G's observations on in Ionia 2/12/58 ff
Old Catholics and 30/9/74, 21/9/79
Osborne House (The Queen) 30/8/54 ff, 12/8/59, 5/8/61, 17/2/64, 27/7/64, 30/1/65, 25/7/65, 23/1/69, 15/2/69, 17/1/72, 18/8/82, 4/8/83, 1/2/84, 1/2/86, 15/8/92
Oscott, St. Mary's College
visit to 18/8/40
O'Shea, Katharine *See* Parnell (Katharine)
O'Shea, William Henry, Capt. (1840–1905), home rule M.P. and husband of Katharine O'Shea 15/5/81, 17/5/81, 15/4/82 ff, 25/4/82, 29/4/82 ff, 9/5/82, 18/1/85 n
divorce case of 17/11/90 n, 21/11/90 ff
G's memoranda on, printed 21/11/90 ff
files petition of divorce 24/12/89 n
G's interview with, memorandum of 5/5/82
land bill 1881 and
Exchequer grant compromise of 13/6/81 c, 14/6/81, 11/4/82
letters from G to, printed 18/9/80, 14/6/81, 11/4/82, 15/4/82, 18/4/82, 6/5/82, 7/5/82
seat for in 1885 election 24/10/85, 18/11/85
wife's attempt to get him under-secretaryship 29/8/82, 1/9/82, 1/11/82, 8/11/82
G's circular to cabinet urging government's debt to him 3/11/82
See also Ireland, Parnell
Ossian, authenticity of 16/10/26, 21/10/26
Oteley Park (C. K. Mainwaring) 16/9/56
otter hunting 22/9/37
Ottoman Empire *See* Turkey
Outram, Zadok *See* servants
Overend & Gurney's bank 18/4/60 n, 19/4/60 n, 21/11/62
1866 panic and 11/5/66
government refuses funds to aid prosecution of 19/6/69 c
Owen's College, Manchester *See* Manchester
Oxford 15/9/25, 19/1/26, 5/12/26, 4/8/28, 16/1/29, 8/1/30, 23/4/30, 14/1/31, 15/4/31, 25/6/31, 21/1/32, 23/1/33, 17/1/34, 8/2/34, 19/5/34, 12/4/41 ff, 12/2/45, 25/10/47, 26/1/49, 20/1/52, 18/11/61, 16/6/63, 31/12/67, 30/1/78
Angel inn, G living at 4/8/28 ff
baptist service at 24/10/30
Dissenting chapel visited 6/3/31
G's family visits 14/5/29 ff, 9/7/31
Headington, development of 4/7/85
King's Arms 14/1/30, 9/7/31
Littlemore church 14/4/41
methodist service at 13/6/30
Oxford Liberal Association
G declines to attend meeting of 26/1/90 n
Parker's bookshop 21/10/29
Port Meadow
G & Phillimore walking on 6/8/31
Saint Peter's church 5/6/31, 14/8/31, 11/9/31, 12/4/41
St. Barnabas's church
internment of Combe in, G fails to secure 2/11/72
Summertown 31/5/57
Water Eaton 30/1/34
See also Cuddesdon, Saint Ebbe's, Saint Mary's
Oxford, University of 16/9/27, 4/8/28 ff, 16/6/93
Address to the Queen 14/7/37
Ashmolean Museum 3/6/57
B.A. taken 26/1/32
Bodleian Library 4/10/28, 15/5/29, 3/6/57, 19/5/63 n, 25/10/92
G's catalogue 'Bibliotheca Homerica' in 16/8/65
G sketches design of rolling-stack bookcases for 5/4/88
later visits to 28/11/83, 5/4/88, 25/10/92
Radcliffe Camera, G hands to the Library 20/11/61 n

Oxford, University of (*cont.*)
Clarendon Press
mechanical and moral improvement of 25/1/31
publishes G's *Butler* 23/12/95, 25/3/96, 3/5/96
visited 25/1/31, 25/10/92, 11/11/92
clergy in
G anxious to increase 24/9/80
Cleveland Commission 27/2/71 n, 17/6/71 c, 20/6/71, 30/6/71, 21/10/71 c, 24/10/71 c, 15/12/71 c, 29/12/71, 10/7/72 c
colleges of
idle to suppose exempted from selfishness 28/3/72
youth may dangerously predominate in 28/3/72
college statutes and 28/3/72
conservatism in 9/9/71
Convocation House 5/2/29, 13/5/30, 21/5/34, 23/10/52
Craven scholarship (G unsuccessful) 5/5/29 ff
Dean Ireland's scholarship (G unsuccessful) 13/3/29, 16/3/29 ff, 8/3/30 ff, 4/3/31, 10/3/31 ff, 16/3/31
Divinity Schools 5/7/48
Encaenia 1/7/29, 23/6/30, 15/6/31, 2/6/57
G less hooted than cheered 20/6/55
Examination Schools of 27/11/83
Final Honours School, G's examinations for
G feels insufficiently examined 17/11/31
Final Honours School (Literae Humaniores) 26/10/31, 7/11/31 ff
First Class in 24/11/31
viva voce exam. by Hampden, Stocker & Garnett 14/11/31
Final Honours School (Mathematics) 9/12/31 ff
First Class in 14/12/31
viva voce exam. by Powell
fourth class, introduction of 13/5/30, 31/5/30
G an old idolater of 27/1/85
G's honorary D. C. L. 5/7/48
non placets rejected 5/7/48
G's matriculation 9/1/28, 22/1/28
Hampden affair, 1836 8/3/36, 21/3/36
Hebrew chair, filling of 4/10/82, 23/10/82
proposed secularisation of 23/10/82
Hegelianism in 16/2/73
history of transformation of needed 2/1/84
home rule and
memorial of support by resident graduates 11/2/88 n
liberalism, conscientious & not violent , in 18/3/70
Literae Humaniores, examination for
possibility of postponing 16/3/31
work plans 17/1/31
local examinations
G speaks for 27/11/61
M.A. taken 17/1/34 ff
Modern History in
Regius chair of 13/2/84, 14/2/84
new buildings for 27/6/45, 8/7/45
Newdigate poetry prize, G enters 30/4/31
new Halls in 1/6/54
Palmerston's D. C. L. 2/7/62
Poetry Professorship election 30/11/41 ff, 15/12/41 ff, 23/12/41 ff
'Popery' in 30/7/38
Proctors, Declaration of Thanks to 11/2/45
professors want increased powers 1/4/54
proposed censure of *Tract 90* 6/2/45, 13/2/45
Pusey House
flourishing of 27/1/85
founding of 21/9/82 n
Puseum visited: G disappointed in 5/7/85
Radcliffe Observatory 3/6/57
reform of 29/1/49, 16/2/49 ff, 20/1/52, 22/1/52, 2/4/53 ff, 4/4/53, 22/10/53, 11/12/53 ff, 27/12/53, 28/12/53, 29/12/53, 31/12/53, 4/1/54, 15/2/54 ff, 7/3/54 ff, 2/4/54 ff, 2/9/81, 3/10/81
commissioners for 14/6/54
deputation of professors 1/4/54
G's draft of 1854 bill 15/12/53, 17/12/53, 20/12/53, 4/1/54, 9/1/54 ff, 25/1/54, 26/1/54, 26/2/54, 27/2/54, 8/3/54, 10/3/54, 14/3/54
G's reforms not intended to lead to decay of theology 4/8/80 n, 3/10/81
Oxford University Bill 1854 17/3/54 ff, 7/4/54 ff, 1/5/54, 11/5/54 ff, 26/5/54 ff, 15/6/54, 5/7/54, 7/7/54, 27/7/54, 2/9/81
poor scholars question 27/1/49
Responsions 20/2/29, 11/6/29, 15/6/29, 23/6/29
revenues of, inquiry into 17/6/71 c, 20/6/71
Romanes lecture, given by G 24/10/92
preparation of 18/12/91 n, 31/8/92 ff, 9/9/92, 19/9/92, 17/10/92, 18/10/92
Royal Commission on 23/4/50, 27/5/52, 19/6/52, 26/7/52 ff, 8/2/54 ff
G opposes 18/7/50
Schools, required attendance at 10/11/28 ff, 7/6/30, 10/11/30, 31/5/31
Selborne commission on 24/9/80, 7/10/80, 9/10/80, 5/12/80, 3/10/81
Sheldonian Theatre 5/7/48, 2/6/57, 2/7/62

Statutes de moribus confirmandis 10/2/28
statutes of colleges studied 20/4/54 ff, 5/3/56 ff
St. Mary's (University Church) 12/10/28 ff, 22/11/29 ff, 14/11/30 ff, 16/1/31 ff, 26/6/31, 16/10/31 ff, 30/1/49
subscription to articles in 6/7/63
subscription to articles on matriculation
G opposes abolition 22/6/54
Taylorian Institute 24/4/78
Rossetti's candidature for Italian chair 14/3/56
tests' abolition 16/3/64, 10/11/69, 13/6/70, 17/6/70, 3/10/81
G opposes 13/6/66
G supports 1/7/68
The Club, G dines with 6/2/90
theology in
G anxious to safeguard 24/9/80
University Museum
G visits with Acland 9/5/59
opening of 20/6/55
University sermons, deficiencies of 23/5/30
Ward's degradation 9/1/45, 13/2/45, 9/6/47, 11/6/47
W. H. G at
G advises immense importance of steady work 27/5/58
writings on by G 27/3/29
See also Cecil, Christ Church and other colleges, clubs, constituencies, details of texts read (in 'Gladstone's Reading'), Gladstone (Herbert), Gladstone (Thomas), Gladstone (William Henry), lectures, Lords (House of), memoranda, Murray's *English Dictionary*, Oxford lectures, Oxford Union Society, Oxford University constituency, Oxford University Press, Radcliffe Camera, Radcliffe Trust, Stanley, Temple (Henry), university tests, University Tests Bill, WEG Essay Club, work
Oxford and Cambridge Club *See* clubs (G member of)
Oxford lectures attended by G
Biscoe's 17/10/31
calculus 14/11/28 ff, 3/10/29 ff
Cardwell's 23/10/28 ff, 22/10/29 ff
divinity 19/10/28 ff, 23/10/29 ff, 22/1/30 ff, 14/5/30 ff
ethics 3/3/30 ff, 15/5/30 ff, 12/5/31 ff
Greek history 3/3/30 ff
hydrostatics 25/10/30
Juvenal 24/10/28 ff
logic 4/1/29 ff, 17/10/31 ff
mathematics 27/10/28 ff, 21/1/29 ff, 26/10/29, 10/5/30 ff, 22/4/31 ff
Mills' 23/2/30 ff
optics 11/5/29 ff, 19/10/31
rhetoric 12/5/29, 24/10/29, 23/1/30 ff
Saunders' 2/2/29
Short's 14/10/28 ff
Sophocles 19/5/29
Thucydides 16/10/28 ff, 22/1/29 ff
Wordsworth's 22/1/31 ff
cancelled 21/2/31
Oxford movement ('Oxfordism') 28/5/37, 22/12/38, 23/4/41, 17/5/41, 31/7/42, 24/10/43, 28/10/43 *See also* Newman, Tractarianism
Oxford Union Society 28/5/29, 18/6/29, 22/10/29, 3/12/29, 4/3/30, 29/12/30, 10/2/31, 3/3/31, 17/5/31 ff, 19/5/31, 27/10/31, 17/11/31, 25/10/52, 5/2/90
fiftieth anniversary, G unable to attend 24/2/73 n
G president of 11/11/30 n, 17/11/30, 22/11/30, 2/12/30, 21/1/31, 27/1/31 n, 3/2/31
G's address on Homer and Assyria to 5/2/90
G secretary of 13/5/30, 17/5/30, 21/5/30, 3/6/30, 30/6/30
G's speeches at 11/2/30, 25/2/30, 18/3/30, 20/5/30, 17/6/30, 28/10/30, 2/12/30, 21/4/31
moves vote of no confidence in Wellington 11/11/30
on Catholic Emancipation 16/2/31
opposing Reform Bill 17/5/31 ff
West Indian slaves 2/5/31
visit of Cambridge men 26/11/29 ff
Oxford University constituency 20/3/47 ff, 22/7/47, 25/7/47 ff, 25/10/47 ff, 18/6/59
calls for religious census 1861 9/7/60
election committee 14/5/47 ff, 7/2/48, 15/2/48, 26/2/48, 2/1/53 ff, 20/5/65 n, 17/6/65 n
G's party for 19/2/48 ff, 20/1/53
G visits 25/10/47
G anticipates defeat in 5/1/53 ff
G considers leaving 19/3/61 n, 9/6/61
G defeated in: a dear dream dispelled 17/7/65
G elected 1/8/47 ff, 5/8/47, 10/7/52, 13/7/52, 30/4/57, 12/2/59 n, 7/4/59 n, 30/6/59 n
G risks bye-election by accepting office in Ionia 18/1/59 n
G sore and demoralised by bye-election in 20/6/59
G uncertain whether to accept 11/5/47 ff
G unopposed in 30/4/57
G visits 25/10/47 ff, 1/11/47 ff, 20/1/52 ff, 22/10/52 ff, 26/1/53 ff, 8/6/53, 16/6/55 ff, 26/1/57 ff, 30/5/57 ff, 12/12/57, 6/5/59 ff, 2/7/62, 16/6/63

Oxford University constituency (*cont.*)
redistribution and 26/11/84 ff
resignation Address (not sent) 10/11/60
See also elections (general/bye)
Oxford University Press 1/10/57, 13/2/79 n, 25/9/86 n, 7/12/89 n
Delegates criticised for including Homer's Hymns with Odyssey 4/11/86
publishes *Studies on Homer* 1/10/57, 5/10/57 ff
See also Oxford (University of, Clarendon Press)

Pacific
defence in 5/2/53
Pacini *See* operas
packet commission inquiry
G's instructions for 24/2/53
Padua 14/6/32, 26/2/59
Paestum 8/5/32
pain
as ground of enjoyment 4/1/43
as instrument of assimilation 3/3/80
as remedy for sin 26/10/45
bars carnal thoughts 19/9/42, 19/7/48
beauty in 18/10/42
discipline of 14/10/62
extent of in childbirth 3/6/40
G's repugnance to 31/12/54
joy of Cranmer in? 4/1/43
needful to G 7/8/51
serious bodily pain rarely experienced 13/9/42, 3/3/80
Palermo 14/10/38 ff
Albion hotel 14/10/38 ff
Palestine
G views with favour plan for introduction of Jews into 27/5/91 n
Palestrina's Improperia
most beautiful piece G ever heard 30/4/46
Paley, archdeacon
analysis of 7/9/30
discussion of 14/1/38
Palladio 20/6/32, 25/6/32
Pall Mall Gazette 19/4/71, 9/1/73, 2/9/81, 26/9/82, 14/8/84, 7/9/84, 27/6/86, 31/7/86, 31/7/93, 5/3/94
bought by liberals 29/4/80 n, 1/5/80
faithful and able ally 22/10/80
forged letter of G published 19/4/71
G's 'clerical' mind and 9/1/73
G's retirement and 31/1/94, 8/2/94
home rule and 18/12/85, 13/7/86
hostility to liberal government its breath of life 6/5/73
'Maiden Tribute' campaign of 15/7/85
G concerned at moral effect of 15/7/85
proposes release of Parnell 5/4/82 n
Palmer, Roundell (1812–1895), 1st Baron Selborne (1872), 1st Earl of Selborne (1882), lord chancellor 1872–4, 1880–5, member of the Engagement, Peelite M.P., unionist and establishmentarian 18/5/31, 9/2/52, 16/6/54 n, 21/5/56, 5/5/57, 5/5/63, 8/3/68, 23/10/68, 9/12/68, 14/2/69, 14/5/70 c, 10/6/71 c, 7/7/74, 13/6/79, 31/8/82, 27/4/86
advises G on Oxford seat 12/7/61
Alabama arbitration and 10/6/72 c, 11/6/72 c, 29/6/72
fee of £6,000 12/10/72
at Hawarden 13/11/75 ff
between ice and ink 4/7/89
controversy with over G's review of Reid's *Life of Forster* 21/9/88 ff
disestablishment and 1/5/75
Gordon and
demand for an expedition 30/7/84
G's Colonial Church Bill and 16/2/52 ff
G's encomium of 17/8/81
home rule and 14/1/86, 27/1/86, 30/1/86
set hostility to 14/1/86
Irish annuities and 8/5/69 c, 13/5/69 n
Irish disestablishment and 19/7/69
land reform and 22/4/73 c
letters from G to, printed 2/11/72, 12/11/72, 26/1/73, 27/1/73, 28/1/73, 2/7/73, 4/7/73, 27/12/73, 21/2/74, 10/5/80, 16/8/80, 18/8/80, 24/9/80, 9/10/80, 1/12/80, 14/12/80, 22/12/80, 21/11/83
Lord Chancellor 1872–4 2/11/72 ff
Lord Chancellor 1880–5 23/4/80 ff
Oxford University bill and 16/6/54 n, 29/6/54
plan for a law school/university 8/7/71 c, 1/12/73 c
leads deputation on 1/2/72
political mishandling of Irish land by 7/4/70, 8/4/70, 12/4/70, 15/4/70
resignation, threat of 16/5/85
sponsors bill abolishing compulsory church rates with G 19/2/68 n, 24/2/68
See also Judicature Bill
Palmerston, Lord *See* Temple (Henry)
Palmer's *Treatise on the Church of Christ*
G's plan for revised edition of 20/3/81, 27/3/81, 19/10/82, 18/11/82, 4/3/83, 12/11/83, 21/11/83, 8/6/84, 17/12/84, 24/10/85, 2/5/92
Panama 1/1/82
Panizzi, Antony, Sir (1797–1879), Italian liberal, Librarian of the British Museum 1856–66 4/11/42, 6/11/44, 1/4/51 ff, 22/3/52, 14/12/53, 18/12/53, 21/1/56, 30/7/56, 2/7/57, 2/11/58,

papers, G's catalogues of 23/8/27, 5/3/29, 2/2/36, 25/11/37, 12/8/75 ff, 10/8/88
arranged for final deposit in Octagon 8/11/87 ff
booklist of those whose letters G keeps 19/10/64
early W. E. G letters sorted 30/11/91
extensive arrangements for sorting of papers 13/8/88 ff
formidable duty of arranging 10/8/88
G overwhelmed by 23/10/93
letters now sorted to 1858 22/10/64
letters of 1871-6 24/5/77
papers ought to be arranged on receipt 8/6/78
parenthood, responsibilites of 29/12/40, 1/5/44
Paris 11/2/32 ff, 28/1/39 ff, 25/9/45 ff, 14/7/49, 8/8/49 ff, 19/10/50, 25/2/51, 6/3/59, 28/9/66, 23/1/67 ff, 14/10/79 ff, 20/2/89, 3/9/89 ff, 15/12/91, 26/2/92 ff, 21/12/92, 10/1/93, 10/2/94
1851 Exposition 9/4/51
Arc de Triomphe
lists defeats as victories 28/1/39
Bibliothèque Nationale 15/10/79
first library in the world, G thinks 16/8/82
Bourse 16/2/32, 24/10/50
British Embassy in 8/8/49, 27/2/83
G meets Tocqueville at 8/8/49
cabdrivers in 15/2/32
cemetery 15/2/32
Chamber of Deputies 13/2/32
china shopping in 7/3/59
Eiffel Tower
G ascends 7/9/89
G with influenza in 29/9/66 ff
Hippodrome 5/9/89
Hôtel Bedford 14/10/79 ff
Hôtel Bristol
G staying at 8/8/49, 28/12/87, 3/9/89
Hôtel Castiglione 6/3/59
Hôtel Victoria 19/10/50
Hôtel Vouillemont 28/9/66
Hôtel Windsor 25/2/51
Indian exhibition in
G's speech at 6/9/89
Louvre 14/2/32, 26/9/45, 14/7/49, 8/8/49, 23/10/50 ff, 7/3/59, 16/10/79 ff, 1/3/83, 27/2/92
closed 29/1/39
Madeleine
shames English works 28/1/39, 14/7/49, 20/10/50, 17/10/79
Maison Quantin (publishers) 3/2/87
Nôtre Dame 15/2/32, 29/1/39, 25/9/45, 26/9/45, 21/10/50, 17/10/79, 26/2/92
Panthéon 18/2/32
Parisians
on the coach, gross language of 29/1/39
restaurants
Café aux Milles Colonnes 14/2/32
Meurice's 12/2/32 ff, 28/1/39 ff
Vefour's 11/2/32, 23/10/50 ff
Sacré Coeur 28/2/92
Sainte Chapelle 9/4/51, 26/2/92
Salle de Danse
attended 15/2/32, 17/2/32
siege of 6/9/70, 12/9/70, 10/1/71
astonishing proposal that Britain supply Paris after surrender 18/11/70, 25/11/70 c, 10/12/70
British protest against bombardment 19/1/71 c
Society of Political Economy of
G's speech in French to 7/9/89
St. Augustin 4/9/89
St. Germain Auxerrois 9/4/51
St. Germain des Prés 9/4/51
Trocadero 4/9/89
Universal Exhibition 1889 6/9/89 ff
Paris, Treaty of
Ionia and 28/12/58
parish councils *See* local government
Parish Councils Bill 31/8/93 c
Parliament, Houses of
new design for 23/3/36, 19/10/42, 27/1/43 n, 2/7/47
parliamentary papers 18/3/53 n
Parnell, Charles Stewart (1846-1891), home rule M.P. and leader 1877-90 26/7/77, 25/6/80, 14/7/80, 11/11/80, 21/1/81, 29/9/81, 5/10/81, 20/5/82, 29/6/82, 20/8/82 n, 15/2/83, 10/3/83 c, 14/3/83, 18/6/83 n, 2/10/83, 26/12/83, 29/12/83, 6/7/84, 26/8/84, 31/1/85, 28/2/85, 30/5/85, 30/6/85, 2/9/85, 2/9/85 n, 5/1/86, 12/5/86 n, 9/7/86 n, 16/11/86, 29/3/87 n, 5/4/87, 10/2/88, 16/7/88, 23/11/88, 22/5/89, 28/5/89, 18/2/90, 11/3/90, 5/12/92, 5/11/93
abominable teaching of 24/11/81
alms bill of 25/6/80, 26/6/80 c
a most satisfactory man 18/5/86 n
arrest of 12/10/81 c, 13/10/81
unimprisonable if declaration of May 1882 made earlier 4/5/82
a Sphinx 29/6/83
Boulogne negotiations and 22/1/91 n, 28/1/91, 7/11/91 n
Carnarvon and 12/12/85
communication with 24/1/86, 29/1/86
absence of becoming undesirable 7/1/86
conservative party and 3/11/85, 8/12/85 n, 13/12/85, 16/12/85 ff, 22/12/85 ff, 26/12/85 ff, 24/1/86

conservative tone of 8/3/88
coolness of head of 30/4/88
death of 7/10/91
enemy of the Empire by acts not motives? 21/9/81
evicted tenants and 22/2/81 c
Fenians and
has stopped supplies to from Paris 9/6/82, 12/6/82
franchise reform and 18/1/84
G denies he has visited Hawarden 21/12/86 n
G discusses with Prince of Wales 3/6/93
G meets at dinner 30/4/88
Government of Ireland Bill and
negotiation on financial clauses of 31/3/86 n, 3/4/86, 5/4/86 n
G's assessment of his motives 1879–82 19/9/82
G's denunciation of, at Leeds 7/10/81 n
G's dinner for 19/3/89, 2/4/89
G's meeting with 2/9/89
G's meeting with on Commission inquiry 21/3/90
G's visit to Ireland
visits farm on Parnell's estate 26/10/77
G too much regards as English-style leader, Morley thinks 15/1/86 n
Hartington overestimates Reform Bill's effect on power of, G thinks 29/12/83
hates England more than loves Ireland, Bright thinks 29/9/81 n
home rule and 8/9/85
discussion at Hawarden of terms of future bill, G's printed memorandum 18/12/89, 23/12/89
G's meetings with after 1886 8/3/88, 3/4/88, 18/12/89 ff
G's meetings with on Government of Ireland Bill 5/4/86, 7/5/86 ?, 18/5/86, 27/5/86
negotiations about delay of the bill 8/5/86, 14/5/86, 18/5/86, 27/5/86
proposes land purchase together with 9/1/86
urges G to declare plan for 3/11/85, 14/11/85, 16/12/85, 24/12/85
worried about Lords opposition to 13/11/85
home rule party leadership and
G's duty to give opinion on 22/11/90
humiliated by Maurice Healy 15/4/91
insight of 21/4/86
invitations to Hawarden 8/8/89, 30/8/89, 4/10/89
Irish local government and
paper of on, G requests copy of 27/6/85, 6/7/85, 4/8/85
'Kilmainham treaty' and 1/5/82 ff
no bargain involved in 1/5/82 c, 15/5/82 n
select committee on 22/5/82, 14/11/82 n, 16/11/82 c
Land Act 1881
will unquestionably obstruct working of 5/9/81
Land Bill 1881
amendment to 13/8/81 c
Land Bill proposal 10/10/82, 7/9/86
Land League, Ladies
has broken up with 29/8/82
Land League and 30/9/80 c, 2/10/80 ff, 7/6/81, 3/10/81 ff
drawing away well-inclined men from Parnell the key to politics 8/9/81
unpopularity of Parnell with Davitt and Dillon 29/8/82
land purchase and 13/7/88
loyal and satisfactory conversation of 2/9/89
most probable reading of: works for law as far as he dare 29/6/83
obstruction in the House and 2/2/81 ff
on 1881 Land Bill 7/6/81
one of the best people to deal with that G has known 19/12/89
O'Shea, Capt.
negotiations with and through 30/4/82 ff, 5/5/82 ff
O'Shea, Mrs. and 15/10/82
prefers the wife to the husband as an organ, G thinks 26/9/82
O'Shea divorce case and 21/3/90
awful matter of 20/11/90
continuance in leadership means end of liberals' common action with Parnell 28/11/90
great dénouement of 6/12/90
G's decision to intervene 23/11/90 ff
G's fear that Parnell will withdraw from public life 21/3/90 n
G's memoranda, printed 21/11/90, 22/11/90, 28/11/90, 30/11/90, 4/12/90, 5/12/90, 29/12/90
letters on to G 'all one way' 21/11/90
Morley, McCarthy and G's undelivered letter 24/11/90 ff, 20/8/91 n
Price's charge against G 5/1/91 n
O'Shea's petition of divorce 24/12/89 n
'Parnellism and crime' 7/3/87 n, 6/7/88
Commission on 12/7/88 n, 18/7/88 ff, 23/7/88, 31/7/88, 1/8/88 ff, 20/8/88, 20/2/89, 23/5/89, 11/2/90, 15/2/90 ff, 20/3/90, 24/3/90
Commission on; G's speech on 3/3/90
G joins in standing ovation for Parnell 1/3/89 n
Pigott's forged letter 28/4/87

Parnell, Charles Stewart (*cont.*)
participation of essential 22/4/82
Phoenix Park murders and 7/5/82 ff
offer of resignation of seat following 7/5/82, 24/11/90
Plan of Campaign and 7/9/86 n, 8/12/86
Prince of Wales and 29/4/85
'Proposed Constitution for Ireland' by 8/8/85, 24/10/85, 1/11/85 ff, 3/11/85
Parnell unwilling to make public 12/12/85 n
smallest proposal acceptable to Ireland 12/12/85 n
prosecution of 21/10/80, 7/11/80, 10/11/80 c, 17/11/80 c, 18/11/80, 19/11/80 c, 25/11/80 c, 26/11/80
probable acquittal of 11/1/81
urgent need for trial of 26/11/80
reckless and suicidal manifesto of 29/11/90
release of 9/4/82 n, 12/4/82, 15/4/82, 1/5/82 c, 2/5/82 c, 10/5/82, 12/5/82
running true 6/5/82, 24/5/82
royal finances and 5/7/89
sagacity of 21/11/90
Secret Societies and
as opposed to as British government, G thinks 12/6/82
speeches of
on colonial government and Irish right to self-rule 2/9/85, 3/9/85, 4/9/85
rather virulent badness of 18/9/85
to be available to cabinet 17/12/80
support in Commons
30–35 6/7/80
not above a dozen 18/9/81
supports National League's attack on liberal party as perfidious etc. 21/11/85 n
to communicate *via* Grosvenor 10/10/82
treasonable practices of? 27/9/81
Ulster and 10/11/85
urgently needed by Morley 8/5/86
visit to Hawarden of 18/12/89 ff
ex-cabinet dicussion of 8/2/90
G's letter to press on, printed 29/11/90
reckless and suicidal manifesto on 29/11/90
See also Chamberlain, Government of Ireland Bill 1886, Harcourt, Hawarden Castle, Herbert, home rule, Ireland, memoranda (printed), Morley, O'Shea
Parnell, Katharine, Mrs., née Page Wood, formerly O'Shea, married 1867 to Capt. O'Shea; divorced by him 1890, married to C. S. Parnell 1891 7/8/85, 18/11/85
communications from wholly uninvited by G 19/9/82
divorce case of
G's memoranda on, printed 21/11/90, 22/11/90, 28/11/90, 30/11/90, 4/12/90, 5/12/90, 29/12/90
G's letter substitutes for an interview 15/6/83
letters from G to, printed 23/5/82, 16/6/82, 23/6/82, 29/6/82, 10/10/82, 1/11/82, 15/6/83, 4/8/85, 8/8/85, 24/10/85, 3/11/85, 12/12/85, 16/12/85, 19/12/85, 22/12/85, 24/12/85, 9/1/86, 24/1/86, 26/1/86, 29/1/86, 8/5/86, 14/5/86
meetings with G 2/6/82, 12/6/82, 29/8/82
G suggests discontinuing 26/9/82
offers to arrange G/Parnell meeting 23/5/82
of use in keeping Parnell on lines of moderation 26/9/82
O'Shea's petition of divorce 24/12/89 n
Parnell's paper on Irish local government and
G's difficulty in obtaining 6/7/85, 4/8/85
Parnell's 'Proposed Constitution for Ireland' and 8/8/85, 24/10/85, 1/11/85 ff, 3/11/85
Parnell urgently needed by Morley 8/5/86
reflects Parnell's views, G presumes 29/8/82
See also Cavendish, Gower, Ireland, Parnell
Parnellism *See* Parnell
party
character of 20/12/45
essentially two parties only 31/5/50
G's unpublished article: 'Party as it was and is. A sketch of the political history of twenty years' 30/3/55 ff
organisation
discussed with C. G 20/10/51
principle of 9/5/41, 5/4/51
the team that draws the coach 1/10/84
See also conservative party, Ireland (home rule party), liberal party, publications
party meetings *See* liberal party
Party Processions Act *See* Ireland
Passionists 28/12/38
passports 2/11/38, 3/12/38, 24/7/49, 17/10/50, 29/10/50
problems with 21/10/50
patents 4/12/82, 7/7/83 c
Patricroft works (Nasmyth) 28/9/54
Patriotic Fund
G commissioner of 18/7/79
patriotism
Pan-Hellenism and 20/1/69
patronage
church 25/9/73, 18/10/73, 12/6/80, 1/12/80, 23/7/81 ff, 17/8/81 ff, 8/9/81 ff, 12/10/81 ff, 17/10/81, 9/1/83, 27/4/83, 9/5/83 n, 16/5/83, 23/12/83, 5/4/84, 20/4/84, 14/9/92
Benson to Canterbury
demarcation between first lord and lord chancellor 3/1/70, 2/11/72

Ewelme rectory case 19/3/71, 22/3/71
G appoints son-in-law to Lincoln deanery 16/1/94 n
G denies chiefly recommending High Churchmen 14/6/83
G encourages Lord Chancellor to appoint liberal clergy 10/9/92
G's list of deserving candidates 3/1/70
King to Lincoln 9/1/84 ff, 27/1/85
King to Oxford as pastoral professor 20/2/73
Mackarness to Oxford 22/9/69, 25/1/70
Temple to Exeter 28/8/69, 22/9/69, 10/10/69, 30/10/69 c, 16/11/69, 21/11/69, 3/1/70, 13/2/70
Temple to London 9/1/85 nf, 27/1/85
Wilberforce to Winchester 12/9/69 n, 22/9/69
effect of civil service examinations on 8/12/69
for relatives 3/4/72
Garter, offers of 8/1/94
Argyll 3/10/83
Bedford 28/8/80
Bedford (declined: old age) 14/8/72
Bessborough (declined) 2/11/93
Breadalbane 2/11/93 n
de Redcliffe 8/11/69 n
Leinster (declined) 8/11/69, 3/10/83 n
Norfolk (declined) 30/8/70
Ripon 8/11/69 n
Rosebery 25/9/92, 3/10/92
Shah of Persia: given, with reluctance 7/6/73 c
Zetland 6/11/72
G discourages Odo Russell from accepting a peerage from tory government 19/9/78
G favours diminution of 12/1/69
government pensions 8/7/81, 22/2/83 ?
honours 3/8/69, 4/8/69, 9/8/69 c, 9/9/69, 6/11/69 n, 29/6/70, 11/3/71 n, 23/3/71 n, 25/5/71, 20/6/71, 5/8/71 n, 9/1/72 n, 31/12/73, 12/2/74, 17/2/74, 23/8/81, 27/8/81, 17/3/82, 15/10/84, 22/5/93, 15/9/93, 28/12/93
Bath, reform of 22/5/71
for G's dentist 2/7/83 n
G seeks to appoint nonconformist peers 4/8/69
G's final honours 16/2/94 ff
Lansdowne's case 8/1/94 ff
medical 19/8/71
Order of Merit, opposed by Granville 21/6/73 c
resignation honours 13/3/73, 12/2/74, 17/2/74, 24/6/85 ff, 29/6/85, 20/7/86 ff
supplications for 4/7/71 n, 19/8/71, 1/11/71 n, 11/8/73 n
judges being made P. C. on retirement 26/1/73
lords lieutenant and deputies 9/11/69, 26/1/71, 24/5/71 n, 15/6/71, 29/6/71 n, 1/4/72, 20/4/72 c, 3/5/72, 1/8/72, 5/11/72, 7/4/73 n, 2/8/73, 4/10/73, 8/7/80, 7/10/92, 11/10/92
nonconformists and 30/12/82
pensions
unsatisfactory character of political pensions 29/5/86
Regius chairs
Divinity 7/11/93
Hebrew 4/10/82, 23/10/82
Modern History (Freeman) 13/2/84, 14/2/84
Royal Bounty Fund 1/9/82, 20/2/84, 21/9/93
use of for emigration 27/3/83
See also peerage, Scotland
Pau 9/1/92
payment of M. Ps. *See* Commons (House of)
peace
conference in London, G unable to take part in 7/7/90 n
England's providential role to promote 20/1/94
G at conclave of peace M. Ps. 24/6/90
G declines to see England set the world in arms 20/1/94
international arbitration 16/6/93
International League of Peace and Liberty 20/9/86
Peace Conference 18/10/93
Peace Preservation Bill *See* Ireland
Peace Society 23/7/50
Boer war and 14/1/81
Herald of Peace and invasion of Egypt 31/8/82
of Holland 14/1/81
Peake, R. B. *See* plays seen
Peckforton Castle (Tollemache) 27/11/56
Peculiar Court
attended by G 9/7/55
Peebles
G's speech at 30/3/80
Peel, Arthur Wellesley (1829–1912), 1st Viscount Peel (1895), liberal M.P., Speaker of the Commons 1884–95 11/10/73, 12/2/74, 9/3/74, 11/3/80, 28/2/85, 3/3/85 ff, 26/6/85, 30/12/85, 5/1/86, 27/1/86, 15/4/86, 2/3/87, 4/3/87, 1/4/87, 22/5/87, 24/2/88, 7/3/88, 21/3/88, 26/7/88, 14/11/88, 21/3/90, 1/3/92, 10/3/92, 4/8/92, 18/12/93
bold judgment of 28/3/90

Peel, Arthur Wellesley (*cont.*)
grave error of 6/9/86
letters from G to, printed 11/10/73, 31/12/73, 16/1/74, 6/2/74, 19/2/74, 28/4/80, 19/12/80, 2/12/83, 31/7/93, 2/3/94
Speakership and 2/12/83 ff, 11/12/83 ff
Peel, Robert, Sir (1788–1850), 2nd Baronet (1830), Prime Minister 1834–5, 1841–5, 1845–6, repealed the Corn Laws 1846 5/2/29, 5/10/30, 29/11/30, 7/7/31, 3/10/31, 1/11/36, 11/5/40, 19/10/49, 27/2/50, 20/3/50, 11/8/71, 5/9/71 n, 20/1/74, 29/7/74, 22/10/80, 23/10/80, 17/12/81, 5/4/82, 31/8/83, 2/1/84, 16/2/84, 28/6/84, 12/6/85, 16/6/85, 30/9/85, 31/12/85, 24/5/86, 23/6/86, 12/11/86, 16/10/93, 5/1/94, 19/3/94
accepts G's resignation 28/1/45
against liberal concession 16/3/44, 25/3/44
annexation of Scinde
unjust and indefensible 3/6/43
announces resignation to cabinet 26/6/46 n
Bank Charter Act and
a baptismal creed 18/5/83
bust of, by C. Benini 27/7/50
bust of, by Fraser 8/4/62
bust of, by Munro 24/2/54
Canada and 13/4/40
considers resignation on sugar duties 15/6/44 ff
conspicuous intellectual greatness of 13/3/42
conversations with
church matters 17/1/43, 20/1/43
on railways 7/7/40
conversation with G on extent of labours 12/7/45
corn laws and 20/1/42, 21/1/42 ff, 5/2/42, 9/2/42 ff, 14/2/42 ff, 2/3/42, 8/11/42, 10/3/43, 13/3/43, 20/12/45, 31/3/57
next change to total repeal 20/12/43
wants new scale 17/8/43
cut foot of 13/7/46
death of 1/7/50, 2/7/50
G misses funeral 9/7/50
G's article on 4/7/50
death of Drummond 25/1/43
declines G's request for diplomatic post with Vatican 12/7/44 n
discussed with J. R. Thursfield 8/3/88
discusses premiership with G 13/7/46
end of his government 2/7/46 ff, 9/7/46, 10/7/46, 13/7/46
France, cultivated alliance with 29/12/70
free trade and 4/6/41, 8/1/42 ff
G at Drayton 18/1/36
G dining with 26/6/33, 14/3/34, 31/3/34, 14/4/34, 29/7/34, 24/1/35, 23/2/35, 11/5/35, 9/12/37, 9/2/39, 1/2/40, 9/7/40, 20/2/41, 13/7/44, 20/3/50
to meet Guizot 29/3/48
G discusses his future with Hope 30/9/46
genesis of Bank Charter Act 13/1/44
G holds hands with 22/12/45
G ignorant of his intentions 10/7/46
government of 1841
formation of 21/8/41 ff
government of 1845
excessive caution of replies to Russell when forming 22/4/80
founded on quicksand 20/12/45
gratified by G's speech: that enough for G 10/3/48
great man commits a great error 17/6/44
G's differences with on religion 9/5/41, 10/10/41, 17/10/41
G's reservations about 7/2/40, 9/4/40
G's view of his position 13/7/46
G thinks position of false, almost immoral 19/10/49
G thinks power coming to 25/2/48
G thinks wrong to resign in 1846 4/10/51
G urges to stay in Parliament 13/7/46
G working on MS letters of (100) 13/6/55
helps with Lady Lincoln 21/6/49, 7/7/49
holds picture party 12/7/48
imposes maximum burden on self 12/7/45
influence on G's career 17/12/34, 20/12/34, 6/3/38, 10/5/80
when speaking officially, 'don't be short' 8/5/83
Irish policy of 4/6/41
Irish policy towards clergy 28/3/69
Life of by Guizot
G declines to review 17/3/57
Lincoln's divorce and 29/5/50 ff
makes no comment on *State and Church* 9/2/39
Maynooth proposals of 11/2/44 ff, 1/3/44, 2/3/44, 25/11/44, 9/1/45
meetings at Peel's 5/3/36, 4/3/37, 28/11/37, 6/12/37, 16/1/38, 25/1/38, 28/2/38, 30/4/38, 22/6/38, 20/7/38, 9/4/39, 13/4/39, 30/4/39, 29/5/39, 5/6/39, 10/6/39, 26/6/39, 16/1/40, 2/5/40, 26/4/41, 1/5/41, 22/5/41, 7/6/41, 4/4/42, 5/5/42, 23/1/43, 16/8/43, 17/8/43, 6/3/45, 8/3/45, 18/4/46, 29/5/46, 27/5/47
on British Guiana 30/6/40
on budget 27/4/43
on Canadian corn 27/4/43, 29/4/43
on China 18/3/40, 24/3/40
on clergy reserves 15/6/40, 20/6/40, 24/6/40, 3/7/40

on corn 20/1/42, 21/1/42, 5/2/42
on New Zealand 21/5/46
on registration 1/3/41
on Stade duties 25/9/42 ff
on sugar duties 1/5/41, 3/5/41, 4/5/41, 7/5/41, 26/2/45
on the Address and dissolution 21/8/41
on Ward's motion on agriculture 13/3/43
vote of no confidence 20/5/41
Memoirs of 3/10/51
G's memorandum on 4/10/51
memorial to 12/7/50 n, 1/3/51, 12/10/53, 20/5/65, 5/3/75
misunderstandings with 5/2/42 ff
MS of, G reading 5/3/55
nation's greatest statesman 2/7/50
Navigations Acts and 11/5/48, 13/2/49, 6/3/49
New Zealand and 13/7/46, 12/2/48
notable speeches of 29/11/30, 7/2/33, 15/2/33, 1/3/33, 23/4/33, 25/4/34, 23/12/34, 24/2/35, 7/4/35, 15/6/35, 15/3/39, 9/4/40, 1/6/40, 18/5/41, 11/3/42, 13/3/42, 6/5/44, 18/2/47, 5/4/48, 9/2/49, 6/7/49, 28/6/50
not best as after-dinner speaker 12/5/38
not favourable to present corn laws 13/5/43
occasional poor judgment of 19/8/43
offers baronetcy to G's father 20/6/46
offers G Cabinet and colonial secretaryship 21/12/45, 22/12/45
offers G Cabinet & Board of Trade 13/5/43 ff
on property tax 26/3/33
on Spanish treaty 7/11/42
on tariffs 10/5/42
Parker's *Peel* 7/4/89, 4/10/90, 23/4/91 ff
G lends MSS for 4/12/86, 4/10/90
pictures of, left to the nation 5/5/71
portraits of
Linnell's portrait of Peel bought by G 9/5/73
praise from 5/6/33
quietness of 19/1/36
refuses to give G office in Ireland 31/8/41, 16/9/41
resignation of 8/4/35, 10/7/46, 13/7/46
Scottish church and 12/6/38
sensible to opponents' cheers 30/6/46
speech at Glasgow 13/1/37
speech on opium only partly acceptable 4/4/43
statue of 3/3/71 n, 23/1/72 c
strictness in use of words 22/4/44
sugar duties and 15/6/44 ff, 10/7/46
requests G not to publish article 24/6/44 n
suggests post for G in Admiralty 31/8/41
tactical lessons to be learned from conduct of 28/4/86
taxed Exchequer excessively for local purposes 17/1/69
the Peelites and 9/12/47, 12/12/48, 5/4/51
the strong man of this Parliament & generation 13/7/46
the Wilmot case and 27/5/47, 29/5/47
tribute to Cobden unworthy 30/6/46, 10/7/46
West Indies relief
unknown attitude to 19/6/48 ff
See also Bank Charter Act, conservative party, corn laws, free trade, Herbert (Sidney), income tax, Maynooth, memoranda (printed), Newman, publications
Peelites
1851 budget and 5/4/51
1857 election and
G tries to avoid tory/Peelite clashes 6/3/57
a bad night for 19/2/57
accused of treason by Otway 15/6/55 n
all along covert party men? 31/3/57
breakup of Aberdeen's ministry and 24/1/55 ff, 31/1/55 ff
concerned about G's vote on Foreign Enlistment Bill 1/7/56 n
conclave on Roebuck 16/7/55, 17/7/55
conditions for party union with liberals 31/3/57
decline to serve on income tax cttee. 15/5/51
disagreement among on Navigation Acts 13/2/49 ff, 6/3/49, 20/3/49, 22/3/49
disposition to vote with Disraeli 19/2/50, 21/2/50
electorally smashed in Flintshire 7/4/57
fall of Derby's ministry and 20/11/52, 23/11/52, 24/11/52 ff
future of in doubt 31/5/50
G favours closer communication among 24/2/52
G fears drifting into general mass of liberal party 24/2/52
good agreement among 18/12/52
G's conversation with Derby on 4/2/57
G sees four distinct shades among 26/3/52
G's letter to Aberdeen on future of, printed 31/3/57
G's memorandum on 29/11/76
G speaks for on Peel's death 3/7/50
G's recollections of 17/2/93, 21/2/93
G unwilling to act independently of 22/5/58, 23/5/58
isolation of 20/1/57

Peelites (*cont.*)
meeting at Clumber 15/1/52 ff
not agreed on practical course 17/1/52
meetings on action in 1859 6/6/59 ff
meetings on finance 5/4/51, 24/5/51, 30/5/51
organisation of 7/12/47, 12/12/48, 16/6/51, 24/2/52 ff, 16/3/52, 18/3/52, 26/3/52, 31/3/52, 20/11/52, 4/12/52
Peelism as if not dead 12/5/57
possibility of joining Palmerston discussed 17/4/56
public duty of 13/3/56
sitting on ministerial side of the Commons 30/4/57
so-called 17/4/56
split on Locke King's reform bill 19/2/57
split on sugar duties 19/6/48 ff, 29/6/48
peerage
bankrupts in 20/1/71 c
declined by G 23/2/74, 2/2/83 n, 14/6/85 n, 19/6/85
G's memorandum on creation of new peerages 14/9/69
life 4/10/82
military 4/10/82
need for decided Liberalism in 17/9/85
reform of 16/3/69 ff
Scottish 17/4/69 c, 29/5/69 c
elections to 18/4/81
See also patronage
Pembroke Lodge (Russell) 22/6/53, 28/6/54, 5/1/60, 21/4/65, 24/6/66, 30/1/69, 18/12/70, 30/7/75, 9/7/77, 20/4/78, 21/5/81, 13/6/88, 29/6/89
G's speech at 13/6/88
Penang
export of arms to Acheen 5/4/73 c
Pendjeh incident *See* Afghanistan
Penicuik 5/1/36, 8/1/36
G's speeches at 24/3/80 ff, 11/7/92
Penmaenmawr 31/8/26, 3/9/55 ff, 3/9/59 ff, 13/9/59, 20/9/59 ff, 27/9/59, 1/9/60, 15/8/61, 15/8/62, 2/9/63, 30/8/64, 10/8/67, 28/8/67, 10/8/68, 10/9/68, 6/8/74, 28/9/82, 19/2/87, 20/10/96
G drawn by working men from station to house 10/8/68
G's grand party at 14/9/64
Orme's Head 23/8/61
quarries at 28/9/59
theft of wine at 18/9/63
See also Gladstone (W. H.)
pen-name, G's *See* Bartholomew Bouverie
Penrhyn Castle (Penrhyn) 31/8/26, 21/9/55, 12/9/61, 13/9/62
Penrhyn quarries 16/9/61
Pentland Firth 1/9/80
Pentre Foelas 1/9/63
peppermint *See* medicines
Pericles' politics 13/5/26
Persia 14/7/57, 16/7/57, 12/6/80 c, 24/10/82 c
boundary with Russia requested 1/3/73 c
British officers for 27/2/69 c
Reuter's concession in 10/11/73 c
Russia and 1834 agreement
not to be changed 5/4/73 c
Russian expansion and 5/3/83 c
Seistan arbitration 15/2/73 c
unacceptable to Persia 1/3/73 c
Shah's visit to U.K.
costs of: a very awkward question 31/1/73
Garter for: given, with reluctance 7/6/73 c
G presented to Shah 19/6/73, 24/6/73
G's reception for 1/7/73
Turkish border with 21/6/73 c, 28/6/73 c
Perth 13/11/33, 27/11/34, 26/10/36, 25/9/40, 7/9/46, 24/1/49, 9/7/57, 24/9/63, 1/12/79, 24/1/80
enthusiastic reception at 29/9/69, 26/9/71
Freedom of 10/8/72 n
G Freeman of 1/12/79
G's speeches in 1/12/79, 24/9/84
Perugia 4/10/38, 2/1/67
Peterborough
Peterborough cathedral 26/9/54
petitions
Bedford 5/3/33
Carrickfergus 1/5/33
Edinburgh 1/5/33, 21/5/33
Irish Church Bill 1833 11/5/33
Ross election 4/7/37 ff
pewrents 8/4/41
Philadelphia and Reading railway *See* railways (G shareholder in)
Philanthropic Society 21/5/48, 30/4/49
Reigate school, G's speech at 24/4/52
philanthropy
black prospects of 29/12/96
Phillimore, Robert Joseph, Judge Sir (1810–1885), 1st Baronet (1881), Peelite M.P., judge, jurist and G's confidant 16/5/26, 30/8/28, 7/7/31, 6/8/31, 21/10/31, 25/3/33, 7/7/36, 9/9/42 ff, 15/11/43, 9/10/44, 2/5/50, 12/3/51, 16/5/51, 19/4/52, 2/1/53 ff, 8/1/53, 13/1/53, 16/1/54, 10/7/55, 12/10/55 n, 8/2/56, 11/7/56, 28/9/56 ff, 5/5/57, 10/3/58, 3/6/58, 1/7/59, 4/7/59, 13/2/60, 19/11/60, 3/8/61, 22/3/64, 19/8/65, 8/2/67 ff, 20/2/68 ff, 16/3/68, 27/5/68, 25/7/69 ff, 10/11/69, 9/12/69, 17/12/69, 31/1/70, 10/5/71, 9/11/71,

10/11/71, 18/12/71, 21/2/72, 1/8/72, 2/2/73, 11/2/73 ff, 21/11/73, 25/1/74, 8/2/74, 7/7/74, 16/7/74, 23/2/75, 19/4/75, 27/5/75, 11/6/75, 17/7/75, 10/11/75, 6/2/76, 7/3/76, 17/2/77, 4/3/77, 10/4/77, 24/6/77, 24/7/77, 3/12/77, 17/1/78, 25/1/78, 5/2/78, 25/3/78, 28/3/78, 31/3/78, 24/7/78, 1/8/78, 1/12/78, 18/3/79, 19/5/79, 29/6/79, 21/7/79, 23/1/80, 25/4/80, 2/5/80, 16/1/81, 23/1/81, 13/2/81, 26/2/81, 21/7/81, 13/11/81, 12/2/82, 26/2/82, 26/3/82, 4/3/83, 18/3/83, 8/4/83, 26/11/83
advises cabinet on *Trent* affair 13/12/61
Alabama, advises cabinet on 8/5/72 c
all with G [on Irish church] 28/4/68
at Cuddesdon 8/6/57
at Hawarden 13/10/55, 27/3/57, 23/10/59 ff, 12/10/61, 19/8/65, 4/8/72, 6/9/75, 7/10/82 ff
advises on the estate 25/8/65
at theatre with G 12/3/70
baronetcy for 14/11/81
'over the moon' about 2/12/81
contemplates resignation 16/6/82
diary of, last surviving entry 16/6/82
funeral of, G unable to attend 9/2/85
G gives 5 reasons against again being Prime Minister 30/3/79
G's candidacy at Oxford and 28/5/47 ff, 24/6/47 ff
G's meeting with Carnarvon at his house 14/2/78
G's Oxford University seat and 18/5/47 ff, 27/1/54 ff, 13/3/57 ff, 18/6/59, 2/3/65
G supports his Tithe Bill 7/5/56
G's verses on his farm 25/12/69
G visiting The Coppice 11/8/60, 28/11/63, 30/9/75, 9/9/79, 21/9/82
Henry Glynne's marriage and 13/2/60 ff, 10/3/60, 17/3/60, 18/3/60, 26/11/60, 27/11/60, 29/11/60
letters from G to, printed 18/3/70
Lushington's judgment and 16/12/55
made judge 25/7/67
meets G on return from Naples 26/2/51
memorial window to 15/7/88
present at G's shooting accident 13/9/42
Queen's Advocate 17/8/62
retirement of 21/3/83
Royal Supremacy and 25/5/50
supports G's plan to retire 5/11/82, 10/12/82
the Denison affair and 24/8/56 ff, 1/9/56
thinks G aged and grave 30/3/79
urges G to have lieutenant in Commons 25/4/80 n
views on U.S.A. and international law 12/10/61
See also Coppice (Henley)
Phillips' auction rooms
Chapman sale 16/2/67, 19/2/67
philosophy, G's writings on 12/12/30
Phoenix Park *See* Ireland, Parnell
phonograph
astonishing performance of 22/11/88
presented to G 24/7/90
recordings of G
by Edison 22/11/88, 24/7/90 ?
by J. Lewis Young for America 7/3/90
for Australia 8/3/90
phonography
demonstration of 18/3/78
See also recordings
photographs of G 28/5/73, 4/9/73, 27/8/74, 18/8/76, 24/6/79, 28/11/79, 16/6/80, 22/12/80, 21/3/81, 13/9/81, 17/8/83, 13/10/87 ff, 13/12/88, 18/12/88, 3/12/89
Acland, Sarah 25/10/92
Alinari of Florence 31/1/88, 3/2/88
at Glamis Castle 22/9/84
at Penmaenmawr
maximum charge of 6d. 21/9/64
Barraud of London 6/5/91
Bassano (frontispiece of Vol. X) 10/3/83
Brewster, Sir D. 13/8/73
Caldesi? 9/7/63
Chancellor (Dublin) 24/10/77, 6/11/77
Claudet 28/7/51, 13/8/53
Dickinson 3/5/71
Downie of Newcastle and London 7/10/62, 22/7/63
G taken on condition of 6d. sale 16/7/67
Elliot and Fry 31/3/79
Fergus (Cannes) 16/2/89
Harcourt, L. V. 3/11/83
Holland of Hull 16/11/86
Jamblin [of Penmaenmawr?] 26/8/68
Lenbach, F. 13/10/79
Lenbach, F. (for portrait) 12/9/74
London Stereoscopic Co. 17/5/88
L. V. Harcourt 21/9/88
Major Shakespeare (in Ionia) 16/2/59, 18/2/59
Maull and Polyblank 3/8/57
Mayall 28/4/55, 19/4/56, 23/7/61, 9/5/66, 26/6/77, 6/6/84, 7/6/84
Maynall 9/5/66, 24/6/69
McLaughlin of Liverpool 14/10/64
Mendelsohn 1/11/84
Millais 7/7/84
Moffat of Edinburgh 13/12/59
Myers, Eveleen 25/4/90
Nottage 25/4/73
Pennant, Miss 16/9/61

photographs of G (*cont.*)
Potter, Rupert 28/7/84 n
Ralph 31/1/87
Rev. Palmer 21/10/89
shameful print of G with Bradlaugh and Besant 18/5/83
treefelling at Hawarden 6/8/77
Walker, S. A. 28/7/62, 26/7/64, 12/9/66, 22/8/81
with C. G 26/7/64
Webster 20/8/84
Whitfield 12/3/80
Whitwell 31/12/68
Williams, T. R. 22/7/61
Winder
in full dress 14/6/64
with 10 grandchildren 6/9/88
Wothly type 22/5/66, 23/5/66
photography
stereoscopes 29/11/62
phrenology 11/8/26, 1/3/28, 13/2/30, 23/12/35, 17/2/75 n
G's head measured at S. Kensington 14/6/90
Physicians, Royal College of
G dining at 5/7/56, 11/7/57
Piacenza 24/9/38
piano-forte, G playing 30/8/25, 10/12/33, 28/12/37
Piccolomini opera company 21/4/57
pickpockets 6/5/32
picnics 2/1/51, 20/8/58, 2/9/62, 17/9/64, 31/7/68, 23/5/88, 11/9/93, 12/9/93, 15/9/93
pictures
Ashburnham collection
government involvement in purchase of 28/2/83, 12/3/83, 14/4/83 c, 26/5/83 c, 2/6/83 c, 13/6/83 c, 23/6/83 c
Blenheim collection
government involvement in purchase of 21/6/84 c, 9/7/84 c, 21/7/86
G buying 20/3/52, 23/3/52
Hern 16/5/72
Linnell's portrait of Peel 9/5/73
Murillo 31/5/53
Warwick Brookes 6/3/71
G buys Clarkson for £100 3/3/68
G's Bellini ('so-called') bought in Rome 6/11/66
G's Brill, restored in Naples 12/12/50, 19/12/50
G's Murillo 25/6/58
lessons on from Lady Schreiber 6/6/72
See also Christie's auction rooms
Piedmont 2/3/32
Pieve di Cadore 29/9/79
Pincher, the dog 12/1/27
Pisa
leaning tower of 14/3/32, 15/3/32
Pitlochry 20/7/92, 8/9/93
Pitt the Younger
fortifications policy of 16/12/59
French Treaty of 27/1/60
French war
excusable but ruinous error 30/1/71, 1/3/71
George III and 16/10/93
MSS of, G working on 19/5/87
reflections on 22/10/33
relationship to G's children 28/2/59
the sinking fund and 21/5/66
Pitt the Elder
conquest of Canada by ended means of retaining British Provinces in N. America 21/12/84
Pius IX
a hardened offender 23/11/69
G's article on: 'Speeches of Pope Pius IX', *Q.R.*, cxxxviii. 266(January 1875) 9/12/74, 3/1/75
G's audience with, printed 22/10/66
publication of in edition of Ricasoli's papers, declined 28/3/93
has done wider and deeper mischief than any other living man 8/12/73
See also cabinet, Italy, Papacy, Roman Catholic Church, Vatican Council
plaid, Scottish, useful in Sicily 6/11/38
plans for action 21/9/40
Plato
bought in Rome 4/6/32
G's memorandum on, printed 15/6/88
Laws, notes on 29/9/37 ff
missing and borrowed 6/10/37, 9/10/37
monstrous views on community of 15/9/32
Phaedo, analysis of 9/11/30, 28/12/30
Republic, analysis of 23/8/32
Timaeus, notes on 8/9/37 ff
writings on by G 16/6/30
See also memoranda, memoranda (printed)
Plautus
G's notes on 23/9/52
plays seen
A Daughter to Marry 31/3/56
Adrienne Lecouvreur (Scribe) 28/7/87
A Man's Shadow 29/3/90
A Midsummer Night's Dream (Shakespeare) 6/8/59, 3/11/70
An Enemy of the People (Ibsen) 19/6/90
Antony and Cleopatra (Shakespeare) 6/12/90
how low our stage has fallen 1/12/73
Antigone (Sophocles) 26/4/90
An Unequal Match 21/10/59
Arrah na Pogue (Boucicault) 13/5/65

A Winter's Tale (Shakespeare) 3/7/56, 17/6/81
Becket (Tennyson) 25/2/93
Captain of the watch (Planché) 14/1/53
Colleen Bawn (Boucicault) 13/11/60, 23/11/60, 17/12/60
Comedy and Tragedy 23/4/85
Conte di Montecristo (Dumas, in Naples) 11/11/50, 18/11/50
Devotion 17/5/84
Diplomacy 29/11/84
Duel (R. B. Peake) 4/5/27
Eilsen Oge 16/8/71
El Gambustino 31/3/56
Elisabetta Regina d'Inghilterra (P. Giacommetti) 9/7/58
  rehearsal attended 10/7/58
Fool's Paradise 19/5/92
Hamlet (Shakespeare) 24/8/27, 29/7/61, 16/4/75, 17/11/76, 19/2/79, 24/3/79
Henry IV (Shakespeare) 22/4/64
Henry VIII (Shakespeare) 11/5/92
Henry V (Shakespeare) 5/5/59
  at Windsor Castle 10/11/53
Hernani(Hugo) 17/10/79
Ici on parle Français 14/3/78
Il bel Demonio 2/12/63
Il Gladiatore (Soumet) 7/7/75
Ingomar (Doyle) 27/4/83
Jack and Jill(pantomime) 3/3/77
Jack's return from Canton 21/10/59
King John (Shakespeare) 31/10/71
King Lear (Shakespeare) 29/5/58, 10/6/58
King's Butterfly 21/11/64
Lady Clare (R. W. Buchanan) 24/4/83
La Gobba 18/11/50
La Suara di Carita Torinese in Roma (in Turin) 2/11/50
le finte Inglesi (Naples) 1/12/38
Le Gendre de M. Poirier(Augier) 20/10/79
Les Anglaises pour rire 21/11/53
Les contes de la reine de Navarre (Sue & Legouvé, in Paris) 22/10/50
Les Fourberies de Scapin(Molière) 20/10/79
Little Don Caesar de Bazan 27/10/76
Little Goody Two Shoes 22/1/63
Louis XI (Delavigne) 11/2/32
Macbeth (Shakespeare) 19/11/64
Maria Stuarda(Schiller) 18/6/56, 27/6/73
Married for Money 16/5/74
Masks and Faces 2/4/81
Merchant of Venice (Shakespeare) 13/7/58, 28/2/80
Money (Lytton) 26/7/75
Much Ado about Nothing (Shakespeare) 25/10/82, 29/1/91
My aunt's husband 19/11/63
My Husband's Ghost 18/8/71
My Milliner's Bill 30/4/84, 17/5/84
My wife's journal 11/2/61
Nos Intimes (Sardou) 19/4/71, 6/4/72
Nursery Chickweed 5/12/64
Olivia 20/7/78
Othello (Shakespeare) 1/10/80, 15/6/81
Our American Cousin 17/11/62
Ours (T. Robinson) 4/2/82
Pair of spectacles 18/3/90
pantomime 5/1/65
Payable on demand 11/8/59
Peril 26/10/76
Phèdre (Racine) 2/3/59, 9/6/80
Phenomenon in a smock frock 24/7/62
Pulcinello (Naples) 20/11/38
Pygmalion and Galatea 23/4/85
Ravenswood (adapted Scott) 2/12/90
Retained for the defence 11/8/59
Richard III (Shakespeare) 4/5/77
Richard II (Shakespeare) 22/4/57, 16/5/57
Rip Van Winckle 9/2/76
Robin Goodfellow (R. C. Carton) 13/1/93
Romeo and Juliet (Shakespeare) 24/7/79, 8/7/82, 8/11/84
Ruy Blaas (Hugo) 5/12/64
Sam's arrival 24/11/62
School for Scandal, The (Sheridan) 17/1/66, 27/9/77
School (T. W. Robertson) 1/11/69
Sophia (R. Buchanan) 13/4/87
The boarding school 18/4/60
The Candidate 10/2/85
The Corsican brothers (Boucicault) 6/8/59, 3/1/81
The Critic (Sheridan) 25/8/60, 16/5/74
The Cup (Tennyson) 3/1/81
The duke's motto 30/5/63, 19/6/63
The emigré's daughter 25/7/50
The evil genius 31/3/56
The first night 25/2/54
The Heir-at-Law 5/9/76
The Hunchback (S. Knowles) 12/8/57
The Isle of St. Tropez 11/2/61
The Lady of Lyons 19/6/79
The lottery ticket 25/2/54
The Lyons Mail 5/3/78
The overland route 18/4/60
The pilgrimage of love 18/4/60
The promise of May (Tennyson) 11/11/82, 14/11/82
The rifle and how to use it 21/10/59
The Rivals (Sheridan) 25/6/84
The Tempest (Shakespeare) 8/8/57
The wandering minstrel 25/2/54
The windmill (E. Morton) 14/1/53
This evening 11/8/58
Ticket of Leave Man 31/3/64, 5/8/75
Trinummus (Plautus) 18/12/60

plays seen (*cont.*)
Two Roses (J. Albery) 16/9/70
G starts campaign against 16/9/70 n
Uncle baby 2/12/63 n
Uncle Dick's Darling 12/3/70
White lady's secret(S. Beazley) 4/5/27
Young Mrs. Winthrop 18/11/84
Zazel 2/7/77
plebiscites 27/4/83
Plockton 1/9/53
ploutocracy 2/9/71 n, 13/9/71, 12/5/74
Queen agrees with G on 21/12/71
Pluralities Bill 29/5/85
Plymouth
G's speeches at 13/7/77, 14/6/89
Plymouth Brethren 20/5/75, 15/12/92
pocket boroughs *See* Reform Bills
poems and verses by G 20/5/26, 18/10/26, 2/2/27, 21/6/27, 14/10/32
African deserts 29/4/30
Art Thou Weary (translation of Latin hymn) 10/10/75
Bedlam 29/7/35
'Box and Cox' verses, printed 21/11/88
Congratulation to the beeches of the Garrol 27/10/34, 31/10/34
death of Anstice 3/3/36
death of Prince Albert 27/12/61 n
Dunottar castle 20/9/34
'Fret not, haste not, droop not, fear not', printed 17/10/90
limericks, printed 10/9/62
on Dante 6/7/36
on his brother's dead child 12/7/36, 19/7/38
on Jessy G 13/5/50
on the nursemaid's aunt 10/11/43
Phillimore's farm 25/12/69
printed in diaries 7/3/79
readings of human life 3/6/37
reread: G uncertain as to merit of 3/11/86
Richard Coeur de Lion 2/9/93 n
selection of verses 20/12/37
sonnets to a young lady 16/6/36
Suttee 27/4/31 ff
the grey mare 11/2/36, 12/12/37
The human heart 4/1/33, 9/12/34
The moorcock's song 6/12/34
the pastor 22/1/38
the Rhône and the Saône 6/6/36
to Judith Fileen 5/10/36
tr. of Dante 28/2/36
Poet Laureateship
filling of 7/10/92 ff, 28/10/92 n, 25/11/92
Ruskin and 7/10/92, 10/10/92, 17/10/92, 15/8/93
Swinburne and 10/10/92
See also Ruskin
poetry
G reciting to Hawardeners 20/11/79
G's reflections on his verses 30/7/58 ff
vice of explanatory notes 31/10/38
poetry, reflections on 20/7/33
poets
G's list of clerical poets 20/12/81
Pola
G visits 22/11/58, 22/2/59
Poland 9/7/33, 24/6/63, 20/7/63
Friends of, complain about G's speech 7/9/88
historical dates of 25/11/33
police 12/2/33, 16/2/33, 4/4/34, 18/9/63
committee on 14/6/70 c
costs of guarding G in Flintshire 7/4/82, 17/9/82, 20/10/82
financing of 2/1/74
G sworn as Special Constable against Chartists 11/3/48, 1/4/48, 12/6/48
metropolitan police 3/5/73 c, 10/4/77, 13/4/77
Police Court
G appears in 11/5/53, 13/5/53, 13/9/79
servants and 23/1/43, 24/1/43, 2/2/43
political economy 12/12/37
and Irish land 5/12/69
discussed with Whewell 25/11/41
G's view of 31/8/46
Harvard University
G declines invitation to lecture on political economy at 15/8/78
See also Manchester School, Paris, Political Economy Club, publications
Political Economy Club
Bank Charter Act amendment 2/2/66
centenary of the *Wealth of Nations*
G's speech at 31/5/76
Coulson on duties 6/4/43
Foxwell on notes 1/7/87
government purchase of railways 3/2/65
Mundella on dangers to British predominance 7/12/77
national issue and small notes 19/4/55
nine hours labour 5/4/72
rate of interest 3/3/65
seignorage 5/2/69
Sidgwick on free trade 10/6/87
Suez Canal shares purchase
generally hostile to 3/3/76
Tooke on tariffs 1/12/42
political hostesses
G's attendance at balls and soireés of
Andalusia, Lady Molesworth 20/6/51, 14/2/52, 26/5/52, 26/2/53, 9/5/57, 3/3/58, 30/3/59, 2/6/59, 14/3/60, 18/6/61, 18/6/62, 10/1/66, 17/2/66, 27/11/67, 10/2/71

Charlotte, Duchess of Beaufort 2/2/38, 20/2/38, 2/3/38, 13/3/38, 10/4/38, 14/4/38, 20/4/38, 23/4/38, 13/7/38, 8/2/39, 26/2/39, 24/4/39, 12/6/39, 15/2/40, 18/3/40, 16/2/41, 8/6/41, 18/12/41, 31/1/42, 17/5/42, 1/7/42, 1/8/42, 13/12/42, 23/1/43, 26/4/43, 21/6/43, 20/12/43, 23/7/44, 8/2/45, 9/4/45, 14/7/45, 20/12/45, 31/1/46, 23/3/46, 17/5/46, 25/5/46, 17/5/47, 24/2/49, 19/7/50, 31/3/51, 15/7/51, 19/7/51, 26/7/51, 5/7/52, 13/3/53, 10/7/53, 5/2/54, 11/2/54

Charlotte, Duchess of Buccleuch 19/6/38, 20/6/38, 6/7/38, 10/7/38, 23/6/42, 25/2/45, 17/4/45, 24/5/49, 16/6/52, 22/6/63, 8/7/63, 16/7/64

Constance, Lady Battersea 4/7/83, 29/4/85

Emily, Lady Palmerston 8/3/51, 15/3/51, 12/4/51, 24/5/51, 14/6/51, 21/6/51, 19/7/51, 26/7/51, 7/2/52, 21/2/52, 28/2/52, 27/3/52, 3/4/52, 8/5/52, 3/6/52, 5/6/52, 19/6/52, 22/11/52, 30/7/53, 13/8/53, 4/3/54, 17/2/55, 24/2/55, 14/3/55, 28/4/55, 12/5/55, 2/2/56, 23/2/56, 14/2/57, 27/3/58, 24/4/58, 19/6/58, 6/3/59, 16/3/59, 30/3/59, 13/4/59, 28/5/59, 2/7/59, 16/7/59, 30/7/59, 10/8/59, 17/11/59, 1/2/60, 9/3/60, 1/8/60, 18/8/60, 20/4/61, 29/6/61, 13/7/61, 17/5/62, 28/6/62, 22/11/62, 25/4/63, 13/5/63, 13/6/63, 20/6/63, 18/7/63, 10/11/63, 14/11/63, 6/2/64, 13/2/64, 9/4/64, 7/5/64, 18/6/64, 22/6/64, 9/7/64, 18/11/64, 11/2/65, 18/3/65, 27/5/65, 3/3/66, 23/2/67, 9/3/67, 22/7/68, 24/2/69, 3/8/69

Frances, Lady Londonderry (2nd wife of 3rd Marquess) 27/5/45, 24/7/45, 9/7/46, 1/7/51

Frances, Lady Salisbury (wife of 1st Marquis) 28/2/35, 14/3/35, 28/3/35, 7/5/36, 16/6/36, 13/3/37, 30/6/37, 2/12/37, 17/2/38, 24/3/38, 23/5/38, 3/7/38

Frances, Lady Waldegrave 27/3/49, 23/5/49, 21/6/49, 4/7/49, 1/4/51, 15/5/51, 28/6/51, 10/2/55, 6/3/58, 8/5/58, 9/5/58, 10/5/58, 11/5/58, 15/6/58, 2/4/59, 28/4/59, 29/4/59, 30/4/59, 19/5/59, 30/5/59, 31/5/59, 17/6/59, 24/6/59, 19/5/60, 17/11/60, 18/11/60, 19/11/60, 8/5/61, 19/6/61, 3/6/63, 22/7/63, 24/2/64, 2/3/64, 27/4/64, 8/2/65, 15/2/65, 28/5/65, 24/3/66, 28/4/66, 23/6/66, 13/3/67, 27/3/67, 10/4/67, 15/6/67, 6/7/67, 7/7/67, 8/7/67, 15/2/68, 29/2/68, 14/3/68, 25/4/68, 23/5/68, 24/5/68, 25/5/68, 26/5/68, 27/5/68, 28/5/68, 29/5/68, 30/5/68, 4/7/68, 5/7/68, 6/7/68, 20/7/68, 14/4/69, 26/2/70, 26/3/70, 22/6/70, 29/6/71, 3/7/71, 30/10/71, 6/12/72, 8/3/73, 3/12/73, 13/3/74, 13/2/75, 5/3/75, 10/2/76, 26/2/76, 27/3/76, 15/7/76, 16/7/76, 17/7/76, 17/2/77, 9/6/77, 10/6/77, 11/6/77, 14/6/77, 20/2/78, 29/3/79

Georgina, Lady Salisbury (wife of 3rd Marquis) 25/5/70, 24/11/70, 31/3/74, 25/6/75, 6/6/83, 30/6/83, 27/10/83, 3/12/84

Harriet, Duchess of Sutherland 10/2/40, 31/1/42, 2/8/45, 16/6/47, 25/7/51, 16/4/53, 7/5/53, 26/12/53, 18/3/54, 20/3/54, 29/3/54, 4/4/54, 11/4/54, 9/5/54, 25/5/54, 7/6/54, 26/7/54, 29/7/54, 30/7/54, 31/7/54, 13/1/55, 30/1/55, 2/2/55, 6/3/55, 27/4/55, 4/5/55, 8/6/55, 16/6/55, 12/7/55, 25/7/55, 27/7/55, 15/2/56, 26/2/56, 25/4/56, 29/5/56, 31/5/56, 19/6/56, 21/6/56, 25/7/56, 12/2/57, 13/2/57, 20/2/57, 21/3/57, 30/5/57, 4/6/57, 5/6/57, 4/7/57, 5/7/57, 6/7/57, 4/12/57, 26/1/58, 27/1/58, 22/2/58, 24/2/58, 11/3/58, 31/3/58, 24/4/58, 12/5/58, 15/3/59, 18/3/59, 11/4/59, 13/4/59, 15/4/59, 6/5/59, 11/6/59, 14/6/59, 17/6/59, 1/7/59, 31/7/59, 2/8/59, 13/8/59, 14/8/59, 15/8/59, 16/8/59, 25/1/60, 27/1/60, 11/3/60, 18/3/60, 29/3/60, 18/4/60, 28/4/60, 29/4/60, 14/5/60, 15/6/60, 1/7/60, 5/7/60, 6/7/60, 18/7/60, 29/7/60, 2/8/60, 4/8/60, 17/8/60, 9/11/60, 13/11/60, 19/11/60, 3/12/60, 7/12/60, 15/12/60, 16/12/60, 18/12/60, 1/7/61, 3/7/61, 6/7/61, 7/7/61, 9/7/61, 10/7/61, 11/7/61, 12/7/61, 22/10/61, 23/10/61, 22/1/62, 20/3/62, 18/4/62, 1/5/62, 8/5/62, 9/5/62, 13/5/62, 23/5/62, 2/6/62, 25/10/62, 12/11/62, 13/11/62, 15/11/62, 19/11/62, 20/11/62, 22/11/62, 23/11/62, 25/11/62, 28/11/62, 30/11/62, 9/12/62, 28/1/63, 1/2/63, 25/2/63, 18/3/63, 25/3/63, 31/3/63, 5/4/63, 8/4/63, 16/4/63, 3/5/63, 23/5/63, 19/6/63, 22/6/63, 25/6/63, 2/7/63, 3/7/63, 6/7/63, 7/7/63, 16/7/63, 23/7/63, 12/11/63, 15/11/63, 19/11/63, 20/11/63, 23/11/63, 25/11/63, 1/12/63, 5/12/63, 7/12/63, 16/12/63, 17/12/63, 20/1/64,

political hostesses (*cont.*)
G's attendance at balls and soirées of (*cont.*)
Harriet, Duchess of Sutherland (*cont.*) 22/1/64, 30/1/64, 6/2/64, 7/2/64, 12/4/64, 13/4/64, 17/4/64, 21/4/64, 29/4/64, 13/5/64, 7/6/64, 12/7/64, 21/7/64, 22/7/64, 11/2/65, 12/2/65, 27/2/65, 1/3/65, 8/3/65, 11/3/65, 15/3/65, 18/3/65, 22/3/65, 29/3/65, 1/4/65, 4/4/65, 9/4/65, 29/4/65, 15/5/65, 26/5/65, 11/7/65, 24/7/65, 26/7/65, 27/7/65, 12/1/66, 13/1/66, 15/1/66, 17/1/66, 20/1/66, 24/1/66, 27/1/66, 28/1/66, 30/1/66, 4/2/66, 5/2/66, 11/2/66, 21/2/66, 4/3/66, 11/3/66, 12/3/66, 15/3/66, 20/3/66, 24/3/66, 27/3/66, 28/3/66, 4/4/66, 7/4/66, 11/4/66, 18/4/66, 25/4/66, 28/4/66, 2/5/66, 5/5/66, 9/5/66, 13/5/66, 16/5/66, 1/6/66, 5/6/66, 12/6/66, 20/6/66, 13/7/66, 25/7/66, 28/7/66, 4/8/66, 13/8/66, 10/11/66, 6/2/67, 9/2/67, 13/2/67, 26/2/67, 1/3/67, 10/4/67, 1/5/67, 23/7/67, 5/8/67, 1/12/67, 2/1/68, 3/1/68, 3/3/68, 2/5/68, 21/6/68, 23/6/68, 20/7/68, 28/10/68, 1/11/84
Ishbel, Lady Aberdeen 21/6/75, 4/3/84, 8/3/84, 11/2/86, 16/2/86
Lady Ashburton 16/5/38, 28/6/38, 2/4/41, 5/5/41, 21/5/51, 18/6/51, 28/4/52, 26/6/52, 28/6/52, 13/7/76, 5/7/78
Lady Carnarvon 2/2/67, 25/4/68, 5/6/69
Lady de Grey/Lady Ripon 13/2/69, 27/2/69, 13/3/69, 24/4/69, 19/2/70, 25/5/71, 7/8/72, 24/6/75, 1/6/80, 9/11/80, 21/2/85
Lady Granville 14/4/69, 20/2/75, 13/3/75, 21/2/79, 6/3/79, 21/5/80, 10/7/80, 21/3/86
Lady Jersey 13/4/35, 2/4/38, 4/6/38, 31/3/41, 11/6/41, 13/5/43, 28/6/44, 1/5/45, 27/3/49, 28/3/51, 2/6/51, 23/6/51, 23/3/52, 28/6/52, 8/7/52, 18/4/56, 2/6/56, 27/3/58, 6/5/58, 19/5/58, 19/6/58, 1/4/59, 21/5/59
Lady John Russell 21/3/49, 20/3/50, 12/3/51, 3/3/52, 8/2/53, 26/1/55, 5/1/60, 21/2/66, 30/7/75, 29/5/76, 17/4/77, 26/2/78, 20/4/78, 7/5/79, 20/5/79, 21/5/81, 22/5/81
Lady Spencer 10/7/68, 19/6/81, 22/4/82, 7/5/82, 20/3/83, 14/4/85
Louisa, Lady Lansdowne 13/6/33, 16/5/34, 3/7/35, 5/5/36, 28/3/38, 6/4/38, 17/5/38, 23/5/38, 6/6/38, 29/6/38, 29/6/49
Louise, Duchess of Manchester 6/12/68, 23/10/70, 15/7/74
Maria, Lady Grey 21/4/49, 25/7/51, 11/2/57
Mary, Lady Salisbury, later Lady Derby 18/6/49, 8/3/52, 22/3/52, 18/6/52, 25/3/58, 21/2/75, 25/6/75, 29/6/75, 10/4/78, 21/5/79, 25/6/79, 8/7/79, 3/3/80, 29/5/80, 30/6/80, 8/1/81, 4/5/81, 8/2/82, 1/3/82, 16/5/82, 24/5/82, 8/11/82, 14/3/83, 18/4/83, 24/1/84, 6/2/84, 25/4/84, 12/11/84, 13/2/85, 25/3/85, 5/5/86, 15/7/86
Mary Anne Disraeli, Lady Beaconsfield 12/5/69, 24/2/72, 9/8/72
Stafford House (after death of Harriet, Duchess of Sutherland) 28/6/69, 4/7/70, 5/7/71, 13/5/73, 8/5/83, 2/6/83, 13/6/84, 7/6/85
politics
basis of G's mind in finance and philanthropy 29/12/96
best part of G's life 31/12/83
Christian politics unrealisable in present state 29/12/43
concession in, importance of 16/4/65 n, 7/1/69
conflicting with private obligations 15/4/40
constant tumult of business 31/12/73
country has suffered from undue prolongation of careers, G thinks 19/2/74
dark prospects of 29/12/96
decline of reverence among conservatives
G's memorandum on, printed 15/8/90
economy out of fashion in 28/1/73
excitement of 22/4/31, 29/12/33, 31/1/40
G far from being an optimist in 10/5/80
G flinches from the Session 7/2/65
G offers his public work before the Eternal Throne 12/4/68
G only held to by the church 16/12/47
G's desire to leave 30/3/39
G's misgivings about direction of 11/2/85
G's politics now summed up in 'Ireland' 12/10/86
G still uncertain of purpose of his life 29/12/57
G telling old stories of 9/8/93
increasing hold of on G 31/12/56
intruding 23/12/32
Ireland's dominance of G's life in 26/4/86
leaving office
somehow makes a void 6/7/66
mainly valuable for good of church 16/8/40
master-violence of 29/12/90
moral sapping of political life 31/12/68
nausea felt on return to 6/2/82
never more anxious or crowded 20/4/85

oracular comment by G to Wilberforce 21/7/65 n
O'Shea divorce case and
G's memoranda on, printed 21/11/90 ff
political serverance
at most once in life only 5/7/73
resembles a change in religion 5/7/73
politicians the most difficult to understand completely 13/8/73
retirement from 31/8/41, 19/3/74 ff, 27/12/74 ff, 7/1/75, 9/1/75, 11/1/75, 14/1/75, 28/12/79, 29/12/79, 31/12/79, 21/4/81, 29/12/90
1872 probably the last of the present cares 31/12/72
agreed that G should wind up Session 3/1/94
at length affected 19/3/94
Carlton House Terrace to be given up at end of present government 13/12/73
change of prospect hits G hard 29/12/90
considered in 1844 8/7/44
discussions/comments on retiring from premiership 23/8/80, 21/4/81, 2/9/81, 29/9/81, 31/10/81 n, 4/11/81 n, 6/11/81, 11/11/81, 2/12/81, 18/12/81, 29/12/81, 10/1/82, 17/5/82, 6/9/82, 24/10/82, 25/11/82, 26/11/82, 10/12/82, 29/12/82, 5/1/83, 28/1/83, 31/1/83, 26/9/83, 13/10/83, 31/12/83, 20/2/84, 31/8/84, 11/2/85, 24/2/85, 6/5/85, 25/5/85, 30/5/85, 16/6/85, 30/6/85, 7/8/85, 16/7/86, 29/12/90
expectation of no rest until the grave 29/12/90
eyesight the solution 23/9/93
G called to walk as Abraham walked 29/12/91
G gives 5 reasons against again being Prime Minister 30/3/79 n
G has passed through death into better life 16/1/75
G urged not to retire 9/9/85, 12/9/85 n, 14/9/85 n, 15/9/85 n
hope of growing more eager 29/12/73
long wooed 31/12/79
minute for ex-cabinet on 16/6/85, 17/6/85
more remote than ever 29/12/76
needed to achieve just balance and true basis 29/12/70
new view of 30/5/85
on the opium question, considered 31/8/41
Parnell and the O'Shea divorce and 29/12/90
prospective work not Parliamentary, except for exceptional circumstances 30/3/75
time come for G to prepare 12/3/73
thoughts on entering 6/7/32 ff, 14/7/32, 30/7/32, 21/7/33
too fascinating? 29/12/30
uneasy day from political anticipation 20/10/65
vocation of absorbs all energies 10/3/86
vortex of 20/5/80
whirl of carries G off balance 3/6/53
See also eyes
poll books 9/1/35
Polsden Lacy (Farquhar) 5/8/54 ff, 17/5/56, 24/3/64
Pompeii 7/5/32 ff, 21/11/38, 8/1/89
Pondicherry *See* India
Ponsonby, Henry Frederick, Gen. Sir (1825–1895), a liberal; the Queen's private secretary 1870–95 22/9/69, 26/9/71 ff, 9/3/72, 16/7/73, 20/8/73, 30/8/73, 14/5/74, 2/5/75, 19/7/75, 8/3/82, 23/9/82, 2/12/82, 11/12/82, 15/12/82, 4/8/83, 18/5/84, 8/9/84, 15/9/84, 29/9/84, 25/11/84, 9/3/85, 18/6/85, 22/6/85 ff, 9/10/85, 1/2/86, 10/2/86, 24/3/86, 25/5/86, 23/2/88, 11/8/92 ff, 13/9/92, 31/10/92 c, 8/9/93 ff, 14/9/93 ff, 29/9/93, 25/10/93, 19/3/94
generous farewell of took the place of the Sovereign's 2/1/96
G's encomium of his abilities 5/3/94
G's final retirement and 19/2/94 ff
home rule and
G's memorandum on, printed 17/5/86
invites G to form 3rd. administration 29/1/86
letters from G to, printed 1/6/80, 22/6/80, 10/1/81, 11/1/81, 21/2/81, 18/3/81, 12/5/81, 24/6/82, 16/8/82, 4/9/82, 14/6/83, 22/6/83, 26/6/83, 22/10/83, 12/11/83, 25/8/84, 29/5/85, 2/6/85, 29/6/85, 16/2/86, 18/2/86, 27/2/86, 27/5/86, 23/8/92, 1/9/92, 18/10/92, 7/11/92, 4/2/94, 19/2/94, 4/3/94, 5/3/94
qualities of
tact and prudence 17/6/87
resignation of the government and 13/3/73 ff
service for recovery of Prince of Wales and 21/12/71, 18/1/72
See also cabinet, Edward VII, Victoria
Pontarlier 1/10/66
Poole
G's speech at 15/6/89
poor law 8/2/41, 3/5/41, 12/2/70 c, 13/10/81, 11/11/92 c, 1/12/93 c
Chalmers' views on 13/12/33
deputation to G on 7/11/93 n

poor law (*cont.*)
Elizabethan Act still in force 1/12/93 c
harmonisation of parish and poor law union 1/3/73 c
report on 4/4/33 ff, 18/3/34 ff
Royal Commission on 2/11/92, 23/11/92 c, 21/12/92, 18/8/93
clerical membership of 8/12/92, 17/12/92 c
female membership of 8/12/92
Queen objects to Arch as Commissioner 21/12/92
sketch on 13/7/37
speech on 21/7/37, 11/6/78
St. Pancras workhouse, G's speech to inmates of 21/8/79
Poor Law Amendment Bill
courage of government in passing 21/8/79 n
G supports 9/5/34
Poor Law Commission
G leads deputation to 12/3/49
Popery 24/9/38
porcelain
bought in Florence 3/10/38
collected 6/1/54, 20/1/54, 25/1/54, 28/1/54, 30/1/54, 5/3/58, 24/3/58, 29/3/58, 31/3/58, 8/4/58 ff, 1/3/59 ff, 9/3/59, 4/4/59, 4/11/59, 8/11/59 ff, 25/4/60
donated to South Kensington museum 23/7/66
G's collection displayed
in Leeds 13/3/68
in Liverpool 13/3/67, 24/5/67, 16/8/72, 25/7/74
in Brighton 3/3/60
in Paris 14/2/32, 20/2/32
in Rome 15/11/66 ff
in Vienna 18/11/58
sales of G's collection 25/3/56, 8/4/63, 1/5/73, 24/2/74, 12/6/75, 23/6/75
by Christie's 24/3/75, 1/4/75 n, 5/4/75, 12/6/75, 21/6/75, 23/6/75
part valued at £2700 24/2/74
shopping in Dresden 13/11/58 ff
pornography
Boccaccio, *Decameron*
G finds dangerous 5/9/50
G reading 15/4/30, 26/10/45, 21/12/47, 13/5/48, 15/5/48, 18/5/48, 11/5/59, 12/5/59, 13/5/59, 18/9/61 ff, 5/9/71
Aretino, at Blenheim 25/11/61 ff
at Dunrobin 15/9/58
at Wilton 21/8/66, 24/8/66, 8/9/66, 25/3/69
Fabliaux 19/7/48, 22/2/49
Kama Sutra 2/5/84
list of occasions 26/10/45
Petronius 15/1/47, 23/7/50
memorandum on 19/7/48
Political Pieces of Charles II 19/7/48
Pseudo Meursius 13/4/52, 14/4/52
Rochester 19/7/48
temptations of 26/10/45
Porte, The *See* Turkey
Portland harbour 19/8/82
Port Madoc 15/9/92
Porto Nuovo *See* Africa
portraits
G commissions portrait of Summerhayes (rescue) from Dyce 6/8/59
portraits of C. Gladstone
Weigall, H. 27/7/88
portraits of G
article on by T. Wemyss Reid 28/7/88
Ber, Mr. 30/1/87 ff
Bradley, W. 2/5/38, 8/5/38, 23/2/41, 25/2/41, 13/3/41, 18/3/41, 27/3/41, 29/4/41, 4/8/42, 6/4/44
Brooks, H. J. 29/3/89
Combe, Miss E. 12/12/37, 21/12/37 ff
Cubley, W. H. (Newark Red Club) 26/1/41, 28/1/41, 1/2/41
Dickinson, G. Lowes (Liverpool College) 14/6/71, 26/5/73, 2/4/74, 18/5/74, 13/7/74, 21/7/74, 17/2/75
Dickson 23/10/43, 25/10/43
Eastham, Mr. 3/7/60
Emslie, A. E. 30/4/90 n
Forbes, J. C. (National Liberal Club) 5/5/91, 30/7/91, 14/8/91
Frith, W. P. (group) 21/11/81, 2/12/81, 25/3/82
Hamilton, J. M. (Louvre; Pennsylvania Academy) 3/9/90, 4/9/90, 5/9/90, 24/9/90
Hargreaves, Mr. 4/12/40, 7/12/40, 8/1/41
Hayter 23/7/33, 29/7/34, 15/4/35
Herbert, J. R. 15/12/73, 18/12/73, 19/12/73, 20/12/73, 22/12/73, 23/12/73, 24/12/73, 2/1/74, 3/1/74, 5/1/74, 6/1/74, 7/1/74, 9/1/74, 10/1/74
Holl, F. M. 31/10/87 ff, 24/3/88, 25/7/88 n
Howard, G. J. (Castle Howard) 5/5/79
Knott, Taverner 1/12/79
Lenbach, F.
1st portrait (Munich) 11/9/74, 14/9/74, 19/9/74, 20/9/74
2nd portrait (National Portrait Gallery, Edinburgh) 11/10/79, 13/10/79
3rd portrait: double portrait with Döllinger(Städtische Galerie, Lenbachhaus, Munich) 31/8/86, 11/9/86
Lewis, George Robert 24/2/45

Lockhart, W. E.? 18/6/89, 20/6/89
Lucas, John (Hawarden) 27/11/43, 30/11/43, 1/12/43, 2/12/43, 4/12/43, 9/12/43, 13/12/43, 12/3/44
Lucy, Charles (V. & A.) 5/4/69
Mansfield, Mr. 29/3/89
Millais, J. E.
1st portrait: displayed at Royal Academy 3/5/79 n
1st portrait (National Portrait Gallery) 18/3/78 n, 26/6/78, 3/7/78, 10/7/78, 17/7/78, 24/7/78, 3/8/78, 6/8/78, 3/7/90 n, 3/11/90 n
1st portrait: viewed by G: surely a very fine work 3/8/78, 21/6/81 n
2nd portrait (Eton College) 7/7/84, 14/7/84, 28/7/84, 31/7/84, 4/8/84, 10/2/85 ?
3rd portrait (Christ Church, Oxford) 10/2/85 ?, 15/6/85, 25/6/85, 13/7/85
4th portrait (Hawarden Castle) 25/6/89 ff, 1/7/89, 10/7/89, 17/7/89, 29/7/91, 30/7/91, 31/7/91
Miller [W. E.?] 21/12/76, 22/12/76, 23/12/76
Mueller (Rome) 10/1/39, 11/1/39, 12/1/39, 14/1/39
on sale in Huddersfield for £20? 27/1/75 n
Phillip, J. 4/12/61, 21/3/62, 28/3/62, 11/3/63
Richmond, George 21/3/43, 25/3/43, 1/4/43, 11/4/43, 8/11/43
Richmond, William Blake
1st (Hawarden) 30/10/67, 31/10/67, 2/11/67, 4/11/67, 5/11/67, 6/11/67, 7/11/67, 8/11/67, 9/11/67, 12/11/67, 13/11/67, 14/11/67
2nd (rejected by Christ Church) 16/1/82, 17/1/82, 18/1/82, 19/1/82, 20/1/82, 21/1/82, 23/1/82
G thinks fine 12/11/67
Roden, W. T. (Birmingham City Art Gallery) 11/9/77, 12/9/77
Rogers, J.? 15/8/43
Selous, H. C. 30/6/51, 19/7/51
Severn, J. 31/12/40 n, 17/4/41, 28/4/41, 12/5/41, 19/5/41, 25/9/41, 9/10/41, 15/8/43
engraved W. H. Mote 31/12/40 n
Thaddeus, J. T. (Reform Club) 27/1/88, 30/1/88, 1/5/88, 7/11/93, 10/11/93, 23/11/93
Tilt, A. J. 10/9/77 n, 13/9/77
Troubetzkoi, Prince P. 4/7/93, 14/7/93
Walker, Elizabeth (engraving) 30/1/44, 29/1/45 ?, 10/6/56
Watts, G. F. 14/6/59, 16/6/59, 23/6/59, 15/8/59, 17/8/59, 18/10/61, 21/10/61, 4/12/61, 19/5/74, 20/7/74, 16/5/76, 30/5/76, 13/6/76, 1/6/78, 26/5/79, 21/7/79
length of sittings a vice in English artists 1/6/78
sittings disrupted by excessive conversation 13/6/76
Weigall, H. 6/3/86
Wells, H. T.? 7/3/87
Westcott, P. 25/11/54, 27/11/54, 29/11/54, 21/12/54, 28/2/55, 5/3/55, 17/3/55, 31/3/55
Portsea
naval review at 11/8/53
Port Sunlight
G's speech at 28/11/91
Portugal 6/6/33, 5/9/80
Congo and 26/5/83 c
debt of 2/4/70 c
Delagoa Bay and
German expansion an idle fear 30/12/84
invasion of by Spain thought possible 15/2/73 c
treaty with 1/1/42, 4/2/43, 10/3/43, 17/8/43, 18/9/43, 4/11/43, 20/11/43, 27/2/44
positivists 16/4/83
possessions
accumulation of
retribution to arrange 2/4/75
Post Office 17/5/61 n, 20/5/61, 22/4/72, 2/6/83 c
G argues for cheap book postage 13/4/55
military recruitment and 10/10/83, 13/11/83 c
telegraph department, funds of 25/7/72, 29/7/73
See also Zanzibar contract
poultices *See* medicines
Poussin, house of 2/1/38
Powerscourt, Enniskerry (Powerscourt) 29/10/77
Powis Castle (Powis) 13/9/56 ff
Prague 16/11/58
G visits Synagogue and Friedhof of 17/11/58
prayer
as remedy for sin 26/10/45
efficacious 23/9/47
ejaculatory 12/10/56
one absorbing prayer: Ireland, Ireland, Ireland 10/4/87
propositions on, printed 9/12/75, 16/12/75
spirit of 9/8/92
to be attached to recurring outward acts 12/10/56
prayer, reflections on 29/2/44 *See also* memoranda (printed; ejaculatory prayer)

prayers
G prays for truth, justice, order, honour, duty, liberty, piety 29/12/72
list of persons to be prayed for 13/4/48
lists of subjects 10/4/87
prayers, family 27/1/28, 25/6/31, 23/12/32, 25/7/33, 11/9/36, 21/8/53, 23/3/79
conducted by G 28/4/33, 29/9/33, 27/3/34, 25/5/34, 17/4/35, 23/2/40 ff, 31/1/41 ff, 23/1/42 ff, 19/3/43 ff, 14/1/44 ff, 19/1/45 ff, 18/1/46 ff, 28/2/47 ff, 5/4/55
G's version of Prayer Book for 17/4/42
See also sermons given by G, widows
prayers written by G 22/12/33
preaching
G's speech on 22/3/77
G street-preaching 25/9/59
See also speeches
Precentor, G as at Fasque 8/11/46, 22/11/46 ff, 28/12/46, 5/4/47, 20/8/47, 28/10/49, 16/12/49
predestination
discussed with C. G 21/7/40
writing on 20/6/30, 26/7/35
premiership
for a brief tenure only 1/2/86
G's length of tenure in 19/2/84, 4/7/84
Hartington advises the Queen to send for G 22/4/80
holder of should not be universal navigator 23/6/86
Midlothian campaign's effect on 23/1/80 n
retirement from
factors delaying 29/9/81
family discussions on 10/1/94, 12/2/94, 27/2/94
G denies imminence of 31/1/94
G's comments on 21/4/81, 2/9/81, 29/9/81, 31/10/81 n, 4/11/81 n, 6/11/81, 11/11/81, 13/11/81 n, 18/11/81, 21/11/81, 2/12/81, 14/12/81, 18/12/81, 29/12/81, 10/1/82, 10/2/82, 16/3/82, 17/5/82, 6/9/82, 24/10/82, 25/11/82, 26/11/82, 10/12/82, 29/12/82, 5/1/83, 28/1/83, 31/1/83, 26/9/83, 13/10/83, 31/12/83, 20/2/84, 31/8/84, 11/2/85, 24/2/85, 6/5/85, 25/5/85, 30/5/85
G's letter to Granville on 31/1/83
G's letter to Spencer on 16/10/82, 24/10/82
G's memoranda on, printed 21/2/94, 22/2/94, 24/2/94, 3/3/94, 10/3/94, 19/3/94
G to wind up present Session 3/1/94
new view of 30/5/85
preparations for house-clearing 16/2/94
Wilberforce tells G he should follow Palmerston 20/10/63
See also governments (G's), offices held, politics (retirement from), Treasury
PreRaphaelites 9/6/54
PreRaphaelitism 12/12/69, 28/10/72, 11/5/75, 15/5/79 n
presbyterian, employed by G 27/2/40
Presbyterianism
found cold & naked by G 14/8/47
timidity of 14/8/47
See also Church of Scotland
Prescott estate *See* Hawarden Castle
Preston
G's speeches at 18/11/68
tory train interrupts 26/9/84, 27/9/84
prices
G expects high prices to slacken in 1873 9/11/72
Prime Minister
Stanley forecasts G's future as 1/6/44
Primrose, Archibald Philip (1847–1929), Lord Dalmeny, 5th Earl of Rosebery (1868); under-secretary at home office (Scotland) 1881; lord privy seal 1885; foreign secretary 1886, 1892–4; chairman of L.C.C. 1889–90; Prime Minister, succeeding G, 1894–5; won the Derby three times 7/4/73, 23/5/73, 5/7/78, 3/12/78, 21/8/79 n, 12/9/79, 25/10/79, 8/3/80, 13/6/80, 6/9/80, 7/9/80, 10/9/80, 12/9/80, 6/5/81 ff, 7/6/81, 27/7/81, 25/1/82, 21/2/82, 18/3/82, 1/4/82, 27/5/82 ff, 4/12/82, 2/7/83 ff, 15/8/83, 27/3/84, 5/4/84, 9/4/84 ff, 16/5/84, 19/3/85, 8/5/85, 22/5/85, 11/6/85, 18/6/85, 14/1/86, 2/2/86, 24/2/86 ff, 27/3/86, 27/5/86, 9/6/86 ff, 29/7/86, 6/5/87, 11/7/87, 8/2/88, 20/2/88, 16/5/88, 20/2/89 ff, 4/3/89, 1/4/89, 5/7/89 ff, 15/7/89, 10/2/90, 16/3/90 ff, 25/6/90 ff, 20/3/91, 21/5/91, 29/3/92 ff, 9/12/92, 8/8/93, 22/9/93 ff
advises G to call party meeting on Ireland 8/12/85 n
ambition of 21/3/90 n
arranges meeting of labour M.P.s with G 30/6/88
as public speaker 1/12/85
at Althorp 7/12/91 ff
at Hawarden 29/10/80 ff, 29/11/81 ff, 5/1/83 ff, 27/10/85 ff, 8/12/85, 11/10/88 ff, 6/1/90 ff, 29/10/91 ff
cabinet and
declines to join 9/11/84, 12/11/84
expects to join 12/12/82, 10/10/84
colonies and 5/3/85

conciliator in coal lock-out 13/11/93 c, 6/12/93
death of Lady Rosebery 22/10/90, 25/11/90
dinner for the Shah given by 5/7/89
disestablishment and 7/11/85, 11/11/85
Egypt and 12/11/84, 25/1/85, 4/2/85, 8/2/85, 26/8/92 ff, 16/1/93 ff, 4/2/93 ff, 15/4/93 ff, 24/5/93 ff, 17/7/93 ff, 22/9/93 ff, 18/12/93
foreign secretary 7/2/86 ff, 28/4/86 ff, 15/8/92 ff
  refuses to be 4/8/92 ff
future full of interest 1/12/85
Garter for 25/9/92, 3/10/92
G at Dalmeny 24/11/79 ff, 16/3/80 ff, 28/3/80 ff, 27/8/84 ff, 24/9/84 ff, 9/11/85 ff, 29/6/92 ff
G at Mentmore 17/4/79 ff, 10/9/80 ff, 6/2/86 ff, 4/8/88 ff, 9/12/91
G dines with on night of resignation 1/3/94
G playing backgammon with 4/11/93
G proposes as British Museum trustee
  prevaricates, then accepts 19/3/83, 27/3/83
G's rescue work and
  opens discussion of its propriety 10/2/82
health of 24/9/84 ff, 30/9/84
home rule and 3/9/85, 13/11/85, 24/12/85, 21/1/86 ff, 20/4/90
  imprudent declaration on 15/3/94
  prefers resignation 1886 8/6/86 n, 10/7/86
  suggests committee to reconsider 1886 bill 7/7/89 n
leadership of Lords and 18/8/92
  declines 13/12/92, 5/1/93
letters from G to, printed 10/7/80, 29/4/81, 17/5/81, 30/7/81, 2/12/81, 10/12/81, 11/12/81, 30/1/82, 19/8/82, 9/9/82, 2/10/82, 7/12/82, 12/12/82, 18/12/82, 8/1/83, 9/3/83, 20/3/83, 27/3/83, 4/4/83, 7/4/83, 7/5/83, 21/7/83, 29/7/83, 1/8/83, 15/11/83, 9/7/84, 11/7/84, 22/7/84, 16/8/84, 23/8/84, 30/9/84, 10/10/84, 12/11/84, 25/1/85, 4/2/85, 8/2/85, 27/6/85, 5/9/85, 10/9/85, 7/11/85, 13/11/85, 1/12/85, 13/12/85, 24/12/85, 1/1/86, 3/1/86, 9/1/86, 10/2/86, 10/3/86, 15/3/86, 22/4/86, 28/4/86, 7/5/86, 21/6/86, 4/7/86, 10/7/86, 17/7/86, 19/7/92, 4/8/92, 15/8/92, 18/8/92, 23/8/92, 24/8/92, 26/8/92, 30/8/92, 3/9/92, 7/9/92, 11/9/92, 13/9/92, 17/9/92, 20/9/92, 21/9/92, 22/9/92, 23/9/92, 24/9/92, 25/9/92, 26/9/92, 27/9/92, 3/10/92, 6/10/92, 7/10/92, 13/10/92, 15/10/92, 21/10/92, 28/10/92, 1/11/92, 2/11/92, 3/11/92, 4/11/92, 6/11/92, 12/11/92, 14/11/92, 21/11/92, 25/11/92, 9/12/92, 11/12/92, 13/12/92, 16/1/93, 17/1/93, 20/1/93, 21/1/93, 22/1/93, 26/1/93, 30/1/93, 1/2/93, 4/2/93, 5/2/93, 6/2/93, 30/3/93, 5/4/93, 6/4/93, 15/4/93, 17/4/93, 24/4/93, 10/5/93, 19/5/93, 24/5/93, 25/5/93, 31/5/93, 9/6/93, 15/6/93, 14/7/93, 15/7/93, 17/7/93, 18/7/93, 19/7/93, 20/7/93, 27/7/93, 3/8/93, 12/8/93, 14/8/93, 11/9/93, 15/9/93, 18/9/93, 22/10/93, 28/10/93, 30/10/93, 5/11/93, 18/12/93, 21/12/93, 11/1/94, 29/1/94, 25/2/94, 4/3/94
lord privy seal 9/2/85 c
lord privy seal and
  angry at not being offered 18/4/81
Midlothian campaigns and 24/11/79 ff, 16/3/80 ff, 5/4/80, 9/11/85 ff, 9/6/86 ff
Midlothian seat and 24/6/78, 8/1/79 n
natural and destined career of 30/7/81, 6/6/83
navy estimates crisis and 18/12/93 ff
notes on G and liberal leadership 28/11/79 n
office offered to 10/7/80
Prime Minister 3/3/94 ff
  G would have preferred Spencer 25/7/94
prospects of 7/4/83, 6/6/83
prospects of brilliant but needs patience 12/12/82
qualities of
  loyalty 24/9/92
  strong self-delusion 28/12/82
  vein of foreign matter in 28/12/82
resigns as liberal leader 20/10/96 n
retirement from public life of 10/12/91
Rosebery Club of Edinburgh 28/11/85
Scottish legislation and 29/4/81, 18/12/82, 7/4/83
  threatens resignation on 28/4/83 n, 7/5/83
Siam and 11/9/93, 18/9/93
South Africa and
  suggested as commissioner for by Harcourt 2/6/83 c, 4/6/83
Spanish anarchy and 1/12/93 c
Uganda and 17/9/92 ff, 29/9/92 c, 7/10/92 ff, 28/10/92, 4/11/92 c, 6/11/92 ff, 9/12/92 ff, 4/2/93 ff, 5/4/93 ff, 20/7/93 c
  carried off by Jingoes of Foreign Office 26/10/92
world tour of 29/7/83, 1/8/83

Primrose, A. P. (*cont.*)
See also cabinet, Dalmeny House, Durdans (Epsom), Ireland, London County Council, Uganda
Prince Edward's Island *See* Canada
Princeton Review 31/12/77
Principalities, Danubian
G's motion on
lost: another broken promise to a people 16/3/58 ff, 22/4/58, 3/5/58, 4/5/58
Printers' Pensions Corporation 5/7/65
Prison Ministers Bill 6/7/72 c, 13/7/72
prisons
convict labour 12/11/80 c, 6/12/80
See also Ireland (Kilmainham), Milbank, Naples (various)
private judgement 2/8/39, 20/10/39, 20/12/40
private secretariat
almost all G's children help in, never with a failure 3/7/86
creation of in opposition undesirable 12/12/79
G doing the work of 21/8/60 ff
G entertained by corps of 19/7/89
G's retirement and 28/2/94, 2/3/94, 6/3/94
Hamilton's article on 4/12/91
none in opposition 3/3/74, 5/3/74, 4/6/77
planning of 21/12/59, 7/1/86
private secretaries, G's
Carmichael, Sir J. (1886) 7/3/86 ff
Cavendish, Lord Frederick (1872–4) 23/7/72
farewell minutes for 27/2/74
Gladstone, S. E.(1865–66) 2/8/65
Gladstone, W. H. (1865–6, 1868–?74) 26/4/65 n, 13/5/65, 4/12/68 n
assisting in the vacations 9/7/59
Godley, J. A. (1872–4, 1880–2) 26/8/72 ff, 11/10/72, 3/8/73, 24/4/80 ff
Gordon, A. (in Ionia) 24/12/58 ff
poor work by 22/1/59, 23/1/59
Gurdon, W. B. (1865–6, 1868–74) 26/4/65 n, 15/5/65, 4/12/68 ff, 17/9/72, 12/8/73, 18/10/73, 12/2/74
Hamilton, E. W. (1873–4, 1880–85) 11/8/73, 5/3/74, 2/5/80 ff
G's tribute to 30/6/85
senior secretary 15/8/82 ff
Herbert, R. G. W. 3/12/54, 11/1/55
Lacaita, J. (in Ionia) 24/12/58 ff
Lawley, F. C. 28/12/52 ff, 16/8/53
appointment to govern S. Australia rescinded 19/7/54
scandal leading to resignation of 10/6/54 ff, 30/7/54, 2/8/54, 3/8/54, 4/8/54
Lyttelton, Spencer (1871–4, 1882–5, 1892–4) 28/11/83 ff, 20/3/86 ff, 14/7/92 ff, 29/9/92 ff
Northcote, S. H. 30/6/42, 21/10/42
Primrose, H. W. (1880, 1886) 28/4/80 ff, 2/2/86, 3/2/86 ff
Rawson, R. W. 6/9/41 ff, 11/12/41
Ryan, C. L. (1859–1865) 24/6/59 n, 29/6/61, 16/7/62, 26/4/65, 12/5/65
Wortley, J. F., assisting 21/12/59, 23/12/59
Seymour, H. (1880–4) 15/8/82 n
Shand, H. G. (1892–4) 18/8/92 ff
Strahan, G. C. (A. D. C in Ionia) 24/1/59, 19/2/59
West, A. E. (1868–72, 1892–4) 23/12/68 ff, 5/3/92 ff
See also Gladstone (Helen), Gladstone (Henry), Gladstone (Herbert), private secretariat
Privy Council
attending birth of royal children 25/5/46
G on education committee of 24/1/53, 4/2/53, 14/3/53, 24/1/54, 26/1/54, 6/2/54, 27/2/54, 19/1/55, 4/3/62, 10/3/62, 15/3/62, 8/4/62, 7/2/71
and Derby's minute 2/4/53
G sworn to 3/9/41
Joint Committee of
dangerous character of 21/7/40
judges being made P. C. on retirement 26/1/73
Judicial Committee of strengthened 17/6/71 c, 5/7/71 c, 12/8/71 c
Privy Seal
G's attempts to reform/abolish 26/5/83 c, 22/8/83 c, 15/2/86
to be held by First Lord 16/2/86 c
See also Fortescue, Primrose
probate duties 1/3/53 ff, 10/1/69 *See also* death duties
processions
avoided and discouraged 6/4/80 ff
exhausting character of 28/9/81
profession, G's decisions on 3/8/30 ff, 30/3/39
property, G's 15/12/55
prophecy 17/2/33
proportional voting *See* franchise, Reform Bills
proposals of marriage by G *See* marriage
prostitutes *See* Gower (Granville), Hamilton, Primrose, rescue work, rescue work (significant cases), Stead
protection 15/9/26, 27/11/46, 31/3/57, 17/2/93
colonial tariffs
colonial control of 16/5/71, 22/5/71
G's correspondence with Pareto on 30/4/92

thought by G to have ended in 1860 in spirit duties 24/8/71
See also fair trade, free trade
protectionists 20/5/41, 8/12/42, 13/3/43, 6/7/49, 27/2/50, 5/4/51
G thinks Derby must bring protectionism to speedy issue 24/2/52
protectorate
definition of 20/1/85 c
Protestant Alliance 6/11/74
Protestant Association 23/6/34 n, 5/3/36 n, 11/5/36
Protestant Defence Association 15/12/70 c
Protestant Home Rule Association 16/2/87 n, 23/10/88 n
Providence
G spoilt child of 16/11/69
purposes of 31/12/56
See also God
provinces, virtues of 30/11/39
Prussia
military system of to be reported on to cabinet 21/9/70, 2/5/71, 11/5/71
normal schools in 24/5/38
religion in 17/12/38
treaty with 18/3/43
Psalms
all read to G by C. G 30/7/92
consolation from 17/7/65, 8/7/86, 9/7/86 ff, 14/4/94
ejaculatory prayer and 12/10/56
G's concordance of 17/6/49, 12/8/49 ff
providentially speaking to G 14/5/43, 17/10/46, 16/9/49, 19/4/53, 3/7/64, 23/3/77, 5/1/83, 24/4/87, 4/9/88
list of occasions 9/5/54
read during insomnia 2/1/85
See also memoranda (printed)
Psyche, statue of, especially admired 2/5/32
ptarmigan, abundance of 6/9/39
publications, Gladstone's
'Address delivered at the distribution of prizes in the Liverpool Collegiate Institute' (1873) 18/12/72, 21/12/72
'Address on the place of Ancient Greece in the providential order of the world' (1865) 3/11/65
'Aggression on Egypt and freedom in the East', *N.C.*, ii. 149 (August 1877) 21/7/77 ff, 8/8/83
republished as pamphlet with preface by G 12/6/84
'A letter to the Earl of Aberdeen on the state prosecutions of the Neapolitan Government' (1851) 9/3/51
reprint of 6/4/59
Tauchnitz edition of 13/11/76 n
'A letter to . . . William Skinner . . . on the functions of laymen in the church (1852) 2/11/51, 7/1/52, 12/1/52
'A Modern "Symposium". Is the popular judgement in politics more than just that of the higher orders?', *N.C.*, iv. 184 (July 1878) 15/6/78, 19/6/78
'An examination of the official reply of the Neapolitan Government' (1852) 24/11/51, 31/12/51, 17/1/52 ff, 30/1/52
'An olive branch from America', *N.C.*, xxii. 611 (November 1887) 31/10/87
'A reply to Dr. Ingram', *Westminster Review* (January 1888) 8/12/87, 20/12/87
'Art Thou Weary?', *C.R.* (December 1875) 10/10/75, 3/12/75
'A second letter to the Earl of Aberdeen on the state prosecutions of the Neapolitan Government' (1851) 12/7/51
'A vindication of Home Rule. A reply to the Duke of Argyll', *N.A.R.* (October 1892) 27/7/92
'British poetry of the nineteenth century', *The Speaker*, 11 January 1890 24/12/89, 11/1/90
Chapter of Autobiography, A (1868) 13/4/68 n, 31/8/68 n, 17/9/68 ff, 13/10/68, 16/10/68, 23/7/86
held back from publication 26/10/68
Church Principles considered in their results (1840) 1/10/39
'Clergy Relief Bill', *Q.R.*, lxxxv. 40 (December 1849) 10/9/49
'Colonel Ingersoll on Christianity', *N.A.R.*, cxlvi. 481 (May 1888) 31/12/87, 28/3/88, 1/6/88
'Count Montalembert on Catholic interests in the nineteenth century', *Q.R.*, xcii. 137 (December 1852) 10/11/52, 16/11/52
reread 15/12/73
'Course of commercial policy at home and abroad', *Foreign and Colonial Quarterly Review*, i 26/11/42
'Daniel O'Connell', *N.C.*, xxv. 148 (January 1889) 26/11/88
'Dawn of creation and of worship', *N.C.*, xviii. 685 (November 1885) 6/10/85
'Dean Hook' (1879) 10/2/79
'Did Dante study at Oxford', *N.C.*, xxxi. 1032 (June 1892) 16/4/92, 30/4/92
'Dr. Döllinger', *The Speaker*, 18 January 1890 13/1/90, 18/1/90
'Dr Döllinger's posthumous remains', *Speaker*, (30 August 1890) 25/8/90

publications, Gladstone's (*cont.*)
'Early memories of Edinburgh and Dr. [Thomas] Chalmers', *Scottish Liberal*, 2, 9, 16 May 1890 29/3/90
'Ecce Homo', *Good Words* (January-March 1868) 20/10/67, 8/12/67
'Electoral facts', *N.C.*, iv. 955 (November 1878) 9/10/78, 18/10/78
'Electoral Facts', *N.C.*, xxx. 329 (September 1891) 5/8/91, 4/9/91
'Electoral facts of 1887', *N.C.*, xxii. 435 (September 1887) 16/8/87
'Electoral facts of today (No. II)', *N.C.*, xxvi. 1056 (December 1889) 5/11/89, 19/11/89
'Ellen Middleton' (anon. review), *English Review*, i. 336 (July 1844) 24/5/44, 7/7/88 n
row over its unauthorised republication 29/12/89 ff
'England's Mission', *N.C.*, iv. 560 (September 1878) 9/8/78, 21/8/78, 22/8/78
'Epithets of movement in Homer', *N.C.*, v. 463 (March 1879) 23/1/79, 4/2/79
'Farini's *Stato Romano* [translated by W. E. Gladstone]', *E.R.*, xcv. 357 (April 1852) 15/11/51, 13/2/52
Financial statements of 1853, 1860–1863 (1863) 1/6/63 ff, 27/5/64
'Foreign affairs: war in Italy', *Q.R.*, cv. 527 (April 1859) 11/4/59
'For the Right', by C. E. Franzos, *N.C.*, xxv. 615 (April 1889) 27/2/89
'France and the late Ministry', *Q.R.*, ciii. 526 (April 1858) 24/3/58, 8/4/58, 9/4/58
'Free Trade', *N.A.R.*, cl. 1 (January 1890) 10/12/88, 3/4/89 ff, 11/4/89, 23/7/89, 5/10/89
'Freetrade, railways, and the growth of commerce', *N.C.*, vii. 367 (February 1880) 13/11/79, 16/12/79, 4/1/80, 5/1/80
'From Oxford to Rome [review of Elizabeth Harris]', *Q.R.*, lxxxi. 131 (June 1847) 13/2/47, 10/3/47, 9/4/47 ff
'Further Notes and Queries on the Irish Demand', *C.R.*, liii. 321 (March 1888) 30/1/88
'Germany, France and England', *E.R.*, cxxxii. 554 (October 1870) 23/8/70 n, 26/8/70, 1/9/70, 23/9/70, 30/9/70
'Giacomo Leopardi', *Q.R.*, lxxxvi. 295 (March 1850) 28/7/49, 9/11/49
Gleanings of past years, 1844–78, 7v. (1879) 6/9/77, 20/9/77, 25/9/77, 6/11/78 ff, 22/11/78 ff, 23/12/78 ff, 8/1/79, 10/1/79 ff, 22/1/79, 16/2/79, 6/5/79, 30/6/79, 8/7/79
partially translated into French by A. Gigot 16/10/80
rather a daring measure 6/11/78
to be published on the Tauchnitz scale 7/11/78
'Greece and the Treaty of Berlin', *N.C.*, v. 1121 (June 1879) 20/5/79
'Homer', *Chambers' Encylopaedia* 7/1/90
Homer, in Macmillan's *Literature Primers*, ed. J. R. Green (1878) 24/8/77 n, 4/10/77 ff, 20/11/77 ff, 5/1/78 ff, 19/1/78 ff, 29/4/78 ff, 11/5/78 ff
'Homer and his successors [Virgil and Tasso] in epic poetry', *Q.R.*, ci. 80 (January 1857) 15/11/56
'Homeric characters in and out of Homer', *Q.R.*, cii. 204 (July 1857) 28/4/57
Homeric Synchronism: an enquiry into the time and place of Homer (1876) 21/9/75, 6/11/75
heavy remaining stock of 11/10/86
'Homerology', *C.R.*, xxii. 632, 803 (March, April 1876) 4/12/75
'Home Rule for Ireland', *Subjects of the Day*, iii. 1 (November 1890) 23/8/90
'Ingram's History of the Irish Union', *N.C.*, xxii. 445 (October 1887) 2/9/87, 27/10/92
Introductory letter to E. de Laveleye, *Protestantism and Catholicism* (1875) 14/4/75
'Is the Church of England worth preserving?', *C.R.*, xxvi. 193 (July 1875) 4/6/75
'Italy and her Church [anon.]', *Church Quarterly Review*, i. 1 (October 1875) 16/7/75
'Italy in 1888–89', *N.C.*, xxv. 763 (May 1889) 18/4/89
Juventus Mundi. The Gods and Men of the Heroic Age (1869) 11/7/67 n, 6/4/68 ff, 29/8/68 n, 7/3/69 ff, 10/4/69, 8/6/69, 9/6/69, 29/5/74
2nd edition of 25/10/69
E. Arnold's review of 17/8/69
'Kin beyond Sea', *N.A.R.*, cxxvii. 179 (September 1878) 21/6/78, 28/6/78, 15/7/78, 18/7/78, 30/11/83 n
reprint of 14/8/78
'Lachmann's *Essays on Homer*', *Q.R.*, lxxxi. 381 (September 1847) 4/6/47
Landmarks of Homeric study, together with an essay on the Assyrian tablets and the Homeric text (1890) 1/1/90, 10/6/90, 16/7/90
'Last words on the county franchise', *N.C.*, iii. 196 (January 1878) 10/12/77, 15/12/77

Later Gleanings. A new series of Gleanings of Past Years (1897) 29/12/96
Lessons in massacre (1877) 26/2/77 ff, 10/3/77
'Lessons of Irish history in the eighteenth century', in J. Bryce, ed., *A handbook of home rule* (1887) 24/9/87
'Letter explaining a sentence', *N.C.*, xxix. 690 (April 1891) 18/3/91
'Letter to Pearsall Smith on International Copyright', *N.C.*, xxii. 602 (November 1887) 15/8/87
'Letter to Samuel Smith, M.P., on female suffrage' (1892) 9/4/92
'Letter to Schenck [on the Confederacy and Gladstone's Newcastle speech], 28 November 1872', *Harper's New Monthly Magazine* (December 1876) 28/11/72, 1/1/76, 19/8/76, 27/9/76 n
'Liberty in the East and West', *N.C.*, iii. 189 (June 1878) 24/5/78
'Life of Bishop Patteson [by C. M. Yonge]', *Q.R.*, cxxxvii. 458 (October 1874) 2/7/74, 19/8/74, 27/9/74
reperusal moves G to tears 14/11/78
'Life of the Prince Consort [review of Martin,i]' by Etonensis, *C.R.*, xxvi. 1 (June 1875) 26/4/75, 9/5/75, 22/5/75, 25/5/75 n
'Life of the Prince Consort [review of Martin,ii], *Church Quarterly Review* (January 1877) 6/11/76, 1/12/76
'Life of the Prince Consort [review of Martin,iii], *Church Quarterly Review* v. 469 (January 1878) 15/12/77, 22/12/77, 26/12/77
really on the Crimean war 26/12/77
'Life of the Revd. Joseph Blanco White', *Q.R.*, lxxvi. 164 (June 1845) 6/5/45, 28/5/45
'"Locksley Hall" and the Jubilee', *N.C.*, xxi. 1 (January 1887) 15/12/86
'Lord Braybrooke', *Gentleman's Magazine*, 2nd. series, iv. 669 (June 1858) 10/5/58, 17/5/58
'Lord John Russell's translation of the Francesca da Rimini', *English Review*, i. 164 (April 1844) 17/2/44
Lo Stato Romano by L. C. Farini, tr. in 4 vols. by G assisted by A. R. Bennett 27/11/50 ff, 21/12/50 ff, 9/9/51 ff, 1/3/52
'Love Odes of Horace. Five specimens', *N.C.*, xxxv. 701 (May 1894) 21/4/94
'Memoir of John Murray', *Murray's Magazine*, (May 1891) 16/4/91
'Memorials of a Southern Planter', *N.C.*, xxvi. 984 (December 1889) 4/11/89
'Montenegro, or Tsernagora: a sketch', *N.C.*, i. 360 (May 1877) 14/4/77, 19/4/77
Russian translation by K. P. Pobedonostsev 14/4/77 n
'Mr. Carnegie's "Gospel of Wealth": a review and a recommendation', *N.C.*, xxviii. 677 (November 1890) 18/9/90, 8/10/90
'Mr. Forster and Ireland', *N.C.*, xxiv. 451 (September 1888) 6/8/88, 9/8/88, 22/8/88
'Mr. Gladstone on Artemis', *Eton College Chronicle*, no. 550, p. 619 (19 March 1891) 7/3/91
'Mr. Lecky and political morality', *N.C.*, xxii. 279 (August 1887) 8/7/87
'Notes and queries on the Irish demand', *N.C.*, xxi. 165 (February 1887) 6/1/87
Notice of Abbé Valin, *Church Quarterly Review*, v. 253 (November 1877) 30/9/77
Notice of N. Loraine, *The church and liberties of England* (1876), *Church Quarterly Review*, ii. 565 (July 1876) 24/6/76, 26/6/76
Obituary of G. W. Lyttelton, *The Guardian*, 26 April 1876 23/4/76
'Olympian Religion', *N.A.R.*, cliv. 231, 365, 489, 613, (February-May 1892) 10/10/91, 5/11/91, 28/12/91
'On an infant who was born, baptised, and died on the same day', *Good Words* (1871), 365 16/4/71
'On books and the housing of them', *N.C.*, xxvii. 384 (March 1890) 17/12/89, 13/2/90
'On epithets of movement in Homer', *N.C.*, v. 463 (March 1879) 8/10/78, 21/3/79
'On the ancient beliefs in a future state', *N.C.*, xxx. 658 (October 1891) 12/9/91
'On the Liberal Party' (1885) 26/8/85 ff, 29/9/85
'On the place of Homer in classical education and in historical inquiry', *Oxford Essays for 1857* (1857) 15/12/56, 23/2/57
'On the Rights and Responsibilities of Labour', *Lloyd's Weekly Newspaper* 28/3/90, 23/4/90
'Our colonies' (1855) 12/11/55
'Phoenicia and Greece', *Q.R.*, cxxiv. 199 (January 1868) 11/11/67, 30/11/67, 21/12/67
'Phoenician affinities of Ithaca', *N.C.*, xxvi. 280 (August 1889) 15/10/88, 1/11/88, 23/11/88, 22/7/89
'Piracy in Borneo and the operations of July, 1849', *C.R.*, xxx. 181 (July 1877) 26/5/77, 6/6/77 ff

publications (Gladstone's) (*cont.*)
'Plain speaking on the Irish Union', *N.C.*, xxvi. 1 (July 1889) 23/5/89, 18/6/89, 21/6/89
Political speeches in Scotland, November and December 1879, ed. J. J. Reid (1879) 24/11/79 n, 20/12/79, 10/1/80, 9/12/80 ff
Political speeches in Scotland, second series (1880) 17/3/80 n
Prayers for family use (1845) 22/12/44, 16/2/45, 2/3/45
given to Salisbury? 12/7/73 n
Preface to 2nd edition of MacKenzie and Irby, *The Slavonic Provinces of Turkey* (1877) 14/12/76, 6/4/77, 7/4/77
Preface to Schliemann's *Mycenae* (1878) 6/9/77 n, 20/9/77 ff, 3/10/77 ff, 10/10/77, 2/11/77
Preface to *The catechism of John Hamilton 1552*, ed. T. G. Law (1884) 27/9/84
'Present aspect of the Church', *Foreign and Colonial Review*, ii (October 1843) 2/9/43
'Proem to Genesis: a plea for a fair trial', *N.C.*, xix. 1 (January 1886) 8/12/85
'Postscript' to Réville's reply, *N.C.*, xix. 176 (January 1886) 26/12/85
'Professor Huxley and the swine-miracle', *N.C.*, xxix. 339 (February 1891) 18/12/90, 25/12/90, 18/1/91
'Prospects political and financial', *Q.R.*, ci. 243 (January 1857) 2/12/56, 15/12/56
Psalter, The, with a concordance (1849) 17/6/49 ff, 19/11/49 ff
'Queen Elizabeth and the Church of England', *N.C.*, xxiv. 764 (November 1888) 18/9/88, 10/10/88
'Rejoinder on authority in matters of opinion', *N.C.*, i. 902 (July 1877) 14/6/77, 20/6/77
'Religion, Achaian and Semitic', *N.C.*, vii. 710 (April 1880) 18/12/79, 12/2/80, 14/3/80
Remarks on the Royal Supremacy (1850) 28/4/50, 25/5/50, 29/4/72
revised edition (1865) 18/12/64
revised edition (1877), with a preface 15/3/77, 28/3/77, 31/3/77
'Remarks upon recent commercial legislation' (1845) 1/3/45, 3/1/61
Review of *Journal de Marie Bashkirtseff, N.C.*, xxvi. 602 (October 1889) 9/8/89
Review of *Memoir of Norman Macleod, Church Quarterly Review* (July 1876) 20/3/76
review of O. Novikov, *Russia and England, N.C.*, vii. 538 (March 1880) 14/2/80, 16/2/80, 21/2/80
MS of given to Buffalo library, U.S.A. 30/9/86, 2/10/86 n
Review of Sir G. C. Lewis, *Essays on the influence of authority*, ed. Sir G Lewis, *N.C.*, i. 2 (March 1877) 8/1/77, 1/2/77
Review of Trevelyan's *Macaulay*, *Q.R.*, cxlii. 1 (July 1876) 23/3/76 n, 3/4/76, 4/6/76 ff, 9/6/76, 12/6/76, 28/6/76, 5/8/76 n
constant interruptions to 10/6/76
Review of vols. v and vi of Lecky's *History of England in the eighteenth century*, *N.C.*, xxi. 919 (June 1887) 16/5/87, 22/5/87
'Richard Monckton Milnes', *The Speaker*, ii. 596 (29 November 1890) 14/11/90
'Ritualism and Ritual', *C.R.*, xxiv. 663 (October 1874) 2/8/74, 19/8/74, 10/9/74
notorious addition to, in Munich 13/9/74
'Robert Elsmere and the Battle of Belief', *N.C.*, xxiii. 766 (May 1888) 6/4/88, 18/4/88, 24/4/88
Rome and the newest fashions in religion. Three tracts (1875) 28/3/75, 11/4/75 ?, 2/7/75 ff, 14/7/75
French translation banned by French government from sale at railways stations 10/11/75
German translation by M. Lossen 13/10/75 n
Tauchnitz edition of 23/7/75 n
'Russian policy and deeds in Turkestan', *C.R.*, xxviii. 873 (November 1876) 19/10/76, 24/10/76, 26/10/76
'Sardinia and Rome', *Q.R.*, xcvii. 41 (June 1855) 29/5/55
'Science and Arts, Utility and Beauty' (1875) 11/11/75, 17/12/75 ff
'Scotch ecclesiastical affairs', *Q.R.*, lxxvii. 220 (December 1845) 20/11/45
'Senti, senti, anima mia [translation of Cowper]', *N.C.*, xiv. 357 (September 1883) 23/7/82
Seven articles on the Bible, *Good Words*, (April-November 1890) 6/1/90 ff, 22/5/90 ff, 26/7/90, 19/8/90
'Soliloquium' 20/10/96
Special aspects of the Irish question. A series of reflections in and since 1886 (1892) 21/6/92
'Speeches of Pope Pius IX', *Q.R.*, cxxxviii. 266 (January 1875) 9/12/74, 19/12/74, 3/1/75
Speeches on parliamentary reform in 1866 (1866) 1/9/66, 14/9/66, 27/9/66
Studies on Homer and the Homeric age (3 v., 1858) 7/7/55 ff, 6/8/55 ff, 7/8/56 ff,

14/10/56 ff, 7/1/57 ff, 22/6/57 ff, 2/9/57 ff, 7/11/57, 24/12/57, 6/1/58, 5/3/58
copies of received 26/3/58
G reading 26/3/58, 24/10/59, 14/8/77
G writes 'Advertisment' for 10/3/58
index of 15/12/57
MS finished 10/2/58
proofs of finished 12/3/58
read by G 27/3/69, 1/4/69
reviews of 20/4/58, 2/7/58, 3/7/58, 12/8/58, 13/8/58, 29/9/58, 21/10/58, 4/11/58, 18/3/59
revised edition never published 11/7/67
W. E. Gladstone's Homerische Studien, frei bearbeitet von Dr. A. Schuster (1863) 2/1/64
Studies subsidiary to the works of Bishop Butler (1896) 23/12/95, 3/5/96
'Substance of a speech on . . . the removal of . . . Jewish disabilities, with a preface [of 22 pp.]' (1847) 24/12/47
'Tennyson's Poems', *Q.R.*, cvi. 454 (October 1859) 14/7/59, 24/8/59, 23/9/59
'The Bill for Divorce', *Q.R.*, (July 1857) 17/6/57
The Bulgarian Horrors and the Question of the East (1876) 28/8/76 ff, 5/9/76
discussed with Granville 5/9/76
Russian translation by K. P. Pobyedonostsev, preface by L. C. Alexander 8/9/76 n
Tauchnitz edition 14/10/76 n, 7/11/76 ff
worked on in British Museum 4/9/76
The Church of England and Ritualism (1875) 28/10/75, 7/11/75
'The colour sense', *N.C.*, ii. 366 (October 1877) 30/8/77
'The conservative collapse; considered in a letter from a Liberal to an old Conservative', signed 'Index', *F.R.*, xxxiii. 607 (May 1880) 13/4/80 ff, 17/4/80, 22/4/80
'The country and the government', *N.C.*, vi. 201 (August 1879) 9/7/79, 19/7/79, 24/7/79
'The county franchise, and Mr. Lowe thereon', *N.C.*, ii. 537 (November 1877) 9/10/77, 15/10/77
'The courses of religious thought', C.R., xxviii. 168 (June 1876) 1/4/76, 2/4/76, 3/4/76 n, 11/5/76
'The declining efficiency of Parliament', *Q.R.*, xcix. 521 (September 1856) 21/7/56 ?, 19/9/56, 23/9/56
'The dominions of Odysseus, and the island group of the Odyssey', *Macmillan's Magazine*, xxxvi. 417 (October 1877) 21/8/77
'The Duke of Argyll on Presbytery', *Q.R.*, lxxxiii. 78 (December 1848) 3/9/48
'The Elizabethan settlement of religion', *F.R.*, xxiv. 1 (July 1888) 1/6/88, 8/6/88, 16/6/88
Cox's reply to 25/8/88 n
'The English Church under Henry the Eighth', *N.C.*, xxvi. 882 (November 1889) 16/9/89
proofs read by Stubbs 16/9/89 n
'The English labourer', *The Weekly Star* (5 February 1892) 4/1/92
'The evangelical movement, its parentage, progress, and issue', *British Quarterly Review* (July 1879) 14/5/79, 30/5/79
'The friends and foes of Russia', *N.C.*, v. 168 (January 1879) 13/12/78, 19/12/78
'The future of the English-speaking races', *Youth's Companion* (November 1888) 22/8/87
'The greater Gods of Olympos. I. Poseidon', *N.C.*, xxi. 460 (March 1887) 7/12/86, 22/2/87
'The greater gods: part II: Apollo', *N.C.*, xxi. 748 (May 1887) 6/3/87, 1/4/87
'The greater gods: part III: Athenê', *N.C.*, xxii. 79 (July 1887) 7/4/87
'The great Olympian sedition', *C.R.*, li. 757 (June 1887) 20/1/87, 22/1/87, 9/5/87, 12/5/87
'The Hellenic factor in the Eastern Question', *C.R.*, xxix. 1 (December 1876) 13/11/76, 21/11/76, 28/11/76
'The history of 1852–1860, and Greville's latest Journals', *E.H.R.*, ii. 281 (April 1887) 20/1/87 n, 3/2/87, 10/2/87, 22/2/87
'The Homeric Herê', *C.R.*, liii. 181 (February 1888) 25/4/87, 16/1/88
'The Idea of a Christian Church [review of Ward]', *Q.R.*, lxxv. 149 (December 1844) 22/9/44, 4/12/44 ff
The impregnable rock of Holy Scripture (1890 and second edition 1892) 6/1/90, 18/8/90, 29/9/90, 9/10/90, 10/11/91 ff, 28/3/92 ff, 28/4/92 ff
The Irish question. I. History of an idea. II. Lessons of the election (1886) 26/7/86, 19/8/86
penny edition of, with addendum 26/7/86 n, 25/9/86, 13/10/86
'The Iris of Homer: and her relation to Genesis ix. 11–17', *C.R.*, xxxii. 11 (April 1878) 15/3/78
'The law of probable evidence and its relation to conduct' (1845, 1879), *N.C.* (May 1879) 26/6/45, 9/3/79 ff, 11/3/79, 19/3/79, 21/3/79, 1/4/79, 13/5/79

publications, Gladstone's (*cont.*)
'The Melbourne government: its acts and persons', *N.C.*, xxvii. 38 (January 1890) 21/11/89, 16/12/89
'The new Parliament and its work', *Q.R.*, ci. 541 (April 1857) 18/3/57 ?, 2/4/57, 14/4/57, 19/4/57, 21/4/57
The Odes of Horace (1894) 14/7/92 ff, 22/8/92 ff, 27/12/92 ff, 5/9/93 ff, 10/3/94 ff, 11/5/94 ff
'The Olympian system versus the solar theory', *N.C.*, vi. 746 (October 1879) 15/8/79
'The past and present administration', *Q.R.*, civ. 515 (October 1858) 6/8/58
'The paths of honour and of shame', *N.C.*, iii. 591 (March 1878) 20/2/78
pamphlet reprint with a preface (1878) 20/2/78 n, 9/3/78
'The Peace to come', *N.C.*, iii. 209 (February 1878) 9/1/78, 15/1/78
'The Phoenician elements in the Homeric Poems', Address to the World Orientalist Congress, *The Times*, 8 September 1892 3/6/92, 22/8/92, 25/8/92 ff, 8/9/92
'The Pitt-Rutland Correspondence', *The Speaker*, i. 363 (5 April 1890) 20/3/90
'The place of heresy and schism in the modern church', *N.C.*, xxxvi. 157 (August 1894) 22/4/94, 21/5/94, 25/7/94
'The place of Homer in history and in Egyptian chronology', *C.R.*, xxiv. 1, 175 (June, July 1874) 30/4/74, 4/5/74 ff, 13/11/75
'The platform, its rise and progress', *N.C.* xxxi. 686 (April 1892) 19/3/92
'The question of divorce', *N.A.R.*, (November 1889) 28/10/89
'The reply of Achilles to the envoys of Agamemnon', *C.R.* (May 1874) 6/4/74
The Romanes Lecture, 1892. An Academic Sketch (1892) 31/8/92, 31/8/92 ff, 17/10/92, 24/10/92, 25/10/92
'The Sclavonic Provinces of the Ottoman Empire', *Eastern Question Association Pamphlets*, 5 (1877) 16/1/77
'The Session and its Sequel', *E.R.*, cxxvi. 540 (October 1867) 26/7/67, 14/9/67, 16/9/67 ff
'The Shield of Achilles', *C.R.* (February 1874) 1/1/74, 9/1/74
'The sixteenth century arraigned before the nineteenth: a study on the Reformation', *C.R.*, xxxiii. 425 (October 1878) 23/8/78, 5/9/78, 6/9/78
'The slicing of Hector', *N.C.*, iv. 752 (October 1878) 11/9/78
The Speeches and Public Addresses of the Rt. Hon. W. E. Gladstone M.P., ed. A. W. Hutton and H. J. Cohen: vol. X (1892), vol. XI (1894) 26/4/90, 23/10/91 ff, 2/4/92, 14/5/92 ff, 2/6/92, 11/6/92, 6/10/92
abandoned 13/6/93
The State in its Relations with the Church (1838) 3/10/31, 1/3/38
3rd edition (1839) 2/2/39
4th edition (2v. 1841) 1/10/39, 9/10/40
German tr. *Der Staat in seinem Verhältnisse zur Kirche*, preface by F. A. G. Tholuck 5/8/43
'The theses of Erastus and the Scottish church establishment', *Foreign and Colonial Review*, iv. 299 (October 1844) 3/9/44
'The Triple Alliance and Italy's place in it', by 'Outidanos', *C.R.*, lvi. 469 (October 1889) 17/8/89, 11/9/89
The Vatican Decrees and their bearing on civil allegiance: *a political expostulation* (1874) 20/10/74, 7/11/74
52,000 sold, 20,500 more printed 27/11/74
application to reprint 14/1/87
cheered in Greenwich 11/11/75
revise of 79th. thousand corrected 2/12/74
shown to de Lisle, Gordon, Acton 28/10/74, 29/10/74
'The war and the peace', *Gentleman's Magazine* (August 1856) 19/7/56, 21/7/56
'The work of universities' [Edinburgh Rectorial] (1860) 20/11/59, 16/4/60
The works of Joseph Butler, 2v. (1896) 12/6/95, 23/12/95, 2/1/96, 25/5/96
Translations, with G. W. Lyttelton (1861) 2/10/57, 7/7/58 ff, 24/10/59 ff, 31/10/60 ff, 22/12/60 ff, 7/2/61
2nd. edition (1863) 24/4/63
'True and false conceptions of the Atonement', *N.C.*, xxxvi. 317 (September 1894) 18/2/94, 18/3/94, 25/7/94, 1/9/94
'Universitas Hominum; or, the Unity of History', *North American Review*, cxlv. 589 (December 1887) 11/6/87, 28/6/87, 1/10/87, 9/11/87
Vaticanism: *an answer to 'Replies and Reproofs'* (1875) 12/12/74, 2/1/75
Döllinger's comments on 19/2/75
Italian translation by Gonzaga 21/7/75 n
proofs corrected by Acton and Oxenham 15/2/74
Wedgwood: *An Address* (1863) 26/10/63
See also Church Principles, *State in its Relations*

with the Church (*The*), letters and articles for the press, *Eton Miscellany*, essays and papers
publications, catalogue of made by G 15/4/68
Public Health Bill 15/6/72 c, 26/6/72 c, 10/7/72 c, 15/7/72, 17/7/72 c, 4/2/73 c
public life 29/12/35
  Christian politics unrealisable in 29/12/43
  exhausts
    personal life and Christian discipline 29/12/78
  G feels no longer fit for, yet bidden to walk in 15/7/92
  G's decision to enter 8/1/32, 15/1/32 ff
  has the best of G 29/12/78
  O'Shea divorce case and
    G's memoranda on, printed 21/11/90 ff
Public Record Office
  control of access to 16/11/86
public schools 24/6/77 n
  speech on, at Marlborough 3/2/77
Public Schools Bill 2/12/64, 14/2/68, 23/6/68
Public Worship Bill 24/6/74, 28/6/74, 17/7/74 ff, 4/8/74, 5/8/74, 28/2/75, 8/4/77
  G's Resolutions on 8/7/74, 9/7/74 ff
    withdrawn 16/7/74
  issues involved almost unhinge G 4/8/74
Punch 12/9/93
  G's dinner with staff of 14/11/88 n, 7/5/89
punishment, eternal/future 27/3/64 ff, 23/7/64, 13/11/64, 14/12/65, 21/6/69, 14/11/75, 8/5/78, 26/1/92
  discussed with Tennyson 2/11/76
  G's writings on 21/8/76 ff
    interrupted by Bulgarian atrocities 28/8/76
purchase abolition *See* army, Lords (House of)
purchase in the army *See* army
purgatory 2/11/38, 1/11/50
Puritanism 17/10/92
Pusey, Edward Bouverie, Rev. Prof. (1800–1882), regius professor of Hebrew, Oxford from 1828, tractarian controversialist 28/9/28, 30/1/34, 1/5/38, 23/7/38, 12/1/40, 12/4/41 ff, 4/7/42, 29/12/44, 17/6/45, 12/12/57, 8/11/74, 30/1/78
  conversions to Rome and 1/4/45
  Daniel the worst written book known to G 27/1/85
  funeral of 21/9/82
  G criticises neutral position of 3/3/47
  Gorham case and 14/3/50 ff, 10/7/51
  G prays for as in spiritual danger 13/4/48
  hardly treated 30/6/43
  letters from G to, printed 10/10/69
  Liddon's *Life* of 19/10/82, 7/1/94 ff
  pours oil on flames 20/3/39
  rationalism of 9/9/71, 31/12/84
  State and Church and 23/7/38, 2/8/38
  Temple, appointment of, seems to have forgiven G 14/11/72
  Tract 90 and 15/4/41
  See also Tracts, Newman, Oxford (University of)
Pusey House *See* Oxford (University of)

Quakers 6/2/74, 27/8/81, 10/10/82, 15/10/93
Quantock Lodge (Taunton) 23/5/63
Quarterly Review *See* publications
Queen Anne's Bounty Board 19/6/58
Queen's College, Oxford
  G dining in 19/11/61
Queens' Colleges *See* Ireland
Queensferry, Edinburgh 13/10/36
Queensferry, Hawarden 9/8/39, 22/9/52, 10/11/52
  G watches Victoria pass in train 14/10/52
quinine *See* medicines

Raby Castle (Cleveland) 6/9/69, 20/9/76
race
  English belief in peculiar aptitude for popular institutions 28/12/58
Racine
  paper on 12/11/33
Radcliffe Camera, Oxford 4/10/28
Radcliffe Trust
  difficulty of gathering quorum 9/7/80
  G as trustee of 25/5/55, 12/2/56, 30/5/56, 22/1/57, 26/1/57, 30/1/57, 5/4/59, 8/4/59, 6/6/59, 27/4/60, 20/7/61, 16/3/63, 3/7/63, 18/3/64, 8/7/67, 10/7/67, 29/6/68, 1/7/69, 19/7/71, 11/7/72, 16/7/73, 13/7/74, 29/6/75, 11/7/76, 13/2/77, 7/7/77, 25/5/78, 12/7/78, 12/7/79, 9/7/80, 1/8/83
    gives Radcliffe Camera to the Bodleian 20/11/61
    resigns trusteeship 24/4/88 n
radicalism
  always linked to liberalism 27/10/85
  Commons infected with by Hartington 6/9/93
  growth of in liberal party 28/10/92
  meeting satisfactory but Radical 3/12/89
  navy estimates and
    those of 1894 the most Radical measure of G's lifetime 25/7/94
  royal finances and 4/7/89
  under-representation in cabinet 5/2/85
  See also Bright, Chamberlain, Commons (House of), Ireland, Labouchere, liberal party, Radical Programme, radicals, republicanism

Radical Programme 20/10/85, 25/10/85, 27/10/85, 4/11/85, 6/11/85
outrageous proposals on disestablishment of 6/11/85
Radley, Oxford
St. Peter's College 31/1/49
Raemoir (Innes) 16/10/49
ragged school
children from to tea 28/2/49
G teaching at 28/2/49
railways 23/2/37, 13/11/79
accidents on 18/11/72 c
Queen's concern about 15/12/70 c
amalgamations of 10/2/72 c, 15/2/72 c, 18/11/72 c
American railways bonds, G's investments in 1/6/74
Chester and Holyhead 25/9/52
conversations on trains 13/10/43, 7/10/50, 21/6/56, 9/7/57, 1/9/58, 15/12/60, 22/11/61, 15/10/63, 10/11/63, 21/10/65, 19/9/67
a lady musician 20/1/70
cabinet on *Alabama* negotiations 21/3/71
geological and coalmining 21/4/73
in Italy 2/3/59
intelligent German 24/11/70
on American civil war 12/1/62
with Bright on Irish land 27/5/69
with Montalembert 21/6/55
with Wiseman and Vaughan 6/8/61
early travel on
Chester 13/7/39
Dover 31/7/44
Eton 22/6/39
London 14/1/40, 25/1/41
Manchester 20/1/32
E. N. R., Gladstones fail to move amndt. against 24/10/48
G as railway arbitrator 13/6/51, 19/7/51, 31/7/51, 18/8/51, 26/8/51, 22/1/52, 2/3/52, 15/9/52, 28/9/52, 5/10/52, 24/10/56, 13/1/57
buys 500 guineas plate as reward for 7/12/57
G learning *Guinevere* by heart in train 14/10/59
government purchase of 6/8/64, 8/9/64 n, 4/5/88 n
G's complaints about stations 25/1/49
G shareholder in
Caledonian 5/2/50, 8/5/50, 22/9/50, 6/3/51, 13/3/51, 14/3/51
Clydesdale Junction 4/2/50, 30/4/50, 7/5/50, 10/5/50
Edinburgh, Perth, Dundee 15/10/49, 23/9/50, 6/5/52, 5/9/65
Metropolitan line 1/2/61 n, 24/5/62, 6/9/65, 23/7/68, 11/4/70 n, 5/4/71, 15/6/71, 19/12/72, 1/6/74, 7/8/74, 16/8/77
Philadelphia and Reading 8/4/79, 9/4/79
Scottish Central 15/1/50, 16/1/50
G's memorandum on redemption of 6/8/64, 19/12/64
G's railway tax scheme 11/2/64
G travels 2nd class 29/1/50
Highland line, fine quality of 9/10/72
how easily taken for granted 14/7/46
impact on the century of 18/6/90 n
inferior branch lines in France 2/10/66
in France
costs of 25/10/50
in Italy
late 9/10/66
L. C. S. 4/10/54 ff
legislation for 8/2/42 ff
London-Bombay railway proposal
government not the proper judge of, but capitalists and engineers 12/9/71
N. Wales, Chester, Birkenhead 30/12/71 n
Railway Dept., memorandum on 25/7/44
Railway Duty Association 26/1/75
rating of 29/3/73 c, 3/4/83 c
Royal Commission on 17/2/65, 14/3/65, 4/5/88
select cttee. proposed for 5/2/44
select committee of 1825
among the curious documents of the age 28/9/54
sleepers (Pullman) 3/6/78
speed of 1/2/49
Hawarden-London 5 hours 10 minutes: quickest journey 21/10/84
Trieste the most beautiful in the world? 20/11/58
Wales-Birkenhead by tunnel
sod cut by G 16/10/84
Wrexham, Mold, Connah's Quay 2/5/65, 5/5/65 ff
C. G cuts sod of 22/10/62
See also cabinet (committees of), France, Lords (House of), memoranda, memoranda (printed), Metropolitan line, select committees (G examined by)
Railways Act 1844 3/7/44
conference on 17/7/44
Parliamentary trains on Sundays defeated 22/7/44
speech on 8/7/44
Ramsau, Bavaria 16/9/74
Ramsay, Edward Bannerman, Dean (1793–1872), Scottish episcopalian; dean of Edinburgh 1841–72 4/6/28, 19/12/33, 4/8/36, 3/1/37, 13/8/37, 2/11/37, 3/11/37, 20/11/37, 26/5/39,

1/10/39, 1/12/40, 6/9/44 ff, 29/12/46, 8/1/50, 16/4/50, 23/9/50, 1/5/51, 11/6/53, 28/5/54, 10/6/56, 28/7/56, 11/12/59 ff, 15/4/60 ff, 11/1/62, 12/1/62, 10/10/63, 23/9/64 ff, 7/10/71 ff, 4/1/73
buries Sir J. G 13/12/51
churchmanship has oozed out of 2/10/64
letters from G to, printed 3/1/70
Scott centenary and
reads out G's tribute to 8/8/71
Trinity College, Glenalmond and 18/9/40 ff, 3/10/40
Ramsgate 12/8/54, 16/8/54, 25/8/54, 2/9/54
St. Augustine's church 11/9/54
Rangemoor, Burton-on-Trent (M. T. Bass) 14/10/65
Ranger's House, Blackheath (Aberdeen) 1/5/52
Rankeillour, Fife (Hope) 29/9/46 ff
Raphael 4/4/32, 4/6/32, 29/9/38, 1/10/38, 4/10/38, 11/12/38, 31/12/38, 1/1/39, 9/1/39, 18/1/39, 30/6/45, 27/11/50, 2/12/50
rates
appeal to magistrates against 25/2/42
incidence of 7/11/72
Peel taxed Exchequer excessively for local purposes 17/1/69
See also church rates, memoranda (printed), poor law, taxation (local)
Rathdrum
Royal Fitzwilliam Hotel 25/10/77
Ravenna 9/6/32 ff
reading
decline in power of 6/9/93
time spent on 6/11/46
reading, lists of 23/4/30 fl, 27/7/30, 10/9/31 fl, 20/7/33 fl, 1/2/37, 28/2/38, 13/4/48
on Irish education 12/4/37
Real Estate Intestacy Bill (Locke King) 13/3/69 c, 10/7/69, 30/11/69, 7/12/69, 9/12/69 c
Rebecca riots *See* Wales
rebellion of 1745 1/7/26, 4/7/26
Receiver General *See* Government of Ireland Bill
recordings of G's voice
for Thomas Edison 22/11/88
See also phonograph
recreation *See* games and sports
Rectorships *See* Glasgow and Edinburgh universities
redistribution 29/1/66
Redistribution Bill 1885 29/1/85
boundary commission for 28/11/84
cumulative vote inadmissable 5/11/84
in Commons 1/12/84 ff, 19/2/85 n, 30/3/85 ff, 28/4/85 cf, 12/5/85 n, 9/6/85 c, 12/6/85
Irish boundary commission, Salisbury's complaints on 24/12/84
negotiations with tories on 5/11/84, 7/11/84 c, 13/11/84 ff
compact, basis of 26/11/84
conferences 7/11/84 c, 13/11/84, 19/11/84, 22/11/84, 26/11/84, 27/11/84 c
memorandum on, printed 28/11/84
single member constituencies and 15/8/84, 29/9/84, 26/10/84, 29/10/84, 26/11/84, 28/11/84
numerical size of 29/9/84, 26/10/84, 5/11/84, 13/11/84, 28/11/84
principle to be generally applied 5/11/84
university seats and 26/11/84, 28/11/84, 29/11/84, 1/12/84
See also cabinet (committees of)
Red River *See* Canada
Redruth
G's speech at 11/6/89
Red Sea 15/6/81 c, 31/8/81
telegraph to 25/1/61, 26/1/61, 28/1/61, 18/10/61, 11/11/61
reform
G's memorandum on cabinet differences over 30/5/60
reform, parliamentary
aspect of public policy lying within reach 31/3/57
See also Reform Bills
reformation
G's articles on 1/6/88, 8/6/88, 16/6/88, 18/9/88, 10/10/88, 16/9/89
dispute with *The Tablet* over 2/11/89, 10/11/89
G's memorandum on, printed 16/8/88
Newman's views of 15/4/41
saved the Pope and the Roman Catholic church from themselves 21/5/69
reformation, history of 10/12/40, 8/9/42, 12/12/80
Reform Bills
1831 24/3/31, 19/4/31 ff, 22/9/31, 3/10/31
antireform fund 27/4/31
meeting at Warwick 4/4/31 ff
pamphlet on by G (unpublished) 5/5/31 ff, 17/7/31
Petition on, written by G 30/5/31 ff, 7/6/31 ff, 1/7/31, 2/7/31
1832 24/4/32, 22/5/32, 25/5/32, 13/6/32, 16/6/32, 6/11/32, 9/11/32
1852
G votes against Hume's motion for 25/3/52

Reform Bills (*cont.*)
1854 23/11/53, 22/12/53
intrinsically considered good 13/2/54
postponement of 27/2/54, 1/3/54, 8/4/54 n
1857 (Locke King)
Peelites split on 19/2/57
1859 16/3/59, 21/3/59
G defends 'small boroughs' 29/3/59, 21/2/93
G opposes Russell's Resolution 29/3/59, 31/3/59
G sorely puzzled by 21/3/59, 24/3/59
G supports 29/3/59 n
1860
G defends in Commons 3/5/60
G on cabinet committee on 12/11/59, 19/11/59, 12/1/60, 16/1/60, 1/12/60
G unwillingly on cabinet committee for 12/11/59
rating v. rent 19/11/59
set back cause of reform 22/12/81
1861
in cabinet 9/2/61
1861 (Baines')
G votes for 10/4/61
1864 (Baines')
G's 'pale of the constitution' speech 11/5/64, 21/5/64
1865 (Baines')
G avoids speaking on but votes for 8/5/65
1866 10/11/65, 16/11/65 n, 22/11/65, 27/12/65, 1/3/66, 2/3/66, 6/3/66, 10/3/66, 23/3/66 ff, 11/6/66
£14 franchise 7/6/66
crowds following G 27/6/66 n, 28/6/66
Dunkellin's amendment 16/6/66, 18/6/66
final points settled 8/3/66
G introduces 12/3/66
G moves 2nd Reading 12/4/66
government defeated 28/5/66
Grosvenor's amendment 16/4/66 ff, 27/4/66
G's dying speech on 19/7/66
G's speeches in Liverpool on 5/4/66, 6/4/66
G's 'time is on our side' speech 27/4/66
heads of settled 21/2/66
householders, compound 15/2/66
householders, ratepaying 2/2/66, 15/2/66, 11/6/66
lodger franchise 2/2/66, 15/2/66
Redistribution Bill 23/3/66 n, 7/5/66
savings banks depositors' franchise 2/2/66
the 'skedaddle' 4/6/66
1866 (Clay's Bill)
G opposes 30/5/66
1867 5/2/67 n
and redistribution 31/5/67, 3/6/67, 15/6/67, 8/4/68, 1/5/68, 13/5/68, 14/5/68
and the Lords 12/7/67, 16/7/67, 1/8/67, 8/8/67, 9/8/67
a smash perhaps without example 12/4/67
battle vitually over 8/7/67
Bright sensible and moderate on 19/3/67
Childers' amendment 16/5/67, 17/5/67 n
compound householders, G beaten on 9/5/67
G opposes 18/3/67
G reserves perfect freedom of action following defeat on 11/5/67 n
G's letter on 13/4/67 ff
G's speeches on 18/3/67, 21/3/67, 25/3/67, 11/4/67, 12/4/67, 9/5/67, 28/5/67
Hodgkinson's amendment 16/5/67, 17/5/67, 20/5/67
Horsman's plurality plan 18/2/67
Instruction moved by Coleridge 27/3/67 n, 1/4/67 n, 3/4/67, 8/4/67
Mill's female suffrage amendment, G opposes 20/5/67 n
minority clauses of 5/3/70 c, 15/6/70, 13/4/71
modification of 12/2/69 c
postal voting, G opposes 20/6/67
registration, G at meeting on 1/5/68
revolt of the 'tea room' 8/4/67 n
Ten Minute Bill, G attacks 25/2/67
third reading, G decides not to speak on 15/7/67
1873 County Household Franchise Bill
G believes county household franchise just & politic, and unavoidable 23/7/73
1875 County Household Franchise Bill
G votes for 7/7/75, 29/6/77, 22/2/78
1884 3/10/83, 13/10/83 ff, 23/1/84, 28/1/84, 4/2/84, 27/2/84
ancient rights franchises and 22/12/83
autumn session for 9/7/84 c, 14/7/84 c, 2/10/84, 3/10/84, 6/10/84 c, 8/10/84 c, 13/10/84, 22/10/84 c, 24/10/84 c
bishops and 2/7/84, 9/7/84
cannot be postponed till 1885 31/12/83, 24/5/84 c
Carnarvon's offer of 'men of weight' compromise 22/10/84 ff
date of efficacy of 31/12/83 c, 24/5/84 c,

31/5/84, 1/10/84, 8/10/84 c, 17/11/84 n
effect on ultra-nationalism 19/10/83
electoral districts and 6/12/83, 22/12/83, 26/12/83
electoral districts: G prefers old divisions 6/12/83, 26/12/83
government committee on redistribution 8/8/84, 9/8/84 c, 15/8/84, 29/9/84
Granville's compromise 8/7/84, 11/7/84
G's campaign for 22/7/84, 16/8/84 ff
G's campaign in Scotland for 29/8/84 ff
in cabinet 25/10/83 ff, 4/1/84 c
in Commons 28/2/84 ff, 7/4/84 ff, 1/5/84, 2/5/84 ff, 26/6/84 ff, 30/6/84, 6/11/84 ff, 11/11/84
in Lords 2/7/84 ff
Ireland and 19/10/83, 22/10/83, 23/10/83, 26/10/83, 3/12/83, 6/12/83, 31/12/83, 1/3/84
Ireland and: 40/- freeholder for? 4/1/84, 14/1/84 n
Ireland must be included 19/10/83
Irish M. Ps. to be reduced? 1/3/84, 6/3/84, 20/3/84
James to draw a Bill 5/11/83, 28/12/83, 4/1/84
Lambert's memorandum and 22/12/83
lodger franchise and 22/12/83, 1/1/84
minorities and 6/12/83, 10/12/83
minorities and: may split the liberal party 6/12/83
minorities and: wide application impossible 31/12/83
need for Lords speedily to pass 19/8/84
next dissolution on old franchise: no 28/4/84 c
occupation franchise and 22/12/83, 1/1/84
one bill for the three kingdoms? 3/10/83
property franchise and 22/12/83, 4/1/84, 10/1/84, 14/1/84
proportional voting and 5/3/84 c, 20/11/84, 1/12/84
redistribution and 22/10/83, 7/11/83, 21/11/83, 22/11/83 c, 3/12/83, 6/12/83, 18/12/83, 22/12/83, 29/12/83, 31/12/83, 21/3/84, 31/5/84, 2/7/84 ff, 30/7/84, 8/8/84, 22/8/84, 11/9/84, 28/9/84, 29/9/84
Redistribution Bill 12/11/83
redistribution not to be linked with franchise 22/11/83 c
registration and 22/12/83
resignation/dissolution on considered 9/7/84, 2/8/84, 25/9/84, 27/9/84, 29/9/84
Rosebery's plan 12/7/84
Royal Assent for: a stage in G's descending life 5/12/84
simplicity the key to success 5/11/83, 9/2/84
single member constituencies 15/8/84 ff
stoppage of a great constitutional hazard 25/8/84
title of 10/1/84
to be accompanied by a heap of local government 15/11/83
women's suffrage and 15/4/84, 9/5/84, 13/5/84, 24/5/84 c, 13/6/84
1893
plans for 20/7/92, 1/8/92
county franchise
Trevelyan's motion on 26/4/72 n
G believes one imminent 5/4/51
See also Bright, cabinet, Cecil, Commons (House of), conservative party, Dilke, Disraeli, franchise, Ireland, liberal party, Lords (House of), memoranda, memoranda (printed), Northcote, Oxford Union Society, redistribution, Redistribution Bill 1885, Russell, Scotland, Temple (Henry), Victoria, Wellesley, women (enfranchisement of)
Reform Club *See* clubs (G member of)
Reformed Church in Switzerland 16/9/38
Reform League
deputation from 11/2/67, 30/3/67
Reform Union
monster deputation from
G gives quasi-manifesto to 11/5/67
Refreshment Houses and Wine Licences Bill 26/3/60 ff, 7/5/60
register
G struck off Flintshire register 29/8/72
registration 1/3/41, 7/8/85 ff, 11/9/85, 14/9/85, 18/9/85, 14/4/86 c
amalgamation of municipal and parliamentary roll 24/1/73 c
Rathbone's bill to be supported 28/6/73 c
See also cabinet (committees of)
Registration Bill 20/7/92, 1/8/92, 31/10/92 c, 25/4/93 ff
Regium Donum *See* Ireland
Regius chairs *See* patronage
religion
census of
clashing with intelligence 24/3/34
crucifix, G given 29/12/96
differences with Peel on 9/5/41
G at service in theatre 23/3/62
G's Homeric studies a service to 10/2/58
G too independent of symbol 29/12/96
religious disabilities
G's memorandum on 2/2/91
value of, among the tumult 20/3/41

vision for outline of a Church 20/3/41
See also memoranda (printed)
Religious Disabilities Bill, G's 2/2/91, 4/2/91, 14/10/93, 26/10/93
religious plans in hand 13/4/48
Rembrandt 11/12/38
Rendel, Stuart (1834–1913), 1st Baron Rendel (1894), G's host and confidant, liberal M.P. and armaments manufacturer 5/3/88, 9/7/88, 25/7/89, 30/1/90, 31/3/90, 30/6/90, 25/11/90, 4/12/90 ff, 19/2/91, 27/4/91, 6/6/91 n, 8/6/91 ff, 28/5/92 ff, 4/8/92 ff, 15/10/92, 12/2/93 ff, 10/3/93 ff, 26/4/93, 28/4/93 ff, 29/7/93, 24/11/93, 8/5/94, 23/1/95
arranges meetings of G and Welsh M.P.s 17/3/86, 16/7/89, 7/6/90
arranging the Gs' Italian holiday 18/11/88 ff, 19/12/88 ff
at Hawarden 13/9/88 ff, 17/8/89 ff, 23/11/89 ff, 14/10/91
G much likes 28/1/87
G's host at Villa Magabi, Valescure 15/1/92 ff
G staying with in Carlton Gardens 29/2/92 ff
G staying with in Whitehall Gardens 13/11/88 ff
G's visit to Swansea and 3/6/87
letters from G to, printed 3/9/92, 13/10/92, 12/11/92, 5/7/93, 2/3/94
marriage of H. N. G to Maud Rendel 25/11/89 ff
navy and 24/1/92
qualities of 16/11/88
kindness more remarkable than aptitudes 19/12/88
sweated labour and 25/12/88
to be informed of G's declining sight 31/1/94
Welsh church and 18/11/88, 5/7/93, 27/11/93
Representation of the People Bills *See* Reform Bills
representative government 9/5/41
believed in by few men 2/7/86
republicanism 23/4/40, 7/9/70 n, 10/9/70, 4/12/71
Bolton Republican Club 5/8/71 c
Bradlaugh and 1/9/71
Labour Representation League deputation 27/9/70
magistrate presiding at Dilke's meeting 29/3/73 c
See also Dilke
rescue work
80/90 talked to indoors or out
increased to 112 24/1/54
only one success 20/1/54
Bewick's comments on prostitutes 2/7/73
chief burden of G's soul 20/1/54
contagious diseases and 18/2/63
Criminal Law Amendment Bill and 31/7/85
dangerous thoughts prompted by 1/9/59
dangers of
paternity suit threatened? 14/6/73
Declaration on absence of infidelity by G to the marriage bed 7/12/96
friends' attempts to stop
Hamilton extracts promise from G 16/7/86
MacColl and Stead warn of conspiracy to blacken G's character 16/7/86 n
Rosebery opens discussion of its propriety 10/2/82
G accosted by prostitutes 15/6/92, 17/6/92
G advises Australia 8/5/57
G checking records of rescue case at Somerset House 19/6/58
G commissions portrait of Summerhayes from Dyce 6/8/59
G favours 18, not 16, as age of consent 31/7/85
G reading *Hamlet* to 13/5/76
G reading 'La Traviata' 4/5/57
G reading on Parisian prostitution 9/7/45, 23/4/67 ff
G writing to cases 10/4/59
in Brighton 9/4/60
in Corfu 4/1/59, 7/1/59, 8/1/59 ff
in Dresden 14/11/58
in Milan 3/3/59
in Nottingham 10/5/75
in Trafalgar Square 21/10/59
leaves G barely conscious morally 19/8/51
letters on burned 16/10/86
literature on 25/11/59 ff
money given to cases 13/1/75, 21/6/79
not within bounds of worldly prudence 10/5/53
one of G's most singular cases 4/11/58
on wedding anniversary
not as it should be 25/7/61
rumours about 7/12/96
Stead's 'Maiden Tribute' and 9/7/85, 15/7/85
Strzelecki's
has sent 260 women to Australia 23/9/61
Victoria, poisoning of her mind on 16/7/86
Wilson's attempt to blackmail G 10/5/53 ff, 13/5/53, 14/6/53, 15/6/53
Wright case 7/12/96 n
See also beauty, journal (G's), Thistlethwayte (Laura)

rescue work, reflections on 19/7/48, 20/1/54
rescue work, significant cases
1828–74 5/8/28 ff, 24/10/29, 22/7/31, 19/11/32, 9/7/45, 10/7/45, 25/5/49, 2/5/50, 4/5/50, 8/7/50, 17/7/50, 4/3/51, 19/3/52, 19/4/52 ff, 3/5/52 ff, 12/10/52 ff, 4/11/52, 30/11/52, 30/12/52, 16/2/53 ff, 9/3/53, 15/3/53, 6/6/53, 8/6/53, 23/6/53 ff, 15/7/53, 14/11/53, 15/11/53 ff, 4/2/54, 29/3/54, 13/5/54 ff, 7/12/54, 23/4/55 ff, 6/6/55, 11/7/55 ff, 27/1/56 n, 4/3/56 ff, 15/4/57, 14/5/57, 1/7/57 ff, 15/7/57 ff, 16/2/58 ff, 6/4/59 ff, 8/11/60 ff, 19/1/61, 22/10/62, 13/2/63 ff, 20/1/64 ff, 2/6/64, 7/11/64, 2/5/65 ff, 7/6/65 ff, 15/12/65, 9/1/66, 24/2/68 ff, 22/4/68, 3/6/68 ff, 26/12/68, 27/1/69 ff, 12/3/69 ff, 7/5/69 ff, 4/9/69 ff, 27/1/70 ff, 22/2/70, 9/3/70, 21/3/70 ff, 8/6/70, 7/9/70, 21/9/70, 29/10/70, 1/12/70 ff, 14/12/70, 24/2/71, 21/3/71 ff, 3/5/71 ff, 9/8/71 ff, 20/8/71, 20/10/71 ff, 29/10/71 ff, 23/1/72 ff, 29/1/72, 28/2/72 ff, 3/4/72, 29/4/72 ff, 16/5/72 ff, 12/7/72 ff, 11/10/72 ff, 4/12/72 ff, 20/2/73 ff, 23/4/73 ff, 27/5/73, 18/6/73 ff, 4/10/73 ff, 12/11/73 ff, 5/12/73, 17/4/74 ff, 17/5/74 ff, 3/8/74, 4/11/75 ff
1875– 7/1/75 ff, 2/3/75 ff, 15/3/75 ff, 25/5/75, 30/6/75 ff, 29/9/75, 8/2/76 ff, 9/2/76 ff, 27/6/76, 12/7/76 ff, 22/7/76 ff, 6/9/76, 28/10/76, 12/2/77 ff, 19/6/77, 28/6/77 ff, 9/7/77, 24/7/77 ff, 5/2/78, 19/3/78 ff, 27/11/78 ff, 22/2/79 ff, 22/4/79 ff, 2/5/79 ff, 9/6/79 ff, 12/7/79 ff, 18/5/80 ff, 16/6/80 ff, 6/7/80, 6/9/80 ff, 22/11/80 ff, 10/1/81 ff, 9/2/81 ff, 4/5/81 ff, 22/6/81 ff, 2/8/81, 22/8/81 ff, 11/10/81, 8/11/81 ff, 26/1/82 ff, 27/1/82 ff, 14/3/82, 6/5/82 ff, 11/8/82 ff, 31/10/82 ?, 13/12/82, 2/6/83 ff, 3/7/83 ff, 22/8/83 ff, 25/10/83 ff, 8/11/83 ff, 25/1/84, 21/10/84, 26/11/84 ff, 17/3/85 ff, 18/4/85 ff, 10/6/85, 27/2/86 ff, 23/3/86 ff, 14/4/86 ff, 8/6/86 ff, 14/6/87, 23/7/87, 12/3/88 ?, 28/4/88, 12/6/88, 19/7/88, 3/12/88, 4/3/89, 24/5/89, 31/5/89, 25/6/89, 16/7/89, 9/9/89, 14/3/90, 14/5/90, 7/6/90, 8/7/90, 8/7/90 ff, 29/7/90 ff, 2/2/91 ff, 9/2/91 ff, 9/4/91, 18/4/91 ff, 15/6/92 ff, 1/3/93, 22/3/93 ?, 24/4/93, 4/8/93 ?, 28/8/93, 24/2/94
Ayscough, Rebecca 31/10/42, 3/11/42, 5/11/44, 27/11/44, 3/12/44, 4/3/45
Beer 14/3/90 ff
Bell
strange, singular, sad 5/8/67, 7/8/67
Blackshaw 9/8/67
Bolton, Mrs. 4/4/82, 5/5/82, 13/5/82, 8/6/82 ff, 9/8/82, 15/9/82, 9/4/83, 18/4/83, 8/6/83, 20/5/84, 19/10/86, 9/2/91, 10/2/91
Bowman 11/3/62 ff
Bramwell 19/11/61, 5/12/61
Burton 18/2/52 ff
Butcher 16/2/63, 28/2/63 ff, 8/6/63
Bywater, Jane 7/2/54, 12/2/54
Campbell 28/7/75 ff
Charrington 30/1/73
Chesterfield, Mrs. 21/6/79, 25/6/79, 28/6/79, 8/7/79, 19/7/79
Clifford 26/4/58, 20/4/61, 26/4/61
Clifton, Emma 23/7/50 ff, 27/7/50, 1/8/50 ff, 2/10/50 ff, 28/2/51 ff, 19/5/52, 22/5/52, 12/10/60, 29/4/63, 5/12/65, 22/3/85 ?
G returns to London to see 15/8/50
G self-bewildered by 22/5/52
G visits lodgings of 1/8/50
Coleti
in Corfu 4/1/59, 7/1/59
Collins, E. 11/6/51 ff, 2/7/51 ff, 7/7/51 ff, 19/8/51, 26/1/52 ff, 13/2/52, 7/5/52, 13/10/52, 6/8/53 ?, 13/8/53 ?, 7/10/53, 7/11/53, 19/11/53, 30/12/53, 3/1/54, 31/1/54, 23/2/54, 26/3/54, 15/7/54, 19/10/54, 23/7/57
G compares to una statua bellissima 1/7/52
going to Australia 10/1/53
G scourges himself after meeting with 13/7/51, 15/7/51, 23/7/51, 19/11/52
G searches Somerset House for records of marriage of 19/6/58, 26/6/58
strange, questionable, or more, meeting with 23/7/51
strange and humbling scene with 13/7/51
Cooper
carried into dreamland by 9/1/82
Cooper, E. 8/5/64 ff, 15/6/68, 8/7/68
wild and untamed 8/5/64
Cornel 27/5/59, 28/5/59
Coward 14/3/47 ff, 22/3/47 ff, 5/5/47 ff, 31/5/47
Cowper, E. (also Throckmorton) 27/11/62, 1/12/62, 2/12/62 ff, 8/12/62, 9/12/62, 20/1/63, 4/3/63, 26/7/63, 28/7/63, 30/7/63, 31/7/63, 16/10/86 ?

rescue work, significant cases (*cont.*)
Cowper, E. (*cont.*)
going to Clewer 31/7/63
spaniel of, G caring for 31/7/63, 1/8/63
Cox/Stanley 2/7/73, 6/3/74
Cray, Mrs. 27/2/86 ff, 21/3/86
Dalton/Phillips (or Phillips/Dalton)
G gains insight into class-life from 20/2/76
reading Longfellow and Shakespeare with 16/2/76
Douglas 2/3/64 ff, 2/2/91 ff
Dumin 18/12/54, 22/12/54, 23/12/54, 24/1/55, 12/2/55, 14/2/55, 12/3/55, 22/3/55
Fitzroy
going to Canada 23/2/74, 25/2/74
French woman
sad and strange 17/1/54
talked to for an hour 12/8/53
Gascoigne, Mrs. 21/7/83 ff, 11/8/83 ff, 25/10/83 ff
G gives *Uncle Tom's Cabin* to 21/10/52
G giving bible to 27/4/56
G giving gifts to 21/6/52
G giving money to 22/6/52, 31/1/53, 12/2/53, 15/2/53
G giving prayer book to 27/4/56
G giving Shakespeare to 29/6/58
G giving Taylor's *Holy Living* to 29/6/52, 12/10/52
Grant 22/4/91
Grassi 14/5/90
Griffin 8/2/54, 12/8/57
G standing outside Argyll Rooms 22/7/50
Gurney 31/5/59, 1/6/59
G visits houses of 4/11/52
Harrington, E. 19/7/53, 9/8/53, 4/10/53, 7/11/53
Hastings, Mrs. H. 6/12/64, 4/1/65, 5/1/65, 18/1/65, 20/1/65, 23/1/65, 19/2/65, 16/5/65, 10/7/65, 22/10/65, 28/10/65, 27/6/66, 18/2/67
G reads whole of *Guinevere* to 16/3/65
Hayes 27/6/62, 1/7/62, 3/7/62, 15/11/62, 5/6/64, 15/11/64
Heaphy, Mrs. 4/10/73 ff
books sent to 6/10/73
Herbert, E. 11/11/63
Herbert, K. 20/11/63, 23/11/63, 29/4/64
for 2 hours 20/11/63
Hicks 12/7/58, 13/7/58, 16/8/58, 9/1/60
Howard 11/8/82 ff
in Hyde Park 25/2/37
Jacobs 20/7/70
Langton 13/4/56
Leslie 23/7/57, 29/7/57
Lester, C. 11/11/62, 16/11/62, 20/1/63
Lightfoot, P. 28/3/51, 9/5/51 ff, 16/7/51, 16/8/53, 9/10/53, 11/3/54, 24/4/54, 2/6/56, 2/7/58
Linwood 25/6/78
Livingstone 20/5/73 ff
Lloyd (80) 2/7/75
Loader, A. 6/7/52, 12/10/52, 4/11/52, 25/2/53, 2/3/53, 9/6/53, 4/10/53, 3/2/54
Louis aet. 15 17/7/54
Lovell 27/5/57, 28/5/57, 29/5/57, 2/7/57 ff, 2/8/57 ff, 24/1/58, 8/3/58, 16/3/58, 24/5/58, 17/7/58, 21/10/58, 15/3/59, 13/6/59, 4/7/59, 12/7/59, 29/8/59, 15/2/60
G scourges himself after meeting with 29/5/57
Macgregor 18/4/77, 21/4/77, 22/4/77, 25/4/77, 12/6/77, 18/7/77, 3/12/77, 28/5/78, 27/11/78, 18/12/78
G buys sewing machine for 14/3/78
Mackay 17/3/58, 20/3/58, 23/3/58
Maclagan 16/7/73
Macready 8/5/69, 12/5/69 ff, 29/5/69
May 26/4/58
Milligan 27/4/56, 23/5/56, 3/6/56, 22/7/56, 16/1/57, 5/5/57
Morgan (82) 28/1/54, 23/7/57
Murray, Mrs. 24/1/60, 22/8/60
Ormond 29/6/66
Osborne 28/12/53, 29/12/53, 25/1/54, 6/6/54, 8/8/54, 1/9/54, 28/3/55
Pearsall, Mrs. de 28/10/59, 15/11/59, 3/1/60, 14/10/60, 20/1/61, 26/5/62
Phillips/Dalton 9/2/76, 12/2/76, 20/2/76 ff, 4/3/76, 11/3/76, 7/7/76, 18/7/76, 25/7/76, 5/9/76, 7/9/76, 5/2/77, 15/3/77, 22/3/77, 26/6/77, 7/7/77, 24/9/77, 11/3/79, 16/5/79, 28/5/79, 9/3/81 ff, 9/9/81, 25/1/82 ff
G read *Hamlet* to 13/5/76
Ponsonby 15/3/90 ff
Rands 22/3/81 ff, 8/11/81 ff
recorded in journal by 'X' 30/12/52 ff
'remember Hooker's torch' 19/11/52, 29/12/53
Ricardo 3/8/81, 5/8/81, 16/8/81, 11/10/81, 10/11/81 ff, 31/1/82, 25/8/82, 18/3/86
Rigby Johnstone 16/6/58, 19/6/58, 26/6/58, 29/6/58, 17/7/58, 12/8/58, 26/4/59
a very singular case 19/6/58
G gives Shakespeare to 29/6/58
Rose, A. 10/7/67, 17/7/67, 25/7/67, 30/7/67
Rumpf, Mrs. C. 27/2/68, 25/3/68, 15/7/68 ff, 30/1/69 ff, 11/2/70, 18/2/70, 29/6/70, 8/9/70, 12/9/70

incredible yet not unsupported account of extraction of 20/8/70
visited in Brixton 26/2/70
Russell 6/7/59, 26/7/59, 24/1/72, 6/3/72 ff, 15/10/72, 2/4/73, 22/3/74, 23/3/74, 14/6/78
Scarsdale, Mrs. 22/8/81 ff, 7/9/81 ff, 10/11/81 ff, 4/7/83 ff, 22/8/89, 2/9/89
Seymour 25/11/62 ff
Shane 28/8/93
Sinclair, Lucy
G sees not without reproach 28/8/66
G writes to from Italy 18/12/66, 5/1/67
smart contest with 30/11/67
Sinclair, Lucy (later Barton) 8/8/66, 10/8/66, 11/9/66, 17/9/66, 27/9/66, 30/1/67 ff, 1/1/68, 27/2/68, 25/4/68, 9/7/69, 11/7/69 ff, 17/1/71, 4/11/74 ?, 5/11/74 ?
ask G to give her away 27/1/71
puts questions to G on her marriage 27/1/71
six in one evening 24/5/71
Somerville 5/3/67, 7/3/67, 11/3/67 ff
Staplyton 16/3/58, 22/3/58, 16/4/58, 20/4/58, 12/8/58, 8/3/59, 29/6/59, 4/7/59
Stewart 19/6/59, 20/6/59, 23/6/59, 29/6/59, 15/10/59
Summerhayes (later Mrs. Dale) 30/7/59, 31/7/59, 2/8/59, 3/8/59, 4/8/59, 6/8/59, 9/8/59, 10/8/59, 11/8/59, 15/8/59, 16/8/59, 17/8/59, 18/8/59, 27/8/59, 29/8/59, 24/9/59, 14/10/59, 16/10/59, 18/10/59, 20/10/59 ff, 27/10/59 ff, 15/11/59 ff, 28/11/59 ff, 18/12/59, 11/4/60, 21/4/60, 1/6/60, 10/8/60, 1/11/60, 25/3/61, 22/7/61, 23/12/61, 5/3/62, 8/3/62 n, 27/11/62, 14/6/67, 20/6/67
at Fine Arts Club 17/7/61
G brings to Downing Street 19/9/59
G commissions picture of from Dyce 6/8/59
G destroys letters of 16/10/86
G reads Tennyson to 16/9/59
G's unflagging interest in 3/8/61
highest degree both of interest and beauty 30/7/59
no common case, for evil or good 26/9/59
scene of rebuke not easily forgotten 17/9/59
thoughts of require to be limited and purged 1/9/59
Tait 9/5/84 ff, 18/5/84, 21/5/84 ff, 20/6/84, 13/4/85
payment to Sisterhood for 4/12/84 n
Taylor 22/2/62 ff
Temple 5/7/65, 7/7/65
three little ones 10/4/59
Trelawney 25/5/59, 11/6/59
G scourges himself after meeting with 25/5/59
Villiers 19/1/61, 21/1/61
Wallace 5/3/86 ff
Watson, E. 13/4/52
Watts 4/2/62
Williams, G. 5/10/53, 26/10/53
Williamson, Mrs. 5/1/60, 11/4/60, 17/8/60, 12/11/60, 29/1/61, 27/7/61, 23/12/61, 10/11/62
Wolfe 10/8/54, 11/8/54, 19/10/54, 17/1/55, 28/3/55, 13/2/56, 11/8/57
Wright 14/11/72 ff
See also journal (G's)
resignation
accepted 28/1/45 ff
Address resigning Oxford University seat (not sent) 10/11/60
G's last shot in the locker 16/7/60
G's resignation *all but* settled 2/6/60
Argyll mediates 4/6/60
G threatens resignation on paper duties 2/7/60
offered 21/1/45
still not dead 18/7/60
See also politics, retirement
resignation considered 3/3/35, 6/3/35
on Maynooth 28/2/44, 2/3/44, 8/7/44, 9/1/45, 21/1/45
pressure on G not to resign 2/3/44
Resina 15/5/32 ff
restlessness
drives G to work on Homer 30/1/62
Retford
G's speech at 11/12/90
retirement
leaves G open to temptation 30/12/45
See also politics (retirement from), resignation
retrenchment 5/2/53, 3/2/57, 6/2/57, 14/2/57, 6/3/57, 10/3/57, 31/3/57, 7/10/64, 3/4/71, 30/8/71, 9/9/71, 29/11/71, 16/7/75, 15/5/76, 7/11/83, 10/11/83 c, 19/1/84, 9/1/85, 7/8/85, 30/9/85, 24/12/86
aspect of public policy lying within reach 31/3/57
better times now! 29/11/62
economy out of fashion 28/1/73
expenditure committee 15/2/73 c, 18/2/73, 10/5/73 c, 24/5/73 c, 21/6/73 c, 6/4/83, 5/5/83 c, 8/5/83
gaining in strength 23/6/62
good prospects for estimates 22/11/62

retrenchment (*cont.*)
government of 1868 has not redeemed election pledges on 9/11/72
G's resolutions on 6/2/57 ff, 14/2/57, 6/3/57
Harcourt's motion on 15/2/73 c, 18/2/73
India Office less economical than the government generally 10/12/73
liberal party and 14/1/75
spirit of economy low 10/1/74
up: for the day? 19/5/62
See also Commons (House of), finance, memoranda (expenditure)
revolutionary war with France 5/10/26
rheumatism *See* illnesses
Rhine
bridges of 23/7/32
disappointing scenery of 23/7/32, 15/8/38
fine scenery of 24/8/38
G drinks from source of 4/7/32
journey up 13/8/38 ff
Rhodes, Cecil John (1853–1902), capitalist and benefactor of liberal party, home ruler, imperialist; prime minister of the Cape 1890–6 14/3/87 ?, 8/7/89 ?, 19/2/91, 3/11/92 ff, 25/11/92, 9/11/93 n, 31/8/93 c
a notable man 19/2/91
liberal party, donations 19/2/91
Rhodes Trust and publication of G's journal 19/2/91 n
Rhyl
G electioneering in 24/3/57
holidays at 21/8/50 ff, 7/9/52 ff
Ribbon Men *See* Ireland
Richard Coeur de Lion, G's poem on 21/6/27, 12/7/27
Richard II, deposition of 18/11/26, 27/10/27
Richmond 24/3/55
Richmond, G. and W. B. *See* portraits of G
riding 21/12/25, 3/1/26 ff, 7/4/26 ff, 4/8/26, 14/8/26, 24/8/27, 23/2/28, 24/6/29, 24/9/29, 17/6/31, 21/11/31, 5/12/31, 18/7/32, 8/9/32, 10/1/33, 3/5/33 ff, 30/8/33, 16/11/33, 10/5/34, 24/6/34 ff, 16/8/34 ff, 13/4/35, 16/12/35, 15/4/36, 14/6/36 ff, 29/7/36, 1/3/37, 29/4/37, 18/11/37 ff, 12/3/38, 13/7/38 ff, 11/4/39, 6/6/39, 16/7/42, 17/4/43 ff, 12/9/44, 11/5/53, 19/5/53 ff, 15/6/53, 28/6/53 ff, 30/7/53, 14/1/54 ff, 7/2/54, 7/3/54, 24/3/54 ff, 5/4/54 ff, 24/6/54 ff, 27/3/55, 26/3/56 ff, 28/4/56 ff, 2/1/57, 28/2/57 ff, 24/4/57, 16/6/60 ff, 28/7/60, 23/8/60, 2/3/61, 6/3/61 ff, 18/4/61 ff, 22/6/61, 28/10/61, 18/12/61 ff, 25/3/62 ff, 2/5/62, 25/2/63 ff, 14/3/63 ff, 21/4/63 ff, 14/3/64 ff, 24/5/64 ff, 17/3/65 ff, 25/5/65 ff, 8/2/66 ff, 24/5/66 ff, 29/3/67 ff, 27/5/67 ff, 23/4/69, 23/3/70 ff, 18/9/91 ?
accidents 11/11/33
at Balmoral 29/9/64
at Chatsworth 31/5/73 ff
G falls from horse in Rotten Row 4/4/63
horse kept at Oxford 2/5/31 ff
in Hyde Park 23/4/33, 4/5/33 ff, 2/7/53, 7/5/61, 14/5/62, 9/7/64, 28/4/70
last: G glad to be quit of luxury & indulgence 4/4/55
with C. G 17/6/39, 19/6/39
See also accidents, Christ Church (Oxford), coach journeys
Rimini 8/6/32 ff
Ripon, Earl of *See* Robinson
ritualism 8/3/77
G assisting in quelling anti-ritualist riot 14/10/60
G at ritualist service 10/3/67
G discourages use of surplice at Fasque 26/9/47
G publishes denial he is ritualist in league with the Pope 24/4/68 n
Green case and 6/9/81 ff, 17/10/81
imprisonment of S. F. Green 6/9/81, 13/9/81, 23/9/81, 16/8/82
prosecution of King 21/6/88
Purchas judgment 25/2/71, 10/3/71, 11/3/71, 19/3/71
G attends Purchas' chapel 7/4/72
royal commission on 6/1/69, 23/1/71, 30/1/72 c
Roanne 27/10/50
Robinson, Frederick John (1782–1859), Viscount Goderich (1827), 1st Earl of Ripon (1833), Prime Minister 1827–8, G's superior as President of Board of Trade 1841–3 3/10/31, 31/8/41, 3/9/41 ff, 22/9/41 ff, 25/9/41 ff, 29/11/41 ff, 11/12/41 ff, 20/1/42, 28/1/42, 1/10/42, 14/2/43, 16/3/43
inadequacies of 28/1/42, 2/2/42 ff, 27/5/43
Robinson, George Frederick Samuel, Lord (1827–1909), Viscount Goderich (1833), 2nd Earl of Ripon & 3rd Earl de Grey (1859), 1st Marquis of Ripon (1871), lord president 1868–73, Indian Viceroy 1880–4, first lord of the Admiralty 1886, colonial secretary 1892–5; convert to Rome 1874 10/2/53, 24/3/56, 9/7/56, 22/6/59, 24/8/60, 3/3/66, 9/7/66, 9/6/68, 8/12/68, 20/2/69 c, 26/6/69 c, 30/6/69, 5/7/71, 2/2/72, 17/4/72, 25/1/73,

Robinson, George Frederick Samuel, Lord (*cont.*)
22/5/73, 6/2/78, 4/12/78, 10/3/80 ff, 18/2/82, 13/6/85, 14/9/85, 14/1/86, 13/2/86, 16/2/86 c, 30/3/86, 27/7/86, 16/11/86, 30/3/87, 21/5/87, 22/6/87, 13/5/88, 21/2/89 ff, 9/3/91, 11/1/93 ff, 3/5/93, 22/11/93 ff, 12/2/94 c
1866 Reform Bill and 19/6/66
at Hawarden 29/9/87 ff, 17/10/89 ff
colonial secretary 14/8/92 ff
conversion to Rome of 21/8/74, 2/10/74
avoids G 24/6/75
G's stiff letter to 4/10/74
rather evades G on meeting, but not rudely 20/3/75
education bill 1870 and 2/10/69, 4/11/69, 5/11/69, 16/5/70, 12/8/71 c, 21/3/73
G at Studley Royal 25/10/87 ff
G's Religious Disabilities Bill and 14/10/93, 26/10/93, 28/10/93
home rule and 2/2/94
Ilbert bill and 17/4/83, 22/5/83, 25/9/83 n, 15/12/83 n, 18/1/84, 4/3/84
cannot be given up 26/5/83 c
finding ways of amending 26/5/83 c
G's feeling on strong and unequivocal 1/6/83
G's feelings on strongly with Ripon 22/5/83
G perplexed at Ripon's handling of 26/12/83
in an impenetrable mist on 21/10/83
not to be postponed 10/10/83, 11/10/83
Indian Viceroy 24/4/80, 3/5/80 c, 19/6/80 c, 9/9/80, 24/7/84
succeeded by Dufferin 7/8/84
successor for 24/7/84
letters from G to, printed 2/10/69, 27/10/69, 4/11/69, 17/4/70, 16/5/70, 3/4/71, 4/4/71, 23/2/72, 21/5/72, 4/3/73, 21/3/73, 10/9/80, 24/11/81, 13/3/82, 1/6/82, 6/9/82, 1/12/82, 17/4/83, 1/6/83, 11/10/83, 18/1/84, 15/5/86, 9/12/86, 14/8/92, 21/8/92, 13/9/92, 30/9/92, 12/10/92, 15/11/92, 12/12/92, 5/4/93, 7/10/93, 10/10/93, 14/10/93, 28/10/93, 4/11/93, 6/11/93, 8/11/93, 2/2/94
marquisate for 25/5/71
Rhodesia and 31/8/93
the War Office and 24/4/63
university reform and 28/3/72
Washington, Treaty of
Fenians and 10/6/71
negotiation of 6/2/71 c, 25/3/71, 28/3/71 c, 1/4/71 c, 3/4/71 ff, 18/4/71 c, 19/4/71 c, 28/4/71, 9/5/71, 21/5/72, 13/6/72
See also Ilbert Bill, India, United States
Robinson, T. *See* plays seen
Rochester 15/10/61
Rockhills (Paxton) 22/5/65
Roebuck committee 24/1/55 ff, 18/2/55
G discusses with Victoria and Albert 18/2/55
G's Resolutions on
drafted but not moved 22/2/55
See also Crimean war, Gordon
Roehampton (Farquhar) 7/7/35, 6/8/35, 13/8/35, 23/8/35 ff
Rogart, Sutherland 21/9/53
Rogers, Frederic, Sir (1811–1889), 1st Baron Blachford (1871), member of the Engagement and Tractarian, permanent undersecretary of the colonial office 13/10/27, 1/12/28 ff, 16/3/46, 9/5/75, 14/3/77, 13/7/78, 27/6/82
chairman of G's London election committee 24/6/59
letters from G to, printed 25/2/72, 9/3/72
See also Engagement (The)
Roman Catholic Church 12/3/26, 3/9/26, 24/9/26, 1/10/26, 10/4/32, 20/7/36, 27/3/81, 19/11/81
aggression, system of 28/2/72
anti-celibacy in 14/3/39
baptisms disgust G 17/3/32, 23/7/32, 29/9/38
breviary of used by G 13/4/84
church building programme of 15/1/39
civil rights of obedient members destroyed by 3/3/74
conventual oaths, G observes 3/6/32
designation of 'Catholic Bishops' by illegal 28/2/72, 1/3/72
discussions on with Wiseman in Rome 6/12/38, 12/12/38, 24/12/38, 7/1/39, 15/1/39
English more ultramontanist than Irish 8/6/65
Episcopal districts of 15/1/39
evolution and 28/9/73
G denies causing Helen G's conversion 28/5/47
Gordon marriage case and 3/5/75, 9/5/75, 30/6/75
G publishes on despite risk of an action 14/7/75
G's article, *The Vatican Decrees* and 20/10/74 ff
G's visit to de Lisle's monastery at Garendon Park 7/10/73 ff

Roman Catholic Church (*cont.*)
G wishes papalists would go forward to Middle Ages 24/12/69
Heathcote's MS on reunion with 18/3/55, 27/3/55
Holy Water, unreasonable claims for 31/5/32
Host, processions of 2/2/32, 19/4/32, 17/10/38, 18/11/50
idolatrous processions 5/5/32
ignorance of C. of E. in 24/4/32
influence on G 13/5/32
Mass
G's strange and fearful interest in 24/12/38
Mass, compared to C. of E. service 1/1/38
miracles 6/4/32, 5/5/32, 22/9/38, 22/12/50
liquefaction 5/5/32, 22/12/50
mummery and devotion in 15/8/38
Old Catholics and
G's memorandum on, printed 30/9/74
ordinations in 21/4/32, 22/12/38
pentitentiary books of 9/7/35, 12/7/35 ff
Prayer Book of
G reading at Eton 24/9/26, 1/10/26
priests inferior 28/2/32
relics in 20/4/32, 24/7/32
sermons in 3/9/38 ff, 20/12/38 ff, 7/1/39 ff, 13/1/39 ff, 27/10/50 ff, 1/11/50 ff, 3/11/50, 10/11/50 ff, 17/11/50, 21/11/50, 24/11/50, 25/11/50
notes made of 29/11/50 n
services observed 5/2/32, 26/8/38, 28/8/38
Sunday school in Milan, G attends 8/7/32
superstition in 16/11/38, 31/7/42
Syllabus of
a great outrage 21/5/69
and ultramontanism 8/1/70
use of crucifixes by 28/2/32, 27/6/32
Vaticanism and
G's pamphlets on 9/12/74 ff, 12/12/74 ff, 2/1/75 ff, 2/2/75 ff, 9/2/75 ff, 12/12/80
G's polemical period hoped over 29/12/75
Wiseman's plan for London College 15/1/39
See also Church of England, colonies, converts to Rome, Jesuits, Papacy, Pius IX, Vatican Council
Roman Catholics
G's Religious Disabilities Bill and 2/2/91, 4/2/91, 14/10/93, 26/10/93
in England
alliance with O'Connell 4/6/41
pray for G and Irish disestablishment 15/7/69
romances
Caroline Farquhar 7/7/35, 8/7/35, 6/8/35, 18/8/35, 22/8/35 ff, 4/9/35, 28/12/35, 13/2/36, 15/2/36, 18/2/36, 24/2/36, 29/2/36, 5/3/36, 9/3/36, 29/3/36, 24/5/36, 4/8/36
arranging correspondence about 21/10/37
See also marriage (proposals of)
Roman Empire 2/12/83
Romanes Lecture *See* Oxford (University of)
Romanism 22/9/38
Rome 29/3/32 ff, 5/10/38 ff, 3/12/38 ff, 22/7/49 ff, 11/10/66 ff, 14/2/89
51 Piazza di Spagna, G occupies 11/10/66 ff
fire in 3/12/66
G ill at 11/12/66 ff
62 Piazza di Spagna, G occupies 5/12/38, 7/12/38 ff
accommodation at
Casa Serny 29/3/32, 5/10/38
American church, G attending 14/11/66 n, 25/11/66
Ara Coeli 8/12/66, 29/12/66
Archaeological Society 8/1/39
Baths of Caracalla 13/4/32, 2/1/38, 17/11/66
capital of Italy
G doubts wisdom of 15/9/70
Capitol 7/1/39, 14/1/39
Castello S. Angelo 27/11/66
catacombs 2/11/66
Jewish 6/11/66
Chiesa Nuova 20/12/38
Colosseum 3/4/32, 3/1/39, 23/10/66
and Melrose 3/1/39
moonlight in 3/1/39
conversations with Abeken 16/12/38, 18/12/38, 21/12/38, 29/12/38
conversations with Padre Venturi 14/12/38, 15/12/38
education in 14/12/38
English College 1/4/32, 14/4/32, 24/4/32, 29/5/32, 6/12/38
G and Manning at Mass in 29/12/38
possible appropriation of 30/4/72
Europa hotel 19/4/32
Forum 5/4/32 ff, 8/10/38, 28/12/38, 3/1/39, 23/10/66, 6/11/66
like City of London 8/10/38
Fratelli delle Scuole Cristiane 14/12/38
Gallarini's gallery 7/11/66 ff
Germans in 16/12/38
Hospitals of 7/11/66
Hotel Russie 4/12/38
list of visits made by G in 30/4/67 fl
Museum Gregorianum Lateranense 16/1/39, 20/11/66

Palazzo Barberini 31/12/38
Palazzo Borghese 18/4/32, 9/1/39
Palazzo Colonna 14/12/38
Palazzo Corsini 12/1/39
Palazzo Doria 7/4/32, 30/5/32, 22/10/66
Palazzo Farnese 17/10/66
Palazzo Rospigliosi 2/6/32, 1/1/39
Palazzo Spada 1/1/39
Pantheon 10/10/38
Philharmonic Society of 3/4/32
poste restante 6/12/38
Propaganda 6/1/39
Quirinal 17/1/39
Romulus & Remus 25/4/32
Saint John Lateran 21/4/32, 31/5/32, 22/12/38, 27/12/38, 11/1/39, 30/10/66
Saint Peter's 31/3/32, 2/4/32, 16/4/32, 17/4/32, 20/4/32, 22/4/32, 4/6/32, 27/7/32, 5/10/38, 6/10/38 ff, 6/12/38, 12/12/38, 13/12/38, 23/7/49, 12/10/66, 22/10/66, 30/11/66, 24/12/66
  G prefers gothic to 31/3/32
  Michael Angelo's Pieta 31/3/32
  view of 17/4/32
  washing of pilgrims' feet 19/4/32 ff
San Agostino 18/1/39
San Clemente 22/12/38, 23/11/66
San Costanza 24/11/66
San Lorenzo in Lucina 25/11/66
San Onofrio 30/11/66
San Pietro in Carcere 5/11/66
San Pietro in Vincolo 11/4/32, 22/12/38
San Prassede 10/1/39
San Silvestro 31/12/38, 6/1/39, 7/1/39, 8/1/39, 9/1/39, 10/1/39, 11/1/39
Santa Maria degli Angeli 9/1/39, 14/10/66
Santa Maria del Popolo 5/1/39, 14/10/66
Santa Maria Maggiore 11/4/32, 10/10/38, 18/12/38, 19/12/38, 20/10/66
Sant' Andrea 20/12/38
sensations on leaving 5/6/32
Serny's hotel, Piazza di Spagna, G staying at 29/3/32, 25/5/32, 22/7/49
Shelley on 30/3/32
studios visited
  Adams' 18/10/66
  Atkin's 24/4/32
  Bienaimé's 29/12/38
  Camuccini's 10/4/32, 2/6/32
  Carta's 11/12/38
  C. Colman's 2/1/39, 30/11/66
  Costa's 21/11/66
  Desoulevay's 11/4/32
  Edward Lear's 2/1/39
  Elsasser's 3/1/39
  Finelli's 1/6/32
  Gibson's 2/4/32 ff, 7/4/32, 23/4/32, 29/5/32, 4/6/32, 8/10/38 ff, 26/12/38, 12/11/66
  Gott's 2/6/32, 4/6/32
  Hosmer's (Miss) 5/12/66, 7/12/66
  Kessels' 1/6/32
  Ketel's 15/1/39
  Koch's 15/1/39
  Leighton's 12/11/66
  Lewis's 16/1/39
  Löwenthal's 18/10/66
  Macdonald's 6/10/38, 1/1/39, 25/10/66
  Macpherson's 23/10/66, 24/10/66
  Overbeck's 8/12/38, 8/12/66
  Penry Williams' 1/6/32
  Richmond, G.& W. B.'s 14/1/39, 29/12/66
  Severn's 16/4/32, 15/12/38, 19/12/38, 3/1/39, 15/1/39
  Tadolini's 24/12/66
  Tenerani's 25/10/66, 8/11/66
  Thorwaldsen's 3/4/32, 29/5/32, 10/10/38
  Vallati's 16/1/39, 12/11/66
  Wellers' 1/6/32
  Wilson's 11/4/32
  Wolff's 1/6/32
  Wyatt's 23/4/32, 26/12/38
Tabulario 14/1/39
Vatican
  Sistine Chapel 2/4/32, 15/4/32, 18/4/32, 19/4/32, 20/4/32, 24/12/38, 31/10/66, 2/11/66
Vatican Library 4/4/32, 16/10/66, 26/11/66
Vatican museum 2/4/32 ff, 28/5/32 ff, 4/6/32, 6/12/38, 13/12/38, 20/12/38, 3/1/39, 10/1/39, 15/1/39, 17/1/39, 15/10/66, 29/10/66
Vatican Treasury 19/11/66
Via Appia 26/4/32
Vigna Palatina 5/4/32
Villa Aldobrandini 23/4/32
Villa Borghese 11/4/32
Villa Ludovisi 15/1/39, 8/11/66
Villa Pamfili Doria 12/1/39, 17/12/66
Ronge movement in Bavaria 4/10/45, 7/10/45
Rosebery, Earl of *See* Primrose
Roseneath, Dumbartonshire (Argyll) 4/6/78
Rossini *See* operas
Rothschild's bank
  offer of guarantee to France of part of war-instalment 4/3/71 c
rotten boroughs *See* Reform Bills
Rotterdam 12/8/38
Roumania *See* Rumania
Roumelia, East 23/9/85, 8/10/85

round game 16/8/67 ff, 30/12/71, 9/1/72 ff, 14/9/72 ff, 26/12/72, 2/1/73 ff, 12/8/74 ff
Round Table *See* Chamberlain, liberal party, memoranda (printed)
Rousseau
house of 28/2/32
memorandum on, printed 24/9/81
tomb of 18/2/32
rowing *See* boating
Royal Academy 27/6/42, 5/5/43, 3/5/45, 1/5/46, 2/5/46, 30/4/47, 1/5/47, 26/6/47, 29/4/48, 4/5/50, 1/5/52, 21/7/53, 29/4/54, 5/5/55, 30/7/56, 1/5/57, 6/5/57, 1/5/58, 30/4/59, 27/7/59, 1/8/60, 4/5/61, 2/5/62, 1/5/63, 30/4/64, 29/4/65, 4/5/66, 1/8/66, 4/5/67, 1/5/68, 2/5/68, 30/4/69, 1/5/69, 30/4/70, 27/4/71, 4/5/72, 2/5/73, 1/5/75, 4/5/77, 5/5/77, 9/7/77, 12/7/78, 13/3/79, 2/5/79, 7/5/79, 25/2/80, 1/5/80, 29/4/81, 30/4/81, 14/5/81, 31/1/82, 28/4/82, 7/3/83, 4/5/83, 31/7/83, 1/5/84, 3/5/84, 2/5/85, 31/7/86, 30/4/87, 4/5/88, 3/5/89, 4/5/89, 24/7/89, 2/5/90, 2/5/91, 31/7/91, 29/4/92, 20/4/93, 28/4/93
accounts of 25/6/84
a good year 3/5/44
G buying at
Madot's 'Slender's wooing by Anne Page' 2/5/57
G hon. Member of 21/11/81
Hunt's 'Scapegoat' awful 3/5/56
noise was tory at dinner of 1/5/69
portrait of E. Ryan a disgrace to the Academy 5/5/72
Royal Bounty Fund *See* patronage
Royal College of Music 28/2/82, 7/5/83
Royal Exchange *See* London
Royal Grants *See* cabinet, Commons (House of), Edward VII, memoranda (printed), Victoria
Royal Holloway College 17/6/73 n
Helen Gladstone declines invitation to head 1/7/86, 22/7/86, 24/7/86
Queen rather hasty about 1/7/86
Royal School of Mines 18/6/77
Royal Society
G dining with 30/11/70, 30/4/79
G Fellow of 19/5/81, 2/3/82
telephone demonstration at 30/4/79
Royal Supremacy *See* Church of England, Supremacy (Royal)
Royal Titles Bill 17/2/76 n, 23/2/76, 8/3/76, 9/3/76, 16/3/76, 17/3/76, 23/3/76, 11/5/76
royalty *See* cabinet, Church of England, Edward VII, monarchy, Victoria
Rubens
better work of 1/1/39
Rubicon, crossed 9/6/32
Rugby 6/3/47, 8/4/79
Rugeley 11/10/81
rules
to be obeyed rather than reason 15/1/47
Rumania 16/2/71
Jews in
British will intervene for with circumspection 15/6/72 c
railway bonds and Germany 29/7/71 c
Rumpf, Mrs. *See* rescue work (significant cases)
running 17/11/29, 11/9/32, 10/1/50
Ruskin, John (1819–1900), art critic and social reformer, Slade professor, Oxford 1870–9, 1883–4 9/6/54, 4/12/77
at Hawarden 12/1/78, 12/10/78 ff
unrivalled guest 15/1/78
comments on Venice justified 6/10/79
G attends his lecture on state of modern art 7/6/67
G painfully anxious about mental breakdown of 10/3/78
G's visit to Ruskin's rooms in Corpus, Oxford 24/4/78
library arrangment and 29/8/78
Poet Laureateship and 7/10/92 ff, 17/10/92, 15/8/93
G's enthusiasm for Ruskin's appointment 10/10/92
political opinions of
restoration of Judaic system, mixture of virtuous absolutism and Christian socialism 14/10/78
See also Corpus Christi College
Russell, John, Lord (1792–1878), 1st Earl Russell (1861), foreign secretary 1852–3, 1859–65, Prime Minister 1846–52, 1865–5 26/11/32 n, 7/2/40, 20/12/45, 10/7/46, 13/7/46, 5/8/46, 16/12/47, 28/6/50, 12/3/51, 5/4/51, 12/3/52, 28/4/52, 1/5/52, 6/5/52, 23/11/52, 30/12/52, 20/1/53, 10/2/53, 28/1/54, 30/1/54, 16/3/54, 21/6/54, 28/6/54, 25/11/54, 14/2/57, 20/7/57, 21/7/57, 12/3/59, 18/6/59, 12/8/59, 30/5/60, 30/6/60, 16/5/62, 3/3/63, 29/1/64, 30/3/65, 4/5/66, 18/5/66, 12/6/66, 4/2/67, 15/2/68, 16/3/68, 4/4/68, 13/11/68, 3/12/68, 26/1/69, 18/4/69, 22/6/70, 23/12/70, 12/1/71, 25/6/71, 2/8/71, 2/3/72, 6/5/72 n, 28/11/72, 30/7/75, 22/4/80, 3/2/83, 16/6/85, 21/5/86, 24/12/86, 28/10/92, 4/3/94, 19/3/94

1853 budget and 11/4/53, 12/4/53, 15/4/53
1854 Reform bill and
modest speech 13/2/54
1860 Reform Bill and 12/1/60, 16/1/60
1861 budget and 11/4/61, 13/4/61, 15/4/61, 13/5/61
handsomely supports G in debate 13/5/61
1866 Reform Bill and 28/4/66
discussions with G on
resignation/dissolution 4/6/66 ff
1867 Reform Bill and 13/2/67, 14/2/67 ff, 17/5/67 ff
accusations against G 17/2/75 n
American civil war and 30/11/61, 26/10/63
another crisis! 14/7/54
as foreign secretary 23/12/52 ff
as potential prime minister 14/2/57, 31/3/57
attempts to form administration 20/12/45 ff
Canada and 8/6/49
clash with Bernal Osborne 15/3/58
degradates cabinet, G thinks 17/12/54
Durham Letter of
read by G in Naples 18/11/50, 9/12/50
Eyre's case and 1/12/65
financial feebleness of his administration 5/4/51
G at Pembroke Lodge 21/4/65, 30/1/69, 18/12/70, 3/12/73
G considers succeeding in City seat of 13/6/61 ff, 12/7/61
G discusses budget with 21/4/65
G expects to succeed Palmerston 20/10/63 n
G opposes his Resolution on reform 29/3/59, 31/3/59
government of
defeated on franchise 28/5/66
in rough waters 18/2/48
resignation avoided 28/4/66
resigns 19/6/66, 25/6/66, 26/6/66
resigns: G favours dissolution 19/6/66, 20/6/66 n, 25/6/66, 26/6/66
G's conversations with 12/3/51
G's letter to on Italy
causes sleepless night 3/1/60
imprudent speech on Ireland by 31/5/53, 1/6/53
Irish land and 4/11/69, 16/12/69
Italian unification and 31/8/59, 30/6/60, 13/10/60 n
juvenile behaviour of, G thinks 31/8/59
Kennedy affair and 9/12/54, 17/12/54
letters from G to, printed 11/1/69, 16/3/69, 4/11/69, 16/12/69, 24/3/70, 12/4/70, 4/7/70, 8/12/73
Lords' reform and 16/3/69
Mill's memorial meeting and 16/5/73
new war office and 25/11/54, 30/11/54, 4/12/54, 6/12/54, 7/12/54
not controlling his party 14/7/43
Oaths Bill of
mistake, and his only 25/5/54
offer to Peelites 10/7/46
old age and
a piteous sight 9/7/77
old age of 29/5/76
a noble wreck 20/4/78
our old men are our youngest, G thinks 5/5/60
outbreak of war and 22/2/54
Peelites meeting to discuss reply to 17/1/52
precipitancy of amounts to disease 10/1/66
questionable language of on Savoy 26/3/60
remarks on nationality and Irish affairs recalled 12/4/70
resignation of
G hears of in Paris 25/2/51
to avoid Cape motion 20/2/52
Roebuck's motion and 24/1/55 ff, 18/2/55 ff
royal commission on imperial security, proposed by Russell 18/6/70 c
Schleswig-Holstein and 26/9/63 n, 5/5/64, 7/5/64 n, 15/6/64 n
speaks better than Peel 7/2/40
statue of 10/5/79
threatened resignation of 31/3/54, 10/4/54, 11/4/54
Walpole's *Life* of 22/10/89 ff
See also cabinet, Crimean war, education, memoranda (printed), Pembroke Lodge, Reform Bills
Russell, Odo William Leopold (1829–1884), 1st Baron Ampthill (1881), secretary in Rome 1858–70, in foreign office 1870, ambassador in Berlin 1871 28/11/66, 11/1/69, 1/12/69, 28/1/70 c, 14/8/70, 10/11/70 c, 17/10/78, 3/7/79, 2/11/80
G discourages from accepting a peerage from tory government 19/9/78
in Rome 22/10/66, 28/11/66, 19/12/66
letters from G to, printed 20/12/69, 3/4/70, 25/2/71, 4/3/71, 3/3/74
letters of interest to G 15/4/69
peerage for 19/9/78, 28/8/80
Straits question and Disraeli 25/2/71, 4/3/71
Vatican Council and 7/11/69, 28/2/70, 22/4/70, 28/4/70

Russia
Afghanistan and 13/3/85 ff, 4/4/85 cf, 11/5/85, 8/6/85 c
gigantic and menacing aspect of 30/4/85
plans for retaliation against aggression in 8/4/85 ff
question amicably settled 2/5/85 c
Alexander II's visit to London
G presented 15/5/74, 20/5/74
assassination of Alexander II 13/3/81 ff
Batoum and 4/7/86
Bulgarian schism and 4/9/72
manipulates 27/11/71
Central Asia 24/8/69
British protest at Khiva expedition 31/1/73
encroachment into 22/1/73 c, 3/5/80 c, 17/5/80 c, 21/8/80 c, 5/3/83 c, 18/2/84 c, 7/3/85 ff
proposed treaty with 10/11/81 c, 1/2/82 c
coronation
British costs at 14/4/83 c, 28/4/83 c
Egypt and 2/1/85 c
famine in
G drafts letter for C. G on 11/2/92
finances of
G's memorandum of Crimean war costs to 7/1/60
Franco-Prussian war and 12/9/70
funds of 2/5/85
guns of not to be distributed 3/11/69 c
Jews in, persecution of 9/1/82, 18/1/82, 22/1/82, 3/3/82
militarism in 20/1/94
nihilism in 10/12/93
Orthodox church in 15/12/38
outbreak of war and
not fighting for Turks but warning off Russia, G thinks 22/2/54
possibility of war with 16/8/43
power of augmented by tory policy 30/1/79
relations with China 3/7/80 c
Siberian exiles and 1/1/90, 17/5/90 n
Straits policy and 1856 Black Sea clauses 4/11/70 c, 10/11/70 c, 11/11/70 c, 16/11/70, 9/5/71
conference on 17/11/70 c, 28/11/70 c, 30/11/70 c, 6/12/70, 11/12/70, 15/12/70 c, 19/1/71 c, 28/1/71 c, 1/2/71 c, 11/2/71 c, 15/2/71 c, 16/2/71 c, 20/2/71 c, 9/5/71
diplomatic outrage of 25/11/70
Gortschakoff circular 28/11/70 c, 30/11/70, 16/2/71, 25/2/71, 4/3/71, 9/5/71
G shocked by Salisbury's Protocol on 4/7/86
trade with during war 14/11/54, 18/11/54
Turkestan and
G's article on 19/10/76 ff
Turkey and 6/1/69
understanding with 19/6/80 c
See also Afghanistan, Balkans, Central Asia, Crimean War, Disraeli, Eastern question, Goschen, India, Novikoff, Orthodox churches, Persia, Turkey
Ruthin church 6/9/56
Ryader 15/7/52

Sabbatarianism *See* Sunday observance
sacerdotalism
G's horror of 16/11/69
Saffron Walden 5/11/59
Said, Viceroy of Egypt *See* Egypt
Saighton Grange, Chester (Wyndham) 5/11/87, 27/10/88
Saint Albans 1/3/75
Saint Andrews, Fife 2/10/46, 23/9/50
Sir J. G building houses in 2/11/46
Saint Andrew's, Liverpool *See* Liverpool
Saint Anne's, Soho 26/5/47 ff
Saint Asaph 8/9/52, 3/8/55, 1/9/75
Saint Catherine's College, Oxford
G's books form basis of library of 9/2/74, 10/2/74
Saint David's, Wales 12/7/52
Saint Deiniol's Library *See* Hawarden, memoranda, memoranda (printed)
Saint Ebbe's church, Oxford 15/11/28, 29/3/29, 28/6/29, 23/5/30
Saint Etienne 26/1/39
Saint George's, Weybridge (Egerton) 6/8/70, 27/4/72, 3/5/73, 5/3/81, 29/4/82
Saint George's in the East
G assisting in quelling anti-ritualist riot 14/10/60
Saint Helen's
G's speech at 16/11/68
Saint James's Square *See* houses
Saint Jean de Luz 26/12/91
Saint John's College, Oxford
G visits library of 1/6/57
Saint Kitt's 11/2/35
Saint Margaret's, Westminster 6/7/34
Saint Martin's, Perthshire (Sir A. Clark) 22/9/84
Saint Martin's College
G speaks at 6/7/67
Saint Mary Hall, Oxford 15/11/28
Saint Paul's, Knightsbridge 16/3/47 ff
Saint Paul's cathedral 13/6/33, 4/6/35, 15/11/52, 18/11/52, 24/11/52, 31/3/74, 2/8/74, 18/4/75, 29/1/82, 22/5/84, 3/4/85, 12/4/87
G petitions for Sunday evening services 2/12/57

reflections on sublimity of 20/3/41
Thanksgiving service for Prince of Wales in 21/12/71 ff, 23/1/72 c, 27/2/72
W. B. Richmond's mosaics for 22/4/93
Saint Paul's School's Apposition 18/5/43, 18/5/47, 26/5/52, 27/5/57
Saint Peter's *See* Rome
Saint Raphael 15/1/92 ff
saints 18/10/43
Saint Thomas's, Toxteth *See* Liverpool
salaries, ministerial 14/8/93
Salerno 7/5/32, 11/11/38
sales of pictures *See* cabinet, Christie's, Sotheby's
Salford
deputation on home rule from 26/6/86
Peel Park 14/10/53
salicine *See* medicines
Salisbury 3/9/66
G's speech at 17/6/89
Salisbury cathedral 1/4/53, 19/1/57, 5/6/57 ff, 30/3/61
Salisbury, Marquis of *See* Cecil
salons *See* political hostesses
Salthill, sock at 13/11/27, 22/11/27
Saltney
G's speech at 26/10/89
Salvation Army 3/3/83
sal-volatile *See* medicines
Salzburg 18/9/74
sanctification, personal
weakly desired by G 19/4/51
Sandringham (Prince of Wales) 30/11/72, 20/11/80, 30/3/83, 29/1/87
liked by G 1/12/72
none of the stiffness of a Court at 1/12/72
Sandwich 15/7/54, 23/5/66
Sandwich Islands 22/2/73 c
Sandycroft
iron works at 18/9/45, 28/8/55
San Felice 23/5/32
San Marino 9/6/32
San Remo 19/1/67
San Sebastian 22/1/94
Sare 4/1/93
Sarzana 13/3/32
Satan 21/2/41, 31/12/43, 19/7/48, 29/12/49
Savernake, Marlborough (Ailesbury) 31/1/77
Savignano 9/6/32
Savings Banks Bill 4/1/60, 26/1/60 ff, 5/3/60 ff, 22/6/60, 20/7/60, 15/8/60 n, 28/1/61, 7/2/61, 8/4/61 ff, 13/2/63, 25/3/63, 10/6/63, 4/6/80, 7/6/80
Savings Banks Monies Bill
G's first financial measure defeated 20/7/60
Savoy
cabinet on 21/3/60
scammony pill *See* medicines
Scandinavia
church affairs in 27/2/38, 2/11/50
home rule and 5/5/86
See also Denmark, Norway, Sweden
Scarisbrick Hall (Scarisbrick) 19/12/67
Pugin met at 20/12/67
Turner should have painted 19/12/67
scarlet fever 2/4/42
Schiller
quoted in journal 29/12/63
Wallenstein 16/10/33
Schleswig-Holstein 26/9/63, 6/10/63 ff, 1/12/63 n, 4/12/63
cabinet 'war party' on 7/5/64
G agrees to division of 5/5/64
schools *See* education
science
G feels a charlatan speaking on 10/10/61
religion and
G's belief in harmony between 5/12/81
Scinde *See* India, Wellesley
Scone Palace 29/9/69
scot and lot voters *See* Newark constituency
Scotland
1874 election and
stands to her colours 9/2/74
Bank Notes Bill 6/2/64, 8/2/64 ff
bottom shown by 27/11/85
Braemar Highland Games, G attends: a very pretty sight 28/8/73
charities in 6/5/71 c
chiefs in
historic role of 19/1/85
coal lock-out in 5/12/93, 6/12/93
county board for 29/4/81
crofters in 3/11/82 c, 27/3/83, 12/12/84, 15/1/85, 19/1/85
Crofters Bill 14/2/85, 16/2/85 c, 27/3/85 c, 16/4/85, 25/4/85, 28/4/85 c, 15/5/85 c, 5/6/85 c, 6/2/86, 14/3/86, 15/3/86
G's historicist analysis of position of 19/1/85
rights of 19/1/85
Royal Commission on 25/11/82, 27/11/82 c, 5/9/84, 14/9/84, 31/10/92 c, 23/11/92 c
disestablishment in 22/12/81, 28/7/85, 27/10/85, 3/11/85 ff, 14/11/85 ff, 15/8/89 n, 13/7/92 ff, 18/7/92, 20/7/92, 1/8/92, 6/9/92, 21/11/92 c, 9/3/93, 26/7/93 n, 25/8/93 n
deputation and 29/11/81, 11/12/81, 29/8/84, 12/7/87
establishment has not another decade to live, G thinks 18/6/78
G's correspondence with Balfour of Burleigh 15/8/89 ff, 30/8/89
G's draft of bill for 20/7/92

Scotland (*cont.*)
disestablishment in (*cont.*)
G votes for 2/5/90
tests for desirability of 2/11/78 n, 23/5/79 n, 29/11/81, 28/7/85
Eastern question and 23/5/78
Education Bill 12/5/54, 27/4/55, 10/5/55 n, 4/7/56, 22/12/68 c, 20/1/71 c, 6/5/71 c, 21/10/71 c, 6/11/71 c, 18/12/71 c, 19/12/71 c, 2/5/72 c, 17/7/72 c, 24/7/72 c, 31/7/72 c
introduced in Lords 11/1/69, 10/4/69 c, 5/6/69 c, 31/7/69 c, 6/8/69 c, 9/8/69 c
Education Board 10/7/69 c
education in 29/6/84, 1/7/84, 12/12/84, 16/2/85 c
capitation grant to 2/1/60
election 1886 and 8/7/86, 9/7/86
defeat will bring forward Scottish questions 10/7/86
emigration from 19/1/85
endowed schools in, commission on 6/11/71
endowments in 20/4/72 c
entails in 31/5/82
cabinet unfavourable to measure on 20/4/72
Feudal Tenure Bill 10/2/72 c
finances of 24/8/93
fisheries of 26/5/83 c, 29/1/94, 12/2/94 c
Game Bill 5/5/80 c
G half a Highlander 23/6/86
government of 15/6/82, 15/3/83, 17/3/83, 20/3/83, 27/3/83, 4/4/83, 5/5/83 c, 7/5/83, 27/6/84 ff, 1/7/84, 27/9/84, 12/12/84, 16/2/85 c, 25/4/85, 27/4/85, 28/4/85 c
need for Scots in cabinet 7/9/84
Grand Committee for? 6/9/92, 6/12/92, 17/12/92 c
highlands of
land values in 19/1/85
home rule and 5/5/86, 23/6/86, 30/11/86, 28/12/86, 7/12/88 n, 4/3/89, 30/11/92, 18/7/93, 20/7/93
G's speeches on 9/4/89, 30/5/89
Intestacy Bill 16/2/70
jealous if too much Irish flavour to liberal proposals for bills 3/2/73
judges in 26/3/81 c, 2/6/81 c
Knox, John
G cautious about subscribing to memorial for 4/1/73
liberal M.P.s of
dinner given by 16/7/87, 25/4/88
local government bill 1882
plan for 10/11/81 c, 30/1/82, 3/2/83
local vote monies and 4/2/81
lord advocate, duties of 18/8/81
meeting with Scottish M.P.s 5/6/86
nationality and 7/12/80
G's speech on 30/5/89
National Library of
deputation on 23/3/65
parliamentary business
arrangements for 7/12/80, 18/12/82, 1/5/84 c
Patronage Bill 3/7/74, 6/7/74, 3/11/74, 16/2/75, 12/3/86
peerage elections and 18/4/81
Permissive Bill Association deputation to G 5/4/92
politics in
character of conservatism 10/5/80
Reform Bill 1867–8 13/5/67, 2/12/67, 1/5/68 n, 20/5/68, 25/5/68, 28/5/68
conclave on 14/2/68, 24/2/68
redistribution 6/6/68, 8/6/68
Reform Bill 1884
G's campaign tour 29/8/84 ff
Royal Bank of Scotland London branch
eventually granted 1/3/73 c, 24/5/73 c, 5/7/73 c
Sabbatarianism in 7/9/83
Scottish business in the Commons/Lords 30/6/69, 15/6/82, 15/3/83, 17/3/83 c, 20/3/83, 27/3/83, 4/4/83, 7/4/83, 5/5/83 c, 7/5/83
Scottish department 20/5/81 c, 5/5/83
Scottish Home Rule Association 7/12/88 n, 9/12/88 n, 24/8/90
Scottish liberal M.P.s 31/1/81
Scottish Universities Bill 14/5/58 n, 16/4/60, 17/4/60 n
G amends to permit unification into national university 5/7/58
Strome Ferry imprisonments 7/9/83
Teinds Bill 31/5/81
teinds in 6/11/71 c
tenants improvements 5/5/80 c
tenants in 25/4/83
Union of
an incorporating union 23/6/86
universities of 15/2/86 c
deputation to G on 14/5/58
tests in 28/4/52
Wallace Monument 16/7/56
whisky industry in 21/3/54
See also Aberdeen, Aviemore, Ballater, Braemar, Brechin, cabinet, Chalmers, Church of Scotland, Commons (House of), Corstorphine, Dalkeith, Dalmeny, Dingwall, Dirleton, Drumguish, Drumlanrig, Drumnadrochit, Drumochtie, Dunblane, Dundee, Dunkeld, Dunottar, Dunrobin, Duns,

Dunster, Edinburgh, Edzell, Episcopal Church of Scotland, Erskine, Fasque, Fettercairn, Flodden Field, Ford Castle, Fordoun, Fort Augustus, Forth Bridge, Free Church of Scotland, Fushie Bridge, Gairloch, Glasgow, Glen, Glen Dye, Glenalmond, Glenquoich, Glenshee, Gore Bridge, Government of Ireland Bill (1886), Grantown-on-Spey, Haddington, Haddo House, home rule, Inveraray, Invercauld, Invergarry, Inverness, Ireland, Kingussie, Kinross, Kirkmichael, Kirkwall, Loch Avon, Loch Lomond, Lochinver, Lochnagar, Mary (Queen of Scots), Melrose, Midlothian, Montrose, Oban, Ossian, Peebles, Penicuik, Pentland Firth, Pitlochry, Primrose (Rosebery), publications, Queensferry, Ramsay (E. B.), Shetland, Skye, St. Andrews, St. Martin's, Tobermory, Trevelyan, Trinity College (Glenalmond), Troon, Trossachs, Tynninghame, walks (long)

Scotsman, The
- correspondent at Hawarden 31/12/77
- home rule and 21/6/86
- offices of, G escapes through 31/3/80

Scott, James Robert Hope- (1812–1873), né Hope (took name Scott 1853), barrister and convert to Rome 1851, G's close friend and confidant 19/1/29, 15/5/29, 24/1/32, 17/4/33, 27/3/34, 22/11/37, 20/2/38, 25/6/38, 13/12/38, 10/10/39, 15/2/40, 17/3/40, 27/5/40, 30/7/40, 20/8/41, 24/12/41, 11/12/42, 29/1/43, 7/12/43, 23/12/45, 2/11/46, 1/9/47, 6/7/48, 27/11/48, 12/1/50 ff, 21/9/50, 6/3/51 ff, 6/12/55, 26/7/57, 20/10/63, 12/4/69, 24/11/72 n, 8/12/82
- Acton's view of different from G's 3/2/84
- advice on Maynooth 29/2/44
- bust of, by Noble 12/7/73
- consulted on G's joining Cabinet 13/5/43, 15/5/43
- conversion to Rome 6/3/51 ff, 19/3/51 ff, 30/3/51, 6/4/51, 7/4/51
  - G unmanned by 19/4/51, 11/5/51
- death and remains of 30/4/73
- dedicates abridgement of Lockhart's *Scott* to G 25/3/71
- doubts about Anglicanism of 22/9/50
- G deletes as executor of will on conversion to Rome 8/3/51
- godfather to W. H. G 16/7/40, 29/9/46
- Gorham case and 11/1/50, 8/3/50 ff
- G's letters from
  - lent to Miss Hope-Scott and Ornsby 13/9/73, 27/7/83
  - read through: over 100 11/9/73
- G's meetings with post-conversion 12/3/55
  - not as in other days 12/3/55
- G's Oxford University seat and 19/5/47
- G's retrospective appraisal of 12/9/73, 17/9/73, 29/9/73
- G thinks acting for Lady Lincoln 12/1/50
- known as 'Jim' 25/11/46, 12/3/55
- letters from G to, printed 25/3/71
- marriage of
  - G hopes will root him to anglicanism 20/7/47
- Ornsby's *Life* of 24/11/83, 2/1/84, 3/2/84
- planning the Engagement 6/11/43
- protection and 27/11/46
- reading MS of *State and Church* 16/7/38, 27/7/38 ff, 2/8/38
- relations with Rome 8/11/41
- revising *State and Church* 4/1/40 ff, 28/1/40 ff
- Roman tendencies of 5/10/46
- speech against Chapters Bill 24/7/40
- Trinity College, Glenalmond and 30/7/40, 28/5/41, 8/6/41, 4/9/41, 19/10/41 ff, 26/5/42 ff

Scott, Walter, Sir (1771–1832), 1st Baronet (1830), novelist
- centenary celebrations for
  - G regrets inability to attend 25/7/71
  - G's tribute read by Ramsay 8/8/71 n
- *Dies Irae* and 14/5/83
- G's comments on 4/12/48
- G's lecture on 3/2/68
- Hope-Scott dedicates abridgement of Lockhart's *Scott* to G 25/3/71
- read to C. G 18/7/39, 26/7/39, 17/6/40, 27/6/40, 30/6/40
- *See also* Napoleon I, plays seen

Scottish Central railway *See* railways (G shareholder in)

scourge
- G deluded by using? 23/7/51
- memorandum of review of use of 22/4/49
- use of on self by G 13/1/49, 11/4/49, 13/4/49, 21/4/49, 29/6/49, 13/6/50, 22/6/50, 13/7/51, 15/7/51, 19/11/52, 9/12/52
  - after meeting with prostitute 13/7/51, 15/7/51, 23/7/51, 29/5/57, 25/5/59
  - list of dates used 26/10/45, 1/6/50, 24/2/52

Scourie 23/9/58

Scribe, E. *See* plays seen

scripture
- teaching in schools 15/6/43, 17/6/43

sculling *See* boating

sculpture 3/9/34 ff *See also* Rome

sculptures
- G's collection of
  - lent to Manchester exhibition 29/6/57

Seacox Heath, Hawkhurst (Goschen) 22/11/84
Seaforth church
  Order in Council for 18/8/70
Seaforth church (St. Thomas) 6/11/53, 26/10/56, 15/11/64 ff, 16/9/65 ff, 9/10/70, 10/10/70, 24/12/70, 25/1/71, 22/12/72, 1/11/78 ff, 20/11/78, 1/12/78 n, 6/12/78 ff, 1/1/79, 17/2/79 n
Seaforth House, Liverpool 2/8/25, 19/7/26, 7/12/26, 3/4/27, 31/7/27, 6/12/27, 10/6/28, 13/12/28, 22/2/29, 22/9/29, 21/12/31, 11/1/34, 15/2/34, 7/8/34, 16/1/36, 5/11/53, 6/11/53, 14/6/55, 10/9/59, 9/4/74 ff, 9/10/83
  G loses £6000 on estate of 18/4/74
  plans for church at 10/9/59
  reduced to desolation by Robertson G 26/7/74
  reflections on boyhood in 8/8/34
  servants' library at 29/9/29, 10/10/29
  valuation of 15/1/52, 20/10/52, 27/10/56
  See also Gladstone (Robertson), Gladstone (Sir John), memoranda
Sealand church consecrated 15/10/67
séances *See* spiritualism
seasickness *See* illnesses
Sebastopol *See* Crimean war
Secretaire(game) 17/8/29
secretaries, private *See* private secretariat, private secretaries (G's)
secret service money 16/8/81, 31/1/84 c, 27/4/86, 29/5/86
  cabinet approval for increase of 7/5/83 c
  G's absolute ignorance of machinery of use of 9/6/82, 18/6/82
  use by ministers of 22/6/82 n
    G never within doors of sublime temple of 6/10/92
    Hand-Book of Home Rule (ed. Bryce) funded from it by G 26/6/86
  used for W. Webster's son's school fees 5/1/92 n
  use of in Ireland 9/6/82, 12/6/82, 18/6/82, 19/6/82 c, 22/6/82
  See also Bryce, cabinet, Harcourt, memoranda (printed)
secularism
  in education
    G's absence of hate or fear of 14/1/75
  secularist hymn book
    contains good sense 24/10/71 n
    G withdraws from the controversy 16/11/71
secularists 16/4/83
sees, amalgamation of 29/4/43 ff
Seidlitz powder *See* medicines
Seistan arbitration *See* Persia
Selborne, Earl of *See* Palmer
select committees
  party balance on 11/3/69
  public accounts 3/6/63, 11/6/73
  See also Commons (House of)
select committees, G examined by
  colonial military expenditure 6/6/61
  Connah's Quay railway 2/5/65, 19/6/82, 12/7/89
  Edmunds' case 27/3/65
  Galway packet 8/5/60
  G. W. railway 5/5/47
  Hoylake railway 11/4/66
  public accounts 2/6/62, 20/3/63
  Scottish Central Railway 8/4/59
  Wrexham & Birkenhead railway 25/4/73
select committees, G on 20/5/33 ff
  aboriginees 27/7/35 ff, 19/2/36, 29/2/36 ff, 25/2/37
  apprenticeship 19/6/37
  Bank Acts 18/2/57 ff, 19/5/57 ff, 3/7/57 ff, 10/7/57, 30/6/58
  Bedford petition 5/3/33 ff
  benefices' resignations 23/5/71
  Blandford's committee on division of parishes 21/2/56 ff
  business of the House 30/6/90 ff
  Ceylon 1/3/49 ff, 25/2/50 ff, 27/5/50 ff
  civil service superannuation 22/3/56
  coalwhippers 6/6/51
  colonial lands 20/7/36 ff
  customs 16/5/51, 20/2/52, 12/3/52 ff
  East India produce 5/5/40 ff, 19/5/40 ff, 19/6/40 ff, 21/7/40 ff
  education 1/8/34, 26/5/35 ff, 30/6/35, 19/2/38, 12/7/38, 2/3/39
  first fruits 1/6/37
  Glasgow lottery 14/4/34 ff, 6/5/34
  Harvey's case 4/6/34 ff, 30/7/34 ff
  Hudson's Bay 18/2/57 ff
  income tax 16/2/61, 19/2/61, 12/3/61 ff, 23/4/61 ff, 4/6/61 ff
    G examines J. S. Mill 18/6/61
  Ipswich election 4/7/35 ff, 21/7/35 ff
  Ireland 19/4/37
  joint stock companies 7/3/44
  Liverpool 4/7/33, 10/7/33, 3/3/34, 12/3/34 ff
  London & York railway 16/5/45
  merchant seamen's pensions 24/4/44 ff
  Newfoundland 2/4/41 ff, 14/5/41 ff
  New Zealand 13/7/40 ff, 22/7/40 ff, 19/2/41 ff
  Nova Scotia 2/6/38
  oaths 6/8/57 ff
  opium 30/4/40 ff
    Jardine 'the rat' examined 18/5/40
  Oxford and Cambridge Bill 8/7/67, 11/7/67

patents 24/6/33
railways 4/5/38 ff, 5/2/44, 23/2/44 ff, 6/5/44
G drafting report 6/5/44
royal grants 15/7/89
shipwrecks 9/5/43 ff, 11/7/43 ff
slave trade prevention 21/3/48 ff, 3/5/48, 1/8/48 ff, 15/6/49
South Australia 15/2/41 ff, 1/3/41 ff
stationery office 6/8/33
Sydney mint 2/6/62
Upper Canada clergy 22/5/37 ff
West Indies 13/7/33, 10/6/36
selfdenial
G's reflections on 30/11/56
selfexamination
of chief besetting sin 26/10/45, 19/7/48
opportunies for at Fasque 17/9/48
self-flagellation *See* scourge
selflove 29/12/43, 31/12/43
inveterate disease of 25/6/39
political campaigns and 28/12/79
Selwyn, George Augustus, Bp. (1809–1878), bishop of New Zealand (1841), bishop of Lichfield (1868) 4/2/26, 19/5/27, 29/5/27, 20/6/27, 25/3/37 ff, 6/5/40, 27/5/40, 30/1/41, 4/6/54, 5/6/54, 30/7/54, 5/8/54 ff, 3/12/54, 24/3/55 ff
as bishop of New Zealand 22/5/41 ff, 17/10/41, 30/10/41, 31/10/41, 10/5/54
funeral of 16/4/78
one of the band of great Bishops 16/4/78
Senna *See* medicines
Serbia 15/11/76
sermons
given by G 28/4/33, 27/3/36, 3/4/36, 23/2/40 ff, 12/4/40, 17/4/40 ff, 7/6/40 ff, 31/1/41 ff, 2/1/42 ff, 29/1/43 ff, 28/1/44 ff, 12/1/45 ff, 18/1/46 ff, 21/3/47 ff, 20/2/48 ff, 11/2/49 ff, 17/3/50 ff, 16/4/51 ff, 8/2/52 ff, 29/1/54 ff, 6/2/55 ff, 11/2/55 ff, 1/6/56, 22/3/57 ff, 27/7/62, 31/1/64 ff, 8/11/68
G street-preaching 25/9/59
on the famine 14/3/47
sermons, notable 17/7/25, 28/1/27, 29/7/27, 7/10/27, 23/12/27, 9/1/31, 14/8/31, 21/8/31, 20/11/31, 18/12/31, 13/5/32, 27/5/32, 10/6/32
Andrews' 28/4/39
Armstrong's 5/6/31
Austin's 17/1/64
Beamish's 4/5/34
Benson's (Lucan, Ireland) 11/11/77
Bethell's 29/10/26, 5/11/26
Blanco White's 22/5/31
Blomfield's 4/2/44
Blunt's 20/3/34
Body's 1/11/69, 15/5/70
Bp. of Nancy's 13/1/39
Brewster's 16/9/49, 13/10/50, 18/12/72
Broad's 25/12/91
Brookfield's 3/3/41
Buckley's 3/7/31, 17/7/31, 24/7/31
Bulteel's 6/2/31, 25/9/31
Butler's 19/2/82
Cavallari's (Sicily) 2/11/38
C. Benson's 26/4/35
Chalmers' 22/10/26, 8/1/34
Champnes' 21/5/26
Chidlow's 1/9/72
Clarke's 9/9/32
Claughton's 8/8/76
Coghlan's 8/3/74
Craig's 13/4/28, 27/4/28
Crowther's 19/6/31
Dale's 5/12/77
Drew's 14/11/86, 4/12/92
Eyton's 11/11/88, 14/10/93
Fortescue's 29/9/69
Garrabé's 27/10/50
Gatzenmeier's (Munich) 20/9/74
Gladstone's 23/7/26 ff, 20/12/85, 13/2/87, 5/6/92
Hall's 2/6/78
H. Hughes' (R. C.) 8/1/39
Hodgson's 8/9/78
Holland's 26/1/73
Hutchinson's (Rome) 23/12/38
Irvine's 11/7/47
Keble's 6/12/29, 26/6/31, 11/11/60
at Hursley 11/11/60
Kingsley's 22/2/60
Liddon's 22/4/77
Lloyd's 14/9/90
Luscombe's 19/2/32
Lyne's 15/3/68
Lyttelton's 1/1/69
MacColl's 12/11/76
Macgregor's 28/3/80
Majendie's 8/5/31, 23/10/31
Malan's 15/7/32
Manning's 25/5/45
Maurice's
striking but half wisdom? 9/6/67
McNeile's 23/10/36
Melvill's 30/6/33, 6/7/34, 25/2/49, 21/3/55, 18/7/69
grand old warhorse 18/7/69
Milne's 8/11/74
Mudge's 13/9/40
Mye's 19/6/87
Newman's 21/6/29, 6/3/31, 24/7/31, 25/9/31, 11/12/31, 22/1/32
Oakeley's 27/11/31

sermons, notable (*cont.*)
Outram's 23/6/89
Percival's 1/9/67
Plumptre's 16/10/25, 24/9/26, 1/10/26, 15/10/26
Ponsonby's 9/11/73
Porteus' 16/8/46
Pusey's 8/11/74
Ramsay's 1/12/33, 8/12/33, 8/10/71
Rawson's 14/8/25, 13/8/26, 3/9/26, 10/9/26, 25/12/31, 8/1/32
Repton's 29/7/32
Ridding's 6/7/90
Roberts' 4/12/25
Roman Catholic 30/9/38, 14/10/38, 21/10/38, 28/10/38, 2/11/38, 5/11/38, 7/12/38, 16/12/38, 30/12/38, 1/1/39, 21/10/66, 2/12/66, 30/12/66
Selwyn's 30/7/54
Sheppard's 14/2/86
Sibthorp's 6/12/29
Sinclair's 3/1/36
Stopford Brooke's
a little perilous 11/6/76
G sorely staggered by 1/4/72
striking but unbalanced and wild? 24/11/67
St. Quentin's 8/4/32
Temple's 13/2/70
Ventura's (Rome) 7/1/39, 10/1/39, 12/1/39, 13/1/39
Wakeford's 31/3/93
Ward's 2/4/37, 25/3/38
Watrin's 20/10/50
Whately's 14/6/29, 13/3/31, 18/9/31
Whipple's 22/7/88
White's 15/3/68
Wickham's 11/7/74, 22/7/83, 12/7/91, 3/8/91
Wigram's 12/4/35
Williamson's 28/4/39
Wright's 13/11/25, 18/6/26, 2/7/26
See also prayers (family)
servants 18/2/37
Augusta Schülte (C. G's maid)
autobiography of 17/10/90
Austin
attending church 24/10/47
Benjamin Kersley
charged with indecent exposure in Hyde Park: G gives evidence for 6/3/71
Best 7/11/34, 4/12/34, 10/12/36, 14/12/36, 26/12/36, 27/12/36, 15/4/39, 18/4/39 ff, 29/4/39, 26/8/43
attends eucharist 3/4/36
G teaches French to 7/11/34 ff
brawls among 9/1/41, 11/1/41
Charles Dickson (valet)
ill in Britain 4/9/67, 24/9/67, 30/9/67
ill in Rome 20/12/66, 23/12/66
confirmation of 16/10/53
Edward 18/10/50
Edwards the coachman 19/11/91
E. Roberts
tried for theft 3/5/43 ff, 11/5/43 ff
George Hall 23/2/37, 6/5/38
and Eucharist 24/3/39
G prepares for confirmation 6/5/38, 13/5/38, 20/5/38, 27/5/38
Giuseppe Lazzara 15/10/38, 1/11/38
pronunciation of 7/11/38
religious views of 28/10/38
Henry (butler) 25/6/68
Henry Scarr (G's footman) 5/12/48
Horsnell (valet) 4/3/33, 20/7/33, 22/7/33
Hurst (Hawarden gamekeeper) 28/10/73
John the groom 1/12/32
library for 24/4/40, 23/5/40
Luigi Lamonica 9/2/32, 30/4/32, 5/6/32, 5/7/32, 6/7/32, 17/7/32
MacCulloch (coachman) 31/1/52, 3/10/53, 5/10/53, 14/8/58
Mary (housemaid)
dies of fever 17/5/61
Michele, muleteer 25/10/38
Miss Scott's funeral 16/10/90
Mrs. Dryden (Hawarden housekeeper) 12/8/73
Mrs. Hampton (housekeeper) 4/2/41, 12/9/54
admits to sex before marrige 31/8/47
Mrs. Pearson 2/9/87
Mrs. Weir (cook)
religion of 3/3/43
police and 23/1/43, 24/1/43
Richard Hayman (Sir J. G's butler) 21/9/47, 2/12/51
Richard Hutchins 11/8/40
Robert 13/10/32, 23/10/32
rules written for 14/2/40, 28/3/43
sex before marrige among 31/8/47
Smith 16/5/90
thefts by 2/2/43, 9/10/46
Tom Jones 18/1/41
given reluctant permission to attend races 25/8/40, 27/12/40
unbelievers found among 14/11/57
William Hampton (butler) 2/2/41, 12/9/54, 18/8/57, 14/5/67, 27/3/70, 31/3/70
a wreck 2/3/70
death of 31/10/70
G reading service with 28/2/41
sex before marriage by 31/8/47, 2/9/47, 4/9/47, 6/9/47

Zadok Outram 22/1/68, 14/8/91
death of 1/12/93 ff, 13/12/93 ff
drink and 14/8/91, 19/11/91
fitted into nooks and crannies of G's life 23/12/93
no longer G's valet 10/10/93
stern alternative put before 9/10/93
to go out of livery 14/8/91
Servants' Provident Society 26/4/47, 26/5/49, 6/6/50
Sestri 16/1/67
Severn, J. *See* portraits of G, Rome (studios)
sex
before marriage among G's servants 31/8/47
G's reading on 23/8/26
Shakers *See* United States
Shakespeare 3/6/82, 10/3/86, 29/12/90
a mighty power 5/5/59
as a great preacher 31/12/80
G promotes readings to highlight neglect of 7/5/72
G's catalogue of books on 18/10/70
See also Irving, journal (G's), plays seen, rescue work, rescue work (significant cases)
shares, G's *See* railways (G shareholder in)
shaving 1/11/38, 14/9/53
Shavington 17/10/72
Sheen House (Wortley) 20/5/59, 23/11/59, 26/2/68, 8/3/68, 2/5/68, 20/6/68, 26/7/68
Sheffield 5/6/78
deputation on home rule from 26/6/86
Sheldonian Theatre *See* Oxford (University of)
Shelley, Percy Bysshe
compared with Wordsworth 27/10/32
G learning 1/11/32
Sheridan, R. B. *See* plays seen
sheriffs, pricking of 12/11/53, 13/11/54, 12/11/59, 12/11/60, 12/11/61, 30/1/63, 12/11/64, 2/2/65, 2/2/70, 25/1/73, 30/1/74, 13/11/82, 6/3/86
Shetland 31/8/85
Shin, Falls of 21/9/58
shipping, Royal Commission on 5/7/84 c
ships 30/1/39
Achilles 1/9/45, 18/8/70
Admiral 10/8/46, 2/10/49
Ariel 29/1/59
Captain
capsizing of 9/9/70, 2/11/70 c, 18/4/71 n
Castore 7/11/50 ff
City of Aberdeen 5/9/35
Commodore 13/8/39
Dublin Castle(Currie's yacht)
voyage on 10/7/77
Duke of Wellington 8/8/36
Giraffe 11/8/38
Grantully Castle(Currie's yacht)
voyage on 26/8/80 ff
Great Eastern
G visits at Holyhead 19/10/59
Independence (U.S.A.)
at Naples 2/12/50
London 15/11/37
Lord Warden 11/8/53
Megaera, H.M.S
beached 5/8/71 c, 7/8/71, 3/11/71 c, 8/11/71 c
Neptune 13/10/38
Osborne(Prince of Wales) 28/8/85
Osprey 3/2/59
Palatine(Wolverton's yacht)
voyage on 19/8/82 ff, 8/9/83 ff
Penelope 18/8/70
Perth 7/8/44
Princess Royal 21/8/43, 27/10/44
Queen of Scotland 17/8/33
Royal Charter 1/10/56
Royal Sovereign 28/7/64
Salamander 1/2/32, 28/7/32
Scamandre 19/7/49
Scourge 18/12/58, 23/12/58
Sunbeam(Brassey) 10/7/77, 8/8/85
voyage to Norway on 8/8/85 ff
Tancrede 20/1/39
Terrible 14/3/46, 21/11/58, 7/12/58 ff, 23/12/58, 11/1/59
Vernon 28/8/32
Vivid 26/2/51
Vulcan 8/8/34, 24/10/36, 11/8/37
shooting 22/12/25, 25/8/27, 28/12/29, 12/8/36, 28/9/36 ff, 18/11/36 ff, 21/12/36, 21/1/37, 4/1/38, 12/1/38, 30/9/40, 13/8/42 ff, 12/8/44 ff, 4/12/44, 24/12/44, 27/12/44, 3/9/46, 22/9/48, 25/10/51
at Audley End 25/9/54
at Drumlanrig 30/9/53
at Dunrobin 13/8/58 ff
at Eaton 27/12/43
birds 20/8/34, 1/10/34, 15/8/37 ff, 8/9/37 ff, 21/8/39 ff, 7/9/40, 29/8/53, 4/6/70
reflections on 11/11/34
continues despite accident 25/8/43 ff
deer 5/9/33 ff, 28/8/34, 12/10/36, 10/10/40 ff, 7/10/43, 12/11/46 ff, 23/8/53, 24/8/53, 25/8/53, 30/8/53, 13/9/58
hares 21/8/39
necessary relief for body & mind 25/8/43
occupation not censured by G's accident 15/9/42
partridge
G shoots off his finger 13/9/42
white hares 28/11/49

shopping 23/11/37, 10/12/38, 25/6/39, 29/4/40, 23/7/40, 26/1/43, 24/9/49, 11/2/53, 27/6/53, 15/8/53, 4/12/54, 12/7/56, 28/7/57, 19/5/58, 9/10/71 ff, 20/5/73, 11/5/76, 17/2/83, 24/8/86, 25/2/90, 6/4/91 ff
for antiquities 19/1/39
Shordley *See* Hawarden Castle
Shrewsbury 16/7/52, 2/1/57
Siam 28/6/80, 20/7/93 c, 30/7/93, 11/9/93, 18/9/93, 22/9/93
Sicily 13/10/38
agriculture in 25/10/38, 31/10/38
Agrigentum 22/10/38
Alcamo 17/10/38
Alicata 23/10/38
beggars in 1/11/38
Bourbon monarchy in 19/10/38
bad reputation of 23/10/38
brigandage in 15/10/38, 1/11/38
Calata Girone 24/10/38
Castelvetrano 18/10/38
Catania 27/10/38
cholera in 26/10/38, 28/10/38
communal life in 20/10/38
comparison of cities with British 3/11/38
cotton exports of 23/10/38
fleas in 17/10/38, 20/10/38, 22/10/38, 31/10/38
G and Kinnaird stuck in 1/11/38
Giardini 31/10/38
Girgenti 20/10/38 ff
guns carried for security 17/10/38, 1/11/38
hints for travel in 6/11/38
Lentini 25/10/38
list of prices in 23/10/38
Messina 1/11/38
minerals in 23/10/38
Mount Etna 24/10/38, 25/10/38, 26/10/38, 27/10/38, 1/11/38
ascent of 29/10/38 ff
mules of 17/10/38 ff, 25/10/38 ff
Victoria and 20/3/94
Palermo 14/10/38 ff
Palma 22/10/38 ff
people of curious but not rude 1/11/38
poor literacy in 15/10/38, 20/10/38
pronunciation in 2/11/38
rice production in 20/10/38
Salemi 18/10/38
Sciacca 19/10/38
Scylla and Charybdis 5/11/38
Segesta 18/10/38
Selinunti, ruins of 19/10/38
Straits of Messina 5/11/38
sulphur monopoly in 7/11/38, 19/11/38
Syracuse 26/10/38
Achradina ruins 26/10/38
Taormina
ruins 31/10/38
temples in 2/11/38
Terra Nuova 23/10/38
things English esteemed in 25/10/38
unspoilt by tourists 15/10/38
visit to planned 6/10/38, 10/10/38, 12/10/38
winegrowing in 17/10/38
Sienna 27/3/32
sight *See* eyes
silk trade 3/2/60
silkworms 16/5/32
Simon de Montford
G's memorandum on 12/3/72
Simplon pass, crossed 11/7/32, 4/8/49
sin
adultery in the heart 22/4/49
backslidings 29/12/67
besetting 1/4/31, 29/12/37, 31/12/39, 15/1/47, 29/12/47, 29/12/52, 29/12/59
list of chief besetting sins 26/10/45, 19/7/48
carnal 19/1/32, 30/3/38
channels of, list of 26/10/45
clinging to 29/12/61
dangers, list of 26/10/45
defaces G's years 31/12/68
delectatio morosa 22/4/49
depth of 29/12/57
disposition to Epicurean indulgence 1/11/55
G barely conscious morally 19/8/51
G's chief sins
impurity and lukewarmness 29/12/50
G's comments on 3/5/29, 16/8/29, 15/11/29, 29/12/29, 19/2/30, 25/4/30, 24/12/30, 7/11/32, 29/12/32, 31/12/32, 25/8/34, 29/12/34, 30/9/35, 28/4/38, 6/2/39, 29/12/41, 1/11/55, 29/12/55, 29/12/89
G's dream about 25/8/34
G's inward temptations losing some of their force 2/1/96
G's shooting accident and 19/9/42
impurity 29/12/54
in missing a division on tests 30/4/44
list of remedies for 26/10/45
mastersins not curbed 29/12/42
memorandum on 19/7/48
not sinful to hope for end to contention? 29/12/91
of those with reflective habits 29/12/43
recollections of sin in childhood 6/11/53
reflections on on marriage day 25/7/39
secret 31/12/83
selfishness 31/12/88

sins mountain high 30/7/92
spiritual sloth 29/12/54
tempest 29/12/54
wrath 29/12/54
See also masturbation, memoranda (printed), temptation
Sinclair, Lucy *See* rescue work (significant cases)
sinecures in army & navy, G votes against Hume's motion 14/2/33
Singapore
export of arms from 10/5/73 c
singing 7/8/26, 26/9/27, 18/9/29, 29/12/30, 24/3/31, 12/7/31, 25/7/31, 30/12/31, 19/1/33, 9/4/33, 9/9/33, 6/12/33, 11/1/38, 18/3/38, 11/2/49, 17/5/52, 18/5/52, 15/8/52, 2/11/52, 6/11/56 ff
at London parties 15/7/34, 14/3/35, 10/8/35, 18/6/36, 23/3/39, 22/5/39, 19/5/57
in G's house 27/6/59
G's voice cracking 23/8/64, 12/12/70
lessons in 24/3/31 ff, 9/4/33 ff, 12/12/33 ff, 29/3/34 ff, 3/8/35
in Italy 3/3/32, 1/5/32, 14/5/32
single member constituencies *See* Reform Bills
Sion College 16/6/46
Sion House (Northumberland) 21/7/42
Sisterhood of Mercy 24/5/48, 23/2/50 *See also* House of Mercy
skating 2/1/54
sketching *See* drawing
Skye, Isle of 31/8/80
crofters land movement in
use of troops against 3/11/82 c
slavery 21/10/30, 2/5/31, 15/5/31, 30/7/32, 6/9/32, 25/9/32, 6/12/32 n, 2/1/33, 11/5/33, 25/7/33, 8/8/35 ff, 16/9/35, 29/3/38, 30/3/38, 1/5/41, 23/8/41, 4/2/76, 24/2/76, 10/10/93, 15/10/93
abolition of 13/2/33, 3/8/33, 1/8/34, 14/12/71 c
Frere sent to Zanzibar as commissioner 12/10/72 c
Brougham's bill for suppression 8/8/43
election difficulties with 25/9/32, 6/12/32, 10/12/32
in Egypt, convention on 10/7/73 c
in United States 31/7/62
in Zanzibar 24/6/71
row with Tooke over 13/2/33
See also Egypt, Gladstone (Sir John), slave trade, Temple (Henry), Zanzibar
slave trade
G perplexed by 25/7/48
G's speech on 19/3/50
sleep
aided by strawberries 1/7/86
disturbed by reading Berlin Protocols 30/7/78
G affected by extraordinary sleepiness 24/7/52
G usually the spoilt child of 8/5/77
interrupted by overwrought brain 18/2/74
interrupted by reflections on rescue work 20/1/54
notes on amount of 20/1/83
oversleeping 25/6/56, 4/7/56, 12/1/83
reflections on 3/11/38, 3/6/59
sleeplessness 2/1/83 ff, 24/4/83, 3/4/84, 11/12/84, 26/12/84 ff, 9/1/85 ff, 31/1/86, 4/5/86, 23/11/92, 28/11/92, 10/12/92, 7/8/93, 21/5/94
caused by black coffee 3/2/74
caused by 'Kilmainham Treaty' 22/5/82
memorandum on, printed
prevents attending church 14/1/83
weakness of old age, unfitting G for Parliament 18/12/93
sleepless night caused by G's letter to Russell on Italy 3/1/60
See also insomnia
smoking after dinner, G stifled by 14/6/79, 26/5/83
Smollett, defects of 17/10/35
smuggling
of tobacco 31/1/63
Sneaton, Whitby (C. Bagnall) 25/8/71
snow 14/2/28, 27/10/36, 24/11/36 ff, 25/12/36 ff, 31/12/36, 29/11/46, 12/12/46 ff, 19/1/50 ff, 18/11/51, 13/2/60, 23/1/67, 11/1/68, 12/12/70, 16/12/74 ff, 25/12/78, 7/12/82, 19/12/86, 29/12/86 ff, 5/1/87 ff, 15/3/87 ff, 26/12/87, 19/2/88, 5/12/92
G snowballing 10/2/47 ff
snowballs thrown at the Gladstones by angry tories in Dover 27/12/87 n
See also medicines
Snowdon
ascent of 15/9/55
Gladstone's Rock on 13/9/92 n
G's speech on slopes of 13/9/92
socialism 4/8/85, 25/10/85
leaning of both parties to, radically disapproved by G 30/9/85
socialist lecturing in Hyde Park 17/4/42
See also Cecil (Salisbury)
Social Science Association
G chairman of committee on natural laws of wages 4/7/68 n
G chairs meeting on natural laws of wages 4/7/68
society
dangers and advantages of 12/1/31, 7/11/32, 29/12/32, 21/2/41
rules of 31/1/40, 22/2/40
Society for Suppression of the Slave Trade 27/5/40, 1/6/40, 23/6/40

Society for the Propagation of the Gospel 24/7/28, 3/8/28, 16/2/38, 16/3/38, 28/2/40, 25/3/40, 24/4/40, 12/6/40, 16/6/40, 11/12/42, 19/3/47, 21/4/47, 11/5/47, 20/5/47, 17/3/48, 7/3/51, 16/4/52, 8/4/56, 18/6/56, 29/9/56, 28/4/64, 3/8/67
Society for the Protection of Ancient Buildings 21/3/79
Society of Antiquaries 24/6/75
Society of Biblical Archaeology
  G attends 3/12/72, 10/6/79
Society of Psychical Research
  G hon. member of 22/8/85 n
soirées *See* political hostesses
Solomon Islands
  Protectorate for 12/12/92, 17/12/92 c
Somerset House
  G checking records of rescue case at 19/6/58
Somerville College, Oxford
  G's visit to 29/11/83
  novel written by member of 31/5/88 n
Sons of the Clergy, festival of 9/5/34
sophistry
  selfwoven, G's awareness of 29/12/49
Sophocles *See* plays seen
sore throats *See* illnesses
sorrow
  G's reflections on 30/11/56
Sotheby's auction rooms 14/5/72, 5/6/72, 7/6/72, 23/5/73, 10/6/73, 12/6/73, 29/3/82
  sale of Gladstone's letters to Farr stopped 17/3/92
  valuing G's London books 24/3/75
Soughton Hall (J. S. Bankes) 17/12/83
soul
  balance of 29/12/65
  disturbed by the waves 29/12/56
  enigma of 29/12/42
  master-violence of politics and 29/12/90
Soumet *See* plays seen
soup kitchen (Soyer's) visited by G & C. G 15/4/48, 17/4/48
South Africa 24/4/83, 7/8/85
  Angra Pequeña
    Germany and 14/6/84 c, 21/6/84 c
  Basutoland and 3/1/82, 6/1/82, 1/2/82 c, 4/3/82, 24/4/83, 23/5/83, 26/5/83 c, 13/6/83 c, 10/11/83 c, 3/1/84 c
    'Home Rule' for? 24/4/83
  Basutos
    disarmament of 12/5/80
  Bechuanaland 6/10/84 c, 28/10/84, 31/10/84 c, 8/11/84, 11/11/84 c
    British obligations to chiefs of 10/3/83 c, 23/5/83, 30/5/83, 2/6/83 c, 23/6/83 c, 9/12/83, 3/1/84 c
    middle course in 12/7/82
    Rhodes and 15/11/92
    Warren expedition to 31/10/84 c, 8/11/84, 11/11/84 c, 27/3/85 c
  Boer states in
    re-incorporation into the Empire 26/10/71
    responsible government for an essential preliminary 26/10/71
  Boer war and 27/12/80 ff, 1/1/81, 14/1/81, 15/1/81 c, 21/1/81, 29/1/81 c, 31/1/81
    Bronkhorstspruit, British defeat at 27/12/80
    Majuba, British defeat at 28/2/81, 2/3/81, 5/3/81 c, 8/3/81 c
    Majuba, British defeat at: the Hand of Judgment? 28/1/81
    Potchefstrom incident and 8/4/81 c, 21/4/81
    sad sad news from 28/2/81
  Cape colony 28/11/37, 16/2/38, 10/7/38, 5/3/52, 3/7/80 c, 24/12/80, 23/6/83 c
    Adderley's motion on 16/2/52 ff
    annexation of Gcalekaland, Tembuland and Bomvanaland to 3/5/80 c
    Basuto war, no British officers to be sent 10/11/80 c
    Basuto war, offer of mediation in 30/12/80 c
    constitution of 5/3/53
    Dutch element, tenacious qualities of 28/1/85
    Frere, recall of 22/5/80 c, 24/5/80 c, 29/5/80 c, 5/6/80 c, 3/7/80 c, 24/7/80 c
    Frere not to be immediately recalled 3/5/80 c, 25/5/80
    postal contract for 22/2/73 c, 25/3/73, 26/4/73 c, 3/5/73 c, 10/5/73 c
    responsible government for approved by 1 vote in cabinet 24/7/72 c
  Cape deputies (including Kruger?) meet G on board *Dublin Castle* 10/7/77
  expansion of British authority along Natal coast
    G heartily supports 30/12/84
  federation of
    encouraged by cabinet 6/11/71 c, 12/5/80 c
    Kruger, letter to on 15/6/80
  Grinqualand West 13/5/71 n
  Grinqualand West established 22/11/72 c
  Kimberley diamond fields, annexation of 11/5/71, 13/5/71 c, 14/12/71 c
  Mashonaland 31/8/93 c, 7/10/93
  Matabeleland war 10/10/93, 14/10/93, 28/10/93, 3/11/93 c, 8/11/93, 9/11/93, 13/11/93 c

Moravians at the Cape 6/6/46
Natal 22/6/83, 11/6/84, 14/3/85
charter for 4/5/72
G establishes executive council in 28/2/46 n
native question in 11/6/84
restoration of responsible government 25/1/82 c, 27/5/82, 2/10/82, 5/10/82
Orange Free State 16/11/83, 11/6/84
Swaziland 7/10/93
cabinet committee on 27/10/92 c, 23/11/92 c
territorial expansion to be avoided 12/5/80 c
Transvaal 8/11/83, 10/11/83 c, 13/11/83 c
annexation of 14/2/81
Ceteywayo vilely used 4/6/81, 29/8/81
Colley's plan wrong 5/2/81, 9/2/81, 15/2/81 c
Commissioner for 15/2/81 c, 12/3/81, 17/3/81, 28/5/81 c, 9/6/81, 24/6/81, 2/6/83 c, 13/6/83 c, 20/6/83, 23/6/83 c
Convention with 23/7/81 c, 26/9/81, 28/9/81, 29/9/81, 6/10/81, 12/10/81 c, 15/10/81, 19/10/81, 30/10/81, 3/11/81, 10/11/81 c, 10/12/81, 30/5/83, 2/6/83 c, 23/6/83 c, 27/10/84
Convention with: best, perhaps only feasible expedient 25/4/83
Convention with: revision of 13/6/83 c, 23/6/83 c, 16/11/83, 17/11/83 c, 20/11/83 c, 22/11/83 c, 21/2/84 c
Convention with: to be given up? 23/5/83
debate in Commons on 18/4/81 ff, 17/5/81, 20/5/81 c, 18/6/81, 23/7/81, 23/7/81 c, 25/7/81 ff
Germany and 17/11/84
G's letter to Kruger 15/6/80
Mapok war and 10/3/83 c
native question and 12/3/81 c, 4/6/81, 9/6/81, 12/6/81, 23/7/81 c
Pretoria, British resident at 12/3/81 c, 17/3/81, 25/5/81, 12/6/81, 23/7/81 c, 23/5/83
suzerainty and 12/3/81 c, 17/3/81, 22/3/81, 29/4/81 c, 24/6/81, 7/7/81, 23/7/81 c
to represented abroad by Britain 24/6/81
visit to of S. G and H. J. G 20/3/77
Zululand and 25/1/82 c, 24/10/82 c, 24/11/82, 27/11/82 c, 5/1/83, 22/6/83, 21/8/83 c, 2/9/83, 28/9/83, 2/10/83, 20/11/83 c, 19/12/83, 3/1/84 c, 14/5/84 c, 11/6/84, 30/7/84, 21/12/84, 30/12/84
Cetewayo's visit to Britain 21/6/82 c, 9/8/82, 12/8/82 n
Cetewayo's visit to Britain: G offers his house for 22/7/82
Cetewayo's visit to Britain: interview with G 9/8/82
Cetewayo vilely used 4/6/81, 29/8/81
return of Cetewayo to 27/5/82, 31/7/82 c, 12/8/82 c, 12/9/82, 2/10/82, 30/5/83, 7/7/83 c, 19/12/83
Zulu rising in 4/4/46 n
Zulu war in
G avoids taking part in debate on 28/3/79
See also British South Africa Company, cabinet (committees of), suzerainty
Southampton 30/8/54
G's speech at 5/6/89
Southborne, Birmingham (Chamberlain) 31/5/77
South Park Hill, Bracknell 1/12/93
Southport
G's speech at 23/10/89
South Sea Company 28/7/53, 9/8/53 *See also* memoranda
Spain
anarchy in 1/12/93 c
Basques and local self-government and 25/9/93
British legation in Madrid sheltering politicians 26/4/73 c
Carlists in
aid to 22/4/73 c
civil war in
British subjects and 30/7/73 c
Italians and 2/8/73, 4/9/73
Malaga, bombardment of, expected 30/7/73
ships and 6/8/73 c, 4/9/73
Cuba and 15/11/73 cf
debt of 28/2/70, 5/3/70 c, 2/4/70 c
decline of, G's commemts on 1/7/55
G crosses border to 26/12/91, 22/1/94
G's writings trnslated into Spanish 6/12/92 n
invasion of Portugal by thought possible 15/2/73 c
Moroccan loan and 26/9/61
most-favoured-nation treaty with 15/11/72 c
republic in
recognise as soon as regularly accepted 15/2/73 c, 22/2/73 c
throne of 7/7/70, 9/7/70 c
treaty with 15/10/42, 7/11/42, 7/2/43, 15/7/45, 5/9/80, 4/1/82, 31/5/82, 10/11/83 c, 17/11/83 c, 7/5/85, 9/5/85 c
West Indies and 28/4/69, 30/4/69 c, 1/5/69 c
Spanish, G learning 12/12/35, 10/8/36, 29/8/37, 31/8/37 ff

Speaker, The *See* publications
Speakership *See* Commons (House of), Denison, Lefevre, Peel (A. W.), Victoria
speeches
2000 a manageable audience 23/10/90
as religious exercise 31/3/35, 23/7/35
audience 'Gladstonized' 12/3/80 n
audience size: 25000 and building of no acoustic merit 31/5/77
below par but put on the steam perforce 30/7/78
by G at bye-election (unprecedented) 11/12/90
catalogue of made by G 15/4/68
delivered from a window 12/3/80
delivered in a kirk 24/3/80
demophilism, Houghton thinks G possessed by 13/9/71
difficulty of a reluctant House 6/5/39
discharge of pentup excitement 15/4/61
edition of G's speeches by Hutton and Cohen 26/4/90, 23/10/91 ff, 2/5/92, 6/10/92
G helping in selection for 23/10/91 ff
egg-flip used to aid voice during 1/9/84
excitement from
rare 3/3/57
frustration of not being called 19/4/39
G dreaming his answer to Disraeli 3/7/64
G giddy during 9/10/62
G's article on Jephson's *The Platform* 19/3/92 ff
G's best off-hand speech (on Italy) 8/8/59
G's eyes almost useless for reading notes for 4/3/93
G's speech on Eastern question to nonconformist ministers
G never addressed an audience better 18/4/78
G's speech on preaching 22/3/77
heckling of 2/9/84
leadership and 1/5/62
legs felt as after a great amount of muscular motion 8/4/86
length of
controlled by the watch 21/10/68
nervous reaction after 26/11/52, 17/12/52
notes for, forgotten 17/3/87
on Parnell Commisssion, less to G's dissatisfaction than usual 3/3/90
Peel's advice on
when speaking officially, 'don't be short' 8/5/83
proofs of
nauseous work of correcting 1/8/87
putting on the steam 3/4/84
reporting of
redictated from *bad* report in *Times* 3/8/78
Swansea visit really a 'progress' 7/6/87
too long, G thinks 18/7/93
speeches, extra-Parliamentary
Aberdeen 26/9/71
Barrow-in-Furness 19/9/67
Bermonsey 20/7/78
Birmingham 31/5/77, 1/6/77, 5/11/88, 7/11/88
Bodmin 12/6/89
Bolton 11/10/64
Carnarvon 13/9/92
Chester 14/1/79, 22/1/90
Dalkeith 26/11/79, 19/3/80, 1/4/80, 21/11/85, 25/10/90
Derby 20/10/87
Dublin
treading on eggs the whole time 7/11/77
Edinburgh 24/11/79 ff, 16/3/80 ff, 29/8/84 ff, 9/11/85 ff, 20/10/90 ff, 21/10/90 ff, 27/9/93
Exeter 13/7/77
Falmouth 11/6/89
Gateshead 8/10/62
Glasgow 1/11/65, 2/7/92
Gore Bridge 4/7/92
Greenwich/Blackheath 27/10/71 c, 28/10/71, 28/1/74, 9/9/76, 30/11/78
G's speech on Eastern question to nonconformist ministers
G never addressed an audience better 18/4/78
Hastings 17/3/91
Hawarden visitors 4/8/77, 18/8/77, 20/8/77, 1/9/77
Holborn restaurant 11/12/91
Holyhead 12/11/77
Lancashire, S. W., electioneering 12/10/68 ff, 20/10/68 ff, 13/11/68 ff
Leeds 6/10/81 ff, 25/10/87
Leith 10/1/62
G's letter to Schenck on 28/11/72
Limehouse 15/12/88
Lincoln 20/5/90
Liverpool 12/10/64, 13/10/64, 18/7/65 ff, 4/8/68
franchise reform 5/4/66, 6/4/66
Liverpool Conservative Association 29/9/36, 4/10/36, 18/10/36
Lowestoft 17/5/90
Manchester 12/3/53, 13/3/53, 23/4/62, 24/4/62, 14/10/64, 18/7/65, 25/6/86, 26/6/86, 2/12/89 ff
Marylebone 27/2/80, 19/7/87
Middlesbrough 9/10/62
Midlothian campaign, 1st. 24/11/79 ff
Midlothian campaign, 2nd. 16/3/80 ff
Midlothian campaign, 3rd. 9/11/85 ff
National Liberal Federation 31/5/77

Newcastle 7/10/62, 1/10/91 ff
G's letter to Schenck on 28/11/72
New Cross/Deptford 2/2/74
Newman Street, London 12/3/80
North London Industrial Exhibition
G presides at 7/11/64
Norwich 17/5/90
Nottingham 27/9/77, 18/10/87, 19/10/87
Oldham 18/12/67
working men 18/12/67, 19/12/67
Oxford
Palmerston Club 30/1/78
Peel Memorial, Manchester 12/10/53
phenomenon of
G has not courted, hopes he does not rely on 14/10/64
Plymouth 13/7/77, 14/6/89
Poole 15/6/89
Port Sunlight 28/11/91
Redruth 11/6/89
reporting of
better done in Scotland 8/7/86
excellently done by *The Times* 5/2/74
Retford 11/12/90
Rhyl (5000) 31/10/78
Ripon 25/10/87
Salisbury 6/9/66
Saltney 26/10/89
Seven Dials 9/4/78
Social Science Association 16/10/58
Southampton 5/6/89
Southport 19/12/67, 23/10/89
St. Austell 12/6/89
St. Pancras 27/2/80
Sunderland 9/10/62
Swansea tour 2/6/87 ff
Swansea visit really a 'progress' 7/6/87
The Wirral 28/11/91
Torquay 10/6/89
Truro 12/6/89
Tunbridge 17/3/91
Wakefield 5/9/71
West Bromwich 8/11/88
West Calder 23/10/90
Whitby 2/9/71, 13/9/71
Woolwich 31/1/74, 30/11/78
Worksop 11/12/90
Yarmouth 19/5/90
See also Bulgarian horrors, France, Italy, Midlothian
speeches by G, principal
aided by prayer 7/4/86
maiden 3/6/33
pleasure in speaking 1/6/36
pours water to cool head before 25/3/51
reporting of 4/6/33 ff, 10/7/33, 19/10/36, 3/4/38, 3/5/53, 16/8/54
speeches made, list of 18/4/38, 30/6/46
Spencer, John Poyntz (1835–1910), 5th Earl Spencer (1857), Irish governor-general 1868–74, 1882–5, lord president 1880–2, 1886; first lord of the Admiralty 1892–5 8/5/67, 22/6/70, 16/7/78, 21/6/79, 4/5/80 ff, 15/6/80, 26/6/80, 3/7/81, 25/4/82, 27/3/83, 24/10/83, 3/12/83, 4/1/84, 7/10/84, 28/4/85, 28/4/85 c, 5/5/85, 25/7/85, 15/3/86 ff, 20/8/86, 9/12/86, 18/12/86, 3/3/87 ff, 30/3/87, 14/5/87, 23/5/87, 11/6/87, 25/7/87, 24/8/87, 26/12/87, 17/2/88, 21/3/88, 9/7/88, 4/12/88, 7/5/91, 28/7/91 ff, 22/3/92, 16/6/92, 27/7/92, 28/9/92 n, 21/11/92 c, 22/1/93, 5/11/93, 22/11/93 ff
Admiralty and 14/2/93 c
G's meeting with on navy estimates 3/1/94
navy estimates crisis and 14/12/93 ff, 2/1/94 ff, 11/1/94 ff, 13/2/94 ff, 23/2/94
alarm at G's meetings with Mrs. O'Shea 26/9/82 n
at Hawarden 14/10/71 ff, 16/10/80, 19/12/81 ff, 14/10/82, 8/12/85 ff, 2/11/87 ff, 2/11/88, 21/8/89
coming liberal government, G's plans for 13/7/92
G at Althorp 12/10/52, 7/11/73 ff, 4/4/79 ff, 7/12/91 ff
Habeas Corpus suspension
insufficiency of Spencer's letter on 7/2/71
home rule and 1/2/74, 13/12/85 n, 15/12/85 ff, 19/12/85 ff, 30/12/85, 12/1/86 ff, 21/1/86, 30/1/86, 20/2/86, 23/3/86, 24/3/86 ff, 4/4/86 ff, 12/6/86 n, 14/6/86, 13/7/92, 23/7/92 ff
G discusses with 14/10/71
linked to land purchase 13/2/86 n
Indian Viceroyalty, offered 26/7/93, 29/7/93, 20/9/93 n
declines 7/8/93
Irish disestablishment and 27/3/69
Irish land and 4/11/69 ff, 21/1/70, 2/3/70, 3/3/70, 15/4/70
land purchase plans 19/12/85, 23/12/85 n, 14/1/86 ff, 12/3/86, 10/4/86 ff, 12/6/86, 14/6/86
Irish lord lieutenant 10/12/68 ff, 27/8/72, 26/4/82 ff, 7/3/83, 10/3/83 c, 18/5/83, 16/7/83, 31/10/84
central board plan and 9/5/85 ff, 1/6/85
exceptional fitness for 20/5/82
G's tribute to 30/6/85
G suggests H. J. G as assistant to 9/5/82
local government and 3/2/83, 1/6/85, 8/6/85 c

Spencer, J.P., Earl Spencer (*cont.*)
Irish lord lieutenant (*cont.*)
Maamstrasna murders 23/8/82, 24/12/82, 8/10/84 c, 31/10/84, 30/6/85, 18/7/85, 21/7/85
to see G's cabinet reports though not a member 24/6/82
visit to Westmeath 12/1/71
Irish university reform and 26/10/72, 28/11/72 c, 1/12/72, 15/2/73
letters from G to, printed 23/1/69, 6/2/69, 27/2/69, 3/3/69, 28/3/69, 28/4/69, 4/11/69, 6/11/69, 7/12/69, 10/12/69, 24/12/69, 21/1/70, 17/2/70, 5/3/70, 15/4/70, 3/9/70, 5/9/70, 14/9/70, 26/9/70, 12/1/71, 26/1/71, 7/2/71, 9/2/71, 25/8/71, 21/6/72, 19/7/72, 1/8/72, 27/8/72, 10/9/72, 26/9/72, 15/2/73, 1/3/73, 1/2/74, 6/2/74, 2/10/80, 15/4/81, 28/6/81, 27/10/81, 3/4/82, 6/5/82, 8/5/82, 9/5/82, 10/5/82, 12/5/82, 13/5/82, 20/5/82, 24/5/82, 12/6/82, 18/6/82, 24/6/82, 19/7/82, 21/7/82, 23/8/82, 29/8/82, 1/9/82, 19/9/82, 26/9/82, 3/10/82, 24/10/82, 1/12/82, 12/12/82, 24/12/82, 24/1/83, 3/2/83, 27/2/83, 22/5/83, 29/6/83, 31/7/83, 2/10/83, 19/10/83, 3/12/83, 6/12/83, 10/12/83, 14/1/84, 20/2/84, 8/4/84, 13/5/84, 17/9/84, 24/12/84, 29/1/85, 21/2/85, 18/3/85, 30/3/85, 9/5/85, 11/5/85, 13/5/85, 16/5/85, 1/6/85, 21/6/85, 27/6/85, 30/6/85, 15/9/85, 4/12/85, 19/12/85, 23/12/85, 28/12/85, 30/12/85, 14/1/86, 13/2/86, 20/2/86, 18/3/86, 24/3/86, 25/3/86, 27/3/86, 19/4/86, 12/6/86, 14/6/86, 4/7/86, 13/7/92, 23/7/92, 26/9/92, 11/12/92, 25/6/93, 7/8/93, 9/12/93, 12/12/93, 15/12/93, 2/1/94, 3/1/94, 4/1/94, 11/1/94, 12/1/94, 13/2/94, 23/2/94
Parnell and 27/6/85
Parnell and the O'Shea divorce case and 28/11/90
premiership and
G's letter to on his intended retirement 16/10/82, 24/10/82
Prime Minister, G would have preferred as 25/7/94
resignation, threat of 16/5/85
See also Althorp, cabinet, Chamberlain, Ireland, navy, Primrose
Spencer House 12/5/55, 21/5/56, 26/5/81, 6/3/86, 25/7/88, 21/2/89
Speyside
G's walk to from Invercauld 1/9/73
Spezia 15/1/67
Sphinx *See* Parnell
spirit duties 11/1/60, 24/2/60, 31/5/85
protection and 24/8/71
See also beer duty, wine duties
spiritualism 10/3/72, 8/7/74 n, 24/2/75, 10/7/77, 4/5/78 n, 7/4/79, 8/4/79, 11/1/85, 18/1/85, 22/8/85, 18/11/86 n, 6/3/88 n
Christianity and 8/4/77 n
G not contemptuous of: is in contented reserve 16/10/78
séances attended by G 29/10/84, 18/11/84
press reports of 7/11/84
Society of Psychical Research, G hon. member of 22/8/85 n
thought-reading demonstration, G attends 10/6/85
Spitalfields School of Design
G chairs meeting at 8/6/48
Spital Old-Hall
G's speech at 28/11/91
Splügen pass 4/7/32, 11/7/32
Spoleto 4/10/38
Sporkenburg castle 1/9/38
sports *See* games and sports
Spring Bank, Headingley, Leeds (J. Kitson) 6/10/81
Stade duties 5/10/41, 25/9/42 ff, 24/10/42 ff, 10/12/42 ff, 16/8/43, 14/11/43 ff, 15/12/43, 24/1/44
might involve European war 12/1/44
Stafford House (Sutherland) 10/2/40, 25/7/51, 16/4/53, 7/5/53, 26/12/53, 18/3/54, 29/3/54, 25/5/54, 27/5/54, 7/6/54, 6/3/55, 27/4/55, 4/5/55, 15/6/55, 12/7/55, 25/7/55, 26/2/56, 29/5/56, 31/5/56, 19/6/56, 13/2/57, 21/3/57, 11/3/58, 31/3/58, 14/6/59, 29/4/60, 5/7/60, 18/7/60, 14/8/60, 25/11/60, 7/12/60, 19/10/61, 20/10/61, 22/10/61, 23/10/61, 24/10/61, 20/3/62, 15/11/62, 19/11/62, 23/11/62, 25/11/62, 12/11/63, 15/11/63, 20/11/63, 22/1/64, 29/3/65, 12/1/66 ff, 5/2/66, 4/3/66, 3/1/68, 3/3/68, 23/6/68, 28/6/69, 4/7/70, 5/7/71, 6/7/72, 15/5/74, 8/5/83, 13/6/84
American civil war debated at 25/11/63
Egyptian Viceroy at 14/7/62
Garibaldi's reception at 13/4/64
meeting commemorating 2/6/83
Neapolitan exiles meeting at 11/4/59
theatre party from 13/11/60
to meet C. Sumner 1/7/59
See also Gower, political hostesses
stamp duty 22/11/59

Stanley, Edward George Geoffrey Smith (1799–1869), Lord Stanley, 14th Earl of Derby (1851), Irish secretary (1830), colonial secretary (1841), chancellor of Oxford University (1852), prime minister 1852, 1858–9, 1866–8 25/7/33, 9/3/38, 30/1/40, 26/2/40, 24/3/40, 12/6/40, 22/2/41, 1/5/41, 3/5/41, 1/3/42, 2/5/45, 27/2/50, 5/4/51, 12/3/52, 27/11/52, 19/2/56, 26/4/56, 21/2/57, 24/2/57, 11/3/57, 9/3/59, 22/4/63, 30/9/85, 21/2/93
as Chancellor of Oxford University 8/6/53, 5/3/56, 5/6/56
G attends installation of 21/10/52
presents petition against reform 15/2/54
Elwin encourages G to negotiate with 20/12/56
fall of his ministry 10/11/52 ff
finest speech yet heard 17/6/50, 11/6/51
forecasts G as prime minister 1/6/44
forming government 25/2/52 ff, 21/2/58 ff
G declines offer of office from 26/2/51
G's conversation with on Peelites and Palmerston 4/2/57
G sends letters on Bentinck row to 26/10/46
G's interview with 26/2/51, 27/11/52
G's view of his ministry 27/11/52
G thinks must bring protectionism to speedy issue 24/2/52
G unwilling to obstruct 27/2/50
letter on reunion (?) to 20/1/57, 23/1/57
makes no comment on *State and Church* 9/2/39
Maynooth, views on 2/3/44, 4/3/44, 25/11/44
conversation with G on 4/3/44
offer of colonial office/board of control to G 22/5/58
rejected after discussion with Aberdeen 23/5/58
offers unspecified office to G 21/2/58, 1/3/58 n
on Canada 15/6/40
on education and Factory Bill 25/7/43
on Peel and tariffs 10/5/42
on Peel's conservatism 2/3/42
on the Italian war 25/4/59
Peel's panegyric on Cobden and 10/7/46
proposal for coalition war government 31/1/55
resignation of 25/2/68
statue of 3/3/71 n
tells G of corn-duty intention 26/2/51
translation of the *Iliad* 5/12/64 ff
G reading aloud 5/12/64
Stanley, Edward Henry (1826–1893), Lord Stanley, 15th Earl of Derby (1869), oscillated between parties, foreign secretary 1866–8, 1874–8 (as tory), colonial secretary 1882–5 as liberal (unionist) 30/6/49, 3/7/49, 21/6/50, 14/10/53, 10/3/58, 22/1/72 c, 20/5/74, 25/6/75, 24/6/77 n, 10/4/78, 20/5/79, 31/5/79, 2/2/81, 3/10/81, 5/10/81, 18/10/81, 26/10/81 ff, 8/2/82, 28/2/82, 22/3/82, 21/6/82 cn, 16/12/82, 25/11/84, 27/3/85, 22/6/85, 7/8/85, 21/1/86, 29/5/86, 31/3/87, 10/5/87, 19/6/89, 4/7/89, 10/3/90, 3/12/90, 17/5/92, 28/9/92 n, 19/12/92
at Hawarden 8/12/55 ff, 1/11/83 ff, 1/10/85
Colonial Secretary 15/12/82 ff, 17/5/84 c, 6/8/84 c
declines offer to join G's cabinet 17/5/82, 24/5/82 n, 31/5/82
Eastern question and 16/2/77 n
Egypt and 19/11/84 c
G at Knowsley 8/10/83 ff
G struck by his ability 30/6/49
Indian secretary
objected to by Victoria 11/12/82 n
proposed as 30/11/82 ff
letters from G to, printed 17/5/82, 25/4/83, 19/5/83, 23/5/83, 30/5/83, 20/6/83, 22/6/83, 2/9/83, 28/9/83, 2/10/83, 23/10/83, 25/10/83, 8/11/83, 29/11/83, 8/12/83, 9/12/83, 19/12/83, 30/12/83, 1/1/84, 11/6/84, 23/10/84, 27/10/84, 7/11/84, 17/11/84, 21/12/84, 24/12/84, 30/12/84, 28/1/85, 14/3/85, 27/3/85, 17/7/85, 14/9/85
Mill's memorial meeting and 16/5/73
premiership of, G anticipates 26/10/81 n
qualities of 9/10/83
resignation of 24/1/78 n, 28/3/78 n, 10/10/83
tells G of his father's resignation 25/2/68
will write his name in English history 12/12/55
See also Knowsley
Stanley, Mary Catherine (1824–1900), née Sackville-West, Lady Salisbury (2nd wife of 2nd Marquis) (1847), Lady Derby (wife of 15th Earl) (1870), political hostess; Salisbury's step-mother 21/5/79, 8/7/79, 29/5/80, 8/1/81, 4/5/81, 27/10/81 ff, 8/2/82, 1/3/82, 16/5/82, 24/5/82, 23/4/83, 6/2/84, 7/11/84, 25/3/85, 6/7/87, 4/7/88, 12/2/90, 6/6/90, 10/3/91, 17/5/92, 28/11/93
Acton's library and 6/6/90

Stanmore, Lord *See* Gordon
Stanmore Park, Middlesex (Wolverton) 24/9/70, 5/8/71
Stansfeld, James, Sir (1820–1898), liberal M.P. and cabinet minister 1/6/63, 17/3/64, 22/1/70, 5/3/71, 30/1/72, 27/4/72 c, 10/7/72 n, 27/1/73 c, 3/5/73 c, 3/2/74, 8/7/79, 16/6/80, 12/12/82, 20/4/83, 5/2/85, 16/2/85 c, 23/3/86, 26/3/86, 27/3/86, 28/6/87, 2/5/88, 12/7/88, 13/5/89, 4/12/90, 28/1/91, 24/3/93 c, 10/11/93
  coal lock-out and 10/11/93
  federal proposal of 5/5/86
  government property 7/6/73 c
  hours of labour and 15/11/72 c
  letters from G to, printed 25/3/93
  local government and 28/11/73 c
State in its Relations with the Church, The
  3rd edition of 2/2/39
  4th edition of (2 vols.) 8/5/39, 4/7/39, 1/10/39 ff, 12/10/39 ff, 9/12/39 ff, 4/1/40 ff, 28/1/40, 21/9/40, 9/10/40 ff, 19/10/40 ff, 7/11/40, 14/12/40 ff, 28/12/40, 8/2/41
    preface to 3/4/41
    proofs of 17/2/41 ff, 29/3/41 ff
  copy of received in Rome 10/1/39
  copy requested by Wiseman 15/1/39
  draft title of 1/3/38
  genesis of? 3/10/31
  German translation by Tholuck 5/8/43
  G reading 6/12/41, 14/4/45, 9/4/68, 17/4/68
  letter on to Matthew Arnold 7/6/70
  Maynooth grant and 25/11/44
  O'Connell's view of 26/2/39
  proofs of 17/8/38 ff, 21/8/38 ff, 7/9/38, 22/9/38
  publication of 17/12/38
    G's responsibility before God for 28/10/38
  reception of 4/2/39, 6/2/39, 26/2/39
  reviews of
    British Critic (Keble) 8/10/39
    Christian Observer 1/5/39
    Eclectic 2/4/39
    Edinburgh Review (Macaulay) 9/4/39, 3/1/40, 13/4/68 n, 16/11/69
    Quarterly Review (Sewell) 10/4/39, 29/12/39, 30/12/39
    The Times 31/12/38
    Westminster Review 30/9/41
  writing of 12/3/37 ff, 30/4/37 ff, 13/5/37 ff, 13/10/37 ff, 14/12/37, 24/12/37 ff, 4/2/38, 11/2/38, 4/7/38, 6/7/38 ff, 27/7/38 ff
    finished 23/7/38 ff
Statistical Society, Royal
  Council of, G on 3/4/52, 19/6/52
  G President of 1868–9 18/2/68
statues of G
  Joy, H. (Bow Vestry) 10/12/78 n
  Theed, W. (Manchester Town Hall) 25/6/77, 2/7/77, 9/7/77, 16/7/77
  Vitalis (Athens) 23/10/83, 26/10/83, 19/7/88 n, 23/4/90 n
Stead, William Thomas (1849–1912), editor, *Northern Echo* (1871), editor, *Pall Mall Gazette* (1883), moral crusader 18/10/76, 3/12/77, 16/10/78, 16/8/81, 9/7/85, 31/3/87, 3/2/91, 4/5/92 n
  Dilke and 8/2/92
  G's rescue work and 16/7/86 n
  interviews G 12/3/92
  letters from G to, printed 18/12/85
  'Maiden Tribute' of 9/7/85, 15/7/85
  navy and 30/9/84
  Parnell and the O'Shea divorce and 26/11/90 ff
  Review of Reviews by
    doubtful morality of 2/3/90
  Tranby Croft affair and 28/6/91
Stelvio pass 19/9/38
  scenery suitable for Dante 19/9/38
St. George's Hill, Weybridge (F. Egerton) 5/4/90, 11/8/93
stick, G using 26/6/83
Stockport 21/4/62
Stocks Commutation Bill 22/4/53 ff
Stoke Holy Cross, Norfolk 16/5/90
Stoke Poges 6/7/57
Stoke (Taunton) 11/2/60, 29/3/62, 7/3/63
Stonehaven 20/8/33, 4/10/49, 1/11/51
  G attends election at 7/8/47
Stonehenge
  noble relic, telling much, concealing more 31/3/53
storms 28/6/26, 2/1/27, 14/1/27, 23/4/27 ff, 26/7/28, 27/8/29, 2/6/32, 11/6/33 ff, 1/11/33, 23/10/34 ff, 14/5/37, 29/9/38, 5/11/38 ff, 24/10/46, 26/9/51, 25/12/52, 27/12/52, 20/10/75, 12/11/77, 30/9/78, 25/10/78, 15/10/81, 22/10/81, 17/11/81, 3/4/82, 22/8/82, 8/12/86, 7/11/90, 12/12/93, 24/12/94
  sirocco 14/10/38
Stourbridge 30/1/47, 14/2/47, 11/2/50
Stourhead House (Hoare) 20/1/77
Stowe 19/4/62
Stowe, Harriet Elizabeth Beecher (1811–1896), author
  G's view of 7/5/53
  Uncle Tom's Cabin
    G gives copies to rescue cases 21/10/52

G thinks great but exaggerated 15/10/52
Stracathro 13/9/33, 13/9/34, 25/9/34, 31/8/36, 16/10/37
Strafford, impeachment of 4/11/26, 30/6/27
Strasbourg 28/9/45, 23/10/45 ff
Cathedral of disappointing 24/10/45
Strathconan (A. J. Balfour) 3/10/72
Stratton Park (Northbrook) 17/11/83
Strawberry Hill (Lady Waldgrave/Carlingford) 8/5/58, 28/4/59, 30/5/59, 17/11/60, 22/7/63, 23/6/66, 6/7/67, 23/5/68, 4/7/68, 22/6/70, 3/12/73, 15/7/76
Lady Waldegrave points out G's errors and defects to him 7/7/67
studios of artists visited
Alma-Tadema 23/2/91
Brock 20/6/76
H. Holiday 12/5/87
Holl 2/4/87
Joy 21/5/84
Leighton 28/3/82
Marochetti 12/7/55, 22/1/62, 20/11/62, 2/5/63
Millais 13/3/73
Munro 13/8/53, 8/5/55, 15/4/56, 13/7/57, 27/7/63
Noble 20/3/54, 23/5/55, 17/3/62, 15/3/66, 9/6/70, 22/5/71, 31/3/73, 12/7/73
busts of Aberdeen and Hope Scott at 12/7/73
Papworth, E. G. 6/6/64
Richmond, G. 9/4/55, 16/5/72
Richmond, W. B. 26/3/74, 29/3/77
Theed 2/8/60
Watts 27/6/63, 25/3/67, 20/7/70, 28/6/71
Westmacott 3/6/44
Woolner 16/4/62, 6/6/64, 1/4/71, 2/4/73, 28/5/75, 15/7/76, 5/5/83
See also Rome, Rome (studios visited)
Studley Royal, Ripon (Lord Ripon) 25/10/87
study
time spent on 6/11/46
Stundists 9/11/92
Sturm und Drang
time of 31/12/84
Stuttgardt 28/9/45, 7/10/45
Suakin *See* Sudan
succession and legacy duties 19/5/53, 13/6/53 ff, 1/7/53 ff, 18/7/53, 25/7/53, 9/8/53, 8/5/57, 9/11/61 n, 5/3/70 c, 11/4/71 ff, 20/4/71, 12/8/73, 19/11/80
1874 budget and 11/8/73, 12/8/73
See also death duties
Sudan 29/5/69 n, 20/11/83 ff, 7/5/85 c, 11/5/85
appointment of Zobeir negatived 21/2/84 c, 5/3/84 c, 15/3/84 c, 16/3/84
Berber and 18/2/84 c, 15/3/84, 29/3/84 c, 2/4/84 c, 21/4/84 c, 23/4/84 c, 28/4/84 c, 13/5/84, 30/7/84, 9/1/85 n, 10/2/85
Berber-Suakin railway 24/5/84 c, 28/5/84, 30/5/84, 2/6/84, 4/6/84, 6/6/84, 10/6/84 c, 10/2/85, 5/4/85, 30/4/85
decision to build 10/6/84 c
likely to lead to permanent occupation 28/5/84
British troops for 21/2/84 c, 29/2/84 c
censure motion on 12/2/84, 27/6/84 c
change of policy in due to Afghan priorities 12/3/85 ff
civilisation v. barbarous Mahometanism 2/4/85
Daily Chronicle and 28/2/85 c
Egypt and 15/9/82, 20/11/83 c, 3/1/84 c
Khartoum not defendable by 3/1/84
serious difficulty anticipated 27/11/83
Turkey to be encouraged into Red Sea ports 3/1/84 c, 4/3/84, 7/3/84 c, 1/5/84 c, 7/5/84 c, 24/5/84 c
evacuation of
plan for 7/2/85, 10/2/85
Gordon's mission to 22/1/84 ff
Harrah, evacuation of 1/5/84 c
Hick's army in destroyed 22/11/83 c
Khartoum 8/2/84, 25/2/84 c, 30/7/84, 6/1/85
consequences of fall of to be borne by Britain alone 9/2/85 c
fall or betrayal of 5/2/85, 6/2/85 c, 7/2/85 c, 10/2/85 n, 11/2/85, 19/2/85 ff
Mahdi and 24/4/84
decision to destroy power at Khartoum of 10/2/85
grounds for an expedition against now untenable 2/4/85
Massowah and
Italy to be excluded 6/10/84 c
payment of south Egypt army by 3/11/82
Red Sea coast, administration of 29/3/84 c
religious war in possible if British troops used 19/8/84
slave trade in 21/2/84 c, 29/2/84 cn, 4/3/84, 5/3/84 c, 7/3/84 c, 15/3/84, 12/3/85 c
Somaliland and 18/2/84 c
Suakin 20/11/83 c, 12/2/84 c, 18/2/84 c, 2/4/84 c, 13/5/84, 24/5/84 c, 6/1/85 ff, 14/1/85, 21/1/85 c, 5/4/85 ff, 30/4/85, 9/5/85 c
expedition to 9/2/85 c
expedition to, unwelcome suggestion of 6/1/85
expedition to: cabinet over-rules G on leadership of 11/2/85 c

Sudan (*cont.*)
Suakin (*cont.*)
grave error in landing at 30/5/85
reinforced by marines 6/2/84 c
tory policy and 4/12/88, 14/12/88
Sudanese fighting to deliver country from the stranger 12/2/84
Tokar garrison and 12/2/84 c
Turkish troops for
no proposal for 9/6/84 c
two grave errors by cabinet in handling of 30/5/85
withdrawal from 20/11/83 c, 22/11/83 c, 5/3/85
Wolseley Governor General of 25/2/85, 28/2/85 c, 12/3/85 c
See also Egypt, Gordon, memoranda, memoranda (printed), Wolseley
Sudbury Hall, Derbyshire (Lord Vernon) 20/10/87
Sue, E. *See* plays seen
Suez canal 24/6/59, 2/1/60, 22/7/69, 24/8/69, 25/11/70 c, 21/2/76, 21/6/82 ff, 3/7/82 c, 25/7/84 c, 20/1/85 c, 15/4/85 c, 10/3/86, 15/3/86
British government's purchase of shares in 26/11/75, 21/2/76
G discusses with Political Economy Club 3/3/76
G expects grave consequences from 27/11/75
British material interest in 6/9/82
British occupation of Egypt and 3/7/82 c, 5/7/82, 8/7/82 c, 13/7/82 c, 29/7/82 c, 31/7/82 c, 15/9/82, 23/6/83 c
negotiations with de Lesseps 18/8/83, 12/9/83
Provisional Agreement on, negotiated and abandoned 23/6/83 c, 30/6/83, 7/7/83 c, 13/7/83 c, 19/7/83 c, 23/7/83 c, 2/8/83
role of cabinet as directors essentially false 18/8/83, 12/9/83
Commission for 20/2/85 c
conference on 1/3/73 c
G discusses at Geographical Society 11/4/59
G's speech on plans for 1/6/58, 2/6/58
neutralisation of 17/9/82
opening of 26/10/69 c
responsibility for rests with Sultan 21/6/82
route available during war?
cabinet committee on 21/5/70 c, 28/5/70 c
second canal planned through Palestine 23/6/83 c, 19/7/83 c
abandoned in favour of wider channel 21/8/83 c
tunnage commission 6/8/73 c
See also Egypt
Suez Canal
neutralisation of, G supports 18/4/69
suffering *See* pain
sugar
Paris sugar conference 20/5/73 n
profits on, G's queries to Fortnum & Mason 30/4/73
sugar duties 15/6/38, 25/6/40, 1/5/41, 18/5/41, 1/12/41 ff, 14/12/41 ff, 4/3/42 ff, 3/6/42, 22/2/43, 17/8/43, 17/11/43, 2/5/44, 11/3/57, 13/4/61, 21/3/62, 23/1/64, 20/4/72, 23/4/72, 25/4/72, 10/5/73 c, 21/5/80, 14/12/87 n
abolition of
abolish income tax and sugar duties, partly paid from death and spirit duties 11/8/73
memorandum summarising means of, printed 19/1/74
article on, unpublished at Peel's request 24/6/44
crisis over 15/6/44 ff
Danish claim 28/6/44, 23/7/44, 8/11/44
G's memorandum on, printed 14/3/72
G's speech on 10/5/41, 22/6/43, 3/6/44, 14/6/44, 24/2/45, 26/2/45
National Association for Abolition of Sugar Bounties 14/12/87 n
Peelites split on 29/6/48
resignation over opposed by G 15/6/44 ff
Venezuela 23/7/44, 29/10/44
See also memoranda, memoranda (printed)
suicide 31/8/60
Zadok Outram's
G really afflicted and alarmed by 3/12/93
Sullivan, Sir Arthur *See* operas (and Dramatis Personae)
Summerhayes (later Mrs. Dale) *See* rescue work (significant cases)
Summertown *See* Oxford
Sumner, J. B., *Records of Creation*, analysis of 11/1/31
sun
eclipse of 1/11/70 n, 2/11/70 c
Sunbeam, S. S. *See* ships
Sunday observance 5/2/32, 11/2/32 ff, 19/2/32, 21/5/32, 14/10/32, 16/5/33, 29/12/33, 14/3/34, 26/6/34, 24/12/34, 21/3/38, 4/8/39, 16/3/69, 15/2/75 n, 22/10/76, 8/6/77, 29/3/84 c
country Sundays unSundaylike 27/8/93
G opposes compulsory cheap trains on Sundays 22/7/44, 27/7/44
G petitions for Sunday evening services 2/12/57

infringements of 23/9/32, 23/6/33, 28/5/35, 16/8/35, 6/6/80
mocked in France 29/1/39
museum opening 20/4/72 c, 26/4/73 c
Ripon and Morley at Hawarden makes a bad Sunday 28/11/86
Strome Ferry imprisonments 7/9/83
Sunday closing/opening 26/5/83 c, 29/6/83
open question in cabinet 19/6/80 c, 4/5/81 c, 13/5/82 c
wretched in France 27/10/50
See also memoranda
Sunday School, G teaching at 10/8/28, 17/8/28, 26/7/29 ff, 30/8/29 ff, 11/7/30, 12/9/30, 31/7/31, 4/12/31
Superannuation Bill 12/1/55 ff, 22/3/56 n, 7/5/56
Supremacy, Royal 6/10/46
Sutherland, Duke and Duchess of *See* Gower
suzerainty
Transvaal and 12/3/81 ff, 29/4/81 c, 24/6/81
Murray's lexicographical note on 29/4/81 n
Swansea 2/6/87
astonishing procession through 4/6/87
G's speeches at 2/6/87 ff
library of, opened by G 6/6/87
the Mumbles, visit to 3/6/87
Swaziland *See* South Africa
Sweden
Dageus Nyheten: articles on G 1/12/87 n
home rule and 22/3/86
Norway, relations with 30/3/93 ff, 10/5/93, 31/5/93, 9/6/93, 23/8/93
treaty with 5/10/42 ff, 27/5/43
Swinburne, A. C.
G much struck by his power 18/12/72
poet laureateship and 7/10/92, 10/10/92, 17/10/92 n
Swindon
G's speech at 7/6/87
Switzerland 3/7/32 ff, 12/7/32 ff, 15/9/38 ff, 5/8/49 ff
army system of 21/12/70
Calvinism in 12/7/32
cleanliness in 17/7/32
sycee silver 2/12/41, 10/12/41
synods 1/11/51, 2/11/51 n, 14/12/51, 23/5/52 n
synonyms, G's dictionary of 25/8/52

table turning 13/9/61 ff, 31/3/69
Tabley House (de Tabley) 11/9/45, 23/10/55, 27/11/68
Tait, Archibald Campbell, Abp. (1811–1882), bishop of London 1856–69, archbishop of Canterbury 1869–82, reformer and anti-ritualist 4/5/64, 7/2/66, 3/7/69 c, 27/8/69, 3/11/69 c, 21/10/71 c, 16/7/73, 27/7/80, 23/1/81, 16/8/82, 9/1/85
Archbishop of Canterbury 11/12/68 n
at Hawarden 18/10/63 ff
at Penmaenmawr 9/9/63
better tone of 23/1/81 n
Burials Bill and Convocation 7/8/80 ff, 9/9/80
church reform and 8/3/72, 9/3/72 c, 27/4/72 c, 9/7/72
death of and succession to 26/8/82 ff, 3/9/82, 2/12/82, 9/12/82, 11/12/82
episcopal conference and 26/10/69 c, 30/10/69 c, 3/11/69 c
Essays and Reviews and 15/3/64
G keeps children from associating with 15/3/64
Irish disestablishment and 14/2/69 n, 15/2/69 c, 19/2/69, 17/7/69 ff
amendments to the bill 3/6/69 ff
Judicature Bill and 4/7/73, 5/7/73 c
lectionary reform and 6/6/71
letters from G to, printed 3/6/69, 21/7/69, 10/1/71, 23/1/71, 6/6/71, 5/11/71, 8/3/72, 5/6/72, 9/7/72, 4/7/73, 17/8/80, 9/9/80, 16/9/80
retirement of bishops and 17/4/69 c
See also Church of England, Public Worship Bill, Victoria
Tarbet 14/8/39
Tarbet House (Sutherland) 26/9/53
tariffs 20/1/42 ff, 10/5/42, 4/7/42 ff *See also* Australia, Board of Trade, budgets, Canada, colonies, France, free trade, Peel, Spain, Stade duties
Tasso
house of 10/5/32
inferior to Dante 18/4/36
Tatton Park (Egerton) 25/11/68
Taunton 24/1/77
taxation
buildings taxes the best 23/4/65
direct 18/12/52, 2/2/85
father tells G to study 16/2/47
European comparisons 23/4/65
gas tax
reserved for wartime 11/4/71
graduated
principle of not objected to by G 19/7/94
G's memorandum, 'paper duty and taxing power of the two Houses' 30/6/60
indirect
cannot be used to finance income tax abolition 2/4/73
indirect taxes and 1871 budget 11/4/71 ff
indirect taxes and 1885 budget 2/2/85

taxation (*cont.*)
local 17/1/69, 5/11/69 c, 11/11/70 c, 25/1/72, 19/4/72, 24/7/72 c, 14/10/72 c, 10/12/72 c, 12/12/72 c, 15/2/73 c, 19/1/81 n, 4/11/81, 24/11/81, 14/4/83 c, 17/4/83, 24/4/83
Goschen's Report 17/9/72, 18/9/72, 24/9/72
plan for 1870 5/11/69 c
plan for 1873 14/10/72 c, 7/11/72, 9/11/72, 3/12/72 c, 7/12/72 c, 10/12/72 c, 12/12/72 c, 22/3/73 c, 5/4/73 c, 22/4/73 n, 26/4/73 c, 6/5/73, 10/5/73 c
plan for 1874 21/11/73 c
need to avoid one-sided reduction in 17/3/72
See also cabinet (committees of), house tax, income tax, match tax
Taymouth Castle, Perthshire (Breadalbane) 1/12/79
tea duties 11/2/57, 6/3/57, 13/4/61, 10/1/69
tedium
G has never known 31/12/56
teeth 31/8/29 ff, 7/10/53, 2/11/93
extracted
in Edinburgh 8/1/50
G's chewing machinery unsatisfactory 24/8/82
G's difficulties with 4/12/27, 15/12/87
G supplied with a frame 7/5/73
toothache 16/7/46 ff, 17/11/47 ff, 25/10/62, 31/5/66, 13/1/73 ff, 15/4/73 ff, 4/2/80 ff
disrupts Reform debate 31/5/66
See also dentist
Tegernsee (Döllinger) 17/9/79 ff, 27/8/86 ff, 27/10/92 n
telegraph
Aden-Gibraltar 3/10/73
Atlantic 2/4/62, 1/8/62, 20/2/65, 12/7/73 c
cable on Irish coast 21/6/73 c
Cape Verde-Sierra Leone
subsidy declined 3/10/73 c
demonstration of 20/3/39, 4/7/40
G and children working the cipher at Hawarden 12/10/70
telegraph department, funds of 25/7/72
misappropriation of 7/6/73 c
See also memoranda
telegraphs
government purchase of
ask for a monopoly 2/2/69 c, 20/3/69 c, 10/4/69 c, 24/4/69 c, 10/7/69 c
Tel-el-Kebir *See* Egypt, Wolseley
telephone
demonstration of 18/3/78, 30/4/79
installed at Hawarden 27/11/80
temper
recorded as bad 20/7/40, 3/7/44
temperance 8/5/69 c, 31/12/80 c, 14/5/88, 5/4/92, 8/4/92, 17/10/92
deputation at Hawarden on 20/1/68
G abstains on 11/3/79
local government and 26/1/84 c
local option 15/1/82, 27/4/83, 20/7/92
G reluctantly agrees to speak on 2/3/80, 5/3/80
open question in cabinet 12/6/80 c, 13/6/81 c
local veto 21/11/92 c, 20/1/93 c
Scottish temperance deputation 29/6/60, 5/4/92
Temple, Henry John (1784–1865), 3rd Viscount Palmerston (1802), Canningite and whig M.P., foreign secretary 1830–4, 1835–41, 1846–51, home secretary 1852–5, prime minister 1855–8, 1859–65 1/2/32, 15/2/32, 21/7/32, 24/3/40, 22/12/41, 7/11/42, 15/7/45, 8/11/51 n, 20/2/52, 25/2/52, 6/5/52, 21/11/52, 22/11/52, 10/2/53, 16/2/53 ff, 19/11/53, 19/12/53, 21/12/53, 28/2/54, 23/2/56, 31/3/57, 2/6/59, 18/6/59, 4/7/59 ff, 24/9/59, 21/1/60 ff, 30/5/60, 3/10/61 ff, 11/11/61 ff, 2/5/62, 27/5/62 n, 29/5/62, 30/5/62, 14/11/62, 27/3/63, 7/10/64, 14/10/72, 28/11/72, 16/3/76, 22/4/80, 17/5/81, 24/10/81, 19/8/84, 21/5/86, 11/10/86, 18/9/92, 21/2/93, 8/4/93, 15/9/93
1854 Reform Bill and 22/2/54
1863 budget and 14/4/63
as home secretary 23/12/52 ff
at Ascot, not at cabinet 12/6/56
at the Manchester exhibition 30/6/57
boundless extravagance of
G opposes 3/2/57
budget explained to by G 10/4/61
causes G displeasure 16/6/64
chairman of Fish Dinner 13/8/53
Cobden treaty and 8/3/60
compromise on fortifications plan and 23/7/60, 25/7/60
death of
Address in Commons on 17/2/66, 22/2/66
makes G giddy 18/10/65
Derby's proposal for a war coalition and 31/1/55
determinded not to make 1861 budget a matter of confidence 13/5/61

diary of, quoted 24/5/60 n, 6/6/60 n
dining with G 3/6/52
discusses ancient pronunciations with G 25/7/63
ecclesiastical patronage and 9/3/60
estimates always settled at dagger's point 28/1/65
exits with propriety 22/2/58
forms government 6/2/55 ff, 13/6/59 ff
funeral of 27/10/65
G attacked for deserting 16/4/57 n
G avoids appearing to attack 18/2/58
G clashes with on China 5/3/57
G deputising for in Commons 10/3/64
G dining with 4/2/54, 19/5/55, 23/1/60, 4/2/61, 5/2/62, 8/3/62
good humour of 2/7/56
G Prime Minister as long as 4/7/84
G proposes health of 10/8/59
great day for his government 15/3/58
great objectives: slave trade suppression & good defences 6/6/60
G's conversation with Derby on 4/2/57
G sees on appointments 1/8/59
G's last shot in the locker 16/7/60
G's memorandum on paper duties repeal 26/5/60
G speaks to order of 13/6/62
G's resignation *all but* settled 2/6/60
G's 'resignation' interview with 6/6/60
G's speech on Baines' Bill and 13/5/64 n, 21/5/64 n
G suggests Wilberforce for York to 28/9/62
G's view of a war-time government led by 4/2/55, 5/2/55, 6/2/55, 9/2/55
G's view of his poor chairmanship of cabinet 6/8/59
G's views on Italian policy of 30/6/59
G thanks for speech 31/1/56
G threatens resignation on paper duties 2/7/60
health of 27/6/63
insolent speech on fall of Kars by 29/4/56
Italian memorandum of 5/1/60 n, 7/1/60
led on the anti-economic host in cabinet 21/12/84
letter of too brusque to send to Victoria 31/8/59
longevity of an exception to Commons' politicians 29/12/96
national monument to, proposed by G 22/2/66
negrophilistic principles, application of 14/10/72
offers G the Exchequer 13/6/59
O'Kane divorce suit 2/11/63
  G thinks must produce fruits 2/11/63
  'she is Kane but is he Able?' 4/11/63 n
  threatens to blaze 4/11/63
our old men are our youngest, G thinks 5/5/60
Oxford, honorary degree from 2/7/62
paper duty and
  new proposal to abandon Resolutions 3/8/60
  ominous letter from 25/6/60
  suggests delay 24/4/60
Peelites discuss possibility of joining 17/4/56
reception for Garibaldi 16/4/64
regards G's memorandum on fortification as absurd 24/5/60 n
remarkable notice of 1861 budget 17/4/61
Roebuck's motion and 24/1/55 ff, 18/2/55 ff
row with over law courts 19/7/61
settles with Derby on Savings Banks Bill 15/8/60, 16/8/60
speeches by 16/2/55
speech on Don Pacifico 25/6/50
statue of 3/3/71 n, 23/1/72 c
tables turned against 23/6/62
the War Office and 24/4/63
thinks 1853 budget impolitic 11/4/53
unequivocally weak bodily and mentally 8/7/64
Wilberforce tells G he should follow him 20/10/63
wild proposal on navy estimates 25/2/61, 27/2/61
wretched defence of government by 26/1/55
See also army, cabinet, liberal party, memoranda, memoranda (printed), navy, Victoria
Temple church 7/11/42, 19/11/42
Temple of Peace *See* Hawarden Castle
temptation
  not resisted 31/3/45, 21/4/48, 12/4/49
tenant right *See* Ireland, Scotland, Wales
tenants
  at Fasque
    merits of 12/11/33
Tenby 9/7/52
Tennyson, Alfred (1809-1892), 1st Baron Tennyson (1884), poet laureate (1850) 16/10/29, 21/5/31 n, 14/7/59, 18/7/59, 13/1/62, 16/12/69, 14/1/72, 19/3/73, 13/5/73, 12/11/75, 16/11/75, 25/9/77, 28/2/78, 7/3/80, 10/6/81
  at Cliveden
    G feels nearer to 5/5/62
    reading *Guinevere* 4/5/62
    reading *Pericles* 2/5/62

Tennyson, Alfred (*cont.*)
at Hawarden 31/10/76 ff
discusses future retribution 2/11/76
read *Harold* for two and a half hours 1/11/76
baronetcy for
declined 28/10/80, 23/10/84 n
Carlyle and 2/9/93
death of 6/10/92 n, 7/10/92
last words of, on G 6/10/92
funeral of, G unable to attend 8/10/92
G learning *Guinevere* by heart in train 14/10/59
G reading aloud 24/11/76, 2/12/76
G reading *Guinevere* to Mrs. Thistlethwayte 10/5/76
G reading *Guinevere* to rescue case 16/3/65
G reading *Princess* to rescue case 16/9/59
G's letters lent for biography of 7/12/92
G's recollections of 27/10/92
G's review of works by 14/7/59 ff, 13/8/59 ff, 24/8/59 ff, 23/9/59
'Locksley Hall; sixty years after' 11/12/86, 15/12/86 ff
partial retraction of remarks 25/11/78
G's version of his epitaph on Sir J. Franklin 12/11/75, 16/11/75
G's visit to Aldworth 22/7/71
Hallam's letters and 26/11/83
letters from G to, printed 28/10/80, 25/9/83, 3/10/83, 26/11/83, 6/7/84, 26/4/86
meetings with 30/3/39, 18/7/59, 12/2/64, 18/2/64, 27/6/64, 22/11/64, 8/12/65, 5/3/73, 24/7/75, 21/2/77, 19/3/77, 26/3/77, 28/3/77, 29/3/77, 7/3/80, 13/3/80, 26/3/81, 29/4/83, 4/7/90
G dining with 21/2/66, 30/3/78, 11/3/82
Montenegro and 19/3/77
obituary of, G declines to write 9/10/92
peerage for 25/9/83, 3/10/83, 26/11/83, 27/12/83
plays of seen 3/1/81
poor reception of *The promise of May* 11/11/82, 14/11/82
readings by
Elaine 20/9/83
Enoch Arden 30/4/62
Guinevere 20/9/83
The Falcon 13/9/83
The Grandmother 22/11/64
'The passing of Arthur' 26/3/81
The promise of May 12/9/83
Tiresias 1/5/83
reads G's translation of Homer 30/7/62
Reform Bill 1884
vote on 3/7/84, 6/7/84
true greatness, genuine simplicity and some eccentricity of 24/7/71
Victoria quotes on death of Albert 19/3/62
voyage to Norway with G on *Pembroke Castle* 8/9/83 ff
well but 'gruff' 4/7/90
See also Hallam, plays seen, publications
terebine *See* medicines
Terni 5/6/32
Test and Corporation Acts
G's paper on 29/2/28, 21/3/28
Thames, river
drainage of 17/7/58, 19/7/58
See also London
Thanksgiving Days 14/4/33
theatre
government subvention of discussed with Kean 12/5/57
National Theatre, call for supported by G 9/3/78
theatres
temptations of 29/12/32
theatres attended
Adelphi 25/7/50, 13/11/60, 23/11/60, 17/12/60, 28/7/87
Alfred 31/10/71
Alhambra 25/9/77
Aquarium 2/7/77
Astley's Amphitheatre 5/4/53
Astley's Circus 12/8/43
Augsburg opera house 29/10/45
Bath 4/5/27
Brighton 6/4/72
Britannia 17/12/60
Charing Cross 19/4/71
Corfu Opera 30/11/58, 27/1/59, 1/2/59
Court 20/7/78, 30/4/84, 17/5/84, 18/11/84
Covent Garden 3/12/27, 15/6/58, 17/6/58, 19/5/59, 16/6/60, 28/1/61, 3/6/61, 4/7/63, 5/1/65, 24/6/70, 8/5/75, 9/6/87, 23/2/89, 15/7/89, 12/6/90
Criterion 14/6/79, 10/2/85
Drury Lane 22/1/63, 22/4/64, 19/11/64, 1/12/73, 12/4/83
Fenice, Venice 24/2/59
Gaiety 12/3/70, 16/5/74, 27/10/76, 9/6/80, 27/4/83
G behind the scenes of 16/5/74
Garrick 18/3/90, 19/5/92, 13/1/93
Globe 14/3/78, 11/11/82, 24/4/83
Globe, Long Acre 3/11/70
Haymarket 31/3/56, 21/10/59, 18/4/60, 25/8/60, 17/11/62, 18/8/71, 7/5/75, 5/9/76, 24/7/79, 2/4/81, 15/6/81, 4/2/82, 29/11/84, 29/3/90, 19/6/90
Her Majesty's 14/5/57, 24/4/66, 10/3/82

Hof (Munich) 11/10/79
Lyceum 30/11/37, 27/1/38, 18/6/56, 30/7/61, 30/5/63, 19/6/63, 2/12/63, 5/11/64, 16/4/75, 19/2/76, 4/5/77, 5/3/78, 19/2/79, 19/6/79, 28/2/80, 3/1/81, 8/7/82, 25/10/82, 10/4/86, 2/12/90, 11/5/92, 22/11/92, 25/2/93
  G behind the scenes at 4/1/81
  saw Miss Terry 'behind' 8/7/82
Metropolitan Music Hall
  show not Athenian 21/7/77
Milan 2/3/59
New Royalty 19/11/63
Nottingham 27/9/77
Olympic 25/2/54, 11/8/59, 24/7/62, 31/3/64
  ballet 31/7/50
Opera house (Florence) 23/3/32
Opera house (Marseilles) 18/7/49
Opera house (Paris) 21/10/50
Prince of Wales 1/11/69, 26/7/75, 26/10/76
Princess's 3/7/56, 22/4/57, 12/5/57, 16/5/57, 8/8/57, 29/5/58, 10/6/58, 13/7/58, 5/5/59, 6/8/59, 29/7/61, 13/5/65, 16/8/71, 9/2/76, 6/12/90
  G behind the scenes at 16/5/57
Royal Grecian, City Road 12/8/57
Royal Olympic 5/8/75
Royal Soho 21/11/53
Sadler's Wells 1/10/80
San Carlino (Naples) 20/11/38, 1/12/38
San Carlos (Naples) 14/11/38, 19/11/38, 9/12/50, 28/12/88
Savoy 14/9/82, 4/12/82, 29/7/85
Schauspielhause (Berlin) 12/11/58
Standard
  for religious service 23/3/62
St. James's 9/7/58, 11/2/61, 17/1/66
  G at rehearsal in 10/7/58
Strand 24/11/62
Teatro Argentina (Rome) 16/10/66
Teatro Carlo Felice (Genoa) 4/11/50, 5/11/50
Teatro de' Fiorentini (Naples) 19/5/32, 11/11/50, 18/11/50
Teatro dell' Vigne (Genoa) 6/11/50
Teatro Gerlino (Turin) 2/11/50
Teatro Metastasio (Rome) 24/11/66
Teatro Nuovo (Naples) 12/11/50
Teatro Ré (Genoa) 30/7/49
Teatro Sannazaro (Naples) 31/1/89
Théatre Français (Paris) 11/2/32, 12/2/32, 22/10/50, 17/10/79, 20/10/79
Theatre Royal (Chester) 5/10/75
Vaudeville 16/9/70, 13/4/87
Victoria Coffee Palace 23/3/87
Vienna opera
  20 minutes long enough 19/11/58
Vienna theatre 18/11/58
  Whitby 28/8/71, 1/9/71
  Windsor Castle 10/11/53
Themistocles 3/12/33
theological writings
  apostolical succession 10/3/37, 22/3/37
  order for almsgiving 9/3/38
  Rule of Faith 19/9/36, 23/9/36
theology
  higher natural theology 21/3/41
  trade, G's reflections on and 1/1/55
  See also Homer, Hooker, memoranda (printed in the *Diaries*), theological writings
Thirty Nine Articles *See* Church of England, memoranda (printed), Oxford (University of)
Thistlethwayte, Laura Eliza Jane Seymour (-1894), née Bell, confidante and intimate correspondent of G, lived at 15 Grosvenor Square and Woodbine Cottage 10/12/64, 29/10/65, 29/4/66, 23/5/66, 19/10/67, 16/2/68, 7/6/68, 26/7/68, 28/12/68, 7/3/69, 23/6/69, 19/10/69, 22/10/69 ff, 28/10/69, 15/11/69 ff, 21/1/70, 4/3/70 ff, 8/4/70 ff, 24/6/70 ff, 3/7/70 ff, 28/10/70 ff, 18/3/71 ff, 29/3/71 ff, 10/5/71, 22/5/71, 27/6/71, 7/7/71, 23/10/71 ff, 2/11/71, 10/11/71 ff, 5/6/72 ff, 13/7/72, 2/8/72, 10/10/72, 25/11/72, 28/1/73 ff, 21/2/73, 31/3/73, 2/10/73, 14/11/73 ff, 29/11/73, 16/1/74, 9/2/74, 19/2/74, 25/2/74 ff, 17/3/74, 20/7/74 ff, 2/8/74, 6/8/74, 6/9/74, 25/9/74, 6/11/74, 7/11/74, 7/1/75, 13/2/75 ff, 22/2/75, 23/2/75 ff, 12/3/75, 26/5/75, 30/6/75, 12/7/75, 1/8/75, 20/1/76, 27/3/76, 4/7/76, 10/7/76, 1/8/76, 6/9/76, 8/9/76, 24/10/76, 9/2/77, 9/3/77, 13/3/77, 31/3/77, 11/6/77, 19/7/77, 25/9/77, 18/3/78, 31/5/78, 5/7/78, 18/10/78, 27/2/79, 10/4/79, 25/4/79, 13/6/79, 23/7/79, 11/9/79, 13/9/79, 27/2/80, 6/5/80, 14/5/80, 11/7/80, 29/9/80, 6/10/80, 23/11/80 ff, 1/1/81 ff, 21/7/81, 8/9/81, 26/1/82, 29/4/82, 20/5/82, 1/8/82, 20/10/82, 17/11/82, 7/3/83, 23/3/83, 9/5/83, 3/7/83, 16/7/83, 26/10/83, 7/2/84, 30/4/84, 26/5/84, 20/6/84, 29/7/84, 8/10/84, 24/10/84, 3/12/84, 21/2/85, 22/5/85, 12/1/86, 19/2/86, 20/3/86, 12/5/86, 19/7/86, 31/7/86, 24/2/87, 10/4/87, 12/5/87, 23/7/87, 10/11/87, 16/6/88, 25/2/89, 18/3/89, 12/4/89, 20/7/89, 14/3/90, 28/6/90, 20/3/92, 2/5/92, 29/9/92, 21/1/93, 10/7/93, 6/8/93, 16/11/93

Thistlethwayte, Laura Eliza Jane Seymour (*cont.*)
autobiography of
G astonished by 25/10/69
G reading 18/9/69, 30/9/69 ff, 5/12/69, 16/1/70
promises G some personal history 2/7/69
told with great modesty 5/10/69
truthful though not quite coherent 5/10/69
Bathhurst, friendship with 26/2/78
birthday of 18/10/69, 18/10/79
bust of G, carving 9/1/75
character of
generous and noble at the base 11/1/75
climax of G's communications with 29/4/71
correspondence with, danger of misapprehension about 25/2/93
cottage of in Hampstead 1/1/84
visited by G 20/7/86, 8/5/88, 20/7/89
death of 17/5/94 n
death of A. F. Thistlethwayte 9/8/87 n, 24/8/87
distressing: much to ruminate on 17/11/72
Duke of Newcastle and 5/2/65
Eastern question and 8/12/76
Egypt, journey to 27/1/72, 11/2/72
as well for G that she goes 11/2/72
embarrasses 27/2/70
essential purity of, G convinced of 19/8/70
extraordinary but interesting scene with 22/3/65
finances of 9/4/89
fusses over small things 19/12/93
G and de Tabley discuss 9/11/69
G at theatre with 16/8/71, 27/10/76, 25/9/77
G believes her 'holy' and 'pure' 28/10/69
G bound to do the best for 25/10/69
G discusses with Argyll 2/7/66
G discusses with C. G 19/12/69
G discusses with Duchess of Sutherland 2/7/66
G discusses with Glyn 20/12/69
G hears at Polytechnic: not to be repeated 30/4/65
G lionised over her pretty room 17/11/69
G lunching with C. G and Mr. and Mrs. 17/6/87
G meeting Shuvalov at her house 26/3/77
G reading *Guinevere* to 10/5/76
G reads H. G's paper on ambition to 12/11/69
G's birthday retrospect on 29/12/69
G's obligations to 29/12/69
G's visit to at Boveridge 11/12/69 ff
she comes to G's rooms at night 12/12/69
G wishes to help but knows not how 1/8/78
health of 17/5/94
interviews with 8/11/69 ff
introduced to C. G 18/5/87
letter of wounds G 20/10/69
letter possibly closing correspondence with 25/6/76
letter to held back for consideration 6/1/70, 19/1/70
married life to be built up into greater fulness 19/1/70
Miss Ponsonby a friend of 17/6/87
MS of her Eastern tour 17/2/73, 19/2/73
mysterious destiny of 9/8/72
older letters of burnt by G 25/2/93
Padwick v. Thistlethwayte(debt suit) 19/4/79
G returns her presents to pay for 28/4/79
G subpoena'd for 1/4/79
painful scene with, G's fault perhaps 19/12/71
places duty and temptation before G 28/10/69
preRaphaelitism and 12/12/69
religion of 5/2/65
singular experiences with 4/8/74
stangely corresponds with G on strangest points 8/4/70
tells G story of her birth 7/6/71
vexing dinner with 3/3/88
visits Downing Street 12/11/69
with G in Cirencester 2/10/75, 3/10/75, 4/10/75
X noted on visit to 31/3/71, 20/4/71, 15/8/71, 18/8/71, 29/10/71, 15/1/72, 16/1/72, 23/1/72, 27/1/72, 31/1/72, 9/2/72, 1/5/72, 6/8/72, 10/10/72, 12/10/72, 14/11/72, 21/1/73, 24/1/73, 14/3/73, 28/3/73, 23/6/73, 31/7/73, 6/8/73, 31/7/74, 6/9/74, 11/1/75, 12/2/75, 24/7/75, 31/7/75, 1/3/76, 13/2/77
See also Gladstone (Catherine), Gladstone (Helen), Kinnaird
Thornes House, Wakefield (Gaskell) 8/9/29, 11/10/32, 4/9/71
thought
as channel of sin 26/10/45
thought-reading 10/6/85
demonstration in Commons, G attends
nonsense to call it imposture 19/6/84
thoughts
carnal and worldly
barred by pain 19/9/42
Thrasymene, Lake 4/10/38
Three Emperors' alliance
G fears revival of 14/10/80

Three F's *See* Ireland (land question)
Thring, Henry, Sir (1818–1907), 1st Baron Thring (1886), parliamentary draftsman; worked with G from 1853 26/1/63, 12/3/63, 4/2/65, 28/5/66, 18/6/66, 26/2/69, 13/7/74, 15/5/82, 10/9/83, 13/7/86 n, 29/7/86, 18/8/86, 30/11/86
drafting bills
Arrears Bill 15/5/82 ff
Ewelme rectory 22/3/71
franchise, 1866 10/3/66
Irish home rule 1886 2/3/86 ff, 2/4/86
Irish land 1870 17/12/69 ff, 10/1/70, 13/1/70, 17/1/70, 29/1/70
Irish land 1881 25/12/80 ff, 11/2/81, 19/2/81, 5/4/81, 25/5/81, 18/8/81
Irish land purchase 1886 5/3/86, 10/3/86 ff, 27/3/86
Irish university, 1873 5/12/72 c, 6/12/72, 11/12/72 ff, 28/1/73
licensing, 1872 21/8/72
nothing to be done without 25/12/80
redistribution, 1866 7/5/66
G's encomium of 18/8/81
letters from G to, printed 22/3/71, 19/2/81, 18/8/81, 2/4/86
not to assist bishops in drafting 8/5/69 c
Thucydides
descriptions of Sicily 26/10/38, 27/10/38, 10/6/81
Tichborne case 24/6/71 c, 1/7/71 c, 22/6/72 c, 3/5/73 c, 11/5/74, 15/4/75 n, 16/4/75 n, 23/4/75
Chile and Australia not to be scoured for witnesses 29/6/72 c
Crown decision to prosecute the Claimant: cabinet divided 29/6/72 c
G sees Tichborne letters 25/4/73
Tilbury 29/8/54
timber duties 6/6/42, 26/1/46, 24/6/53
timber duty
beaten on 20/6/53
time
an age of shocks 29/12/60
claims of family finances on 24/9/48
December a notable month for G
list of events 31/12/68
great clock of 31/12/54
G's reflections on his half-century 29/12/59
G's resistance to passage of 29/12/59
G wishes to lay hands on and stop 29/12/59
hours spent in devotion, work etc., recorded 23/8/45, 31/8/45, 18/9/46
hours spent in recreation etc., recorded 24/2/45 ff
hours spent reading 6/11/46
hours spent working(14) 20/3/46
interruption of usual habits of, as cause of sin 26/10/45
never better spent than on Eastern question 16/5/77
not enough time 5/11/40
stream of 31/12/58
Turkish ideas of 3/2/59
use of 13/8/44, 3/6/59
Times, The 15/7/52, 20/2/57, 4/2/69, 27/2/69, 2/1/93
Albert exults in Italian policy of 5/1/60
anarchy, accuses G of toiling for 29/12/89
antitractarianism of 20/11/44
changes tone on Irish land 7/9/69
correspondent at Hawarden 31/12/77
excellent reporting of G's speeches by 5/2/74
G accused of treason by 24/12/82
'Parnellism and crime' 7/3/87 n, 6/7/88
Pigott's forged letter 28/4/87
reviews *State and Church* 31/12/38
supposed status as government organ to be denied 27/10/80
virtually Disraeli's paper 6/5/73
Wilberforce's salary and 6/10/69
See also letters, Parnell ('Parnellism and crime')
Tintagel (Lord Hayter) 13/6/89
Tintoretto 19/6/32 ff
tithes 22/3/34, 2/7/38, 19/7/38, 11/7/56
Titian 4/5/32, 19/6/32, 23/11/32, 2/10/38, 11/12/38, 31/12/38, 15/1/39, 21/5/41
Tivoli 17/4/32
tobacco duties 1/1/63, 31/1/63, 13/2/63, 16/2/63, 18/3/63, 28/3/81, 7/3/82
See also memoranda (printed)
Tobermory, Mull 31/8/80, 11/9/83
Tokar *See* Sudan
Tolpuddle martyrs, petition on 21/4/34
Tolquhon Castle 2/10/58
tombs, inscriptions on 28/5/32
Tor Abbey 31/8/32
tories of Queen Anne's reign, G voting against 29/9/27
Torquay 16/8/32 ff, 23/9/32, 12/7/77
Kent's cavern 3/9/32 ff, 19/9/32
tory party *See* conservative party
Totness 12/7/77
Toul, striking church at 27/9/45
Toulouse 12/1/92 ff
tourists, refreshing absence of on Deeside 6/9/39
Toxteth *See* Liverpool
Tractarians 30/3/41, 31/7/42, 11/6/82, 18/6/82, 27/6/82, 5/10/84
Tracts for the Times
read & comments on 27/10/33, 10/11/33, 2/1/34, 19/11/37, 12/12/38, 15/1/39, 30/8/40, 14/12/40, 15/4/41, 19/4/41, 15/10/43, 14/4/65

Tracts for the Times (*cont.*)
Tract 90 17/3/41 n, 10/6/41
ominous 12/3/41
proposed censure of 6/2/45, 8/2/45, 11/2/45, 13/2/45
Trade, Board of 31/8/41 ff, 18/10/43 ff
arrangement of business of 25/9/41
declining duties of 21/5/80
farewell to 3/2/45
G President of 13/5/43, 15/5/43 ff
G Vice-President of 31/8/41 ff
mem. on state of business 1/2/45
Railway Dept., memorandum on 25/7/44
trade unions 27/6/33, 4/4/34, 21/4/34, 9/2/67, 8/10/68 n, 24/5/69 n, 3/7/69 c, 5/7/69, 2/11/70 c
Agricultural Labourers' Union 4/12/73 n
bill for
to prevent violence; law to play no part in economic matters 28/1/71 c
demonstrations in Edinburgh by against legislation 3/9/73
deputation of 15/2/68, 18/2/68
difficult to justify use of soldiers in case of strikes 3/9/72
Farrer v. Close 3/7/69 cn
gas stokers' case 15/1/73, 22/1/73 c
cabinet recommends reduction of sentences 22/1/73 c
general election and 3/9/73 n
G fears danger of labouring classes thinking monopolistically 5/11/72
legal status of 25/1/71 c, 28/1/71 c, 6/5/71 c, 3/9/73, 27/9/73, 3/10/73 c, 26/11/73 c, 1/12/73 c
conspiracy and 26/11/73 c, 1/12/73 c
Lowe's bill to amend legislation on 3/9/73, 27/9/73, 3/10/73 c, 26/11/73 c, 1/12/73 c
non-interference, doctrine of 27/10/72
non-union movement 9/2/67
protection of funds of 10/7/69 c
strike at Aston colliery, Hawarden estate
miners accept 10 per cent wage reduction 9/6/74 ff, 12/6/74
Trades Union Congress
parliamentary committee of 8/1/81
troops used for harvesting at Woodstock 3/9/72, 27/10/72, 5/11/72
See also cabinet, coal, eight hours question, liberal party, Lowe, Manchester School, Mundella, political economy, wages, working classes
Trafalgar Square *See* London
tramways 19/2/70 c
Tranby Croft affair *See* Edward VII
translations
Euripides' Hecuba 23/3/93 n
'Hark my soul' 23/7/82 ff, 5/8/82 ff, 16/8/83, 31/10/83
Horace 14/7/92 ff, 6/1/93 ff, 5/9/93 ff, 23/9/93 ff, 23/10/93 ff, 30/11/93 ff, 11/12/93 ff, 6/1/94 ff, 22/1/94 ff, 1/3/94 ff
finished 3/3/94
G disgusted by IV. 1 16/12/93
principles of 29/9/93
'Rock of Ages' 9/3/45, 18/3/45
See also Homer, Horace
transportation 3/4/38
Transvaal *See* South Africa
travel
by train, how easy 14/7/46
See also passports
travels abroad 1/2/32 ff, 11/8/38 ff, 25/9/45 ff, 13/7/49 ff, 18/10/50 ff, 8/4/51 ff, 8/11/58 ff, 28/9/66 ff, 7/9/74 ff, 14/9/79 ff, 12/1/80 ff, 17/1/83 ff, 28/12/87 ff, 19/12/88 ff, 3/9/89 ff, 15/12/91 ff, 21/12/92 ff, 13/1/94 ff, 8/1/95 ff, 2/1/96 ff
Albania 2/2/59
Austria 27/6/32 ff, 16/11/58, 24/9/79, 11/9/86
Baden 19/7/32
Belgium 1/2/32, 25/7/32, 8/11/58, 25/8/86
Denmark 16/9/83 ff
France 10/2/32, 25/9/45, 14/7/49, 18/10/50, 8/4/51, 6/3/59, 28/9/66, 14/10/79 ff, 18/1/83 ff, 28/12/87, 4/2/88, 15/2/89, 3/9/89, 15/12/91 ff, 21/12/92 ff, 14/1/94 ff, 8/1/95, 2/1/96
Germany 18/7/32 ff, 14/8/38 ff, 28/9/45 ff, 7/9/74 ff, 15/9/79 ff, 10/10/79 ff, 12/1/80 ff, 25/8/86 ff
Greece 17/12/58 ff
Holland 11/8/38 ff
Italy 2/3/32 ff, 19/9/38 ff, 19/7/49 ff, 23/2/59 ff, 6/10/66 ff, 27/9/79 ff, 30/12/87 ff, 22/12/88 ff
list of miles covered 9/8/49
Norway 15/9/83, 11/8/85 ff
Papal states 28/3/32
Savoy 28/2/32
Spain 26/12/91, 22/1/94
Switzerland 3/7/32 ff, 20/12/88
Treasury
conversion of funds 19/2/53, 9/3/53, 2/4/53
anxious days 23/5/53
establishment of 2/1/66
Exchequer Bills 19/2/53
financial secretary of
duties of 11/6/73

First Lord of, G as 3/12/68 ff, 23/4/80 ff, 1/12/86 ff, 15/8/92 ff
G's index of subjects and progress 17/2/53
G's memorandum on powers of 2/12/62
G's plan for Ministry of Finance and 16/2/56, 20/2/56
India, control of finance of 22/11/71
india rubber and 17/4/69 c
jurisdiction of 10/8/71
Lords of sitting as a court 10/5/69
reorganisation of 21/2/54, 4/10/60, 2/8/69
superannuation and 24/6/59
See also budgets, civil service, finance, Lowe
Treasury Board 20/12/34, 9/1/35 ff, 22/1/53 ff *See also* cabinet (committees of)
treaties
G opposes Commons' debate on before ratification 14/2/73
treating
law habitually violated 2/6/41
treefelling
at Dalmeny 3/4/80
at Hagley 30/12/68, 17/1/76
at Hawarden 1852–74 29/10/52, 2/8/58, 5/8/58 ff, 24/8/58 ff, 9/11/67, 10/11/67 ff, 4/12/67 ff, 21/12/67 ff, 6/1/68 ff, 9/4/68 ff, 16/9/68 ff, 4/11/68 ff, 1/1/69 ff, 24/5/69, 12/10/69 ff, 22/11/69 ff, 1/1/70 ff, 17/1/70 ff, 16/4/70 ff, 18/4/70 ff, 19/9/70 ff, 7/10/70 ff, 17/11/70 ff, 3/12/70 ff, 20/12/70 ff, 8/4/71 ff, 9/9/71 ff, 13/10/71 ff, 13/11/71 ff, 23/12/71 ff, 20/5/72 ff, 19/8/72 ff, 15/9/72 ff, 22/10/72 ff, 19/12/72 ff, 27/12/72 ff, 6/1/73, 12/4/73 ff, 16/8/73 ff, 10/9/73 ff, 10/10/73, 24/10/73 ff, 2/1/74 ff, 7/4/74 ff, 13/4/74, 27/4/74 ff, 28/5/74 ff, 31/8/74 ff, 28/9/74 ff, 24/11/74
and General Grey's telegram 1/12/68
closing the season 3/6/74
first lesson in 31/7/58
H. N. G felled together with tree 27/12/67
splinter in G's eye 23/12/67, 25/12/67
yew felled in error 24/11/71
at Hawarden 1875- 6/1/75 ff, 18/5/75 ff, 13/8/75 ff, 3/9/75 ff, 6/10/75 ff, 9/12/75, 1/1/76 ff, 20/4/76, 21/4/76, 28/4/76 ff, 5/8/76, 13/10/76 ff, 1/1/77 ff, 18/5/77 ff, 3/8/77, 2/10/77 ff, 13/11/77 ff, 26/12/77 ff, 2/1/78 ff, 22/1/78 ff, 30/4/78 ff, 20/8/78 ff, 8/10/78 ff, 6/11/78 ff, 16/1/79 ff, 12/2/79 ff, 12/8/79 ff, 3/9/79 ff, 4/11/79 ff, 9/12/79 ff, 3/1/80 ff, 30/1/80 ff, 17/4/80, 29/11/80 ff, 27/12/80, 20/4/81 ff, 22/9/81, 3/10/81 ff, 15/10/81 ff, 15/11/81 ff, 5/12/81 ff, 15/4/82 ff, 7/9/82 ff, 19/12/82 ff, 18/5/83 ff, 22/5/83 ff, 29/8/83 ff, 29/9/83 ff, 30/10/83 ff, 6/12/83 ff, 8/1/84 ff, 30/5/84, 30/5/84 ff, 2/10/84 ff, 10/12/84 ff, 28/5/85, 26/9/85 ff, 13/10/85 ff, 7/12/85 ff, 16/12/85 ff, 4/1/86 ff, 22/4/86 ff, 28/9/86 ff, 5/11/86 ff, 1/1/87 ff, 4/2/87 ff, 28/5/87 ff, 6/9/87, 4/10/87, 31/10/87 ff, 5/12/87 ff, 26/9/88 ff, 1/11/88 ff, 29/11/88, 10/12/88 ff, 30/4/89, 25/9/89 ff, 21/10/89 ff, 30/11/89 ff, 7/10/90, 14/11/90 ff, 2/12/91
G no longer equal to true woodman's work 22/9/81
last fall? 28/5/85
non sum qualis eram 3/10/81
at Holmbury 5/4/77
at Penmaenmawr 4/9/62
at Raby Castle 22/9/76
at Sandringham 31/3/83
at the Glen, Innerleithen 5/11/90
at Walmer 4/6/70
at Wanborough 12/8/86
at Wellington College 3/11/79
at Windsor Castle 22/12/71
at Woburn, assisted by the duke 22/10/78
at Wollaton Hall 11/5/75
finger bruised in course of 29/1/68
G interesting grand-son in 30/11/89
G playing second fiddle at 20/11/89
splinters from collected by visitors 4/8/77 n
under C. G's orders 4/10/87
See also accidents
treeplanting
at Aston Clinton 3/4/88
at Dalmeny 1/12/79
at Hawarden 20/2/80
at Newnham, Cambridge 31/1/87
trees
Fredville oak, Barfreston 16/9/54
Trefnant, church at 28/9/55
Trentham (Sutherland) 8/12/59, 3/11/68
Trevelyan, George Otto, Sir (1838–1928), 2nd Baronet (1886), liberal M.P. and historian, Irish secretary 1882–4, Chancellor of the Duchy 1884–5, Scottish secretary 1886, 1892–5 20/7/65, 14/12/65, 23/3/76, 23/5/76, 7/5/77 n, 12/11/80, 3/5/82, 8/5/82 ff, 10/6/82 c, 22/7/84, 26/8/84, 27/2/85, 9/3/85, 28/4/85 c, 11/5/85, 8/6/85 c, 8/3/87, 9/7/90, 4/12/90, 31/3/91, 9/4/92, 14/8/92 ff, 4/8/93, 20/2/94
at Hawarden 13/10/83 ff

Trevelyan, George Otto, Sir (*cont.*)
Chancellor of the Duchy 15/10/84
determined on including Ireland in 1884 Reform Bill 23/10/83
disestablishment and 9/3/86
Edinburgh Rectorship and 18/10/83
Glasgow election and 3/8/87
home rule and 21/1/86
Ireland and
resignation on 15/3/86, 22/3/86, 26/3/86 c, 27/3/86
Irish secretary 9/5/82 ff, 13/5/82 ff, 23/8/83
cabinet and 17/9/84
letters from G to, printed 7/11/82, 5/12/82, 30/12/82, 10/3/83, 7/4/83, 23/8/83, 23/10/83, 12/3/86, 15/3/86, 27/3/86, 6/10/92
reconciliation to liberal party of 23/5/87, 25/5/87, 26/5/87
trials
G as witness 12/5/43
See also Birmingham, Egypt, Ireland, Land League, O'Connell, Old Bailey, Parnell
Trieste
G visits 20/11/58
G decides not to visit 22/6/32
trigonometry 8/8/28 ff, 15/7/31
Tring Park (Rothschild) 28/2/91, 26/8/93
unSabbatical life at 1/3/91
Trinity College, Glenalmond
Council meeting in Edinburgh, G at 17/11/74
estimates for 25/8/40
G drafts fundamental laws for 2/6/45
G persuades Wordsworth to be Warden 31/5/46
G's speech on classical education at 9/7/57
Jubilee of 30/9/91 ff
G's speech at 1/10/91
loan to by G 25/3/55 n, 3/10/55, 1/6/74
opening of 7/9/46, 8/9/46
origin of 30/7/40
Oscott visited as model for 18/8/40
plans for 1/10/40 ff, 14/10/40 ff, 28/10/40 ff, 10/5/41, 28/5/41, 8/6/41, 12/6/41, 10/12/41, 1/5/42, 26/5/42, 23/8/42, 14/11/42, 28/6/45 ff, 3/9/45 ff, 9/6/46, 12/6/46, 17/6/54
Dyce's designs for 22/1/43
subcommittee for 11/4/43 ff
visits to 24/8/42, 11/9/48, 25/10/48, 30/4/51, 23/10/51, 8/7/57, 9/10/63, 30/9/91
Wardenship of 2/7/45, 3/1/95
See also Gladstone (Sir John), Scott (J. R. H.-)
Trinity College, Oxford 23/5/31, 25/10/52, 27/1/57
Trinity House 29/11/42, 8/6/46, 4/6/53, 21/6/54, 5/6/61, 3/7/69, 24/7/80
G Elder Brother of 16/11/61 n, 25/6/62, 5/7/76
Triple Alliance 30/8/92
G surprised that conditions of not known to Foreign Office 11/9/92
naval expansion a further movement towards 9/1/94 c
triremes 3/5/32 n
Troon 12/9/48
Trossachs 15/8/39
Troubetzkoi, Prince *See* portraits of G
truck
commission on 14/6/70 c
Truro
G's speech at 12/6/89
trusteeships
British Museum 8/4/53
Clarendon Trust, Oxford 16/7/58
Cobden's MSS 20/6/77, 24/10/81 n
Colonial Bishoprics Fund 27/4/41
Dee/Hawarden Embankment Trust 15/10/57, 21/4/76, 30/10/83, 16/8/88, 29/5/90, 20/10/93
Marlborough Trust 24/6/68
National Portrait Gallery 28/6/60
Newcastle Trust 1/7/56
Radcliffe Trust 25/5/55
River Dee Trust 11/8/56, 26/8/75 ff, 9/5/88
See also institutions and trusts by own names
Truth 7/9/84
Tunbridge Wells
G's speech at 17/3/91
Tunis 12/6/80 c, 13/5/81 c, 20/5/81 c, 13/6/81 c, 15/6/81 c
Salisbury and 13/4/81
Tupper, Martin Farquhar (1810–1889), G's friend while at Christ Church, Oxford, versifier and author of *Proverbial Philosophy* 2/4/29, 22/11/29, 14/1/31, 31/5/31 ff, 25/1/33, 12/4/44, 17/5/58, 20/11/65, 19/6/76, 11/9/88 n
better if had not written 19/3/47
death of 28/11/89 n
G sees at Albury 16/5/56
letters from G to, printed 2/4/83
pension for
discussed with the Queen 11/11/69
Turin 2/3/32, 1/11/50, 2/3/59, 30/12/87
china shopping in 3/3/59
dankest air in Italy in 2/11/50
decline of friars in 2/11/50
Europa Hotel 1/11/50
has gaiety of a capital 2/11/50
Palazzo Madama 2/11/50
Shroud of 2/3/32
Superga 3/11/50
See also Italy

Turkey 7/10/53, 25/10/53, 24/4/69, 17/11/69, 28/10/70, 2/11/70 c, 23/9/85, 11/1/94
aggression at Aden by 15/11/73 c
Albert's minute on shown to G 25/10/53
Anglo-Turkish Convention 1878
announcement of a new Asiatic Empire, G thinks 8/7/78, 10/7/78
astounding announcement of the new Asiatic Empire 8/7/78
Balkan policy of, printed memorandum 14/5/80, 21/5/80
budget of 12/12/63
Bulgaria and 24/8/92
Bulgarian schism and 4/9/72
Christian subjects in
G's concern for vindicated 8/2/76
coercion of over Smyrna 30/6/80, 25/9/80, 27/9/80, 30/9/80 c
Conference on Turco-Greek relations 6/1/69, 11/1/69, 13/1/69, 26/1/69 c, 2/2/69 c
Egypt and 21/6/82 cf, 24/3/85 c, 10/3/86, 18/7/93 ff
federal system better for than unitary centralisation, G thinks 18/10/69
Fuad's testament 18/10/69
German officers in 17/7/80 c
Greece and 22/12/68 c, 6/1/69
G visits Albania 2/2/59
impression most saddening: indolence, decay, stagnation 2/2/59
liberty, local, to be promoted in 6/1/69
loan to 20/7/55, 22/2/64, 23/11/75, 6/5/76, 21/7/76, 17/7/77 n
significant division on 20/7/55
may go to pieces 4/11/69
Midhat's constitution!!! 5/1/77
military convention with, proposed 5/8/82 c, 13/9/82 c
Mohometan rule in Europe not permanent, G thinks 13/11/71
permission for cartridges for, withdrawn 7/12/69 c
Straits policy and 1856 Black Sea clauses
conference on 4/11/70 c, 10/11/70 c, 11/11/70 c, 16/11/70, 17/11/70 c, 28/11/70 c, 30/11/70 c, 6/12/70 ff, 19/1/71 c, 28/1/71 c, 1/2/71 c, 11/2/71 c, 15/2/71 c, 16/2/71, 20/2/71, 9/5/71
Sultan of
at end of his dodges 3/10/80
bottomless pit of fraud and falsehood 19/9/80, 26/10/80, 4/9/82
Sultan's visit to Britain
G much pleased by his manner 20/7/67
suzereignty and local autonomy in favoured by G 6/1/69, 18/1/69, 8/7/76 n, 31/7/76 n, 24/7/80
Treaty of 1856 and 2/11/70 c, 4/11/70 c
treaty with 18/12/43
See also Eastern Question, Egypt, memoranda, memoranda (printed)
Tynninghame House, Dunbar (Haddington) 4/1/37
typewriters 19/5/93 n, 24/5/93
tyrannicide 10/10/27
tyranny in Naples
unparalled at this moment 13/2/51
Tyre, G's prize essay on 10/4/30 ff, 26/4/30
Tyrol 26/6/32 ff

Uganda 17/9/92 ff, 29/9/92 c, 4/11/92 ff, 5/1/93, 4/2/93, 20/3/93 ff, 5/4/93 ff, 20/7/93 c, 15/9/93
Commissioner for 4/11/92 c, 7/11/92 c, 18/11/92 ff, 21/11/92, 23/11/92 c, 4/2/93
evacuation of proposed 20/9/92, 24/9/92, 29/9/92 c
G favours proposal to attach to Zanzibar 21/10/92 ff, 2/11/92 ff, 9/12/92
G's meeting with Stanley and McKinnon on 23/6/90
G's memoranda on, printed 20/9/92, 24/9/92, 30/9/92
Macdonald Report on 30/9/92 c, 20/7/93
massacres in 17/9/92
missionaries and 20/9/92, 23/9/92 ff
publication of papers on 23/9/92, 13/10/92, 4/2/93
railway to 3/2/92, 29/9/92
Rhodes's offer to administer, declined 4/11/92 c, 12/11/92, 14/11/92
Ruwenzori mountains
G complains at Stanley's names for 23/6/90 n
See also British East Africa Company, cabinet (committees of), Cecil, Harcourt, jingoism, Labouchere, memoranda (printed), Primrose
Ulster *See* Ireland
ultramontanism 8/6/65, 18/5/75
anti-social power of 8/1/70
effect of on British education 1/12/69
Manzoni and 24/9/38
no parallel in the religious world 8/6/71
pertinacity and awful longevity of 7/6/71
Vatican Council and 1/12/69, 19/11/72
See also Manning (H. E.), Roman Catholic Church, Vaticanism
umbrellas 6/11/38
prices of in Naples 28/11/50
unemployment 16/2/86, 18/12/88 n, 18/8/93 c *See also* trade unions, working classes

Union Castle shipping co.
contract for Zanzibar and the Cape 22/2/73 c, 28/7/73
See also Zanzibar contract
unitarianism 14/11/34, 5/11/35 n, 17/6/38, 14/8/68 n
G denies he was baptized a unitarian 23/3/68 n
See also Ireland
Unitarians
1854 Oxford bill and 3/4/54
decline of 16/8/83
in Ireland 21/7/43
in Liverpool 7/11/53
See also Gladstone (Robertson)
United Kingdom
Chamberlain's plan of National Councils for 11/7/85
United Presbyterians 2/4/80
United States
Academy of Arts and Sciences
G elected a member 14/2/74 n
Alabama arbitration 1/7/71 c, 25/1/72 c, 16/3/72 c, 19/3/72, 5/4/72 c, 9/4/72 c, 17/4/72 n, 3/6/72, 8/6/72 c, 11/6/72 c, 12/6/72 c, 13/6/72, 15/6/72 c, 16/6/72 c, 17/6/72, 22/6/72 c, 26/6/72 c, 29/6/72 c, 24/5/73 c, 26/5/73
bristles with difficulty 27/5/72
British case for 4/12/71, 19/1/72 c, 27/1/72 c, 30/1/72 c, 2/2/72 c, 10/2/72 c, 24/2/72 c, 2/3/72 c, 5/4/72 c, 9/4/72 c, 13/4/72 c, 24/4/72, 2/5/72 c, 6/5/72 c, 8/5/72 c, 10/5/72 c, 13/5/72 c
cabinet now hardly ever out of 10/6/72
Cockburn to be British arbitrator 1/7/71 c
Emperor of Germany as Arbitrator 20/8/72
offer made by British cabinet 5/6/72 c
payment of 19/12/72, 31/1/73, 2/4/73, 4/9/73
Alabama incident 14/9/63, 17/12/68 ff, 11/2/69, 22/3/69, 30/3/69, 24/8/69, 23/10/69, 25/10/69, 26/10/69 c, 28/10/69, 25/11/69, 7/12/69 c, 9/12/69 c, 24/12/69, 25/12/69, 21/1/70 c, 15/5/70, 21/5/70 c, 13/6/70, 10/11/70 c, 28/1/71 c, 11/3/71 c, 21/3/71, 1/4/71 ff, 24/1/72, 6/2/72, 28/11/72, 29/1/73
arbitration on, need for 21/10/69, 5/12/69
arbitration on, proposed 28/11/70 c
discussed with nonconformists 13/2/68
Motley withdrawn from 15/10/69, 21/10/69
need for Britain's statement of her case 18/5/69
U.S.A. proposes cession of Canada as indemnity 27/6/69 c
Alexandra incident 28/11/63
American Exhibition in London
G watching Buffalo Bill at 28/4/87
American Free Trade League, G member of 19/4/69 n
Americans in Paris, questionable behaviour of 28/1/39
Anglo-American Committee 15/12/70 c
Anglo-Saxons and 13/6/71
art exhibition 11/5/89, 13/5/89
Baillie's motion on 17/4/56
Boston Household Arts Society
G's loan of jewel collection to 16/8/72
Burke a magazine of wisdom on 18/12/85
Canadian/American disputes
commission on 6/1/71 c, 28/1/71 c, 1/2/71 c, 16/3/71, 17/3/71 c, 1/4/71 c, 3/4/71 ff, 17/4/71 c, 19/4/71 c, 22/4/71 c, 28/4/71, 9/5/71, 20/5/71
civil service in
poor appointment system of 16/10/80
civil war in 23/11/61, 24/1/62, 28/11/62 n, 28/4/71
Britain decides not to mediate 12/11/62
Confederate pamphlets read 21/7/62
Fredericksburg: will end the madness? 27/12/62
G's memorandum advocating European intervention 23/10/62, 24/10/62
G's memorandum expecting European intervention 7/7/62
G's Newcastle speech on 7/10/62, 17/10/62, 1/2/72 n, 28/11/72
G's Newcastle speech on: letter to Schenck explaining, printed 28/11/72
Victoria and Albert anti-Northern 28/11/61
commercial policy towards 5/6/43, 19/8/43
Confederacy
G denies subscribing to Confederate Loan 4/10/65
G opposes Roebuck's motion to recognise 30/6/63
G's letter to Schenck explaining his attitude to, printed 28/11/72
Confederate agent
G meets 30/7/62, 31/7/62, 8/4/65
Confederate bonds 27/11/71 ff
Confederate 'nation'
G's speech on 7/10/62, 17/10/62
Confederates
G meets 14/11/65

Congress of
  and national religion 9/5/41
Constitution of
  G declines invitation to centenary celebrations of 20/7/87
cookery in, G's views attacked 26/3/79
cotton bonds and 14/12/71 c, 18/12/71 c
Fenianism and
  G fears may be formidable in 22/10/66
Fenians and 23/2/66
  'dregs of Irishism (our creation)' 28/12/92
Fenians in 15/5/70, 13/6/70, 5/9/70, 14/9/70, 21/10/71 c, 26/8/72, 10/5/82 c, 10/10/82, 17/3/83 c, 28/4/83 c, 8/8/83 c
  British protests at dynamiting in U.K. by 29/2/84
  Haggerty case 5/6/69 c, 19/6/69 c
finances of 5/1/70
free trade and 5/1/70
friendship with, G speaks on to group of Americans 28/11/72
Harvard University
  G declines invitation to lecture on political economy at 15/8/78
home rulers in 12/4/89 n
home rule support in 30/11/85
international law and 12/10/61
Irish in
  G's appeal to 2/9/93
Land League and
  case of U. S. citizens arrested 31/3/82, 3/4/82
mail contracts with 20/3/69
McKinley tariff
  G's speech on at Dundee 29/10/90
Molly Maguires and 11/7/82, 19/7/82, 21/7/82, 5/12/82, 27/2/83
New York, social centre of 26/12/92
New York Historical Society
  attack on G's comments on American cookery 26/2/79 n
New York Mail and Express 31/7/89
New York Press Association 19/5/87
New York World testimonial presentation 9/7/87
Oneida incident 9/7/70 c
Peabody's remains to be shipped to 10/11/69 c
proposes union of Canada with 24/1/70, 25/1/70 c, 28/1/70 c
Puritanism and 17/10/92
railways bonds, G's investments in 1/6/74
recruitment to 17/4/56, 26/4/56, 31/5/56, 6/6/56, 13/6/56, 16/6/56, 17/6/56, 30/6/56
Samuel Gilbert incident 21/10/71 c, 25/10/71 c
San Juan convention 21/1/70 c, 16/3/71 c, 1/4/71 c, 22/4/71 c, 27/11/71, 18/11/72 c
Shakers in 15/8/75
slavery in 1/5/50
  G's mem. for cabinet on 31/7/62
taste in
  G's criticisms of 26/12/75 n
Trent incident 28/11/61 n, 13/12/61, 20/1/62, 5/2/94, 13/2/94
Vaticanism and 10/3/75
Virginius incident 15/11/73 c, 17/11/73 c, 21/11/73 c, 26/11/73 c, 28/11/73 c
Washington, Treaty of
  commissioners over-anxious to settle 13/4/71
  Fenians and 10/6/71 c
  indirect claims and the *Alabama* 2/2/72 c, 3/2/72 c, 15/2/72 n, 17/2/72 c, 28/2/72, 16/3/72 c, 19/3/72 c, 9/4/72 c, 24/4/72, 27/4/72 c, 2/5/72 c, 6/5/72 c, 8/5/72 c, 10/5/72 c, 13/5/72 c, 28/5/72 c, 5/6/72 c, 8/6/72 c, 10/6/72 c, 12/6/72 c, 13/6/72, 15/6/72, 17/6/72
  supplemental article for 19/3/72 c
Washington treaty 28/7/43
See also Canada, publications, Washington (George)
United Universities Club 28/5/63
unity in the Church
  ruling force in G's life 8/10/38
universal church 24/9/38, 8/10/38
universities
  endowments of, British compared with European 6/2/83
Universities Elections Bill
  G opposes 12/7/61
Universities' Mission to Central Africa (U. M. C. A)
  G addresses meeting at Cambridge 1/11/59
University College, Oxford 5/7/48
  H. J. G at 21/4/72
University College London
  Italian chair
    G assists endowment of 31/10/91 n
university extension movement
  G speaks for 19/2/79
university reform 10/11/53, 11/11/53 *See also* Cambridge (University of), Edinburgh (University of), Ireland, London (University of), Manchester (Owen's College), Nottingham (College), Oxford (University of), Royal Holloway College, Scotland (Scottish Universities Bill), Scotland (universities of)

university seats
abolition of 20/7/92, 1/8/92
redistribution and 26/11/84 ff
university tests 9/4/34 n, 17/4/34, 26/4/34, 20/6/34 ff, 23/7/34, 28/7/34
1854 bill and 3/4/54
speech on 28/7/34
subscription to articles on matriculation
G opposes abolition 22/6/54
University Tests Bill 10/11/69, 3/2/70, 24/3/70, 1/12/70, 4/12/70, 13/1/71, 18/1/71, 24/2/71, 27/2/71, 6/5/71 c, 13/5/71 c, 22/5/71
deputation on 18/1/71, 19/1/71 c
G opposes 14/6/65
headships not to be reserved 23/6/70 c
Lords' amendments to 25/4/71, 13/5/71 c, 23/5/71, 12/6/71
Salisbury's Resolutions on 22/4/71 c, 25/4/71, 6/5/71 c
Unkel, Bavaria 15/9/74
unworthiness
G's deep, deep, deep 29/12/60
Upleatham, Guisborough (Zetland) 9/10/62
Urie House (Capt. Barclay) 1/11/51
utilitarianism 23/3/41

vaccination
G vaccinated 28/12/27
Society for Compulsory Vaccination 2/5/87 n
Vale Royal Abbey (Delamere) 1/9/40
Valescure, St. Raphael 15/1/92 ff
Van Diemen's Land *See* Australia, memoranda
vanity, dangers of 2/4/38
Vatican
G suggests diplomatic post for self at 12/7/44 n
renewal of relations with 18/4/44 ff, 7/7/44, 8/7/44
Vatican Council 21/5/69, 24/8/69, 7/11/69, 29/12/69, 8/1/70 ff, 16/1/70 ff, 24/2/70, 1/3/70, 13/3/70, 18/4/70, 28/4/70
Döllinger and 10/10/69
effect of on English education bill 16/4/70
French troops in Rome and 13/3/70
G favours clear European declaration on civil rights 7/9/69
G urges British caution towards 21/5/69
G wish papalists would go forward to Middle Ages 24/12/69
infallibility and 23/11/69, 8/1/70, 30/9/74
Old Catholics and
G's memorandum on, printed 30/9/74
See also Acton, cabinet, Döllinger, France, Italy, Manning, Papacy, Pius IX, publications, Russell (Odo), Wodehouse
Vaud
visit to & impression of 5/3/32, 6/3/32
Vaudois
G's interest in 3/3/32, 4/3/32
Venice 15/6/32 ff, 23/2/59 ff, 30/9/79 ff
Armenian convent visited 8/10/79
Arsenal of 16/6/32, 20/6/32
Burano 7/10/79
churches and galleries of 19/6/32 ff
Clerle's café 2/10/79 ff
Doge's Palace, Library & Prison 20/6/32, 24/2/59, 3/10/79
Fenice theatre 24/2/59
Florian's café 25/2/59, 1/10/79 ff
Frari church 25/2/59
glass manufacturers of 22/6/32
gondola, ride in 18/6/32, 30/9/79
Grand Hotel 30/9/79 ff
Lido, like Seaforth 21/6/32
not what it was in 1832: but still much 23/2/59
Palazzo Morosini 9/10/79
picturesque character of 25/6/32
St. Mark's 15/6/32 ff, 23/2/59, 24/2/59, 1/10/79 ff
Torcello 7/10/79
Ventnor 11/7/77
ventriloquism 1/1/87
Verdi *See* operas
Verona 25/6/32, 28/2/59
verses *See* memoranda (printed), poems, poetry
vertigo *See* illnesses
Vesuvius, ascent of 14/5/32 ff, 29/11/38, 4/12/50
vice, suppression of 2/6/36
Vicenza, Palladian villas of 25/6/32, 26/2/59
Victoria, Queen (1819–1901), Queen of Great Britain and Ireland (1837), Empress of India (1876) 28/5/34 n, 4/5/35 n, 19/8/43, 3/4/54, 3/1/60, 10/12/62, 30/1/65, 18/11/65 ff, 10/1/68, 11/9/69 ff, 19/9/69 ff, 29/2/72, 1/3/72, 14/4/72, 12/3/77, 10/3/80, 12/9/80, 23/9/80, 9/2/81, 28/5/81, 11/4/84, 7/8/84, 8/9/84 ff, 23/5/85, 18/6/85, 20/6/85, 29/6/85, 10/2/86, 4/4/86, 22/5/87, 4/7/89, 27/7/89, 17/1/94, 27/7/96
accepts G's resignation as Chancellor with great pain 28/2/55
accepts Salisbury's resignation 'with regret' 12/8/92 n
accident to 7/10/63 ff
Albert's death and
G ill fitted to discuss 16/3/62, 19/3/62
American civil war and
anti-Northern 28/11/61
Angeli's portrait of 10/7/75, 12/3/85

approves Lords' rejection of paper duties repeal 22/5/60
at Balmoral 25/9/63 ff
attacked by Fenian with unloaded pistol 29/2/72
O'Connor to be sent abroad 13/4/72 c, 3/12/72 c
attacked by R. Maclean 3/3/82 ff
attitude to Liberalism of 10/3/94
audiences with 5/8/61, 6/12/68, 9/12/68, 4/3/69, 11/3/69, 18/6/69, 11/11/69, 14/11/69, 5/2/70, 22/2/70, 10/4/70, 18/5/70, 6/7/70, 9/8/70, 29/11/70, 8/2/71, 24/3/71, 17/5/71, 1/10/71, 17/1/72, 23/6/72, 27/11/72, 5/2/73, 19/3/73, 8/4/73, 13/5/73, 26/6/73, 9/8/73, 2/12/73, 26/1/74, 17/2/74, 23/4/80, 28/4/80, 3/5/80, 12/5/80, 19/5/80, 28/6/80, 12/7/80, 27/11/80, 18/2/81, 30/3/81, 15/5/81, 27/6/81, 30/11/81, 8/3/82, 10/3/82, 12/5/82, 29/6/82, 18/8/82, 11/12/82, 16/12/82, 3/3/83, 21/3/83, 10/7/83, 5/8/83, 25/11/83, 1/2/84, 4/3/84, 19/5/84, 11/3/85, 19/5/85, 1/2/86, 5/3/86, 24/3/86, 25/5/86, 25/11/92, 21/2/93, 10/3/93, 11/3/93, 8/5/93
after Albert's death 19/3/62
G's final audience as Prime Minister 28/2/94, 3/3/94, 10/3/94, 19/3/94
in nothing helpful 15/8/92
Mordaunt divorce case discussed at 22/2/70
notes for, printed 4/3/84, 25/11/92
occurences of 1872 lead her to 'shut up' 27/11/72
on formation of government 6/12/68, 23/4/80, 1/2/86, 15/8/92
on retirement/resignation 3/2/45, 10/7/46, 26/6/66, 13/3/73, 17/2/74, 26/6/85, 30/7/86
on Thanksgiving service for recovery of Prince of Wales 21/12/71
Queen raises question of dissolution 13/5/73
Ayrton, fired hot shot into 9/7/71
Balkans and 1/12/85
Battenburg interest and 1/12/85
Boer war and
row over settlement 22/3/81 n, 17/5/81
cabinet ministers and
letters sent to on honours but not on political office 28/12/82
church patronage, influence over 11/8/81 ff
charges G with recommending mostly High Churchmen 14/6/83
concern and pain caused her by G 23/4/80
Contagious Diseases Acts and 26/6/82
coronation of 24/6/38, 28/6/38
Crawford divorce and 29/7/86, 1/8/86
crown's private estates and 14/6/73 cf, 5/7/73 c, 19/7/73 c, 21/7/73 n
death of Gordon and
telegraph 'en clair' to G, Granville and Hartington 5/2/85
death of Peel and 1/7/50
declines to accept Aberdeen's resignation 25/1/55
Denmark and 16/6/64
disestablishment and 7/11/93
Disraeli's mischievous speech on her incapacity 1/10/71
dissolution and 20/1/74 ff, 26/1/74, 17/5/86
Egypt and 17/5/84 c, 23/1/93 c
elasticity of mind of 19/3/62
embarrassed, G thinks 9/3/87
essentially fair 17/4/69
expects reduction in G's honours list 22/5/93
fondness of for C. G 17/1/72
Franco-Prussian war and
regrets anti-German feeling 11/2/71 n
strong German sympathies 12/9/70
G always outside an iron ring 30/11/81
G discusses Roebuck committee with 18/2/55
G discusses seclusion of with Duchess of Sutherland 18/1/65
G dreading personal introduction to 10/4/42
G dreams of breakfasting with 2/1/96
G kisses hands with as Ionian commissioner 5/11/58
good-natured archness of 23/4/80
Gordon's letters and 25/3/88
grace of manner and movement 3/6/41
G receives on visit to S. Kensington museum 14/4/58
G requests permission to publish letters on 'Kilmainham Treaty' 24/9/88
Grey's anxieties about 3/12/68
G's assessment of his relations with 10/3/94
G's distress at her handling of his resignation 3/3/94 ff
G's election defeat will be a great relief 8/7/86
G's final resignation as Prime Minster and 21/2/94 ff
intends not to ask his advice about his successor 28/2/94
Queen at highest point of cheerfulness over 28/2/94
G's relations with sad in themselves 2/1/96
G's retirement
looks forward to as a day of relief, G thinks 28/12/82

Victoria, Queen (*cont.*)
G's talks with on Neapolitan horrors 7/4/51
G's *Vatican* pamphlet, has not read 9/7/75
G visits at Osborne 31/8/54
G watches pass in train 14/10/52
has different measures for different political parties 28/7/86
holds G at arms length 12/7/80
home rule and 31/12/85, 20/3/86, 24/3/86
dissolution on 18/5/86
G's memoranda on, printed 17/5/86, 20/9/92 ff, 28/10/92
requests Goschen to form administration to avoid 29/1/86 n
Ilbert Bill and 22/10/83
Indian guard for 5/3/83 c, 10/3/83 c
Irish disestablishment and 6/12/68, 13/12/68, 23/1/69, 24/1/69, 17/7/69 ff
Jubilee 1887
will dislike his speech, G thinks 10/9/87
Kandahar, withdrawal from 7/9/80, 18/9/80
interference with cabinet's policy on 7/1/81, 10/1/81
kind but under restraint with G 9/7/75
knights, prevents G recommending 18/9/92, 15/9/93
Lansdowne dukedom and 8/1/94 ff, 29/1/94
letter of scant kindness from 14/2/74
liberal appointments and
attempts to exclude Childers from the War Office 23/4/80
attempts to exclude Clarendon and De Tabley 28/11/68 ff, 20/3/94
excludes Derby from India Office 11/12/82 ff
excludes Dilke from the Duchy 11/12/82 ff, 19/12/82
limits cabinet information for Prince of Wales 7/11/92 n
lordship-in-waiting
tries to appoint to without consulting premier 1/5/84 c
mind poisoned against G by stories about rescue work 16/7/86 n
Mordaunt divorce case: asks G to speak to Prince seriously 22/1/70
mystery in her relations with G since 1844 10/3/94, 19/3/94
naturalness of 4/1/54
need to start subjects, not merely giving replies 11/7/83
objects to Elgin as Viceroy 14/8/93
objects to G electioneering beyond his constituency 27/6/86
offers Abergeldie to G as let 27/8/64
offers of peerage to G, declined 23/2/74
opposes G's resignation honours 28/7/86
Parliament and
demands nightly report on proceedings of 27/1/93
Phipps' death, shock of 24/2/66, 25/2/66
police to report on her probable reception 17/1/72
Poor Law Commission and
objects to Arch as Commissioner 21/12/92
prejudices of never original 17/4/69
public duty, visible discharge of needed 25/6/71
purchase abolition and
Cambridge's vote 10/7/71 ff
Queen's Speech and
expects changes in wording of on Irish government 29/1/93
railway accidents, concern about 15/12/70 c, 19/3/73, 25/8/73, 4/10/73 c
reclusiveness of 3/2/69 n, 10/4/69, 25/5/69, 4/7/69, 5/2/70
early retirement to Balmoral 9/8/71 c, 10/8/71
fanciful ideas about ill-health 11/6/69
results of showing in practical form 13/4/71
Reform Bill 1884 and 18/7/84 n
compromise on 7/11/84 n, 11/11/84 c, 14/11/84, 25/11/84
G's memorandum on, printed 19/8/84
opposed to a dissolution 31/10/84
regency if Prince of Wales dies 11/12/71 c
resignation of Beaconfield's government and 20/4/80 ff
Hartington's report of audience on 22/4/80
resignation of the government and
accepts 13/3/73
Roman Catholic church, views on 19/3/62
royal finances
income tax: Dilke's inquiry 25/1/72 c
income tax not paid on certain schedules by 11/12/71 c
'What does she do with it?', circulated to cabinet 9/9/71, 21/9/71 n
royal marriages and 28/8/73 ff
royal residence in Ireland 22/12/68 c, 21/6/71, 24/6/71 c, 1/7/71 c, 5/7/71 c, 27/8/72, 28/8/72, 12/10/72 c
G's audience on 25/6/71
Russell's dispatch on Italian unification and 31/8/59
Schleswig-Holstein and 26/9/63, 6/10/63
Sicilian mule and 20/3/94

simple and noble qualities of 17/2/64
speaks goodhumouredly of Garibaldi 1/10/64
strength of character of 19/3/62
tells G to prepare a large budget 14/11/59
the Eastern question and 9/11/53, 11/11/53
too ready for rupture with France 21/6/69
Uganda and 8/10/92
unwilling to read long papers 17/11/69
warm about G. C. Lewis' death 18/4/63
warns G not to overwork 18/4/63
Welsh disestablishment and 26/2/93
Wolseley's title
row over 4/3/81, 18/3/81, 24/3/81 ff, 19/5/81, 21/5/81, 25/5/81 ff, 31/8/81, 25/10/81
See also Balmoral, budgets, cabinet, Commons (House of), Court, Edward VII, Government of Ireland Bill, Gower, India, Ireland, Jubilee, Mill, Osborne, Ponsonby, Tennyson, Wellesley (G. V.), Windsor Castle
Victoria Cross
G attends delivery of 4/1/60
Vienna
G visits 18/11/58 ff
Villiers, George William Frederick (1800–1870), 4th Earl of Clarendon (1838), foreign secretary 1853–8, 1865–6, 1868–70 5/10/48, 15/3/54, 30/8/54, 31/8/54, 1/9/54, 10/3/55, 30/5/59, 9/6/66, 12/6/66, 4/4/68, 13/6/68, 13/3/69, 21/9/92, 23/9/92, 4/3/94, 19/3/94
Alabama incident and 11/2/69 ff, 24/8/69 ff, 5/12/69 ff
civil service reform and 31/12/69
conversation on coming government 13/7/68
G promises foreign secretaryship to? 13/7/68 n
Crimean speeches of 6/7/76
death of 27/6/70
delightful hospitality of 6/11/69
disarmament and 9/4/70
foreign secretary 5/12/68
Queen attempts to prevent appointment 28/11/68, 29/11/68, 2/12/68, 3/12/68, 5/12/68, 20/3/94
full and free talk with 30/5/59
health of 13/3/70, 25/6/70
in Rome 2/11/66 ff, 10/11/66 ff
Irish land and 25/9/69 ff, 10/11/69 ff
comments on G's memorandum 22/3/70
dislikes quasi-menaces to get bill through 22/4/70 n
G's critique of his speech on 6/10/69
letters from G to, printed 6/1/69, 11/1/69, 13/1/69, 15/1/69, 18/1/69, 20/1/69, 30/1/69, 11/2/69, 18/2/69, 9/3/69, 22/3/69, 30/3/69, 15/4/69, 17/4/69, 18/4/69, 28/4/69, 19/5/69, 21/5/69, 25/5/69, 21/6/69, 22/7/69, 24/8/69, 7/9/69, 25/9/69, 6/10/69, 8/10/69, 15/10/69, 18/10/69, 21/10/69, 23/10/69, 25/10/69, 27/10/69, 28/10/69, 4/11/69, 5/11/69, 10/11/69, 17/11/69, 20/11/69, 23/11/69, 25/11/69, 1/12/69, 5/12/69, 24/12/69, 25/12/69, 29/12/69, 31/12/69, 5/1/70, 13/1/70, 16/1/70, 24/1/70, 16/2/70, 18/2/70, 23/2/70, 24/2/70, 28/2/70, 13/3/70, 24/3/70, 5/4/70, 9/4/70, 14/4/70, 18/4/70, 22/4/70, 28/4/70, 15/5/70, 23/5/70, 7/6/70, 13/6/70, 15/6/70
Vatican Council and 21/5/69 ff, 13/3/70 ff
See also United States
Vincentius *See* memoranda (printed)
Virgil
accuracy of account of Etna 31/10/38
Sicilian farming and 1/11/38
Sicilian life compared with *Georgics* 18/10/38, 19/10/38 ff
tomb of 18/5/32
visits abroad *See* travels
voice
loss of 9/3/37 ff, 23/8/84, 16/6/85 ff, 6/7/85, 3/9/85, 27/6/86, 18/4/87, 19/4/87
favourable report on 29/10/85
treatment for 16/7/85, 20/7/85 ff
Voltaire
tomb of 18/2/32
villa of 14/7/32
Volunteers 11/1/69, 30/11/70 c
G at review of 1/6/68
a noble spectacle 23/6/60
in Brighton 2/4/66
in Hawarden 11/10/60
in Mold 25/9/62
G presenting prizes to 30/11/61, 10/11/64, 4/10/70
review at Chester
G praises while calming alarms 5/11/60
rifle match at Queensferry 6/8/62
See also army, Hawarden, London (Hyde Park), Militia
voting
G struck off Flintshire register 29/8/72
voting system *See* Commons (House of), franchise, Lords (House of), redistribution, Reform Bills
voyages
on *Dublin Castle* (Currie's yacht) 10/7/77 ff
Cape deputies met on 10/7/77

voyages (*cont.*)
on *Grantully Castle* (Currie's yacht) 26/8/80 ff
on *Palatine* (Wolverton's yacht) 19/8/82 ff
on *Pembroke Castle* (Currie's yacht) 8/9/83 ff
on *Sunbeam* (Brassey's yacht) 8/8/85 ff
on *Tantallon Castle* (Currie's yacht) 2/4/95, 12/6/95
on *The Garland* (Mrs. Yorke) 8/6/89 ff

Waddesdon (Rothschild) 1/8/85
Wadebridge
pin-shot cartridge thrown at G (unexploded) 13/6/89 n
wages
government has no direct power to raise 20/10/69
government wages
need for minimum rates in? 16/12/92, 17/12/92 c
G proposes cost of living index based on lodging, fuel, clothing, food, travel, books, newspapers 20/12/72
machinery the one legitimate and wholesome check on 23/8/73
wages in docklands 4/2/73 c, 8/2/73 c
Wagner, Richard *See* operas
Waitangi, Treaty of *See* New Zealand
Waldenses *See* Vaudois
Wales
amalgamation of sees in 13/5/43, 29/5/43
Anglican church in 20/12/91 ff
bishops for 14/10/69, 18/12/82 ff
G's search for Welsh-speaking bishops 5/1/70 ff, 12/1/70, 16/1/70 n, 21/2/70, 25/2/70, 11/3/70
six times more trouble than English 28/12/82
Church of England in 17/9/92
strength of in 17th century 13/5/83
will hold own with dissenters in open intellectual field 24/10/70
clerical education in 3/11/75
Cymmrodorion Society
G addresses on pottery 12/5/77
delicacy of singing in 6/9/88
disestablishment and 9/3/86, 23/2/87, 6/10/88 n, 2/7/90 n, 20/7/92, 1/8/92, 3/9/92, 23/10/92, 31/10/92 c, 21/11/92 c, 15/2/93, 10/11/93, 27/11/93
G pairs on division on 20/2/91
G's argument with Lloyd George on priority for 29/5/90
inseparable from disendowment, G thinks 17/9/92
Memorial from Welsh M.P.s to G on 5/7/93
Eastern question and 8/5/78
education in 18/3/82 c, 28/4/85 c, 15/5/85 c, 15/2/86 c
benefit to church of 24/10/70
G meeting with Welsh members on 20/6/79
Eisteddfodd of 27/8/72 n
G addresses at Mold 19/8/73
G's addresses at Wrexham 4/9/88
row about, G defusing 1/9/88, 4/9/88
election 1886 and 8/7/86
defeat will bring forward Welsh questions 10/7/86
Established Church (Wales) Bill 23/2/93 ff
Victoria and 26/2/93
G's tours of 31/8/26 ff, 9/7/52 ff, 10/9/55 ff, 6/9/56 ff
speaking tour of S. Wales 2/6/87 ff
home rule and 1/7/86
Land League in? 13/1/82
land reform and 20/7/92, 12/11/92
liberal party in 1/4/72
middle class in 14/4/71
M.P.s of meeting G at Rendel's 17/3/86, 16/7/89, 7/6/90
nonconformity in 13/5/83
G's argument with Lloyd George on 29/5/90 n
politics of 21/9/86 n
Rebecca riots in 13/1/82
Reform Bill 1884 and 29/10/84
religious and linguistic cleavage harms landlord/tenant relations 13/1/82
rents in 13/10/92
South Wales Federation 24/1/87
University of Wales 1/7/79
deputation on 21/6/71
difficulties of government support for 14/4/71
G favourable to after inquiry 24/10/70, 14/4/71
G sees difficulties in establishing 11/6/69
money for Aberystwyth 18/7/84 c
Welsh language 4/10/56 n, 28/12/82, 5/10/87
does not make favourable impressions 23/9/55
G modifies his opinion on 19/8/73
G's translation of Bp. Morgan's preface to Welsh Bible 28/9/75 ff, 14/10/75
service in, G attends 23/9/55, 2/9/60
singing in, noble 16/9/61
See also Aberystwyth, Asquith, Cardiff, Carnaervon, Conway, Flintshire, Hawarden, Lampeter, Mold, Newport, nonconformists, Penmaenmawr, Penrhyn, Snowdon, St. David's, Swansea, Wrexham
Wales, Prince of *See* Edward VII
Wales, Princess of *See* Alexandra

walks, long 4/10/28, 29/4/29, 17/12/33, 5/9/84, 6/9/84
Aboyne Castle–Kirriemuir 6/10/71
Balmoral–Lochnagar 6/10/63
Braemar–Ben Macdhui 9/9/36, 11/9/84
Braemar–Ben-na-Buird 4/9/39
Braemar–Loch Avon 5/9/39
Braemar–Lochnagar 8/9/36, 3/9/39
Ivercauld (Deeside)–Kingussie via Glen Feshie 1/9/73
Mount Etna 29/10/38 ff
Oxford–Leamington 25/6/30, 19/3/31
Penmaenmawr–Llanrwst 28/9/60
Snowdon 15/9/55
Vesuvius 14/5/32, 29/11/38
Wallachia 4/5/58, 23/11/70
Wallenburg 18/7/32
Walmer Castle, Kent (Granville) 10/8/69, 1/6/70, 11/8/70, 23/8/70, 3/9/81
Walmer (Warden of Cinque Ports) 15/9/54, 27/10/76
Wellington's room at 15/9/54
Walpole, Sir Robert, G's view of 4/3/26, 11/7/26, 6/2/27, 10/2/27, 13/12/37
Walsall 24/12/40, 19/1/41
Wanborough (West) 9/8/86
Warren's Hotel *See* London
Warrington 12/10/68
wars *See* Afghanistan, army, Ashantee, Bright, budgets, Cavendish, China, Crimean war, Eastern Question, Egypt, France, Franco-Prussian war, Germany, Gold Coast, Gower, India, liberal party, Maxim gun, navy, Peace Society, revolutionary war, Russia, South Africa, Spain (civil war), Sudan, United States (civil war), Victoria, Wolseley
Warwick 1/10/50
Warwick castle 2/8/28, 23/11/32
Washington, George
above most modern greatness 4/12/48
G declines to write on 20/12/89 n
G declines to write on for *America* 30/11/88 n
greatness of 4/10/84 n
Roman qualities of 4/12/48
Washington, Treaty of *See* Disraeli, United States
Water Eaton *See* Oxford
Watts, G. F. *See* portraits of G
Wavertree
G's speech at 14/11/68
weather
service of humiliation for 5/9/79
See also heatwaves, snow, storms
Weber *See* operas
Weekly Star *See* publications
WEG Essay Society 20/10/29, 22/10/29 ff, 31/10/29, 28/11/29, 5/12/29, 6/2/30, 27/2/30, 6/3/30, 13/3/30, 8/5/30, 15/5/30 n, 29/5/30, 5/6/30, 30/10/30, 6/11/30, 13/11/30, 12/2/31, 19/2/31, 5/3/31, 12/3/31, 23/4/31, 6/5/31, 7/5/31, 14/5/31 n, 21/5/31, 18/11/31
G President of 30/1/30, 29/1/31
G reads to 13/2/30, 20/2/30, 1/5/30, 22/11/30, 28/5/31
on Plato and Aristotle 22/1/31
G Secretary of 7/10/29
weight, G's
10 stone 13.8 lb. 20/2/47
11 stone 10.5 lb. 15/9/61
11 stone 11 lb. 21/11/80
11 stone 11 lb. 31/12/78 fl
11 stone 3 lb. 16/2/47
12 stone 9 lb. ('proh pudor') 3/1/93
Welbeck (Portland) 15/3/74
Wellesley, Arthur (1769–1852), 1st Duke of Wellington (1814), commander-in-chief, prime minister 1828–30, 1834; in cabinet 1841–6 20/1/36, 18/6/36, 28/11/37, 3/5/41, 22/5/41, 4/7/42, 22/11/43, 28/10/44, 18/3/46, 9/6/46, 24/2/52, 11/8/71, 12/11/86, 28/10/92
death of, G astounded by 16/9/52
foreign policy of 28/10/30
funeral of 18/11/52
German views of 21/7/32
influence over Peel on India 27/6/43
lying in state of 12/11/52
Maynooth grant and 12/2/44 ff
on China and the ministry 18/3/40, 12/5/40
on Ireland 15/5/43, 27/5/43, 22/4/81
expects war in 8/6/43
reform and 11/11/30, 25/5/32
statue of 26/5/83 c, 8/8/83 c, 22/1/84 c, 22/4/84 c, 1/5/84 c
supports annexation of Scinde 24/6/43
ultra-alarmist, regarded as in Peel cabinet 5/1/94
vigour of 18/3/40
whigs chuckling at 12/5/40
See also Oxford Union Society
Wellesley, Gerald Valerian, Dean (1809–1892), dean of Windsor (1854) 18/2/26, 16/7/36, 25/10/53, 19/3/62, 13/7/67, 22/4/68, 27/6/68, 28/4/69, 26/6/69, 13/6/70, 14/4/72, 23/6/72, 9/7/75 ff, 16/5/80, 9/8/80 ff, 27/11/80, 18/6/81 ff, 17/7/81, 29/7/81, 25/6/82, 15/7/82 ff, 20/11/82, 12/3/85
at Hawarden 21/10/69
death of, G much affected by 18/9/82 ff, 2/10/82
his life the most precious in the Church of England 19/9/82

Wellesley, Gerald Valerian, Dean (*cont.*)
G discusses episcopal appointments with 25/2/56
G's latin epitaph for 14/8/84, 21/8/84
G's respect for 14/11/59
G staying with at Windsor 12/11/59 ff, 18/3/71, 14/4/72, 23/6/72, 2/5/75, 26/6/75 ff, 13/4/78 ff, 31/5/79
letters from G to, printed 10/1/72, 23/7/81, 8/8/81, 9/8/81, 11/8/81, 17/8/81, 20/9/81, 12/10/81, 13/10/81, 26/6/82, 26/8/82, 27/8/82, 29/8/82, 3/9/82
Victoria and 27/6/69, 17/7/69, 7/5/71
and Irish church, G discusses 28/6/68
Wellington, Duke of *See* Wellesley
Wellington College
G defends in Commons 1/4/79
G's lecture at 3/11/79
G visiting 11/7/74, 1/4/76, 31/10/79, 19/7/84, 16/7/93
Wellington Museum 4/8/57
Wells
bishop's palace 22/1/77
cathedral 17/8/66, 22/1/77 ff
quality of music in 7/1/94
Wensleydale peerage case 7/2/56 n
Wentworth, Rotherham (Fitzwilliam) 30/11/75
Werneth Park, Oldham (J. T. Platt) 17/12/67
Wesleyan Missionary Society, G declines to attend 9/3/37
Wesleyans 16/12/39 *See also* nonconformists
West, Algernon Edward, Sir (1832–1921), Knight (1886), commissioner of inland revenue 1872, chairman 1881, G's private secretary 1868–72, 1892–4 (unofficial) 1/4/69, 11/5/69, 2/11/69, 11/3/70, 4/4/70, 19/5/70, 9/6/70, 29/9/70, 4/2/71, 11/5/71, 1/6/71, 1/11/71, 9/7/72, 17/10/73, 28/11/73, 16/2/76, 7/6/76, 25/7/77, 22/1/80, 26/2/80, 21/4/80 ff, 13/5/80, 2/10/80, 3/4/81, 12/11/81, 27/1/82 ff, 5/6/82 ff, 27/6/82, 2/11/82, 7/3/83 ff, 15/11/83, 2/1/84, 22/5/84, 13/11/84, 21/2/85, 20/5/85, 26/1/86, 13/4/86, 25/1/87, 20/3/87, 26/5/87, 9/2/88, 3/4/89, 12/5/90, 12/12/91, 1/7/92 ff, 28/9/92 ff, 16/12/92 ff, 11/1/93 ff, 10/7/93 ff, 24/9/93 ff, 15/11/93 ff, 1/12/93 ff
acts as go-between with tories 12/7/86
at Hawarden 13/11/78 ff, 28/10/89 ff, 9/1/91 ff, 29/10/91 n
Commissioner of Inland Revenue 9/7/72 n, 5/3/92 n
G at Wanborough with 9/8/86 ff
Gordon, the Queen and 25/3/88
G's secretary 23/12/68 ff, 5/3/92 ff
G staying with 4/4/76
in Biarritz with G 28/12/91 ff
letters from G to, printed 10/12/73, 28/9/80, 1/7/81, 13/3/82, 1/4/82, 24/6/82, 12/7/86
marriage of 31/7/90
navy estimates crisis and 20/1/94 ff
on voyage to Norway with G on *Pembroke Castle* 9/9/83 ff
Reform Bill 1884
conferences on 13/11/84 ff
with G in Biarritz 14/1/94 ff
West Calder
G's speeches at 2/4/80, 7/7/92
West Country
G's speech-tour of 8/6/89 ff
West Indies 12/7/28, 21/4/29, 5/2/33, 30/4/33, 11/5/33, 13/5/33 ff, 11/7/33 ff, 20/7/33, 11/10/33, 1/8/34, 27/3/38, 22/3/39 ff
Abolition of Slavery bill 14/5/33, 3/6/33, 25/7/33 ff
apprentices in 22/3/36, 6/4/38, 22/5/38, 23/5/38, 25/5/38, 28/5/38
British Guiana 8/8/37, 24/10/39, 31/12/39, 1/1/40
concurrent endowment and, G expects a speech uncorked on from Disraeli 16/7/73
Demerara
Sir J. G's properties 30/8/39, 20/9/39
deputation on 22/7/33
education in 3/2/35 ff, 8/2/35, 27/2/35, 21/3/35 ff, 16/5/35, 8/1/36, 16/2/38
given coup de grace 27/2/45
G offers to go to 19/4/38, 26/4/38
immigration to 25/2/46
Jamaica 9/2/39, 25/3/39
Jamaica conveyance executed at Liverpool 31/10/56
Leeward Islands
federation of 25/3/71 c
relief for 19/6/48 ff, 22/6/48
Resolutions on 1/6/33 ff, 10/6/33
Vreedenhoop estate 3/6/33 n, 7/6/33 ff, 10/6/33
West Indian Federation 25/1/71 c
West Indian loan 3/2/53, 19/6/54
writings on 1/3/34
See also Jamaica, memoranda, slavery
Westmeath *See* Ireland
Westminster, Palace of
Westminster Hall, plans for 14/7/84 c
See also Commons (House of), Lords (House of), Parliament
Westminster Abbey 10/2/33, 1/7/34, 23/3/37, 16/6/38, 28/6/38, 25/3/41, 1/6/41, 19/8/41, 5/12/41 ff, 25/7/42,

24/3/43, 5/6/43, 29/6/47, 28/11/47, 23/9/49, 16/3/50, 12/4/54, 14/4/54, 25/4/54, 17/5/57, 24/1/58, 19/7/60, 4/4/63, 25/1/73, 4/8/85, 3/6/86
Chapter House restoration 21/7/71
fabric of 5/5/83 c
G petitions for Sunday evening services 2/12/57
Jubilee service in 21/6/87
one of the few sublime churches 24/3/83
poor restoration of 29/6/48
Westminster Conservative Association 23/4/36
Westminster Constitutional Club 16/1/35, 19/1/35
Westminster Gazette 20/2/94, 23/2/94
Westminster Review *See* publications
Westminster School
G attends play at 18/12/60, 19/12/71
Westwood Park (Pakington) 10/1/57
Whately, Richard (1787–1863), archbishop of Dublin 1831 15/11/28, 23/11/28, 14/6/29, 17/2/30, 18/9/31 *See also* sermons
whey 4/2/28 ff
whiggery 2/12/33, 16/10/35, 21/4/49
a check to socialism 27/10/85
disintegration of Liberal aristocracy promotes radicalism 10/11/85
G's visit to Woburn 21/10/78 ff
liberal peers' defection will advance democracy and endanger stability 14/4/86
tendancy to reaction in 17/9/85
timid and reactionary attitudes of 30/9/85
whigs and radicals should be able to combine in liberal party 13/11/82
whig government
defeat of 20/6/40
whig party 20/12/45, 5/4/51
whip, use of by G for scourging *See* discipline, journal (G's), rescue work, scourge
whist *See* card games
Whitby 22/8/71
Whiteboys *See* Ireland
Whittinghame, East Lothian (A. J. Balfour) 14/11/74
Wickham, Agnes (1842–1931), née Gladstone, G's daughter 18/10/42, 9/11/42, 29/12/43, 18/10/46, 18/11/47, 18/10/48, 1/1/49, 18/10/52, 18/10/53, 27/9/59, 18/10/67, 4/10/69, 18/10/72, 18/5/73, 18/8/73 n, 18/3/74, 5/4/74, 24/6/74, 23/3/75, 1/4/76, 17/5/76, 29/7/76, 18/10/76, 26/12/76, 1/9/78, 1/1/79, 18/10/79, 31/10/79, 19/7/84 ff, 25/12/84, 18/10/86, 9/11/86, 22/12/86, 24/1/87, 29/5/89 ff, 27/6/89, 2/9/90 ff, 18/10/92, 18/10/93, 7/4/94 ff
A. Gordon wishes to marry 4/10/61
at Wellington 11/7/74, 1/4/76, 31/10/79, 19/7/84
beauty in illness of 22/9/47
confirmed by Hamilton in Salisbury cathedral 6/6/57, 7/6/57
critical condition of 19/9/47 ff
engagement of 26/8/73, 6/9/73 ff
fever and erysipelas 18/9/47 ff
erysipelas returns 21/10/47 ff, 21/9/51
thanksgiving for recovery from 21/9/52, 21/9/64, 21/9/75, 21/9/77, 21/9/78
G discusses confirmation and future life with 30/11/56
G gives desk to, memento for illness 19/12/47
G's inscription on her recovery 28/9/47
G teaching Italian to 31/10/50 ff
G teaching scripture to 23/3/48 ff
in Italy 8/1/67
marriage of 27/12/73
measles of 7/1/56
naughtiness of 26/11/48
pregnancy of 26/3/75
presented at Drawing Room 24/3/60
pure character of 20/9/47
qualities of 1/1/48, 26/10/50, 18/10/57
really ill 19/1/47 ff, 18/9/47
recovery of 24/9/47 ff
relief of by A. Munro 12/3/55
scarlet fever of 11/7/69
stealing sugar 16/7/48
temper of 3/8/52, 1/5/57
with G in Ionia 24/11/58 ff
working the telegraph cipher at Hawarden 12/10/70
See also childrearing, Hawarden, illnesses
Widnes
G's speech at 16/11/68
widows
list of, prayed for by G 13/4/48
Wigan
choir of sings at Hawarden 6/9/88
G as possible candidate for 28/2/46, 9/3/46, 17/3/46 n
Wilberforce, Samuel, Bp. (1805–1873), bishop of Oxford (1845), bishop of Winchester (1869) 2/9/30, 10/2/31, 2/5/39, 4/3/47, 26/4/50, 25/3/51, 24/5/51, 21/1/52, 22/1/52, 10/10/53, 12/10/53, 13/10/53, 9/5/54, 1/2/56, 4/7/57, 5/7/57, 24/1/58, 15/5/58, 17/6/59, 2/11/59, 24/1/60, 23/6/60, 18/3/62, 19/3/62, 25/6/65, 14/6/66, 20/2/68, 17/6/68, 18/8/69, 19/8/69, 3/11/69, 6/6/70, 15/3/71, 2/5/71, 28/7/71, 18/5/73, 25/12/82, 28/12/82, 27/9/83, 12/3/92 n
acharné with Disraeli 11/12/68

Wilberforce, Samuel, Bp. (*cont.*)
at Hawarden 19/7/52, 20/10/55, 4/11/56 ff, 12/10/57 ff, 21/7/58, 20/10/63, 23/8/64 ff, 24/10/68 ff
at Penmaenmawr 25/8/62, 30/8/64
biography of 30/8/75 n, 6/8/79, 3/9/79, 22/11/80, 19/12/80, 6/7/82
confirms G's children
Helen G 20/10/63
S. G 8/5/59
Court of Appeal and 23/11/64
death of; fall from his horse 19/7/73
inquest for, G attends 21/7/73
education bill and 7/6/70
Education Minute and 14/11/61
evangelising of S. London
G unable to assist Wilberforce in 9/1/73
G consults on church appointments 11/12/68
G proposes to Palmerston for York 28/9/62
G's letter requesting support for Irish land bill in Lords 20/6/70
G's Oxford University seat and 18/5/47 ff
G speaks in praise of 9/6/57
G's reflections on his life 31/12/79, 6/7/82
Irish disestablishment and 25/1/69 n, 27/2/69
G hopes will lead party of concession 7/1/69
G urges need for support 21/1/69, 12/6/69
letters from G to, printed 21/1/69, 12/6/69, 21/3/70, 20/6/70, 26/9/70, 10/3/71, 20/5/71, 11/3/72, 9/1/73
memorial to 18/11/73
oracular comment by G to 21/7/65 n
playing whist with G 19/8/69
politics of 6/7/82
resembles Macaulay 1/6/40
Scottish Office and 1/5/62
tells G he should follow Palmerston 20/10/63
See also Church of England, Ireland, patronage, politics
Wilde, Oscar Fingall O'Flahertie Wills (1856–1900), dramatist; admired G's politics, Eighty Club member 29/10/77 n, 14/7/88
G declines to sign a memorial by 1/11/88
meeting with G 3/8/81
sends G his *Poems* 26/7/81
will, G's 14/1/34, 22/2/45, 27/4/47, 9/6/47, 16/12/55, 29/8/60, 9/10/61, 15/1/64, 25/4/81, 31/12/81
1st version 1/8/40, 21/1/47, 22/1/47
2nd version 8/1/85, 29/9/86
discussed with C. G 4/2/44
G deletes Hope as executor, on conversion to Rome 8/4/51
last (third) will 4/9/96, 20/9/96
new codicil executed 19/9/50, 26/12/61
increasing amounts left to children 11/1/73
new will necessary 21/11/49, 29/7/50 ff, 21/9/85 ff
draft of finished 29/7/5, 24/5/50
reviewed 31/1/76
dispositions satisfactory for present 29/12/67
statement of G's income and property 26/12/56
testamentary memorandum, printed 1/1/79
See also memoranda (printed)
will and self-determination
G's memorandum on, printed 2/3/91
Wilmslow
G's mathematical tuition with Turner at 24/1/28 ff
G's return to old haunts of 3/12/89
Wilton House (Pembroke) 29/3/53, 17/1/57 ff, 28/3/61, 20/8/66, 29/8/66, 25/3/69
Herbert's funeral at 9/8/61
services (Roman Catholic) at 22/8/66 ff
Wimborne
G's speech at 15/6/89
Winchester 30/5/46, 8/5/83, 19/11/83
Windsor 9/3/87
Windsor Castle
Deanery of
G staying at 20/6/52, 3/6/54, 12/11/59 ff, 1/5/75, 13/4/78 ff
dinners at need enlivening 11/7/83
fête at 9/3/74
games for money at 9/1/45
G staying at 9/1/45, 31/12/45, 12/1/53, 23/10/53 ff, 9/11/53, 4/1/54, 30/11/54, 3/12/55, 22/10/59, 3/1/60, 1/12/60, 28/11/61, 19/3/62, 10/12/62, 18/4/63, 5/12/63, 18/11/65, 24/2/66, 13/7/67, 27/6/68, 12/12/68, 26/6/69, 13/11/69, 16/11/69, 9/4/70, 29/11/70, 12/2/71, 18/3/71, 6/5/71, 24/6/71, 8/7/71, 13/4/72, 22/6/72, 9/12/72, 8/4/73, 9/7/73, 2/12/73, 9/3/74, 26/6/75, 9/7/75, 13/4/78, 15/5/80, 9/8/80, 18/6/81, 16/7/81, 30/11/81, 8/3/82, 26/4/82, 15/7/82, 11/7/83, 24/11/83, 14/6/84, 25/11/84, 11/3/85, 19/5/85, 25/11/92, 21/2/93, 2/3/94
pictures at 10/1/45
St. George's Chapel 16/6/48
whist at 8/4/73, 2/12/73
wine duties 5/4/53, 6/4/53, 11/1/60, 26/2/60, 27/2/60, 28/2/60, 3/10/61,

Wolseley, Garnet Joseph, Sir (*cont.*)
letters from G to, printed 22/2/74, 15/9/82
relief of Gordon 13/4/84 n, 27/1/85
2000 white umbrellas needed 9/1/85 n
can relieve Khartoum and later crush Osman Digna 9/1/85 n
death of Gordon ought to kill 'old Gladstone' 5/2/85 n
failure of 6/2/85 c, 7/2/85 c, 11/2/85 cf
plan for 13/5/84, 27/5/84 c
prays Gordon has been killed 5/2/85 n
Suakin proposals unsatisfactory 6/1/85
simple unconscious manner of 28/10/82
Sudan and 10/2/84 n
Afghan crisis requires cabinet to change policy on 12/3/85 ff
effect of Pendjeh incident on 8/4/85 ff
expedition to destroy Mahdi's power at Khartoum 10/2/85, 1/4/85, 2/4/85, 5/4/85, 8/4/85, 11/4/85, 15/4/85 c, 25/4/85 c, 29/4/85, 5/5/85, 7/5/85 c, 9/5/85 c
expedition to relieve Gordon 23/8/84 ff, 8/10/84 c
Governor General of 25/2/85, 28/2/85 c, 12/3/85 c
Tel-el-Kebir
peerage for 15/9/82
title for
row with the Queen over 4/3/81 ff, 18/3/81, 24/3/81 ff, 19/5/81, 21/5/81, 25/5/81 ff, 31/8/81, 25/10/81
See also Egypt, Gordon, memoranda, Sudan, Victoria
Wolsey, Cardinal, deposition of 11/11/26
Wolverhampton 15/1/34, 12/8/51, 10/11/88
Wolverton, Lord *See* Glyn
womanhood, burden of 18/10/42
women
anti-feminist literature
G disseminates 31/1/70
at the Commons 22/3/41, 14/2/42
churching of 25/6/40, 24/11/42, 19/8/45, 21/12/47, 28/4/52, 4/2/54
degrees for 21/4/77 n
disabilities of
open question in cabinet 26/4/73 c
divorced women at Court, position of 31/3/81
education of, G's speech on 17/7/90 n
eligibility of for County Councils
deputation to G on 18/3/91
emancipation of
G's sympathy for Crepaz' views 3/10/92
enfranchisement of 3/5/71, 15/4/84, 9/5/84, 13/5/84, 24/5/84 c, 10/6/84 c, 13/6/84 n, 27/9/84 n
1884 Reform Bill and 15/4/84, 9/5/84, 13/5/84, 24/5/84 c, 13/6/84 n
G declines to see Jacob Bright's deputation on 15/4/71
G not strongly opposed to every form of 9/5/84
G's abandoned article on 24/4/91, 30/4/91
G's *Letter* to S. Smith on 9/4/92
Lords and 13/5/84
open question in cabinet 25/2/86 c
opposed, but not to be a cabinet question 7/5/70 c, 12/5/70
resist equalisation of for married/single women in local elections 21/11/93 c
uncomfortably small majority against, G thinks 27/4/92
femininity, characteristics of 4/1/40
G presented with diploma of Naples' society for the perfection of women 11/10/75 n
G's horror of giving inner pain to 20/10/69
G's visits to women's colleges
Somerville and Lady Margaret Hall, Oxford 29/11/83
Newnham, Cambridge 31/1/87
higher education of 5/4/83
judge more by signs than proofs 5/11/38
Ladies' League, G at meeting of 19/5/87
Ladies' memorial to the Queen on Bulgarian horrors 13/9/76
Mary G the most womanish of the daughters 23/11/57
Marylebone Women's Liberal Association
G's speech to 16/4/88
Mill's *Subjection*
G reading and commenting 2/6/69, 3/6/69
Palmerston's letter to Victoria too brusque for a woman 31/8/59
purification through childbirth 3/6/40
Royal Commission on Poor Law
female membership of 8/12/92
superiority and inferiority of 5/9/34
thoughts on 5/3/35, 15/2/40
women doctors: short enabling act for 1/12/73 c
Women's Liberal Federation 10/5/88
C. G's difficulties as President of 17/4/92 ff, 27/4/92, 1/5/92
G's speech to 22/5/89
See also beauty, memoranda (printed), Reform Bills
Wood, Charles, Sir (1800–1885), 1st Viscount Halifax (1866), whig M.P.; lord privy seal in cabinet 1870–4 9/3/33 ?, 12/3/53, 28/6/53, 16/11/63, 14/3/68, 26/11/69, 14/8/70, 21/8/70, 10/5/71, 27/6/71, 21/8/71, 13/6/72, 24/9/72, 23/2/74, 8/3/74, 27/3/74, 6/7/75,

16/3/76, 15/3/77, 29/3/78, 21/4/80 ff, 10/10/81, 27/10/81, 23/3/83, 2/7/83
formation of G's first cabinet and 28/11/68 ff
letters from G to, printed 29/3/69, 2/12/69, 10/2/70, 29/7/70, 12/9/70, 13/4/71, 26/4/71, 15/11/71, 4/12/71, 2/5/72, 28/8/72, 2/9/72, 8/9/72, 10/12/73, 9/2/81, 18/9/81, 20/5/82, 2/8/83, 27/4/86
refuses to join G's cabinet 6/12/68
supports Palmerston against paper duty repeal 5/5/60
wood, price of 27/4/86
Wood, William Page, Sir (1801–1881), 1st Baron Hatherley (1868), lord chancellor 1868–72 7/7/77, 17/7/78
letters from G to, printed 10/7/69, 10/12/69, 3/1/70, 3/2/70, 2/8/70, 10/9/70, 11/3/71, 16/3/71, 19/3/71, 18/7/71
Woodard schools 2/11/76
G speaks for in Oxford 22/11/61
woodcutting *See* treefelling
Woodlands, Consilla (Annaly) 10/11/77
Woodstock
troops used for harvesting at 3/9/72, 27/10/72, 5/11/72
woodturning 4/2/28, 25/2/28 ff
woollens duties 23/9/41 ff
Worcester 5/10/75
Wordsworth, William (1770–1850), poet 16/5/36, 8/6/36 n, 21/6/36, 24/6/36
comments on *Peter Bell* 8/8/40
compared with Shelley 27/10/32
work
G advises immense importance of steady work at Oxford 27/5/58
G shrinking from public business 1/10/64
hours spent on
14 20/3/46
15 18/2/53
17 30/5/53
usual till 2. 30 a.m. 6/4/53
misliked work more difficult 24/7/55
time spent preparing for examinations 17/1/31
Victoria warns G not to overwork 18/4/63
working classes 7/1/61, 26/9/71, 21/6/86
as factory inspectors 8/1/81 n
brought to tea with G by Hall 31/3/64, 21/7/64
comparatively well-off 16/2/86
cost of living, index of, G proposes 20/12/72
danger of their thinking monopolistically 5/11/72
deputation of working men on museum opening hours 26/1/65
Eastern question and 9/4/78, 10/4/78
Edinburgh workmen's deputation 21/6/86
gardening by 19/8/75
G's article on 28/3/90, 23/4/90
G at Victoria Coffee Palace entertainment 23/3/87
Gs drawn by working men from station to house 10/8/68
G's speech in Seven Dials
mixed reception of 9/4/78
impolicy of taxing locomotion of 19/12/72
importance of Commons' representation to G 27/1/74
in Edinburgh 23/12/35
labour M.P.s
'a good lot' 30/6/88
G meeting 26/4/87, 30/6/88
labour question, speech on 4/7/92
legislation for 20/9/71 n, 9/5/80
no fear of 30/5/60
no fear of labouring classes on G's part 3/9/73
not idolised by G 10/5/80
rural labourers
G's article on 4/1/92
sweated labour and 25/12/88
unemployment and 16/2/86
working men's clubs, virtues of 1/4/72 n
working men's exhibition in Islington, G visits 7/9/70
G speaks at closing ceremony of 1/11/70
Workmen's Hyde Park Demonstration Committee
'fountain' of G's Bulgarian pamphlet 23/8/76 n
Workmen's Neutrality Committee
G's speech to abandoned (jingoism) 19/2/78
See also deputations, eight hours question, trade unions, wages
Worksop 22/12/39, 14/3/74, 12/4/79
G's speech at 11/12/90
Worksop Manor (Foley) 29/10/64, 12/5/75
world
increasing ties that bind G to 31/12/56
Worsley (Ellesmere) 27/9/54
Worsley Hall, Manchester (Egerton) 14/10/64
Wotton House (Evelyn) 17/5/56
Wrest Park, Bedfordshire (Cowper) 24/10/78
Wrexham 18/9/56, 22/10/62
exhibition in 20/11/76
G's speech to Eisteddfodd in 1/9/88 n, 4/9/88
Wrexham, Mold, Connah's Quay railway *See* railways

Wycombe Abbey (Carrington) 15/8/35, 11/9/76

Yarmouth 3/9/80
G's speech at 19/5/90
York 6/1/47, 11/10/76
Bishopthorpe Palace 11/1/47
Blue Coat school 6/1/47
G's speech at 16/3/80
York House, Twickenham (Grant Duff) 17/5/79, 9/7/81
York Minster 19/12/34, 1/12/39, 13/1/47 ff, 11/10/62, 22/8/71, 11/10/76
service in, painful 6/1/47
Yorkshire
moral atmosphere clearer than London 30/11/39
Young England group
discussed by G, Herbert, Lincoln 5/8/44
G gives party for all members of 11/2/46
mistakes of 13/10/43
Youth's Companion *See* publications

Zadok *See* servants (Outram, Zadok)
Zanzibar 22/4/73 c, 27/11/82 c, 5/3/83 c, 21/4/83 c, 14/12/84, 28/4/86
Frere sent to as commissioner 12/10/72 c
mail contract
and the 'scandals' 11/6/73, 14/6/73 c, 16/6/73 n, 19/6/73 n, 25/7/73 c, 28/7/73, 30/7/73 c
slave trade in 24/6/71 c, 10/5/73 c, 15/11/73 c
no slave market on island to be permitted 14/5/73 c
Sultan to be required to sign treaty 14/5/73 c
See also cabinet
Zollverein 2/7/44
colonies and 29/12/71, 27/1/72 c, 9/2/72
iron duties 12/8/43, 17/10/43, 24/8/44
See also memoranda
Zoological society 13/6/36
Zoz, cartoon of G in 12/11/77
Zululand *See* South Africa